RAPID REVIEW
Chapter Content

PLANT ASSETS (Chapter 10)

Presentation

Tangible Assets	Intangible Assets
Property, plant, and equipment	Intangible assets (Patents, copyrights, trademarks, franchises, goodwill)
Natural resources	

Computation of Annual Depreciation Expense

Straight-line	$\frac{\text{Cost} - \text{Salvage value}}{\text{Useful life (in years)}}$
Units-of-activity	$\frac{\text{Depreciable cost}}{\text{Useful life (in units)}} \times$ Units of activity during year
Declining-balance	Book value at beginning of year × Declining balance rate* *Declining-balance rate = 1 ÷ Useful life (in years)

Note: If depreciation is calculated for partial periods, the straight-line and declining-balance methods must be adjusted for the relevant proportion of the year. Multiply the annual depreciation expense by the number of months expired in the year divided by 12 months.

SHAREHOLDERS' EQUITY (Chapter 13)

Comparison of Equity Accounts

Proprietorship	Partnership	Corporation
Owner's equity Name, Capital	Partner's equity Name, Capital Name, Capital	Stockholders' equity Common stock Retained earnings

No-Par Value vs. Par Value Stock Journal Entries

No-Par Value	Par Value
Cash Common Stock	Cash Common Stock (par value) Paid-in Capital in Excess of Par Value

DIVIDENDS (Chapter 14)

Comparison of Dividend Effects

	Cash	Common Stock	Retained Earnings
Cash dividend	↓	No effect	↓
Stock dividend	No effect	↑	↓
Stock split	No effect	No effect	No effect

BONDS (Chapter 15)

Premium	Market interest rate < Contractual interest rate
Face Value	Market interest rate = Contractual interest rate
Discount	Market interest rate > Contractual interest rate

INVESTMENTS (Chapter 16)

Comparison of Long-Term Bond Investment and Liability Journal Entries

Event	Investor	Investee
Purchase / issue of bonds	Debt Investments Cash	Cash Bonds Payable
Interest receipt / payment	Cash Interest Revenue	Interest Expense Cash

Comparison of Cost and Equity Methods of Accounting for Long-Term Stock Investments

Event	Cost	Equity
Acquisition	Stock Investments Cash	Stock Investments Cash
Investee reports earnings	No entry	Stock Investments Investment Revenue
Investee pays dividends	Cash Dividend Revenue	Cash Stock Investments

Trading and Available-for-Sale Securities

Trading	Report at fair value with changes reported in net income.
Available-for-sale	Report at fair value with changes reported in the stockholders' equity section.

STATEMENT OF CASH FLOWS (Chapter 17)

Cash flows from operating activities (**indirect method**)

Net income			
Add:	Losses on disposals of assets	$ X	
	Amortization and depreciation	X	
	Decreases in current assets	X	
	Increases in current liabilities	X	
Deduct:	Gains on disposals of assets	(X)	
	Increases in current assets	(X)	
	Decreases in current liabilities	(X)	
Net cash provided (used) by operating activities			$ X

Cash flows from operating activities (**direct method**)

Cash receipts (Examples: from sales of goods and services to customers, from receipts of interest and dividends on loans and investments)	$ X	
Cash payments (Examples: to suppliers, for operating expenses, for interest, for taxes)	(X)	
Cash provided (used) by operating activities		$ X

PRESENTATION OF NON-TYPICAL ITEMS (Chapter 18)

Prior period adjustments (Chapter 14)	Statement of retained earnings (adjustment of beginning retained earnings)
Discontinued operations	Income statement (presented separately after "Income from continuing operations")
Extraordinary items	Income statement (presented separately after "Income before extraordinary items")
Changes in accounting principle	In most instances, use the new method in current period and restate previous years results using new method. For changes in depreciation and amortization methods, use the new method in the current period, but do not restate previous periods.

Read 684-688

RAPID REVIEW
Chapter Content

MANAGERIAL ACCOUNTING (Chapter 19)

Characteristics of Managerial Accounting

Primary Users	Internal users
Reports	Internal reports issued as needed
Purpose	Special purpose for a particular user
Content	Pertains to subunits, may be detailed, use of relevant data
Verification	No independent audits

Types of Manufacturing Costs

Direct materials	Raw materials directly associated with finished product
Direct labor	Work of employees directly associated with turning raw materials into finished product
Manufacturing overhead	Costs indirectly associated with manufacture of finished product

JOB ORDER AND PROCESS COSTING (Chapters 20 and 21)

Types of Accounting Systems

Job order	Costs are assigned to each unit or each batch of goods
Process cost	Costs are applied to similar products that are mass-produced in a continuous fashion

Job Order and Process Cost Flow

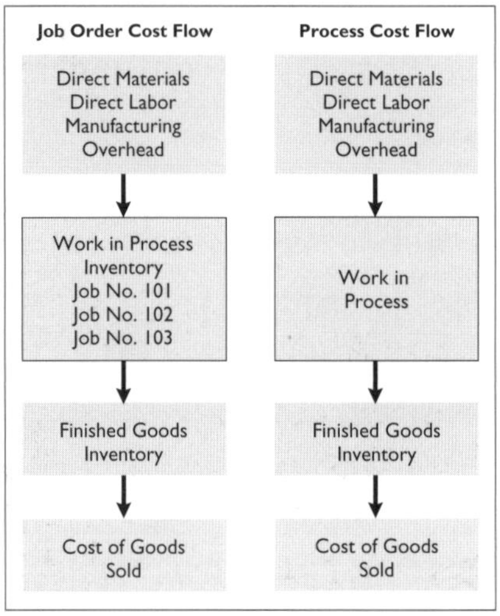

COST-VOLUME-PROFIT (Chapter 22)

Types of Costs

Variable costs	Vary in total directly and proportionately with changes in activity level
Fixed costs	Remain the same in total regardless of change in activity level
Mixed costs	Contain both a fixed and a variable element

CVP Income Statement Format

	Total	Per Unit
Sales	$xx	$xx
Variable costs	xx	xx
Contribution margin	xx	$xx
Fixed costs	xx	
Net income	$xx	

Breakeven Point

Breakeven point in units = Fixed costs ÷ Contribution margin per unit

Target Net Income

Required sales in units = (Fixed costs + Target net income) ÷ Contribution margin per unit

BUDGETS (Chapter 23)

Components of the Master Budget

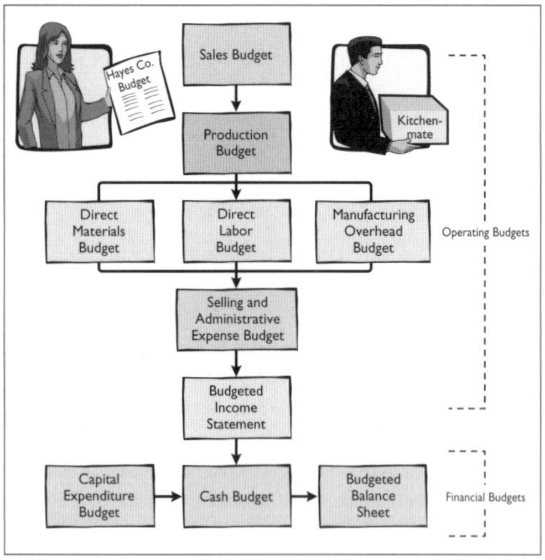

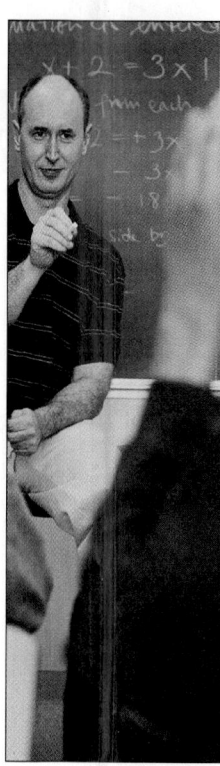

TO THE INSTRUCTOR

WileyPLUS is built around the activities you perform

Prepare & Present

Create outstanding class presentations using a wealth of resources, such as PowerPoint™ slides, interactive simulations, and more. Plus you can easily upload any materials you have created into your course, and combine them with the resources contained in *WileyPLUS*.

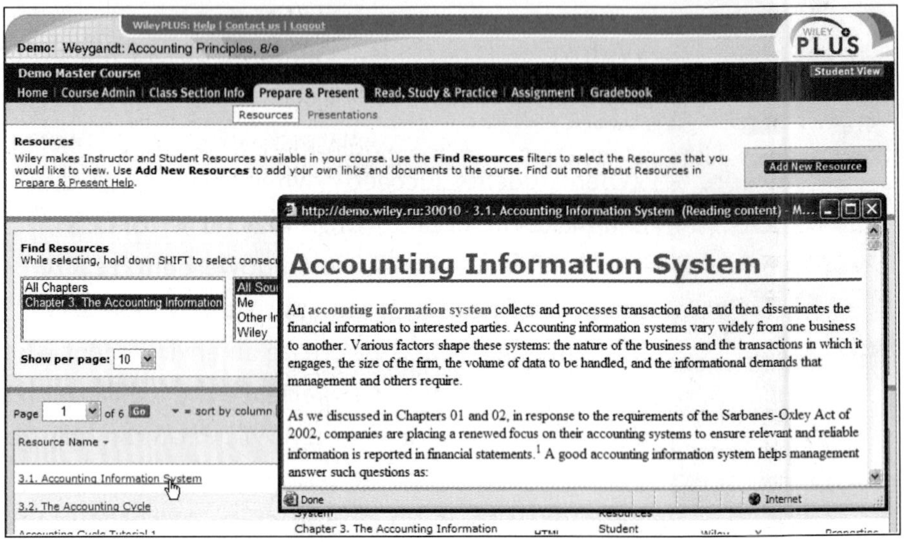

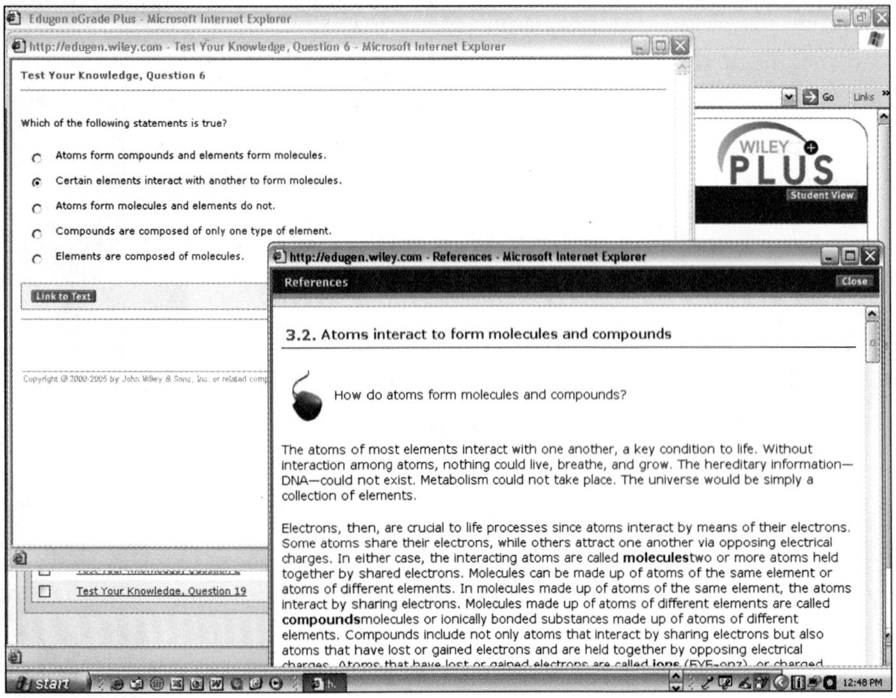

Create Assignments

Automate the assigning and grading of homework or quizzes by using the provided question banks, or by writing your own. Student results will be automatically graded and recorded in your gradebook. *WileyPLUS* also links homework problems to relevant sections of the online text, hints, or solutions—context-sensitive help where students need it most!

in your class each day. With Wiley**PLUS** you will:

Track Student Progress

Keep track of your students' progress via an instructor's gradebook, which allows you to analyze individual and overall class results. This gives you an accurate and realistic assessment of your students' progress and level of understanding.

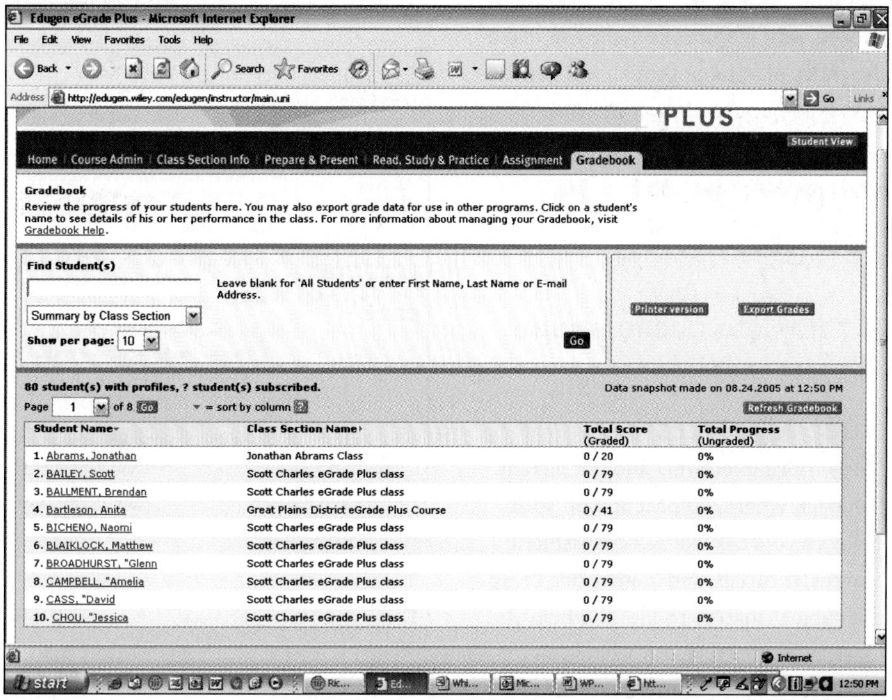

Now Available with WebCT and Blackboard!

Now you can seamlessly integrate all of the rich content and resources available with *WileyPLUS* with the power and convenience of your WebCT or Blackboard course. You and your students get the best of both worlds with single sign-on, an integrated gradebook, list of assignments and roster, and more. If your campus is using another course management system, contact your local Wiley Representative.

"I studied more for this class than I would have without *WileyPLUS*."

Melissa Lawler, *Western Washington Univ.*

For more information on what *WileyPLUS* can do to help your students reach their potential, please visit

www.wiley.com/college/wileyplus

82% of students surveyed said it made them better prepared for tests. *

* Based on a spring 2005 survey of 972 student users of *WileyPLUS*

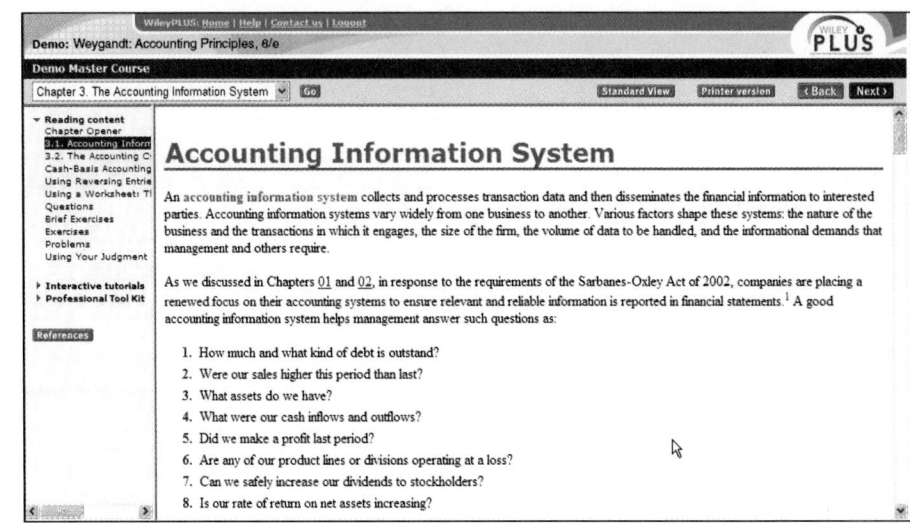

8th Edition

Accounting Principles

Jerry J. Weygandt PhD, CPA

Arthur Andersen Alumni Professor of Accounting
University of Wisconsin
Madison, Wisconsin

Donald E. Kieso PhD, CPA

KPMG Emeritus Professor of Accountancy
Northern Illinois University
DeKalb, Illinois

Paul D. Kimmel PhD, CPA

Associate Professor of Accounting
University of Wisconsin—Milwaukee
Milwaukee, Wisconsin

BICENTENNIAL 1807 WILEY 2007 BICENTENNIAL

John Wiley & Sons, Inc.

Dedicated to
Amaya, Christina, and Max, and their grandmother Enid
Morgan, Cole, and Erin, and their grandmother Donna
Croix, Marais, and Kale, and their mother Merlynn

Publisher Donald Fowley
Executive Editor Christopher DeJohn
Associate Editor Brian Kamins
Executive Marketing Manager Clay Stone
Senior Production Editor Valerie A. Vargas
Senior Media Editor Allie K. Morris
Development Editor Ann Torbert
Production Management Ingrao Associates
Creative Director Harry Nolan
Senior Designer Madelyn Lesure
Project Editor Ed Brislin
Text and Cover Designer Jerry Wilke
Senior Photo Editor Elle Wagner
Senior Illustration Editor Sandra Rigby
Editorial Assistant Karolina Zarychta
Marketing Assistant Tierra Morgan
Cover Photo © Peter Turner/The Image Bank/Getty Images

This book was set in Times Ten by GTS/Techbooks and printed and bound by Von Hoffmann Press.
The cover was printed by Von Hoffmann Press.

We are grateful for permission to use the following material: The PepsiCo logo throughout the text and the PepsiCo 2005 Annual Report in Appendix A. Pepsi is a registered trademark of PepsiCo, Inc. Used with permission. The Coca-Cola 2005 Annual Report in Appendix B: Printed with permission of The Coca-Cola Company.

ISBN: 978-0471-98019-3

Printed in the United States of America

10 9 8 7 6 5 4 3 2 1

STUDENT OWNERS MANUAL

How to Use the Study Aids in This Book

Chapter 7

Accounting Information Systems

STUDY OBJECTIVES

After studying this chapter, you should be able to:

1 Identify the basic concepts of an accounting information system.
2 Describe the nature and purpose of a subsidiary ledger.
3 Explain how companies use special journals in journalizing.
4 Indicate how companies post a multi-column journal.

✓ The Navigator

✓ The Navigator

Scan **Study Objectives**	■
Read **Feature Story**	■
Read **Preview**	■
Read text and answer **Before You Go On** p. 297 ■ p. 311 ■	
Work **Demonstration Problem**	■
Review **Summary of Study Objectives**	■
Answer **Self-Study Questions**	■
Complete **Assignments**	■

The Navigator is a learning system designed to guide you through the chapter and help you succeed in learning the material. It consists of (1) a checklist at the beginning of the chapter, which outlines text features and study aids you will need, and (2) a series of check boxes that prompt you to use the chapter's learning aids and set priorities as you study.

Feature Story

QUICKBOOKS® HELPS THIS RETAILER SELL GUITARS

Starting a small business requires many decisions. For example, you have to decide where to locate, how much space you need, how much inventory to have, how many employees to hire, and where to advertise. Small business owners are typically so concerned about the product and sales side of their business that they often do not give enough thought to something that is critical to their success—how to keep track of financial results.

Small business owners today can choose either manual or computerized accounting systems. For example, Paul and Laura West are the owners of the first independent dealership of Carvin guitars and professional audio equipment. When they founded their company, in Sacramento, California, they

290

The **Feature Story** helps you picture how the chapter topic relates to the real world of accounting and business. References to the Feature Story throughout the chapter will help you put new ideas in context, organize them, and remember them.

Study Objectives at the beginning of each chapter give you a framework for learning the specific concepts in the chapter. Each study objective reappears in the margin where the concept is discussed. You can review the study objectives in the **Summary** at the end of the chapter text.

decided to purchase a computerized accounting system that would integrate many aspects of their retail operations. They wanted their accounting software to manage their inventory of guitars and amplifiers, ring up sales, record and report financial data, and process credit card and debit card transactions. They evaluated a number of options and chose QuickBooks® by Intuit Inc.

QuickBooks®, like most other popular software packages, has programs designed for the needs of a specific business, which in this case is retailing. This QuickBooks® retailing package automatically collects sales information from its point-of-sale scanning devices. It also keeps track of inventory levels and automatically generates purchase orders for popular items when re-order points are reached. It even supports sales efforts by compiling a customer database from which the Wests send out targeted direct mailings to potential customers. The computerized system enables data files to be emailed to the company's accountant. This keeps costs down and makes it easier and more efficient to generate financial reports as needed. The Wests believe that the investment in the computerized system has saved them time and money and allowed them to spend more time on other aspects of their business.

Source: Intuit Inc., "QuickBooks® and ProAdvisor® Help Make Guitar Store a Hit," *Journal of Accountancy*, May 2006, p. 101.

✓ The Navigator

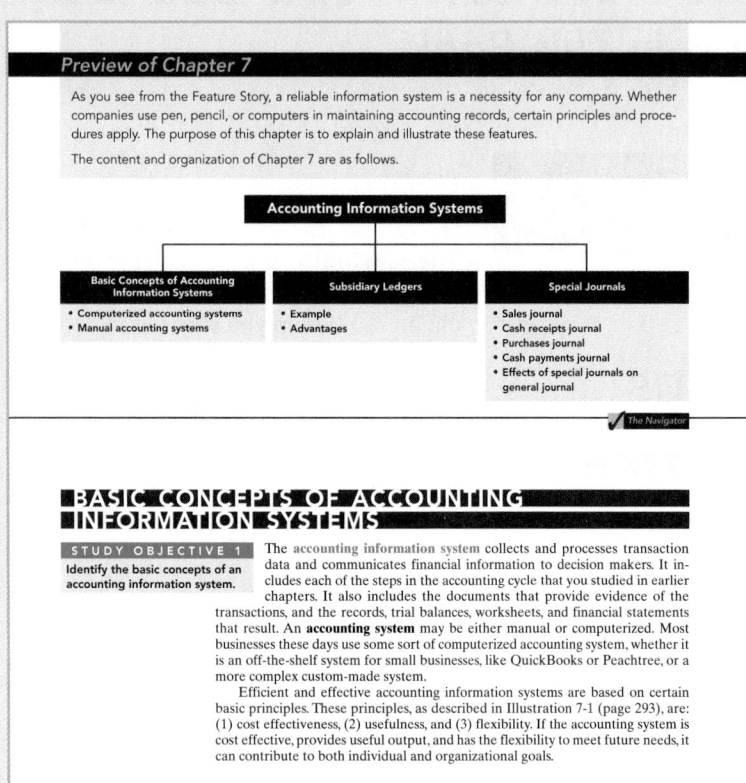

Preview of Chapter 7

As you see from the Feature Story, a reliable information system is a necessity for any company. Whether companies use pen, pencil, or computers in maintaining accounting records, certain principles and procedures apply. The purpose of this chapter is to explain and illustrate these features.

The content and organization of Chapter 7 are as follows.

Accounting Information Systems

Basic Concepts of Accounting Information Systems	Subsidiary Ledgers	Special Journals
• Computerized accounting systems • Manual accounting systems	• Example • Advantages	• Sales journal • Cash receipts journal • Purchases journal • Cash payments journal • Effects of special journals on general journal

The Navigator

The **Preview** links the Feature Story with the major topics of the chapter and describes the purpose of the chapter.

A **graphic outline** provides a visual preview of the chapter topics. Together, the narrative and visual previews help you organize the information you are learning.

BASIC CONCEPTS OF ACCOUNTING INFORMATION SYSTEMS

STUDY OBJECTIVE 1

Identify the basic concepts of an accounting information system.

The accounting information system collects and processes transaction data and communicates financial information to decision makers. It includes each of the steps in the accounting cycle that you studied in earlier chapters. It also includes the documents that provide evidence of the transactions, and the records, trial balances, worksheets, and financial statements that result. An **accounting system** may be either manual or computerized. Most businesses these days use some sort of computerized accounting system, whether it is an off-the-shelf system for small businesses, like QuickBooks or Peachtree, or a more complex custom-made system.

Efficient and effective accounting information systems are based on certain basic principles. These principles, as described in Illustration 7-1 (page 293), are: (1) cost effectiveness, (2) usefulness, and (3) flexibility. If the accounting system is cost effective, provides useful output, and has the flexibility to meet future needs, it can contribute to both individual and organizational goals.

Study Objectives reappear in the margins next to the text discussion of the related topic. End-of-chapter assignments are keyed to study objectives.

Helpful Hints in the margins further clarify concepts being discussed. They are like having an instructor with you as you read.

Ethics Notes point out ethical issues related to the nearby text discussion.

202 Chapter 5 Accounting for Merchandising Operations

HELPFUL HINT

The merchandiser credits the Sales account only for sales of goods held for resale. Sales of assets not held for resale, such as equipment or land, are credited directly to the asset account.

For internal decision-making purposes, merchandising companies may use more than one sales account. For example, PW Audio Supply may decide to keep separate sales accounts for its sales of TV sets, DVD recorders, and satellite radio receivers. Wal-Mart might use separate accounts for sporting goods, children's clothing, and hardware—or it might have even more narrowly defined accounts. By using separate sales accounts for major product lines, rather than a single combined sales account, company management can more closely monitor sales trends and respond more strategically to changes in sales patterns. For example, if HDTV sales are increasing while DVD-player sales are decreasing, PW Audio Supply might reevaluate both its advertising and pricing policies on these items to ensure they are optimal.

ETHICS NOTE

Many companies are trying to improve the quality of their financial reporting. For example, General Electric now provides more detail on its revenues and operating profits.

On its income statement presented to outside investors, a merchandising company normally would provide only a single sales figure—the sum of all of its individual sales accounts. This is done for two reasons. First, providing detail on all of its individual sales accounts would add considerable length to its income statement. Second, companies do not want their competitors to know the details of their operating results. However, Microsoft recently expanded its disclosure of revenue from three to five types. The reason: The additional categories will better enable financial statement users to evaluate the growth of the company's consumer and Internet businesses.

Sales Returns and Allowances

We now look at the "flipside" of purchase returns and allowances, which the seller records as sales returns and allowances. PW Audio Supply's entries to record credit for returned goods involve (1) an increase in Sales Returns and Allowances and a decrease in Accounts Receivable at the $300 selling price, and (2) an increase in

ETHICS INSIGHT

Curbing Fraudulent Activity with Software

The Sarbanes-Oxley Act (SOX) of 2002 requires that companies demonstrate that they have adequate controls in place to detect significant fraudulent behavior by employees. As of November 2005 about 15% of publicly traded companies reported at least one material weakness in their controls that needed to be remedied.

The SOX requirements have created a huge market for software that can monitor and trace every recorded transaction and adjusting entry. This enables companies to pinpoint who used the accounting system and *when* they used it. These systems also require "electronic signatures" by employees for all significant transactions. Such signatures verify that employees have followed all required procedures, and that all actions are properly authorized. SOX-related technology spending was estimated to be approximately $2 billion in 2005. One firm that specializes in compliance software had 10 clients prior to SOX and 250 after SOX.

Source: W. M. Bulkeley and C. Forelle, "Anti-Crime Program: How Corporate Scandals Gave Tech Firms a New Business Line," *Wall Street Journal*, December 9, 2005, p. A1.

? Why might this software help reduce fraudulent activity by employees?

***Insight* examples** give you more glimpses into how actual companies make decisions using accounting information. These high-interest boxes focus on various themes—ethics, international, investor concerns, and management.

A **critical thinking question** asks you to apply your accounting learning to the story in the example. *Guideline answers* appear at the end of the chapter.

Accounting Across the Organization examples show the use of accounting by people in non-accounting functions—such as finance, marketing, or management.

Guideline answers to the critical thinking questions appear at the end of the chapter.

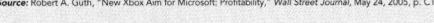

ACCOUNTING ACROSS THE ORGANIZATION

New Xbox Contributes to Profitability

Bryan Lee is head of finance at Microsoft's Home and Entertainment Division. In recent years the division has lost over $4 billion, mostly due to losses on the original Xbox videogame player. With the new Xbox 360 videogame player, Mr. Lee hopes the division will become profitable. He has set strict goals for sales, revenue, and profit. "A manager seeking to spend more on a feature such as a disk drive has to find allies in the group to cut spending elsewhere, or identify new revenue to offset the increase," he explains.

For example, Microsoft originally designed the new Xbox to have 256 megabytes of memory. But the design department said that amount of memory wouldn't support the best special effects. The purchasing department said that adding more memory would cost $30—which is 10% of the estimated selling price of $300. But the marketing department "determined that adding the memory would let Microsoft reduce marketing costs and attract more game developers, boosting royalty revenue. It would also extend the life of the console, generating more sales." Microsoft doubled the memory to 512 megabytes.

Source: Robert A. Guth, "New Xbox Aim for Microsoft: Profitability," *Wall Street Journal*, May 24, 2005, p. C1.

? In what ways is this Microsoft division using accounting to assist in its effort to become more profitable?

Review It questions marked with the PepsiCo icon direct you to find information in PepsiCo, Inc.'s 2005 annual report, printed in Appendix A. Answers to these questions appear on the last page of the chapter.

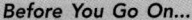

Before You Go On...

REVIEW IT

1. What are the two criteria for classifying a debt as a current liability?
2. Identify the liabilities classified as current by PepsiCo. The answer to this question appears on page 511.
3. What entries does a company make for an interest-bearing note payable?
4. How do retailers record sales taxes? Identify three unearned revenues.
5. How may the liquidity of a company be analyzed?
6. What are the accounting guidelines for contingent liabilities?

DO IT

You and several classmates are studying for the next accounting examination. They ask you to answer the following questions: (1) How is the sales tax amount determined when the cash register total includes sales taxes? (2) When should a company record a contingency in the accounts?

Action Plan

- Remove the sales tax from the total sales.
- Identify the criteria for recording and disclosing contingent liabilities.

Solution

(1) First, divide the total proceeds by 100% plus the sales tax percentage to find the sales amount. Second, subtract the sales amount from the total proceeds to determine the sales taxes.
(2) A company should record a contingency when it is *probable* that it will incur a liability *and* it can *reasonably* estimate the amount.

Related exercise material: *BE11-3, BE11-6, E11-3, E11-5, and E11-6.*

The Navigator

Before You Go On sections follow each key topic. **Review It** questions prompt you to stop and review the key points you have just studied. If you cannot answer these questions, you should go back and read the section again.

Brief **Do It** exercises ask you to put to work your newly acquired knowledge. They outline an **Action Plan** necessary to complete the exercise, and they show a **Solution**.

Accounting equation analyses appear next to key journal entries. They will help you understand the impact of an accounting transaction on the components of the accounting equation, on the owner's equity accounts, and on the company's cash flows.

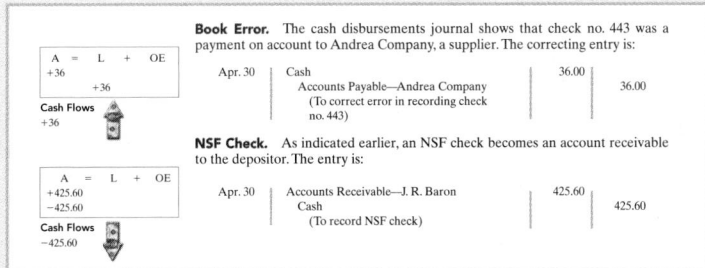

Book Error. The cash disbursements journal shows that check no. 443 was a payment on account to Andrea Company, a supplier. The correcting entry is:

A	=	L	+	OE
+36				
		+36		

Cash Flows
+36

Apr. 30	Cash	36.00	
	Accounts Payable—Andrea Company		36.00
	(To correct error in recording check no. 443)		

NSF Check. As indicated earlier, an NSF check becomes an account receivable to the depositor. The entry is:

A	=	L	+	OE
+425.60				
−425.60				

Cash Flows
−425.60

Apr. 30	Accounts Receivable—J. R. Baron	425.60	
	Cash		425.60
	(To record NSF check)		

Owner's Equity

The content of the owner's equity section varies with the form of business organization. In a proprietorship, there is one capital account. In a partnership, there is a capital account for each partner. Corporations divide owners' equity into two accounts—Capital Stock and Retained Earnings. Corporations record stockholders' investments in the company by debiting an asset account and crediting the Capital Stock account. They record in the Retained Earnings account income retained for use in the business. Corporations combine the Capital Stock and Retained Earnings accounts and report them on the balance sheet as **stockholders' equity**. (We'll learn more about these corporation accounts in later chapters.) Nordstrom, Inc. recently reported its stockholders' equity section as follows.

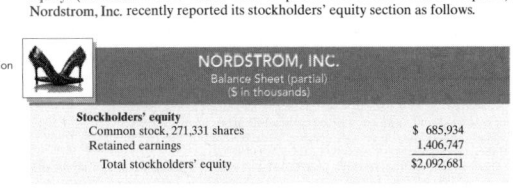

Illustration 4-23
Stockholders' equity section

NORDSTROM, INC.
Balance Sheet (partial)
($ in thousands)

Stockholders' equity	
Common stock, 271,331 shares	$ 685,934
Retained earnings	1,406,747
Total stockholders' equity	$2,092,681

Be sure to read **ALL ABOUT YOU: *Your Personal Balance Sheet*** on page 165 for information on how topics in this chapter apply to you.

Financial statements appear regularly. Those from actual companies are identified by a company logo or a photo.

An ***All About You* feature** links some aspect of the chapter topic to your personal life, and often to some financial situation you are likely to face now or in the near future. We offer our own *opinions* about the situation near the end of the chapter.

all about YOU

Should You Be Carrying Plastic?

Smart business people carefully consider their use of credit. They evaluate who they lend to, and how they finance their own operations. They know that getting overextended on credit can destroy their business.

Individuals need to evaluate their personal credit positions using the same thought processes used by business people. Some of you might consider the idea of not having a credit card a ridiculous proposition. But the reality is that the misuse of credit cards brings financial hardship to millions of Americans each year. Credit card companies aggressively market their cards with images of glamour and happiness. But there isn't much glamour in paying an 18% to 21% interest rate, and there is very little happiness to be found in filing for personal bankruptcy.

About the Numbers

Presented below is a chart that shows the major causes of personal financial problems. Note the excessive use of credit, which is cited as the number-one cause. This often translates into addiction to credit cards.

Causes of Personal Financial Problems

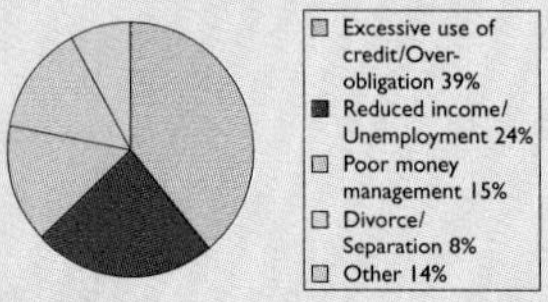

Source: Debt Solutions of America, *www.becomedebtfree.com* (accessed May 2006).

Some Facts

* About 70% of undergraduates at 4-year colleges carry at least one credit card in their own name. Approximately 22% of college students got their first credit cards in high school.
* The average monthly debt on a college student's charge account, according to one study, is close to $2,000.
* In a recent year, Americans charged more than $1 trillion in purchases with their credit cards. That was more than they spent in cash.
* During one quarter in 2006, the percentage of delinquent credit card payments rose to 5% from 4.3%. Card write-offs increased from 5.6% to 6.4%. Until this year, both numbers were declining.
* Significant increases in consumer bankruptcy filings occurred in every region of the country. There were 2,043,535 new filings in 2005, up 31.6% from 1,552,967 in 2004—that is, one in every 53 households filed a bankruptcy petition.

What Do You Think?

Should you cut up your credit card(s)?

YES: Americans are carrying huge personal debt burdens. Credit cards encourage unnecessary, spontaneous expenditures. The interest rates on credit cards are extremely high, which causes debt problems to escalate exponentially.

NO: Credit cards are a necessity for transactions in today's economy. In fact, many transactions are difficult or impossible to carry out without a credit card. People should learn to use credit cards responsibly.

Sources: Debtsmart, *www.debtsmart.com/pages/debt_stats.html*; Robin Marantz Henig, "Teen Credit Cards Actually Teach Responsibility," *USAToday.com*, July 30, 2001.

Demonstration Problem

WILEY PLUS

Cassandra Wilson Company uses a six-column cash receipts journal with the following columns:

Cash (Dr.)
Sales Discounts (Dr.)
Accounts Receivable (Cr.)
Sales (Cr.)
Other Accounts (Cr.)
Cost of Goods Sold (Dr.) and Merchandise Inventory (Cr.)

Cash receipts transactions for the month of July 2008 are as follows.

July 3 Cash sales total $5,800 (cost, $3,480).
5 Received a check for $6,370 from Jeltz Company in payment of an invoice dated June 26 for $6,500, terms 2/10, n/30.
9 Cassandra Wilson, the proprietor, made an additional investment of $5,000 in cash in the business.
10 Cash sales total $12,519 (cost, $7,511).
12 Received a check for $7,275 from R. Eliot & Co. in payment of a $7,500 invoice dated July 3, terms 3/10, n/30.
15 Received a customer advance of $700 cash for future sales.
20 Cash sales total $15,472 (cost, $9,283).
22 Received a check for $5,880 from Beck Company in payment of $6,000 invoice dated July 13, terms 2/10, n/30.
29 Cash sales total $17,660 (cost, $10,596).
31 Received cash of $200 on interest earned for July.

Instructions

(a) Journalize the transactions in the cash receipts journal.
(b) Contrast the posting of the Accounts Receivable and Other Accounts columns.

action plan

✓ Record all cash receipts in the cash receipts journal.
✓ The "account credited" indicates items posted individually to the subsidiary ledger or general ledger.
✓ Record cash sales in the cash receipts journal—not in the sales journal.
✓ The total debits must equal the total credits.

Solution to Demonstration Problem

(a) CASSANDRA WILSON COMPANY
Cash Receipts Journal

Date	Account Credited	Ref.	Cash Dr.	Sales Discounts Dr.	Accounts Receivable Cr.	Sales Cr.	Other Accoun Cr.
2008							
7/3			5,800			5,800	
5	Jeltz Company		6,370	130	6,500		
9	C. Wilson, Capital		5,000				5,000

A **Demonstration Problem** is a review of key concepts and a warm-up before you begin homework. These sample problems provide you with an **Action Plan** in the margin that lists the strategies needed to approach and solve the problem.

The **Solution to the Demonstration Problem** demonstrates both the form and content of complete answers.

SUMMARY OF STUDY OBJECTIVES

WILEY PLUS

1 **Describe the steps in determining inventory quantities.** The steps are (1) take a physical inventory of goods on hand and (2) determine the ownership of goods in transit or on consignment.

2 **Explain the accounting for inventories and apply the inventory cost flow methods.** The primary basis of accounting for inventories is cost. Cost of goods available for sale includes (a) cost of beginning inventory and (b) cost of goods purchased. The inventory cost flow methods are: specific identification and three assumed cost flow methods—FIFO, LIFO, and average-cost.

3 **Explain the financial effects of the inventory cost flow assumptions.** Companies may allocate the cost of goods available for sale to cost of goods sold and ending inventory by specific identification or by a method based on an assumed cost flow. When prices are rising, the first-in, first-out (FIFO) method results in lower cost of goods sold and higher net income than the other methods. The reverse is true when prices are falling. In the balance sheet, FIFO results in an ending inventory that is closest to current value; inventory under LIFO is the farthest from current value. LIFO results in the lowest income taxes.

4 **Explain the lower-of-cost-or-market basis of accounting for inventories.** Companies may use the lower-of-cost-or-market (LCM) basis when the current replacement cost (market) is less than cost. Under LCM, companies recognize the loss in the period in which the price decline occurs.

5 **Indicate the effects of inventory errors on the financial statements.** *In the income statement of the current year:* (a) An error in beginning inventory will have a reverse effect on net income. (b) An error in ending inventory will have a similar effect on net income. If ending inventory errors are not corrected in the following period, their effect on net income for that period is reversed, and total net income for the two years will be correct.

In the balance sheet: Ending inventory errors will have the same effect on total assets and total stockholders' equity and no effect on liabilities.

6 **Compute and interpret the inventory turnover ratio.** The inventory turnover ratio is cost of goods sold divided by average inventory. To convert it to average days in inventory, divide 365 days by the inventory turnover ratio.

The Navigator

The **Summary of Study Objectives** reviews the main points related to the study objectives. It provides you with an opportunity to review what you have learned and to see how the key topics within the chapter fit together.

GLOSSARY

Accounting information system A system that collects and processes transaction data, and communicates financial information to decision makers. (p. 292).

Accounts payable (creditors') subsidiary ledger A subsidiary ledger that collects transaction data of individual creditors. (p. 295).

Accounts receivable (customers') subsidiary ledger A subsidiary ledger that collects transaction data of individual customers. (p. 295).

Cash payments (disbursements) journal A special journal that records all cash paid. (p. 307).

Cash receipts journal A special journal that records all cash received. (p. 301).

Control account An account in the general ledger that summarizes subsidiary ledger. (p. 295).

Manual accounting system A system in which someone performs each of the steps in the accounting cycle by hand. (p. 295).

Purchases journal A special journal that records all purchases of merchandise on account. (p. 305).

Sales journal A special journal that records all sales of merchandise on account. (p. 299).

Special journal A journal that records similar types of transactions, such as all credit sales. (p. 298).

Subsidiary ledger A group of accounts with a common characteristic. (p. 295).

The **Glossary** defines all the **key terms** and **concepts** introduced in the chapter. Page references help you find any terms you need to study further.

The **WileyPLUS icon** here and throughout the end-of-chapter material identifies resources for further reading, study, and practice that can be accessed via WileyPLUS.

SELF-STUDY QUESTIONS

Answers are at the end of the chapter.

1. The basic principles of an accounting information system include all of the following *except*:
   a. cost effectiveness.
   b. flexibility.
   c. useful output.
   d. periodicity.
2. Which of the following is *not* an advantage of computerized accounting systems?
   a. Data is entered only once in computerized accounting systems.
   b. Computerized accounting systems provide up-to-date information.
   c. Computerized accounting systems eliminate entering of transaction information.
   d. Computerized accounting systems eliminate many errors resulting from human intervention.
3. Which of the following is *incorrect* concerning subsidiary ledgers?
   a. The purchases ledger is a common subsidiary ledger for creditor accounts.
   b. The accounts receivable ledger is a subsidiary ledger.
   c. A subsidiary ledger is a group of accounts with a common characteristic.
   d. An advantage of the subsidiary ledger is that it permits a division of labor in posting.
4. A sales journal will be used for:

	Credit Sales	Cash Sales	Sales Discounts
a.	no	yes	yes
b.	yes	no	yes
c.	yes	no	
d.	yes	yes	

Self-Study Questions provide a practice test, keyed to study objectives, with which you can check your knowledge of important chapter topics. *Answers* appear on the last page of the chapter.

Questions focus your study on understanding concepts and relationships from the chapter. Use them to help prepare for class discussion and tests.

QUESTIONS

1. (a) "The steps in the accounting cycle for a merchandising company are different from the accounting cycle for a service company." Do you agree or disagree? (b) Is the measurement of net income for a merchandising company conceptually the same as for a service company? Explain.
2. Why is the normal operating cycle for a merchandising company likely to be longer than for a service company?
3. (a) How do the components of revenues and expenses differ between merchandising and service companies? (b) Explain the income measurement process in a merchandising company.
4. How does income measurement differ between a merchandising and a service company?
5. When is cost of goods sold determined in a perpetual inventory system?

Give the journal entry on July 24 to record payment of the balance due within the discount period using a perpetual inventory system.

9. Joan Roland believes revenues from credit sales may be earned before they are collected in cash. Do you agree? Explain.
10. (a) What is the primary source document for recording (1) cash sales, (2) credit sales. (b) Using XXs for amounts, give the journal entry for each of the transactions in part (a).
11. A credit sale is made on July 10 for $900, terms 2/10, n/30. On July 12, $100 of goods are returned for credit. Give the journal entry on July 19 to record the receipt of the balance due within the discount period.
12. Explain why the Merchandise Inventory account will usually require adjustment at year-end.

Brief Exercises focus on one study objective at a time. They help build confidence in your basic skills and knowledge.

BRIEF EXERCISES

BE4-1 The steps in using a worksheet are presented in random order below. List the steps in the proper order by placing numbers 1–5 in the blank spaces.

List the steps in preparing a worksheet. (SO 1)

(a) _____ Prepare a trial balance on the worksheet.
(b) _____ Enter adjusted balances.
(c) _____ Extend adjusted balances to appropriate statement columns.
(d) _____ Total the statement columns, compute net income (loss), and complete the worksheet.
(e) _____ Enter adjustment data.

BE4-2 The ledger of Ley Company includes the following unadjusted balances: Prepaid Insurance $3,000, Service Revenue $58,000, and Salaries Expense $25,000. Adjusting entries are required for **(a)** expired insurance $1,200; **(b)** services provided $1,100, but unbilled and uncollected; and **(c)** accrued salaries payable $800. Enter the unadjusted balances and adjustments into a worksheet and complete the worksheet for all accounts. *Note:* You will need to add the following accounts: Accounts Receivable, Salaries Payable, and Insurance Expense.

Prepare partial worksheet. (SO 1)

BE4-3 The following selected accounts appear in the adjusted trial balance columns of the worksheet for Batan Company: Accumulated Depreciation; Depreciation Expense; N. Batan, Capital; N. Batan, Drawing; Service Revenue; Supplies; and Accounts Payable. Indicate the financial statement column (income statement Dr., balance sheet Cr., etc.) to which each balance should be extended.

Identify worksheet columns for selected accounts. (SO 1)

EXERCISES

Analyze statements about accounting and the recording process. (SO 1)

E2-1 Josh Cephus has prepared the following list of stateme

1. An account is an accounting record of either a specific ass
2. An account shows only increases, not decreases, in the item it relates to.
3. Some items, such as Cash and Accounts Receivable, are combined into one account.
4. An account has a left, or credit side, and a right, or debit side.
5. A simple form of an account consisting of just the account title, the left side, and the right side, is called a T-account.

Instructions
Identify each statement as true or false. If false, indicate how to correct the statement.

Identify debits, credits, and normal balances. (SO 2)

E2-2 Selected transactions for D. Reyes, an interior decorator, in her first month of business, are as follows.

Jan. 2 Invested $10,000 cash in business.
3 Purchased used car for $4,000 cash for use in business.
9 Purchased supplies on account for $500.
11 Billed customers $1,800 for services performed.
16 Paid $200 cash for advertising.
20 Received $700 cash from customers billed on January 11.
23 Paid creditor $300 cash on balance owed.
28 Withdrew $1,000 cash for personal use by owner.

Instructions
For each transaction indicate the following.
(a) The basic type of account debited and credited (asset, liability, owner's equity).
(b) The specific account debited and credited (cash, rent expense, service revenue, etc.).
(c) Whether the specific account is increased or decreased.
(d) The normal balance of the specific account.

Exercises are slightly more difficult than Brief Exercises, and may combine two or more study objectives. They help you continue to build confidence in your ability to combine and use the material learned in the chapter.

EXERCISES: SET B

Visit the book's website at **www.wiley.com/college/weygandt**, and choose the Student Companion site, to access Exercise Set B.

A set of **B Exercises**, closely related to the Exercises in the book, appears at the book's *companion website*, for additional practice.

Each **Problem** helps you pull together and apply several concepts from the chapter.

An icon identifies **Exercises** and **Problems** that can be solved using Excel templates at the student website.

Selected problems, identified by this icon, can be solved using the **General Ledger Software (GLS)** package.

Problems marked with the **Peachtree** icon can be worked using *Peachtree Complete Accounting® to Accompany Accounting Principles.*

Check figures in the margin provide key numbers to let you know you're on the right track as you work the problems.

PROBLEMS: SET A

WILEY PLUS

Journalize purchase and sales transactions under a perpetual inventory system.

(SO 2, 3)

P5-1A Sansomite Co. distributes suitcases to retail stores and extends credit terms of 1/10, n/30 to all of its customers. At the end of June, Sansomite's inventory consisted of 40 suitcases purchased at $30 each. During the month of July the following merchandising transactions occurred.

July 1 Purchased 60 suitcases on account for $30 each from Trunk Manufacturers, FOB destination, terms 2/10, n/30. The appropriate party also made a cash payment of $100 for freight on this date.
3 Sold 40 suitcases on account to Satchel World for $50 each.
9 Paid Trunk Manufacturers in full.
12 Received payment in full from Satchel World.
17 Sold 30 suitcases on account to The Going Concern for $50 each.
18 Purchased 60 suitcases on account for $1,700 from Kingman Manufacturers, FOB shipping point, terms 1/10, n/30. The appropriate party also made a cash payment of $100 for freight on this date.
20 Received $300 credit (including freight) for 10 suitcases returned to Kingman Manufacturers.
21 Received payment in full from The Going Concern.
22 Sold 45 suitcases on account to Fly-By-Night for $50 each.
30 Paid Kingman Manufacturers in full.
31 Granted Fly-By-Night $200 credit for 4 suitcases returned costing $120.

Sansomite's chart of accounts includes the following: No. 101 Cash, No. 112 Accounts Receivable, No. 120 Merchandise Inventory, No. 201 Accounts Payable, No. 401 Sales, No. 412 Sales Returns and Allowances, No. 414 Sales Discounts, No. 505 Cost of Goods Sold.

Instructions

Journalize the transactions for the month of July for Sansomite using a perpetual inventory system.

Journalize, post, and prepare a partial income statement.

(SO 2, 3, 5, 6)

GLS Peachtree

P5-2A Olaf Distributing Company completed the following merchandising transactions in the month of April. At the beginning of April, the ledger of Olaf showed Cash of $9,000 and M. Olaf, Capital of $9,000.

Apr. 2 Purchased merchandise on account from Dakota Supply Co. $6,900, terms 1/10, n/30.
4 Sold merchandise on account $5,500, FOB destination, terms 1/10, n/30. The cost of the merchandise sold was $4,100.
5 Paid $240 freight on April 4 sale.
6 Received credit from Dakota Supply Co. for merchandise returned $500.
11 Paid Dakota Supply Co. in full, less discount.
13 Received collections in full, less discounts, from customers billed on April 4.
14 Purchased merchandise for cash $3,800.
16 Received refund from supplier for returned goods on cash purchase of April 14, $500.
18 Purchased merchandise from Skywalker Distributors $4,500, FOB shipping point, terms 2/10, n/30.
20 Paid freight on April 18 purchase $100.
23 Sold merchandise for cash $6,400. The merchandise sold had a cost of $5,120.
26 Purchased merchandise for cash $2,300.
27 Paid Skywalker Distributors in full, less discount.
29 Made refunds to cash customers for defective merchandise $90. The returned merchandise had a scrap value of $30.
30 Sold merchandise on account $3,700, terms n/30. The cost of the merchandise sold was $2,800.

Olaf Company's chart of accounts includes the following: No. 101 Cash, No. 112 Accounts Receivable, No. 120 Merchandise Inventory, No. 201 Accounts Payable, No. 301 M. Olaf, Capital, No. 401 Sales, No. 412 Sales Returns and Allowances, No. 414 Sales Discounts, No. 505 Cost of Goods Sold, and No. 644 Freight-out.

Instructions

(a) Journalize the transactions using a perpetual inventory system.
(b) Enter the beginning cash and capital balances, and post the transactions. (Use J1 for the journal reference.)
(c) Prepare the income statement through gross profit for the month of April 2008.

PROBLEMS: SET B

Journalize purchase and sales transactions under a perpetual inventory system.

(SO 2, 3)

P5-1B Sorvino Book Warehouse distributes hardcover books to retail stores and extends credit terms of 2/10, n/30 to all of its customers. At the end of May, Sorvino's inventory consisted of 240 books purchased at $1,200. During the month of June the following merchandising transactions occurred.

June 1 Purchased 180 books on account for $5 each from Atkinson Publishers, FOB destination, terms 2/10, n/30. The appropriate party also made a cash payment of $50 for the freight on this date.
3 Sold 120 books on account to Readers-R-Us for $10 each.
6 Received $50 credit for 10 books returned to Atkinson Publishers.
9 Paid Atkinson Publishers in full, less discount.
15 Received payment in full from Readers-R-Us.
17 Sold 150 books on account to Bargain Books for $10 each.
20 Purchased 120 books on account for $5 each from Bookem Publishers, FOB destination, terms 2/15, n/30. The appropriate party also made a cash payment of $50 for the freight on this date.
24 Received payment in full from Bargain Books.
26 Paid Bookem Publishers in full, less discount.
28 Sold 110 books on account to Read-n-Weep Bookstore for $10 each.
30 Granted Read-n-Weep Bookstore $150 credit for 15 books returned costing $75.

Sorvino Book Warehouse's chart of accounts includes the following: No. 101 Cash, No. 112 Accounts Receivable, No. 120 Merchandise Inventory, No. 201 Accounts Payable, No. 401 Sales, No. 412 Sales Returns and Allowances, No. 414 Sales Discounts, No. 505 Cost of Goods Sold.

Instructions

Journalize the transactions for the month of June for Sorvino Book Warehouse using a perpetual inventory system.

In the book, two similar sets of **Problems—A** and **B**—are keyed to the same study objectives.

An additional parallel set of **C Problems** appears at the book's companion site.

Comprehensive Problems in six chapters combine concepts covered across multiple chapters.

PROBLEMS: SET C

Visit the book's website at **www.wiley.com/college/weygandt**, and choose the Student Companion site, to access Problem Set C.

COMPREHENSIVE PROBLEM: CHAPTERS 2 TO 4

Julie Molony opened Julie's Maids Cleaning Service on July 1, 2008. During July, the company completed the following transactions.

July 1 Invested $14,000 cash in the business.
1 Purchased a used truck for $10,000, paying $3,000 cash and the balance on account.
3 Purchased cleaning supplies for $800 on account.
5 Paid $1,800 on a one-year insurance policy, effective July 1.
12 Billed customers $3,800 for cleaning services.
18 Paid $1,000 of amount owed on truck, and $400 of amount owed on cleaning supplies.
20 Paid $1,600 for employee salaries.
21 Collected $1,400 from customers billed on July 12.
25 Billed customers $1,500 for cleaning services.

CONTINUING COOKIE CHRONICLE

CCC1 Natalie Koebel spent much of her childhood learning the art of cookie-making from her grandmother. They passed many happy hours mastering every type of cookie imaginable and later creating new recipes that were both healthy and delicious. Now at the start of her second year in college, Natalie is investigating various possibilities for starting her own business as part of the requirements of the entrepreneurship program in which she is enrolled.

A long-time friend insists that Natalie has to somehow include cookies in her business plan. After a series of brainstorming sessions, Natalie settles on the idea of operating a cookie-making school. She will start on a part-time basis and offer her services in people's homes. Now that she has started thinking about it, the possibilities seem endless. During the fall, she will concentrate on holiday cookies. She will offer individual lessons and group sessions (which will probably be more entertainment than education for the participants). Natalie also decides to include children in her target market.

The first difficult decision is coming up with the perfect name for her business. In the end, she settles on "Cookie Creations" and then moves on to more important issues.

Instructions

(a) What form of business organization—proprietorship, partnership, or corporation—do you recommend that Natalie use for her business? Discuss the benefits and weaknesses of each form and give the reasons for your choice.

(b) Will Natalie need accounting information? If yes, what information will she need and why? How often will she need this information?

(c) Identify specific asset, liability, and equity accounts that Cookie Creations will likely use to record its business transactions.

(d) Should Natalie open a separate bank account for the business? Why or why not?

The **Continuing Cookie Chronicle** exercise follows the continuing saga of accounting for a small business begun by an entrepreneurial student.

BROADENING YOUR PERSPECTIVE

FINANCIAL REPORTING AND ANALYSIS

Financial Reporting Problem

PepsiCo, Inc.

BYP1-1 The actual financial statements of PepsiCo, as presented in the company's 2005 Annual Report, are contained in Appendix A (at the back of the textbook).

Instructions

Refer to PepsiCo's financial statements and answer the following questions.

(a) What were PepsiCo's total assets at December 31, 2005? At December 25, 2004?

(b) How much cash (and cash equivalents) did PepsiCo have on December 31, 2005?

(c) What amount of accounts payable did PepsiCo report on December 31, 2005? On December 25, 2004?

(d) What were PepsiCo's net sales in 2003? In 2004? In 2005?

(e) What is the amount of the change in PepsiCo's net income

The **Broadening Your Perspective** section helps you pull together concepts from the chapter and apply them to real-world business situations.

The **Financial Reporting Problem** focuses on reading and understanding the financial statements of PepsiCo, Inc., which are printed in Appendix A.

Comparative Analysis Problem

PepsiCo, Inc. vs. The Coca-Cola Company

BYP5-2 PepsiCo's financial statements are presented in Appendix A. Coca-Cola's financial statements are presented in Appendix B.

Instructions

(a) Based on the information contained in these financial statements, determine each of the following for each company.
  (1) Gross profit for 2005.
  (2) Gross profit rate for 2005.
  (3) Operating income for 2005.
  (4) Percent change in operating income from 2004 to 2005.

(b) What conclusions concerning the relative profitability of the two companies can you draw from these data?

A **Comparative Analysis Problem** compares and contrasts the financial reporting of PepsiCo with its competitor The Coca-Cola Company.

Exploring the Web

BYP5-3 No financial decision maker should ever rely solely on the financial information reported in the annual report to make decisions. It is important to keep abreast of financial news. This activity demonstrates how to search for financial news on the Web.

Address: biz.yahoo.com/i, or go to **www.wiley.com/college/weygandt**

Steps:

1. Type in either PepsiCo or Coca-Cola.
2. Choose **News**.
3. Select an article that sounds interesting to you.

Instructions

(a) What was the source of the article? (For example, Reuters, Businesswire, PR Newswire.)

(b) Pretend that you are a personal financial planner and that one of your clients owns stock in the company. Write a brief memo to your client, summarizing the article and explaining the implications of the article for their investment.

Exploring the Web exercises guide you to websites where you can find and analyze information related to the chapter topic.

CRITICAL THINKING

Decision Making Across the Organization

BYP5-4 Three years ago, Carrie Dungy and her brother-in-law Luke Barber opened FedCo Department Store. For the first two years, business was good, but the following condensed income results for 2007 were disappointing.

FEDCO DEPARTMENT STORE
Income Statement
For the Year Ended December 31, 2007

Net sales		$700,000
Cost of goods sold		553,000
Gross profit		147,000
Operating expenses		
Selling expenses	$100,000	
Administrative expenses	20,000	120,000
Net income		$ 27,000

Decision Making Across the Organization helps you build decision-making skills by analyzing accounting information in a less structured situation. These cases require teams of students to evaluate a manager's decision or lead to a decision among alternative courses of action.

Communication Activity

BYP8-5 As a new auditor for the CPA firm of Croix, Marais, and Kale, you have been assigned to review the internal controls over mail cash receipts of Manhattan Company. Your review reveals the following: Checks are promptly endorsed "For Deposit Only," but no list of the checks is prepared by the person opening the mail. The mail is opened either by the cashier or by the employee who maintains the accounts receivable records. Mail receipts are deposited in the bank weekly by the cashier.

Instructions

Write a letter to Jerry Mays, owner of the Manhattan Company, explaining the weaknesses in internal control and your recommendations for improving the system.

Communication Activities help you build business communication skills by asking you to engage in real-world business situations using writing, speaking, or presentation skills.

Ethics Cases ask you to reflect on typical ethical dilemmas, analyze the stakeholders and the issues involved, and decide on an appropriate course of action.

Ethics Case

BYP3-6 Bluestem Company is a pesticide manufacturer. Its sales declined greatly this year due to the passage of legislation outlawing the sale of several of Bluestem's chemical pesticides. In the coming year, Bluestem will have environmentally safe and competitive chemicals to replace these discontinued products. Sales in the next year are expected to greatly exceed any prior year's. The decline in sales and profits appears to be a one-year aberration. But even so, the company president fears a large dip in the current year's profits. He believes that such a dip could cause a significant drop in the market price of Bluestem's stock and make the company a takeover target.

To avoid this possibility, the company president calls in Cathi Bell, controller, to discuss this period's year-end adjusting entries. He urges her to accrue every possible revenue and to defer as many expenses as possible. He says to Cathi, "We need the revenues this year, and next year can easily absorb expenses deferred from this year. We can't let our stock price be hammered down!" Cathi didn't get around to recording the adjusting entries until January 17, but she dated the entries December 31 as if they were recorded then. Cathi also made every effort to comply with the president's request.

Instructions

(a) Who are the stakeholders in this situation?
(b) What are the ethical considerations of (1) the president's request and (2) Cathi's dating the adjusting entries December 31?
(c) Can Cathi accrue revenues and defer expenses and still be ethical?

The **"All About You" Activity** offers another opportunity to explore the All About You topic in a homework assignment.

"All About You" Activity

BYP3-7 In the **All About You** feature in this chapter (p. 113), you learned how important it is that companies report or disclose information about all liabilities, including potential liabilities related to environmental clean-up. There are many situations in which you will be asked to provide personal financial information about your assets, liabilities, revenue, and expenses. Sometimes you will face difficult decisions regarding what to disclose and how to disclose it.

Instructions

Suppose that you are putting together a loan application to purchase a home. Based on your income and assets, you qualify for the mortgage loan, but just barely. How would you address each of the following situations in reporting your financial position for the loan application? Provide responses for each of the following questions.

(a) You signed a guarantee for a bank loan that a friend took out for $20,000. If your friend doesn't pay, you will have to pay. Your friend has made all of the payments so far, and it appears he will be able to pay in the future.
(b) You were involved in an auto accident in which you were at fault. There is the possibility that you may have to pay as much as $50,000 as part of a settlement. The issue will not be resolved before the bank processes your mortgage request.
(c) The company at which you work isn't doing very well, and it has recently laid off employees. You are still employed, but it is quite possible that you will lose your job in the next few months.

Answers to Insight and Accounting Across the Organization Questions

p. 386 Be Sure to Read the Fine Print
Q: Why are credit card companies willing to offer relaxed repayment options?
A: *Credit card companies generate their income primarily from interest charges on cardholders' balances. The larger the outstanding balances, the greater the interest income.*

p. 392 When Investors Ignore Warning Signs
Q: When would it be appropriate for a company to lower its allowance for doubtful accounts as a percentage of its receivables?
A: *It could do so if the company's collection experience had improved, or was expected to improve, and therefore the company expected lower defaults as a percentage of receivables.*

p. 395 How Does a Credit Card Work?
Q: Assume that Nordstrom prepares a bank reconciliation at the end of each month. If some credit card sales have not been processed by the bank, how should Nordstrom treat these transactions on its bank reconciliation?
A: *Nordstrom would treat the credit card receipts as deposits in transit. It has already recorded the receipts as cash. Its bank will increase Nordstrom's cash account when it receives the receipts.*

p. 400 Who Gets Credit?
Q: How would reported net income likely differ during the first year of this promotion if Mitsubishi used the direct write-off method versus the allowance method?
A: *Under the direct write-off method, Mitsubishi would not record bad debt expense until a customer defaulted on a loan. Under the allowance method, it would estimate how many of its loans would default rather than waiting until they default. The direct write-off method would have resulted in higher net income during the first year of the promotion.*

Authors' Comments on *All About You:* Should You Be Carrying Plastic? (p. 403)

We aren't going to tell you to cut up your credit card. Well, we aren't going to tell *all* of you to do so. Credit cards, when used properly, can serve a very useful purpose. They provide great convenience, are widely accepted, and can be a source of security in an emergency. But too many Americans use credit cards inappropriately. When businesses purchase short-term items such as inventory and supplies, they use short-term credit, which they expect to pay back very quickly. The same should be true of your credit card. When you make purchases of everyday items, you should completely pay off those items within a month or two. If you don't, you are living beyond your means, and you will soon dig yourself a deep financial pit.

Longer-term items should not be purchased with credit cards, since the interest rate is too high. If you currently have a large balance on your credit card(s), we encourage you to cut up your card(s) until you have paid off your balance(s).

Answers to Insight and Accounting Across the Organization questions offer guideline answers for questions in the boxed real-world examples.

Authors' Comments on *All About You* provide the author's opinions and further discussion about financial literacy topic in the chapter.

The **Answer to PepsiCo Review It Question**, based on the PepsiCo financial statements, appears here.

Answers to Self-Study Questions provide feedback on your understanding of the chapter's basic concepts.

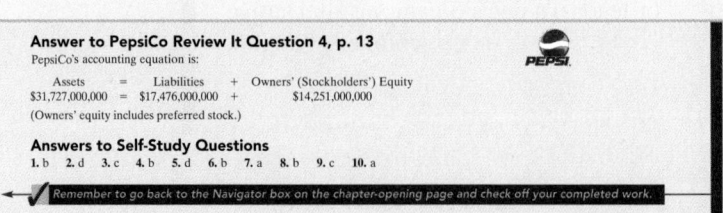

Answer to PepsiCo Review It Question 4, p. 13

PepsiCo's accounting equation is:

Assets	=	Liabilities	+	Owners' (Stockholders') Equity
$31,727,000,000	=	$17,476,000,000	+	$14,251,000,000

(Owners' equity includes preferred stock.)

Answers to Self-Study Questions

1. b **2.** d **3.** c **4.** b **5.** d **6.** b **7.** a **8.** b **9.** c **10.** a

Remember to go back to the Navigator box on the chapter-opening page and check off your completed work.

After you complete your homework assignments, it's a good idea to go back to **The Navigator** checklist at the start of the chapter to see if you have used all the chapter's study aids.

SPECIAL STUDENT SUPPLEMENTS

That Help You Get the Best Grade You Can

The Accounting Principles Website

The book's website at **www.wiley.com/college/weygandt** provides a wealth of materials that will help you develop a conceptual understanding and increase your ability to solve problems. For example, you will find PowerPoint™ presentations and web quizzing. Be sure to check the site often.

Working Papers

Working papers are partially completed accounting forms (templates) for all end-of-chapter brief exercises, exercises, problems, and cases. They are a convenient resource for organizing and completing homework assignments, and they demonstrate how to correctly set up solution formats. The Working Papers are available in various groupings, so take care to order the set that matches the book you are using (check the number of chapters in your book). Also available on CD-ROM is an electronic version of the print working papers, which are Excel-formatted templates that will help you learn to properly format and present end-of-chapter textbook solutions.

Study Guide

The Study Guide is a comprehensive review of accounting. It guides you through chapter content, tied to study objectives. Each chapter of the Study Guide includes a chapter review (20 to 30 key points); a demonstration problem; and for extra practice, true/false, multiple-choice, and matching questions, and additional exercises, with solutions. The Study Guide is an excellent tool for use on a regular basis during the course and also when preparing for exams. The Study Guide is available in two volumes, Volume I for Chapters 1–12 and Volume II for Chapters 13–26.

Problem-Solving Survival Guide

This tutorial is designed to improve your success rates in solving homework assignments and exam questions. Each chapter includes an overview of key topics; a purpose statement and link to study objectives for each homework assignment; numerous review tips to alert you to common pitfalls and misconceptions; and reminders to concepts and principles. Multiple-choice exercises and cases similar to common homework assignments or exam questions enhance your problem-solving proficiency. Solutions not only explain answers but also discuss an approach to similar types of accounting problems. The Problem-Solving Survival Guide comes in two volumes, Volume I (Chapters 1–12) and Volume II (Chapters 13–26).

General Ledger Software for Windows

GLS The General Ledger Software program allows you to use a computerized accounting system to solve the end-of-chapter text problems that are identified by the icon shown here.

Peachtree Complete® Accounting

A workbook and accompanying CD teach you how to use Peachtree Complete® Accounting Software. Selected problems in the book, denoted by the Peachtree icon, can be solved using this supplementary software package.

Solving Accounting Principles Problems Using Excel

A manual guides you step-by-step from an introduction to computers and Excel, to completion of preprogrammed spreadsheets, to design of your own spreadsheets. Accompanying spreadsheet templates allow you to complete selected end-of-chapter exercises and problems, identified by the icon shown here.

Practice Sets

Practice sets expose you to real-world simulations of maintaining a complete set of accounting records for a business. They integrate the business events, accounting concepts, procedures, and records covered within the textbook, and they reinforce the concepts and procedures learned. Four different practice sets are available: Campus Cycle Shop; Heritage Home Furniture; University Bookstore; and Custom Party Associates.

For more information on any of these student supplements, check with your professor or bookstore, or go to the companion website at **www.wiley.com/college/weygandt**.

ABOUT THE AUTHORS

Jerry J. Weygandt, PhD, CPA, is Arthur Andersen Alumni Professor of Accounting at the University of Wisconsin—Madison. He holds a Ph.D. in accounting from the University of Illinois. Articles by Professor Weygandt have appeared in the *Accounting Review, Journal of Accounting Research, Accounting Horizons, Journal of Accountancy,* and other academic and professional journals. These articles have examined such financial reporting issues as accounting for price-level adjustments, pensions, convertible securities, stock option contracts, and interim reports. Professor Weygandt is author of other accounting and financial reporting books and is a member of the American Accounting Association, the American Institute of Certified Public Accountants, and the Wisconsin Society of Certified Public Accountants. He has seved on numerous committees of the American Accounting Association and as a member of the editorial board of the *Accounting Review*; he also has served as President and Secretary-Treasurer of the American Accounting Association. In addition, he has been actively involved with the American Institute of Certified Public Accountants and has been a member of the Accounting Standards Executive Committee (AcSEC) of that organization. He has served on the FASB task force that examined the reporting issues related to accounting for income taxes and served as a trustee of the Financial Accounting Foundation. Professor Weygandt has received the Chancellor's Award for Excellence in Teaching and the Beta Gamma Sigma Dean's Teaching Award. He is on the board of directors of M & I Bank of Southern Wisconsin. He is the recipient of the Wisconsin Institute of CPA's Outstanding Educator's Award and the Lifetime Achievement Award. In 2001 he received the American Accounting Association's Outstanding Accounting Educator Award.

Donald E. Kieso, PhD, CPA, received his bachelor's degree from Aurora University and his doctorate in accounting from the University of Illinois. He has served as chairman of the Department of Accountancy and is currently the KPMG Emeritus Professor of Accountancy at Northern Illinois University. He has public accounting experience with Price Waterhouse & Co. (San Francisco and Chicago) and Arthur Andersen & Co. (Chicago) and research experience with the Research Division of the American Institute of Certified Public Accountants (New York). He has done postdoctorate work as a Visiting Scholar at the University of California at Berkeley and is a recipient of NIU's Teaching Excellence Award and four Golden Apple Teaching Awards. Professor Kieso is the author of other accounting and business books and is a member of the American Accounting Association, the American Institute of Certified Public Accountants, and the Illinois CPA Society. He has served as a member of the Board of Directors of the Illinois CPA Society, the AACSB's Accounting Accreditation Committees, the State of Illinois Comptroller's Commission, as Secretary-Treasurer of the Federation of Schools of Accountancy, and as Secretary-Treasurer of the American Accounting Association. Professor Kieso is currently serving on the Board of Trustees and Executive Committee of Aurora University, as a member of the Board of Directors of Kishwaukee Community Hospital, and as Treasurer and Director of Valley West Community Hospital. From 1989 to 1993 he served as a charter member of the national Accounting Education Change Commission. He is the recipient of the Outstanding Accounting Educator Award from the Illinois CPA Society, the FSA's Joseph A. Silvoso Award of Merit, the NIU Foundation's Humanitarian Award for Service to Higher Education, a Distinguished Service Award from the Illinois CPA Society, and in 2003 an honorary doctorate from Aurora University.

Paul D. Kimmel, PhD, CPA, received his bachelor's degree from the University of Minnesota and his doctorate in accounting from the University of Wisconsin. He is an Associate Professor at the University of Wisconsin—Milwaukee, and has public accounting experience with Deloitte & Touche (Minneapolis). He was the recipient of the UWM School of Business Advisory Council Teaching Award, the Reggie Taite Excellence in Teaching Award, and a three-time winner of the Outstanding Teaching Assistant Award at the University of Wisconsin. He is also a recipient of the Elijah Watts Sells Award for Honorary Distinction for his results on the CPA exam. He is a member of the American Accounting Association and the Institute of Management Accountants and has published articles in *Accounting Review, Accounting Horizons, Advances in Management Accounting, Managerial Finance, Issues in Accounting Education, Journal of Accounting Education*, as well as other journals. His research interests include accounting for financial instruments and innovation in accounting education. He has published papers and given numerous talks on incorporating critical thinking into accounting education, and helped prepare a catalog of critical thinking resources for the Federated Schools of Accountancy.

HOW DO I LEARN BEST?

This questionnaire aims to find out something about your preferences for the way you work with information. You will have a preferred learning style, and one part of that learning style is your preference for the intake and output of ideas and information.

Choose the answer which best explains your preference. You can select more than one response if a single answer does not match your perception. Leave blank any question that does not apply.

1. You are about to give directions to a person who is standing with you. She is staying in a hotel in town and wants to visit your house later. She has a rental car. You would:
- **a.** draw or provide a map on paper.
- **b.** tell her the directions.
- **c.** write down the directions (without a map).
- **d.** pick her up from the hotel in a car.

2. You are not sure whether a word should be spelled "dependent" or "dependant." You would:
- **c.** look it up in the dictionary.
- **a.** see the word in your mind and choose by the way it looks
- **b.** sound it out in your mind.
- **d.** write both versions down on paper and choose one.

3. You have just received a copy of your itinerary for a world trip. This is of interest to some friends. You would:
- **b.** phone, text, or email them and tell them about it.
- **c.** send them a copy of the printed itinerary.
- **a.** show them on a map of the world.
- **d.** describe what you plan to do at each place on the itinerary.

4. You are going to cook something as a special treat for your family. You would:
- **d.** cook something familiar without the need for instructions.
- **a.** thumb through the cookbook looking for ideas from the pictures.
- **c.** refer to a specific cookbook where there is a good recipe.

5. A group of tourists has been assigned to you to find out about wildlife reserves or parks. You would:
- **d.** drive them to a wildlife reserve or park.
- **a.** show them slides and photographs.
- **c.** give them pamphlets or a book on wildlife reserves or parks.
- **b.** give them a talk on wildlife reserves or parks.

6. You are about to purchase a new CD player. Other than price, what would most influence your decision?
- **b.** The salesperson telling you what you want to know.
- **c.** Reading the details about it.
- **d.** Playing with the controls and listening to it.
- **a.** It looks really smart and fashionable.

7. Recall a time in your life when you learned how to do something like playing a new board game. Try to avoid choosing a very physical skill, e.g. riding a bike. You learned best by:
- **a.** visual clues – pictures, diagrams and charts.
- **c.** written instructions.
- **b.** listening to somebody explaining it.
- **d.** doing it or trying it.

8. You have a knee problem. You would prefer that the doctor:
- **b.** told you what was wrong.
- **a.** showed you a diagram of what was wrong.
- **d.** used a model of a knee to show you what was wrong.

9. You are about to learn to use a new program on a computer. You would:
- **d.** sit down at the keyboard and experiment with the program.
- **c.** read the manual that came with the program.
- **b.** telephone or text a friend and ask questions about the program.

10. You are staying in a hotel and have a rental car. You would like to visit friends whose address/location you do not know. You would like them to:
- **a.** draw you a map on paper or provide a map from the Internet.
- **b.** tell you the directions.
- **c.** write down the directions (without a map).
- **d.** pick you up from the hotel in a car.

11. Apart from the price, what would most influence your decision to buy a particular textbook?
- **d.** You have used a copy before.
- **b.** A friend talking about it.
- **c.** Quickly reading parts of it.
- **a.** The way it looks is appealing.

12. A new movie has arrived in town. What would most influence your decision to go (or not go)?
- **b.** You heard a review about it on the radio.
- **c.** You read a review about it.
- **a.** You saw a preview of it.

13. You prefer a teacher who likes to use:
- **c.** a textbook, handouts, and reading.
- **a.** flow diagrams, charts, and graphs.
- **d.** field trips, models, laboratories, and practical sessions.
- **b.** class or email discussion, online chat groups, and guest speakers.

	a.	**b.**	**c.**	**d.**
Count your choices:	❑	❑	❑	❑
	V	**A**	**R**	**K**

Now match the letter or letters you have recorded most to the same letter or letters in the Learning Styles Chart. You may have more than one learning style preference—many people do. Next to each letter in the chart are suggestions that will refer you to different learning aids throughout this text.

LEARNING STYLES CHART

	Intake: *To take in the information*	*To make a study package*
Visual **V**	• Pay close attention to charts, drawings, and handouts your instructors use. • Underline. • Use different colors. • Use symbols, flow charts, graphs, different arrangements on the page, white spaces.	Convert your lecture notes into "page pictures." To do this: • Use the "Intake" strategies. • Reconstruct images in different ways. • Redraw pages from memory. • Replace words with symbols and initials. • Look at your pages.
Aural **A**	• Attend lectures and tutorials. • Discuss topics with students and instructors. • Explain new ideas to other people. • Use a tape recorder. • Leave spaces in your lecture notes for later recall. • Describe overheads, pictures, and visuals to somebody who was not in class.	You may take poor notes because you prefer to listen. Therefore: • Expand your notes by talking with others and with information from your textbook. • Tape-record summarized notes and listen. • Read summarized notes out loud. • Explain your notes to another "aural" person.
Reading/ Writing **R**	• Use lists and headings. • Use dictionaries, glossaries, and definitions. • Read handouts, textbooks, and supplementary library readings. • Use lecture notes.	• Write out words again and again. • Reread notes silently. • Rewrite ideas and principles into other words. • Turn charts, diagrams, and other illustrations into statements.
Kinesthetic **K**	• Use all your senses. • Go to labs, take field trips. • Listen to real-life examples. • Pay attention to applications. • Use hands-on approaches. • Use trial-and-error methods.	You may take poor notes because topics do not seem concrete or relevant. Therefore: • Put examples in your summaries. • Use case studies and applications to help with principles and abstract concepts. • Talk about your notes with another "kinesthetic" person. • Use pictures and photographs that illustrate an idea.

Source: Adapted from VARK pack. © Copyright 2001–2006 Neil D. Fleming. This material may be used for faculty or student development if attribution is given. It may not be published in either paper or electronic form without consent of the authors. There is a VARK website at **www.vark-learn.com.**

Visual

V

The Navigator/Feature Story/Preview
Infographics/Illustrations
Accounting Equation Analyses
Highlighted words
Graph in *All About You*
Demonstration Problem/Action Plan
Questions/Exercises/Problems
Financial Reporting Problem
Comparative Analysis Problem
Exploring the Web

- Recall your "page pictures."
- Draw diagrams where appropriate.
- Practice turning your visuals back into words.

Aural

A

Preview
Insight Boxes
Review It/Do It/Action Plan
"What Do You Think?" in *All About You*
Summary of Study Objectives
Glossary
Demonstration Problem/Action Plan
Self-Study Questions
Questions/Exercises/Problems
Financial Reporting Problem
Comparative Analysis Problem
Exploring the Web
Group Decision Case
Communication Activity
Ethics Case

- Talk with the instructor.
- Spend time in quiet places recalling the ideas.
- Practice writing answers to old exam questions.
- Say your answers out loud.

Reading/ Writing

R

The Navigator/Feature Story/Study Objectives/Preview
Review It/Do It/Action Plan
Summary of Study Objectives
Glossary/Self-Study Questions
Questions/Exercises/Problems
Writing Problems
Financial Reporting Problem
Comparative Analysis Problem
"All About You" Activity
Exploring the Web
Group Decision Case
Communication Activity

- Write exam answers.
- Practice with multiple-choice questions.
- Write paragraphs, beginnings and endings.
- Write your lists in outline form.
- Arrange your words into hierarchies and points.

Kinesthetic

K

The Navigator/Feature Story/Preview
Infographics/Illustrations
Review It/Do It/Action Plan
Summary of Study Objectives
Demonstration Problem/Action Plan
Self-Study Questions
Questions/Exercises/Problems
Financial Reporting Problem
Comparative Analysis Problem
Exploring the Web
Group Decision Case
Communication Activity
"All About You" Activity

- Write practice answers.
- Role-play the exam situation.

For all learning styles: Be sure to use the book's website to enhance your understanding of the concepts and procedures of the text.

www.wiley.com/college/weygandt

ACKNOWLEDGMENTS

From the first edition and onward, we have benefited greatly from feedback provided by numerous instructors and students of accounting principles courses throughout the country. We offer our thanks to those many people for their criticism, constructive suggestions, and innovative ideas. We are indebted to the following reviewers and focus group participants for their contributions to the most recent editions of the book.

Seventh Edition

Matt Anderson, *Michigan State University;* Yvonne Baker, *Cincinnati State Tech Community College;* Peter Battelle, *University of Vermont;* Michael Blackett, *National American University;* David Boyd, *Arkansas State University;* Leon Button, *Scottsdale Community College;* Trudy Chiaravelli, *Lansing Community College;* Kenneth Couvillion, *San Joaquin Delta College.*

Thomas Davies, *University of South Dakota;* Peggy DeJong, *Kirkwood Community College;* Kevin Dooley, *Kapi'olani Community College;* Edmond Douville, *Indiana University Northwest;* Pamela Druger, *Augustana College;* John Eagan, *Erie Community College;* Richard Ellison, *Middlesex Community College;* Richard Ghio, *San Joaquin Delta College.*

Jeannie Harrington, *Middle Tennessee State University;* William Harvey, *Henry Ford Community College;* Zach Holmes, *Oakland Community College;* Paul Holt, *Texas A&M–Kingsville;* Verne Ingram, *Red Rocks Community College;* Mark Johnston, *Washtenaw Community College;* Shirly Kleiner, *Johnson County Community College;* Jo Koehn, *Central Missouri State University.*

Robert Laycock, *Montgomery College;* Maureen McBeth, *College of DuPage;* Jerry Martens, *Community College of Aurora;* Shea Mears, *Des Moines Area Community College;* Pam Meyer, *University of Louisiana–Lafayette;* Robin Nelson, *Community College of Southern Nevada;* George Palz, *Erie Community College;* Bill Rencher, *Seminole Community College;* Renee Rigoni, *Monroe Community College;* Jill Russell, *Camden County College.*

Alice Sineath, *Forsyth Tech Community College;* Jeff Slater, *North Shore Community College;* Ken Sinclair, *Lehigh University;* James Smith, *Ivy Tech State College;* Carol Springer, *Georgia State University;* Lynda Thompson, *Massasoit Community College;* Sue Van Boven, *Paradise Valley Community College;* and Christian Widmer, *Tidewater Community College.*

Eighth Edition

Sylvia Allen, *Los Angeles Valley College*; Alan Applebaum, *Broward Community College*; Juanita Ardavany, *Los Angeles Valley College*; Jim Benedum, *Milwaukee Area Technical College;* Bernard Bieg, *Bucks County College*; Barry Bomboy, *J. Sargeant Reynolds Community College;* Greg Brookins, *Santa Monica College;* Kent D. Bowen, *Butler County Community College*; Kurt H. Buerger, *Angelo State University.*

Steve Carlson, *University of North Dakota;* Fatma Cebenoyan, *Hunter College;* Shifei Chung, *Rowan University;* Siu Chung, *Los Angeles Valley College;* Lisa Cole, *Johnson County Community College;* Alan B. Czyzewski, *Indiana State University*; John Delaney, *Augustana College*; Pamela Druger, *Augustana College*; Russell Dunn, *Broward Community College;* Mary Falkey, *Prince George Community College;* Raymond Gardner, *Ocean County College.*

Amy Haas, *Kingsborough Community College, CUNY;* Bonnie Harrison, *College of Southern Maryland*; Michelle Heard, *Metropolitan Community College;* Ruth Henderson, *Union Community College;* Ed Hess, *Butler County Community College*; Kathy Hill, *Leeward Community College*; Patty Holmes, *Des Moines Area Community College*; Audrey Hunter, *Broward Community College.*

Joanne Johnson, *Caldwell Community College*; Naomi Karolinski, *Monroe Community College*; Anil Khatri, *Bowie State University*; Ken Koerber, *Bucks County Community College*; Adriana Kulakowski, *Mynderse Academy*; Natasha Librizzi, *Madison Area Technical College*; William P. Lovell, *Cayuga Community College/ Fulton Campus.*

Melanie Mackey, *Ocean County College;* Francis T. McCloskey, *Community College of Philadelphia* Chris McNamara, *Finger Lakes Community College*; Edwin Mah, *University of Maryland, University College*; Thomas Marsh, *Northern Virginia Community College—Annandale;* Cathy Montesarchio, *Broward Community College*; Robin Nelson, *Community College of Southern Nevada;* Joseph M. Nicassio, *Westmoreland County Community College;* Michael O'Neill, *Seattle Central Community College.*

Mike Palma, *Gwinnett Tech*; Michael Papke, *Kellogg Community College*; Ruth Parks, *Kellogg Community College*; Al Partington, *Los Angeles Pierce College;* Jennifer Patty, *Des Moines Area Community College*; Jan Pitera, *Broome Community College*; Laura M. Prosser, *Black Hills State University;* Jenny Resnick, Santa Monica College; Renee Rigoni, *Monroe Community College;* Kathie Rogers, *SUNY Suffolk;* Al Ruggiero, *SUNY Suffolk.*

Roger Sands, *Milwaukee Area Technical College;* Marcia Sandvold, *Des Moines Area Community College;* Kent Schneider, *East Tennessee State University*; Karen Searle; Paul J. Shinal, *Cayuga Community College*; Leon Singleton, *Santa Monica College*; Michael S. Skaff, *College of the Sequoias*; Lois Slutsky, *Broward Community College*; Dan Small, *J. Sargeant Reynolds Community College;* Lee Smart, *Southwest Tennessee Community College;* Jeff

Spoelman, *Grand Rapids Community College;* Norman Sunderman, *Angelo State University*.

Donald Terpstra, *Jefferson Community College*; Wanda Wong, *Chabot College*; Pat Walczak, *Lansing Community College;* Carol N. Welsh, *Rowan University*; Idalene Williams, *Metropolitan Community College;* Gloria Worthy, *Southwest Tennessee Community College;* and Cathy Xanthaky, *Middlesex Community College*

Special Thanks

Our thanks also go to the authors of the Eighth Edition supplements:

Mel Coe, *DeVry Institute of Technology, Atlanta* – Peachtree Workbook

Joan Cook, *Milwaukee Area Technical College* – Heritage Home Furniture Practice Set

Larry Falcetto, *Emporia State University* – Test Bank, Instructor's Manual, Campus Cycle Practice Set

Coby Harmon, University of California, Santa Barbara – PowerPoint Presentations

Marilyn Hunt, *University of Central Florida* – Problem-Solving Survival Guide

Douglas W. Kieso, *Aurora University* – Study Guide

Rex A. Schildhouse, Miramar College, *San Diego Community College District Campus* – Peachtree Workbook, Excel Workbook and Templates

Dick Wasson, *Southwestern College* – Excel Working Papers, Working Papers

We also thank those who have ensured the accuracy of our supplements:

Cynthia Ash, *Davenport University*
Irene Bembenista, *Davenport University*
Jack Borke, *University of Wisconsin – Platteville*
Terry Elliott, *Morehead State University*
James Emig, *Villanova University*
Larry Falcetto, *Emporia State University*
A. Anthony Falgiani, *Western Illinois University*
Lori Grady, *Bucks County Community College*
Jennifer Laudermilch, *PricewaterhouseCoopers*
Kevin McNelis, *New Mexico State University*
Barbara Muller, *Arizona State University*
Anne Oppegard, *Augustana College*
Renee Rigoni, *Monroe Community College*
Paul Robertson, *Henderson State University*
Rex A. Schildhouse, Miramar College, *San Diego Community College District*
Alice Sineath, *Forsyth Tech Community College*
Teresa Speck, *St. Mary's University*
Sheila Viel, *University of Wisconsin–Milwaukee*
Dick Wasson, *Southwestern College*
Bernie Weinrich, *Lindenwood University*

In addition, special recognition goes to Karen Huffman of Palomar College for her assessment of the text's pedagogy and her suggestions on how to increase its helpfulness to students; to Gary R., Morrison of Wayne State University for his review of the instructional design; and to Nancy Galli of Palomar College for her work on learning styles. Thanks also to "perpetual reviewers" Robert Benjamin of Taylor University; Charles Malone, Tammy Wend, and Carol Wysocki, all of Columbia Basin College; and William Gregg of Montgomery College for their continuing interest in the book and their regular contributions of ideas to improve it. Finally, special thanks to Wayne Higley of Buena Vista University for his technical proofing.

Our thanks to the publishing "pros" who contribute to our efforts to publish high-quality products that benefit both teachers and students: project editor Ed Brislin, associate editor Brian Kamins, editorial assistant Karolina Zarychta, senior media editor Allie Morris, senior production editor Valerie Vargas, director of production and manufacturing Pam Kennedy, vice president of higher education production and manufacturing Ann Berlin, designer Maddy Lesure, illustration editor Sandra Rigby, photo editor Elle Wagner, project manager Suzanne Ingrao of Ingrao Associates, permissions editor Karyn Morrison, product manager Jane Shifflet at TechBooks, and project manager Kim Nichols at Elm Street Publishing Services. They provided innumerable services that helped this project take shape.

We wish to acknowledge the outstanding work of our development editor, Ann Torbert, whose expertise, encouragement, and patience have helped us immeasurably.

We also appreciate the exemplary support and professional commitment given us by Executive Editor Chris DeJohn. A special thanks to Susan Elbe, who has been our publisher for many years and who has provided exceptional support, and guidance. We wish her well in her new assignment, and we look forward to working with her in her new role.

Finally, our thanks for the support provided by Joe Heider, Vice President of Product and e-Business Development, Bonnie Lieberman, Senior Vice President of the College Division, and Will Pesce, President and Chief Executive Officer.

We thank PepsiCo, Inc. and The Coca-Cola Company for permitting us the use of their 2005 annual reports for our specimen financial statements and accompanying notes.

We will appreciate suggestions and comments from users—instructors and students alike. You can send your thoughts to us via email at:

AccountingAuthors@yahoo.com.

Jerry J. Weygandt
Madison, Wisconsin

Donald E. Kieso
DeKalb, Illinois

Paul D. Kimmel
Milwaukee, Wisconsin

BRIEF CONTENTS

APPENDIXES

DETAILED CONTENTS

all about Y✻U

quick guide

The new ***"All About You"*** features, one in each chapter, promote financial literacy. They are intended to get students thinking and talking about how accounting impacts their personal lives. Students are more likely to understand the accounting concept being made within the textbook when accounting material is linked to a familiar topic. Each *All About You* box presents a high-interest issue related to the chapter topic, offers facts about it, poses a situation for students to think about, and offers brief opposing answers as a starting place for further discussion. As a feedback mechanism, the authors' comments and opinions about the situation appear at the end of the chapter.

An ***"All About You"*** *Activity*, located in the *Broadening Your Perspective* section near the end of the assignment material, offers further opportunity to explore aspects of a high-interest topic in a homework assignment.

CHAPTER 1 Accounting in Action

Ethics: Managing Personal Financial Reporting

Compares filing for financial aid, especially the FAFSA form, to corporate financial reporting. Presents facts about student debt loads. Asks whether students should present a negative financial picture to increase the chance of receiving financial aid. *AAY Activity* further examines ethics of financial aid and corporate reporting.

CHAPTER 2 The Recording Process

Your Personal Annual Report

Likens a student's résumé to a company's annual report. Presents facts about prominent people with inaccurate résumés. Asks students to consider whether firing Radio Shack's CEO for résumé falsehoods was warranted. *AAY Activity* explores short-term career goals and résumé presentation.

CHAPTER 3 Adjusting the Accounts

Is Your Old Computer a Liability?

Discusses the responsibility for disposing of old electronic equipment and presents facts about the extent of that problem nationally. Asks if companies should consider environmental clean-up costs as liabilities. *AAY Activity* asks students to evaluate different liability-disclosure scenarios.

CHAPTER 4 Completing the Accounting Cycle

Your Personal Balance Sheet

Walks students through identification of personal assets and personal liabilities. Presents facts about Americans' wealth and attitudes toward saving versus spending. Asks if college is a good time to prepare a personal balance sheet. *AAY Activity* gives students practice preparing a personal balance sheet.

CHAPTER 5 Accounting for Merchandising Operations

When Is a Sale Not a Sale?

Discusses channel stuffing as a way to manipulate revenue recognition. Presents facts about companies that improperly recognized revenue and the percentage that restated earnings to correct errors. Asks students to think through what they would do if a boss asked them to engage in channel stuffing. *AAY Activity* presents ethical situations related to revenue recognition.

CHAPTER 6 Inventories

Employee Theft—An Inside Job

Discusses the problem of inventory theft, and how companies keep it in check. Presents facts about inventory theft. Asks for students' opinions on the use of video cameras to reduce theft. *AAY Activity* involves an Internet search for stories on inventory fraud.

CHAPTER 7 Accounting Information Systems

Keeping Track of the Documents in Your Life

Discusses personal record-keeping and documents students may need to keep. Presents facts about what records to keep, and where, as well as back-up contingencies. Asks students to think about their own record-keeping. *AAY Activity* explores a general ledger software program.

CHAPTER 8 Internal Control and Cash

Protecting Yourself from Identity Theft

Likens corporate internal controls to individuals' efforts to protect themselves from identity thieves. Presents facts about how thieves obtain stolen data and how they use it. Asks students about the safety of storing personal financial data on computers. *AAY Activity* asks students to take an online quiz on identity theft.

CHAPTER 9 Accounting for Receivables

Should You Be Carrying Plastic?

Discusses the need for individuals to evaluate their credit positions as thoughtfully as companies do. Presents facts about college-student debt, Americans' use of credit cards, and recent bankruptcy filings. Asks whether students should cut up their credit cards. *AAY Activity* asks students to evaluate credit card terms.

CHAPTER 10 Plant Assets, Natural Resources, and Intangible Assets

Buying a Wreck of Your Own

Presents information about costs and financing of new versus used cars. Asks whether students could improve their economic well-being by buying a used car. The *AAY Activity* tests knowledge of famous trade names.

CHAPTER 11 Current Liabilities and Payroll Accounting

Your Boss Wants to Know If You Jogged Today

Discusses ways to contain cost of health-care benefits. Presents facts on costs and spending on health care. Asks students to consider whose responsibility it is to maintain healthy lifestyles to control health-care costs. *AAY Activity* looks at an employee's other major cost—taxes—and has students calculate various types of taxes.

CHAPTER 12 Accounting for Partnerships

How Well Do You Know Your Partner?

Focuses on the importance of the right business partner. Presents facts about partnerships and other forms of business organization. Asks students to evaluate the risks of a possible partnership siutation. *AAY Activity* asks students to research organizational forms of local businesses.

CHAPTER 13 Corporations: Organization and Capital Stock Transactions

Home-Equity Loans

Compares equity-reducing transactions of companies to use of home-equity loans by individuals. Presents facts about home-equity loans, including tax benefits and variable interest rates. Asks students to assess use of a home-equity loan for a dream vacation. *AAY Activity* asks students to navigate through an annual report like a shareholder would.

CHAPTER 14 Corporations: Dividends, Retained Earnings, and Income Reporting

Corporations Have Governance Structures—Do You?

Discusses the idea of codes of ethics in business and at college. Presents facts about use and abuse of codes of ethics in the workplace, and responses of stockholders. Asks students for opinions on whether schools' codes of ethics serve a useful purpose. *AAY Activity* has students evaluate a code of ethics, and make recommendations to improve it.

CHAPTER 15 Long-Term Liabilities

The Risks of Adjustable Rates

Describes benefits and drawbacks of adjustable-rate mortgages (ARMs). Presents facts about use of ARMs and fixed-rate mortgages. Asks students to evaluate a home-buying scenario and whether to use adjustable-rate financing. *AAY Activity* has students research articles about warning signs of personal-debt trouble.

CHAPTER 16 Investments

A Good Day to Start Saving

Lists excuses not to save, and encourages students to begin saving now. Presents facts about U.S. savings rates and the difference made by starting early. Asks students to assess whether to pay off credit cards before contributing to a 401(k). *AAY Activity* sends students to the SEC's websites to define investment terms and for a quiz on investment "smarts."

CHAPTER 17 The Statement of Cash Flows

Where Does the Money Go?

Discusses the need to know how one spends one's cash. Presents facts about college students' spending patterns. Asks students to analyze a personal cash flow statement and decide whether, and where, cuts should be made. *AAY Activity* has students read an article at The Motley Fool site and discuss how much money to set aside for short-term needs.

CHAPTER 18 Financial Statement Analysis

Should I Play the Market Yet?

Discusses when to begin investing in the stock market. Presents facts about stock ownership in the U.S. Asks students to decide whether a young working person should invest in her employer's stock. *AAY Activity* asks students to complete a questionnaire about appropriate types of mutual funds.

CHAPTER 19 Managerial Accounting

Outsourcing and Jobs

Discusses trends in outsourcing. Presents facts about outsourcing by U.S. companies and top foreign employers in the U.S. Asks students to assess the outsourcing of tax-prep services overseas. *AAY Activity* has students identify personal situations to which managerial accounting techniques apply.

CHAPTER 20 Job Order Cost Accounting

Minding Your Own Business

Focuses on how small business owners calculate product costs. Presents facts about sole proprietorships and franchises. Poses a start-up business idea and asks students to evaluate the cost of labor input. *AAY Activity* sends students to SBA website to take quiz on readiness to start a small business.

CHAPTER 21 Process Cost Accounting

Wal-Mart Is on the Phone

Describes cost accounting for a small company with a possible Wal-Mart deal. Presents facts about Wal-Mart's desirability as an outlet and potential risks for its suppliers. Ask students to evaluate whether a small company should accept a distribution offer. *AAY Activity* asks students to identify activities and cost drivers in a service company.

CHAPTER 22 Cost-Volume-Profit

A Hybrid Dilemma

Explores the cost tradeoffs of hybrid vehicles. Presents facts about sales, costs, and fuel efficiency of hybrid vehicles. Asks students to evaluate the pros and cons of buying a hybrid vehicle. *AAY Activity* asks students to do a break-even analysis on the decision to buy a hybrid.

CHAPTER 23 Budgetary Planning

Avoiding Personal Financial Disaster

Explores personal budgets for college students. Presents facts about the average family budget. Asks students to look at a budgeting calculator and consider whether student loans should be considered a source of income. *AAY Activity* has students compute and analyze a personal budget, using assumed data.

CHAPTER 24 Budgetary Control and Responsibility Accounting

Budgeting for Housing Costs

Applies performance evaluation to personal budgeting, via control of routine expenses, especially housing costs. Presents facts about expenses for childrearing, medical, and housing costs. Asks students to consider the pros and cons of buying a house immediately out of college. *AAY Activity* explores the strategy of "envelope budgeting."

CHAPTER 25 Performance Evaluation Through Standard Costs

Balancing Costs and Quality in Health Care

Applies the concept of standard costs to balancing costs and quality in health care. Presents facts about medical costs and incentives for physicians to reduce costs and maintain quality care. Asks students to consider whether doctors should have to meet standard-cost targets. *AAY Activity* explores using standardized tests to measure college students' learning.

CHAPTER 26 Incremental Analysis and Capital Budgeting

What Is a Degree Worth?

Explores the decision to stay in college as an example of incremental analysis and capital budgeting. Presents facts about the cost of college, and benefits of a college education. Asks students to consider the value of a college education. *AAY Activity* applies incremental analysis to the problem of chronic homelessness.

BICENTENNIAL 1807 WILEY 2007 BICENTENNIAL

The Wiley Bicentennial–Knowledge for Generations

Each generation has its unique needs and aspirations. When Charles Wiley first opened his small printing shop in lower Manhattan in 1807, it was a generation of boundless potential searching for an identity. And we were there, helping to define a new American literary tradition. Over half a century later, in the midst of the Second Industrial Revolution, it was a generation focused on building the future. Once again, we were there, supplying the critical scientific, technical, and engineering knowledge that helped frame the world. Throughout the 20th Century, and into the new millennium, nations began to reach out beyond their own borders and a new international community was born. Wiley was there, expanding its operations around the world to enable a global exchange of ideas, opinions, and know-how.

For 200 years, Wiley has been an integral part of each generation's journey, enabling the flow of information and understanding necessary to meet their needs and fulfill their aspirations. Today, bold new technologies are changing the way we live and learn. Wiley will be there, providing you the must-have knowledge you need to imagine new worlds, new possibilities, and new opportunities.

Generations come and go, but you can always count on Wiley to provide you the knowledge you need, when and where you need it!

William J. Pesce
President and Chief Executive Officer

Peter Booth Wiley
Chairman of the Board

8th Edition

Accounting Principles

Jerry J. Weygandt PhD, CPA
Arthur Andersen Alumni Professor of Accounting
University of Wisconsin
Madison, Wisconsin

Donald E. Kieso PhD, CPA
KPMG Emeritus Professor of Accountancy
Northern Illinois University
DeKalb, Illinois

Paul D. Kimmel PhD, CPA
Associate Professor of Accounting
University of Wisconsin—Milwaukee
Milwaukee, Wisconsin

BICENTENNIAL 1807 WILEY 2007 BICENTENNIAL

John Wiley & Sons, Inc.

8th Edition

Accounting Principles

Accounting in Action

STUDY OBJECTIVES

After studying this chapter, you should be able to:

1 Explain what accounting is.
2 Identify the users and uses of accounting.
3 Understand why ethics is a fundamental business concept.
4 Explain generally accepted accounting principles and the cost principle.
5 Explain the monetary unit assumption and the economic entity assumption.
6 State the accounting equation, and define assets, liabilities, and owner's equity.
7 Analyze the effects of business transactions on the accounting equation.
8 Understand the four financial statements and how they are prepared.

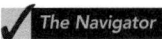

✓ The Navigator

***Study Objectives** give you a framework for learning the specific concepts covered in the chapter.*

✓ The Navigator

Scan **Study Objectives**	■
Read **Feature Story**	■
Read **Preview**	■
Read text and answer **Before You Go On** p. 7 ■ p. 13 ■ p. 20 ■ p. 24 ■	
Work **Demonstration Problem**	■
Review **Summary of Study Objectives**	■
Answer **Self-Study Questions**	■
Complete **Assignments**	■

***The Navigator** is a learning system designed to prompt you to use the learning aids in the chapter and set priorities as you study.*

Feature Story

KNOWING THE NUMBERS

Consider this quote from Harold Geneen, the former chairman of IT&T: "To be good at your business, you have to know the numbers—cold." Success in any business comes back to the numbers. You will rely on them to make decisions, and managers will use them to evaluate your performance. That is true whether your job involves marketing, production, management, or information systems.

In business, accounting and financial statements are the means for communicating the numbers. If you don't know how to read financial statements, you can't really know your business.

When Jack Stack and 11 other managers purchased Springfield ReManufacturing Corporation (SRC) (*www.srcreman.com*) for 10 cents a share, it was a failing

division of International Harvester. Stack had 119 employees who were counting on him for their livelihood, and he knew that the company was on the verge of financial failure.

Stack decided that the company's only chance of survival was to encourage every employee to think like a businessperson and to act like an owner. To accomplish this, all employees at SRC took basic accounting courses and participated in weekly reviews of the company's financial statements. SRC survived, and eventually thrived. To this day, every employee (now numbering more than 1,000) undergoes this same training.

Many other companies have adopted this approach, which is called "open-book management." Even in companies that do not practice open-book management, employers generally assume that managers in all areas of the company are "financially literate."

Taking this course will go a long way to making you financially literate. In this book you will learn how to read and prepare financial statements, and how to use basic tools to evaluate financial results. Appendixes A and B provide real financial statements of two well-known companies, PepsiCo and The Coca-Cola Company. Throughout this textbook we attempt to increase your familiarity with financial reporting by providing numerous references, questions, and exercises that encourage you to explore these financial statements.

__The Feature Story__ helps you picture how the chapter topic relates to the real world of accounting and business. You will find references to the story throughout the chapter.

✓ The Navigator

Inside Chapter 1...

__"Inside Chapter x"__ lists boxes in the chapter that should be of special interest to you.

Preview of Chapter 1

The opening story about Springfield ReManufacturing Corporation highlights the importance of having good financial information to make effective business decisions. Whatever one's pursuits or occupation, the need for financial information is inescapable. You cannot earn a living, spend money, buy on credit, make an investment, or pay taxes without receiving, using, or dispensing financial information. Good decision making depends on good information.

The purpose of this chapter is to show you that accounting is the system used to provide useful financial information. The content and organization of Chapter 1 are as follows.

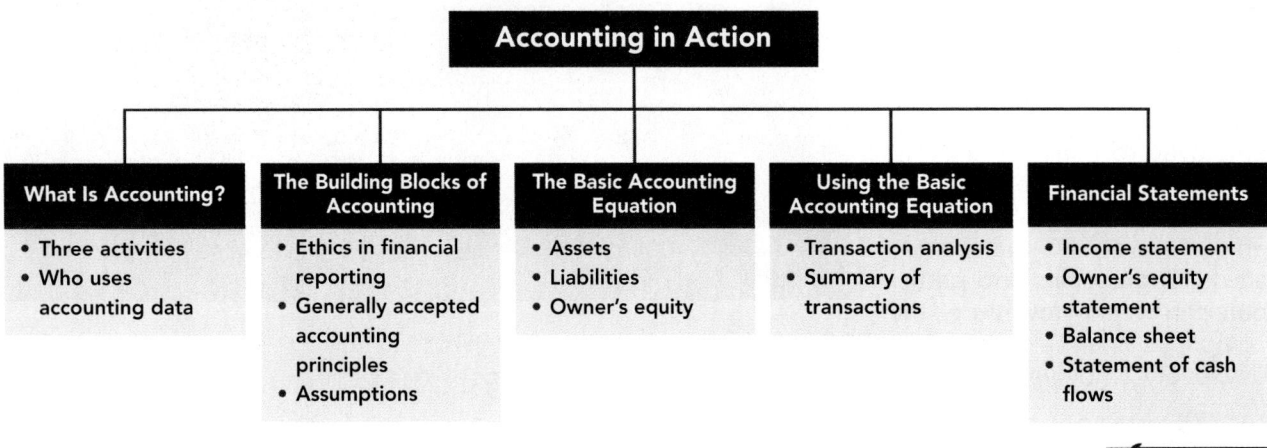

Accounting in Action

- **What Is Accounting?**
  - Three activities
  - Who uses accounting data
- **The Building Blocks of Accounting**
  - Ethics in financial reporting
  - Generally accepted accounting principles
  - Assumptions
- **The Basic Accounting Equation**
  - Assets
  - Liabilities
  - Owner's equity
- **Using the Basic Accounting Equation**
  - Transaction analysis
  - Summary of transactions
- **Financial Statements**
  - Income statement
  - Owner's equity statement
  - Balance sheet
  - Statement of cash flows

✓ The Navigator

*The **Preview** describes and outlines the major topics and subtopics you will see in the chapter.*

WHAT IS ACCOUNTING?

STUDY OBJECTIVE 1

Explain what accounting is.

Why is accounting so popular? What consistently ranks as one of the top career opportunities in business? What frequently rates among the most popular majors on campus? What was the undergraduate degree chosen by Nike founder Phil Knight, Home Depot co-founder Arthur Blank, former acting director of the Federal Bureau of Investigation (FBI) Thomas Pickard, and numerous members of Congress? Accounting.[1] Why did these people choose accounting? They wanted to understand what was happening financially to their organizations. Accounting is the financial information system that provides these insights. In short, to understand your organization, you have to know the numbers.

Accounting consists of three basic activities—it **identifies**, **records**, and **communicates** the economic events of an organization to interested users. Let's take a closer look at these three activities.

Three Activities

To **identify** economic events, a company selects the **economic events relevant to its business**. Examples of economic events are the sale of snack chips by PepsiCo, providing of telephone services by AT & T, and payment of wages by Ford Motor Company.

[1]The appendix to this chapter describes job opportunities for accounting majors and explains why accounting is such a popular major.

Once a company like PepsiCo identifies economic events, it **records** those events in order to provide a history of its financial activities. Recording consists of keeping a **systematic, chronological diary of events**, measured in dollars and cents. In recording, PepsiCo also classifies and summarizes economic events.

Finally, PepsiCo **communicates** the collected information to interested users by means of **accounting reports**. The most common of these reports are called **financial statements**. To make the reported financial information meaningful, PepsiCo reports the recorded data in a standardized way. It accumulates information resulting from similar transactions. For example, PepsiCo accumulates all sales transactions over a certain period of time and reports the data as one amount in the company's financial statements. Such data are said to be reported **in the aggregate**. By presenting the recorded data in the aggregate, the accounting process simplifies a multitude of transactions and makes a series of activities understandable and meaningful.

A vital element in communicating economic events is the accountant's ability to **analyze** and **interpret** the reported information. Analysis involves use of ratios, percentages, graphs, and charts to highlight significant financial trends and relationships. Interpretation involves **explaining the uses, meaning, and limitations of reported data**. Appendix A of this textbook shows the financial statements of PepsiCo, Inc.; Appendix B illustrates the financial statements of The Coca-Cola Company. We refer to these statements at various places throughout the text. At this point, they probably strike you as complex and confusing. By the end of this course, you'll be surprised at your ability to understand, analyze, and interpret them.

Illustration 1-1 summarizes the activities of the accounting process.

Illustration 1-1
Accounting process

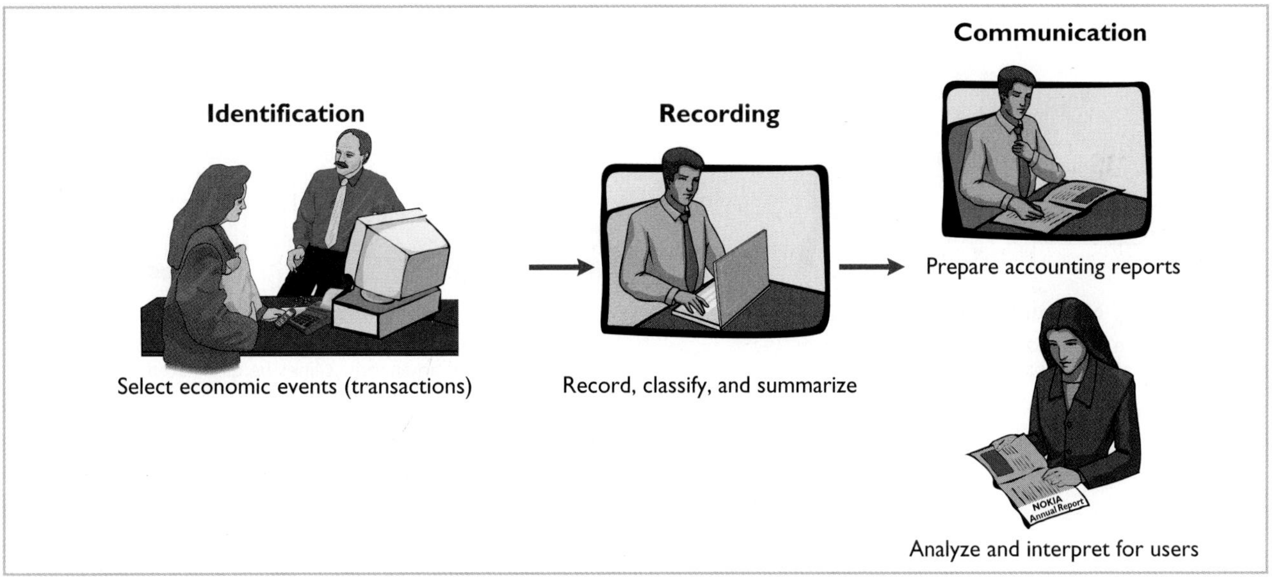

You should understand that the accounting process **includes** the bookkeeping function. **Bookkeeping** usually involves **only** the recording of economic events. It is therefore just one part of the accounting process. In total, accounting involves **the entire process of identifying, recording, and communicating economic events.**[2]

***Essential terms** are printed in blue when they first appear, and are defined in the end-of-chapter glossary.*

[2]The origins of accounting are generally attributed to the work of Luca Pacioli, an Italian Renaissance mathematician. Pacioli was a close friend and tutor to Leonardo da Vinci and a contemporary of Christopher Columbus. In his 1494 text *Summa de Arithmetica, Geometria, Proportione et Proportionalite,* Pacioli described a system to ensure that financial information was recorded efficiently and accurately.

Who Uses Accounting Data

STUDY OBJECTIVE 2

Identify the users and uses of accounting.

The information that a user of financial information needs depends upon the kinds of decisions the user makes. There are two broad groups of users of financial information: internal users and external users.

INTERNAL USERS

Internal users of accounting information are those individuals inside a company who plan, organize, and run the business. These include *marketing managers, production supervisors, finance directors, and company officers.* In running a business, internal users must answer many important questions, as shown in Illustration 1-2.

Illustration 1-2

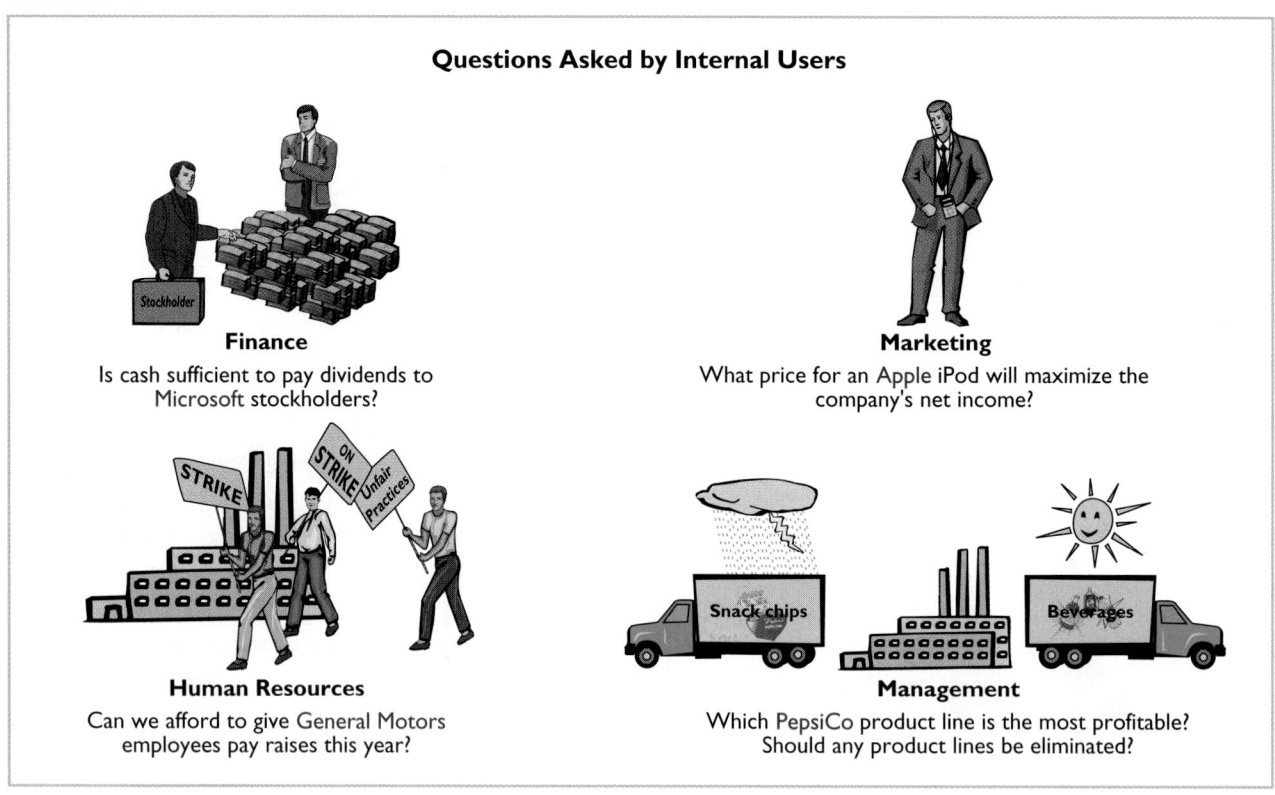

Questions Asked by Internal Users

Finance

Is cash sufficient to pay dividends to Microsoft stockholders?

Marketing

What price for an Apple iPod will maximize the company's net income?

Human Resources

Can we afford to give General Motors employees pay raises this year?

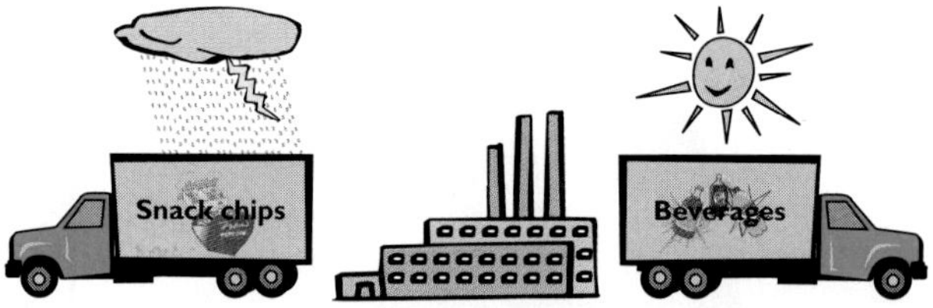

Management

Which PepsiCo product line is the most profitable? Should any product lines be eliminated?

To answer these and other questions, internal users need detailed information on a timely basis. **Managerial accounting** provides internal reports to help users make decisions about their companies. Examples are financial comparisons of operating alternatives, projections of income from new sales campaigns, and forecasts of cash needs for the next year.

EXTERNAL USERS

External users are individuals and organizations outside a company who want financial information about the company. There are several types of external users. The two most common types of external users are investors and creditors. **Investors** (owners) use accounting information to make decisions to buy, hold, or sell stock. **Creditors** (such as suppliers and bankers) use accounting information to evaluate the risks of granting credit or lending money. Illustration 1-3 shows some questions that may be asked by investors and creditors.

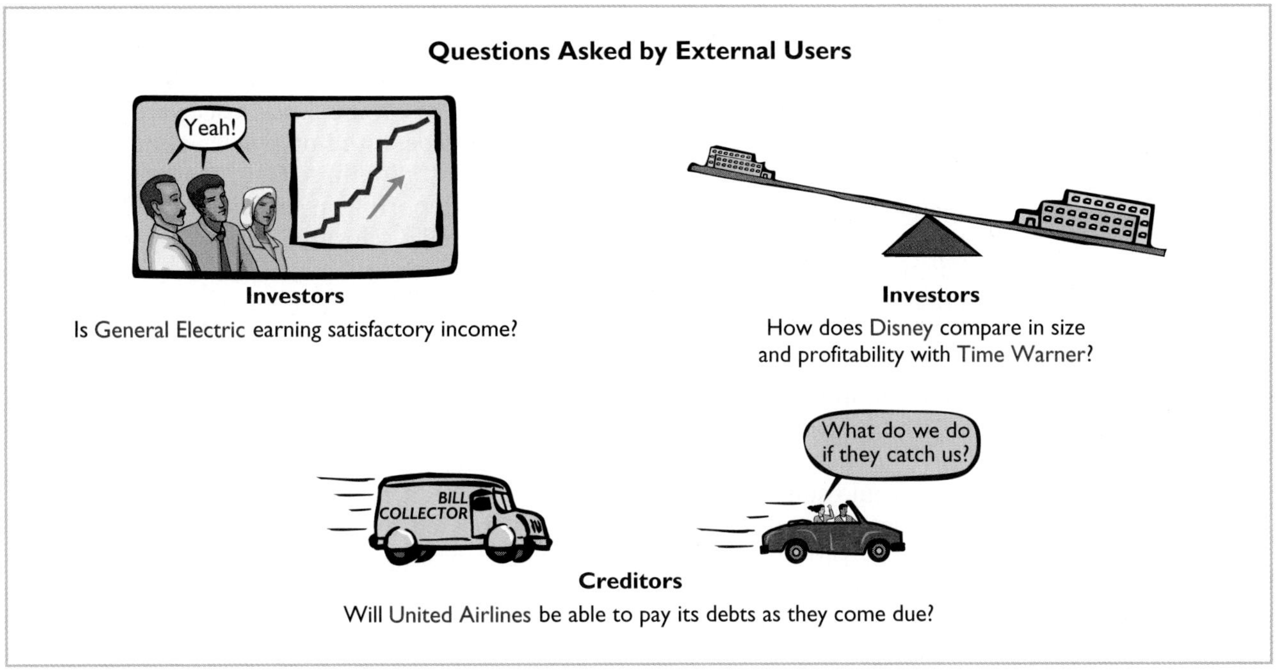

Questions Asked by External Users
Yeah!

Will United Airlines be able to pay its debts as they come due?

Illustration 1-3

Ethics Notes help sensitize you to some of the ethical issues in accounting.

Financial accounting answers these questions. It provides economic and financial information for investors, creditors, and other external users. The information needs of external users vary considerably. **Taxing authorities** (such as the Internal Revenue Service) want to know whether the company complies with tax laws. **Regulatory agencies**, such as the Securities and Exchange Commission and the Federal Trade Commission, want to know whether the company is operating within prescribed rules. **Customers** are interested in whether a company like General Motors will continue to honor product warranties and support its product lines. **Labor unions** such as the Major League Baseball Players Association want to know whether the owners can pay increased wages and benefits.

ETHICS NOTE

The IRS and the SEC require companies to retain records that can be audited.

Before You Go On...

1. What is accounting?
2. What does it mean to analyze and interpret financial information?
3. What is the difference between bookkeeping and accounting?
4. Identify specific internal and external users of accounting.

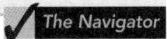

✓ The Navigator

THE BUILDING BLOCKS OF ACCOUNTING

Is General Electric earning satisfactory income?

How does Disney compare in size and profitability with Time Warner?
What do we do if they catch us?
BILL COLLECTOR

A doctor follows certain standards in treating a patient's illness. An architect follows certain standards in designing a building. An accountant follows certain standards in reporting financial information. For these standards to work, a fundamental business concept must be at work—ethical behavior.

Ethics In Financial Reporting

STUDY OBJECTIVE 3

Understand why ethics is a fundamental business concept.

People won't gamble in a casino if they think it is rigged. Similarly, people won't play the stock market if they think stock prices are rigged. In recent years the financial press has been full of articles about financial scandals at Enron, WorldCom, HealthSouth, AIG, and others. As more scandals came to light, mistrust of financial reporting in general grew. One article in the *Wall Street Journal* noted that "repeated disclosures about questionable accounting practices have bruised investors' faith in the reliability of earnings reports, which in turn has sent stock prices tumbling."[3] Imagine trying to carry on a business or invest money if you could not depend on the financial statements to be honestly prepared. Information would have no credibility. There is no doubt that a sound, well-functioning economy depends on accurate and dependable financial reporting.

United States regulators and lawmakers were very concerned that the economy would suffer if investors lost confidence in corporate accounting because of unethical financial reporting. Congress passed the **Sarbanes-Oxley Act of 2002** (SOX, or Sarbox) to reduce unethical corporate behavior and decrease the likelihood of future corporate scandals. As a result of SOX, top management must now certify the accuracy of financial information. In addition, top management now faces much more severe penalties for fraudulent financial activity. Also, SOX calls for increased independence of the outside auditors who review the accuracy of corporate financial statements, and increased responsibility of boards of directors in their oversight role.

The standards of conduct by which one's actions are judged as right or wrong, honest or dishonest, fair or not fair, are **ethics**. Effective financial reporting depends on sound ethical behavior. To sensitize you to ethical situations and to give you practice at solving ethical dilemmas, we address ethics in a number of ways in this book: (1) A number of the *Feature Stories* and other parts of the text discuss the central importance of ethical behavior to financial reporting. (2) *Ethics Insight boxes* and *Ethics Notes* highlight ethics situations and issues in actual business settings. (3) Many of the *All About You* boxes (near the chapter Summary) focus on ethical issues you may face in your college and early-career years. (4) At the end of the chapter, an *Ethics Case* simulates a business situation and asks you to put yourself in the position of a decision maker in that case.

When analyzing these various ethics cases, as well as experiences in your own life, it is useful to apply the three steps outlined in Illustration 1-4.

Illustration 1-4
Steps in analyzing ethics cases

Solving an Ethical Dilemma

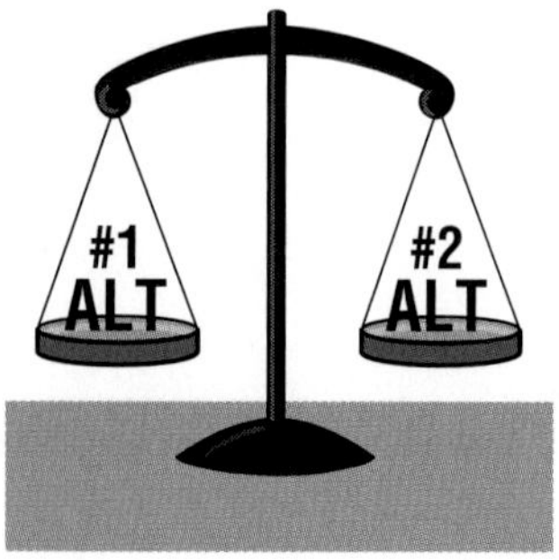

1. Recognize an ethical situation and the ethical issues involved.
Use your personal ethics to identify ethical situations and issues. Some businesses and professional organizations provide written codes of ethics for guidance in some business situations.

2. Identify and analyze the principal elements in the situation.
Identify the *stakeholders*—persons or groups who may be harmed or benefited. Ask the question: What are the responsibilities and obligations of the parties involved?

3. Identify the alternatives, and weigh the impact of each alternative on various stakeholders.
Select the most ethical alternative, considering all the consequences. Sometimes there will be one right answer. Other situations involve more than one right solution; these situations require an evaluation of each and a selection of the best alternative.

[3] "U.S. Share Prices Slump," *Wall Street Journal*, February 21, 2002.

INTERNATIONAL INSIGHT

Chinese Investors Lack Confidence in Financial Reports

Concern over the quality and integrity of financial reporting is not limited to the United States. Recently the Chinese Ministry of Finance reprimanded a large accounting firm for preparing fraudulent financial reports for a number of its publicly traded companies. Afterward, a news agency, run by the Chinese government, noted that investors and analysts actually felt that the punishment of the firm was not adequate. In fact, a recent survey of investors in China found that less than 10% had full confidence in companies' annual reports. As a result of these concerns the Chinese Institute of Certified Public Accountants vowed to strengthen its policing of its members.

? What has been done in the United States to improve the quality and integrity of financial reporting and to build investor confidence in financial reports?

***Insight** boxes provide examples of business situations from various perspectives—ethics, investor, and international. Guideline answers are provided on the last page of the chapter.*

Generally Accepted Accounting Principles

The accounting profession has developed standards that are generally accepted and universally practiced. This common set of standards is called **generally accepted accounting principles (GAAP)**. These standards indicate how to report economic events.

STUDY OBJECTIVE 4

Explain generally accepted accounting principles and the cost principle.

The **Securities and Exchange Commission (SEC)** is the agency of the U.S. government that oversees U.S. financial markets and accounting standard-setting bodies. The primary accounting standard-setting body in the United States is the **Financial Accounting Standards Board (FASB)**. Many countries outside of the United States have adopted the accounting standards issued by the **International Accounting Standards Board (IASB)**. In recent years the FASB and IASB have worked closely to try to minimize the differences in their standards.

One important principle is the cost principle. The **cost principle** (or historical cost principle) dictates that companies record assets at their cost. This is true not only at the time the asset is purchased, but also over the time the asset is held. For example, if Best Buy purchases land for $30,000, the company initially reports it on the balance sheet at $30,000. But what does Best Buy do if, by the end of the next year, the land had increased in value to $40,000? Under the cost principle it continues to report the land at $30,000.

Critics contend the cost principle is irrelevant. They argue that market value (the value determined by the market at any particular time) is more useful to financial decision makers. Proponents of the cost principle counter that cost is the best measure. The reason: Cost can be easily verified, whereas market value is often subjective. Recently, the FASB has changed some accounting rules and now requires that certain investment securities be recorded at their market value. In choosing between cost and market value, the FASB weighed the **reliability** of cost figures versus the **relevance** of market value.

Assumptions

STUDY OBJECTIVE 5

Explain the monetary unit assumption and the economic entity assumption.

Assumptions provide a foundation for the accounting process. Two main assumptions are the **monetary unit assumption** and the **economic entity assumption**.

MONETARY UNIT ASSUMPTION

The **monetary unit assumption** requires that companies include in the accounting records only transaction data that can be expressed in terms of money. This assumption enables accounting to quantify (measure) economic events. The monetary unit assumption is vital to applying the cost principle.

This assumption prevents the inclusion of some relevant information in the accounting records. For example, the health of the owner, the quality of service, and the morale of employees are not included. The reason: Companies cannot quantify this information in terms of money. Though this information is important, only events that can be measured in money are recorded.

ETHICS NOTE

The importance of the economic entity assumption is illustrated by scandals involving Adelphia. In this case, senior company employees entered into transactions that blurred the line between the employee's financial interests and those of the company. For example, Aldephia guaranteed over $2 billion of loans to the founding family.

ECONOMIC ENTITY ASSUMPTION

An economic entity can be any organization or unit in society. It may be a company (such as General Electric Company), a governmental unit (the state of Ohio), a municipality (Seattle), a school district (St. Louis District 48), or a church (Southern Baptist). The **economic entity assumption** requires that the activities of the entity be kept separate and distinct from the activities of its owner and all other economic entities. To illustrate, Sally Rider, owner of Sally's Boutique, must keep her personal living costs separate from the expenses of the Boutique. Similarly, PepsiCo, Coca-Cola, and Cadbury-Schweppes are segregated into separate economic entities for accounting purposes.

Proprietorship. A business owned by one person is generally a **proprietorship**. The owner is often the manager/operator of the business. Small service-type businesses (plumbing companies, beauty salons, and auto repair shops), farms, and small retail stores (antique shops, clothing stores, and used-book stores) are often sole proprietorships. **Usually only a relatively small amount of money (capital) is necessary to start in business as a proprietorship. The owner (proprietor) receives any profits, suffers any losses, and is personally liable for all debts of the business.** There is no legal distinction between the business as an economic unit and the owner, but the accounting records of the business activities are kept separate from the personal records and activities of the owner.

Partnership. A business owned by two or more persons associated as partners is a **partnership**. In most respects a partnership is like a proprietorship except that more than one owner is involved. Typically a partnership agreement (written or oral) sets forth such terms as initial investment, duties of each partner, division of net income (or net loss), and settlement to be made upon death or withdrawal of a partner. Each partner generally has unlimited personal liability for the debts of the partnership. **Like a proprietorship, for accounting purposes the partnership transactions must be kept separate from the personal activities of the partners.** Partnerships are often used to organize retail and service-type businesses, including professional practices (lawyers, doctors, architects, and certified public accountants).

Corporation. A business organized as a separate legal entity under state corporation law and having ownership divided into transferable shares of stock is a **corporation**. The holders of the shares (stockholders) **enjoy limited liability**; that is, they are not personally liable for the debts of the corporate entity. Stockholders **may transfer all or part of their shares to other investors at any time** (i.e., sell their shares). The ease with which ownership can change adds to the attractiveness of investing in a corporation. Because ownership can be transferred without dissolving the corporation, the corporation **enjoys an unlimited life**.

Although the combined number of proprietorships and partnerships in the United States is more than five times the number of corporations, the revenue produced by corporations is eight times greater. Most of the largest enterprises in the United States—for example, ExxonMobil, General Motors, Wal-Mart, Citigroup, and Microsoft—are corporations.

ACCOUNTING ACROSS THE ORGANIZATION

How Will Accounting Help Me?

One question that students frequently ask is, "How will the study of accounting help me?" It should help you a great deal, because a working knowledge of accounting is desirable for virtually **every field** of endeavor. Some examples of how accounting is used in other careers include:

General management: Imagine running Ford Motors, Massachusetts General Hospital, Northern Virginia Community College, a McDonald's franchise, a Trek bike shop. All general managers need to understand where the enterprise's cash comes from and where it goes in order to make wise business decisions.

Marketing: A marketing specialist at a company like Procter & Gamble develops strategies to help the sales force be successful. But making a sale is meaningless unless it is a profitable sale. Marketing people must be sensitive to costs and benefits, which accounting helps them quantify and understand.

Finance: Do you want to be a banker for Bank of America, an investment analyst for Goldman Sachs, a stock broker for Merrill Lynch? These fields rely heavily on accounting. In all of them you will regularly examine and analyze financial statements. In fact, it is difficult to get a good finance job without two or three courses in accounting.

Real estate: Are you interested in being a real estate broker for Prudential Real Estate? Because a third party—the bank—is almost always involved in financing a real estate transaction, brokers must understand the numbers involved: Can the buyer afford to make the payments to the bank? Does the cash flow from an industrial property justify the purchase price? What are the tax benefits of the purchase?

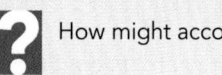

? How might accounting help you?

Accounting Across the Organization stories demonstrate applications of accounting information in various business functions.

THE BASIC ACCOUNTING EQUATION

STUDY OBJECTIVE 6

State the accounting equation, and define assets, liabilities, and owner's equity.

The two basic elements of a business are what it owns and what it owes. **Assets** are the resources a business owns. For example, The Coca-Cola Company has total assets of approximately $29.4 billion. Liabilities and owner's equity are the rights or claims against these resources. Thus, Coca-Cola has $29.4 billion of claims against its $29.4 billion of assets. Claims of those to whom the company owes money (creditors) are called **liabilities**. Claims of owners are called **owner's equity**. Coca-Cola has liabilities of $13.1 billion and owners' equity of $16.4 billion.

We can express the relationship of assets, liabilities, and owner's equity as an equation, as follows.

Illustration 1-5
The basic accounting equation

Assets	=	Liabilities	+	Owner's Equity

This relationship is the **basic accounting equation**. Assets must equal the sum of liabilities and owner's equity. Liabilities appear before owner's equity in the basic accounting equation because they are paid first if a business is liquidated.

The accounting equation applies to all **economic entities** regardless of size, nature of business, or form of business organization. It applies to a small proprietorship such as a corner grocery store as well as to a giant corporation such as Kellogg. The equation provides the **underlying framework** for recording and summarizing economic events.

Let's look in more detail at the categories in the basic accounting equation.

Assets

As noted above, **assets** are resources a business owns. The business uses its assets in carrying out such activities as production and sales. The common characteristic possessed by all assets is the capacity to provide future services or benefits. In a business, that service potential or future economic benefit eventually results in cash inflows (receipts). For example, Campus Pizza owns a delivery truck that provides economic benefits from delivering pizzas. Other assets of Campus Pizza are tables, chairs, jukebox, cash register, oven, tableware, and, of course, cash.

Liabilities

Liabilities are claims against assets—that is, existing debts and obligations. Businesses of all sizes usually borrow money and purchase merchandise on credit. These economic activities result in payables of various sorts:

Campus Pizza, for instance, purchases cheese, sausage, flour, and beverages on credit from suppliers. These obligations are called **accounts payable**.

Campus Pizza also has a **note payable** to First National Bank for the money borrowed to purchase the delivery truck.

Campus Pizza may also have **wages payable** to employees and **sales and real estate taxes payable** to the local government.

All of these persons or entities to whom Campus Pizza owes money are its **creditors**.

Creditors may legally force the liquidation of a business that does not pay its debts. In that case, the law requires that creditor claims be paid before ownership claims.

Owner's Equity

The ownership claim on total assets is **owner's equity**. It is equal to total assets minus total liabilities. Here is why: The assets of a business are claimed by either creditors or owners. To find out what belongs to owners, we subtract the creditors' claims (the liabilities) from assets. The remainder is the owner's claim on the assets—the owner's equity. Since the claims of creditors must be paid **before** ownership claims, owner's equity is often referred to as **residual equity**.

INCREASES IN OWNER'S EQUITY

In a proprietorship, owner's investments and revenues increase owner's equity.

Investments by Owner. **Investments by owner** are the assets the owner puts into the business. These investments increase owner's equity.

Revenues. Revenues are the **gross increase in owner's equity resulting from business activities entered into for the purpose of earning income**. Generally, revenues result from selling merchandise, performing services, renting property, and lending money. Common sources of revenue are: sales, fees, services, commissions, interest, dividends, royalties, and rent.

Revenues usually result in an increase in an asset. They may arise from different sources and are called various names depending on the nature of the business. Campus Pizza, for instance, has two categories of sales revenues—pizza sales and beverage sales.

Helpful Hints further clarify concepts being discussed.

HELPFUL HINT

In some places we use the term *owner's equity* and in others we use *owners' equity*. *Owner's* refers to one owner (the case with a sole proprietorship), and *owners'* refers to multiple owners (the case with partnerships or corporations).

DECREASES IN OWNER'S EQUITY

In a proprietorship, owner's drawings and expenses decrease owner's equity.

Drawings. An owner may withdraw cash or other assets for personal use. We use a separate classification called drawings to determine the total withdrawals for each accounting period. **Drawings decrease owner's equity.**

Expenses. Expenses are the cost of assets consumed or services used in the process of earning revenue. They are **decreases in owner's equity that result from operating the business**. For example, Campus Pizza recognizes the following expenses: cost of ingredients (meat, flour, cheese, tomato paste, mushrooms, etc.); cost of beverages; wages expense; utility expense (electric, gas, and water expense); telephone expense; delivery expense (gasoline, repairs, licenses, etc.); supplies expense (napkins, detergents, aprons, etc.); rent expense; interest expense; and property tax expense.

In summary, owner's equity is increased by an owner's investments and by revenues from business operations. Owner's equity is decreased by an owner's withdrawals of assets and by expenses. Illustration 1-6 shows these relationships.

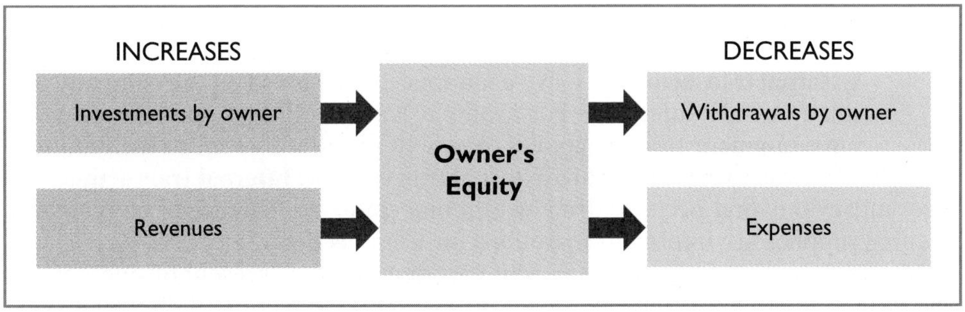

Illustration 1-6
Increases and decreases in owner's equity

Before You Go On...

REVIEW IT

1. Why is ethics a fundamental business concept?
2. What are generally accepted accounting principles? Give an example.
3. Explain the monetary unit and the economic entity assumptions.
4. The accounting equation is: Assets = Liabilities + Owner's Equity. Replacing the words in that equation with dollar amounts, what is PepsiCo's accounting equation at December 31, 2005? (*Hint:* Owner's equity is equivalent to shareholders' equity. The answer to this question appears on page 45.)
5. What are assets, liabilities, and owner's equity?

Review It questions encourage you to stop and think about what you have just learned. Sometimes these questions stand alone; other times they are accompanied by practice exercises.

Review It questions marked with this icon require that you use PepsiCo's Annual Report.

*The **Do It** exercises, like the one here, ask you to put newly acquired knowledge to work. They outline the Action Plan necessary to complete the exercise and show a Solution.*

DO IT

Classify the following items as investment by owner (I), owner's drawings (D), revenues (R), or expenses (E). Then indicate whether each item increases or decreases owner's equity:

(1) Rent Expense, (2) Service Revenue,
(3) Drawings, (4) Salaries Expense.

Action Plan

- Review the rules for changes in owner's equity: Investments and revenues increase owner's equity. Expenses and drawings decrease owner's equity.
- Understand the sources of revenue: the sale of merchandise, performance of services, rental of property, and lending of money.
- Understand what causes expenses: the consumption of assets or services.
- Recognize that drawings are withdrawals of cash or other assets from the business for personal use.

Solution

1. Rent Expense is an expense (E); it decreases owner's equity.
2. Service Revenue is revenue (R); it increases owner's equity.
3. Drawings is owner's drawings (D); it decreases owner's equity.
4. Salaries Expense is an expense (E); it decreases owner's equity.

Related exercise material: *BE1-1, BE1-2, BE1-3, BE1-4, E1-1, E1-2, E1-3, E1-4, E1-5, E1-6, and E1-7.*

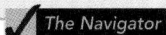

The Navigator

USING THE BASIC ACCOUNTING EQUATION

STUDY OBJECTIVE 7
Analyze the effects of business transactions on the accounting equation.

Transactions (business transactions) are a business's economic events recorded by accountants. Transactions may be external or internal. **External transactions** involve economic events between the company and some outside enterprise. For example, Campus Pizza's purchase of cooking equipment from a supplier, payment of monthly rent to the landlord, and sale of pizzas to customers are external transactions. **Internal transactions** are economic events that occur entirely within one company. The use of cooking and cleaning supplies are internal transactions for Campus Pizza.

A company may carry on many activities that do not represent business transactions. Examples are hiring employees, answering the telephone, talking with customers, and placing orders for merchandise. Some of these activities, however, may lead to business transactions: Employees will earn wages, and suppliers will deliver ordered merchandise. The company must analyze each event to find out if it has an effect on the components of the accounting equation. If it does, the company will record the transaction. Illustration 1-7 (page 15) demonstrates the transaction-identification process.

Each transaction must have a dual effect on the accounting equation. For example, if an asset is increased, there must be a corresponding:

1. Decrease in another asset, or
2. Increase in a specific liability, or
3. Increase in owner's equity.

Two or more items could be affected when an asset is increased. For example, as one asset is increased $10,000, another asset could decrease $6,000 and a specific

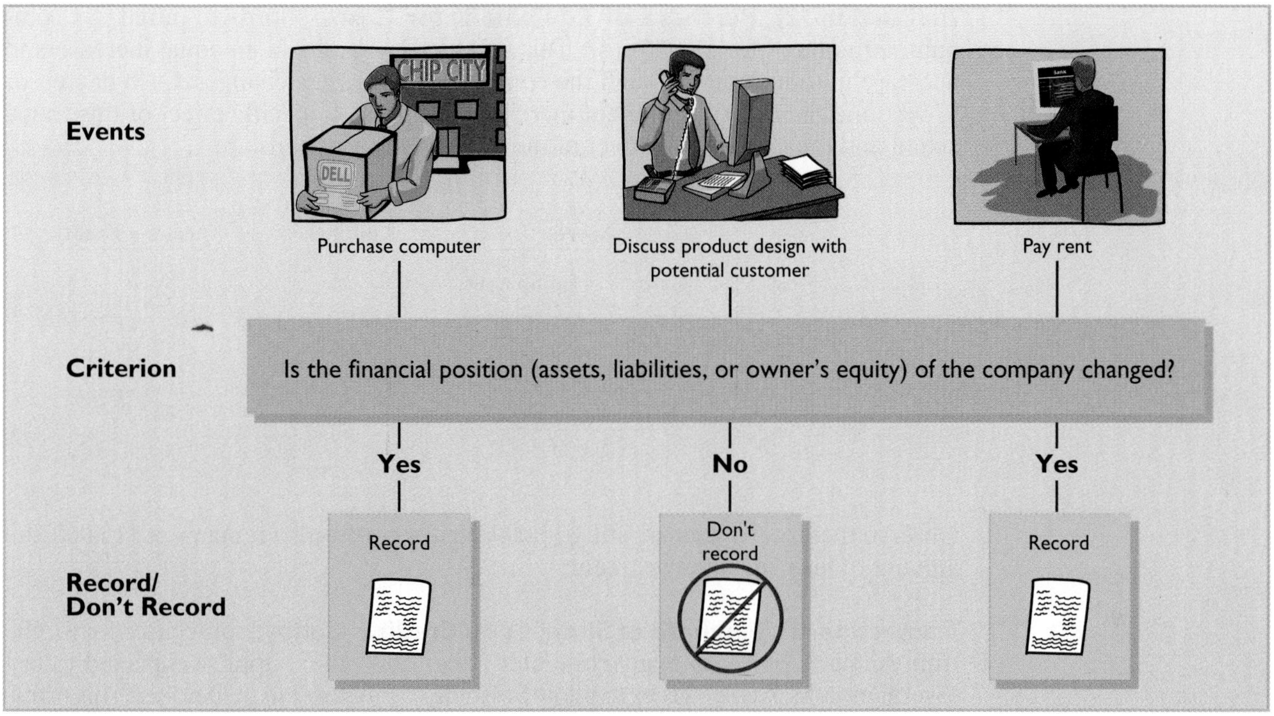

Illustration 1-7
Transaction-identification process

liability could increase $4,000. Any change in a liability or ownership claim is subject to similar analysis.

Transaction Analysis

The following examples are business transactions for a computer programming business during its first month of operations. You will want to study these transactions until you are sure you understand them. They are not difficult, but understanding them is important to your success in this course. The ability to analyze transactions in terms of the basic accounting equation is essential in accounting.

Transaction (1). Investment By Owner. Ray Neal decides to open a computer programming service which he names Softbyte. On September 1, 2008, he invests $15,000 cash in the business. This transaction results in an equal increase in assets and owner's equity. The asset Cash increases $15,000, as does the owner's equity, identified as R. Neal, Capital. The effect of this transaction on the basic equation is:

	Assets	=	**Liabilities**	+	**Owner's Equity**	
	Cash	=			R. Neal, Capital	
(1)	**+$15,000**	=			**+$15,000**	**Investment**

Observe that the equality of the basic equation has been maintained. Note also that the source of the increase in owner's equity (Investment) is indicated. Why does this matter? Because investments by the owner do not represent revenues, and they are excluded in determining net income. Therefore it is necessary to make clear that the increase is an investment rather than revenue from operations.

Transaction (2). Purchase of Equipment for Cash. Softbyte purchases computer equipment for $7,000 cash. This transaction results in an equal increase and decrease in total assets, though the composition of assets changes: Cash decreases $7,000, and the asset Equipment increases $7,000. The specific effect of this transaction and the cumulative effect of the first two transactions are:

		Assets		=	**Liabilities** + **Owner's Equity**
		Cash +	Equipment	=	R. Neal, Capital
	Old Bal.	$15,000			$15,000
(2)		**−7,000**	**+$7,000**		
	New Bal.	$ 8,000	$7,000	=	$15,000
		$15,000			

Observe that total assets are still $15,000. Neal's equity also remains at $15,000, the amount of his original investment.

Transaction (3). Purchase of Supplies on Credit. Softbyte purchases for $1,600 from Acme Supply Company computer paper and other supplies expected to last several months. Acme agrees to allow Softbyte to pay this bill in October. This transaction is a purchase on account (a credit purchase). Assets increase because of the expected future benefits of using the paper and supplies, and liabilities increase by the amount due Acme Company. The asset Supplies increase $1,600, and the liability Accounts Payable increase by the same amount. The effect on the equation is:

		Assets			=	**Liabilities**	+	**Owner's Equity**
		Cash +	Supplies +	Equipment	=	Accounts Payable	+	R. Neal, Capital
	Old Bal.	$8,000		$7,000				$15,000
(3)			**+$1,600**			**+$1,600**		
	New Bal.	$8,000 +	$1,600 +	$7,000	=	$1,600	+	$15,000
			$16,600				$16,600	

Total assets are now $16,600. This total is matched by a $1,600 creditor's claim and a $15,000 ownership claim.

Transaction (4). Services Provided for Cash. Softbyte receives $1,200 cash from customers for programming services it has provided. This transaction represents Softbyte's principal revenue-producing activity. Recall that **revenue increases owner's equity**. In this transaction, Cash increases $1,200, and R. Neal, Capital increases $1,200. The new balances in the equation are:

		Assets			=	**Liabilities**	+	**Owner's Equity**	
		Cash +	Supplies +	Equipment	=	Accounts Payable	+	R. Neal, Capital	
	Old Bal.	$8,000	$1,600	$7,000		$1,600		$15,000	
(4)		**+$1,200**						**+1,200**	**Service Revenue**
	New Bal.	$9,200 +	$1,600 +	$7,000	=	$1,600	+	$16,200	
			$17,800				$17,800		

The two sides of the equation balance at $17,800. The title Service Revenue indicates the source of the increase in owner's equity. Service Revenue is included in determining Softbyte's net income.

Transaction (5). Purchase of Advertising on Credit. Softbyte receives a bill for $250 from the *Daily News* for advertising but postpones payment until a later date. This transaction results in an increase in liabilities and a decrease in owner's equity. The specific items involved are Accounts Payable and R. Neal, Capital. The effect on the equation is:

		Assets						=	Liabilities	+	Owner's Equity	
		Cash	+	Supplies	+	Equipment		=	Accounts Payable	+	R. Neal, Capital	
	Old Bal.	$9,200		$1,600		$7,000			$1,600		$16,200	
(5)									**+250**		**−250**	**Advertising Expense**
	New Bal.	$9,200	+	$1,600	+	$7,000		=	$1,850	+	$15,950	
				$17,800						$17,800		

The two sides of the equation still balance at $17,800. Owner's equity decreases when Softbyte incurs the expense. In addition, the specific cause of the decrease (advertising expense) is noted. Expenses do not have to be paid in cash at the time they are incurred. When Softbyte pays at a later date, the liability Accounts Payable will decrease and the asset Cash will decrease [see Transaction (8)]. The cost of advertising is an expense (rather than an asset) because the company has used the benefits. Advertising Expense is included in determining net income.

Transaction (6). Services Provided for Cash and Credit. Softbyte provides $3,500 of programming services for customers. The company receives cash of $1,500 from customers, and it bills the balance of $2,000 on account. This transaction results in an equal increase in assets and owner's equity. Three specific items are affected: Cash increases $1,500; Accounts Receivable increases $2,000; and R. Neal, Capital increases $3,500. The new balances are as follows.

		Assets							=	Liabilities	+	Owner's Equity	
		Cash	+	Accounts Receivable	+	Supplies	+	Equipment	=	Accounts Payable	+	R. Neal, Capital	
	Old Bal.	$9,200				$1,600		$7,000		$1,850		$15,950	
(6)		**+1,500**		**+$2,000**								**+3,500**	**Service Revenue**
	New Bal.	$10,700	+	$2,000	+	$1,600	+	$7,000	=	$1,850	+	$19,450	
					$21,300						$21,300		

Why increase owner's equity $3,500 when the company has collected only $1,500? We do so because the inflow of assets resulting from the earning of revenues does not have to be in the form of cash. Owner's equity is increased when revenues are earned; Softbyte earns revenues when it provides the service. When it later receives collections on account, Softbyte will increase Cash and will decrease Accounts Receivable [see Transaction (9)].

Transaction (7). Payment of Expenses. Softbyte pays the following Expenses in cash for September: store rent $600, salaries of employees $900, and utilities $200. These payments result in an equal decrease in assets and owner's equity. Cash decreases $1,700, and R. Neal, Capital decreases by the same amount. The effect of these payments on the equation is:

		Assets				=	Liabilities	+	Owner's Equity	
		Cash	+ Accounts Receivable	+ Supplies	+ Equipment	=	Accounts Payable	+	R. Neal, Capital	
	Old Bal.	$10,700	$2,000	$1,600	$7,000		$1,850		$19,450	
(7)		−1,700							−600	Rent Expense
									−900	Salaries Expense
									−200	Utilities Expense
	New Bal.	$9,000	+ $2,000	+ $1,600	+ $7,000	=	$1,850	+	$17,750	
				$19,600				$19,600		

The two sides of the equation now balance at $19,600. Three lines in the analysis indicate the different types of expenses that have been incurred.

Transaction (8). Payment of Accounts Payable. Softbyte pays its $250 *Daily News* bill in cash. The company previously [in Transaction (5)] recorded the bill as an increase in Accounts Payable and a decrease in owner's equity. This payment "on account" decreases the asset Cash by $250 and also decreases the liability Accounts Payable by $250. The effect of this transaction on the equation is:

		Assets				=	Liabilities	+	Owner's Equity
		Cash	+ Accounts Receivable	+ Supplies	+ Equipment	=	Accounts Payable	+	R. Neal, Capital
	Old Bal.	$9,000	$2,000	$1,600	$7,000		$1,850		$17,750
(8)		−250					−250		
	New Bal.	$8,750	+ $2,000	+ $1,600	+ $7,000	=	$1,600	+	$17,750
				$19,350				$19,350	

Observe that the payment of a liability related to an expense that has previously been recorded does not affect owner's equity. The company recorded this expense in Transaction (5) and should not record it again.

Transaction (9). Receipt of Cash on Account. Softbyte receives $600 in cash from customers who had been billed for services [in Transaction (6)]. This does not change total assets, but it changes the composition of those assets. Cash increases $600 and Accounts Receivable decreases $600. The new balances are:

		Assets				=	Liabilities	+	Owner's Equity
		Cash	+ Accounts Receivable	+ Supplies	+ Equipment	=	Accounts Payable	+	R. Neal, Capital
	Old Bal.	$8,750	$2,000	$1,600	$7,000		$1,600		$17,750
(9)		+600	−600						
	New Bal.	$9,350	+ $1,400	+ $1,600	+ $7,000	=	$1,600	+	$17,750
				$19,350				$19,350	

Note that the collection of an account receivable for services previously billed and recorded does not affect owner's equity. Softbyte already recorded this revenue in Transaction (6) and should not record it again.

Transaction (10). Withdrawal of Cash by Owner. Ray Neal withdraws $1,300 in cash from the business for his personal use. This transaction results in an equal decrease in assets and owner's equity. Both Cash and R. Neal, Capital decrease $1,300, as shown below.

	Assets							=	Liabilities	+	Owner's Equity	
	Cash	+	Accounts Receivable	+	Supplies	+	Equipment	=	Accounts Payable	+	R. Neal, Capital	
Old Bal.	$9,350		$1,400		$1,600		$7,000		$1,600		$17,750	
(10)	**−1,300**										**−1,300**	**Drawings**
New Bal.	$8,050	+	$1,400	+	$1,600	+	$7,000	=	$1,600	+	$16,450	
			$18,050							$18,050		

Observe that the effect of a cash withdrawal by the owner is the opposite of the effect of an investment by the owner. **Owner's drawings are not expenses.** Like owner's investment, the company excludes them in determining net income.

Summary of Transactions

Illustration 1-8 summarizes the September transactions of Softbyte. It indicates the transaction number, the specific effects of the transaction, and the balances after each transaction.

Illustration 1-8
Tabular summary of Softbyte transactions

	Assets							=	Liabilities	+	Owner's Equity	
Transaction	Cash	+	Accounts Receivable	+	Supplies	+	Equipment	=	Accounts Payable	+	R. Neal, Capital	
(1)	+$15,000										+$15,000	**Investment**
(2)	−7,000						+$7,000					
	8,000					+	7,000	=			15,000	
(3)					+$1,600				+$1,600			
	8,000			+	1,600	+	7,000	=	1,600	+	15,000	
(4)	+1,200										+1,200	**Service Revenue**
	9,200			+	1,600	+	7,000	=	1,600	+	16,200	
(5)									+250		−250	**Advertising Expense**
	9,200			+	1,600	+	7,000	=	1,850	+	15,950	
(6)	+1,500		+$2,000								+3,500	**Service Revenue**
	10,700	+	2,000	+	1,600	+	7,000	=	1,850	+	19,450	
(7)	−1,700										−600	**Rent Expense**
											−900	**Salaries Expense**
											−200	**Utilities Expense**
	9,000	+	2,000	+	1,600	+	7,000	=	1,850	+	17,750	
(8)	−250								−250			
	8,750	+	2,000	+	1,600	+	7,000	=	1,600	+	17,750	
(9)	+600		−600									
	9,350	+	1,400	+	1,600	+	7,000	=	1,600	+	17,750	
(10)	−1,300										−1,300	**Drawings**
	$8,050	+	$1,400	+	$1,600	+	$7,000	=	$1,600	+	$16,450	
			$18,050						$18,050			

Illustration 1-8 demonstrates some significant facts, listed below.

1. Each transaction is analyzed in terms of its effect on:
   (a) the three components of the basic accounting equation.
   (b) specific types (kinds) of items within each component.
2. The two sides of the equation must always be equal.
3. The causes of each change in the owner's claim on assets are indicated in the owner's equity column.

There! You made it through transaction analysis. If you feel a bit shaky on any of the transactions, it might be a good idea at this point to get up, take a short break, and come back again for a 10- to 15-minute review of the transactions, to make sure you understand them before you go on to the next section.

Before You Go On...

REVIEW IT

1. What is an example of an external transaction? What is an example of an internal transaction?
2. If an asset increases, what are the three possible effects on the basic accounting equation?

DO IT

A tabular analysis of the transactions made by Roberta Mendez & Co., a certified public accounting firm, for the month of August appears below. Each increase and decrease in owner's equity is explained.

	Assets			=	**Liabilities**	+	**Owner's Equity**	
	Cash	+	Office Equipment	=	Accounts Payable	+	R. Mendez, Capital	
1.	+$25,000						+25,000	Investment
2.			+7,000		+7,000			
3.	+8,000						+8,000	Service Revenue
4.	−850						−850	Rent Expense

Describe each transaction that occurred for the month.

Action Plan

- Analyze the tabular analysis to determine the nature and effect of each transaction.
- Keep the accounting equation in balance.
- Remember that a change in an asset will require a change in another asset, a liability, or in owner's equity.

Solution

1. The owner invested $25,000 of cash in the business.
2. The company purchased $7,000 of office equipment on credit.
3. The company received $8,000 of cash in exchange for services performed.
4. The company paid $850 for this month's rent.

Related exercise material: *BE1-5, BE1-6, BE1-7, BE1-8, E1-6, E1-7, E1-8, E1-10, and E1-11.*

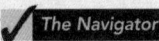

The Navigator

FINANCIAL STATEMENTS

Companies prepare four financial statements from the summarized accounting data:

STUDY OBJECTIVE 8

Understand the four financial statements and how they are prepared.

1. An **income statement** presents the revenues and expenses and resulting net income or net loss for a specific period of time.
2. An **owner's equity statement** summarizes the changes in owner's equity for a specific period of time.
3. A **balance sheet** reports the assets, liabilities, and owner's equity at a specific date.
4. A **statement of cash flows** summarizes information about the cash inflows (receipts) and outflows (payments) for a specific period of time.

Alternative Terminology notes present synonymous terms you may come across in practice or in later courses.

These statements provide relevant financial data for internal and external users.

Illustration 1-9 (page 22) shows the financial statements of Softbyte. Note that the statements are interrelated: **(1) Net income of $2,750 on the income statement is added to the beginning balance of owner's capital in the owner's equity statement. (2) Owner's capital of $16,450 at the end of the reporting period shown in the owner's equity statement is reported on the balance sheet. (3) Cash of $8,050 on the balance sheet is reported on the statement of cash flows.**

HELPFUL HINT

The income statement, owner's equity statement, and statement of cash flows are all for a *period* of time, whereas the balance sheet is for a *point* in time.

Also, explanatory notes and supporting schedules are an integral part of every set of financial statements. We illustrate these notes and schedules in later chapters of this textbook.

Be sure to carefully examine the format and content of each statement in Illustration 1-9. We describe the essential features of each in the following sections.

Income Statement

The income statement reports the revenues and expenses for a specific period of time. (In Softbyte's case, this is "For the Month Ended September 30, 2008.") Softbyte's income statement is prepared from the data appearing in the owner's equity column of Illustration 1-8.

ALTERNATIVE TERMINOLOGY

The income statement is sometimes referred to as the *statement of operations, earnings statement,* or *profit and loss statement.*

The income statement lists revenues first, followed by expenses. Finally the statement shows net income (or net loss). **Net income** results when revenues exceed expenses. A **net loss** occurs when expenses exceed revenues.

Although practice varies, we have chosen in our illustrations and homework solutions to list expenses in order of magnitude. (We will consider alternative formats for the income statement in later chapters.)

Note that the income statement does **not** include investment and withdrawal transactions between the owner and the business in measuring net income. For example, as explained earlier, the withdrawal by Ray Neal of cash from Softbyte was not regarded as a business expense.

Owner's Equity Statement

The owner's equity statement reports the changes in owner's equity for a specific period of time. The time period is the same as that covered by the income statement. Data for the preparation of the owner's equity statement come from the owner's equity column of the tabular summary (Illustration 1-8) and from the income statement. The first line of the statement shows the beginning owner's equity amount.

Illustration 1-9
Financial statements and their interrelationships

HELPFUL HINT
The heading of each statement identifies the company, the type of statement, and the specific date or time period covered by the statement.

HELPFUL HINT
Note that final sums are double-underlined.

HELPFUL HINT
1. Net income is computed first and is needed to determine the ending balance in owner's equity.
2. The ending balance in owner's equity is needed in preparing the balance sheet.
3. The cash shown on the balance sheet is needed in preparing the statement of cash flows.

SOFTBYTE
Income Statement
For the Month Ended September 30, 2008

Revenues		
Service revenue		$ 4,700
Expenses		
Salaries expense	$900	
Rent expense	600	
Advertising expense	250	
Utilities expense	200	
Total expenses		1,950
Net income		**$ 2,750** (1)

SOFTBYTE
Owner's Equity Statement
For the Month Ended September 30, 2008

R. Neal, Capital September 1		$ -0-
Add: Investments	$15,000	
Net income	**2,750**	17,750
		17,750
Less: Drawings		1,300
R. Neal, Capital, September 30		**$16,450** (2)

SOFTBYTE
Balance Sheet
September 30, 2008

Assets

Cash (3)	**$ 8,050**
Accounts receivable	1,400
Supplies	1,600
Equipment	7,000
Total assets	$18,050

Liabilities and Owner's Equity

Liabilities	
Accounts payable	$ 1,600
Owner's equity	
R. Neal, Capital	**16,450**
Total liabilities and owner's equity	$18,050

SOFTBYTE
Statement of Cash Flows
For the Month Ended September 30, 2008

Cash flows from operating activities		
Cash receipts from revenues		$ 3,300
Cash payments for expenses		(1,950)
Net cash provided by operating activities		1,350
Cash flows from investing activities		
Purchase of equipment		(7,000)
Cash flows from financing activities		
Investments by owner	$15,000	
Drawings by owner	(1,300)	13,700
Net increase in cash		8,050
Cash at the beginning of the period		0
Cash at the end of the period		**$ 8,050**

Then come the owner's investments, net income, and the owner's drawings. This statement indicates the reasons why owner's equity has increased or decreased during the period.

What if Softbyte reported a net loss in its first month? Let's assume that during the month of September 2008, Softbyte lost $10,000. Illustration 1-10 shows the presentation of a net loss in the owner's equity statement.

Illustration 1-10
Presentation of net loss

SOFTBYTE Owner's Equity Statement For the Month Ended September 30, 2008		
R. Neal, Capital, September 1		$ -0-
Add: Investments		15,000
		15,000
Less: Drawings	$ 1,300	
Net loss	**10,000**	11,300
R. Neal, Capital, September 30		$ 3,700

If the owner makes any additional investments, the company reports them in the owner's equity statement as investments.

Balance Sheet

Softbyte's balance sheet reports the assets, liabilities, and owner's equity at a specific date (in Softbyte's case, September 30, 2008). The company prepares the balance sheet from the column headings and the month-end data shown in the last line of the tabular summary (Illustration 1-8).

Observe that the balance sheet lists assets at the top, followed by liabilities and owner's equity. Total assets must equal total liabilities and owner's equity. Softbyte reports only one liability—accounts payable—in its balance sheet. In most cases, there will be more than one liability. When two or more liabilities are involved, a customary way of listing is as follows.

Illustration 1-11
Presentation of liabilities

Liabilities	
Notes payable	$10,000
Accounts payable	63,000
Salaries payable	18,000
Total liabilities	$91,000

The balance sheet is a snapshot of the company's financial condition at a specific moment in time (usually the month-end or year-end).

ACCOUNTING ACROSS THE ORGANIZATION

What Do Delta Air Lines, Walt Disney, and Dunkin' Donuts Have in Common?

Not every company uses December 31 as the accounting year-end. Why do companies choose the particular year-ends that they do? Many choose to end the accounting year when inventory or operations are at a low. Compiling accounting information requires much time and effort by managers, so companies would rather do it when they aren't as busy operating the business. Also, inventory is easier and less costly to count when it is low. Some companies whose year-ends differ from December 31 are Delta Air Lines, June 30; Walt Disney Productions, September 30; and Dunkin' Donuts Inc., October 31.

? What year-end would you likely use if you owned a ski resort and ski rental business? What if you owned a college bookstore? Why choose those year-ends?

HELPFUL HINT

Investing activities pertain to investments made by the company, not investments made by the owner.

Statement of Cash Flows

The statement of cash flows provides information on the cash receipts and payments for a specific period of time. The statement of cash flows reports (1) the cash effects of a company's operations during a period, (2) its investing transactions, (3) its financing transactions, (4) the net increase or decrease in cash during the period, and (5) the cash amount at the end of the period.

Reporting the sources, uses, and change in cash is useful because investors, creditors, and others want to know what is happening to a company's most liquid resource. The statement of cash flows provides answers to the following simple but important questions.

1. Where did cash come from during the period?
2. What was cash used for during the period?
3. What was the change in the cash balance during the period?

As shown in Softbyte's statement of cash flows, cash increased $8,050 during the period. Net cash flow provided from operating activities increased cash $1,350. Cash flow from investing transactions decreased cash $7,000. And cash flow from financing transactions increased cash $13,700. At this time, you need not be concerned with how these amounts are determined. Chapter 17 will examine the statement of cash flows in detail.

Before You Go On...

REVIEW IT

1. What are the income statement, owner's equity statement, balance sheet, and statement of cash flows?
2. How are the financial statements interrelated?

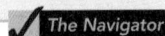

✓ The Navigator

Be sure to read **ALL ABOUT YOU: *Ethics: Managing Personal Financial Reporting*** on page 25 for information on how topics in this chapter apply to you.

Ethics: Managing Personal Financial Reporting

When companies need money, they go to investors or creditors. Before investors or creditors will give a company cash, they want to know the company's financial position and performance. They want to see the company's financial statements—the balance sheet and the income statement. When students need money for school, they often apply for financial aid. When you apply for financial aid, you must submit your own version of a financial statement—the Free Application for Federal Student Aid (FAFSA) form.

The FAFSA form asks how much you make (based on your federal income tax return) and how much your parents make. The purpose is to find out how much you own and how much you owe. Why do the Department of Education and your school want this information? Simple: They want to know whether you really need the money. Schools and government-loan funds have limited resources, and they want to make sure that the money goes to those who need it the most. The bottom line is: The worse off you look financially, the more likely you are to get money.

The question is: Should you intentionally make yourself look worse off than you are?

The federal share of assistance is declining
Sources of financial aid as a percentage of total aid used to finance postsecondary expenses

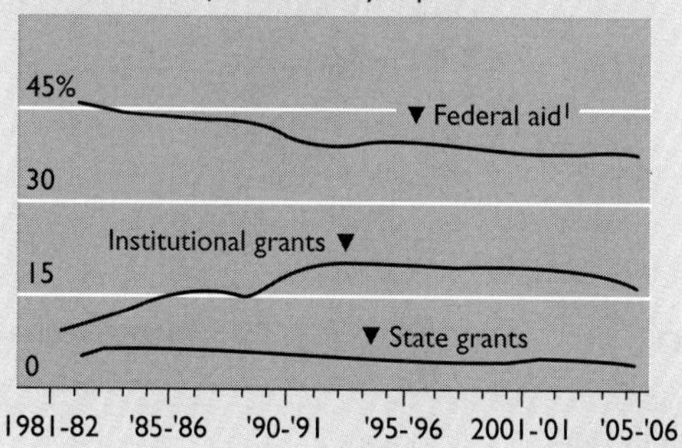

Source for graph: College Board, *Princeton Review,* as reported in "College Admissions: Is Gate Open or Closed?," *Wall Street Journal,* March 25, 2006, p. A7.

Some Facts

* After adjusting for inflation, private-college tuition and fees have increased 37% over the past decade; public-college tuition has risen 54%.
* Two-thirds (65.6%) of undergraduate students graduate with some debt.
* Among graduating seniors, the average debt load is $19,202, according to an analysis of data from the Department of Education's National Postsecondary Student Aid Study. That does not include any debt that their parents might incur.
* Colleges are required to audit the FAFSA forms of at least one-third of their students; some audit 100%. (Compare that to the IRS, which audits a very small percentage of tax returns.) Thus, if you lie on your financial aid forms, there's a very good chance you'll get caught.

Additional information regarding scholarships and loans is available at ***www.finaid.org/.*** You might find especially interesting the section that discusses how to maximize your chances of obtaining financial aid at ***www.finaid.org/fafsa/maximize.phtml.***

What Do You Think?

Consider the following and decide what action you would take:

Suppose you have $4,000 in cash and $4,000 in credit card bills. The more cash and other assets that you have, the less likely you are to get financial aid. Also, if you have a lot of consumer debt (credit card bills), schools are not more likely to loan you money. To increase your chances of receiving aid, should you use the cash to pay off your credit card bills, and therefore make yourself look "worse off" to the financial aid decision makers?

YES: You are playing within the rules. You are not hiding assets. You are simply restructuring your assets and liabilities to best conform with the preferences that are built into the federal aid formulas.

NO: You are engaging in a transaction solely to take advantage of a loophole in the federal aid rules. In doing so, you are potentially depriving someone who is actually worse off than you from receiving aid.

Sources: "College Admissions: Is Gate Open or Closed?," *Wall Street Journal,* March 25, 2006, P. A7; *www.finaid.org.*

The authors' comments on this situation appear on page 45.

*Demonstration Problems are a final review of the chapter. The **Action Plan** gives tips about how to approach the problem, and the **Solution** demonstrates both the form and content of complete answers.*

Demonstration Problem

WILEY PLUS

Joan Robinson opens her own law office on July 1, 2008. During the first month of operations, the following transactions occurred.

1. Invested $10,000 in cash in the law practice.
2. Paid $800 for July rent on office space.
3. Purchased office equipment on account $3,000.
4. Provided legal services to clients for cash $1,500.
5. Borrowed $700 cash from a bank on a note payable.
6. Performed legal services for client on account $2,000.
7. Paid monthly expenses: salaries $500, utilities $300, and telephone $100.

Instructions

(a) Prepare a tabular summary of the transactions.

(b) Prepare the income statement, owner's equity statement, and balance sheet at July 31 for Joan Robinson, Attorney at Law.

action plan

- Remember that assets must equal liabilities and owner's equity after each transaction.
- Investments and revenues increase owner's equity.
- Expenses decrease owner's equity.
- The income statement shows revenues and expenses for a period of time.
- The owner's equity statement shows the changes in owner's equity for a period of time.
- The balance sheet reports assets, liabilities, and owner's equity at a specific date.

Solution to Demonstration Problem

(a)

	Assets			=	Liabilities		+	Owner's Equity	
Trans-action	Cash	+ Accounts Receivable	+ Equipment	=	Notes Payable	+ Accounts Payable	+	Joan Robinson, Capital	
(1)	+$10,000							+$10,000	Investment
(2)	−800							−800	Rent Expense
	9,200			=				9,200	
(3)			+$3,000			+$3,000			
	9,200		+ 3,000	=		3,000	+	9,200	
(4)	+1,500							+1,500	Service Revenue
	10,700		+ 3,000	=		3,000	+	10,700	
(5)	+700				+$700				
	11,400		+ 3,000	=	700	+ 3,000	+	10,700	
(6)		+$2,000						+2,000	Service Revenue
	11,400 +	2,000 +	3,000	=	700	+ 3,000	+	12,700	
(7)	−900							−500	Salaries Expense
								−300	Utilities Expense
								−100	Telephone Expense
	$10,500 +	$2,000 +	$3,000	=	$700	+ $3,000	+	$11,800	

(b)

JOAN ROBINSON
Attorney at Law
Income Statement
For the Month Ended July 31, 2008

Revenues		
Service revenue		$3,500
Expenses		
Rent expense	$800	
Salaries expense	500	
Utilities expense	300	
Telephone expense	100	
Total expenses		1,700
Net income		$1,800

JOAN ROBINSON
Attorney at Law
Owner's Equity Statement
For the Month Ended July 31, 2008

Joan Robinson, Capital, July 1		$ -0-
Add: Investments	$10,000	
Net income	1,800	11,800
Joan Robinson, Capital, July 31		$11,800

JOAN ROBINSON
Attorney at Law
Balance Sheet
July 31, 2008

Assets	
Cash	$10,500
Accounts receivable	2,000
Equipment	3,000
Total assets	$15,500
Liabilities and Owner's Equity	
Liabilities	
Notes payable	$ 700
Accounts payable	3,000
Total liabilities	3,700
Owner's equity	
Joan Robinson, Capital	11,800
Total liabilities and owner's equity	$15,500

The Navigator

*This would be a good time to return to the **Student Owner's Manual** at the beginning of the book (or look at it for the first time if you skipped it before) to read about the various types of assignment materials that appear at the end of each chapter. Knowing the purpose of the different assignments will help you appreciate what each contributes to your accounting skills and competencies.*

SUMMARY OF STUDY OBJECTIVES

WILEY PLUS

1 **Explain what accounting is.** Accounting is an information system that identifies, records, and communicates the economic events of an organization to interested users.

2 **Identify the users and uses of accounting.** The major users and uses of accounting are: (a) Management uses accounting information in planning, controlling, and evaluating business operations. (b) Investors (owners) decide whether to buy, hold, or sell their financial interests on the basis of accounting data. (c) Creditors (suppliers and bankers) evaluate the risks of granting credit or lending money on the basis of accounting information. Other groups that use accounting information are taxing authorities, regulatory agencies, customers, labor unions, and economic planners.

3 **Understand why ethics is a fundamental business concept.** Ethics are the standards of conduct by which actions are judged as right or wrong. If you cannot depend on the honesty of the individuals you deal with, effective communication and economic activity would be impossible, and information would have no credibility.

4 **Explain generally accepted accounting principles and the cost principle.** Generally accepted accounting principles are a common set of standards used by accountants. The cost principle states that companies should record assets at their cost.

5 **Explain the monetary unit assumption and the economic entity assumption.** The monetary unit assumption requires that companies include in the accounting records only transaction data that can be expressed in terms of money. The economic entity assumption requires that the activities of each economic entity be kept separate from the activities of its owner and other economic entities.

6 **State the accounting equation, and define assets, liabilities, and owner's equity.** The basic accounting equation is:

Assets = Liabilities + Owner's Equity

Assets are resources owned by a business. Liabilities are creditorship claims on total assets. Owner's equity is the ownership claim on total assets.

7 **Analyze the effects of business transactions on the accounting equation.** Each business transaction must have a dual effect on the accounting equation. For example, if an individual asset increases, there must be a corresponding (1) decrease in another asset, or (2) increase in a specific liability, or (3) increase in owner's equity.

8 **Understand the four financial statements and how they are prepared.** An income statement presents the revenues and expenses of a company for a specified period of time. An owner's equity statement summarizes the changes in owner's equity that have occurred for a specific period of time. A balance sheet reports the assets, liabilities, and owner's equity of a business at a specific date. A statement of cash flows summarizes information about the cash inflows (receipts) and outflows (payments) for a specific period of time.

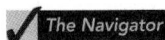

The Navigator

GLOSSARY

WILEY PLUS

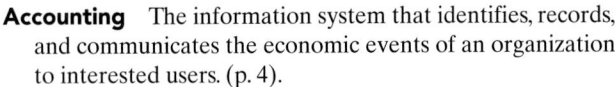

Accounting The information system that identifies, records, and communicates the economic events of an organization to interested users. (p. 4).

Assets Resources a business owns. (p. 12).

Balance sheet A financial statement that reports the assets, liabilities, and owner's equity at a specific date. (p. 21).

Basic accounting equation Assets = Liabilities + Owner's Equity. (p. 12).

Bookkeeping A part of accounting that involves only the recording of economic events. (p. 5).

Corporation A business organized as a separate legal entity under state corporation law, having ownership divided into transferable shares of stock. (p. 10).

Cost principle An accounting principle that states that companies should record assets at their cost. (p. 9).

Drawings Withdrawal of cash or other assets from an unincorporated business for the personal use of the owner(s). (p. 13).

Economic entity assumption An assumption that requires that the activities of the entity be kept separate and distinct from the activities of its owner and all other economic entities. (p. 10).

Ethics The standards of conduct by which one's actions are judged as right or wrong, honest or dishonest, fair or not fair. (p. 8).

Expenses The cost of assets consumed or services used in the process of earning revenue. (p. 13).

Financial accounting The field of accounting that provides economic and financial information for investors, creditors, and other external users. (p. 7).

Financial Accounting Standards Board (FASB) A private organization that establishes generally accepted accounting principles (GAAP). (p. 9).

Generally accepted accounting principles (GAAP) Common standards that indicate how to report economic events. (p. 9).

Income statement A financial statement that presents the revenues and expenses and resulting net income or net loss of a company for a specific period of time. (p. 21).

International Accounting Standards Board (IASB) An accounting standard-setting body that issues standards adopted by many countries outside of the United States. (p. 9).

Investments by owner The assets an owner puts into the business. (p. 12).

Liabilities Creditor claims on total assets. (p. 12).

Managerial accounting The field of accounting that provides internal reports to help users make decisions about their companies. (p. 6).

Monetary unit assumption An assumption stating that companies include in the accounting records only transaction data that can be expressed in terms of money. (p. 10).

Net income The amount by which revenues exceed expenses. (p. 21).

Net loss The amount by which expenses exceed revenues. (p. 21).

Owner's equity The ownership claim on total assets. (p. 12).

Owner's equity statement A financial statement that summarizes the changes in owner's equity for a specific period of time. (p. 21).

Partnership A business owned by two or more persons associated as partners. (p. 10).

Proprietorship A business owned by one person. (p. 10).

Revenues The gross increase in owner's equity resulting from business activities entered into for the purpose of earning income. (p. 13).

Sarbanes-Oxley Act of 2002 (SOX) Law passed by Congress in 2002 intended to reduce unethical corporate behavior. (p. 8).

Securities and Exchange Commission (SEC) A governmental agency that requires companies to file financial reports in accordance with generally accepted accounting principles. (p. 9).

Statement of cash flows A financial statement that summarizes information about the cash inflows (receipts) and cash outflows (payments) for a specific period of time. (p. 21).

Transactions The economic events of a business that are recorded by accountants. (p. 14).

APPENDIX Accounting Career Opportunities

STUDY OBJECTIVE 9

Explain the career opportunities in accounting.

Why is accounting such a popular major and career choice? First, there are a lot of jobs. In many cities in recent years, the demand for accountants exceeded the supply. Not only are there a lot of jobs, but there are a wide array of opportunities. As observed by one accounting organization, "accounting is one degree with 360 degrees of opportunity."

Accounting is also hot because it is obvious that accounting matters. Interest in accounting has increased, ironically, because of the attention caused by the accounting failures of companies such as Enron and WorldCom. These widely publicized scandals revealed the important role that accounting plays in society. Most people want to make a difference, and an accounting career provides many opportunities to contribute to society. Finally, the Sarbanes-Oxley Act of 2002 (SOX) (see page 8) significantly increased the accounting and internal control requirements for corporations. This dramatically increased demand for professionals with accounting training.

Accountants are in such demand that it is not uncommon for accounting students to have accepted a job offer a year before graduation. As the following discussion reveals, the job options of people with accounting degrees are virtually unlimited.

Public Accounting

Individuals in **public accounting** offer expert service to the general public, in much the same way that doctors serve patients and lawyers serve clients. A major portion of public accounting involves **auditing**. In auditing, a certified public accountant (CPA) examines company financial statements and provides an opinion as to how accurately the financial statements present the company's results and financial position. Analysts, investors, and creditors rely heavily on these "audit opinions," which CPAs have the exclusive authority to issue.

Taxation is another major area of public accounting. The work that tax specialists perform includes tax advice and planning, preparing tax returns, and representing clients before governmental agencies such as the Internal Revenue Service.

A third area in public accounting is **management consulting**. It ranges from installing basic accounting software or highly complex enterprise resource planning systems, to providing support services for major marketing projects or merger and acquisition activities.

Many CPAs are entrepreneurs. They form small- or medium-sized practices that frequently specialize in tax or consulting services.

Private Accounting

Instead of working in public accounting, you might choose to be an employee of a for-profit company such as Starbucks, Google, or Kellogg. In **private** (or **managerial**) **accounting**, you would be involved in activities such as cost accounting (finding the cost of producing specific products), budgeting, accounting information system design and support, or tax planning and preparation. You might also be a member of your company's internal audit team. In response to SOX, the internal auditors' job of reviewing the company's operations to ensure compliance with company policies and to increase efficiency has taken on increased importance.

Alternatively, many accountants work for not-for-profit organizations such as the Red Cross or the Bill and Melinda Gates Foundation, or for museums, libraries, or performing arts organizations.

Opportunities in Government

Another option is to pursue one of the many accounting opportunities in governmental agencies. For example, the Internal Revenue Service (IRS), Federal Bureau of Investigation (FBI), and the Securities and Exchange Commission (SEC) all employ accountants. The FBI has a stated goal that at least 15% of its new agents should be CPAs. There is also a very high demand for accounting educators at public colleges and universities and in state and local governments.

Forensic Accounting

Forensic accounting uses accounting, auditing, and investigative skills to conduct investigations into theft and fraud. It is listed among the top 20 career paths of the future. The job of forensic accountants is to catch the perpetrators of the estimated $600 billion per year of theft and fraud occurring at U.S. companies. This includes tracing money-laundering and identity-theft activities as well as tax evasion. Insurance companies hire forensic accountants to detect insurance frauds such as arson, and law offices employ forensic accountants to identify marital assets in divorces.

"Show Me the Money"

How much can a new accountant make? Salary estimates are constantly changing, and salaries vary considerably across the country. At the time this text was written, the following general information was available from Robert Half and Co.

Illustration 1A-1
Salary estimates for jobs in public and corporate accounting

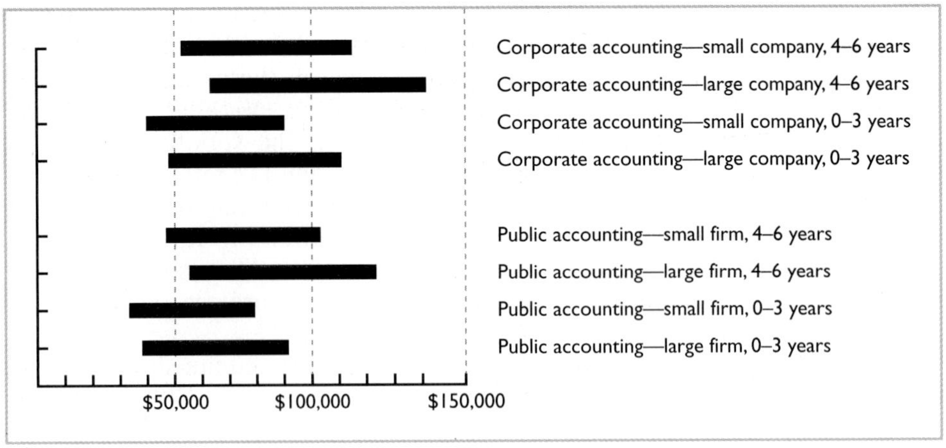

The average salary for a first-year partner in a CPA firm is close to $130,000, with experienced partners often making substantially more. On the corporate side, controllers (the head accountant) can earn $150,000, while chief financial officers can earn as much as $350,000.

For up-to-date salary estimates, as well as a wealth of additional information regarding accounting as a career, check out *www.startheregoplaces.com*.

SUMMARY OF STUDY OBJECTIVE FOR APPENDIX

9 Explain the career opportunities in accounting. Accounting offers many different jobs in fields such as public and private accounting, government, and forensic accounting. Accounting is a popular major because there are many different types of jobs, with unlimited potential for career advancement.

GLOSSARY FOR APPENDIX

Auditing The examination of financial statements by a certified public accountant in order to express an opinion as to the fairness of presentation. (p. 29).

Forensic accounting An area of accounting that uses accounting, auditing, and investigative skills to conduct investigations into theft and fraud. (p. 30).

Management consulting An area of public accounting ranging from development of accounting and computer systems to support services for marketing projects and merger and acquisition activities. (p. 29).

Private (or managerial) accounting An area of accounting within a company that involves such activities as cost accounting, budgeting, design and support of accounting information systems, and tax planning and preparation. (p. 29).

Public accounting An area of accounting in which the accountant offers expert service to the general public. (p. 29).

Taxation An area of public accounting involving tax advice, tax planning, preparing tax returns, and representing clients before governmental agencies. (p. 29).

SELF-STUDY QUESTIONS

WILEY PLUS

Answers are at the end of the chapter.

(SO 1) **1.** Which of the following is *not* a step in the accounting process?
a. identification. **c.** recording.
b. verification. **d.** communication.

(SO 2) **2.** Which of the following statements about users of accounting information is *incorrect*?
a. Management is an internal user.
b. Taxing authorities are external users.
c. Present creditors are external users.
d. Regulatory authorities are internal users.

(SO 4) **3.** The cost principle states that:
a. assets should be initially recorded at cost and adjusted when the market value changes.
b. activities of an entity are to be kept separate and distinct from its owner.
c. assets should be recorded at their cost.
d. only transaction data capable of being expressed in terms of money be included in the accounting records.

(SO 5) **4.** Which of the following statements about basic assumptions is *correct*?
a. Basic assumptions are the same as accounting principles.
b. The economic entity assumption states that there should be a particular unit of accountability.
c. The monetary unit assumption enables accounting to measure employee morale.
d. Partnerships are not economic entities.

(SO 6) **5.** Net income will result during a time period when:
a. assets exceed liabilities.
b. assets exceed revenues.
c. expenses exceed revenues.
d. revenues exceed expenses.

6. Performing services on account will have the following effects on the components of the basic accounting equation: (SO 7)
a. increase assets and decrease owner's equity.
b. increase assets and increase owner's equity.
c. increase assets and increase liabilities.
d. increase liabilities and increase owner's equity.

7. As of December 31, 2008, Stoneland Company has assets of $3,500 and owner's equity of $2,000. What are the liabilities for Stoneland Company as of December 31, 2008? (SO 7)
a. $1,500. **b.** $1,000. **c.** $2,500. **d.** $2,000.

8. On the last day of the period, Jim Otto Company buys a $900 machine on credit. This transaction will affect the: (SO 8)
a. income statement only.
b. balance sheet only.
c. income statement and owner's equity statement only.
d. income statement, owner's equity statement, and balance sheet.

9. The financial statement that reports assets, liabilities, and owner's equity is the: (SO 8)
a. income statement.
b. owner's equity statement.
c. balance sheet.
d. statement of cash flow.

***10.** Services provided by a public accountant include: (SO 9)
a. auditing, taxation, and management consulting.
b. auditing, budgeting, and management consulting.
c. auditing, budgeting, and cost accounting.
d. internal auditing, budgeting, and management consulting.

Go to the book's website, **www.wiley.com/college/weygandt**, for Additional Self-Study questions.

✓ The Navigator

QUESTIONS

1. "Accounting is ingrained in our society and it is vital to our economic system." Do you agree? Explain.

2. Identify and describe the steps in the accounting process.

3. (a) Who are internal users of accounting data?(b) How does accounting provide relevant data to these users?

4. What uses of financial accounting information are made by (a) investors and (b) creditors?

5. "Bookkeeping and accounting are the same." Do you agree? Explain.

6. Karen Sommers Travel Agency purchased land for \$90,000 cash on December 10, 2008. At December 31, 2008, the land's value has increased to \$93,000. What amount should be reported for land on Karen Sommers's balance sheet at December 31, 2008? Explain.
7. What is the monetary unit assumption?
8. What is the economic entity assumption?
9. What are the three basic forms of business organizations for profit-oriented enterprises?
10. Maria Gonzalez is the owner of a successful printing shop. Recently her business has been increasing, and Maria has been thinking about changing the organization of her business from a proprietorship to a corporation. Discuss some of the advantages Maria would enjoy if she were to incorporate her business.
11. What is the basic accounting equation?
12. **(a)** Define the terms assets, liabilities, and owner's equity.
    (b) What items affect owner's equity?
13. Which of the following items are liabilities of Stanley Jewelry Stores?
    (a) Cash.
    (b) Accounts payable.
    (c) Drawings.
    (d) Accounts receivable.
    (e) Supplies.
    (f) Equipment.
    (g) Salaries payable.
    (h) Service revenue.
    (i) Rent expense.
14. Can a business enter into a transaction in which only the left side of the basic accounting equation is affected? If so, give an example.
15. Are the following events recorded in the accounting records? Explain your answer in each case.
    (a) The owner of the company dies.
    (b) Supplies are purchased on account.
    (c) An employee is fired.
    (d) The owner of the business withdraws cash from the business for personal use.
16. Indicate how the following business transactions affect the basic accounting equation.
    (a) Paid cash for janitorial services.
    (b) Purchased equipment for cash.
    (c) Invested cash in the business.
    (d) Paid accounts payable in full.
17. Listed below are some items found in the financial statements of Alex Greenspan Co. Indicate in which financial statement(s) the following items would appear.
    (a) Service revenue.
    (b) Equipment.
    (c) Advertising expense.
    (d) Accounts receivable.
    (e) Alex Greenspan, Capital.
    (f) Wages payable.
18. In February 2008, Paula King invested an additional \$10,000 in her business, King's Pharmacy, which is organized as a proprietorship. King's accountant, Lance Jones, recorded this receipt as an increase in cash and revenues. Is this treatment appropriate? Why or why not?
19. "A company's net income appears directly on the income statement and the owner's equity statement, and it is included indirectly in the company's balance sheet." Do you agree? Explain.
20. Garcia Enterprises had a capital balance of \$168,000 at the beginning of the period. At the end of the accounting period, the capital balance was \$198,000.
    (a) Assuming no additional investment or withdrawals during the period, what is the net income for the period?
    (b) Assuming an additional investment of \$13,000 but no withdrawals during the period, what is the net income for the period?
21. Summarized operations for J. R. Ross Co. for the month of July are as follows.

    Revenues earned: for cash \$20,000; on account \$70,000.

    Expenses incurred: for cash \$26,000; on account \$40,000.

    Indicate for J. R. Ross Co. (a) the total revenues, (b) the total expenses, and (c) net income for the month of July.

The Navigator

BRIEF EXERCISES

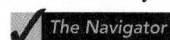

WILEY PLUS

Use basic accounting equation. (SO 6)

BE1-1 Presented below is the basic accounting equation. Determine the missing amounts.

	Assets	=	Liabilities	+	Owner's Equity
(a)	\$90,000		\$50,000		?
(b)	?		\$40,000		\$70,000
(c)	\$94,000		?		\$60,000

Use basic accounting equation. (SO 6)

BE1-2 Given the accounting equation, answer each of the following questions.

(a) The liabilities of McGlone Company are \$120,000 and the owner's equity is \$232,000. What is the amount of McGlone Company's total assets?

(b) The total assets of Company are \$190,000 and its owner's equity is \$80,000. What is the amount of its total liabilities?

(c) The total assets of McGlone Co. are \$800,000 and its liabilities are equal to one half of its total assets. What is the amount of McGlone Co.'s owner's equity?

Use basic accounting equation. (SO 6)

BE1-3 At the beginning of the year, Hernandez Company had total assets of \$800,000 and total liabilities of \$500,000. Answer the following questions.

(a) If total assets increased \$150,000 during the year and total liabilities decreased \$80,000, what is the amount of owner's equity at the end of the year?

(b) During the year, total liabilities increased $100,000 and owner's equity decreased $70,000. What is the amount of total assets at the end of the year?

(c) If total assets decreased $80,000 and owner's equity increased $120,000 during the year, what is the amount of total liabilities at the end of the year?

BE1-4 Indicate whether each of the following items is an asset (A), liability (L), or part of owner's equity (OE).

Identify assets, liabilities, and owner's equity.
(SO 6)

_______**(a)** Accounts receivable
_______**(b)** Salaries payable
_______**(c)** Equipment
_______**(d)** Office supplies
_______**(e)** Owner's investment
_______**(f)** Notes payable

BE1-5 Presented below are three business transactions. On a sheet of paper, list the letters (a), (b), (c) with columns for assets, liabilities, and owner's equity. For each column, indicate whether the transactions increased (+), decreased (−), or had no effect (NE) on assets, liabilities, and owner's equity.

Determine effect of transactions on basic accounting equation.
(SO 7)

(a) Purchased supplies on account.
(b) Received cash for providing a service.
(c) Paid expenses in cash.

BE1-6 Follow the same format as BE1-5 above. Determine the effect on assets, liabilities, and owner's equity of the following three transactions.

Determine effect of transactions on basic accounting equation.
(SO 7)

(a) Invested cash in the business.
(b) Withdrawal of cash by owner.
(c) Received cash from a customer who had previously been billed for services provided.

BE1-7 Classify each of the following items as owner's drawing (D), revenue (R), or expense (E).

Classify items affecting owner's equity.
(SO 7)

_______**(a)** Advertising expense
_______**(b)** Commission revenue
_______**(c)** Insurance expense
_______**(d)** Salaries expense
_______**(e)** Bergman, Drawing
_______**(f)** Rent revenue
_______**(g)** Utilities expense

BE1-8 Presented below are three transactions. Mark each transaction as affecting owner's investment (I), owner's drawings (D), revenue (R), expense (E), or not affecting owner's equity (NOE).

Determine effect of transactions on basic owner's equity.
(SO 7)

_______**(a)** Received cash for services performed
_______**(b)** Paid cash to purchase equipment
_______**(c)** Paid employee salaries.

BE1-9 In alphabetical order below are balance sheet items for Lopez Company at December 31, 2008. Kim Lopez is the owner of Lopez Company. Prepare a balance sheet, following the format of Illustration 1-9.

Prepare a balance sheet.
(SO 8)

Accounts payable	$90,000
Accounts receivable	$72,500
Cash	$49,000
Kim Lopez, Capital	$31,500

BE1-10 Indicate whether the following items would appear on the income statement (IS), balance sheet (BS), or owner's equity statement (OE).

Determine where items appear on financial statements.
(SO 8)

_______**(a)** Notes payable
_______**(b)** Advertising expense
_______**(c)** Trent Buchanan, Capital
_______**(d)** Cash
_______**(e)** Service revenue

EXERCISES

WILEY PLUS

E1-1 Urlacher Company performs the following accounting tasks during the year.

Classify the three activities of accounting.
(SO 1)

______Analyzing and interpreting information.
______Classifying economic events.
______Explaining uses, meaning, and limitations of data.
______Keeping a systematic chronological diary of events.
______Measuring events in dollars and cents.
______Preparing accounting reports.

______Reporting information in a standard format.
______Selecting economic activities relevant to the company.
______Summarizing economic events.

Accounting is "an information system that **identifies, records,** and **communicates** the economic events of an organization to interested users."

Instructions
Categorize the accounting tasks performed by Urlacher as relating to either the identification (I), recording (R), or communication (C) aspects of accounting.

Identify users of accounting information.
(SO 2)

E1-2 **(a)** The following are users of financial statements.

______Customers
______Internal Revenue Service
______Labor unions
______Marketing manager
______Production supervisor
______Securities and Exchange Commission
______Store manager
______Suppliers
______Vice-president of finance

Instructions
Identify the users as being either **external users** or **internal users.**

(b) The following questions could be asked by an internal user or an external user.

______Can we afford to give our employees a pay raise?
______Did the company earn a satisfactory income?
______Do we need to borrow in the near future?
______How does the company's profitability compare to other companies?
______What does it cost us to manufacture each unit produced?
______Which product should we emphasize?
______Will the company be able to pay its short-term debts?

Instructions
Identify each of the questions as being more likely asked by an **internal user** or an **external user.**

Discuss ethics and the cost principle.
(SO 3)

E1-3 Larry Smith, president of Smith Company, has instructed Ron Rivera, the head of the accounting department for Smith Company, to report the company's land in the company's accounting reports at its market value of $170,000 instead of its cost of $100,000. Smith says, "Showing the land at $170,000 will make our company look like a better investment when we try to attract new investors next month."

Instructions
Explain the ethical situation involved for Ron Rivera, identifying the stakeholders and the alternatives.

Use accounting concepts.
(SO 4, 5)

E1-4 The following situations involve accounting principles and assumptions.

1. Grossman Company owns buildings that are worth substantially more than they originally cost. In an effort to provide more relevant information, Grossman reports the buildings at market value in its accounting reports.
2. Jones Company includes in its accounting records only transaction data that can be expressed in terms of money.
3. Caleb Borke, owner of Caleb's Cantina, records his personal living costs as expenses of the Cantina.

Instructions
For each of the three situations, say if the accounting method used is correct or incorrect. If correct, identify which principle or assumption supports the method used. If incorrect, identify which principle or assumption has been violated.

Classify accounts as assets, liabilities, and owner's equity.
(SO 6)

E1-5 Meredith Cleaners has the following balance sheet items.

Accounts payable	Accounts receivable
Cash	Notes payable
Cleaning equipment	Salaries payable
Cleaning supplies	Karin Meredith, Capital

Instructions
Classify each item as an asset, liability, or owner's equity.

E1-6 Selected transactions for Evergreen Lawn Care Company are listed below.

Analyze the effect of transactions.
(SO 6, 7)

1. Made cash investment to start business.
2. Paid monthly rent.
3. Purchased equipment on account.
4. Billed customers for services performed.
5. Withdrew cash for owner's personal use.
6. Received cash from customers billed in (4).
7. Incurred advertising expense on account.
8. Purchased additional equipment for cash.
9. Received cash from customers when service was performed.

Instructions
List the numbers of the above transactions and describe the effect of each transaction on assets, liabilities, and owner's equity. For example, the first answer is: (1) Increase in assets and increase in owner's equity.

E1-7 Brandon Computer Timeshare Company entered into the following transactions during May 2008.

Analyze the effect of transactions on assets, liabilities, and owner's equity.
(SO 6, 7)

1. Purchased computer terminals for $20,000 from Digital Equipment on account.
2. Paid $4,000 cash for May rent on storage space.
3. Received $15,000 cash from customers for contracts billed in April.
4. Provided computer services to Fisher Construction Company for $3,000 cash.
5. Paid Northern States Power Co. $11,000 cash for energy usage in May.
6. Brandon invested an additional $32,000 in the business.
7. Paid Digital Equipment for the terminals purchased in (1) above.
8. Incurred advertising expense for May of $1,200 on account.

Instructions
Indicate with the appropriate letter whether each of the transactions above results in:

(a) an increase in assets and a decrease in assets.
(b) an increase in assets and an increase in owner's equity.
(c) an increase in assets and an increase in liabilities.
(d) a decrease in assets and a decrease in owner's equity.
(e) a decrease in assets and a decrease in liabilities.
(f) an increase in liabilities and a decrease in owner's equity.
(g) an increase in owner's equity and a decrease in liabilities.

E1-8 An analysis of the transactions made by S. Moses & Co., a certified public accounting firm, for the month of August is shown below. Each increase and decrease in owner's equity is explained.

Analyze transactions and compute net income.
(SO 7)

	Cash	+	Accounts Receivable	+	Supplies	+	Office Equipment	=	Accounts Payable	+	Owner's Equity S. Moses, Capital	
1.	+$15,000										+$15,000	Investment
2.	−2,000						+$5,000		+$3,000			
3.	−750				+$750							
4.	+4,600		+$3,700								+8,300	Service Revenue
5.	−1,500								−1,500			
6.	−2,000										−2,000	Drawings
7.	−650										−650	Rent Expense
8.	+450		−450									
9.	−4,900										−4,900	Salaries Expense
10.									+500		−500	Utilities Expense

Instructions
(a) Describe each transaction that occurred for the month.
(b) Determine how much owner's equity increased for the month.
(c) Compute the amount of net income for the month.

Prepare financial statements.
(SO 8)

E1-9 An analysis of transactions for S. Moses & Co. was presented in E1–8.

Instructions

Prepare an income statement and an owner's equity statement for August and a balance sheet at August 31, 2008.

Determine net income (or loss).
(SO 7)

E1-10 Lily Company had the following assets and liabilities on the dates indicated.

December 31	Total Assets	Total Liabilities
2007	$400,000	$250,000
2008	$460,000	$300,000
2009	$590,000	$400,000

Lily began business on January 1, 2007, with an investment of $100,000.

Instructions

From an analysis of the change in owner's equity during the year, compute the net income (or loss) for:

(a) 2007, assuming Lily's drawings were $15,000 for the year.
(b) 2008, assuming Lily made an additional investment of $50,000 and had no drawings in 2008.
(c) 2009, assuming Lily made an additional investment of $15,000 and had drawings of $30,000 in 2009.

Analyze financial statements items.
(SO 6, 7)

E1-11 Two items are omitted from each of the following summaries of balance sheet and income statement data for two proprietorships for the year 2008, Craig Cantrel and Mills Enterprises.

	Craig Cantrel	Mills Enterprises
Beginning of year:		
Total assets	$ 95,000	$129,000
Total liabilities	85,000	(c)
Total owner's equity	(a)	80,000
End of year:		
Total assets	160,000	180,000
Total liabilities	120,000	50,000
Total owner's equity	40,000	130,000
Changes during year in owner's equity:		
Additional investment	(b)	25,000
Drawings	24,000	(d)
Total revenues	215,000	100,000
Total expenses	175,000	55,000

Instructions

Determine the missing amounts.

Prepare income statement and owner's equity statement.
(SO 8)

E1-12 The following information relates to Linda Stanley Co. for the year 2008.

Linda Stanley, Capital, January 1, 2008	$ 48,000	Advertising expense	$ 1,800
Linda Stanley, Drawing during 2008	6,000	Rent expense	10,400
Service revenue	62,500	Utilities expense	3,100
Salaries expense	30,000		

Instructions

After analyzing the data, prepare an income statement and an owner's equity statement for the year ending December 31, 2008.

Correct an incorrectly prepared balance sheet.
(SO 8)

E1-13 Mary Close is the bookkeeper for Mendez Company. Mary has been trying to get the balance sheet of Mendez Company to balance. Mendez's balance sheet is shown on page 37.

MENDEZ COMPANY
Balance Sheet
December 31, 2008

Assets		Liabilities	
Cash	$15,000	Accounts payable	$20,000
Supplies	8,000	Accounts receivable	(8,500)
Equipment	46,000	Mendez, Capital	67,500
Mendez, Drawing	10,000	Total liabilities and	
Total assets	$79,000	owner's equity	$79,000

Instructions
Prepare a correct balance sheet.

Compute net income and prepare a balance sheet.
(SO 8)

E1-14 Jan Nab is the sole owner of Deer Park, a public camping ground near the Lake Mead National Recreation Area. Jan has compiled the following financial information as of December 31, 2008.

Revenues during 2008—camping fees	$140,000	Market value of equipment	$140,000
Revenues during 2008—general store	50,000	Notes payable	60,000
Accounts payable	11,000	Expenses during 2008	150,000
Cash on hand	23,000	Supplies on hand	2,500
Original cost of equipment	105,500		

Instructions
(a) Determine Jan Nab's net income from Deer Park for 2008.
(b) Prepare a balance sheet for Deer Park as of December 31, 2008.

Prepare an income statement.
(SO 8)

E1-15 Presented below is financial information related to the 2008 operations of Summers Cruise Company.

Maintenance expense	$ 95,000
Property tax expense (on dock facilities)	10,000
Salaries expense	142,000
Advertising expense	3,500
Ticket revenue	325,000

Instructions
Prepare the 2008 income statement for Summers Cruise Company.

Prepare an owner's equity statement.
(SO 8)

E1-16 Presented below is information related to the sole proprietorship of Kevin Johnson, attorney.

Legal service revenue—2008	$350,000
Total expenses—2008	211,000
Assets, January 1, 2008	85,000
Liabilities, January 1, 2008	62,000
Assets, December 31, 2008	168,000
Liabilities, December 31, 2008	85,000
Drawings—2008	?

Instructions
Prepare the 2008 owner's equity statement for Kevin Johnson's legal practice.

EXERCISES: SET B

Visit the book's website at **www.wiley.com/college/weygandt,** and choose the Student Companion site, to access Exercise Set B.

PROBLEMS: SET A

Analyze transactions and compute net income.

(SO 6, 7)

P1-1A Barone's Repair Shop was started on May 1 by Nancy Barone. A summary of May transactions is presented below.

1. Invested $10,000 cash to start the repair shop.
2. Purchased equipment for $5,000 cash.
3. Paid $400 cash for May office rent.
4. Paid $500 cash for supplies.
5. Incurred $250 of advertising costs in the *Beacon News* on account.
6. Received $5,100 in cash from customers for repair service.
7. Withdrew $1,000 cash for personal use.
8. Paid part-time employee salaries $2,000.
9. Paid utility bills $140.
10. Provided repair service on account to customers $750.
11. Collected cash of $120 for services billed in transaction (10).

Instructions

(a) Ending capital $12,060

(b) Net income $3,060

(a) Prepare a tabular analysis of the transactions, using the following column headings: Cash, Accounts Receivable, Supplies, Equipment, Accounts Payable, and Nancy Barone, Capital. Revenue is called Service Revenue.

(b) From an analysis of the column Nancy Barone, Capital, compute the net income or net loss for May.

Analyze transactions and prepare income statement, owner's equity statement, and balance sheet.

(SO 6, 7, 8)

P1-2A Maria Gonzalez opened a veterinary business in Nashville, Tennessee, on August 1. On August 31, the balance sheet showed Cash $9,000, Accounts Receivable $1,700, Supplies $600, Office Equipment $6,000, Accounts Payable $3,600, and M. Gonzalez, Capital $13,700. During September the following transactions occurred.

1. Paid $2,900 cash on accounts payable.
2. Collected $1,300 of accounts receivable.
3. Purchased additional office equipment for $2,100, paying $800 in cash and the balance on account.
4. Earned revenue of $8,000, of which $2,500 is paid in cash and the balance is due in October.
5. Withdrew $1,000 cash for personal use.
6. Paid salaries $1,700, rent for September $900, and advertising expense $300.
7. Incurred utilities expense for month on account $170.
8. Received $10,000 from Capital Bank–money borrowed on a note payable.

Instructions

(a) Ending capital $17,630

(b) Net income $4,930
Total assets $29,800

(a) Prepare a tabular analysis of the September transactions beginning with August 31 balances. The column headings should be as follows: Cash + Accounts Receivable + Supplies + Office Equipment = Notes Payable + Accounts Payable + M. Gonzalez, Capital.

(b) Prepare an income statement for September, an owner's equity statement for September, and a balance sheet at September 30.

Prepare income statement, owner's equity statement, and balance sheet.

(SO 8)

P1-3A On May 1, Jeff Wilkins started Skyline Flying School, a company that provides flying lessons, by investing $45,000 cash in the business. Following are the assets and liabilities of the company on May 31, 2008, and the revenues and expenses for the month of May.

Cash	$ 5,600	Notes Payable	$30,000
Accounts Receivable	7,200	Rent Expense	1,200
Equipment	64,000	Repair Expense	400
Lesson Revenue	7,500	Fuel Expense	2,500
Advertising Expense	500	Insurance Expense	400
		Accounts Payable	800

Jeff Wilkins made no additional investment in May, but he withdrew $1,500 in cash for personal use.

Instructions

(a) Net income $2,500
Owner's equity $46,000
Total assets $76,800

(a) Prepare an income statement and owner's equity statement for the month of May and a balance sheet at May 31.

(b) Prepare an income statement and owner's equity statement for May assuming the following data are not included above: (1) $900 of revenue was earned and billed but not collected at May 31, and (2) $1,500 of fuel expense was incurred but not paid.

(b) Net income $1,900
Owner's equity $45,400

P1-4A Mark Miller started his own delivery service, Miller Deliveries, on June 1, 2008. The following transactions occurred during the month of June.

Analyze transactions and prepare financial statements.

(SO 6, 7, 8)

June 1 Mark invested $10,000 cash in the business.
2 Purchased a used van for deliveries for $12,000. Mark paid $2,000 cash and signed a note payable for the remaining balance.
3 Paid $500 for office rent for the month.
5 Performed $4,400 of services on account.
9 Withdrew $200 cash for personal use.
12 Purchased supplies for $150 on account.
15 Received a cash payment of $1,250 for services provided on June 5.
17 Purchased gasoline for $100 on account.
20 Received a cash payment of $1,500 for services provided.
23 Made a cash payment of $500 on the note payable.
26 Paid $250 for utilities.
29 Paid for the gasoline purchased on account on June 17.
30 Paid $1,000 for employee salaries.

Instructions

(a) Show the effects of the previous transactions on the accounting equation using the following format.

(a) Ending capital $13,850

	Assets								=	Liabilities			+	Owner's Equity
Date	Cash	+	Accounts Receivable	+	Supplies	+	Delivery Van		=	Notes Payable	+	Accounts Payable	+	M. Miller Capital

Include explanations for any changes in the M. Miller, Capital account in your analysis.

(b) Prepare an income statement for the month of June.

(c) Prepare a balance sheet at June 30, 2008.

(b) Net income $4,050
(c) Cash $8,200

P1–5A Financial statement information about four different companies is as follows.

Determine financial statement amounts and prepare owner's equity statement.

(SO 7, 8)

	Karma Company	Yates Company	McCain Company	Dench Company
January 1, 2008				
Assets	$ 95,000	$110,000	(g)	$170,000
Liabilities	50,000	(d)	75,000	(j)
Owner's equity	(a)	60,000	45,000	90,000
December 31, 2008				
Assets	(b)	137,000	200,000	(k)
Liabilities	55,000	75,000	(h)	80,000
Owner's equity	60,000	(e)	130,000	170,000
Owner's equity changes in year				
Additional investment	(c)	15,000	10,000	15,000
Drawings	25,000	(f)	14,000	20,000
Total revenues	350,000	420,000	(i)	520,000
Total expenses	320,000	385,000	342,000	(l)

Instructions

(a) Determine the missing amounts. (*Hint:* For example, to solve for (a), Assets − Liabilities = Owner's equity = $45,000.)

(b) Prepare the owner's equity statement for Yates Company.

(c) Write a memorandum explaining the sequence for preparing financial statements and the interrelationship of the owner's equity statement to the income statement and balance sheet.

PROBLEMS: SET B

Analyze transactions and compute net income.

(SO 6, 7)

P1-1B On April 1, Jenny Russo established Matrix Travel Agency. The following transactions were completed during the month.

1. Invested $10,000 cash to start the agency.
2. Paid $400 cash for April office rent.
3. Purchased office equipment for $2,500 cash.
4. Incurred $300 of advertising costs in the *Chicago Tribune,* on account.
5. Paid $600 cash for office supplies.
6. Earned $9,500 for services rendered: $3,000 cash is received from customers, and the balance of $6,500 is billed to customers on account.
7. Withdrew $200 cash for personal use.
8. Paid *Chicago Tribune* amount due in transaction (4).
9. Paid employees' salaries $2,200.
10. Received $4,000 in cash from customers who have previously been billed in transaction (6).

Instructions

(a) Ending capital $16,400

(a) Prepare a tabular analysis of the transactions using the following column headings: Cash, Accounts Receivable, Supplies, Office Equipment, Accounts Payable, and Jenny Russo, Capital.

(b) Net income $6,600

(b) From an analysis of the column Jenny Russo, Capital, compute the net income or net loss for April.

Analyze transactions and prepare income statement, owner's equity statement, and balance sheet.

(SO 6, 7, 8)

P1-2B Cindy Belton opened a law office, Cindy Belton, Attorney at Law, on July 1, 2008. On July 31, the balance sheet showed Cash $4,000, Accounts Receivable $1,500, Supplies $500, Office Equipment $5,000, Accounts Payable $4,200, and Cindy Belton, Capital $6,800. During August the following transactions occurred.

1. Collected $1,400 of accounts receivable.
2. Paid $2,700 cash on accounts payable.
3. Earned revenue of $9,000 of which $3,000 is collected in cash and the balance is due in September.
4. Purchased additional office equipment for $1,000, paying $400 in cash and the balance on account.
5. Paid salaries $3,000, rent for August $900, and advertising expenses $350.
6. Withdrew $750 in cash for personal use.
7. Received $2,000 from Standard Federal Bank—money borrowed on a note payable.
8. Incurred utility expenses for month on account $250.

Instructions

(a) Ending capital $10,550

(a) Prepare a tabular analysis of the August transactions beginning with July 31 balances. The column headings should be as follows: Cash + Accounts Receivable + Supplies + Office Equipment = Notes Payable + Accounts Payable + Cindy Belton, Capital.

(b) Net income $4,500
Total assets $14,900

(b) Prepare an income statement for August, an owner's equity statement for August, and a balance sheet at August 31.

Prepare income statement, owner's equity statement, and balance sheet.

(SO 8)

P1-3B On June 1, Michelle Bullock started Divine Cosmetics Co., a company that provides individual skin care treatment, by investing $26,200 cash in the business. Following are the assets and liabilities of the company at June 30 and the revenues and expenses for the month of June.

Cash	$11,000	Notes Payable	$13,000
Accounts Receivable	4,000	Accounts Payable	1,200
Service Revenue	6,000	Supplies Expense	1,600
Cosmetic Supplies	2,000	Gas and Oil Expense	800
Advertising Expense	500	Utilities Expense	300
Equipment	25,000		

Michelle made no additional investment in June, but withdrew $1,200 in cash for personal use during the month.

Instructions

(a) Net income $2,800
Owner's equity $27,800
Total assets $42,000
(b) Net income $3,500
Owner's equity $28,500

(a) Prepare an income statement and owner's equity statement for the month of June and a balance sheet at June 30, 2008.

(b) Prepare an income statement and owner's equity statement for June assuming the following data are not included above: (1) $800 of revenue was earned and billed but not collected at June 30, and (2) $100 of gas and oil expense was incurred but not paid.

P1-4B Laura Geller started her own consulting firm, Geller Consulting, on May 1, 2008. The following transactions occurred during the month of May.

Analyze transactions and prepare financial statements.

(SO 6, 7, 8)

May 1 Geller invested $8,000 cash in the business.
2 Paid $800 for office rent for the month.
3 Purchased $500 of supplies on account.
5 Paid $50 to advertise in the *County News.*
9 Received $3,000 cash for services provided.
12 Withdrew $700 cash for personal use.
15 Performed $5,300 of services on account.
17 Paid $3,000 for employee salaries.
20 Paid for the supplies purchased on account on May 3.
23 Received a cash payment of $3,000 for services provided on account on May 15.
26 Borrowed $5,000 from the bank on a note payable.
29 Purchased office equipment for $2,800 on account.
30 Paid $150 for utilities.

Instructions

(a) Show the effects of the previous transactions on the accounting equation using the following format.

(a) Ending capital $11,600

	Assets							=	Liabilities				Owner's Equity
Date	Cash	+	Accounts Receivable	+	Supplies	+	Office Equipment	=	Notes Payable	+	Accounts Payable	+	L. Geller Capital

Include explanations for any changes in the L. Geller, Capital account in your analysis.

(b) Prepare an income statement for the month of May.
(c) Prepare a balance sheet at May 31, 2008.

(b) Net income $4,300
(c) Cash $13,800

P1-5B Financial statement information about four different companies is as follows.

Determine financial statement amounts and prepare owner's equity statement.

(SO 7, 8)

	McKane Company	Selara Company	Gordon Company	Hindi Company
January 1, 2008				
Assets	$ 80,000	$90,000	(g)	$150,000
Liabilities	50,000	(d)	75,000	(j)
Owner's equity	(a)	50,000	49,000	100,000
December 31, 2008				
Assets	(b)	117,000	180,000	(k)
Liabilities	55,000	72,000	(h)	80,000
Owner's equity	40,000	(e)	100,000	145,000
Owner's equity changes in year				
Additional investment	(c)	8,000	10,000	15,000
Drawings	10,000	(f)	12,000	10,000
Total revenues	350,000	400,000	(i)	500,000
Total expenses	335,000	385,000	360,000	(l)

Instructions

(a) Determine the missing amounts. (*Hint:* For example, to solve for (a), Assets – Liabilities = Owner's equity = $30,000.)
(b) Prepare the owner's equity statement for McKane Company.
(c) Write a memorandum explaining the sequence for preparing financial statements and the interrelationship of the owner's equity statement to the income statement and balance sheet.

PROBLEMS: SET C

Visit the book's website at **www.wiley.com/college/weygandt,** and choose the Student Companion site, to access Problem Set C.

CONTINUING COOKIE CHRONICLE

*The **Continuing Cookie Chronicle** starts in this chapter and continues in every chapter. You also can find this problem at the book's Student Companion site.*

CCC1 Natalie Koebel spent much of her childhood learning the art of cookie-making from her grandmother. They passed many happy hours mastering every type of cookie imaginable and later creating new recipes that were both healthy and delicious. Now at the start of her second year in college, Natalie is investigating various possibilities for starting her own business as part of the requirements of the entrepreneurship program in which she is enrolled.

A long-time friend insists that Natalie has to somehow include cookies in her business plan. After a series of brainstorming sessions, Natalie settles on the idea of operating a cookie-making school. She will start on a part-time basis and offer her services in people's homes. Now that she has started thinking about it, the possibilities seem endless. During the fall, she will concentrate on holiday cookies. She will offer individual lessons and group sessions (which will probably be more entertainment than education for the participants). Natalie also decides to include children in her target market.

The first difficult decision is coming up with the perfect name for her business. In the end, she settles on "Cookie Creations" and then moves on to more important issues.

Instructions

(a) What form of business organization—proprietorship, partnership, or corporation—do you recommend that Natalie use for her business? Discuss the benefits and weaknesses of each form and give the reasons for your choice.

(b) Will Natalie need accounting information? If yes, what information will she need and why? How often will she need this information?

(c) Identify specific asset, liability, and equity accounts that Cookie Creations will likely use to record its business transactions.

(d) Should Natalie open a separate bank account for the business? Why or why not?

BROADENING YOUR PERSPECTIVE

FINANCIAL REPORTING AND ANALYSIS

Financial Reporting Problem

PepsiCo, Inc.

BYP1-1 The actual financial statements of PepsiCo, as presented in the company's 2005 Annual Report, are contained in Appendix A (at the back of the textbook).

Instructions

Refer to PepsiCo's financial statements and answer the following questions.

(a) What were PepsiCo's total assets at December 31, 2005? At December 25, 2004?

(b) How much cash (and cash equivalents) did PepsiCo have on December 31, 2005?

(c) What amount of accounts payable did PepsiCo report on December 31, 2005? On December 25, 2004?

(d) What were PepsiCo's net sales in 2003? In 2004? In 2005?

(e) What is the amount of the change in PepsiCo's net income from 2004 to 2005?

Comparative Analysis Problem

PepsiCo, Inc. vs. The Coca-Cola Company

BYP1-2 PepsiCo's financial statements are presented in Appendix A. The Coca-Cola Company's financial statements are presented in Appendix B.

Instructions

(a) Based on the information contained in these financial statements, determine the following for each company.

(1) Total assets at December 31, 2005, for PepsiCo, and for Coca-Cola at December 31, 2005.
(2) Accounts (notes) receivable, net at December 31, 2005, for PepsiCo and at December 31, 2005, for Coca-Cola.
(3) Net sales for year ended in 2005.
(4) Net income for year ended in 2005.

(b) What conclusions concerning the two companies can be drawn from these data?

Exploring the Web

BYP1-3 This exercise will familiarize you with skill requirements, job descriptions, and salaries for accounting careers.

Address: www.careers-in-accounting.com, or go to **www.wiley.com/college/weygandt**

Instructions

Go to the site shown above. Answer the following questions.

(a) What are the three broad areas of accounting (from "Skills and Talents Required")?
(b) List eight skills required in accounting.
(c) How do the three accounting areas differ in terms of these eight required skills?
(d) Explain one of the key job functions in accounting.
(e) Based on the *Smart Money* survey, what is the salary range for a junior staff accountant with Deloitte & Touche?

CRITICAL THINKING

Decision Making Across the Organization

BYP1-4 Mary and Jack Gray, local golf stars, opened the Chip-Shot Driving Range on March 1, 2008, by investing $25,000 of their cash savings in the business. A caddy shack was constructed for cash at a cost of $8,000, and $800 was spent on golf balls and golf clubs. The Grays leased five acres of land at a cost of $1,000 per month and paid the first month's rent. During the first month, advertising costs totaled $750, of which $150 was unpaid at March 31, and $400 was paid to members of the high-school golf team for retrieving golf balls. All revenues from customers were deposited in the company's bank account. On March 15, Mary and Jack withdrew a total of $1,000 in cash for personal living expenses. A $100 utility bill was received on March 31 but was not paid. On March 31, the balance in the company's bank account was $18,900.

Mary and Jack thought they had a pretty good first month of operations. But, their estimates of profitability ranged from a loss of $6,100 to net income of $2,450.

Instructions

With the class divided into groups, answer the following.

(a) How could the Grays have concluded that the business operated at a loss of $6,100? Was this a valid basis on which to determine net income?
(b) How could the Grays have concluded that the business operated at a net income of $2,450? (*Hint:* Prepare a balance sheet at March 31.) Was this a valid basis on which to determine net income?
(c) Without preparing an income statement, determine the actual net income for March.
(d) What was the revenue earned in March?

Communication Activity

BYP1-5 Lynn Benedict, the bookkeeper for New York Company, has been trying to get the balance sheet to balance. The company's balance sheet is shown on page 44.

NEW YORK COMPANY
Balance Sheet
For the Month Ended December 31, 2008

Assets		Liabilities	
Equipment	$25,500	Don Wenger, Capital	$26,000
Cash	9,000	Accounts receivable	(6,000)
Supplies	2,000	Don Wenger, Drawing	(2,000)
Accounts payable	(8,000)	Notes payable	10,500
	$28,500		$28,500

Instructions
Explain to Lynn Benedict in a memo why the original balance sheet is incorrect, and what should be done to correct it.

Ethics Case

BYP1-6 After numerous campus interviews, Steve Baden, a senior at Great Northern College, received two office interview invitations from the Baltimore offices of two large firms. Both firms offered to cover his out-of-pocket expenses (travel, hotel, and meals). He scheduled the interviews for both firms on the same day, one in the morning and one in the afternoon. At the conclusion of each interview, he submitted to both firms his total out-of-pocket expenses for the trip to Baltimore: mileage $112 (280 miles at $0.40), hotel $130, meals $36, parking and tolls $18, for a total of $296. He believes this approach is appropriate. If he had made two trips, his cost would have been two times $296. He is also certain that neither firm knew he had visited the other on that same trip. Within ten days Steve received two checks in the mail, each in the amount of $296.

Instructions
(a) Who are the stakeholders (affected parties) in this situation?
(b) What are the ethical issues in this case?
(c) What would you do in this situation?

* "All About You" Activity

BYP1-7 As discussed in the **All About You** feature in this chapter (p. 25), some people are tempted to make their finances look worse to get financial aid. Companies sometimes also manage their financial numbers in order to accomplish certain goals. Earnings management is the planned timing of revenues, expenses, gains, and losses to smooth out bumps in net income. In managing earnings, companies' actions vary from being within the range of ethical activity, to being both unethical and illegal attempts to mislead investors and creditors.

Instructions
Provide responses for each of the following questions.
(a) Discuss whether you think each of the following actions (adapted from *www.finaid.org/fafsa/maximize.phtml*) to increase the chances of receiving financial aid is ethical.
  (i) Spend down the student's assets and income first, before spending parents' assets and income.
  (ii) Accelerate necessary expenses to reduce available cash. For example, if you need a new car, buy it before applying for financial aid.
  (iii) State that a truly financially dependent child is independent.
  (iv) Have a parent take an unpaid leave of absence for long enough to get below the "threshold" level of income.
(b) What are some reasons why a *company* might want to overstate its earnings?
(c) What are some reasons why a *company* might want to understate its earnings?
(d) Under what circumstances might an otherwise ethical person decide to illegally overstate or understate earnings?

Answers to Insight and Accounting Across the Organization Questions

p. 9 Chinese Investors Lack Confidence in Financial Reports

Q: What has been done in the United States to improve the quality and integrity of financial reporting and to build investor confidence in financial reports?

A: *Congress passed new laws to legislate fair business behavior and accounting and auditing practices. The* Sarbanes-Oxley Act of 2002 *increased the resources for the government to combat fraud and to curb poor reporting practices. It introduced sweeping changes to the structure and practice of the accounting and auditing professions and increased the responsibility of corporate boards and officers.*

p. 11 How Will Accounting Help Me?

Q: How might accounting help you?

A: *You will need to understand financial reports in any enterprise with which you are associated. Whether you become a business manager, doctor, lawyer, social worker, teacher, engineer, architect, or entrepreneur, a working knowledge of accounting is relevant.*

p. 24 What Do Delta Air Lines, Walt Disney, and Dunkin' Donuts Have in Common?

Q: What year-end would you likely use if you owned a ski resort and ski rental business?

A: *Probable choices for a ski resort would be between May 31 and August 31.*

Q: What if you owned a college bookstore?

A: *For a college bookstore, a likely year-end would be June 30.*

Q: Why choose those year-ends?

A: *The optimum accounting year-end, especially for seasonal businesses, is a point when inventory and activities are lowest.*

Authors' Comments on *All About You: Ethics: Managing Personal Financial Reporting* (p. 25)

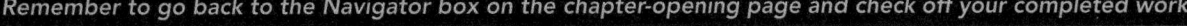

In this chapter you saw that there are very specific rules governing the recording of assets, liabilities, revenues, and expenses. However, within these rules there is a lot of room for judgment. It would not be at all unusual for two experienced accountants, when faced with identical situations, to arrive at different results.

Similarly, in reporting your financial situation for financial aid there is a lot of room for judgment. The question is, what kinds of actions are both permissible and ethical, and what kinds of actions are illegal and unethical? It might be argued that paying off your credit card debt to reduce your assets is legal and ethical. It is true that you have intentionally changed the nature of your assets in order to improve your chances of getting aid. You did so, however, through a legitimate transaction. In fact, given the high interest rates charged on credit card bills, it would probably be a good idea to use the cash to pay off your bills even if you aren't applying for aid.

Now, consider an alternative situation. Suppose that you have $10,000 in cash, and you have a sibling who is five years younger than you. Should you "give" the cash to your sibling while you are being considered for financial aid? This would give the appearance of substantially reducing your assets, and thus increase the likelihood that you will receive aid. Most people would argue that this is unethical, and it is probably illegal.

When completing your FAFSA form, don't ignore the following warning on the front of the form: "If you get Federal student aid based on incorrect information, you will have to pay it back; you may also have to pay fines and fees. If you purposely give false or misleading information on your application, you may be fined $20,000, sent to prison, or both."

Answer to PepsiCo Review It Question 4, p. 13

PepsiCo's accounting equation is:

Assets	=	Liabilities	+	Owners' (Stockholders') Equity
$31,727,000,000	=	$17,476,000,000	+	$14,251,000,000

(Owners' equity includes preferred stock.)

Answers to Self-Study Questions

1. b **2.** d **3.** c **4.** b **5.** d **6.** b **7.** a **8.** b **9.** c **10.** a

Remember to go back to the Navigator box on the chapter-opening page and check off your completed work.

Chapter 2

The Recording Process

STUDY OBJECTIVES

After studying this chapter, you should be able to:

1. Explain what an account is and how it helps in the recording process.
2. Define debits and credits and explain their use in recording business transactions.
3. Identify the basic steps in the recording process.
4. Explain what a journal is and how it helps in the recording process.
5. Explain what a ledger is and how it helps in the recording process.
6. Explain what posting is and how it helps in the recording process.
7. Prepare a trial balance and explain its purposes.

The Navigator

The Navigator

- Scan **Study Objectives**
- Read **Feature Story**
- Read **Preview**
- Read text and answer **Before You Go On** p. 52 p. 56 p. 65 p. 69
- Work **Demonstration Problem**
- Review **Summary of Study Objectives**
- Answer **Self-Study Questions**
- Complete **Assignments**

Feature Story

ACCIDENTS HAPPEN

How organized are you financially? Take a short quiz. Answer *yes* or *no* to each question:

- Does your wallet contain so many cash machine receipts that you've been declared a walking fire hazard?
- Is your wallet such a mess that it is often faster to fish for money in the crack of your car seat than to dig around in your wallet?
- Was LeBron James playing high school basketball the last time you balanced your checkbook?

If you think it is hard to keep track of the many transactions that make up *your* life, imagine what it is like for a major corporation like Fidelity Investments (*www.fidelity.com*). Fidelity is one of the largest mutual fund management firms in the world. If you had your life savings invested at Fidelity Investments, you might be just slightly displeased if, when you called to find out your balance, the representative said, "You know, I kind of remember someone with a name like yours sending us some money—now what did we do with that?"

To ensure the accuracy of your balance and the security of your funds, Fidelity Investments, like all other companies large and small, relies on a sophisticated accounting information system. That's not to say that Fidelity or any other company is error-free. In fact, if you've ever really messed up your checkbook register, you may take some comfort from one accountant's mistake at Fidelity Investments. The accountant failed to include a minus sign while doing a calculation, making what was actually a $1.3 billion loss look like a $1.3 billion gain! Fortunately, like most accounting errors, it was detected before any real harm was done.

No one expects that kind of mistake at a company like Fidelity, which has sophisticated computer systems and top investment managers. In explaining the mistake to shareholders, a spokesperson wrote, "Some people have asked how, in this age of technology, such a mistake could be made. While many of our processes are computerized, accounting systems are complex and dictate that some steps must be handled manually by our managers and accountants, and people can make mistakes."

✓ The Navigator

Inside Chapter 2...

Preview of Chapter 2

In Chapter 1, we analyzed business transactions in terms of the accounting equation, and we presented the cumulative effects of these transactions in tabular form. Imagine a company like Fidelity Investments (as in the Feature Story) using the same tabular format as Softbyte to keep track of its transactions. In a single day, Fidelity engages in thousands of business transactions. To record each transaction this way would be impractical, expensive, and unnecessary. Instead, companies use a set of procedures and records to keep track of transaction data more easily. This chapter introduces and illustrates these basic procedures and records.

The content and organization of Chapter 2 are as follows.

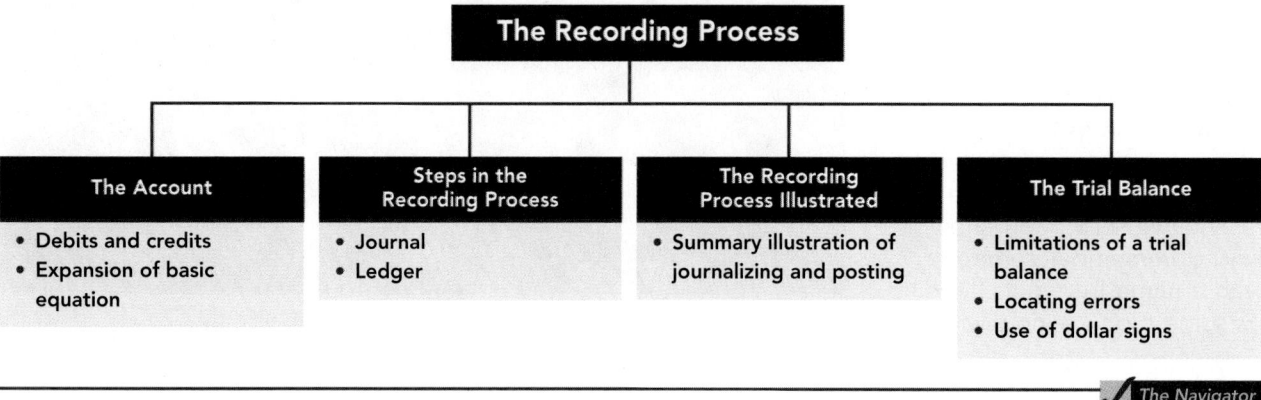

The Recording Process

The Account
- Debits and credits
- Expansion of basic equation

Steps in the Recording Process
- Journal
- Ledger

The Recording Process Illustrated
- Summary illustration of journalizing and posting

The Trial Balance
- Limitations of a trial balance
- Locating errors
- Use of dollar signs

The Navigator

THE ACCOUNT

STUDY OBJECTIVE 1

Explain what an account is and how it helps in the recording process.

An **account** is an accounting record of increases and decreases in a specific asset, liability, or owner's equity item. For example, Softbyte (the company discussed in Chapter 1) would have separate accounts for Cash, Accounts Receivable, Accounts Payable, Service Revenue, and Salaries Expense. In its simplest form, an account consists of three parts: (1) a title, (2) a left or debit side, and (3) a right or credit side. Because the format of an account resembles the letter T, we refer to it as a **T account**. Illustration 2-1 shows the basic form of an account.

Illustration 2-1
Basic form of account

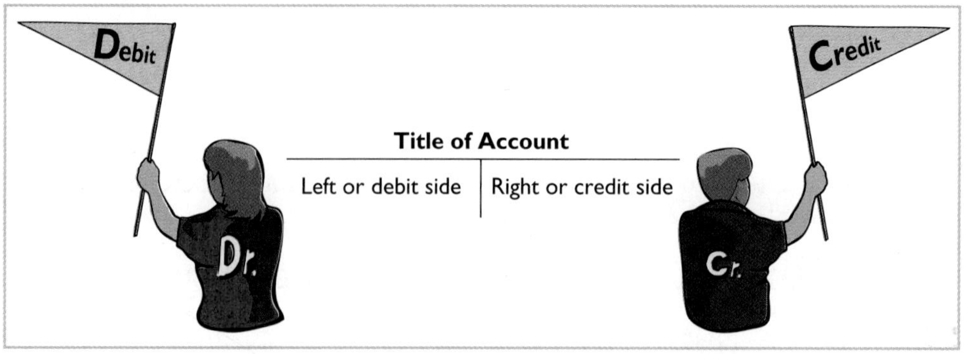

The T account is a standard shorthand in accounting, which helps make clear the effects of transactions on individual accounts. We will use it often throughout this book to explain basic accounting relationships.

Debits and Credits

STUDY OBJECTIVE 2

Define debits and credits and explain their use in recording business transactions.

The terms debit and credit are directional signals: **Debit** indicates left, and **credit** indicates right. They indicate which side of a T account a number will be recorded on. Entering an amount on the left side of an account is called **debiting** the account; making an entry on the right side is **crediting** the account. We commonly abbreviate debit as Dr. and credit as Cr.

Having debits on the left and credits on the right is an accounting custom, or rule, like the custom of driving on the right-hand side of the road in the United States. **This rule applies to all accounts.**

Illustration 2-2 shows the recording of debits and credits in an account for the cash transactions of Softbyte. The data are taken from the cash column of the tabular summary in Illustration 1-8 (from page 19), which is reproduced here.

Illustration 2-2
Tabular summary compared to account form

Tabular Summary

Cash
$15,000
−7,000
1,200
1,500
−1,700
−250
600
−1,300
$ 8,050

Account Form

Cash			
(Debits)	15,000	**(Credits)**	7,000
	1,200		1,700
	1,500		250
	600		1,300
Balance **(Debit)**	8,050		

In the tabular summary, every positive item represents Softbyte's receipt of cash; every negative amount represents a payment of cash. In the account form we record the increases in cash as debits, and the decreases in cash as credits. Having increases on one side and decreases on the other helps determine the total of each side as well as the overall account balance. The balance, a debit of $8,050, indicates that Softbyte has had $8,050 more increases than decreases in cash.

When the totals of the two sides of an account are compared, an account will have a **debit balance** if the total of the debit amounts exceeds the credits. An account will have a **credit balance** if the credit amounts exceed the debits. The account in Illustration 2-2 has a debit balance.

DEBIT AND CREDIT PROCEDURE

In Chapter 1 you learned the effect of a transaction on the basic accounting equation. Remember that each transaction must affect two or more accounts to keep the basic accounting equation in balance. In other words, for each transaction, debits must equal credits in the accounts. The equality of debits and credits provides the basis for the **double-entry system** of recording transactions.

In the double-entry system the dual (two-sided) effect of each transaction is recorded in appropriate accounts. This system provides a logical method for recording transactions. It also helps ensure the accuracy of the recorded amounts. The sum of all the debits to the accounts must equal the sum of all the credits.

The double-entry system for determining the equality of the accounting equation is much more efficient than the plus/minus procedure used in Chapter 1. On the following pages, we will illustrate debit and credit procedures in the double-entry system.

Assets and Liabilities. Both sides of the accounting equation (Assets = Liabilities + Owner's equity) must be equal. It follows, then, that we must record increases and decreases in assets opposite from each other. In Illustration 2-2, Softbyte entered increases in cash—an asset—on the left side, and decreases in cash on the right side. Therefore, we must enter increases in liabilities on the right or credit side, and decreases in liabilities on the left or debit side. Illustration 2-3 summarizes the effects that debits and credits have on assets and liabilities.

Illustration 2-3
Debit and credit effects—assets and liabilities

Debits	Credits
Increase assets	Decrease assets
Decrease liabilities	Increase liabilities

Debits to a specific asset account should exceed the credits to that account. Credits to a liability account should exceed debits to that account. **The normal balance of an account is on the side where an increase in the account is recorded.** Thus, asset accounts normally show debit balances, and liability accounts normally show credit balances. Illustration 2-4 shows the normal balances for assets and liabilities.

Illustration 2-4
Normal balances—assets and liabilities

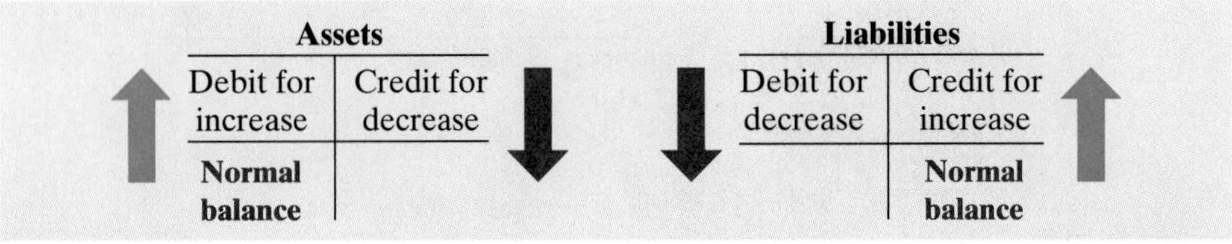

Knowing the normal balance in an account may help you trace errors. For example, a credit balance in an asset account such as Land would indicate a recording error. Similarly, a debit balance in a liability account such as Wages Payable would indicate an error. Occasionally, though, an abnormal balance may be correct. The Cash account, for example, will have a credit balance when a company has overdrawn its bank balance (i.e., written a "bad" check). (Notice that when we are referring to a specific account, we capitalize its name.)

Owner's Equity. As Chapter 1 indicated, owner's investments and revenues increase owner's equity. Owner's drawings and expenses decrease owner's equity. Companies keep accounts for each of these types of transactions, as explained below.

Owner's Capital. Investments by owners are credited to the Owner's Capital account. Credits increase this account, and debits decrease it. For example, when an owner invests cash in the business, the company debits (increases) Cash and credits (increases) Owner's Capital. When the owner's investment in the business is reduced, Owner's Capital is debited (decreased).

Illustration 2-5 shows the rules of debit and credit for the Owner's Capital account.

Illustration 2-5
Debit and credit effects—Owner's Capital

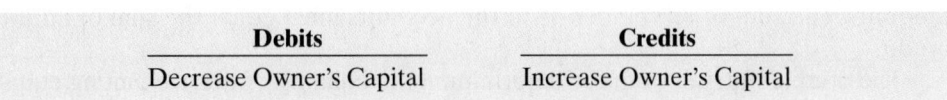

Debits	Credits
Decrease Owner's Capital	Increase Owner's Capital

We can diagram the normal balance in Owner's Capital as follows.

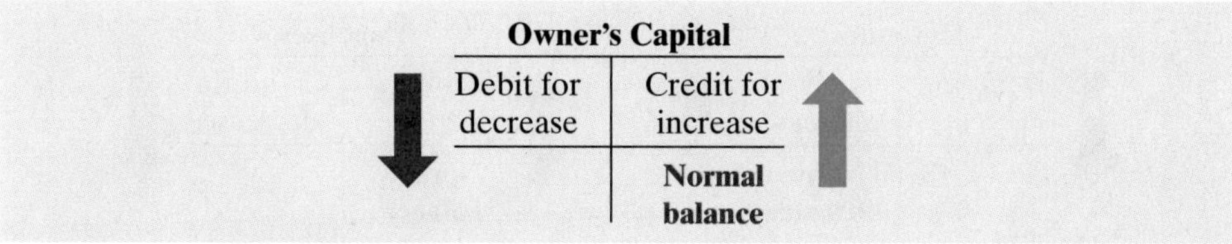

Illustration 2-6
Normal balance—Owner's Capital

Owner's Drawing. An owner may withdraw cash or other assets for personal use. Withdrawals could be debited directly to Owner's Capital to indicate a decrease in owner's equity. However, it is preferable to use a separate account, called Owner's Drawing. This separate account makes it easier to determine total withdrawals for each accounting period. Owner's Drawing is increased by debits and decreased by credits. Normally, the drawing account will have a debit balance.

Illustration 2-7 shows the rules of debit and credit for the drawing account.

Debits	Credits
Increase Owner's Drawing	Decrease Owner's Drawing

Illustration 2-7
Debit and credit effects—Owner's Drawing

We can diagram the normal balance as follows.

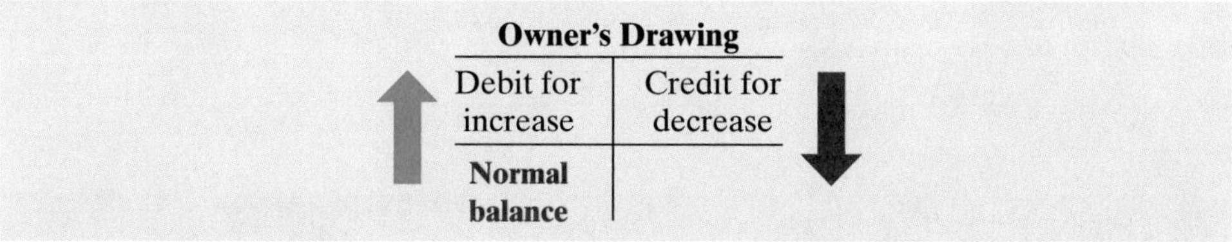

Illustration 2-8
Normal balance—Owner's Drawing

The Drawing account decreases owner's equity. It is not an income statement account like revenues and expenses.

Revenues and Expenses. The purpose of earning revenues is to benefit the owner(s) of the business. When a company earns revenues, owner's equity increases. Therefore, **the effect of debits and credits on revenue accounts is the same as their effect on Owner's Capital**. Revenue accounts are increased by credits and decreased by debits.

Expenses have the opposite effect: expenses decrease owner's equity. Since expenses decrease net income, and revenues increase it, it is logical that the increase and decrease sides of expense accounts should be the reverse of revenue accounts. Thus, expense accounts are increased by debits and decreased by credits.

Illustration 2-9 shows the rules of debits and credits for revenues and expenses.

HELPFUL HINT

Because revenues increase owner's equity, a revenue account has the same debit/credit rules as the Owner's Capital account. Expenses have the opposite effect.

Debits	Credits
Decrease revenues	Increase revenues
Increase expenses	Decrease expenses

Illustration 2-9
Debit and credit effects—revenues and expenses

Credits to revenue accounts should exceed debits. Debits to expense accounts should exceed credits. Thus, revenue accounts normally show credit balances, and expense accounts normally show debit balances. We can diagram the normal balances as follows.

Illustration 2-10
Normal balances—revenues and expenses

Revenues	
Debit for decrease	Credit for increase
	Normal balance

Expenses	
Debit for increase	Credit for decrease
Normal balance	

HELPFUL HINT
You may want to bookmark Illustration 2-11. You probably will refer to it often.

Expansion of the Basic Equation

You have already learned the basic accounting equation. Illustration 2-11 expands this equation by showing the accounts that comprise owner's equity. In addition, it illustrates the debit/credit rules and effects on each type of account. Study this diagram carefully. It will help you understand the fundamentals of the double-entry system.

Basic Equation: Assets = Liabilities + Owner's Equity

	Assets		=	Liabilities		+	Owner's Capital		−	Owner's Drawing		+	Revenues		−	Expenses	
Expanded Basic Equation																	
Debit / Credit Effects	Dr. +	Cr. −		Dr. −	Cr. +		Dr. −	Cr. +		Dr. +	Cr. −		Dr. −	Cr. +		Dr. +	Cr. −

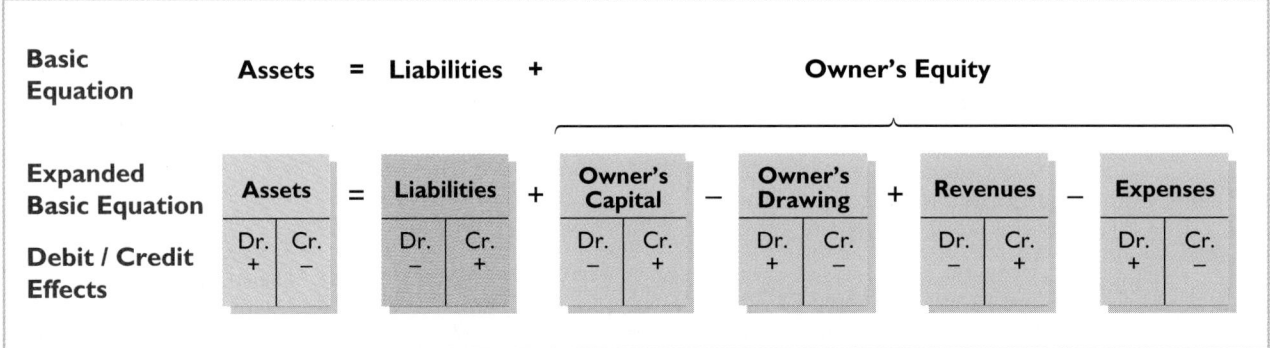

Illustration 2-11
Expanded basic equation and debit/credit rules and effects

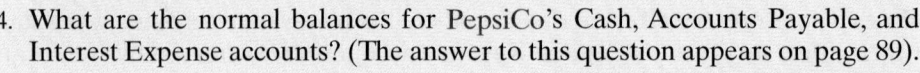

Before You Go On...

REVIEW IT

1. What do the terms *debit* and *credit* mean?
2. What are the debit and credit effects on assets, liabilities, and owner's capital?
3. What are the debit and credit effects on revenues, expenses, and owner's drawing?
4. What are the normal balances for PepsiCo's Cash, Accounts Payable, and Interest Expense accounts? (The answer to this question appears on page 89).

DO IT

Kate Browne has just rented space in a shopping mall. In this space, she will open a hair salon, to be called "Hair It Is." A friend has advised Kate to set up a double-entry set of accounting records in which to record all of her business transactions.

Identify the balance sheet accounts that Kate will likely need to record the transactions needed to open her business. Indicate whether the normal balance of each account is a debit or a credit.

Action Plan

- Determine the types of accounts needed: Kate will need asset accounts for each different type of asset she invests in the business, and liability accounts for any debts she incurs.
- Understand the types of owner's equity accounts: Only Owner's Capital will be needed when Kate begins the business. Other owner's equity accounts will be needed later.

Solution Kate would likely need the following accounts in which to record the transactions necessary to ready her hair salon for opening day:

Cash (debit balance)
Equipment (debit balance)
Supplies (debit balance)
Accounts Payable (credit balance)
If she borrows money: Notes payable (credit balance)
K. Browne, Capital (credit balance)

Related exercise material: *BE2-1, BE2-2, BE2-5, E2-1, E2-2, and E2-4.*

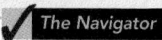

✓ The Navigator

STEPS IN THE RECORDING PROCESS

STUDY OBJECTIVE 3
Identify the basic steps in the recording process.

In practically every business, there are three basic steps in the recording process:

1. Analyze each transaction for its effects on the accounts.
2. Enter the transaction information in a *journal*.
3. Transfer the journal information to the appropriate accounts in the *ledger*.

Although it is possible to enter transaction information directly into the accounts without using a journal, few businesses do so.

The recording process begins with the transaction. **Business documents**, such as a sales slip, a check, a bill, or a cash register tape, provide evidence of the transaction. The company analyzes this evidence to determine the transaction's effects on specific accounts. The company then enters the transaction in the journal. Finally, it transfers the journal entry to the designated accounts in the ledger. Illustration 2-12 shows the recording process.

Illustration 2-12
The recording process

The steps in the recording process occur repeatedly. We illustrated the first step, the analysis of transactions, in Chapter 1, and will give further examples in this and later chapters. The other two steps in the recording process are explained in the next sections.

The Journal

STUDY OBJECTIVE 4
Explain what a journal is and how it helps in the recording process.

Companies initially record transactions in chronological order (the order in which they occur). Thus, the **journal** is referred to as the book of original entry. For each transaction the journal shows the debit and credit effects on specific accounts.

Companies may use various kinds of journals, but every company has the most basic form of journal, a **general journal**. Typically, a general journal has spaces for dates, account titles and explanations, references, and two amount columns. See the format of the journal in Illustration 2-13, below. Whenever we use the term "journal" in this textbook without a modifying adjective, we mean the general journal.

The journal makes several significant contributions to the recording process:

1. It discloses in one place the complete effects of a transaction.
2. It provides a chronological record of transactions.
3. It helps to prevent or locate errors because the debit and credit amounts for each entry can be easily compared.

JOURNALIZING

Entering transaction data in the journal is known as **journalizing**. Companies make separate journal entries for each transaction. A complete entry consists of: (1) the date of the transaction, (2) the accounts and amounts to be debited and credited, and (3) a brief explanation of the transaction.

Illustration 2-13 shows the technique of journalizing, using the first two transactions of Softbyte. On September 1, Ray Neal invested $15,000 cash in the business, and Softbyte purchased computer equipment for $7,000 cash. The number J1 indicates that these two entries are recorded on the first page of the journal. Illustration 2-13 shows the standard form of journal entries for these two transactions. (The boxed numbers correspond to explanations in the list below the illustration.)

Illustration 2-13
Technique of journalizing

GENERAL JOURNAL J1

Date		Account Titles and Explanation	Ref.	Debit	Credit
2008			[5]		
Sept. 1	[2]	Cash		15,000	
[1]	[3]	R. Neal, Capital			15,000
	[4]	(Owner's investment of cash in business)			
1		Computer Equipment		7,000	
		Cash			7,000
		(Purchase of equipment for cash)			

[1] The date of the transaction is entered in the Date column.

[2] The debit account title (that is, the account to be debited) is entered first at the extreme left margin of the column headed "Account Titles and Explanation," and the amount of the debit is recorded in the Debit column.

[3] The credit account title (that is, the account to be credited) is indented and entered on the next line in the column headed "Account Titles and Explanation," and the amount of the credit is recorded in the Credit column.

[4] A brief explanation of the transaction appears on the line below the credit account title. A space is left between journal entries. The blank space separates individual journal entries and makes the entire journal easier to read.

[5] The column titled Ref. (which stands for Reference) is left blank when the journal entry is made. This column is used later when the journal entries are transferred to the ledger accounts.

It is important to use correct and specific account titles in journalizing. The main criterion is that each title must appropriately describe the content of the account. For example, a company might use Delivery Equipment, Delivery Trucks, or Trucks as the account title used for the cost of delivery trucks. Once a company chooses the specific title to use, it should record under that account title all later transactions involving the account.[1]

SIMPLE AND COMPOUND ENTRIES

Some entries involve only two accounts, one debit and one credit. (See, for example, the entries in Illustration 2-13.) An entry like these is considered a **simple entry**. Some transactions, however, require more than two accounts in journalizing. An entry that requires three or more accounts is a **compound entry**. To illustrate, assume that on July 1, Butler Company purchases a delivery truck costing $14,000. It pays $8,000 cash now and agrees to pay the remaining $6,000 on account (to be paid later). The compound entry is as follows.

Illustration 2-14
Compound journal entry

GENERAL JOURNAL J1

Date	Account Titles and Explanation	Ref.	Debit	Credit
2008				
July 1	Delivery Equipment		14,000	
	Cash			8,000
	Accounts Payable			6,000
	(Purchased truck for cash with balance on account)			

In a compound entry, the standard format requires that all debits be listed before the credits.

ACCOUNTING ACROSS THE ORGANIZATION

New Xbox Contributes to Profitability

Bryan Lee is head of finance at Microsoft's Home and Entertainment Division. In recent years the division has lost over $4 billion, mostly due to losses on the original Xbox videogame player. With the new Xbox 360 videogame player, Mr. Lee hopes the division will become profitable. He has set strict goals for sales, revenue, and profit. "A manager seeking to spend more on a feature such as a disk drive has to find allies in the group to cut spending elsewhere, or identify new revenue to offset the increase," he explains.

For example, Microsoft originally designed the new Xbox to have 256 megabytes of memory. But the design department said that amount of memory wouldn't support the best special effects. The purchasing department said that adding more memory would cost $30—which is 10% of the estimated selling price of $300. But the marketing department "determined that adding the memory would let Microsoft reduce marketing costs and attract more game developers, boosting royalty revenue. It would also extend the life of the console, generating more sales." Microsoft doubled the memory to 512 megabytes.

Source: Robert A. Guth, "New Xbox Aim for Microsoft: Profitability," *Wall Street Journal*, May 24, 2005, p. C1.

? In what ways is this Microsoft division using accounting to assist in its effort to become more profitable?

[1] In homework problems, you should use specific account titles when they are given. When account titles are not given, you may select account titles that identify the nature and content of each account. The account titles used in journalizing should not contain explanations such as Cash Paid or Cash Received.

Before You Go On...

REVIEW IT

1. What is the sequence of the steps in the recording process?
2. How does the journal benefit the recording process?
3. What is the standard form and content of a journal entry made in the general journal?

DO IT

Kate Browne engaged in the following activities in establishing her salon, Hair It Is:

1. Opened a bank account in the name of Hair It Is and deposited $20,000 of her own money in this account as her initial investment.
2. Purchased equipment on account (to be paid in 30 days) for a total cost of $4,800.
3. Interviewed three persons for the position of hair stylist.

In what form (type of record) should Kate record these three activities? Prepare the entries to record the transactions.

Action Plan

- Understand which activities need to be recorded and which do not. Any that have economic effects should be recorded in a journal.
- Analyze the effects of transactions on asset, liability, and owner's equity accounts.

Solution Each transaction that is recorded is entered in the general journal. The three activities would be recorded as follows.

1. Cash	20,000	
K. Browne, Capital		20,000
(Owner's investment of cash in business)		
2. Equipment	4,800	
Accounts Payable		4,800
(Purchase of equipment on account)		
3. No entry because no transaction has occurred.		

Related exercise material: *BE2-3, BE2-6, E2-3, E2-5, E2-6, and E2-7.*

✓ The Navigator

The Ledger

STUDY OBJECTIVE 5

Explain what a ledger is and how it helps in the recording process.

The entire group of accounts maintained by a company is the **ledger**. The ledger keeps in one place all the information about changes in specific account balances.

Companies may use various kinds of ledgers, but every company has a general ledger. A **general ledger** contains all the asset, liability, and owner's equity accounts, as shown in Illustration 2-15 (page 57), for J. Lind Company. Whenever we use the term "ledger" in this textbook without a modifying adjective, we mean the general ledger.

Companies arrange the ledger in the sequence in which they present the accounts in the financial statements, beginning with the balance sheet accounts. First in order are the asset accounts, followed by liability accounts, owner's capital, owner's drawing, revenues, and expenses. Each account is numbered for easier identification.

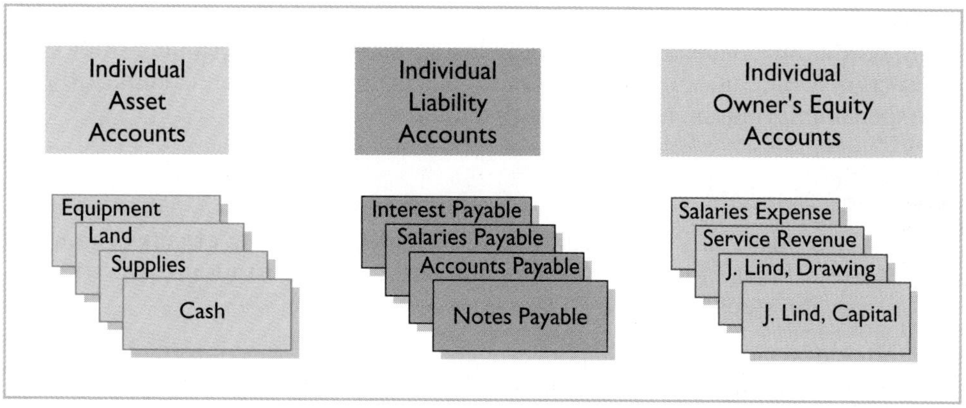

Illustration 2-15
The general ledger, which contains all of a company's accounts

The ledger provides the balance in each of the accounts. For example, the Cash account shows the amount of cash available to meet current obligations. The Accounts Receivable account shows amounts due from customers. Accounts Payable shows amounts owed to creditors.

ACCOUNTING ACROSS THE ORGANIZATION

What Would Sam Do?

In his autobiography Sam Walton described the double-entry accounting system he used when Wal-Mart was just getting started: "We kept a little pigeonhole on the wall for the cash receipts and paperwork of each [Wal-Mart] store. I had a blue binder ledger book for each store. When we added a store, we added a pigeonhole. We did this at least up to twenty stores. Then once a month, the bookkeeper and I would enter the merchandise, enter the sales, enter the cash, and balance it."

Source: Sam Walton, *Made in America* (New York: Doubleday, 1992), p. 53.

? Why did Sam Walton keep separate pigeonholes and blue binders? Why bother to keep separate records for each store?

STANDARD FORM OF ACCOUNT

The simple T-account form used in accounting textbooks is often very useful for illustration purposes. However, in practice, the account forms used in ledgers are much more structured. Illustration 2-16 shows a typical form, using assumed data from a cash account.

CASH — **NO. 101**

Date	Explanation	Ref.	Debit	Credit	Balance
2008					
June 1			25,000		25,000
2				8,000	17,000
3			4,200		21,200
9			7,500		28,700
17				11,700	17,000
20				250	16,750
30				7,300	9,450

Illustration 2-16
Three-column form of account

This is called the **three-column form of account**. It has three money columns—debit, credit, and balance. The balance in the account is determined after each transaction. Companies use the explanation space and reference columns to provide special information about the transaction.

POSTING

STUDY OBJECTIVE 6

Explain what posting is and how it helps in the recording process.

Transferring journal entries to the ledger accounts is called **posting**. This phase of the recording process accumulates the effects of journalized transactions into the individual accounts. Posting involves the following steps.

1. In the ledger, enter, in the appropriate columns of the account(s) debited, the date, journal page, and debit amount shown in the journal.
2. In the reference column of the journal, write the account number to which the debit amount was posted.
3. In the ledger, enter, in the appropriate columns of the account(s) credited, the date, journal page, and credit amount shown in the journal.
4. In the reference column of the journal, write the account number to which the credit amount was posted.

Illustration 2-17 shows these four steps using Softbyte's first journal entry. The boxed numbers indicate the sequence of the steps.

Illustration 2-17
Posting a journal entry

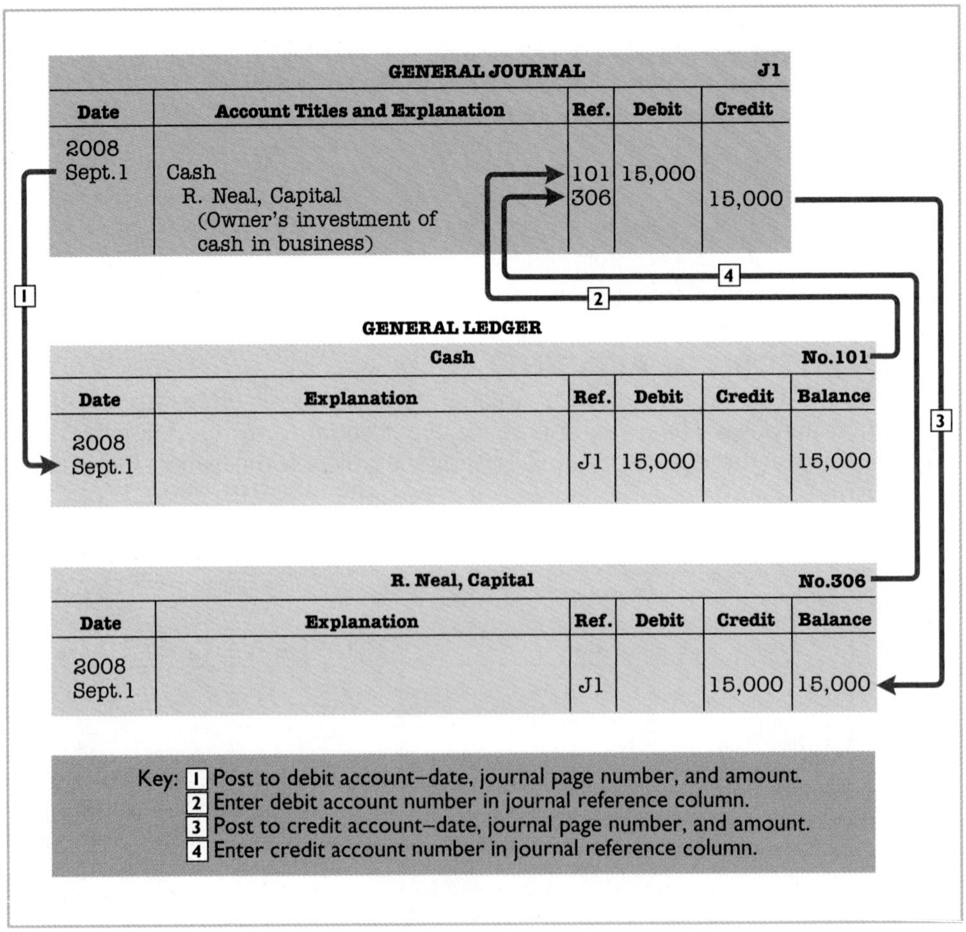

Posting should be performed in chronological order. That is, the company should post all the debits and credits of one journal entry before proceeding to the next journal entry. Postings should be made on a timely basis to ensure that the ledger is up to date.[2]

The reference column **of a ledger** account indicates the journal page from which the transaction was posted.[3] The explanation space of the ledger account is used infrequently because an explanation already appears in the journal.

CHART OF ACCOUNTS

The number and type of accounts differ for each company. The number of accounts depends on the amount of detail management desires. For example, the management of one company may want a single account for all types of utility expense. Another may keep separate expense accounts for each type of utility, such as gas, electricity, and water. Similarly, a small company like Softbyte will have fewer accounts than a corporate giant like Dell. Softbyte may be able to manage and report its activities in twenty to thirty accounts, while Dell may require thousands of accounts to keep track of its worldwide activities.

Most companies have a **chart of accounts**. This chart lists the accounts and the account numbers that identify their location in the ledger. The numbering system that identifies the accounts usually starts with the balance sheet accounts and follows with the income statement accounts.

In this and the next two chapters, we will be explaining the accounting for Pioneer Advertising Agency (a service company). Accounts 101–199 indicate asset accounts; 200–299 indicate liabilities; 301–350 indicate owner's equity accounts; 400–499, revenues; 601–799, expenses; 800–899, other revenues; and 900–999, other expenses. Illustration 2-18 shows Pioneer's chart of accounts. (C. R. Byrd is Pioneer's owner.) Accounts listed in red are used in this chapter; accounts shown in black are explained in later chapters.

Illustration 2-18
Chart of accounts

PIONEER ADVERTISING AGENCY
Chart of Accounts

Assets	Owner's Equity
101 Cash	**301 C. R. Byrd, Capital**
112 Accounts Receivable	**306 C. R. Byrd, Drawing**
126 Advertising Supplies	350 Income Summary
130 Prepaid Insurance	
157 Office Equipment	**Revenues**
158 Accumulated Depreciation—Office Equipment	**400 Service Revenue**
Liabilities	**Expenses**
200 Notes Payable	631 Advertising Supplies Expense
201 Accounts Payable	711 Depreciation Expense
209 Unearned Revenue	722 Insurance Expense
212 Salaries Payable	**726 Salaries Expense**
230 Interest Payable	**729 Rent Expense**
	905 Interest Expense

[2] In homework problems, you can journalize all transactions before posting any of the journal entries.

[3] After the last entry has been posted, the accountant should scan the reference column **in the journal**, to confirm that all postings have been made.

You will notice that there are gaps in the numbering system of the chart of accounts for Pioneer Advertising. Gaps are left to permit the insertion of new accounts as needed during the life of the business.

THE RECORDING PROCESS ILLUSTRATED

Illustrations 2-19 through 2-28 show the basic steps in the recording process, using the October transactions of Pioneer Advertising Agency. Pioneer's accounting period is a month. A basic analysis and a debit-credit analysis precede the journalizing and posting of each transaction. For simplicity, we use the T-account form in the illustrations instead of the standard account form.

Study these transaction analyses carefully. **The purpose of transaction analysis is first to identify the type of account involved, and then to determine whether to make a debit or a credit to the account.** You should always perform this type of analysis before preparing a journal entry. Doing so will help you understand the journal entries discussed in this chapter as well as more complex journal entries in later chapters.

In addition, an Accounting Cycle Tutorial at the book's website, **www.wiley.com/college/weygandt**, provides an interactive presentation of the steps in the accounting cycle, using the examples in the illustrations on the following pages.

Illustration 2-19
Investment of cash by owner

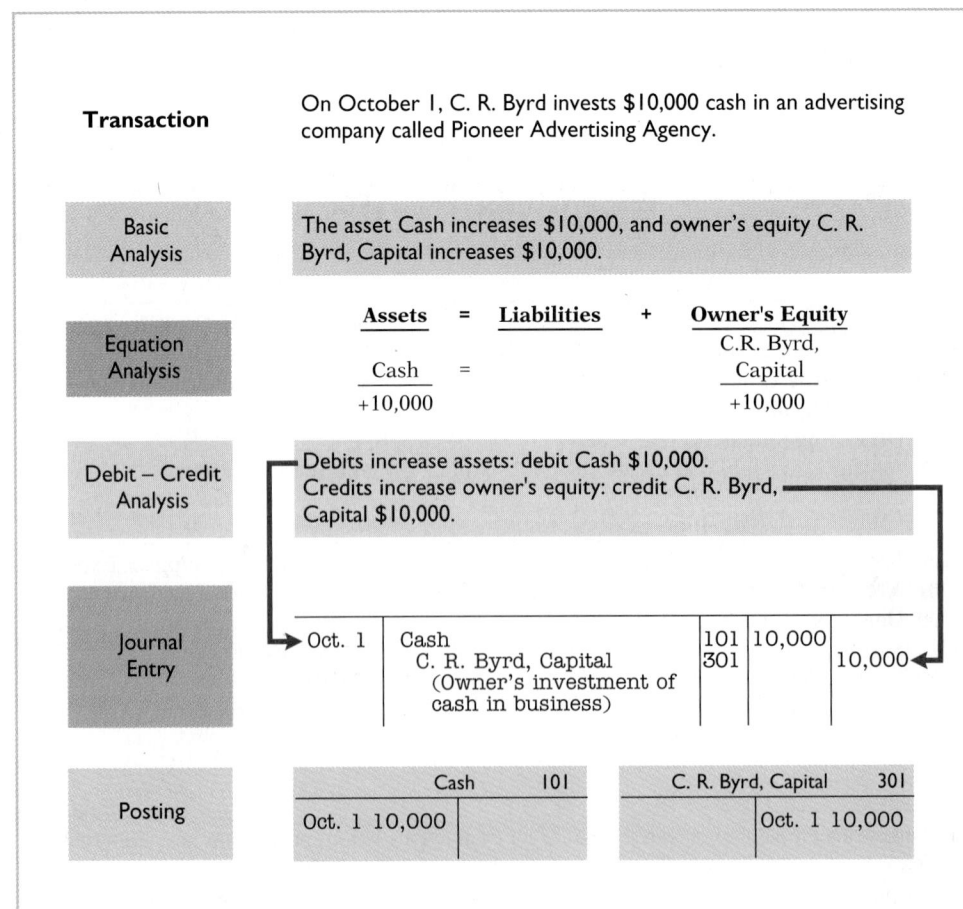

Transaction: On October 1, C. R. Byrd invests $10,000 cash in an advertising company called Pioneer Advertising Agency.

Basic Analysis: The asset Cash increases $10,000, and owner's equity C. R. Byrd, Capital increases $10,000.

Equation Analysis:

Assets	=	Liabilities	+	Owner's Equity
				C.R. Byrd,
Cash	=			Capital
+10,000				+10,000

Debit – Credit Analysis: Debits increase assets: debit Cash $10,000.
Credits increase owner's equity: credit C. R. Byrd, Capital $10,000.

Journal Entry:

Oct. 1	Cash	101	10,000	
	C. R. Byrd, Capital	301		10,000
	(Owner's investment of cash in business)			

Posting:

Cash	101
Oct. 1 10,000	

C. R. Byrd, Capital	301
	Oct. 1 10,000

HELPFUL HINT
Follow these steps:
1. Determine what type of account is involved.
2. Determine what items increased or decreased and by how much.
3. Translate the increases and decreases into debits and credits.

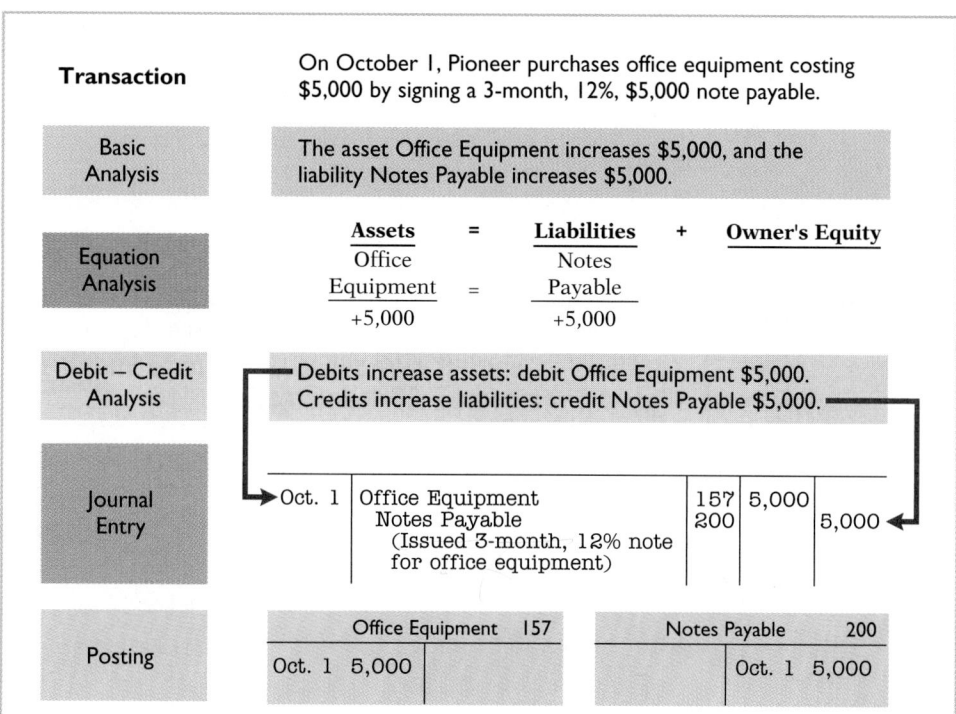

Illustration 2-20
Purchase of office equipment

Transaction

On October 1, Pioneer purchases office equipment costing $5,000 by signing a 3-month, 12%, $5,000 note payable.

Basic Analysis

The asset Office Equipment increases $5,000, and the liability Notes Payable increases $5,000.

Equation Analysis

Assets	=	Liabilities	+	Owner's Equity
Office Equipment	=	Notes Payable		
+5,000		+5,000		

Debit – Credit Analysis

Debits increase assets: debit Office Equipment $5,000.
Credits increase liabilities: credit Notes Payable $5,000.

Journal Entry

Oct. 1	Office Equipment	157	5,000	
	Notes Payable	200		5,000
	(Issued 3-month, 12% note for office equipment)			

Posting

Office Equipment 157	
Oct. 1 5,000	

Notes Payable 200	
	Oct. 1 5,000

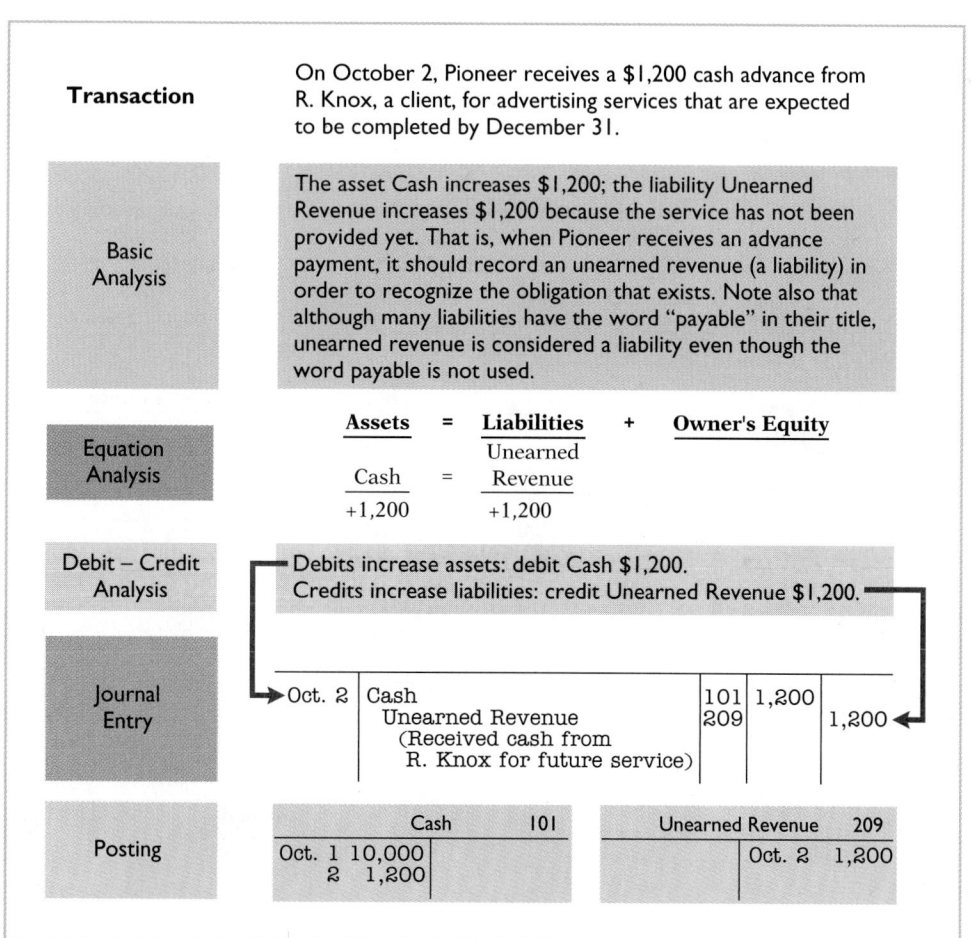

Illustration 2-21
Receipt of cash for future service

Transaction

On October 2, Pioneer receives a $1,200 cash advance from R. Knox, a client, for advertising services that are expected to be completed by December 31.

Basic Analysis

The asset Cash increases $1,200; the liability Unearned Revenue increases $1,200 because the service has not been provided yet. That is, when Pioneer receives an advance payment, it should record an unearned revenue (a liability) in order to recognize the obligation that exists. Note also that although many liabilities have the word "payable" in their title, unearned revenue is considered a liability even though the word payable is not used.

Equation Analysis

Assets	=	Liabilities	+	Owner's Equity
Cash	=	Unearned Revenue		
+1,200		+1,200		

Debit – Credit Analysis

Debits increase assets: debit Cash $1,200.
Credits increase liabilities: credit Unearned Revenue $1,200.

Journal Entry

Oct. 2	Cash	101	1,200	
	Unearned Revenue	209		1,200
	(Received cash from R. Knox for future service)			

Posting

Cash 101	
Oct. 1 10,000	
2 1,200	

Unearned Revenue 209	
	Oct. 2 1,200

Illustration 2-22
Payment of monthly rent

Transaction
On October 3, Pioneer pays office rent for October in cash, $900.

Basic Analysis
The expense account Rent Expense increases $900 because the payment pertains only to the current month; the asset Cash decreases $900.

Equation Analysis

Assets	=	Liabilities	+	Owner's Equity
Cash	=			Rent Expense
-900				-900

Debit – Credit Analysis
Debits increase expenses: debit Rent Expense $900.
Credits decrease assets: credit Cash $900.

Journal Entry

Oct. 3	Rent Expense	729	900	
	Cash	101		900
	(Paid October rent)			

Posting

Cash			101
Oct. 1	10,000	Oct. 3	900
2	1,200		

Rent Expense			729
Oct. 3	900		

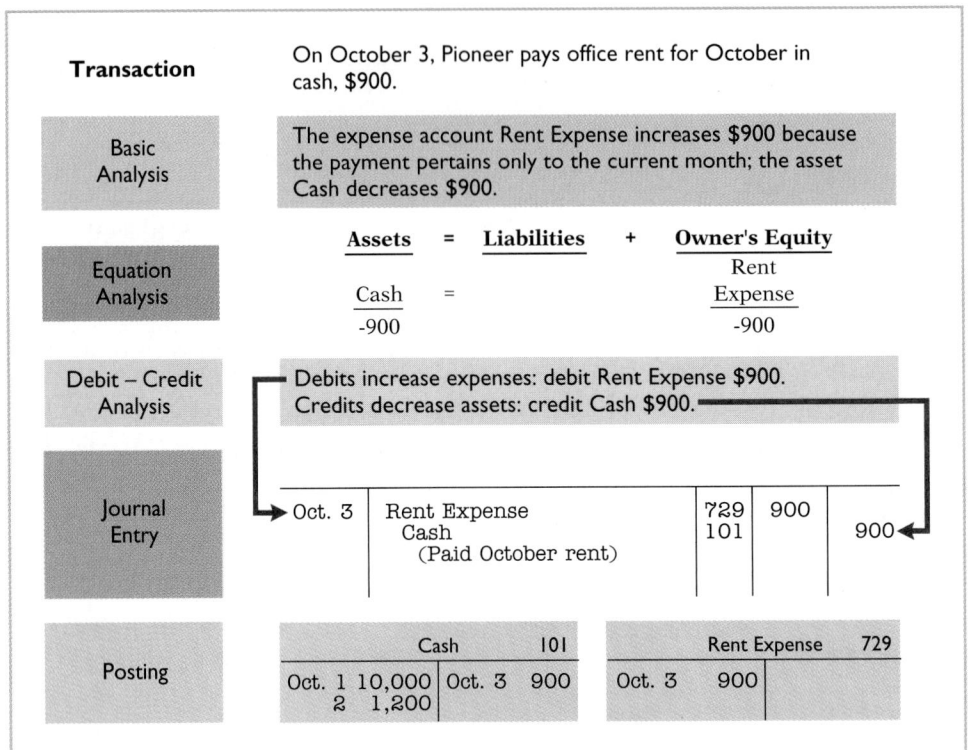

Illustration 2-23
Payment for insurance

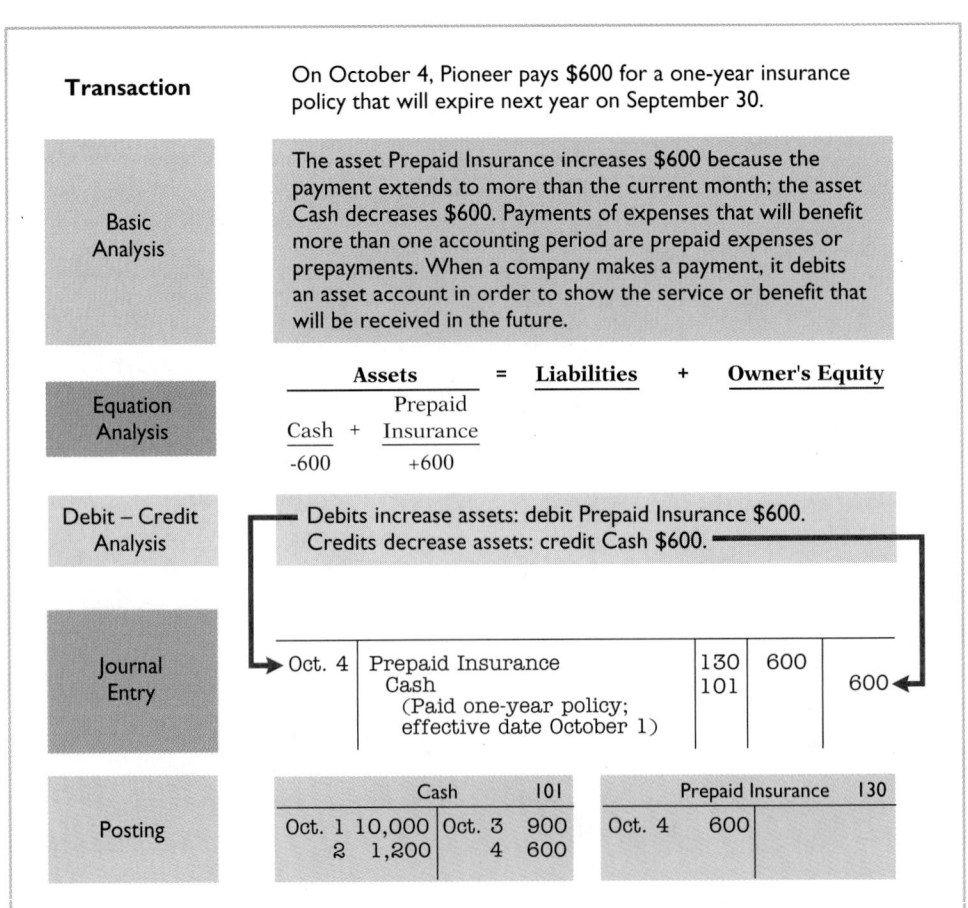

Transaction
On October 4, Pioneer pays $600 for a one-year insurance policy that will expire next year on September 30.

Basic Analysis
The asset Prepaid Insurance increases $600 because the payment extends to more than the current month; the asset Cash decreases $600. Payments of expenses that will benefit more than one accounting period are prepaid expenses or prepayments. When a company makes a payment, it debits an asset account in order to show the service or benefit that will be received in the future.

Equation Analysis

Assets			=	Liabilities	+	Owner's Equity
Cash	+	Prepaid Insurance				
-600		+600				

Debit – Credit Analysis
Debits increase assets: debit Prepaid Insurance $600.
Credits decrease assets: credit Cash $600.

Journal Entry

Oct. 4	Prepaid Insurance	130	600	
	Cash	101		600
	(Paid one-year policy; effective date October 1)			

Posting

Cash			101
Oct. 1	10,000	Oct. 3	900
2	1,200	4	600

Prepaid Insurance			130
Oct. 4	600		

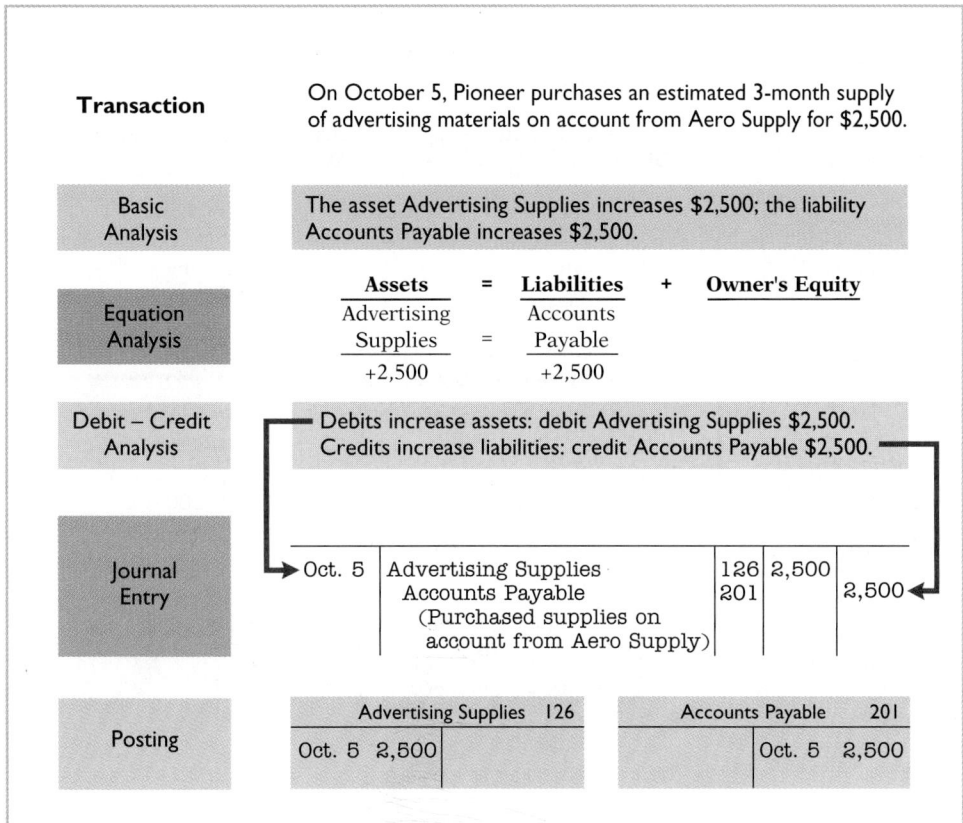

Illustration 2-24
Purchase of supplies on credit

Transaction: On October 5, Pioneer purchases an estimated 3-month supply of advertising materials on account from Aero Supply for $2,500.

Basic Analysis: The asset Advertising Supplies increases $2,500; the liability Accounts Payable increases $2,500.

Equation Analysis:

Assets	=	Liabilities	+	Owner's Equity
Advertising Supplies	=	Accounts Payable		
+2,500		+2,500		

Debit – Credit Analysis: Debits increase assets: debit Advertising Supplies $2,500. Credits increase liabilities: credit Accounts Payable $2,500.

Journal Entry:

Oct. 5	Advertising Supplies	126	2,500	
	Accounts Payable	201		2,500
	(Purchased supplies on account from Aero Supply)			

Posting:

Advertising Supplies 126	
Oct. 5 2,500	

Accounts Payable 201	
	Oct. 5 2,500

Illustration 2-25
Hiring of employees

Event: On October 9, Pioneer hires four employees to begin work on October 15. Each employee is to receive a weekly salary of $500 for a 5-day work week, payable every 2 weeks—first payment made on October 26.

Basic Analysis: A business transaction has not occurred. There is only an agreement between the employer and the employees to enter into a business transaction beginning on October 15. Thus, a debit–credit analysis is not needed because there is no accounting entry. (See transaction of October 26 for first entry.)

Illustration 2-26
Withdrawal of cash by owner

Transaction — On October 20, C. R. Byrd withdraws $500 cash for personal use.

Basic Analysis — The owner's equity account C. R. Byrd, Drawing, increases $500; the asset Cash decreases $500.

Equation Analysis

Assets	=	Liabilities	+	Owner's Equity
Cash	=			C.R. Byrd, Drawing
-500				-500

Debit – Credit Analysis — Debits increase drawings: debit C. R. Byrd, Drawing $500. Credits decrease assets: credit Cash $500.

Journal Entry

Oct. 20	C. R. Byrd, Drawing	306	500	
	Cash	101		500
	(Withdrew cash for personal use)			

Posting

Cash			101
Oct. 1	10,000	Oct. 3	900
2	1,200	4	600
		20	500

C. R. Byrd, Drawing			306
Oct. 20	500		

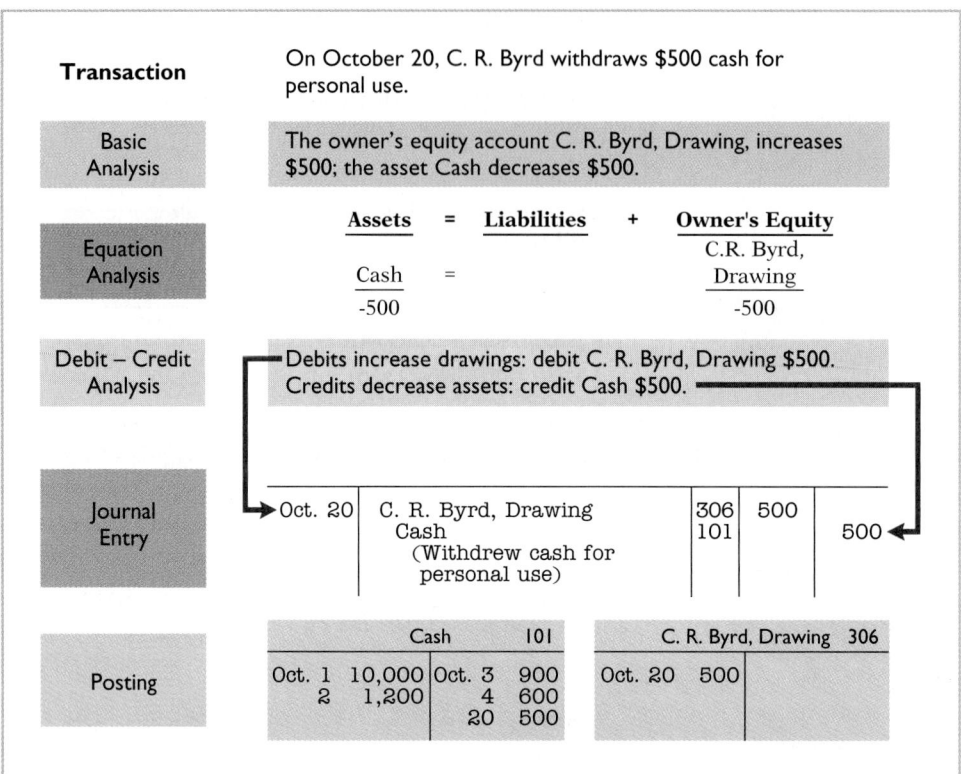

Illustration 2-27
Payment of salaries

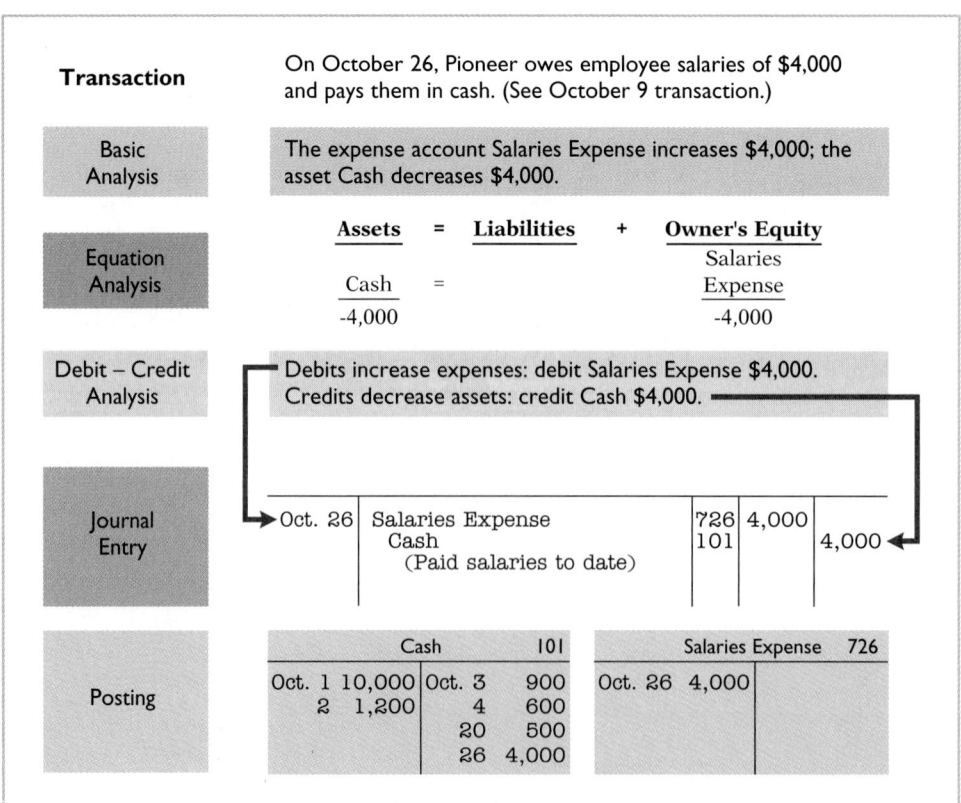

Transaction — On October 26, Pioneer owes employee salaries of $4,000 and pays them in cash. (See October 9 transaction.)

Basic Analysis — The expense account Salaries Expense increases $4,000; the asset Cash decreases $4,000.

Equation Analysis

Assets	=	Liabilities	+	Owner's Equity
Cash	=			Salaries Expense
-4,000				-4,000

Debit – Credit Analysis — Debits increase expenses: debit Salaries Expense $4,000. Credits decrease assets: credit Cash $4,000.

Journal Entry

Oct. 26	Salaries Expense	726	4,000	
	Cash	101		4,000
	(Paid salaries to date)			

Posting

Cash			101
Oct. 1	10,000	Oct. 3	900
2	1,200	4	600
		20	500
		26	4,000

Salaries Expense			726
Oct. 26	4,000		

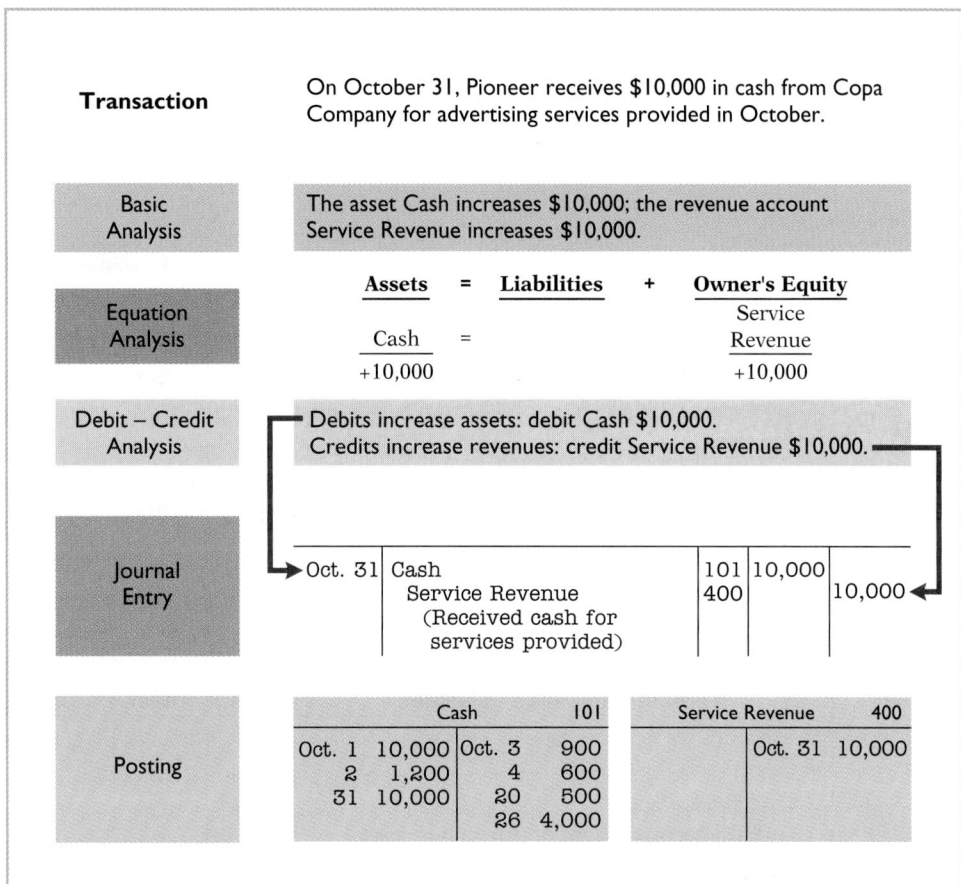

Illustration 2-28
Receipt of cash for services provided

Transaction

On October 31, Pioneer receives $10,000 in cash from Copa Company for advertising services provided in October.

Basic Analysis

The asset Cash increases $10,000; the revenue account Service Revenue increases $10,000.

Equation Analysis

Assets	=	**Liabilities**	+	**Owner's Equity**
Cash	=			Service Revenue
+10,000				+10,000

Debit – Credit Analysis

Debits increase assets: debit Cash $10,000.
Credits increase revenues: credit Service Revenue $10,000.

Journal Entry

Oct. 31	Cash	101	10,000	
	Service Revenue	400		10,000
	(Received cash for services provided)			

Posting

Cash			101
Oct. 1	10,000	Oct. 3	900
2	1,200	4	600
31	10,000	20	500
		26	4,000

Service Revenue			400
		Oct. 31	10,000

Before You Go On...

REVIEW IT

1. How does journalizing differ from posting?
2. What is the purpose of (a) the ledger and (b) a chart of accounts?

DO IT

Kate Brown recorded the following transactions in a general journal during the month of March.

Mar. 4	Cash	2,280	
	Service Revenue		2,280
Mar. 15	Wages Expense	400	
	Cash		400
Mar. 19	Utilities Expense	92	
	Cash		92

Post these entries to the Cash account of the general ledger to determine the ending balance in cash. The beginning balance in cash on March 1 was $600.

Action Plan

- Recall that posting involves transferring the journalized debits and credits to specific accounts in the ledger.
- Determine the ending balance by netting the total debits and credits.

Solution

Cash

3/1	600	3/15	400
3/4	2,280	3/19	92
3/31 Bal.	2,388		

Related exercise material: *BE2-7, BE2-8, E2-8, and E2-12.*

The Navigator

Summary Illustration of Journalizing and Posting

Illustration 2-29 shows the journal for Pioneer Advertising Agency for October. Illustration 2-30, on page 67, shows the ledger, with all balances in color.

Illustration 2-29
General journal entries

GENERAL JOURNAL — PAGE J1

Date	Account Titles and Explanation	Ref.	Debit	Credit
2008				
Oct. 1	Cash	101	10,000	
	C. R. Byrd, Capital	301		10,000
	(Owner's investment of cash in business)			
1	Office Equipment	157	5,000	
	Notes Payable	200		5,000
	(Issued 3-month, 12% note for office equipment)			
2	Cash	101	1,200	
	Unearned Revenue	209		1,200
	(Received cash from R. Knox for future service)			
3	Rent Expense	729	900	
	Cash	101		900
	(Paid October rent)			
4	Prepaid Insurance	130	600	
	Cash	101		600
	(Paid one-year policy; effective date October 1)			
5	Advertising Supplies	126	2,500	
	Accounts Payable	201		2,500
	(Purchased supplies on account from Aero Supply)			
20	C. R. Byrd, Drawing	306	500	
	Cash	101		500
	(Withdrew cash for personal use)			
26	Salaries Expense	726	4,000	
	Cash	101		4,000
	(Paid salaries to date)			
31	Cash	101	10,000	
	Service Revenue	400		10,000
	(Received cash for services provided)			

GENERAL LEDGER

Cash — No. 101

Date	Explanation	Ref.	Debit	Credit	Balance
2008					
Oct. 1		J1	10,000		10,000
2		J1	1,200		11,200
3		J1		900	10,300
4		J1		600	9,700
20		J1		500	9,200
26		J1		4,000	5,200
31		J1	10,000		**15,200**

Advertising Supplies — No. 126

Date	Explanation	Ref.	Debit	Credit	Balance
2008					
Oct. 5		J1	2,500		**2,500**

Prepaid Insurance — No. 130

Date	Explanation	Ref.	Debit	Credit	Balance
2008					
Oct. 4		J1	600		**600**

Office Equipment — No. 157

Date	Explanation	Ref.	Debit	Credit	Balance
2008					
Oct. 1		J1	5,000		**5,000**

Notes Payable — No. 200

Date	Explanation	Ref.	Debit	Credit	Balance
2008					
Oct. 1		J1		5,000	**5,000**

Accounts Payable — No. 201

Date	Explanation	Ref.	Debit	Credit	Balance
2008					
Oct. 5		J1		2,500	**2,500**

Unearned Revenue — No. 209

Date	Explanation	Ref.	Debit	Credit	Balance
2008					
Oct. 2		J1		1,200	**1,200**

C.R. Byrd, Capital — No. 301

Date	Explanation	Ref.	Debit	Credit	Balance
2008					
Oct. 1		J1		10,000	**10,000**

C.R. Byrd, Drawing — No. 306

Date	Explanation	Ref.	Debit	Credit	Balance
2008					
Oct. 20		J1	500		**500**

Service Revenue — No. 400

Date	Explanation	Ref.	Debit	Credit	Balance
2008					
Oct. 31		J1		10,000	**10,000**

Salaries Expense — No. 726

Date	Explanation	Ref.	Debit	Credit	Balance
2008					
Oct. 26		J1	4,000		**4,000**

Rent Expense — No. 729

Date	Explanation	Ref.	Debit	Credit	Balance
2008					
Oct. 3		J1	900		**900**

Illustration 2-30
General ledger

THE TRIAL BALANCE

STUDY OBJECTIVE 7
Prepare a trial balance and explain its purposes.

A **trial balance** is a list of accounts and their balances at a given time. Customarily, companies prepare a trial balance at the end of an accounting period. They list accounts in the order in which they appear in the ledger. Debit balances appear in the left column and credit balances in the right column.

The primary purpose of a trial balance is to prove (check) that the debits equal the credits after posting. The sum of the debit balances in the trial balance should equal the sum of the credit balances. If the debits and credits do not agree, the company can use the trial balance to uncover errors in journalizing and posting. In addition, the trial balance is useful in preparing financial statements, as we will explain in the next two chapters.

The steps for preparing a trial balance are:

1. List the account titles and their balances.
2. Total the debit and credit columns.
3. Prove the equality of the two columns.

Illustration 2-31 shows the trial balance prepared from Pioneer Advertising's ledger. Note that the total debits equal the total credits.

Illustration 2-31
A trial balance

PIONEER ADVERTISING AGENCY
Trial Balance
October 31, 2008

	Debit	Credit
Cash	$15,200	
Advertising Supplies	2,500	
Prepaid Insurance	600	
Office Equipment	5,000	
Notes Payable		$ 5,000
Accounts Payable		2,500
Unearned Revenue		1,200
C. R. Byrd, Capital		10,000
C. R. Byrd, Drawing	500	
Service Revenue		10,000
Salaries Expense	4,000	
Rent Expense	900	
	$28,700	**$28,700**

A trial balance is a necessary checkpoint for uncovering certain types of errors. For example, if only the debit portion of a journal entry has been posted, the trial balance would bring this error to light.

Limitations of a Trial Balance

A trial balance does not guarantee freedom from recording errors. Numerous errors may exist even though the trial balance columns agree. For example, the trial balance may balance even when (1) a transaction is not journalized, (2) a correct journal entry is not posted, (3) a journal entry is posted twice, (4) incorrect accounts are used in journalizing or posting, or (5) offsetting errors are made in recording the amount of a transaction. As long as equal debits and credits are posted, even to the wrong account or in the wrong amount, the total debits will equal the total credits. **The trial balance does not prove that the company has recorded all transactions or that the ledger is correct.**

ETHICS NOTE

An *error* is the result of an unintentional mistake; it is neither ethical nor unethical. An *irregularity* is an intentional misstatement, which *is* viewed as unethical.

Locating Errors

Errors in a trial balance generally result from mathematical mistakes, incorrect postings, or simply transcribing data incorrectly. What do you do if you are faced with a trial balance that does not balance? First determine the amount of the difference between the two columns of the trial balance. After this amount is known, the following steps are often helpful:

1. If the error is $1, $10, $100, or $1,000, re-add the trial balance columns and recompute the account balances.
2. If the error is divisible by 2, scan the trial balance to see whether a balance equal to half the error has been entered in the wrong column.
3. If the error is divisible by 9, retrace the account balances on the trial balance to see whether they are incorrectly copied from the ledger. For example, if a balance was $12 and it was listed as $21, a $9 error has been made. Reversing the order of numbers is called a **transposition error**.
4. If the error is not divisible by 2 or 9, scan the ledger to see whether an account balance in the amount of the error has been omitted from the trial balance, and scan the journal to see whether a posting of that amount has been omitted.

Use of Dollar Signs

Note that dollar signs do not appear in journals or ledgers. Dollar signs are typically used only in the trial balance and the financial statements. Generally, a dollar sign is shown only for the first item in the column and for the total of that column. A single line is placed under the column of figures to be added or subtracted; the total amount is double-underlined to indicate the final sum.

ETHICS INSIGHT

Sarbanes-Oxley Comes to the Rescue

While most companies record transactions very carefully, the reality is that mistakes still happen: Bank regulators fined Bank One Corporation (now Chase) $1.8 million; they felt that the unreliability of the bank's accounting system caused it to violate regulatory requirements. Also, in recent years Fannie Mae, the government-chartered mortgage association, announced large accounting errors. These announcements caused investors, regulators, and politicians to fear larger, undetected problems. Such problems could spill over into the home-mortgage market, which depends on Fannie Mae to buy hundreds of billions of dollars of mortgages each year. Finally, before a major overhaul of its accounting system, the financial records of Waste Management Company were in such disarray that of the company's 57,000 employees, 10,000 were receiving pay slips that were in error.

The Sarbanes-Oxley Act of 2002 was created to minimize the occurrence of errors like these by increasing every employee's responsibility for accurate financial reporting.

? In order for these companies to prepare and issue financial statements, their accounting equations (debits and credits) must have been in balance at year-end. How could these errors or misstatements have occurred?

Before You Go On...

REVIEW IT

1. What is a trial balance, and what is its primary purpose?
2. How is a trial balance prepared?
3. What are the limitations of a trial balance?

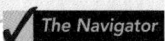

✓ The Navigator

Be sure to read **ALL ABOUT YOU: *Your Personal Annual Report*** on page 70 for information on how topics in this chapter apply to you.

Your Personal Annual Report

If you haven't already done so, in the not-too-distant future you will prepare a résumé. In some ways your résumé is like a company's annual report. Its purpose is to enable others to evaluate your past, in an effort to predict your future.

A résumé is your opportunity to create a positive first impression. It is important that it be impressive—but it should also be accurate. In order to increase their job prospects, some people are tempted to "inflate" their résumés by overstating the importance of some past accomplishments or positions. In fact, you might even think that "everybody does it" and that if you don't do it, you will be at a disadvantage.

Some Facts

Before you turn your résumé into a world-class work of fiction, consider the following:

* David Edmondson, the president and CEO of well-known electronics retailer Radio Shack, overstated his accomplishments by claiming that he had earned a bachelor's of science degree, when in fact he had not. Apparently his employer had not done a background check to ensure the accuracy of his résumé.
* A chief financial officer of Veritas Software lied about having an M.B.A. from Stanford University.
* A former president of the U.S. Olympic Committee, lied about having a Ph.D. from Arizona State University. When the truth was discovered, she resigned.
* The University of Notre Dame discovered that its football coach, George O'Leary, lied about his education and football history. He was forced to resign after only five days.

About the Numbers

- A survey by Automatic Data Processing reported that 40% of applicants misrepresented their education or employment history.
- A survey by the Society for Human Resource Management of human resource professionals reported the following responses to the question, "*When investigating the backgrounds of job candidates, how important or unimportant is the discovery of inaccuracies in the job candidate's résumé on your decision to extend a job offer?*"

Importance of Résumé Inaccuracies on the Hiring Decision

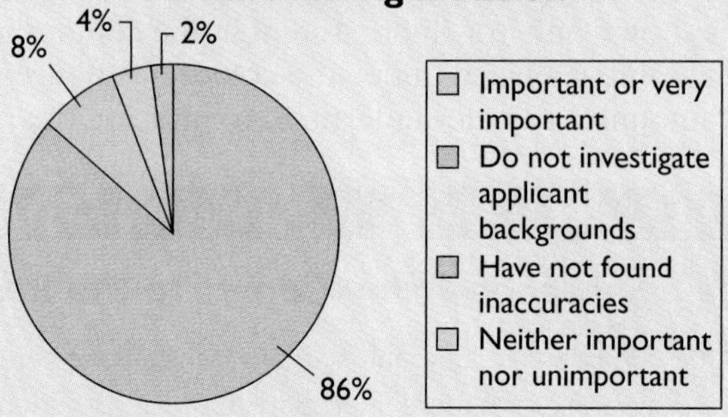

Source: Society for Human Resource Management, press release, August 31, 2004, *http://www.shrm.org/press/ntu_published/cms_009624.asp.*

What Do You Think?

Using Radio Shack as an example, what should the company have done when it learned of the falsehoods on Mr. Edmondson's résumé? Should Radio Shack have fired him?

NO: Mr. Edmondson had been a Radio Shack employee for 11 years. He had served the company in a wide variety of positions, and had earned the position of CEO through exceptional performance. While the fact that he lied 11 years earlier on his résumé was unfortunate, his service since then made this past transgression irrelevant. In addition, the company was in the midst of a massive restructuring, which included closing 700 of its 7,000 stores. It could not afford additional upheaval at this time.

YES: Radio Shack is a publicly traded company. Investors, creditors, employees, and others doing business with the company will not trust it if its leader is known to have poor integrity. The "tone at the top" is vital to creating an ethical organization.

Sources: E. White and T. Herrick, "Ethical Breaches Pose Dilemma for Boards: When to Fire a CEO?" *Wall Street Journal,* February 15, 2006; and T. Hanrahan, "Résumé Trouble," *Wall Street Journal,* March 3, 2006.

Tips on resume writing can be found at many websites, such as ***http://resume.monster.com/.***

The authors' comments on this situation appear on page 89.

Demonstration Problem

Bob Sample opened the Campus Laundromat on September 1, 2008. During the first month of operations the following occurred.

Sept. 1 Invested $20,000 cash in the business.
2 Paid $1,000 cash for store rent for September.
3 Purchased washers and dryers for $25,000, paying $10,000 in cash and signing a $15,000, 6-month, 12% note payable.
4 Paid $1,200 for a one-year accident insurance policy.
10 Received a bill from the *Daily News* for advertising the opening of the laundromat $200.
20 Withdrew $700 cash for personal use.
30 Determined that cash receipts for laundry services for the month were $6,200.

The chart of accounts for the company is the same as that for Pioneer Advertising Agency plus the following: No. 154 Laundry Equipment and No. 610 Advertising Expense.

Instructions

(a) Journalize the September transactions. (Use J1 for the journal page number.)
(b) Open ledger accounts and post the September transactions.
(c) Prepare a trial balance at September 30, 2008.

Solution to Demonstration Problem

(a) GENERAL JOURNAL **J1**

Date	Account Titles and Explanation	Ref.	Debit	Credit
2008				
Sept. 1	Cash	101	20,000	
	Bob Sample, Capital	301		20,000
	(Owner's investment of cash in business)			
2	Rent Expense	729	1,000	
	Cash	101		1,000
	(Paid September rent)			
3	Laundry Equipment	154	25,000	
	Cash	101		10,000
	Notes Payable	200		15,000
	(Purchased laundry equipment for cash and 6-month, 12% note payable)			
4	Prepaid Insurance	130	1,200	
	Cash	101		1,200
	(Paid one-year insurance policy)			
10	Advertising Expense	610	200	
	Accounts Payable	201		200
	(Received bill from *Daily News* for advertising)			
20	Bob Sample, Drawing	306	700	
	Cash	101		700
	(Withdrew cash for personal use)			
30	Cash	101	6,200	
	Service Revenue	400		6,200
	(Received cash for services provided)			

action plan

- ✓ Make separate journal entries for each transaction.
- ✓ In journalizing, make sure debits equal credits.
- ✓ In journalizing, use specific account titles taken from the chart of accounts.
- ✓ Provide appropriate description of each journal entry.
- ✓ Arrange ledger in statement order, beginning with the balance sheet accounts.
- ✓ Post in chronological order.
- ✓ Use numbers in the reference column to indicate the amount has been posted.
- ✓ In the trial balance, list accounts in the order in which they appear in the ledger.
- ✓ List debit balances in the left column, and credit balances in the right column.

(b) GENERAL LEDGER

Cash — No. 101

Date	Explanation	Ref.	Debit	Credit	Balance
2008					
Sept. 1		J1	20,000		20,000
2		J1		1,000	19,000
3		J1		10,000	9,000
4		J1		1,200	7,800
20		J1		700	7,100
30		J1	6,200		13,300

Prepaid Insurance — No. 130

Date	Explanation	Ref.	Debit	Credit	Balance
2008					
Sept. 4		J1	1,200		1,200

Laundry Equipment — No. 154

Date	Explanation	Ref.	Debit	Credit	Balance
2008					
Sept. 3		J1	25,000		25,000

Notes Payable — No. 200

Date	Explanation	Ref.	Debit	Credit	Balance
2008					
Sept. 3		J1		15,000	15,000

Accounts Payable — No. 201

Date	Explanation	Ref.	Debit	Credit	Balance
2008					
Sept. 10		J1		200	200

Bob Sample, Capital — No. 301

Date	Explanation	Ref.	Debit	Credit	Balance
2008					
Sept. 1		J1		20,000	20,000

Bob Sample, Drawing — No. 306

Date	Explanation	Ref.	Debit	Credit	Balance
2008					
Sept. 20		J1	700		700

Service Revenue — No. 400

Date	Explanation	Ref.	Debit	Credit	Balance
2008					
Sept. 30		J1		6,200	6,200

Advertising Expense — No. 610

Date	Explanation	Ref.	Debit	Credit	Balance
2008					
Sept. 10		J1	200		200

Rent Expense — No. 729

Date	Explanation	Ref.	Debit	Credit	Balance
2008					
Sept. 2		J1	1,000		1,000

(c) CAMPUS LAUNDROMAT
Trial Balance
September 30, 2008

	Debit	Credit
Cash	$13,300	
Prepaid Insurance	1,200	
Laundry Equipment	25,000	
Notes Payable		$15,000
Accounts Payable		200
Bob Sample, Capital		20,000
Bob Sample, Drawing	700	
Service Revenue		6,200
Advertising Expense	200	
Rent Expense	1,000	
	$41,400	$41,400

The Navigator

SUMMARY OF STUDY OBJECTIVES

WILEY PLUS

1 **Explain what an account is and how it helps in the recording process.** An account is a record of increases and decreases in specific asset, liability, and owner's equity items.

2 **Define debits and credits and explain their use in recording business transactions.** The terms debit and credit are synonymous with left and right. Assets, drawings,

and expenses are increased by debits and decreased by credits. Liabilities, owner's capital, and revenues are increased by credits and decreased by debits.

3 **Identify the basic steps in the recording process.** The basic steps in the recording process are: (a) analyze each transaction for its effects on the accounts, (b) enter the transaction information in a journal, (c) transfer the journal information to the appropriate accounts in the ledger.

4 **Explain what a journal is and how it helps in the recording process.** The initial accounting record of a transaction is entered in a journal before the data are entered in the accounts. A journal (a) discloses in one place the complete effects of a transaction, (b) provides a chronological record of transactions, and (c) prevents or locates errors because the debit and credit amounts for each entry can be easily compared.

5 **Explain what a ledger is and how it helps in the recording process.** The ledger is the entire group of accounts maintained by a company. The ledger keeps in one place all the information about changes in specific account balances.

6 **Explain what posting is and how it helps in the recording process.** Posting is the transfer of journal entries to the ledger accounts. This phase of the recording process accumulates the effects of journalized transactions in the individual accounts.

7 **Prepare a trial balance and explain its purposes.** A trial balance is a list of accounts and their balances at a given time. Its primary purpose is to prove the equality of debits and credits after posting. A trial balance also uncovers errors in journalizing and posting and is useful in preparing financial statements.

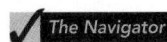

✓ The Navigator

GLOSSARY

WILEY PLUS

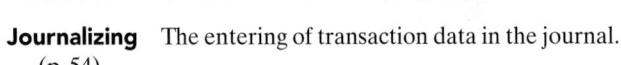

Account A record of increases and decreases in specific asset, liability, or owner's equity items. (p. 48).

Chart of accounts A list of accounts and the account numbers that identify their location in the ledger. (p. 59).

Compound entry A journal entry that involves three or more accounts. (p. 55).

Credit The right side of an account. (p. 49).

Debit The left side of an account. (p. 49).

Double-entry system A system that records in appropriate accounts the dual effect of each transaction. (p. 49).

General journal The most basic form of journal. (p. 54).

General ledger A ledger that contains all asset, liability, and owner's equity accounts. (p. 56).

Journal An accounting record in which transactions are initially recorded in chronological order. (p. 53).

Journalizing The entering of transaction data in the journal. (p. 54).

Ledger The entire group of accounts maintained by a company. (p. 56).

Normal balance An account balance on the side where an increase in the account is recorded. (p. 50)

Posting The procedure of transferring journal entries to the ledger accounts. (p. 58).

Simple entry A journal entry that involves only two accounts. (p. 55).

T account The basic form of an account. (p. 48).

Three-column form of account A form with columns for debit, credit, and balance amounts in an account. (p. 58).

Trial balance A list of accounts and their balances at a given time. (p. 67).

SELF-STUDY QUESTIONS

WILEY PLUS

Answers are at the end of the chapter.

(SO 1) **1.** Which of the following statements about an account is true?
- **a.** In its simplest form, an account consists of two parts.
- **b.** An account is an individual accounting record of increases and decreases in specific asset, liability, and owner's equity items.
- **c.** There are separate accounts for specific assets and liabilities but only one account for owner's equity items.
- **d.** The left side of an account is the credit or decrease side.

(SO 2) **2.** Debits:
- **a.** increase both assets and liabilities.
- **b.** decrease both assets and liabilities.
- **c.** increase assets and decrease liabilities.
- **d.** decrease assets and increase liabilities.

3. A revenue account: (SO 2)
- **a.** is increased by debits.
- **b.** is decreased by credits.
- **c.** has a normal balance of a debit.
- **d.** is increased by credits.

4. Accounts that normally have debit balances are: (SO 2)
- **a.** assets, expenses, and revenues.
- **b.** assets, expenses, and owner's capital.
- **c.** assets, liabilities, and owner's drawings.
- **d.** assets, owner's drawings, and expenses.

5. Which of the following is *not* part of the recording process? (SO 3)
- **a.** Analyzing transactions.
- **b.** Preparing a trial balance.
- **c.** Entering transactions in a journal.
- **d.** Posting transactions.

(SO 4) **6.** Which of the following statements about a journal is *false*?
a. It is not a book of original entry.
b. It provides a chronological record of transactions.
c. It helps to locate errors because the debit and credit amounts for each entry can be readily compared.
d. It discloses in one place the complete effect of a transaction.

(SO 5) **7.** A ledger:
a. contains only asset and liability accounts.
b. should show accounts in alphabetical order.
c. is a collection of the entire group of accounts maintained by a company.
d. is a book of original entry.

(SO 6) **8.** Posting:
a. normally occurs before journalizing.
b. transfers ledger transaction data to the journal.
c. is an optional step in the recording process.
d. transfers journal entries to ledger accounts.

9. A trial balance: (SO 7)
a. is a list of accounts with their balances at a given time.
b. proves the mathematical accuracy of journalized transactions.
c. will not balance if a correct journal entry is posted twice.
d. proves that all transactions have been recorded.

10. A trial balance will not balance if: (SO 7)
a. a correct journal entry is posted twice.
b. the purchase of supplies on account is debited to Supplies and credited to Cash.
c. a $100 cash drawing by the owner is debited to Owner's Drawing for $1,000 and credited to Cash for $100.
d. a $450 payment on account is debited to Accounts Payable for $45 and credited to Cash for $45.

Go to the book's website, **www.wiley.com/college/ weygandt,** for Additional Self-Study questions.

The Navigator

QUESTIONS

1. Describe the parts of a T account.

2. "The terms *debit* and *credit* mean increase and decrease, respectively." Do you agree? Explain.

3. Jeff Hiller, a fellow student, contends that the double-entry system means each transaction must be recorded twice. Is Jeff correct? Explain.

4. Maria Alvarez, a beginning accounting student, believes debit balances are favorable and credit balances are unfavorable. Is Maria correct? Discuss.

5. State the rules of debit and credit as applied to (a) asset accounts, (b) liability accounts, and (c) the owner's equity accounts (revenue, expenses, owner's drawing, and owner's capital).

6. What is the normal balance for each of the following accounts? (a) Accounts Receivable. (b) Cash. (c) Owner's Drawing. (d) Accounts Payable. (e) Service Revenue. (f) Salaries Expense. (g) Owner's Capital.

7. Indicate whether each of the following accounts is an asset, a liability, or an owner's equity account and whether it has a normal debit or credit balance: (a) Accounts Receivable, (b) Accounts Payable, (c) Equipment, (d) Owner's Drawing, (e) Supplies.

8. For the following transactions, indicate the account debited and the account credited.
(a) Supplies are purchased on account.
(b) Cash is received on signing a note payable.
(c) Employees are paid salaries in cash.

9. Indicate whether the following accounts generally will have (a) debit entries only, (b) credit entries only, or (c) both debit and credit entries.
(1) Cash.
(2) Accounts Receivable.
(3) Owner's Drawing.
(4) Accounts Payable.
(5) Salaries Expense.
(6) Service Revenue.

10. What are the basic steps in the recording process?

11. What are the advantages of using a journal in the recording process?

12. (a) When entering a transaction in the journal, should the debit or credit be written first?
(b) Which should be indented, the debit or credit?

13. Describe a compound entry, and provide an example.

14. (a) Should business transaction debits and credits be recorded directly in the ledger accounts?
(b) What are the advantages of first recording transactions in the journal and then posting to the ledger?

15. The account number is entered as the last step in posting the amounts from the journal to the ledger. What is the advantage of this step?

16. Journalize the following business transactions.
(a) Hector Molina invests $9,000 cash in the business.
(b) Insurance of $800 is paid for the year.
(c) Supplies of $2,000 are purchased on account.
(d) Cash of $7,500 is received for services rendered.

17. (a) What is a ledger?
(b) What is a chart of accounts and why is it important?

18. What is a trial balance and what are its purposes?

19. Jim Benes is confused about how accounting information flows through the accounting system. He believes the flow of information is as follows.
(a) Debits and credits posted to the ledger.
(b) Business transaction occurs.
(c) Information entered in the journal.
(d) Financial statements are prepared.
(e) Trial balance is prepared.

Is Jim correct? If not, indicate to Jim the proper flow of the information.

20. Two students are discussing the use of a trial balance. They wonder whether the following errors, each considered separately, would prevent the trial balance from balancing.
   (a) The bookkeeper debited Cash for $600 and credited Wages Expense for $600 for payment of wages.
   (b) Cash collected on account was debited to Cash for $900 and Service Revenue was credited for $90.

   What would you tell them?

BRIEF EXERCISES

Indicate debit and credit effects and normal balance.
(SO 2)

BE2-1 For each of the following accounts indicate the effects of (a) a debit and (b) a credit on the accounts and (c) the normal balance of the account.

1. Accounts Payable.
2. Advertising Expense.
3. Service Revenue.
4. Accounts Receivable.
5. A. J. Ritter, Capital.
6. A. J. Ritter, Drawing.

Identify accounts to be debited and credited.
(SO 2)

BE2-2 Transactions for the Hank Norris Company for the month of June are presented below. Identify the accounts to be debited and credited for each transaction.

June 1 Hank Norris invests $5,000 cash in a small welding business of which he is the sole proprietor.
2 Purchases equipment on account for $900.
3 $800 cash is paid to landlord for June rent.
12 Bills J. Kronsnoble $300 for welding work done on account.

Journalize transactions.
(SO 4)

BE2-3 Using the data in BE2-2, journalize the transactions. (You may omit explanations.)

Identify and explain steps in recording process.
(SO 3)

BE2-4 Tom Oslow, a fellow student, is unclear about the basic steps in the recording process. Identify and briefly explain the steps in the order in which they occur.

Indicate basic and debit-credit analysis.
(SO 2)

BE2-5 T. J. Carlin has the following transactions during August of the current year. Indicate (a) the effect on the accounting equation and (b) the debit-credit analysis illustrated on pages 60–65 of the text.

Aug. 1 Opens an office as a financial advisor, investing $8,000 in cash.
4 Pays insurance in advance for 6 months, $1,800 cash.
16 Receives $800 from clients for services provided.
27 Pays secretary $1,000 salary.

Journalize transactions.
(SO 4)

BE2-6 Using the data in BE2-5, journalize the transactions. (You may omit explanations.)

Post journal entries to T accounts.
(SO 6)

BE2-7 Selected transactions for the Finney Company are presented in journal form below. Post the transactions to T accounts. Make one T account for each item and determine each account's ending balance.

J1

Date	Account Titles and Explanation	Ref.	Debit	Credit
May 5	Accounts Receivable		5,000	
	Service Revenue			5,000
	(Billed for services provided)			
12	Cash		2,400	
	Accounts Receivable			2,400
	(Received cash in payment of account)			
15	Cash		3,000	
	Service Revenue			3,000
	(Received cash for services provided)			

Post journal entries to standard form of account.
(SO 6)

BE2-8 Selected journal entries for the Finney Company are presented in BE2-7. Post the transactions using the standard form of account.

Prepare a trial balance.
(SO 7)

BE2-9 From the ledger balances given below, prepare a trial balance for the Cleland Company at June 30, 2008. List the accounts in the order shown on page 59 of the text. All account balances are normal.

Accounts Payable $9,000, Cash $8,800, Cleland, Capital $20,000, Cleland, Drawing $1,200, Equipment $17,000, Service Revenue $8,000, Accounts Receivable $3,000, Salaries Expense $6,000, and Rent Expense $1,000.

Prepare a correct trial balance.
(SO 7)

BE2-10 An inexperienced bookkeeper prepared the following trial balance. Prepare a correct trial balance, assuming all account balances are normal.

KWUN COMPANY
Trial Balance
December 31, 2008

	Debit	Credit
Cash	$14,800	
Prepaid Insurance		$3,500
Accounts Payable		3,000
Unearned Revenue	2,200	
P. Kwun, Capital		13,000
P. Kwun, Drawing		4,500
Service Revenue		25,600
Salaries Expense	18,600	
Rent Expense		2,400
	$35,600	$52,000

EXERCISES

WILEY PLUS

Analyze statements about accounting and the recording process.
(SO 1)

E2-1 Josh Cephus has prepared the following list of statements about accounts.

1. An account is an accounting record of either a specific asset or a specific liability.
2. An account shows only increases, not decreases, in the item it relates to.
3. Some items, such as Cash and Accounts Receivable, are combined into one account.
4. An account has a left, or credit side, and a right, or debit side.
5. A simple form of an account consisting of just the account title, the left side, and the right side, is called a T-account.

Instructions

Identify each statement as true or false. If false, indicate how to correct the statement.

Identify debits, credits, and normal balances.
(SO 2)

E2-2 Selected transactions for D. Reyes, an interior decorator, in her first month of business, are as follows.

Jan. 2 Invested $10,000 cash in business.
3 Purchased used car for $4,000 cash for use in business.
9 Purchased supplies on account for $500.
11 Billed customers $1,800 for services performed.
16 Paid $200 cash for advertising.
20 Received $700 cash from customers billed on January 11.
23 Paid creditor $300 cash on balance owed.
28 Withdrew $1,000 cash for personal use by owner.

Instructions

For each transaction indicate the following.

(a) The basic type of account debited and credited (asset, liability, owner's equity).
(b) The specific account debited and credited (cash, rent expense, service revenue, etc.).
(c) Whether the specific account is increased or decreased.
(d) The normal balance of the specific account.

Use the following format, in which the January 2 transaction is given as an example.

	Account Debited				Account Credited			
Date	(a) Basic Type	(b) Specific Account	(c) Effect	(d) Normal Balance	(a) Basic Type	(b) Specific Account	(c) Effect	(d) Normal Balance
Jan. 2	Asset	Cash	Increase	Debit	Owner's Equity	D. Reyes, Capital	Increase	Credit

E2-3 Data for D. Reyes, interior decorator, are presented in E2-2.

Journalize transactions.

(SO 4)

Instructions

Journalize the transactions using journal page J1. (You may omit explanations.)

E2-4 Presented below is information related to Hanshew Real Estate Agency.

Analyze transactions and determine their effect on accounts.

(SO 2)

Oct. 1 Pete Hanshew begins business as a real estate agent with a cash investment of $15,000.
2 Hires an administrative assistant.
3 Purchases office furniture for $1,900, on account.
6 Sells a house and lot for B. Kidman; bills B. Kidman $3,200 for realty services provided.
27 Pays $700 on the balance related to the transaction of October 3.
30 Pays the administrative assistant $2,500 in salary for October.

Instructions

Prepare the debit-credit analysis for each transaction as illustrated on pages 60–65.

E2-5 Transaction data for Hanshew Real Estate Agency are presented in E2-4.

Journalize transactions.

(SO 4)

Instructions

Journalize the transactions. (You may omit explanations.)

E2-6 Konerko Industries had the following transactions.

Analyze transactions and journalize.

(SO 2, 3, 4)

1. Borrowed $5,000 from the bank by signing a note.
2. Paid $2,500 cash for a computer.
3. Purchased $700 of supplies on account.

Instructions

(a) Indicate what accounts are increased and decreased by each transaction.
(b) Journalize each transaction.

E2-7 Rowand Enterprises had the following selected transactions.

Analyze transactions and journalize.

(SO 2, 3, 4)

1. Aaron Rowand invested $4,000 cash in the business.
2. Paid office rent of $1,100.
3. Performed consulting services and billed a client $5,200.
4. Aaron Rowand withdrew $700 cash for personal use.

Instructions

(a) Indicate the effect each transaction has on the basic accounting equation (Assets = Liabilities + Owner's Equity), using plus and minus signs.
(b) Journalize each transaction.

E2-8 Josie Feeney has prepared the following list of statements about the general ledger.

Analyze statements about the ledger.

(SO 5)

1. The general ledger contains all the asset and liability accounts, but no owner's equity accounts.
2. The general ledger is sometimes referred to as simply the ledger.
3. The accounts in the general ledger are arranged in alphabetical order.
4. Each account in the general ledger is numbered for easier identification.
5. The general ledger is a book of original entry.

Instructions

Identify each statement as true or false. If false, indicate how to correct the statement.

Post journal entries and prepare a trial balance.
(SO 6, 7)

E2-9 Selected transactions from the journal of Teresa Gonzalez, investment broker, are presented below.

Date	Account Titles and Explanation	Ref.	Debit	Credit
Aug. 1	Cash		5,000	
	Teresa Gonzalez, Capital			5,000
	(Owner's investment of cash in business)			
10	Cash		2,400	
	Service Revenue			2,400
	(Received cash for services provided)			
12	Office Equipment		5,000	
	Cash			1,000
	Notes Payable			4,000
	(Purchased office equipment for cash and notes payable)			
25	Accounts Receivable		1,600	
	Service Revenue			1,600
	(Billed clients for services provided)			
31	Cash		900	
	Accounts Receivable			900
	(Receipt of cash on account)			

Instructions

(a) Post the transactions to T accounts.
(b) Prepare a trial balance at August 31, 2008.

Journalize transactions from account data and prepare a trial balance.
(SO 4, 7)

E2-10 The T accounts below summarize the ledger of Simon Landscaping Company at the end of the first month of operations.

Cash — No. 101

4/1	15,000	4/15	600
4/12	900	4/25	1,500
4/29	400		
4/30	1,000		

Unearned Revenue — No. 205

		4/30	1,000

Accounts Receivable — No. 112

4/7	3,200	4/29	400

J. Simon, Capital — No. 301

		4/1	15,000

Supplies — No. 126

4/4	1,800		

Service Revenue — No. 400

		4/7	3,200
		4/12	900

Accounts Payable — No. 201

4/25	1,500	4/4	1,800

Salaries Expense — No. 726

4/15	600		

Instructions

(a) Prepare the complete general journal (including explanations) from which the postings to Cash were made.
(b) Prepare a trial balance at April 30, 2008.

Journalize transactions from account data and prepare a trial balance.
(SO 4, 7)

E2-11 Presented below and on the next page is the ledger for Heerey Co.

Cash — No. 101

10/1	5,000	10/4	400
10/10	650	10/12	1,500
10/10	4,000	10/15	250
10/20	500	10/30	300
10/25	2,000	10/31	500

Heerey, Capital — No. 301

		10/1	5,000
		10/25	2,000

Heerey, Drawing — No. 306

10/30	300		

Accounts Receivable			No. 112
10/6	800	10/20	500
10/20	940		

Supplies			No. 126
10/4	400		

Furniture			No. 149
10/3	2,000		

Notes Payable			No. 200
		10/10	4,000

Accounts Payable			No. 201
10/12	1,500	10/3	2,000

Service Revenue			No. 407
		10/6	800
		10/10	650
		10/20	940

Store Wages Expense			No. 628
10/31	500		

Rent Expense			No. 729
10/15	250		

Instructions

(a) Reproduce the journal entries for the transactions that occurred on October 1, 10, and 20, and provide explanations for each.

(b) Determine the October 31 balance for each of the accounts above, and prepare a trial balance at October 31, 2008.

Prepare journal entries and post using standard account form.
(SO 4, 6)

E2-12 Selected transactions for Tina Cordero Company during its first month in business are presented below.

Sept. 1 Invested $10,000 cash in the business.
5 Purchased equipment for $12,000 paying $5,000 in cash and the balance on account.
25 Paid $3,000 cash on balance owed for equipment.
30 Withdrew $500 cash for personal use.

Cordero's chart of accounts shows: No. 101 Cash, No. 157 Equipment, No. 201 Accounts Payable, No. 301 Tina Cordero, Capital, No. 306 Tina Cordero, Drawing.

Instructions

(a) Journalize the transactions on page J1 of the journal.

(b) Post the transactions using the standard account form.

Analyze errors and their effects on trial balance.
(SO 7)

E2-13 The bookkeeper for Sam Kaplin Equipment Repair made a number of errors in journalizing and posting, as described below.

1. A credit posting of $400 to Accounts Receivable was omitted.
2. A debit posting of $750 for Prepaid Insurance was debited to Insurance Expense.
3. A collection from a customer of $100 in payment of its account owed was journalized and posted as a debit to Cash $100 and a credit to Service Revenue $100.
4. A credit posting of $300 to Property Taxes Payable was made twice.
5. A cash purchase of supplies for $250 was journalized and posted as a debit to Supplies $25 and a credit to Cash $25.
6. A debit of $475 to Advertising Expense was posted as $457.

Instructions

For each error:

(a) Indicate whether the trial balance will balance.

(b) If the trial balance will not balance, indicate the amount of the difference.

(c) Indicate the trial balance column that will have the larger total.

Consider each error separately. Use the following form, in which error (1) is given as an example.

Error	(a) In Balance	(b) Difference	(c) Larger Column
(1)	No	$400	debit

Prepare a trial balance.

(SO 2, 7)

E2-14 The accounts in the ledger of Sanford Delivery Service contain the following balances on July 31, 2008.

Accounts Receivable	$ 7,642	Prepaid Insurance	$1,968
Accounts Payable	8,396	Repair Expense	961
Cash	?	Service Revenue	10,610
Delivery Equipment	49,360	Sanford, Drawing	700
Gas and Oil Expense	758	Sanford, Capital	44,636
Insurance Expense	523	Salaries Expense	4,428
Notes Payable	18,450	Salaries Payable	815

Instructions

Prepare a trial balance with the accounts arranged as illustrated in the chapter and fill in the missing amount for Cash.

EXERCISES: SET B

Visit the book's website at **www.wiley.com/college/weygandt**, and choose the Student Companion site, to access Exercise Set B.

PROBLEMS: SET A

Journalize a series of transactions.

(SO 2, 4)

GLS Peachtree

P2-1A Frontier Park was started on April 1 by C. J. Mendez. The following selected events and transactions occurred during April.

Apr. 1 Mendez invested $40,000 cash in the business.
4 Purchased land costing $30,000 for cash.
8 Incurred advertising expense of $1,800 on account.
11 Paid salaries to employees $1,500.
12 Hired park manager at a salary of $4,000 per month, effective May 1.
13 Paid $1,500 cash for a one-year insurance policy.
17 Withdrew $1,000 cash for personal use.
20 Received $5,700 in cash for admission fees.
25 Sold 100 coupon books for $25 each. Each book contains 10 coupons that entitle the holder to one admission to the park.
30 Received $8,900 in cash admission fees.
30 Paid $900 on balance owed for advertising incurred on April 8.

Mendez uses the following accounts: Cash; Prepaid Insurance; Land; Accounts Payable; Unearned Admission Revenue; C. J. Mendez, Capital; C. J. Mendez, Drawing; Admission Revenue; Advertising Expense; and Salaries Expense.

Instructions

Journalize the April transactions.

Journalize transactions, post, and prepare a trial balance.

(SO 2, 4, 6, 7)

GLS

P2-2A Jane Kent is a licensed CPA. During the first month of operations of her business, the following events and transactions occurred.

May 1 Kent invested $25,000 cash.
2 Hired a secretary-receptionist at a salary of $2,000 per month.
3 Purchased $2,500 of supplies on account from Read Supply Company.
7 Paid office rent of $900 cash for the month.
11 Completed a tax assignment and billed client $2,100 for services provided.
12 Received $3,500 advance on a management consulting engagement.
17 Received cash of $1,200 for services completed for H. Arnold Co.
31 Paid secretary-receptionist $2,000 salary for the month.
31 Paid 40% of balance due Read Supply Company.

Jane uses the following chart of accounts: No. 101 Cash, No. 112 Accounts Receivable, No. 126 Supplies, No. 201 Accounts Payable, No. 205 Unearned Revenue, No. 301 Jane Kent, Capital, No. 400 Service Revenue, No. 726 Salaries Expense, and No. 729 Rent Expense.

Instructions

(a) Journalize the transactions.
(b) Post to the ledger accounts.
(c) Prepare a trial balance on May 31, 2008.

Trial balance totals $33,300

P2-3A Jack Shellenkamp owns and manages a computer repair service, which had the following trial balance on December 31, 2007 (the end of its fiscal year).

Journalize and post transactions and prepare a trial balance.

(SO 2, 4, 6, 7)

BYTE REPAIR SERVICE
Trial Balance
December 31, 2007

Cash	$ 8,000	
Accounts Receivable	15,000	
Parts Inventory	13,000	
Prepaid Rent	3,000	
Shop Equipment	21,000	
Accounts Payable		$19,000
Jack Shellenkamp, Capital		41,000
	$60,000	$60,000

Summarized transactions for January 2008 were as follows:

1. Advertising costs, paid in cash, $1,000.
2. Additional repair parts inventory acquired on account $4,000.
3. Miscellaneous expenses, paid in cash, $2,000.
4. Cash collected from customers in payment of accounts receivable $14,000.
5. Cash paid to creditors for accounts payable due $15,000.
6. Repair parts used during January $4,000. (*Hint*: Debit this to Repair Parts Expense.)
7. Repair services performed during January: for cash $6,000; on account $9,000.
8. Wages for January, paid in cash, $3,000.
9. Jack's drawings during January were $3,000.

Instructions

(a) Open T accounts for each of the accounts listed in the trial balance, and enter the opening balances for 2008.
(b) Prepare journal entries to record each of the January transactions.
(c) Post the journal entries to the accounts in the ledger. (Add accounts as needed.)
(d) Prepare a trial balance as of January 31, 2008.

Trial balance totals $64,000

P2-4A The trial balance of the Sterling Company shown below does not balance.

Prepare a correct trial balance.

(SO 7)

STERLING COMPANY
Trial Balance
May 31, 2008

	Debit	Credit
Cash	$5,850	
Accounts Receivable		$2,750
Prepaid Insurance	700	
Equipment	8,000	
Accounts Payable		4,500
Property Taxes Payable	560	
M. Sterling, Capital		11,700
Service Revenue	6,690	
Salaries Expense	4,200	
Advertising Expense		1,100
Property Tax Expense	800	
	$26,800	$20,050

Your review of the ledger reveals that each account has a normal balance. You also discover the following errors (page 82).

1. The totals of the debit sides of Prepaid Insurance, Accounts Payable, and Property Tax Expense were each understated $100.
2. Transposition errors were made in Accounts Receivable and Service Revenue. Based on postings made, the correct balances were $2,570 and $6,960, respectively.
3. A debit posting to Salaries Expense of $200 was omitted.
4. A $1,000 cash drawing by the owner was debited to M. Sterling, Capital for $1,000 and credited to Cash for $1,000.
5. A $520 purchase of supplies on account was debited to Equipment for $520 and credited to Cash for $520.
6. A cash payment of $450 for advertising was debited to Advertising Expense for $45 and credited to Cash for $45.
7. A collection from a customer for $210 was debited to Cash for $210 and credited to Accounts Payable for $210.

Instructions

Trial balance totals $24,930

Prepare a correct trial balance. Note that the chart of accounts includes the following: M. Sterling, Drawing, and Supplies. (*Hint:* It helps to prepare the correct journal entry for the transaction described and compare it to the mistake made.)

Journalize transactions, post, and prepare a trial balance.

(SO 2, 4, 6, 7)

GLS Peachtree

P2-5A The Lake Theater is owned by Tony Carpino. All facilities were completed on March 31. At this time, the ledger showed: No. 101 Cash $6,000; No. 140 Land $10,000; No. 145 Buildings (concession stand, projection room, ticket booth, and screen) $8,000; No. 157 Equipment $6,000; No. 201 Accounts Payable $2,000; No. 275 Mortgage Payable $8,000; and No. 301 Tony Carpino, Capital $20,000. During April, the following events and transactions occurred.

Apr. 2 Paid film rental of $800 on first movie.
3 Ordered two additional films at $1,000 each.
9 Received $2,800 cash from admissions.
10 Made $2,000 payment on mortgage and $1,000 for accounts payable due.
11 Lake Theater contracted with R. Wynns Company to operate the concession stand. Wynns is to pay 17% of gross concession receipts (payable monthly) for the right to operate the concession stand.
12 Paid advertising expenses $500.
20 Received one of the films ordered on April 3 and was billed $1,000. The film will be shown in April.
25 Received $5,200 cash from admissions.
29 Paid salaries $2,000.
30 Received statement from R. Wynns showing gross concession receipts of $1,000 and the balance due to The Lake Theater of $170 ($1,000 × 17%) for April. Wynns paid one-half of the balance due and will remit the remainder on May 5.
30 Prepaid $900 rental on special film to be run in May.

In addition to the accounts identified above, the chart of accounts shows: No. 112 Accounts Receivable, No. 136 Prepaid Rentals, No. 405 Admission Revenue, No. 406 Concession Revenue, No. 610 Advertising Expense, No. 632 Film Rental Expense, and No. 726 Salaries Expense.

Instructions

Trial balance totals $36,170

(a) Enter the beginning balances in the ledger as of April 1. Insert a check mark (✓) in the reference column of the ledger for the beginning balance.
(b) Journalize the April transactions.
(c) Post the April journal entries to the ledger. Assume that all entries are posted from page 1 of the journal.
(d) Prepare a trial balance on April 30, 2008.

PROBLEMS: SET B

Journalize a series of transactions.

(SO 2, 4)

GLS

P2-1B Surepar Miniature Golf and Driving Range was opened on March 1 by Jerry Glover. The following selected events and transactions occurred during March:

Mar. 1 Invested $50,000 cash in the business.
3 Purchased Lee's Golf Land for $38,000 cash. The price consists of land $23,000, building $9,000, and equipment $6,000. (Make one compound entry.)

5 Advertised the opening of the driving range and miniature golf course, paying advertising expenses of $1,600.
6 Paid cash $1,480 for a one-year insurance policy.
10 Purchased golf clubs and other equipment for $2,600 from Palmer Company payable in 30 days.
18 Received $800 in cash for golf fees earned.
19 Sold 100 coupon books for $15 each. Each book contains 10 coupons that enable the holder to play one round of miniature golf or to hit one bucket of golf balls.
25 Withdrew $2,000 cash for personal use.
30 Paid salaries of $600.
30 Paid Palmer Company in full.
31 Received $500 cash for fees earned.

Jerry Glover uses the following accounts: Cash; Prepaid Insurance; Land; Buildings; Equipment; Accounts Payable; Unearned Revenue; Jerry Glover, Capital; Jerry Glover, Drawing; Golf Revenue; Advertising Expense; and Salaries Expense.

Instructions
Journalize the March transactions.

Journalize transactions, post, and prepare a trial balance.
(SO 2, 4, 6, 7)
GLS

P2-2B Rosa Perez is a licensed architect. During the first month of the operation of her business, the following events and transactions occurred.

April 1 Invested $30,000 cash.
1 Hired a secretary-receptionist at a salary of $500 per week payable monthly.
2 Paid office rent for the month $800.
3 Purchased architectural supplies on account from Halo Company $1,500.
10 Completed blueprints on a carport and billed client $1,200 for services.
11 Received $500 cash advance from R. Welk for the design of a new home.
20 Received $1,500 cash for services completed and delivered to P. Donahue.
30 Paid secretary-receptionist for the month $2,000.
30 Paid $600 to Halo Company for accounts payable due.

Rosa uses the following chart of accounts: No. 101 Cash, No. 112 Accounts Receivable, No. 126 Supplies, No. 201 Accounts Payable, No. 205 Unearned Revenue, No. 301 Rosa Perez, Capital, No. 400 Service Revenue, No. 726 Salaries Expense, and No. 729 Rent Expense.

Instructions
(a) Journalize the transactions.
(b) Post to the ledger accounts.
(c) Prepare a trial balance on April 30, 2008.

Trial balance totals $34,100

Journalize transactions, post, and prepare a trial balance.
(SO 2, 4, 6, 7)

P2-3B Slocombe Services was formed on May 1, 2008. The following transactions took place during the first month.

Transactions on May 1:

1. Ronald Slocombe invested $100,000 cash in the company, as its sole owner.
2. Hired two employees to work in the warehouse. They will each be paid a salary of $3,000 per month.
3. Signed a 2-year rental agreement on a warehouse; paid $36,000 cash in advance for the first year.
4. Purchased furniture and equipment costing $60,000. A cash payment of $20,000 was made immediately; the remainder will be paid in 6 months.
5. Paid $3,000 cash for a one-year insurance policy on the furniture and equipment.

Transactions during the remainder of the month:

6. Purchased basic office supplies for $1,000 cash.
7. Purchased more office supplies for $3,000 on account.
8. Total revenues earned were $30,000—$10,000 cash and $20,000 on account.
9. Paid $800 to suppliers for accounts payable due.
10. Received $5,000 from customers in payment of accounts receivable.
11. Received utility bills in the amount of $400, to be paid next month.
12. Paid the monthly salaries of the two employees, totalling $6,000.

Instructions
(a) Prepare journal entries to record each of the events listed.

Trial balance totals $172,600

(b) Post the journal entries to T accounts.
(c) Prepare a trial balance as of May 31, 2008.

Prepare a correct trial balance.
(SO 7)

P2-4B The trial balance of Don Kelso Co. shown below does not balance.

DON KELSO CO.
Trial Balance
June 30, 2008

	Debit	Credit
Cash		$ 2,840
Accounts Receivable	$ 3,231	
Supplies	800	
Equipment	3,000	
Accounts Payable		2,666
Unearned Revenue	1,200	
D. Kelso, Capital		9,000
D. Kelso, Drawing	800	
Service Revenue		2,380
Salaries Expense	3,400	
Office Expense	910	
	$13,341	$16,886

Each of the listed accounts has a normal balance per the general ledger. An examination of the ledger and journal reveals the following errors.

1. Cash received from a customer in payment of its account was debited for $470, and Accounts Receivable was credited for the same amount. The actual collection was for $740.
2. The purchase of a printer on account for $340 was recorded as a debit to Supplies for $340 and a credit to Accounts Payable for $340.
3. Services were performed on account for a client for $890. Accounts Receivable was debited for $890, and Service Revenue was credited for $89.
4. A debit posting to Salaries Expense of $600 was omitted.
5. A payment of a balance due for $206 was credited to Cash for $206 and credited to Accounts Payable for $260.
6. The withdrawal of $500 cash for Kelso's personal use was debited to Salaries Expense for $500 and credited to Cash for $500.

Instructions

Trial balance totals $15,581

Prepare a correct trial balance. (*Hint:* It helps to prepare the correct journal entry for the transaction described and compare it to the mistake made).

Journalize transactions, post, and prepare a trial balance.
(SO 2, 4, 6, 7)
GLS

P2-5B The Quinn Theater, owned by Mike Quinn, will begin operations in March. The Quinn will be unique in that it will show only triple features of sequential theme movies. As of March 1, the ledger of Quinn showed: No. 101 Cash $16,000; No. 140 Land $42,000; No. 145 Buildings (concession stand, projection room, ticket booth, and screen) $18,000; No. 157 Equipment $16,000; No. 201 Accounts Payable $12,000; and No. 301 M. Quinn, Capital $80,000. During the month of March the following events and transactions occurred.

Mar. 2 Rented the three *Star Wars* movies (*Star Wars, The Empire Strikes Back,* and *The Return of the Jedi*) to be shown for the first 3 weeks of March. The film rental was $6,000; $3,000 was paid in cash and $3,000 will be paid on March 10.
3 Ordered the first three *Star Trek* movies to be shown the last 10 days of March. It will cost $300 per night.
9 Received $6,500 cash from admissions.
10 Paid balance due on *Star Wars* movies rental and $4,000 on March 1 accounts payable.
11 Quinn Theater contracted with M. Brewer Company to operate the concession stand. Brewer is to pay 10% of gross concession receipts (payable monthly) for the right to operate the concession stand.
12 Paid advertising expenses $800.
20 Received $7,200 cash from customers for admissions.

20 Received the *Star Trek* movies and paid the rental fee of $3,000.
31 Paid salaries of $4,800.
31 Received statement from M. Brewer showing gross receipts from concessions of $8,000 and the balance due to Quinn Theater of $800 ($8,000 × 10%) for March. Brewer paid one-half the balance due and will remit the remainder on April 5.
31 Received $11,000 cash from customers for admissions.

In addition to the accounts identified above, the chart of accounts includes: No. 112 Accounts Receivable, No. 405 Admission Revenue, No. 406 Concession Revenue, No. 610 Advertising Expense, No. 632 Film Rental Expense, and No. 726 Salaries Expense.

Instructions

(a) Enter the beginning balances in the ledger. Insert a check mark (✓) in the reference column of the ledger for the beginning balance.
(b) Journalize the March transactions.
(c) Post the March journal entries to the ledger. Assume that all entries are posted from page 1 of the journal.
(d) Prepare a trial balance on March 31, 2008.

Trial balance totals $113,500

PROBLEMS: SET C

Visit the book's website at **www.wiley.com/college/weygandt**, and choose the Student Companion site, to access Problem Set C.

CONTINUING COOKIE CHRONICLE

(*Note*: This is a continuation of the Cookie Chronicle from Chapter 1.)

CCC2 After researching the different forms of business organization, Natalie Koebel decides to operate "Cookie Creations" as a proprietorship. She then starts the process of getting the business running.

Go to the book's website,
www.wiley.com/college/weygandt,
to see the completion of this problem.

BROADENING YOUR PERSPECTIVE

FINANCIAL REPORTING AND ANALYSIS

Financial Reporting Problem

PepsiCo, Inc.

BYP2-1 The financial statements of PepsiCo are presented in Appendix A. The notes accompanying the statements contain the following selected accounts, stated in millions of dollars.

Accounts Payable	$1,799	Income Taxes Payable	$ 546
Accounts Receivable	3,261	Interest Expense	256
Property, Plant, and Equipment	8,681	Inventory	1,693

Instructions

(a) Answer the following questions.
  (1) What is the increase and decrease side for each account?
  (2) What is the normal balance for each account?
(b) Identify the probable other account in the transaction and the effect on that account when:
  (1) Accounts Receivable is decreased.
  (2) Accounts Payable is decreased.
  (3) Inventory is increased.

(c) Identify the other account(s) that ordinarily would be involved when:
- **(1)** Interest Expense is increased.
- **(2)** Property, Plant, and Equipment is increased.

Comparative Analysis Problem

PepsiCo, Inc. vs. The Coca-Cola Company

BYP2-2 PepsiCo's financial statements are presented in Appendix A. Coca-Cola's financial statements are presented in Appendix B.

Instructions

(a) Based on the information contained in the financial statements, determine the normal balance of the listed accounts for each company.

PepsiCo	Coca-Cola
1. Inventory	**1.** Accounts Receivable
2. Property, Plant, and Equipment	**2.** Cash and Cash Equivalents
3. Accounts Payable	**3.** Cost of Goods Sold
4. Interest Expense	**4.** Sales (revenue)

(b) Identify the other account ordinarily involved when:
- **(1)** Accounts Receivable is increased.
- **(2)** Wages Payable is decreased.
- **(3)** Property, Plant, and Equipment is increased.
- **(4)** Interest Expense is increased.

Exploring the Web

BYP2-3 Much information about specific companies is available on the World Wide Web. Such information includes basic descriptions of the company's location, activities, industry, financial health, and financial performance.

Address: biz.yahoo.com/i, or go to **www.wiley.com/college/weygandt**

Steps

1. Type in a company name, or use index to find company name.
2. Choose **Profile**. Perform instructions (a)–(c) below.
3. Click on the company's specific industry to identify competitors. Perform instructions (d)–(g) below.

Instructions

Answer the following questions.

(a) What is the company's industry?
(b) What was the company's total sales?
(c) What was the company's net income?
(d) What are the names of four of the company's competitors?
(e) Choose one of these competitors.
(f) What is this competitor's name? What were its sales? What was its net income?
(g) Which of these two companies is larger by size of sales? Which one reported higher net income?

CRITICAL THINKING

Decision Making Across the Organization

BYP2-4 Lisa Ortega operates Ortega Riding Academy. The academy's primary sources of revenue are riding fees and lesson fees, which are paid on a cash basis. Lisa also boards horses for owners, who are billed monthly for boarding fees. In a few cases, boarders pay in advance of expected use. For its revenue transactions, the academy maintains the following accounts: No. 1 Cash, No. 5 Boarding Accounts Receivable, No. 27 Unearned Boarding Revenue, No. 51 Riding Revenue, No. 52 Lesson Revenue, and No. 53 Boarding Revenue.

The academy owns 10 horses, a stable, a riding corral, riding equipment, and office equipment. These assets are accounted for in accounts No. 11 Horses, No. 12 Building, No. 13 Riding Corral, No. 14 Riding Equipment, and No. 15 Office Equipment.

For its expenses, the academy maintains the following accounts: No. 6 Hay and Feed Supplies, No. 7 Prepaid Insurance, No. 21 Accounts Payable, No. 60 Salaries Expense, No. 61 Advertising Expense, No. 62 Utilities Expense, No. 63 Veterinary Expense, No. 64 Hay and Feed Expense, and No. 65 Insurance Expense.

Lisa makes periodic withdrawals of cash for personal living expenses. To record Lisa's equity in the business and her drawings, two accounts are maintained: No. 50 Lisa Ortega, Capital, and No. 51 Lisa Ortega, Drawing.

During the first month of operations an inexperienced bookkeeper was employed. Lisa Ortega asks you to review the following eight entries of the 50 entries made during the month. In each case, the explanation for the entry is correct.

May 1	Cash	18,000	
	Lisa Ortega, Capital		18,000
	(Invested $18,000 cash in business)		
5	Cash	250	
	Riding Revenue		250
	(Received $250 cash for lessons provided)		
7	Cash	300	
	Boarding Revenue		300
	(Received $300 for boarding of horses beginning June 1)		
14	Riding Equipment	80	
	Cash		800
	(Purchased desk and other office equipment for $800 cash)		
15	Salaries Expense	400	
	Cash		400
	(Issued check to Lisa Ortega for personal use)		
20	Cash	148	
	Riding Revenue		184
	(Received $184 cash for riding fees)		
30	Veterinary Expense	75	
	Accounts Payable		75
	(Received bill of $75 from veterinarian for services rendered)		
31	Hay and Feed Expense	1,700	
	Cash		1,700
	(Purchased an estimated 2 months' supply of feed and hay for $1,700 on account)		

Instructions

With the class divided into groups, answer the following.

(a) Identify each journal entry that is correct. For each journal entry that is incorrect, prepare the entry that should have been made by the bookkeeper.

(b) Which of the incorrect entries would prevent the trial balance from balancing?

(c) What was the correct net income for May, assuming the bookkeeper reported net income of $4,500 after posting all 50 entries?

(d) What was the correct cash balance at May 31, assuming the bookkeeper reported a balance of $12,475 after posting all 50 entries (and the only errors occurred in the items listed above)?

Communication Activity

BYP2-5 Woderson's Maid Company offers home cleaning service. Two recurring transactions for the company are billing customers for services rendered and paying employee salaries. For example, on March 15, bills totaling $6,000 were sent to customers and $2,000 was paid in salaries to employees.

Instructions

Write a memo to your instructor that explains and illustrates the steps in the recording process for each of the March 15 transactions. Use the format illustrated in the text under the heading, "The Recording Process Illustrated" (p. 60).

Ethics Case

BYP2-6 Mary Jansen is the assistant chief accountant at Casey Company, a manufacturer of computer chips and cellular phones. The company presently has total sales of $20 million. It is the end of the first quarter. Mary is hurriedly trying to prepare a general ledger trial balance so that quarterly financial statements can be prepared and released to management and the regulatory agencies. The total credits on the trial balance exceed the debits by $1,000. In order to meet the 4 p.m. deadline, Mary decides to force the debits and credits into balance by adding the amount of the difference to the Equipment account. She chose Equipment because it is one of the larger account balances; percentage-wise, it will be the least misstated. Mary "plugs" the difference! She believes that the difference will not affect anyone's decisions. She wishes that she had another few days to find the error but realizes that the financial statements are already late.

Instructions

(a) Who are the stakeholders in this situation?
(b) What are the ethical issues involved in this case?
(c) What are Mary's alternatives?

"All About You" Activity

BYP2-7 Every company needs to plan in order to move forward. Its top management must consider where it wants the company to be in three to five years. Like a company, you need to think about where you want to be three to five years from now, and you need to start taking steps now in order to get there. With some forethought, you can help yourself avoid a situation, like those described in the **All About You** feature in this chapter (p. 70), in which your résumé seems to need creative writing.

Instructions

Provide responses to each of the following items.

(a) Where would you like to be working in three to five years? Describe your plan for getting there by identifying between five and 10 specific steps that you need to take in order to get there.
(b) In order to get the job you want, you will need a résumé. Your résumé is the equivalent of a company's annual report. It needs to provide relevant and reliable information about your past accomplishments so that employers can decide whether to "invest" in you. Do a search on the Internet to find a good résumé format. What are the basic elements of a résumé?
(c) A company's annual report provides information about a company's accomplishments. In order for investors to use the annual report, the information must be reliable; that is, users must have faith that the information is accurate and believable. How can you provide assurance that the information on your résumé is reliable?
(d) Prepare a résumé assuming that you have accomplished the five to 10 specific steps you identified in part (a). Also, provide evidence that would give assurance that the information is reliable.

Answers to Insight and Accounting Across the Organization Questions

p. 55. New Xbox Contributes to Profitability

Q: In what ways is this Microsoft division using accounting to assist in its effort to become more profitable?

A: *The division has used accounting to set very strict sales, revenue, and profit goals. In addition, the division managers use accounting to keep a tight rein on product costs. Also, accounting serves as the basis of communication, so that the marketing managers and product designers can work with production managers, engineers, and accountants to achieve an exciting product within specified cost constraints.*

p. 57 What Would Sam Do?

Q: Why did Sam Walton keep separate pigeonholes and blue binders?

A: *Using separate pigeonholes and blue binders for each store enabled Walton to accumulate and track the performance of each individual store easily.*

Q: Why bother to keep separate records for each store?

A: *Keeping separate records for each store provided Walton with more information about performance of individual stores and managers, and greater control. Walton would want and need the same advantages if he were starting his business today. The difference is that he might now use a computerized system for small businesses.*

p. 69 Sarbanes-Oxley Comes to the Rescue

Q: In order for these companies to prepare and issue financial statements, their accounting equations (debits and credits) must have been in balance at year-end. How could these errors or misstatements have occurred?

A: *A company's accounting equation (as expressed in its books) can be in balance yet its financial statements have errors or misstatements because of the following: entire transactions were not recorded, transactions were recorded at wrong amounts; transactions were recorded in the wrong accounts; transactions were recorded in the wrong accounting period. Audits of financial statements uncover some, but not all, errors or misstatements.*

Authors' Comments on *All About You: Buffing Up Your Résumé* (p. 70)

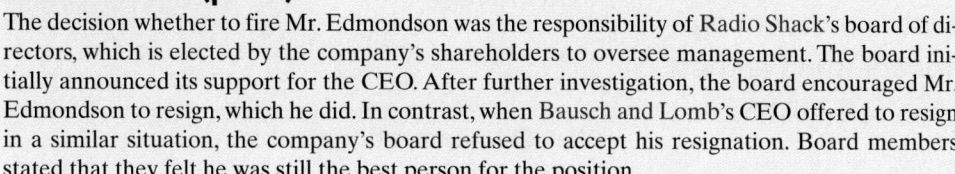

The decision whether to fire Mr. Edmondson was the responsibility of Radio Shack's board of directors, which is elected by the company's shareholders to oversee management. The board initially announced its support for the CEO. After further investigation, the board encouraged Mr. Edmondson to resign, which he did. In contrast, when Bausch and Lomb's CEO offered to resign in a similar situation, the company's board refused to accept his resignation. Board members stated that they felt he was still the best person for the position.

Radio Shack says that although it did a reference check at the time of Mr. Edmondson's hiring, it did not check his educational credentials. Under the Sarbanes-Oxley Act of 2002, companies must now perform thorough background checks as part of a check of internal controls. The bottom line: Your résumé must be a fair and accurate depiction of your past.

Answer to PepsiCo Review It Question 4, p. 52

Normal balances for PepsiCo (or any company) are: Cash—debit; Accounts Payable—credit; Interest Expense—debit.

Answers to Self-Study Questions

1. b **2.** c **3.** d **4.** d **5.** b **6.** a **7.** c **8.** d **9.** a **10.** c

Remember to go back to the Navigator box on the chapter-opening page and check off your completed work.

Adjusting the Accounts

STUDY OBJECTIVES

After studying this chapter, you should be able to:

1 Explain the time period assumption.
2 Explain the accrual basis of accounting.
3 Explain the reasons for adjusting entries.
4 Identify the major types of adjusting entries.
5 Prepare adjusting entries for deferrals.
6 Prepare adjusting entries for accruals.
7 Describe the nature and purpose of an adjusted trial balance.

The Navigator

✓ The Navigator

Scan **Study Objectives**	■
Read **Feature Story**	■
Read **Preview**	■
Read text and answer **Before You Go On** p. 95 ■ p. 102 ■ p. 107 ■ p. 112 ■	
Work **Demonstration Problem**	■
Review **Summary of Study Objectives**	■
Answer **Self-Study Questions**	■
Complete **Assignments**	■

Feature Story

WHAT WAS YOUR PROFIT?

The accuracy of the financial reporting system depends on answers to a few fundamental questions: At what point has revenue been earned? At what point is the earnings process complete? When have expenses really been incurred?

During the 1990s' boom in the stock prices of dot-com companies, many dot-coms earned most of their revenue from selling advertising space on their websites. To boost reported revenue, some dot-coms began swapping website ad space. Company A would put an ad for its website on company B's website, and company B would put an ad for its website on company A's website. No money changed hands, but each company recorded revenue (for the value of the space that it gave the other company on its site). This practice did little to boost net income, and it resulted in no additional cash flow—but it did boost *reported revenue*. Regulators eventually put an end to this misleading practice.

Another type of transgression results from companies recording revenues or expenses in the wrong year. In fact, shifting revenues and expenses is one of the most common abuses of financial accounting. Xerox, for example, admitted reporting billions of dollars of lease revenue in periods earlier than it should have been reported. And WorldCom stunned the financial markets with its admission that it had boosted net income by billions of dollars by delaying the recognition of expenses until later years.

Unfortunately, revelations such as these have become all too common in the corporate world. It is no wonder that a U.S. Trust survey of affluent Americans reported that 85% of respondents believed that there should be tighter regulation of financial disclosures; 66% said they did not trust the management of publicly traded companies.

Why did so many companies violate basic financial reporting rules and sound ethics? Many speculate that as stock prices climbed, executives were under increasing pressure to meet higher and higher earnings expectations. If actual results weren't as good as hoped for, some gave in to temptation and "adjusted" their numbers to meet market expectations.

✓ The Navigator

Inside Chapter 3...

Preview of Chapter 3

In Chapter 1 you learned a neat little formula: Net income = Revenues − Expenses. In Chapter 2 you learned some rules for recording revenue and expense transactions. Guess what? Things are not really that nice and neat. In fact, it is often difficult for companies to determine in what time period they should report some revenues and expenses. In other words, in measuring net income, timing is everything.

The content and organization of Chapter 3 are as follows.

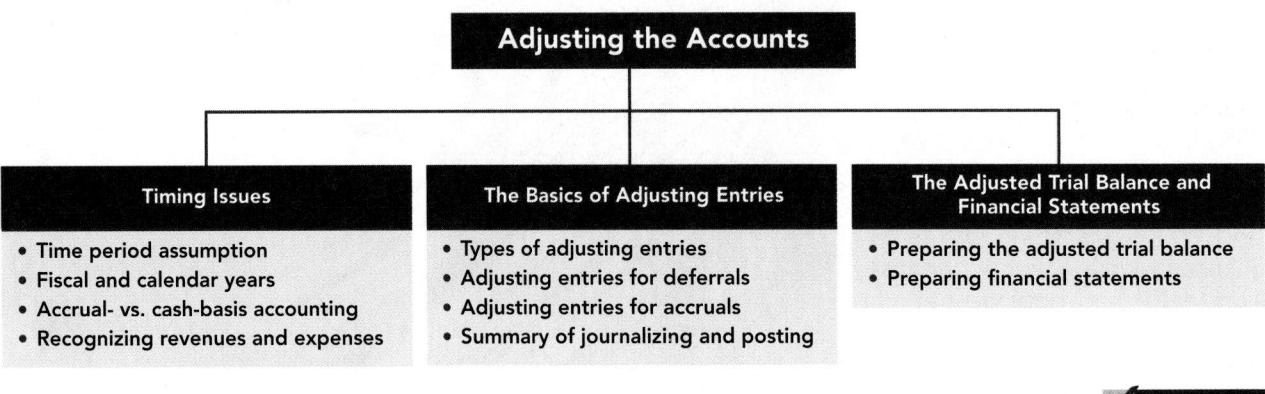

Adjusting the Accounts

Timing Issues
- Time period assumption
- Fiscal and calendar years
- Accrual- vs. cash-basis accounting
- Recognizing revenues and expenses

The Basics of Adjusting Entries
- Types of adjusting entries
- Adjusting entries for deferrals
- Adjusting entries for accruals
- Summary of journalizing and posting

The Adjusted Trial Balance and Financial Statements
- Preparing the adjusted trial balance
- Preparing financial statements

The Navigator

TIMING ISSUES

STUDY OBJECTIVE 1

Explain the time period assumption.

We would need no adjustments if we could wait to prepare financial statements until a company ended its operations. At that point, we could easily determine its final balance sheet and the amount of lifetime income it earned. The following story illustrates one way to compute lifetime income.

A grocery store owner from the "old country" kept his accounts payable on a spindle, accounts receivable on a note pad, and cash in a cigar box. His daughter, having just passed the CPA exam, chided the father: "I don't understand how you can run your business this way. How do you know what your profits are?"

"Well," the father replied, "when I got off the boat 40 years ago, I had nothing but the pants I was wearing. Today your brother is a doctor, your sister is a college professor, and you are a CPA. Your mother and I have a nice car, a well-furnished house, and a lake home. We have a good business, and everything is paid for. So, you add all that together, subtract the pants, and there's your profit."

Time Period Assumption

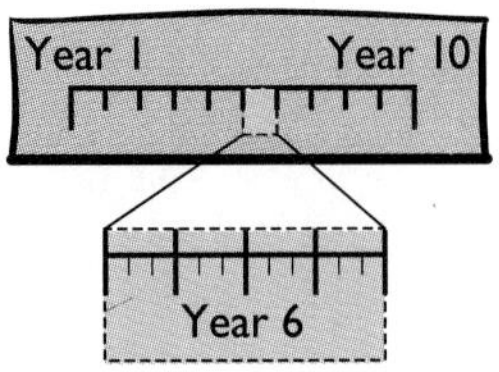

Selecting an Accounting Time Period

Although the old grocer may be correct in his evaluation, it is impractical to wait so long for the results of operations. All companies find it desirable to report the results of their activities on a frequent basis. For example, management usually wants monthly financial statements, and the Internal Revenue Service requires all businesses to file annual tax returns. Therefore, **accountants divide the economic life of a business into artificial time periods**. This convenient assumption is referred to as the **time period assumption**.

Many business transactions affect more than one of these arbitrary time periods. For example, the airplanes purchased by Northwest Air Lines five years ago are still in use today. We must determine the relevance of each business transaction to specific accounting periods. (How much of the cost of an airplane contributed to operations this year?)

ALTERNATIVE TERMINOLOGY

The time period assumption is also called the *periodicity assumption.*

Fiscal and Calendar Years

Both small and large companies prepare financial statements periodically in order to assess their financial condition and results of operations. **Accounting time periods are generally a month, a quarter, or a year.** Monthly and quarterly time periods are called interim periods. Most large companies must prepare both quarterly and annual financial statements.

An accounting time period that is one year in length is a fiscal year. A fiscal year usually begins with the first day of a month and ends twelve months later on the last day of a month. Most businesses use the calendar year (January 1 to December 31) as their accounting period. Some do not. Companies whose fiscal year differs from the calendar year include Delta Air Lines, June 30, and Walt Disney Productions, September 30. Sometimes a company's year-end will vary from year to year. For example, PepsiCo's fiscal year ends on the Friday closest to December 31, which was December 25 in 2004 and December 30 in 2005.

Accrual- vs. Cash-Basis Accounting

STUDY OBJECTIVE 2

Explain the accrual basis of accounting.

What you will learn in this chapter is accrual-basis accounting. Under the accrual basis, companies record transactions **in the periods in which the events occur**. For example, using the accrual basis to determine net income means companies recognize revenues when earned (rather than when they receive cash). It also means recognizing expenses when incurred (rather than when paid).

An alternative to the accrual basis is the cash basis. Under cash-basis accounting, companies record revenue when they receive cash. They record an expense when they pay out cash. The cash basis seems appealing due to its simplicity, but it often produces misleading financial statements. It fails to record revenue that a company has earned but for which it has not received the cash. Also, it does not match expenses with earned revenues. **Cash-basis accounting is not in accordance with generally accepted accounting principles (GAAP).**

Individuals and some small companies do use cash-basis accounting. The cash basis is justified for small businesses because they often have few receivables and payables. Medium and large companies use accrual-basis accounting.

Recognizing Revenues and Expenses

It can be difficult to determine the amount of revenues and expenses to report in a given accounting period. Two principles help in this task: the revenue recognition principle and the matching principle.

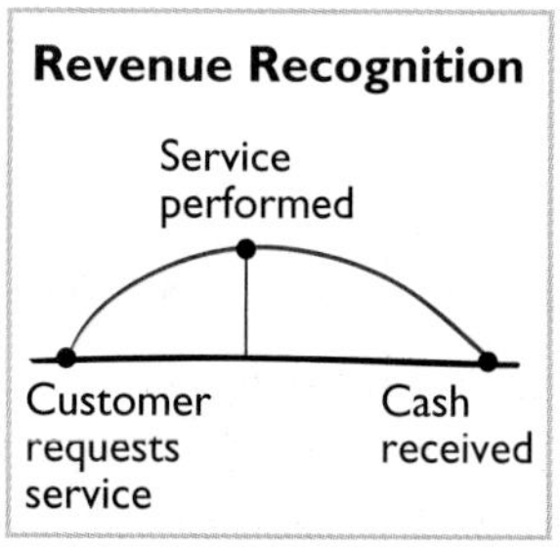

REVENUE RECOGNITION PRINCIPLE

The revenue recognition principle dictates that companies recognize revenue in the accounting period in which it is earned. In a service enterprise, revenue is considered to be earned at the time the service is performed. To illustrate, assume that Dave's Dry Cleaning cleans clothing on June 30 but customers do not claim and pay for their clothes until the first week of July. Under the revenue recognition principle, Dave's earns revenue in June when it performed the service, rather than in July when it received the cash. At June 30, Dave's would report a receivable on its balance sheet and revenue in its income statement for the service performed.

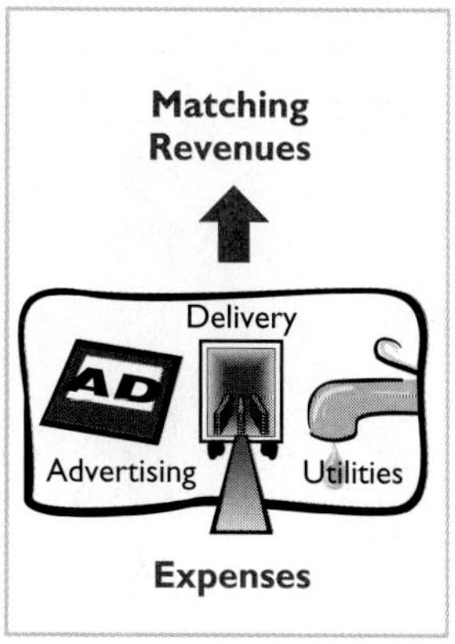

MATCHING PRINCIPLE

Accountants follow a simple rule in recognizing expenses: "Let the expenses follow the revenues." That is, expense recognition is tied to revenue recognition. In the dry cleaning example, this principle means that Dave's should report the salary expense incurred in performing the June 30 cleaning service in the income statement for the same period in which it recognizes the service revenue. The critical issue in expense recognition is when the expense makes its contribution to revenue. This may or may not be the same period in which the expense is paid. If Dave's does not pay the salary incurred on June 30 until July, it would report salaries payable on its June 30 balance sheet.

This practice of expense recognition is referred to as the **matching principle**. It dictates that efforts (expenses) be matched with accomplishments (revenues). Illustration 3-1 summarizes the revenue and expense recognition principles.

Illustration 3-1
GAAP relationships in revenue and expense recognition

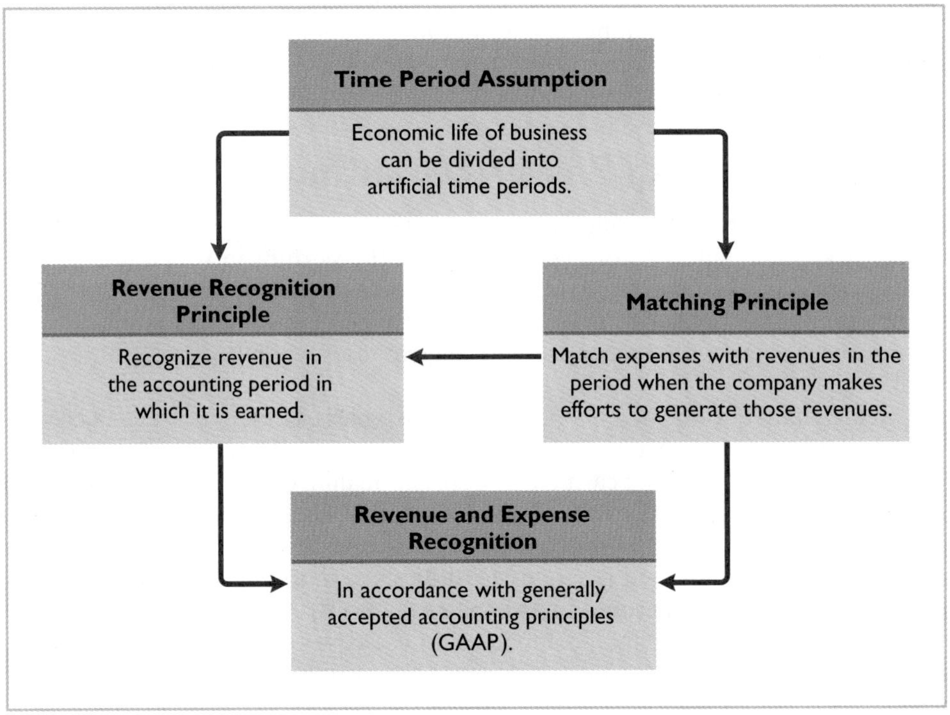
Time Period Assumption
Economic life of business can be divided into artificial time periods.
Revenue Recognition Principle
Recognize revenue in the accounting period in which it is earned.
Matching Principle
Match expenses with revenues in the period when the company makes efforts to generate those revenues.
Revenue and Expense Recognition
In accordance with generally accepted accounting principles (GAAP).

ACCOUNTING ACROSS THE ORGANIZATION

How Long Will "The Force" Be with Us?

Suppose you are filmmaker George Lucas and you spent $11 million to produce Twentieth Century Fox's film *Star Wars*. Over what period should the studio expense the cost?

Yes, it should expense the cost over the economic life of the film. But what *is* its economic life? You must estimate how much revenue you will earn from box office sales, video sales, television, and games and toys—a period that could be less than a year or more than 20 years, as is the case for *Star Wars*. Originally released in 1977, and rereleased in 1997, domestic revenues total over $500 million for *Star Wars* and continue to grow.

What accounting principle does this example illustrate? How will financial results be affected if the expenses are recognized over a period that is *less than* that used for revenues? What if the expenses are recognized over a period that is *longer than* that used for revenues?

Before You Go On...

REVIEW IT

1. What is the relevance of the time period assumption to accounting?
2. What are the revenue recognition and matching principles?

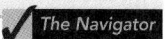

The Navigator

THE BASICS OF ADJUSTING ENTRIES

STUDY OBJECTIVE 3

Explain the reasons for adjusting entries.

In order for revenues and expenses to be reported in the correct period, companies make adjusting entries at the end of the accounting period. **Adjusting entries** **ensure that the revenue recognition and matching principles are followed.** Adjusting entries make it possible to report correct amounts on the balance sheet and on the income statement.

The trial balance—the first summarization of the transaction data—may not contain up-to-date and complete data. This is true for several reasons:

1. Some events are not recorded daily because it is not efficient to do so. For example, companies do not record the daily use of supplies or the earning of wages by employees.
2. Some costs are not recorded during the accounting period because they expire with the passage of time rather than as a result of daily transactions. Examples are rent, insurance, and charges related to the use of equipment.
3. Some items may be unrecorded. An example is a utility bill that the company will not receive until the next accounting period.

www.wiley.com/college/weygandt

Accounting Cycle Tutorial—Making Adjusting Entries

A company must make adjusting entries every time it prepares financial statements. It analyzes each account in the trial balance to determine whether it is complete and up-to-date. For example, the company may need to make inventory counts of supplies. It may also need to prepare supporting schedules of insurance policies, rental agreements, and other contractual commitments. Because the adjusting and closing process can be time-consuming, companies often prepare adjusting entries after the balance sheet date, but date them as of the balance sheet date.

HELPFUL HINT

Adjusting entries are needed to enable financial statements to conform to GAAP.

Types of Adjusting Entries

STUDY OBJECTIVE 4

Identify the major types of adjusting entries.

Adjusting entries are classified as either **deferrals** or **accruals**. As Illustration 3-2 shows, each of these classes has two subcategories.

Deferrals

1. **Prepaid Expenses.** Expenses paid in cash and recorded as assets before they are used or consumed.
2. **Unearned Revenues.** Cash received and recorded as liabilities before revenue is earned.

Accruals

1. **Accrued Revenues.** Revenues earned but not yet received in cash or recorded.
2. **Accrued Expenses.** Expenses incurred but not yet paid in cash or recorded.

Illustration 3-2
Categories of adjusting entries

The following pages explain each type of adjustment and show examples. Each example is based on the October 31 trial balance of Pioneer Advertising Agency, from Chapter 2 and reproduced in Illustration 3-3.

Illustration 3-3
Trial balance

PIONEER ADVERTISING AGENCY
Trial Balance
October 31, 2008

	Debit	Credit
Cash	$15,200	
Advertising Supplies	2,500	
Prepaid Insurance	600	
Office Equipment	5,000	
Notes Payable		$ 5,000
Accounts Payable		2,500
Unearned Revenue		1,200
C. R. Byrd, Capital		10,000
C. R. Byrd, Drawing	500	
Service Revenue		10,000
Salaries Expense	4,000	
Rent Expense	900	
	$28,700	**$28,700**

We assume that Pioneer Advertising uses an accounting period of one month, and thus it makes monthly adjusting entries. The entries are dated October 31.

Adjusting Entries for Deferrals

STUDY OBJECTIVE 5
Prepare adjusting entries for deferrals.

Deferrals are either prepaid expenses or unearned revenues. Companies make adjustments for deferrals to record the portion of the deferral that represents the **expense incurred or the revenue earned** in the current period.

PREPAID EXPENSES

Companies record payments of expenses that will benefit more than one accounting period as assets called **prepaid expenses** or **prepayments**. When expenses are prepaid, an asset account is increased (debited) to show the service or benefit that the company will receive in the future. Examples of common prepayments are insurance, supplies, advertising, and rent. In addition, companies make prepayments when they purchase buildings and equipment.

Prepaid expenses are costs that expire either with the passage of time (e.g., rent and insurance) **or through use** (e.g., supplies). The expiration of these costs does not require daily journal entries. Companies postpone recognizing these costs until they prepare financial statements. At each statement date, they make adjusting entries: (1) to record the expenses that apply to the current accounting period, and (2) to show the unexpired costs in the asset accounts.

Prior to adjustment for prepaid expenses, assets are overstated and expenses are understated. As shown in Illustration 3-4, **an adjusting entry for prepaid expense increases (debits) an expense account and a decreases (credits) an asset account**.

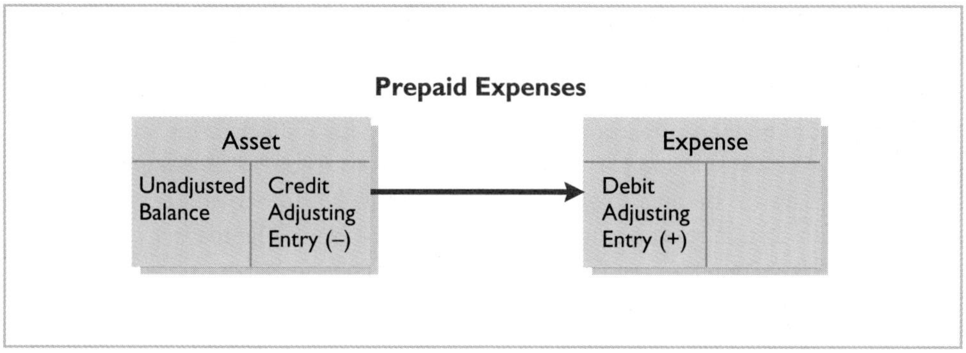

Illustration 3-4
Adjusting entries for prepaid expenses

On the next few pages, we will look in more detail at some specific types of prepaid expenses, beginning with supplies.

Supplies. Businesses use various types of supplies such as paper, envelopes, and printer cartridges. Companies generally debit supplies to an asset account when they acquire them. In the course of operations, supplies are used, but companies postpone recognizing their use until the adjustment process. At the end of the accounting period, a company counts the remaining supplies. The difference between the balance in the Supplies (asset) account and the supplies on hand represents the supplies used (an expense) for the period.

Pioneer Advertising Agency purchased advertising supplies costing $2,500 on October 5. Pioneer recorded that transaction by increasing (debiting) the asset Advertising Supplies. This account shows a balance of $2,500 in the October 31 trial balance. An inventory count at the close of business on October 31 reveals that $1,000 of supplies are still on hand. Thus, the cost of supplies used is $1,500 ($2,500 − $1,000). Pioneer makes the following adjusting entry.

Oct. 31	Advertising Supplies Expense	1,500	
	Advertising Supplies		1,500
	(To record supplies used)		

A	=	L	+	OE
				−1,500 Exp
−1,500				

Cash Flows
no effect

Equation analyses summarize the effects of the transaction on the elements of the accounting equation.

After the adjusting entry is posted, the two supplies accounts show:

Illustration 3-5
Supplies accounts after adjustment

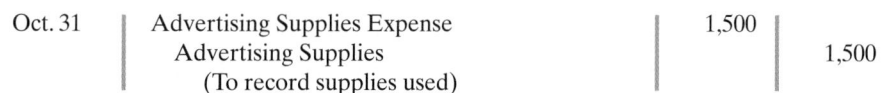

Advertising Supplies				Advertising Supplies Expense		
10/5	2,500	10/31 **Adj.**	**1,500**	10/31 **Adj.**	**1,500**	
10/31 Bal.	1,000					

The asset account Advertising Supplies now shows a balance of $1,000, which is equal to the cost of supplies on hand at the statement date. In addition, Advertising Supplies Expense shows a balance of $1,500, which equals the cost of supplies used in October. **If Pioneer does not make the adjusting entry, October expenses will be understated and net income overstated by $1,500. Also, both assets and owner's equity will be overstated by $1,500 on the October 31 balance sheet.**

ACCOUNTING ACROSS THE ORGANIZATION

Companies Change Advertising Treatment

The method of accounting for advertising costs affects sales and marketing executives. In the past, companies sometimes recorded as assets the costs of media advertising for burgers, bleaches, athletic shoes, and other products. They then expensed those costs in subsequent periods as sales took place. The reasoning behind this treatment was that long ad campaigns provided benefits over multiple accounting periods. Today the accounting profession no longer allows this treatment because it decided that the benefits were too difficult to measure.

Instead, companies now must expense advertising costs when the advertising takes place. The issue is important because the outlays for advertising can be substantial. Recent big spenders: The Coca-Cola Company spent $2.2 billion, PepsiCo., Inc. $1.7 billion, Nike, Inc. $1,378 million, and Limited Brands $484 million.

? Why might the new accounting method cause companies sometimes to spend less on advertising?

Insurance

Oct.4
Insurance purchased; record asset

Insurance Policy			
Oct $50	Nov $50	Dec $50	Jan $50
Feb $50	March $50	April $50	May $50
June $50	July $50	Aug $50	Sept $50
I YEAR $600			

Oct.31
Insurance expired; record insurance expense

Insurance. Companies purchase insurance to protect themselves from losses due to fire, theft, and other unforeseen events. Insurance must be paid in advance. Insurance premiums (payments) normally are recorded as an increase (a debit) to the asset account Prepaid Insurance. At the financial statement date companies increase (debit) Insurance Expense and decrease (credit) Prepaid Insurance for the cost that has expired during the period.

On October 4, Pioneer Advertising Agency paid $600 for a one-year fire insurance policy. Coverage began on October 1. Pioneer recorded the payment by increasing (debiting) Prepaid Insurance. This account shows a balance of $600 in the October 31 trial balance. Insurance of $50 ($600 ÷ 12) expires each month. Thus, Pioneer makes the following adjusting entry.

A	=	L	+	OE
				−50 Exp
−50				

Cash Flows
no effect

Oct. 31	Insurance Expense	50	
	Prepaid Insurance		50
	(To record insurance expired)		

After Pioneer posts the adjusting entry, the accounts show:

Illustration 3-6
Insurance accounts after adjustment

Prepaid Insurance			
10/4	600	10/31 **Adj.**	**50**
10/31 Bal.	550		

Insurance Expense			
10/31 **Adj.**	**50**		

The asset Prepaid Insurance shows a balance of $550. This amount represents the unexpired cost for the remaining 11 months of coverage. The $50 balance in Insurance Expense equals the insurance cost that has expired in October. If Pioneer does not make this adjustment, October expenses will be understated and net income overstated by $50. Also, both assets and owner's equity will be overstated by $50 on the October 31 balance sheet.

Depreciation. Companies typically own buildings, equipment, and vehicles. These long-lived assets provide service for a number of years. Thus, each is recorded as an asset, rather than an expense, in the year it is acquired. As explained in Chapter 1, companies record such assets **at cost**, as required by the cost principle. The term of service is referred to as the **useful life**.

According to the matching principle, companies then report a portion of the cost of a long-lived asset as an expense during each period of the asset's useful life. **Depreciation** is the process of allocating the cost of an asset to expense over its useful life in a rational and systematic manner.

Depreciation
Oct.2
Office equipment purchased; record asset
Office Equipment
Oct $40
Nov $40
Dec $40
Jan $40
Feb $40
March $40
April $40
May $40
June $40
July $40
Aug $40
Sept $40
Depreciation = $480/year
Oct.31
Depreciation recognized; record depreciation expense

Need for Depreciation Adjustment. From an accounting standpoint, acquiring long-lived assets is essentially a long-term prepayment for services. Companies need to make periodic adjusting entries for depreciation, just as they do for other prepaid expenses. These entries recognize the cost that has been used (an expense) during the period and report the unexpired cost (an asset) at the end of the period.

When a company acquires a long-lived asset, it does not know its exact useful life. The asset may be useful for a longer or shorter time than expected, depending on various factors. Thus, **depreciation is an estimate** rather than a factual measurement of expired cost. A common procedure in computing depreciation expense is to divide the cost of the asset by its useful life. For example, if cost is \$10,000 and useful life is expected to be 10 years, annual depreciation is \$1,000.[1]

Pioneer Advertising estimates depreciation on the office equipment to be \$480 a year, or \$40 per month. Thus, Pioneer makes the following adjusting entry to record depreciation for October.

Oct. 31	Depreciation Expense	40	
	Accumulated Depreciation—Office Equipment		40
	(To record monthly depreciation)		

A	=	L	+	OE
				−40 Exp
−40				

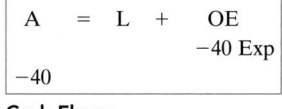

Cash Flows
no effect

After the adjusting entry is posted, the accounts show:

Office Equipment

10/1	5,000		

Accumulated Depreciation—Office Equipment

		10/31 **Adj.**	**40**

Depreciation Expense

10/31 **Adj.**	**40**		

Illustration 3-7
Accounts after adjustment for depreciation

The balance in the accumulated depreciation account will increase \$40 each month. After journalizing and posting the adjusting entry at November 30, the balance will be \$80; at December 31, \$120; and so on.

Statement Presentation. Accumulated Depreciation—Office Equipment is a **contra asset account**. That means that it is offset against an asset account on the balance sheet. This accumulated depreciation account appears just after the account it offsets (in this case, Office Equipment) on the balance sheet. Its normal balance is a credit.

HELPFUL HINT
All contra accounts have increases, decreases, and normal balances *opposite to the account to which* they relate.

An alternative to using a contra asset account would be to decrease (credit) the asset account (e.g., Office Equipment) directly for the depreciation each month. But use of the contra account is preferable for a simple reason: it discloses *both* the original cost of the equipment *and* the total cost that has expired to date.

[1] Chapter 10 addresses the computation of depreciation expense in detail.

In the balance sheet, Pioneer deducts Accumulated Depreciation—Office Equipment from the related asset account, as follows.

Illustration 3-8
Balance sheet presentation of accumulated depreciation

Office equipment	$5,000	
Less: Accumulated depreciation—office equipment	40	**$4,960**

ALTERNATIVE TERMINOLOGY

Book value is sometimes referred to as *carrying value* or *unexpired cost*.

The difference between the cost of any depreciable asset and its related accumulated depreciation is its **book value**. In Illustration 3-8, the book value of the equipment at the balance sheet date is $4,960. The book value of an asset generally differs from its **market value**—the price at which the asset could be sold in the marketplace. Remember that depreciation is a means of cost allocation, not a matter of market valuation.

Depreciation expense identifies that portion of the asset's cost that has expired during the period (in this case, in October). As for other prepaid adjustments, the omission of this adjusting entry would cause total assets, total owner's equity, and net income to be overstated and depreciation expense to be understated.

If the company owns additional long-lived assets, such as store equipment or buildings, it records depreciation expense on each of those items. It also establishes related accumulated depreciation accounts, such as: Accumulated Depreciation—Store Equipment; and Accumulated Depreciation—Buildings.

Illustration 3-9 summarizes the accounting for prepaid expenses.

Illustration 3-9
Accounting for prepaid expenses

ACCOUNTING FOR PREPAID EXPENSES

Examples	Reason for Adjustment	Accounts Before Adjustment	Adjusting Entry
Insurance, supplies, advertising, rent, depreciation	Prepaid expenses recorded in asset accounts have been used.	Assets overstated. Expenses understated.	Dr. Expenses Cr. Assets

Unearned Revenues

Oct.2

Thank you in advance for your work
I will finish by Dec. 31
$1,200

Cash is received in advance; liability is recorded

Oct.31
Some service has been provided; some revenue is recorded

UNEARNED REVENUES

Companies record cash received before revenue is earned by increasing a liability account called **unearned revenues**. Examples are rent, magazine subscriptions, and customer deposits for future service. Airlines such as United, American, and Delta, for instance, treat receipts from the sale of tickets as unearned revenue until they provide the flight service. Similarly, colleges consider tuition received prior to the start of a semester as unearned revenue.

Unearned revenues are the opposite of prepaid expenses. Indeed, unearned revenue on the books of one company is likely to be a prepayment on the books of the company that made the advance payment. For example, a landlord will have unearned rent revenue when a tenant has prepaid rent.

When a company receives cash for future services, it increases (credits) an unearned revenue account (a liability) to recognize the liability. Later, the company earns revenues by providing service. It may not be practical to make daily journal entries as the revenue is earned. Instead, we delay recognizing earned revenue until the end of the period. Then the company makes an adjusting entry to record the revenue that has been earned and to show the liability that remains. Typically, prior to adjustment, liabilities are overstated and revenues are understated. Therefore, as shown in Illustration 3-10, the adjusting entry for unearned revenues results in a decrease (a debit) to a liability account and an increase (a credit) to a revenue account.

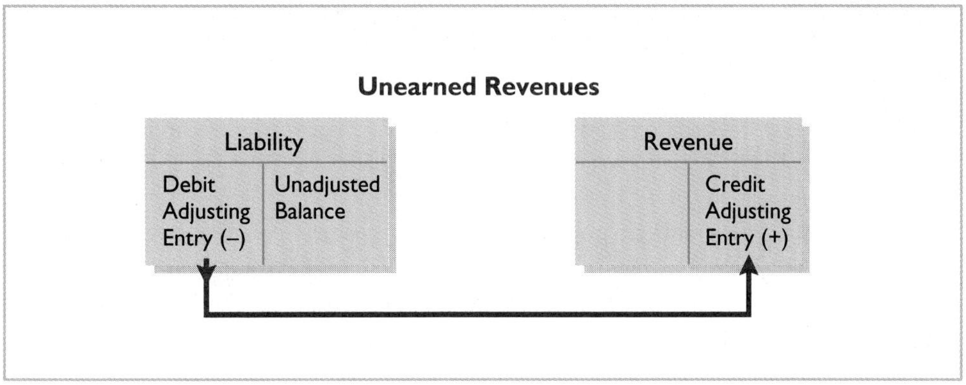

Illustration 3-10
Adjusting entries for unearned revenues

Pioneer Advertising Agency received $1,200 on October 2 from R. Knox for advertising services expected to be completed by December 31. Pioneer credited the payment to Unearned Service Revenue; this account shows a balance of $1,200 in the October 31 trial balance. Analysis reveals that the company earned $400 of those fees in October. Thus, it makes the following adjusting entry.

ALTERNATIVE TERMINOLOGY

Unearned revenue is sometimes referred to as *deferred revenue.*

Oct. 31	Unearned Revenue	400	
	Service Revenue		400
	(To record revenue for services provided)		

A	=	L	+	OE
		−400		
				+400 Rev

Cash Flows
no effect

After the company posts the adjusting entry, the accounts show:

Unearned Revenue

10/31 **Adj.**	**400**	10/2	1,200
		10/31 Bal.	800

Service Revenue

		10/31 Bal.	10,000
		31 **Adj.**	**400**

Illustration 3-11
Revenue accounts after prepayments adjustment

The liability Unearned Revenue now shows a balance of $800. That amount represents the remaining prepaid advertising services to be performed in the future. At the same time, Service Revenue shows total revenue of $10,400 earned in October. Without this adjustment, revenues and net income are understated by $400 in the income statement. Also, liabilities are overstated and owner's equity understated by $400 on the October 31 balance sheet.

Illustration 3-12 summarizes the accounting for unearned revenues.

ACCOUNTING FOR UNEARNED REVENUES

Examples	Reason for Adjustment	Accounts Before Adjustment	Adjusting Entry
Rent, magazine subscriptions, customer deposits for future service	Unearned revenues recorded in liability accounts have been earned.	Liabilities overstated. Revenues understated.	Dr. Liabilities Cr. Revenues

Illustration 3-12
Accounting for unearned revenues

ACCOUNTING ACROSS THE ORGANIZATION

Turning Gift Cards into Revenue

Those of you interested in marketing know that gift cards are among the hottest tools in merchandising today. Customers purchase gift cards and give them to someone for later use. In a recent year gift-card sales topped $95 billion.

Although these programs are popular with marketing executives, they create accounting questions. Should revenue be recorded at the time the gift card is sold, or when it is used by the customer? How should expired gift cards be accounted for? In its 2004 balance sheet Best Buy reported unearned revenue related to gift cards of $300 million.

Source: Robert Berner, "Gift Cards: No Gift to Investors," *Business Week* (March 14, 2005), p. 86.

? Suppose that Robert Jones purchases a $100 gift card at Best Buy on December 24, 2007, and gives it to his wife, Devon, on December 25, 2007. On January 3, 2008, Devon uses the card to purchase $100 worth of CDs. When do you think Best Buy should recognize revenue, and why?

Before You Go On...

REVIEW IT

1. What are the four types of adjusting entries?
2. What is the effect on assets, owner's equity, expenses, and net income if a company does not make a prepaid expense adjusting entry?
3. What is the effect on liabilities, owner's equity, revenues, and net income if a company does not make an unearned revenue adjusting entry?
4. Using PepsiCo's Consolidated Statement of Income, what was the amount of depreciation expense for 2005 and 2004? (See Note 4 to the financial statements.) The answer to this question appears on page 138.

DO IT

The ledger of Hammond, Inc. on March 31, 2008, includes the following selected accounts before adjusting entries.

	Debit	Credit
Prepaid Insurance	3,600	
Office Supplies	2,800	
Office Equipment	25,000	
Accumulated Depreciation—Office Equipment		5,000
Unearned Revenue		9,200

An analysis of the accounts shows the following.

1. Insurance expires at the rate of $100 per month.
2. Supplies on hand total $800.
3. The office equipment depreciates $200 a month.
4. One-half of the unearned revenue was earned in March.

Prepare the adjusting entries for the month of March.

Action Plan

- Make adjusting entries at the end of the period for revenues earned and expenses incurred in the period.

- Don't forget to make adjusting entries for prepayments. Failure to adjust for prepayments leads to overstatement of the asset or liability and related understatement of the expense or revenue.

Solution

1. Insurance Expense	100	
Prepaid Insurance		100
(To record insurance expired)		
2. Office Supplies Expense	2,000	
Office Supplies		2,000
(To record supplies used)		
3. Depreciation Expense	200	
Accumulated Depreciation—Office Equipment		200
(To record monthly depreciation)		
4. Unearned Revenue	4,600	
Service Revenue		4,600
(To record revenue for services provided)		

Related exercise material: *BE3-3, BE3-4, BE3-5, and BE3-6.*

✓ The Navigator

Adjusting Entries for Accruals

STUDY OBJECTIVE 6
Prepare adjusting entries for accruals.

The second category of adjusting entries is **accruals**. Companies make adjusting entries for accruals to record revenues earned and expenses incurred in the current accounting period that have not been recognized through daily entries.

ACCRUED REVENUES

Revenues earned but not yet recorded at the statement date are accrued revenues. Accrued revenues may accumulate (accrue) with the passing of time, as in the case of interest revenue and rent revenue. Or they may result from services that have been performed but are neither billed nor collected. The former are unrecorded because the earning process (e.g., of interest and rent) does not involve daily transactions. The latter may be unrecorded because the company has provided only a portion of the total service.

Accrued Revenues
Oct.31
My fee is $200
Revenue and receivable are recorded for unbilled services
Nov.10
$
Cash is received; receivable is reduced

An adjusting entry for accrued revenues serves two purposes: (1) It shows the receivable that exists at the balance sheet date, and (2) it records the revenues earned during the period. Prior to adjustment, both assets and revenues are understated. Therefore, as Illustration 3-13 shows, **an adjusting entry for accrued revenues increases (debits) an asset account and increases (credits) a revenue account**.

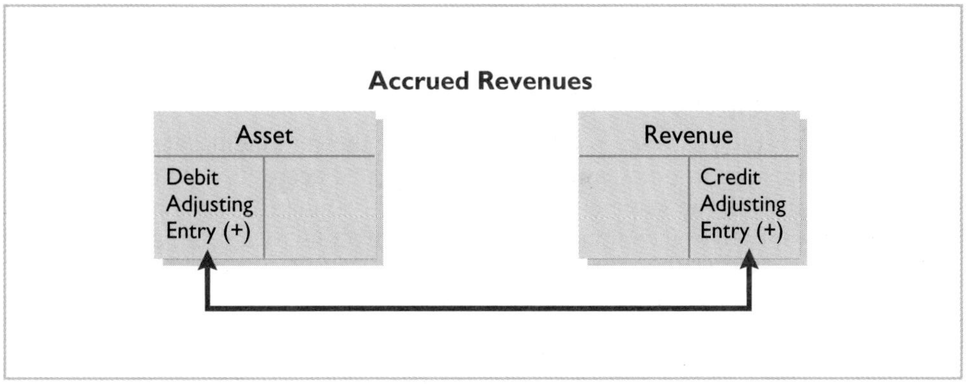

Illustration 3-13
Adjusting entries for accrued revenues

In October Pioneer Advertising Agency earned $200 for advertising services that have not been recorded. Pioneer makes the following adjusting entry on October 31.

A	=	L	+	OE
+200				
				+200 Rev

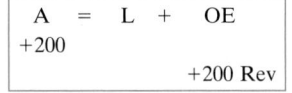

Cash Flows
no effect

Oct. 31	Accounts Receivable	200	
	Service Revenue		200
	(To record revenue for services provided)		

After Pioneer posts the adjusting entry, the accounts show:

Illustration 3-14
Receivable and revenue accounts after accrual adjustment

Accounts Receivable

10/31 **Adj.** **200**	

Service Revenue

	10/31 10,000
	31 400
	31 **Adj.** **200**
	10/31 Bal. 10,600

ETHICS NOTE

Computer Associates International was accused of backdating sales—that is, saying that a sale that occurred at the beginning of one quarter occurred at the end of the previous quarter, in order to achieve the previous quarter's sales targets.

The asset Accounts Receivable indicates that clients owe $200 at the balance sheet date. The balance of $10,600 in Service Revenue represents the total revenue Pioneer earned during the month ($10,000 + $400 + $200). Without the adjusting entry, assets and owner's equity on the balance sheet, and revenues and net income on the income statement, are understated.

On November 10, Pioneer receives cash of $200 for the services performed in October and makes the following entry.

A	=	L	+	OE
+200				
−200				

Cash Flows
+200

Nov. 10	Cash	200	
	Accounts Receivable		200
	(To record cash collected on account)		

The company records collection of cash on account with a debit (increase) to Cash and a credit (decrease) to Accounts Receivable.

Illustration 3-15 summarizes the accounting for accrued revenues.

Illustration 3-15
Accounting for accrued revenues

ACCOUNTING FOR ACCRUED REVENUES

Examples	Reason for Adjustment	Accounts Before Adjustment	Adjusting Entry
Interest, rent, services performed but not collected	Revenues have been earned but not yet received in cash or recorded.	Assets understated. Revenues understated.	Dr. Assets Cr. Revenues

ACCRUED EXPENSES

ALTERNATIVE TERMINOLOGY

Accrued expenses are also called *accrued liabilities*.

Expenses incurred but not yet paid or recorded at the statement date are **accrued expenses**. Interest, rent, taxes, and salaries are typical accrued expenses. Accrued expenses result from the same causes as accrued revenues. In fact, an accrued expense on the books of one company is an accrued revenue to another company. For example, Pioneer's $200 accrual of revenue is an accrued expense to the client that received the service.

An adjusting entry for accrued expenses serves two purposes: (1) It records the obligations that exist at the balance sheet date, and (2) it recognizes the expenses of the current accounting period. Prior to adjustment, both liabilities and expenses are understated. Therefore, as Illustration 3-16 shows, **an adjusting entry for accrued expenses increases (debits) an expense account and increases (credits) a liability account**.

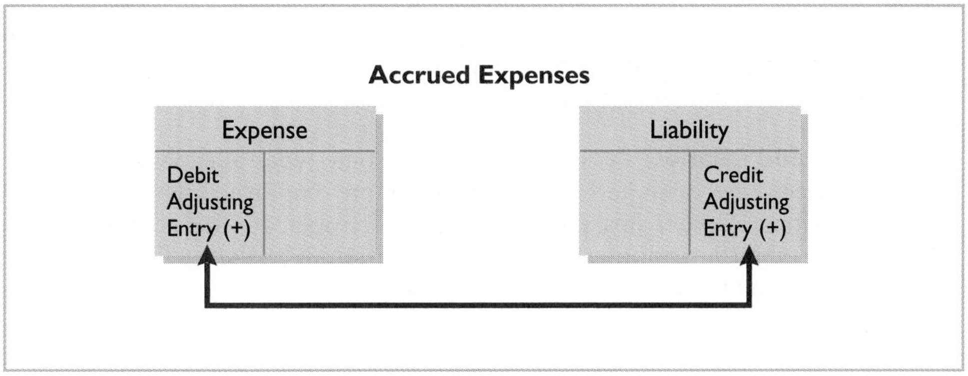

Illustration 3-16
Adjusting entries for accrued expenses

On the next few pages, we will look in more detail at some specific types of accrued expenses, beginning with accrued interest.

Accrued Interest. Pioneer Advertising Agency signed a $5,000, 3-month note payable on October 1. The note requires Pioneer to pay interest at an annual rate of 12%.

Three factors determine the amount of interest accumulation: (1) the face value of the note, (2) the interest rate, which is always expressed as an annual rate, and (3) the length of time the note is outstanding. For Pioneer, the total interest due on the note at its due date is $150 ($5,000 face value × 12% interest rate × 3/12 time period). The interest is thus $50 per month. Illustration 3-17 shows the formula for computing interest and its application to Pioneer Advertising Agency for the month of October.[2] Note that the time period is expressed as a fraction of a year.

HELPFUL HINT
Interest is a cost of borrowing money that accumulates with the passage of time.

Face Value of Note	×	Annual Interest Rate	×	Time in Terms of One Year	=	Interest
$5,000	×	12%	×	1/12	=	**$50**

Illustration 3-17
Formula for computing interest

Pioneer makes the following accrued expense adjusting entry on October 31.

Oct. 31	Interest Expense	50	
	Interest Payable		50
	(To record interest on notes payable)		

A	=	L	+	OE
				−50 Exp
		+50		

Cash Flows
no effect

After the company posts this adjusting entry, the accounts show:

Interest Expense		Interest Payable	
10/31 **Adj.**	**50**		
			10/31 **Adj.** **50**

Illustration 3-18
Interest accounts after adjustment

[2] We will consider the computation of interest in more depth in later chapters.

Interest Expense shows the interest charges for the month of October. Interest Payable shows the amount of interest owed at the statement date. (As of October 31, they are the same because October is the first month of the note payable.) Pioneer will not pay the interest until the note comes due at the end of three months. Companies use the Interest Payable account, instead of crediting (increasing) Notes Payable, in order to disclose the two types of obligations—interest and principal—in the accounts and statements. Without this adjusting entry, liabilities and interest expense are understated, and net income and owner's equity are overstated.

ETHICS NOTE

A report released by Fannie Mae's board of directors stated that improper adjusting entries at the mortgage-finance company resulted in delayed recognition of expenses caused by interest-rate changes. The motivation for such accounting apparently was the desire to hit earnings estimates.

Accrued Salaries. Companies pay for some types of expenses after the services have been performed. Examples are employee salaries and commissions. Pioneer last paid salaries on October 26; the next payday is November 9. As the calendar in Illustration 3-19 shows, three working days remain in October (October 29–31).

Illustration 3-19
Calendar showing Pioneer's pay periods

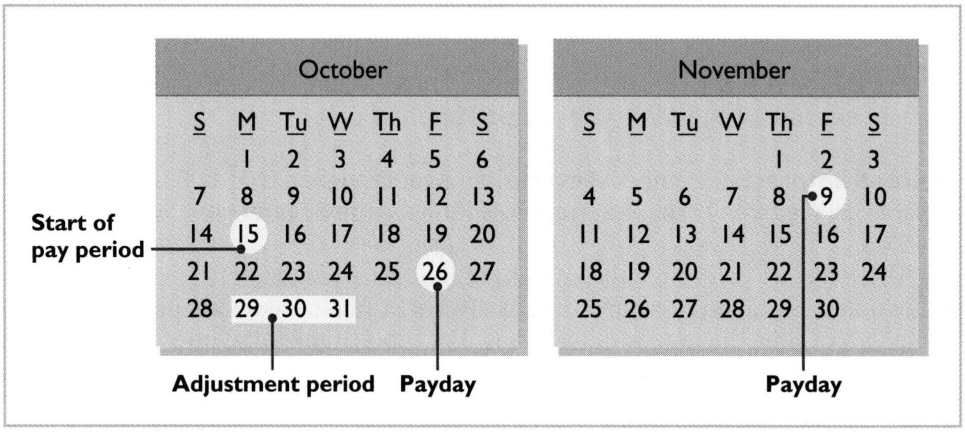

At October 31, the salaries for the last three days of the month represent an accrued expense and a related liability. The employees receive total salaries of $2,000 for a five-day work week, or $400 per day. Thus, accrued salaries at October 31 are $1,200 ($400 × 3). Pioneer makes the following adjusting entry:

A	=	L	+	OE
				−1,200 Exp
		+1,200		

Cash Flows
no effect

Oct. 31	Salaries Expense	1,200	
	Salaries Payable		1,200
	(To record accrued salaries)		

After the company posts this adjusting entry, the accounts show:

Illustration 3-20
Salary accounts after adjustment

Salaries Expense			
10/26	4,000		
31 **Adj.**	**1,200**		
10/31 Bal.	5,200		

Salaries Payable			
		10/31 **Adj.**	**1,200**

After this adjustment, the balance in Salaries Expense of $5,200 (13 days × $400) is the actual salary expense for October. The balance in Salaries Payable of $1,200 is the amount of the liability for salaries Pioneer owes as of October 31. Without the $1,200 adjustment for salaries, Pioneer's expenses are understated $1,200, and its liabilities are understated $1,200.

Pioneer Advertising pays salaries every two weeks. The next payday is November 9, when the company will again pay total salaries of $4,000. The payment will consist of $1,200 of salaries payable at October 31 plus $2,800 of salaries expense for November (7 working days as shown in the November calendar × $400). Therefore, Pioneer makes the following entry on November 9.

Nov. 9	Salaries Payable	1,200	
	Salaries Expense	2,800	
	Cash		4,000
	(To record November 9 payroll)		

A	=	L	+	OE
		−1,200		
				−2,800 Exp
−4,000				

Cash Flows
−4,000

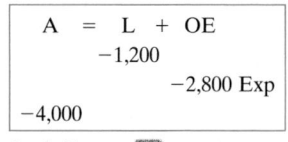

This entry eliminates the liability for Salaries Payable that Pioneer recorded in the October 31 adjusting entry. It also records the proper amount of Salaries Expense for the period between November 1 and November 9.

Illustration 3-21 summarizes the accounting for accrued expenses.

Illustration 3-21
Accounting for accrued expenses

ACCOUNTING FOR ACCRUED EXPENSES

Examples	Reason for Adjustment	Accounts Before Adjustment	Adjusting Entry
Interest, rent, salaries	Expenses have been incurred but not yet paid in cash or recorded.	Expenses understated. Liabilities understated.	Dr. Expenses Cr. Liabilities

Before You Go On...

REVIEW IT

1. What is the effect on assets, owner's equity, revenues, and net income if an accrued revenue adjusting entry is not made?
2. What is the effect on liabilities, owner's equity, expenses, and net income if an accrued expense adjusting entry is not made?

DO IT

Calvin and Hobbes are the new owners of Micro Computer Services. At the end of August 2008, their first month of ownership, Calvin and Hobbes are trying to prepare monthly financial statements. They have the following information for the month.

1. At August 31, Calvin and Hobbes owed employees $800 in salaries that the company will pay on September 1.
2. On August 1, Calvin and Hobbes borrowed $30,000 from a local bank on a 15-year note. The annual interest rate is 10%.
3. Service revenue unrecorded in August totaled $1,100.

Prepare the adjusting entries needed at August 31, 2008.

Action Plan

- Make adjusting entries at the end of the period for revenues earned and expenses incurred in the period.
- Don't forget to make adjusting entries for accruals. Adjusting entries for accruals will increase both a balance sheet and an income statement account.

Solution

1. Salaries Expense	800	
Salaries Payable		800
(To record accrued salaries)		
2. Interest Expense	250	
Interest Payable		250
(To record interest)		
($30,000 × 10% × 1/12 = $250)		
3. Accounts Receivable	1,100	
Service Revenue		1,100
(To record revenue for services provided)		

Related exercise material: *BE3-7, E3-5, E3-6, E3-7, E3-8, E3-9, E3-10, E3-11, E3-12, and E3-13.*

✓ The Navigator

Summary of Journalizing and Posting

Illustrations 3-22 and 3-23 show the journalizing and posting of adjusting entries for Pioneer Advertising Agency on October 31. The ledger identifies all adjustments by the reference J2 because they have been recorded on page 2 of the general journal. The company may insert a center caption "Adjusting Entries" between the last transaction entry and the first adjusting entry in the journal. When you review the general ledger in Illustration 3-23, note that the entries highlighted in color are the adjustments.

Illustration 3-22
General journal showing adjusting entries

HELPFUL HINT
(1) Adjusting entries should not involve debits or credits to cash.
(2) Evaluate whether the adjustment makes sense. For example, an adjustment to recognize supplies used should increase supplies expense.
(3) Double-check all computations.
(4) Each adjusting entry affects one balance sheet account and one income statement account.

GENERAL JOURNAL — J2

Date	Account Titles and Explanation	Ref.	Debit	Credit
2008	Adjusting Entries			
Oct. 31	Advertising Supplies Expense	631	1,500	
	Advertising Supplies	126		1,500
	(To record supplies used)			
31	Insurance Expense	722	50	
	Prepaid Insurance	130		50
	(To record insurance expired)			
31	Depreciation Expense	711	40	
	Accumulated Depreciation—Office Equipment	158		40
	(To record monthly depreciation)			
31	Unearned Revenue	209	400	
	Service Revenue	400		400
	(To record revenue for services provided)			
31	Accounts Receivable	112	200	
	Service Revenue	400		200
	(To record revenue for services provided)			
31	Interest Expense	905	50	
	Interest Payable	230		50
	(To record interest on notes payable)			
31	Salaries Expense	726	1,200	
	Salaries Payable	212		1,200
	(To record accrued salaries)			

Illustration 3-23
General ledger after adjustment

GENERAL LEDGER

Cash — No. 101

Date	Explanation	Ref.	Debit	Credit	Balance
2008					
Oct. 1		J1	10,000		10,000
2		J1	1,200		11,200
3		J1		900	10,300
4		J1		600	9,700
20		J1		500	9,200
26		J1		4,000	5,200
31		J1	10,000		15,200

Accounts Receivable — No. 112

Date	Explanation	Ref.	Debit	Credit	Balance
2008					
Oct. 31	**Adj. entry**	**J2**	**200**		**200**

Advertising Supplies — No. 126

Date	Explanation	Ref.	Debit	Credit	Balance
2008					
Oct. 5		J1	2,500		2,500
31	**Adj. entry**	**J2**		**1,500**	**1,000**

Prepaid Insurance — No. 130

Date	Explanation	Ref.	Debit	Credit	Balance
2008					
Oct. 4		J1	600		600
31	**Adj. entry**	**J2**		**50**	**550**

Office Equipment — No. 157

Date	Explanation	Ref.	Debit	Credit	Balance
2008					
Oct. 1		J1	5,000		5,000

Accumulated Depreciation—Office Equipment — No. 158

Date	Explanation	Ref.	Debit	Credit	Balance
2008					
Oct. 31	**Adj. entry**	**J2**		**40**	**40**

Notes Payable — No. 200

Date	Explanation	Ref.	Debit	Credit	Balance
2008					
Oct. 1		J1		5,000	5,000

Accounts Payable — No. 201

Date	Explanation	Ref.	Debit	Credit	Balance
2008					
Oct. 5		J1		2,500	2,500

Unearned Revenue — No. 209

Date	Explanation	Ref.	Debit	Credit	Balance
2008					
Oct. 2		J1		1,200	1,200
31	**Adj. entry**	**J2**	**400**		**800**

Salaries Payable — No. 212

Date	Explanation	Ref.	Debit	Credit	Balance
2008					
Oct. 31	**Adj. entry**	**J2**		**1,200**	**1,200**

Interest Payable — No. 230

Date	Explanation	Ref.	Debit	Credit	Balance
2008					
Oct. 31	**Adj. entry**	**J2**		**50**	**50**

C. R. Byrd, Capital — No. 301

Date	Explanation	Ref.	Debit	Credit	Balance
2008					
Oct. 1		J1		10,000	10,000

C. R. Byrd, Drawing — No. 306

Date	Explanation	Ref.	Debit	Credit	Balance
2008					
Oct. 20		J1	500		500

Service Revenue — No. 400

Date	Explanation	Ref.	Debit	Credit	Balance
2008					
Oct. 31		J1		10,000	10,000
31	**Adj. entry**	**J2**		**400**	**10,400**
31	**Adj. entry**	**J2**		**200**	**10,600**

Advertising Supplies Expense — No. 631

Date	Explanation	Ref.	Debit	Credit	Balance
2008					
Oct. 31	**Adj. entry**	**J2**	**1,500**		**1,500**

Depreciation Expense — No. 711

Date	Explanation	Ref.	Debit	Credit	Balance
2008					
Oct. 31	**Adj. entry**	**J2**	**40**		**40**

Insurance Expense — No. 722

Date	Explanation	Ref.	Debit	Credit	Balance
2008					
Oct. 31	**Adj. entry**	**J2**	**50**		**50**

Salaries Expense — No. 726

Date	Explanation	Ref.	Debit	Credit	Balance
2008					
Oct. 26		J1	4,000		4,000
31	**Adj. entry**	**J2**	**1,200**		**5,200**

Rent Expense — No. 729

Date	Explanation	Ref.	Debit	Credit	Balance
2008					
Oct. 3		J1	900		900

Interest Expense — No. 905

Date	Explanation	Ref.	Debit	Credit	Balance
2008					
Oct. 31	**Adj. entry**	**J2**	**50**		**50**

THE ADJUSTED TRIAL BALANCE AND FINANCIAL STATEMENTS

STUDY OBJECTIVE 7

Describe the nature and purpose of an adjusted trial balance.

The company has journalized and posted all adjusting entries. Next it prepares another trial balance from the ledger accounts. This is called an **adjusted trial balance**. Its purpose is to **prove the equality** of the total debit balances and the total credit balances in the ledger after all adjustments. The accounts in the adjusted trial balance contain all data that the company needs to prepare financial statements.

Preparing the Adjusted Trial Balance

Illustration 3-24 presents the adjusted trial balance for Pioneer Advertising Agency, prepared from the ledger accounts in Illustration 3-23. The amounts highlighted in color are those affected by the adjusting entries. Compare these amounts to those in the unadjusted trial balance in Illustration 3-3 on page 96.

Illustration 3-24
Adjusted trial balance

PIONEER ADVERTISING AGENCY
Adjusted Trial Balance
October 31, 2008

	Dr.	Cr.
Cash	$15,200	
Accounts Receivable	**200**	
Advertising Supplies	**1,000**	
Prepaid Insurance	**550**	
Office Equipment	5,000	
Accumulated Depreciation—Office Equipment		$ **40**
Notes Payable		5,000
Accounts Payable		2,500
Unearned Revenue		**800**
Salaries Payable		**1,200**
Interest Payable		**50**
C. R. Byrd, Capital		10,000
C. R. Byrd, Drawing	500	
Service Revenue		**10,600**
Salaries Expense	**5,200**	
Advertising Supplies Expense	**1,500**	
Rent Expense	900	
Insurance Expense	**50**	
Interest Expense	**50**	
Depreciation Expense	**40**	
	$30,190	$30,190

Preparing Financial Statements

Companies can prepare financial statements directly from the adjusted trial balance. Illustrations 3-25 (below) and 3-26 (on page 112) show the interrelationships of data in the adjusted trial balance and the financial statements.

As Illustration 3-25 shows, companies first prepare the income statement from the revenue and expense accounts. Next, they use the owner's capital and drawing accounts and the net income (or net loss) from the income statement to prepare the owner's equity statement. As Illustration 3-26 (page 112) shows, companies then prepare the balance sheet from the asset and liability accounts and the ending owner's capital balance as reported in the owner's equity statement.

PIONEER ADVERTISING AGENCY
Adjusted Trial Balance
October 31, 2008

Account	Debit	Credit
Cash	$15,200	
Accounts Receivable	200	
Advertising Supplies	1,000	
Prepaid Insurance	550	
Office Equipment	5,000	
Accumulated Depreciation—Office Equipment		$ 40
Notes Payable		5,000
Accounts Payable		2,500
Unearned Revenue		800
Salaries Payable		1,200
Interest Payable		50
C. R. Byrd, Capital		10,000
C. R. Byrd, Drawing	500	
Service Revenue		**10,600**
Salaries Expense	**5,200**	
Advertising Supplies Expense	**1,500**	
Rent Expense	**900**	
Insurance Expense	**50**	
Interest Expense	**50**	
Depreciation Expense	**40**	
	$30,190	$30,190

PIONEER ADVERTISING AGENCY
Income Statement
For the Month Ended October 31, 2008

Revenues		
Service Revenue		$10,600
Expenses		
Salaries expense	$5,200	
Advertising supplies expense	1,500	
Rent expense	900	
Insurance expense	50	
Interest expense	50	
Depreciation expense	40	
Total expenses		7,740
Net income		$ 2,860

PIONEER ADVERTISING AGENCY
Owner's Equity Statement
For the Month Ended October 31, 2008

C. R. Byrd; Capital, October 1	$ -0-
Add: Investments by owners	10,000
C. R. Byrd, Capital	10,000
Net income	2,860
	12,860
Less: Drawings	500
C. R. Byrd, Capital, October 31	$12,360

To balance sheet

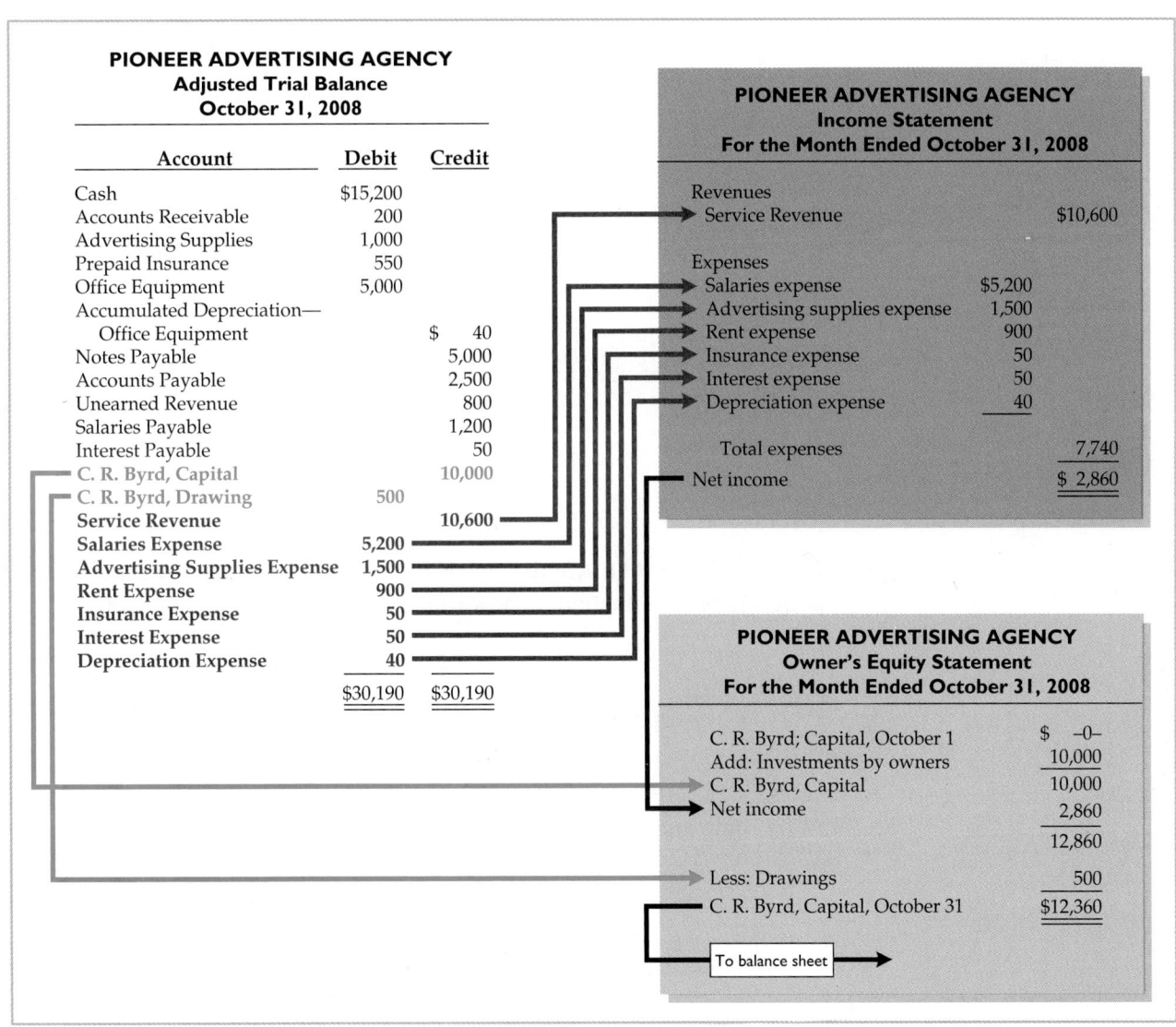

Illustration 3-25
Preparation of the income statement and owner's equity statement from the adjusted trial balance

PIONEER ADVERTISING AGENCY
Adjusted Trial Balance
October 31, 2008

Account	Debit	Credit
Cash	$15,200	
Accounts Receivable	200	
Advertising Supplies	1,000	
Prepaid Insurance	550	
Office Equipment	5,000	
Accumulated Depreciation—Office Equipment		$ 40
Notes Payable		5,000
Accounts Payable		2,500
Unearned Revenue		800
Salaries Payable		1,200
Interest Payable		50
C. R. Byrd, Capital		10,000
C. R. Byrd, Drawing	500	
Service Revenue		10,600
Salaries Expense	5,200	
Advertising Supplies Expense	1,500	
Rent Expense	900	
Insurance Expense	50	
Interest Expense	50	
Depreciation Expense	40	
	$30,190	$30,190

PIONEER ADVERTISING AGENCY
Balance Sheet
October 31, 2008

Assets		
Cash		$15,200
Accounts receivable		200
Advertising supplies		1,000
Prepaid insurance		550
Office equipment	$5,000	
Less: Accumulated depreciation	40	4,960
Total assets		$21,910
Liabilities and Owner's Equity		
Liabilities		
Notes payable		$ 5,000
Accounts payable		2,500
Unearned revenue		800
Salaries payable		1,200
Interest payable		50
Total liabilities		9,550
Owner's equity		
C. R. Byrd, Capital		12,360
Total liabilities and owner's equity		$21,910

Capital Balance at Oct. 31 from Owner's Equity Statement in Illustration 3-25

Illustration 3-26
Preparation of the balance sheet from the adjusted trial balance

Be sure to read **ALL ABOUT YOU: *Is Your Old Computer a Liability?*** on page 113 for information on how topics in this chapter apply to you.

Before You Go On...

REVIEW IT

1. What is the purpose of an adjusted trial balance?
2. How do companies prepare an adjusted trial balance?

The Navigator

Is Your Old Computer a Liability?

Do you have an old computer or two in your garage? How about an old TV that needs replacing? Many people do. Approximately 163,000 computers and televisions become obsolete *each day*. Yet, in a recent year, only 11% of computers were recycled. It is estimated that 75% of all computers ever sold are sitting in storage somewhere, waiting to be disposed of. Each of these old TVs and computers is loaded with lead, cadmium, mercury, and other toxic chemicals. If you have one these electronic gadgets, you have a responsibility, and a probable cost, for disposing of it.

What about companies? Many have potential pollution or environmental-disposal problems—not only for electronic gadgets, but also for the lead paint or asbestos they sold. How do we fit these issues into the accounting equation? Are these costs and related liabilities that companies should report?

In the past, two arguments were made for excluding pollution and environmental costs from the financial statements of product manufacturers. First, companies argued that pollution wasn't their responsibility. If it wasn't their responsibility, then there was no liability. Second, even if there was a liability, companies argued that they could not easily estimate its amount.

These arguments may be as out-of-date as last year's cell phone model. Increasingly, states are putting environmental liabilities into the accounting equation by passing laws that hold companies responsible for the toxic waste from their discarded products. Also, courts are levying steep fines for environmental cleanup caused by product waste.

Some Facts

* California adds $6 to $10 of sales tax to the cost of computers and televisions to fund recycling programs.
* Each cathode ray tube (CRT) monitor contains 4–6 pounds of lead. Consumer electronic products account for about 40% of the lead found in landfills.
* Environmental groups put a resolution on Apple Computer's 2006 shareholder meeting agenda requiring the company to study how it can increase recycling.
* The average household has two to three old computers in its garage or storage area.

About the Numbers

The nearby chart shows the amount of electronic products, in millions of tons, in storage, now being recycled, and in landfills.

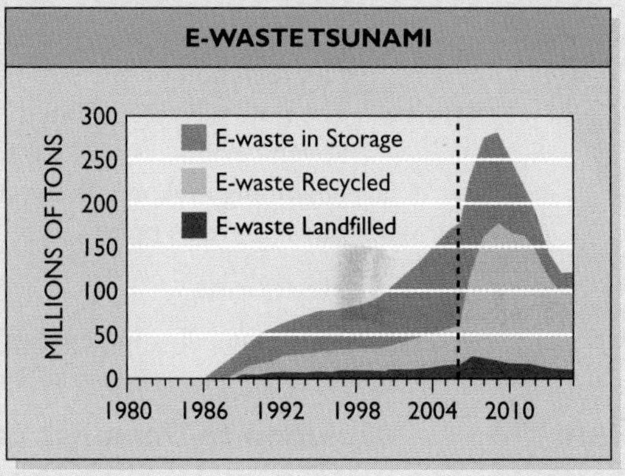

Source for graph: Silicon Valley Toxics Coalition, "Poison PCs and Toxic TVs," *www.svtc.org/cleancc/pubs/ppcttv2004.pdf*, p. 5.

What Do You Think?

Should companies accrue for environmental clean-up costs as liabilities on their financial statements?

YES: As more states impose laws holding companies responsible, and as more courts levy pollution-related fines, it becomes increasingly likely that companies will have to pay large amounts in the future.

NO: The amounts still are too difficult to estimate. Putting inaccurate estimates on the financial statements reduces their usefulness. Instead, why not charge the costs later, when the actual environmental clean-up or disposal occurs, at which time the company knows the actual cost?

Sources: Lorraine Woellert, "HP Wants Your Old PCs Back," *Business Week*, April 10, 2006, pp. 82-83; "Poison PCs and Toxic TVs: E-waste Tsunami to Roll Across the U.S.: Are We Prepared?" 2004 report of the Silicon Valley Toxics Coalition.

The authors' comments on this situation appear on page 138.

Demonstration Problem

Terry Thomas opens the Green Thumb Lawn Care Company on April 1. At April 30, the trial balance shows the following balances for selected accounts.

Prepaid Insurance	$ 3,600
Equipment	28,000
Notes Payable	20,000
Unearned Revenue	4,200
Service Revenue	1,800

Analysis reveals the following additional data.

1. Prepaid insurance is the cost of a 2-year insurance policy, effective April 1.
2. Depreciation on the equipment is $500 per month.
3. The note payable is dated April 1. It is a 6-month, 12% note.
4. Seven customers paid for the company's 6 months' lawn service package of $600 beginning in April. The company performed services for these customers in April.
5. Lawn services provided other customers but not recorded at April 30 totaled $1,500.

Instructions

Prepare the adjusting entries for the month of April. Show computations.

action plan

- Note that adjustments are being made for one month.
- Make computations carefully.
- Select account titles carefully.
- Make sure debits are made first and credits are indented.
- Check that debits equal credits for each entry.

Solution to Demonstration Problem

GENERAL JOURNAL J1

Date	Account Titles and Explanation	Ref.	Debit	Credit
	Adjusting Entries			
Apr. 30	Insurance Expense		150	
	Prepaid Insurance			150
	(To record insurance expired: $3,600 ÷ 24 = $150 per month)			
30	Depreciation Expense		500	
	Accumulated Depreciation—Equipment			500
	(To record monthly depreciation)			
30	Interest Expense		200	
	Interest Payable			200
	(To record interest on notes payable: $20,000 × 12% × 1/12 = $200)			
30	Unearned Revenue		700	
	Service Revenue			700
	(To record service revenue: $600 ÷ 6 = $100; $100 per month × 7 = $700)			
30	Accounts Receivable		1,500	
	Service Revenue			1,500
	(To record revenue for services provided)			

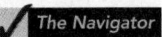

The Navigator

SUMMARY OF STUDY OBJECTIVES

1 **Explain the time period assumption.** The time period assumption assumes that the economic life of a business is divided into artificial time periods.

2 **Explain the accrual basis of accounting.** Accrual-basis accounting means that companies record events that change a company's financial statements in the periods in which those events occur, rather than in the periods in which the company receives or pays cash.

3 **Explain the reasons for adjusting entries.** Companies make adjusting entries at the end of an accounting period.

Such entries ensure that companies record revenues in the period in which they are earned and that they recognize expenses in the period in which they are incurred.

4 **Identify the major types of adjusting entries.** The major types of adjusting entries are deferrals (prepaid expenses and unearned revenues), and accruals (accrued revenues and accrued expenses).

5 **Prepare adjusting entries for deferrals.** Deferrals are either prepaid expenses or unearned revenues. Companies make adjusting entries for deferrals to record the portion of the prepayment that represents the expense incurred or the revenue earned in the current accounting period.

6 **Prepare adjusting entries for accruals.** Accruals are either accrued revenues or accrued expenses. Companies make adjusting entries for accruals to record revenues earned and expenses incurred in the current accounting period that have not been recognized through daily entries.

7 **Describe the nature and purpose of an adjusted trial balance.** An adjusted trial balance shows the balances of all accounts, including those that have been adjusted, at the end of an accounting period. Its purpose is to prove the equality of the total debit balances and total credit balances in the ledger after all adjustments.

The Navigator

GLOSSARY

WILEY PLUS

Accrual-basis accounting Accounting basis in which companies record transactions that change a company's financial statements in the periods in which the events occur. (p. 93).

Accruals Adjusting entries for either accrued revenues or accrued expenses. (p. 95).

Accrued expenses Expenses incurred but not yet paid in cash or recorded. (p. 104).

Accrued revenues Revenues earned but not yet received in cash or recorded. (p. 103).

Adjusted trial balance A list of accounts and their balances after the company has made all adjustments. (p. 110).

Adjusting entries Entries made at the end of an accounting period to ensure that companies follow the revenue recognition and matching principles. (p. 95).

Book value The difference between the cost of a depreciable asset and its related accumulated depreciation. (p. 100).

Calendar year An accounting period that extends from January 1 to December 31. (p. 93).

Cash-basis accounting Accounting basis in which companies record revenue when they receive cash and an expense when they pay cash. (p. 93).

Contra asset account An account offset against an asset account on the balance sheet. (p. 99).

Deferrals Adjusting entries for either prepaid expenses or unearned revenues. (p. 95).

Depreciation The allocation of the cost of an asset to expense over its useful life in a rational and systematic manner. (p. 99).

Fiscal year An accounting period that is one year in length. (p. 93).

Interim periods Monthly or quarterly accounting time periods. (p. 93).

Matching principle The principle that companies match efforts (expenses) with accomplishments (revenues). (p. 94).

Prepaid expenses Expenses paid in cash that benefit more than one accounting period and that are recorded as assets. (p. 96).

Revenue recognition principle The principle that companies recognize revenue in the accounting period in which it is earned. (p. 93).

Time period assumption An assumption that accountants can divide the economic life of a business into artificial time periods. (p. 92).

Unearned revenues Cash received and recorded as liabilities before revenue is earned. (p. 100).

Useful life The length of service of a productive facility. (p. 99).

APPENDIX Alternative Treatment of Prepaid Expenses and Unearned Revenues

STUDY OBJECTIVE 8

Prepare adjusting entries for the alternative treatment of deferrals.

In discussing adjusting entries for prepaid expenses and unearned revenues, we illustrated transactions for which companies made the initial entries to balance sheet accounts. In the case of prepaid expenses, the company debited the prepayment to an asset account. In the case of unearned revenue, the company credited a liability account to record the cash received.

Some companies use an alternative treatment: (1) When a company prepays an expense, it debits that amount to an expense account. (2) When it receives payment for future services, it credits the amount to a revenue account. In this appendix, we describe the circumstances that justify such entries and the different adjusting entries that may be required. This alternative treatment of prepaid expenses and unearned revenues has the same effect on the financial statements as the procedures described in the chapter.

Prepaid Expenses

Prepaid expenses become expired costs either through the passage of time (e.g., insurance) or through consumption (e.g., advertising supplies). If, at the time of purchase, the company expects to consume the supplies before the next financial statement date, **it may choose to debit (increase) an expense account rather than an asset account.** This alternative treatment is simply more convenient.

Assume that Pioneer Advertising expects that it will use before the end of the month all of the supplies purchased on October 5. A debit of $2,500 to Advertising Supplies Expense (rather than to the asset account Advertising Supplies) on October 5 will eliminate the need for an adjusting entry on October 31. At October 31, the Advertising Supplies Expense account will show a balance of $2,500, which is the cost of supplies used between October 5 and October 31.

But what if the company does not use all the supplies? For example, what if an inventory of $1,000 of advertising supplies remains on October 31? Obviously, the company would need to make an adjusting entry. Prior to adjustment, the expense account Advertising Supplies Expense is overstated $1,000, and the asset account Advertising Supplies is understated $1,000. Thus Pioneer makes the following adjusting entry.

A	=	L	+	OE
+1,000				
				+1,000 Exp

Cash Flows
no effect

Oct. 31	Advertising Supplies	1,000	
	Advertising Supplies Expense		1,000
	(To record supplies inventory)		

After the company posts the adjusting entry, the accounts show:

Illustration 3A-1
Prepaid expenses accounts after adjustment

Advertising Supplies		Advertising Supplies Expense	
10/31 **Adj.** **1,000**		10/5 2,500	10/31 **Adj.** **1,000**
		10/31 **Bal.** **1,500**	

After adjustment, the asset account Advertising Supplies shows a balance of $1,000, which is equal to the cost of supplies on hand at October 31. In addition, Advertising Supplies Expense shows a balance of $1,500. This is equal to the cost of supplies used between October 5 and October 31. Without the adjusting entry expenses are overstated and net income is understated by $1,000 in the October income statement. Also, both assets and owner's equity are understated by $1,000 on the October 31 balance sheet.

Illustration 3A-2 compares the entries and accounts for advertising supplies in the two adjustment approaches.

Illustration 3A-2
Adjustment approaches—a comparison

Prepayment Initially Debited to Asset Account (per chapter)				**Prepayment Initially Debited to Expense Account (per appendix)**			
Oct. 5	Advertising Supplies	2,500		Oct. 5	Advertising Supplies Expense	2,500	
	Accounts Payable		2,500		Accounts Payable		2,500
Oct. 31	Advertising Supplies Expense	1,500		Oct. 31	Advertising Supplies	1,000	
	Advertising Supplies		1,500		Advertising Supplies Expense		1,000

After Pioneer posts the entries, the accounts appear as follows.

Illustration 3A-3
Comparison of accounts

(per chapter) Advertising Supplies

10/5	2,500	10/31	**Adj.**	**1,500**
10/31 **Bal.**	**1,000**			

(per appendix) Advertising Supplies

10/31 **Adj.**	**1,000**	

Advertising Supplies Expense (per chapter)

10/31 **Adj.**	**1,500**	

Advertising Supplies Expense (per appendix)

10/5	2,500	10/31	**Adj.**	**1,000**
10/31 **Bal.**	**1,500**			

Note that the account balances under each alternative are the same at October 31: Advertising Supplies $1,000, and Advertising Supplies Expense $1,500.

Unearned Revenues

Unearned revenues become earned either through the passage of time (e.g., unearned rent) or through providing the service (e.g., unearned fees). Similar to the case for prepaid expenses, companies may credit (increase) a revenue account when they receive cash for future services.

To illustrate, assume that Pioneer Advertising received $1,200 for future services on October 2. Pioneer expects to perform the services before October 31.[3] In such a case, the company credits Service Revenue. If it in fact earns the revenue before October 31, no adjustment is needed.

HELPFUL HINT
The required adjusted balances here are Service Revenue $400 and Unearned Revenue $800.

However, if at the statement date Pioneer has not performed $800 of the services, it would make an adjusting entry. Without the entry, the revenue account Service Revenue is overstated $800, and the liability account Unearned Revenue is understated $800. Thus, Pioneer makes the following adjusting entry.

Oct. 31	Service Revenue	800	
	Unearned Revenue		800
	(To record unearned revenue)		

A	=	L	+	OE
				−800 Rev
		+800		

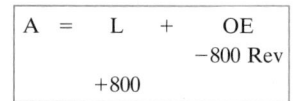

Cash Flows
no effect

After Pioneer posts the adjusting entry, the accounts show:

Illustration 3A-4
Unearned revenue accounts after adjustment

Unearned Revenue

	10/31	**Adj.**	**800**

Service Revenue

10/31 **Adj.**	**800**	10/2	1,200
		10/31 **Bal.**	**400**

The liability account Unearned Revenue shows a balance of $800. This equals the services that will be provided in the future. In addition, the balance in Service Revenue equals the services provided in October. Without the adjusting entry, both revenues and net income are overstated by $800 in the October income statement. Also, liabilities are understated by $800, and owner's equity is overstated by $800 on the October 31 balance sheet.

Illustration 3A-5 compares the entries and accounts for service revenue earned and unearned in the two adjustment approaches.

[3]This example focuses only on the alternative treatment of unearned revenues. In the interest of simplicity, we have ignored the entries to Service Revenue pertaining to the immediate earning of revenue ($10,000) and the adjusting entry for accrued revenue ($200).

Illustration 3A-5
Adjustment approaches—a comparison

Unearned Revenue Initially Credited to Liability Account (per chapter)				Unearned Revenue Initially Credited to Revenue Account (per appendix)			
Oct. 2	Cash	1,200		Oct. 2	Cash	1,200	
	Unearned Revenue		1,200		Service Revenue		1,200
Oct. 31	Unearned Revenue	400		Oct. 31	Service Revenue	800	
	Service Revenue		400		Unearned Revenue		800

After Pioneer posts the entries, the accounts appear as follows.

Illustration 3A-6
Comparison of accounts

(per chapter) Unearned Revenue

Debit		Credit	
10/31 **Adj.**	**400**	10/2	1,200
		10/31 **Bal.**	**800**

(per appendix) Unearned Revenue

Debit		Credit	
		10/31 **Adj.**	**800**

(per chapter) Service Revenue

Debit		Credit	
		10/31 **Adj.**	**400**

(per appendix) Service Revenue

Debit		Credit	
10/31 **Adj.**	**800**	10/2	1,200
		10/31 **Bal.**	**400**

Note that the balances in the accounts are the same under the two alternatives: Unearned Revenue $800, and Service Revenue $400.

Summary of Additional Adjustment Relationships

Illustration 3A-7
Summary of basic relationships for deferrals

Illustration 3A-7 provides a summary of basic relationships for deferrals.

Type of Adjustment	Reason for Adjustment	Account Balances before Adjustment	Adjusting Entry
1. Prepaid expenses	(a) Prepaid expenses initially recorded in asset accounts have been used.	Assets overstated Expenses understated	Dr. Expenses Cr. Assets
	(b) **Prepaid expenses initially recorded in expense accounts have not been used.**	**Assets understated** **Expenses overstated**	**Dr. Assets** **Cr. Expenses**
2. Unearned revenues	(a) Unearned revenues initially recorded in liability accounts have been earned.	Liabilities overstated Revenues understated	Dr. Liabilities Cr. Revenues
	(b) **Unearned revenues initially recorded in revenue accounts have not been earned.**	**Liabilities understated** **Revenues overstated**	**Dr. Revenues** **Cr. Liabilities**

Alternative adjusting entries **do not apply** to accrued revenues and accrued expenses because **no entries occur before companies make these types of adjusting entries**.

SUMMARY OF STUDY OBJECTIVE FOR APPENDIX

WILEY PLUS

8 **Prepare adjusting entries for the alternative treatment of deferrals.** Companies may initially debit prepayments to an expense account. Likewise, they may credit unearned revenues to a revenue account. At the end of the period, these accounts may be overstated. The adjusting entries for prepaid expenses are a debit to an asset account and a credit to an expense account. Adjusting entries for unearned revenues are a debit to a revenue account and a credit to a liability account.

*__Note:__ All asterisked Questions, Exercises, and Problems relate to material in the appendix to the chapter.

SELF-STUDY QUESTIONS

Answers are at the end of the chapter.

(SO 1) **1.** The time period assumption states that:
a. revenue should be recognized in the accounting period in which it is earned.
b. expenses should be matched with revenues.
c. the economic life of a business can be divided into artificial time periods.
d. the fiscal year should correspond with the calendar year.

(SO 2) **2.** The principle or assumption dictating that efforts (expenses) be matched with accomplishments (revenues) is the:
a. matching principle.
b. cost assumption.
c. periodicity principle.
d. revenue recognition principle.

(SO 2) **3.** One of the following statements about the accrual basis of accounting is *false*. That statement is:
a. Events that change a company's financial statements are recorded in the periods in which the events occur.
b. Revenue is recognized in the period in which it is earned.
c. This basis is in accord with generally accepted accounting principles.
d. Revenue is recorded only when cash is received, and expense is recorded only when cash is paid.

(SO 3) **4.** Adjusting entries are made to ensure that:
a. expenses are recognized in the period in which they are incurred.
b. revenues are recorded in the period in which they are earned.
c. balance sheet and income statement accounts have correct balances at the end of an accounting period.
d. all of the above.

(SO 4) **5.** Each of the following is a major type (or category) of adjusting entries *except:*
a. prepaid expenses.
b. accrued revenues.
c. accrued expenses.
d. earned revenues.

(SO 5) **6.** The trial balance shows Supplies $1,350 and Supplies Expense $0. If $600 of supplies are on hand at the end of the period, the adjusting entry is:

a. Supplies	600	
Supplies Expense		600
b. Supplies	750	
Supplies Expense		750
c. Supplies Expense	750	
Supplies		750
d. Supplies Expense	600	
Supplies		600

7. Adjustments for unearned revenues: (SO 5)
a. decrease liabilities and increase revenues.
b. have an assets and revenues account relationship.
c. increase assets and increase revenues.
d. decrease revenues and decrease assets.

8. Adjustments for accrued revenues: (SO 6)
a. have a liabilities and revenues account relationship.
b. have an assets and revenues account relationship.
c. decrease assets and revenues.
d. decrease liabilities and increase revenues.

9. Kathy Siska earned a salary of $400 for the last week of September. She will be paid on October 1. The adjusting entry for Kathy's employer at September 30 is: (SO 6)
a. No entry is required.

b. Salaries Expense	400	
Salaries Payable		400
c. Salaries Expense	400	
Cash		400
d. Salaries Payable	400	
Cash		400

10. Which of the following statements is *incorrect* concerning the adjusted trial balance? (SO 7)
a. An adjusted trial balance proves the equality of the total debit balances and the total credit balances in the ledger after all adjustments are made.
b. The adjusted trial balance provides the primary basis for the preparation of financial statements.
c. The adjusted trial balance lists the account balances segregated by assets and liabilities.
d. The adjusted trial balance is prepared after the adjusting entries have been journalized and posted.

***11.** The trial balance shows Supplies $0 and Supplies Expense $1,500. If $800 of supplies are on hand at the end of the period, the adjusting entry is: (SO 8)
a. Debit Supplies $800 and credit Supplies Expense $800.
b. Debit Supplies Expense $800 and credit Supplies $800.
c. Debit Supplies $700 and credit Supplies Expense $700.
d. Debit Supplies Expense $700 and credit Supplies $700.

Go to the book's website, **www.wiley.com/college/weygandt**, for Additional Self-Study questions.

The Navigator

QUESTIONS

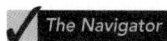

1. (a) How does the time period assumption affect an accountant's analysis of business transactions?
(b) Explain the terms *fiscal year, calendar year*, and *interim periods*.

2. State two generally accepted accounting principles that relate to adjusting the accounts.

3. Rick Marsh, a lawyer, accepts a legal engagement in March, performs the work in April, and is paid in May. If Marsh's law firm prepares monthly financial statements, when should it recognize revenue from this engagement? Why?

4. Why do accrual-basis financial statements provide more useful information than cash-basis statements?
5. In completing the engagement in question 3, Marsh pays no costs in March, $2,000 in April, and $2,500 in May (incurred in April). How much expense should the firm deduct from revenues in the month when it recognizes the revenue? Why?
6. "Adjusting entries are required by the cost principle of accounting." Do you agree? Explain.
7. Why may a trial balance not contain up-to-date and complete financial information?
8. Distinguish between the two categories of adjusting entries, and identify the types of adjustments applicable to each category.
9. What is the debit/credit effect of a prepaid expense adjusting entry?
10. "Depreciation is a valuation process that results in the reporting of the fair market value of the asset." Do you agree? Explain.
11. Explain the differences between depreciation expense and accumulated depreciation.
12. Shinn Company purchased equipment for $18,000. By the current balance sheet date, $6,000 had been depreciated. Indicate the balance sheet presentation of the data.
13. What is the debit/credit effect of an unearned revenue adjusting entry?
14. A company fails to recognize revenue earned but not yet received. Which of the following accounts are involved in the adjusting entry: (a) asset, (b) liability, (c) revenue, or (d) expense? For the accounts selected, indicate whether they would be debited or credited in the entry.
15. A company fails to recognize an expense incurred but not paid. Indicate which of the following accounts is debited and which is credited in the adjusting entry: (a) asset, (b) liability, (c) revenue, or (d) expense.
16. A company makes an accrued revenue adjusting entry for $900 and an accrued expense adjusting entry for $700. How much was net income understated prior to these entries? Explain.
17. On January 9, a company pays $5,000 for salaries, of which $2,000 was reported as Salaries Payable on December 31. Give the entry to record the payment.
18. For each of the following items before adjustment, indicate the type of adjusting entry (prepaid expense, unearned revenue, accrued revenue, and accrued expense) that is needed to correct the misstatement. If an item could result in more than one type of adjusting entry, indicate each of the types.
    (a) Assets are understated.
    (b) Liabilities are overstated.
    (c) Liabilities are understated.
    (d) Expenses are understated.
    (e) Assets are overstated.
    (f) Revenue is understated.
19. One-half of the adjusting entry is given below. Indicate the account title for the other half of the entry.
    (a) Salaries Expense is debited.
    (b) Depreciation Expense is debited.
    (c) Interest Payable is credited.
    (d) Supplies is credited.
    (e) Accounts Receivable is debited.
    (f) Unearned Service Revenue is debited.
20. "An adjusting entry may affect more than one balance sheet or income statement account." Do you agree? Why or why not?
21. Why is it possible to prepare financial statements directly from an adjusted trial balance?

*22. Adel Company debits Supplies Expense for all purchases of supplies and credits Rent Revenue for all advanced rentals. For each type of adjustment, give the adjusting entry.

BRIEF EXERCISES

WILEY PLUS

Indicate why adjusting entries are needed.
(SO 3)

BE3-1 The ledger of Dey Company includes the following accounts. Explain why each account may require adjustment.

(a) Prepaid Insurance
(b) Depreciation Expense
(c) Unearned Revenue
(d) Interest Payable

Identify the major types of adjusting entries.
(SO 4)

BE3-2 Nunez Company accumulates the following adjustment data at December 31. Indicate **(a)** the type of adjustment (prepaid expense, accrued revenues and so on), and **(b)** the status of accounts before adjustment (overstated or understated).

1. Supplies of $100 are on hand.
2. Services provided but not recorded total $900.
3. Interest of $200 has accumulated on a note payable.
4. Rent collected in advance totaling $800 has been earned.

Prepare adjusting entry for supplies.
(SO 5)

BE3-3 Windsor Advertising Company's trial balance at December 31 shows Advertising Supplies $6,700 and Advertising Supplies Expense $0. On December 31, there are $2,700 of supplies on hand. Prepare the adjusting entry at December 31, and using T accounts, enter the balances in the accounts, post the adjusting entry, and indicate the adjusted balance in each account.

BE3-4 At the end of its first year, the trial balance of Denton Company shows Equipment $30,000 and zero balances in Accumulated Depreciation—Equipment and Depreciation Expense. Depreciation for the year is estimated to be $5,000. Prepare the adjusting entry for depreciation at December 31, post the adjustments to T accounts, and indicate the balance sheet presentation of the equipment at December 31.

Prepare adjusting entry for depreciation.

(SO 5)

BE3-5 On July 1, 2008, Spahn Co. pays $18,000 to Randle Insurance Co. for a 3-year insurance contract. Both companies have fiscal years ending December 31. For Spahn Co., journalize and post the entry on July 1 and the adjusting entry on December 31.

Prepare adjusting entry for prepaid expense.

(SO 5)

BE3-6 Using the data in BE3-5, journalize and post the entry on July 1 and the adjusting entry on December 31 for Randle Insurance Co. Randle uses the accounts Unearned Insurance Revenue and Insurance Revenue.

Prepare adjusting entry for unearned revenue.

(SO 5)

BE3-7 The bookkeeper for Oglesby Company asks you to prepare the following accrued adjusting entries at December 31.

Prepare adjusting entries for accruals.

(SO 6)

1. Interest on notes payable of $400 is accrued.
2. Services provided but not recorded total $1,500.
3. Salaries earned by employees of $900 have not been recorded.

Use the following account titles: Service Revenue, Accounts Receivable, Interest Expense, Interest Payable, Salaries Expense, and Salaries Payable.

BE3-8 The trial balance of Bair Company includes the following balance sheet accounts. Identify the accounts that may require adjustment. For each account that requires adjustment, indicate **(a)** the type of adjusting entry (prepaid expenses, unearned revenues, accrued revenues, and accrued expenses) and **(b)** the related account in the adjusting entry.

Analyze accounts in an unadjusted trial balance.

(SO 4)

Accounts Receivable	Interest Payable
Prepaid Insurance	Unearned Service Revenue
Accumulated Depreciation—Equipment	

BE3-9 The adjusted trial balance of Harmony Company at December 31, 2008, includes the following accounts: S. Harmony, Capital $15,600; S. Harmony, Drawing $6,000; Service Revenue $35,400; Salaries Expense $16,000; Insurance Expense $2,000; Rent Expense $4,000; Supplies Expense $1,500; and Depreciation Expense $1,300. Prepare an income statement for the year.

Prepare an income statement from an adjusted trial balance.

(SO 7)

BE3-10 Partial adjusted trial balance data for Harmony Company is presented in BE3-9. The balance in S. Harmony, Capital is the balance as of January 1. Prepare an owner's equity statement for the year assuming net income is $10,600 for the year.

Prepare an owner's equity statement from an adjusted trial balance.

(SO 7)

***BE3-11** Duncan Company records all prepayments in income statement accounts. At April 30, the trial balance shows Supplies Expense $2,800, Service Revenue $9,200, and zero balances in related balance sheet accounts. Prepare the adjusting entries at April 30 assuming **(a)** $1,000 of supplies on hand and **(b)** $3,000 of service revenue should be reported as unearned.

Prepare adjusting entries under alternative treatment of deferrals.

(SO 8)

EXERCISES

WILEY PLUS

E3-1 Jo Seacat has prepared the following list of statements about the time period assumption.

Explain the time period assumption.

(SO 1)

1. Adjusting entries would not be necessary if a company's life were not divided into artificial time periods.
2. The IRS requires companies to file annual tax returns.
3. Accountants divide the economic life of a business into artificial time periods, but each transaction affects only one of these periods.
4. Accounting time periods are generally a month, a quarter, or a year.
5. A time period lasting one year is called an interim period.
6. All fiscal years are calendar years, but not all calendar years are fiscal years.

Instructions

Identify each statement as true or false. If false, indicate how to correct the statement.

E3-2 On numerous occasions, proposals have surfaced to put the federal government on the accrual basis of accounting. This is no small issue. If this basis were used, it would mean that billions in unrecorded liabilities would have to be booked, and the federal deficit would increase substantially.

Distinguish between cash and accrual basis of accounting.

(SO 2)

Instructions

(a) What is the difference between accrual-basis accounting and cash-basis accounting?
(b) Why would politicians prefer the cash basis over the accrual basis?
(c) Write a letter to your senator explaining why the federal government should adopt the accrual basis of accounting.

Compute cash and accrual accounting income.
(SO 2)

E3-3 Conan Industries collected $100,000 from customers in 2008. Of the amount collected, $25,000 was from revenue earned on account in 2007. In addition, Conan earned $40,000 of revenue in 2008, which will not be collected until 2009.

Conan Industries also paid $70,000 for expenses in 2008. Of the amount paid, $30,000 was for expenses incurred on account in 2007. In addition, Conan incurred $42,000 of expenses in 2008, which will not be paid until 2009.

Instructions

(a) Compute 2008 cash-basis net income.
(b) Compute 2008 accrual-basis net income.

Identify the type of adjusting entry needed.
(SO 4)

E3-4 Emeril Corporation encounters the following situations:

1. Emeril collects $1,000 from a customer in 2008 for services to be performed in 2009.
2. Emeril incurs utility expense which is not yet paid in cash or recorded.
3. Emeril's employees worked 3 days in 2008, but will not be paid until 2009.
4. Emeril earned service revenue but has not yet received cash or recorded the transaction.
5. Emeril paid $2,000 rent on December 1 for the 4 months starting December 1.
6. Emeril received cash for future services and recorded a liability until the revenue was earned.
7. Emeril performed consulting services for a client in December 2008. On December 31, it billed the client $1,200.
8. Emeril paid cash for an expense and recorded an asset until the item was used up.
9. Emeril purchased $900 of supplies in 2008; at year-end, $400 of supplies remain unused.
10. Emeril purchased equipment on January 1, 2008; the equipment will be used for 5 years.
11. Emeril borrowed $10,000 on October 1, 2008, signing an 8% one-year note payable.

Instructions

Identify what type of adjusting entry (prepaid expense, unearned revenue, accrued expense, accrued revenue) is needed in each situation, at December 31, 2008.

Prepare adjusting entries from selected data.
(SO 5, 6)

E3-5 Drew Carey Company has the following balances in selected accounts on December 31, 2008.

Accounts Receivable	$ -0-
Accumulated Depreciation—Equipment	-0-
Equipment	7,000
Interest Payable	-0-
Notes Payable	10,000
Prepaid Insurance	2,100
Salaries Payable	-0-
Supplies	2,450
Unearned Consulting Revenue	40,000

All the accounts have normal balances. The information below has been gathered at December 31, 2008.

1. Drew Carey Company borrowed $10,000 by signing a 12%, one-year note on September 1, 2008.
2. A count of supplies on December 31, 2008, indicates that supplies of $800 are on hand.
3. Depreciation on the equipment for 2008 is $1,000.
4. Drew Carey Company paid $2,100 for 12 months of insurance coverage on June 1, 2008.
5. On December 1, 2008, Drew Carey collected $40,000 for consulting services to be performed from December 1, 2008, through March 31, 2009.
6. Drew Carey performed consulting services for a client in December 2008. The client will be billed $4,200.
7. Drew Carey Company pays its employees total salaries of $9,000 every Monday for the preceding 5-day week (Monday through Friday). On Monday, December 29, employees were paid for the week ending December 26. All employees worked the last 3 days of 2008.

Instructions

Prepare adjusting entries for the seven items described on page 122.

E3-6 Affleck Company accumulates the following adjustment data at December 31.

Identify types of adjustments and account relationships.

(SO 4, 5, 6)

1. Services provided but not recorded total $750.
2. Store supplies of $300 have been used.
3. Utility expenses of $225 are unpaid.
4. Unearned revenue of $260 has been earned.
5. Salaries of $900 are unpaid.
6. Prepaid insurance totaling $350 has expired.

Instructions

For each of the above items indicate the following.

(a) The type of adjustment (prepaid expense, unearned revenue, accrued revenue, or accrued expense).

(b) The status of accounts before adjustment (overstatement or understatement).

E3-7 The ledger of Piper Rental Agency on March 31 of the current year includes the following selected accounts before adjusting entries have been prepared.

Prepare adjusting entries from selected account data.

(SO 5, 6)

	Debit	Credit
Prepaid Insurance	$ 3,600	
Supplies	2,800	
Equipment	25,000	
Accumulated Depreciation—Equipment		$ 8,400
Notes Payable		20,000
Unearned Rent		9,900
Rent Revenue		60,000
Interest Expense	-0-	
Wages Expense	14,000	

An analysis of the accounts shows the following.

1. The equipment depreciates $400 per month.
2. One-third of the unearned rent was earned during the quarter.
3. Interest of $500 is accrued on the notes payable.
4. Supplies on hand total $700.
5. Insurance expires at the rate of $200 per month.

Instructions

Prepare the adjusting entries at March 31, assuming that adjusting entries are made **quarterly**. Additional accounts are: Depreciation Expense, Insurance Expense, Interest Payable, and Supplies Expense.

E3-8 Andy Wright, D.D.S., opened a dental practice on January 1, 2008. During the first month of operations the following transactions occurred.

Prepare adjusting entries.

(SO 5, 6)

1. Performed services for patients who had dental plan insurance. At January 31, $875 of such services was earned but not yet recorded.
2. Utility expenses incurred but not paid prior to January 31 totaled $520.
3. Purchased dental equipment on January 1 for $80,000, paying $20,000 in cash and signing a $60,000, 3-year note payable. The equipment depreciates $400 per month. Interest is $500 per month.
4. Purchased a one-year malpractice insurance policy on January 1 for $12,000.
5. Purchased $1,600 of dental supplies. On January 31, determined that $400 of supplies were on hand.

Instructions

Prepare the adjusting entries on January 31. Account titles are: Accumulated Depreciation—Dental Equipment, Depreciation Expense, Service Revenue, Accounts Receivable, Insurance Expense, Interest Expense, Interest Payable, Prepaid Insurance, Supplies, Supplies Expense, Utilities Expense, and Utilities Payable.

Prepare adjusting entries.
(SO 5, 6)

E3-9 The trial balance for Pioneer Advertising Agency is shown in Illustration 3-3, p. 96. In lieu of the adjusting entries shown in the text at October 31, assume the following adjustment data.

1. Advertising supplies on hand at October 31 total $500.
2. Expired insurance for the month is $100.
3. Depreciation for the month is $50.
4. Unearned revenue earned in October totals $600.
5. Services provided but not recorded at October 31 are $300.
6. Interest accrued at October 31 is $70.
7. Accrued salaries at October 31 are $1,500.

Instructions
Prepare the adjusting entries for the items above.

Prepare correct income statement.
(SO 2, 5, 6, 7)

E3-10 The income statement of Benning Co. for the month of July shows net income of $1,400 based on Service Revenue $5,500, Wages Expense $2,300, Supplies Expense $1,200, and Utilities Expense $600. In reviewing the statement, you discover the following.

1. Insurance expired during July of $400 was omitted.
2. Supplies expense includes $200 of supplies that are still on hand at July 31.
3. Depreciation on equipment of $150 was omitted.
4. Accrued but unpaid wages at July 31 of $300 were not included.
5. Services provided but unrecorded totaled $500.

Instructions
Prepare a correct income statement for July 2008.

Analyze adjusted data.
(SO 4, 5, 6, 7)

E3-11 A partial adjusted trial balance of Sila Company at January 31, 2008, shows the following.

SILA COMPANY
Adjusted Trial Balance
January 31, 2008

	Debit	Credit
Supplies	$ 850	
Prepaid Insurance	2,400	
Salaries Payable		$ 800
Unearned Revenue		750
Supplies Expense	950	
Insurance Expense	400	
Salaries Expense	1,800	
Service Revenue		2,000

Instructions
Answer the following questions, assuming the year begins January 1.

(a) If the amount in Supplies Expense is the January 31 adjusting entry, and $500 of supplies was purchased in January, what was the balance in Supplies on January 1?
(b) If the amount in Insurance Expense is the January 31 adjusting entry, and the original insurance premium was for one year, what was the total premium and when was the policy purchased?
(c) If $3,500 of salaries was paid in January, what was the balance in Salaries Payable at December 31, 2007?
(d) If $1,600 was received in January for services performed in January, what was the balance in Unearned Revenue at December 31, 2007?

Journalize basic transactions and adjusting entries.
(SO 5, 6, 7)

E3-12 Selected accounts of Tabor Company are shown below and on page 125.

Supplies Expense

7/31	800		

Supplies

7/1 Bal.	1,100	7/31	800
7/10	400		

Salaries Payable

		7/31	1,200

Accounts Receivable			
7/31	500		

Unearned Revenue			
7/31	900	7/1 Bal.	1,500
		7/20	1,000

Salaries Expense			
7/15	1,200		
7/31	1,200		

Service Revenue			
		7/14	2,000
		7/31	900
		7/31	500

Instructions
After analyzing the accounts, journalize **(a)** the July transactions and **(b)** the adjusting entries that were made on July 31. (*Hint:* July transactions were for cash.)

E3-13 The trial balances before and after adjustment for Garcia Company at the end of its fiscal year are presented below.

Prepare adjusting entries from analysis of trial balances.
(SO 5, 6, 7)

GARCIA COMPANY
Trial Balance
August 31, 2008

	Before Adjustment		After Adjustment	
	Dr.	**Cr.**	**Dr.**	**Cr.**
Cash	$10,400		$10,400	
Accounts Receivable	8,800		9,800	
Office Supplies	2,300		700	
Prepaid Insurance	4,000		2,500	
Office Equipment	14,000		14,000	
Accumulated Depreciation—Office Equipment		$ 3,600		$ 4,500
Accounts Payable		5,800		5,800
Salaries Payable		–0–		1,100
Unearned Rent		1,500		600
T. Garcia, Capital		15,600		15,600
Service Revenue		34,000		35,000
Rent Revenue		11,000		11,900
Salaries Expense	17,000		18,100	
Office Supplies Expense	–0–		1,600	
Rent Expense	15,000		15,000	
Insurance Expense	–0–		1,500	
Depreciation Expense	–0–		900	
	$71,500	$71,500	$74,500	$74,500

Instructions
Prepare the adjusting entries that were made.

E3-14 The adjusted trial balance for Garcia Company is given in E3-13.

Prepare financial statements from adjusted trial balance.
(SO 7)

Instructions
Prepare the income and owner's equity statements for the year and the balance sheet at August 31.

E3-15 The following data are taken from the comparative balance sheets of Girard Billiards Club, which prepares its financial statements using the accrual basis of accounting.

Record transactions on accrual basis; convert revenue to cash receipts.
(SO 5, 6)

December 31	2008	2007
Fees receivable from members	$14,000	$ 9,000
Unearned fees revenue	17,000	25,000

Fees are billed to members based upon their use of the club's facilities. Unearned fees arise from the sale of gift certificates, which members can apply to their future use of club facilities.

The 2008 income statement for the club showed that fees revenue of $153,000 was earned during the year.

Instructions

(*Hint:* You will probably find it helpful to use T accounts to analyze these data.)

(a) Prepare journal entries for each of the following events that took place during 2008.
- **(1)** Fees receivable from 2007 were all collected.
- **(2)** Gift certificates outstanding at the end of 2007 were all redeemed.
- **(3)** An additional $35,000 worth of gift certificates were sold during 2008. A portion of these was used by the recipients during the year; the remainder was still outstanding at the end of 2008.
- **(4)** Fees for 2008 for services provided to members were billed to members.
- **(5)** Fees receivable for 2008 (i.e., those billed in item [4] above) were partially collected.

(b) Determine the amount of cash received by the club, with respect to fees, during 2008.

Journalize adjusting entries.
(SO 8)

***E3-16** Colin Mochrie Company has the following balances in selected accounts on December 31, 2008.

Consulting Revenue	$40,000
Insurance Expense	2,100
Supplies Expense	2,450

All the accounts have normal balances. Colin Mochrie Company debits prepayments to expense accounts when paid, and credits unearned revenues to revenue accounts when received. The following information below has been gathered at December 31, 2008.

1. Colin Mochrie Company paid $2,100 for 12 months of insurance coverage on June 1, 2008.
2. On December 1, 2008, Colin Mochrie Company collected $40,000 for consulting services to be performed from December 1, 2008, through March 31, 2009.
3. A count of supplies on December 31, 2008, indicates that supplies of $800 are on hand.

Instructions

Prepare the adjusting entries needed at December 31, 2008.

Journalize transactions and adjusting entries.
(SO 8)

***E3-17** At Natasha Company, prepayments are debited to expense when paid, and unearned revenues are credited to revenue when received. During January of the current year, the following transactions occurred.

Jan.	2	Paid $1,800 for fire insurance protection for the year.
	10	Paid $1,700 for supplies.
	15	Received $6,100 for services to be performed in the future.

On January 31, it is determined that $2,500 of the services fees have been earned and that there are $800 of supplies on hand.

Instructions

(a) Journalize and post the January transactions. (Use T accounts.)
(b) Journalize and post the adjusting entries at January 31.
(c) Determine the ending balance in each of the accounts.

EXERCISES: SET B

Visit the book's website at **www.wiley.com/college/weygandt**, and choose the Student Companion site, to access Exercise Set B.

PROBLEMS: SET A

Prepare adjusting entries, post to ledger accounts, and prepare adjusted trial balance.
(SO 5, 6, 7)

P3-1A Tony Masasi started his own consulting firm, Masasi Company, on June 1, 2008. The trial balance at June 30 is shown on page 127.

MASASI COMPANY
Trial Balance
June 30, 2008

Account Number		Debit	Credit
101	Cash	$ 7,150	
112	Accounts Receivable	6,000	
126	Supplies	2,000	
130	Prepaid Insurance	3,000	
157	Office Equipment	15,000	
201	Accounts Payable		$ 4,500
209	Unearned Service Revenue		4,000
301	T. Masasi, Capital		21,750
400	Service Revenue		7,900
726	Salaries Expense	4,000	
729	Rent Expense	1,000	
		$38,150	$38,150

In addition to those accounts listed on the trial balance, the chart of accounts for Masasi Company also contains the following accounts and account numbers: No. 158 Accumulated Depreciation—Office Equipment, No. 244 Utilities Payable, No. 212 Salaries Payable, No. 711 Depreciation Expense, No. 722 Insurance Expense, No. 732 Utilities Expense, and No. 631 Supplies Expense.

Other data:

1. Supplies on hand at June 30 are $600.
2. A utility bill for $150 has not been recorded and will not be paid until next month.
3. The insurance policy is for a year.
4. $2,500 of unearned service revenue has been earned at the end of the month.
5. Salaries of $2,000 are accrued at June 30.
6. The office equipment has a 5-year life with no salvage value. It is being depreciated at $250 per month for 60 months.
7. Invoices representing $1,000 of services performed during the month have not been recorded as of June 30.

Instructions

(a) Prepare the adjusting entries for the month of June. Use J3 as the page number for your journal.
(b) Post the adjusting entries to the ledger accounts. Enter the totals from the trial balance as beginning account balances and place a check mark in the posting reference column.
(c) Prepare an adjusted trial balance at June 30, 2008.

(c) Adj. trial balance $41,550

Prepare adjusting entries, post, and prepare adjusted trial balance, and financial statements.

(SO 5, 6, 7)

P3-2A Neosho River Resort opened for business on June 1 with eight air-conditioned units. Its trial balance before adjustment on August 31 is as follows.

NEOSHO RIVER RESORT
Trial Balance
August 31, 2008

Account Number		Debit	Credit
101	Cash	$ 19,600	
126	Supplies	3,300	
130	Prepaid Insurance	6,000	
140	Land	25,000	
143	Cottages	125,000	
149	Furniture	26,000	
201	Accounts Payable		$ 6,500
208	Unearned Rent		7,400
275	Mortgage Payable		80,000
301	P. Harder, Capital		100,000
306	P. Harder, Drawing	5,000	
429	Rent Revenue		80,000
622	Repair Expense	3,600	
726	Salaries Expense	51,000	
732	Utilities Expense	9,400	
		$273,900	$273,900

In addition to those accounts listed on the trial balance, the chart of accounts for Neosho River Resort also contains the following accounts and account numbers: No. 112 Accounts Receivable, No. 144 Accumulated Depreciation—Cottages, No. 150 Accumulated Depreciation—Furniture, No. 212 Salaries Payable, No. 230 Interest Payable, No. 620 Depreciation Expense—Cottages, No. 621 Depreciation Expense—Furniture, No. 631 Supplies Expense, No. 718 Interest Expense, and No. 722 Insurance Expense.

Other data:

1. Insurance expires at the rate of $400 per month.
2. A count on August 31 shows $600 of supplies on hand.
3. Annual depreciation is $6,000 on cottages and $2,400 on furniture.
4. Unearned rent of $4,100 was earned prior to August 31.
5. Salaries of $400 were unpaid at August 31.
6. Rentals of $1,000 were due from tenants at August 31. (Use Accounts Receivable.)
7. The mortgage interest rate is 9% per year. (The mortgage was taken out on August 1.)

(c) Adj. trial balance $278,000

(d) Net income $14,100
Ending capital balance $109,100
Total assets $199,900

Instructions

(a) Journalize the adjusting entries on August 31 for the 3-month period June 1–August 31.

(b) Prepare a ledger using the three-column form of account. Enter the trial balance amounts and post the adjusting entries. (Use J1 as the posting reference.)

(c) Prepare an adjusted trial balance on August 31.

(d) Prepare an income statement and an owner's equity statement for the 3 months ending August 31 and a balance sheet as of August 31.

Prepare adjusting entries and financial statements.

(SO 5, 6, 7)

P3-3A Fernetti Advertising Agency was founded by John Fernetti in January of 2007. Presented below are both the adjusted and unadjusted trial balances as of December 31, 2008.

FERNETTI ADVERTISING AGENCY
Trial Balance
December 31, 2008

	Unadjusted		Adjusted	
	Dr.	**Cr.**	**Dr.**	**Cr.**
Cash	$ 11,000		$ 11,000	
Accounts Receivable	20,000		22,500	
Art Supplies	8,600		5,000	
Prepaid Insurance	3,350		2,500	
Printing Equipment	60,000		60,000	
Accumulated Depreciation		$ 28,000		$ 34,000
Accounts Payable		5,000		5,000
Interest Payable		-0-		150
Notes Payable		5,000		5,000
Unearned Advertising Fees		7,200		5,600
Salaries Payable		-0-		1,300
J. Fernetti, Capital		25,500		25,500
J. Fernetti, Drawing	12,000		12,000	
Advertising Revenue		58,600		62,700
Salaries Expense	10,000		11,300	
Insurance Expense			850	
Interest Expense	350		500	
Depreciation Expense			6,000	
Art Supplies Expense			3,600	
Rent Expense	4,000		4,000	
	$129,300	$129,300	$139,250	$139,250

Instructions

(a) Journalize the annual adjusting entries that were made.

(b) Prepare an income statement and a statement of owner's equity for the year ending December 31, 2008, and a balance sheet at December 31.

(c) Answer the following questions.

(1) If the note has been outstanding 6 months, what is the annual interest rate on that note?

(2) If the company paid $12,500 in salaries in 2008, what was the balance in Salaries Payable on December 31, 2007?

(b) Net income $36,450
Ending capital $49,950
Total assets $67,000

(c) (1) 6%
(2) $2,500

P3-4A A review of the ledger of Remington Company at December 31, 2008, produces the following data pertaining to the preparation of annual adjusting entries.

Preparing adjusting entries.

(SO 5, 6)

1. Salaries Payable $0. There are eight salaried employees. Salaries are paid every Friday for the current week. Five employees receive a salary of $800 each per week, and three employees earn $600 each per week. December 31 is a Tuesday. Employees do not work weekends. All employees worked the last 2 days of December.

1. Salaries expense $2,320

2. Unearned Rent $324,000. The company began subleasing office space in its new building on November 1. At December 31, the company had the following rental contracts that are paid in full for the entire term of the lease.

2. Rent revenue $74,000

Date	Term (in months)	Monthly Rent	Number of Leases
Nov. 1	6	$4,000	5
Dec. 1	6	$8,500	4

3. Prepaid Advertising $15,000. This balance consists of payments on two advertising contracts. The contracts provide for monthly advertising in two trade magazines. The terms of the contracts are as follows.

3. Advertising expense $4,800

Contract	Date	Amount	Number of Magazine Issues
A650	May 1	$5,400	12
B974	Oct. 1	9,600	24

The first advertisement runs in the month in which the contract is signed.

4. Notes Payable $120,000. This balance consists of a note for one year at an annual interest rate of 9%, dated June 1.

4. Interest expense $6,300

Instructions

Prepare the adjusting entries at December 31, 2008. (Show all computations.)

P3-5A On September 1, 2008, the account balances of Rand Equipment Repair were as follows.

Journalize transactions and follow through accounting cycle to preparation of financial statements.

(SO 5, 6, 7)

No.	Debits		No.	Credits	
101	Cash	$ 4,880	154	Accumulated Depreciation	$ 1,500
112	Accounts Receivable	3,520	201	Accounts Payable	3,400
126	Supplies	2,000	209	Unearned Service Revenue	1,400
153	Store Equipment	15,000	212	Salaries Payable	500
			301	J. Rand, Capital	18,600
		$25,400			$25,400

During September the following summary transactions were completed.

Sept. 8 Paid $1,400 for salaries due employees, of which $900 is for September.
10 Received $1,200 cash from customers on account.
12 Received $3,400 cash for services performed in September.
15 Purchased store equipment on account $3,000.
17 Purchased supplies on account $1,200.
20 Paid creditors $4,500 on account.
22 Paid September rent $500.
25 Paid salaries $1,250.
27 Performed services on account and billed customers for services provided $1,500.
29 Received $650 from customers for future service.

Adjustment data consist of:

1. Supplies on hand $1,200.
2. Accrued salaries payable $400.
3. Depreciation is $100 per month.
4. Unearned service revenue of $1,450 is earned.

Instructions

(a) Enter the September 1 balances in the ledger accounts.
(b) Journalize the September transactions.
(c) Post to the ledger accounts. Use J1 for the posting reference. Use the following accounts: No. 407 Service Revenue, No. 615 Depreciation Expense, No. 631 Supplies Expense, No. 726 Salaries Expense, and No. 729 Rent Expense.
(d) Prepare a trial balance at September 30.
(e) Journalize and post adjusting entries.
(f) Prepare an adjusted trial balance.
(g) Prepare an income statement and an owner's equity statement for September and a balance sheet at September 30.

(d) Trial balance $30,150
(f) Adj. trial balance $30,650
(g) Net income $1,200
Ending capital $19,800
Total assets $23,900

Prepare adjusting entries, adjusted trial balance, and financial statements using appendix.

(SO 5, 6, 7, 8)

***P3-6A** Givens Graphics Company was organized on January 1, 2008, by Sue Givens. At the end of the first 6 months of operations, the trial balance contained the following accounts.

Debits		Credits	
Cash	$ 9,500	Notes Payable	$ 20,000
Accounts Receivable	14,000	Accounts Payable	9,000
Equipment	45,000	Sue Givens, Capital	22,000
Insurance Expense	1,800	Graphic Revenue	52,100
Salaries Expense	30,000	Consulting Revenue	6,000
Supplies Expense	3,700		
Advertising Expense	1,900		
Rent Expense	1,500		
Utilities Expense	1,700		
	$109,100		$109,100

Analysis reveals the following additional data.

1. The $3,700 balance in Supplies Expense represents supplies purchased in January. At June 30, $1,300 of supplies was on hand.
2. The note payable was issued on February 1. It is a 9%, 6-month note.
3. The balance in Insurance Expense is the premium on a one-year policy, dated March 1, 2008.
4. Consulting fees are credited to revenue when received. At June 30, consulting fees of $1,500 are unearned.

5. Graphic revenue earned but unrecorded at June 30 totals $2,000.
6. Depreciation is $2,000 per year.

Instructions

(a) Journalize the adjusting entries at June 30. (Assume adjustments are recorded every 6 months.)
(b) Prepare an adjusted trial balance.
(c) Prepare an income statement and owner's equity statement for the 6 months ended June 30 and a balance sheet at June 30.

(b) Adj. trial balance $112,850
(c) Net income $18,750
Ending capital $40,750
Total assets $72,000

PROBLEMS: SET B

P3-1B Linda Ace started her own consulting firm, Modine Consulting, on May 1, 2008. The trial balance at May 31 is as follows.

Prepare adjusting entries, post to ledger accounts, and prepare an adjusted trial balance.

(SO 5, 6, 7)

MODINE CONSULTING
Trial Balance
May 31, 2008

Account Number		Debit	Credit
101	Cash	$ 7,700	
112	Accounts Receivable	4,000	
126	Supplies	1,500	
130	Prepaid Insurance	4,800	
149	Office Furniture	9,600	
201	Accounts Payable		$ 3,500
209	Unearned Service Revenue		3,000
301	L. Ace, Capital		19,100
400	Service Revenue		6,000
726	Salaries Expense	3,000	
729	Rent Expense	1,000	
		$31,600	$31,600

In addition to those accounts listed on the trial balance, the chart of accounts for Modine Consulting also contains the following accounts and account numbers: No. 150 Accumulated Depreciation—Office Furniture, No. 229 Travel Payable, No. 212 Salaries Payable, No. 717 Depreciation Expense, No. 722 Insurance Expense, No. 736 Travel Expense, and No. 631 Supplies Expense.

Other data:

1. $500 of supplies have been used during the month.
2. Travel expense incurred but not paid on May 31, 2008, $200.
3. The insurance policy is for 2 years.
4. $1,000 of the balance in the unearned service revenue account remains unearned at the end of the month.
5. May 31 is a Wednesday, and employees are paid on Fridays. Modine Consulting has two employees, who are paid $700 each for a 5-day work week.
6. The office furniture has a 5-year life with no salvage value. It is being depreciated at $160 per month for 60 months.
7. Invoices representing $1,000 of services performed during the month have not been recorded as of May 31.

Instructions

(a) Prepare the adjusting entries for the month of May. Use J4 as the page number for your journal.

(b) Post the adjusting entries to the ledger accounts. Enter the totals from the trial balance as beginning account balances and place a check mark in the posting reference column.

(c) Adj. trial balance $33,800

(c) Prepare an adjusted trial balance at May 31, 2008.

Prepare adjusting entries, post, and prepare adjusted trial balance, and financial statements.

(SO 5, 6, 7)

GLS

P3-2B The Elston Motel opened for business on May 1, 2008. Its trial balance before adjustment on May 31 is as follows.

ELSTON MOTEL
Trial Balance
May 31, 2008

Account Number		Debit	Credit
101	Cash	$ 2,500	
126	Supplies	1,900	
130	Prepaid Insurance	2,400	
140	Land	15,000	
141	Lodge	70,000	
149	Furniture	16,800	
201	Accounts Payable		$ 5,300
208	Unearned Rent		3,600
275	Mortgage Payable		40,000
301	Mary Lerner, Capital		55,000
429	Rent Revenue		9,200
610	Advertising Expense	500	
726	Salaries Expense	3,000	
732	Utilities Expense	1,000	
		$113,100	$113,100

In addition to those accounts listed on the trial balance, the chart of accounts for Elston Motel also contains the following accounts and account numbers: No. 142 Accumulated Depreciation—Lodge, No. 150 Accumulated Depreciation—Furniture, No. 212 Salaries Payable, No. 230 Interest Payable, No. 619 Depreciation Expense—Lodge, No. 621 Depreciation Expense—Furniture, No. 631 Supplies Expense, No. 718 Interest Expense, and No. 722 Insurance Expense.

Other data:

1. Insurance expires at the rate of $200 per month.
2. A count of supplies shows $500 of unused supplies on May 31.
3. Annual depreciation is $3,600 on the lodge and $3,000 on furniture.
4. The mortgage interest rate is 12%. (The mortgage was taken out on May 1.)
5. Unearned rent of $2,500 has been earned.
6. Salaries of $800 are accrued and unpaid at May 31.

Instructions

(a) Journalize the adjusting entries on May 31.

(c) Adj. trial balance $114,850

(d) Net income $3,850
Ending capital balance $58,850
Total assets $106,450

(b) Prepare a ledger using the three-column form of account. Enter the trial balance amounts and post the adjusting entries. (Use J1 as the posting reference.)

(c) Prepare an adjusted trial balance on May 31.

(d) Prepare an income statement and an owner's equity statement for the month of May and a balance sheet at May 31.

P3-3B Ortega Co. was organized on July 1, 2008. Quarterly financial statements are prepared. The unadjusted and adjusted trial balances as of September 30 are shown below.

Prepare adjusting entries and financial statements.

(SO 5, 6, 7)

ORTEGA CO.
Trial Balance
September 30, 2008

	Unadjusted		Adjusted	
	Dr.	**Cr.**	**Dr.**	**Cr.**
Cash	$ 6,700		$ 6,700	
Accounts Receivable	400		900	
Supplies	1,200		1,000	
Prepaid Rent	1,500		900	
Equipment	15,000		15,000	
Accumulated Depreciation—Equipment				$ 350
Notes Payable		$ 5,000		5,000
Accounts Payable		1,510		1,510
Salaries Payable				600
Interest Payable				50
Unearned Rent		900		500
Jose Ortega, Capital		14,000		14,000
Jose Ortega, Drawing	600		600	
Commission Revenue		14,000		14,500
Rent Revenue		400		800
Salaries Expense	9,000		9,600	
Rent Expense	900		1,500	
Depreciation Expense			350	
Supplies Expense			200	
Utilities Expense	510		510	
Interest Expense			50	
	$35,810	$35,810	$37,310	$37,310

Instructions

(a) Journalize the adjusting entries that were made.

(b) Prepare an income statement and an owner's equity statement for the 3 months ending September 30 and a balance sheet at September 30.

(b) Net income $3,090
Ending capital $16,490
Total assets $24,150

(c) If the note bears interest at 12%, how many months has it been outstanding?

P3-4B A review of the ledger of Yoda Company at December 31, 2008, produces the following data pertaining to the preparation of annual adjusting entries.

Prepare adjusting entries

(SO 5, 6)

1. Prepaid Insurance $8,600. The company has separate insurance policies on its buildings and its motor vehicles. Policy B4564 on the building was purchased on July 1, 2007, for $6,000. The policy has a term of 3 years. Policy A2958 on the vehicles was purchased on January 1, 2008, for $3,600. This policy has a term of 2 years.

1. Insurance expense $3,800

2. Unearned Subscriptions $49,000. The company began selling magazine subscriptions in 2008 on an annual basis. The magazine is published monthly. The selling price of a subscription is $50. A review of subscription contracts reveals the following.

2. Subscription revenue $7,000

Subscription Date	Number of Subscriptions
October 1	200
November 1	300
December 1	480
	980

3. Notes Payable $60,000. This balance consists of a note for 6 months at an annual interest rate of 9%, dated September 1.

3. Interest expense $1,800

4. Salaries expense $2,850

4. Salaries Payable $0. There are eight salaried employees. Salaries are paid every Friday for the current week. Five employees receive a salary of $500 each per week, and three employees earn $750 each per week. December 31 is a Wednesday. Employees do not work weekends. All employees worked the last 3 days of December.

Instructions

Prepare the adjusting entries at December 31, 2008.

Journalize transactions and follow through accounting cycle to preparation of financial statements.

(SO 5, 6, 7)

GLS

P3-5B On November 1, 2008, the account balances of Rondeli Equipment Repair were as follows.

No.	Debits		No.	Credits	
101	Cash	$ 2,790	154	Accumulated Depreciation	$ 500
112	Accounts Receivable	2,510	201	Accounts Payable	2,100
126	Supplies	2,000	209	Unearned Service Revenue	1,400
153	Store Equipment	10,000	212	Salaries Payable	500
			301	P. Rondeli, Capital	12,800
		$17,300			$17,300

During November the following summary transactions were completed.

Nov. 8 Paid $1,100 for salaries due employees, of which $600 is for November.
10 Received $1,200 cash from customers on account.
12 Received $1,400 cash for services performed in November.
15 Purchased store equipment on account $3,000.
17 Purchased supplies on account $500.
20 Paid creditors on account $2,500.
22 Paid November rent $300.
25 Paid salaries $1,300.
27 Performed services on account and billed customers for services provided $400.
29 Received $550 from customers for future service.

Adjustment data consist of:

1. Supplies on hand $500.
2. Accrued salaries payable $500.
3. Depreciation for the month is $100.
4. Unearned service revenue of $1,150 is earned.

Instructions

(a) Enter the November 1 balances in the ledger accounts.
(b) Journalize the November transactions.
(c) Post to the ledger accounts. Use J1 for the posting reference. Use the following accounts: No. 407 Service Revenue, No. 615 Depreciation Expense, No. 631 Supplies Expense, No. 726 Salaries Expense, and No. 729 Rent Expense.
(d) Prepare a trial balance at November 30.
(e) Journalize and post adjusting entries.
(f) Prepare an adjusted trial balance.
(g) Prepare an income statement and an owner's equity statement for November and a balance sheet at November 30.

(d) Trial balance $20,150
(f) Adj. trial balance $20,750
(g) Net loss $1,850; Ending capital $10,950; Total assets $15,350

PROBLEMS: SET C

Visit the book's website at **www.wiley.com/college/weygandt**, and choose the Student Companion site, to access Problem Set C.

CONTINUING COOKIE CHRONICLE

(*Note*: This is a continuation of the Cookie Chronicle from Chapters 1 and 2.)

CCC3 It is the end of November and Natalie has been in touch with her grandmother. Her grandmother asked Natalie how well things went in her first month of business. Natalie, too, would like to know if she has been profitable or not during November. Natalie realizes that in order to determine Cookie Creations' income, she must first make adjustments.

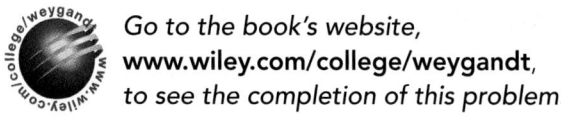

Go to the book's website,
www.wiley.com/college/weygandt,
to see the completion of this problem.

BROADENING YOUR PERSPECTIVE

FINANCIAL REPORTING AND ANALYSIS

Financial Reporting Problem

PepsiCo, Inc.

BYP3-1 The financial statements of PepsiCo are presented in Appendix A at the end of this textbook.

Instructions

(a) Using the consolidated financial statements and related information, identify items that may result in adjusting entries for prepayments.

(b) Using the consolidated financial statements and related information, identify items that may result in adjusting entries for accruals.

(c) Using the Selected Financial Data and 5-Year Summary, what has been the trend since 2001 for net income?

Comparative Analysis Problem

PepsiCo, Inc. vs. The Coca-Cola Company

BYP3-2 PepsiCo's financial statements are presented in Appendix A. Coca-Cola's financial statements are presented in Appendix B.

Instructions

Based on information contained in these financial statements, determine the following for each company.

(a) Net increase (decrease) in property, plant, and equipment (net) from 2004 to 2005.

(b) Increase (decrease) in selling, general, and administrative expenses from 2004 to 2005.

(c) Increase (decrease) in long-term debt (obligations) from 2004 to 2005.

(d) Increase (decrease) in net income from 2004 to 2005.

(e) Increase (decrease) in cash and cash equivalents from 2004 to 2005.

Exploring the Web

BYP3-3 A wealth of accounting-related information is available via the Internet. For example the Rutgers Accounting Web offers access to a great variety of sources.

Address: www.accounting.rutgers.edu/ or go to **www.wiley.com/college/weygandt**

Steps: Click on **Accounting Resources**. (*Note*: Once on this page, you may have to click on the **text only** box to access the available information.)

Instructions

(a) List the categories of information available through the **Accounting Resources** page.

(b) Select any one of these categories and briefly describe the types of information available.

CRITICAL THINKING

Decision Making Across the Organization

BYP3-4 Happy Camper Park was organized on April 1, 2007, by Amaya Berge. Amaya is a good manager but a poor accountant. From the trial balance prepared by a part-time bookkeeper, Amaya prepared the following income statement for the quarter that ended March 31, 2008.

HAPPY CAMPER PARK
Income Statement
For the Quarter Ended March 31, 2008

Revenues		
Rental revenue		$90,000
Operating expenses		
Advertising	$ 5,200	
Wages	29,800	
Utilities	900	
Depreciation	800	
Repairs	4,000	
Total operating expenses		40,700
Net income		$49,300

Amaya thought that something was wrong with the statement because net income had never exceeded $20,000 in any one quarter. Knowing that you are an experienced accountant, she asks you to review the income statement and other data.

You first look at the trial balance. In addition to the account balances reported above in the income statement, the ledger contains the following additional selected balances at March 31, 2008.

Supplies	$ 6,200
Prepaid Insurance	7,200
Notes Payable	12,000

You then make inquiries and discover the following.

1. Rental revenues include advanced rentals for summer occupancy $15,000.
2. There were $1,700 of supplies on hand at March 31.
3. Prepaid insurance resulted from the payment of a one-year policy on January 1, 2008.
4. The mail on April 1, 2008, brought the following bills: advertising for week of March 24, $110; repairs made March 10, $260; and utilities, $180.
5. There are four employees, who receive wages totaling $300 per day. At March 31, 2 days' wages have been incurred but not paid.
6. The note payable is a 3-month, 10% note dated January 1, 2008.

Instructions

With the class divided into groups, answer the following.

(a) Prepare a correct income statement for the quarter ended March 31, 2008.

(b) Explain to Amaya the generally accepted accounting principles that she did not recognize in preparing her income statement and their effect on her results.

Communication Activity

BYP3-5 In reviewing the accounts of Keri Ann Co. at the end of the year, you discover that adjusting entries have not been made.

Instructions

Write a memo to Keri Ann Nickels, the owner of Keri Ann Co., that explains the following: the nature and purpose of adjusting entries, why adjusting entries are needed, and the types of adjusting entries that may be made.

Ethics Case

BYP3-6 Bluestem Company is a pesticide manufacturer. Its sales declined greatly this year due to the passage of legislation outlawing the sale of several of Bluestem's chemical pesticides. In the coming year, Bluestem will have environmentally safe and competitive chemicals to replace these discontinued products. Sales in the next year are expected to greatly exceed any prior year's. The decline in sales and profits appears to be a one-year aberration. But even so, the company president fears a large dip in the current year's profits. He believes that such a dip could cause a significant drop in the market price of Bluestem's stock and make the company a takeover target.

To avoid this possibility, the company president calls in Cathi Bell, controller, to discuss this period's year-end adjusting entries. He urges her to accrue every possible revenue and to defer as many expenses as possible. He says to Cathi, "We need the revenues this year, and next year can easily absorb expenses deferred from this year. We can't let our stock price be hammered down!" Cathi didn't get around to recording the adjusting entries until January 17, but she dated the entries December 31 as if they were recorded then. Cathi also made every effort to comply with the president's request.

Instructions

(a) Who are the stakeholders in this situation?

(b) What are the ethical considerations of (1) the president's request and (2) Cathi's dating the adjusting entries December 31?

(c) Can Cathi accrue revenues and defer expenses and still be ethical?

"All About You" Activity

BYP3-7 In the **All About You** feature in this chapter (p. 113), you learned how important it is that companies report or disclose information about all liabilities, including potential liabilities related to environmental clean-up. There are many situations in which you will be asked to provide personal financial information about your assets, liabilities, revenue, and expenses. Sometimes you will face difficult decisions regarding what to disclose and how to disclose it.

Instructions

Suppose that you are putting together a loan application to purchase a home. Based on your income and assets, you qualify for the mortgage loan, but just barely. How would you address each of the following situations in reporting your financial position for the loan application? Provide responses for each of the following questions.

(a) You signed a guarantee for a bank loan that a friend took out for $20,000. If your friend doesn't pay, you will have to pay. Your friend has made all of the payments so far, and it appears he will be able to pay in the future.

(b) You were involved in an auto accident in which you were at fault. There is the possibility that you may have to pay as much as $50,000 as part of a settlement. The issue will not be resolved before the bank processes your mortgage request.

(c) The company at which you work isn't doing very well, and it has recently laid off employees. You are still employed, but it is quite possible that you will lose your job in the next few months.

Answers to Insight and Accounting Across the Organization Questions

p. 94 How Long Will "The Force" Be with Us?

Q: What accounting principle does this example illustrate?

A: *This situation demonstrates the difficulty of matching expenses to revenues.*

Q: How will financial results be affected if the expenses are recognized over a period that is *less than* that used for revenues?

A: *If expenses are recognized over a period that is* less than *that used for revenues, earnings will be understated during the early years and overstated during the later years.*

Q: What if the expenses are recognized over a period that is *longer than* that used for revenues?

A: *If the expenses are recognized over a period that is longer than that used for revenues, earnings will be overstated during the early years and understated in later years. In either case, management and stockholders could be misled.*

p. 98 Companies Change Advertising Treatment

Q: Why might the new accounting method cause companies sometimes to spend less on advertising?

A: *Under the old approach companies could delay to future periods the expensing of advertising costs. Under that approach, money spent this period did not necessarily immediately reduce income. Under the new approach, a dollar spent on advertising immediately reduces this year's income. If the company is concerned that it might not hit this year's earnings target, it might decide to reduce its advertising spending.*

p. 102 Turning Gift Cards into Revenue

Q: Suppose that Robert Jones purchases a $100 gift card at Best Buy on December 24, 2007, and gives it to his wife, Devon, on December 25, 2007. On January 3, 2008, Devon uses the card to purchase $100 worth of CDs. When do you think Best Buy should recognize revenue, and why?

A: *According to the revenue recognition principle, companies should recognize revenue when earned. In this case revenue is not earned until Best Buy provides the goods. Thus, when Best Buy receives cash in exchange for the gift card on December 24, 2007, it should recognize a liability, Unearned Revenue, for $100. On January 3, 2008, when Devon Jones exchanges the card for merchandise, Best Buy should recognize revenue and eliminate $100 from the balance in the Unearned Revenue account.*

* Authors' Comments on *All About You*: Is Your Old Computer a Liability? (p. 113)

The balance sheet should provide a fair representation of what a company owns and what it owes. If significant obligations of the company are not reported on the balance sheet, the company's net worth (its equity) will be overstated. While it is true that it is not possible to estimate the *exact* amount of future environmental clean-up costs, it is becoming clear that companies will be held accountable.

Therefore, it doesn't seem reasonable to not accrue for environmental costs. Recognition of these liabilities provides a more accurate picture of the company's financial position. It also has the potential to improve the environment. As companies are forced to report these amounts on their financial statements, they will start to look for more effective and efficient means to reduce toxic waste, and therefore reduce their costs.

Answer to PepsiCo Review It Question 4, p. 102

Per Note 4, PepsiCo's 2005 depreciation expense is $1,103 million; 2004 depreciation expense was $1,062 million.

Answers to Self-Study Questions

1. c **2.** a **3.** d **4.** d **5.** d **6.** c **7.** a **8.** b **9.** b **10.** c ***11.** a

Remember to go back to the Navigator box on the chapter-opening page and check off your completed work.

Chapter 4

Completing the Accounting Cycle

STUDY OBJECTIVES

After studying this chapter, you should be able to:

1 Prepare a worksheet.
2 Explain the process of closing the books.
3 Describe the content and purpose of a post-closing trial balance.
4 State the required steps in the accounting cycle.
5 Explain the approaches to preparing correcting entries.
6 Identify the sections of a classified balance sheet.

The Navigator

The Navigator

Scan **Study Objectives**	☐
Read **Feature Story**	☐
Read **Preview**	☐
Read text and answer **Before You Go On** p. 148 ☐ p. 158 ☐ p. 166 ☐	
Work **Demonstration Problem**	☐
Review **Summary of Study Objectives**	☐
Answer **Self-Study Questions**	☐
Complete **Assignments**	☐

Feature Story

EVERYONE LIKES TO WIN

When Ted Castle was a hockey coach at the University of Vermont, his players were self-motivated by their desire to win. Hockey was a game you either won or lost. But at Rhino Foods, Inc., a bakery-foods company he founded in Burlington, Vermont, he discovered that manufacturing-line workers were not so self-motivated. Ted thought, what if he turned the food-making business into a game, with rules, strategies, and trophies?

Ted knew that in a game knowing the score is all-important. He felt that only if the employees know the score—know exactly how the business is doing daily, weekly, monthly—could he turn food-making into a game. But Rhino is a closely held, family-owned business, and its financial statements and profits were confidential. Ted wondered, should he open Rhino's books to the employees?

A consultant put Ted's concerns in perspective when he said, "Imagine you're playing touch football. You play for an hour or two, and the whole time I'm sitting there with a book, keeping score. All of a sudden I blow the whistle, and I say, 'OK, that's it. Everybody go home.' I close my book and walk away. How would you feel?" Ted opened his books and revealed the financial statements to his employees.

The next step was to teach employees the rules and strategies of how to "win" at making food. The first lesson: "Your opponent at Rhino is expenses. You must cut and control expenses." Ted and his staff distilled those lessons into daily scorecards—production reports and income statements—that keep Rhino's employees up-to-date on the game. At noon each day, Ted posts the previous day's results at the entrance to the production room. Everyone checks whether they made or lost money on what they produced the day before. And it's not just an academic exercise: There's a bonus check for each employee at the end of every four-week "game" that meets profitability guidelines.

Rhino has flourished since the first game. Employment has increased from 20 to 130 people, while both revenues and profits have grown dramatically.

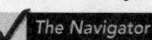

The Navigator

Inside Chapter 4...

Preview of Chapter 4

At Rhino Foods, Inc., financial statements help employees understand what is happening in the business. In Chapter 3, we prepared financial statements directly from the adjusted trial balance. However, with so many details involved in the end-of-period accounting procedures, it is easy to make errors. One way to minimize errors in the records and to simplify the end-of-period procedures is to use a worksheet.

In this chapter we will explain the role of the worksheet in accounting. We also will study the remaining steps in the accounting cycle, especially the closing process, again using Pioneer Advertising Agency as an example. Then we will consider correcting entries and classified balance sheets. The content and organization of Chapter 4 are as follows.

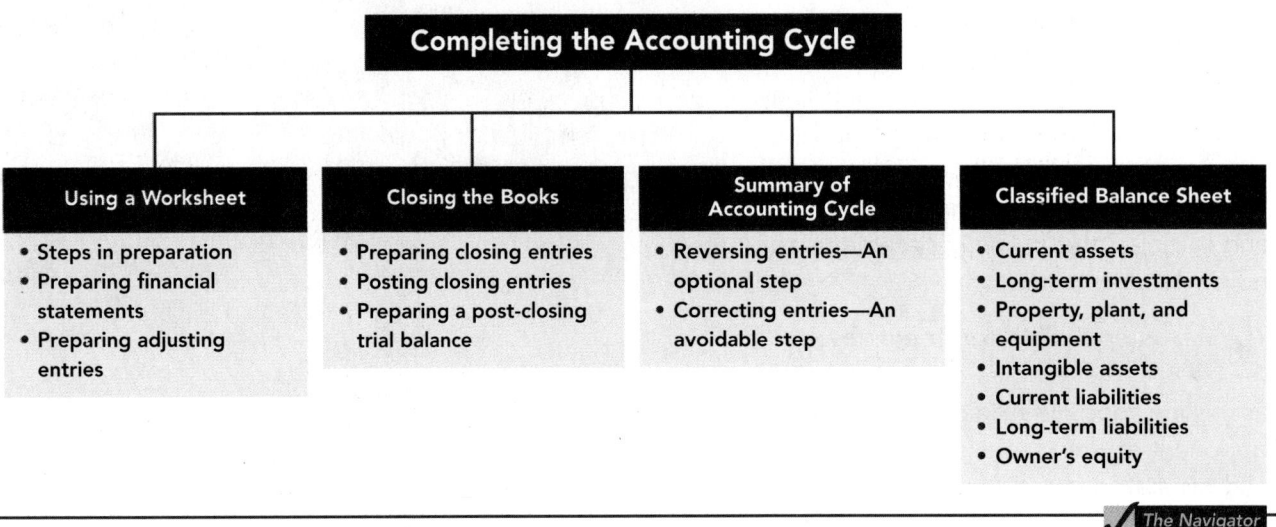

Completing the Accounting Cycle

Using a Worksheet
- Steps in preparation
- Preparing financial statements
- Preparing adjusting entries

Closing the Books
- Preparing closing entries
- Posting closing entries
- Preparing a post-closing trial balance

Summary of Accounting Cycle
- Reversing entries—An optional step
- Correcting entries—An avoidable step

Classified Balance Sheet
- Current assets
- Long-term investments
- Property, plant, and equipment
- Intangible assets
- Current liabilities
- Long-term liabilities
- Owner's equity

The Navigator

USING A WORKSHEET

STUDY OBJECTIVE 1
Prepare a worksheet.

A **worksheet** is a multiple-column form that companies use in the adjustment process and in preparing financial statements. As its name suggests, the worksheet is a working tool. **It is not a permanent accounting record**; it is neither a journal nor a part of the general ledger. The worksheet is merely a device used in preparing adjusting entries and the financial statements. Companies generally computerize worksheets using an electronic spreadsheet program such as Excel.

Illustration 4-1 shows the basic form of a worksheet and the five steps for preparing it. Each step is performed in sequence. **The use of a worksheet is optional.** When a company chooses to use one, it prepares financial statements from the worksheet. It enters the adjustments in the worksheet columns and then journalizes and posts the adjustments after it has prepared the financial statements. Thus, worksheets make it possible to provide the financial statements to management and other interested parties at an earlier date.

Steps in Preparing a Worksheet

We will use the October 31 trial balance and adjustment data of Pioneer Advertising, from Chapter 3, to illustrate how to prepare a worksheet. We describe

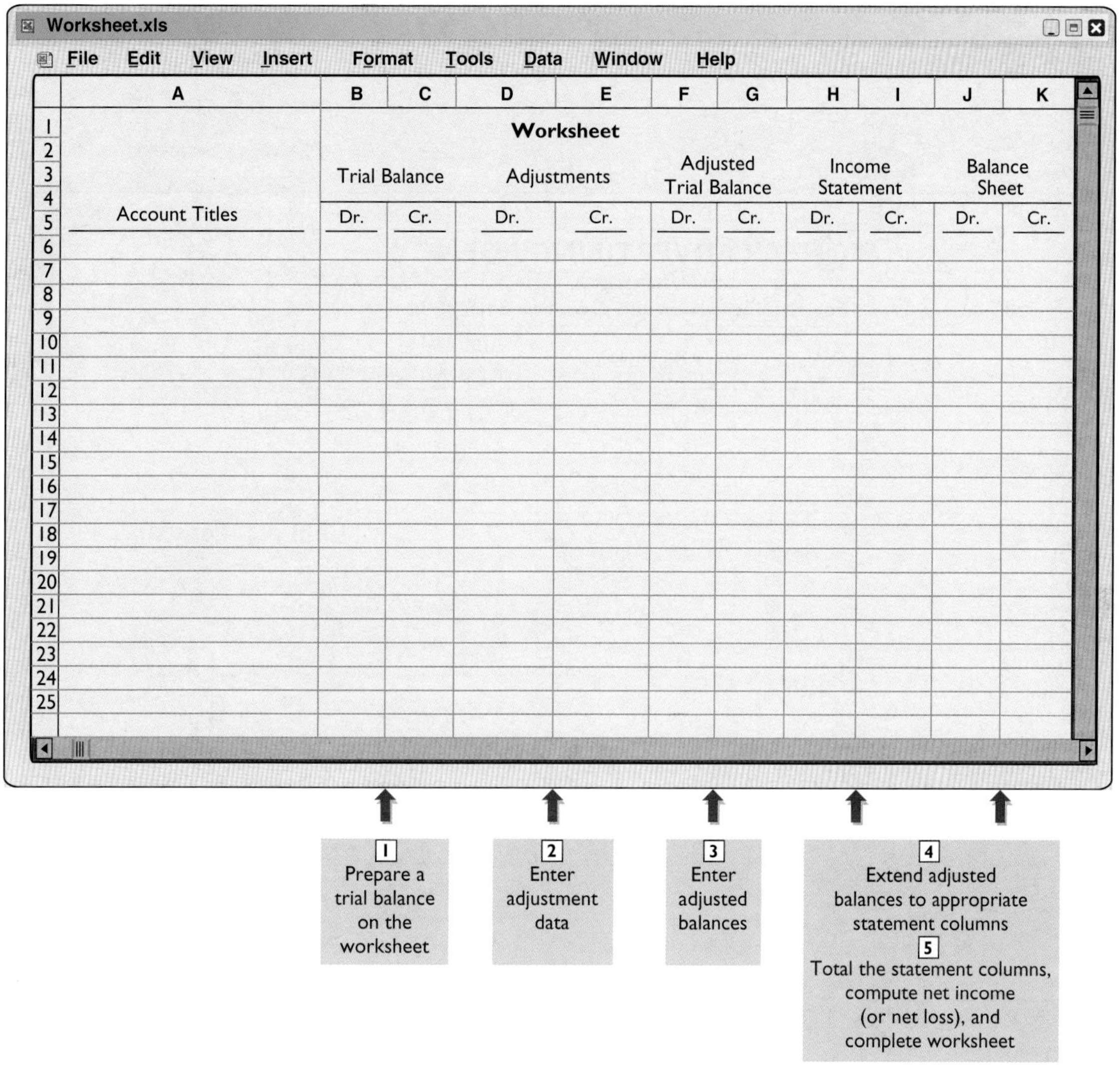

Illustration 4-1
Form and procedure for a worksheet

each step of the process and demonstrate these steps in Illustrations 4-2 and transparencies 4-3A, B, C, and D.

STEP 1. PREPARE A TRIAL BALANCE ON THE WORKSHEET

Enter all ledger accounts with balances in the account titles space. Enter debit and credit amounts from the ledger in the trial balance columns. Illustration 4-2 shows the worksheet trial balance for Pioneer Advertising Agency.

STEP 2. ENTER THE ADJUSTMENTS IN THE ADJUSTMENTS COLUMNS

Turn over the first transparency, Illustration 4-3A. When using a worksheet, enter all adjustments in the adjustments columns. In entering the adjustments, use applicable trial balance accounts. If additional accounts are needed, insert them on the lines immediately below the trial balance totals. A different letter identifies the debit and credit for each adjusting entry. The term used to describe this process is **keying**. **Companies do not journalize the adjustments until after they complete the worksheet and prepare the financial statements.**

(**Note:** Text continues on page 145, following acetate overlays.)

Illustration 4-2
Preparing a trial balance

Pioneer Advertising.xls

File Edit View Insert Format Tools Data Window Help

PIONEER ADVERTISING AGENCY
Worksheet
For the Month Ended October 31, 2008

	A	B	C	D	E	F	G	H	I	J	K
		Trial Balance		Adjustments		Adjusted Trial Balance		Income Statement		Balance Sheet	
	Account Titles	Dr.	Cr.	Dr.	Cr.	Dr.	Cr.	Dr.	Cr.	Dr.	Cr.
8	Cash	15,200									
9	Advertising Supplies	2,500									
10	Prepaid Insurance	600									
11	Office Equipment	5,000									
12	Notes Payable		5,000								
13	Accounts Payable		2,500								
14	Unearned Revenue		1,200								
15	C. R. Byrd, Capital		10,000								
16	C. R. Byrd, Drawing	500									
17	Service Revenue		10,000								
18											
19	Salaries Expense	4,000									
20	Rent Expense	900									
21	Totals	28,700	28,700								

Include all accounts with balances from ledger.

Trial balance amounts come directly from ledger accounts.

The adjustments for Pioneer Advertising Agency are the same as the adjustments illustrated on page 108. They are keyed in the adjustments columns of the worksheet as follows.

(a) Pioneer debits an additional account, Advertising Supplies Expense, $1,500 for the cost of supplies used, and credits Advertising Supplies $1,500.

(b) Pioneer debits an additional account, Insurance Expense, $50 for the insurance that has expired, and credits Prepaid Insurance $50.

(c) The company needs two additional depreciation accounts. It debits Depreciation Expense $40 for the month's depreciation, and credits Accumulated Depreciation—Office Equipment $40.

(d) Pioneer debits Unearned Revenue $400 for services provided, and credits Service Revenue $400.

(e) Pioneer debits an additional account, Accounts Receivable, $200 for services provided but not billed, and credits Service Revenue $200.

(f) The company needs two additional accounts relating to interest. It debits Interest Expense $50 for accrued interest, and credits Interest Payable $50.

(g) Pioneer debits Salaries Expense $1,200 for accrued salaries, and credits an additional account, Salaries Payable, $1,200.

After Pioneer has entered all the adjustments, the adjustments columns are totaled to prove their equality.

STEP 3. ENTER ADJUSTED BALANCES IN THE ADJUSTED TRIAL BALANCE COLUMNS

Turn over the second transparency, Illustration 4-3B. Pioneer determines the adjusted balance of an account by combining the amounts entered in the first four columns of the worksheet for each account. For example, the Prepaid Insurance account in the trial balance columns has a $600 debit balance and a $50 credit in the adjustments columns. The result is a $550 debit balance recorded in the adjusted trial balance columns. **For each account, the amount in the adjusted trial balance columns is the balance that will appear in the ledger after journalizing and posting the adjusting entries.** The balances in these columns are the same as those in the adjusted trial balance in Illustration 3-24 (page 110).

After Pioneer has entered all account balances in the adjusted trial balance columns, the columns are totaled to prove their equality. If the column totals do not agree, the financial statement columns will not balance and the financial statements will be incorrect.

STEP 4. EXTEND ADJUSTED TRIAL BALANCE AMOUNTS TO APPROPRIATE FINANCIAL STATEMENT COLUMNS

Turn over the third transparency, Illustration 4-3C. The fourth step is to extend adjusted trial balance amounts to the income statement and balance sheet columns of the worksheet. Pioneer enters balance sheet accounts in the appropriate balance sheet debit and credit columns. For instance, it enters Cash in the balance sheet debit column, and Notes Payable in the credit column. Pioneer extends Accumulated Depreciation to the balance sheet credit column; the reason is that accumulated depreciation is a contra-asset account with a credit balance.

Because the worksheet does not have columns for the owner's equity statement, Pioneer extends the balance in owner's capital to the balance sheet credit column. In addition, it extends the balance in owner's drawing to the balance sheet debit column because it is an owner's equity account with a debit balance.

The company enters the expense and revenue accounts such as Salaries Expense and Service Revenue in the appropriate income statement columns. Illustration 4-3C shows all of these extensions.

HELPFUL HINT

Every adjusted trial balance amount must be extended to one of the four statement columns.

STEP 5. TOTAL THE STATEMENT COLUMNS, COMPUTE THE NET INCOME (OR NET LOSS), AND COMPLETE THE WORKSHEET

Turn over the fourth transparency, Illustration 4-3D. The company now must total each of the financial statement columns. The net income or loss for the period is the difference between the totals of the two income statement columns. If total credits exceed total debits, the result is net income. In such a case, as shown in Illustration 4-3D, the company inserts the words "Net Income" in the account titles space. It then enters the amount in the income statement debit column and the balance sheet credit column. **The debit amount balances the income statement columns; the credit amount balances the balance sheet columns.** In addition, the credit in the balance sheet column indicates the increase in owner's equity resulting from net income.

What if total debits in the income statement columns exceed total credits? In that case, the company has a net loss. It enters the amount of the net loss in the income statement credit column and the balance sheet debit column.

After entering the net income or net loss, the company determines new column totals. The totals shown in the debit and credit income statement columns will match. So will the totals shown in the debit and credit balance sheet columns. If either the income statement columns or the balance sheet columns are not equal after the net income or net loss has been entered, there is an error in the worksheet. Illustration 4-3D shows the completed work sheet for Pioneer Advertising Agency.

Preparing Financial Statements from a Worksheet

After a company has completed a worksheet, it has at hand all the data required for preparation of financial statements. The income statement is prepared from the income statement columns. The balance sheet and owner's equity statement are prepared from the balance sheet columns. Illustration 4-4 shows the financial statements prepared from Pioneer's worksheet. At this point, the company has not journalized or posted adjusting entries. Therefore, ledger balances for some accounts are not the same as the financial statement amounts.

Accounting Cycle Tutorial—Preparing Financial Statements and Closing the Books

The amount shown for owner's capital on the worksheet is the account balance **before considering drawings and net income (or loss)**. When the owner has made no additional investments of capital during the period, this worksheet amount for owner's capital is the balance at the beginning of the period.

Using a worksheet, companies can prepare financial statements before they journalize and post adjusting entries. **However, the completed worksheet is not a substitute for formal financial statements.** The format of the data in the financial statement columns of the worksheet is not the same as the format of the financial statements. **A worksheet is essentially a working tool of the accountant;** companies do not distribute it to management and other parties.

Preparing Adjusting Entries from a Worksheet

HELPFUL HINT
Note that writing the explanation to the adjustment at the bottom of the worksheet is not required.

A worksheet is not a journal, and it cannot be used as a basis for posting to ledger accounts. To adjust the accounts, the company must journalize the adjustments and post them to the ledger. **The adjusting entries are prepared from the adjustments columns of the worksheet.** The reference letters in the adjustments columns and the explanations of the adjustments at the bottom of the worksheet help identify

Illustration 4-4
Financial statements from a worksheet

PIONEER ADVERTISING AGENCY
Income Statement
For the Month Ended October 31, 2008

Revenues		
Service revenue		$10,600
Expenses		
Salaries expense	$5,200	
Advertising supplies expense	1,500	
Rent expense	900	
Insurance expense	50	
Interest expense	50	
Depreciation expense	40	
Total expenses		7,740
Net income		$ 2,860

PIONEER ADVERTISING AGENCY
Owner's Equity Statement
For the Month Ended October 31, 2008

C. R. Byrd, Capital, October 1		$ -0-
Add: Investments	$10,000	
Net income	2,860	12,860
		12,860
Less: Drawings		500
C. R. Byrd, Capital, October 31		$12,360

PIONEER ADVERTISING AGENCY
Balance Sheet
October 31, 2008

Assets		
Cash		$15,200
Accounts receivable		200
Advertising supplies		1,000
Prepaid insurance		550
Office equipment	$5,000	
Less: Accumulated depreciation	40	4,960
Total assets		$21,910
Liabilities and Owner's Equity		
Liabilities		
Notes payable		$ 5,000
Accounts payable		2,500
Interest payable		50
Unearned revenue		800
Salaries payable		1,200
Total liabilities		9,550
Owner's equity		
C. R. Byrd, Capital		12,360
Total liabilities and owner's equity		$21,910

the adjusting entries. The journalizing and posting of adjusting entries **follows** the preparation of financial statements when a worksheet is used. The adjusting entries on October 31 for Pioneer Advertising Agency are the same as those shown in Illustration 3-22 (page 108).

Before You Go On...

REVIEW IT

1. What are the five steps in preparing a worksheet?
2. How is net income or net loss shown in a worksheet?
3. How does a worksheet relate to preparing financial statements and adjusting entries?

DO IT

Susan Elbe is preparing a worksheet. Explain to Susan how she should extend the following adjusted trial balance accounts to the financial statement columns of the worksheet:

Cash	Julie Kerr, Drawing
Accumulated Depreciation	Service Revenue
Accounts Payable	Salaries Expense

Action Plan

- Extend asset balances to the balance sheet debit column. Extend liability balances to the balance sheet credit column. Extend accumulated depreciation to the balance sheet credit column.
- Extend the drawing account to the balance sheet debit column.
- Extend expenses to the income statement debit column.
- Extend revenue accounts to the income statement credit column.

Solution

Income statement debit column—Salaries Expense
Income statement credit column—Service Revenue
Balance sheet debit column—Cash; Julie Kerr, Drawing
Balance sheet credit column—Accumulated Depreciation; Accounts Payable

Related exercise material: *BE4-1, BE4-2, BE4-3, E4-1, E4-2, E4-5, and E4-6.*

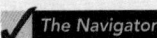

✓ The Navigator

CLOSING THE BOOKS

STUDY OBJECTIVE 2

Explain the process of closing the books.

At the end of the accounting period, the company makes the accounts ready for the next period. This is called **closing the books**. In closing the books, the company distinguishes between temporary and permanent accounts.

ALTERNATIVE TERMINOLOGY

Temporary accounts are sometimes called *nominal accounts*, and permanent accounts are sometimes called *real accounts*.

Temporary accounts relate only to a given accounting period. They include all income statement accounts and the owner's drawing account. The company closes all temporary accounts at the end of the period.

In contrast, **permanent accounts** relate to one or more future accounting periods. They consist of all balance sheet accounts, including the owner's capital account. Permanent accounts are not closed from period to period. Instead, the company carries forward the balances of permanent accounts into the next accounting period. Illustration 4-5 identifies the accounts in each category.

TEMPORARY These accounts are closed	PERMANENT These accounts are not closed
All revenue accounts	All asset accounts
All expense accounts	All liability accounts
Owner's drawing account	Owner's capital account

Illustration 4-5
Temporary versus permanent accounts

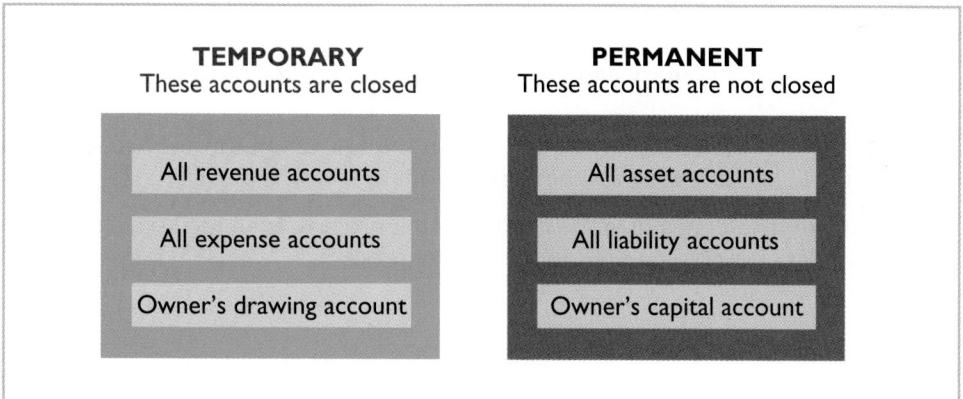

HELPFUL HINT
A contra-asset account, such as accumulated depreciation, is a permanent account also.

Preparing Closing Entries

At the end of the accounting period, the company transfers temporary account balances to the permanent owner's equity account, Owner's Capital, by means of closing entries.[1]

Closing entries formally recognize in the ledger the transfer of net income (or net loss) and owner's drawing to owner's capital. The owner's equity statement shows the results of these entries. **Closing entries also produce a zero balance in each temporary account.** The temporary accounts are then ready to accumulate data in the next accounting period separate from the data of prior periods. Permanent accounts are not closed.

Journalizing and posting closing entries is a required step in the accounting cycle. (See Illustration 4-12 on page 156.) The company performs this step after it has prepared financial statements. In contrast to the steps in the cycle that you have already studied, companies generally journalize and post closing entries **only at the end of the annual accounting period**. Thus, all temporary accounts will contain data for the entire year.

In preparing closing entries, companies could close each income statement account directly to owner's capital. However, to do so would result in excessive detail in the permanent Owner's Capital account. Instead, companies close the revenue and expense accounts to another temporary account, Income Summary, and they transfer the resulting net income or net loss from this account to owner's capital.

Companies **record closing entries in the general journal**. A center caption, Closing Entries, inserted in the journal between the last adjusting entry and the first closing entry, identifies these entries. Then the company posts the closing entries to the ledger accounts.

Companies generally prepare closing entries directly from the adjusted balances in the ledger. They could prepare separate closing entries for each

[1]We explain closing entries for a partnership and for a corporation in Chapters 12 and 13, respectively.

nominal account, but the following four entries accomplish the desired result more efficiently:

1. Debit each revenue account for its balance, and credit Income Summary for total revenues.
2. Debit Income Summary for total expenses, and credit each expense account for its balance.
3. Debit Income Summary and credit Owner's Capital for the amount of net income.
4. Debit Owner's Capital for the balance in the Owner's Drawing account, and credit Owner's Drawing for the same amount.

HELPFUL HINT

Owner's Drawing is closed directly to Capital and *not* to Income Summary because Owner's Drawing is not an expense.

Illustration 4-6 presents a diagram of the closing process. In it, the boxed numbers refer to the four entries required in the closing process.

Illustration 4-6
Diagram of closing process—proprietorship

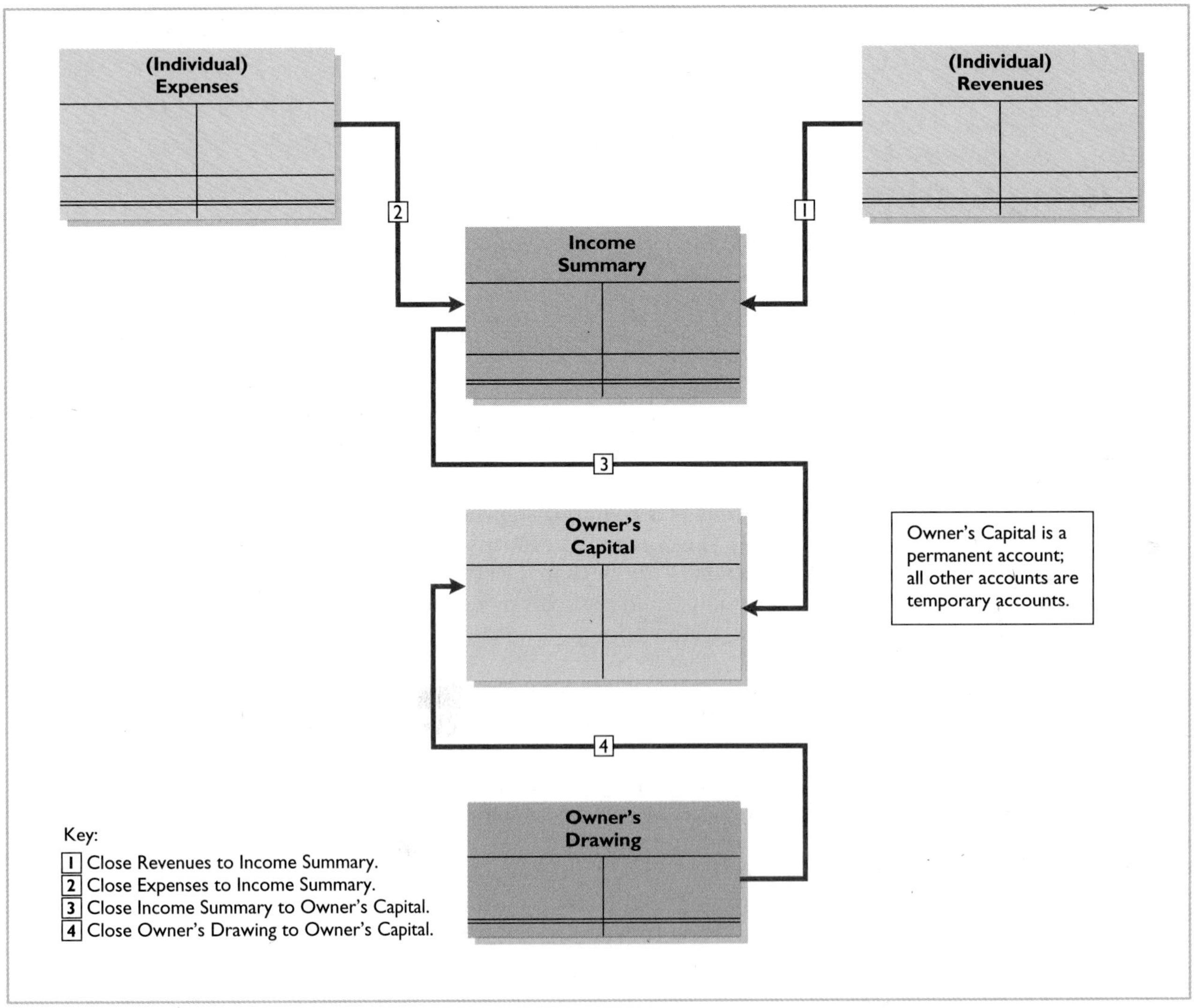

If there were a net loss (because expenses exceeded revenues), entry 3 in Illustration 4-6 would be reversed: there would be a credit to Income Summary and a debit to Owner's Capital.

CLOSING ENTRIES ILLUSTRATED

In practice, companies generally prepare closing entries only at the end of the annual accounting period. However, to illustrate the journalizing and posting of closing entries, we will assume that Pioneer Advertising Agency closes its books monthly. Illustration 4-7 shows the closing entries at October 31. (The numbers in parentheses before each entry correspond to the four entries diagrammed in Illustration 4-6.)

Illustration 4-7
Closing entries journalized

GENERAL JOURNAL — J3

Date	Account Titles and Explanation	Ref.	Debit	Credit
	Closing Entries			
2008	(1)			
Oct. 31	Service Revenue	400	10,600	
	Income Summary	350		10,600
	(To close revenue account)			
	(2)			
31	Income Summary	350	7,740	
	Advertising Supplies Expense	631		1,500
	Depreciation Expense	711		40
	Insurance Expense	722		50
	Salaries Expense	726		5,200
	Rent Expense	729		900
	Interest Expense	905		50
	(To close expense accounts)			
	(3)			
31	Income Summary	350	2,860	
	C. R. Byrd, Capital	301		2,860
	(To close net income to capital)			
	(4)			
31	C. R. Byrd, Capital	301	500	
	C. R. Byrd, Drawing	306		500
	(To close drawings to capital)			

Note that the amounts for Income Summary in entries (1) and (2) are the totals of the income statement credit and debit columns, respectively, in the worksheet.

A couple of cautions in preparing closing entries: (1) Avoid unintentionally doubling the revenue and expense balances rather than zeroing them. (2) Do not close Owner's Drawing through the Income Summary account. **Owner's Drawing is not an expense, and it is not a factor in determining net income.**

Posting Closing Entries

Illustration 4-8 (page 152) shows the posting of the closing entries and the ruling of the accounts. Note that all temporary accounts have zero balances after posting the closing entries. In addition, notice that the balance in owner's capital (C. R. Byrd, Capital) represents the total equity of the owner at the end of the accounting period. This balance is shown on the balance sheet and is the ending capital reported on the owner's equity statement, as shown in Illustration 4-4 on

HELPFUL HINT
The balance in Income Summary before it is closed must equal the net income or net loss for the period.

page 147. Pioneer uses the Income Summary account only in closing. It does not journalize and post entries to this account during the year.

As part of the closing process, Pioneer totals, balances, and double-rules its temporary accounts—revenues, expenses, and owner's drawing, as shown in T account form in Illustration 4-8. It does not close its permanent accounts—assets, liabilities, and owner's capital. Instead, Pioneer draws a single rule beneath the current-period entries for the permanent accounts. The account balance is then entered below the single rule and is carried forward to the next period. (For example, see C. R. Byrd, Capital.)

Illustration 4-8
Posting of closing entries

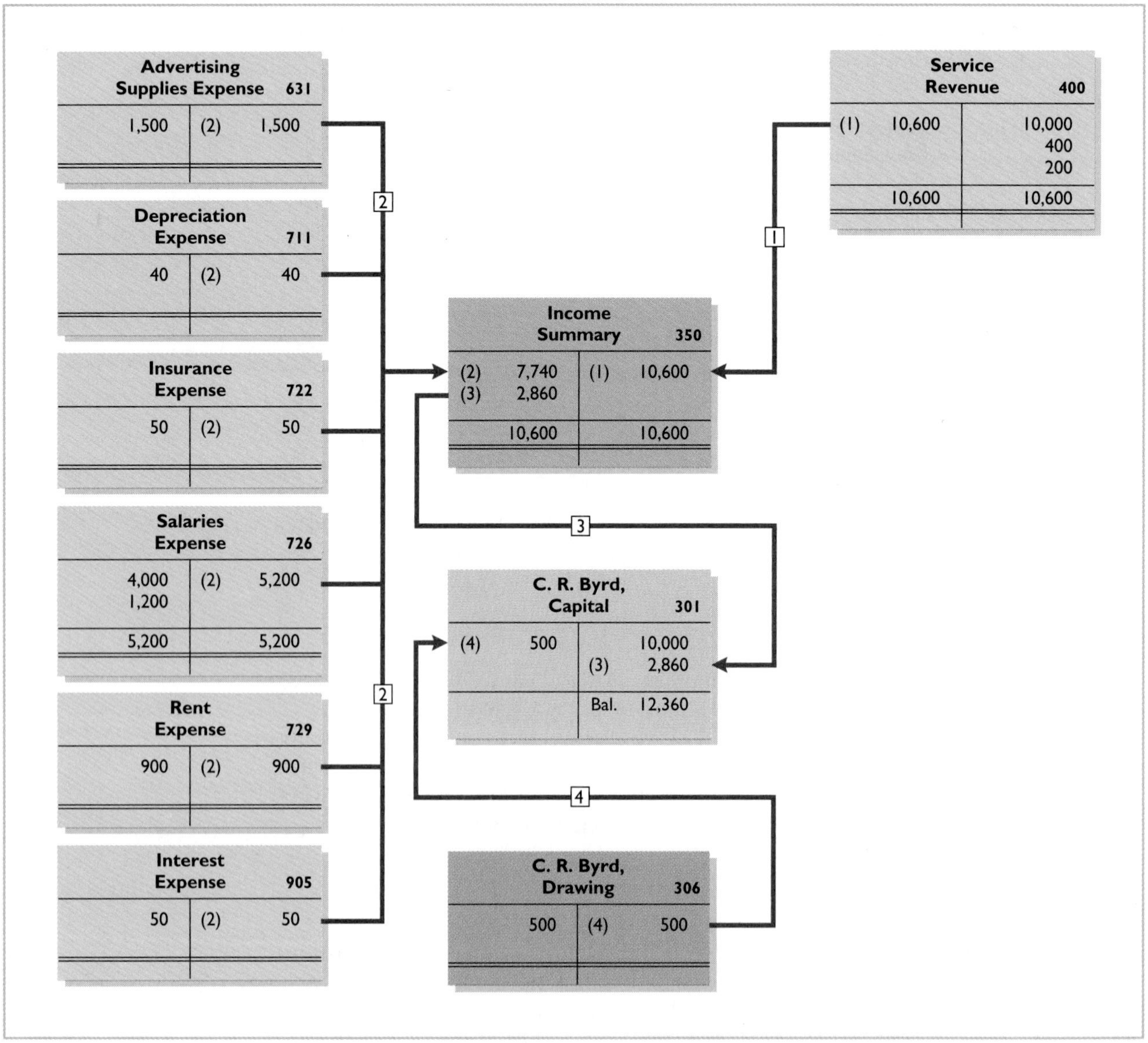

ACCOUNTING ACROSS THE ORGANIZATION

Cisco Performs the Virtual Close

Technology has dramatically shortened the closing process. Recent surveys have reported that the average company now takes only six to seven days to close, rather than 20 days. But a few companies do much better. Cisco Systems can perform a "virtual close"—closing within 24 hours on any day in the quarter. The same is true at Lockheed Martin Corp., which improved its closing time by 85% in just the last few years. Not very long ago it took 14 to 16 days. Managers at these companies emphasize that this increased speed has not reduced the accuracy and completeness of the data.

This is not just showing off. Knowing exactly where you are financially all of the time allows the company to respond faster than competitors. It also means that the hundreds of people who used to spend 10 to 20 days a quarter tracking transactions can now be more usefully employed on things such as mining data for business intelligence to find new business opportunities.

Source: "Reporting Practices: Few Do It All," *Financial Executive*, November 2003, p. 11.

? Who else benefits from a shorter closing process?

Preparing a Post-Closing Trial Balance

STUDY OBJECTIVE 3

Describe the content and purpose of a post-closing trial balance.

After Pioneer has journalized and posted all closing entries, it prepares another trial balance, called a **post-closing trial balance**, from the ledger. The post-closing trial balance lists permanent accounts and their balances after journalizing and posting of closing entries. The purpose of the post-closing trial balance is **to prove the equality of the permanent account balances carried forward into the next accounting period**. Since all temporary accounts will have zero balances, **the post-closing trial balance will contain only permanent—balance sheet—accounts.**

Illustration 4-9 shows the post-closing trial balance for Pioneer Advertising Agency.

Illustration 4-9
Post-closing trial balance

PIONEER ADVERTISING AGENCY
Post-Closing Trial Balance
October 31, 2008

	Debit	Credit
Cash	$15,200	
Accounts Receivable	200	
Advertising Supplies	1,000	
Prepaid Insurance	550	
Office Equipment	5,000	
Accumulated Depreciation—Office Equipment		$ 40
Notes Payable		5,000
Accounts Payable		2,500
Unearned Revenue		800
Salaries Payable		1,200
Interest Payable		50
C. R. Byrd, Capital		12,360
	$21,950	**$21,950**

Pioneer prepares the post-closing trial balance from the permanent accounts in the ledger. Illustration 4-10 shows the permanent accounts in Pioneer's general ledger.

A post-closing trial balance provides evidence that the company has properly journalized and posted the closing entries. It also shows that the accounting equation is in balance at the end of the accounting period. However, like the trial balance, it does not prove that Pioneer has recorded all transactions or that the ledger is correct. For example, the post-closing trial balance will balance if a transaction is not journalized and posted or if a transaction is journalized and posted twice.

Illustration 4-10
General ledger, permanent accounts

(Permanent Accounts Only)

GENERAL LEDGER

Cash — No. 101

Date	Explanation	Ref.	Debit	Credit	Balance
2008					
Oct. 1		J1	10,000		10,000
2		J1	1,200		11,200
3		J1		900	10,300
4		J1		600	9,700
20		J1		500	9,200
26		J1		4,000	5,200
31		J1	10,000		**15,200**

Accounts Receivable — No. 112

Date	Explanation	Ref.	Debit	Credit	Balance
2008					
Oct. 31	Adj. entry	J2	**200**		**200**

Advertising Supplies — No. 126

Date	Explanation	Ref.	Debit	Credit	Balance
2008					
Oct. 5		J1	2,500		2,500
31	Adj. entry	J2		**1,500**	**1,000**

Prepaid Insurance — No. 130

Date	Explanation	Ref.	Debit	Credit	Balance
2008					
Oct. 4		J1	600		600
31	Adj. entry	J2		**50**	**550**

Office Equipment — No. 157

Date	Explanation	Ref.	Debit	Credit	Balance
2008					
Oct. 1		J1	5,000		**5,000**

Accumulated Depreciation—Office Equipment — No. 158

Date	Explanation	Ref.	Debit	Credit	Balance
2008					
Oct. 31	Adj. entry	J2		**40**	**40**

Notes Payable — No. 200

Date	Explanation	Ref.	Debit	Credit	Balance
2008					
Oct. 1		J1		5,000	**5,000**

Accounts Payable — No. 201

Date	Explanation	Ref.	Debit	Credit	Balance
2008					
Oct. 5		J1		2,500	**2,500**

Unearned Revenue — No. 209

Date	Explanation	Ref.	Debit	Credit	Balance
2008					
Oct. 2		J1		1,200	1,200
31	Adj. entry	J2	400		**800**

Salaries Payable — No. 212

Date	Explanation	Ref.	Debit	Credit	Balance
2008					
Oct. 31	Adj. entry	J2		**1,200**	**1,200**

Interest Payable — No. 230

Date	Explanation	Ref.	Debit	Credit	Balance
2008					
Oct. 31	Adj. entry	J2		**50**	**50**

C. R. Byrd, Capital — No. 301

Date	Explanation	Ref.	Debit	Credit	Balance
2008					
Oct. 1		J1		10,000	10,000
31	**Closing entry**	**J3**		**2,860**	**12,860**
31	**Closing entry**	**J3**	**500**		**12,360**

Note: The permanent accounts for Pioneer Advertising Agency are shown here; Illustration 4-11 shows the temporary accounts. Both permanent and temporary accounts are part of the general ledger; they are segregated here to aid in learning.

The remaining accounts in the general ledger are temporary accounts, shown in Illustration 4-11. After Pioneer correctly posts the closing entries, each temporary account has a zero balance. These accounts are double-ruled to finalize the closing process.

Illustration 4-11
General ledger, temporary accounts

(Temporary Accounts Only)

GENERAL LEDGER

C. R. Byrd, Drawing — No. 306

Date	Explanation	Ref.	Debit	Credit	Balance
2008					
Oct. 20		J1	500		500
31	**Closing entry**	**J3**		**500**	**–0–**

Income Summary — No. 350

Date	Explanation	Ref.	Debit	Credit	Balance
2008					
Oct. 31	**Closing entry**	**J3**		**10,600**	**10,600**
31	**Closing entry**	**J3**	**7,740**		**2,860**
31	**Closing entry**	**J3**	**2,860**		**–0–**

Service Revenue — No. 400

Date	Explanation	Ref.	Debit	Credit	Balance
2008					
Oct. 31		J1		10,000	10,000
31	Adj. entry	J2		**400**	10,400
31	Adj. entry	J2		**200**	10,600
31	**Closing entry**	**J3**	**10,600**		**–0–**

Advertising Supplies Expense — No. 631

Date	Explanation	Ref.	Debit	Credit	Balance
2008					
Oct. 31	Adj. entry	J2	**1,500**		1,500
31	**Closing entry**	**J3**		**1,500**	**–0–**

Depreciation Expense — No. 711

Date	Explanation	Ref.	Debit	Credit	Balance
2008					
Oct. 31	Adj. entry	J2	**40**		40
31	**Closing entry**	**J3**		**40**	**–0–**

Insurance Expense — No. 722

Date	Explanation	Ref.	Debit	Credit	Balance
2008					
Oct. 31	Adj. entry	J2	**50**		50
31	**Closing entry**	**J3**		**50**	**–0–**

Salaries Expense — No. 726

Date	Explanation	Ref.	Debit	Credit	Balance
2008					
Oct. 26		J1	4,000		4,000
31	Adj. entry	J2	**1,200**		5,200
31	**Closing entry**	**J3**		**5,200**	**–0–**

Rent Expense — No. 729

Date	Explanation	Ref.	Debit	Credit	Balance
2008					
Oct. 3		J1	900		900
31	**Closing entry**	**J3**		**900**	**–0–**

Interest Expense — No. 905

Date	Explanation	Ref.	Debit	Credit	Balance
2008					
Oct. 31	Adj. entry	J2	**50**		50
31	**Closing entry**	**J3**		**50**	**–0–**

Note: The temporary accounts for Pioneer Advertising Agency are shown here; Illustration 4-10 shows the permanent accounts. Both permanent and temporary accounts are part of the general ledger; they are segregated here to aid in learning.

SUMMARY OF THE ACCOUNTING CYCLE

STUDY OBJECTIVE 4
State the required steps in the accounting cycle.

Illustration 4-12 (page 156) summarizes the steps in the accounting cycle. You can see that the cycle begins with the analysis of business transactions and ends with the preparation of a post-closing trial balance. Companies perform the steps in the cycle in sequence and repeat these steps in each accounting period.

Steps 1–3 may occur daily during the accounting period, as explained in Chapter 2. Companies perform Steps 4–7 on a periodic basis, such as monthly, quarterly, or annually. Steps 8 and 9—closing entries, and a post-closing trial balance—usually take place only at the end of a company's **annual** accounting period.

Illustration 4-12
Steps in the accounting cycle

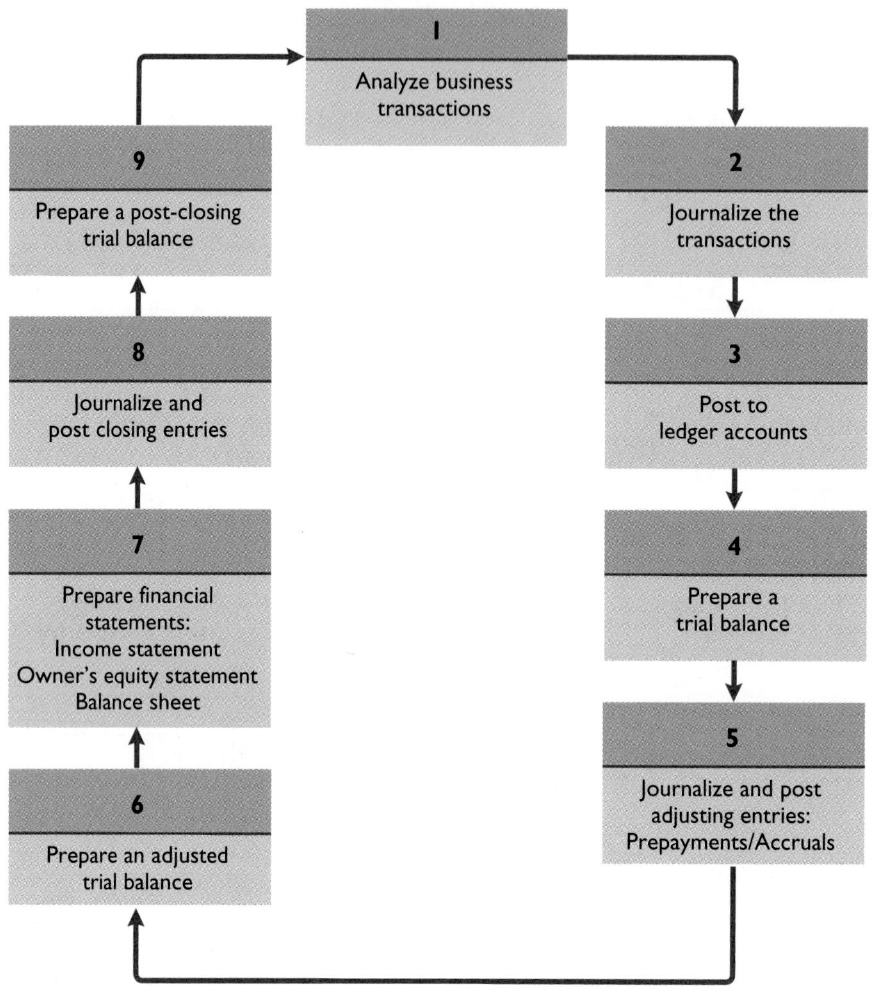

Optional steps: If a worksheet is prepared, steps 4, 5, and 6 are incorporated in the worksheet. If reversing entries are prepared, they occur between steps 9 and 1 as discussed below.

There are also two **optional steps** in the accounting cycle. As you have seen, companies may use a worksheet in preparing adjusting entries and financial statements. In addition, they may use reversing entries, as explained below.

Reversing Entries—An Optional Step

Some accountants prefer to reverse certain adjusting entries by making a **reversing entry** at the beginning of the next accounting period. A reversing entry is the exact opposite of the adjusting entry made in the previous period. **Use of reversing entries is an optional bookkeeping procedure; it is not a required step in the accounting cycle.** Accordingly, we have chosen to cover this topic in an appendix at the end of the chapter.

Correcting Entries—An Avoidable Step

STUDY OBJECTIVE 5
Explain the approaches to preparing correcting entries.

Unfortunately, errors may occur in the recording process. Companies should correct errors, **as soon as they discover them**, by journalizing and posting **correcting entries**. If the accounting records are free of errors, no correcting entries are needed.

You should recognize several differences between correcting entries and adjusting entries. First, adjusting entries are an integral part of the accounting cycle. Correcting entries, on the other hand, are unnecessary if the records are error-free. Second, companies journalize and post adjustments **only at the end of an accounting period**. In contrast, companies make correcting entries **whenever they discover an error**. Finally, adjusting entries always affect at least one balance sheet account and one income statement account. In contrast, correcting entries may involve any combination of accounts in need of correction. **Correcting entries must be posted before closing entries.**

ETHICS NOTE

When companies find errors in previously released income statements, they restate those numbers. Perhaps because of the increased scrutiny caused by Sarbanes-Oxley, in 2005 companies filed a record 1,195 restatements.

To determine the correcting entry, it is useful to compare the incorrect entry with the correct entry. Doing so helps identify the accounts and amounts that should—and should not—be corrected. After comparison, the accountant makes an entry to correct the accounts. The following two cases for Mercato Co. illustrate this approach.

CASE 1

On May 10, Mercato Co. journalized and posted a $50 cash collection on account from a customer as a debit to Cash $50 and a credit to Service Revenue $50. The company discovered the error on May 20, when the customer paid the remaining balance in full.

Illustration 4-13
Comparison of entries

Incorrect Entry (May 10)			Correct Entry (May 10)		
Cash	50		Cash	50	
Service Revenue		50	Accounts Receivable		50

Comparison of the incorrect entry with the correct entry reveals that the debit to Cash $50 is correct. However, the $50 credit to Service Revenue should have been credited to Accounts Receivable. As a result, both Service Revenue and Accounts Receivable are overstated in the ledger. Mercato makes the following correcting entry.

Illustration 4-14
Correcting entry

Correcting Entry

May 20	Service Revenue	50	
	Accounts Receivable		50
	(To correct entry of May 10)		

A	=	L	+	OE
				−50 Rev
−50				

Cash Flows
no effect

CASE 2

On May 18, Mercato purchased on account office equipment costing $450. The transaction was journalized and posted as a debit to Delivery Equipment $45 and a credit to Accounts Payable $45. The error was discovered on June 3, when Mercato received the monthly statement for May from the creditor.

Illustration 4-15
Comparison of entries

Incorrect Entry (May 18)			Correct Entry (May 18)		
Delivery Equipment	45		Office Equipment	450	
Accounts Payable		45	Accounts Payable		450

Comparison of the two entries shows that three accounts are incorrect. Delivery Equipment is overstated $45; Office Equipment is understated $450; and Accounts Payable is understated $405. Mercato makes the following correcting entry.

Illustration 4-16
Correcting entry

A	=	L	+	OE
+450				
−45				
		+405		

Cash Flows
no effect

Correcting Entry

June 3	Office Equipment	450	
	Delivery Equipment		45
	Accounts Payable		405
	(To correct entry of May 18)		

Instead of preparing a correcting entry, **it is possible to reverse the incorrect entry and then prepare the correct entry**. This approach will result in more entries and postings than a correcting entry, but it will accomplish the desired result.

ACCOUNTING ACROSS THE ORGANIZATION

Yale Express Loses Some Transportation Bills

Yale Express, a short-haul trucking firm, turned over much of its cargo to local truckers to complete deliveries. Yale collected the entire delivery charge; when billed by the local trucker, Yale sent payment for the final phase to the local trucker. Yale used a cutoff period of 20 days into the next accounting period in making its adjusting entries for accrued liabilities. That is, it waited 20 days to receive the local truckers' bills to determine the amount of the unpaid but incurred delivery charges as of the balance sheet date.

On the other hand, Republic Carloading, a nationwide, long-distance freight forwarder, frequently did not receive transportation bills from truckers to whom it passed on cargo until months after the year-end. In making its year-end adjusting entries, Republic waited for months in order to include all of these outstanding transportation bills.

When Yale Express merged with Republic Carloading, Yale's vice president employed the 20-day cutoff procedure for both firms. As a result, millions of dollars of Republic's accrued transportation bills went unrecorded. When the company detected the error and made correcting entries, these and other errors changed a reported profit of $1.14 million into a loss of $1.88 million!

? What might Yale Express's vice president have done to produce more accurate financial statements without waiting months for Republic's outstanding transportation bills?

Before You Go On...

REVIEW IT

1. How do permanent accounts differ from temporary accounts?
2. What four different types of entries do companies make in closing the books?
3. What are the content and purpose of a post-closing trial balance?
4. What are the required and optional steps in the accounting cycle?

DO IT

The worksheet for Hancock Company shows the following in the financial statement columns:

R. Hancock, Drawing $15,000
R. Hancock, Capital $42,000
Net income $18,000

Prepare the closing entries at December 31 that affect owner's capital.

Action Plan

- Remember to make closing entries in the correct sequence.
- Make the first two entries to close revenues and expenses.
- Make the third entry to close net income to owner's capital.
- Make the final entry to close owner's drawing to owner's capital.

Solution

Dec. 31	Income Summary	18,000	
	R. Hancock, Capital		18,000
	(To close net income to capital)		
31	R. Hancock, Capital	15,000	
	R. Hancock, Drawing		15,000
	(To close drawings to capital)		

Related exercise material: *BE4-4, BE4-5, BE4-6, BE4-7, BE4-8, E4-4, E4-7, E4-8, E4-10, and E4-11.*

The Navigator

THE CLASSIFIED BALANCE SHEET

STUDY OBJECTIVE 6

Identify the sections of a classified balance sheet.

The balance sheet presents a snapshot of a company's financial position at a point in time. To improve users' understanding of a company's financial position, companies often group similar assets and similar liabilities together. This is useful because it tells you that items within a group have similar economic characteristics. A **classified balance sheet** generally contains the standard classifications listed in Illustration 4-17.

Illustration 4-17
Standard balance sheet classifications

Assets	Liabilities and Owner's Equity
Current assets	Current liabilities
Long-term investments	Long-term liabilities
Property, plant, and equipment	Owner's (Stockholders') equity
Intangible assets	

These groupings help readers determine such things as (1) whether the company has enough assets to pay its debts as they come due, and (2) the claims of short- and long-term creditors on the company's total assets. Many of these groupings can be seen in the balance sheet of Franklin Corporation shown in Illustration 4-18 (page 160). In the sections that follow, we explain each of these groupings.

Current Assets

Current assets are assets that a company expects to convert to cash or use up within one year. In Illustration 4-18, Franklin Corporation had current assets of $22,100. For most businesses the cutoff for classification as current assets is one year from the balance sheet date. For example, accounts receivable are current assets because the company will collect them and convert them to cash within one year. Supplies is a current asset because the company expects to use it up in operations within one year.

Illustration 4-18
Classified balance sheet

FRANKLIN CORPORATION
Balance Sheet
October 31, 2008

Assets			
Current assets			
Cash		$ 6,600	
Short-term investments		2,000	
Accounts receivable		7,000	
Notes receivable		1,000	
Inventories		3,000	
Supplies		2,100	
Prepaid insurance		400	
Total current assets			$22,100
Long-term investments			
Investment in stock of Walters Corp.		5,200	
Investment in real estate		2,000	7,200
Property, plant, and equipment			
Land		10,000	
Office equipment	$24,000		
Less: Accumulated depreciation	5,000	19,000	29,000
Intangible assets			
Patents			3,100
Total assets			$61,400
Liabilities and Owner's Equity			
Current liabilities			
Notes payable		$11,000	
Accounts payable		2,100	
Salaries payable		1,600	
Unearned revenue		900	
Interest payable		450	
Total current liabilities			$16,050
Long-term liabilities			
Mortgage note payable		10,000	
Notes payable		1,300	
Total long-term liabilities			11,300
Total liabilities			27,350
Owner's equity			
B. Franklin, Capital			34,050
Total liabilities and owner's equity			$61,400

HELPFUL HINT

Recall that the accounting equation is Assets = Liabilities + Owner's Equity.

Some companies use a period longer than one year to classify assets and liabilities as current because they have an operating cycle longer than one year. The **operating cycle** of a company is the average time that it takes to purchase inventory, sell it on account, and then collect cash from customers. For most businesses this cycle takes less than a year, so they use a one-year cutoff. But, for some businesses, such as vineyards or airplane manufacturers, this period may be longer than a year. **Except where noted, we will assume that companies use one year to determine whether an asset or liability is current or long-term.**

Common types of current assets are (1) cash, (2) short-term investments (such as short-term U.S. government securities), (3) receivables (notes receivable, accounts receivable, and interest receivable), (4) inventories, and (5) prepaid expenses (insurance and supplies). **On the balance sheet, companies usually list these items in the order in which they expect to convert them into cash.**

Illustration 4-19 presents the current assets of The Coca-Cola Company.

Illustration 4-19
Current assets section

The Coca-Cola Company

THE COCA-COLA COMPANY
Balance Sheet (partial)
(in millions)

Current assets	
Cash and cash equivalents	$ 6,707
Short-term investments	61
Trade accounts receivable	2,171
Inventories	1,420
Prepaid expenses and other assets	1,735
Total current assets	$12,094

As explained later in the chapter, a company's current assets are important in assessing its short-term debt-paying ability.

Long-Term Investments

Long-term investments are generally investments in stocks and bonds of other companies that are normally held for many years. This category also includes investments in long-term assets such as land or buildings that a company is not currently using in its operating activities. In Illustration 4-18 Franklin Corporation reported total long-term investments of $7,200 on its balance sheet.

ALTERNATIVE TERMINOLOGY

Long-term investments are often referred to simply as *investments*.

Yahoo! Inc. reported long-term investments in its balance sheet as shown in Illustration 4-20.

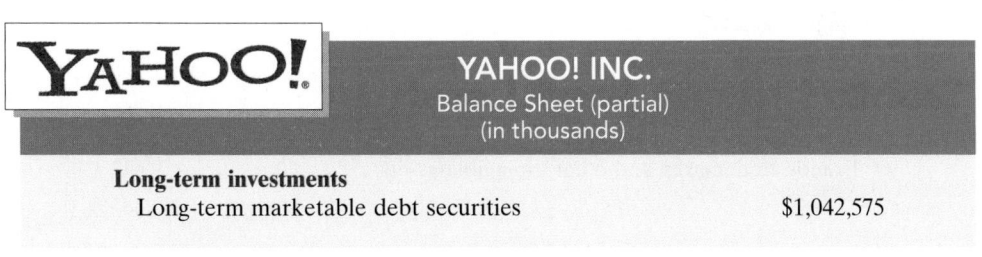

Illustration 4-20
Long-term investments section

YAHOO!

YAHOO! INC.
Balance Sheet (partial)
(in thousands)

Long-term investments	
Long-term marketable debt securities	$1,042,575

Property, Plant, and Equipment

ALTERNATIVE TERMINOLOGY

Property, plant, and equipment is sometimes called *fixed assets.*

Property, plant, and equipment are assets with relatively long useful lives that a company is currently using in operating the business. This category includes land, buildings, machinery and equipment, delivery equipment, and furniture. In Illustration 4-18 Franklin Corporation reported property, plant, and equipment of $29,000.

Depreciation is the practice of allocating the cost of assets to a number of years. Companies do this by systematically assigning a portion of an asset's cost as an expense each year (rather than expensing the full purchase price in the year of purchase). The assets that the company depreciates are reported on the balance sheet at cost less accumulated depreciation. The **accumulated depreciation** account shows the total amount of depreciation that the company has expensed thus far in the asset's life. In Illustration 4-18 Franklin Corporation reported accumulated depreciation of $5,000.

Illustration 4-21 presents the property, plant, and equipment of ski and sporting goods manufacturer K2, Inc.

Illustration 4-21
Property, plant, and equipment section

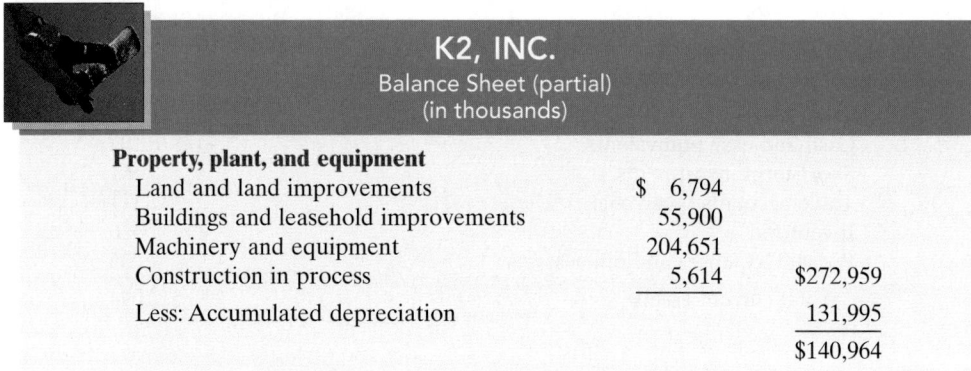

K2, INC.
Balance Sheet (partial)
(in thousands)

Property, plant, and equipment		
Land and land improvements	$ 6,794	
Buildings and leasehold improvements	55,900	
Machinery and equipment	204,651	
Construction in process	5,614	$272,959
Less: Accumulated depreciation		131,995
		$140,964

Intangible Assets

HELPFUL HINT

Sometimes intangible assets are reported under a broader heading called *"Other assets."*

Many companies have assets that do not have physical substance yet often are very valuable. We call these assets **intangible assets**. One common intangible asset is goodwill. Other intangibles include patents, copyrights, and trademarks or trade names that give the company **exclusive right** of use for a specified period of time. Franklin Corporation reported intangible assets of $3,100.

Illustration 4-22 shows how media giant Time Warner, Inc. reported its intangible assets.

Illustration 4-22
Intangible assets section

TIME WARNER, INC.
Balance Sheet (partial)
(in millions)

Intangible assets	
Film library	$ 3,361
Customer lists	868
Cable television franchises	29,751
Sports franchises	262
Brands, trademarks, and other intangible assets	9,643
	$43,885

INTERNATIONAL INSIGHT

Big Changes Are Coming to Chinese Balance Sheets

Beginning in 2007 many Chinese companies will be following International Financial Reporting Standards to prepare financial statements. Many people say that the largest change will occur on Chinese balance sheets. The new standards will require the companies to report a market value for many assets, including things like plant and equipment. (This, of course, is not in accordance with the cost principle, which U.S. GAAP follows.)

Chinese authorities hope that adopting international standards will give investors more confidence in the validity of Chinese financial reports.

Source: James T. Areddy, "Adding Up Chinese Data", *Wall Street Journal*, February 27, 2006, p. C10.

? What are the potential benefits and challenges presented by reporting assets like plant and equipment at their market value rather than historical cost?

Current Liabilities

In the liabilities and stockholders' equity section of the balance sheet, the first grouping is current liabilities. **Current liabilities** are obligations that the company is to pay within the coming year. Common examples are accounts payable, wages payable, bank loans payable, interest payable, and taxes payable. Also included as current liabilities are current maturities of long-term obligations—payments to be made within the next year on long-term obligations. In Illustration 4-18 Franklin Corporation reported five different types of current liabilities, for a total of $16,050.

Within the current liabilities section, companies usually list notes payable first, followed by accounts payable. Other items then follow in the order of their magnitude. *In your homework, you should present notes payable first, followed by accounts payable, and then other liabilities in order of magnitude.*

Illustration 4-23 shows the current liabilities section adapted from the balance sheet of Marcus Corporation.

Illustration 4-23
Current liabilities section

MARCUS CORPORATION
Balance Sheet (partial)
(in thousands)

Current liabilities	
Notes payable	$ 2,066
Accounts payable	17,516
Current maturities of long-term debt	26,321
Taxes payable	14,889
Other current liabilities	14,809
Accrued compensation payable	8,614
Total current liabilities	$84,215

Users of financial statements look closely at the relationship between current assets and current liabilities. This relationship is important in evaluating a company's

liquidity—its ability to pay obligations expected to be due within the next year. When current assets exceed current liabilities at the balance sheet date, the likelihood for paying the liabilities is favorable. When the reverse is true, short-term creditors may not be paid, and the company may ultimately be forced into bankruptcy.

Long-Term Liabilities

Long-term liabilities are obligations that a company expects to pay **after** one year. Liabilities in this category include bonds payable, mortgages payable, long-term notes payable, lease liabilities, and pension liabilities. Many companies report long-term debt maturing after one year as a single amount in the balance sheet and show the details of the debt in notes that accompany the financial statements. Others list the various types of long-term liabilities. In Illustration 4-18 Franklin Corporation reported long-term liabilities of $11,300. *In your homework, list long-term liabilities in the order of their magnitude.*

Illustration 4-24 shows the long-term liabilities that Northwest Airlines Corporation reported in its balance sheet.

Illustration 4-24
Long-term liabilities section

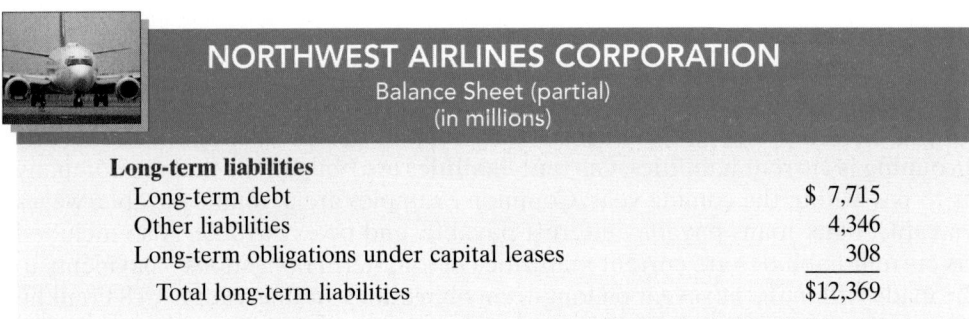

NORTHWEST AIRLINES CORPORATION
Balance Sheet (partial)
(in millions)

Long-term liabilities	
Long-term debt	$ 7,715
Other liabilities	4,346
Long-term obligations under capital leases	308
Total long-term liabilities	$12,369

Owner's Equity

The content of the owner's equity section varies with the form of business organization. In a proprietorship, there is one capital account. In a partnership, there is a capital account for each partner. Corporations divide owners' equity into two accounts—Capital Stock and Retained Earnings. Corporations record stockholders' investments in the company by debiting an asset account and crediting the Capital Stock account. They record in the Retained Earnings account income retained for use in the business. Corporations combine the Capital Stock and Retained Earnings accounts and report them on the balance sheet as **stockholders' equity**. (We'll learn more about these corporation accounts in later chapters.) Nordstrom, Inc. recently reported its stockholders' equity section as follows.

Illustration 4-25
Stockholders' equity section

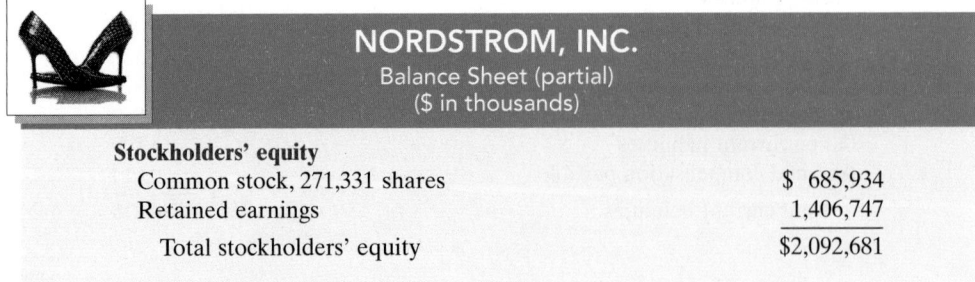

NORDSTROM, INC.
Balance Sheet (partial)
($ in thousands)

Stockholders' equity	
Common stock, 271,331 shares	$ 685,934
Retained earnings	1,406,747
Total stockholders' equity	$2,092,681

Be sure to read **ALL ABOUT YOU: *Your Personal Balance Sheet*** on page 165 for information on how topics in this chapter apply to you.

Your Personal Balance Sheet

By now you should be pretty comfortable with how to prepare a company's balance sheet. Maybe it is time for us to look at your personal financial position.

What are your personal assets? These are the items of value that you own. Some of your assets are *liquid*—cash or items that are easily converted to cash. Others, like cars, real estate, and some types of investments, are less liquid. Some assets, like houses and investments, tend to rise in value over time, which increases your net worth. Other assets, such as cars, tend to fall in value over time, decreasing your net worth.

What are your personal liabilities—the amounts that you owe to others? Student loans, car loans, credit card bills, and amounts owed to relatives are all personal liabilities. These liabilities are either current (to be repaid within 12 months) or long-term.

The difference between your assets and liabilities is, to use the terminology of the accounting equation, your "owner's equity." In personal finance terminology, this is your *net worth.* Having a high net worth does not guarantee happiness—but most believe that it is better than being broke. By monitoring your personal balance sheet, you can begin to take control of your financial future.

Some Facts

* 48% of Americans think they know how much wealth they have.
* 2005 was the first year since the Depression when Americans spent more money than they made.
* The total net worth of U.S. households hit a record of $51.09 trillion during 2005.
* Economists note that a rise in house prices actually results in a fall in individual savings. It has been documented that a $1,000 rise in the value of a home results in a $50 fall in savings per year, presumably because homeowners feel more wealthy and therefore spend more (save less).
* When asked about very important wealth-building strategies for all Americans, 16% said "win the lottery."

About the Numbers

Your ability to make good financial decisions is often influenced by your attitudes toward saving versus spending. The authors of a recent study conclude that "people commonly fall prey to psychologically driven impulses that affect their financial decisions." For example, when individuals were asked whether could they save 20% of their household income, nearly half said they couldn't. But, when asked if they could spend less, well more than half (71%) said they could live comfortably on 80% of their income. This clearly is inconsistent thinking: If you can live on 80% of your current income, you can save 20% of your current income.

"How much could you save?"

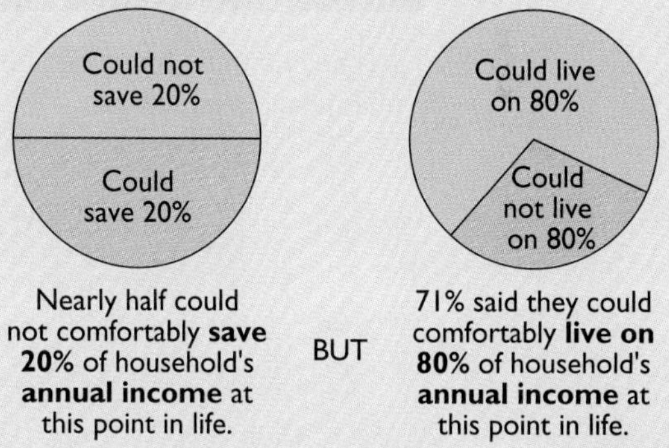
Could not save 20%
Could save 20%
Nearly half could not comfortably **save 20%** of household's **annual income** at this point in life.
BUT
Could live on 80%
Could not live on 80%
71% said they could comfortably **live on 80%** of household's **annual income** at this point in life.

Source: Northwestern Mutual Life, *www.nmfn.com/contentassets/pdfs/fin_misbehav.pdf,* p. 6.

What Do You Think?

Should you prepare a personal balance sheet?

YES: In order to attain your desired financial objectives, you need to set goals early. The personal balance sheet provides a benchmark by which you can measure progress toward your financial goals. You need to do it now so that you begin to develop good financial habits. It provides a mechanism so that you don't allow your finances to get too "out-of-whack" while you are in school. That is, you don't want to dig too deep a hole.

NO: Your financial situation right now bears very little resemblance to what it will look like after you graduate. At that point, you will have a better job, and you won't have to pay tuition. Right now, you're just "bleeding cash."

Sources: Andrew Blackman, "How to Calculate Your Savings Rate; For Americans in 2005, Earnings Didn't Keep Pace with Boom in Spending," *Wall Street Journal,* January 3, 2006, p. D2; "Financial Planners Share Views on Saving," Consumer Federation of America and Financial Planning Association, January 2006.

The authors' comments on this situation appear on page 191.

Before You Go On...

REVIEW IT

1. What are the major sections in a classified balance sheet?
2. Using the PepsiCo annual report, determine its current liabilities at December 31, 2005, and December 25, 2004. Were current liabilities higher or lower than current assets in these two years? The answer to this question appears on page 191.

The Navigator

Demonstration Problem

At the end of its first month of operations, Watson Answering Service has the following unadjusted trial balance.

WATSON ANSWERING SERVICE
August 31, 2008
Trial Balance

	Debit	Credit
Cash	$ 5,400	
Accounts Receivable	2,800	
Prepaid Insurance	2,400	
Supplies	1,300	
Equipment	60,000	
Notes Payable		$40,000
Accounts Payable		2,400
Ray Watson, Capital		30,000
Ray Watson, Drawing	1,000	
Service Revenue		4,900
Salaries Expense	3,200	
Utilities Expense	800	
Advertising Expense	400	
	$77,300	$77,300

Other data:

1. Insurance expires at the rate of $200 per month.
2. $1,000 of supplies are on hand at August 31.
3. Monthly depreciation on the equipment is $900.
4. Interest of $500 on the notes payable has accrued during August.

Instructions

(a) Prepare a worksheet.
(b) Prepare a classified balance sheet assuming $35,000 of the notes payable are long-term.
(c) Journalize the closing entries.

action plan

- ✔ In completing the worksheet, be sure to (a) key the adjustments; (b) start at the top of the adjusted trial balance columns and extend adjusted balances to the correct statement columns; and (c) enter net income (or net loss) in the proper columns.
- ✔ In preparing a classified balance sheet, know the contents of each of the sections.
- ✔ In journalizing closing entries, remember that there are only four entries and that owner's drawing is closed to owner's capital.

Solution to Demonstration Problem

(a)

WATSON ANSWERING SERVICE
Worksheet
For the Month Ended August 31, 2008

	Trial Balance		Adjustments		Adjusted Trial Balance		Income Statement		Balance Sheet	
Account Titles	**Dr.**	**Cr.**	**Dr.**	**Cr.**	**Dr.**	**Cr.**	**Dr.**	**Cr.**	**Dr.**	**Cr.**
Cash	5,400				5,400				5,400	
Accounts Receivable	2,800				2,800				2,800	
Supplies	1,300			(b) 300	1,000				1,000	
Prepaid Insurance	2,400			(a) 200	2,200				2,200	
Equipment	60,000				60,000				60,000	
Notes Payable		40,000				40,000				40,000
Accounts Payable		2,400				2,400				2,400
Ray Watson, Capital		30,000				30,000				30,000
Ray Watson, Drawing	1,000				1,000				1,000	
Service Revenue		4,900				4,900		4,900		
Salaries Expense	3,200				3,200		3,200			
Utilities Expense	800				800		800			
Advertising Expense	400				400		400			
Totals	77,300	77,300								
Insurance Expense			(a) 200		200		200			
Supplies Expense			(b) 300		300		300			
Depreciation Expense			(c) 900		900		900			
Accumulated Depreciation—Equipment				(c) 900		900				900
Interest Expense			(d) 500		500		500			
Interest Payable				(d) 500		500				500
Totals			1,900	1,900	78,700	78,700	6,300	4,900	72,400	73,800
Net Loss								1,400	1,400	
Totals							6,300	6,300	73,800	73,800

Explanation: (a) Insurance expired, (b) Supplies used, (c) Depreciation expensed, (d) Interest accrued.

(b)

WATSON ANSWERING SERVICE
Balance Sheet
August 31, 2008

Assets

Current assets		
Cash		$ 5,400
Accounts receivable		2,800
Supplies		1,000
Prepaid insurance		2,200
Total current assets		11,400
Property, plant, and equipment		
Equipment	$60,000	
Less: Accumulated depreciation—equipment	900	59,100
Total assets		$70,500

Liabilities and Owner's Equity

Current liabilities		
Notes payable	$ 5,000	
Accounts payable	2,400	
Interest payable	500	
Total current liabilities	7,900	
Long-term liabilities		
Notes payable	35,000	
Total liabilities	42,900	
Owner's equity		
Ray Watson, Capital	27,600*	
Total liabilities and owner's equity	$70,500	

*Ray Watson, Capital, $30,000 less drawings $1,000 and net loss $1,400.

(c)

Date	Account Titles and Explanation	Debit	Credit
Aug. 31	Service Revenue	4,900	
	Income Summary		4,900
	(To close revenue account)		
31	Income Summary	6,300	
	Salaries Expense		3,200
	Depreciation Expense		900
	Utilities Expense		800
	Interest Expense		500
	Advertising Expense		400
	Supplies Expense		300
	Insurance Expense		200
	(To close expense accounts)		
31	Ray Watson, Capital	1,400	
	Income Summary		1,400
	(To close net loss to capital)		
31	Ray Watson, Capital	1,000	
	Ray Watson, Drawing		1,000
	(To close drawings to capital)		

The Navigator

SUMMARY OF STUDY OBJECTIVES

WILEY PLUS

1 **Prepare a worksheet.** The steps in preparing a worksheet are: (a) Prepare a trial balance on the worksheet. (b) Enter the adjustments in the adjustments columns. (c) Enter adjusted balances in the adjusted trial balance columns. (d) Extend adjusted trial balance amounts to appropriate financial statement columns. (e) Total the statement columns, compute net income (or net loss), and complete the worksheet.

2 **Explain the process of closing the books.** Closing the books occurs at the end of an accounting period. The process is to journalize and post closing entries and then rule and balance all accounts. In closing the books, companies make separate entries to close revenues and expenses to Income Summary, Income Summary to Owner's Capital, and Owner's Drawings to Owner's Capital. Only temporary accounts are closed.

3 **Describe the content and purpose of a post-closing trial balance.** A post-closing trial balance contains the balances in permanent accounts that are carried forward to the next accounting period. The purpose of this trial balance is to prove the equality of these balances.

4 **State the required steps in the accounting cycle.** The required steps in the accounting cycle are: (1) analyze business transactions, (2) journalize the transactions, (3) post to ledger accounts, (4) prepare a trial balance, (5) journalize and post adjusting entries, (6) prepare an adjusted trial balance, (7) prepare financial statements, (8) journalize and post closing entries, and (9) prepare a post-closing trial balance.

5 **Explain the approaches to preparing correcting entries.** One way to determine the correcting entry is to compare the incorrect entry with the correct entry. After comparison, the

company makes a correcting entry to correct the accounts. An alternative to a correcting entry is to reverse the incorrect entry and then prepare the correct entry.

6 **Identify the sections of a classified balance sheet.** A classified balance sheet categorizes assets as current assets; long-term investments; property, plant, and equipment; and intangibles. Liabilities are classified as either current or long-term. There is also an owner's (owners') equity section, which varies with the form of business organization.

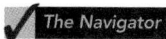

The Navigator

GLOSSARY

WILEY PLUS

Classified balance sheet A balance sheet that contains a number of standard classifications or sections. (p. 159).

Closing entries Entries made at the end of an accounting period to transfer the balances of temporary accounts to a permanent owner's equity account, Owner's Capital. (p. 149).

Correcting entries Entries to correct errors made in recording transactions. (p. 156).

Current assets Assets that a company expects to convert to cash or use up within one year. (p. 160).

Current liabilities Obligations that a company expects to pay from existing current assets within the coming year. (p. 163).

Income Summary A temporary account used in closing revenue and expense accounts. (p. 149).

Intangible assets Noncurrent assets that do not have physical substance. (p. 162).

Liquidity The ability of a company to pay obligations expected to be due within the next year. (p. 164).

Long-term investments Generally, investments in stocks and bonds of other companies that companies normally hold for many years. Also includes long-term assets, such as land and buildings, not currently being used in operations. (p. 161).

Long-term liabilities Obligations that a company expects to pay after one year. (p. 164).

Operating cycle The average time that it takes to go from cash to cash in producing revenues. (p. 161).

Permanent (real) accounts Accounts that relate to one or more accounting periods. Consist of all balance sheet accounts. Balances are carried forward to next accounting period. (p. 148).

Post-closing trial balance A list of permanent accounts and their balances after a company has journalized and posted closing entries. (p. 153).

Property, plant, and equipment Assets with relatively long useful lives, currently being used in operations. (p. 162).

Reversing entry An entry, made at the beginning of the next accounting period, that is the exact opposite of the adjusting entry made in the previous period. (p. 156).

Stockholders' equity The ownership claim of shareholders on total assets. It is to a corporation what owner's equity is to a proprietorship. (p. 164).

Temporary (nominal) accounts Accounts that relate only to a given accounting period. Consist of all income statement accounts and owner's drawing account. All temporary accounts are closed at end of accounting period. (p. 148).

Worksheet A multiple-column form that may be used in making adjusting entries and in preparing financial statements. (p. 142).

APPENDIX Reversing Entries

STUDY OBJECTIVE 7
Prepare reversing entries.

After preparing the financial statements and closing the books, it is often helpful to reverse some of the adjusting entries before recording the regular transactions of the next period. Such entries are **reversing entries**. Companies make **a reversing entry at the beginning of the next accounting period**. Each reversing entry **is the exact opposite of the adjusting entry made in the previous period**. The recording of reversing entries is an **optional step** in the accounting cycle.

The purpose of reversing entries is to simplify the recording of a subsequent transaction related to an adjusting entry. For example, in Chapter 3 (page 107), the payment of salaries after an adjusting entry resulted in two debits: one to Salaries Payable and the other to Salaries Expense. With reversing entries, the company can debit the entire subsequent payment to Salaries Expense. **The use of reversing entries does not change the amounts reported in the financial statements.** What it does is simplify the recording of subsequent transactions.

Reversing Entries Example

Companies most often use reversing entries to reverse two types of adjusting entries: accrued revenues and accrued expenses. To illustrate the optional use of reversing entries for accrued expenses, we will use the salaries expense transactions for Pioneer Advertising Agency. The transaction and adjustment data are as follows.

1. October 26 (initial salary entry): Pioneer pays $4,000 of salaries earned between October 15 and October 26.
2. October 31 (adjusting entry): Salaries earned between October 29 and October 31 are $1,200. The company will pay these in the November 9 payroll.
3. November 9 (subsequent salary entry): Salaries paid are $4,000. Of this amount, $1,200 applied to accrued wages payable and $2,800 was earned between November 1 and November 9.

Illustration 4A-1 shows the entries with and without reversing entries.

Illustration 4A-1
Comparative entries—not reversing vs. reversing

Without Reversing Entries (per chapter)				**With Reversing Entries (per appendix)**			
	Initial Salary Entry				Initial Salary Entry		
Oct. 26	Salaries Expense	4,000		Oct. 26	(Same entry)		
	Cash		4,000				
	Adjusting Entry				Adjusting Entry		
Oct. 31	Salaries Expense	1,200		Oct. 31	(Same entry)		
	Salaries Payable		1,200				
	Closing Entry				Closing Entry		
Oct. 31	Income Summary	5,200		Oct. 31	(Same entry)		
	Salaries Expense		5,200				
	Reversing Entry				Reversing Entry		
Nov. 1	No reversing entry is made.			Nov. 1	**Salaries Payable**	**1,200**	
					Salaries Expense		**1,200**
	Subsequent Salary Entry				Subsequent Salary Entry		
Nov. 9	Salaries Payable	1,200		Nov. 9	**Salaries Expense**	**4,000**	
	Salaries Expense	2,800			**Cash**		**4,000**
	Cash		4,000				

The first three entries are the same whether or not Pioneer uses reversing entries. The last two entries are different. The November 1 **reversing entry** eliminates the $1,200 balance in Salaries Payable created by the October 31 adjusting entry. The reversing entry also creates a $1,200 credit balance in the Salaries Expense account. As you know, it is unusual for an expense account to have a credit balance. The balance is correct in this instance, though, because it anticipates that the entire amount of the first salary payment in the new accounting period will be debited to Salaries Expense. This debit will eliminate the credit balance. The resulting debit balance in the expense account will equal the salaries expense incurred in the new accounting period ($2,800 in this example).

If Pioneer makes reversing entries, it can debit all cash payments of expenses to the expense account. This means that on November 9 (and every payday) Pioneer can debit Salaries Expense for the amount paid, without regard to any accrued salaries payable. Being able to make the **same entry each time** simplifies the recording process: The company can record subsequent transactions as if the related adjusting entry had never been made.

Illustration 4A-2 shows the posting of the entries with reversing entries.

Illustration 4A-2
Postings with reversing entries

Salaries Expense				Salaries Payable			
10/26 Paid	4,000	10/31 Closing	5,200	**11/1 Reversing**	**1,200**	10/31 Adjusting	1,200
31 Adjusting	1,200						
	5,200		5,200				
11/9 Paid	4,000	**11/1 Reversing**	**1,200**				

A company can also use reversing entries for accrued revenue adjusting entries. For Pioneer Advertising, the adjusting entry was: Accounts Receivable (Dr.) $200 and Service Revenue (Cr.) $200. Thus, the reversing entry on November 1 is:

Nov. 1	Service Revenue	200	
	Accounts Receivable		200
	(To reverse October 31 adjusting entry)		

A	=	L	+	OE
				−200 Rev
−200				

Cash Flows
no effect

When Pioneer collects the accrued service revenue, it debits Cash and credits Service Revenue.

SUMMARY OF STUDY OBJECTIVE FOR APPENDIX

WILEY PLUS

7 Prepare reversing entries. Reversing entries are the opposite of the adjusting entries made in the preceding period. Some companies choose to make reversing entries at the beginning of a new accounting period to simplify the recording of later transactions related to the adjusting entries. In most cases, only accrued adjusting entries are reversed.

*__Note:__ All asterisked Questions, Exercises, and Problems relate to material in the appendix to the chapter.

SELF-STUDY QUESTIONS

WILEY PLUS

Answers are at the end of the chapter.

(SO 1) **1.** Which of the following statements is *incorrect* concerning the worksheet?
a. The worksheet is essentially a working tool of the accountant.
b. The worksheet is distributed to management and other interested parties.
c. The worksheet cannot be used as a basis for posting to ledger accounts.
d. Financial statements can be prepared directly from the worksheet before journalizing and posting the adjusting entries.

2. In a worksheet, net income is entered in the following columns: (SO 1)
a. income statement (Dr) and balance sheet (Dr).
b. income statement (Cr) and balance sheet (Dr).
c. income statement (Dr) and balance sheet (Cr).
d. income statement (Cr) and balance sheet (Cr).

3. An account that will have a zero balance after closing entries have been journalized and posted is: (SO 2)
a. Service Revenue.
b. Advertising Supplies.
c. Prepaid Insurance.
d. Accumulated Depreciation.

(SO 2) **4.** When a net loss has occurred, Income Summary is:
a. debited and Owner's Capital is credited.
b. credited and Owner's Capital is debited.
c. debited and Owner's Drawing is credited.
d. credited and Owner's Drawing is debited.

(SO 2) **5.** The closing process involves separate entries to close (1) expenses, (2) drawings, (3) revenues, and (4) income summary. The correct sequencing of the entries is:
a. (4), (3), (2), (1)
b. (1), (2), (3), (4)
c. (3), (1), (4), (2)
d. (3), (2), (1), (4)

(SO 3) **6.** Which types of accounts will appear in the post-closing trial balance?
a. Permanent (real) accounts.
b. Temporary (nominal) accounts.
c. Accounts shown in the income statement columns of a work sheet.
d. None of the above.

(SO 4) **7.** All of the following are required steps in the accounting cycle *except*:
a. journalizing and posting closing entries.
b. preparing financial statements.
c. journalizing the transactions.
d. preparing a work sheet.

(SO 5) **8.** Cash of $100 received at the time the service was provided was journalized and posted as a debit to Cash $100 and a credit to Accounts Receivable $100. Assuming the incorrect entry is not reversed, the correcting entry is:
a. debit Service Revenue $100 and credit Accounts Receivable $100.
b. debit Accounts Receivable $100 and credit Service Revenue $100.
c. debit Cash $100 and credit Service Revenue $100.
d. debit Accounts Receivable $100 and credit Cash $100.

9. In a classified balance sheet, assets are usually classified using the following categories: (SO 6)
a. current assets; long-term assets; property, plant, and equipment; and intangible assets.
b. current assets; long-term investments; property, plant, and equipment; and other assets.
c. current assets; long-term investments; tangible assets; and intangible assets.
d. current assets; long-term investments; property, plant, and equipment; and intangible assets.

10. Current assets are listed: (SO 6)
a. by liquidity.
b. by importance.
c. by longevity.
d. alphabetically.

***11.** On December 31, Frank Voris Company correctly made an adjusting entry to recognize $2,000 of accrued salaries payable. On January 8 of the next year, total salaries of $3,400 were paid. Assuming the correct reversing entry was made on January 1, the entry on January 8 will result in a credit to Cash $3,400 and the following debit(s): (SO 7)
a. Salaries Payable $1,400, and Salaries Expense $2,000.
b. Salaries Payable $2,000 and Salaries Expense $1,400.
c. Salaries Expense $3,400.
d. Salaries Payable $3,400.

Go to the book's website, **www.wiley.com/college/weygandt**, for additional Self-Study Questions.

The Navigator

QUESTIONS

1. "A worksheet is a permanent accounting record and its use is required in the accounting cycle." Do you agree? Explain.
2. Explain the purpose of the worksheet.
3. What is the relationship, if any, between the amount shown in the adjusted trial balance column for an account and that account's ledger balance?
4. If a company's revenues are $125,000 and its expenses are $113,000, in which financial statement columns of the worksheet will the net income of $12,000 appear? When expenses exceed revenues, in which columns will the difference appear?
5. Why is it necessary to prepare formal financial statements if all of the data are in the statement columns of the worksheet?
6. Identify the account(s) debited and credited in each of the four closing entries, assuming the company has net income for the year.
7. Describe the nature of the Income Summary account and identify the types of summary data that may be posted to this account.
8. What are the content and purpose of a post-closing trial balance?
9. Which of the following accounts would not appear in the post-closing trial balance? Interest Payable; Equipment; Depreciation Expense; Jennifer Shaeffer, Drawing; Unearned Revenue; Accumulated Depreciation—Equipment; and Service Revenue.
10. Distinguish between a reversing entry and an adjusting entry. Are reversing entries required?
11. Indicate, in the sequence in which they are made, the three required steps in the accounting cycle that involve journalizing.
12. Identify, in the sequence in which they are prepared, the three trial balances that are often used to report financial information about a company.
13. How do correcting entries differ from adjusting entries?
14. What standard classifications are used in preparing a classified balance sheet?
15. What is meant by the term "operating cycle?"
16. Define current assets. What basis is used for arranging individual items within the current assets section?

17. Distinguish between long-term investments and property, plant, and equipment.

18. (a) What is the term used to describe the owner's equity section of a corporation? (b) Identify the two owners' equity accounts in a corporation and indicate the purpose of each.

*19. Sanchez Company prepares reversing entries. If the adjusting entry for interest payable is reversed, what type of an account balance, if any, will there be in Interest Payable and Interest Expense after the reversing entry is posted?

*20. At December 31, accrued salaries payable totaled $3,500. On January 10, total salaries of $8,000 are paid. (a) Assume that reversing entries are made at January 1. Give the January 10 entry, and indicate the Salaries Expense account balance after the entry is posted. (b) Repeat part (a) assuming reversing entries are not made.

BRIEF EXERCISES

WILEY PLUS

BE4-1 The steps in using a worksheet are presented in random order below. List the steps in the proper order by placing numbers 1–5 in the blank spaces.

List the steps in preparing a worksheet.
(SO 1)

(a) _____ Prepare a trial balance on the worksheet.
(b) _____ Enter adjusted balances.
(c) _____ Extend adjusted balances to appropriate statement columns.
(d) _____ Total the statement columns, compute net income (loss), and complete the worksheet.
(e) _____ Enter adjustment data.

BE4-2 The ledger of Ley Company includes the following unadjusted balances: Prepaid Insurance $3,000, Service Revenue $58,000, and Salaries Expense $25,000. Adjusting entries are required for **(a)** expired insurance $1,200; **(b)** services provided $1,100, but unbilled and uncollected; and **(c)** accrued salaries payable $800. Enter the unadjusted balances and adjustments into a worksheet and complete the worksheet for all accounts. *Note:* You will need to add the following accounts: Accounts Receivable, Salaries Payable, and Insurance Expense.

Prepare partial worksheet.
(SO 1)

BE4-3 The following selected accounts appear in the adjusted trial balance columns of the worksheet for Batan Company: Accumulated Depreciation; Depreciation Expense; N. Batan, Capital; N. Batan, Drawing; Service Revenue; Supplies; and Accounts Payable. Indicate the financial statement column (income statement Dr., balance sheet Cr., etc.) to which each balance should be extended.

Identify worksheet columns for selected accounts.
(SO 1)

BE4-4 The ledger of Swann Company contains the following balances: D. Swann, Capital $30,000; D. Swann, Drawing $2,000; Service Revenue $50,000; Salaries Expense $27,000; and Supplies Expense $4,000. Prepare the closing entries at December 31.

Prepare closing entries from ledger balances.
(SO 2)

BE4-5 Using the data in BE4-4, enter the balances in T accounts, post the closing entries, and rule and balance the accounts.

Post closing entries; rule and balance T accounts.
(SO 2)

BE4-6 The income statement for Crestwood Golf Club for the month ending July 31 shows Green Fee Revenue $13,600, Salaries Expense $8,200, Maintenance Expense $2,500, and Net Income $2,900. Prepare the entries to close the revenue and expense accounts. Post the entries to the revenue and expense accounts, and complete the closing process for these accounts using the three-column form of account.

Journalize and post closing entries using the three-column form of account.
(SO 2)

BE4-7 Using the data in BE4-3, identify the accounts that would be included in a post-closing trial balance.

Identify post-closing trial balance accounts.
(SO 3)

BE4-8 The steps in the accounting cycle are listed in random order below. List the steps in proper sequence, assuming no worksheet is prepared, by placing numbers 1–9 in the blank spaces.

List the required steps in the accounting cycle in sequence.
(SO 4)

(a) _____ Prepare a trial balance.
(b) _____ Journalize the transactions.
(c) _____ Journalize and post closing entries.
(d) _____ Prepare financial statements.
(e) _____ Journalize and post adjusting entries.
(f) _____ Post to ledger accounts.
(g) _____ Prepare a post-closing trial balance.
(h) _____ Prepare an adjusted trial balance.
(i) _____ Analyze business transactions.

Prepare correcting entries.
(SO 5)

BE4-9 At Batavia Company, the following errors were discovered after the transactions had been journalized and posted. Prepare the correcting entries.

1. A collection on account from a customer for $780 was recorded as a debit to Cash $780 and a credit to Service Revenue $780.
2. The purchase of store supplies on account for $1,570 was recorded as a debit to Store Supplies $1,750 and a credit to Accounts Payable $1,750.

Prepare the current assets section of a balance sheet.
(SO 6)

BE4-10 The balance sheet debit column of the worksheet for Diaz Company includes the following accounts: Accounts Receivable $12,500; Prepaid Insurance $3,600; Cash $15,400; Supplies $5,200, and Short-term Investments $6,700. Prepare the current assets section of the balance sheet, listing the accounts in proper sequence.

Classify accounts on balance sheet.
(SO 6)

BE4-11 The following are the major balance sheet classifications:

Current assets (CA)	Current liabilities (CL)
Long-term investments (LTI)	Long-term liabilities (LTL)
Property, plant, and equipment (PPE)	Owner's equity (OE)
Intangible assets (IA)	

Match each of the following accounts to its proper balance sheet classification.

_____ Accounts payable	_____ Income tax payable
_____ Accounts receivable	_____ Investment in long-term bonds
_____ Accumulated depreciation	_____ Land
_____ Building	_____ Merchandise inventory
_____ Cash	_____ Patent
_____ Copyrights	_____ Supplies

Prepare reversing entries.
(SO 7)

***BE4-12** At October 31, Nathan Company made an accrued expense adjusting entry of $1,400 for salaries. Prepare the reversing entry on November 1, and indicate the balances in Salaries Payable and Salaries Expense after posting the reversing entry.

EXERCISES

WILEY PLUS

Complete the worksheet.
(SO 1)

E4-1 The trial balance columns of the worksheet for Briscoe Company at June 30, 2008, are as follows.

BRISCOE COMPANY
Worksheet
for the Month Ended June 30, 2008

	Trial Balance	
Account Titles	**Dr.**	**Cr.**
Cash	$2,320	
Accounts Receivable	2,440	
Supplies	1,880	
Accounts Payable		$1,120
Unearned Revenue		240
Lenny Briscoe, Capital		3,600
Service Revenue		2,400
Salaries Expense	560	
Miscellaneous Expense	160	
	$7,360	$7,360

Other data:

1. A physical count reveals $300 of supplies on hand.
2. $100 of the unearned revenue is still unearned at month-end.
3. Accrued salaries are $280.

Instructions
Enter the trial balance on a worksheet and complete the worksheet.

Complete the worksheet.
(SO 1)

E4-2 The adjusted trial balance columns of the worksheet for Goode Company are as follows.

GOODE COMPANY
Worksheet (partial)
for the Month Ended April 30, 2008

Account Titles	Adjusted Trial Balance Dr.	Adjusted Trial Balance Cr.	Income Statement Dr.	Income Statement Cr.	Balance Sheet Dr.	Balance Sheet Cr.
Cash	13,752					
Accounts Receivable	7,840					
Prepaid Rent	2,280					
Equipment	23,050					
Accumulated Depreciation		4,921				
Notes Payable		5,700				
Accounts Payable		5,672				
T. Goode, Capital		30,960				
T. Goode, Drawing	3,650					
Service Revenue		15,590				
Salaries Expense	10,840					
Rent Expense	760					
Depreciation Expense	671					
Interest Expense	57					
Interest Payable		57				
Totals	62,900	62,900				

Instructions
Complete the worksheet.

Prepare financial statements from worksheet.
(SO 1, 6)

E4-3 Worksheet data for Goode Company are presented in E4-2. The owner did not make any additional investments in the business in April.

Instructions
Prepare an income statement, an owner's equity statement, and a classified balance sheet.

Journalize and post closing entries and prepare a post-closing trial balance.
(SO 2, 3)

E4-4 Worksheet data for Goode Company are presented in E4-2.

Instructions
(a) Journalize the closing entries at April 30.
(b) Post the closing entries to Income Summary and T. Goode, Capital. Use T accounts.
(c) Prepare a post-closing trial balance at April 30.

Prepare adjusting entries from a worksheet, and extend balances to worksheet columns.
(SO 1)

E4-5 The adjustments columns of the worksheet for Mears Company are shown below.

Account Titles	Adjustments Debit	Adjustments Credit
Accounts Receivable	600	
Prepaid Insurance		400
Accumulated Depreciation		900
Salaries Payable		500
Service Revenue		600
Salaries Expense	500	
Insurance Expense	400	
Depreciation Expense	900	
	2,400	2,400

Instructions

(a) Prepare the adjusting entries.

(b) Assuming the adjusted trial balance amount for each account is normal, indicate the financial statement column to which each balance should be extended.

Derive adjusting entries from worksheet data.

(SO 1)

E4-6 Selected worksheet data for Nicholson Company are presented below.

Account Titles	Trial Balance		Adjusted Trial Balance	
	Dr.	Cr.	Dr.	Cr.
Accounts Receivable	?		34,000	
Prepaid Insurance	26,000		20,000	
Supplies	7,000		?	
Accumulated Depreciation		12,000		?
Salaries Payable		?		5,000
Service Revenue		88,000		97,000
Insurance Expense			?	
Depreciation Expense			10,000	
Supplies Expense			5,000	
Salaries Expense	?		49,000	

Instructions

(a) Fill in the missing amounts.

(b) Prepare the adjusting entries that were made.

Prepare closing entries, and prepare a post-closing trial balance.

(SO 2, 3)

E4-7 Emil Skoda Company had the following adjusted trial balance.

EMIL SKODA COMPANY
Adjusted Trial Balance
for the Month Ended June 30, 2008

Account Titles	Adjusted Trial Balance	
	Debits	Credits
Cash	$3,712	
Accounts Receivable	3,904	
Supplies	480	
Accounts Payable		$1,792
Unearned Revenue		160
Emil Skoda, Capital		5,760
Emil Skoda, Drawing	300	
Service Revenue		4,064
Salaries Expense	1,344	
Miscellaneous Expense	256	
Supplies Expense	2,228	
Salaries Payable		448
	$12,224	$12,224

Instructions

(a) Prepare closing entries at June 30, 2008.

(b) Prepare a post-closing trial balance.

Journalize and post closing entries, and prepare a post-closing trial balance.

(SO 2, 3)

E4-8 Apachi Company ended its fiscal year on July 31, 2008. The company's adjusted trial balance as of the end of its fiscal year is as shown at the top of page 177.

APACHI COMPANY
Adjusted Trial Balance
July 31, 2008

No.	Account Titles	Debits	Credits
101	Cash	$ 14,840	
112	Accounts Receivable	8,780	
157	Equipment	15,900	
167	Accumulated Depreciation		$ 7,400
201	Accounts Payable		4,220
208	Unearned Rent Revenue		1,800
301	B. J. Apachi, Capital		45,200
306	B. J. Apachi, Drawing	16,000	
404	Commission Revenue		65,000
429	Rent Revenue		6,500
711	Depreciation Expense	4,000	
720	Salaries Expense	55,700	
732	Utilities Expense	14,900	
		$130,120	$130,120

Instructions

(a) Prepare the closing entries using page J15.

(b) Post to B. J. Apachi, Capital and No. 350 Income Summary accounts. (Use the three-column form.)

(c) Prepare a post-closing trial balance at July 31.

E4-9 The adjusted trial balance for Apachi Company is presented in E4-8.

Prepare financial statements.

(SO 6)

Instructions

(a) Prepare an income statement and an owner's equity statement for the year. Apachi did not make any capital investments during the year.

(b) Prepare a classified balance sheet at July 31.

E4-10 Josh Borke has prepared the following list of statements about the accounting cycle.

Answer questions related to the accounting cycle.

(SO 4)

1. "Journalize the transactions" is the first step in the accounting cycle.
2. Reversing entries are a required step in the accounting cycle.
3. Correcting entries do not have to be part of the accounting cycle.
4. If a worksheet is prepared, some steps of the accounting cycle are incorporated into the worksheet.
5. The accounting cycle begins with the analysis of business transactions and ends with the preparation of a post-closing trial balance.
6. All steps of the accounting cycle occur daily during the accounting period.
7. The step of "post to the ledger accounts" occurs before the step of "journalize the transactions."
8. Closing entries must be prepared before financial statements can be prepared.

Instructions

Identify each statement as true of false. If false, indicate how to correct the statement.

E4-11 Selected accounts for Nina's Salon are presented below. All June 30 postings are from closing entries.

Prepare closing entries.

(SO 2)

Salaries Expense

6/10	3,200	6/30	8,800
6/28	5,600		

Service Revenue

6/30	15,100	6/15	6,700
		6/24	8,400

Nina Cole, Capital

6/30	2,500	6/1	12,000
		6/30	2,000
		Bal.	11,500

Supplies Expense

6/12	600	6/30	1,300
6/24	700		

Rent Expense

6/1	3,000	6/30	3,000

Nina Cole, Drawing

6/13	1,000	6/30	2,500
6/25	1,500		

Instructions

(a) Prepare the closing entries that were made.

(b) Post the closing entries to Income Summary.

Prepare correcting entries.
(SO 5)

E4-12 Max Weinberg Company discovered the following errors made in January 2008.

1. A payment of Salaries Expense of $600 was debited to Equipment and credited to Cash, both for $600.
2. A collection of $1,000 from a client on account was debited to Cash $100 and credited to Service Revenue $100.
3. The purchase of equipment on account for $980 was debited to Equipment $890 and credited to Accounts Payable $890.

Instructions

(a) Correct the errors by reversing the incorrect entry and preparing the correct entry.

(b) Correct the errors without reversing the incorrect entry.

Prepare correcting entries.
(SO 5)

E4-13 Mason Company has an inexperienced accountant. During the first 2 weeks on the job, the accountant made the following errors in journalizing transactions. All entries were posted as made.

1. A payment on account of $630 to a creditor was debited to Accounts Payable $360 and credited to Cash $360.
2. The purchase of supplies on account for $560 was debited to Equipment $56 and credited to Accounts Payable $56.
3. A $400 withdrawal of cash for M. Mason's personal use was debited to Salaries Expense $400 and credited to Cash $400.

Instructions

Prepare the correcting entries.

Prepare a classified balance sheet.
(SO 6)

E4-14 The adjusted trial balance for Karr Bowling Alley at December 31, 2008, contains the following accounts.

Debits		Credits	
Building	$128,800	Sue Karr, Capital	$115,000
Accounts Receivable	14,520	Accumulated Depreciation—Building	42,600
Prepaid Insurance	4,680	Accounts Payable	12,300
Cash	18,040	Note Payable	97,780
Equipment	62,400	Accumulated Depreciation—Equipment	18,720
Land	64,000	Interest Payable	2,600
Insurance Expense	780	Bowling Revenues	14,180
Depreciation Expense	7,360		$303,180
Interest Expense	2,600		
	$303,180		

Instructions

(a) Prepare a classified balance sheet; assume that $13,900 of the note payable will be paid in 2009.

(b) Comment on the liquidity of the company.

Classify accounts on balance sheet.
(SO 6)

E4-15 The following are the major balance sheet classifications.

Current assets (CA)	Current liabilities (CL)
Long-term investments (LTI)	Long-term liabilities (LTL)
Property, plant, and equipment (PPE)	Owner's equity (OE)
Intangible assets (IA)	

Instructions

Classify each of the following accounts taken from Roberts Company's balance sheet.

______ Accounts payable	______ Accumulated depreciation
______ Accounts receivable	______ Buildings.

______ Cash	______ Land
______ Roberts, Capital	______ Long-term debt
______ Patents	______ Supplies
______ Salaries payable	______ Office equipment
______ Inventories	______ Prepaid expenses
______ Investments	

E4-16 The following items were taken from the financial statements of R. Stevens Company. (All dollars are in thousands.)

Prepare a classified balance sheet.

(SO 6)

Long-term debt	$ 943	Accumulated depreciation	5,655
Prepaid expenses	880	Accounts payable	1,444
Property, plant, and equipment	11,500	Notes payable after 2009	368
Long-term investments	264	R. Stevens, Capital	13,063
Short-term investments	3,690	Accounts receivable	1,696
Notes payable in 2009	481	Inventories	1,256
Cash	$ 2,668		

Instructions

Prepare a classified balance sheet in good form as of December 31, 2008.

E4-17 These financial statement items are for B. Snyder Company at year-end, July 31, 2008.

Prepare financial statements.

(SO 1, 6)

Salaries payable	$ 2,080	Note payable (long-term)	$ 1,800
Salaries expense	51,700	Cash	24,200
Utilities expense	22,600	Accounts receivable	9,780
Equipment	18,500	Accumulated depreciation	6,000
Accounts payable	4,100	B. Snyder, Drawing	4,000
Commission revenue	61,100	Depreciation expense	4,000
Rent revenue	8,500	B. Snyder, Capital (beginning of the year)	51,200

Instructions

(a) Prepare an income statement and an owner's equity statement for the year. The owner did not make any new investments during the year.

(b) Prepare a classified balance sheet at July 31.

***E4-18** LaBamba Company pays salaries of $10,000 every Monday for the preceding 5-day week (Monday through Friday). Assume December 31 falls on a Tuesday, so LaBamba's employes have worked 2 days without being paid.

Use reversing entries.

(SO 7)

Instructions

(a) Assume the company does not use reversing entries. Prepare the December 31 adjusting entry and the entry on Monday, January 6, when LaBamba pays the payroll.

(b) Assume the company does use reversing entries. Prepare the December 31 adjusting entry, the January 1 reversing entry, and the entry on Monday, January 6, when LaBamba pays the payroll.

***E4-19** On December 31, the adjusted trial balance of Oslo Employment Agency shows the following selected data.

Prepare closing and reversing entries.

(SO 2, 4, 7)

Accounts Receivable	$24,000	Commission Revenue	$92,000
Interest Expense	7,800	Interest Payable	1,500

Analysis shows that adjusting entries were made to (1) accrue $4,500 of commission revenue and (2) accrue $1,500 interest expense.

Instructions

(a) Prepare the closing entries for the temporary accounts at December 31.

(b) Prepare the reversing entries on January 1.

(c) Post the entries in (a) and (b). Rule and balance the accounts. (Use T accounts.)

(d) Prepare the entries to record (1) the collection of the accrued commissions on January 10 and (2) the payment of all interest due ($2,500) on January 15.

(e) Post the entries in (d) to the temporary accounts.

EXERCISES: SET B

Visit the book's website at **www.wiley.com/college/weygandt**, and choose the Student Companion site, to access Exercise Set B.

PROBLEMS: SET A

Prepare worksheet, financial statements, and adjusting and closing entries.

(SO 1, 2, 3, 6)

P4-1A Thomas Magnum began operations as a private investigator on January 1, 2008. The trial balance columns of the worksheet for Thomas Magnum, P.I. at March 31 are as follows.

THOMAS MAGNUM, P.I.
Worksheet
For the Quarter Ended March 31, 2008

Account Titles	Trial Balance Dr.	Trial Balance Cr.
Cash	11,400	
Accounts Receivable	5,620	
Supplies	1,050	
Prepaid Insurance	2,400	
Equipment	30,000	
Notes Payable		10,000
Accounts Payable		12,350
T. Magnum, Capital		20,000
T. Magnum, Drawing	600	
Service Revenue		13,620
Salaries Expense	2,200	
Travel Expense	1,300	
Rent Expense	1,200	
Miscellaneous Expense	200	
	55,970	55,970

Other data:

1. Supplies on hand total $380.
2. Depreciation is $1,000 per quarter.
3. Interest accrued on 6-month note payable, issued January 1, $300.
4. Insurance expires at the rate of $200 per month.
5. Services provided but unbilled at March 31 total $530.

Instructions

(a) Adjusted trial balance $57,800

(b) Net income $6,680
Total assets $48,730

(a) Enter the trial balance on a worksheet and complete the worksheet.
(b) Prepare an income statement and owner's equity statement for the quarter and a classified balance sheet at March 31. T. Magnum did not make any additional investments in the business during the quarter ended March 31, 2008.
(c) Journalize the adjusting entries from the adjustments columns of the worksheet.
(d) Journalize the closing entries from the financial statement columns of the worksheet.

Complete worksheet; prepare financial statements, closing entries, and post-closing trial balance.

(SO 1, 2, 3, 6)

GLS Peachtree

P4-2A The adjusted trial balance columns of the worksheet for Porter Company are as follows.

PORTER COMPANY
Worksheet
For the Year Ended December 31, 2008

Account No.	Account Titles	Adjusted Trial Balance Dr.	Adjusted Trial Balance Cr.
101	Cash	18,800	
112	Accounts Receivable	16,200	
126	Supplies	2,300	

Account No.	Account Titles	Adjusted Trial Balance Dr.	Adjusted Trial Balance Cr.
130	Prepaid Insurance	4,400	
151	Office Equipment	44,000	
152	Accumulated Depreciation—Office Equipment		20,000
200	Notes Payable		20,000
201	Accounts Payable		8,000
212	Salaries Payable		2,600
230	Interest Payable		1,000
301	B. Porter, Capital		36,000
306	B. Porter, Drawing	12,000	
400	Service Revenue		77,800
610	Advertising Expense	12,000	
631	Supplies Expense	3,700	
711	Depreciation Expense	8,000	
722	Insurance Expense	4,000	
726	Salaries Expense	39,000	
905	Interest Expense	1,000	
	Totals	165,400	165,400

Instructions

(a) Complete the worksheet by extending the balances to the financial statement columns.

(a) Net income $10,100

(b) Prepare an income statement, owner's equity statement, and a classified balance sheet. $10,000 of the notes payable become due in 2009. B. Porter did not make any additional investments in the business during 2008.

(b) Current assets $41,700
Current liabilities $21,600

(c) Prepare the closing entries. Use J14 for the journal page.

(d) Post the closing entries. Use the three-column form of account. Income Summary is account No. 350.

(e) Prepare a post-closing trial balance.

(e) Post-closing trial balance $85,700

P4-3A The completed financial statement columns of the worksheet for Woods Company are shown below.

Prepare financial statements, closing entries, and post-closing trial balance.

(SO 1, 2, 3, 6)

WOODS COMPANY
Worksheet
For the Year Ended December 31, 2008

Account No.	Account Titles	Income Statement Dr.	Income Statement Cr.	Balance Sheet Dr.	Balance Sheet Cr.
101	Cash			8,200	
112	Accounts Receivable			7,500	
130	Prepaid Insurance			1,800	
157	Equipment			28,000	
167	Accumulated Depreciation				8,600
201	Accounts Payable				11,700
212	Salaries Payable				3,000
301	S. Woods, Capital				34,000
306	S. Woods, Drawing			7,200	
400	Service Revenue		44,000		
622	Repair Expense	5,400			
711	Depreciation Expense	2,800			
722	Insurance Expense	1,200			
726	Salaries Expense	35,200			
732	Utilities Expense	4,000			
	Totals	48,600	44,000	52,700	57,300
	Net Loss		4,600	4,600	
		48,600	48,600	57,300	57,300

(a) Net loss $4,600
Ending capital $22,200
Total assets $36,900

(d) Post-closing trial balance $45,500

Instructions

(a) Prepare an income statement, owner's equity statement, and a classified balance sheet. S. Woods made an additional investment in the business of $4,000 during 2008.
(b) Prepare the closing entries.
(c) Post the closing entries and rule and balance the accounts. Use T accounts. Income Summary is account No. 350.
(d) Prepare a post-closing trial balance.

Complete worksheet; prepare classified balance sheet, entries, and post-closing trial balance.

(SO 1, 2, 3, 6)

P4-4A Disney Amusement Park has a fiscal year ending on September 30. Selected data from the September 30 worksheet are presented below.

DISNEY AMUSEMENT PARK
Worksheet
For the Year Ended September 30, 2008

	Trial Balance		Adjusted Trial Balance	
	Dr.	**Cr.**	**Dr.**	**Cr.**
Cash	41,400		41,400	
Supplies	18,600		1,200	
Prepaid Insurance	31,900		8,900	
Land	80,000		80,000	
Equipment	120,000		120,000	
Accumulated Depreciation		36,200		42,200
Accounts Payable		14,600		14,600
Unearned Admissions Revenue		3,700		2,000
Mortgage Note Payable		50,000		50,000
L. Disney, Capital		109,700		109,700
L. Disney, Drawing	14,000		14,000	
Admissions Revenue		277,500		279,200
Salaries Expense	105,000		105,000	
Repair Expense	30,500		30,500	
Advertising Expense	9,400		9,400	
Utilities Expense	16,900		16,900	
Property Taxes Expense	18,000		21,000	
Interest Expense	6,000		10,000	
Totals	491,700	491,700		
Insurance Expense			23,000	
Supplies Expense			17,400	
Interest Payable				4,000
Depreciation Expense			6,000	
Property Taxes Payable				3,000
Totals			504,700	504,700

(a) Net income $40,000

(b) Total current assets $51,500

(e) Post-closing trial balance $251,500

Instructions

(a) Prepare a complete worksheet.
(b) Prepare a classified balance sheet. (*Note*: $10,000 of the mortgage note payable is due for payment in the next fiscal year.)
(c) Journalize the adjusting entries using the worksheet as a basis.
(d) Journalize the closing entries using the worksheet as a basis.
(e) Prepare a post-closing trial balance.

Complete all steps in accounting cycle.

(SO 1, 2, 3, 4, 6)

GLS Peachtree

P4-5A Laura Eddy opened Eddy's Carpet Cleaners on March 1. During March, the following transactions were completed.

Mar.	1	Invested $10,000 cash in the business.
	1	Purchased used truck for $6,000, paying $3,000 cash and the balance on account.
	3	Purchased cleaning supplies for $1,200 on account.
	5	Paid $1,200 cash on one-year insurance policy effective March 1.

14 Billed customers $4,800 for cleaning services.
18 Paid $1,500 cash on amount owed on truck and $500 on amount owed on cleaning supplies.
20 Paid $1,800 cash for employee salaries.
21 Collected $1,400 cash from customers billed on March 14.
28 Billed customers $2,500 for cleaning services.
31 Paid gas and oil for month on truck $200.
31 Withdrew $700 cash for personal use.

The chart of accounts for Eddy's Carpet Cleaners contains the following accounts: No. 101 Cash, No. 112 Accounts Receivable, No. 128 Cleaning Supplies, No. 130 Prepaid Insurance, No. 157 Equipment, No. 158 Accumulated Depreciation—Equipment, No. 201 Accounts Payable, No. 212 Salaries Payable, No. 301 L. Eddy, Capital, No. 306, L. Eddy, Drawing, No. 350 Income Summary, No. 400 Service Revenue, No. 633 Gas & Oil Expense, No. 634 Cleaning Supplies Expense, No. 711 Depreciation Expense, No. 722 Insurance Expense, and No. 726 Salaries Expense.

Instructions

(a) Journalize and post the March transactions. Use page J1 for the journal and the three-column form of account.
(b) Prepare a trial balance at March 31 on a worksheet.
(c) Enter the following adjustments on the worksheet and complete the worksheet.
  (1) Earned but unbilled revenue at March 31 was $700.
  (2) Depreciation on equipment for the month was $250.
  (3) One-twelfth of the insurance expired.
  (4) An inventory count shows $400 of cleaning supplies on hand at March 31.
  (5) Accrued but unpaid employee salaries were $500.
(d) Prepare the income statement and owner's equity statement for March and a classified balance sheet at March 31.
(e) Journalize and post adjusting entries. Use page J2 for the journal.
(f) Journalize and post closing entries and complete the closing process. Use page J3 for the journal.
(g) Prepare a post-closing trial balance at March 31.

(b) Trial balance $19,500
(c) Adjusted trial balance $20,950
(d) Net income $4,350
Total assets $16,350
(g) Post-closing trial balance $16,600

P4-6A Joe Edmonds, CPA, was retained by Fox Cable to prepare financial statements for April 2008. Edmonds accumulated all the ledger balances per Fox's records and found the following.

Analyze errors and prepare correcting entries and trial balance.

(SO 5)

FOX CABLE
Trial Balance
April 30, 2008

	Debit	Credit
Cash	$ 4,100	
Accounts Receivable	3,200	
Supplies	800	
Equipment	10,600	
Accumulated Depreciation		$ 1,350
Accounts Payable		2,100
Salaries Payable		700
Unearned Revenue		890
A. Manion, Capital		12,900
Service Revenue		5,450
Salaries Expense	3,300	
Advertising Expense	600	
Miscellaneous Expense	290	
Depreciation Expense	500	
	$23,390	$23,390

Joe Edmonds reviewed the records and found the following errors.

1. Cash received from a customer on account was recorded as $960 instead of $690.
2. A payment of $65 for advertising expense was entered as a debit to Miscellaneous Expense $65 and a credit to Cash $65.
3. The first salary payment this month was for $1,900, which included $700 of salaries payable on March 31. The payment was recorded as a debit to Salaries Expense $1,900 and a credit to Cash $1,900. (No reversing entries were made on April 1.)
4. The purchase on account of a printer costing $290 was recorded as a debit to Supplies and a credit to Accounts Payable for $290.
5. A cash payment of repair expense on equipment for $95 was recorded as a debit to Equipment $59 and a credit to Cash $59.

Instructions

(a) Prepare an analysis of each error showing (1) the incorrect entry, (2) the correct entry, and (3) the correcting entry. Items 4 and 5 occurred on April 30, 2008.

Trial balance $22,690

(b) Prepare a correct trial balance.

PROBLEMS: SET B

Prepare a worksheet, financial statements, and adjusting and closing entries.

(SO 1, 2, 3, 6)

P4-1B The trial balance columns of the worksheet for Everlast Roofing at March 31, 2008, are as follows.

EVERLAST ROOFING
Worksheet
For the Month Ended March 31, 2008

Account Titles	Trial Balance Dr.	Trial Balance Cr.
Cash	2,500	
Accounts Receivable	1,800	
Roofing Supplies	1,100	
Equipment	6,000	
Accumulated Depreciation—Equipment		700
Accounts Payable		1,400
Unearned Revenue		300
J. Watt, Capital		7,000
J. Watt, Drawing	600	
Service Revenue		3,500
Salaries Expense	700	
Miscellaneous Expense	200	
	12,900	12,900

Other data:

1. A physical count reveals only $240 of roofing supplies on hand.
2. Depreciation for March is $200.
3. Unearned revenue amounted to $130 after adjustment on March 31.
4. Accrued salaries are $350.

Instructions

(a) Adjusted trial balance $13,450

(b) Net income $1,360
Total assets $9,640

(a) Enter the trial balance on a worksheet and complete the worksheet.

(b) Prepare an income statement and owner's equity statement for the month of March and a classified balance sheet at March 31. J. Watt did not make any additional investments in the business in March.

(c) Journalize the adjusting entries from the adjustments columns of the worksheet.

(d) Journalize the closing entries from the financial statement columns of the worksheet.

P4-2B The adjusted trial balance columns of the worksheet for Sparks Company, owned by Billy Sparks, are as follows.

Complete worksheet; prepare financial statements, closing entries, and post-closing trial balance.

(SO 1, 2, 3, 6)

GLS

SPARKS COMPANY
Worksheet
For the Year Ended December 31, 2008

Account No.	Account Titles	Adjusted Trial Balance Dr.	Adjusted Trial Balance Cr.
101	Cash	11,600	
112	Accounts Receivable	15,400	
126	Supplies	2,000	
130	Prepaid Insurance	2,800	
151	Office Equipment	34,000	
152	Accumulated Depreciation—Office Equipment		8,000
200	Notes Payable		20,000
201	Accounts Payable		9,000
212	Salaries Payable		3,500
230	Interest Payable		800
301	B. Sparks, Capital		25,000
306	B. Sparks, Drawing	10,000	
400	Service Revenue		85,000
610	Advertising Expense	12,000	
631	Supplies Expense	5,700	
711	Depreciation Expense	8,000	
722	Insurance Expense	5,000	
726	Salaries Expense	44,000	
905	Interest Expense	800	
	Totals	151,300	151,300

Instructions

(a) Complete the worksheet by extending the balances to the financial statement columns.

(b) Prepare an income statement, owner's equity statement, and a classified balance sheet. (*Note:* $10,000 of the notes payable become due in 2009.) Billy Sparks did not make any additional investments in the business during the year.

(c) Prepare the closing entries. Use J14 for the journal page.

(d) Post the closing entries. Use the three-column form of account. Income Summary is No. 350.

(e) Prepare a post-closing trial balance.

(a) Net income $9,500

(b) Current assets $31,800; Current liabilities $23,300

(e) Post-closing trial balance $65,800

P4-3B The completed financial statement columns of the worksheet for Molinda Company are shown below and on the next page.

Prepare financial statements, closing entries, and post-closing trial balance.

(SO 1, 2, 3, 6)

MOLINDA COMPANY
Worksheet
For the Year Ended December 31, 2008

Account No.	Account Titles	Income Statement Dr.	Income Statement Cr.	Balance Sheet Dr.	Balance Sheet Cr.
101	Cash			22,400	
112	Accounts Receivable			13,500	
130	Prepaid Insurance			3,500	
157	Equipment			26,000	
167	Accumulated Depreciation				5,600
201	Accounts Payable				11,300
212	Salaries Payable				3,000
301	Ann Molinda, Capital				36,000
306	Ann Molinda, Drawing			14,000	
400	Service Revenue		69,000		
622	Repair Expense	2,000			

Account No.	Account Titles	Income Statement Dr.	Income Statement Cr.	Balance Sheet Dr.	Balance Sheet Cr.
711	Depreciation Expense	2,600			
722	Insurance Expense	2,200			
726	Salaries Expense	37,000			
732	Utilities Expense	1,700			
	Totals	45,500	69,000	79,400	55,900
	Net Income	23,500			23,500
		69,000	69,000	79,400	79,400

(a) Ending capital $45,500; Total current assets $39,400

(d) Post-closing trial balance $65,400

Instructions

(a) Prepare an income statement, owner's equity statement, and a classified balance sheet.
(b) Prepare the closing entries. Ann did not make any additional investments during the year.
(c) Post the closing entries and rule and balance the accounts. Use T accounts. Income Summary is account No. 350.
(d) Prepare a post-closing trial balance.

Complete worksheet; prepare classified balance sheet, entries, and post-closing trial balance.

(SO 1, 2, 3, 6)

P4-4B Pettengill Management Services began business on January 1, 2008, with a capital investment of $120,000. The company manages condominiums for owners (Service Revenue) and rents space in its own office building (Rent Revenue). The trial balance and adjusted trial balance columns of the worksheet at the end of the first year are as follows.

PETTENGILL MANAGEMENT SERVICES
Worksheet
For the Year Ended December 31, 2008

Account Titles	Trial Balance Dr.	Trial Balance Cr.	Adjusted Trial Balance Dr.	Adjusted Trial Balance Cr.
Cash	11,500		11,500	
Accounts Receivable	23,600		23,600	
Prepaid Insurance	3,100		1,400	
Land	56,000		56,000	
Building	106,000		106,000	
Equipment	49,000		49,000	
Accounts Payable		10,400		10,400
Unearned Rent Revenue		5,000		2,800
Mortgage Note Payable		100,000		100,000
G. Pettengill, Capital		120,000		120,000
G. Pettengill, Drawing	18,000		18,000	
Service Revenue		75,600		75,600
Rent Revenue		24,000		26,200
Salaries Expense	35,000		35,000	
Advertising Expense	17,000		17,000	
Utilities Expense	15,800		15,800	
Totals	335,000	335,000		
Insurance Expense			1,700	
Depreciation Expense—Building			2,500	
Accumulated Depreciation—Building				2,500
Depreciation Expense—Equipment			3,900	
Accumulated Depreciation—Equipment				3,900
Interest Expense			9,000	
Interest Payable				9,000
Totals			350,400	350,400

(a) Net income $16,900

(b) Total current assets $36,500

Instructions

(a) Prepare a complete worksheet.
(b) Prepare a classified balance sheet. (*Note*: $10,000 of the mortgage note payable is due for payment next year.)

(c) Journalize the adjusting entries.
(d) Journalize the closing entries.
(e) Prepare a post-closing trial balance.

(e) Post-closing trial balance $247,500

P4-5B Lee Choi opened Choi's Window Washing on July 1, 2008. During July the following transactions were completed.

Complete all steps in accounting cycle.

(SO 1, 2, 3, 4, 6)

GLS

July	1	Choi invested $12,000 cash in the business.
	1	Purchased used truck for $6,000, paying $3,000 cash and the balance on account.
	3	Purchased cleaning supplies for $1,300 on account.
	5	Paid $2,400 cash on one-year insurance policy effective July 1.
	12	Billed customers $2,500 for cleaning services.
	18	Paid $1,000 cash on amount owed on truck and $800 on amount owed on cleaning supplies.
	20	Paid $1,200 cash for employee salaries.
	21	Collected $1,400 cash from customers billed on July 12.
	25	Billed customers $5,000 for cleaning services.
	31	Paid gas and oil for month on truck $200.
	31	Withdrew $900 cash for personal use.

The chart of accounts for Choi's Window Washing contains the following accounts: No. 101 Cash, No. 112 Accounts Receivable, No. 128 Cleaning Supplies, No. 130 Prepaid Insurance, No. 157 Equipment, No. 158 Accumulated Depreciation—Equipment, No. 201 Accounts Payable, No. 212 Salaries Payable, No. 301 Lee Choi, Capital, No. 306 Lee Choi, Drawing, No. 350 Income Summary, No. 400 Service Revenue, No. 633 Gas & Oil Expense, No. 634 Cleaning Supplies Expense, No. 711 Depreciation Expense, No. 722 Insurance Expense, and No. 726 Salaries Expense.

Instructions

(a) Journalize and post the July transactions. Use page J1 for the journal and the three-column form of account.
(b) Prepare a trial balance at July 31 on a worksheet.
(c) Enter the following adjustments on the worksheet and complete the worksheet.
  (1) Services provided but unbilled and uncollected at July 31 were $1,500.
  (2) Depreciation on equipment for the month was $300.
  (3) One-twelfth of the insurance expired.
  (4) An inventory count shows $400 of cleaning supplies on hand at July 31.
  (5) Accrued but unpaid employee salaries were $600.
(d) Prepare the income statement and owner's equity statement for July and a classified balance sheet at July 31.
(e) Journalize and post adjusting entries. Use page J2 for the journal.
(f) Journalize and post closing entries and complete the closing process. Use page J3 for the journal.
(g) Prepare a post-closing trial balance at July 31.

(b) Trial balance $22,000

(c) Adjusted trial balance $24,400

(d) Net income $5,600; Total assets $19,800

(g) Post-closing trial balance $20,100

PROBLEMS: SET C

Visit the book's website at **www.wiley.com/college/weygandt**, and choose the Student Companion site, to access Problem Set C.

COMPREHENSIVE PROBLEM: CHAPTERS 2 TO 4

Julie Molony opened Julie's Maids Cleaning Service on July 1, 2008. During July, the company completed the following transactions.

July	1	Invested $14,000 cash in the business.
	1	Purchased a used truck for $10,000, paying $3,000 cash and the balance on account.
	3	Purchased cleaning supplies for $800 on account.
	5	Paid $1,800 on a one-year insurance policy, effective July 1.
	12	Billed customers $3,800 for cleaning services.
	18	Paid $1,000 of amount owed on truck, and $400 of amount owed on cleaning supplies.
	20	Paid $1,600 for employee salaries.
	21	Collected $1,400 from customers billed on July 12.
	25	Billed customers $1,500 for cleaning services.

31 Paid gas and oil for the month on the truck, $400.
31 Withdrew $600 cash for personal use.

The chart of accounts for Julie's Maids Cleaning Service contains the following accounts: No. 101 Cash, No. 112 Accounts Receivable, No. 128 Cleaning Supplies, No. 130 Prepaid Insurance, No. 157 Equipment, No. 158 Accumulated Depreciation—Equipment, No. 201 Accounts Payable, No. 212 Salaries Payable, No. 301, Julie Molony, Capital, No. 306 Julie Molony, Drawing, No. 350 Income Summary, No. 400 Service Revenue, No. 633 Gas & Oil Expense, No. 634 Cleaning Supplies Expense, No. 711 Depreciation Expense, No. 722 Insurance Expense, and No. 726 Salaries Expense.

Instructions

(a) Journalize and post the July transactions. Use page J1 for the journal.

(b) Trial balance totals $25,700

(b) Prepare a trial balance at July 31 on a worksheet.

(c) Enter the following adjustments on the worksheet, and complete the worksheet.
- **(1)** Earned but unbilled fees at July 31 were $1,300.
- **(2)** Depreciation on equipment for the month was $200.
- **(3)** One-twelfth of the insurance expired.
- **(4)** An inventory count shows $100 of cleaning supplies on hand at July 31.
- **(5)** Accrued but unpaid employee salaries were $500.

(d) Net income $3,050
Total assets $23,350

(d) Prepare the income statement and statement of owner's equity for July, and a classified balance sheet at July 31, 2008.

(e) Journalize and post the adjusting entries. Use page J2 for the journal.

(f) Journalize and post the closing entries, and complete the closing process. Use page J3 for the journal.

(g) Trial balance totals $23,550

(g) Prepare a post-closing trial balance at July 31.

CONTINUING COOKIE CHRONICLE

(*Note*: This is a continuation of the Cookie Chronicle from Chapters 1 through 3.)

CCC4 Natalie had a very busy December. At the end of the month after journalizing and posting the December transactions and adjusting entries, Natalie prepared an adjusted trial balance. Using that information, she wants to prepare financial statements for the year-end, closing entries, and a post-closing trial balance.

Go to the book's website,
www.wiley.com/college/weygandt,
to see the completion of this problem.

BROADENING YOUR PERSPECTIVE

FINANCIAL REPORTING AND ANALYSIS

Financial Reporting Problem

PepsiCo, Inc.

BYP4-1 Appendix A at the end of this textbook presents the financial statements of PepsiCo.

Instructions

Answer the following questions using the Consolidated Balance Sheet and the Notes to Consolidated Financial Statements section.

(a) What were PepsiCo's total current assets at December 31, 2005 and December 25, 2004?

(b) Are assets that PepsiCo included under current assets listed in proper order? Explain.

(c) How are PepsiCo's assets classified?

(d) What are "cash equivalents"?
(e) What were PepsiCo 's total current liabilities at December 31, 2005 and December 25, 2004?

Comparative Analysis Problem

PepsiCo, Inc. vs. The Coca-Cola Company

BYP4-2 Appendix A presents PepsiCo's financial statements. Appendix B presents Coca-Cola's financial statements.

Instructions

(a) Based on the information contained in these financial statements, determine each of the following for PepsiCo at December 31, 2005, and for Coca-Cola at December 31, 2005.
  (1) Total current assets.
  (2) Net amount of property, plant, and equipment (land, buildings, and equipment).
  (3) Total current liabilities.
  (4) Total stockholders' (shareholders') equity.
(b) What conclusions concerning the companies' respective financial positions can be drawn?

Exploring the Web

BYP4-3 Numerous companies have established home pages on the Internet, e.g., Capt'n Eli Root Beer Company **(www.captneli.com/rootbeer.php)** and Kodak **(www.kodak.com)**.

Instructions

Examine the home pages of any two companies and answer the following questions.

(a) What type of information is available?
(b) Is any accounting-related information presented?
(c) Would you describe the home page as informative, promotional, or both? Why?

CRITICAL THINKING

Decision Making Across the Organization

BYP4-4 Whitegloves Janitorial Service was started 2 years ago by Nancy Kohl. Because business has been exceptionally good, Nancy decided on July 1, 2008, to expand operations by acquiring an additional truck and hiring two more assistants. To finance the expansion, Nancy obtained on July 1, 2008, a $25,000, 10% bank loan, payable $10,000 on July 1, 2009, and the balance on July 1, 2010. The terms of the loan require the borrower to have $10,000 more current assets than current liabilities at December 31, 2008. If these terms are not met, the bank loan will be refinanced at 15% interest. At December 31, 2008, the accountant for Whitegloves Janitorial Service Inc. prepared the balance sheet shown on page 190.

Nancy presented the balance sheet to the bank's loan officer on January 2, 2009, confident that the company had met the terms of the loan. The loan officer was not impressed. She said, "We need financial statements audited by a CPA." A CPA was hired and immediately realized that the balance sheet had been prepared from a trial balance and not from an adjusted trial balance. The adjustment data at the balance sheet date consisted of the following.

(1) Earned but unbilled janitorial services were $3,700.
(2) Janitorial supplies on hand were $2,500.
(3) Prepaid insurance was a 3-year policy dated January 1, 2008.
(4) December expenses incurred but unpaid at December 31, $500.
(5) Interest on the bank loan was not recorded.
(6) The amounts for property, plant, and equipment presented in the balance sheet were reported net of accumulated depreciation (cost less accumulated depreciation). These amounts were $4,000 for cleaning equipment and $5,000 for delivery trucks as of January 1, 2008. Depreciation for 2008 was $2,000 for cleaning equipment and $5,000 for delivery trucks.

WHITEGLOVES JANITORIAL SERVICE
Balance Sheet
December 31, 2008

Assets		**Liabilities and Owner's Equity**	
Current assets		Current liabilities	
Cash	$ 6,500	Notes payable	$10,000
Accounts receivable	9,000	Accounts payable	2,500
Janitorial supplies	5,200	Total current liabilities	12,500
Prepaid insurance	4,800	Long-term liability	
Total current assets	25,500	Notes payable	15,000
Property, plant, and equipment		Total liabilities	27,500
Cleaning equipment (net)	22,000	Owner's equity	
Delivery trucks (net)	34,000	Nancy Kohl, Capital	54,000
Total property, plant, and equipment	56,000		
Total assets	$81,500	Total liabilities and owner's equity	$81,500

Instructions

With the class divided into groups, answer the following.

(a) Prepare a correct balance sheet.
(b) Were the terms of the bank loan met? Explain.

Communication Activity

BYP4-5 The accounting cycle is important in understanding the accounting process.

Instructions

Write a memo to your instructor that lists the steps of the accounting cycle in the order they should be completed. End with a paragraph that explains the optional steps in the cycle.

Ethics Case

BYP4-6 As the controller of Breathless Perfume Company, you discover a misstatement that overstated net income in the prior year's financial statements. The misleading financial statements appear in the company's annual report which was issued to banks and other creditors less than a month ago. After much thought about the consequences of telling the president, Jerry McNabb, about this misstatement, you gather your courage to inform him. Jerry says, "Hey! What they don't know won't hurt them. But, just so we set the record straight, we'll adjust this year's financial statements for last year's misstatement. We can absorb that misstatement better in this year than in last year anyway! Just don't make such a mistake again."

Instructions

(a) Who are the stakeholders in this situation?
(b) What are the ethical issues in this situation?
(c) What would you do as a controller in this situation?

* "All About You" Activity

BYP4-7 Companies prepare balance sheets in order to know their financial position at a specific point in time. This enables them to make a comparison to their position at previous points in time, and gives them a basis for planning for the future. As discussed in the **All About You** feature in this chapter, in order to evaluate your financial position you need to prepare a personal balance sheet. Assume that you have compiled the following information regarding your finances. (*Hint:* Some of the items might not be used in your personal balance sheet.)

Amount owed on student loan balance (long-term)	$5,000
Balance in checking account	1,200
Certificate of deposit (6-month)	3,000
Annual earnings from part-time job	11,300

Automobile	7,000
Balance on automobile loan (current portion)	1,500
Balance on automobile loan (long-term portion)	4,000
Home computer	800
Amount owed to you by younger brother	300
Balance in money market account	1,800
Annual tuition	6,400
Video and stereo equipment	1,250
Balance owed on credit card (current portion)	150
Balance owed on credit card (long-term portion)	1,650

Instructions

Prepare a personal balance sheet using the format you have learned for a classified balance sheet for a company. For the capital account, use M. Y. Own, Capital.

Answers to Insight and Accounting Across the Organization Questions

p. 153 Cisco Performs the Virtual Close

Q: Who else benefits from a shorter closing process?

A: *Investors benefit from a shorter closing process. The shorter the closing, the sooner the company can report its financial results. This means that the financial information is more timely, and therefore more relevant to investors.*

p. 158 Yale Express Loses Some Transportation Bills

Q: What might Yale Express's vice president have done to produce more accurate financial statements without waiting months for Republic's outstanding transportation bills?

A: *Yale's vice president could have engaged his accountants and auditors to prepare an adjusting entry based on an estimate of the outstanding transportation bills. (The estimate could have been made using past experience and the current volume of business.)*

p. 163 Big Changes Are Coming to Chinese Balance Sheets

Q: What are the potential benefits and challenges presented by reporting assets like plant and equipment at market value rather than historical cost?

A: *Reporting assets at market value will provide investors with more relevant information. Most investors are more interested in what an asset is currently worth than in what it originally cost. However, determining the market value of some assets can be very subjective. Some companies may take advantage of this in order to obtain more desirable accounting results.*

Authors' Comments on *All About You:* Your Personal Balance Sheet (p. 165)

By deciding to go to school after high school, you have taken a big step toward improving your long-term personal finances. Post-high-school education increases your job opportunities, which increases your earning potential.

Although it is true that your earnings will probably increase considerably when you graduate, you should not wait until graduation to lay the groundwork for a sound financial plan. If you do not monitor your finances closely while you are in school, you could easily dig a deep hole that would be difficult to get out of. Controlling your spending now will give you better control of your personal finances by the time you graduate. A first step toward taking control of your finances is preparing a personal balance sheet. In later chapters we discuss topics that will give you the tools that you need to improve your financial position.

Software is available to help you identify your assets and liabilities and determine your net worth. See for example the net worth calculator at *http://www.bygpub.com/finance/NetWorthCalc.htm.*

Answers to PepsiCo Review It Question 2, p. 166

PepsiCo's current liabilities in 2005 were $9,406 million. Current liabilities in 2004 were $6,752 million. In both 2005 and 2004, current liabilities were less than current assets.

Answers to Self-Study Questions

1. b **2.** c **3.** a **4.** b **5.** c **6.** a **7.** d **8.** b **9.** d **10.** a **11.** c

Remember to go back to the Navigator box on the chapter-opening page and check off your completed work.

Chapter 5

Accounting for Merchandising Operations

STUDY OBJECTIVES

After studying this chapter, you should be able to:

1. Identify the differences between service and merchandising companies.
2. Explain the recording of purchases under a perpetual inventory system.
3. Explain the recording of sales revenues under a perpetual inventory system.
4. Explain the steps in the accounting cycle for a merchandising company.
5. Distinguish between a multiple-step and a single-step income statement.
6. Explain the computation and importance of gross profit.
7. Determine cost of goods sold under a periodic inventory system.

The Navigator

The Navigator

Scan **Study Objectives**

Read **Feature Story**

Read **Preview**

Read text and answer **Before You Go On**
p. 201 p. 203 p. 206 p. 212 p. 214

Work **Demonstration Problem**

Review **Summary of Study Objectives**

Answer **Self-Study Questions**

Complete **Assignments**

Feature Story

WHO DOESN'T SHOP AT WAL-MART?

In his book *The End of Work,* Jeremy Rifkin notes that until the 20th century the word *consumption* evoked negative images. To be labeled a "consumer" was an insult. In fact, one of the deadliest diseases in history, tuberculosis, was often referred to as "consumption." Twentieth-century merchants realized, however, that in order to prosper, they had to convince people of the need for things not previously needed. For example, General Motors made annual changes in its cars so that people would be discontented with the cars they already owned. Thus began consumerism.

Today consumption describes the U.S. lifestyle in a nutshell. We consume twice as much today per person as we did at the end of World War II. The amount of U.S. retail space per person is vastly greater than that of any other country. It appears that we live to shop.

The first great retail giant was Sears, Roebuck and Company. It started as a catalog company enabling people in rural areas to buy things by mail. For decades it was the uncontested merchandising leader.

Today Wal-Mart (*www.walmart.com*) is the undisputed champion provider of basic (and perhaps not-so-basic) human needs. Wal-Mart opened its first store in 1962, and it now has more than 6,000 stores, serving more than 100 million customers every week. A key cause of Wal-Mart's incredible growth is its amazing system of inventory control and distribution. Wal-Mart has a management information system that employs six satellite channels, from which company computers receive 8.4 million updates every minute on what items customers buy and the relationship among items sold to each person.

Measured by sales revenues, Wal-Mart is the largest company in the world. In six years it went from selling almost no groceries to being America's largest grocery retailer.

It would appear that things have never looked better at Wal-Mart. On the other hand, a *Wall Street Journal* article entitled "How to Sell More to Those Who Think It's Cool to Be Frugal" suggests that consumerism as a way of life might be dying. Don't bet your wide-screen TV on it, though.

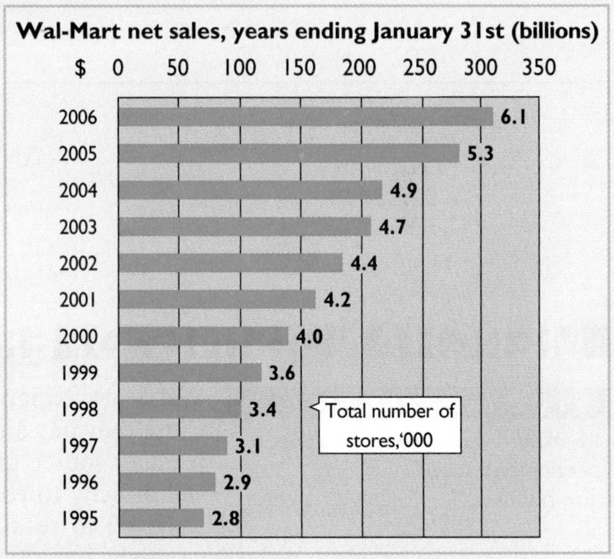

Sources: "How Big Can It Grow?" *The Economist*, April 17, 2004, pp. 67–69; and *www.walmart.com* (accessed May 1, 2006).

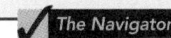

The Navigator

Inside Chapter 5...

Preview of Chapter 5

Merchandising is one of the largest and most influential industries in the United States. It is likely that a number of you will work for a merchandiser. Therefore, understanding the financial statements of merchandising companies is important. In this chapter you will learn the basics about reporting merchandising transactions. In addition, you will learn how to prepare and analyze a commonly used form of the income statement—the multiple-step income statement. The content and organization of the chapter are as follows.

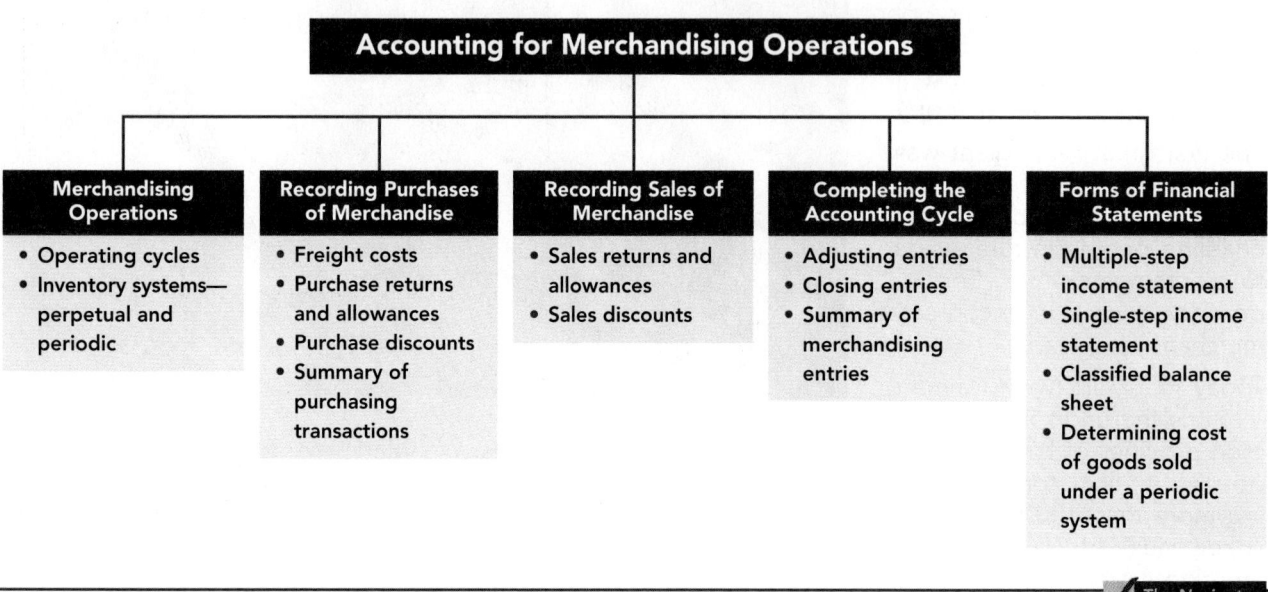

Accounting for Merchandising Operations

Merchandising Operations
- Operating cycles
- Inventory systems—perpetual and periodic

Recording Purchases of Merchandise
- Freight costs
- Purchase returns and allowances
- Purchase discounts
- Summary of purchasing transactions

Recording Sales of Merchandise
- Sales returns and allowances
- Sales discounts

Completing the Accounting Cycle
- Adjusting entries
- Closing entries
- Summary of merchandising entries

Forms of Financial Statements
- Multiple-step income statement
- Single-step income statement
- Classified balance sheet
- Determining cost of goods sold under a periodic system

✓ The Navigator

MERCHANDISING OPERATIONS

STUDY OBJECTIVE 1

Identify the differences between service and merchandising companies.

Wal-Mart, Kmart, and Target are called merchandising companies because they buy and sell merchandise rather than perform services as their primary source of revenue. Merchandising companies that purchase and sell directly to consumers are called **retailers**. Merchandising companies that sell to retailers are known as **wholesalers**. For example, retailer Walgreens might buy goods from wholesaler McKesson; retailer Office Depot might buy office supplies from wholesaler United Stationers. The primary source of revenues for merchandising companies is the sale of merchandise, often referred to simply as **sales revenue** or **sales**. A merchandising company has two categories of expenses: cost of goods sold and operating expenses.

Cost of goods sold is the total cost of merchandise sold during the period. This expense is directly related to the revenue recognized from the sale of goods. Illustration 5-1 (page 195) shows the income measurement process for a merchandising company. The items in the two blue boxes are unique to a merchandising company; they are not used by a service company.

Operating Cycles

The operating cycle of a merchandising company ordinarily is longer than that of a service company. The purchase of merchandise inventory and its eventual sale

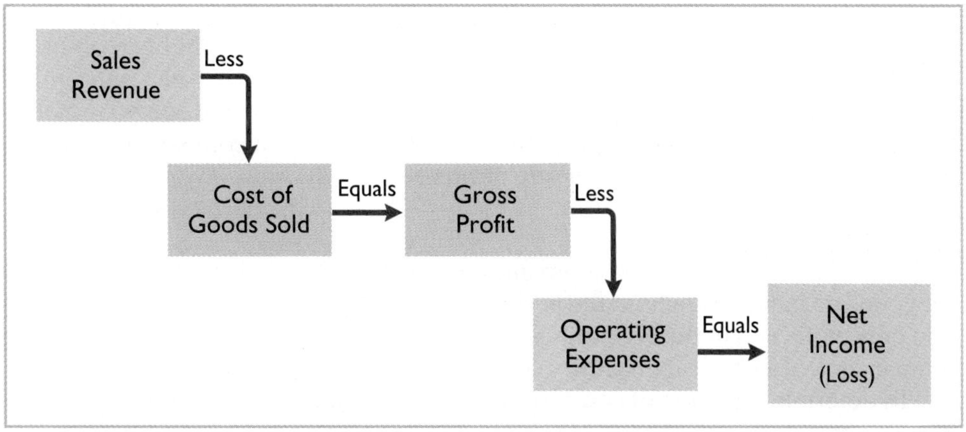

Illustration 5-1
Income measurement process for a merchandising company

lengthen the cycle. Illustration 5-2 contrasts the operating cycles of service and merchandising companies. Note that the added asset account for a merchandising company is the Merchandise Inventory account. Companies report merchandise inventory as a current asset on the balance sheet.

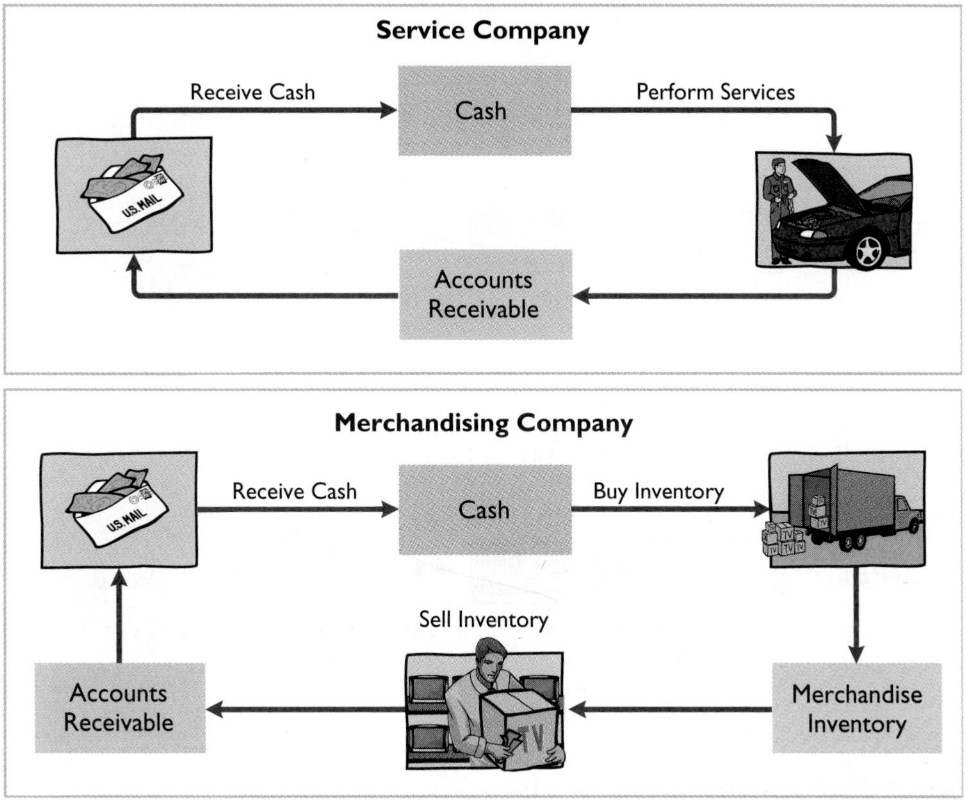

Illustration 5-2
Operating cycles for a service company and a merchandising company

Inventory Systems

A merchandising company keeps track of its inventory to determine what is available for sale and what has been sold. Companies use one of two systems to account for inventory: a **perpetual inventory system** or a **periodic inventory system**.

PERPETUAL SYSTEM

In a **perpetual inventory system**, companies keep detailed records of the cost of each inventory purchase and sale. These records continuously—perpetually—show

HELPFUL HINT
For control purposes companies take a physical inventory count under the perpetual system, even though it is not needed to determine cost of goods sold.

the inventory that should be on hand for every item. For example, a Ford dealership has separate inventory records for each automobile, truck, and van on its lot and showroom floor. Similarly, a Kroger grocery store uses bar codes and optical scanners to keep a daily running record of every box of cereal and every jar of jelly that it buys and sells. Under a perpetual inventory system, a company determines the cost of goods sold **each time a sale occurs**.

PERIODIC SYSTEM

In a **periodic inventory system**, companies do not keep detailed inventory records of the goods on hand throughout the period. Instead, they determine the cost of goods sold **only at the end of the accounting period**—that is, periodically. At that point, the company takes a physical inventory count to determine the cost of goods on hand.

To determine the cost of goods sold under a periodic inventory system, the following steps are necessary:

1. Determine the cost of goods on hand at the beginning of the accounting period.
2. Add to it the cost of goods purchased.
3. Subtract the cost of goods on hand at the end of the accounting period.

Illustration 5-3 graphically compares the sequence of activities and the timing of the cost of goods sold computation under the two inventory systems.

Illustration 5-3
Comparing perpetual and periodic inventory systems

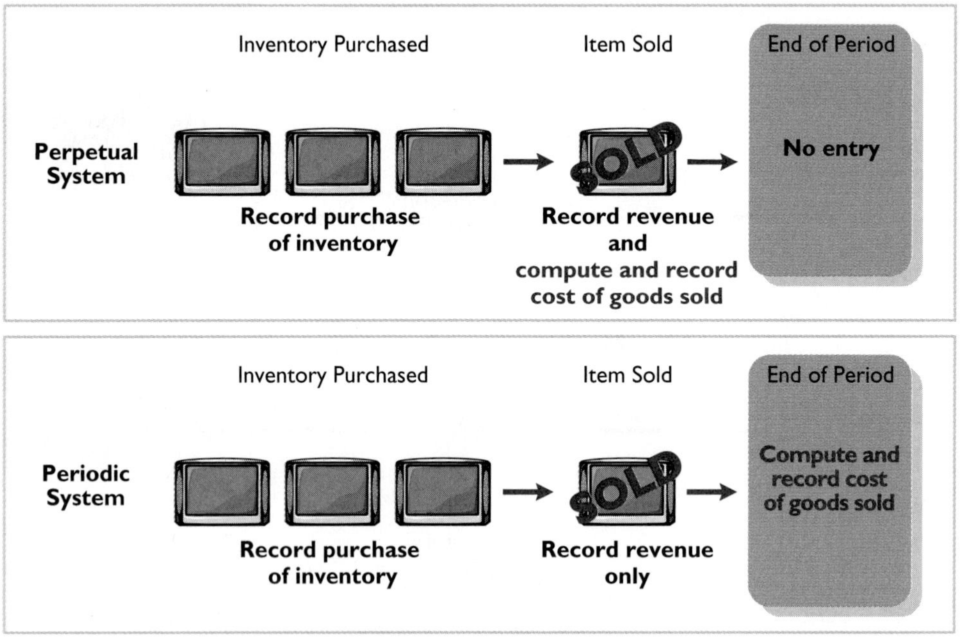

ADDITIONAL CONSIDERATIONS

Companies that sell merchandise with high unit values, such as automobiles, furniture, and major home appliances, have traditionally used perpetual systems. The growing use of computers and electronic scanners has enabled many more companies to install perpetual inventory systems. The perpetual inventory system is so named because the accounting records continuously—perpetually—show the quantity and cost of the inventory that should be on hand at any time.

A perpetual inventory system provides better control over inventories than a periodic system. Since the inventory records show the quantities that should be on hand, the company can count the goods at any time to see whether the amount of goods actually on hand agrees with the inventory records. If shortages are uncovered, the company can investigate immediately. Although a perpetual inventory system requires additional clerical work and additional cost to maintain the subsidiary records, a computerized system can minimize this cost. As noted in the Feature Story, much of Wal-Mart's success is attributed to its sophisticated inventory system.

Some businesses find it either unnecessary or uneconomical to invest in a computerized perpetual inventory system. Many small merchandising businesses, in particular, find that a perpetual inventory system costs more than it is worth. Managers of these businesses can control their merchandise and manage day-to-day operations using a periodic inventory system.

Because the perpetual inventory system is growing in popularity and use, we illustrate it in this chapter. Appendix 5A describes the journal entries for the periodic system.

INVESTOR INSIGHT

Morrow Snowboards Improves Its Stock Appeal

Investors are often eager to invest in a company that has a hot new product. However, when snowboard maker Morrow Snowboards, Inc., issued shares of stock to the public for the first time, some investors expressed reluctance to invest in Morrow because of a number of accounting control problems. To reduce investor concerns, Morrow implemented a perpetual inventory system to improve its control over inventory. In addition, it stated that it would perform a physical inventory count every quarter until it felt that the perpetual inventory system was reliable.

? If a perpetual system keeps track of inventory on a daily basis, why do companies ever need to do a physical count?

RECORDING PURCHASES OF MERCHANDISE

STUDY OBJECTIVE 2

Explain the recording of purchases under a perpetual inventory system.

Companies purchase inventory using cash or credit (on account). They normally record purchases when they receive the goods from the seller. Business documents provide written evidence of the transaction. A canceled check or a cash register receipt, for example, indicate the items purchased and amounts paid for each cash purchase. Companies record cash purchases by an increase in Merchandise Inventory and a decrease in Cash.

A **purchase invoice** should support each credit purchase. This invoice indicates the total purchase price and other relevant information. The purchaser uses the copy of the sales invoice sent by the seller as a purchase invoice. In Illustration 5-4 (page 198), for example, Sauk Stereo (the buyer) uses as a purchase invoice the sales invoice prepared by PW Audio Supply, Inc. (the seller).

Sauk Stereo makes the following journal entry to record its purchase from PW Audio Supply. The entry increases (debits) Merchandise Inventory and increases (credits) Accounts Payable.

May	4	Merchandise Inventory	3,800	
		Accounts Payable		3,800
		(To record goods purchased on account from PW Audio Supply)		

A	=	L	+	OE
+3,800				
		+3,800		

Cash Flows
no effect

Under the perpetual inventory system, companies record in the Merchandise Inventory account the purchase of goods they intend to sell. Thus, Wal-Mart would

Illustration 5-4
Sales invoice used as purchase invoice by Sauk Stereo

INVOICE NO. 731

PW Audio Supply, Inc.
27 Circle Drive
Harding, Michigan 48281

SOLD TO

Firm Name: Sauk Stereo
Attention of: James Hoover, Purchasing Agent
Address: 125 Main Street
City: Chelsea State: Illinois Zip: 60915

Date 5/4/08	Salesperson Malone	Terms 2/10, n/30	Freight Paid by Buyer	
Catalog No.	**Description**	**Quantity**	**Price**	**Amount**
X572Y9820	Printed Circuit Board-prototype	1	2,300	$2,300
A2547Z45	Production Model Circuits	5	300	1,500
IMPORTANT: ALL RETURNS MUST BE MADE WITHIN 10 DAYS			**TOTAL**	$3,800

HELPFUL HINT

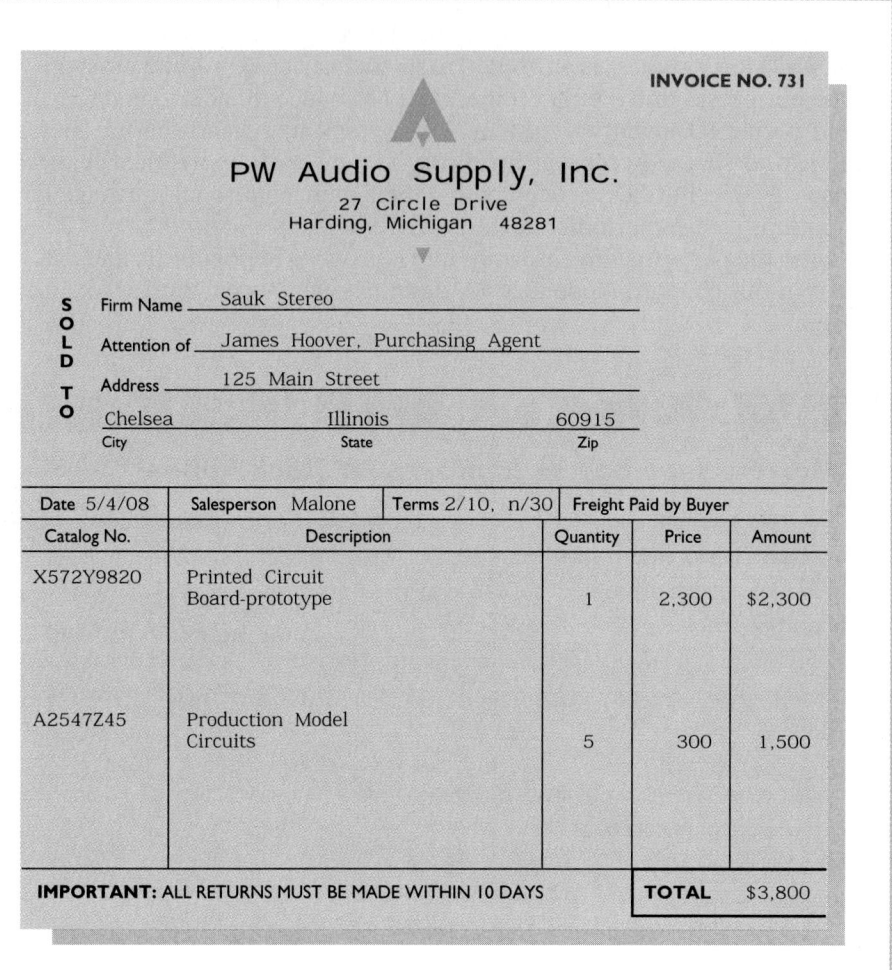

To better understand the contents of this invoice, identify these items:

1. **Seller**
2. **Invoice date**
3. **Purchaser**
4. **Salesperson**
5. **Credit terms**
6. **Freight terms**
7. **Goods sold: catalog number, description, quantity, price per unit**
8. **Total invoice amount**

increase (debit) Merchandise Inventory for clothing, sporting goods, and anything else purchased for resale to customers.

Not all purchases are debited to Merchandise Inventory, however. Companies record purchases of assets acquired for use and not for resale, such as supplies, equipment, and similar items, as increases to specific asset accounts rather than to Merchandise Inventory. For example, to record the purchase of materials used to make shelf signs or for cash register receipt paper, Wal-Mart would increase Supplies.

Freight Costs

The sales agreement should indicate who—the seller or the buyer—is to pay for transporting the goods to the buyer's place of business. When a common carrier such as a railroad, trucking company, or airline transports the goods, the carrier prepares a freight bill in accord with the sales agreement.

Freight terms are expressed as either FOB shipping point or FOB destination. The letters FOB mean **free on board**. Thus, **FOB shipping point** means that the seller places the goods free on board the carrier, and the buyer pays the freight costs. Conversely, **FOB destination** means that the seller places the goods free on board to the buyer's place of business, and the seller pays the freight. For example, the sales invoice in Illustration 5-4 (above) indicates that the buyer (Sauk Stereo) pays the freight charges.

When the purchaser incurs the freight costs, it debits (increases) the account Merchandise Inventory for those costs. For example, if upon delivery of the goods on May 6, Sauk Stereo pays Acme Freight Company $150 for freight charges, the entry on Sauk Stereo's books is:

May 6	Merchandise Inventory	150	
	Cash		150
	(To record payment of freight on goods purchased)		

A	=	L	+	OE
+150				
−150				

Cash Flows
−150

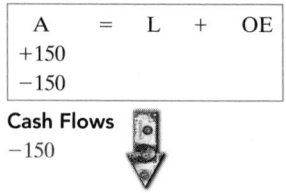

In contrast, **freight costs incurred by the seller on outgoing merchandise are an operating expense to the seller.** These costs increase an expense account titled Freight-out or Delivery Expense. If the freight terms on the invoice in Illustration 5-4 had required PW Audio Supply to pay the freight charges, the entry by PW Audio Supply would have been:

May 4	Freight-out (or Delivery Expense)	150	
	Cash		150
	(To record payment of freight on goods sold)		

A	=	L	+	OE
				−150 Exp
−150				

Cash Flows
−150

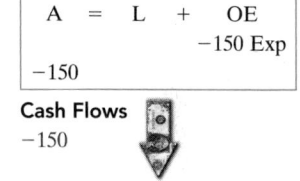

When the seller pays the freight charges, it will usually establish a higher invoice price for the goods to cover the shipping expense.

Purchase Returns and Allowances

A purchaser may be dissatisfied with the merchandise received because the goods are damaged or defective, of inferior quality, or do not meet the purchaser's specifications. In such cases, the purchaser may return the goods to the seller for credit if the sale was made on credit, or for a cash refund if the purchase was for cash. This transaction is known as a **purchase return**. Alternatively, the purchaser may choose to keep the merchandise if the seller is willing to grant an allowance (deduction) from the purchase price. This transaction is known as a **purchase allowance**.

Assume that on May 8 Sauk Stereo returned to PW Audio Supply goods costing $300. The following entry by Sauk Stereo for the returned merchandise decreases (debits) Accounts Payable and decreases (credits) Merchandise Inventory.

May 8	Accounts Payable	300	
	Merchandise Inventory		300
	(To record return of goods purchased from PW Audio Supply)		

A	=	L	+	OE
		−300		
−300				

Cash Flows
no effect

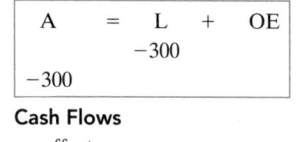

Because Sauk Stereo increased Merchandise Inventory when the goods were received, Merchandise Inventory is decreased when Sauk returns the goods (or when it is granted an allowance).

Purchase Discounts

The credit terms of a purchase on account may permit the buyer to claim a cash discount for prompt payment. The buyer calls this cash discount a **purchase discount**. This incentive offers advantages to both parties: The purchaser saves money, and the seller shortens the operating cycle by more quickly converting the accounts receivable into cash.

Credit terms specify the amount of the cash discount and time period in which it is offered. They also indicate the time period in which the purchaser is expected

HELPFUL HINT
The term *net* in "net 30" means the remaining amount due after subtracting any sales returns and allowances and partial payments.

to pay the full invoice price. In the sales invoice in Illustration 5-4 (page 198) credit terms are 2/10, n/30, which is read "two-ten, net thirty." This means that the buyer may take a 2% cash discount on the invoice price less ("net of") any returns or allowances, if payment is made within 10 days of the invoice date (the **discount period**). If the buyer does not pay in that time, the invoice price, less any returns or allowances, is due 30 days from the invoice date.

Alternatively, the discount period may extend to a specified number of days following the month in which the sale occurs. For example, 1/10 EOM (end of month) means that a 1% discount is available if the invoice is paid within the first 10 days of the next month.

When the seller elects not to offer a cash discount for prompt payment, credit terms will specify only the maximum time period for paying the balance due. For example, the invoice may state the time period as n/30, n/60, or n/10 EOM. This means, respectively, that the buyer must pay the net amount in 30 days, 60 days, or within the first 10 days of the next month.

When the buyer pays an invoice within the discount period, the amount of the discount decreases Merchandise Inventory. Why? Because companies record inventory at cost and, by paying within the discount period, the merchandiser has reduced that cost. To illustrate, assume Sauk Stereo pays the balance due of $3,500 (gross invoice price of $3,800 less purchase returns and allowances of $300) on May 14, the last day of the discount period. The cash discount is $70 ($3,500 × 2%), and Sauk Stereo pays $3,430 ($3,500 − $70). The entry Sauk makes to record its May 14 payment decreases (debits) Accounts Payable by the amount of the gross invoice price, reduces (credits) Merchandise Inventory by the $70 discount, and reduces (credits) Cash by the net amount owed.

A	=	L	+	OE
		−3,500		
−3,430				
−70				

Cash Flows
−3,430

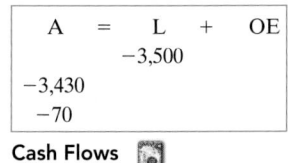

May 14	Accounts Payable	3,500	
	Cash		3,430
	Merchandise Inventory		70
	(To record payment within discount period)		

If Sauk Stereo failed to take the discount, and instead made full payment of $3,500 on June 3, it would debit Accounts Payable and credit Cash for $3,500 each.

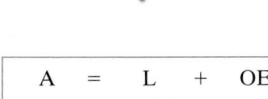

A	=	L	+	OE
		−3,500		
−3,500				

Cash Flows
−3,500

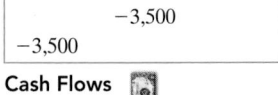

June 3	Accounts Payable	3,500	
	Cash		3,500
	(To record payment with no discount taken)		

As a rule, a company usually should take all available discounts. Passing up the discount may be viewed as **paying interest** for use of the money. For example, passing up the discount offered by PW Audio would be comparable to Sauk Stereo paying an interest rate of 2% for the use of $3,500 for 20 days. This is the equivalent of an annual interest rate of approximately 36.5% (2% × 365/20). Obviously, it would be better for Sauk Stereo to borrow at prevailing bank interest rates of 6% to 10% than to lose the discount.

Summary of Purchasing Transactions

The following T account (with transaction descriptions in blue) provides a summary of the effect of the previous transactions on Merchandise Inventory. Sauk originally purchased $3,800 worth of inventory for resale. It then returned $300 of goods. It paid $150 in freight charges, and finally, it received a $70 discount off the balance owed because it paid within the discount period. This results in a balance in Merchandise Inventory of $3,580.

Merchandise Inventory

Purchase	May 4	3,800	May 8	300	Purchase return
Freight-in	6	150	14	70	Purchase discount
Balance		3,580			

Before You Go On...

REVIEW IT

1. How does a merchandising company measure net income differently from a service company?
2. In what ways is a perpetual inventory system different from a periodic system?
3. Under the perpetual inventory system, what entries do companies make to record purchases, purchase returns and allowances, purchase discounts, and freight costs?

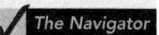

✓ The Navigator

RECORDING SALES OF MERCHANDISE

STUDY OBJECTIVE 3

Explain the recording of sales revenues under a perpetual inventory system.

Companies record sales revenues, like service revenues, when earned, in compliance with the revenue recognition principle. Typically, companies earn sales revenues when the goods transfer from the seller to the buyer. At this point the sales transaction is complete and the sales price established.

Sales may be made on credit or for cash. A **business document** should support every sales transaction, to provide written evidence of the sale. **Cash register tapes** provide evidence of cash sales. A **sales invoice**, like the one shown in Illustration 5-4 (page 198), provides support for a credit sale. The original copy of the invoice goes to the customer, and the seller keeps a copy for use in recording the sale. The invoice shows the date of sale, customer name, total sales price, and other relevant information.

The seller makes two entries for each sale. The first entry records the sale: The seller increases (debits) Cash (or Accounts Receivable, if a credit sale), and also increases (credits) Sales for the invoice price of the goods. The second entry records the cost of the merchandise sold: The seller increases (debits) Cost of Goods Sold, and also decreases (credits) Merchandise Inventory for the cost of those goods. As a result, the Merchandise Inventory account will show at all times the amount of inventory that should be on hand.

To illustrate a credit sales transaction, PW Audio Supply records its May 4 sale of $3,800 to Sauk Stereo (see Illustration 5-4) as follows. (Here, we assume the merchandise cost PW Audio Supply $2,400.)

May	4	Accounts Receivable	3,800	
		Sales		3,800
		(To record credit sale to Sauk Stereo per invoice #731)		

A	=	L	+	OE
+3,800				+3,800 Rev

Cash Flows
no effect

	4	Cost of Goods Sold	2,400	
		Merchandise Inventory		2,400
		(To record cost of merchandise sold on invoice #731 to Sauk Stereo)		

A	=	L	+	OE
				−2,400 Exp
−2,400				

Cash Flows
no effect

HELPFUL HINT
The merchandiser credits the Sales account only for sales of goods held for resale. Sales of assets not held for resale, such as equipment or land, are credited directly to the asset account.

For internal decision-making purposes, merchandising companies may use more than one sales account. For example, PW Audio Supply may decide to keep separate sales accounts for its sales of TV sets, DVD recorders, and satellite radio receivers. Wal-Mart might use separate accounts for sporting goods, children's clothing, and hardware—or it might have even more narrowly defined accounts. By using separate sales accounts for major product lines, rather than a single combined sales account, company management can more closely monitor sales trends and respond more strategically to changes in sales patterns. For example, if HDTV sales are increasing while DVD-player sales are decreasing, PW Audio Supply might reevaluate both its advertising and pricing policies on these items to ensure they are optimal.

On its income statement presented to outside investors, a merchandising company normally would provide only a single sales figure—the sum of all of its individual sales accounts. This is done for two reasons. First, providing detail on all of its individual sales accounts would add considerable length to its income statement. Second, companies do not want their competitors to know the details of their operating results. However, Microsoft recently expanded its disclosure of revenue from three to five types. The reason: The additional categories will better enable financial statement users to evaluate the growth of the company's consumer and Internet businesses.

ETHICS NOTE
Many companies are trying to improve the quality of their financial reporting. For example, General Electric now provides more detail on its revenues and operating profits.

Sales Returns and Allowances

We now look at the "flipside" of purchase returns and allowances, which the seller records as **sales returns and allowances**. PW Audio Supply's entries to record credit for returned goods involve (1) an increase in Sales Returns and Allowances and a decrease in Accounts Receivable at the $300 selling price, and (2) an increase in Merchandise Inventory (assume a $140 cost) and a decrease in Cost of Goods Sold as shown below. (We have assumed that the goods were not defective. If they were defective, PW Audio would make an adjustment to the inventory account to reflect their decline in value.)

A	=	L	+	OE
				−300 Rev
−300				

Cash Flows
no effect

May 8	Sales Returns and Allowances	300	
	Accounts Receivable		300
	(To record credit granted to Sauk Stereo for returned goods)		

A	=	L	+	OE
+140				
				+140 Exp

Cash Flows
no effect

8	Merchandise Inventory	140	
	Cost of Goods Sold		140
	(To record cost of goods returned)		

If Sauk returns goods because they are damaged or defective, then PW Audio Supply's entry to Merchandise Inventory and Cost of Goods Sold should be for the estimated value of the returned goods, rather than their cost. For example, if the returned goods were defective and had a scrap value of $50, PW Audio would debit Merchandise Inventory for $50, and would credit Cost of Goods Sold for $50.

Sales Returns and Allowances is a **contra-revenue account** to Sales. The normal balance of Sales Returns and Allowances is a debit. Companies use a contra account, instead of debiting Sales, to disclose in the accounts and in the income statement the amount of sales returns and allowances. Disclosure of this information is important to management: Excessive returns and allowances may suggest problems—inferior merchandise, inefficiencies in filling orders, errors in billing customers, or delivery or shipment mistakes. Moreover, a decrease (debit) recorded directly to Sales would obscure the relative importance of sales returns and allowances as a percentage of sales. It also could distort comparisons between total sales in different accounting periods.

ACCOUNTING ACROSS THE ORGANIZATION

Should Publishers Have Liberal Return Policies?

In most industries sales returns are relatively minor. In the publishing industry, however, bookstores are allowed to return unsold hardcover books to the publisher. Marketing managers at the publishing companies argue that these generous return policies are necessary to encourage bookstores to buy a broader range of books, instead of focusing just on "sure things."

But with returns of hardcover books now exceeding 34% of sales, this generous return policy is taking its toll on net income. Production and inventory managers are quick to point out the many costs of excess returns. Publishers must pay to have the books shipped back to their warehouse, sorted, and then shipped to discounters. If the discounters don't sell them, the books are repackaged again, shipped back to the publisher, and destroyed. Some bookstores and publishers have proposed adopting a "no returns" policy, but no company wants to be the first to implement it.

Source: Jeffrey A Trachtenberg, "Quest for Best Seller Creates a Pileup of Returned Books," *Wall Street Journal* (June 3, 2005), p. A1.

? If a company expects significant returns, what are the implications for revenue recognition?

Sales Discounts

As mentioned earlier, the seller may offer the customer a cash discount—called by the seller a **sales discount**—for the prompt payment of the balance due. It is based on the invoice price less returns and allowances, if any. The seller increases (debits) the Sales Discounts account for discounts that are taken. For example, PW Audio Supply makes the following entry to record the cash receipt on May 14 from Sauk Stereo within the discount period.

May 14	Cash	3,430	
	Sales Discounts	70	
	Accounts Receivable		3,500
	(To record collection within 2/10, n/30 discount period from Sauk Stereo)		

A	=	L	+	OE
+3,430				
				−70 Rev
−3,500				

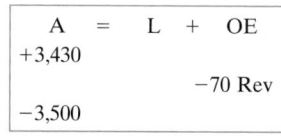

Cash Flows
+3,430

Like Sales Returns and Allowances, Sales Discounts is a **contra-revenue account** to Sales. Its normal balance is a debit. PW Audio uses this account, instead of debiting sales, to disclose the amount of cash discounts taken by customers. If Sauk Stereo does not take the discount, PW Audio Supply increases Cash for $3,500 and decreases Accounts Receivable for the same amount at the date of collection.

Before You Go On...

REVIEW IT

1. Under a perpetual inventory system, what are the two entries that a selling company must record at the time of each sale?
2. Why is it important to use the Sales Returns and Allowances account, rather than simply reducing the Sales account, when purchasers return goods?

DO IT

On September 5, De La Hoya Company buys merchandise on account from Junot Diaz Company. The selling price of the goods is $1,500, and the cost to Diaz Company was $800. On September 8, De La Hoya returns defective goods with a selling price of $200 and a scrap value of $80. Record the transactions on the books of both companies.

Action Plan

- Purchaser records goods at cost.
- Seller records both the sale and the cost of goods sold at the time of the sale.
- When goods are returned, purchaser reduces Merchandise Inventory, but seller records the return in a contra account, Sales Returns and Allowances.

Solution

De La Hoya Company

Sept.	5	Merchandise Inventory	1,500	
		Accounts Payable		1,500
		(To record goods purchased on account)		
Sept.	8	Accounts Payable	200	
		Merchandise Inventory		200
		(To record return of defective goods)		

Junot Diaz Company

Sept.	5	Accounts Receivable	1,500	
		Sales		1,500
		(To record credit sale)		
	5	Cost of Goods Sold	800	
		Merchandise Inventory		800
		(To record cost of goods sold on account)		
Sept.	8	Sales Returns and Allowances	200	
		Accounts Receivable		200
		(To record credit granted for receipt of returned goods)		
	8	Merchandise Inventory	80	
		Cost of Goods Sold		80
		(To record scrap value of goods returned)		

Related exercise material: *BE5-2, BE5-3, BE5-4, E5-2, E5-3, E5-4, and E5-5.*

✓ The Navigator

COMPLETING THE ACCOUNTING CYCLE

STUDY OBJECTIVE 4

Explain the steps in the accounting cycle for a merchandising company.

Up to this point, we have illustrated the basic entries for transactions relating to purchases and sales in a perpetual inventory system. Now we consider the remaining steps in the accounting cycle for a merchandising company. Each of the required steps described in Chapter 4 for service companies apply to merchandising companies. Appendix 5B to this chapter shows use of a worksheet by a merchandiser (an optional step).

Adjusting Entries

A merchandising company generally has the same types of adjusting entries as a service company. However, a merchandiser using a perpetual system will require one additional adjustment to make the records agree with the actual inventory on hand. Here's why: At the end of each period, for control purposes, a merchandising company that uses a perpetual system will take a physical count of its goods on hand. The company's unadjusted balance in Merchandise Inventory usually does not agree with the actual amount of inventory on hand. The perpetual inventory records may be incorrect due to recording errors, theft, or waste. Thus, the company needs to adjust the perpetual records to make the recorded inventory amount agree with the inventory on hand. **This involves adjusting Merchandise Inventory and Cost of Goods Sold.**

For example, suppose that PW Audio Supply has an unadjusted balance of $40,500 in Merchandise Inventory. Through a physical count, PW Audio determines that its actual merchandise inventory at year-end is $40,000. The company would make an adjusting entry to debit Cost of Goods Sold for $500 and to credit Merchandise Inventory for $500.

Closing Entries

A merchandising company, like a service company, closes to Income Summary all accounts that affect net income. In journalizing, the company credits all temporary accounts with debit balances, and debits all temporary accounts with credit balances, as shown below for PW Audio Supply. Note that PW Audio closes Cost of Goods Sold to Income Summary.

Dec. 31	Sales	480,000	
	Income Summary		480,000
	(To close income statement accounts with credit balances)		
31	Income Summary	450,000	
	Sales Returns and Allowances		12,000
	Sales Discounts		8,000
	Cost of Goods Sold		316,000
	Store Salaries Expense		45,000
	Administrative Salaries Expense		19,000
	Freight-out		7,000
	Advertising Expense		16,000
	Utilities Expense		17,000
	Depreciation Expense		8,000
	Insurance Expense		2,000
	(To close income statement accounts with debit balances)		
31	Income Summary	30,000	
	R.A. Lamb, Capital		30,000
	(To close net income to capital)		
31	R.A. Lamb, Capital	15,000	
	R.A. Lamb, Drawing		15,000
	(To close drawings to capital)		

HELPFUL HINT

The easiest way to prepare the first two closing entries is to identify the temporary accounts by their balances and then prepare one entry for the credits and one for the debits.

After PW Audio has posted the closing entries, all temporary accounts have zero balances. In addition, R.A. Lamb, Capital has a credit balance of $98,000: Beginning balance + Net income − Drawings ($83,000 + $30,000 − $15,000).

Summary of Merchandising Entries

Illustration 5-5 summarizes the entries for the merchandising accounts using a perpetual inventory system.

Illustration 5-5
Daily recurring and adjusting and closing entries

	Transactions	Daily Recurring Entries	Dr.	Cr.
Sales Transactions	Selling merchandise to customers.	Cash or Accounts Receivable	XX	
		Sales		XX
		Cost of Goods Sold	XX	
		Merchandise Inventory		XX
	Granting sales returns or allowances to customers.	Sales Returns and Allowances	XX	
		Cash or Accounts Receivable		XX
		Merchandise Inventory	XX	
		Cost of Goods Sold		XX
	Paying freight costs on sales; FOB destination.	Freight-out	XX	
		Cash		XX
	Receiving payment from customers within discount period.	Cash	XX	
		Sales Discounts	XX	
		Accounts Receivable		XX
Purchase Transactions	Purchasing merchandise for resale.	Merchandise Inventory	XX	
		Cash or Accounts Payable		XX
	Paying freight costs on merchandise purchased; FOB shipping point.	Merchandise Inventory	XX	
		Cash		XX
	Receiving purchase returns or allowances from suppliers.	Cash or Accounts Payable	XX	
		Merchandise Inventory		XX
	Paying suppliers within discount period.	Accounts Payable	XX	
		Merchandise Inventory		XX
		Cash		XX
	Events	**Adjusting and Closing Entries**		
	Adjust because book amount is higher than the inventory amount determined to be on hand.	Cost of Goods Sold	XX	
		Merchandise Inventory		XX
	Closing temporary accounts with credit balances.	Sales	XX	
		Income Summary		XX
	Closing temporary accounts with debit balances.	Income Summary	XX	
		Sales Returns and Allowances		XX
		Sales Discounts		XX
		Cost of Goods Sold		XX
		Freight-out		XX
		Expenses		XX

Before You Go On...

REVIEW IT

1. Why do merchandising companies usually need to make an adjustment to the Merchandise Inventory account?
2. What merchandising account(s) will appear in the post-closing trial balance?

DO IT

The trial balance of Celine's Sports Wear Shop at December 31 shows Merchandise Inventory $25,000, Sales $162,400, Sales Returns and Allowances $4,800, Sales Discounts $3,600, Cost of Goods Sold $110,000, Rental Revenue $6,000, Freight-out $1,800, Rent Expense $8,800, and Salaries and Wages Expense $22,000. Prepare the closing entries for the above accounts.

Action Plan

- Close all temporary accounts with credit balances to Income Summary by debiting these accounts.
- Close all temporary accounts with debit balances to Income Summary by crediting these accounts.

Solution The two closing entries are:

Dec. 31	Sales	162,400	
	Rental Revenue	6,000	
	Income Summary		168,400
	(To close accounts with credit balances)		
31	Income Summary	151,000	
	Cost of Goods Sold		110,000
	Sales Returns and Allowances		4,800
	Sales Discounts		3,600
	Freight-out		1,800
	Rent Expense		8,800
	Salaries and Wages Expense		22,000
	(To close accounts with debit balances)		

Related exercise material: *BE5-5, BE5-6, E5-6, E5-7, and E5-8.*

✓ The Navigator

FORMS OF FINANCIAL STATEMENTS

STUDY OBJECTIVE 5

Distinguish between a multiple-step and a single-step income statement.

Merchandising companies widely use the classified balance sheet introduced in Chapter 4 and one of two forms for the income statement. This section explains the use of these financial statements by merchandisers.

Multiple-Step Income Statement

The **multiple-step income statement** is so named because it shows several steps in determining net income. Two of these steps relate to the company's principal operating activities. A multiple-step statement also distinguishes between **operating** and **non-operating activities**. Finally, the statement also highlights intermediate components of income and shows subgroupings of expenses.

INCOME STATEMENT PRESENTATION OF SALES

The multiple-step income statement begins by presenting **sales revenue**. It then deducts contra-revenue accounts—sales returns and allowances, and sales discounts—to arrive at **net sales**. Illustration 5-6 (page 208) presents the sales revenues section for PW Audio Supply, using assumed data.

Illustration 5-6
Computation of net sales

PW AUDIO SUPPLY
Income Statement (partial)

Sales revenues		
Sales		$480,000
Less: Sales returns and allowances	$12,000	
Sales discounts	8,000	20,000
Net sales		**$460,000**

This presentation discloses the key data about the company's principal revenue-producing activities.

GROSS PROFIT

STUDY OBJECTIVE 6
Explain the computation and importance of gross profit.

From Illustration 5-1, you learned that companies deduct from sales revenue the cost of goods sold in order to determine **gross profit**. For this computation, companies use **net sales** as the amount of sales revenue. On the basis of the sales data in Illustration 5-6 (net sales of $460,000) and cost of goods sold under the perpetual inventory system (assume $316,000), PW Audio's gross profit is $144,000, computed as follows.

Illustration 5-7
Computation of gross profit

Net sales	$460,000
Cost of goods sold	316,000
Gross profit	**$144,000**

We also can express a company's gross profit as a percentage, called the **gross profit rate**. To do so, we divide the amount of gross profit by net sales. For PW Audio, the **gross profit rate** is 31.3%, computed as follows.

Illustration 5-8
Gross profit rate formula and computation

Gross Profit	÷	Net Sales	=	Gross Profit Rate
$144,000	÷	$460,000	=	**31.3%**

Analysts generally consider the gross profit **rate** to be more useful than the gross profit **amount**. The rate expresses a more meaningful (qualitative) relationship between net sales and gross profit. For example, a gross profit of $1,000,000 may sound impressive. But if it is the result of a gross profit rate of only 7%, it is not so impressive. The gross profit rate tells how many cents of each sales dollar go to gross profit.

Gross profit represents the **merchandising profit** of a company. It is not a measure of the overall profitability, because operating expenses are not yet deducted. But managers and other interested parties closely watch the amount and trend of gross profit. They compare current gross profit with amounts reported in past periods. They also compare the company's gross profit rate with rates of competitors and with industry averages. Such comparisons provide information about the effectiveness of a company's purchasing function and the soundness of its pricing policies.

OPERATING EXPENSES AND NET INCOME

Operating expenses are the next component in measuring a merchandising company's net income. They are the expenses incurred in the process of earning sales revenue. These expenses are similar in merchandising and service enterprises. At

PW Audio, operating expenses were $114,000. The company's net income is determined by subtracting operating expenses from gross profit. Thus, net income is $30,000, as calculated below.

Gross profit	$144,000
Operating expenses	**114,000**
Net income	$ 30,000

Illustration 5-9
Operating expenses in computing net income

The net income amount is the so-called "bottom line" of a company's income statement.

SUBGROUPING OF OPERATING EXPENSES

Larger companies often subdivide operating expenses into selling expenses and administrative expenses. **Selling expenses** are those associated with making sales. They include expenses for sales promotion and expenses of completing the sale, such as delivery and shipping. **Administrative expenses** (sometimes called general expenses) relate to general operating activities such as personnel management, accounting, and store security.

When companies use these subgroupings, they may need to prorate some expenses (e.g., 70% to selling and 30% to administrative expenses). For example, if a company uses a store building for both selling and general functions, it will need to allocate to the two categories building expenses such as depreciation, utilities, and property taxes.

Any reasonable classification of expenses that serves to inform those who use the statement is satisfactory. The present tendency in statements prepared for management's internal use is to present in considerable detail expense data grouped along lines of responsibility.

NONOPERATING ACTIVITIES

Nonoperating activities consist of various revenues and expenses and gains and losses that are unrelated to the company's main line of operations. When nonoperating items are included, the label "**Income from operations**" (or "Operating income") precedes them. This label clearly identifies the results of the company's normal operations, an amount determined by subtracting cost of goods sold and operating expenses from net sales. The results of nonoperating activities are shown in the categories "**Other revenues and gains**" and "**Other expenses and losses.**" Illustration 5-10 lists examples of each.

Other Revenues and Gains
Interest revenue from notes receivable and marketable securities.
Dividend revenue from investments in capital stock.
Rent revenue from subleasing a portion of the store.
Gain from the sale of property, plant, and equipment.
Other Expenses and Losses
Interest expense on notes and loans payable.
Casualty losses from recurring causes, such as vandalism and accidents.
Loss from the sale or abandonment of property, plant, and equipment.
Loss from strikes by employees and suppliers.

Illustration 5-10
Other items of nonoperating activities

Merchandising companies report the nonoperating activities in the income statement immediately after the company's primary operating activities. Illustration 5-11 (page 211) shows these sections for PW Audio Supply, Inc., using assumed data.

In the nonoperating activities sections, companies generally report items at the net amount. Thus, if a company received a $2,500 insurance settlement on vandalism losses of $2,700, it reports the loss at $200. Note, too, that the company nets the results of the two nonoperating sections. (For example, PW Audio shows an amount for $1,600, which is the net of the two nonoperating activities amounts.) This difference is added to or subtracted from income from operations to determine net income. Companies often combine these two nonoperating activities sections into a single "Other revenues and expenses" section.

ETHICS NOTE

Companies manage earnings in various ways. ConAgra Foods recorded a nonrecurring gain for $186 million from the sale of Pilgrim's Pride stock to help meet an earnings projection for the quarter.

Illustration 5-11
Multiple-step income statement—nonoperating sections and subgroupings of operating expenses

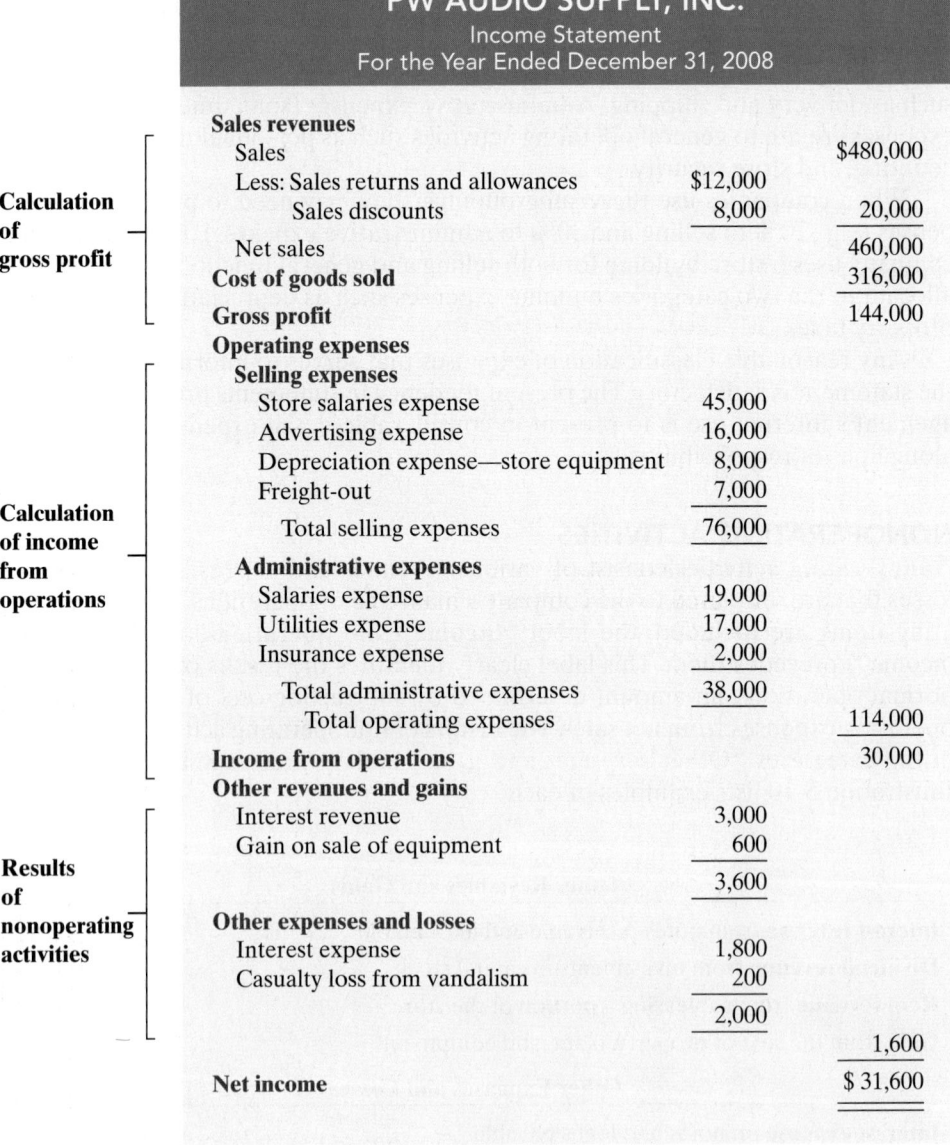

PW AUDIO SUPPLY, INC.
Income Statement
For the Year Ended December 31, 2008

Calculation of gross profit	**Sales revenues**		
	Sales		$480,000
	Less: Sales returns and allowances	$12,000	
	Sales discounts	8,000	20,000
	Net sales		460,000
	Cost of goods sold		316,000
	Gross profit		144,000
Calculation of income from operations	**Operating expenses**		
	Selling expenses		
	Store salaries expense	45,000	
	Advertising expense	16,000	
	Depreciation expense—store equipment	8,000	
	Freight-out	7,000	
	Total selling expenses	76,000	
	Administrative expenses		
	Salaries expense	19,000	
	Utilities expense	17,000	
	Insurance expense	2,000	
	Total administrative expenses	38,000	
	Total operating expenses		114,000
	Income from operations		30,000
Results of nonoperating activities	**Other revenues and gains**		
	Interest revenue	3,000	
	Gain on sale of equipment	600	
		3,600	
	Other expenses and losses		
	Interest expense	1,800	
	Casualty loss from vandalism	200	
		2,000	
			1,600
	Net income		$ 31,600

The distinction between operating and nonoperating activities is crucial to many external users of financial data. These users view operating income as sustainable and many nonoperating activities as nonrecurring. Therefore, when forecasting next year's income, analysts put the most weight on this year's operating income, and less weight on this year's nonoperating activities.

ETHICS INSIGHT

For IBM, What Is Operating?

After Enron, increased investor criticism and regulator scrutiny forced many companies to improve the clarity of their financial disclosures. For example, IBM announced it would provide more detail of its "Other gains and losses." It had previously included these items in its selling, general, and administrative expenses, with little disclosure.

Disclosing other gains and losses in a separate line item on the income statement will not have any effect on bottom-line income. However, analysts complained that burying these details in the selling, general, and administrative expense line reduced their ability to fully understand how well IBM was performing. For example, previously if IBM sold one of its buildings at a gain, it would include this gain in the selling, general, and administrative expense line item, thus reducing that expense. This made it appear that the company had done a better job of controlling operating expenses than it actually had.

Other companies that also recently announced changes to increase the informativeness of their income statements include PepsiCo and General Electric.

? Why have investors and analysts demanded more accuracy in isolating "Other gains and losses" from operating items?

Single-Step Income Statement

Another income statement format is the **single-step income statement**. The statement is so named because only one step—subtracting total expenses from total revenues—is required in determining net income.

A single-step statement classifies all data under two categories: revenues and expenses. **Revenues** include both operating revenues and other revenues and gains. **Expenses** include cost of goods sold, operating expenses, and other expenses and losses. Illustration 5-12 (page 212) shows a single-step statement for PW Audio Supply.

There are two primary reasons for using the single-step format: (1) A company does not realize any type of profit or income until total revenues exceed total expenses, so it makes sense to divide the statement into these two categories. (2) The format is simpler and easier to read. *For homework problems, however, you should use the single-step format only when specifically instructed to do so.*

Classified Balance Sheet

In the balance sheet, merchandising companies report merchandise inventory as a current asset immediately below accounts receivable. Recall from Chapter 4 that companies generally list current asset items in the order of their closeness to cash (liquidity). Merchandise inventory is less close to cash than accounts receivable, because the goods must first be sold and then collection made from the customer. Illustration 5-13 (page 212) presents the assets section of a classified balance sheet for PW Audio Supply.

Illustration 5-12
Single-step income statement

PW AUDIO SUPPLY
Income Statement
For the Year Ended December 31, 2008

Revenues		
Net sales		$460,000
Interest revenue		3,000
Gain on sale of equipment		600
Total revenues		463,600
Expenses		
Cost of goods sold	$316,000	
Selling expenses	76,000	
Administrative expenses	38,000	
Interest expense	1,800	
Casualty loss from vandalism	200	
Total expenses		432,000
Net income		$ 31,600

Illustration 5-13
Assets section of a classified balance sheet

HELPFUL HINT
The $40,000 is the *cost* of the inventory on hand, not its expected selling price.

PW AUDIO SUPPLY
Balance Sheet (Partial)
December 31, 2008

Assets

Current assets		
Cash		$ 9,500
Accounts receivable		16,100
Merchandise inventory		40,000
Prepaid insurance		1,800
Total current assets		67,400
Property, plant, and equipment		
Store equipment	$80,000	
Less: Accumulated depreciation—store equipment	24,000	56,000
Total assets		$123,400

Before You Go On...

REVIEW IT

1. Determine PepsiCo's gross profit rate for 2005 and 2004. Indicate whether it increased or decreased from 2004 to 2005. The answer to this question appears on page 241.
2. What are nonoperating activities? How do companies report them in the income statement?
3. How does a single-step income statement differ from a multiple-step income statement?

The Navigator

Be sure to read **ALL ABOUT YOU: *When Is a Sale a Sale?*** on page 213 for information on how topics in this chapter apply to you.

When Is a Sale a Sale?

Two interesting questions about merchandising are, "When is a sale not really a sale?" and "Why does it matter?" The answer for the second question is easy. If sales increase, net income increases. Managers' bonuses and stock prices generally increase when net income increases. Therefore, managers want sales to increase, and they feel much pressure at year-end to make sure this happens.

The first question is more difficult to answer. As the chapter indicates, a sale generally occurs when the seller has earned the revenue. But what do we mean by "earning the revenue"? Sometimes, to achieve higher sales figures, managers resort to reducing sales prices at year-end. Others may go even further. One example is a practice called *channel stuffing*. This involves shipping more goods to a customer than the customer needs. This practice boosts reported sales in that quarter. In the next quarter, however, the customer frequently returns a large portion of the extra goods, or at the very least, buys fewer goods because of the inventory already on hand.

About the Numbers

Presented below is a pie chart to illustrate that revenue recognition issues often require companies to correct—restate—their financial statements.

Oops! Total 2004 Restatements by Error Category

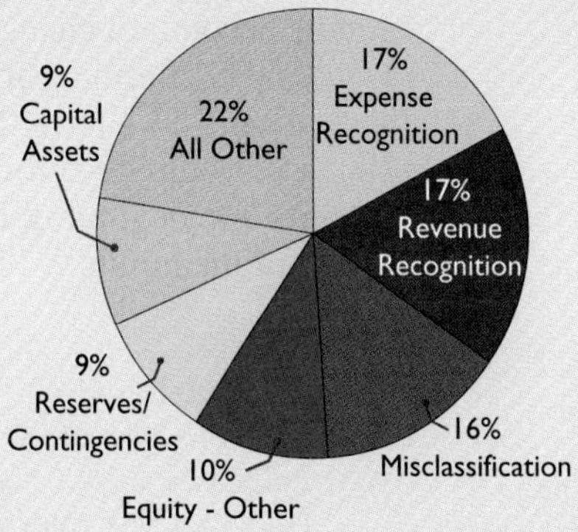

Source for chart: Terry Baldwin and Daniel Yoo, "Restatements—Traversing Shaky Ground: An Analysis for Investors," Glass Lewis & Co., June 2, 2005, p. 9, Graph 7.

Some Facts

* In early 2005 the shareholders of Krispy Kreme Doughnuts filed a lawsuit against management, alleging that at the end of accounting quarters the company was shipping twice as many doughnuts to wholesale customers than ordered.
* The SEC investigated claims that Harley-Davidson was shipping motorcycles to dealers in excess of dealer requests, in order to give the appearance of continued strong sales.
* In a recent lawsuit settlement, pharmaceutical company Bristol-Myers Squibb paid a $150 million fine for an alleged channel stuffing scheme that began in 1991 and did not end until 2001.
* An SEC investigation concluded that The Coca-Cola Company shipped $1.2 of excessive beverage concentrate to bottlers in Japan during a three-year period. The bottlers' inventories surged 62% during this time, while their sales increased only 11%.

What Do You Think?

Suppose that at the end of the year, your boss asks you to ship twice as many goods to your customers as they ordered. If you don't do so, you won't make your sales goal, and you won't get your bonus. You ask yourself, "Is channel stuffing an ethical business practice?"

YES: Motorcycles and pharmaceuticals can't be sold if they are sitting in the manufacturer's warehouse. They should be shipped to dealers and retailers so they have a chance of being sold to customers.

NO: If goods are intentionally shipped to customers when the customer hasn't requested them, and the seller has a high expectation that the goods will be returned, then this clearly is not a real sale. Management is providing a distorted picture of the company's sales performance, and thus misleading investors about the company's success.

Sources: Betsy McKay and Chad Terhune, "Coca-Cola Settles Regulatory Probe," *Wall Street Journal*, April 19, 2005, p. A3; Jay Hancock, "Check Those 4th-Quarter Earnings for Plumping," *The Baltimore Sun*, January 9, 2005, p. 1D.

The authors' comments on this situation appear on p. 242.

DETERMINING COST OF GOODS SOLD UNDER A PERIODIC SYSTEM

STUDY OBJECTIVE 7

Determine cost of goods sold under a periodic inventory system.

As shown in Illustration 5–3 (page 196), determining cost of goods sold is different under the periodic inventory system. When a company uses a perpetual inventory system, it records all transactions affecting inventory (such as purchases, freight costs, returns, and discounts) directly to the Merchandise Inventory account. In addition, at the time of each sale the perpetual system requires a reduction in Merchandise Inventory and an increase in Cost of Goods Sold.

Under a periodic system, however, the company uses **separate accounts** to record purchases, freight costs, returns, and discounts. Also, the company does not maintain a running account of changes in inventory. Instead, at the end of the period, it calculates the balance in ending inventory, as well as the cost of goods sold for the period. Illustration 5-14 shows the calculation of cost of goods sold for PW Audio Supply, using a periodic inventory system. Note that it includes (here, in blue type) separate amounts for beginning inventory, cost of goods purchased, and ending inventory. These are the inputs to the cost of goods sold computation under a periodic system.

Illustration 5-14
Cost of goods sold for a merchandising company using a periodic inventory system

Cost of goods sold				
Inventory, January 1			$36,000	
Purchases		$325,000		
Less: Purchase returns and allowances	$10,400			
Purchase discounts	6,800	17,200		
Net purchases		307,800		
Add: Freight-in		12,200		
Cost of goods purchased			320,000	
Cost of goods available for sale			356,000	
Inventory, December 31			40,000	
Cost of goods sold				**316,000**

HELPFUL HINT

Reading from right to left, the second column identifies the primary items that make up cost of goods sold of $316,000. The third column explains cost of goods purchased of $320,000. The fourth column reports contra-purchase items of $17,200.

A company reports merchandise inventory in the current assets section whether it uses a periodic or a perpetual system.

Appendix 5A provides further detail on the use of the periodic system.

Before You Go On...

REVIEW IT

1. Name two basic systems of accounting for inventory.
2. What accounts are used in determining the cost of goods purchased?
3. What is included in cost of goods available for sale?

DO IT

Aerosmith Company's accounting records show the following at year-end: Purchase Discounts $3,400; Freight-in $6,100; Sales $240,000; Purchases $162,500; Beginning Inventory $18,000; Ending Inventory $20,000; Sales Discounts $10,000; Purchase Returns $5,200; and Operating Expenses $57,000. Compute the following amounts for Aerosmith Company: net sales, cost of goods purchased, cost of goods sold, gross profit, and net income.

Action Plan

- Understand the relationships of the cost components in measuring net income for a merchandising company.

- Compute net sales.
- Compute cost of goods purchased.
- Compute cost of goods sold.
- Compute gross profit.
- Compute net income.

Solution

Net sales:

Sales − Sales discounts = Net sales
\$240,000 − \$10,000 = \$230,000

Cost of goods purchased:

Purchases − Purchase returns − Purchase discounts + Freight-in = Cost of goods purchased
\$162,500 − \$5,200 − \$3,400 + \$6,100 = \$160,000

Cost of goods sold:

Beginning inventory + Cost of goods purchased − Ending inventory = Cost of goods sold
\$18,000 + \$160,000 − \$20,000 = \$158,000

Gross profit:

Net sales − Cost of goods sold = Gross profit
\$230,000 − \$158,000 = \$72,000

Net income:

Gross profit − Operating expenses = Net income
\$72,000 − \$57,000 = \$15,000

Related exercise material: *BE5-10, BE5-11, E5-13, E5-14, and E5-15.*

The Navigator

Demonstration Problem

WILEY PLUS

The adjusted trial balance columns of Falcetto Company's worksheet for the year ended December 31, 2008, are as follows.

Debit		Credit	
Cash	14,500	Accumulated Depreciation	18,000
Accounts Receivable	11,100	Notes Payable	25,000
Merchandise Inventory	29,000	Accounts Payable	10,600
Prepaid Insurance	2,500	Larry Falcetto, Capital	81,000
Store Equipment	95,000	Sales	536,800
Larry Falcetto, Drawing	12,000	Interest Revenue	2,500
Sales Returns and Allowances	6,700		673,900
Sales Discounts	5,000		
Cost of Goods Sold	363,400		
Freight-out	7,600		
Advertising Expense	12,000		
Store Salaries Expense	56,000		
Utilities Expense	18,000		
Rent Expense	24,000		
Depreciation Expense	9,000		
Insurance Expense	4,500		
Interest Expense	3,600		
	673,900		

Instructions

Prepare an income statement assuming Falcetto Company does not use subgroupings for operating expenses.

action plan

- ✔ Remember that the key components of the income statement are net sales, cost of goods sold, gross profit, total operating expenses, and net income (loss). Report these components in the right-hand column of the income statement.
- ✔ Put nonoperating items after income from operations.

Solution to Demonstration Problem

FALCETTO COMPANY
Income Statement
For the Year Ended December 31, 2008

Sales revenues		
Sales		$536,800
Less: Sales returns and allowances	$6,700	
Sales discounts	5,000	11,700
Net sales		525,100
Cost of goods sold		363,400
Gross profit		161,700
Operating expenses		
Store salaries expense	56,000	
Rent expense	24,000	
Utilities expense	18,000	
Advertising expense	12,000	
Depreciation expense	9,000	
Freight-out	7,600	
Insurance expense	4,500	
Total operating expenses		131,100
Income from operations		30,600
Other revenues and gains		
Interest revenue	2,500	
Other expenses and losses		
Interest expense	3,600	1,100
Net income		$ 29,500

The Navigator

SUMMARY OF STUDY OBJECTIVES

WILEY PLUS

1 **Identify the differences between service and merchandising companies.** Because of inventory, a merchandising company has sales revenue, cost of goods sold, and gross profit. To account for inventory, a merchandising company must choose between a perpetual and a periodic inventory system.

2 **Explain the recording of purchases under a perpetual inventory system.** The company debits the Merchandise Inventory account for all purchases of merchandise and freight-in, and credits it for purchase discounts and purchase returns and allowances.

3 **Explain the recording of sales revenues under a perpetual inventory system.** When a merchandising company sells inventory, it debits Accounts Receivable (or Cash), and credits Sales for the **selling price** of the merchandise. At the same time, it debits Cost of Goods Sold, and credits Merchandise Inventory for the **cost** of the inventory items sold.

4 **Explain the steps in the accounting cycle for a merchandising company.** Each of the required steps in the accounting cycle for a service company applies to a merchandising company. A worksheet is again an optional step. Under a perpetual inventory system, the company must adjust the Merchandise Inventory account to agree with the physical count.

5 **Distinguish between a multiple-step and a single-step income statement.** A multiple-step income statement shows numerous steps in determining net income, including nonoperating activities sections. A single-step income statement classifies all data under two categories, revenues or expenses, and determines net income in one step.

6 **Explain the computation and importance of gross profit.** Merchandising companies compute gross profit by subtracting cost of goods sold from net sales. Gross profit represents the merchandising profit of a company. Managers and other interested parties closely watch the amount and trend of gross profit.

7 **Determine cost of goods sold under a periodic inventory system.** (a) Determine the cost of goods on hand at the beginning of the accounting period. (b) Add to it the cost of goods purchased. (c) Subtract the cost of goods on hand at the end of the accounting period.

The Navigator

GLOSSARY

Administrative expenses Expenses relating to general operating activities such as personnel management, accounting, and store security. (p. 209).

Contra-revenue account An account that is offset against a revenue account on the income statement. (p. 202).

Cost of goods sold The total cost of merchandise sold during the period. (p. 194).

FOB destination Freight terms indicating that the seller places the goods free on board to the buyer's place of business, and the seller pays the freight. (p. 198).

FOB shipping point Freight terms indicating that the seller places goods free on board the carrier, and the buyer pays the freight costs. (p. 198).

Gross profit The excess of net sales over the cost of goods sold. (p. 208).

Gross profit rate Gross profit expressed as a percentage, by dividing the amount of gross profit by net sales. (p. 208).

Income from operations Income from a company's principal operating activity; determined by subtracting cost of goods sold and operating expenses from net sales. (p. 209).

Multiple-step income statement An income statement that shows several steps in determining net income. (p. 207).

Net sales Sales less sales returns and allowances and less sales discounts. (p. 207).

Nonoperating activities Various revenues, expenses, gains, and losses that are unrelated to a company's main line of operations. (p. 209).

Operating expenses Expenses incurred in the process of earning sales revenues. (p. 208).

Other expenses and losses A nonoperating-activities section of the income statement that shows expenses from auxiliary operations and losses unrelated to the company's operations. (p. 209).

Other revenues and gains A nonoperating-activities section of the income statement that shows revenues from auxiliary operations and gains unrelated to the company's operations. (p. 209).

Periodic inventory system An inventory system under which the company does not keep detailed inventory records throughout the accounting period but determines the cost of goods sold only at the end of an accounting period. (p. 196).

Perpetual inventory system An inventory system under which the company keeps detailed records of the cost of each inventory purchase and sale and the records continuously show the inventory that should be on hand. (p. 195).

Purchase allowance A deduction made to the selling price of merchandise, granted by the seller so that the buyer will keep the merchandise. (p. 199).

Purchase discount A cash discount claimed by a buyer for prompt payment of a balance due. (p. 199).

Purchase invoice A document that supports each credit purchase. (p. 197).

Purchase return A return of goods from the buyer to the seller for a cash or credit refund. (p. 199).

Sales discount A reduction given by a seller for prompt payment of a credit sale. (p. 203).

Sales invoice A document that supports each credit sale. (p. 201).

Sales returns and allowances Purchase returns and allowances from the seller's perspective. See *Purchase return* and *Purchase allowance,* above. (p. 202).

Sales revenue (Sales) The primary source of revenue in a merchandising company. (p. 194).

Selling expenses Expenses associated with making sales. (p. 209).

Single-step income statement An income statement that shows only one step in determining net income. (p. 211).

APPENDIX 5A Periodic Inventory System

STUDY OBJECTIVE 8

Explain the recording of purchases and sales of inventory under a periodic inventory system.

As described in this chapter, companies may use one of two basic systems of accounting for inventories: (1) the perpetual inventory system or (2) the periodic inventory system. In the chapter we focused on the characteristics of the perpetual inventory system. In this appendix we discuss and illustrate the **periodic inventory system**. One key difference between the two systems is the point at which the company computes cost of goods sold. For a visual reminder of this difference, you may want to refer back to Illustration 5-3 on page 196.

Recording Merchandise Transactions

In a **periodic inventory system**, companies record revenues from the sale of merchandise when sales are made, just as in a perpetual system. Unlike the perpetual system, however, companies **do not attempt on the date of sale to record the cost of the merchandise sold.** Instead, they take a physical inventory count at the **end of the period** to determine (1) the cost of the merchandise then on hand and (2) the cost of the goods sold during the period. And, **under a periodic system, companies record purchases of merchandise in the Purchases account rather than the Merchandise Inventory account**. Also, in a periodic system, purchase returns and allowances, purchase discounts, and freight costs on purchases are recorded in separate accounts.

To illustrate the recording of merchandise transactions under a periodic inventory system, we will use purchase/sale transactions between PW Audio Supply, Inc. and Sauk Stereo, as illustrated for the perpetual inventory system in this chapter.

HELPFUL HINT
Be careful not to debit purchases of equipment or supplies to a Purchases account.

Recording Purchases of Merchandise

On the basis of the sales invoice (Illustration 5-4, shown on page 198) and receipt of the merchandise ordered from PW Audio Supply, Sauk Stereo records the $3,800 purchase as follows.

May 4	Purchases	3,800	
	Accounts Payable		3,800
	(To record goods purchased on account from PW Audio Supply)		

Purchases is a temporary account whose normal balance is a debit.

FREIGHT COSTS

When the purchaser directly incurs the freight costs, it debits the account Freight-in (or Transportation-in). For example, if Sauk pays Haul-It Freight Company $150 for freight charges on its purchase from PW Audio Supply on May 6, the entry on Sauk's books is:

May 6	Freight-in (Transportation-in)	150	
	Cash		150
	(To record payment of freight on goods purchased)		

ALTERNATIVE TERMINOLOGY
Freight-in is also called *transportation-in.*

Like Purchases, Freight-in is a temporary account whose normal balance is a debit. **Freight-in is part of cost of goods purchased.** The reason is that cost of goods purchased should include any freight charges necessary to bring the goods to the purchaser. Freight costs are not subject to a purchase discount. Purchase discounts apply to the invoice cost of the merchandise.

PURCHASE RETURNS AND ALLOWANCES

Sauk Stereo returns $300 of goods to PW Audio Supply and prepares the following entry to recognize the return.

May 8	Accounts Payable	300	
	Purchase Returns and Allowances		300
	(To record return of goods purchased from PW Audio Supply)		

Purchase Returns and Allowances is a temporary account whose normal balance is a credit.

PURCHASE DISCOUNTS

On May 14 Sauk Stereo pays the balance due on account to PW Audio Supply, taking the 2% cash discount allowed by PW Audio for payment within 10 days. Sauk Stereo records the payment and discount as follows.

May 14	Accounts Payable ($3,800 − $300)	3,500	
	Purchase Discounts ($3,500 × .02)		70
	Cash		3,430
	(To record payment within the discount period)		

Purchase Discounts is a temporary account whose normal balance is a credit.

Recording Sales of Merchandise

The seller, PW Audio Supply, records the sale of $3,800 of merchandise to Sauk Stereo on May 4 (sales invoice No. 731, Illustration 5-4, page 198) as follows.

May 4	Accounts Receivable	3,800	
	Sales		3,800
	(To record credit sales per invoice #731 to Sauk Stereo)		

SALES RETURNS AND ALLOWANCES

To record the returned goods received from Sauk Stereo on May 8, PW Audio Supply records the $300 sales return as follows.

May 8	Sales Returns and Allowances	300	
	Accounts Receivable		300
	(To record credit granted to Sauk Stereo for returned goods)		

SALES DISCOUNTS

On May 14, PW Audio Supply receives payment of $3,430 on account from Sauk Stereo. PW Audio honors the 2% cash discount and records the payment of Sauk's account receivable in full as follows.

May 14	Cash	3,430	
	Sales Discounts ($3,500 × .02)	70	
	Accounts Receivable ($3,800 − $300)		3,500
	(To record collection within 2/10, n/30 discount period from Sauk Stereo)		

COMPARISON OF ENTRIES—PERPETUAL VS. PERIODIC

The following display summarizes the periodic inventory entries shown in this appendix and compares them to the perpetual-system entries from the chapter. Entries that differ in the two systems are shown in color.

ENTRIES ON SAUK STEREO'S BOOKS

Transaction		Perpetual Inventory System			Periodic Inventory System		
May 4	Purchase of merchandise on credit.	Merchandise Inventory Accounts Payable	3,800	 3,800	**Purchases** Accounts Payable	**3,800**	 3,800
May 6	Freight costs on purchases.	Merchandise Inventory Cash	150	 150	**Freight-in** Cash	**150**	 150
May 8	Purchase returns and allowances.	Accounts Payable Merchandise Inventory	300	 300	Accounts Payable **Purchase Returns and Allowances**	300	 **300**
May 14	Payment on account with a discount.	Accounts Payable Cash Merchandise Inventory	3,500	 3,430 70	Accounts Payable Cash **Purchase Discounts**	3,500	 3,430 **70**

ENTRIES ON PW AUDIO SUPPLY'S BOOKS

Transaction		Perpetual Inventory System			Periodic Inventory System		
May 4	Sale of merchandise on credit.	Accounts Receivable Sales Revenue	3,800	 3,800	Accounts Receivable Sales Revenue	3,800	 3,800
		Cost of Goods Sold Merchandise Inventory	2,400	 2,400	**No entry for cost of goods sold**		
May 8	Return of merchandise sold.	Sales Returns and Allowances Accounts Receivable	300	 300	Sales Returns and Allowances Accounts Receivable	300	 300
		Merchandise Inventory Cost of Goods Sold	140	 140	**No entry**		
May 14	Cash received on account with a discount.	Cash Sales Discounts Accounts Receivable	3,430 70	 3,500	Cash Sales Discounts Accounts Receivable	3,430 70	 3,500

SUMMARY OF STUDY OBJECTIVE FOR APPENDIX 5A

WILEY PLUS

8 Explain the recording of purchases and sales of inventory under a periodic inventory system. In recording purchases under a periodic system, companies must make entries for (a) cash and credit purchases, (b) purchase returns and allowances, (c) purchase discounts, and (d) freight costs. In recording sales, companies must make entries for (a) cash and credit sales, (b) sales returns and allowances, and (c) sales discounts.

APPENDIX 5B Worksheet for a Merchandising Company

STUDY OBJECTIVE 9

Prepare a worksheet for a merchandising company.

Using a Worksheet

As indicated in Chapter 4, a worksheet enables companies to prepare financial statements before they journalize and post adjusting entries. The steps in preparing a worksheet for a merchandising company are the same as for a service enterprise (see page 142). Illustration 5B-1 shows the worksheet for PW Audio Supply (excluding nonoperating items). The unique accounts for a merchandiser using a perpetual inventory system are in boldface letters and in red.

PW Audio Supply.xls

File Edit View Insert Format Tools Data Window Help

PW AUDIO SUPPLY
Worksheet
For the Year Ended December 31, 2008

	A	B	C	D	E	F	G	H	I	J	K
		Trial Balance		Adjustments		Adjusted Trial Balance		Income Statement		Balance Sheet	
7	Accounts	Dr.	Cr.	Dr.	Cr.	Dr.	Cr.	Dr.	Cr.	Dr.	Cr.
8	Cash	9,500				9,500				9,500	
9	Accounts Receivable	16,100				16,100				16,100	
10	**Merchandise Inventory**	**40,500**			(a) 500	**40,000**				**40,000**	
11	Prepaid Insurance	3,800			(b) 2,000	1,800				1,800	
12	Store Equipment	80,000				80,000				80,000	
13	Accumulated Depreciation		16,000		(c) 8,000		24,000				24,000
14	Accounts Payable		20,400				20,400				20,400
15	R. A. Lamb, Capital		83,000				83,000				83,000
16	R. A. Lamb, Drawing	15,000				15,000				15,000	
17	**Sales**		**480,000**				**480,000**		**480,000**		
18	**Sales Returns and Allowances**	**12,000**				**12,000**		**12,000**			
19	**Sales Discounts**	**8,000**				**8,000**		**8,000**			
20	**Cost of Goods Sold**	**315,500**		(a) 500		**316,000**		**316,000**			
21	Freight-out	7,000				7,000		7,000			
22	Advertising Expense	16,000				16,000		16,000			
23	Admin. Sal. Exp.	19,000				19,000		19,000			
24	Store Salaries Expense	40,000		(d) 5,000		45,000		45,000			
25	Utilities Expense	17,000				17,000		17,000			
26	Totals	599,400	599,400								
27	Insurance Expense			(b) 2,000		2,000		2,000			
28	Depreciation Expense			(c) 8,000		8,000		8,000			
29	Salaries Payable				(d) 5,000		5,000				5,000
30	Totals			15,500	15,500	612,400	612,400	450,000	480,000	162,400	132,400
31	Net Income							30,000			30,000
32	Totals							480,000	480,000	162,400	162,400
33											
34											

Key: (a) Adjustment to inventory on hand, (b) Insurance expired, (c) Depreciation expense, (d) Salaries accrued.

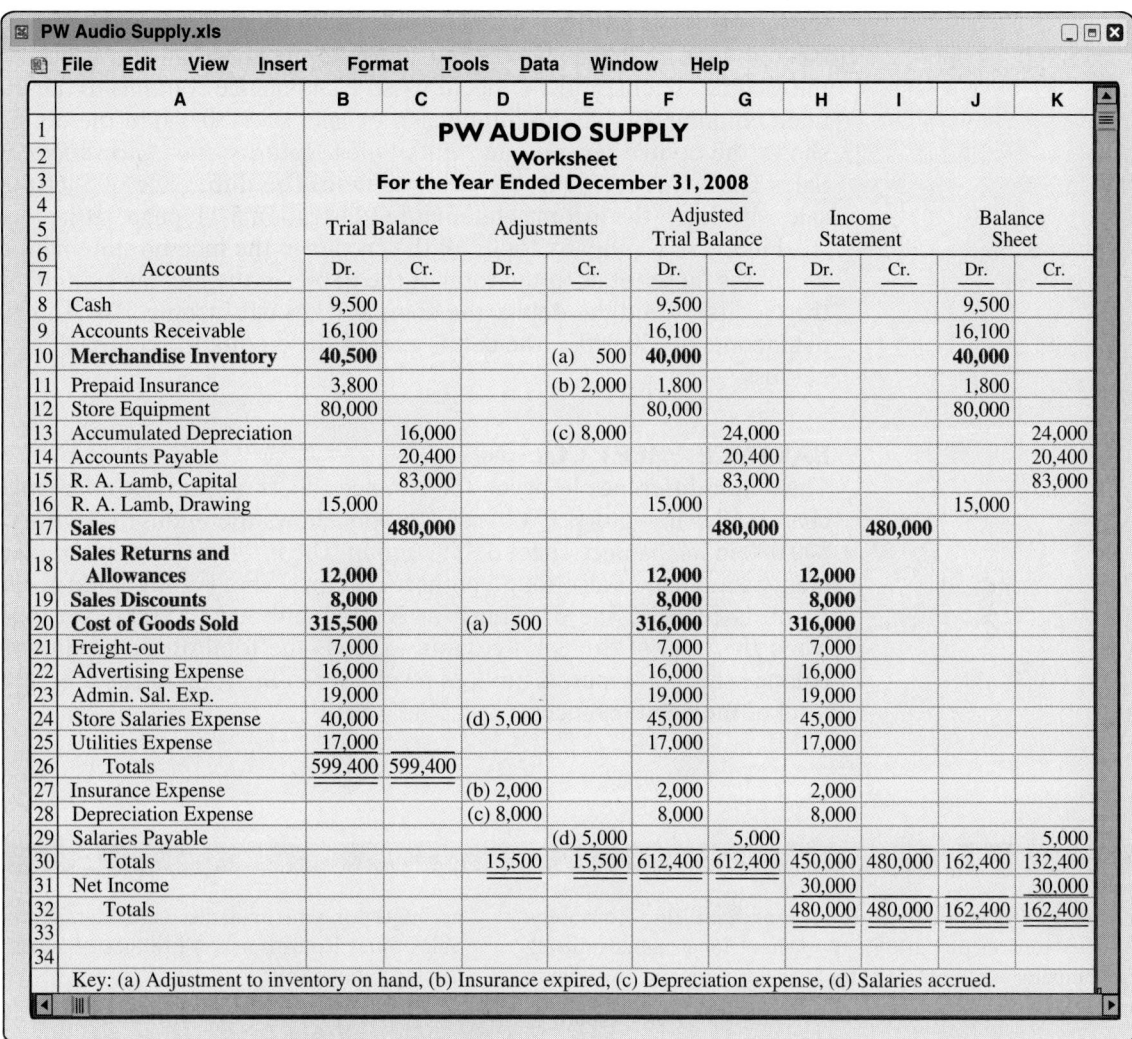

Illustration 5B-1 Worksheet for merchandising company

TRIAL BALANCE COLUMNS

Data for the trial balance come from the ledger balances of PW Audio Supply at December 31. The amount shown for Merchandise Inventory, $40,500, is the year-end inventory amount from the perpetual inventory system.

ADJUSTMENTS COLUMNS

A merchandising company generally has the same types of adjustments as a service company. As you see in the worksheet, adjustments (b), (c), and (d) are for insurance, depreciation, and salaries. Pioneer Advertising Agency, as illustrated in Chapters 3 and 4 also had these adjustments. Adjustment (a) was required to adjust the perpetual inventory carrying amount to the actual count.

After PW Audio enters all adjustments data on the worksheet, it establishes the equality of the adjustments column totals. It then extends the balances in all accounts to the adjusted trial balance columns.

ADJUSTED TRIAL BALANCE

The adjusted trial balance shows the balance of all accounts after adjustment at the end of the accounting period.

INCOME STATEMENT COLUMNS

Next, the merchandising company transfers the accounts and balances that affect the income statement from the adjusted trial balance columns to the income statement columns. PW Audio Supply shows sales of $480,000 in the credit column. It shows the contra-revenue accounts Sales Returns and Allowances $12,000 and Sales Discounts $8,000 in the debit column. The difference of $460,000 is the net sales shown on the income statement (Illustration 5-11, page 210).

Finally, the company totals all the credits in the income statement column and compares those totals to the total of the debits in the income statement column. If the credits exceed the debits, the company has net income. PW Audio Supply has net income of $30,000. If the debits exceed the credits, the company would report a net loss.

BALANCE SHEET COLUMNS

The major difference between the balance sheets of a service company and a merchandiser is inventory. PW Audio Supply shows the ending inventory amount of $40,000 in the balance sheet debit column. The information to prepare the owner's equity statement is also found in these columns. That is, the capital account of R. A. Lamb is $83,000. The drawings for R. A. Lamb are $15,000. Net income results when the total of the debit column exceeds the total of the credit column in the balance sheet columns. A net loss results when the total of the credits exceeds the total of the debit balances.

SUMMARY OF STUDY OBJECTIVE

9 **Prepare a worksheet for a merchandising company.** The steps in preparing a worksheet for a merchandising company are the same as for a service company. The unique accounts for a merchandiser are Merchandise Inventory, Sales, Sales Returns and Allowances, Sales Discounts, and Cost of Goods Sold.

*__Note__: All **asterisked** Questions, Exercises, and Problems relate to material in the appendices to the chapter.

SELF-STUDY QUESTIONS

WILEY PLUS

Answers are at the end of the chapter.

(SO 1) **1.** Gross profit will result if:
- **a.** operating expenses are less than net income.
- **b.** sales revenues are greater than operating expenses.
- **c.** sales revenues are greater than cost of goods sold.
- **d.** operating expenses are greater than cost of goods sold.

(SO 2) **2.** Under a perpetual inventory system, when goods are purchased for resale by a company:
- **a.** purchases on account are debited to Merchandise Inventory.
- **b.** purchases on account are debited to Purchases.
- **c.** purchase returns are debited to Purchase Returns and Allowances.
- **d.** freight costs are debited to Freight-out.

(SO 3) **3.** The sales accounts that normally have a debit balance are:
- **a.** Sales Discounts.
- **b.** Sales Returns and Allowances.
- **c.** both (a) and (b).
- **d.** neither (a) nor (b).

4. A credit sale of $750 is made on June 13, terms 2/10, net/30. A return of $50 is granted on June 16. The amount received as payment in full on June 23 is: (SO 3)
- **a.** $700.
- **b.** $686.
- **c.** $685.
- **d.** $650.

5. Which of the following accounts will normally appear in the ledger of a merchandising company that uses a perpetual inventory system? (SO 2)
- **a.** Purchases.
- **b.** Freight-in.
- **c.** Cost of Goods Sold.
- **d.** Purchase Discounts.

(SO 5) **6.** The multiple-step income statement for a merchandising company shows each of the following features *except*:
a. gross profit.
b. cost of goods sold.
c. a sales revenue section.
d. investing activities section.

(SO 6) **7.** If sales revenues are $400,000, cost of goods sold is $310,000, and operating expenses are $60,000, the gross profit is:
a. $30,000.
b. $90,000.
c. $340,000.
d. $400,000.

(SO 5) **8.** A single-step income statement:
a. reports gross profit.
b. does not report cost of goods sold.
c. reports sales revenues and "Other revenues and gains" in the revenues section of the income statement.
d. reports operating income separately.

(SO 5) **9.** Which of the following appears on both a single-step and a multiple-step income statement?
a. merchandise inventory.
b. gross profit.
c. income from operations.
d. cost of goods sold.

(SO 7) **10.** In determining cost of goods sold:
a. purchase discounts are deducted from net purchases.
b. freight-out is added to net purchases.
c. purchase returns and allowances are deducted from net purchases.
d. freight-in is added to net purchases.

11. If beginning inventory is $60,000, cost of goods purchased is $380,000, and ending inventory is $50,000, cost of goods sold is: (SO 7)
a. $390,000.
b. $370,000.
c. $330,000.
d. $420,000.

***12.** When goods are purchased for resale by a company using a periodic inventory system: (SO 8)
a. purchases on account are debited to Merchandise Inventory.
b. purchases on account are debited to Purchases.
c. purchase returns are debited to Purchase Returns and Allowances.
d. freight costs are debited to Purchases.

***13.** In a worksheet, Merchandise Inventory is shown in the following columns: (SO 9)
a. Adjusted trial balance debit and balance sheet debit.
b. Income statement debit and balance sheet debit.
c. Income statement credit and balance sheet debit.
d. Income statement credit and adjusted trial balance debit.

Go to the book's website, **www.wiley.com/college/weygandt**, for Additional Self-Study questions.

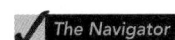

The Navigator

QUESTIONS

1. (a)"The steps in the accounting cycle for a merchandising company are different from the accounting cycle for a service company." Do you agree or disagree? (b) Is the measurement of net income for a merchandising company conceptually the same as for a service company? Explain.
2. Why is the normal operating cycle for a merchandising company likely to be longer than for a service company?
3. (a) How do the components of revenues and expenses differ between merchandising and service companies? (b) Explain the income measurement process in a merchandising company.
4. How does income measurement differ between a merchandising and a service company?
5. When is cost of goods sold determined in a perpetual inventory system?
6. Distinguish between FOB shipping point and FOB destination. Identify the freight terms that will result in a debit to Merchandise Inventory by the purchaser and a debit to Freight-out by the seller.
7. Explain the meaning of the credit terms 2/10, n/30.
8. Goods costing $2,000 are purchased on account on July 15 with credit terms of 2/10, n/30. On July 18 a $200 credit memo is received from the supplier for damaged goods. Give the journal entry on July 24 to record payment of the balance due within the discount period using a perpetual inventory system.
9. Joan Roland believes revenues from credit sales may be earned before they are collected in cash. Do you agree? Explain.
10. (a) What is the primary source document for recording (1) cash sales, (2) credit sales. (b) Using XXs for amounts, give the journal entry for each of the transactions in part (a).
11. A credit sale is made on July 10 for $900, terms 2/10, n/30. On July 12, $100 of goods are returned for credit. Give the journal entry on July 19 to record the receipt of the balance due within the discount period.
12. Explain why the Merchandise Inventory account will usually require adjustment at year-end.
13. Prepare the closing entries for the Sales account, assuming a balance of $200,000 and the Cost of Goods Sold account with a $145,000 balance.
14. What merchandising account(s) will appear in the post-closing trial balance?
15. Reese Co. has sales revenue of $105,000, cost of goods sold of $70,000, and operating expenses of $20,000. What is its gross profit and its gross profit rate?

16. Ann Fort Company reports net sales of $800,000, gross profit of $370,000, and net income of $240,000. What are its operating expenses?
17. Identify the distinguishing features of an income statement for a merchandising company.
18. Identify the sections of a multiple-step income statement that relate to (a) operating activities, and (b) nonoperating activities.
19. Distinguish between the types of functional groupings of operating expenses. What problem is created by these groupings?
20. How does the single-step form of income statement differ from the multiple-step form?
21. Identify the accounts that are added to or deducted from Purchases to determine the cost of goods purchased. For each account, indicate whether it is added or deducted.
*22. Goods costing $3,000 are purchased on account on July 15 with credit terms of 2/10, n/30. On July 18 a $200 credit was received from the supplier for damaged goods. Give the journal entry on July 24 to record payment of the balance due within the discount period, assuming a periodic inventory system.
*23. Indicate the columns of the work sheet in which (a) merchandise inventory and (b) cost of goods sold will be shown.

BRIEF EXERCISES

Compute missing amounts in determining net income.
(SO 1)

BE5-1 Presented below are the components in Waegelain Company's income statement. Determine the missing amounts.

	Sales	Cost of Goods Sold	Gross Profit	Operating Expenses	Net Income
(a)	$75,000	?	$30,000	?	$10,800
(b)	$108,000	$70,000	?	?	$29,500
(c)	?	$71,900	$79,600	$39,500	?

Journalize perpetual inventory entries.
(SO 2, 3)

BE5-2 Hollins Company buys merchandise on account from Gordon Company. The selling price of the goods is $780, and the cost of the goods is $520. Both companies use perpetual inventory systems. Journalize the transaction on the books of both companies.

Journalize sales transactions.
(SO 3)

BE5-3 Prepare the journal entries to record the following transactions on Monroe Company's books using a perpetual inventory system.

(a) On March 2, Monroe Company sold $900,000 of merchandise to Churchill Company, terms 2/10, n/30. The cost of the merchandise sold was $620,000.
(b) On March 6, Churchill Company returned $120,000 of the merchandise purchased on March 2 because it was defective. The cost of the returned merchandise was $90,000.
(c) On March 12, Monroe Company received the balance due from Churchill Company.

Journalize purchase transactions.
(SO 2)

BE5-4 From the information in BE5-3, prepare the journal entries to record these transactions on Churchill Company's books under a perpetual inventory system.

Prepare adjusting entry for merchandise inventory.
(SO 4)

BE5-5 At year-end the perpetual inventory records of Garbo Company showed merchandise inventory of $98,000. The company determined, however, that its actual inventory on hand was $96,500. Record the necessary adjusting entry.

Prepare closing entries for merchandise accounts.
(SO 4)

BE5-6 Bleeker Company has the following merchandise account balances: Sales $195,000, Sales Discounts $2,000, Cost of Goods Sold $105,000, and Merchandise Inventory $40,000. Prepare the entries to record the closing of these items to Income Summary.

Prepare sales revenues section of income statement.
(SO 5)

BE5-7 Maulder Company provides the following information for the month ended October 31, 2008: Sales on credit $280,000, cash sales $100,000, sales discounts $13,000, sales returns and allowances $11,000. Prepare the sales revenues section of the income statement based on this information.

Contrast presentation in multiple-step and single-step income statements.
(SO 5)

BE5-8 Explain where each of the following items would appear on (1) a multiple-step income statement, and on (2) a single-step income statement: **(a)** gain on sale of equipment, **(b)** casualty loss from vandalism, and **(c)** cost of goods sold.

Compute net sales, gross profit, income from operations, and gross profit rate.
(SO 5, 6)

BE5-9 Assume Baja Company has the following account balances: Sales $510,000, Sales Returns and Allowances $15,000, Cost of Goods Sold $350,000, Selling Expenses $70,000, and Administrative Expenses $40,000. Compute the following: **(a)** net sales, **(b)** gross profit, **(c)** income from operations, and **(d)** gross profit rate. (Round to one decimal place.)

BE5-10 Assume that Alshare Company uses a periodic inventory system and has these account balances: Purchases $450,000; Purchase Returns and Allowances $11,000; Purchase Discounts $8,000; and Freight-in $16,000. Determine net purchases and cost of goods purchased.

Compute net purchases and cost of goods purchased.
(SO 7)

BE5-11 Assume the same information as in BE5-10 and also that Alshare Company has beginning inventory of $60,000, ending inventory of $90,000, and net sales of $630,000. Determine the amounts to be reported for cost of goods sold and gross profit.

Compute cost of goods sold and gross profit.
(SO 6, 7)

***BE5-12** Prepare the journal entries to record these transactions on Allied Company's books using a periodic inventory system.

Journalize purchase transactions.
(SO, 8)

(a) On March 2, Allied Company purchased $1,000,000 of merchandise from B. Streisand Company, terms 2/10, n/30.
(b) On March 6 Allied Company returned $130,000 of the merchandise purchased on March 2 because it was defective.
(c) On March 12 Allied Company paid the balance due to B. Streisand Company.

***BE5-13** Presented below is the format of the worksheet presented in the chapter.

Identify worksheet columns for selected accounts.
(SO 9)

Trial Balance		**Adjustments**		**Adjusted Trial Balance**		**Income Statement**		**Balance Sheet**	
Dr.	Cr.	Dr.	Cr.	Dr.	Cr.	Dr.	Cr.	Dr.	Cr.

Indicate where the following items will appear on the worksheet: **(a)** Cash, **(b)** Merchandise Inventory, **(c)** Sales, **(d)** Cost of goods sold.

Example:
Cash: Trial balance debit column; Adjusted trial balance debit column; and Balance sheet debit column.

EXERCISES

WILEY PLUS

E5-1 Mr. Wellington has prepared the following list of statements about service companies and merchandisers.

Answer general questions on inventory.
(SO 1)

1. Measuring net income for a merchandiser is conceptually the same as for a service company.
2. For a merchandiser, sales less operating expenses is called gross profit.
3. For a merchandiser, the primary source of revenues is the sale of inventory.
4. Sales salaries is an example of an operating expense.
5. The operating cycle of a merchandiser is the same as that of a service company.
6. In a perpetual inventory system, no detailed inventory records of goods on hand are maintained.
7. In a periodic inventory system, the cost of goods sold is determined only at the end of the accounting period.
8. A periodic inventory system provides better control over inventories than a perpetual system.

Instructions
Identify each statement as true or false. If false, indicate how to correct the statement.

E5-2 Information related to Steffens Co. is presented below.

Journalize purchases transactions.
(SO 2)

1. On April 5, purchased merchandise from Bryant Company for $25,000 terms 2/10, net/30, FOB shipping point.
2. On April 6 paid freight costs of $900 on merchandise purchased from Bryant.
3. On April 7, purchased equipment on account for $26,000.
4. On April 8, returned damaged merchandise to Bryant Company and was granted a $4,000 credit for returned merchandise.
5. On April 15 paid the amount due to Bryant Company in full.

Instructions

(a) Prepare the journal entries to record these transactions on the books of Steffens Co. under a perpetual inventory system.

(b) Assume that Steffens Co. paid the balance due to Bryant Company on May 4 instead of April 15. Prepare the journal entry to record this payment.

Journalize perpetual inventory entries.
(SO 2, 3)

E5-3 On September 1, Howe Office Supply had an inventory of 30 calculators at a cost of $18 each. The company uses a perpetual inventory system. During September, the following transactions occurred.

Sept. 6 Purchased 80 calculators at $20 each from DeVito Co. for cash.
9 Paid freight of $80 on calculators purchased from DeVito Co.
10 Returned 2 calculators to DeVito Co. for $42 credit (including freight) because they did not meet specifications.
12 Sold 26 calculators costing $21 (including freight) for $31 each to Mega Book Store, terms n/30.
14 Granted credit of $31 to Mega Book Store for the return of one calculator that was not ordered.
20 Sold 30 calculators costing $21 for $31 each to Barbara's Card Shop, terms n/30.

Instructions

Journalize the September transactions.

Prepare purchase and sale entries.
(SO 2, 3)

E5-4 On June 10, Meredith Company purchased $8,000 of merchandise from Leinert Company, FOB shipping point, terms 2/10, n/30. Meredith pays the freight costs of $400 on June 11. Damaged goods totaling $300 are returned to Leinert for credit on June 12. The scrap value of these goods is $150. On June 19, Meredith pays Leinert Company in full, less the purchase discount. Both companies use a perpetual inventory system.

Instructions

(a) Prepare separate entries for each transaction on the books of Meredith Company.

(b) Prepare separate entries for each transaction for Leinert Company. The merchandise purchased by Meredith on June 10 had cost Leinert $5,000.

Journalize sales transactions.
(SO 3)

E5-5 Presented below are transactions related to Wheeler Company.

1. On December 3, Wheeler Company sold $500,000 of merchandise to Hashmi Co., terms 2/10, n/30, FOB shipping point. The cost of the merchandise sold was $350,000.
2. On December 8, Hashmi Co. was granted an allowance of $27,000 for merchandise purchased on December 3.
3. On December 13, Wheeler Company received the balance due from Hashmi Co.

Instructions

(a) Prepare the journal entries to record these transactions on the books of Wheeler Company using a perpetual inventory system.

(b) Assume that Wheeler Company received the balance due from Hashmi Co. on January 2 of the following year instead of December 13. Prepare the journal entry to record the receipt of payment on January 2.

Prepare sales revenues section and closing entries.
(SO 4, 5)

E5-6 The adjusted trial balance of Zambrana Company shows the following data pertaining to sales at the end of its fiscal year October 31, 2008: Sales $800,000, Freight-out $16,000, Sales Returns and Allowances $25,000, and Sales Discounts $15,000.

Instructions

(a) Prepare the sales revenues section of the income statement.

(b) Prepare separate closing entries for (1) sales, and (2) the contra accounts to sales.

Prepare adjusting and closing entries.
(SO 4)

E5-7 Peter Kalle Company had the following account balances at year-end: cost of goods sold $60,000; merchandise inventory $15,000; operating expenses $29,000; sales $108,000; sales discounts $1,200; and sales returns and allowances $1,700. A physical count of inventory determines that merchandise inventory on hand is $14,100.

Instructions

(a) Prepare the adjusting entry necessary as a result of the physical count.

(b) Prepare closing entries.

E5-8 Presented is information related to Rogers Co. for the month of January 2008.

Prepare adjusting and closing entries.

(SO 4)

Ending inventory per perpetual records	$ 21,600	Salary expense	$ 61,000
Ending inventory actually on hand	21,000	Sales discounts	10,000
Cost of goods sold	218,000	Sales returns and allowances	13,000
Freight-out	7,000	Sales	350,000
Insurance expense	12,000		
Rent expense	20,000		

Instructions

(a) Prepare the necessary adjusting entry for inventory.
(b) Prepare the necessary closing entries.

E5-9 In its income statement for the year ended December 31, 2008, Pele Company reported the following condensed data.

Prepare multiple-step and single-step income statements.

(SO 5)

Administrative expenses	$ 435,000	Selling expenses	$ 490,000
Cost of goods sold	1,289,000	Loss on sale of equipment	10,000
Interest expense	70,000	Net sales	2,312,000
Interest revenue	28,000		

Instructions

(a) Prepare a multiple-step income statement.
(b) Prepare a single-step income statement.

E5-10 An inexperienced accountant for Blaufuss Company made the following errors in recording merchandising transactions.

Prepare correcting entries for sales and purchases.

(SO 2, 3)

1. A $175 refund to a customer for faulty merchandise was debited to Sales $175 and credited to Cash $175.
2. A $180 credit purchase of supplies was debited to Merchandise Inventory $180 and credited to Cash $180.
3. A $110 sales discount was debited to Sales.
4. A cash payment of $20 for freight on merchandise purchases was debited to Freight-out $200 and credited to Cash $200.

Instructions

Prepare separate correcting entries for each error, assuming that the incorrect entry is not reversed. (Omit explanations.)

E5-11 In 2008, Walter Payton Company had net sales of $900,000 and cost of goods sold of $540,000. Operating expenses were $230,000, and interest expense was $11,000. Payton prepares a multiple-step income statement.

Compute various income measures.

(SO 5, 6)

Instructions

(a) Compute Payton's gross profit.
(b) Compute the gross profit rate. Why is this rate computed by financial statement users?
(c) What is Payton's income from operations and net income?
(d) If Payton prepared a single-step income statement, what amount would it report for net income?
(e) In what section of its classified balance sheet should Payton report merchandise inventory?

E5-12 Presented below is financial information for two different companies.

Compute missing amounts and compute gross profit rate.

(SO 5, 6)

	Nam Company	Mayo Company
Sales	$90,000	(d)
Sales returns	(a)	$ 5,000
Net sales	84,000	100,000
Cost of goods sold	56,000	(e)
Gross profit	(b)	41,500
Operating expenses	15,000	(f)
Net income	(c)	15,000

Instructions
(a) Determine the missing amounts on page 227.
(b) Determine the gross profit rates. (Round to one decimal place.)

Prepare cost of goods sold section.
(SO 7)

E5-13 The trial balance of G. Durler Company at the end of its fiscal year, August 31, 2008, includes these accounts: Merchandise Inventory $17,200; Purchases $149,000; Sales $190,000; Freight-in $4,000; Sales Returns and Allowances $3,000; Freight-out $1,000; and Purchase Returns and Allowances $2,000. The ending merchandise inventory is $25,000.

Instructions
Prepare a cost of goods sold section for the year ending August 31 (periodic inventory).

Compute various income statement items.
(SO 7)

E5-14 On January 1, 2008, Rachael Ray Corporation had merchandise inventory of $50,000. At December 31, 2008, Rachael Ray had the following account balances.

Freight-in	$ 4,000
Purchases	500,000
Purchase discounts	6,000
Purchase returns and allowances	2,000
Sales	800,000
Sales discounts	5,000
Sales returns and allowances	10,000

At December 31, 2008, Rachael Ray determines that its ending inventory is $60,000.

Instructions
(a) Compute Rachael Ray's 2008 gross profit.
(b) Compute Rachael Ray's 2008 operating expenses if net income is $130,000 and there are no nonoperating activities.

Prepare cost of goods sold section.
(SO 7)

E5-15 Below is a series of cost of goods sold sections for companies B, F, L, and R.

	B	F	L	R
Beginning inventory	$ 150	$ 70	$1,000	$ (j)
Purchases	1,600	1,080	(g)	43,590
Purchase returns and allowances	40	(d)	290	(k)
Net purchases	(a)	1,030	6,210	41,090
Freight-in	110	(e)	(h)	2,240
Cost of goods purchased	(b)	1,280	7,940	(l)
Cost of goods available for sale	1,820	1,350	(i)	49,530
Ending inventory	310	(f)	1,450	6,230
Cost of goods sold	(c)	1,230	7,490	43,300

Instructions
Fill in the lettered blanks to complete the cost of goods sold sections.

Journalize purchase transactions.
(SO 8)

***E5-16** This information relates to Martinez Co.

1. On April 5 purchased merchandise from D. Norlan Company for $20,000, terms 2/10, net/30, FOB shipping point.
2. On April 6 paid freight costs of $900 on merchandise purchased from D. Norlan Company.
3. On April 7 purchased equipment on account for $26,000.
4. On April 8 returned some of April 5 merchandise to D. Norlan Company which cost $2,800.
5. On April 15 paid the amount due to D. Norlan Company in full.

Instructions
(a) Prepare the journal entries to record these transactions on the books of Martinez Co. using a periodic inventory system.
(b) Assume that Martinez Co. paid the balance due to D. Norlan Company on May 4 instead of April 15. Prepare the journal entry to record this payment.

Journalize purchase transactions.
(SO 8)

***E5-17** Presented below is information related to Chevalier Co.

1. On April 5, purchased merchandise from Paris Company for $22,000, terms 2/10, net/30, FOB shipping point.

2. On April 6, paid freight costs of $800 on merchandise purchased from Paris.
3. On April 7, purchased equipment on account from Wayne Higley Mfg. Co. for $26,000.
4. On April 8, returned damaged merchandise to Paris Company and was granted a $4,000 allowance.
5. On April 15, paid the amount due to Paris Company in full.

Instructions

(a) Prepare the journal entries to record these transactions on the books of Chevalier Co. using a periodic inventory system.

(b) Assume that Chevalier Co. paid the balance due to Paris Company on May 4 instead of April 15. Prepare the journal entry to record this payment.

***E5-18** Presented below are selected accounts for Carpenter Company as reported in the worksheet at the end of May 2008.

Complete worksheet. (SO 9)

Accounts	Adjusted Trial Balance		Income Statement		Balance Sheet	
	Dr.	Cr.	Dr.	Cr.	Dr.	Cr.
Cash	9,000					
Merchandise Inventory	76,000					
Sales		450,000				
Sales Returns and Allowances	10,000					
Sales Discounts	9,000					
Cost of Goods Sold	300,000					

Instructions

Complete the worksheet by extending amounts reported in the adjusted trial balance to the appropriate columns in the work sheet. Do not total individual columns.

***E5-19** The trial balance columns of the worksheet for Green Company at June 30, 2008, are as follows.

Prepare a worksheet. (SO 9)

GREEN COMPANY
Worksheet
For the Month Ended June 30, 2008

Account Titles	Trial Balance Debit	Trial Balance Credit
Cash	$ 2,320	
Accounts Receivable	2,440	
Merchandise Inventory	11,640	
Accounts Payable		$ 1,120
Ed Green, Capital		3,600
Sales		42,400
Cost of Goods Sold	20,560	
Operating Expenses	10,160	
	$47,120	$47,120

Other data:
Operating expenses incurred on account which have not yet been recorded total $1,500.

Instructions

Enter the trial balance on a worksheet and complete the worksheet.

EXERCISES: SET B

Visit the book's website at **www.wiley.com/college/weygandt**, and choose the Student Companion site, to access Exercise Set B.

PROBLEMS: SET A

WILEY PLUS

Journalize purchase and sales transactions under a perpetual inventory system.

(SO 2, 3)

P5-1A Sansomite Co. distributes suitcases to retail stores and extends credit terms of 1/10, n/30 to all of its customers. At the end of June, Sansomite's inventory consisted of 40 suitcases purchased at $30 each. During the month of July the following merchandising transactions occurred.

July 1 Purchased 60 suitcases on account for $30 each from Trunk Manufacturers, FOB destination, terms 2/10, n/30. The appropriate party also made a cash payment of $100 for freight on this date.
3 Sold 40 suitcases on account to Satchel World for $50 each.
9 Paid Trunk Manufacturers in full.
12 Received payment in full from Satchel World.
17 Sold 30 suitcases on account to The Going Concern for $50 each.
18 Purchased 60 suitcases on account for $1,700 from Kingman Manufacturers, FOB shipping point, terms 1/10, n/30. The appropriate party also made a cash payment of $100 for freight on this date.
20 Received $300 credit (including freight) for 10 suitcases returned to Kingman Manufacturers.
21 Received payment in full from The Going Concern.
22 Sold 45 suitcases on account to Fly-By-Night for $50 each.
30 Paid Kingman Manufacturers in full.
31 Granted Fly-By-Night $200 credit for 4 suitcases returned costing $120.

Sansomite's chart of accounts includes the following: No. 101 Cash, No. 112 Accounts Receivable, No. 120 Merchandise Inventory, No. 201 Accounts Payable, No. 401 Sales, No. 412 Sales Returns and Allowances, No. 414 Sales Discounts, No. 505 Cost of Goods Sold.

Instructions

Journalize the transactions for the month of July for Sansomite using a perpetual inventory system.

Journalize, post, and prepare a partial income statement.

(SO 2, 3, 5, 6)

GLS Peachtree

P5-2A Olaf Distributing Company completed the following merchandising transactions in the month of April. At the beginning of April, the ledger of Olaf showed Cash of $9,000 and M. Olaf, Capital of $9,000.

Apr. 2 Purchased merchandise on account from Dakota Supply Co. $6,900, terms 1/10, n/30.
4 Sold merchandise on account $5,500, FOB destination, terms 1/10, n/30. The cost of the merchandise sold was $4,100.
5 Paid $240 freight on April 4 sale.
6 Received credit from Dakota Supply Co. for merchandise returned $500.
11 Paid Dakota Supply Co. in full, less discount.
13 Received collections in full, less discounts, from customers billed on April 4.
14 Purchased merchandise for cash $3,800.
16 Received refund from supplier for returned goods on cash purchase of April 14, $500.
18 Purchased merchandise from Skywalker Distributors $4,500, FOB shipping point, terms 2/10, n/30.
20 Paid freight on April 18 purchase $100.
23 Sold merchandise for cash $6,400. The merchandise sold had a cost of $5,120.
26 Purchased merchandise for cash $2,300.
27 Paid Skywalker Distributors in full, less discount.
29 Made refunds to cash customers for defective merchandise $90. The returned merchandise had a scrap value of $30.
30 Sold merchandise on account $3,700, terms n/30. The cost of the merchandise sold was $2,800.

Olaf Company's chart of accounts includes the following: No. 101 Cash, No. 112 Accounts Receivable, No. 120 Merchandise Inventory, No. 201 Accounts Payable, No. 301 M. Olaf, Capital, No. 401 Sales, No. 412 Sales Returns and Allowances, No. 414 Sales Discounts, No. 505 Cost of Goods Sold, and No. 644 Freight-out.

Instructions

(a) Journalize the transactions using a perpetual inventory system.
(b) Enter the beginning cash and capital balances, and post the transactions. (Use J1 for the journal reference.)
(c) Prepare the income statement through gross profit for the month of April 2008.

(c) Gross profit $3,465

P5-3A Maine Department Store is located near the Village Shopping Mall. At the end of the company's fiscal year on December 31, 2008, the following accounts appeared in two of its trial balances.

Prepare financial statements and adjusting and closing entries.

(SO 4, 5)

	Unadjusted	Adjusted		Unadjusted	Adjusted
Accounts Payable	$ 79,300	$ 79,300	Interest Payable		$ 8,000
Accounts Receivable	50,300	50,300	Interest Revenue	$ 4,000	4,000
Accumulated Depr.—Building	42,100	52,500	Merchandise Inventory	75,000	75,000
Accumulated Depr.—Equipment	29,600	42,900	Mortgage Payable	80,000	80,000
Building	190,000	190,000	Office Salaries Expense	32,000	32,000
Cash	23,800	23,800	Prepaid Insurance	9,600	2,400
B. Maine, Capital	176,600	176,600	Property Tax Expense		4,800
Cost of Goods Sold	412,700	412,700	Property Taxes Payable		4,800
Depr. Expense—Building		10,400	Sales Salaries Expense	76,000	76,000
Depr. Expense—Equipment		13,300	Sales	628,000	628,000
B. Maine, Drawing	28,000	28,000	Sales Commissions Expense	10,200	14,500
Equipment	110,000	110,000	Sales Commissions Payable		4,300
Insurance Expense		7,200	Sales Returns and Allowances	8,000	8,000
Interest Expense	3,000	11,000	Utilities Expense	11,000	12,000
			Utilities Expense Payable		1,000

Analysis reveals the following additional data.

1. Insurance expense and utilities expense are 60% selling and 40% administrative.
2. $20,000 of the mortgage payable is due for payment next year.
3. Depreciation on the building and property tax expense are administrative expenses; depreciation on the equipment is a selling expense.

Instructions

(a) Prepare a multiple-step income statement, an owner's equity statement, and a classified balance sheet.

(b) Journalize the adjusting entries that were made.

(c) Journalize the closing entries that are necessary.

(a) Net income $30,100
Capital $178,700
Total assets $356,100

P5-4A J. Hafner, a former professional tennis star, operates Hafner's Tennis Shop at the Miller Lake Resort. At the beginning of the current season, the ledger of Hafner's Tennis Shop showed Cash $2,500, Merchandise Inventory $1,700, and J. Hafner, Capital $4,200. The following transactions were completed during April.

Journalize, post, and prepare a trial balance.

(SO 2, 3, 4)

Apr.	4	Purchased racquets and balls from Wellman Co. $840, FOB shipping point, terms 2/10, n/30.
	6	Paid freight on purchase from Wellman Co. $40.
	8	Sold merchandise to members $1,150, terms n/30. The merchandise sold had a cost of $790.
	10	Received credit of $40 from Wellman Co. for a damaged racquet that was returned.
	11	Purchased tennis shoes from Venus Sports for cash, $420.
	13	Paid Wellman Co. in full.
	14	Purchased tennis shirts and shorts from Serena's Sportswear $900, FOB shipping point, terms 3/10, n/60.
	15	Received cash refund of $50 from Venus Sports for damaged merchandise that was returned.
	17	Paid freight on Serena's Sportswear purchase $30.
	18	Sold merchandise to members $810, terms n/30. The cost of the merchandise sold was $530.
	20	Received $500 in cash from members in settlement of their accounts.
	21	Paid Serena's Sportswear in full.
	27	Granted an allowance of $30 to members for tennis clothing that did not fit properly.
	30	Received cash payments on account from members, $660.

The chart of accounts for the tennis shop includes the following: No. 101 Cash, No. 112 Accounts Receivable, No. 120 Merchandise Inventory, No. 201 Accounts Payable, No. 301 J. Hafner, Capital, No. 401 Sales, No. 412 Sales Returns and Allowances, No. 505 Cost of Goods Sold.

Instructions

(a) Journalize the April transactions using a perpetual inventory system.

(b) Enter the beginning balances in the ledger accounts and post the April transactions. (Use J1 for the journal reference.)

(c) Total debits $6,160

(c) Prepare a trial balance on April 30, 2008.

Determine cost of goods sold and gross profit under periodic approach.

(SO 6, 7)

P5-5A At the end of Gordman Department Store's fiscal year on December 31, 2008, these accounts appeared in its adjusted trial balance.

Freight-in	$5,600
Merchandise Inventory	40,500
Purchases	447,000
Purchase Discounts	12,000
Purchase Returns and Allowances	6,400
Sales	718,000
Sales Returns and Allowances	8,000

Additional facts:

1. Merchandise inventory on December 31, 2008, is $75,000.
2. Note that Gordman Department Store uses a periodic system.

Instructions

Gross profit $310,300

Prepare an income statement through gross profit for the year ended December 31, 2008.

Calculate missing amounts and assess profitability.

(SO 6, 7)

P5-6A Kristen Montana operates a retail clothing operation. She purchases all merchandise inventory on credit and uses a periodic inventory system. The accounts payable account is used for recording inventory purchases only; all other current liabilities are accrued in separate accounts. You are provided with the following selected information for the fiscal years 2005, 2006, 2007, and 2008.

	2005	2006	2007	2008
Inventory (ending)	$ 13,000	$ 11,300	$ 14,700	$ 12,200
Accounts payable (ending)	20,000			
Sales		225,700	227,600	219,500
Purchases of merchandise inventory on account		146,000	145,000	129,000
Cash payments to suppliers		135,000	161,000	127,000

Instructions

(a) 2007 $141,600

(a) Calculate cost of goods sold for each of the 2006, 2007, and 2008 fiscal years.

(b) Calculate the gross profit for each of the 2006, 2007, and 2008 fiscal years.

(c) 2007 Ending accts payable $15,000

(c) Calculate the ending balance of accounts payable for each of the 2006, 2007, and 2008 fiscal years.

(d) Sales declined in fiscal 2008. Does that mean that profitability, as measured by the gross profit rate, necessarily also declined? Explain, calculating the gross profit rate for each fiscal year to help support your answer. (Round to one decimal place.)

Journalize, post, and prepare trial balance and partial income statement using periodic approach.

(SO 7, 8)

GLS

***P5-7A** At the beginning of the current season, the ledger of Village Tennis Shop showed Cash $2,500; Merchandise Inventory $1,700; and Angie Wilbert, Capital $4,200. The following transactions were completed during April.

Apr.	4	Purchased racquets and balls from Denton Co. $740, terms 3/10, n/30.
	6	Paid freight on Denton Co. purchase $60.
	8	Sold merchandise to members $900, terms n/30.
	10	Received credit of $40 from Denton Co. for a damaged racquet that was returned.
	11	Purchased tennis shoes from Newbee Sports for cash $300.
	13	Paid Denton Co. in full.
	14	Purchased tennis shirts and shorts from Venus's Sportswear $600, terms 2/10, n/60.
	15	Received cash refund of $50 from Newbee Sports for damaged merchandise that was returned.
	17	Paid freight on Venus's Sportswear purchase $30.
	18	Sold merchandise to members $1,000, terms n/30.
	20	Received $500 in cash from members in settlement of their accounts.
	21	Paid Venus's Sportswear in full.
	27	Granted an allowance of $30 to members for tennis clothing that did not fit properly.
	30	Received cash payments on account from members $500.

The chart of accounts for the tennis shop includes Cash; Accounts Receivable; Merchandise Inventory; Accounts Payable; Angie Wilbert, Capital; Sales; Sales Returns and Allowances; Purchases; Purchase Returns and Allowances; Purchase Discounts; and Freight-in.

Instructions

(a) Journalize the April transactions using a periodic inventory system.

(b) Using T accounts, enter the beginning balances in the ledger accounts and post the April transactions.

(c) Prepare a trial balance on April 30, 2008.

(d) Prepare an income statement through gross profit, assuming merchandise inventory on hand at April 30 is $2,296.

(c) Tot. trial balance $6,223
(d) Gross profit $ 859

***P5-8A** The trial balance of Terry Manning Fashion Center contained the following accounts at November 30, the end of the company's fiscal year.

Complete accounting cycle beginning with a worksheet.
(SO 4, 5, 6, 9)

TERRY MANNING FASHION CENTER
Trial Balance
November 30, 2008

	Debit	Credit
Cash	$ 28,700	
Accounts Receivable	30,700	
Merchandise Inventory	44,700	
Store Supplies	6,200	
Store Equipment	85,000	
Accumulated Depreciation—Store Equipment		$ 22,000
Delivery Equipment	48,000	
Accumulated Depreciation—Delivery Equipment		6,000
Notes Payable		51,000
Accounts Payable		48,500
Terry Manning, Capital		110,000
Terry Manning, Drawing	12,000	
Sales		755,200
Sales Returns and Allowances	8,800	
Cost of Goods Sold	497,400	
Salaries Expense	140,000	
Advertising Expense	24,400	
Utilities Expense	14,000	
Repair Expense	12,100	
Delivery Expense	16,700	
Rent Expense	24,000	
Totals	$992,700	$992,700

Adjustment data:

1. Store supplies on hand totaled $2,500.
2. Depreciation is $9,000 on the store equipment and $5,000 on the delivery equipment.
3. Interest of $4,080 is accrued on notes payable at November 30.
4. Merchandise inventory actually on hand is $44,400.

Other data:

1. Salaries expense is 70% selling and 30% administrative.
2. Rent expense and utilities expense are 80% selling and 20% administrative.
3. $30,000 of notes payable are due for payment next year.
4. Repair expense is 100% administrative.

Instructions

(a) Enter the trial balance on a worksheet, and complete the worksheet.

(b) Prepare a multiple-step income statement and an owner's equity statement for the year, and a classified balance sheet as of November 30, 2008.

(c) Journalize the adjusting entries.

(d) Journalize the closing entries.

(e) Prepare a post-closing trial balance.

(a) Adj. trial balance $1,010,780
Net loss $4,280
(b) Gross profit $248,700
Total assets $197,300

PROBLEMS: SET B

Journalize purchase and sales transactions under a perpetual inventory system.

(SO 2, 3)

P5-1B Sorvino Book Warehouse distributes hardcover books to retail stores and extends credit terms of 2/10, n/30 to all of its customers. At the end of May, Sorvino's inventory consisted of 240 books purchased at $1,200. During the month of June the following merchandising transactions occurred.

June 1 Purchased 180 books on account for $5 each from Atkinson Publishers, FOB destination, terms 2/10, n/30. The appropriate party also made a cash payment of $50 for the freight on this date.
3 Sold 120 books on account to Readers-R-Us for $10 each.
6 Received $50 credit for 10 books returned to Atkinson Publishers.
9 Paid Atkinson Publishers in full, less discount.
15 Received payment in full from Readers-R-Us.
17 Sold 150 books on account to Bargain Books for $10 each.
20 Purchased 120 books on account for $5 each from Bookem Publishers, FOB destination, terms 2/15, n/30. The appropriate party also made a cash payment of $50 for the freight on this date.
24 Received payment in full from Bargain Books.
26 Paid Bookem Publishers in full, less discount.
28 Sold 110 books on account to Read-n-Weep Bookstore for $10 each.
30 Granted Read-n-Weep Bookstore $150 credit for 15 books returned costing $75.

Sorvino Book Warehouse's chart of accounts includes the following: No. 101 Cash, No. 112 Accounts Receivable, No. 120 Merchandise Inventory, No. 201 Accounts Payable, No. 401 Sales, No. 412 Sales Returns and Allowances, No. 414 Sales Discounts, No. 505 Cost of Goods Sold.

Instructions

Journalize the transactions for the month of June for Sorvino Book Warehouse using a perpetual inventory system.

Journalize, post, and prepare a partial income statement.

(SO 2, 3, 5, 6)

GLS

P5-2B Newson Hardware Store completed the following merchandising transactions in the month of May. At the beginning of May, the ledger of Newson showed Cash of $10,000 and John Newson, Capital of $10,000.

May 1 Purchased merchandise on account from Mesa Wholesale Supply $8,000, terms 2/10, n/30.
2 Sold merchandise on account $4,000, terms 1/10, n/30. The cost of the merchandise sold was $3,100.
5 Received credit from Mesa Wholesale Supply for merchandise returned $600.
9 Received collections in full, less discounts, from customers billed on sales of $4,000 on May 2.
10 Paid Mesa Wholesale Supply in full, less discount.
11 Purchased supplies for cash $900.
12 Purchased merchandise for cash $2,700.
15 Received refund for poor quality merchandise from supplier on cash purchase $230.
17 Purchased merchandise from Sherrick Distributors $2,500, FOB shipping point, terms 2/10, n/30.
19 Paid freight on May 17 purchase $250.
24 Sold merchandise for cash $6,200. The merchandise sold had a cost of $4,600.
25 Purchased merchandise from Duffy Inc. $1,000, FOB destination, terms 2/10, n/30.
27 Paid Sherrick Distributors in full, less discount.
29 Made refunds to cash customers for defective merchandise $100. The returned merchandise had a scrap value of $20.
31 Sold merchandise on account $1,600, terms n/30. The cost of the merchandise sold was $1,120.

Newson Hardware's chart of accounts includes the following: No. 101 Cash, No. 112 Accounts Receivable, No. 120 Merchandise Inventory, No. 126 Supplies, No. 201 Accounts Payable, No. 301 John Newson, Capital, No. 401 Sales, No. 412 Sales Returns and Allowances, No. 414 Sales Discounts, No. 505 Cost of Goods Sold.

Instructions

(a) Journalize the transactions using a perpetual inventory system.
(b) Enter the beginning cash and capital balances and post the transactions. (Use J1 for the journal reference.)
(c) Prepare an income statement through gross profit for the month of May 2008.

(c) Gross profit $2,860

P5-3B Huffman Department Store is located in midtown Metropolis. During the past several years, net income has been declining because of suburban shopping centers. At the end of the company's fiscal year on November 30, 2008, the following accounts appeared in two of its trial balances.

Prepare financial statements and adjusting and closing entries.

(SO 4, 5)

	Unadjusted	Adjusted		Unadjusted	Adjusted
Accounts Payable	$ 47,310	$ 47,310	Interest Revenue	$ 5,000	$ 5,000
Accounts Receivable	11,770	11,770	Merchandise Inventory	36,200	36,200
Accumulated Depr.—Delivery Equip.	15,680	19,680	Notes Payable	46,000	46,000
Accumulated Depr.—Store Equip.	32,300	41,800	Prepaid Insurance	13,500	4,500
Cash	8,000	8,000	Property Tax Expense		3,500
M. Huffman, Capital	84,200	84,200	Property Taxes Payable		3,500
Cost of Goods Sold	633,220	633,220	Rent Expense	19,000	19,000
Delivery Expense	8,200	8,200	Salaries Expense	120,000	120,000
Delivery Equipment	57,000	57,000	Sales	850,000	850,000
Depr. Expense—Delivery Equip.		4,000	Sales Commissions Expense	8,000	14,000
Depr. Expense—Store Equip.		9,500	Sales Commissions Payable		6,000
M. Huffman, Drawing	12,000	12,000	Sales Returns and Allowances	10,000	10,000
Insurance Expense		9,000	Store Equip.	125,000	125,000
Interest Expense	8,000	8,000	Utilities Expense	10,600	10,600

Analysis reveals the following additional data.

1. Salaries expense is 75% selling and 25% administrative.
2. Insurance expense is 50% selling and 50% administrative.
3. Rent expense, utilities expense, and property tax expense are administrative expenses.
4. Notes payable are due in 2011.

Instructions

(a) Prepare a multiple-step income statement, an owner's equity statement, and a classified balance sheet.
(b) Journalize the adjusting entries that were made.
(c) Journalize the closing entries that are necessary.

(a) Net income $5,980
Capital $78,180
Total assets $180,990

P5-4B Mike Palmer, a former professional golf star, operates Mike's Pro Shop at Bay Golf Course. At the beginning of the current season on April 1, the ledger of Mike's Pro Shop showed Cash $2,500, Merchandise Inventory $3,500, and M. Palmer, Capital $6,000. The following transactions were completed during April.

Journalize, post, and prepare a trial balance.

(SO 2, 3, 4)

GLS

Apr. 5 Purchased golf bags, clubs, and balls on account from Ramos Co. $1,500, FOB shipping point, terms 2/10, n/60.
7 Paid freight on Ramos purchase $80.
9 Received credit from Ramos Co. for merchandise returned $100.
10 Sold merchandise on account to members $1,100, terms n/30. The merchandise sold had a cost of $810.
12 Purchased golf shoes, sweaters, and other accessories on account from Penguin Sportswear $860, terms 1/10, n/30.
14 Paid Ramos Co. in full, less discount.
17 Received credit from Penguin Sportswear for merchandise returned $60.
20 Made sales on account to members $700, terms n/30. The cost of the merchandise sold was $490.
21 Paid Penguin Sportswear in full, less discount.
27 Granted an allowance to members for clothing that did not fit properly $40.
30 Received payments on account from members $1,000.

The chart of accounts for the pro shop includes the following: No. 101 Cash, No. 112 Accounts Receivable, No. 120 Merchandise Inventory, No. 201 Accounts Payable, No. 301 M. Palmer, Capital, No. 401 Sales, No. 412 Sales Returns and Allowances, No. 505 Cost of Goods Sold.

Instructions

(a) Journalize the April transactions using a perpetual inventory system.

(b) Enter the beginning balances in the ledger accounts and post the April transactions. (Use J1 for the journal reference.)

(c) Total debits $7,800

(c) Prepare a trial balance on April 30, 2008.

Determine cost of goods sold and gross profit under periodic approach.

(SO 6, 7)

P5-5B At the end of Duckwall Department Store's fiscal year on November 30, 2008, these accounts appeared in its adjusted trial balance.

Freight-in	$ 5,060
Merchandise Inventory	44,360
Purchases	650,000
Purchase Discounts	7,000
Purchase Returns and Allowances	3,000
Sales	900,000
Sales Returns and Allowances	20,000

Additional facts:

1. Merchandise inventory on November 30, 2008, is $36,200.
2. Note that Duckwall Department Store uses a periodic system.

Instructions

Gross profit $226,780

Prepare an income statement through gross profit for the year ended November 30, 2008.

Calculate missing amounts and assess profitability.

(SO 6, 7)

P5-6B Howit Inc. operates a retail operation that purchases and sells snowmobiles, amongst other outdoor products. The company purchases all merchandise inventory on credit and uses a periodic inventory system. The accounts payable account is used for recording inventory purchases only; all other current liabilities are accrued in separate accounts. You are provided with the following selected information for the fiscal years 2005 through 2008, inclusive.

	2005	2006	2007	2008
Income Statement Data				
Sales		$96,850	$ (e)	$82,220
Cost of goods sold		(a)	25,140	25,990
Gross profit		69,640	61,540	(i)
Operating expenses		63,500	(f)	52,060
Net income		$ (b)	$ 4,570	$ (j)
Balance Sheet Data				
Merchandise inventory	$13,000	$ (c)	$14,700	$ (k)
Accounts payable	5,800	6,500	4,600	(l)
Additional Information				
Purchases of merchandise inventory on account		$25,890	$ (g)	$24,050
Cash payments to suppliers		(d)	(h)	24,650

Instructions

(c) $11,680
(g) $28,160
(i) $56,230

(a) Calculate the missing amounts.

(b) Sales declined over the 3-year fiscal period, 2006–2008. Does that mean that profitability necessarily also declined? Explain, computing the gross profit rate and the profit margin ratio for each fiscal year to help support your answer. (Round to one decimal place.)

***P5-7B** At the beginning of the current season on April 1, the ledger of Four Oaks Pro Shop showed Cash $2,500; Merchandise Inventory $3,500; and Phil Mickel, Capital $6,000. These transactions occured during April 2008.

Journalize, post, and prepare trial balance and partial income statement using periodic approach.

(SO 7, 8)

GLS

Apr. 5 Purchased golf bags, clubs, and balls on account from Hardee Co. $2,200, FOB shipping point, terms 2/10, n/60.
7 Paid freight on Hardee Co. purchases $80.
9 Received credit from Hardee Co. for merchandise returned $200.
10 Sold merchandise on account to members $950, terms n/30.
12 Purchased golf shoes, sweaters, and other accessories on account from Arrow Sportswear $460, terms 1/10, n/30.
14 Paid Hardee Co. in full.
17 Received credit from Arrow Sportswear for merchandise returned $60.
20 Made sales on account to members $1,000, terms n/30.
21 Paid Arrow Sportswear in full.
27 Granted credit to members for clothing that did not fit properly $75.
30 Received payments on account from members $1,100.

The chart of accounts for the pro shop includes Cash; Accounts Receivable, Merchandise Inventory; Accounts Payable; Phil Mickel, Capital; Sales; Sales Returns and Allowances; Purchases; Purchase Returns and Allowances; Purchase Discounts, and Freight-in.

Instructions

(a) Journalize the April transactions using a periodic inventory system.
(b) Using T accounts, enter the beginning balances in the ledger accounts and post the April transactions.
(c) Prepare a trial balance on April 30, 2008.
(d) Prepare an income statement through gross profit, assuming merchandise inventory on hand at April 30 is $4,524.

(c) Tot. trial balance $8,254
Gross profit $463

PROBLEMS: SET C

Visit the book's website at **www.wiley.com/college/weygandt**, and choose the Student Companion site, to access Problem Set C.

CONTINUING COOKIE CHRONICLE

(*Note:* This is a continuation of the Cookie Chronicle from Chapters 1 through 4.)

CCC5 Because Natalie has had such a successful first few months, she is considering other opportunities to develop her business. One opportunity is the sale of fine European mixers. The owner of Kzinski Supply Company has approached Natalie to become the exclusive U.S. distributor of these fine mixers in her state. The current cost of a mixer is approximately $525 (U.S.), and Natalie would sell each one for $1,050. Natalie comes to you for advice on how to account for these mixers.

Go to the book's website, www.wiley.com/college/weygandt, to see the completion of this problem.

BROADENING YOUR PERSPECTIVE

FINANCIAL REPORTING AND ANALYSIS

Financial Reporting Problem

PepsiCo, Inc.

BYP5-1 The financial statements of PepsiCo are presented in Appendix A at the end of this textbook.

Instructions

Answer the following questions using the Consolidated Statement of Income.

(a) What was the percentage change in (1) sales and in (2) net income from 2003 to 2004 and from 2004 to 2005?

(b) What was the company's gross profit rate in 2003, 2004, and 2005?

(c) What was the company's percentage of net income to net sales in 2003, 2004, and 2005? Comment on any trend in this percentage.

Comparative Analysis Problem

PepsiCo, Inc. vs. The Coca-Cola Company

BYP5-2 PepsiCo's financial statements are presented in Appendix A. Coca-Cola's financial statements are presented in Appendix B.

Instructions

(a) Based on the information contained in these financial statements, determine each of the following for each company.
- **(1)** Gross profit for 2005.
- **(2)** Gross profit rate for 2005.
- **(3)** Operating income for 2005.
- **(4)** Percent change in operating income from 2004 to 2005.

(b) What conclusions concerning the relative profitability of the two companies can you draw from these data?

Exploring the Web

BYP5-3 No financial decision maker should ever rely solely on the financial information reported in the annual report to make decisions. It is important to keep abreast of financial news. This activity demonstrates how to search for financial news on the Web.

Address: biz.yahoo.com/i, or go to **www.wiley.com/college/weygandt**

Steps:
1. Type in either PepsiCo or Coca-Cola.
2. Choose **News**.
3. Select an article that sounds interesting to you.

Instructions

(a) What was the source of the article? (For example, Reuters, Businesswire, PR Newswire.)

(b) Pretend that you are a personal financial planner and that one of your clients owns stock in the company. Write a brief memo to your client, summarizing the article and explaining the implications of the article for their investment.

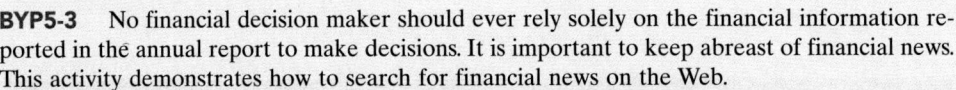

CRITICAL THINKING

Decision Making Across the Organization

BYP5-4 Three years ago, Carrie Dungy and her brother-in-law Luke Barber opened FedCo Department Store. For the first two years, business was good, but the following condensed income results for 2007 were disappointing.

FEDCO DEPARTMENT STORE
Income Statement
For the Year Ended December 31, 2007

Net sales		$700,000
Cost of goods sold		553,000
Gross profit		147,000
Operating expenses		
Selling expenses	$100,000	
Administrative expenses	20,000	120,000
Net income		$ 27,000

Carrie believes the problem lies in the relatively low gross profit rate (gross profit divided by net sales) of 21%. Luke believes the problem is that operating expenses are too high.

Carrie thinks the gross profit rate can be improved by making both of the following changes. She does not anticipate that these changes will have any effect on operating expenses.

1. Increase average selling prices by 17%. This increase is expected to lower sales volume so that total sales will increase only 6%.
2. Buy merchandise in larger quantities and take all purchase discounts. These changes are expected to increase the gross profit rate by 3 percentage points.

Luke thinks expenses can be cut by making both of the following changes. He feels that these changes will not have any effect on net sales.

1. Cut 2007 sales salaries of $60,000 in half and give sales personnel a commission of 2% of net sales.
2. Reduce store deliveries to one day per week rather than twice a week; this change will reduce 2007 delivery expenses of $30,000 by 40%.

Carrie and Luke come to you for help in deciding the best way to improve net income.

Instructions

With the class divided into groups, answer the following.

(a) Prepare a condensed income statement for 2008 assuming (1) Carrie's changes are implemented and (2) Luke's ideas are adopted.
(b) What is your recommendation to Carrie and Luke?
(c) Prepare a condensed income statement for 2008 assuming both sets of proposed changes are made.

Communication Activity

BYP5-5 The following situation is in chronological order.

1. Flutie decides to buy a surfboard.
2. He calls Surfing USA Co. to inquire about their surfboards.
3. Two days later he requests Surfing USA Co. to make him a surfboard.
4. Three days later, Surfing USA Co. sends him a purchase order to fill out.
5. He sends back the purchase order.
6. Surfing USA Co. receives the completed purchase order.
7. Surfing USA Co. completes the surfboard.
8. Flutie picks up the surfboard.
9. Surfing USA Co. bills Flutie.
10. Surfing USA Co. receives payment from Flutie.

Instructions

In a memo to the president of Surfing USA Co., answer the following.

(a) When should Surfing USA Co. record the sale?
(b) Suppose that with his purchase order, Flutie is required to make a down payment. Would that change your answer?

Ethics Case

BYP5-6 Laura McAntee was just hired as the assistant treasurer of Dorchester Stores. The company is a specialty chain store with nine retail stores concentrated in one metropolitan area. Among other things, the payment of all invoices is centralized in one of the departments Laura will manage. Her primary responsibility is to maintain the company's high credit rating by paying all bills when due and to take advantage of all cash discounts.

Danny Feeney, the former assistant treasurer who has been promoted to treasurer, is training Laura in her new duties. He instructs Laura that she is to continue the practice of preparing all checks "net of discount" and dating the checks the last day of the discount period. "But," Danny continues, "we always hold the checks at least 4 days beyond the discount period before mailing them. That way we get another 4 days of interest on our money. Most of our creditors need our business and don't complain. And, if they scream about our missing the discount period, we blame it on the mail room or the post office. We've only lost one discount out of every hundred we take that way. I think everybody does it. By the way, welcome to our team!"

Instructions
(a) What are the ethical considerations in this case?
(b) Who are the stakeholders that are harmed or benefitted in this situation?
(c) Should Laura continue the practice started by Danny? Does she have any choice?

"All About You" Activity

BYP5-7 In the **All About You** feature in this chapter (page 213), you learned about channel stuffing—intentionally shipping customers more goods than they requested in order to boost reported sales. Channel stuffing is just one type of challenge to proper revenue recognition. There are many situations in business where it is difficult to determine the proper period in which to record revenue.

Suppose that after graduation with a degree in finance, you take a job as a manager at a consumer electronics store called Atlantis Electronics. The company has expanded rapidly in order to compete with Best Buy and Circuit City.

Instructions
Provide a response to the questions below. In each case provide reasoning to support your conclusion.

(a) Atlantis Electronics operates a website. It earns revenue from fees collected from advertisements placed on its site. It recently rented space on its site worth $50,000 to Lester Consumer Goods for a 2-year period. Rather than pay cash, Lester will provide space on Lester's website worth $50,000 to Atlantis for the same 2-year period. Since the amount given and received by each party is equal, no cash will change hands. How should each company record the $50,000 of advertising space? Should Atlantis record $50,000 of revenue for the advertising space given to Lester, or should it recognize no revenue at all?
(b) Atlantis has also begun selling gift cards for its electronic products. The cards are available in any dollar amount, and allow the holder of the card to purchase an item for up to 2 years from the time the card is purchased. If the card is not used during that 2 years, it expires. At what point should the revenue from the gift cards be recognized? Should the revenue be recognized at the time the card is sold, or should it be recorded when the card is redeemed?
(c) Atlantis sells extended warranties along with many of its electronics. It sells a stereo for $1,000 and a related 3-year extended warranty for $150 to cover maintenance and repair of the stereo. When should the $1,000 be recognized as revenue—at the time of sale, or at the time that the 3-year warranty is completed? At what time should the $150 for the 3-year warranty be recorded as revenue—at the time of sale, equally over the 3-year period, or at the end of the 3-year period?

Answers to Insight and Accounting Across the Organization Questions

p. 197 Morrow Snowboards Improves Its Stock Appeal
Q: If a perpetual system keeps track of inventory on a daily basis, why do companies ever need to do a physical count?
A: *A perpetual system keeps track of all sales and purchases on a continuous basis. This provides a constant record of the number of units in the inventory. However, if employees make errors in recording sales or purchases, the inventory value will not be correct. As a consequence, all companies do a physical count of inventory at least once a year.*

p. 203 Should Publishers Have Liberal Return Policies?
Q: If a company expects significant returns, what are the implications for revenue recognition?
A: *If a company expects significant returns, it should make an adjusting entry at the end of the year reducing sales by the estimated amount of sales returns. This is necessary so as not to overstate the amount of revenue recognized in the period.*

p. 210 For IBM, What Is Operating?
Q: Why have investors and analysts demanded more accuracy in isolating "Other gains and losses" from operating items?
A: *Greater accuracy in the classification of operating versus nonoperating ("Other gains and losses") items permits investors and analysts to judge the real operating margin, the results of continuing operations, and management's ability to control operating expenses.*

Authors' Comments on *All About You:* When Is a Sale a Sale? (p. 213)

Channel stuffing represents a difficult area for accounting. Some instances are clearly attempts by management to overstate sales. For example, Sunbeam Corporation shipped $1.5 million of barbeque grills to a distributor; all were eventually returned. In many other instances, though, it might be argued that although such sales tactics are *aggressive*, it isn't clear that they are illegal or unethical business practices, or even that they violate good accounting. Even in the situation related to The Coca-Cola Company, the SEC concluded that the sales were "technically legitimate" but that Coke had not adequately disclosed the existence of these sales, nor discussed the potential negative impact they might have on future periods.

In general, if the company makes an accurate estimate of the amount of expected returns, then the shipping of excess goods is of little concern. In fact, in some industries, such as magazine and book sales, significant returns are expected and routinely estimated.

Answer to PepsiCo Review It Question 1, p. 212

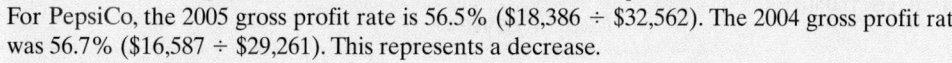

For PepsiCo, the 2005 gross profit rate is 56.5% ($18,386 ÷ $32,562). The 2004 gross profit rate was 56.7% ($16,587 ÷ $29,261). This represents a decrease.

Answers to Self-Study Questions

1. c **2.** a **3.** c **4.** b **5.** c **6.** d **7.** b **8.** c **9.** d **10.** d **11.** a ***12.** b ***13.** a

Remember to go back to the Navigator box on the chapter-opening page and check off your completed work.

Chapter 6

Inventories

STUDY OBJECTIVES

After studying this chapter, you should be able to:

1 Describe the steps in determining inventory quantities.

2 Explain the accounting for inventories and apply the inventory cost flow methods.

3 Explain the financial effects of the inventory cost flow assumptions.

4 Explain the lower-of-cost-or-market basis of accounting for inventories.

5 Indicate the effects of inventory errors on the financial statements.

6 Compute and interpret the inventory turnover ratio.

✓ *The Navigator*

✓ The Navigator

Scan **Study Objectives**	■
Read **Feature Story**	■
Read **Preview**	■
Read text and answer **Before You Go On** p. 247 ■ p. 256 ■ p. 260 ■	
Work **Demonstration Problems**	■
Review **Summary of Study Objectives**	■
Answer **Self-Study Questions**	■
Complete **Assignments**	■

Feature Story

WHERE IS THAT SPARE BULLDOZER BLADE?

Let's talk inventory—big, bulldozer-size inventory. Caterpillar Inc. (*www.cat.com*) is the world's largest manufacturer of construction and mining equipment, diesel and natural gas engines, and industrial gas turbines. It sells its products in over 200 countries, making it one of the most successful U.S. exporters. More than 70% of its productive assets are located domestically, and nearly 50% of its sales are foreign.

During the 1980s Caterpillar's profitability suffered, but today it is very successful. A big part of this turnaround can be attributed to effective management of its inventory. Imagine what a bulldozer costs. Now imagine what it costs Caterpillar to have too many bulldozers sitting around in inventory—a situation the company definitely wants to avoid. Conversely, Caterpillar must make sure it has enough inventory to meet demand.

During a recent 7-year period, Caterpillar's sales increased by 100%, while its inventory increased by only 50%. To achieve this dramatic reduction in the amount of resources tied up in inventory, while continuing to meet customers' needs, Caterpillar used a two-pronged approach. First, it completed a factory modernization program, which dramatically increased its production efficiency. The program reduced by 60% the amount of inventory the company processed at any one time. It also reduced by an incredible 75% the time it takes to manufacture a part.

Second, Caterpillar dramatically improved its parts distribution system. It ships more than 100,000 items daily from its 23 distribution centers strategically located around the world (10 *million* square feet of warehouse space—remember, we're talking bulldozers). The company can virtually guarantee that it can get any part to anywhere in the world within 24 hours. Although this network services 550,000 part numbers, Caterpillar is able to ship 99.7% of its orders within hours. In fact, Caterpillar's distribution system is so advanced that it created a subsidiary, Caterpillar Logistics Services, Inc., that warehouses and distributes other companies' products. This subsidiary distributes products as diverse as running shoes, computer software, and auto parts all around the world.

In short, how Caterpillar manages and accounts for its inventory goes a long way in explaining how profitable it is.

✓ The Navigator

Inside Chapter 6...

Preview of Chapter 6

In the previous chapter, we discussed the accounting for merchandise inventory using a perpetual inventory system. In this chapter, we explain the methods used to calculate the cost of inventory on hand at the balance sheet date and the cost of goods sold.

The content and organization of this chapter are as follows.

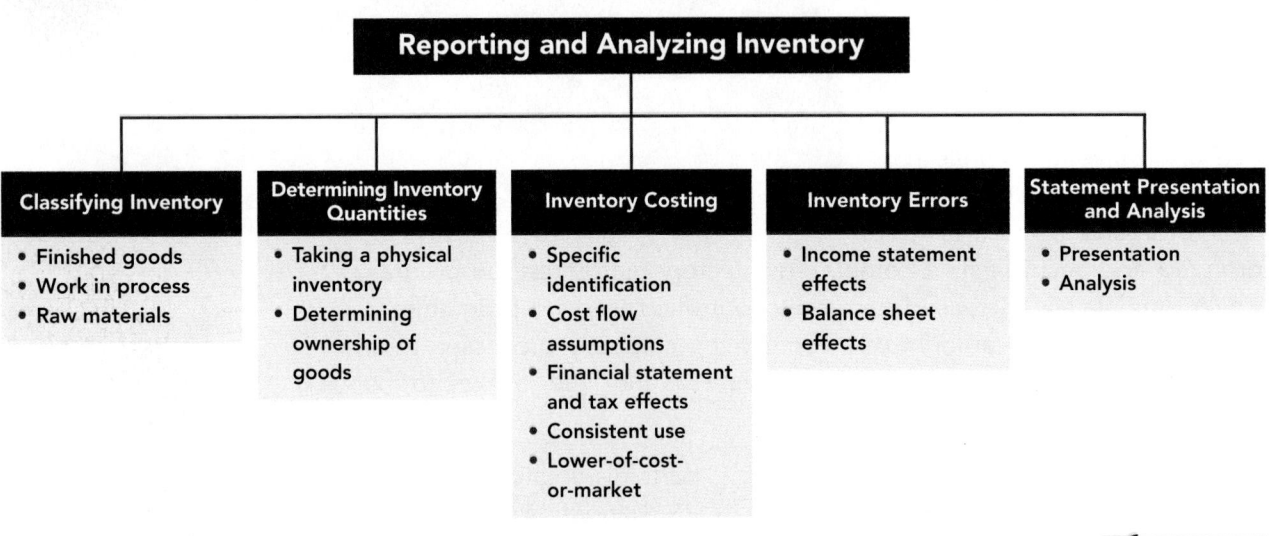

Reporting and Analyzing Inventory

- **Classifying Inventory**
  - Finished goods
  - Work in process
  - Raw materials
- **Determining Inventory Quantities**
  - Taking a physical inventory
  - Determining ownership of goods
- **Inventory Costing**
  - Specific identification
  - Cost flow assumptions
  - Financial statement and tax effects
  - Consistent use
  - Lower-of-cost-or-market
- **Inventory Errors**
  - Income statement effects
  - Balance sheet effects
- **Statement Presentation and Analysis**
  - Presentation
  - Analysis

✓ *The Navigator*

CLASSIFYING INVENTORY

How a company classifies its inventory depends on whether the firm is a merchandiser or a manufacturer. In a **merchandising** company, such as those described in Chapter 5, inventory consists of many different items. For example, in a grocery store, canned goods, dairy products, meats, and produce are just a few of the inventory items on hand. These items have two common characteristics: (1) They are owned by the company, and (2) they are in a form ready for sale to customers in the ordinary course of business. Thus, merchandisers need only one inventory classification, **merchandise inventory**, to describe the many different items that make up the total inventory.

In a **manufacturing** company, some inventory may not yet be ready for sale. As a result, manufacturers usually classify inventory into three categories: finished goods, work in process, and raw materials. **Finished goods inventory** is manufactured items that are completed and ready for sale. **Work in process** is that portion of manufactured inventory that has been placed into the production process but is not yet complete. **Raw materials** are the basic goods that will be used in production but have not yet been placed into production.

HELPFUL HINT

Regardless of the classification, companies report all inventories under Current Assets on the balance sheet.

For example, Caterpillar classifies earth-moving tractors completed and ready for sale as **finished goods**. It classifies the tractors on the assembly line in various stages of production as **work in process**. The steel, glass, tires, and other components that are on hand waiting to be used in the production of tractors are identified as **raw materials**.

By observing the levels and changes in the levels of these three inventory types, financial statement users can gain insight into management's production plans. For example, low levels of raw materials and high levels of finished goods suggest that management believes it has enough inventory on hand, and production will be slowing down—perhaps in anticipation of a recession. On the other hand, high levels of raw materials and low levels of finished goods probably indicate that management is planning to step up production.

Many companies have significantly lowered inventory levels and costs using **just-in-time (JIT) inventory** methods. Under a just-in-time method, companies manufacture or purchase goods just in time for use. Dell is famous for having developed a system for making computers in response to individual customer requests. Even though it makes each computer to meet each customer's particular specifications, Dell is able to assemble the computer and put it on a truck in less than 48 hours. By integrating its information systems with those of its suppliers, Dell reduced its inventories to nearly zero. This is a huge advantage in an industry where products become obsolete nearly overnight.

The accounting concepts discussed in this chapter apply to the inventory classifications of both merchandising and manufacturing companies. Our focus here is on merchandise inventory.

ACCOUNTING ACROSS THE ORGANIZATION

How Wal-Mart Tracks Inventory

Wal-Mart improved its inventory control in 2004 with the introduction of electronic product codes (EPCs). Much like bar codes, which tell a retailer the number of boxes of a specific product it has, EPCs go a step farther, helping to distinguish one box of a specific product from another. EPCs use radio frequency identification (RFID) technology, the same technology behind keyless remotes used to unlock car doors.

Companies currently use EPCs to track shipments from supplier to distribution center to store. Other potential uses include help with monitoring product expiration dates and acting quickly on product recalls. Wal-Mart also anticipates faster returns and warranty processing using EPCs. This technology will further assist Wal-Mart managers in their efforts to ensure that their stores have just the right type of inventory, in just the right amount, in just the right place.

? Why is inventory control important to managers such as those at Wal-Mart?

DETERMINING INVENTORY QUANTITIES

STUDY OBJECTIVE 1

Describe the steps in determining inventory quantities.

No matter whether they are using a periodic or perpetual inventory system, all companies need to determine inventory quantities at the end of the accounting period. When using a perpetual system, companies take a physical inventory for two purposes: The first purpose is to check the accuracy of their perpetual inventory records. The second is to determine the amount of inventory lost due to wasted raw materials, shoplifting, or employee theft.

Companies using a periodic inventory system must take a physical inventory for two *different* purposes: to determine the inventory on hand at the balance sheet date, and to determine the cost of goods sold for the period.

Determining inventory quantities involves two steps: (1) taking a physical inventory of goods on hand and (2) determining the ownership of goods.

Taking a Physical Inventory

Taking a physical inventory involves actually counting, weighing, or measuring each kind of inventory on hand. In many companies, taking an inventory is a formidable task. Retailers such as Target, True Value Hardware, or Home Depot have thousands of different inventory items. An inventory count is generally more accurate when goods are not being sold or received during the counting. Consequently, companies often "take inventory" when the business is closed or when business is slow. Many retailers close early on a chosen day in January—after the holiday sales and returns, when inventories are at their lowest level—to count inventory. Recall from Chapter 5 that Wal-Mart had a year-end of January 31. Companies take the physical inventory at the end of the accounting period.[1]

ETHICS INSIGHT

"Fill 'Em Up—With Water, Not Oil"

Over the years inventory has played a role in many fraud cases. A classic case involved salad oil. Management of a salad-oil company filled storage tanks mostly with water. Since oil rises to the top, the auditors thought the tanks were full of oil. In addition, management said they had more tanks than they really did—they repainted numbers on the tanks to confuse auditors.

More recently, managers at women's apparel maker Leslie Fay were convicted of falsifying inventory records to boost net income—and consequently to boost management bonuses.

? What effect does an overstatement of inventory have on a company's financial statements?

Determining Ownership of Goods

One challenge in computing inventory quantities is determining what inventory a company owns. To determine ownership of goods, two questions must be answered: Do all of the goods included in the count belong to the company? Does the company own any goods that were not included in the count?

GOODS IN TRANSIT

A complication in determining ownership is **goods in transit** (on board a truck, train, ship, or plane) at the end of the period. The company may have purchased goods that have not yet been received, or it may have sold goods that have not yet been delivered. To arrive at an accurate count, the company must determine ownership of these goods.

Goods in transit should be included in the inventory of the company that has legal title to the goods. Legal title is determined by the terms of the sale, as shown in Illustration 6-1 and described below.

1. When the terms are **FOB (free on board) shipping point**, ownership of the goods passes to the buyer when the public carrier accepts the goods from the seller.
2. When the terms are **FOB destination**, ownership of the goods remains with the seller until the goods reach the buyer.

If goods in transit at the statement date are ignored, inventory quantities may be seriously miscounted. Assume, for example, that Hargrove Company has 20,000 units of inventory on hand on December 31. It also has the following goods in transit: (1) sales of 1,500 units shipped December 31 FOB destination, and (2) purchases of 2,500 units shipped FOB shipping point by the seller on December 31. Hargrove has legal title to both the 1,500 units sold and the 2,500 units purchased. If the

[1]To estimate the cost of inventory when a physical inventory cannot be taken (e.g., the inventory is destroyed) or when it is inconvenient (e.g., during interim periods), companies can use estimation methods. We discuss these methods—gross profit method and retail inventory method—in Appendix 6B.

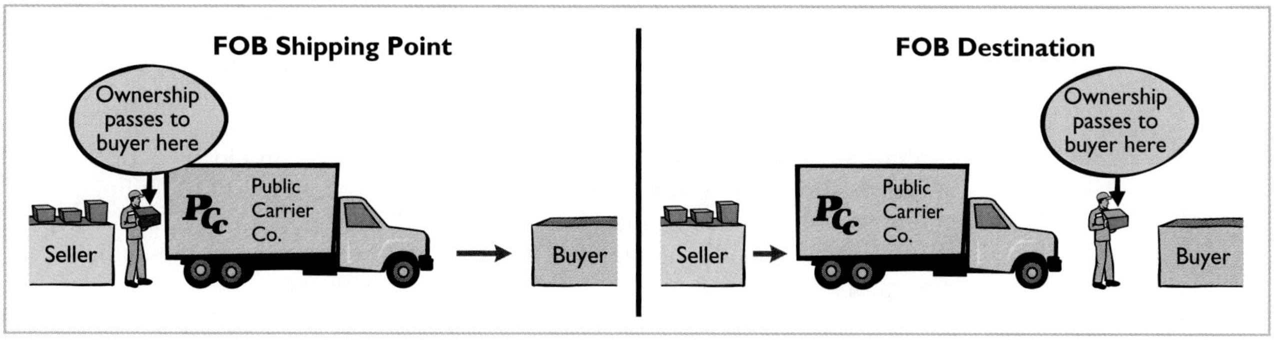

Illustration 6-1
Terms of sale

company ignores the units in transit, it would understate inventory quantities by 4,000 units (1,500 + 2,500).

As we will see later in the chapter, inaccurate inventory counts affect not only the inventory amount shown on the balance sheet but also the cost of goods sold calculation on the income statement.

ETHICS NOTE

Employees of Craig Consumer Electronics **allegedly overstated the company's inventory figures by improperly classifying defective goods as either new or refurbished. They also were accused of stating that the company owned goods from suppliers when in fact the company did not own the shipments, or the shipments did not even exist.**

CONSIGNED GOODS

In some lines of business, it is common to hold the goods of other parties and try to sell the goods for them for a fee, but without taking ownership of the goods. These are called **consigned goods**.

For example, you might have a used car that you would like to sell. If you take the item to a dealer, the dealer might be willing to put the car on its lot and charge you a commission if it is sold. Under this agreement the dealer **would not take ownership** of the car, which would still belong to you. Therefore, if an inventory count were taken, the car would not be included in the dealer's inventory.

Many car, boat, and antique dealers sell goods on consignment to keep their inventory costs down and to avoid the risk of purchasing an item that they won't be able to sell. Today even some manufacturers are making consignment agreements with their suppliers in order to keep their inventory levels low.

Before You Go On...

REVIEW IT

1. What steps are involved in determining inventory quantities?
2. How is ownership determined for goods in transit at the balance sheet date?
3. Who has title to consigned goods?

DO IT

Hasbeen Company completed its inventory count. It arrived at a total inventory value of $200,000. As a new member of Hasbeen's accounting department, you have been given the information listed below. Discuss how this information affects the reported cost of inventory.

1. Hasbeen included in the inventory goods held on consignment for Falls Co., costing $15,000.
2. The company did not include in the count purchased goods of $10,000 which were in transit (terms: FOB shipping point).
3. The company did not include in the count sold inventory with a cost of $12,000 which was in transit (terms: FOB shipping point).

Action Plan
- Apply the rules of ownership to goods held on consignment.
- Apply the rules of ownership to goods in transit FOB shipping point.

Solution The goods of $15,000 held on consignment should be deducted from the inventory count. The goods of $10,000 purchased FOB shipping point should be added to the inventory count. Sold goods of $12,000 which were in transit FOB shipping point should not be included in the ending inventory. Thus, inventory should be carried at $195,000.

Related exercise material: *BE6-1, E6-1, and E6-2.*

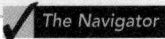

The Navigator

INVENTORY COSTING

STUDY OBJECTIVE 2

Explain the accounting for inventories and apply the inventory cost flow methods.

After a company has determined the quantity of units of inventory, it applies unit costs to the quantities to compute the total cost of the inventory and the cost of goods sold. This process can be complicated if a company has purchased inventory items at different times and at different prices.

For example, assume that Crivitz TV Company purchases three identical 46-inch TVs on different dates at costs of $700, $750, and $800. During the year Crivitz sold two sets at $1,200 each. These facts are summarized in Illustration 6-2.

Illustration 6-2
Data for inventory costing example

Purchases			
February 3	1 TV	at	$700
March 5	1 TV	at	$750
May 22	1 TV	at	$800
Sales			
June 1	2 TVs	for	$2,400 ($1,200 × 2)

Cost of goods sold will differ depending on which two TVs the company sold. For example, it might be $1,450 ($700 + $750), or $1,500 ($700 + $800), or $1,550 ($750 + $800). In this section we discuss alternative costing methods available to Crivitz.

Specific Identification

If Crivitz sold the TVs it purchased on February 3 and May 22, then its cost of goods sold is $1,500 ($700 + $800), and its ending inventory is $750. If Crivitz can positively identify which particular units it sold and which are still in ending inventory, it can use the **specific identification method** of inventory costing (see Illustration 6-3, page 249). Using this method, companies can accurately determine ending inventory and cost of goods sold.

Specific identification requires that companies keep records of the original cost of each individual inventory item. Historically, specific identification was possible only when a company sold a limited variety of high-unit-cost items that could be identified clearly from the time of purchase through the time of sale. Examples of such products are cars, pianos, or expensive antiques.

Today, bar coding, electronic product codes, and radio frequency identification make it theoretically possible to do specific identification with nearly any type of product. The reality is, however, that this practice is still relatively

ETHICS NOTE

A major disadvantage of the specific identification method is that management may be able to manipulate net income. For example, it can boost net income by selling units purchased at a low cost, or reduce net income by selling units purchased at a high cost.

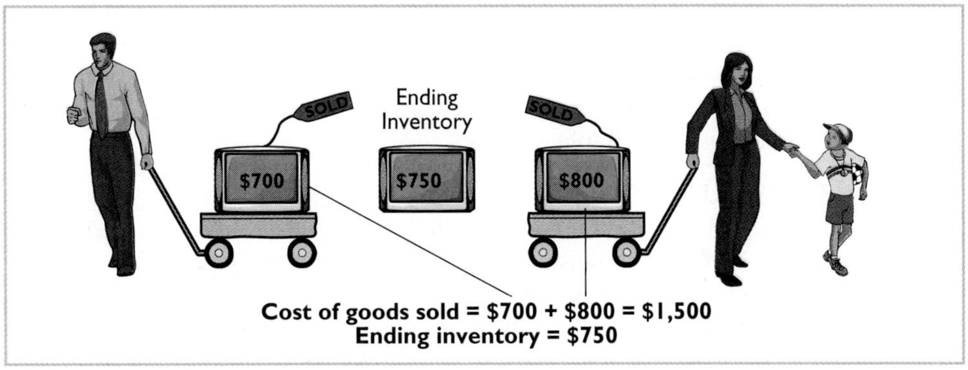

Illustration 6-3
Specific identification method

rare. Instead, rather than keep track of the cost of each particular item sold, most companies make assumptions, called **cost flow assumptions**, about which units were sold.

Cost Flow Assumptions

Because specific identification is often impractical, other cost flow methods are permitted. These differ from specific identification in that they **assume** flows of costs that may be unrelated to the physical flow of goods. There are three assumed cost flow methods:

1. First-in, first-out (FIFO)
2. Last-in, first-out (LIFO)
3. Average-cost

There is no accounting requirement that the cost flow assumption be consistent with the physical movement of the goods. Company management selects the appropriate cost flow method.

To illustrate these three inventory cost flow methods, we will assume that Houston Electronics uses a periodic inventory system and has the information shown in Illustration 6-4 for its Astro condenser.[2] (An appendix to this chapter presents the use of these methods under a perpetual system.)

Illustration 6-4
Cost of goods available for sale

HOUSTON ELECTRONICS
Astro Condensers

Date	Explanation	Units	Unit Cost	Total Cost
Jan. 1	Beginning inventory	100	$10	$ 1,000
Apr. 15	Purchase	200	11	2,200
Aug. 24	Purchase	300	12	3,600
Nov. 27	Purchase	400	13	5,200
	Total	1,000		$12,000

The company had a total of 1,000 units available that it could have sold during the period. The total cost of these units was $12,000. A physical inventory at the end

[2]We have chosen to use the periodic approach for a number of reasons. First, many companies that use a perpetual inventory system use it to keep track of units on hand, but then determine cost of goods sold at the end of the period using one of the three cost flow approaches applied under essentially a periodic approach. In addition, because of the complexity, few companies use average cost on a perpetual basis. Also, most companies that use perpetual LIFO employ dollar-value LIFO, which is presented in more advanced texts. Furthermore, FIFO gives the same results under either perpetual or periodic. And finally, it is easier to demonstrate the cost flow assumptions under the periodic system, which makes it more pedagogically appropriate.

of the year determined that during the year Houston sold 550 units and had 450 units in inventory at December 31. The question then is how to determine what prices to use to value the goods sold and the ending inventory. The sum of the cost allocated to the units sold plus the cost of the units in inventory must be $12,000, the total cost of all goods available for sale.

FIRST-IN, FIRST-OUT (FIFO)

The **FIFO (first-in, first-out) method** assumes that the **earliest goods** purchased are the first to be sold. FIFO often parallels the actual physical flow of merchandise; it generally is good business practice to sell the oldest units first. Under the FIFO method, therefore, the **costs** of the earliest goods purchased are the first to be recognized in determining cost of goods sold. (This does not necessarily mean that the oldest units *are* sold first, but that the costs of the oldest units are *recognized* first. In a bin of picture hangers at the hardware store, for example, no one really knows, nor would it matter, which hangers are sold first.) Illustration 6-5 shows the allocation of the cost of goods available for sale at Houston Electronics under FIFO.

Illustration 6-5
Allocation of costs—FIFO method

HELPFUL HINT
Note the sequencing of the allocation: (1) Compute ending inventory, and (2) determine cost of goods sold.

HELPFUL HINT
Another way of thinking about the calculation of FIFO ending inventory is the *LISH assumption*—last in still here.

COST OF GOODS AVAILABLE FOR SALE

Date	Explanation	Units	Unit Cost	Total Cost
Jan. 1	Beginning inventory	100	$10	$ 1,000
Apr. 15	Purchase	200	11	2,200
Aug. 24	Purchase	300	12	3,600
Nov. 27	Purchase	400	13	5,200
	Total	1,000		**$12,000**

STEP 1: ENDING INVENTORY

Date	Units	Unit Cost	Total Cost
Nov. 27	400	$13	$5,200
Aug. 24	50	12	600
Total	450		**$5,800**

STEP 2: COST OF GOODS SOLD

Cost of goods available for sale	$12,000
Less: Ending inventory	5,800
Cost of goods sold	**$ 6,200**

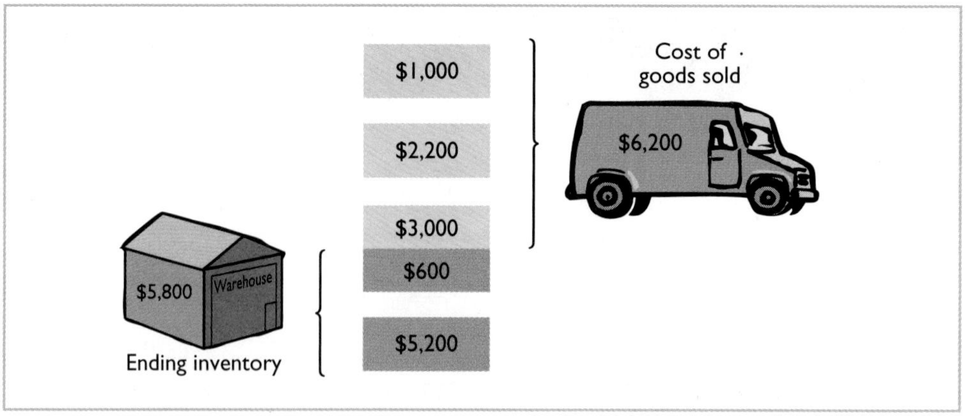

Under FIFO, since it is assumed that the first goods purchased were the first goods sold, ending inventory is based on the prices of the most recent units purchased. That is, **under FIFO, companies obtain the cost of the ending inventory by taking the unit cost of the most recent purchase and working backward until all units of inventory have been costed**. In this example, Houston Electronics prices the 450 units of ending inventory using the *most recent* prices. The last purchase was 400 units at $13 on November 27. The remaining 50 units are priced using the unit cost of the second most recent purchase, $12, on August 24. Next, Houston

Electronics calculates cost of goods sold by subtracting the cost of the units **not sold** (ending inventory) from the cost of all goods available for sale.

Illustration 6-6 demonstrates that companies also can calculate cost of goods sold by pricing the 550 units sold using the prices of the first 550 units acquired. Note that of the 300 units purchased on August 24, only 250 units are assumed sold. This agrees with our calculation of the cost of ending inventory, where 50 of these units were assumed unsold and thus included in ending inventory.

Illustration 6-6
Proof of cost of goods sold

Date	Units	Unit Cost	Total Cost
Jan. 1	100	$10	$1,000
Apr. 15	200	11	2,200
Aug. 24	250	12	3,000
Total	550		**$6,200**

LAST-IN, FIRST-OUT (LIFO)

The **LIFO (last-in, first-out) method** assumes that the **latest goods** purchased are the first to be sold. LIFO seldom coincides with the actual physical flow of inventory. (Exceptions include goods stored in piles, such as coal or hay, where goods are removed from the top of the pile as they are sold.) Under the LIFO method, the **costs** of the latest goods purchased are the first to be recognized in determining cost of goods sold. Illustration 6-7 shows the allocation of the cost of goods available for sale at Houston Electronics under LIFO.

Illustration 6-7
Allocation of costs—LIFO method

COST OF GOODS AVAILABLE FOR SALE

Date	Explanation	Units	Unit Cost	Total Cost
Jan. 1	Beginning inventory	100	$10	$ 1,000
Apr. 15	Purchase	200	11	2,200
Aug. 24	Purchase	300	12	3,600
Nov. 27	Purchase	400	13	5,200
	Total	1,000		**$12,000**

STEP 1: ENDING INVENTORY

Date	Units	Unit Cost	Total Cost
Jan. 1	100	$10	$1,000
Apr. 15	200	11	2,200
Aug. 24	150	12	1,800
Total	450		**$5,000**

STEP 2: COST OF GOODS SOLD

Cost of goods available for sale	$12,000
Less: Ending inventory	5,000
Cost of goods sold	**$ 7,000**

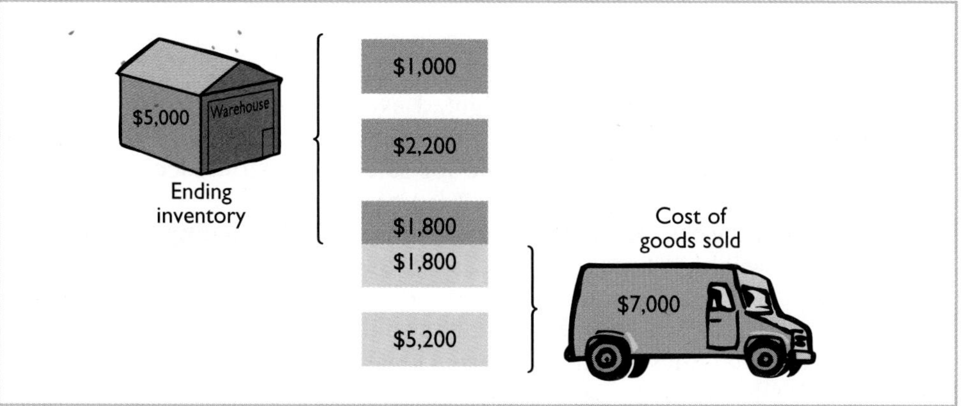

HELPFUL HINT
Another way of thinking about the calculation of LIFO ending inventory is the *FISH assumption*—first in still here.

Under LIFO, since it is assumed that the first goods sold were those that were most recently purchased, ending inventory is based on the prices of the oldest units purchased. That is, **under LIFO, companies obtain the cost of the ending inventory by taking the unit cost of the earliest goods available for sale and working forward until all units of inventory have been costed.** In this example, Houston Electronics prices the 450 units of ending inventory using the *earliest* prices. The first purchase was 100 units at $10 in the January 1 beginning inventory. Then 200 units were purchased at $11. The remaining 150 units needed are priced at $12 per unit (August 24 purchase). Next, Houston Electronics calculates cost of goods sold by subtracting the cost of the units **not sold** (ending inventory) from the cost of all goods available for sale.

Illustration 6-8 demonstrates that companies also can calculate cost of goods sold by pricing the 550 units sold using the prices of the last 550 units acquired. Note that of the 300 units purchased on August 24, only 150 units are assumed sold. This agrees with our calculation of the cost of ending inventory, where 150 of these units were assumed unsold and thus included in ending inventory.

Illustration 6-8
Proof of cost of goods sold

Date	Units	Unit Cost	Total Cost
Nov. 27	400	$13	$5,200
Aug. 24	150	12	1,800
Total	550		**$7,000**

Under a periodic inventory system, which we are using here, **all goods purchased during the period are assumed to be available for the first sale, regardless of the date of purchase.**

AVERAGE-COST

The **average-cost method** allocates the cost of goods available for sale on the basis of the **weighted average unit cost** incurred. The average-cost method assumes that goods are similar in nature. Illustration 6-9 presents the formula and a sample computation of the weighted-average unit cost.

Illustration 6-9
Formula for weighted average unit cost

Cost of Goods Available for Sale	÷	Total Units Available for Sale	=	Weighted Average Unit Cost
$12,000	÷	1,000	=	**$12.00**

The company then applies the weighted average unit cost to the units on hand to determine the cost of the ending inventory. Illustration 6-10 shows the allocation of the cost of goods available for sale at Houston Electronics using average cost.

We can verify the cost of goods sold under this method by multiplying the units sold times the weighted average unit cost (550 × $12 = $6,600). Note that this method does not use the average of the unit costs. That average is $11.50 ($10 + $11 + $12 + $13 = $46; $46 ÷ 4). The average cost method instead uses the average **weighted by** the quantities purchased at each unit cost.

Illustration 6-10
Allocation of costs—average-cost method

COST OF GOODS AVAILABLE FOR SALE

Date	Explanation	Units	Unit Cost	Total Cost
Jan. 1	Beginning inventory	100	$10	$ 1,000
Apr. 15	Purchase	200	11	2,200
Aug. 24	Purchase	300	12	3,600
Nov. 27	Purchase	400	13	5,200
	Total	1,000		$12,000

STEP 1: ENDING INVENTORY

$12,000	÷	1,000	=	$12.00
		Unit		Total
Units		Cost		Cost
450		$12.00		$5,400

STEP 2: COST OF GOODS SOLD

Cost of goods available for sale	$12,000
Less: Ending inventory	5,400
Cost of goods sold	$ 6,600

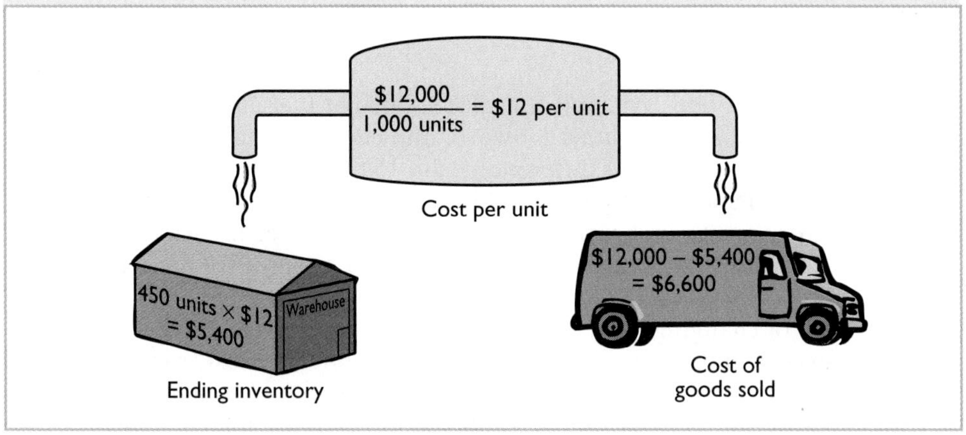

Financial Statement and Tax Effects of Cost Flow Methods

STUDY OBJECTIVE 3
Explain the financial effects of the inventory cost flow assumptions.

Each of the three assumed cost flow methods is acceptable for use. For example, Reebok International Ltd. and Wendy's International currently use the FIFO method of inventory costing. Campbell Soup Company, Krogers, and Walgreen Drugs use LIFO for part or all of their inventory. Bristol-Myers Squibb, Starbucks, and Motorola use the average-cost method. In fact, a company may also use more than one cost flow method at the same time. Black & Decker Manufacturing Company, for example, uses LIFO for domestic inventories and FIFO for foreign inventories. Illustration 6-11 (in the margin) shows the use of the three cost flow methods in the 600 largest U.S. companies.

The reasons companies adopt different inventory cost flow methods are varied, but they usually involve one of three factors: (1) income statement effects, (2) balance sheet effects, or (3) tax effects.

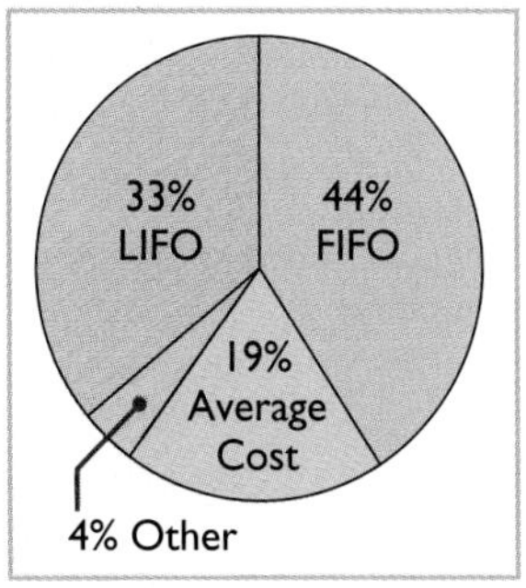

Illustration 6-11
Use of cost flow methods in major U.S. companies

INCOME STATEMENT EFFECTS

To understand why companies might choose a particular cost flow method, let's examine the effects of the different cost flow assumptions on the financial statements of Houston Electronics. The condensed income statements in Illustration 6-12 (page 254) assume that Houston sold its 550 units for $11,500, had operating expenses of $2,000, and is subject to an income tax rate of 30%.

Illustration 6-12
Comparative effects of cost flow methods

HOUSTON ELECTRONICS
Condensed Income Statements

	FIFO	LIFO	Average Cost
Sales	$11,500	$11,500	$11,500
Beginning inventory	1,000	1,000	1,000
Purchases	11,000	11,000	11,000
Cost of goods available for sale	12,000	12,000	12,000
Ending inventory	**5,800**	**5,000**	**5,400**
Cost of goods sold	6,200	7,000	6,600
Gross profit	5,300	4,500	4,900
Operating expenses	2,000	2,000	2,000
Income before income taxes[3]	3,300	2,500	2,900
Income tax expense (30%)	990	750	870
Net income	**$ 2,310**	**$ 1,750**	**$ 2,030**

Note the cost of goods available for sale ($12,000) is the same under each of the three inventory cost flow methods. However, the ending inventories and the costs of goods sold are different. This difference is due to the unit costs that the company allocated to cost of goods sold and to ending inventory. Each dollar of difference in ending inventory results in a corresponding dollar difference in income before income taxes. For Houston, an $800 difference exists between FIFO and LIFO cost of goods sold.

In periods of changing prices, the cost flow assumption can have a significant impact on income and on evaluations based on income. In most instances, prices are rising (inflation). In a period of inflation, FIFO produces a higher net income because the lower unit costs of the first units purchased are matched against revenues. In a period of rising prices (as is the case in the Houston example), FIFO reports the highest net income ($2,310) and LIFO the lowest ($1,750); average cost falls in the middle ($2,030). If prices are falling, the results from the use of FIFO and LIFO are reversed: FIFO will report the lowest net income and LIFO the highest.

To management, higher net income is an advantage: It causes external users to view the company more favorably. In addition, management bonuses, if based on net income, will be higher. Therefore, when prices are rising (which is usually the case), companies tend to prefer FIFO because it results in higher net income.

Some argue that the use of LIFO in a period of inflation enables the company to avoid reporting **paper** (or **phantom**) **profit** as economic gain. To illustrate, assume that Kralik Company buys 200 units of a product at $20 per unit on January 10 and 200 more on December 31 at $24 each. During the year, Kralik sells 200 units at $30 each. Illustration 6-13 shows the results under FIFO and LIFO.

Illustration 6-13
Income statement effects compared

	FIFO	LIFO
Sales (200 × $30)	$6,000	$6,000
Cost of goods sold	**4,000 (200 × $20)**	**4,800 (200 × $24)**
Gross profit	$2,000	$1,200

[3]We are assuming that Houston Electronics is a corporation, and corporations are required to pay income taxes.

Under LIFO, Kralik Company has recovered the current replacement cost ($4,800) of the units sold. Thus, the gross profit in economic terms is real. However, under FIFO, the company has recovered only the January 10 cost ($4,000). To replace the units sold, it must reinvest $800 (200 × $4) of the gross profit. Thus, $800 of the gross profit is said to be phantom or illusory. As a result, reported net income is also overstated in real terms.

BALANCE SHEET EFFECTS

A major advantage of the FIFO method is that in a period of inflation, the costs allocated to ending inventory will approximate their current cost. For example, for Houston Electronics, 400 of the 450 units in the ending inventory are costed under FIFO at the higher November 27 unit cost of $13.

Conversely, a major shortcoming of the LIFO method is that in a period of inflation, the costs allocated to ending inventory may be significantly understated in terms of current cost. The understatement becomes greater over prolonged periods of inflation if the inventory includes goods purchased in one or more prior accounting periods. For example, Caterpillar has used LIFO for 50 years. Its balance sheet shows ending inventory of $4,675 million. But the inventory's actual current cost if FIFO had been used is $6,799 million.

HELPFUL HINT

A tax rule, often referred to as the *LIFO conformity rule*, requires that if companies use LIFO for tax purposes they must also use it for financial reporting purposes. This means that if a company chooses the LIFO method to reduce its tax bills, it will also have to report lower net income in its financial statements.

TAX EFFECTS

We have seen that both inventory on the balance sheet and net income on the income statement are higher when companies use FIFO in a period of inflation. Yet, many companies have selected LIFO. Why? The reason is that LIFO results in the lowest income taxes (because of lower net income) during times of rising prices. For example, at Houston Electronics, income taxes are $750 under LIFO, compared to $990 under FIFO. The tax savings of $240 makes more cash available for use in the business.

Using Inventory Cost Flow Methods Consistently

Whatever cost flow method a company chooses, it should use that method consistently from one accounting period to another. This approach is often referred to as the **consistency principle**, which means that a company uses the same accounting principles and methods from year to year. Consistent application enhances the comparability of financial statements over successive time periods. In contrast, using the FIFO method one year and the LIFO method the next year would make it difficult to compare the net incomes of the two years.

Although consistent application is preferred, it does not mean that a company may *never* change its inventory costing method. When a company adopts a different method, it should disclose in the financial statements the change and its effects on net income. Illustration 6-14 shows a typical disclosure, using information from financial statements of Quaker Oats (now a unit of PepsiCo).

Illustration 6-14
Disclosure of change in cost flow method

QUAKER OATS
Notes to the Financial Statements

Note 1: Effective July 1, the Company adopted the LIFO cost flow assumption for valuing the majority of U.S. Grocery Products inventories. The Company believes that the use of the LIFO method better matches current costs with current revenues. The effect of this change on the current year was to decrease net income by $16.0 million.

Lower-of-Cost-or-Market

STUDY OBJECTIVE 4

Explain the lower-of-cost-or-market basis of accounting for inventories.

The value of inventory for companies selling high-technology or fashion goods can drop very quickly due to changes in technology or fashions. These circumstances sometimes call for inventory valuation methods other than those presented so far. For example, purchasing managers at Ford decided to make a large purchase of palladium, a precious metal used in vehicle emission devices. They made this purchase because they feared a future shortage. The shortage did not materialize, and by the end of the year the price of palladium had plummeted. Ford's inventory was then worth $1 billion less than its original cost. Do you think Ford's inventory should have been stated at cost, in accordance with the cost principle, or at its lower replacement cost?

As you probably reasoned, this situation requires a departure from the cost basis of accounting. When the value of inventory is lower than its cost, companies can "write down" the inventory to its market value. This is done by valuing the inventory at the **lower-of-cost-or-market (LCM)** in the period in which the price decline occurs. LCM is an example of the accounting concept of **conservatism**, which means that the best choice among accounting alternatives is the method that is least likely to overstate assets and net income.

Companies apply LCM to the items in inventory after they have used one of the cost flow methods (specific identification, FIFO, LIFO, or average cost) to determine cost. Under the LCM basis, market is defined as **current replacement cost**, not selling price. For a merchandising company, market is the cost of purchasing the same goods at the present time from the usual suppliers in the usual quantities. Current replacement cost is used because a decline in the replacement cost of an item usually leads to a decline in the selling price of the item.

To illustrate the application of LCM, assume that Ken Tuckie TV has the following lines of merchandise with costs and market values as indicated. LCM produces the results shown in Illustration 6-15. Note that the amounts shown in the final column are the lower of cost or market amounts for each item.

Illustration 6-15
Computation of lower-of-cost-or-market

	Cost	Market	Lower-of-Cost-or-Market
Flatscreen TVs	$ 60,000	$ 55,000	$ 55,000
Satellite radios	45,000	52,000	45,000
DVD recorders	48,000	45,000	45,000
DVDs	15,000	14,000	14,000
Total inventory	$168,000	$166,000	**$159,000**

Before You Go On...

REVIEW IT

1. What factors should management consider in selecting an inventory cost flow method?
2. What inventory cost flow method does PepsiCo use for its inventories? (*Hint:* You will need to examine the notes for PepsiCo's financial statements.) The answers to these questions appear on page 289.
3. Which inventory cost flow method produces the highest net income in a period of rising prices? Which results in the lowest income taxes?
4. When should inventory be reported at a value other than cost?

DO IT

The accounting records of Shumway Ag Implement show the following data.

Beginning inventory	4,000 units at \$ 3
Purchases	6,000 units at \$ 4
Sales	7,000 units at \$12

Determine the cost of goods sold during the period under a periodic inventory system using (a) the FIFO method, (b) the LIFO method, and (c) the average-cost method.

Action Plan

- Understand the periodic inventory system.
- Allocate costs between goods sold and goods on hand (ending inventory) for each cost flow method.
- Compute cost of goods sold for each cost flow method.

Solution

Cost of goods available for sale = (4,000 × \$3) + (6,000 × \$4) = \$36,000
Ending inventory = 10,000 − 7,000 = 3,000 units
(a) FIFO: \$36,000 − (3,000 × \$4) = \$24,000
(b) LIFO: \$36,000 − (3,000 × \$3) = 27,000
(c) Average-cost: [(4,000 @ \$3) + (6,000 @ \$4)] ÷ 10,000
= (\$12,000 + \$24,000) ÷ 10,000
= \$3.60 per unit; 7,000 @ \$3.60 = \$25,200

Related exercise material: *BE6-3, BE6-4, BE6-5, E6-3, E6-4, E6-5, E6-6, E6-7, and E6-8.*

The Navigator

INVENTORY ERRORS

STUDY OBJECTIVE 5
Indicate the effects of inventory errors on the financial statements.

Unfortunately, errors occasionally occur in accounting for inventory. In some cases, errors are caused by failure to count or price the inventory correctly. In other cases, errors occur because companies do not properly recognize the transfer of legal title to goods that are in transit. When errors occur, they affect both the income statement and the balance sheet.

Income Statement Effects

As you know, both the beginning and ending inventories appear in the income statement. The ending inventory of one period automatically becomes the beginning inventory of the next period. Thus, inventory errors affect the computation of cost of goods sold and net income in two periods.

The effects on cost of goods sold can be computed by entering incorrect data in the formula in Illustration 6-16 and then substituting the correct data.

Beginning Inventory	+	Cost of Goods Purchased	−	Ending Inventory	=	Cost of Goods Sold

Illustration 6-16
Formula for cost of goods sold

If the error understates *beginning* inventory, cost of goods sold will be understated. If the error understates *ending* inventory, cost of goods sold will be overstated. Illustration 6-17 (page 258) shows the effects of inventory errors on the current year's income statement.

Illustration 6-17
Effects of inventory errors on current year's income statement

Inventory Error	Cost of Goods Sold	Net Income
Understate beginning inventory	Understated	Overstated
Overstate beginning inventory	Overstated	Understated
Understate ending inventory	Overstated	Understated
Overstate ending inventory	Understated	Overstated

ETHICS NOTE

Inventory fraud increases during recessions. Such fraud includes pricing inventory at amounts in excess of its actual value, or claiming to have inventory when no inventory exists. Inventory fraud usually overstates ending inventory, thereby understating cost of goods sold and creating higher income.

So far, the effects of inventory errors are fairly straightforward. Now, though, comes the (at first) surprising part: An error in the ending inventory of the current period will have a **reverse effect on net income of the next accounting period**. Illustration 6-18 shows this effect. As you study the illustration, you will see that the reverse effect comes from the fact that understating ending inventory in 2008 results in understating beginning inventory in 2009 and overstating net income in 2009.

Over the two years, though, total net income is correct because the errors **offset each other**. Notice that total income using incorrect data is \$35,000 (\$22,000 + \$13,000), which is the same as the total income of \$35,000 (\$25,000 + \$10,000) using correct data. Also note in this example that an error in the beginning inventory does not result in a corresponding error in the ending inventory for that period. The correctness of the ending inventory depends entirely on the accuracy of taking and costing the inventory at the balance sheet date under the periodic inventory system.

Illustration 6-18
Effects of inventory errors on two years' income statements

SAMPLE COMPANY
Condensed Income Statements

	2008				2009			
	Incorrect		Correct		Incorrect		Correct	
Sales		\$80,000		\$80,000		\$90,000		\$90,000
Beginning inventory	\$20,000		\$20,000		**\$12,000**		**\$15,000**	
Cost of goods purchased	40,000		40,000		68,000		68,000	
Cost of goods available for sale	60,000		60,000		80,000		83,000	
Ending inventory	**12,000**		**15,000**		23,000		23,000	
Cost of goods sold		48,000		45,000		57,000		60,000
Gross profit		32,000		35,000		33,000		30,000
Operating expenses		10,000		10,000		20,000		20,000
Net income		\$22,000		\$25,000		\$13,000		\$10,000

\$(3,000) Net income understated

\$3,000 Net income overstated

The errors cancel. Thus the combined total income for the 2-year period is correct.

Balance Sheet Effects

Companies can determine the effect of ending inventory errors on the balance sheet by using the basic accounting equation: Assets = Liabilities + Stockholders' equity. Errors in the ending inventory have the effects shown in Illustration 6-19.

Ending Inventory Error	Assets	Liabilities	Stockholders' Equity
Overstated	Overstated	No effect	Overstated
Understated	Understated	No effect	Understated

Illustration 6-19
Effects of ending inventory errors on balance sheet

STATEMENT PRESENTATION AND ANALYSIS

Presentation

As indicated in Chapter 5, inventory is classified as a current asset after receivables in the balance sheet. In a multiple-step income statement, cost of goods sold is subtracted from sales. There also should be disclosure of (1) the major inventory classifications, (2) the basis of accounting (cost, or lower of cost or market), and (3) the costing method (FIFO, LIFO, or average).

Wal-Mart, for example, in its January 31, 2006, balance sheet reported inventories of $32,191 million under current assets. The accompanying notes to the financial statements, as shown in Illustration 6-20, disclosed the following information.

WAL★MART

WAL-MART STORES, INC.
Notes to the Financial Statements

Note 1. Summary of Significant Accounting Policies
Inventories

The company values inventories at the lower-of-cost-or-market as determined primarily by the retail method of accounting, using the last-in, first-out ("LIFO") method for substantially all merchandise inventories in the United States, except SAM'S CLUB merchandise and merchandise in our distribution warehouses, which is based on cost LIFO method. Inventories of foreign operations are primarily valued by the retail method of accounting, using the first-in, first-out ("FIFO") method. At January 31, 2006 and 2005, our inventories valued at LIFO approximate those inventories as if they were valued at FIFO.

Illustration 6-20
Inventory disclosures by Wal-Mart

As indicated in this note, Wal-Mart values its inventories at the lower-of-cost-or-market using LIFO and FIFO.

Analysis

The amount of inventory carried by a company has significant economic consequences. And inventory management is a double-edged sword that requires constant attention. On the one hand, management wants to have a great variety and quantity on hand so that customers have a wide selection and items are always in stock. But such a policy may incur high carrying costs (e.g., investment, storage, insurance, obsolescence, and damage). On the other hand, low inventory levels lead to stockouts and lost sales. Common ratios used to manage and evaluate inventory levels are inventory turnover and a related measure, days in inventory.

STUDY OBJECTIVE 6
Compute and interpret the inventory turnover ratio.

Inventory turnover measures the number of times on average the inventory is sold during the period. Its purpose is to measure the liquidity of the inventory. The inventory turnover is computed by dividing cost of goods sold by the average inventory during the period. Unless seasonal factors are significant, average inventory can be computed from the beginning and ending inventory balances. For example, Wal-Mart reported in its 2006 annual report a beginning inventory of $29,762 million, an ending inventory of $32,191 million, and cost of goods sold for the year ended January 31, 2006, of $240,391 million. The inventory turnover formula and computation for Wal-Mart are shown below.

Illustration 6-21
Inventory turnover formula and computation for Wal-Mart

Cost of Goods Sold	÷	Average Inventory	=	Inventory Turnover
$240,391	÷	$\frac{\$29,762 + \$32,191}{2}$	=	**7.8 times**

A variant of the inventory turnover ratio is **days in inventory**. This measures the average number of days inventory is held. It is calculated as 365 divided by the inventory turnover ratio. For example, Wal-Mart's inventory turnover of 7.8 times divided into 365 is approximately 47 days. This is the approximate time that it takes a company to sell the inventory once it arrives at the store.

There are typical levels of inventory in every industry. Companies that are able to keep their inventory at lower levels and higher turnovers and still satisfy customer needs are the most successful.

ACCOUNTING ACROSS THE ORGANIZATION

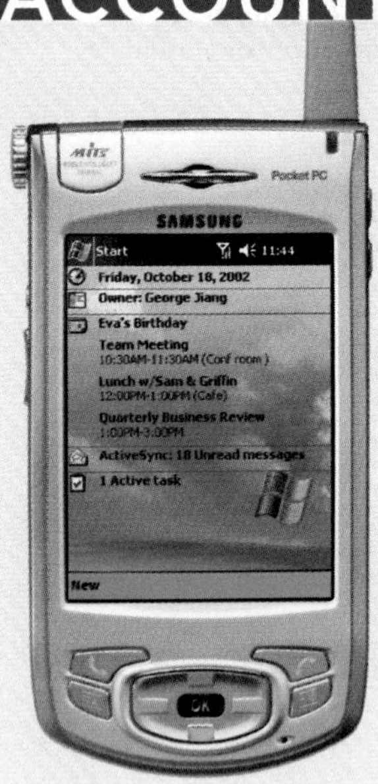

Samsung Uses a Different Strategy

Demand for cell phones typically falls during the first quarter of each year. It is a widely held principle that a company should cut back its production and inventory levels when it anticipates that demand will decrease. Thus many industry observers were surprised when Samsung Electronics Co. chose to increase production during the first quarter of the year, for the third year in a row.

Why did Samsung do this? Its executives felt that this approach would enable it to stand out against competitors by putting "a slew of new cell phones on shelves next to graying models from its rivals." It is clear that even with just-in-time inventory techniques and highly efficient inventory systems, management still must make many critical strategic decisions regarding inventory.

Source: Evan Ramstad, "Samsung to Report Whether Counterintuitive Move Paid Off," *Wall Street Journal,* April 24, 2005, p. B3.

? If Samsung isn't successful in selling the units, what steps will it have to take, and how will this show up in its financial statements?

Before You Go On...

REVIEW IT

1. How do inventory errors affect financial statements?
2. What is the purpose of the inventory turnover ratio?
3. What is the relationship between the inventory turnover ratio and average days in inventory?

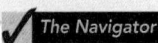

The Navigator

Be sure to read **ALL ABOUT YOU: *Employee Theft—An Inside Job*** on page 261 for information on how topics in this chapter apply to you.

Employee Theft—An Inside Job

Inventory theft is a huge problem for many businesses. Few employees would be as bold as the character in a Johnny Cash song, who while working on an assembly line in Detroit, steals an entire car, one piece at a time, over the course of many years (*www.lyricsdomain.com/10/johnny_cash/one_piece_at_a_time.html*). Nonetheless, at most companies, employees are the primary culprits. While you might think that a free pizza or steak at the end of your shift isn't hurting anybody, the statistics below show that such pilferage really adds up.

Many companies use sophisticated technologies to monitor their customers and employees in order to keep their inventory from walking off. Examples include closed-circuit video cameras and radio frequency identification (RFID). Other companies use techniques that don't rely on technology, such as taking frequent (in some cases daily) inventory counts, having employees keep all personal belongings and bags in a separate changing room, and making surprise checks of employees' bags as they leave. An increasing number of companies are setting up 800 numbers that employees or customers can call to report suspicious behavior, sometimes for a reward.

Some Facts

* The National Food Service Security Council estimates that employee theft costs U.S. restaurants $15 billion to $25 billion annually.
* The average supermarket has inventory shrinkage losses of 2.28% of sales, or $224,808 per year. Average net profit is only 1.1% of sales, so inventory shrinkage is twice the level of profits.
* Fear of getting caught and being fired ranks among one of the top reasons employees give, in surveys of reasons why they do not steal from their employer.
* Tips from customers are the No. 1 way that many stores catch thieving employees.
* The average employee caught stealing costs his or her company $1,341, while the average loss from a shoplifting incident is only $207.

About the Numbers

Where Did the Inventory Go?

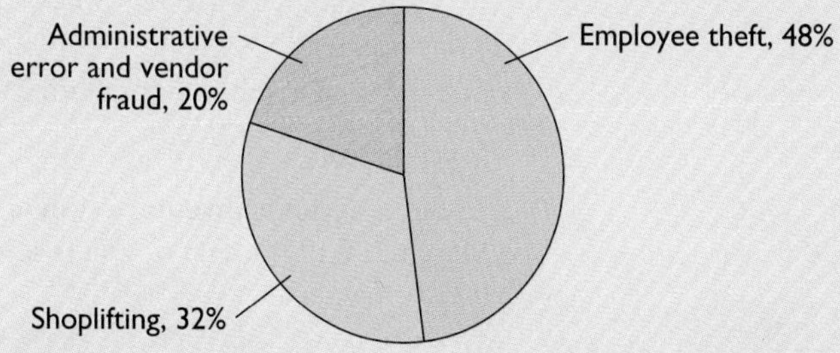

Source: Data from 2003 National Retail Security Survey, University of Florida.

What Do You Think?

Suppose you own a number of wine shops selling mid-level as well as expensive bottled wine. You have been experiencing significant losses from theft at your stores. You suspect that it is a combination of both employee and customer theft. Assuming that it would be cost-effective, would you install video cameras to reduce both employee theft and customer theft?

YES: Most employees and customers are honest. However, some will steal if given the opportunity. Management has a responsibility to employ reasonable, cost-effective approaches to safeguard company assets.

NO: The use of video technology to monitor employees and customers sends a message of distrust. You run the risk of alienating your employees (who may well figure out a way around the cameras anyway). Cameras might also reduce the welcoming atmosphere for your customers, who might find the cameras offensive.

Sources: Bob Ingram, "Shrink Has Shrunk," *Supermarket Business*, September 15, 2000, p. 65; Lisa Bertagnoli, "Wrapping up Shrink," *Restaurants & Institutions*, May 1, 2005, pp. 89–90; Naomi R. Kooker, "Taking Aim at Crime," *Nation's Restaurant News*, May 22, 2000, pp. 114–118.

The authors' comments on this situation appear on page 289.

Demonstration Problem 1

Gerald D. Englehart Company has the following inventory, purchases, and sales data for the month of March.

Inventory: March 1		200 units @ $4.00	$ 800
Purchases:			
	March 10	500 units @ $4.50	2,250
	March 20	400 units @ $4.75	1,900
	March 30	300 units @ $5.00	1,500
Sales:			
	March 15	500 units	
	March 25	400 units	

The physical inventory count on March 31 shows 500 units on hand.

Instructions

Under a **periodic inventory system**, determine the cost of inventory on hand at March 31 and the cost of goods sold for March under (a) (FIFO), (b) (LIFO), and (c) average-cost.

action plan

- ✓ Compute the cost of inventory under the periodic FIFO method by allocating to the units on hand the **latest costs**.
- ✓ Compute the cost of inventory under the periodic LIFO method by allocating to the units on hand the **earliest costs**.
- ✓ Compute the cost of inventory under the periodic average-cost method by allocating to the units on hand a **weighted-average cost**.

Solution to Demonstration Problem 1

The cost of goods available for sale is $6,450, as follows.

Inventory:		200 units @ $4.00	$ 800
Purchases:			
	March 10	500 units @ $4.50	2,250
	March 20	400 units @ $4.75	1,900
	March 30	300 units @ $5.00	1,500
Total cost of goods available for sale			$6,450

Under a **periodic inventory system**, the cost of goods sold under each cost flow method is as follows.

FIFO Method

Ending inventory:

Date	Units	Unit Cost	Total Cost	
March 30	300	$5.00	$1,500	
March 20	200	4.75	950	$2,450

Cost of goods sold: $6,450 − $2,450 = $4,000

LIFO Method

Ending inventory:

Date	Units	Unit Cost	Total Cost	
March 1	200	$4.00	$ 800	
March 10	300	4.50	1,350	$2,150

Cost of goods sold: $6,450 − $2,150 = $4,300

Average-Cost Method

Average unit cost: $6,450 ÷ 1,400 = $4.607
Ending inventory: 500 × $4.607 = $2,303.50

Cost of goods sold: $6,450 − $2,303.50 = $4,146.50

The Navigator

SUMMARY OF STUDY OBJECTIVES

1 **Describe the steps in determining inventory quantities.** The steps are (1) take a physical inventory of goods on hand and (2) determine the ownership of goods in transit or on consignment.

2 **Explain the accounting for inventories and apply the inventory cost flow methods.** The primary basis of accounting for inventories is cost. Cost of goods available for sale includes (a) cost of beginning inventory and (b) cost of goods purchased. The inventory cost flow methods are: specific identification and three assumed cost flow methods—FIFO, LIFO, and average-cost.

3 **Explain the financial effects of the inventory cost flow assumptions.** Companies may allocate the cost of goods available for sale to cost of goods sold and ending inventory by specific identification or by a method based on an assumed cost flow. When prices are rising, the first-in, first-out (FIFO) method results in lower cost of goods sold and higher net income than the other methods. The reverse is true when prices are falling. In the balance sheet, FIFO results in an ending inventory that is closest to current value; inventory under LIFO is the farthest from current value. LIFO results in the lowest income taxes.

4 **Explain the lower-of-cost-or-market basis of accounting for inventories.** Companies may use the lower-of-cost-or-market (LCM) basis when the current replacement cost (market) is less than cost. Under LCM, companies recognize the loss in the period in which the price decline occurs.

5 **Indicate the effects of inventory errors on the financial statements.** *In the income statement of the current year:* (a) An error in beginning inventory will have a reverse effect on net income. (b) An error in ending inventory will have a similar effect on net income. If ending inventory errors are not corrected in the following period, their effect on net income for that period is reversed, and total net income for the two years will be correct.

In the balance sheet: Ending inventory errors will have the same effect on total assets and total stockholders' equity and no effect on liabilities.

6 **Compute and interpret the inventory turnover ratio.** The inventory turnover ratio is cost of goods sold divided by average inventory. To convert it to average days in inventory, divide 365 days by the inventory turnover ratio.

The Navigator

GLOSSARY

Average-cost method Inventory costing method that uses the weighted average unit cost to allocate to ending inventory and cost of goods sold the cost of goods available for sale. (p. 252).

Conservatism Concept that dictates that when in doubt, choose the method that will be least likely to overstate assets and net income. (p. 256).

Consigned goods Goods held for sale by one party (the consignee) although ownership of the goods is retained by another party (the consignor). (p. 247).

Consistency principle Dictates that a company use the same accounting principles and methods from year to year. (p. 255).

Current replacement cost The current cost to replace an inventory item. (p. 256).

Days in inventory Measure of the average number of days inventory is held; calculated as 365 divided by inventory turnover ratio. (p. 260).

Finished goods inventory Manufactured items that are completed and ready for sale. (p. 244).

First-in, first-out (FIFO) method Inventory costing method that assumes that the costs of the earliest goods purchased are the first to be recognized as cost of goods sold. (p. 250).

FOB (free on board) destination Freight terms indicating that ownership of the goods passes to the buyer when the public carrier accepts the goods from the seller. (p. 246).

FOB (free on board) shipping point Freight terms indicating that ownership of the goods remains with the seller until the goods reach the buyer. (p. 246).

Inventory turnover ratio A ratio that measures the number of times on average the inventory sold during the period; computed by dividing cost of goods sold by the average inventory during the period. (p. 259).

Just-in-time (JIT) inventory method Inventory system in which companies manufacture or purchase goods just in time for use. (p. 245).

Last-in, first-out (LIFO) method Inventory costing method that assumes the costs of the latest units purchased are the first to be allocated to cost of goods sold. (p. 251).

Lower-of-cost-or-market (LCM) basis A basis whereby inventory is stated at the lower of either its cost or its market value as determined by current replacement cost. (p. 256).

Raw materials Basic goods that will be used in production but have not yet been placed into production. (p. 244).

Specific identification method An actual physical flow costing method in which items still in inventory are specifically costed to arrive at the total cost of the ending inventory. (p. 248).

Weighted average unit cost Average cost that is weighted by the number of units purchased at each unit cost. (p. 252).

Work in process That portion of manufactured inventory that has been placed into the production process but is not yet complete. (p. 244).

APPENDIX 6A Inventory Cost Flow Methods in Perpetual Inventory Systems

STUDY OBJECTIVE 7

Apply the inventory cost flow methods to perpetual inventory records.

What inventory cost flow methods do companies employ if they use a perpetual inventory system? Simple—they can use any of the inventory cost flow methods described in the chapter. To illustrate the application of the three assumed cost flow methods (FIFO, LIFO, and average-cost), we will use the data shown in Illustration 6A-1 and in this chapter for Houston Electronic's Astro Condenser.

Illustration 6A-1
Inventoriable units and costs

HOUSTON ELECTRONICS
Astro Condensers

Date	Explanation	Units	Unit Cost	Total Cost	Balance in Units
1/1	Beginning inventory	100	$10	$ 1,000	100
4/15	Purchases	200	11	2,200	300
8/24	Purchases	300	12	3,600	600
9/10	Sale	550			50
11/27	Purchases	400	13	5,200	450
				$12,000	

First-In, First-Out (FIFO)

Under FIFO, the company charges to cost of goods sold the cost of the earliest goods on hand **prior to each sale**. Therefore, the cost of goods sold on September 10 consists of the units on hand January 1 and the units purchased April 15 and August 24. Illustration 6A-2 shows the inventory under a FIFO method perpetual system.

Illustration 6A-2
Perpetual system—FIFO

Date	Purchases		Cost of Goods Sold	Balance (in units and cost)	
January 1				(100 @ $10)	$ 1,000
April 15	(200 @ $11)	$2,200		(100 @ $10) (200 @ $11)	$ 3,200
August 24	(300 @ $12)	$3,600		(100 @ $10) (200 @ $11) (300 @ $12)	$ 6,800
September 10			(100 @ $10) (200 @ $11) (250 @ $12) **$6,200**	(50 @ $12)	$ 600
November 27	(400 @ $13)	$5,200		(50 @ $12) (400 @ $13)	**$5,800**

Cost of goods sold ($6,200)

Ending inventory ($5,800)

The ending inventory in this situation is $5,800, and the cost of goods sold is $6,200 [(100 @ $10) + (200 @ $11) + (250 @ $12)].

Compare Illustrations 6-5 (page 250) and 6A-2. You can see that the results under FIFO in a perpetual system are the **same as in a periodic system**. In both cases, the ending inventory is $5,800 and cost of goods sold is $6,200. Regardless of the system, the first costs in are the costs assigned to cost of goods sold.

Last-In, First-Out (LIFO)

Under the LIFO method using a perpetual system, the company charges to cost of goods sold the cost of the most recent purchase prior to sale. Therefore, the cost of the goods sold on September 10 consists of all the units from the August 24 and April 15 purchases plus 50 of the units in beginning inventory. Illustration 6A-3 shows the computation of the ending inventory under the LIFO method.

Illustration 6A-3
Perpetual system—LIFO

Date	Purchases		Cost of Goods Sold	Balance (in units and cost)	
January 1				(100 @ $10)	$1,000
April 15	(200 @ $11)	$2,200		(100 @ $10) (200 @ $11)	$3,200
August 24	(300 @ $12)	$3,600		(100 @ $10) (200 @ $11) (300 @ $12)	$6,800
September 10			(300 @ $12) (200 @ $11) (50 @ $10) **$6,300**	(50 @ $10)	$ 500
November 27	(400 @ $13)	$5,200		(50 @ $10) (400 @ $13)	**$5,700**

Cost of goods sold ($6,300)
Ending inventory ($5,700)

The use of LIFO in a perpetual system will usually produce cost allocations that differ from those using LIFO in a periodic system. In a perpetual system, the company allocates the latest units purchased *prior to each sale* to cost of goods sold. In contrast, in a periodic system, the latest units purchased *during the period* are allocated to cost of goods sold. Thus, when a purchase is made after the last sale, the LIFO periodic system will apply this purchase to the previous sale. Compare Illustrations 6-8 (page 252) and 6A-3. Illustration 6-8 shows that the 400 units at $13 purchased on November 27 applied to the sale of 550 units on September 10. Under the LIFO perpetual system in Illustration 6A-3, the 400 units at $13 purchased on November 27 are all applied to the ending inventory.

The ending inventory in this LIFO perpetual illustration is $5,700, and cost of goods sold is $6,300, as compared to the LIFO periodic illustration (on page 251) where the ending inventory is $5,000 and cost of goods sold is $7,000.

Average-Cost

The average-cost method in a perpetual inventory system is called the **moving-average method**. Under this method the company computes a new average **after each purchase**, by dividing the cost of goods available for sale by the units on hand. They then apply the average cost to: (1) the units sold, to determine the cost of goods sold, and (2) the remaining units on hand, to determine the ending inventory amount. Illustration 6A-4 shows the application of the average-cost method by Houston Electronics.

Illustration 6A-4
Perpetual system—average-cost method

Date	Purchases		Cost of Goods Sold	Balance (in units and cost)	
January 1				(100 @ $10)	$1,000
April 15	(200 @ $11)	$2,200		(300 @ $10.667)	$3,200
August 24	(300 @ $12)	$3,600		(600 @ $11.333)	$6,800
September 10			(550 @ $11.333) **$6,233**	(50 @ $11.333)	$ 567
November 27	(400 @ $13)	$5,200		(450 @ $12.816)	**$5,767**

Cost of goods sold ($6,233)
Ending inventory ($5,767)

As indicated above, Houston Electronics computes **a new average each time it makes a purchase**. On April 15, after it buys 200 units for $2,200, a total of 300 units costing $3,200 ($1,000 + $2,200) are on hand. The average unit cost is $10.667 ($3,200 ÷ 300). On August 24, after Houston Electronics buys 300 units for $3,600, a total of 600 units costing $6,800 ($1,000 + $2,200 + $3,600) are on hand, at an average cost per unit of $11.333 ($6,800 ÷ 600). Houston Electronics uses this unit cost of $11.333 in costing sales until it makes another purchase, when the company computes a new unit cost. Accordingly, the unit cost of the 550 units sold on September 10 is $11.333, and the total cost of goods sold is $6,233. On November 27, following the purchase of 400 units for $5,200, there are 450 units on hand costing $5,767 ($567 + $5,200) with a new average cost of $12.816 ($5,767 ÷ 450).

Compare this moving-average cost under the perpetual inventory system to Illustration 6-10 (on page 253) showing the weighted-average method under a periodic inventory system.

Demonstration Problem 2

Demonstration Problem 1 on page 262 showed cost of goods sold computations under a periodic inventory system. Now let's assume that Gerald D. Englehart Company uses a perpetual inventory system. The company has the same inventory, purchases, and sales data for the month of March as shown earlier:

Inventory:	March 1	200 units @ $4.00	$ 800
Purchases:	March 10	500 units @ $4.50	2,250
	March 20	400 units @ $4.75	1,900
	March 30	300 units @ $5.00	1,500
Sales:	March 15	500 units	
	March 25	400 units	

The physical inventory count on March 31 shows 500 units on hand.

Instructions

Under a **perpetual inventory system**, determine the cost of inventory on hand at March 31 and the cost of goods sold for March under (a) FIFO, (b) LIFO, and (c) average-cost.

action plan

- Compute the cost of goods sold under the perpetual FIFO method by allocating to the goods sold the **earliest** cost of goods purchased.
- Compute the cost of goods sold under the perpetual LIFO method by allocating to the goods sold the **latest** cost of goods purchased.
- Compute the cost of goods sold under the perpetual average-cost method by allocating to the goods sold a **moving-average** cost.

Solution to Demonstration Problem 2

The cost of goods available for sale is $6,450, as follows.

Inventory:		200 units @ $4.00	$ 800
Purchases:	March 10	500 units @ $4.50	2,250
	March 20	400 units @ $4.75	1,900
	March 30	300 units @ $5.00	1,500
Total cost of goods available for sale			$6,450

Under a **perpetual inventory system**, the cost of goods sold under each cost flow method is as follows.

FIFO Method

Date	Purchases	Cost of Goods Sold	Balance
March 1			(200 @ $4.00) $ 800
March 10	(500 @ $4.50) $2,250		(200 @ $4.00) (500 @ $4.50) } $3,050
March 15		(200 @ $4.00) (300 @ $4.50) $2,150	(200 @ $4.50) $ 900

Date	Purchases	Cost of Goods Sold	Balance
March 20	(400 @ $4.75) $1,900		(200 @ $4.50) (400 @ $4.75) } $2,800
March 25		(200 @ $4.50) (200 @ $4.75) $1,850	(200 @ $4.75) $ 950
March 30	(300 @ $5.00) $1,500		(200 @ $4.75) (300 @ $5.00) } $2,450
	Ending inventory, $2,450	Cost of goods sold: $2,150 + $1,850 = $4,000	

LIFO Method

Date	Purchases	Cost of Goods Sold	Balance
March 1			(200 @ $4.00) $ 800
March 10	(500 @ $4.50) $2,250		(200 @ $4.00) (500 @ $4.50) } $3,050
March 15		(500 @ $4.50) $2,250	(200 @ $4.00) $ 800
March 20	(400 @ $4.75) $1,900		(200 @ $4.00) (400 @ $4.75) } $2,700
March 25		(400 @ $4.75) $1,900	(200 @ $4.00) $ 800
March 30	(300 @ $5.00) $1,500		(200 @ $4.00) (300 @ $5.00) } $2,300
	Ending inventory, $2,300	Cost of goods sold: $2,250 + $1,900 = $4,150	

Moving-Average Cost Method

Date	Purchases	Cost of Goods Sold	Balance
March 1			(200 @ $ 4.00) $ 800
March 10	(500 @ $4.50) $2,250		(700 @ $4.357) $3,050
March 15		(500 @ $4.357) $2,179	(200 @ $4.357) $ 871
March 20	(400 @ $4.75) $1,900		(600 @ $4.618) $2,771
March 25		(400 @ $4.618) $1,847	(200 @ $4.618) $ 924
March 30	(300 @ $5.00) $1,500		(500 @ $4.848) $2,424
	Ending inventory, $2,424	Cost of goods sold: $2,179 + $1,847 = $4,026	

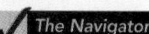

The Navigator

SUMMARY OF STUDY OBJECTIVE FOR APPENDIX 6A

WILEY PLUS

7 **Apply the inventory cost flow methods to perpetual inventory records.** Under FIFO and a perpetual inventory system, companies charge to cost of goods sold the cost of the earliest goods on hand prior to each sale. Under LIFO and a perpetual system, companies charge to cost of goods sold the cost of the most recent purchase prior to sale. Under the moving-average (average cost) method and a perpetual system, companies compute a new average cost after each purchase.

APPENDIX 6B Estimating Inventories

STUDY OBJECTIVE 8

Describe the two methods of estimating inventories.

In the chapter we assumed that a company would be able to physically count its inventory. What if it cannot? What if the inventory were destroyed by fire or flood, for example? In that case, the company would use an estimate.

Two circumstances explain why companies sometimes estimate inventories. First, a casualty such as fire, flood, or earthquake may make it impossible to take a physical inventory. Second, managers may want monthly or quarterly financial statements, but a physical inventory is taken only annually. The need for estimating inventories occurs primarily with a periodic inventory system because of the absence of perpetual inventory records.

There are two widely used methods of estimating inventories: (1) the gross profit method, and (2) the retail inventory method.

Gross Profit Method

The **gross profit method** estimates the cost of ending inventory by applying a gross profit rate to net sales. This method is relatively simple, but effective. It will detect large errors. Accountants, auditors, and managers frequently use the gross profit method to test the reasonableness of the ending inventory amount.

To use this method, a company needs to know its net sales, cost of goods available for sale, and gross profit rate. With the gross profit rate, the company can estimate its gross profit for the period. Illustration 6B-1 shows the formulas for using the gross profit method.

Illustration 6B-1
Gross profit method formulas

Step 1:	Net Sales	−	Estimated Gross Profit	=	Estimated Cost of Goods Sold
Step 2:	Cost of Goods Available for Sale	−	Estimated Cost of Goods Sold	=	Estimated Cost of Ending Inventory

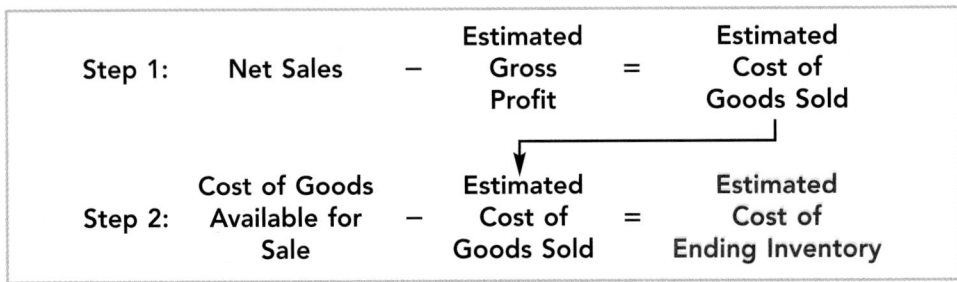

To illustrate, assume that Kishwaukee Company wishes to prepare an income statement for the month of January. Its records show net sales of $200,000, beginning inventory $40,000, and cost of goods purchased $120,000. In the preceding year, the company realized a 30% gross profit rate. It expects to earn the same rate this year. Given these facts and assumptions, Kishwaukee can compute the estimated cost of the ending inventory at January 31 under the gross profit method as follows.

Illustration 6B-2
Example of gross profit method

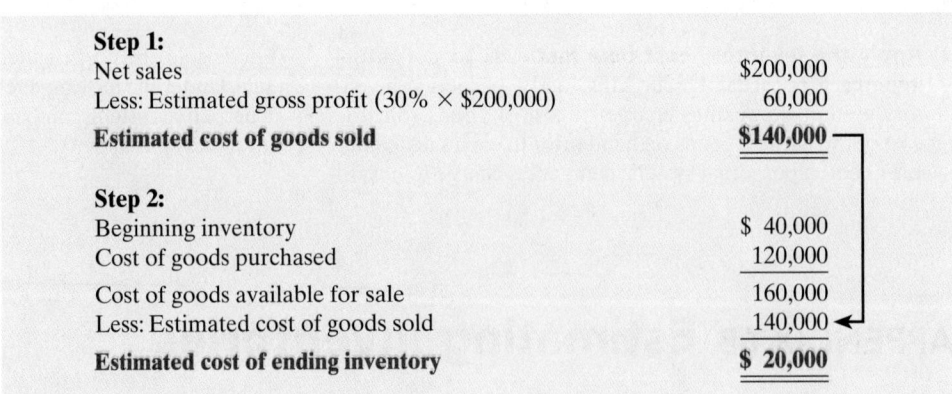

Step 1:	
Net sales	$200,000
Less: Estimated gross profit (30% × $200,000)	60,000
Estimated cost of goods sold	**$140,000**
Step 2:	
Beginning inventory	$ 40,000
Cost of goods purchased	120,000
Cost of goods available for sale	160,000
Less: Estimated cost of goods sold	140,000
Estimated cost of ending inventory	**$ 20,000**

The gross profit method is based on the assumption that the gross profit rate will remain constant. But it may not remain constant, due to a change in merchandising policies or in market conditions. In such cases, the company should adjust the rate to reflect current operating conditions. In some cases, companies can obtain a more accurate estimate by applying this method on a department or product-line basis.

Note that companies should not use the gross profit method to prepare financial statements at the end of the year. These statements should be based on a physical inventory count.

Retail Inventory Method

A retail store such as Home Depot, Ace Hardware, or Wal-Mart has thousands of different types of merchandise at low unit costs. In such cases it is difficult and time-consuming to apply unit costs to inventory quantities. An alternative is to use the **retail inventory method** to estimate the cost of inventory. Most retail companies can establish a relationship between cost and sales price. The company then applies the cost-to-retail percentage to the ending inventory at retail prices to determine inventory at cost.

Under the retail inventory method, a company's records must show both the cost and retail value of the goods available for sale. Illustration 6B-3 presents the formulas for using the retail inventory method.

Illustration 6B-3
Retail inventory method formulas

Step 1:	Goods Available for Sale at Retail	−	Net Sales	=	Ending Inventory at Retail
Step 2:	Goods Available for Sale at Cost	÷	Goods Available for Sale at Retail	=	Cost-to-Retail Ratio
Step 3:	Ending Inventory at Retail	×	Cost-to-Retail Ratio	=	Estimated Cost of Ending Inventory

We can demonstrate the logic of the retail method by using unit-cost data. Assume that Ortiz Inc. has marked 10 units purchased at \$7 to sell for \$10 per unit. Thus, the cost-to-retail ratio is 70% (\$70 ÷ \$100). If four units remain unsold, their retail value is \$40 (4 × \$10), and their cost is \$28 (\$40 × 70%). This amount agrees with the total cost of goods on hand on a per unit basis (4 × \$7).

Illustration 6B-4 shows application of the retail method for Valley West Co. Note that it is not necessary to take a physical inventory to determine the estimated cost of goods on hand at any given time.

Illustration 6B-4
Application of retail inventory method

	At Cost	At Retail
Beginning inventory	\$14,000	\$ 21,500
Goods purchased	61,000	78,500
Goods available for sale	\$75,000	100,000
Net sales		70,000
Step (1) Ending inventory at retail =		**\$ 30,000**
Step (2) Cost-to-retail ratio \$75,000 ÷ \$100,000 = 75%		
Step (3) Estimated cost of ending inventory = \$30,000 × 75% =	**\$22,500**	

HELPFUL HINT
In determining inventory at retail, companies use selling prices of the units.

The retail inventory method also facilitates taking a physical inventory at the end of the year. Valley West can value the goods on hand at the prices marked on the merchandise, and then apply the cost-to-retail ratio to the goods on hand at retail to determine the ending inventory at cost.

The major disadvantage of the retail method is that it is an averaging technique. Thus, it may produce an incorrect inventory valuation if the mix of the ending inventory is not representative of the mix in the goods available for sale. Assume, for example, that the cost-to-retail ratio of 75% for Valley West Co. consists of equal proportions of inventory items that have cost-to-retail ratios of 70%, 75%, and 80%. If the ending inventory contains only items with a 70% ratio, an incorrect inventory cost will result. Companies can minimize this problem by applying the retail method on a department or product-line basis.

SUMMARY OF STUDY OBJECTIVE FOR APPENDIX 6B

WILEY PLUS

8 **Describe the two methods of estimating inventories.** The two methods of estimating inventories are the gross profit method and the retail inventory method. Under the gross profit method, companies apply a gross profit rate to net sales to determine estimated cost of goods sold. They then subtract estimated cost of goods sold from cost of goods available for sale to determine the estimated cost of the ending inventory.

Under the retail inventory method, companies compute a cost-to-retail ratio by dividing the cost of goods available for sale by the retail value of the goods available for sale. They then apply this ratio to the ending inventory at retail to determine the estimated cost of the ending inventory.

GLOSSARY FOR APPENDIX 6B

WILEY PLUS

Gross profit method A method for estimating the cost of the ending inventory by applying a gross profit rate to net sales and subtracting the result from cost of goods available for sale. (p. 268).

Retail inventory method A method for estimating the cost of the ending inventory by applying a cost-to-retail ratio to the ending inventory at retail. (p. 269).

*__Note:__ All **asterisked** Questions, Exercises, and Problems relate to material in the appendixes to the chapter.

SELF-STUDY QUESTIONS

WILEY PLUS

Answers are at the end of the chapter.

(SO 1) 1. Which of the following should *not* be included in the physical inventory of a company?
 a. Goods held on consignment from another company.
 b. Goods shipped on consignment to another company.
 c. Goods in transit from another company shipped FOB shipping point.
 d. None of the above.

(SO 2) 2. Cost of goods available for sale consist of two elements: beginning inventory and
 a. ending inventory.
 b. cost of goods purchased.
 c. cost of goods sold.
 d. all of the above.

(SO 2) 3. Tinker Bell Company has the following:

	Units	Unit Cost
Inventory, Jan. 1	8,000	$11
Purchase, June 19	13,000	12
Purchase, Nov. 8	5,000	13

If Tinker Bell has 9,000 units on hand at December 31, the cost of the ending inventory under FIFO is:
 a. $99,000. c. $113,000.
 b. $108,000. d. $117,000.

4. Using the data in (3) above, the cost of the ending inventory under LIFO is: (SO 2)
 a. $113,000. c. $99,000.
 b. $108,000. d. $100,000.

5. In periods of rising prices, LIFO will produce: (SO 3)
 a. higher net income than FIFO.
 b. the same net income as FIFO.
 c. lower net income than FIFO.
 d. higher net income than average costing.

6. Factors that affect the selection of an inventory costing method do *not* include: (SO 3)
 a. tax effects.
 b. balance sheet effects.
 c. income statement effects.
 d. perpetual vs. periodic inventory system.

(SO 4) **7.** Rickety Company purchased 1,000 widgets and has 200 widgets in its ending inventory at a cost of $91 each and a current replacement cost of $80 each. The ending inventory under lower of cost or market is:
a. $91,000.
b. $80,000.
c. $18,200.
d. $16,000.

(SO 5) **8.** Atlantis Company's ending inventory is understated $4,000. The effects of this error on the current year's cost of goods sold and net income, respectively, are:
a. understated, overstated.
b. overstated, understated.
c. overstated, overstated.
d. understated, understated.

(SO 6) **9.** Which of these would cause the inventory turnover ratio to increase the most?
a. Increasing the amount of inventory on hand.
b. Keeping the amount of inventory on hand constant but increasing sales.
c. Keeping the amount of inventory on hand constant but decreasing sales.
d. Decreasing the amount of inventory on hand and increasing sales.

***10.** Songbird Company has sales of $150,000 and cost of goods available for sale of $135,000. If the gross profit rate is 30%, the estimated cost of the ending inventory under the gross profit method is: (SO 8)
a. $15,000.
b. $30,000.
c. $45,000.
d. $75,000.

***11.** In a perpetual inventory system, (SO 7)
a. LIFO cost of goods sold will be the same as in a periodic inventory system.
b. average costs are based entirely on unit cost averages.
c. a new average is computed under the average cost method after each sale.
d. FIFO cost of goods sold will be the same as in a periodic inventory system.

Go to the book's website,
www.wiley.com/college/weygandt,
for Additional Self-Study questions.

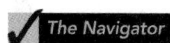

✓ The Navigator

QUESTIONS

1. "The key to successful business operations is effective inventory management." Do you agree? Explain.

2. An item must possess two characteristics to be classified as inventory by a merchandiser. What are these two characteristics?

3. Your friend Tom Witt has been hired to help take the physical inventory in Hawkeye Hardware Store. Explain to Tom Witt what this job will entail.

4. (a) Reeves Company ships merchandise to Cox Company on December 30. The merchandise reaches the buyer on January 6. Indicate the terms of sale that will result in the goods being included in (1) Reeves's December 31 inventory, and (2) Cox's December 31 inventory.
(b) Under what circumstances should Reeves Company include consigned goods in its inventory?

5. Jim's Hat Shop received a shipment of hats for which it paid the wholesaler $2,970. The price of the hats was $3,000 but Jim's was given a $30 cash discount and required to pay freight charges of $50. In addition, Jim's paid $130 to cover the travel expenses of an employee who negotiated the purchase of the hats. What amount will Jim's record for inventory? Why?

6. Identify the distinguishing features of an income statement for a merchandiser.

7. David Shannon believes that the allocation of inventoriable costs should be based on the actual physical flow of the goods. Explain to David why this may be both impractical and inappropriate.

8. What is a major advantage and a major disadvantage of the specific identification method of inventory costing?

9. "The selection of an inventory cost flow method is a decision made by accountants." Do you agree? Explain. Once a method has been selected, what accounting requirement applies?

10. Which assumed inventory cost flow method:
(a) usually parallels the actual physical flow of merchandise?
(b) assumes that goods available for sale during an accounting period are identical?
(c) assumes that the latest units purchased are the first to be sold?

11. In a period of rising prices, the inventory reported in Plato Company's balance sheet is close to the current cost of the inventory. Cecil Company's inventory is considerably below its current cost. Identify the inventory cost flow method being used by each company. Which company has probably been reporting the higher gross profit?

12. Casey Company has been using the FIFO cost flow method during a prolonged period of rising prices. During the same time period, Casey has been paying out all of its net income as dividends. What adverse effects may result from this policy?

13. Peter Lunde is studying for the next accounting mid-term examination. What should Peter know about (a) departing from the cost basis of accounting for inventories and (b) the meaning of "market" in the lower-of-cost-or-market method?

14. Garitson Music Center has 5 CD players on hand at the balance sheet date. Each cost $400. The current replacement cost is $380 per unit. Under the lower-of-cost-or-market basis of accounting for inventories, what value should be reported for the CD players on the balance sheet? Why?

15. Ruthie Stores has 20 toasters on hand at the balance sheet data. Each cost $27. The current replacement cost is

$30 per unit. Under the lower-of-cost-or-market basis of accounting for inventories, what value should Ruthie report for the toasters on the balance sheet? Why?

16. Mintz Company discovers in 2008 that its ending inventory at December 31, 2007, was $7,000 understated. What effect will this error have on (a) 2007 net income, (b) 2008 net income, and (c) the combined net income for the 2 years?

17. Willingham Company's balance sheet shows Inventories $162,800. What additional disclosures should be made?

18. Under what circumstances might inventory turnover be too high? That is, what possible negative consequences might occur?

***19.** "When perpetual inventory records are kept, the results under the FIFO and LIFO methods are the same as they would be in a periodic inventory system." Do you agree? Explain.

***20.** How does the average-cost method of inventory costing differ between a perpetual inventory system and a periodic inventory system?

***21.** When is it necessary to estimate inventories?

***22.** Both the gross profit method and the retail inventory method are based on averages. For each method, indicate the average used, how it is determined, and how it is applied.

***23.** Maureen Company has net sales of $400,000 and cost of goods available for sale of $300,000. If the gross profit rate is 35%, what is the estimated cost of the ending inventory? Show computations.

***24.** Milo Shoe Shop had goods available for sale in 2008 with a retail price of $120,000. The cost of these goods was $84,000. If sales during the period were $80,000, what is the ending inventory at cost using the retail inventory method?

BRIEF EXERCISES

WILEY PLUS

Identify items to be included in taking a physical inventory.
(SO 1)

BE6-1 Smart Company identifies the following items for possible inclusion in the taking of a physical inventory. Indicate whether each item should be included or excluded from the inventory taking.

(a) Goods shipped on consignment by Smart to another company.
(b) Goods in transit from a supplier shipped FOB destination.
(c) Goods sold but being held for customer pickup.
(d) Goods held on consignment from another company.

Identify the components of goods available for sale.
(SO 2)

BE6-2 The ledger of Gomez Company includes the following items: **(a)** Freight-in, **(b)** Purchase Returns and Allowances, **(c)** Purchases, **(d)** Sales Discounts, **(e)** Purchase Discounts. Identify which items are included in goods available for sale.

Compute ending inventory using FIFO and LIFO.
(SO 2)

BE6-3 In its first month of operations, Quirk Company made three purchases of merchandise in the following sequence: (1) 300 units at $6, (2) 400 units at $7, and (3) 200 units at $8. Assuming there are 360 units on hand, compute the cost of the ending inventory under the **(a)** FIFO method and **(b)** LIFO method. Quirk uses a periodic inventory system.

Compute the ending inventory using average-cost.
(SO 2)

BE6-4 Data for Quirk Company are presented in BE6-3. Compute the cost of the ending inventory under the average-cost method, assuming there are 360 units on hand.

Explain the financial statement effect of inventory cost flow assumptions.
(SO 3)

BE6-5 The management of Hoyt Corp. is considering the effects of various inventory-costing methods on its financial statements and its income tax expense. Assuming that the price the company pays for inventory is increasing, which method will:

(a) provide the highest net income?
(b) provide the highest ending inventory?
(c) result in the lowest income tax expense?
(d) result in the most stable earnings over a number of years?

Explain the financial statement effect of inventory cost flow assumptions.
(SO 3)

BE6-6 In its first month of operation, Gulletson Company purchased 100 units of inventory for $6, then 200 units for $7, and finally 150 units for $8. At the end of the month, 180 units remained. Compute the amount of phantom profit that would result if the company used FIFO rather than LIFO. Explain why this amount is referred to as phantom profit. The company uses the periodic method.

Determine the LCM valuation using inventory categories.
(SO 4)

BE6-7 Alou Appliance Center accumulates the following cost and market data at December 31.

Inventory Categories	Cost Data	Market Data
Cameras	$12,000	$12,100
Camcorders	9,500	9,700
VCRs	14,000	12,800

Compute the lower-of-cost-or-market valuation for the company's total inventory.

BE6-8 Cody Company reports net income of $90,000 in 2008. However, ending inventory was understated $10,000. What is the correct net income for 2008? What effect, if any, will this error have on total assets as reported in the balance sheet at December 31, 2008?

Determine correct income statement amounts.
(SO 5)

BE6-9 At December 31, 2008, the following information was available for J. Graff Company: ending inventory $40,000, beginning inventory $60,000, cost of goods sold $270,000, and sales revenue $380,000. Calculate inventory turnover and days in inventory for J. Graff Company.

Compute inventory turnover and days in inventory.
(SO 6)

***BE6-10** Jensen's Department Store uses a perpetual inventory system. Data for product E2-D2 include the following purchases.

Apply cost flow methods to perpetual inventory records.
(SO 7)

Date	Number of Units	Unit Price
May 7	50	$10
July 28	30	13

On June 1 Jensen's sold 30 units, and on August 27, 40 more units. Prepare the perpetual inventory schedule for the above transactions using (1) FIFO, (2) LIFO, and (3) average-cost.

***BE6-11** At May 31, Creole Company has net sales of $330,000 and cost of goods available for sale of $230,000. Compute the estimated cost of the ending inventory, assuming the gross profit rate is 35%.

Apply the gross profit method.
(SO 8)

***BE6-12** On June 30, Fabre Fabrics has the following data pertaining to the retail inventory method: Goods available for sale: at cost $35,000, at retail $50,000; net sales $40,000, and ending inventory at retail $8,000. Compute the estimated cost of the ending inventory using the retail inventory method.

Apply the retail inventory method.
(SO 8)

EXERCISES

WILEY PLUS

E6-1 Premier Bank and Trust is considering giving Lima Company a loan. Before doing so, they decide that further discussions with Lima's accountant may be desirable. One area of particular concern is the inventory account, which has a year-end balance of $297,000. Discussions with the accountant reveal the following.

Determine the correct inventory amount.
(SO 1)

1. Lima sold goods costing $38,000 to Comerica Company, FOB shipping point, on December 28. The goods are not expected to arrive at Comerica until January 12. The goods were not included in the physical inventory because they were not in the warehouse.
2. The physical count of the inventory did not include goods costing $95,000 that were shipped to Lima FOB destination on December 27 and were still in transit at year-end.
3. Lima received goods costing $22,000 on January 2. The goods were shipped FOB shipping point on December 26 by Galant Co. The goods were not included in the physical count.
4. Lima sold goods costing $35,000 to Emerick Co., FOB destination, on December 30. The goods were received at Emerick on January 8. They were not included in Lima's physical inventory.
5. Lima received goods costing $44,000 on January 2 that were shipped FOB destination on December 29. The shipment was a rush order that was supposed to arrive December 31. This purchase was included in the ending inventory of $297,000.

Instructions
Determine the correct inventory amount on December 31.

E6-2 Kale Thompson, an auditor with Sneed CPAs, is performing a review of Strawser Company's inventory account. Strawser did not have a good year and top management is under pressure to boost reported income. According to its records, the inventory balance at year-end was $740,000. However, the following information was not considered when determining that amount.

Determine the correct inventory amount.
(SO 1)

1. Included in the company's count were goods with a cost of $250,000 that the company is holding on consignment. The goods belong to Superior Corporation.
2. The physical count did not include goods purchased by Strawser with a cost of $40,000 that were shipped FOB destination on December 28 and did not arrive at Strawser's warehouse until January 3.

3. Included in the inventory account was $17,000 of office supplies that were stored in the warehouse and were to be used by the company's supervisors and managers during the coming year.
4. The company received an order on December 29 that was boxed and was sitting on the loading dock awaiting pick-up on December 31. The shipper picked up the goods on January 1 and delivered them on January 6. The shipping terms were FOB shipping point. The goods had a selling price of $40,000 and a cost of $30,000. The goods were not included in the count because they were sitting on the dock.
5. On December 29 Strawser shipped goods with a selling price of $80,000 and a cost of $60,000 to District Sales Corporation FOB shipping point. The goods arrived on January 3. District Sales had only ordered goods with a selling price of $10,000 and a cost of $8,000. However, a sales manager at Strawser had authorized the shipment and said that if District wanted to ship the goods back next week, it could.
6. Included in the count was $40,000 of goods that were parts for a machine that the company no longer made. Given the high-tech nature of Strawser's products, it was unlikely that these obsolete parts had any other use. However, management would prefer to keep them on the books at cost, "since that is what we paid for them, after all."

Instructions

Prepare a schedule to determine the correct inventory amount. Provide explanations for each item above, saying why you did or did not make an adjustment for each item.

Calculate cost of goods sold using specific identification and FIFO.

(SO 2, 3)

E6-3 On December 1, Bargain Electronics Ltd. has three DVD players left in stock. All are identical, all are priced to sell at $150. One of the three DVD players left in stock, with serial #1012, was purchased on June 1 at a cost of $100. Another, with serial #1045, was purchased on November 1 for $90. The last player, serial #1056, was purchased on November 30 for $80.

Instructions

(a) Calculate the cost of goods sold using the FIFO periodic inventory method assuming that two of the three players were sold by the end of December, Bargain Electronic's year-end.

(b) If Bargain Electronics used the specific identification method instead of the FIFO method, how might it alter its earnings by "selectively choosing" which particular players to sell to the two customers? What would Bargain's cost of goods sold be if the company wished to minimize earnings? Maximize earnings?

(c) Which inventory method do you recommend that Bargain use? Explain why.

Compute inventory and cost of goods sold using FIFO and LIFO.

(SO 2)

E6-4 Boarders sells a snowboard, Xpert, that is popular with snowboard enthusiasts. Below is information relating to Boarders's purchases of Xpert snowboards during September. During the same month, 121 Xpert snowboards were sold. Boarders uses a periodic inventory system.

Date	Explanation	Units	Unit Cost	Total Cost
Sept. 1	Inventory	26	$ 97	$ 2,522
Sept. 12	Purchases	45	102	4,590
Sept. 19	Purchases	20	104	2,080
Sept. 26	Purchases	50	105	5,250
	Totals	141		$14,442

Instructions

(a) Compute the ending inventory at September 30 and cost of goods sold using the FIFO and LIFO methods. Prove the amount allocated to cost of goods sold under each method.

(b) For both FIFO and LIFO, calculate the sum of ending inventory and cost of goods sold. What do you notice about the answers you found for each method?

Compute inventory and cost of goods sold using FIFO and LIFO.

(SO 2)

E6-5 Catlet Co. uses a periodic inventory system. Its records show the following for the month of May, in which 65 units were sold.

		Units	Unit Cost	Total Cost
May 1	Inventory	30	$ 8	$240
15	Purchases	25	11	275
24	Purchases	35	12	420
	Totals	90		$935

Instructions

Compute the ending inventory at May 31 and cost of goods sold using the FIFO and LIFO methods. Prove the amount allocated to cost of goods sold under each method.

Compute inventory and cost of goods sold using FIFO and LIFO.

(SO 2, 3)

E6-6 Yount Company reports the following for the month of June.

		Units	Unit Cost	Total Cost
June 1	Inventory	200	$5	$1,000
12	Purchase	300	6	1,800
23	Purchase	500	7	3,500
30	Inventory	120		

Instructions

(a) Compute the cost of the ending inventory and the cost of goods sold under (1) FIFO and (2) LIFO.
(b) Which costing method gives the higher ending inventory? Why?
(c) Which method results in the higher cost of goods sold? Why?

Compute inventory under FIFO, LIFO, and average-cost.

(SO 2, 3)

E6-7 Jones Company had 100 units in beginning inventory at a total cost of $10,000. The company purchased 200 units at a total cost of $26,000. At the end of the year, Jones had 80 units in ending inventory.

Instructions

(a) Compute the cost of the ending inventory and the cost of goods sold under (1) FIFO, (2) LIFO, and (3) average-cost.
(b) Which cost flow method would result in the highest net income?
(c) Which cost flow method would result in inventories approximating current cost in the balance sheet?
(d) Which cost flow method would result in Jones paying the least taxes in the first year?

Compute inventory and cost of goods sold using average-cost.

(SO 2, 3)

E6-8 Inventory data for Yount Company are presented in E6-6.

Instructions

(a) Compute the cost of the ending inventory and the cost of goods sold using the average-cost method.
(b) Will the results in (a) be higher or lower than the results under (1) FIFO and (2) LIFO?
(c) Why is the average unit cost not $6?

Determine ending inventory under LCM.

(SO 4)

E6-9 Americus Camera Shop uses the lower-of-cost-or-market basis for its inventory. The following data are available at December 31.

Item	Units	Unit Cost	Market
Cameras:			
Minolta	5	$170	$156
Canon	6	150	152
Light meters:			
Vivitar	12	125	115
Kodak	14	120	135

Instructions

Determine the amount of the ending inventory by applying the lower-of-cost-or-market basis.

Compute lower-of-cost-or-market.

(SO 4)

E6-10 Conan Company applied FIFO to its inventory and got the following results for its ending inventory.

VCRs	100 units at a cost per unit of $65
DVD players	150 units at a cost per unit of $75
iPods	125 units at a cost per unit of $80

The cost of purchasing units at year-end was VCRs $71, DVD players $69, and iPods $78.

Instructions

Determine the amount of ending inventory at lower-of-cost-or-market.

Determine effects of inventory errors.
(SO 5)

E6-11 Lebo Hardware reported cost of goods sold as follows.

	2008	2009
Beginning inventory	$ 20,000	$ 30,000
Cost of goods purchased	150,000	175,000
Cost of goods available for sale	170,000	205,000
Ending inventory	30,000	35,000
Cost of goods sold	$140,000	$170,000

Lebo made two errors: (1) 2008 ending inventory was overstated $3,000, and (2) 2009 ending inventory was understated $6,000.

Instructions
Compute the correct cost of goods sold for each year.

Prepare correct income statements.
(SO 5)

E6-12 Staley Watch Company reported the following income statement data for a 2-year period.

	2008	2009
Sales	$210,000	$250,000
Cost of goods sold		
Beginning inventory	32,000	44,000
Cost of goods purchased	173,000	202,000
Cost of goods available for sale	205,000	246,000
Ending inventory	44,000	52,000
Cost of goods sold	161,000	194,000
Gross profit	$ 49,000	$ 56,000

Staley uses a periodic inventory system. The inventories at January 1, 2008, and December 31, 2009, are correct. However, the ending inventory at December 31, 2008, was overstated $5,000.

Instructions
(a) Prepare correct income statement data for the 2 years.
(b) What is the cumulative effect of the inventory error on total gross profit for the 2 years?
(c) Explain in a letter to the president of Staley Company what has happened—i.e., the nature of the error and its effect on the financial statements.

Compute inventory turnover, days in inventory, and gross profit rate.
(SO 6)

E6-13 This information is available for Santo's Photo Corporation for 2007, 2008, and 2009.

	2007	2008	2009
Beginning inventory	$ 100,000	$ 300,000	$ 400,000
Ending inventory	300,000	400,000	480,000
Cost of goods sold	900,000	1,120,000	1,300,000
Sales	1,200,000	1,600,000	1,900,000

Instructions
Calculate inventory turnover, days in inventory, and gross profit rate (from Chapter 5) for Santo's Photo Corporation for 2007, 2008, 2009. Comment on any trends.

Compute inventory turnover and days in inventory.
(SO 6)

E6-14 The cost of goods sold computations for O'Brien Company and Weinberg Company are shown below.

	O'Brien Company	Weinberg Company
Beginning inventory	$ 45,000	$ 71,000
Cost of goods purchased	200,000	290,000
Cost of goods available for sale	245,000	361,000
Ending inventory	55,000	69,000
Cost of goods sold	$190,000	$292,000

Instructions

(a) Compute inventory turnover and days in inventory for each company.
(b) Which company moves its inventory more quickly?

***E6-15** Klugman Appliance uses a perpetual inventory system. For its flat-screen television sets, the January 1 inventory was 3 sets at $600 each. On January 10, Klugman purchased 6 units at $660 each. The company sold 2 units on January 8 and 4 units on January 15.

Apply cost flow methods to perpetual records.

(SO 7)

Instructions

Compute the ending inventory under (1) FIFO, (2) LIFO, and (3) average-cost.

***E6-16** Yount Company reports the following for the month of June.

Calculate inventory and cost of goods sold using three cost flow methods in a perpetual inventory system.

(SO 7)

Date	Explanation	Units	Unit Cost	Total Cost
June 1	Inventory	200	$5	$1,000
12	Purchase	300	6	1,800
23	Purchase	500	7	3,500
30	Inventory	120		

Instructions

(a) Calculate the cost of the ending inventory and the cost of goods sold for each cost flow assumption, using a perpetual inventory system. Assume a sale of 400 units occurred on June 15 for a selling price of $8 and a sale of 480 units on June 27 for $9.
(b) How do the results differ from E6-6 and E6-8?
(c) Why is the average unit cost not $6 [($5 + $6 + $7) ÷ 3 = $6]?

***E6-17** Information about Boarders is presented in E6-4. Additional data regarding Boarders' sales of Xpert snowboards are provided below. Assume that Boarders uses a perpetual inventory system.

Apply cost flow methods to perpetual records.

(SO 7)

Date		Units	Unit Price	Total Cost
Sept. 5	Sale	12	$199	$ 2,388
Sept. 16	Sale	50	199	9,950
Sept. 29	Sale	59	209	12,331
	Totals	121		$24,669

Instructions

(a) Compute ending inventory at September 30 using FIFO, LIFO, and average cost.
(b) Compare ending inventory using a perpetual inventory system to ending inventory using a periodic inventory system (from E6-4).
(c) Which inventory cost flow method (FIFO, LIFO) gives the same ending inventory value under both periodic and perpetual? Which method gives different ending inventory values?

***E6-18** Doc Gibbs Company reported the following information for November and December 2008.

Use the gross profit method to estimate inventory.

(SO 8)

	November	December
Cost of goods purchased	$500,000	$ 610,000
Inventory, beginning-of-month	100,000	120,000
Inventory, end-of-month	120,000	????
Sales	800,000	1,000,000

Doc Gibbs's ending inventory at December 31 was destroyed in a fire.

Instructions

(a) Compute the gross profit rate for November.
(b) Using the gross profit rate for November, determine the estimated cost of inventory lost in the fire.

***E6-19** The inventory of Faber Company was destroyed by fire on March 1. From an examination of the accounting records, the following data for the first 2 months of the year are obtained: Sales $51,000, Sales Returns and Allowances $1,000, Purchases $31,200, Freight-in $1,200, and Purchase Returns and Allowances $1,400.

Determine merchandise lost using the gross profit method of estimating inventory.

(SO 8)

Instructions

Determine the merchandise lost by fire, assuming:

(a) A beginning inventory of $20,000 and a gross profit rate of 40% on net sales.

(b) A beginning inventory of $30,000 and a gross profit rate of 30% on net sales.

Determine ending inventory at cost using retail method.

(SO 8)

***E6-20** Quayle Shoe Store uses the retail inventory method for its two departments, Women's Shoes and Men's Shoes. The following information for each department is obtained.

Item	Women's Department	Men's Department
Beginning inventory at cost	$ 32,000	$ 45,000
Cost of goods purchased at cost	148,000	136,300
Net sales	178,000	185,000
Beginning inventory at retail	46,000	60,000
Cost of goods purchased at retail	179,000	185,000

Instructions

Compute the estimated cost of the ending inventory for each department under the retail inventory method.

EXERCISES: SET B

Visit the book's website at **www.wiley.com/college/weygandt**, and choose the Student Companion site, to access Exercise Set B.

PROBLEMS: SET A

Determine items and amounts to be recorded in inventory.

(SO 1)

P6-1A Heath Limited is trying to determine the value of its ending inventory at February 28, 2008, the company's year end. The accountant counted everything that was in the warehouse as of February 28, which resulted in an ending inventory valuation of $48,000. However, she didn't know how to treat the following transactions so she didn't record them.

(a) On February 26, Heath shipped to a customer goods costing $800. The goods were shipped FOB shipping point, and the receiving report indicates that the customer received the goods on March 2.

(b) On February 26, Seller Inc. shipped goods to Heath FOB destination. The invoice price was $350. The receiving report indicates that the goods were received by Heath on March 2.

(c) Heath had $500 of inventory at a customer's warehouse "on approval." The customer was going to let Heath know whether it wanted the merchandise by the end of the week, March 4.

(d) Heath also had $400 of inventory on consignment at a Jasper craft shop.

(e) On February 26, Heath ordered goods costing $750. The goods were shipped FOB shipping point on February 27. Heath received the goods on March 1.

(f) On February 28, Heath packaged goods and had them ready for shipping to a customer FOB destination. The invoice price was $350; the cost of the items was $250. The receiving report indicates that the goods were received by the customer on March 2.

(g) Heath had damaged goods set aside in the warehouse because they are no longer saleable. These goods originally cost $400 and, originally, Heath expected to sell these items for $600.

Instructions

For each of the above transactions, specify whether the item in question should be included in ending inventory, and if so, at what amount. For each item that is not included in ending inventory, indicate who owns it and what account, if any, it should have been recorded in.

Determine cost of goods sold and ending inventory using FIFO, LIFO, and average-cost with analysis.

(SO 2, 3)

P6-2A Glanville Distribution markets CDs of the performing artist Harrilyn Clooney. At the beginning of March, Glanville had in beginning inventory 1,500 Clooney CDs with a unit cost of $7. During March Glanville made the following purchases of Clooney CDs.

March 5	3,000 @ $8	March 21	4,000 @ $10
March 13	5,500 @ $9	March 26	2,000 @ $11

During March 12,500 units were sold. Glanville uses a periodic inventory system.

Instructions

(a) Determine the cost of goods available for sale.

(b) Determine (1) the ending inventory and (2) the cost of goods sold under each of the assumed cost flow methods (FIFO, LIFO, and average-cost). Prove the accuracy of the cost of goods sold under the FIFO and LIFO methods.

(c) Which cost flow method results in (1) the highest inventory amount for the balance sheet and (2) the highest cost of goods sold for the income statement?

(b)(2) Cost of goods sold:
FIFO $109,000
LIFO $119,500
Average $114,062

Determine cost of goods sold and ending inventory using FIFO, LIFO, and average-cost with analysis.

(SO 2, 3)

P6-3A Eddings Company had a beginning inventory of 400 units of Product XNA at a cost of $8.00 per unit. During the year, purchases were:

Feb. 20	600 units at $9	Aug. 12	300 units at $11
May 5	500 units at $10	Dec. 8	200 units at $12

Eddings Company uses a periodic inventory system. Sales totaled 1,500 units.

Instructions

(a) Determine the cost of goods available for sale.

(b) Determine (1) the ending inventory, and (2) the cost of goods sold under each of the assumed cost flow methods (FIFO, LIFO, and average). Prove the accuracy of the cost of goods sold under the FIFO and LIFO methods.

(c) Which cost flow method results in (1) the lowest inventory amount for the balance sheet, and (2) the lowest cost of goods sold for the income statement?

(b) Cost of goods sold:
FIFO $13,600
LIFO $15,200
Average $14,475

Compute ending inventory, prepare income statements, and answer questions using FIFO and LIFO.

(SO 2, 3)

P6-4A The management of Morales Co. is reevaluating the appropriateness of using its present inventory cost flow method, which is average-cost. They request your help in determining the results of operations for 2008 if either the FIFO method or the LIFO method had been used. For 2008, the accounting records show the following data.

Inventories		Purchases and Sales	
Beginning (15,000 units)	$32,000	Total net sales (215,000 units)	$865,000
Ending (30,000 units)		Total cost of goods purchased (230,000 units)	595,000

Purchases were made quarterly as follows.

Quarter	Units	Unit Cost	Total Cost
1	60,000	$2.40	$144,000
2	50,000	2.50	125,000
3	50,000	2.60	130,000
4	70,000	2.80	196,000
	230,000		$595,000

Operating expenses were $147,000, and the company's income tax rate is 34%.

Instructions

(a) Prepare comparative condensed income statements for 2008 under FIFO and LIFO. (Show computations of ending inventory.)

(b) Answer the following questions for management.

(1) Which cost flow method (FIFO or LIFO) produces the more meaningful inventory amount for the balance sheet? Why?

(2) Which cost flow method (FIFO or LIFO) produces the more meaningful net income? Why?

(3) Which cost flow method (FIFO or LIFO) is more likely to approximate actual physical flow of the goods? Why?

(4) How much additional cash will be available for management under LIFO than under FIFO? Why?

(5) Will gross profit under the average-cost method be higher or lower than (a) FIFO and (b) LIFO? (*Note*: It is not necessary to quantify your answer.)

(a) Net income
FIFO $115,500
LIFO $104,940
(b)(4) $5,440

Calculate ending inventory, cost of goods sold, gross profit, and gross profit rate under periodic method; compare results.

(SO 2, 3)

P6-5A You are provided with the following information for Pavey Inc. for the month ended October 31, 2008. Pavey uses a periodic method for inventory.

Date	Description	Units	Unit Cost or Selling Price
October 1	Beginning inventory	60	$25
October 9	Purchase	120	26
October 11	Sale	100	35
October 17	Purchase	70	27
October 22	Sale	60	40
October 25	Purchase	80	28
October 29	Sale	110	40

Instructions

(a)(iii) Gross profit:
LIFO $3,050
FIFO $3,230
Average $3,141

(a) Calculate (i) ending inventory, (ii) cost of goods sold, (iii) gross profit, and (iv) gross profit rate under each of the following methods.
  (1) LIFO.
  (2) FIFO.
  (3) Average-cost.

(b) Compare results for the three cost flow assumptions.

Compare specific identification, FIFO and LIFO under periodic method; use cost flow assumption to influence earnings.

(SO 2, 3)

P6-6A You have the following information for Bernelli Diamonds. Bernelli Diamonds uses the periodic method of accounting for its inventory transactions. Bernelli only carries one brand and size of diamonds—all are identical. Each batch of diamonds purchased is carefully coded and marked with its purchase cost.

March 1	Beginning inventory 150 diamonds at a cost of $300 per diamond.
March 3	Purchased 200 diamonds at a cost of $350 each.
March 5	Sold 180 diamonds for $600 each.
March 10	Purchased 350 diamonds at a cost of $375 each.
March 25	Sold 400 diamonds for $650 each.

Instructions

(a) Gross profit:
(1) Maximum $166,750
(2) Minimum $157,750

(a) Assume that Bernelli Diamonds uses the specific identification cost flow method.
  (1) Demonstrate how Bernelli Diamonds could maximize its gross profit for the month by specifically selecting which diamonds to sell on March 5 and March 25.
  (2) Demonstrate how Bernelli Diamonds could minimize its gross profit for the month by selecting which diamonds to sell on March 5 and March 25.

(b) Assume that Bernelli Diamonds uses the FIFO cost flow assumption. Calculate cost of goods sold. How much gross profit would Bernelli Diamonds report under this cost flow assumption?

(c) Assume that Bernelli Diamonds uses the LIFO cost flow assumption. Calculate cost of goods sold. How much gross profit would the company report under this cost flow assumption?

(d) Which cost flow method should Bernelli Diamonds select? Explain.

Compute ending inventory, prepare income statements, and answer questions using FIFO and LIFO.

(SO 2, 3)

P6-7A The management of Utley Inc. asks your help in determining the comparative effects of the FIFO and LIFO inventory cost flow methods. For 2008 the accounting records show these data.

Inventory, January 1 (10,000 units)	$ 35,000
Cost of 120,000 units purchased	504,500
Selling price of 100,000 units sold	665,000
Operating expenses	130,000

Units purchased consisted of 35,000 units at $4.00 on May 10; 60,000 units at $4.20 on August 15; and 25,000 units at $4.50 on November 20. Income taxes are 28%.

Instructions

Gross profit:
FIFO $259,000
LIFO $240,500

(a) Prepare comparative condensed income statements for 2008 under FIFO and LIFO. (Show computations of ending inventory.)

(b) Answer the following questions for management in the form of a business letter.
  (1) Which inventory cost flow method produces the most meaningful inventory amount for the balance sheet? Why?

(2) Which inventory cost flow method produces the most meaningful net income? Why?
(3) Which inventory cost flow method is most likely to approximate the actual physical flow of the goods? Why?
(4) How much more cash will be available for management under LIFO than under FIFO? Why?
(5) How much of the gross profit under FIFO is illusionary in comparison with the gross profit under LIFO?

Calculate cost of goods sold and ending inventory for FIFO, average-cost, and LIFO under the perpetual system; compare gross profit under each assumption.

(SO 7)

***P6-8A** Vasquez Ltd. is a retailer operating in Edmonton, Alberta. Vasquez uses the perpetual inventory method. All sales returns from customers result in the goods being returned to inventory; the inventory is not damaged. Assume that there are no credit transactions; all amounts are settled in cash. You are provided with the following information for Vasquez Ltd. for the month of January 2008.

Date	Description	Quantity	Unit Cost or Selling Price
December 31	Ending inventory	150	$17
January 2	Purchase	100	21
January 6	Sale	150	40
January 9	Sale return	10	40
January 9	Purchase	75	24
January 10	Purchase return	15	24
January 10	Sale	50	45
January 23	Purchase	100	28
January 30	Sale	110	50

Instructions

(a) For each of the following cost flow assumptions, calculate (i) cost of goods sold, (ii) ending inventory, and (iii) gross profit.
(1) LIFO. **(2)** FIFO. **(3)** Moving-average-cost.
(b) Compare results for the three cost flow assumptions.

Gross profit:
LIFO $6,330
FIFO $7,500
Average $7,090

Determine ending inventory under a perpetual inventory system.

(SO 7)

***P6-9A** Sandoval Appliance Mart began operations on May 1. It uses a perpetual inventory system. During May the company had the following purchases and sales for its Model 25 Sureshot camera.

	Purchases		
Date	**Units**	**Unit Cost**	**Sales Units**
May 1	7	$150	
4			4
8	8	$170	
12			5
15	6	$185	
20			3
25			4

Instructions

(a) Determine the ending inventory under a perpetual inventory system using (1) FIFO, (2) average-cost, and (3) LIFO.
(b) Which costing method produces (1) the highest ending inventory valuation and (2) the lowest ending inventory valuation?

(a) FIFO $925
Average $874
LIFO $790

Estimate inventory loss using gross profit method.

(SO 8)

***P6-10A** Saffordville Company lost 70% of its inventory in a fire on March 25, 2008. The accounting records showed the following gross profit data for February and March.

	February	March (to 3/25)
Net sales	$300,000	$250,000
Net purchases	197,800	191,000
Freight-in	2,900	4,000
Beginning inventory	4,500	13,200
Ending inventory	13,200	?

Saffordville Company is fully insured for fire losses but must prepare a report for the insurance company.

Instructions

(a) Compute the gross profit rate for the month of February.

(b) Using the gross profit rate for February, determine both the estimated total inventory and inventory lost in the fire in March.

Compute ending inventory using retail method.

(SO 8)

***P6-11A** Neer Department Store uses the retail inventory method to estimate its monthly ending inventories. The following information is available for two of its departments at August 31, 2008.

	Sporting Goods		Jewelry and Cosmetics	
	Cost	**Retail**	**Cost**	**Retail**
Net sales		$1,000,000		$1,160,000
Purchases	$675,000	1,066,000	$741,000	1,158,000
Purchase returns	(26,000)	(40,000)	(12,000)	(20,000)
Purchase discounts	(12,360)	—	(2,440)	—
Freight-in	9,000	—	14,000	—
Beginning inventory	47,360	74,000	39,440	62,000

At December 31, Neer Department Store takes a physical inventory at retail. The actual retail values of the inventories in each department are Sporting Goods $95,000, and Jewelry and Cosmetics $44,000.

Instructions

(a) Determine the estimated cost of the ending inventory for each department on **August 31**, 2008, using the retail inventory method.

(b) Compute the ending inventory at cost for each department at **December 31**, assuming the cost-to-retail ratios are 60% for Sporting Goods and 64% for Jewelry and Cosmetics.

PROBLEMS: SET B

Determine items and amounts to be recorded in inventory.

(SO 1)

Peachtree

P6-1B Slaymakker Country Limited is trying to determine the value of its ending inventory as of February 28, 2008, the company's year-end. The following transactions occurred, and the accountant asked your help in determining whether they should be recorded or not.

(a) On February 26, Slaymakker shipped goods costing $800 to a customer and charged the customer $1,000. The goods were shipped with terms FOB destination and the receiving report indicates that the customer received the goods on March 2.

(b) On February 26, Seller Inc. shipped goods to Slaymakker under terms FOB shipping point. The invoice price was $350 plus $25 for freight. The receiving report indicates that the goods were received by Slaymakker on March 2.

(c) Slaymakker had $500 of inventory isolated in the warehouse. The inventory is designated for a customer who has requested that the goods be shipped on March 10.

(d) Also included in Slaymakker's warehouse is $400 of inventory that Craft Producers shipped to Slaymakker on consignment.

(e) On February 26, Slaymakker issued a purchase order to acquire goods costing $750. The goods were shipped with terms FOB destination on February 27. Slaymakker received the goods on March 2.

(f) On February 26, Slaymakker shipped goods to a customer under terms FOB shipping point. The invoice price was $350 plus $25 for freight; the cost of the items was $300. The receiving report indicates that the goods were received by the customer on March 2.

Instructions

For each of the above transactions, specify whether the item in question should be included in ending inventory, and if so, at what amount.

Determine cost of goods sold and ending inventory using FIFO, LIFO, and average-cost with analysis.

(SO 2, 3)

P6-2B Carrington Distribution markets CDs of the performing artist Christina Spears. At the beginning of October, Carrington had in beginning inventory 1,000 Spears CDs with a unit cost of $5. During October Carrington made the following purchases of Spears CDs.

Oct. 3	3,500 @ $6	Oct. 19	2,000 @ $8
Oct. 9	4,000 @ $7	Oct. 25	2,000 @ $9

During October 9,500 units were sold. Carrington uses a periodic inventory system.

Instructions

(a) Determine the cost of goods available for sale.

(b) Determine (1) the ending inventory and (2) the cost of goods sold under each of the assumed cost flow methods (FIFO, LIFO, and average-cost). Prove the accuracy of the cost of goods sold under the FIFO and LIFO methods.

(c) Which cost flow method results in (1) the highest inventory amount for the balance sheet and (2) the highest cost of goods sold for the income statement?

(b)(2) Cost of goods sold:
FIFO $62,000
LIFO $71,000
Average $66,880

P6-3B Shellankamp Company had a beginning inventory on January 1 of 100 units of Product WD-44 at a cost of $21 per unit. During the year, the following purchases were made.

Determine cost of goods sold and ending inventory, using FIFO, LIFO, and average-cost with analysis.

(SO 2, 3)

Mar. 15	300 units at $24	Sept. 4	300 units at $28
July 20	200 units at $25	Dec. 2	100 units at $30

800 units were sold. Shellankamp Company uses a periodic inventory system.

Instructions

(a) Determine the cost of goods available for sale.

(b) Determine (1) the ending inventory, and (2) the cost of goods sold under each of the assumed cost flow methods (FIFO, LIFO, and average-cost). Prove the accuracy of the cost of goods sold under the FIFO and LIFO methods.

(c) Which cost flow method results in (1) the highest inventory amount for the balance sheet, and (2) the highest cost of goods sold for the income statement?

(b)(2) Cost of goods sold:
FIFO $19,900
LIFO $21,200
Average $20,560

P6-4B The management of Groneman Inc. is reevaluating the appropriateness of using its present inventory cost flow method, which is average-cost. The company requests your help in determining the results of operations for 2008 if either the FIFO or the LIFO method had been used. For 2008 the accounting records show these data:

Compute ending inventory, prepare income statements, and answer questions using FIFO and LIFO.

(SO 2, 3)

Inventories		Purchases and Sales	
Beginning (10,000 units)	$22,800	Total net sales (220,000 units)	$865,000
Ending (20,000 units)		Total cost of goods purchased (230,000 units)	578,500

Purchases were made quarterly as follows.

Quarter	Units	Unit Cost	Total Cost
1	60,000	$2.30	$138,000
2	50,000	2.50	125,000
3	50,000	2.60	130,000
4	70,000	2.65	185,500
	230,000		$578,500

Operating expenses were $147,000, and the company's income tax rate is 32%.

Instructions

(a) Prepare comparative condensed income statements for 2008 under FIFO and LIFO. (Show computations of ending inventory.)

(a) Gross profit:
FIFO $316,700
LIFO $309,500

(b) Answer the following questions for management.

(1) Which cost flow method (FIFO or LIFO) produces the more meaningful inventory amount for the balance sheet? Why?

(2) Which cost flow method (FIFO or LIFO) produces the more meaningful net income? Why?

(3) Which cost flow method (FIFO or LIFO) is more likely to approximate the actual physical flow of goods? Why?

(4) How much more cash will be available for management under LIFO than under FIFO? Why?

(5) Will gross profit under the average-cost method be higher or lower than FIFO? Than LIFO? (*Note*: It is not necessary to quantify your answer.)

Calculate ending inventory, cost of goods sold, gross profit, and gross profit rate under periodic method; compare results.

(SO 2, 3)

P6-5B You are provided with the following information for Charlote Inc. for the month ended June 30, 2008. Charlote uses the periodic method for inventory.

Date	Description	Quantity	Unit Cost or Selling Price
June 1	Beginning inventory	25	$60
June 4	Purchase	85	64
June 10	Sale	70	90
June 11	Sale return	10	90
June 18	Purchase	35	68
June 18	Purchase return	5	68
June 25	Sale	40	95
June 28	Purchase	20	72

(a)(iii) Gross profit:
LIFO $2,520
FIFO $2,900
Average $2,687.50

Instructions

(a) Calculate (i) ending inventory, (ii) cost of goods sold, (iii) gross profit, and (iv) gross profit rate under each of the following methods.
(1) LIFO. **(2)** FIFO. **(3)** Average-cost.

(b) Compare results for the three cost flow assumptions.

Compare specific identification, FIFO, and LIFO under periodic method; use cost flow assumption to justify price increase.

(SO 2, 3)

P6-6B You are provided with the following information for Rondelli Inc. Rondelli Inc. uses the periodic method of accounting for its inventory transactions.

March 1 Beginning inventory 1,500 litres at a cost of 40¢ per litre.
March 3 Purchased 2,000 litres at a cost of 45¢ per litre.
March 5 Sold 1,800 litres for 60¢ per litre.
March 10 Purchased 3,500 litres at a cost of 49¢ per litre.
March 20 Purchased 2,000 litres at a cost of 55¢ per litre.
March 30 Sold 4,500 litres for 70¢ per litre.

Instructions

(a) Prepare partial income statements through gross profit, and calculate the value of ending inventory that would be reported on the balance sheet, under each of the following cost flow assumptions.

(a)(1) Gross profit:
Specific identification $1,256

(1) Specific identification method assuming:
(i) the March 5 sale consisted of 900 litres from the March 1 beginning inventory and 900 litres from the March 3 purchase; and
(ii) the March 30 sale consisted of the following number of units sold from beginning inventory and each purchase: 400 litres from March 1; 500 litres from March 3; 2,600 litres from March 10; 1,000 litres from March 20.

(2) FIFO $1,358
(3) LIFO $1,055

(2) FIFO.
(3) LIFO.

(b) How can companies use a cost flow method to justify price increases? Which cost flow method would best support an argument to increase prices?

Compute ending inventory, prepare income statements, and answer questions using FIFO and LIFO.

(SO 2, 3)

P6-7B The management of Dains Co. asks your help in determining the comparative effects of the FIFO and LIFO inventory cost flow methods. For 2008, the accounting records show the following data.

Inventory, January 1 (10,000 units)	$ 37,000
Cost of 110,000 units purchased	479,000
Selling price of 90,000 units sold	630,000
Operating expenses	120,000

Units purchased consisted of 40,000 units at $4.20 on May 10; 50,000 units at $4.40 on August 15; and 20,000 units at $4.55 on November 20. Income taxes are 30%.

Instructions

(a) Net income
FIFO $90,300
LIFO $80,500

(a) Prepare comparative condensed income statements for 2008 under FIFO and LIFO. (Show computations of ending inventory.)

(b) Answer the following questions for management.
(1) Which inventory cost flow method produces the most meaningful inventory amount for the balance sheet? Why?

(2) Which inventory cost flow method produces the most meaningful net income? Why?
(3) Which inventory cost flow method is most likely to approximate actual physical flow of the goods? Why?
(4) How much additional cash will be available for management under LIFO than under FIFO? Why?
(5) How much of the gross profit under FIFO is illusory in comparison with the gross profit under LIFO?

***P6-8B** Fechter Inc. is a retailer operating in Dartmouth, Nova Scotia. Fechter uses the perpetual inventory method. All sales returns from customers result in the goods being returned to inventory; the inventory is not damaged. Assume that there are no credit transactions; all amounts are settled in cash. You are provided with the following information for Fechter Inc. for the month of January 2008.

Calculate cost of goods sold and ending inventory under LIFO, FIFO, and average-cost under the perpetual system; compare gross profit under each assumption.

(SO 7)

Date	Description	Quantity	Unit Cost or Selling Price
January 1	Beginning inventory	50	$12
January 5	Purchase	100	14
January 8	Sale	80	25
January 10	Sale return	10	25
January 15	Purchase	30	18
January 16	Purchase return	5	18
January 20	Sale	75	25
January 25	Purchase	10	20

Instructions

(a) For each of the following cost flow assumptions, calculate (i) cost of goods sold, (ii) ending inventory, and (iii) gross profit.
(1) LIFO. **(2)** FIFO. **(3)** Moving-average-cost.
(b) Compare results for the three cost flow assumptions.

Gross profit:
LIFO $1,535
FIFO $1,695
Average $1,608

***P6-9B** Falco Co. began operations on July 1. It uses a perpetual inventory system. During July the company had the following purchases and sales.

Determine ending inventory under a perpetual inventory system.

(SO 7)

	Purchases		
Date	Units	Unit Cost	Sales Units
July 1	4	$ 90	
July 6			3
July 11	5	$ 99	
July 14			2
July 21	6	$106	
July 27			5

Instructions

(a) Determine the ending inventory under a perpetual inventory system using (1) FIFO, (2) average-cost, and (3) LIFO.
(b) Which costing method produces the highest ending inventory valuation?

(a) Ending inventory
FIFO $530
Avg. $513
LIFO $493

***P6-10B** Hannigan Company lost all of its inventory in a fire on December 26, 2008. The accounting records showed the following gross profit data for November and December.

Compute gross profit rate and inventory loss using gross profit method.

(SO 8)

	November	December (to 12/26)
Net sales	$500,000	$400,000
Beginning inventory	34,100	31,100
Purchases	334,975	246,000
Purchase returns and allowances	11,800	5,000
Purchase discounts	7,577	6,000
Freight-in	6,402	3,700
Ending inventory	31,100	?

Hannigan is fully insured for fire losses but must prepare a report for the insurance company.

Instructions

(a) Compute the gross profit rate for November.

(b) Using the gross profit rate for November, determine the estimated cost of the inventory lost in the fire.

Compute ending inventory using retail method.
(SO 8)

***P6-11B** Frontenac Books uses the retail inventory method to estimate its monthly ending inventories. The following information is available for two of its departments at October 31, 2008.

	Hardcovers		Paperbacks	
	Cost	**Retail**	**Cost**	**Retail**
Beginning inventory	$ 256,000	$ 400,000	$ 65,000	$ 90,000
Purchases	1,180,000	1,825,000	266,000	380,000
Freight-in	4,000		2,000	
Purchase discounts	16,000		4,000	
Net sales		1,827,000		385,000

At December 31, Frontenac Books takes a physical inventory at retail. The actual retail values of the inventories in each department are Hardcovers $395,000 and Paperbacks $88,000.

Instructions

(a) Determine the estimated cost of the ending inventory for each department at **October 31**, 2008, using the retail inventory method.

(b) Compute the ending inventory at cost for each department at **December 31**, assuming the cost-to-retail ratios for the year are 65% for hardcovers and 70% for paperbacks.

PROBLEMS: SET C

Visit the book's website at **www.wiley.com/college/weygandt**, and choose the Student Companion site, to access Problem Set C.

CONTINUING COOKIE CHRONICLE

(*Note:* This is a continuation of the Cookie Chronicle from Chapters 1 through 5.)

CCC6 Natalie is busy establishing both divisions of her business (cookie classes and mixer sales) and completing her business degree. Her goals for the next 11 months are to sell one mixer per month and to give two to three classes per week.

The cost of the fine European mixers is expected to increase. Natalie has just negotiated new terms with Kzinski that include shipping costs in the negotiated purchase price (mixers will be shipped FOB destination). Natalie must choose a cost flow assumption for her mixer inventory.

Go to the book's website,
www.wiley.com/college/weygandt,
to see the completion of this problem.

BROADENING YOUR PERSPECTIVE

FINANCIAL REPORTING AND ANALYSIS

Financial Reporting Problem

PepsiCo, Inc.

BYP6-1 The notes that accompany a company's financial statements provide informative details that would clutter the amounts and descriptions presented in the statements. Refer to the financial statements of PepsiCo and the Notes to Consolidated Financial Statements in Appendix A.

Instructions
Answer the following questions. Complete the requirements in millions of dollars, as shown in PepsiCo's annual report.

(a) What did PepsiCo report for the amount of inventories in its consolidated balance sheet at December 31, 2005? At December 25, 2004?
(b) Compute the dollar amount of change and the percentage change in inventories between 2004 and 2005. Compute inventory as a percentage of current assets at December 31, 2005.
(c) How does PepsiCo value its inventories? Which inventory cost flow method does PepsiCo use? (See Notes to the Financial Statements.)
(d) What is the cost of sales (cost of goods sold) reported by PepsiCo for 2005, 2004, and 2003? Compute the percentage of cost of sales to net sales in 2005.

Comparative Analysis Problem
PepsiCo, Inc. vs. The Coca-Cola Company

BYP6-2 PepsiCo's financial statements are presented in Appendix A. Coca-Cola's financial statements are presented in Appendix B.

Instructions
(a) Based on the information contained in these financial statements, compute the following 2005 ratios for each company.
(1) Inventory turnover ratio
(2) Days in inventory
(b) What conclusions concerning the management of the inventory can you draw from these data?

Exploring the Web

BYP6-3 A company's annual report usually will identify the inventory method used. Knowing that, you can analyze the effects of the inventory method on the income statement and balance sheet.

Address: www.cisco.com, or go to **www.wiley.com/college/weygandt**

Instructions
Answer the following questions based on the current year's Annual Report on Cisco's Web site.

(a) At Cisco's fiscal year-end, what was the inventory on the balance sheet?
(b) How has this changed from the previous fiscal year-end?
(c) How much of the inventory was finished goods?
(d) What inventory method does Cisco use?

CRITICAL THINKING

Decision Making Across the Organization

BYP6-4 On April 10, 2008, fire damaged the office and warehouse of Inwood Company. Most of the accounting records were destroyed, but the following account balances were determined as of March 31, 2008: Merchandise Inventory, January 1, 2008, \$80,000; Sales (January 1–March 31, 2008), \$180,000; Purchases (January 1–March 31, 2008) \$94,000.

The company's fiscal year ends on December 31. It uses a periodic inventory system.

From an analysis of the April bank statement, you discover cancelled checks of \$4,200 for cash purchases during the period April 1–10. Deposits during the same period totaled \$18,500. Of that amount, 60% were collections on accounts receivable, and the balance was cash sales.

Correspondence with the company's principal suppliers revealed \$12,400 of purchases on account from April 1 to April 10. Of that amount, \$1,600 was for merchandise in transit on April 10 that was shipped FOB destination.

Correspondence with the company's principal customers produced acknowledgments of credit sales totaling \$37,000 from April 1 to April 10. It was estimated that \$5,600 of credit sales will never be acknowledged or recovered from customers.

Inwood Company reached an agreement with the insurance company that its fire-loss claim should be based on the average of the gross profit rates for the preceding 2 years. The financial statements for 2006 and 2007 showed the following data.

	2007	2006
Net sales	$600,000	$480,000
Cost of goods purchased	404,000	356,000
Beginning inventory	60,000	40,000
Ending inventory	80,000	60,000

Inventory with a cost of $17,000 was salvaged from the fire.

Instructions

With the class divided into groups, answer the following.

(a) Determine the balances in (1) Sales and (2) Purchases at April 10.

*__(b)__ Determine the average profit rate for the years 2006 and 2007. (*Hint*: Find the gross profit rate for each year and divide the sum by 2.)

*__(c)__ Determine the inventory loss as a result of the fire, using the gross profit method.

Communication Activity

BYP6-5 You are the controller of Small Toys Inc. Janice LeMay, the president, recently mentioned to you that she found an error in the 2007 financial statements which she believes has corrected itself. She determined, in discussions with the Purchasing Department, that 2007 ending inventory was overstated by $1 million. Janice says that the 2008 ending inventory is correct. Thus she assumes that 2008 income is correct. Janice says to you, "What happened has happened—there's no point in worrying about it anymore."

Instructions

You conclude that Janice is incorrect. Write a brief, tactful memo to Janice, clarifying the situation.

Ethics Case

BYP6-6 B. J. Ortiz Wholesale Corp. uses the LIFO method of inventory costing. In the current year, profit at B. J. Ortiz is running unusually high. The corporate tax rate is also high this year, but it is scheduled to decline significantly next year. In an effort to lower the current year's net income and to take advantage of the changing income tax rate, the president of B. J. Ortiz Wholesale instructs the plant accountant to recommend to the purchasing department a large purchase of inventory for delivery 3 days before the end of the year. The price of the inventory to be purchased has doubled during the year, and the purchase will represent a major portion of the ending inventory value.

Instructions

(a) What is the effect of this transaction on this year's and next year's income statement and income tax expense? Why?

(b) If B. J. Ortiz Wholesale had been using the FIFO method of inventory costing, would the president give the same directive?

(c) Should the plant accountant order the inventory purchase to lower income? What are the ethical implications of this order?

"All About You" Activity

BYP6-7 Some of the largest business frauds ever perpetrated have involved the misstatement of inventory. Two classics were at Leslie Fay Cos, and McKesson Corporation.

Instructions

There is considerable information regarding inventory frauds available on the Internet. Search for information about one of the two cases mentioned above, or inventory fraud at any other company, and prepare a short explanation of the nature of the inventory fraud.

Answers to Insight and Accounting Across the Organization Questions

p. 245 How Wal-Mart Tracks Inventory

Q: Why is inventory control important to managers such as those at Wal-Mart?

A: *In the very competitive environment of discount retailing, where Wal-Mart is the major player, small differences in price matter to the customer. Wal-Mart sells a high volume of inventory at a low gross profit rate. When operating in a high-volume, low-margin environment, small cost savings can mean the difference between being profitable or going out of business.*

p. 246 "Fill 'Em Up—With Water, Not Oil"

Q: What effect does an overstatement of inventory have on a company's financial statements?

A: *The balance sheet looks stronger because inventory and retained earnings are overstated. The income statement looks better because cost of goods sold is understated and income is overstated.*

p. 260 Samsung Uses a Different Strategy

Q. If Samsung isn't successful in selling the units, what steps will it have to take, and how will this show up in its financial statements?

A. *If Samsung increases production, but then can't sell the units, its finished goods inventory will increase. Because cell phones are constantly changing, Samsung would want to take steps to sell off the inventory before it becomes obsolete. Thus, it would need to offer big discounts. Such a strategy would get its inventory down to desirable levels, but would severely depress the company's gross profit.*

Authors' Comments on *All About You*: Employee Theft—An Inside Job (p. 261)

Opinions regarding video technology differ greatly. One chief operating officer of a pub and restaurant chain says his company considers them "Big Brother-ish and demeaning." However, others feel that they are sometimes the only effective option. When properly implemented, theft-reduction procedures don't need to offend employees or customers. Wal-Mart has long employed senior citizens as greeters at its stores. Many people don't realize that these "greeters" are actually part of Wal-Mart's anti-shoplifting efforts.

Also, the need for video cameras depends, in part, on the nature of the product. In business environments where the inventory is of lower value, and/or not easily stolen, other techniques can be effective. However, in the case of expensive inventory items that can be easily concealed (such as expensive bottles of wine), reliance on video surveillance may be necessary.

Answer to PepsiCo Review It Question 2, p. 256

PepsiCo uses the average, FIFO, and LIFO methods to account for its inventories.

Answers to Self-Study Questions

1. a **2.** b **3.** c **4.** d **5.** c **6.** d **7.** d **8.** b **9.** d ***10.** b ***11.** d

Remember to go back to the Navigator box on the chapter-opening page and check off your completed work.

Chapter 7

Accounting Information Systems

STUDY OBJECTIVES

After studying this chapter, you should be able to:

1 Identify the basic concepts of an accounting information system.

2 Describe the nature and purpose of a subsidiary ledger.

3 Explain how companies use special journals in journalizing.

4 Indicate how companies post a multi-column journal.

The Navigator

The Navigator

Scan **Study Objectives**	■
Read **Feature Story**	■
Read **Preview**	■
Read text and answer **Before You Go On** p. 297 ■ p. 311 ■	
Work **Demonstration Problem**	■
Review **Summary of Study Objectives**	■
Answer **Self-Study Questions**	■
Complete **Assignments**	■

Feature Story

QUICKBOOKS® HELPS THIS RETAILER SELL GUITARS

Starting a small business requires many decisions. For example, you have to decide where to locate, how much space you need, how much inventory to have, how many employees to hire, and where to advertise. Small business owners are typically so concerned about the product and sales side of their business that they often do not give enough thought to something that is critical to their success—how to keep track of financial results.

Small business owners today can choose either manual or computerized accounting systems. For example, Paul and Laura West are the owners of the first independent dealership of Carvin guitars and professional audio equipment. When they founded their company, in Sacramento, California, they decided to purchase a computerized accounting system that would integrate many aspects of their retail operations. They wanted their accounting software to manage their inventory of guitars and amplifiers, ring up sales, record and report financial data, and process credit card and debit card transactions. They evaluated a number of options and chose QuickBooks® by Intuit Inc.

QuickBooks®, like most other popular software packages, has programs designed for the needs of a specific business, which in this case is retailing. This QuickBooks® retailing package automatically collects sales information from its point-of-sale scanning devices. It also keeps track of inventory levels and automatically generates purchase orders for popular items when re-order points are reached. It even supports sales efforts by compiling a customer database from which the Wests send out targeted direct mailings to potential customers. The computerized system enables data files to be emailed to the company's accountant. This keeps costs down and makes it easier and more efficient to generate financial reports as needed. The Wests believe that the investment in the computerized system has saved them time and money and allowed them to spend more time on other aspects of their business.

Source: Intuit Inc., "QuickBooks® and ProAdvisor® Help Make Guitar Store a Hit," *Journal of Accountancy*, May 2006, p. 101.

The Navigator

Inside Chapter 7...

Preview of Chapter 7

As you see from the Feature Story, a reliable information system is a necessity for any company. Whether companies use pen, pencil, or computers in maintaining accounting records, certain principles and procedures apply. The purpose of this chapter is to explain and illustrate these features.

The content and organization of Chapter 7 are as follows.

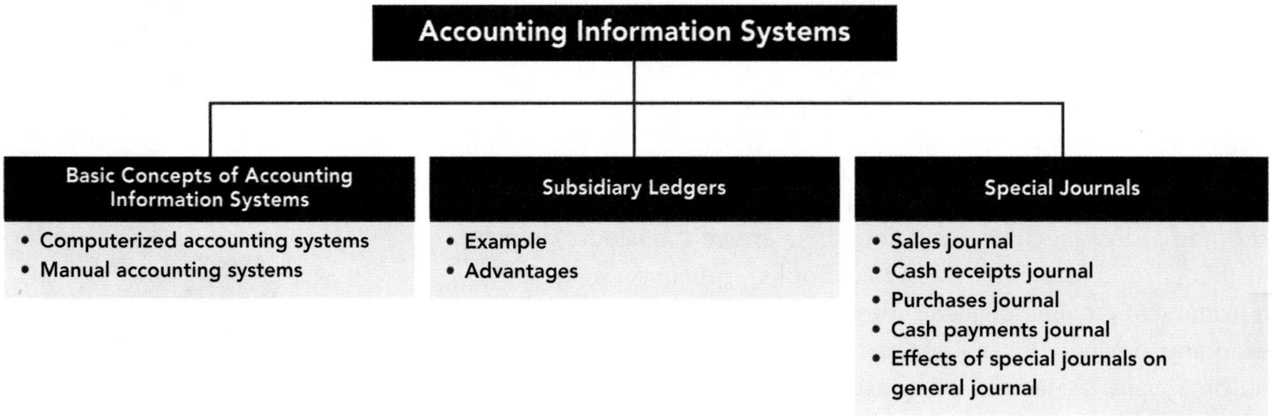

The Navigator

BASIC CONCEPTS OF ACCOUNTING INFORMATION SYSTEMS

STUDY OBJECTIVE 1

Identify the basic concepts of an accounting information system.

The **accounting information system** collects and processes transaction data and communicates financial information to decision makers. It includes each of the steps in the accounting cycle that you studied in earlier chapters. It also includes the documents that provide evidence of the transactions, and the records, trial balances, worksheets, and financial statements that result. An **accounting system** may be either manual or computerized. Most businesses these days use some sort of computerized accounting system, whether it is an off-the-shelf system for small businesses, like QuickBooks or Peachtree, or a more complex custom-made system.

Efficient and effective accounting information systems are based on certain basic principles. These principles, as described in Illustration 7-1 (page 293), are: (1) cost effectiveness, (2) usefulness, and (3) flexibility. If the accounting system is cost effective, provides useful output, and has the flexibility to meet future needs, it can contribute to both individual and organizational goals.

Computerized Accounting Systems

Many small businesses eventually replace their manual accounting system with a computerized general ledger accounting system. **General ledger accounting systems** are software programs that integrate the various accounting functions related to sales, purchases, receivables, payables, cash receipts and disbursements, and payroll. They also generate financial statements. Computerized systems have a number of advantages over manual systems. First, the company typically enters data only once in a computerized system. Second, because the computer does most steps automatically, many errors resulting from human intervention in a manual system,

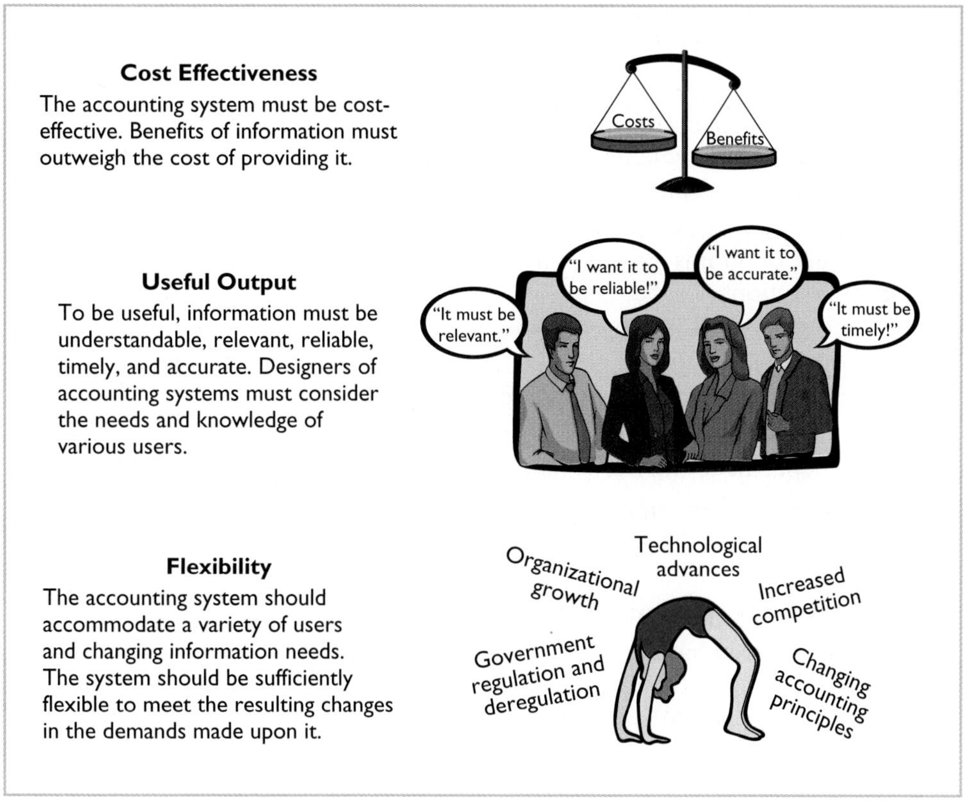
Cost Effectiveness
The accounting system must be cost-effective. Benefits of information must outweigh the cost of providing it.
Costs
Benefits
Useful Output
To be useful, information must be understandable, relevant, reliable, timely, and accurate. Designers of accounting systems must consider the needs and knowledge of various users.
"It must be relevant."
"I want it to be reliable!"
"I want it to be accurate."
"It must be timely!"
Flexibility
The accounting system should accommodate a variety of users and changing information needs. The system should be sufficiently flexible to meet the resulting changes in the demands made upon it.
Organizational growth
Technological advances
Increased competition
Government regulation and deregulation
Changing accounting principles

Illustration 7-1
Principles of an efficient and effective accounting information system

such as errors in posting or preparation of financial statements, are eliminated. Computerized systems also provide information up-to-the-minute. More timely information results in better business decisions. Many different general ledger software packages are available.

CHOOSING A SOFTWARE PACKAGE

To identify the right software for your business, you must understand your company's operations. For example, consider its needs with regard to inventory, billing, payroll, and cash management. In addition, the company might have specific needs that are not supported by all software systems. For example, you might want to track employees' hours on individual jobs or to extract information for determining sales commissions. Choosing the right system is critical because installation of even a basic system is time-consuming, and learning a new system will require many hours of employee time.

ENTRY-LEVEL SOFTWARE

Software publishers tend to classify businesses into groups based on revenue and the number of employees. Companies with revenues of less than $5 million and up to 20 employees generally use **entry-level programs**. The two leading entry-level programs are Intuit's QuickBooks and Sage Software's Peachtree. These programs control more than 90% of the market. Each of these entry-level programs comes in many different industry-specific versions. For example, some are designed for very specific industry applications such as restaurants, retailing, construction, manufacturing, or nonprofit. *(Both QuickBooks and Peachtree, as well as this textbook's general ledger system, can be used in working many of the problems in this textbook.)*

Quality entry-level packages typically involve more than recording transactions and preparing financial statements. Here are some common features and benefits:

- **Easy data access and report preparation.** Users can easily access information related to specific customers or suppliers. For example, you can view all transactions, invoices, payments, as well as contact information for a specific client.
- **Audit trail.** As a result of the Sarbanes-Oxley Act, companies are now far more concerned that their accounting system minimizes opportunities for fraud. Many programs provide an "audit trail" that enables the tracking of all transactions.
- **Internal controls.** Some systems have an internal accounting review that identifies suspicious transactions or likely mistakes such as wrong account numbers or duplicate transactions.
- **Customization.** This feature enables the company to create data fields specific to the needs of its business.
- **Network-compatibility.** Multiple users in the company can access the system at the same time.

ETHICS NOTE

Entire books and movies have used computer-system tampering as a major theme. Most programmers would agree that tamper-proofing and debugging programs are the most difficult and time-consuming phases of their jobs.

ENTERPRISE RESOURCE PLANNING SYSTEMS

Enterprise resource planning (ERP) systems are typically used by manufacturing companies with more than 500 employees and $500 million in sales. The best-known of these systems are SAP (the most widely used) by SAP AG, J.D. Edwards' ERP, and Oracle's Financials. ERP systems go far beyond the functions of an entry-level general ledger package. They integrate all aspects of the organization, including accounting, sales, human resource management, and manufacturing. Because of the complexity of an ERP system, implementation can take three years and cost five times as much as the purchase price of the system. Purchase and implementation of ERP systems can cost from $250,000 to as much as $50 million for the largest multinational corporations.

ETHICS INSIGHT

Curbing Fraudulent Activity with Software

The Sarbanes-Oxley Act (SOX) of 2002 requires that companies demonstrate that they have adequate controls in place to detect significant fraudulent behavior by employees. As of November 2005 about 15% of publicly traded companies reported at least one material weakness in their controls that needed to be remedied.

The SOX requirements have created a huge market for software that can monitor and trace every recorded transaction and adjusting entry. This enables companies to pinpoint *who* used the accounting system and *when* they used it. These systems also require "electronic signatures" by employees for all significant transactions. Such signatures verify that employees have followed all required procedures, and that all actions are properly authorized. SOX-related technology spending was estimated to be approximately $2 billion in 2005. One firm that specializes in compliance software had 10 clients prior to SOX and 250 after SOX.

Source: W. M. Bulkeley and C. Forelle, "Anti-Crime Program: How Corporate Scandals Gave Tech Firms a New Business Line," *Wall Street Journal*, December 9, 2005, p. A1.

? Why might this software help reduce fraudulent activity by employees?

Manual Accounting Systems

Manual accounting systems perform each of the steps in the accounting cycle by hand. For example, someone manually enters each accounting transaction in the journal and manually posts each to the ledger. Other manual computations must be made to obtain ledger account balances and to prepare a trial balance and financial statements. In the remainder of this chapter, we illustrate the use of a manual system.

You might be wondering, "Why cover manual accounting systems if the real world uses computerized systems?" First, small businesses still abound. Most of them begin operations with manual accounting systems and convert to computerized systems as the business grows. You may work in a small business, or start your own someday, so it is useful to know how a manual system works. Second, to understand what computerized accounting systems do, you also need to understand manual accounting systems.

The manual accounting system represented in the first six chapters of this textbook is satisfactory in a company with a low volume of transactions. However, in most companies, it is necessary to add additional ledgers and journals to the accounting system to record transaction data efficiently.

SUBSIDIARY LEDGERS

STUDY OBJECTIVE 2

Describe the nature and purpose of a subsidiary ledger.

Imagine a business that has several thousand charge (credit) customers and shows the transactions with these customers in only one general ledger account—Accounts Receivable. It would be nearly impossible to determine the balance owed by an individual customer at any specific time. Similarly, the amount payable to one creditor would be difficult to locate quickly from a single Accounts Payable account in the general ledger.

Instead, companies use subsidiary ledgers to keep track of individual balances. A **subsidiary ledger** is a group of accounts with a common characteristic (for example, all accounts receivable). It is an addition to, and an expansion of, the general ledger. The subsidiary ledger frees the general ledger from the details of individual balances.

Two common subsidiary ledgers are:

1. The **accounts receivable** (or **customers'**) **subsidiary ledger**, which collects transaction data of individual customers.
2. The **accounts payable** (or **creditors'**) **subsidiary ledger**, which collects transaction data of individual creditors.

In each of these subsidiary ledgers, companies usually arrange individual accounts in alphabetical order.

A general ledger account summarizes the detailed data from a subsidiary ledger. For example, the detailed data from the accounts receivable subsidiary ledger are summarized in Accounts Receivable in the general ledger. The general ledger account that summarizes subsidiary ledger data is called a **control account**. Illustration 7-2 (page 296) presents an overview of the relationship of subsidiary ledgers to the general ledger. There, the general ledger control accounts and subsidiary ledger accounts are in green. Note that cash and owner's capital in this illustration are not control accounts because there are no subsidiary ledger accounts related to these accounts.

At the end of an accounting period, each general ledger control account balance must equal the composite balance of the individual accounts in the related subsidiary ledger. For example, the balance in Accounts Payable in Illustration 7-2 must equal the total of the subsidiary balances of Creditors X + Y + Z.

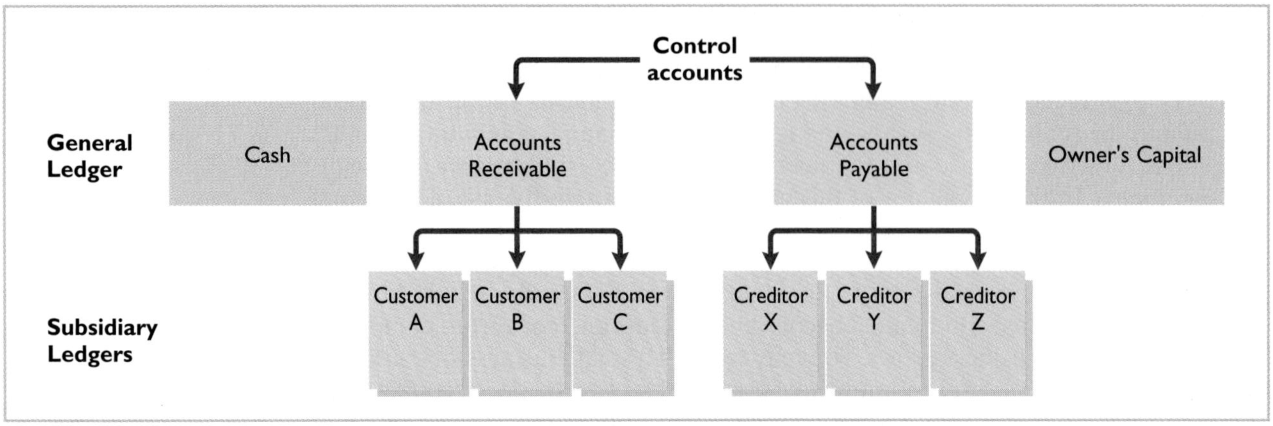

Illustration 7-2
Relationship of general ledger and subsidiary ledgers

Subsidiary Ledger Example

Illustration 7-3 provides an example of a control account and subsidiary ledger for Pujols Enterprises. (Due to space considerations, the explanation column in these accounts is not shown in this and subsequent illustrations.) Illustration 7-3 is based on the transactions listed in Illustration 7-4.

Illustration 7-3
Relationship between general and subsidiary ledgers

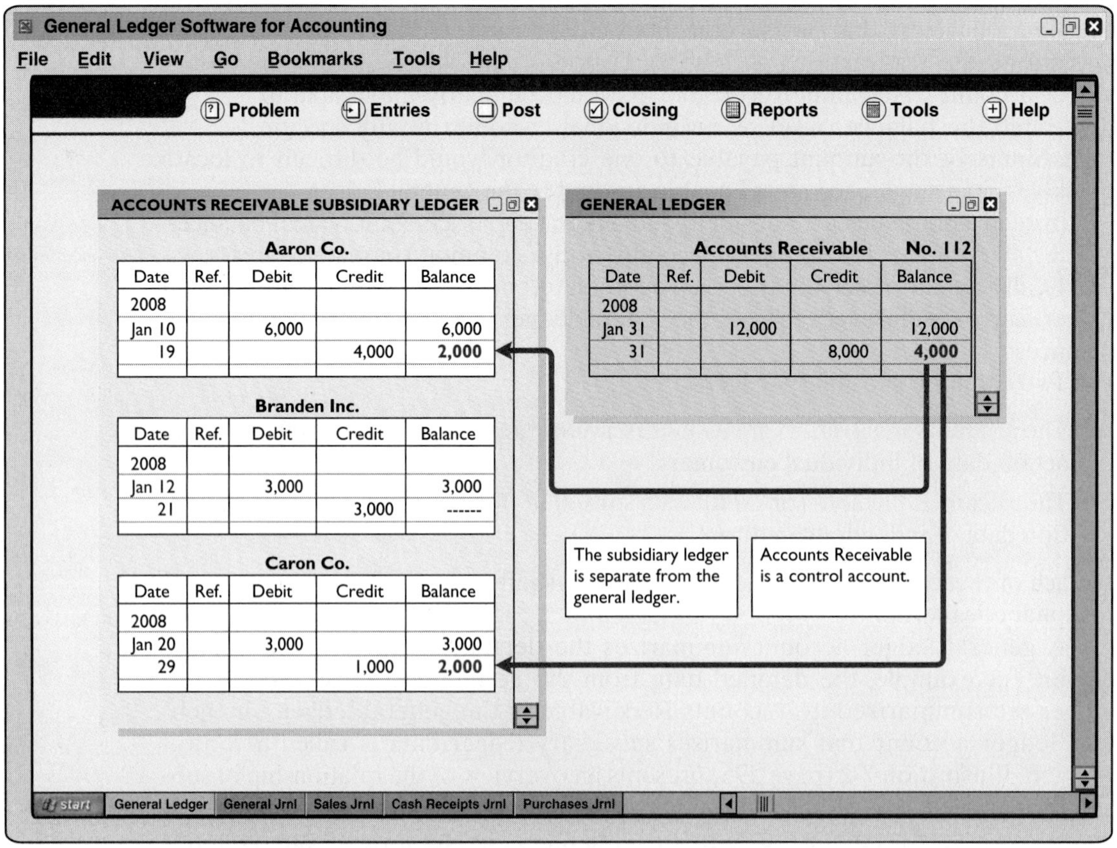

Illustration 7-4
Sales and collection transactions

Credit Sales			Collections on Account		
Jan. 10	Aaron Co.	$ 6,000	Jan. 19	Aaron Co.	$ 4,000
12	Branden Inc.	3,000	21	Branden Inc.	3,000
20	Caron Co.	3,000	29	Caron Co.	1,000
		$12,000			$ 8,000

Pujols can reconcile the total debits ($12,000) and credits ($8,000) in Accounts Receivable in the general ledger to the detailed debits and credits in the subsidiary accounts. Also, the balance of $4,000 in the control account agrees with the total of the balances in the individual accounts (Aaron Co. $2,000 + Branden Inc. $0 + Caron Co. $2,000) in the subsidiary ledger.

As Illustration 7-3 shows, companies make monthly postings to the control accounts in the general ledger. This practice allows them to prepare monthly financial statements. Companies post to the individual accounts in the subsidiary ledger daily. Daily posting ensures that account information is current. This enables the company to monitor credit limits, bill customers, and answer inquiries from customers about their account balances.

Advantages of Subsidiary Ledgers

Subsidiary ledgers have several advantages:

1. **They show in a single account transactions affecting one customer or one creditor**, thus providing up-to-date information on specific account balances.
2. **They free the general ledger of excessive details.** As a result, a trial balance of the general ledger does not contain vast numbers of individual account balances.
3. **They help locate errors in individual accounts** by reducing the number of accounts in one ledger and by using control accounts.
4. **They make possible a division of labor** in posting. One employee can post to the general ledger while someone else posts to the subsidiary ledgers.

ACCOUNTING ACROSS THE ORGANIZATION

"I'm John Smith, a.k.a. 13695071642"

Rather than relying on customer or creditor names in a subsidiary ledger, a computerized system expands the account number of the control account in a prespecified manner. For example, if Accounts Receivable was numbered 10010, the first account in the accounts receivable subsidiary ledger might be numbered 10010–0001. Most systems allow inquiries about specific accounts in the subsidiary ledger (by account number) or about the control account. With the latter, the system would automatically total all the subsidiary accounts whenever an inquiry to the control account was made.

? Why use numbers to identify names in a computerized system?

Before You Go On...

REVIEW IT

1. What basic concepts are followed in designing and developing an effective accounting information system?
2. What are the advantages of a computerized accounting system?
3. What is a subsidiary ledger, and what purpose does it serve?

DO IT

Presented on page 298 is information related to Sims Company for its first month of operations. Determine the balances that appear in the accounts payable subsidiary ledger. What Accounts Payable balance appears in the general ledger at the end of January?

Credit Purchases			Cash Paid		
Jan. 5	Devon Co.	$11,000	Jan. 9	Devon Co.	$7,000
11	Shelby Co.	7,000	14	Shelby Co.	2,000
22	Taylor Co.	14,000	27	Taylor Co.	9,000

Action Plan

- Subtract cash paid from credit purchases to determine the balances in the accounts payable subsidiary ledger.
- Sum the individual balances to determine the Accounts Payable balance.

Solution Subsidiary ledger balances:
Devon Co. $4,000 ($11,000 − $7,000)
Shelby Co. $5,000 ($7,000 − $2,000)
Taylor Co. $5,000 ($14,000 − $9,000).
General ledger Accounts Payable balance: $14,000 ($4,000 + $5,000 + $5,000).

Related exercise material: *BE7-4, BE7-5, E7-1, E7-2, E7-4, and E7-5.*

The Navigator

SPECIAL JOURNALS

STUDY OBJECTIVE 3

Explain how companies use special journals in journalizing.

So far you have learned to journalize transactions in a two-column general journal and post each entry to the general ledger. This procedure is satisfactory in only the very smallest companies. To expedite journalizing and posting, most companies use special journals **in addition to the general journal.**

Companies use **special journals** to record similar types of transactions. Examples are all sales of merchandise on account, or all cash receipts. The types of transactions that occur frequently in a company determine what special journals the company uses. Most merchandising enterprises record daily transactions using the journals shown in Illustration 7-5.

Illustration 7-5
Use of special journals and the general journal

Sales Journal	Cash Receipts Journal	Purchases Journal	Cash Payments Journal	General Journal
Used for: All sales of merchandise on account	Used for: All cash received (including cash sales)	Used for: All purchases of merchandise on account	Used for: All cash paid (including cash purchases)	Used for: Transactions that cannot be entered in a special journal, including correcting, adjusting, and closing entries

If a transaction cannot be recorded in a special journal, the company records it in the general journal. For example, if a company had special journals for only the four types of transactions listed above, it would record purchase returns and allowances in the general journal. Similarly, **correcting, adjusting, and closing entries are recorded in the general journal.** In some situations, companies might use special journals other than those listed above. For example, when sales returns and allowances are frequent, a company might use a special journal to record these transactions.

Special journals **permit greater division of labor** because several people can record entries in different journals at the same time. For example, one employee may journalize all cash receipts, and another may journalize all credit sales. Also, the use of special journals **reduces the time needed to complete the posting process.** With special journals, companies may post some accounts monthly, instead of daily, as we will illustrate later in the chapter. On the following pages, we discuss the four special journals shown in Illustration 7-5.

Sales Journal

In the **sales journal**, companies record **sales of merchandise on account**. Cash sales of merchandise go in the cash receipts journal. Credit sales of assets other than merchandise go in the general journal.

JOURNALIZING CREDIT SALES

To demonstrate use of a sales journal, we will use data for Karns Wholesale Supply, which uses a **perpetual inventory system**. Under this system, each entry in the sales journal results in one entry **at selling price** and another entry **at cost**. The entry at selling price is a debit to Accounts Receivable (a control account) and a credit of equal amount to Sales. The entry at cost is a debit to Cost of Goods Sold and a credit of equal amount to Merchandise Inventory (a control account). Using a sales journal with two amount columns, the company can show on only one line a sales transaction at both selling price and cost. Illustration 7-6 shows this two-column sales journal of Karns Wholesale Supply, using assumed credit sales transactions (for sales invoices 101–107).

HELPFUL HINT
Postings are also made daily to individual ledger accounts in the inventory subsidiary ledger to maintain a perpetual inventory.

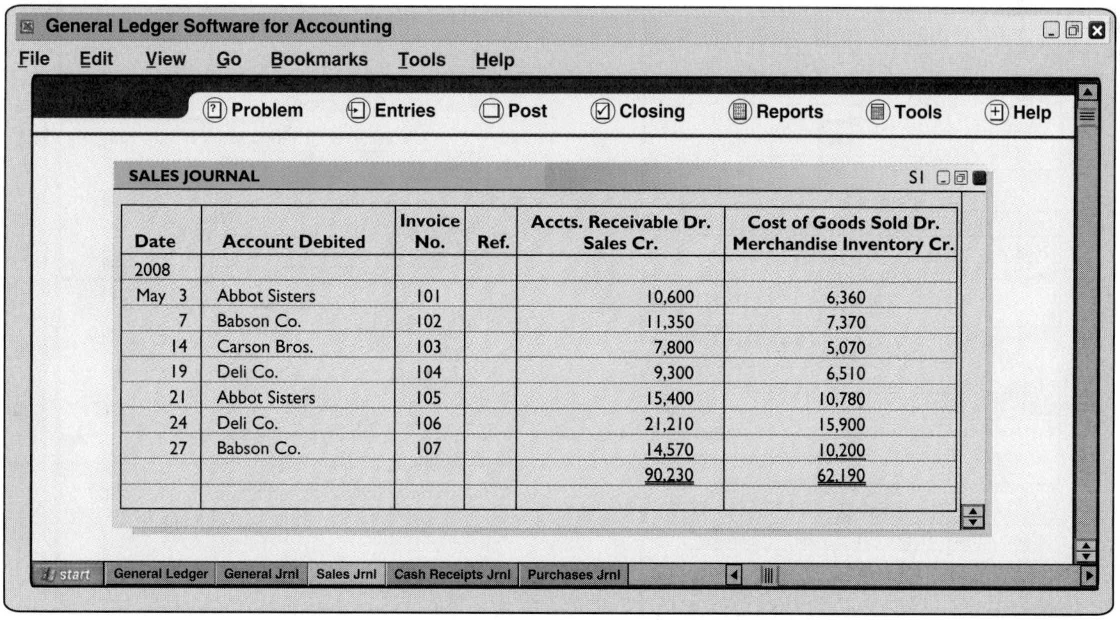

SALES JOURNAL — S1

Date	Account Debited	Invoice No.	Ref.	Accts. Receivable Dr. Sales Cr.	Cost of Goods Sold Dr. Merchandise Inventory Cr.
2008					
May 3	Abbot Sisters	101		10,600	6,360
7	Babson Co.	102		11,350	7,370
14	Carson Bros.	103		7,800	5,070
19	Deli Co.	104		9,300	6,510
21	Abbot Sisters	105		15,400	10,780
24	Deli Co.	106		21,210	15,900
27	Babson Co.	107		14,570	10,200
				90,230	62,190

Illustration 7-6
Journalizing the sales journal—perpetual inventory system

Note that, unlike the general journal, an explanation is not required for each entry in a special journal. Also, note that use of prenumbered invoices ensures that all invoices are journalized. Finally, note that the reference (Ref.) column is not used in journalizing. It is used in posting the sales journal, as explained in the next section.

POSTING THE SALES JOURNAL

Companies make daily postings from the sales journal **to the individual accounts receivable** in the subsidiary ledger. Posting **to the general ledger** is done **monthly**. Illustration 7-7 shows both the daily and monthly postings.

Illustration 7-7
Posting the sales journal

General Ledger Software for Accounting

File Edit View Go Bookmarks Tools Help

Problem | Entries | Post | Closing | Reports | Tools | Help

SALES JOURNAL S1

Date	Account Debited	Invoice No.	Ref.	Accts. Receivable Dr. Sales Cr.	Cost of Goods Sold Dr. Merchandise Inventory Cr.
2008					
May 3	Abbot Sisters	101	√	10,600	6,360
7	Babson Co.	102	√	11,350	7,370
14	Carson Bros.	103	√	7,800	5,070
19	Deli Co.	104	√	9,300	6,510
21	Abbot Sisters	105	√	15,400	10,780
24	Deli Co.	106	√	21,210	15,900
27	Babson Co.	107	√	14,570	10,200
				90,230	62,190
				(112) / (401)	(505) / (120)

At the end of the accounting period, the company posts totals to the general ledger.

The company posts individual amounts to the subsidiary ledger daily.

ACCOUNTS RECEIVABLE SUBSIDIARY LEDGER

Abbot Sisters

Date	Ref.	Debit	Credit	Balance
2008				
May 3	S1	10,600		10,600
21	S1	15,400		26,000

Babson Co.

Date	Ref.	Debit	Credit	Balance
2008				
May 7	S1	11,350		11,350
27	S1	14,570		25,920

Carson Bros.

Date	Ref.	Debit	Credit	Balance
2008				
May 14	S1	7,800		7,800

Deli Co.

Date	Ref.	Debit	Credit	Balance
2008				
May 19	S1	9,300		9,300
24	S1	21,210		30,510

GENERAL LEDGER

Accounts Receivable No. 112

Date	Ref.	Debit	Credit	Balance
2008				
May 31	S1	90,230		90,230

Merchandise Inventory No. 120

Date	Ref.	Debit	Credit	Balance
2008				
May 31	S1		62,190	62,190[1]

Sales No. 401

Date	Ref.	Debit	Credit	Balance
2008				
May 31	S1		90,230	90,230

Cost of Goods Sold No. 505

Date	Ref.	Debit	Credit	Balance
2008				
May 31	S1	62,190		62,190

The subsidiary ledger is separate from the general ledger.

Accounts Receivable is a control account.

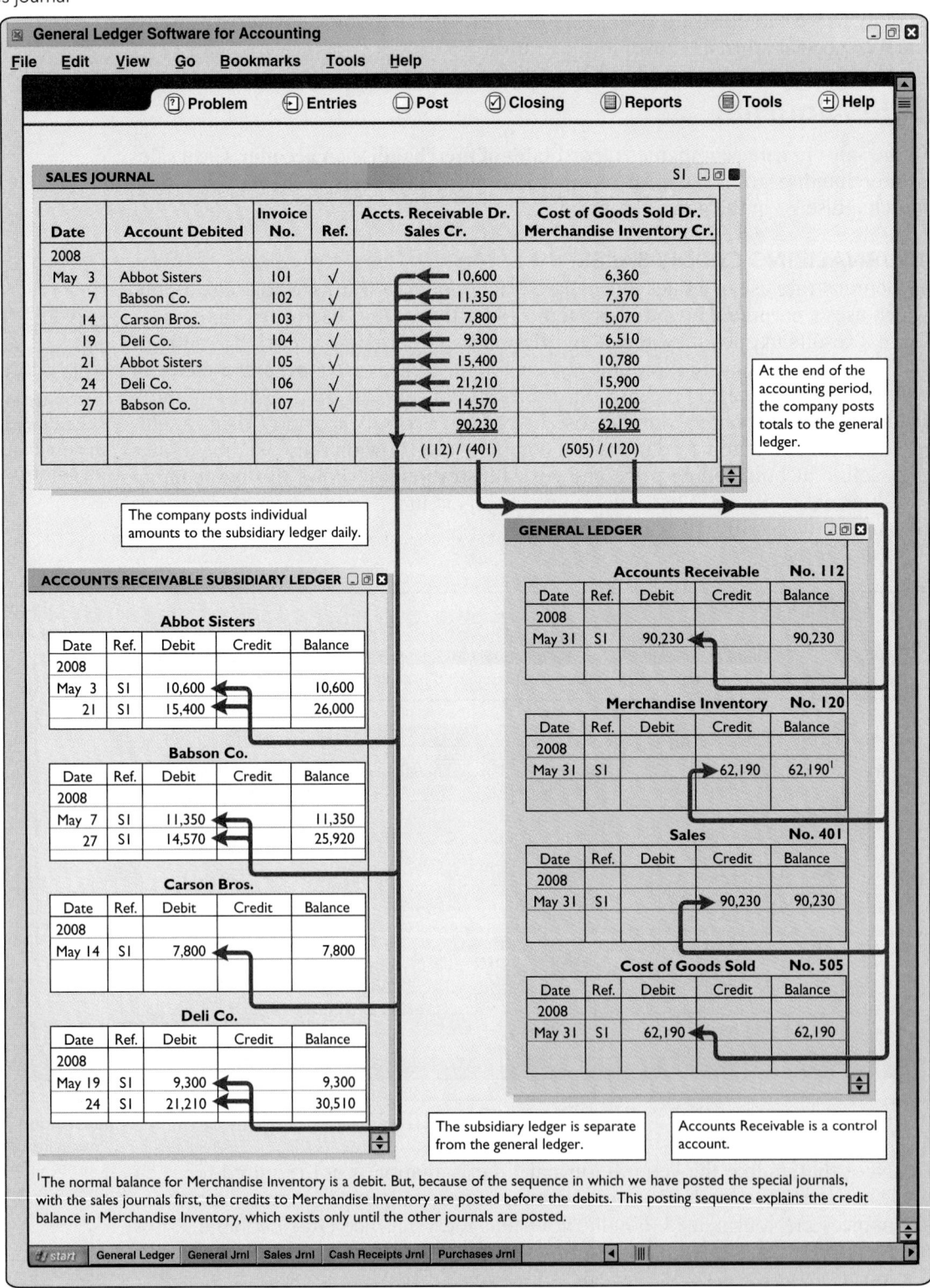

[1]The normal balance for Merchandise Inventory is a debit. But, because of the sequence in which we have posted the special journals, with the sales journals first, the credits to Merchandise Inventory are posted before the debits. This posting sequence explains the credit balance in Merchandise Inventory, which exists only until the other journals are posted.

start | General Ledger | General Jrnl | Sales Jrnl | Cash Receipts Jrnl | Purchases Jrnl

A check mark (✓) is inserted in the reference posting column to indicate that the daily posting to the customer's account has been made. If the subsidiary ledger accounts were numbered, the account number would be entered in place of the check mark. At the end of the month, Karns posts the column totals of the sales journal to the general ledger. Here, the column totals are as follows: From the selling-price column, a debit of $90,230 to Accounts Receivable (account No. 112), and a credit of $90,230 to Sales (account No. 401). From the cost column, a debit of $62,190 to Cost of Goods Sold (account No. 505), and a credit of $62,190 to Merchandise Inventory (account No. 120). Karns inserts the account numbers below the column totals to indicate that the postings have been made. In both the general ledger and subsidiary ledger accounts, the reference **S1** indicates that the posting came from page 1 of the sales journal.

PROVING THE LEDGERS

The next step is to "prove" the ledgers. To do so, Karns must determine two things: (1) The total of the general ledger debit balances must equal the total of the general ledger credit balances. (2) The sum of the subsidiary ledger balances must equal the balance in the control account. Illustration 7-8 shows the proof of the postings from the sales journal to the general and subsidiary ledger.

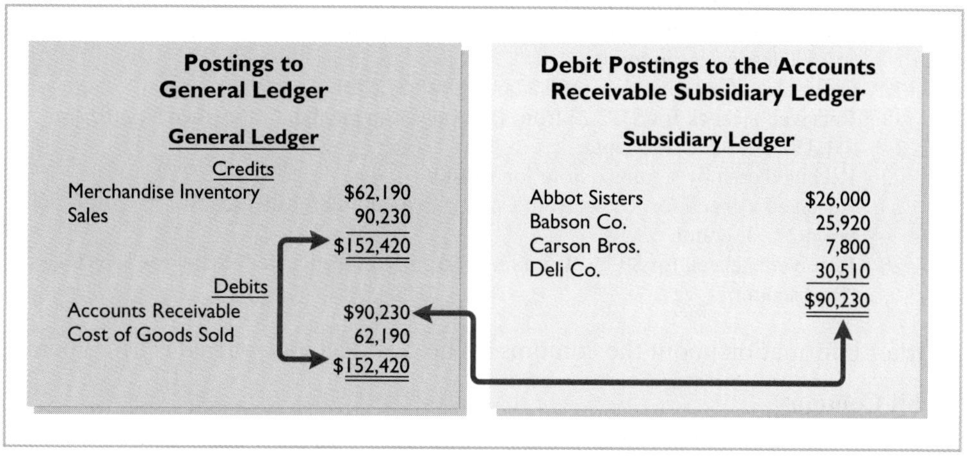

Illustration 7-8
Proving the equality of the postings from the sales journal

ADVANTAGES OF THE SALES JOURNAL

The use of a special journal to record sales on account has a number of advantages. First, the one-line entry for each sales transaction saves time. In the sales journal, it is not necessary to write out the four account titles for each transaction. Second, only totals, rather than individual entries, are posted to the general ledger. This saves posting time and reduces the possibilities of errors in posting. Finally, a division of labor results, because one individual can take responsibility for the sales journal.

Cash Receipts Journal

In the **cash receipts journal**, companies record all receipts of cash. The most common types of cash receipts are cash sales of merchandise and collections of accounts receivable. Many other possibilities exist, such as receipt of money from bank loans and cash proceeds from disposal of equipment. A one- or two-column cash receipts journal would not have space enough for all possible cash receipt transactions. Therefore, companies use a multiple-column cash receipts journal.

Generally, a cash receipts journal includes the following columns: debit columns for Cash and Sales Discounts, and credit columns for Accounts Receivable, Sales, and "Other" accounts. Companies use the "Other Accounts" category when the cash receipt does not involve a cash sale or a collection of accounts receivable. Under a perpetual inventory system, each sales entry also is accompanied by an entry that debits Cost of Goods Sold and credits Merchandise Inventory for the cost of the merchandise sold. Illustration 7-9 (page 303) shows a six-column cash receipts journal.

Companies may use additional credit columns if these columns significantly reduce postings to a specific account. For example, a loan company, such as Household International, receives thousands of cash collections from customers. Using separate credit columns for Loans Receivable and Interest Revenue, rather than the Other Accounts credit column, would reduce postings.

JOURNALIZING CASH RECEIPTS TRANSACTIONS

To illustrate the journalizing of cash receipts transactions, we will continue with the May transactions of Karns Wholesale Supply. Collections from customers relate to the entries recorded in the sales journal in Illustration 7-6. The entries in the cash receipts journal are based on the following cash receipts.

May	1	D. A. Karns makes an investment of $5,000 in the business.
	7	Cash sales of merchandise total $1,900 (cost, $1,240).
	10	Received a check for $10,388 from Abbot Sisters in payment of invoice No. 101 for $10,600 less a 2% discount.
	12	Cash sales of merchandise total $2,600 (cost, $1,690).
	17	Received a check for $11,123 from Babson Co. in payment of invoice No. 102 for $11,350 less a 2% discount.
	22	Received cash by signing a note for $6,000.
	23	Received a check for $7,644 from Carson Bros. in full for invoice No. 103 for $7,800 less a 2% discount.
	28	Received a check for $9,114 from Deli Co. in full for invoice No. 104 for $9,300 less a 2% discount.

Further information about the columns in the cash receipts journal is listed below.

Debit Columns:

1. **Cash.** Karns enters in this column the amount of cash actually received in each transaction. The column total indicates the total cash receipts for the month.
2. **Sales Discounts.** Karns includes a Sales Discounts column in its cash receipts journal. By doing so, it does not need to enter sales discount items in the general journal. As a result, the cash receipts journal shows on one line the collection of an account receivable within the discount period.

HELPFUL HINT
When is an account title entered in the "Account Credited" column of the cash receipts journal? Answer: A *subsidiary ledger* account is entered when the entry involves a collection of accounts receivable. A *general ledger* account is entered when the account is not shown in a special column (and an amount must be entered in the Other Accounts column). Otherwise, no account is shown in the "Account Credited" column.

Credit Columns:

3. **Accounts Receivable.** Karns uses the Accounts Receivable column to record cash collections on account. The amount entered here is the amount to be credited to the individual customer's account.
4. **Sales.** The Sales column records all cash sales of merchandise. Cash sales of other assets (plant assets, for example) are not reported in this column.
5. **Other Accounts.** Karns uses the Other Accounts column whenever the credit is other than to Accounts Receivable or Sales. For example, in the first entry, Karns enters $5,000 as a credit to D. A. Karns, Capital. This column is often referred to as the sundry accounts column.

Debit and Credit Column:

6. **Cost of Goods Sold and Merchandise Inventory.** This column records debits to Cost of Goods Sold and credits to Merchandise Inventory.

Illustration 7-9
Journalizing and posting the cash receipts journal

General Ledger Software for Accounting

File Edit View Go Bookmarks Tools Help

Problem | Entries | Post | Closing | Reports | Tools | Help

CASH RECEIPTS JOURNAL CR1

Date	Account Credited	Ref.	Cash Dr.	Sales Discounts Dr.	Accounts Receivable Cr.	Sales Cr.	Other Accounts Cr.	Cost of Goods Sold Dr. Mdse. Inv. Cr.
2008								
May 1	D.A. Karns, Capital	301	5,000				5,000	
7			1,900			1,900		1,240
10	Abbot Sisters	√	10,388	212	10,600			
12			2,600			2,600		1,690
17	Babson Co.	√	11,123	227	11,350			
22	Notes Payable	200	6,000				6,000	
23	Carson Bros.	√	7,644	156	7,800			
28	Deli Co.	√	9,114	186	9,300			
			53,769	781	39,050	4,500	11,000	2,930
			(101)	(414)	(112)	(401)	(x)	(505)/(120)

The company posts individual amounts to the subsidiary ledger daily.

At the end of the accounting period, the company posts totals to the general ledger.

ACCOUNTS RECEIVABLE SUBSIDIARY LEDGER

Abbot Sisters

Date	Ref.	Debit	Credit	Balance
2008				
May 3	S1	10,600		10,600
10	CR1		10,600	--------
21	S1	15,400		15,400

Babson Co.

Date	Ref.	Debit	Credit	Balance
2008				
May 7	S1	11,350		11,350
17	CR1		11,350	--------
27	S1	14,570		14,570

Carson Bros.

Date	Ref.	Debit	Credit	Balance
2008				
May 14	S1	7,800		7,800
23	CR1		7,800	-------

Deli Co.

Date	Ref.	Debit	Credit	Balance
2008				
May 19	S1	9,300		9,300
24	S1	21,210		30,510
28	CR1		9,300	21,210

The subsidiary ledger is separate from the general ledger.

Accounts Receivable is a control account.

GENERAL LEDGER

Cash No. 101

Date	Ref.	Debit	Credit	Balance
2008				
May 31	CR1	53,769		53,769

Accounts Receivable No. 112

Date	Ref.	Debit	Credit	Balance
2008				
May 31	S1	90,230		90,230
31	CR1		39,050	51,180

Merchandise Inventory No. 120

Date	Ref.	Debit	Credit	Balance
2008				
May 31	S1		62,190	62,190
31	CR1		2,930	65,120

Notes Payable No. 200

Date	Ref.	Debit	Credit	Balance
2008				
May 22	CR1		6,000	6,000

D.A. Karns, Capital No. 301

Date	Ref.	Debit	Credit	Balance
2008				
May 1	CR1		5,000	5,000

Sales No. 401

Date	Ref.	Debit	Credit	Balance
2008				
May 31	S1		90,230	90,230
31	CR1		4,500	94,730

Sales Discounts No. 414

Date	Ref.	Debit	Credit	Balance
2008				
May 31	CR1	781		781

Cost of Goods Sold No. 505

Date	Ref.	Debit	Credit	Balance
2008				
May 31	S1	62,190		62,190
31	CR1	2,930		65,120

start | General Ledger | General Jrnl | Sales Jrnl | Cash Receipts Jrnl | Purchases Jrnl

In a multi-column journal, generally only one line is needed for each entry. Debit and credit amounts for each line must be equal. When Karns journalizes the collection from Abbot Sisters on May 10, for example, three amounts are indicated. Note also that the Account Credited column identifies both general ledger and subsidiary ledger account titles. General ledger accounts are illustrated in the May 1 and May 22 entries. A subsidiary account is illustrated in the May 10 entry for the collection from Abbot Sisters.

When Karns has finished journalizing a multi-column journal, it totals the amount columns and compares the totals to prove the equality of debits and credits. Illustration 7-10 shows the proof of the equality of Karns's cash receipts journal.

Illustration 7-10
Proving the equality of the cash receipts journal

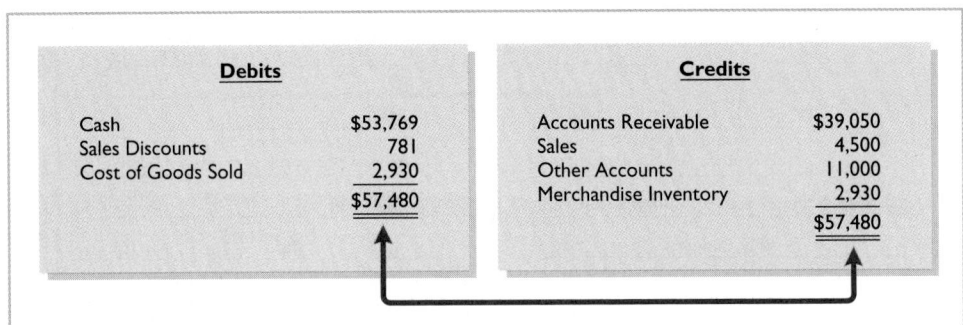

Debits	
Cash	$53,769
Sales Discounts	781
Cost of Goods Sold	2,930
	$57,480

Credits	
Accounts Receivable	$39,050
Sales	4,500
Other Accounts	11,000
Merchandise Inventory	2,930
	$57,480

Totaling the columns of a journal and proving the equality of the totals is called **footing** and **cross-footing** a journal.

POSTING THE CASH RECEIPTS JOURNAL

Posting a multi-column journal involves the following steps.

STUDY OBJECTIVE 4
Indicate how companies post a multi-column journal.

1. **At the end of the month**, the company posts all column totals, except for the Other Accounts total, to the account title(s) specified in the column heading (such as Cash or Accounts Receivable). The company then enters account numbers below the column totals to show that they have been posted. For example, Karns has posted cash to account No. 101, accounts receivable to account No. 112, merchandise inventory to account No. 120, sales to account No. 401, sales discounts to account No. 414, and cost of goods sold to account No. 505.
2. The company **separately posts the individual amounts comprising the Other Accounts total** to the general ledger accounts specified in the Account Credited column. See, for example, the credit posting to D. A. Karns, Capital: The total amount of this column has not been posted. The symbol (X) is inserted below the total to this column to indicate that the amount has not been posted.
3. The individual amounts in a column, posted in total to a control account (Accounts Receivable, in this case), are posted **daily to the subsidiary ledger** account specified in the Account Credited column. See, for example, the credit posting of $10,600 to Abbot Sisters.

The symbol **CR**, used in both the subsidiary and general ledgers, identifies postings from the cash receipts journal.

PROVING THE LEDGERS

After posting of the cash receipts journal is completed, Karns proves the ledgers. As shown in Illustration 7-11, the general ledger totals agree. Also, the sum of the subsidiary ledger balances equals the control account balance.

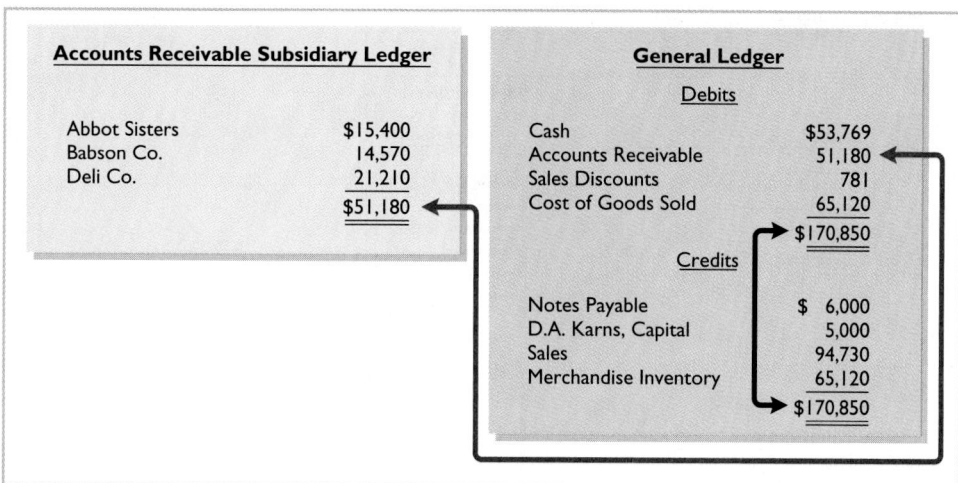

Illustration 7-11
Proving the ledgers after posting the sales and the cash receipts journals

Accounts Receivable Subsidiary Ledger

Abbot Sisters	$15,400
Babson Co.	14,570
Deli Co.	21,210
	$51,180

General Ledger

Debits	
Cash	$53,769
Accounts Receivable	51,180
Sales Discounts	781
Cost of Goods Sold	65,120
	$170,850
Credits	
Notes Payable	$ 6,000
D.A. Karns, Capital	5,000
Sales	94,730
Merchandise Inventory	65,120
	$170,850

Purchases Journal

In the **purchases journal**, companies record all purchases of merchandise on account. Each entry in this journal results in a debit to Merchandise Inventory and a credit to Accounts Payable. Illustration 7-13 (on page 306) shows the purchases journal for Karns Wholesale Supply.

When using a one-column purchases journal (as in Illustration 7-13), a company cannot journalize other types of purchases on account or cash purchases in it. For example, using the purchases journal shown in Illustration 7-13, Karns would have to record credit purchases of equipment or supplies in the general journal. Likewise, all cash purchases would be entered in the cash payments journal. As illustrated later, companies that make numerous credit purchases for items other than merchandise often expand the purchases journal to a multi-column format. (See Illustration 7-15.)

JOURNALIZING CREDIT PURCHASES OF MERCHANDISE

The journalizing procedure is similar to that for a sales journal. Companies make entries in the purchases journal from purchase invoices. In contrast to the sales journal, the purchases journal may not have an invoice number column, because invoices received from different suppliers will not be in numerical sequence. To ensure that they record all purchase invoices, some companies consecutively number each invoice upon receipt and then use an internal document number column in the purchases journal. The entries for Karns Wholesale Supply are based on the assumed credit purchases listed in Illustration 7-12.

Illustration 7-12
Credit purchases transactions

Date	Supplier	Amount
5/6	Jasper Manufacturing Inc.	$11,000
5/10	Eaton and Howe Inc.	7,200
5/14	Fabor and Son	6,900
5/19	Jasper Manufacturing Inc.	17,500
5/26	Fabor and Son	8,700
5/29	Eaton and Howe Inc.	12,600

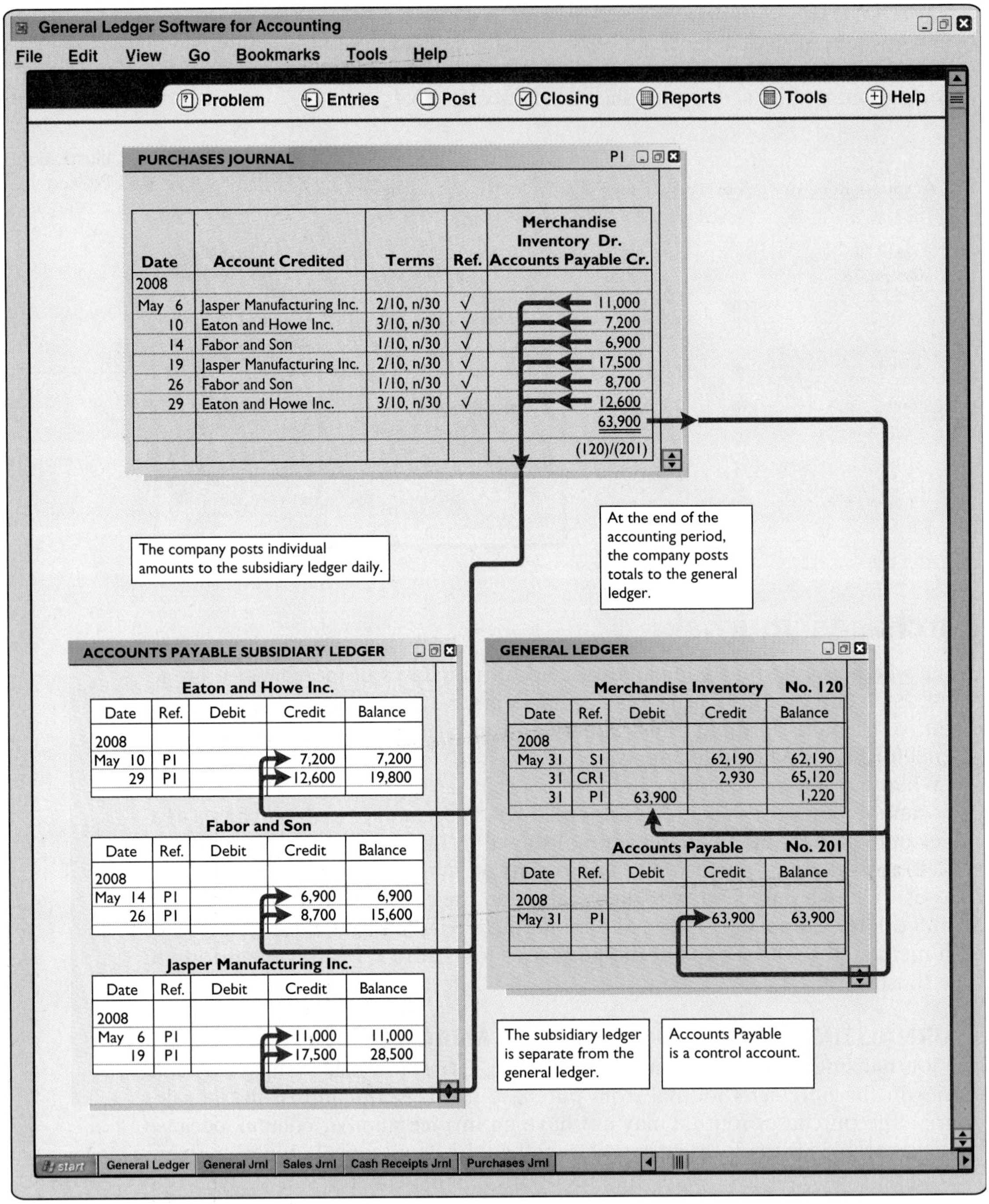

PURCHASES JOURNAL P1

Date	Account Credited	Terms	Ref.	Merchandise Inventory Dr. Accounts Payable Cr.
2008				
May 6	Jasper Manufacturing Inc.	2/10, n/30	√	11,000
10	Eaton and Howe Inc.	3/10, n/30	√	7,200
14	Fabor and Son	1/10, n/30	√	6,900
19	Jasper Manufacturing Inc.	2/10, n/30	√	17,500
26	Fabor and Son	1/10, n/30	√	8,700
29	Eaton and Howe Inc.	3/10, n/30	√	12,600
				63,900
				(120)/(201)

ACCOUNTS PAYABLE SUBSIDIARY LEDGER

Eaton and Howe Inc.

Date	Ref.	Debit	Credit	Balance
2008				
May 10	P1		7,200	7,200
29	P1		12,600	19,800

Fabor and Son

Date	Ref.	Debit	Credit	Balance
2008				
May 14	P1		6,900	6,900
26	P1		8,700	15,600

Jasper Manufacturing Inc.

Date	Ref.	Debit	Credit	Balance
2008				
May 6	P1		11,000	11,000
19	P1		17,500	28,500

GENERAL LEDGER

Merchandise Inventory No. 120

Date	Ref.	Debit	Credit	Balance
2008				
May 31	S1		62,190	62,190
31	CR1		2,930	65,120
31	P1	63,900		1,220

Accounts Payable No. 201

Date	Ref.	Debit	Credit	Balance
2008				
May 31	P1		63,900	63,900

Illustration 7-13
Journalizing and posting the purchases journal

HELPFUL HINT
Postings to subsidiary ledger accounts are done daily because it is often necessary to know a current balance for the subsidiary accounts.

POSTING THE PURCHASES JOURNAL

The procedures for posting the purchases journal are similar to those for the sales journal. In this case, Karns makes **daily** postings to the **accounts payable ledger**; it makes **monthly** postings to Merchandise Inventory and Accounts Payable in the general ledger. In both ledgers, Karns uses **P1** in the reference column to show that the postings are from page 1 of the purchases journal.

Proof of the equality of the postings from the purchases journal to both ledgers is shown in Illustration 7-14.

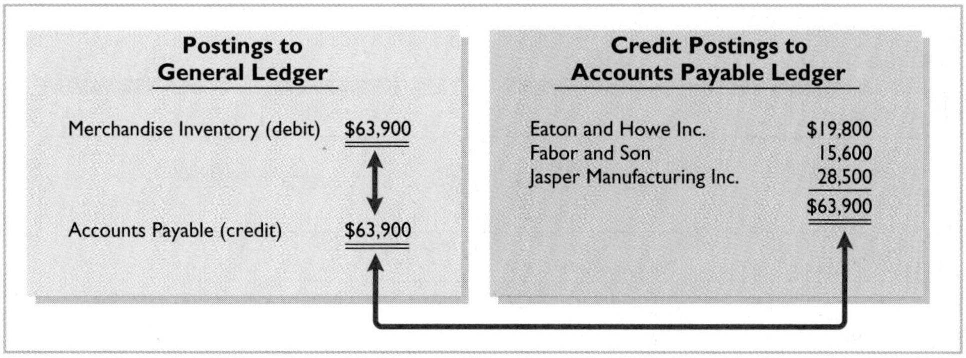

Postings to General Ledger
Merchandise Inventory (debit) $63,900
Accounts Payable (credit) $63,900
Credit Postings to Accounts Payable Ledger
Eaton and Howe Inc. $19,800
Fabor and Son 15,600
Jasper Manufacturing Inc. 28,500
$63,900

Illustration 7-14
Proving the equality of the purchases journal

EXPANDING THE PURCHASES JOURNAL

As noted earlier, some companies expand the purchases journal to include all types of purchases on account. Instead of one column for merchandise inventory and accounts payable, they use a multiple-column format. This format usually includes a credit column for Accounts Payable and debit columns for purchases of Merchandise Inventory, Office Supplies, Store Supplies, and Other Accounts. Illustration 7-15 shows a multi-column purchases journal for Hanover Co. The posting procedures are similar to those shown earlier for posting the cash receipts journal.

HELPFUL HINT
A single-column purchases journal needs only to be footed to prove the equality of debits and credits.

Illustration 7-15
Multi-column purchases journal

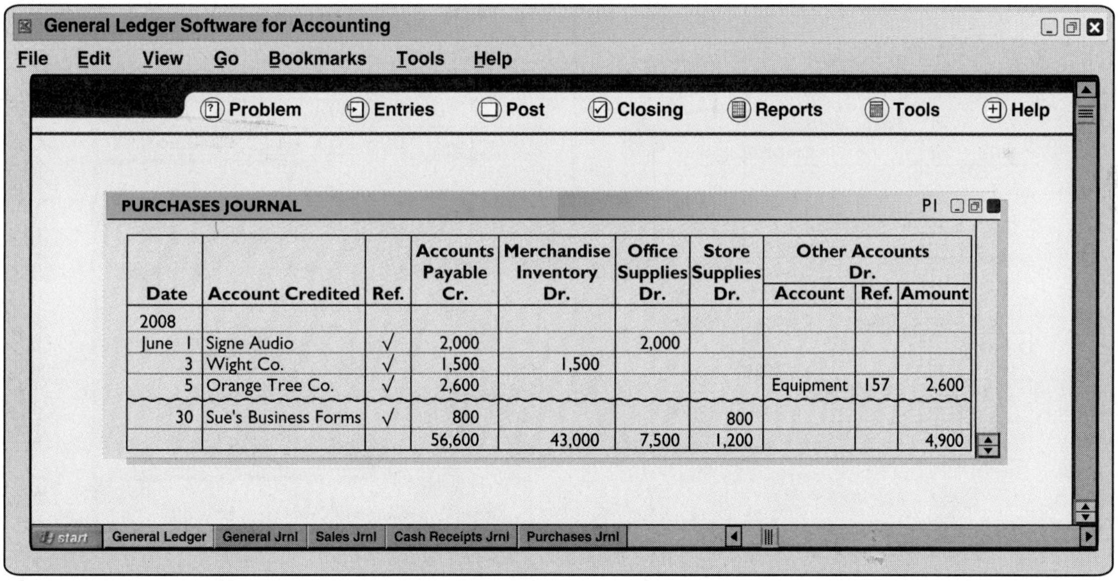

Date	Account Credited	Ref.	Accounts Payable Cr.	Merchandise Inventory Dr.	Office Supplies Dr.	Store Supplies Dr.	Other Accounts Dr. Account	Ref.	Amount
2008									
June 1	Signe Audio	√	2,000		2,000				
3	Wight Co.	√	1,500	1,500					
5	Orange Tree Co.	√	2,600				Equipment	157	2,600
30	Sue's Business Forms	√	800			800			
			56,600	43,000	7,500	1,200			4,900

Cash Payments Journal

In a **cash payments (cash disbursements) journal**, companies record all disbursements of cash. Entries are made from prenumbered checks. Because companies make cash payments for various purposes, the cash payments journal has multiple columns. Illustration 7-16 (page 308) shows a four-column journal.

JOURNALIZING CASH PAYMENTS TRANSACTIONS

The procedures for journalizing transactions in this journal are similar to those for the cash receipts journal. Karns records each transaction on one line, and for each line there must be equal debit and credit amounts. The entries in the cash payments

General Ledger Software for Accounting

File Edit View Go Bookmarks Tools Help

Problem | Entries | Post | Closing | Reports | Tools | Help

CASH PAYMENTS JOURNAL CP1

Date	Ck. No.	Account Debited	Ref.	Other Accounts Dr.	Accounts Payable Dr.	Merchandise Inventory Cr.	Cash Cr.
2008							
May 1	101	Prepaid Insurance	130	1,200			1,200
3	102	Mdse. Inventory	120	100			100
8	103	Mdse. Inventory	120	4,400			4,400
10	104	Jasper Manuf. Inc.	√		11,000	220	10,780
19	105	Eaton & Howe Inc.	√		7,200	216	6,984
23	106	Fabor and Son	√		6,900	69	6,831
28	107	Jasper Manuf. Inc.	√		17,500	350	17,150
30	108	D.A. Karns, Drawing	306	500			500
				6,200	42,600	855	47,945
				(x)	(201)	(120)	(101)

The company posts individual amounts to the subsidiary ledger daily.

At the end of the accounting period, the company posts totals to the general ledger.

ACCOUNTS PAYABLE SUBSIDIARY LEDGER

Eaton and Howe Inc.

Date	Ref.	Debit	Credit	Balance
2008				
May 10	P1		7,200	7,200
19	CP1	7,200		-------
29	P1		12,600	12,600

Fabor and Son

Date	Ref.	Debit	Credit	Balance
2008				
May 14	P1		6,900	6,900
23	CP1	6,900		-------
26	P1		8,700	8,700

Jasper Manufacturing Inc.

Date	Ref.	Debit	Credit	Balance
2008				
May 6	P1		11,000	11,000
10	CP1	11,000		--------
19	P1		17,500	17,500
28	CP1	17,500		--------

The subsidiary ledger is separate from the general ledger.

Accounts Receivable is a control account.

GENERAL LEDGER

Cash **No. 101**

Date	Ref.	Debit	Credit	Balance
2008				
May 31	CR1	53,769		53,769
31	CP1		47,945	5,824

Merchandise Inventory **No. 120**

Date	Ref.	Debit	Credit	Balance
2008				
May 3	CP1	100		100
8	CP1	4,400		4,500
31	S1		62,190	57,690
31	CR1		2,930	60,620
31	P1	63,900		3,280
31	CP1		855	2,425

Prepaid Insurance **No. 130**

Date	Ref.	Debit	Credit	Balance
2008				
May 1	CP1	1,200		1,200

Accounts Payable **No. 201**

Date	Ref.	Debit	Credit	Balance
2008				
May 31	P1		63,900	63,900
31	CP1	42,600		21,300

D.A. Karns, Drawing **No. 306**

Date	Ref.	Debit	Credit	Balance
2008				
May 30	CP1	500		500

start | General Ledger | General Jrnl | Sales Jrnl | Cash Receipts Jrnl | Purchases Jrnl

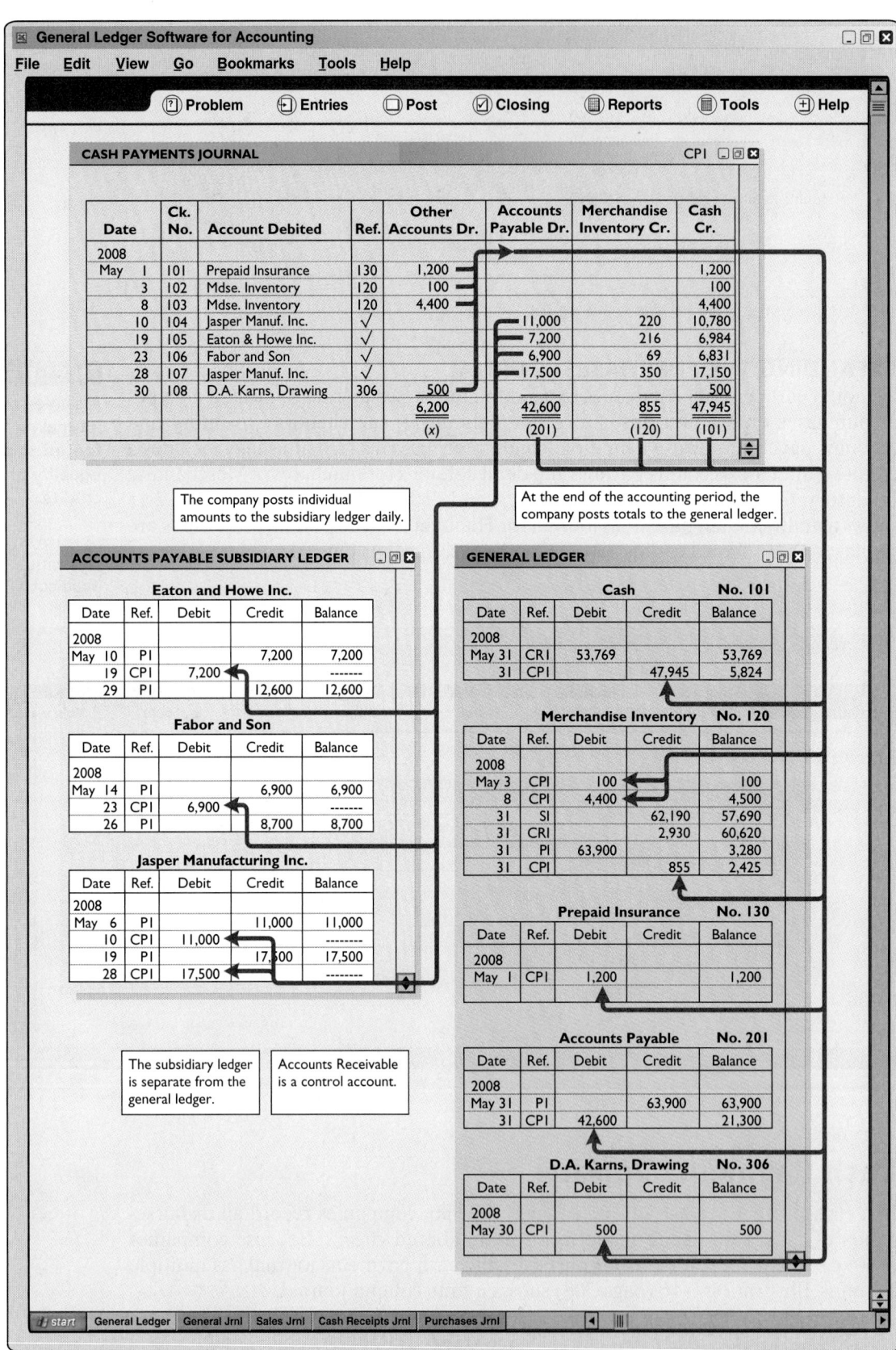

Illustration 7-16
Journalizing and posting the cash payments journal

journal in Illustration 7-16 are based on the following transactions for Karns Wholesale Supply.

May 1 Issued check No. 101 for $1,200 for the annual premium on a fire insurance policy.
3 Issued check No. 102 for $100 in payment of freight when terms were FOB shipping point.
8 Issued check No. 103 for $4,400 for the purchase of merchandise.
10 Sent check No. 104 for $10,780 to Jasper Manufacturing Inc. in payment of May 6 invoice for $11,000 less a 2% discount.
19 Mailed check No. 105 for $6,984 to Eaton and Howe Inc. in payment of May 10 invoice for $7,200 less a 3% discount.
23 Sent check No. 106 for $6,831 to Fabor and Son in payment of May 14 invoice for $6,900 less a 1% discount.
28 Sent check No. 107 for $17,150 to Jasper Manufacturing Inc. in payment of May 19 invoice for $17,500 less a 2% discount.
30 Issued check No. 108 for $500 to D. A. Karns as a cash withdrawal for personal use.

Note that whenever Karns enters an amount in the Other Accounts column, it must identify a specific general ledger account in the Account Debited column. The entries for checks No. 101, 102, 103, and 108 illustrate this situation. Similarly, Karns must identify a subsidiary account in the Account Debited column whenever it enters an amount in the Accounts Payable column. See, for example, the entry for check No. 104.

After Karns journalizes the cash payments journal, it totals the columns. The totals are then balanced to prove the equality of debits and credits.

POSTING THE CASH PAYMENTS JOURNAL

The procedures for posting the cash payments journal are similar to those for the cash receipts journal. Karns posts the amounts recorded in the Accounts Payable column individually to the subsidiary ledger and in total to the control account. It posts Merchandise Inventory and Cash only in total at the end of the month. Transactions in the Other Accounts column are posted individually to the appropriate account(s) affected. The company does not post totals for the Other Accounts column.

Illustration 7-16 shows the posting of the cash payments journal. Note that Karns uses the symbol **CP** as the posting reference. After postings are completed, the company proves the equality of the debit and credit balances in the general ledger. In addition, the control account balances should agree with the subsidiary ledger total balance. Illustration 7-17 shows the agreement of these balances.

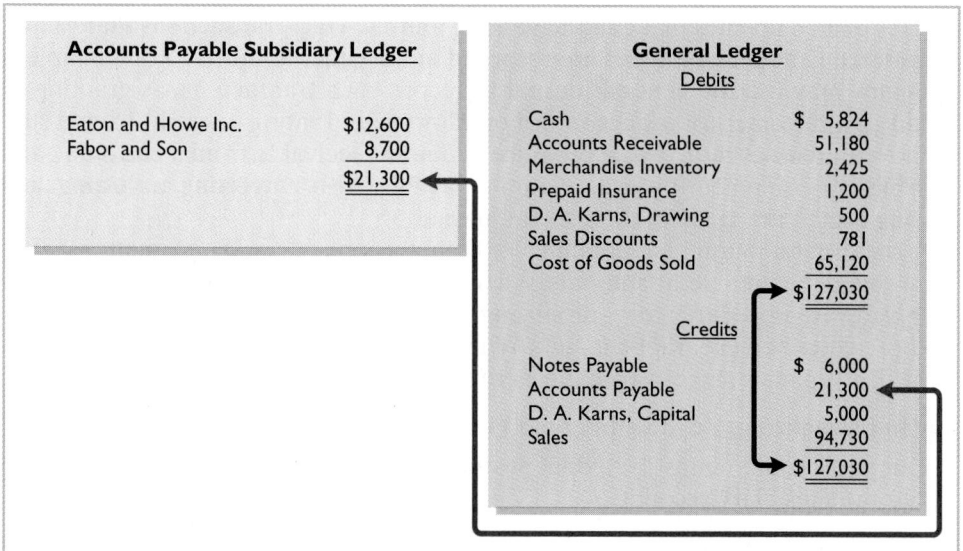

Illustration 7-17
Proving the ledgers after postings from the sales, cash receipts, purchases, and cash payments journals

Accounts Payable Subsidiary Ledger

Eaton and Howe Inc.	$12,600
Fabor and Son	8,700
	$21,300

General Ledger

Debits	
Cash	$ 5,824
Accounts Receivable	51,180
Merchandise Inventory	2,425
Prepaid Insurance	1,200
D. A. Karns, Drawing	500
Sales Discounts	781
Cost of Goods Sold	65,120
	$127,030

Credits	
Notes Payable	$ 6,000
Accounts Payable	21,300
D. A. Karns, Capital	5,000
Sales	94,730
	$127,030

ETHICS INSIGHT

How Do Employees Steal?

A recent study by the Association of Certified Fraud Examiners found that two-thirds of all employee thefts involved a fraudulent disbursement by an employee. The most common form (52% of cases) was fraudulent billing schemes. In these, the employee causes the company to issue a payment to the employee by submitting a bill for nonexistent goods or services, purchases of personal goods by the employee, or inflated invoices. The following graph shows various types of fraudulent disbursements and the median loss from each.

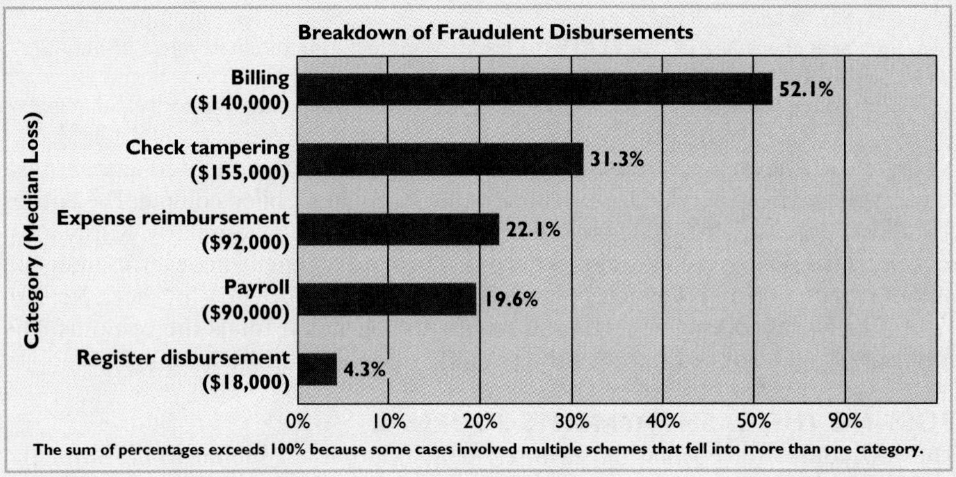

Source: 2004 Report to the Nation on Occupational Fraud and Abuse, Association of Certified Fraud Examiners, *www.cfenet.com/pdfs/2004RttN.pdf*, p. 14.

? How can companies reduce the likelihood of fraudulent disbursements?

Effects of Special Journals on the General Journal

Special journals for sales, purchases, and cash substantially reduce the number of entries that companies make in the general journal. **Only transactions that cannot be entered in a special journal are recorded in the general journal.** For example, a company may use the general journal to record such transactions as granting of credit to a customer for a sales return or allowance, granting of credit from a supplier for purchases returned, acceptance of a note receivable from a customer, and purchase of equipment by issuing a note payable. Also, **correcting, adjusting, and closing entries are made in the general journal**.

The general journal has columns for date, account title and explanation, reference, and debit and credit amounts. When control and subsidiary accounts are not involved, the procedures for journalizing and posting of transactions are the same as those described in earlier chapters. When control and subsidiary accounts *are* involved, companies make two changes from the earlier procedures:

1. In **journalizing**, they identify both the control and the subsidiary accounts.
2. In **posting**, there must be a **dual posting**: once to the control account and once to the subsidiary account.

To illustrate, assume that on May 31, Karns Wholesale Supply returns $500 of merchandise for credit to Fabor and Son. Illustration 7-18 shows the entry in the general journal and the posting of the entry. Note that if Karns receives cash instead of credit on this return, then it would record the transaction in the cash receipts journal.

Illustration 7-18
Journalizing and posting the general journal

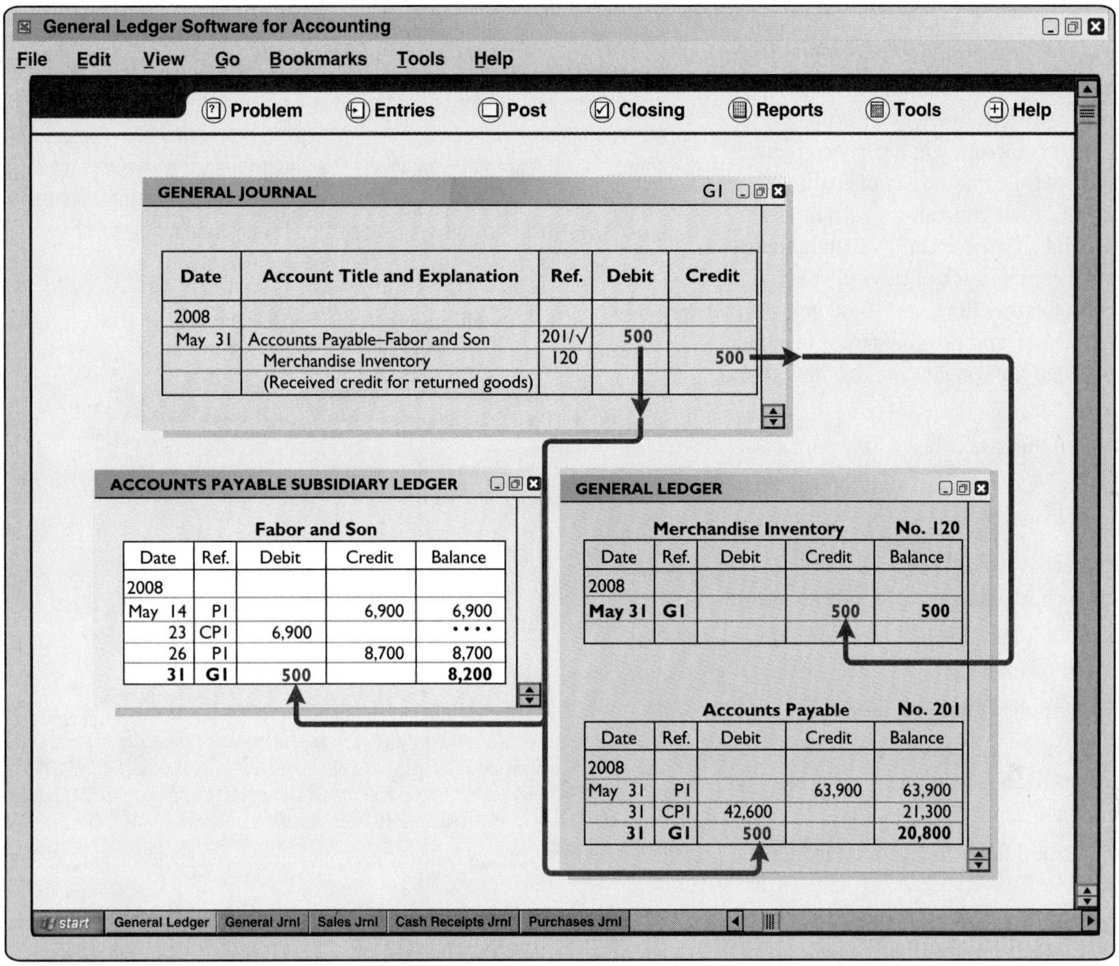

GENERAL JOURNAL G1

Date	Account Title and Explanation	Ref.	Debit	Credit
2008				
May 31	Accounts Payable–Fabor and Son	201/√	500	
	Merchandise Inventory	120		500
	(Received credit for returned goods)			

ACCOUNTS PAYABLE SUBSIDIARY LEDGER

Fabor and Son

Date	Ref.	Debit	Credit	Balance
2008				
May 14	P1		6,900	6,900
23	CP1	6,900		••••
26	P1		8,700	8,700
31	**G1**	**500**		**8,200**

GENERAL LEDGER

Merchandise Inventory No. 120

Date	Ref.	Debit	Credit	Balance
2008				
May 31	**G1**		**500**	**500**

Accounts Payable No. 201

Date	Ref.	Debit	Credit	Balance
2008				
May 31	P1		63,900	63,900
31	CP1	42,600		21,300
31	**G1**	**500**		**20,800**

Note that the general journal indicates two accounts (Accounts Payable, and Fabor and Son) for the debit, and two postings ("201/✓") in the reference column. One debit is posted to the control account and another debit to the creditor's account in the subsidiary ledger.

Before You Go On...

REVIEW IT

1. What types of special journals do companies frequently use to record transactions? Why do they use special journals?
2. Explain how companies post transactions recorded in the sales journal and the cash receipts journal.
3. Indicate the types of transactions that companies record in the general journal when they use special journals.

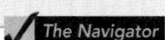

✓ *The Navigator*

Be sure to read **ALL ABOUT YOU: *Keeping Track of the Documents in Your Life*** on page 312 for information on how topics in this chapter apply to you.

Keeping Track of the Documents in Your Life

In this chapter you learned about the inner workings of basic accounting systems that companies use to keep track of all of their important financial information. Although you aren't a company, you *are* an economic entity. Each day you engage in a variety of economic transactions, some of which generate important financial or personal documents. Unfortunately, many of us do a poor job keeping track of this information. With just a little bit of extra effort, you could get your financial records in order, and possibly save yourself a lot of future grief. What are some of the documents and records in your life?

* Social Security card, birth certificate, passport
* Check book and bank statements, loan information (including school loans)
* Credit card statements and receipts
* Apartment lease or home title and property tax records
* Automobile records (purchase, loans, registration, repair records and receipts)
* Insurance records (policy numbers, medical information)
* W-2 forms, receipts for tax-deductible items, income tax returns from past years
* Receipts for major purchases (e.g., computer) and related warranties

Some Facts

* You can keep financial and personal records in file cabinets, on your home computer, or in a safe-deposit box at a bank. Where to keep records depends on the particular characteristics of each record. Highly sensitive or non-replaceable documents should be kept in a safe-deposit box; day-to-day records of a non-sensitive nature can go in home files.
* Hurricane Katrina caused hundreds of thousands of people to lose personal and financial records, including medical, dental, and tax records, birth certificates, and Social Security cards, as well as credit cards and driver's licenses.
* Signing up for direct payroll deposit as well as automatic bill payment can be a useful precautionary step against possible disaster. Many of your financial transactions will continue to take place while you are trying to put the rest of your life back together.
* Online services are available to back up your data over an Internet connection to a computer located somewhere distant. If disaster strikes, your files are safe.

About the Numbers

Probably no official document produces more anxiety than tax returns. Many people wonder how long they should keep old tax returns and supporting documentation. The graph below shows the time frame within which the IRS must initiate an audit. To ensure that you have adequate documentation, many tax experts suggest that you keep supporting tax documents for seven years.

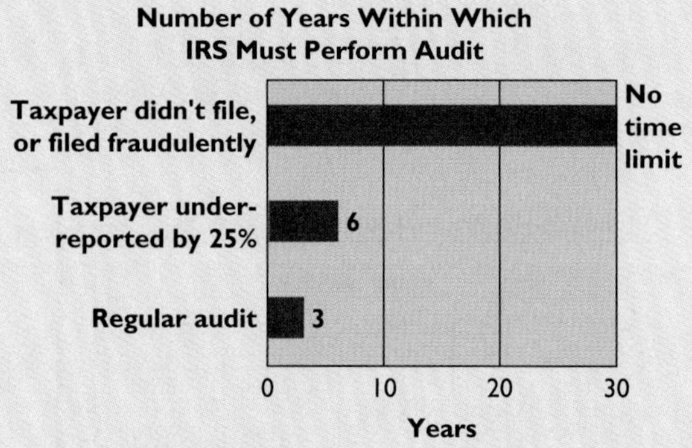

Sources: "Fires, Floods and Other Misfortunes: Are You Prepared Financially?" Federal Deposit Insurance Corporation, *www.fdic.gov/consumers/consumer/news/cnwin0506/misfortunes.html;* "How to Organize Financial Records," SmartPros, *http://accounting.smartpros.com/x32643.xml;* Ann Papmehl, "Emergency Planning: Where to Keep Your Important Papers," *CMA Management,* June 2002, pp. 43-44.

What Do You Think

Do you really need to take the time to organize your financial documents?

YES: Everyone engages in financial transactions each day. For a variety of reasons (such as for tax reporting or job applications), we need to maintain adequate documentation of these transactions.

NO: I lead a relatively uncomplicated life, and I can usually (well, some of the time) find the documents that I need when I need them.

The authors' comments on this situation appear on page 334.

Demonstration Problem

Cassandra Wilson Company uses a six-column cash receipts journal with the following columns:

Cash (Dr.)
Sales Discounts (Dr.)
Accounts Receivable (Cr.)
Sales (Cr.)
Other Accounts (Cr.)
Cost of Goods Sold (Dr.) and Merchandise Inventory (Cr.)

Cash receipts transactions for the month of July 2008 are as follows.

July 3 Cash sales total $5,800 (cost, $3,480).
5 Received a check for $6,370 from Jeltz Company in payment of an invoice dated June 26 for $6,500, terms 2/10, n/30.
9 Cassandra Wilson, the proprietor, made an additional investment of $5,000 in cash in the business.
10 Cash sales total $12,519 (cost, $7,511).
12 Received a check for $7,275 from R. Eliot & Co. in payment of a $7,500 invoice dated July 3, terms 3/10, n/30.
15 Received a customer advance of $700 cash for future sales.
20 Cash sales total $15,472 (cost, $9,283).
22 Received a check for $5,880 from Beck Company in payment of $6,000 invoice dated July 13, terms 2/10, n/30.
29 Cash sales total $17,660 (cost, $10,596).
31 Received cash of $200 on interest earned for July.

Instructions

(a) Journalize the transactions in the cash receipts journal.
(b) Contrast the posting of the Accounts Receivable and Other Accounts columns.

action plan

- Record all cash receipts in the cash receipts journal.
- The "account credited" indicates items posted individually to the subsidiary ledger or general ledger.
- Record cash sales in the cash receipts journal—not in the sales journal.
- The total debits must equal the total credits.

Solution to Demonstration Problem

(a)

CASSANDRA WILSON COMPANY
Cash Receipts Journal

CR1

Date	Account Credited	Ref.	Cash Dr.	Sales Discounts Dr.	Accounts Receivable Cr.	Sales Cr.	Other Accounts Cr.	Cost of Goods Sold Dr. Mdse. Inv. Cr.
2008								
7/3			5,800			5,800		3,480
5	Jeltz Company		6,370	130	6,500			
9	C. Wilson, Capital		5,000				5,000	
10			12,519			12,519		7,511
12	R. Eliot & Co.		7,275	225	7,500			
15	Unearned Revenue		700				700	
20			15,472			15,472		9,283
22	Beck Company		5,880	120	6,000			
29			17,660			17,660		10,596
31	Interest Revenue		200				200	
			76,876	475	20,000	51,451	5,900	30,870

(b) The Accounts Receivable column is posted as a credit to Accounts Receivable. The individual amounts are credited to the customers' accounts identified in the Account Credited column, which are maintained in the accounts receivable subsidiary ledger.

The amounts in the Other Accounts column are posted individually. They are credited to the account titles identified in the Account Credited column.

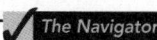

The Navigator

SUMMARY OF STUDY OBJECTIVES

1 **Identify the basic concepts of an accounting information system.** The basic principles in developing an accounting information system are cost effectiveness, useful output, and flexibility. Most companies use a computerized accounting system. Smaller companies use entry-level software such as QuickBooks or Peachtree. Larger companies use custom-made software packages which often integrate all aspects of the organization.

2 **Describe the nature and purpose of a subsidiary ledger.** A subsidiary ledger is a group of accounts with a common characteristic. It facilitates the recording process by freeing the general ledger from details of individual balances.

3 **Explain how companies use special journals in journalizing.** Companies use special journals to group similar types of transactions. In a special journal, generally only one line is used to record a complete transaction.

4 **Indicate how companies post a multi-column journal.** In posting a multi-column journal:

(a) Companies post all column totals except for the Other Accounts column once at the end of the month to the account title specified in the column heading.

(b) Companies do not post the total of the Other Accounts column. Instead, the individual amounts comprising the total are posted separately to the general ledger accounts specified in the Account Credited (Debited) column.

(c) The individual amounts in a column posted in total to a control account are posted daily to the subsidiary ledger accounts specified in the Account Credited (Debited) column.

The Navigator

GLOSSARY

Accounting information system A system that collects and processes transaction data, and communicates financial information to decision makers. (p. 292).

Accounts payable (creditors') subsidiary ledger A subsidiary ledger that collects transaction data of individual creditors. (p. 295).

Accounts receivable (customers') subsidiary ledger A subsidiary ledger that collects transaction data of individual customers. (p. 295).

Cash payments (disbursements) journal A special journal that records all cash paid. (p. 307).

Cash receipts journal A special journal that records all cash received. (p. 301).

Control account An account in the general ledger that summarizes subsidiary ledger. (p. 295).

Manual accounting system A system in which someone performs each of the steps in the accounting cycle by hand. (p. 295).

Purchases journal A special journal that records all purchases of merchandise on account. (p. 305).

Sales journal A special journal that records all sales of merchandise on account. (p. 299).

Special journal A journal that records similar types of transactions, such as all credit sales. (p. 298).

Subsidiary ledger A group of accounts with a common characteristic. (p. 295).

SELF-STUDY QUESTIONS

Answers are at the end of the chapter.

(SO 1) **1.** The basic principles of an accounting information system include all of the following *except*:
a. cost effectiveness.
b. flexibility.
c. useful output.
d. periodicity.

(SO 1) **2.** Which of the following is *not* an advantage of computerized accounting systems?
a. Data is entered only once in computerized accounting systems.
b. Computerized accounting systems provide up-to-date information.
c. Computerized accounting systems eliminate entering of transaction information.
d. Computerized accounting systems eliminate many errors resulting from human intervention.

3. Which of the following is *incorrect* concerning subsidiary ledgers? (SO 2)
a. The purchases ledger is a common subsidiary ledger for creditor accounts.
b. The accounts receivable ledger is a subsidiary ledger.
c. A subsidiary ledger is a group of accounts with a common characteristic.
d. An advantage of the subsidiary ledger is that it permits a division of labor in posting.

4. A sales journal will be used for: (SO 3)

	Credit Sales	Cash Sales	Sales Discounts
a.	no	yes	yes
b.	yes	no	yes
c.	yes	no	no
d.	yes	yes	no

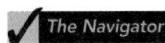

(SO 3, 4) **5.** Which of the following statements is *correct*?
a. The sales discount column is included in the cash receipts journal.
b. The purchases journal records all purchases of merchandise whether for cash or on account.
c. The cash receipts journal records sales on account.
d. Merchandise returned by the buyer is recorded by the seller in the purchases journal.

(SO 4) **6.** Which of the following is *incorrect* concerning the posting of the cash receipts journal?
a. The total of the Other Accounts column is not posted.
b. All column totals except the total for the Other Accounts column are posted once at the end of the month to the account title(s) specified in the column heading.
c. The totals of all columns are posted daily to the accounts specified in the column heading.
d. The individual amounts in a column posted in total to a control account are posted daily to the subsidiary ledger account specified in the Account Credited column.

(SO 4) **7.** Postings from the purchases journal to the subsidiary ledger are generally made:
a. yearly.
b. monthly.
c. weekly.
d. daily.

8. Which statement is *incorrect* regarding the general journal? (SO 3)
a. Only transactions that cannot be entered in a special journal are recorded in the general journal.
b. Dual postings are always required in the general journal.
c. The general journal may be used to record acceptance of a note receivable in payment of an account receivable.
d. Correcting, adjusting, and closing entries are made in the general journal.

9. When companies use special journals: (SO 3)
a. they record all purchase transactions in the purchases journal.
b. they record all cash received, except from cash sales, in the cash receipts journal.
c. they record all cash disbursements in the cash payments journal.
d. a general journal is not necessary.

10. If a customer returns goods for credit, the selling company normally makes an entry in the: (SO 3)
a. cash payments journal.
b. sales journal.
c. general journal.
d. cash receipts journal.

Go to the book's website, **www.wiley.com/college/weygandt**, for Additional Self-Study questions.

✓ The Navigator

QUESTIONS

1. (a) What is an accounting information system? (b) "An accounting information system applies only to a manual system." Do you agree? Explain.
2. Certain principles should be followed in the development of an accounting information system. Identify and explain each of the principles.
3. What are common features of computerized accounting packages beyond recording transactions and preparing financial statements?
4. How does an enterprise resource planning (ERP) system differ from an entry-level computerized accounting system?
5. What are the advantages of using subsidiary ledgers?
6. (a) When do companies normally post to (1) the subsidiary accounts and (2) the general ledger control accounts? (b) Describe the relationship between a control account and a subsidiary ledger.
7. Identify and explain the four special journals discussed in the chapter. List an advantage of using each of these journals rather than using only a general journal.
8. Thogmartin Company uses special journals. It recorded in a sales journal a sale made on account to R. Peters for $435. A few days later, R. Peters returns $70 worth of merchandise for credit. Where should Thogmartin Company record the sales return? Why?
9. A $500 purchase of merchandise on account from Lore Company was properly recorded in the purchases journal. When posted, however, the amount recorded in the subsidiary ledger was $50. How might this error be discovered?
10. Why would special journals used in different businesses not be identical in format? What type of business would maintain a cash receipts journal but not include a column for accounts receivable?
11. The cash and the accounts receivable columns in the cash receipts journal were mistakenly overadded by $4,000 at the end of the month. (a) Will the customers' ledger agree with the Accounts Receivable control account? (b) Assuming no other errors, will the trial balance totals be equal?
12. One column total of a special journal is posted at month-end to only two general ledger accounts. One of these two accounts is Accounts Receivable. What is the name of this special journal? What is the other general ledger account to which that same month-end total is posted?
13. In what journal would the following transactions be recorded? (Assume that a two-column sales journal and a single-column purchases journal are used.)
    (a) Recording of depreciation expense for the year.
    (b) Credit given to a customer for merchandise purchased on credit and returned.
    (c) Sales of merchandise for cash.
    (d) Sales of merchandise on account.
    (e) Collection of cash on account from a customer.
    (f) Purchase of office supplies on account.

14. In what journal would the following transactions be recorded? (Assume that a two-column sales journal and a single-column purchases journal are used.)
    (a) Cash received from signing a note payable.
    (b) Investment of cash by the owner of the business.
    (c) Closing of the expense accounts at the end of the year.
    (d) Purchase of merchandise on account.
    (e) Credit received for merchandise purchased and returned to supplier.
    (f) Payment of cash on account due a supplier.
15. What transactions might be included in a multiple-column purchases journal that would not be included in a single-column purchases journal?
16. Give an example of a transaction in the general journal that causes an entry to be posted twice (i.e., to two accounts), one in the general ledger, the other in the subsidiary ledger. Does this affect the debit/credit equality of the general ledger?
17. Give some examples of appropriate general journal transactions for an organization using special journals.

BRIEF EXERCISES

Identify basic concepts of an accounting information system. (SO 1)

BE7-1 Indicate whether each of the following statements is true or false.

1. When designing an accounting system, we need to think about the needs and knowledge of both the top managers and various other users.
2. When the environment changes as a result of technological advances, increased competition, or government regulation, an accounting system does not have to be sufficiently flexible to meet the changes in order to save money.
3. In developing an accounting system, cost is relevant. The benefits obtained from the information disseminated must outweigh the cost of providing it.

Identify basic concepts of an accounting information system. (SO 1)

BE 7-2 Here is a list of words or phrases related to computerized accounting systems.

1. Entry-level software.
2. Enterprise resource planning system.
3. Network-compatible.
4. Audit trail.
5. Internal control.

Instructions

Match each word or phrase with the best description of it.

______**(a)** Allows multiple users to access the system at the same time.
______**(b)** Enables the tracking of all transactions.
______**(c)** Identifies suspicious transactions or likely mistakes such as wrong account numbers or duplicate transactions.
______**(d)** Large-scale computer systems that integrate all aspects of the organization including, accounting, sales, human resource management, and manufacturing.
______**(e)** System for companies with revenues of less than $5 million and up to 20 employees.

Identify basic concepts of an accounting information system. (SO 1)

BE 7-3 Beka Borke has prepared the following list of statements about accounting information systems.

1. The accounting information system includes each of the steps of the accounting cycle, the documents that provide evidence of transactions that have occurred, and the accounting records.
2. The benefits obtained from information provided by the accounting information system need not outweigh the cost of providing that information.
3. Designers of accounting systems must consider the needs and knowledge of various users.
4. If an accounting information system is cost-effective and provides useful output, it does not need to be flexible.

Instructions

Identify each statement as true or false. If false, indicate how to correct the statement.

Identify subsidiary ledger balances. (SO 2)

BE7-4 Presented below is information related to Kienholz Company for its first month of operations. Identify the balances that appear in the accounts receivable subsidiary ledger and the accounts receivable balance that appears in the general ledger at the end of January.

Credit Sales			Cash Collections		
Jan. 7	Agler Co.	$10,000	Jan. 17	Agler Co.	$7,000
15	Barto Co.	6,000	24	Barto Co.	4,000
23	Maris Co.	9,000	29	Maris Co.	9,000

BE7-5 Identify in what ledger (general or subsidiary) each of the following accounts is shown.

Identify subsidiary ledger accounts.
(SO 2)

1. Rent Expense
2. Accounts Receivable—Char
3. Notes Payable
4. Accounts Payable—Thebeau

BE7-6 Identify the journal in which each of the following transactions is recorded.

Identify special journals.
(SO 3)

1. Cash sales
2. Owner withdrawal of cash
3. Cash purchase of land
4. Credit sales
5. Purchase of merchandise on account
6. Receipt of cash for services performed

BE7-7 Indicate whether each of the following debits and credits is included in the cash receipts journal. (Use "Yes" or "No" to answer this question.)

Identify entries to cash receipts journal.
(SO 3)

1. Debit to Sales
2. Credit to Merchandise Inventory
3. Credit to Accounts Receivable
4. Debit to Accounts Payable

BE7-8 Galindo Co. uses special journals and a general journal. Identify the journal in which each of the following transactions is recorded.

Identify transactions for special journals.
(SO 3)

(a) Purchased equipment on account.
(b) Purchased merchandise on account.
(c) Paid utility expense in cash.
(d) Sold merchandise on account.

BE7-9 Identify the special journal(s) in which the following column headings appear.

Identify transactions for special journals.
(SO 3)

1. Sales Discounts Dr.
2. Accounts Receivable Cr.
3. Cash Dr.
4. Sales Cr.
5. Merchandise Inventory Dr.

BE7-10 Kidwell Computer Components Inc. uses a multi-column cash receipts journal. Indicate which column(s) is/are posted only in total, only daily, or both in total and daily.

Indicate postings to cash receipts journal.
(SO 4)

1. Accounts Receivable
2. Sales Discounts
3. Cash
4. Other Accounts

EXERCISES

WILEY PLUS

E7-1 Donahue Company uses both special journals and a general journal as described in this chapter. On June 30, after all monthly postings had been completed, the Accounts Receivable control account in the general ledger had a debit balance of $320,000; the Accounts Payable control account had a credit balance of $77,000.

Determine control account balances, and explain posting of special journals.
(SO 2, 4)

The July transactions recorded in the special journals are summarized below. No entries affecting accounts receivable and accounts payable were recorded in the general journal for July.

Sales journal	Total sales $161,400
Purchases journal	Total purchases $56,400
Cash receipts journal	Accounts receivable column total $131,000
Cash payments journal	Accounts payable column total $47,500

Instructions

(a) What is the balance of the Accounts Receivable control account after the monthly postings on July 31?
(b) What is the balance of the Accounts Payable control account after the monthly postings on July 31?
(c) To what account(s) is the column total of $161,400 in the sales journal posted?
(d) To what account(s) is the accounts receivable column total of $131,000 in the cash receipts journal posted?

E7-2 Presented below is the subsidiary accounts receivable account of Jeremy Dody.

Explain postings to subsidiary ledger.
(SO 2)

Date	Ref.	Debit	Credit	Balance
2008				
Sept. 2	S31	61,000		61,000
9	G4		14,000	47,000
27	CR8		47,000	—

Instructions

Write a memo to Andrea Barden, chief financial officer, that explains each transaction.

Post various journals to control and subsidiary accounts.
(SO 2, 4)

E7-3 On September 1 the balance of the Accounts Receivable control account in the general ledger of Seaver Company was $10,960. The customers' subsidiary ledger contained account balances as follows: Ruiz $1,440, Kingston $2,640, Bannister $2,060, Crampton $4,820. At the end of September the various journals contained the following information.

Sales journal: Sales to Crampton $800; to Ruiz $1,260; to Iman $1,330; to Bannister $1,100.
Cash receipts journal: Cash received from Bannister $1,310; from Crampton $2,300; from Iman $380; from Kingston $1,800; from Ruiz $1,240.
General journal: An allowance is granted to Crampton $220.

Instructions

(a) Set up control and subsidiary accounts and enter the beginning balances. Do not construct the journals.
(b) Post the various journals. Post the items as individual items or as totals, whichever would be the appropriate procedure. (No sales discounts given.)
(c) Prepare a list of customers and prove the agreement of the controlling account with the subsidiary ledger at September 30, 2008.

Determine control and subsidiary ledger balances for accounts receivable.
(SO 2)

E7-4 Yu Suzuki Company has a balance in its Accounts Receivable control account of $11,000 on January 1, 2008. The subsidiary ledger contains three accounts: Smith Company, balance $4,000; Green Company, balance $2,500; and Koyan Company. During January, the following receivable-related transactions occurred.

	Credit Sales	Collections	Returns
Smith Company	$9,000	$8,000	$ -0-
Green Company	7,000	2,500	3,000
Koyan Company	8,500	9,000	-0-

Instructions

(a) What is the January 1 balance in the Koyan Company subsidiary account?
(b) What is the January 31 balance in the control account?
(c) Compute the balances in the subsidiary accounts at the end of the month.
(d) Which January transaction would not be recorded in a special journal?

Determine control and subsidiary ledger balances for accounts payable.
(SO 2)

E7-5 Nobo Uematsu Company has a balance in its Accounts Payable control account of $8,250 on January 1, 2008. The subsidiary ledger contains three accounts: Jones Company, balance $3,000; Brown Company, balance $1,875; and Aatski Company. During January, the following receivable-related transactions occurred.

	Purchases	Payments	Returns
Jones Company	$6,750	$6,000	$ -0-
Brown Company	5,250	1,875	2,250
Aatski Company	6,375	6,750	-0-

Instructions

(a) What is the January 1 balance in the Aatski Company subsidiary account?
(b) What is the January 31 balance in the control account?
(c) Compute the balances in the subsidiary accounts at the end of the month.
(d) Which January transaction would not be recorded in a special journal?

Record transactions in sales and purchases journal.
(SO 2, 3)

E7-6 Montalvo Company uses special journals and a general journal. The following transactions occurred during September 2008.

Sept. 2 Sold merchandise on account to T. Hossfeld, invoice no. 101, $720, terms n/30. The cost of the merchandise sold was $420.
10 Purchased merchandise on account from L. Rincon $600, terms 2/10, n/30.
12 Purchased office equipment on account from R. Press $6,500.
21 Sold merchandise on account to P. Lowther, invoice no. 102 for $800, terms 2/10, n/30. The cost of the merchandise sold was $480.

25 Purchased merchandise on account from W. Barone $860, terms n/30.
27 Sold merchandise to S. Miller for $700 cash. The cost of the merchandise sold was $400.

Instructions

(a) Prepare a sales journal (see Illustration 7-7) and a single-column purchase journal (see Illustration 7-13). (Use page 1 for each journal.)

(b) Record the transaction(s) for September that should be journalized in the sales journal and the purchases journal.

Record transactions in cash receipts and cash payments journal.

(SO 2, 3)

E7-7 Pherigo Co. uses special journals and a general journal. The following transactions occurred during May 2008.

May 1 I. Pherigo invested $50,000 cash in the business.
2 Sold merchandise to B. Sherrick for $6,300 cash. The cost of the merchandise sold was $4,200.
3 Purchased merchandise for $7,200 from J. DeLeon using check no. 101.
14 Paid salary to H. Potter $700 by issuing check no. 102.
16 Sold merchandise on account to K. Kimbell for $900, terms n/30. The cost of the merchandise sold was $630.
22 A check of $9,000 is received from M. Moody in full for invoice 101; no discount given.

Instructions

(a) Prepare a multiple-column cash receipts journal (see Illustration 7-9) and a multiple-column cash payments journal (see Illustration 7-16). (Use page 1 for each journal.)

(b) Record the transaction(s) for May that should be journalized in the cash receipts journal and cash payments journal.

Explain journalizing in cash journals.

(SO 3)

E7-8 Wick Company uses the columnar cash journals illustrated in the textbook. In April, the following selected cash transactions occurred.

1. Made a refund to a customer for the return of damaged goods.
2. Received collection from customer within the 3% discount period.
3. Purchased merchandise for cash.
4. Paid a creditor within the 3% discount period.
5. Received collection from customer after the 3% discount period had expired.
6. Paid freight on merchandise purchased.
7. Paid cash for office equipment.
8. Received cash refund from supplier for merchandise returned.
9. Withdrew cash for personal use of owner.
10. Made cash sales.

Instructions

Indicate **(a)** the journal, and **(b)** the columns in the journal that should be used in recording each transaction.

Journalize transactions in general journal and post.

(SO 2, 4)

E7-9 Velasquez Company has the following selected transactions during March.

Mar. 2 Purchased equipment costing $9,400 from Chang Company on account.
5 Received credit of $410 from Lyden Company for merchandise damaged in shipment to Velasquez.
7 Issued credit of $400 to Higley Company for merchandise the customer returned. The returned merchandise had a cost of $260.

Velasquez Company uses a one-column purchases journal, a sales journal, the columnar cash journals used in the text, and a general journal.

Instructions

(a) Journalize the transactions in the general journal.

(b) In a brief memo to the president of Velasquez Company, explain the postings to the control and subsidiary accounts from each type of journal.

Indicate journalizing in special journals.

(SO 3)

E7-10 Below are some typical transactions incurred by Kwun Company.

1. Payment of creditors on account.
2. Return of merchandise sold for credit.

3. Collection on account from customers.
4. Sale of land for cash.
5. Sale of merchandise on account.
6. Sale of merchandise for cash.
7. Received credit for merchandise purchased on credit.
8. Sales discount taken on goods sold.
9. Payment of employee wages.
10. Income summary closed to owner's capital.
11. Depreciation on building.
12. Purchase of office supplies for cash.
13. Purchase of merchandise on account.

Instructions

For each transaction, indicate whether it would normally be recorded in a cash receipts journal, cash payments journal, sales journal, single-column purchases journal, or general journal.

Explain posting to control account and subsidiary ledger.
(SO 2, 4)

E7-11 The general ledger of Sanchez Company contained the following Accounts Payable control account (in T-account form). Also shown is the related subsidiary ledger.

GENERAL LEDGER

Accounts Payable

Feb. 15	General journal	1,400	Feb. 1	Balance	26,025
28	?	?	5	General journal	265
			11	General journal	550
			28	Purchases	13,400
			Feb. 28	Balance	9,500

ACCOUNTS PAYABLE LEDGER

Perez

	Feb. 28 Bal. 4,600

Tebbetts

	Feb. 28 Bal. ?

Zerbe

	Feb. 28 Bal. 2,300

Instructions

(a) Indicate the missing posting reference and amount in the control account, and the missing ending balance in the subsidiary ledger.
(b) Indicate the amounts in the control account that were dual-posted (i.e., posted to the control account and the subsidiary accounts).

Prepare purchases and general journals.
(SO 2, 3)

E7-12 Selected accounts from the ledgers of Lockhart Company at July 31 showed the following.

GENERAL LEDGER

Store Equipment No. 153

Date	Explanation	Ref.	Debit	Credit	Balance
July 1		G1	3,900		3,900

Accounts Payable No. 201

Date	Explanation	Ref.	Debit	Credit	Balance
July 1		G1		3,900	3,900
15		G1		400	4,300
18		G1	100		4,200
25		G1	200		4,000
31		P1		8,300	12,300

Merchandise Inventory No. 120

Date	Explanation	Ref.	Debit	Credit	Balance
July 15		G1	400		400
18		G1		100	300
25		G1		200	100
31		P1	8,300		8,400

ACCOUNTS PAYABLE LEDGER

Albin Equipment Co.

Date	Explanation	Ref.	Debit	Credit	Balance
July 1		G1		3,900	3,900

Drago Co.

Date	Explanation	Ref.	Debit	Credit	Balance
July 14		P1		1,100	1,100
25		G1	200		900

Brian Co.

Date	Explanation	Ref.	Debit	Credit	Balance
July 3		P1		2,400	2,400
20		P1		700	3,100

Erik Co.

Date	Explanation	Ref.	Debit	Credit	Balance
July 12		P1		500	500
21		P1		600	1,100

Chacon Corp

Date	Explanation	Ref.	Debit	Credit	Balance
July 17		P1		1,400	1,400
18		G1	100		1,300
29		P1		1,600	2,900

Heinen Inc.

Date	Explanation	Ref.	Debit	Credit	Balance
July 15		G1		400	400

Instructions

From the data prepare:

(a) the single-column purchases journal for July.

(b) the general journal entries for July.

Determine correct posting amount to control account.

(SO 4)

E7-13 Kansas Products uses both special journals and a general journal as described in this chapter. Kansas also posts customers' accounts in the accounts receivable subsidiary ledger. The postings for the most recent month are included in the subsidiary T accounts below.

Bargo

	Debit	Credit
Bal.	340	250
	200	

Leary

	Debit	Credit
Bal.	150	150
	240	

Carol

	Debit	Credit
Bal.	–0–	145
	145	

Paul

	Debit	Credit
Bal.	120	120
	190	
	150	

Instructions

Determine the correct amount of the end-of-month posting from the sales journal to the Accounts Receivable control account.

Compute balances in various accounts.

(SO 4)

E7-14 Selected account balances for Matisyahu Company at January 1, 2008, are presented below.

Accounts Payable	$14,000
Accounts Receivable	22,000
Cash	17,000
Inventory	13,500

Matisyahu's sales journal for January shows a total of $100,000 in the selling price column, and its one-column purchases journal for January shows a total of $72,000.

The column totals in Matisyahu's cash receipts journal are: Cash Dr. $61,000; Sales Discounts Dr. $1,100; Accounts Receivable Cr. $45,000; Sales Cr. $6,000; and Other Accounts Cr. $11,100.

The column totals in Matisyahu's cash payments journal for January are: Cash Cr. $55,000; Inventory Cr. $1,000; Accounts Payable Dr. $46,000; and Other Accounts Dr. $10,000. Matisyahu's total cost of goods sold for January is $63,600.

Accounts Payable, Accounts Receivable, Cash, Inventory, and Sales are not involved in the "Other Accounts" column in either the cash receipts or cash payments journal, and are not involved in any general journal entries.

Instructions

Compute the January 31 balance for Matisyahu in the following accounts.

(a) Accounts Payable.
(b) Accounts Receivable.
(c) Cash.
(d) Inventory.
(e) Sales.

EXERCISES: SET B

Visit the book's website at **www.wiley.com/college/weygandt**, and choose the Student Companion site, to access Exercise Set B.

PROBLEMS: SET A

Journalize transactions in cash receipts journal; post to control account and subsidiary ledger.
(SO 2, 3, 4)

GLS Peachtree®

P7-1A Grider Company's chart of accounts includes the following selected accounts.

101 Cash	401 Sales
112 Accounts Receivable	414 Sales Discounts
120 Merchandise Inventory	505 Cost of Goods Sold
301 O. Grider, Capital	

On April 1 the accounts receivable ledger of Grider Company showed the following balances: Ogden $1,550, Chelsea $1,200, Eggleston Co. $2,900, and Baez $1,800. The April transactions involving the receipt of cash were as follows.

Apr. 1 The owner, O. Grider, invested additional cash in the business $7,200.
4 Received check for payment of account from Baez less 2% cash discount.
5 Received check for $920 in payment of invoice no. 307 from Eggleston Co.
8 Made cash sales of merchandise totaling $7,245. The cost of the merchandise sold was $4,347.
10 Received check for $600 in payment of invoice no. 309 from Ogden.
11 Received cash refund from a supplier for damaged merchandise $740.
23 Received check for $1,500 in payment of invoice no. 310 from Eggleston Co.
29 Received check for payment of account from Chelsea.

Instructions

(a) Balancing totals $21,205

(a) Journalize the transactions above in a six-column cash receipts journal with columns for Cash Dr., Sales Discounts Dr., Accounts Receivable Cr., Sales Cr., Other Accounts Cr., and Cost of Goods Sold Dr./Merchandise Inventory Cr. Foot and crossfoot the journal.
(b) Insert the beginning balances in the Accounts Receivable control and subsidiary accounts, and post the April transactions to these accounts.
(c) Prove the agreement of the control account and subsidiary account balances.

(c) Accounts Receivable $1,430

Journalize transactions in cash payments journal; post to control account and subsidiary ledgers.
(SO 2, 3, 4)

GLS

P7-2A Ming Company's chart of accounts includes the following selected accounts.

101 Cash	201 Accounts Payable
120 Merchandise Inventory	306 T. Ming, Drawing
130 Prepaid Insurance	505 Cost of Goods Sold
157 Equipment	

On October 1 the accounts payable ledger of Ming Company showed the following balances: Bovary Company $2,700, Nyman Co. $2,500, Pyron Co. $1,800, and Sims Company $3,700. The October transactions involving the payment of cash were as follows.

Oct. 1 Purchased merchandise, check no. 63, $300.
3 Purchased equipment, check no. 64, $800.
5 Paid Bovary Company balance due of $2,700, less 2% discount, check no. 65, $2,646.
10 Purchased merchandise, check no. 66, $2,250.
15 Paid Pyron Co. balance due of $1,800, check no. 67.
16 T. Ming, the owner, pays his personal insurance premium of $400, check no. 68.
19 Paid Nyman Co. in full for invoice no. 610, $1,600 less 2% cash discount, check no. 69, $1,568.
29 Paid Sims Company in full for invoice no. 264, $2,500, check no. 70.

Instructions

(a) Journalize the transactions above in a four-column cash payments journal with columns for Other Accounts Dr., Accounts Payable Dr., Merchandise Inventory Cr., and Cash Cr. Foot and crossfoot the journal.

(a) Balancing totals $12,350

(b) Insert the beginning balances in the Accounts Payable control and subsidiary accounts, and post the October transactions to these accounts.

(c) Prove the agreement of the control account and the subsidiary account balances.

(c) Accounts Payable $2,100

Journalize transactions in multi-column purchases journal; post to the general and subsidiary ledgers.

(SO 2, 3, 4)

P7-3A The chart of accounts of Lopez Company includes the following selected accounts.

112 Accounts Receivable	401 Sales
120 Merchandise Inventory	412 Sales Returns and Allowances
126 Supplies	505 Cost of Goods Sold
157 Equipment	610 Advertising Expense
201 Accounts Payable	

In July the following selected transactions were completed. All purchases and sales were on account. The cost of all merchandise sold was 70% of the sales price.

July 1 Purchased merchandise from Fritz Company $8,000.
2 Received freight bill from Wayward Shipping on Fritz purchase $400.
3 Made sales to Pinick Company $1,300, and to Wayne Bros. $1,500.
5 Purchased merchandise from Moon Company $3,200.
8 Received credit on merchandise returned to Moon Company $300.
13 Purchased store supplies from Cress Supply $720.
15 Purchased merchandise from Fritz Company $3,600 and from Anton Company $3,300.
16 Made sales to Sager Company $3,450 and to Wayne Bros. $1,570.
18 Received bill for advertising from Lynda Advertisements $600.
21 Sales were made to Pinick Company $310 and to Haddad Company $2,800.
22 Granted allowance to Pinick Company for merchandise damaged in shipment $40.
24 Purchased merchandise from Moon Company $3,000.
26 Purchased equipment from Cress Supply $900.
28 Received freight bill from Wayward Shipping on Moon purchase of July 24, $380.
30 Sales were made to Sager Company $5,600.

Instructions

(a) Journalize the transactions above in a purchases journal, a sales journal, and a general journal. The purchases journal should have the following column headings: Date, Account Credited (Debited), Ref., Accounts Payable Cr., Merchandise Inventory Dr., and Other Accounts Dr.

(a) Purchases journal—
Accounts Payable $24,100
Sales column total $16,530

(b) Post to both the general and subsidiary ledger accounts. (Assume that all accounts have zero beginning balances.)

(c) Prove the agreement of the control and subsidiary accounts.

(c) Accounts Receivable $16,490
Accounts Payable $23,800

Journalize transactions in special journals.

(SO 2, 3, 4)

P7-4A Selected accounts from the chart of accounts of Boyden Company are shown below.

101 Cash	401 Sales
112 Accounts Receivable	412 Sales Returns and Allowances
120 Merchandise Inventory	414 Sales Discounts
126 Supplies	505 Cost of Goods Sold
157 Equipment	726 Salaries Expense
201 Accounts Payable	

The cost of all merchandise sold was 60% of the sales price. During January, Boyden completed the following transactions.

Jan. 3 Purchased merchandise on account from Wortham Co. $10,000.
4 Purchased supplies for cash $80.
4 Sold merchandise on account to Milam $5,250, invoice no. 371, terms 1/10, n/30.
5 Returned $300 worth of damaged goods purchased on account from Wortham Co. on January 3.
6 Made cash sales for the week totaling $3,150.
8 Purchased merchandise on account from Noyes Co. $4,500.
9 Sold merchandise on account to Connor Corp. $6,400, invoice no. 372, terms 1/10, n/30.

11 Purchased merchandise on account from Betz Co. $3,700.
13 Paid in full Wortham Co. on account less a 2% discount.
13 Made cash sales for the week totaling $6,260.
15 Received payment from Connor Corp. for invoice no. 372.
15 Paid semi-monthly salaries of $14,300 to employees.
17 Received payment from Milam for invoice no. 371.
17 Sold merchandise on account to Bullock Co. $1,200, invoice no. 373, terms 1/10, n/30.
19 Purchased equipment on account from Murphy Corp. $5,500.
20 Cash sales for the week totaled $3,200.
20 Paid in full Noyes Co. on account less a 2% discount.
23 Purchased merchandise on account from Wortham Co. $7,800.
24 Purchased merchandise on account from Forgetta Corp. $5,100.
27 Made cash sales for the week totaling $4,230.
30 Received payment from Bullock Co. for invoice no. 373.
31 Paid semi-monthly salaries of $13,200 to employees.
31 Sold merchandise on account to Milam $9,330, invoice no. 374, terms 1/10, n/30.

Boyden Company uses the following journals.

1. Sales journal.
2. Single-column purchases journal.
3. Cash receipts journal with columns for Cash Dr., Sales Discounts Dr., Accounts Receivable Cr., Sales Cr., Other Accounts Cr., and Cost of Goods Sold Dr./Merchandise Inventory Cr.
4. Cash payments journal with columns for Other Accounts Dr., Accounts Payable Dr., Merchandise Inventory Cr., and Cash Cr.
5. General journal.

Instructions

(a) Sales journal $22,180
Purchases journal $31,100
Cash receipts journal balancing total $29,690
Cash payments journal balancing total $41,780

Using the selected accounts provided:

(a) Record the January transactions in the appropriate journal noted.
(b) Foot and crossfoot all special journals.
(c) Show how postings would be made by placing ledger account numbers and checkmarks as needed in the journals. (Actual posting to ledger accounts is not required.)

Journalize in sales and cash receipts journals; post; prepare a trial balance; prove control to subsidiary; prepare adjusting entries; prepare an adjusted trial balance.

(SO 2, 3, 4)

P7-5A Presented below are the purchases and cash payments journals for Reyes Co. for its first month of operations.

PURCHASES JOURNAL P1

Date	Account Credited	Ref.	Merchandise Inventory Dr. Accounts Payable Cr.
July 4	G. Clemens		6,800
5	A. Ernst		8,100
11	J. Happy		5,920
13	C. Tabor		15,300
20	M. Sneezy		7,900
			44,020

CASH PAYMENTS JOURNAL CP1

Date	Account Debited	Ref.	Other Accounts Dr.	Accounts Payable Dr.	Merchandise Inventory Cr.	Cash Cr.
July 4	Store Supplies		600			600
10	A. Ernst			8,100	81	8,019
11	Prepaid Rent		6,000			6,000
15	G. Clemens			6,800		6,800
19	Reyes, Drawing		2,500			2,500
21	C. Tabor			15,300	153	15,147
			9,100	30,200	234	39,066

In addition, the following transactions have not been journalized for July. The cost of all merchandise sold was 65% of the sales price.

July	1	The founder, D. Reyes, invests $80,000 in cash.
	6	Sell merchandise on account to Ewing Co. $6,200 terms 1/10, n/30.
	7	Make cash sales totaling $6,000.
	8	Sell merchandise on account to S. Beauty $3,600, terms 1/10, n/30.
	10	Sell merchandise on account to W. Pitts $4,900, terms 1/10, n/30.
	13	Receive payment in full from S. Beauty.
	16	Receive payment in full from W. Pitts.
	20	Receive payment in full from Ewing Co.
	21	Sell merchandise on account to H. Prince $5,000, terms 1/10, n/30.
	29	Returned damaged goods to G. Clemens and received cash refund of $420.

Instructions

(a) Open the following accounts in the general ledger.

101 Cash	306 Reyes, Drawing
112 Accounts Receivable	401 Sales
120 Merchandise Inventory	414 Sales Discounts
127 Store Supplies	505 Cost of Goods Sold
131 Prepaid Rent	631 Supplies Expense
201 Accounts Payable	729 Rent Expense
301 Reyes, Capital	

(b) Journalize the transactions that have not been journalized in the sales journal, the cash receipts journal (see Illustration 7-9), and the general journal.

(c) Post to the accounts receivable and accounts payable subsidiary ledgers. Follow the sequence of transactions as shown in the problem.

(d) Post the individual entries and totals to the general ledger.

(e) Prepare a trial balance at July 31, 2008.

(f) Determine whether the subsidiary ledgers agree with the control accounts in the general ledger.

(g) The following adjustments at the end of July are necessary.

(1) A count of supplies indicates that $140 is still on hand.

(2) Recognize rent expense for July, $500.

Prepare the necessary entries in the general journal. Post the entries to the general ledger.

(h) Prepare an adjusted trial balance at July 31, 2008.

(b) Sales journal total $19,700
Cash receipts journal balancing totals $101,120

(e) Totals $119,520

(f) Accounts Receivable $5,000
Accounts Payable $13,820

(h) Totals $119,520

P7-6A The post-closing trial balance for Cortez Co. is as follows.

Journalize in special journals; post; prepare a trial balance.

(SO 2, 3, 4)

GLS

CORTEZ CO.
Post-Closing Trial Balance
December 31, 2008

	Debit	Credit
Cash	$ 41,500	
Accounts Receivable	15,000	
Notes Receivable	45,000	
Merchandise Inventory	23,000	
Equipment	6,450	
Accumulated Depreciation—Equipment		$ 1,500
Accounts Payable		43,000
B. Cortez, Capital		86,450
	$130,950	$130,950

The subsidiary ledgers contain the following information: (1) accounts receivable—J. Anders $2,500, F. Cone $7,500, T. Dudley $5,000; (2) accounts payable—J. Feeney $10,000, D. Goodman $18,000, and K. Inwood $15,000. The cost of all merchandise sold was 60% of the sales price.

The transactions for January 2009 are as follows.

Jan. 3 Sell merchandise to M. Rensing $5,000, terms 2/10, n/30.
5 Purchase merchandise from E. Vietti $2,000, terms 2/10, n/30.
7 Receive a check from T. Dudley $3,500.
11 Pay freight on merchandise purchased $300.
12 Pay rent of $1,000 for January.
13 Receive payment in full from M. Rensing.
14 Post all entries to the subsidiary ledgers. Issued credit of $300 to J. Aders for returned merchandise.
15 Send K. Inwood a check for $14,850 in full payment of account, discount $150.
17 Purchase merchandise from G. Marley $1,600, terms 2/10, n/30.
18 Pay sales salaries of $2,800 and office salaries $2,000.
20 Give D. Goodman a 60-day note for $18,000 in full payment of account payable.
23 Total cash sales amount to $9,100.
24 Post all entries to the subsidiary ledgers. Sell merchandise on account to F. Cone $7,400, terms 1/10, n/30.
27 Send E. Vietti a check for $950.
29 Receive payment on a note of $40,000 from B. Lemke.
30 Post all entries to the subsidiary ledgers. Return merchandise of $300 to G. Marley for credit.

Instructions

(a) Open general and subsidiary ledger accounts for the following.

101 Cash	301 B. Cortez, Capital
112 Accounts Receivable	401 Sales
115 Notes Receivable	412 Sales Returns and Allowances
120 Merchandise Inventory	414 Sales Discounts
157 Equipment	505 Cost of Goods Sold
158 Accumulated Depreciation—Equipment	726 Sales Salaries Expense
200 Notes Payable	727 Office Salaries Expense
201 Accounts Payable	729 Rent Expense

(b) Sales journal $12,400
Purchases journal $3,600
Cash receipts journal (balancing) $57,600
Cash payments journal (balancing) $22,050
(d) Totals $139,800
(e) Accounts Receivable $18,600
Accounts Payable $12,350

(b) Record the January transactions in a sales journal, a single-column purchases journal, a cash receipts journal (see Illustration 7-9), a cash payments journal (see Illustration 7-16), and a general journal.

(c) Post the appropriate amounts to the general ledger.

(d) Prepare a trial balance at January 31, 2009.

(e) Determine whether the subsidiary ledgers agree with controlling accounts in the general ledger.

PROBLEMS: SET B

Journalize transactions in cash receipts journal; post to control account and subsidiary ledger.

(SO 2, 3, 4)

GLS

P7-1B Darby Company's chart of accounts includes the following selected accounts.

101 Cash	401 Sales
112 Accounts Receivable	414 Sales Discounts
120 Merchandise Inventory	505 Cost of Goods Sold
301 J. Darby, Capital	

On June 1 the accounts receivable ledger of Darby Company showed the following balances: Deering & Son $2,500, Farley Co. $1,900, Grinnell Bros. $1,600, and Lenninger Co. $1,300. The June transactions involving the receipt of cash were as follows.

June 1 The owner, J. Darby, invested additional cash in the business $10,000.
3 Received check in full from Lenninger Co. less 2% cash discount.
6 Received check in full from Farley Co. less 2% cash discount.
7 Made cash sales of merchandise totaling $6,135. The cost of the merchandise sold was $4,090.
9 Received check in full from Deering & Son less 2% cash discount.
11 Received cash refund from a supplier for damaged merchandise $320.

15 Made cash sales of merchandise totaling $4,500. The cost of the merchandise sold was $3,000.
20 Received check in full from Grinnell Bros. $1,600.

Instructions

(a) Journalize the transactions above in a six-column cash receipts journal with columns for Cash Dr., Sales Discounts Dr., Accounts Receivable Cr., Sales Cr., Other Accounts Cr., and Cost of Goods Sold Dr./Merchandise Inventory Cr. Foot and crossfoot the journal.

(a) Balancing totals $28,255

(b) Insert the beginning balances in the Accounts Receivable control and subsidiary accounts, and post the June transactions to these accounts.

(c) Prove the agreement of the control account and subsidiary account balances.

(c) Accounts Receivable $0

P7-2B Gonya Company's chart of accounts includes the following selected accounts.

Journalize transactions in cash payments journal; post to the general and subsidiary ledgers.

(SO 2, 3, 4)

GLS

101 Cash	157 Equipment
120 Merchandise Inventory	201 Accounts Payable
130 Prepaid Insurance	306 B. Gonya, Drawing

On November 1 the accounts payable ledger of Gonya Company showed the following balances: A. Hess & Co. $4,500, C. Kimberlin $2,350, G. Ruttan $1,000, and Wex Bros. $1,500. The November transactions involving the payment of cash were as follows.

Nov. 1 Purchased merchandise, check no. 11, $1,140.
3 Purchased store equipment, check no. 12, $1,700.
5 Paid Wex Bros. balance due of $1,500, less 1% discount, check no. 13, $1,485.
11 Purchased merchandise, check no. 14, $2,000.
15 Paid G. Ruttan balance due of $1,000, less 3% discount, check no. 15, $970.
16 B. Gonya, the owner, withdrew $500 cash for own use, check no. 16.
19 Paid C. Kimberlin in full for invoice no. 1245, $1,150 less 2% discount, check no. 17, $1,127.
25 Paid premium due on one-year insurance policy, check no. 18, $3,000.
30 Paid A. Hess & Co. in full for invoice no. 832, $3,500, check no. 19.

Instructions

(a) Journalize the transactions above in a four-column cash payments journal with columns for Other Accounts Dr., Accounts Payable Dr., Merchandise Inventory Cr., and Cash Cr. Foot and crossfoot the journal.

(a) Balancing totals $15,490

(b) Insert the beginning balances in the Accounts Payable control and subsidiary accounts, and post the November transactions to these accounts.

(c) Prove the agreement of the control account and the subsidiary account balances.

(c) Accounts Payable $2,200

P7-3B The chart of accounts of Emley Company includes the following selected accounts.

Journalize transactions in multi-column purchases journal; post to the general and subsidiary ledgers.

(SO 2, 3, 4)

GLS

112 Accounts Receivable	401 Sales
120 Merchandise Inventory	412 Sales Returns and Allowances
126 Supplies	505 Cost of Goods Sold
157 Equipment	610 Advertising Expense
201 Accounts Payable	

In May the following selected transactions were completed. All purchases and sales were on account except as indicated. The cost of all merchandise sold was 65% of the sales price.

May 2 Purchased merchandise from Younger Company $7,500.
3 Received freight bill from Ruden Freight on Younger purchase $360.
5 Sales were made to Ellie Company $1,980, DeShazer Bros. $2,700, and Liu Company $1,500.
8 Purchased merchandise from Utley Company $8,000 and Zeider Company $8,700.
10 Received credit on merchandise returned to Zeider Company $500.
15 Purchased supplies from Rodriquez Supply $900.
16 Purchased merchandise from Younger Company $4,500, and Utley Company $7,200.
17 Returned supplies to Rodriquez Supply, receiving credit $100. (*Hint*: Credit Supplies.)
18 Received freight bills on May 16 purchases from Ruden Freight $500.
20 Returned merchandise to Younger Company receiving credit $300.
23 Made sales to DeShazer Bros. $2,400 and to Liu Company $3,600.
25 Received bill for advertising from Amster Advertising $900.

26 Granted allowance to Liu Company for merchandise damaged in shipment $200.
28 Purchased equipment from Rodriquez Supply $500.

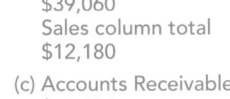

(a) Purchases journal—Accounts Payable, Cr. $39,060
Sales column total $12,180
(c) Accounts Receivable $11,980
Accounts Payable $38,160

Instructions

(a) Journalize the transactions above in a purchases journal, a sales journal, and a general journal. The purchases journal should have the following column headings: Date, Account Credited (Debited), Ref., Accounts Payable Cr., Merchandise Inventory Dr., and Other Accounts Dr.

(b) Post to both the general and subsidiary ledger accounts. (Assume that all accounts have zero beginning balances.)

(c) Prove the agreement of the control and subsidiary accounts.

Journalize transactions in special journals.

(SO 2, 3, 4)

GLS

P7-4B Selected accounts from the chart of accounts of Litke Company are shown below.

101 Cash	201 Accounts Payable
112 Accounts Receivable	401 Sales
120 Merchandise Inventory	414 Sales Discounts
126 Supplies	505 Cost of Goods Sold
140 Land	610 Advertising Expense
145 Buildings	

The cost of all merchandise sold was 70% of the sales price. During October, Litke Company completed the following transactions.

Oct. 2 Purchased merchandise on account from Camacho Company $16,500.
4 Sold merchandise on account to Enos Co. $7,700. Invoice no. 204, terms 2/10, n/30.
5 Purchased supplies for cash $80.
7 Made cash sales for the week totaling $9,160.
9 Paid in full the amount owed Camacho Company less a 2% discount.
10 Purchased merchandise on account from Finn Corp. $3,500.
12 Received payment from Enos Co. for invoice no. 204.
13 Returned $210 worth of damaged goods purchased on account from Finn Corp. on October 10.
14 Made cash sales for the week totaling $8,180.
16 Sold a parcel of land for $27,000 cash, the land's original cost.
17 Sold merchandise on account to G. Richter & Co. $5,350, invoice no. 205, terms 2/10, n/30.
18 Purchased merchandise for cash $2,125.
21 Made cash sales for the week totaling $8,200.
23 Paid in full the amount owed Finn Corp. for the goods kept (no discount).
25 Purchased supplies on account from Robinson Co. $260.
25 Sold merchandise on account to Hunt Corp. $5,220, invoice no. 206, terms 2/10, n/30.
25 Received payment from G. Richter & Co. for invoice no. 205.
26 Purchased for cash a small parcel of land and a building on the land to use as a storage facility. The total cost of $35,000 was allocated $21,000 to the land and $14,000 to the building.
27 Purchased merchandise on account from Kudro Co. $8,500.
28 Made cash sales for the week totaling $7,540.
30 Purchased merchandise on account from Camacho Company $14,000.
30 Paid advertising bill for the month from the *Gazette*, $400.
30 Sold merchandise on account to G. Richter & Co. $4,600, invoice no. 207, terms 2/10, n/30.

Litke Company uses the following journals.

1. Sales journal.
2. Single-column purchases journal.
3. Cash receipts journal with columns for Cash Dr., Sales Discounts Dr., Accounts Receivable Cr., Sales Cr., Other Accounts Cr., and Cost of Goods Sold Dr./Merchandise Inventory Cr.
4. Cash payments journal with columns for Other Accounts Dr., Accounts Payable Dr., Merchandise Inventory Cr., and Cash Cr.
5. General journal.

Instructions

Using the selected accounts provided:

(a) Record the October transactions in the appropriate journals.

(b) Foot and crossfoot all special journals.

(c) Show how postings would be made by placing ledger account numbers and check marks as needed in the journals. (Actual posting to ledger accounts is not required.)

(b) Sales journal $22,870
Purchases journal $42,500
Cash receipts journal—Cash, Dr. $72,869
Cash payments journal, Cash, Cr. $57,065

P7-5B Presented below are the sales and cash receipts journals for Wyrick Co. for its first month of operations.

Journalize in purchases and cash payments journals; post; prepare a trial balance; prove control to subsidiary; prepare adjusting entries; prepare an adjusted trial balance.

(SO 2, 3, 4)

GLS

SALES JOURNAL S1

Date	Account Debited	Ref.	Accounts Receivable Dr. Sales Cr.	Cost of Goods Sold Dr. Merchandise Inventory Cr.
Feb. 3	S. Arndt		5,500	3,630
9	C. Boyd		6,500	4,290
12	F. Catt		8,000	5,280
26	M. Didde		7,000	4,620
			27,000	17,820

CASH RECEIPTS JOURNAL CR1

Date	Account Credited	Ref.	Cash Dr.	Sales Discounts Dr.	Accounts Receivable Cr.	Sales Cr.	Other Accounts Cr.	Cost of Goods Sold Dr. Merchandise Inventory Cr.
Feb. 1	A. Wyrick, Capital		30,000				30,000	
2			6,500			6,500		4,290
13	S. Arndt		5,445	55	5,500			
18	Merchandise Inventory		150				150	
26	C. Boyd		6,500		6,500			
			48,595	55	12,000	6,500	30,150	4,290

In addition, the following transactions have not been journalized for February 2008.

Feb. 2 Purchased merchandise on account from J. Vopat for $4,600, terms 2/10, n/30.
7 Purchased merchandise on account from P. Kneiser for $30,000, terms 1/10, n/30.
9 Paid cash of $1,250 for purchase of supplies.
12 Paid $4,508 to J. Vopat in payment for $4,600 invoice, less 2% discount.
15 Purchased equipment for $7,000 cash.
16 Purchased merchandise on account from J. Nunez $2,400, terms 2/10, n/30.
17 Paid $29,700 to P. Kneiser in payment of $30,000 invoice, less 1% discount.
20 A. Wyrick withdrew cash of $1,100 from business for personal use.
21 Purchased merchandise on account from G. Reedy for $7,800, terms 1/10, n/30.
28 Paid $2,400 to J. Nunez in payment of $2,400 invoice.

Instructions

(a) Open the following accounts in the general ledger.

101 Cash
112 Accounts Receivable
120 Merchandise Inventory
126 Supplies
157 Equipment
158 Accumulated Depreciation—Equipment
201 Accounts Payable
301 A. Wyrick, Capital
306 A. Wyrick, Drawing
401 Sales
414 Sales Discounts
505 Cost of Goods Sold
631 Supplies Expense
711 Depreciation Expense

(b) Purchases journal total $44,800
Cash payments journal—Cash, Cr. $45,958

(e) Totals $71,300

(f) Accounts Receivable $15,000
Accounts Payable $7,800

(h) Totals $71,500

(b) Journalize the transactions that have not been journalized in a one-column purchases journal and the cash payments journal (see Illustration 7-16).

(c) Post to the accounts receivable and accounts payable subsidiary ledgers. Follow the sequence of transactions as shown in the problem.

(d) Post the individual entries and totals to the general ledger.

(e) Prepare a trial balance at February 28, 2008.

(f) Determine that the subsidiary ledgers agree with the control accounts in the general ledger.

(g) The following adjustments at the end of February are necessary.

(1) A count of supplies indicates that $300 is still on hand.

(2) Depreciation on equipment for February is $200.

Prepare the adjusting entries and then post the adjusting entries to the general ledger.

(h) Prepare an adjusted trial balance at February 28, 2008.

PROBLEMS: SET C

Visit the book's website at **www.wiley.com/college/weygandt**, and choose the Student Companion site, to access Problem Set C.

COMPREHENSIVE PROBLEM: CHAPTERS 3 TO 7

Packard Company has the following opening account balances in its general and subsidiary ledgers on January 1 and uses the periodic inventory system. All accounts have normal debit and credit balances.

General Ledger

Account Number	Account Title	January 1 Opening Balance
101	Cash	$33,750
112	Accounts Receivable	13,000
115	Notes Receivable	39,000
120	Merchandise Inventory	20,000
125	Office Supplies	1,000
130	Prepaid Insurance	2,000
157	Equipment	6,450
158	Accumulated Depreciation	1,500
201	Accounts Payable	35,000
301	I. Packard, Capital	78,700

Accounts Receivable Subsidiary Ledger

Customer	January 1 Opening Balance
R. Draves	$1,500
B. Hachinski	7,500
S. Ingles	4,000

Accounts Payable Subsidiary Ledger

Creditor	January 1 Opening Balance
S. Kosko	$ 9,000
R. Mikush	15,000
D. Moreno	11,000

Jan. 3 Sell merchandise on account to B. Remy $3,100, invoice no. 510, and J. Fine $1,800, invoice no. 511.
5 Purchase merchandise on account from S. Yost $3,000 and D. Laux $2,700.
7 Receive checks for $4,000 from S. Ingles and $2,000 from B. Hachinski.
8 Pay freight on merchandise purchased $180.
9 Send checks to S. Kosko for $9,000 and D. Moreno for $11,000.
9 Issue credit of $300 to J. Fine for merchandise returned.
10 Summary cash sales total $15,500.
11 Sell merchandise on account to R. Draves for $1,900, invoice no. 512, and to S. Ingles $900, invoice no. 513.
Post all entries to the subsidiary ledgers.

12 Pay rent of $1,000 for January.
13 Receive payment in full from B. Remy and J. Fine.
15 Withdraw $800 cash by I. Packard for personal use.
16 Purchase merchandise on account from D. Moreno for $15,000, from S. Kosko for $13,900, and from S. Yost for $1,500.
17 Pay $400 cash for office supplies.
18 Return $200 of merchandise to S. Kosko and receive credit.
20 Summary cash sales total $17,500.
21 Issue $15,000 note to R. Mikush in payment of balance due.
21 Receive payment in full from S. Ingles.
Post all entries to the subsidiary ledgers.
22 Sell merchandise on account to B. Remy for $3,700, invoice no. 514, and to R. Draves for $800, invoice no. 515.
23 Send checks to D. Moreno and S. Kosko in full payment.
25 Sell merchandise on account to B. Hachinski for $3,500, invoice no. 516, and to J. Fine for $6,100, invoice no. 517.
27 Purchase merchandise on account from D. Moreno for $12,500, from D. Laux for $1,200, and from S. Yost for $2,800.
28 Pay $200 cash for office supplies.
31 Summary cash sales total $22,920.
31 Pay sales salaries of $4,300 and office salaries of $3,600.

Instructions

(a) Record the January transactions in the appropriate journal—sales, purchases, cash receipts, cash payments, and general.

(b) Post the journals to the general and subsidiary ledgers. Add and number new accounts in an orderly fashion as needed.

(c) Prepare a trial balance at January 31, 2008, using a worksheet. Complete the worksheet using the following additional information.
  (1) Office supplies at January 31 total $700.
  (2) Insurance coverage expires on October 31, 2008.
  (3) Annual depreciation on the equipment is $1,500.
  (4) Interest of $30 has accrued on the note payable.
  (5) Merchandise inventory at January 31 is $15,000.

(c) Trial balance totals $196,820; Adj. T/B totals $196,975

(d) Prepare a multiple-step income statement and a statement of owner's equity for January and a classified balance sheet at the end of January.

(d) Net income $9,685 Total assets $126,315

(e) Prepare and post the adjusting and closing entries.

(f) Prepare a post-closing trial balance, and determine whether the subsidiary ledgers agree with the control accounts in the general ledger.

(f) Post-closing T/B totals $127,940

BROADENING YOUR PERSPECTIVE

FINANCIAL REPORTING AND ANALYSIS

Financial Reporting Problem—Mini Practice Set

BYP7-1 **(You will need the working papers that accompany this textbook in order to work this mini practice set.)**

Bluma Co. uses a perpetual inventory system and both an accounts receivable and an accounts payable subsidiary ledger. Balances related to both the general ledger and the subsidiary ledger for Bluma are indicated in the working papers. Presented below are a series of transactions for Bluma Co. for the month of January. Credit sales terms are 2/10, n/30. The cost of all merchandise sold was 60% of the sales price.

Jan. 3 Sell merchandise on account to B. Richey $3,100, invoice no. 510, and to J. Forbes $1,800, invoice no. 511.
5 Purchase merchandise from S. Vogel $5,000 and D. Lynch $2,200, terms n/30.

7 Receive checks from S. LaDew $4,000 and B. Garcia $2,000 after discount period has lapsed.
8 Pay freight on merchandise purchased $235.
9 Send checks to S. Hoyt for $9,000 less 2% cash discount, and to D. Omara for $11,000 less 1% cash discount.
9 Issue credit of $300 to J. Forbes for merchandise returned.
10 Summary daily cash sales total $15,500.
11 Sell merchandise on account to R. Dvorak $1,600, invoice no. 512, and to S. LaDew $900, invoice no. 513.
12 Pay rent of $1,000 for January.
13 Receive payment in full from B. Richey and J. Forbes less cash discounts.
15 Withdraw $800 cash by M. Bluma for personal use.
15 Post all entries to the subsidiary ledgers.
16 Purchase merchandise from D. Omara $18,000, terms 1/10, n/30; S. Hoyt $14,200, terms 2/10, n/30; and S. Vogel $1,500, terms n/30.
17 Pay $400 cash for office supplies.
18 Return $200 of merchandise to S. Hoyt and receive credit.
20 Summary daily cash sales total $20,100.
21 Issue $15,000 note, maturing in 90 days, to R. Moses in payment of balance due.
21 Receive payment in full from S. LaDew less cash discount.
22 Sell merchandise on account to B. Richey $2,700, invoice no. 514, and to R. Dvorak $1,300, invoice no. 515.
22 Post all entries to the subsidiary ledgers.
23 Send checks to D. Omara and S. Hoyt in full payment less cash discounts.
25 Sell merchandise on account to B. Garcia $3,500, invoice no. 516, and to J. Forbes $6,100, invoice no. 517.
27 Purchase merchandise from D. Omara $14,500, terms 1/10, n/30; D. Lynch $1,200, terms n/30; and S. Vogel $5,400, terms n/30.
27 Post all entries to the subsidiary ledgers.
28 Pay $200 cash for office supplies.
31 Summary daily cash sales total $21,300.
31 Pay sales salaries $4,300 and office salaries $3,800.

Instructions

(a) Record the January transactions in a sales journal, a single-column purchases journal, a cash receipts journal as shown on page 303, a cash payments journal as shown on page 308, and a two-column general journal.

(b) Post the journals to the general ledger.

(c) Prepare a trial balance at January 31, 2008, in the trial balance columns of the worksheet. Complete the worksheet using the following additional information.

(1) Office supplies at January 31 total $900.
(2) Insurance coverage expires on October 31, 2008.
(3) Annual depreciation on the equipment is $1,500.
(4) Interest of $50 has accrued on the note payable.

(d) Prepare a multiple-step income statement and an owner's equity statement for January and a classified balance sheet at the end of January.

(e) Prepare and post adjusting and closing entries.

(f) Prepare a post-closing trial balance, and determine whether the subsidiary ledgers agree with the control accounts in the general ledger.

Exploring the Web

BYP7-2 Great Plains' Accounting is one of the leading accounting software packages. Information related to this package is found at its website.

Address: www.microsoft.com/dynamics/gp/product/demos.mspx, or go to **www.wiley.com/college/weygandt**

Steps

1. Go to the site shown above.
2. Choose **General Ledger**. Perform instruction (a) on page 333.
3. Choose **Accounts Payable**. Perform instruction (b) on page 333.

Instructions

(a) What are three key features of the general ledger module highlighted by the company?

(b) What are three key features of the payables management module highlighted by the company?

CRITICAL THINKING

Decision Making Across the Organization

BYP7-3 Hughey & Payne is a wholesaler of small appliances and parts. Hughey & Payne is operated by two owners, Rich Hughey and Kristen Payne. In addition, the company has one employee, a repair specialist, who is on a fixed salary. Revenues are earned through the sale of appliances to retailers (approximately 75% of total revenues), appliance parts to do-it-yourselfers (10%), and the repair of appliances brought to the store (15%). Appliance sales are made on both a credit and cash basis. Customers are billed on prenumbered sales invoices. Credit terms are always net/30 days. All parts sales and repair work are cash only.

Merchandise is purchased on account from the manufacturers of both the appliances and the parts. Practically all suppliers offer cash discounts for prompt payments, and it is company policy to take all discounts. Most cash payments are made by check. Checks are most frequently issued to suppliers, to trucking companies for freight on merchandise purchases, and to newspapers, radio, and TV stations for advertising. All advertising bills are paid as received. Rich and Kristen each make a monthly drawing in cash for personal living expenses. The salaried repairman is paid twice monthly. Hughey & Payne currently has a manual accounting system.

Instructions

With the class divided into groups, answer the following.

(a) Identify the special journals that Hughey & Payne should have in its manual system. List the column headings appropriate for each of the special journals.

(b) What control and subsidiary accounts should be included in Hughey & Payne manual system? Why?

Communication Activity

BYP7-4 Barb Doane, a classmate, has a part-time bookkeeping job. She is concerned about the inefficiencies in journalizing and posting transactions. Jim Houser is the owner of the company where Barb works. In response to numerous complaints from Barb and others, Jim hired two additional bookkeepers a month ago. However, the inefficiencies have continued at an even higher rate. The accounting information system for the company has only a general journal and a general ledger. Jim refuses to install an electronic accounting system.

Instructions

Now that Barb is an expert in manual accounting information systems, she decides to send a letter to Jim Houser explaining (1) why the additional personnel did not help and (2) what changes should be made to improve the efficiency of the accounting department. Write the letter that you think Barb should send.

Ethics Case

BYP7-5 Roniger Products Company operates three divisions, each with its own manufacturing plant and marketing/sales force. The corporate headquarters and central accounting office are in Roniger, and the plants are in Freeport, Rockport, and Bayport, all within 50 miles of Roniger. Corporate management treats each division as an independent profit center and encourages competition among them. They each have similar but different product lines. As a competitive incentive, bonuses are awarded each year to the employees of the fastest growing and most profitable division.

Jose Molina is the manager of Roniger's centralized computer accounting operation that enters the sales transactions and maintains the accounts receivable for all three divisions. Jose came up in the accounting ranks from the Bayport division where his wife, several relatives, and many friends still work.

As sales documents are entered into the computer, the originating division is identified by code. Most sales documents (95%) are coded, but some (5%) are not coded or are coded incorrectly. As the manager, Jose has instructed the data-entry personnel to assign the Bayport code to all uncoded and incorrectly coded sales documents. This is done he says, "in order to expedite processing and to keep the computer files current since they are updated daily." All receivables and cash collections for all three divisions are handled by Roniger as one subsidiary accounts receivable ledger.

Instructions

(a) Who are the stakeholders in this situation?
(b) What are the ethical issues in this case?
(c) How might the system be improved to prevent this situation?

"All About You" Activity

BYP7-6 In this chapter you learned about a basic manual accounting information system. Computerized accounting systems range from the very basic and inexpensive to the very elaborate and expensive. Even the most sophisticated systems are based on the fundamental structures and relationships that you learned in this chapter.

Instructions

Go to the book companion site for this text, **www.wiley.com/weygandt**, and review the demonstration that is provided for the general ledger software package that is used with this text. Prepare a brief explanation of how the general ledger system works—that is, how it is used, and what information it provides.

Answers to Insight and Accounting Across the Organization Questions

p. 294 Curbing Fraudulent Activity with Software

Q: Why might this software help reduce fraudulent activity by employees?

A: *By pinpointing who used the accounting system and when they used it, the software can hold employees more accountable for their actions. Companies hope that this will reduce efforts by employees to enter false accounting entries, change the dates of transactions, or create unauthorized expenditures. If employees do engage in these activities, there will be significant evidence of their activities.*

p. 297 "I'm John Smith, a.k.a. 13695071642"

Q: Why use numbers to identify names in a computerized system?

A: *Computerized systems process numbers faster than letters. Also, letters sometimes cause problems because you may have two people with the same name. Computerized systems avoid this problem by giving different customers, including those with the same names, different account numbers.*

p. 310 How Do Employees Steal?

Q: How can companies reduce the likelihood of fraudulent disbursements?

A: *Some common-sense approaches are to make sure only certain designated individuals can sign checks. In addition, make sure that different personnel approve payments and make payments. The next chapter will provide even more sophisticated approaches to reduce fraudulent disbursements.*

Authors' Comments on *All About You:* Keeping Track of the Documents in Your Life (p. 312)

We feel that every person or household should develop a system for maintaining personal financial records. Why? For one thing, once implemented, a basic system can greatly reduce the frustration of managing your financial affairs. Of equal importance, managing your documents can significantly reduce the complications and hardship experienced when trying to put your life back in order after a fire, theft, or death of a relative. It would also be of great assistance to your loved ones should you die unexpectedly.

How do you organize such a system? At a minimum you should have a home file cabinet with separate files for each type of document, organized in an intuitive fashion. In addition, you might consider a safe-deposit box for very important documents and records that you wouldn't want to lose in a fire or theft. Also, you can store many of your documents and records on your home computer. However, if you store information in your computer, make sure that you have proper security and backup (a topic we will address in a later chapter). For simple, specific directions on how to organize your records, we suggest you look at *www.ehow.com/how_560_keep-financial-records.html*.

Answers to Self-Study Questions

1. d **2.** c **3.** a **4.** c **5.** a **6.** c **7.** d **8.** b **9.** c **10.** c

Remember to go back to the Navigator box on the chapter-opening page and check off your completed work.

Chapter 8

Internal Control and Cash

STUDY OBJECTIVES

After studying this chapter, you should be able to:

1. Define internal control.
2. Identify the principles of internal control.
3. Explain the applications of internal control principles to cash receipts.
4. Explain the applications of internal control principles to cash disbursements.
5. Describe the operation of a petty cash fund.
6. Indicate the control features of a bank account.
7. Prepare a bank reconciliation.
8. Explain the reporting of cash.

The Navigator

The Navigator

Scan **Study Objectives**	☐
Read **Feature Story**	☐
Read **Preview**	☐
Read text and answer **Before You Go On** p. 345 ☐ p. 349 ☐ p. 353 ☐ p. 360 ☐ p. 363 ☐	☐
Work **Demonstration Problem**	☐
Review **Summary of Study Objectives**	☐
Answer **Self-Study Questions**	☐
Complete **Assignments**	☐

Feature Story

MINDING THE MONEY IN MOOSE JAW

If you're ever looking for a cappuccino in Moose Jaw, Saskatchewan, stop by Stephanie's Gourmet Coffee and More, located on Main Street. Staff there serve, on average, 650 cups of coffee a day, including both regular and specialty coffees, not to mention soups, Italian sandwiches, and a wide assortment of gourmet cheesecakes.

"We've got high school students who come here, and students from the community college," says owner/manager Stephanie Mintenko, who has run the place since opening it in 1995. "We have customers who are retired, and others who are working people and have only 30 minutes for lunch. We have to be pretty quick."

That means that the cashiers have to be efficient. Like most businesses where purchases are low-cost and high-volume, cash control has to be simple.

"We have an electronic cash register, but it's not the fancy new kind where you just punch in the item," explains Ms. Mintenko. "You have to punch in the prices." The machine does keep track of sales in several categories, however. Cashiers punch a button to indicate whether each item is a beverage, a meal, or a charge for the cafe's Internet connections. An internal tape in the machine keeps a record of all transactions; the customer receives a receipt only upon request.

There is only one cash register. "Up to three of us might operate it on any given shift, including myself," says Ms. Mintenko.

She and her staff do two "cashouts" each day—one with the shift change at 5:00 p.m. and one when the shop closes at 10:00 p.m. At each cashout, they count the cash in the register drawer. That amount, minus the cash change carried forward (the float), should match the shift total on the register tape. If there's a discrepancy, they do another count. Then, if necessary, "we go through the whole tape to find the mistake," she explains. "It usually turns out to be someone who punched in $18 instead of $1.80, or something like that."

Ms. Mintenko sends all the cash tapes and float totals to a bookkeeper, who double-checks everything and provides regular reports. "We try to keep the accounting simple, so we can concentrate on making great coffee and food."

The Navigator

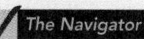

Inside Chapter 8...

Preview of Chapter 8

As the story about recording cash sales at Stephanie's Gourmet Coffee and More indicates, control of cash is important. Companies also need controls to safeguard other types of assets. For example, Stephanie's undoubtedly has controls to prevent the theft of food and supplies, and controls to prevent the theft of tableware and dishes from its kitchen.

In this chapter, we explain the essential features of an internal control system and then describe how those controls apply to cash. The applications include some controls with which you may be already familiar. Toward the end of the chapter, we describe the use of a bank and explain how companies report cash on the balance sheet.

The content and organization of Chapter 8 are as follows.

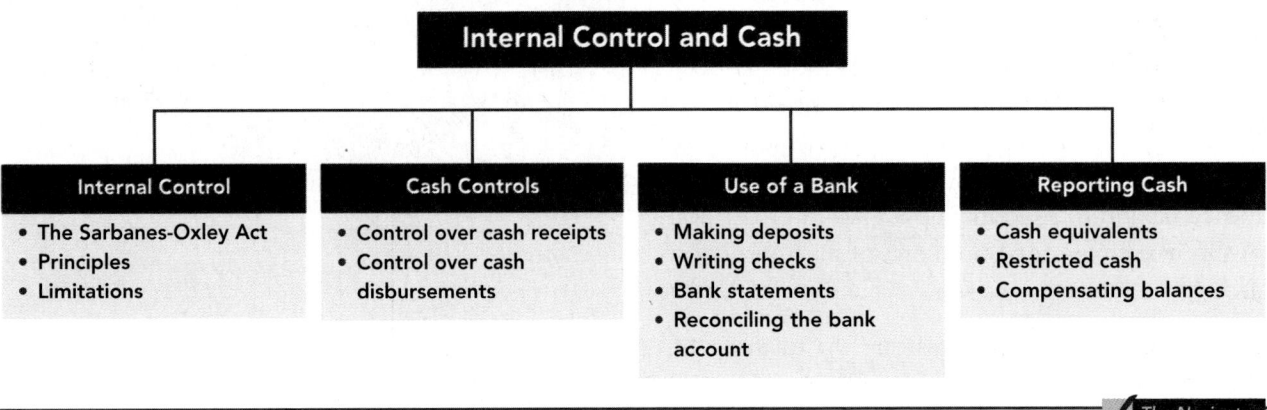

Internal Control and Cash

Internal Control	Cash Controls	Use of a Bank	Reporting Cash
• The Sarbanes-Oxley Act • Principles • Limitations	• Control over cash receipts • Control over cash disbursements	• Making deposits • Writing checks • Bank statements • Reconciling the bank account	• Cash equivalents • Restricted cash • Compensating balances

✓ The Navigator

INTERNAL CONTROL

STUDY OBJECTIVE 1

Define internal control.

Could there be dishonest employees where you work? Unfortunately, sometimes the answer is yes. For example, in addition to the highly publicized frauds at Enron, WorldCom, Tyco, and Global Crossing, the financial press recently reported the following.

> A bookkeeper in a small company diverted $750,000 of bill payments to a personal bank account over a three-year period.
>
> A shipping clerk with 28 years of service shipped $125,000 of merchandise to himself.
>
> A computer operator embezzled $21 million from Wells Fargo Bank over a two-year period.
>
> A church treasurer "borrowed" $150,000 of church funds to finance a friend's business dealings.

These situations emphasize the need for organizations to have good systems of internal control.

Internal control consists of all the related methods and measures adopted within an organization to:

1. **Safeguard its assets** from employee theft, robbery, and unauthorized use.
2. **Enhance the accuracy and reliability of its accounting records.** This is done by reducing the risk of **errors** (unintentional mistakes) and **irregularities** (intentional mistakes and misrepresentations) in the accounting process.

Under the Sarbanes-Oxley Act, all publicly traded U.S. corporations are **required** to maintain an adequate system of internal control. Companies that fail to comply are subject to fines, and company officers may be imprisoned.

The Sarbanes-Oxley Act

"Better get those controls under control" was a comment often made after the numerous corporate scandals of recent years. As a result, Congress passed the Sarbanes-Oxley Act of 2002 (SOX). One of the most important laws to be passed in decades, SOX forces companies to pay more attention to internal controls.

SOX imposes more responsibilities on corporate executives and boards of directors to ensure that companies' internal controls are reliable and effective. Under one part of the law, companies must develop sound principles of control over financial reporting. They must continually verify that these controls are working. In addition, independent outside auditors must attest to the level of internal control. SOX also created the **Public Company Accounting Oversight Board (PCAOB)**, which now establishes auditing standards and regulates auditor activity.

One poll found that about 60% of investors believe that SOX will help safeguard their stock investments. Many say they would be unlikely to invest in a company that fails to follow SOX requirements. Although some corporate executives have criticized the time and expense involved in following the requirements of the law, SOX appears to be working well. For example, the chief accounting officer of Eli Lily noted that SOX triggered a comprehensive review of how the company documents its controls. This review uncovered redundancies and also pointed out controls that needed to be added. In short, it added up to time and money well spent. And the finance chief at General Electric noted, "We have seen value in SOX. It helps build investors' trust and gives them more confidence."[1]

Principles of Internal Control

STUDY OBJECTIVE 2

Identify the principles of internal control.

To safeguard assets and enhance the accuracy and reliability of accounting records, companies follow specific control principles. These measures vary with the size and nature of the business and with management's control philosophy. The six principles listed in Illustration 8-1 (page 340) apply to most enterprises. They are explained in the following sections.

ESTABLISHMENT OF RESPONSIBILITY

An essential principle of internal control is to assign responsibility to specific employees. **Control is most effective when only one person is responsible for a given task.**

To illustrate, assume that the cash on hand at the end of the day in a Safeway supermarket is $10 short of the cash rung up on the cash register. If only one person has operated the register, the shift manager can quickly determine responsibility for the shortage. If two or more individuals have worked the register, it may be impossible to determine who is responsible for the error unless each person is assigned a separate cash drawer and register key. In the Feature Story, the principle of establishing responsibility does not appear to be strictly applied by Stephanie's, since three people operate the cash register on any given shift. To quickly identify any shortages, employees at Stephanie's perform two cashouts each day.

Transfer of cash drawers

[1]"Corporate Regulation Must Be Working—There's a Backlash," *Wall Street Journal,* June 16, 2004, p. C1; and Judith Burns, "Is Sarbanes-Oxley Working?" *Wall Street Journal,* June 21, 2004, pp. R8–R9.

Illustration 8-1
Principles of internal control

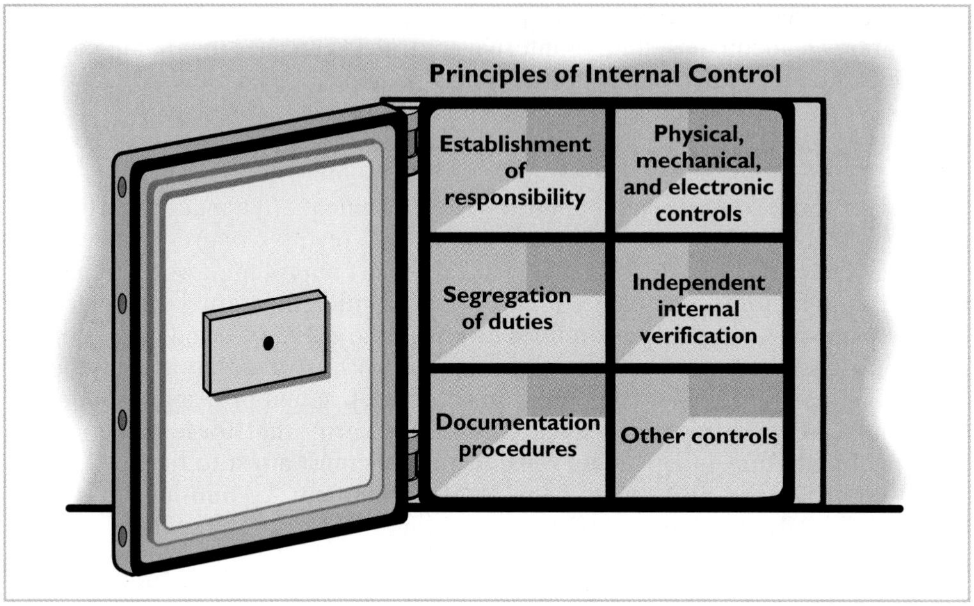

Establishing responsibility includes authorization and approval of transactions. For example, the vice president of sales should have the authority to establish policies for making credit sales. The policies ordinarily will require written credit department approval of credit sales.

SEGREGATION OF DUTIES

Segregation of duties (also called separation of functions) is indispensable in an internal control system. There are two common applications of this principle:

1. Different individuals should be responsible for related activities.
2. The responsibility for record keeping for an asset should be separate from the physical custody of that asset.

The rationale for segregation of duties is this: **The work of one employee should, without a duplication of effort, provide a reliable basis for evaluating the work of another employee.**

Related Activities. In both purchasing and selling, companies should assign related activities to different individuals. **Making one individual responsible for all of the related activities increases the potential for errors and irregularities.**

Related *purchasing activities* include ordering merchandise, receiving the goods, and paying (or authorizing payment) for the merchandise. For example, a dishonest employee could place orders with friends or with suppliers who give kickbacks. An employee could do only a cursory count and inspection of delivered goods, which could lead to errors and poor-quality merchandise. An employee might authorize payment without a careful review of the invoice, or even worse, might approve fictitious invoices for payment. When a company assigns responsibility for ordering, receiving, and paying to different individuals, it minimizes the risk of such abuses.

Similarly, companies should assign related *sales activities* to different individuals. Related selling activities include making a sale, shipping (or delivering) the goods to the customer, billing the customer, and receiving payment. Various frauds are possible when one person handles related sales transactions. A salesperson could make sales at unauthorized prices to increase sales commissions. A shipping clerk could ship goods to himself. A billing clerk could understate the amount billed for sales made to friends and relatives. These abuses are less likely to occur when companies divide the sales tasks: the salespeople make the sale; the shipping department ships the goods on the basis of the sales order; and the billing department prepares the sales invoice after comparing the sales order with the report of goods shipped.

INTERNATIONAL INSIGHT

This Was a Penalty to Take Seriously

It's said that accountants' predecessors were the scribes of ancient Egypt, who kept the pharaohs' books. They inventoried grain, gold, and other assets. Unfortunately, some fell victim to temptation and stole from their leader, as did other employees of the king. The solution was to have two scribes independently record each transaction—perhaps the first instance of internal control. As long as the scribes' totals agreed exactly, there was no problem. But if the totals were materially different, both scribes would be put to death. That proved to be a great incentive for them to carefully check all the numbers and make sure the help wasn't stealing. In fact, fraud prevention and detection became the royal accountants' main duty.

Source: Joseph T. Wells, "So That's Why It's Called a Pyramid Scheme," *Journal of Accountancy* (October 2000), p. 91. Copyright © 2000 from the *Journal of Accountancy by the American Institute of Certified Public Accountants, Inc.* Opinions of the authors are their own and do not necessarily reflect policies of the AICPA. Reprinted with permission.

? Which principle of internal control was implemented in ancient Egypt? Who do you think investors today expect to detect and prevent fraud?

Record Keeping Separate from Physical Custody. To provide a valid basis of accountability for an asset, the accountant should have neither physical custody of the asset nor access to it. Likewise, the custodian of the asset should not maintain or have access to the accounting records. **The custodian of the asset is not likely to convert the asset to personal use when one employee maintains the record of the asset, and a different employee has physical custody of the asset.** The separation of accounting responsibility from the custody of assets is especially important for cash and inventories because these assets are very vulnerable to unauthorized use or misappropriation.

Illustration 8-2 shows the segregation of duties concept.

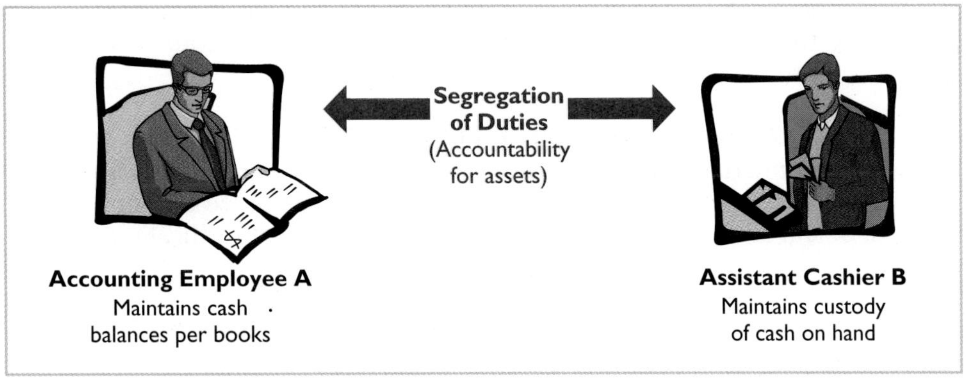

Illustration 8-2
The segregation of duties (accountability for assets) principle

Prenumbered invoices

DOCUMENTATION PROCEDURES

Documents provide evidence that transactions and events have occurred. At Stephanie's Gourmet Coffee and More, the cash register tape is the restaurant's documentation for the sale and the amount of cash received. Similarly, a shipping document indicates that the goods have been shipped, and a sales invoice indicates that the company has billed the customer for the goods. By requiring signatures (or initials) on the documents, the company can identify the individual(s) responsible for the transaction or event. Companies should document transactions when the transaction occurs. They generally develop documentation of events, such as those leading to adjusting entries, when the adjustments are made.

Companies should establish procedures for documents. First, whenever possible, companies should use **prenumbered documents, and all documents should be accounted for**. Prenumbering helps to prevent a transaction from being recorded more than once, or conversely, from not being recorded at all. Second, the control system should require that employees **promptly forward source documents for accounting entries to the accounting department. This control measure helps to ensure timely recording of the transaction** and contributes directly to the accuracy and reliability of the accounting records.

ACCOUNTING ACROSS THE ORGANIZATION

SOX Boosts the Role of Human Resources

The human resources (HR) department has always played an important role in internal control by carefully screening potential hires. The Sarbanes-Oxley Act has increased HR's role in a number of ways. Under SOX, a company needs to keep track of employees' degrees and certifications to ensure that employees continue to meet the specified requirements of a job. Also, to ensure proper employee supervision and proper separation of duties, companies must develop and monitor an organizational chart. When one corporation went through this exercise it found that out of 17,000 employees, there were 400 people who did not report to anyone, and they had 35 people who reported to each other. In addition, if an employee complains of an unfair firing and mentions financial issues at the company, HR must refer the case to the company audit committee and possibly to its legal counsel.

? Why would unsupervised employees or employees who report to each other represent potential internal control threats?

PHYSICAL, MECHANICAL, AND ELECTRONIC CONTROLS

ETHICS NOTE

Program controls built into the computer prevent intentional or unintentional errors or unauthorized access. To prevent unauthorized access, the computer system may require that users enter passwords or correctly answer random personal questions.

Use of physical, mechanical, and electronic controls is essential. *Physical controls* relate to the safeguarding of assets. *Mechanical* and *electronic controls* also safeguard assets and enhance the accuracy and reliability of the accounting records. Illustration 8-3 shows examples of these controls.

INDEPENDENT INTERNAL VERIFICATION

Most internal control systems provide for **independent internal verification**. This principle involves the review of data prepared by employees. To obtain maximum benefit from independent internal verification:

1. Companies should verify records periodically or on a surprise basis.
2. An employee who is independent of the personnel responsible for the information should make the verification.

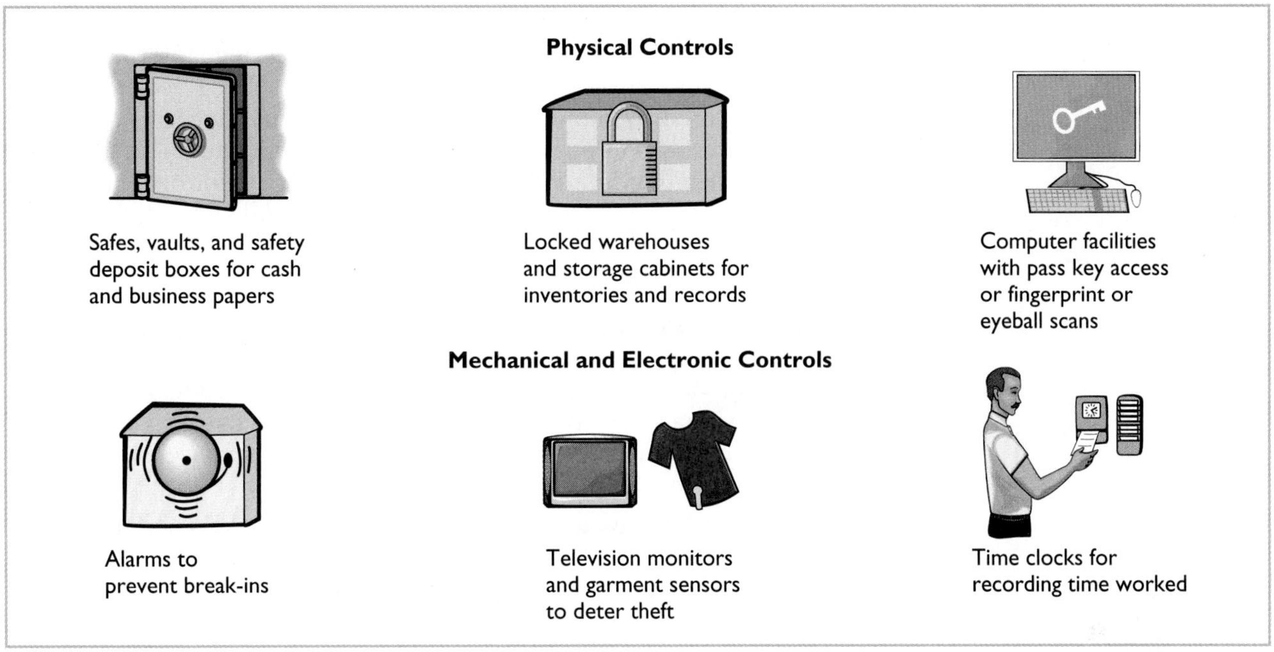
Physical Controls
Safes, vaults, and safety deposit boxes for cash and business papers
Locked warehouses and storage cabinets for inventories and records
Computer facilities with pass key access or fingerprint or eyeball scans
Mechanical and Electronic Controls
Alarms to prevent break-ins
Television monitors and garment sensors to deter theft
Time clocks for recording time worked

Illustration 8-3
Physical, mechanical, and electronic controls

3. Discrepancies and exceptions should be reported to a management level that can take appropriate corrective action.

Independent internal verification is especially useful in comparing recorded accountability with existing assets. The reconciliation of the cash register tape with the cash in the register at Stephanie's Gourmet Coffee and More is an example of this internal control principle. Another common example is the reconciliation of a company's cash balance per books with the cash balance per bank. Illustration 8-4 shows the relationship between this principle and the segregation of duties principle.

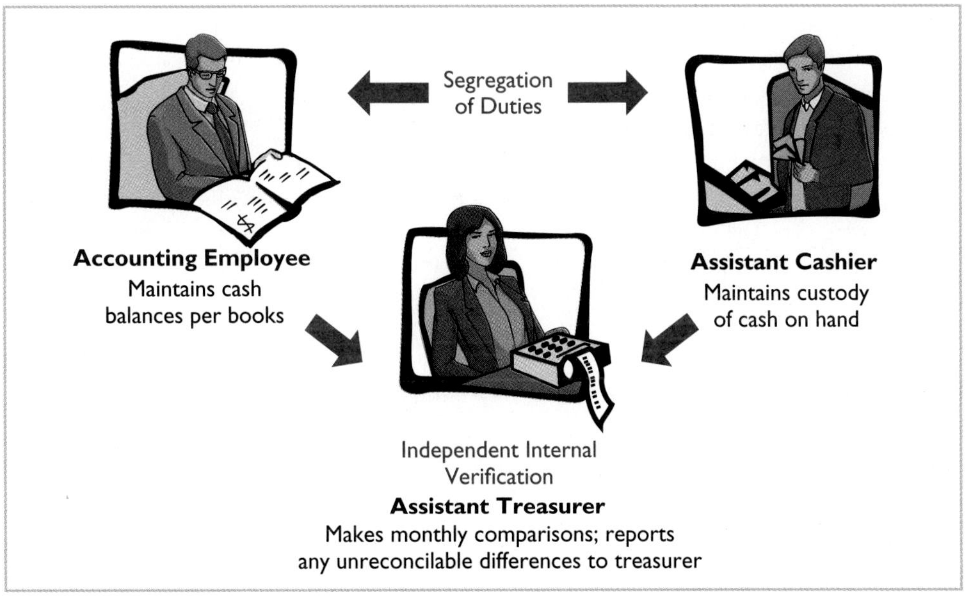
Segregation of Duties
Accounting Employee
Maintains cash balances per books
Assistant Cashier
Maintains custody of cash on hand
Independent Internal Verification
Assistant Treasurer
Makes monthly comparisons; reports any unreconcilable differences to treasurer

Illustration 8-4
Comparison of segregation of duties principle with independent internal verification principle

Large companies often assign independent internal verification to internal auditors. **Internal auditors** are company employees who continuously evaluate the effectiveness of the company's internal control systems. They review the activities of departments and individuals to determine whether prescribed internal controls are being followed. They also recommend improvements when needed. In fact, most fraud is discovered by the company through internal mechanisms such as existing internal controls and internal audits. For example, the alleged fraud at WorldCom, involving billions of dollars, was uncovered by an internal auditor.

OTHER CONTROLS

Other control measures include the following.

1. **Bond employees who handle cash.** Bonding involves obtaining insurance protection against misappropriation of assets by employees. It contributes to the safeguarding of cash in two ways: First, the insurance company carefully screens all individuals before adding them to the policy and may reject risky applicants. Second, bonded employees know that the insurance company will vigorously prosecute all offenders.
2. **Rotate employees' duties and require employees to take vacations.** These measures deter employees from attempting thefts since they will not be able to permanently conceal their improper actions. Many banks, for example, have discovered embezzlements when the perpetrator was on vacation or assigned to a new position.
3. **Conduct thorough background checks.** Many believe that the most important and inexpensive measure any business can take to reduce employee theft and fraud is for the human resources department to conduct thorough background checks. Two tips: (1) Check to see whether job applicants actually graduated from the schools they list. (2) Never use the telephone numbers for previous employers given on the reference sheet; always look them up yourself.

INVESTOR INSIGHT

Poor Internal Control Can Hammer Stock Price

Poor internal controls can cost a company money even if no theft occurs. For example, Eastman Kodak Co., SunTrust Banks Inc., and Toys "R" Us Inc. all recently reported material weaknesses in internal controls. When a company announces that it has deficiencies in its internal controls, its stock price often falls.

Under the Sarbanes-Oxley Act companies must evaluate their internal controls systems and report on any deficiencies. Some analysts estimate that as many as 10% of all publicly traded companies will report weaknesses in their internal controls. The estimate for smaller companies is even higher.

Source: William M. Bulkeley and Robert Tomsho, "Kodak to Get Auditors Adverse View," *Wall Street Journal Online*, January 27, 2005.

? Why would a company's stock price fall if it reports deficiencies in its internal controls?

Limitations of Internal Control

Companies generally design their systems of internal control to provide **reasonable assurance** of proper safeguarding of assets and reliability of the accounting records. The concept of reasonable assurance rests on the premise that the costs of establishing control procedures should not exceed their expected benefit.

To illustrate, consider shoplifting losses in retail stores. Stores could eliminate such losses by having a security guard stop and search customers as they leave the store. But store managers have concluded that the negative effects of such a procedure cannot be justified. Instead, stores have attempted to control shoplifting losses by less costly procedures: They post signs saying, "We reserve the right to inspect all packages" and "All shoplifters will be prosecuted." They use hidden TV cameras and store detectives to monitor customer activity, and they install sensor equipment at exits.

HELPFUL HINT

Controls may vary with the risk level of the activity. For example, management may consider cash to be high risk and maintaining inventories in the stockroom as low risk. Thus management would have stricter controls for cash.

The **human element** is an important factor in every system of internal control. A good system can become ineffective as a result of employee fatigue, carelessness, or indifference. For example, a receiving clerk may not bother to count goods received and may just "fudge" the counts. Occasionally, two or more individuals may work together to get around prescribed controls. Such **collusion** can significantly impair the effectiveness of a system, eliminating the protection offered by segregation of duties. No system of internal control is perfect.

The size of the business also may impose limitations on internal control. A small company, for example, may find it difficult to segregate duties or to provide for independent internal verification.

Before You Go On...

REVIEW IT

1. What are the two primary objectives of internal control?
2. Identify and describe the principles of internal control.
3. What are the limitations of internal control?

DO IT

Li Song owns a small retail store. Li wants to establish good internal control procedures but is confused about the difference between segregation of duties and independent internal verification. Explain the differences to Li.

Action Plan

- Understand and explain the differences between (1) segregation of duties and (2) independent internal verification.

Solution Segregation of duties involves assigning responsibility so that the work of one employee evaluates the work of another employee. Segregation of duties occurs daily in executing and recording transactions.

In contrast, independent internal verification involves reviewing, comparing, and reconciling data prepared by employees. Independent internal verification occurs *after the fact*, as in the case of reconciling cash register totals at the end of the day with cash on hand.

Related exercise material: *BE8-1, BE8-2, BE8-3, and E8-1.*

✓ *The Navigator*

CASH CONTROLS

Just as cash is the beginning of a company's operating cycle, so it is also usually the starting point for a company's system of internal control. Cash is the one asset that is readily convertible into any other type of asset. It also is easily concealed and transported, and is highly desired. Because of these characteristics, **cash is the asset most susceptible to improper diversion and use**. In addition, because of the large volume of cash transactions, numerous errors may occur in executing and recording them. To safeguard cash and to ensure the accuracy of the accounting records for cash, effective internal control over cash is imperative.

Cash consists of coins, currency (paper money), checks, money orders, and money on hand or on deposit in a bank or similar depository. The general rule is that cash is whatever the bank will accept for deposit.

In the next sections we explain the application of internal control principles to cash receipts and cash disbursements.

Internal Control over Cash Receipts

STUDY OBJECTIVE 3

Explain the applications of internal control principles to cash receipts.

Cash receipts come from a variety of sources: cash sales; collections on account from customers; the receipt of interest, rent, and dividends; investments by owners; bank loans; and proceeds from the sale of noncurrent assets. Illustration 8-5 shows how the internal control principles explained earlier apply to cash receipts transactions.

Illustration 8-5
Application of internal control principles to cash receipts

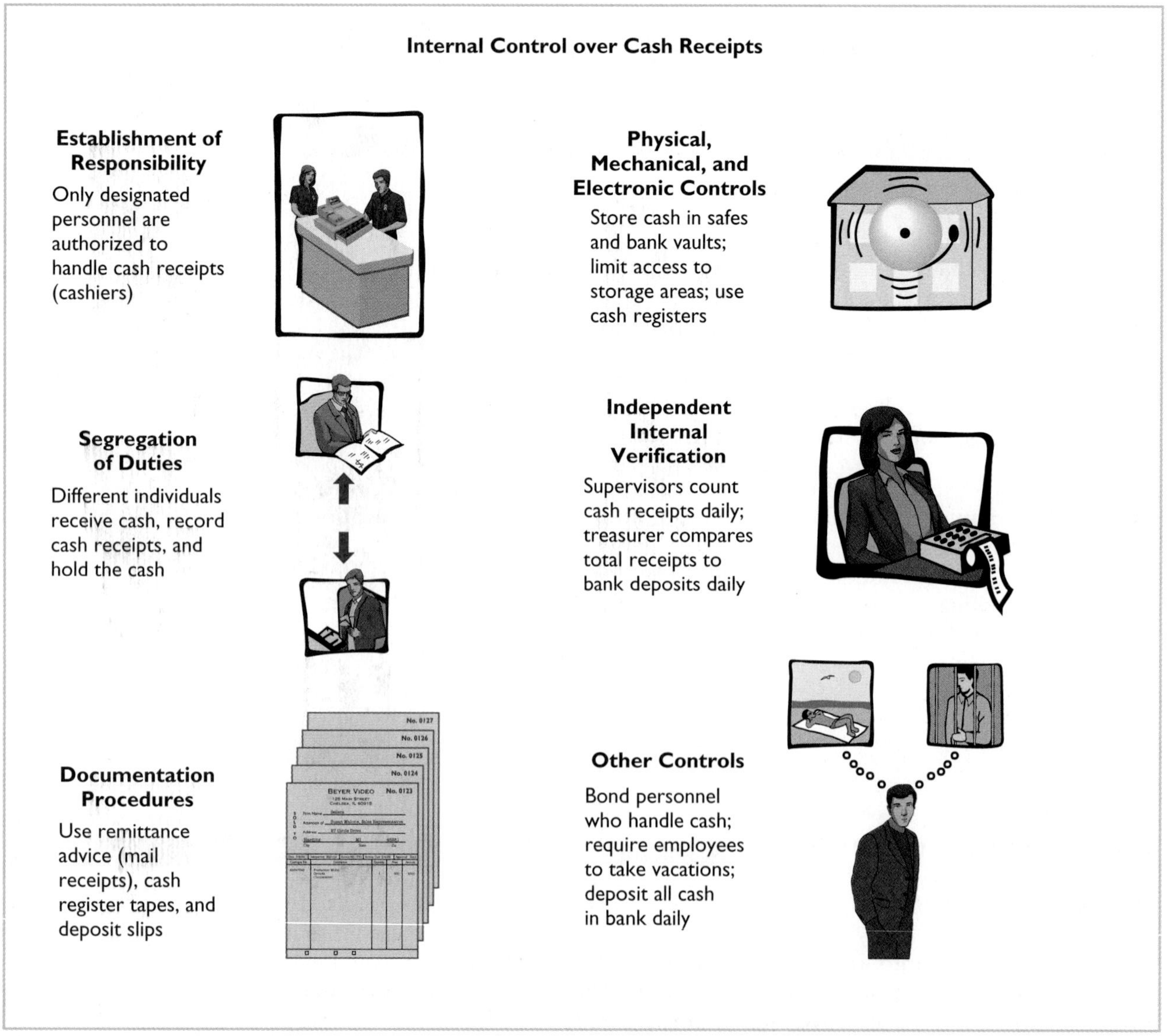
Internal Control over Cash Receipts
Establishment of Responsibility
Only designated personnel are authorized to handle cash receipts (cashiers)
Physical, Mechanical, and Electronic Controls
Store cash in safes and bank vaults; limit access to storage areas; use cash registers
Segregation of Duties
Different individuals receive cash, record cash receipts, and hold the cash
Independent Internal Verification
Supervisors count cash receipts daily; treasurer compares total receipts to bank deposits daily
Documentation Procedures
Use remittance advice (mail receipts), cash register tapes, and deposit slips
No. 0127
No. 0126
No. 0125
No. 0124
No. 0123
BEYER VIDEO
Other Controls
Bond personnel who handle cash; require employees to take vacations; deposit all cash in bank daily

As you might expect, companies vary considerably in how they apply these principles. To illustrate internal control over cash receipts, we will examine control measures for a retail store with both over-the-counter and mail receipts.

OVER-THE-COUNTER RECEIPTS

In retail businesses, control of over-the-counter receipts centers on cash registers that are visible to customers. Supermarkets and discount stores such as Wal-Mart, typically place cash registers in check-out lines near the exit. In stores such as Sears, Roebuck & Co. and JCPenney, each department has its own cash register. A cash sale is "rung up" on a cash register **with the amount clearly visible to the customer**. This measure prevents the cashier from ringing up a lower amount and pocketing the difference. The customer receives an itemized cash register receipt slip and is expected to count the change received.

The cash register keeps a tape locked in the register until a supervisor or manager removes it. This tape accumulates the daily transactions and totals. When the tape is removed, the supervisor compares the total with the amount of cash in the register. The tape should show all registered receipts accounted for. The supervisor reports his or her findings on a cash count sheet which both the cashier and supervisor sign. Illustration 8-6 shows a typical cash count sheet.

Illustration 8-6
Cash count sheet

Store No. 8	Date March 8, 2008
1. Opening cash balance	$ 50.00
2. Cash sales per tape (attached)	6,956.20
3. Total cash to be accounted for	7,006.20
4. Cash on hand	6,996.10
5. Cash (short) or over	$ (10.10)
6. Ending cash balance	$ 50.00
7. Cash for deposit (Line 4 – Line 6)	$6,946.10
Cashier J. Cruse	Supervisor M. Braun

Next, the supervisor gives the count sheets, register tapes, and cash to the head cashier. This person prepares a daily cash summary showing the total cash received and the amount from each source, such as cash sales and collections on account. The head cashier sends one copy of the summary to the accounting department for entry. A second copy goes to the treasurer's office for later comparison with the daily bank deposit.

The head cashier prepares a deposit slip (see Illustration 8-10 on page 354) and makes the bank deposit. The total amount deposited should equal the total receipts on the daily cash summary. This will ensure that the head cashier has placed all receipts in the custody of the bank. In accepting the bank deposit, the bank stamps (authenticates) the duplicate deposit slip and sends it to the company treasurer, who compares the amount of the cash deposit with the daily cash summary.

Illustration 8-7 (page 348) graphically presents these measures for cash sales. It shows the activities of the sales department separately from those of the cashier's department to indicate the segregation of duties in handling cash.

Illustration 8-7
Executing over-the-counter cash sales

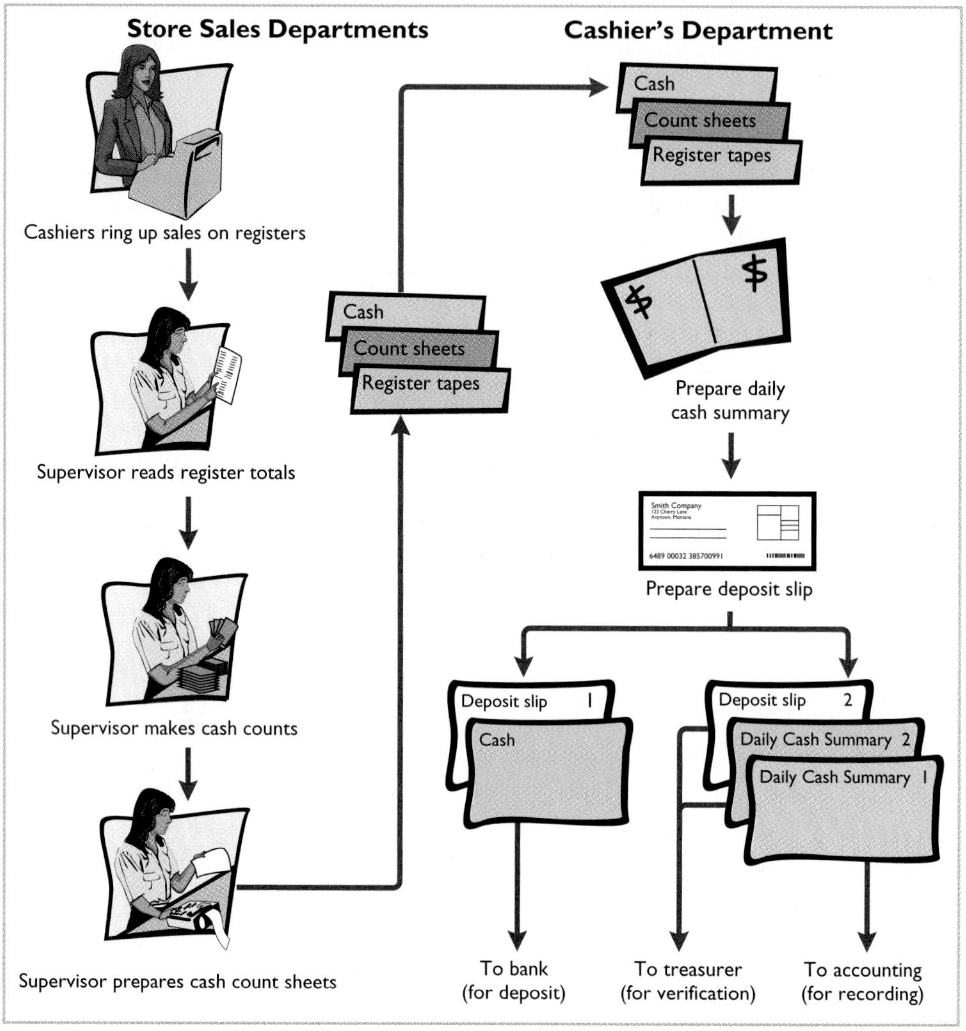

HELPFUL HINT
Flowcharts such as this one enhance the understanding of the flow of documents, the processing steps, and the internal control procedures.

MAIL RECEIPTS

As an individual customer, you may be more familiar with over-the-counter receipts than with mail receipts. However, mail receipts resulting from billings and credit sales are by far the most common way that companies receive cash. Think, for example, of the number of checks received through the mail daily by a national retailer such as J. Crew or American Eagle Outfitters.

All mail receipts should be opened in the presence of two mail clerks. These receipts are generally in the form of checks or money orders. A remittance advice stating the purpose of the check frequently comes with the check (sometimes attached to the check, but often a part of the bill that the customer tears off and returns). A mail clerk should endorse each check "For Deposit Only" by use of a company stamp. This **restrictive endorsement** reduces the likelihood that someone could divert the check to personal use. Banks will not give an individual cash when presented with a check that has this type of endorsement.

The mail-receipt clerks prepare, in duplicate, a list of the checks received each day. This list shows the name of the check issuer, the purpose of the payment, and the amount of the check. Each mail clerk signs the list to establish responsibility for the data. The original copy of the list, along with the checks and remittance advices, are then sent to the cashier's department. There, the cashier adds the checks to the over-the-counter receipts (if any) in preparing the daily cash summary (remember, checks are cash) and in making the daily bank deposit. Also, the mail-receipt clerks send a copy of the list to the treasurer's office for comparison with the total mail receipts shown on the daily cash summary. This copy ensures that all mail receipts have been included.

Before You Go On...

REVIEW IT

1. How do the principles of internal control apply to cash receipts?
2. What procedures do companies use for over-the-counter receipts?

Do It

L. R. Cortez is concerned about the control over cash receipts in his fast-food restaurant, Big Cheese. The restaurant has two cash registers. At no time do more than two employees take customer orders and ring up sales. Work shifts for employees range from 4 to 8 hours. Cortez asks your help in installing a good system of internal control over cash receipts.

Action Plan

- Differentiate among the internal control principles of (1) establishing responsibility, (2) using electronic controls, and (3) independent internal verification.
- Design an effective system of internal control over cash receipts.

Solution Cortez should assign a cash register to each employee at the start of each work shift, with register totals set at zero. Each employee should be instructed to use only the assigned register and to ring up all sales. At the end of each work shift, Cortez or a supervisor/manager should total the register and make a cash count to see whether all cash is accounted for.

Related exercise material: *BE8-4 and E8-2.*

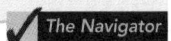

✓ The Navigator

Internal Control over Cash Disbursements

STUDY OBJECTIVE 4

Explain the applications of internal control principles to cash disbursements.

Companies disburse cash for a variety of reasons, such as to pay expenses and liabilities or to purchase assets. **Generally, internal control over cash disbursements is more effective when companies pay by check, rather than by cash.** One exception is **for incidental amounts that are paid out of petty cash.**[2]

Companies generally issue checks only after following specified control procedures. Illustration 8-8 (page 350) shows how principles of internal control apply to cash disbursements.

VOUCHER SYSTEM

Most medium and large companies use vouchers as part of their internal control over cash disbursements. A **voucher system** is a network of approvals by authorized individuals, acting independently, to ensure that all disbursements by check are proper.

The system begins with the authorization to incur a cost or expense. It ends with the issuance of a check for the liability incurred. A **voucher** is an authorization form prepared for each expenditure. Companies require vouchers for all types of cash disbursements except those from petty cash.

[2] We explain the operation of a petty cash fund on pages 351–353.

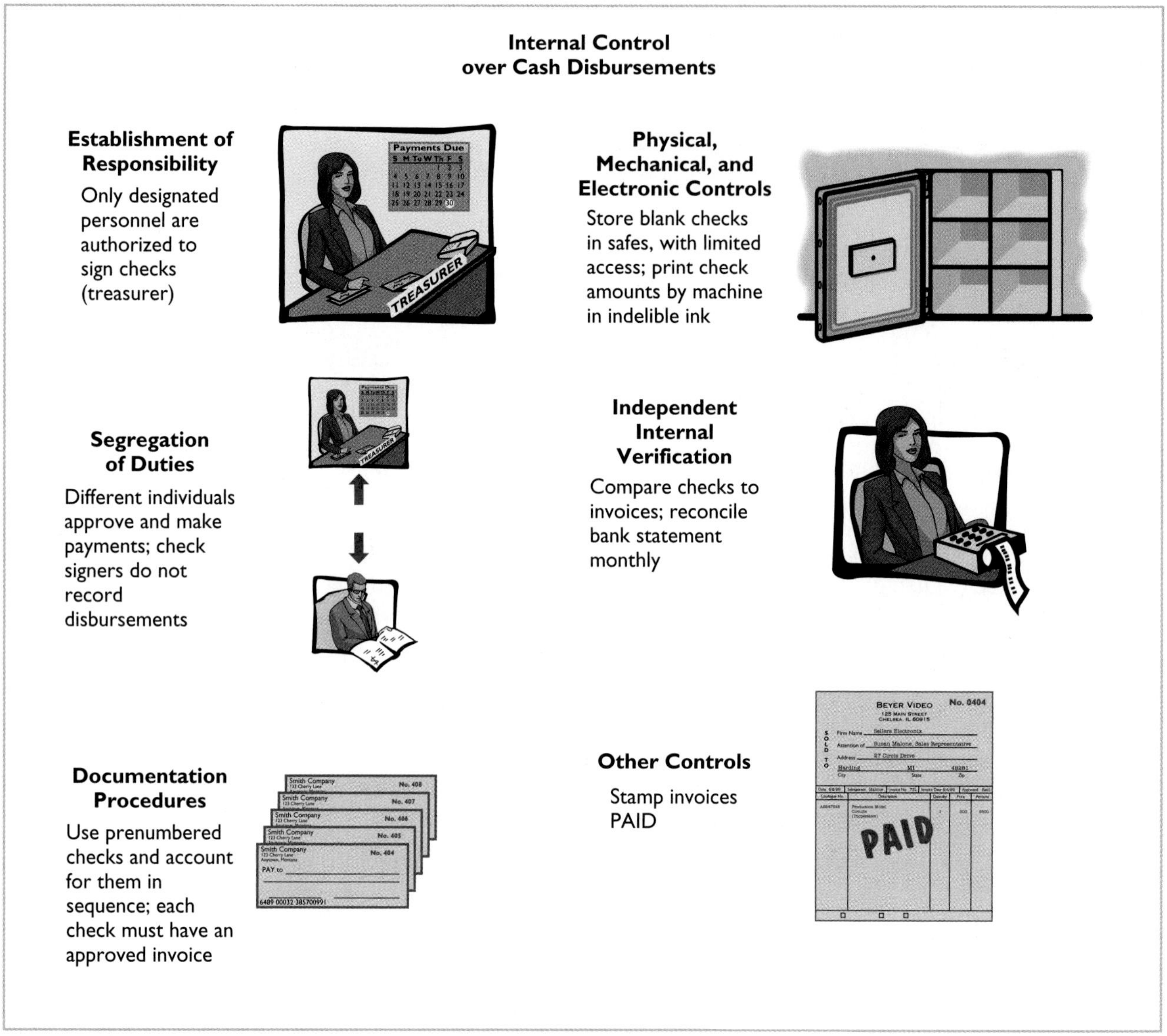
Internal Control
over Cash Disbursements
Establishment of Responsibility
Only designated personnel are authorized to sign checks (treasurer)
Payments Due
TREASURER
Physical, Mechanical, and Electronic Controls
Store blank checks in safes, with limited access; print check amounts by machine in indelible ink
Segregation of Duties
Different individuals approve and make payments; check signers do not record disbursements
Independent Internal Verification
Compare checks to invoices; reconcile bank statement monthly
Documentation Procedures
Use prenumbered checks and account for them in sequence; each check must have an approved invoice
Smith Company
No. 408
No. 407
No. 406
No. 405
No. 404
PAY to
Other Controls
Stamp invoices PAID
BEYER VIDEO
No. 0404
PAID

Illustration 8-8
Application of internal control principles to cash disbursements

The starting point in preparing a voucher is to fill in the appropriate information about the liability on the face of the voucher. The vendor's invoice provides most of the needed information. Then, an employee in accounts payable records the voucher (in a journal called a **voucher register**) and files it according to the date on which it is to be paid. The company issues and sends a check on that date, and stamps the voucher "paid." The paid voucher is sent to the accounting department for recording (in a journal called the **check register**). A voucher system involves two journal entries, one to issue the voucher and a second to pay the voucher.

ELECTRONIC FUNDS TRANSFER (EFT) SYSTEM

Accounting for and controlling cash is an expensive and time-consuming process. The cost to process a check through a bank system is about $1 per check and is increasing. In contrast, it costs only 35¢ if a customer pays by credit card over the telephone, and only 1¢ if the customer pays by credit card via a computer.

It is not surprising, therefore, that companies and banks have developed approaches to transfer funds among parties without the use of paper (deposit tickets, checks, etc.). Such procedures, called **electronic funds transfers (EFT)**, are disbursement systems that use wire, telephone, or computers to transfer cash balances from one location to another. Use of EFT is quite common. For example, many employees receive no formal payroll checks from their employers. Instead, employers send electronic payroll data to the appropriate banks. Also, individuals now frequently make regular payments such as those for house, car, and utilities by EFT.

PETTY CASH FUND

STUDY OBJECTIVE 5
Describe the operation of a petty cash fund.

As you learned earlier in the chapter, better internal control over cash disbursements is possible when companies make payments by check. However, using checks to pay small amounts is both impractical and a nuisance. For instance, a company would not want to write checks to pay for postage due, working lunches, or taxi fares. A common way of handling such payments, while maintaining satisfactory control, is to use a **petty cash fund** to pay relatively small amounts. The operation of a petty cash fund, often called an **imprest system**, involves three steps: (1) establishing the fund, (2) making payments from the fund, and (3) replenishing the fund.[3]

Establishing The Fund. In establishing a petty cash fund, a company appoints a petty cash custodian who will be responsible for the fund. Next it determines the size of the fund. Ordinarily, a company expects the amount in the fund to cover anticipated disbursements for a three- to four-week period.

To establish the fund, a company issues a check payable to the petty cash custodian for the stipulated amount. For example, if Laird Company decides to establish a $100 fund on March 1, the journal entry is:

Mar. 1	Petty Cash	100	
	Cash		100
	(To establish a petty cash fund)		

A	=	L	+	OE
+100				
−100				

Cash Flows
no effect

The fund custodian cashes the check and places the proceeds in a locked petty cash box or drawer. Most petty cash funds are established on a fixed-amount basis. The company will make no additional entries to the Petty Cash account unless management changes the stipulated amount of the fund. For example, if Laird Company decides on July 1 to increase the size of the fund to $250, it would debit Petty Cash $150 and credit Cash $150.

Making Payments from the Fund. The petty cash fund custodian has the authority to make payments from the fund that conform to prescribed management policies. Usually, management limits the size of expenditures that come from petty cash. Likewise, it may not permit use of the fund for certain types of transactions (such as making short-term loans to employees).

Each payment from the fund must be documented on a prenumbered petty cash receipt (or petty cash voucher), as shown in Illustration 8-9 (page 352). Note that the signatures of both the fund custodian and the person receiving payment are required on the receipt. If other supporting documents such as a freight bill or invoice are available, they should be attached to the petty cash receipt.

The fund custodian keeps the receipts in the petty cash box until the fund is replenished. The sum of the petty cash receipts and the money in the fund should equal the established total at all times. Management can (and should) make surprise counts at any time to determine whether the fund is being maintained correctly.

The company does not make an accounting entry to record a payment when it is made from petty cash. Instead, the company recognizes the accounting effects of each payment when it replenishes the fund.

[3]The term "imprest" means an advance of money for a designated purpose.

Illustration 8-9
Petty cash receipt

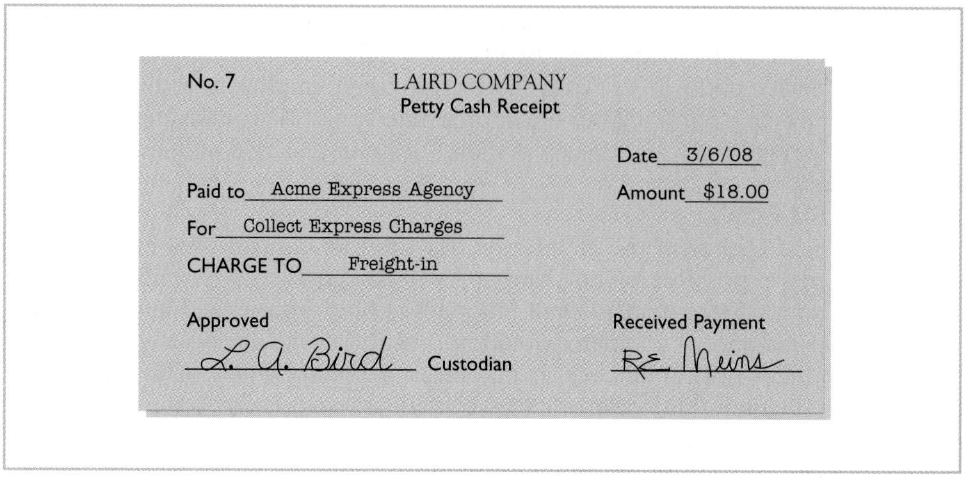
No. 7
LAIRD COMPANY
Petty Cash Receipt

Date 3/6/08
Paid to Acme Express Agency
Amount $18.00
For Collect Express Charges
CHARGE TO Freight-in

Approved
L. A. Bird Custodian
Received Payment
R.E. Meins

Replenishing the Fund. When the money in the petty cash fund reaches a minimum level, the company replenishes the fund. The petty cash custodian initiates a request for reimbursement. He or she prepares a schedule (or summary) of the payments that have been made and sends the schedule, supported by petty cash receipts and other documentation, to the treasurer's office. Someone in the treasurer's office examines the receipts and supporting documents to verify that they were proper payments from the fund. The treasurer then approves the request and issues a check to restore the fund to its established amount. At the same time, all supporting documentation is stamped "paid" so that it cannot be submitted again for payment.

To illustrate, assume that on March 15 Laird's petty cash custodian requests a check for $87. The fund contains $13 cash and petty cash receipts for postage $44, freight-out $38, and miscellaneous expenses $5. The general journal entry to record the check is:

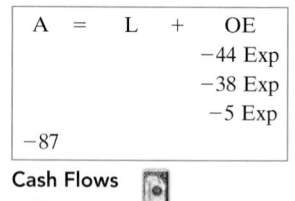

A	=	L	+	OE
				−44 Exp
				−38 Exp
				−5 Exp
−87				

Cash Flows
−87

Mar. 15	Postage Expense	44	
	Freight-out	38	
	Miscellaneous Expense	5	
	Cash		87
	(To replenish petty cash fund)		

Note that the reimbursement entry does not affect the Petty Cash account. Replenishment changes the composition of the fund by replacing the petty cash receipts with cash. It does not change the balance in the fund.

HELPFUL HINT
Cash over and short situations result from mathematical errors or from failure to keep accurate records.

Occasionally, in replenishing a petty cash fund, the company may need to recognize a cash shortage or overage. This results when the total of the cash plus receipts in the petty cash box does not equal the established amount of the petty cash fund. To illustrate, assume that Laird's petty cash custodian has only $12 in cash in the fund plus the receipts as listed. The request for reimbursement would, therefore, be for $88, and Laird would make the following entry:

A	=	L	+	OE
				−44 Exp
				−38 Exp
				−5 Exp
				−1 Exp
−88				

Cash Flows
−88

Mar. 15	Postage Expense	44	
	Freight-out	38	
	Miscellaneous Expense	5	
	Cash Over and Short	1	
	Cash		88
	(To replenish petty cash fund)		

Conversely, if the custodian has $14 in cash, the reimbursement request would be for $86, and the company would credit Cash Over and Short for $1 (overage). A company reports a debit balance in Cash Over and Short in the income statement as miscellaneous expense. It reports a credit balance in the account as miscellaneous revenue. The company closes Cash Over and Short to Income Summary at the end of the year.

Companies should replenish a petty cash fund at the end of the accounting period, regardless of the cash in the fund. Replenishment at this time is necessary in order to recognize the effects of the petty cash payments on the financial statements.

ETHICS NOTE

Internal control over a petty cash fund is strengthened by: (1) having a supervisor make surprise counts of the fund to confirm whether the paid vouchers and fund cash equal the imprest amount, and (2) canceling or mutilating the paid vouchers so they cannot be resubmitted for reimbursement.

Before You Go On...

REVIEW IT

1. How do the principles of internal control apply to cash disbursements?
2. What are the entries required in a petty cash system?

The Navigator

USE OF A BANK

STUDY OBJECTIVE 6

Indicate the control features of a bank account.

The use of a bank contributes significantly to good internal control over cash. A company can safeguard its cash by using a bank as a depository and as a clearing house for checks received and written. Use of a bank minimizes the amount of currency that a company must keep on hand. Also, use of a bank facilitates the control of cash because it creates a double record of all bank transactions—one by the company and the other by the bank. The asset account Cash maintained by the company should have the same balance as the bank's liability account for that company. A **bank reconciliation** compares the bank's balance with the company's balance and explains any differences to make them agree.

Many companies have more than one bank account. For efficiency of operations and better control, national retailers like Wal-Mart and Target may have regional bank accounts. Large companies, with tens of thousands of employees, may have a payroll bank account, as well as one or more general bank accounts. Also, a company may maintain several bank accounts in order to have more than one source for short-term loans when needed.

Making Bank Deposits

An authorized employee, such as the head cashier, should make a company's bank deposits. Each deposit must be documented by a deposit slip (ticket), as shown in Illustration 8-10 (page 354).

Deposit slips are prepared in duplicate. The bank retains the original; the depositor keeps the duplicate, machine-stamped by the bank to establish its authenticity.

Writing Checks

Most of us write checks, without thinking very much about them. A **check** is a written order signed by the depositor directing the bank to pay a specified sum of money to a designated recipient. There are three parties to a check: (1) the **maker** (or drawer) who issues the check, (2) the **bank** (or payer) on which the check is

Illustration 8-10
Deposit slip

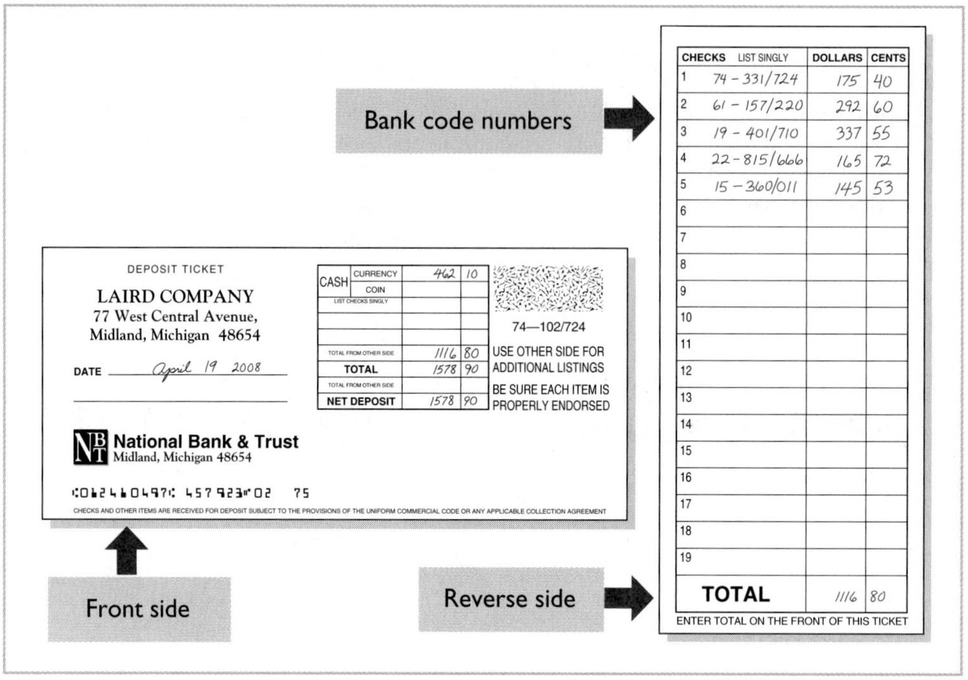

drawn, and (3) the **payee** to whom the check is payable. A check is a **negotiable instrument** that one party can transfer to another party by endorsement. Each check should be accompanied by an explanation of its purpose. In many companies, a remittance advice attached to the check, as shown in Illustration 8-11 explains the check's purpose.

Illustration 8-11
Check with remittance advice

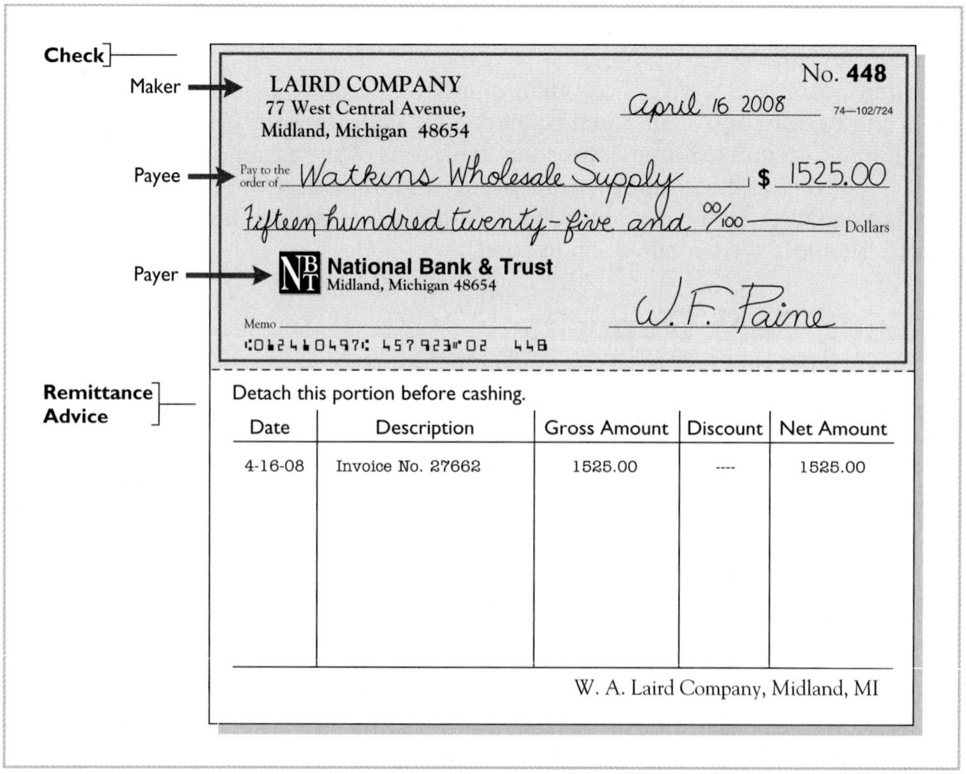

It is important to know the balance in the checking account at all times. To keep the balance current, the depositor should enter each deposit and check on running-balance memo forms provided by the bank or on the check stubs in the checkbook.

ACCOUNTING ACROSS THE ORGANIZATION

Cash? What Cash?

Cash is virtually obsolete. Today, many people use debit cards and credit cards to pay for most of their purchases. But debit cards are usable only at specified locations, and credit cards are cumbersome for small transactions. They are no good for transferring cash between individuals or to small companies that do not want to pay credit card fees. Digital cash may be the next online wave.

There are many digital-cash companies. One of the most flexible appears to be PayPal (*www.paypal.com*). PayPal became popular with users of the auction site eBay, because it allows them to transfer funds to each other as easily as sending e-mail. (PayPal is now owned by eBay, though it is operated as an independent site.)

Source: Mathew Ingram, "Will Digital Cash Work This Time?" *The Globe and Mail*, March 18, 2000, p. N4.

? Will "cash" be obsolete in terms of financial statement reporting?

Bank Statements

If you have a personal checking account, you are probably familiar with bank statements. A **bank statement** shows the depositor's bank transactions and balances.[4] Each month, a depositor receives a statement from the bank. Illustration 8-12 (page 356) presents a typical bank statement. It shows: (1) checks paid and other debits that reduce the balance in the depositor's account, (2) deposits and other credits that increase the balance in the account, and (3) the account balance after each day's transactions.

HELPFUL HINT
Essentially, the bank statement is a copy of the bank's records sent to the customer for periodic review.

The bank statement lists in numerical sequence all "paid" checks, along with the date the check was paid and its amount. Upon paying a check, the bank stamps the check "paid"; a paid check is sometimes referred to as a **canceled** check. On the statement the bank also includes memoranda explaining other debits and credits it made to the depositor's account.

DEBIT MEMORANDUM

Some banks charge a monthly fee for their services. Often they charge this fee only when the average monthly balance in a checking account falls below a specified amount. They identify the fee, called a **bank service charge**, on the bank statement by a symbol such as **SC**. The bank also sends with the statement a debit memorandum explaining the charge noted on the statement. Other debit memoranda may also be issued for other bank services such as the cost of printing checks, issuing traveler's checks, and wiring funds to other locations. The symbol **DM** is often used for such charges.

[4]Our presentation assumes that the depositor makes all adjustments at the end of the month. In practice, a company may also make journal entries during the month as it receives information from the bank regarding its account.

Illustration 8-12
Bank statement

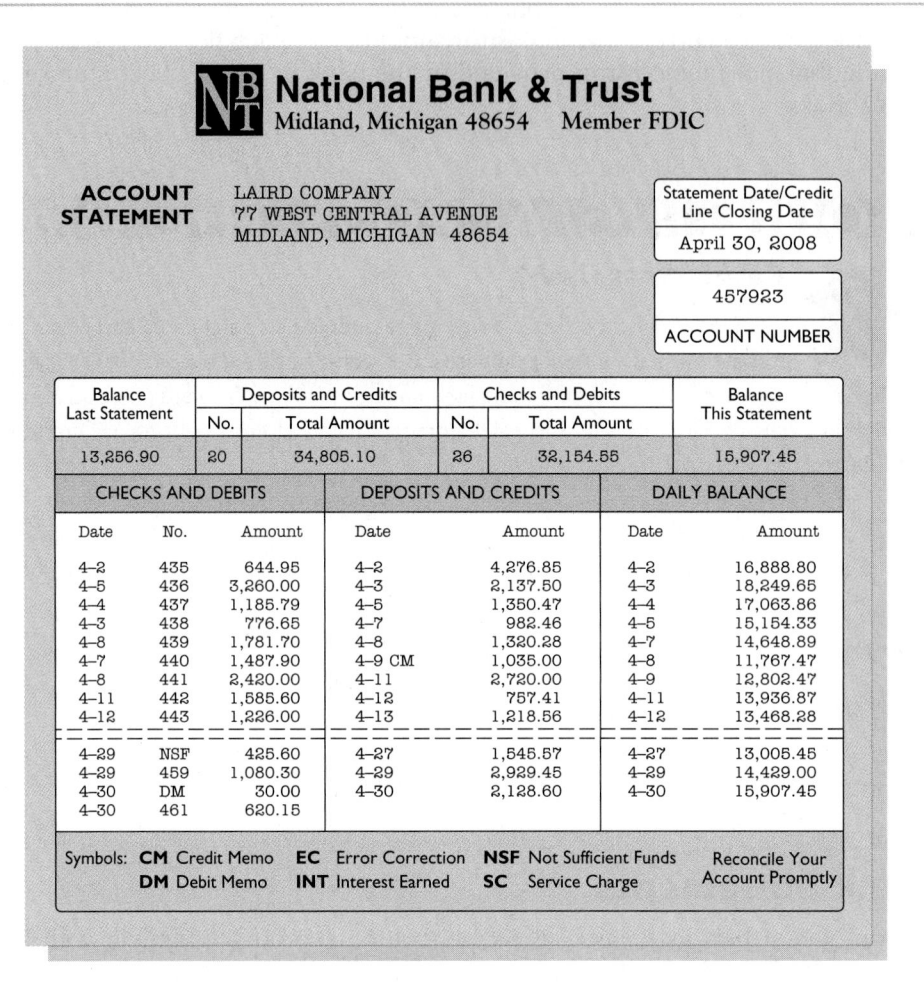

National Bank & Trust
Midland, Michigan 48654 Member FDIC

ACCOUNT STATEMENT

LAIRD COMPANY
77 WEST CENTRAL AVENUE
MIDLAND, MICHIGAN 48654

Statement Date/Credit Line Closing Date
April 30, 2008

457923
ACCOUNT NUMBER

Balance Last Statement	Deposits and Credits		Checks and Debits		Balance This Statement
	No.	Total Amount	No.	Total Amount	
13,256.90	20	34,805.10	26	32,154.55	15,907.45

CHECKS AND DEBITS			DEPOSITS AND CREDITS		DAILY BALANCE	
Date	No.	Amount	Date	Amount	Date	Amount
4-2	435	644.95	4-2	4,276.85	4-2	16,888.80
4-5	436	3,260.00	4-3	2,137.50	4-3	18,249.65
4-4	437	1,185.79	4-5	1,350.47	4-4	17,063.86
4-3	438	776.65	4-7	982.46	4-5	15,154.33
4-8	439	1,781.70	4-8	1,320.28	4-7	14,648.89
4-7	440	1,487.90	4-9 CM	1,035.00	4-8	11,767.47
4-8	441	2,420.00	4-11	2,720.00	4-9	12,802.47
4-11	442	1,585.60	4-12	757.41	4-11	13,936.87
4-12	443	1,226.00	4-13	1,218.56	4-12	13,468.28
4-29	NSF	425.60	4-27	1,545.57	4-27	13,005.45
4-29	459	1,080.30	4-29	2,929.45	4-29	14,429.00
4-30	DM	30.00	4-30	2,128.60	4-30	15,907.45
4-30	461	620.15				

Symbols: **CM** Credit Memo **EC** Error Correction **NSF** Not Sufficient Funds
DM Debit Memo **INT** Interest Earned **SC** Service Charge

Reconcile Your Account Promptly

HELPFUL HINT
The bank *credits* to the customer's account every deposit it receives. The reverse occurs when the bank "pays" a check issued by a company on its checking account balance: Payment reduces the bank's liability. Thus the bank *debits* check payments to the customer's account with the bank.

Banks also use a debit memorandum when a deposited check from a customer "bounces" because of insufficient funds. For example, assume that Scott Company, a customer of Laird Company, sends a check for $800 to Laird Company for services provided. Unfortunately, Scott does not have sufficient funds at its bank to pay for these services. In such a case, Scott's bank marks the check NSF (not sufficient funds) and returns it to Laird's (the depositor's) bank. Laird's bank then debits Laird's account, as shown by the symbol NSF on the bank statement in Illustration 8-12 (above). The bank sends the NSF check and debit memorandum to Laird as notification of the charge. Laird then records an Account Receivable from Scott Company (the writer of the bad check) and reduces cash for the NSF check.

CREDIT MEMORANDUM

Sometimes a depositor asks the bank to collect its notes receivable. In such a case, the bank will credit the depositor's account for the cash proceeds of the note. This is illustrated by the symbol **CM** on the Laird Company bank statement. The bank issues and sends with the statement a credit memorandum to explain the entry. Many banks also offer interest on checking accounts. The interest earned may be indicated on the bank statement by the symbol **CM** or **INT**.

Reconciling the Bank Account

STUDY OBJECTIVE 7
Prepare a bank reconciliation.

The bank and the depositor maintain independent records of the depositor's checking account. People tend to assume that the respective balances will always agree. In fact, the two balances are seldom the same at any given time. Therefore it is necessary to make the balance per books agree with the balance per bank—a process called **reconciling the bank account**. The lack of agreement between the two balances has two causes:

1. **Time lags** that prevent one of the parties from recording the transaction in the same period as the other party.
2. **Errors** by either party in recording transactions.

Time lags occur frequently. For example, several days may elapse between the time a company mails a check to a payee and the date the bank pays the check. Similarly, when the depositor uses the bank's night depository to make its deposits, there will be a difference of at least one day between the time the depositor records the deposit and the time the bank does so. A time lag also occurs whenever the bank mails a debit or credit memorandum to the depositor.

The incidence of errors depends on the effectiveness of the internal controls of the depositor and the bank. Bank errors are infrequent. However, either party could accidentally record a $450 check as $45 or $540. In addition, the bank might mistakenly charge a check to a wrong account by keying in an incorrect account name or number.

RECONCILIATION PROCEDURE

The bank reconciliation should be prepared by an employee who has no other responsibilities pertaining to cash. If a company fails to follow this internal control principle of independent internal verification, cash embezzlements may go unnoticed. For example, a cashier who prepares the reconciliation can embezzle cash and conceal the embezzlement by misstating the reconciliation. Thus, the bank accounts would reconcile, and the embezzlement would not be detected.

In reconciling the bank account, it is customary to reconcile the balance per books and balance per bank to their adjusted (correct or true) cash balances. The starting point in preparing the reconciliation is to enter the balance per bank statement and balance per books on the reconciliation schedule. The company then makes various adjustments, as shown in Illustration 8-13 (page 358).

The following steps should reveal all the reconciling items that cause the difference between the two balances.

Step 1. Deposits in transit. Compare the individual deposits listed on the bank statement with deposits in transit from the preceding bank reconciliation and with the deposits per company records or duplicate deposit slips. Deposits recorded by the depositor that have not been recorded by the bank are the **deposits in transit**. Add these deposits to the balance per bank.

HELPFUL HINT
Deposits in transit and outstanding checks are reconciling items because of time lags.

Step 2. Outstanding checks. Compare the paid checks shown on the bank statement with (a) checks outstanding from the previous bank reconciliation, and (b) checks issued by the company as recorded in the cash payments journal (or in the check register in your personal checkbook). Issued checks recorded by the company but that have not yet been paid by the bank are **outstanding checks**. Deduct outstanding checks from the balance per the bank.

Step 3. Errors. Note any errors discovered in the foregoing steps and list them in the appropriate section of the reconciliation schedule. For example, if the company mistakenly recorded as $169 a paid check correctly written

Illustration 8-13
Bank reconciliation procedures

for $196, it would deduct the error of $27 from the balance per books. All errors made by the depositor are reconciling items in determining the adjusted cash balance per books. In contrast, all errors made by the bank are reconciling items in determining the adjusted cash balance per the bank.

HELPFUL HINT
Note in the bank statement on page 356 that checks no. 459 and 461 have been paid but check no. 460 is not listed. Thus, this check is outstanding. If a complete bank statement were provided, checks no. 453 and 457 would also not be listed. The amounts for these three checks are obtained from the company's cash payments records.

Step 4. Bank memoranda. Trace bank memoranda to the depositor's records. List in the appropriate section of the reconciliation schedule any unrecorded memoranda. For example, the company would deduct from the balance per books a $5 debit memorandum for bank service charges. Similarly, it would add to the balance per books $32 of interest earned.

BANK RECONCILIATION ILLUSTRATED

The bank statement for Laird Company, in Illustration 8-12, shows a balance per bank of $15,907.45 on April 30, 2008. On this date the balance of cash per books is $11,589.45. Using the four reconciliation steps, Laird determines the following reconciling items.

Step 1. Deposits in transit: April 30 deposit (received by bank on May 1).	$2,201.40
Step 2. Outstanding checks: No. 453, $3,000.00; no. 457, $1,401.30; no. 460, $1,502.70.	5,904.00
Step 3. Errors: Laird wrote check no. 443 for $1,226.00 and the bank correctly paid that amount. However, Laird recorded the check as $1,262.00.	36.00
Step 4. Bank memoranda:	
a. Debit—NSF check from J. R. Baron for $425.60	425.60
b. Debit—Charge for printing company checks $30.00	30.00
c. Credit—Collection of note receivable for $1,000 plus interest earned $50, less bank collection fee $15.00	1,035.00

Illustration 8-14 shows Laird's bank reconciliation.

Illustration 8-14
Bank reconciliation

LAIRD COMPANY Bank Reconciliation April 30, 2008		
Cash balance per bank statement		$15,907.45
Add: Deposits in transit		2,201.40
		18,108.85
Less: Outstanding checks		
No. 453	$3,000.00	
No. 457	1,401.30	
No. 460	1,502.70	5,904.00
Adjusted cash balance per bank		**$12,204.85**
Cash balance per books		$11,589.45
Add: Collection of note receivable $1,000, plus interest earned $50, less collection fee $15	$1,035.00	
Error in recording check no. 443	36.00	1,071.00
		12,660.45
Less: NSF check	425.60	
Bank service charge	30.00	455.60
Adjusted cash balance per books		**$12,204.85**

ALTERNATIVE TERMINOLOGY

The terms *adjusted balance, true cash balance,* and *correct cash balance* are used interchangeably.

HELPFUL HINT

The entries that follow are adjusting entries. In prior chapters, Cash was an account that did not require adjustment. That was a simplifying assumption for learning purposes, because we had not yet explained a bank reconciliation.

ENTRIES FROM BANK RECONCILIATION

The company records each reconciling item used to determine the **adjusted cash balance per books. If the company does not journalize and post these items, the Cash account will not show the correct balance.** Laird Company would make the following entries on April 30.

Collection of Note Receivable. This entry involves four accounts. Assuming that the interest of $50 has not been accrued and the collection fee is charged to Miscellaneous Expense, the entry is:

Apr. 30	Cash	1,035.00	
	Miscellaneous Expense	15.00	
	Notes Receivable		1,000.00
	Interest Revenue		50.00
	(To record collection of note receivable by bank)		

A	=	L	+	OE
+1,035				
				−15 Exp
−1,000				
				+50 Rev

Cash Flows
+1,035

Book Error. The cash disbursements journal shows that check no. 443 was a payment on account to Andrea Company, a supplier. The correcting entry is:

A	=	L	+	OE
+36				
		+36		

Cash Flows
+36

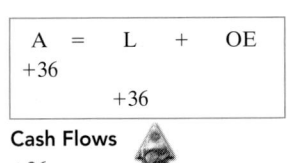

Apr. 30	Cash	36.00	
	Accounts Payable—Andrea Company		36.00
	(To correct error in recording check no. 443)		

NSF Check. As indicated earlier, an NSF check becomes an account receivable to the depositor. The entry is:

A	=	L	+	OE
+425.60				
−425.60				

Cash Flows
−425.60

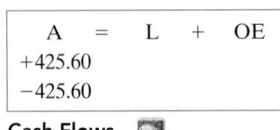

Apr. 30	Accounts Receivable—J. R. Baron	425.60	
	Cash		425.60
	(To record NSF check)		

Bank Service Charges. Depositors debit check printing charges (DM) and other bank service charges (SC) to Miscellaneous Expense, because they are usually nominal in amount. The entry is:

A	=	L	+	OE
				−30 Exp
−30				

Cash Flows
−30

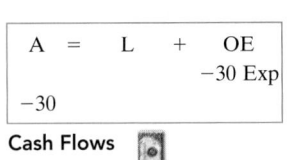

Apr. 30	Miscellaneous Expense	30.00	
	Cash		30.00
	(To record charge for printing company checks)		

Instead of making four separate entries, Laird could combine them into one compound entry.

After Laird has posted the entries, the Cash account will show the following.

Illustration 8-15
Adjusted balance in cash account

Cash			
Apr. 30 Bal.	11,589.45	Apr. 30	425.60
30	1,035.00	30	30.00
30	36.00		
Apr. 30 Bal.	**12,204.85**		

The adjusted cash balance in the ledger should agree with the adjusted cash balance per books in the bank reconciliation in Illustration 8-14.

What entries does the bank make? If the company discovers any bank errors in preparing the reconciliation, it should notify the bank. The bank then can make the necessary corrections in its records. The bank does not make any entries for deposits in transit or outstanding checks. Only when these items reach the bank will the bank record these items.

Before You Go On...

REVIEW IT

1. Why is it necessary to reconcile a bank account?
2. What steps are involved in the reconciliation procedure?
3. What information does a bank reconciliation include?

DO IT

Sally Kist owns Linen Kist Fabrics. Sally asks you to explain how she should treat the following reconciling items when reconciling the company's bank account: (1) a debit memorandum for an NSF check, (2) a credit memorandum for a note collected by the bank, (3) outstanding checks, and (4) a deposit in transit.

Action Plan
- Understand the purpose of a bank reconciliation.
- Identify time lags and explain how they cause reconciling items.

Solution Sally should treat the reconciling items as follows.
(1) NSF check: Deduct from balance per books.
(2) Collection of note: Add to balance per books.
(3) Outstanding checks: Deduct from balance per bank.
(4) Deposit in transit: Add to balance per bank.

Related exercise material: *BE8-8, BE8-9, BE8-10, BE8-11, E8-9, E8-10, E8-11, E8-12, and E8-13.*

✓ The Navigator

REPORTING CASH

STUDY OBJECTIVE 8
Explain the reporting of cash.

On the balance sheet, companies often combine cash on hand, cash in banks, and petty cash and report the total simply as **Cash**. Because it is the most liquid asset owned by a company, cash is listed first in the current assets section of the balance sheet. Some companies use the term "Cash and cash equivalents" in reporting cash, as shown in Illustration 8-16.

Illustration 8-16
Presentation of cash and cash equivalents

EASTMAN KODAK COMPANY
Balance Sheets (partial)

	2005	2004
Current assets (in millions)		
Cash and cash equivalents	$1,255	$1,665

Cash equivalents are short-term, highly liquid investments that can be converted into a specific amount of cash. At the time of purchase, they typically have maturities of three months or less. They include money market funds, bank certificates of deposit, and U.S. Treasury bills and notes.

A company may have cash that is restricted for a special purpose. An example is a payroll bank account for paying salaries and wages. Another would be a plant expansion cash fund for financing new construction. Companies should report **restricted cash** separately on the balance sheet. If a company expects to use the restricted cash **within the next year**, the amount should be reported as a current asset. Otherwise, it should be reported as a noncurrent asset. Since a payroll bank account will be used as early as the next payday, it is reported as a current asset. In contrast, unless the new construction will begin within the next year, cash for plant expansion would be classified as a noncurrent asset (long-term investment).

When making loans to depositors, banks commonly require borrowers to maintain minimum cash balances. These minimum balances, called **compensating balances**, provide the bank with support for the loans. They are a restriction on the use of cash that may affect a company's liquidity. Thus, companies should disclose compensating balances in the notes to the financial statements.

Be sure to read **ALL ABOUT YOU: *Protecting Yourself from Identity Theft*** on page 362 for information on how topics in this chapter apply to you.

Protecting Yourself from Identity Theft

As a result of the Sarbanes-Oxley Act, companies have done a lot to improve their internal controls to help protect themselves from both internal and external thieves. What have you done lately to shore up your own personal internal controls? You've heard the stories about hackers cleaning out people's online investment accounts or running up credit card bills that would take you most of your life to pay off. (If you don't have a credit card, they'll open an account for you.) The identity thieves aren't going away. So what can you do to protect yourself? Many of the same common-sense controls discussed in this chapter can be implemented in your personal life.

Some Facts

* Identity thieves determine your identity by going through your mail or trash, stealing your credit cards, redirecting mail through change of address forms, or acquiring personal information you share on unsecured sites. In a recent year, more than 7 million people were victims of identity theft.
* During a single computer-virus outbreak, called the "Hearse," thieves stole 90,000 pieces of personal data.
* The average identity-theft victim spends 600 hours clearing up his or her finances and financial and other records to recover from the crime.
* Victims incur an average of $1,400 in out-of-pocket expenses.
* Consumers have $1.7 trillion worth of assets with online brokerage firms. Many of the largest identity theft losses have been the result of thieves completely cleaning out online brokerage accounts.
* The Federal Trade Commission reports identify theft is the No. 1 fraud complaint among consumers. Phoenix and Las Vegas top the list for identity theft per capita.

About the Numbers

The following chart shows the most common survey responses from victims of identity theft when asked how their information was used by the thieves. (Note that respondents chose more than one type of use.)

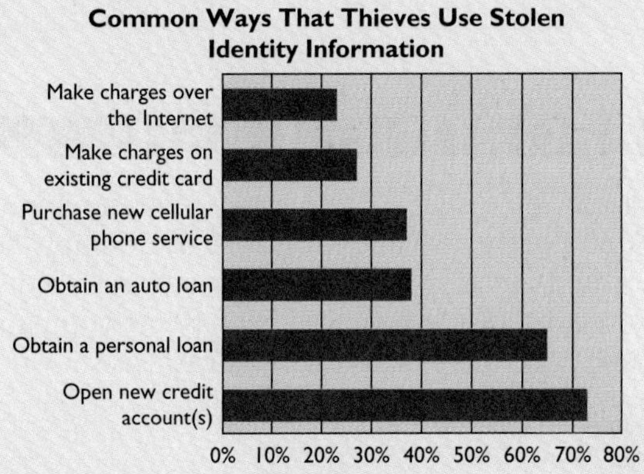

Source: The Identity Theft Resource Center, *Identity Theft: The Aftermath 2003*, *www.idtheftcenter.org/idaftermath.pdf* (accessed May 2006).

What Do You Think

Do you feel it is safe to store personal financial data (such as Social Security numbers and bank and credit account numbers) on your computer?

YES: I have anti-virus software that will detect and stop any intruder.

NO: Even the best anti-virus software does not detect every kind of intruder.

Sources: Amy Borrus, "Invasion of the Stock Hackers," *Business Week*, November 14, 2005, pp. 38-40; Brian Grow, "Nasty, Brutish, and Sneaky," *Business Week*, April 10, 2006, p. 37; Federal Trade Commission, *www.consumer.gov/idtheft/*.

The authors' comments on this situation appear on page 381.

Before You Go On...

REVIEW IT

1. What do companies generally report as cash on the balance sheet?
2. What are cash equivalents? What are compensating balances? What is restricted cash?
3. At what amount does PepsiCo report cash and cash equivalents in its 2005 consolidated balance sheet? The answer to this question appears on page 381.

The Navigator

Demonstration Problem

Poorten Company's bank statement for May 2008 shows the following data.

Balance 5/1	$12,650	Balance 5/31	$14,280
Debit memorandum:		Credit memorandum:	
NSF check	$175	Collection of note receivable	$505

The cash balance per books at May 31 is $13,319. Your review of the data reveals the following.

1. The NSF check was from Copple Co., a customer.
2. The note collected by the bank was a $500, 3-month, 12% note. The bank charged a $10 collection fee. No interest has accrued.
3. Outstanding checks at May 31 total $2,410.
4. Deposits in transit at May 31 total $1,752.
5. A Poorten Company check for $352, dated May 10, cleared the bank on May 25. The company recorded this check, which was a payment on account, for $325.

Instructions

(a) Prepare a bank reconciliation at May 31.
(b) Journalize the entries required by the reconciliation.

Solution to Demonstration Problem

(a)

POORTEN COMPANY
Bank Reconciliation
May 31, 2008

Cash balance per bank statement		$14,280
Add: Deposits in transit		1,752
		16,032
Less: Outstanding checks		2,410
Adjusted cash balance per bank		$13,622
Cash balance per books		$13,319
Add: Collection of note receivable $500, plus $15 interest, less collection fee $10		505
		13,824
Less: NSF check	$175	
Error in recording check	27	202
Adjusted cash balance per books		$13,622

action plan

- ✓ Follow the four steps in the reconciliation procedure. (pp. 357–358).
- ✓ Work carefully to minimize mathematical errors in the reconciliation.
- ✓ Prepare adjusting entries from reconciling items per books.
- ✓ Make sure the cash ledger balance after posting the reconciling entries agrees with the adjusted cash balance per books.

(b)

May 31	Cash	505	
	Miscellaneous Expense	10	
	Notes Receivable		500
	Interest Revenue		15
	(To record collection of note by bank)		
31	Accounts Receivable—Copple Co.	175	
	Cash		175
	(To record NSF check from Copple Co.)		
31	Accounts Payable	27	
	Cash		27
	(To correct error in recording check)		

The Navigator

SUMMARY OF STUDY OBJECTIVES

WILEY PLUS

1 **Define internal control.** Internal control is the related methods and procedures adopted within an organization to safeguard its assets and to enhance the accuracy and reliability of its accounting records.

2 **Identify the principles of internal control.** The principles of internal control are: establishment of responsibility; segregation of duties; documentation procedures; physical, mechanical, and electronic controls; independent internal verification; and other controls such as bonding and requiring employees to take vacations.

3 **Explain the applications of internal control principles to cash receipts.** Internal controls over cash receipts include: (a) designating specific personnel to handle cash; (b) assigning different individuals to receive cash, record cash, and maintain custody of cash; (c) using remittance advices for mail receipts, cash register tapes for over-the-counter receipts, and deposit slips for bank deposits; (d) using company safes and bank vaults to store cash with access limited to authorized personnel, and using cash registers in executing over-the-counter receipts; (e) making independent daily counts of register receipts and daily comparison of total receipts with total deposits; and (f) bonding personnel that handle cash and requiring them to take vacations.

4 **Explain the applications of internal control principles to cash disbursements.** Internal controls over cash disbursements include: (a) having specific individuals such as the treasurer authorized to sign checks; (b) assigning different individuals to approve items for payment, pay the items, and record the payment; (c) using prenumbered checks and accounting for all checks, with each check supported by an approved invoice; (d) storing blank checks in a safe or vault with access restricted to authorized personnel, and using a checkwriting machine to imprint amounts on checks; (e) comparing each check with the approved invoice before issuing the check, and making monthly reconciliations of bank and book balances; and (f) after payment, stamping each approved invoice "paid."

5 **Describe the operation of a petty cash fund.** Companies operate a petty cash fund to pay relatively small amounts of cash. They must establish the fund, make payments from the fund, and replenish the fund when the cash in the fund reaches a minimum level.

6 **Indicate the control features of a bank account.** A bank account contributes to good internal control by providing physical controls for the storage of cash. It minimizes the amount of currency that a company must keep on hand, and it creates a double record of a depositor's bank transactions.

7 **Prepare a bank reconciliation.** It is customary to reconcile the balance per books and balance per bank to their adjusted balances. The steps in the reconciling process are to determine deposits in transit, outstanding checks, errors by the depositor or the bank, and unrecorded bank memoranda.

8 **Explain the reporting of cash.** Companies list cash first in the current assets section of the balance sheet. In some cases, they report cash together with cash equivalents. Cash restricted for a special purpose is reported separately as a current asset or as a noncurrent asset, depending on when the cash is expected to be used.

The Navigator

GLOSSARY

WILEY PLUS

Bank reconciliation The process of comparing the bank's balance of an account with the company's balance and explaining any differences to make them agree. (p. 353).

Bank service charge A fee charged by a bank for the use of its services. (p. 355).

Bank statement A monthly statement from the bank that shows the depositor's bank transactions and balances. (p. 355).

Bonding Obtaining insurance protection against misappropriation of assets by employees. (p. 344).

Cash Resources that consist of coins, currency, checks, money orders, and money on hand or on deposit in a bank or similar depository. (p. 346).

Cash equivalents Short-term, highly liquid investments that can be converted to a specific amount of cash. (p. 361).

Check A written order signed by a bank depositor, directing the bank to pay a specified sum of money to a designated recipient. (p. 353).

Compensating balances Minimum cash balances required by a bank in support of bank loans. (p. 361).

Deposits in transit Deposits recorded by the depositor but not yet been recorded by the bank. (p. 357).

Electronic funds transfer (EFT) A disbursement system that uses wire, telephone, or computers to transfer funds from one location to another. (p. 350).

Internal auditors Company employees who continuously evaluate the effectiveness of the company's internal control system. (p. 343).

Internal control All of the related methods and measures adopted within an organization to safeguard its assets and enhance the accuracy and reliability of its accounting records. (p. 338).

NSF check A check that is not paid by a bank because of insufficient funds in a customer's bank account. (p. 356).

Outstanding checks Checks issued and recorded by a company but not yet paid by the bank. (p. 357).

Petty cash fund A cash fund used to pay relatively small amounts. (p. 351).

Restricted cash Cash that must be used for a special purpose. (p. 361).

Sarbanes-Oxley Act Regulations passed by Congress in 2002 to try to reduce unethical corporate behavior. (p. 339).

Voucher An authorization form prepared for each payment in a voucher system. (p. 349).

Voucher system A network of approvals by authorized individuals acting independently to ensure that all disbursements by check are proper. (p. 349).

SELF-STUDY QUESTIONS

WILEY PLUS

Answers are at the end of the chapter.

(SO 1) **1.** An organization uses internal control to enhance the accuracy and reliability of its accounting records and to:
a. safeguard its assets.
b. prevent fraud.
c. produce correct financial statements.
d. deter employee dishonesty.

(SO 2) **2.** The principles of internal control do *not* include:
a. establishment of responsibility.
b. documentation procedures.
c. management responsibility.
d. independent internal verification.

(SO 2) **3.** Physical controls do *not* include:
a. safes and vaults to store cash.
b. independent bank reconciliations.
c. locked warehouses for inventories.
d. bank safety deposit boxes for important papers.

(SO 3) **4.** Which of the following items in a cash drawer at November 30 is *not* cash?
a. Money orders.
b. Coins and currency.
c. A customer check dated December 1.
d. A customer check dated November 28.

(SO 3) **5.** Permitting only designated personnel to handle cash receipts is an application of the principle of:
a. segregation of duties.
b. establishment of responsibility.
c. independent check.
d. other controls.

(SO 4) **6.** The use of prenumbered checks in disbursing cash is an application of the principle of:
a. establishment of responsibility.
b. segregation of duties.
c. physical, mechanical, and electronic controls.
d. documentation procedures.

7. A company writes a check to replenish a \$100 petty cash fund when the fund contains receipts of \$94 and \$3 in cash. In recording the check, the company should: (SO 5)
a. debit Cash Over and Short for \$3.
b. debit Petty Cash for \$94.
c. credit Cash for \$94.
d. credit Petty Cash for \$3.

8. The control features of a bank account do *not* include: (SO 6)
a. having bank auditors verify the correctness of the bank balance per books.
b. minimizing the amount of cash that must be kept on hand.
c. providing a double record of all bank transactions.
d. safeguarding cash by using a bank as a depository.

9. In a bank reconciliation, deposits in transit are: (SO 7)
a. deducted from the book balance.
b. added to the book balance.
c. added to the bank balance.
d. deducted from the bank balance.

10. The reconciling item in a bank reconciliation that will result in an adjusting entry by the depositor is: (SO 7)
a. outstanding checks.
b. deposit in transit.
c. a bank error.
d. bank service charges.

11. Which of the following statements correctly describes the reporting of cash? (SO 8)
a. Cash cannot be combined with cash equivalents.
b. Restricted cash funds may be combined with Cash.
c. Cash is listed first in the current assets section.
d. Restricted cash funds cannot be reported as a current asset.

Go to the book's website, **www.wiley.com/college/weygandt**, for Additional Self-Study questions.

✓ The Navigator

QUESTIONS

1. "Internal control is concerned only with enhancing the accuracy of the accounting records." Do you agree? Explain.
2. What principles of internal control apply to most organizations?
3. At the corner grocery store, all sales clerks make change out of one cash register drawer. Is this a violation of internal control? Why?
4. Meg Lucas is reviewing the principle of segregation of duties. What are the two common applications of this principle?
5. How do documentation procedures contribute to good internal control?
6. What internal control objectives are met by physical, mechanical, and electronic controls?
7. (a) Explain the control principle of independent internal verification. (b) What practices are important in applying this principle?
8. The management of Sewell Company asks you, as the company accountant, to explain (a) the concept of reasonable assurance in internal control and (b) the importance of the human factor in internal control.
9. McCartney Fertilizer Co. owns the following assets at the balance sheet date.

Cash in bank savings account	$ 8,000
Cash on hand	850
Cash refund due from the IRS	1,000
Checking account balance	12,000
Postdated checks	500

What amount should McCartney report as cash in the balance sheet?

10. What principle(s) of internal control is (are) involved in making daily cash counts of over-the-counter receipts?
11. Jacobs Department Stores has just installed new electronic cash registers in its stores. How do cash registers improve internal control over cash receipts?
12. At Hummel Wholesale Company, two mail clerks open all mail receipts. How does this strengthen internal control?
13. "To have maximum effective internal control over cash disbursements, all payments should be made by check." Is this true? Explain.
14. Joe Griswold Company's internal controls over cash disbursements provide for the treasurer to sign checks imprinted by a checkwriting machine in indelible ink after comparing the check with the approved invoice. Identify the internal control principles that are present in these controls.
15. How do the principles of (a) physical, mechanical, and electronic controls and (b) other controls apply to cash disbursements?
16. (a) What is a voucher system? (b) What principles of internal control apply to a voucher system?
17. What is the essential feature of an electronic funds transfer (EFT) procedure?
18. (a) Identify the three activities that pertain to a petty cash fund, and indicate an internal control principle that is applicable to each activity. (b) When are journal entries required in the operation of a petty cash fund?
19. "The use of a bank contributes significantly to good internal control over cash." Is this true? Why or why not?
20. Lori Figgs is confused about the lack of agreement between the cash balance per books and the balance per the bank. Explain the causes for the lack of agreement to Lori, and give an example of each cause.
21. What are the four steps involved in finding differences between the balance per books and balance per bank?
22. Kristen Hope asks your help concerning an NSF check. Explain to Kristen (a) what an NSF check is, (b) how it is treated in a bank reconciliation, and (c) whether it will require an adjusting entry.
23. (a) "Cash equivalents are the same as cash." Do you agree? Explain. (b) How should restricted cash funds be reported on the balance sheet?

BRIEF EXERCISES

WILEY PLUS

Indicate internal control concepts.
(SO 1)

BE8-1 Jim Gaffigan has prepared the following list of statements about internal control.

1. One of the objectives of internal control is to safeguard assets from employee theft, robbery, and unauthorized use.
2. One of the objectives of internal control is to enhance the accuracy and reliability of the accounting records.
3. No laws require U.S. corporations to maintain an adequate system of internal control.

Instructions

Identify each statement as true or false. If false, indicate how to correct the statement.

Explain the importance of internal control.
(SO 1)

BE8-2 Heather Bailiff is the new owner of Ready Parking. She has heard about internal control but is not clear about its importance for her business. Explain to Heather the two purposes of internal control and give her one application of each purpose for Ready Parking.

Identify internal control principles.
(SO 2)

BE8-3 The internal control procedures in Weiser Company provide that:

(a) Employees who have physical custody of assets do not have access to the accounting records.

(b) Each month the assets on hand are compared to the accounting records by an internal auditor.
(c) A prenumbered shipping document is prepared for each shipment of goods to customers.

Identify the principles of internal control that are being followed.

BE8-4 Knobloch Company has the following internal control procedures over cash receipts. Identify the internal control principle that is applicable to each procedure.

Identify the internal control principles applicable to cash receipts.
(SO 3)

1. All over-the-counter receipts are registered on cash registers.
2. All cashiers are bonded.
3. Daily cash counts are made by cashier department supervisors.
4. The duties of receiving cash, recording cash, and custody of cash are assigned to different individuals.
5. Only cashiers may operate cash registers.

BE8-5 Mingenback Company has the following internal control procedures over cash disbursements. Identify the internal control principle that is applicable to each procedure.

Identify the internal control principles applicable to cash disbursements.
(SO 4)

1. Company checks are prenumbered.
2. The bank statement is reconciled monthly by an internal auditor.
3. Blank checks are stored in a safe in the treasurer's office.
4. Only the treasurer or assistant treasurer may sign checks.
5. Check signers are not allowed to record cash disbursement transactions.

Prepare entry to replenish a petty cash fund.
(SO 5)

BE8-6 On March 20, Terrell's petty cash fund of $100 is replenished when the fund contains $7 in cash and receipts for postage $52, freight-out $26, and travel expense $10. Prepare the journal entry to record the replenishment of the petty cash fund.

Identify the control features of a bank account.
(SO 6)

BE8-7 Gary Cunningham is uncertain about the control features of a bank account. Explain the control benefits of **(a)** a check and **(b)** a bank statement.

BE8-8 The following reconciling items are applicable to the bank reconciliation for Stormont Company: (1) outstanding checks, (2) bank debit memorandum for service charge, (3) bank credit memorandum for collecting a note for the depositor, (4) deposits in transit. Indicate how each item should be shown on a bank reconciliation.

Indicate location of reconciling items in a bank reconciliation.
(SO 7)

Identify reconciling items that require adjusting entries.
(SO 7)

BE8-9 Using the data in BE8-8, indicate **(a)** the items that will result in an adjustment to the depositor's records and **(b)** why the other items do not require adjustment.

BE8-10 At July 31, Kuhlmann Company has the following bank information: cash balance per bank $7,420, outstanding checks $762, deposits in transit $1,120, and a bank service charge $20. Determine the adjusted cash balance per bank at July 31.

Prepare partial bank reconciliation.
(SO 7)

BE8-11 At August 31, Felipe Company has a cash balance per books of $8,500 and the following additional data from the bank statement: charge for printing Felipe Company checks $35, interest earned on checking account balance $40, and outstanding checks $800. Determine the adjusted cash balance per books at August 31.

Prepare partial bank reconciliation.
(SO 7)

BE8-12 Quirk Company has the following cash balances: Cash in Bank $15,742, Payroll Bank Account $6,000, and Plant Expansion Fund Cash $25,000. Explain how each balance should be reported on the balance sheet.

Explain the statement presentation of cash balances.
(SO 8)

EXERCISES

WILEY PLUS

E8-1 Sue Merando is the owner of Merando's Pizza. Merando's is operated strictly on a carry-out basis. Customers pick up their orders at a counter where a clerk exchanges the pizza for cash. While at the counter, the customer can see other employees making the pizzas and the large ovens in which the pizzas are baked.

Identify the principles of internal control.
(SO 2)

Instructions

Identify the six principles of internal control and give an example of each principle that you might observe when picking up your pizza. (*Note*: It may not be possible to observe all the principles.)

E8-2 The following control procedures are used at Gonzales Company for over-the-counter cash receipts.

Identify internal control weaknesses over cash receipts and suggest improvements.
(SO 2, 3)

1. To minimize the risk of robbery, cash in excess of $100 is stored in an unlocked attaché case in the stock room until it is deposited in the bank.

2. All over-the-counter receipts are registered by three clerks who use a cash register with a single cash drawer.
3. The company accountant makes the bank deposit and then records the day's receipts.
4. At the end of each day, the total receipts are counted by the cashier on duty and reconciled to the cash register total.
5. Cashiers are experienced; they are not bonded.

Instructions

(a) For each procedure, explain the weakness in internal control, and identify the control principle that is violated.
(b) For each weakness, suggest a change in procedure that will result in good internal control.

Identify internal control weaknesses over cash disbursements and suggest improvements.
(SO 2, 4)

E8-3 The following control procedures are used in Benton's Boutique Shoppe for cash disbursements.

1. The company accountant prepares the bank reconciliation and reports any discrepancies to the owner.
2. The store manager personally approves all payments before signing and issuing checks.
3. Each week, Benton leaves 100 company checks in an unmarked envelope on a shelf behind the cash register.
4. After payment, bills are filed in a paid invoice folder.
5. The company checks are unnumbered.

Instructions

(a) For each procedure, explain the weakness in internal control, and identify the internal control principle that is violated.
(b) For each weakness, suggest a change in the procedure that will result in good internal control.

Identify internal control weaknesses for cash disbursements and suggest improvements.
(SO 4)

E8-4 At Hutchingson Company, checks are not prenumbered because both the puchasing agent and the treasurer are authorized to issue checks. Each signer has access to unissued checks kept in an unlocked file cabinet. The purchasing agent pays all bills pertaining to goods purchased for resale. Prior to payment, the purchasing agent determines that the goods have been received and verifies the mathematical accuracy of the vendor's invoice. After payment, the invoice is filed by vendor, and the purchasing agent records the payment in the cash disbursements journal. The treasurer pays all other bills following approval by authorized employees. After payment, the treasurer stamps all bills PAID, files them by payment date, and records the checks in the cash disbursements journal. Hutchingson Company maintains one checking account that is reconciled by the treasurer.

Instructions

(a) List the weaknesses in internal control over cash disbursements.
(b) Write a memo to the company treasurer indicating your recommendations for improvement.

Indicate whether procedure is good or weak internal control.
(SO 2, 3, 4)

E8-5 Listed below are five procedures followed by The Beat Company.

1. Several individuals operate the cash register using the same register drawer.
2. A monthly bank reconciliation is prepared by someone who has no other cash responsibilities.
3. Ellen May writes checks and also records cash payment journal entries.
4. One individual orders inventory, while a different individual authorizes payments.
5. Unnumbered sales invoices from credit sales are forwarded to the accounting department every four weeks for recording.

Instructions

Indicate whether each procedure is an example of good internal control or of weak internal control. If it is an example of good internal control, indicate which internal control principle is being followed. If it is an example of weak internal control, indicate which internal control principle is violated. Use the table below.

Procedure	IC Good or Weak?	Related Internal Control Principle
1.		
2.		
3.		
4.		
5.		

E8-6 Listed below are five procedures followed by Collins Company.

Indicate whether procedure is good or weak internal control.
(SO 2, 3, 4)

1. Employees are required to take vacations.
2. Any member of the sales department can approve credit sales.
3. Jethro Bodine ships goods to customers, bills customers, and receives payment from customers.
4. Total cash receipts are compared to bank deposits daily by someone who has no other cash responsibilities.
5. Time clocks are used for recording time worked by employees.

Instructions

Indicate whether each procedure is an example of good internal control or of weak internal control. If it is an example of good internal control, indicate which internal control principle is being followed. If it is an example of weak internal control, indicate which internal control principle is violated. Use the table below.

Procedure	IC Good or Weak?	Related Internal Control Principle
1.		
2.		
3.		
4.		
5.		

E8-7 James Hughes Company established a petty cash fund on May 1, cashing a check for $100. The company reimbursed the fund on June 1 and July 1 with the following results.

Prepare journal entries for a petty cash fund.
(SO 5)

June 1: Cash in fund $2.75. Receipts: delivery expense $31.25; postage expense $39.00; and miscellaneous expense $25.00.

July 1: Cash in fund $3.25. Receipts: delivery expense $21.00; entertainment expense $51.00; and miscellaneous expense $24.75.

On July 10, James Hughes increased the fund from $100 to $150.

Instructions

Prepare journal entries for James Hughes Company for May 1, June 1, July 1, and July 10.

E8-8 Lincolnville Company uses an imprest petty cash system. The fund was established on March 1 with a balance of $100. During March the following petty cash receipts were found in the petty cash box.

Prepare journal entries for a petty cash fund.
(SO 5)

Date	Receipt No.	For	Amount
3/5	1	Stamp Inventory	$39
7	2	Freight-out	21
9	3	Miscellaneous Expense	6
11	4	Travel Expense	24
14	5	Miscellaneous Expense	5

The fund was replenished on March 15 when the fund contained $3 in cash. On March 20, the amount in the fund was increased to $150.

Instructions

Journalize the entries in March that pertain to the operation of the petty cash fund.

E8-9 Anna Pelo is unable to reconcile the bank balance at January 31. Anna's reconciliation is as follows.

Prepare bank reconciliation and adjusting entries.
(SO 7)

Cash balance per bank	$3,560.20
Add: NSF check	690.00
Less: Bank service charge	25.00
Adjusted balance per bank	$4,225.20
Cash balance per books	$3,875.20
Less: Deposits in transit	530.00
Add: Outstanding checks	930.00
Adjusted balance per books	$4,275.20

Instructions

(a) Prepare a correct bank reconciliation.
(b) Journalize the entries required by the reconciliation.

Determine outstanding checks.
(SO 7)

E8-10 On April 30, the bank reconciliation of Galena Company shows three outstanding checks: no. 254, $650, no. 255, $820, and no. 257, $410. The May bank statement and the May cash payments journal show the following.

Bank Statement		
Checks Paid		
Date	**Check No.**	**Amount**
5/4	254	650
5/2	257	410
5/17	258	159
5/12	259	275
5/20	261	500
5/29	263	480
5/30	262	750

Cash Payments Journal		
Checks Issued		
Date	**Check No.**	**Amount**
5/2	258	159
5/5	259	275
5/10	260	890
5/15	261	500
5/22	262	750
5/24	263	480
5/29	264	560

Instructions

Using step 2 in the reconciliation procedure, list the outstanding checks at May 31.

Prepare bank reconciliation and adjusting entries.
(SO 7)

E8-11 The following information pertains to Family Video Company.

1. Cash balance per bank, July 31, $7,263.
2. July bank service charge not recorded by the depositor $28.
3. Cash balance per books, July 31, $7,284.
4. Deposits in transit, July 31, $1,500.
5. Bank collected $900 note for Family in July, plus interest $36, less fee $20. The collection has not been recorded by Family, and no interest has been accrued.
6. Outstanding checks, July 31, $591.

Instructions

(a) Prepare a bank reconciliation at July 31.
(b) Journalize the adjusting entries at July 31 on the books of Family Video Company.

Prepare bank reconciliation and adjusting entries.
(SO 7)

E8-12 The information below relates to the Cash account in the ledger of Robertson Company.

Balance September 1—$17,150; Cash deposited—$64,000.
Balance September 30—$17,404; Checks written—$63,746.

The September bank statement shows a balance of $16,422 on September 30 and the following memoranda.

Credits		Debits	
Collection of $1,500 note plus interest $30	$1,530	NSF check: J. E. Hoover	$425
Interest earned on checking account	$45	Safety deposit box rent	$65

At September 30, deposits in transit were $4,450, and outstanding checks totaled $2,383.

Instructions

(a) Prepare the bank reconciliation at September 30.
(b) Prepare the adjusting entries at September 30, assuming (1) the NSF check was from a customer on account, and (2) no interest had been accrued on the note.

Compute deposits in transit and outstanding checks for two bank reconciliations.
(SO 7)

E8-13 The cash records of Givens Company show the following four situations.

1. The June 30 bank reconciliation indicated that deposits in transit total $720. During July the general ledger account Cash shows deposits of $15,750, but the bank statement indicates that only $15,600 in deposits were received during the month.
2. The June 30 bank reconciliation also reported outstanding checks of $680. During the month of July, Givens Company books show that $17,200 of checks were issued. The bank statement showed that $16,400 of checks cleared the bank in July.

3. In September, deposits per the bank statement totaled $26,700, deposits per books were $25,400, and deposits in transit at September 30 were $2,100.
4. In September, cash disbursements per books were $23,700, checks clearing the bank were $25,000, and outstanding checks at September 30 were $2,100.

There were no bank debit or credit memoranda. No errors were made by either the bank or Givens Company.

Instructions

Answer the following questions.

(a) In situation (1), what were the deposits in transit at July 31?
(b) In situation (2), what were the outstanding checks at July 31?
(c) In situation (3), what were the deposits in transit at August 31?
(d) In situation (4), what were the outstanding checks at August 31?

Show presentation of cash in financial statements.

(SO 8)

E8-14 Lipkus Company has recorded the following items in its financial records.

Cash in bank	$ 47,000
Cash in plant expansion fund	100,000
Cash on hand	12,000
Highly liquid investments	34,000
Petty cash	500
Receivables from customers	89,000
Stock investments	61,000

The cash in bank is subject to a compensating balance of $5,000. The highly liquid investments had maturities of 3 months or less when they were purchased. The stock investments will be sold in the next 6 to 12 months. The plant expansion project will begin in 3 years.

Instructions

(a) What amount should Lipkus report as "Cash and cash equivalents" on its balance sheet?
(b) Where should the items not included in part (a) be reported on the balance sheet?
(c) What disclosures should Lipkus make in its financial statements concerning "cash and cash equivalents"?

EXERCISES: SET B

Visit the book's website at **www.wiley.com/college/weygandt**, and choose the Student Companion site, to access Exercise Set B.

PROBLEMS: SET A

Identify internal control principles over cash disbursements.

(SO 2, 4)

P8-1A Luby Office Supply Company recently changed its system of internal control over cash disbursements. The system includes the following features.

Instead of being unnumbered and manually prepared, all checks must now be prenumbered and written by using the new checkwriting machine purchased by the company. Before a check can be issued, each invoice must have the approval of Sally Morgan, the purchasing agent, and John Countryman, the receiving department supervisor. Checks must be signed by either Ann Lynn, the treasurer, or Bob Skabo, the assistant treasurer. Before signing a check, the signer is expected to compare the amount of the check with the amount on the invoice.

After signing a check, the signer stamps the invoice PAID and inserts within the stamp, the date, check number, and amount of the check. The "paid" invoice is then sent to the accounting department for recording.

Blank checks are stored in a safe in the treasurer's office. The combination to the safe is known only by the treasurer and assistant treasurer. Each month, the bank statement is reconciled with the bank balance per books by the assistant chief accountant.

Instructions

Identify the internal control principles and their application to cash disbursements of Luby Office Supply Company.

Journalize and post petty cash fund transactions.

(SO 5)

GLS Peachtree

P8-2A Winningham Company maintains a petty cash fund for small expenditures. The following transactions occurred over a 2-month period.

July 1 Established petty cash fund by writing a check on Cubs Bank for $200.

15 Replenished the petty cash fund by writing a check for $196.00. On this date the fund consisted of $4.00 in cash and the following petty cash receipts: freight-out $94.00, postage expense $42.40, entertainment expense $46.60, and miscellaneous expense $11.20.

31 Replenished the petty cash fund by writing a check for $192.00. At this date, the fund consisted of $8.00 in cash and the following petty cash receipts: freight-out $82.10, charitable contributions expense $45.00, postage expense $25.50, and miscellaneous expense $39.40.

Aug. 15 Replenished the petty cash fund by writing a check for $187.00. On this date, the fund consisted of $13.00 in cash and the following petty cash receipts: freight-out $75.60, entertainment expense $43.00, postage expense $33.00, and miscellaneous expense $37.00.

16 Increased the amount of the petty cash fund to $300 by writing a check for $100.

31 Replenished petty cash fund by writing a check for $284.00. On this date, the fund consisted of $16 in cash and the following petty cash receipts: postage expense $140.00, travel expense $95.60, and freight-out $47.10.

Instructions

(a) July 15, Cash short $1.80

(b) Aug. 31 balance $300

(a) Journalize the petty cash transactions.
(b) Post to the Petty Cash account.
(c) What internal control features exist in a petty cash fund?

Prepare a bank reconciliation and adjusting entries.

(SO 7)

P8-3A On May 31, 2008, James Logan Company had a cash balance per books of $6,781.50. The bank statement from Farmers State Bank on that date showed a balance of $6,404.60. A comparison of the statement with the cash account revealed the following facts.

1. The statement included a debit memo of $40 for the printing of additional company checks.
2. Cash sales of $836.15 on May 12 were deposited in the bank. The cash receipts journal entry and the deposit slip were incorrectly made for $886.15. The bank credited Logan Company for the correct amount.
3. Outstanding checks at May 31 totaled $576.25. Deposits in transit were $1,916.15.
4. On May 18, the company issued check No. 1181 for $685 to Barry Trest, on account. The check, which cleared the bank in May, was incorrectly journalized and posted by Logan Company for $658.
5. A $2,500 note receivable was collected by the bank for Logan Company on May 31 plus $80 interest. The bank charged a collection fee of $20. No interest has been accrued on the note.
6. Included with the cancelled checks was a check issued by Bridgetown Company to Tom Lujak for $800 that was incorrectly charged to Logan Company by the bank.
7. On May 31, the bank statement showed an NSF charge of $680 for a check issued by Sandy Grifton, a customer, to Logan Company on account.

Instructions

(a) Adjusted cash balance per bank $8,544.50

(a) Prepare the bank reconciliation at May 31, 2008.
(b) Prepare the necessary adjusting entries for Logan Company at May 31, 2008.

Prepare a bank reconciliation and adjusting entries from detailed data.

(SO 7)

P8-4A The bank portion of the bank reconciliation for Backhaus Company at November 30, 2008, was as follows.

BACKHAUS COMPANY
Bank Reconciliation
November 30, 2008

Cash balance per bank		$14,367.90
Add: Deposits in transit		2,530.20
		16,898.10
Less: Outstanding checks		
Check Number	Check Amount	
3451	$2,260.40	
3470	720.10	
3471	844.50	
3472	1,426.80	
3474	1,050.00	6,301.80
Adjusted cash balance per bank		$10,596.30

The adjusted cash balance per bank agreed with the cash balance per books at November 30.

The December bank statement showed the following checks and deposits.

Bank Statement

Checks			Deposits	
Date	**Number**	**Amount**	**Date**	**Amount**
12-1	3451	$ 2,260.40	12-1	$ 2,530.20
12-2	3471	844.50	12-4	1,211.60
12-7	3472	1,426.80	12-8	2,365.10
12-4	3475	1,640.70	12-16	2,672.70
12-8	3476	1,300.00	12-21	2,945.00
12-10	3477	2,130.00	12-26	2,567.30
12-15	3479	3,080.00	12-29	2,836.00
12-27	3480	600.00	12-30	1,025.00
12-30	3482	475.50	Total	$18,152.90
12-29	3483	1,140.00		
12-31	3485	540.80		
	Total	$15,438.70		

The cash records per books for December showed the following.

Cash Payments Journal

Date	Number	Amount	Date	Number	Amount
12-1	3475	$1,640.70	12-20	3482	$ 475.50
12-2	3476	1,300.00	12-22	3483	1,140.00
12-2	3477	2,130.00	12-23	3484	798.00
12-4	3478	621.30	12-24	3485	450.80
12-8	3479	3,080.00	12-30	3486	1,889.50
12-10	3480	600.00	Total		$14,933.20
12-17	3481	807.40			

Cash Receipts Journal

Date	Amount
12-3	$ 1,211.60
12-7	2,365.10
12-15	2,672.70
12-20	2,954.00
12-25	2,567.30
12-28	2,836.00
12-30	1,025.00
12-31	1,690.40
Total	$17,322.10

The bank statement contained two memoranda:

1. A credit of $4,145 for the collection of a $4,000 note for Backhaus Company plus interest of $160 and less a collection fee of $15. Backhaus Company has not accrued any interest on the note.
2. A debit of $572.80 for an NSF check written by D. Chagnon, a customer. At December 31, the check had not been redeposited in the bank.

At December 31 the cash balance per books was $12,485.20, and the cash balance per the bank statement was $20,154.30. The bank did not make any errors, but two errors were made by Backhaus Company.

Instructions

(a) Using the four steps in the reconciliation procedure, prepare a bank reconciliation at December 31.

(a) Adjusted balance per books $15,958.40

(b) Prepare the adjusting entries based on the reconciliation. (*Hint*: The correction of any errors pertaining to recording checks should be made to Accounts Payable. The correction of any errors relating to recording cash receipts should be made to Accounts Receivable.)

Prepare a bank reconciliation and adjusting entries.

(SO 7)

Peachtree

P8-5A Haverman Company maintains a checking account at the Commerce Bank. At July 31, selected data from the ledger balance and the bank statement are shown on page 374.

	Cash in Bank	
	Per Books	**Per Bank**
Balance, July 1	$17,600	$16,800
July receipts	81,400	
July credits		82,470
July disbursements	77,150	
July debits		74,756
Balance, July 31	$21,850	$24,514

Analysis of the bank data reveals that the credits consist of $79,000 of July deposits and a credit memorandum of $3,470 for the collection of a $3,400 note plus interest revenue of $70. The July debits per bank consist of checks cleared $74,700 and a debit memorandum of $56 for printing additional company checks.

You also discover the following errors involving July checks: (1) A check for $230 to a creditor on account that cleared the bank in July was journalized and posted as $320. (2) A salary check to an employee for $255 was recorded by the bank for $155.

The June 30 bank reconciliation contained only two reconciling items: deposits in transit $7,000 and outstanding checks of $6,200.

(a) Adjusted balance per books $25,354

Instructions

(a) Prepare a bank reconciliation at July 31.

(b) Journalize the adjusting entries to be made by Haverman Company at July 31, 2008. Assume that interest on the note has not been accrued.

Identify internal control weaknesses in cash receipts and cash disbursements.

(SO 2, 3, 4)

P8-6A Emporia Middle School wants to raise money for a new sound system for its auditorium. The primary fund-raising event is a dance at which the famous disc jockey Obnoxious Ed will play classic and not-so-classic dance tunes. Tom Wickman, the music and theater instructor, has been given the responsibility for coordinating the fund-raising efforts. This is Tom's first experience with fund-raising. He decides to put the eighth-grade choir in charge of the event; he will be a relatively passive observer.

Tom had 500 unnumbered tickets printed for the dance. He left the tickets in a box on his desk and told the choir students to take as many tickets as they thought they could sell for $5 each. In order to ensure that no extra tickets would be floating around, he told them to dispose of any unsold tickets. When the students received payment for the tickets, they were to bring the cash back to Tom, and he would put it in a locked box in his desk drawer.

Some of the students were responsible for decorating the gymnasium for the dance. Tom gave each of them a key to the money box and told them that if they took money out to purchase materials, they should put a note in the box saying how much they took and what it was used for. After 2 weeks the money box appeared to be getting full, so Tom asked Luke Gilmor to count the money, prepare a deposit slip, and deposit the money in a bank account Tom had opened.

The day of the dance, Tom wrote a check from the account to pay the DJ. Obnoxious Ed, however, said that he accepted only cash and did not give receipts. So Tom took $200 out of the cash box and gave it to Ed. At the dance Tom had Mel Harris working at the entrance to the gymnasium, collecting tickets from students and selling tickets to those who had not prepurchased them. Tom estimated that 400 students attended the dance.

The following day Tom closed out the bank account, which had $250 in it, and gave that amount plus the $180 in the cash box to Principal Foran. Principal Foran seemed surprised that, after generating roughly $2,000 in sales, the dance netted only $430 in cash. Tom did not know how to respond.

Instructions

Identify as many internal control weaknesses as you can in this scenario, and suggest how each could be addressed.

PROBLEMS: SET B

Identify internal control weaknesses over cash receipts.

(SO 2, 3)

P8-1B Starr Theater is located in the Zurbrugg Mall. A cashier's booth is located near the entrance to the theater. Two cashiers are employed. One works from 1–5 P.M., the other from 5–9 P.M. Each cashier is bonded. The cashiers receive cash from customers and operate a machine that ejects serially numbered tickets. The rolls of tickets are inserted and locked into the machine by the theater manager at the beginning of each cashier's shift.

After purchasing a ticket, the customer takes the ticket to an usher stationed at the entrance of the theater lobby some 60 feet from the cashier's booth. The usher tears the ticket in half, admits the customer, and returns the ticket stub to the customer. The other half of the ticket is dropped into a locked box by the usher.

At the end of each cashier's shift, the theater manager removes the ticket rolls from the machine and makes a cash count. The cash count sheet is initialed by the cashier. At the end of the day, the manager deposits the receipts in total in a bank night deposit vault located in the mall. The manager also sends copies of the deposit slip and the initialed cash count sheets to the theater company treasurer for verification and to the company's accounting department. Receipts from the first shift are stored in a safe located in the manager's office.

Instructions

(a) Identify the internal control principles and their application to the cash receipts transactions of the Starr Theater.

(b) If the usher and cashier decide to collaborate to misappropriate cash, what actions might they take?

Journalize and post petty cash fund transactions.

(SO 5)

GLS

P8-2B Cushenberry Company maintains a petty cash fund for small expenditures. The following transactions occurred over a 2-month period.

July 1 Established petty cash fund by writing a check on Landmark Bank for $200.

15 Replenished the petty cash fund by writing a check for $194.30. On this date the fund consisted of $5.70 in cash and the following petty cash receipts: freight-out $94.00, postage expense $42.40, entertainment expense $45.90, and miscellaneous expense $10.70.

31 Replenished the petty cash fund by writing a check for $192.00. At this date, the fund consisted of $8.00 in cash and the following petty cash receipts: freight-out $82.10, charitable contributions expense $30.00, postage expense $47.80, and miscellaneous expense $32.10.

Aug. 15 Replenished the petty cash fund by writing a check for $188.00. On this date, the fund consisted of $12.00 in cash and the following petty cash receipts: freight-out $74.40, entertainment expense $41.50, postage expense $33.00, and miscellaneous expense $36.00.

16 Increased the amount of the petty cash fund to $300 by writing a check for $100.

31 Replenished petty cash fund by writing a check for $283.00. On this date, the fund consisted of $17 in cash and the following petty cash receipts: postage expense $145.00, entertainment expense $90.60, and freight-out $46.00.

Instructions

(a) Journalize the petty cash transactions.

(b) Post to the Petty Cash account.

(c) What internal control features exist in a petty cash fund?

(a) July 15 Cash short $1.30
(b) Aug. 31 balance $300

Prepare a bank reconciliation and adjusting entries.

(SO 7)

P8-3B Flint Hills Genetics Company of Lawrence, Kansas, spreads herbicides and applies liquid fertilizer for local farmers. On May 31, 2008, the company's cash account per its general ledger showed the following balance.

CASH NO. 101

Date	Explanation	Ref.	Debit	Credit	Balance
May 31	Balance				6,781.50

The bank statement from Lawrence State Bank on that date showed the following balance.

LAWRENCE STATE BANK

Checks and Debits	Deposits and Credits	Daily Balance
XXX	XXX	5/31 6,804.60

A comparison of the details on the bank statement with the details in the cash account revealed the following facts.

1. The statement included a debit memo of $40 for the printing of additional company checks.
2. Cash sales of $836.15 on May 12 were deposited in the bank. The cash receipts journal entry and the deposit slip were incorrectly made for $846.15. The bank credited Flint Hills Genetics Company for the correct amount.

3. Outstanding checks at May 31 totaled $515.25, and deposits in transit were $936.15.
4. On May 18, the company issued check no. 1181 for $685 to M. Datz, on account. The check, which cleared the bank in May, was incorrectly journalized and posted by Flint Hills Genetics Company for $658.
5. A $2,000 note receivable was collected by the bank for Flint Hills Genetics Company on May 31 plus $80 interest. The bank charged a collection fee of $25. No interest has been accrued on the note.
6. Included with the cancelled checks was a check issued by Bohr Company to Fred Mertz for $600 that was incorrectly charged to Flint Hills Genetics Company by the bank.
7. On May 31, the bank statement showed an NSF charge of $934 for a check issued by Tyler Gricius, a customer, to Flint Hills Genetics Company on account.

Instructions

(a) Adj. cash bal. $7,825.50

(a) Prepare the bank reconciliation at May 31, 2008.
(b) Prepare the necessary adjusting entries for Flint Hills Genetics Company at May 31, 2008.

Prepare a bank reconciliation and adjusting entries from detailed data.

(SO 7)

P8-4B The bank portion of the bank reconciliation for Conlin Company at October 31, 2008 was as follows.

CONLIN COMPANY
Bank Reconciliation
October 31, 2008

Cash balance per bank			$11,444.70
Add: Deposits in transit			1,530.20
			12,974.90
Less: Outstanding checks			
	Check Number	Check Amount	
	2451	$1,260.40	
	2470	720.10	
	2471	844.50	
	2472	503.60	
	2474	1,050.00	4,378.60
Adjusted cash balance per bank			$ 8,596.30

The adjusted cash balance per bank agreed with the cash balance per books at October 31.
The November bank statement showed the following checks and deposits:

Bank Statement

Checks			Deposits	
Date	**Number**	**Amount**	**Date**	**Amount**
11-1	2470	$ 720.10	11-1	$ 1,530.20
11-2	2471	844.50	11-4	1,211.60
11-5	2474	1,050.00	11-8	990.10
11-4	2475	1,640.70	11-13	2,575.00
11-8	2476	2,830.00	11-18	1,472.70
11-10	2477	600.00	11-21	2,945.00
11-15	2479	1,750.00	11-25	2,567.30
11-18	2480	1,330.00	11-28	1,650.00
11-27	2481	695.40	11-30	1,186.00
11-30	2483	575.50	Total	$16,127.90
11-29	2486	900.00		
	Total	$12,936.20		

The cash records per books for November showed the following.

Cash Payments Journal					
Date	Number	Amount	Date	Number	Amount
11-1	2475	$1,640.70	11-20	2483	$ 575.50
11-2	2476	2,830.00	11-22	2484	829.50
11-2	2477	600.00	11-23	2485	974.80
11-4	2478	538.20	11-24	2486	900.00
11-8	2479	1,570.00	11-29	2487	398.00
11-10	2480	1,330.00	11-30	2488	1,200.00
11-15	2481	695.40	Total		$14,694.10
11-18	2482	612.00			

Cash Receipts Journal	
Date	Amount
11-3	$ 1,211.60
11-7	990.10
11-12	2,575.00
11-17	1,472.70
11-20	2,954.00
11-24	2,567.30
11-27	1,650.00
11-29	1,186.00
11-30	2,338.00
Total	$16,944.70

The bank statement contained two bank memoranda:

1. A credit of $2,505.00 for the collection of a $2,400 note for Conlin Company plus interest of $120 and less a collection fee of $15. Conlin Company has not accrued any interest on the note.
2. A debit for the printing of additional company checks $72.

At November 30, the cash balance per books was $10,846.90, and the cash balance per the bank statement was $17,069.40. The bank did not make any errors, but two errors were made by Conlin Company.

Instructions

(a) Using the four steps in the reconciliation procedure described on page 357, prepare a bank reconciliation at November 30.

(a) Adjusted cash balance per bank $13,090.90

(b) Prepare the adjusting entries based on the reconciliation. (*Hint*: The correction of any errors pertaining to recording checks should be made to Accounts Payable. The correction of any errors relating to recording cash receipts should be made to Accounts Receivable).

Prepare a bank reconciliation and adjusting entries.

(SO 7)

P8-5B Baumgardner Company's bank statement from Last National Bank at August 31, 2008, shows the following information.

Balance, August 1	$17,400	Bank credit memoranda:	
August deposits	73,110	Collection of note receivable plus $130 interest	$6,930
Checks cleared in August	71,500	Interest earned	32
Balance, August 31	25,932	Bank debit memorandum:	
		Safety deposit box rent	40

A summary of the Cash account in the ledger for August shows: Balance, August 1, $16,900; receipts $77,000; disbursements $73,570; and balance, August 31, $20,330. Analysis reveals that the only reconciling items on the July 31 bank reconciliation were a deposit in transit for $4,000 and outstanding checks of $4,500. The deposit in transit was the first deposit recorded by the bank in August. In addition, you determine that there were two errors involving company checks drawn in August: (1) A check for $240 to a creditor on account that cleared the bank in August was journalized and posted for $420. (2) A salary check to an employee for $275 was recorded by the bank for $278.

Instructions

(a) Prepare a bank reconciliation at August 31.

(a) Adjusted balance per books $27,432

(b) Journalize the adjusting entries to be made by Baumgardner Company at August 31. Assume that interest on the note has not been accrued by the company.

Prepare comprehensive bank reconciliation with theft and internal control deficiencies.

(SO 2, 3, 4, 7)

P8-6B Richardson Company is a very profitable small business. It has not, however, given much consideration to internal control. For example, in an attempt to keep clerical and office expenses to a minimum, the company has combined the jobs of cashier and bookkeeper. As a result, Jake Stickyfingers handles all cash receipts, keeps the accounting records, and prepares the monthly bank reconciliations.

The balance per the bank statement on October 31, 2008, was $18,180. Outstanding checks were: no. 62 for $126.75, no. 183 for $150, no. 284 for $253.25, no. 862 for $190.71, no. 863 for

$226.80, and no. 864 for $165.28. Included with the statement was a credit memorandum of $400 indicating the collection of a note receivable for Richardson Company by the bank on October 25. This memorandum has not been recorded by Richardson Company.

The company's ledger showed one cash account with a balance of $21,892.72. The balance included undeposited cash on hand. Because of the lack of internal controls, Stickyfingers took for personal use all of the undeposited receipts in excess of $3,795.51. He then prepared the following bank reconciliation in an effort to conceal his theft of cash.

BANK RECONCILIATION

Cash balance per books, October 31		$21,892.72
Add: Outstanding checks		
No. 862	$190.71	
No. 863	226.80	
No. 864	165.28	482.79
		22,375.51
Less: Undeposited receipts		3,795.51
Unadjusted balance per bank, October 31		18,580.00
Less: Bank credit memorandum		400.00
Cash balance per bank statement, October 31		$18,180.00

Instructions

(a) Adjusted balance per books $20,862.72

(a) Prepare a correct bank reconciliation. (*Hint*: Deduct the amount of the theft from the adjusted balance per books.)

(b) Indicate the three ways that Stickyfingers attempted to conceal the theft and the dollar amount pertaining to each method.

(c) What principles of internal control were violated in this case?

PROBLEMS: SET C

Visit the book's website at **www.wiley.com/college/weygandt**, and choose the Student Companion site, to access Problem Set C.

CONTINUING COOKIE CHRONICLE

(Note: This is a continuation of the Cookie Chronicle from Chapters 1 through 6.)

CCC8 Part 1 Natalie is struggling to keep up with the recording of her accounting transactions. She is spending a lot of time marketing and selling mixers and giving her cookie classes. Her friend John is an accounting student who runs his own accounting service. He has asked Natalie if she would like to have him do her accounting. John and Natalie meet and discuss her business.

Part 2 Natalie decides that she cannot afford to hire John to do her accounting. One way that she can ensure that her cash account does not have any errors and is accurate and up-to-date is to prepare a bank reconciliation at the end of each month. Natalie would like you to help her.

Go to the book's website, www.wiley.com/college/weygandt, to see the completion of this problem.

BROADENING YOUR PERSPECTIVE

FINANCIAL REPORTING AND ANALYSIS

Financial Reporting Problem

PepsiCo, Inc.

BYP8-1 The financial statements of PepsiCo, Inc, are presented in Appendix A at the end of this textbook.

Instructions

(a) What comments, if any, are made about cash in the report of the independent auditors?
(b) What data about cash and cash equivalents are shown in the consolidated balance sheet?
(c) In its notes to Consolidated Financial Statements, how does PepsiCo define cash equivalents?
(d) In management's letter that assumes "Responsibility for Financial Reporting," what does PepsiCo's management say about internal control? (See page A3 in Appendix A of the back of the book.)

Comparative Analysis Problem

PepsiCo, Inc. vs. The Coca-Cola Company

BYP8-2 PepsiCo's financial statements are presented in Appendix A. Coca-Cola's financial statements are presented in Appendix B.

Instructions

(a) Based on the information contained in these financial statements, determine each of the following for each company:
   (1) Cash and cash equivalents balance at December 31, 2005, for PepsiCo and at December 31, 2005, for Coca-Cola.
   (2) Increase (decrease) in cash and cash equivalents from 2004 to 2005.
   (3) Cash provided by operating activities during the year ended December 2005 (from statement of cash flows).
(b) What conclusions concerning the management of cash can be drawn from these data?

Exploring the Web

BYP8-3 All organizations should have systems of internal control. Universities are no exception. This site discusses the basics of internal control in a university setting.

Address: **www.bc.edu/offices/audit/controls**, or go to **www.wiley.com/college/weygandt**

Steps: Go to the site shown above.

Instructions

The front page of this site provides links to pages that answer six critical questions. Use these links to answer the following questions.

(a) In a university setting who has responsibility for evaluating the adequacy of the system of internal control?
(b) What do reconciliations ensure in the university setting? Who should review the reconciliation?
(c) What are some examples of physical controls?
(d) What are two ways to accomplish inventory counts?

CRITICAL THINKING

Decision Making Across the Organization

BYP8-4 The board of trustees of a local church is concerned about the internal accounting controls for the offering collections made at weekly services. The trustees ask you to serve on a three-person audit team with the internal auditor of a local college and a CPA who has just joined the church.

At a meeting of the audit team and the board of trustees you learn the following.

1. The church's board of trustees has delegated responsibility for the financial management and audit of the financial records to the finance committee. This group prepares the annual budget and approves major disbursements. It is not involved in collections or record keeping. No audit has been made in recent years because the same trusted employee has kept church records and served as financial secretary for 15 years. The church does not carry any fidelity insurance.
2. The collection at the weekly service is taken by a team of ushers who volunteer to serve one month. The ushers take the collection plates to a basement office at the rear of the church. They hand their plates to the head usher and return to the church service. After all plates have been turned in, the head usher counts the cash received. The head usher then places

the cash in the church safe along with a notation of the amount counted. The head usher volunteers to serve for 3 months.

3. The next morning the financial secretary opens the safe and recounts the collection. The secretary withholds $150–$200 in cash, depending on the cash expenditures expected for the week, and deposits the remainder of the collections in the bank. To facilitate the deposit, church members who contribute by check are asked to make their checks payable to "Cash."
4. Each month, the financial secretary reconciles the bank statement and submits a copy of the reconciliation to the board of trustees. The reconciliations have rarely contained any bank errors and have never shown any errors per books.

Instructions

With the class divided into groups, answer the following.

(a) Indicate the weaknesses in internal accounting control over the handling of collections.

(b) List the improvements in internal control procedures that you plan to make at the next meeting of the audit team for (1) the ushers, (2) the head usher, (3) the financial secretary, and (4) the finance committee.

(c) What church policies should be changed to improve internal control?

Communication Activity

BYP8-5 As a new auditor for the CPA firm of Croix, Marais, and Kale, you have been assigned to review the internal controls over mail cash receipts of Manhattan Company. Your review reveals the following: Checks are promptly endorsed "For Deposit Only," but no list of the checks is prepared by the person opening the mail. The mail is opened either by the cashier or by the employee who maintains the accounts receivable records. Mail receipts are deposited in the bank weekly by the cashier.

Instructions

Write a letter to Jerry Mays, owner of the Manhattan Company, explaining the weaknesses in internal control and your recommendations for improving the system.

Ethics Case

BYP8-6 You are the assistant controller in charge of general ledger accounting at Riverside Bottling Company. Your company has a large loan from an insurance company. The loan agreement requires that the company's cash account balance be maintained at $200,000 or more, as reported monthly.

At June 30 the cash balance is $80,000, which you report to Gena Schmitt, the financial vice president. Gena excitedly instructs you to keep the cash receipts book open for one additional day for purposes of the June 30 report to the insurance company. Gena says, "If we don't get that cash balance over $200,000, we'll default on our loan agreement. They could close us down, put us all out of our jobs!" Gena continues, "I talked to Oconto Distributors (one of Riverside's largest customers) this morning. They said they sent us a check for $150,000 yesterday. We should receive it tomorrow. If we include just that one check in our cash balance, we'll be in the clear. It's in the mail!"

Instructions

(a) Who will suffer negative effects if you do not comply with Gena Schmitt's instructions? Who will suffer if you do comply?

(b) What are the ethical considerations in this case?

(c) What alternatives do you have?

* "All About You" Activity

BYP8-7 The **All About You** feature in this chapter (page 362) indicates potential security risks that may arise from your personal computer. It is important to keep in mind, however, that there are also many other ways that your identity can be stolen other than from your computer. The federal government provides many resources to help protect you from identity thieves.

Instructions

Go to **http://onguardonline.gov/idtheft.html**, and click on ID Theft Faceoff. Complete the quiz provided there.

Answers to Insight and Accounting Across the Organization Questions

p. 341 This Was a Penalty to Take Seriously

Q: Which principle of internal control was implemented in ancient Egypt?

A: *The system in ancient Egypt used the principle of independent internal verification.*

Q: Who do you think investors today expect to detect and prevent fraud?

A: *Today, investors probably expect independent auditors to detect and prevent fraud. In reality, management is assigned this important responsibility. Auditors attest to compliance with GAAP and specifically state that financial statements and the system of internal control are management's responsibility.*

p. 342 SOX Boosts the Role of Human Resources

Q: Why would unsupervised employees or employees who report to each other represent potential internal control threats?

A. *An unsupervised employee may have a fraudulent job (or may even be a fictitious person—e.g., a person drawing a paycheck without working). Or, if two employees supervise each other, there is no real separation of duties, and they can conspire to defraud the company.*

p. 344 Poor Internal Control Can Hammer Stock Price

Q. Why would a company's stock price fall if it reports deficiencies in its internal controls?

A. *Internal controls protect against employee theft, but they also provide protection against manipulation of accounting numbers. If a company has poor internal controls, investors will have less confidence that its financial statements are accurate. As a consequence, its stock price might suffer.*

p. 355 Cash? What Cash?

Q: Will "cash" be obsolete in terms of financial statement reporting?

A: *Cash, as the most liquid asset, will continue to be reported on balance sheets, and cash flows will still be reported on the statement of cash flows. Coins and currency may be less popular, but cash in the form of virtual cash (balances or deposits in accounts) will exist in a big way and will continue to appear in financial statements.*

Authors' Comments on *All About You:* Protecting Yourself from Identity Theft p. 362

Most experts discourage storing sensitive financial information on your computer. In recent years there have been countless examples of hackers penetrating sophisticated corporate systems to steal personal data. If hackers can beat sophisticated systems, it is unlikely that you can do better.

The Federal Trade Commission recommends that you frequently update your anti-virus software. Use a firewall program and a secure browser that encrypts all online transactions. If you do store financial information on your computer, make sure that it is password-protected with a password that is an unrecognizable combination of upper- and lower-case letters, numbers, and symbols. Change the password periodically. When you dispose of your old computer, make sure that you use a wiping utility to destroy all information on the hard drive.

Be careful, too, not to focus all of your internal control efforts on your computer. Most identity theft still derives from very non-technical sources—such as your trash can. You should take the following steps to minimize non-computer-related risks: Use passwords on your credit card, bank, and phone accounts. Make sure that all personal information in your home is in a secure place, especially if you have roommates or employ outside help. Don't give out personal information unless you initiated the contact or you are sure you know whom you are dealing with. Deposit outgoing mail in post-office collection boxes (not in your mailbox with the red flag up), and promptly remove all mail from your mailbox. Use a cross-cut shredder to shred all charge receipts, insurance forms, bank statements, etc. that might reveal personal information.

Answer to PepsiCo Review It Question 3, p. 363

PepsiCo reports cash and cash equivalents on its balance sheet for 2005 of $1,716 million.

Answers to Self-Study Questions

1. a **2.** c **3.** b **4.** c **5.** b **6.** d **7.** a **8.** a **9.** c **10.** d **11.** c

Remember to go back to the Navigator box on the chapter-opening page and check off your completed work.

Chapter 9

Accounting for Receivables

STUDY OBJECTIVES

After studying this chapter, you should be able to:

1 Identify the different types of receivables.

2 Explain how companies recognize accounts receivable.

3 Distinguish between the methods and bases companies use to value accounts receivable.

4 Describe the entries to record the disposition of accounts receivable.

5 Compute the maturity date of and interest on notes receivable.

6 Explain how companies recognize notes receivable.

7 Describe how companies value notes receivable.

8 Describe the entries to record the disposition of notes receivable.

9 Explain the statement presentation and analysis of receivables. ✓ The Navigator

✓ *The Navigator*

Scan **Study Objectives**	■
Read **Feature Story**	■
Read **Preview**	■
Read text and answer **Before You Go On** p. 392 ■ p. 395 ■ p. 400 ■ p. 402	■
Work **Demonstration Problem**	■
Review **Summary of Study Objectives**	■
Answer **Self-Study Questions**	■
Complete **Assignments**	■

Feature Story

A DOSE OF CAREFUL MANAGEMENT KEEPS RECEIVABLES HEALTHY

"Sometimes you have to know when to be very tough, and sometimes you can give them a bit of a break," says Vivi Su. She's not talking about her children, but about the customers of a subsidiary of pharmaceutical company Whitehall-Robins (www.whitehall-robins.com), where she works as supervisor of credit and collections.

For example, while the company's regular terms are 1/15, n/30 (1% discount if paid within 15 days), a customer might ask for and receive a few days of grace and still get the discount. Or a customer might place orders above its credit limit, in which case, depending on its payment history and the circumstances, Ms. Su might authorize shipment of the goods anyway.

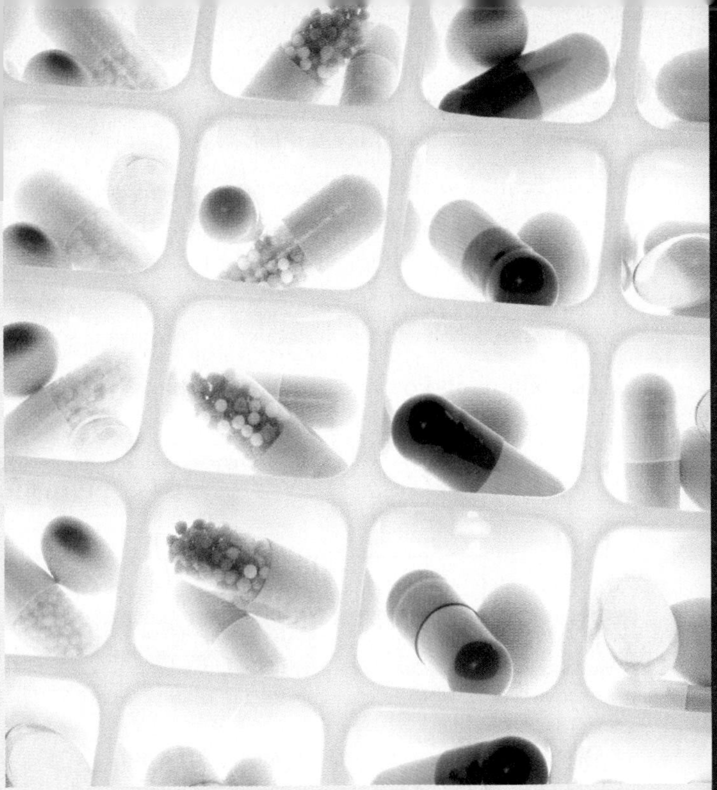

Nearly all of the company's sales come through the credit accounts Ms. Su manages. The process starts with the decision to grant a customer an account in the first place, Ms. Su explains. The sales rep gives the customer a credit application. "My department reviews this application very carefully; a customer needs to supply three good references, and we also run a check with a credit firm like Equifax. If we accept them, then based on their size and history, we assign a credit limit."

Once accounts are established, the company supervises them very carefully. "I get an aging report every single day," says Ms. Su.

"The rule of thumb is that we should always have at least 85% of receivables current—meaning they were billed less than 30 days ago," she continues. "But we try to do even better than that—I like to see 90%." Similarly, her guideline is never to have more than 5% of receivables at over 90 days. But long before that figure is reached, "we jump on it," she says firmly.

At 15 days overdue, Whitehall-Robins phones the client. Often there's a reasonable explanation for the delay—an invoice may have gone astray, or the payables clerk is away. "But if a customer keeps on delaying, and tells us several times that it'll only be a few more days, we know there's a problem," says Ms. Su. After 45 days, "I send a letter. Then a second notice is sent in writing. After the third and final notice, the client has 10 days to pay, and then I hand it over to a collection agency, and it's out of my hands."

Ms. Su knows that management of receivables is crucial to the profitability of Whitehall-Robins. "Receivables are generally the second-largest asset of any company (after its capital assets)," she points out. "So it's no wonder we keep a very close eye on them."

✓ The Navigator

Inside Chapter 9...

Preview of Chapter 9

As indicated in the Feature Story, receivables are a significant asset for many pharmaceutical companies. Because a significant portion of sales in the United States are done on credit, receivables are significant to companies in other industries as well. As a consequence, companies must pay close attention to their receivables and manage them carefully. In this chapter you will learn what journal entries companies make when they sell products, when they collect cash from those sales, and when they write off accounts they cannot collect.

The content and organization of the chapter are as follows.

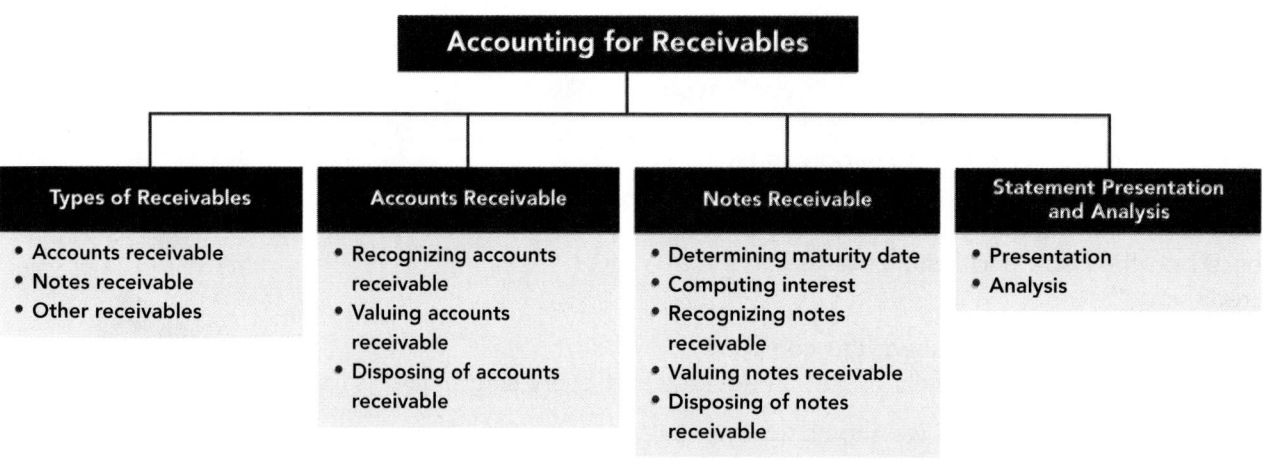

Accounting for Receivables

Types of Receivables
- Accounts receivable
- Notes receivable
- Other receivables

Accounts Receivable
- Recognizing accounts receivable
- Valuing accounts receivable
- Disposing of accounts receivable

Notes Receivable
- Determining maturity date
- Computing interest
- Recognizing notes receivable
- Valuing notes receivable
- Disposing of notes receivable

Statement Presentation and Analysis
- Presentation
- Analysis

The Navigator

TYPES OF RECEIVABLES

STUDY OBJECTIVE 1

Identify the different types of receivables.

The term **receivables** refers to amounts due from individuals and other companies. Receivables are claims that are expected to be collected in cash. They are frequently classified as (1) accounts receivable, (2) notes receivable, and (3) other receivables.

Accounts receivable are amounts owed by customers on account. They result from the sale of goods and services. Companies generally expect to collect these receivables within 30 to 60 days. Accounts receivable are the most significant type of claim held by a company.

Notes receivable are claims for which formal instruments of credit are issued as proof of the debt. A note receivable normally extends for time periods of 60–90 days or longer and requires the debtor to pay interest. Notes and accounts receivable that result from sales transactions are often called **trade receivables**.

Other receivables include nontrade receivables. Examples are interest receivable, loans to company officers, advances to employees, and income taxes refundable. These do not generally result from the operations of the business. Therefore companies generally classify and report them as separate items in the balance sheet.

ETHICS NOTE

Companies report receivables from employees separately in the financial statements. The reason: Sometimes those assets are not the result of an "arm's-length" transaction.

ACCOUNTS RECEIVABLE

Three accounting issues associated with accounts receivable are:

1. **Recognizing** accounts receivable.
2. **Valuing** accounts receivable.
3. **Disposing of** accounts receivable.

Recognizing Accounts Receivable

STUDY OBJECTIVE 2

Explain how companies recognize accounts receivable.

Recognizing accounts receivable is relatively straightforward. In Chapter 5 we saw how the sale of merchandise affects accounts receivable. To review, assume that Jordache Co. on July 1, 2008, sells merchandise on account to Polo Company for $1,000 terms 2/10, n/30. On July 5, Polo returns merchandise worth $100 to Jordache Co. On July 11, Jordache receives payment from Polo Company for the balance due. The journal entries to record these transactions on the books of Jordache Co. are as follows.

July 1	Accounts Receivable—Polo Company	1,000	
	Sales		1,000
	(To record sales on account)		
July 5	Sales Returns and Allowances	100	
	Accounts Receivable—Polo Company		100
	(To record merchandise returned)		
July 11	Cash ($900−$18)	882	
	Sales Discounts ($900 × .02)	18	
	Accounts Receivable—Polo Company		900
	(To record collection of accounts receivable)		

HELPFUL HINT

These entries are the same as those described in Chapter 5. For simplicity, we have omitted inventory and cost of goods sold from this set of journal entries and from end-of-chapter material.

The opportunity to receive a cash discount usually occurs when a manufacturer sells to a wholesaler or a wholesaler sells to a retailer. The selling company gives a discount in these situations either to encourage prompt payment or for competitive reasons.

Retailers rarely grant cash discounts to customers. In fact, when you use a retailer's credit card (Sears, for example), instead of giving a discount, the retailer charges interest on the balance due if not paid within a specified period (usually 25–30 days).

To illustrate, assume that you use your J.C. Penney Company credit card to purchase clothing with a sales price of $300. J.C. Penney will make the following entry at the date of sale.

Accounts Receivable	300	
Sales		300
(To record sale of merchandise)		

A	=	L	+	OE
+300				
				+300 Rev

Cash Flows
no effect

J.C. Penney will send you a monthly statement of this transaction and any others that have occurred during the month. If you do not pay in full within 30 days, J.C. Penney adds an interest (financing) charge to the balance due. Although interest rates vary by region and over time, a common rate for retailers is 18% per year (1.5% per month).

The seller recognizes interest revenue when it adds financing charges. Assuming that you owe $300 at the end of the month, and J.C. Penney charges 1.5% per month on the balance due, the adjusting entry to record interest revenue of $4.50 ($300 × 1.5%) is as follows.

Accounts Receivable	4.50	
Interest Revenue		4.50
(To record interest on amount due)		

A	=	L	+	OE
+4.50				
				+4.50 Rev

Cash Flows
no effect

Interest revenue is often substantial for many retailers.

ACCOUNTING ACROSS THE ORGANIZATION

Be Sure to Read the Fine Print

Interest rates on most credit cards are quite high, sometimes 18% or higher. As a result, consumers often look for companies that charge lower rates. Be careful—some companies offer lower interest rates but have eliminated the standard 25-day grace period before finance charges kick in. Other companies encourage consumers to increase their debt by advertising that only a $1 minimum payment is due on a $1,000 account balance. The less you pay off, the more interest they earn! Several banks market a credit card that allows cardholders to skip a payment twice a year. However, the outstanding balance continues to incur interest. Other credit card companies calculate finance charges on two-month, rather than one-month, averages, a practice that often translates into higher interest charges. In short, read the fine print in your credit agreement.

? Why are credit card companies willing to offer relaxed payment options?

Valuing Accounts Receivable

STUDY OBJECTIVE 3

Distinguish between the methods and bases companies use to value accounts receivable.

Once companies record receivables in the accounts, the next question is: How should they report receivables in the financial statements? Companies report accounts receivable on the balance sheet as an asset. But determining the **amount** to report is sometimes difficult because some receivables will become uncollectible.

Each customer must satisfy the credit requirements of the seller before the credit sale is approved. Inevitably, though, some accounts receivable become uncollectible. For example, a customer may not be able to pay because of a decline in its sales revenue due to a downturn in the economy. Similarly, individuals may be laid off from their jobs or faced with unexpected hospital bills. Companies record credit losses as debits to Bad Debts Expense (or Uncollectible Accounts Expense). Such losses are a normal and necessary risk of doing business on a credit basis.

Two methods are used in accounting for uncollectible accounts: (1) the direct write-off method and (2) the allowance method. The following sections explain these methods.

DIRECT WRITE-OFF METHOD FOR UNCOLLECTIBLE ACCOUNTS

Under the direct write-off method, when a company determines a particular account to be uncollectible, it charges the loss to Bad Debts Expense. Assume, for example, that on December 12 Warden Co. writes off as uncollectible M. E. Doran's $200 balance. The entry is:

A	=	L	+	OE
				−200 Exp
−200				

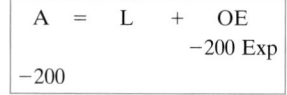

Cash Flows
no effect

Dec. 12	Bad Debts Expense	200	
	Accounts Receivable—M. E. Doran		200
	(To record write-off of M. E. Doran account)		

Under this method, Bad Debts Expense will show only **actual losses** from uncollectibles. The company will report accounts receivable at its gross amount.

Although this method is simple, its use can reduce the usefulness of both the income statement and balance sheet. Consider the following example. Assume that in 2008, Quick Buck Computer Company decided it could increase its revenues by offering computers to college students without requiring any money down and with no credit-approval process. On campuses across the country it distributed one million computers with a selling price of $800 each. This increased Quick Buck's revenues and receivables by $800 million. The promotion was a huge success! The 2008 balance sheet and income statement looked great. Unfortunately, during 2009, nearly 40% of the customers defaulted on their loans. This made the 2009 income statement and balance sheet look terrible. Illustration 9-1 shows the effect of these events on the financial statements if the direct write-off method is used.

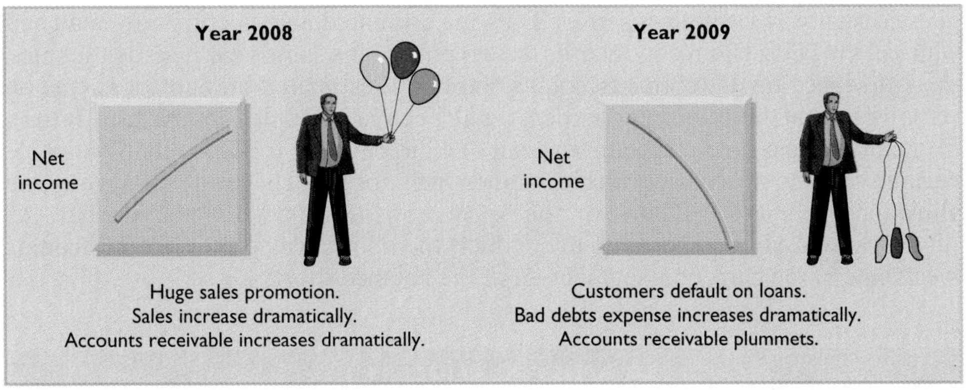

Illustration 9-1
Effects of direct write-off method

Under the direct write-off method, companies often record bad debts expense in a period different from the period in which they record the revenue. The method does not attempt to match bad debts expense to sales revenues in the income statement. Nor does the direct write-off method show accounts receivable in the balance sheet at the amount the company actually expects to receive. **Consequently, unless bad debts losses are insignificant, the direct write-off method is not acceptable for financial reporting purposes.**

ALLOWANCE METHOD FOR UNCOLLECTIBLE ACCOUNTS

The **allowance method** of accounting for bad debts involves estimating uncollectible accounts at the end of each period. This provides better matching on the income statement. It also ensures that companies state receivables on the balance sheet at their cash (net) realizable value. **Cash (net) realizable value** is the net amount the company expects to receive in cash. It excludes amounts that the company estimates it will not collect. Thus, this method reduces receivables in the balance sheet by the amount of estimated uncollectible receivables.

GAAP requires the allowance method for financial reporting purposes when bad debts are material in amount. This method has three essential features:

HELPFUL HINT
In this context, *material* means significant or important to financial statement users.

1. Companies **estimate** uncollectible accounts receivable. They match this estimated expense **against revenues** in the same accounting period in which they record the revenues.
2. Companies debit estimated uncollectibles to Bad Debts Expense and credit them to Allowance for Doubtful Accounts (a contra-asset account) through an adjusting entry at the end of each period.
3. When companies write off a specific account, they debit actual uncollectibles to Allowance for Doubtful Accounts and credit that amount to Accounts Receivable.

Recording Estimated Uncollectibles. To illustrate the allowance method, assume that Hampson Furniture has credit sales of $1,200,000 in 2008. Of this amount, $200,000 remains uncollected at December 31. The credit manager estimates that $12,000 of these sales will be uncollectible. The adjusting entry to record the estimated uncollectibles is:

A	=	L	+	OE
				−12,000 Exp
−12,000				

Cash Flows
no effect

Dec. 31	Bad Debts Expense	12,000	
	Allowance for Doubtful Accounts		12,000
	(To record estimate of uncollectible accounts)		

Hampson reports Bad Debts Expense in the income statement as an operating expense (usually as a selling expense). Thus, the estimated uncollectibles are matched with sales in 2008. Hampson records the expense in the same year it made the sales.

Allowance for Doubtful Accounts shows the estimated amount of claims on customers that the company expects will become uncollectible in the future. Companies use a contra account instead of a direct credit to Accounts Receivable because they do not know which customers will not pay. The credit balance in the allowance account will absorb the specific write-offs when they occur. As Illustration 9-2 shows, the company deducts the allowance account from accounts receivable in the current assets section of the balance sheet.

Illustration 9-2
Presentation of allowance for doubtful accounts

HAMPSON FURNITURE
Balance Sheet (partial)

Current assets		
Cash		$ 14,800
Accounts receivable	**$200,000**	
Less: Allowance for doubtful accounts	**12,000**	**188,000**
Merchandise inventory		310,000
Prepaid expense		25,000
Total current assets		$537,800

HELPFUL HINT
Cash realizable value is sometimes referred to as *accounts receivable (net).*

The amount of $188,000 in Illustration 9-2 represents the expected **cash realizable value** of the accounts receivable at the statement date. **Companies do not close Allowance for Doubtful Accounts at the end of the fiscal year.**

Recording the Write-Off of an Uncollectible Account. As described in the Feature Story, companies use various methods of collecting past-due accounts, such as letters, calls, and legal action. When they have exhausted all means of collecting a past-due account and collection appears impossible, the company should write off the account. In the credit card industry, for example, it is standard practice to write off accounts that are 210 days past due. To prevent premature or unauthorized write-offs, management should formally approve, in writing, each write-off. To maintain good internal control, companies should not give authorization to write off accounts to someone who also has daily responsibilities related to cash or receivables.

To illustrate a receivables write-off, assume that the financial vice-president of Hampson Furniture authorizes a write-off of the $500 balance owed by R. A. Ware on March 1, 2009. The entry to record the write-off is:

A	=	L	+	OE
+500				
−500				

Cash Flows
no effect

Mar. 1	Allowance for Doubtful Accounts	500	
	Accounts Receivable—R. A. Ware		500
	(Write-off of R. A. Ware account)		

Bad Debts Expense does not increase when the write-off occurs. **Under the allowance method, companies debit every bad debt write-off to the allowance account rather than to Bad Debts Expense.** A debit to Bad Debts Expense would be incorrect because the company has already recognized the expense when it made the adjusting entry for estimated bad debts. Instead, the entry to record the write-off of an uncollectible account reduces both Accounts Receivable and the Allowance for Doubtful Accounts. After posting, the general ledger accounts will appear as in Illustration 9-3.

Illustration 9-3
General ledger balances after write-off

Accounts Receivable		**Allowance for Doubtful Accounts**	
Jan. 1 Bal. 200,000	Mar. 1 **500**	Mar. 1 **500**	Jan. 1 Bal. 12,000
Mar. 1 Bal. 199,500			Mar. 1 Bal. 11,500

A write-off affects **only balance sheet accounts**—not income statement accounts. The write-off of the account reduces both Accounts Receivable and Allowance for Doubtful Accounts. Cash realizable value in the balance sheet, therefore, remains the same, as Illustration 9-4 shows.

Illustration 9-4
Cash realizable value comparison

	Before Write-off	**After Write-off**
Accounts receivable	$200,000	$199,500
Allowance for doubtful accounts	12,000	11,500
Cash realizable value	**$188,000**	**$188,000**

Recovery of an Uncollectible Account. Occasionally, a company collects from a customer after it has written off the account as uncollectible. The company makes two entries to record the recovery of a bad debt: (1) It reverses the entry made in writing off the account. This reinstates the customer's account. (2) It journalizes the collection in the usual manner.

To illustrate, assume that on July 1, R. A. Ware pays the $500 amount that Hampson had written off on March 1. These are the entries:

	(1)		
July 1	Accounts Receivable—R. A. Ware	500	
	Allowance for Doubtful Accounts		500
	(To reverse write-off of R. A. Ware account)		

A	=	L	+	OE
+500				
−500				

Cash Flows
no effect

	(2)		
July 1	Cash	500	
	Accounts Receivable—R. A. Ware		500
	(To record collection from R. A. Ware)		

A	=	L	+	OE
+500				
−500				

Cash Flows
+500

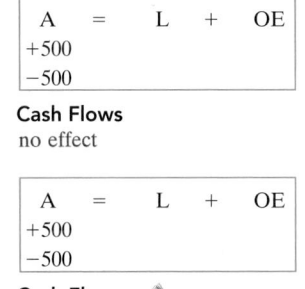

Note that the recovery of a bad debt, like the write-off of a bad debt, affects **only balance sheet accounts**. The net effect of the two entries above is a debit to Cash and a credit to Allowance for Doubtful Accounts for $500. Accounts Receivable and the Allowance for Doubtful Accounts both increase in entry (1) for two reasons: First, the company made an error in judgment when it wrote off the account receivable. Second, after R. A. Ware did pay, Accounts Receivable in the general ledger and Ware's account in the subsidiary ledger should show the collection for possible future credit purposes.

Bases Used For Allowance Method. To simplify the preceding explanation, we assumed we knew the amount of the expected uncollectibles. In "real life," companies must estimate that amount when they use the allowance method. Two bases are used to determine this amount: **(1) percentage of sales**, and **(2) percentage of receivables**. Both bases are generally accepted. The choice is a management decision. It depends on the relative emphasis that management wishes to give to expenses and revenues on the one hand or to cash realizable value of the accounts receivable on the other. The choice is whether to emphasize income statement or balance sheet relationships. Illustration 9-5 compares the two bases.

Illustration 9-5
Comparison of bases for estimating uncollectibles

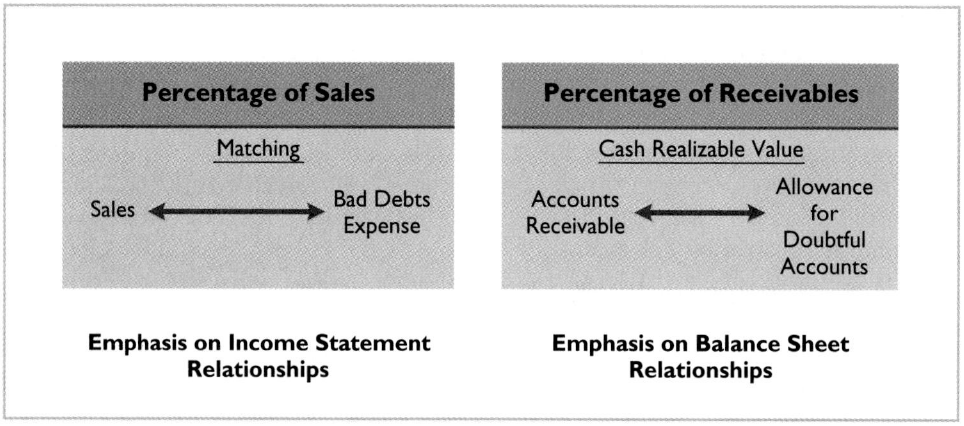

The percentage-of-sales basis results in a better matching of expenses with revenues—an income statement viewpoint. The percentage-of-receivables basis produces the better estimate of cash realizable value—a balance sheet viewpoint. Under both bases, the company must determine its past experience with bad debt losses.

Percentage-of-Sales. In the **percentage-of-sales basis**, management estimates what percentage of credit sales will be uncollectible. This percentage is based on past experience and anticipated credit policy.

The company applies this percentage to either total credit sales or net credit sales of the current year. To illustrate, assume that Gonzalez Company elects to use the percentage-of-sales basis. It concludes that 1% of net credit sales will become uncollectible. If net credit sales for 2008 are $800,000, the estimated bad debts expense is $8,000 (1% × $800,000). The adjusting entry is:

A	=	L	+	OE
				−8,000 Exp
−8,000				

Cash Flows
no effect

Dec. 31	Bad Debts Expense	8,000	
	Allowance for Doubtful Accounts		8,000
	(To record estimated bad debts for year)		

After the adjusting entry is posted, assuming the allowance account already has a credit balance of $1,723, the accounts of Gonzalez Company will show the following:

Illustration 9-6
Bad debts accounts after posting

Bad Debts Expense			Allowance for Doubtful Accounts	
Dec. 31 Adj.	**8,000**		Jan. 1 Bal.	1,723
			Dec. 31 Adj.	**8,000**
			Dec. 31 Bal.	9,723

This basis of estimating uncollectibles emphasizes the matching of expenses with revenues. As a result, Bad Debts Expense will show a direct percentage relationship to the sales base on which it is computed. **When the company makes the adjusting entry, it disregards the existing balance in Allowance for Doubtful Accounts.** The adjusted balance in this account should be a reasonable approximation of the realizable value of the receivables. If actual write-offs differ significantly from the amount estimated, the company should modify the percentage for future years.

Percentage-of-Receivables. Under the **percentage-of-receivables basis**, management estimates what percentage of receivables will result in losses from uncollectible accounts. The company prepares an **aging schedule**, in which it classifies customer balances by the length of time they have been unpaid. Because of its emphasis on time, the analysis is often called **aging the accounts receivable**. In the opening story, Whitehall-Robins prepared an aging report daily.

After the company arranges the accounts by age, it determines the expected bad debt losses. It applies percentages based on past experience to the totals in each category. The longer a receivable is past due, the less likely it is to be collected. Thus, the estimated percentage of uncollectible debts increases as the number of days past due increases. Illustration 9-7 shows an aging schedule for Dart Company. Note that the estimated percentage uncollectible increases from 2 to 40% as the number of days past due increases.

Worksheet.xls

File Edit View Insert Format Tools Data Window Help

	A	B	C	D	E	F	G
1–2			Not	Number of Days Past Due			
3	Customer	Total	Yet Due	1–30	31–60	61–90	Over 90
4	T. E. Adert	$ 600		$ 300		$ 200	$ 100
5	R. C. Bortz	300	$ 300				
6	B. A. Carl	450		200	$ 250		
7	O. L. Diker	700	500			200	
8	T. O. Ebbet	600			300		300
9	Others	36,950	26,200	5,200	2,450	1,600	1,500
10		$39,600	$27,000	$5,700	$3,000	$2,000	$1,900
11	Estimated Percentage Uncollectible		2%	4%	10%	20%	40%
12	Total Estimated Bad Debts	$ 2,228	$ 540	$ 228	$ 300	$ 400	$ 760
13							

Illustration 9-7
Aging schedule

HELPFUL HINT
The older categories have higher percentages because the longer an account is past due, the less likely it is to be collected.

Total estimated bad debts for Dart Company ($2,228) represent the amount of existing customer claims the company expects will become uncollectible in the future. This amount represents the **required balance** in Allowance for Doubtful Accounts at the balance sheet date. **The amount of the bad debt adjusting entry is the difference between the required balance and the existing balance in the allowance account.** If the trial balance shows Allowance for Doubtful Accounts with a credit balance of $528, the company will make an adjusting entry for $1,700 ($2,228 − $528), as shown here.

Dec. 31	Bad Debts Expense	1,700	
	Allowance for Doubtful Accounts		1,700
	(To adjust allowance account to total estimated uncollectibles)		

A	=	L	+	OE
				−1,700 Exp
−1,700				

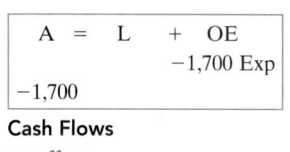

Cash Flows
no effect

After the adjusting entry is posted, the accounts of the Dart Company will show:

Illustration 9-8
Bad debts accounts after posting

Bad Debts Expense		Allowance for Doubtful Accounts	
Dec. 31 Adj. **1,700**			Bal. 528
			Dec. 31 Adj. **1,700**
			Bal. 2,228

Occasionally the allowance account will have a **debit balance** prior to adjustment. This occurs when write-offs during the year have exceeded previous provisions for bad debts. In such a case the company **adds the debit balance to the required balance** when it makes the adjusting entry. Thus, if there had been a $500 debit balance in the allowance account before adjustment, the adjusting entry would have been for $2,728 ($2,228 + $500) to arrive at a credit balance of $2,228. The percentage-of-receivables basis will normally result in the better approximation of cash realizable value.

INVESTOR INSIGHT

When Investors Ignore Warning Signs

Recently Nortel Networks announced that half of its previous year's earnings were "fake." Should investors have seen this coming? Well, there were issues in its annual report that should at least have caused investors to ask questions. The company had cut its allowance for doubtful accounts on all receivables from $1,253 million to $544 million, even though its total balance of receivables remained relatively unchanged.

This reduction in bad debts expense was responsible for a very large part of the company's earnings that year. At the time it was unclear whether Nortel might have set the reserves too high originally and needed to reduce them, or whether it slashed the allowance to artificially boost earnings. But one thing is certain—when a company makes an accounting change of this magnitude, investors need to ask questions.

Source: Jonathan Weil, "Outside Audit: At Nortel, Warning Signs Existed Months Ago," *Wall Street Journal*, May, 18, 2004, p. C3.

? When would it be appropriate for a company to lower its allowance for doubtful accounts as a percentage of its receivables?

Before You Go On...

REVIEW IT

1. What is the primary criticism of the direct write-off method?
2. Explain the difference between the percentage of sales and the percentage of receivables methods.
3. What percentage does PepsiCo's allowance for doubtful accounts represent as a percent of its gross receivables? (*Hint:* See PepsiCo's Note 14.) The answer to this question appears on page 421.

PEPSI

DO IT

Brule Co. has been in business 5 years. The ledger at the end of the current year shows: Accounts Receivable $30,000, Sales $180,000, and Allowance for

Doubtful Accounts with a debit balance of $2,000. Bad debts are estimated to be 10% of receivables. Prepare the entry to adjust the Allowance for Doubtful Accounts.

Action Plan

- Report receivables at their cash (net) realizable value.
- Estimate the amount the company does not expect to collect.
- Consider the existing balance in the allowance account when using the percentage-of-receivables basis.

Solution The following entry should be made to bring the balance in the Allowance for Doubtful Accounts up to a balance of $3,000 (0.1 × $30,000):

Bad Debts Expense	5,000	
Allowance for Doubtful Accounts		5,000
(To record estimate of uncollectible accounts)		

Related exercise material: *BE9-3, BE9-4, BE9-5, BE9-6, BE9-7, E9-3, E9-4, E9-5, and E9-6.*

The Navigator

Disposing of Accounts Receivable

STUDY OBJECTIVE 4

Describe the entries to record the disposition of accounts receivable.

In the normal course of events, companies collect accounts receivable in cash and remove the receivables from the books. However, as credit sales and receivables have grown in significance, the "normal course of events" has changed. Companies now frequently sell their receivables to another company for cash, thereby shortening the cash-to-cash operating cycle.

Companies sell receivables for two major reasons. First, **they may be the only reasonable source of cash.** When money is tight, companies may not be able to borrow money in the usual credit markets. Or, if money is available, the cost of borrowing may be prohibitive.

A second reason for selling receivables is that **billing and collection are often time-consuming and costly**. It is often easier for a retailer to sell the receivables to another party with expertise in billing and collection matters. Credit card companies such as MasterCard, Visa, and Discover specialize in billing and collecting accounts receivable.

SALE OF RECEIVABLES

A common sale of receivables is a sale to a factor. A **factor** is a finance company or bank that buys receivables from businesses and then collects the payments directly from the customers. Factoring is a multibillion dollar business.

Factoring arrangements vary widely. Typically the factor charges a commission to the company that is selling the receivables. This fee ranges from 1–3% of the amount of receivables purchased. To illustrate, assume that Hendredon Furniture factors $600,000 of receivables to Federal Factors. Federal Factors assesses a service charge of 2% of the amount of receivables sold. The journal entry to record the sale by Hendredon Furniture is as follows.

Cash	588,000	
Service Charge Expense (2% × $600,000)	12,000	
Accounts Receivable		600,000
(To record the sale of accounts receivable)		

A	=	L	+	OE
+588,000				
				−12,000 Exp
−600,000				

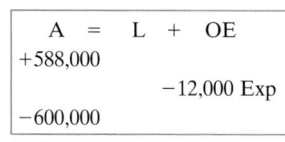

Cash Flows
+588,000

If the company often sells its receivables, it records the service charge expense (such as that incurred by Hendredon) as selling expense. If the company infrequently sells receivables, it may report this amount in the "Other expenses and losses" section of the income statement.

CREDIT CARD SALES

Over one billion credit cards are in use in the United States—more than three credit cards for every man, woman, and child in this country. Visa, MasterCard, and American Express are the national credit cards that most individuals use. Three parties are involved when national credit cards are used in retail sales: (1) the credit card issuer, who is independent of the retailer, (2) the retailer, and (3) the customer. A retailer's acceptance of a national credit card is another form of selling (factoring) the receivable.

Illustration 9-9 shows the major advantages of national credit cards to the retailer. In exchange for these advantages, the retailer pays the credit card issuer a fee of 2–6% of the invoice price for its services.

Illustration 9-9
Advantages of credit cards to the retailer

Accounting for Credit Card Sales. The retailer generally considers sales from the use of national credit card sales as *cash sales*. The retailer must pay to the bank that issues the card a fee of 2 to 4% for processing the transactions. The retailer records the credit card slips in a similar manner as checks deposited from a cash sale.

To illustrate, Anita Ferreri purchases $1,000 of compact discs for her restaurant from Karen Kerr Music Co., using her Visa First Bank Card. First Bank charges a service fee of 3%. The entry to record this transaction by Karen Kerr Music is as follows.

Cash	970	
Service Charge Expense	30	
Sales		1,000
(To record Visa credit card sales)		

A	=	L	+	OE
+970				
				−30 Exp
				+1,000 Rev

Cash Flows
+970

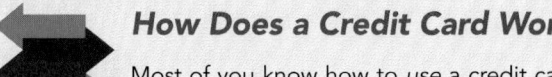

ACCOUNTING ACROSS THE ORGANIZATION

How Does a Credit Card Work?

Most of you know how to *use* a credit card, but do you know what happens in the transaction and how the transaction is processed? Suppose that you use a Visa card to purchase some new ties at Nordstrom. The salesperson swipes your card, and the swiping machine reads the information on the magnetic strip on the back of the card. The salesperson then types in the amount of the purchase. The machine contacts the Visa computer, which routes the call back to the bank that issued your Visa card. The issuing bank verifies that the account exists, that the card is not stolen, and that you have not exceeded your credit limit. At this point, the slip is printed, which you sign.

Visa acts as the clearing agent for the transaction. It transfers funds from the issuing bank to Nordstrom's bank account. Generally this transfer of funds, from sale to the receipt of funds in the merchant's account, takes two to three days.

In the meantime, Visa puts a pending charge on your account for the amount of the tie purchase; that amount counts immediately against your available credit limit. At the end of the billing period, Visa sends you an invoice (your credit card bill) which shows the various charges you made, and the amounts that Visa expended on your behalf, for the month. You then must "pay the piper" for your stylish new ties.

? Assume that Nordstrom prepares a bank reconciliation at the end of each month. If some credit card sales have not been processed by the bank, how should Nordstrom treat these transactions on its bank reconciliation?

Before You Go On...

REVIEW IT

1. Why do companies sell their receivables?
2. What is the journal entry when a company sells its receivables to a factor?
3. How do companies report sales using Visa or MasterCard?

DO IT

Mehl Wholesalers Co. has been expanding faster than it can raise capital. According to its local banker, the company has reached its debt ceiling. Mehl's customers are slow in paying (60–90 days), but its suppliers (creditors) are demanding 30-day payment. Mehl has a cash flow problem.

Mehl needs $120,000 in cash to safely cover next Friday's employee payroll. Its balance of outstanding receivables totals $750,000. What might Mehl do to alleviate this cash crunch? Record the entry that Mehl would make when it raises the needed cash.

Action Plan

- To speed up the collection of cash, sell receivables to a factor.
- Calculate service charge expense as a percentage of the factored receivables.

Solution Assuming that Mehl Wholesalers factors $125,000 of its accounts receivable at a 1% service charge, it would make the following entry.

Cash	123,750	
Service Charge Expense	1,250	
Accounts Receivable		125,000
(To record sale of receivables to factor)		

Related exercise material: *BE9-8, E9-7, E9-8, and E9-9.*

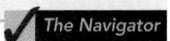

The Navigator

NOTES RECEIVABLE

Companies may also grant credit in exchange for a promissory note. A **promissory note** is a written promise to pay a specified amount of money on demand or at a definite time. Notes receivable give the payee a stronger legal claim to assets than accounts receivable. Promissory notes may be used: (1) when individuals and companies lend or borrow money, (2) when the amount of the transaction and the credit period exceed normal limits, or (3) in settlement of accounts receivable.

In a promissory note, the party making the promise to pay is called the **maker**. The party to whom payment is to be made is called the **payee**. The note may specifically identify the payee by name or may designate the payee simply as the bearer of the note. In the note shown in Illustration 9-10, Calhoun Company is the maker, Wilma Company is the payee. To Wilma Company, the promissory note is a note receivable; to Calhoun Company, it is a note payable.

Illustration 9-10
Promissory note

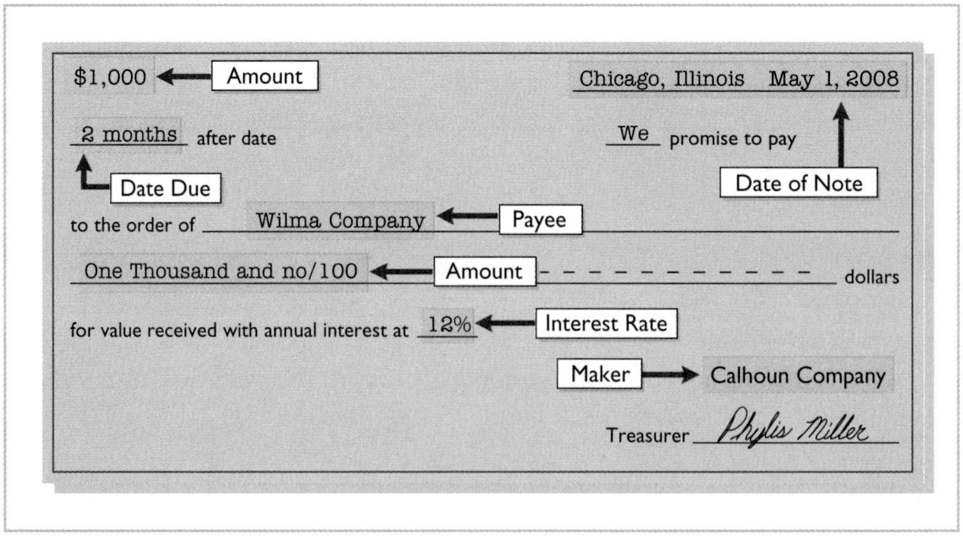

HELPFUL HINT

Who are the two key parties to a note, and what entry does each party make when the note is issued?

Answer:

1. **The maker, Calhoun Company, credits Notes Payable.**
2. **The payee, Wilma Company, debits Notes Receivable.**

Like accounts receivable, notes receivable can be readily sold to another party. Promissory notes are negotiable instruments (as are checks), which means that they can be transferred to another party by endorsement.

Companies frequently accept notes receivable from customers who need to extend the payment of an account receivable. They often require such notes from high-risk customers. In some industries (such as the pleasure boat industry), all credit sales are supported by notes. The majority of notes originate from loans.

The basic issues in accounting for notes receivable are the same as those for accounts receivable:

1. **Recognizing** notes receivable.
2. **Valuing** notes receivable.
3. **Disposing of** notes receivable.

On the following pages, we will look at these issues. Before we do, we need to consider two issues that did not apply to accounts receivable: maturity date and computing interest.

Determining the Maturity Date

STUDY OBJECTIVE 5

Compute the maturity date of and interest on notes receivable.

When the life of a note is expressed in terms of months, you find the date when it matures by counting the months from the date of issue. For example, the maturity date of a three-month note dated May 1 is August 1. A note drawn on the last day of a month matures on the last day of a subsequent month. That is, a July 31 note due in two months matures on September 30.

When the due date is stated in terms of days, you need to count the exact number of days to determine the maturity date. In counting, **omit the date the note is issued but include the due date**. For example, the maturity date of a 60-day note dated July 17 is September 15, computed as follows.

Term of note		60 days
July (31−17)	14	
August	31	45
Maturity date: September		**15**

Illustration 9-11
Computation of maturity date

Illustration 9-12 shows three ways of stating the maturity date of a promissory note.

Illustration 9-12
Maturity date of different notes

Computing Interest

As indicated in Chapter 3, the basic formula for computing interest on an interest-bearing note is:

Illustration 9-13
Formula for computing interest

Face Value of Note	×	Annual Interest Rate	×	Time in Terms of One Year	=	Interest

HELPFUL HINT
The interest rate specified is the *annual* rate.

The interest rate specified in a note is an **annual** rate of interest. There are many different ways to calculate interest. The time factor in the formula in Illustration 9-13 expresses the fraction of a year that the note is outstanding. When the maturity date is stated in days, the time factor is often the number of days divided by 360. When the due date is stated in months, the time factor is the number of months divided by 12. Illustration 9-14 shows computation of interest for various time periods.

Illustration 9-14
Computation of interest

Terms of Note	Interest Computation Face × Rate × Time = Interest
\$ 730, 18%, 120 days	\$ 730 × 18% × 120/360 = \$ 43.80
\$1,000, 15%, 6 months	\$1,000 × 15% × 6/12 = \$ 75.00
\$2,000, 12%, 1 year	\$2,000 × 12% × 1/1 = \$240.00

The computation above assumed 360 days for the length of the year. Financial instruments actually use 365 days. In order to simplify calculations in our illustrations, we have assumed 360 days. *For homework problems, assume 360 days.*

Recognizing Notes Receivable

STUDY OBJECTIVE 6
Explain how companies recognize notes receivable.

To illustrate the basic entry for notes receivable, we will use the \$1,000, two-month, 12% promissory note on page 396. Assuming that Calhoun Company wrote the note to settle an open account, Wilma Company makes the following entry for the receipt of the note.

A	=	L	+	OE
+1,000				
−1,000				

Cash Flows
no effect

May 1	Notes Receivable	1,000	
	Accounts Receivable—Calhoun Company		1,000
	(To record acceptance of Calhoun Company note)		

The company records the note receivable at its **face value**, the amount shown on the face of the note. No interest revenue is reported when the note is accepted, because the revenue recognition principle does not recognize revenue until earned. Interest is earned (accrued) as time passes.

If a company lends money using a note, the entry is a debit to Notes Receivable and a credit to Cash in the amount of the loan.

Valuing Notes Receivable

STUDY OBJECTIVE 7
Describe how companies value notes receivable.

Valuing short-term notes receivable is the same as valuing accounts receivable. Like accounts receivable, companies report short-term notes receivable at their **cash (net) realizable value**. The notes receivable allowance account is Allowance for Doubtful Accounts. The estimations involved in determining cash realizable value and in recording bad debts expense and the related allowance are done similarly to accounts receivable.

Disposing of Notes Receivable

STUDY OBJECTIVE 8

Describe the entries to record the disposition of notes receivable.

Notes may be held to their maturity date, at which time the maker must pay the face value plus accrued interest. Sometimes the maker of the note defaults and the payee must make an adjustment to the accounts. At other times the holder of the note speeds up the conversion to cash by selling the note receivable.

HONOR OF NOTES RECEIVABLE

A note is **honored** when its maker pays it in full at its maturity date. For an interest-bearing note, the amount due at maturity is the face value of the note plus interest for the length of time specified on the note.

To illustrate, assume that Betty Co. lends Wayne Higley Inc. $10,000 on June 1, accepting a five-month, 9% interest-bearing note. Interest will be $375 ($10,000 × 9% × 5/12). The maturity value will be $10,375. To obtain payment, Betty Co. (the payee) must present the note either to Wayne Higley Inc. (the maker) or to the maker's designated agent, such as a bank. Assuming that Betty Co. presents the note to Wayne Higley Inc. on the maturity date, Betty Co.'s entry to record the collection is:

Nov. 1	Cash	10,375	
	Notes Receivable		10,000
	Interest Revenue		375
	(To record collection of Higley Inc. note)		

A	=	L	+	OE
+10,375				
−10,000				
				+375 Rev

Cash Flows
+10,375

If Betty Co. prepares financial statements as of September 30, it must accrue interest. In this case, Betty Co. would make the adjusting entry shown below to record 4 months' interest ($300).

Sept. 30	Interest Receivable ($10,000 × 9% × 4/12)	300	
	Interest Revenue		300
	(To accrue 4 months' interest)		

A	=	L	+	OE
+300				
				+300 Rev

Cash Flows
no effect

When interest has been accrued, the company must credit Interest Receivable at maturity. In addition, since an additional month has passed, it must record one month of interest revenue. The entry by Betty Co. to record the honoring of the Wayne Higley Inc. note on November 1 is:

Nov. 1	Cash	10,375	
	Notes Receivable		10,000
	Interest Receivable		300
	Interest Revenue ($10,000 × 9% × 1/12)		75
	(To record collection of note at maturity)		

A	=	L	+	OE
+10,375				
−10,000				
−300				
				+75 Rev

Cash Flows
+10,375

In this case, Betty Co. credits Interest Receivable because the receivable was established in the adjusting entry of September 30.

DISHONOR OF NOTES RECEIVABLE

A **dishonored note** is a note that is not paid in full at maturity. A dishonored note receivable is no longer negotiable. However, the payee still has a claim against the maker of the note. Therefore the note holder usually transfers the Notes Receivable account to an Account Receivable.

To illustrate, assume that Wayne Higley Inc. on November 1 indicates that it cannot pay at the present time. The entry to record the dishonor of the note depends on whether Betty Co. expects eventual collection. If it does expect eventual collection, Betty Co. debits the amount due (face value and interest) on the note to Accounts Receivable. It would make the following entry at the time the note is dishonored (assuming no previous accrual of interest).

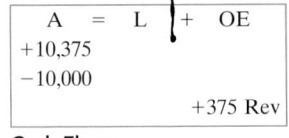

A	=	L	+	OE
+10,375				
−10,000				
				+375 Rev

Cash Flows
no effect

Nov. 1	Accounts Receivable—Wayne Higley Inc.	10,375	
	Notes Receivable		10,000
	Interest Revenue		375
	(To record the dishonor of Higley Inc. note)		

If instead, on November 1, there is no hope of collection, the note holder would write off the face value of the note by debiting the Allowance for Doubtful Accounts. No interest revenue would be recorded because collection will not occur.

ACCOUNTING ACROSS THE ORGANIZATION

Who Gets Credit?

Management must decide to whom it will grant credit. This is one of the hardest, and most critical, decisions that it makes. Consider the case of Mitsubishi Motors. It had been floundering, reporting large losses for a number of years in a row. Then management came up with what appeared to be a great plan. It began a marketing campaign aimed at giving Mitsubishi a hip image (think flashy ads with loud music), thus making its vehicles attractive to single people in their early twenties. The company combined this campaign with easy credit-terms—so called "zero-zero-zero" deals. This meant no down-payment, no payments for the first six months, and 0% financing.

The plan worked great—sort of. Sales took off. But then the twenty-somethings started defaulting on their loans. Soon Mitsubishi's losses were even bigger than before. It has since refocused its ads and credit terms. It now focuses on people who are "young at heart" (as opposed to just young)—and "economically safer."

Source: Todd Zaun, "Bad Loans Bump Mitsubishi Motors Off Road to Recovery," *Wall Street Journal*, November 12, 2003.

? How would reported net income likely differ during the first year of this promotion if Mitsubishi used the direct write-off method versus the allowance method?

SALE OF NOTES RECEIVABLE

The accounting for the sale of notes receivable is recorded similarly to the sale of accounts receivable. The accounting entries for the sale of notes receivable are left for a more advanced course.

Before You Go On...

REVIEW IT

1. What is the basic formula for computing interest?
2. At what value do companies report notes receivable on the balance sheet?
3. Explain the difference between honoring and dishonoring a note receivable.

DO IT

Gambit Stores accepts from Leonard Co. a $3,400, 90-day, 12% note dated May 10 in settlement of Leonard's overdue account. What is the maturity date of the note? What is the entry made by Gambit at the maturity date, assuming Leonard pays the note and interest in full at that time?

Action Plan

- Count the exact number of days to determine the maturity date. Omit the date the note is issued, but include the due date.
- Determine whether interest was accrued. The entry here assumes that no interest has been previously accrued on this note.

Solution The maturity date is August 8, computed as follows.

Term of note:		90 days
May (31–10)	21	
June	30	
July	31	82
Maturity date: August		8

The interest payable at maturity date is $102, computed as follows.

Face	× Rate	× Time	= Interest
$3,400	× 12%	× 90/360	= $102

The entry recorded by Gambit Stores at the maturity date is:

Cash	3,502	
Notes Receivable		3,400
Interest Revenue		102
(To record collection of Leonard note)		

Related exercise material: *BE9-9, BE9-10, BE9-11, E9-10, E9-11, E9-12, and E9-13.*

The Navigator

STATEMENT PRESENTATION AND ANALYSIS

Presentation

STUDY OBJECTIVE 9

Explain the statement presentation and analysis of receivables.

Companies should identify in the balance sheet or in the notes to the financial statements each of the major types of receivables. Short-term receivables appear in the current assets section of the balance sheet, below short-term investments. Short-term investments appear before receivables, because short-term investments are more liquid (nearer to cash). Companies report both the gross amount of receivables and the allowance for doubtful accounts.

In a multiple-step income statement, companies report bad debts expense and service charge expense as selling expenses in the operating expenses section. Interest revenue appears under "Other revenues and gains" in the nonoperating activities section of the income statement.

Analysis

Investors and corporate managers compute financial ratios to evaluate the liquidity of a company's accounts receivable. They use the **accounts receivable turnover ratio** to assess the liquidity of the receivables. This ratio measures the number of times, on average, the company collects accounts receivable during the period. It is computed by dividing net credit sales (net sales less cash sales) by the average net accounts receivable during the year. Unless seasonal factors are significant, average net accounts receivable outstanding can be computed from the beginning and ending balances of net accounts receivable.

For example, in 2005 Cisco Systems had net sales of $24,801 million for the year. It had a beginning accounts receivable (net) balance of $1,825 million and an ending accounts receivable (net) balance of $2,216 million. Assuming that Cisco's sales were all on credit, its accounts receivable turnover ratio is computed as follows.

Illustration 9-15
Accounts receivable turnover ratio and computation

Net Credit Sales	÷	Average Net Accounts Receivable	=	Accounts Receivable Turnover
$24,801	÷	$\frac{\$1,825 + \$2,216}{2}$	=	**12.3 times**

The result indicates an accounts receivable turnover ratio of 12.3 times per year. The higher the turnover ratio the more liquid the company's receivables.

A variant of the accounts receivable turnover ratio that makes the liquidity even more evident is its conversion into an **average collection period** in terms of days. This is done by dividing the turnover ratio into 365 days. For example, Cisco's turnover of 12.3 times is divided into 365 days, as shown in Illustration 9-16, to obtain approximately 29.7 days. This means that it takes Cisco about 30 days to collect its accounts receivable.

Illustration 9-16
Average collection period for receivables formula and computation

Days in Year	÷	Accounts Receivable Turnover	=	Average Collection Period in Days
365 days	÷	12.3 times	=	**29.7 days**

Companies frequently use the average collection period to assess the effectiveness of a company's credit and collection policies. The general rule is that the collection period should not greatly exceed the credit term period (that is, the time allowed for payment).

Before You Go On...

REVIEW IT

1. Explain where companies report accounts and notes receivable on the balance sheet.
2. Where do companies report bad debts expense, service charge expense, and interest revenue on the multiple-step income statement?

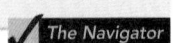

The Navigator

Be sure to read **ALL ABOUT YOU: *Should You Be Carrying Plastic?*** on page 403 for information on how topics in this chapter apply to you.

Should You Be Carrying Plastic?

Smart business people carefully consider their use of credit. They evaluate who they lend to, and how they finance their own operations. They know that getting overextended on credit can destroy their business.

Individuals need to evaluate their personal credit positions using the same thought processes used by business people. Some of you might consider the idea of not having a credit card a ridiculous proposition. But the reality is that the misuse of credit cards brings financial hardship to millions of Americans each year. Credit card companies aggressively market their cards with images of glamour and happiness. But there isn't much glamour in paying an 18% to 21% interest rate, and there is very little happiness to be found in filing for personal bankruptcy.

Some Facts

* About 70% of undergraduates at 4-year colleges carry at least one credit card in their own name. Approximately 22% of college students got their first credit cards in high school.
* The average monthly debt on a college student's charge account, according to one study, is close to $2,000.
* In a recent year, Americans charged more than $1 trillion in purchases with their credit cards. That was more than they spent in cash.
* During one quarter in 2006, the percentage of delinquent credit card payments rose to 5% from 4.3%. Card write-offs increased from 5.6% to 6.4%. Until this year, both numbers were declining.
* Significant increases in consumer bankruptcy filings occurred in every region of the country. There were 2,043,535 new filings in 2005, up 31.6% from 1,552,967 in 2004—that is, one in every 53 households filed a bankruptcy petition.

About the Numbers

Presented below is a chart that shows the major causes of personal financial problems. Note the excessive use of credit, which is cited as the number-one cause. This often translates into addiction to credit cards.

Causes of Personal Financial Problems

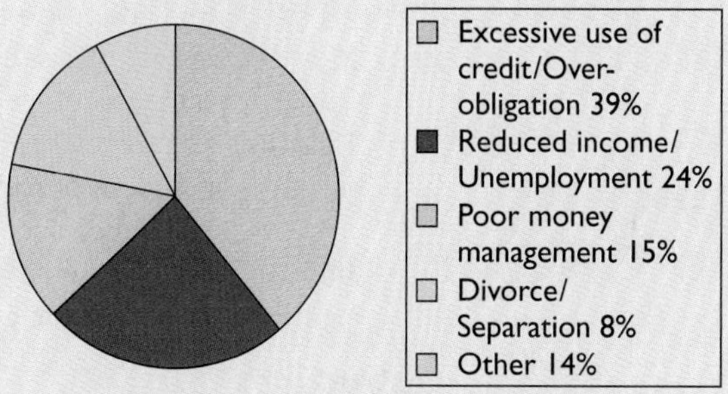

Source: Debt Solutions of America, *www.becomedebtfree.com* (accessed May 2006).

What Do You Think?

Should you cut up your credit card(s)?

YES: Americans are carrying huge personal debt burdens. Credit cards encourage unnecessary, spontaneous expenditures. The interest rates on credit cards are extremely high, which causes debt problems to escalate exponentially.

NO: Credit cards are a necessity for transactions in today's economy. In fact, many transactions are difficult or impossible to carry out without a credit card. People should learn to use credit cards responsibly.

Sources: Debtsmart, *www.debtsmart.com/pages/debt_stats.html*; Robin Marantz Henig, "Teen Credit Cards Actually Teach Responsibility," *USAToday.com*, July 30, 2001.

The authors' comments on this situation appear on page 421.

Demonstration Problem

The following selected transactions relate to Falcetto Company.

Mar.	1	Sold $20,000 of merchandise to Potter Company, terms 2/10, n/30.
	11	Received payment in full from Potter Company for balance due.
	12	Accepted Juno Company's $20,000, 6-month, 12% note for balance due.
	13	Made Falcetto Company credit card sales for $13,200.
	15	Made Visa credit card sales totaling $6,700. A 3% service fee is charged by Visa.
Apr.	11	Sold accounts receivable of $8,000 to Harcot Factor. Harcot Factor assesses a service charge of 2% of the amount of receivables sold.
	13	Received collections of $8,200 on Falcetto Company credit card sales and added finance charges of 1.5% to the remaining balances.
May	10	Wrote off as uncollectible $16,000 of accounts receivable. Falcetto uses the percentage-of-sales basis to estimate bad debts.
June	30	Credit sales recorded during the first 6 months total $2,000,000. The bad debt percentage is 1% of credit sales. At June 30, the balance in the allowance account is $3,500.
July	16	One of the accounts receivable written off in May was from J. Simon, who pays the amount due, $4,000, in full.

Instructions

Prepare the journal entries for the transactions.

Solution to Demonstration Problem

Mar. 1	Accounts Receivable–Potter	20,000	
	Sales		20,000
	(To record sales on account)		
Mar. 11	Cash	19,600	
	Sales Discounts (2% × $20,000)	400	
	Accounts Receivable—Potter		20,000
	(To record collection of accounts receivable)		
Mar. 12	Notes Receivable	20,000	
	Accounts Receivable—Juno		20,000
	(To record acceptance of Juno Company note)		
Mar. 13	Accounts Receivable	13,200	
	Sales		13,200
	(To record company credit card sales)		
Mar. 15	Cash	6,499	
	Service Charge Expense (3% × $6,700)	201	
	Sales		6,700
	(To record credit card sales)		
Apr. 11	Cash	7,840	
	Service Charge Expense (2% × $8,000)	160	
	Accounts Receivable		8,000
	(To record sale of receivables to factor)		
Apr. 13	Cash	8,200	
	Accounts Receivable		8,200
	(To record collection of accounts receivable)		

action plan

- ✓ Generally, record accounts receivable at invoice price.
- ✓ Recognize that sales returns and allowances and cash discounts reduce the amount received on accounts receivable.
- ✓ Record a service charge expense on the seller's books when accounts receivable are sold.
- ✓ Prepare an adjusting entry for bad debts expense.
- ✓ Ignore any balance in the allowance account under the percentage-of-sales basis. Recognize the balance in the allowance account under the percentage-of-receivables basis.
- ✓ Record write-offs of accounts receivable only in balance sheet accounts.

	Accounts Receivable [($13,200 − $8,200) × 1.5%]	75	
	Interest Revenue		75
	(To record interest on amount due)		
May 10	Allowance for Doubtful Accounts	16,000	
	Accounts Receivable		16,000
	(To record write-off of accounts receivable)		
June 30	Bad Debts Expense ($2,000,000 × 1%)	20,000	
	Allowance for Doubtful Accounts		20,000
	(To record estimate of uncollectible accounts)		
July 16	Accounts Receivable—J. Simon	4,000	
	Allowance for Doubtful Accounts		4,000
	(To reverse write-off of accounts receivable)		
	Cash	4,000	
	Accounts Receivable—J. Simon		4,000
	(To record collection of accounts receivable)		

The Navigator

SUMMARY OF STUDY OBJECTIVES

WILEY PLUS

1 **Identify the different types of receivables.** Receivables are frequently classified as (1) accounts, (2) notes, and (3) other. Accounts receivable are amounts customers owe on account. Notes receivable are claims for which lenders issue formal instruments of credit as proof of the debt. Other receivables include nontrade receivables such as interest receivable, loans to company officers, advances to employees, and income taxes refundable.

2 **Explain how companies recognize accounts receivable.** Companies record accounts receivable at invoice price. They are reduced by sales returns and allowances. Cash discounts reduce the amount received on accounts receivable. When interest is charged on a past due receivable, the company adds this interest to the accounts receivable balance and recognizes it as interest revenue.

3 **Distinguish between the methods and bases companies use to value accounts receivable.** There are two methods of accounting for uncollectible accounts: the allowance method and the direct write-off method. Companies may use either the percentage-of-sales or the percentage-of-receivables basis to estimate uncollectible accounts using the allowance method. The percentage-of-sales basis emphasizes the matching principle. The percentage-of-receivables basis emphasizes the cash realizable value of the accounts receivable. An aging schedule is often used with this basis.

4 **Describe the entries to record the disposition of accounts receivable.** When a company collects an account receivable, it credits Accounts Receivable. When a company sells (factors) an account receivable, a service charge expense reduces the amount received.

5 **Compute the maturity date of and interest on notes receivable.** For a note stated in months, the maturity date is found by counting the months from the date of issue. For a note stated in days, the number of days is counted, omitting the issue date and counting the due date. The formula for computing interest is: Face value × Interest rate × Time.

6 **Explain how companies recognize notes receivable.** Companies record notes receivable at face value. In some cases, it is necessary to accrue interest prior to maturity. In this case, companies debit Interest Receivable and credit Interest Revenue.

7 **Describe how companies value notes receivable.** As with accounts receivable, companies report notes receivable at their cash (net) realizable value. The notes receivable allowance account is the Allowance for Doubtful Accounts. The computation and estimations involved in valuing notes receivable at cash realizable value, and in recording the proper amount of bad debts expense and related allowance are similar to those for accounts receivable.

8 **Describe the entries to record the disposition of notes receivable.** Notes can be held to maturity. At that time the face value plus accrued interest is due, and the note is removed from the accounts. In many cases, the holder of the note speeds up the conversion by selling the receivable to another party (a factor). In some situations, the maker of the note dishonors the note (defaults), in which case the company transfers the note and accrued interest to an account receivable or writes off the note.

9 **Explain the statement presentation and analysis of receivables.** Companies should identify in the balance sheet

or in the notes to the financial statements each major type of receivable. Short-term receivables are considered current assets. Companies report the gross amount of receivables and the allowance for doubtful accounts. They report bad debts and service charge expenses in the multiple-step income statement as operating (selling) expenses; interest revenue appears under other revenues and gains in the nonoperating activities section of the statement. Managers and investors evaluate accounts receivable for liquidity by computing a turnover ratio and an average collection period.

The Navigator

GLOSSARY

WILEY PLUS

Accounts receivable Amounts owed by customers on account. (p. 384).

Accounts receivable turnover ratio A measure of the liquidity of accounts receivable; computed by dividing net credit sales by average net accounts receivable. (p. 401).

Aging the accounts receivable The analysis of customer balances by the length of time they have been unpaid. (p. 391).

Allowance method A method of accounting for bad debts that involves estimating uncollectible accounts at the end of each period. (p. 387).

Average collection period The average amount of time that a receivable is outstanding; calculated by dividing 365 days by the accounts receivables turnover ratio. (p. 402).

Bad Debts Expense An expense account to record uncollectible receivables. (p. 386).

Cash (net) realizable value The net amount a company expects to receive in cash. (p. 387).

Direct write-off method A method of accounting for bad debts that involves expensing accounts at the time they are determined to be uncollectible. (p. 386).

Dishonored note A note that is not paid in full at maturity. (p. 399).

Factor A finance company or bank that buys receivables from businesses and then collects the payments directly from the customers. (p. 393).

Maker The party in a promissory note who is making the promise to pay. (p. 396).

Notes receivable Claims for which formal instruments of credit are issued as proof of the debt. (p. 384).

Other receivables Various forms of nontrade receivables, such as interest receivable and income taxes refundable. (p. 384).

Payee The party to whom payment of a promissory note is to be made. (p. 396).

Percentage-of-receivables basis Management estimates what percentage of receivables will result in losses from uncollectible accounts. (p. 391).

Percentage-of-sales basis Management estimates what percentage of credit sales will be uncollectible. (p. 390).

Promissory note A written promise to pay a specified amount of money on demand or at a definite time. (p. 396).

Receivables Amounts due from individuals and other companies. (p. 384).

Trade receivables Notes and accounts receivable that result from sales transactions. (p. 384).

SELF-STUDY QUESTIONS

WILEY PLUS

Answers are at the end of the chapter.

(SO 2) **1.** Buehler Company on June 15 sells merchandise on account to Chaz Co. for $1,000, terms 2/10, n/30. On June 20, Chaz Co. returns merchandise worth $300 to Buehler Company. On June 24, payment is received from Chaz Co. for the balance due. What is the amount of cash received?
- **a.** $700.
- **b.** $680.
- **c.** $686.
- **d.** None of the above.

(SO 3) **2.** Which of the following approaches for bad debts is best described as a balance sheet method?
- **a.** Percentage-of-receivables basis.
- **b.** Direct write-off method.
- **c.** Percentage-of-sales basis.
- **d.** Both a and b.

(SO 3) **3.** Net sales for the month are $800,000, and bad debts are expected to be 1.5% of net sales. The company uses the percentage-of-sales basis. If the Allowance for Doubtful Accounts has a credit balance of $15,000 before adjustment, what is the balance after adjustment?
- **a.** $15,000.
- **b.** $27,000.
- **c.** $23,000.
- **d.** $31,000.

4. In 2008, Roso Carlson Company had net credit sales of $750,000. On January 1, 2008, Allowance for Doubtful Accounts had a credit balance of $18,000. During 2008, $30,000 of uncollectible accounts receivable were written off. Past experience indicates that 3% of net credit sales become uncollectible. What should be the adjusted balance of Allowance for Doubtful Accounts at December 31, 2008? (SO 3)
- **a.** $10,050.
- **b.** $10,500.
- **c.** $22,500.
- **d.** $40,500.

(SO 3) **5.** An analysis and aging of the accounts receivable of Prince Company at December 31 reveals the following data.

Accounts receivable	$800,000
Allowance for doubtful accounts per books before adjustment	50,000
Amounts expected to become uncollectible	65,000

The cash realizable value of the accounts receivable at December 31, after adjustment, is:

a. $685,000.
b. $750,000.
c. $800,000.
d. $735,000.

(SO 6) **6.** One of the following statements about promissory notes is incorrect. The *incorrect* statement is:

a. The party making the promise to pay is called the maker.
b. The party to whom payment is to be made is called the payee.
c. A promissory note is not a negotiable instrument.
d. A promissory note is often required from high-risk customers.

(SO 4) **7.** Which of the following statements about Visa credit card sales is *incorrect*?

a. The credit card issuer makes the credit investigation of the customer.
b. The retailer is not involved in the collection process.
c. Two parties are involved.
d. The retailer receives cash more quickly than it would from individual customers on account.

(SO 4) **8.** Blinka Retailers accepted $50,000 of Citibank Visa credit card charges for merchandise sold on July 1. Citibank charges 4% for its credit card use. The entry to record this transaction by Blinka Retailers will include a credit to Sales of $50,000 and a debit(s) to:

a. Cash	$48,000
and Service Charge Expense	2,000
b. Accounts Receivable	$48,000
and Service Charge Expense	$2,000
c. Cash	$50,000
d. Accounts Receivable	$50,000

9. Foti Co. accepts a $1,000, 3-month, 12% promissory note in settlement of an account with Bartelt Co. The entry to record this transaction is as follows. (SO 6)

a. Notes Receivable	1,030	
Accounts Receivable		1,030
b. Notes Receivable	1,000	
Accounts Receivable		1,000
c. Notes Receivable	1,000	
Sales		1,000
d. Notes Receivable	1,020	
Accounts Receivable		1,020

10. Ginter Co. holds Kolar Inc.'s $10,000, 120-day, 9% note. The entry made by Ginter Co. when the note is collected, assuming no interest has been previously accrued, is: (SO 8)

a. Cash	10,300	
Notes Receivable		10,300
b. Cash	10,000	
Notes Receivable		10,000
c. Accounts Receivable	10,300	
Notes Receivable		10,000
Interest Revenue		300
d. Cash	10,300	
Notes Receivable		10,000
Interest Revenue		300

Go to the book's website, **www.wiley.com/college/weygandt**, for additional Self-Study Questions.

The Navigator

QUESTIONS

1. What is the difference between an account receivable and a note receivable?

2. What are some common types of receivables other than accounts receivable and notes receivable?

3. Texaco Oil Company issues its own credit cards. Assume that Texaco charges you $40 on an unpaid balance. Prepare the journal entry that Texaco makes to record this revenue.

4. What are the essential features of the allowance method of accounting for bad debts?

5. Jerry Gatewood cannot understand why cash realizable value does not decrease when an uncollectible account is written off under the allowance method. Clarify this point for Jerry Gatewood.

6. Distinguish between the two bases that may be used in estimating uncollectible accounts.

7. Eaton Company has a credit balance of $3,500 in Allowance for Doubtful Accounts. The estimated bad debts expense under the percentage-of-sales basis is $4,100. The total estimated uncollectibles under the percentage-of-receivables basis is $5,800. Prepare the adjusting entry under each basis.

8. How are bad debts accounted for under the direct write-off method? What are the disadvantages of this method?

9. DeVito Company accepts both its own credit cards and national credit cards. What are the advantages of accepting both types of cards?

10. An article recently appeared in the *Wall Street Journal* indicating that companies are selling their receivables at a record rate. Why are companies selling their receivables?

11. Pinkston Textiles decides to sell $600,000 of its accounts receivable to First Factors Inc. First Factors assesses a service charge of 3% of the amount of receivables sold. Prepare the journal entry that Pinkston Textiles makes to record this sale.

12. Your roommate is uncertain about the advantages of a promissory note. Compare the advantages of a note receivable with those of an account receivable.

13. How may the maturity date of a promissory note be stated?

14. Indicate the maturity date of each of the following promissory notes:

Date of Note	Terms
(a) March 13	one year after date of note
(b) May 4	3 months after date
(c) June 20	30 days after date
(d) July 1	60 days after date

15. Compute the missing amounts for each of the following notes.

	Principal	Annual Interest Rate	Time	Total Interest
(a)	?	9%	120 days	$ 600
(b)	$30,000	10%	3 years	?
(c)	$60,000	?	5 months	$2,000
(d)	$45,000	8%	?	$1,200

16. In determining interest revenue, some financial institutions use 365 days per year and others use 360 days. Why might a financial institution use 360 days?

17. Cain Company dishonors a note at maturity. What actions by Cain may occur with the dishonoring of the note?

18. General Motors Corporation has accounts receivable and notes receivable. How should the receivables be reported on the balance sheet?

19. The accounts receivable turnover ratio is 8.14, and average net receivables during the period are $400,000. What is the amount of net credit sales for the period?

BRIEF EXERCISES

WILEY PLUS

Identify different types of receivables.
(SO 1)

BE9-1 Presented below are three receivables transactions. Indicate whether these receivables are reported as accounts receivable, notes receivable, or other receivables on a balance sheet.

(a) Sold merchandise on account for $64,000 to a customer.
(b) Received a promissory note of $57,000 for services performed.
(c) Advanced $10,000 to an employee.

Record basic accounts receivable transactions.
(SO 2)

BE9-2 Record the following transactions on the books of Keyser Co.

(a) On July 1, Keyser Co. sold merchandise on account to Maxfield Inc. for $15,200, terms 2/10, n/30.
(b) On July 8, Maxfield Inc. returned merchandise worth $3,800 to Keyser Co.
(c) On July 11, Maxfield Inc. paid for the merchandise.

Prepare entry for allowance method and partial balance sheet.
(SO 3, 9)

BE9-3 During its first year of operations, Henley Company had credit sales of $3,000,000; $600,000 remained uncollected at year-end. The credit manager estimates that $35,000 of these receivables will become uncollectible.

(a) Prepare the journal entry to record the estimated uncollectibles.
(b) Prepare the current assets section of the balance sheet for Henley Company. Assume that in addition to the receivables it has cash of $90,000, merchandise inventory of $130,000, and prepaid expenses of $7,500.

Prepare entry for write-off; determine cash realizable value.
(SO 3)

BE9-4 At the end of 2008, Delong Co. has accounts receivable of $700,000 and an allowance for doubtful accounts of $54,000. On January 24, 2009, the company learns that its receivable from Ristau Inc. is not collectible, and management authorizes a write-off of $5,400.

(a) Prepare the journal entry to record the write-off.
(b) What is the cash realizable value of the accounts receivable (1) before the write-off and (2) after the write-off?

Prepare entries for collection of bad debts write-off.
(SO 3)

BE9-5 Assume the same information as BE9-4. On March 4, 2009, Delong Co. receives payment of $5,400 in full from Ristau Inc. Prepare the journal entries to record this transaction.

Prepare entry using percentage-of-sales method.
(SO 3)

BE9-6 Nieto Co. elects to use the percentage-of-sales basis in 2008 to record bad debts expense. It estimates that 2% of net credit sales will become uncollectible. Sales are $800,000 for 2008, sales returns and allowances are $45,000, and the allowance for doubtful accounts has a credit balance of $9,000. Prepare the adjusting entry to record bad debts expense in 2008.

Prepare entry using percentage-of-receivables method.
(SO 3)

BE9-7 Linhart Co. uses the percentage-of-receivables basis to record bad debts expense. It estimates that 1% of accounts receivable will become uncollectible. Accounts receivable are $450,000 at the end of the year, and the allowance for doubtful accounts has a credit balance of $1,500.

(a) Prepare the adjusting journal entry to record bad debts expense for the year.
(b) If the allowance for doubtful accounts had a debit balance of $800 instead of a credit balance of $1,500, determine the amount to be reported for bad debts expense.

BE9-8 Presented below are two independent transactions.

Prepare entries to dispose of accounts receivable.

(SO 4)

(a) St. Pierre Restaurant accepted a Visa card in payment of a $150 lunch bill. The bank charges a 4% fee. What entry should St. Pierre make?
(b) Jamar Company sold its accounts receivable of $60,000. What entry should Jamar make, given a service charge of 3% on the amount of receivables sold?

BE9-9 Compute interest and find the maturity date for the following notes.

Compute interest and determine maturity dates on notes.

(SO 5)

	Date of Note	Principal	Interest Rate (%)	Terms
(a)	June 10	$80,000	6%	60 days
(b)	July 14	$50,000	7%	90 days
(c)	April 27	$12,000	8%	75 days

BE9-10 Presented below are data on three promissory notes. Determine the missing amounts.

Determine maturity dates and compute interest and rates on notes.

(SO 5)

	Date of Note	Terms	Maturity Date	Principal	Annual Interest Rate	Total Interest
(a)	April 1	60 days	?	$600,000	9%	?
(b)	July 2	30 days	?	90,000	?	$600
(c)	March 7	6 months	?	120,000	10%	?

BE9-11 On January 10, 2008, Edmunds Co. sold merchandise on account to Jeff Gallup for $13,600, n/30. On February 9, Jeff Gallup gave Edmunds Co. a 10% promissory note in settlement of this account. Prepare the journal entry to record the sale and the settlement of the account receivable.

Prepare entry for notes receivable exchanged for account receivable.

(SO 6)

BE9-12 The financial statements of Minnesota Mining and Manufacturing Company (3M) report net sales of $20.0 billion. Accounts receivable (net) are $2.7 billion at the beginning of the year and $2.8 billion at the end of the year. Compute 3M's receivables turnover ratio. Compute 3M's average collection period for accounts receivable in days.

Compute ratios to analyze receivables.

(SO 9)

EXERCISES

WILEY PLUS

E9-1 Presented below are selected transactions of Pale Force Company. Pale Force sells in large quantities to other companies and also sells its product in a small retail outlet.

Journalize entries related to accounts receivable.

(SO 2)

March 1 Sold merchandise on account to CC Company for $3,000, terms 2/10, n/30.
3 CC Company returned merchandise worth $500 to Pale Force.
9 Pale Force collected the amount due from CC Company from the March 1 sale.
15 Pale Force sold merchandise for $400 in its retail outlet. The customer used his Pale Force credit card.
31 Pale Force added 1.5% monthly interest to the customer's credit card balance.

Instructions
Prepare journal entries for the transactions above.

E9-2 Presented below are two independent situations.

Journalize entries for recognizing accounts receivable.

(SO 2)

(a) On January 6, Arneson Co. sells merchandise on account to Cortez Inc. for $9,000, terms 2/10, n/30. On January 16, Cortez Inc. pays the amount due. Prepare the entries on Arneson's books to record the sale and related collection.
(b) On January 10, Mary Dawes uses her Pierson Co. credit card to purchase merchandise from Pierson Co. for $9,000. On February 10, Dawes is billed for the amount due of $9,000. On February 12, Dawes pays $5,000 on the balance due. On March 10, Dawes is billed for the amount due, including interest at 2% per month on the unpaid balance as of February 12. Prepare the entries on Pierson Co.'s books related to the transactions that occurred on January 10, February 12, and March 10.

E9-3 The ledger of Hixson Company at the end of the current year shows Accounts Receivable $120,000, Sales $840,000, and Sales Returns and Allowances $30,000.

Journalize entries to record allowance for doubtful accounts using two different bases.

(SO 3)

Instructions

(a) If Hixson uses the direct write-off method to account for uncollectible accounts, journalize the adjusting entry at December 31, assuming Hixson determines that Fell's $1,400 balance is uncollectible.

(b) If Allowance for Doubtful Accounts has a credit balance of $2,100 in the trial balance, journalize the adjusting entry at December 31, assuming bad debts are expected to be (1) 1% of net sales, and (2) 10% of accounts receivable.

(c) If Allowance for Doubtful Accounts has a debit balance of $200 in the trial balance, journalize the adjusting entry at December 31, assuming bad debts are expected to be (1) 0.75% of net sales and (2) 6% of accounts receivable.

Determine bad debts expense; prepare the adjusting entry for bad debts expense.

(SO 3)

E9-4 Ingles Company has accounts receivable of $93,100 at March 31. An analysis of the accounts shows the following.

Month of Sale	Balance, March 31
March	$60,000
February	17,600
January	8,500
Prior to January	7,000
	$93,100

Credit terms are 2/10, n/30. At March 31, Allowance for Doubtful Accounts has a credit balance of $1,200 prior to adjustment. The company uses the percentage-of-receivables basis for estimating uncollectible accounts. The company's estimate of bad debts is as follows.

Age of Accounts	Estimated Percentage Uncollectible
1–30 days	2.0%
30–60 days	5.0%
60–90 days	30.0%
Over 90 days	50.0%

Instructions

(a) Determine the total estimated uncollectibles.

(b) Prepare the adjusting entry at March 31 to record bad debts expense.

Journalize write-off and recovery.

(SO 3)

E9-5 At December 31, 2007, Braddock Company had a balance of $15,000 in the Allowance for Doubtful Accounts. During 2008, Braddock wrote off accounts totaling $13,000. One of those accounts ($1,800) was later collected. At December 31, 2008, an aging schedule indicated that the balance in the Allowance for Doubtful Accounts should be $19,000.

Instructions

Prepare journal entries to record the 2008 transactions of Braddock Company.

Journalize percentage of sales basis, write-off, recovery.

(SO 3)

E9-6 On December 31, 2008, Jarnigan Co. estimated that 2% of its net sales of $400,000 will become uncollectible. The company recorded this amount as an addition to Allowance for Doubtful Accounts. On May 11, 2009, Jarnigan Co. determined that Terry Frye's account was uncollectible and wrote off $1,100. On June 12, 2009, Frye paid the amount previously written off.

Instructions

Prepare the journal entries on December 31, 2008, May 11, 2009, and June 12, 2009.

Journalize entries for the sale of accounts receivable.

(SO 4)

E9-7 Presented below are two independent situations.

(a) On March 3, Cornwell Appliances sells $680,000 of its receivables to Marsh Factors Inc. Marsh Factors assesses a finance charge of 3% of the amount of receivables sold. Prepare the entry on Cornwell Appliances' books to record the sale of the receivables.

(b) On May 10, Dale Company sold merchandise for $3,500 and accepted the customer's America Bank MasterCard. America Bank charges a 4% service charge for credit card sales. Prepare the entry on Dale Company's books to record the sale of merchandise.

Journalize entries for credit card sales.

(SO 4)

E9-8 Presented below are two independent situations.

(a) On April 2, Nancy Hansel uses her J. C. Penney Company credit card to purchase merchandise from a J. C. Penney store for $1,500. On May 1, Hansel is billed for the $1,500 amount due. Hansel pays $700 on the balance due on May 3. On June 1, Hansel receives a bill for the amount due, including interest at 1.0% per month on the unpaid balance as of May 3. Prepare the entries on J. C. Penney Co.'s books related to the transactions that occurred on April 2, May 3, and June 1.

(b) On July 4, Kimble's Restaurant accepts a Visa card for a $200 dinner bill. Visa charges a 3% service fee. Prepare the entry on Kimble's books related to this transaction.

Journalize credit card sales, and indicate the statement presentation of financing charges and service charge expense.

(SO 4)

E9-9 Topeka Stores accepts both its own and national credit cards. During the year the following selected summary transactions occurred.

Jan. 15 Made Topeka credit card sales totaling $18,000. (There were no balances prior to January 15.)
20 Made Visa credit card sales (service charge fee 2%) totaling $4,300.
Feb. 10 Collected $10,000 on Topeka credit card sales.
15 Added finance charges of 1% to Topeka credit card balance.

Instructions

(a) Journalize the transactions for Topeka Stores.
(b) Indicate the statement presentation of the financing charges and the credit card service charge expense for Topeka Stores.

Journalize entries for notes receivable transactions.

(SO 5, 6)

E9-10 Orosco Supply Co. has the following transactions related to notes receivable during the last 2 months of 2008.

Nov. 1 Loaned $15,000 cash to Sally Givens on a 1-year, 10% note.
Dec. 11 Sold goods to John Countryman, Inc., receiving a $6,750, 90-day, 8% note.
16 Received a $4,000, 6-month, 9% note in exchange for Bob Reber's outstanding accounts receivable.
31 Accrued interest revenue on all notes receivable.

Instructions

(a) Journalize the transactions for Orosco Supply Co.
(b) Record the collection of the Givens note at its maturity in 2009.

Journalize entries for notes receivable.

(SO 5, 6)

E9-11 Record the following transactions for Sandwich Co. in the general journal.

<u>2008</u>

May 1 Received a $7,500, 1-year, 10% note in exchange for Julia Gonzalez's outstanding accounts receivable.
Dec. 31 Accrued interest on the Gonzalez note.
Dec. 31 Closed the interest revenue account.

<u>2009</u>

May 1 Received principal plus interest on the Gonzalez note. (No interest has been accrued in 2009.)

Prepare entries for note receivable transactions.

(SO 5, 6, 8)

E9-12 Singletary Company had the following select transactions.

Apr. 1, 2008 Accepted Wilson Company's 1-year, 12% note in settlement of a $20,000 account receivable.
July 1, 2008 Loaned $25,000 cash to Richard Dent on a 9-month, 10% note.
Dec. 31, 2008 Accrued interest on all notes receivable.
Apr. 1, 2009 Received principal plus interest on the Wilson note.
Apr. 1, 2009 Richard Dent dishonored its note; Singletary expects it will eventually collect.

Instructions

Prepare journal entries to record the transactions. Singletary prepares adjusting entries once a year on December 31.

Journalize entries for dishonor of notes receivable.

(SO 5, 8)

E9-13 On May 2, Kleinsorge Company lends $7,600 to Everhart, Inc., issuing a 6-month, 9% note. At the maturity date, November 2, Everhart indicates that it cannot pay.

Instructions

(a) Prepare the entry to record the issuance of the note.
(b) Prepare the entry to record the dishonor of the note, assuming that Kleinsorge Company expects collection will occur.
(c) Prepare the entry to record the dishonor of the note, assuming that Kleinsorge Company does not expect collection in the future.

Determine missing amounts related to sales and accounts receivable.
(SO 2, 4, 9)

E9-14 The following information pertains to Napa Merchandising Company.

Merchandise inventory at end of year	$33,000
Accounts receivable at beginning of year	24,000
Cash sales made during the year	18,000
Gross profit on sales	20,000
Accounts receivable written off during the year	1,000
Purchases made during the year	60,000
Accounts receivable collected during the year	78,000
Merchandise inventory at beginning of year	36,000

Instructions

(a) Calculate the amount of credit sales made during the year. (*Hint:* You will need to use income statement relationships—introduced in Chapter 5—in order to determine this.)

(b) Calculate the balance of accounts receivable at the end of the year.

Compute receivables turnover and average collection period.
(SO 9)

E9-15 Bledel Company had accounts receivable of $100,000 on January 1, 2008. The only transactions that affected accounts receivable during 2008 were net credit sales of $1,000,000, cash collections of $900,000, and accounts written off of $30,000.

Instructions

(a) Compute the ending balance of accounts receivable.

(b) Compute the accounts receivable turnover ratio for 2008.

(c) Compute the average collection period in days.

EXERCISES: SET B

Visit the book's website at **www.wiley.com/college/weygandt**, and choose the Student Companion site, to access Exercise Set B.

PROBLEMS: SET A

Prepare journal entries related to bad debts expense.
(SO 2, 3, 9)

P9-1A At December 31, 2007, Leis Co. reported the following information on its balance sheet.

Accounts receivable	$960,000
Less: Allowance for doubtful accounts	80,000

During 2008, the company had the following transactions related to receivables.

1. Sales on account	$3,200,000
2. Sales returns and allowances	50,000
3. Collections of accounts receivable	2,810,000
4. Write-offs of accounts receivable deemed uncollectible	90,000
5. Recovery of bad debts previously written off as uncollectible	24,000

Instructions

(a) Prepare the journal entries to record each of these five transactions. Assume that no cash discounts were taken on the collections of accounts receivable.

(b) Accounts receivable $1,210,000
ADA $14,000

(c) Bad debts expense $101,000

(b) Enter the January 1, 2008, balances in Accounts Receivable and Allowance for Doubtful Accounts, post the entries to the two accounts (use T accounts), and determine the balances.

(c) Prepare the journal entry to record bad debts expense for 2008, assuming that an aging of accounts receivable indicates that expected bad debts are $115,000.

(d) Compute the accounts receivable turnover ratio for 2008.

Compute bad debts amounts.
(SO 3)

P9-2A Information related to Hermesch Company for 2008 is summarized below.

Total credit sales	$2,200,000
Accounts receivable at December 31	825,000
Bad debts written off	33,000

Instructions

(a) What amount of bad debts expense will Hermesch Company report if it uses the direct write-off method of accounting for bad debts?

(b) Assume that Hermesch Company estimates its bad debts expense to be 2% of credit sales. What amount of bad debts expense will Hermesch record if it has an Allowance for Doubtful Accounts credit balance of $4,000?

(c) Assume that Hermesch Company estimates its bad debts expense based on 6% of accounts receivable. What amount of bad debts expense will Hermesch record if it has an Allowance for Doubtful Accounts credit balance of $3,000?

(d) Assume the same facts as in (c), except that there is a $3,000 debit balance in Allowance for Doubtful Accounts. What amount of bad debts expense will Hermesch record?

(e) What is the weakness of the direct write-off method of reporting bad debts expense?

Journalize entries to record transactions related to bad debts.

(SO 2, 3)

P9-3A Presented below is an aging schedule for Zillmann Company.

Worksheet.xls

	A	B	C	D	E	F	G
1							
2			Not	Number of Days Past Due			
3	Customer	Total	Yet Due	1–30	31–60	61–90	Over 90
4	Arndt	$ 22,000		$10,000	$12,000		
5	Blair	40,000	$ 40,000				
6	Chase	57,000	16,000	6,000		$35,000	
7	Drea	34,000					$34,000
8	Others	132,000	96,000	16,000	14,000		6,000
9		$285,000	$152,000	$32,000	$26,000	$35,000	$40,000
10	Estimated Percentage Uncollectible		3%	6%	13%	25%	60%
11	Total Estimated Bad Debts	$ 42,610	$ 4,560	$ 1,920	$ 3,380	$ 8,750	$24,000
12							

At December 31, 2008, the unadjusted balance in Allowance for Doubtful Accounts is a credit of $12,000.

Instructions

(a) Journalize and post the adjusting entry for bad debts at December 31, 2008.

(a) Bad debts expense $30,610

(b) Journalize and post to the allowance account the following events and transactions in the year 2009.

(1) On March 31, a $1,000 customer balance originating in 2008 is judged uncollectible.

(2) On May 31, a check for $1,000 is received from the customer whose account was written off as uncollectible on March 31.

(c) Journalize the adjusting entry for bad debts on December 31, 2009, assuming that the unadjusted balance in Allowance for Doubtful Accounts is a debit of $800 and the aging schedule indicates that total estimated bad debts will be $28,600.

(c) Bad debts expense $29,400

Journalize transactions related to bad debts.

(SO 2, 3)

P9-4A Wall Inc. uses the allowance method to estimate uncollectible accounts receivable. The company produced the following aging of the accounts receivable at year end.

Worksheet.xls

	A	B	C	D	E	F	G
1							
2			Number of Days Outstanding				
3		Total	0–30	31–60	61–90	91–120	Over 120
4	Accounts receivable	$375,000	$220,000	$90,000	$40,000	$10,000	$15,000
5	% uncollectible		1%	4%	5%	8%	10%
6	Estimated bad debts						
7							

Instructions

(a) Calculate the total estimated bad debts based on the above information.

(a) Tot. est. bad debts $10,100

(b) Prepare the year-end adjusting journal entry to record the bad debts using the aged uncollectible accounts receivable determined in (a). Assume the current balance in Allowance for Doubtful Accounts is a $8,000 debit.

(c) Of the above accounts, $5,000 is determined to be specifically uncollectible. Prepare the journal entry to write off the uncollectible account.
(d) The company collects $5,000 subsequently on a specific account that had previously been determined to be uncollectible in (c). Prepare the journal entry(ies) necessary to restore the account and record the cash collection.
(e) Comment on how your answers to (a)–(d) would change if Wall Inc. used 3% of *total* accounts receivable, rather than aging the accounts receivable. What are the advantages to the company of aging the accounts receivable rather than applying a percentage to total accounts receivable?

Journalize entries to record transactions related to bad debts.

(SO 3)

P9-5A At December 31, 2008, the trial balance of Worcester Company contained the following amounts before adjustment.

	Debits	Credits
Accounts Receivable	$385,000	
Allowance for Doubtful Accounts		$ 2,000
Sales		950,000

Instructions
(a) Based on the information given, which method of accounting for bad debts is Worcester Company using—the direct write-off method or the allowance method? How can you tell?

(b) (2) $9,500

(b) Prepare the adjusting entry at December 31, 2008, for bad debts expense under each of the following independent assumptions.
  (1) An aging schedule indicates that $11,750 of accounts receivable will be uncollectible.
  (2) The company estimates that 1% of sales will be uncollectible.
(c) Repeat part (b) assuming that instead of a credit balance there is an $2,000 debit balance in Allowance for Doubtful Accounts.
(d) During the next month, January 2009, a $3,000 account receivable is written off as uncollectible. Prepare the journal entry to record the write-off.
(e) Repeat part (d) assuming that Worcester uses the direct write-off method instead of the allowance method in accounting for uncollectible accounts receivable.
(f) What type of account is Allowance for Doubtful Accounts? How does it affect how accounts receivable is reported on the balance sheet at the end of the accounting period?

Prepare entries for various notes receivable transactions.

(SO 2, 4, 5, 8, 9)

GLS Peachtree

P9-6A Mendosa Company closes its books monthly. On September 30, selected ledger account balances are:

Notes Receivable	$33,000
Interest Receivable	$ 170

Notes Receivable include the following.

Date	Maker	Face	Term	Interest
Aug. 16	Chang Inc.	$ 8,000	60 days	8%
Aug. 25	Hughey Co.	9,000	60 days	10%
Sept. 30	Skinner Corp.	16,000	6 months	9%

Interest is computed using a 360-day year. During October, the following transactions were completed.

Oct. 7 Made sales of $6,900 on Mendosa credit cards.
12 Made sales of $900 on MasterCard credit cards. The credit card service charge is 3%.
15 Added $460 to Mendosa customer balance for finance charges on unpaid balances.
15 Received payment in full from Chang Inc. on the amount due.
24 Received notice that the Hughey note has been dishonored. (Assume that Hughey is expected to pay in the future.)

Instructions
(a) Journalize the October transactions and the October 31 adjusting entry for accrued interest receivable.

(b) Accounts receivable $16,510

(c) Total receivables $32,630

(b) Enter the balances at October 1 in the receivable accounts. Post the entries to all of the receivable accounts.
(c) Show the balance sheet presentation of the receivable accounts at October 31.

Prepare entries for various receivable transactions.

(SO 2, 4, 5, 6, 7, 8)

P9-7A On January 1, 2008, Kloppenberg Company had Accounts Receivable $139,000, Notes Receivable $25,000, and Allowance for Doubtful Accounts $13,200. The note receivable is from

Sara Rogers Company. It is a 4-month, 12% note dated December 31, 2007. Kloppenberg Company prepares financial statements annually. During the year the following selected transactions occurred.

Jan.	5	Sold $20,000 of merchandise to Dedonder Company, terms n/15.
	20	Accepted Dedonder Company's $20,000, 3-month, 9% note for balance due.
Feb.	18	Sold $8,000 of merchandise to Ludwig Company and accepted Ludwig's $8,000, 6-month, 9% note for the amount due.
Apr.	20	Collected Dedonder Company note in full.
	30	Received payment in full from Sara Rogers Company on the amount due.
May	25	Accepted Jenks Inc.'s $4,000, 3-month, 7% note in settlement of a past-due balance on account.
Aug.	18	Received payment in full from Ludwig Company on note due.
	25	The Jenks Inc. note was dishonored. Jenks Inc. is not bankrupt; future payment is anticipated.
Sept.	1	Sold $12,000 of merchandise to Lena Torme Company and accepted a $12,000, 6-month, 10% note for the amount due.

Instructions

Journalize the transactions.

PROBLEMS: SET B

P9-1B At December 31, 2007, Pickeril Imports reported the following information on its balance sheet.

Prepare journal entries related to bad debts expense.

(SO 2, 3, 9)

Accounts receivable	$1,000,000
Less: Allowance for doubtful accounts	60,000

During 2008, the company had the following transactions related to receivables.

1. Sales on account	$2,570,000
2. Sales returns and allowances	40,000
3. Collections of accounts receivable	2,300,000
4. Write-offs of accounts receivable deemed uncollectible	65,000
5. Recovery of bad debts previously written off as uncollectible	25,000

Instructions

(a) Prepare the journal entries to record each of these five transactions. Assume that no cash discounts were taken on the collections of accounts receivable.

(b) Enter the January 1, 2008, balances in Accounts Receivable and Allowance for Doubtful Accounts. Post the entries to the two accounts (use T accounts), and determine the balances.

(c) Prepare the journal entry to record bad debts expense for 2008, assuming that an aging of accounts receivable indicates that estimated bad debts are $90,000.

(d) Compute the accounts receivable turnover ratio for the year 2008.

(b) Accounts receivable $1,165,000 ADA $20,000

(c) Bad debts expense $70,000

P9-2B Information related to Hively Company for 2008 is summarized below.

Compute bad debts amounts.

(SO 3)

Total credit sales	$1,540,000
Accounts receivable at December 31	520,000
Bad debts written off	26,000

Instructions

(a) What amount of bad debts expense will Hively Company report if it uses the direct write-off method of accounting for bad debts?

(b) Assume that Hively Company decides to estimate its bad debts expense to be 2% of credit sales. What amount of bad debts expense will Hively record if Allowance for Doubtful Accounts has a credit balance of $3,000?

(c) Assume that Hively Company decides to estimate its bad debts expense based on 5% of accounts receivable. What amount of bad debts expense will Hively Company record if Allowance for Doubtful Accounts has a credit balance of $4,000?

(d) Assume the same facts as in (c), except that there is a $2,000 debit balance in Allowance for Doubtful Accounts. What amount of bad debts expense will Hively record?

(e) What is the weakness of the direct write-off method of reporting bad debts expense?

Journalize entries to record transactions related to bad debts.

(SO 2, 3)

P9-3B Presented below is an aging schedule for Lawrenz Company.

Worksheet.xls

Customer	Total	Not Yet Due	Number of Days Past Due 1–30	31–60	61–90	Over 90
Akers	$ 20,000		$ 9,000	$11,000		
Baietto	30,000	$ 30,000				
Comer	50,000	15,000	5,000		$30,000	
DeJong	38,000					$38,000
Others	126,000	92,000	15,000	13,000		6,000
	$264,000	$137,000	$29,000	$24,000	$30,000	$44,000
Estimated Percentage Uncollectible		2%	5%	10%	24%	50%
Total Estimated Bad Debts	$ 35,790	$ 2,740	$ 1,450	$ 2,400	$ 7,200	$22,000

At December 31, 2008, the unadjusted balance in Allowance for Doubtful Accounts is a credit of $10,000.

Instructions

(a) Bad debts expense $25,790

(c) Bad debts expense $29,500

(a) Journalize and post the adjusting entry for bad debts at December 31, 2008.

(b) Journalize and post to the allowance account the following events and transactions in the year 2009.

 (1) March 1, an $1,100 customer balance originating in 2008 is judged uncollectible.

 (2) May 1, a check for $1,100 is received from the customer whose account was written off as uncollectible on March 1.

(c) Journalize the adjusting entry for bad debts on December 31, 2009. Assume that the unadjusted balance in Allowance for Doubtful Accounts is a debit of $1,200, and the aging schedule indicates that total estimated bad debts will be $28,300.

Journalize transactions related to bad debts.

(SO 2, 3)

P9-4B The following represents selected information taken from a company's aging schedule to estimate uncollectible accounts receivable at year end.

Worksheet.xls

	Total	Number of Days Outstanding 0–30	31–60	61–90	91–120	Over 120
Accounts receivable	$260,000	$100,000	$60,000	$50,000	$30,000	$20,000
% uncollectible		1%	5%	7.5%	10%	15%
Estimated bad debts						

Instructions

(a) Tot. est. bad debts $13,750

(a) Calculate the total estimated bad debts based on the above information.

(b) Prepare the year-end adjusting journal entry to record the bad debts using the allowance method and the aged uncollectible accounts receivable determined in (a). Assume the current balance in the Allowance for Doubtful Accounts account is a $10,000 credit.

(c) Of the above accounts, $2,000 is determined to be specifically uncollectible. Prepare the journal entry to write off the uncollectible accounts.

(d) The company subsequently collects $1,000 on a specific account that had previously been determined to be uncollectible in (c). Prepare the journal entry(ies) necessary to restore the account and record the cash collection.

(e) Explain how establishing an allowance account satisfies the matching principle.

P9-5B At December 31, 2008, the trial balance of Schnakenberg Company contained the following amounts before adjustment.

Journalize entries to record transactions related to bad debts.

(SO 3)

	Debits	Credits
Accounts Receivable	$350,000	
Allowance for Doubtful Accounts		$ 1,500
Sales		850,000

Instructions

(a) Prepare the adjusting entry at December 31, 2008, to record bad debts expense under each of the following independent assumptions.

(1) An aging schedule indicates that $17,550 of accounts receivable will be uncollectible.

(2) The company estimates that 2% of sales will be uncollectible.

(a) (2) $17,000

(b) Repeat part (a) assuming that instead of a credit balance, there is a $1,500 debit balance in Allowance for Doubtful Accounts.

(c) During the next month, January 2009, a $4,500 account receivable is written off as uncollectible. Prepare the journal entry to record the write-off.

(d) Repeat part (c) assuming that Schnakenberg Company uses the direct write-off method instead of the allowance method in accounting for uncollectible accounts receivable.

(e) What are the advantages of using the allowance method in accounting for uncollectible accounts as compared to the direct write-off method?

P9-6B Schottenheimer Co. closes its books monthly. On June 30, selected ledger account balances are:

Prepare entries for various notes receivable transactions.

(SO 2, 4, 5, 8, 9)

GLS

Notes Receivable	$46,000
Interest Receivable	$ 300

Notes Receivable include the following.

Date	Maker	Face	Term	Interest
May 16	Baylor Inc.	$ 6,000	60 days	10%
May 25	Felter Co.	25,000	60 days	9%
June 30	ERV Corp.	15,000	6 months	8%

During July, the following transactions were completed.

July 5 Made sales of $6,200 on Schottenheimer Co. credit cards.
14 Made sales of $700 on Visa credit cards. The credit card service charge is 3%.
14 Added $440 to Schottenheimer Co. credit card customer balances for finance charges on unpaid balances.
15 Received payment in full from Baylor Inc. on the amount due.
25 Received notice that the Felter Co. note has been dishonored. (Assume that Felter Co. is expected to pay in the future.)

Instructions

(a) Journalize the July transactions and the July 31 adjusting entry for accrued interest receivable. (Interest is computed using 360 days.)

(b) Enter the balances at July 1 in the receivable accounts. Post the entries to all of the receivable accounts.

(b) Accounts receivable $32,015

(c) Show the balance sheet presentation of the receivable accounts at July 31.

(c) Total receivables $47,115

P9-7B On January 1, 2008, Frybendall Company had Accounts Receivable $56,900 and Allowance for Doubtful Accounts $4,700. Frybendall Company prepares financial statements annually. During the year the following selected transactions occurred.

Prepare entries for various receivable transactions.

(SO 2, 4, 5, 6, 7, 8)

Jan. 5 Sold $6,300 of merchandise to Klosterman Company, terms n/30.
Feb. 2 Accepted a $6,300, 4-month, 10% promissory note from Klosterman Company for the balance due.
12 Sold $7,800 of merchandise to Menard Company and accepted Menard's $7,800, 2-month, 10% note for the balance due.
26 Sold $4,000 of merchandise to Louk Co., terms n/10.
Apr. 5 Accepted a $4,000, 3-month, 8% note from Louk Co. for the balance due.
12 Collected Menard Company note in full.
June 2 Collected Klosterman Company note in full.

July 5 Louk Co. dishonors its note of April 5. It is expected that Louk will eventually pay the amount owed.

15 Sold $7,000 of merchandise to Peck Co. and accepted Peck's $7,000, 3-month, 12% note for the amount due.

Oct. 15 Peck Co.'s note was dishonored. Peck Co. is bankrupt, and there is no hope of future settlement.

Instructions

Journalize the transactions.

PROBLEMS: SET C

Visit the book's website at **www.wiley.com/college/weygandt**, and choose the Student Companion site, to access Problem Set C.

CONTINUING COOKIE CHRONICLE

(*Note:* This is a continuation of the Cookie Chronicle from Chapters 1 through 8.)

CCC9 One of Natalie's friends, Curtis Lesperance, runs a coffee shop where he sells specialty coffees and prepares and sells muffins and cookies. He is eager to buy one of Natalie's fine European mixers, which would enable him to make larger batches of muffins and cookies. However, Curtis cannot afford to pay for the mixer for at least 30 days. He asks Natalie if she would be willing to sell him the mixer on credit. Natalie comes to you for advice.

Go to the book's website, ***www.wiley.com/college/weygandt****, to see the completion of this problem.*

BROADENING YOUR PERSPECTIVE

FINANCIAL REPORTING AND ANALYSIS

Financial Reporting Problem
SEK Company

BYP9-1 SEK Company sells office equipment and supplies to many organizations in the city and surrounding area on contract terms of 2/10, n/30. In the past, over 75% of the credit customers have taken advantage of the discount by paying within 10 days of the invoice date.

The number of customers taking the full 30 days to pay has increased within the last year. Current indications are that less than 60% of the customers are now taking the discount. Bad debts as a percentage of gross credit sales have risen from the 2.5% provided in past years to about 4.5% in the current year.

The company's Finance Committee has requested more information on the collections of accounts receivable. The controller responded to this request with the report reproduced below.

SEK COMPANY
Accounts Receivable Collections
May 31, 2008

The fact that some credit accounts will prove uncollectible is normal. Annual bad debts write-offs have been 2.5% of gross credit sales over the past 5 years. During the last fiscal year, this percentage increased to slightly less than 4.5%. The current Accounts Receivable balance is $1,400,000. The condition of this balance in terms of age and probability of collection is as follows.

Proportion of Total	Age Categories	Probability of Collection
62%	not yet due	98%
20%	less than 30 days past due	96%
9%	30 to 60 days past due	94%
5%	61 to 120 days past due	91%
2½%	121 to 180 days past due	75%
1½%	over 180 days past due	30%

The Allowance for Doubtful Accounts had a credit balance of $29,500 on June 1, 2007. SEK has provided for a monthly bad debts expense accrual during the current fiscal year based on the assumption that 4.5% of gross credit sales will be uncollectible. Total gross credit sales for the 2007–08 fiscal year amounted to $2,900,000. Write-offs of bad accounts during the year totaled $102,000.

Instructions

(a) Prepare an accounts receivable aging schedule for SEK Company using the age categories identified in the controller's report to the Finance Committee showing the following.
  (1) The amount of accounts receivable outstanding for each age category and in total.
  (2) The estimated amount that is uncollectible for each category and in total.
(b) Compute the amount of the year-end adjustment necessary to bring Allowance for Doubtful Accounts to the balance indicated by the age analysis. Then prepare the necessary journal entry to adjust the accounting records.
(c) In a recessionary environment with tight credit and high interest rates:
  (1) Identify steps SEK Company might consider to improve the accounts receivable situation.
  (2) Then evaluate each step identified in terms of the risks and costs involved.

Comparative Analysis Problem

PepsiCo, Inc. vs. The Coca-Cola Company

BYP9-2 PepsiCo's financial statements are presented in Appendix A. Coca-Cola's financial statements are presented in Appendix B.

Instructions

(a) Based on the information in these financial statements, compute the following 2005 ratios for each company. (Assume all sales are credit sales. Also, see PepsiCo's Note 14.)
  (1) Accounts receivable turnover ratio.
  (2) Average collection period for receivables.
(b) What conclusions about managing accounts receivable can you draw from these data?

Exploring the Web

BYP9-3 **Purpose:** To learn more about factoring services.

Address: **www.invoicefinancial.com**, or go to **www.wiley.com/college/weygandt**

Steps: Go to the website and answer the following questions.

(a) What are some of the benefits of factoring?
(b) What is the range of the percentages of the typical discount rate?
(c) If a company factors its receivables, what percentage of the value of the receivables can it expect to receive from the factor in the form of cash, and how quickly will it receive the cash?

CRITICAL THINKING

Decision Making Across the Organization

BYP9-4 Molly and Joe Mayne own Campus Fashions. From its inception Campus Fashions has sold merchandise on either a cash or credit basis, but no credit cards have been accepted. During the past several months, the Maynes have begun to question their sales policies. First, they have lost some sales because of refusing to accept credit cards. Second, representatives of two metropolitan banks have been persuasive in almost convincing them to accept their national credit cards. One bank, City National Bank, has stated that its credit card fee is 4%.

The Maynes decide that they should determine the cost of carrying their own credit sales. From the accounting records of the past 3 years they accumulate the following data.

	2008	2007	2006
Net credit sales	$500,000	$600,000	$400,000
Collection agency fees for slow-paying customers	2,450	2,500	2,400
Salary of part-time accounts receivable clerk	4,100	4,100	4,100

Credit and collection expenses as a percentage of net credit sales are: uncollectible accounts 1.6%, billing and mailing costs 0.5%, and credit investigation fee on new customers 0.15%.

Molly and Joe also determine that the average accounts receivable balance outstanding during the year is 5% of net credit sales. The Maynes estimate that they could earn an average of 8% annually on cash invested in other business opportunities.

Instructions

With the class divided into groups, answer the following.

(a) Prepare a table showing, for each year, total credit and collection expenses in dollars and as a percentage of net credit sales.

(b) Determine the net credit and collection expense in dollars and as a percentage of sales after considering the revenue not earned from other investment opportunities.

(c) Discuss both the financial and nonfinancial factors that are relevant to the decision.

Communication Activity

BYP9-5 Rene Mai, a friend of yours, overheard a discussion at work about changes her employer wants to make in accounting for uncollectible accounts. Rene knows little about accounting, and she asks you to help make sense of what she heard. Specifically, she asks you to explain the differences between the percentage-of-sales, percentage-of-receivables, and the direct write-off methods for uncollectible accounts.

Instructions

In a letter of one page (or less), explain to Rene the three methods of accounting for uncollectibles. Be sure to discuss differences among these methods.

Ethics Case

BYP9-6 The controller of Ruiz Co. believes that the yearly allowance for doubtful accounts for Ruiz Co. should be 2% of net credit sales. The president of Ruiz Co., nervous that the stockholders might expect the company to sustain its 10% growth rate, suggests that the controller increase the allowance for doubtful accounts to 4%. The president thinks that the lower net income, which reflects a 6% growth rate, will be a more sustainable rate for Ruiz Co.

Instructions

(a) Who are the stakeholders in this case?

(b) Does the president's request pose an ethical dilemma for the controller?

(c) Should the controller be concerned with Ruiz Co.'s growth rate? Explain your answer.

* "All About You" Activity

BYP9-7 As the **All About You** feature in this chapter (page 403) indicates, credit card usage in the United States is substantial. Many startup companies use credit cards as a way to help meet short-term financial needs. The most common forms of debt for startups are use of credit cards and loans from relatives.

Suppose that you start up Brothers Sandwich Shop. You invested your savings of $20,000 and borrowed $70,000 from your relatives. Although sales in the first few months are good, you see that you may not have sufficient cash to pay expenses and maintain your inventory at acceptable levels, at least in the short term. You decide you may need to use one or more credit cards to fund the possible cash shortfall.

Instructions

(a) Go to the Web and find two sources that provide insight into how to compare credit card terms.

(b) Develop a list, in descending order of importance, as to what features are most important to you in selecting a credit card for your business.

(c) Examine the features of your present credit card. (If you do not have a credit card, select a likely one online for this exercise.) Given your analysis above, what are the three major disadvantages of your present credit card?

Answers to Insight and Accounting Across the Organization Questions

p. 386 Be Sure to Read the Fine Print

Q: Why are credit card companies willing to offer relaxed repayment options?

A: *Credit card companies generate their income primarily from interest charges on cardholders' balances. The larger the outstanding balances, the greater the interest income.*

p. 392 When Investors Ignore Warning Signs

Q: When would it be appropriate for a company to lower its allowance for doubtful accounts as a percentage of its receivables?

A: *It could do so if the company's collection experience had improved, or was expected to improve, and therefore the company expected lower defaults as a percentage of receivables.*

p. 395 How Does a Credit Card Work?

Q: Assume that Nordstrom prepares a bank reconciliation at the end of each month. If some credit card sales have not been processed by the bank, how should Nordstrom treat these transactions on its bank reconciliation?

A: *Nordstrom would treat the credit card receipts as deposits in transit. It has already recorded the receipts as cash. Its bank will increase Nordstrom's cash account when it receives the receipts.*

p. 400 Who Gets Credit?

Q: How would reported net income likely differ during the first year of this promotion if Mitsubishi used the direct write-off method versus the allowance method?

A: *Under the direct write-off method, Mitsubishi would not record bad debt expense until a customer defaulted on a loan. Under the allowance method, it would estimate how many of its loans would default rather than waiting until they default. The direct write-off method would have resulted in higher net income during the first year of the promotion.*

Authors' Comments on *All About You:* Should You Be Carrying Plastic? (p. 403)

We aren't going to tell you to cut up your credit card. Well, we aren't going to tell *all* of you to do so. Credit cards, when used properly, can serve a very useful purpose. They provide great convenience, are widely accepted, and can be a source of security in an emergency. But too many Americans use credit cards inappropriately. When businesses purchase short-term items such as inventory and supplies, they use short-term credit, which they expect to pay back very quickly. The same should be true of your credit card. When you make purchases of everyday items, you should completely pay off those items within a month or two. If you don't, you are living beyond your means, and you will soon dig yourself a deep financial pit.

Longer-term items should not be purchased with credit cards, since the interest rate is too high. If you currently have a large balance on your credit card(s), we encourage you to cut up your card(s) until you have paid off your balance(s).

Answer to PepsiCo Review It Question 3, p. 392

According to Note 14, PepsiCo's gross receivables were $3,336 million. Its allowance for doubtful accounts was $75 million. Therefore, the allowance is 2.2% of the gross receivables balance.

Answers to Self-Study Questions

1. c **2.** a **3.** b **4.** b **5.** d **6.** c **7.** c **8.** a **9.** b **10.** d

Remember to go back to the Navigator box on the chapter-opening page and check off your completed work.

Chapter 10

Plant Assets, Natural Resources, and Intangible Assets

STUDY OBJECTIVES

After studying this chapter, you should be able to:

1 Describe how the cost principle applies to plant assets.
2 Explain the concept of depreciation.
3 Compute periodic depreciation using different methods.
4 Describe the procedure for revising periodic depreciation.
5 Distinguish between revenue and capital expenditures, and explain the entries for each.
6 Explain how to account for the disposal of a plant asset.
7 Compute periodic depletion of natural resources.
8 Explain the basic issues related to accounting for intangible assets.
9 Indicate how plant assets, natural resources, and intangible assets are reported.

The Navigator

The Navigator

Scan **Study Objectives**	☐
Read **Feature Story**	☐
Read **Preview**	☐
Read text and answer **Before You Go On** p. 428 ☐ p. 435 ☐ p. 439 ☐ p. 447	☐
Work **Demonstration Problems**	☐
Review **Summary of Study Objectives**	☐
Answer **Self-Study Questions**	☐
Complete **Assignments**	☐

Feature Story

HOW MUCH FOR A RIDE TO THE BEACH?

It's spring break. Your plane has landed, you've finally found your bags, and you're dying to hit the beach—but first you need a "vehicular unit" to get

you there. As you turn away from baggage claim you see a long row of rental agency booths. Many are names you are familiar with—Hertz, Avis, and Budget. But a booth at the far end catches your eye—Rent-A-Wreck (*www.rent-a-wreck.com*). Now there's a company making a clear statement!

Any company that relies on equipment to generate revenues must make decisions about what kind of equipment to buy, how long to keep it, and how vigorously to maintain it. Rent-A-Wreck has decided to rent used rather than new cars and trucks. It rents these vehicles across the United States, Europe, and Asia. While the big-name agencies push vehicles with that "new car smell," Rent-A-Wreck competes on price. The message is simple: Rent a used car and save some cash. It's not a message that appeals to everyone. If you're a marketing executive wanting to impress a big client, you probably don't want to pull up in a Rent-A-Wreck car. But if you want to get from point A to point B for the minimum cash per mile, then they are playing your tune. The company's message seems to be getting across to the right clientele. Revenues have increased significantly.

When you rent a car from Rent-A-Wreck, you are renting from an independent business person who has paid a "franchise fee" for the right to use the Rent-A-Wreck name. In order to gain a franchise, he or she must meet financial and other criteria, and must agree to run the rental agency according to rules prescribed by Rent-A-Wreck. Some of these rules require that each franchise maintain its cars in a reasonable fashion. This ensures that, though you won't be cruising down Daytona Beach's Atlantic Avenue in a Mercedes convertible, you can be reasonably assured that you won't be calling a towtruck.

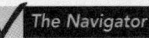

The Navigator

Inside Chapter 10...

Preview of Chapter 10

The accounting for long-term assets has important implications for a company's reported results. In this chapter, we explain the application of the cost principle of accounting to property, plant, and equipment, such as Rent-A-Wreck vehicles, as well as to natural resources and intangible assets such as the "Rent-A-Wreck" trademark. We also describe the methods that companies may use to allocate an asset's cost over its useful life. In addition, we discuss the accounting for expenditures incurred during the useful life of assets, such as the cost of replacing tires and brake pads on rental cars.

The content and organization of Chapter 10 are as follows.

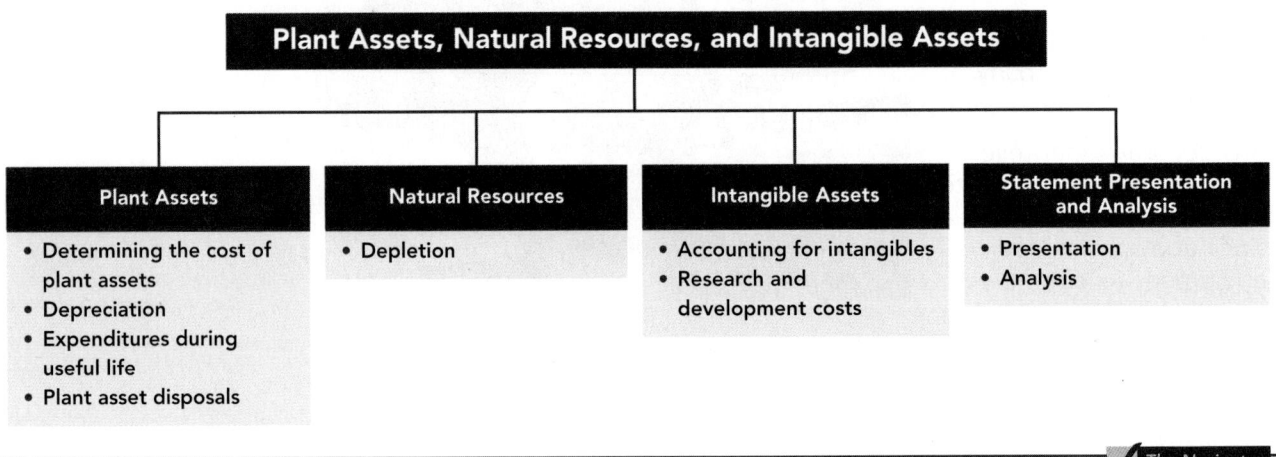

Plant Assets, Natural Resources, and Intangible Assets

Plant Assets
- Determining the cost of plant assets
- Depreciation
- Expenditures during useful life
- Plant asset disposals

Natural Resources
- Depletion

Intangible Assets
- Accounting for intangibles
- Research and development costs

Statement Presentation and Analysis
- Presentation
- Analysis

The Navigator

SECTION 1 Plant Assets

Plant assets are resources that have three characteristics: they have a physical substance (a definite size and shape), are used in the operations of a business, and are not intended for sale to customers. They are also called **property, plant, and equipment**; **plant and equipment**; and **fixed assets**. These assets are expected to provide services to the company for a number of years. Except for land, plant assets decline in service potential over their useful lives.

Because plant assets play a key role in ongoing operations, companies keep plant assets in good operating condition. They also replace worn-out or outdated plant assets, and expand productive resources as needed. Many companies have substantial investments in plant assets. Illustration 10-1 shows the

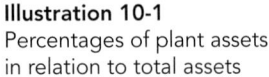

Illustration 10-1
Percentages of plant assets in relation to total assets

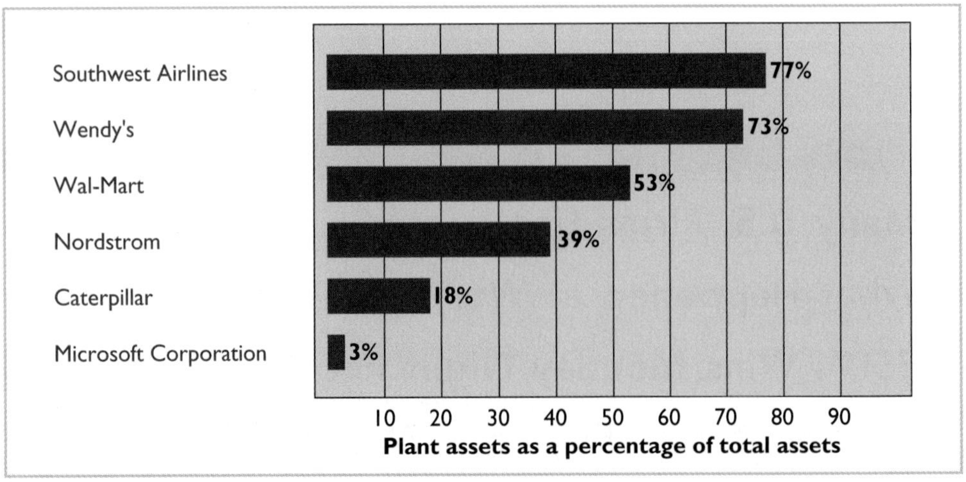

percentages of plant assets in relation to total assets of companies in a number of industries.

DETERMINING THE COST OF PLANT ASSETS

STUDY OBJECTIVE 1

Describe how the cost principle applies to plant assets.

The cost principle requires that companies record plant assets at cost. Thus Rent-A-Wreck records its vehicles at cost. **Cost consists of all expenditures necessary to acquire the asset and make it ready for its intended use.** For example, the cost of factory machinery includes the purchase price, freight costs paid by the purchaser, and installation costs. Once cost is established, the company uses that amount as the basis of accounting for the plant asset over its useful life.

In the following sections, we explain the application of the cost principle to each of the major classes of plant assets.

Land

Companies acquire **land** for use as a site upon which to build a manufacturing plant or office. The cost of land includes (1) the cash purchase price, (2) closing costs such as title and attorney's fees, (3) real estate brokers' commissions, and (4) accrued property taxes and other liens assumed by the purchaser. For example, if the cash price is $50,000 and the purchaser agrees to pay accrued taxes of $5,000, the cost of the land is $55,000.

Companies record as debits (increases) to the Land account all necessary costs incurred to make land **ready for its intended use**. When a company acquires vacant land, these costs include expenditures for clearing, draining, filling, and grading. Sometimes the land has a building on it that must be removed before construction of a new building. In this case, the company debits to the Land account all demolition and removal costs, less any proceeds from salvaged materials.

HELPFUL HINT

Management's intended use is important in applying the cost principle.

To illustrate, assume that Hayes Manufacturing Company acquires real estate at a cash cost of $100,000. The property contains an old warehouse that is razed at a net cost of $6,000 ($7,500 in costs less $1,500 proceeds from salvaged materials). Additional expenditures are the attorney's fee, $1,000, and the real estate broker's commission, $8,000. The cost of the land is $115,000, computed as follows.

Illustration 10-2
Computation of cost of land

Land	
Cash price of property	$100,000
Net removal cost of warehouse	6,000
Attorney's fee	1,000
Real estate broker's commission	8,000
Cost of land	**$115,000**

When Hayes records the acquisition, it debits Land for $115,000 and credits Cash for $115,000.

Land Improvements

Land improvements are structural additions made to land. Examples are driveways, parking lots, fences, landscaping, and underground sprinklers. The cost of land improvements includes all expenditures necessary to make the improvements ready for their intended use. For example, the cost of a new parking lot for Home Depot includes the amount paid for paving, fencing, and lighting. Thus Home Depot debits to Land Improvements the total of all of these costs.

Land improvements have limited useful lives, and their maintenance and replacement are the responsibility of the company. Because of their limited useful life, companies expense (depreciate) the cost of land improvements over their useful lives.

Buildings

Buildings are facilities used in operations, such as stores, offices, factories, warehouses, and airplane hangars. Companies debit to the Buildings account all necessary expenditures related to the purchase or construction of a building. When a building is **purchased**, such costs include the purchase price, closing costs (attorney's fees, title insurance, etc.) and real estate broker's commission. Costs to make the building ready for its intended use include expenditures for remodeling and replacing or repairing the roof, floors, electrical wiring, and plumbing. When a new building is **constructed**, cost consists of the contract price plus payments for architects' fees, building permits, and excavation costs.

In addition, companies charge certain interest costs to the Buildings account: Interest costs incurred to finance the project are included in the cost of the building when a significant period of time is required to get the building ready for use. In these circumstances, interest costs are considered as necessary as materials and labor. However, the inclusion of interest costs in the cost of a constructed building is **limited to the construction period**. When construction has been completed, the company records subsequent interest payments on funds borrowed to finance the construction as debits (increases) to Interest Expense.

Equipment

Equipment includes assets used in operations, such as store check-out counters, office furniture, factory machinery, delivery trucks, and airplanes. The cost of equipment, such as Rent-A-Wreck vehicles, consists of the **cash purchase price**, **sales taxes**, **freight charges, and insurance during transit paid by the purchaser**. It also includes expenditures required in assembling, installing, and testing the unit. However, Rent-A-Wreck does not include motor vehicle licenses and accident insurance on company vehicles in the cost of equipment. These costs represent annual recurring expenditures and do not benefit future periods. Thus, they are treated as expenses as they are incurred.

To illustrate, assume Merten Company purchases factory machinery at a cash price of $50,000. Related expenditures are for sales taxes $3,000, insurance during shipping $500, and installation and testing $1,000. The cost of the factory machinery is $54,500, computed as follows.

Illustration 10-3
Computation of cost of factory machinery

Factory Machinery

Cash price	$50,000
Sales taxes	3,000
Insurance during shipping	500
Installation and testing	1,000
Cost of factory machinery	**$54,500**

Merten makes the following summary entry to record the purchase and related expenditures:

Factory Machinery	54,500	
Cash		54,500
(To record purchase of factory machine)		

A	=	L	+	OE
+54,500				
−54,500				

Cash Flows
−54,500

For another example, assume that Lenard Company purchases a delivery truck at a cash price of $22,000. Related expenditures consist of sales taxes $1,320, painting and lettering $500, motor vehicle license $80, and a three-year accident insurance policy $1,600. The cost of the delivery truck is $23,820, computed as follows.

Illustration 10-4
Computation of cost of delivery truck

Delivery Truck	
Cash price	$22,000
Sales taxes	1,320
Painting and lettering	500
Cost of delivery truck	**$23,820**

Lenard treats the cost of the motor vehicle license as an expense, and the cost of the insurance policy as a prepaid asset. Thus, Lenard makes the following entry to record the purchase of the truck and related expenditures:

Delivery Truck	23,820	
License Expense	80	
Prepaid Insurance	1,600	
Cash		25,500
(To record purchase of delivery truck and related expenditures)		

A	=	L	+	OE
+23,820				
				−80 Exp
+1,600				
−25,500				

Cash Flows
−25,500

ACCOUNTING ACROSS THE ORGANIZATION

Many U.S. Firms Use Leases

Leasing is big business for U.S. companies. For example, business investment in equipment in 2004 totaled $709 billion. Leasing accounted for about 31% of all business investment ($218 billion).

Who does the most leasing? Interestingly major banks, such as Continental Bank, J.P. Morgan Leasing, and US Bancorp Equipment Finance, are the major lessors. Also, many companies have established separate leasing companies, such as Boeing Capital Corporation, Dell Financial Services, and John Deere Capital Corporation. And, as an excellent example of the magnitude of leasing, leased planes account for nearly 40% of the U.S. fleet of commercial airlines. In addition, leasing is becoming increasingly common in the hotel industry. Marriott, Hilton, and InterContinental are increasingly choosing to lease hotels that are owned by someone else.

? Why might airline managers choose to lease rather than purchase their planes?

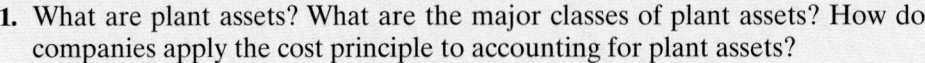

Before You Go On...

REVIEW IT

1. What are plant assets? What are the major classes of plant assets? How do companies apply the cost principle to accounting for plant assets?
2. What classifications and amounts are shown in PepsiCo's Note 4 to explain its total property, plant, and equipment (net) of $8,681,000,000? The answer to this question appears on p. 469.

DO IT

Assume that Drummond Heating and Cooling Co. purchases a delivery truck for $15,000 cash, plus sales taxes of $900 and delivery costs to the dealer of $500. The buyer also pays $200 for painting and lettering, $600 for an annual insurance policy, and $80 for a motor vehicle license. Explain how each of these costs would be accounted for.

Action Plan

- Identify expenditures made in order to get delivery equipment ready for its intended use.
- Treat operating costs as expenses.

Solution The first four payments ($15,000, $900, $500, and $200) are expenditures necessary to make the truck ready for its intended use. Thus, the cost of the truck is $16,600. The payments for insurance and the license are operating costs and therefore are expensed.

Related exercise material: *BE10-1, BE10-2, E10-1, E10-2, and E10-3.*

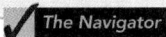

The Navigator

DEPRECIATION

STUDY OBJECTIVE 2

Explain the concept of depreciation.

As explained in Chapter 3, **depreciation is the process of allocating to expense the cost of a plant asset over its useful (service) life in a rational and systematic manner**. Cost allocation enables companies to properly match expenses with revenues in accordance with the matching principle (see Illustration 10-5).

Illustration 10-5
Depreciation as an allocation concept

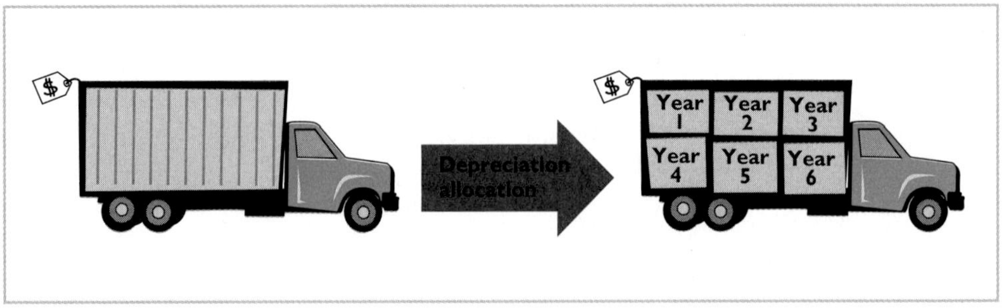

It is important to understand that **depreciation is a process of cost allocation, not a process of asset valuation**. No attempt is made to measure the change in an asset's market value during ownership. So, the **book value** (cost less accumulated depreciation) of a plant asset may be quite different from its market value.

Depreciation applies to three classes of plant assets: land improvements, buildings, and equipment. Each asset in these classes is considered to be a **depreciable asset**. Why? Because the usefulness to the company and revenue-producing ability of each asset will decline over the asset's useful life. Depreciation **does not apply to land** because its usefulness and revenue-producing ability generally remain intact over time. In fact, in many cases, the usefulness of land is greater over time because of the scarcity of good land sites. Thus, **land is not a depreciable asset**.

ETHICS NOTE

When a business is acquired, proper allocation of the purchase price to various asset classes is important, since different depreciation treatment can materially affect income. For example, buildings are depreciated, but land is not.

During a depreciable asset's useful life its revenue-producing ability declines because of **wear and tear**. A delivery truck that has been driven 100,000 miles will be less useful to a company than one driven only 800 miles.

Revenue-producing ability may also decline because of obsolescence. **Obsolescence** is the process of becoming out of date before the asset physically wears out. For example, major airlines moved from Chicago's Midway Airport to Chicago-O'Hare International Airport because Midway's runways were too short for jumbo jets. Similarly, many companies replace their computers long before they originally planned to do so because improvements in new computing technology make the old computers obsolete.

Recognizing depreciation on an asset does not result in an accumulation of cash for replacement of the asset. The balance in Accumulated Depreciation represents the total amount of the asset's cost that the company has charged to expense. It is not a cash fund.

Note that the concept of depreciation is consistent with the going-concern assumption. The **going-concern assumption** states that the company will continue in operation for the foreseeable future. If a company does not use a going-concern assumption, then plant assets should be stated at their market value. In that case, depreciation of these assets is not needed.

Factors in Computing Depreciation

Three factors affect the computation of depreciation:

1. **Cost.** Earlier, we explained the issues affecting the cost of a depreciable asset. Recall that companies record plant assets at cost, in accordance with the cost principle.
2. **Useful life.** **Useful life** is an estimate of the expected *productive life*, also called *service life*, of the asset. Useful life may be expressed in terms of time, units of activity (such as machine hours), or units of output. Useful life is an estimate. In making the estimate, management considers such factors as the intended use of the asset, its expected repair and maintenance, and its vulnerability to obsolescence. Past experience with similar assets is often helpful in deciding on expected useful life. We might reasonably expect Rent-A-Wreck and Avis to use different estimated useful lives for their vehicles.
3. **Salvage value.** **Salvage value** is an estimate of the asset's value at the end of its useful life. This value may be based on the asset's worth as scrap or on its expected trade-in value. Like useful life, salvage value is an estimate. In making the estimate, management considers how it plans to dispose of the asset and its experience with similar assets.

ALTERNATIVE TERMINOLOGY

Another term sometimes used for salvage value is *residual value*.

Illustration 10-6 (on page 430) summarizes the three factors used in computing depreciation.

Illustration 10-6
Three factors in computing depreciation

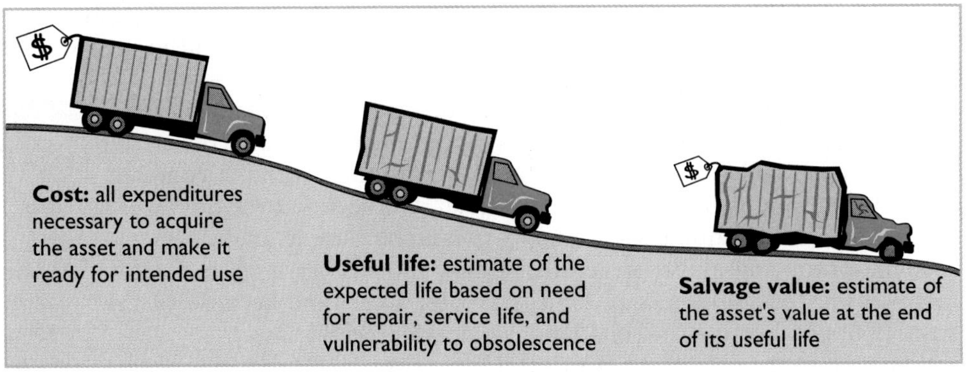

$
Cost: all expenditures necessary to acquire the asset and make it ready for intended use
Useful life: estimate of the expected life based on need for repair, service life, and vulnerability to obsolescence
$
Salvage value: estimate of the asset's value at the end of its useful life

HELPFUL HINT
Depreciation expense is reported on the income statement. Accumulated depreciation is reported on the balance sheet as a deduction from plant assets.

Depreciation Methods

STUDY OBJECTIVE 3
Compute periodic depreciation using different methods.

Depreciation is generally computed using one of the following methods:

1. Straight-line
2. Units-of-activity
3. Declining-balance

Each method is acceptable under generally accepted accounting principles. Management selects the method(s) it believes to be appropriate. The objective is to select the method that best measures an asset's contribution to revenue over its useful life. Once a company chooses a method, it should apply it consistently over the useful life of the asset. Consistency enhances the comparability of financial statements. Depreciation affects the balance sheet through accumulated depreciation and the income statement through depreciation expense.

We will compare the three depreciation methods using the following data for a small delivery truck purchased by Barb's Florists on January 1, 2008.

Illustration 10-7
Delivery truck data

Cost	$13,000
Expected salvage value	$ 1,000
Estimated useful life in years	5
Estimated useful life in miles	100,000

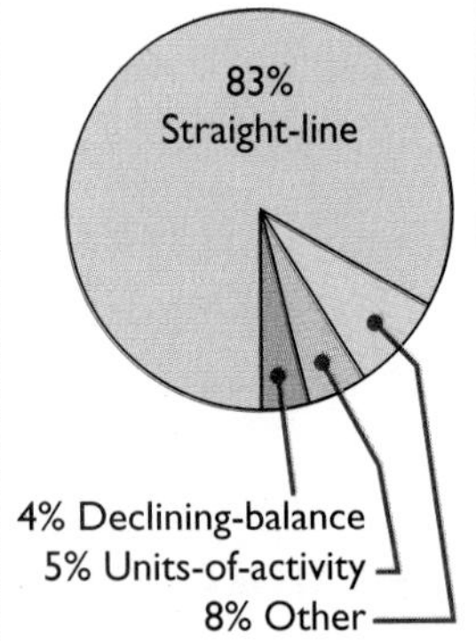

Illustration 10-8
Use of depreciation methods in 600 large U.S. companies

Illustration 10-8 (in the margin) shows the use of the primary depreciation methods in 600 of the largest companies in the United States.

STRAIGHT-LINE

Under the **straight-line method**, companies expense the same amount of depreciation for each year of the asset's useful life. It is measured solely by the passage of time.

In order to compute depreciation expense under the straight-line method, companies need to determine depreciable cost. **Depreciable cost** is the cost of the asset less its salvage value. It represents the total amount subject to depreciation. Under the straight-line method, to determine annual depreciation expense, we divide depreciable cost by the asset's useful life. Illustration 10-9 shows the computation of the first year's depreciation expense for Barb's Florists.

Alternatively, we also can compute an annual **rate** of depreciation. In this case, the rate is 20% (100% ÷ 5 years). When a company uses an annual straight-line rate, it applies the percentage rate to the depreciable cost of the asset. Illustration 10-10 shows a **depreciation schedule** using an annual rate.

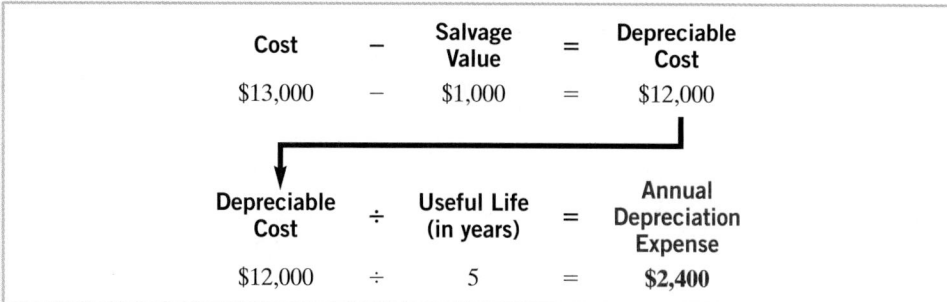

Illustration 10-9
Formula for straight-line method

Cost	−	Salvage Value	=	Depreciable Cost
$13,000	−	$1,000	=	$12,000

Depreciable Cost	÷	Useful Life (in years)	=	Annual Depreciation Expense
$12,000	÷	5	=	**$2,400**

Illustration 10-10
Straight-line depreciation schedule

BARB'S FLORISTS

	Computation					End of Year	
Year	Depreciable Cost	×	Depreciation Rate	=	Annual Depreciation Expense	Accumulated Depreciation	Book Value
2008	$12,000		20%		**$2,400**	$ 2,400	$10,600*
2009	12,000		20		**2,400**	4,800	8,200
2010	12,000		20		**2,400**	7,200	5,800
2011	12,000		20		**2,400**	9,600	3,400
2012	12,000		20		**2,400**	12,000	**1,000**

*Book Value = Cost − Accumulated depreciation = ($13,000 − $2,400).

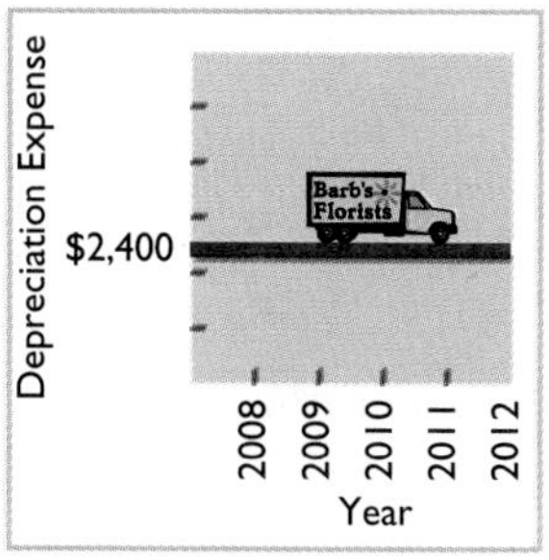

Note that the depreciation expense of $2,400 is the same each year. The book value (computed as cost minus accumulated depreciation) at the end of the useful life is equal to the expected $1,000 salvage value.

What happens to these computations for an asset purchased **during** the year, rather than on January 1? In that case, it is necessary to **prorate the annual depreciation** on a time basis. If Barb's Florists had purchased the delivery truck on April 1, 2008, the company would own the truck for nine months of the first year (April–December). Thus, depreciation for 2008 would be $1,800 ($12,000 × 20% × 9/12 of a year).

The straight-line method predominates in practice. Such large companies as Campbell Soup, Marriott, and General Mills use the straight-line method. It is simple to apply, and it matches expenses with revenues when the use of the asset is reasonably uniform throughout the service life. For simplicity, Rent-A-Wreck is probably using the straight-line method of depreciation for its vehicles.

UNITS-OF-ACTIVITY

Under the **units-of-activity method**, useful life is expressed in terms of the total units of production or use expected from the asset, rather than as a time period. The units-of-activity method is ideally suited to factory machinery. Manufacturing companies can measure production in units of output or in machine hours. This method can also be used for such assets as delivery equipment (miles driven) and airplanes (hours in use). The units-of-activity method is generally not suitable for buildings or furniture, because depreciation for these assets is more a function of time than of use.

To use this method, companies estimate the total units of activity for the entire useful life, and then divide these units into depreciable cost. The resulting number represents the depreciation cost per unit. The depreciation cost per unit is then applied to the units of activity during the year to determine the annual depreciation expense.

ALTERNATIVE TERMINOLOGY

Another term often used is the *units-of-production method.*

HELPFUL HINT

Under any method, depreciation stops when the asset's book value equals expected salvage value.

To illustrate, assume that Barb's Florists drives its delivery truck 15,000 miles in the first year. Illustration 10-11 shows the units-of-activity formula and the computation of the first year's depreciation expense.

Illustration 10-11
Formula for units-of-activity method

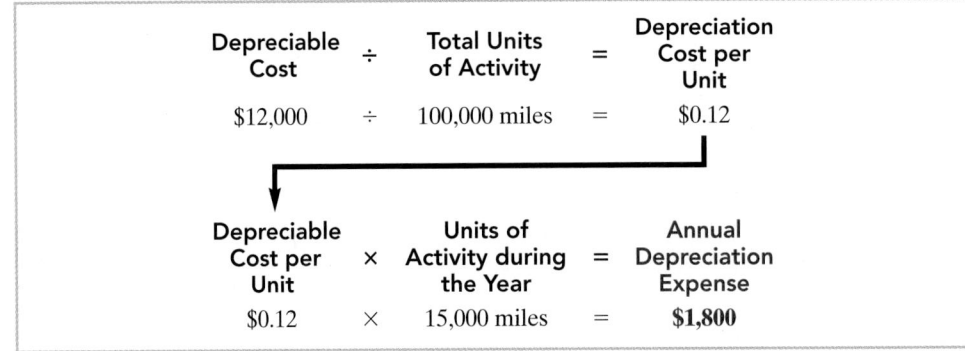

Depreciable Cost	÷	Total Units of Activity	=	Depreciation Cost per Unit
$12,000	÷	100,000 miles	=	$0.12

Depreciable Cost per Unit	×	Units of Activity during the Year	=	Annual Depreciation Expense
$0.12	×	15,000 miles	=	**$1,800**

The units-of-activity depreciation schedule, using assumed mileage, is as follows.

Illustration 10-12
Units-of-activity depreciation schedule

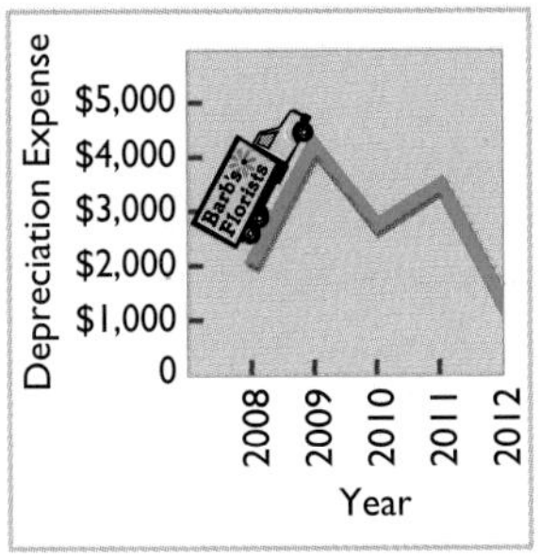

BARB'S FLORISTS

	Computation					End of Year	
Year	**Units of Activity**	×	**Depreciation Cost/Unit**	=	**Annual Depreciation Expense**	**Accumulated Depreciation**	**Book Value**
2008	15,000		$0.12		**$1,800**	$ 1,800	$11,200*
2009	30,000		0.12		**3,600**	5,400	7,600
2010	20,000		0.12		**2,400**	7,800	5,200
2011	25,000		0.12		**3,000**	10,800	2,200
2012	10,000		0.12		**1,200**	12,000	**1,000**

*($13,000 − $1,800).

This method is easy to apply for assets purchased mid-year. In such a case, the company computes the depreciation using the productivity of the asset for the partial year.

The units-of-activity method is not nearly as popular as the straight-line method (see Illustration 10-8, page 430), primarily because it is often difficult for companies to reasonably estimate total activity. However, some very large companies, such as Chevron and Boise Cascade (a forestry company), do use this method. When the productivity of an asset varies significantly from one period to another, the units-of-activity method results in the best matching of expenses with revenues.

DECLINING-BALANCE

The **declining-balance method** produces a decreasing annual depreciation expense over the asset's useful life. The method is so named because the periodic depreciation is based on a **declining book value** (cost less accumulated depreciation) of the asset. With this method, companies compute annual depreciation expense by multiplying the book value at the beginning of the year by the declining-balance depreciation rate. **The depreciation rate remains constant from year to year, but the book value to which the rate is applied declines each year.**

At the beginning of the first year, book value is the cost of the asset. This is so because the balance in accumulated depreciation at the beginning of the asset's useful life is zero. In subsequent years, book value is the difference between cost and accumulated depreciation to date. Unlike the other depreciation methods, the declining-balance method does not use depreciable cost. That is, **it ignores salvage value in determining the amount to which the declining-balance rate is applied**. Salvage value, however, does limit the total depreciation that can be taken. Depreciation stops when the asset's book value equals expected salvage value.

A common declining-balance rate is double the straight-line rate. The method is often called the **double-declining-balance method**. If Barb's Florists uses the double-declining-balance method, it uses a depreciation rate of 40% (2 × the straight-line rate of 20%). Illustration 10-13 shows the declining-balance formula and the computation of the first year's depreciation on the delivery truck.

Book Value at Beginning of Year	×	Declining-Balance Rate	=	Annual Depreciation Expense
$13,000	×	40%	=	**$5,200**

Illustration 10-13 Formula for declining-balance method

The depreciation schedule under this method is as follows.

Illustration 10-14 Double-declining-balance depreciation schedule

BARB'S FLORISTS

	Computation					End of Year	
Year	Book Value Beginning of Year	×	Depreciation Rate	=	Annual Depreciation Expense	Accumulated Depreciation	Book Value
2008	$13,000		40%		**$5,200**	$ 5,200	$7,800
2009	7,800		40		**3,120**	8,320	4,680
2010	4,680		40		**1,872**	10,192	2,808
2011	2,808		40		**1,123**	11,315	1,685
2012	1,685		40		**685***	12,000	**1,000**

*Computation of $674 ($1,685 × 40%) is adjusted to $685 in order for book value to equal salvage value.

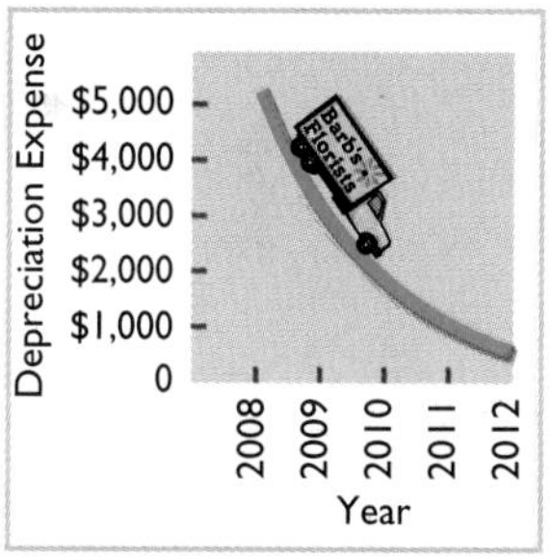

The delivery equipment is 69% depreciated ($8,320 ÷ $12,000) at the end of the second year. Under the straight-line method, the truck would be depreciated 40% ($4,800 ÷ $12,000) at that time. Because the declining-balance method produces higher depreciation expense in the early years than in the later years, it is considered an **accelerated-depreciation method**. The declining-balance method is compatible with the matching principle. It matches the higher depreciation expense in early years with the higher benefits received in these years. It also recognizes lower depreciation expense in later years, when the asset's contribution to revenue is less. Some assets lose usefulness rapidly because of obsolescence. In these cases, the declining-balance method provides the most appropriate depreciation amount.

HELPFUL HINT

The method recommended for an asset that is expected to be significantly more productive in the first half of its useful life is the declining-balance method.

When a company purchases an asset during the year, it must pro-rate the first year's declining-balance depreciation on a time basis. For example, if Barb's Florists had purchased the truck on April 1, 2008, depreciation for 2008 would become $3,900 ($13,000 × 40% × 9/12). The book value at the beginning of 2009 is then $9,100 ($13,000 − $3,900), and the 2009 depreciation is $3,640 ($9,100 × 40%). Subsequent computations would follow from those amounts.

COMPARISON OF METHODS

Illustration 10-15 compares annual and total depreciation expense under each of the three methods for Barb's Florists.

Illustration 10-15
Comparison of depreciation methods

Year	Straight-Line	Units-of-Activity	Declining-Balance
2008	$ 2,400	$ 1,800	$ 5,200
2009	2,400	3,600	3,120
2010	2,400	2,400	1,872
2011	2,400	3,000	1,123
2012	2,400	1,200	685
	$12,000	**$12,000**	**$12,000**

Annual depreciation varies considerably among the methods, but **total depreciation is the same for the five-year period** under all three methods. Each method is acceptable in accounting, because each recognizes in a rational and systematic manner the decline in service potential of the asset. Illustration 10-16 graphs the depreciation expense pattern under each method.

Illustration 10-16
Patterns of depreciation

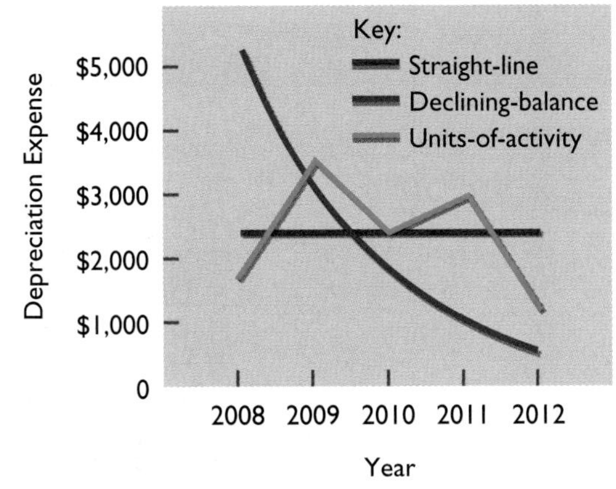

Depreciation and Income Taxes

The Internal Revenue Service (IRS) allows corporate taxpayers to deduct depreciation expense when they compute taxable income. However, the IRS does not require the taxpayer to use the same depreciation method on the tax return that is used in preparing financial statements.

Many corporations use straight-line in their financial statements to maximize net income. At the same time, they use a special accelerated-depreciation method on their tax returns to minimize their income taxes. Taxpayers must use on their tax returns either the straight-line method or a special accelerated-depreciation method called the **Modified Accelerated Cost Recovery System** (MACRS).

Revising Periodic Depreciation

STUDY OBJECTIVE 4
Describe the procedure for revising periodic depreciation.

Depreciation is one example of the use of estimation in the accounting process. Management should periodically review annual depreciation expense. If wear and tear or obsolescence indicate that annual depreciation estimates are inadequate or excessive, the company should change the amount of depreciation expense.

When a change in an estimate is required, the company makes the change in **current and future years. It does not change depreciation in prior periods.** The rationale is that continual restatement of prior periods would adversely affect confidence in financial statements.

To determine the new annual depreciation expense, the company first computes the asset's depreciable cost at the time of the revision. It then allocates the revised depreciable cost to the remaining useful life.

To illustrate, assume that Barb's Florists decides on January 1, 2011, to extend the useful life of the truck one year because of its excellent condition. The company has used the straight-line method to depreciate the asset to date, and book value is $5,800 ($13,000 − $7,200). The new annual depreciation is $1,600, computed as follows.

Illustration 10-17
Revised depreciation computation

Book value, 1/1/11	$5,800	
Less: Salvage value	1,000	
Depreciable cost	$4,800	
Remaining useful life	3 years	(2011–2013)
Revised annual depreciation ($4,800 ÷ 3)	**$1,600**	

HELPFUL HINT
Use a step-by-step approach: (1) determine new depreciable cost; (2) divide by remaining useful life.

Barb's Florists makes no entry for the change in estimate. On December 31, 2011, during the preparation of adjusting entries, it records depreciation expense of $1,600. Companies must describe in the financial statements significant changes in estimates.

Before You Go On...

REVIEW IT

1. What is the relationship, if any, of depreciation to (a) cost allocation, (b) asset valuation, and (c) cash accumulation?
2. Explain the factors that affect the computation of depreciation.
3. What are the formulas for computing annual depreciation under each of the depreciation methods?
4. How do the methods differ in terms of their effects on annual depreciation over the useful life of the asset?
5. Do companies make revisions of periodic depreciation to prior periods? Explain.

DO IT

On January 1, 2008, Iron Mountain Ski Corporation purchased a new snow-grooming machine for $50,000. The machine is estimated to have a 10-year life with a $2,000 salvage value. What journal entry would Iron Mountain Ski Corporation make at December 31, 2008, if it uses the straight-line method of depreciation?

Action Plan

- Calculate depreciable cost (Cost − Salvage value).
- Divide the depreciable cost by the estimated useful life.

Solution

$$\text{Depreciation expense} = \frac{\text{Cost} - \text{Salvage value}}{\text{Useful life}} = \frac{\$50{,}000 - \$2{,}000}{10} = \$4{,}800$$

The entry to record the first year's depreciation would be:

Dec. 31	Depreciation Expense	4,800	
	Accumulated Depreciation		4,800
	(To record annual depreciation on snow-grooming machine)		

Related exercise material: *BE10-3, BE10-4, BE10-5, BE10-6, BE10-7, E10-5, E10-6, E10-7, and E10-8.*

The Navigator

EXPENDITURES DURING USEFUL LIFE

STUDY OBJECTIVE 5

Distinguish between revenue and capital expenditures, and explain the entries for each.

During the useful life of a plant asset, a company may incur costs for ordinary repairs, additions, or improvements. **Ordinary repairs** are expenditures to **maintain** the operating efficiency and productive life of the unit. They usually are fairly small amounts that occur frequently. Examples are motor tune-ups and oil changes, the painting of buildings, and the replacing of worn-out gears on machinery. Companies record such repairs as debits to Repair (or Maintenance) Expense as they are incurred. Because they are immediately charged as an expense against revenues, these costs are often referred to as **revenue expenditures**.

Additions and improvements are costs incurred to **increase** the operating efficiency, productive capacity, or useful life of a plant asset. They are usually material in amount and occur infrequently. Additions and improvements increase the company's investment in productive facilities. Companies generally debit these amounts to the plant asset affected. They are often referred to as **capital expenditures**. Most major U.S. corporations disclose annual capital expenditures.

Companies must use good judgment in deciding between a revenue expenditure and capital expenditure. For example, assume that Rodriguez Co. purchases a number of wastepaper baskets. Although the proper accounting would appear to be to capitalize and then depreciate these wastepaper baskets over their useful life, it would be more usual for Rodriguez to expense them immediately. This practice is justified on the basis of **materiality**. Materiality refers to the impact of an item's size on a company's financial operations. The **materiality principle** states that if an item would not make a difference in decision making, the company does not have to follow GAAP in reporting that item.

ETHICS INSIGHT

What Happened at WorldCom?

In what could become one of the largest accounting frauds in history, WorldCom announced the discovery of $7 billion in expenses improperly booked as capital expenditures, a gimmick that boosted profit over a recent five-quarter period. If these expenses had been recorded properly, WorldCom, one of the biggest stock market stars of the 1990s, would have reported a net loss for 2001, as well as for the first quarter of 2002. Instead, WorldCom reported a profit of $1.4 billion for 2001 and $130 million for the first quarter of 2002. As a result of these problems, WorldCom declared bankruptcy, to the dismay of its investors and creditors.

What erroneous accounting entries (accounts debited and credited) did WorldCom make? What is the correcting entry that should be recorded, and what is its effect on WorldCom's financial statements?

PLANT ASSET DISPOSALS

Companies dispose of plant assets in three ways—retirement, sale, or exchange—as Illustration 10-18 shows. Whatever the method, at the time of disposal the company must determine the book value of the plant asset. As noted earlier, book value is the difference between the cost of a plant asset and the accumulated depreciation to date.

STUDY OBJECTIVE 6

Explain how to account for the disposal of a plant asset.

Illustration 10-18
Methods of plant asset disposal

At the time of disposal, the company records depreciation for the fraction of the year to the date of disposal. The book value is then eliminated by two entries: (1) debiting (decreasing) Accumulated Depreciation for the total depreciation to date, and (2) crediting (decreasing) the asset account for the cost of the asset. In this chapter we examine the accounting for the retirement and sale of plant assets. In the appendix to the chapter we discuss and illustrate the accounting for exchanges of plant assets.

Retirement of Plant Assets

To illustrate the retirement of plant assets, assume that Hobart Enterprises retires its computer printers, which cost $32,000. The accumulated depreciation on these printers is $32,000. The equipment, therefore, is fully depreciated (zero book value). The entry to record this retirement is as follows.

Accumulated Depreciation—Printing Equipment	32,000	
Printing Equipment		32,000
(To record retirement of fully depreciated equipment)		

A	=	L	+	OE
+32,000				
−32,000				

Cash Flows
no effect

What happens if a fully depreciated plant asset is still useful to the company? In this case, the asset and its accumulated depreciation continue to be reported on the balance sheet, without further depreciation adjustment, until the company retires the asset. Reporting the asset and related accumulated depreciation on the balance sheet informs the financial statement reader that the asset is still in use. Once fully depreciated, no additional depreciation should be taken, even if an asset is still being used. In no situation can the accumulated depreciation on a plant asset exceed its cost.

HELPFUL HINT

When a company disposes of a plant asset, the company must remove from the accounts all amounts related to the asset. This includes the original cost in the asset account and the total depreciation to date in the accumulated depreciation account.

If a company retires a plant asset before it is fully depreciated, and no cash is received for scrap or salvage value, a loss on disposal occurs. For example, assume that Sunset Company discards delivery equipment that cost $18,000 and has accumulated depreciation of $14,000. The entry is as follows.

Accumulated Depreciation—Delivery Equipment	14,000	
Loss on Disposal	4,000	
Delivery Equipment		18,000
(To record retirement of delivery equipment at a loss)		

A	=	L	+	OE
+14,000				
				−4,000 Exp
−18,000				

Cash Flows
no effect

Companies report a loss on disposal in the "Other expenses and losses" section of the income statement.

Sale of Plant Assets

In a disposal by sale, the company compares the book value of the asset with the proceeds received from the sale. If the proceeds of the sale **exceed** the book value of the plant asset, **a gain on disposal occurs**. If the proceeds of the sale **are less than** the book value of the plant asset sold, **a loss on disposal occurs**.

Only by coincidence will the book value and the fair market value of the asset be the same when the asset is sold. Gains and losses on sales of plant assets are therefore quite common. For example, Delta Airlines reported a $94,343,000 gain on the sale of five Boeing B727-200 aircraft and five Lockheed L-1011-1 aircraft.

GAIN ON DISPOSAL

To illustrate a gain, assume that on July 1, 2008, Wright Company sells office furniture for $16,000 cash. The office furniture originally cost $60,000. As of January 1, 2008, it had accumulated depreciation of $41,000. Depreciation for the first six months of 2008 is $8,000. Wright records depreciation expense and updates accumulated depreciation to July 1 with the following entry.

A	=	L	+	OE
				−8,000 Exp
−8,000				

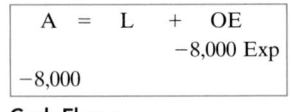

Cash Flows
no effect

July 1	Depreciation Expense	8,000	
	Accumulated Depreciation—Office Furniture		8,000
	(To record depreciation expense for the first 6 months of 2008)		

After the accumulated depreciation balance is updated, the company computes the gain or loss. Illustration 10-19 shows this computation for Wright Company, which has a gain on disposal of $5,000.

Illustration 10-19
Computation of gain on disposal

Cost of office furniture	$60,000
Less: Accumulated depreciation ($41,000 + $8,000)	49,000
Book value at date of disposal	11,000
Proceeds from sale	16,000
Gain on disposal	**$ 5,000**

Wright records the sale and the gain on disposal as follows.

A	=	L	+	OE
+16,000				
+49,000				
−60,000				
				+5,000 Rev

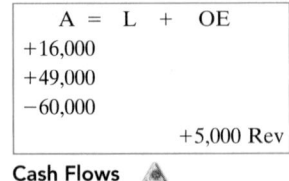

Cash Flows
+16,000

July 1	Cash	16,000	
	Accumulated Depreciation—Office Furniture	49,000	
	Office Furniture		60,000
	Gain on Disposal		5,000
	(To record sale of office furniture at a gain)		

Companies report a gain on disposal in the "Other revenues and gains" section of the income statement.

LOSS ON DISPOSAL

Assume that instead of selling the office furniture for $16,000, Wright sells it for $9,000. In this case, Wright computes a loss of $2,000 as follows:

Illustration 10-20
Computation of loss on disposal

Cost of office furniture	$60,000
Less: Accumulated depreciation	49,000
Book value at date of disposal	11,000
Proceeds from sale	9,000
Loss on disposal	**$ 2,000**

Wright records the sale and the loss on disposal as follows.

July 1	Cash	9,000	
	Accumulated Depreciation—Office Furniture	49,000	
	Loss on Disposal	2,000	
	Office Furniture		60,000
	(To record sale of office furniture at a loss)		

A	=	L	+	OE
+9,000				
+49,000				
				−2,000 Exp
−60,000				

Cash Flows
+9,000

Companies report a loss on disposal in the "Other expenses and losses" section of the income statement.

Before You Go On...

REVIEW IT

1. How does a capital expenditure differ from a revenue expenditure?
2. What is the proper accounting for the retirement and sale of plant assets?

DO IT

Overland Trucking has an old truck that cost $30,000. The truck has accumulated depreciation of $16,000 and a fair value of $17,000. Overland has decided to sell the truck. (a) What is the entry that Overland Trucking would make to record the sale of the truck for $17,000 cash? (b) What is the entry that Overland trucking would make to record the sale of the truck for $10,000 cash?

Action Plan

- At the time of disposal, determine the book value of the asset.
- Compare the asset's book value with the proceeds received to determine whether a gain or loss has occurred.

Solution

(a) Sale of truck for cash at a gain:

Cash	17,000	
Accumulated Depreciation—Truck	16,000	
Truck		30,000
Gain on Disposal [$17,000 − ($30,000 − $16,000)]		3,000
(To record sale of truck at a gain)		

(b) Sale of truck for cash at a loss:

Cash	10,000	
Loss on Disposal [$10,000 − ($30,000 − $16,000)]	4,000	
Accumulated Depreciation—Truck	16,000	
Truck		30,000
(To record sale of truck at a loss)		

Related exercise material: *BE10-9, BE10-10, E10-9, and E10-10.*

✓ The Navigator

SECTION 2 Natural Resources

HELPFUL HINT
On a balance sheet, natural resources may be described more specifically as *timberlands, mineral deposits, oil reserves*, and so on.

Natural resources consist of standing timber and underground deposits of oil, gas, and minerals. These long-lived productive assets have two distinguishing characteristics: (1) They are physically extracted in operations (such as mining, cutting, or pumping). (2) They are replaceable only by an act of nature.

The acquisition cost of a natural resource is the price needed to acquire the resource **and** prepare it for its intended use. For an already-discovered resource, such as an existing coal mine, cost is the price paid for the property.

The allocation of the cost of natural resources to expense in a rational and systematic manner over the resource's useful life is called **depletion**. (That is, *depletion* is to natural resources as *depreciation* is to plant assets.) **Companies generally use the units-of-activity method** (learned earlier in the chapter) **to compute depletion**. The reason is that **depletion generally is a function of the units extracted during the year**.

STUDY OBJECTIVE 7
Compute periodic depletion of natural resources.

Under the units-of-activity method, companies divide the total cost of the natural resource minus salvage value by the number of units estimated to be in the resource. The result is a **depletion cost per unit of product**. They then multiply the depletion cost per unit by the number of units extracted and sold. The result is the **annual depletion expense**. Illustration 10-21 shows the formula to compute depletion expense.

Illustration 10-21
Formula to compute depletion expense

Total Cost minus Salvage Value	÷	Total Estimated Units	=	Depletion Cost per Unit
Depletion Cost per Unit	×	Number of Units Extracted and Sold	=	Annual Depletion Expense

ETHICS NOTE
Investors were stunned at news that Royal Dutch/Shell Group had significantly overstated its reported oil reserves—and perhaps had done so intentionally.

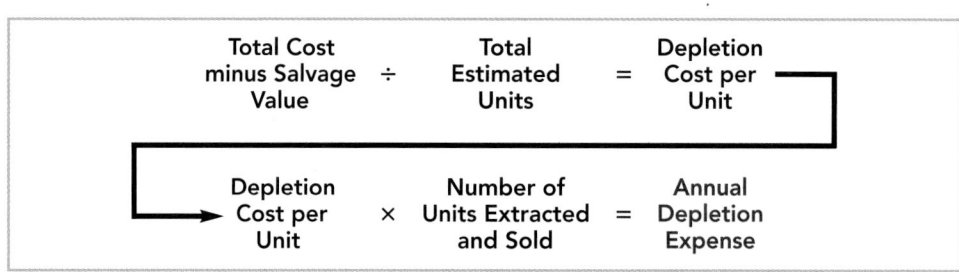

To illustrate, assume that Lane Coal Company invests $5 million in a mine estimated to have 10 million tons of coal and no salvage value. In the first year, Lane extracts and sells 800,000 tons of coal. Using the formulas above, Lane computes the depletion expense as follows:

$$\$5{,}000{,}000 \div 10{,}000{,}000 = \$0.50 \text{ depletion cost per ton}$$

$$\$0.50 \times 800{,}000 = \$400{,}000 \text{ annual depletion expense}$$

Lane records depletion expense for the first year of operation as follows.

A	=	L	+	OE
				−400,000 Exp
−400,000				

Cash Flows
no effect

Dec. 31	Depletion Expense	400,000	
	Accumulated Depletion		400,000
	(To record depletion expense on coal deposits)		

The company reports the account Depletion Expense as a part of the cost of producing the product. Accumulated Depletion is a contra-asset account, similar to accumulated depreciation. It is deducted from the cost of the natural resource in the balance sheet, as Illustration 10-22 shows.

Illustration 10-22
Statement presentation of accumulated depletion

LANE COAL COMPANY
Balance Sheet (partial)

Coal mine	$5,000,000	
Less: Accumulated depletion	**400,000**	$4,600,000

Many companies do not use an Accumulated Depletion account. In such cases, the company credits the amount of depletion directly to the natural resources account.

Sometimes, a company will extract natural resources in one accounting period but not sell them until a later period. In this case, the company does not expense the depletion until it sells the resource. It reports the amount not sold as inventory in the current assets section.

SECTION 3 Intangible Assets

Intangible assets are rights, privileges, and competitive advantages that result from the ownership of long-lived assets that do not possess physical substance. Evidence of intangibles may exist in the form of contracts or licenses. Intangibles may arise from the following sources:

1. Government grants, such as patents, copyrights, and trademarks.
2. Acquisition of another business, in which the purchase price includes a payment for the company's favorable attributes (called *goodwill*).
3. Private monopolistic arrangements arising from contractual agreements, such as franchises and leases.

Some widely known intangibles are Microsoft's patents, McDonald's franchises, Apple's trade name iPod, J.K. Rowlings' copyrights on the Harry Potter books, and the trademark Rent-A-Wreck in the Feature Story.

ACCOUNTING FOR INTANGIBLE ASSETS

STUDY OBJECTIVE 8
Explain the basic issues related to accounting for intangible assets.

Companies record intangible assets at cost. Intangibles are categorized as having either a limited life or an indefinite life. If an intangible has a **limited life**, the company allocates its cost over the asset's useful life using a process similar to depreciation. The process of allocating the cost of intangibles is referred to as **amortization**. The cost of intangible assets with **indefinite lives should not be amortized**.

HELPFUL HINT
Amortization is to intangibles what *depreciation* is to plant assets and *depletion* is to natural resources.

To record amortization of an intangible asset, a company increases (debits) Amortization Expense, and decreases (credits) the specific intangible asset. (Unlike depreciation, no contra account, such as Accumulated Amortization, is usually used.)

Intangible assets are typically amortized on a straight-line basis. For example, the legal life of a patent is 20 years. Companies **amortize the cost of a patent over its 20-year life or its useful life, whichever is shorter**. To illustrate the computation of patent amortization, assume that National Labs purchases a patent at a cost of $60,000. If National estimates the useful life of the patent to be eight years, the annual amortization expense is $7,500 ($60,000 ÷ 8). National records the annual amortization as follows.

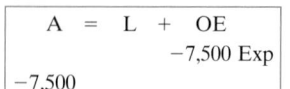

A	=	L	+	OE
				−7,500 Exp
−7,500				

Cash Flows
no effect

Dec. 31	Amortization Expense—Patent	7,500	
	Patent		7,500
	(To record patent amortization)		

Companies classify Amortization Expense—Patents as an operating expense in the income statement.

There is a difference between intangible assets and plant assets in determining cost. For plant assets, cost includes both the purchase price of the asset and the costs incurred in designing and constructing the asset. In contrast, cost for an intangible asset includes **only the purchase price**. Companies expense any costs incurred in developing an intangible asset.

Patents

A **patent** is an exclusive right issued by the U.S. Patent Office that enables the recipient to manufacture, sell, or otherwise control an invention for a period of 20 years from the date of the grant. A patent is nonrenewable. But companies can extend the legal life of a patent by obtaining new patents for improvements or other changes in the basic design. **The initial cost of a patent is the cash or cash equivalent price paid to acquire the patent.**

The saying, "A patent is only as good as the money you're prepared to spend defending it" is very true. Many patents are subject to litigation. Any legal costs an owner incurs in successfully defending a patent in an infringement suit are considered necessary to establish the patent's validity. **The owner adds those costs to the Patent account and amortizes them over the remaining life of the patent.**

The patent holder amortizes the cost of a patent over its 20-year legal life or its useful life, whichever is shorter. Companies consider obsolescence and inadequacy in determining useful life. These factors may cause a patent to become economically ineffective before the end of its legal life.

Copyrights

The federal government grants **copyrights** which give the owner the exclusive right to reproduce and sell an artistic or published work. Copyrights extend for the life of the creator plus 70 years. The cost of a copyright is the **cost of acquiring and defending it**. The cost may be only the $10 fee paid to the U.S. Copyright Office. Or it may amount to much more if an infringement suit is involved.

The useful life of a copyright generally is significantly shorter than its legal life. Therefore, copyrights usually are amortized over a relatively short period of time.

Trademarks and Trade Names

A **trademark** or **trade name** is a word, phrase, jingle, or symbol that identifies a particular enterprise or product. Trade names like Wheaties, Game Boy, Frappuccino, Kleenex, Windows, Coca-Cola, and Jeep create immediate product identification. They also generally enhance the sale of the product. The creator or original user may obtain exclusive legal right to the trademark or trade name by registering it with the U.S. Patent Office. Such registration provides 20 years of protection. The registration may be renewed indefinitely as long as the trademark or trade name is in use.

If a company purchases the trademark or trade name, its cost is the purchase price. If a company develops and maintains the trademark or trade name, any costs related to these activities are expensed as incurred. Because trademarks and trade names have indefinite lives, they are not amortized.

Franchises and Licenses

When you fill up your tank at the corner Shell station, eat lunch at Taco Bell, or rent a car from Rent-A-Wreck, you are dealing with franchises. A **franchise** is a contractual arrangement between a franchisor and a franchisee. The franchisor grants the franchisee the right to sell certain products, provide specific services, or use certain trademarks or trade names, usually within a designated geographical area.

Another type of franchise is that entered into between a governmental body (commonly municipalities) and a company. This franchise permits the company to use public property in performing its services. Examples are the use of city streets for a bus line or taxi service, use of public land for telephone and electric lines, and the use of airwaves for radio or TV broadcasting. Such operating rights are referred to as **licenses**.

When a company can identify costs with the purchase of a franchise or license, it should recognize an intangible asset. Companies should amortize the cost of a limited-life franchise (or license) over its useful life. If the life is indefinite, the cost is not amortized. Annual payments made under a franchise agreement are recorded as **operating expenses** in the period in which they are incurred.

ACCOUNTING ACROSS THE ORGANIZATION

ESPN Wins Monday Night Football Franchise

What is a well-known franchise worth? Recently ESPN outbid its rivals for the right to broadcast Monday Night Football. At a price of $1.1 billion per year—nearly twice what rival ABC paid in previous years—it isn't clear who won and who lost.

When bidding for a unique franchise like Monday Night Football, management must consider many factors to determine a price. As part of the deal, ESPN also got wireless rights and Spanish-language telecasts. By its estimation, ESPN will generate a profit of $200 million per year from Monday Night Football. ABC was losing $150 million per year.

Another factor in the decision was ESPN management's concern that if ESPN didn't win the bid, a buyer would emerge that would use Monday Night Football as a launching pad for a new sports network. ESPN doesn't want any more competitors than it already has. It is hard to put a price tag on the value of keeping the competition to a minimum.

Source: Ronald Grover and Tom Lowry, "A Ball ESPN Couldn't Afford to Drop," *BusinessWeek*, May 2, 2005, p. 42.

? How should ESPN account for the $1.1 billion per year franchise fee?

Goodwill

Usually, the largest intangible asset that appears on a company's balance sheet is goodwill. **Goodwill** represents the value of all favorable attributes that relate to a company. These include exceptional management, desirable location, good customer relations, skilled employees, high-quality products, and harmonious relations with labor unions. Goodwill is unique: Unlike assets such as investments and plant assets, which can be sold *individually* in the marketplace, goodwill can be identified only with the business as a whole.

If goodwill can be identified only with the business as a whole, how can its amount be determined? One could try to put a dollar value on the factors listed above (exceptional management, desirable location, and so on). But the results would be very subjective, and such subjective valuations would not contribute to the reliability of financial statements. **Therefore, companies record goodwill only when an entire business is purchased. In that case, goodwill is the excess of cost over the fair market value of the net assets (assets less liabilities) acquired.**

In recording the purchase of a business, the company debits (increases) the net assets at their fair market values, credits (decreases) cash for the purchase price, and debits goodwill for the difference. **Goodwill is not amortized** (because it is considered to have an indefinite life). Companies report goodwill in the balance sheet under intangible assets.

RESEARCH AND DEVELOPMENT COSTS

HELPFUL HINT
Research and development (R&D) costs are not intangible assets. But because they may lead to patents and copyrights, we discuss them in this section.

Research and development costs are expenditures that may lead to patents, copyrights, new processes, and new products. Many companies spend considerable sums of money on research and development (R&D). For example, in a recent year IBM spent over $5.1 billion on R&D.

Research and development costs present accounting problems. For one thing, it is sometimes difficult to assign the costs to specific projects. Also, there are uncertainties in identifying the extent and timing of future benefits. As a result, companies usually record R&D costs **as an expense when incurred**, whether the research and development is successful or not.

To illustrate, assume that Laser Scanner Company spent $3 million on R&D. This expenditure resulted in two highly successful patents, obtained with $20,000 in lawyers' fees. The company would add the lawyers' fees to the patent account. The R&D costs, however, cannot be included in the cost of the patent. Instead, the company would record the R&D costs as an expense when incurred.

Many disagree with this accounting approach. They argue that expensing R&D costs leads to understated assets and net income. Others, however, argue that capitalizing these costs will lead to highly speculative assets on the balance sheet. It is difficult to determine who is right. The controversy illustrates how difficult it can be to establish proper guidelines for financial reporting.

STATEMENT PRESENTATION AND ANALYSIS

Presentation

STUDY OBJECTIVE 9
Indicate how plant assets, natural resources, and intangible assets are reported.

Usually companies combine plant assets and natural resources under "Property, plant, and equipment" in the balance sheet. They show intangibles separately. Companies disclose either in the balance sheet or the notes the balances of the major classes of assets, such as land, buildings, and equipment, and accumulated depreciation by major classes or in total. In addition, they should describe the depreciation and amortization methods that were used, as well as disclose the amount of depreciation and amortization expense for the period.

Illustration 10-23 shows the financial statement presentation of property, plant, and equipment and intangibles by The Procter & Gamble Company (P&G) in its 2005 balance sheet. The notes to P&G's financial statements present greater details about the accounting for its long-term tangible and intangible assets.

Illustration 10-24 shows another comprehensive presentation of property, plant, and equipment, from the balance sheet of Owens-Illinois. The notes to the financial statements of Owens-Illinois identify the major classes of property, plant, and equipment. They also indicate that depreciation and amortization are by the straight-line method, and depletion is by the units-of-activity method.

Analysis

Using ratios, we can analyze how efficiently a company uses its assets to generate sales. The **asset turnover ratio** analyzes the productivity of a company's assets. It tells us how many dollars of sales a company generates for each dollar invested in assets. This ratio is computed by dividing net sales by average total assets for

Illustration 10-23
P&G's presentation of property, plant, and equipment, and intangible assets

P&G

THE PROCTER & GAMBLE COMPANY
Balance Sheet (partial)
(in millions)

	June 30	
	2005	**2004**
Property, plant, and equipment		
Buildings	$ 5,292	$ 5,206
Machinery and equipment	20,397	19,456
Land	636	642
	26,325	25,304
Accumulated depreciation	(11,993)	(11,196)
Net property, plant, and equipment	14,332	14,108
Goodwill and other intangible assets		
Goodwill	19,816	19,610
Trademarks and other intangible assets, net	4,347	4,290
Net goodwill and other intangible assets	$24,163	$23,900

Illustration 10-24
Owens-Illinois' presentation of property, plant, and equipment, and intangible assets

OWENS-ILLINOIS

OWENS-ILLINOIS, INC.
Balance Sheet (partial)
(in millions)

Property, plant, and equipment			
Timberlands, at cost, less accumulated depletion		$ 95.4	
Buildings and equipment, at cost	$2,207.1		
Less: Accumulated depreciation	1,229.0	978.1	
Total property, plant, and equipment			$1,073.5
Intangibles			
Patents			410.0
Total			$1,483.5

the period. The formula in Illustration 10-25 shows the computation of the asset turnover ratio for The Procter & Gamble Company. P&G's net sales for 2005 were $56,741 million. Its total ending assets were $61,527 million, and beginning assets were $57,048 million.

Illustration 10-25
Asset turnover formula and computation

Net Sales	÷	Average Total Assets	=	Asset Turnover Ratio
$56,741	÷	$\frac{\$61,527 + \$57,048}{2}$	=	**.96 times**

Thus, each dollar invested in assets produced $0.96 in sales for P&G. If a company is using its assets efficiently, each dollar of assets will create a high amount of sales. This ratio varies greatly among different industries—from those that are asset intensive (utilities) to those that are not (services).

Be sure to read **ALL ABOUT YOU: *Buying a Wreck of Your Own*** on page 446 for information on how topics in this chapter apply to you.

Buying a Wreck of Your Own

The opening story to this chapter discusses car rental company Rent-A-Wreck. Recall that Rent-A-Wreck determined it can maximize its profitability by buying and renting used, rather than new, cars. What about *you*? Could you maximize your economic well-being by buying a used car rather than a new one?

Some Facts

* In a recent year, nearly 17 million new cars were sold in the U.S., compared to sales of 44 million used cars.
* The cost of an average new car has risen in recent years, to about $22,000. The price of the average used car has actually been falling, and is now about $8,100.
* Financial institutions typically require a down payment of at least 10% of the value of a vehicle on a vehicle loan. Thus, the average new car will require a much higher down payment. However, interest rates on used-car loans are higher than on new-car loans.
* A new car typically loses at least 30% of its value during the first two years, and about 40 to 50% after three years. Some brands maintain their value better than others.
* The price of new cars has increased faster than average annual incomes in recent years.
* To keep monthly car payments down, car companies will now provide financing for up to six years. (It used to be two or three years.) With such a long loan, you might end up "upside down on the loan"—that is, you might actually owe more money than the car is worth if you decide to sell the car before the end of the loan.

About the Numbers

There are many costs to consider in deciding whether to buy a new or used car. These costs include the down payment, monthly loan payments, insurance, maintenance and repair costs, and state (department of motor vehicle) fees. The graph below compares the total costs over five years for the typical new versus used car.

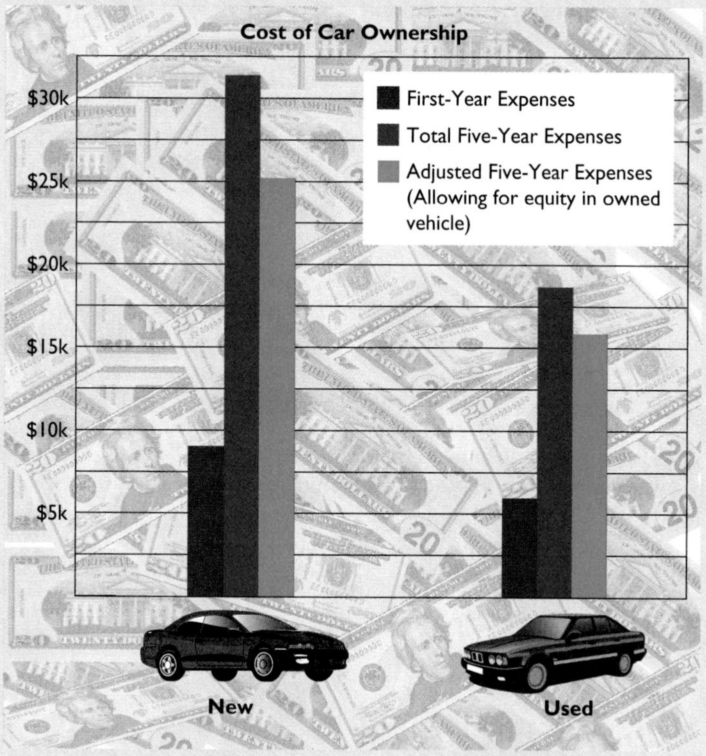

Source for graph: Phillip Reed, "Compare the Costs: Buying vs. Leasing vs. Buying a Used Car," *www.edmunds.com/advice/buying/articles/47079/article.html* (accessed May 2006).

What Do You Think?

Should you buy a new car?

YES: I have enough stress in my life. I don't want to worry about my car breaking down—and if it does break down, I want it to be covered by a warranty. Besides, I have an image to maintain—I don't want to be seen in anything less than the latest styling and the latest technology.

NO: I'm a college student, and I need to keep my costs down. Also, used cars are a lot more dependable than they used to be. In addition, my self-image is strong enough that I don't need a fancy new car to feel good about myself (despite what the car advertisements say).

Source: Michelle Krebs, "Should You Buy New or Used?" *www.cars.com/go/advice,* May 3, 2005.

The authors' comments on this situation appear on page 469.

Before You Go On...

REVIEW IT

1. How is depletion expense computed?
2. What are the main differences between accounting for intangible assets and for plant assets?
3. Identify the major types of intangibles and the proper accounting for them.
4. Explain the accounting for research and development costs.
5. What ratio may be computed to analyze property, plant, and equipment?

The Navigator

Demonstration Problem 1

WILEY PLUS

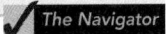

DuPage Company purchases a factory machine at a cost of $18,000 on January 1, 2008. DuPage expects the machine to have a salvage value of $2,000 at the end of its 4-year useful life.

During its useful life, the machine is expected to be used 160,000 hours. Actual annual hourly use was: 2008, 40,000; 2009, 60,000; 2010, 35,000; and 2011, 25,000.

Instructions

Prepare depreciation schedules for the following methods: (a) straight-line, (b) units-of-activity, and (c) declining-balance using double the straight-line rate.

Solution to Demonstration Problem 1

action plan

- ✓ Under the straight-line method, apply the depreciation rate to depreciable cost.
- ✓ Under the units-of-activity method, compute the depreciation cost per unit by dividing depreciable cost by total units of activity.
- ✓ Under the declining-balance method, apply the depreciation rate to **book value** at the beginning of the year.

(a)

Straight-Line Method

	Computation					End of Year	
Year	Depreciable Cost*	×	Depreciation Rate	=	Annual Depreciation Expense	Accumulated Depreciation	Book Value
2008	$16,000		25%		$4,000	$ 4,000	$14,000**
2009	16,000		25%		4,000	8,000	10,000
2010	16,000		25%		4,000	12,000	6,000
2011	16,000		25%		4,000	16,000	2,000

*$18,000 − $2,000.
**$18,000 − $4,000.

(b)

Units-of-Activity Method

	Computation					End of Year	
Year	Units of Activity	×	Depreciation Cost/Unit	=	Annual Depreciation Expense	Accumulated Depreciation	Book Value
2008	40,000		$0.10*		$4,000	$ 4,000	$14,000
2009	60,000		0.10		6,000	10,000	8,000
2010	35,000		0.10		3,500	13,500	4,500
2011	25,000		0.10		2,500	16,000	2,000

*($18,000 − $2,000) ÷ 160,000.

(c)

Declining-Balance Method

	Computation				End of Year	
Year	Book Value Beginning of Year	×	Depreciation Rate*	= Annual Depreciation Expense	Accumulated Depreciation	Book Value
2008	$18,000		50%	$9,000	$ 9,000	$9,000
2009	9,000		50%	4,500	13,500	4,500
2010	4,500		50%	2,250	15,750	2,250
2011	2,250		50%	250**	16,000	2,000

*¼ × 2.
**Adjusted to $250 because ending book value should not be less than expected salvage value.

The Navigator

Demonstration Problem 2

WILEY PLUS

On January 1, 2006, Skyline Limousine Co. purchased a limo at an acquisition cost of $28,000. The vehicle has been depreciated by the straight-line method using a 4-year service life and a $4,000 salvage value. The company's fiscal year ends on December 31.

Instructions

Prepare the journal entry or entries to record the disposal of the limousine assuming that it was:
(a) Retired and scrapped with no salvage value on January 1, 2010.
(b) Sold for $5,000 on July 1, 2009.

Solution to Demonstration Problem 2

(a)	1/1/10	Accumulated Depreciation—Limousine	24,000	
		Loss on Disposal	4,000	
		Limousine		28,000
		(To record retirement of limousine)		
(b)	7/1/09	Depreciation Expense	3,000	
		Accumulated Depreciation—Limousine		3,000
		(To record depreciation to date of disposal)		
	7/1/09	Cash	5,000	
		Accumulated Depreciation—Limousine	21,000	
		Loss on Disposal	2,000	
		Limousine		28,000
		(To record sale of limousine)		

action plan

- ✔ At the time of disposal, determine the book value of the asset.
- ✔ Recognize any gain or loss from disposal of the asset.
- ✔ Remove the book value of the asset from the records by debiting Accumulated Depreciation for the total depreciation to date of disposal and crediting the asset account for the cost of the asset.

The Navigator

SUMMARY OF STUDY OBJECTIVES

WILEY PLUS

1 Describe how the cost principle applies to plant assets. The cost of plant assets includes all expenditures necessary to acquire the asset and make it ready for its intended use. Cost is measured by the cash or cash equivalent price paid.

2 Explain the concept of depreciation. Depreciation is the allocation of the cost of a plant asset to expense over its useful (service) life in a rational and systematic manner. Depreciation is not a process of valuation, nor is it a process that results in an accumulation of cash.

3 Compute periodic depreciation using different methods. Three depreciation methods are:

Method	Effect on Annual Depreciation	Formula
Straight-line	Constant amount	Depreciable cost ÷ Useful life (in years)
Units-of-activity	Varying amount	Depreciation cost per unit × Units of activity during the year
Declining-balance	Decreasing amount	Book value at beginning of year × Declining-balance rate

4 Describe the procedure for revising periodic depreciation. Companies make revisions of periodic depreciation in present and future periods, not retroactively. They determine the new annual depreciation by dividing the depreciable cost at the time of the revision by the remaining useful life.

5 Distinguish between revenue and capital expenditures, and explain the entries for each. Companies incur revenue expenditures to maintain the operating efficiency and productive life of an asset. They debit these expenditures to Repair Expense as incurred. Capital expenditures increase the operating efficiency, productive capacity, or expected useful life of the asset. Companies generally debit these expenditures to the plant asset affected.

6 Explain how to account for the disposal of a plant asset. The accounting for disposal of a plant asset through retirement or sale is as follows:

(a) Eliminate the book value of the plant asset at the date of disposal.

(b) Record cash proceeds, if any.

(c) Account for the difference between the book value and the cash proceeds as a gain or loss on disposal.

7 Compute periodic depletion of natural resources. Companies compute depletion cost per unit by dividing the total cost of the natural resource minus salvage value by the number of units estimated to be in the resource. They then multiply the depletion cost per unit by the number of units extracted and sold.

8 Explain the basic issues related to accounting for intangible assets. The process of allocating the cost of an intangible asset is referred to as amortization. The cost of intangible assets with indefinite lives are not amortized. Companies normally use the straight-line method for amortizing intangible assets.

9 Indicate how plant assets, natural resources, and intangible assets are reported. Companies usually combine plant assets and natural resources under property, plant, and equipment; they show intangibles separately under intangible assets. Either within the balance sheet or in the notes, companies should disclose the balances of the major classes of assets, such as land, buildings, and equipment, and accumulated depreciation by major classes or in total. They also should describe the depreciation and amortization methods used, and should disclose the amount of depreciation and amortization expense for the period. The asset turnover ratio measures the productivity of a company's assets in generating sales.

The Navigator

GLOSSARY

WILEY PLUS

Accelerated-depreciation method Depreciation method that produces higher depreciation expense in the early years than in the later years. (p. 433).

Additions and improvements Costs incurred to increase the operating efficiency, productive capacity, or useful life of a plant asset. (p. 436).

Amortization The allocation of the cost of an intangible asset to expense over its useful life in a systematic and rational manner. (p. 441).

Asset turnover ratio A measure of how efficiently a company uses its assets to generate sales; calculated as net sales divided by average total assets. (p. 444).

Capital expenditures Expenditures that increase the company's investment in productive facilities. (p. 436).

Copyright Exclusive grant from the federal government that allows the owner to reproduce and sell an artistic or published work. (p. 442).

Declining-balance method Depreciation method that applies a constant rate to the declining book value of the asset and produces a decreasing annual depreciation expense over the useful life of the asset. (p. 432).

Depletion The allocation of the cost of a natural resource to expense in a rational and systematic manner over the resource's useful life. (p. 440).

Depreciation The process of allocating to expense the cost of a plant asset over its useful (service) life in a rational and systematic manner. (p. 428).

Depreciable cost The cost of a plant asset less its salvage value. (p. 430).

Franchise (license) A contractual arrangement under which the franchisor grants the franchisee the right to sell certain products, provide specific services, or use certain trademarks or trade names, usually within a designated geographical area. (p. 443).

Going-concern assumption States that the company will continue in operation for the foreseeable future. (p. 429).

Goodwill The value of all favorable attributes that relate to a business enterprise. (p. 443).

Intangible assets Rights, privileges, and competitive advantages that result from the ownership of long-lived assets that do not possess physical substance. (p. 441).

Licenses Operating rights to use public property, granted to a business enterprise by a governmental agency. (p. 443).

Materiality principle If an item would not make a difference in decision making, a company does not have to follow GAAP in reporting it. (p. 436).

Natural resources Assets that consist of standing timber and underground deposits of oil, gas, or minerals. (p. 440).

Ordinary repairs Expenditures to maintain the operating efficiency and productive life of the unit. (p. 436).

Patent An exclusive right issued by the U.S. Patent Office that enables the recipient to manufacture, sell, or otherwise control an invention for a period of 20 years from the date of the grant. (p. 442).

Plant assets Tangible resources that are used in the operations of the business and are not intended for sale to customers. (p. 424).

Research and development (R&D) costs Expenditures that may lead to patents, copyrights, new processes, or new products. (p. 444).

Revenue expenditures Expenditures that are immediately charged against revenues as an expense. (p. 436).

Salvage value An estimate of an asset's value at the end of its useful life. (p. 429).

Straight-line method Depreciation method in which periodic depreciation is the same for each year of the asset's useful life. (p. 430).

Trademark (trade name) A word, phrase, jingle, or symbol that identifies a particular enterprise or product. (p. 442).

Units-of-activity method Depreciation method in which useful life is expressed in terms of the total units of production or use expected from an asset. (p. 431).

Useful life An estimate of the expected productive life, also called service life, of an asset. (p. 429).

APPENDIX Exchange of Plant Assets

STUDY OBJECTIVE 10

Explain how to account for the exchange of plant assets.

Ordinarily, companies record a gain or loss on the exchange of plant assets. The rationale for recognizing a gain or loss is that most exchanges have **commercial substance**. An exchange has commercial substance if the future cash flows change as a result of the exchange.

To illustrate, Ramos Co. exchanges some of its equipment for land held by Brodhead Inc. It is likely that the timing and amount of the cash flows arising from the land will differ significantly from the cash flows arising from the equipment. As a result, both Ramos and Brodhead are in different economic positions. Therefore **the exchange has commercial substance**, and the companies recognize a gain or loss in the exchange. Because most exchanges have commercial substance (even when similar assets are exchanged), we illustrate only this type of situation, for both a loss and a gain.

Loss Treatment

To illustrate an exchange that results in a loss, assume that Roland Company exchanged a set of used trucks plus cash for a new semi-truck. The used trucks have a combined book value of $42,000 (cost $64,000 less $22,000 accumulated depreciation). Roland's purchasing agent, experienced in the second-hand market, indicates that the used trucks have a fair market value of $26,000. In addition to the trucks, Roland must pay $17,000 for the semi-truck. Roland computes the cost of the semi-truck as follows

Illustration 10A-1
Cost of semi-truck

Fair value of used trucks	$26,000
Cash paid	17,000
Cost of semi-truck	$43,000

Roland incurs a loss on disposal of $16,000 on this exchange. The reason is that the book value of the used trucks is greater than the fair market value of these trucks. The computation is as follows.

Book value of used trucks ($64,000−$22,000)	$42,000
Fair market value of used trucks	26,000
Loss on disposal	**$16,000**

Illustration 10A-2
Computation of loss on disposal

In recording an exchange at a loss, three steps are required: (1) Eliminate the book value of the asset given up, (2) record the cost of the asset acquired, and (3) recognize the loss on disposal. Roland Company thus records the exchange on the loss as follows.

Semi-truck	43,000	
Accumulated Depreciation—Used Trucks	22,000	
Loss on Disposal	16,000	
Used Trucks		64,000
Cash		17,000
(To record exchange of used trucks for semi-truck.)		

A	=	L	+	OE
+43,000				
+22,000				
				−16,000 Exp
−64,000				
−17,000				

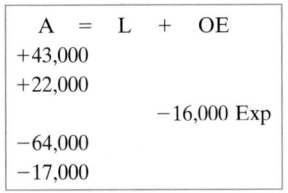

Cash Flows
−17,000

Gain Treatment

To illustrate a gain situation, assume that Mark Express Delivery decides to exchange its old delivery equipment plus cash of $3,000 for new delivery equipment. The book value of the old delivery equipment is $12,000 (cost $40,000 less accumulated depreciation $28,000). The fair market value of the old delivery equipment is $19,000.

The cost of the new asset is the fair market value of the old asset exchanged plus any cash paid (or other consideration given up). The cost of the new delivery equipment is $22,000 computed as follows.

Fair market value of old delivery equipment	$19,000
Cash paid	3,000
Cost of new delivery equipment	**$22,000**

Illustration 10A-3
Cost of new delivery equipment

A gain results when the fair market value of the old delivery equipment is greater than its book value. For Mark Express there is a gain of $7,000 on disposal, computed as follows.

Fair market value of old delivery equipment	$19,000
Book value of old delivery equipment ($40,000−$28,000)	12,000
Gain on disposal	**$ 7,000**

Illustration 10A-4
Computation of gain on disposal

Mark Express Delivery records the exchange as follows.

Delivery Equipment (new)	22,000	
Accumulated Depreciation—Delivery Equipment (old)	28,000	
Delivery Equipment (old)		40,000
Gain on Disposal		7,000
Cash		3,000
(To record exchange of old delivery equipment for new delivery equipment)		

A	=	L	+	OE
+22,000				
+28,000				
−40,000				
				+7,000 Rev
−3,000				

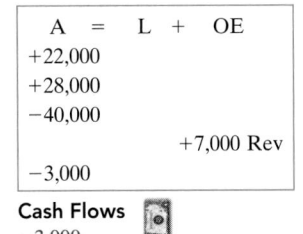

Cash Flows
−3,000

In recording an exchange at a gain, the following three steps are involved: (1) Eliminate the book value of the asset given up, (2) record the cost of the asset acquired, and (3) recognize the gain on disposal. Accounting for exchanges of plant assets becomes more complex if the transaction does not have commercial substance. This issue is discussed in more advanced accounting classes.

SUMMARY OF STUDY OBJECTIVE FOR APPENDIX

WILEY PLUS

10 Explain how to account for the exchange of plant assets. Ordinarily companies record a gain or loss on the exchange of plant assets. The rationale for recognizing a gain or loss is that most exchanges have commercial substance. An exchange has commercial substance if the future cash flows change as a result of the exchange.

*__Note:__ All **asterisked** Questions, Exercises, and Problems relate to material in the appendix to the chapter.

SELF-STUDY QUESTIONS

WILEY PLUS

Answers are at the end of the chapter.

(SO 1) **1.** Erin Danielle Company purchased equipment and incurred the following costs.

Cash price	$24,000
Sales taxes	1,200
Insurance during transit	200
Installation and testing	400
Total costs	$25,800

What amount should be recorded as the cost of the equipment?

a. $24,000.
b. $25,200.
c. $25,400.
d. $25,800.

(SO 2) **2.** Depreciation is a process of:

a. valuation.
b. cost allocation.
c. cash accumulation.
d. appraisal.

(SO 3) **3.** Micah Bartlett Company purchased equipment on January 1, 2007, at a total invoice cost of $400,000. The equipment has an estimated salvage value of $10,000 and an estimated useful life of 5 years. The amount of accumulated depreciation at December 31, 2008, if the straight-line method of depreciation is used, is:

a. $80,000.
b. $160,000.
c. $78,000.
d. $156,000.

(SO 3) **4.** Ann Torbert purchased a truck for $11,000 on January 1, 2007. The truck will have an estimated salvage value of $1,000 at the end of 5 years. Using the units-of-activity method, the balance in accumulated depreciation at December 31, 2008, can be computed by the following formula:

a. ($11,000 ÷ Total estimated activity) × Units of activity for 2008.
b. ($10,000 ÷ Total estimated activity) × Units of activity for 2008.
c. ($11,000 ÷ Total estimated activity) × Units of activity for 2007 and 2008.
d. ($10,000 ÷ Total estimated activity) × Units of activity for 2007 and 2008.

5. When there is a change in estimated depreciation: (SO 4)

a. previous depreciation should be corrected.
b. current and future years' depreciation should be revised.
c. only future years' depreciation should be revised.
d. None of the above.

6. Additions to plant assets are: (SO 5)

a. revenue expenditures.
b. debited to a Repair Expense account.
c. debited to a Purchases account.
d. capital expenditures.

7. Maggie Sharrer Company expects to extract 20 million tons of coal from a mine that cost $12 million. If no salvage value is expected, and 2 million tons are mined and sold in the first year, the entry to record depletion will include a: (SO 7)

a. debit to Accumulated Depletion of $2,000,000.
b. credit to Depletion Expense of $1,200,000.
c. debit to Depletion Expense of $1,200,000.
d. credit to Accumulated Depletion of $2,000,000.

8. Martha Beyerlein Company incurred $150,000 of research and development costs in its laboratory to develop a patent granted on January 2, 2008. On July 31, 2008, Beyerlein paid $35,000 for legal fees in a successful defense of the patent. The total amount debited to Patents through July 31, 2008, should be: (SO 8)

a. $150,000.
b. $35,000.
c. $185,000.
d. $170,000.

9. Indicate which of the following statements is *true*. (SO 9)

a. Since intangible assets lack physical substance, they need be disclosed only in the notes to the financial statements.
b. Goodwill should be reported as a contra-account in the owner's equity section.
c. Totals of major classes of assets can be shown in the balance sheet, with asset details disclosed in the notes to the financial statements.
d. Intangible assets are typically combined with plant assets and natural resources and shown in the property, plant, and equipment section.

(SO 10) *10. Schopenhauer Company exchanged an old machine, with a book value of $39,000 and a fair market value of $35,000, and paid $10,000 cash for a similar new machine. The transaction has commercial substance. At what amount should the machine acquired in the exchange be recorded on Schopenhauer's books?
a. $45,000.
b. $46,000.
c. $49,000.
d. $50,000.

*11. In exchanges of assets in which the exchange has commercial substance: (SO 10)
a. neither gains nor losses are recognized immediately.
b. gains, but not losses, are recognized immediately.
c. losses, but not gains, are recognized immediately.
d. both gains and losses are recognized immediately.

Go to the book's website, **www.wiley.com/college/ weygandt,** for Additional Self-Study questions.

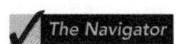

The Navigator

QUESTIONS

1. Tim Hoover is uncertain about the applicability of the cost principle to plant assets. Explain the principle to Tim.
2. What are some examples of land improvements?
3. Dain Company acquires the land and building owned by Corrs Company. What types of costs may be incurred to make the asset ready for its intended use if Dain Company wants to use (a) only the land, and (b) both the land and the building?
4. In a recent newspaper release, the president of Keene Company asserted that something has to be done about depreciation. The president said, "Depreciation does not come close to accumulating the cash needed to replace the asset at the end of its useful life." What is your response to the president?
5. Robert is studying for the next accounting examination. He asks your help on two questions: (a) What is salvage value? (b) Is salvage value used in determining periodic depreciation under each depreciation method? Answer Robert's questions.
6. Contrast the straight-line method and the units-of-activity method as to (a) useful life, and (b) the pattern of periodic depreciation over useful life.
7. Contrast the effects of the three depreciation methods on annual depreciation expense.
8. In the fourth year of an asset's 5-year useful life, the company decides that the asset will have a 6-year service life. How should the revision of depreciation be recorded? Why?
9. Distinguish between revenue expenditures and capital expenditures during useful life.
10. How is a gain or loss on the sale of a plant asset computed?
11. Mendez Corporation owns a machine that is fully depreciated but is still being used. How should Mendez account for this asset and report it in the financial statements?
12. What are natural resources, and what are their distinguishing characteristics?
13. Explain what depletion is and how it is computed.
14. What are the similarities and differences between the terms depreciation, depletion, and amortization?
15. Pendergrass Company hires an accounting intern who says that intangible assets should always be amortized over their legal lives. Is the intern correct? Explain.
16. Goodwill has been defined as the value of all favorable attributes that relate to a business enterprise. What types of attributes could result in goodwill?
17. Kenny Sain, a business major, is working on a case problem for one of his classes. In the case problem, the company needs to raise cash to market a new product it developed. Joe Morris, an engineering major, takes one look at the company's balance sheet and says, "This company has an awful lot of goodwill. Why don't you recommend that they sell some of it to raise cash?" How should Kenny respond to Joe?
18. Under what conditions is goodwill recorded?
19. Often research and development costs provide companies with benefits that last a number of years. (For example, these costs can lead to the development of a patent that will increase the company's income for many years.) However, generally accepted accounting principles require that such costs be recorded as an expense when incurred. Why?
20. McDonald's Corporation reports total average assets of $28.9 billion and net sales of $20.5 billion. What is the company's asset turnover ratio?
21. Resco Corporation and Yapan Corporation operate in the same industry. Resco uses the straight-line method to account for depreciation; Yapan uses an accelerated method. Explain what complications might arise in trying to compare the results of these two companies.
22. Lopez Corporation uses straight-line depreciation for financial reporting purposes but an accelerated method for tax purposes. Is it acceptable to use different methods for the two purposes? What is Lopez's motivation for doing this?
23. You are comparing two companies in the same industry. You have determined that May Corp. depreciates its plant assets over a 40-year life, whereas Won Corp. depreciates its plant assets over a 20-year life. Discuss the implications this has for comparing the results of the two companies.
24. Wade Company is doing significant work to revitalize its warehouses. It is not sure whether it should capitalize these costs or expense them. What are the implications for current-year net income and future net income of expensing versus capitalizing these costs?

***25.** When assets are exchanged in a transaction involving commercial substance, how is the gain or loss on disposal computed?

***26.** Tatum Refrigeration Company trades in an old machine on a new model when the fair market value of the old machine is greater than its book value. The transaction has commercial substance. Should Tatum recognize a gain on disposal? If the fair market value of the old machine is less than its book value, should Tatum recognize a loss on disposal?

BRIEF EXERCISES

Determine the cost of land. (SO 1)

BE10-1 The following expenditures were incurred by Obermeyer Company in purchasing land: cash price $70,000, accrued taxes $3,000, attorneys' fees $2,500, real estate broker's commission $2,000, and clearing and grading $3,500. What is the cost of the land?

Determine the cost of a truck. (SO 1)

BE10-2 Neeley Company incurs the following expenditures in purchasing a truck: cash price $30,000, accident insurance $2,000, sales taxes $1,500, motor vehicle license $100, and painting and lettering $400. What is the cost of the truck?

Compute straight-line depreciation. (SO 3)

BE10-3 Conlin Company acquires a delivery truck at a cost of $42,000. The truck is expected to have a salvage value of $6,000 at the end of its 4-year useful life. Compute annual depreciation for the first and second years using the straight-line method.

Compute depreciation and evaluate treatment. (SO 3)

BE10-4 Ecklund Company purchased land and a building on January 1, 2008. Management's best estimate of the value of the land was $100,000 and of the building $200,000. But management told the accounting department to record the land at $220,000 and the building at $80,000. The building is being depreciated on a straight-line basis over 20 years with no salvage value. Why do you suppose management requested this accounting treatment? Is it ethical?

Compute declining-balance depreciation. (SO 3)

BE10-5 Depreciation information for Conlin Company is given in BE10-3. Assuming the declining-balance depreciation rate is double the straight-line rate, compute annual depreciation for the first and second years under the declining-balance method.

Compute depreciation using the units-of-activity method. (SO 3)

BE10-6 Speedy Taxi Service uses the units-of-activity method in computing depreciation on its taxicabs. Each cab is expected to be driven 150,000 miles. Taxi no. 10 cost $33,500 and is expected to have a salvage value of $500. Taxi no. 10 is driven 30,000 miles in year 1 and 20,000 miles in year 2. Compute the depreciation for each year.

Compute revised depreciation. (SO 4)

BE10-7 On January 1, 2008, the Ramirez Company ledger shows Equipment $29,000 and Accumulated Depreciation $9,000. The depreciation resulted from using the straight-line method with a useful life of 10 years and salvage value of $2,000. On this date, the company concludes that the equipment has a remaining useful life of only 4 years with the same salvage value. Compute the revised annual depreciation.

Prepare entries for delivery truck costs. (SO 5)

BE10-8 Firefly Company had the following two transactions related to its delivery truck.

1. Paid $45 for an oil change.
2. Paid $400 to install special shelving units, which increase the operating efficiency of the truck.

Prepare Firefly's journal entries to record these two transactions.

Prepare entries for disposal by retirement. (SO 6)

BE10-9 Prepare journal entries to record the following.

(a) Gomez Company retires its delivery equipment, which cost $41,000. Accumulated depreciation is also $41,000 on this delivery equipment. No salvage value is received.

(b) Assume the same information as (a), except that accumulated depreciation for Gomez Company is $39,000, instead of $41,000.

Prepare entries for disposal by sale. (SO 6)

BE10-10 Chan Company sells office equipment on September 30, 2008, for $20,000 cash. The office equipment originally cost $72,000 and as of January 1, 2008, had accumulated depreciation of $42,000. Depreciation for the first 9 months of 2008 is $5,250. Prepare the journal entries to **(a)** update depreciation to September 30, 2008, and **(b)** record the sale of the equipment.

Prepare depletion expense entry and balance sheet presentation for natural resources. (SO 7)

BE10-11 Olpe Mining Co. purchased for $7 million a mine that is estimated to have 35 million tons of ore and no salvage value. In the first year, 6 million tons of ore are extracted and sold.

(a) Prepare the journal entry to record depletion expense for the first year.

(b) Show how this mine is reported on the balance sheet at the end of the first year.

BE10-12 Galena Company purchases a patent for $120,000 on January 2, 2008. Its estimated useful life is 10 years.

Prepare patent expense entry and balance sheet presentation for intangibles.
(SO 8)

(a) Prepare the journal entry to record patent expense for the first year.
(b) Show how this patent is reported on the balance sheet at the end of the first year.

BE10-13 Information related to plant assets, natural resources, and intangibles at the end of 2008 for Spain Company is as follows: buildings $1,100,000; accumulated depreciation—buildings $650,000; goodwill $410,000; coal mine $500,000; accumulated depletion—coal mine $108,000. Prepare a partial balance sheet of Spain Company for these items.

Classify long-lived assets on balance sheet.
(SO 9)

BE10-14 In its 2005 annual report Target reported beginning total assets of $32.2 billion; ending total assets of $35.0 billion; property and equipment (net) of $19.4 billion; and net sales of $51.2 billion. Compute Target's asset turnover ratio.

Analyze long-lived assets.
(SO 9)

***BE10-15** Rivera Company exchanges old delivery equipment for new delivery equipment. The book value of the old delivery equipment is $31,000 (cost $61,000 less accumulated depreciation $30,000). Its fair market value is $19,000, and cash of $5,000 is paid. Prepare the entry to record the exchange, assuming the transaction has commercial substance.

Prepare entry for disposal by exchange.
(SO 10)

***BE10-16** Assume the same information as BE10-15, except that the fair market value of the old delivery equipment is $38,000. Prepare the entry to record the exchange.

Prepare entry for disposal by exchange.
(SO 10)

EXERCISES

E10-1 The following expenditures relating to plant assets were made by Spaulding Company during the first 2 months of 2008.

Determine cost of plant acquisitions.
(SO 1)

1. Paid $5,000 of accrued taxes at time plant site was acquired.
2. Paid $200 insurance to cover possible accident loss on new factory machinery while the machinery was in transit.
3. Paid $850 sales taxes on new delivery truck.
4. Paid $17,500 for parking lots and driveways on new plant site.
5. Paid $250 to have company name and advertising slogan painted on new delivery truck.
6. Paid $8,000 for installation of new factory machinery.
7. Paid $900 for one-year accident insurance policy on new delivery truck.
8. Paid $75 motor vehicle license fee on the new truck.

Instructions

(a) Explain the application of the cost principle in determining the acquisition cost of plant assets.
(b) List the numbers of the foregoing transactions, and opposite each indicate the account title to which each expenditure should be debited.

E10-2 Trudy Company incurred the following costs.

Determine property, plant, and equipment costs.
(SO 1)

1. Sales tax on factory machinery purchased	$5,000
2. Painting of and lettering on truck immediately upon purchase	700
3. Installation and testing of factory machinery	2,000
4. Real estate broker's commission on land purchased	3,500
5. Insurance premium paid for first year's insurance on new truck	880
6. Cost of landscaping on property purchased	7,200
7. Cost of paving parking lot for new building constructed	17,900
8. Cost of clearing, draining, and filling land	13,300
9. Architect's fees on self-constructed building	10,000

Instructions

Indicate to which account Trudy would debit each of the costs.

E10-3 On March 1, 2008, Penner Company acquired real estate on which it planned to construct a small office building. The company paid $80,000 in cash. An old warehouse on the property was razed at a cost of $8,600; the salvaged materials were sold for $1,700. Additional expenditures before construction began included $1,100 attorney's fee for work concerning the land purchase, $5,000 real estate broker's fee, $7,800 architect's fee, and $14,000 to put in driveways and a parking lot.

Determine acquisition costs of land.
(SO 1)

Instructions

(a) Determine the amount to be reported as the cost of the land.

(b) For each cost not used in part (a), indicate the account to be debited.

Understand depreciation concepts.

(SO 2)

E10-4 Chris Rock has prepared the following list of statements about depreciation.

1. Depreciation is a process of asset valuation, not cost allocation.
2. Depreciation provides for the proper matching of expenses with revenues.
3. The book value of a plant asset should approximate its market value.
4. Depreciation applies to three classes of plant assets: land, buildings, and equipment.
5. Depreciation does not apply to a building because its usefulness and revenue-producing ability generally remain intact over time.
6. The revenue-producing ability of a depreciable asset will decline due to wear and tear and to obsolescence.
7. Recognizing depreciation on an asset results in an accumulation of cash for replacement of the asset.
8. The balance in accumulated depreciation represents the total cost that has been charged to expense.
9. Depreciation expense and accumulated depreciation are reported on the income statement.
10. Four factors affect the computation of depreciation: cost, useful life, salvage value, and residual value.

Instructions

Identify each statement as true or false. If false, indicate how to correct the statement.

Compute depreciation under units-of-activity method.

(SO 3)

E10-5 Younger Bus Lines uses the units-of-activity method in depreciating its buses. One bus was purchased on January 1, 2008, at a cost of $168,000. Over its 4-year useful life, the bus is expected to be driven 100,000 miles. Salvage value is expected to be $8,000.

Instructions

(a) Compute the depreciation cost per unit.

(b) Prepare a depreciation schedule assuming actual mileage was: 2008, 26,000; 2009, 32,000; 2010, 25,000; and 2011, 17,000.

Determine depreciation for partial periods.

(SO 3)

E10-6 Kelm Company purchased a new machine on October 1, 2008, at a cost of $120,000. The company estimated that the machine will have a salvage value of $12,000. The machine is expected to be used for 10,000 working hours during its 5-year life.

Instructions

Compute the depreciation expense under the following methods for the year indicated.

(a) Straight-line for 2008.

(b) Units-of-activity for 2008, assuming machine usage was 1,700 hours.

(c) Declining-balance using double the straight-line rate for 2008 and 2009.

Compute depreciation using different methods.

(SO 3)

E10-7 Brainiac Company purchased a delivery truck for $30,000 on January 1, 2008. The truck has an expected salvage value of $2,000, and is expected to be driven 100,000 miles over its estimated useful life of 8 years. Actual miles driven were 15,000 in 2008 and 12,000 in 2009.

Instructions

(a) Compute depreciation expense for 2008 and 2009 using (1) the straight-line method, (2) the units-of-activity method, and (3) the double-declining balance method.

(b) Assume that Brainiac uses the straight-line method.

(1) Prepare the journal entry to record 2008 depreciation.

(2) Show how the truck would be reported in the December 31, 2008, balance sheet.

Compute revised annual depreciation.

(SO 4)

E10-8 Jerry Grant, the new controller of Blackburn Company, has reviewed the expected useful lives and salvage values of selected depreciable assets at the beginning of 2008. His findings are as follows.

Type of Asset	Date Acquired	Cost	Accumulated Depreciation 1/1/08	Useful Life in Years		Salvage Value	
				Old	Proposed	Old	Proposed
Building	1/1/02	$800,000	$114,000	40	50	$40,000	$37,000
Warehouse	1/1/03	100,000	25,000	25	20	5,000	3,600

All assets are depreciated by the straight-line method. Blackburn Company uses a calendar year in preparing annual financial statements. After discussion, management has agreed to accept Jerry's proposed changes.

Instructions

(a) Compute the revised annual depreciation on each asset in 2008. (Show computations.)
(b) Prepare the entry (or entries) to record depreciation on the building in 2008.

E10-9 Presented below are selected transactions at Ingles Company for 2008.

Journalize entries for disposal of plant assets.
(SO 6)

Jan. 1 Retired a piece of machinery that was purchased on January 1, 1998. The machine cost $62,000 on that date. It had a useful life of 10 years with no salvage value.
June 30 Sold a computer that was purchased on January 1, 2005. The computer cost $40,000. It had a useful life of 5 years with no salvage value. The computer was sold for $14,000.
Dec. 31 Discarded a delivery truck that was purchased on January 1, 2004. The truck cost $39,000. It was depreciated based on a 6-year useful life with a $3,000 salvage value.

Instructions

Journalize all entries required on the above dates, including entries to update depreciation, where applicable, on assets disposed of. Ingles Company uses straight-line depreciation. (Assume depreciation is up to date as of December 31, 2007.)

E10-10 Beka Company owns equipment that cost $50,000 when purchased on January 1, 2005. It has been depreciated using the straight-line method based on estimated salvage value of $5,000 and an estimated useful life of 5 years.

Journalize entries for disposal of equipment.
(SO 6)

Instructions

Prepare Beka Company's journal entries to record the sale of the equipment in these four independent situations.

(a) Sold for $28,000 on January 1, 2008.
(b) Sold for $28,000 on May 1, 2008.
(c) Sold for $11,000 on January 1, 2008.
(d) Sold for $11,000 on October 1, 2008.

E10-11 On July 1, 2008, Hurtig Inc. invested $720,000 in a mine estimated to have 800,000 tons of ore of uniform grade. During the last 6 months of 2008, 100,000 tons of ore were mined and sold.

Journalize entries for natural resources depletion.
(SO 7)

Instructions

(a) Prepare the journal entry to record depletion expense.
(b) Assume that the 100,000 tons of ore were mined, but only 80,000 units were sold. How are the costs applicable to the 20,000 unsold units reported?

E10-12 The following are selected 2008 transactions of Franco Corporation.

Prepare adjusting entries for amortization.
(SO 8)

Jan. 1 Purchased a small company and recorded goodwill of $150,000. Its useful life is indefinite.
May 1 Purchased for $90,000 a patent with an estimated useful life of 5 years and a legal life of 20 years.

Instructions

Prepare necessary adjusting entries at December 31 to record amortization required by the events above.

E10-13 Herzogg Company, organized in 2008, has the following transactions related to intangible assets.

Prepare entries to set up appropriate accounts for different intangibles; amortize intangible assets.
(SO 8)

1/2/08	Purchased patent (7-year life)	$560,000
4/1/08	Goodwill purchased (indefinite life)	360,000
7/1/08	10-year franchise; expiration date 7/1/2018	440,000
9/1/08	Research and development costs	185,000

Instructions

Prepare the necessary entries to record these intangibles. All costs incurred were for cash. Make the adjusting entries as of December 31, 2008, recording any necessary amortization and reflecting all balances accurately as of that date.

E10-14 During 2008 Nasra Corporation reported net sales of $4,900,000 and net income of $1,500,000. Its balance sheet reported average total assets of $1,400,000.

Calculate asset turnover ratio.
(SO 9)

Instructions

Calculate the asset turnover ratio.

Journalize entries for exchanges.

(SO 10)

***E10-15** Presented below are two independent transactions. Both transactions have commercial substance.

1. Sidney Co. exchanged old trucks (cost $64,000 less $22,000 accumulated depreciation) plus cash of $17,000 for new trucks. The old trucks had a fair market value of $36,000.
2. Lupa Inc. trades its used machine (cost $12,000 less $4,000 accumulated depreciation) for a new machine. In addition to exchanging the old machine (which had a fair market value of $9,000), Lupa also paid cash of $3,000.

Instructions

(a) Prepare the entry to record the exchange of assets by Sidney Co.
(b) Prepare the entry to record the exchange of assets by Lupa Inc.

Journalize entries for the exchange of plant assets.

(SO 10)

***E10-16** Coran's Delivery Company and Enright's Express Delivery exchanged delivery trucks on January 1, 2008. Coran's truck cost $22,000. It has accumulated depreciation of $15,000 and a fair market value of $4,000. Enright's truck cost $10,000. It has accumulated depreciation of $8,000 and a fair market value of $4,000. The transaction has commercial substance.

Instructions

(a) Journalize the exchange for Coran's Delivery Company.
(b) Journalize the exchange for Enright's Express Delivery.

EXERCISES: SET B

Visit the book's website at **www.wiley.com/college/weygandt**, and choose the Student Companion site, to access Exercise Set B.

PROBLEMS: SET A

Determine acquisition costs of land and building.

(SO 1)

P10-1A Diaz Company was organized on January 1. During the first year of operations, the following plant asset expenditures and receipts were recorded in random order.

Debits

1. Cost of filling and grading the land	$ 4,000
2. Full payment to building contractor	700,000
3. Real estate taxes on land paid for the current year	5,000
4. Cost of real estate purchased as a plant site (land $100,000 and building $45,000)	145,000
5. Excavation costs for new building	35,000
6. Architect's fees on building plans	10,000
7. Accrued real estate taxes paid at time of purchase of real estate	2,000
8. Cost of parking lots and driveways	14,000
9. Cost of demolishing building to make land suitable for construction of new building	15,000
	$930,000

Credits

10. Proceeds from salvage of demolished building	$ 3,500

Instructions

Analyze the foregoing transactions using the following column headings. Insert the number of each transaction in the Item space, and insert the amounts in the appropriate columns. For amounts entered in the Other Accounts column, also indicate the account titles.

Totals
Land $162,500
Building $745,000

Item	Land	Building	Other Accounts

Compute depreciation under different methods.

(SO 3)

P10-2A In recent years, Juresic Transportation purchased three used buses. Because of frequent turnover in the accounting department, a different accountant selected the depreciation method for each bus, and various methods were selected. Information concerning the buses is summarized on the next page.

Bus	Acquired	Cost	Salvage Value	Useful Life in Years	Depreciation Method
1	1/1/06	$ 96,000	$ 6,000	5	Straight-line
2	1/1/06	120,000	10,000	4	Declining-balance
3	1/1/07	80,000	8,000	5	Units-of-activity

For the declining-balance method, the company uses the double-declining rate. For the units-of-activity method, total miles are expected to be 120,000. Actual miles of use in the first 3 years were: 2007, 24,000; 2008, 34,000; and 2009, 30,000.

Instructions

(a) Compute the amount of accumulated depreciation on each bus at December 31, 2008.

(a) Bus 2, 2007, $90,000

(b) If bus no. 2 was purchased on April 1 instead of January 1, what is the depreciation expense for this bus in (1) 2006 and (2) 2007?

Compute depreciation under different methods.

(SO 3)

P10-3A On January 1, 2008, Pele Company purchased the following two machines for use in its production process.

Machine A: The cash price of this machine was $38,000. Related expenditures included: sales tax $1,700, shipping costs $150, insurance during shipping $80, installation and testing costs $70, and $100 of oil and lubricants to be used with the machinery during its first year of operations. Pele estimates that the useful life of the machine is 5 years with a $5,000 salvage value remaining at the end of that time period. Assume that the straight-line method of depreciation is used.

Machine B: The recorded cost of this machine was $160,000. Pele estimates that the useful life of the machine is 4 years with a $10,000 salvage value remaining at the end of that time period.

Instructions

(a) Prepare the following for Machine A.
  (1) The journal entry to record its purchase on January 1, 2008.
  (2) The journal entry to record annual depreciation at December 31, 2008.

(b) Calculate the amount of depreciation expense that Pele should record for machine B each year of its useful life under the following assumptions.
  (1) Pele uses the straight-line method of depreciation.
  (2) Pele uses the declining-balance method. The rate used is twice the straight-line rate.
  (3) Pele uses the units-of-activity method and estimates that the useful life of the machine is 125,000 units. Actual usage is as follows: 2008, 45,000 units; 2009, 35,000 units; 2010, 25,000 units; 2011, 20,000 units.

(b) (2) 2008 DDB depreciation $80,000

(c) Which method used to calculate depreciation on machine B reports the highest amount of depreciation expense in year 1 (2008)? The highest amount in year 4 (2011)? The highest total amount over the 4-year period?

Calculate revisions to depreciation expense.

(SO 3, 4)

P10-4A At the beginning of 2006, Lehman Company acquired equipment costing $90,000. It was estimated that this equipment would have a useful life of 6 years and a residual value of $9,000 at that time. The straight-line method of depreciation was considered the most appropriate to use with this type of equipment. Depreciation is to be recorded at the end of each year.

During 2008 (the third year of the equipment's life), the company's engineers reconsidered their expectations, and estimated that the equipment's useful life would probably be 7 years (in total) instead of 6 years. The estimated residual value was not changed at that time. However, during 2011 the estimated residual value was reduced to $5,000.

Instructions

Indicate how much depreciation expense should be recorded each year for this equipment, by completing the following table.

Year	Depreciation Expense	Accumulated Depreciation
2006		
2007		
2008		
2009		
2010		
2011		
2012		

2012 depreciation expense, $12,800

Journalize a series of equipment transactions related to purchase, sale, retirement, and depreciation.

(SO 3, 6, 9)

P10-5A At December 31, 2008, Jimenez Company reported the following as plant assets.

Land		$ 4,000,000
Buildings	$28,500,000	
Less: Accumulated depreciation—buildings	12,100,000	16,400,000
Equipment	48,000,000	
Less: Accumulated depreciation—equipment	5,000,000	43,000,000
Total plant assets		$63,400,000

During 2009, the following selected cash transactions occurred.

April 1	Purchased land for $2,130,000.
May 1	Sold equipment that cost $780,000 when purchased on January 1, 2005. The equipment was sold for $450,000.
June 1	Sold land purchased on June 1, 1999, for $1,500,000. The land cost $400,000.
July 1	Purchased equipment for $2,000,000.
Dec. 31	Retired equipment that cost $500,000 when purchased on December 31, 1999. No salvage value was received.

Instructions

(a) Journalize the above transactions. The company uses straight-line depreciation for buildings and equipment. The buildings are estimated to have a 50-year life and no salvage value. The equipment is estimated to have a 10-year useful life and no salvage value. Update depreciation on assets disposed of at the time of sale or retirement.

(b) Record adjusting entries for depreciation for 2009.

(c) Prepare the plant assets section of Jimenez's balance sheet at December 31, 2009.

(b) Depreciation Expense—building $570,000; equipment $4,772,000
(c) Total plant assets $61,270,000

Record disposals.

(SO 6)

P10-6A Puckett Co. has office furniture that cost $75,000 and that has been depreciated $50,000. Record the disposal under the following assumptions.

(a) It was scrapped as having no value.

(b) It was sold for $21,000.

(c) It was sold for $31,000.

Prepare entries to record transactions related to acquisition and amortization of intangibles; prepare the intangible assets section.

(SO 8, 9)

P10-7A The intangible assets section of Redeker Company at December 31, 2008, is presented below.

Patent ($70,000 cost less $7,000 amortization)	$63,000
Franchise ($48,000 cost less $19,200 amortization)	28,800
Total	$91,800

The patent was acquired in January 2008 and has a useful life of 10 years. The franchise was acquired in January 2005 and also has a useful life of 10 years. The following cash transactions may have affected intangible assets during 2009.

Jan. 2	Paid $45,000 legal costs to successfully defend the patent against infringement by another company.
Jan.–June	Developed a new product, incurring $140,000 in research and development costs. A patent was granted for the product on July 1. Its useful life is equal to its legal life.
Sept. 1	Paid $50,000 to an extremely large defensive lineman to appear in commercials advertising the company's products. The commercials will air in September and October.
Oct. 1	Acquired a franchise for $100,000. The franchise has a useful life of 50 years.

Instructions

(a) Prepare journal entries to record the transactions above.

(b) Prepare journal entries to record the 2009 amortization expense.

(c) Prepare the intangible assets section of the balance sheet at December 31, 2009.

(b) Amortization Expense—Patents $12,000
Amortization Expense—Franchise $5,300
(c) Total intangible assets $219,500

Prepare entries to correct errors made in recording and amortizing intangible assets.

(SO 8)

P10-8A Due to rapid turnover in the accounting department, a number of transactions involving intangible assets were improperly recorded by the Thorne Company in 2008.

1. Thorne developed a new manufacturing process, incurring research and development costs of $136,000. The company also purchased a patent for $60,000. In early January, Thorne capitalized $196,000 as the cost of the patents. Patent amortization expense of $9,800 was recorded based on a 20-year useful life.

2. On July 1, 2008, Thorne purchased a small company and as a result acquired goodwill of $92,000. Thorne recorded a half-year's amortization in 2008, based on a 50-year life ($920 amortization). The goodwill has an indefinite life.

Instructions

Prepare all journal entries necessary to correct any errors made during 2008. Assume the books have not yet been closed for 2008.

1. R&D Exp. $136,000

P10-9A Lebo Company and Ritter Corporation, two corporations of roughly the same size, are both involved in the manufacture of in-line skates. Each company depreciates its plant assets using the straight-line approach. An investigation of their financial statements reveals the following information.

Calculate and comment on asset turnover ratio.

(SO 9)

	Lebo Co.	Ritter Corp.
Net income	$ 800,000	$1,000,000
Sales	1,200,000	1,080,000
Average total assets	2,500,000	2,000,000
Average plant assets	1,800,000	1,000,000

Instructions

(a) For each company, calculate the asset turnover ratio.

(b) Based on your calculations in part (a), comment on the relative effectiveness of the two companies in using their assets to generate sales and produce net income.

PROBLEMS: SET B

P10-1B Selmon Company was organized on January 1. During the first year of operations, the following plant asset expenditures and receipts were recorded in random order.

Determine acquisition costs of land and building.

(SO 1)

Debits

1. Accrued real estate taxes paid at time of purchase of real estate	$ 2,000
2. Real estate taxes on land paid for the current year	3,000
3. Full payment to building contractor	600,000
4. Excavation costs for new building	22,000
5. Cost of real estate purchased as a plant site (land $100,000 and building $25,000)	125,000
6. Cost of parking lots and driveways	15,000
7. Architect's fees on building plans	10,000
8. Installation cost of fences around property	4,000
9. Cost of demolishing building to make land suitable for construction of new building	24,000
	$805,000

Credit

10. Proceeds from salvage of demolished building	$ 2,500

Instructions

Analyze the foregoing tranactions using the following column headings. Insert the number of each transaction in the Item space, and insert the amounts in the appropriate columns. For amounts entered in the Other Accounts column, also indicate the account title.

Item	Land	Building	Other Accounts

Totals
Land $148,500
Building $632,000

P10-2B In recent years, Escobar Company purchased three machines. Because of heavy turnover in the accounting department, a different accountant was in charge of selecting the depreciation method for each machine, and various methods were selected. Information concerning the machines is summarized on the next page.

Compute depreciation under different methods.

(SO 3)

Machine	Acquired	Cost	Salvage Value	Useful Life in Years	Depreciation Method
1	1/1/05	$86,000	$ 6,000	10	Straight-line
2	1/1/06	100,000	10,000	8	Declining-balance
3	11/1/08	78,000	6,000	6	Units-of-activity

For the declining-balance method, the company uses the double-declining rate. For the units-of-activity method, total machine hours are expected to be 24,000. Actual hours of use in the first 3 years were: 2008, 1,000; 2009, 4,500; and 2010, 5,000.

Instructions

(a) Machine 2, 2007, $18,750

(a) Compute the amount of accumulated depreciation on each machine at December 31, 2008.
(b) If machine 2 had been purchased on April 1 instead of January 1, what would be the depreciation expense for this machine in (1) 2006 and (2) 2007?

Compute depreciation under different methods.
(SO 3)

P10-3B On January 1, 2008, Guthrie Company purchased the following two machines for use in its production process.

Machine A: The cash price of this machine was $46,500. Related expenditures included: sales tax $2,200, shipping costs $175, insurance during shipping $75, installation and testing costs $50, and $90 of oil and lubricants to be used with the machinery during its first year of operation. Guthrie estimates that the useful life of the machine is 4 years with a $5,000 salvage value remaining at the end of that time period.

Machine B: The recorded cost of this machine was $120,000. Guthrie estimates that the useful life of the machine is 4 years with a $8,000 salvage value remaining at the end of that time period.

Instructions

(a) (2) $11,000

(a) Prepare the following for Machine A.
  (1) The journal entry to record its purchase on January 1, 2008.
  (2) The journal entry to record annual depreciation at December 31, 2008, assuming the straight-line method of depreciation is used.
(b) Calculate the amount of depreciation expense that Guthrie should record for machine B each year of its useful life under the following assumption.
  (1) Guthrie uses the straight-line method of depreciation.
  (2) Guthrie uses the declining-balance method. The rate used is twice the straight-line rate.
  (3) Guthrie uses the units-of-activity method and estimates the useful life of the machine is 25,000 units. Actual usage is as follows: 2008, 6,500 units; 2009, 7,500 units; 2010, 6,000 units; 2011, 5,000 units.
(c) Which method used to calculate depreciation on machine B reports the lowest amount of depreciation expense in year 1 (2008)? The lowest amount in year 4 (2011)? The lowest total amount over the 4-year period?

Calculate revisions to depreciation expense.
(SO 3, 4)

P10-4B At the beginning of 2006, Hadaway Company acquired equipment costing $80,000. It was estimated that this equipment would have a useful life of 6 years and a residual value of $8,000 at that time. The straight-line method of depreciation was considered the most appropriate to use with this type of equipment. Depreciation is to be recorded at the end of each year.

During 2008 (the third year of the equipment's life), the company's engineers reconsidered their expectations, and estimated that the equipment's useful life would probably be 7 years (in total) instead of 6 years. The estimated residual value was not changed at that time. However, during 2011 the estimated residual value was reduced to $4,000.

Instructions

Indicate how much depreciation expense should be recorded for this equipment each year by completing the following table.

Year	Depreciation Expense	Accumulated Depreciation
2006		
2007		
2008		
2009		
2010		
2011		
2012		

2012 depreciation expense, $11,600

Journalize a series of equipment transactions related to purchase, sale, retirement, and depreciation.

(SO 3, 6, 9)

P10-5B At December 31, 2008, Yockey Company reported the following as plant assets.

Land		$ 3,000,000
Buildings	$26,500,000	
Less: Accumulated depreciation—buildings	12,100,000	14,400,000
Equipment	40,000,000	
Less: Accumulated depreciation—equipment	5,000,000	35,000,000
Total plant assets		$52,400,000

During 2009, the following selected cash transactions occurred.

April 1	Purchased land for $2,200,000.
May 1	Sold equipment that cost $600,000 when purchased on January 1, 2005. The equipment was sold for $360,000.
June 1	Sold land purchased on June 1, 1999, for $1,800,000. The land cost $600,000.
July 1	Purchased equipment for $1,800,000.
Dec. 31	Retired equipment that cost $500,000 when purchased on December 31, 1999. No salvage value was received.

Instructions

(a) Journalize the above transactions. Yockey uses straight-line depreciation for buildings and equipment. The buildings are estimated to have a 50-year useful life and no salvage value. The equipment is estimated to have a 10-year useful life and no salvage value. Update depreciation on assets disposed of at the time of sale or retirement.

(b) Record adjusting entries for depreciation for 2009.

(c) Prepare the plant assets section of Yockey's balance sheet at December 31, 2009.

(b) Depreciation expense—Building $530,000; Equipment $3,980,000
(c) Total plant assets $50,880,000

Record disposals.

(SO 6)

P10-6B Riggs Co. has delivery equipment that cost $50,000 and that has been depreciated $24,000. Record the disposal under the following assumptions.

(a) It was scrapped as having no value.
(b) It was sold for $31,000.
(c) It was sold for $18,000.

Prepare entries to record transactions related to acquisition and amortization of intangibles; prepare the intangible assets section.

(SO 8, 9)

P10-7B The intangible assets section of Justen Company at December 31, 2008, is presented below.

Patent ($60,000 cost less $6,000 amortization)	$54,000
Copyright ($36,000 cost less $14,400 amortization)	21,600
Total	$75,600

The patent was acquired in January 2008 and has a useful life of 10 years. The copyright was acquired in January 2005 and also has a useful life of 10 years. The following cash transactions may have affected intangible assets during 2009.

Jan. 2	Paid $27,000 legal costs to successfully defend the patent against infringement by another company.
Jan.–June	Developed a new product, incurring $140,000 in research and development costs. A patent was granted for the product on July 1. Its useful life is equal to its legal life.
Sept. 1	Paid $75,000 to a quarterback to appear in commercials advertising the company's products. The commercials will air in September and October.
Oct. 1	Acquired a copyright for $120,000. The copyright has a useful life of 50 years.

Instructions

(a) Prepare journal entries to record the transactions above.
(b) Prepare journal entries to record the 2009 amortization expense for intangible assets.
(c) Prepare the intangible assets section of the balance sheet at December 31, 2009.
(d) Prepare the note to the financials on Justen's intangibles as of December 31, 2009.

(b) Amortization Expense—Patents $9,000; Amortization Expense—Copyrights $4,200
(c) Total intangible assets, $209,400

Prepare entries to correct errors made in recording and amortizing intangible assets.

(SO 8)

P10-8B Due to rapid turnover in the accounting department, a number of transactions involving intangible assets were improperly recorded by Duby Company in 2008.

1. Duby developed a new manufacturing process, incurring research and development costs of $95,000. The company also purchased a patent for $40,000. In early January, Duby capitalized $135,000 as the cost of the patents. Patent amortization expense of $6,750 was recorded based on a 20-year useful life.

2. On July 1, 2008, Duby purchased a small company and as a result acquired goodwill of $80,000. Duby recorded a half-year's amortization in 2008, based on a 50-year life ($800 amortization). The goodwill has an indefinite life.

R&D Exp. $95,000

Instructions

Prepare all journal entries necessary to correct any errors made during 2008. Assume the books have not yet been closed for 2008.

Calculate and comment on asset turnover ratio.

(SO 9)

P10-9B Gavin Corporation and Keady Corporation, two corporations of roughly the same size, are both involved in the manufacture of canoes and sea kayaks. Each company depreciates its plant assets using the straight-line approach. An investigation of their financial statements reveals the following information.

	Gavin Corp.	Keady Corp.
Net income	$ 400,000	$ 420,000
Sales	1,300,000	1,140,000
Average total assets	2,000,000	1,500,000
Average plant assets	1,500,000	800,000

Instructions

(a) For each company, calculate the asset turnover ratio.

(b) Based on your calculations in part (a), comment on the relative effectiveness of the two companies in using their assets to generate sales and produce net income.

PROBLEMS: SET C

Visit the book's website at **www.wiley.com/college/weygandt**, and choose the Student Companion site, to access Problem Set C.

COMPREHENSIVE PROBLEM: CHAPTERS 3 TO 10

Winterschid Company's trial balance at December 31, 2008, is presented below. All 2008 transactions have been recorded except for the items described on page 465.

	Debit	Credit
Cash	$ 28,000	
Accounts Receivable	36,800	
Notes Receivable	10,000	
Interest Receivable	–0–	
Merchandise Inventory	36,200	
Prepaid Insurance	3,600	
Land	20,000	
Building	150,000	
Equipment	60,000	
Patent	9,000	
Allowance for Doubtful Accounts		$ 500
Accumulated Depreciation—Building		50,000
Accumulated Depreciation—Equipment		24,000
Accounts Payable		27,300
Salaries Payable		–0–
Unearned Rent		6,000
Notes Payable (short-term)		11,000
Interest Payable		–0–
Notes Payable (long-term)		35,000
Winterschid, Capital		113,600
Winterschid, Drawing	12,000	
Sales		900,000

Interest Revenue		–0–
Rent Revenue		–0–
Gain on Disposal		–0–
Bad Debts Expense	–0–	
Cost of Goods Sold	630,000	
Depreciation Expense—Buildings	–0–	
Depreciation Expense—Equipment	–0–	
Insurance Expense	–0–	
Interest Expense	–0–	
Other Operating Expenses	61,800	
Amortization Expense—Patents	–0–	
Salaries Expense	110,000	
Total	$1,167,400	$1,167,400

Unrecorded transactions

1. On May 1, 2008, Winterschid purchased equipment for $13,200 plus sales taxes of $600 (all paid in cash).
2. On July 1, 2008, Winterschid sold for $3,500 equipment which originally cost $5,000. Accumulated depreciation on this equipment at January 1, 2008, was $1,800; 2008 depreciation prior to the sale of equipment was $450.
3. On December 31, 2008, Winterschid sold for $9,000 on account inventory that cost $6,300.
4. Winterschid estimates that uncollectible accounts receivable at year-end is $4,000.
5. The note receivable is a one-year, 8% note dated April 1, 2008. No interest has been recorded.
6. The balance in prepaid insurance represents payment of a $3,600 6-month premium on September 1, 2008.
7. The building is being depreciated using the straight-line method over 30 years. The salvage value is $30,000.
8. The equipment owned prior to this year is being depreciated using the straight-line method over 5 years. The salvage value is 10% of cost.
9. The equipment purchased on May 1, 2008, is being depreciated using the straight-line method over 5 years, with a salvage value of $1,800.
10. The patent was acquired on January 1, 2008, and has a useful life of 10 years from that date.
11. Unpaid salaries at December 31, 2008, total $2,200.
12. The unearned rent of $6,000 was received on December 1, 2008, for 3 months rent.
13. Both the short-term and long-term notes payable are dated January 1, 2008, and carry a 9% interest rate. All interest is payable in the next 12 months.

Instructions

(a) Prepare journal entries for the transactions listed above.
(b) Prepare an updated December 31, 2008, trial balance.
(c) Prepare a 2008 income statement and an owner's equity statement.
(d) Prepare a December 31, 2008, classified balance sheet.

CONTINUING COOKIE CHRONICLE

(Note: This is a continuation of the Cookie Chronicle from Chapters 1 through 9.)

CCC10

Natalie is also thinking of buying a van that will be used only for business. Natalie is concerned about the impact of the van's cost on her income statement and balance sheet. She has come to you for advice on calculating the van's depreciation.

Go to the book's website,
www.wiley.com/college/weygandt,
to see the completion of this problem.

BROADENING YOUR PERSPECTIVE

FINANCIAL REPORTING AND ANALYSIS

Financial Reporting Problem

PepsiCo, Inc.

BYP10-1 The financial statements and the Notes to Consolidated Financial Statements of PepsiCo are presented in Appendix A.

Instructions

Refer to PepsiCo's financial statements and answer the following questions.

(a) What was the total cost and book value of property, plant, and equipment at December 31, 2005?
(b) What method or methods of depreciation are used by the company for financial reporting purposes?
(c) What was the amount of depreciation and amortization expense for each of the three years 2003–2005?
(d) Using the statement of cash flows, what is the amount of capital spending in 2005 and 2004?
(e) Where does the company disclose its intangible assets, and what types of intangibles did it have at December 31, 2005?

Comparative Analysis Problem

PepsiCo, Inc. vs. The Coca-Cola Company

BYP10-2 PepsiCo's financial statements are presented in Appendix A. Coca-Cola's financial statements are presented in Appendix B.

Instructions

(a) Compute the asset turnover ratio for each company for 2005.
(b) What conclusions concerning the efficiency of assets can be drawn from these data?

Exploring the Web

BYP10-3 A company's annual report identifies the amount of its plant assets and the depreciation method used.

Address: www.reportgallery.com, or go to **www.wiley.com/college/weygandt**

Steps

1. From Report Gallery Homepage, choose **Search by Alphabet**, and pick a letter.
2. Select a particular company.
3. Choose the most recent **Annual Report**.
4. Follow instructions below.

Instructions

(a) What is the name of the company?
(b) At fiscal year-end, what is the net amount of its plant assets?
(c) What is the accumulated depreciation?
(d) Which method of depreciation does the company use?

CRITICAL THINKING

Decision Making Across the Organization

BYP10-4 Reimer Company and Lingo Company are two proprietorships that are similar in many respects. One difference is that Reimer Company uses the straight-line method and Lingo

Company uses the declining-balance method at double the straight-line rate. On January 2, 2006, both companies acquired the following depreciable assets.

Asset	Cost	Salvage Value	Useful Life
Building	$320,000	$20,000	40 years
Equipment	110,000	10,000	10 years

Including the appropriate depreciation charges, annual net income for the companies in the years 2006, 2007, and 2008 and total income for the 3 years were as follows.

	2006	2007	2008	Total
Reimer Company	$84,000	$88,400	$90,000	$262,400
Lingo Company	68,000	76,000	85,000	229,000

At December 31, 2008, the balance sheets of the two companies are similar except that Lingo Company has more cash than Reimer Company.

Sally Vogts is interested in buying one of the companies. She comes to you for advice.

Instructions

With the class divided into groups, answer the following.

(a) Determine the annual and total depreciation recorded by each company during the 3 years.

(b) Assuming that Lingo Company also uses the straight-line method of depreciation instead of the declining-balance method as in (a), prepare comparative income data for the 3 years.

(c) Which company should Sally Vogts buy? Why?

Communication Activity

BYP10-5 The following was published with the financial statements to American Exploration Company.

> **AMERICAN EXPLORATION COMPANY**
> Notes to the Financial Statements
>
> **Property, Plant, and Equipment**—The Company accounts for its oil and gas exploration and production activities using the successful efforts method of accounting. Under this method, acquisition costs for proved and unproved properties are capitalized when incurred.... The costs of drilling exploratory wells are capitalized pending determination of whether each well has discovered proved reserves. If proved reserves are not discovered, such drilling costs are charged to expense.... Depletion of the cost of producing oil and gas properties is computed on the units-of-activity method.

Instructions

Write a brief memo to your instructor discussing American Exploration Company's note regarding property, plant, and equipment. Your memo should address what is meant by the "successful efforts method" and "units-of-activity method."

Ethics Case

BYP10-6 Buster Container Company is suffering declining sales of its principal product, nonbiodegradeable plastic cartons. The president, Dennis Harwood, instructs his controller, Shelly McGlone, to lengthen asset lives to reduce depreciation expense. A processing line of automated plastic extruding equipment, purchased for $3.1 million in January 2008, was originally estimated to have a useful life of 8 years and a salvage value of $300,000. Depreciation has been recorded for 2 years on that basis. Dennis wants the estimated life changed to 12 years total, and the straight-line method continued. Shelly is hesitant to make the change, believing it is unethical to increase net income in this manner. Dennis says, "Hey, the life is only an estimate, and I've heard that our competition uses a 12-year life on their production equipment."

Instructions

(a) Who are the stakeholders in this situation?

(b) Is the change in asset life unethical, or is it simply a good business practice by an astute president?

(c) What is the effect of Dennis Harwood's proposed change on income before taxes in the year of change?

"All About You" Activity

BYP10-7 Both the **All About You** story and the Feature Story at the beginning of the chapter discussed the company Rent-A-Wreck. Note that the tradename Rent-A-Wreck is a very important asset to the company, as it creates immediate product identification. As indicated in the chapter, companies invest substantial sums to ensure that their product is well-known to the consumer. Test your knowledge of who owns some famous brands and their impact on the financial statements.

Instructions

(a) Provide an answer to the five multiple-choice questions below.

(1) Which company owns both Taco Bell and Pizza Hut?
(a) McDonald's. **(c)** Yum Brands.
(b) CKE. **(d)** Wendy's.

(2) Dairy Queen belongs to:
(a) Breyer. **(c)** GE.
(b) Berkshire Hathaway. **(d)** The Coca-Cola Company.

(3) Phillip Morris, the cigarette maker, is owned by:
(a) Altria. **(c)** Boeing.
(b) GE. **(d)** ExxonMobil.

(4) AOL, a major Internet provider, belongs to:
(a) Microsoft. **(c)** NBC.
(b) Cisco. **(d)** Time Warner.

(5) ESPN, the sports broadcasting network, is owned by:
(a) Procter & Gamble. **(c)** Walt Disney.
(b) Altria. **(d)** The Coca-Cola Company.

(b) How do you think the value of these brands is reported on the appropriate company's balance sheet?

Answers to Insight and Accounting Across the Organization Questions

p. 427 Many U.S. Firms Use Leases

Q: Why might airline managers choose to lease rather than purchase their planes?

A: *The reasons for leasing include favorable tax treatment, better financing options, increased flexibility, reduced risk of obsolescence, and low airline income.*

p. 436 What Happened at WorldCom?

Q: What erroneous accounting entries (accounts debited and credited) were made by WorldCom?

A: *WorldCom erroneously debited Assets and credited Cash/Accounts Payable.*

Q: What is the correcting entry that should be recorded, and what is its effect on WorldCom's financial statements?

A: *The correcting entry would be a debit to Expenses and a credit to Assets. This correction would decrease reported income and assets and increase expenses.*

p. 443 ESPN Wins Monday Night Football Franchise

Q: How should ESPN account for the $1.1 billion per year franchise fee?

A: *Since this is an annual franchise fee, ESPN should expense it each year, rather than capitalizing and amortizing it.*

Authors' Comments on *All About You: Buying a Wreck of Your Own* (p. 446)

As the data in the box suggest, this decision can have significant implications for your personal budget. For many college students, vehicle costs are among their biggest expenses—and vehicle expenses often offer the greatest opportunities for savings. But for many people their vehicle choice is not just about how to get around. Some view their car as an expression of their personality. That said, many people simply don't realize just how much this particular expression of their personality is actually costing them.

You should approach this decision using the skills you have acquired in your business studies. Evaluate your transportation needs, collect information about all of your alternatives, and understand exactly what the real costs are of each. For example, everyone knows that the original purchase price of a new car is higher than a used car, but few people stop to consider the fact that insurance costs and annual motor vehicle costs on a new vehicle are also much higher.

We cannot tell you whether a new or used car is right for you, but we do hope that we have convinced you to carefully consider all aspects of the financial implications of your decision the next time you shop for new wheels. In later chapters we will provide you with additional tools to help you evaluate this decision.

Answer to PepsiCo Review It Question 2, p. 428

PepsiCo reports the following categories and amounts under the heading "Property, plant, and equipment (net)": Land and improvements $685,000,000; Buildings and improvements $3,736,000,000; Machinery and equipment, including fleet and software $11,658,000,000; and Construction in progress $1,066,000,000. In addition, accumulated depreciation of $8,464,000,000 was deducted.

Answers to Self-Study Questions

1. d **2.** b **3.** d **4.** d **5.** b **6.** d **7.** c **8.** b **9.** c **10.** a **11.** d

Remember to go back to the Navigator box on the chapter-opening page and check off your completed work.

Chapter 11

Current Liabilities and Payroll Accounting

STUDY OBJECTIVES

After studying this chapter, you should be able to:

1. Explain a current liability, and identify the major types of current liabilities.
2. Describe the accounting for notes payable.
3. Explain the accounting for other current liabilities.
4. Explain the financial statement presentation and analysis of current liabilities.
5. Describe the accounting and disclosure requirements for contingent liabilities.
6. Compute and record the payroll for a pay period.
7. Describe and record employer payroll taxes.
8. Discuss the objectives of internal control for payroll.

The Navigator

The Navigator

Scan **Study Objectives**	■
Read **Feature Story**	■
Read **Preview**	■
Read text and answer **Before You Go On** p. 480 ■ p. 486 ■ p. 490	■
Work **Demonstration Problem**	■
Review **Summary of Study Objectives**	■
Answer **Self-Study Questions**	■
Complete **Assignments**	■

Feature Story

FINANCING HIS DREAMS

What would you do if you had a great idea for a new product, but couldn't come up with the cash to get the business off the ground? Small businesses often cannot attract investors. Nor can they obtain traditional debt financing through bank loans or bond issuances. Instead, they often resort to unusual, and costly, forms of nontraditional financing.

Such was the case for Wilbert Murdock. Murdock grew up in a New York housing project, and always had great ambitions. This ambitious spirit led him

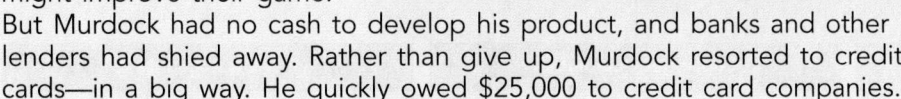

into some business ventures that failed: a medical diagnostic tool, a device to eliminate carpal-tunnel syndrome, custom-designed sneakers, and a device to keep people from falling asleep while driving.

Another idea was computerized golf clubs that analyze a golfer's swing and provide immediate feedback. Murdock saw great potential in the idea: Many golfers are willing to shell out considerable sums of money for devices that might improve their game. But Murdock had no cash to develop his product, and banks and other lenders had shied away. Rather than give up, Murdock resorted to credit cards—in a big way. He quickly owed $25,000 to credit card companies.

While funding a business with credit cards might sound unusual, it isn't. A recent study found that one-third of businesses with fewer than 20 employees financed at least part of their operations with credit cards. As Murdock explained, credit cards are an appealing way to finance a start-up because "credit-card companies don't care how the money is spent." However, they do care how they are paid. And so Murdock faced high interest charges and a barrage of credit card collection letters.

Murdock's debt forced him to sacrifice nearly everything in order to keep his business afloat. His car stopped running, he barely had enough money to buy food, and he lived and worked out of a dimly lit apartment in his mother's basement. Through it all he tried to maintain a positive spirit, joking that, if he becomes successful, he might some day get to appear in an American Express commercial.

Source: Rodney Ho, "Banking on Plastic: To Finance a Dream, Many Entrepreneurs Binge on Credit Cards," *Wall Street Journal*, March 9, 1998, p. A1.

The Navigator

Inside Chapter 11...

Preview of Chapter 11

Inventor-entrepreneur Wilbert Murdock, as you can tell from the Feature Story, had to use multiple credit cards to finance his business ventures. Murdock's credit card debts would be classified as *current liabilities* because they are due every month. Yet by making minimal payments and paying high interest each month, Murdock used this credit source long-term. Some credit card balances remain outstanding for years as they accumulate interest.

In Chapter 4, we defined liabilities as creditors' claims on total assets and as existing debts and obligations. These claims, debts, and obligations must be settled or paid at some time **in the future** by the transfer of assets or services. The future date on which they are due or payable (maturity date) is a significant feature of liabilities. This "future date" feature gives rise to two basic classifications of liabilities: (1) current liabilities and (2) long-term liabilities. We will explain current liabilities, along with payroll accounting, in this chapter. We will explain long-term liabilities in Chapter 15.

The content and organization of Chapter 11 are as follows.

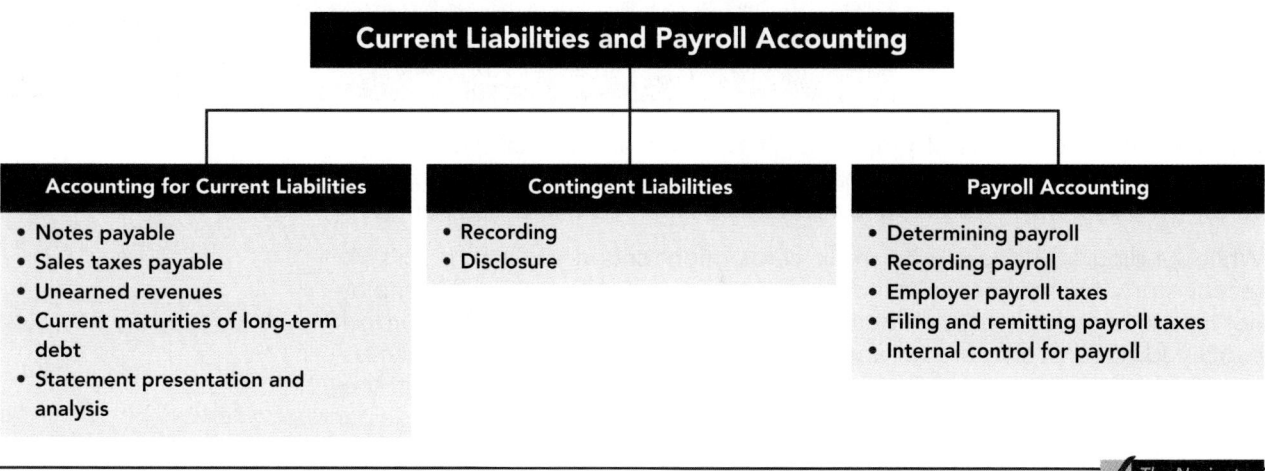

Current Liabilities and Payroll Accounting

Accounting for Current Liabilities
- Notes payable
- Sales taxes payable
- Unearned revenues
- Current maturities of long-term debt
- Statement presentation and analysis

Contingent Liabilities
- Recording
- Disclosure

Payroll Accounting
- Determining payroll
- Recording payroll
- Employer payroll taxes
- Filing and remitting payroll taxes
- Internal control for payroll

The Navigator

ACCOUNTING FOR CURRENT LIABILITIES

STUDY OBJECTIVE 1
Explain a current liability, and identify the major types of current liabilities.

As explained in Chapter 4, a **current liability** is a debt with two key features: (1) The company reasonably expects to pay the debt from existing current assets or through the creation of other current liabilities. (2) The company will pay the debt within one year or the operating cycle, whichever is longer. Debts that do not meet **both criteria** are classified as long-term liabilities. Most companies pay current liabilities within one year out of current assets, rather than by creating other liabilities.

Companies must carefully monitor the relationship of current liabilities to current assets. This relationship is critical in evaluating a company's short-term debt-paying ability. A company that has more current liabilities than current assets may not be able to meet its current obligations when they become due.

Current liabilities include notes payable, accounts payable, and unearned revenues. They also include accrued liabilities such as taxes, salaries and wages, and interest payable. In previous chapters we explained the entries for accounts payable and adjusting entries for some current liabilities. In the following sections, we discuss other types of current liabilities.

Notes Payable

STUDY OBJECTIVE 2

Describe the accounting for notes payable.

Companies record obligations in the form of written promissory notes, called **notes payable**. Notes payable are often used instead of accounts payable because they give the lender formal proof of the obligation in case legal remedies are needed to collect the debt. Notes payable usually require the borrower to pay interest. Companies frequently issue them to meet short-term financing needs.

Notes are issued for varying periods. **Those due for payment within one year of the balance sheet date are usually classified as current liabilities.**

To illustrate the accounting for notes payable, assume that First National Bank agrees to lend $100,000 on March 1, 2008, if Cole Williams Co. signs a $100,000, 12%, four-month note. With an interest-bearing promissory note, the amount of assets received upon issuance of the note generally equals the note's face value. Cole Williams Co. therefore will receive $100,000 cash and will make the following journal entry.

Mar. 1	Cash	100,000	
	Notes Payable		100,000
	(To record issuance of 12%, 4-month note to First National Bank)		

A	=	L	+	OE
+100,000				
		+100,000		

Cash Flows
+100,000

Interest accrues over the life of the note, and the company must periodically record that accrual. If Cole Williams Co. prepares financial statements on June 30, it makes an adjusting entry at June 30 to recognize interest expense and interest payable of $4,000 ($100,000 × 12% × 4/12). Illustration 11-1 shows the formula for computing interest, and its application to Cole Williams Co.'s note.

Face Value of Note	×	Annual Interest Rate	×	Time in Terms of One Year	=	Interest
$100,000	×	12%	×	4/12	=	**$4,000**

Illustration 11-1
Formula for computing interest

Cole Williams makes an adjusting entry as follows:

June 30	Interest Expense	4,000	
	Interest Payable		4,000
	(To accrue interest for 4 months on First National Bank note)		

A	=	L	+	OE
				−4,000 Exp
		+4,000		

Cash Flows
no effect

In the June 30 financial statements, the current liabilities section of the balance sheet will show notes payable $100,000 and interest payable $4,000. In addition, the company will report interest expense of $4,000 under "Other expenses and losses" in the income statement. If Cole Williams Co. prepared financial statements monthly, the adjusting entry at the end of each month would have been $1,000 ($100,000 × 12% × 1/12).

At maturity (July 1, 2008), Cole Williams Co. must pay the face value of the note ($100,000) plus $4,000 interest ($100,000 × 12% × 4/12). It records payment of the note and accrued interest as shown on the next page.

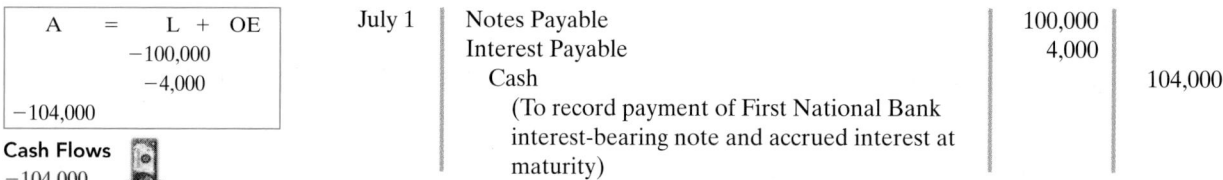

A	=	L	+	OE
		−100,000		
		−4,000		
−104,000				

Cash Flows
−104,000

Date	Account Titles and Explanation	Debit	Credit
July 1	Notes Payable	100,000	
	Interest Payable	4,000	
	Cash		104,000
	(To record payment of First National Bank interest-bearing note and accrued interest at maturity)		

Sales Taxes Payable

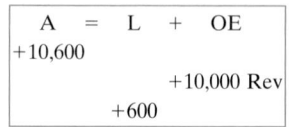

STUDY OBJECTIVE 3

Explain the accounting for other current liabilities.

As a consumer, you know that many of the products you purchase at retail stores are subject to sales taxes. Many states also are now collecting sales taxes on purchases made on the Internet. Sales taxes are expressed as a stated percentage of the sales price. The retailer collects the tax from the customer when the sale occurs. Periodically (usually monthly), the retailer remits the collections to the state's department of revenue.

Under most state sales tax laws, the selling company must ring up separately on the cash register the amount of the sale and the amount of the sales tax collected. (Gasoline sales are a major exception.) The company then uses the cash register readings to credit Sales and Sales Taxes Payable. For example, if the March 25 cash register reading for Cooley Grocery shows sales of $10,000 and sales taxes of $600 (sales tax rate of 6%), the journal entry is:

A	=	L	+	OE
+10,600				
				+10,000 Rev
		+600		

Cash Flows
+10,600

Date	Account Titles and Explanation	Debit	Credit
Mar. 25	Cash	10,600	
	Sales		10,000
	Sales Taxes Payable		600
	(To record daily sales and sales taxes)		

When the company remits the taxes to the taxing agency, it debits Sales Taxes Payable and credits Cash. The company does not report sales taxes as an expense. It simply forwards to the government the amount paid by the customers. Thus, Cooley Grocery serves only as a **collection agent** for the taxing authority.

Sometimes companies do not ring up sales taxes separately on the cash register. To determine the amount of sales in such cases, divide total receipts by 100% plus the sales tax percentage. To illustrate, assume that in the above example Cooley Grocery rings up total receipts of $10,600. The receipts from the sales are equal to the sales price (100%) plus the tax percentage (6% of sales), or 1.06 times the sales total. We can compute the sales amount as follows.

HELPFUL HINT

Alternatively, Cooley could find the tax by multiplying sales by the sales tax rate ($10,000 × .06).

$$\$10,600 \div 1.06 = \$10,000$$

Thus, Cooley Grocery could find the sales tax amount it must remit to the state ($600) by subtracting sales from total receipts ($10,600 − $10,000).

Unearned Revenues

A magazine publisher, such as Sports Illustrated, receives customers' checks when they order magazines. An airline company, such as American Airlines, receives cash when it sells tickets for future flights. Through these transactions, both companies have incurred **unearned revenues**—revenues that are received before the company delivers goods or provides services. How do companies account for unearned revenues?

1. When a company receives the advance payment, it debits Cash, and credits a current liability account identifying the source of the unearned revenue.
2. When the company earns the revenue, it debits the Unearned Revenue account, and credits an earned revenue account.

To illustrate, assume that Superior University sells 10,000 season football tickets at $50 each for its five-game home schedule. The university makes the following entry for the sale of season tickets:

Aug. 6	Cash	500,000	
	Unearned Football Ticket Revenue		500,000
	(To record sale of 10,000 season tickets)		

A	=	L	+	OE
+500,000				
		+500,000		

Cash Flows
+500,000

As the school completes each of the five home games, it earns one-fifth of the revenue. The following entry records the revenue earned.

Sept. 7	Unearned Football Ticket Revenue	100,000	
	Football Ticket Revenue		100,000
	(To record football ticket revenue earned)		

A	=	L	+	OE
		−100,000		
				+100,000 Rev

Cash Flows
no effect

Organizations report any balance in an unearned revenue account (in Unearned Football Ticket Revenue, for example) as a current liability in the balance sheet. As they earn the revenue, a transfer from unearned revenue to earned revenue occurs. Unearned revenue is material for some companies. In the airline industry, for example, tickets sold for future flights represent almost 30% of total current liabilities. At United Air Lines, unearned ticket revenue is the largest current liability, recently amounting to over $1.5 billion.

Illustration 11-2 shows specific unearned and earned revenue accounts used in selected types of businesses.

Illustration 11-2
Unearned and earned revenue accounts

Type of Business	Account Title: Unearned Revenue	Account Title: Earned Revenue
Airline	Unearned Passenger Ticket Revenue	Passenger Revenue
Magazine publisher	Unearned Subscription Revenue	Subscription Revenue
Hotel	Unearned Rental Revenue	Rental Revenue
Insurance company	Unearned Premium Revenue	Premium Revenue

Current Maturities of Long-Term Debt

Companies often have a portion of long-term debt that comes due in the current year. That amount is considered a current liability. For example, assume that Wendy Construction issues a five-year interest-bearing $25,000 note on January 1, 2008. Each January 1, starting January 1, 2009, $5,000 of the note is due to be paid. When Wendy Construction prepares financial statements on December 31, 2008, it should report $5,000 as a current liability. It would report the remaining $20,000 on the note as a long-term liability. Current maturities of long-term debt are often termed **long-term debt due within one year**.

It is not necessary to prepare an adjusting entry to recognize the current maturity of long-term debt. The company will recognize the proper statement classification of each balance sheet account when it prepares the balance sheet.

Statement Presentation and Analysis

STUDY OBJECTIVE 4
Explain the financial statement presentation and analysis of current liabilities.

PRESENTATION

As indicated in Chapter 4, current liabilities are the first category under liabilities on the balance sheet. Each of the principal types of current liabilities is listed separately. In addition, companies disclose the terms of notes payable and other key information about the individual items in the notes to the financial statements.

Companies seldom list current liabilities in the order of liquidity. The reason is that varying maturity dates may exist for specific obligations such as notes payable. A more common method of presenting current liabilities is to list them by **order of magnitude**, with the largest ones first. Or, as a matter of custom, many companies show notes payable first, and then accounts payable, regardless of amount. Then the remaining current liabilities are listed by magnitude. (*Use this approach in your homework.*) The following adapted excerpt from the balance sheet of Caterpillar Inc. illustrates its order of presentation.

Illustration 11-3
Balance sheet presentation of current liabilities

CATERPILLAR®

CATERPILLAR INC.
Balance Sheet
December 31, 2004
(in millions)

Assets	
Current assets	$20,856
Property, plant and equipment (net)	7,682
Other long-term assets	14,553
Total assets	$43,091
Liabilities and Stockholders' Equity	
Current liabilities	
Short-term borrowings (notes payable)	**$ 4,157**
Accounts payable	**3,990**
Accrued expenses	**1,847**
Accrued wages, salaries, and employee benefits	**1,730**
Customer advances	**555**
Dividends payable	**141**
Deferred and current income taxes payable	**259**
Long-term debt due within one year	**3,531**
Total current liabilities	**16,210**
Noncurrent liabilities	19,414
Total liabilities	35,624
Stockholders' equity	7,467
Total liabilities and stockholders' equity	$43,091

HELPFUL HINT

For other examples of current liabilities sections, refer to the PepsiCo **and** Coca-Cola **balance sheets in Appendixes A and B.**

ANALYSIS

Use of current and noncurrent classifications makes it possible to analyze a company's liquidity. **Liquidity** refers to the ability to pay maturing obligations and meet unexpected needs for cash. The relationship of current assets to current liabilities is critical in analyzing liquidity. We can express this relationship as a dollar amount (working capital) and as a ratio (the current ratio).

The excess of current assets over current liabilities is **working capital**. Illustration 11-4 on the next page shows the formula for the computation of Caterpillar's working capital (dollar amounts in millions).

Current Assets	−	Current Liabilities	=	Working Capital
$20,856	−	$16,210	=	**$4,646**

Illustration 11-4
Working capital formula and computation

As an absolute dollar amount, working capital offers limited informational value. For example, $1 million of working capital may be far more than needed for a small company but be inadequate for a large corporation. Also, $1 million of working capital may be adequate for a company at one time but inadequate at another time.

The **current ratio** permits us to compare the liquidity of different-sized companies and of a single company at different times. The current ratio is calculated as current assets divided by current liabilities. The formula for this ratio is illustrated below, along with its computation using Caterpillar's current asset and current liability data (dollar amounts in millions).

Current Assets	÷	Current Liabilities	=	Current Ratio
$20,856	÷	$16,210	=	**1.29:1**

Illustration 11-5
Current ratio formula and computation

Historically, companies and analysts considered a current ratio of 2:1 to be the standard for a good credit rating. In recent years, however, many healthy companies have maintained ratios well below 2:1 by improving management of their current assets and liabilities. Caterpillar's ratio of 1.29:1 is adequate but certainly below the standard of 2:1.

CONTINGENT LIABILITIES

STUDY OBJECTIVE 5

Describe the accounting and disclosure requirements for contingent liabilities.

With notes payable, interest payable, accounts payable, and sales taxes payable, we know that an obligation to make a payment exists. But suppose that your company is involved in a dispute with the Internal Revenue Service (IRS) over the amount of its income tax liability. Should you report the disputed amount as a liability on the balance sheet? Or suppose your company is involved in a lawsuit which, if you lose, might result in bankruptcy. How should you report this major contingency? The answers to these questions are difficult, because these liabilities are dependent—contingent—upon some future event. In other words, a **contingent liability** is a potential liability that may become an actual liability in the future.

How should companies report contingent liabilities? They use the following guidelines:

1. If the contingency is **probable** (if it is *likely* to occur) **and** the amount can be **reasonably estimated**, the liability should be recorded in the accounts.
2. If the contingency is only **reasonably possible** (if it *could* happen), then it needs to be disclosed only in the notes that accompany the financial statements.
3. If the contingency is **remote** (if it is *unlikely* to occur), it need not be recorded or disclosed.

ACCOUNTING ACROSS THE ORGANIZATION

Contingencies: How Big Are They?

Contingent liabilities abound in the real world. Consider the following: Manville Corp. filed for bankruptcy when it was hit by billions of dollars in asbestos product-liability claims. Companies having multiple toxic waste sites are faced with cleanup costs that average $10 to $30 million and can reach as high as $500 million depending on the type of waste. For life and health insurance companies and their stockholders, the cost of diseases such as diabetes, Alzheimer's, and AIDS is like an iceberg: Everyone wonders how big such costs really are and what damage they might do in the future. And frequent-flyer programs are so popular that airlines at one time owed participants more than 3 million round-trip domestic tickets. That's enough to fly at least 5.4 billion miles—free for the passengers, but at what future cost to the airlines?

? Why do you think most companies disclose, but do not record, contingent liabilities?

Recording a Contingent Liability

Product warranties are an example of a contingent liability that companies should record in the accounts. Warranty contracts result in future costs that companies may incur in replacing defective units or repairing malfunctioning units. Generally, a manufacturer, such as Black & Decker, knows that it will incur some warranty costs. From prior experience with the product, the company usually can reasonably estimate the anticipated cost of servicing (honoring) the warranty.

The accounting for warranty costs is based on the matching principle. **The estimated cost of honoring product warranty contracts should be recognized as an expense in the period in which the sale occurs.** To illustrate, assume that in 2008 Denson Manufacturing Company sells 10,000 washers and dryers at an average price of $600 each. The selling price includes a one-year warranty on parts. Denson expects that 500 units (5%) will be defective and that warranty repair costs will average $80 per unit. In 2008, the company honors warranty contracts on 300 units, at a total cost of $24,000.

At December 31, it is necessary to accrue the estimated warranty costs on the 2008 sales. Denson computes the estimated warranty liability as follows.

Illustration 11-6
Computation of estimated product warranty liability

Number of units sold	10,000
Estimated rate of defective units	× 5%
Total estimated defective units	500
Average warranty repair cost	× $80
Estimated product warranty liability	**$40,000**

The company makes the following adjusting entry.

A	=	L	+	OE
				−40,000 Exp
		+40,000		

Cash Flows
no effect

Dec. 31	Warranty Expense	40,000	
	Estimated Warranty Liability		40,000
	(To accrue estimated warranty costs)		

Denson records those repair costs incurred in 2008 to honor warranty contracts on 2008 sales as shown below.

Jan. 1– Dec. 31	Estimated Warranty Liability Repair Parts (To record honoring of 300 warranty contracts on 2008 sales)	24,000	 24,000

A	=	L	+	OE
		−24,000		
−24,000				

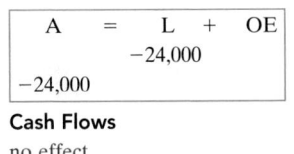

Cash Flows
no effect

The company reports warranty expense of $40,000 under selling expenses in the income statement. It classifies estimated warranty liability of $16,000 ($40,000 − $24,000) as a current liability on the balance sheet.

In the following year, Denson should debit to Estimated Warranty Liability all expenses incurred in honoring warranty contracts on 2008 sales. To illustrate, assume that the company replaces 20 defective units in January 2009, at an average cost of $80 in parts and labor. The summary entry for the month of January 2009 is:

Jan. 31	Estimated Warranty Liability Repair Parts (To record honoring of 20 warranty contracts on 2008 sales)	1,600	 1,600

A	=	L	+	OE
		−1,600		
−1,600				

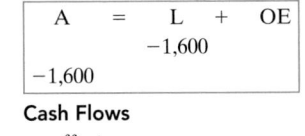

Cash Flows
no effect

Disclosure of Contingent Liabilities

When it is probable that a company will incur a contingent liability but it cannot reasonably estimate the amount, or when the contingent liability is only reasonably possible, only disclosure of the contingency is required. Examples of contingencies that may require disclosure are pending or threatened lawsuits and assessment of additional income taxes pending an IRS audit of the tax return.

The disclosure should identify the nature of the item and, if known, the amount of the contingency and the expected outcome of the future event. Disclosure is usually accomplished through a note to the financial statements, as illustrated by the following.

YAHOO!

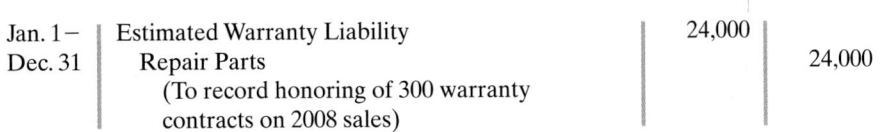

YAHOO! INC.
Notes to the Financial Statements

Contingencies. From time to time, third parties assert patent infringement claims against the company. Currently the company is engaged in several lawsuits regarding patent issues and has been notified of a number of other potential patent disputes. In addition, from time to time the company is subject to other legal proceedings and claims in the ordinary course of business, including claims for infringement of trademarks, copyrights and other intellectual property rights.... The Company does not believe, based on current knowledge, that any of the foregoing legal proceedings or claims are likely to have a material adverse effect on the financial position, results of operations or cash flows.

Illustration 11-7
Disclosure of contingent liability

The required disclosure for contingencies is a good example of the use of the full-disclosure principle. The **full-disclosure principle** requires that companies disclose all circumstances and events that would make a difference to financial statement users. Some important financial information, such as contingencies, is not easily reported in the financial statements. Reporting information on contingencies in the notes to the financial statements will help investors be aware of events that can affect the financial health of a company.

Before You Go On...

REVIEW IT

1. What are the two criteria for classifying a debt as a current liability?
2. Identify the liabilities classified as current by PepsiCo. The answer to this question appears on page 511.
3. What entries does a company make for an interest-bearing note payable?
4. How do retailers record sales taxes? Identify three unearned revenues.
5. How may the liquidity of a company be analyzed?
6. What are the accounting guidelines for contingent liabilities?

DO IT

You and several classmates are studying for the next accounting examination. They ask you to answer the following questions: (1) How is the sales tax amount determined when the cash register total includes sales taxes? (2) When should a company record a contingency in the accounts?

Action Plan

- Remove the sales tax from the total sales.
- Identify the criteria for recording and disclosing contingent liabilities.

Solution

(1) First, divide the total proceeds by 100% plus the sales tax percentage to find the sales amount. Second, subtract the sales amount from the total proceeds to determine the sales taxes.
(2) A company should record a contingency when it is *probable* that it will incur a liability *and* it can *reasonably* estimate the amount.

Related exercise material: *BE11-3, BE11-6, E11-3, E11-5, and E11-6.*

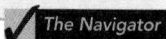

The Navigator

PAYROLL ACCOUNTING

Payroll and related fringe benefits often make up a large percentage of current liabilities. Employee compensation is often the most significant expense that a company incurs. For example, Costco recently reported total employees of 103,000 and labor and fringe benefits costs which approximated 70% of the company's total cost of operations.

Payroll accounting involves more than paying employees' wages. Companies are required by law to maintain payroll records for each employee, to file and pay payroll taxes, and to comply with state and federal tax laws related to employee compensation.

The term "payroll" pertains to both salaries and wages. Managerial, administrative, and sales personnel are generally paid **salaries**. Salaries are often expressed in terms of a specified amount per month or per year rather than an hourly rate. Store clerks, factory employees, and manual laborers are normally paid **wages**. Wages are based on a rate per hour or on a piecework basis (such as per unit of product). Frequently, people use the terms "salaries" and "wages" interchangeably.

The term "payroll" does not apply to payments made for services of professionals such as certified public accountants, attorneys, and architects. Such professionals are independent contractors rather than salaried employees. Payments to them are called **fees**. This distinction is important because government regulations relating to the payment and reporting of payroll taxes apply only to employees.

Determining the Payroll

STUDY OBJECTIVE 6

Compute and record the payroll for a pay period.

Determining the payroll involves computing three amounts: (1) gross earnings, (2) payroll deductions, and (3) net pay.

GROSS EARNINGS

Gross earnings is the total compensation earned by an employee. It consists of wages or salaries, plus any bonuses and commissions.

Companies determine total **wages** for an employee by multiplying the hours worked by the hourly rate of pay. In addition to the hourly pay rate, most companies are required by law to pay hourly workers a minimum of 1½ times the regular hourly rate for overtime work in excess of eight hours per day or 40 hours per week. In addition, many employers pay overtime rates for work done at night, on weekends, and on holidays.

For example, assume that Michael Jordan, an employee of Academy Company, worked 44 hours for the weekly pay period ending January 14. His regular wage is $12 per hour. For any hours in excess of 40, the company pays at one-and-a-half times the regular rate. Academy computes Jordan's gross earnings (total wages) as follows.

Illustration 11-8
Computation of total wages

Type of Pay	Hours	×	Rate	=	Gross Earnings
Regular	40	×	$12	=	$480
Overtime	4	×	18	=	72
Total wages					**$552**

This computation assumes that Jordan receives 1½ times his regular hourly rate ($12 × 1.5) for his overtime hours. Union contracts often require that overtime rates be as much as twice the regular rates.

An employee's **salary** is generally based on a monthly or yearly rate. The company then prorates these rates to its payroll periods (e.g., biweekly or monthly). Most executive and administrative positions are salaried. Federal law does not require overtime pay for employees in such positions.

Many companies have **bonus** agreements for employees. One survey found that over 94% of the largest U.S. manufacturing companies offer annual bonuses to key executives. Bonus arrangements may be based on such factors as increased sales or net income. Companies may pay bonuses in cash and/or by granting employees the opportunity to acquire shares of company stock at favorable prices (called stock option plans).

ETHICS NOTE

Bonuses often reward outstanding individual performance, but successful corporations also need considerable teamwork. A challenge is to motivate individuals while preventing an unethical employee from taking another's idea for his or her own advantage.

PAYROLL DEDUCTIONS

As anyone who has received a paycheck knows, gross earnings are usually very different from the amount actually received. The difference is due to **payroll deductions**.

Payroll deductions may be mandatory or voluntary. Mandatory deductions are required by law and consist of FICA taxes and income taxes. Voluntary deductions are at the option of the employee. Illustration 11-9 (page 482) summarizes common types of payroll deductions. Such deductions do not result in payroll tax expense to the employer. The employer is merely a collection agent, and subsequently transfers the deducted amounts to the government and designated recipients.

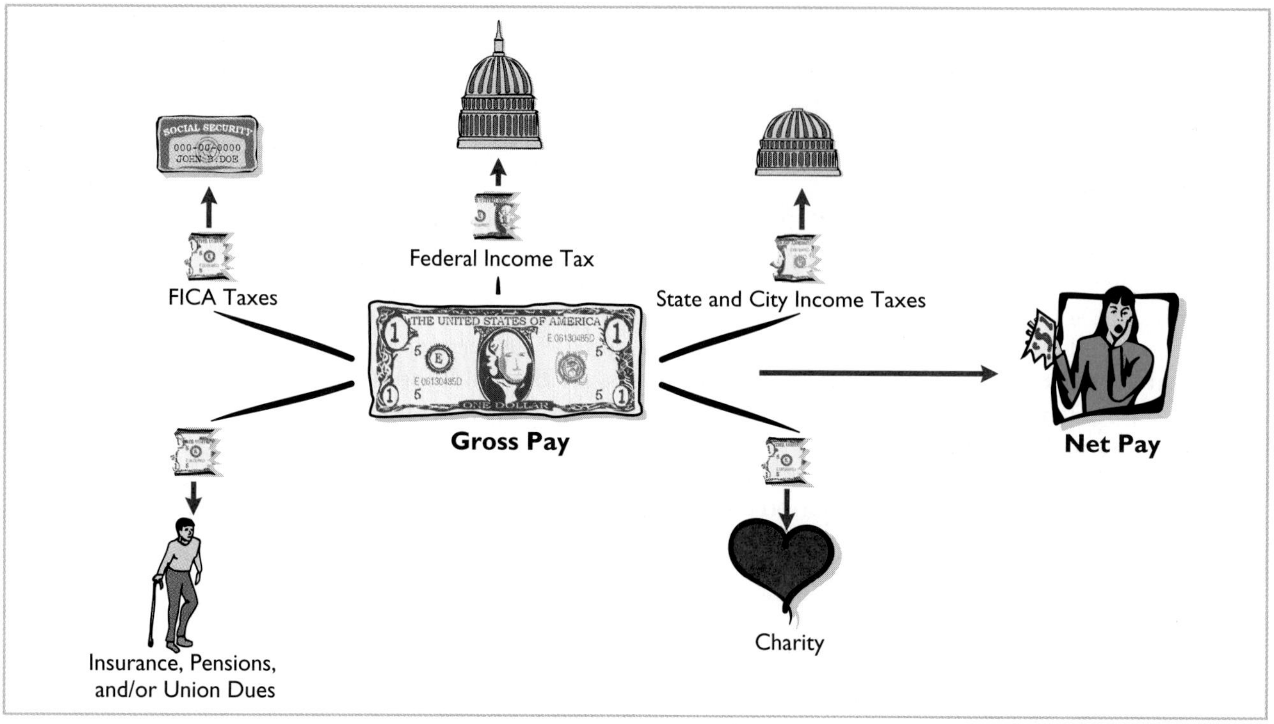

Illustration 11-9
Payroll deductions

FICA Taxes. In 1937 Congress enacted the Federal Insurance Contribution Act (FICA). **FICA taxes are designed to provide workers with supplemental retirement, employment disability, and medical benefits.** In 1965, Congress extended benefits to include Medicare for individuals over 65 years of age. The benefits are financed by a tax levied on employees' earnings. FICA taxes are commonly referred to as **Social Security taxes**.

Congress sets the tax rate and the tax base for FICA taxes. When FICA taxes were first imposed, the rate was 1% on the first $3,000 of gross earnings, or a maximum of $30 per year. The rate and base have changed dramatically since that time! In 2006, the rate was 7.65% (6.2% Social Security plus 1.45% Medicare) on the first $94,200 of gross earnings for each employee.[1] For purpose of illustration in this chapter, we will assume a rate of 8% on the first $90,000 of gross earnings, or a maximum of $7,200. Using the 8% rate, the FICA withholding for Jordan for the weekly pay period ending January 14 is $44.16 ($552 × 8%).

Income Taxes. Under the U.S. pay-as-you-go system of federal income taxes, employers are required to withhold income taxes from employees each pay period. Three variables determine the amount to be withheld: (1) the employee's gross earnings; (2) the number of allowances claimed by the employee; and (3) the length of the pay period. The number of allowances claimed typically includes the employee, his or her spouse, and other dependents.

Withholding tables furnished by the Internal Revenue Service indicate the amount of income tax to be withheld. Withholding amounts are based on gross wages and the number of allowances claimed. Separate tables are provided for weekly, biweekly, semimonthly, and monthly pay periods. Illustration 11-10 shows the withholding tax table for Michael Jordan (assuming he earns $552 per week and claims two allowances). For a weekly salary of $552 with two allowances, the income tax to be withheld is $49.

[1]The Medicare provision also includes a tax of 1.45% on gross earnings in excess of $94,200. In the interest of simplification, we ignore this 1.45% charge in our end-of-chapter assignment material. We assume zero FICA withholdings on gross earnings above $90,000.

Illustration 11-10
Withholding tax table

MARRIED Persons — **WEEKLY** Payroll Period
(For Wages Paid in 2008)

If the wages are —		And the number of withholding allowances claimed is —										
At least	But less than	0	1	2	3	4	5	6	7	8	9	10
		The amount of income tax to be withheld is —										
490	**500**	56	48	40	32	24	17	9	1	0	0	0
500	**510**	57	49	42	34	26	18	10	3	0	0	0
510	**520**	59	51	43	35	27	20	12	4	0	0	0
520	**530**	60	52	45	37	29	21	13	6	0	0	0
530	**540**	62	54	46	38	30	23	15	7	0	0	0
540	**550**	63	55	48	40	32	24	16	9	1	0	0
550	**560**	65	57	**49**	41	33	26	18	10	2	0	0
560	**570**	66	58	51	43	35	27	19	12	4	0	0
570	**580**	68	60	52	44	36	29	21	13	5	0	0
580	**590**	69	61	54	46	38	30	22	15	7	0	0
590	**600**	71	63	55	47	39	32	24	16	8	1	0
600	**610**	72	64	57	49	41	33	25	18	10	2	0
610	**620**	74	66	58	50	42	35	27	19	11	4	0
620	**630**	75	67	60	52	44	36	28	21	13	5	0
630	**640**	77	69	61	53	45	38	30	22	14	7	0
640	**650**	78	70	63	55	47	39	31	24	16	8	0
650	**660**	80	72	64	56	48	41	33	25	17	10	2
660	**670**	81	73	66	58	50	42	34	27	19	11	3
670	**680**	83	75	67	59	51	44	36	28	20	13	5
680	**690**	84	76	69	61	53	45	37	30	22	14	6

In addition, most states (and some cities) require **employers** to withhold income taxes from employees' earnings. As a rule, the amounts withheld are a percentage (specified in the state revenue code) of the amount withheld for the federal income tax. Or they may be a specified percentage of the employee's earnings. For the sake of simplicity, we have assumed that Jordan's wages are subject to state income taxes of 2%, or \$11.04 (2% × \$552) per week.

There is no limit on the amount of gross earnings subject to income tax withholdings. In fact, under our progressive system of taxation, the higher the earnings, the higher the percentage of income withheld for taxes.

Other Deductions. Employees may voluntarily authorize withholdings for charitable, retirement, and other purposes. All voluntary deductions from gross earnings should be authorized in writing by the employee. The authorization(s) may be made individually or as part of a group plan. Deductions for charitable organizations, such as the United Way, or for financial arrangements, such as U.S. savings bonds and repayment of loans from company credit unions, are made individually. Deductions for union dues, health and life insurance, and pension plans are often made on a group basis. We will assume that Jordan has weekly voluntary deductions of \$10 for the United Way and \$5 for union dues.

NET PAY

Academy determines **net pay** by subtracting payroll deductions from gross earnings. Illustration 11-11 (page 484) shows the computation of Jordan's net pay for the pay period.

ALTERNATIVE TERMINOLOGY

Net pay is also called *take-home pay.*

Assuming that Michael Jordan's wages for each week during the year are \$552, total wages for the year are \$28,704 (52 × \$552). Thus, all of Jordan's wages are subject to FICA tax during the year. In comparison, let's assume that Jordan's department head earns \$1,800 per week, or \$93,600 for the year. Since only the first

Illustration 11-11
Computation of net pay

Gross earnings		$552.00
Payroll deductions:		
FICA taxes	$44.16	
Federal income taxes	49.00	
State income taxes	11.04	
United Way	10.00	
Union dues	5.00	119.20
Net pay		**$432.80**

$90,000 is subject to FICA taxes, the maximum FICA withholdings on the department head's earnings would be $7,200 ($90,000 × 8%).

ACCOUNTING ACROSS THE ORGANIZATION

Taxes Are the Largest Slice of the Pie

In 2006, Americans worked 77 days to afford their federal taxes and 39 more days to afford state and local taxes, according to the Tax Foundation. Each year this foundation calculates the mathematical average of tax collections in the United States, using a formula that divides the year's total tax collections (federal, state, and local taxes) by all income earned (the "national income"). The resulting national "tax burden" varies each year, and the tax burden also varies by state.

National taxation in 2006 was a bigger burden than average expenditures on housing and household operation (62 days), health and medical care (52 days), food (30 days), transportation (30 days), recreation (22 days), or clothing and accessories (14 days).

Source: *www.taxfoundation.org/taxfreedomday* (accessed June 2006). For a map of tax burden by states, see Figure 6 at that site.

If the information on 2006 taxation depicted your spending patterns, on what date (starting on January 1) will you have earned enough to pay all of your taxes? This date is often referred to as Tax Freedom Day.

Recording the Payroll

Recording the payroll involves maintaining payroll department records, recognizing payroll expenses and liabilities, and recording payment of the payroll.

MAINTAINING PAYROLL DEPARTMENT RECORDS

To comply with state and federal laws, an employer must keep a cumulative record of each employee's gross earnings, deductions, and net pay during the year. The record that provides this information is the **employee earnings record**. Illustration 11-12 (page 485) shows Michael Jordan's employee earnings record.

Companies keep a separate earnings record for each employee, and update these records after each pay period. The employer uses the cumulative payroll data on the earnings record to: (1) determine when an employee has earned the maximum earnings subject to FICA taxes, (2) file state and federal payroll tax returns (as explained later), and (3) provide each employee with a statement of gross earnings and tax withholdings for the year. Illustration 11-16 on page 490 shows this statement.

In addition to employee earnings records, many companies find it useful to prepare a **payroll register**. This record accumulates the gross earnings, deductions, and net pay by employee for each pay period. It provides the documentation for

Academy Company.xls

File Edit View Insert Format Tools Data Window Help

ACADEMY COMPANY
Employee Earnings Record
For the Year 2008

Name	Michael Jordan	Address	2345 Mifflin Ave.
Social Security Number	329-36-9547		Hampton, Michigan 48292
Date of Birth	December 24, 1962	Telephone	555-238-9051
Date Employed	September 1, 2003	Date Employment Ended	
Sex	Male	Exemptions	2
Single ____	Married x		

2008 Period Ending	Total Hours	Gross Earnings: Regular	Overtime	Total	Cumulative	Deductions: FICA	Fed. Inc. Tax	State Inc. Tax	United Way	Union Dues	Total	Payment: Net Amount	Check No.
1/7	42	480.00	36.00	516.00	516.00	41.28	43.00	10.32	10.00	5.00	109.60	406.40	974
1/14	**44**	**480.00**	**72.00**	**552.00**	**1,068.00**	**44.16**	**49.00**	**11.04**	**10.00**	**5.00**	**119.20**	**432.80**	**1028**
1/21	43	480.00	54.00	534.00	1,602.00	42.72	46.00	10.68	10.00	5.00	114.40	419.60	1077
1/28	42	480.00	36.00	516.00	2,118.00	41.28	43.00	10.32	10.00	5.00	109.60	406.40	1133
Jan. Total		1,920.00	198.00	2,118.00		169.44	181.00	42.36	40.00	20.00	452.80	1,665.20	

Illustration 11-12
Employee earnings record

preparing a paycheck for each employee. Illustration 11-13 presents Academy Company's payroll register. It shows the data for Michael Jordan in the wages section. In this example, Academy Company's total weekly payroll is $17,210, as shown in the gross earnings column.

Illustration 11-13
Payroll register

Academy Company.xls

File Edit View Insert Format Tools Data Window Help

ACADEMY COMPANY
Payroll Register
For the Week Ending January 14, 2008

Employee	Total Hours	Earnings: Regular	Over-time	Gross	Deductions: FICA	Federal Income Tax	State Income Tax	United Way	Union Dues	Total	Paid: Net Pay	Check No.	Accounts Debited: Office Salaries Expense	Wages Expense
Office Salaries														
Arnold, Patricia	40	580.00		580.00	46.40	61.00	11.60	15.00		134.00	446.00	998	580.00	
Canton, Matthew	40	590.00		590.00	47.20	63.00	11.80	20.00		142.00	448.00	999	590.00	
Mueller, William	40	530.00		530.00	42.40	54.00	10.60	11.00		118.00	412.00	1000	530.00	
Subtotal		5,200.00		5,200.00	416.00	1,090.00	104.00	120.00		1,730.00	3,470.00		5,200.00	
Wages														
Bennett, Robin	42	480.00	36.00	516.00	41.28	43.00	10.32	18.00	5.00	117.60	398.40	1025		516.00
Jordan, Michael	**44**	**480.00**	**72.00**	**552.00**	**44.16**	**49.00**	**11.04**	**10.00**	**5.00**	**119.20**	**432.80**	**1028**		**552.00**
Milroy, Lee	43	480.00	54.00	534.00	42.72	46.00	10.68	10.00	5.00	114.40	419.60	1029		534.00
Subtotal		11,000.00	1,010.00	12,010.00	960.80	2,400.00	240.20	301.50	115.00	4,017.50	7,992.50			12,010.00
Total		16,200.00	1,010.00	17,210.00	1,376.80	3,490.00	344.20	421.50	115.00	5,747.50	11,462.50		5,200.00	12,010.00

Note that this record is a listing of each employee's payroll data for the pay period. In some companies, a payroll register is a journal or book of original entry. Postings are made from it directly to ledger accounts. In other companies, the payroll register is a memorandum record that provides the data for a general journal entry and subsequent posting to the ledger accounts. At Academy Company, the latter procedure is followed.

RECOGNIZING PAYROLL EXPENSES AND LIABILITIES

From the payroll register in Illustration 11-13, Academy Company makes a journal entry to record the payroll. For the week ending January 14 the entry is:

A	=	L	+	OE
				−5,200.00 Exp
				−12,010.00 Exp
		+1,376.80		
		+3,490.00		
		+344.20		
		+421.50		
		+115.00		
		+11,462.50		

Cash Flows
no effect

Jan. 14	Office Salaries Expense	5,200.00	
	Wages Expense	12,010.00	
	FICA Taxes Payable		1,376.80
	Federal Income Taxes Payable		3,490.00
	State Income Taxes Payable		344.20
	United Way Payable		421.50
	Union Dues Payable		115.00
	Salaries and Wages Payable		11,462.50
	(To record payroll for the week ending January 14)		

The company credits specific liability accounts for the mandatory and voluntary deductions made during the pay period. In the example, Academy debits Office Salaries Expense for the gross earnings of salaried office workers, and it debits Wages Expense for the gross earnings of employees who are paid at an hourly rate. Other companies may debit other accounts such as Store Salaries or Sales Salaries. The amount credited to Salaries and Wages Payable is the sum of the individual checks the employees will receive.

RECORDING PAYMENT OF THE PAYROLL

A company makes payments by check (or electronic funds transfer) either from its regular bank account or a payroll bank account. Each paycheck is usually accompanied by a detachable **statement of earnings** document. This shows the employee's gross earnings, payroll deductions, and net pay, both for the period and for the year-to-date. Academy Company uses its regular bank account for payroll checks. Illustration 11-14 (on page 487) shows the paycheck and statement of earnings for Michael Jordan.

Following payment of the payroll, the company enters the check numbers in the payroll register. Academy Company records payment of the payroll as follows.

A	=	L	+	OE
		−11,462.50		
−11,462.50				

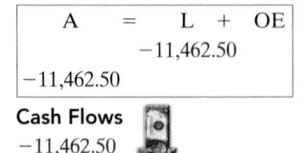

Cash Flows
−11,462.50

Jan. 14	Salaries and Wages Payable	11,462.50	
	Cash		11,462.50
	(To record payment of payroll)		

When a company uses currency in payment, it prepares one check for the payroll's total amount of net pay. The company cashes this check, and inserts the coins and currency in individual pay envelopes for disbursement to individual employees.

Before You Go On...

REVIEW IT

1. What are the primary sources of gross earnings?
2. What payroll deductions are (a) mandatory and (b) voluntary?

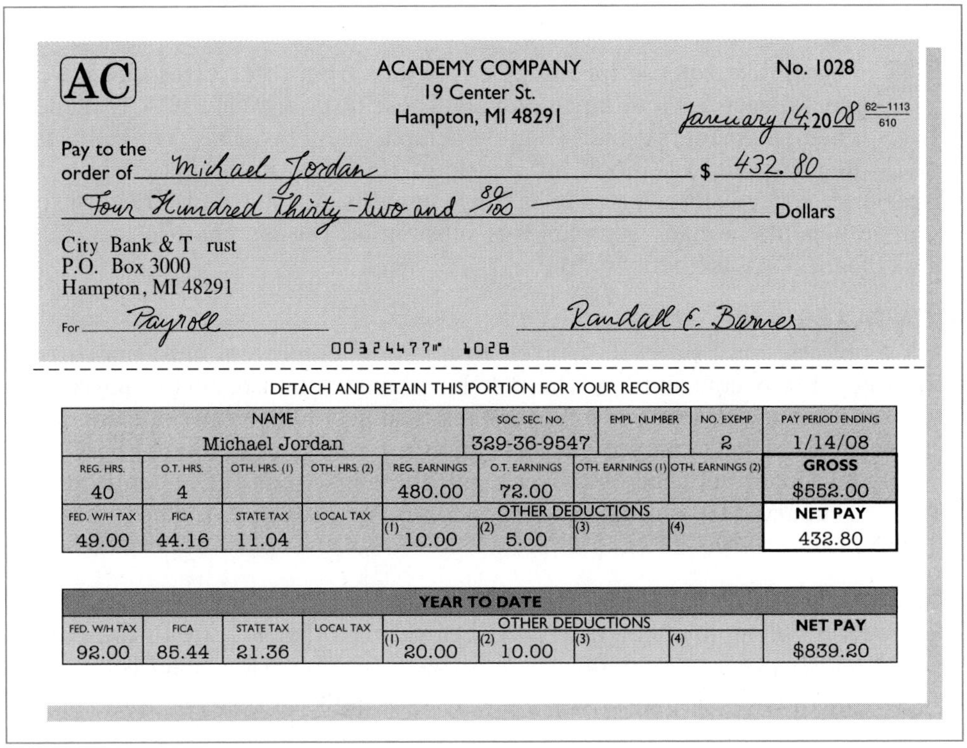

AC

ACADEMY COMPANY
19 Center St.
Hampton, MI 48291

No. 1028

January 14, 2008   62—1113 / 610

Pay to the order of Michael Jordan $ 432.80

Four Hundred Thirty-two and 80/100 Dollars

City Bank & T rust
P.O. Box 3000
Hampton, MI 48291

For Payroll   Randall E. Barnes

00324477⑈ ⑆028

DETACH AND RETAIN THIS PORTION FOR YOUR RECORDS

NAME	SOC. SEC. NO.	EMPL. NUMBER	NO. EXEMP	PAY PERIOD ENDING
Michael Jordan	329-36-9547		2	1/14/08

REG. HRS.	O.T. HRS.	OTH. HRS. (1)	OTH. HRS. (2)	REG. EARNINGS	O.T. EARNINGS	OTH. EARNINGS (1)	OTH. EARNINGS (2)	GROSS
40	4			480.00	72.00			$552.00

FED. W/H TAX	FICA	STATE TAX	LOCAL TAX	OTHER DEDUCTIONS (1)	(2)	(3)	(4)	NET PAY
49.00	44.16	11.04		10.00	5.00			432.80

YEAR TO DATE

FED. W/H TAX	FICA	STATE TAX	LOCAL TAX	OTHER DEDUCTIONS (1)	(2)	(3)	(4)	NET PAY
92.00	85.44	21.36		20.00	10.00			$839.20

Illustration 11-14
Paycheck and statement of earnings

HELPFUL HINT

Do any of the income tax liabilities result in payroll tax expense for the employer?

Answer: No. The employer is acting only as a collection agent for the government.

3. What account titles do companies use in recording a payroll, assuming only mandatory payroll deductions are involved?

DO IT

Your cousin Stan is establishing a house-cleaning business and will have a number of employees working for him. He is aware that documentation procedures are an important part of internal control. But he is unsure about the difference between an employee earnings record and a payroll register. He asks you to explain the principal differences, because he wants to be sure that he sets up the proper payroll procedures.

Action Plan

- Determine the earnings and deductions data that must be recorded and reported for each employee.
- Design a record that will accumulate earnings and deductions data and will serve as a basis for journal entries to be prepared and posted to the general ledger accounts.
- Explain the difference between the employee earnings record and the payroll register.

Solution An employee earnings record is kept for *each* employee. It shows gross earnings, payroll deductions, and net pay for each pay period, as well as cumulative payroll data for that employee. In contrast, a payroll register is a listing of *all* employees' gross earnings, payroll deductions, and net pay for each pay period. It is the documentation for preparing paychecks and for recording the payroll. Of course, Stan will need to keep both documents.

Related exercise material: *BE11-7, BE11-8, E11-10, E11-11, and E11-13.*

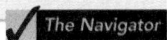

The Navigator

Employer Payroll Taxes

STUDY OBJECTIVE 7

Describe and record employer payroll taxes.

Payroll tax expense for businesses results from three taxes that governmental agencies levy **on employers**. These taxes are: (1) FICA, (2) federal unemployment tax, and (3) state unemployment tax. These taxes plus such items as paid vacations and pensions (discussed in the appendix to this chapter) are collectively referred to as **fringe benefits**. As indicated earlier, the cost of fringe benefits in many companies is substantial. The pie chart in the margin shows the pieces of the benefits "pie."

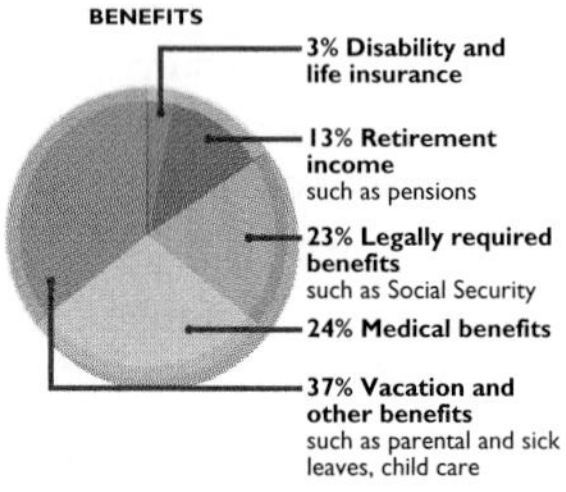

FICA TAXES

Each employee must pay FICA taxes. In addition, employers must match each employee's FICA contribution. The matching contribution results in **payroll tax expense** to the employer. The employer's tax is subject to the same rate and maximum earnings as the employee's. The company uses the same account, FICA Taxes Payable, to record both the employee's and the employer's FICA contributions. For the January 14 payroll, Academy Company's FICA tax contribution is $1,376.80 ($17,210.00 × 8%).

FEDERAL UNEMPLOYMENT TAXES

The Federal Unemployment Tax Act (FUTA) is another feature of the federal Social Security program. **Federal unemployment taxes** provide benefits for a limited period of time to employees who lose their jobs through no fault of their own. The FUTA tax rate is 6.2% of taxable wages. The taxable wage base is the first $7,000 of wages paid to each employee in a calendar year. Employers who pay the state unemployment tax on a timely basis will receive an offset credit of up to 5.4%. Therefore, the net federal tax rate is generally 0.8% (6.2%–5.4%). This rate would equate to a maximum of $56 of federal tax per employee per year (.008 × $7,000). State tax rates are based on state law.

HELPFUL HINT

Both the employer and employee pay FICA taxes. Federal unemployment taxes and (in most states) the state unemployment taxes are borne entirely by the employer.

The **employer** bears the entire federal unemployment tax. There is no deduction or withholding from employees. Companies use the account Federal Unemployment Taxes Payable to recognize this liability. The federal unemployment tax for Academy Company for the January 14 payroll is $137.68 ($17,210.00 × 0.8%).

STATE UNEMPLOYMENT TAXES

All states have unemployment compensation programs under state unemployment tax acts (SUTA). Like federal unemployment taxes, **state unemployment taxes** provide benefits to employees who lose their jobs. These taxes are levied on employers.[2] The basic rate is usually 5.4% on the first $7,000 of wages paid to an employee during the year. The state adjusts the basic rate according to the employer's experience rating: Companies with a history of stable employment may pay less than 5.4%. Companies with a history of unstable employment may pay more than the basic rate. Regardless of the rate paid, the company's credit on the federal unemployment tax is still 5.4%.

Companies use the account State Unemployment Taxes Payable for this liability. The state unemployment tax for Academy Company for the January 14 payroll is $929.34 ($17,210.00 × 5.4%). Illustration 11-15 (page 489) summarizes the types of employer payroll taxes.

RECORDING EMPLOYER PAYROLL TAXES

Companies usually record employer payroll taxes at the same time they record the payroll. The entire amount of gross pay ($17,210.00) shown in the payroll register in Illustration 11-13 is subject to each of the three taxes mentioned above.

[2] In a few states, the employee is also required to make a contribution. *In this textbook, including the homework, we will assume that the tax is only on the employer.*

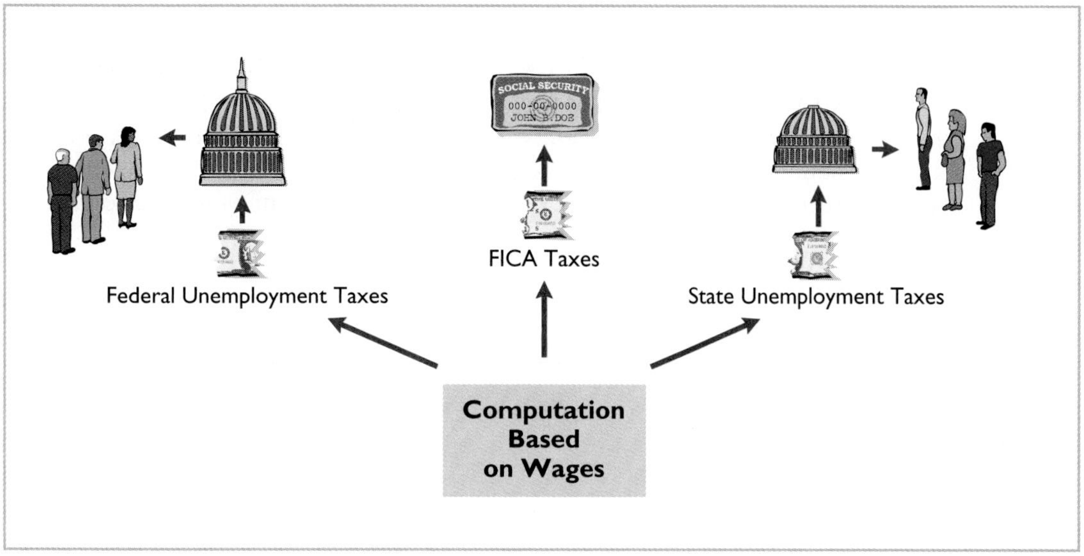

Illustration 11-15
Employer payroll taxes

Accordingly, Academy records the payroll tax expense associated with the January 14 payroll with the following entry.

Jan. 14	Payroll Tax Expense	2,443.82	
	FICA Taxes Payable		1,376.80
	Federal Unemployment Taxes Payable		137.68
	State Unemployment Taxes Payable		929.34
	(To record employer's payroll taxes on January 14 payroll)		

A	=	L	+	OE
				−2,443.82 Exp
		+1,376.80		
		+137.68		
		+929.34		

Cash Flows
no effect

Note that Academy uses separate liability accounts instead of a single credit to Payroll Taxes Payable. Why? Because these liabilities are payable to different taxing authorities at different dates. Companies classify the liability accounts in the balance sheet as current liabilities since they will be paid within the next year. They classify Payroll Tax Expense on the income statement as an operating expense.

Filing and Remitting Payroll Taxes

Preparation of payroll tax returns is the responsibility of the payroll department. The treasurer's department makes the tax payment. Much of the information for the returns is obtained from employee earnings records.

For purposes of reporting and remitting to the IRS, the Company combines the FICA taxes and federal income taxes that it withheld. **Companies must report the taxes quarterly**, no later than one month following the close of each quarter. The remitting requirements depend on the amount of taxes withheld and the length of the pay period. Companies remit funds through deposits in either a Federal Reserve bank or an authorized commercial bank.

Companies generally file and remit federal unemployment taxes **annually** on or before January 31 of the subsequent year. Earlier payments are required when the tax exceeds a specified amount. Companies usually must file and pay state unemployment taxes by the **end of the month following each quarter**. When payroll taxes are paid, companies debit payroll liability accounts, and credit Cash.

Employers also must provide each employee with a **Wage and Tax Statement (Form W-2)** by January 31 following the end of a calendar year. This statement shows gross earnings, FICA taxes withheld, and income taxes withheld for the year. The required W-2 form for Michael Jordan, using assumed annual data, is shown in Illustration 11-16. The employer must send a copy of each employee's Wage and Tax Statement (Form W-2) to the Social Security Administration. This agency subsequently furnishes the Internal Revenue Service with the income data required.

Illustration 11-16
W-2 form

Form **W-2 Wage and Tax Statement** — Calendar Year **2008**

1 Control number		OMB No. 1545-0008	
2 Employer's name, address and ZIP code Academy Company 19 Center St. Hampton, MI 48291		3 Employer's identification number 36-2167852	4 Employer's State number
		5 Stat. employee ☐ Deceased ☐ Legal rep. ☐ 942 emp. ☐ Subtotal ☐ Void ☐	
		6 Allocated tips	7 Advance EIC payment
8 Employee's social security number 329-36-9547	9 Federal income tax withheld $2,248.00	10 Wages, tips, other compensation $26,300.00	11 Social security tax withheld $2,104.00
12 Employee's name, address, and ZIP code Michael Jordan 2345 Mifflin Ave. Hampton, MI 48292		13 Social security wages $26,300.00	14 Social security tips
		16	
		17 State income tax $526.00 · 18 State wages, tips, etc.	19 Name of State Michigan
		20 Local income tax · 21 Local wages, tips, etc.	22 Name of locality

Internal Control for Payroll

STUDY OBJECTIVE 8
Discuss the objectives of internal control for payroll.

Chapter 8 introduced internal control. As applied to payrolls, the objectives of internal control are (1) to safeguard company assets against unauthorized payments of payrolls, and (2) to ensure the accuracy and reliability of the accounting records pertaining to payrolls.

Irregularities often result if internal control is lax. Methods of theft involving payroll include overstating hours, using unauthorized pay rates, adding fictitious employees to the payroll, continuing terminated employees on the payroll, and distributing duplicate payroll checks. Moreover, inaccurate records will result in incorrect paychecks, financial statements, and payroll tax returns.

Payroll activities involve four functions: hiring employees, timekeeping, preparing the payroll, and paying the payroll. For effective internal control, companies should assign these four functions to different departments or individuals. Illustration 11-17 (page 491) highlights these functions and illustrates their internal control features.

Before You Go On...

REVIEW IT

1. What payroll taxes do governments levy on employers?
2. What accounts are involved in accruing employer payroll taxes?
3. Identify an internal control feature that applies to each payroll function.

Payroll Function		Payroll Function	
Hiring Employees	**Internal control feature:** Human Resources department documents and authorizes employment. **Fraud prevented:** Fictitious employees are not added to payroll.	**Preparing the Payroll**	**Internal control feature:** Two (or more) employees verify payroll amounts; supervisor approves. **Fraud prevented:** Payroll calculations are accurate and relevant.
Timekeeping	**Internal control feature:** Supervisors monitor hours worked through time cards and time reports. **Fraud prevented:** Employee works appropriate hours.	**Paying the Payroll**	**Internal control feature:** Treasurer signs and distributes prenumbered checks. **Fraud prevented:** Checks are not lost from theft; endorsed check provides proof of payment.

Illustration 11-17
Internal Control for Payroll

DO IT

In January, the payroll supervisor determines that gross earnings for Halo Company are $70,000. All earnings are subject to 8% FICA taxes, 5.4% state unemployment taxes, and 0.8% federal unemployment taxes. Halo asks you to record the employer's payroll taxes.

Action Plan

- Compute the employer's payroll taxes on the period's gross earnings.
- Identify the expense account(s) to be debited.
- Identify the liability account(s) to be credited.

Solution The entry to record the employer's payroll taxes is:

Payroll Tax Expense	9,940	
FICA Taxes Payable ($70,000 × 8%)		5,600
Federal Unemployment Taxes Payable ($70,000 × 0.8%)		560
State Unemployment Taxes Payable ($70,000 × 5.4%)		3,780
(To record employer's payroll taxes on January payroll)		

Related exercise material: *BE11-10, E11-12, and E11-14.*

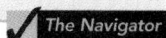

The Navigator

Be sure to read **ALL ABOUT YOU: *Your Boss Wants to Know If You Jogged Today*** on page 492 for information on how topics in this chapter apply to you.

all about YOU

Your Boss Wants to Know If You Jogged Today

As you saw in this chapter, compensation packages often include fringe benefits in addition to basic salary. Health insurance is one benefit that many employers offer. In recent years, as the cost of health insurance has sky-rocketed, many employers either have shifted some of the cost of health insurance onto employees, or have discontinued health insurance coverage altogether.

Some Facts

* Health-care spending in the U.S. was $1.9 trillion in 2004, and is projected to be $2.9 trillion by 2009. It is four times the amount spent on national defense and represents 16% of U.S. gross domestic product.
* About 45 million Americans are without any form of health insurance. Many of these people are employed, but their jobs don't provide a health-care benefit.
* For employers, the average cost of health-care benefits per employee is about $6,700 per year.
* The rate of increase of employer health-care costs has slowed somewhat as employers raised the employee share of premiums and raised deductibles (the amount of a bill that the employee pays before insurance coverage begins).
* More than 30% of small employers have a deductible of $1,000 for employee health insurance.

About the Numbers

As the graph below shows, private health insurance, such as that provided by employers, pays for less than half of health-care costs in the U.S. If employers continue to cut their health-care benefits, more of the burden will shift to the government or to individuals as out-of-pocket costs.

The Nation's Health-Care Dollar: Where it Comes From*

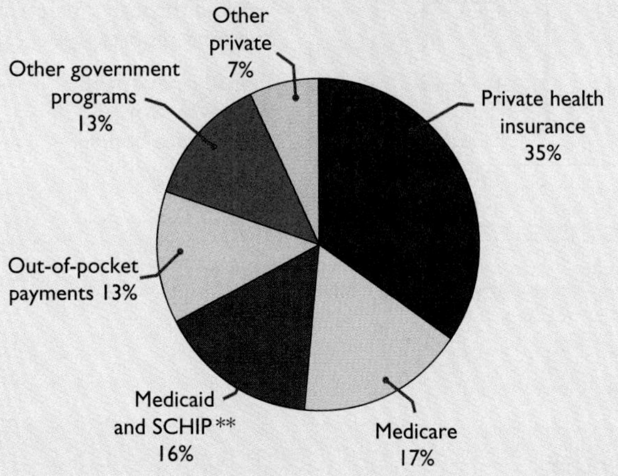

* Does not add to 100% due to rounding.
** State Children's Health Insurance Program.

Source: Data for 2004, from Centers for Medicare and Medicaid Services, Office of the Actuary, National Health Statistics Group.

What Do You Think?

Suppose you own a business. About a quarter of your employees smoke, and an even higher percentage are overweight. You decide to implement a mandatory health program that requires employees to quit smoking and to exercise regularly, with regular monitoring. If employees do not participate in the program, they will have to pay their own insurance premiums. Is this fair?

YES: It is the responsibility of management to try to maximize a company's profit. Employees with unhealthy habits drive up the cost of health insurance because they require more frequent and more costly medical attention.

NO: What people do on their own time is their own business. This represents an invasion of privacy, and is a form of discrimination.

Source: Dee Gill, "Get Healthy . . . Or Else," *Inc.* Magazine, April 2006; "Health Insurance Cost," The National Coalition on Health Care, *www.nchc.org/facts/cost.shtml* (accessed May 2006).

The authors' comments on this situation appear on page 511.

Demonstration Problem

Indiana Jones Company had the following selected transactions.

Feb. 1 Signs a $50,000, 6-month, 9%-interest-bearing note payable to CitiBank and receives $50,000 in cash.

10 Cash register sales total $43,200, which includes an 8% sales tax.

28 The payroll for the month consists of Sales Salaries $32,000 and Office Salaries $18,000. All wages are subject to 8% FICA taxes. A total of $8,900 federal income taxes are withheld. The salaries are paid on March 1.

28 The company develops the following adjustment data.

1. Interest expense of $375 has been incurred on the note.
2. Employer payroll taxes include 8% FICA taxes, a 5.4% state unemployment tax, and a 0.8% federal unemployment tax.
3. Some sales were made under warranty. Of the units sold under warranty, 350 are expected to become defective. Repair costs are estimated to be $40 per unit.

Instructions

(a) Journalize the February transactions.
(b) Journalize the adjusting entries at February 28.

Solution to Demonstration Problem

(a) Feb. 1	Cash	50,000	
	Notes Payable		50,000
	(Issued 6-month, 9%-interest-bearing note to CitiBank)		
10	Cash	43,200	
	Sales ($43,200 ÷ 1.08)		40,000
	Sales Taxes Payable ($40,000 × 8%)		3,200
	(To record sales and sales taxes payable)		
28	Sales Salaries Expense	32,000	
	Office Salaries Expense	18,000	
	FICA Taxes Payable (8% × $50,000)		4,000
	Federal Income Taxes Payable		8,900
	Salaries Payable		37,100
	(To record February salaries)		
(b) Feb. 28	Interest Expense	375	
	Interest Payable		375
	(To record accrued interest for February)		
28	Payroll Tax Expense	7,100	
	FICA Taxes Payable		4,000
	Federal Unemployment Taxes Payable (0.8% × $50,000)		400
	State Unemployment Taxes Payable (5.4% × $50,000)		2,700
	(To record employer's payroll taxes on February payroll)		
28	Warranty Expense (350 × $40)	14,000	
	Estimated Warranty Liability		14,000
	(To record estimated product warranty liability)		

The Navigator

action plan

- ✓ To determine sales, divide the cash register total by 100% plus the sales tax percentage.
- ✓ Base payroll taxes on gross earnings.
- ✓ Expense warranty costs in the period in which the sale occurs.

SUMMARY OF STUDY OBJECTIVES

WILEY PLUS

1 Explain a current liability, and identify the major types of current liabilities. A current liability is a debt that a company can reasonably expect to pay (1) from existing current assets or through the creation of other current liabilities, and (2) within one year or the operating cycle, whichever is longer. The major types of current liabilities are notes payable, accounts payable, sales taxes payable, unearned revenues, and accrued liabilities such as taxes, salaries and wages, and interest payable.

2 Describe the accounting for notes payable. When a promissory note is interest-bearing, the amount of assets received upon the issuance of the note is generally equal to the face value of the note. Interest expense accrues over the life of the note. At maturity, the amount paid equals the face value of the note plus accrued interest.

3 Explain the accounting for other current liabilities. Companies record sales taxes payable at the time the related sales occur. The company serves as a collection agent for the taxing authority. Sales taxes are not an expense to the company. Companies initially record unearned revenues in an Unearned Revenue account. As the company earns the revenue, a transfer from unearned revenue to earned revenue occurs. Companies report the current maturities of long-term debt as a current liability in the balance sheet.

4 Explain the financial statement presentation and analysis of current liabilities. Companies should report the nature and amount of each current liability in the balance sheet or in schedules in the notes accompanying the statements. The liquidity of a company may be analyzed by computing working capital and the current ratio.

5 Describe the accounting and disclosure requirements for contingent liabilities. If the contingency is *probable* (likely to occur) and the amount is reasonably estimable, the company should record the liability in the accounts. If the contingency is only *reasonably possible* (it could happen), then it should be disclosed only in the notes to the financial statements. If the possibility that the contingency will happen is *remote* (unlikely to occur), it need not be recorded or disclosed.

6 Compute and record the payroll for a pay period. The computation of the payroll involves gross earnings, payroll deductions, and net pay. In recording the payroll, companies debit salaries (or wages) expense for gross earnings, credit individual tax and other liability accounts for payroll deductions, and credit salaries (wages) payable for net pay. When the payroll is paid, companies debit Salaries and Wages Payable, and credit Cash.

7 Describe and record employer payroll taxes. Employer payroll taxes consist of FICA, federal unemployment taxes, and state unemployment taxes. The taxes are usually accrued at the time the company records the payroll, by debiting Payroll Tax Expense and crediting separate liability accounts for each type of tax.

8 Discuss the objectives of internal control for payroll. The objectives of internal control for payroll are (1) to safeguard company assets against unauthorized payments of payrolls, and (2) to ensure the accuracy of the accounting records pertaining to payrolls.

✓ The Navigator

GLOSSARY

WILEY PLUS

Bonus Compensation to management and other personnel, based on factors such as increased sales or the amount of net income. (p. 481).

Contingent liability A potential liability that may become an actual liability in the future. (p. 477).

Current ratio A measure of a company's liquidity; computed as current assets divided by current liabilities. (p. 477).

Employee earnings record A cumulative record of each employee's gross earnings, deductions, and net pay during the year. (p. 484).

Federal unemployment taxes Taxes imposed on the employer by the federal government that provide benefits for a limited time period to employees who lose their jobs through no fault of their own. (p. 488).

Fees Payments made for the services of professionals. (p. 480).

FICA taxes Taxes designed to provide workers with supplemental retirement, employment disability, and medical benefits. (p. 482).

Full-disclosure principle Requires that companies disclose all circumstances and events that would make a difference to financial statement users. (p. 479).

Gross earnings Total compensation earned by an employee. (p. 481).

Net pay Gross earnings less payroll deductions. (p. 483).

Notes payable Obligations in the form of written promissory notes. (p. 473).

Payroll deductions Deductions from gross earnings to determine the amount of a paycheck. (p. 481).

Payroll register A payroll record that accumulates the gross earnings, deductions, and net pay by employee for each pay period. (p. 484).

Salaries Employee pay based on a fixed amount rather than an hourly rate. (p. 480).

Statement of earnings A document attached to a paycheck that indicates the employee's gross earnings, payroll deductions, and net pay. (p. 486).

State unemployment taxes Taxes imposed on the employer by states that provide benefits to employees who lose their jobs. (p. 488).

Wage and Tax Statement (Form W-2) A form showing gross earnings, FICA taxes withheld, and income taxes withheld, prepared annually by an employer for each employee. (p. 490).

Wages Amounts paid to employees based on a rate per hour or on a piece-work basis. (p. 480).

Working capital A measure of a company's liquidity; computed as current assets minus current liabilities. (p. 476).

APPENDIX Additional Fringe Benefits

STUDY OBJECTIVE 9

Identify additional fringe benefits associated with employee compensation.

In addition to the three payroll-tax fringe benefits, employers incur other substantial fringe benefit costs. Two of the most important are paid absences and post-retirement benefits.

Paid Absences

Employees often are given rights to receive compensation for absences when they meet certain conditions of employment. The compensation may be for paid vacations, sick pay benefits, and paid holidays. When the payment for such absences is **probable** and the amount can be **reasonably estimated**, the company should accrue a liability for paid future absences. When the amount cannot be reasonably estimated, the company should instead disclose the potential liability. Ordinarily, vacation pay is the only paid absence that is accrued. The other types of paid absences are only disclosed.[3]

To illustrate, assume that Academy Company employees are entitled to one day's vacation for each month worked. If 30 employees earn an average of $110 per day in a given month, the accrual for vacation benefits in one month is $3,300. Academy records the liability at the end of the month by the following adjusting entry.

Jan. 31	Vacation Benefits Expense	3,300	
	Vacation Benefits Payable		3,300
	(To accrue vacation benefits expense)		

A	=	L	+	OE
				−3,300 Exp
		+3,300		

Cash Flows
no effect

This accrual is required by the matching principle. Academy would report Vacation Benefits Expense as an operating expense in the income statement, and Vacation Benefits Payable as a current liability in the balance sheet.

Later, when Academy pays vacation benefits, it debits Vacation Benefits Payable and credits Cash. For example, if the above benefits for 10 employees are paid in July, the entry is:

July 31	Vacation Benefits Payable	1,100	
	Cash		1,100
	(To record payment of vacation benefits)		

A	=	L	+	OE
		−1,100		
−1,100				

Cash Flows
−1,100

The magnitude of unpaid absences has gained employers' attention. Consider the case of an assistant superintendent of schools who worked for 20 years and rarely took a vacation or sick day. A month or so before she retired, the school district discovered that she was due nearly $30,000 in accrued benefits. Yet the school district had never accrued the liability.

---

[3]The typical U.S. company provides an average of 12 days of paid vacations for its employees, at an average cost of 5% of gross earnings.

Post-Retirement Benefits

Post-retirement benefits are benefits that employers provide to retired employees for (1) pensions and (2) health care and life insurance. Companies account for both types of post-retirement benefits on the accrual basis. The cost of post-retirement benefits is getting steep. For example, General Motor's pension and health-care costs for retirees in a recent year totaled $6.2 billion, or approximately $1,784 per vehicle produced.

The average American has debt of approximately $10,000 (not counting the mortgage on their home) and has little in the way of savings. What will happen at retirement for these people? The picture is not pretty—people are living longer, the future of Social Security is unclear, and companies are cutting back on post-retirement benefits. This situation may lead to one of the great social and moral dilemmas this country faces in the next 40 years. The more you know about post-retirement benefits, the better you will understand the issues involved in this dilemma.

PENSIONS

A **pension plan** is an agreement whereby employers provide benefits (payments) to employees after they retire. The most popular type of pension plan used is the 401(k) plan. A 401(k) plan works as follows: As an employee, you can contribute up to a certain percentage of your pay into a 401(k) plan, and your employer will match a percentage of your contribution. These contributions are then generally invested in stocks and bonds through mutual funds. These funds will grow without being taxed and can be withdrawn beginning at age 59-1/2. If you must access the funds earlier, you may be able to do so, but a penalty usually occurs along with a payment of tax on the proceeds. Any time you have the opportunity to be involved in a 401(k) plan, you should avail yourself of this benefit!

The accounting for a 401(k) plan by the company is straightforward. When the company makes a contribution on behalf of the employee, it debits Pension Expense and credits Cash for the amount contributed. For example, Mark Hatfield, an employee of Veri Company, contributes $11,000 to his 401(k) plan. Veri Company matches this contribution, and records the expense with the following entry.

Pension Expense	11,000	
Cash		11,000
(To record contribution to 401(k) plan.)		

If the pension expense is not funded during the year, the company credits Pension Liability.

A 401(k) plan is often referred to as a **defined-contribution plan**. In a defined-contribution plan, the plan defines the contribution that an employer will make but not the benefit that the employee will receive at retirement.

The other type of pension plan is a **defined-benefit plan**. In a defined-benefit plan, the employer agrees to pay a defined amount to retirees, based on employees meeting certain eligibility standards. The amount of the benefit is usually based on years of service and average salary over a period of years. Employers are at risk with defined-benefit plans because they must contribute enough to meet the cost of benefits that the plan defines. Many large companies have defined-benefit plans. The accounting for these plans is complex. Many companies are starting to utilize 401(k) plans more extensively instead.

Post-Retirement Health-Care and Life Insurance Benefits

Providing medical and related health-care benefits for retirees was at one time an inexpensive and highly effective way of generating employee goodwill. This practice has now turned into one of corporate America's most worrisome financial problems. Runaway medical costs, early retirement, and increased longevity are sending the liability for retiree health plans through the roof.

Companies estimate and expense post-retirement costs during the working years of the employee because the company benefits from the employee's services during this period. However, the company rarely sets up funds to meet the cost of the future benefits. It follows a pay-as-you-go basis for these costs. The major reason is that the company does not receive a tax deduction until it actually pays the medical bill.

SUMMARY OF STUDY OBJECTIVE FOR APPENDIX

WILEY PLUS

9 **Identify additional fringe benefits associated with employee compensation.** Additional fringe benefits associated with wages are paid absences (paid vacations, sick pay benefits, and paid holidays), and post-retirement benefits (pensions and health care and life insurance).

GLOSSARY FOR APPENDIX

WILEY PLUS

Pension plan An agreement whereby an employer provides benefits to employees after they retire. (p. 496).

Post-retirement benefits Payments by employers to retired employees for health care, life insurance, and pensions. (p. 496).

*__Note:__ All **asterisked** Questions, Exercises, and Problems relate to material in the appendix to the chapter.

SELF-STUDY QUESTIONS

WILEY PLUS

Answers are at the end of the chapter.

(SO 1) **1.** The time period for classifying a liability as current is one year or the operating cycle, whichever is:
a. longer.
b. shorter.
c. probable.
d. possible.

(SO 1) **2.** To be classified as a current liability, a debt must be expected to be paid:
a. out of existing current assets.
b. by creating other current liabilities.
c. within 2 years.
d. both (a) and (b).

(SO 2) **3.** Maggie Sharrer Company borrows $88,500 on September 1, 2008, from Sandwich State Bank by signing an $88,500, 12%, one-year note. What is the accrued interest at December 31, 2008?
a. $2,655.
b. $3,540.
c. $4,425.
d. $10,620.

(SO 3) **4.** Becky Sherrick Company has total proceeds from sales of $4,515. If the proceeds include sales taxes of 5%, the amount to be credited to Sales is:
a. $4,000.
b. $4,300.
c. $4,289.25.
d. No correct answer given.

5. Working capital is calculated as: (SO 4)
a. current assets minus current liabilities.
b. total assets minus total liabilities.
c. long-term liabilities minus current liabilities.
d. both (b) and (c).

6. A contingent liability should be recorded in the accounts when: (SO 5)
a. it is probable the contingency will happen, but the amount cannot be reasonably estimated.
b. it is reasonably possible the contingency will happen, and the amount can be reasonably estimated.
c. it is probable the contingency will happen, and the amount can be reasonably estimated.
d. it is reasonably possible the contingency will happen, but the amount cannot be reasonably estimated.

7. At December 31, Hanes Company prepares an adjusting entry for a product warranty contract. Which of the following accounts is/are included in the entry? (SO 5)
a. Miscellaneous Expense.
b. Estimated Warranty Liability.
c. Repair Parts/Wages Payable.
d. Both (a) and (b).

8. Andy Manion earns $14 per hour for a 40-hour week and $21 per hour for any overtime work. If Manion works 45 hours in a week, gross earnings are: (SO 6)
a. $560.
b. $630.
c. $650.
d. $665.

(SO 7) **9.** Employer payroll taxes do *not* include:
a. federal unemployment taxes.
b. state unemployment taxes.
c. federal income taxes.
d. FICA taxes.

(SO 8) **10.** The department that should pay the payroll is the:
a. timekeeping department.
b. human resources department.
c. payroll department.
d. treasurer's department.

***11.** Which of the following is *not* an additional fringe benefit? (SO 9)
a. Post-retirement pensions.
b. Paid absences.
c. Paid vacations.
d. Salaries.

Go to the book's website, **www.wiley.com/college/weygandt**, for additional Self-Study Questions.

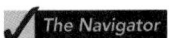

The Navigator

QUESTIONS

1. Jill Loomis believes a current liability is a debt that can be expected to be paid in one year. Is Jill correct? Explain.
2. Frederickson Company obtains $40,000 in cash by signing a 9%, 6-month, $40,000 note payable to First Bank on July 1. Frederickson's fiscal year ends on September 30. What information should be reported for the note payable in the annual financial statements?
3. (a) Your roommate says, "Sales taxes are reported as an expense in the income statement." Do you agree? Explain.
   (b) Planet Hollywood has cash proceeds from sales of $7,400. This amount includes $400 of sales taxes. Give the entry to record the proceeds.
4. Baylor University sold 10,000 season football tickets at $80 each for its five-game home schedule. What entries should be made (a) when the tickets were sold, and (b) after each game?
5. What is liquidity? What are two measures of liquidity?
6. What is a contingent liability? Give an example of a contingent liability that is usually recorded in the accounts.
7. Under what circumstances is a contingent liability disclosed only in the notes to the financial statements? Under what circumstances is a contingent liability not recorded in the accounts nor disclosed in the notes to the financial statements?
8. What is the difference between gross pay and net pay? Which amount should a company record as wages or salaries expense?
9. Which payroll tax is levied on both employers and employees?
10. Are the federal and state income taxes withheld from employee paychecks a payroll tax expense for the employer? Explain your answer.
11. What do the following acronyms stand for: FICA, FUTA, and SUTA?
12. What information is shown in a W-2 statement?
13. Distinguish between the two types of payroll deductions and give examples of each.
14. What are the primary uses of the employee earnings record?
15. (a) Identify the three types of employer payroll taxes.
    (b) How are tax liability accounts and payroll tax expense accounts classified in the financial statements?
16. You are a newly hired accountant with Batista Company. On your first day, the controller asks you to identify the main internal control objectives related to payroll accounting. How would you respond?
17. What are the four functions associated with payroll activities?

*18. Identify two additional types of fringe benefits associated with employees' compensation.

*19. Often during job interviews, the candidate asks the potential employer about the firm's paid absences policy. What are paid absences? How are they accounted for?

*20. What are two types of post-retirement benefits?

*21. Explain how a 401(k) plan works.

*22. What is the difference between a defined-contribution pension plan and a defined-benefit pension plan?

BRIEF EXERCISES

WILEY PLUS

Identify whether obligations are current liabilities.
(SO 1)

BE11-1 Buffaloe Company has the following obligations at December 31: (a) a note payable for $100,000 due in 2 years, (b) a 10-year mortgage payable of $300,000 payable in ten $30,000 annual payments, (c) interest payable of $15,000 on the mortgage, and (d) accounts payable of $60,000. For each obligation, indicate whether it should be classified as a current liability. (Assume an operating cycle of less than one year.)

BE11-2 Hanna Company borrows $80,000 on July 1 from the bank by signing a $80,000, 10%, one-year note payable.

Prepare entries for an interest-bearing note payable.
(SO 2)

(a) Prepare the journal entry to record the proceeds of the note.
(b) Prepare the journal entry to record accrued interest at December 31, assuming adjusting entries are made only at the end of the year.

BE11-3 Leister Auto Supply does not segregate sales and sales taxes at the time of sale. The register total for March 16 is $15,540. All sales are subject to a 5% sales tax. Compute sales taxes payable, and make the entry to record sales taxes payable and sales.

Compute and record sales taxes payable.
(SO 3)

BE11-4 Emporia State University sells 4,000 season basketball tickets at $180 each for its 12-game home schedule. Give the entry to record (a) the sale of the season tickets and (b) the revenue earned by playing the first home game.

Prepare entries for unearned revenues.
(SO 3)

BE11-5 Yahoo! Inc.'s 2004 financial statements contain the following selected data (in thousands).

Analyze liquidity.
(SO 4)

Current assets	$4,090,475
Total assets	9,178,201
Current liabilities	1,180,707
Total liabilities	2,076,755

Compute the following ratios.

(a) Working capital.
(b) Current ratio.

BE11-6 On December 1, Diaz Company introduces a new product that includes a one-year warranty on parts. In December, 1,000 units are sold. Management believes that 5% of the units will be defective and that the average warranty costs will be $80 per unit. Prepare the adjusting entry at December 31 to accrue the estimated warranty cost.

Prepare adjusting entry for warranty costs.
(SO 5)

BE11-7 Cindy Neuer's regular hourly wage rate is $16, and she receives an hourly rate of $24 for work in excess of 40 hours. During a January pay period, Cindy works 47 hours. Cindy's federal income tax withholding is $95, and she has no voluntary deductions. Compute Cindy Neuer's gross earnings and net pay for the pay period.

Compute gross earnings and net pay.
(SO 6)

BE11-8 Data for Cindy Neuer are presented in BE11-7. Prepare the journal entries to record **(a)** Cindy's pay for the period and **(b)** the payment of Cindy's wages. Use January 15 for the end of the pay period and the payment date.

Record a payroll and the payment of wages.
(SO 6)

BE11-9 In January, gross earnings in Vega Company totaled $70,000. All earnings are subject to 8% FICA taxes, 5.4% state unemployment taxes, and 0.8% federal unemployment taxes. Prepare the entry to record January payroll tax expense.

Record employer payroll taxes.
(SO 7)

BE11-10 Rodriquez Company has the following payroll procedures.

Identify payroll functions.
(SO 8)

(a) Supervisor approves overtime work.
(b) The human resources department prepares hiring authorization forms for new hires.
(c) A second payroll department employee verifies payroll calculations.
(d) The treasurer's department pays employees.

Identify the payroll function to which each procedure pertains.

***BE11-11** At Tagaci Company employees are entitled to one day's vacation for each month worked. In January, 80 employees worked the full month. Record the vacation pay liability for January assuming the average daily pay for each employee is $120.

Record estimated vacation benefits.
(SO 9)

EXERCISES

WILEY PLUS

E11-1 Rob Judson Company had the following transactions involving notes payable.

Prepare entries for interest-bearing notes.
(SO 2)

July 1, 2008	Borrows $50,000 from Third National Bank by signing a 9-month, 12% note.
Nov. 1, 2008	Borrows $60,000 from DeKalb State Bank by signing a 3-month, 10% note.
Dec. 31, 2008	Prepares adjusting entries.
Feb. 1, 2009	Pays principal and interest to DeKalb State Bank.
Apr. 1, 2009	Pays principal and interest to Third National Bank.

Instructions

Prepare journal entries for each of the transactions shown on the previous page.

Prepare entries for interest-bearing notes.
(SO 2)

E11-2 On June 1, Melendez Company borrows $90,000 from First Bank on a 6-month, $90,000, 12% note.

Instructions

(a) Prepare the entry on June 1.
(b) Prepare the adjusting entry on June 30.
(c) Prepare the entry at maturity (December 1), assuming monthly adjusting entries have been made through November 30.
(d) What was the total financing cost (interest expense)?

Journalize sales and related taxes.
(SO 3)

E11-3 In providing accounting services to small businesses, you encounter the following situations pertaining to cash sales.

1. Warkentinne Company rings up sales and sales taxes separately on its cash register. On April 10, the register totals are sales $30,000 and sales taxes $1,500.
2. Rivera Company does not segregate sales and sales taxes. Its register total for April 15 is $23,540, which includes a 7% sales tax.

Instructions

Prepare the entry to record the sales transactions and related taxes for each client.

Journalize unearned subscription revenue.
(SO 3)

E11-4 Guyer Company publishes a monthly sports magazine, *Fishing Preview*. Subscriptions to the magazine cost $20 per year. During November 2008, Guyer sells 12,000 subscriptions beginning with the December issue. Guyer prepares financial statements quarterly and recognizes subscription revenue earned at the end of the quarter. The company uses the accounts Unearned Subscriptions and Subscription Revenue.

Instructions

(a) Prepare the entry in November for the receipt of the subscriptions.
(b) Prepare the adjusting entry at December 31, 2008, to record subscription revenue earned in December 2008.
(c) Prepare the adjusting entry at March 31, 2009, to record subscription revenue earned in the first quarter of 2009.

Record estimated liability and expense for warranties.
(SO 5)

E11-5 Hiatt Company sells automatic can openers under a 75-day warranty for defective merchandise. Based on past experience, Hiatt estimates that 3% of the units sold will become defective during the warranty period. Management estimates that the average cost of replacing or repairing a defective unit is $20. The units sold and units defective that occurred during the last 2 months of 2008 are as follows.

Month	Units Sold	Units Defective Prior to December 31
November	30,000	600
December	32,000	400

Instructions

(a) Determine the estimated warranty liability at December 31 for the units sold in November and December.
(b) Prepare the journal entries to record the estimated liability for warranties and the costs incurred in honoring 1,000 warranty claims. (Assume actual costs of $20,000.)
(c) Give the entry to record the honoring of 500 warranty contracts in January at an average cost of $20.

Record and disclose contingent liabilities.
(SO 5)

E11-6 Brad Hoey Company is involved in a lawsuit as a result of an accident that took place September 5, 2008. The lawsuit was filed against Brad Hoey on November 1, 2008, and claims damages of $1,000,000.

Instructions

(a) At December 31, 2008, Brad Hoey's attorneys feel it is remote that Brad Hoey will lose the lawsuit. How should the company account for the effects of the lawsuit?

(b) Assume instead that at December 31, 2008, Brad Hoey's attorneys feel it is probable that Brad Hoey will lose the lawsuit, and be required to pay $1,000,000. How should the company account for this lawsuit?

(c) Assume instead that at December 31, 2008, Brad Hoey's attorneys feel it is reasonably possible that Brad Hoey could lose the lawsuit, and be required to pay $1,000,000. How should the company account for this lawsuit?

E11-7 Jewett Online Company has the following liability accounts after posting adjusting entries: Accounts Payable $63,000, Unearned Ticket Revenue $24,000, Estimated Warranty Liability $18,000, Interest Payable $8,000, Mortgage Payable $120,000, Notes Payable $80,000, and Sales Taxes Payable $10,000. Assume the company's operating cycle is less than 1 year, ticket revenue will be earned within 1 year, warranty costs are expected to be incurred within 1 year, and the notes mature in 3 years.

Prepare the current liability section of the balance sheet.
(SO 1, 2, 3, 4, 5)

Instructions

(a) Prepare the current liabilities section of the balance sheet, assuming $30,000 of the mortgage is payable next year.

(b) Comment on Jewett Online Company's liquidity, assuming total current assets are $300,000.

E11-8 Kroger Co.'s 2005 financial statements contained the following selected data (in millions).

Calculate liquidity ratios.
(SO 4)

Current assets	$ 6,466	Accounts receivable	$680
Total assets	20,482	Interest expense	510
Current liabilities	6,715	Income tax expense	567
Total liabilities	16,092	Net income	958
Cash	210		

Instructions

Compute these values:

(a) Working capital.

(b) Current ratio.

E11-9 The following financial data were reported by 3M Company for 2004 and 2005 (dollars in millions).

Calculate current ratio and working capital before and after paying accounts payable.
(SO 4)

3M COMPANY
Balance Sheets (partial)

	2005	2004
Current assets		
Cash and cash equivalents	$1,072	$2,757
Accounts receivable, net	2,838	2,792
Inventories	2,162	1,897
Other current assets	1,043	1,274
Total current assets	$7,115	$8,720
Current liabilities	$5,238	$6,071

Instructions

(a) Calculate the current ratio and working capital for 3M for 2004 and 2005.

(b) Suppose that at the end of 2005 3M management used $200 million cash to pay off $200 million of accounts payable. How would its current ratio and working capital have changed?

E11-10 Joyce Kieffer's regular hourly wage rate is $15, and she receives a wage of 1½ times the regular hourly rate for work in excess of 40 hours. During a March weekly pay period Joyce worked 42 hours. Her gross earnings prior to the current week were $6,000. Joyce is married and claims three withholding allowances. Her only voluntary deduction is for group hospitalization insurance at $25 per week.

Compute net pay and record pay for one employee.
(SO 6)

Instructions

(a) Compute the following amounts for Joyce's wages for the current week.
   (1) Gross earnings.
   (2) FICA taxes. (Assume an 8% rate on maximum of $90,000.)
   (3) Federal income taxes withheld. (Use the withholding table in the text, page 483.)
   (4) State income taxes withheld. (Assume a 2.0% rate.)
   (5) Net pay.

(b) Record Joyce's pay, assuming she is an office computer operator.

Compute maximum FICA deductions.
(SO 6)

E11-11 Employee earnings records for Medenciy Company reveal the following gross earnings for four employees through the pay period of December 15.

C. Ogle	$83,500	D. Delgado	$86,100
L. Jeter	$87,600	T. Spivey	$90,000

For the pay period ending December 31, each employee's gross earnings is $4,000. The FICA tax rate is 8% on gross earnings of $90,000.

Instructions

Compute the FICA withholdings that should be made for each employee for the December 31 pay period. (Show computations.)

Prepare payroll register and record payroll and payroll tax expense.
(SO 6, 7)

E11-12 Alvamar Company has the following data for the weekly payroll ending January 31.

	Hours							Federal	
Employee	**M**	**T**	**W**	**T**	**F**	**S**	**Hourly Rate**	**Income Tax Withholding**	**Health Insurance**
M. Hashmi	8	8	9	8	10	3	$12	$34	$10
E. Benson	8	8	8	8	8	2	13	37	25
K. Kern	9	10	8	8	9	0	15	58	25

Employees are paid 1½ times the regular hourly rate for all hours worked in excess of 40 hours per week. FICA taxes are 8% on the first $90,000 of gross earnings. Alvamar Company is subject to 5.4% state unemployment taxes and 0.8% federal unemployment taxes on the first $7,000 of gross earnings.

Instructions

(a) Prepare the payroll register for the weekly payroll.

(b) Prepare the journal entries to record the payroll and Alvamar's payroll tax expense.

Compute missing payroll amounts and record payroll.
(SO 6)

E11-13 Selected data from a February payroll register for Gerfield Company are presented below. Some amounts are intentionally omitted.

Gross earnings:		State income taxes	$(3)
Regular	$8,900	Union dues	100
Overtime	(1)		
Total	(2)	Total deductions	(4)
Deductions:		Net pay	$7,660
FICA taxes	$ 800	Accounts debited:	
Federal income taxes	1,140	Warehouse wages	(5)
		Store wages	$4,000

FICA taxes are 8%. State income taxes are 3% of gross earnings.

Instructions

(a) Fill in the missing amounts.

(b) Journalize the February payroll and the payment of the payroll.

Determine employer's payroll taxes; record payroll tax expense.
(SO 7)

E11-14 According to a payroll register summary of Ruiz Company, the amount of employees' gross pay in December was $850,000, of which $90,000 was not subject to FICA tax and $750,000 was not subject to state and federal unemployment taxes.

Instructions

(a) Determine the employer's payroll tax expense for the month, using the following rates: FICA 8%, state unemployment 5.4%, federal unemployment 0.8%.

(b) Prepare the journal entry to record December payroll tax expense.

***E11-15** Cerner Company has two fringe benefit plans for its employees:

Prepare adjusting entries for fringe benefits.

(SO 9)

1. It grants employees 2 days' vacation for each month worked. Ten employees worked the entire month of March at an average daily wage of $120 per employee.
2. In its pension plan the company recognizes 10% of gross earnings as a pension expense. Gross earnings in March were $40,000. No contribution has been made to the pension fund.

Instructions

Prepare the adjusting entries at March 31.

***E11-16** Serenity Corporation has 20 employees who each earn $120 a day. The following information is available.

Prepare journal entries for fringe benefits.

(SO 9)

1. At December 31, Serenity recorded vacation benefits. Each employee earned 5 vacation days during the year.
2. At December 31, Serenity recorded pension expense of $100,000, and made a contribution of $70,000 to the pension plan.
3. In January, 18 employees used one vacation day each.

Instructions

Prepare Serenity's journal entries to record these transactions.

EXERCISES: SET B

Visit the book's website at **www.wiley.com/college/weygandt**, and choose the Student Companion site, to access Exercise Set B.

PROBLEMS: SET A

P11-1A On January 1, 2008, the ledger of Mane Company contains the following liability accounts.

Prepare current liability entries, adjusting entries, and current liabilities section.

(SO 1, 2, 3, 4, 5)

GLS Peachtree

Accounts Payable	$52,000
Sales Taxes Payable	7,700
Unearned Service Revenue	16,000

During January the following selected transactions occurred.

Jan. 5 Sold merchandise for cash totaling $22,680, which includes 8% sales taxes.
12 Provided services for customers who had made advance payments of $10,000. (Credit Service Revenue.)
14 Paid state revenue department for sales taxes collected in December 2007 ($7,700).
20 Sold 800 units of a new product on credit at $50 per unit, plus 8% sales tax. This new product is subject to a 1-year warranty.
21 Borrowed $18,000 from UCLA Bank on a 3-month, 8%, $18,000 note.
25 Sold merchandise for cash totaling $12,420, which includes 8% sales taxes.

Instructions

(a) Journalize the January transactions.
(b) Journalize the adjusting entries at January 31 for (1) the outstanding notes payable, and (2) estimated warranty liability, assuming warranty costs are expected to equal 7% of sales of the new product. (*Hint:* Use one-third of a month for the UCLA Bank note.)
(c) Prepare the current liabilities section of the balance sheet at January 31, 2008. Assume no change in accounts payable.

(c) Current liability total $84,640

P11-2A The following are selected transactions of Winsky Company. Winsky prepares financial statements quarterly.

Journalize and post note transactions; show balance sheet presentation.

(SO 2)

Jan. 2 Purchased merchandise on account from Yokum Company, $30,000, terms 2/10, n/30.
Feb. 1 Issued a 9%, 2-month, $30,000 note to Yokum in payment of account.
Mar. 31 Accrued interest for 2 months on Yokum note.

Apr. 1 Paid face value and interest on Yokum note.
July 1 Purchased equipment from Korsak Equipment paying $11,000 in cash and signing a 10%, 3-month, $40,000 note.
Sept. 30 Accrued interest for 3 months on Korsak note.
Oct. 1 Paid face value and interest on Korsak note.
Dec. 1 Borrowed $15,000 from the Otago Bank by issuing a 3-month, 8% interest-bearing note with a face value of $15,000.
Dec. 31 Recognized interest expense for 1 month on Otago Bank note.

Instructions

(a) Prepare journal entries for the above transactions and events.
(b) Post to the accounts Notes Payable, Interest Payable, and Interest Expense.
(c) Show the balance sheet presentation of notes and interest payable at December 31.
(d) $1,550
(d) What is total interest expense for the year?

Prepare payroll register and payroll entries.
(SO 6, 7)

P11-3A Del Hardware has four employees who are paid on an hourly basis plus time-and-a half for all hours worked in excess of 40 a week. Payroll data for the week ended March 15, 2008, are presented below.

Employee	Hours Worked	Hourly Rate	Federal Income Tax Withholdings	United Fund
Joe Devena	40	$15.00	$?	$5.00
Mary Keener	42	15.00	?	5.00
Andy Dye	44	13.00	60	8.00
Kim Shen	46	13.00	61	5.00

Devena and Keener are married. They claim 0 and 4 withholding allowances, respectively. The following tax rates are applicable: FICA 8%, state income taxes 3%, state unemployment taxes 5.4%, and federal unemployment 0.8%. The first three employees are sales clerks (store wages expense). The fourth employee performs administrative duties (office wages expense).

Instructions

(a) Net pay $1,944.20; Store wages expense $1,843
(b) Payroll tax expense $352.16
(d) Cash paid $636.80

(a) Prepare a payroll register for the weekly payroll. (Use the wage-bracket withholding table in the text for federal income tax withholdings.)
(b) Journalize the payroll on March 15, 2008, and the accrual of employer payroll taxes.
(c) Journalize the payment of the payroll on March 16, 2008.
(d) Journalize the deposit in a Federal Reserve bank on March 31, 2008, of the FICA and federal income taxes payable to the government.

Journalize payroll transactions and adjusting entries.
(SO 6, 7, 9)

P11-4A The following payroll liability accounts are included in the ledger of Armitage Company on January 1, 2008.

FICA Taxes Payable	$760.00
Federal Income Taxes Payable	1,204.60
State Income Taxes Payable	108.95
Federal Unemployment Taxes Payable	288.95
State Unemployment Taxes Payable	1,954.40
Union Dues Payable	870.00
U.S. Savings Bonds Payable	360.00

In January, the following transactions occurred.

Jan. 10 Sent check for $870.00 to union treasurer for union dues.
12 Deposited check for $1,964.60 in Federal Reserve bank for FICA taxes and federal income taxes withheld.
15 Purchased U.S. Savings Bonds for employees by writing check for $360.00.
17 Paid state income taxes withheld from employees.
20 Paid federal and state unemployment taxes.
31 Completed monthly payroll register, which shows office salaries $26,600, store wages $28,400, FICA taxes withheld $4,400, federal income taxes payable $2,158, state income taxes payable $454, union dues payable $400, United Fund contributions payable $1,888, and net pay $45,700.
31 Prepared payroll checks for the net pay and distributed checks to employees.

At January 31, the company also makes the following accrued adjustments pertaining to employee compensation.

1. Employer payroll taxes: FICA taxes 8%, federal unemployment taxes 0.8%, and state unemployment taxes 5.4%.
*2. Vacation pay: 6% of gross earnings.

Instructions

(a) Journalize the January transactions.
(b) Journalize the adjustments pertaining to employee compensation at January 31.

(b) Payroll tax expense $7,810; Vacation benefits expense $3,300

P11-5A For the year ended December 31, 2008, Blasing Electrical Repair Company reports the following summary payroll data.

Prepare entries for payroll and payroll taxes; prepare W-2 data.

(SO 6, 7)

Gross earnings:	
Administrative salaries	$200,000
Electricians' wages	370,000
Total	$570,000
Deductions:	
FICA taxes	$ 38,800
Federal income taxes withheld	174,400
State income taxes withheld (3%)	17,100
United Fund contributions payable	27,500
Hospital insurance premiums	17,200
Total	$275,000

Blasing Company's payroll taxes are: FICA 8%, state unemployment 2.5% (due to a stable employment record), and 0.8% federal unemployment. Gross earnings subject to FICA taxes total $485,000, and unemployment taxes total $135,000.

Instructions

(a) Prepare a summary journal entry at December 31 for the full year's payroll.
(b) Journalize the adjusting entry at December 31 to record the employer's payroll taxes.
(c) The W-2 Wage and Tax Statement requires the following dollar data.

(a) Wages Payable $295,000
(b) Payroll tax expense $43,255

Wages, Tips, Other Compensation	Federal Income Tax Withheld	State Income Tax Withheld	FICA Wages	FICA Tax Withheld

Complete the required data for the following employees.

Employee	Gross Earnings	Federal Income Tax Withheld
Jane Eckman	$59,000	$28,500
Sharon Bishop	26,000	10,200

PROBLEMS: SET B

P11-1B On January 1, 2008, the ledger of Payless Software Company contains the following liability accounts.

Prepare current liability entries, adjusting entries, and current liabilities section.

(SO 1, 2, 3, 4, 5)

GLS

Accounts Payable	$42,500
Sales Taxes Payable	5,800
Unearned Service Revenue	15,000

During January the following selected transactions occurred.

Jan. 1 Borrowed $30,000 in cash from Amsterdam Bank on a 4-month, 8%, $30,000 note.
5 Sold merchandise for cash totaling $10,400, which includes 4% sales taxes.
12 Provided services for customers who had made advance payments of $9,000. (Credit Service Revenue.)
14 Paid state treasurer's department for sales taxes collected in December 2007, $5,800.
20 Sold 900 units of a new product on credit at $52 per unit, plus 4% sales tax. This new product is subject to a 1-year warranty.
25 Sold merchandise for cash totaling $18,720, which includes 4% sales taxes.

Instructions

(a) Journalize the January transactions.

(b) Journalize the adjusting entries at January 31 for (1) the outstanding notes payable, and (2) estimated warranty liability, assuming warranty costs are expected to equal 5% of sales of the new product.

(c) Current liability total $84,032

(c) Prepare the current liabilities section of the balance sheet at January 31, 2008. Assume no change in accounts payable.

Journalize and post note transactions and show balance sheet presentation.

(SO 2)

P11-2B The following are selected transactions of Zimmer Company. Zimmer prepares financial statements *quarterly.*

Jan. 2	Purchased merchandise on account from Alicea Company, $18,000, terms 2/10, n/30.
Feb. 1	Issued a 10%, 2-month, $18,000 note to Alicea in payment of account.
Mar. 31	Accrued interest for 2 months on Alicea note.
Apr. 1	Paid face value and interest on Alicea note.
July 1	Purchased equipment from Vincent Equipment paying $11,000 in cash and signing a 10%, 3-month, $24,000 note.
Sept. 30	Accrued interest for 3 months on Vincent note.
Oct. 1	Paid face value and interest on Vincent note.
Dec. 1	Borrowed $10,000 from the Associated Bank by issuing a 3-month, 12%-interest-bearing note with a face value of $10,000.
Dec. 31	Recognized interest expense for 1 month on Associated Bank note.

Instructions

(a) Prepare journal entries for the above transactions and events.

(b) Post to the accounts, Notes Payable, Interest Payable, and Interest Expense.

(c) Show the balance sheet presentation of notes and interest payable at December 31.

(d) $1,000

(d) What is total interest expense for the year?

Prepare payroll register and payroll entries.

(SO 6, 7)

P11-3B Hiller Drug Store has four employees who are paid on an hourly basis plus time-and-a-half for all hours worked in excess of 40 a week. Payroll data for the week ended February 15, 2008, are presented below.

Employees	Hours Worked	Hourly Rate	Federal Income Tax Withholdings	United Fund
L. Steck	39	$15.00	$?	$–0–
S. Jabar	42	13.00	?	5.00
M. Cape	44	12.00	61	7.50
L. Wild	46	12.00	46	5.00

Steck and Jabar are married. They claim 2 and 4 withholding allowances, respectively. The following tax rates are applicable: FICA 8%, state income taxes 3%, state unemployment taxes 5.4%, and federal unemployment 0.8%. The first three employees are sales clerks (store wages expense). The fourth employee performs administrative duties (office wages expense).

Instructions

(a) Net pay $1,821.26; Store wages expense $1,696.00

(b) Payroll tax expense $324.33

(d) Cash paid $559.44

(a) Prepare a payroll register for the weekly payroll. (Use the wage-bracket withholding table in the text for federal income tax withholdings.)

(b) Journalize the payroll on February 15, 2008, and the accrual of employer payroll taxes.

(c) Journalize the payment of the payroll on February 16, 2008.

(d) Journalize the deposit in a Federal Reserve bank on February 28, 2008, of the FICA and federal income taxes payable to the government.

Journalize payroll transactions and adjusting entries.

(SO 6, 7, 9)

GLS

P11-4B The following payroll liability accounts are included in the ledger of Pettiegrew Company on January 1, 2008.

FICA Taxes Payable	$ 662.20
Federal Income Taxes Payable	1,254.60
State Income Taxes Payable	102.15
Federal Unemployment Taxes Payable	312.00
State Unemployment Taxes Payable	1,954.40
Union Dues Payable	250.00
U.S. Savings Bonds Payable	350.00

In January, the following transactions occurred.

Jan. 10 Sent check for $250.00 to union treasurer for union dues.
12 Deposited check for $1,916.80 in Federal Reserve bank for FICA taxes and federal income taxes withheld.
15 Purchased U.S. Savings Bonds for employees by writing check for $350.00.
17 Paid state income taxes withheld from employees.
20 Paid federal and state unemployment taxes.
31 Completed monthly payroll register, which shows office salaries $22,600, store wages $27,400, FICA taxes withheld $4,000, federal income taxes payable $1,970, state income taxes payable $430, union dues payable $400, United Fund contributions payable $1,800, and net pay $41,400.
31 Prepared payroll checks for the net pay and distributed checks to employees.

At January 31, the company also makes the following accruals pertaining to employee compensation.

1. Employer payroll taxes: FICA taxes 8%, state unemployment taxes 5.4%, and federal unemployment taxes 0.8%.
***2.** Vacation pay: 5% of gross earnings.

Instructions

(a) Journalize the January transactions.
(b) Journalize the adjustments pertaining to employee compensation at January 31.

(b) Payroll tax expense $7,100.00; Vacation benefits expense $2,500

P11-5B For the year ended December 31, 2008, R. Uhlman Company reports the following summary payroll data.

Prepare entries for payroll and payroll taxes; prepare W-2 data.

(SO 6, 7)

Gross earnings:	
Administrative salaries	$200,000
Electricians' wages	320,000
Total	$520,000
Deductions:	
FICA taxes	$ 36,000
Federal income taxes withheld	159,000
State income taxes withheld (3%)	15,600
United Fund contributions payable	25,000
Hospital insurance premiums	15,800
Total	$251,400

R. Uhlman Company's payroll taxes are: FICA 8%, state unemployment 2.5% (due to a stable employment record), and 0.8% federal unemployment. Gross earnings subject to FICA taxes total $450,000, and unemployment taxes total $120,000.

Instructions

(a) Prepare a summary journal entry at December 31 for the full year's payroll.
(b) Journalize the adjusting entry at December 31 to record the employer's payroll taxes.
(c) The W-2 Wage and Tax Statement requires the dollar data shown below.

(a) Wages Payable $268,600
(b) Payroll tax expense $39,960

Wages, Tips, Other Compensation	Federal Income Tax Withheld	State Income Tax Withheld	FICA Wages	FICA Tax Withheld

Complete the required data for the following employees.

Employee	Gross Earnings	Federal Income Tax Withheld
R. Lopez	$60,000	$27,500
K. Vopat	27,000	11,000

PROBLEMS: SET C

Visit the book's website at **www.wiley.com/college/weygandt**, and choose the Student Companion site, to access Problem Set C.

CONTINUING COOKIE CHRONICLE

(*Note:* This is a continuation of the Cookie Chronicle from Chapters 1 through 10.)

CCC11 Recall that Cookie Creations sells fine European mixers that it purchases from Kzinski Supply Co. Kzinski warrants the mixers to be free of defects in material and workmanship for a period of one year from the date of original purchase. If the mixer has such a defect, Kzinski will repair or replace the mixer free of charge for parts and labor.

Go to the book's website, ***www.wiley.com/college/weygandt****, to see the completion of this problem.*

BROADENING YOUR PERSPECTIVE

FINANCIAL REPORTING AND ANALYSIS

Financial Reporting Problem

PepsiCo, Inc.

BYP11-1 The financial statements of PepsiCo. and the Notes to Consolidated Financial Statements appear in Appendix A.

Instructions

Refer to PepsiCo's financial statements and answer the following questions about current and contingent liabilities and payroll costs.

(a) What were PepsiCo's total current liabilities at December 31, 2005? What was the increase/decrease in PepsiCo's total current liabilities from the prior year?

(b) In PepsiCo's Note 2 ("Our Significant Accounting Policies"), the company explains the nature of its contingencies. Under what conditions does PepsiCo recognize (record and report) liabilities for contingencies?

(c) What were the components of total current liabilities on December 31, 2005?

Comparative Analysis Problem

PepsiCo, Inc. vs. The Coca-Cola Company

BYP11-2 PepsiCo's financial statements are presented in Appendix A. Coca-Cola's financial statements are presented in Appendix B.

Instructions

(a) At December 31, 2005, what was PepsiCo's largest current liability account? What were its total current liabilities? At December 31, 2005, what was Coca-Cola's largest current liability account? What were its total current liabilities?

(b) Based on information contained in those financial statements, compute the following 2005 values for each company.

(1) Working capital.

(2) Current ratio.

(c) What conclusions concerning the relative liquidity of these companies can be drawn from these data?

Exploring the Web

BYP11-3 The Internal Revenue Service provides considerable information over the Internet. The following demonstrates how useful one of its sites is in answering payroll tax questions faced by employers.

Address: www.irs.ustreas.gov/formspubs/index.html, or go to **www.wiley.com/college/weygandt**

Steps

1. Go to the site shown above.
2. Choose **View Online, Tax Publications.**
3. Choose **Publication 15, Circular E, Employer's Tax Guide.**

Instructions

Answer each of the following questions.

(a) How does the government define "employees"?
(b) What are the special rules for Social Security and Medicare regarding children who are employed by their parents?
(c) How can an employee obtain a Social Security card if he or she doesn't have one?
(d) Must employees report to their employer tips received from customers? If so, what is the process?
(e) Where should the employer deposit Social Security taxes withheld or contributed?

CRITICAL THINKING

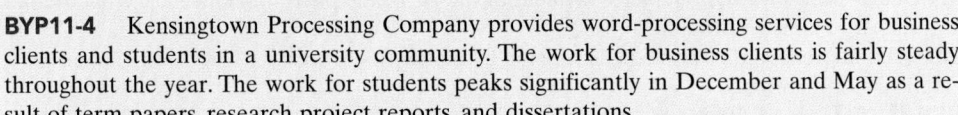

Decision Making Across the Organization

BYP11-4 Kensingtown Processing Company provides word-processing services for business clients and students in a university community. The work for business clients is fairly steady throughout the year. The work for students peaks significantly in December and May as a result of term papers, research project reports, and dissertations.

Two years ago, the company attempted to meet the peak demand by hiring part-time help. However, this led to numerous errors and considerable customer dissatisfaction. A year ago, the company hired four experienced employees on a permanent basis instead of using part-time help. This proved to be much better in terms of productivity and customer satisfaction. But, it has caused an increase in annual payroll costs and a significant decline in annual net income.

Recently, Valarie Flynn, a sales representative of Metcalfe Services Inc., has made a proposal to the company. Under her plan, Metcalfe Services will provide up to four experienced workers at a daily rate of $75 per person for an 8-hour workday. Metcalfe workers are not available on an hourly basis. Kensingtown Processing would have to pay only the daily rate for the workers used.

The owner of Kensingtown Processing, Donna Bell, asks you, as the company's accountant, to prepare a report on the expenses that are pertinent to the decision. If the Metcalfe plan is adopted, Donna will terminate the employment of two permanent employees and will keep two permanent employees. At the moment, each employee earns an annual income of $21,000. Kensingtown Processing pays 8% FICA taxes, 0.8% federal unemployment taxes, and 5.4% state unemployment taxes. The unemployment taxes apply to only the first $7,000 of gross earnings. In addition, Kensingtown Processing pays $40 per month for each employee for medical and dental insurance.

Donna indicates that if the Metcalfe Services plan is accepted, her needs for temporary workers will be as follows.

Months	Number of Employees	Working Days per Month
January–March	2	20
April–May	3	25
June–October	2	18
November–December	3	23

Instructions

With the class divided into groups, answer the following.

(a) Prepare a report showing the comparative payroll expense of continuing to employ permanent workers compared to adopting the Metcalfe Services Inc. plan.
(b) What other factors should Donna consider before finalizing her decision?

Communication Activity

BYP11-5 Jack Quaney, president of the Ramsberg Company, has recently hired a number of additional employees. He recognizes that additional payroll taxes will be due as a result of this hiring, and that the company will serve as the collection agent for other taxes.

Instructions

In a memorandum to Jack Quaney, explain each of the taxes, and identify the taxes that result in payroll tax expense to Ramsberg Company.

Ethics Case

BYP11-6 Daniel Longan owns and manages Daniel's Restaurant, a 24-hour restaurant near the city's medical complex. Daniel employs 9 full-time employees and 16 part-time employees. He pays all of the full-time employees by check, the amounts of which are determined by Daniel's public accountant, Gina Watt. Daniel pays all of his part-time employees in currency. He computes their wages and withdraws the cash directly from his cash register.

Gina has repeatedly urged Daniel to pay all employees by check. But as Daniel has told his competitor and friend, Steve Hill, who owns the Greasy Diner, "First of all, my part-time employees prefer the currency over a check, and secondly I don't withhold or pay any taxes or workmen's compensation insurance on those wages because they go totally unrecorded and unnoticed."

Instructions

(a) Who are the stakeholders in this situation?

(b) What are the legal and ethical considerations regarding Daniel's handling of his payroll?

(c) Gina Watt is aware of Daniel's payment of the part-time payroll in currency. What are her ethical responsibilities in this case?

(d) What internal control principle is violated in this payroll process?

"All About You" Activity

BYP11-7 As indicated in the **All About You** story, "Your Boss Wants to Know If You Jogged Today," medical costs are substantial and rising. But will medical costs be your most substantial expense over your lifetime? Not likely. Will it be housing or food? Again, not likely. The answer is in the *Accounting Across the Organization* box on page 484: taxes. On average, Americans work 77 days to afford their federal taxes. Companies, too, have large tax burdens. They look very hard at tax issues in deciding where to build their plants and where to locate their administrative headquarters.

Instructions

(a) Determine what your state income taxes are if your taxable income is $60,000 and you file as a single taxpayer in the state in which you live.

(b) Assume that you own a home worth $200,000 in your community and the tax rate is 2.1%. Compute the property taxes you would pay.

(c) Assume that the total gasoline bill for your automobile is $1,200 a year (400 gallons at $3 per gallon). What are the amounts of state and federal taxes that you pay on the $1,200?

(d) Assume that your purchases for the year total $9,000. Of this amount, $5,000 was for food and prescription drugs. What is the amount of sales tax you would pay on these purchases? (Note that many states do not have a sales tax for food or prescription drug purchases. Does yours?).

(e) Determine what your Social Security taxes are if your income is $60,000.

(f) Determine what your federal income taxes are if your taxable income is $60,000 and you file as a single taxpayer.

(g) Determine your *total* taxes paid based on the above calculations, and determine the percentage of income that you would pay in taxes based on the following formula: Total taxes paid ÷ Total income.

Answers to Insight and Accounting Across the Organization Questions

p. 478 Contingencies: How Big Are They?

Q: Why do you think most companies disclose, but do not record, contingent liabilities?

A: *In many cases, it is probable that companies have a contingent liability. But the amount of the liability is often difficult to determine. If it cannot be determined, the company is not required to accrue it as a liability.*

p. 484 Taxes Are the Largest Slice of the Pie

Q: If the information on 2006 taxation depicted your spending patterns, on what date (starting on January 1) will you have earned enough to pay all of your taxes?

A: *As indicated in the story, it takes 116 (77 + 39) days to pay your taxes. Thus, April 26 is Tax Freedom Day. Tax Freedom Day for the past 26 years has occurred in April, except for the year 2000 when it occurred in May.*

Authors' Comments on *All About You:* Your Boss Wants to Know If You Jogged Today (p. 492)

On the one hand, a company's insurance premiums would be substantially lower if its employees did not smoke and if they were in better shape. Some argue that employees with unhealthy habits place a burden on healthy employees because they increase the share of insurance premiums that all employees have to pay, and because unhealthy employees miss more days of work. On the other hand, some argue that this approach discriminates in favor of "healthy" people. Also, it is not illegal to smoke or to be overweight. Should an employer really be able to dictate against non-illegal behavior that employees do on their own time? The cost of health care is a huge problem in the U.S., with no easy answers.

Answer to PepsiCo Review It Question 2, p. 480

Under the heading of current liabilities, PepsiCo has listed short-term obligations, accounts payable and other current liabilities, and income taxes payable.

Answers to Self-Study Questions

1. a **2.** d **3.** b **4.** b **5.** a **6.** c **7.** b **8.** d **9.** c **10.** d **11.** d

Remember to go back to the Navigator box on the chapter-opening page and check off your completed work.

Chapter 12

Accounting for Partnerships

STUDY OBJECTIVES

After studying this chapter, you should be able to:

1 Identify the characteristics of the partnership form of business organization.

2 Explain the accounting entries for the formation of a partnership.

3 Identify the bases for dividing net income or net loss.

4 Describe the form and content of partnership financial statements.

5 Explain the effects of the entries to record the liquidation of a partnership.

✓ *The Navigator*

✓ The Navigator

Scan **Study Objectives**	■
Read **Feature Story**	■
Read **Preview**	■
Read text and answer **Before You Go On** p. 518 ■ p. 524 ■ p. 531 ■	
Work **Demonstration Problem**	■
Review **Summary of Study Objectives**	■
Answer **Self-Study Questions**	■
Complete **Assignments**	■

Feature Story

FROM TRIALS TO THE TOP TEN

In 1990 Cliff Chenfield and Craig Balsam gave up the razors, ties, and six-figure salaries they had become accustomed to as New York lawyers. Instead, they set up a partnership, Razor & Tie Music *(www.razorandtie.com)*, in Cliff's living room. Ten years later, it became the only record company in the country that had achieved success in selling music both on television and in stores. Razor & Tie's entertaining and effective TV commercials have yielded unprecedented sales for multi-artist music compilations. At the same time, its hot retail label has been behind some of the most recent original, progressive releases.

Razor & Tie may be best known for its wildly popular *Kidz Bop* CD series, the top-selling children's audio product in the United States. Advertised on Nickelodeon, the Cartoon Network, and elsewhere, *Kidz Bop* titles have sold over 7 million copies. Seven of the 11 releases in the series have "gone Gold."

Razor & Tie got its start with its first TV release, *Those Fabulous '70s* (100,000 copies sold), followed by *Disco Fever* (over 300,000 sold). These albums generated so much publicity that partners Cliff and Craig were guests on dozens of TV interview shows.

After restoring the respectability of the oft-maligned music of the 1970s, the partners forged into the musical '80s with the same zeal that elicited success with their first releases. In 1993, Razor & Tie released *Totally '80s*, a collection of Top-10 singles from the 1980s that has sold over 450,000 units. Featuring the tag line, "The greatest hits from the decade when communism died and music videos were born," *Totally '80s* was the best-selling direct-response album in the country in 1993.

In 1995, Razor & Tie broke into the contemporary music world with *Living in the '90s*, the most successful record in the history of the company. Featuring a number of songs that were still hits on the radio at the time the package initially aired, *Living in the '90s* was a blockbuster. It received Gold certification in less than nine months and rewrote the rules on direct-response albums. For the first time, contemporary music was available through an album offered only through direct-response spots. Razor & Tie pursued that same strategy with its 2002 introduction of the *Kidz Bop* titles.

How has Razor & Tie carved out its sizable piece of the market? Through the complementary talents of the two partners. Their imagination and savvy, along with exciting new releases planned for the coming years, ensure Razor & Tie continued growth.

✓ The Navigator

Inside Chapter 12...

Preview of Chapter 12

It is not surprising that when Cliff Chenfield and Craig Balsam began Razor & Tie, they decided to use the partnership form of organization. Both saw the need for hands-on control of their product and its promotion. In this chapter, we will discuss reasons why businesses select the partnership form of organization. We also will explain the major issues in accounting for partnerships.

The content and organization of Chapter 12 are as follows.

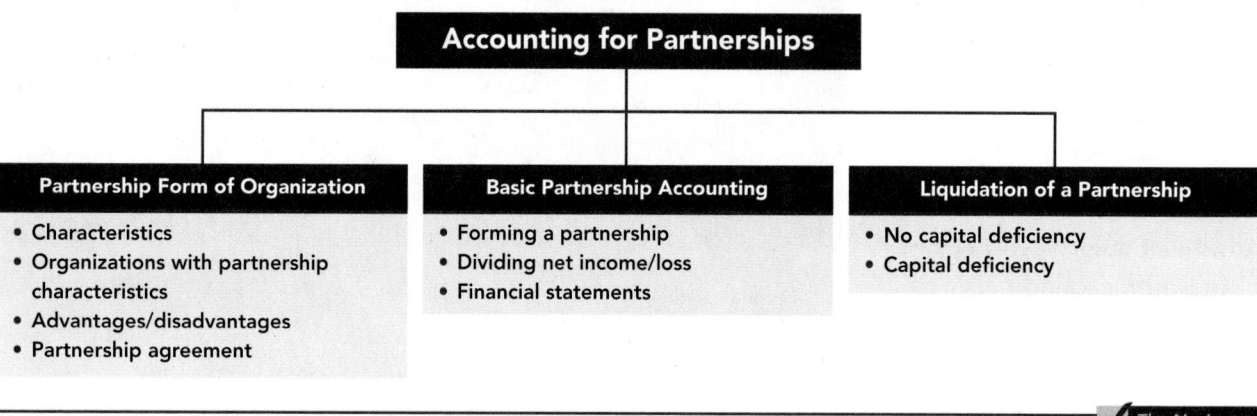

Accounting for Partnerships

Partnership Form of Organization
- Characteristics
- Organizations with partnership characteristics
- Advantages/disadvantages
- Partnership agreement

Basic Partnership Accounting
- Forming a partnership
- Dividing net income/loss
- Financial statements

Liquidation of a Partnership
- No capital deficiency
- Capital deficiency

The Navigator

PARTNERSHIP FORM OF ORGANIZATION

A **partnership** is an association of two or more persons to carry on as co-owners of a business for profit. Partnerships are sometimes used in small retail, service, or manufacturing companies. Also accountants, lawyers, and doctors find it desirable to form partnerships with other professionals in the field.

Characteristics of Partnerships

STUDY OBJECTIVE 1

Identify the characteristics of the partnership form of business organization.

Partnerships are fairly easy to form. People form partnerships simply by a verbal agreement, or more formally, by written agreement. We explain the principal characteristics of partnerships in the following sections.

Association of Individuals

ASSOCIATION OF INDIVIDUALS

A partnership is a legal entity. A partnership can own property (land, buildings, equipment), and can sue or be sued. **A partnership also is an accounting entity.** Thus, the personal assets, liabilities, and transactions of the partners are excluded from the accounting records of the partnership, just as they are in a proprietorship.

The net income of a partnership is not taxed as a separate entity. But, a partnership must file an information tax return showing partnership net income and each partner's share of that net income. Each partner's share is taxable at **personal tax rates**, regardless of the amount of net income each withdraws from the business during the year.

Mutual Agency

MUTUAL AGENCY

Mutual agency means that each partner acts on behalf of the partnership when engaging in partnership business. The act of any partner is binding on all other partners. This is true even when partners act beyond the scope of their authority, so long as the act appears to be appropriate for the partnership. For example, a partner of a grocery store who purchases a delivery truck creates a binding contract in the name of the partnership, even if the partnership agreement denies this authority. On the other hand, if a partner in a law firm purchased a snowmobile for the partnership, such an act would not be binding on the partnership. The purchase is clearly outside the scope of partnership business.

LIMITED LIFE

Corporations have unlimited life. Partnerships do not. A partnership may be ended voluntarily at any time through the acceptance of a new partner or the withdrawal of a partner. It may be ended involuntarily by the death or incapacity of a partner. Partnership dissolution occurs whenever a partner withdraws or a new partner is admitted. Dissolution does not necessarily mean that the business ends. If the continuing partners agree, operations can continue without interruption by forming a new partnership.

Limited Life

UNLIMITED LIABILITY

Each partner is **personally and individually liable** for all partnership liabilities. Creditors' claims attach first to partnership assets. If these are insufficient, the claims then attach to the personal resources of any partner, irrespective of that partner's equity in the partnership. Because each partner is responsible for all the debts of the partnership, each partner is said to have **unlimited liability**.

Unlimited Liability

CO-OWNERSHIP OF PROPERTY

Partners jointly own partnership assets. If the partnership is dissolved, each partner has a claim on total assets equal to the balance in his or her respective capital account. This claim does not attach to **specific assets** that an individual partner contributed to the firm. Similarly, if a partner invests a building in the partnership valued at $100,000 and the building is later sold at a gain of $20,000, the partners all share in the gain.

Partnership net income (or net loss) is also co-owned. **If the partnership contract does not specify to the contrary, all net income or net loss is shared equally by the partners.** As you will see later, though, partners may agree to unequal sharing of net income or net loss.

Co-ownership of Property

Organizations with Partnership Characteristics

If you are starting a business with a friend and each of you has little capital and your business is not risky, you probably want to use a partnership. As indicated above, the partnership is easy to establish and its cost is minimal. These types of partnerships are often called **regular partnerships**. However if your business is risky—say, roof repair or providing some type of professional service—you will want to limit your liability and not use a regular partnership. As a result, special forms of business organizations with partnership characteristics are now often used to provide protection from unlimited liability for people who wish to work together in some activity.

The special partnership forms are: limited partnerships, limited liability partnerships, and limited liability companies. These special forms use the same accounting procedures as those described for a regular partnership. In addition, for taxation purposes, all the profits and losses pass through these organizations (similar to the regular partnership) to the owners, who report their share of partnership net income or losses on their personal tax returns.

LIMITED PARTNERSHIPS

In a limited partnership, one or more partners have **unlimited liability** and one or more partners have **limited liability** for the debts of the firm. Those with unlimited liability are **general partners**. Those with limited liability are **limited partners**. Limited partners are responsible for the debts of the partnership up to the limit of their investment in the firm.

The words "Limited Partnership," or "Ltd.," or "LP" identify this type of organization. For the privilege of limited liability, the limited partner usually accepts less compensation than a general partner and exercises less influence in the affairs of the firm. If the limited partners get involved in management, they risk their liability protection.

LIMITED LIABILITY PARTNERSHIP

Most states allow professionals such as lawyers, doctors, and accountants to form a **limited liability partnership** or "LLP." The LLP is designed to protect innocent partners from malpractice or negligence claims resulting from the acts of another partner. LLPs generally carry large insurance policies as protection against malpractice suits. These professional partnerships vary in size from a medical partnership of three to five doctors, to 150 to 200 partners in a large law firm, to more than 2,000 partners in an international accounting firm.

LIMITED LIABILITY COMPANIES

A hybrid form of business organization with certain features like a corporation and others like a limited partnership is the **limited liability company**, or "LLC." An LLC usually has a limited life. The owners, called **members**, have limited liability like owners of a corporation. Whereas limited partners do not actively participate in the management of a limited partnership (LP), the members of a limited liability company (LLC) can assume an active management role. For income tax purposes, the IRS usually classifies an LLC as a partnership.

ACCOUNTING ACROSS THE ORGANIZATION

Limited Liability Companies Gain in Popularity

The proprietorship form of business organization is still the most popular, followed by the corporate form. But whenever a group of individuals wants to form a partnership, the limited liability company is usually the popular choice.

One other form of business organization is a *subchapter S corporation*. A subchapter S corporation has many of the characteristics of a partnership—especially, taxation as a partnership—but it is losing its popularity. The reason: It involves more paperwork and expense than a limited liability company, which in most cases offers similar advantages.

? Why do you think that the use of the limited liability company is gaining in popularity?

Illustration 12-1 summarizes different forms of organizations that have partnership characteristics.

Advantages and Disadvantages of Partnerships

Why do people choose partnerships? One major advantage of a partnership is to combine the skills and resources of two or more individuals. In addition, partnerships are easily formed and are relatively free from government regulations and restrictions. A partnership does not have to contend with the "red tape" that a

Illustration 12-1
Different forms of organizations with partnership characteristics

	Major Advantages	Major Disadvantages
Regular Partnership  General Partners	Simple and inexpensive to create and operate.	Owners (partners) personally liable for business debts.
Limited Partnership  General Partners / Limited Partners	Limited partners have limited personal liability for business debts as long as they do not participate in management. General partners can raise cash without involving outside investors in management of business.	General partners personally liable for business debts. More expensive to create than regular partnership. Suitable mainly for companies that invest in real estate.
Limited Liability Partnership 	Mostly of interest to partners in old-line professions such as law, medicine, and accounting. Owners (partners) are not personally liable for the malpractice of other partners.	Unlike a limited liability company, owners (partners) remain personally liable for many types of obligations owed to business creditors, lenders, and landlords.. Often limited to a short list of professions.
Limited Liability Company 	Owners have limited personal liability for business debts even if they participate in management.	More expensive to create than regular partnership.

Source: *www.nolo.com* (accessed June 2006).

corporation must face. Also, partners generally can make decisions quickly on substantive business matters without having to consult a board of directors.

On the other hand, partnerships also have some major disadvantages. **Unlimited liability** is particularly troublesome. Many individuals fear they may lose not only their initial investment but also their personal assets, if those assets are needed to pay partnership creditors.

Illustration 12-2 summarizes the advantages and disadvantages of the regular partnership form of business organization. As indicated in the previous section, different types of partnership forms have evolved to reduce some of the disadvantages.

Illustration 12-2
Advantages and disadvantages of a partnership

Advantages	Disadvantages
Combining skills and resources of two or more individuals	Mutual agency
Ease of formation	Limited life
Freedom from governmental regulations and restrictions	Unlimited liability
Ease of decision making	

ETHICS NOTE

A well-developed partnership agreement reduces ethical conflict among partners. It specifies in clear and concise language the process by which the partners will resolve ethical and legal problems. This issue is especially significant when the partnership experiences financial distress.

The Partnership Agreement

Ideally, the agreement of two or more individuals to form a partnership should be expressed in a written contract, called the **partnership agreement** or **articles of co-partnership**. The partnership agreement contains such basic information as the name and principal location of the firm, the purpose of the business, and date of inception. In addition, it should specify relationships among the partners, such as:

1. Names and capital contributions of partners.
2. Rights and duties of partners.
3. Basis for sharing net income or net loss.
4. Provision for withdrawals of assets.
5. Procedures for submitting disputes to arbitration.
6. Procedures for the withdrawal or addition of a partner.
7. Rights and duties of surviving partners in the event of a partner's death.

We cannot overemphasize the importance of a written contract. The agreement should attempt to anticipate all possible situations, contingencies, and disagreements. The help of a lawyer is highly desirable in preparing the agreement.

ACCOUNTING ACROSS THE ORGANIZATION

How to Part Ways Nicely

What should you do when you and your business partner do not agree on things, to the point where you are no longer on speaking terms? Given how heated business situations can get, this is not an unusual occurrence. Unfortunately, in many instances the partners do everything they can to undermine the other partner, eventually destroying the business. In some instances people even steal from the partnership because they either feel that they "deserve it" or they assume that the other partners are stealing from them.

It would be much better to follow the example of Jennifer Appel and her partner. They found that after opening a successful bakery and writing a cookbook, they couldn't agree on how the business should be run. The other partner bought out Ms. Appel's share of the business, and Ms. Appel went on to start her own style of bakery, which she ultimately franchised.

Source: Paulette Thomas, "As Partnership Sours, Parting Is Sweet," *Wall Street Journal*, July 6, 2004, p. A20.

? How can partnership conflicts be minimized and more easily resolved?

Before You Go On...

REVIEW IT

1. What are the distinguishing characteristics of a partnership?
2. What are the principal advantages and disadvantages of a partnership? Why is PepsiCo not a partnership? The answer to this question appears on page 552.
3. What is the difference between a regular partnership and a limited liability company?
4. What are the major items in a partnership agreement?

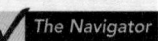

✓ The Navigator

BASIC PARTNERSHIP ACCOUNTING

We now turn to the basic accounting for partnerships. The major accounting issues relate to forming the partnership, dividing income or loss, and preparing financial statements.

Forming a Partnership

STUDY OBJECTIVE 2

Explain the accounting entries for the formation of a partnership.

Each partner's initial investment in a partnership is entered in the partnership records. The partnership should record these investments at the **fair market value of the assets at the date of their transfer to the partnership**. All partners must agree to the values assigned.

To illustrate, assume that A. Rolfe and T. Shea combine their proprietorships to start a partnership named U.S. Software. The firm will specialize in developing financial modeling software packages. Rolfe and Shea have the following assets prior to the formation of the partnership.

Illustration 12-3
Book and market values of assets invested

	Book Value		Market Value	
	A. Rolfe	T. Shea	A. Rolfe	T. Shea
Cash	$ 8,000	$ 9,000	**$ 8,000**	**$ 9,000**
Office equipment	5,000		**4,000**	
Accumulated depreciation	(2,000)			
Accounts receivable		4,000		**4,000**
Allowance for doubtful accounts		(700)		**(1,000)**
	$11,000	$12,300	**$12,000**	**$12,000**

*Items under **owners' equity (OE)** in the accounting equation analyses (in margins) are not labeled in this partnership chapter. Nearly all affect partners' **capital** accounts.*

The partnership records the investments as follows.

Investment of A. Rolfe

Cash	8,000	
Office Equipment	4,000	
A. Rolfe, Capital		12,000
(To record investment of Rolfe)		

A	=	L	+	OE
+8,000				
+4,000				
				+12,000

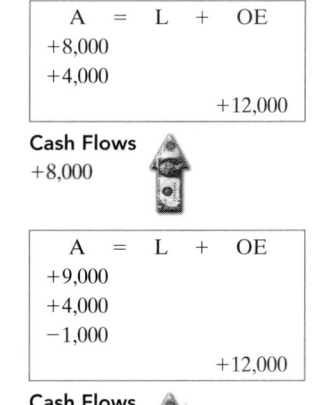

Cash Flows
+8,000

Investment of T. Shea

Cash	9,000	
Accounts Receivable	4,000	
Allowance for Doubtful Accounts		1,000
T. Shea, Capital		12,000
(To record investment of Shea)		

A	=	L	+	OE
+9,000				
+4,000				
−1,000				
				+12,000

Cash Flows
+9,000

Note that the partnership records neither the original cost of the office equipment ($5,000) nor its book value ($5,000 − $2,000). It records the equipment at its fair market value, $4,000. The partnership does not carry forward any accumulated depreciation from the books of previous entities (in this case, the two proprietorships).

In contrast, the gross claims on customers ($4,000) are carried forward to the partnership. The partnership adjusts the allowance for doubtful accounts to $1,000, to arrive at a cash (net) realizable value of $3,000. A partnership may start with an allowance for doubtful accounts because it will continue to collect existing accounts receivable, some of which are expected to be uncollectible. In addition, this procedure maintains the control and subsidiary relationship between Accounts Receivable and the accounts receivable subsidiary ledger.

After formation of the partnership, the accounting for transactions is similar to any other type of business organization. For example, the partners record all transactions with outside parties, such as the purchase or sale of merchandise inventory and the payment or receipt of cash, the same as would a sole proprietor.

The steps in the accounting cycle described in Chapter 4 for a proprietorship also apply to a partnership. For example, the partnership prepares a trial balance and journalizes and posts adjusting entries. A worksheet may be used. There are minor differences in journalizing and posting closing entries and in preparing financial statements, as we explain in the following sections. The differences occur because there is more than one owner.

Dividing Net Income or Net Loss

Partners equally share partnership net income or net loss unless the partnership contract indicates otherwise. The same basis of division usually applies to both net income and net loss. It is customary to refer to this basis as the **income ratio**, the **income and loss ratio**, or the **profit and loss (P&L) ratio**. Because of its wide acceptance, we will use the term **income ratio** to identify the basis for dividing net income and net loss. The partnership recognizes a partner's share of net income or net loss in the accounts through closing entries.

CLOSING ENTRIES

As in the case of a proprietorship, a partnership must make four entries in preparing closing entries. The entries are:

1. Debit each revenue account for its balance, and credit Income Summary for total revenues.
2. Debit Income Summary for total expenses, and credit each expense account for its balance.
3. Debit Income Summary for its balance, and credit each partner's capital account for his or her share of net income. Or, credit Income Summary, and debit each partner's capital account for his or her share of net loss.
4. Debit each partner's capital account for the balance in that partner's drawing account, and credit each partner's drawing account for the same amount.

The first two entries are the same as in a proprietorship. The last two entries are different because (1) there are two or more owners' capital and drawing accounts, and (2) it is necessary to divide net income (or net loss) among the partners.

To illustrate the last two closing entries, assume that AB Company has net income of $32,000 for 2008. The partners, L. Arbor and D. Barnett, share net income and net loss equally. Drawings for the year were Arbor $8,000 and Barnett $6,000. The last two closing entries are:

A	=	L	+	OE
				−32,000
				+16,000
				+16,000

Cash Flows
no effect

Date	Account	Debit	Credit
Dec. 31	Income Summary	32,000	
	L. Arbor, Capital ($32,000 × 50%)		16,000
	D. Barnett, Capital ($32,000 × 50%)		16,000
	(To transfer net income to partners' capital accounts)		

A	=	L	+	OE
				−8,000
				−6,000
				+8,000
				+6,000

Cash Flows
no effect

Date	Account	Debit	Credit
Dec. 31	L. Arbor, Capital	8,000	
	D. Barnett, Capital	6,000	
	L. Arbor, Drawing		8,000
	D. Barnett, Drawing		6,000
	(To close drawing accounts to capital accounts)		

Assume that the beginning capital balance is $47,000 for Arbor and $36,000 for Barnett. After posting the closing entries, the capital and drawing accounts will appear as shown in Illustration 12-4.

L. Arbor, Capital

12/31 **Clos.**	**8,000**	1/1 Bal.	47,000
		12/31 **Clos.**	**16,000**
		12/31 Bal.	55,000

D. Barnett, Capital

12/31 **Clos.**	**6,000**	1/1 Bal.	36,000
		12/31 **Clos.**	**16,000**
		12/31 Bal.	46,000

L. Arbor, Drawing

12/31 Bal.	8,000	12/31 **Clos.**	**8,000**

D. Barnett, Drawing

12/31 Bal.	6,000	12/31 **Clos.**	**6,000**

Illustration 12-4
Partners' capital and drawing accounts after closing

As in a proprietorship, the partners' capital accounts are permanent accounts; their drawing accounts are temporary accounts. Normally, the capital accounts will have credit balances, and the drawing accounts will have debit balances. Drawing accounts are debited when partners withdraw cash or other assets from the partnership for personal use.

INCOME RATIOS

STUDY OBJECTIVE 3
Identify the bases for dividing net income or net loss.

As noted earlier, the partnership agreement should specify the basis for sharing net income or net loss. The following are typical income ratios.

1. A fixed ratio, expressed as a proportion (6:4), a percentage (70% and 30%), or a fraction (2/3 and 1/3).
2. A ratio based either on capital balances at the beginning of the year or on average capital balances during the year.
3. Salaries to partners and the remainder on a fixed ratio.
4. Interest on partners' capital balances and the remainder on a fixed ratio.
5. Salaries to partners, interest on partners' capital, and the remainder on a fixed ratio.

The objective is to settle on a basis that will equitably reflect the partners' capital investment and service to the partnership.

A **fixed ratio** is easy to apply, and it may be an equitable basis in some circumstances. Assume, for example, that Hughes and Lane are partners. Each contributes the same amount of capital, but Hughes expects to work full-time in the partnership and Lane expects to work only half-time. Accordingly, the partners agree to a fixed ratio of 2/3 to Hughes and 1/3 to Lane.

A **ratio based on capital balances** may be appropriate when the funds invested in the partnership are considered the critical factor. Capital ratios may also be equitable when the partners hire a manager to run the business and do not plan to take an active role in daily operations.

The three remaining ratios (items 3, 4, and 5) give specific recognition to differences among partners. These ratios provide salary allowances for time worked and interest allowances for capital invested. Then, the partnership allocates any remaining net income or net loss on a fixed ratio.

Salaries to partners and interest on partners' capital are not expenses of the partnership. Therefore, these items do not enter into the matching of expenses with revenues and the determination of net income or net loss. For a partnership, as for other entities, salaries expense pertains to the cost of services performed by employees. Likewise, interest expense relates to the cost of borrowing from creditors. But partners, as owners, are not considered either **employees** or **creditors**. When the partnership agreement permits the partners to make monthly withdrawals of cash based on their "salary," the partnership debits these withdrawals to the partner's drawing account.

SALARIES, INTEREST, AND REMAINDER ON A FIXED RATIO

Under income ratio (5) in the list above, the partnership must apply salaries and interest **before** it allocates the remainder on the specified fixed ratio. **This is true even if the provisions exceed net income. It is also true even if the partnership has suffered a net loss for the year.** The partnership's income statement should show, below net income, detailed information concerning the division of net income or net loss.

To illustrate, assume that King and Lee are co-partners in the Kingslee Company. The partnership agreement provides for: (1) salary allowances of $8,400 to King and $6,000 to Lee, (2) interest allowances of 10% on capital balances at the beginning of the year, and (3) the remainder equally. Capital balances on January 1 were King $28,000, and Lee $24,000. In 2008, partnership net income is $22,000. The division of net income is as follows.

Illustration 12-5
Income statement with division of net income

KINGSLEE COMPANY
Income Statement (partial)
For the Year Ended December 31, 2008

Sales	$200,000
Net income	$ 22,000

Division of Net Income

	Sara King	Ray Lee	Total
Salary allowance	$ 8,400	$6,000	$14,400
Interest allowance on partners' capital			
Sara King ($28,000 × 10%)	2,800		
Ray Lee ($24,000 × 10%)		2,400	
Total interest allowance			5,200
Total salaries and interest	11,200	8,400	19,600
Remaining income, $2,400			
($22,000 − $19,600)			
Sara King ($2,400 × 50%)	1,200		
Ray Lee ($2,400 × 50%)		1,200	
Total remainder			2,400
Total division of net income	**$12,400**	**$9,600**	**$22,000**

Kingslee records the division of net income as follows.

A	=	L	+	OE
				−22,000
				+12,400
				+9,600

Cash Flows
no effect

Dec. 31	Income Summary	22,000	
	Sara King, Capital		12,400
	Ray Lee, Capital		9,600
	(To close net income to partners' capital)		

Now let's look at a situation in which the salary and interest allowances *exceed* net income. Assume that Kingslee Company's net income is only $18,000. In this case, the salary and interest allowances will create a deficiency of $1,600 ($19,600 − $18,000). The computations of the allowances are the same as those in the preceding example. Beginning with total salaries and interest, we complete the division of net income as shown in Illustration 12-6.

Illustration 12-6
Division of net income—income deficiency

	Sara King	Ray Lee	Total
Total salaries and interest	$11,200	$8,400	$19,600
Remaining deficiency ($1,600)			
($18,000 − $19,600)			
Sara King ($1,600 × 50%)	(800)		
Ray Lee ($1,600 × 50%)		(800)	
Total remainder			(1,600)
Total division	**$10,400**	**$7,600**	**$18,000**

ACCOUNTING ACROSS THE ORGANIZATION

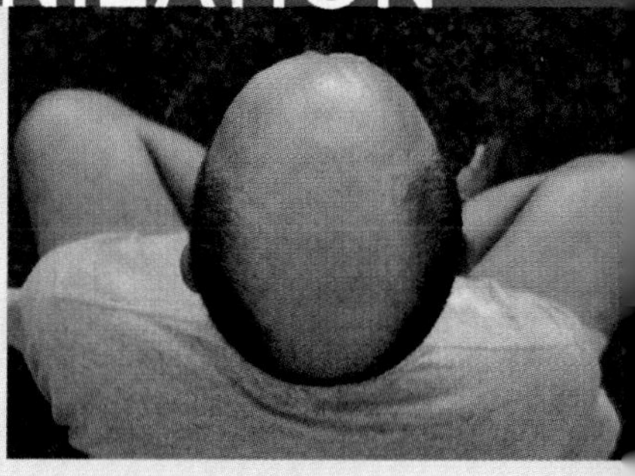

Start-Up Seeks to Share R&D Costs, and Profits

A biotech company named Curis has a promising new product to combat baldness. In order to bring the product to market, the company decided to form partnerships with some much larger companies in order minimize its legal exposure and maximize its research firepower. Says CEO Daniel Passeri, "Any quality-of-life drug is going to be looked at very carefully" by the U.S. Food and Drug Administration (FDA). "The FDA is likely to require big safety studies—broader than we can subsidize ourselves." The company had struggled to minimize its losses during the years when its research and development costs were huge and its sales were minimal. Although the company would have liked to retain all of the profits from its new product for itself, forming partnerships with other companies seemed like its only viable option.

Source: Arlene Weintraub, "Bristling with Promise," *BusinessWeek*, May 15, 2005, p. 57.

? What advantages does Curis achieve by forming agreements with other companies?

Partnership Financial Statements

STUDY OBJECTIVE 4
Describe the form and content of partnership financial statements.

The financial statements of a partnership are similar to those of a proprietorship. The differences are due to the number of owners involved. The income statement for a partnership is identical to the income statement for a proprietorship except for the division of net income, as shown earlier.

The owners' equity statement for a partnership is called the **partners' capital statement**. It explains the changes in each partner's capital account and in total partnership capital during the year. Illustration 12-7 (page 524) shows the partners' capital statement for Kingslee Company. It is based on the division of $22,000 of net income in Illustration 12-5. The statement includes assumed data for the additional investment and drawings. The partnership prepares the partners' capital statement from the income statement and the partners' capital and drawing accounts.

Illustration 12-7
Partners' capital statement

HELPFUL HINT
As in a proprietorship, partners' capital may change due to (1) additional investment, (2) drawings, and (3) net income or net loss.

KINGSLEE COMPANY
Partners' Capital Statement
For the Year Ended December 31, 2008

	Sara King	Ray Lee	Total
Capital, January 1	$28,000	$24,000	$52,000
Add: Additional investment	2,000		2,000
Net income	12,400	9,600	22,000
	42,400	33,600	76,000
Less: Drawings	7,000	5,000	12,000
Capital, December 31	**$35,400**	**$28,600**	**$64,000**

The balance sheet for a partnership is the same as for a proprietorship except for the owner's equity section. For a partnership, the balance sheet shows the capital balances of each partner. The owners' equity section for Kingslee Company would show the following.

Illustration 12-8
Owners' equity section of a partnership balance sheet

KINGSLEE COMPANY
Balance Sheet (partial)
December 31, 2008

Total liabilities (assumed amount)		$115,000
Owners' equity		
Sara King, Capital	$35,400	
Ray Lee, Capital	28,600	
Total owners' equity		64,000
Total liabilities and owners' equity		$179,000

Before You Go On...

REVIEW IT

1. How should a partnership value a partner's initial investment of assets?
2. What are the closing entries for a partnership?
3. What types of income ratios might a partnership use?
4. How do partnership financial statements differ from proprietorship financial statements?

DO IT

LeeMay Company reports net income of $57,000. The partnership agreement provides for salaries of $15,000 to L. Lee and $12,000 to R. May. They will share the remainder on a 60:40 basis (60% to Lee). L. Lee asks your help to divide the net income between the partners and to prepare the closing entry.

Action Plan

- Compute net income exclusive of any salaries to partners and interest on partners' capital.
- Deduct salaries to partners from net income.

- Apply the partners' income ratios to the remaining net income.
- Prepare the closing entry distributing net income or net loss among the partners' capital accounts.

Solution The division of net income is as follows.

	L. Lee	R. May	Total
Salary allowance	$15,000	$12,000	$27,000
Remaining income $30,000 ($57,000 − $27,000)			
L. Lee (60% × $30,000)	18,000		
R. May (40% × $30,000)		12,000	
Total remaining income			30,000
Total division of net income	$33,000	$24,000	$57,000

The closing entry for net income therefore is:

Income Summary	57,000	
L. Lee, Capital		33,000
R. May, Capital		24,000
(To close net income to partners' capital accounts)		

Related exercise material: *BE12-3, BE12-4, BE12-5, E12-4, and E12-5.*

The Navigator

LIQUIDATION OF A PARTNERSHIP

STUDY OBJECTIVE 5

Explain the effects of the entries to record the liquidation of a partnership.

Liquidation of a business involves selling the assets of the firm, paying liabilities, and distributing any remaining assets. Liquidation may result from the sale of the business by mutual agreement of the partners, from the death of a partner, or from bankruptcy. **Partnership liquidation** ends both the legal and economic life of the entity.

From an accounting standpoint, the partnership should complete the accounting cycle for the final operating period prior to liquidation. This includes preparing adjusting entries and financial statements. It also involves preparing closing entries and a post-closing trial balance. Thus, only balance sheet accounts should be open as the liquidation process begins.

In liquidation, the sale of noncash assets for cash is called **realization**. Any difference between book value and the cash proceeds is called the **gain or loss on realization**. To liquidate a partnership, it is necessary to:

1. Sell noncash assets for cash and recognize a gain or loss on realization.
2. Allocate gain/loss on realization to the partners based on their income ratios.
3. Pay partnership liabilities in cash.
4. Distribute remaining cash to partners on the basis of their **capital balances**.

Each of the steps must be performed in sequence. The partnership must pay creditors **before** partners receive any cash distributions. Also, an accounting entry must record each step.

When a partnership is liquidated, all partners may have credit balances in their capital accounts. This situation is called **no capital deficiency**. Or, one or more partners may have a debit balance in the capital account. This situation is termed a **capital deficiency**. To illustrate each of these conditions, assume that Ace Company is liquidated when its ledger shows the following assets, liabilities, and owners' equity accounts.

Illustration 12-9
Account balances prior to liquidation

Assets		Liabilities and Owners' Equity	
Cash	$ 5,000	Notes payable	$15,000
Accounts receivable	15,000	Accounts payable	16,000
Inventory	18,000	R. Arnet, Capital	15,000
Equipment	35,000	P. Carey, Capital	17,800
Accum. depr.—equipment	(8,000)	W. Eaton, Capital	1,200
	$65,000		$65,000

No Capital Deficiency

The partners of Ace Company agree to liquidate the partnership on the following terms: (1) The partnership will sell its noncash assets to Jackson Enterprises for $75,000 cash. (2) The partnership will pay its partnership liabilities. The income ratios of the partners are 3 : 2 : 1, respectively. The steps in the liquidation process are as follows.

1. Ace sells the noncash assets (accounts receivable, inventory, and equipment) for $75,000. The book value of these assets is $60,000 ($15,000 + $18,000 + $35,000 − $8,000). Thus Ace realizes a gain of $15,000 on the sale. The entry is:

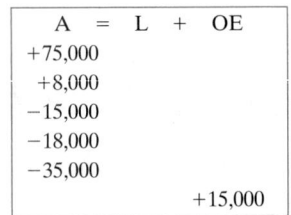

A	=	L	+	OE
+75,000				
+8,000				
−15,000				
−18,000				
−35,000				
				+15,000

Cash Flows
+75,000

(1)

Cash	75,000	
Accumulated Depreciation–Equipment	8,000	
Accounts Receivable		15,000
Inventory		18,000
Equipment		35,000
Gain on Realization		15,000
(To record realization of noncash assets)		

2. Ace allocates the $15,000 gain on realization to the partners on their income ratios, which are 3:2:1. The entry is:

A	=	L	+	OE
				−15,000
				+7,500
				+5,000
				+2,500

Cash Flows
no effect

(2)

Gain on Realization	15,000	
R. Arnet, Capital ($15,000 × 3/6)		7,500
P. Carey, Capital ($15,000 × 2/6)		5,000
W. Eaton, Capital ($15,000 × 1/6)		2,500
(To allocate gain to partners' capital accounts)		

3. Partnership liabilities consist of Notes Payable $15,000 and Accounts Payable $16,000. Ace pays creditors in full by a cash payment of $31,000. The entry is:

A	=	L	+	OE
		−15,000		
		−16,000		
−31,000				

Cash Flows
−31,000

(3)

Notes Payable	15,000	
Accounts Payable	16,000	
Cash		31,000
(To record payment of partnership liabilities)		

4. Ace distributes the remaining cash to the partners on the basis of **their capital balances**. After posting the entries in the first three steps, all partnership accounts, including Gain on Realization, will have zero balances except for four accounts: Cash $49,000; R. Arnet, Capital $22,500; P. Carey, Capital $22,800; and W. Eaton, Capital $3,700, as shown on the next page.

Cash				R. Arnet, Capital		P. Carey, Capital		W. Eaton, Capital	
Bal.	5,000	(3)	31,000		Bal. 15,000		Bal. 17,800		Bal. 1,200
(1)	75,000				(2) 7,500		(2) 5,000		(2) 2,500
Bal.	**49,000**				**Bal. 22,500**		**Bal. 22,800**		**Bal. 3,700**

Illustration 12-10
Ledger balances before distribution of cash

Ace records the distribution of cash as follows.

(4)

	Debit	Credit
R. Arnet, Capital	22,500	
P. Carey, Capital	22,800	
W. Eaton, Capital	3,700	
Cash		49,000
(To record distribution of cash to partners)		

A	=	L	+	OE
				−22,500
				−22,800
				−3,700
−49,000				

Cash Flows
−49,000

After posting this entry, all partnership accounts will have zero balances.

A word of caution: **Partnerships should not distribute remaining cash to partners on the basis of their income-sharing ratios.** On this basis, Arnet would receive three-sixths, or $24,500, which would produce an erroneous debit balance of $2,000. The income ratio is the proper basis for allocating net income or loss. **It is not a proper basis for making the final distribution of cash to the partners.**

SCHEDULE OF CASH PAYMENTS

The **schedule of cash payments** shows the distribution of cash to the partners in a partnership liquidation. A cash payments schedule is sometimes prepared to determine the distribution of cash to the partners in the liquidation of a partnership. The schedule of cash payments is organized around the basic accounting equation. Illustration 12-11 shows the schedule for Ace Company. The numbers in parentheses refer to the four required steps in the liquidation of a partnership. They also identify the accounting entries that Ace must make. The cash payments schedule is especially useful when the liquidation process extends over a period of time.

ALTERNATIVE TERMINOLOGY

The schedule of cash payments is sometimes called a *safe cash payments schedule.*

Illustration 12-11
Schedule of cash payments, no capital deficiency

ACE Company.xls
File Edit View Insert Format Tools Data Window Help

ACE COMPANY
Schedule of Cash Payments

	Item		Cash	+	Noncash Assets	=	Liabilities	+	R. Arnet Capital	+	P. Carey Capital	+	W. Eaton Capital
3	Balances before liquidation		5,000	+	60,000	=	31,000	+	15,000	+	17,800	+	1,200
4	**Sales of noncash assets and allocation of gain**	(1)&(2)	**75,000**	+	**(60,000)**	=			**7,500**	+	**5,000**	+	**2,500**
5	New balances		80,000	+	−0−	=	31,000	+	22,500	+	22,800	+	3,700
6	**Pay liabilities**	(3)	**(31,000)**			=	**(31,000)**						
7	New balances		49,000	+	−0−	=	−0−	+	22,500	+	22,800	+	3,700
8	**Cash distribution to partners**	(4)	**(49,000)**			=			**(22,500)**	+	**(22,800)**	+	**(3,700)**
9	Final balances		−0−		−0−		−0−		−0−		−0−		−0−

Capital Deficiency

A capital deficiency may result from recurring net losses, excessive drawings, or losses from realization suffered during liquidation. To illustrate, assume that Ace Company is on the brink of bankruptcy. The partners decide to liquidate by having a "going-out-of-business" sale. They sell merchandise at substantial discounts, and sell the equipment at auction. Cash proceeds from these sales and collections from customers total only $42,000. Thus, the loss from liquidation is $18,000 ($60,000 – $42,000). The steps in the liquidation process are as follows.

1. The entry for the realization of noncash assets is:

A	=	L	+	OE
+42,000				
+8,000				
				−18,000
−15,000				
−18,000				
−35,000				

Cash Flows
+42,000

(1)

Cash	42,000	
Accumulated Depreciation—Equipment	8,000	
Loss on Realization	18,000	
Accounts Receivable		15,000
Inventory		18,000
Equipment		35,000
(To record realization of noncash assets)		

2. Ace allocates the loss on realization to the partners on the basis of their income ratios. The entry is:

A	=	L	+	OE
				−9,000
				−6,000
				−3,000
				+18,000

Cash Flows
no effect

(2)

R. Arnet, Capital ($18,000 × 3/6)	9,000	
P. Carey, Capital ($18,000 × 2/6)	6,000	
W. Eaton, Capital ($18,000 × 1/6)	3,000	
Loss on Realization		18,000
(To allocate loss on realization to partners)		

3. Ace pays the partnership liabilities. This entry is the same as the previous one.

A	=	L	+	OE
		−15,000		
		−16,000		
−31,000				

Cash Flows
−31,000

(3)

Notes Payable	15,000	
Accounts Payable	16,000	
Cash		31,000
(To record payment of partnership liabilities)		

4. After posting the three entries, two accounts will have debit balances—Cash $16,000, and W. Eaton, Capital $1,800. Two accounts will have credit balances—R. Arnet, Capital $6,000, and P. Carey, Capital $11,800. All four accounts are shown below.

Illustration 12-12
Ledger balances before distribution of cash

Cash (Dr.)		Cash (Cr.)		R. Arnet, Capital (Dr.)		R. Arnet, Capital (Cr.)		P. Carey, Capital (Dr.)		P. Carey, Capital (Cr.)		W. Eaton, Capital (Dr.)		W. Eaton, Capital (Cr.)	
Bal.	5,000	(3)	31,000	(2)	9,000	Bal.	15,000	(2)	6,000	Bal.	17,800	(2)	3,000	Bal.	1,200
(1)	42,000														
Bal.	**16,000**					**Bal.**	**6,000**			**Bal.**	**11,800**	**Bal.**	**1,800**		

Eaton has a capital deficiency of $1,800, and so owes the partnership $1,800. Arnet and Carey have a legally enforceable claim for that amount against Eaton's personal assets. Note that the distribution of cash is still made on the basis of capital balances. But the amount will vary depending on how Eaton settles the deficiency. Two alternatives are presented in the following sections.

PAYMENT OF DEFICIENCY

If the partner with the capital deficiency pays the amount owed the partnership, the deficiency is eliminated. To illustrate, assume that Eaton pays $1,800 to the partnership. The entry is:

A	=	L	+	OE
+1,800				
				+1,800

Cash Flows
+1,800

(a)

Cash	1,800	
W. Eaton, Capital		1,800
(To record payment of capital deficiency by Eaton)		

After posting this entry, account balances are as follows.

Illustration 12-13
Ledger balances after paying capital deficiency

Cash		R. Arnet, Capital		P. Carey, Capital		W. Eaton, Capital	
Bal. 5,000	(3) 31,000	(2) 9,000	Bal. 15,000	(2) 6,000	Bal. 17,800	(2) 3,000	Bal. 1,200
(1) 42,000							(a) 1,800
(a) 1,800			**Bal. 6,000**		**Bal. 11,800**		
Bal. 17,800							**Bal. -0-**

The cash balance of $17,800 is now equal to the credit balances in the capital accounts (Arnet $6,000 + Carey $11,800). Ace now distributes cash on the basis of these balances. The entry is:

R. Arnet, Capital	6,000	
P. Carey, Capital	11,800	
Cash		17,800
(To record distribution of cash to the partners)		

A	=	L	+	OE
				−6,000
				−11,800
−17,800				

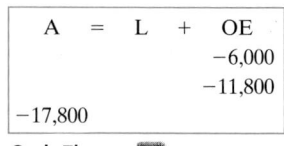

Cash Flows
−17,800

After posting this entry, all accounts will have zero balances.

NONPAYMENT OF DEFICIENCY

If a partner with a capital deficiency is unable to pay the amount owed to the partnership, the partners with credit balances must absorb the loss. The partnership allocates the loss on the basis of the income ratios that exist between the partners with credit balances.

The income ratios of Arnet and Carey are 3 : 2, or 3/5 and 2/5, respectively. Thus, Ace would make the following entry to remove Eaton's capital deficiency.

(a)

R. Arnet, Capital ($1,800 × 3/5)	1,080	
P. Carey, Capital ($1,800 × 2/5)	720	
W. Eaton, Capital		1,800
(To record write-off of capital deficiency)		

A	=	L	+	OE
				−1,080
				−720
				+1,800

Cash Flows
no effect

After posting this entry, the cash and capital accounts will have the following balances.

Cash		R. Arnet, Capital		P. Carey, Capital		W. Eaton, Capital	
Bal. 5,000	(3) 31,000	(2) 9,000	Bal. 15,000	(2) 6,000	Bal. 17,800	(2) 3,000	Bal. 1,200
(1) 42,000		(a) 1,080		(a) 720			(a) 1,800
Bal. 16,000			**Bal. 4,920**		**Bal. 11,080**		**Bal. -0-**

Illustration 12-14
Ledger balances after nonpayment of capital deficiency

The cash balance ($16,000) now equals the sum of the credit balances in the capital accounts (Arnet $4,920 + Carey $11,080). Ace records the distribution of cash as:

R. Arnet, Capital	4,920	
P. Carey, Capital	11,080	
Cash		16,000
(To record distribution of cash to the partners)		

A	=	L	+	OE
				−4,920
				−11,080
−16,000				

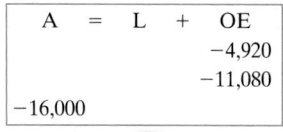

Cash Flows
−16,000

After posting this entry, all accounts will have zero balances.

Be sure to read **ALL ABOUT YOU: *How Well Do You Know Your Partner?*** on page 530 for information on how topics in this chapter apply to you.

How Well Do You Know Your Partner?

As noted in this chapter, the partnership form of organization is popular for a variety of reasons. A partnership is easy to form, and it has significant tax advantages over the corporate form. But the partnership form is not without its faults. Chief among these is that, in a standard partnership, each partner can be held fully responsible for all of the partnership's obligations—not just his or her share. Because of this, choosing a partner is a big decision, and choosing the wrong partner can have devastating consequences.

Some Facts

* There are about 1.7 million business partnerships in the United States, with an average of 9 partners per partnership.
* Over 72% of all small businesses are sole proprietors. Only 6% are partnerships (including limited liability companies that choose to file tax returns as partnerships).
* A partnership is simple to set up because no legal documents are needed. Partnerships are often formed by an oral agreement between the parties. Potential problems can be averted down the road by drawing up a written legal partnership agreement.

About the Numbers

The following graph shows that the most rapid growth in business organizations is occurring in limited liability companies (LLCs). The LLC form is the choice of most new businesses.

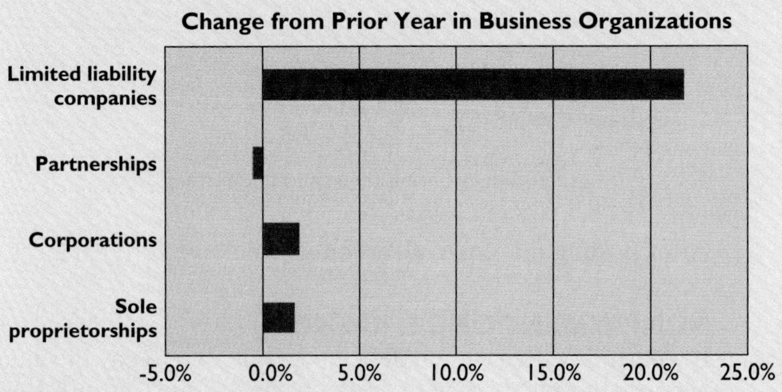

Source of graph: *www.BizStats.com* (accessed June 2006).

What Do You Think?

Suppose that your best friend has approached you about forming a partnership to design and build websites. You have a degree in computer programming, and your friend has a degree in marketing. You are very interested in starting the business. You know you have the technical abilities, but you dread having to be a salesperson. Your friend, on the other hand, has always been outgoing and assertive—the perfect salesperson. Your friend also, however, has an extremely bad credit history, including having filed for personal bankruptcy. Should you form the partnership?

YES: This is a great opportunity. What could be better than working with your best friend?

NO: If the partnership has financial trouble, and your friend cannot pay, then, as a partner you will be responsible for all of the firm's debts, not just your half.

Sources: BizStats.com; Darrell Zahorsky, "Creating a Winning Business Partnership," *www.sbinformation.about.com* (accessed June 2006); *www.askinc@inc.com* (accessed June 2006); *Inc.* Magazine, December 2005, p. 64.

The authors' comments on this situation appear on page 552.

Before You Go On...

REVIEW IT

1. What are the steps in liquidating a partnership?
2. What basis do partnerships use in making final distribution of cash to partners?

The Navigator

Demonstration Problem

On January 1, 2008, the capital balances in Hollingsworth Company are Lois Holly $26,000, and Jim Worth $24,000. In 2008 the partnership reports net income of $30,000. The income ratio provides for salary allowances of $12,000 for Holly and $10,000 to Worth and the remainder equally. Neither partner had any drawings in 2008.

Instructions

(a) Prepare a schedule showing the distribution of net income in 2008.
(b) Journalize the division of 2008 net income to the partners.

Solution to Demonstration Problem

(a) Net income 30,000

Division of Net Income

	Lois Holly	Jim Worth	Total
Salary allowance	$12,000	$10,000	$22,000
Remaining income $8,000 ($30,000 − $22,000)			
Lois Holly ($8,000 × 50%)	4,000		
Jim Worth ($8,000 × 50%)		4,000	
Total remainder			8,000
Total division of net income	$16,000	$14,000	$30,000

(b)

Date	Account	Debit	Credit
12/31/08	Income Summary	30,000	
	Lois Holly, Capital		16,000
	Jim Worth, Capital		14,000
	(To close net income to partners' capital)		

The Navigator

action plan

- Compute the net income of the partnership.
- Allocate the partners' salaries.
- Divide the remaining net income among the partners, applying the income/loss ratio.
- Journalize the division of net income in a closing entry.

SUMMARY OF STUDY OBJECTIVES

1 **Identify the characteristics of the partnership form of business organization.** The principal characteristics of a partnership are: (a) association of individuals, (b) mutual agency, (c) limited life, (d) unlimited liability, and (e) co-ownership of property.

2 **Explain the accounting entries for the formation of a partnership.** When formed, a partnership records each partner's initial investment at the fair market value of the assets at the date of their transfer to the partnership.

3 **Identify the bases for dividing net income or net loss.** Partnerships divide net income or net loss on the basis of the income ratio, which may be (a) a fixed ratio, (b) a ratio based on beginning or average capital balances, (c) salaries to partners and the remainder on a fixed ratio, (d) interest

on partners' capital and the remainder on a fixed ratio, and (e) salaries to partners, interest on partners' capital, and the remainder on a fixed ratio.

4 **Describe the form and content of partnership financial statements.** The financial statements of a partnership are similar to those of a proprietorship. The principal differences are: (a) The partnership shows the division of net income on the income statement. (b) The owners' equity statement is called a partners' capital statement. (c) The partnership reports each partner's capital on the balance sheet.

5 **Explain the effects of the entries to record the liquidation of a partnership.** When a partnership is liquidated, it is necessary to record the (a) sale of noncash assets, (b) allocation of the gain or loss on realization, (c) payment of partnership liabilities, and (d) distribution of cash to the partners on the basis of their capital balances.

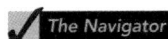

The Navigator

GLOSSARY

WILEY PLUS

Capital deficiency A debit balance in a partner's capital account after allocation of gain or loss. (p. 525).

General partner A partner who has unlimited liability for the debts of the firm. (p. 516).

Income ratio The basis for dividing net income and net loss in a partnership. (p. 520).

Limited liability company A form of business organization, usually classified as a partnership for tax purposes and usually with limited life, in which partners, who are called *members*, have limited liability. (p. 516).

Limited liability partnership A partnership of professionals in which partners are given limited liability and the public is protected from malpractice by insurance carried by the partnership. (p. 516).

Limited partner A partner whose liability for the debts of the firm is limited to that partner's investment in the firm. (p. 516).

Limited partnership A partnership in which one or more general partners have unlimited liability and one or more partners have limited liability for the obligations of the firm. (p. 515).

No capital deficiency All partners have credit balances after allocation of gain or loss. (p. 525).

Partners' capital statement The owners' equity statement for a partnership which shows the changes in each partner's capital account and in total partnership capital during the year. (p. 523).

Partnership An association of two or more persons to carry on as co-owners of a business for profit. (p. 514).

Partnership agreement A written contract expressing the voluntary agreement of two or more individuals in a partnership. (p. 518).

Partnership dissolution A change in partners due to withdrawal or admission, which does not necessarily terminate the business. (p. 515).

Partnership liquidation An event that ends both the legal and economic life of a partnership. (p. 525).

Schedule of cash payments A schedule showing the distribution of cash to the partners in a partnership liquidation. (p. 527).

APPENDIX Admission and Withdrawal of Partners

The chapter explained how the basic accounting for a partnership works. We now look at how to account for a common occurrence in partnerships—the addition or withdrawal of a partner.

Admission of a Partner

STUDY OBJECTIVE 6

Explain the effects of the entries when a new partner is admitted.

The admission of a new partner results in the **legal dissolution** of the existing partnership and the beginning of a new one. From an economic standpoint, however, the admission of a new partner (or partners) may be of minor significance in the continuity of the business. For example, in large public accounting or law firms, partners are admitted annually without any change in operating policies. **To recognize the economic effects, it is necessary only to open a capital account for each new partner.** In the entries illustrated in this appendix, we assume that the accounting records of the predecessor firm will continue to be used by the new partnership.

A new partner may be admitted either by (1) purchasing the interest of one or more existing partners or (2) investing assets in the partnership, as shown in Illustration 12A-1. The former affects only the capital accounts of the partners who are parties to the transaction. The latter increases both net assets and total capital of the partnership.

Admission of Partner through:

Illustration 12A-1
Procedures in adding partners

PURCHASE OF A PARTNER'S INTEREST

The **admission** of a partner **by purchase of an interest** is a personal transaction between one or more existing partners and the new partner. Each party acts as an individual separate from the partnership entity. The individuals involved negotiate the price paid. It may be equal to or different from the capital equity acquired. The purchase price passes directly from the new partner to the partners who are giving up part or all of their ownership claims.

Any money or other consideration exchanged is the personal property of the participants and **not** the property of the partnership. Upon purchase of an interest, the new partner acquires each selling partner's capital interest and income ratio.

Accounting for the purchase of an interest is straightforward. The partnership records record only the changes in partners' capital. **Partners' capital accounts are debited for any ownership claims sold.** At the same time, the new partner's capital account is credited for the capital equity purchased. Total assets, total liabilities, and total capital remain unchanged, as do all individual asset and liability accounts.

To illustrate, assume that L. Carson agrees to pay $10,000 each to C. Ames and D. Barker for 33⅓% (one-third) of their interest in the Ames–Barker partnership. At the time of the admission of Carson, each partner has a $30,000 capital balance. Both partners, therefore, give up $10,000 of their capital equity. The entry to record the admission of Carson is:

C. Ames, Capital	10,000	
D. Barker, Capital	10,000	
L. Carson, Capital		20,000
(To record admission of Carson by purchase)		

HELPFUL HINT
In a purchase of an interest, the partnership is not a participant in the transaction. In this transaction, the new partner contributes *no* cash to the partnership.

Illustration 12A-2
Ledger balances after purchase of a partner's interest

The effect of this transaction on net assets and partners' capital is shown below.

Net Assets		C. Ames, Capital		D. Barker, Capital		L. Carson, Capital	
60,000		**10,000**	30,000	**10,000**	30,000		**20,000**
			Bal. 20,000		Bal. 20,000		

Note that net assets remain unchanged at $60,000, and each partner has a $20,000 capital balance. Ames and Barker continue as partners in the firm, but the capital interest of each has changed. The cash paid by Carson goes directly to the individual partners and not to the partnership.

Regardless of the amount paid by Carson for the one-third interest, the entry is exactly the same. If Carson pays $12,000 each to Ames and Barker for one-third of the partnership, the partnership still makes the entry shown on the bottom of page 533.

INVESTMENT OF ASSETS IN A PARTNERSHIP

The admission of a partner by an investment of assets is a transaction between the new partner and the partnership. Often referred to simply as **admission by investment**, the transaction **increases both the net assets and total capital of the partnership**.

Assume, for example, that instead of purchasing an interest, Carson invests $30,000 in cash in the Ames–Barker partnership for a 33⅓% capital interest. In such a case, the entry is:

Cash	30,000	
L. Carson, Capital		30,000
(To record admission of Carson by investment)		

Illustration 12A-3
Ledger balances after investment of assets

The effects of this transaction on the partnership accounts would be:

Net Assets		C. Ames, Capital		D. Barker, Capital		L. Carson, Capital	
60,000			30,000		30,000		**30,000**
30,000							
Bal. 90,000							

Note that both net assets and total capital have increased by $30,000.

Remember that Carson's one-third capital interest might not result in a one-third income ratio. The new partnership agreement should specify Carson's income ratio, and it may or may not be equal to the one-third capital interest.

The comparison of the net assets and capital balances in Illustration 12A-4 shows the different effects of the purchase of an interest and admission by investment.

Illustration 12A-4
Comparison of purchase of an interest and admission by investment

Purchase of an Interest		Admission by Investment	
Net Assets	**$60,000**	**Net Assets**	**$90,000**
Capital		Capital	
C. Ames	$20,000	C. Ames	$30,000
D. Barker	20,000	D. Barker	30,000
L. Carson	20,000	L. Carson	30,000
Total capital	**$60,000**	**Total capital**	**$90,000**

When a new partner purchases an interest, the total net assets and total capital of the partnership *do not change*. When a partner is admitted by investment, both the total net assets and the total capital *change*.

In the case of admission by investment, further complications occur when the new partner's investment differs from the capital equity acquired. When those amounts are not the same, the difference is considered a **bonus** either to (1) the existing (old) partners or (2) the new partner.

Bonus to Old Partners For both personal and business reasons, the existing partners may be unwilling to admit a new partner without receiving a bonus. In an established firm, existing partners may insist on a bonus as compensation for the work they have put into the company over the years. Two accounting factors underlie the business reason: First, total partners' capital equals the **book value** of the recorded net assets of the partnership. When the new partner is admitted, the fair market values of assets such as land and buildings may be higher than their book values. The bonus will help make up the difference between fair market value and book value. Second, when the partnership has been profitable, goodwill may exist. But, the partnership balance sheet does not report goodwill. In such cases, the new partner is usually willing to pay the bonus to become a partner.

A bonus to old partners results when the new partner's investment in the firm is greater than the capital credit on the date of admittance. The bonus results in **an increase in the capital balances of the old partners. The partnership allocates the bonus to them on the basis of their income ratios before the admission of the new partner.**

To illustrate, assume that the Bart–Cohen partnership, owned by Sam Bart and Tom Cohen, has total capital of $120,000. Lea Eden acquires a 25% ownership (capital) interest in the partnership by making a cash investment of $80,000. The procedure for determining Eden's capital credit and the bonus to the old partners is as follows.

1. **Determine the total capital of the new partnership:** Add the new partner's investment to the total capital of the old partnership. In this case the total capital of the new firm is $200,000, computed as follows.

Total capital of existing partnership	$120,000
Investment by new partner, Eden	80,000
Total capital of new partnership	$200,000

2. **Determine the new partner's capital credit:** Multiply the total capital of the new partnership by the new partner's ownership interest. Eden's capital credit is $50,000 ($200,000 × 25%).
3. **Determine the amount of bonus:** Subtract the new partner's capital credit from the new partner's investment. The bonus in this case is $30,000 ($80,000 − $50,000).
4. **Allocate the bonus to the old partners on the basis of their income ratios:** Assuming the ratios are Bart 60%, and Cohen 40%, the allocation is: Bart $18,000 ($30,000 × 60%) and Cohen $12,000 ($30,000 × 40%).

The entry to record the admission of Eden is:

Cash	80,000	
Sam Bart, Capital		18,000
Tom Cohen, Capital		12,000
Lea Eden, Capital		50,000
(To record admission of Eden and bonus to old partners)		

A	=	L	+	OE
+80,000				
				+18,000
				+12,000
				+50,000

Cash Flows
+80,000

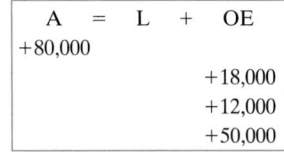

Bonus to New Partner A bonus to a new partner results when the new partner's investment in the firm is less than his or her capital credit. This may occur when the new partner possesses resources or special attributes that the partnership wants. For example, the new partner may be able to supply cash that the firm urgently needs for expansion or to meet maturing debts. Or the new partner may be a recognized expert or authority in a relevant field. Thus, an engineering firm may be willing to give a renowned engineer a bonus to join the firm. The partners of a restaurant may offer a bonus to a sports celebrity in order to add the athlete's name to the partnership. A bonus to a new partner may also result when recorded book values on the partnership books are higher than their market values.

A bonus to a new partner results in a **decrease in the capital balances of the old partners. The amount of the decrease for each partner is based on the income ratios before the admission of the new partner.** To illustrate, assume that Lea Eden invests $20,000 in cash for a 25% ownership interest in the Bart–Cohen partnership. The computations for Eden's capital credit and the bonus are as follows, using the four procedures described in the preceding section.

Illustration 12A-5
Computation of capital credit and bonus to new partner

1. Total capital of Bart–Cohen partnership		$120,000
Investment by new partner, Eden		20,000
Total capital of new partnership		$140,000
2. **Eden's capital credit** (25% × $140,000)		**$ 35,000**
3. **Bonus to Eden** ($35,000 − $20,000)		**$ 15,000**
4. Allocation of bonus to old partners:		
Bart ($15,000 × 60%)	$9,000	
Cohen ($15,000 × 40%)	6,000	$ 15,000

The partnership records the admission of Eden as follows:

A	=	L	+	OE
+20,000				
				−9,000
				−6,000
				+35,000

Cash Flows
+20,000

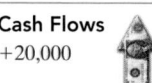

Cash	20,000	
Sam Bart, Capital	9,000	
Tom Cohen, Capital	6,000	
Lea Eden, Capital		35,000
(To record Eden's admission and bonus)		

Withdrawal of a Partner

STUDY OBJECTIVE 7

Describe the effects of the entries when a partner withdraws from the firm.

Now let's look at the opposite situation—the withdrawal of a partner. A partner may withdraw from a partnership **voluntarily**, by selling his or her equity in the firm. Or, he or she may withdraw **involuntarily**, by reaching mandatory retirement age or by dying. The withdrawal of a partner, like the admission of a partner, legally dissolves the partnership. The legal effects may be recognized by dissolving the firm. However, it is customary to record only the economic effects of the partner's withdrawal, while the firm continues to operate and reorganizes itself legally.

As indicated earlier, the partnership agreement should specify the terms of withdrawal. As Illustration 12A-6 shows, the withdrawal of a partner may be accomplished by (1) payment from partners' personal assets or (2) payment from partnership assets. The former affects only the partners' capital accounts. The latter decreases total net assets and total capital of the partnership.

Illustration 12A-6
Procedures in partnership withdrawal

Withdrawal of Partner through:

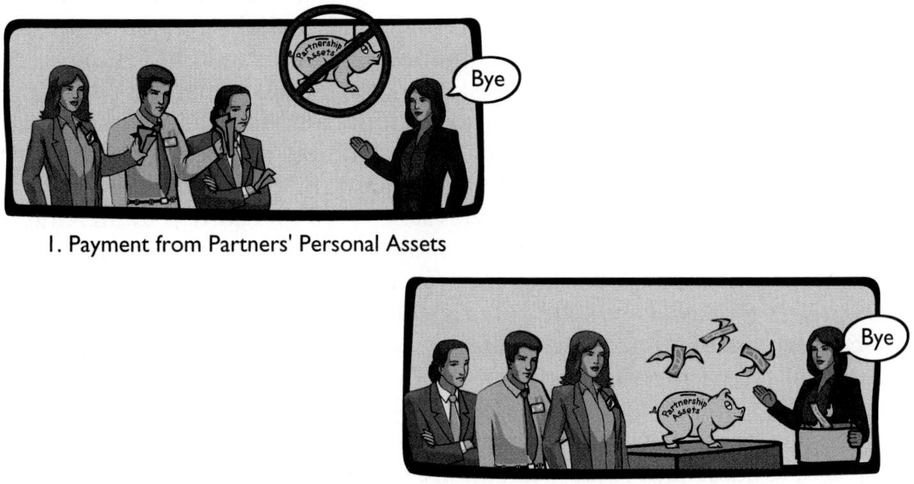

1. Payment from Partners' Personal Assets

2. Payment from Partnership Assets

PAYMENT FROM PARTNERS' PERSONAL ASSETS

Withdrawal by payment from partners' personal assets is a personal transaction between the partners. **It is the direct opposite of admitting a new partner who purchases a partner's interest.** The remaining partners pay the retiring partner directly from their personal assets. **Partnership assets are not involved in any way, and total capital does not change.** The effect on the partnership is limited to changes in the partners' capital balances.

To illustrate, assume that partners Morz, Nead, and Odom have capital balances of $25,000, $15,000, and $10,000, respectively. Morz and Nead agree to buy out Odom's interest. Each of them agrees to pay Odom $8,000 in exchange for one-half of Odom's total interest of $10,000. The entry to record the withdrawal is:

J. Odom, Capital	10,000	
A. Morz, Capital		5,000
M. Nead, Capital		5,000
(To record purchase of Odom's interest)		

A	=	L	+	OE
				−10,000
				+5,000
				+5,000

Cash Flows
no effect

The effect of this entry on the partnership accounts is shown below.

Net Assets		A. Morz, Capital		M. Nead, Capital		J. Odom, Capital	
50, 000			25,000		15,000	**10,000**	10,000
			5,000		**5,000**		Bal. –0–
			Bal. 30,000		Bal. 20,000		

Illustration 12A-7
Ledger balances after payment from partners' personal assets

Note that net assets and total capital remain the same at $50,000.

What about the $16,000 paid to Odom? You've probably noted that it is not recorded. The entry debited Odom's capital only for $10,000, not for the $16,000 that she received. Similarly, both Morz and Nead credit their capital accounts for only $5,000, not for the $8,000 they each paid.

After Odom's withdrawal, Morz and Nead will share net income or net loss equally unless they specifically indicate another income ratio in the partnership agreement.

PAYMENT FROM PARTNERSHIP ASSETS

Withdrawal by payment from partnership assets is a transaction that involves the partnership. **Both partnership net assets and total capital decrease as a result.** Using partnership assets to pay for a withdrawing partner's interest is the **reverse** of admitting a partner through the investment of assets in the partnership.

Many partnership agreements provide that the amount paid should be based on the fair market value of the assets at the time of the partner's withdrawal. When this basis is required, some maintain that any differences between recorded asset balances and their fair market values should be (1) recorded by an adjusting entry, and (2) allocated to all partners on the basis of their income ratios. This position has serious flaws. Recording the revaluations violates the cost principle, which requires that assets be stated at original cost. It also is a departure from the going-concern assumption, which assumes the entity will continue indefinitely. The terms of the partnership contract should not dictate the accounting for this event.

In accounting for a withdrawal by payment from partnership assets, the partnership should not record asset revaluations. Instead, it should consider any difference between the amount paid and the withdrawing partner's capital balance as **a bonus** to the retiring partner or to the remaining partners.

Bonus to Retiring Partner A partnership may pay a bonus to a retiring partner when:

1. The fair market value of partnership assets is more than their book value,
2. There is unrecorded goodwill resulting from the partnership's superior earnings record, or
3. The remaining partners are eager to remove the partner from the firm.

The partnership deducts the bonus from the remaining partners' capital balances on the basis of their income ratios at the time of the withdrawal.

To illustrate, assume that the following capital balances exist in the RST partnership: Roman \$50,000, Sand \$30,000, and Terk \$20,000. The partners share income in the ratio of 3 : 2 : 1, respectively. Terk retires from the partnership and receives a cash payment of \$25,000 from the firm. The procedure for determining the bonus to the retiring partner and the allocation of the bonus to the remaining partners is as follows.

HELPFUL HINT

Compare this entry to the one on page 539.

1. **Determine the amount of the bonus:** Subtract the retiring partner's capital balance from the cash paid by the partnership. The bonus in this case is \$5,000 (\$25,000 – \$20,000).
2. **Allocate the bonus to the remaining partners on the basis of their income ratios:** The ratios of Roman and Sand are 3 : 2. Thus, the allocation of the \$5,000 bonus is: Roman \$3,000 (\$5,000 × 3/5) and Sand \$2,000 (\$5,000 × 2/5).

The partnership records the withdrawal of Terk as follows.

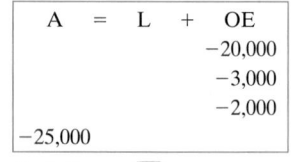

A	=	L	+	OE
				−20,000
				−3,000
				−2,000
−25,000				

Cash Flows
−25,000

B. Terk, Capital	20,000	
F. Roman, Capital	3,000	
D. Sand, Capital	2,000	
Cash		25,000
(To record withdrawal of and bonus to Terk)		

The remaining partners, Roman and Sand, will recover the bonus given to Terk as the partnership sells or uses the undervalued assets.

Bonus to Remaining Partners The retiring partner may give a bonus to the remaining partners when:

1. Recorded assets are overvalued,
2. The partnership has a poor earnings record, or
3. The partner is eager to leave the partnership.

In such cases, the cash paid to the retiring partner will be less than the retiring partner's capital balance. **The partnership allocates (credits) the bonus to the capital accounts of the remaining partners on the basis of their income ratios.**

To illustrate, assume (instead of the example above) that the partnership pays Terk only $16,000 for her $20,000 equity when she withdraws from the partnership. In that case:

1. The bonus to remaining partners is $4,000 ($20,000 − $16,000).
2. The allocation of the $4,000 bonus is: Roman $2,400 ($4,000 × 3/5) and Sand $1,600 ($4,000 × 2/5).

HELPFUL HINT
Compare this entry to the one on page 538.

Under these circumstances, the entry to record the withdrawal is:

B. Terk, Capital	20,000	
F. Roman, Capital		2,400
D. Sand, Capital		1,600
Cash		16,000
(To record withdrawal of Terk and bonus to remaining partners)		

A	=	L	+	OE
				−20,000
				+2,400
				+1,600
−16,000				

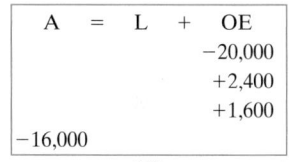

Cash Flows
−16,000

Note that if Sand had withdrawn from the partnership, Roman and Terk would divide any bonus on the basis of their income ratio, which is 3 : 1 or 75% and 25%.

DEATH OF A PARTNER

The death of a partner dissolves the partnership. But partnership agreements usually contain a provision for the surviving partners to continue operations. When a partner dies, it usually is necessary to determine the partner's equity at the date of death. This is done by (1) determining the net income or loss for the year to date, (2) closing the books, and (3) preparing financial statements. The partnership agreement may also require an independent audit of the financial statements and a revaluation of assets by an appraisal firm.

The surviving partners may agree to purchase the deceased partner's equity from their personal assets. Or they may use partnership assets to settle with the deceased partner's estate. In both instances, the entries to record the withdrawal of the partner are similar to those presented earlier.

To facilitate payment from partnership assets, some partnerships obtain life insurance policies on each partner, with the partnership named as the beneficiary. The partnership then uses the proceeds from the insurance policy on the deceased partner to settle with the estate.

SUMMARY OF STUDY OBJECTIVES FOR APPENDIX

WILEY PLUS

6 **Explain the effects of the entries when a new partner is admitted.** The entry to record the admittance of a new partner by purchase of a partner's interest affects only partners' capital accounts. The entries to record the admittance by investment of assets in the partnership (a) increase both net assets and total capital and (b) may result in recognition of a bonus to either the old partners or the new partner.

7 **Describe the effects of the entries when a partner withdraws from the firm.** The entry to record a withdrawal from the firm when the partners pay from their personal assets affects only partners' capital accounts. The entry to record a withdrawal when payment is made from partnership assets (a) decreases net assets and total capital and (b) may result in recognizing a bonus either to the retiring partner or the remaining partners.

GLOSSARY FOR APPENDIX

WILEY PLUS

Admission by investment Admission of a partner by investing assets in the partnership, causing both partnership net assets and total capital to increase. (p. 534).

Admission by purchase of an interest Admission of a partner in a personal transaction between one or more existing partners and the new partner; does not change total partnership assets or total capital. (p. 533).

Withdrawal by payment from partners' personal assets Withdrawal of a partner in a personal transaction between partners; does not change total partnership assets or total capital. (p. 537).

Withdrawal by payment from partnership assets Withdrawal of a partner in a transaction involving the partnership, causing both partnership net assets and total capital to decrease. (p. 538).

***Note:** All **asterisked** Questions, Exercises, and Problems relate to material in the appendix to the chapter.

SELF-STUDY QUESTIONS

WILEY PLUS

Answers are at the end of the chapter.

(SO 1) **1.** Which of the following is *not* a characteristic of a partnership?
- **a.** Taxable entity
- **b.** Co-ownership of property
- **c.** Mutual agency
- **d.** Limited life

(SO 1) **2.** The advantages of a partnership do *not* include:
- **a.** ease of formation.
- **b.** unlimited liability.
- **c.** freedom from government regulation.
- **d.** ease of decision making.

(SO 2) **3.** Upon formation of a partnership, each partner's initial investment of assets should be recorded at their:
- **a.** book values.
- **b.** cost.
- **c.** market values.
- **d.** appraised values.

(SO 3) **4.** The NBC Company reports net income of $60,000. If partners N, B, and C have an income ratio of 50%, 30%, and 20%, respectively, C's share of the net income is:
- **a.** $30,000.
- **b.** $12,000.
- **c.** $18,000.
- **d.** No correct answer is given.

(SO 3) **5.** Using the data in (4) above, what is B's share of net income if the percentages are applicable after each partner receives a $10,000 salary allowance?
- **a.** $12,000
- **b.** $20,000
- **c.** $19,000
- **d.** $21,000

(SO 4) **6.** Which of the following statements about partnership financial statements is true?
- **a.** Details of the distribution of net income are shown in the owners' equity statement.
- **b.** The distribution of net income is shown on the balance sheet.
- **c.** Only the total of all partner capital balances is shown in the balance sheet.
- **d.** The owners' equity statement is called the partners' capital statement.

7. In the liquidation of a partnership it is necessary to (1) distribute cash to the partners, (2) sell noncash assets, (3) allocate any gain or loss on realization to the partners, and (4) pay liabilities. These steps should be performed in the following order: (SO 5)
- **a.** (2), (3), (4), (1).
- **b.** (2), (3), (1), (4).
- **c.** (3), (2), (1), (4).
- **d.** (3), (2), (4), (1).

***8.** Louisa Santiago purchases 50% of Leo Lemon's capital interest in the K & L partnership for $22,000. If the capital balance of Kate Kildare and Leo Lemon are $40,000 and $30,000, respectively, Santiago's capital balance following the purchase is: (SO 6)
- **a.** $22,000.
- **b.** $35,000.
- **c.** $20,000.
- **d.** $15,000.

***9.** Capital balances in the MEM partnership are Mary Capital $60,000, Ellen Capital $50,000, and Mills Capital $40,000, and income ratios are 5 : 3 : 2, respectively. The MEMO partnership is formed by admitting Oleg to the firm with a cash investment of $60,000 for a 25% capital interest. The bonus to be credited to Mills Capital in admitting Oleg is: (SO 6)
- **a.** $10,000.
- **b.** $7,500.
- **c.** $3,750.
- **d.** $1,500.

***10.** Capital balances in the MURF partnership are Molly Capital $50,000, Ursula Capital $40,000, Ray Capital $30,000, and Fred Capital $20,000, and income ratios are 4 : 3 : 2 : 1, respectively. Fred withdraws from the firm following payment of $29,000 in cash from the partnership. Ursula's capital balance after recording the withdrawal of Fred is: (SO 7)
- **a.** $36,000.
- **b.** $37,000.
- **c.** $38,000.
- **d.** $40,000.

Go to the book's website,
www.wiley.com/college/weygandt,
for Additional Self-Study questions.

The Navigator

QUESTIONS

1. The characteristics of a partnership include the following: (a) association of individuals, (b) limited life, and (c) co-ownership of property. Explain each of these terms.
2. Jerry Kerwin is confused about the partnership characteristics of (a) mutual agency and (b) unlimited liability. Explain these two characteristics for Jerry.
3. Brent Houghton and Dick Kreibach are considering a business venture. They ask you to explain the advantages and disadvantages of the partnership form of organization.
4. Why might a company choose to use a limited partnership?
5. Sampson and Stevens form a partnership. Sampson contributes land with a book value of $50,000 and a fair market value of $65,000. Sampson also contributes equipment with a book value of $52,000 and a fair market value of $57,000. The partnership assumes a $20,000 mortgage on the land. What should be the balance in Sampson's capital account upon formation of the partnership?
6. W. Mantle, N. Cash, and W. DiMaggio have a partnership called Outlaws. A dispute has arisen among the partners. Mantle has invested twice as much in assets as the other two partners, and he believes net income and net losses should be shared in accordance with the capital ratios. The partnership agreement does not specify the division of profits and losses. How will net income and net loss be divided?
7. Blue and Grey are discussing how income and losses should be divided in a partnership they plan to form. What factors should be considered in determining the division of net income or net loss?
8. M. Carson and R. Leno have partnership capital balances of $40,000 and $80,000, respectively. The partnership agreement indicates that net income or net loss should be shared equally. If net income for the partnership is $36,000, how should the net income be divided?
9. S. McMurray and F. Kohl share net income and net loss equally. (a) Which account(s) is (are) debited and credited to record the division of net income between the partners? (b) If S. McMurray withdraws $30,000 in cash for personal use in lieu of salary, which account is debited and which is credited?
10. Partners T. Evans and R. Meloy are provided salary allowances of $30,000 and $25,000, respectively. They divide the remainder of the partnership income in a ratio of 60 : 40. If partnership net income is $45,000, how much is allocated to Evans and Meloy?
11. Are the financial statements of a partnership similar to those of a proprietorship? Discuss.
12. How does the liquidation of a partnership differ from the dissolution of a partnership?
13. Bobby Donal and Bill Spader are discussing the liquidation of a partnership. Bobby maintains that all cash should be distributed to partners on the basis of their income ratios. Is he correct? Explain.
14. In continuing their discussion from Question 13, Bill says that even in the case of a capital deficiency, all cash should still be distributed on the basis of capital balances. Is Bill correct? Explain.
15. Lowery, Keegan, and Feeney have income ratios of 5 : 3 : 2 and capital balances of $34,000, $31,000, and $28,000, respectively. Noncash assets are sold at a gain. After creditors are paid, $109,000 of cash is available for distribution to the partners. How much cash should be paid to Keegan?
16. Before the final distribution of cash, account balances are: Cash $23,000; S. Penn, Capital $19,000 (Cr.); L. Pattison, Capital $12,000 (Cr.); and M. Jeter, Capital $8,000 (Dr.). Jeter is unable to pay any of the capital deficiency. If the income-sharing ratios are 5 : 3 : 2, respectively, how much cash should be paid to L. Pattison?

*17. Linda Ratzlaff decides to purchase from an existing partner for $50,000 a one-third interest in a partnership. What effect does this transaction have on partnership net assets?

*18. Steve Renn decides to invest $25,000 in a partnership for a one-sixth capital interest. How much do the partnership's net assets increase? Does Renn also acquire a one-sixth income ratio through this investment?

*19. Kate Robidou purchases for $72,000 Grant's interest in the Sharon-Grant partnership. Assuming that Grant has a $66,000 capital balance in the partnership, what journal entry is made by the partnership to record this transaction?

*20. Tracy Harper has a $39,000 capital balance in a partnership. She sells her interest to Kim Remington for $45,000 cash. What entry is made by the partnership for this transaction?

*21. Debbie Perry retires from the partnership of Garland, Newlin, and Perry. She receives $85,000 of partnership assets in settlement of her capital balance of $77,000. Assuming that the income-sharing ratios are 5 : 3 : 2, respectively, how much of Perry's bonus is debited to Newlin's capital account?

*22. Your roommate argues that partnership assets should be revalued in situations like those in question 21. Why is this generally not done?

*23. How is a deceased partner's equity determined?

BRIEF EXERCISES

WILEY PLUS

BE12-1 Jennifer DeVine and Stanley Farrin decide to organize the ALL-Star partnership. DeVine invests $15,000 cash, and Farrin contributes $10,000 cash and equipment having a book value of $3,500. Prepare the entry to record Farrin's investment in the partnership, assuming the equipment has a fair market value of $5,000.

Journalize entries in forming a partnership.

(SO 2)

Prepare portion of opening balance sheet for partnership. (SO 2)

BE12-2 Beck and Cey decide to merge their proprietorships into a partnership called Fresh Start Company. The balance sheet of Cey Co. shows:

Accounts receivable	$16,000	
Less: Allowance for doubtful accounts	1,200	$14,800
Equipment	20,000	
Less: Accumulated depreciation	7,000	13,000

The partners agree that the net realizable value of the receivables is $13,500 and that the fair market value of the equipment is $11,000. Indicate how the four accounts should appear in the opening balance sheet of the partnership.

Journalize the division of net income using fixed income ratios. (SO 3)

BE12-3 Held Bond Co. reports net income of $70,000. The income ratios are Held 60% and Bond 40%. Indicate the division of net income to each partner, and prepare the entry to distribute the net income.

Compute division of net income with a salary allowance and fixed ratios. (SO 3)

BE12-4 ESU Co. reports net income of $55,000. Partner salary allowances are Espino $15,000, Sears $5,000, and Utech $5,000. Indicate the division of net income to each partner, assuming the income ratio is 50 : 30 : 20, respectively.

Show division of net income when allowances exceed net income. (SO 3)

BE12-5 Joe & Sam Co. reports net income of $28,000. Interest allowances are Joe $7,000 and Sam $5,000; salary allowances are Joe $15,000 and Sam $10,000; the remainder is shared equally. Show the distribution of income on the income statement.

Journalize final cash distribution in liquidation. (SO 5)

BE12-6 After liquidating noncash assets and paying creditors, account balances in the Heartley Co. are Cash $19,000, A Capital (Cr.) $8,000, L Capital (Cr.) $7,000, and F Capital (Cr.) $4,000. The partners share income equally. Journalize the final distribution of cash to the partners.

Journalize admission by purchase of an interest. (SO 6)

***BE12-7** In Alpha Co. capital balances are: Ace $30,000, Bly $25,000, and Cox $20,000. The partners share income equally. Day is admitted to the firm by purchasing one-half of Cox's interest for $13,000. Journalize the admission of Day to the partnership.

Journalize admission by investment. (SO 6)

***BE12-8** In Decker Co., capital balances are Menke $40,000 and Hibbett $50,000. The partners share income equally. Kosko is admitted to the firm with a 45% interest by an investment of cash of $52,000. Journalize the admission of Kosko.

Journalize withdrawal paid by personal assets. (SO 7)

***BE12-9** Capital balances in Midway Co. are Messer $40,000, Isch $30,000, and Denny $18,000. Messer and Isch each agree to pay Denny $12,000 from their personal assets. Messer and Isch each receive 50% of Denny's equity. The partners share income equally. Journalize the withdrawal of Denny.

Journalize withdrawal paid by partnership assets. (SO 7)

***BE12-10** Data pertaining to Midway Co. are presented in BE12-9. Instead of payment from personal assets, assume that Denny receives $24,000 from partnership assets in withdrawing from the firm. Journalize the withdrawal of Denny.

EXERCISES

WILEY PLUS

Identify characteristics of partnership. (SO 1)

E12-1 Shani Davis has prepared the following list of statements about partnerships.

1. A partnership is an association of three or more persons to carry on as co-owners of a business for profit.
2. The legal requirements for forming a partnership can be quite burdensome.
3. A partnership is not an entity for financial reporting purposes.
4. The net income of a partnership is taxed as a separate entity.
5. The act of any partner is binding on all other partners, even when partners perform business acts beyond the scope of their authority.
6. Each partner is personally and individually liable for all partnership liabilities.
7. When a partnership is dissolved, the assets legally revert to the original contributor.
8. In a limited partnership, one or more partners have unlimited liability and one or more partners have limited liability for the debts of the firm.
9. Mutual agency is a major advantage of the partnership form of business.

Instructions

Identify each statement on page 542 as true or false. If false, indicate how to correct the statement.

E12-2 K. Meissner, S. Cohen, and E. Hughes are forming a partnership. Meissner is transferring $50,000 of personal cash to the partnership. Cohen owns land worth $15,000 and a small building worth $80,000, which she transfers to the partnership. Hughes transfers to the partnership cash of $9,000, accounts receivable of $32,000 and equipment worth $19,000. The partnership expects to collect $29,000 of the accounts receivable.

Journalize entry for formation of a partnership.

(SO 2)

Instructions

(a) Prepare the journal entries to record each of the partners' investments.
(b) What amount would be reported as total owners' equity immediately after the investments?

E12-3 Jack Herington has owned and operated a proprietorship for several years. On January 1, he decides to terminate this business and become a partner in the firm of Herington and Kaspar. Herington's investment in the partnership consists of $12,000 in cash, and the following assets of the proprietorship: accounts receivable $14,000 less allowance for doubtful accounts of $2,000, and equipment $20,000 less accumulated depreciation of $4,000. It is agreed that the allowance for doubtful accounts should be $3,000 for the partnership. The fair market value of the equipment is $13,500.

Journalize entry for formation of a partnership.

(SO 2)

Instructions

Journalize Herington's admission to the firm of Kaspar and Herington.

E12-4 F. Calvert and G. Powers have capital balances on January 1 of $50,000 and $40,000, respectively. The partnership income-sharing agreement provides for (1) annual salaries of $20,000 for Calvert and $12,000 for Powers, (2) interest at 10% on beginning capital balances, and (3) remaining income or loss to be shared 60% by Calvert and 40% by Powers.

Prepare schedule showing distribution of net income and closing entry.

(SO 3)

Instructions

(a) Prepare a schedule showing the distribution of net income, assuming net income is (1) $50,000 and (2) $36,000.
(b) Journalize the allocation of net income in each of the situations above.

E12-5 O. Guillen (beginning capital, $60,000) and K. Williams (beginning capital $90,000) are partners. During 2008, the partnership earned net income of $70,000, and Guillen made drawings of $18,000 while Williams made drawings of $24,000.

Prepare journal entries to record allocation of net income.

(SO 3)

Instructions

(a) Assume the partnership income-sharing agreement calls for income to be divided 45% to Guillen and 55% to Williams. Prepare the journal entry to record the allocation of net income.
(b) Assume the partnership income-sharing agreement calls for income to be divided with a salary of $30,000 to Guillen and $25,000 to Williams, with the remainder divided 45% to Guillen and 55% to Williams. Prepare the journal entry to record the allocation of net income.
(c) Assume the partnership income-sharing agreement calls for income to be divided with a salary of $40,000 to Guillen and $35,000 to Williams, interest of 10% on beginning capital, and the remainder divided 50%–50%. Prepare the journal entry to record the allocation of net income.
(d) Compute the partners' ending capital balances under the assumption in part (c).

E12-6 For Starrite Co., beginning capital balances on January 1, 2008, are Gary Stark $20,000 and Jim Nyland $18,000. During the year, drawings were Stark $8,000 and Nyland $5,000. Net income was $30,000, and the partners share income equally.

Prepare partners' capital statement and partial balance sheet.

(SO 4)

Instructions

(a) Prepare the partners' capital statement for the year.
(b) Prepare the owners' equity section of the balance sheet at December 31, 2008.

E12-7 Moe, Larry, and Curly are forming The Stooges Partnership. Moe is transferring $30,000 of personal cash and equipment worth $25,000 to the partnership. Larry owns land worth $18,000 and a small building worth $75,000, which he transfers to the partnership. There is a long-term mortgage of $20,000 on the land and building, which the partnership assumes. Curly transfers cash of $7,000, accounts receivable of $36,000, supplies worth $3,000, and equipment worth $22,000 to the partnership. The partnership expects to collect $32,000 of the accounts receivable.

Prepare a classified balance sheet of a partnership.

(SO 4)

Instructions
Prepare a classified balance sheet for the partnership after the partners' investments on December 31, 2008.

Prepare cash distribution schedule.
(SO 5)

E12-8 The Best Company at December 31 has cash $20,000, noncash assets $100,000, liabilities $55,000, and the following capital balances: Rodriguez $45,000 and Escobedo $20,000. The firm is liquidated, and $110,000 in cash is received for the noncash assets. Rodriguez and Escobedo income ratios are 60% and 40%, respectively.

Instructions
Prepare a cash distribution schedule.

Journalize transactions in a liquidation.
(SO 5)

E12-9 Data for The Best partnership are presented in E12-8.

Instructions
Prepare the entries to record:

(a) The sale of noncash assets.
(b) The allocation of the gain or loss on liquidation to the partners.
(c) Payment of creditors.
(d) Distribution of cash to the partners.

Journalize transactions with a capital deficiency.
(SO 5)

E12-10 Prior to the distribution of cash to the partners, the accounts in the NJF Company are: Cash $28,000, Newell Capital (Cr.) $17,000, Jennings Capital (Cr.) $15,000, and Farley Capital (Dr.) $4,000. The income ratios are 5 : 3 : 2, respectively.

Instructions
(a) Prepare the entry to record (1) Farley's payment of $4,000 in cash to the partnership and (2) the distribution of cash to the partners with credit balances.
(b) Prepare the entry to record (1) the absorption of Farley's capital deficiency by the other partners and (2) the distribution of cash to the partners with credit balances.

Journalize admission of a new partner by purchase of an interest.
(SO 6)

***E12-11** J. Lynn, M. Oller, and F. Tate share income on a 5 : 3 : 2 basis. They have capital balances of $30,000, $26,000, and $18,000, respectively, when Doc Duran is admitted to the partnership.

Instructions
Prepare the journal entry to record the admission of Doc Duran under each of the following assumptions.

(a) Purchase of 50% of Lynn's equity for $19,000.
(b) Purchase of 50% of Oller's equity for $12,000.
(c) Purchase of 33⅓% of Tate's equity for $9,000.

Journalize admission of a new partner by investment.
(SO 6)

***E12-12** G. Olde and R. Young share income on a 6 : 4 basis. They have capital balances of $100,000 and $70,000, respectively, when K. Twener is admitted to the partnership.

Instructions
Prepare the journal entry to record the admission of K. Twener under each of the following assumptions.

(a) Investment of $90,000 cash for a 30% ownership interest with bonuses to the existing partners.
(b) Investment of $50,000 cash for a 30% ownership interest with a bonus to the new partner.

Journalize withdrawal of a partner with payment from partners' personal assets.
(SO 7)

***E12-13** B. Cates, V. Elder, and S. Nguyen have capital balances of $50,000, $40,000, and $32,000, respectively. Their income ratios are 5 : 3 : 2. Nguyen withdraws from the partnership under each of the following independent conditions.

1. Cates and Elder agree to purchase Nguyen's equity by paying $17,000 each from their personal assets. Each purchaser receives 50% of Nguyen's equity.
2. Elder agrees to purchase all of Nguyen's equity by paying $22,000 cash from her personal assets.
3. Cates agrees to purchase all of Nguyen's equity by paying $26,000 cash from her personal assets.

Instructions
Journalize the withdrawal of Nguyen under each of the assumptions above.

***E12-14** H. Barrajas, T. Dingler, and R. Fisk have capital balances of $95,000, $75,000, and $60,000, respectively. They share income or loss on a 5 : 3 : 2 basis. Fisk withdraws from the partnership under each of the following conditions.

Journalize withdrawal of a partner with payment from partnership assets.

(SO 7)

1. Fisk is paid $68,000 in cash from partnership assets, and a bonus is granted to the retiring partner.
2. Fisk is paid $56,000 in cash from partnership assets, and bonuses are granted to the remaining partners.

Instructions

Journalize the withdrawal of Fisk under each of the assumptions above.

***E12-15** Carson, Letterman, and O'Brien are partners who share profits and losses 50%, 30%, and 20%, respectively. Their capital balances are $100,000, $60,000, and $40,000, respectively.

Journalize entry for admission and withdrawal of partners.

(SO 6, 7)

Instructions

(a) Assume Stewart joins the partnership by investing $80,000 for a 25% interest with bonuses to the existing partners. Prepare the journal entry to record his investment.

(b) Assume instead that Carson leaves the partnership. Carson is paid $120,000 with a bonus to the retiring partner. Prepare the journal entry to record Carson's withdrawal.

EXERCISES: SET B

Visit the book's website at **www.wiley.com/college/weygandt**, and choose the Student Companion site, to access Exercise Set B.

PROBLEMS: SET A

P12-1A The post-closing trial balances of two proprietorships on January 1, 2008, are presented below.

Prepare entries for formation of a partnership and a balance sheet.

(SO 2, 4)

GLS Peachtree

	Patrick Company		Samuelson Company	
	Dr.	Cr.	Dr.	Cr.
Cash	$ 14,000		$12,000	
Accounts receivable	17,500		26,000	
Allowance for doubtful accounts		$ 3,000		$ 4,400
Merchandise inventory	26,500		18,400	
Equipment	45,000		29,000	
Accumulated depreciation—equipment		24,000		11,000
Notes payable		18,000		15,000
Accounts payable		22,000		31,000
Patrick, Capital		36,000		
Samuelson, Capital				24,000
	$103,000	$103,000	$85,400	$85,400

Patrick and Samuelson decide to form a partnership, Pasa Company, with the following agreed upon valuations for noncash assets.

	Patrick Company	Samuelson Company
Accounts receivable	$17,500	$26,000
Allowance for doubtful accounts	4,500	4,000
Merchandise inventory	28,000	20,000
Equipment	23,000	16,000

All cash will be transferred to the partnership, and the partnership will assume all the liabilities of the two proprietorships. Further, it is agreed that Patrick will invest an additional $5,000 in cash, and Samuelson will invest an additional $19,000 in cash.

(a) Patrick, Capital $38,000 Samuelson, Capital $24,000

(c) Total assets $172,000

Instructions

(a) Prepare separate journal entries to record the transfer of each proprietorship's assets and liabilities to the partnership.
(b) Journalize the additional cash investment by each partner.
(c) Prepare a balance sheet for the partnership on January 1, 2008.

Journalize divisions of net income and prepare a partners' capital statement.

(SO 3, 4)

P12-2A At the end of its first year of operations on December 31, 2008, CNU Company's accounts show the following.

Partner	Drawings	Capital
Reese Caplin	$23,000	$48,000
Phyllis Newell	14,000	30,000
Betty Uhrich	10,000	25,000

The capital balance represents each partner's initial capital investment. Therefore, net income or net loss for 2008 has not been closed to the partners' capital accounts.

(a) (1) Caplin $18,000
(2) Caplin $19,000
(3) Caplin $15,700

(c) Caplin $40,700

Instructions

(a) Journalize the entry to record the division of net income for the year 2008 under each of the following independent assumptions.
(1) Net income is $30,000. Income is shared 6 : 3 : 1.
(2) Net income is $37,000. Caplin and Newell are given salary allowances of $15,000 and $10,000, respectively. The remainder is shared equally.
(3) Net income is $19,000. Each partner is allowed interest of 10% on beginning capital balances. Caplin is given a $12,000 salary allowance. The remainder is shared equally.
(b) Prepare a schedule showing the division of net income under assumption (3) above.
(c) Prepare a partners' capital statement for the year under assumption (3) above.

Prepare entries with a capital deficiency in liquidation of a partnership.

(SO 5)

GLS Peachtree

P12-3A The partners in New Yorker Company decide to liquidate the firm when the balance sheet shows the following.

NEW YORKER COMPANY
Balance Sheet
May 31, 2008

Assets		Liabilities and Owners' Equity	
Cash	$ 27,500	Notes payable	$ 13,500
Accounts receivable	25,000	Accounts payable	27,000
Allowance for doubtful accounts	(1,000)	Wages payable	4,000
Merchandise inventory	34,500	M. Mantle, Capital	33,000
Equipment	21,000	W. Mays, Capital	21,000
Accumulated depreciation—equipment	(5,500)	D. Snider, Capital	3,000
Total	$101,500	Total	$101,500

The partners share income and loss 5 : 3 : 2. During the process of liquidation, the following transactions were completed in the following sequence.

1. A total of $55,000 was received from converting noncash assets into cash.
2. Liabilities were paid in full.
3. D. Snider paid his capital deficiency.
4. Cash was paid to the partners with credit balances.

(a) Loss on realization $19,000
Cash paid: to Mantle $23,500; to Mays $15,300

Instructions

(a) Prepare the entries to record the transactions.
(b) Post to the cash and capital accounts.
(c) Assume that Snider is unable to pay the capital deficiency.
(1) Prepare the entry to allocate Snider's debit balance to Mantle and Mays.
(2) Prepare the entry to record the final distribution of cash.

Journalize admission of a partner under different assumptions.

(SO 6)

***P12-4A** At April 30, partners' capital balances in SKG Company are: S. Seger $52,000, J. Kensington $54,000, and T. Gomez $18,000. The income sharing ratios are 5:4:1, respectively. On May 1, the SKGA Company is formed by admitting D. Atchley to the firm as a partner.

Instructions

(a) Journalize the admission of Atchley under each of the following independent assumptions.

(1) Atchley purchases 50% of Gomez's ownership interest by paying Gomez $16,000 in cash.

(2) Atchley purchases 33⅓% of Kensington's ownership interest by paying Kensington $15,000 in cash.

(3) Atchley invests $66,000 for a 30% ownership interest, and bonuses are given to the old partners.

(4) Atchley invests $46,000 for a 30% ownership interest, which includes a bonus to the new partner.

(b) Kensington's capital balance is $32,000 after admitting Atchley to the partnership by investment. If Kensington's ownership interest is 20% of total partnership capital, what were (1) Atchley's cash investment and (2) the bonus to the new partner?

(a) (1) Atchley $9,000
(2) Atchley $18,000
(3) Atchley $57,000
(4) Atchley $51,000

***P12-5A** On December 31, the capital balances and income ratios in FAD Company are as follows.

Journalize withdrawal of a partner under different assumptions.

(SO 7)

Partner	Capital Balance	Income Ratio
J. Fagan	$60,000	50%
P. Ames	40,000	30%
K. Durham	26,000	20%

Instructions

(a) Journalize the withdrawal of Durham under each of the following assumptions.

(1) Each of the continuing partners agrees to pay $18,000 in cash from personal funds to purchase Durham's ownership equity. Each receives 50% of Durham's equity.

(2) Ames agrees to purchase Durham's ownership interest for $25,000 cash.

(3) Durham is paid $34,000 from partnership assets, which includes a bonus to the retiring partner.

(4) Durham is paid $22,000 from partnership assets, and bonuses to the remaining partners are recognized.

(b) If Ames's capital balance after Durham's withdrawal is $42,400 what were (1) the total bonus to the remaining partners and (2) the cash paid by the partnership to Durham?

(a) (1) Ames, Capital $13,000
(2) Ames, Capital $26,000
(3) Bonus $8,000
(4) Bonus $4,000

PROBLEMS: SET B

P12-1B The post-closing trial balances of two proprietorships on January 1, 2008, are presented below.

Prepare entries for formation of a partnership and a balance sheet.

(SO 2, 4)

GLS

	Free Company		Will Company	
	Dr.	**Cr.**	**Dr.**	**Cr.**
Cash	$ 9,500		$ 6,000	
Accounts receivable	15,000		23,000	
Allowance for doubtful accounts		$ 2,500		$ 4,000
Merchandise inventory	28,000		17,000	
Equipment	50,000		30,000	
Accumulated depreciation—equipment		24,000		13,000
Notes payable		25,000		
Accounts payable		20,000		37,000
Free, Capital		31,000		
Will, Capital				22,000
	$102,500	$102,500	$76,000	$76,000

Free and Will decide to form a partnership, Free-Will Company, with the following agreed upon valuations for noncash assets.

	Free Company	Will Company
Accounts receivable	$15,000	$23,000
Allowance for doubtful accounts	3,500	5,000
Merchandise inventory	32,000	21,000
Equipment	28,000	18,000

All cash will be transferred to the partnership, and the partnership will assume all the liabilities of the two proprietorships. Further, it is agreed that Free will invest an additional $3,000 in cash, and Will will invest an additional $13,000 in cash.

Instructions

(a) Free, Capital $36,000 Will, Capital $26,000

(c) Total assets $160,000

(a) Prepare separate journal entries to record the transfer of each proprietorship's assets and liabilities to the partnership.
(b) Journalize the additional cash investment by each partner.
(c) Prepare a balance sheet for the partnership on January 1, 2008.

Journalize divisions of net income and prepare a partners' capital statement.

(SO 3, 4)

P12-2B At the end of its first year of operations on December 31, 2008, the RAF Company's accounts show the following.

Partner	Drawings	Capital
J. Reno	$12,000	$33,000
L. Augustine	9,000	20,000
J. Fritz	4,000	10,000

The capital balance represents each partner's initial capital investment. Therefore, net income or net loss for 2008 has not been closed to the partners' capital accounts.

Instructions

(a) (1) Reno $20,000 (2) Reno $14,000 (3) Reno $22,200

(c) Reno $43,200

(a) Journalize the entry to record the division of net income for 2008 under each of the following independent assumptions.
   (1) Net income is $40,000. Income is shared 5:3:2.
   (2) Net income is $30,000. Reno and Augustine are given salary allowances of $11,000 and $10,000, respectively. The remainder is shared equally.
   (3) Net income is $27,000. Each partner is allowed interest of 10% on beginning capital balances. Reno is given an $18,000 salary allowance. The remainder is shared equally.
(b) Prepare a schedule showing the division of net income under assumption (3) above.
(c) Prepare a partners' capital statement for the year under assumption (3) above.

Prepare entries and schedule of cash payments in liquidation of a partnership

(SO 5)

P12-3B The partners in Shawnee Company decide to liquidate the firm when the balance sheet shows the following.

SHAWNEE COMPANY
Balance Sheet
April 30, 2008

Assets		Liabilities and Owners' Equity	
Cash	$28,000	Notes payable	$16,000
Accounts receivable	19,000	Accounts payable	24,000
Allowance for doubtful accounts	(1,000)	Wages payable	2,000
Merchandise inventory	28,000	Neeley, Capital	23,000
Equipment	17,000	Hannah, Capital	11,200
Accumulated depreciation—equipment	(10,000)	Doonan, Capital	4,800
Total	$81,000	Total	$81,000

The partners share income and loss 5:3:2. During the process of liquidation, the transactions below were completed in the following sequence.

1. A total of $43,000 was received from converting noncash assets into cash.
2. Liabilities were paid in full.
3. Cash was paid to the partners with credit balances.

Instructions

(a) Loss on realization $10,000 Cash paid: to Neeley $18,000; to Doonan $2,800

(a) Prepare a cash distribution schedule.
(b) Prepare the entries to record the transactions.
(c) Post to the cash and capital accounts.

Journalize admission of a partner under different assumptions.

(SO 6)

***P12-4B** At April 30, partners' capital balances in ANR Company are: Alexander $49,000. Norrison $26,000, and Rothlisberger $24,000. The income-sharing ratios are 5:3:2, respectively. On May 1, the ANRW Company is formed by admitting Wamser to the firm as a partner.

Instructions

(a) Journalize the admission of Wamser under each of the following independent assumptions.

(1) Wamser purchases 50% of Rothlisberger's ownership interest by paying Rothlisberger $9,000 in cash.

(2) Wamser purchases 50% of Norrison's ownership interest by paying Norrison $15,000 in cash.

(3) Wamser invests $46,000 cash in the partnership for a 40% ownership interest that includes a bonus to the new partner.

(4) Wamser invests $30,000 in the partnership for a 20% ownership interest, and bonuses are given to the old partners.

(b) Rothlisberger's capital balance is $27,000 after admitting Wamser to the partnership by investment. If Rothlisberger's ownership interest is 15% of total partnership capital, what were (1) Wamser's cash investment and (2) the total bonus to the old partners?

(a) (1) Wamser Capital $12,000
(2) Wamser $13,000
(3) Wamser $58,000
(4) Wamser $25,800

***P12-5B** On December 31, the capital balances and income ratios in the Poker Company are as follows.

Journalize withdrawal of a partner under different assumptions.

(SO 7)

GLS

Partner	Capital Balance	Income Ratio
A. King	$70,000	60%
L. Queen	30,000	30
B. Jack	20,000	10

Instructions

(a) Journalize the withdrawal of Jack under each of the following independent assumptions.

(1) Each of the remaining partners agrees to pay $13,000 in cash from personal funds to purchase Jack's ownership equity. Each receives 50% of Jack's equity.

(2) Queen agrees to purchase Jack's ownership interest for $18,000 in cash.

(3) From partnership assets, Jack is paid $26,000, which includes a bonus to the retiring partner.

(4) Jack is paid $11,000 from partnership assets. Bonuses to the remaining partners are recognized.

(b) If Queen's capital balance after Jack's withdrawal is $32,000, what were (1) the total bonus to the remaining partners and (2) the cash paid by the partnership to Jack?

(a) (1) Queen, Capital $10,000
(2) Queen, Capital $20,000
(3) Bonus $6,000
(4) Bonus $9,000

PROBLEMS: SET C

Visit the book's website at **www.wiley.com/college/weygandt**, and choose the Student Companion site, to access Problem Set C.

CONTINUING COOKIE CHRONICLE

(*Note:* This is a continuation of the Cookie Chronicle from Chapters 1 through 11.)

CCC12 Natalie's high school friend, Katy Peterson, has been operating a bakery for approximately 18 months. Because Natalie has been so successful operating Cookie Creations, Katy would like to have Natalie become her partner. Katy believes that together they will create a thriving cookie-making business. Natalie is quite happy with her current business set-up. Up until now, she had not considered joining forces with anyone. However, Natalie thinks that it may be a good idea to establish a partnership with Katy, and decides to look into it.

Go to the book's website, www.wiley.com/college/weygandt, to see the completion of this problem.

BROADENING YOUR PERSPECTIVE

FINANCIAL REPORTING AND ANALYSIS

Exploring the Web

BYP12-1 This exercise is an introduction to the Big Four accounting firms, all of which are partnerships.

Addresses

Deloitte & Touche	**www.deloitte.com/**
Ernst & Young	**www.ey.com/**
KPMG	**www.us.kpmg.com/**
PricewaterhouseCoopers	**www.pw.com/**

or go to **www.wiley.com/college/weygandt**

Steps

1. Select a firm that is of interest to you.
2. Go to the firm's homepage.

Instructions

(a) Name two services provided by the firm.
(b) What is the firm's total annual revenue?
(c) How many clients does it service?
(d) How many people are employed by the firm?
(e) How many partners are there in the firm?

CRITICAL THINKING

Decision Making Across the Organization

BYP12-2 Richard Powers and Jane Keckley, two professionals in the finance area, have worked for Eberhart Leasing for a number of years. Eberhart Leasing is a company that leases high-tech medical equipment to hospitals. Richard and Jane have decided that, with their financial expertise, they might start their own company to provide consulting services to individuals interested in leasing equipment. One form of organization they are considering is a partnership.

If they start a partnership, each individual plans to contribute $50,000 in cash. In addition, Richard has a used IBM computer that originally cost $3,700, which he intends to invest in the partnership. The computer has a present market value of $1,500.

Although both Richard and Jane are financial wizards, they do not know a great deal about how a partnership operates. As a result, they have come to you for advice.

Instructions

With the class divided into groups, answer the following.

(a) What are the major disadvantages of starting a partnership?
(b) What type of document is needed for a partnership, and what should this document contain?
(c) Both Richard and Jane plan to work full-time in the new partnership. They believe that net income or net loss should be shared equally. However, they are wondering how they can provide compensation to Richard Powers for his additional investment of the computer. What would you tell them?
(d) Richard is not sure how the computer equipment should be reported on his tax return. What would you tell him?
(e) As indicated above, Richard and Jane have worked together for a number of years. Richard's skills complement Jane's and vice versa. If one of them dies, it will be very difficult for the other to maintain the business, not to mention the difficulty of paying the deceased partner's estate for his or her partnership interest. What would you advise them to do?

Communication Activity

BYP12-3 You are an expert in the field of forming partnerships. Daniel Ortman and Sue Stafford want to establish a partnership to start "Pasta Shop," and they are going to meet with you to discuss their plans. Prior to the meeting you will send them a memo discussing the issues they need to consider before their visit.

Instructions

Write a memo in good form to be sent to Ortman and Stafford.

Ethics Case

BYP12-4 Elizabeth and Laurie operate a beauty salon as partners who share profits and losses equally. The success of their business has exceeded their expectations; the salon is operating quite profitably. Laurie is anxious to maximize profits and schedules appointments from 8 a.m. to 6 p.m. daily, even sacrificing some lunch hours to accommodate regular customers. Elizabeth schedules her appointments from 9 a.m. to 5 p.m. and takes long lunch hours. Elizabeth regularly makes significantly larger withdrawals of cash than Laurie does, but, she says, "Laurie, you needn't worry, I never make a withdrawal without you knowing about it, so it is properly recorded in my drawing account and charged against my capital at the end of the year." Elizabeth's withdrawals to date are double Laurie's.

Instructions

(a) Who are the stakeholders in this situation?
(b) Identify the problems with Elizabeth's actions and discuss the ethical considerations of her actions.
(c) How might the partnership agreement be revised to accommodate the differences in Elizabeth's and Laurie's work and withdrawal habits?

"All About You" Activity

BYP12-5 As the **All About You** feature in this chapter (p. 530) indicates, the partnership form of organization has advantages and disadvantages. The chapter noted that different types of partnerships have been developed to minimize some of these disadvantages. Alternatively, an individual or company can choose the proprietorship or corporate form of organization.

*

Instructions

Go to two local businesses that are different, such as a restaurant, a retailer, a construction company, a professional office (dentist, doctor, etc.), and find the answers to the following questions.

(a) What form of organization do you use in your business?
(b) What do you believe are the two major advantages of this form of organization for your business?
(c) What do you believe are the two major disadvantages of this form of organization for your business?
(d) Do you believe that eventually you may choose another form of organization?
(e) Did you have someone help you form this organization (attorney, accountant, relative, etc.)?

Answers to Insight and Accounting Across the Organization Questions

?

p. 516 Limited Liability Companies Gain in Popularity

Q: Why do you think that the use of the limited liability company is gaining in popularity?

A: *The LLC is gaining in popularity because owners in such companies have limited liability for business debts even if they participate in management. As a result, the LLC form has a distinct advantage over regular partnerships. In addition, the other limited type partnerships discussed in Illustration 12-1 are restrictive as to their use. As a result, it is not surprising that limited liability companies are now often used as the form of organization when individuals want to set up a partnership.*

p. 518 How to Part Ways Nicely

Q: How can partnership conflicts be minimized and more easily resolved?

A: *First, it is important to develop a business plan that all parties agree to. Second, it is vital to have a well-thought-out partnership agreement. Third, it can be useful to set up a board of mutually agreed upon and respected advisors to consult when making critical decisions.*

p. 523 Start-Up Seeks to Share R&D Costs, and Profits

Q: What advantages does Curis achieve by forming agreements with other companies?

A: *Research and development for new pharmaceutical products can be extremely costly. In addition, product lawsuits from negative side-effects can completely wipe out a company. By forming agreements with much larger companies, Curis expands its research capabilities and legal defense resources.*

Authors' Comments on *All About You:* How Well Do You Know Your Partner? (p. 530)

The answer to this question depends in part on the cause of your friend's financial hardship. Was it bad luck, or irresponsibility? A high percentage of personal bankruptcies in the United States are the result of an inability to pay medical bills. If this was the case with your friend, then your concerns would be lessened. On the other hand, if the personal bankruptcy was the result of irresponsible spending, then perhaps your friend would not be a good person to own a business with.

If you do decide to form the business, you might need to consider a different organizational form to ensure that you do not get stuck with an undue portion of the legal liability. If limiting your legal liability is a concern, then you should investigate the option of forming a limited liability company. Under this form, you can avoid the legal liabilities of a partnership, but you can still get the benefits of partnership taxation, along with a very flexible organizational structure. This option is not available in all states, and is not allowable for certain types of businesses.

Answer to PepsiCo Review It Question 2, p. 518

Mutual agency, limited life, unlimited liability, and co-ownership of property are major characteristics of a partnership. As a company like PepsiCo becomes very large, it becomes difficult to remain as a partnership because of these factors. Unlimited liability is particularly troublesome because owners may lose not only their initial investment but also their personal assets, if those assets are needed to pay partnership creditors. Also, it is much easier to change owners of a corporation than it is to change owners in a partnership.

Answers to Self-Study Questions

1. a **2.** b **3.** c **4.** b **5.** c **6.** d **7.** a ***8.** d ***9.** d ***10.** b

Remember to go back to the Navigator box on the chapter-opening page and check off your completed work.

Chapter 13

Corporations: Organization and Capital Stock Transactions

STUDY OBJECTIVES

After studying this chapter, you should be able to:

1. Identify the major characteristics of a corporation.
2. Differentiate between paid-in capital and retained earnings.
3. Record the issuance of common stock.
4. Explain the accounting for treasury stock.
5. Differentiate preferred stock from common stock.
6. Prepare a stockholders' equity section.
7. Compute book value per share.

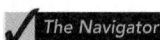

The Navigator

The Navigator

- Scan **Study Objectives**
- Read **Feature Story**
- Read **Preview**
- Read text and answer **Before You Go On**
  p. 562 p. 565 p. 568 p. 572 p. 576
- Work **Demonstration Problem**
- Review **Summary of Study Objectives**
- Answer **Self-Study Questions**
- Complete **Assignments**

Feature Story

"HAVE YOU DRIVEN A FORD LATELY?"

A company that has produced such renowned successes as the Model T and the Mustang, and such a dismal failure as the Edsel, would have some interesting tales to tell. Henry Ford was a defiant visionary from the day he formed Ford Motor Company (*www.ford.com*) in 1903. His goal from day one was to design a car he could mass-produce and sell at a price that was affordable to the masses. In short order he accomplished this goal. By 1920,

60% of all vehicles on U.S. roads were Fords.

Henry Ford was intolerant of anything that stood between him and success. In the early years Ford had issued shares to the public in order to finance the company's exponential growth. In 1916 he decided not to pay a dividend in order to increase the funds available to expand the company.

The shareholders sued. Henry Ford's reaction was swift and direct: If the shareholders didn't see things his way, he would get rid of them. In 1919 the Ford family purchased 100 percent of the outstanding shares of Ford, eliminating any outside "interference." It was over 35 years before the company again issued shares to the public.

Ford Motor Company has continued to evolve and grow over the years into one of the largest international corporations. Today there are nearly a billion shares of publicly traded Ford stock outstanding. But some aspects of the company have changed very little: The chairman and chief executive of the company is a member of the Ford family. Also, the Ford family still retains a significant stake in Ford Motor Company. In a move Henry Ford might have supported, top management recently decided to centralize decision making—that is, to have more key decisions made by top management, rather than by division managers. And, reminiscent of Henry Ford's most famous car, the company is attempting to make a "global car"—a mass-produced car that can be sold around the world with only minor changes.

✓ The Navigator

Inside Chapter 13...

Preview of Chapter 13

Corporations like Ford Motor Company have substantial resources. In fact, the corporation is the dominant form of business organization in the United States in terms of number of employees and dollar volume of sales and earnings. All of the 500 largest companies in the United States are corporations. In this chapter we will explain the essential features of a corporation and the accounting for a corporation's capital stock transactions. In Chapter 14 we will look at other issues related to accounting for corporations.

The content and organization of Chapter 13 are as follows.

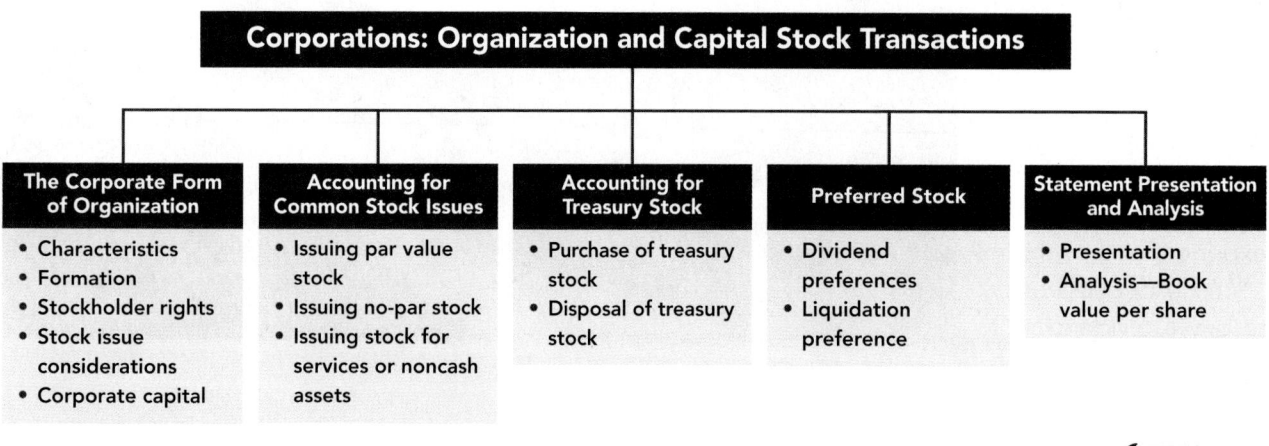

Corporations: Organization and Capital Stock Transactions

The Corporate Form of Organization
- Characteristics
- Formation
- Stockholder rights
- Stock issue considerations
- Corporate capital

Accounting for Common Stock Issues
- Issuing par value stock
- Issuing no-par stock
- Issuing stock for services or noncash assets

Accounting for Treasury Stock
- Purchase of treasury stock
- Disposal of treasury stock

Preferred Stock
- Dividend preferences
- Liquidation preference

Statement Presentation and Analysis
- Presentation
- Analysis—Book value per share

The Navigator

THE CORPORATE FORM OF ORGANIZATION

In 1819, Chief Justice John Marshall defined a corporation as "an artificial being, invisible, intangible, and existing only in contemplation of law." This definition is the foundation for the prevailing legal interpretation that a **corporation** is an **entity separate and distinct from its owners**.

A corporation is created by law, and its continued existence depends upon the statutes of the state in which it is incorporated. As a legal entity, a corporation has most of the rights and privileges of a person. The major exceptions relate to privileges that only a living person can exercise, such as the right to vote or to hold public office. A corporation is subject to the same duties and responsibilities as a person. For example, it must abide by the laws, and it must pay taxes.

Two common ways to classify corporations are by purpose and by ownership. A corporation may be organized for the purpose of making a **profit**, or it may be **not-for-profit**. For-profit corporations include such well-known companies as McDonald's, Ford Motor Company, PepsiCo, and Google. Not-for-profit corporations are organized for charitable, medical, or educational purposes. Examples are the Salvation Army, the American Cancer Society, and the Bill & Melinda Gates Foundation.

Classification by **ownership** distinguishes between publicly held and privately held corporations. A **publicly held corporation** may have thousands of stockholders. Its stock is regularly traded on a national securities exchange such as the New York Stock Exchange. Most of the largest U.S. corporations are publicly held. Examples of publicly held corporations are Intel, IBM, Caterpillar Inc., and General Electric.

ALTERNATIVE TERMINOLOGY

Privately held corporations are also referred to as *closely held corporations.*

In contrast, a **privately held corporation** usually has only a few stockholders, and does not offer its stock for sale to the general public. Privately held companies are generally much smaller than publicly held companies, although some notable exceptions exist. Cargill Inc., a private corporation that trades in grain and other commodities, is one of the largest companies in the United States.

Characteristics of a Corporation

A number of characteristics distinguish corporations from proprietorships and partnerships. We explain the most important of these characteristics below.

STUDY OBJECTIVE 1
Identify the major characteristics of a corporation.

SEPARATE LEGAL EXISTENCE

As an entity separate and distinct from its owners, the corporation acts under its own name rather than in the name of its stockholders. Ford Motor Company may buy, own, and sell property. It may borrow money, and may enter into legally binding contracts in its own name. It may also sue or be sued, and it pays its own taxes.

Remember that in a partnership the acts of the owners (partners) bind the partnership. In contrast, the acts of its owners (stockholders) do not bind the corporation unless such owners are **agents** of the corporation. For example, if you owned shares of Ford Motor Company stock, you would not have the right to purchase automobile parts for the company unless you were appointed as an agent of the company, such as a purchasing manager.

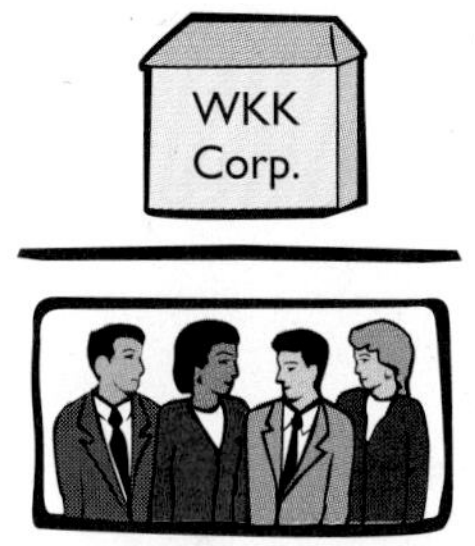

Stockholders
Legal existence separate from owners

LIMITED LIABILITY OF STOCKHOLDERS

Since a corporation is a separate legal entity, creditors have recourse only to corporate assets to satisfy their claims. The liability of stockholders is normally limited to their investment in the corporation. Creditors have no legal claim on the personal assets of the owners unless fraud has occurred. Even in the event of bankruptcy, stockholders' losses are generally limited to their capital investment in the corporation.

Stockholders
Limited liability of stockholders

TRANSFERABLE OWNERSHIP RIGHTS

Shares of capital stock give ownership in a corporation. These shares are transferable units. Stockholders may dispose of part or all of their interest in a corporation simply by selling their stock. Remember that the transfer of an ownership interest in a partnership requires the consent of each owner. In contrast, the transfer of stock is entirely at the discretion of the stockholder. It does not require the approval of either the corporation or other stockholders.

The transfer of ownership rights between stockholders normally has no effect on the daily operating activities of the corporation. Nor does it affect the corporation's assets, liabilities, and total ownership equity. The transfer of these ownership rights is a transaction between individual owners. After it first issues the capital stock, the company does not participate in such transfers.

Transferable ownership rights

ABILITY TO ACQUIRE CAPITAL

It is relatively easy for a corporation to obtain capital through the issuance of stock. Investors buy stock in a corporation to earn money over time as the share price grows, and because a stockholder has limited liability and shares of stock are readily transferable. Also, individuals can become stockholders by investing relatively small amounts of money. In sum, the ability of a successful corporation to obtain capital is virtually unlimited.

Ability to acquire capital

CONTINUOUS LIFE

The life of a corporation is stated in its charter. The life may be perpetual, or it may be limited to a specific number of years. If it is limited, the company can extend the life through renewal of the charter. Since a corporation is a separate legal entity, its

Continuous life

continuance as a going concern is not affected by the withdrawal, death, or incapacity of a stockholder, employee, or officer. As a result, a successful enterprise can have a continuous and perpetual life.

CORPORATION MANAGEMENT

As in Ford Motor Company, stockholders legally own the corporation. But they manage the corporation indirectly through a board of directors they elect. The board, in turn, formulates the operating policies for the company. The board also selects officers, such as a president and one or more vice presidents, to execute policy and to perform daily management functions.

Illustration 13-1 presents a typical organization chart showing the delegation of responsibility. The chief executive officer (CEO) has overall responsibility for managing the business. As the organization chart shows, the CEO delegates responsibility to other officers.

Illustration 13-1
Corporation organization chart

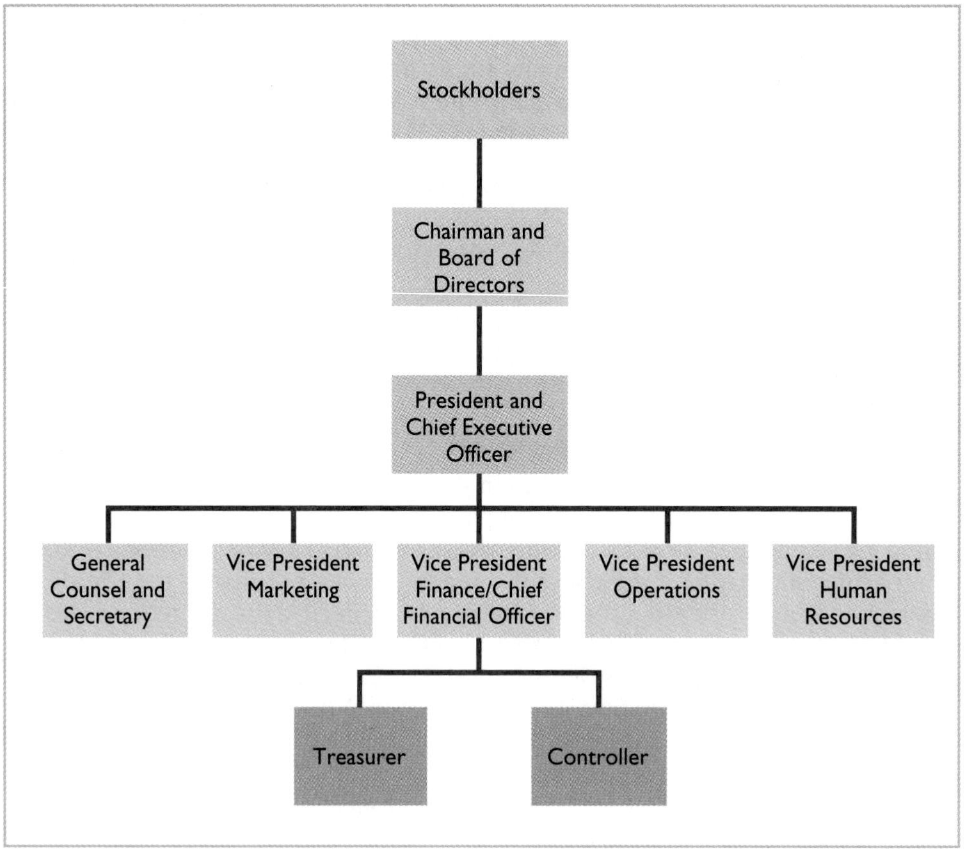

The chief accounting officer is the **controller**. The controller's responsibilities include (1) maintaining the accounting records, (2) maintaining an adequate system of internal control, and (3) preparing financial statements, tax returns, and internal reports. The **treasurer** has custody of the corporation's funds and is responsible for maintaining the company's cash position.

The organizational structure of a corporation enables a company to hire professional managers to run the business. On the other hand, the separation of ownership and management prevents owners from having an active role in managing the company, which some owners like to have.

ETHICS NOTE

Managers who are not owners are often compensated based on the performance of the firm. They thus may be tempted to exaggerate firm performance by inflating income figures.

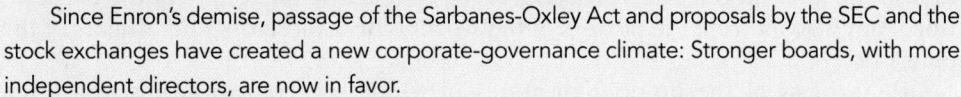

ETHICS INSIGHT

Directors Take on More Accountability

In the wake of Enron's collapse, the members of Enron's board of directors were questioned and scrutinized to determine what they knew, and when they knew it. A *Wall Street Journal* story reported that Enron's board contends it was "kept in the dark" by management and by Arthur Andersen—Enron's longtime auditors—and didn't learn about the company's troublesome accounting until October 2001. But, the *Wall Street Journal* reported that according to outside attorneys, "directors on at least two occasions waived Enron's ethical code of conduct to approve partnerships between Enron and its chief financial officer. Those partnerships kept significant debt off of Enron's books and masked actual company finances."

Since Enron's demise, passage of the Sarbanes-Oxley Act and proposals by the SEC and the stock exchanges have created a new corporate-governance climate: Stronger boards, with more independent directors, are now in favor.

Source: Carol Hymowitz, "Serving on a Board Now Means Less Talk, More Accountability," *Wall Street Journal*, January 29, 2002.

? Was Enron's board of directors fulfilling its role in a corporate organization when it waived Enron's ethical code on two occasions?

GOVERNMENT REGULATIONS

A corporation is subject to numerous state and federal regulations. State laws usually prescribe the requirements for issuing stock, the distributions of earnings permitted to stockholders, and the effects of retiring stock. Federal securities laws govern the sale of capital stock to the general public. Also, most publicly held corporations are required to make extensive disclosure of their financial affairs to the Securities and Exchange Commission (SEC) through quarterly and annual reports. In addition, when a corporation lists its stock on organized securities exchanges, it must comply with the reporting requirements of these exchanges. Government regulations are designed to protect the owners of the corporation.

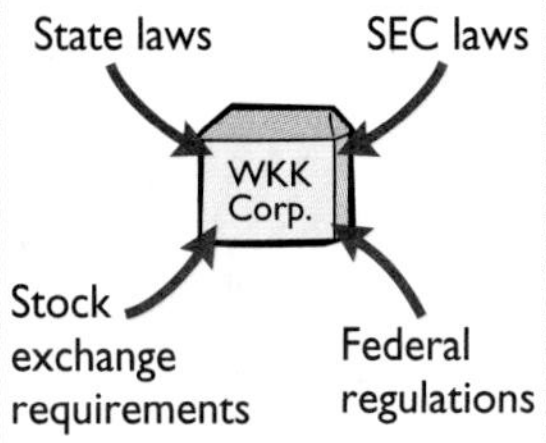

Government regulations

ADDITIONAL TAXES

Neither proprietorships nor partnerships pay income taxes separate from the owner's share of earnings. Sole proprietors and partners report earnings on their personal income tax returns and pay taxes on this amount. Corporations, on the other hand, must pay federal and state income taxes **as a separate legal entity**. These taxes are substantial.

Additional taxes

In addition, stockholders must pay taxes on cash dividends (pro rata distributions of net income). Thus, many argue that the government taxes corporate income **twice (double taxation)**—once at the corporate level, and again at the individual level.

In summary, we can identify the following advantages and disadvantages of a corporation compared to a proprietorship and a partnership.

Illustration 13-2
Advantages and disadvantages of a corporation

Advantages	Disadvantages
Separate legal existence	Corporation management—separation of ownership and management
Limited liability of stockholders	Government regulations
Transferable ownership rights	Additional taxes
Ability to acquire capital	
Continuous life	
Corporation management—professional managers	

Forming a Corporation

The initial step in forming a corporation is to file an application with the Secretary of State in the state in which incorporation is desired. The application contains such information as: (1) the name and purpose of the proposed corporation; (2) amounts, kinds, and number of shares of capital stock to be authorized; (3) the names of the incorporators; and (4) the shares of stock to which each has subscribed.

After the state approves the application, it grants a **charter**. The charter may be an approved copy of the application form, or it may be a separate document containing the same basic data. The issuance of the charter creates the corporation. Upon receipt of the charter, the corporation develops its by-laws. The **by-laws** establish the internal rules and procedures for conducting the affairs of the corporation. They also indicate the powers of the stockholders, directors, and officers of the enterprise.[1]

ALTERNATIVE TERMINOLOGY

The charter is often referred to as the *articles of incorporation.*

Regardless of the number of states in which a corporation has operating divisions, it is incorporated in only one state. It is to the company's advantage to incorporate in a state whose laws are favorable to the corporate form of business organization. General Motors, for example, is incorporated in Delaware, whereas Qualcomm is a New Jersey corporation. Many corporations choose to incorporate in states with rules favorable to existing management. For example, Gulf Oil at one time changed its state of incorporation to Delaware to thwart possible unfriendly takeovers. There, state law allows boards of directors to approve certain defensive tactics against takeovers without a vote by shareholders.

Corporations engaged in interstate commerce must also obtain a license from each state in which they do business. The license subjects the corporation's operating activities to the corporation laws of the state.

Costs incurred in the formation of a corporation are called **organization costs**. These costs include legal and state fees, and promotional expenditures involved in the organization of the business. **Corporations expense organization costs as incurred.** To determine the amount and timing of future benefits is so difficult that it is standard procedure to take a conservative approach of expensing these costs immediately.

Ownership Rights of Stockholders

When chartered, the corporation may begin selling ownership rights in the form of shares of stock. When a corporation has only one class of stock, it is **common stock**. Each share of common stock gives the stockholder the ownership rights pictured in Illustration 13-3. A corporation's articles of incorporation or its by-laws state the ownership rights of a share of stock.

Proof of stock ownership is evidenced by a form known as a **stock certificate**. As Illustration 13-4 shows, the face of the certificate shows the name of the corporation, the stockholder's name, the class and special features of the stock, the number of shares owned, and the signatures of authorized corporate officials. Prenumbered certificates facilitate accountability. They may be issued for any quantity of shares.

[1]Following approval by two-thirds of the stockholders, the by-laws become binding upon all stockholders, directors, and officers. Legally, a corporation is regulated first by the laws of the state, second by its charter, and third by its by-laws. Corporations must take care to ensure that the provisions of the by-laws are not in conflict with either state laws or the charter.

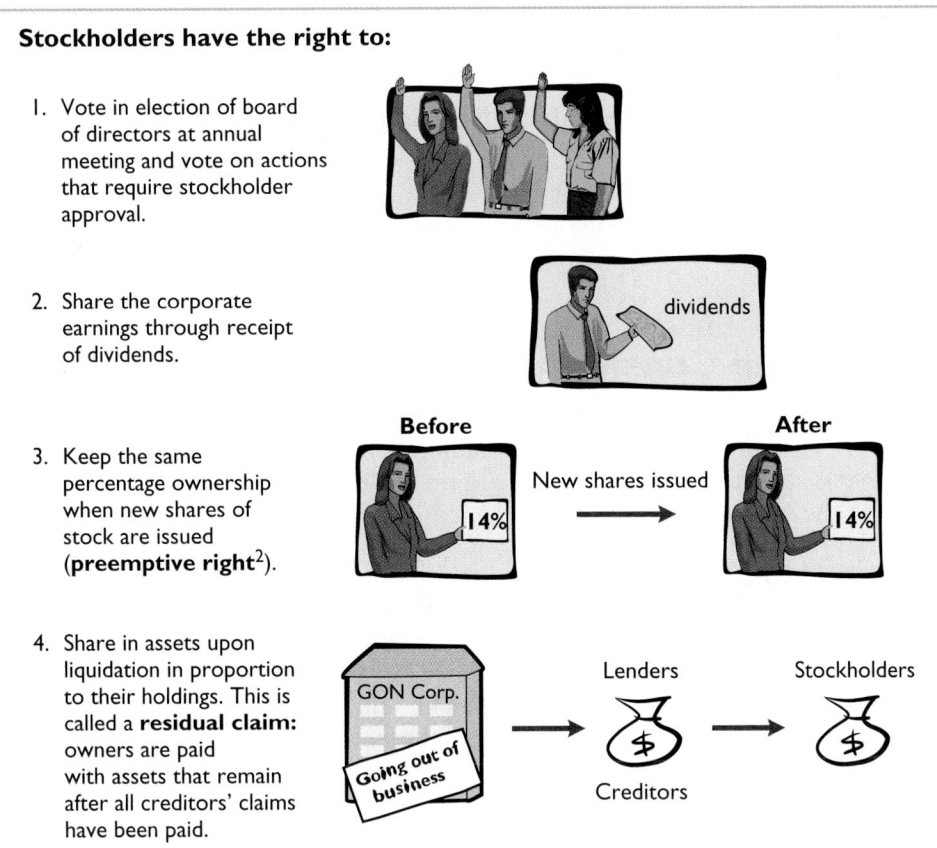

Illustration 13-3
Ownership rights of stockholders

Stockholders have the right to:

1. Vote in election of board of directors at annual meeting and vote on actions that require stockholder approval.

2. Share the corporate earnings through receipt of dividends.

3. Keep the same percentage ownership when new shares of stock are issued (**preemptive right**[2]).

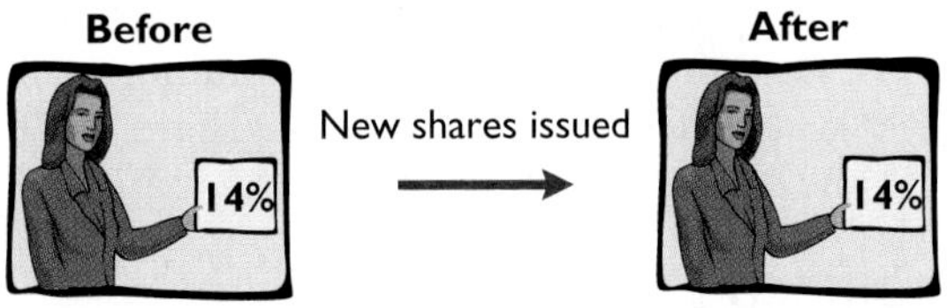

4. Share in assets upon liquidation in proportion to their holdings. This is called a **residual claim:** owners are paid with assets that remain after all creditors' claims have been paid.

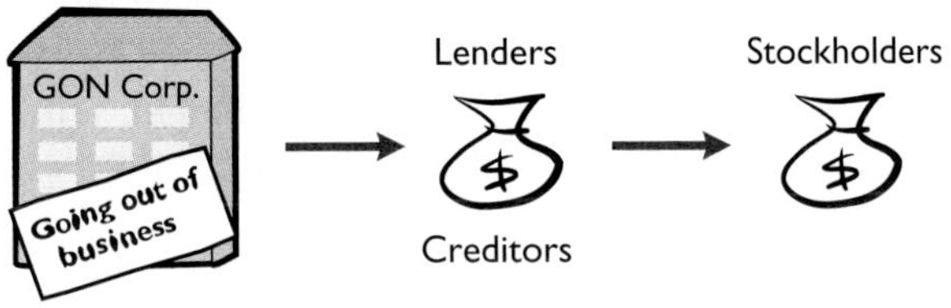

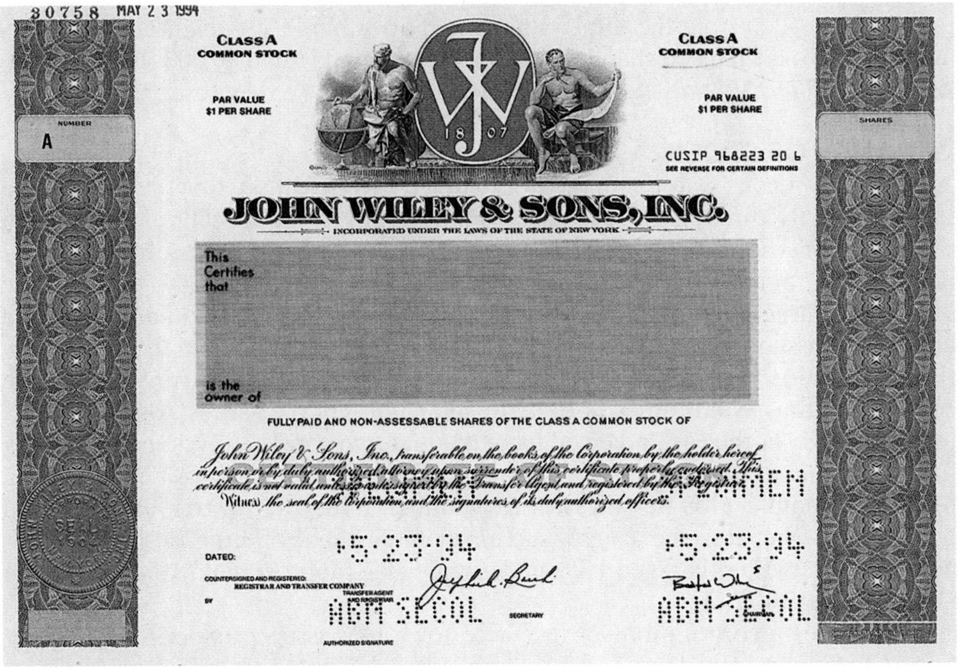

Illustration 13-4
A stock certificate

[2]A number of companies have eliminated the preemptive right, because they believe it makes an unnecessary and cumbersome demand on management. For example, by stockholder approval, IBM has dropped its preemptive right for stockholders.

Before You Go On...

REVIEW IT

1. What are the advantages and disadvantages of a corporation compared to a proprietorship and a partnership?
2. Identify the principal steps in forming a corporation.
3. What rights are inherent in owning a share of stock in a corporation?

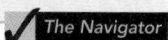

The Navigator

Stock Issue Considerations

In considering the issuance of stock, a corporation must resolve a number of basic questions: How many shares should it authorize for sale? How should it issue the stock? At what price should it issue the shares? What value should the corporation assign to the stock? These questions are addressed in the following sections.

AUTHORIZED STOCK

The charter indicates the amount of stock that a corporation is **authorized** to sell. The total amount of **authorized stock** at the time of incorporation normally anticipates both initial and subsequent capital needs. As a result, the number of shares authorized generally exceeds the number initially sold. If it sells all authorized stock, a corporation must obtain consent of the state to amend its charter before it can issue additional shares.

The authorization of capital stock does not result in a formal accounting entry. This event has no immediate effect on either corporate assets or stockholders' equity. However, the number of authorized shares is often reported in the stockholders' equity section. It is then simple to determine the number of unissued shares that the corporation can issue without amending the charter: subtract the total shares issued from the total authorized. For example, if Advanced Micro was authorized to sell 100,000 shares of common stock and issued 80,000 shares, 20,000 shares would remain unissued.

Indirect Issuance

ISSUANCE OF STOCK

A corporation can issue common stock **directly** to investors. Or it can issue the stock **indirectly** through an investment banking firm that specializes in bringing securities to market. Direct issue is typical in closely held companies. Indirect issue is customary for a publicly held corporation.

In an indirect issue, the investment banking firm may agree to **underwrite** the entire stock issue. In this arrangement, the investment banker buys the stock from the corporation at a stipulated price and resells the shares to investors. The corporation thus avoids any risk of being unable to sell the shares. Also, it obtains immediate use of the cash received from the underwriter. The investment banking firm, in turn, assumes the risk of reselling the shares, in return for an underwriting fee.[3] For example, Google (the world's number 1 Internet search engine) used underwriters when it issued a highly successful initial public offering, raising $1.67 billion. The underwriters charged a 3% underwriting fee (approximately $50 million) on Google's stock offering.

How does a corporation set the price for a new issue of stock? Among the factors to be considered are: (1) the company's anticipated future earnings, (2) its

[3] Alternatively, the investment banking firm may agree only to enter into a **best-efforts** contract with the corporation. In such cases, the banker agrees to sell as many shares as possible at a specified price. The corporation bears the risk of unsold stock. Under a best-efforts arrangement, the banking firm is paid a fee or commission for its services.

expected dividend rate per share, (3) its current financial position, (4) the current state of the economy, and (5) the current state of the securities market. The calculation can be complex and is properly the subject of a finance course.

MARKET VALUE OF STOCK

The stock of publicly held companies is traded on organized exchanges. The interaction between buyers and sellers determines the prices per share. In general, the prices set by the marketplace tend to follow the trend of a company's earnings and dividends. But, factors beyond a company's control, such as an oil embargo, changes in interest rates, and the outcome of a presidential election, may cause day-to-day fluctuations in market prices.

INVESTOR INSIGHT

How to Read Stock Quotes

The volume of trading on national and international exchanges is heavy. Shares in excess of a billion are often traded daily on the New York Stock Exchange (NYSE) alone. For each listed stock, the *Wall Street Journal* and other financial media report the total volume of stock traded for a given day, the high and low price for the day, the closing market price, and the net change for the day. A recent stock quote for PepsiCo, listed on the NYSE under the ticker symbol PEP, is shown below.

Stock	Volume	High	Low	Close	Net Change
PepsiCo	4,305,600	60.30	59.32	60.02	+0.41

These numbers indicate that PepsiCo's trading volume was 4,305,600 shares. The high, low, and closing prices for that date were $60.30, $59.32, and $60.02, respectively. The net change for the day was an increase of $0.41 per share.

? For stocks traded on organized stock exchanges, how are the dollar prices per share established? What factors might influence the price of shares in the marketplace?

The trading of capital stock on securities exchanges involves the transfer of **already issued shares** from an existing stockholder to another investor. These transactions have **no impact** on a corporation's stockholders' equity.

PAR AND NO-PAR VALUE STOCKS

Par value stock is capital stock to which the charter has assigned a value per share. Years ago, par value determined the **legal capital** per share that a company must retain in the business for the protection of corporate creditors; that amount was not available for withdrawal by stockholders. Thus, in the past, most states required the corporation to sell its shares at par or above.

However, par value was often immaterial relative to the value of the company's stock—even at the time of issue. Thus, its usefulness as a protective device to creditors was questionable. For example, Reebok's par value is $0.01 per share, yet a new issue in 2006 would have sold at a **market value** in the $33 per share range. Thus, par has no relationship with market value; in the vast majority of cases, it is an immaterial amount. As a consequence, today many states do not require a par value. Instead, they use other means to determine legal capital to protect creditors.

No-par value stock is capital stock to which the charter has not assigned a value. No-par value stock is quite common today. For example, Nike, Procter & Gamble, and North American Van Lines all have no-par stock. In many states the board of directors assigns a **stated value** to no-par shares.

Corporate Capital

STUDY OBJECTIVE 2

Differentiate between paid-in capital and retained earnings.

Owners' equity is identified by various names: **stockholders' equity**, **shareholders' equity**, or **corporate capital**. The stockholders' equity section of a corporation's balance sheet consists of two parts: (1) paid-in (contributed) capital and (2) retained earnings (earned capital).

The distinction between **paid-in capital** and **retained earnings** is important from both a legal and a financial point of view. Legally, corporations can make distributions of earnings (declare dividends) out of retained earnings in all states. However, in many states they cannot declare dividends out of paid-in capital. Management, stockholders, and others often look to retained earnings for the continued existence and growth of the corporation.

PAID-IN CAPITAL

Paid-in capital is the total amount of cash and other assets paid in to the corporation by stockholders in exchange for capital stock. As noted earlier, when a corporation has only one class of stock, it is **common stock**.

RETAINED EARNINGS

Retained earnings is net income that a corporation retains for future use. Net income is recorded in Retained Earnings by a closing entry that debits Income Summary and credits Retained Earnings. For example, assuming that net income for Delta Robotics in its first year of operations is $130,000, the closing entry is:

A	=	L	+	SE
				−130,000 Inc
				+130,000 RE

Cash Flows
no effect

Income Summary	130,000	
Retained Earnings		130,000
(To close Income Summary and transfer net income to retained earnings)		

If Delta Robotics has a balance of $800,000 in common stock at the end of its first year, its stockholders' equity section is as follows.

Illustration 13-5
Stockholders' equity section

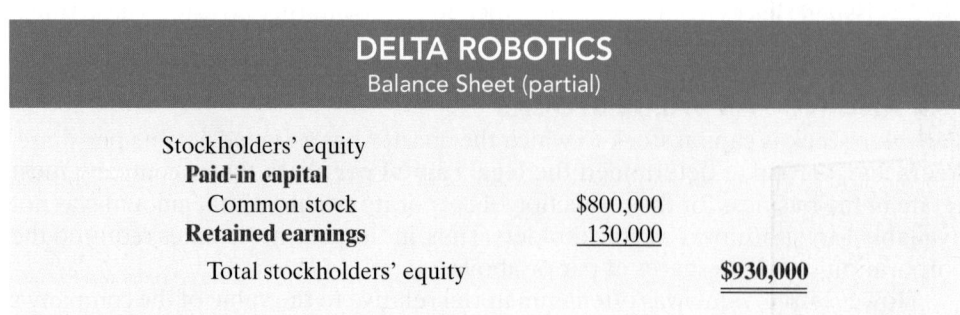

DELTA ROBOTICS
Balance Sheet (partial)

Stockholders' equity		
Paid-in capital		
Common stock	$800,000	
Retained earnings	130,000	
Total stockholders' equity		**$930,000**

The following illustration compares the owners' equity (stockholders' equity) accounts reported on a balance sheet for a proprietorship, a partnership, and a corporation.

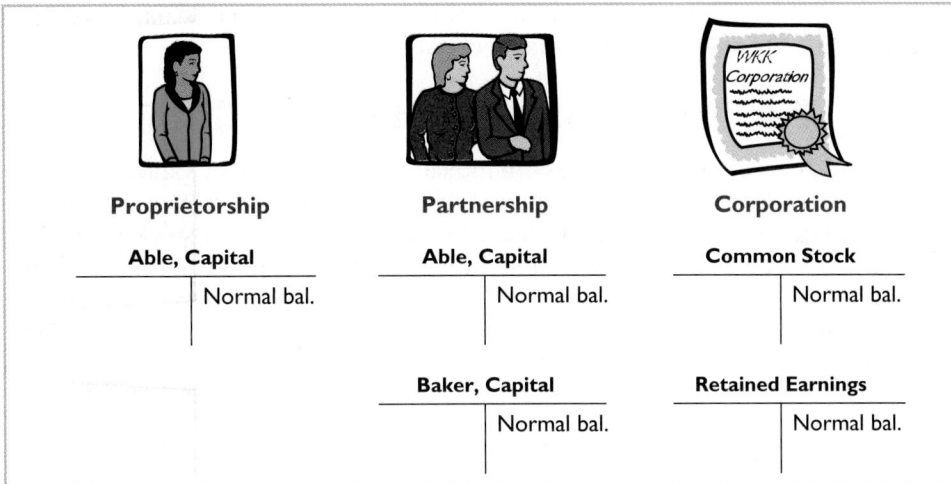

Illustration 13-6
Comparison of owners' equity accounts

Proprietorship

Able, Capital	
	Normal bal.

Partnership

Able, Capital	
	Normal bal.

Baker, Capital	
	Normal bal.

Corporation

Common Stock	
	Normal bal.

Retained Earnings	
	Normal bal.

Before You Go On...

REVIEW IT

1. Of what significance to a corporation is the amount of authorized stock?
2. What alternative approaches may a corporation use in issuing stock?
3. Distinguish between par value and market value.

DO IT

At the end of its first year of operation, Doral Corporation has $750,000 of common stock and net income of $122,000. Prepare (a) the closing entry for net income and (b) the stockholders' equity section at year-end.

Action Plan

- Record net income in Retained Earnings by a closing entry in which Income Summary is debited and Retained Earnings is credited.
- In the stockholders' equity section, show (1) paid-in capital and (2) retained earnings.

Solution

(a) Income Summary	122,000	
Retained Earnings		122,000
(To close Income Summary and transfer net income to retained earnings)		

(b) Stockholders' equity		
Paid-in capital		
Common stock	$750,000	
Retained earnings	122,000	
Total stockholders' equity		$872,000

Related exercise material: *BE13-2.*

✓ *The Navigator*

ACCOUNTING FOR COMMON STOCK ISSUES

STUDY OBJECTIVE 3

Record the issuance of common stock.

Let's now look at how to account for issues of common stock. The primary objectives in accounting for the issuance of common stock are: (1) to identify the specific sources of paid-in capital, and (2) to maintain the distinction between paid-in capital and retained earnings. **The issuance of common stock affects only paid-in capital accounts.**

Issuing Par Value Common Stock for Cash

As discussed earlier, par value does not indicate a stock's market value. Therefore, the cash proceeds from issuing par value stock may be equal to, greater than, or less than par value. When the company records issuance of common stock for cash, it credits to Common Stock the par value of the shares. It records in a separate paid-in capital account the portion of the proceeds that is above or below par value.

To illustrate, assume that Hydro-Slide, Inc. issues 1,000 shares of $1 par value common stock at par for cash. The entry to record this transaction is:

A	=	L	+	SE
+1,000				
				+1,000 CS

Cash Flows
+1,000

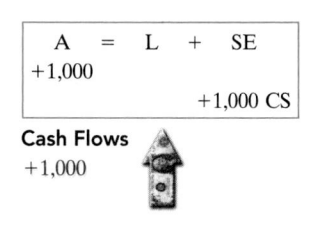

Cash	1,000	
Common Stock		1,000
(To record issuance of 1,000 shares of $1 par common stock at par)		

If Hydro-Slide issues an additional 1,000 shares of the $1 par value common stock for cash at $5 per share, the entry is:

A	=	L	+	SE
+5,000				
				+1,000 CS
				+4,000 CS

Cash Flows
+5,000

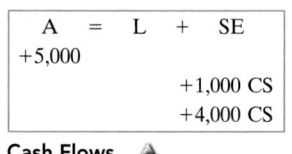

Cash	5,000	
Common Stock		1,000
Paid-in Capital in Excess of Par Value		4,000
(To record issuance of 1,000 shares of $1 par common stock)		

The total paid-in capital from these two transactions is $6,000, and the legal capital is $2,000. Assuming Hydro-Slide, Inc. has retained earnings of $27,000, Illustration 13-7 shows the company's stockholders' equity section.

Illustration 13-7
Stockholders' equity—paid-in capital in excess of par value

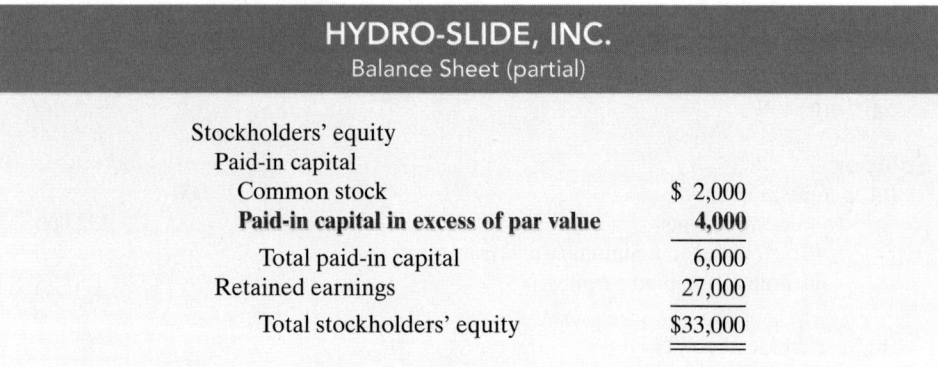

HYDRO-SLIDE, INC.
Balance Sheet (partial)

Stockholders' equity	
Paid-in capital	
Common stock	$ 2,000
Paid-in capital in excess of par value	**4,000**
Total paid-in capital	6,000
Retained earnings	27,000
Total stockholders' equity	$33,000

ALTERNATIVE TERMINOLOGY

Paid-in Capital in Excess of Par is also called *Premium on Stock*.

When a corporation issues stock for less than par value, it debits the account Paid-in Capital in Excess of Par Value, if a credit balance exists in this account. If a credit balance does not exist, then the corporation debits to Retained Earnings the amount less than par. This situation occurs only rarely: Most states do not permit the sale of common stock below par value, because stockholders may be held personally liable for the difference between the price paid upon original sale and par value.

Issuing No-Par Common Stock for Cash

When no-par common stock has a stated value, the entries are similar to those illustrated for par value stock. The corporation credits the stated value to Common Stock. Also, when the selling price of no-par stock exceeds stated value, the corporation credits the excess to Paid-in Capital in Excess of Stated Value.

For example, assume that instead of $1 par value stock, Hydro-Slide, Inc. has $5 stated value no-par stock and the company issues 5,000 shares at $8 per share for cash. The entry is:

Cash	40,000	
Common Stock		25,000
Paid-in Capital in Excess of Stated Value		15,000
(To record issue of 5,000 shares of $5 stated value no-par stock)		

A	=	L	+	SE
+40,000				
				+25,000 CS
				+15,000 CS

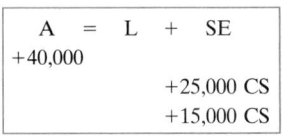

Cash Flows
+40,000

Hydro-Slide, Inc. reports Paid-in Capital in Excess of Stated Value as part of paid-in capital in the stockholders' equity section.

What happens when no-par stock does not have a stated value? In that case, the corporation credits the entire proceeds to Common Stock. Thus, if Hydro-Slide does not assign a stated value to its no-par stock, it would record the issuance of the 5,000 shares at $8 per share for cash as follows.

Cash	40,000	
Common Stock		40,000
(To record issue of 5,000 shares of no-par stock)		

A	=	L	+	SE
+40,000				
				+40,000 CS

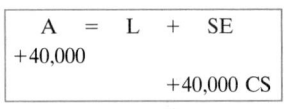

Cash Flows
+40,000

Issuing Common Stock for Services or Noncash Assets

Corporations also may issue stock for services (compensation to attorneys or consultants) or for noncash assets (land, buildings, and equipment). In such cases, what cost should be recognized in the exchange transaction? To comply with the **cost principle**, in a noncash transaction **cost is the cash equivalent price**. Thus, **cost is either the fair market value of the consideration given up, or the fair market value of the consideration received**, whichever is more clearly determinable.

To illustrate, assume that attorneys have helped Jordan Company incorporate. They have billed the company $5,000 for their services. They agree to accept 4,000 shares of $1 par value common stock in payment of their bill. At the time of the exchange, there is no established market price for the stock. In this case, the market value of the consideration received, $5,000, is more clearly evident. Accordingly, Jordan Company makes the following entry:

Organization Expense	5,000	
Common Stock		4,000
Paid-in Capital in Excess of Par Value		1,000
(To record issuance of 4,000 shares of $1 par value stock to attorneys)		

A	=	L	+	SE
				−5,000 Exp
				+4,000 CS
				+1,000 CS

Cash Flows
no effect

As explained on page 560, organization costs are expensed as incurred.

In contrast, assume that Athletic Research Inc. is an existing publicly held corporation. Its $5 par value stock is actively traded at $8 per share. The company issues 10,000 shares of stock to acquire land recently advertised for sale at $90,000. The most clearly evident value in this noncash transaction is the market price of the consideration given, $80,000. The company records the transaction as follows.

Land	80,000	
Common Stock		50,000
Paid-in Capital in Excess of Par Value		30,000
(To record issuance of 10,000 shares of $5 par value stock for land)		

A	=	L	+	SE
+80,000				
				+50,000 CS
				+30,000 CS

Cash Flows
no effect

As illustrated in these examples, **the par value of the stock is never a factor in determining the cost of the assets received**. This is also true of the stated value of no-par stock.

Before You Go On...

REVIEW IT

1. Explain the accounting for par and no-par common stock issued for cash.
2. Explain the accounting for the issuance of stock for services or noncash assets.
3. What is the par or stated value per share of PepsiCo's common stock? How many shares has PepsiCo issued at December 31, 2005? The answers to these questions appear on page 593.

DO IT

Cayman Corporation begins operations on March 1 by issuing 100,000 shares of $10 par value common stock for cash at $12 per share. On March 15 it issues 5,000 shares of common stock to attorneys in settlement of their bill of $50,000 for organization costs. Journalize the issuance of the shares, assuming the stock is not publicly traded.

Action Plan

- In issuing shares for cash, credit Common Stock for par value per share.
- Credit any additional proceeds in excess of par value to a separate paid-in capital account.
- When stock is issued for services, use the cash equivalent price.
- For the cash equivalent price use either the fair market value of what is given up or the fair market value of what is received, whichever is more clearly determinable.

Solution

Mar. 1	Cash	1,200,000	
	Common Stock		1,000,000
	Paid-in Capital in Excess of Par Value		200,000
	(To record issuance of 100,000 shares at $12 per share)		
Mar. 15	Organization Expense	50,000	
	Common Stock		50,000
	(To record issuance of 5,000 shares for attorneys' fees)		

Related exercise material: *BE13-3, BE13-4, BE13-5, E13-3, E13-4, and E13-6.*

The Navigator

ACCOUNTING FOR TREASURY STOCK

STUDY OBJECTIVE 4

Explain the accounting for treasury stock.

Treasury stock is a corporation's own stock that it has issued and subsequently reacquired from shareholders, but not retired. A corporation may acquire treasury stock for various reasons:

1. To reissue the shares to officers and employees under bonus and stock compensation plans.
2. To signal to the stock market that management believes the stock is underpriced, in the hope of enhancing its market value.

3. To have additional shares available for use in the acquisition of other companies.
4. To reduce the number of shares outstanding and thereby increase earnings per share.
5. To rid the company of disgruntled investors, perhaps to avoid a takeover, as illustrated in the Ford Motor Company Feature Story.

HELPFUL HINT
Treasury shares do not have dividend rights or voting rights.

Many corporations have treasury stock. One survey of 600 U.S. companies found that approximately two-thirds have treasury stock.[4] Buybacks are becoming more popular. For example, ExxonMobil Corp., Microsoft Corp., and Time Warner Inc. purchased a combined $14.37 billion of their shares in the first quarter of 2005.

Purchase of Treasury Stock

Companies generally account for treasury stock by **the cost method**. This method uses the cost of the shares purchased to value the treasury stock. Under the cost method, the company debits **Treasury Stock** for the **price paid to reacquire the shares**.

When the company disposes of the shares, it credits to Treasury Stock **the same amount** it paid to reacquire the shares. To illustrate, assume that on January 1, 2008, the stockholders' equity section of Mead, Inc. has 100,000 shares of $5 par value common stock outstanding (all issued at par value) and Retained Earnings of $200,000. The stockholders' equity section before purchase of treasury stock is as follows.

Illustration 13-8
Stockholders' equity with no treasury stock

MEAD, INC.
Balance Sheet (partial)

Stockholders' equity	
Paid-in capital	
Common stock, $5 par value, 100,000 shares issued and outstanding	$500,000
Retained earnings	200,000
Total stockholders' equity	$700,000

On February 1, 2008, Mead acquires 4,000 shares of its stock at $8 per share. The entry is:

Feb. 1	Treasury Stock	32,000	
	Cash		32,000
	(To record purchase of 4,000 shares of treasury stock at $8 per share)		

A	=	L	+	SE
				−32,000 TS
−32,000				

Cash Flows
−32,000

Note that Mead debits Treasury Stock for the cost of the shares purchased. Is the original paid-in capital account, Common Stock, affected? No, because the number of issued shares does not change. In the stockholders' equity section of the balance sheet, Mead deducts treasury stock from total paid-in capital and retained earnings. Treasury Stock is a **contra stockholders' equity account**. Thus, the acquisition of treasury stock reduces stockholders' equity.

[4] *Accounting Trends & Techniques 2005* (New York: American Institute of Certified Public Accountants).

The stockholders' equity section of Mead, Inc. after purchase of treasury stock is as follows.

Illustration 13-9
Stockholders' equity with treasury stock

MEAD, INC.
Balance Sheet (partial)

Stockholders' equity	
Paid-in capital	
Common stock, $5 par value, 100,000 shares issued and 96,000 shares outstanding	$500,000
Retained earnings	200,000
Total paid-in capital and retained earnings	700,000
Less: Treasury stock (4,000 shares)	**32,000**
Total stockholders' equity	$668,000

ETHICS NOTE

The purchase of treasury stock reduces the cushion for creditors and preferred stockholders. A restriction for the cost of treasury stock purchased is often required. The restriction is usually applied to retained earnings.

In the balance sheet, Mead discloses both the number of shares issued (100,000) and the number in the treasury (4,000). The difference between these two amounts is the number of shares of stock outstanding (96,000). The term **outstanding stock** means the number of shares of issued stock that are being held by stockholders.

Some maintain that companies should report treasury stock as an asset because it can be sold for cash. Under this reasoning, companies should also show unissued stock as an asset, clearly an erroneous conclusion. Rather than being an asset, treasury stock reduces stockholder claims on corporate assets. This effect is correctly shown by reporting treasury stock as a deduction from total paid-in capital and retained earnings.

ACCOUNTING ACROSS THE ORGANIZATION

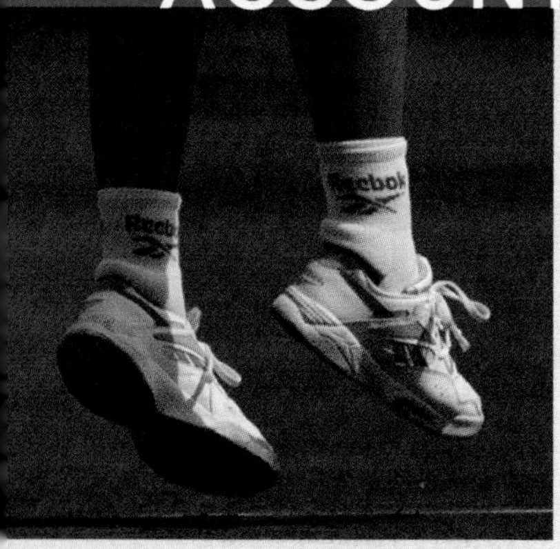

Why Did Reebok Buy Its Own Stock?

In a bold (and some would say risky) move, Reebok at one time bought back nearly a *third* of its shares. This repurchase of shares dramatically reduced Reebok's available cash. In fact, the company borrowed significant funds to accomplish the repurchase. In a press release, management stated that it was repurchasing the shares because it believed its stock was severely underpriced. The repurchase of so many shares was meant to signal management's belief in good future earnings.

Skeptics, however, suggested that Reebok's management was repurchasing shares to make it less likely that another company would acquire Reebok (in which case Reebok's top managers would likely lose their jobs). By depleting its cash, Reebok became a less likely acquisition target. Acquiring companies like to purchase companies with large cash balances so they can pay off debt used in the acquisition.

? What signal might a large stock repurchase send to investors regarding management's belief about the company's growth opportunities?

Disposal of Treasury Stock

Treasury stock is usually sold or retired. The accounting for its sale differs when treasury stock is sold above cost than when it is sold below cost.

SALE OF TREASURY STOCK ABOVE COST

If the selling price of the treasury shares is equal to their cost, the company records the sale of the shares by a debit to Cash and a credit to Treasury Stock. When the selling price of the shares is greater than their cost, the company credits the difference to Paid-in Capital from Treasury Stock.

To illustrate, assume that on July 1, Mead sells for $10 per share the 1,000 shares of its treasury stock, previously acquired at $8 per share. The entry is as follows.

HELPFUL HINT

Treasury stock transactions are classified as capital stock transactions. As in the case when stock is issued, the income statement is not involved.

July 1	Cash	10,000	
	Treasury Stock		8,000
	Paid-in Capital from Treasury Stock		2,000
	(To record sale of 1,000 shares of treasury stock above cost)		

A	=	L	+	SE
+10,000				
				+8,000 TS
				+2,000 TS

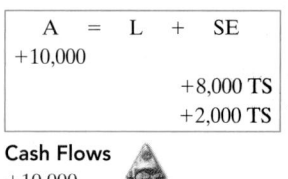

Cash Flows
+10,000

Mead does not record a $2,000 gain on sale of treasury stock for two reasons: (1) Gains on sales occur when **assets** are sold, and treasury stock is not an asset. (2) A corporation does not realize a gain or suffer a loss from stock transactions with its own stockholders. Thus, companies should not include in net income any paid-in capital arising from the sale of treasury stock. Instead, they report Paid-in Capital from Treasury Stock separately on the balance sheet, as a part of paid-in capital.

SALE OF TREASURY STOCK BELOW COST

When a company sells treasury stock below its cost, it usually debits to Paid-in Capital from Treasury Stock the excess of cost over selling price. Thus, if Mead, Inc. sells an additional 800 shares of treasury stock on October 1 at $7 per share, it makes the following entry.

Oct. 1	Cash	5,600	
	Paid-in Capital from Treasury Stock	800	
	Treasury Stock		6,400
	(To record sale of 800 shares of treasury stock below cost)		

A	=	L	+	SE
+5,600				
				−800 TS
				+6,400 TS

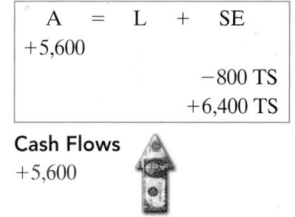

Cash Flows
+5,600

Observe the following from the two sales entries: (1) Mead credits Treasury Stock at cost in each entry. (2) Mead uses Paid-in Capital from Treasury Stock for the difference between cost and the resale price of the shares. (3) The original paid-in capital account, Common Stock, is not affected. **The sale of treasury stock increases both total assets and total stockholders' equity.**

After posting the foregoing entries, the treasury stock accounts will show the following balances on October 1.

Illustration 13-10
Treasury stock accounts

Treasury Stock			
Feb. 1	32,000	July 1	8,000
		Oct. 1	6,400
Oct. 1 Bal.	17,600		

Paid-in Capital from Treasury Stock			
Oct. 1	800	July 1	2,000
		Oct. 1 Bal.	1,200

When a company fully depletes the credit balance in Paid-in Capital from Treasury Stock, it debits to Retained Earnings any additional excess of cost over selling price. To illustrate, assume that Mead, Inc. sells its remaining 2,200 shares at $7 per share on December 1. The excess of cost over selling price is $2,200 [2,200 × ($8 − $7)]. In this case, Mead debits $1,200 of the excess to Paid-in

Capital from Treasury Stock. It debits the remainder to Retained Earnings. The entry is:

A	=	L	+	SE
+15,400				
				−1,200 TS
				−1,000 RE
				+17,600 TS

Cash Flows
+15,400

Dec. 1	Cash	15,400	
	Paid-in Capital from Treasury Stock	1,200	
	Retained Earnings	1,000	
	Treasury Stock		17,600
	(To record sale of 2,200 shares of treasury stock at $7 per share)		

Before You Go On...

REVIEW IT

1. What is treasury stock, and why do companies acquire it?
2. How do companies record treasury stock?
3. Where do companies report treasury stock in the financial statements? Does a company record gains and losses on treasury stock transactions? Explain.
4. How many shares of treasury stock did PepsiCo have at December 31, 2005 and at December 25, 2004? The answer to this question appears on page 593.

DO IT

Santa Anita Inc. purchases 3,000 shares of its $50 par value common stock for $180,000 cash on July 1. It will hold the shares in the treasury until resold. On November 1, the corporation sells 1,000 shares of treasury stock for cash at $70 per share. Journalize the treasury stock transactions.

Action Plan

- Record the purchase of treasury stock at cost.
- When treasury stock is sold above its cost, credit the excess of the selling price over cost to Paid-in Capital from Treasury Stock.
- When treasury stock is sold below its cost, debit the excess of cost over selling price to Paid-in Capital from Treasury Stock.

Solution

July 1	Treasury Stock	180,000	
	Cash		180,000
	(To record the purchase of 3,000 shares at $60 per share)		
Nov. 1	Cash	70,000	
	Treasury Stock		60,000
	Paid-in Capital from Treasury Stock		10,000
	(To record the sale of 1,000 shares at $70 per share)		

Related exercise material: *BE13-6, E13-6, and E13-7.*

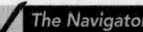

✓ The Navigator

PREFERRED STOCK

STUDY OBJECTIVE 5
Differentiate preferred stock from common stock.

To appeal to more investors, a corporation may issue an additional class of stock, called preferred stock. **Preferred stock** has provisions that give it some preference or priority over common stock. Typically, preferred stockholders have a priority as to (1) distributions of earnings (dividends) and (2) assets in the event of liquidation. However, they generally do not have voting rights.

Like common stock, corporations may issue preferred stock for cash or for noncash assets. The entries for these transactions are similar to the entries for common stock. When a corporation has more than one class of stock, each paid-in capital account title should identify the stock to which it relates. A company might have the following accounts: Preferred Stock, Common Stock, Paid-in Capital in Excess of Par Value—Preferred Stock, and Paid-in Capital in Excess of Par Value—Common Stock. For example, if Stine Corporation issues 10,000 shares of $10 par value preferred stock for $12 cash per share, the entry to record the issuance is:

Cash	120,000	
Preferred Stock		100,000
Paid-in Capital in Excess of Par Value–Preferred Stock		20,000
(To record the issuance of 10,000 shares of $10 par value preferred stock)		

A	=	L	+	SE
+120,000				
				+100,000 PS
				+20,000 PS

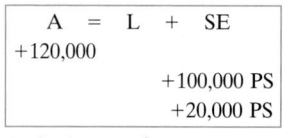

Cash Flows
+120,000

Preferred stock may have either a par value or no-par value. In the stockholders' equity section of the balance sheet, companies list preferred stock first because of its dividend and liquidation preferences over common stock.

We discuss various features associated with the issuance of preferred stock on the following pages.

Dividend Preferences

As noted earlier, **preferred stockholders have the right to receive dividends before common stockholders**. For example, if the dividend rate on preferred stock is $5 per share, common shareholders will not receive any dividends in the current year until preferred stockholders have received $5 per share. The first claim to dividends does not, however, guarantee the payment of dividends. Dividends depend on many factors, such as adequate retained earnings and availability of cash. If a company does not pay dividends to preferred stockholders, it cannot of course pay dividends to common stockholders.

I hope there is some money left when it's my turn.
Preferred stockholders
Common stockholders

Dividend Preference

The per share dividend amount is stated as a percentage of the preferred stock's par value or as a specified amount. For example, at one time Crane Company specified a 3¾% dividend on its $100 par value preferred ($100 × 3¾% = $3.75 per share). PepsiCo has a $5.46 series of no-par preferred stock.

CUMULATIVE DIVIDEND

Preferred stock often contains a cumulative dividend feature. This means that preferred stockholders must be paid both current-year dividends and any unpaid prior-year dividends before common stockholders receive dividends. When preferred stock is cumulative, preferred dividends not declared in a given period are called **dividends in arrears**.

To illustrate, assume that Scientific Leasing has 5,000 shares of 7%, $100 par value, cumulative preferred stock outstanding. The annual dividend is $35,000 (5,000 × $7 per share), but dividends are two years in arrears. In this case, preferred stockholders are entitled to receive the following dividends in the current year.

Dividends in arrears ($35,000 × 2)	$ 70,000
Current-year dividends	35,000
Total preferred dividends	**$105,000**

Illustration 13-11
Computation of total dividends to preferred stock

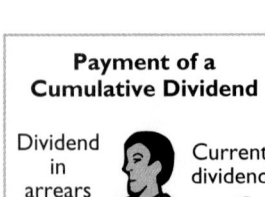

Payment of a Cumulative Dividend

Preferred stockholders

The company cannot pay dividends to common stockholders until it pays the entire preferred dividend. In other words, companies cannot pay dividends to common stockholders while any preferred stock is in arrears.

Are dividends in arrears considered a liability? **No—no payment obligation exists until the board of directors declares a dividend**. However, companies should disclose in the notes to the financial statements the amount of dividends in arrears. Doing so enables investors to assess the potential impact of this commitment on the corporation's financial position.

Companies that are unable to meet their dividend obligations are not looked upon favorably by the investment community. As a financial officer noted in discussing one company's failure to pay its cumulative preferred dividend for a period of time, "Not meeting your obligations on something like that is a major black mark on your record." The accounting entries for preferred stock dividends are explained in Chapter 14.

Liquidation Preference

Most preferred stocks also have a preference on corporate assets if the corporation fails. This feature provides security for the preferred stockholder. The preference to assets may be for the par value of the shares or for a specified liquidating value. For example, EarthLink's preferred stock entitles its holders to receive $20.83 per share, plus accrued and unpaid dividends, in the event of involuntary liquidation. The liquidation preference establishes the respective claims of creditors and preferred stockholders.

STATEMENT PRESENTATION AND ANALYSIS

STUDY OBJECTIVE 6

Prepare a stockholders' equity section.

Companies report paid-in capital and retained earnings in the stockholders' equity section of the balance sheet. They identify the specific sources of paid-in capital. Within paid-in capital, companies use the following classifications.

ALTERNATIVE TERMINOLOGY

Paid-in capital is sometimes called *contributed capital.*

1. **Capital stock.** This category consists of preferred and common stock. Preferred stock appears before common stock because of its preferential rights. Companies report par value, shares authorized, shares issued, and shares outstanding for each class of stock.
2. **Additional paid-in capital.** This category includes the excess of amounts paid in over par or stated value and paid-in capital from treasury stock.

Presentation

The stockholders' equity section of Connally Inc. in Illustration 13-12 (next page) includes most of the accounts discussed in this chapter. The disclosures pertaining to Connally's common stock indicate that: the company issued 400,000 shares; 100,000 shares are unissued (500,000 authorized less 400,000 issued); and 390,000 shares are outstanding (400,000 issued less 10,000 shares in treasury).

Published annual reports often combine and report as a single amount the individual sources of additional paid-in capital, as shown in Illustration 13-13 (next page). In addition, authorized shares are sometimes not reported.

In practice, companies sometimes use the term "Capital surplus" in place of "Additional paid-in capital," and "Earned surplus" in place of "Retained earnings." The use of the term "surplus" suggests that the company has available an excess amount of funds. Such is not necessarily the case. Therefore, **the term**

Illustration 13-12
Stockholders' equity section

CONNALLY INC.
Balance Sheet (partial)

Stockholders' equity		
Paid-in capital		
Capital stock		
9% preferred stock, $100 par value cumulative, 10,000 shares authorized, 6,000 shares issued and outstanding		$ 600,000
Common stock, no par, $5 stated value, 500,000 shares authorized, 400,000 shares issued, and 390,000 outstanding		2,000,000
Total capital stock		2,600,000
Additional paid-in capital		
In excess of par value—preferred stock	$ 30,000	
In excess of stated value—common stock	860,000	
From treasury stock	140,000	
Total additional paid-in capital		1,030,000
Total paid-in capital		3,630,000
Retained earnings		1,058,000
Total paid-in capital and retained earnings		4,688,000
Less: Treasury stock—common (10,000 shares) (at cost)		(80,000)
Total stockholders' equity		$4,608,000

Illustration 13-13
Published stockholders' equity section

Kellogg's

KELLOGG COMPANY
Balance Sheet (partial)
($ in millions)

Stockholders' equity	
Common stock, $0.25 par value, 1,000,000,000 shares authorized	
Issued: 418,451,198 shares	$ 104.6
Capital in excess of par value	58.9
Retained earnings	3,266.1
Treasury stock, at cost 13,121,446 shares	(569.8)
Accumulated other comprehensive income	(576.1)
Total stockholders' equity	$2,283.7

"surplus" should not be employed in accounting. Unfortunately, a number of financial statements still do use it.

Analysis—Book Value Per Share

STUDY OBJECTIVE 7
Compute book value per share.

You have learned about a number of per share amounts in this chapter. Another per share amount of some importance is **book value per share**. It represents **the equity a common stockholder has in the net assets of the corporation** from owning one share of stock. Remember that the net assets of a corporation must be equal to total stockholders' equity. Therefore, the formula for computing book value per share when a company has only one class of stock outstanding is:

Illustration 13-14
Book value per share formula

Total Stockholders' Equity	÷	Number of Common Shares Outstanding	=	Book Value per Share

Thus, if Marlo Corporation has total stockholders' equity of $1,500,000 (common stock $1,000,000 and retained earnings $500,000) and 50,000 shares of common stock outstanding, book value per share is $30 ($1,500,000 ÷ 50,000).[5]

BOOK VALUE VERSUS MARKET VALUE

Be sure you understand that **book value per share generally does not equal market value per share**. Book value generally is based on recorded costs. Market value reflects the subjective judgments of thousands of stockholders and prospective investors about a company's potential for future earnings and dividends.

Market value per share may exceed book value per share, but that fact does not necessarily mean that the stock is overpriced. The correlation between book value and the annual range of a company's market value per share is often remote, as indicated by the following recent data.

Illustration 13-15
Book and market values compared

Company	Book Value (year-end)	Market Range (for year 2005)
The Limited, Inc.	$13.38	$31.03–$22.89
H. J. Heinz Company	$ 7.48	$40.61–$34.53
Cisco Systems	$ 3.66	$21.24–$17.01
Wal-Mart Stores	$12.79	$50.87–$42.31

Book value per share is useful in determining the trend of a stockholder's per share equity in a corporation. It is also significant in many contracts and in court cases where the rights of individual parties are based on cost information.

Before You Go On...

REVIEW IT

1. Identify the classifications within the paid-in capital section and the totals stated in the stockholders' equity section of a balance sheet.
2. What is the method for computing book value per share when only common stock is outstanding?

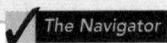

The Navigator

Be sure to read **ALL ABOUT YOU: *Home-Equity Loans*** on the next page for information on how topics in this chapter apply to you.

[5]When a company has both preferred and common stock, the computation of book value is a bit more complex. Since preferred stockholders have a prior claim on net assets over common stockholders, their equity must be deducted from total stockholders' equity.

Home-Equity Loans

In this chapter you learned that companies sometimes reduce their stockholders' equity by buying treasury stock or paying dividends. They do this for a variety of reasons—some good, and some not so good. Individuals who own homes sometimes engage in equity reducing transactions by using home-equity loans. Home-equity loans use the equity existing in the home as collateral for borrowing additional monies.

Many banks encourage people to take out home-equity loans. As a result of the dramatic increase in home values in the United States in recent years, many people have significant equity in their homes. Thus, many people have chosen to use home-equity loans to finance vacations, new cars, improvements to the home, educational pursuits, and so on, or to consolidate debt. However, by taking out a home-equity loan, a homeowner is reducing the equity in that home.

Some Facts

* PNC Financial Services Group Inc. offered gifts—in some cases, two airline tickets—to borrowers who took out a new home-equity loan.
* Many banks are extending the length of home-equity loans. Regions Financial Corp. introduced a fixed-rate home-equity loan with a term of up to 15 years. It had previously been five years.
* While home-equity loans tend to have fixed rates, home-equity lines of credit, which allow the homeowner to borrow up to a certain amount whenever they want to, have variable rates. Rates on home-equity lines of credit averaged 8.33% in April 2006, versus about 14% for credit card debt.
* Home-equity loan interest is tax deductible (like home mortgage interest). Interest on car loans, most student loans, and credit cards is not.

About the Numbers

Home-equity loans can be very tempting. Suppose that you wanted to borrow $5,000 to take a vacation. You could spread your payments over 15 years and you would have to pay only about $50 per month. But look what your total payments would be over the life of the 15-year loan. Some vacation!

Amount of Monthly Payment on a $5,000, 9% Loan

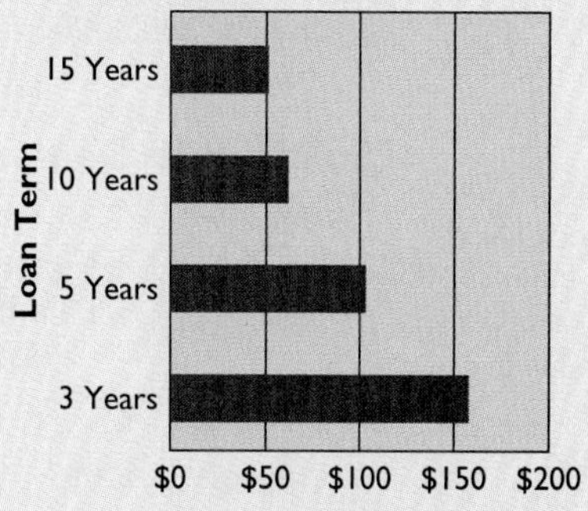

Total Cost Over Life of $5,000, 9% Loan

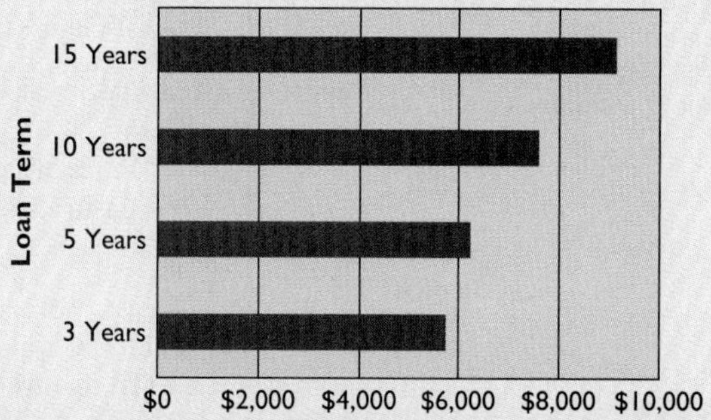

Source: Data from Marc Eisenson and Nancy Castleman, "When Mining Your Home for Money, Beware of Fool's Gold," Good Advice Press, *www.goodadvicepress.com/omhomeequity.htm* (accessed June 20, 2006).

What Do You Think?

Your home has increased in value by $50,000 during the last five years. You have very little savings outside of the equity in your home. You desperately need a vacation, and you are considering taking out a $5,000 home-equity loan to finance a two-week dream vacation in Europe. Is this is a bad idea?

YES: This represents a significant portion of your savings. Home-equity loans should be used to finance investments of a lasting nature, not items of a fleeting nature like vacations.

NO: You need a vacation. If you use a little of the equity in your home now, you can make it up when your house increases in value in the future.

Source: Ruth Simon, "Lenders Push Home-Equity Deals," *Wall Street Journal,* April 27, 2006, page D1; Marc Eisenson and Nancy Castleman, "When Mining Your Home for Money, Beware of Fool's Gold," Good Advice Press, *www.goodadvicepress.com/omhomeequity.htm* (accessed June 20, 2006).

The authors' comments on this situation appear on page 593.

Demonstration Problem

The Rolman Corporation is authorized to issue 1,000,000 shares of $5 par value common stock. In its first year, the company has the following stock transactions.

Jan. 10	Issued 400,000 shares of stock at $8 per share.
July 1	Issued 100,000 shares of stock for land. The land had an asking price of $900,000. The stock is currently selling on a national exchange at $8.25 per share.
Sept. 1	Purchased 10,000 shares of common stock for the treasury at $9 per share.
Dec. 1	Sold 4,000 shares of the treasury stock at $10 per share.

Instructions

(a) Journalize the transactions.

(b) Prepare the stockholders' equity section assuming the company had retained earnings of $200,000 at December 31.

action plan

- When common stock has a par value, credit Common Stock for par value.
- Use fair market value in a noncash transaction.
- Debit and credit the Treasury Stock account at cost.
- Record differences between the cost and selling price of treasury stock in stockholders' equity accounts, not as gains or losses.

Solution to Demonstration Problem

(a) Jan. 10	Cash	3,200,000	
	Common Stock		2,000,000
	Paid-in Capital in Excess of Par Value		1,200,000
	(To record issuance of 400,000 shares of $5 par value stock)		
July 1	Land	825,000	
	Common Stock		500,000
	Paid-in Capital in Excess of Par Value		325,000
	(To record issuance of 100,000 shares of $5 par value stock for land)		
Sept. 1	Treasury Stock	90,000	
	Cash		90,000
	(To record purchase of 10,000 shares of treasury stock at cost)		
Dec. 1	Cash	40,000	
	Treasury Stock		36,000
	Paid-in Capital from Treasury Stock		4,000
	(To record sale of 4,000 shares of treasury stock above cost)		

(b)

ROLMAN CORPORATION
Balance Sheet (partial)

Stockholders' equity		
Paid-in capital		
Capital stock		
Common stock, $5 par value, 1,000,000 shares authorized, 500,000 shares issued, 494,000 shares outstanding		$2,500,000
Additional paid-in capital		
In excess of par value	$1,525,000	
From treasury stock	4,000	
Total additional paid-in capital		1,529,000
Total paid-in capital		4,029,000
Retained earnings		200,000
Total paid-in capital and retained earnings		4,229,000
Less: Treasury stock (6,000 shares)		(54,000)
Total stockholders' equity		$4,175,000

The Navigator

SUMMARY OF STUDY OBJECTIVES

1 **Identify the major characteristics of a corporation.** The major characteristics of a corporation are separate legal existence, limited liability of stockholders, transferable ownership rights, ability to acquire capital, continuous life, corporation management, government regulations, and additional taxes.

2 **Differentiate between paid-in capital and retained earnings.** Paid-in capital is the total amount paid in on capital stock. It is often called contributed capital. Retained earnings is net income retained in a corporation. It is often called earned capital.

3 **Record the issuance of common stock.** When companies record the issuance of common stock for cash, they credit the par value of the shares to Common Stock. They record in a separate paid-in capital account the portion of the proceeds that is above or below par value. When no-par common stock has a stated value, the entries are similar to those for par value stock. When no-par stock does not have a stated value, companies credit the entire proceeds to Common Stock.

4 **Explain the accounting for treasury stock.** The cost method is generally used in accounting for treasury stock. Under this approach, companies debit Treasury Stock at the price paid to reacquire the shares. They credit the same amount to Treasury Stock when they sell the shares. The difference between the sales price and cost is recorded in stockholders' equity accounts, not in income statement accounts.

5 **Differentiate preferred stock from common stock.** Preferred stock has contractual provisions that give it priority over common stock in certain areas. Typically, preferred stockholders have a preference (1) to dividends and (2) to assets in liquidation. They usually do not have voting rights.

6 **Prepare a stockholders' equity section.** In the stockholders' equity section, companies report paid-in capital and retained earnings and identify specific sources of paid-in capital. Within paid-in capital, two classifications are shown: capital stock and additional paid-in capital. If a corporation has treasury stock, it deducts the cost of treasury stock from total paid-in capital and retained earnings to obtain total stockholders' equity.

7 **Compute book value per share.** Book value per share represents the equity a common stockholder has in the net assets of a corporation from owning one share of stock. When there is only common stock outstanding, the formula for computing book value is: Total stockholders' equity ÷ Number of common shares outstanding = Book value per share.

The Navigator

GLOSSARY

Authorized stock The amount of stock that a corporation is authorized to sell as indicated in its charter. (p. 562).

Book value per share The equity a common stockholder has in the net assets of the corporation from owning one share of stock. (p. 575).

By-laws The internal rules and procedures for conducting the affairs of a corporation. (p. 560).

Charter A document that creates a corporation. (p. 560).

Corporation A business organized as a legal entity separate and distinct from its owners under state corporation law. (p. 556).

Cumulative dividend A feature of preferred stock entitling the stockholder to receive current and unpaid prior-year dividends before common stockholders receive dividends. (p. 573).

No-par value stock Capital stock that has not been assigned a value in the corporate charter. (p. 564).

Organization costs Costs incurred in the formation of a corporation. (p. 560).

Outstanding stock Capital stock that has been issued and is being held by stockholders. (p. 570).

Paid-in capital Total amount of cash and other assets paid in to the corporation by stockholders in exchange for capital stock. (p. 564).

Par value stock Capital stock that has been assigned a value per share in the corporate charter. (p. 563).

Preferred stock Capital stock that has some preferences over common stock. (p. 572).

Privately held corporation A corporation that has only a few stockholders and whose stock is not available for sale to the general public. (p. 556).

Publicly held corporation A corporation that may have thousands of stockholders and whose stock is regularly traded on a national securities exchange. (p. 556).

Retained earnings Net income that is retained in the corporation. (p. 564).

Stated value The amount per share assigned by the board of directors to no-par stock. (p. 564).

Treasury stock A corporation's own stock that has been issued and subsequently reacquired from shareholders by the corporation but not retired. (p. 568).

SELF-STUDY QUESTIONS

WILEY PLUS

Answers are at the end of the chapter.

(SO 1) **1.** Which of the following is *not* a major advantage of a corporation?
a. Separate legal existence.
b. Continuous life.
c. Government regulations.
d. Transferable ownership rights.

(SO 1) **2.** A major disadvantage of a corporation is:
a. limited liability of stockholders.
b. additional taxes.
c. transferable ownership rights.
d. none of the above.

(SO 2) **3.** Which of the following statements is *false*?
a. Ownership of common stock gives the owner a voting right.
b. The stockholders' equity section begins with paid-in capital.
c. The authorization of capital stock does not result in a formal accounting entry.
d. Legal capital per share applies to par value stock but not to no-par value stock.

(SO 2) **4.** The account Retained Earnings is:
a. a subdivision of paid-in capital.
b. net income retained in the corporation.
c. reported as an expense in the income statement.
d. closed to capital stock.

(SO 3) **5.** ABC Corporation issues 1,000 shares of $10 par value common stock at $12 per share. In recording the transaction, credits are made to:
a. Common Stock $10,000 and Paid-in Capital in Excess of Stated Value $2,000.
b. Common Stock $12,000.
c. Common Stock $10,000 and Paid-in Capital in Excess of Par Value $2,000.
d. Common Stock $10,000 and Retained Earnings $2,000.

(SO 4) **6.** XYZ, Inc. sells 100 shares of $5 par value treasury stock at $13 per share. If the cost of acquiring the shares was $10 per share, the entry for the sale should include credits to:
a. Treasury Stock $1,000 and Paid-in Capital from Treasury Stock $300.
b. Treasury Stock $500 and Paid-in Capital from Treasury Stock $800.
c. Treasury Stock $1,000 and Retained Earnings $300.
d. Treasury Stock $500 and Paid-in Capital in Excess of Par Value $800.

7. In the stockholders' equity section, the cost of treasury stock is deducted from: (SO 4)
a. total paid-in capital and retained earnings.
b. retained earnings.
c. total stockholders' equity.
d. common stock in paid-in capital.

8. Preferred stock may have priority over common stock *except* in: (SO 5)
a. dividends.
b. assets in the event of liquidation.
c. cumulative dividend features.
d. voting.

9. Which of the following is *not* reported under additional paid-in capital? (SO 6)
a. Paid-in capital in excess of par value.
b. Common stock.
c. Paid-in capital in excess of stated value.
d. Paid-in capital from treasury stock.

10. The ledger of JFK, Inc. shows common stock, common treasury stock, and no preferred stock. For this company, the formula for computing book value per share is: (SO 7)
a. Total paid-in capital and retained earnings divided by the number of shares of common stock issued.
b. Common stock divided by the number of shares of common stock issued.
c. Total stockholders' equity divided by the number of shares of common stock outstanding.
d. Total stockholders' equity divided by the number of shares of common stock issued.

Go to the book's website, **www.wiley.com/college/weygandt**, for Additional Self-Study questions.

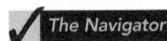

The Navigator

QUESTIONS

1. Eric Fink, a student, asks your help in understanding the following characteristics of a corporation: (a) separate legal existence, (b) limited liability of stockholders, and (c) transferable ownership rights. Explain these characteristics to Eric.

2. (a) Your friend Vicky Biel cannot understand how the characteristic of corporation management is both an advantage and a disadvantage. Clarify this problem for Vicky.
(b) Identify and explain two other disadvantages of a corporation.

3. (a) The following terms pertain to the forming of a corporation: (1) charter, (2) by-laws, and (3) organization costs. Explain the terms.
(b) Linda Merando believes a corporation must be incorporated in the state in which its headquarters office is located. Is Linda correct? Explain.

4. What are the basic ownership rights of common stockholders in the absence of restrictive provisions?

5. (a) What are the two principal components of stockholders' equity?
(b) What is paid-in capital? Give three examples.

6. How do the financial statements for a corporation differ from the statements for a proprietorship?
7. The corporate charter of Hawes Corporation allows the issuance of a maximum of 100,000 shares of common stock. During its first two years of operations, Hawes sold 70,000 shares to shareholders and reacquired 7,000 of these shares. After these transactions, how many shares are authorized, issued, and outstanding?
8. Which is the better investment—common stock with a par value of $5 per share, or common stock with a par value of $20 per share? Why?
9. What factors help determine the market value of stock?
10. What effect does the issuance of stock at a price above par value have on the issuer's net income? Explain.
11. Why is common stock usually not issued at a price that is less than par value?
12. Land appraised at $80,000 is purchased by issuing 1,000 shares of $20 par value common stock. The market price of the shares at the time of the exchange, based on active trading in the securities market, is $95 per share. Should the land be recorded at $20,000, $80,000, or $95,000? Explain.
13. For what reasons might a company like IBM repurchase some of its stock (treasury stock)?
14. Kwun, Inc. purchases 1,000 shares of its own previously issued $5 par common stock for $12,000. Assuming the shares are held in the treasury, what effect does this transaction have on (a) net income, (b) total assets, (c) total paid-in capital, and (d) total stockholders' equity?
15. The treasury stock purchased in question 14 is resold by Kwun, Inc. for $18,000. What effect does this transaction have on (a) net income, (b) total assets, (c) total paid-in capital, and (d) total stockholders' equity?
16. **(a)** What are the principal differences between common stock and preferred stock?
    (b) Preferred stock may be cumulative. Discuss this feature.
    (c) How are dividends in arrears presented in the financial statements?
17. What is the formula for computing book value per share when a corporation has only common stock?
18. Ruiz Inc.'s common stock has a par value of $1, a book value of $29, and a current market value of $15. Explain why these amounts are all different.
19. Indicate how each of the following accounts should be classified in the stockholders' equity section.
    (a) Common stock
    (b) Paid-in capital in excess of par value
    (c) Retained earnings
    (d) Treasury stock
    (e) Paid-in capital from treasury stock
    (f) Paid-in capital in excess of stated value
    (g) Preferred stock

BRIEF EXERCISES

WILEY PLUS

BE13-1 Ken Fritz is studying for his accounting midterm examination. Identify for Ken the advantages and disadvantages of the corporate form of business organization.

List the advantages and disadvantages of a corporation. (SO 1)

BE13-2 At December 31, Kunkel Corporation reports net income of $450,000. Prepare the entry to close net income.

Prepare closing entries for a corporation. (SO 2)

BE13-3 On May 10, Mazili Corporation issues 2,000 shares of $10 par value common stock for cash at $18 per share. Journalize the issuance of the stock.

Prepare entries for issuance of par value common stock. (SO 3)

BE13-4 On June 1, Mendoza Inc. issues 3,000 shares of no-par common stock at a cash price of $6 per share. Journalize the issuance of the shares assuming the stock has a stated value of $1 per share.

Prepare entries for issuance of no-par value common stock. (SO 3)

BE13-5 Kane Inc.'s $10 par value common stock is actively traded at a market value of $15 per share. Kane issues 5,000 shares to purchase land advertised for sale at $85,000. Journalize the issuance of the stock in acquiring the land.

Prepare entries for issuance of stock in a noncash transaction. (SO 3)

BE13-6 On July 1, Goetz Corporation purchases 500 shares of its $5 par value common stock for the treasury at a cash price of $8 per share. On September 1, it sells 300 shares of the treasury stock for cash at $11 per share. Journalize the two treasury stock transactions.

Prepare entries for treasury stock transactions. (SO 4)

BE13-7 Acker Inc. issues 5,000 shares of $100 par value preferred stock for cash at $130 per share. Journalize the issuance of the preferred stock.

Prepare entries for issuance of preferred stock. (SO 5)

BE13-8 Ermler Corporation has the following accounts at December 31: Common Stock, $10 par, 5,000 shares issued, $50,000; Paid-in Capital in Excess of Par Value $20,000; Retained Earnings $45,000; and Treasury Stock—Common, 500 shares, $11,000. Prepare the stockholders' equity section of the balance sheet.

Prepare stockholders' equity section. (SO 6)

BE13-9 The balance sheet for Gambino Inc. shows the following: total paid-in capital and retained earnings $870,000, total stockholders' equity $820,000, common stock issued 44,000 shares, and common stock outstanding 40,000 shares. Compute the book value per share.

Compute book value per share. (SO 7)

EXERCISES

Identify characteristics of a corporation.
(SO 1)

E13-1 Jeff Lynne has prepared the following list of statements about corporations.

1. A corporation is an entity separate and distinct from its owners.
2. As a legal entity, a corporation has most of the rights and privileges of a person.
3. Most of the largest U.S. corporations are privately held corporations.
4. Corporations may buy, own, and sell property; borrow money; enter into legally binding contracts; and sue and be sued.
5. The net income of a corporation is not taxed as a separate entity.
6. Creditors have a legal claim on the personal assets of the owners of a corporation if the corporation does not pay its debts.
7. The transfer of stock from one owner to another requires the approval of either the corporation or other stockholders.
8. The board of directors of a corporation legally owns the corporation.
9. The chief accounting officer of a corporation is the controller.
10. Corporations are subject to less state and federal regulations than partnerships or proprietorships.

Instructions
Identify each statement as true or false. If false, indicate how to correct the statement.

Identify characteristics of a corporation.
(SO 1, 2)

E13-2 Jeff Lynne (see E13-1) has studied the information you gave him in that exercise and has come to you with more statements about corporation.

1. Corporation management is both an advantage and a disadvantage of a corporation compared to a proprietorship or a partnership.
2. Limited liability of stockholders, government regulations, and additional taxes are the major disadvantages of a corporation.
3. When a corporation is formed, organization costs are recorded as an asset.
4. Each share of common stock gives the stockholder the ownership rights to vote at stockholder meetings, share in corporate earnings, keep the same percentage ownership when new shares of stock are issued, and share in assets upon liquidation.
5. The number of issued shares is always greater than or equal to the number of authorized shares.
6. A journal entry is required for the authorization of capital stock.
7. Publicly held corporations usually issue stock directly to investors.
8. The trading of capital stock on a securities exchange involves the transfer of already issued shares from an existing stockholder to another investor.
9. The market value of common stock is usually the same as its par value.
10. Retained earnings is the total amount of cash and other assets paid in to the corporation by stockholders in exchange for capital stock.

Instructions
Identify each statement as true or false. If false, indicate how to correct the statement.

Journalize issuance of common stock.
(SO 3)

E13-3 During its first year of operations, Harlan Corporation had the following transactions pertaining to its common stock.

Jan. 10 Issued 70,000 shares for cash at $5 per share.
July 1 Issued 40,000 shares for cash at $7 per share.

Instructions
(a) Journalize the transactions, assuming that the common stock has a par value of $5 per share.
(b) Journalize the transactions, assuming that the common stock is no-par with a stated value of $1 per share.

Journalize issuance of common stock.
(SO 3)

E13-4 Grossman Corporation issued 1,000 shares of stock.

Instructions
Prepare the entry for the issuance under the following assumptions.

(a) The stock had a par value of $5 per share and was issued for a total of $52,000.
(b) The stock had a stated value of $5 per share and was issued for a total of $52,000.

(c) The stock had no par or stated value and was issued for a total of $52,000.
(d) The stock had a par value of $5 per share and was issued to attorneys for services during incorporation valued at $52,000.
(e) The stock had a par value of $5 per share and was issued for land worth $52,000.

E13-5 Leone Co. had the following transactions during the current period.

Journalize issuance of common and preferred stock and purchase of treasury stock.
(SO 3, 4, 5)

Mar. 2 Issued 5,000 shares of $5 par value common stock to attorneys in payment of a bill for $30,000 for services provided in helping the company to incorporate.
June 12 Issued 60,000 shares of $5 par value common stock for cash of $375,000.
July 11 Issued 1,000 shares of $100 par value preferred stock for cash at $110 per share.
Nov. 28 Purchased 2,000 shares of treasury stock for $80,000.

Instructions
Journalize the transactions.

E13-6 As an auditor for the CPA firm of Bunge and Dodd, you encounter the following situations in auditing different clients.

Journalize noncash common stock transactions.
(SO 3)

1. Desi Corporation is a closely held corporation whose stock is not publicly traded. On December 5, the corporation acquired land by issuing 5,000 shares of its $20 par value common stock. The owners' asking price for the land was $120,000, and the fair market value of the land was $115,000.
2. Lucille Corporation is a publicly held corporation whose common stock is traded on the securities markets. On June 1, it acquired land by issuing 20,000 shares of its $10 par value stock. At the time of the exchange, the land was advertised for sale at $250,000. The stock was selling at $12 per share.

Instructions
Prepare the journal entries for each of the situations above.

E13-7 On January 1, 2008, the stockholders' equity section of Nunez Corporation shows: Common stock ($5 par value) $1,500,000; paid-in capital in excess of par value $1,000,000; and retained earnings $1,200,000. During the year, the following treasury stock transactions occurred.

Journalize treasury stock transactions.
(SO 4)

Mar. 1 Purchased 50,000 shares for cash at $15 per share.
July 1 Sold 10,000 treasury shares for cash at $17 per share.
Sept. 1 Sold 8,000 treasury shares for cash at $14 per share.

Instructions
(a) Journalize the treasury stock transactions.
(b) Restate the entry for September 1, assuming the treasury shares were sold at $12 per share.

E13-8 Mad City Corporation purchased from its stockholders 5,000 shares of its own previously issued stock for $250,000. It later resold 2,000 shares for $54 per share, then 2,000 more shares for $49 per share, and finally 1,000 shares for $40 per share.

Journalize treasury stock transactions.
(SO 4)

Instructions
Prepare journal entries for the purchase of the treasury stock and the three sales of treasury stock.

E13-9 Polzin Corporation is authorized to issue both preferred and common stock. The par value of the preferred is $50. During the first year of operations, the company had the following events and transactions pertaining to its preferred stock.

Journalize preferred stock transactions and indicate statement presentation.
(SO 5, 6)

Feb. 1 Issued 20,000 shares for cash at $53 per share.
July 1 Issued 12,000 shares for cash at $57 per share.

Instructions
(a) Journalize the transactions.
(b) Post to the stockholders' equity accounts.
(c) Indicate the financial statement presentation of the related accounts.

E13-10 AI Corporation issued 100,000 shares of $20 par value, cumulative, 8% preferred stock on January 1, 2007, for $2,100,000. In December 2009, AI declared its first dividend of $500,000.

Differentiate between preferred and common stock.
(SO 5)

Instructions

(a) Prepare AI's journal entry to record the issuance of the preferred stock.

(b) If the preferred stock is *not* cumulative, how much of the $500,000 would be paid to **common** stockholders?

(c) If the preferred stock is cumulative, how much of the $500,000 would be paid to **common** stockholders?

Prepare correct entries for capital stock transactions.

(SO 3, 4, 5)

E13-11 Roemer Corporation recently hired a new accountant with extensive experience in accounting for partnerships. Because of the pressure of the new job, the accountant was unable to review his textbooks on the topic of corporation accounting. During the first month, the accountant made the following entries for the corporation's capital stock.

May 2	Cash	130,000	
	Capital Stock		130,000
	(Issued 10,000 shares of $10 par value common stock at $13 per share)		
10	Cash	600,000	
	Capital Stock		600,000
	(Issued 10,000 shares of $50 par value preferred stock at $60 per share)		
15	Capital Stock	15,000	
	Cash		15,000
	(Purchased 1,000 shares of common stock for the treasury at $15 per share)		
31	Cash	8,000	
	Capital Stock		5,000
	Gain on Sale of Stock		3,000
	(Sold 500 shares of treasury stock at $16 per share)		

Instructions

On the basis of the explanation for each entry, prepare the entry that should have been made for the capital stock transactions.

Prepare a stockholders' equity section.

(SO 6)

E13-12 The following stockholders' equity accounts, arranged alphabetically, are in the ledger of Freeze Corporation at December 31, 2008.

Common Stock ($5 stated value)	$1,700,000
Paid-in Capital in Excess of Par Value—Preferred Stock	280,000
Paid-in Capital in Excess of Stated Value—Common Stock	900,000
Preferred Stock (8%, $100 par, noncumulative)	500,000
Retained Earnings	1,134,000
Treasury Stock—Common (10,000 shares)	120,000

Instructions

Prepare the stockholders' equity section of the balance sheet at December 31, 2008.

Answer questions about stockholders' equity section.

(SO 3, 4, 5, 6)

E13-13 The stockholders' equity section of Jarvis Corporation at December 31 is as follows.

JARVIS CORPORATION

Balance Sheet (partial)

Paid-in capital	
Preferred stock, cumulative, 10,000 shares authorized, 6,000 shares issued and outstanding	$ 300,000
Common stock, no par, 750,000 shares authorized, 600,000 shares issued	1,200,000
Total paid-in capital	1,500,000
Retained earnings	1,858,000
Total paid-in capital and retained earnings	3,358,000
Less: Treasury stock (10,000 common shares)	(64,000)
Total stockholders' equity	$3,294,000

Instructions

From a review of the stockholders' equity section, as chief accountant, write a memo to the president of the company answering the following questions.

(a) How many shares of common stock are outstanding?
(b) Assuming there is a stated value, what is the stated value of the common stock?
(c) What is the par value of the preferred stock?
(d) If the annual dividend on preferred stock is $30,000, what is the dividend rate on preferred stock?
(e) If dividends of $60,000 were in arrears on preferred stock, what would be the balance in Retained Earnings?

Prepare a stockholders' equity section.
(SO 6)

E13-14 In a recent year, the stockholders' equity section of Aluminum Company of America (Alcoa) showed the following (in alphabetical order): additional paid-in capital $6,101, common stock $925, preferred stock $55, retained earnings $7,428, and treasury stock 2,828. All dollar data are in millions.

The preferred stock has 557,740 shares authorized, with a par value of $100 and an annual $3.75 per share cumulative dividend preference. At December 31, 557,649 shares of preferred are issued and 546,024 shares are outstanding. There are 1.8 billion shares of $1 par value common stock authorized, of which 924.6 million are issued and 844.8 million are outstanding at December 31.

Instructions

Prepare the stockholders' equity section, including disclosure of all relevant data.

Classify stockholders' equity accounts.
(SO 6)

E13-15 The ledger of Mathis Corporation contains the following accounts: Common Stock, Preferred Stock, Treasury Stock—Common, Paid-in Capital in Excess of Par Value—Preferred Stock, Paid-in Capital in Excess of Stated Value—Common Stock, Paid-in Capital from Treasury Stock, and Retained Earnings.

Instructions

Classify each account using the following table headings.

	Paid-in Capital			
Account	**Capital Stock**	**Additional**	**Retained Earnings**	**Other**

Compute book value per share.
(SO 7)

E13-16 At December 31, Penny Corporation has total stockholders' equity of $5,500,000. There are no shares of preferred stock outstanding. At year-end, 250,000 shares of common stock are outstanding and 20,000 shares are in treasury.

Instructions

Compute the book value per share of common stock.

EXERCISES: SET B

Visit the book's website at **www.wiley.com/college/weygandt**, and choose the Student Companion site, to access Exercise Set B.

PROBLEMS: SET A

Journalize stock transactions, post, and prepare paid-in capital section.
(SO 3, 5, 6)

P13-1A Franco Corporation was organized on January 1, 2008. It is authorized to issue 10,000 shares of 8%, $100 par value preferred stock, and 500,000 shares of no-par common stock with a stated value of $2 per share. The following stock transactions were completed during the first year.

Jan. 10 Issued 80,000 shares of common stock for cash at $4 per share.
Mar. 1 Issued 5,000 shares of preferred stock for cash at $105 per share.
Apr. 1 Issued 24,000 shares of common stock for land. The asking price of the land was $90,000. The fair market value of the land was $85,000.

May 1 Issued 80,000 shares of common stock for cash at $4.50 per share.
Aug. 1 Issued 10,000 shares of common stock to attorneys in payment of their bill of $30,000 for services provided in helping the company organize.
Sept. 1 Issued 10,000 shares of common stock for cash at $5 per share.
Nov. 1 Issued 1,000 shares of preferred stock for cash at $109 per share.

Instructions

(a) Journalize the transactions.
(b) Post to the stockholders' equity accounts. (Use J5 as the posting reference.)
(c) Prepare the paid-in capital section of stockholders' equity at December 31, 2008.

(c) Total paid-in capital $1,479,000

Journalize and post treasury stock transactions, and prepare stockholders' equity section.

(SO 4, 6)

P13-2A Jacobsen Corporation had the following stockholders' equity accounts on January 1, 2008: Common Stock ($5 par) $500,000, Paid-in Capital in Excess of Par Value $200,000, and Retained Earnings $100,000. In 2008, the company had the following treasury stock transactions.

Mar. 1 Purchased 5,000 shares at $9 per share.
June 1 Sold 1,000 shares at $12 per share.
Sept. 1 Sold 2,000 shares at $10 per share.
Dec. 1 Sold 1,000 shares at $6 per share.

Jacobsen Corporation uses the cost method of accounting for treasury stock. In 2008, the company reported net income of $30,000.

Instructions

(a) Journalize the treasury stock transactions, and prepare the closing entry at December 31, 2008, for net income.
(b) Open accounts for (1) Paid-in Capital from Treasury Stock, (2) Treasury Stock, and (3) Retained Earnings. Post to these accounts using J10 as the posting reference.
(c) Prepare the stockholders' equity section for Jacobsen Corporation at December 31, 2008.

(b) Treasury Stock $9,000
(c) Total stockholders' equity $823,000

Journalize and post transactions, prepare stockholders' equity section.

(SO 2, 3, 4, 5, 6)

GLS

P13-3A The stockholders' equity accounts of Neer Corporation on January 1, 2008, were as follows.

Preferred Stock (8%, $50 par, cumulative, 10,000 shares authorized)	$ 400,000
Common Stock ($1 stated value, 2,000,000 shares authorized)	1,000,000
Paid-in Capital in Excess of Par Value—Preferred Stock	100,000
Paid-in Capital in Excess of Stated Value—Common Stock	1,450,000
Retained Earnings	1,816,000
Treasury Stock—Common (10,000 shares)	50,000

During 2008, the corporation had the following transactions and events pertaining to its stockholders' equity.

Feb. 1 Issued 25,000 shares of common stock for $120,000.
Apr. 14 Sold 6,000 shares of treasury stock—common for $33,000.
Sept. 3 Issued 5,000 shares of common stock for a patent valued at $35,000.
Nov. 10 Purchased 1,000 shares of common stock for the treasury at a cost of $6,000.
Dec. 31 Determined that net income for the year was $452,000.

No dividends were declared during the year.

Instructions

(a) Journalize the transactions and the closing entry for net income.
(b) Enter the beginning balances in the accounts, and post the journal entries to the stockholders' equity accounts. (Use J5 for the posting reference.)
(c) Prepare a stockholders' equity section at December 31, 2008, including the disclosure of the preferred dividends in arrears.

(c) Total stockholders' equity $5,350,000

Journalize and post stock transactions, and prepare stockholders' equity section.

(SO 2, 3, 5, 6)

GLS Peachtree

P13-4A Vargas Corporation is authorized to issue 20,000 shares of $50 par value, 10% preferred stock and 125,000 shares of $3 par value common stock. On January 1, 2008, the ledger contained the following stockholders' equity balances.

Preferred Stock (10,000 shares)	$500,000
Paid-in Capital in Excess of Par Value—Preferred	75,000
Common Stock (70,000 shares)	210,000
Paid-in Capital in Excess of Par Value—Common	700,000
Retained Earnings	300,000

During 2008, the following transactions occurred.

Feb.	1	Issued 2,000 shares of preferred stock for land having a fair market value of $125,000.
Mar.	1	Issued 1,000 shares of preferred stock for cash at $65 per share.
July	1	Issued 16,000 shares of common stock for cash at $7 per share.
Sept.	1	Issued 400 shares of preferred stock for a patent. The asking price of the patent was $30,000. Market values were preferred stock $70 and patent indeterminable.
Dec.	1	Issued 8,000 shares of common stock for cash at $7.50 per share.
Dec.	31	Net income for the year was $260,000. No dividends were declared.

Instructions

(a) Journalize the transactions and the closing entry for net income.

(b) Enter the beginning balances in the accounts, and post the journal entries to the stockholders' equity accounts. (Use J2 for the posting reference.)

(c) Prepare a stockholders' equity section at December 31, 2008.

(c) Total stockholders' equity $2,435,000

Prepare stockholders' equity section.

(SO 6)

P13-5A The following stockholders' equity accounts arranged alphabetically are in the ledger of Tyner Corporation at December 31, 2008.

Common Stock ($5 stated value)	$2,000,000
Paid-in Capital from Treasury Stock	10,000
Paid-in Capital in Excess of Stated Value—Common Stock	1,600,000
Paid-in Capital in Excess of Par Value—Preferred Stock	679,000
Preferred Stock (8%, $50 par, noncumulative)	800,000
Retained Earnings	1,748,000
Treasury Stock—Common (10,000 shares)	130,000

Instructions

Prepare a stockholders' equity section at December 31, 2008.

Total stockholders' equity $6,707,000

Prepare entries for stock transactions and prepare stockholders' equity section.

(SO 3, 4, 5, 6)

P13-6A Palmaro Corporation has been authorized to issue 20,000 shares of $100 par value, 10%, noncumulative preferred stock and 1,000,000 shares of no-par common stock. The corporation assigned a $2.50 stated value to the common stock. At December 31, 2008, the ledger contained the following balances pertaining to stockholders' equity.

Preferred Stock	$120,000
Paid-in Capital in Excess of Par Value—Preferred	20,000
Common Stock	1,000,000
Paid-in Capital in Excess of Stated Value—Common	1,800,000
Treasury Stock—Common (1,000 shares)	13,000
Paid-in Capital from Treasury Stock	500
Retained Earnings	82,000

The preferred stock was issued for land having a fair market value of $140,000. All common stock issued was for cash. In November, 1,500 shares of common stock were purchased for the treasury at a per share cost of $13. In December, 500 shares of treasury stock were sold for $14 per share. No dividends were declared in 2008.

Instructions

(a) Prepare the journal entries for the:

- **(1)** Issuance of preferred stock for land.
- **(2)** Issuance of common stock for cash.
- **(3)** Purchase of common treasury stock for cash.
- **(4)** Sale of treasury stock for cash.

(b) Prepare the stockholders' equity section at December 31, 2008.

(b) Total stockholders' equity $3,009,500

PROBLEMS: SET B

Journalize stock transactions, post, and prepare paid-in capital section.

(SO 3, 5, 6)

GLS

P13-1B Scribner Corporation was organized on January 1, 2008. It is authorized to issue 20,000 shares of 6%, $50 par value preferred stock, and 500,000 shares of no-par common stock with a stated value of $1 per share. The following stock transactions were completed during the first year.

Jan.	10	Issued 100,000 shares of common stock for cash at $3 per share.
Mar.	1	Issued 10,000 shares of preferred stock for cash at $55 per share.

Apr. 1 Issued 25,000 shares of common stock for land. The asking price of the land was $90,000. The company's estimate of fair market value of the land was $75,000.
May 1 Issued 75,000 shares of common stock for cash at $4 per share.
Aug. 1 Issued 10,000 shares of common stock to attorneys in payment of their bill for $50,000 for services provided in helping the company organize.
Sept. 1 Issued 5,000 shares of common stock for cash at $6 per share.
Nov. 1 Issued 2,000 shares of preferred stock for cash at $60 per share.

Instructions

(a) Journalize the transactions.
(b) Post to the stockholders' equity accounts. (Use J1 as the posting reference.)
(c) Prepare the paid-in capital section of stockholders' equity at December 31, 2008.

(c) Total paid-in capital $1,425,000

Journalize and post treasury stock transactions, and prepare stockholders' equity section.

(SO 4, 6)

P13-2B Inwood Corporation had the following stockholders' equity accounts on January 1, 2008: Common Stock ($1 par) $400,000, Paid-in Capital in Excess of Par Value $500,000, and Retained Earnings $100,000. In 2008, the company had the following treasury stock transactions.

Mar. 1 Purchased 5,000 shares at $8 per share.
June 1 Sold 1,000 shares at $10 per share.
Sept. 1 Sold 2,000 shares at $9 per share.
Dec. 1 Sold 1,000 shares at $5 per share.

Inwood Corporation uses the cost method of accounting for treasury stock. In 2008, the company reported net income of $50,000.

Instructions

(a) Journalize the treasury stock transactions, and prepare the closing entry at December 31, 2008, for net income.
(b) Open accounts for (1) Paid-in Capital from Treasury Stock, (2) Treasury Stock, and (3) Retained Earnings. Post to these accounts using J12 as the posting reference.
(c) Prepare the stockholders' equity section for Inwood Corporation at December 31, 2008.

(b) Treasury Stock $8,000
(c) Total stockholders' equity $1,043,000

Journalize and post transactions, prepare stockholders' equity section.

(SO 2, 3, 4, 5, 6)

GLS

P13-3B The stockholders' equity accounts of Litke Corporation on January 1, 2008, were as follows.

Preferred Stock (10%, $100 par, noncumulative, 5,000 shares authorized)	$ 300,000
Common Stock ($5 stated value, 300,000 shares authorized)	1,000,000
Paid-in Capital in Excess of Par Value—Preferred Stock	20,000
Paid-in Capital in Excess of Stated Value—Common Stock	425,000
Retained Earnings	488,000
Treasury Stock—Common (5,000 shares)	35,000

During 2008, the corporation had the following transactions and events pertaining to its stockholders' equity.

Feb. 1 Issued 3,000 shares of common stock for $24,000.
Mar. 20 Purchased 1,500 additional shares of common treasury stock at $7 per share.
June 14 Sold 4,000 shares of treasury stock—common for $36,000.
Sept. 3 Issued 2,000 shares of common stock for a patent valued at $17,000.
Dec. 31 Determined that net income for the year was $320,000.

Instructions

(a) Journalize the transactions and the closing entry for net income.
(b) Enter the beginning balances in the accounts and post the journal entries to the stockholders' equity accounts. (Use J1 as the posting reference.)
(c) Prepare a stockholders' equity section at December 31, 2008.

(c) Total stockholders' equity $2,584,500

Journalize and post stock transactions, and prepare stockholders' equity section.

(SO 2, 3, 5, 6)

GLS

P13-4B Mendez Corporation is authorized to issue 10,000 shares of $50 par value, 10% preferred stock and 200,000 shares of $2 par value common stock. On January 1, 2008, the ledger contained the following stockholders' equity balances.

Preferred Stock (4,000 shares)	$200,000
Paid-in Capital in Excess of Par Value—Preferred	60,000
Common Stock (70,000 shares)	140,000
Paid-in Capital in Excess of Par Value—Common	700,000
Retained Earnings	300,000

During 2008, the following transactions occurred.

Feb.	1	Issued 1,000 shares of preferred stock for land having a fair market value of $65,000.
Mar.	1	Issued 2,000 shares of preferred stock for cash at $60 per share.
July	1	Issued 20,000 shares of common stock for cash at $5.80 per share.
Sept.	1	Issued 800 shares of preferred stock for a patent. The asking price of the patent was $60,000. Market values were preferred stock $65 and patent, indeterminable.
Dec.	1	Issued 10,000 shares of common stock for cash at $6 per share.
Dec.	31	Net income for the year was $210,000. No dividends were declared.

Instructions

(a) Journalize the transactions and the closing entry for net income.

(b) Enter the beginning balances in the accounts, and post the journal entries to the stockholders' equity accounts. (Use J2 as the posting reference.)

(c) Prepare a stockholders' equity section at December 31, 2008.

(c) Total stockholders' equity $2,023,000

Prepare stockholders' equity section.

(SO 6)

P13-5B The following stockholders' equity accounts arranged alphabetically are in the ledger of Parnell Corporation at December 31, 2008.

Common Stock ($10 stated value)	$1,200,000
Paid-in Capital from Treasury Stock	6,000
Paid-in Capital in Excess of Stated Value—Common Stock	690,000
Paid-in Capital in Excess of Par Value—Preferred Stock	288,400
Preferred Stock (8%, $100 par, noncumulative)	400,000
Retained Earnings	876,000
Treasury Stock—Common (8,000 shares)	88,000

Instructions

Prepare a stockholders' equity section at December 31, 2008.

Total stockholders' equity $3,372,400

Prepare entries for stock transactions and prepare stockholders' equity section.

(SO 3, 4, 5, 6)

P13-6B Colyer Corporation has been authorized to issue 40,000 shares of $100 par value, 8%, noncumulative preferred stock and 2,000,000 shares of no-par common stock. The corporation assigned a $5 stated value to the common stock. At December 31, 2008, the ledger contained the following balances pertaining to stockholders' equity.

Preferred Stock	$ 240,000
Paid-in Capital in Excess of Par Value—Preferred	56,000
Common Stock	2,000,000
Paid-in Capital in Excess of Stated Value—Common	5,200,000
Treasury Stock—Common (1,000 shares)	24,000
Paid-in Capital from Treasury Stock	2,000
Retained Earnings	560,000

The preferred stock was issued for land having a fair market value of $296,000. All common stock issued was for cash. In November, 1,500 shares of common stock were purchased for the treasury at a per share cost of $24. In December, 500 shares of treasury stock were sold for $28 per share. No dividends were declared in 2008.

Instructions

(a) Prepare the journal entries for the:

(1) Issuance of preferred stock for land.

(2) Issuance of common stock for cash.

(3) Purchase of common treasury stock for cash.

(4) Sale of treasury stock for cash.

(b) Prepare the stockholders' equity section at December 31, 2008.

(b) Total stockholders' equity $8,034,000

PROBLEMS: SET C

Visit the book's website at **www.wiley.com/college/weygandt**, and choose the Student Companion site, to access Problem Set C.

CONTINUING COOKIE CHRONICLE

(*Note:* This is a continuation of the Cookie Chronicle from Chapters 1 through 12.)

CCC13 Natalie's friend, Curtis Lesperance, decides to meet with Natalie after hearing that her discussions about a possible business partnership with her friend Katy Peterson have failed. Because Natalie has been so successful with Cookie Creations and Curtis has been just as successful with his coffee shop, they both conclude that they could benefit from each other's business expertise. Curtis and Natalie next evaluate the different types of business organization, and because of the advantage of limited personal liability, decide to form a corporation. Natalie and Curtis are very excited about this new business venture. They come to you with information about their businesses and with a number of questions.

Go to the book's website, **www.wiley.com/college/weygandt,** *to see the completion of this problem.*

BROADENING YOUR PERSPECTIVE

FINANCIAL REPORTING AND ANALYSIS

Financial Reporting Problem:
PepsiCo, Inc.

BYP13-1 The stockholders' equity section for PepsiCo is shown in Appendix A. You will also find data relative to this problem on other pages of the appendix.

Instructions

(a) What is the par or stated value per share of PepsiCo's common stock?
(b) What percentage of PepsiCo's authorized common stock was issued at December 31, 2005?
(c) How many shares of common stock were outstanding at December 31, 2005, and at December 25, 2004?
(d) What was book value per share at December 31, 2005, and at December 25, 2004?
(e) What was the high and low market price per share in the fourth quarter of fiscal 2005, as reported under Selected Financial Data?

Comparative Analysis Problem:
PepsiCo, Inc. vs. The Coca-Cola Company

BYP13-2 PepsiCo's financial statements are presented in Appendix A. Coca-Cola's financial statements are presented in Appendix B.

Instructions

(a) Based on the information contained in these financial statements, compute the 2005 book value per share for each company. (*Hint:* Use the value reported for "common shareholders' equity" as the numerator for PepsiCo.)
(b) Compare the market value per share for each company to the book value per share at year-end 2005. Assume that the market value of Coca-Cola's stock was $40.31 at year-end 2005.
(c) Why are book value and market value per share different?

Exploring the Web

BYP13-3 SEC filings of publicly traded companies are available to view online.

Address: http://biz.yahoo.com/i, or go to **www.wiley.com/college/weygandt**

Steps

1. Pick a company and type in the company's name.
2. Choose **Quote**.

Instructions

Answer the following questions.

(a) What company did you select?
(b) What is its stock symbol?
(c) What was the stock's trading range today?
(d) What was the stock's trading range for the year?

CRITICAL THINKING

Decision Making Across the Organization

BYP13-4 The stockholders' meeting for Strauder Corporation has been in progress for some time. The chief financial officer for Strauder is presently reviewing the company's financial statements and is explaining the items that comprise the stockholders' equity section of the balance sheet for the current year. The stockholders' equity section of Strauder Corporation at December 31, 2008, is as follows.

STRAUDER CORPORATION
Balance Sheet (partial)
December 31, 2008

Paid-in capital		
Capital stock		
Preferred stock, authorized 1,000,000 shares cumulative, $100 par value, $8 per share, 6,000 shares issued and outstanding		$ 600,000
Common stock, authorized 5,000,000 shares, $1 par value, 3,000,000 shares issued, and 2,700,000 outstanding		3,000,000
Total capital stock		3,600,000
Additional paid-in capital		
In excess of par value—preferred stock	$ 50,000	
In excess of par value—common stock	25,000,000	
Total additional paid-in capital		25,050,000
Total paid-in capital		28,650,000
Retained earnings		900,000
Total paid-in capital and retained earnings		29,550,000
Less: Common treasury stock (300,000 shares)		9,300,000
Total stockholders' equity		$20,250,000

At the meeting, stockholders have raised a number of questions regarding the stockholders' equity section.

Instructions

With the class divided into groups, answer the following questions as if you were the chief financial officer for Strauder Corporation.

(a) "What does the cumulative provision related to the preferred stock mean?"
(b) "I thought the common stock was presently selling at $29.75, but the company has the stock stated at $1 per share. How can that be?"
(c) "Why is the company buying back its common stock? Furthermore, the treasury stock has a debit balance because it is subtracted from stockholders' equity. Why is treasury stock not reported as an asset if it has a debit balance?"
(d) "Why is it necessary to show additional paid-in capital? Why not just show common stock at the total amount paid in?"

Communication Activity

BYP13-5 Sid Hosey, your uncle, is an inventor who has decided to incorporate. Uncle Sid knows that you are an accounting major at U.N.O. In a recent letter to you, he ends with the question, "I'm filling out a state incorporation application. Can you tell me the difference in the following terms: (1) authorized stock, (2) issued stock, (3) outstanding stock, (4) preferred stock?"

Instructions

In a brief note, differentiate for Uncle Sid among the four different stock terms. Write the letter to be friendly, yet professional.

Ethics Case

BYP13-6 The R&D division of Marco Chemical Corp. has just developed a chemical for sterilizing the vicious Brazilian "killer bees" which are invading Mexico and the southern states of the United States. The president of Marco is anxious to get the chemical on the market to boost Marco's profits. He believes his job is in jeopardy because of decreasing sales and profits. Marco has an opportunity to sell this chemical in Central American countries, where the laws are much more relaxed than in the United States.

The director of Marco's R&D division strongly recommends further testing in the laboratory for side-effects of this chemical on other insects, birds, animals, plants, and even humans. He cautions the president, "We could be sued from all sides if the chemical has tragic side-effects that we didn't even test for in the labs." The president answers, "We can't wait an additional year for your lab tests. We can avoid losses from such lawsuits by establishing a separate wholly owned corporation to shield Marco Corp. from such lawsuits. We can't lose any more than our investment in the new corporation, and we'll invest just the patent covering this chemical. We'll reap the benefits if the chemical works and is safe, and avoid the losses from lawsuits if it's a disaster." The following week Marco creates a new wholly owned corporation called Brecht Inc., sells the chemical patent to it for $10, and watches the spraying begin.

Instructions

(a) Who are the stakeholders in this situation?
(b) Are the president's motives and actions ethical?
(c) Can Marco shield itself against losses of Brecht Inc.?

* "All About You" Activity

BYP13-7 A high percentage of Americans own stock in corporations. As a shareholder in a corporation, you will receive an annual report. One of the goals of this course is for you to learn how to navigate your way around an annual report.

Instructions

Use the annual report provided in Appendix A to answer the following questions.

(a) What CPA firm performed the audit of PepsiCo's financial statements?
(b) What was the amount of PepsiCo's earnings per share in 2005?
(c) What are the company's net sales to foreign countries?
(d) What were net sales in 2001?
(e) How many shares of treasury stock did the company have at the end of 2005?
(f) How much cash did PepsiCo spend on capital expenditures in 2005?
(g) Over what life does the company depreciate its buildings?
(h) What was the total amount of dividends paid in 2005?

? Answers to Insight and Accounting Across the Organization Questions

p. 559 Directors Take on More Accountability

Q: Was Enron's board of directors fulfilling its role in a corporate organization when it waived Enron's ethical code on two occasions?

A: *The board of directors is elected by the owners (stockholders) of the corporation to manage the corporation. One of its roles is to formulate the ethical and operating policies for the* *company and to assume an oversight responsibility on behalf of the stockholders and other third parties. It was the responsibility of the board of directors to enforce the corporation's ethical code, not to waive it.*

p. 563 How to Read Stock Quotes

Q: For stocks traded on organized stock exchanges, how are the dollar prices per share established?

A: *The dollar prices per share are established by the interaction between buyers and sellers of the shares.*

Q: What factors might influence the price of shares in the marketplace?

A: *The price of shares is influenced by a company's earnings and dividends as well as by factors beyond a company's control, such as changes in interest rates, labor strikes, scarcity of supplies or resources, and politics. The number of willing buyers and sellers (demand and supply) also plays a part in the price of shares.*

p. 570 Why Did Reebok Buy Its Own Stock?

Q: What signal might a large stock repurchase send to investors regarding management's belief about the company's growth opportunities?

A: *When a company has many growth opportunities it will normally conserve its cash in order to be better able to fund expansion. A large use of cash to buy back stock (and essentially shrink the company) would suggest that management was not optimistic about its growth opportunities.*

Authors' Comments on *All About You:* Home Equity Loans (p. 577)

The reasons why people reduce the equity in their homes with home-equity loans are as varied as the reasons why companies reduce their stockholders' equity by buying treasury stock or paying dividends. There are good and bad reasons to buy treasury stock and pay dividends, and there are good and bad reasons to use a home-equity loan.

Suppose you are considering putting an addition on your house which would increase its value. That may be a good use of a home-equity loan, since it increases the value of your investment. Or suppose that you need to buy a new car. Financing the purchase with a home-equity loan can make good financial sense, since the interest on a home-equity loan is tax-deductible, while the interest on a car loan is not. But you should be sure you repay the home-equity loan over the same time period that you would have repaid the car loan. As the graphs in the box show, if you spread the loan over a long period you could end up owing more money than the car is worth when it comes time to sell it.

Borrowing against the equity in your home to go on a vacation is not a financially prudent thing to do. If you want to go on a vacation, you should set up a separate travel fund as part of your personal budget, and go on the vacation only when you can actually afford it.

The bottom line is this: Reducing equity, either corporate or personal, increases reliance on debt and therefore increases risk. It is a decision that should be carefully considered.

Answers to PepsiCo Review It Question 3, p. 568, and Question 4, p. 572

3. The par value of PepsiCo's common stock is $0.0166 per share. On December 31, 2005, PepsiCo had issued 1,782 million shares.

4. Treasury shares held by PepsiCo on December 31, 2005, were 126 million, and on December 25, 2004, were 103 million.

Answers to Self-Study Questions

1. c **2.** b **3.** d **4.** b **5.** c **6.** a **7.** a **8.** d **9.** b **10.** c

Remember to go back to the Navigator box on the chapter-opening page and check off your completed work.

Chapter 14

Corporations: Dividends, Retained Earnings, and Income Reporting

STUDY OBJECTIVES

After studying this chapter, you should be able to:

1. Prepare the entries for cash dividends and stock dividends.
2. Identify the items reported in a retained earnings statement.
3. Prepare and analyze a comprehensive stockholders' equity section.
4. Describe the form and content of corporation income statements.
5. Compute earnings per share.

The Navigator

The Navigator

Scan **Study Objectives**	■
Read **Feature Story**	■
Read **Preview**	■
Read text and answer **Before You Go On** p. 603 ■ p. 608 ■ p. 611 ■	
Work **Demonstration Problem**	■
Review **Summary of Study Objectives**	■
Answer **Self-Study Questions**	■
Complete **Assignments**	■

Feature Story

WHAT'S COOKING?

What major U.S. corporation got its start 35 years ago with a waffle iron? Hint: It doesn't sell food. Another hint: Swoosh. Another hint: "Just do it." That's right, Nike (*www.nike.com*). In 1971 Nike cofounder Bill Bowerman put a piece of rubber into a kitchen waffle iron, and the trademark waffle sole was born.

Nike was cofounded by Bowerman and Phil Knight, a member of Bowerman's University of Oregon track team. Each began in the shoe business independently

during the early 1960s. Bowerman got his start by making hand-crafted running shoes for his university track team. Knight, after completing graduate school, started a small business importing low-cost, high-quality shoes from Japan. In 1964 the two joined forces. Each contributed $500, and formed Blue Ribbon Sports, a partnership.

At first they marketed Japanese shoes. It wasn't until 1971 that the company began manufacturing its own line of shoes. With the new shoes came a new corporate name—Nike—the Greek goddess of victory. It is hard to imagine that the company that now enlists promoters such as Tiger Woods, Maria Sharapova, Dwayne Wade, and Lance Armstrong at one time had part-time employees selling shoes out of car trunks.

By 1980 Nike was sufficiently established that it was able to issue its first stock to the public. In that same year it also created a stock ownership program that allowed its employees to share in the company's success. Since then Nike has enjoyed phenomenal growth. Sales in 2005 were $13.74 billion. Its dividend per share to shareholders increased from 15 cents per share in 1992 to 95 cents per share in 2005.

Nike is not alone in its quest for the top of the sport shoe world. Reebok (*www.reebok.com*) pushes Nike every step of the way. It's a race to see who will dominate the sports shoe industry. Currently Nike is outpacing Reebok. But is the race over? Probably not. The shoe market is fickle, with new styles becoming popular almost daily. Whether one of these two giants, or some other shoe brand, does eventually take control of the planet remains to be seen. Meanwhile the shareholders sit anxiously in the stands as this Olympic-size drama unfolds.

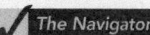

✓ *The Navigator*

Inside Chapter 14...

Preview of Chapter 14

As indicated in the Feature Story, a profitable corporation like Nike often distributes substantial portions of corporate income to owners (stockholders), in the form of dividends. In addition, it often reinvests a portion of its earnings in the business. This chapter discusses dividends, retained earnings, corporation income statements, and earnings per share.

The content and organization of Chapter 14 are as follows.

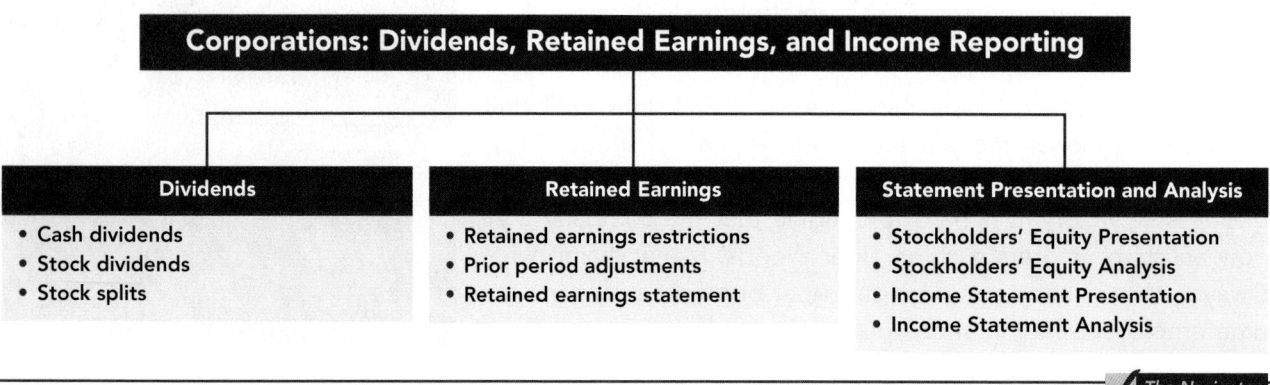

Corporations: Dividends, Retained Earnings, and Income Reporting

Dividends
- Cash dividends
- Stock dividends
- Stock splits

Retained Earnings
- Retained earnings restrictions
- Prior period adjustments
- Retained earnings statement

Statement Presentation and Analysis
- Stockholders' Equity Presentation
- Stockholders' Equity Analysis
- Income Statement Presentation
- Income Statement Analysis

The Navigator

DIVIDENDS

STUDY OBJECTIVE 1

Prepare the entries for cash dividends and stock dividends.

A dividend is a corporation's distribution of cash or stock to its stockholders on a pro rata (proportional) basis. Investors are very interested in a company's dividend policies and practices. Dividends can take four forms: cash, property, scrip (a promissory note to pay cash), or stock. Cash dividends predominate in practice. Also, companies declare stock dividends with some frequency. These two forms of dividends will be the focus of discussion in this chapter.

Dividends may be expressed in two ways: (1) as a percentage of the par or stated value of the stock, or (2) as a dollar amount per share. The financial press generally reports **dividends as a dollar amount per share**. For example, Boeing Company's dividend rate is $1.05 a share, Hershey Foods Corp.'s is $0.93, and Nike's is $0.95.

Cash Dividends

A **cash dividend** is a pro rata distribution of cash to stockholders. For a corporation to pay a cash dividend, it must have:

1. **Retained earnings.** The legality of a cash dividend depends on the laws of the state in which the company is incorporated. Payment of cash dividends from retained earnings is legal in all states. In general, cash dividend distributions from only the balance in common stock (legal capital) are illegal.

   A dividend declared out of paid-in capital is termed a **liquidating dividend**. Such a dividend reduces or "liquidates" the amount originally paid in by stockholders. Statutes vary considerably with respect to cash dividends based on paid-in capital in excess of par or stated value. Many states permit such dividends.
2. **Adequate cash.** The legality of a dividend and the ability to pay a dividend are two different things. For example, Nike, with retained earnings of over $3

billion, could legally declare a dividend of at least $3 billion. But Nike's cash balance is only $198 million.

Before declaring a cash dividend, a company's board of directors must carefully consider both current and future demands on the company's cash resources. In some cases, current liabilities may make a cash dividend inappropriate. In other cases, a major plant expansion program may warrant only a relatively small dividend.

3. **A declaration of dividends.** A company does not pay dividends unless its board of directors decides to do so, at which point the board "declares" the dividend. The board of directors has full authority to determine the amount of income to distribute in the form of a dividend and the amount to retain in the business. Dividends do not accrue like interest on a note payable, and they are not a liability until declared.

The amount and timing of a dividend are important issues. The payment of a large cash dividend could lead to liquidity problems for the company. On the other hand, a small dividend or a missed dividend may cause unhappiness among stockholders. Many stockholders expect to receive a reasonable cash payment from the company on a periodic basis. Many companies declare and pay cash dividends quarterly.

ENTRIES FOR CASH DIVIDENDS

Three dates are important in connection with dividends: (1) the declaration date, (2) the record date, and (3) the payment date. Normally, there are two to four weeks between each date. Companies make accounting entries on two of the dates—the declaration date and the payment date.

On the **declaration date**, the board of directors formally declares (authorizes) the cash dividend and announces it to stockholders. Declaration of a cash dividend **commits the corporation to a legal obligation**. The obligation is binding and cannot be rescinded. The company makes an entry to recognize the decrease in retained earnings and the increase in the liability Dividends Payable.

To illustrate, assume that on December 1, 2008, the directors of Media General declare a 50¢ per share cash dividend on 100,000 shares of $10 par value common stock. The dividend is $50,000 (100,000 × 50¢) The entry to record the declaration is:

Declaration Date

Dec. 1	Retained Earnings	50,000	
	Dividends Payable		50,000
	(To record declaration of cash dividend)		

A	=	L	+	SE
				−50,000 Div
		+50,000		

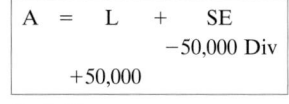

Cash Flows
no effect

Dividends Payable is a current liability: it will normally be paid within the next several months.

Instead of debiting Retained Earnings, the company may debit the account Dividends. This account provides additional information in the ledger. Also, a company may have separate dividend accounts for each class of stock. When using a dividend account, the company transfers the balance of that account to Retained Earnings at the end of the year by a closing entry. Whichever account is used for the dividend declaration, the effect is the same: Retained earnings decreases, and a current liability increases. *For homework problems, you should use the Retained Earnings account for recording dividend declarations.*

At the **record date**, the company determines ownership of the outstanding shares for dividend purposes. The records maintained by the corporation supply this information. In the interval between the declaration date and the record date, the corporation updates its stock ownership records. For Media General, the

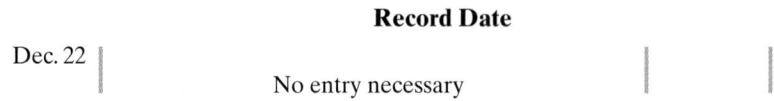

HELPFUL HINT
The purpose of the record date is to identify the persons or entities that will receive the dividend, not to determine the amount of the dividend liability.

record date is December 22. No entry is required on this date because the corporation's liability recognized on the declaration date is unchanged.

Record Date

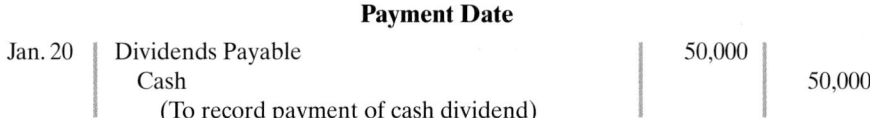

Dec. 22	No entry necessary		

On the **payment date**, the company mails dividend checks to the stockholders and records the payment of the dividend. Assuming that the payment date is January 20 for Media General, the entry on that date is:

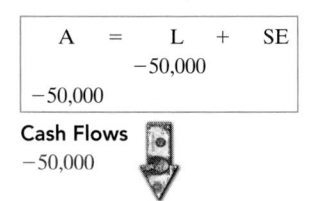

A	=	L	+	SE
		−50,000		
−50,000				

Cash Flows
−50,000

Payment Date

Jan. 20	Dividends Payable	50,000	
	Cash		50,000
	(To record payment of cash dividend)		

Note that payment of the dividend reduces both current assets and current liabilities. It has no effect on stockholders' equity. The **cumulative effect** of the **declaration and payment** of a cash dividend is to **decrease both stockholders' equity and total assets**. Illustration 14-1 summarizes the three important dates associated with dividends for Media General.

Illustration 14-1
Key dividend dates

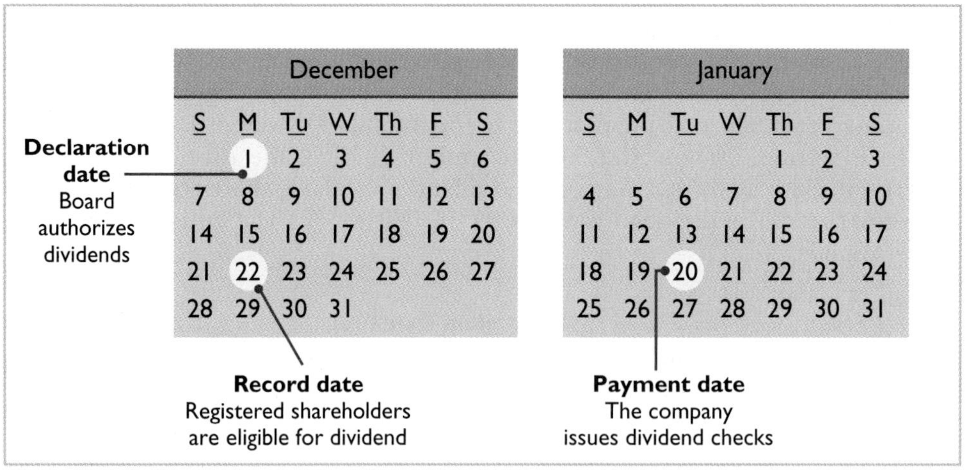

ALLOCATING CASH DIVIDENDS BETWEEN PREFERRED AND COMMON STOCK

As explained in Chapter 13, preferred stock has priority over common stock in regard to dividends. Holders of cumulative preferred stock must be paid any unpaid prior-year dividends before common stockholders receive dividends.

To illustrate, assume that at December 31, 2008, IBR Inc. has 1,000 shares of 8%, $100 par value cumulative preferred stock. It also has 50,000 shares of $10 par value common stock outstanding. The dividend per share for preferred stock is $8 ($100 par value × 8%). The required annual dividend for preferred stock is therefore $8,000 (1,000 × $8). At December 31, 2008, the directors declare a $6,000 cash dividend. In this case, the entire dividend amount goes to preferred stockholders because of their dividend preference. The entry to record the declaration of the dividend is:

Dec. 31	Retained Earnings	6,000	
	Dividends Payable		6,000
	(To record $6 per share cash dividend to preferred stockholders)		

A	=	L	+	SE
				−6,000 Div
		+6,000		

Cash Flows
no effect

Because of the cumulative feature, dividends of $2 per share are in arrears on preferred stock for 2008. The company must pay these dividends to preferred stockholders before it can pay any future dividends to common stockholders. IBR should disclose dividends in arrears in the financial statements.

At December 31, 2009, IBR declares a $50,000 cash dividend. The allocation of the dividend to the two classes of stock is as follows.

Total dividend		$50,000
Allocated to preferred stock		
Dividends in arrears, 2008 (1,000 × $2)	**$2,000**	
2009 dividend (1,000 × $8)	**8,000**	10,000
Remainder allocated to common stock		$40,000

Illustration 14-2
Allocating dividends to preferred and common stock

The entry to record the declaration of the dividend is:

Dec. 31	Retained Earnings	50,000	
	Dividends Payable		50,000
	(To record declaration of cash dividends of $10,000 to preferred stock and $40,000 to common stock)		

A	=	L	+	SE
				−50,000 Div
		+50,000		

Cash Flows
no effect

What if IBR's preferred stock were not cumulative? In that case preferred stockholders would have received only $8,000 in dividends in 2009. Common stockholders would have received $42,000.

ACCOUNTING ACROSS THE ORGANIZATION

Why Are Companies Increasing Their Dividends?

The decision whether to pay a cash dividend, and how much to pay, is a very important management decision. During 2004 cash dividend payments were a record $181 billion—not including a one-time $32.6 billion dividend by Microsoft. The $181 billion does include a 44% dividend increase by Wal-Mart and a doubling of the dividend payment by Intel.

One explanation for the increase is that Congress lowered, from 39% to 15%, the tax rate paid by investors on dividends received, making dividends more attractive to investors. Another driving force for the dividend increases was that companies were sitting on record amounts of cash. Because they did not see a lot of good expansion opportunities, companies decided to return the cash to shareholders.

Bigger dividends are still possible in the future. Large companies paid out 34% of their earnings as dividends in 2004—well below the historical average payout of 54% of earnings.

Source: Alan Levinsohn, "Divine Dividends," *Strategic Finance,* May 2005, pp. 59–60.

? What factors must management consider in deciding how large a dividend to pay?

Stock Dividends

A **stock dividend** is a pro rata distribution to stockholders of the corporation's own stock. Whereas a company pays cash in a cash dividend, a company issues shares of stock in a stock dividend. **A stock dividend results in a decrease in retained earnings and an increase in paid-in capital.** Unlike a cash dividend, a stock dividend does not decrease total stockholders' equity or total assets.

To illustrate, assume that you have a 2% ownership interest in Cetus Inc.; you own 20 of its 1,000 shares of common stock. If Cetus declares a 10% stock dividend, it would issue 100 shares (1,000 × 10%) of stock. You would receive two shares (2% × 100). Would your ownership interest change? No, it would remain at 2% (22 ÷ 1,100). **You now own more shares of stock, but your ownership interest has not changed.** Illustration 14-3 shows the effect of a stock dividend for stockholders.

Illustration 14-3
Effect of stock dividend for stockholders

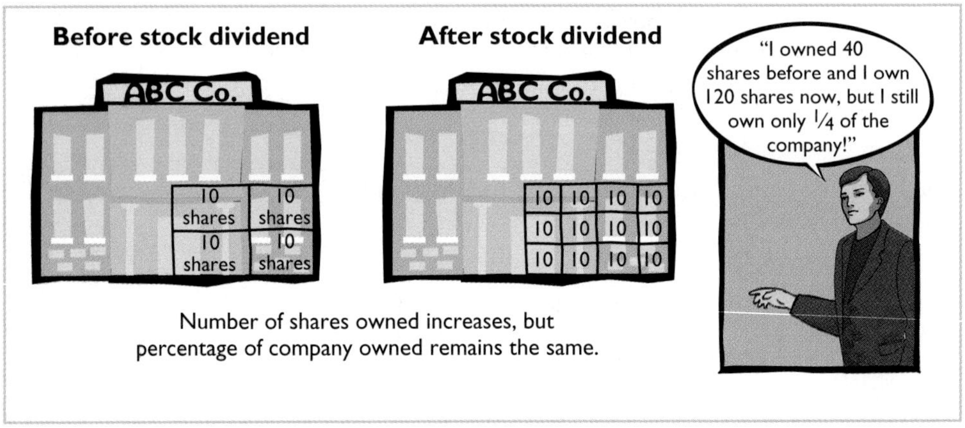

The company has disbursed no cash, and has assumed no liabilities. What are the purposes and benefits of a stock dividend? Corporations issue stock dividends generally for one or more of the following reasons.

1. To satisfy stockholders' dividend expectations without spending cash.
2. To increase the marketability of the corporation's stock. When the number of shares outstanding increases, the market price per share decreases. Decreasing the market price of the stock makes it easier for smaller investors to purchase the shares.
3. To emphasize that a portion of stockholders' equity has been permanently reinvested in the business (and is unavailable for cash dividends).

When the dividend is declared, the board of directors determines the size of the stock dividend and the value assigned to each dividend. Generally, if the company issues a **small stock dividend** (less than 20–25% of the corporation's issued stock), the value assigned to the dividend is the fair market value per share. This treatment is based on the assumption that a small stock dividend will have little effect on the market price of the outstanding shares. Many stockholders consider small stock dividends to be distributions of earnings equal to the fair market value of the shares distributed. If a company issues a **large stock dividend** (greater than 20–25%), the value assigned to the dividend is the par or stated value. Small stock dividends predominate in practice. Thus, we will illustrate only entries for small stock dividends.

ENTRIES FOR STOCK DIVIDENDS

To illustrate the accounting for small stock dividends, assume that Medland Corporation has a balance of $300,000 in retained earnings. It declares a 10% stock dividend on its 50,000 shares of $10 par value common stock. The current fair market value of its stock is $15 per share. The number of shares to be issued is 5,000 (10% × 50,000). Therefore the total amount to be debited to Retained Earnings is $75,000 (5,000 × $15). The entry to record the declaration of the stock dividend is as follows.

Retained Earnings	75,000	
Common Stock Dividends Distributable		50,000
Paid-in Capital in Excess of Par Value		25,000
(To record declaration of 10% stock dividend)		

A	=	L	+	SE
				−75,000 Div
				+50,000 CS
				+25,000 CS

Cash Flows
no effect

Medland debits Retained Earnings for the fair market value of the stock issued ($15 × 5,000). It credits to Common Stock Dividends Distributable the par value of the dividend shares ($10 × 5,000), and credits to Paid-in Capital in Excess of Par Value the excess over par ($5 × 5,000).

Common Stock Dividends Distributable is a **stockholders' equity account.** It is not a liability because assets will not be used to pay the dividend. If the company prepares a balance sheet before it issues the dividend shares, it reports the distributable account under Paid-in capital as shown in Illustration 14-4.

Paid-in capital		
Common stock	$500,000	
Common stock dividends distributable	**50,000**	$550,000

Illustration 14-4
Statement presentation of common stock dividends distributable

When Medland issues the dividend shares, it debits Common Stock Dividends Distributable, and credits Common Stock, as follows.

Common Stock Dividends Distributable	50,000	
Common Stock		50,000
(To record issuance of 5,000 shares in a stock dividend)		

A	=	L	+	SE
				−50,000 CS
				+50,000 CS

Cash Flows
no effect

EFFECTS OF STOCK DIVIDENDS

How do stock dividends affect stockholders' equity? They **change the composition of stockholders' equity**, because they transfer to paid-in capital a portion of retained earnings. However, **total stockholders' equity remains the same**. Stock dividends also have no effect on the par or stated value per share. But the number of shares outstanding increases, and the book value per share decreases. Illustration 14-5 shows these effects for Medland Corporation.

	Before Dividend	**After Dividend**
Stockholders' equity		
Paid-in capital		
Common stock, $10 par	$500,000	$550,000
Paid-in capital in excess of par value	—	25,000
Total paid-in capital	500,000	575,000
Retained earnings	300,000	225,000
Total stockholders' equity	**$800,000**	**$800,000**
Outstanding shares	**50,000**	**55,000**
Book value per share	**$16.00**	**$14.55**

Illustration 14-5
Stock dividend effects

In this example, total paid-in capital increases by $75,000, and retained earnings decreases by the same amount. Note also that total stockholders' equity remains unchanged at $800,000.

Stock Splits

A **stock split**, like a stock dividend, involves issuance of additional shares to stockholders according to their percentage ownership. **A stock split results in a reduction in the par or stated value per share.** The purpose of a stock split is to increase the marketability of the stock by lowering its market value per share.

The effect of a split on market value is generally *inversely proportional* to the size of the split. For example, after a recent 2-for-1 stock split, the market value of Nike's stock fell from $111 to approximately $55. The lower market value stimulated market activity, and within one year the stock was trading above $100 again.

HELPFUL HINT

A stock split changes the par value per share but does not affect any balances in stockholders' equity.

In a stock split, the number of shares increases in the same proportion that par or stated value per share decreases. For example, in a 2-for-1 split, one share of $10 par value stock is exchanged for two shares of $5 par value stock. **A stock split does not have any effect on total paid-in capital, retained earnings, or total stockholders' equity.** But the number of shares outstanding increases, and book value per share decreases. Illustration 14-6 shows these effects for Medland Corporation, assuming that it splits its 50,000 shares of common stock on a 2-for-1 basis.

Illustration 14-6
Stock split effects

	Before Stock Split	After Stock Split
Stockholders' equity		
Paid-in capital		
Common stock	$500,000	$500,000
Paid-in capital in excess of par value	–0–	–0–
Total paid-in capital	500,000	500,000
Retained earnings	300,000	300,000
Total stockholders' equity	**$800,000**	**$800,000**
Outstanding shares	**50,000**	**100,000**
Book value per share	**$16.00**	**$8.00**

A stock split does not affect the balances in any stockholders' equity accounts. Therefore **it is not necessary to journalize a stock split**.

Illustration 14-7 summarizes the significant differences between stock splits and stock dividends.

Illustration 14-7
Differences between the effects of stock splits and stock dividends

Item	Stock Split	Stock Dividend
Total paid-in capital	No change	Increase
Total retained earnings	No change	Decrease
Total par value (common stock)	No change	Increase
Par value per share	Decrease	No change

INVESTOR INSIGHT

Would You Pay $92,100 for One Share of Stock?

A handful of U.S. companies have no intention of keeping their stock trading in a range accessible to mere mortals. These companies never split their stock, no matter how high their stock price gets. The king is investment company Berkshire Hathaway's Class A stock, which sells for a pricey $92,100—per share! The company's Class B stock is a relative bargain at roughly $3,071 per share.

How does the effect on share price following a stock split compare to the effect on share price of treasury shares acquired?

Before You Go On...

REVIEW IT

1. What entries do companies make for cash dividends on (a) the declaration date, (b) the record date, and (c) the payment date?
2. Distinguish between a small and large stock dividend, and indicate the basis for valuing each kind of dividend.
3. Contrast the effects of a small stock dividend and a 2-for-1 stock split on (a) stockholders' equity, (b) outstanding shares, and (c) book value per share.
4. What were the amounts of the dividends PepsiCo declared per share of common stock during the years 2001 to 2005? Is the trend in dividends consistent with the company's net income trend during that period? The answers to these questions appear on page 628.

DO IT

Sing CD Company has had five years of record earnings. Due to this success, the market price of its 500,000 shares of $2 par value common stock has tripled from $15 per share to $45. During this period, paid-in capital remained the same at $2,000,000. Retained earnings increased from $1,500,000 to $10,000,000. CEO Joan Elbert is considering either (1) a 10% stock dividend or (2) a 2-for-1 stock split. She asks you to show the before-and-after effects of each option on (a) retained earnings and (b) book value per share.

Action Plan

- Calculate the stock dividend's effect on retained earnings by multiplying the number of new shares times the market price of the stock (or par value for a large stock dividend).
- Recall that a stock dividend increases the number of shares without affecting total equity, thus decreasing the book value per share.
- Recall that a stock split only increases the number of shares outstanding and decreases the par value per share.

Solution

(a) (1) The stock dividend amount is $2,250,000 [(500,000 × 10%) × $45]. The new balance in retained earnings is $7,750,000 ($10,000,000 – $2,250,000).

(2) The retained earnings balance after the stock split would be the same as it was before the split: $10,000,000.

(b) The book value effects are as follows:

	Original Balances	After Dividend	After Split
Paid-in capital	$ 2,000,000	$ 4,250,000	$ 2,000,000
Retained earnings	10,000,000	7,750,000	10,000,000
Total stockholders' equity	$12,000,000	$12,000,000	$12,000,000
Shares outstanding	500,000	550,000	1,000,000
Book value per share	$24	$21.82	$12

Related exercise material: *BE14-2, BE14-3, E14-3, and E14-4.*

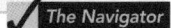

The Navigator

RETAINED EARNINGS

STUDY OBJECTIVE 2

Identify the items reported in a retained earnings statement.

As you learned in Chapter 13, **retained earnings** is net income that a company retains for use in the business. The balance in retained earnings is part of the stockholders' claim on the total assets of the corporation. It does not, though, represent a claim on any specific asset. Nor can the amount of retained earnings be associated with the balance of any asset account. For example, a $100,000 balance in retained earnings does not mean that there should be $100,000 in cash. The reason is that the company may have used the cash resulting from the excess of revenues over expenses to purchase buildings, equipment, and other assets.

To demonstrate that retained earnings and cash may be quite different, Illustration 14-8 shows recent amounts of retained earnings and cash in selected companies.

Illustration 14-8
Retained earnings and cash balances

Company	(in millions) Retained Earnings	Cash
Disney Co.	$17,775	$1,723
Intel Corp.	29,810	7,324
Kellogg Co.	3,266.1	219.1
Amazon.com	(2,027)	1,013

HELPFUL HINT

Remember that Retained Earnings is a stockholders' equity account, whose normal balance is a credit.

Remember from Chapter 13 that when a company has net income, it closes net income to retained earnings. The closing entry is a debit to Income Summary and a credit to Retained Earnings.

When a company has a **net loss** (expenses exceed revenues), it also closes this amount to retained earnings. The closing entry in this case is a debit to Retained Earnings and a credit to Income Summary. This is done even if it results in a debit balance in Retained Earnings. **Companies do not debit net losses to paid-in capital accounts.** To do so would destroy the distinction between paid-in and earned capital. A debit balance in Retained Earnings is identified as a **deficit**. It is reported as a deduction in the stockholders' equity section, as shown below.

Illustration 14-9
Stockholders' equity with deficit

Balance Sheet (partial)

Stockholders' equity	
Paid-in capital	
Common stock	$800,000
Retained earnings (deficit)	**(50,000)**
Total stockholders' equity	$750,000

Retained Earnings Restrictions

The balance in retained earnings is generally available for dividend declarations. Some companies state this fact. For example, Lockheed Martin Corporation states the following in the notes to its financial statements.

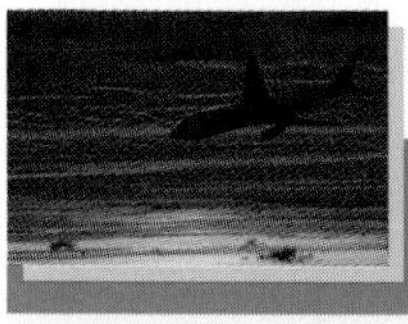

LOCKHEED MARTIN CORPORATION
Notes to the Financial Statements

Illustration 14-10
Disclosure of unrestricted retained earnings

At December 31, retained earnings were unrestricted and available for dividend payments.

In some cases, there may be **retained earnings restrictions**. These make a portion of the retained earnings balance currently unavailable for dividends. Restrictions result from one or more of the following causes.

1. **Legal restrictions.** Many states require a corporation to restrict retained earnings for the cost of treasury stock purchased. The restriction keeps intact the corporation's legal capital that is being temporarily held as treasury stock. When the company sells the treasury stock, the restriction is lifted.
2. **Contractual restrictions.** Long-term debt contracts may restrict retained earnings as a condition for the loan. The restriction limits the use of corporate assets for payment of dividends. Thus, it increases the likelihood that the corporation will be able to meet required loan payments.
3. **Voluntary restrictions.** The board of directors may voluntarily create retained earnings restrictions for specific purposes. For example, the board may authorize a restriction for future plant expansion. By reducing the amount of retained earnings available for dividends, the company makes more cash available for the planned expansion.

Companies generally disclose **retained earnings restrictions** in the notes to the financial statements. For example, Tektronix Inc., a manufacturer of electronic measurement devices, had total retained earnings of $774 million, but the unrestricted portion was only $223.8 million.

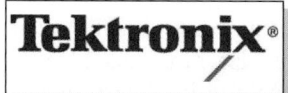

Tektronix®

TEKTRONIX INC.
Notes to the Financial Statements

Illustration 14-11
Disclosure of restriction

Certain of the Company's debt agreements require compliance with debt covenants. Management believes that the Company is in compliance with such requirements. The Company had unrestricted retained earnings of $223.8 million after meeting those requirements.

Prior Period Adjustments

Suppose that a corporation has closed its books and issued financial statements. The corporation then discovers that it made a material error in reporting net income of a prior year. How should the company record this situation in the accounts and report it in the financial statements?

The correction of an error in previously issued financial statements is known as a **prior period adjustment**. The company makes the correction directly to Retained

Earnings, because the effect of the error is now in this account. The net income for the prior period has been recorded in retained earnings through the journalizing and posting of closing entries.

To illustrate, assume that General Microwave discovers in 2008 that it understated depreciation expense in 2007 by $300,000 due to computational errors. These errors overstated both net income for 2007 and the current balance in retained earnings. The entry for the prior period adjustment, ignoring all tax effects, is as follows.

A	=	L	+	SE
				−300,000 RE
−300,000				

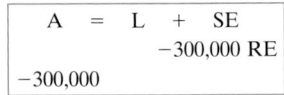

Cash Flows
no effect

	Debit	Credit
Retained Earnings	300,000	
Accumulated Depreciation		300,000
(To adjust for understatement of depreciation in a prior period)		

A debit to an income statement account in 2008 is incorrect because the error pertains to a prior year.

Companies report prior period adjustments in the retained earnings statement.[1] They add (or deduct, as the case may be) these adjustments from the beginning retained earnings balance. This results in an adjusted beginning balance. For example, assuming a beginning balance of $800,000 in retained earnings, General Microwave reports the prior period adjustment as follows.

Illustration 14-12
Statement presentation of prior period adjustments

GENERAL MICROWAVE
Retained Earnings Statement (partial)

Balance, January 1, as reported	$ 800,000
Correction for overstatement of net income in prior period (depreciation error)	**(300,000)**
Balance, January 1, as adjusted	$ 500,000

Again, reporting the correction in the current year's income statement would be incorrect because it applies to a prior year's income statement.

Retained Earnings Statement

The **retained earnings statement** shows the changes in retained earnings during the year. The company prepares the statement from the Retained Earnings account. Illustration 14-13 shows (in account form) transactions that affect retained earnings.

Illustration 14-13
Debits and credits to retained earnings

Retained Earnings (Debits)	Retained Earnings (Credits)
1. Net loss	1. Net income
2. Prior period adjustments for overstatement of net income	2. Prior period adjustments for understatement of net income
3. Cash dividends and stock dividends	
4. Some disposals of treasury stock	

As indicated, net income increases retained earnings, and a net loss decreases retained earnings. Prior period adjustments may either increase or decrease retained earnings. Both cash dividends and stock dividends decrease retained earnings. The

[1]A complete retained earnings statement is shown in Illustration 14-14 on the next page.

circumstances under which treasury stock transactions decrease retained earnings are explained in Chapter 13, page 571.

A complete retained earnings statement for Graber Inc., based on assumed data, is as follows.

Illustration 14-14
Retained earnings statement

GRABER INC.
Retained Earnings Statement
For the Year Ended December 31, 2008

Balance, January 1, as reported		$1,050,000
Correction for understatement of net income in prior period (inventory error)		50,000
Balance, January 1, as adjusted		1,100,000
Add: Net income		360,000
		1,460,000
Less: Cash dividends	$100,000	
Stock dividends	200,000	300,000
Balance, December 31		$1,160,000

STATEMENT PRESENTATION AND ANALYSIS

Stockholders' Equity Presentation

STUDY OBJECTIVE 3
Prepare and analyze a comprehensive stockholders' equity section.

Illustration 14-15 presents the stockholders' equity section of Graber Inc.'s balance sheet. Note the following: (1) "Common stock dividends distributable" is shown under "Capital stock," in "Paid-in capital." (2) A note (Note R) discloses a retained earnings restriction.

Illustration 14-15
Comprehensive stockholders' equity section

GRABER INC.
Balance Sheet (partial)

Stockholders' equity		
Paid-in capital		
Capital stock		
9% Preferred stock, $100 par value, cumulative, callable at $120, 10,000 shares authorized, 6,000 shares issued and outstanding		$ 600,000
Common stock, no par, $5 stated value, 500,000 shares authorized, 400,000 shares issued and 390,000 outstanding	$2,000,000	
Common stock dividends distributable	**50,000**	2,050,000
Total capital stock		2,650,000
Additional paid-in capital		
In excess of par value—preferred stock	30,000	
In excess of stated value—common stock	1,050,000	
Total additional paid-in capital		1,080,000
Total paid-in capital		3,730,000
Retained earnings **(see Note R)**		1,160,000
Total paid-in capital and retained earnings		4,890,000
Less: Treasury stock—common (10,000 shares)		80,000
Total stockholders' equity		$4,810,000

Note R: Retained earnings is restricted for the cost of treasury stock, $80,000.

Instead of presenting a detailed stockholders' equity section in the balance sheet and a retained earnings statement, many companies prepare a **stockholders' equity statement**. This statement shows the changes (1) in each stockholders' equity account and (2) in total that occurred during the year. An example of a stockholders' equity statement appears in PepsiCo's financial statements in Appendix A (page A8).

Stockholders' Equity Analysis

Investors and analysts can measure profitability from the viewpoint of the common stockholder by the **return on common stockholders' equity**. This ratio shows how many dollars of net income the company earned for each dollar invested by the stockholders. It is computed by dividing **net income available to common stockholders** (which is net income minus preferred stock dividends) by average common stockholders' equity.

To illustrate, Kellogg Company's beginning-of-the-year and end-of-the-year common stockholders' equity were $1,443.2 and $2,257.2 million respectively. Its net income was $890.6 million, and no preferred stock was outstanding. The return on common stockholders' equity ratio is computed as follows.

Illustration 14-16
Return on common stockholders' equity ratio and computation

Net Income Available to Common Stockholders	÷	Average Common Stockholders' Equity	=	Return on Common Stockholders' Equity
($890.6 − $0)	÷	$\frac{(\$1,443.2 + \$2,257.2)}{2}$	=	**48.1%**

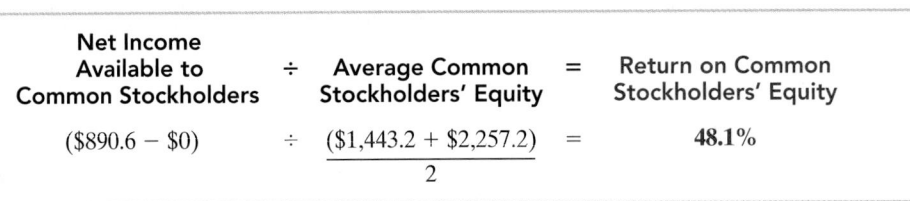

As shown above, if a company has preferred stock, we would deduct the amount of **preferred dividends** from the company's net income to compute income available to common stockholders. Also, the par value of preferred stock is deducted from total average stockholders' equity to arrive at the amount of common stockholders' equity.

Before You Go On...

REVIEW IT

1. How do companies generally report retained earnings restrictions?
2. What is a prior period adjustment, and how is it reported?
3. What are the principal sources of debits and credits to Retained Earnings?
4. How do companies report stock dividends distributable in the stockholders' equity section?
5. Explain the return on common stockholders' equity ratio.

DO IT

Vega Corporation has retained earnings of $5,130,000 on January 1, 2008. During the year, Vega earns $2,000,000 of net income. It declares and pays a $250,000 cash dividend. In 2008, Vega records an adjustment of $180,000 due to the understatement of 2007 depreciation expense from a mathematical error. Prepare a retained earnings statement for 2008.

Action Plan

- Recall that a retained earnings statement begins with retained earnings, as reported at the end of the previous year.
- Add or subtract any prior period adjustments to arrive at the adjusted beginning figure.
- Add net income and subtract dividends declared to arrive at the ending balance in retained earnings.

Solution

VEGA CORPORATION
Retained Earnings Statement
For the Year Ended December 31, 2008

Balance, January 1, as reported	$5,130,000
Correction for overstatement of net income in prior period (depreciation error)	(180,000)
Balance, January 1, as adjusted	4,950,000
Add: Net income	2,000,000
	6,950,000
Less: Cash dividends	250,000
Balance, December 31	$6,700,000

Related exercise material: *BE14-4, BE14-5, BE14-6, BE14-7, E14-8, E14-9, E14-10, and E14-11.*

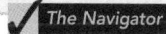

The Navigator

Income Statement Presentation

STUDY OBJECTIVE 4

Describe the form and content of corporation income statements.

Income statements for **corporations are the same as the statements for proprietorships or partnerships except for one thing: the reporting of income taxes.** For income tax purposes, corporations are a separate legal entity. As a result, corporations report **income tax expense** in a separate section of the corporation income statement, before net income. The condensed income statement for Leads Inc. in Illustration 14-17 shows a typical presentation. Note that the corporation reports income before income taxes as one line item and income tax expense as another.

Illustration 14-17
Income statement with income taxes

LEADS INC.
Income Statement
For the Year Ended December 31, 2008

Sales	$800,000
Cost of goods sold	600,000
Gross profit	200,000
Operating expenses	50,000
Income from operations	150,000
Other revenues and gains	10,000
Other expenses and losses	(4,000)
Income before income taxes	**156,000**
Income tax expense	**46,800**
Net income	$109,200

Companies record income tax expense and the related liability for income taxes payable as part of the adjusting process. Using the data for Leads Inc., in Illustration 14-17, the adjusting entry for income tax expense at December 31, 2008, is:

A	=	L	+	SE
				−46,800 Exp
		+46,800		

Cash Flows
no effect

Income Tax Expense	46,800	
Income Taxes Payable		46,800
(To record income taxes for 2008)		

The income statement of PepsiCo in Appendix A presents another illustration of income taxes.

Income Statement Analysis

STUDY OBJECTIVE 5
Compute earnings per share.

The financial press frequently reports earnings data. Stockholders and potential investors widely use these data in evaluating the profitability of a company. A convenient measure of earnings is **earnings per share (EPS)**, which indicates the net income earned by each share of outstanding **common stock**.

EPS AND PREFERRED DIVIDENDS

The existence of preferred dividends slightly complicates the calculation of EPS. When a corporation has both preferred and common stock, we must subtract the current year's preferred dividend from net income, to arrive at **income available to common stockholders**. Illustration 14-18 shows the formula for computing EPS.

Illustration 14-18
Formula for earnings per share

$$\frac{\text{Net Income minus Preferred Dividends}}{} \div \text{Weighted-Average of Common Shares Outstanding} = \text{Earnings per Share}$$

ETHICS NOTE
In order to meet market expectations for EPS, some managers engage in elaborate treasury stock transactions. These transactions can be very costly for the remaining shareholders.

To illustrate, assume that Rally Inc. reports net income of \$211,000 on its 102,500 weighted-average common shares.[2] During the year it also declares a \$6,000 dividend on its preferred stock. Therefore, the amount Rally has available for common stock dividends is \$205,000 (\$211,000 − \$6,000). Earnings per share is \$2 (\$205,000 ÷ 102,500). If the preferred stock is cumulative, Rally deducts the dividend for the current year, whether or not it is declared. Remember that companies report **earnings per share only for common stock**.

Investors often attempt to link earnings per share to the market price per share of a company's stock.[3] Because of the importance of earnings per share, most companies must report it on the face of the income statement. Generally companies

[2]The calculation of the weighted average of common shares outstanding is discussed in advanced accounting courses.

[3]The ratio of the market price per share to the earnings per share is called the *price/earnings (P/E) ratio*. The financial media report this ratio for common stocks listed on major stock exchanges.

simply report this amount below net income on the statement. For Rally Inc. the presentation is as follows.

Illustration 14-19
Basic earnings per share disclosure

RALLY INC. Income Statement (partial)	
Net income	$211,000
Earnings per share	**$2.00**

INVESTOR INSIGHT

Yahoo! and Costco Feel the Impact of Earnings per Share

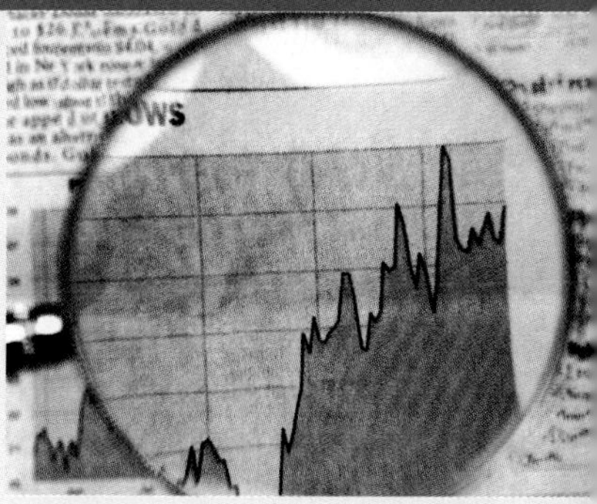

When a company publicly announces its latest earnings per share figure, a change in the company's stock price will often follow. The change in stock price will be most pronounced if the company's net income figure differs from what investors were expecting. When Yahoo! announced earnings per share that exceeded investor expectations, its stock price jumped 14% in a single day. When retail giant Costco Wholesale Corporation announced earnings per share only 1 cent below analysts' expectations, its stock price fell 22% in a single day. To avoid "earnings surprises" and the resultant wide swings in share prices, companies continually try to keep investors informed.

? Why do you think the prices of these companies changed as indicated?

Before You Go On...

REVIEW IT

1. What is the unique feature of a corporation income statement?
2. Explain the components of the formula for computing earnings per share when there is only common stock and outstanding shares are unchanged during the year.
3. What effects may preferred stock have on the formula for computing earnings per share?

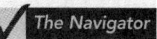

✓ The Navigator

Be sure to read **ALL ABOUT YOU: *Corporations Have Governance Structures—Do You?*** on page 612 for information on how topics in this chapter apply to you.

Corporations Have Governance Structures—Do You?

As discussed previously in this text, the scandals and bankruptcies at Enron, WorldCom, and other companies brought many changes to the way America does business. One of the primary lessons has been that companies need to take corporate governance and management oversight more seriously. As part of this effort, many companies have developed a code of ethics. The purpose of a code of ethics is to clearly specify standards of conduct to deter wrongdoing and promote honest and ethical conduct. It also is intended to be an expression by top management of its "tone at the top" —that is, to indicate that top management takes ethics seriously. Many other organizations, including university student groups, also have formulated ethics codes.

Some Facts

* Under Sarbanes-Oxley, a company must disclose in its annual report whether it has a code of ethics. It must also disclose any changes to or waivers of the code of ethics.
* Enron had a code of ethics. In a number of instances, Enron's board of directors knowingly waived requirements of the code so that the CFO could set up and run special purpose entities. Ultimately these waivers contributed to Enron's downfall.
* In some instances U.S. federal prosecutors have pressured companies to not pay the legal-defense bills of employees accused of wrong-doing, thus making it harder for the employees to defend themselves.
* In a recent survey of 1,436 workers, 34% said that they have seen unethical activities at their workplace, but only 47% said they are likely to report these activities. Many cited fear of retaliation by their bosses as the reason for not reporting.

About the Numbers

Stockholders often lose money as a result of unethical behavior by management. When they do, they often file lawsuits against the company in an effort to recoup these losses. The graph below shows just how expensive these class-action lawsuits can be for companies.

Top Class-Action Securities Settlements

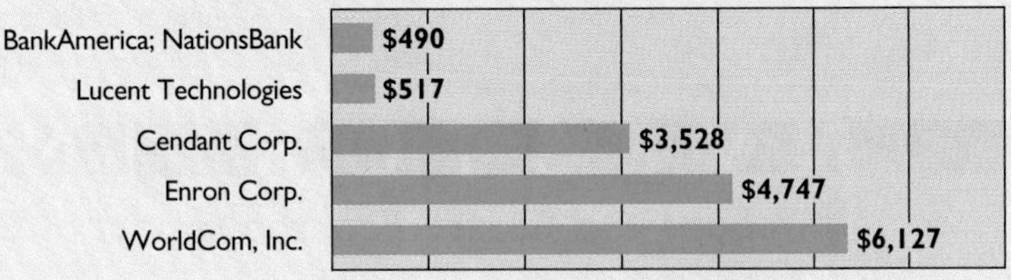

Dollars in Millions

Source: Elaine Buckberg, Todd Foster, and Ronald I. Miller, "Recent Trends in Shareholder Class Action Litigation: Are WorldCom and Enron the New Standard?" NERA Economic Consulting, *www.nera.com* (accessed June 26, 2006).

What Do You Think

Many universities have become concerned about student cheating. In particular, the prevalence of digital documents on the Internet has made it very easy to plagiarize. Many schools now have student ethics codes. Do you think that these ethics codes serve a useful purpose?

YES: Anything that will reduce unethical behavior is a good thing. An ethics code establishes what is and is not acceptable behavior, which helps universities maintain ethical standards for academic work and weed out those students who try to get ahead by non-ethical means.

NO: The existence of an ethics code won't affect student behavior. If students have a propensity to cheat, a document that tells them what is and is not good behavior is not going to be a deterrent. Students already know what cheating is, and that it is wrong.

Sources: "Whistleblowing Workers: Becoming an Endangered Species?" *HR Focus*, June 2006, p. 9; Lauren Etter, "The Enron Trial Finally Begins," *Wall Street Journal*, February 4, 2006, p. A7.

The authors' comments on this situation appear on page 627.

Demonstration Problem

On January 1, 2008, Hayslett Corporation had the following stockholders' equity accounts.

Common Stock ($10 par value, 260,000 shares issued and outstanding)	$2,600,000
Paid-in Capital in Excess of Par Value	1,500,000
Retained Earnings	3,200,000

During the year, the following transactions occurred.

April 1 Declared a $1.50 cash dividend per share to stockholders of record on April 15, payable May 1.
May 1 Paid the dividend declared in April.
June 1 Announced a 2-for-1 stock split. Prior to the split, the market price per share was $24.
Aug. 1 Declared a 10% stock dividend to stockholders of record on August 15, distributable August 31. On August 1, the market price of the stock was $10 per share.
31 Issued the shares for the stock dividend.
Dec. 1 Declared a $1.50 per share dividend to stockholders of record on December 15, payable January 5, 2009.
31 Determined that net income for the year was $600,000.

Instructions

(a) Journalize the transactions and the closing entry for net income.
(b) Prepare a stockholders' equity section at December 31.

Solution to Demonstration Problem

(a) Apr. 1	Retained Earnings (260,000 × $1.50)	390,000	
	Dividends Payable		390,000
May 1	Dividends Payable	390,000	
	Cash		390,000
June 1	Memo—two-for-one stock split increases number of shares to 520,000 (260,000 × 2) and reduces par value to $5 per share.		
Aug. 1	Retained Earnings (52,000* × $10)	520,000	
	Common Stock Dividends Distributable (52,000 × $5)		260,000
	Paid-in Capital in Excess of Par Value (52,000 × $5)		260,000
	*520,000 × .10		
31	Common Stock Dividends Distributable	260,000	
	Common Stock		260,000
Dec. 1	Retained Earnings (572,000** × $1.50)	858,000	
	Dividends Payable		858,000
	**(260,000 × 2) + 52,000		
31	Income Summary	600,000	
	Retained Earnings		600,000

action plan

- ✓ Award dividends to outstanding shares only.
- ✓ Adjust the par value and number of shares for stock splits, but make no journal entry.
- ✓ Use market value of stock to determine the value of a small stock dividend.
- ✓ Close Income Summary to Retained Earnings.

(b) HAYSLETT CORPORATION

Stockholders' equity	
Paid-in capital	
Capital stock	
Common stock, $5 par value, 572,000 shares issued and outstanding	$2,860,000
Additional paid-in capital in excess of par value	1,760,000
Total paid-in capital	4,620,000
Retained earnings	2,032,000
Total stockholders' equity	$6,652,000

The Navigator

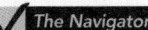

SUMMARY OF STUDY OBJECTIVES

WILEY PLUS

1 **Prepare the entries for cash dividends and stock dividends.** Companies make entries for both cash and stock dividends at the declaration date and at the payment date. At the *declaration date* the entries are: cash dividend—debit Retained Earnings, and credit Dividends Payable; small stock dividend—debit Retained Earnings, credit Paid-in Capital in Excess of Par (or Stated) Value, and credit Common Stock Dividends Distributable. At the *payment date,* the entries for cash and stock dividends are: cash dividend—debit Dividends Payable and credit Cash; small stock dividend—debit Common Stock Dividends Distributable and credit Common Stock.

2 **Identify the items reported in a retained earnings statement.** Companies report each of the individual debits and credits to retained earnings in the retained earnings statement. Additions consist of net income and prior period adjustments to correct understatements of prior years' net income. Deductions consist of net loss, adjustments to correct overstatements of prior years' net income, cash and stock dividends, and some disposals of treasury stock.

3 **Prepare and analyze a comprehensive stockholders' equity section.** A comprehensive stockholders' equity section includes all stockholders' equity accounts. It consists of two sections: paid-in capital and retained earnings. It should also include notes to the financial statements that explain any restrictions on retained earnings and any dividends in arrears. One measure of profitability is the return on common stockholders' equity. It is calculated by dividing net income minus preferred stock dividends by average common stockholders' equity.

4 **Describe the form and content of corporation income statements.** The form and content of corporation income statements are similar to the statements of proprietorships and partnerships with one exception: Corporations must report income taxes or income tax expense in a separate section before net income in the income statement.

5 **Compute earnings per share.** Companies compute earnings per share by dividing net income by the weighted-average number of common shares outstanding during the period. When preferred stock dividends exist, they must be deducted from net income in order to calculate EPS.

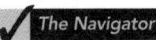

The Navigator

GLOSSARY

WILEY PLUS

Cash dividend A pro rata distribution of cash to stockholders. (p. 596).

Declaration date The date the board of directors formally declares a dividend and announces it to stockholders. (p. 597).

Deficit A debit balance in retained earnings. (p. 604).

Dividend A corporation's distribution of cash or stock to its stockholders on a pro rata (proportional) basis. (p. 596).

Earnings per share The net income earned by each share of outstanding common stock. (p 610)

Liquidating dividend A dividend declared out of paid-in capital. (p. 596).

Payment date The date dividend checks are mailed to stockholders. (p. 598).

Prior period adjustment The correction of an error in previously issued financial statements. (p. 605).

Record date The date when ownership of outstanding shares is determined for dividend purposes. (p. 597).

Retained earnings Net income that is retained in the business. (p. 604).

Retained earnings restrictions Circumstances that make a portion of retained earnings currently unavailable for dividends. (p. 605).

Retained earnings statement A financial statement that shows the changes in retained earnings during the year. (p. 606).

Return on common stockholders' equity A measure of profitability that shows how many dollars of net income were earned for each dollar invested by the owners; computed as net income minus preferred dividends divided by average common stockholders' equity. (p. 608).

Stock dividend A pro rata distribution to stockholders of the corporation's own stock. (p. 600).

Stockholders' equity statement A statement that shows the changes in each stockholders' equity account and in total stockholders' equity during the year. (p. 608).

Stock split The issuance of additional shares of stock to stockholders according to their percentage ownership; is accompanied by a reduction in the par or stated value per share. (p. 602).

SELF-STUDY QUESTIONS

WILEY PLUS

Answers are at the end of the chapter.

(SO 1) **1.** Entries for cash dividends are required on the:
- **a.** declaration date and the payment date.
- **b.** record date and the payment date.
- **c.** declaration date, record date, and payment date.
- **d.** declaration date and the record date.

(SO 1) **2.** Which of the following statements about small stock dividends is true?
- **a.** A debit to Retained Earnings for the par value of the shares issued should be made.
- **b.** A small stock dividend decreases total stockholders' equity.
- **c.** Market value per share should be assigned to the dividend shares.
- **d.** A small stock dividend ordinarily will have no effect on book value per share of stock.

(SO 1) **3.** Which of the following statements about a 3-for-1 stock split is true?
- **a.** It will triple the market value of the stock.
- **b.** It will triple the amount of total stockholders' equity.
- **c.** It will have no effect on total stockholders' equity.
- **d.** It requires the company to distribute cash.

(SO 2) **4.** Which of the following can cause a restriction in retained earnings?
- **a.** State laws regarding treasury stock.
- **b.** Long-term debt contract terms.
- **c.** Authorizations by the board of directors in light of planned expansion of corporate facilities.
- **d.** All of the above.

(SO 2) **5.** All *but one* of the following is reported in a retained earnings statement. The exception is:
- **a.** cash and stock dividends.
- **b.** net income and net loss.
- **c.** some disposals of treasury stock below cost.
- **d.** sales of treasury stock above cost.

(SO 2) **6.** A prior period adjustment is:
- **a.** reported in the income statement as a nontypical item.
- **b.** a correction of an error that is made directly to retained earnings.
- **c.** reported directly in the stockholders' equity section.
- **d.** reported in the retained earnings statement as an adjustment of the ending balance of retained earnings.

7. In the stockholders' equity section, Common Stock Dividends Distributable is reported as a(n): (SO 3)
- **a.** deduction from total paid-in capital and retained earnings.
- **b.** addition to additional paid-in capital.
- **c.** deduction from retained earnings.
- **d.** addition to capital stock.

8. Corporation income statements may be the same as the income statements for unincorporated companies *except* for: (SO 4)
- **a.** gross profit.
- **b.** income tax expense.
- **c.** operating income.
- **d.** net sales.

9. The return on common stockholders' equity is defined as: (SO 3)
- **a.** Net income divided by total assets.
- **b.** Cash dividends divided by average common stockholders' equity.
- **c.** Income available to common stockholders divided by average common stockholders' equity.
- **d.** None of these is correct.

10. The income statement for Nadeen, Inc. shows income before income taxes $700,000, income tax expense $210,000, and net income $490,000. If Nadeen has 100,000 shares of common stock outstanding throughout the year, earnings per share is: (SO 5)
- **a.** $7.00.
- **b.** $4.90.
- **c.** $2.10.
- **d.** No correct answer is given.

Go to the book's website,
www.wiley.com/college/weygandt,
for Additional Self-Study questions.

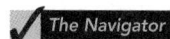

The Navigator

QUESTIONS

1. (a) What is a dividend? (b) "Dividends must be paid in cash." Do you agree? Explain.
2. Sue DeVine maintains that adequate cash is the only requirement for the declaration of a cash dividend. Is Sue correct? Explain.
3. (a) Three dates are important in connection with cash dividends. Identify these dates, and explain their significance to the corporation and its stockholders.
   (b) Identify the accounting entries that are made for a cash dividend and the date of each entry.
4. Conger Inc. declares a $45,000 cash dividend on December 31, 2008. The required annual dividend on preferred stock is $10,000. Determine the allocation of the dividend to preferred and common stockholders assuming the preferred stock is cumulative and dividends are 1 year in arrears.
5. Contrast the effects of a cash dividend and a stock dividend on a corporation's balance sheet.
6. Todd Huebner asks, "Since stock dividends don't change anything, why declare them?" What is your answer to Todd?
7. Meenen Corporation has 30,000 shares of $10 par value common stock outstanding when it announces a 2-for-1 stock split. Before the split, the stock had a market price of $120 per share. After the split, how many shares of stock will be outstanding? What will be the approximate market price per share?
8. The board of directors is considering either a stock split or a stock dividend. They understand that total stockholders' equity will remain the same under either action. However, they are not sure of the different effects of the two types of actions on other aspects of stockholders' equity. Explain the differences to the directors.
9. What is a prior period adjustment, and how is it reported in the financial statements?
10. KSU Corporation has a retained earnings balance of $210,000 on January 1. During the year, a prior period adjustment of $50,000 is recorded because of the understatement of depreciation in the prior period. Show the retained earnings statement presentation of these data.
11. What is the purpose of a retained earnings restriction? Identify the possible causes of retained earnings restrictions.
12. How are retained earnings restrictions generally reported in the financial statements?
13. Identify the events that result in debits and credits to retained earnings.
14. Juan Ortega believes that both the beginning and ending balances in retained earnings are shown in the stockholders' equity section. Is Juan correct? Discuss.
15. Gene Remington, who owns many investments in common stock, says, "I don't care what a company's net income is. The stock price tells me everything I need to know!" How do you respond to Gene?
16. What is the unique feature of a corporation income statement? Illustrate this feature, using assumed data.
17. Why must preferred stock dividends be subtracted from net income in computing earnings per share?

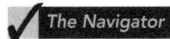

✓ The Navigator

BRIEF EXERCISES

Prepare entries for a cash dividend.
(SO 1)

BE14-1 Eidman Corporation has 80,000 shares of common stock outstanding. It declares a $1 per share cash dividend on November 1 to stockholders of record on December 1. The dividend is paid on December 31. Prepare the entries on the appropriate dates to record the declaration and payment of the cash dividend.

Prepare entries for a stock dividend.
(SO 1)

BE14-2 Tidwell Corporation has 50,000 shares of $10 par value common stock outstanding. It declares a 10% stock dividend on December 1 when the market value per share is $16. The dividend shares are issued on December 31. Prepare the entries for the declaration and payment of the stock dividend.

Show before and after effects of a stock dividend.
(SO 1)

BE14-3 The stockholders' equity section of O'Vear Corporation consists of common stock ($10 par) $2,000,000 and retained earnings $500,000. A 10% stock dividend (20,000 shares) is declared when the market value per share is $14. Show the before and after effects of the dividend on the following.

(a) The components of stockholders' equity.
(b) Shares outstanding.
(c) Book value per share.

Prepare a retained earnings statement.
(SO 2)

BE14-4 For the year ending December 31, 2008, Kerns Inc. reports net income $140,000 and dividends $85,000. Prepare the retained earnings statement for the year assuming the balance in retained earnings on January 1, 2008, was $220,000.

Prepare a retained earnings statement.
(SO 2)

BE14-5 The balance in retained earnings on January 1, 2008, for Persinger Inc, was $800,000. During the year, the corporation paid cash dividends of $90,000 and distributed a stock dividend of $8,000. In addition, the company determined that it had understated its depreciation expense in prior years by $50,000. Net income for 2008 was $120,000. Prepare the retained earnings statement for 2008.

BE14-6 SUPERVALU, one of the largest grocery retailers in the United States, is headquartered in Minneapolis. The following financial information (in millions) was taken from the company's 2005 annual report. Net sales $19,543; net income $386; beginning stockholders' equity $2,210; ending stockholders' equity $2,510. Compute the return on common stockholders' equity ratio.

Calculate the return on common stockholders' equity.
(SO 3)

BE14-7 Fuentes Corporation reported net income of $152,000, declared dividends on common stock of $50,000, and had an ending balance in retained earnings of $360,000. Stockholders' equity was $700,000 at the beginning of the year and $820,000 at the end of the year. Compute the return on common stockholders' equity.

Compute return on common stockholders' equity.
(SO 3)

BE14-8 The following information is available for Dixen Corporation for the year ended December 31, 2008: Cost of goods sold $205,000; Sales $450,000; Other revenues and gains $50,000; Operating expenses $75,000. Assuming a corporate tax rate of 30%, prepare an income statement for the company.

Prepare a corporate income statement.
(SO 4)

BE14-9 Quayle Corporation reports net income of $380,000 and a weighted average of 200,000 shares of common stock outstanding for the year. Compute the earnings per share of common stock.

Compute earnings per share.
(SO 5)

BE14-10 Income and common stock data for Quayle Corporation are presented in BE14-9. Assume also that Quayle has cumulative preferred stock dividends for the current year of $20,000 that were declared and paid. Compute the earnings per share of common stock.

Compute earnings per share with cumulative preferred stock.
(SO 5)

EXERCISES

WILEY PLUS

E14-1 On January 1, Molini Corporation had 95,000 shares of no-par common stock issued and outstanding. The stock has a stated value of $5 per share. During the year, the following occurred.

Journalize cash dividends; indicate statement presentation.
(SO 1)

Apr. 1	Issued 25,000 additional shares of common stock for $17 per share.
June 15	Declared a cash dividend of $1 per share to stockholders of record on June 30.
July 10	Paid the $1 cash dividend.
Dec. 1	Issued 2,000 additional shares of common stock for $19 per share.
15	Declared a cash dividend on outstanding shares of $1.20 per share to stockholders of record on December 31.

Instructions

(a) Prepare the entries, if any, on each of the three dividend dates.

(b) How are dividends and dividends payable reported in the financial statements prepared at December 31?

E14-2 Perez Corporation was organized on January 1, 2007. During its first year, the corporation issued 2,000 shares of $50 par value preferred stock and 100,000 shares of $10 par value common stock. At December 31, the company declared the following cash dividends: 2007, $6,000, 2008, $12,000, and 2009, $28,000.

Allocate cash dividends to preferred and common stock.
(SO 1)

Instructions

(a) Show the allocation of dividends to each class of stock, assuming the preferred stock dividend is 7% and not cumulative.

(b) Show the allocation of dividends to each class of stock, assuming the preferred stock dividend is 8% and cumulative.

(c) Journalize the declaration of the cash dividend at December 31, 2009, under part (b).

E14-3 On January 1, 2008, Deweese Corporation had $1,000,000 of common stock outstanding that was issued at par. It also had retained earnings of $750,000. The company issued 40,000 shares of common stock at par on July 1 and earned net income of $400,000 for the year.

Journalize stock dividends.
(SO 1)

Instructions

Journalize the declaration of a 15% stock dividend on December 10, 2008, for the following independent assumptions.

1. Par value is $10, and market value is $18.
2. Par value is $5, and market value is $20.

Compare effects of a stock dividend and a stock split.
(SO 1)

E14-4 On October 31, the stockholders' equity section of Huth Company consists of common stock $300,000 and retained earnings $900,000. Huth is considering the following two courses of action: (1) declaring a 5% stock dividend on the 30,000, $10 par value shares outstanding, or (2) effecting a 2-for-1 stock split that will reduce par value to $5 per share. The current market price is $14 per share.

Instructions

Prepare a tabular summary of the effects of the alternative actions on the components of stockholders' equity, outstanding shares, and book value per share. Use the following column headings: Before Action, After Stock Dividend, and After Stock Split.

Compute book value per share; indicate account balances after a stock dividend.
(SO 1, 3)

E14-5 On October 1, Kosko Corporation's stockholders' equity is as follows.

Common stock, $5 par value	$400,000
Paid-in capital in excess of par value	25,000
Retained earnings	155,000
Total stockholders' equity	$580,000

On October 1, Kosko declares and distributes a 10% stock dividend when the market value of the stock is $15 per share.

Instructions

(a) Compute the book value per share (1) before the stock dividend and (2) after the stock dividend. (Round to two decimals.)
(b) Indicate the balances in the three stockholders' equity accounts after the stock dividend shares have been distributed.

Indicate the effects on stockholders' equity components.
(SO 1, 2, 3)

E14-6 During 2008, Jester Corporation had the following transactions and events.

1. Declared a cash dividend.
2. Issued par value common stock for cash at par value.
3. Completed a 2-for-1 stock split in which $10 par value stock was changed to $5 par value stock.
4. Declared a small stock dividend when the market value was higher than par value.
5. Made a prior period adjustment for overstatement of net income.
6. Issued the shares of common stock required by the stock dividend declaration in item no. 4 above.
7. Paid the cash dividend in item no. 1 above.
8. Issued par value common stock for cash above par value.

Instructions

Indicate the effect(s) of each of the foregoing items on the subdivisions of stockholders' equity. Present your answer in tabular form with the following columns. Use (I) for increase, (D) for decrease, and (NE) for no effect. Item no. 1 is given as an example.

	Paid-in Capital		
Item	Capital Stock	Additional	Retained Earnings
1	NE	NE	D

Prepare correcting entries for dividends and a stock split.
(SO 1)

E14-7 Before preparing financial statements for the current year, the chief accountant for Reynolds Company discovered the following errors in the accounts.

1. The declaration and payment of $50,000 cash dividend was recorded as a debit to Interest Expense $50,000 and a credit to Cash $50,000.
2. A 10% stock dividend (1,000 shares) was declared on the $10 par value stock when the market value per share was $18. The only entry made was: Retained Earnings (Dr.) $10,000 and Dividend Payable (Cr.) $10,000. The shares have not been issued.

3. A 4-for-1 stock split involving the issue of 400,000 shares of $5 par value common stock for 100,000 shares of $20 par value common stock was recorded as a debit to Retained Earnings $2,000,000 and a credit to Common Stock $2,000,000.

Instructions
Prepare the correcting entries at December 31.

Prepare a retained earnings statement.
(SO 2)

E14-8 On January 1, 2008, Felter Corporation had retained earnings of $550,000. During the year, Felter had the following selected transactions.

1. Declared cash dividends $120,000.
2. Corrected overstatement of 2007 net income because of depreciation error $40,000.
3. Earned net income $350,000.
4. Declared stock dividends $60,000.

Instructions
Prepare a retained earnings statement for the year.

Prepare a retained earnings statement.
(SO 2)

E14-9 Sasha Company reported retained earnings at December 31, 2007, of $310,000. Sasha had 200,000 shares of common stock outstanding throughout 2008.

The following transactions occurred during 2008.

1. An error was discovered: in 2006, depreciation expense was recorded at $70,000, but the correct amount was $50,000.
2. A cash dividend of $0.50 per share was declared and paid.
3. A 5% stock dividend was declared and distributed when the market price per share was $15 per share.
4. Net income was $285,000.

Instructions
Prepare a retained earnings statement for 2008.

Prepare stockholders' equity section.
(SO 3)

E14-10 Kelly Groucutt Company reported the following balances at December 31, 2007: common stock $400,000; paid-in capital in excess of par value $100,000; retained earnings $250,000. During 2008, the following transactions affected stockholder's equity.

1. Issued preferred stock with a par value of $125,000 for $200,000.
2. Purchased treasury stock (common) for $40,000.
3. Earned net income of $140,000.
4. Declared and paid cash dividends of $56,000.

Instructions
Prepare the stockholders' equity section of Kelly Groucutt Company's December 31, 2008, balance sheet.

Prepare a stockholders' equity section.
(SO 3)

E14-11 The following accounts appear in the ledger of Ortiz Inc. after the books are closed at December 31.

Common Stock, no par, $1 stated value, 400,000 shares authorized; 300,000 shares issued	$ 300,000
Common Stock Dividends Distributable	30,000
Paid-in Capital in Excess of Stated Value—Common Stock	1,200,000
Preferred Stock, $5 par value, 8%, 40,000 shares authorized; 30,000 shares issued	150,000
Retained Earnings	800,000
Treasury Stock (10,000 common shares)	74,000
Paid-in Capital in Excess of Par Value—Preferred Stock	344,000

Instructions
Prepare the stockholders' equity section at December 31, assuming retained earnings is restricted for plant expansion in the amount of $100,000.

Prepare an income statement and compute earnings per share.
(SO 4, 5)

E14-12 The following information is available for Patel Corporation for the year ended December 31, 2008: Sales $800,000; Other revenues and gains $92,000; Operating expenses $110,000; Cost of goods sold $465,000; Other expenses and losses $32,000; Preferred stock dividends $30,000. The company's tax rate was 20%, and it had 50,000 shares outstanding during the entire year.

Instructions

(a) Prepare a corporate income statement.
(b) Calculate earnings per share.

Prepare an income statement and compute return on equity.
(SO 3, 4)

E14-13 In 2008, Mike Singletary Corporation had net sales of $600,000 and cost of goods sold of $360,000. Operating expenses were $153,000, and interest expense was $7,500. The corporation's tax rate is 30%. The corporation declared preferred dividends of $15,000 in 2008, and its average common stockholders' equity during the year was $200,000.

Instructions

(a) Prepare an income statement for Mike Singletary Corporation.
(b) Compute Mike Singletary Corporation's return on common stockholders' equity for 2008.

Compute EPS.
(SO 4, 5)

E14-14 McCoy Corporation has outstanding at December 31, 2008, 50,000 shares of $20 par value, cumulative, 8% preferred stock and 200,000 shares of $5 par value common stock. All shares were outstanding the entire year. During 2008, McCoy earned total revenues of $2,000,000 and incurred total expenses (except income taxes) of $1,200,000. McCoy's income tax rate is 30%.

Instructions

Compute McCoy's 2008 earnings per share.

Calculate ratios to evaluate earnings performance.
(SO 3, 5)

E14-15 The following financial information is available for Cheney Corporation.

	2008	2007
Average common stockholders' equity	$1,200,000	$900,000
Dividends paid to common stockholders	50,000	30,000
Dividends paid to preferred stockholders	20,000	20,000
Net income	290,000	200,000
Market price of common stock	20	15

The weighted average number of shares of common stock outstanding was 80,000 for 2007 and 100,000 for 2008.

Instructions

Calculate earnings per share and return on common stockholders' equity for 2008 and 2007.

Calculate ratios to evaluate earnings performance.
(SO 3, 5)

E14-16 This financial information is available for Hoyle Corporation.

	2008	2007
Average common stockholders' equity	$1,800,000	$1,900,000
Dividends paid to common stockholders	90,000	70,000
Dividends paid to preferred stockholders	20,000	20,000
Net income	290,000	248,000
Market price of common stock	20	25

The weighted-average number of shares of common stock outstanding was 180,000 for 2007 and 150,000 for 2008.

Instructions

Calculate earnings per share and return on common stockholders' equity for 2008 and 2007.

Compute earnings per share under different assumptions.
(SO 5)

E14-17 At December 31, 2008, Cali Corporation has 2,000 shares of $100 par value, 8%, preferred stock outstanding and 100,000 shares of $10 par value common stock issued. Cali's net income for the year is $241,000.

Instructions

Compute the earnings per share of common stock under the following independent situations. (Round to two decimals.)

(a) The dividend to preferred stockholders was declared. There has been no change in the number of shares of common stock outstanding during the year.
(b) The dividend to preferred stockholders was not declared. The preferred stock is cumulative. Cali held 10,000 shares of common treasury stock throughout the year.

EXERCISES: SET B

Visit the book's website at **www.wiley.com/college/weygandt**, and choose the Student Companion site, to access Exercise Set B.

PROBLEMS: SET A

P14-1A On January 1, 2008, Carolinas Corporation had the following stockholders' equity accounts.

Prepare dividend entries and stockholders' equity section.
(SO 1, 3)

Common Stock ($20 par value, 60,000 shares issued and outstanding)	$1,200,000
Paid-in Capital in Excess of Par Value	200,000
Retained Earnings	600,000

During the year, the following transactions occurred.

Feb. 1 Declared a $1 cash dividend per share to stockholders of record on February 15, payable March 1.
Mar. 1 Paid the dividend declared in February.
Apr. 1 Announced a 2-for-1 stock split. Prior to the split, the market price per share was $36.
July 1 Declared a 10% stock dividend to stockholders of record on July 15, distributable July 31. On July 1, the market price of the stock was $13 per share.
31 Issued the shares for the stock dividend.
Dec. 1 Declared a $0.50 per share dividend to stockholders of record on December 15, payable January 5, 2009.
31 Determined that net income for the year was $350,000.

Instructions
(a) Journalize the transactions and the closing entry for net income.
(b) Enter the beginning balances, and post the entries to the stockholders' equity accounts. (*Note*: Open additional stockholders' equity accounts as needed.)
(c) Prepare a stockholders' equity section at December 31.

(c) Total stockholders' equity $2,224,000

P14-2A The stockholders' equity accounts of Hashmi Company at January 1, 2008, are as follows.

Journalize and post transactions; prepare retained earnings statement and stockholders' equity section.
(SO 1, 2, 3)

Preferred Stock, 6%, $50 par	$600,000
Common Stock, $5 par	800,000
Paid-in Capital in Excess of Par Value—Preferred Stock	200,000
Paid-in Capital in Excess of Par Value—Common Stock	300,000
Retained Earnings	800,000

There were no dividends in arrears on preferred stock. During 2008, the company had the following transactions and events.

July 1 Declared a $0.50 cash dividend on common stock.
Aug. 1 Discovered $25,000 understatement of 2007 depreciation. Ignore income taxes.
Sept. 1 Paid the cash dividend declared on July 1.
Dec. 1 Declared a 10% stock dividend on common stock when the market value of the stock was $18 per share.
15 Declared a 6% cash dividend on preferred stock payable January 15, 2009.
31 Determined that net income for the year was $355,000.
31 Recognized a $200,000 restriction of retained earnings for plant expansion.

Instructions
(a) Journalize the transactions, events, and closing entries.
(b) Enter the beginning balances in the accounts, and post to the stockholders' equity accounts. (*Note*: Open additional stockholders' equity accounts as needed.)
(c) Prepare a retained earnings statement for the year.
(d) Prepare a stockholders' equity section at December 31, 2008.

(c) Ending balance $726,000
(d) Total stockholders' equity $2,914,000

Prepare retained earnings statement and stockholders' equity section, and compute earnings per share.

(SO 1, 2, 3, 5)

P14-3A The post-closing trial balance of Dold Corporation at December 31, 2008, contains the following stockholders' equity accounts.

Preferred Stock (15,000 shares issued)	$ 750,000
Common Stock (250,000 shares issued)	2,500,000
Paid-in Capital in Excess of Par Value—Preferred	250,000
Paid-in Capital in Excess of Par Value—Common	400,000
Common Stock Dividends Distributable	250,000
Retained Earnings	1,042,000

A review of the accounting records reveals the following.

1. No errors have been made in recording 2008 transactions or in preparing the closing entry for net income.
2. Preferred stock is $50 par, 6%, and cumulative; 15,000 shares have been outstanding since January 1, 2007.
3. Authorized stock is 20,000 shares of preferred, 500,000 shares of common with a $10 par value.
4. The January 1 balance in Retained Earnings was $1,170,000.
5. On July 1, 20,000 shares of common stock were sold for cash at $16 per share.
6. On September 1, the company discovered an understatement error of $90,000 in computing depreciation in 2007. The net of tax effect of $63,000 was properly debited directly to Retained Earnings.
7. A cash dividend of $250,000 was declared and properly allocated to preferred and common stock on October 1. No dividends were paid to preferred stockholders in 2007.
8. On December 31, a 10% common stock dividend was declared out of retained earnings on common stock when the market price per share was $16.
9. Net income for the year was $585,000.
10. On December 31, 2008, the directors authorized disclosure of a $200,000 restriction of retained earnings for plant expansion. (Use Note X.)

Instructions

(a) Reproduce the Retained Earnings account for the year.
(b) Prepare a retained earnings statement for the year.
(c) Prepare a stockholders' equity section at December 31.
(d) Compute the earnings per share of common stock using 240,000 as the weighted average shares outstanding for the year.
(e) Compute the allocation of the cash dividend to preferred and common stock.

(c) Total stockholders' equity, $5,192,000

Prepare the stockholders' equity section, reflecting dividends and stock split.

(SO 1, 2, 3)

P14-4A On January 1, 2008, Pattini Corporation had the following stockholders' equity accounts.

Common Stock (no par value, 90,000 shares issued and outstanding)	$1,400,000
Retained Earnings	500,000

During the year, the following transactions occurred.

Feb. 1	Declared a $1 cash dividend per share to stockholders of record on February 15, payable March 1.
Mar. 1	Paid the dividend declared in February.
Apr. 1	Announced a 4-for-1 stock split. Prior to the split, the market price per share was $36.
July 1	Declared a 5% stock dividend to stockholders of record on July 15, distributable July 31. On July 1, the market price of the stock was $13 per share.
31	Issued the shares for the stock dividend.
Dec. 1	Declared a $0.50 per share dividend to stockholders of record on December 15, payable January 5, 2009.
31	Determined that net income for the year was $350,000.

Instructions

Prepare the stockholders' equity section of the balance sheet at: (a) March 31, (b) June 30, (c) September 30, and (d) December 31, 2008.

(d) Total stockholders' equity $1,971,000

Prepare the stockholders' equity section, reflecting various events.

(SO 1, 3)

P14-5A On January 1, 2008, Yadier Inc. had the following stockholders' equity account balances.

Common Stock, no-par value (500,000 shares issued)	$1,500,000
Common Stock Dividends Distributable	200,000
Retained Earnings	600,000

During 2008, the following transactions and events occurred.

1. Issued 50,000 shares of common stock as a result of a 10% stock dividend declared on December 15, 2007.
2. Issued 30,000 shares of common stock for cash at $6 per share.
3. Corrected an error that had understated the net income for 2006 by $70,000.
4. Declared and paid a cash dividend of $80,000.
5. Earned net income of $300,000.

Instructions

Prepare the stockholders' equity section of the balance sheet at December 31, 2008.

Total stockholders' equity $2,770,000

PROBLEMS: SET B

Prepare dividend entries and stockholders' equity section.

(SO 1, 3)

GLS

P14-1B On January 1, 2008, Verlin Corporation had the following stockholders' equity accounts.

Common Stock ($10 par value, 100,000 shares issued and outstanding)	$1,000,000
Paid-in Capital in Excess of Par Value	200,000
Retained Earnings	540,000

During the year, the following transactions occurred.

Jan. 15 Declared a $1 cash dividend per share to stockholders of record on January 31, payable February 15.
Feb. 15 Paid the dividend declared in January.
Apr. 15 Declared a 10% stock dividend to stockholders of record on April 30, distributable May 15. On April 15, the market price of the stock was $15 per share.
May 15 Issued the shares for the stock dividend.
July 1 Announced a 2-for-1 stock split. The market price per share prior to the announcement was $17. (The new par value is $5.)
Dec. 1 Declared a $0.50 per share cash dividend to stockholders of record on December 15, payable January 10, 2009.
31 Determined that net income for the year was $250,000.

Instructions

(a) Journalize the transactions and the closing entry for net income.
(b) Enter the beginning balances, and post the entries to the stockholders' equity accounts. (*Note*: Open additional stockholders' equity accounts as needed.)
(c) Prepare a stockholders' equity section at December 31.

(c) Total stockholders' equity $1,780,000

Journalize and post transactions; prepare retained earnings statement and stockholders' equity section.

(SO 1, 2, 3)

GLS

P14-2B The stockholders' equity accounts of Holmes Inc., at January 1, 2008, are as follows.

Preferred Stock, $100 par, 7%	$500,000
Common Stock, $10 par	800,000
Paid-in Capital in Excess of Par Value—Preferred Stock	100,000
Paid-in Capital in Excess of Par Value—Common Stock	200,000
Retained Earnings	500,000

There were no dividends in arrears on preferred stock. During 2008, the company had the following transactions and events.

July 1 Declared a $0.50 cash dividend on common stock.
Aug. 1 Discovered a $72,000 overstatement of 2007 depreciation. Ignore income taxes.
Sept. 1 Paid the cash dividend declared on July 1.
Dec. 1 Declared a 10% stock dividend on common stock when the market value of the stock was $16 per share.
15 Declared a 7% cash dividend on preferred stock payable January 31, 2009.
31 Determined that net income for the year was $350,000.

Instructions

(a) Journalize the transactions and the closing entry for net income.
(b) Enter the beginning balances in the accounts and post to the stockholders' equity accounts. (*Note*: Open additional stockholders' equity accounts as needed.)

(c) Ending balance $719,000
(d) Total stockholders' equity $2,447,000

(c) Prepare a retained earnings statement for the year.
(d) Prepare a stockholders' equity section at December 31, 2008.

Prepare retained earnings statement and stockholders' equity section, and compute earnings per share.
(SO 1, 2, 3, 5)

P14-3B The ledger of Taguci Corporation at December 31, 2008, after the books have been closed, contains the following stockholders' equity accounts.

Preferred Stock (10,000 shares issued)	$1,000,000
Common Stock (400,000 shares issued)	2,000,000
Paid-in Capital in Excess of Par Value—Preferred	200,000
Paid-in Capital in Excess of Stated Value—Common	1,180,000
Common Stock Dividends Distributable	200,000
Retained Earnings	2,330,000

A review of the accounting records reveals the following.

1. No errors have been made in recording 2008 transactions or in preparing the closing entry for net income.
2. Preferred stock is 6%, $100 par value, noncumulative, and callable at $125. Since January 1, 2007, 10,000 shares have been outstanding; 20,000 shares are authorized.
3. Common stock is no-par with a stated value of $5 per share; 600,000 shares are authorized.
4. The January 1 balance in Retained Earnings was $2,450,000.
5. On October 1, 100,000 shares of common stock were sold for cash at $8 per share.
6. A cash dividend of $600,000 was declared and properly allocated to preferred and common stock on November 1. No dividends were paid to preferred stockholders in 2007.
7. On December 31, a 10% common stock dividend was declared out of retained earnings on common stock when the market price per share was $9.
8. Net income for the year was $840,000.
9. On December 31, 2008, the directors authorized disclosure of a $100,000 restriction of retained earnings for plant expansion. (Use Note A.)

Instructions

(a) Reproduce the Retained Earnings account (T-account) for the year.
(b) Prepare a retained earnings statement for the year.
(c) Prepare a stockholders' equity section at December 31.
(d) Compute the earnings per share of common stock using 325,000 as the weighted average shares outstanding for the year.
(e) Compute the allocation of the cash dividend to preferred and common stock.

(c) Total stockholders' equity: $6,910,000

Prepare the stockholders' equity section, reflecting dividends and stock split.
(SO 1, 2, 3)

P14-4B On January 1, 2008, Erwin Corporation had the following stockholders' equity accounts.

Common Stock (no-par value, 150,000 shares issued and outstanding)	$2,800,000
Retained Earnings	1,000,000

During the year, the following transactions occurred.

Feb. 1 Declared a $1 cash dividend per share to stockholders of record on February 15, payable March 1.
Mar. 1 Paid the dividend declared in February.
Apr. 1 Announced a 4-for-1 stock split. Prior to the split, the market price per share was $36.
July 1 Declared a 5% stock dividend to stockholders of record on July 15, distributable July 31. On July 1, the market price of the stock was $13 per share.
31 Issued the shares for the stock dividend.
Dec. 1 Declared a $0.50 per share dividend to stockholders of record on December 15, payable January 5, 2009.
31 Determined that net income for the year was $700,000.

Instructions

Prepare the stockholders' equity section of the balance sheet at: (a) March 31, (b) June 30, (c) September 30, and (d) December 31, 2008.

(d) Total, stockholders' equity $4,035,000

Prepare the stockholders' equity section, reflecting various events.
(SO 1, 3)

P14-5B On January 1, 2008, Morales Inc. had the following shareholders' equity balances.

Common Stock, no-par value (1,000,000 shares issued)	$3,000,000
Common Stock Dividends Distributable	400,000
Retained Earnings	1,200,000

During 2008, the following transactions and events occurred.

1. Issued 100,000 shares of common stock as a result of a 10% stock dividend declared on December 15, 2007.
2. Issued 40,000 shares of common stock for cash at $5 per share.
3. Corrected an error that had understated the net income for 2006 by $140,000.
4. Declared and paid a cash dividend of $500,000.
5. Earned net income of $600,000.

Instructions

Prepare the stockholders' equity section of the balance sheet at December 31, 2008.

Total stockholders' equity $5,040,000

PROBLEMS: SET C

Visit the book's website at **www.wiley.com/college/weygandt**, and choose the Student Companion site, to access Problem Set C.

CONTINUING COOKIE CHRONICLE

(Note: This is a continuation of the Cookie Chronicle from Chapters 1 through 13.)

CCC14 After establishing their company's fiscal year end to be October 31, Natalie and Curtis began operating Cookie & Coffee Creations Inc. on November 1, 2008. On that date, they issued both preferred and common stock. After the first year of operations, Natalie and Curtis want to prepare financial information for the year.

Go to the book's website, **www.wiley.com/college/weygandt,** *to see the completion of this problem.*

BROADENING YOUR PERSPECTIVE

FINANCIAL REPORTING AND ANALYSIS

Financial Reporting Problem: PepsiCo, Inc.

BYP14-1 The financial statements of PepsiCo are presented in Appendix A.

Instructions

Refer to PepsiCo's financial statements and answer the following questions.

What amount did PepsiCo declare in dividends on common stock in the year ended December 31, 2005? How does this amount compare with dividends declared on common stock in the year ended December 25, 2004?

Comparative Analysis Problem: PepsiCo, Inc. vs. The Coca-Cola Company

BYP14-2 PepsiCo's financial statements are presented in Appendix A. Coca-Cola's financial statements are presented in Appendix B.

Instructions

(a) Compute earnings per share and return on common stockholders' equity for both companies for the year ending December 31, 2005. Assume PepsiCo's weighted average shares were 1,669 million and Coca-Cola's weighted average shares were 2,392 million. Can these measures be used to compare the profitability of the two companies? Why or why not?

(b) What was the total amount of dividends paid by each company in 2005?

Exploring the Web

BYP14-3 Use the stockholders' equity section of an annual report and identify the major components.

Address: www.reportgallery.com, or go to **www.wiley.com/college/weygandt**

Steps

1. From Report Gallery Homepage, choose **Search by Alphabet**, and choose a letter.
2. Select a particular company.
3. Choose Annual Report.
4. Follow instructions below.

Instructions

Answer the following questions.

(a) What is the company's name?
(b) What classes of capital stock has the company issued?
(c) For each class of stock:
 (1) How many shares are authorized, issued, and/or outstanding?
 (2) What is the par value?
(d) What are the company's retained earnings?
(e) Has the company acquired treasury stock? How many shares?

CRITICAL THINKING

Decision Making Across the Organization

BYP14-4 The stockholders' equity accounts of Fernandez, Inc., at January 1, 2008, are as follows.

Preferred Stock, no par, 4,000 shares issued	$400,000
Common Stock, no par, 140,000 shares issued	700,000
Retained Earnings	500,000

During 2008, the company had the following transactions and events.

July 1	Declared a $0.50 cash dividend on common stock.
Aug. 1	Discovered a $72,000 overstatement of 2007 depreciation expense. (Ignore income taxes.)
Sept. 1	Paid the cash dividend declared on July 1.
Dec. 1	Declared a 10% stock dividend on common stock when the market value of the stock was $12 per share.
15	Declared a $9 per share cash dividend on preferred stock, payable January 31, 2009.
31	Determined that net income for the year was $320,000.

Instructions

With the class divided into groups, answer the following questions.

(a) Prepare a retained earnings statement for the year. There are no preferred dividends in arrears.
(b) Discuss why the overstatement of 2007 depreciation expense is not treated as an adjustment of the current year's income.
(c) Discuss the reasons why a company might decide to issue a stock dividend rather than a cash dividend.

Communication Activity

BYP14-5 In the past year, Cormier Corporation declared a 10% stock dividend, and Fegan, Inc. announced a 2-for-1 stock split. Your parents own 100 shares of each company's $50 par value common stock. During a recent phone call, your parents ask you, as an accounting student, to explain the differences between the two events.

Instructions

Write a letter to your parents that explains the effects of the two events to them as stockholders and the effects of each event on the financial statements of each corporation.

Ethics Case

BYP14-6 Garcia Corporation has paid 60 consecutive quarterly cash dividends (15 years). The last 6 months, however, have been a cash drain on the company, as profit margins have been greatly narrowed by increasing competition. With a cash balance sufficient to meet only day-to-day operating needs, the president, Tom Henson, has decided that a stock dividend instead of a cash dividend should be declared. He tells Garcia's financial vice president, Andrea Lane, to issue a press release stating that the company is extending its consecutive dividend record with the issuance of a 5% stock dividend. "Write the press release convincing the stockholders that the stock dividend is just as good as a cash dividend," he orders. "Just watch our stock rise when we announce the stock dividend; it must be a good thing if that happens."

Instructions

(a) Who are the stakeholders in this situation?
(b) Is there anything unethical about Henson's intentions or actions?
(c) What is the effect of a stock dividend on a corporation's stockholders' equity accounts? Which would you rather receive as a stockholder—a cash dividend or a stock dividend? Why?

"All About You" Activity

BYP14-7 In the **All About You** feature in this chapter (p. 612), you learned that in response to the Sarbanes-Oxley Act, many companies have implemented formal ethics codes. Many other organizations also have ethics codes.

Instructions

Obtain the ethics code from an organization that you belong to (e.g., student organization, business school, employer, or a volunteer organization). Evaluate the ethics code based on how clearly it identifies proper and improper behavior. Discuss its strengths, and how it might be improved.

Answers to Insight and Accounting Across the Organization Questions

p. 599 Why Are Companies Increasing Their Dividends?

Q: What factors must management consider in deciding how large a dividend to pay?

A: *Management must consider the size of its retained earnings balance, the amount of available cash, its expected near-term cash needs, its growth opportunities, and what level of dividend it will be able to sustain based upon its expected future earnings.*

p. 603 Would You Pay $92,100 for One Share of Stock?

Q: How does the effect on share price following a stock split compare to the effect on share price of treasury shares acquired?

A: *A stock split and the acquisition of treasury shares have the opposite effects on share price: A stock split* decreases *the share price, whereas the acquisition of treasury shares* increases *the share price.*

p. 611 Yahoo! and Costco Feel the Impact of Earnings per Share

Q: Why do you think the prices of these companies changed as indicated?

A: *Stock prices are a function of expected future cash flows. The price of a company's stock is based on investors' expectations of a certain level of future cash flows. If the company exceeds these expectations, its stock price will rise. If it does not meet these expectations, the stock price will fall.*

Authors' Comments on *All About You:* Corporations Have Governance Structures—Do You? p. 612

Before we address the usefulness of a student code of ethics, let's first ask whether a corporate code of ethics will ensure that employees no longer commit fraud. The answer is, "Clearly not." Does that mean a code of ethics is a waste of time? No. A code of ethics is a useful statement by the leaders of an organization about what kind of behavior is expected of the members of that organization. It provides a concrete reference point by which wrongdoing can be identified and evaluated.

Now, suppose that you were taking an exam and that you observed a number of people cheating. It would be very frustrating if you thought that your instructor, the school administrators, and other students didn't care that people were cheating. Ultimately this would encourage even more people to cheat. But if the school has defined unethical behavior, stated that it won't be tolerated, and created the necessary mechanisms for detecting and punishing unethical behavior, then it has begun the first steps in creating a more ethical environment. For an example of an ethics code for university students, see the ethics section of the Student Resources at **www.bus.wisc.edu/accounting**.

Answers to PepsiCo Review It Question 4, p. 603

Dividends per share of common stock declared by PepsiCo were $0.575 in 2001; $0.595 in 2002; $0.630 in 2003; $0.850 in 2004; and $1.01 in 2005. During this same period net income increased in a similar fashion, except from 2004 and 2005 when net income declined.

Answers to Self-Study Questions

1. a **2.** c **3.** c **4.** d **5.** d **6.** b **7.** d **8.** b **9.** c **10.** b

Remember to go back to the Navigator box on the chapter-opening page and check off your completed work.

Chapter 15

Long-Term Liabilities

STUDY OBJECTIVES

After studying this chapter, you should be able to:

1. Explain why bonds are issued.
2. Prepare the entries for the issuance of bonds and interest expense.
3. Describe the entries when bonds are redeemed or converted.
4. Describe the accounting for long-term notes payable.
5. Contrast the accounting for operating and capital leases.
6. Identify the methods for the presentation and analysis of long-term liabilities.

The Navigator

The Navigator

Scan **Study Objectives**	☐
Read **Feature Story**	☐
Read **Preview**	☐
Read text and answer **Before You Go On** p. 637 ☐ p. 640 ☐ p. 642 ☐ p. 647	☐
Work **Demonstration Problem**	☐
Review **Summary of Study Objectives**	☐
Answer **Self-Study Questions**	☐
Complete **Assignments**	☐

Feature Story

THANK GOODNESS FOR BANKRUPTCY

One piece of baggage America's first settlers carried with them from England was the belief that not repaying one's debts was a moral failure. As in England, the colonists' penalty for such wickedness was often prison.

The theory behind jailing debtors was that the threat of incarceration might persuade them to reveal hidden assets. Or their families might take pity and pay their ransom. But if the debtor was truly penniless, he could be sentenced to what amounted to life in prison. Unlike murderers, rapists, and thieves, the debtors were also responsible for paying their own upkeep, thus putting them even further into debt. . . .

The colonies gradually developed more forgiving laws on debt, recognizing that owing money could be the result of bad luck rather than evidence of fraud or indolence. "Crops fail, prices fall, ships sink, warehouses burn, owners die, partners steal, pirates pillage, wars ravage, and people simply

make mistakes," wrote Bruce Mann in his 2002 book *Republic of Debtors.* "Failure was the down side of entrepreneurial risk. This made failure the potential common fate of all merchants." . . .

Colonial lawmakers began taking a more charitable view toward debtors, but they were likelier to excuse a rich defaulter than a poor one. . . . Indeed, when some large speculative financial schemes collapsed after the Revolutionary War, many wealthy men were suddenly bankrupt. One of them, Robert Morris, who had signed the Declaration of Independence and provided critical financing for the war, lost his fortune speculating on land. Sentenced to debtors' prison in Philadelphia, Morris rented the best room in the jail and outfitted it with a settee, writing desks, a bed, a trunk of clothes and other comforts of home.

However lavishly they could outfit their prison cells, though, rich and poor faced the same dim future. There was no way an insolvent could get a fresh start—the "holy grail of debt relief," as Mr. Mann put it. In prison or out, debtors were expected to repay every penny they owed their creditors, even if it took them the rest of their lives. . . .

Congress passed a bankruptcy law in 1800 but then repealed it three years later. Not until 1831 did New York abolish prison for most debtors; Pennsylvania kept its debtors' prisons open until 1842. . . .

Source: Excerpted from Cynthia Crossen, "Early Debtors Faced Jail at Own Expense Until All Was Repaid," *Wall Street Journal*, January 30, 2006, p. B1. By permission.

✓ The Navigator

Inside Chapter 15...

Preview of Chapter 15

As you can see from the Feature Story, having liabilities can be dangerous in difficult economic times. In this chapter we will explain the accounting for the major types of long-term liabilities reported on the balance sheet. **Long-term liabilities** are obligations that are expected to be paid after one year. These liabilities may be bonds, long-term notes, or lease obligations.

The content and organization of Chapter 15 are as follows.

Long-Term Liabilities

Bonds Basics
- Types of bonds
- Issuing procedures
- Trading
- Market value

Accounting for Bond Issues
- Issuing bonds at face value
- Discount or premium
- Issuing bonds at a discount
- Issuing bonds at a premium

Accounting for Bond Retirements
- Redeeming bonds at maturity
- Redeeming bonds before maturity
- Converting bonds into common stock

Accounting for Other Long-Term Liabilities
- Long-term notes payable
- Lease liabilities

Statement Presentation and Analysis
- Presentation
- Analysis

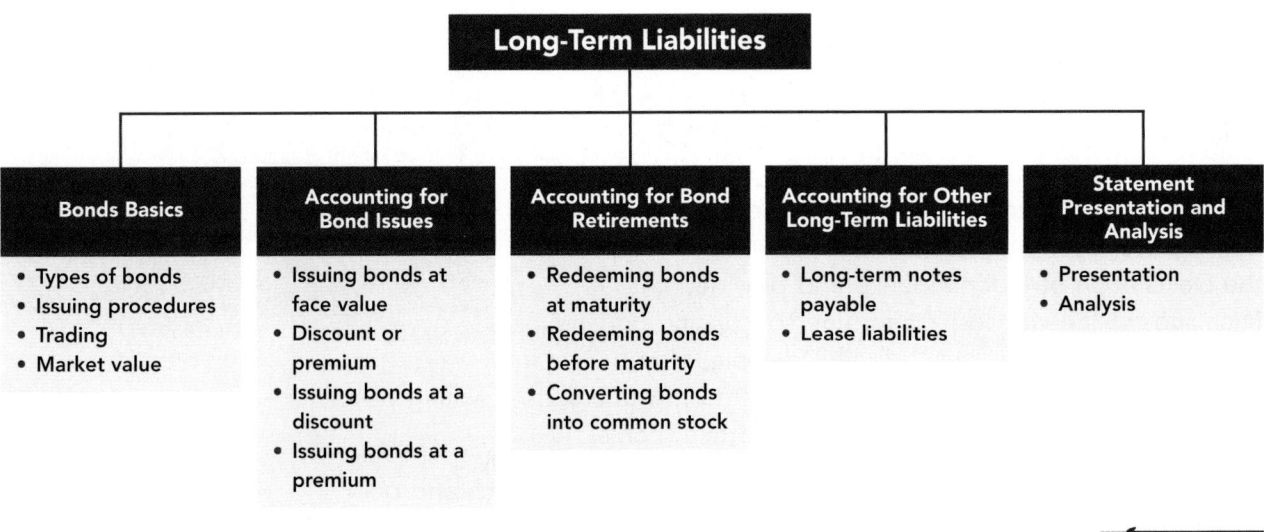

The Navigator

BOND BASICS

STUDY OBJECTIVE 1
Explain why bonds are issued.

Bonds are a form of interest-bearing notes payable. To obtain **large amounts of long-term capital**, corporate management usually must decide whether to issue common stock (equity financing) or bonds. Bonds offer three advantages over common stock, as shown in Illustration 15-1.

Illustration 15-1
Advantages of bond financing over common stock

Bond Financing	Advantages
	1. **Stockholder control is not affected.** Bondholders do not have voting rights, so current owners (stockholders) retain full control of the company.
	2. **Tax savings result.** Bond interest is deductible for tax purposes; dividends on stock are not.
	3. **Earnings per share may be higher.** Although bond interest expense reduces net income, earnings per share on common stock often is higher under bond financing because no additional shares of common stock are issued.

As the illustration shows, one reason to issue bonds is that they do not affect stockholder control. Because bondholders do not have voting rights, owners can raise capital with bonds and still maintain corporate control. In addition, bonds are attractive to corporations because the cost of bond interest is tax-deductible. As a result of this tax treatment, which stock dividends do not offer, bonds may result in lower cost of capital than equity financing.

To illustrate the third advantage, on earnings per share, assume that Microsystems, Inc. is considering two plans for financing the construction of a new $5 million plant. Plan A involves issuance of 200,000 shares of common stock at the current market price of $25 per share. Plan B involves issuance of $5 million, 8% bonds at face value. Income before interest and taxes on the new plant will be $1.5 million. Income taxes are expected to be 30%. Microsystems currently has 100,000 shares of common stock outstanding. Illustration 15-2 shows the alternative effects on earnings per share.

Illustration 15-2
Effects on earnings per share—stocks vs. bonds

	Plan A Issue Stock	Plan B Issue Bonds
Income before interest and taxes	$1,500,000	$1,500,000
Interest (8% × $5,000,000)	—	400,000
Income before income taxes	1,500,000	1,100,000
Income tax expense (30%)	450,000	330,000
Net income	$1,050,000	$ 770,000
Outstanding shares	300,000	100,000
Earnings per share	**$3.50**	**$7.70**

Note that net income is $280,000 less ($1,050,000 − $770,000) with long-term debt financing (bonds). However, earnings per share is higher because there are 200,000 fewer shares of common stock outstanding.

One disadvantage in using bonds is that the company must **pay interest** on a periodic basis. In addition, the company must also **repay the principal** at the due date. A company with fluctuating earnings and a relatively weak cash position may have great difficulty making interest payments when earnings are low.

A corporation may also obtain long-term financing from notes payable and leasing. However, notes payable and leasing are seldom sufficient to furnish the amount of funds needed for plant expansion and major projects like new buildings.

Bonds are sold in relatively small denominations (usually $1,000 multiples). As a result of their size, and the variety of their features, bonds attract many investors.

HELPFUL HINT
Besides corporations, governmental agencies and universities also issue bonds to raise capital.

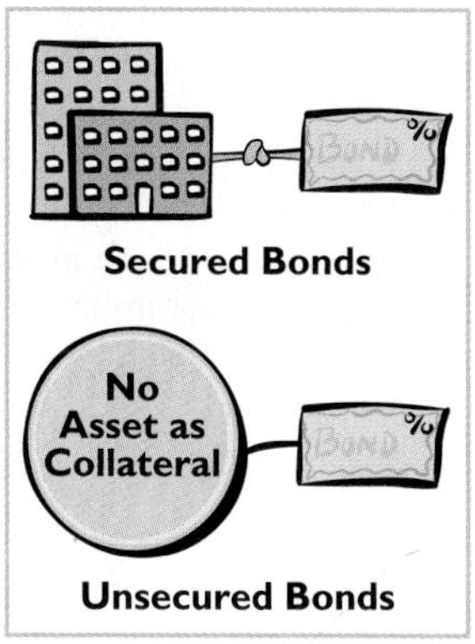

Types of Bonds

Bonds may have many different features. In the following sections, we describe the types of bonds commonly issued.

SECURED AND UNSECURED BONDS

Secured bonds have specific assets of the issuer pledged as collateral for the bonds. A bond secured by real estate, for example, is called a **mortgage bond**. A bond secured by specific assets set aside to retire the bonds is called a **sinking fund bond**.

Unsecured bonds, also called **debenture bonds**, are issued against the general credit of the borrower. Companies with good credit ratings use these bonds extensively. For example, in a recent annual report, DuPont reported over $2 billion of debenture bonds outstanding.

TERM AND SERIAL BONDS

Bonds that mature—are due for payment—at a single specified future date are **term bonds**. In contrast, bonds that mature in installments are **serial bonds**.

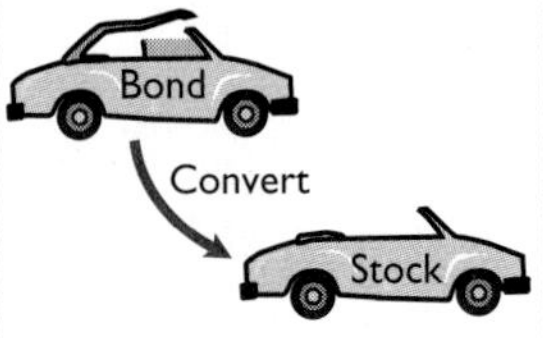

Convertible Bonds

Callable Bonds

REGISTERED AND BEARER BONDS

Bonds issued in the name of the owner are **registered bonds**. Interest payments on registered bonds are made by check to bondholders of record. Bonds not registered are **bearer** (or **coupon**) **bonds**. Holders of bearer bonds must send in coupons to receive interest payments. Most bonds issued today are registered bonds.

CONVERTIBLE AND CALLABLE BONDS

Bonds that can be converted into common stock at the bondholder's option are **convertible bonds**. The conversion feature generally is attractive to bond buyers. Bonds that the issuing company can retire at a stated dollar amount prior to maturity are **callable bonds**. A call feature is included in nearly all corporate bond issues.

Issuing Procedures

State laws grant corporations the power to issue bonds. Both the board of directors and stockholders usually must approve bond issues. **In authorizing the bond issue, the board of directors must stipulate the number of bonds to be authorized, total face value, and contractual interest rate.** The total bond authorization often exceeds the number of bonds the company originally issues. This gives the corporation the flexibility to issue more bonds, if needed, to meet future cash requirements.

The **face value** is the amount of principal the issuing company must pay at the maturity date. The **contractual interest rate**, often referred to as the **stated rate**, is the rate used to determine the amount of cash interest the borrower pays and the investor receives. Usually the contractual rate is stated as an annual rate. Interest is generally paid semiannually.

The terms of the bond issue are set forth in a legal document called a **bond indenture**. The indenture shows the terms and summarizes the rights of the bondholders and their trustees, and the obligations of the issuing company. The **trustee** (usually a financial institution) keeps records of each bondholder, maintains custody of unissued bonds, and holds conditional title to pledged property.

In addition, the issuing company arranges for the printing of **bond certificates**. The indenture and the certificate are separate documents. As shown in Illustration 15-3, a bond certificate provides the following information: name of the issuer, face value, contractual interest rate, and maturity date. An investment company that specializes in selling securities generally sells the bonds for the issuing company.

ETHICS NOTE

Some companies try to minimize the amount of debt reported on their balance sheet by not reporting certain types of commitments as liabilities. This subject is of intense interest in the financial community.

Bond Trading

Bondholders have the opportunity to convert their holdings into cash at any time by selling the bonds at the current market price on national securities exchanges. **Bond prices are quoted as a percentage of the face value of the bond, which is usually $1,000.** A $1,000 bond with a quoted price of 97 means that the selling price of

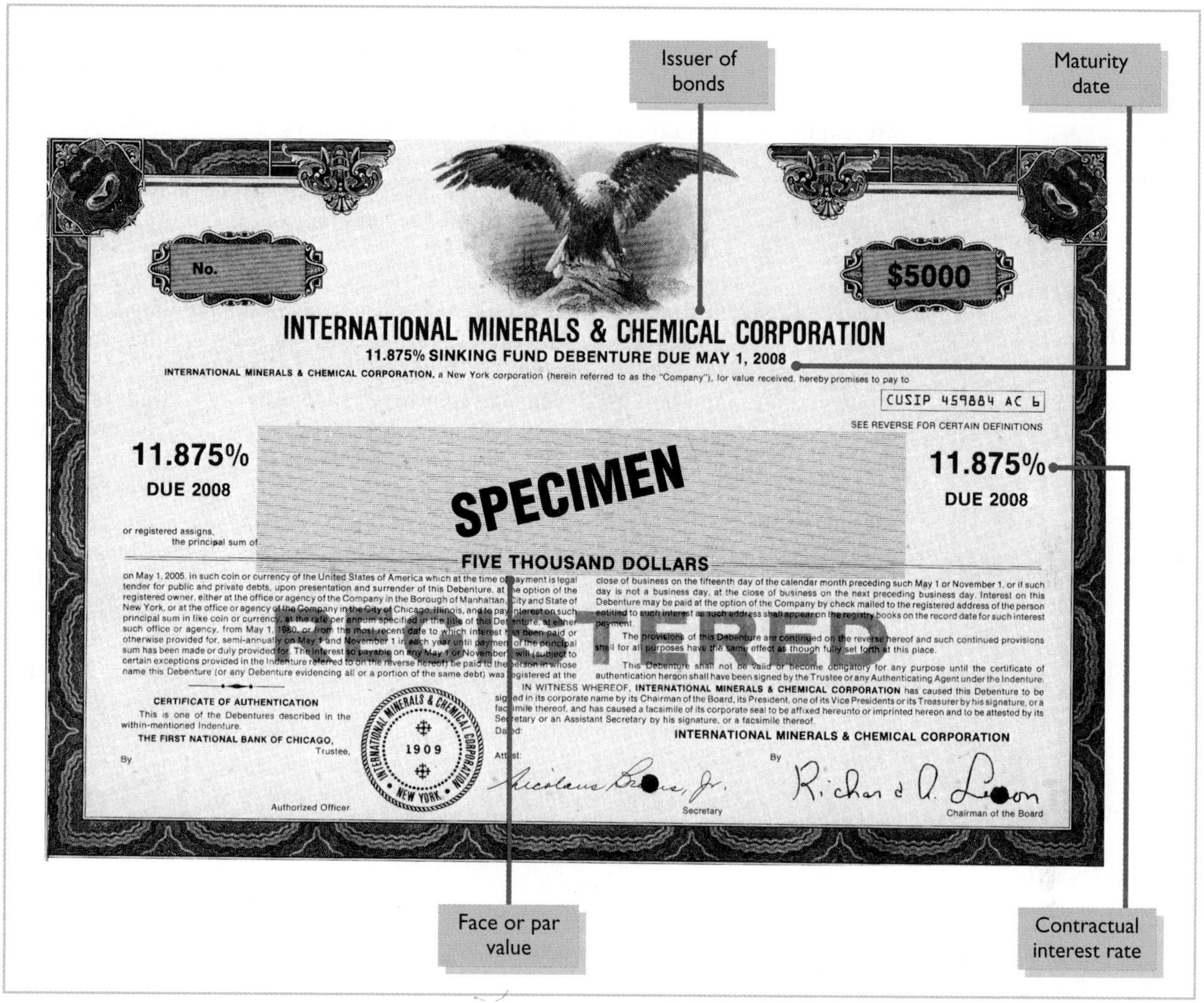

Illustration 15-3
Bond certificate

the bond is 97% of face value, or $970. Newspapers and the financial press publish bond prices and trading activity daily as illustrated by the following.

Illustration 15-4
Market information for bonds

Bonds	Maturity	Close	Yield	Est. Volume (000)
Boeing Co. 5.125	Feb. 15, 2011	96.595	5.747	33,965

This bond listing indicates that Boeing Co. has outstanding 5.125%, $1,000 bonds that mature in 2011. They currently yield a 5.747% return. On this day, $33,965,000 of these bonds were traded. At the close of trading, the price was 96.595% of face value, or $965.95.

A corporation makes journal entries **only when it issues or buys back bonds**, or when bondholders convert bonds into common stock. For example, DuPont **does not journalize** transactions between its bondholders and other investors. If Tom Smith sells his DuPont bonds to Faith Jones, DuPont does not journalize the transaction. (DuPont or its trustee does, however, keep records of the names of bondholders in the case of registered bonds.)

HELPFUL HINT

(1) What is the price of a $1,000 bond trading at 95¼?
(2) What is the price of a $1,000 bond trading at 101⅞?
Answers: (1) $952.50.
(2) $1,018.75.

Determining the Market Value of Bonds

Same dollars at different times are not equal.

If you were an investor wanting to purchase a bond, how would you determine how much to pay? To be more specific, assume that Coronet, Inc. issues a **zero-interest bond** (pays no interest) with a face value of $1,000,000 due in 20 years. For this bond, the only cash you receive is a million dollars at the end of 20 years. Would you pay a million dollars for this bond? We hope not! A million dollars received 20 years from now is not the same as a million dollars received today.

The reason you should not pay a million dollars for Coronet's bond relates to what is called the **time value of money**. If you had a million dollars today, you would invest it. From that investment, you would earn interest such that at the end of 20 years, you would have much more than a million dollars. If someone is going to pay you a million dollars 20 years from now, you would want to find its equivalent today. In other words, you would want to determine how much you must invest today at current interest rates to have a million dollars in 20 years. The amount that must be invested today at a given rate of interest over a specified time is called **present value**.

The present value of a bond is the value at which it should sell in the marketplace. Market value therefore is a function of the three factors that determine present value: (1) the dollar amounts to be received, (2) the length of time until the amounts are received, and (3) the market rate of interest. The **market interest rate** is the rate investors demand for loaning funds. Appendix 15A discusses the process of finding the present value for bonds. Appendix C near the end of the book also provides additional material for time value of money computations.

ACCOUNTING ACROSS THE ORGANIZATION

When to Go Long-Term

A decision that all companies must make is to what extent to rely on short-term versus long-term financing. The critical nature of this decision was highlighted in the fall of 2001, after the World Trade Center disaster. Prior to September 11, short-term interest rates had been extremely low relative to long-term rates. In order to minimize interest costs, many companies were relying very heavily on short-term financing to purchase things they normally would have used long-term debt for. The problem with short-term financing is that it requires companies to continually find new financing as each loan comes due. This makes them vulnerable to sudden changes in the economy.

After September 11, lenders and short-term investors became very reluctant to loan money. This put the squeeze on many companies: as short-term loans came due, they were unable to refinance. Some were able to get other financing, but at extremely high rates (for example, 12% as compared to 3%). Others were unable to get loans and instead had to sell assets to generate cash for their immediate needs.

Source: Henny Sender, "Firms Feel Consequences of Short-Term Borrowing," *Wall Street Journal Online* (October 12, 2001).

Based on this story, what is a good general rule to use in choosing between short-term and long-term financing?

Before You Go On...

REVIEW IT

1. What are the advantages of bond versus stock financing?
2. What are secured versus unsecured bonds, term versus serial bonds, registered versus bearer bonds, and callable versus convertible bonds?
3. Explain the terms face value, contractual interest rate, and bond indenture.
4. Explain why you would prefer to receive $1 million today rather than five years from now.

The Navigator

ACCOUNTING FOR BOND ISSUES

STUDY OBJECTIVE 2

Prepare the entries for the issuance of bonds and interest expense.

Bonds may be issued at face value, below face value (at a discount), or above face value (at a premium).

Issuing Bonds at Face Value

To illustrate the accounting for bonds, assume that on January 1, 2008, Candlestick Corporation issues $100,000, five-year, 10% bonds at 100 (100% of face value). The entry to record the sale is:

Jan. 1	Cash	100,000	
	Bonds Payable		100,000
	(To record sale of bonds at face value)		

A	=	L	+	SE
+100,000				
		+100,000		

Cash Flows
+100,000

Candlestick reports bonds payable in the long-term liabilities section of the balance sheet because the maturity date is more than one year away.

Over the term (life) of the bonds, companies make entries to record bond interest. Interest on bonds payable is computed in the same manner as interest on notes payable, as explained in Chapter 11 (page 473). Assume that interest is payable semiannually on January 1 and July 1 on the bonds described above. In that case, Candlestick must pay interest of $5,000 ($100,000 × 10% × 6/12) on July 1, 2008. The entry for the payment, assuming no previous accrual of interest, is:

July 1	Bond Interest Expense	5,000	
	Cash		5,000
	(To record payment of bond interest)		

A	=	L	+	SE
				−5,000 Exp
−5,000				

Cash Flows
−5,000

At December 31, Candlestick recognizes the $5,000 of interest expense incurred since July 1 with the following adjusting entry:

Dec. 31	Bond Interest Expense	5,000	
	Bond Interest Payable		5,000
	(To accrue bond interest)		

A	=	L	+	SE
				−5,000 Exp
		+5,000		

Cash Flows
no effect

Companies classify bond interest payable as a current liability, because it is scheduled for payment within the next year. When Candlestick pays the interest on January 1, 2009, it debits (decreases) Bond Interest Payable and credits (decreases) Cash for $5,000.

Discount or Premium on Bonds

In the Candlestick illustrations above, we assumed that the contractual (stated) interest rate paid on the bonds and the market (effective) interest rate were the same.

Recall that the **contractual interest rate** is the rate applied to the face (par) value to arrive at the interest paid in a year. The **market interest rate** is the rate investors demand for loaning funds to the corporation. When the contractual interest rate and the market interest rate are the same, bonds sell **at face value**.

However, market interest rates change daily. The type of bond issued, the state of the economy, current industry conditions, and the company's performance all affect market interest rates. Contractual and market interest rates often differ. As a result, bonds often sell below or above face value.

To illustrate, suppose that a company issues 10% bonds at a time when other bonds of similar risk are paying 12%. Investors will not be interested in buying the 10% bonds, so their value will fall below their face value. In this case, we say the 10% bonds are **selling at a discount**. As a result of the decline in the bonds' selling price, the actual interest rate incurred by the company increases to the level of the current market interest rate.

Conversely, if the market rate of interest is **lower than** the contractual interest rate, investors will have to pay more than face value for the bonds. That is, if the market rate of interest is 8% but the contractual interest rate on the bonds is 10%, the issuer will require more funds from the investor. In these cases, **bonds sell at a premium**. Illustration 15-5 shows these relationships graphically.

Illustration 15-5
Interest rates and bond prices

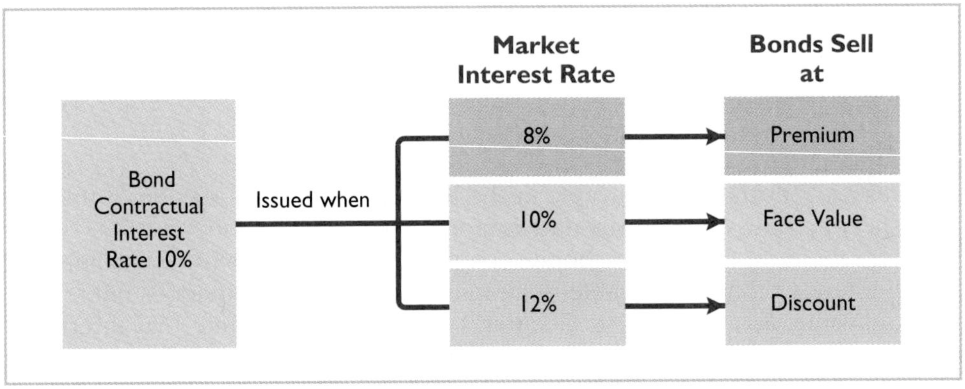

Issuing bonds at an amount different from face value is quite common. By the time a company prints the bond certificates and markets the bonds, it will be a coincidence if the market rate and the contractual rate are the same. Thus, the sale of bonds at a discount does not mean that the issuer's financial strength is suspect. Nor does the sale of bonds at a premium indicate exceptional financial strength.

HELPFUL HINT

Discount on Bonds Payable	
Increase Debit ↓ Normal Balance	Decrease Credit

Issuing Bonds at a Discount

To illustrate issuance of bonds at a discount, assume that on January 1, 2008, Candlestick, Inc. sells $100,000, five-year, 10% bonds for $92,639 (92.639% of face value). Interest is payable on July 1 and January 1. The entry to record the issuance is:

A	=	L	+	SE
+92,639				
		−7,361		
		+100,000		

Cash Flows
+92,639

Jan. 1	Cash	92,639	
	Discount on Bonds Payable	7,361	
	Bonds Payable		100,000
	(To record sale of bonds at a discount)		

Although Discount on Bonds Payable has a debit balance, **it is not an asset**. Rather, it is a **contra account**. This account is **deducted from bonds payable** on the balance sheet, as shown in Illustration 15-6.

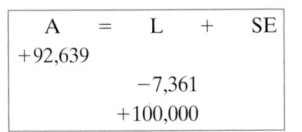

CANDLESTICK, INC. Balance Sheet (partial)		
Long-term liabilities		
Bonds payable	$100,000	
Less: Discount on bonds payable	**7,361**	$92,639

Illustration 15-6
Statement presentation of discount on bonds payable

The $92,639 represents the **carrying (or book) value** of the bonds. On the date of issue this amount equals the market price of the bonds.

The issuance of bonds below face value—at a discount—causes the total cost of borrowing to differ from the bond interest paid. That is, the issuing corporation must pay not only the contractual interest rate over the term of the bonds, but also the face value (rather than the issuance price) at maturity. Therefore, the difference between the issuance price and face value of the bonds—the discount—is an **additional cost of borrowing**. The company records this additional cost as **bond interest expense** over the life of the bonds. Appendixes 15B and 15C show the procedures for recording this additional cost.

The total cost of borrowing $92,639 for Candlestick, Inc. is $57,361, computed as follows.

HELPFUL HINT
Carrying value (book value) of bonds issued at a discount is determined by subtracting the balance of the discount account from the balance of the Bonds Payable account.

Bonds Issued at a Discount	
Semiannual interest payments	
($100,000 × 10% × ½ = $5,000; $5,000 × 10)	$50,000
Add: Bond discount ($100,000 − $92,639)	7,361
Total cost of borrowing	**$57,361**

Illustration 15-7
Total cost of borrowing—bonds issued at a discount

Alternatively, we can compute the total cost of borrowing as follows.

Bonds Issued at a Discount	
Principal at maturity	$100,000
Semiannual interest payments ($5,000 × 10)	50,000
Cash to be paid to bondholders	150,000
Cash received from bondholders	92,639
Total cost of borrowing	**$ 57,361**

Illustration 15-8
Alternative computation of total cost of borrowing—bonds issued at a discount

Issuing Bonds at a Premium

To illustrate the issuance of bonds at a premium, we now assume the Candlestick, Inc. bonds described above sell for $108,111 (108.111% of face value) rather than for $92,639. The entry to record the sale is:

Jan. 1	Cash	108,111	
	Bonds Payable		100,000
	Premium on Bonds Payable		8,111
	(To record sale of bonds at a premium)		

A	=	L	+	SE
+108,111				
		+100,000		
		+8,111		

Cash Flows
+108,111

Candlestick adds the premium on bonds payable **to the bonds payable amount** on the balance sheet, as shown in Illustration 15-9 on the next page.

Illustration 15-9
Statement presentation of bond premium

CANDLESTICK, INC.
Balance Sheet (partial)

Long-term liabilities		
Bonds payable	$100,000	
Add: Premium on bonds payable	**8,111**	$108,111

HELPFUL HINT

Premium on Bonds Payable

Decrease Debit	Increase Credit ↓ Normal Balance

The sale of bonds above face value causes the total cost of borrowing to be **less than the bond interest paid**. The bond premium is considered to be **a reduction in the cost of borrowing**. The company credits the bond premium to Bond Interest Expense over the life of the bonds. Appendixes 15B and 15C show the procedures for recording this reduction in the cost of borrowing. The total cost of borrowing $108,111 for Candlestick, Inc. is computed as follows.

Illustration 15-10
Total cost of borrowing—bonds issued at a premium

Bonds Issued at a Premium

Semiannual interest payments ($100,000 × 10% × ½ = $5,000; $5,000 × 10)	$50,000
Less: Bond premium ($108,111 − $100,000)	8,111
Total cost of borrowing	**$41,889**

Alternatively, we can compute the cost of borrowing as follows.

Illustration 15-11
Alternative computation of total cost of borrowing—bonds issued at a premium

Bonds Issued at a Premium

Principal at maturity	$100,000
Semiannual interest payments ($5,000 × 10)	50,000
Cash to be paid to bondholders	150,000
Cash received from bondholders	108,111
Total cost of borrowing	**$ 41,889**

Before You Go On...

REVIEW IT

1. What entry would a company make to record the issuance of bonds payable of $1 million at 100? At 96? At 102?
2. Why do bonds sell at a discount? At a premium? At face value?

Related exercise material: *BE15-2, BE15-3, BE15-4, E15-3, E15-4, and E15-7.*

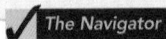

✓ The Navigator

ACCOUNTING FOR BOND RETIREMENTS

STUDY OBJECTIVE 3

Describe the entries when bonds are redeemed or converted.

An issuing corporation retires bonds either when it redeems the bonds or when bondholders convert them into common stock. We explain the entries for these transactions in the following sections.

Redeeming Bonds at Maturity

Regardless of the issue price of bonds, the book value of the bonds at maturity will equal their face value. Assuming that the company pays and records separately the interest for the last interest period, Candlestick records the redemption of its bonds at maturity as follows:

Bonds Payable	100,000	
Cash		100,000
(To record redemption of bonds at maturity)		

A	=	L	+	SE
		−100,000		
−100,000				

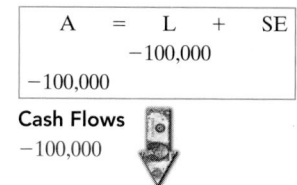

Cash Flows
−100,000

Redeeming Bonds before Maturity

Bonds also may be redeemed before maturity. A company may decide to retire bonds before maturity to reduce interest cost and to remove debt from its balance sheet. A company should retire debt early only if it has sufficient cash resources.

When a company retires bonds before maturity, it is necessary to: (1) eliminate the carrying value of the bonds at the redemption date; (2) record the cash paid; and (3) recognize the gain or loss on redemption. The carrying value of the bonds is the face value of the bonds less unamortized bond discount or plus unamortized bond premium at the redemption date.

HELPFUL HINT

Question: A bond is redeemed prior to its maturity date. Its carrying value exceeds its redemption price. Will the retirement result in a gain or a loss on redemption?
Answer: Gain.

To illustrate, assume that Candlestick, Inc. has sold its bonds at a premium. At the end of the eighth period, Candlestick retires these bonds at 103 after paying the semiannual interest. Assume also that the carrying value of the bonds at the redemption date is $101,623. Candlestick makes the following entry to record the redemption at the end of the eighth interest period (January 1, 2012):

Jan. 1	Bonds Payable	100,000	
	Premium on Bonds Payable	1,623	
	Loss on Bond Redemption	1,377	
	Cash		103,000
	(To record redemption of bonds at 103)		

A	=	L	+	SE
		−100,000		
		−1,623		
				−1,377 Exp
−103,000				

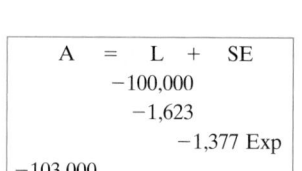

Cash Flows
−103,000

Note that the loss of $1,377 is the difference between the cash paid of $103,000 and the carrying value of the bonds of $101,623.

Converting Bonds into Common Stock

Convertible bonds have features that are attractive both to bondholders and to the issuer. The conversion often gives bondholders an opportunity to benefit if the market price of the common stock increases substantially. Until conversion, though, the bondholder receives interest on the bond. For the issuer of convertible bonds, the bonds sell at a higher price and pay a lower rate of interest than comparable debt securities without the conversion option. Many corporations, such as USAir, USX Corp., and DaimlerChrysler Corporation, have convertible bonds outstanding.

When the issuing company records a conversion, the company ignores the current market prices of the bonds and stock. Instead, the company transfers the **carrying value** of the bonds to paid-in capital accounts. **No gain or loss is recognized.**

To illustrate, assume that on July 1 Saunders Associates converts $100,000 bonds sold at face value into 2,000 shares of $10 par value common stock. Both the bonds and the common stock have a market value of $130,000. Saunders makes the following entry to record the conversion:

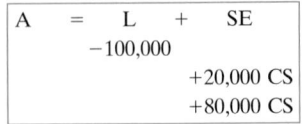

A	=	L	+	SE
		−100,000		
				+20,000 CS
				+80,000 CS

Cash Flows
no effect

July 1	Bonds Payable	100,000	
	Common Stock		20,000
	Paid-in Capital in Excess of Par Value		80,000
	(To record bond conversion)		

Note that the company does not consider the current market price of the bonds and stock ($130,000) in making the entry. This method of recording the bond conversion is often referred to as the **carrying (or book) value method**.

Before You Go On...

REVIEW IT

1. Explain the accounting for redemption of bonds at maturity, before maturity by payment in cash, and by conversion into common stock.
2. Did PepsiCo redeem any of its debt during the fiscal year ended December 31, 2005? (*Hint:* Examine PepsiCo's statement of cash flows. The answer to this question appears on page 680.)

DO IT

R & B Inc. issued $500,000, 10-year bonds at a premium. Prior to maturity, when the carrying value of the bonds is $508,000, the company retires the bonds at 102. Prepare the entry to record the redemption of the bonds.

Action Plan

- Determine and eliminate the carrying value of the bonds.
- Record the cash paid.
- Compute and record the gain (loss) (the difference between the first two items).

Solution There is a loss on redemption: The cash paid, $510,000 ($500,000 × 102%), is greater than the carrying value of $508,000. The entry is:

Bonds Payable	500,000	
Premium on Bonds Payable	8,000	
Loss on Bond Redemption	2,000	
Cash		510,000
(To record redemption of bonds at 102)		

Related exercise material: *BE15-5, E15-5, E15-6, E15-8, and E15-9.*

The Navigator

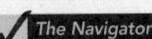

ACCOUNTING FOR OTHER LONG-TERM LIABILITIES

Other common types of long-term obligations are notes payable and lease liabilities. The accounting for these liabilities is explained in the following sections.

Long-Term Notes Payable

STUDY OBJECTIVE 4

Describe the accounting for long-term notes payable.

The use of notes payable in long-term debt financing is quite common. **Long-term notes payable** are similar to short-term interest-bearing notes payable except that the term of the notes exceeds one year.

A long-term note may be secured by a **mortgage** that pledges title to specific assets as security for a loan. Individuals widely use **mortgage notes payable** to purchase homes, and many small and some large companies use them to acquire plant assets. At one time, approximately 18% of McDonald's long-term debt related to mortgage notes on land, buildings, and improvements.

Mortgage loan terms may stipulate either a **fixed** or an **adjustable** interest rate. The interest rate on a fixed-rate mortgage remains the same over the life of the mortgage. The interest rate on an adjustable-rate mortgage is adjusted periodically to reflect changes in the market rate of interest. Typically, the terms require the borrower to make installment payments over the term of the loan. Each payment consists of (1) interest on the unpaid balance of the loan and (2) a reduction of loan principal. The interest decreases each period, while the portion applied to the loan principal increases.

Companies initially record mortgage notes payable at face value. They subsequently make entries for each installment payment. To illustrate, assume that Porter Technology Inc. issues a $500,000, 12%, 20-year mortgage note on December 31, 2008, to obtain needed financing for a new research laboratory. The terms provide for semiannual installment payments of $33,231 (not including real estate taxes and insurance). The installment payment schedule for the first two years is as follows.

Illustration 15-12
Mortgage installment payment schedule

Semiannual Interest Period	(A) Cash Payment	(B) Interest Expense (D) × 6%	(C) Reduction of Principal (A) − (B)	(D) Principal Balance (D) − (C)
12/31/08				$500,000
06/30/09	$33,231	$30,000	$3,231	496,769
12/31/09	33,231	29,806	3,425	493,344
06/30/10	33,231	29,601	3,630	489,714
12/31/10	33,231	29,383	3,848	485,866

Porter records the mortgage loan and first installment payment as follows.

Dec. 31	Cash	500,000	
	Mortgage Notes Payable		500,000
	(To record mortgage loan)		

A	=	L	+	SE
+500,000				
		+500,000		

Cash Flows
+500,000

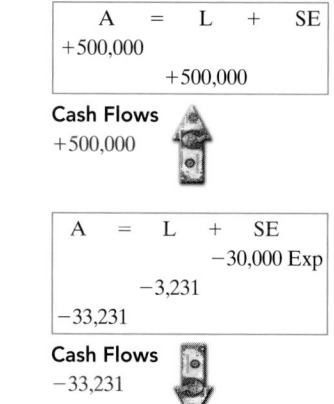

June 30	Interest Expense	30,000	
	Mortgage Notes Payable	3,231	
	Cash		33,231
	(To record semiannual payment on mortgage)		

A	=	L	+	SE
				−30,000 Exp
		−3,231		
−33,231				

Cash Flows
−33,231

In the balance sheet, the company reports the reduction in principal for the next year as a current liability, and it classifies the remaining unpaid principal balance as a long-term liability. At December 31, 2009, the total liability is $493,344. Of that amount, $7,478 ($3,630 + $3,848) is current, and $485,866 ($493,344 − $7,478) is long-term.

ACCOUNTING ACROSS THE ORGANIZATION

Search for Your Best Rate

Companies spend a great deal of time shopping for the best loan terms. You should do the same. Suppose that you have a used car that you are planning to trade in on the purchase of a new car. Experts suggest that you view this deal as three separate transactions: (1) the purchase of a new car, (2) the trade in or sale of an old car, and (3) shopping for an interest rate.

Studies suggest that too many people neglect transaction number 3. One survey found that 63% of people planned on shopping for the best car-loan interest rate online the next time they bought a car. But a separate study found that only 15% of people who bought a car actually shopped around for the best online rate. Too many people simply take the interest rate offered at the car dealership. Many lenders will pre-approve you for a loan up to a specific dollar amount, and many will then give you a blank check (negotiable for up to that amount) that you can take to the car dealer.

Source: Ron Lieber, "How to Haggle the Best Car Loan," *Wall Street Journal*, March 25, 2006, p. B1.

? What should you do if the dealer "trash-talks" your lender, or refuses to sell you the car for the agreed-upon price unless you get your car loan through the dealer?

Lease Liabilities

STUDY OBJECTIVE 5

Contrast the accounting for operating and capital leases.

As indicated in Chapter 10, a lease is a contractual arrangement between a lessor (owner of the property) and a lessee (renter of the property). It grants the right to use specific property for a period of time in return for cash payments. Leasing is big business. U.S. companies leased an estimated \$125 billion of capital equipment in a recent year. This represents approximately one-third of equipment financed that year. The two most common types of leases are operating leases and capital leases.

OPERATING LEASES

The renting of an apartment and the rental of a car at an airport are examples of **operating leases. In an operating lease the intent is temporary use of the property by the lessee, while the lessor continues to own the property.**

In an operating lease, the lessee records the lease (or rental) payments as an expense. The lessor records the payments as revenue. For example, assume that a sales representative for Western Inc. leases a car from Hertz Car Rental at the Los Angeles airport and that Hertz charges a total of \$275. Western, the lessee, records the rental as follows:

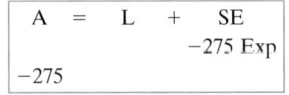

A	=	L	+	SE
				−275 Exp
−275				

Cash Flows
−275

Car Rental Expense	275	
Cash		275
(To record payment of lease rental charge)		

The lessee may incur other costs during the lease period. For example, in the case above, Western will generally incur costs for gas. Western would report these costs as an expense.

CAPITAL LEASES

In most lease contracts, the lessee makes a periodic payment and records that payment in the income statement as rent expense. In some cases, however, the lease contract transfers to the lessee substantially all the benefits and risks of ownership. Such a lease is in effect a purchase of the property. This type of lease is a **capital lease**. Its name comes from the fact that the company capitalizes the present value of the cash payments for the lease and records that amount as an asset. Illustration 15-13 indicates the major difference between operating and capital leases.

Illustration 15-13
Types of leases

HELPFUL HINT
A capital lease situation is one that, although legally a rental case, is *in substance* an installment purchase by the lessee. Accounting standards require that substance over form be used in such a situation.

If **any one** of the following conditions exists, the lessee must record a lease **as an asset**—that is, as a capital lease:

1. **The lease transfers ownership of the property to the lessee.** *Rationale:* If during the lease term the lessee receives ownership of the asset, the lessee should report the leased asset as an asset on its books.
2. **The lease contains a bargain purchase option.** *Rationale:* If during the term of the lease the lessee can purchase the asset at a price substantially below its fair market value, the lessee will exercise this option. Thus, the lessee should report the lease as a leased asset on its books.
3. **The lease term is equal to 75% or more of the economic life of the leased property.** *Rationale:* If the lease term is for much of the asset's useful life, the lessee should report the asset as a leased asset on its books.
4. **The present value of the lease payments equals or exceeds 90% of the fair market value of the leased property.** *Rationale:* If the present value of the lease payments is equal to or almost equal to the fair market value of the asset, the lessee has essentially purchased the asset. As a result, the lessee should report the leased asset as an asset on its books.

To illustrate, assume that Gonzalez Company decides to lease new equipment. The lease period is four years; the economic life of the leased equipment is estimated to be five years. The present value of the lease payments is $190,000, which is equal to the fair market value of the equipment. There is no transfer of ownership during the lease term, nor is there any bargain purchase option.

In this example, Gonzalez has essentially purchased the equipment. Conditions 3 and 4 have been met. First, the lease term is 75% or more of the economic life of the asset. Second, the present value of cash payments is equal to the equipment's fair market value. Gonzalez records the transaction as follows.

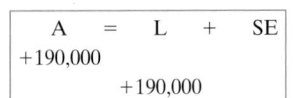

A	=	L	+	SE
+190,000				
		+190,000		

Cash Flows
no effect

Leased Asset—Equipment	190,000	
Lease Liability		190,000
(To record leased asset and lease liability)		

The lessee reports a leased asset on the balance sheet under plant assets. It reports the lease liability on the balance sheet as a liability. **The portion of the lease liability expected to be paid in the next year is a current liability. The remainder is classified as a long-term liability.**

ETHICS NOTE

Accounting standard setters are attempting to rewrite rules on lease accounting because of concerns that abuse of the current standards is reducing the usefulness of financial statements.

Most lessees do not like to report leases on their balance sheets. Why? Because the lease liability increases the company's total liabilities. This, in turn, may make it more difficult for the company to obtain needed funds from lenders. As a result, companies attempt to keep leased assets and lease liabilities off the balance sheet by structuring leases so as not to meet any of the four conditions mentioned on page 645. The practice of keeping liabilities off the balance sheet is referred to as **off-balance-sheet financing**.

STATEMENT PRESENTATION AND ANALYSIS

Presentation

STUDY OBJECTIVE 6

Identify the methods for the presentation and analysis of long-term liabilities.

Companies report long-term liabilities in a separate section of the balance sheet immediately following current liabilities, as shown in Illustration 15-14. Alternatively, companies may present summary data in the balance sheet, with detailed data (interest rates, maturity dates, conversion privileges, and assets pledged as collateral) shown in a supporting schedule. Companies report the current maturities of long-term debt under current liabilities if they are to be paid from current assets.

Illustration 15-14
Balance sheet presentation of long-term liabilities

LAX CORPORATION
Balance Sheet (partial)

Long-term liabilities		
Bonds payable 10% due in 2015	$1,000,000	
Less: Discount on bonds payable	80,000	$ 920,000
Mortgage notes payable, 11%, due in 2021 and secured by plant assets		500,000
Lease liability		440,000
Total long-term liabilities		$1,860,000

Analysis

Long-term creditors and stockholders are interested in a company's long-run solvency. Of particular interest is the company's ability to pay interest as it comes due and to repay the face value of the debt at maturity. Debt to total assets and times interest earned are two ratios that provide information about debt-paying ability and long-run solvency.

The **debt to total assets ratio** measures the percentage of the total assets provided by creditors. As shown in the formula in Illustration 15-15, it is computed by dividing total debt (both current and long-term liabilities) by total assets. The higher the percentage of debt to total assets, the greater the risk that the company may be unable to meet its maturing obligations.

The **times interest earned ratio** indicates the company's ability to meet interest payments as they come due. It is computed by dividing income before income taxes and interest expense by interest expense.

To illustrate these ratios, we will use data from Kellogg Company's 2005 annual report. The company had total liabilities of $8,290.8 million, total assets of $10,574.5 million, interest expense of $300.3 million, income taxes of $444.7 million, and net income of $980.4 million. Kellogg's debt to total assets ratio and times interest earned ratio are shown below.

Illustration 15-15
Debt to total assets and times interest earned ratios, with computations

Total Debt	÷	Total Assets	=	Debt to Total Assets
$8,290.8	÷	$10,574.5	=	**78.4%**
Income before Income Taxes and Interest Expense	÷	**Interest Expense**	=	**Times Interest Earned**
$980.4 + $444.7 + $300.3	÷	$300.3	=	**5.75 times**

Kellogg has a relatively high debt to total assets percentage of 78.4%. Its interest coverage of 5.75 times is considered safe.

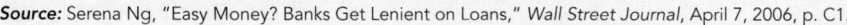

INVESTOR INSIGHT

They Thought It Was Easy Money

Lending markets change over time. Sometimes it is easy to borrow money, while at other times the credit market dries up. During the spring of 2006 many observers noted that money was flowing very freely. This was a concern to some analysts, who noted that many lenders had cut back on the number and restrictiveness of loan covenants that they required of borrowers. *Covenants* are performance hurdles that companies agree to in order to obtain a loan. For example, many loan covenants specify required values for debt to total assets or times interest earned measures that must be maintained while the debt is outstanding. In the words of one observer, "Credit quality is still strong, but this trend of shrinking covenants is laying the groundwork for the next round of credit problems."

Source: Serena Ng, "Easy Money? Banks Get Lenient on Loans," *Wall Street Journal*, April 7, 2006, p. C1.

? What do you think happens when a company violates its debt covenants?

Before You Go On...

REVIEW IT

1. Explain the accounting for long-term mortgage notes payable.
2. What is the difference in accounting for an operating lease versus a capital lease? Explain the four conditions used to determine whether the lease contract transfers substantially all the benefits and risks of ownership.
3. What ratios may be computed to analyze a company's long-run solvency?

✓ The Navigator

Be sure to read **ALL ABOUT YOU: *The Risks of Adjustable Rates*** on page 648 for information on how topics in this chapter apply to you.

The Risks of Adjustable Rates

As home prices rose rapidly between 2000 and 2005, many people found that they could not afford to buy a home using traditional fixed interest rate loans. Lenders encouraged some people to use less-conventional loans such as ARMs—adjustable-rate mortgages.

The lender periodically adjusts the interest rate on an ARM to reflect changes in market interest rates. The advantage of ARMs to home buyers is that the initial rate on an ARM is below the rate charged on a fixed-rate loan. This can enable the buyer to purchase a home that he or she otherwise could not afford. If market interest rates rise, however, the rate on the ARM can rise well above the initial rate. This will result in much higher mortgage payments. Rising rates can be a problem for homeowners who have not planned for them.

Some Facts

* 35% of people with ARMs do not know how much the rate could increase at one time, and 41% are not sure of the maximum rate they could face.
* 28% of people with ARMs do not know which index of interest rates is used to determine their adjustments.
* ARMs represented about one-third of all loans granted during 2004 and 2005, which was substantially higher than most previous years.
* Borrowers with less income or education were more likely not to know their mortgage terms. Borrowers with less income faced the largest change in their ARM payment, as a percentage of income, when interest rates changed.

About the Numbers

Although a high percentage of loans granted during 2004 and 2005 were adjustable-rate loans, these loans still represent a relatively small percentage of all loans outstanding. Many people who are initially granted an adjustable-rate loan subsequently refinance their loan to get a fixed-rate loan that will offer no unpleasant surprises in later years.

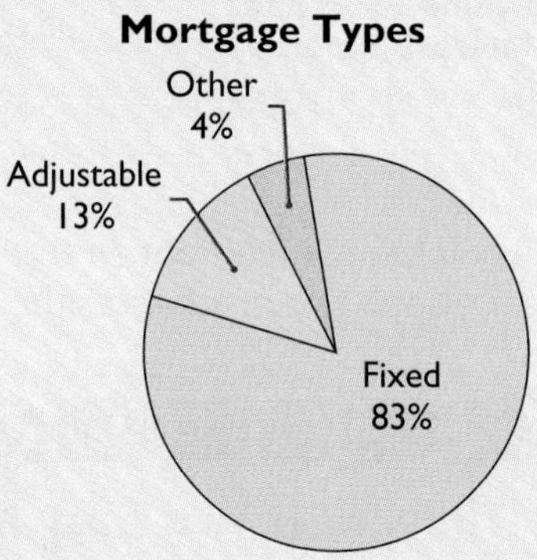

Source: Brian Bucks and Karen Pence, "Do Homeowners Know Their House Values and Mortgage Terms?," Federal Reserve Board of Governors, January 2006, *www.federalreserve.gov/pubs/feds/2006/200603/200603pap.pdf.*

What Do You Think?

Suppose that you are planning to buy your first home for $200,000. The payment on a 30-year, 7% fixed-rate loan of $180,000 (after a down payment of $20,000) would be $1,198 per month, which is more than you qualify for with the lender. The lender has suggested that you could instead use an ARM. The interest rate would be 5.5%, resulting in payments of $1,022 per month for the first three years. After that, the interest rate would be adjusted annually and could increase by as much as 2% each year, with an upper-end rate of 10.5%. Should you buy the home using adjustable-rate financing?

YES: House prices are just going to keep going up, up, up. If you don't get into the market now, you may never be able to.

NO: This nontraditional loan has too much uncertainty tied to it. If interest rates go up, your payment could get so high that you wouldn't be able to make the payment, in which case you would lose the house.

Sources: James R. Hagerty, "The Home-Mortgage Muddle; Some Borrowers Are Confused by Terms of Adjustable-Rate Loans," *Wall Street Journal*, March 11, 2006, p. B4.

The authors' comments on this situation appear on page 680.

Demonstration Problem

Snyder Software Inc. has successfully developed a new spreadsheet program. To produce and market the program, the company needed $2 million of additional financing. On January 1, 2009, Snyder borrowed money as follows.

1. Snyder issued $500,000, 11%, 10-year convertible bonds. The bonds sold at face value and pay semiannual interest on January 1 and July 1. Each $1,000 bond is convertible into 30 shares of Snyder's $20 par value common stock.
2. Snyder issued $1 million, 10%, 10-year bonds at face value. Interest is payable semiannually on January 1 and July 1.
3. Snyder also issued a $500,000, 12%, 15-year mortgage note payable. The terms provide for semiannual installment payments of $36,324 on June 30 and December 31.

Instructions

1. For the convertible bonds, prepare journal entries for:
   (a) The issuance of the bonds on January 1, 2009.
   (b) Interest expense on July 1 and December 31, 2009.
   (c) The payment of interest on January 1, 2010.
   (d) The conversion of all bonds into common stock on January 1, 2010, when the market value of the common stock was $67 per share.
2. For the 10-year, 10% bonds:
   (a) Journalize the issuance of the bonds on January 1, 2009.
   (b) Prepare the journal entries for interest expense in 2009. Assume no accrual of interest on July 1.
   (c) Prepare the entry for the redemption of the bonds at 101 on January 1, 2012, after paying the interest due on this date.
3. For the mortgage note payable:
   (a) Prepare the entry for the issuance of the note on January 1, 2009.
   (b) Prepare a payment schedule for the first four installment payments.
   (c) Indicate the current and noncurrent amounts for the mortgage note payable at December 31, 2009.

Solution to Demonstration Problem

1. (a) 2009

Jan. 1	Cash	500,000	
	Bonds Payable		500,000
	(To record issue of 11%, 10-year convertible bonds at face value)		

(b) 2009

July 1	Bond Interest Expense	27,500	
	Cash ($500,000 × 0.055)		27,500
	(To record payment of semiannual interest)		
Dec. 31	Bond Interest Expense	27,500	
	Bond Interest Payable		27,500
	(To record accrual of semiannual bond interest)		

action plan

✔ Compute interest semiannually (six months).

✔ Record the accrual and payment of interest on appropriate dates.

✔ Record the conversion of the bonds into common stock by removing the book (carrying) value of the bonds from the liability account.

Date	Account Titles and Explanation	Debit	Credit
(c) 2010			
Jan. 1	Bond Interest Payable	27,500	
	Cash		27,500
	(To record payment of accrued interest)		
(d) Jan. 1	Bonds Payable	500,000	
	Common Stock		300,000*
	Paid-in Capital in Excess of Par Value		200,000
	(To record conversion of bonds into common stock)		
	*($500,000 ÷ $1,000 = 500 bonds; 500 × 30 = 15,000 shares; 15,000 × $20 = $300,000)		

action plan

- Record the issuance of the bonds.
- Compute interest expense for each period.
- Compute the loss on bond redemption as the excess of the cash paid over the carrying value of the redeemed bonds.

2.

Date	Account Titles and Explanation	Debit	Credit
(a) 2009			
Jan. 1	Cash	1,000,000	
	Bonds Payable		1,000,000
	(To record issuance of bonds)		
(b) 2009			
July 1	Bond Interest Expense	50,000	
	Cash		50,000
	(To record payment of semiannual interest)		
Dec. 31	Bond Interest Expense	50,000	
	Bond Interest Payable		50,000
	(To record accrual of semiannual interest)		
(c) 2012			
Jan. 1	Bonds Payable	1,000,000	
	Loss on Bond Redemption	10,000*	
	Cash		1,010,000
	(To record redemption of bonds at 101)		
	*($1,010,000 − $1,000,000)		

action plan

- Compute periodic interest expense on a mortgage note, recognizing that as the principal amount decreases, so does the interest expense.
- Record mortgage payments, recognizing that each payment consists of (1) interest on the unpaid loan balance and (2) a reduction of the loan principal.

3.

Date	Account Titles and Explanation	Debit	Credit
(a) 2009			
Jan. 1	Cash	500,000	
	Mortgage Notes Payable		500,000
	(To record issuance of mortgage note payable)		

(b)

Semiannual Interest Period	Cash Payment	Interest Expense	Reduction of Principal	Principal Balance
Issue date				$500,000
1	$36,324	$30,000	$6,324	493,676
2	36,324	29,621	6,703	486,973
3	36,324	29,218	7,106	479,867
4	36,324	28,792	7,532	472,335

(c) Current liability $14,638 ($7,106 + $7,532)
Long-term liability $472,335

The Navigator

SUMMARY OF STUDY OBJECTIVES

WILEY PLUS

1 **Explain why bonds are issued.** Companies may sell bonds to investors to raise long-term capital. Bonds offer the following advantages over common stock: (a) stockholder control is not affected, (b) tax savings result, (c) earnings per share of common stock may be higher.

2 **Prepare the entries for the issuance of bonds and interest expense.** When companies issue bonds, they debit Cash for the cash proceeds, and credit Bonds Payable for the face value of the bonds. The account Premium on Bonds Payable shows a bond premium; Discount on Bonds Payable shows a bond discount.

3 **Describe the entries when bonds are redeemed or converted.** When bondholders redeem bonds at maturity, the issuing company credits Cash and debits Bonds Payable for the face value of the bonds. When bonds are redeemed before maturity, the issuing company (a) eliminates the carrying value of the bonds at the redemption date, (b) records the cash paid, and (c) recognizes the gain or loss on redemption. When bonds are converted to common stock, the issuing company transfers the carrying (or book) value of the bonds to appropriate paid-in capital accounts; no gain or loss is recognized.

4 **Describe the accounting for long-term notes payable.** Each payment consists of (1) interest on the unpaid balance of the loan and (2) a reduction of loan principal. The interest decreases each period, while the portion applied to the loan principal increases.

5 **Contrast the accounting for operating and capital leases.** For an operating lease, the lessee (renter) records lease (rental) payments as an expense. For a capital lease, the lessee records the asset and related obligation at the present value of the future lease payments.

6 **Identify the methods for the presentation and analysis of long-term liabilities.** Companies should report the nature and amount of each long-term debt in the balance sheet or in the notes accompanying the financial statements. Stockholders and long-term creditors are interested in a company's long-run solvency. Debt to total assets and times interest earned are two ratios that provide information about debt-paying ability and long-run solvency.

The Navigator

GLOSSARY

WILEY PLUS

Bearer (coupon) bonds Bonds not registered. (p. 634).

Bond certificate A legal document that indicates the name of the issuer, the face value of the bonds, and such other data as the contractual interest rate and maturity date of the bonds. (p. 634).

Bond indenture A legal document that sets forth the terms of the bond issue. (p. 634).

Bonds A form of interest-bearing notes payable issued by corporations, universities, and governmental entities. (p. 632).

Callable bonds Bonds that are subject to retirement at a stated dollar amount prior to maturity at the option of the issuer. (p. 634).

Capital lease A contractual arrangement that transfers substantially all the benefits and risks of ownership to the lessee so that the lease is in effect a purchase of the property. (p. 645).

Contractual interest rate Rate used to determine the amount of cash interest the borrower pays and the investor receives. (p. 634).

Convertible bonds Bonds that permit bondholders to convert them into common stock at their option. (p. 634).

Debenture bonds Bonds issued against the general credit of the borrower. Also called unsecured bonds. (p. 634).

Debt to total assets ratio A solvency measure that indicates the percentage of total assets provided by creditors; computed as total debt divided by total assets. (p. 646).

Discount (on a bond) The difference between the face value of a bond and its selling price, when the bond is sold for less than its face value. (p. 638).

Face value Amount of principal the issuer must pay at the maturity date of the bond. (p. 634).

Long-term liabilities Obligations expected to be paid after one year. (p. 632).

Market interest rate The rate investors demand for loaning funds to the corporation. (p. 636).

Mortgage bond A bond secured by real estate. (p. 633).

Mortgage note payable A long-term note secured by a mortgage that pledges title to specific assets as security for a loan. (p. 643).

Operating lease A contractual arrangement giving the lessee temporary use of the property, with continued ownership of the property by the lessor. (p. 644).

Premium (on a bond) The difference between the selling price and the face value of a bond, when the bond is sold for more than its face value. (p. 638).

Registered bonds Bonds issued in the name of the owner. (p. 634).

Secured bonds Bonds that have specific assets of the issuer pledged as collateral. (p. 633).

Serial bonds Bonds that mature in installments. (p. 634).

Sinking fund bonds Bonds secured by specific assets set aside to retire them. (p. 633).

Term bonds Bonds that mature at a single specified future date. (p. 634).

Times interest earned ratio A solvency measure that indicates a company's ability to meet interest payments; computed by dividing income before income taxes and interest expense by interest expense. (p. 647).

Unsecured bonds Bonds issued against the general credit of the borrower. Also called debenture bonds. (p. 634).

APPENDIX 15A Present Value Concepts Related to Bond Pricing

Congratulations! You have a winning lottery ticket and the state has provided you with three possible options for payment. They are:

1. Receive $10,000,000 in three years.
2. Receive $7,000,000 immediately.
3. Receive $3,500,000 at the end of each year for three years.

Which of these options would you select? The answer is not easy to determine at a glance. To make a dollar-maximizing choice, you must perform present value computations. A present value computation is based on the concept of time value of money. Time value of money concepts are useful for the lottery situation and for pricing other amounts to be received in the future. This appendix discusses how to use present value concepts to price bonds. It also will tell you how to determine what option you should take as a lottery winner.

Present Value of Face Value

STUDY OBJECTIVE 7

Compute the market price of a bond.

To illustrate present value concepts, assume that you are willing to invest a sum of money that will yield $1,000 at the end of one year. In other words, what amount would you need to invest today to have $1,000 one year from now? If you want to earn 10%, the investment (or present value) is $909.09 ($1,000 ÷ 1.10). Illustration 15A-1 shows the computation.

Illustration 15A-1
Present value computation—$1,000 discounted at 10% for one year

Present value	×	(1 + Interest rate)	=	Future amount
Present value	×	(1 + 10%)	=	$1,000
Present value			=	$1,000 ÷ 1.10
Present value			=	**$909.09**

The future amount ($1,000), the interest rate (10%), and the number of periods (1) are known. We can depict the variables in this situation as shown in the time diagram in Illustration 15A-2.

Illustration 15A-2
Finding present value if discounted for one period

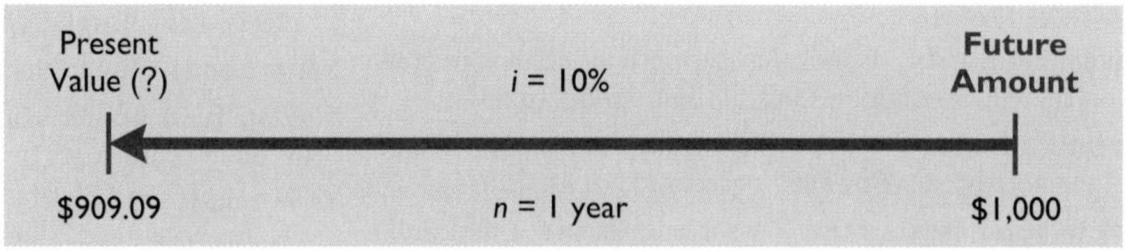

If you are to receive the single future amount of $1,000 **in two years**, discounted at 10%, its present value is $826.45 [($1,000 ÷ 1.10) ÷ 1.10], depicted as follows.

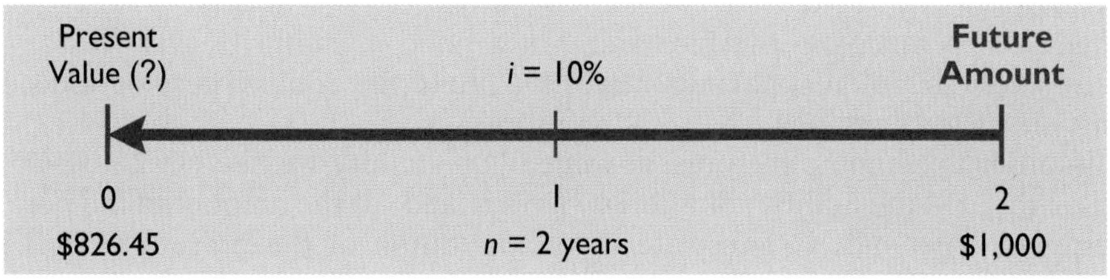

Illustration 15A-3
Finding present value if discounted for two periods

We also can determine the present value of 1 through tables that show the present value of 1 for *n* periods. In Table 15A-1 below, *n* is the number of discounting periods involved. The percentages are the periodic interest rates, and the 5-digit decimal numbers in the respective columns are the factors for the present value of 1.

When using Table 15A-1, we multiply the future amount by the present value factor specified at the intersection of the number of periods and the interest rate. For example, the present value factor for 1 period at an interest rate of 10% is .90909, which equals the $909.09 ($1,000 × .90909) computed in Illustration 15A-1.

TABLE 15A-1
Present Value of 1

(*n*) Periods	4%	5%	6%	8%	9%	10%	11%	12%	15%
1	.96154	.95238	.94340	.92593	.91743	.90909	.90090	.89286	.86957
2	.92456	.90703	.89000	.85734	.84168	.82645	.81162	.79719	.75614
3	.88900	.86384	.83962	.79383	.77218	.75132	.73119	.71178	.65752
4	.85480	.82270	.79209	.73503	.70843	.68301	.65873	.63552	.57175
5	.82193	.78353	.74726	.68058	.64993	.62092	.59345	.56743	.49718
6	.79031	.74622	.70496	.63017	.59627	.56447	.53464	.50663	.43233
7	.75992	.71068	.66506	.58349	.54703	.51316	.48166	.45235	.37594
8	.73069	.67684	.62741	.54027	.50187	.46651	.43393	.40388	.32690
9	.70259	.64461	.59190	.50025	.46043	.42410	.39092	.36061	.28426
10	.67556	.61391	.55839	.46319	.42241	.38554	.35218	.32197	.24719

For two periods at an interest rate of 10%, the present value factor is .82645, which equals the $826.45 ($1,000 × .82645) computed previously.

Let's now go back to our lottery example. Given the present value concepts just learned, we can determine whether receiving $10,000,000 in three years is better than receiving $7,000,000 today, assuming the appropriate discount rate is 9%. The computation is as follows.

$10,000,000 × PV of 1 due in 3 years at 9% =	
$10,000,000 × .77218 (Table 15A-1)	$7,721,800
Amount to be received from state immediately	7,000,000
Difference	$ 721,800

Illustration 15A-4
Present value of $10,000,000 to be received in three years

What this computation shows you is that you would be $721,800 better off receiving the $10,000,000 at the end of three years rather than taking $7,000,000 immediately.

Present Value of Interest Payments (Annuities)

In addition to receiving the face value of a bond at maturity, an investor also receives periodic interest payments over the life of the bonds. These periodic payments are called **annuities**.

In order to compute the present value of an annuity, we need to know: (1) the interest rate, (2) the number of interest periods, and (3) the amount of the periodic receipts or payments. To illustrate the computation of the present value of an annuity, assume that you will receive $1,000 cash annually for three years and the interest rate is 10%. The time diagram in Illustration 15A-5 depicts this situation.

Illustration 15A-5
Time diagram for a three-year annuity

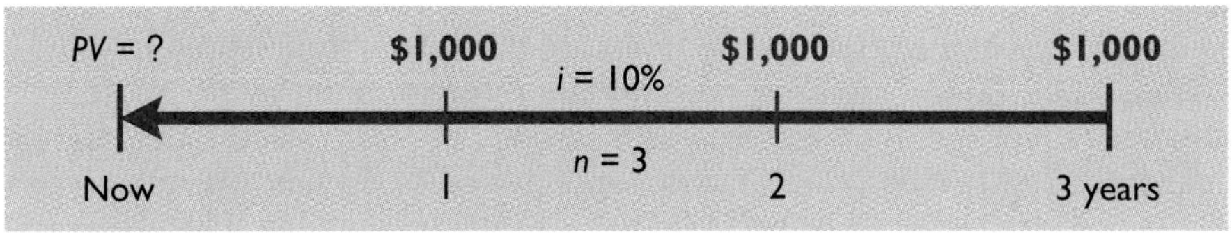

The present value in this situation may be computed as follows.

Illustration 15A-6
Present value of a series of future amounts computation

Future Amount	×	Present Value of 1 Factor at 10%	=	Present Value
$1,000 (1 year away)		.90909		$ 909.09
1,000 (2 years away)		.82645		826.45
1,000 (3 years away)		.75132		751.32
		2.48686		**$2,486.86**

We also can use annuity tables to value annuities. As illustrated in Table 15A-2 below, these tables show the present value of 1 to be received periodically for a given number of periods.

TABLE 15A-2
Present Value of an Annuity of 1

(*n*) Periods	**4%**	**5%**	**6%**	**8%**	**9%**	**10%**	**11%**	**12%**	**15%**
1	.96154	.95238	.94340	.92593	.91743	.90909	.90090	.89286	.86957
2	1.88609	1.85941	1.83339	1.78326	1.75911	1.73554	1.71252	1.69005	1.62571
3	2.77509	2.72325	2.67301	2.57710	2.53130	2.48685	2.44371	2.40183	2.28323
4	3.62990	3.54595	3.46511	3.31213	3.23972	3.16986	3.10245	3.03735	2.85498
5	4.45182	4.32948	4.21236	3.99271	3.88965	3.79079	3.69590	3.60478	3.35216
6	5.24214	5.07569	4.91732	4.62288	4.48592	4.35526	4.23054	4.11141	3.78448
7	6.00205	5.78637	5.58238	5.20637	5.03295	4.86842	4.71220	4.56376	4.16042
8	6.73274	6.46321	6.20979	5.74664	5.53482	5.33493	5.14612	4.96764	4.48732
9	7.43533	7.10782	6.80169	6.24689	5.99525	5.75902	5.53705	5.32825	4.77158
10	8.11090	7.72173	7.36009	6.71008	6.41766	6.14457	5.88923	5.65022	5.01877

From Table 15A-2 you can see that the present value factor of an annuity of 1 for three periods at 10% is 2.48685.[1] This present value factor is the total of the three individual present value factors as shown in Illustration 15A-6. Applying this amount to the annual cash flow of $1,000 produces a present value of $2,486.85.

Let's now go back to our lottery example. We determined that you would get more money if you wait and take the $10,000,000 in three years rather than take $7,000,000 immediately. But there is still another option—to receive $3,500,000 at the end of **each year** for three years (an annuity). The computation to evaluate this option (again assuming a 9% discount rate) is as follows.

$3,500,000 × PV of 1 due yearly for 3 years at 9% =	
$3,500,000 × 2.53130 (Table 15A-2)	$8,859,550
Present value of $10,000,000 to be received in 3 years	7,721,800
Difference	$1,137,750

Illustration 15A-7
Present value of lottery payments to be received over three years

If you take the annuity of $3,500,000 for each of 3 years, you will be $1,137,750 richer as a result.

Time Periods and Discounting

We have used an **annual** interest rate to determine present value. Present value computations may also be done over shorter periods of time, such as monthly, quarterly, or semiannually. When the time frame is less than one year, it is necessary to convert the annual interest rate to the shorter time frame.

Assume, for example, that the investor in Illustration 15A-6 received $500 **semiannually** for three years instead of $1,000 annually. In this case, the number of periods becomes 6 (3 × 2), the interest rate is 5% (10% ÷ 2), the present value factor from Table 15A-2 is 5.07569, and the present value of the future cash flows is $2,537.85 (5.07569 × $500). This amount is slightly higher than the $2,486.86 computed in Illustration 15A-6 because interest is computed twice during the same year. That is, interest is earned on the first half year's interest.

Computing the Present Value of a Bond

The present value (or market price) of a bond is a function of three variables: (1) the payment amounts, (2) the length of time until the amounts are paid, and (3) the interest (discount) rate.

The first variable (dollars to be paid) is made up of two elements: (1) a series of interest payments (an annuity), and (2) the principal amount (a single sum). To compute the present value of the bond, we must discount both the interest payments and the principal amount.

When the investor's interest (discount) rate is equal to the bond's contractual interest rate, the present value of the bonds will equal the face value of the bonds. To illustrate, assume a bond issue of 10%, five-year bonds with a face value of $100,000 with interest payable **semiannually** on January 1 and July 1. If the discount rate is the same as the contractual rate, the bonds will sell **at face value**. In this case, the investor will receive: (1) $100,000 at maturity and (2) a series of ten $5,000 interest payments [$100,000 × (10% ÷ 2)] over the term of the bonds. The length of time is expressed in terms of interest periods (in this case, 10) and the discount rate per interest period (5%). The time diagram in Illustration 15A-8 (page 656) depicts the variables involved in this discounting situation.

[1]The difference of .00001 between 2.48686 and 2.48685 is due to rounding.

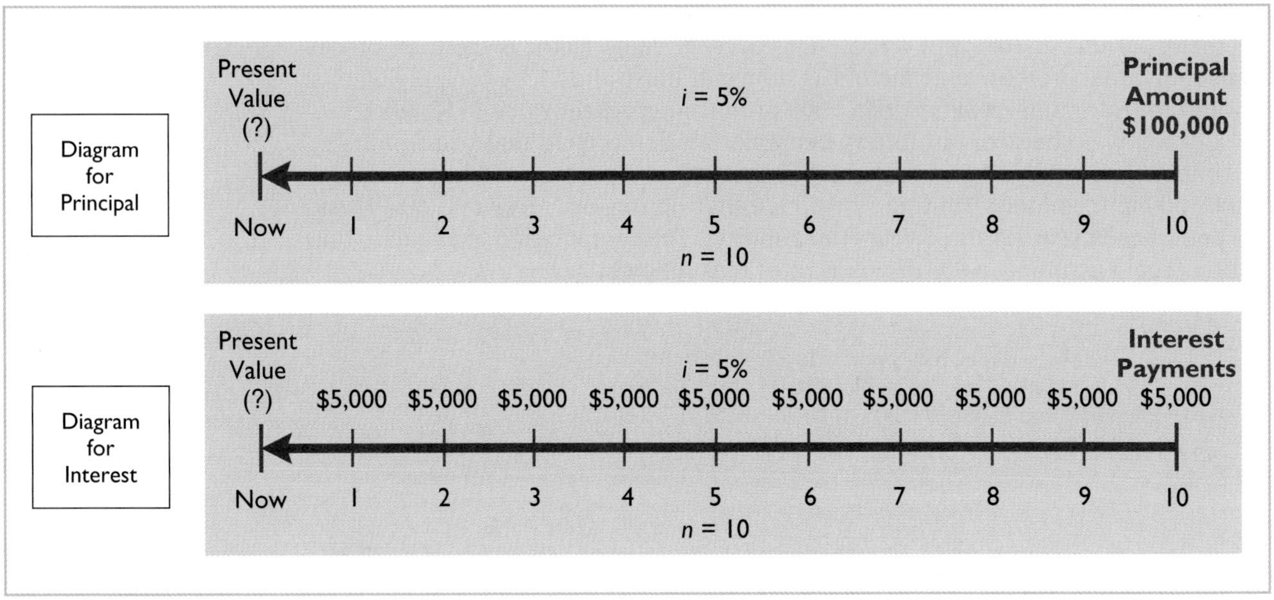

Illustration 15A-8
Time diagram for the present value of a 10%, five-year bond paying interest semiannually

The computation of the present value of Candlestick's bonds, assuming they were issued at face value (page 637), is shown below.

Illustration 15A-9
Present value of principal and interest (face value)

10% Contractual Rate—10% Discount Rate	
Present value of principal to be received at maturity	
$100,000 × PV of 1 due in 10 periods at 5%	
$100,000 × .61391 (Table 15A-1)	$ 61,391
Present value of interest to be received periodically over the term of the bonds	
$5,000 × PV of 1 due periodically for 10 periods at 5%	
$5,000 × 7.72173 (Table 15A-2)	38,609*
Present value of bonds	**$100,000**

*(Rounded).

Now assume that the investor's required rate of return is 12%, not 10%. The future amounts are again $100,000 and $5,000, respectively. But now we must use a discount rate of 6% (12% ÷ 2). The present value of Candlestick's bonds issued at a discount (page 638) is $92,639 as computed below.

Illustration 15A-10
Present value of principal and interest (discount)

10% Contractual Rate—12% Discount Rate	
Present value of principal to be received at maturity	
$100,000 × .55839 (Table 15A-1)	$55,839
Present value of interest to be received periodically over the term of the bonds	
$5,000 × 7.36009 (Table 15A-2)	36,800
Present value of bonds	**$92,639**

If the discount rate is 8% and the contractual rate is 10%, the present value of Candlestick's bonds issued at a premium (page 639) is $108,111, computed as follows.

10% Contractual Rate—8% Discount Rate	
Present value of principal to be received at maturity	
$100,000 × .67556 (Table 15A-1)	$67,556
Present value of interest to be received periodically over the term of the bonds	
$5,000 × 8.11090 (Table 15A-2)	40,555
Present value of bonds	**$108,111**

Illustration 15A-11
Present value of principal and interest (premium)

SUMMARY OF STUDY OBJECTIVE FOR APPENDIX 15A

7 **Compute the market price of a bond.** Time value of money concepts are useful for pricing bonds. The present value (or market price) of a bond is a function of three variables: (1) the payment amounts, (2) the length of time until the amounts are paid, and (3) the interest rate.

APPENDIX 15B Effective-Interest Method of Bond Amortization

STUDY OBJECTIVE 8
Apply the effective-interest method of amortizing bond discount and bond premium.

Under the effective-interest method, the amortization of bond discount or bond premium results in periodic interest expense equal to a **constant percentage** of the carrying value of the bonds. The effective-interest method results in varying amounts of amortization and interest expense per period but **a constant percentage rate**.

The following steps are required under the effective-interest method.

1. Compute the **bond interest expense**. To do so, multiply the carrying value of the bonds at the beginning of the interest period by the effective-interest rate.
2. Compute the **bond interest paid** (or accrued). To do so, multiply the face value of the bonds by the contractual interest rate.
3. Compute the **amortization amount**. To do so, determine the difference between the amounts computed in steps (1) and (2).

Illustration 15B-1 depicts these steps.

(1) Bond Interest Expense		(2) Bond Interest Paid		(3)
(Carrying Value of Bonds at Beginning of Period × Effective Interest Rate)	−	(Face Amount of Bonds × Contractual Interest Rate)	=	Amortization Amount

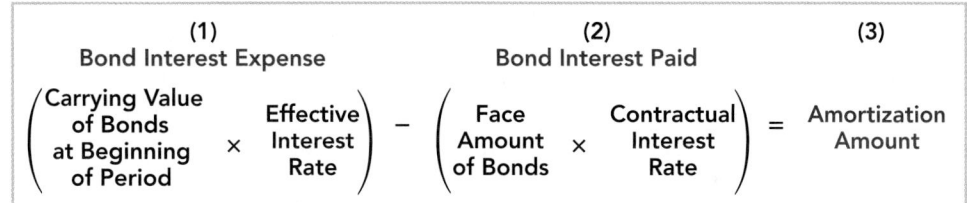

Illustration 15B-1
Computation of amortization—effective-interest method

When the difference between the straight-line method of amortization (Appendix 15C) and the effective-interest method is material, GAAP requires the use of the effective-interest method.

Amortizing Bond Discount

To illustrate the effective-interest method of bond discount amortization, assume that Candlestick, Inc. issues $100,000 of 10%, five-year bonds on January 1, 2008, with interest payable each July 1 and January 1 (pages 638–639). The bonds sell for $92,639 (92.639% of face value). This sales price results in bond discount of $7,361 ($100,000 − $92,639) and an effective-interest rate of 12%. A bond discount amortization schedule, as shown in Illustration 15B-2 (page 658), facilitates the recording of interest expense and the discount amortization. Note that interest expense as a percentage of carrying value remains constant at 6%.

Candlestick Inc.xls

File Edit View Insert Format Tools Data Window Help

CANDLESTICK, INC.
Bond Discount Amortization
Effective-Interest Method—Semiannual Interest Payments
10% Bonds Issued at 12%

Semiannual Interest Periods	(A) Interest to Be Paid (5% × $100,000)	(B) Interest Expense to Be Recorded (6% × Preceding Bond Carrying Value)		(C) Discount Amortization (B) − (A)	(D) Unamortized Discount (D) − (C)	(E) Bond Carrying Value ($100,000 − D)
Issue date					$7,361	$92,639
1	**$ 5,000**	**$ 5,558**	**(6% × $92,639)**	**$ 558**	**6,803**	**93,197**
2	5,000	5,592	(6% × $93,197)	592	6,211	93,789
3	5,000	5,627	(6% × $93,789)	627	5,584	94,416
4	5,000	5,665	(6% × $94,416)	665	4,919	95,081
5	5,000	5,705	(6% × $95,081)	705	4,214	95,786
6	5,000	5,747	(6% × $95,786)	747	3,467	96,533
7	5,000	5,792	(6% × $96,533)	792	2,675	97,325
8	5,000	5,840	(6% × $97,325)	840	1,835	98,165
9	5,000	5,890	(6% × $98,165)	890	945	99,055
10	5,000	5,945*	(6% × $99,055)	945	−0−	100,000
	$50,000	$57,361		$7,361		

Column **(A)** remains constant because the face value of the bonds ($100,000) is multiplied by the semiannual contractual interest rate (5%) each period.

Column **(B)** is computed as the preceding bond carrying value times the semiannual effective-interest rate (6%).

Column **(C)** indicates the discount amortization each period.

Column **(D)** decreases each period until it reaches zero at maturity.

Column **(E)** increases each period until it equals face value at maturity.

*$2 difference due to rounding.

Illustration 15B-2
Bond discount amortization schedule

We have highlighted columns (A), (B), and (C) in the amortization schedule to emphasize their importance. These three columns provide the numbers for each period's journal entries. They are the primary reason for preparing the schedule.

For the first interest period, the computations of bond interest expense and the bond discount amortization are:

Illustration 15B-3
Computation of bond discount amortization

Bond interest expense ($92,639 × 6%)	$5,558
Contractual interest ($100,000 × 5%)	5,000
Bond discount amortization	**$ 558**

Candlestick records the payment of interest and amortization of bond discount on July 1, 2008, as follows.

A	=	L	+	SE
				−5,558 Exp
		+558		
−5,000				

Cash Flows
−5,000

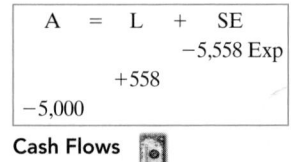

July 1	Bond Interest Expense	5,558	
	Discount on Bonds Payable		558
	Cash		5,000
	(To record payment of bond interest and amortization of bond discount)		

For the second interest period, bond interest expense will be $5,592 ($93,197 × 6%), and the discount amortization will be $592. At December 31, Candlestick makes the following adjusting entry.

Dec. 31	Bond Interest Expense	5,592	
	Discount on Bonds Payable		592
	Bond Interest Payable		5,000
	(To record accrued interest and amortization of bond discount)		

A	=	L	+	SE
				−5,592 Exp
		+592		
		+5,000		

Cash Flows
no effect

Total bond interest expense for 2008 is $11,150 ($5,558 + $5,592). On January 1, Candlestick records payment of the interest by a debit to Bond Interest Payable and a credit to Cash.

Amortizing Bond Premium

The amortization of bond premium by the effective-interest method is similar to the procedures described for bond discount. For example, assume that Candlestick, Inc. issues $100,000, 10%, five-year bonds on January 1, 2008, with interest payable on July 1 and January 1 (pages 639–640). In this case, the bonds sell for $108,111. This sales price results in bond premium of $8,111 and an effective-interest rate of 8%. Illustration 15-4 shows the bond premium amortization schedule.

HELPFUL HINT

When a bond sells for $108,111, it is quoted as 108.111% of face value. Note that $108,111 can be proven as shown in Appendix 15A.

Illustration 15B-4
Bond premium amortization schedule

Candlestick Inc.xls

File Edit View Insert Format Tools Data Window Help

CANDLESTICK, INC.
Bond Premium Amortization
Effective-Interest Method—Semiannual Interest Payments
10% Bonds Issued at 8%

Semiannual Interest Periods	(A) Interest to Be Paid (5% × $100,000)	(B) Interest Expense to Be Recorded (4% × Preceding Bond Carrying Value)		(C) Premium Amortization (A) − (B)	(D) Unamortized Premium (D) − (C)	(E) Bond Carrying Value ($100,000 + D)
Issue date					$8,111	$108,111
1	**$ 5,000**	**$ 4,324**	**(4% × $108,111)**	**$ 676**	**7,435**	**107,435**
2	5,000	4,297	(4% × $107,435)	703	6,732	106,732
3	5,000	4,269	(4% × $106,732)	731	6,001	106,001
4	5,000	4,240	(4% × $106,001)	760	5,241	105,241
5	5,000	4,210	(4% × $105,241)	790	4,451	104,451
6	5,000	4,178	(4% × $104,451)	822	3,629	103,629
7	5,000	4,145	(4% × $103,629)	855	2,774	102,774
8	5,000	4,111	(4% × $102,774)	889	1,885	101,885
9	5,000	4,075	(4% × $101,885)	925	960	100,960
10	5,000	4,040*	(4% × $100,960)	960	−0−	100,000
	$50,000	$41,889		$8,111		

Column **(A)** remains constant because the face value of the bonds ($100,000) is multiplied by the semiannual contractual interest rate (5%) each period.
Column **(B)** is computed as the carrying value of the bonds times the semiannual effective-interest rate (4%).
Column **(C)** indicates the premium amortization each period.
Column **(D)** decreases each period until it reaches zero at maturity.
Column **(E)** decreases each period until it equals face value at maturity.

*$2 difference due to rounding.

For the first interest period, the computations of bond interest expense and the bond premium amortization are:

Illustration 15B-5
Computation of bond premium amortization

Bond interest expense ($108,111 × 4%)	$4,324
Contractual interest ($100,000 × 5%)	5,000
Bond premium amortization	**$ 676**

Candlestick records payments on the first interest date as follows.

A	=	L	+	SE
				−4,324 Exp
		−676		
−5,000				

Cash Flows
−5,000

July 1	Bond Interest Expense	4,324	
	Premium on Bonds Payable	676	
	Cash		5,000
	(To record payment of bond interest and amortization of bond premium)		

For the second interest period, interest expense will be $4,297, and the premium amortization will be $703. Total bond interest expense for 2008 is $8,621 ($4,324 + $4,297).

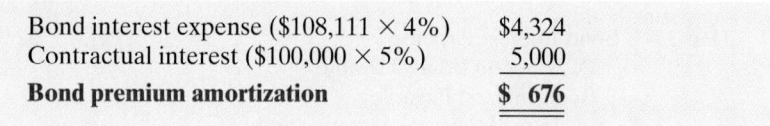

Demonstration Problem for Appendix15B

WILEY PLUS

Gardner Corporation issues $1,750,000, 10-year, 12% bonds on January 1, 2008, at $1,820,000, to yield 10%. The bonds pay semiannual interest July 1 and January 1. Gardner uses the effective-interest method of amortization.

Instructions

(a) Prepare the journal entry to record the issuance of the bonds.
(b) Prepare the journal entry to record the payment of interest on July 1, 2008.

action plan

- ✓ Compute interest expense by multiplying bond carrying value at the beginning of the period by the effective-interest rate.
- ✓ Compute credit to cash (or bond interest payable) by multiplying the face value of the bonds by the contractual interest rate.
- ✓ Compute bond premium or discount amortization, which is the difference between interest expense and cash paid.
- ✓ Interest expense decreases when the effective-interest method is used for bonds issued at a premium. The reason is that a constant percentage is applied to a decreasing book value to compute interest expense.

Solution to Demonstration Problem

(a) 2008

Jan. 1	Cash	1,820,000	
	Bonds Payable		1,750,000
	Premium on Bonds Payable		70,000
	(To record issuance of bonds at a premium)		

(b) 2008

July 1	Bond Interest Expense	91,000*	
	Premium on Bonds Payable	14,000**	
	Cash		105,000
	(To record payment of semiannual interest and amortization of bond premium)		
	*($1,820,000 × 5%)		
	**($105,000 − $91,000)		

✓ The Navigator

WILEY PLUS

SUMMARY OF STUDY OBJECTIVE FOR APPENDIX 15B

8 **Apply the effective-interest method of amortizing bond discount and bond premium.** The effective-interest method results in varying amounts of amortization and interest expense per period but a *constant percentage rate* of interest. When the difference between the straight-line and effective-interest method is material, GAAP requires the use of the effective-interest method.

GLOSSARY FOR APPENDIX 15B

Effective-interest method of amortization A method of amortizing bond discount or bond premium that results in periodic interest expense equal to a constant percentage of the carrying value of the bonds. (p. 657).

APPENDIX 15C Straight-Line Amortization

Amortizing Bond Discount

STUDY OBJECTIVE 9

Apply the straight-line method of amortizing bond discount and bond premium.

To follow the matching principle, companies should allocate bond discount systematically to each period in which the bonds are outstanding. The **straight-line method of amortization** allocates the **same amount to interest expense** in each interest period. The amount is determined using the formula in Illustration 15C-1.

Bond Discount	÷	Number of Interest Periods	=	Bond Discount Amortization

Illustration 15C-1
Formula for straight-line method of bond discount amortization

In the Candlestick, Inc. example (page 638), the company sold $100,000, five-year, 10% bonds on January 1, 2008, for $92,639. This price resulted in a $7,361 bond discount ($100,000 − $92,639). Interest is payable on July 1 and January 1. The bond discount amortization for each interest period is $736 ($7,361 ÷ 10). Candlestick records the payment of bond interest and the amortization of bond discount on the first interest date (July 1, 2008) as follows.

July 1	Bond Interest Expense	5,736	
	Discount on Bonds Payable		736
	Cash		5,000
	(To record payment of bond interest and amortization of bond discount)		

A	=	L	+	SE
				−5,736 Exp
		+736		
−5,000				

Cash Flows
−5,000

At December 31, Candlestick makes the following adjusting entry.

Dec. 31	Bond Interest Expense	5,736	
	Discount on Bonds Payable		736
	Bond Interest Payable		5,000
	(To record accrued bond interest and amortization of bond discount)		

A	=	L	+	SE
				−5,736 Exp
		+736		
		+5,000		

Cash Flows
no effect

Over the term of the bonds, the balance in Discount on Bonds Payable will decrease annually by the **same amount** until it has a zero balance at the maturity date of the bonds. Thus, the carrying value of the bonds at maturity will be equal to the face value.

It is useful to prepare a bond discount amortization schedule as shown in Illustration 15C-2 (page 662). The schedule shows interest expense, discount amortization, and the carrying value of the bond for each interest period. As indicated, the interest expense recorded **each period** for the Candlestick bond is $5,736. Also note that the carrying value of the bond increases $736 each period until it reaches its face value $100,000 at the end of period 10.

Illustration 15C-2
Bond discount amortization schedule

Candlestick Inc.xls
File Edit View Insert Format Tools Data Window Help

CANDLESTICK, INC.
Bond Discount Amortization
Straight-Line Method—Semiannual Interest Payments

Semiannual Interest Periods	(A) Interest to Be Paid (5% × $100,000)	(B) Interest Expense to Be Recorded (A) + (C)	(C) Discount Amortization ($7,361 ÷ 10)	(D) Unamortized Discount (D) − (C)	(E) Bond Carrying Value ($100,000 − D)
Issue date				$7,361	$92,639
1	$ 5,000	$ 5,736	$ 736	6,625	93,375
2	5,000	5,736	736	5,889	94,111
3	5,000	5,736	736	5,153	94,847
4	5,000	5,736	736	4,417	95,583
5	5,000	5,736	736	3,681	96,319
6	5,000	5,736	736	2,945	97,055
7	5,000	5,736	736	2,209	97,791
8	5,000	5,736	736	1,473	98,527
9	5,000	5,736	736	737	99,263
10	5,000	5,737*	737*	−0−	100,000
	$50,000	$57,361	$7,361		

Column (**A**) remains constant because the face value of the bonds ($100,000) is multiplied by the semiannual contractual interest rate (5%) each period.
Column (**B**) is computed as the interest paid (Column A) plus the discount amortization (Column C).
Column (**C**) indicates the discount amortization each period.
Column (**D**) decreases each period by the same amount until it reaches zero at maturity.
Column (**E**) increases each period by the same amount of discount amortization until it equals the face value at maturity.

*One dollar difference due to rounding.

We have highlighted columns (A), (B), and (C) in the amortization schedule to emphasize their importance. These three columns provide the numbers for each period's journal entries. They are the primary reason for preparing the schedule.

Amortizing Bond Premium

The amortization of bond premium parallels that of bond discount. Illustration 15C-3 presents the formula for determining bond premium amortization under the straight-line method.

Illustration 15C-3
Formula for straight-line method of bond premium amortization

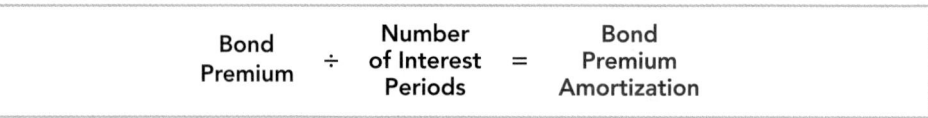

Bond Premium ÷ **Number of Interest Periods** = **Bond Premium Amortization**

Continuing our example, assume that Candlestick sells the bonds for $108,111, rather than $92,639 (page 639). This sale price results in a bond premium of $8,111 ($108,111 − $100,000). The bond premium amortization for each interest period is $811 ($8,111 ÷ 10). Candlestick records the first payment of interest on July 1 as follows.

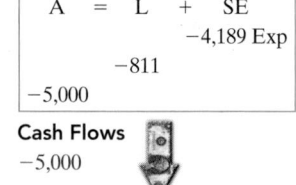

A	=	L	+	SE
				−4,189 Exp
		−811		
−5,000				

Cash Flows
−5,000

July 1	Bond Interest Expense	4,189	
	Premium on Bonds Payable	811	
	Cash		5,000
	(To record payment of bond interest and amortization of bond premium)		

At December 31, the company makes the following adjusting entry.

Dec. 31	Bond Interest Expense	4,189	
	Premium on Bonds Payable	811	
	Bond Interest Payable		5,000
	(To record accrued bond interest and amortization of bond premium)		

A	=	L	+	SE
				−4,189 Exp
		−811		
		+5,000		

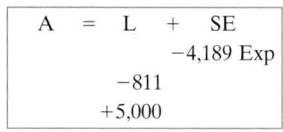

Cash Flows
no effect

Over the term of the bonds, the balance in Premium on Bonds Payable will decrease annually **by the same amount** until it has a zero balance at maturity.

It is useful to prepare a bond premium amortization schedule as shown in Illustration 15C-4. It shows interest expense, premium amortization, and the carrying value of the bond. The interest expense recorded each period for the Candlestick bond is $4,189. Also note that the carrying value of the bond decreases $811 each period until it reaches its face value $100,000 at the end of period 10.

Illustration 15C-4
Bond premium amortization schedule

Candlestick Inc.xls

CANDLESTICK, INC.
Bond Premium Amortization
Straight-Line Method—Semiannual Interest Payments

Semiannual Interest Periods	(A) Interest to Be Paid (5% × $100,000)	(B) Interest Expense to Be Recorded (A) − (C)	(C) Premium Amortization ($8,111 ÷ 10)	(D) Unamortized Premium (D) − (C)	(E) Bond Carrying Value ($100,000 + D)
Issue date				$8,111	$108,111
1	$ 5,000	$ 4,189	$ 811	7,300	107,300
2	5,000	4,189	811	6,489	106,489
3	5,000	4,189	811	5,678	105,678
4	5,000	4,189	811	4,867	104,867
5	5,000	4,189	811	4,056	104,056
6	5,000	4,189	811	3,245	103,245
7	5,000	4,189	811	2,434	102,434
8	5,000	4,189	811	1,623	101,623
9	5,000	4,189	811	812	100,812
10	5,000	4,188*	812*	−0−	100,000
	$50,000	$41,889	$8,111		

Column **(A)** remains constant because the face value of the bonds ($100,000) is multiplied by the semiannual contractual interest rate (5%) each period.
Column **(B)** is computed as the interest paid (Column A) less the premium amortization (Column C).
Column **(C)** indicates the premium amortization each period.
Column **(D)** decreases each period by the same amount until it reaches zero at maturity.
Column **(E)** decreases each period by the amount of premium amortization until it equals the face value at maturity.

*One dollar difference due to rounding.

Demonstration Problem for Appendix 15C

Glenda Corporation issues $1,750,000, 10-year, 12% bonds on January 1, 2008, for $1,820,000 to yield 10%. The bonds pay semiannual interest July 1 and January 1. Glenda uses the straight-line method of amortization.

Instructions

(a) Prepare the journal entry to record the issuance of the bonds.
(b) Prepare the journal entry to record the payment of interest on July 1, 2008.

action plan

- Compute credit to cash (or bond interest payable) by multiplying the face value of the bonds by the contractual interest rate.
- Compute bond premium or discount amortization by dividing bond premium or discount by the total number of periods.
- Understand that interest expense decreases when bonds are issued at a premium. The reason is that the amortization of premium reduces the total cost of borrowing.

Solution to Demonstration Problem

(a) 2008

Jan. 1	Cash	1,820,000	
	Bonds Payable		1,750,000
	Premium on Bonds Payable		70,000

(b) 2008

July 1	Bond Interest Expense	101,500**	
	Premium on Bonds Payable	3,500*	
	Cash		105,000
	*$70,000 ÷ 20		
	**$105,000 – $3,500		

The Navigator

WILEY PLUS

SUMMARY OF STUDY OBJECTIVE FOR APPENDIX 15C

9 Apply the straight-line method of amortizing bond discount and bond premium. The straight-line method of amortization results in a *constant amount* of amortization and interest expense per period.

GLOSSARY FOR APPENDIX 15C

WILEY PLUS

Straight-line method of amortization. A method of amortizing bond discount or bond premium that results in allocating the same amount to interest expense in each interest period. (p. 661)

*__Note__: All asterisked Questions, Exercises, and Problems relate to material in the appendices to the chapter.

SELF-STUDY QUESTIONS

WILEY PLUS

Answers are at the end of the chapter.

(SO 1) **1.** The term used for bonds that are unsecured is:
a. callable bonds.
b. indenture bonds.
c. debenture bonds.
d. bearer bonds.

(SO 2) **2.** Karson Inc. issues 10-year bonds with a maturity value of $200,000. If the bonds are issued at a premium, this indicates that:
a. the contractual interest rate exceeds the market interest rate.
b. the market interest rate exceeds the contractual interest rate.
c. the contractual interest rate and the market interest rate are the same.
d. no relationship exists between the two rates.

(SO 3) **3.** Gester Corporation retires its $100,000 face value bonds at 105 on January 1, following the payment of semiannual interest. The carrying value of the bonds at the redemption date is $103,745. The entry to record the redemption will include a:
a. credit of $3,745 to Loss on Bond Redemption.
b. debit of $3,745 to Premium on Bonds Payable.
c. credit of $1,255 to Gain on Bond Redemption.
d. debit of $5,000 to Premium on Bonds Payable.

4. Colson Inc. converts $600,000 of bonds sold at face value into 10,000 shares of common stock, par value $1. Both the bonds and the stock have a market value of $760,000. What amount should be credited to Paid-in Capital in Excess of Par as a result of the conversion? (SO 3)
a. $10,000.
b. $160,000.
c. $600,000.
d. $590,000.

5. Andrews Inc. issues a $497,000, 10% 3-year mortgage note on January 1. The note will be paid in three annual installments of $200,000, each payable at the end of the year. What is the amount of interest expense that should be recognized by Andrews Inc. in the second year? (SO 4)
a. $16,567.
b. $49,700.
c. $34,670.
d. $346,700.

6. Lease A does not contain a bargain purchase option, but the lease term is equal to 90 percent of the estimated economic life of the leased property. Lease B does not transfer (SO 5) ownership of the property to the lessee by the end of the lease term, but the lease term is equal to 75 percent of the estimated economic life of the leased property. How should the lessee classify these leases?

	Lease A	**Lease B**
a.	Operating lease	Capital lease
b.	Operating lease	Operating lease
c.	Capital lease	Operating lease
d.	Capital lease	Capital lease

(SO 8) ***7.** On January 1, Besalius Inc. issued $1,000,000, 9% bonds for $939,000. The market rate of interest for these bonds is 10%. Interest is payable annually on December 31. Besalius uses the effective-interest method of amortizing bond discount. At the end of the first year, Besalius should report unamortized bond discount of:

a. $54,900. **c.** $51,610.
b. $57,100. **d.** $51,000.

(SO 8) ***8.** On January 1, Dias Corporation issued $1,000,000, 14%, 5-year bonds with interest payable on July 1 and January 1. The bonds sold for $1,098,540. The market rate of interest for these bonds was 12%. On the first interest date, using the effective-interest method, the debit entry to Bond Interest Expense is for:

a. $60,000. **c.** $65,912.
b. $76,898. **d.** $131,825.

***9.** On January 1, Hurley Corporation issues $500,000, 5-year, 12% bonds at 96 with interest payable on July 1 and January 1. The entry on July 1 to record payment of bond interest and the amortization of bond discount using the straight-line method will include a: (SO 9)

a. debit to Interest Expense $30,000.
b. debit to Interest Expense $60,000.
c. credit to Discount on Bonds Payable $4,000.
d. credit to Discount on Bonds Payable $2,000.

***10.** For the bonds issued in question 9, above, what is the carrying value of the bonds at the end of the third interest period? (SO 9)

a. $486,000. **c.** $472,000.
b. $488,000. **d.** $464,000.

Go to the book's website, **www.wiley.com/college/weygandt**, for Additional Self-Study questions.

The Navigator

QUESTIONS

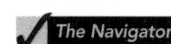

1. (a) What are long-term liabilities? Give three examples. (b) What is a bond?
2. (a) As a source of long-term financing, what are the major advantages of bonds over common stock? (b) What are the major disadvantages in using bonds for long-term financing?
3. Contrast the following types of bonds: (a) secured and unsecured, (b) term and serial, (c) registered and bearer, and (d) convertible and callable.
4. The following terms are important in issuing bonds: (a) face value, (b) contractual interest rate, (c) bond indenture, and (d) bond certificate. Explain each of these terms.
5. Describe the two major obligations incurred by a company when bonds are issued.
6. Assume that Koslowski Inc. sold bonds with a par value of $100,000 for $104,000. Was the market interest rate equal to, less than, or greater than the bonds' contractual interest rate? Explain.
7. If a 7%, 10-year, $800,000 bond is issued at par and interest is paid semiannually, what is the amount of the interest payment at the end of the first semiannual period?
8. If the Bonds Payable account has a balance of $900,000 and the Discount on Bonds Payable account has a balance of $40,000, what is the carrying value of the bonds?
9. Which accounts are debited and which are credited if a bond issue originally sold at a premium is redeemed before maturity at 97 immediately following the payment of interest?
10. Henricks Corporation is considering issuing a convertible bond. What is a convertible bond? Discuss the advantages of a convertible bond from the standpoint of (a) the bondholders and (b) the issuing corporation.
11. Tim Brown, a friend of yours, has recently purchased a home for $125,000, paying $25,000 down and the remainder financed by a 10.5%, 20-year mortgage, payable at $998.38 per month. At the end of the first month, Tim receives a statement from the bank indicating that only $123.38 of principal was paid during the month. At this rate, he calculates that it will take over 67 years to pay off the mortgage. Is he right? Discuss.
12. (a) What is a lease agreement? (b) What are the two most common types of leases? (c) Distinguish between the two types of leases.
13. Clooney Company rents a warehouse on a month-to-month basis for the storage of its excess inventory. The company periodically must rent space when its production greatly exceeds actual sales. What is the nature of this type of lease agreement, and what accounting treatment should be used?
14. Rondelli Company entered into an agreement to lease 12 computers from Estes Electronics Inc. The present value of the lease payments is $186,300. Assuming that this is a capital lease, what entry would Rondelli Company make on the date of the lease agreement?
15. In general, what are the requirements for the financial statement presentation of long-term liabilities?

***16.** Laura Hiatt is discussing the advantages of the effective-interest method of bond amortization with her accounting staff. What do you think Laura is saying?

***17.** Markham Corporation issues $500,000 of 9%, 5-year bonds on January 1, 2008, at 104. If Markham uses the effective-interest method in amortizing the premium, will the annual interest expense increase or decrease over the life of the bonds? Explain.

*18. Tina Cruz and Dale Commons are discussing how the market price of a bond is determined. Tina believes that the market price of a bond is solely a function of the amount of the principal payment at the end of the term of a bond. Is she right? Discuss.

*19. Explain the straight-line method of amortizing discount and premium on bonds payable.

*20. DeWeese Corporation issues $400,000 of 8%, 5-year bonds on January 1, 2008, at 105. Assuming that the straight-line method is used to amortize the premium, what is the total amount of interest expense for 2008?

BRIEF EXERCISES

Compare bond versus stock financing.
(SO 1)

BE15-1 Mareska Inc. is considering two alternatives to finance its construction of a new $2 million plant.

(a) Issuance of 200,000 shares of common stock at the market price of $10 per share.
(b) Issuance of $2 million, 8% bonds at par.

Complete the following table, and indicate which alternative is preferable.

	Issue Stock	Issue Bond
Income before interest and taxes	$700,000	$700,000
Interest expense from bonds		
Income before income taxes	$	$
Income tax expense (30%)		
Net income	$	$
Outstanding shares		500,000
Earnings per share		

Prepare entries for bonds issued at face value.
(SO 2)

BE15-2 Pruitt Corporation issued 3,000, 8%, 5-year, $1,000 bonds dated January 1, 2008, at 100.
(a) Prepare the journal entry to record the sale of these bonds on January 1, 2008.
(b) Prepare the journal entry to record the first interest payment on July 1, 2008 (interest payable semiannually), assuming no previous accrual of interest.
(c) Prepare the adjusting journal entry on December 31, 2008, to record interest expense.

Prepare entries for bonds sold at a discount and a premium.
(SO 2)

BE15-3 Ratzlaff Company issues $2 million, 10-year, 8% bonds at 97, with interest payable on July 1 and January 1.

(a) Prepare the journal entry to record the sale of these bonds on January 1, 2008.
(b) Assuming instead that the above bonds sold for 104, prepare the journal entry to record the sale of these bonds on January 1, 2008.

Prepare entries for bonds issued.
(SO 2)

BE15-4 Halloway Company has issued three different bonds during 2008. Interest is payable semiannually on each of these bonds.

1. On January 1, 2008, 1,000, 8%, 5-year, $1,000 bonds dated January 1, 2008, were issued at face value.
2. On July 1, $800,000, 9%, 5-year bonds dated July 1, 2008, were issued at 102.
3. On September 1, $200,000, 7%, 5-year bonds dated September 1, 2008, were issued at 98.

Prepare the journal entry to record each bond transaction at the date of issuance.

Prepare entry for redemption of bonds.
(SO 3)

BE15-5 The balance sheet for Lemay Company reports the following information on July 1, 2008.

Long-term liabilities		
Bonds payable	$1,000,000	
Less: Discount on bonds payable	60,000	$940,000

Lemay decides to redeem these bonds at 101 after paying semiannual interest. Prepare the journal entry to record the redemption on July 1, 2008.

Prepare entries for long-term notes payable.
(SO 4)

BE15-6 Pickeril Inc. issues a $600,000, 10%, 10-year mortgage note on December 31, 2008, to obtain financing for a new building. The terms provide for semiannual installment payments of $48,145. Prepare the entry to record the mortgage loan on December 31, 2008, and the first installment payment.

BE15-7 Prepare the journal entries that the lessee should make to record the following transactions.

Contrast accounting for operating and capital lease.

(SO 5)

1. The lessee makes a lease payment of $80,000 to the lessor in an operating lease transaction.
2. Veatch Company leases a new building from Joel Construction, Inc. The present value of the lease payments is $700,000. The lease qualifies as a capital lease.

BE15-8 Presented below are long-term liability items for Molini Company at December 31, 2008. Prepare the long-term liabilities section of the balance sheet for Molini Company.

Prepare statement presentation of long-term liabilities.

(SO 6)

Bonds payable, due 2010	$500,000
Lease liability	70,000
Notes payable, due 2013	80,000
Discount on bonds payable	45,000

***BE15-9** (a) What is the present value of $10,000 due 8 periods from now, discounted at 10%?
(b) What is the present value of $20,000 to be received at the end of each of 6 periods, discounted at 8%?

Determine present value.

(SO 7)

***BE15-10** Presented below is the partial bond discount amortization schedule for Morales Corp. Morales uses the effective-interest method of amortization.

Use effective-interest method of bond amortization.

(SO 8)

Semiannual Interest Periods	Interest to Be Paid	Interest Expense to Be Recorded	Discount Amortization	Unamortized Discount	Bond Carrying Value
Issue date				$62,311	$937,689
1	$45,000	$46,884	$1,884	60,427	939,573
2	45,000	46,979	1,979	58,448	941,552

Instructions

(a) Prepare the journal entry to record the payment of interest and the discount amortization at the end of period 1.
(b) Explain why interest expense is greater than interest paid.
(c) Explain why interest expense will increase each period.

***BE15-11** Deane Company issues $5 million, 10-year, 9% bonds at 96, with interest payable on July 1 and January 1. The straight-line method is used to amortize bond discount.

Prepare entries for bonds issued at a discount.

(SO 9)

(a) Prepare the journal entry to record the sale of these bonds on January 1, 2008.
(b) Prepare the journal entry to record interest expense and bond discount amortization on July 1, 2008, assuming no previous accrual of interest.

***BE15-12** Coates Inc. issues $3 million, 5-year, 10% bonds at 102, with interest payable on July 1 and January 1. The straight-line method is used to amortize bond premium.

Prepare entries for bonds issued at a premium.

(SO 9)

(a) Prepare the journal entry to record the sale of these bonds on January 1, 2008.
(b) Prepare the journal entry to record interest expense and bond premium amortization on July 1, 2008, assuming no previous accrual of interest.

EXERCISES

E15-1 Jim Thome has prepared the following list of statements about bonds.

Evaluate statements about bonds.

(SO 1)

1. Bonds are a form of interest-bearing notes payable.
2. When seeking long-term financing, an advantage of issuing bonds over issuing common stock is that stockholder control is not affected.
3. When seeking long-term financing, an advantage of issuing common stock over issuing bonds is that tax savings result.
4. Secured bonds have specific assets of the issuer pledged as collateral for the bonds.
5. Secured bonds are also known as debenture bonds.
6. Bonds that mature in installments are called term bonds.
7. A conversion feature may be added to bonds to make them more attractive to bond buyers.
8. The rate used to determine the amount of cash interest the borrower pays is called the stated rate.
9. Bond prices are usually quoted as a percentage of the face value of the bond.
10. The present value of a bond is the value at which it should sell in the marketplace.

Instructions

Identify each statement on page 667 as true or false. If false, indicate how to correct the statement.

Compare two alternatives of financing—issuance of common stock vs. issuance of bonds.
(SO 1)

E15-2 Northeast Airlines is considering two alternatives for the financing of a purchase of a fleet of airplanes. These two alternatives are:

1. Issue 60,000 shares of common stock at $45 per share. (Cash dividends have not been paid nor is the payment of any contemplated).
2. Issue 10%, 10-year bonds at par for $2,700,000.

It is estimated that the company will earn $800,000 before interest and taxes as a result of this purchase. The company has an estimated tax rate of 30% and has 90,000 shares of common stock outstanding prior to the new financing.

Instructions

Determine the effect on net income and earnings per share for these two methods of financing.

Prepare entries for issuance of bonds, and payment and accrual of bond interest.
(SO 2)

E15-3 On January 1, Neuer Company issued $500,000, 10%, 10-year bonds at par. Interest is payable semiannually on July 1 and January 1.

Instructions

Present journal entries to record the following.

(a) The issuance of the bonds.
(b) The payment of interest on July 1, assuming that interest was not accrued on June 30.
(c) The accrual of interest on December 31.

Prepare entries for bonds issued at face value.
(SO 2)

E15-4 On January 1, Flory Company issued $300,000, 8%, 5-year bonds at face value. Interest is payable semiannually on July 1 and January 1.

Instructions

Prepare journal entries to record the following events.

(a) The issuance of the bonds.
(b) The payment of interest on July 1, assuming no previous accrual of interest.
(c) The accrual of interest on December 31.

Prepare entries for bonds issued at face value.
(SO 2, 3)

E15-5 Jaurez Company issued $400,000 of 9%, 10-year bonds on January 1, 2008, at face value. Interest is payable semiannually on July 1 and January 1.

Instructions

Prepare the journal entries to record the following events.

(a) The issuance of the bonds.
(b) The payment of interest on July 1, assuming no previous accrual of interest.
(c) The accrual of interest on December 31.
(d) The redemption of bonds at maturity, assuming interest for the last interest period has been paid and recorded.

Prepare entries for issuance, retirement, and conversion of bonds.
(SO 2, 3)

E15-6 Nocioni Company issued $1,000,000 of bonds on January 1, 2008.

Instructions

(a) Prepare the journal entry to record the issuance of the bonds if they are issued at (1) 100, (2), 98, and (3) 103.
(b) Prepare the journal entry to record the retirement of the bonds at maturity, assuming the bonds were issued at 100.
(c) Prepare the journal entry to record the retirement of the bonds before maturity at 98. Assume the balance in Premium on Bonds Payable is $9,000.
(d) Prepare the journal entry to record the conversion of the bonds into 30,000 shares of $10 par value common stock. Assume the bonds were issued at par.

Prepare entries to record issuance of bonds at discount and premium.
(SO 2)

E15-7 Deng Company issued $500,000 of 5-year, 8% bonds at 97 on January 1, 2008. The bonds pay interest twice a year.

Instructions

(a) **(1)** Prepare the journal entry to record the issuance of the bonds.
(2) Compute the total cost of borrowing for these bonds.
(b) Repeat the requirements from part **(a)**, assuming the bonds were issued at 105.

E15-8 The following section is taken from Budke Corp.'s balance sheet at December 31, 2007.

Prepare entries for bond interest and redemption.

(SO 2, 3)

Current liabilities	
Bond interest payable	$ 72,000
Long-term liabilities	
Bonds payable, 9%, due January 1, 2012	1,600,000

Interest is payable semiannually on January 1 and July 1. The bonds are callable on any interest date.

Instructions

(a) Journalize the payment of the bond interest on January 1, 2008.

(b) Assume that on January 1, 2008, after paying interest, Budke calls bonds having a face value of $600,000. The call price is 104. Record the redemption of the bonds.

(c) Prepare the entry to record the payment of interest on July 1, 2008, assuming no previous accrual of interest on the remaining bonds.

E15-9 Presented below are three independent situations.

Prepare entries for redemption of bonds and conversion of bonds into common stock.

(SO 3)

1. Sigel Corporation retired $130,000 face value, 12% bonds on June 30, 2008, at 102. The carrying value of the bonds at the redemption date was $117,500. The bonds pay semiannual interest, and the interest payment due on June 30, 2008, has been made and recorded.
2. Diaz Inc. retired $150,000 face value, 12.5% bonds on June 30, 2008, at 98. The carrying value of the bonds at the redemption date was $151,000. The bonds pay semiannual interest, and the interest payment due on June 30, 2008, has been made and recorded.
3. Haas Company has $80,000, 8%, 12-year convertible bonds outstanding. These bonds were sold at face value and pay semiannual interest on June 30 and December 31 of each year. The bonds are convertible into 30 shares of Haas $5 par value common stock for each $1,000 worth of bonds. On December 31, 2008, after the bond interest has been paid, $20,000 face value bonds were converted. The market value of Haas common stock was $44 per share on December 31, 2008.

Instructions

For each independent situation above, prepare the appropriate journal entry for the redemption or conversion of the bonds.

E15-10 Leoni Co. receives $240,000 when it issues a $240,000, 10%, mortgage note payable to finance the construction of a building at December 31, 2008. The terms provide for semiannual installment payments of $20,000 on June 30 and December 31.

Prepare entries to record mortgage note and installment payments.

(SO 4)

Instructions

Prepare the journal entries to record the mortgage loan and the first two installment payments.

E15-11 TPol Company borrowed $300,000 on January 1, 2008, by issuing a $300,000, 8% mortgage note payable. The terms call for semiannual installment payments of $20,000 on June 30 and December 31.

Prepare entries to record mortgage note and installment payments.

(SO 4)

Instructions

(a) Prepare the journal entries to record the mortgage loan and the first two installment payments.

(b) Indicate the amount of mortgage note payable to be reported as a current liability and as a long-term liability at December 31, 2008.

E15-12 Presented below are two independent situations.

Prepare entries for operating lease and capital lease.

(SO 5)

1. Speedy Car Rental leased a car to Mayfield Company for one year. Terms of the operating lease agreement call for monthly payments of $500.
2. On January 1, 2008, Olsen Inc. entered into an agreement to lease 20 computers from Gage Electronics. The terms of the lease agreement require three annual rental payments of $30,000 (including 10% interest) beginning December 31, 2008. The present value of the three rental payments is $74,606. Olsen considers this a capital lease.

Instructions

(a) Prepare the appropriate journal entry to be made by Mayfield Company for the first lease payment.

(b) Prepare the journal entry to record the lease agreement on the books of Olsen Inc. on January 1, 2008.

Prepare long-term liabilities section.

(SO 6)

E15-13 The adjusted trial balance for Gilligan Corporation at the end of the current year contained the following accounts.

Bond Interest Payable	$ 9,000
Lease Liability	89,500
Bonds Payable, due 2013	180,000
Premium on Bonds Payable	32,000

Instructions

Prepare the long-term liabilities section of the balance sheet.

Compute debt to total assets and times interest earned ratios.

(SO 6)

E15-14 Seven Corporation reports the following amounts in their 2008 financial statements:

	At December 31, 2008	For the Year 2008
Total assets	$1,000,000	
Total liabilities	620,000	
Total stockholders' equity	?	
Interest expense		$ 7,000
Income tax expense		100,000
Net income		150,000

Instructions

(a) Compute the December 31, 2008, balance in stockholders' equity.
(b) Compute the debt to total assets ratio at December 31, 2008.
(c) Compute times interest earned for 2008.

Compute market price of bonds.

(SO 7)

***E15-15** Banzai Corporation is issuing $200,000 of 8%, 5-year bonds when potential bond investors want a return of 10%. Interest is payable semiannually.

Instructions

Compute the market price (present value) of the bonds.

Prepare entries for issuance of bonds, payment of interest, and amortization of discount using effective-interest method

(SO 8)

***E15-16** Hrabik Corporation issued $600,000, 9%, 10-year bonds on January 1, 2008, for $562,613. This price resulted in an effective-interest rate of 10% on the bonds. Interest is payable semiannually on July 1 and January 1. Hrabik uses the effective-interest method to amortize bond premium or discount.

Instructions

Prepare the journal entries to record the following. (Round to the nearest dollar.)

(a) The issuance of the bonds.
(b) The payment of interest and the discount amortization on July 1, 2008, assuming that interest was not accrued on June 30.
(c) The accrual of interest and the discount amortization on December 31, 2008.

Prepare entries for issuance of bonds, payment of interest, and amortization of premium using effective-interest method.

(SO 8)

***E15-17** Siburo Company issued $300,000, 11%, 10-year bonds on January 1, 2008, for $318,694. This price resulted in an effective-interest rate of 10% on the bonds. Interest is payable semiannually on July 1 and January 1. Siburo uses the effective-interest method to amortize bond premium or discount.

Instructions

Prepare the journal entries to record the following. (Round to the nearest dollar).

(a) The issuance of the bonds.
(b) The payment of interest and the premium amortization on July 1, 2008, assuming that interest was not accrued on June 30.
(c) The accrual of interest and the premium amortization on December 31, 2008.

Prepare entries to record issuance of bonds, payment of interest, amortization of premium, and redemption at maturity.

(SO 3, 9)

***E15-18** Patino Company issued $400,000, 9%, 20-year bonds on January 1, 2008, at 103. Interest is payable semiannually on July 1 and January 1. Patino uses straight-line amortization for bond premium or discount.

Instructions

Prepare the journal entries to record the following.

(a) The issuance of the bonds.
(b) The payment of interest and the premium amortization on July 1, 2008, assuming that interest was not accrued on June 30.

(c) The accrual of interest and the premium amortization on December 31, 2008.
(d) The redemption of the bonds at maturity, assuming interest for the last interest period has been paid and recorded.

***E15-19** Joseph Company issued $800,000, 11%, 10-year bonds on December 31, 2007, for $730,000. Interest is payable semiannually on June 30 and December 31. Joseph Company uses the straight-line method to amortize bond premium or discount.

Prepare entries to record issuance of bonds, payment of interest, amortization of discount, and redemption at maturity.
(SO 3, 9)

Instructions
Prepare the journal entries to record the following.
(a) The issuance of the bonds.
(b) The payment of interest and the discount amortization on June 30, 2008.
(c) The payment of interest and the discount amortization on December 31, 2008.
(d) The redemption of the bonds at maturity, assuming interest for the last interest period has been paid and recorded.

EXERCISES: SET B

Visit the book's website at **www.wiley.com/college/weygandt**, and choose the Student Companion site, to access Exercise Set B.

PROBLEMS: SET A

WILEY PLUS

P15-1A On May 1, 2008, Newby Corp. issued $600,000, 9%, 5-year bonds at face value. The bonds were dated May 1, 2008, and pay interest semiannually on May 1 and November 1. Financial statements are prepared annually on December 31.

Prepare entries to record issuance of bonds, interest accrual, and bond redemption.
(SO 2, 3, 6)

Instructions
(a) Prepare the journal entry to record the issuance of the bonds.
(b) Prepare the adjusting entry to record the accrual of interest on December 31, 2008.
(c) Show the balance sheet presentation on December 31, 2008.
(d) Prepare the journal entry to record payment of interest on May 1, 2009, assuming no accrual of interest from January 1, 2009, to May 1, 2009.
(d) Int. exp. $18,000
(e) Prepare the journal entry to record payment of interest on November 1, 2009.
(f) Assume that on November 1, 2009, Newby calls the bonds at 102. Record the redemption of the bonds.
(f) Loss $12,000

P15-2A Kusmaul Electric sold $500,000, 10%, 10-year bonds on January 1, 2008. The bonds were dated January 1 and paid interest on January 1 and July 1. The bonds were sold at 104.

Prepare entries to record issuance of bonds, interest accrual, and bond redemption.
(SO 2, 3, 6)

Instructions
(a) Prepare the journal entry to record the issuance of the bonds on January 1, 2008.
(b) At December 31, 2008, the balance in the Premium on Bonds Payable account is $18,000. Show the balance sheet presentation of accrued interest and the bond liability at December 31, 2008.
(c) On January 1, 2010, when the carrying value of the bonds was $516,000, the company redeemed the bonds at 105. Record the redemption of the bonds assuming that interest for the period has already been paid.
(c) Loss $9,000

P15-3A Fordyce Electronics issues a $400,000, 8%, 10-year mortgage note on December 31, 2007. The proceeds from the note are to be used in financing a new research laboratory. The terms of the note provide for semiannual installment payments, exclusive of real estate taxes and insurance, of $29,433. Payments are due June 30 and December 31.

Prepare installment payments schedule and journal entries for a mortgage note payable.
(SO 4)

Instructions
(a) Prepare an installment payments schedule for the first 2 years.
(b) Prepare the entries for (1) the loan and (2) the first two installment payments.
(b) June 30 Mortgage Notes Payable $13,433
(c) Show how the total mortgage liability should be reported on the balance sheet at December 31, 2008.
(c) Current liability—2008: $29,639

Analyze three different lease situations and prepare journal entries.

(SO 5)

P15-4A Presented below are three different lease transactions that occurred for Kear Inc. in 2008. Assume that all lease contracts start on January 1, 2008. In no case does Kear receive title to the properties leased during or at the end of the lease term.

	Lessor		
	Jansen Delivery	**Flood Co.**	**Louis Auto**
Type of property	Computer	Delivery equipment	Automobile
Yearly rental	$ 6,000	$ 4,200	$ 3,700
Lease term	6 years	4 years	2 years
Estimated economic life	7 years	7 years	5 years
Fair market value of lease asset	$33,000	$19,000	$11,000
Present value of the lease rental payments	$31,000	$13,000	$ 6,400
Bargain purchase option	None	None	None

Instructions

(a) Which of the leases above are operating leases and which are capital leases? Explain.
(b) How should the lease transaction for Flood Co. be recorded in 2008?
(c) How should the lease transaction for Jansen Delivery be recorded on January 1, 2008?

Prepare entries to record issuance of bonds, payment of interest, and amortization of bond premium using effective-interest method.

(SO 2, 8)

***P15-5A** On July 1, 2008, Atwater Corporation issued $2,000,000 face value, 10%, 10-year bonds at $2,271,813. This price resulted in an effective-interest rate of 8% on the bonds. Atwater uses the effective-interest method to amortize bond premium or discount. The bonds pay semi-annual interest July 1 and January 1.

Instructions

(Round all computations to the nearest dollar.)

(a) Prepare the journal entry to record the issuance of the bonds on July 1, 2008.
(b) Prepare an amortization table through December 31, 2009 (3 interest periods) for this bond issue.

(c) Amortization $9,127

(c) Prepare the journal entry to record the accrual of interest and the amortization of the premium on December 31, 2008.

(d) Amortization $9,493

(d) Prepare the journal entry to record the payment of interest and the amortization of the premium on July 1, 2009, assuming no accrual of interest on June 30.

(e) Amortization $9,872

(e) Prepare the journal entry to record the accrual of interest and the amortization of the premium on December 31, 2009.

Prepare entries to record issuance of bonds, payment of interest, and amortization of discount using effective-interest method. In addition, answer questions.

(SO 2, 8)

***P15-6A** On July 1, 2008, Rossillon Company issued $4,000,000 face value, 8%, 10-year bonds at $3,501,514. This price resulted in an effective-interest rate of 10% on the bonds. Rossillon uses the effective-interest method to amortize bond premium or discount. The bonds pay semiannual interest July 1 and January 1.

Instructions

(Round all computations to the nearest dollar.)

(a) Prepare the journal entries to record the following transactions.
  (1) The issuance of the bonds on July 1, 2008.
  (2) The accrual of interest and the amortization of the discount on December 31, 2008.

(a) (3) Amortization $15,830

  (3) The payment of interest and the amortization of the discount on July 1, 2009, assuming no accrual of interest on June 30.

(a) (4) Amortization $16,621

  (4) The accrual of interest and the amortization of the discount on December 31, 2009.

(b) Bond carrying value $3,549,041

(b) Show the proper balance sheet presentation for the liability for bonds payable on the December 31, 2009, balance sheet.
(c) Provide the answers to the following questions in letter form.
  (1) What amount of interest expense is reported for 2009?
  (2) Would the bond interest expense reported in 2009 be the same as, greater than, or less than the amount that would be reported if the straight-line method of amortization were used?
  (3) Determine the total cost of borrowing over the life of the bond.
  (4) Would the total bond interest expense be greater than, the same as, or less than the total interest expense that would be reported if the straight-line method of amortization were used?

***P15-7A** Soprano Electric sold $3,000,000, 10%, 10-year bonds on January 1, 2008. The bonds were dated January 1 and pay interest July 1 and January 1. Soprano Electric uses the straight-line method to amortize bond premium or discount. The bonds were sold at 104. Assume no interest is accrued on June 30.

Prepare entries to record issuance of bonds, interest accrual, and straight-line amortization for 2 years.

(SO 6, 9)

Instructions

(a) Prepare the journal entry to record the issuance of the bonds on January 1, 2008.
(b) Prepare a bond premium amortization schedule for the first 4 interest periods.
(c) Prepare the journal entries for interest and the amortization of the premium in 2008 and 2009.
(d) Show the balance sheet presentation of the bond liability at December 31, 2009.

(b) Amortization $6,000
(d) Premium on bonds payable $96,000

***P15-8A** Elkins Company sold $2,500,000, 8%, 10-year bonds on July 1, 2008. The bonds were dated July 1, 2008, and pay interest July 1 and January 1. Elkins Company uses the straight-line method to amortize bond premium or discount. Assume no interest is accrued on June 30.

Prepare entries to record issuance of bonds, interest, and straight-line amortization of bond premium and discount.

(SO 6, 9)

Instructions

(a) Prepare all the necessary journal entries to record the issuance of the bonds and bond interest expense for 2008, assuming that the bonds sold at 104.
(b) Prepare journal entries as in part (a) assuming that the bonds sold at 98.
(c) Show balance sheet presentation for each bond issue at December 31, 2008.

(a) Amortization $5,000
(b) Amortization $2,500
(c) Premium on bonds payable $95,000
Discount on bonds payable $47,500

***P15-9A** The following is taken from the Pinkston Company balance sheet.

Prepare entries to record interest payments, straight-line premium amortization, and redemption of bonds.

(SO 2, 3, 9)

PINKSTON COMPANY
Balance Sheet (partial)
December 31, 2008

Current liabilities		
Bond interest payable (for 6 months from July 1 to December 31)		$ 105,000
Long-term liabilities		
Bonds payable, 7% due January 1, 2019	$3,000,000	
Add: Premium on bonds payable	200,000	$3,200,000

Interest is payable semiannually on January 1 and July 1. The bonds are callable on any semiannual interest date. Pinkston uses straight-line amortization for any bond premium or discount. From December 31, 2008, the bonds will be outstanding for an additional 10 years (120 months).

Instructions

(a) Journalize the payment of bond interest on January 1, 2009.
(b) Prepare the entry to amortize bond premium and to pay the interest due on July 1, 2009, assuming no accrual of interest on June 30.
(c) Assume that on July 1, 2009, after paying interest, Pinkston Company calls bonds having a face value of $1,200,000. The call price is 101. Record the redemption of the bonds.
(d) Prepare the adjusting entry at December 31, 2009, to amortize bond premium and to accrue interest on the remaining bonds.

(b) Amortization $10,000
(c) Gain $64,000
(d) Amortization $6,000

PROBLEMS: SET B

P15-1B On June 1, 2008, Logsdon Corp. issued $1,500,000, 8%, 5-year bonds at face value. The bonds were dated June 1, 2008, and pay interest semiannually on June 1 and December 1. Financial statements are prepared annually on December 31.

Prepare entries to record issuance of bonds, interest accrual, and bond redemption.

(SO 2, 3, 6)

Instructions

(a) Prepare the journal entry to record the issuance of the bonds.
(b) Prepare the adjusting entry to record the accrual of interest on December 31, 2008.
(c) Show the balance sheet presentation on December 31, 2008.
(d) Prepare the journal entry to record payment of interest on June 1, 2009, assuming no accrual of interest from January 1, 2009, to June 1, 2009.
(e) Prepare the journal entry to record payment of interest on December 1, 2009.
(f) Assume that on December 1, 2009, Logsdon calls the bonds at 102. Record the redemption of the bonds.

(d) Int. exp. $50,000
(f) Loss $30,000

Prepare entries to record issuance of bonds, interest accrual, and bond redemption.

(SO 2, 3, 6)

P15-2B Merendo Co. sold $600,000, 9%, 10-year bonds on January 1, 2008. The bonds were dated January 1, and interest is paid on January 1 and July 1. The bonds were sold at 105.

Instructions

(a) Prepare the journal entry to record the issuance of the bonds on January 1, 2008.

(b) At December 31, 2008, the balance in the Premium on Bonds Payable account is $27,000. Show the balance sheet presentation of accrued interest and the bond liability at December 31, 2008.

(c) Loss $6,000

(c) On January 1, 2010, when the carrying value of the bonds was $624,000, the company redeemed the bonds at 105. Record the redemption of the bonds assuming that interest for the period has already been paid.

Prepare installment payments schedule and journal entries for a mortgage note payable.

(SO 4)

P15-3B Egan Electronics issues an $500,000, 8%, 10-year mortgage note on December 31, 2008, to help finance a plant expansion program. The terms provide for semiannual installment payments, not including real estate taxes and insurance, of $36,791. Payments are due June 30 and December 31.

Instructions

(a) Prepare an installment payments schedule for the first 2 years.

(b) June 30 Mortgage Notes Payable $16,791

(b) Prepare the entries for (1) the mortgage loan and (2) the first two installment payments.

(c) Current liability—2009: $37,049

(c) Show how the total mortgage liability should be reported on the balance sheet at December 31, 2009.

Analyze three different lease situations and prepare journal entries.

(SO 5)

P15-4B Presented below are three different lease transactions in which Gomez Enterprises engaged in 2008. Assume that all lease transactions start on January 1, 2008. In no case does Gomez receive title to the properties leased during or at the end of the lease term.

	Lessor		
	Schoen Co.	**Didde Co.**	**Krumme Inc.**
Type of property	Bulldozer	Truck	Furniture
Bargain purchase option	None	None	None
Lease term	4 years	6 years	3 years
Estimated economic life	8 years	7 years	5 years
Yearly rental	$13,000	$18,000	$ 4,000
Fair market value of leased asset	$80,000	$86,000	$27,500
Present value of the lease rental payments	$48,000	$74,000	$12,000

Instructions

(a) Identify the leases above as operating or capital leases. Explain.

(b) How should the lease transaction for Didde Co. be recorded on January 1, 2008?

(c) How should the lease transaction for Krumme Inc. be recorded in 2008?

Prepare entries to record issuance of bonds, payment of interest, and amortization of bond discount using effective-interest method.

(SO 2, 8)

***P15-5B** On July 1, 2008, Matlock Satellites issued $2,700,000 face value, 9%, 10-year bonds at $2,531,760. This price resulted in an effective-interest rate of 10% on the bonds. Matlock uses the effective-interest method to amortize bond premium or discount. The bonds pay semiannual interest July 1 and January 1.

Instructions

(Round all computations to the nearest dollar.)

(a) Prepare the journal entry to record the issuance of the bonds on July 1, 2008.

(b) Prepare an amortization table through December 31, 2009 (3 interest periods) for this bond issue.

(c) Amortization $5,088

(c) Prepare the journal entry to record the accrual of interest and the amortization of the discount on December 31, 2008.

(d) Amortization $5,342

(d) Prepare the journal entry to record the payment of interest and the amortization of the discount on July 1, 2009, assuming that interest was not accrued on June 30.

(e) Amortization $5,610

(e) Prepare the journal entry to record the accrual of interest and the amortization of the discount on December 31, 2009.

Prepare entries to record issuance of bonds, payment of interest, and amortization of premium using effective-interest method. In addition, answer questions.

(SO 2, 8)

***P15-6B** On July 1, 2008, S. Posadas Chemical Company issued $3,000,000 face value, 10%, 10-year bonds at $3,407,720. This price resulted in an 8% effective-interest rate on the bonds. Posadas uses the effective-interest method to amortize bond premium or discount. The bonds pay semiannual interest on each July 1 and January 1.

Instructions

(Round all computations to the nearest dollar.)

(a) Prepare the journal entries to record the following transactions.

(1) The issuance of the bonds on July 1, 2008.

(2) The accrual of interest and the amortization of the premium on December 31, 2008.

(3) The payment of interest and the amortization of the premium on July 1, 2009, assuming no accrual of interest on June 30.

(4) The accrual of interest and the amortization of the premium on December 31, 2009.

(b) Show the proper balance sheet presentation for the liability for bonds payable on the December 31, 2009, balance sheet.

(c) Provide the answers to the following questions in letter form.

(1) What amount of interest expense is reported for 2009?

(2) Would the bond interest expense reported in 2009 be the same as, greater than, or less than the amount that would be reported if the straight-line method of amortization were used?

(3) Determine the total cost of borrowing over the life of the bond.

(4) Would the total bond interest expense be greater than, the same as, or less than the total interest expense if the straight-line method of amortization were used?

(a) (2) Amortization $13,691
(a) (3) Amortization $14,239
(a) (4) Amortization $14,808
(b) Bond carrying value $3,364,982

Prepare entries to record issuance of bonds, interest accrual, and straight-line amortization for 2 years.

(SO 6, 9)

***P15-7B** Roeder Company sold $4,000,000, 9%, 20-year bonds on January 1, 2008. The bonds were dated January 1, 2008, and pay interest on January 1 and July 1. Roeder Company uses the straight-line method to amortize bond premium or discount. The bonds were sold at 96. Assume no interest is accrued on June 30.

Instructions

(a) Prepare the journal entry to record the issuance of the bonds on January 1, 2008.

(b) Prepare a bond discount amortization schedule for the first 4 interest periods.

(c) Prepare the journal entries for interest and the amortization of the discount in 2008 and 2009.

(d) Show the balance sheet presentation of the bond liability at December 31, 2009.

(b) Amortization $4,000
(d) Discount on bonds payable $144,000

Prepare entries to record issuance of bonds, interest, and straight-line amortization of bond premium and discount.

(SO 6, 9)

***P15-8B** Karjala Corporation sold $5,000,000, 8%, 10-year bonds on January 1, 2008. The bonds were dated January 1, 2008, and pay interest on July 1 and January 1. Karjala Corporation uses the straight-line method to amortize bond premium or discount. Assume no interest is accrued on June 30.

Instructions

(a) Prepare all the necessary journal entries to record the issuance of the bonds and bond interest expense for 2008, assuming that the bonds sold at 103.

(b) Prepare journal entries as in part (a) assuming that the bonds sold at 96.

(c) Show balance sheet presentation for each bond issue at December 31, 2008.

(a) Amortization $7,500
(b) Amortization $10,000
(c) Premium on bonds payable $135,000
Discount on bonds payable $180,000

Prepare entries to record interest payments, straight-line discount amortization, and redemption of bonds.

(SO 2, 3, 9)

***P15-9B** The following is taken from the Magana Corp. balance sheet.

MAGANA CORPORATION
Balance Sheet (partial)
December 31, 2008

Current liabilities		
Bond interest payable (for 6 months from July 1 to December 31)		$ 84,000
Long-term liabilities		
Bonds payable, 7%, due January 1, 2019	$2,400,000	
Less: Discount on bonds payable	90,000	$2,310,000

Interest is payable semiannually on January 1 and July 1. The bonds are callable on any semiannual interest date. Magana uses straight-line amortization for any bond premium or discount. From December 31, 2008, the bonds will be outstanding for an additional 10 years (120 months).

Instructions

(Round all computations to the nearest dollar).

(a) Journalize the payment of bond interest on January 1, 2009.

(b) Amortization $4,500

(b) Prepare the entry to amortize bond discount and to pay the interest due on July 1, 2009, assuming that interest was not accrued on June 30.

(c) Loss $36,500

(c) Assume that on July 1, 2009, after paying interest, Magana Corp. calls bonds having a face value of $800,000. The call price is 101. Record the redemption of the bonds.

(d) Amortization $3,000

(d) Prepare the adjusting entry at December 31, 2009, to amortize bond discount and to accrue interest on the remaining bonds.

PROBLEMS: SET C

Visit the book's website at **www.wiley.com/college/weygandt**, and choose the Student Companion site, to access Problem Set C.

COMPREHENSIVE PROBLEM: CHAPTERS 13–15

Nordham Corporation's trial balance at December 31, 2008, is presented below. All 2008 transactions have been recorded except for the items described below and on the next page.

	Debit	Credit
Cash	$ 23,000	
Accounts Receivable	51,000	
Merchandise Inventory	22,700	
Land	65,000	
Building	95,000	
Equipment	40,000	
Allowance for Doubtful Accounts		$ 450
Accumulated Depreciation—Building		30,000
Accumulated Depreciation—Equipment		14,400
Accounts Payable		19,300
Bond Interest Payable		–0–
Dividends Payable		–0–
Unearned Rent Revenue		8,000
Bonds Payable (10%)		50,000
Common Stock ($10 par)		30,000
Paid-in Capital in Excess of Par—Common Stock		6,000
Preferred Stock ($20 par)		–0–
Paid-in Capital in Excess of Par—Preferred Stock		–0–
Retained Earnings		75,050
Treasury Stock	–0–	
Dividends	–0–	
Sales		570,000
Rent Revenue		–0–
Bad Debts Expense	–0–	
Bond Interest Expense	2,500	
Cost of Goods Sold	400,000	
Depreciation Expense—Buildings	–0–	
Depreciation Expense—Equipment	–0–	
Other Operating Expenses	39,000	
Salaries Expense	65,000	
Total	$803,200	$803,200

Unrecorded transactions

1. On January 1, 2008, Nordham issued 1,000 shares of $20 par, 6% preferred stock for $22,000.
2. On January 1, 2008, Nordham also issued 1,000 shares of common stock for $23,000.
3. Nordham reacquired 300 shares of its common stock on July 1, 2008, for $49 per share.

4. On December 31, 2008, Nordham declared the annual preferred stock dividend and a $1.50 per share dividend on the outstanding common stock, all payable on January 15, 2009.
5. Nordham estimates that uncollectible accounts receivable at year-end is $5,100.
6. The building is being depreciated using the straight-line method over 30 years. The salvage value is $5,000.
7. The equipment is being depreciated using the straight-line method over 10 years. The salvage value is $4,000.
8. The unearned rent was collected on October 1, 2008. It was receipt of 4 months' rent in advance (October 1, 2008 through January 31, 2009).
9. The 10% bonds payable pay interest every January 1 and July 1. The interest for the 6 months ended December 31, 2008, has not been paid or recorded.

Instructions

(Ignore income taxes.)

(a) Prepare journal entries for the transactions listed above.
(b) Prepare an updated December 31, 2008, trial balance, reflecting the unrecorded transactions.
(c) Prepare a multiple-step income statement for the year ending December 31, 2008.
(d) Prepare a statement of retained earnings for the year ending December 31, 2008.
(e) Prepare a classified balance sheet as of December 31, 2008.

CONTINUING COOKIE CHRONICLE

(Note: This is a continuation of the Cookie Chronicle from Chapters 1 through 14.)

CCC15 Natalie and Curtis have been experiencing great demand for their cookies and muffins. As a result, they are now thinking about buying a commercial oven. They know which oven they want and how much it will cost. They have some cash set aside for the purchase and will need to borrow the rest. They met with a bank manager to discuss their options.

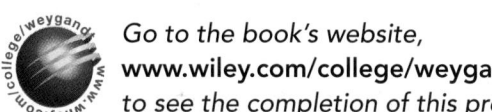

Go to the book's website,
www.wiley.com/college/weygandt,
to see the completion of this problem.

BROADENING YOUR PERSPECTIVE

FINANCIAL REPORTING AND ANALYSIS

Financial Reporting Problem:
PepsiCo, Inc.

BYP15-1 Refer to the financial statements of PepsiCo and the Notes to Consolidated Financial Statements in Appendix A.

Instructions

(a) What was PepsiCo's total long-term debt at December 31, 2005? What was the increase/decrease in total long-term debt from the prior year? What does Note 9 to the financial statements indicate about the composition of PepsiCo's long-term debt obligation?
(b) What type of leases, operating or capital, does PepsiCo report? (See Note 9.) Are these leases reported on PepsiCo's financial statements?
(c) What are the total long-term contractual commitments that PepsiCo reports as of December 31, 2005? (See Note 9.)

Comparative Analysis Problem:
PepsiCo, Inc. vs. The Coca-Cola Company

BYP15-2 PepsiCo's financial statements are presented in Appendix A. Coca-Cola's financial statements are presented in Appendix B.

Instructions

(a) Based on the information contained in these financial statements, compute the following 2005 ratios for each company.
  (1) Debt to total assets.
  (2) Times interest earned.

(b) What conclusions concerning the companies' long-run solvency can be drawn from these ratios?

(c) Which company has reported the greater amount of future long-term commitments for the 5 succeeding years?

Exploring the Web

BYP15-3 Bond or debt securities pay a stated rate of interest. This rate of interest is dependent on the risk associated with the investment. Moody's Investment Service provides ratings for companies that issue debt securities.

Address: www.moodys.com, or go to **www.wiley.com/college/weygandt**

Steps: From Moody's homepage, choose **About Moody's**.

Instructions

(a) What year did Moody's introduce the first bond rating? (See Moody's History.)

(b) What is the total amount of debt securities that Moody's analysts "track"? (See **An Introduction**.)

(c) What characteristics must debt ratings have in order to be useful to the capital markets? (See **Understand Risk: The Truth About Credit Ratings**.)

CRITICAL THINKING

Decision Making Across the Organization

***BYP15-4** On January 1, 2006, Carlin Corporation issued $2,400,000 of 5-year, 8% bonds at 95; the bonds pay interest semiannually on July 1 and January 1. By January 1, 2008, the market rate of interest for bonds of risk similar to those of Carlin Corporation had risen. As a result the market value of these bonds was $2,000,000 on January 1, 2008—below their carrying value. Andrea Carlin, president of the company, suggests repurchasing all of these bonds in the open market at the $2,000,000 price. To do so the company will have to issue $2,000,000 (face value) of new 10-year, 11% bonds at par. The president asks you, as controller, "What is the feasibility of my proposed repurchase plan?"

Instructions

With the class divided into groups, answer the following.

(a) What is the carrying value of the outstanding Carlin Corporation 5-year bonds on January 1, 2008? (Assume straight-line amortization.)

(b) Prepare the journal entry to retire the 5-year bonds on January 1, 2008. Prepare the journal entry to issue the new 10-year bonds.

(c) Prepare a short memo to the president in response to her request for advice. List the economic factors that you believe should be considered for her repurchase proposal.

Communication Activity

BYP15-5 Joe Penner, president of the Penner Corporation, is considering the issuance of bonds to finance an expansion of his business. He has asked you to (1) discuss the advantages of bonds over common stock financing, (2) indicate the types of bonds he might issue, and (3) explain the issuing procedures used in bond transactions.

Instructions
Write a memo to the president, answering his request.

Ethics Case

BYP15-6 Sam Farr is the president, founder, and majority owner of Galena Medical Corporation, an emerging medical technology products company. Galena is in dire need of additional capital to keep operating and to bring several promising products to final development, testing, and production. Sam, as owner of 51% of the outstanding stock, manages the company's operations. He places heavy emphasis on research and development and on long-term growth. The other principal stockholder is Jill Hutton who, as a nonemployee investor, owns 40% of the stock. Jill would like to deemphasize the R&D functions and emphasize the marketing function, to maximize short-run sales and profits from existing products. She believes this strategy would raise the market price of Galena's stock.

All of Sam's personal capital and borrowing power is tied up in his 51% stock ownership. He knows that any offering of additional shares of stock will dilute his controlling interest because he won't be able to participate in such an issuance. But, Jill has money and would likely buy enough shares to gain control of Galena. She then would dictate the company's future direction, even if it meant replacing Sam as president and CEO.

The company already has considerable debt. Raising additional debt will be costly, will adversely affect Galena's credit rating, and will increase the company's reported losses due to the growth in interest expense. Jill and the other minority stockholders express opposition to the assumption of additional debt, fearing the company will be pushed to the brink of bankruptcy. Wanting to maintain his control and to preserve the direction of "his" company, Sam is doing everything to avoid a stock issuance. He is contemplating a large issuance of bonds, even if it means the bonds are issued with a high effective-interest rate.

Instructions
(a) Who are the stakeholders in this situation?
(b) What are the ethical issues in this case?
(c) What would you do if you were Sam?

"All About You" Activity

BYP15-7 Numerous articles have been written that identify early warning signs that you might be getting into trouble with your personal debt load. You can find many good articles on this topic on the Web.

Instructions
Find an article that identifies early warning signs of personal debt trouble. Write up a summary of the article and bring your summary and the article to class to share.

Answers to Insight and Accounting Across the Organization Questions

p. 636 When to Go Long-Term
Q: Based on this story, what is a good general rule to use in choosing between short-term and long-term financing?
A: *In general, it is best to finance short-term assets with short-term liabilities and long-term assets with long-term liabilities, in order to reduce the likelihood of a liquidity crunch such as this.*

p. 644 Search for Your Best Rate
Q: What should you do if the dealer "trash-talks" your lender, or refuses to sell you the car for the agreed-upon price unless you get your car loan through the dealer?
A: *Experts suggest that if the dealer "trash-talks" your lender or refuses to sell you the car at the agreed-upon price unless you get your financing through the dealer, get up and leave, and buy your car somewhere else.*

p. 647 They Thought It Was Easy Money

Q: What do you think happens when a company violates its debt covenants?

A: *If a company violates its debt covenants the lender can "call the loan." This means that the company is required to repay the loan immediately, even though the maturity date of the loan has not been reached. In practice, many lenders will renegotiate the terms of the loan rather than force the company to repay immediately.*

Authors' Comments on *All About You*: The Risks of Adjustable Rates (p. 648)

A big part of the American dream is home ownership. In the past, homes have enjoyed a relatively steady and safe increase in value; thus many people are eager to quit renting and become homeowners.

But home ownership is not without risks. In recent years home prices increased so much that economists expect that in some parts of the country home prices could fall by as much as 30%. In the example above, if the house lost 30% of its value it would be worth only $140,000—much less than the amount owed. Another risk is that, as interest rates increase, people with adjustable-rate mortgages can experience huge increases in their mortgage payments. In the example given here, if the loan rate hit the cap of 10.5%, the monthly payment would jump to $1,647. That represents a 61% increase. We don't want to discourage you from home ownership, but we do want to encourage you to get educated about mortgage terms.

Answer to PepsiCo Review It Question 2, p. 642

An examination of PepsiCo's statement of cash flows indicates the following reductions of debt: payments of long-term debt, $177 million, and payments of short-term borrowings of more than 3 months, $85 million.

Answers to Self-Study Questions

1. c **2.** a **3.** b **4.** d **5.** c **6.** d ***7.** b ***8.** c ***9.** d ***10.** a

Remember to go back to the Navigator box on the chapter-opening page and check off your completed work.

Chapter 16

Investments

STUDY OBJECTIVES

After studying this chapter, you should be able to:

1 Discuss why corporations invest in debt and stock securities.

2 Explain the accounting for debt investments.

3 Explain the accounting for stock investments.

4 Describe the use of consolidated financial statements.

5 Indicate how debt and stock investments are reported in financial statements.

6 Distinguish between short-term and long-term investments.

The Navigator

The Navigator

Scan **Study Objectives**	■
Read **Feature Story**	■
Read **Preview**	■
Read text and answer **Before You Go On** p. 687 ■ p. 692 ■ p. 698	■
Work **Demonstration Problem**	■
Review **Summary of Study Objectives**	■
Answer **Self-Study Questions**	■
Complete **Assignments**	■

Feature Story

"IS THERE ANYTHING ELSE WE CAN BUY?"

In a rapidly changing world you must change rapidly or suffer the consequences. In business, change requires investment.

A case in point is found in the entertainment industry. Technology is bringing about innovations so quickly that it is nearly impossible to guess which technologies will last and which will soon fade away. For example, will both satellite TV and cable TV survive, or will just one succeed, or will both be replaced by something else? Or consider the publishing industry. Will paper newspapers and magazines be replaced by online news via the World Wide Web? If you are a publisher, you have to make your best guess about what the future holds and invest accordingly.

Time Warner, Inc. (*www.timewarner.com*) lives at the center of this arena. It is not an environment for the timid, and Time Warner's philosophy is anything but timid. It might be characterized as, "If we can't beat you, we will buy you." Its mantra is "invest, invest, invest." A list of Time Warner's holdings gives an idea of its reach. Magazines: *People, Time, Life, Sports Illustrated, Fortune*. Book publishers: Time-Life Books, Book-of-the-Month Club, Little, Brown & Co, Sunset Books. Television and movies: Warner Bros. ("ER," "Without a Trace," the WB Network), HBO, and movies like *Harry Potter and the Goblet of Fire, and Batman Begins.* Broadcasting: TNT, CNN news, and Turner's library of thousands of classic movies. Internet: America Online, and AOL Anywhere. Time Warner owns more information and entertainment copyrights and brands than any other company in the world.

So what has Time Warner's aggressive acquisition spree meant for the bottom line? It has left the company with an accumulated deficit of approximately $93 billion. Some of the acquisitions have not come cheap, resulting in large amounts of reported goodwill and related intangible assets. The merger of America Online (AOL) with Time Warner was billed as a merger of equals. But, it was AOL's phenomenal growth and astronomical stock price that made this merger possible. Unfortunately, investors involved in this merger have faired poorly. From a high of $95.80, Time Warner's stock price recently sold at $17.08 per share.

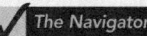

✓ The Navigator

Inside Chapter 16...

Preview of Chapter 16

Time Warner's management believes in aggressive growth through investing in the stock of existing companies. Besides purchasing stock, companies also purchase other securities such as bonds issued by corporations or by governments. Companies can make investments for a short or long period of time, as a passive investment, or with the intent to control another company. As you will see in this chapter, the way in which a company accounts for its investments is determined by a number of factors.

The content and organization of Chapter 16 are as follows.

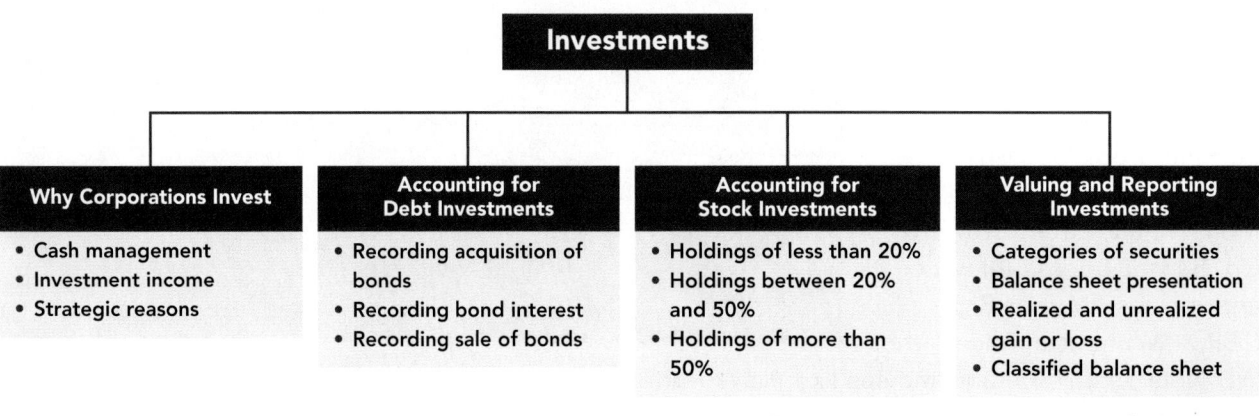

Investments

Why Corporations Invest
- Cash management
- Investment income
- Strategic reasons

Accounting for Debt Investments
- Recording acquisition of bonds
- Recording bond interest
- Recording sale of bonds

Accounting for Stock Investments
- Holdings of less than 20%
- Holdings between 20% and 50%
- Holdings of more than 50%

Valuing and Reporting Investments
- Categories of securities
- Balance sheet presentation
- Realized and unrealized gain or loss
- Classified balance sheet

The Navigator

WHY CORPORATIONS INVEST

STUDY OBJECTIVE 1

Discuss why corporations invest in debt and stock securities.

Corporations purchase investments in debt or stock securities generally for one of three reasons. First, a corporation may **have excess cash** that it does not need for the immediate purchase of operating assets. For example, many companies experience seasonal fluctuations in sales. A Cape Cod marina has more sales in the spring and summer than in the fall and winter. At the end of an operating cycle, the marina may have cash on hand that is temporarily idle until the start of another operating cycle. It may invest the excess funds to earn a greater return than it would get by just holding the funds in the bank. Illustration 16-1 depicts the role that such temporary investments play in the operating cycle.

Illustration 16-1
Temporary investments and the operating cycle

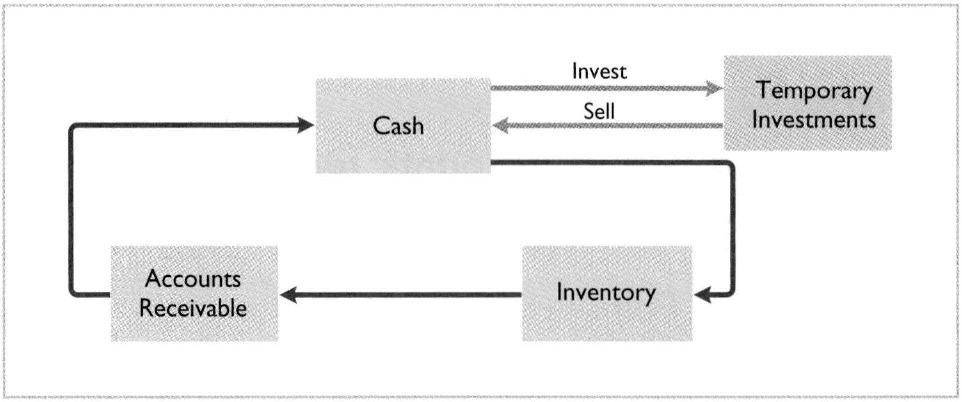

Excess cash may also result from economic cycles. For example, when the economy is booming, General Electric generates considerable excess cash. It uses some of this cash to purchase new plant and equipment and pays out some of the cash in dividends. But it may also invest excess cash in liquid assets in anticipation of a future downturn in the economy. It can then liquidate these investments during a recession, when sales slow and cash is scarce.

When investing excess cash for short periods of time, corporations invest in low-risk, highly liquid securities—most often short-term government securities. It is generally not wise to invest short-term excess cash in shares of common stock because stock investments can experience rapid price changes. If you did invest your short-term excess cash in stock and the price of the stock declined significantly just before you needed cash again, you would be forced to sell your stock investment at a loss.

A second reason some companies purchase investments is to generate **earnings from investment income**. For example, banks make most of their earnings by lending money, but they also generate earnings by investing in debt. Conversely, mutual stock funds invest primarily in equity securities in order to benefit from stock-price appreciation and dividend revenue.

Third, companies also invest for **strategic reasons**. A company can exercise some influence over a customer or supplier by purchasing a significant, but not controlling, interest in that company. Or, a company may purchase a noncontrolling interest in another company in a related industry in which it wishes to establish a presence. For example, Time Warner initially purchased an interest of less than 20% in Turner Broadcasting to have a stake in Turner's expanding business opportunities. At a later date Time Warner acquired the remaining 80%. Subsequently, Time Warner merged with AOL and became AOL Time Warner, Inc. Now, it is again just Time Warner, Inc., having dropped the "AOL" from its name in late 2003.

A corporation may also choose to purchase a controlling interest in another company. For example, in the *Accounting Across the Organization* box on page 691, Philip Morris purchased Kraft Foods. Such purchases might be done to enter a new industry without incurring the tremendous costs and risks associated with starting from scratch. Or a company might purchase another company in its same industry.

In summary, businesses invest in other companies for the reasons shown in Illustration 16-2.

Illustration 16-2
Why corporations invest

Reason	Typical Investment
To house excess cash until needed 	Low-risk, high-liquidity, short-term securities such as government-issued securities
To generate earnings 	Debt securities (banks and other financial institutions); and stock securities (mutual funds and pension funds)
To meet strategic goals 	Stocks of companies in a related industry or in an unrelated industry that the company wishes to enter

ACCOUNTING FOR DEBT INVESTMENTS

STUDY OBJECTIVE 2

Explain the accounting for debt investments.

Debt investments are investments in government and corporation bonds. In accounting for debt investments, companies make entries to record (1) the acquisition, (2) the interest revenue, and (3) the sale.

Recording Acquisition of Bonds

At acquisition, the cost principle applies. Cost includes all expenditures necessary to acquire these investments, such as the price paid plus brokerage fees (commissions), if any.

Assume, for example, that Kuhl Corporation acquires 50 Doan Inc. 8%, 10-year, $1,000 bonds on January 1, 2008, for $54,000, including brokerage fees of $1,000. The entry to record the investment is:

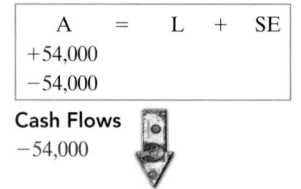

A	=	L	+	SE
+54,000				
−54,000				

Cash Flows
−54,000

Jan. 1	Debt Investments	54,000	
	Cash		54,000
	(To record purchase of 50 Doan Inc. bonds)		

Recording Bond Interest

The Doan, Inc. bonds pay interest of $2,000 semiannually on July 1 and January 1 ($50,000 × 8% × ½). The entry for the receipt of interest on July 1 is:

A	=	L	+	SE
+2,000				
				+2,000 Rev

Cash Flows
+2,000

July 1	Cash	2,000	
	Interest Revenue		2,000
	(To record receipt of interest on Doan Inc. bonds		

If Kuhl Corporation's fiscal year ends on December 31, it accrues the interest of $2,000 earned since July 1. The adjusting entry is:

A	=	L	+	SE
+2,000				
				+2,000 Rev

Cash Flows
no effect

Dec. 31	Interest Receivable	2,000	
	Interest Revenue		2,000
	(To accrue interest on Doan Inc. bonds)		

Kuhl reports Interest Receivable as a current asset in the balance sheet. It reports Interest Revenue under "Other revenues and gains" in the income statement.

Kuhl reports receipt of the interest on January 1 as follows.

A	=	L	+	SE
+2,000				
−2,000				

Cash Flows
+2,000

Jan. 1	Cash	2,000	
	Interest Receivable		2,000
	(To record receipt of accrued interest)		

A credit to Interest Revenue at this time is incorrect because the company earned and accrued interest revenue in the *preceding* accounting period.

Recording Sale of Bonds

When Kuhl sells the bonds, it credits the investment account for the cost of the bonds. Kuhl records as a gain or loss any difference between the net proceeds from the sale (sales price less brokerage fees) and the cost of the bonds.

Assume, for example, that Kuhl Corporation receives net proceeds of $58,000 on the sale of the Doan Inc. bonds on January 1, 2009, after receiving the interest due. Since the securities cost $54,000, the company realizes a gain of $4,000. It records the sale as:

Jan. 1	Cash	58,000	
	Debt Investments		54,000
	Gain on Sale of Debt Investments		4,000
	(To record sale of Doan Inc. bonds)		

A	=	L	+	SE
+58,000				
−54,000				
				+4,000 Rev

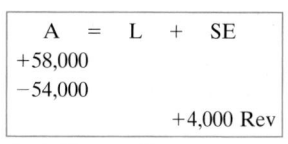

Cash Flows
+58,000

Kuhl reports the gain on sale of debt investments under "Other revenues and gains" in the income statement and reports losses under "Other expenses and losses."

Before You Go On...

REVIEW IT

1. Why might a company make investments in debt or stock securities?
2. What entries are required in accounting for debt investments?
3. How do companies report gains and losses from the sale of bonds in the income statement?

DO IT

Waldo Corporation had the following transactions pertaining to debt investments.

Jan. 1 Purchased 30, $1,000 Hillary Co. 10% bonds for $30,000, plus brokerage fees of $900. Interest is payable semiannually on July 1 and January 1.
July 1 Received semiannual interest on Hillary Co. bonds.
July 1 Sold 15 Hillary Co. bonds for $15,000, less $400 brokerage fees.

(a) Journalize the transactions, and **(b)** prepare the adjusting entry for the accrual of interest on December 31.

Action Plan

- Record bond investments at cost.
- Record interest when received and/or accrued.
- When bonds are sold, credit the investment account for the cost of the bonds.
- Record any difference between the cost and the net proceeds as a gain or loss.

Solution

(a) Jan. 1	Debt Investments	30,900	
	Cash		30,900
	(To record purchase of 30 Hillary Co. bonds)		
July 1	Cash	1,500	
	Interest Revenue ($30,000 × .10 × 6/12)		1,500
	(To record receipt of interest on Hillary Co. bonds)		
July 1	Cash	14,600	
	Loss on Sale of Debt Investments	850	
	Debt Investments ($30,900 × 15/30)		15,450
	(To record sale of 15 Hillary Co. bonds)		
(b) Dec. 31	Interest Receivable	750	
	Interest Revenue ($15,000 × .10 × 6/12)		750
	(To accrue interest on Hillary Co. bonds)		

Related exercise material: *BE16-1, E16-2, and E16-3.*

The Navigator

ACCOUNTING FOR STOCK INVESTMENTS

STUDY OBJECTIVE 3

Explain the accounting for stock investments.

Stock investments are investments in the capital stock of other corporations. When a company holds stock (and/or debt) of several different corporations, the group of securities is identified as an **investment portfolio**.

The accounting for investments in common stock depends on the extent of the investor's influence over the operating and financial affairs of the issuing corporation (the **investee**). Illustration 16-3 shows the general guidelines.

Illustration 16-3
Accounting guidelines for stock investments

	Investor's Ownership Interest in Investee's Common Stock	Presumed Influence on Investee	Accounting Guidelines
	Less than 20%	Insignificant	Cost method
	Between 20% and 50%	Significant	Equity method
	More than 50%	Controlling	Consolidated financial statements

Companies are required to use judgment instead of blindly following the guidelines.[1] On the following pages we will explain the application of each guideline.

Holdings of Less than 20%

HELPFUL HINT

The entries for investments in common stock also apply to investments in preferred stock.

In accounting for stock investments of less than 20%, companies use the cost method. Under the **cost method**, companies record the investment at cost, and recognize revenue only when cash dividends are received.

RECORDING ACQUISITION OF STOCK INVESTMENTS

At acquisition, the cost principle applies. Cost includes all expenditures necessary to acquire these investments, such as the price paid plus any brokerage fees (commissions).

Assume, for example, that on July 1, 2008, Sanchez Corporation acquires 1,000 shares (10% ownership) of Beal Corporation common stock. Sanchez pays $40 per share plus brokerage fees of $500. The entry for the purchase is:

A	=	L	+	SE
+40,500				
−40,500				

Cash Flows
−40,500

July 1	Stock Investments	40,500	
	Cash		40,500
	(To record purchase of 1,000 shares of Beal Corporation common stock)		

[1]Among the questions that are considered in determining an investor's influence are these: (1) Does the investor have representation on the investee's board? (2) Does the investor participate in the investee's policy-making process? (3) Are there material transactions between the investor and investee? (4) Is the common stock held by other stockholders concentrated or dispersed?

RECORDING DIVIDENDS

During the time Sanchez owns the stock, it makes entries for any cash dividends received. If Sanchez receives a $2 per share dividend on December 31, the entry is:

Dec. 31	Cash (1,000 × $2)	2,000	
	Dividend Revenue		2,000
	(To record receipt of a cash dividend)		

A	=	L	+	SE
+2,000				
				+2,000 Rev

Cash Flows
+2,000

Sanchez reports Dividend Revenue under "Other revenues and gains" in the income statement. Unlike interest on notes and bonds, dividends do not accrue. Therefore, companies do not make adjusting entries to accrue dividends.

RECORDING SALE OF STOCK

When a company sells a stock investment, it recognizes as a gain or a loss the difference between the net proceeds from the sale (sales price less brokerage fees) and the cost of the stock.

Assume that Sanchez Corporation receives net proceeds of $39,500 on the sale of its Beal stock on February 10, 2009. Because the stock cost $40,500, Sanchez incurred a loss of $1,000. The entry to record the sale is:

Feb. 10	Cash	39,500	
	Loss on Sale of Stock Investments	1,000	
	Stock Investments		40,500
	(To record sale of Beal common stock)		

A	=	L	+	SE
+39,500				
				−1,000 Exp
−40,500				

Cash Flows
+39,500

Sanchez reports the loss under "Other expenses and losses" in the income statement. It would show a gain on sale under "Other revenues and gains."

Holdings Between 20% and 50%

When an investor company owns only a small portion of the shares of stock of another company, the investor cannot exercise control over the investee. But, when an investor owns between 20% and 50% of the common stock of a corporation, it is presumed that the investor has significant influence over the financial and operating activities of the investee. The investor probably has a representative on the investee's board of directors, and through that representative, may exercise some control over the investee. The investee company in some sense becomes part of the investor company.

For example, even prior to purchasing all of Turner Broadcasting, Time Warner owned 20% of Turner. Because it exercised significant control over major decisions made by Turner, Time Warner used an approach called the equity method. Under the **equity method**, **the investor records its share of the net income of the investee in the year when it is earned**. An alternative might be to delay recognizing the investor's share of net income until the investee declares a cash dividend. But that approach would ignore the fact that the investor and investee are, in some sense, one company, making the investor better off by the investee's earned income.

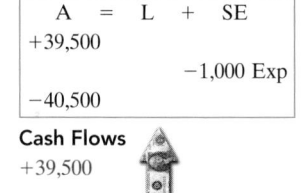

HELPFUL HINT
Under the equity method, the investor recognizes revenue on the accrual basis—i.e., when it is earned by the investee.

Under the equity method, the investor company initially records the investment in common stock at cost. After that, it **annually adjusts** the investment account to show the investor's equity in the investee. Each year, the investor does the following: (1) It increases (debits) the investment account and increases (credits) revenue for its share of the investee's net income.[2] (2) The investor also decreases

[2] Or, the investor increases (debits) a loss account and decreases (credits) the investment account for its share of the investee's net loss.

(credits) the investment account for the amount of dividends received. The investment account is reduced for dividends received, because payment of a dividend decreases the net assets of the investee.

RECORDING ACQUISITION OF STOCK INVESTMENTS

Assume that Milar Corporation acquires 30% of the common stock of Beck Company for $120,000 on January 1, 2008. Milar records this transaction as:

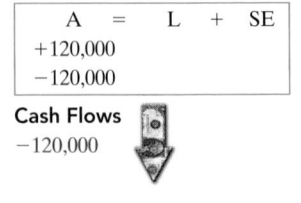

A	=	L	+	SE
+120,000				
−120,000				

Cash Flows
−120,000

Jan. 1	Stock Investments	120,000	
	Cash		120,000
	(To record purchase of Beck common stock)		

RECORDING REVENUE AND DIVIDENDS

For 2008, Beck reports net income of $100,000. It declares and pays a $40,000 cash dividend. Milar records (1) its share of Beck's income, $30,000 (30% × $100,000) and (2) the reduction in the investment account for the dividends received, $12,000 ($40,000 × 30%). The entries are:

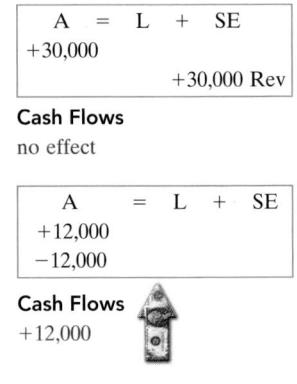

A	=	L	+	SE
+30,000				
				+30,000 Rev

Cash Flows
no effect

	(1)		
Dec. 31	Stock Investments	30,000	
	Revenue from Investment in Beck Company		30,000
	(To record 30% equity in Beck's 2008 net income)		

A	=	L	+	SE
+12,000				
−12,000				

Cash Flows
+12,000

	(2)		
Dec. 31	Cash	12,000	
	Stock Investments		12,000
	(To record dividends received)		

After Milar posts the transactions for the year, its investment and revenue accounts will show the following.

Illustration 16-4
Investment and revenue accounts after posting

Stock Investments			
Jan. 1	120,000	Dec. 31	**12,000**
Dec. 31	**30,000**		
Dec. 31 Bal.	138,000		

Revenue from Investment in Beck Company			
		Dec. 31	**30,000**

During the year, the net increase in the investment account was $18,000. As indicated above, the investment account increased by $30,000 due to Milar's share of Beck's income, and it decreased by $12,000 due to dividends received from Beck. In addition, Milar reports $30,000 of revenue from its investment, which is 30% of Beck's net income of $100,000.

Note that the difference between reported revenue under the cost method and reported revenue under the equity method can be significant. For example, Milar would report only $12,000 of dividend revenue (30% × $40,000) if it used the cost method.

STUDY OBJECTIVE 4
Describe the use of consolidated financial statements.

Holdings of More than 50%

A company that owns more than 50% of the common stock of another entity is known as the **parent company**. The entity whose stock the parent company owns is called the **subsidiary (affiliated) company**. Because of its stock ownership, the parent company has a **controlling interest** in the subsidiary.

When a company owns more than 50% of the common stock of another company, it usually prepares **consolidated financial statements**. These statements present the total assets and liabilities controlled by the parent company. They also present the total revenues and expenses of the subsidiary companies. Companies prepare consolidated statements **in addition to** the financial statements for the parent and individual subsidiary companies.

As noted earlier, when Time Warner had a 20% investment in Turner, it reported this investment in a single line item—Other Investments. After the merger, Time Warner instead consolidated Turner's results with its own. Under this approach, Time Warner included Turner's individual assets and liabilities with its own: its plant and equipment were added to Time Warner's plant and equipment, its receivables were added to Time Warner's receivables, and so on.

HELPFUL HINT

If parent (A) has three wholly owned subsidiaries (B, C, & D), there are four separate legal entities. From the viewpoint of the shareholders of the parent company, there is only one economic entity.

ACCOUNTING ACROSS THE ORGANIZATION

How Altria Group Accounts for Kraft Foods

Altria Group Inc. (formerly Philip Morris) owns 98.3% of the common stock of Kraft Foods, Inc. The common stockholders of Altria elect the board of directors of the company, who, in turn, select the officers and managers of the company. Altria's board of directors controls the property owned by the corporation, which includes the common stock of Kraft. Thus, they are in a position to elect the board of directors of Kraft and, in effect, control its operations. These relationships are graphically illustrated here.

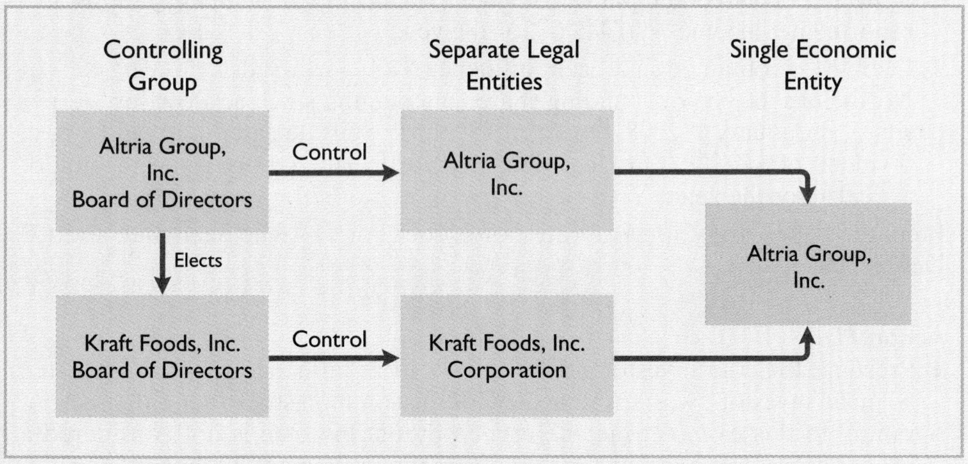

? Where on Altria Group's balance sheet will you find its investment in Kraft Foods, Inc.?

Consolidated statements are useful to the stockholders, board of directors, and managers of the parent company. These statements indicate the magnitude and scope of operations of the companies under common control. For example, regulators and the courts undoubtedly used the consolidated statements of AT&T to determine whether a breakup of AT&T was in the public interest. Listed at the top of page 692 are three companies that prepare consolidated statements and some of the companies they have owned. One, Disney, is Time Warner's arch rival.

Illustration 16-5
Examples of consolidated companies and their subsidiaries

Toys "R" Us, Inc.	Cendant	The Disney Company
Kids "R" Us	Howard Johnson	Capital Cities/ABC, Inc.
Babies "R" Us	Ramada Inn	Disneyland, Disney World
Imaginarium	Century 21	Mighty Ducks
Toysrus.com	Coldwell Banker	Anaheim Angels
	Avis	ESPN

Before You Go On...

REVIEW IT

1. What are the accounting entries for stock investments of less than 20%?
2. What entries are made under the equity method when (a) the investor receives a cash dividend from the investee and (b) the investee reports net income for the year?
3. What is the purpose of consolidated financial statements?
4. What does PepsiCo state regarding its accounting policy involving consolidated financial statements? The answer to this question appears on page 717.

DO IT

Presented below are two independent situations.

1. Rho Jean Inc. acquired 5% of the 400,000 shares of common stock of Stillwater Corp. at a total cost of $6 per share on May 18, 2008. On August 30, Stillwater declared and paid a $75,000 dividend. On December 31, Stillwater reported net income of $244,000 for the year.
2. Debbie, Inc. obtained significant influence over North Sails by buying 40% of North Sails' 60,000 outstanding shares of common stock at a cost of $12 per share on January 1, 2008. On April 15, North Sails declared and paid a cash dividend of $45,000. On December 31, North Sails reported net income of $120,000 for the year.

Prepare all necessary journal entries for 2008 for (1) Rho Jean Inc. and (2) Debbie, Inc.

Action Plan

- Presume that the investor has relatively little influence over the investee when an investor owns less than 20% of the common stock of another corporation. In this case, net income earned by the investee is not considered a proper basis for recognizing income from the investment by the investor.
- Presume significant influence for investments of 20%–50%. Therefore, record the investor's share of the net income of the investee.

Solution

(1) May 18	Stock Investments (20,000 × $6)	120,000	
	Cash		120,000
	(To record purchase of 20,000 shares of Stillwater Co. stock)		
Aug. 30	Cash	3,750	
	Dividend Revenue ($75,000 × 5%)		3,750
	(To record receipt of cash dividend)		

(2) Jan. 1	Stock Investments (60,000 × 40% × $12)	288,000	
	Cash		288,000
	(To record purchase of 24,000 shares of North Sails' stock)		
Apr. 15	Cash	18,000	
	Stock Investments ($45,000 × 40%)		18,000
	(To record receipt of cash dividend)		
Dec. 31	Stock Investments ($120,000 × 40%)	48,000	
	Revenue from Investment in North Sails		48,000
	(To record 40% equity in North Sails' net income)		

Related exercise material: *BE16-2, BE16-3, E16-4, E16-5, E16-6, E16-7, and E16-8.*

✓ The Navigator

VALUING AND REPORTING INVESTMENTS

STUDY OBJECTIVE 5

Indicate how debt and stock investments are reported in financial statements.

The value of debt and stock investments may fluctuate greatly during the time they are held. For example, in one 12-month period, the stock price of Dell Computer Corp. hit a high of $41.99 and a low of $23.60. In light of such price fluctuations, how should companies value investments at the balance sheet date? Valuation could be at cost, at fair value (market value), or at the lower-of-cost-or-market value.

Many people argue that fair value offers the best approach because it represents the expected cash realizable value of securities. Fair value is the amount for which a security could be sold in a normal market. Others counter that, unless a security is going to be sold soon, the fair value is not relevant because the price of the security will likely change again.

Categories of Securities

For purposes of valuation and reporting at a financial statement date, companies classify debt and stock investments into three categories:

1. Trading securities are bought and held primarily for sale in the near term to generate income on short-term price differences.
2. Available-for-sale securities are held with the intent of selling them sometime in the future.
3. Held-to-maturity securities are debt securities that the investor has the intent and ability to hold to maturity.[3]

Illustration 16-6 (on page 694) shows the valuation guidelines for these securities. **These guidelines apply to all debt securities and all stock investments in which the holdings are less than 20%.**

TRADING SECURITIES

Companies hold trading securities with the intention of selling them in a short period (generally less than a month). *Trading* means frequent buying and selling. Companies report trading securities at fair value, and report changes from cost as part of net income. The changes are reported as **unrealized gains or losses** because

[3]This category is provided for completeness. The accounting and valuation issues related to held-to-maturity securities are discussed in more advanced accounting courses.

Trading
"We'll sell within ten days."
At fair value with changes reported in net income
Available-for-sale
"We'll hold the stock for a while to see how it performs."
At fair value with changes reported in the stockholders' equity section
Held-to-maturity
"We intend to hold until maturity."
At amortized cost

Illustration 16-6
Valuation guidelines

the securities have not been sold. The unrealized gain or loss is the difference between the **total cost** of trading securities and their **total fair value**. Companies classify trading securities as current assets.

Illustration 16-7 shows the cost and fair values for investments Pace classified as trading securities on December 31, 2008. Pace has an unrealized gain of $7,000 because total fair value of $147,000 is $7,000 greater than total cost of $140,000.

Illustration 16-7
Valuation of trading securities

Trading Securities, December 31, 2008

Investments	Cost	Fair Value	Unrealized Gain (Loss)
Yorkville Company bonds	$ 50,000	$ 48,000	$ (2,000)
Kodak Company stock	90,000	99,000	9,000
Total	$140,000	$147,000	**$ 7,000**

HELPFUL HINT
The fact that trading securities are short-term investments increases the likelihood that they will be sold at fair value (the company may not be able to time their sale) and the likelihood that there will be realized gains or losses.

Pace records fair value and unrealized gain or loss through an adjusting entry at the time it prepares financial statements. In this entry, the company uses a valuation allowance account, Market Adjustment—Trading, to record the difference between the total cost and the total fair value of the securities. The adjusting entry for Pace Corporation is:

A	=	L	+	SE
+7,000				
				+7,000 Rev

Cash Flows
no effect

Dec. 31	Market Adjustment—Trading	7,000	
	Unrealized Gain—Income		7,000
	(To record unrealized gain on trading securities)		

Use of a Market Adjustment—Trading account enables Pace to maintain a record of the investment cost. It needs actual cost to determine the gain or loss realized when it sells the securities. Pace adds the Market Adjustment—Trading balance to the cost of the investments to arrive at a fair value for the trading securities.

The fair value of the securities is the amount Pace reports on its balance sheet. It reports the unrealized gain in the income statement in the "Other revenues and gains" section. The term "Income" in the account title indicates that the gain affects net income.

If the total cost of the trading securities is greater than total fair value, an unrealized loss has occurred. In such a case, the adjusting entry is a debit to Unrealized Loss—Income and a credit to Market Adjustment—Trading. Companies report the unrealized loss under "Other expenses and losses" in the income statement.

The market adjustment account is carried forward into future accounting periods. The company does not make any entry to the account until the end of each reporting period. At that time, the company adjusts the balance in the account to the difference between cost and fair value. For trading securities, it closes the Unrealized Gain (Loss)—Income account at the end of the reporting period.

ACCOUNTING ACROSS THE ORGANIZATION

And the Correct Way to Report Investments Is...?

The accompanying graph presents an estimate of the percentage of companies on the major exchanges that have investments in the equity of other entities.

As the graph indicates, many companies have equity investments of some type. These investments can be substantial. For example, the total amount of equity-method investments appearing on company balance sheets is approximately $403 billion, and the amount shown in the income statements in any one year for all companies is approximately $38 billion.

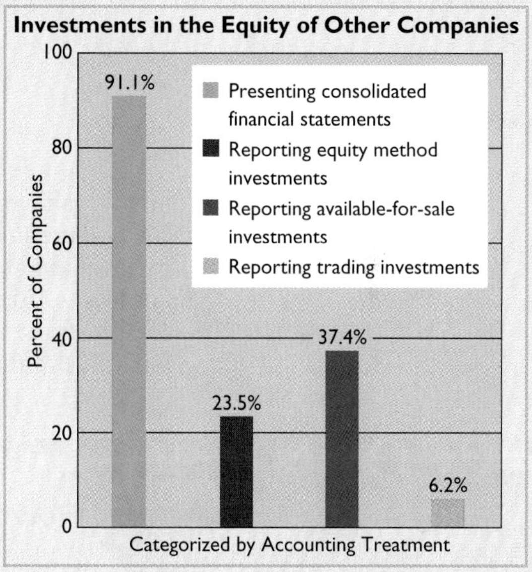

Source: "Report and Recommendations Pursuant to Section 401(c) of the Sarbanes-Oxley Act of 2002 on Arrangements with Off-Balance Sheet Implications, Special Purpose Entities, and Transparency of Filings by Issuers," United States Securities and Exchange Commission—Office of Chief Accountant, Office of Economic Analyses, Division of Corporation Finance (June 2005), pp. 36–39.

? Why might the use of the equity method not lead to full disclosure in the financial statements?

AVAILABLE-FOR-SALE SECURITIES

As indicated earlier, companies hold available-for-sale securities with the intent of selling these investments sometime in the future. If the intent is to sell the securities within the next year or operating cycle, the investor classifies the securities as current assets in the balance sheet. Otherwise, it classifies them as long-term assets in the investments section of the balance sheet.

Companies report available-for-sale securities at fair value. The procedure for determining fair value and the unrealized gain or loss for these securities is the same as for trading securities. To illustrate, assume that Ingrao Corporation has two securities that it classifies as available-for-sale. Illustration 16-8 provides information on their valuation. There is an unrealized loss of $9,537 because total cost of $293,537 is $9,537 more than total fair value of $284,000.

ETHICS NOTE

Some managers seem to hold their available-for-sale securities that have experienced losses, while selling those that have gains, thus increasing income. Do you think this is ethical?

Illustration 16-8
Valuation of available-for-sale securities

Available-for-Sale Securities, December 31, 2008

Investments	Cost	Fair Value	Unrealized Gain (Loss)
Campbell Soup Corporation 8% bonds	$ 93,537	$103,600	$10,063
Hershey Corporation stock	200,000	180,400	(19,600)
Total	$293,537	$284,000	**$(9,537)**

Both the adjusting entry and the reporting of the unrealized gain or loss for Ingrao's available-for-sale securities differ from those illustrated for trading securities. The differences result because Ingrao does not expect to sell these securities in the near term. Thus, prior to actual sale it is more likely that changes in fair value may change either unrealized gains or losses. Therefore, Ingrao does not report an unrealized gain or loss in the income statement. Instead, it reports it as a **separate component of stockholders' equity**.

In the adjusting entry, Ingrao identifies the market adjustment account with available-for-sale securities, and it identifies the unrealized gain or loss account with stockholders' equity. Ingrao records the unrealized loss of $9,537 as follows:

A	=	L	+	SE
				−9,537 Exp
−9,537				

Cash Flows
no effect

Dec. 31	Unrealized Gain or Loss—Equity	9,537	
	Market Adjustment—Available-for-Sale		9,537
	(To record unrealized loss on available-for-sale securities)		

If total fair value exceeds total cost, Ingrao debits Market Adjustment—Available for Sale and credits Unrealized Gain or Loss—Equity.

For available-for-sale securities, the company carries forward the Unrealized Gain or Loss—Equity account to future periods. At each future balance sheet date, Ingrao adjusts the market adjustment account to show the difference between cost and fair value at that time.

ACCOUNTING ACROSS THE ORGANIZATION

How Fair Is Fair?

In the fall of 2000, Wall Street brokerage firm Morgan Stanley told investors that rumors of big losses in its bond portfolio were "greatly exaggerated." As it turns out, Morgan Stanley also was exaggerating.

Recently, the SEC accused Morgan Stanley of violating securities laws by overstating the value of certain bonds by $75 million. The overvaluations stemmed more from wishful thinking than reality, the SEC said. "In effect, Morgan Stanley valued its positions at the price at which it thought a willing buyer and seller should enter into an exchange, rather than at a price at which a willing buyer and a willing seller would enter into a current exchange," the SEC wrote.

The SEC also noted that Morgan Stanley in some instances used its own more optimistic assumptions as a substitute for external pricing sources. "What that is saying is: 'Fair value is what you want the value to be. Pick a number...' That's especially troublesome."

? What do you believe is a major concern in valuing securities at fair value in the financial statements?

Balance Sheet Presentation

In the balance sheet, companies classify investments as either short-term or long-term.

SHORT-TERM INVESTMENTS

STUDY OBJECTIVE 6

Distinguish between short-term and long-term investments.

Short-term investments (also called **marketable securities**) are securities held by a company that are (1) **readily marketable** and (2) **intended to be converted into cash** within the next year or operating cycle, whichever is longer. Investments that do not meet **both criteria** are classified as **long-term investments**.

Readily Marketable. **An investment is readily marketable when it can be sold easily whenever the need for cash arises.** Short-term paper[4] meets this criterion. It can be readily sold to other investors. Stocks and bonds traded on organized securities exchanges, such as the New York Stock Exchange, are readily marketable. They can be bought and sold daily. In contrast, there may be only a limited market for the securities issued by small corporations, and no market for the securities of a privately held company.

HELPFUL HINT
Trading securities are always classified as short-term. Available-for-sale securities can be either short-term or long-term.

Intent to Convert. **Intent to convert means that management intends to sell the investment within the next year or operating cycle, whichever is longer.** Generally, this criterion is satisfied when the investment is considered a resource that the investor will use whenever the need for cash arises. For example, a ski resort may invest idle cash during the summer months with the intent to sell the securities to buy supplies and equipment shortly before the winter season. This investment is considered short-term even if lack of snow cancels the next ski season and eliminates the need to convert the securities into cash as intended.

Because of their high liquidity, short-term investments appear immediately below Cash in the "Current assets" section of the balance sheet. They are reported at fair value. For example, Pace Corporation would report its trading securities as shown in Illustration 16-9.

Illustration 16-9
Presentation of short-term investments

PACE CORPORATION Balance Sheet (partial)	
Current assets	
Cash	$ 21,000
Short-term investments, at fair value	147,000

HELPFUL HINT
In a recent survey of 600 large U.S. companies, 242 reported short-term investments.

LONG-TERM INVESTMENTS

Companies generally report long-term investments in a separate section of the balance sheet immediately below "Current assets," as shown later in Illustration 16-12 (page 699). Long-term investments in available-for-sale securities are reported at fair value. Investments in common stock accounted for under the equity method are reported at their equity value.

Presentation of Realized and Unrealized Gain or Loss

Companies must present in the financial statements gains and losses on investments, whether realized or unrealized. In the income statement, companies report gains and losses in the nonoperating activities section under the categories listed in Illustration 16-10. Interest and dividend revenue are also reported in that section.

Illustration 16-10
Nonoperating items related to investments

Other Revenue and Gains	Other Expenses and Losses
Interest Revenue	Loss on Sale of Investments
Dividend Revenue	Unrealized Loss—Income
Gain on Sale of Investments	
Unrealized Gain—Income	

[4]**Short-term paper** includes (1) certificates of deposit (CDs) issued by banks, (2) money market certificates issued by banks and savings and loan associations, (3) Treasury bills issued by the U.S. government, and (4) commercial paper (notes) issued by corporations with good credit ratings.

As indicated earlier, companies report an unrealized gain or loss on available-for-sale securities as a separate component of stockholders' equity. To illustrate, assume that Dawson Inc. has common stock of $3,000,000, retained earnings of $1,500,000, and an unrealized loss on available-for-sale securities of $100,000. Illustration 16-11 shows the balance sheet presentation of the unrealized loss.

Illustration 16-11
Unrealized loss in stockholders' equity section

DAWSON INC. Balance Sheet (partial)	
Stockholders' equity	
Common stock	$3,000,000
Retained earnings	1,500,000
Total paid-in capital and retained earnings	4,500,000
Less: Unrealized loss on available-for-sale securities	**(100,000)**
Total stockholders' equity	$4,400,000

Note that the loss decreases stockholders' equity. An unrealized gain is added to stockholders' equity. Reporting the unrealized gain or loss in the stockholders' equity section serves two purposes: (1) It reduces the volatility of net income due to fluctuations in fair value. (2) It informs the financial statement user of the gain or loss that would occur if the securities were sold at fair value.

Companies must report items such as this, which affect stockholders' equity but are not included in the calculation of net income, as part of a more inclusive measure called *comprehensive income*. We discuss comprehensive income briefly in Chapter 18.

Classified Balance Sheet

We have presented many sections of classified balance sheets in this and preceding chapters. The classified balance sheet in Illustration 16-12 includes, in one place, key topics from previous chapters: the issuance of par value common stock, restrictions of retained earnings, and issuance of long-term bonds. From this chapter, the statement includes (highlighted in red) short-term and long-term investments. The investments in short-term securities are considered trading securities. The long-term investments in stock of less than 20% owned companies are considered available-for-sale securities. Illustration 16-12 also includes a long-term investment reported at equity and descriptive notations within the statement, such as the basis for valuing merchandise and one note to the statement.

Before You Go On...

REVIEW IT

1. What is the proper valuation and reporting of trading and available-for-sale securities on a balance sheet?
2. Explain how companies report the unrealized gain or loss for both trading and available-for-sale securities.
3. Explain where to report short- and long-term investments on a balance sheet.

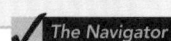

The Navigator

Be sure to read **ALL ABOUT YOU: *A Good Day to Start Saving*** on page 700 for information on how topics in this chapter apply to you.

Illustration 16-12
Classified balance sheet

PACE CORPORATION
Balance Sheet
December 31, 2008

Assets

Current assets			
Cash			$ 21,000
Short-term investments, at fair value			**147,000**
Accounts receivable		$ 84,000	
Less: Allowance for doubtful accounts		4,000	80,000
Merchandise inventory, at FIFO cost			43,000
Prepaid insurance			23,000
Total current assets			314,000
Investments			
Investments in stock of less than 20% owned companies, at fair value		**50,000**	
Investment in stock of 20–50% owned company, at equity		**150,000**	
Total investments			200,000
Property, plant, and equipment			
Land		200,000	
Buildings	$800,000		
Less: Accumulated depreciation	200,000	600,000	
Equipment	180,000		
Less: Accumulated depreciation	54,000	126,000	
Total property, plant, and equipment			926,000
Intangible assets			
Goodwill			270,000
Total assets			$1,710,000

Liabilities and Stockholders' Equity

Current liabilities		
Accounts payable		$185,000
Federal income taxes payable		60,000
Bond interest payable		10,000
Total current liabilities		255,000
Long-term liabilities		
Bonds payable, 10%, due 2019	$ 300,000	
Less: Discount on bonds	10,000	
Total long-term liabilities		290,000
Total liabilities		545,000
Stockholders' equity		
Paid-in capital		
Common stock, $10 par value, 200,000 shares authorized, 80,000 shares issued and outstanding	800,000	
Paid-in capital in excess of par value	100,000	
Total paid-in capital	900,000	
Retained earnings (Note 1)	255,000	
Total paid-in capital and retained earnings	1,155,000	
Add: Unrealized gain on available-for-sale securities	**10,000**	
Total stockholders' equity		1,165,000
Total liabilities and stockholders' equity		$1,710,000

Note 1. Retained earnings of $100,000 is restricted for plant expansion.

A Good Day to Start Saving

Compared to citizens in many other nations, Americans are very poor savers. It isn't that we don't know that we should save. It is just that we would rather spend. When *is* a good time to get serious about saving? Maybe you should start saving when you've graduated and have a good job, but then there will be those student loans to pay off, and your car loans as well. Maybe you should start after you've purchased your first home—and furnished it. Oh, and you might have kids, so you might wait until after they've gone off to college. You get the picture: there's always a reason not to start saving. Given that, *today* is as good a day as any to start saving.

Some Facts

* Only about 48% of people in their twenties whose employers have a 401(k) plan participate in that plan. [401(k) plans allow you to put part of your pre-tax salary into investments. The investment and its earnings are not taxed until you withdraw them in retirement.] Many employers automatically enroll employees in 401(k) plans when they hire them.
* Only 40% of working couples currently are covered by pension plans, but 61% of workers expect to get income from a company pension plan.
* More than half of workers age 55 and older have less than $50,000 in retirement savings.
* 80% of individuals between the ages of 18 to 26 said that, if given $10,000, they would deposit the money into a traditional bank savings account rather than invest in the stock market. Many stated that they are intimidated by the stock market, and choose to give up the added returns the stock market offers over the long run, rather than face the market.

About the Numbers

The message to start saving early has been presented in many different ways. The chart below presents the facts in very blunt terms. When you are 25 years old, if you start putting $300 per month into an investment earning 8%, by the age of 65 you will have accumulated more than $1 million. But if you wait until age 55, you will accumulate only about $55,000. Notice the sharp drop-off between ages 25 and 35.

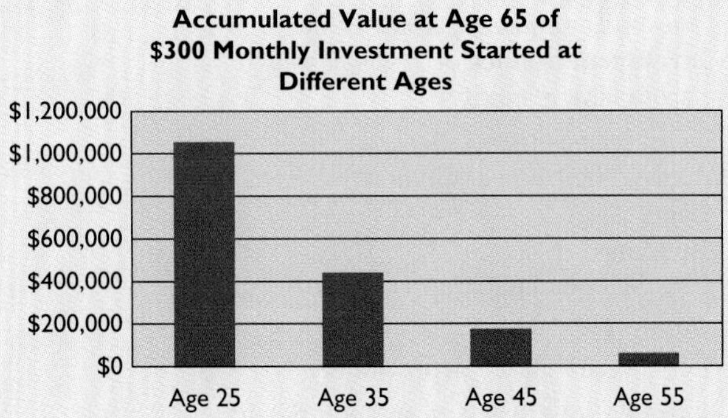

What Do You Think?

You've got $3,000 in credit card bills at an 18% interest rate. Your employer has a 401(k) plan in which it will match your contributions, up to 10% of your annual salary. Should you pay off your credit card bills before you start putting money into the 401(k)?

YES: Paying off an 18% debt, and thus avoiding 18% interest payments, is essentially equivalent to earning 18% on investments. Reducing your debts reduces your financial vulnerability.

NO: You need to get in the savings habit as soon as possible. You should take part of the money you would have used to pay off your debt each month and instead put it into the 401(k).

Sources: Kelly Greene, "Workers' Views On Retirement May Be Too Rosy," *Wall Street Journal*, April 4, 2006, p. D2; Ron Lieber, "Getting Younger Folk to Save," *Wall Street Journal*, June 17, 2006, p. B1; Eric A. Henon, "Why and How Generation Y Saves and Spends," *Benefits & Compensation Digest*, February 2006, pp. 30–32.

The authors' comments on this situation appear on page 717.

Demonstration Problem

WILEY PLUS

In its first year of operations, DeMarco Company had the following selected transactions in stock investments that are considered trading securities.

June 1	Purchased for cash 600 shares of Sanburg common stock at $24 per share, plus $300 brokerage fees.
July 1	Purchased for cash 800 shares of Cey common stock at $33 per share, plus $600 brokerage fees.
Sept. 1	Received a $1 per share cash dividend from Cey Corporation.
Nov. 1	Sold 200 shares of Sanburg common stock for cash at $27 per share, less $150 brokerage fees.
Dec. 15	Received a $0.50 per share cash dividend on Sanburg common stock.

At December 31, the fair values per share were: Sanburg $25 and Cey $30.

Instructions

(a) Journalize the transactions.

(b) Prepare the adjusting entry at December 31 to report the securities at fair value.

Solution to Demonstration Problem

(a) June 1	Stock Investments	14,700	
	Cash (600 × $24) + $300		14,700
	(To record purchase of 600 shares of Sanburg common stock)		
July 1	Stock Investments	27,000	
	Cash (800 × $33) + $600		27,000
	(To record purchase of 800 shares of Cey common stock)		
Sept. 1	Cash (800 × $1.00)	800	
	Dividend Revenue		800
	(To record receipt of $1 per share cash dividend from Cey Corporation)		
Nov. 1	Cash (200 × $27) − $150	5,250	
	Stock Investments ($14,700 × 200/600)		4,900
	Gain on Sale of Stock Investments		350
	(To record sale of 200 shares of Sanburg common stock)		
Dec. 15	Cash (600 − 200) × $0.50	200	
	Dividend Revenue		200
	(To record receipt of $0.50 per share dividend from Sanburg Corporation)		
(b) Dec. 31	Unrealized Loss—Income	2,800	
	Market Adjustment—Trading		2,800
	(To record unrealized loss on trading securities)		

Investment	Cost	Fair Value	Unrealized Gain (Loss)
Sanburg common stock	$ 9,800	$10,000	$ 200
Cey common stock	27,000	24,000	(3,000)
Totals	$36,800	$34,000	$(2,800)

The Navigator

action plan

- Include the price paid plus brokerage fees in the cost of the investment.
- Compute the gain or loss on sales as the difference between net selling price and the cost of the securities.
- Base the adjustment to fair value on the total difference between the cost and the fair value of the securities.

SUMMARY OF STUDY OBJECTIVES

WILEY PLUS

1 **Discuss why corporations invest in debt and stock securities.** Corporations invest for three primary reasons: (a) They have excess cash. (b) They view investments as a significant revenue source. (c) They have strategic goals such as gaining control of a competitor or moving into a new line of business.

2 **Explain the accounting for debt investments.** Companies record investments in debt securities when they purchase bonds, receive or accrue interest, and sell the bonds. They report gains or losses on the sale of bonds in the "Other revenues and gains" or "Other expenses and losses" sections of the income statement.

3 **Explain the accounting for stock investments.** Companies record investments in common stock when they purchase the stock, receive dividends, and sell the stock. When ownership is less than 20%, the cost method is used. When ownership is between 20% and 50%, the equity method should be used. When ownership is more than 50%, companies prepare consolidated financial statements.

4 **Describe the use of consolidated financial statements.** When a company owns more than 50% of the common stock of another company, it usually prepares consolidated financial statements. These statements indicate the magnitude and scope of operations of the companies under common control.

5 **Indicate how debt and stock investments are reported in financial statements.** Investments in debt and stock securities are classified as trading, available-for-sale, or held-to-maturity securities for valuation and reporting purposes. Trading securities are reported as current assets at fair value, with changes from cost reported in net income. Available-for-sale securities are also reported at fair value, with the changes from cost reported in stockholders' equity. Available-for-sale securities are classified as short-term or long-term depending on their expected future sale date.

6 **Distinguish between short-term and long-term investments.** Short-term investments are securities that are (a) readily marketable and (b) intended to be converted to cash within the next year or operating cycle, whichever is longer. Investments that do not meet both criteria are classified as long-term investments.

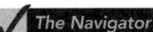

The Navigator

GLOSSARY

WILEY PLUS

Available-for-sale securities Securities that are held with the intent of selling them sometime in the future. (p. 693).

Consolidated financial statements Financial statements that present the assets and liabilities controlled by the parent company and the total revenues and expenses of the subsidiary companies. (p. 691).

Controlling interest Ownership of more than 50% of the common stock of another entity. (p. 691).

Cost method An accounting method in which the investment in common stock is recorded at cost, and revenue is recognized only when cash dividends are received. (p. 688).

Debt investments Investments in government and corporation bonds. (p. 686).

Equity method An accounting method in which the investment in common stock is initially recorded at cost, and the investment account is then adjusted annually to show the investor's equity in the investee. (p. 689).

Fair value Amount for which a security could be sold in a normal market. (p. 693).

Held-to-maturity securities Debt securities that the investor has the intent and ability to hold to their maturity date. (p. 693).

Investment portfolio A group of stocks and/or debt securities in different corporations held for investment purposes. (p. 688).

Long-term investments Investments that are not readily marketable or that management does not intend to convert into cash within the next year or operating cycle, whichever is longer. (p. 696).

Parent company A company that owns more than 50% of the common stock of another entity. (p. 690).

Short-term investments Investments that are readily marketable and intended to be converted into cash within the next year or operating cycle, whichever is longer. (p. 696).

Stock investments Investments in the capital stock of other corporations. (p. 688).

Subsidiary (affiliated) company A company in which more than 50% of its stock is owned by another company. (p. 690).

Trading securities Securities bought and held primarily for sale in the near term to generate income on short-term price differences. (p. 693).

SELF-STUDY QUESTIONS

Answers are at the end of the chapter.

(SO 2) **1.** Debt investments are initially recorded at:
a. cost.
b. cost plus accrued interest.
c. fair value.
d. None of the above.

(SO 2) **2.** Hanes Company sells debt investments costing $26,000 for $28,000, plus accrued interest that has been recorded. In journalizing the sale, credits are to:
a. Debt Investments and Loss on Sale of Debt Investments.
b. Debt Investments, Gain on Sale of Debt Investments, and Bond Interest Receivable.
c. Stock Investments and Bond Interest Receivable.
d. No correct answer given.

(SO 3) **3.** Pryor Company receives net proceeds of $42,000 on the sale of stock investments that cost $39,500. This transaction will result in reporting in the income statement a:
a. loss of $2,500 under "Other expenses and losses."
b. loss of $2,500 under "Operating expenses."
c. gain of $2,500 under "Other revenues and gains."
d. gain of $2,500 under "Operating revenues."

(SO 3) **4.** The equity method of accounting for long-term investments in stock should be used when the investor has significant influence over an investee and owns:
a. between 20% and 50% of the investee's common stock.
b. 20% or more of the investee's common stock.
c. more than 50% of the investee's common stock.
d. less than 20% of the investee's common stock.

(SO 4) **5.** Which of the following statements is *not true*? Consolidated financial statements are useful to:
a. determine the profitability of specific subsidiaries.
b. determine the total profitability of enterprises under common control.
c. determine the breadth of a parent company's operations.
d. determine the full extent of total obligations of enterprises under common control.

6. At the end of the first year of operations, the total cost of the trading securities portfolio is $120,000. Total fair value is $115,000. The financial statements should show: (SO 5)
a. a reduction of an asset of $5,000 and a realized loss of $5,000.
b. a reduction of an asset of $5,000 and an unrealized loss of $5,000 in the stockholders' equity section.
c. a reduction of an asset of $5,000 in the current assets section and an unrealized loss of $5,000 in "Other expenses and losses."
d. a reduction of an asset of $5,000 in the current assets section and a realized loss of $5,000 in "Other expenses and losses."

7. In the balance sheet, a debit balance in Unrealized Gain or Loss—Equity is reported as a: (SO 5)
a. contra asset account.
b. contra stockholders' equity account.
c. loss in the income statement.
d. loss in the retained earnings statement.

8. Short-term debt investments must be readily marketable and be expected to be sold within: (SO 6)
a. 3 months from the date of purchase.
b. the next year or operating cycle, whichever is shorter.
c. the next year or operating cycle, whichever is longer.
d. the operating cycle.

Go to the book's website, **www.wiley.com/college/ weygandt**, for Additional Self-Study questions.

The Navigator

QUESTIONS

1. What are the reasons that corporations invest in securities?

2. (a) What is the cost of an investment in bonds? (b) When is interest on bonds recorded?

3. Tino Martinez is confused about losses and gains on the sale of debt investments. Explain to Tino (a) how the gain or loss is computed, and (b) the statement presentation of the gains and losses.

4. Olindo Company sells Gish's bonds costing $40,000 for $45,000, including $500 of accrued interest. In recording the sale, Olindo books a $5,000 gain. Is this correct? Explain.

5. What is the cost of an investment in stock?

6. To acquire Kinston Corporation stock, R. Neal pays $62,000 in cash, plus $1,200 broker's fees. What entry should be made for this investment, assuming the stock is readily marketable?

7. (a) When should a long-term investment in common stock be accounted for by the equity method? (b) When is revenue recognized under this method?

8. Rijo Corporation uses the equity method to account for its ownership of 30% of the common stock of Pippen Packing. During 2008 Pippen reported a net income of $80,000 and declares and pays cash dividends of $10,000. What recognition should Rijo Corporation give to these events?

9. What constitutes "significant influence" when an investor's financial interest is below the 50% level?

10. Distinguish between the cost and equity methods of accounting for investments in stocks.

11. What are consolidated financial statements?

12. What are the valuation guidelines for investments at a balance sheet date?

13. Tina Eddings is the controller of Mendez Inc. At December 31, the company's investments in trading securities cost $74,000. They have a fair value of $70,000. Indicate how Tina would report these data in the financial statements prepared on December 31.
14. Using the data in question 13, how would Tina report the data if the investment were long-term and the securities were classified as available-for-sale?
15. Hashmi Company's investments in available-for-sale securities at December 31 show total cost of $195,000 and total fair value of $205,000. Prepare the adjusting entry.
16. Using the data in question 15, prepare the adjusting entry assuming the securities are classified as trading securities.
17. What is the proper statement presentation of the account Unrealized Loss—Equity?
18. What purposes are served by reporting Unrealized Gains (Losses)—Equity in the stockholders' equity section?
19. Altoona Wholesale Supply owns stock in Key Corporation. Altoona intends to hold the stock indefinitely because of some negative tax consequences if sold. Should the investment in Key be classified as a short-term investment? Why or why not?

BRIEF EXERCISES

WILEY PLUS

Journalize entries for debt investments.
(SO 2)

BE16-1 Coffey Corporation purchased debt investments for $52,000 on January 1, 2008. On July 1, 2008, Coffey received cash interest of $2,340. Journalize the purchase and the receipt of interest. Assume that no interest has been accrued.

Journalize entries for stock investments.
(SO 3)

BE16-2 On August 1, Wade Company buys 1,000 shares of Morgan common stock for $35,000 cash, plus brokerage fees of $700. On December 1, Wade sells the stock investments for $40,000 in cash. Journalize the purchase and sale of the common stock.

Record transactions under the equity method of accounting.
(SO 3)

BE16-3 Kayser Company owns 25% of Fort Company. For the current year Fort reports net income of $180,000 and declares and pays a $50,000 cash dividend. Record Kayser's equity in Fort's net income and the receipt of dividends from Fort.

Prepare adjusting entry using fair value.
(SO 5)

BE16-4 The cost of the trading securities of Cepeda Company at December 31, 2008, is $62,000. At December 31, 2008, the fair value of the securities is $59,000. Prepare the adjusting entry to record the securities at fair value.

Indicate statement presentation using fair value.
(SO 5, 6)

BE16-5 For the data presented in BE16-4, show the financial statement presentation of the trading securities and related accounts.

Prepare adjusting entry using fair value.
(SO 5)

BE16-6 Garrett Corporation holds as a long-term investment available-for-sale stock securities costing $72,000. At December 31, 2008, the fair value of the securities is $66,000. Prepare the adjusting entry to record the securities at fair value.

Indicate statements presentation using fair value.
(SO 5, 6)

BE16-7 For the data presented in BE16-6, show the financial statement presentation of the available-for-sale securities and related accounts. Assume the available-for-sale securities are noncurrent.

Prepare investments section of balance sheet.
(SO 5, 6)

BE16-8 Gowdy Corporation has the following long-term investments: (1) Common stock of Dixen Co. (10% ownership) held as available-for-sale securities, cost $108,000, fair value $115,000. (2) Common stock of Ely Inc. (30% ownership), cost $210,000, equity $270,000. Prepare the investments section of the balance sheet.

EXERCISES

WILEY PLUS

Understand debt and stock investments.
(SO 1)

E16-1 Max Weinberg is studying for an accounting test and has developed the following questions about investments.

1. What are three reasons why companies purchase investments in debt or stock securities?
2. Why would a corporation have excess cash that it does not need for operations?
3. What is the typical investment when investing cash for short periods of time?
4. What is the typical investment when investing cash to generate earnings?

5. Why would a company invest in securities that provide no current cash flows?
6. What is the typical investment when investing cash for strategic reasons?

Instructions
Provide answers for Max.

Journalize debt investment transactions and accrue interest.
(SO 2)

E16-2 Foren Corporation had the following transactions pertaining to debt investments.

Jan. 1 Purchased 50 8%, $1,000 Choate Co. bonds for $50,000 cash plus brokerage fees of $900. Interest is payable semiannually on July 1 and January 1.
July 1 Received semiannual interest on Choate Co. bonds.
July 1 Sold 30 Choate Co. bonds for $34,000 less $500 brokerage fees.

Instructions
(a) Journalize the transactions.
(b) Prepare the adjusting entry for the accrual of interest at December 31.

Journalize debt investment transactions, accrue interest, and record sale.
(SO 2)

E16-3 EmmyLou Company purchased 70 Harris Company 12%, 10-year, $1,000 bonds on January 1, 2008, for $73,000. EmmyLou Company also had to pay $500 of broker's fees. The bonds pay interest semiannually. On January 1, 2009, after receipt of interest, EmmyLou Company sold 40 of the bonds for $40,100.

Instructions
Prepare the journal entries to record the transactions described above.

Journalize stock investment transactions.
(SO 3)

E16-4 Dossett Company had the following transactions pertaining to stock investments.

Feb. 1 Purchased 600 shares of Goetz common stock (2%) for $6,000 cash, plus brokerage fees of $200.
July 1 Received cash dividends of $1 per share on Goetz common stock.
Sept. 1 Sold 300 shares of Goetz common stock for $4,400, less brokerage fees of $100.
Dec. 1 Received cash dividends of $1 per share on Goetz common stock.

Instructions
(a) Journalize the transactions.
(b) Explain how dividend revenue and the gain (loss) on sale should be reported in the income statement.

Journalize transactions for investments in stocks.
(SO 3)

E16-5 Wyrick Inc. had the following transactions pertaining to investments in common stock.

Jan. 1 Purchased 2,500 shares of Murphy Corporation common stock (5%) for $140,000 cash plus $2,100 broker's commission.
July 1 Received a cash dividend of $3 per share.
Dec. 1 Sold 500 shares of Murphy Corporation common stock for $32,000 cash, less $800 broker's commission.
Dec. 31 Received a cash dividend of $3 per share.

Instructions
Journalize the transactions.

Journalize transactions for investments in stocks.
(SO 3)

E16-6 On February 1, Neil Company purchased 500 shares (2% ownership) of Young Company common stock for $30 per share plus brokerage fees of $400. On March 20, Neil Company sold 100 shares of Young stock for $2,900, less a $50 brokerage fee. Neil received a dividend of $1.00 per share on April 25. On June 15, Neil sold 200 shares of Young stock for $7,400, less a $90 brokerage fee. On July 28, Neil received a dividend of $1.25 per share.

Instructions
Prepare the journal entries to record the transactions described above.

Journalize and post transactions, and contrast cost and equity method results.
(SO 3)

E16-7 On January 1 Kwun Corporation purchased a 25% equity in Connors Corporation for $180,000. At December 31 Connors declared and paid a $60,000 cash dividend and reported net income of $200,000.

Instructions
(a) Journalize the transactions.
(b) Determine the amount to be reported as an investment in Connors stock at December 31.

Journalize entries under cost and equity methods.

(SO 3)

E16-8 Presented below are two independent situations.

1. Heath Cosmetics acquired 15% of the 200,000 shares of common stock of Van Fashion at a total cost of $13 per share on March 18, 2008. On June 30, Van declared and paid a $60,000 dividend. On December 31, Van reported net income of $122,000 for the year. At December 31, the market price of Van Fashion was $15 per share. The stock is classified as available-for-sale.
2. Yoder, Inc., obtained significant influence over Parks Corporation by buying 30% of Parks 30,000 outstanding shares of common stock at a total cost of $9 per share on January 1, 2008. On June 15, Parks declared and paid a cash dividend of $30,000. On December 31, Parks reported a net income of $80,000 for the year.

Instructions

Prepare all the necessary journal entries for 2008 for (a) Heath Cosmetics and (b) Yoder, Inc.

Understand the usefulness of consolidated statements.

(SO 4)

E16-9 Ryan Company purchased 70% of the outstanding common stock of Wayne Corporation.

Instructions

(a) Explain the relationship between Ryan Company and Wayne Corporation.
(b) How should Ryan account for its investment in Wayne?
(c) Why is the accounting treatment described in **(b)** useful?

Prepare adjusting entry to record fair value, and indicate statement presentation.

(SO 5, 6)

E16-10 At December 31, 2008, the trading securities for Natoli, Inc. are as follows.

Security	Cost	Fair Value
A	$17,500	$16,000
B	12,500	14,000
C	23,000	19,000
	$53,000	$49,000

Instructions

(a) Prepare the adjusting entry at December 31, 2008, to report the securities at fair value.
(b) Show the balance sheet and income statement presentation at December 31, 2008, after adjustment to fair value.

Prepare adjusting entry to record fair value, and indicate statement presentation.

(SO 5, 6)

E16-11 Data for investments in stock classified as trading securities are presented in E16-10. Assume instead that the investments are classified as available-for-sale securities. They have the same cost and fair value. The securities are considered to be a long-term investment.

Instructions

(a) Prepare the adjusting entry at December 31, 2008, to report the securities at fair value.
(b) Show the statement presentation at December 31, 2008, after adjustment to fair value.
(c) M. Linquist, a member of the board of directors, does not understand the reporting of the unrealized gains or losses. Write a letter to Mr. Linquist explaining the reporting and the purposes that it serves.

Prepare adjusting entries for fair value, and indicate statement presentation for two classes of securities.

(SO 5, 6)

E16-12 McGee Company has the following data at December 31, 2008.

Securities	Cost	Fair Value
Trading	$120,000	$124,000
Available-for-sale	100,000	94,000

The available-for-sale securities are held as a long-term investment.

Instructions

(a) Prepare the adjusting entries to report each class of securities at fair value.
(b) Indicate the statement presentation of each class of securities and the related unrealized gain (loss) accounts.

EXERCISES: SET B

www.wiley.com/college/weygandt

Visit the book's website at **www.wiley.com/college/weygandt**, and choose the Student Companion site, to access Exercise Set B.

PROBLEMS: SET A

P16-1A Davison Carecenters Inc. provides financing and capital to the health-care industry, with a particular focus on nursing homes for the elderly. The following selected transactions relate to bonds acquired as an investment by Davison, whose fiscal year ends on December 31.

Journalize debt investment transactions and show financial statement presentation.

(SO 2, 5, 6)

2008

Jan. 1 Purchased at par $2,000,000 of Hannon Nursing Centers, Inc., 10-year, 8% bonds dated January 1, 2008, directly from Hannon.
July 1 Received the semiannual interest on the Hannon bonds.
Dec. 31 Accrual of interest at year-end on the Hannon bonds.

(Assume that all intervening transactions and adjustments have been properly recorded and that the number of bonds owned has not changed from December 31, 2008, to December 31, 2010.)

2011

Jan. 1 Received the semiannual interest on the Hannon bonds.
Jan. 1 Sold $1,000,000 Hannon bonds at 106. The broker deducted $6,000 for commissions and fees on the sale.
July 1 Received the semiannual interest on the Hannon bonds.
Dec. 31 Accrual of interest at year-end on the Hannon bonds.

Instructions

(a) Journalize the listed transactions for the years 2008 and 2011.

(a) Gain on sale of debt investment $54,000

(b) Assume that the fair value of the bonds at December 31, 2008, was $2,200,000. These bonds are classified as available-for-sale securities. Prepare the adjusting entry to record these bonds at fair value.

(c) Based on your analysis in part (b), show the balance sheet presentation of the bonds and interest receivable at December 31, 2008. Assume the investments are considered long-term. Indicate where any unrealized gain or loss is reported in the financial statements.

P16-2A In January 2008, the management of Noble Company concludes that it has sufficient cash to permit some short-term investments in debt and stock securities. During the year, the following transactions occurred.

Journalize investment transactions, prepare adjusting entry, and show statement presentation.

(SO 2, 3, 5, 6)

GLS Peachtree

Feb. 1 Purchased 600 shares of Hiens common stock for $31,800, plus brokerage fees of $600.
Mar. 1 Purchased 800 shares of Pryce common stock for $20,000, plus brokerage fees of $400.
Apr. 1 Purchased 50 $1,000, 7% Roy bonds for $50,000, plus $1,000 brokerage fees. Interest is payable semiannually on April 1 and October 1.
July 1 Received a cash dividend of $0.60 per share on the Hiens common stock.
Aug. 1 Sold 200 shares of Hiens common stock at $58 per share less brokerage fees of $200.
Sept. 1 Received a $1 per share cash dividend on the Pryce common stock.
Oct. 1 Received the semiannual interest on the Roy bonds.
Oct. 1 Sold the Roy bonds for $50,000 less $1,000 brokerage fees.

At December 31, the fair value of the Hiens common stock was $55 per share. The fair value of the Pryce common stock was $24 per share.

Instructions

(a) Journalize the transactions and post to the accounts Debt Investments and Stock Investments. (Use the T-account form.)

(a) Gain on stock sale $600

(b) Prepare the adjusting entry at December 31, 2008, to report the investment securities at fair value. All securities are considered to be trading securities.

(c) Show the balance sheet presentation of investment securities at December 31, 2008.

(d) Identify the income statement accounts and give the statement classification of each account.

P16-3A On December 31, 2008, Ramey Associates owned the following securities, held as a long-term investment. The securities are not held for influence or control of the investee.

Journalize transactions and adjusting entry for stock investments.

(SO 3, 5, 6)

Common Stock	Shares	Cost
Hurst Co.	2,000	$60,000
Pine Co.	5,000	45,000
Scott Co.	1,500	30,000

On December 31, 2008, the total fair value of the securities was equal to its cost. In 2009, the following transactions occurred.

July 1	Received $1 per share semiannual cash dividend on Pine Co. common stock.
Aug. 1	Received $0.50 per share cash dividend on Hurst Co. common stock.
Sept. 1	Sold 1,500 shares of Pine Co. common stock for cash at $8 per share, less brokerage fees of $300.
Oct. 1	Sold 800 shares of Hurst Co. common stock for cash at $33 per share, less brokerage fees of $500.
Nov. 1	Received $1 per share cash dividend on Scott Co. common stock.
Dec. 15	Received $0.50 per share cash dividend on Hurst Co. common stock.
31	Received $1 per share semiannual cash dividend on Pine Co. common stock.

At December 31, the fair values per share of the common stocks were: Hurst Co. $32, Pine Co. $8, and Scott Co. $18.

Instructions

(a) Journalize the 2009 transactions and post to the account Stock Investments. (Use the T-account form.)

(b) Unrealized loss $4,100

(b) Prepare the adjusting entry at December 31, 2009, to show the securities at fair value. The stock should be classified as available-for-sale securities.

(c) Show the balance sheet presentation of the investments at December 31, 2009. At this date, Ramey Associates has common stock $1,500,000 and retained earnings $1,000,000.

Prepare entries under the cost and equity methods, and tabulate differences.

(SO 3)

P16-4A Glaser Services acquired 30% of the outstanding common stock of Nickels Company on January 1, 2008, by paying $800,000 for the 45,000 shares. Nickels declared and paid $0.30 per share cash dividends on March 15, June 15, September 15, and December 15, 2008. Nickels reported net income of $320,000 for the year. At December 31, 2008, the market price of Nickels common stock was $24 per share.

Instructions

(a) Total dividend revenue $54,000

(a) Prepare the journal entries for Glaser Services for 2008 assuming Glaser cannot exercise significant influence over Nickels. (Use the cost method and assume that Nickels common stock should be classified as a trading security.)

(b) Revenue from investments $96,000

(b) Prepare the journal entries for Glaser Services for 2008, assuming Glaser can exercise significant influence over Nickels. Use the equity method.

(c) In tabular form, indicate the investment and income statement account balances at December 31, 2008, under each method of accounting.

Journalize stock investment transactions and show statement presentation.

(SO 3, 5, 6)

P16-5A The following securities are in Pascual Company's portfolio of long-term available-for-sale securities at December 31, 2008.

	Cost
1,000 shares of Abel Corporation common stock	$52,000
1,400 shares of Frey Corporation common stock	84,000
1,200 shares of Weiss Corporation preferred stock	33,600

On December 31, 2008, the total cost of the portfolio equaled total fair value. Pascual had the following transactions related to the securities during 2009.

Jan. 20	Sold 1,000 shares of Abel Corporation common stock at $55 per share less brokerage fees of $600.
28	Purchased 400 shares of $70 par value common stock of Rosen Corporation at $78 per share, plus brokerage fees of $480.
30	Received a cash dividend of $1.15 per share on Frey Corp. common stock.
Feb. 8	Received cash dividends of $0.40 per share on Weiss Corp. preferred stock.
18	Sold all 1,200 shares of Weiss Corp. preferred stock at $27 per share less brokerage fees of $360.
July 30	Received a cash dividend of $1.00 per share on Frey Corp. common stock.
Sept. 6	Purchased an additional 900 shares of $10 par value common stock of Rosen Corporation at $82 per share, plus brokerage fees of $1,200.
Dec. 1	Received a cash dividend of $1.50 per share on Rosen Corporation common stock.

At December 31, 2009, the fair values of the securities were:

Frey Corporation common stock	$64 per share
Rosen Corporation common stock	$72 per share

Pascual Company uses separate account titles for each investment, such as "Investment in Frey Corporation Common Stock."

Instructions

(a) Prepare journal entries to record the transactions.
(b) Post to the investment accounts. (Use T accounts.)
(c) Prepare the adjusting entry at December 31, 2009 to report the portfolio at fair value.
(d) Show the balance sheet presentation at December 31, 2009.

(a) Loss on sale of preferred stock $1,560
(c) Unrealized loss $7,480

P16-6A The following data, presented in alphabetical order, are taken from the records of Urbina Corporation.

Prepare a balance sheet.
(SO, 5, 6)

Accounts payable	$ 240,000
Accounts receivable	140,000
Accumulated depreciation—building	180,000
Accumulated depreciation—equipment	52,000
Allowance for doubtful accounts	6,000
Bonds payable (10%, due 2016)	500,000
Buildings	950,000
Cash	42,000
Common stock ($10 par value; 500,000 shares authorized, 150,000 shares issued)	1,500,000
Dividends payable	80,000
Equipment	275,000
Goodwill	200,000
Income taxes payable	120,000
Investment in Flott common stock (10% ownership), at cost	278,000
Investment in Portico common stock (30% ownership), at equity	380,000
Land	390,000
Market adjustment—available-for-sale securities (Dr)	8,000
Merchandise inventory	170,000
Notes payable (due 2009)	70,000
Paid-in capital in excess of par value	130,000
Premium on bonds payable	40,000
Prepaid insurance	16,000
Retained earnings	103,000
Short-term stock investment, at fair value (and cost)	180,000
Unrealized gain—available-for-sale securities	8,000

The investment in Flott common stock is considered to be a long-term available-for-sale security.

Instructions

Prepare a balance sheet at December 31, 2008.

Total assets $2,791,000

PROBLEMS: SET B

P16-1B Marshall Farms is a grower of hybrid seed corn for DeKalb Genetics Corporation. It has had two exceptionally good years and has elected to invest its excess funds in bonds. The following selected transactions relate to bonds acquired as an investment by Marshall Farms, whose fiscal year ends on December 31.

Journalize debt investment transactions and show financial statement presentation.
(SO 2, 5, 6)

2008

Jan. 1 Purchased at par $600,000 of Kenner Corporation 10-year, 9% bonds dated January 1, 2008, directly from the issuing corporation.
July 1 Received the semiannual interest on the Kenner bonds.
Dec. 31 Accrual of interest at year-end on the Kenner bonds.

(Assume that all intervening transactions and adjustments have been properly recorded and the number of bonds owned has not changed from December 31, 2008, to December 31, 2010.)

2011

Jan. 1 Received the semiannual interest on the Kenner bonds.
Jan. 1 Sold $300,000 Kenner bonds at 114. The broker deducted $7,000 for commissions and fees on the sale.
July 1 Received the semiannual interest on the Kenner bonds.
Dec. 31 Accrual of interest at year-end on the Kenner bonds.

Instructions

(a) Gain on sale of debt investments $35,000

(a) Journalize the listed transactions for the years 2008 and 2011.
(b) Assume that the fair value of the bonds at December 31, 2008, was $580,000. These bonds are classified as available-for-sale securities. Prepare the adjusting entry to record these bonds at fair value.
(c) Based on your analysis in part (b) show the balance sheet presentation of the bonds and interest receivable at December 31, 2008. Assume the investments are considered long-term. Indicate where any unrealized gain or loss is reported in the financial statements.

Journalize investment transactions, prepare adjusting entry, and show statement presentation.

(SO 2, 3, 5, 6)

GLS

P16-2B In January 2008, the management of Pandya Company concludes that it has sufficient cash to purchase some short-term investments in debt and stock securities. During the year, the following transactions occurred.

Feb. 1 Purchased 600 shares of EMP common stock for $40,000, plus brokerage fees of $800.
Mar. 1 Purchased 500 shares of SEK common stock for $15,000, plus brokerage fees of $300.
Apr. 1 Purchased 60 $1,000, 9% CRE bonds for $60,000, plus $1,200 brokerage fees. Interest is payable semiannually on April 1 and October 1.
July 1 Received a cash dividend of $0.60 per share on the EMP common stock.
Aug. 1 Sold 300 shares of EMP common stock at $72 per share, less brokerage fees of $350.
Sept. 1 Received a $1 per share cash dividend on the SEK common stock.
Oct. 1 Received the semiannual interest on the CRE bonds.
Oct. 1 Sold the CRE bonds for $64,000, less $1,000 brokerage fees.

At December 31, the fair value of the EMP common stock was $66 per share. The fair value of the SEK common stock was $29 per share.

Instructions

(a) Journalize the transactions and post to the accounts Debt Investments and Stock Investments. (Use the T-account form.)

(b) Unrealized loss $1,400

(b) Prepare the adjusting entry at December 31, 2008, to report the investments at fair value. All securities are considered to be trading securities.
(c) Show the balance sheet presentation of investment securities at December 31, 2008.
(d) Identify the income statement accounts and give the statement classification of each account.

Journalize transactions and adjusting entry for stock investments.

(SO 3, 5, 6)

GLS

P16-3B On December 31, 2008, Hastco Associates owned the following securities, held as long-term investments.

Common Stock	Shares	Cost
Agee Co.	3,000	$60,000
Burns Co.	6,000	36,000
Corea Co.	1,200	24,000

On this date, the total fair value of the securities was equal to its cost. The securities are not held for influence or control over the investees. In 2009, the following transactions occurred.

July 1 Received $1 per share semiannual cash dividend on Burns Co. common stock.
Aug. 1 Received $0.50 per share cash dividend on Agee Co. common stock.
Sept. 1 Sold 2,000 shares of Burns Co. common stock for cash at $8 per share, less brokerage fees of $300.
Oct. 1 Sold 600 shares of Agee Co. common stock for cash at $28 per share, less brokerage fees of $600.
Nov. 1 Received $1 per share cash dividend on Corea Co. common stock.
Dec. 15 Received $0.50 per share cash dividend on Agee Co. common stock.
31 Received $1 per share semiannual cash dividend on Burns Co. common stock.

At December 31, the fair values per share of the common stocks were: Agee Co. $18, Burns Co. $6, and Corea Co. $19.

Instructions

(a) Journalize the 2009 transactions and post to the account Stock Investments. (Use the T-account form.)

(a) Gain on sale, $3,700 and $4,200

(b) Prepare the adjusting entry at December 31, 2009, to show the securities at fair value. The stock should be classified as available-for-sale securities.

(c) Show the balance sheet presentation of the investments at December 31, 2009. At this date, Hastco Associates has common stock $2,000,000 and retained earnings $1,200,000.

P16-4B Keady's Concrete acquired 30% of the outstanding common stock of Washburn, Inc. on January 1, 2008, by paying $1,600,000 for 60,000 shares. Washburn declared and paid a $0.50 per share cash dividend on June 30 and again on December 31, 2008. Washburn reported net income of $600,000 for the year. At December 31, 2008, the market price of Washburn's common stock was $30 per share.

Prepare entries under the cost and equity methods, and tabulate differences.

(SO 3)

Instructions

(a) Prepare the journal entries for Keady's Concrete for 2008 assuming Keady's cannot exercise significant influence over Washburn. (Use the cost method and assume Washburn common stock should be classified as available-for-sale.)

(a) Total dividend revenue $60,000

(b) Prepare the journal entries for Keady's Concrete for 2008, assuming Keady's can exercise significant influence over Washburn. (Use the equity method.)

(b) Revenue from investments $180,000

(c) In tabular form, indicate the investment and income account balances at December 31, 2008, under each method of accounting.

P16-5B The following are in Madisen Company's portfolio of long-term available-for-sale securities at December 31, 2008.

Journalize stock investment transactions and show statement presentation.

(SO 3, 5, 6)

	Cost
500 shares of Bonds Corporation common stock	$26,000
700 shares of Mays Corporation common stock	42,000
600 shares of Dukakis Corporation preferred stock	16,800

On December 31, the total cost of the portfolio equaled total fair value. Madisen Company had the following transactions related to the securities during 2009.

Jan.	7	Sold 500 shares of Bonds Corporation common stock at $56 per share, less brokerage fees of $700.
	10	Purchased 200 shares, $70 par value common stock of Petengill Corporation at $78 per share, plus brokerage fees of $240.
	26	Received a cash dividend of $1.15 per share on Mays Corporation common stock.
Feb.	2	Received cash dividends of $0.40 per share on Dukakis Corporation preferred stock.
	10	Sold all 600 shares of Dukakis Corporation preferred stock at $26 per share less brokerage fees of $180.
July	1	Received a cash dividend of $1.00 per share on Mays Corporation common stock.
Sept.	1	Purchased an additional 600 shares of the $70 par value common stock of Petengill Corporation at $75 per share, plus brokerage fees of $900.
Dec.	15	Received a cash dividend of $1.50 per share on Petengill Corporation common stock.

At December 31, 2009, the fair values of the securities were:

Mays Corporation common stock	$63 per share
Petengill Corporation common stock	$72 per share

Madisen uses separate account titles for each investment, such as Investment in Mays Corporation Common Stock.

Instructions

(a) Prepare journal entries to record the transactions.

(a) Loss on sale $1,380

(b) Post to the investment accounts. (Use T accounts.)

(c) Prepare the adjusting entry at December 31, 2009, to report the portfolio at fair value.

(c) Unrealized loss $2,040

(d) Show the balance sheet presentation at December 31, 2009.

P16-6B The following data, presented in alphabetical order, are taken from the records of Manning Corporation.

Prepare a balance sheet.

(SO 5, 6)

Accounts payable	$ 250,000
Accounts receivable	90,000
Accumulated depreciation—building	180,000
Accumulated depreciation—equipment	52,000
Allowance for doubtful accounts	6,000
Bonds payable (10%, due 2018)	400,000
Buildings	900,000
Cash	142,000
Common stock ($5 par value; 500,000 shares authorized, 300,000 shares issued)	1,500,000
Discount on bonds payable	20,000
Dividends payable	50,000
Equipment	275,000
Goodwill	200,000
Income taxes payable	120,000
Investment in Tabares Inc. stock (30% ownership), at equity	600,000
Land	520,000
Merchandise inventory	170,000
Notes payable (due 2009)	70,000
Paid-in capital in excess of par value	200,000
Prepaid insurance	16,000
Retained earnings	290,000
Short-term stock investment, at fair value (and cost)	185,000

Instructions

Total assets $2,860,000

Prepare a balance sheet at December 31, 2008.

PROBLEMS: SET C

Visit the book's website at **www.wiley.com/college/weygandt**, and choose the Student Companion site, to access Problem Set C.

COMPREHENSIVE PROBLEM: CHAPTERS 12 TO 16

Part I

Mindy Feldkamp and her two colleagues, Oscar Lopez and Lori Melton, are personal trainers at an upscale health spa/resort in Tampa, Florida. They want to start a health club that specializes in health plans for people in the 50+ age range. The growing population in this age range and strong consumer interest in the health benefits of physical activity have convinced them they can profitably operate their own club. In addition to many other decisions, they need to determine what type of business organization they want. Oscar believes there are more advantages to the corporate form than a partnership, but he hasn't yet convinced Mindy and Lori. They have come to you, a small business consulting specialist, seeking information and advice regarding the choice of starting a partnership versus a corporation.

Instructions

(a) Prepare a memo (dated May 26, 2007) that describes the advantages and disadvantages of both partnerships and corporations. Advise Mindy, Oscar, and Lori regarding which organizational form you believe would better serve their purposes. Make sure to include reasons supporting your advice.

Part II

After deciding to incorporate, each of the three investors receives 20,000 shares of $2 par common stock on June 12, 2007, in exchange for their co-owned building ($200,000 market value) and $100,000 total cash they contributed to the business. The next decision that Mindy, Oscar, and Lori need to make is how to obtain financing for renovation and equipment. They understand the difference between equity securities and debt securities, but do not understand the tax, net income, and earnings per share consequences of equity versus debt financing on the future of their business.

Instructions

(b) Prepare notes for a discussion with the three entrepreneurs in which you will compare the consequences of using equity versus debt financing. As part of your notes, show the differences in interest and tax expense assuming $1,400,000 is financed with common stock, and then alternatively with debt. Assume that when common stock is used, 140,000 shares will be issued. When debt is used, assume the interest rate on debt is 9%, the tax rate is 32%, and income before interest and taxes is $300,000. (You may want to use an electronic spreadsheet.)

Part III

During the discussion about financing, Lori mentions that one of her clients, Roberto Marino, has approached her about buying a significant interest in the new club. Having an interested investor sways the three to issue equity securities to provide the financing they need. On July 21, 2007, Mr. Marino buys 90,000 shares at a price of $10 per share.

The club, LifePath Fitness, opens on January 12, 2008, and after a slow start, begins to produce the revenue desired by the owners. The owners decide to pay themselves a stock dividend, since cash has been less than abundant since they opened their doors. The 10% stock dividend is declared by the owners on July 27, 2008. The market value of the stock is $3 on the declaration date. The date of record is July 31, 2008 (there have been no changes in stock ownership since the initial issuance), and the issue date is August 15, 2008. By the middle of the fourth quarter of 2008, the cash flow of LifePath Fitness has improved to the point that the owners feel ready to pay themselves a cash dividend. They declare a $0.05 cash dividend on December 4, 2008. The record date is December 14, 2008, and the payment date is December 24, 2008.

Instructions

(c) **(1)** Record all of the transactions related to the common stock of LifePath Fitness during the years 2007 and 2008. **(2)** Indicate how many shares are issued and outstanding after the stock dividend is issued.

Part IV

Since the club opened, a major concern has been the pool facilities. Although the existing pool is adequate, Mindy, Oscar, and Lori all desire to make LifePath a cutting-edge facility. Until the end of 2008, financing concerns prevented this improvement. However, because there has been steady growth in clientele, revenue, and income since the fourth quarter of 2008, the owners have explored possible financing options. They are hesitant to issue stock and change the ownership mix because they have been able to work together as a team with great effectiveness. They have formulated a plan to issue secured term bonds to raise the needed $600,000 for the pool facilities. By the end of April 2009 everything was in place for the bond issue to go ahead. On June 1, 2009, the bonds were issued for $548,000. The bonds pay semiannual interest of 3% (6% annual) on December 1 and June 1 of each year. The bonds mature in 10 years, and amortization is computed using the straight-line method.

Instructions

(d) Record **(1)** the issuance of the secured bonds, **(2)** the interest payment made on December 1, 2009, **(3)** the adjusting entry required at December 31, 2009, and **(4)** the interest payment made on June 1, 2010.

Part V

Mr. Marino's purchase of LifePath Fitness was done through his business. The investment has always been accounted for using the cost method on his firm's books. However, early in 2010 he decided to take his company public. He is preparing an IPO (initial public offering), and he needs to have the firm's financial statements audited. One of the issues to be resolved is to restate the investment in LifePath Fitness using the equity method, since Mr. Marino's ownership percentage is greater than 20%.

Instructions

(e) **(1)** Give the entries that would have been made on Marino's books if the equity method of accounting for investments had been used since the initial investment. Assume the following data for LifePath.

	2007	2008	2009
Net income	$30,000	$70,000	$105,000
Total cash dividends	$ 2,100	$20,000	$ 50,000

(2) Compute the balance in the LifePath Investment account at the end of 2009.

CONTINUING COOKIE CHRONICLE

(Note: This is a continuation of the Cookie Chronicle from Chapters 1 through 15.)

CCC 16 Natalie has been approached by Ken Thornton, a shareholder of The Beanery Coffee Inc. Ken wants to retire and would like to sell his 1,000 shares in The Beanery Coffee, which represents 20% of all shares issued. The Beanery is currently operated by Ken's twin daughters, who each own 40% of the common shares. The Beanery not only operates a coffee shop but also roasts and sells beans to retailers, under the name "Rocky Mountain Beanery."

Ken has met with Curtis and Natalie to discuss the business operation. All have concluded that there would be many advantages for Cookie & Coffee Creations Inc. to acquire an interest in The Beanery Coffee. Despite the apparent advantages, Natalie and Curtis are still not convinced that they should participate in this business venture.

Go to the book's website, ***www.wiley.com/college/weygandt,*** *to see the completion of this problem.*

BROADENING YOUR PERSPECTIVE

FINANCIAL REPORTING AND ANALYSIS

Financial Reporting Problem: Pepsico, Inc.

BYP16-1 The annual report of PepsiCo. is presented in Appendix A.

Instructions

(a) See Note 1 to the financial statements and indicate what the consolidated financial statements include.

(b) Using PepsiCo's consolidated statement of cash flows, determine how much was spent for capital acquisitions during the current year.

Comparative Analysis Problem: PepsiCo, Inc. vs. The Coca-Cola Company

BYP16-2 PepsiCo's financial statements are presented in Appendix A. Coca-Cola's financial statements are presented in Appendix B.

Instructions

(a) Based on the information contained in these financial statements, determine each of the following for each company.

   (1) Net cash used for investing (investment) activities for the current year (from the statement of cash flows).

   (2) Cash used for capital expenditures during the current year.

(b) Each of PepsiCo's financial statements is labeled "consolidated." What has been consolidated? That is, from the contents of PepsiCo's annual report, identify by name the corporations that have been consolidated (parent and subsidiaries).

Exploring the Web

BYP16-3 Most publicly traded companies are analyzed by numerous analysts. These analysts often don't agree about a company's future prospects. In this exercise you will find analysts' ratings about companies and make comparisons over time and across companies in the same industry. You will also see to what extent the analysts experienced "earnings surprises." Earnings surprises can cause changes in stock prices.

Address: biz.yahoo.com/i, or go to **www.wiley.com/college/weygandt**

Steps

1. Choose a company.
2. Use the index to find the company's name.
3. Choose **Research**.

Instructions

(a) How many analysts rated the company?
(b) What percentage rated it a strong buy?
(c) What was the average rating for the week?
(d) Did the average rating improve or decline relative to the previous week?
(e) How do the analysts rank this company among all the companies in its industry?
(f) What was the amount of the earnings surprise percentage during the last quarter?

CRITICAL THINKING

Decision Making Across the Organization

BYP16-4 At the beginning of the question and answer portion of the annual stockholders' meeting of Kemper Corporation, stockholder Mike Kerwin asks, "Why did management sell the holdings in UMW Company at a loss when this company has been very profitable during the period its stock was held by Kemper?"

Since president Tony Chavez has just concluded his speech on the recent success and bright future of Kemper, he is taken aback by this question and responds, "I remember we paid $1,300,000 for that stock some years ago, and I am sure we sold that stock at a much higher price. You must be mistaken."

Kerwin retorts, "Well, right here in footnote number 7 to the annual report it shows that 240,000 shares, a 30% interest in UMW, were sold on the last day of the year. Also, it states that UMW earned $520,000 this year and paid out $160,000 in cash dividends. Further, a summary statement indicates that in past years, while Kemper held UMW stock, UMW earned $1,240,000 and paid out $440,000 in dividends. Finally, the income statement for this year shows a loss on the sale of UMW stock of $180,000. So, I doubt that I am mistaken."

Red-faced, president Chavez turns to you.

Instructions

With the class divided into groups, answer the following.

(a) What dollar amount did Kemper receive upon the sale of the UMW stock?
(b) Explain why both stockholder Kerwin and president Chavez are correct.

Communication Activity

BYP16-5 Bunge Corporation has purchased two securities for its portfolio. The first is a stock investment in Longley Corporation, one of its suppliers. Bunge purchased 10% of Longley with the intention of holding it for a number of years, but has no intention of purchasing more shares. The second investment was a purchase of debt securities. Bunge purchased the debt securities because its analysts believe that changes in market interest rates will cause these securities to increase in value in a short period of time. Bunge intends to sell the securities as soon as they have increased in value.

Instructions

Write a memo to Max Scholes, the chief financial officer, explaining how to account for each of these investments. Explain what the implications for reported income are from this accounting treatment.

Ethics Case

BYP16-6 Bartlet Financial Services Company holds a large portfolio of debt and stock securities as an investment. The total fair value of the portfolio at December 31, 2008, is greater than total cost. Some securities have increased in value and others have decreased. Deb Faust, the financial vice president, and Jan McCabe, the controller, are in the process of classifying for the first time the securities in the portfolio.

Faust suggests classifying the securities that have increased in value as trading securities in order to increase net income for the year. She wants to classify the securities that have decreased in value as long-term available-for-sale securities, so that the decreases in value will not affect 2008 net income.

McCabe disagrees. She recommends classifying the securities that have decreased in value as trading securities and those that have increased in value as long-term available-for-sale securities. McCabe argues that the company is having a good earnings year and that recognizing the losses now will help to smooth income for this year. Moreover, for future years, when the company may not be as profitable, the company will have built-in gains.

Instructions

(a) Will classifying the securities as Faust and McCabe suggest actually affect earnings as each says it will?

(b) Is there anything unethical in what Faust and McCabe propose? Who are the stakeholders affected by their proposals?

(c) Assume that Faust and McCabe properly classify the portfolio. Assume, at year-end, that Faust proposes to sell the securities that will increase 2008 net income, and that McCabe proposes to sell the securities that will decrease 2008 net income. Is this unethical?

* "All About You" Activity

BYP16-7 The Securities and Exchange Commission (SEC) is the primary regulatory agency of U.S. financial markets. Its job is to ensure that the markets remain fair for all investors. The following SEC sites provide useful information for investors.

Address: **www.sec.gov/answers.shtml** and **http://www.sec.gov/investor/tools/quiz.htm**, or go to **www.wiley.com/college/weygandt**.

Instructions

(a) Go to the first SEC site and find the definition of the following terms.
 (i) Ask price.
 (ii) Margin account.
 (iii) Prospectus.
 (iv) Index fund.

(b) Go to the second SEC site and take the short quiz.

? Answers to Insight and Accounting Across the Organization Questions

p. 691 How Altria Group Accounts for Kraft Foods

Q: Where on Altria Group's balance sheet will you find its investment in Kraft Foods, Inc.?

A: *Because Altria owns 98.3% of Kraft, Altria Group does not report Kraft in the investment section of its balance sheet. Instead, Kraft's assets and liabilities are included and commingled with the assets and liabilities of Altria Group.*

p. 695 And the Correct Way to Report Investments Is . . . ?

Q: Why might the use of the equity method not lead to full disclosure in the financial statements?

A: *Under the equity method, the investment in common stock of another company is initially recorded at cost. After that, the investment account is adjusted at each reporting date to show the investor's equity in the investee. However, on the investor's balance sheet, only the investment account is shown. The pro-rata share of the investee's assets and liabilities are not reported. Because the pro-rata share of the investee's assets and liabilities are not shown, some argue that the full disclosure principle is violated.*

p. 696 How Fair Is Fair?

Q: What do you believe is a major concern in valuing securities at fair value in the financial statements?

A: *Some question the relevance of fair value measures for investments in securities, arguing in favor of reporting based on cost. They believe that cost provides relevant information: it focuses on the decision to acquire the asset, the earning effects of that decision that will be realized over time, and the ultimate recoverable value of the asset. They argue that fair value ignores those concepts. Instead, fair value focuses on the effects of transactions and events that do not involve the company, reflecting opportunity gains and losses whose recognition in the financial statements is, in their view, not appropriate until realized.*

Authors' Comments on *All About You:* A Good Day to Start Saving (p. 700)

We believe that the correct answer to this situation is both *yes* and *no*. Here is what we propose: You need to cut up your credit cards, and then pay down your credit card debt. You should prepare a budget and figure out an affordable monthly payment that will pay off your debt as fast as possible. After you have paid off the credit card, you should continue to make this same payment into some form of savings account. If your employer has a 401(k) plan, then you should put the payment into that, since it has significant tax advantages. Otherwise set up an Individual Retirement Account (IRA). Most local banks or brokerage houses would be happy to help you set up an account.

A final note: All of us want to have financial security when we retire. We don't want to be a burden to anyone. That means that we should, whenever possible, participate in any tax-advantaged savings programs available to us, such as the 401(k) and IRAs. This is especially true given the concerns that many people have about the long-term viability of Social Security.

Answer to PepsiCo Review It Question 4, page 692

In Note 1, the following statement is made regarding PepsiCo's consolidation policy:

> Our financial statements include the consolidated accounts of PepsiCo, Inc. and the affiliates that we control. In addition, we include our share of the results of certain other affiliates based on our economic ownership interest. We do not control these other affiliates, as our ownership in these other affiliates is generally less than fifty percent. Our share of the net income of noncontrolled bottling affiliates is reported in our income statement as bottling equity income. Bottling equity income also includes any changes in our ownership interests of these affiliates. In 2005, bottling equity income includes $126 million of pre-tax gains on our sales of PBG stock. See Note 8 for additional information on our noncontrolled bottling affiliates. Our share of other noncontrolled affiliates is included in division operating profit. Intercompany balances and transactions are eliminated.

Answers to Self-Study Questions

1. a **2.** b **3.** c **4.** a **5.** a **6.** c **7.** b **8.** c

Remember to go back to the Navigator box on the chapter-opening page and check off your completed work.

Chapter 17

Statement of Cash Flows

STUDY OBJECTIVES

After studying this chapter, you should be able to:

1. Indicate the usefulness of the statement of cash flows.
2. Distinguish among operating, investing, and financing activities.
3. Prepare a statement of cash flows using the indirect method.
4. Analyze the statement of cash flows.

The Navigator

The Navigator

- Scan **Study Objectives**
- Read **Feature Story**
- Read **Preview**
- Read text and answer **Before You Go On** p. 724 p. 726 p. 734 p. 739
- Work **Demonstration Problem 1**
- Review **Summary of Study Objectives**
- Work **Demonstration Problem 2**
- Answer **Self-Study Questions**
- Complete **Assignments**

Feature Story

GOT CASH?

In today's environment, companies must be ready to respond to changes quickly in order to survive and thrive. They need to produce new products and expand into new markets continually. To do this takes cash—lots and lots of cash. Keeping lots of cash available is a real challenge for a young company. It requires careful cash management and attention to cash flow.

One company that managed cash successfully in its early years was Microsoft (*www.microsoft.com*). During those years the company paid much of its payroll with stock options (rights to purchase company stock in the future at a given price) instead of cash. This strategy conserved cash, and turned more than a thousand of its employees into millionaires during the company's first 20 years of business.

In recent years Microsoft has had a different kind of cash problem. Now that it has reached a more "mature" stage in life, it generates so much cash—roughly $1 billion per month—that it cannot always figure out what to do with it. By 2004 Microsoft had accumulated $60 billion.

The company said it was accumulating cash to invest in new opportunities, buy other companies, and pay off pending lawsuits. But for years, the federal government has blocked attempts by Microsoft to buy anything other than small firms because it feared that purchase of a large firm would only increase Microsoft's monopolistic position. In addition, even the largest estimates of Microsoft's legal obligations related to pending lawsuits would use up only about $6 billion in cash.

Microsoft's stockholders have complained for years that holding all this cash was putting a drag on the company's profitability. Why? Because Microsoft had the cash invested in very low-yielding government securities. Stockholders felt that the company either should find new investment projects that would bring higher returns, or return some of the cash to stockholders.

Finally, in July 2004 Microsoft announced a plan to return cash to stockholders, by paying a special one-time $32 billion dividend in December 2004. This special dividend was so large that, according to the U.S. Commerce Department, it caused total personal income in the United States to rise by 3.7% in one month—the largest monthly increase ever recorded by the agency. (It also made the holiday season brighter, especially for retailers in the Seattle area.) Microsoft also doubled its regular annual dividend to $3.50 per share. Further, it announced that it would spend another $30 billion over the next four years buying treasury stock. These actions will help to deplete some of its massive cash horde, but as you will see in this chapter, for a cash-generating machine like Microsoft, the company will be anything but cash-starved.

Source: "Business: An End to Growth? Microsoft's Cash Bonanza," *The Economist*, July 23, 2005, p. 61.

The Navigator

Inside Chapter 17...

Preview of Chapter 17

The balance sheet, income statement, and retained earnings statement do not always show the whole picture of the financial condition of a company or institution. In fact, looking at the financial statements of some well-known companies, a thoughtful investor might ask questions like these: How did Eastman Kodak finance cash dividends of $649 million in a year in which it earned only $17 million? How could United Airlines purchase new planes that cost $1.9 billion in a year in which it reported a net loss of over $2 billion? How did the companies that spent a combined fantastic $3.4 trillion on mergers and acquisitions in a recent year finance those deals? Answers to these and similar questions can be found in this chapter, which presents the statement of cash flows.

The content and organization of this chapter are as follows.

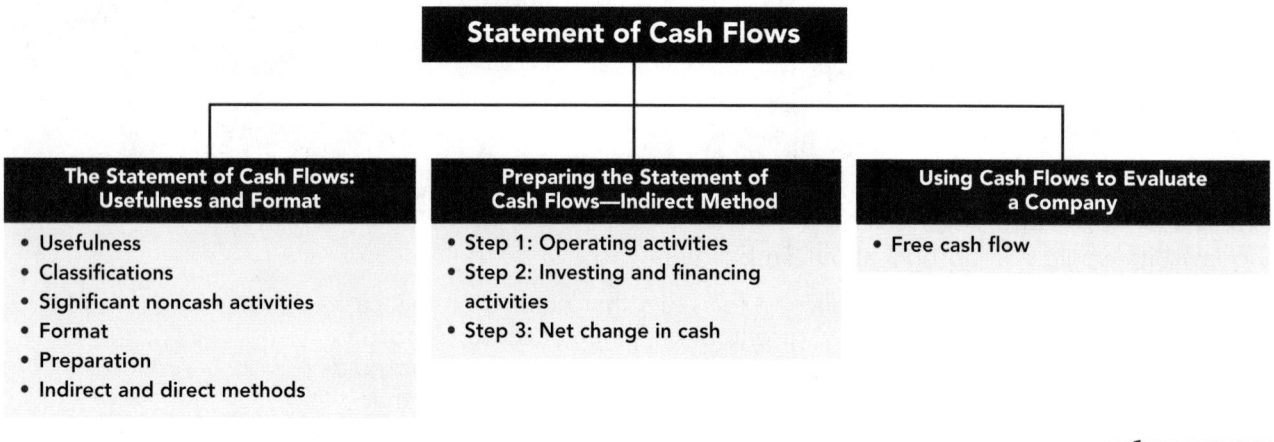

Statement of Cash Flows

The Statement of Cash Flows: Usefulness and Format
- Usefulness
- Classifications
- Significant noncash activities
- Format
- Preparation
- Indirect and direct methods

Preparing the Statement of Cash Flows—Indirect Method
- Step 1: Operating activities
- Step 2: Investing and financing activities
- Step 3: Net change in cash

Using Cash Flows to Evaluate a Company
- Free cash flow

The Navigator

THE STATEMENT OF CASH FLOWS: USEFULNESS AND FORMAT

The balance sheet, income statement, and retained earnings statement provide only limited information about a company's cash flows (cash receipts and cash payments). For example, comparative balance sheets show the increase in property, plant, and equipment during the year. But they do not show how the additions were financed or paid for. The income statement shows net income. But it does not indicate the amount of cash generated by operating activities. The retained earnings statement shows cash dividends declared but not the cash dividends paid during the year. None of these statements presents a detailed summary of where cash came from and how it was used.

Usefulness of the Statement of Cash Flows

STUDY OBJECTIVE 1

Indicate the usefulness of the statement of cash flows.

The **statement of cash flows** reports the cash receipts, cash payments, and net change in cash resulting from operating, investing, and financing activities during a period. The information in a statement of cash flows should help investors, creditors, and others assess:

1. **The entity's ability to generate future cash flows.** By examining relationships between items in the statement of cash flows, investors can make predictions of the amounts, timing, and uncertainty of future cash flows better than they can from accrual basis data.

2. **The entity's ability to pay dividends and meet obligations.** If a company does not have adequate cash, it cannot pay employees, settle debts, or pay dividends. Employees, creditors, and stockholders should be particularly interested in this statement, because it alone shows the flows of cash in a business.
3. **The reasons for the difference between net income and net cash provided (used) by operating activities.** Net income provides information on the success or failure of a business enterprise. However, some financial statement users are critical of accrual-basis net income because it requires many estimates. As a result, users often challenge the reliability of the number. Such is not the case with cash. Many readers of the statement of cash flows want to know the reasons for the difference between net income and net cash provided by operating activities. Then they can assess for themselves the reliability of the income number.
4. **The cash investing and financing transactions during the period.** By examining a company's investing and financing transactions, a financial statement reader can better understand why assets and liabilities changed during the period.

ETHICS NOTE

Though we would discourage reliance on cash flows to the exclusion of accrual accounting, comparing cash from operations to net income can reveal important information about the "quality" of reported net income. Such a comparison can reveal the extent to which net income provides a good measure of actual performance.

Classification of Cash Flows

STUDY OBJECTIVE 2

Distinguish among operating, investing, and financing activities.

The statement of cash flows classifies cash receipts and cash payments as operating, investing, and financing activities. Transactions and other events characteristic of each kind of activity are as follows.

1. **Operating activities** include the cash effects of transactions that create revenues and expenses. They thus enter into the determination of net income.
2. **Investing activities** include (a) acquiring and disposing of investments and property, plant, and equipment, and (b) lending money and collecting the loans.
3. **Financing activities** include (a) obtaining cash from issuing debt and repaying the amounts borrowed, and (b) obtaining cash from stockholders, repurchasing shares, and paying dividends.

The operating activities category is the most important. It shows the cash provided by company operations. This source of cash is generally considered to be the best measure of a company's ability to generate sufficient cash to continue as a going concern.

Illustration 17-1 (page 722) lists typical cash receipts and cash payments within each of the three classifications. **Study the list carefully.** It will prove very useful in solving homework exercises and problems.

Note the following general guidelines:

1. Operating activities involve income statement items.
2. Investing activities involve cash flows resulting from changes in investments and long-term asset items.
3. Financing activities involve cash flows resulting from changes in long-term liability and stockholders' equity items.

Companies classify as operating activities some cash flows related to investing or financing activities. For example, receipts of investment revenue (interest and dividends) are classified as operating activities. So are payments of interest to lenders. Why are these considered operating activities? **Because companies report these items in the income statement, where results of operations are shown.**

Illustration 17-1
Typical receipt and payment classifications

Operating activities

Investing activities

Financing activities

TYPES OF CASH INFLOWS AND OUTFLOWS

Operating activities—Income statement items
Cash inflows:
From sale of goods or services.
From interest received and dividends received.
Cash outflows:
To suppliers for inventory.
To employees for services.
To government for taxes.
To lenders for interest.
To others for expenses.

Investing activities—Changes in investments and long-term assets
Cash inflows:
From sale of property, plant, and equipment.
From sale of investments in debt or equity securities of other entities.
From collection of principal on loans to other entities.
Cash outflows:
To purchase property, plant, and equipment.
To purchase investments in debt or equity securities of other entities.
To make loans to other entities.

Financing activities—Changes in long-term liabilities and stockholders' equity
Cash inflows:
From sale of common stock.
From issuance of long-term debt (bonds and notes).
Cash outflows:
To stockholders as dividends.
To redeem long-term debt or reacquire capital stock (treasury stock).

Significant Noncash Activities

Not all of a company's significant activities involve cash. Examples of significant noncash activities are:

1. Direct issuance of common stock to purchase assets.
2. Conversion of bonds into common stock.
3. Direct issuance of debt to purchase assets.
4. Exchanges of plant assets.

Companies do not report in the body of the statement of cash flows significant financing and investing activities that do not affect cash. Instead, they report these activities in either a **separate schedule** at the bottom of the statement of cash flows or in a **separate note or supplementary schedule** to the financial statements. The reporting of these noncash activities in a separate schedule satisfies the **full disclosure principle**.

In solving homework assignments you should present significant noncash investing and financing activities in a separate schedule at the bottom of the statement of cash flows. (See the last entry in Illustration 17-2, at the bottom of page 723, for an example.)

HELPFUL HINT
Do not include noncash investing and financing activities in the body of the statement of cash flows. Report this information in a separate schedule.

ACCOUNTING ACROSS THE ORGANIZATION

Net *What?*

Net income is not the same as net cash provided by operating activities. Below are some results from recent annual reports (dollars in millions). Note the wide disparity among these companies, all of which engaged in retail merchandising.

Company	Net Income	Net Cash Provided by Operating Activities
Kohl's Corporation	$ 730	$ 948
Wal-Mart Stores, Inc.	10,267	15,044
J. C. Penney Company, Inc.	524	61
Costco Wholesale Corp.	882	2,099
Target Corporation	3,198	3,195

? In general, why do differences exist between net income and net cash provided by operating activities?

Format of the Statement of Cash Flows

The general format of the statement of cash flows presents the results of the three activities discussed previously—operating, investing, and financing—plus the significant noncash investing and financing activities. Illustration 17–2 shows a widely used form of the statement of cash flows.

Illustration 17-2
Format of statement of cash flows

COMPANY NAME
Statement of Cash Flows
Period Covered

Cash flows from operating activities		
(List of individual items)	XX	
Net cash provided (used) by operating activities		XXX
Cash flows from investing activities		
(List of individual inflows and outflows)	XX	
Net cash provided (used) by investing activities		XXX
Cash flows from financing activities		
(List of individual inflows and outflows)	XX	
Net cash provided (used) by financing activities		XXX
Net increase (decrease) in cash		XXX
Cash at beginning of period		XXX
Cash at end of period		XXX
Noncash investing and financing activities		
(List of individual noncash transactions)		XXX

The cash flows from operating activities section always appears first, followed by the investing activities section and then the financing activities section.

Before You Go On...

REVIEW IT

1. Why is the statement of cash flows useful?
2. What are the major classifications of cash flows on the statement of cash flows?
3. What are some examples of significant noncash activities?
4. What is the general format of the statement of cash flows? In what sequence are the three types of business activities presented?
5. In its 2005 statement of cash flows, what amounts did PepsiCo report for net cash (a) provided by operating activities, (b) used for investing activities, and (c) used for financing activities? The answer to this question appears on page 777.

DO IT

During its first week, Duffy & Stevenson Company had these transactions.

1. Issued 100,000 shares of $5 par value common stock for $800,000 cash.
2. Borrowed $200,000 from Castle Bank, signing a 5-year note bearing 8% interest.
3. Purchased two semi-trailer trucks for $170,000 cash.
4. Paid employees $12,000 for salaries and wages.
5. Collected $20,000 cash for services provided.

Classify each of these transactions by type of cash flow activity.

Action Plan

- Identify the three types of activities used to report all cash inflows and outflows.
- Report as operating activities the cash effects of transactions that create revenues and expenses and enter into the determination of net income.
- Report as investing activities transactions that (a) acquire and dispose of investments and productive long-lived assets and (b) lend money and collect loans.
- Report as financing activities transactions that (a) obtain cash from issuing debt and repay the amounts borrowed and (b) obtain cash from stockholders and pay them dividends.

Solution

1. Financing activity
2. Financing activity
3. Investing activity
4. Operating activity
5. Operating activity

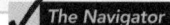

The Navigator

Preparing the Statement of Cash Flows

Companies prepare the statement of cash flows differently from the three other basic financial statements. First, it is not prepared from an adjusted trial balance. It requires detailed information concerning the changes in account balances that occurred between two points in time. An adjusted trial balance will not provide the necessary data. Second, the statement of cash flows deals with cash receipts and payments. As a result, the company **must adjust** the effects of the use of accrual accounting **to determine cash flows**.

The information to prepare this statement usually comes from three sources:

- **Comparative balance sheets.** Information in the comparative balance sheets indicates the amount of the changes in assets, liabilities, and stockholders' equities from the beginning to the end of the period.
- **Current income statement.** Information in this statement helps determine the amount of cash provided or used by operations during the period.
- **Additional information.** Such information includes transaction data that are needed to determine how cash was provided or used during the period.

Preparing the statement of cash flows from these data sources involves three major steps, explained in Illustration 17-3 below.

Illustration 17-3
Three major steps in preparing the statement of cash flows

Step 1: Determine net cash provided/used by operating activities by converting net income from an accrual basis to a cash basis.

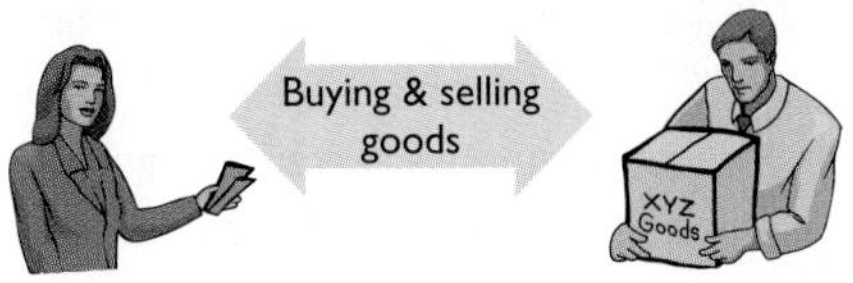

This step involves analyzing not only the current year's income statement but also comparative balance sheets and selected additional data.

Step 2: Analyze changes in noncurrent asset and liability accounts and record as investing and financing activities, or disclose as noncash transactions.

This step involves analyzing comparative balance sheet data and selected additional information for their effects on cash.

Step 3: Compare the net change in cash on the statement of cash flows with the change in the cash account reported on the balance sheet to make sure the amounts agree.

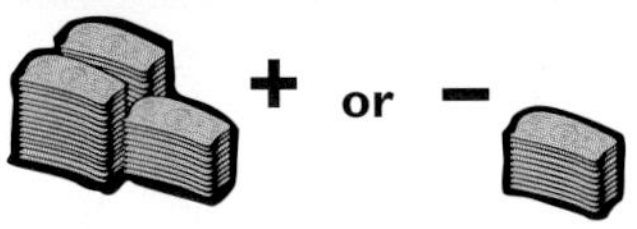

The difference between the beginning and ending cash balances can be easily computed from comparative balance sheets.

Indirect and Direct Methods

In order to perform step 1, a company **must convert net income from an accrual basis to a cash basis**. This conversion may be done by either of two methods: (1) the indirect method or (2) the direct method. **Both methods arrive at the same total amount** for "Net cash provided by operating activities." They differ in **how** they arrive at the amount.

The **indirect method** adjusts net income for items that do not affect cash. A great majority of companies (98.8%) use this method, as shown in the nearby chart.[1] Companies favor the indirect method for two reasons: (1) It is easier and

Usage of Methods

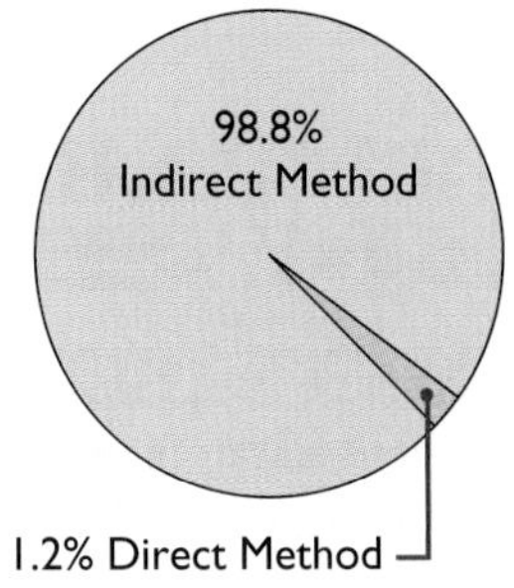

[1] *Accounting Trends and Techniques—2005* (New York: American Institute of Certified Public Accountants, 2005).

less costly to prepare, and (2) it focuses on the differences between net income and net cash flow from operating activities.

The **direct method** shows operating cash receipts and payments, making it more consistent with the objective of a statement of cash flows. The FASB has expressed a preference for the direct method, but allows the use of either method.

The next section illustrates the more popular indirect method. Appendix 17B illustrates the direct method.

INVESTOR INSIGHT

Cash Flow Isn't Always What It Seems

Some managers have taken actions that artificially increase cash flow from operating activities. They do this by moving negative amounts out of the operating section and into the investing or financing section.

For example, WorldCom, Inc. disclosed that it had improperly capitalized expenses: It had moved $3.8 billion of cash outflows from the "Cash from operating activities" section of the cash flow statement to the "Investing activities" section, thereby greatly enhancing cash provided by operating activities. Similarly, Dynegy, Inc. restated its cash flow statement because it had improperly included in operating activities, instead of in financing activities, $300 million from natural gas trading. The restatement resulted in a drop of 37% in cash flow from operating activities.

Source: Henny Sender, "Sadly, These Days Even Cash Flow Isn't Always What It Seems To Be," *Wall Street Journal*, May 8, 2002.

? For what reasons might managers at WorldCom and at Dynegy take the actions noted above?

Before You Go On...

REVIEW IT

1. What are the three major steps in preparing a statement of cash flows?
2. What is the primary difference between the indirect and direct approaches to the statement of cash flows?
3. Which method of preparing the statement of cash flows is more commonly used in practice?

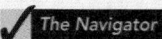

The Navigator

PREPARING THE STATEMENT OF CASH FLOWS—INDIRECT METHOD

STUDY OBJECTIVE 3

Prepare a statement of cash flows using the indirect method.

To explain how to prepare a statement of cash flows using the indirect method, we use financial information from Computer Services Company. Illustration 17-4 presents Computer Services' current and previous-year balance sheets, its current-year income statement, and related financial information for the current year.

Illustration 17-4
Comparative balance sheets, income statement, and additional information for Computer Services Company

COMPUTER SERVICES COMPANY
Comparative Balance Sheets
December 31

Assets	2008	2007	Change in Account Balance Increase/Decrease
Current assets			
Cash	$ 55,000	$ 33,000	$ 22,000 Increase
Accounts receivable	20,000	30,000	10,000 Decrease
Merchandise inventory	15,000	10,000	5,000 Increase
Prepaid expenses	5,000	1,000	4,000 Increase
Property, plant, and equipment			
Land	130,000	20,000	110,000 Increase
Building	160,000	40,000	120,000 Increase
Accumulated depreciation—building	(11,000)	(5,000)	6,000 Increase
Equipment	27,000	10,000	17,000 Increase
Accumulated depreciation—equipment	(3,000)	(1,000)	2,000 Increase
Total assets	$398,000	$138,000	
Liabilities and Stockholders' Equity			
Current liabilities			
Accounts payable	$ 28,000	$ 12,000	$ 16,000 Increase
Income tax payable	6,000	8,000	2,000 Decrease
Long-term liabilities			
Bonds payable	130,000	20,000	110,000 Increase
Stockholders' equity			
Common stock	70,000	50,000	20,000 Increase
Retained earnings	164,000	48,000	116,000 Increase
Total liabilities and stockholders' equity	$398,000	$138,000	

COMPUTER SERVICES COMPANY
Income Statement
For the Year Ended December 31, 2008

Revenues		$507,000
Cost of goods sold	$150,000	
Operating expenses (excluding depreciation)	111,000	
Depreciation expense	9,000	
Loss on sale of equipment	3,000	
Interest expense	42,000	315,000
Income before income tax		192,000
Income tax expense		47,000
Net income		$145,000

Additional information for 2008:

1. The company declared and paid a $29,000 cash dividend.
2. Issued $110,000 of long-term bonds in direct exchange for land.
3. A building costing $120,000 was purchased for cash. Equipment costing $25,000 was also purchased for cash.
4. The company sold equipment with a book value of $7,000 (cost $8,000, less accumulated depreciation $1,000) for $4,000 cash.
5. Issued common stock for $20,000 cash.
6. Depreciation expense was comprised of $6,000 for building and $3,000 for equipment.

We will now apply the three steps to the information provided for Computer Services Company.

Step 1: Operating Activities

DETERMINE NET CASH PROVIDED/USED BY OPERATING ACTIVITIES BY CONVERTING NET INCOME FROM AN ACCRUAL BASIS TO A CASH BASIS

To determine net cash provided by operating activities under the indirect method, companies **adjust net income in numerous ways**. A useful starting point is to understand **why** net income must be converted to net cash provided by operating activities.

Under generally accepted accounting principles, most companies use the accrual basis of accounting. As you have learned, this basis requires that companies record revenue when earned and record expenses when incurred. Earned revenues may include credit sales for which the company has not yet collected cash. Expenses incurred may include some items that it has not yet paid in cash. Thus, under the accrual basis of accounting, net income is not the same as net cash provided by operating activities.

Therefore, under the **indirect method**, companies must adjust net income to convert certain items to the cash basis. The indirect method (or reconciliation method) starts with net income and converts it to net cash provided by operating activities. Illustration 17-5 lists the three types of adjustments.

Illustration 17-5
Three types of adjustments to convert net income to net cash provided by operating activities

Net Income	+/−	Adjustments	=	Net Cash Provided/ Used by Operating Activities
		• **Add back noncash expenses**, such as depreciation expense, amortization, or depletion. • **Deduct gains and add losses** that resulted from investing and financing activities. • **Analyze changes** to noncash current asset and current liability accounts.		

HELPFUL HINT
Depreciation is similar to any other expense in that it reduces net income. It differs in that it does not involve a current cash outflow; that is why it must be *added back* to net income to arrive at cash provided by operating activities.

We explain the three types of adjustments in the next three sections.

DEPRECIATION EXPENSE

Computer Services' income statement reports depreciation expense of $9,000. Although depreciation expense reduces net income, it does not reduce cash. In other words, depreciation expense is a noncash charge. The company must add it back to net income to arrive at net cash provided by operating activities. Computer Services reports depreciation expense as follows in the statement of cash flows.

Illustration 17-6
Adjustment for depreciation

Cash flows from operating activities	
Net income	$145,000
Adjustments to reconcile net income to net cash provided by operating activities:	
Depreciation expense	**9,000**
Net cash provided by operating activities	$154,000

As the first adjustment to net income in the statement of cash flows, companies frequently list depreciation and similar noncash charges such as amortization of intangible assets, depletion expense, and bad debt expense.

LOSS ON SALE OF EQUIPMENT

Illustration 17-1 states that the investing activities section should report cash received from the sale of plant assets. Because of this, **companies must eliminate from net income all gains and losses related to the disposal of plant assets, to arrive at cash provided by operating activities.**

In our example, Computer Services' income statement reports a $3,000 loss on the sale of equipment (book value $7,000, less $4,000 cash received from sale of equipment). The company's loss of $3,000 should not be included in the operating activities section of the statement of cash flows. Illustration 17-7 shows that the $3,000 loss is eliminated by adding $3,000 back to net income to arrive at net cash provided by operating activities.

Cash flows from operating activities		
Net income		$145,000
Adjustments to reconcile net income to net cash provided by operating activities:		
Depreciation expense	$9,000	
Loss on sale of equipment	**3,000**	12,000
Net cash provided by operating activities		$157,000

Illustration 17-7
Adjustment for loss on sale of equipment

If a gain on sale occurs, the company deducts the gain from its net income in order to determine net cash provided by operating activities. **In the case of either a gain or a loss, companies report as a source of cash in the investing activities section of the statement of cash flows the actual amount of cash received from the sale.**

CHANGES TO NONCASH CURRENT ASSET AND CURRENT LIABILITY ACCOUNTS

A final adjustment in reconciling net income to net cash provided by operating activities involves examining all changes in current asset and current liability accounts. The accrual accounting process records revenues in the period earned and expenses in the period incurred. For example, companies use Accounts Receivable to record amounts owed to the company for sales that have been made but for which cash collections have not yet been received. They use the Prepaid Insurance account to reflect insurance that has been paid for, but which has not yet expired, and therefore has not been expensed. Similarly, the Salaries Payable account reflects salaries expense that has been incurred by the company but has not been paid.

As a result, we need to adjust net income for these accruals and prepayments to determine net cash provided by operating activities. Thus we must analyze the change in each current asset and current liability account to determine its impact on net income and cash.

CHANGES IN NONCASH CURRENT ASSETS. The adjustments required for changes in noncash current asset accounts are as follows: **Deduct from net income increases in current asset accounts, and add to net income decreases in current asset accounts, to arrive at net cash provided by operating activities.** We can observe these relationships by analyzing the accounts of Computer Services Company.

Decrease in Accounts Receivable. Computer Services Company's accounts receivable decreased by $10,000 (from $30,000 to $20,000) during the period. For Computer Services this means that cash receipts were $10,000 higher than revenues. The Accounts Receivable account in Illustration 17-8 shows that Computer Services Company had $507,000 in revenues (as reported on the income statement), but it collected $517,000 in cash. As shown in Illustration 17-9 (below), to adjust net income to net cash provided by operating activities, the company adds to net income the decrease of $10,000 in accounts receivable.

Illustration 17-8
Analysis of accounts receivable

Accounts Receivable

1/1/08	Balance	30,000	**Receipts from customers**	**517,000**
	Revenues	**507,000**		
12/31/08	Balance	20,000		

When the Accounts Receivable balance increases, cash receipts are lower than revenue earned under the accrual basis. Therefore, the company deducts from net income the amount of the increase in accounts receivable, to arrive at net cash provided by operating activities.

Increase in Merchandise Inventory. Computer Services Company's Merchandise Inventory balance increased $5,000 (from $10,000 to $15,000) during the period. The change in the Merchandise Inventory account reflects the difference between the amount of inventory purchased and the amount sold. For Computer Services this means that the cost of merchandise purchased exceeded the cost of goods sold by $5,000. As a result, cost of goods sold does not reflect $5,000 of cash payments made for merchandise. The company deducts from net income this inventory increase of $5,000 during the period, to arrive at net cash provided by operating activities (see Illustration 17-9). If inventory decreases, the company adds to net income the amount of the change, to arrive at net cash provided by operating activities.

Increase in Prepaid Expenses. Computer Services' prepaid expenses increased during the period by $4,000. This means that cash paid for expenses is higher than expenses reported on an accrual basis. In other words, the company has made cash payments in the current period, but will not charge expenses to income until future periods (as charges to the income statement). To adjust net income to net cash provided by operating activities, the company deducts from net income the $4,000 increase in prepaid expenses (see Illustration 17-9).

Illustration 17-9
Adjustments for changes in current asset accounts

Cash flows from operating activities		
Net income		$145,000
Adjustments to reconcile net income to net cash provided by operating activities:		
Depreciation expense	$ 9,000	
Loss on sale of equipment	3,000	
Decrease in accounts receivable	**10,000**	
Increase in merchandise inventory	**(5,000)**	
Increase in prepaid expenses	**(4,000)**	13,000
Net cash provided by operating activities		$158,000

If prepaid expenses decrease, reported expenses are higher than the expenses paid. Therefore, the company adds to net income the decrease in prepaid expenses, to arrive at net cash provided by operating activities.

CHANGES IN CURRENT LIABILITIES. The adjustments required for changes in current liability accounts are as follows: **Add to net income increases in current liability accounts, and deduct from net income decreases in current liability accounts, to arrive at net cash provided by operating activities.**

Increase in Accounts Payable. For Computer Services Company, Accounts Payable increased by $16,000 (from $12,000 to $28,000) during the period. That means the company received $16,000 more in goods than it actually paid for. As shown in Illustration 17-10 (below), to adjust net income to determine net cash provided by operating activities, the company adds to net income the $16,000 increase in Accounts Payable.

Decrease in Income Taxes Payable. When a company incurs income tax expense but has not yet paid its taxes, it records income tax payable. A change in the Income Tax Payable account reflects the difference between income tax expense incurred and income tax actually paid. Computer Services' Income Tax Payable account decreased by $2,000. That means the $47,000 of income tax expense reported on the income statement was $2,000 less than the amount of taxes paid during the period of $49,000. As shown in Illustration 17-10, to adjust net income to a cash basis, the company must reduce net income by $2,000.

Illustration 17-10
Adjustments for changes in current liability accounts

Cash flows from operating activities		
Net income		$145,000
Adjustments to reconcile net income to net cash provided by operating activities:		
Depreciation expense	$ 9,000	
Loss on sale of equipment	3,000	
Decrease in accounts receivable	10,000	
Increase in merchandise inventory	(5,000)	
Increase in prepaid expenses	(4,000)	
Increase in accounts payable	**16,000**	
Decrease in income tax payable	**(2,000)**	27,000
Net cash provided by operating activities		$172,000

Illustration 17-10 shows that, after starting with net income of $145,000, the sum of all of the adjustments to net income was $27,000. This resulted in net cash provided by operating activities of $172,000.

Summary of Conversion to Net Cash Provided by Operating Activities—Indirect Method

As shown in the previous illustrations, the statement of cash flows prepared by the indirect method starts with net income. It then adds or deducts items to arrive at net cash provided by operating activities. The required adjustments are of three types:

1. Noncash charges such as depreciation, amortization, and depletion.
2. Gains and losses on the sale of plant assets.
3. Changes in noncash current asset and current liability accounts.

Illustration 17-11 (page 732) provides a summary of these changes.

Illustration 17-11
Adjustments required to convert net income to net cash provided by operating activities

		Adjustment Required to Convert Net Income to Net Cash Provided by Operating Activities
Noncash Charges	Depreciation expense	Add
	Patent amortization expense	Add
	Depletion expense	Add
Gains and Losses	Loss on sale of plant asset	Add
	Gain on sale of plant asset	Deduct
Changes in Current Assets and Current Liabilities	Increase in current asset account	Deduct
	Decrease in current asset account	Add
	Increase in current liability account	Add
	Decrease in current liability account	Deduct

ACCOUNTING ACROSS THE ORGANIZATION

GM Must Sell More Cars

Market share matters—and it shows up in the accounting numbers. Just ask General Motors. In recent years GM has seen its market share erode until, at 25.6% of the market, the company reached the point where it actually consumed more cash than it generated. It isn't time to panic yet—GM has about $20 billion in cash on hand—but it is time to come up with a plan.

To address immediate cash needs, GM management may have to quit paying its $1.1 billion annual dividend, and it may have to sell off some assets and businesses. But in the long term, GM must either increase its market share, or shrink its operations to fit its sales figures. The following table shows net income and cash provided by operating activities at various market-share levels.

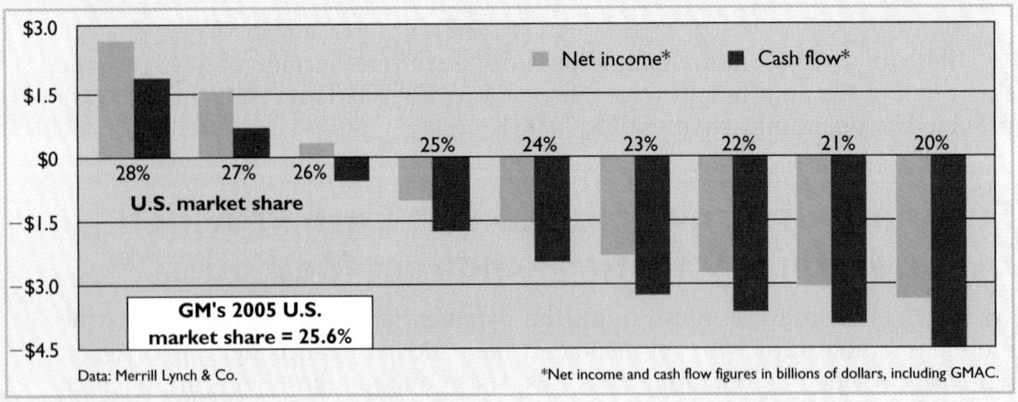

Source: David Welch and Dan Beucke, "Why GM's Plan Won't Work," *Business Week*, May 9, 2005, pp. 85–93.

Why does GM's cash provided by operating activities drop so precipitously when the company's sales figures decline?

Step 2: Investing and Financing Activities

ANALYZE CHANGES IN NONCURRENT ASSET AND LIABILITY ACCOUNTS AND RECORD AS INVESTING AND FINANCING ACTIVITIES, OR AS NONCASH INVESTING AND FINANCING ACTIVITIES

Increase in Land. As indicated from the change in the Land account and the additional information, the company purchased land of $110,000 through the issuance of long-term bonds. The issuance of bonds payable for land has no effect on cash. But it is a significant noncash investing and financing activity that merits disclosure in a separate schedule. (See Illustration 17-13 on page 734.)

HELPFUL HINT
The investing and financing activities are measured and reported in the same way under both the direct and indirect methods.

Increase in Building. As the additional data indicate, Computer Services Company acquired an office building for $120,000 cash. This is a cash outflow reported in the investing section. (See Illustration 17-13 on page 734.)

Increase in Equipment. The Equipment account increased $17,000. The additional information explains that this was a net increase that resulted from two transactions: (1) a purchase of equipment of $25,000, and (2) the sale for $4,000 of equipment costing $8,000. These transactions are investing activities. The company should report each transaction separately. Thus it reports the purchase of equipment as an outflow of cash for $25,000. It reports the sale as an inflow of cash for $4,000. The T account below shows the reasons for the change in this account during the year.

Illustration 17-12
Analysis of equipment

Equipment

1/1/08 Balance	10,000	Cost of equipment sold	8,000
Purchase of equipment	**25,000**		
12/31/08 Balance	27,000		

The following entry shows the details of the equipment sale transaction.

Cash	4,000	
Accumulated Depreciation	1,000	
Loss on Sale of Equipment	3,000	
Equipment		8,000

A	=	L	+	SE
+4,000				
+1,000				
				−3,000 Exp
−8,000				

Cash Flows
+4,000

Increase in Bonds Payable. The Bonds Payable account increased $110,000. As indicated in the additional information, the company acquired land from the issuance of these bonds. It reports this noncash transaction in a separate schedule at the bottom of the statement.

Increase in Common Stock. The balance sheet reports an increase in Common Stock of $20,000. The additional information section notes that this increase resulted from the issuance of new shares of stock. This is a cash inflow reported in the financing section.

HELPFUL HINT
When companies issue stocks or bonds for cash, the actual proceeds will appear in the statement of cash flows as a financing inflow (rather than the par value of the stocks or face value of bonds).

Increase in Retained Earnings. Retained earnings increased $116,000 during the year. This increase can be explained by two factors: (1) Net income of $145,000 increased retained earnings. (2) Dividends of $29,000 decreased retained earnings. The company adjusts net income to net cash provided by operating activities in the operating activities section. Payment of the dividends (not the declaration) is a **cash outflow that the company reports as a financing activity**.

STATEMENT OF CASH FLOWS—2008

Using the previous information, we can now prepare a statement of cash flows for 2008 for Computer Services Company as shown in Illustration 17-13.

Illustration 17-13
Statement of cash flows, 2008—indirect method

HELPFUL HINT
Note that in the investing and financing activities sections, positive numbers indicate cash inflows (receipts), and negative numbers indicate cash outflows (payments).

COMPUTER SERVICES COMPANY
Statement of Cash Flows—Indirect Method
For the Year Ended December 31, 2008

Cash flows from operating activities		
Net income		$145,000
Adjustments to reconcile net income to net cash provided by operating activities:		
Depreciation expense	$ 9,000	
Loss on sale of equipment	3,000	
Decrease in accounts receivable	10,000	
Increase in merchandise inventory	(5,000)	
Increase in prepaid expenses	(4,000)	
Increase in accounts payable	16,000	
Decrease in income tax payable	(2,000)	27,000
Net cash provided by operating activities		172,000
Cash flows from investing activities		
Purchase of building	(120,000)	
Purchase of equipment	(25,000)	
Sale of equipment	4,000	
Net cash used by investing activities		(141,000)
Cash flows from financing activities		
Issuance of common stock	20,000	
Payment of cash dividends	(29,000)	
Net cash used by financing activities		(9,000)
Net increase in cash		22,000
Cash at beginning of period		33,000
Cash at end of period		$ 55,000
Noncash investing and financing activities		
Issuance of bonds payable to purchase land		$110,000

Step 3: Net Change in Cash

COMPARE THE NET CHANGE IN CASH ON THE STATEMENT OF CASH FLOWS WITH THE CHANGE IN THE CASH ACCOUNT REPORTED ON THE BALANCE SHEET TO MAKE SURE THE AMOUNTS AGREE

Illustration 17-13 indicates that the net change in cash during the period was an increase of $22,000. This agrees with the change in Cash account reported on the balance sheet in Illustration 17-4 (page 727).

Before You Go On...

REVIEW IT

1. What is the format of the operating activities section?
2. Where is depreciation expense shown on a statement of cash flows?
3. Where are significant noncash investing and financing activities shown?

DO IT

Use the information on page 735 to prepare a statement of cash flows using the indirect method.

REYNOLDS COMPANY
Comparative Balance Sheets
December 31

Assets	**2008**	**2007**	**Change Increase/Decrease**
Cash	$ 54,000	$ 37,000	$ 17,000 Increase
Accounts receivable	68,000	26,000	42,000 Increase
Inventories	54,000	-0-	54,000 Increase
Prepaid expenses	4,000	6,000	2,000 Decrease
Land	45,000	70,000	25,000 Decrease
Buildings	200,000	200,000	-0-
Accumulated depreciation—buildings	(21,000)	(11,000)	10,000 Increase
Equipment	193,000	68,000	125,000 Increase
Accumulated depreciation—equipment	(28,000)	(10,000)	18,000 Increase
Totals	$569,000	$386,000	
Liabilities and Stockholders' Equity			
Accounts payable	$ 23,000	$ 40,000	$ 17,000 Decrease
Accrued expenses payable	10,000	-0-	10,000 Increase
Bonds payable	110,000	150,000	40,000 Decrease
Common stock ($1 par)	220,000	60,000	160,000 Increase
Retained earnings	206,000	136,000	70,000 Increase
Totals	$569,000	$386,000	

REYNOLDS COMPANY
Income Statement
For the Year Ended December 31, 2008

Revenues		$890,000
Cost of goods sold	$465,000	
Operating expenses	221,000	
Interest expense	12,000	
Loss on sale of equipment	2,000	700,000
Income before income taxes		190,000
Income tax expense		65,000
Net income		$125,000

Additional information:

1. Operating expenses include depreciation expense of $33,000 and charges from prepaid expenses of $2,000.
2. Land was sold at its book value for cash.
3. Cash dividends of $55,000 were declared and paid in 2008.
4. Interest expense of $12,000 was paid in cash.
5. Equipment with a cost of $166,000 was purchased for cash. Equipment with a cost of $41,000 and a book value of $36,000 was sold for $34,000 cash.
6. Bonds of $10,000 were redeemed at their book value for cash. Bonds of $30,000 were converted into common stock.
7. Common stock ($1 par) of $130,000 was issued for cash.
8. Accounts payable pertain to merchandise suppliers.

Action Plan

- Determine net cash provided/used by operating activities by adjusting net income for items that did not affect cash.

- Determine net cash provided/used by investing activities and financing activities.
- Determine the net increase/decrease in cash.

Solution

REYNOLDS COMPANY
Statement of Cash Flows—Indirect Method
For the Year Ended December 31, 2008

Cash flows from operating activities		
Net income		$125,000
Adjustments to reconcile net income to net cash provided by operating activities:		
Depreciation expense	$ 33,000	
Loss on sale of equipment	2,000	
Increase in accounts receivable	(42,000)	
Increase in inventories	(54,000)	
Decrease in prepaid expenses	2,000	
Decrease in accounts payable	(17,000)	
Increase in accrued expenses payable	10,000	(66,000)
Net cash provided by operating activities		59,000
Cash flows from investing activities		
Sale of land	25,000	
Sale of equipment	34,000	
Purchase of equipment	(166,000)	
Net cash used by investing activities		(107,000)
Cash flows from financing activities		
Redemption of bonds	(10,000)	
Sale of common stock	130,000	
Payment of dividends	(55,000)	
Net cash provided by financing activities		65,000
Net increase in cash		17,000
Cash at beginning of period		37,000
Cash at end of period		$ 54,000
Noncash investing and financing activities		
Conversion of bonds into common stock		$ 30,000

Related exercise material: *BE17-4, BE17-5, BE17-6, BE17-7, E17-4, E17-5, and E17-6.*

✓ The Navigator

HELPFUL HINT

1. Determine net cash provided/used by operating activities, recognizing that operating activities generally relate to changes in current assets and current liabilities.
2. Determine net cash provided/used by investing activities, recognizing that investing activities generally relate to changes in noncurrent assets.
3. Determine net cash provided/used by financing activities, recognizing that financing activities generally relate to changes in long-term liabilities and stockholders' equity accounts.

USING CASH FLOWS TO EVALUATE A COMPANY

STUDY OBJECTIVE 4

Analyze the statement of cash flows.

Traditionally, investors and creditors have most commonly used ratios based on accrual accounting. These days, cash-based ratios are gaining increased acceptance among analysts.

Free Cash Flow

In the statement of cash flows, cash provided by operating activities is intended to indicate the cash-generating capability of the company. Analysts have noted, however, that **cash provided by operating activities fails to take into account that a company must invest in new fixed assets** just to maintain its current level of operations. Companies also must at least **maintain dividends at current levels** to satisfy investors. The measurement of free cash flow provides additional insight regarding a company's cash-generating ability. **Free cash flow** describes the cash remaining from operations after adjustment for capital expenditures and dividends.

Consider the following example: Suppose that MPC produced and sold 10,000 personal computers this year. It reported $100,000 cash provided by operating activities. In order to maintain production at 10,000 computers, MPC invested $15,000 in equipment. It chose to pay $5,000 in dividends. Its free cash flow was $80,000 ($100,000 − $15,000 − $5,000). The company could use this $80,000 either to purchase new assets to expand the business or to pay an $80,000 dividend and continue to produce 10,000 computers. In practice, free cash flow is often calculated with the formula in Illustration 17-14. Alternative definitions also exist.

Illustration 17-14
Free cash flow

Free Cash Flow	=	Cash Provided by Operating Activities	−	Capital Expenditures	−	Cash Dividends

Illustration 17-15 provides basic information excerpted from the 2004 statement of cash flows of Microsoft Corporation.

Illustration 17-15
Microsoft cash flow information ($ in millions)

MICROSOFT CORPORATION
Statement of Cash Flows (partial)
2004

Cash provided by operating activities		$14,626
Cash flows from investing activities		
Additions to property and equipment	$ (1,109)	
Purchases of investments	(92,495)	
Sales of investments	85,302	
Acquisitions of companies	(4)	
Maturities of investments	5,561	
Cash used by investing activities		(2,745)
Cash paid for dividends		(1,729)

Microsoft's free cash flow is calculated as shown in Illustration 17-16.

Illustration 17-16
Calculation of Microsoft's free cash flow ($ in millions)

Cash provided by operating activities	$14,626
Less: Expenditures on property, plant, and equipment	1,109
Dividends paid	1,729
Free cash flow	$11,788

This is a tremendous amount of cash generated in a single year. It is available for the acquisition of new assets, the retirement of stock or debt, or the payment of dividends. Also note that this amount far exceeds Microsoft's 2004 net income of $8,168 million. This lends additional credibility to Microsoft's income number as an indicator of potential future performance. If anything, Microsoft's net income might understate its actual performance.

Oracle Corporation is one of the world's largest sellers of database software and information management services. Like Microsoft, its success depends on continuing to improve its existing products while developing new products to keep pace with rapid changes in technology. Oracle's free cash flow for 2004 was $2,988 million. This is impressive, but significantly less than Microsoft's amazing ability to generate cash.

Be sure to read **ALL ABOUT YOU: *Where Does the Money Go?*** on page 738 for information on how topics in this chapter apply to you.

Where Does the Money Go?

When a company's cash flow from operating activities does not cover its cash needs, it must borrow money. In the short term this is OK, but in the long-term it can spell disaster. Sooner or later the company needs to increase its cash from operations or cut back on its expenditures, or it will go broke. Guess what? The same is true for you and me.

Where do you spend your cash? Most of us know how much we spend each month on rent and car payments. But how much do you spend each month on soda, coffee, pizza, video rentals, music downloads, and your cell phone service? Don't think it matters? Suppose you spend an average of only $4 per day on unneeded "incidentals." That's $120 a month, or almost $1,500 per year.

Some Facts

* College students spend about $200 billion per year on consumer products. Of that amount, $41 billion is "discretionary" in nature.
* More than 70% of college students own a cell phone, and 71% own a car.
* College students spend more than $8 billion per year purchasing DVDs, CDs, music downloads, and video games.
* Annual spending on travel by college students is about $4.6 billion.
* 78% of college students work, earning an average of $821 per month.

About the Numbers

College students spend an average of $287 per month on discretionary items (defined as anything other than tuition, room/board, rent, books, and school fees). A large chunk of that—more than $11 billion—is spent on beverages and snack foods. Maybe this would be a good place to start cutting your expenditures.

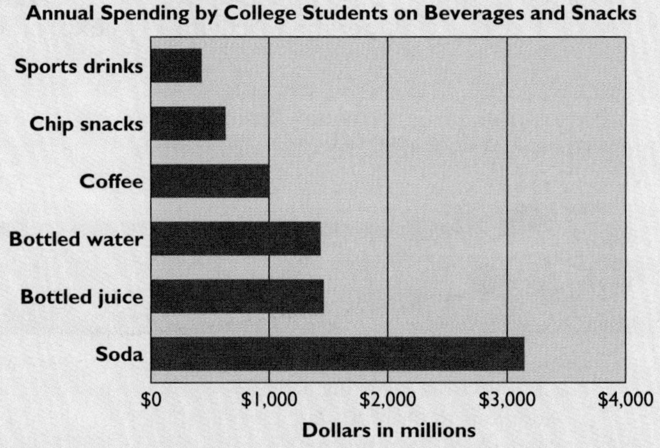

Source: "College Students Spend $200 Billion per Year," HarrisInteractive, *www.harrisinteractive.com/news/allnewsbydate.asp?NewsID=480* (accessed May 2006).

What Do You Think?

Let's say that you live on campus and own a car. You use the car for pleasure and to drive to a job that is three miles away. Suppose your annual cash flow statement includes the following items.

Cash inflows:	
Wages	$ 9,000
Student loans	5,000
Credit card debt	4,000
Cash outflows:	
Tuition, books, room, and board	13,000
Vehicle costs	2,000
Vacation	2,000
Cell phone service	500
Snacks and beverages	500

Should you get rid of your car and cell phone, quit eating snacks, and give up the idea of a vacation?

YES: At this rate you will accumulate nearly $40,000 in debts by the time you graduate. It is not fun to spend most of the paycheck of your post-graduation job paying off the debts you accumulated while in school.

NO: Give me a break. A person has to have some fun. Life wouldn't be worth living if I couldn't be drinking a Starbucks while cruising down the road talking on my cell phone.

Sources: Becky Ebenkamp, "College Communications 101," *Brandweek*, August 22-29, 2005, p. 16.

The authors' comments on this situation appear on page 777.

Before You Go On...

REVIEW IT

1. What is the difference between cash from operations and free cash flow?
2. What does it mean if a company has negative free cash flow?

The Navigator

Demonstration Problem 1

WILEY PLUS

The income statement for the year ended December 31, 2008, for John Kosinski Manufacturing Company contains the following condensed information.

JOHN KOSINSKI MANUFACTURING COMPANY
Income Statement

Revenues		$6,583,000
Operating expenses (excluding depreciation)	$4,920,000	
Depreciation expense	880,000	5,800,000
Income before income taxes		783,000
Income tax expense		353,000
Net income		$ 430,000

Included in operating expenses is a $24,000 loss resulting from the sale of machinery for $270,000 cash. Machinery was purchased at a cost of $750,000.

The following balances are reported on Kosinski's comparative balance sheets at December 31.

JOHN KOSINSKI MANUFACTURING COMPANY
Comparative, Balance Sheets (partial)

	2008	2007
Cash	$672,000	$130,000
Accounts receivable	775,000	610,000
Inventories	834,000	867,000
Accounts payable	521,000	501,000

Income tax expense of $353,000 represents the amount paid in 2008. Dividends declared and paid in 2008 totaled $200,000.

Instructions

Prepare the statement of cash flows using the indirect method.

Solution to Demonstration Problem 1

JOHN KOSINSKI MANUFACTURING COMPANY
Statement of Cash Flows—Indirect Method
For the Year Ended December 31, 2008

Cash flows from operating activities		
Net income		$ 430,000
Adjustments to reconcile net income to net cash provided by operating activities:		
Depreciation expense	$ 880,000	
Loss on sale of machinery	24,000	
Increase in accounts receivable	(165,000)	
Decrease in inventories	33,000	
Increase in accounts payable	20,000	792,000
Net cash provided by operating activities		1,222,000

action plan

- ✓ Determine net cash from operating activities. Operating activities generally relate to changes in current assets and current liabilities.
- ✓ Determine net cash from investing activities. Investing activities generally relate to changes in noncurrent assets.
- ✓ Determine net cash from financing activities. Financing activities generally relate to changes in long-term liabilities and stockholders' equity accounts.

Cash flows from investing activities		
Sale of machinery	270,000	
Purchase of machinery	(750,000)	
Net cash used by investing activities		(480,000)
Cash flows from financing activities		
Payment of cash dividends		(200,000)
Net increase in cash		542,000
Cash at beginning of period		130,000
Cash at end of period		$ 672,000

The Navigator

SUMMARY OF STUDY OBJECTIVES

WILEY PLUS

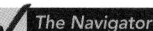

1 **Indicate the usefulness of the statement of cash flows.** The statement of cash flows provides information about the cash receipts, cash payments, and net change in cash resulting from the operating, investing, and financing activities of a company during the period.

2 **Distinguish among operating, investing, and financing activities.** Operating activities include the cash effects of transactions that enter into the determination of net income. Investing activities involve cash flows resulting from changes in investments and long-term asset items. Financing activities involve cash flows resulting from changes in long-term liability and stockholders' equity items.

3 **Prepare a statement of cash flows using the indirect method.** The preparation of a statement of cash flows involves three major steps: (1) Determine net cash provided/used by operating activities by converting net income from an accrual basis to a cash basis. (2) Analyze changes in noncurrent asset and liability accounts and record as investing and financing activities, or disclose as noncash transactions. (3) Compare the net change in cash on the statement of cash flows with the change in the cash account reported on the balance sheet to make sure the amounts agree.

4 **Analyze the statement of cash flows.** Free cash flow indicates the amount of cash a company generated during the current year that is available for the payment of additional dividends or for expansion.

The Navigator

GLOSSARY

WILEY PLUS

Direct method A method of determining net cash provided by operating activities by adjusting each item in the income statement from the accrual basis to the cash basis. (p. 726)

Financing activities Cash flow activities that include (a) obtaining cash from issuing debt and repaying the amounts borrowed and (b) obtaining cash from stockholders, repurchasing shares, and paying dividends. (p. 721).

Free cash flow Cash provided by operating activities adjusted for capital expenditures and dividends paid. (p. 737).

Indirect method A method of preparing a statement of cash flows in which net income is adjusted for items that do not affect cash, to determine net cash provided by operating activities. (pp. 725, 728).

Investing activities Cash flow activities that include (a) purchasing and disposing of investments and property, plant, and equipment using cash and (b) lending money and collecting the loans. (p. 721).

Operating activities Cash flow activities that include the cash effects of transactions that create revenues and expenses and thus enter into the determination of net income. (p. 721).

Statement of cash flows A basic financial statement that provides information about the cash receipts, cash payments, and net change in cash during a period, resulting from operating, investing, and financing activities. (p. 720).

APPENDIX 17A Using a Worksheet to Prepare the Statement of Cash Flows—Indirect Method

STUDY OBJECTIVE 5

Explain how to use a worksheet to prepare the statement of cash flows using the indirect method.

When preparing a statement of cash flows, companies may need to make numerous adjustments of net income. In such cases, they often use **a worksheet to assemble and classify the data that will appear on the statement**. The worksheet is merely an aid in preparing the statement. Its use is optional. Illustration 17A-1 shows the skeleton format of the worksheet for preparation of the statement of cash flows.

Illustration 17A-1
Format of worksheet

XYZ Company.xls

File Edit View Insert Format Tools Data Window Help

	A	B	C	D	E
1					
2	**XYZ COMPANY**				
3	**Worksheet**				
4	**Statement of Cash Flows For the Year Ended . . .**				
5					
6		**End of**			**End of**
7		**Last Year**	**Reconciling Items**		**Current Year**
8	**Balance Sheet Accounts**	**Balances**	**Debit**	**Credit**	**Balances**
9	Debit balance accounts	XX	XX	XX	XX
10		XX	XX	XX	XX
11	Totals	XXX			XXX
12	Credit balance accounts	XX	XX	XX	XX
13		XX	XX	XX	XX
14	Totals	XXX			XXX
15	**Statement of Cash**				
16	**Flows Effects**				
17	Operating activities				
18	Net income		XX		
19	Adjustments to net income		XX	XX	
20	Investing activities				
21	Receipts and payments		XX	XX	
22	Financing activities				
23	Receipts and payments		XX	XX	
24	Totals		XXX	XXX	
25	Increase (decrease) in cash		(XX)	XX	
26	Totals		XXX	XXX	
27					

The following guidelines are important in preparing a worksheet.

1. In the balance sheet accounts section, **list accounts with debit balances separately from those with credit balances**. This means, for example, that Accumulated Depreciation appears under credit balances and not as a contra account under debit balances. Enter the beginning and ending balances of each account in the appropriate columns. Enter as reconciling items in the two middle columns the transactions that caused the change in the account balance during the year.

   After all reconciling items have been entered, each line pertaining to a balance sheet account should "foot across." That is, the beginning balance plus or minus the reconciling item(s) must equal the ending balance. When this agreement exists for all balance sheet accounts, all changes in account balances have been reconciled.

2. The bottom portion of the worksheet consists of the operating, investing, and financing activities sections. It provides the information necessary to prepare the formal statement of cash flows. **Enter inflows of cash as debits in the reconciling columns. Enter outflows of cash as credits in the reconciling columns.** Thus, in this section, the sale of equipment for cash at book value appears as a debit under investing activities. Similarly, the purchase of land for cash appears as a credit under investing activities.
3. **The reconciling items shown in the worksheet are not entered in any journal or posted to any account.** They do not represent either adjustments or corrections of the balance sheet accounts. They are used only to facilitate the preparation of the statement of cash flows.

Preparing the Worksheet

As in the case of worksheets illustrated in earlier chapters, preparing a worksheet involves a series of prescribed steps. The steps in this case are:

1. Enter in the balance sheet accounts section the balance sheet accounts and their beginning and ending balances.
2. Enter in the reconciling columns of the worksheet the data that explain the changes in the balance sheet accounts other than cash and their effects on the statement of cash flows.
3. Enter on the cash line and at the bottom of the worksheet the increase or decrease in cash. This entry should enable the totals of the reconciling columns to be in agreement.

To illustrate the preparation of a worksheet, we will use the 2008 data for Computer Services Company. Your familiarity with these data (from the chapter) should help you understand the use of a worksheet. For ease of reference, the comparative balance sheets, income statement, and selected data for 2008 are presented in Illustration 17A-2 (on page 743).

DETERMINING THE RECONCILING ITEMS

Companies can use one of several approaches to determine the reconciling items. For example, they can first complete the changes affecting net cash provided by operating activities, and then can determine the effects of financing and investing transactions. Or, they can analyze the balance sheet accounts in the order in which they are listed on the worksheet. We will follow this latter approach for Computer Services, except for cash. As indicated in step 3, **cash is handled last**.

Accounts Receivable The decrease of $10,000 in accounts receivable means that cash collections from revenues are higher than the revenues reported in the income statement. To convert net income to net cash provided by operating activities, we add the decrease of $10,000 to net income. The entry in the reconciling columns of the worksheet is:

(a)	Operating—Decrease in Accounts Receivable	10,000	
	Accounts Receivable		10,000

Merchandise Inventory Computer Services Company's Merchandise Inventory balance increases $5,000 during the period. The Merchandise Inventory account reflects the difference between the amount of inventory that the company purchased and the amount that it sold. For Computer Services this means that the cost of merchandise purchased exceeds the cost of goods sold by $5,000. As a

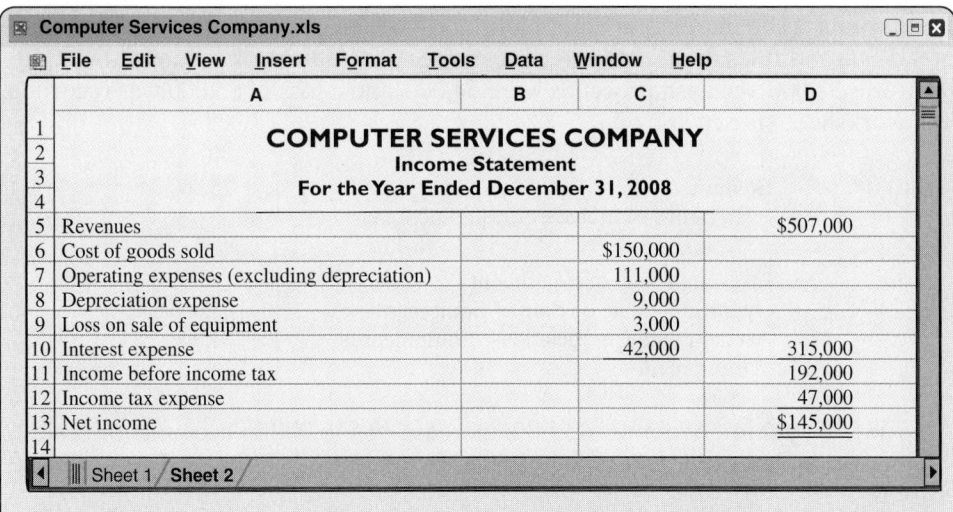

Illustration 17A-2
Comparative balance sheets, income statement, and additional information for Computer Services Company

Computer Services Company.xls

File Edit View Insert Format Tools Data Window Help

COMPUTER SERVICES COMPANY
Comparative Balance Sheets
December 31

Assets	2008	2007	Change in Account Balance Increase/Decrease
Current assets			
Cash	$ 55,000	$ 33,000	$ 22,000 Increase
Accounts receivable	20,000	30,000	10,000 Decrease
Merchandise inventory	15,000	10,000	5,000 Increase
Prepaid expenses	5,000	1,000	4,000 Increase
Property, plant, and equipment			
Land	130,000	20,000	110,000 Increase
Building	160,000	40,000	120,000 Increase
Accumulated depreciation—building	(11,000)	(5,000)	6,000 Increase
Equipment	27,000	10,000	17,000 Increase
Accumulated depreciation—equipment	(3,000)	(1,000)	2,000 Increase
Total	$398,000	$138,000	
Liabilities and Stockholders' Equity			
Current liabilities			
Accounts payable	$ 28,000	$ 12,000	$ 16,000 Increase
Income tax payable	6,000	8,000	2,000 Decrease
Long-term liabilities			
Bonds payable	130,000	20,000	110,000 Increase
Stockholders' equity			
Common stock	70,000	50,000	20,000 Increase
Retained earnings	164,000	48,000	116,000 Increase
Total liabilities and stockholders' equity	$398,000	$138,000	

Sheet 1 / Sheet 2

Computer Services Company.xls

File Edit View Insert Format Tools Data Window Help

COMPUTER SERVICES COMPANY
Income Statement
For the Year Ended December 31, 2008

Revenues			$507,000
Cost of goods sold		$150,000	
Operating expenses (excluding depreciation)		111,000	
Depreciation expense		9,000	
Loss on sale of equipment		3,000	
Interest expense		42,000	315,000
Income before income tax			192,000
Income tax expense			47,000
Net income			$145,000

Sheet 1 / Sheet 2

Additional information for 2008:

1. The company declared and paid a $29,000 cash dividend.
2. Issued $110,000 of long-term bonds in direct exchange for land.
3. A building costing $120,000 was purchased for cash. Equipment costing $25,000 was also purchased for cash.
4. The company sold equipment with a book value of $7,000 (cost $8,000, less accumulated depreciation $1,000) for $4,000 cash.
5. Issued common stock for $20,000 cash.
6. Depreciation expense was comprised of $6,000 for building and $3,000 for equipment.

result, cost of goods sold does not reflect $5,000 of cash payments made for merchandise. We deduct this inventory increase of $5,000 during the period from net income to arrive at net cash provided by operating activities. The worksheet entry is:

(b)	Merchandise Inventory	5,000	
	Operating—Increase in Merchandise Inventory		5,000

Prepaid Expenses An increase of $4,000 in prepaid expenses means that expenses deducted in determining net income are less than expenses that were paid in cash. We deduct the increase of $4,000 from net income in determining net cash provided by operating activities. The worksheet entry is:

(c)	Prepaid Expenses	4,000	
	Operating—Increase in Prepaid Expenses		4,000

HELPFUL HINT
These amounts are asterisked in the worksheet to indicate that they result from a significant noncash transaction.

Land The increase in land of $110,000 resulted from a purchase through the issuance of long-term bonds. The company should report this transaction as a significant noncash investing and financing activity. The worksheet entry is:

(d)	Land	110,000	
	Bonds Payable		110,000

Building The cash purchase of a building for $120,000 is an investing activity cash outflow. The entry in the reconciling columns of the worksheet is:

(e)	Building	120,000	
	Investing—Purchase of Building		120,000

Equipment The increase in equipment of $17,000 resulted from a cash purchase of $25,000 and the sale of equipment costing $8,000. The book value of the equipment was $7,000, the cash proceeds were $4,000, and a loss of $3,000 was recorded. The worksheet entries are:

(f)	Equipment	25,000	
	Investing—Purchase of Equipment		25,000
(g)	Investing—Sale of Equipment	4,000	
	Operating—Loss on Sale of Equipment	3,000	
	Accumulated Depreciation—Equipment	1,000	
	Equipment		8,000

Accounts Payable We must add the increase of $16,000 in accounts payable to net income to determine net cash provided by operating activities. The worksheet entry is:

(h)	Operating—Increase in Accounts Payable	16,000	
	Accounts Payable		16,000

Income Taxes Payable When a company incurs income tax expense but has not yet paid its taxes, it records income tax payable. A change in the Income Tax Payable account reflects the difference between income tax expense incurred and income tax actually paid. Computer Services' Income Tax Payable account decreases by $2,000. That means the $47,000 of income tax expense reported on the income statement was $2,000 less than the amount of taxes paid during the period of $49,000. To adjust net income to a cash basis, we must reduce net income by $2,000. The worksheet entry is:

(i)	Income Taxes Payable	2,000	
	Operating—Decrease in Income Taxes Payable		2,000

Bonds Payable The increase of $110,000 in this account resulted from the issuance of bonds for land. This is a significant noncash investing and financing activity. Worksheet entry (d) above is the only entry necessary.

Common Stock The balance sheet reports an increase in Common Stock of $20,000. The additional information section notes that this increase resulted from the issuance of new shares of stock. This is a cash inflow reported in the financing section. The worksheet entry is:

(j)	Financing—Issuance of Common Stock	20,000	
	Common Stock		20,000

Accumulated Depreciation—Building, and Accumulated Depreciation—Equipment Increases in these accounts of $6,000 and $3,000, respectively, resulted from depreciation expense. Depreciation expense is a **noncash charge that we must add to net income** to determine net cash provided by operating activities. The worksheet entries are:

(k)	Operating—Depreciation Expense—Building	6,000	
	Accumulated Depreciation—Building		6,000
(l)	Operating—Depreciation Expense—Equipment	3,000	
	Accumulated Depreciation—Equipment		3,000

Retained Earnings The $116,000 increase in retained earnings resulted from net income of $145,000 and the declaration and payment of a $29,000 cash dividend. Net income is included in net cash provided by operating activities, and the dividends are a financing activity cash outflow. The entries in the reconciling columns of the worksheet are:

(m)	Operating—Net Income	145,000	
	Retained Earnings		145,000
(n)	Retained Earnings	29,000	
	Financing—Payment of Dividends		29,000

Disposition of Change in Cash The firm's cash increased $22,000 in 2008. The final entry on the worksheet, therefore, is:

(o)	Cash	22,000	
	Increase in Cash		22,000

As shown in the worksheet, we enter the increase in cash in the reconciling credit column as a **balancing** amount. This entry should complete the reconciliation of the changes in the balance sheet accounts. Also, it should permit the totals of the reconciling columns to be in agreement. When all changes have been explained and the reconciling columns are in agreement, the reconciling columns are ruled to complete the worksheet. The completed worksheet for Computer Services Company is shown in Illustration 17A-3 (page 746).

Illustration 17A-3
Completed worksheet—indirect method

Computer Services Company.xls

File Edit View Insert Format Tools Data Window Help

	A	B	C	D	E
1	**COMPUTER SERVICES COMPANY**				
2	**Worksheet**				
3	**Statement of Cash Flows For the Year Ended December 31, 2008**				
4					
5		**Balance**	**Reconciling Items**		**Balance**
6	**Balance Sheet Accounts**	**12/31/07**	**Debit**	**Credit**	**12/31/08**
7	Debits				
8	Cash	33,000	(o) 22,000		55,000
9	Accounts Receivable	30,000		(a) 10,000	20,000
10	Merchandise Inventory	10,000	(b) 5,000		15,000
11	Prepaid Expenses	1,000	(c) 4,000		5,000
12	Land	20,000	(d) 110,000*		130,000
13	Building	40,000	(e) 120,000		160,000
14	Equipment	10,000	(f) 25,000	(g) 8,000	27,000
15	Total	144,000			412,000
16	Credits				
17	Accounts Payable	12,000		(h) 16,000	28,000
18	Income Taxes Payable	8,000	(i) 2,000		6,000
19	Bonds Payable	20,000		(d) 110,000*	130,000
20	Accumulated Depreciation—Building	5,000		(k) 6,000	11,000
21	Accumulated Depreciation—Equipment	1,000	(g) 1,000	(l) 3,000	3,000
22	Common Stock	50,000		(j) 20,000	70,000
23	Retained Earnings	48,000	(n) 29,000	(m) 145,000	164,000
24	Total	144,000			412,000
25	**Statement of Cash Flows Effects**				
26	Operating activities				
27	Net income		(m) 145,000		
28	Decrease in accounts receivable		(a) 10,000		
29	Increase in merchandise inventory			(b) 5,000	
30	Increase in prepaid expenses			(c) 4,000	
31	Increase in accounts payable		(h) 16,000		
32	Decrease in income taxes payable			(i) 2,000	
33	Depreciation expense—building		(k) 6,000		
34	Depreciation expense—equipment		(l) 3,000		
35	Loss on sale of equipment		(g) 3,000		
36	Investing activities				
37	Purchase of building			(e) 120,000	
38	Purchase of equipment			(f) 25,000	
39	Sale of equipment		(g) 4,000		
40	Financing activities				
41	Issuance of common stock		(j) 20,000		
42	Payment of dividends			(n) 29,000	
43	Totals		525,000	503,000	
44	Increase in cash			(o) 22,000	
45	Totals		525,000	525,000	
46					

* Significant noncash investing and financing activity.

SUMMARY OF STUDY OBJECTIVE FOR APPENDIX 17A

5 **Explain how to use a worksheet to prepare the statement of cash flows using the indirect method.** When there are numerous adjustments, a worksheet can be a helpful tool in preparing the statement of cash flows. Key guidelines for using a worksheet are: (1) List accounts with debit balances separately from those with credit balances. (2) In the reconciling columns in the bottom portion of the worksheet, show cash inflows as debits and cash outflows as credits. (3) Do not enter reconciling items in any journal or account, but use them only to help prepare the statement of cash flows.

The steps in preparing the worksheet are: (1) Enter beginning and ending balances of balance sheet accounts. (2) Enter debits and credits in reconciling columns. (3) Enter the increase or decrease in cash in two places as a balancing amount.

APPENDIX 17B Statement of Cash Flows—Direct Method

To explain and illustrate the direct method, we will use the transactions of Juarez Company for 2008, to prepare a statement of cash flows. Illustration 17B-1 presents information related to 2008 for Juarez Company.

STUDY OBJECTIVE 6

Prepare a statement of cash flows using the direct method.

Illustration 17B-1
Comparative balance sheets, income statement, and additional information for Juarez Company

JUAREZ COMPANY
Comparative Balance Sheets
December 31

Assets	2008	2007	Change Increase/Decrease
Cash	$191,000	$159,000	$ 32,000 Increase
Accounts receivable	12,000	15,000	3,000 Decrease
Inventory	170,000	160,000	10,000 Increase
Prepaid expenses	6,000	8,000	2,000 Decrease
Land	140,000	80,000	60,000 Increase
Equipment	160,000	-0-	160,000 Increase
Accumulated depreciation—equipment	(16,000)	-0-	16,000 Increase
Total	$663,000	$422,000	
Liabilities and Stockholders' Equity			
Accounts payable	$ 52,000	$ 60,000	$ 8,000 Decrease
Accrued expenses payable	15,000	20,000	5,000 Decrease
Income taxes payable	12,000	-0-	12,000 Increase
Bonds payable	130,000	-0-	130,000 Increase
Common stock	360,000	300,000	60,000 Increase
Retained earnings	94,000	42,000	52,000 Increase
Total	$663,000	$422,000	

JUAREZ COMPANY
Income Statement
For the Year Ended December 31, 2008

Revenues		$975,000
Cost of goods sold	$660,000	
Operating expenses (excluding depreciation)	176,000	
Depreciation expense	18,000	
Loss on sale of store equipment	1,000	855,000
Income before income taxes		120,000
Income tax expense		36,000
Net income		$ 84,000

Additional information:

1. In 2008, the company declared and paid a $32,000 cash dividend.
2. Bonds were issued at face value for $130,000 in cash.
3. Equipment costing $180,000 was purchased for cash.
4. Equipment costing $20,000 was sold for $17,000 cash when the book value of the equipment was $18,000.
5. Common stock of $60,000 was issued to acquire land.

Preparing the Statement of Cash Flows—Direct Method

To prepare a statement of cash flows under the direct approach, we will apply the three steps outlined in Illustration 17-3 (page 725).

STEP 1: OPERATING ACTIVITIES

DETERMINE NET CASH PROVIDED/USED BY OPERATING ACTIVITIES BY CONVERTING NET INCOME FROM AN ACCRUAL BASIS TO A CASH BASIS

Under the **direct method**, companies compute net cash provided by operating activities by **adjusting each item in the income statement** from the accrual basis to the cash basis. To simplify and condense the operating activities section, companies **report only major classes of operating cash receipts and cash payments**. For these major classes, the difference between cash receipts and cash payments is the net cash provided by operating activities. These relationships are as shown in Illustration 17B-2.

Illustration 17B-2
Major classes of cash receipts and payments

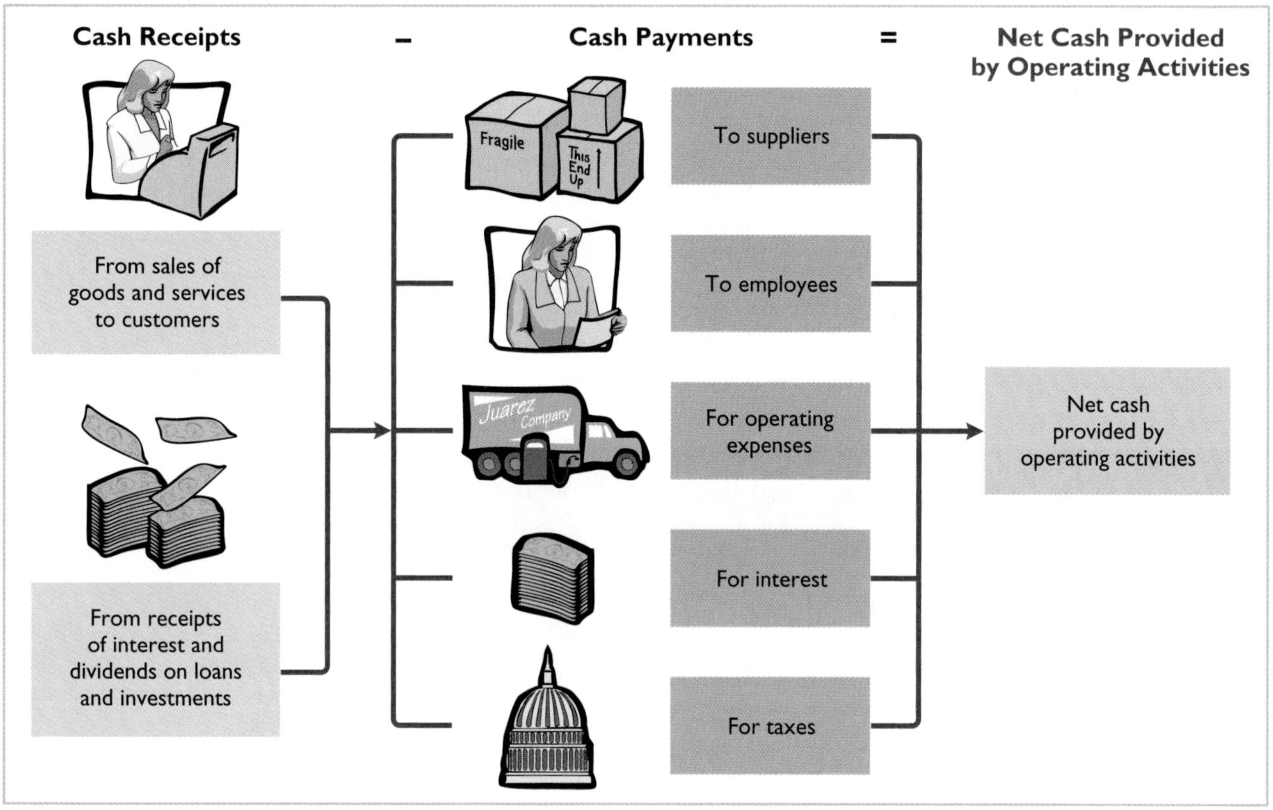

An efficient way to apply the direct method is to analyze the items reported in the income statement in the order in which they are listed. We then determine cash receipts and cash payments related to these revenues and expenses. The following pages present the adjustments required to prepare a statement of cash flows for Juarez Company using the direct approach.

Cash Receipts From Customers. The income statement for Juarez Company reported revenues from customers of $975,000. How much of that was cash receipts? To answer that, companies need to consider the change in accounts receivable during the year. When accounts receivable increase during the year, revenues on an accrual basis are higher than cash receipts from customers. Operations led to revenues, but not all of these revenues resulted in cash receipts.

To determine the amount of cash receipts, the company deducts from sales revenues the increase in accounts receivable. On the other hand, there may be a decrease in accounts receivable. That would occur if cash receipts from customers exceeded sales revenues. In that case, the company adds to sales revenues the decrease in accounts receivable.

For Juarez Company, accounts receivable decreased $3,000. Thus, cash receipts from customers were $978,000, computed as shown in Illustration 17B-3.

Revenues from sales	$ 975,000
Add: Decrease in accounts receivable	3,000
Cash receipts from customers	**$ 978,000**

Illustration 17B-3
Computation of cash receipts from customers

Juarez can also determine cash receipts from customers from an analysis of the Accounts Receivable account, as shown in Illustration 17B-4.

Accounts Receivable

1/1/08	Balance	15,000	**Receipts from customers**	**978,000**
	Revenues from sales	975,000		
12/31/08	Balance	12,000		

Illustration 17B-4
Analysis of accounts receivable

HELPFUL HINT
The T account shows that revenue plus decrease in receivables equals cash receipts.

Illustration 17B-5 shows the relationships among cash receipts from customers, revenues from sales, and changes in accounts receivable.

Cash Receipts from Customers	=	Revenues from Sales	+ Decrease in Accounts Receivable or − Increase in Accounts Receivable

Illustration 17B-5
Formula to compute cash receipts from customers—direct method

Cash Payments to Suppliers. Juarez Company reported cost of goods sold of $660,000 on its income statement. How much of that was cash payments to suppliers? To answer that, it is first necessary to find purchases for the year. To find purchases, companies adjust cost of goods sold for the change in inventory. When inventory increases during the year, purchases for the year have exceeded cost of goods sold. As a result, to determine the amount of purchases, the company adds to cost of goods sold the increase in inventory.

In 2008, Juarez Company's inventory increased $10,000. It computes purchases as follows.

Cost of goods sold	$660,000
Add: Increase in inventory	10,000
Purchases	**$670,000**

Illustration 17B-6
Computation of purchases

After computing purchases, a company can determine cash payments to suppliers. This is done by adjusting purchases for the change in accounts payable.

When accounts payable increase during the year, purchases on an accrual basis are higher than they are on a cash basis. As a result, to determine cash payments to suppliers, a company deducts from purchases the increase in accounts payable. On the other hand, if cash payments to suppliers exceed purchases, there will be a decrease in accounts payable. In that case, a company adds to purchases the decrease in accounts payable.

For Juarez Company, cash payments to suppliers were $678,000, computed as follows.

Illustration 17B-7
Computation of cash payments to suppliers

Purchases	$670,000
Add: Decrease in accounts payable	8,000
Cash payments to suppliers	**$678,000**

Juarez also can determine cash payments to suppliers from an analysis of the Accounts Payable account, as shown in Illustration 17B-8.

Illustration 17B-8
Analysis of accounts payable

Accounts Payable

Payments to suppliers	**678,000**	1/1/08	Balance	60,000
			Purchases	670,000
		12/31/08	Balance	52,000

HELPFUL HINT
The T account shows that purchases plus decrease in accounts payable equals payments to suppliers.

Illustration 17B-9 shows the relationships among cash payments to suppliers, cost of goods sold, changes in inventory, and changes in accounts payable.

Illustration 17B-9
Formula to compute cash payments to suppliers—direct method

$$\text{Cash Payments to Suppliers} = \text{Cost of Goods Sold} \begin{cases} + \text{ Increase in Inventory} \\ \text{or} \\ - \text{ Decrease in Inventory} \end{cases} \begin{cases} + \text{ Decrease in Accounts Payable} \\ \text{or} \\ - \text{ Increase in Accounts Payable} \end{cases}$$

Cash Payments for Operating Expenses. Juarez reported on its income statement operating expenses of $176,000. How much of that amount was cash paid for operating expenses? To answer that, we need to adjust this amount for any changes in prepaid expenses and accrued expenses payable. For example, if prepaid expenses increased during the year, cash paid for operating expenses is higher than operating expenses reported on the income statement. To convert operating expenses to cash payments for operating expenses, a company adds the increase to operating expenses. On the other hand, if prepaid expenses decrease during the year, it deducts the decrease from operating expenses.

Companies must also adjust operating expenses for changes in accrued expenses payable. When accrued expenses payable increase during the year, operating expenses on an accrual basis are higher than they are in a cash basis. As a result, to determine cash payments for operating expenses, a company deducts from operating expenses an increase in accrued expenses payable. On the other hand, a company adds to operating expenses a decrease in accrued expenses payable because cash payments exceed operating expenses.

Juarez Company's cash payments for operating expenses were $179,000, computed as follows.

Operating expenses	$176,000
Deduct: Decrease in prepaid expenses	(2,000)
Add: Decrease in accrued expenses payable	5,000
Cash payments for operating expenses	**$179,000**

Illustration 17B-10
Computation of cash payments for operating expenses

Illustration 17B-11 shows the relationships among cash payments for operating expenses, changes in prepaid expenses, and changes in accrued expenses payable.

Cash Payments for Operating Expenses = **Operating Expenses** { **+ Increase in Prepaid Expense** or **− Decrease in Prepaid Expense** } { **+ Decrease in Accrued Expenses Payable** or **− Increase in Accrued Expenses Payable** }

Illustration 17B-11
Formula to compute cash payments for operating expenses—direct method

Depreciation Expense and Loss on Sale of Equipment. Companies show operating expenses exclusive of depreciation. Juarez's depreciation expense in 2008 was $18,000. Depreciation expense is not shown on a statement of cash flows because it is a noncash charge. If the amount for operating expenses includes depreciation expense, the company must reduce operating expenses by the amount of depreciation to determine cash payments for operating expenses.

The loss on sale of equipment of $1,000 is also a noncash charge. The loss on sale of equipment reduces net income, but it does not reduce cash. Thus, companies do not report on a statement of cash flows the loss on sale of equipment.

Other charges to expense that do not require the use of cash, such as the amortization of intangible assets, depletion expense, and bad debt expense, are treated in the same manner as depreciation.

Cash Payments For Income Taxes. Juarez reported income tax expense of $36,000 on the income statement. Income taxes payable, however, increased $12,000. This increase means that the company has not yet paid $12,000 of the income taxes. As a result, income taxes paid were less than income taxes reported in the income statement. Cash payments for income taxes were, therefore, $24,000 as shown below.

Income tax expense	$36,000
Deduct: Increase in income taxes payable	12,000
Cash payments for income taxes	**$24,000**

Illustration 17B-12
Computation of cash payments for income taxes

Illustration 17B-13 shows the relationships among cash payments for income taxes, income tax expense, and changes in income taxes payable.

Cash Payments for Income Taxes = **Income Tax Expense** { **+ Decrease in Income Taxes Payable** or **− Increase in Income Taxes Payable** }

Illustration 17B-13
Formula to compute cash payments for income taxes—direct method

The operating activities section of the statement of cash flows of Juarez Company is shown in Illustration 17B-14.

Illustration 17B-14
Operating activities section of the statement of cash flows

Cash flows from operating activities		
Cash receipts from customers		$978,000
Less: Cash payments:		
To suppliers	$678,000	
For operating expenses	179,000	
For income taxes	24,000	881,000
Net cash provided by operating activities		$ 97,000

When a company uses the direct method, it must also provide in a **separate schedule** (not shown here) the net cash flows from operating activities as computed under the indirect method.

STEP 2: INVESTING AND FINANCING ACTIVITIES

ANALYZE CHANGES IN NONCURRENT ASSET AND LIABILITY ACCOUNTS AND RECORD AS INVESTING AND FINANCING ACTIVITIES, OR AS SIGNIFICANT NONCASH TRANSACTIONS

Increase in Land. Juarez's land increased $60,000. The additional information section indicates that the company issued common stock to purchase the land. The issuance of common stock for land has no effect on cash. But it is a **significant noncash investing and financing transaction**. This transaction requires disclosure in a separate schedule at the bottom of the statement of cash flows.

Increase in Equipment. The comparative balance sheets show that equipment increased $160,000 in 2008. The additional information in Illustration 17B-1 indicated that the increase resulted from two investing transactions: (1) Juarez purchased for cash equipment costing $180,000. And (2) it sold for $17,000 cash equipment costing $20,000, whose book value was $18,000. The relevant data for the statement of cash flows is the cash paid for the purchase and the cash proceeds from the sale. For Juarez Company, the investing activities section will show the following: The $180,000 purchase of equipment as an outflow of cash, and the $17,000 sale of equipment as an inflow of cash. The company **should not net** the two amounts. **Both individual outflows and inflows of cash should be shown.**

The analysis of the changes in equipment should include the related Accumulated Depreciation account. These two accounts for Juarez Company are shown in Illustration 17B-15.

Illustration 17B-15
Analysis of equipment and related accumulated depreciation

Equipment

1/1/08	Balance	–0–	Cost of equipment sold	20,000
	Cash purchase	**180,000**		
12/31/08	Balance	160,000		

Accumulated Depreciation—Equipment

Sale of equipment	2,000	1/1/08	Balance	–0–
			Depreciation expense	18,000
		12/31/08	Balance	16,000

Increase in Bonds Payable. Bonds Payable increased $130,000. The additional information in Illustration 17B-1 indicated that Juarez issued, for $130,000 cash, bonds with a face value of $130,000. The issuance of bonds is a financing activity. For Juarez Company, there is an inflow of cash of $130,000 from the issuance of bonds.

Increase in Common Stock. The Common Stock account increased $60,000. The additional information indicated that Juarez acquired land from the issuance of common stock. This transaction is a **significant noncash investing and financing transaction** which the company should report separately at the bottom of the statement.

Increase in Retained Earnings. The $52,000 net increase in Retained Earnings resulted from net income of $84,000 and the declaration and payment of a cash dividend of $32,000. Companies **do not report net income in the statement of cash flows under the direct method.** Cash dividends paid of $32,000 are reported in the financing activities section as an outflow of cash.

Statement of Cash Flows—2008 Illustration 17B-16 shows the statement of cash flows for Juarez.

Illustration 17B-16
Statement of cash flows, 2008—direct method

JUAREZ COMPANY
Statement of Cash Flows—Direct Method
For the Year Ended December 31, 2008

Cash flows from operating activities		
Cash receipts from customers		$ 978,000
Less: Cash payments:		
To suppliers	$ 678,000	
For operating expenses	179,000	
For income taxes	24,000	881,000
Net cash provided by operating activities		97,000
Cash flows from investing activities		
Purchase of equipment	(180,000)	
Sale of equipment	17,000	
Net cash used by investing activities		(163,000)
Cash flows from financing activities		
Issuance of bonds payable	130,000	
Payment of cash dividends	(32,000)	
Net cash provided by financing activities		98,000
Net increase in cash		32,000
Cash at beginning of period		159,000
Cash at end of period		$ 191,000
Noncash investing and financing activities		
Issuance of common stock to purchase land		$ 60,000

STEP 3: NET CHANGE IN CASH

COMPARE THE NET CHANGE IN CASH ON THE STATEMENT OF CASH FLOWS WITH THE CHANGE IN THE CASH ACCOUNT REPORTED ON THE BALANCE SHEET TO MAKE SURE THE AMOUNTS AGREE

Illustration 17B-16 indicates that the net change in cash during the period was an increase of $32,000. This agrees with the change in balances in the cash account reported on the balance sheets in Illustration 17B-1 (page 747).

SUMMARY OF STUDY OBJECTIVE FOR APPENDIX 17B

6 **Prepare a statement of cash flows using the direct method.** The preparation of the statement of cash flows involves three major steps: (1) Determine net cash provided/used by operating activities by converting net income from an accrual basis to a cash basis. (2) Analyze changes in noncurrent asset and liability accounts and record as investing and financing activities, or disclose as noncash transactions. (3) Compare the net change in cash on the statement of cash flows with the change in the cash account reported on the balance sheet to make sure the amounts agree. The direct method reports cash receipts less cash payments to arrive at net cash provided by operating activities.

GLOSSARY FOR APPENDIX 17B

Direct method A method of determining net cash provided by operating activities by adjusting each item in the income statement from the accrual basis to the cash basis. (pp. 748)

Demonstration Problem 2

The income statement for Kosinski Manufacturing Company contains the following condensed information.

KOSINSKI MANUFACTURING COMPANY
Income Statement
For the Year Ended December 31, 2008

Revenues		$6,583,000
Operating expenses, excluding depreciation	$4,920,000	
Depreciation expense	880,000	5,800,000
Income before income taxes		783,000
Income tax expense		353,000
Net income		$ 430,000

Included in operating expenses is a $24,000 loss resulting from the sale of machinery for $270,000 cash. Machinery was purchased at a cost of $750,000. The following balances are reported on Kosinski's comparative balance sheet at December 31.

	2008	2007
Cash	$672,000	$130,000
Accounts receivable	775,000	610,000
Inventories	834,000	867,000
Accounts payable	521,000	501,000

Income tax expense of $353,000 represents the amount paid in 2008. Dividends declared and paid in 2008 totaled $200,000.

Instructions

Prepare the statement of cash flows using the direct method.

KOSINSKI MANUFACTURING COMPANY

Statement of Cash Flows—Direct Method
For the Year Ended December 31, 2008

Cash flows from operating activities		
Cash collections from customers		$6,418,000*
Cash payments:		
For operating expenses	$4,843,000**	
For income taxes	353,000	5,196,000
Net cash provided by operating activities		1,222,000
Cash flows from investing activities		
Sale of machinery	270,000	
Purchase of machinery	(750,000)	
Net cash used by investing activities		(480,000)
Cash flows from financing activities		
Payment of cash dividends	(200,000)	
Net cash used by financing activities		(200,000)
Net increase in cash		542,000
Cash at beginning of period		130,000
Cash at end of period		$ 672,000

Direct-Method Computations:

*Computation of cash collections from customers:	
Revenues per the income statement	$6,583,000
Deduct: Increase in accounts receivable	(165,000)
Cash collections from customers	$6,418,000
**Computation of cash payments for operating expenses:	
Operating expenses per the income statement	$4,920,000
Deduct: Loss from sale of machinery	(24,000)
Deduct: Decrease in inventories	(33,000)
Deduct: Increase in accounts payable	(20,000)
Cash payments for operating expenses	$4,843,000

action plan

✓ Determine net cash from operating activities. Each item in the income statement must be adjusted to the cash basis.

✓ Determine net cash from investing activities. Investing activities generally relate to changes in noncurrent assets.

✓ Determine net cash from financing activities. Financing activities generally relate to changes in long-term liabilities and stockholders' equity accounts.

✓ The Navigator

Note: All Questions, Exercises, and Problems marked with an asterisk relate to material in the appendices to the chapter.

SELF-STUDY QUESTIONS

WILEY PLUS

Answers are at the end of the chapter.

(SO 1) **1.** Which of the following is *incorrect* about the statement of cash flows?
a. It is a fourth basic financial statement.
b. It provides information about cash receipts and cash payments of an entity during a period.
c. It reconciles the ending cash account balance to the balance per the bank statement.
d. It provides information about the operating, investing, and financing activities of the business.

(SO 2) **2.** The statement of cash flows classifies cash receipts and cash payments by these activities:
a. operating and nonoperating.
b. investing, financing, and operating.
c. financing, operating, and nonoperating.
d. investing, financing, and nonoperating.

3. Which is an example of a cash flow from an operating activity? (SO 2)
a. Payment of cash to lenders for interest.
b. Receipt of cash from the sale of capital stock.
c. Payment of cash dividends to the company's stockholders.
d. None of the above.

4. Which is an example of a cash flow from an investing activity? (SO 2)
a. Receipt of cash from the issuance of bonds payable.
b. Payment of cash to repurchase outstanding capital stock.

c. Receipt of cash from the sale of equipment.
d. Payment of cash to suppliers for inventory.

(SO 2) 5. Cash dividends paid to stockholders are classified on the statement of cash flows as:
a. operating activities.
b. investing activities.
c. a combination of (a) and (b).
d. financing activities.

(SO 2) 6. Which is an example of a cash flow from a financing activity?
a. Receipt of cash from sale of land.
b. Issuance of debt for cash.
c. Purchase of equipment for cash.
d. None of the above

(SO 2) 7. Which of the following is *incorrect* about the statement of cash flows?
a. The direct method may be used to report cash provided by operations.
b. The statement shows the cash provided (used) for three categories of activity.
c. The operating section is the last section of the statement.
d. The indirect method may be used to report cash provided by operations.

Questions 8 and 9 apply only to the indirect method.

(SO 3) 8. Net income is $132,000, accounts payable increased $10,000 during the year, inventory decreased $6,000 during the year, and accounts receivable increased $12,000 during the year. Under the indirect method, what is net cash provided by operating activities?
a. $102,000. c. $124,000.
b. $112,000. d. $136,000.

(SO 3) 9. Items that are added back to net income in determining cash provided by operating activities under the indirect method do *not* include:
a. depreciation expense.
b. an increase in inventory.
c. amortization expense.
d. loss on sale of equipment.

10. The statement of cash flows should *not* be used to evaluate an entity's ability to: (SO 4)
a. earn net income.
b. generate future cash flows.
c. pay dividends.
d. meet obligations.

11. Free cash flow provides an indication of a company's ability to: (SO 4)
a. generate net income.
b. generate cash to pay dividends.
c. generate cash to invest in new capital expenditures.
d. both (b) and (c).

*12. In a worksheet for the statement of cash flows, a decrease in accounts receivable is entered in the reconciling columns as a credit to Accounts Receivable and a debit in the: (SO 5)
a. investing activities section.
b. operating activities section.
c. financing activities section.
d. None of the above.

Questions 13 and 14 apply only to the direct method.

*13. The beginning balance in accounts receivable is $44,000, the ending balance is $42,000, and sales during the period are $129,000. What are cash receipts from customers? (SO 6)
a. $127,000. c. $131,000.
b. $129,000. d. $141,000.

*14. Which of the following items is reported on a cash flow statement prepared by the direct method? (SO 6)
a. Loss on sale of building.
b. Increase in accounts receivable.
c. Depreciation expense.
d. Cash payments to suppliers.

Go to the book's website, **www.wiley.com/college/weygandt**, for Additional Self-Study questions.

The Navigator

QUESTIONS

1. **(a)** What is a statement of cash flows?
(b) John Norris maintains that the statement of cash flows is an optional financial statement. Do you agree? Explain.
2. What questions about cash are answered by the statement of cash flows?
3. Distinguish among the three types of activities reported in the statement of cash flows.
4. **(a)** What are the major sources (inflows) of cash in a statement of cash flows?
(b) What are the major uses (outflows) of cash?
5. Why is it important to disclose certain noncash transactions? How should they be disclosed?
6. Wilma Flintstone and Barny Rublestone were discussing the format of the statement of cash flows of Hart Candy Co. At the bottom of Hart Candy's statement of cash flows was a separate section entitled "Noncash investing and financing activities." Give three examples of significant noncash transactions that would be reported in this section.
7. Why is it necessary to use comparative balance sheets, a current income statement, and certain transaction data in preparing a statement of cash flows?
8. Contrast the advantages and disadvantages of the direct and indirect methods of preparing the statement of cash flows. Are both methods acceptable? Which method is preferred by the FASB? Which method is more popular?
9. When the total cash inflows exceed the total cash outflows in the statement of cash flows, how and where is this excess identified?
10. Describe the indirect method for determining net cash provided (used) by operating activities.

11. Why is it necessary to convert accrual-based net income to cash-basis income when preparing a statement of cash flows?
12. The president of Ferneti Company is puzzled. During the last year, the company experienced a net loss of $800,000, yet its cash increased $300,000 during the same period of time. Explain to the president how this could occur.
13. Identify five items that are adjustments to convert net income to net cash provided by operating activities under the indirect method.
14. Why and how is depreciation expense reported in a statement prepared using the indirect method?
15. Why is the statement of cash flows useful?
16. During 2008 Doubleday Company converted $1,700,000 of its total $2,000,000 of bonds payable into common stock. Indicate how the transaction would be reported on a statement of cash flows, if at all.

*17. Why is it advantageous to use a worksheet when preparing a statement of cash flows? Is a worksheet required to prepare a statement of cash flows?

*18. Describe the direct method for determining net cash provided by operating activities.

*19. Give the formulas under the direct method for computing (a) cash receipts from customers and (b) cash payments to suppliers.

*20. Garcia Inc. reported sales of $2 million for 2008. Accounts receivable decreased $200,000 and accounts payable increased $300,000. Compute cash receipts from customers, assuming that the receivable and payable transactions related to operations.

*21. In the direct method, why is depreciation expense not reported in the cash flows from operating activities section?

BRIEF EXERCISES

WILEY PLUS

BE17-1 Each of these items must be considered in preparing a statement of cash flows for Kiner Co. for the year ended December 31, 2008. For each item, state how it should be shown in the statement of cash flows for 2008.

Indicate statement presentation of selected transactions.
(SO 2)

(a) Issued bonds for $200,000 cash.
(b) Purchased equipment for $150,000 cash.
(c) Sold land costing $20,000 for $20,000 cash.
(d) Declared and paid a $50,000 cash dividend.

BE17-2 Classify each item as an operating, investing, or financing activity. Assume all items involve cash unless there is information to the contrary.

Classify items by activities.
(SO 2)

(a) Purchase of equipment.
(b) Sale of building.
(c) Redemption of bonds.
(d) Depreciation.
(e) Payment of dividends.
(f) Issuance of capital stock.

BE17-3 The following T account is a summary of the cash account of Edmonds Company.

Identify financing activity transactions.
(SO 2)

Cash (Summary Form)

Balance, Jan. 1	8,000		
Receipts from customers	364,000	Payments for goods	200,000
Dividends on stock investments	6,000	Payments for operating expenses	140,000
Proceeds from sale of equipment	36,000	Interest paid	10,000
Proceeds from issuance of		Taxes paid	8,000
bonds payable	300,000	Dividends paid	50,000
Balance, Dec. 31	306,000		

What amount of net cash provided (used) by financing activities should be reported in the statement of cash flows?

BE17-4 Martinez, Inc. reported net income of $2.5 million in 2008. Depreciation for the year was $160,000, accounts receivable decreased $350,000, and accounts payable decreased $280,000. Compute net cash provided by operating activities using the indirect method.

Compute cash provided by operating activities—indirect method.
(SO 3)

BE17-5 The net income for Adcock Co. for 2008 was $280,000. For 2008 depreciation on plant assets was $70,000, and the company incurred a loss on sale of plant assets of $12,000. Compute net cash provided by operating activities under the indirect method.

Compute cash provided by operating activities—indirect method.
(SO 3)

BE17-6 The comparative balance sheets for Goltra Company show these changes in noncash current asset accounts: accounts receivable decrease $80,000, prepaid expenses increase $28,000, and inventories increase $30,000. Compute net cash provided by operating activities using the indirect method assuming that net income is $200,000.

Compute net cash provided by operating activities—indirect method.
(SO 3)

Determine cash received from sale of equipment.
(SO 3)

BE17-7 The T accounts for Equipment and the related Accumulated Depreciation for Pettengill Company at the end of 2008 are shown here.

Equipment

Beg. bal.	80,000	Disposals	22,000
Acquisitions	41,600		
End. bal.	99,600		

Accumulated Depreciation

Disposals	5,500	Beg. bal.	44,500
		Depr. exp.	12,000
		End. bal.	51,000

In addition, Pettengill Company's income statement reported a loss on the sale of equipment of $5,500. What amount was reported on the statement of cash flows as "cash flow from sale of equipment"?

Calculate free cash flow.
(SO 4)

BE17-8 In a recent year, Cypress Semiconductor Corporation reported cash provided by operating activities of $155,793,000, cash used in investing of $207,826,000, and cash used in financing of $33,372,000. In addition, cash spent for fixed assets during the period was $132,280,000. No dividends were paid. Calculate free cash flow.

Calculate free cash flow.
(SO 4)

BE17-9 Lott Corporation reported cash provided by operating activities of $360,000, cash used by investing activities of $250,000, and cash provided by financing activities of $70,000. In addition, cash spent for capital assets during the period was $200,000. No dividends were paid. Calculate free cash flow.

Calculate free cash flow.
(SO 4)

BE17-10 Alliance Atlantis Communications Inc. reported a $35.8 million increase in operating cash flow for its first quarter of 2005. Alliance reported cash provided by operating activities of $45,600,000 and revenues of $264,800,000. Cash spent on plant asset additions during the quarter was $1,600,000. Calculate free cash flow.

Calculate and analyze free cash flow.
(SO 4)

BE17-11 The management of Radar Inc. is trying to decide whether it can increase its dividend. During the current year it reported net income of $875,000. It had cash provided by operating activities of $734,000, paid cash dividends of $70,000, and had capital expenditures of $280,000. Compute the company's free cash flow, and discuss whether an increase in the dividend appears warranted. What other factors should be considered?

Indicate entries in worksheet.
(SO 5)

***BE17-12** During the year, prepaid expenses decreased $6,600, and accrued expenses increased $2,400. Indicate how the changes in prepaid expenses and accrued expenses payable should be entered in the reconciling columns of a worksheet. Assume that beginning balances were: Prepaid expenses $18,600 and Accrued expenses payable $8,200.

Compute receipts from customers—direct method.
(SO 6)

***BE17-13** Columbia Sportswear Company had accounts receivable of $206,024,000 at the beginning of a recent year, and $267,653,000 at year-end. Sales revenues were $1,095,307,000 for the year. What is the amount of cash receipts from customers?

Compute cash payments for income taxes—direct method.
(SO 6)

***BE17-14** Young Corporation reported income taxes of $340,000,000 on its 2008 income statement and income taxes payable of $277,000,000 at December 31, 2007, and $522,000,000 at December 31, 2008. What amount of cash payments were made for income taxes during 2008?

Compute cash payments for operating expenses—direct method.
(SO 6)

***BE17-15** Flynn Corporation reports operating expenses of $80,000 excluding depreciation expense of $15,000 for 2008. During the year prepaid expenses decreased $6,600 and accrued expenses payable increased $4,400. Compute the cash payments for operating expenses in 2008.

EXERCISES

WILEY PLUS

Classify transactions by type of activity.
(SO 2)

E17-1 Pioneer Corporation had these transactions during 2008.

(a) Issued $50,000 par value common stock for cash.
(b) Purchased a machine for $30,000, giving a long-term note in exchange.
(c) Issued $200,000 par value common stock upon conversion of bonds having a face value of $200,000.
(d) Declared and paid a cash dividend of $18,000.
(e) Sold a long-term investment with a cost of $15,000 for $15,000 cash.
(f) Collected $16,000 of accounts receivable.
(g) Paid $18,000 on accounts payable.

Instructions

Analyze the transactions and indicate whether each transaction resulted in a cash flow from operating activities, investing activities, financing activities, or noncash investing and financing activities.

Classify transactions by type of activity.

(SO 2)

E17-2 An analysis of comparative balance sheets, the current year's income statement, and the general ledger accounts of Gagliano Corp. uncovered the following items. Assume all items involve cash unless there is information to the contrary.

(a) Payment of interest on notes payable.
(b) Exchange of land for patent.
(c) Sale of building at book value.
(d) Payment of dividends.
(e) Depreciation.
(f) Receipt of dividends on investment in stock.
(g) Receipt of interest on notes receivable.
(h) Issuance of capital stock.
(i) Amortization of patent.
(j) Issuance of bonds for land.
(k) Purchase of land.
(l) Conversion of bonds into common stock.
(m) Loss on sale of land.
(n) Retirement of bonds.

Instructions

Indicate how each item should be classified in the statement of cash flows using these four major classifications: operating activity (indirect method), investing activity, financing activity, and significant noncash investing and financing activity.

Prepare journal entry and determine effect on cash flows.

(SO 2)

E17-3 Rachael Ray Corporation had the following transactions.

1. Sold land (cost $12,000) for $15,000.
2. Issued common stock for $20,000.
3. Recorded depreciation of $17,000.
4. Paid salaries of $9,000.
5. Issued 1,000 shares of $1 par value common stock for equipment worth $8,000.
6. Sold equipment (cost $10,000, accumulated depreciation $7,000) for $1,200.

Instructions

For each transaction above, **(a)** prepare the journal entry, and **(b)** indicate how it would affect the statement of cash flows.

Prepare the operating activities section—indirect method.

(SO 3)

E17-4 Villa Company reported net income of $195,000 for 2008. Villa also reported depreciation expense of $45,000 and a loss of $5,000 on the sale of equipment. The comparative balance sheet shows a decrease in accounts receivable of $15,000 for the year, a $17,000 increase in accounts payable, and a $4,000 decrease in prepaid expenses.

Instructions

Prepare the operating activities section of the statement of cash flows for 2008. Use the indirect method.

Prepare the operating activities section—indirect method.

(SO 3)

E17-5 The current sections of Bellinham Inc.'s balance sheets at December 31, 2007 and 2008, are presented here.

Bellinham's net income for 2008 was $153,000. Depreciation expense was $24,000.

	2008	2007
Current assets		
Cash	$105,000	$ 99,000
Accounts receivable	110,000	89,000
Inventory	158,000	172,000
Prepaid expenses	27,000	22,000
Total current assets	$400,000	$382,000
Current liabilities		
Accrued expenses payable	$ 15,000	$ 5,000
Accounts payable	85,000	92,000
Total current liabilities	$100,000	$ 97,000

Instructions

Prepare the net cash provided by operating activities section of the company's statement of cash flows for the year ended December 31, 2008, using the indirect method.

Prepare partial statement of cash flows—indirect method.

(SO 3)

E17-6 The three accounts shown below appear in the general ledger of Cesar Corp. during 2008.

Equipment

Date		Debit	Credit	Balance
Jan. 1	Balance			160,000
July 31	Purchase of equipment	70,000		230,000
Sept. 2	Cost of equipment constructed	53,000		283,000
Nov. 10	Cost of equipment sold		49,000	234,000

Accumulated Depreciation—Equipment

Date		Debit	Credit	Balance
Jan. 1	Balance			71,000
Nov. 10	Accumulated depreciation on equipment sold	30,000		41,000
Dec. 31	Depreciation for year		28,000	69,000

Retained Earnings

Date		Debit	Credit	Balance
Jan. 1	Balance			105,000
Aug. 23	Dividends (cash)	14,000		91,000
Dec. 31	Net income		67,000	158,000

Instructions

From the postings in the accounts, indicate how the information is reported on a statement of cash flows using the indirect method. The loss on sale of equipment was $5,000. (*Hint:* Cost of equipment constructed is reported in the investing activities section as a decrease in cash of $53,000.)

Prepare statement of cash flows and compute free cash flow.

(SO 3, 4)

E17-7 Scully Corporation's comparative balance sheets are presented below.

SCULLY CORPORATION
Comparative Balance Sheets
December 31

	2008	2007
Cash	$ 14,300	$ 10,700
Accounts receivable	21,200	23,400
Land	20,000	26,000
Building	70,000	70,000
Accumulated depreciation	(15,000)	(10,000)
Total	$110,500	$120,100
Accounts payable	$12,370	$31,100
Common stock	75,000	69,000
Retained earnings	23,130	20,000
Total	$110,500	$120,100

Additional information:

1. Net income was $22,630. Dividends declared and paid were $19,500.
2. All other changes in noncurrent account balances had a direct effect on cash flows, except the change in accumulated depreciation. The land was sold for $4,900.

Instructions

(a) Prepare a statement of cash flows for 2008 using the indirect method.
(b) Compute free cash flow.

E17-8 Here are comparative balance sheets for Taguchi Company.

Prepare a statement of cash flows—indirect method.
(SO 3)

TAGUCHI COMPANY
Comparative Balance Sheets
December 31

Assets	2008	2007
Cash	$ 73,000	$ 22,000
Accounts receivable	85,000	76,000
Inventories	170,000	189,000
Land	75,000	100,000
Equipment	260,000	200,000
Accumulated depreciation	(66,000)	(32,000)
Total	$597,000	$555,000
Liabilities and Stockholders' Equity		
Accounts payable	$ 39,000	$ 47,000
Bonds payable	150,000	200,000
Common stock ($1 par)	216,000	174,000
Retained earnings	192,000	134,000
Total	$597,000	$555,000

Additional information:

1. Net income for 2008 was $103,000.
2. Cash dividends of $45,000 were declared and paid.
3. Bonds payable amounting to $50,000 were redeemed for cash $50,000.
4. Common stock was issued for $42,000 cash.
5. No equipment was sold during 2008.

Instructions

Prepare a statement of cash flows for 2008 using the indirect method.

E17-9 Muldur Corporation's comparative balance sheets are presented below.

Prepare statement of cash flows and compute free cash flow.
(SO 3, 4)

MULDUR CORPORATION
Comparative Balance Sheets
December 31

	2008	2007
Cash	$ 15,200	$ 17,700
Accounts receivable	25,200	22,300
Investments	20,000	16,000
Equipment	60,000	70,000
Accumulated depreciation	(14,000)	(10,000)
Total	$106,400	$116,000
Accounts payable	$ 14,600	$ 11,100
Bonds payable	10,000	30,000
Common stock	50,000	45,000
Retained earnings	31,800	29,900
Total	$106,400	$116,000

Additional information:

1. Net income was $18,300. Dividends declared and paid were $16,400.
2. Equipment which cost $10,000 and had accumulated depreciation of $1,200 was sold for $3,300.
3. All other changes in noncurrent account balances had a direct effect on cash flows, except the change in accumulated depreciation.

Instructions

(a) Prepare a statement of cash flows for 2008 using the indirect method.
(b) Compute free cash flow.

Prepare a worksheet.

(SO 5)

***E17-10** Comparative balance sheets for Eddie Murphy Company are presented below.

EDDIE MURPHY COMPANY
Comparative Balance Sheets
December 31

Assets	2008	2007
Cash	$ 63,000	$ 22,000
Accounts receivable	85,000	76,000
Inventories	180,000	189,000
Land	75,000	100,000
Equipment	260,000	200,000
Accumulated depreciation	(66,000)	(42,000)
Total	$597,000	$545,000

Liabilities and Stockholders' Equity		
Accounts payable	$ 34,000	$ 47,000
Bonds payable	150,000	200,000
Common stock ($1 par)	214,000	164,000
Retained earnings	199,000	134,000
Total	$597,000	$545,000

Additional information:

1. Net income for 2008 was $125,000.
2. Cash dividends of $60,000 were declared and paid.
3. Bonds payable amounting to $50,000 were redeemed for cash $50,000.
4. Common stock was issued for $50,000 cash.
5. Depreciation expense was $24,000.
6. Sales for the year were $978,000.

Instructions

Prepare a worksheet for a statement of cash flows for 2008 using the indirect method. Enter the reconciling items directly on the worksheet, using letters to cross-reference each entry.

Compute cash provided by operating activities—direct method.

(SO 6)

***E17-11** Hairston Company completed its first year of operations on December 31, 2008. Its initial income statement showed that Hairston had revenues of $192,000 and operating expenses of $78,000. Accounts receivable and accounts payable at year-end were $60,000 and $23,000, respectively. Assume that accounts payable related to operating expenses. Ignore income taxes.

Instructions

Compute net cash provided by operating activities using the direct method.

Compute cash payments—direct method.

(SO 6)

***E17-12** The 2004 income statement for McDonald's Corporation shows cost of goods sold $4,852.7 million and operating expenses (including depreciation expense of $1,201 million) $10,671.5 million. The comparative balance sheet for the year shows that inventory increased $18.1 million, prepaid expenses increased $56.3 million, accounts payable (merchandise suppliers) increased $136.9 million, and accrued expenses payable increased $160.9 million.

Instructions

Using the direct method, compute (a) cash payments to suppliers and (b) cash payments for operating expenses.

***E17-13** The 2008 accounting records of Verlander Transport reveal these transactions and events.

Compute cash flow from operating activities—direct method.

(SO 6)

Payment of interest	$ 10,000	Collection of accounts receivable	$182,000
Cash sales	48,000	Payment of salaries and wages	53,000
Receipt of dividend revenue	18,000	Depreciation expense	16,000
Payment of income taxes	12,000	Proceeds from sale of vehicles	12,000
Net income	38,000	Purchase of equipment for cash	22,000
Payment of accounts payable for merchandise	115,000	Loss on sale of vehicles	3,000
		Payment of dividends	14,000
Payment for land	74,000	Payment of operating expenses	28,000

Instructions

Prepare the cash flows from operating activities section using the direct method. (Not all of the items will be used.)

***E17-14** The following information is taken from the 2008 general ledger of Pierzynski Company.

Calculate cash flows—direct method.

(SO 6)

Rent	Rent expense	$ 40,000
	Prepaid rent, January 1	5,900
	Prepaid rent, December 31	9,000
Salaries	Salaries expense	$ 54,000
	Salaries payable, January 1	10,000
	Salaries payable, December 31	8,000
Sales	Revenue from sales	$170,000
	Accounts receivable, January 1	16,000
	Accounts receivable, December 31	7,000

Instructions

In each case, compute the amount that should be reported in the operating activities section of the statement of cash flows under the direct method.

EXERCISES: SET B

Visit the book's website at **www.wiley.com/college/weygandt**, and choose the Student Companion site, to access Exercise Set B.

PROBLEMS: SET A

P17-1A You are provided with the following transactions that took place during a recent fiscal year.

Distinguish among operating, investing, and financing activities.

(SO 2)

Transaction	Where Reported on Statement	Cash Inflow, Outflow, or No Effect?
(a) Recorded depreciation expense on the plant assets.		
(b) Recorded and paid interest expense.		
(c) Recorded cash proceeds from a sale of plant assets.		
(d) Acquired land by issuing common stock.		
(e) Paid a cash dividend to preferred stockholders.		
(f) Distributed a stock dividend to common stockholders.		
(g) Recorded cash sales.		
(h) Recorded sales on account.		
(i) Purchased inventory for cash.		
(j) Purchased inventory on account.		

Instructions

Complete the table indicating whether each item (1) should be reported as an operating (O) activity, investing (I) activity, financing (F) activity, or as a noncash (NC) transaction reported in a separate schedule, and (2) represents a cash inflow or cash outflow or has no cash flow effect. Assume use of the indirect approach.

Determine cash flow effects of changes in equity accounts.

(SO 3)

P17-2A The following account balances relate to the stockholders' equity accounts of Gore Corp. at year-end.

	2008	2007
Common stock, 10,500 and 10,000 shares, respectively, for 2008 and 2007	$160,000	$140,000
Preferred stock, 5,000 shares	125,000	125,000
Retained earnings	300,000	260,000

A small stock dividend was declared and issued in 2008. The market value of the shares was $10,500. Cash dividends were $15,000 in both 2008 and 2007. The common stock has no par or stated value.

Instructions

(a) Net income $65,500

(a) What was the amount of net income reported by Gore Corp. in 2008?

(b) Determine the amounts of any cash inflows or outflows related to the common stock and dividend accounts in 2008.

(c) Indicate where each of the cash inflows or outflows identified in (b) would be classified on the statement of cash flows.

Prepare the operating activities section—indirect method.

(SO 3)

P17-3A The income statement of Elbert Company is presented here.

ELBERT COMPANY
Income Statement
For the Year Ended November 30, 2008

Sales		$7,700,000
Cost of goods sold		
Beginning inventory	$1,900,000	
Purchases	4,400,000	
Goods available for sale	6,300,000	
Ending inventory	1,400,000	
Total cost of goods sold		4,900,000
Gross profit		2,800,000
Operating expenses		
Selling expenses	450,000	
Administrative expenses	700,000	1,150,000
Net income		$1,650,000

Additional information:

1. Accounts receivable increased $250,000 during the year, and inventory decreased $500,000.
2. Prepaid expenses increased $150,000 during the year.
3. Accounts payable to suppliers of merchandise decreased $340,000 during the year.
4. Accrued expenses payable decreased $100,000 during the year.
5. Administrative expenses include depreciation expense of $90,000.

Cash from operations $1,400,000

Instructions

Prepare the operating activities section of the statement of cash flows for the year ended November 30, 2008, for Elbert Company, using the indirect method.

Prepare the operating activities section—direct method.

(SO 6)

***P17-4A** Data for Elbert Company are presented in P17-3A.

Instructions

Prepare the operating activities section of the statement of cash flows using the direct method.

Cash from operations
$1,400,000

Prepare the operating activities section—indirect method.

(SO 3)

P17-5A Grania Company's income statement contained the condensed information below.

GRANIA COMPANY
Income Statement
For the Year Ended December 31, 2008

Revenues		$970,000
Operating expenses, excluding depreciation	$624,000	
Depreciation expense	60,000	
Loss on sale of equipment	16,000	700,000
Income before income taxes		270,000
Income tax expense		40,000
Net income		$230,000

Grania's balance sheet contained the comparative data at December 31, shown below.

	2008	2007
Accounts receivable	$75,000	$60,000
Accounts payable	41,000	28,000
Income taxes payable	11,000	7,000

Accounts payable pertain to operating expenses.

Instructions

Prepare the operating activities section of the statement of cash flows using the indirect method.

Cash from operations
$308,000

Prepare the operating activities section—direct method.

(SO 6)

Cash from operations
$308,000

***P17-6A** Data for Grania Company are presented in P17-5A.

Instructions

Prepare the operating activities section of the statement of cash flows using the direct method.

Prepare a statement of cash flows—indirect method, and compute free cash flow.

(SO 3, 4)

P17-7A Presented below are the financial statements of Weller Company.

WELLER COMPANY
Comparative Balance Sheets
December 31

Assets	**2008**	**2007**
Cash	$ 35,000	$ 20,000
Accounts receivable	33,000	14,000
Merchandise inventory	27,000	20,000
Property, plant, and equipment	60,000	78,000
Accumulated depreciation	(29,000)	(24,000)
Total	$126,000	$108,000
Liabilities and Stockholders' Equity		
Accounts payable	$ 29,000	$ 15,000
Income taxes payable	7,000	8,000
Bonds payable	27,000	33,000
Common stock	18,000	14,000
Retained earnings	45,000	38,000
Total	$126,000	$108,000

WELLER COMPANY
Income Statement
For the Year Ended December 31, 2008

Sales		$242,000
Cost of goods sold		175,000
Gross profit		67,000
Selling expenses	$18,000	
Administrative expenses	6,000	24,000
Income from operations		43,000
Interest expense		3,000
Income before income taxes		40,000
Income tax expense		8,000
Net income		$ 32,000

Additional data:

1. Dividends declared and paid were $25,000.
2. During the year equipment was sold for $8,500 cash. This equipment cost $18,000 originally and had a book value of $8,500 at the time of sale.
3. All depreciation expense, $14,500, is in the selling expense category.
4. All sales and purchases are on account.

Instructions

(a) Cash from operations $33,500

(a) Prepare a statement of cash flows using the indirect method.
(b) Compute free cash flow.

Prepare a statement of cash flows—direct method, and compute free cash flow.

(SO 4, 6)

***P17-8A** Data for Weller Company are presented in P17-7A. Further analysis reveals the following.

1. Accounts payable pertain to merchandise suppliers.
2. All operating expenses except for depreciation were paid in cash.

Instructions

(a) Cash from operations $33,500

(a) Prepare a statement of cash flows for Weller Company using the direct method.
(b) Compute free cash flow.

Prepare a statement of cash flows—indirect method.

(SO 3)

P17-9A Condensed financial data of Arma Inc. follow.

ARMA INC.
Comparative Balance Sheets
December 31

Assets	**2008**	**2007**
Cash	$ 90,800	$ 48,400
Accounts receivable	92,800	33,000
Inventories	112,500	102,850
Prepaid expenses	28,400	26,000
Investments	138,000	114,000
Plant assets	270,000	242,500
Accumulated depreciation	(50,000)	(52,000)
Total	$682,500	$514,750
Liabilities and Stockholders' Equity		
Accounts payable	$112,000	$ 67,300
Accrued expenses payable	16,500	17,000
Bonds payable	110,000	150,000
Common stock	220,000	175,000
Retained earnings	224,000	105,450
Total	$682,500	$514,750

ARMA INC.
Income Statement
For the Year Ended December 31, 2008

Sales		$392,780
Less:		
Cost of goods sold	$135,460	
Operating expenses, excluding depreciation	12,410	
Depreciation expense	46,500	
Income taxes	27,280	
Interest expense	4,730	
Loss on sale of plant assets	7,500	233,880
Net income		$158,900

Additional information:

1. New plant assets costing $85,000 were purchased for cash during the year.
2. Old plant assets having an original cost of $57,500 were sold for $1,500 cash.
3. Bonds matured and were paid off at face value for cash.
4. A cash dividend of $40,350 was declared and paid during the year.

Instructions

Prepare a statement of cash flows using the indirect method.

Cash from operations $185,250

***P17-10A** Data for Arma Inc. are presented in P17-9A. Further analysis reveals that accounts payable pertain to merchandise creditors.

Prepare a statement of cash flows—direct method.

(SO 6)

Instructions

Prepare a statement of cash flows for Arma Inc. using the direct method.

Cash from operations $185,250

P17-11A The comparative balance sheets for Ramirez Company as of December 31 are presented below.

Prepare a statement of cash flows—indirect method.

(SO 3)

RAMIREZ COMPANY
Comparative Balance Sheets
December 31

Assets	2008	2007
Cash	$ 71,000	$ 45,000
Accounts receivable	44,000	62,000
Inventory	151,450	142,000
Prepaid expenses	15,280	21,000
Land	105,000	130,000
Equipment	228,000	155,000
Accumulated depreciation—equipment	(45,000)	(35,000)
Building	200,000	200,000
Accumulated depreciation—building	(60,000)	(40,000)
Total	$709,730	$680,000
Liabilities and Stockholders' Equity		
Accounts payable	$ 47,730	$ 40,000
Bonds payable	260,000	300,000
Common stock, $1 par	200,000	160,000
Retained earnings	202,000	180,000
Total	$709,730	$680,000

Additional information:

1. Operating expenses include depreciation expense of $42,000 and charges from prepaid expenses of $5,720.
2. Land was sold for cash at book value.

3. Cash dividends of $15,000 were paid.
4. Net income for 2008 was $37,000.
5. Equipment was purchased for $95,000 cash. In addition, equipment costing $22,000 with a book value of $10,000 was sold for $6,000 cash.
6. Bonds were converted at face value by issuing 40,000 shares of $1 par value common stock.

Cash from operations $105,000

Instructions

Prepare a statement of cash flows for the year ended December 31, 2008, using the indirect method.

Prepare a worksheet—indirect method.

(SO 5)

***P17-12A** Condensed financial data of Oprah Company appear below.

OPRAH COMPANY
Comparative Balance Sheets
December 31

Assets	**2008**	**2007**
Cash	$ 92,700	$ 47,250
Accounts receivable	90,800	57,000
Inventories	121,900	102,650
Investments	84,500	87,000
Plant assets	250,000	205,000
Accumulated depreciation	(49,500)	(40,000)
	$590,400	$458,900

Liabilities and Stockholders' Equity		
Accounts payable	$ 57,700	$ 48,280
Accrued expenses payable	12,100	18,830
Bonds payable	100,000	70,000
Common stock	250,000	200,000
Retained earnings	170,600	121,790
	$590,400	$458,900

OPRAH COMPANY
Income Statement
For the Year Ended December 31, 2008

Sales		$297,500
Gain on sale of plant assets		8,750
		306,250
Less:		
Cost of goods sold	$99,460	
Operating expenses (excluding depreciation expense)	14,670	
Depreciation expense	49,700	
Income taxes	7,270	
Interest expense	2,940	174,040
Net income		$132,210

Additional information:

1. New plant assets costing $92,000 were purchased for cash during the year.
2. Investments were sold at cost.
3. Plant assets costing $47,000 were sold for $15,550, resulting in gain of $8,750.
4. A cash dividend of $83,400 was declared and paid during the year.

Reconciling items total $610,210

Instructions

Prepare a worksheet for the statement of cash flows using the indirect method. Enter the reconciling items directly in the worksheet columns, using letters to cross-reference each entry.

PROBLEMS: SET B

P17-1B You are provided with the following transactions that took place during a recent fiscal year.

Distinguish among operating, investing, and financing activities.

(SO 2)

Transaction	Where Reported on Statement	Cash Inflow, Outflow, or No Effect?
(a) Recorded depreciation expense on the plant assets.		
(b) Incurred a loss on disposal of plant assets.		
(c) Acquired a building by paying cash.		
(d) Made principal repayments on a mortgage.		
(e) Issued common stock.		
(f) Purchased shares of another company to be held as a long-term equity investment.		
(g) Paid dividends to common stockholders.		
(h) Sold inventory on credit. The company uses a perpetual inventory system.		
(i) Purchased inventory on credit.		
(j) Paid wages to employees.		

Instructions

Complete the table indicating whether each item (1) should be reported as an operating (O) activity, investing (I) activity, financing (F) activity, or as a noncash (NC) transaction reported in a separate schedule, and (2) represents a cash inflow or cash outflow or has no cash flow effect. Assume use of the indirect approach.

P17-2B The following selected account balances relate to the plant asset accounts of Zambia Inc. at year-end.

Determine cash flow effects of changes in plant asset accounts.

(SO 3)

	2008	2007
Accumulated depreciation—buildings	$337,500	$300,000
Accumulated depreciation—equipment	144,000	96,000
Buildings	750,000	750,000
Depreciation expense	101,500	85,500
Equipment	300,000	240,000
Land	100,000	70,000
Loss on sale of equipment	3,000	0

Additional information:

1. Zambia purchased $85,000 of equipment and $30,000 of land for cash in 2008.
2. Zambia also sold equipment in 2008.
3. Depreciation expense in 2008 was $37,500 on building and $64,000 on equipment.

Instructions

(a) Determine the amounts of any cash inflows or outflows related to the plant asset accounts in 2008.

(a) Cash proceeds $6,000

(b) Indicate where each of the cash inflows or outflows identified in (a) would be classified on the statement of cash flows.

P17-3B The income statement of Marquette Company is presented on page 770.

Prepare the operating activities section—indirect method.

(SO 3)

Additional information:

1. Accounts receivable decreased $520,000 during the year, and inventory increased $140,000.
2. Prepaid expenses increased $175,000 during the year.
3. Accounts payable to merchandise suppliers increased $50,000 during the year.
4. Accrued expenses payable increased $165,000 during the year.

MARQUETTE COMPANY
Income Statement
For the Year Ended December 31, 2008

Sales		$5,400,000
Cost of goods sold		
Beginning inventory	$1,780,000	
Purchases	3,430,000	
Goods available for sale	5,210,000	
Ending inventory	1,920,000	
Total cost of goods sold		3,290,000
Gross profit		2,110,000
Operating expenses		
Selling expenses	420,000	
Administrative expense	525,000	
Depreciation expense	105,000	
Amortization expense	20,000	1,070,000
Net income		$1,040,000

Instructions

Prepare the operating activities section of the statement of cash flows for the year ended December 31, 2008, for Marquette Company, using the indirect method.

Cash from operations $1,585,000

Prepare the operating activities section—direct method.

(SO 6)

***P17-4B** Data for Marquette Company are presented in P17-3B.

Instructions

Prepare the operating activities section of the statement of cash flows using the direct method.

Cash from operations $1,585,000

Prepare the operating activities section—indirect method.

(SO 3)

P17-5B The income statement of Shapiro Inc. reported the following condensed information.

SHAPIRO INC.
Income Statement
For the Year Ended December 31, 2008

Revenues	$545,000
Operating expenses	400,000
Income from operations	145,000
Income tax expense	47,000
Net income	$ 98,000

Shapiro's balance sheet contained these comparative data at December 31.

	2008	2007
Accounts receivable	$50,000	$75,000
Accounts payable	30,000	51,000
Income taxes payable	10,000	4,000

Shapiro has no depreciable assets. Accounts payable pertain to operating expenses.

Instructions

Prepare the operating activities section of the statement of cash flows using the indirect method.

Cash from operations $108,000

Prepare the operating activities section—direct method.

(SO 6)

***P17-6B** Data for Shapiro Inc. are presented in P17-5B.

Instructions

Prepare the operating activities section of the statement of cash flows using the direct method.

Cash from operations $108,000

P17-7B Presented below are the financial statements of Molina Company.

Prepare a statement of cash flows—indirect method, and compute free cash flow.

(SO 3, 4)

MOLINA COMPANY
Comparative Balance Sheets
December 31

Assets		**2008**		**2007**
Cash		$ 28,000		$ 33,000
Accounts receivable		23,000		14,000
Merchandise inventory		41,000		25,000
Property, plant, and equipment	$ 70,000		$ 78,000	
Less: Accumulated depreciation	(27,000)	43,000	(24,000)	54,000
Total		$135,000		$126,000

Liabilities and Stockholders' Equity	**2008**	**2007**
Accounts payable	$ 31,000	$ 43,000
Income taxes payable	26,000	20,000
Bonds payable	20,000	10,000
Common stock	25,000	25,000
Retained earnings	33,000	28,000
Total	$135,000	$126,000

MOLINA COMPANY
Income Statement
For the Year Ended December 31, 2008

Sales		$286,000
Cost of goods sold		194,000
Gross profit		92,000
Selling expenses	$28,000	
Administrative expenses	9,000	37,000
Income from operations		55,000
Interest expense		7,000
Income before income taxes		48,000
Income tax expense		10,000
Net income		$ 38,000

Additional data:

1. Dividends of $33,000 were declared and paid.
2. During the year equipment was sold for $10,000 cash. This equipment cost $13,000 originally and had a book value of $10,000 at the time of sale.
3. All depreciation expense, $6,000, is in the selling expense category.
4. All sales and purchases are on account.
5. Additional equipment was purchased for $5,000 cash.

Instructions

(a) Prepare a statement of cash flows using the indirect method.
(b) Compute free cash flow.

(a) Cash from operations $13,000

***P17-8B** Data for Molina Company are presented in P17-7B. Further analysis reveals the following.

Prepare a statement of cash flows—direct method, and compute free cash flow.

(SO 4, 6)

1. Accounts payable pertains to merchandise creditors.
2. All operating expenses except for depreciation are paid in cash.

Instructions

(a) Prepare a statement of cash flows using the direct method.
(b) Compute free cash flow.

(a) Cash from operations $13,000

Prepare a statement of cash flows—indirect method.

(SO 3)

P17-9B Condensed financial data of Yaeger Company are shown below.

YAEGER COMPANY
Comparative Balance Sheets
December 31

Assets	**2008**	**2007**
Cash	$ 97,700	$ 33,400
Accounts receivable	70,800	37,000
Inventories	121,900	102,650
Investments	89,500	107,000
Plant assets	310,000	205,000
Accumulated depreciation	(49,500)	(40,000)
Total	$640,400	$445,050
Liabilities and Stockholders' Equity		
Accounts payable	$ 62,700	$ 48,280
Accrued expenses payable	15,100	18,830
Bonds payable	140,000	70,000
Common stock	250,000	200,000
Retained earnings	172,600	107,940
Total	$640,400	$445,050

YAEGER COMPANY
Income Statement
For the Year Ended December 31, 2008

Sales		$297,500
Gain on sale of plant assets		5,000
		302,500
Less:		
Cost of goods sold	$99,460	
Operating expenses, excluding depreciation expense	14,670	
Depreciation expense	35,500	
Income taxes	27,270	
Interest expense	2,940	179,840
Net income		$122,660

Additional information:

1. New plant assets costing $141,000 were purchased for cash during the year.
2. Investments were sold at cost.
3. Plant assets costing $36,000 were sold for $15,000, resulting in a gain of $5,000.
4. A cash dividend of $58,000 was declared and paid during the year.

Cash from operations $110,800

Instructions
Prepare a statement of cash flows using the indirect method.

Prepare a statement of cash flows—direct method.

(SO 6)

***P17-10B** Data for Yaeger Company are presented in P17-9B. Further analysis reveals that accounts payable pertain to merchandise creditors.

Cash from operations $110,800

Instructions
Prepare a statement of cash flows for Yaeger Company using the direct method.

P17-11B Presented below are the comparative balance sheets for Lewis Company at December 31.

Prepare a statement of cash flows—indirect method.

(SO 3)

LEWIS COMPANY
Comparative Balance Sheets
December 31

Assets	**2008**	**2007**
Cash	$ 31,000	$ 57,000
Accounts receivable	77,000	64,000
Inventory	192,000	140,000
Prepaid expenses	12,140	16,540
Land	100,000	150,000
Equipment	215,000	175,000
Accumulated depreciation—equipment	(70,000)	(42,000)
Building	250,000	250,000
Accumulated depreciation—building	(70,000)	(50,000)
Total	$737,140	$760,540
Liabilities and Stockholders' Equity		
Accounts payable	$ 58,000	$ 45,000
Bonds payable	235,000	265,000
Common stock, $1 par	280,000	250,000
Retained earnings	164,140	200,540
Total	$737,140	$760,540

Additional information:

1. Operating expenses include depreciation expense $65,000 and charges from prepaid expenses of $4,400.
2. Land was sold for cash at cost.
3. Cash dividends of $69,290 were paid.
4. Net income for 2007 was $32,890.
5. Equipment was purchased for $80,000 cash. In addition, equipment costing $40,000 with a book value of $23,000 was sold for $25,000 cash.
6. Bonds were converted at face value by issuing 30,000 shares of $1 par value common stock.

Instructions

Prepare a statement of cash flows for 2008 using the indirect method.

Cash from operations $48,290

PROBLEMS: SET C

Visit the book's website at **www.wiley.com/college/weygandt** and choose the Student Companion site to access Problem Set C.

CONTINUING COOKIE CHRONICLE

(*Note:* This is a continuation of the Cookie Chronicle from Chapters 1 through 16.)

CCC17 Natalie has prepared the balance sheet and income statement of Cookie & Coffee Creations Inc. and would like you to prepare the cash flow statement.

Go to the book's website,
www.wiley.com/college/weygandt,
to see the completion of this problem.

BROADENING YOUR PERSPECTIVE

FINANCIAL REPORTING AND ANALYSIS

Financial Reporting Problem: PepsiCo, Inc.

BYP17-1 Refer to the financial statements of PepsiCo, presented in Appendix A, and answer the following questions.

(a) What was the amount of net cash provided by operating activities for the year ended December 31, 2005? For the year ended December 25, 2004?
(b) What was the amount of increase or decrease in cash and cash equivalents for the year ended December 31, 2005? For the year ended December 25, 2004?
(c) Which method of computing net cash provided by operating activities does PepsiCo use?
(d) From your analysis of the 2005 statement of cash flows, did the change in accounts and notes receivable require or provide cash? Did the change in inventories require or provide cash? Did the change in accounts payable and other current liabilities require or provide cash?
(e) What was the net outflow or inflow of cash from investing activities for the year ended December 31, 2005?
(f) What was the amount of interest paid in the year ended December 31, 2005? What was the amount of income taxes paid in the year ended December 31, 2005? (See Note 14.)

Comparative Analysis Problem: PepsiCo, Inc. vs. The Coca-Cola Company

BYP17-2 PepsiCo's financial statements are presented in Appendix A. Coca-Cola's financial statements are presented in Appendix B.

Instructions

(a) Based on the information contained in these financial statements, compute free cash flow for each company.
(b) What conclusions concerning the management of cash can be drawn from these data?

Exploring the Web

BYP17-3 Purpose: Learn about the SEC.

Address:www.sec.gov/index.html, or go to **www.wiley.com/college/weygandt**

From the SEC homepage, choose **About the SEC**.

Instructions

Answer the following questions.

(a) How many enforcement actions does the SEC take each year against securities law violators? What are typical infractions?
(b) After the Depression, Congress passed the Securities Acts of 1933 and 1934 to improve investor confidence in the markets. What two "common sense" notions are these laws based on?
(c) Who was the President of the United States at the time of the creation of the SEC? Who was the first SEC Chairperson?

BYP17-4 Purpose: Use the Internet to view SEC filings.

Address: biz.yahoo.com/i, or go to **www.wiley.com/college/weygandt**

Steps

1. Type in a company name.
2. Choose **Profile**.
3. Choose **SEC**. (This will take you to Yahoo-Edgar Online.)

Instructions
Answer the following questions.

(a) What company did you select?
(b) Which filing is the most recent? What is the date?
(c) What other recent SEC filings are available for your viewing?

CRITICAL THINKING

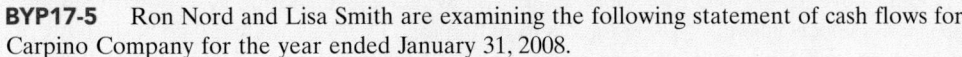

Decision Making Across the Organization

BYP17-5 Ron Nord and Lisa Smith are examining the following statement of cash flows for Carpino Company for the year ended January 31, 2008.

CARPINO COMPANY
Statement of Cash Flows
For the Year Ended January 31, 2008

Sources of cash	
From sales of merchandise	$380,000
From sale of capital stock	420,000
From sale of investment (purchased below)	80,000
From depreciation	55,000
From issuance of note for truck	20,000
From interest on investments	6,000
Total sources of cash	961,000
Uses of cash	
For purchase of fixtures and equipment	330,000
For merchandise purchased for resale	258,000
For operating expenses (including depreciation)	160,000
For purchase of investment	75,000
For purchase of truck by issuance of note	20,000
For purchase of treasury stock	10,000
For interest on note payable	3,000
Total uses of cash	856,000
Net increase in cash	$ 105,000

Ron claims that Carpino's statement of cash flows is an excellent portrayal of a superb first year with cash increasing $105,000. Lisa replies that it was not a superb first year. Rather, she says, the year was an operating failure, that the statement is presented incorrectly, and that $105,000 is not the actual increase in cash. The cash balance at the beginning of the year was $140,000.

Instructions
With the class divided into groups, answer the following.

(a) Using the data provided, prepare a statement of cash flows in proper form using the indirect method. The only noncash items in the income statement are depreciation and the gain from the sale of the investment.
(b) With whom do you agree, Ron or Lisa? Explain your position.

Communication Activity

BYP17-6 Kyle Benson, the owner-president of Computer Services Company, is unfamiliar with the statement of cash flows that you, as his accountant, prepared. He asks for further explanation.

Instructions
Write him a brief memo explaining the form and content of the statement of cash flows as shown in Illustration 17-13 (page 734).

Ethics Case

BYP17-7 Tappit Corp. is a medium-sized wholesaler of automotive parts. It has 10 stockholders who have been paid a total of $1 million in cash dividends for 8 consecutive years. The board's policy requires that, for this dividend to be declared, net cash provided by operating activities as reported in Tappit's current year's statement of cash flows must exceed $1 million. President and CEO Willie Morton's job is secure so long as he produces annual operating cash flows to support the usual dividend.

At the end of the current year, controller Robert Jennings presents president Willie Morton with some disappointing news: The net cash provided by operating activities is calculated by the indirect method to be only $970,000. The president says to Robert, "We must get that amount above $1 million. Isn't there some way to increase operating cash flow by another $30,000?" Robert answers, "These figures were prepared by my assistant. I'll go back to my office and see what I can do." The president replies, "I know you won't let me down, Robert."

Upon close scrutiny of the statement of cash flows, Robert concludes that he can get the operating cash flows above $1 million by reclassifying a $60,000, 2-year note payable listed in the financing activities section as "Proceeds from bank loan—$60,000." He will report the note instead as "Increase in payables—$60,000" and treat it as an adjustment of net income in the operating activities section. He returns to the president, saying, "You can tell the board to declare their usual dividend. Our net cash flow provided by operating activities is $1,030,000." "Good man, Robert! I knew I could count on you," exults the president.

Instructions

(a) Who are the stakeholders in this situation?

(b) Was there anything unethical about the president's actions? Was there anything unethical about the controller's actions?

(c) Are the board members or anyone else likely to discover the misclassification?

* "All About You" Activity

BYP17-8 In this chapter you learned that companies prepare a statement of cash flows in order to keep track of their sources and uses of cash and to help them plan for their future cash needs. Planning for your own short- and long-term cash needs is every bit as important as it is for a company.

Instructions

Read the article provided at **www.fool.com/savings/shortterm/02.htm**, and answer the following questions.

(a) Describe the three factors that determine how much money you should set aside for short-term needs.

(b) How many months of living expenses does the article suggest to set aside?

(c) Estimate how much you should set aside based upon your current situation. Are you closer to Cliff's scenario or to Prudence's?

? Answers to Insight and Accounting Across the Organization Questions

p. 723 Net *What?*

Q: In general, why do differences exist between net income and net cash provided by operating activities?

A: *The differences are explained by differences in the timing of the reporting of revenues and expenses under accrual accounting versus cash. Under accrual accounting, companies report revenues when earned, even if cash hasn't been received, and they report expenses when incurred, even if cash hasn't been paid.*

p. 726 Cash Flow Isn't Always What It Seems

Q: For what reasons might managers at WorldCom and at Dynegy take the actions noted above?

A: *Analysts increasingly use cash-flow-based measures of income, such as cash flow provided by operations, in addition to net income. More investors now focus on cash flow from operations, and some compensation contracts now have bonuses tied to cash-flow numbers. Thus, some managers have taken actions that artificially increase cash flow from operations.*

p. 732 GM Must Sell More Cars

Q: Why does GM's cash provided by operating activities drop so precipitously when the company's sales figures decline?

A: *GM's cash inflow is directly related to how many cars it sells. But many of its cash outflows are not tied to sales—they are "fixed." For example, many of its employee payroll costs are very rigid due to labor contracts. Therefore, even though sales (and therefore cash inflows) fall, these cash outflows don't decline.*

Authors' Comments on *All About You*: Where Does the Money Go? (p. 738)

There are really two issues to consider here. The first centers on the problems associated with accumulating debt to support discretionary expenditures. If you think that you will simply pay off your debts when you graduate, consider the fact that it is not unusual for people to spend 10 years to pay off the debts they accumulated during college.

A second issue relates to the impact that working so many hours can have on your academic performance. Research shows that college students today spend more hours working at jobs and fewer hours studying than at any time in the past. This same research shows that academic performance declines when students work too many hours at their jobs. If you could cut back on your discretionary expenditures, you could quit working so many hours, which would mean that you would do better in school, which would mean that you would have a better shot at a good job after college.

The bottom line: While we think that borrowing to invest in yourself through your education makes good sense, we think that borrowing to support a Starbucks habit is a bad idea. For more ideas on how to get your cash flow under control, see *http://financialplan.about.com/cs/college/a/MoneyCollege.htm*.

Answer to PepsiCo Review It Question 4, p. 724

In its 2005 statement of cash flows, PepsiCo reported:

(1) net cash provided by operating activities of $5.852 billion;
(2) net cash used for investing activities of $3.517 million; and
(3) net cash used for financing activities of $1.878 billion.

Answers to Self-Study Questions

1. c 2. b 3. a 4. c 5. d 6. b 7. c 8. d 9. b 10. a 11. d *12. b *13. c *14. d

Remember to go back to the Navigator box on the chapter-opening page and check off your completed work.

Chapter 18

Financial Statement Analysis

STUDY OBJECTIVES

After studying this chapter, you should be able to:

1 Discuss the need for comparative analysis.
2 Identify the tools of financial statement analysis.
3 Explain and apply horizontal analysis.
4 Describe and apply vertical analysis.
5 Identify and compute ratios used in analyzing a firm's liquidity, profitability, and solvency.
6 Understand the concept of earning power, and how irregular items are presented.
7 Understand the concept of quality of earnings.

The Navigator

The Navigator

Scan **Study Objectives**
Read **Feature Story**
Read **Preview**
Read text and answer **Before You Go On** p. 787 p. 798 p. 803 p. 806
Work **Demonstration Problems**
Review **Summary of Study Objectives**
Answer **Self-Study Questions**
Complete **Assignments**

Feature Story

"FOLLOW THAT STOCK!"

If you thought cab drivers with cell phones were scary, how about a cab driver with a trading desk in the front seat?

When a stoplight turns red or traffic backs up, New York City cabby Carlos Rubino morphs into a day trader, scanning real-time quotes of his favorite stocks as they spew across a PalmPilot mounted next to the steering wheel. "It's kind of stressful," he says, "but I like it."

Itching to know how a particular stock is doing? Mr. Rubino is happy to look up quotes for passengers. Yahoo! and Amazon.com are two of the most requested ones. He even lets customers use his laptop computer to send urgent e-mails from the back seat. Aware of a local law prohibiting cabbies from using cell phones while they're driving, Mr. Rubino extends that rule to his trading. "I stop the cab at the side of the road if I have to make a trade," he says. "Safety first."

Originally from São Paulo, Brazil, Mr. Rubino has been driving his cab since 1987, and started trading stocks a few years ago. His curiosity grew as he began to educate himself by reading business publications. The Wall Street brokers he picks up are usually impressed with his knowledge, he says. But the feeling generally isn't mutual. Some of them "don't know much," he says. "They buy what people tell them to buy—they're like a toll collector."

Mr. Rubino is an enigma to his fellow cab drivers. A lot of his colleagues say they want to trade too. "But cab drivers are a little cheap," he says. "The [real-time] quotes cost $100 a month. The wireless Internet access is $54 a month."

Will he give up his brokerage firm on wheels for a stationary job? Not likely. Though he claims a 70% return on his investments in some months, he says he makes $1,300 and up a week driving his cab—more than he does trading. Besides, he adds, "Why go somewhere and have a boss?"

Source: Excerpted from Barbara Boydston, "With This Cab, People Jump in and Shout, 'Follow that Stock!'," *Wall Street Journal*, August 18, 1999, p. C1. Reprinted by permission of the Wall Street Journal © 1999 Dow Jones & Company, Inc. All Rights Reserved Worldwide.

✓ The Navigator

Inside Chapter 18...

Preview of Chapter 18

We can learn an important lesson from the Feature Story: Experience is the best teacher. By now you have learned a significant amount about financial reporting by U.S. companies. Using some of the basic decision tools presented in this book, you can perform a rudimentary analysis on any U.S. company and draw basic conclusions about its financial health. Although it would not be wise for you to bet your life savings on a company's stock relying solely on your current level of knowledge, we strongly encourage you to practice your new skills wherever possible. Only with practice will you improve your ability to interpret financial numbers.

Before unleashing you on the world of high finance, we will present a few more important concepts and techniques, as well as provide you with one more comprehensive review of corporate financial statements. We use all of the decision tools presented in this text to analyze a single company—J.C. Penney Company, one of the country's oldest and largest retail store chains.

The content and organization of Chapter 18 are as follows.

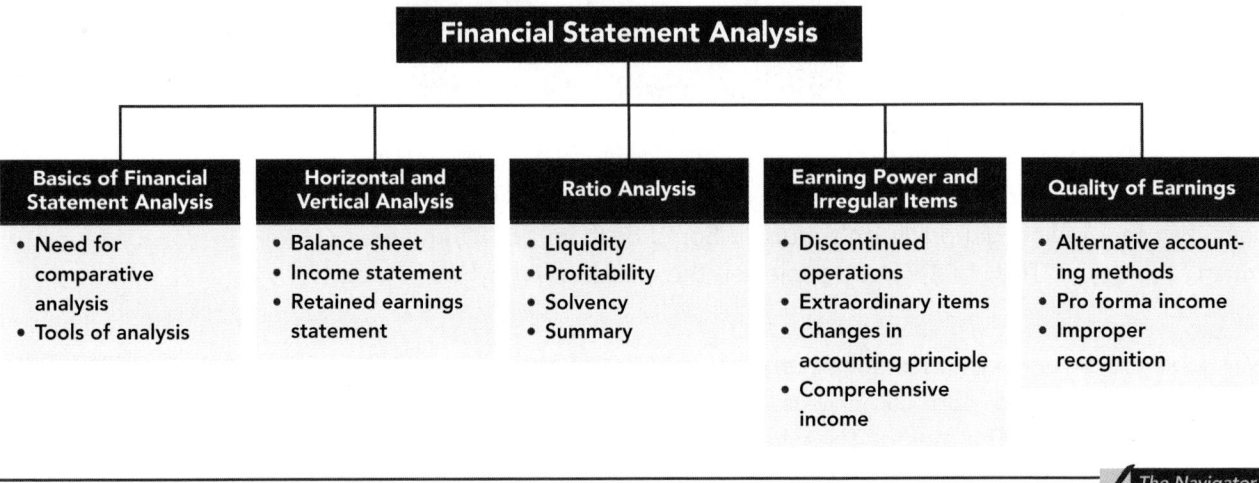

Financial Statement Analysis

Basics of Financial Statement Analysis
- Need for comparative analysis
- Tools of analysis

Horizontal and Vertical Analysis
- Balance sheet
- Income statement
- Retained earnings statement

Ratio Analysis
- Liquidity
- Profitability
- Solvency
- Summary

Earning Power and Irregular Items
- Discontinued operations
- Extraordinary items
- Changes in accounting principle
- Comprehensive income

Quality of Earnings
- Alternative accounting methods
- Pro forma income
- Improper recognition

The Navigator

BASICS OF FINANCIAL STATEMENT ANALYSIS

Analyzing financial statements involves evaluating three characteristics: a company's liquidity, profitability, and solvency. A **short-term creditor**, such as a bank, is primarily interested in liquidity—the ability of the borrower to pay obligations when they come due. The liquidity of the borrower is extremely important in evaluating the safety of a loan. A **long-term creditor**, such as a bondholder, looks to profitability and solvency measures that indicate the company's ability to survive over a long period of time. Long-term creditors consider such measures as the amount of debt in the company's capital structure and its ability to meet interest payments. Similarly, **stockholders** look at the profitability and solvency of the company. They want to assess the likelihood of dividends and the growth potential of the stock.

Need for Comparative Analysis

STUDY OBJECTIVE 1

Discuss the need for comparative analysis.

Every item reported in a financial statement has significance. When J.C. Penney Company, Inc. reports cash of $3,016 million on its balance sheet, we know the company had that amount of cash on the balance sheet date. But, we do not know whether the amount represents an increase over prior years, or whether it is adequate in relation to the company's need for cash. To obtain such information, we need to compare the amount of cash with other financial statement data.

Comparisons can be made on a number of different bases. Three are illustrated in this chapter:

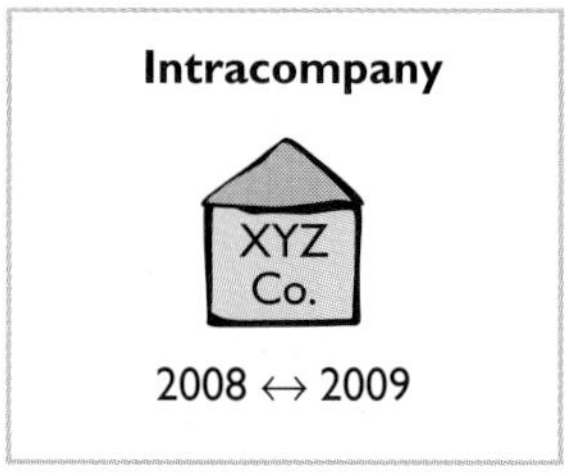

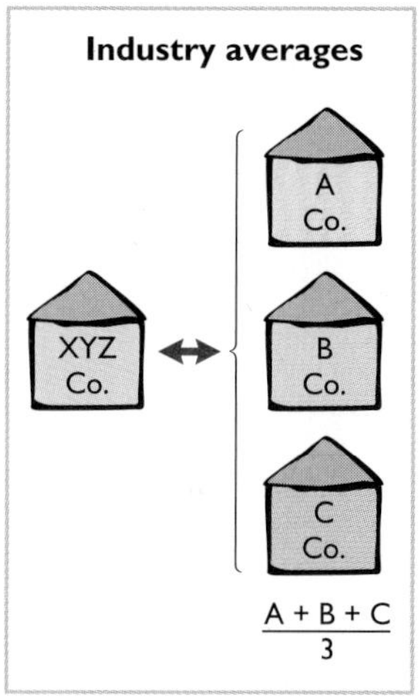

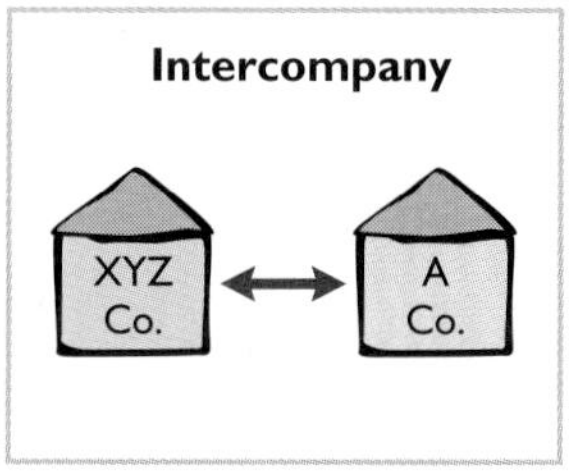

1. **Intracompany basis.** This basis compares an item or financial relationship **within a company** in the current year with the same item or relationship in one or more prior years. For example, J.C. Penney can compare its cash balance at the end of the current year with last year's balance to find the amount of the increase or decrease. Likewise, J.C. Penney can compare the percentage of cash to current assets at the end of the current year with the percentage in one or more prior years. Intracompany comparisons are useful in detecting changes in financial relationships and significant trends.
2. **Industry averages.** This basis compares an item or financial relationship of a company with **industry averages** (or **norms**) published by financial ratings organizations such as Dun & Bradstreet, Moody's, and Standard & Poor's. For example, J.C. Penney's net income can be compared with the average net income of all companies in the retail chain-store industry. Comparisons with industry averages provide information as to a company's relative performance within the industry.
3. **Intercompany basis.** This basis compares an item or financial relationship of one company with the same item or relationship in **one or more competing companies**. Analysts make these comparisons on the basis of the published financial statements of the individual companies. For example, we can compare J.C. Penney's total sales for the year with the total sales of a major competitor such as Kmart. Intercompany comparisons are useful in determining a company's competitive position.

Tools of Analysis

STUDY OBJECTIVE 2

Identify the tools of financial statement analysis.

We use various tools to evaluate the significance of financial statement data. Three commonly used tools are these:

- **Horizontal analysis** evaluates a series of financial statement data over a period of time.
- **Vertical analysis** evaluates financial statement data by expressing each item in a financial statement as a percent of a base amount.
- **Ratio analysis** expresses the relationship among selected items of financial statement data.

Horizontal analysis is used primarily in intracompany comparisons. Two features in published financial statements facilitate this type of comparison: First, each of the basic financial statements presents comparative financial data for a minimum of two years. Second, a summary of selected financial data is presented for a series of five to ten years or more. *Vertical analysis* is used in both intra- and intercompany comparisons. *Ratio analysis* is used in all three types of comparisons. In the following sections, we explain and illustrate each of the three types of analysis.

HORIZONTAL ANALYSIS

STUDY OBJECTIVE 3

Explain and apply horizontal analysis.

Horizontal analysis, also called **trend analysis**, is a technique for evaluating a series of financial statement data over a period of time. Its purpose is to determine the increase or decrease that has taken place. This change may be expressed as either an amount or a percentage. For example, the recent net sales figures of J.C. Penney Company are as follows.

Illustration 18-1
J.C. Penney Company's net sales

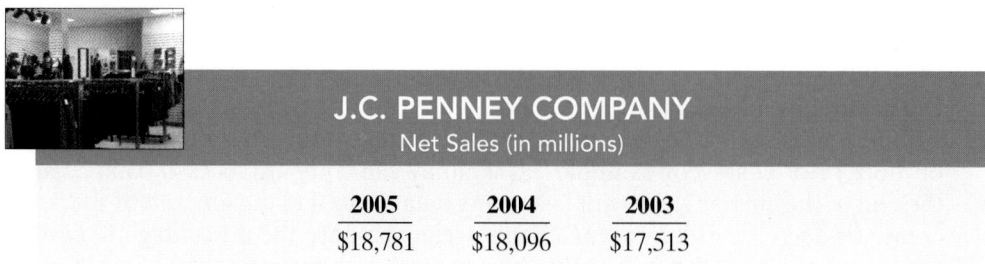

J.C. PENNEY COMPANY Net Sales (in millions)		
2005	**2004**	**2003**
$18,781	$18,096	$17,513

If we assume that 2003 is the base year, we can measure all percentage increases or decreases from this base period amount as follows.

Illustration 18-2
Formula for horizontal analysis of changes since base period

$$\text{Change Since Base Period} = \frac{\text{Current Year Amount} - \text{Base Year Amount}}{\text{Base Year Amount}}$$

For example, we can determine that net sales for J.C. Penney increased from 2003 to 2004 approximately 3.3% [($18,096 − $17,513) ÷ $17,513]. Similarly, we can determine that net sales increased from 2003 to 2005 approximately 7.2% [($18,781 − $17,513) ÷ $17,513].

Alternatively, we can express current year sales as a percentage of the base period. We do this by dividing the current year amount by the base year amount, as shown below.

Illustration 18-3
Formula for horizontal analysis of current year in relation to base year

$$\text{Current Results in Relation to Base Period} = \frac{\text{Current Year Amount}}{\text{Base Year Amount}}$$

Illustration 18-4 presents this analysis for J.C. Penney for a three-year period using 2003 as the base period.

Illustration 18-4
Horizontal analysis of J.C. Penney Company's net sales in relation to base period

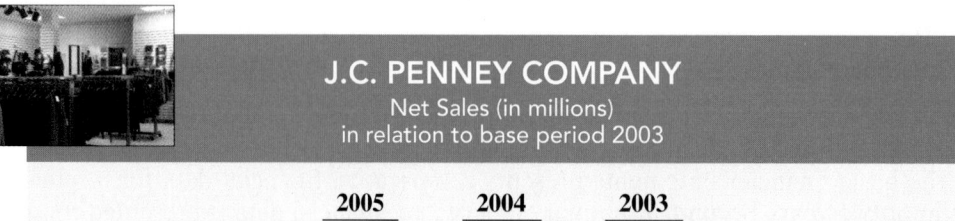

J.C. PENNEY COMPANY Net Sales (in millions) in relation to base period 2003		
2005	**2004**	**2003**
$18,781	$18,096	$17,513
107.2%	103.3%	100.0%

Balance Sheet

To further illustrate horizontal analysis, we will use the financial statements of Quality Department Store Inc., a fictional retailer. Illustration 18-5 presents a horizontal analysis of its two-year condensed balance sheets, showing dollar and percentage changes.

Illustration 18-5
Horizontal analysis of balance sheets

QUALITY DEPARTMENT STORE INC.
Condensed Balance Sheets
December 31

	2005	2004	Increase or (Decrease) during 2005 Amount	Percent
Assets				
Current assets	$1,020,000	$ 945,000	**$ 75,000**	**7.9%**
Plant assets (net)	800,000	632,500	**167,500**	**26.5%**
Intangible assets	15,000	17,500	**(2,500)**	**(14.3%)**
Total assets	$1,835,000	$1,595,000	**$240,000**	**15.0%**
Liabilities				
Current liabilities	$ 344,500	$ 303,000	**$ 41,500**	**13.7%**
Long-term liabilities	487,500	497,000	**(9,500)**	**(1.9%)**
Total liabilities	832,000	800,000	**32,000**	**4.0%**
Stockholders' Equity				
Common stock, $1 par	275,400	270,000	**5,400**	**2.0%**
Retained earnings	727,600	525,000	**202,600**	**38.6%**
Total stockholders' equity	1,003,000	795,000	**208,000**	**26.2%**
Total liabilities and stockholders' equity	$1,835,000	$1,595,000	**$240,000**	**15.0%**

The comparative balance sheets in Illustration 18-5 show that a number of significant changes have occurred in Quality Department Store's financial structure from 2004 to 2005:

- In the assets section, plant assets (net) increased $167,500, or 26.5%.
- In the liabilities section, current liabilities increased $41,500, or 13.7%.
- In the stockholders' equity section, retained earnings increased $202,600, or 38.6%.

These changes suggest that the company expanded its asset base during 2005 and **financed this expansion primarily by retaining income** rather than assuming additional long-term debt.

Income Statement

Illustration 18-6 (page 784) presents a horizontal analysis of the two-year condensed income statements of Quality Department Store Inc. for the years 2005 and 2004. Horizontal analysis of the income statements shows the following changes:

- Net sales increased $260,000, or 14.2% ($260,000 ÷ $1,837,000).
- Cost of goods sold increased $141,000, or 12.4% ($141,000 ÷ $1,140,000).
- Total operating expenses increased $37,000, or 11.6% ($37,000 ÷ $320,000).

Overall, gross profit and net income were up substantially. Gross profit increased 17.1%, and net income, 26.5%. Quality's profit trend appears favorable.

Illustration 18-6
Horizontal analysis of income statements

QUALITY DEPARTMENT STORE INC.
Condensed Income Statements
For the Years Ended December 31

	2005	2004	Increase or (Decrease) during 2005 Amount	Percent
Sales	$2,195,000	$1,960,000	$235,000	12.0%
Sales returns and allowances	98,000	123,000	(25,000)	(20.3%)
Net sales	2,097,000	1,837,000	260,000	14.2%
Cost of goods sold	1,281,000	1,140,000	141,000	12.4%
Gross profit	816,000	697,000	119,000	17.1%
Selling expenses	253,000	211,500	41,500	19.6%
Administrative expenses	104,000	108,500	(4,500)	(4.1%)
Total operating expenses	357,000	320,000	37,000	11.6%
Income from operations	459,000	377,000	82,000	21.8%
Other revenues and gains				
Interest and dividends	9,000	11,000	(2,000)	(18.2%)
Other expenses and losses				
Interest expense	36,000	40,500	(4,500)	(11.1%)
Income before income taxes	432,000	347,500	84,500	24.3%
Income tax expense	168,200	139,000	29,200	21.0%
Net income	$ 263,800	$ 208,500	$ 55,300	26.5%

HELPFUL HINT
Note that though the amount column is additive (the total is $55,300), the percentage column is not additive (26.5% is not the total). A separate percentage has been calculated for each item.

Retained Earnings Statement

Illustration 18-7 presents a horizontal analysis of Quality Department Store's comparative retained earnings statements. Analyzed horizontally, net income increased $55,300, or 26.5%, whereas dividends on the common stock increased only $1,200, or 2%. We saw in the horizontal analysis of the balance sheet that ending retained earnings increased 38.6%. As indicated earlier, the company retained a significant portion of net income to finance additional plant facilities.

Illustration 18-7
Horizontal analysis of retained earnings statements

QUALITY DEPARTMENT STORE INC.
Retained Earnings Statements
For the Years Ended December 31

	2005	2004	Increase or (Decrease) during 2005 Amount	Percent
Retained earnings, Jan. 1	$525,000	$376,500	$148,500	39.4%
Add: Net income	263,800	208,500	55,300	26.5%
	788,800	585,000	203,800	
Deduct: Dividends	61,200	60,000	1,200	2.0%
Retained earnings, Dec. 31	$727,600	$525,000	$202,600	38.6%

Horizontal analysis of changes from period to period is relatively straightforward and is quite useful. But complications can occur in making the computations. If an item has no value in a base year or preceding year but does have a value in the next year, we cannot compute a percentage change. Similarly, if a negative amount appears in the base or preceding period and a positive amount exists the following year (or vice versa), no percentage change can be computed.

VERTICAL ANALYSIS

STUDY OBJECTIVE 4
Describe and apply vertical analysis.

Vertical analysis, also called **common-size analysis**, is a technique that expresses each financial statement item as a percent of a base amount. On a balance sheet we might say that current assets are 22% of total assets—*total assets* being the base amount. Or on an income statement, we might say that selling expenses are 16% of net sales—*net sales* being the base amount.

Balance Sheet

Illustration 18-8 presents the vertical analysis of Quality Department Store Inc.'s comparative balance sheets. The base for the asset items is **total assets**. The base for the liability and stockholders' equity items is **total liabilities and stockholders' equity**.

Illustration 18-8
Vertical analysis of balance sheets

QUALITY DEPARTMENT STORE INC.
Condensed Balance Sheets
December 31

	2005		2004	
	Amount	**Percent**	**Amount**	**Percent**
Assets				
Current assets	$1,020,000	**55.6%**	$ 945,000	**59.2%**
Plant assets (net)	800,000	**43.6%**	632,500	**39.7%**
Intangible assets	15,000	**0.8%**	17,500	**1.1%**
Total assets	$1,835,000	**100.0%**	$1,595,000	**100.0%**
Liabilities				
Current liabilities	$ 344,500	**18.8%**	$ 303,000	**19.0%**
Long-term liabilities	487,500	**26.5%**	497,000	**31.2%**
Total liabilities	832,000	**45.3%**	800,000	**50.2%**
Stockholders' Equity				
Common stock, $1 par	275,400	**15.0%**	270,000	**16.9%**
Retained earnings	727,600	**39.7%**	525,000	**32.9%**
Total stockholders' equity	1,003,000	**54.7%**	795,000	**49.8%**
Total liabilities and stockholders' equity	$1,835,000	**100.0%**	$1,595,000	**100.0%**

HELPFUL HINT
The formula for calculating these balance sheet percentages is:

$$\frac{\text{Each item on B/S}}{\text{Total assets}} = \%$$

Vertical analysis shows the relative size of each category in the balance sheet. It also can show the **percentage change** in the individual asset, liability, and stockholders' equity items. For example, we can see that current assets decreased from 59.2% of total assets in 2004 to 55.6% in 2005 (even though the absolute dollar amount increased $75,000 in that time). Plant assets (net) have increased from 39.7% to 43.6% of total assets. Retained earnings have increased from 32.9% to 39.7% of total liabilities and stockholders' equity. These results reinforce the earlier observations that **Quality is choosing to finance its growth through retention of earnings rather than through issuing additional debt**.

Income Statement

Illustration 18-9 (page 786) shows vertical analysis of Quality's income statements. Cost of goods sold as a percentage of net sales declined 1% (62.1% vs. 61.1%), and total operating expenses declined 0.4% (17.4% vs. 17.0%). As a result, it is not surprising to see net income as a percent of net sales increase from 11.4% to 12.6%. Quality appears to be a profitable enterprise that is becoming even more successful.

Illustration 18-9
Vertical analysis of income statements

QUALITY DEPARTMENT STORE INC.
Condensed Income Statements
For the Years Ended December 31

	2005		2004	
	Amount	**Percent**	**Amount**	**Percent**
Sales	$2,195,000	104.7%	$1,960,000	106.7%
Sales returns and allowances	98,000	4.7%	123,000	6.7%
Net sales	2,097,000	100.0%	1,837,000	100.0%
Cost of goods sold	1,281,000	61.1%	1,140,000	62.1%
Gross profit	816,000	38.9%	697,000	37.9%
Selling expenses	253,000	12.0%	211,500	11.5%
Administrative expenses	104,000	5.0%	108,500	5.9%
Total operating expenses	357,000	17.0%	320,000	17.4%
Income from operations	459,000	21.9%	377,000	20.5%
Other revenues and gains				
Interest and dividends	9,000	0.4%	11,000	0.6%
Other expenses and losses				
Interest expense	36,000	1.7%	40,500	2.2%
Income before income taxes	432,000	20.6%	347,500	18.9%
Income tax expense	168,200	8.0%	139,000	7.5%
Net income	$ 263,800	12.6%	$ 208,500	11.4%

HELPFUL HINT
The formula for calculating these income statement percentages is:

$$\frac{\text{Each item on I/S}}{\text{Net sales}} = \%$$

An associated benefit of vertical analysis is that it enables you to compare companies of different sizes. For example, Quality's main competitor is a JC Penney store in a nearby town. Using vertical analysis, we can compare the condensed income statements of Quality Department Store Inc. (a small retail company) with J.C. Penney Company, Inc. (a giant international retailer), as shown in Illustration 18-10.

Illustration 18-10
Intercompany income statement comparison

CONDENSED INCOME STATEMENTS
(in thousands)

	Quality Department Store Inc.		J. C. Penney Company[1]	
	Dollars	**Percent**	**Dollars**	**Percent**
Net sales	$2,097	100.0%	$18,781,000	100.0%
Cost of goods sold	1,281	61.1%	11,405,000	60.7%
Gross profit	816	38.9%	7,376,000	39.3%
Selling and administrative expenses	357	17.0%	5,799,000	30.9%
Income from operations	459	21.9%	1,577,000	8.4%
Other expenses and revenues (including income taxes)	195	9.3%	489,000	2.6%
Net income	$ 264	12.6%	$ 1,088,000	5.8%

[1] *2005 Annual Report* J.C. Penney Company, Inc. (Dallas, Texas).

J.C. Penney's net sales are 8,956 times greater than the net sales of relatively tiny Quality Department Store. But vertical analysis eliminates this difference in size. The percentages show that Quality's and J.C. Penney's gross profit rates were comparable at 38.9% and 39.3%. However, the percentages related to income from operations were significantly different at 21.9% and 8.4%. This disparity can be attributed to Quality's selling and administrative expense percentage (17%) which is much lower than J.C. Penney's (30.9%). Although J.C. Penney earned net income more than 4,121 times larger than Quality's, J.C. Penney's net income as a **percent of each sales dollar** (5.8%) is only 46% of Quality's (12.6%).

Before You Go On...

REVIEW IT

1. What are the different tools that might be used to compare financial information?
2. What is horizontal analysis?
3. What is vertical analysis?
4. Identify the specific sections in PepsiCo's 2005 Annual Report where horizontal and vertical analysis of financial data is presented. The answer to this question is provided on page 829.

DO IT

Summary financial information for Rosepatch Company is as follows.

	December 31, 2008	December 31, 2007
Current assets	$234,000	$180,000
Plant assets (net)	756,000	420,000
Total assets	$990,000	$600,000

Compute the amount and percentage changes in 2008 using horizontal analysis, assuming 2007 is the base year.

Action Plan

- Find the percentage change by dividing the amount of the increase by the 2007 amount (base year).

Solution

	Increase in 2008	
	Amount	Percent
Current assets	$ 54,000	30% [($234,000 − $180,000) ÷ $180,000]
Plant assets (net)	336,000	80% [($756,000 − $420,000) ÷ $420,000]
Total assets	$390,000	65% [($990,000 − $600,000) ÷ $600,000]

Related exercise material: *BE18-2, BE18-3, BE18-5, BE18-6, BE18-7, E18-1, E18-3, and E18-4.*

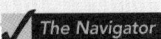

The Navigator

RATIO ANALYSIS

Ratio analysis expresses the relationship among selected items of financial statement data. A **ratio** expresses the mathematical relationship between one quantity and another. The relationship is expressed in terms of either a percentage, a rate, or a simple proportion. To illustrate, in 2005 Nike, Inc., had current assets of $6,351.1

STUDY OBJECTIVE 5

Identify and compute ratios used in analyzing a firm's liquidity, profitability, and solvency.

million and current liabilities of $1,999.2 million. We can find the relationship between these two measures by dividing current assets by current liabilities. The alternative means of expression are:

Percentage:	Current assets are 318% of current liabilities.
Rate:	Current assets are 3.18 times current liabilities.
Proportion:	The relationship of current assets to liabilities is 3.18:1.

To analyze the primary financial statements, we can use ratios to evaluate liquidity, profitability, and solvency. Illustration 18-11 describes these classifications.

Illustration 18-11
Financial ratio classifications

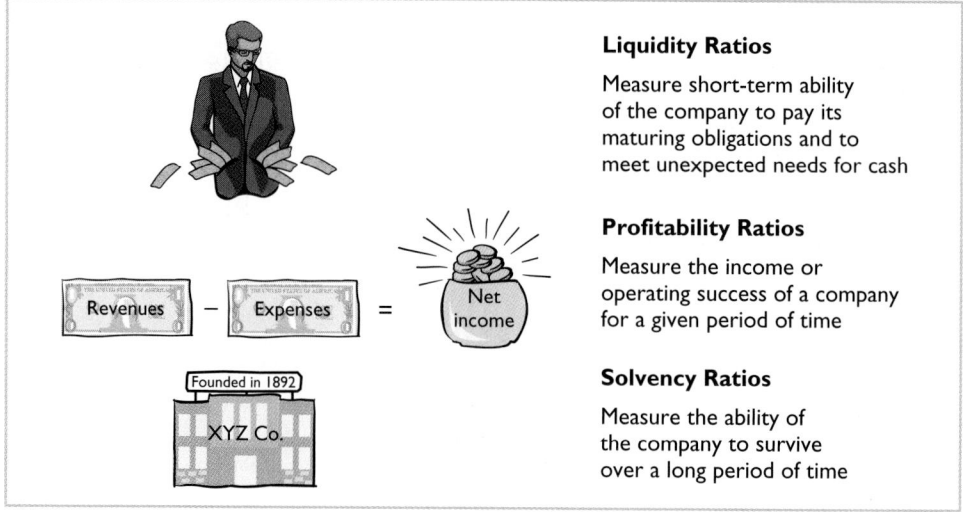

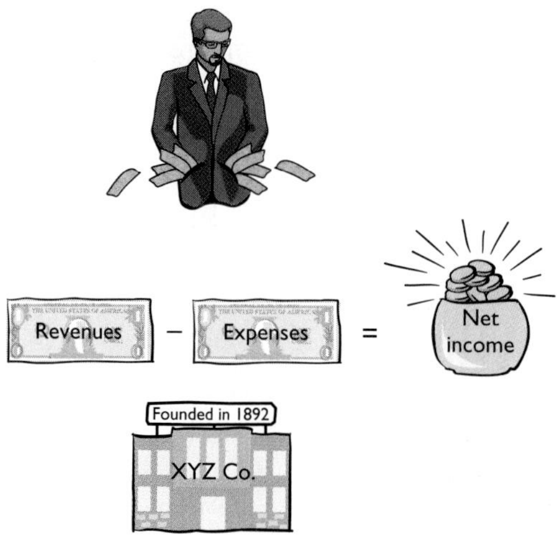

Liquidity Ratios

Measure short-term ability of the company to pay its maturing obligations and to meet unexpected needs for cash

Profitability Ratios

Measure the income or operating success of a company for a given period of time

Solvency Ratios

Measure the ability of the company to survive over a long period of time

Ratios can provide clues to underlying conditions that may not be apparent from individual financial statement components. However, a single ratio by itself is not very meaningful. Thus, in the discussion of ratios we will use the following types of comparisons.

1. **Intracompany comparisons** for two years for Quality Department Store.
2. **Industry average comparisons** based on median ratios for department stores.
3. **Intercompany comparisons** based on J.C. Penney Company as Quality Department Store's principal competitor.

Liquidity Ratios

Liquidity ratios measure the short-term ability of the company to pay its maturing obligations and to meet unexpected needs for cash. Short-term creditors such as bankers and suppliers are particularly interested in assessing liquidity. The ratios we can use to determine the enterprise's short-term debt-paying ability are the current ratio, the acid-test ratio, receivables turnover, and inventory turnover.

1. CURRENT RATIO

The **current ratio** is a widely used measure for evaluating a company's liquidity and short-term debt-paying ability. The ratio is computed by dividing current assets by current liabilities. Illustration 18-12 shows the 2005 and 2004 current ratios for Quality Department Store and comparative data.

$$\text{Current Ratio} = \frac{\text{Current Assets}}{\text{Current Liabilities}}$$

Quality Department Store

2005	2004
$\frac{\$1,020,000}{\$344,500} = 2.96:1$	$\frac{\$945,000}{\$303,000} = 3.12:1$
Industry average	J.C. Penney Company
1.28:1	5.72:1

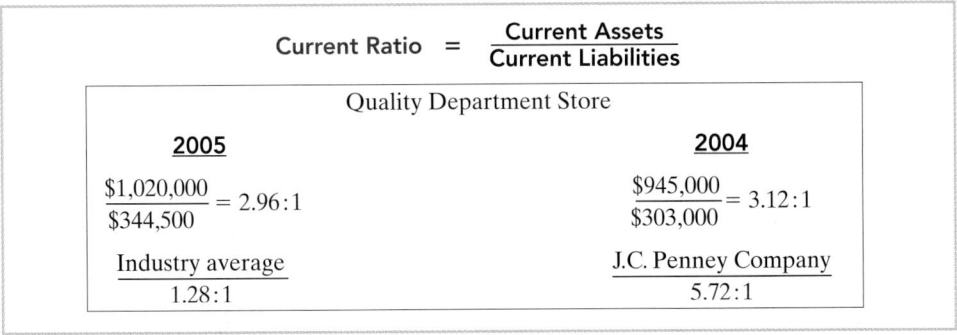

Illustration 18-12
Current ratio

HELPFUL HINT

Can any company operate successfully without working capital? Yes, if it has very predictable cash flows and solid earnings. A number of companies (e.g., Whirlpool, American Standard, **and** Campbell's Soup) **are pursuing this goal. The rationale: Less money tied up in working capital means more money to invest in the business.**

What does the ratio actually mean? The 2005 ratio of 2.96:1 means that for every dollar of current liabilities, Quality has $2.96 of current assets. Quality's current ratio has decreased in the current year. But, compared to the industry average of 1.28:1, Quality appears to be reasonably liquid. J.C. Penney has a very high current ratio of 5.72 which indicates it has considerable current assets relative to its current liabilities.

The current ratio is sometimes referred to as the **working capital ratio**; **working capital** is current assets minus current liabilities. The current ratio is a more dependable indicator of liquidity than working capital. Two companies with the same amount of working capital may have significantly different current ratios.

The current ratio is only one measure of liquidity. It does not take into account the **composition** of the current assets. For example, a satisfactory current ratio does not disclose the fact that a portion of the current assets may be tied up in slow-moving inventory. A dollar of cash would be more readily available to pay the bills than a dollar of slow-moving inventory.

ACCOUNTING ACROSS THE ORGANIZATION

How to Manage the Current Ratio

The apparent simplicity of the current ratio can have real-world limitations. An addition of equal amounts to both the numerator and the denominator causes the ratio to change.

Assume, for example, that a company has $2,000,000 of current assets and $1,000,000 of current liabilities. Its current ratio is 2:1. If it purchases $1,000,000 of inventory on account, it will have $3,000,000 of current assets and $2,000,000 of current liabilities. Its current ratio will decrease to 1.5:1. If, instead, the company pays off $500,000 of its current liabilities, it will have $1,500,000 of current assets and $500,000 of current liabilities, and its current ratio will increase to 3:1. Thus, any trend analysis should be done with care, because the ratio is susceptible to quick changes and is easily influenced by management.

? How might management influence the company's current ratio?

2. ACID-TEST RATIO

The **acid-test (quick) ratio** is a measure of a company's immediate short-term liquidity. We compute this ratio by dividing the sum of cash, short-term investments, and net receivables by current liabilities. Thus, it is an important complement to the current ratio. For example, assume that the current assets of Quality Department Store for 2005 and 2004 consist of the items shown in Illustration 18-13 (page 790).

ALTERNATIVE TERMINOLOGY

The acid-test ratio is also called the *quick ratio.*

Illustration 18-13
Current assets of Quality Department Store

QUALITY DEPARTMENT STORE INC.
Balance Sheet (partial)

	2005	2004
Current assets		
Cash	**$ 100,000**	**$155,000**
Short-term investments	**20,000**	**70,000**
Receivables (net*)	**230,000**	**180,000**
Inventory	620,000	500,000
Prepaid expenses	50,000	40,000
Total current assets	$1,020,000	$945,000

*Allowance for doubtful accounts is $10,000 at the end of each year.

Cash, short-term investments, and receivables (net) are highly liquid compared to inventory and prepaid expenses. The inventory may not be readily saleable, and the prepaid expenses may not be transferable to others. Thus, the acid-test ratio measures **immediate** liquidity. The 2005 and 2004 acid-test ratios for Quality Department Store and comparative data are as follows.

Illustration 18-14
Acid-test ratio

$$\text{Acid-Test Ratio} = \frac{\text{Cash + Short-Term Investments + Receivables (Net)}}{\text{Current Liabilities}}$$

Quality Department Store

2005	2004
$\frac{\$100,000 + \$20,000 + \$230,000}{\$344,500} = 1.02:1$	$\frac{\$155,000 + \$70,000 + \$180,000}{\$303,000} = 1.34:1$
Industry average	J.C. Penney Company
0.33:1	1.19:1

The ratio has declined in 2005. Is an acid-test ratio of 1.02:1 adequate? This depends on the industry and the economy. When compared with the industry average of 0.33:1 and Penney's of 1.19:1, Quality's acid-test ratio seems adequate.

3. RECEIVABLES TURNOVER

We can measure liquidity by how quickly a company can convert certain assets to cash. How liquid, for example, are the receivables? The ratio used to assess the liquidity of the receivables is **receivables turnover**. It measures the number of times, on average, the company collects receivables during the period. We compute receivables turnover by dividing net credit sales (net sales less cash sales) by the average net receivables. Unless seasonal factors are significant, average net receivables can be computed from the beginning and ending balances of the net receivables.[2]

Assume that all sales are credit sales. The balance of net receivables at the beginning of 2004 is $200,000. Illustration 18-15 shows the receivables turnover for Quality Department Store and comparative data. Quality's receivables turnover improved in 2005. The turnover of 10.2 times is substantially lower than J.C. Penney's 69 times, but is similar to the department store industry's average of 10.8 times.

[2] If seasonal factors are significant, the average receivables balance might be determined by using monthly amounts.

Illustration 18-15
Receivables turnover

$$\text{Receivables Turnover} = \frac{\text{Net Credit Sales}}{\text{Average Net Receivables}}$$

Quality Department Store

2005	2004
$\frac{\$2{,}097{,}000}{\left[\frac{\$180{,}000 + \$230{,}000}{2}\right]} = 10.2$ times	$\frac{\$1{,}837{,}000}{\left[\frac{\$200{,}000 + \$180{,}000}{2}\right]} = 9.7$ times
Industry average	J.C. Penney Company
10.8 times	69 times

Average Collection Period. A popular variant of the receivables turnover ratio is to convert it to an **average collection period** in terms of days. To do so, we divide the receivables turnover ratio into 365 days. For example, the receivables turnover of 10.2 times divided into 365 days gives an average collection period of approximately 36 days. This means that receivables are collected on average every 36 days, or about every 5 weeks. Analysts frequently use the average collection period to assess the effectiveness of a company's credit and collection policies. The general rule is that the collection period should not greatly exceed the credit term period (the time allowed for payment).

4. INVENTORY TURNOVER

Inventory turnover measures the number of times, on average, the inventory is sold during the period. Its purpose is to measure the liquidity of the inventory. We compute the inventory turnover by dividing cost of goods sold by the average inventory. Unless seasonal factors are significant, we can use the beginning and ending inventory balances to compute average inventory.

Assuming that the inventory balance for Quality Department Store at the beginning of 2004 was $450,000, its inventory turnover and comparative data are as shown in Illustration 18-16. Quality's inventory turnover declined slightly in 2005. The turnover of 2.3 times is relatively low compared with the industry average of 6.7 and J.C. Penney's 3.6. Generally, the faster the inventory turnover, the less cash a company has tied up in inventory and the less the chance of inventory obsolescence.

Illustration 18-16
Inventory turnover

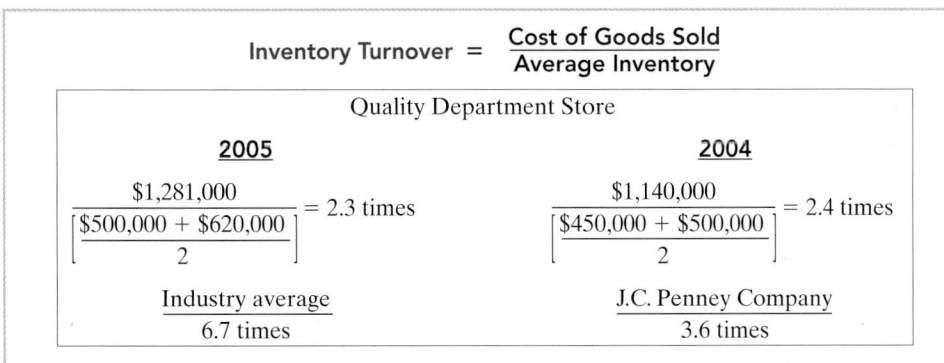

$$\text{Inventory Turnover} = \frac{\text{Cost of Goods Sold}}{\text{Average Inventory}}$$

Quality Department Store

2005	2004
$\frac{\$1{,}281{,}000}{\left[\frac{\$500{,}000 + \$620{,}000}{2}\right]} = 2.3$ times	$\frac{\$1{,}140{,}000}{\left[\frac{\$450{,}000 + \$500{,}000}{2}\right]} = 2.4$ times
Industry average	J.C. Penney Company
6.7 times	3.6 times

Days in Inventory. A variant of inventory turnover is the **days in inventory**. We calculate it by dividing the inventory turnover into 365. For example, Quality's 2005 inventory turnover of 2.3 times divided into 365 is approximately 159 days. An average selling time of 159 days is also relatively high compared with the industry average of 54.5 days (365 ÷ 6.7) and J.C. Penney's 101.4 days (365 ÷ 3.6).

Inventory turnover ratios vary considerably among industries. For example, grocery store chains have a turnover of 10 times and an average selling period of 37 days. In contrast, jewelry stores have an average turnover of 1.3 times and an average selling period of 281 days.

Profitability Ratios

Profitability ratios measure the income or operating success of a company for a given period of time. Income, or the lack of it, affects the company's ability to obtain debt and equity financing. It also affects the company's liquidity position and the company's ability to grow. As a consequence, both creditors and investors are interested in evaluating earning power—profitability. Analysts frequently use profitability as the ultimate test of management's operating effectiveness.

ALTERNATIVE TERMINOLOGY

Profit margin is also called the *rate of return on sales.*

5. PROFIT MARGIN

Profit margin is a measure of the percentage of each dollar of sales that results in net income. We can compute it by dividing net income by net sales. Illustration 18-17 shows Quality Department Store's profit margin and comparative data.

Illustration 18-17
Profit margin

$$\text{Profit Margin} = \frac{\text{Net Income}}{\text{Net Sales}}$$

Quality Department Store

2005	2004
$\frac{\$263,800}{\$2,097,000} = 12.6\%$	$\frac{\$208,500}{\$1,837,000} = 11.4\%$
Industry average	J.C. Penney Company
3.6%	3.7%

Quality experienced an increase in its profit margin from 2004 to 2005. Its profit margin is unusually high in comparison with the industry average of 3.6% and J.C. Penney's 3.7%.

High-volume (high inventory turnover) enterprises such as grocery stores (Safeway or Kroger) and discount stores (Kmart or Wal-Mart) generally experience low profit margins. In contrast, low-volume enterprises such as jewelry stores (Tiffany & Co.) or airplane manufacturers (Boeing Co.) have high profit margins.

6. ASSET TURNOVER

Asset turnover measures how efficiently a company uses its assets to generate sales. It is determined by dividing net sales by average assets. The resulting number shows the dollars of sales produced by each dollar invested in assets. Unless seasonal factors are significant, we can use the beginning and ending balance of total assets to determine average total assets. Assuming that total assets at the beginning of 2004 were $1,446,000, the 2005 and 2004 asset turnover for Quality Department Store and comparative data are Shown in Illustration 18-18.

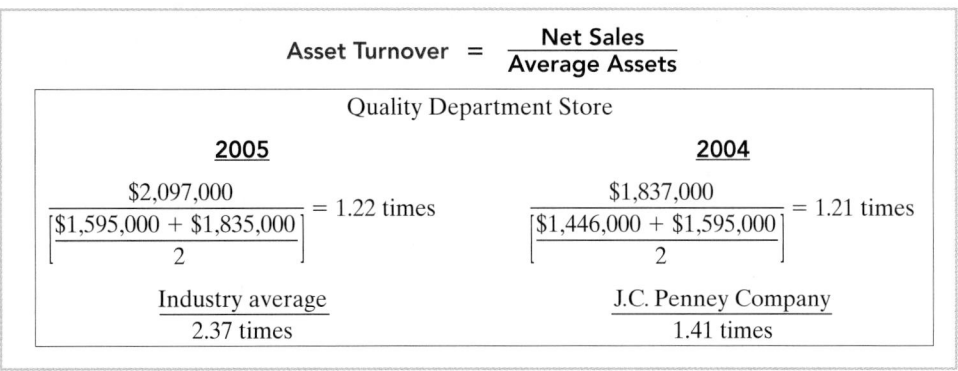

Illustration 18-18
Asset turnover

$$\text{Asset Turnover} = \frac{\text{Net Sales}}{\text{Average Assets}}$$

Quality Department Store

2005	2004
$\frac{\$2{,}097{,}000}{\left[\frac{\$1{,}595{,}000 + \$1{,}835{,}000}{2}\right]} = 1.22\text{ times}$	$\frac{\$1{,}837{,}000}{\left[\frac{\$1{,}446{,}000 + \$1{,}595{,}000}{2}\right]} = 1.21\text{ times}$
Industry average	J.C. Penney Company
2.37 times	1.41 times

Asset turnover shows that in 2005 Quality generated sales of $1.22 for each dollar it had invested in assets. The ratio changed little from 2004 to 2005. Quality's asset turnover is below the industry average of 2.37 times and J.C. Penney's ratio of 1.41 times.

Asset turnover ratios vary considerably among industries. For example, a large utility company like Consolidated Edison (New York) has a ratio of 0.49 times, and the large grocery chain Kroger Stores has a ratio of 4.34 times.

7. RETURN ON ASSETS

An overall measure of profitability is **return on assets**. We compute this ratio by dividing net income by average assets. The 2005 and 2004 return on assets for Quality Department Store and comparative data are shown below.

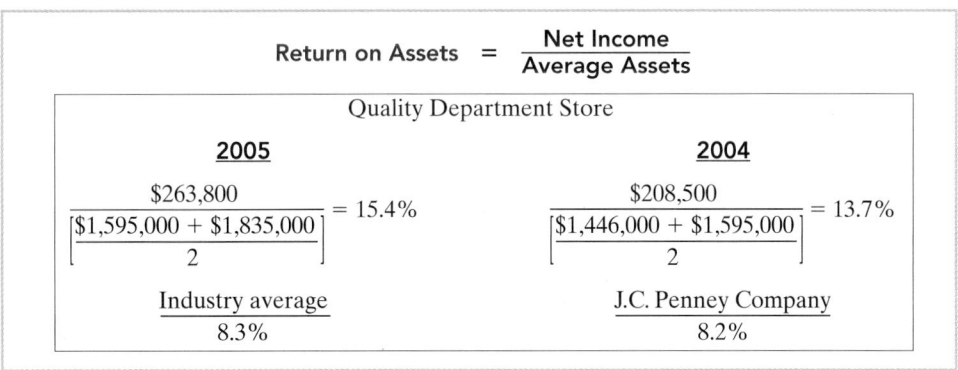

Illustration 18-19
Return on assets

$$\text{Return on Assets} = \frac{\text{Net Income}}{\text{Average Assets}}$$

Quality Department Store

2005	2004
$\frac{\$263{,}800}{\left[\frac{\$1{,}595{,}000 + \$1{,}835{,}000}{2}\right]} = 15.4\%$	$\frac{\$208{,}500}{\left[\frac{\$1{,}446{,}000 + \$1{,}595{,}000}{2}\right]} = 13.7\%$
Industry average	J.C. Penney Company
8.3%	8.2%

Quality's return on assets improved from 2004 to 2005. Its return of 15.4% is very high compared with the department store industry average of 8.3% and J.C. Penney's 8.2%.

8. RETURN ON COMMON STOCKHOLDERS' EQUITY

Another widely used profitability ratio is **return on common stockholders' equity**. It measures profitability from the common stockholders' viewpoint. This ratio shows how many dollars of net income the company earned for each dollar invested by the owners. We compute it by dividing net income by average common stockholders' equity. Assuming that common stockholders' equity at the beginning of 2004 was $667,000, Illustration 18-20 shows the 2005 and 2004 ratios for Quality Department Store and comparative data.

Illustration 18-20
Return on common stockholders' equity

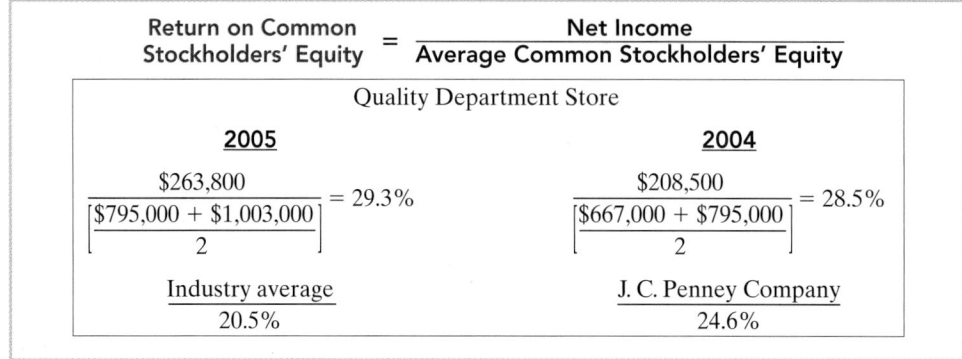

$$\text{Return on Common Stockholders' Equity} = \frac{\text{Net Income}}{\text{Average Common Stockholders' Equity}}$$

Quality Department Store

2005	2004
$\dfrac{\$263{,}800}{\left[\dfrac{\$795{,}000 + \$1{,}003{,}000}{2}\right]} = 29.3\%$	$\dfrac{\$208{,}500}{\left[\dfrac{\$667{,}000 + \$795{,}000}{2}\right]} = 28.5\%$
Industry average: 20.5%	J. C. Penney Company: 24.6%

Quality's rate of return on common stockholders' equity is high at 29.3%, considering an industry average of 20.5% and a rate of 24.6% for J.C. Penney.

With Preferred Stock. When a company has preferred stock, we must deduct **preferred dividend** requirements from net income to compute income available to common stockholders. Similarly, we deduct the par value of preferred stock (or call price, if applicable) from total stockholders' equity to determine the amount of common stockholders' equity used in this ratio. The ratio then appears as follows.

Illustration 18-21
Return on common stockholders' equity with preferred stock

$$\text{Return on Common Stockholders' Equity} = \frac{\text{Net Income} - \text{Preferred Dividends}}{\text{Average Common Stockholders' Equity}}$$

Note that Quality's rate of return on stockholders' equity (29.3%) is substantially higher than its rate of return on assets (15.4%). The reason is that Quality has made effective use of **leverage**. **Leveraging** or **trading on the equity** at a gain means that the company has borrowed money at a lower rate of interest than it is able to earn by using the borrowed money. Leverage enables Quality Department Store to use money supplied by nonowners to increase the return to the owners. A comparison of the rate of return on total assets with the rate of interest paid for borrowed money indicates the profitability of trading on the equity. Quality Department Store earns more on its borrowed funds than it has to pay in the form of interest. Thus the return to stockholders exceeds the return on the assets, due to benefits from the positive leveraging.

9. EARNINGS PER SHARE (EPS)

Earnings per share (EPS) is a measure of the net income earned on each share of common stock. It is computed by dividing net income by the number of weighted average common shares outstanding during the year. A measure of net income earned on a per share basis provides a useful perspective for determining profitability. Assuming that there is no change in the number of outstanding shares during 2004 and that the 2005 increase occurred midyear, Illustration 18-22 shows the net income per share for Quality Department Store for 2005 and 2004.

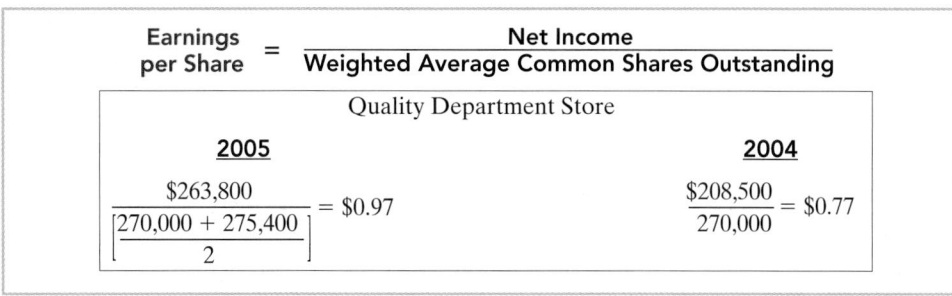

Illustration 18-22
Earnings per share

$$\text{Earnings per Share} = \frac{\text{Net Income}}{\text{Weighted Average Common Shares Outstanding}}$$

Quality Department Store

2005	2004
$\frac{\$263,800}{\left[\frac{270,000 + 275,400}{2}\right]} = \$0.97$	$\frac{\$208,500}{270,000} = \$0.77$

Note that no industry or J.C. Penney data are presented. Such comparisons are not meaningful because of the wide variations in the number of shares of outstanding stock among companies. The only meaningful EPS comparison is an intracompany trend comparison: Quality's earnings per share increased 20 cents per share in 2005. This represents a 26% increase over the 2004 earnings per share of 77 cents.

The terms "earnings per share" and "net income per share" refer to the amount of net income applicable to each share of **common stock**. Therefore, in computing EPS, if there are preferred dividends declared for the period, we must deduct them from net income to determine income available to the common stockholders.

10. PRICE-EARNINGS RATIO

The **price-earnings (P-E) ratio** is an oft-quoted measure of the ratio of the market price of each share of common stock to the earnings per share. The price-earnings (P-E) ratio reflects investors' assessments of a company's future earnings. We compute it by dividing the market price per share of the stock by earnings per share. Assuming that the market price of Quality Department Store Inc. stock is $8 in 2004 and $12 in 2005, the price-earnings ratio computation is as follows.

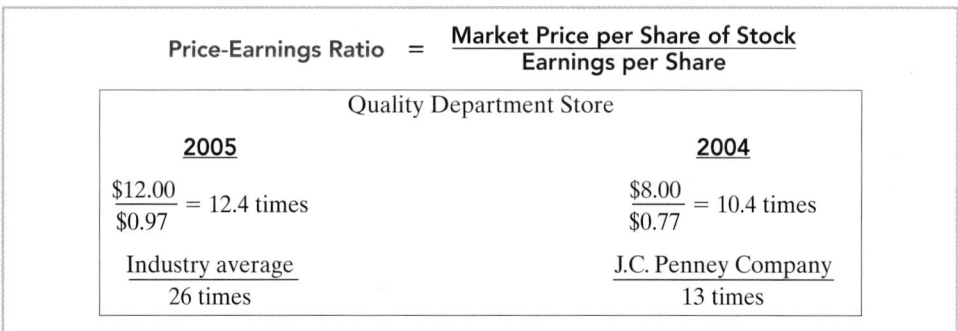

Illustration 18-23
Price-earnings ratio

$$\text{Price-Earnings Ratio} = \frac{\text{Market Price per Share of Stock}}{\text{Earnings per Share}}$$

Quality Department Store

2005	2004
$\frac{\$12.00}{\$0.97} = 12.4 \text{ times}$	$\frac{\$8.00}{\$0.77} = 10.4 \text{ times}$
Industry average	J.C. Penney Company
26 times	13 times

In 2005 each share of Quality's stock sold for 12.4 times the amount that the company earned on each share. Quality's price-earnings ratio is lower than the industry average of 26 times, but almost the same as the ratio of 13 times for J.C. Penney. The average price-earnings ratio for the stocks that constitute the Standard and Poor's 500 Index (500 largest U.S. firms) in early 2006 was a little less than 20 times.

11. PAYOUT RATIO

The **payout ratio** measures the percentage of earnings distributed in the form of cash dividends. We compute it by dividing cash dividends by net income. Companies that have high growth rates generally have low payout ratios because they reinvest most of their net income into the business. The 2005 and 2004 payout ratios for Quality Department Store are computed as shown in Illustration 18-24 (page 796).

Illustration 18-24
Payout ratio

$$\text{Payout Ratio} = \frac{\text{Cash Dividends}}{\text{Net Income}}$$

Quality Department Store

2005	2004
$\frac{\$61,200}{\$263,800} = 23.2\%$	$\frac{\$60,000}{\$208,500} = 28.8\%$
Industry average	J.C. Penney Company
16.0%	12.0%

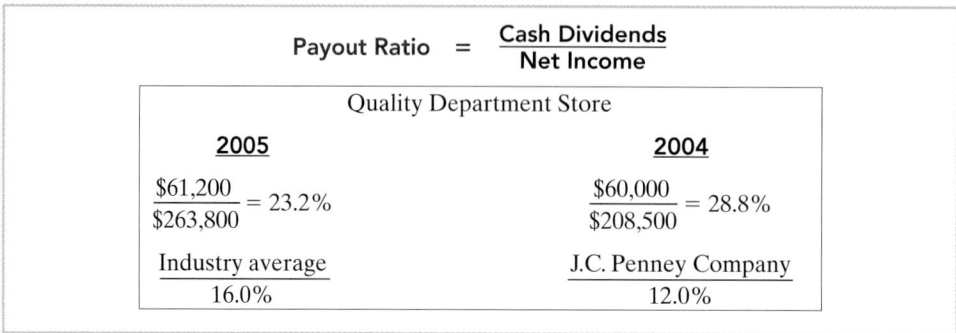

Quality's payout ratio is higher than J.C. Penney's payout ratio of 12.0%. As indicated earlier (page 785), Quality funded its purchase of plant assets through retention of earnings but still is able to pay dividends.

Solvency Ratios

Solvency ratios measure the ability of a company to survive over a long period of time. Long-term creditors and stockholders are particularly interested in a company's ability to pay interest as it comes due and to repay the face value of debt at maturity. Debt to total assets and times interest earned are two ratios that provide information about debt-paying ability.

12. DEBT TO TOTAL ASSETS RATIO

The **debt to total assets ratio** measures the percentage of the total assets that creditors provide. We compute it by dividing total debt (both current and long-term liabilities) by total assets. This ratio indicates the company's degree of leverage. It also provides some indication of the company's ability to withstand losses without impairing the interests of creditors. The higher the percentage of debt to total assets, the greater the risk that the company may be unable to meet its maturing obligations. The 2005 and 2004 ratios for Quality Department Store and comparative data are as follows.

Illustration 18-25
Debt to total assets ratio

$$\text{Debt to Total Assets Ratio} = \frac{\text{Total Debt}}{\text{Total Assets}}$$

Quality Department Store

2005	2004
$\frac{\$832,000}{\$1,835,000} = 45.3\%$	$\frac{\$800,000}{\$1,595,000} = 50.2\%$
Industry average	J.C. Penney Company
40.1%	67.8%

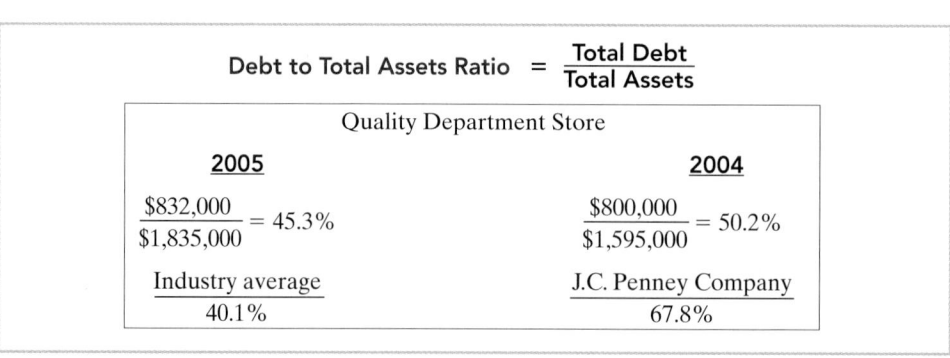

A ratio of 45.3% means that creditors have provided 45.3% of Quality Department Store's total assets. Quality's 45.3% is above the industry average of 40.1%. It is considerably below the high 67.8% ratio of J.C. Penney. The lower the ratio, the more equity "buffer" there is available to the creditors. Thus, from the creditors' point of view, a low ratio of debt to total assets is usually desirable.

The adequacy of this ratio is often judged in the light of the company's earnings. Generally, companies with relatively stable earnings (such as public utilities) have higher debt to total assets ratios than cyclical companies with widely fluctuating earnings (such as many high-tech companies).

13. TIMES INTEREST EARNED

Times interest earned provides an indication of the company's ability to meet interest payments as they come due. We compute it by dividing income before interest expense and income taxes by interest expense. Illustration 18-26 shows the 2005 and 2004 ratios for Quality Department Store and comparative data. Note that times interest earned uses income before income taxes and interest expense. This represents the amount available to cover interest. For Quality Department Store the 2005 amount of $468,000 is computed by taking the income before income taxes of $432,000 and adding back the $36,000 of interest expense.

ALTERNATIVE TERMINOLOGY

Times interest earned is also called *interest coverage*.

Illustration 18-26
Times interest earned

$$\text{Times Interest Earned} = \frac{\text{Income before Income Taxes and Interest Expense}}{\text{Interest Expense}}$$

Quality Department Store

2005	2004
$\frac{\$468,000}{\$36,000} = 13$ times	$\frac{\$388,000}{\$40,500} = 9.6$ times
Industry average	J.C. Penney Company
12 times	10.2 times

Quality's interest expense is well covered at 13 times, compared with the industry average of 12 times and J.C. Penney's 10.2 times.

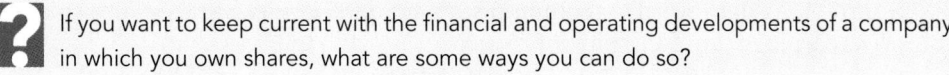

INVESTOR INSIGHT

Keeping Up to Date as an Investor

Today, investors have access to information provided by corporate managers that used to be available only to professional analysts. Corporate managers have always made themselves available to security analysts for questions at the end of every quarter. Now, because of a combination of new corporate disclosure requirements by the Securities and Exchange Commission and technologies that make communication to large numbers of people possible at a very low price, the average investor can listen in on these discussions. For example, one individual investor, Matthew Johnson, a Nortel Networks local area network engineer in Belfast, Northern Ireland, "stayed up past midnight to listen to Apple Computer's recent Internet conference call. Hearing the company's news 'from the dog's mouth,' he says 'gave me better information' than hunting through chat-rooms."

Source: Jeff D. Opdyke, "Individuals Pick Up on Conference Calls," *Wall Street Journal*, November 20, 2000.

? If you want to keep current with the financial and operating developments of a company in which you own shares, what are some ways you can do so?

Summary of Ratios

Illustration 18-27
Summary of liquidity, profitability, and solvency ratios

Illustration 18-27 summarizes the ratios discussed in this chapter. The summary includes the formula and purpose or use of each ratio.

Ratio	Formula	Purpose or Use
Liquidity Ratios		
1. Current ratio	Current assets / Current liabilities	Measures short-term debt-paying ability.
2. Acid-test (quick) ratio	(Cash + Short-term investments + Receivables (net)) / Current liabilities	Measures immediate short-term liquidity.
3. Receivables turnover	Net credit sales / Average net receivables	Measures liquidity of receivables.
4. Inventory turnover	Cost of goods sold / Average inventory	Measures liquidity of inventory.
Profitability Ratios		
5. Profit margin	Net income / Net sales	Measures net income generated by each dollar of sales.
6. Asset turnover	Net sales / Average assets	Measures how efficiently assets are used to generate sales.
7. Return on assets	Net income / Average assets	Measures overall profitability of assets.
8. Return on common stockholders' equity	Net income / Average common stockholders' equity	Measures profitability of owners' investment.
9. Earnings per share (EPS)	Net income / Weighted average common shares outstanding	Measures net income earned on each share of common stock.
10. Price-earnings (P-E) ratio	Market price per share of stock / Earnings per share	Measures the ratio of the market price per share to earnings per share.
11. Payout ratio	Cash dividends / Net income	Measures percentage of earnings distributed in the form of cash dividends.
Solvency Ratios		
12. Debt to total assets ratio	Total debt / Total assets	Measures the percentage of total assets provided by creditors.
13. Times interest earned	Income before income taxes and interest expense / Interest expense	Measures ability to meet interest payments as they come due.

Before You Go On...

REVIEW IT

1. What are liquidity ratios? Explain the current ratio, acid-test ratio, receivables turnover, and inventory turnover.
2. What are profitability ratios? Explain the profit margin, asset turnover ratio, return on assets, return on common stockholders' equity, earnings per share, price-earnings ratio, and payout ratio.
3. What are solvency ratios? Explain the debt to total assets ratio and times interest earned.

DO IT

Selected financial data for Drummond Company at December 31, 2008, are as follows: cash $60,000; receivables (net) $80,000; inventory $70,000; current liabilities $140,000. Compute the current and acid-test ratios.

Action Plan

- Use the formula for the current ratio: Current assets ÷ Current liabilities.
- Use the formula for the acid-test ratio: Cash + Short-term investments + Receivables (net) ÷ Current liabilities.

Solution The current ratio is 1.5:1 ($210,000 ÷ $140,000). The acid-test ratio is 1:1 ($140,000 ÷ $140,000).

Related exercise material: *BE18-9, BE18-10, BE18-11, BE18-12, BE18-13, E18-5, E18-6, E18-7, E18-8, E18-9, E18-10, and E18-11.*

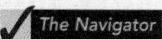

The Navigator

EARNING POWER AND IRREGULAR ITEMS

STUDY OBJECTIVE 6

Understand the concept of earning power, and how irregular items are presented.

Users of financial statements are interested in the concept of earning power. **Earning power** means the normal level of income to be obtained in the future. Earning power differs from actual net income by the amount of irregular revenues, expenses, gains, and losses. Users are interested in earning power because it helps them derive an estimate of future earnings without the "noise" of irregular items.

For users of financial statements to determine earning power or regular income, the "irregular" items are separately identified on the income statement. Companies report two types of "irregular" items.

1. Discontinued operations.
2. Extraordinary items.

These "irregular" items are reported net of income taxes. That is, the income statement first reports income tax on the income before "irregular" items. Then the amount of tax for each of the listed "irregular" items is computed. The general concept is "let the tax follow income or loss."

Discontinued Operations

Discontinued operations refers to the disposal of a **significant component** of a business. Examples involve stopping an entire activity or eliminating a major class of customers. For example, Kmart reported as discontinued operations its decision to terminate its interest in four business activities, including PACE Membership Warehouse and PayLess Drug Stores Northwest.

Following the disposal of a significant component, the company should report on its income statement both income from continuing operations and income (or loss) from discontinued operations. **The income (loss) from discontinued operations consists of two parts: the income (loss) from operations** and **the gain (loss) on disposal of the segment**.

To illustrate, assume that during 2008 Acro Energy Inc. has income before income taxes of $800,000. During 2008 Acro discontinued and sold its unprofitable chemical division. The loss in 2008 from chemical operations (net of $60,000 taxes) was $140,000. The loss on disposal of the chemical division (net of $30,000 taxes) was $70,000. Assuming a 30% tax rate on income, Illustration 18-28 shows Acro's income statement presentation.

Illustration 18-28
Statement presentation of discontinued operations

HELPFUL HINT
Observe the dual disclosures: (1) The results of operations of the discontinued division must be eliminated from the results of continuing operations. (2) The company must also report the disposal of the operation.

ACRO ENERGY INC.
Income Statement (partial)
For the Year Ended December 31, 2008

Income before income taxes		$800,000
Income tax expense		240,000
Income from continuing operations		560,000
Discontinued operations		
Loss from operations of chemical division, net of $60,000 income tax saving	**$140,000**	
Loss from disposal of chemical division, net of $30,000 income tax saving	**70,000**	**210,000**
Net income		$350,000

Note that the statement uses the caption "Income from continuing operations," and adds a new section "Discontinued operations". **The new section reports both the operating loss and the loss on disposal net of applicable income taxes.** This presentation clearly indicates the separate effects of continuing operations and discontinued operations on net income.

Extraordinary Items

Extraordinary items are events and transactions that meet two conditions: They are (1) **unusual in nature,** and (2) **infrequent in occurrence**. To be *unusual*, the item should be abnormal and only incidentally related to the company's customary activities. To be *infrequent*, the item should not be reasonably expected to recur in the foreseeable future.

A company must evaluate both criteria in terms of its operating environment. Thus, Weyerhaeuser Co. reported the $36 million in damages to its timberland caused by the volcanic eruption of Mount St. Helens as an extraordinary item. The eruption was both unusual and infrequent. In contrast, Florida Citrus Company does not report frost damage to its citrus crop as an extraordinary item, because frost damage is not infrequent. Illustration 18-29 shows the classification of extraordinary and ordinary items.

Companies report extraordinary items net of taxes in a separate section of the income statement, immediately below discontinued operations. To illustrate, assume that in 2008 a foreign government expropriated property held as an investment by Acro Energy Inc. If the loss is $70,000 before applicable income taxes of $21,000, the income statement will report a deduction of $49,000, as shown in Illustration 18-30 (page 801). When there is an extraordinary item to report, the company adds the caption "Income before extraordinary item" immediately before the section for the extraordinary item. This presentation clearly indicates the effect of the extraordinary item on net income.

What if a transaction or event meets one (but not both) of the criteria for an extraordinary item? In that case the company reports it under either "Other revenues and gains" or "Other expenses and losses" at its gross amount (not net of

Extraordinary items		Ordinary items	
1. Effects of major natural casualties, if rare in the area.		1. Effects of major natural casualties, not uncommon in the area.	
2. Expropriation (takeover) of property by a foreign government.		2. Write-down of inventories or write-off of receivables.	
3. Effects of a newly enacted law or regulation, such as a property condemnation action.		3. Losses attributable to labor strikes.	
		4. Gains or losses from sales of property, plant, or equipment.	

Illustration 18-29
Examples of extraordinary and ordinary items

tax). This is true, for example, of gains (losses) resulting from the sale of property, plant, and equipment, as explained in Chapter 10. It is quite common for companies to use the label "Nonrecurring charges" for losses that do not meet the extraordinary item criteria.

Illustration 18-30
Statement presentation of extraordinary items

ACRO ENERGY INC.
Income Statement (partial)
For the Year Ended December 31, 2008

Income before income taxes		$800,000
Income tax expense		240,000
Income from continuing operations		560,000
Discontinued operations		
Loss from operations of chemical division, net of $60,000 income tax saving	$140,000	
Loss from disposal of chemical division, net of $30,000 income tax saving	70,000	210,000
Income before extraordinary item		350,000
Extraordinary item		
Expropriation of investment, net of $21,000 income tax saving		**49,000**
Net income		$301,000

HELPFUL HINT
If there are no discontinued operations, the third line of the income statement would be labeled "Income before extraordinary item."

INVESTOR INSIGHT

What Is Extraordinary?

Many companies these days are incurring restructuring charges as a result of attempting to reduce costs. Are these costs ordinary or extraordinary? Some companies report "one-time" restructuring charges over and over. Case in point: Toothpaste and diapers giant Procter & Gamble Co. reported a restructuring charge in 12 consecutive quarters, and Motorola had "special" charges 14 quarters in a row. On the other hand, some companies take a restructuring charge only once in five years. The one-size-fits-all classification therefore will not work. There appears to be no substitute for a careful analysis of the numbers that comprise net income.

? If a company takes a large restructuring charge, what is the effect on the company's current income statement versus future ones?

Changes in Accounting Principle

ETHICS NOTE

Changes in accounting principle should result in financial statements that are more informative for statement users. They should *not* be used to artificially improve the reported performance or financial position of the corporation.

For ease of comparison, users of financial statements expect companies to prepare such statements on a basis **consistent** with the preceding period. A **change in accounting principle** occurs when the principle used in the current year is different from the one used in the preceding year. Accounting rules permit a change when management can show that the new principle is preferable to the old principle. An example is a change in inventory costing methods (such as FIFO to average cost).

Companies report most changes in accounting principle retroactively. That is, they report both the current period and previous periods using the new principle. As a result the same principle applies in all periods. This treatment improves the ability to compare results across years.

Comprehensive Income

The income statement reports most revenues, expenses, gains, and losses recognized during the period. However, over time, specific exceptions to this general practice have developed. Certain items now bypass income and are reported directly in stockholders' equity.

For example, in Chapter 16 you learned that companies do not include in income any unrealized gains and losses on available-for-sale securities. Instead, they report such gains and losses in the balance sheet as adjustments to stockholders' equity. Why are these gains and losses on available-for-sale securities excluded from net income? Because disclosing them separately (1) reduces the volatility of net income due to fluctuations in fair value, yet (2) informs the financial statement user of the gain or loss that would be incurred if the securities were sold at fair value.

Many analysts have expressed concern over the significant increase in the number of items that bypass the income statement. They feel that such reporting has reduced the usefulness of the income statement. To address this concern, in addition to reporting net income, a company must also report comprehensive income. **Comprehensive income** includes all changes in stockholders' equity during a period except those resulting from investments by stockholders and distributions to stockholders. A number of alternative formats for reporting comprehensive income are allowed. These formats are discussed in advanced accounting courses.

Before You Go On...

REVIEW IT

1. What are the similarities and differences in reporting material items not typical of regular operations?
2. What is included in comprehensive income?

DO IT

In its proposed 2008 income statement, AIR Corporation reports income before income taxes $400,000, extraordinary loss $100,000, income taxes (30%) $120,000, and net income $210,000. Prepare a correct income statement, beginning with income before income taxes.

Action Plan

- Recall that the loss is extraordinary because it meets the criteria of being both unusual and infrequent.
- Disclose the income tax effect of each component of income, beginning with income before any irregular items.
- Report irregular items net of any income tax effect.

Solution

AIR CORPORATION
Income Statement (partial)

Income before income taxes	$400,000
Income tax expense (30%)	120,000
Income before extraordinary item	280,000
Extraordinary loss net of $30,000 income tax saving	70,000
Net income	$210,000

Related exercise material: *BE18-14, BE18-15, E18-12, and E18-13.*

The Navigator

QUALITY OF EARNINGS

STUDY OBJECTIVE 7
Understand the concept of quality of earnings.

In evaluating the financial performance of a company, the quality of a company's earnings is of extreme importance to analysts. A company that has a high **quality of earnings** provides full and transparent information that will not confuse or mislead users of the financial statements.

The issue of quality of earnings has taken on increasing importance because recent accounting scandals suggest that some companies are spending too much time managing their income and not enough time managing their business. Here are some of the factors affecting quality of earnings.

Alternative Accounting Methods

Variations among companies in the application of generally accepted accounting principles may hamper comparability and reduce quality of earnings. For example, one company may use the FIFO method of inventory costing, while another company in the same industry may use LIFO. If inventory is a significant asset to both companies, it is unlikely that their current ratios are comparable. For example, if General Motors Corporation had used FIFO instead of LIFO for inventory valuation, its inventories in a recent year would have been 26% higher, which significantly affects the current ratio (and other ratios as well).

In addition to differences in inventory costing methods, differences also exist in reporting such items as depreciation, depletion, and amortization. Although these differences in accounting methods might be detectable from reading the notes to the financial statements, adjusting the financial data to compensate for the different methods is often difficult, if not impossible.

Pro Forma Income

Companies whose stock is publicly traded are required to present their income statement following generally accepted accounting principles (GAAP). In recent years, many companies have also reported a second measure of income, called pro forma income. **Pro forma income** usually excludes items that the company thinks are unusual or nonrecurring. For example, in a recent year, Cisco Systems (a high-tech company) reported a quarterly net loss under GAAP of $2.7 billion. Cisco reported pro forma income for the same quarter as a profit of $230 million. This large difference in profits between GAAP income numbers and pro forma income is not unusual these days. For example, during one recent 9-month period the 100 largest firms on the Nasdaq stock exchange reported a total pro forma income of $19.1 billion, but a total loss as measured by GAAP of $82.3 billion—a difference of about $100 billion!

To compute pro forma income, companies generally can exclude any items they deem inappropriate for measuring their performance. Many analysts and investors are critical of the practice of using pro forma income because these numbers often make companies look better than they really are. As the financial press noted, pro forma numbers might be called EBS, which stands for "earnings before bad stuff." Companies, on the other hand, argue that pro forma numbers more clearly indicate sustainable income because they exclude unusual and nonrecurring expenses. "Cisco's technique gives readers of financial statements a clear picture of Cisco's normal business activities," the company said in a statement issued in response to questions about its pro forma income accounting.

Recently, the SEC provided some guidance on how companies should present pro forma information. Stay tuned: Everyone seems to agree that pro forma numbers can be useful if they provide insights into determining a company's sustainable income. However, many companies have abused the flexibility that pro forma numbers allow and have used the measure as a way to put their companies in a good light.

Improper Recognition

Because some managers have felt pressure from Wall Street to continually increase earnings, they have manipulated the earnings numbers to meet these expectations. The most common abuse is the improper recognition of revenue. One practice that companies are using is *channel stuffing*: Offering deep discounts on their products to customers, companies encourage their customers to buy early (stuff the channel) rather than later. This lets the company report good earnings in the current period, but it often leads to a disaster in subsequent periods because customers have no need for additional goods. To illustrate, Bristol-Myers Squibb recently indicated that it used sales incentives to encourage wholesalers to buy more drugs than needed to meet patients' demands. As a result, the company had to issue revised financial statements showing corrected revenues and income.

Another practice is the improper capitalization of operating expenses. The classic case is WorldCom. It capitalized over $7 billion dollars of operating expenses so that it would report positive net income. In other situations, companies fail to report all their liabilities. Enron had promised to make payments on certain contracts if financial difficulty developed, but these guarantees were not reported as liabilities. In addition, disclosure was so lacking in transparency that it was impossible to understand what was happening at the company.

Be sure to read **ALL ABOUT YOU: *Should I Play the Market Yet?*** on the next page for information on how topics in this chapter apply to you.

all about YOU

Should I Play the Market Yet?

In this chapter you learned how to use many tools for performing a financial analysis of a company. Sometimes companies fail even though they have a good product and good sales growth. All too often the cause of failure is something that should have caused only momentary discomfort. But if a company lacks sufficient liquidity, a momentary hiccup can be fatal. This is true for individuals as well.

For example, the decision to invest in common stock can be risky. As a company's net income changes, its stock price can be volatile. You must take this into consideration when deciding whether to buy stock. You don't want to be in a situation where you have to sell a stock whose price has fallen in order to raise cash to pay your bills.

Some Facts

* 83.4 million Americans own stock investments, either through mutual funds or individual stocks; 89% of stock investors own stock mutual funds.
* 44% of the people who own stock bought their first stock before 1990.
* The typical equity investor is in his or her late 40s, is married, is employed, and has a household income in the low $60,000s.
* 58% of people who own stock said that they rely on professional financial advisors when making decisions regarding the purchase and sale of stock.
* 46% of people who own stock used the Internet to check stock prices, and 38% use it to read online financial publications.

About the Numbers

The percentage of Americans who buy stock, either through mutual funds or individual shares, has increased significantly in recent years. A big part of this increase is due to the increasing prevalence of employer-sponsored retirement plans, such as 401(k) plans.

Equity Ownership in the U.S., 1983–2002, Selected Years
(number and percent of U.S. households)

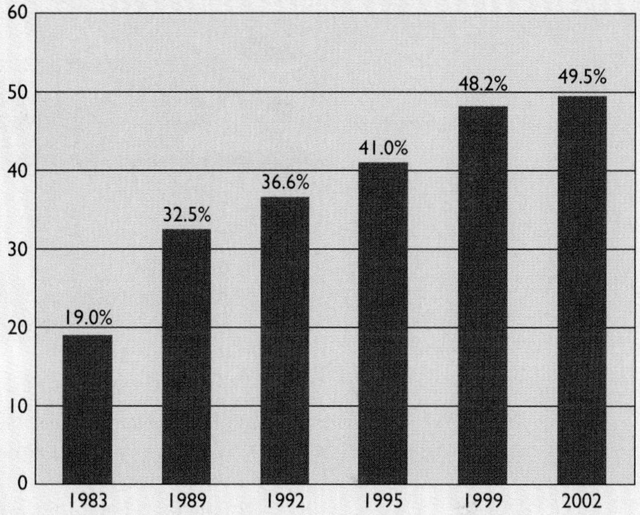

	1983	1989	1992	1995	1999	2002
U.S. Households (*millions*)	15.9	30.2	34.6	40.6	49.2	52.7

Source: "Equity Ownership in America," Investment Company Institute and the Securities Industry Association, 2002, p. 1.

What Do You Think?

Rachael West has been working at her new job for six months. She has a good salary, with lots of opportunities for growth. She has already accumulated $8,000 in savings, which right now is sitting in a bank savings account earning very little interest. She has decided to take $7,000 out of this savings account and buy common stock of her employer, a young company that has been in business for two years. Rachael's liquid assets, including her savings account, total $10,000. Her monthly expenses are approximately $3,000. Should Rachael make this investment?

YES: She has a good income, and this is a great opportunity for her to get in on the ground floor of her employer's fast-growing company.

NO: She shouldn't invest all of her money in one company, particularly the company at which she works.

Source: "Equity Ownership in America," Investment Company Institute and the Securities Industry Association, 2002.

The authors' comments on this situation appear on p. 828.

Before You Go On...

REVIEW IT

1. What is meant by *quality of earnings?*
2. Give examples of alternative accounting methods that hamper comparability.
3. What is pro forma income and why are analysts often critical of this number?

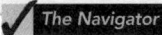

The Navigator

Demonstration Problem 1

The condensed financial statements ot The Estée Lauder Companies, Inc., for the years ended June 30, 2005 and 2004, are presented below.

THE ESTÉE LAUDER COMPANIES, INC.
Balance Sheets
June 30

	(in millions)	
Assets	**2005**	**2004**
Current assets		
Cash and cash equivalents	$ 553.3	$ 611.6
Accounts receivable (net)	776.6	664.9
Inventories	768.3	653.5
Prepaid expenses and other current assets	204.4	269.2
Total current assets	2,302.6	2,199.2
Property, plant, and equipment (net)	694.2	647.0
Investments	12.3	12.6
Intangibles and other assets	876.7	849.3
Total assets	$3,885.8	$3,708.1
Liabilities and Stockholders' Equity		
Current liabilities	$1,497.7	$1,322.0
Long-term liabilities	679.5	637.1
Stockholders' equity—common	1,708.6	1,749.0
Total liabilities and stockholders' equity	$3,885.8	$3,708.1

THE ESTÉE LAUDER COMPANIES, INC.
Income Statements
For the Year Ended June 30

	(in millions)	
	2005	**2004**
Revenues	$6,336.3	$5,790.4
Costs and expenses		
Cost of goods sold	1,617.4	1,476.3
Selling and administrative expenses	4,007.6	3,679.0
Interest expense	13.9	27.1
Total costs and expenses	5,638.9	5,182.4
Income before income taxes	697.4	608.0
Income tax expense	291.3	232.6
Net income	$ 406.1	$ 375.4

Instructions

Compute the following ratios for 2005 and 2004.

(a) Current ratio.
(b) Inventory turnover. (Inventory on 6/30/03 was $599.0.)
(c) Profit margin ratio.
(d) Return on assets. (Assets on 6/30/03 were $3,349.9.)
(e) Return on common stockholders' equity. (Equity on 6/30/03 was $1,795.9.)
(f) Debt to total assets ratio.
(g) Times interest earned.

Solution to Demonstration Problem 1

	2005	2004
(a) Current ratio:		
$2,302.6 ÷ $1,497.7 =	1.5:1	
$2,199.2 ÷ $1,322.0 =		1.7:1
(b) Inventory turnover:		
$1,617.4 ÷ [($768.3 + $653.5) ÷ 2] =	2.3 times	
$1,476.3 ÷ [($653.5 + $599.0) ÷ 2] =		2.4 times
(c) Profit margin:		
$406.1 ÷ $6,336.3	6.4%	
$375.4 ÷ $5,790.4		6.5%
(d) Return on assets:		
$406.1 ÷ [($3,885.8 + $3,708.1) ÷ 2] =	10.7%	
$375.4 ÷ [($3,708.1 + $3,349.9) ÷ 2] =		10.6%
(e) Return on common stockholders' equity:		
$406.1 ÷ [($1,708.6 + $1,749.0) ÷ 2] =	23.5%	
$375.4 ÷ [($1,749.0 + $1,795.9) ÷ 2] =		21.2%
(f) Debt to total assets ratio:		
($1,497.7 + $679.5) ÷ $3,885.8 =	56.0%	
($1,322.0 + $637.1) ÷ $3,708.1 =		52.8%
(g) Times interest earned:		
($406.1 + $291.3 + $13.9) ÷ $13.9 =	51.2 times	
($375.4 + $232.6 + $27.1) ÷ $27.1 =		23.4 times

action plan

✓ Remember that the current ratio includes all current assets. The acid-test ratio uses only cash, short-term investments, and net receivables.

✓ Use average balances for turnover ratios like inventory, receivables, and assets.

✓ The Navigator

Demonstration Problem 2

WILEY PLUS

The events and transactions of Dever Corporation for the year ending December 31, 2008, resulted in the following data.

Cost of goods sold	$2,600,000
Net sales	4,400,000
Other expenses and losses	9,600
Other revenues and gains	5,600
Selling and administrative expenses	1,100,000
Income from operations of plastics division	70,000
Gain from disposal of plastics division	500,000
Loss from tornado disaster (extraordinary loss)	600,000

Analysis reveals that:

1. All items are before the applicable income tax rate of 30%.
2. The plastics division was sold on July 1.
3. All operating data for the plastics division have been segregated.

Instructions

Prepare an income statement for the year.

action plan

- Report material items not typical of operations in separate sections, net of taxes.
- Associate income taxes with the item that affects the taxes.
- Apply the corporate tax rate to income before income taxes to determine tax expense.
- Recall that all data presented in determining income before income taxes are the same as for unincorporated companies.

Solution to Demonstration Problem 2

DEVER CORPORATION
Income Statement
For the Year Ended December 31, 2008

Net sales		$4,400,000
Cost of goods sold		2,600,000
Gross profit		1,800,000
Selling and administrative expenses		1,100,000
Income from operations		700,000
Other revenues and gains	$5,600	
Other expenses and losses	9,600	4,000
Income before income taxes		696,000
Income tax expense ($696,000 × 30%)		208,800
Income from continuing operations		487,200
Discontinued operations		
Income from operations of plastics division, net of $21,000 income taxes ($70,000 × 30%)	49,000	
Gain from disposal of plastics division, net of $150,000 income taxes ($500,000 × 30%)	350,000	399,000
Income before extraordinary item		886,200
Extraordinary item		
Tornado loss, net of $180,000 income tax saving ($600,000 × 30%)		420,000
Net income		$ 466,200

The Navigator

SUMMARY OF STUDY OBJECTIVES

WILEY PLUS

1 **Discuss the need for comparative analysis.** There are three bases of comparison: (1) Intracompany, which compares an item or financial relationship with other data within a company. (2) Industry, which compares company data with industry averages. (3) Intercompany, which compares an item or financial relationship of a company with data of one or more competing companies.

2 **Identify the tools of financial statement analysis.** Financial statements can be analyzed horizontally, vertically, and with ratios.

3 **Explain and apply horizontal analysis.** Horizontal analysis is a technique for evaluating a series of data over a period of time to determine the increase or decrease that has taken place, expressed as either an amount or a percentage.

4 **Describe and apply vertical analysis.** Vertical analysis is a technique that expresses each item within a financial statement in terms of a percentage of a relevant total or a base amount.

5 **Identify and compute ratios used in analyzing a firm's liquidity, profitability, and solvency.** The formula and purpose of each ratio was presented in Illustration 18-27 (page 798).

6 **Understand the concept of earning power, and how irregular items are presented.** Earning power refers to a company's ability to sustain its profits from operations. "Irregular items"—discontinued operations and extraordinary items—are presented net of tax below income from continuing operations to highlight their unusual nature.

7 **Understand the concept of quality of earnings.** A high quality of earnings provides full and transparent information that will not confuse or mislead users of the financial statements. Issues related to quality of earnings are (1) alternative accounting methods, (2) pro forma income, and (3) improper recognition.

The Navigator

GLOSSARY

WILEY PLUS

Acid-test (quick) ratio A measure of a company's immediate short-term liquidity; computed by dividing the sum of cash, short-term investments, and net receivables by current liabilities. (p. 789).

Asset turnover A measure of how efficiently a company uses its assets to generate sales; computed by dividing net sales by average assets. (p. 792).

Change in accounting principle The use of a principle in the current year that is different from the one used in the preceding year. (p. 802).

Comprehensive income Includes all changes in stockholders' equity during a period except those resulting from investments by stockholders and distributions to stockholders. (p. 802).

Current ratio A measure used to evaluate a company's liquidity and short-term debt-paying ability; computed by dividing current assets by current liabilities. (p. 788).

Debt to total assets ratio Measures the percentage of total assets provided by creditors; computed by dividing total debt by total assets. (p. 796).

Discontinued operations The disposal of a significant segment of a business. (p. 799).

Earnings per share (EPS) The net income earned on each share of common stock; computed by dividing net income by the number of weighted average common shares outstanding. (p. 794).

Extraordinary items Events and transactions that are unusual in nature and infrequent in occurrence. (p. 800).

Horizontal analysis A technique for evaluating a series of financial statement data over a period of time, to determine the increase (decrease) that has taken place, expressed as either an amount or a percentage. (p. 781).

Inventory turnover A measure of the liquidity of inventory; computed by dividing cost of goods sold by average inventory. (p. 791).

Leveraging See Trading on the equity.

Liquidity ratios Measures of the short-term ability of the enterprise to pay its maturing obligations and to meet unexpected needs for cash. (p. 788).

Payout ratio Measures the percentage of earnings distributed in the form of cash dividends; computed by dividing cash dividends by net income. (p. 795).

Price-earnings (P-E) ratio Measures the ratio of the market price of each share of common stock to the earnings per share; computed by dividing the market price of the stock by earnings per share. (p. 795).

Profit margin Measures the percentage of each dollar of sales that results in net income; computed by dividing net income by net sales. (p. 792).

Profitability ratios Measures of the income or operating success of an enterprise for a given period of time. (p. 792).

Pro forma income A measure of income that usually excludes items that a company thinks are unusual or nonrecurring. (p. 804).

Quality of earnings Indicates the level of full and transparent information provided to users of the financial statements (p. 803).

Ratio An expression of the mathematical relationship between one quantity and another. The relationship may be expressed either as a percentage, a rate, or a simple proportion. (p. 787).

Ratio analysis A technique for evaluating financial statements that expresses the relationship between selected financial statement data. (p. 787).

Receivables turnover A measure of the liquidity of receivables; computed by dividing net credit sales by average net receivables. (p. 790).

Return on assets An overall measure of profitability; computed by dividing net income by average assets. (p. 793).

Return on common stockholders' equity Measures the dollars of net income earned for each dollar invested by the owners; computed by dividing net income by average common stockholders' equity. (p. 793).

Solvency ratios Measures of the ability of the enterprise to survive over a long period of time. (p. 796).

Times interest earned Measures a company's ability to meet interest payments as they come due; computed by dividing income before interest expense and income taxes by interest expense. (p. 797).

Trading on the equity Borrowing money at a lower rate of interest than can be earned by using the borrowed money. (p. 794).

Vertical analysis A technique for evaluating financial statement data that expresses each item within a financial statement as a percent of a base amount. (p. 785).

SELF-STUDY QUESTIONS

WILEY PLUS

Answers are at the end of the chapter.

(SO 1) **1.** Comparisons of data within a company are an example of the following comparative basis:
a. Industry averages.
b. Intracompany.
c. Intercompany.
d. Both (b) and (c).

(SO 3) **2.** In horizontal analysis, each item is expressed as a percentage of the:
a. net income amount.
b. stockholders' equity amount.
c. total assets amount.
d. base year amount.

3. In vertical analysis, the base amount for depreciation expense is generally: (SO 4)
a. net sales.
b. depreciation expense in a previous year.
c. gross profit.
d. fixed assets.

4. The following schedule is a display of what type of analysis? (SO 4)

	Amount	Percent
Current assets	$200,000	25%
Property, plant, and equipment	600,000	75%
Total assets	$800,000	

a. Horizontal analysis.
b. Differential analysis.
c. Vertical analysis.
d. Ratio analysis.

(SO 3) 5. Sammy Corporation reported net sales of $300,000, $330,000, and $360,000 in the years, 2006, 2007, and 2008, respectively. If 2006 is the base year, what is the trend percentage for 2008?
a. 77%.
b. 108%.
c. 120%.
d. 130%.

(SO 5) 6. Which of the following measures is an evaluation of a firm's ability to pay current liabilities?
a. Acid-test ratio.
b. Current ratio.
c. Both (a) and (b).
d. None of the above.

(SO 5) 7. A measure useful in evaluating the efficiency in managing inventories is:
a. inventory turnover.
b. average days to sell inventory.
c. Both (a) and (b).
d. None of the above.

(SO 6) 8. In reporting discontinued operations, the income statement should show in a special section:
a. gains and losses on the disposal of the discontinued segment.
b. gains and losses from operations of the discontinued segment.
c. Both (a) and (b).
d. Neither (a) nor (b).

9. Scout Corporation has income before taxes of $400,000 and an extraordinary loss of $100,000. If the income tax rate is 25% on all items, the income statement should show income before extraordinary items and extraordinary items, respectively, of: (SO 6)
a. $325,000 and $100,000.
b. $325,000 and $75,000.
c. $300,000 and $100,000
d. $300,000 and $75,000.

10. Which situation below might indicate a company has a low quality of earnings? (SO 7)
a. The same accounting principles are used each year.
b. Revenue is recognized when earned.
c. Maintenance costs are expensed as incurred.
d. The company is continually reporting pro forma income numbers.

Go to the book's website, **www.wiley.com/college/weygandt**, for Additional Self-Study questions.

The Navigator

QUESTIONS

1. (a) Juan Marichal believes that the analysis of financial statements is directed at two characteristics of a company: liquidity and profitability. Is Juan correct? Explain.
   (b) Are short-term creditors, long-term creditors, and stockholders interested primarily in the same characteristics of a company? Explain.
2. (a) Distinguish among the following bases of comparison: (1) intracompany, (2) industry averages, and (3) intercompany.
   (b) Give the principal value of using each of the three bases of comparison.
3. Two popular methods of financial statement analysis are horizontal analysis and vertical analysis. Explain the difference between these two methods.
4. (a) If Leonard Company had net income of $360,000 in 2008 and it experienced a 24.5% increase in net income for 2009, what is its net income for 2009?
   (b) If six cents of every dollar of Leonard revenue is net income in 2008, what is the dollar amount of 2008 revenue?
5. What is a ratio? What are the different ways of expressing the relationship of two amounts? What information does a ratio provide?
6. Name the major ratios useful in assessing (a) liquidity and (b) solvency.
7. Raphael Ochoa is puzzled. His company had a profit margin of 10% in 2008. He feels that this is an indication that the company is doing well. Cindy Lore, his accountant, says that more information is needed to determine the firm's financial well-being. Who is correct? Why?
8. What do the following classes of ratios measure? (a) Liquidity ratios. (b) Profitability ratios. (c) Solvency ratios.
9. What is the difference between the current ratio and the acid-test ratio?
10. Donte Company, a retail store, has a receivables turnover of 4.5 times. The industry average is 12.5 times. Does Donte have a collection problem with its receivables?
11. Which ratios should be used to help answer the following questions?
    (a) How efficient is a company in using its assets to produce sales?
    (b) How near to sale is the inventory on hand?
    (c) How many dollars of net income were earned for each dollar invested by the owners?
    (d) How able is a company to meet interest charges as they fall due?
12. The price-earnings ratio of General Motors (automobile builder) was 8, and the price-earnings ratio of Microsoft (computer software) was 38. Which company did the stock market favor? Explain.

13. What is the formula for computing the payout ratio? Would you expect this ratio to be high or low for a growth company?
14. Holding all other factors constant, indicate whether each of the following changes generally signals good or bad news about a company.
    (a) Increase in profit margin.
    (b) Decrease in inventory turnover.
    (c) Increase in the current ratio.
    (d) Decrease in earnings per share.
    (e) Increase in price-earnings ratio.
    (f) Increase in debt to total assets ratio.
    (g) Decrease in times interest earned.
15. The return on assets for Tresh Corporation is 7.6%. During the same year Tresh's return on common stockholders' equity is 12.8%. What is the explanation for the difference in the two rates?
16. Which two ratios do you think should be of greatest interest to:
    (a) A pension fund considering the purchase of 20-year bonds?
    (b) A bank contemplating a short-term loan?
    (c) A common stockholder?
17. Why must preferred stock dividends be subtracted from net income in computing earnings per share?
18. (a) What is meant by trading on the equity?
    (b) How would you determine the profitability of trading on the equity?
19. Hillman Inc. has net income of $160,000, weighted average shares of common stock outstanding of 50,000, and preferred dividends for the period of $40,000. What is Hillman's earnings per share of common stock? Kate Hillman, the president of Hillman Inc., believes the computed EPS of the company is high. Comment.
20. Why is it important to report discontinued operations separately from income from continuing operations?
21. You are considering investing in Shawnee Transportation. The company reports 2008 earnings per share of $6.50 on income before extraordinary items and $4.75 on net income. Which EPS figure would you consider more relevant to your investment decision? Why?
22. STL Inc. reported 2007 earnings per share of $3.20 and had no extraordinary items. In 2008, EPS on income before extraordinary items was $2.99, and EPS on net income was $3.49. Is this a favorable trend?
23. Indicate which of the following items would be reported as an extraordinary item in Mordica Corporation's income statement.
    (a) Loss from damages caused by volcano eruption.
    (b) Loss from sale of temporary investments.
    (c) Loss attributable to a labor strike.
    (d) Loss caused when manufacture of a product was prohibited by the Food and Drug Administration.
    (e) Loss from flood damage. (The nearby Black River floods every 2 to 3 years.)
    (f) Write-down of obsolete inventory.
    (g) Expropriation of a factory by a foreign government.
24. Identify and explain factors that affect quality of earnings.

BRIEF EXERCISES

WILEY PLUS

Follow the rounding procedures used in the chapter.

BE18-1 You recently received a letter from your Uncle Frank. A portion of the letter is presented below.

Discuss need for comparative analysis.
(SO 1)

> You know that I have a significant amount of money I saved over the years. I am thinking about starting an investment program. I want to do the investing myself, based on my own research and analysis of financial statements. I know that you are studying accounting, so I have a couple of questions for you. I have heard that different users of financial statements are interested in different characteristics of companies. Is this true, and, if so, why? Also, some of my friends, who are already investing, have told me that comparisons involving a company's financial data can be made on a number of different bases. Can you explain these bases to me?

Instructions
Write a letter to your Uncle Frank which answers his questions.

BE18-2 Drew Carey Corporation reported the following amounts in 2007, 2008, and 2009.

Identify and use tools of financial statement analysis.
(SO 2, 3, 4, 5)

	2007	2008	2009
Current assets	$200,000	$230,000	$240,000
Current liabilities	$160,000	$168,000	$184,000
Total assets	$500,000	$600,000	$620,000

Instructions
(a) Identify and describe the three tools of financial statement analysis. **(b)** Perform each of the three types of analysis on Drew Carey's current assets.

Prepare horizontal analysis.
(SO 3)

BE18-3 Using the following data from the comparative balance sheet of Rodenbeck Company, illustrate horizontal analysis.

	December 31, 2009	December 31, 2008
Accounts receivable	$ 520,000	$ 400,000
Inventory	$ 840,000	$ 600,000
Total assets	$ 3,000,000	$2,500,000

Prepare vertical analysis.
(SO 4)

BE18-4 Using the same data presented above in BE18-3 for Rodenbeck Company, illustrate vertical analysis.

Calculate percentage of change.
(SO 3)

BE18-5 Net income was $500,000 in 2007, $450,000 in 2008, and $522,000 in 2009. What is the percentage of change from **(a)** 2007 to 2008 and **(b)** 2008 to 2009? Is the change an increase or a decrease?

Calculate net income.
(SO 3)

BE18-6 If Soule Company had net income of $585,000 in 2009 and it experienced a 30% increase in net income over 2008, what was its 2008 net income?

Calculate change in net income.
(SO 3)

BE18-7 Horizontal analysis (trend analysis) percentages for Epstein Company's sales, cost of goods sold, and expenses are shown below.

Horizontal Analysis	2009	2008	2007
Sales	96.2	106.8	100.0
Cost of goods sold	102.0	97.0	100.0
Expenses	109.6	98.4	100.0

Did Epstein's net income increase, decrease, or remain unchanged over the 3-year period?

Calculate change in net income.
(SO 4)

BE18-8 Vertical analysis (common size) percentages for Charles Company's sales, cost of goods sold, and expenses are shown below.

Vertical Analysis	2009	2008	2007
Sales	100.0	100.0	100.0
Cost of goods sold	59.2	62.4	64.5
Expenses	25.0	25.6	27.5

Did Charles's net income as a percent of sales increase, decrease, or remain unchanged over the 3-year period? Provide numerical support for your answer.

Calculate liquidity ratios.
(SO 5)

BE18-9 Selected condensed data taken from a recent balance sheet of Perkins Inc. are as follows.

PERKINS INC.
Balance Sheet (partial)

Cash	$ 8,041,000
Short-term investments	4,947,000
Accounts receivable	12,545,000
Inventories	14,814,000
Other current assets	5,571,000
Total current assets	$45,918,000
Total current liabilities	$40,644,000

What are the **(a)** working capital, **(b)** current ratio, and **(c)** acid-test ratio?

Calculate profitability ratios.
(SO 5)

BE18-10 McLaren Corporation has net income of $11.44 million and net revenue of $80 million in 2008. Its assets are $14 million at the beginning of the year and $18 million at the end of the year. What are McLaren's **(a)** asset turnover and **(b)** profit margin?

BE18-11 The following data are taken from the financial statements of Morino Company.

Evaluate collection of accounts receivable.
(SO 5)

	2009	2008
Accounts receivable (net), end of year	$ 550,000	$ 520,000
Net sales on account	3,960,000	3,100,000

Terms for all sales are 1/10, n/60.

(a) Compute for each year (1) the receivables turnover and (2) the average collection period. At the end of 2007, accounts receivable (net) was $480,000.

(b) What conclusions about the management of accounts receivable can be drawn from these data?

BE18-12 The following data are from the income statements of Huntsinger Company.

Evaluate management of inventory.
(SO 5)

	2009	2008
Sales	$6,420,000	$6,240,000
Beginning inventory	980,000	860,000
Purchases	4,340,000	4,661,000
Ending inventory	1,020,000	980,000

(a) Compute for each year (1) the inventory turnover and (2) the average days to sell the inventory. **(b)** What conclusions concerning the management of the inventory can be drawn from these data?

BE18-13 Gladow Company has owners' equity of $400,000 and net income of $66,000. It has a payout ratio of 20% and a rate of return on assets of 15%. How much did Gladow pay in cash dividends, and what were its average assets?

Calculate profitability ratios.
(SO 5)

BE18-14 An inexperienced accountant for Ming Corporation showed the following in the income statement: income before income taxes and extraordinary item $400,000, and extraordinary loss from flood (before taxes) $70,000. The extraordinary loss and taxable income are both subject to a 30% tax rate. Prepare a correct income statement.

Prepare income statement including extraordinary items.
(SO 6)

BE18-15 On June 30, Reeves Corporation discontinued its operations in Mexico. During the year, the operating loss was $300,000 before taxes. On September 1, Reeves disposed of the Mexico facility at a pretax loss of $120,000. The applicable tax rate is 30%. Show the discontinued operations section of the income statement.

Prepare discontinued operations section of income statement.
(SO 6)

EXERCISES

WILEY PLUS

Follow the rounding procedures used in the chapter.

E18-1 Financial information for Blevins Inc. is presented below.

Prepare horizontal analysis.
(SO 3)

	December 31, 2009	December 31, 2008
Current assets	$125,000	$100,000
Plant assets (net)	396,000	330,000
Current liabilities	91,000	70,000
Long-term liabilities	133,000	95,000
Common stock, $1 par	161,000	115,000
Retained earnings	136,000	150,000

Instructions

Prepare a schedule showing a horizontal analysis for 2009 using 2008 as the base year.

E18-2 Operating data for Gallup Corporation are presented below.

Prepare vertical analysis.
(SO 4)

	2009	2008
Sales	$750,000	$600,000
Cost of goods sold	465,000	390,000
Selling expenses	120,000	72,000
Administrative expenses	60,000	54,000
Income tax expense	33,000	24,000
Net income	72,000	60,000

Instructions

Prepare a schedule showing a vertical analysis for 2009 and 2008.

Prepare horizontal and vertical analyses.
(SO 3, 4)

E18-3 The comparative condensed balance sheets of Conard Corporation are presented below.

CONARD CORPORATION
Comparative Condensed Balance Sheets
December 31

	2009	2008
Assets		
Current assets	$ 74,000	$ 80,000
Property, plant, and equipment (net)	99,000	90,000
Intangibles	27,000	40,000
Total assets	$200,000	$210,000
Liabilities and stockholders' equity		
Current liabilities	$ 42,000	$ 48,000
Long-term liabilities	143,000	150,000
Stockholders' equity	15,000	12,000
Total liabilities and stockholders' equity	$200,000	$210,000

Instructions

(a) Prepare a horizontal analysis of the balance sheet data for Conard Corporation using 2008 as a base.

(b) Prepare a vertical analysis of the balance sheet data for Conard Corporation in columnar form for 2009.

Prepare horizontal and vertical analyses.
(SO 3, 4)

E18-4 The comparative condensed income statements of Hendi Corporation are shown below.

HENDI CORPORATION
Comparative Condensed Income Statements
For the Years Ended December 31

	2009	2008
Net sales	$600,000	$500,000
Cost of goods sold	483,000	420,000
Gross profit	117,000	80,000
Operating expenses	57,200	44,000
Net income	$ 59,800	$ 36,000

Instructions

(a) Prepare a horizontal analysis of the income statement data for Hendi Corporation using 2008 as a base. (Show the amounts of increase or decrease.)

(b) Prepare a vertical analysis of the income statement data for Hendi Corporation in columnar form for both years.

Compute liquidity ratios and compare results.
(SO 5)

E18-5 Nordstrom, Inc. operates department stores in numerous states. Selected financial statement data for the year ending January 29, 2005, are as follows.

NORDSTROM, INC.
Balance Sheet (partial)

(in millions)	End-of-Year	Beginning-of-Year
Cash and cash equivalents	$ 361	$ 340
Receivables (less allowance of 19 and 20)	646	667
Merchandise inventory	917	902
Prepaid expenses	53	46
Other current assets	595	570
Total current assets	$2,572	$2,525
Total current liabilities	$1,341	$1,123

For the year, net sales were $7,131, and cost of goods sold was $4,559 (in millions).

Instructions

(a) Compute the four liquidity ratios at the end of the year.

(b) Using the data in the chapter, compare Nordstrom's liquidity with (1) that of J.C. Penney Company, and (2) the industry averages for department stores.

E18-6 Leach Incorporated had the following transactions occur involving current assets and current liabilities during February 2008.

Perform current and acid-test ratio analysis.

(SO 5)

Feb.	3	Accounts receivable of $15,000 are collected.
	7	Equipment is purchased for $28,000 cash.
	11	Paid $3,000 for a 3-year insurance policy.
	14	Accounts payable of $12,000 are paid.
	18	Cash dividends of $5,000 are declared.

Additional information:

1. As of February 1, 2008, current assets were $130,000, and current liabilities were $50,000.
2. As of February 1, 2008, current assets included $15,000 of inventory and $2,000 of prepaid expenses.

Instructions

(a) Compute the current ratio as of the beginning of the month and after each transaction.

(b) Compute the acid-test ratio as of the beginning of the month and after each transaction.

E18-7 Bennis Company has the following comparative balance sheet data.

Compute selected ratios.

(SO 5)

BENNIS COMPANY
Balance Sheets
December 31

	2009	2008
Cash	$ 15,000	$ 30,000
Receivables (net)	70,000	60,000
Inventories	60,000	50,000
Plant assets (net)	200,000	180,000
	$345,000	$320,000
Accounts payable	$50,000	$60,000
Mortgage payable (15%)	100,000	100,000
Common stock, $10 par	140,000	120,000
Retained earnings	55,000	40,000
	$345,000	$320,000

Additional information for 2009:

1. Net income was $25,000.
2. Sales on account were $410,000. Sales returns and allowances were $20,000.
3. Cost of goods sold was $198,000.
4. The allowance for doubtful accounts was $2,500 on December 31, 2009, and $2,000 on December 31, 2008.

Instructions

Compute the following ratios at December 31, 2009.

(a) Current.

(b) Acid-test.

(c) Receivables turnover.

(d) Inventory turnover.

E18-8 Selected comparative statement data for Willingham Products Company are presented on the next page. All balance sheet data are as of December 31.

Compute selected ratios.

(SO 5)

	2009	2008
Net sales	$760,000	$720,000
Cost of goods sold	480,000	440,000
Interest expense	7,000	5,000
Net income	50,000	42,000
Accounts receivable	120,000	100,000
Inventory	85,000	75,000
Total assets	580,000	500,000
Total common stockholders' equity	430,000	325,000

Instructions

Compute the following ratios for 2009.

(a) Profit margin.
(b) Asset turnover.
(c) Return on assets.
(d) Return on common stockholders' equity.

Compute selected ratios.
(SO 5)

E18-9 The income statement for Christensen, Inc., appears below.

CHRISTENSEN, INC.
Income Statement
For the Year Ended December 31, 2008

Sales	$400,000
Cost of goods sold	230,000
Gross profit	170,000
Expenses (including $16,000 interest and $24,000 income taxes)	105,000
Net income	$ 65,000

Additional information:

1. The weighted average common shares outstanding in 2008 were 30,000 shares.
2. The market price of Christensen, Inc. stock was $13 in 2008.
3. Cash dividends of $26,000 were paid, $5,000 of which were to preferred stockholders.

Instructions

Compute the following ratios for 2008.

(a) Earnings per share.
(b) Price-earnings.
(c) Payout.
(d) Times interest earned.

Compute amounts from ratios.
(SO 5)

E18-10 Rees Corporation experienced a fire on December 31, 2009, in which its financial records were partially destroyed. It has been able to salvage some of the records and has ascertained the following balances.

	December 31, 2009	December 31, 2008
Cash	$ 30,000	$ 10,000
Receivables (net)	72,500	126,000
Inventory	200,000	180,000
Accounts payable	50,000	90,000
Notes payable	30,000	60,000
Common stock, $100 par	400,000	400,000
Retained earnings	113,500	101,000

Additional information:

1. The inventory turnover is 3.5 times.
2. The return on common stockholders' equity is 24%. The company had no additional paid-in capital.
3. The receivables turnover is 8.8 times.
4. The return on assets is 20%.
5. Total assets at December 31, 2008, were $605,000.

Instructions

Compute the following for Rees Corporation.

(a) Cost of goods sold for 2009.
(b) Net sales (credit) for 2009.
(c) Net income for 2009.
(d) Total assets at December 31, 2009.

E18-11 Scully Corporation's comparative balance sheets are presented below.

Compute ratios.
(SO 5)

SCULLY CORPORATION
Balance Sheets
December 31

	2008	2007
Cash	$ 4,300	$ 3,700
Accounts receivable	21,200	23,400
Inventory	10,000	7,000
Land	20,000	26,000
Building	70,000	70,000
Accumulated depreciation	(15,000)	(10,000)
Total	$110,500	$120,100
Accounts payable	$ 12,370	$ 31,100
Common stock	75,000	69,000
Retained earnings	23,130	20,000
Total	$110,500	$120,100

Scully's 2008 income statement included net sales of $100,000, cost of goods sold of $60,000, and net income of $15,000.

Instructions

Compute the following ratios for 2008.

(a) Current ratio.
(b) Acid-test ratio.
(c) Receivables turnover.
(d) Inventory turnover.
(e) Profit margin.
(f) Asset turnover.
(g) Return on assets.
(h) Return on common stockholders' equity.
(i) Debt to total assets ratio.

E18-12 For its fiscal year ending October 31, 2008, Molini Corporation reports the following partial data.

Prepare a correct income statement.
(SO 6)

Income before income taxes	$540,000
Income tax expense (30% × $390,000)	117,000
Income before extraordinary items	423,000
Extraordinary loss from flood	150,000
Net income	$273,000

The flood loss is considered an extraordinary item. The income tax rate is 30% on all items.

Instructions

(a) Prepare a correct income statement, beginning with income before income taxes.
(b) Explain in memo form why the income statement data are misleading.

E18-13 Yadier Corporation has income from continuing operations of $290,000 for the year ended December 31, 2008. It also has the following items (before considering income taxes).

Prepare income statement.
(SO 6)

1. An extraordinary loss of $80,000.
2. A gain of $30,000 on the discontinuance of a division.

3. A correction of an error in last year's financial statements that resulted in a $20,000 understatement of 2007 net income.

Assume all items are subject to income taxes at a 30% tax rate.

Instructions

(a) Prepare an income statement, beginning with income from continuing operations.
(b) Indicate the statement presentation of any item not included in (a) above.

EXERCISES: SET B

Visit the book's website at **www.wiley.com/college/weygandt**, and choose the Student Companion site, to access Exercise Set B.

PROBLEMS

Follow the rounding procedures used in the chapter.

Prepare vertical analysis and comment on profitability.
(SO 4, 5)

P18-1 Comparative statement data for Douglas Company and Maulder Company, two competitors, appear below. All balance sheet data are as of December 31, 2009, and December 31, 2008.

	Douglas Company		Maulder Company	
	2009	**2008**	**2009**	**2008**
Net sales	$1,549,035		$339,038	
Cost of goods sold	1,080,490		241,000	
Operating expenses	302,275		79,000	
Interest expense	8,980		2,252	
Income tax expense	54,500		6,650	
Current assets	325,975	$312,410	83,336	$ 79,467
Plant assets (net)	521,310	500,000	139,728	125,812
Current liabilities	65,325	75,815	35,348	30,281
Long-term liabilities	108,500	90,000	29,620	25,000
Common stock, $10 par	500,000	500,000	120,000	120,000
Retained earnings	173,460	146,595	38,096	29,998

Instructions

(a) Prepare a vertical analysis of the 2009 income statement data for Douglas Company and Maulder Company in columnar form.
(b) Comment on the relative profitability of the companies by computing the return on assets and the return on common stockholders' equity ratios for both companies.

Compute ratios from balance sheet and income statement.
(SO 5)

P18-2 The comparative statements of Villa Tool Company are presented below.

VILLA TOOL COMPANY
Income Statement
For the Year Ended December 31

	2009	**2008**
Net sales	$1,818,500	$1,750,500
Cost of goods sold	1,011,500	996,000
Gross profit	807,000	754,500
Selling and administrative expense	516,000	479,000
Income from operations	291,000	275,500
Other expenses and losses		
Interest expense	18,000	14,000
Income before income taxes	273,000	261,500
Income tax expense	81,000	77,000
Net income	$ 192,000	$ 184,500

VILLA TOOL COMPANY
Balance Sheets
December 31

Assets	2009	2008
Current assets		
Cash	$ 60,100	$ 64,200
Short-term investments	69,000	50,000
Accounts receivable (net)	117,800	102,800
Inventory	123,000	115,500
Total current assets	369,900	332,500
Plant assets (net)	600,300	520,300
Total assets	$970,200	$852,800
Liabilities and Stockholders' Equity		
Current liabilities		
Accounts payable	$160,000	$145,400
Income taxes payable	43,500	42,000
Total current liabilities	203,500	187,400
Bonds payable	200,000	200,000
Total liabilities	403,500	387,400
Stockholders' equity		
Common stock ($5 par)	280,000	300,000
Retained earnings	286,700	165,400
Total stockholders' equity	566,700	465,400
Total liabilities and stockholders' equity	$970,200	$852,800

All sales were on account. The allowance for doubtful accounts was $3,200 on December 31, 2009, and $3,000 on December 31, 2008.

Instructions

Compute the following ratios for 2009. (Weighted average common shares in 2009 were 57,000.)

(a) Earnings per share.
(b) Return on common stockholders' equity.
(c) Return on assets.
(d) Current.
(e) Acid-test.
(f) Receivables turnover.
(g) Inventory turnover.
(h) Times interest earned.
(i) Asset turnover.
(j) Debt to total assets.

P18-3 Condensed balance sheet and income statement data for Kersenbrock Corporation appear below.

Perform ratio analysis, and evaluate financial position and operating results.

(SO 5)

KERSENBROCK CORPORATION
Balance Sheets
December 31

	2009	2008	2007
Cash	$ 25,000	$ 20,000	$ 18,000
Receivables (net)	50,000	45,000	48,000
Other current assets	90,000	95,000	64,000
Investments	75,000	70,000	45,000
Plant and equipment (net)	400,000	370,000	358,000
	$640,000	$600,000	$533,000
Current liabilities	$ 75,000	$ 80,000	$ 70,000
Long-term debt	80,000	85,000	50,000
Common stock, $10 par	340,000	310,000	300,000
Retained earnings	145,000	125,000	113,000
	$640,000	$600,000	$533,000

KERSENBROCK CORPORATION
Income Statement
For the Year Ended December 31

	2009	2008
Sales	$740,000	$700,000
Less: Sales returns and allowances	40,000	50,000
Net sales	700,000	650,000
Cost of goods sold	420,000	400,000
Gross profit	280,000	250,000
Operating expenses (including income taxes)	235,000	220,000
Net income	$ 45,000	$ 30,000

Additional information:

1. The market price of Kersenbrock's common stock was $4.00, $5.00, and $8.00 for 2007, 2008, and 2009, respectively.
2. All dividends were paid in cash.

Instructions

(a) Compute the following ratios for 2008 and 2009.
  (1) Profit margin.
  (2) Asset turnover.
  (3) Earnings per share. (Weighted average common shares in 2009 were 32,000 and in 2008 were 31,000.)
  (4) Price-earnings.
  (5) Payout.
  (6) Debt to total assets.

(b) Based on the ratios calculated, discuss briefly the improvement or lack thereof in financial position and operating results from 2008 to 2009 of Kersenbrock Corporation.

Compute ratios, and comment on overall liquidity and profitability.
(SO 5)

P18-4 Financial information for Hanshew Company is presented below.

HANSHEW COMPANY
Balance Sheets
December 31

Assets	2009	2008
Cash	$ 70,000	$ 65,000
Short-term investments	52,000	40,000
Receivables (net)	98,000	80,000
Inventories	125,000	135,000
Prepaid expenses	29,000	23,000
Land	130,000	130,000
Building and equipment (net)	180,000	175,000
	$684,000	$648,000
Liabilities and Stockholders' Equity		
Notes payable	$100,000	$100,000
Accounts payable	48,000	42,000
Accrued liabilities	50,000	40,000
Bonds payable, due 2012	150,000	150,000
Common stock, $10 par	200,000	200,000
Retained earnings	136,000	116,000
	$684,000	$648,000

HANSHEW COMPANY
Income Statement
For the Years Ended December 31

	2009	2008
Sales	$850,000	$790,000
Cost of goods sold	620,000	575,000
Gross profit	230,000	215,000
Operating expenses	187,000	173,000
Net income	$ 43,000	$ 42,000

Additional information:

1. Inventory at the beginning of 2008 was $118,000.
2. Receivables (net) at the beginning of 2008 were $88,000. The allowance for doubtful accounts was $4,000 at the end of 2009, $3,800 at the end of 2008, and $3,700 at the beginning of 2008.
3. Total assets at the beginning of 2008 were $630,000.
4. No common stock transactions occurred during 2008 or 2009.
5. All sales were on account.

Instructions

(a) Indicate, by using ratios, the change in liquidity and profitability of Hanshew Company from 2008 to 2009. (*Note*: Not all profitability ratios can be computed.)

(b) Given below are three independent situations and a ratio that may be affected. For each situation, compute the affected ratio (1) as of December 31, 2009, and (2) as of December 31, 2010, after giving effect to the situation. Net income for 2010 was $50,000. Total assets on December 31, 2010, were $700,000.

Situation	Ratio
(1) 18,000 shares of common stock were sold at par on July 1, 2010.	Return on common stockholders' equity
(2) All of the notes payable were paid in 2010. The only change in liabilities was that the notes payable were paid.	Debt to total assets
(3) Market price of common stock was $9 on December 31, 2009, and $12.80 on December 31, 2010.	Price-earnings ratio

P18-5 Selected financial data of Target and Wal-Mart for 2005 are presented here (in millions).

Compute selected ratios, and compare liquidity, profitability, and solvency for two companies.

(SO 5)

	Target Corporation	Wal-Mart Stores, Inc.
	Income Statement Data for Year	
Net sales	$45,682	$285,222
Cost of goods sold	31,445	219,793
Selling and administrative expenses	10,480	51,354
Interest expense	570	986
Other income (expense)	1,157	2,767
Income tax expense	1,146	5,589
Net income	$ 3,198	$ 10,267
	Balance Sheet Data (End of Year)	
Current assets	$13,922	$ 38,491
Noncurrent assets	18,371	81,732
Total assets	$32,293	$120,223
Current liabilities	$ 8,220	$ 42,888
Long-term debt	11,044	27,939
Total stockholders' equity	13,029	49,396
Total liabilities and stockholders' equity	$32,293	$120,223

	Beginning-of-Year Balances	
Total assets	$31,416	$105,405
Total stockholders' equity	11,132	43,623
Current liabilities	8,314	40,364
Total liabilities	20,284	61,782
	Other Data	
Average net receivables	$4,845	$ 1,485
Average inventory	4,958	28,030
Net cash provided by operating activities	3,821	15,044

Instructions

(a) For each company, compute the following ratios.

(1) Current.
(2) Receivables turnover.
(3) Average collection period.
(4) Inventory turnover.
(5) Days in inventory.
(6) Profit margin.
(7) Asset turnover.
(8) Return on assets.
(9) Return on common stockholders' equity.
(10) Debt to total assets.
(11) Times interest earned.

(b) Compare the liquidity, solvency, and profitability of the two companies.

Compute numerous ratios.
(SO 5)

P18-6 The comparative statements of Dillon Company are presented below.

DILLON COMPANY
Income Statement
For Year Ended December 31

	2009	2008
Net sales (all on account)	$600,000	$520,000
Expenses		
Cost of goods sold	415,000	354,000
Selling and administrative	120,800	114,800
Interest expense	7,800	6,000
Income tax expense	18,000	14,000
Total expenses	561,600	488,800
Net income	$ 38,400	$ 31,200

DILLON COMPANY
Balance Sheets
December 31

Assets	2009	2008
Current assets		
Cash	$ 21,000	$ 18,000
Short-term investments	18,000	15,000
Accounts receivable (net)	86,000	74,000
Inventory	90,000	70,000
Total current assets	215,000	177,000
Plant assets (net)	423,000	383,000
Total assets	$638,000	$560,000

Liabilities and Stockholders' Equity		
Current liabilities		
Accounts payable	$122,000	$110,000
Income taxes payable	23,000	20,000
Total current liabilities	145,000	130,000
Long-term liabilities		
Bonds payable	120,000	80,000
Total liabilities	265,000	210,000
Stockholders' equity		
Common stock ($5 par)	150,000	150,000
Retained earnings	223,000	200,000
Total stockholders' equity	373,000	350,000
Total liabilities and stockholders' equity	$638,000	$560,000

Additional data:

The common stock recently sold at $19.50 per share.
The year-end balance in the allowance for doubtful accounts was $3,000 for 2009 and $2,400 for 2008.

Instructions

Compute the following ratios for 2009.

(a) Current.
(b) Acid-test.
(c) Receivables turnover.
(d) Inventory turnover.
(e) Profit margin.
(f) Asset turnover.
(g) Return on assets.
(h) Return on common stockholders' equity.
(i) Earnings per share.
(j) Price-earnings.
(k) Payout.
(l) Debt to total assets.
(m) Times interest earned.

P18-7 Presented below is an incomplete income statement and an incomplete comparative balance sheet of Cotte Corporation.

Compute missing information given a set of ratios.

(SO 5)

COTTE CORPORATION
Income Statement
For the Year Ended December 31, 2009

Sales	$11,000,000
Cost of goods sold	?
Gross profit	?
Operating expenses	1,665,000
Income from operations	?
Other expenses and losses	
Interest expense	?
Income before income taxes	?
Income tax expense	560,000
Net income	$?

COTTE CORPORATION
Balance Sheets
December 31

Assets	2009	2008
Current assets		
Cash	$ 450,000	$ 375,000
Accounts receivable (net)	?	950,000
Inventory	?	1,720,000
Total current assets	?	3,045,000
Plant assets (net)	4,620,000	3,955,000
Total assets	$?	$7,000,000
Liabilities and Stockholders' Equity		
Current liabilities	$?	$ 825,000
Long-term notes payable	?	2,800,000
Total liabilities	?	3,625,000
Common stock, $1 par	3,000,000	3,000,000
Retained earnings	400,000	375,000
Total stockholders' equity	3,400,000	3,375,000
Total liabilities and stockholders' equity	$?	$7,000,000

Additional information:

1. The receivables turnover for 2009 is 10 times.
2. All sales are on account.
3. The profit margin for 2009 is 14.5%.
4. Return on assets is 22% for 2009.
5. The current ratio on December 31, 2009, is 3.0.
6. The inventory turnover for 2009 is 4.8 times.

Instructions

Compute the missing information given the ratios above. Show computations. (*Note*: Start with one ratio and derive as much information as possible from it before trying another ratio. List all missing amounts under the ratio used to find the information.)

Prepare income statement with discontinued operations and extraordinary loss.

(SO 6)

P18-8 Cheaney Corporation owns a number of cruise ships and a chain of hotels. The hotels, which have not been profitable, were discontinued on September 1, 2008. The 2008 operating results for the company were as follows.

Operating revenues	$12,850,000
Operating expenses	8,700,000
Operating income	$ 4,150,000

Analysis discloses that these data include the operating results of the hotel chain, which were: operating revenues $2,000,000 and operating expenses $2,400,000. The hotels were sold at a gain of $200,000 before taxes. This gain is not included in the operating results. During the year, Cheaney suffered an extraordinary loss of $800,000 before taxes, which is not included in the operating results. In 2008, the company had other revenues and gains of $100,000, which are not included in the operating results. The corporation is in the 30% income tax bracket.

Instructions

Prepare a condensed income statement.

Prepare income statement with nontypical items.

(SO 6)

P18-9 The ledger of LaRussa Corporation at December 31, 2008, contains the following summary data.

Net sales	$1,700,000	Cost of goods sold	$1,100,000
Selling expenses	120,000	Administrative expenses	150,000
Other revenues and gains	20,000	Other expenses and losses	28,000

Your analysis reveals the following additional information that is not included in the above data.

1. The entire puzzles division was discontinued on August 31. The income from operations for this division before income taxes was $20,000. The puzzles division was sold at a loss of $90,000 before income taxes.
2. On May 15, company property was expropriated for an interstate highway. The settlement resulted in an extraordinary gain of $120,000 before income taxes.
3. The income tax rate on all items is 30%.

Instructions

Prepare an income statement for the year ended December 31, 2008. Use the format illustrated in Demonstration Problem 2 (p. 808).

PROBLEMS: SET B

Visit the book's website at **www.wiley.com/college/weygandt**, and choose the Student Companion site, to access Problem Set B.

CONTINUING COOKIE CHRONICLE

(Note: This is a continuation of the Cookie Chronicle from Chapters 1-17.)

CCC18 Natalie and Curtis have comparative balance sheets and income statements for Cookie & Coffee Creations Inc. They have been told that they can use these financial statements to prepare horizontal and vertical analyses, and to calculate financial ratios, to analyze how their business is doing and to make some decisions they have been considering.

Go to the book's website, www.wiley.com/college/weygandt, to see the completion of this problem.

BROADENING YOUR PERSPECTIVE

FINANCIAL REPORTING AND ANALYSIS

Financial Reporting Problem

PepsiCo, Inc.

BYP18-1 Your parents are considering investing in PepsiCo, common stock. They ask you, as an accounting expert, to make an analysis of the company for them. Fortunately, excerpts from a current annual report of PepsiCo are presented in Appendix A of this textbook. Note that all dollar amounts are in millions.

Instructions

(Follow the approach in the chapter for rounding numbers.)

(a) Make a 5-year trend analysis, using 2001 as the base year, of (1) net sales and (2) net income. Comment on the significance of the trend results.

(b) Compute for 2005 and 2004 the (1) profit margin, (2) asset turnover, (3) return on assets, and (4) return on common stockholders' equity. How would you evaluate PepsiCo's profitability? Total assets at December 27, 2003, were $25,327, and total stockholders' equity at December 27, 2003, was $11,896.

(c) Compute for 2005 and 2004 the (1) debt to total assets and (2) times interest earned ratio. How would you evaluate PepsiCo's long-term solvency?

(d) What information outside the annual report may also be useful to your parents in making a decision about PepsiCo, Inc.?

Comparative Analysis Problem
PepsiCo, Inc. vs. The Coca-Cola Company

BYP18-2 PepsiCo's financial statements are presented in Appendix A. Coca-Cola Company's financial statements are presented in Appendix B.

Instructions

(a) Based on the information contained in these financial statements, determine each of the following for each company.

(1) The percentage increase (decrease) in (i) net sales and (ii) net income from 2004 to 2005.

(2) The percentage increase in (i) total assets and (ii) total common stockholders' (shareholders') equity from 2004 to 2005.

(3) The basic earnings per share and price-earnings ratio for 2005. (For Coca-Cola, use the basic earnings per share.) Coca-Cola's common stock had a market price of $43.60 at the end of fiscal-year 2005.

(b) What conclusions concerning the two companies can be drawn from these data?

Exploring the Web

BYP18-3 The Management Discussion and Analysis section of an annual report addresses corporate performance for the year, and sometimes uses financial ratios to support its claims.

Address: www.ibm.com/investor/tools/index.phtml or go to **www.wiley.com/college/weygandt**

Steps

1. From IBM's Investor Tools, choose **Investment Guides**.
2. Choose **Guide to Annual Reports**.
3. Choose **Anatomy of an Annual Report**.

Instructions

Using the information from the above site, answer the following questions.

(a) What are the optional elements that are often included in an annual report?

(b) What are the elements of an annual report that are required by the SEC?

(c) Describe the contents of the Management Discussion.

(d) Describe the contents of the Auditors' Report.

(e) Describe the contents of the Selected Financial Data.

CRITICAL THINKING

Decision Making Across the Organization

BYP18-4 As the CPA for Carismo Manufacturing Inc., you have been asked to develop some key ratios from the comparative financial statements. This information is to be used to convince creditors that the company is solvent and will continue as a going concern. The data requested and the computations developed from the financial statements follow.

	2008	2007
Current ratio	3.1 times	2.1 times
Acid-test ratio	.8 times	1.4 times
Asset turnover	2.8 times	2.2 times
Net income	Up 32%	Down 8%
Earnings per share	$3.30	$2.50
Book value per share	Up 8%	Up 11%

Instructions

With the class divided into groups, answer the following.

Carismo Manufacturing Inc. asks you to prepare a list of brief comments stating how each of these items supports the solvency and going-concern potential of the business. The company wishes to use these comments to support its presentation of data to its creditors. You are to prepare the comments as requested, giving the implications and the limitations of each item separately. Then prepare a collective inference that may be drawn from the individual items about Carismo's solvency and going-concern potential.

BYP18-5 General Dynamics develops, produces, and supports innovative, reliable, and highly sophisticated military and commercial products. In July of a recent year, the corporation announced that its Quincy Shipbuilding Division (Quincy) will be closed following the completion of the Maritime Prepositioning Ship construction program.

Prior to discontinuance, the operating results of Quincy were net sales $246.8 million, income from operations before income taxes $28.3 million, and income taxes $12.5 million. The corporation's loss on disposition of Quincy was $5.0 million, net of $4.3 million income tax benefits.

From its other operating activities, General Dynamics' financial results were net sales $8,163.8 million, cost of goods sold $6,958.8 million, and selling and administrative expenses $537.0 million. In addition, the corporation had interest expense of $17.2 million and interest revenue of $3.6 million. Income taxes were $282.9 million.

General Dynamics had an average of 42.3 million shares of common stock outstanding during the year.

Instructions

With the class divided into groups, answer the following.

(a) Prepare the income statement for the year, assuming that the year ended on December 31, 2008. Show earnings per share data on the income statement. All dollars should be stated in millions, except for per share amounts. (For example, $8 million would be shown as $8.0)

(b) In the preceding year, Quincy's earnings were $51.6 million before income taxes of $22.8 million. For comparative purposes, General Dynamics reported earnings per share of $0.61 from discontinued operations for Quincy in the preceding year.

(1) What was the average number of common shares outstanding during the preceding year?

(2) If earnings per share from continuing operations was $7.47, what was income from continuing operations during the preceding year? (Round to two decimals.)

Communication Activity

BYP18-6 Beth Harlan is the CEO of Lafferty's Electronics. Harlan is an expert engineer but a novice in accounting. She asks you to explain (1) the bases for comparison in analyzing Lafferty's financial statements, and (2) the factors affecting quality of earnings.

Instructions

Write a letter to Beth Harlan that explains the bases for comparison and factors affecting quality of earnings.

Ethics Case

BYP18-7 Jack McClintock, president of McClintock Industries, wishes to issue a press release to bolster his company's image and maybe even its stock price, which has been gradually falling. As controller, you have been asked to provide a list of twenty financial ratios along with some other operating statistics relative to McClintock Industries' first quarter financials and operations.

Two days after you provide the ratios and data requested, Jeremy Phelps, the public relations director of McClintock, asks you to prove the accuracy of the financial and operating data contained in the press release written by the president and edited by Jeremy. In the press release, the president highlights the sales increase of 25% over last year's first quarter and the positive change in the current ratio from 1.5:1 last year to 3:1 this year. He also emphasizes that production was up 50% over the prior year's first quarter.

You note that the press release contains only positive or improved ratios and none of the negative or deteriorated ratios. For instance, no mention is made that the debt to total assets ratio has increased from 35% to 55%, that inventories are up 89%, and that while the current ratio improved, the acid-test ratio fell from 1:1 to .5:1. Nor is there any mention that the reported profit for the quarter would have been a loss had not the estimated lives of McClintock's plant and machinery been increased by 30%. Jeremy emphasized, "The prez wants this release by early this afternoon."

Instructions

(a) Who are the stakeholders in this situation?
(b) Is there anything unethical in president McClintock's actions?
(c) Should you as controller remain silent? Does Jeremy have any responsibility?

"All About You" Activity

BYP18-8 In this chapter you learned how to use many tools for performing a financial analysis of a company. When making personal investments, however, it is most likely that you won't be buying stocks and bonds in individual companies. Instead, when most people want to invest in stock, they buy mutual funds. By investing in a mutual fund, you reduce your risk because the fund diversifies by buying the stock of a variety of different companies, bonds, and other investments, depending on the stated goals of the fund.

Before you invest in a fund, you will need to decide what type of fund you want. For example, do you want a fund that has the potential of high growth (but also high risk), or are you looking for lower risk and a steady stream of income? Do you want a fund that invests only in U.S. companies, or do you want one that invests globally? Many resources are available to help you with these types of decisions.

Instructions

Go to **http://web.archive.org/web/20050210200843/http://www.cnb1.com/invallocmdl.htm** and complete the investment allocation questionnaire. Add up your total points to determine the type of investment fund that would be appropriate for you.

Answers to Insight and Accounting Across the Organization Questions

p. 789 How to Manage the Current Ratio

Q: How might management influence the company's current ratio?

A: *Management can affect the current ratio by speeding up or withholding payments on accounts payable just before the balance sheet date. Management can alter the cash balance by increasing or decreasing long-term assets or long-term debt, or by issuing or purchasing equity shares.*

p. 797 Keeping Up to Date as an Investor

Q: If you want to keep current with the financial and operating developments of a company in which you own shares, what are some ways you can do so?

A: *You can obtain current information on your investments through a company's Web site, financial magazines and newspapers, CNBC television programs, investment letters, and a stockbroker.*

p. 802 What Is Extraordinary?

Q: If a company takes a large restructuring charge, what is the effect on the company's current income statement versus future ones?

A: *The current period's net income can be greatly diminished by a large restructuring charge, while the net income in future periods can be enhanced because they are relieved of costs (i.e., depreciation and labor expenses) that would have been charged to them.*

Authors' Comments on *All About You:* Should I Play the Market Yet? (p. 805)

For a number of reasons, it is probably a bad idea for Rachael to buy her employer's stock. First, if Rachael is going to invest in the stock market, she should diversify her investments across a number of different companies. Second, you should never have more than a small portion of your total investment portfolio invested in your employer. Suppose that your employer starts to do poorly, the stock price falls, and you get laid off. You lose on two counts: You don't have income, and your net worth has been affected adversely by the drop in the stock price. (This exact situation happened to thousands of Enron employees, who not only lost their jobs, but their retirement savings as well, as Enron's stock plummeted). Third, after purchasing her employer's stock, Rachael's liquidity would be negatively affected: She would have only $3,000 of remaining liquid assets.

If Rachel invests $7,000, she actually has only enough liquid assets to cover one month's worth of expenses. It is true that she could sell her stock, but if it has fallen in value, she will be reluctant to sell. In short, if she were to buy the stock, her financial flexibility would be very limited.

The bottom line is that we think that Rachael *should* invest in something that offers a higher return than her bank savings account, but we question whether she has enough liquidity to invest in individual stocks. We would recommend that she put some money in a stock mutual fund, some in a short-term CD, and the rest in a money-market fund.

Answer to PepsiCo Review It Question 4, p. 787

PepsiCo presents horizontal analyses in its "Financial Highlights" section and its Management's Discussion and Analysis section. Vertical analysis is used in discussions presented in the Management's Discussion and Analysis section.

Answers to Self-Study Questions

1. b **2.** d **3.** a **4.** c **5.** c **6.** c **7.** c **8.** c **9.** d **10.** d

Remember to go back to the Navigator box on the chapter-opening page and check off your completed work.

Chapter 19

Managerial Accounting

STUDY OBJECTIVES

After studying this chapter, you should be able to:

1. Explain the distinguishing features of managerial accounting.
2. Identify the three broad functions of management.
3. Define the three classes of manufacturing costs.
4. Distinguish between product and period costs.
5. Explain the difference between a merchandising and a manufacturing income statement.
6. Indicate how cost of goods manufactured is determined.
7. Explain the difference between a merchandising and a manufacturing balance sheet.
8. Identify trends in managerial accounting.

The Navigator

The Navigator

Scan **Study Objectives**	☐
Read **Feature Story**	☐
Read **Preview**	☐
Read text and answer **Before You Go On** p. 836 ☐ p. 839 ☐ p. 844 ☐ p. 847	☐
Work **Demonstration Problems**	☐
Review **Summary of Study Objectives**	☐
Answer **Self-Study Questions**	☐
Complete **Assignments**	☐

Feature Story

WHAT A DIFFERENCE A DAY MAKES

In January 1998 Compaq Computer (*www.compaq.com*) had just become the largest seller of personal computers, and it was *Forbes* magazine's "company of the year." Its chief executive, Eckhard Pfeiffer, was riding high. But during the next two years Compaq lost $2 billion. The company was in chaos, and Mr. Pfeiffer was out of a job. What happened?

First, Dell happened. Dell Computer (www.dell.com) pioneered a new way of making and selling personal computers. Its customers "custom design" their computer over the Internet or phone. Dell reengineered its "supply chain": It coordinated its efforts with its suppliers and streamlined its order-taking and production process. It can ship a computer within two days of taking an order. Personal computers lose 1 percent of their value every week they sit on a shelf. Thus, having virtually no inventory is a great advantage to Dell. Compaq tried to adopt Dell's approach, but with limited success.

The second shock to Compaq came when it acquired a company even larger than itself—Digital Equipment. Digital was famous as much for its technical service as it was for its products. Mr. Pfeiffer believed that the purchase of Digital, with its huge and respected technical sales force, opened new opportunities for Compaq as a global service company. Now it could sell to and service high-end corporate customers. But combining the two companies proved to be hugely expensive and extremely complicated. Ultimately Compaq decided to merge with Hewlett-Packard (*www.hp.com*) in order to survive.

But now Hewlett-Packard is looking over its shoulder for Dell. Why? Because recently Dell moved into the computer printer business—a segment that Hewlett-Packard has long dominated. Dell currently sells only 2 million printers per year, compared to Hewlett-Packard's 42 million. But many analysts predict that by employing the same techniques that it used in its PC business, Dell will soon take a major share of the printer business—and in the process drive down prices and force some less-nimble competitors out of business.

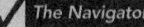

✓ The Navigator

Inside Chapter 19...

Preview of Chapter 19

This chapter focuses on issues illustrated in the Feature Story about Compaq Computer and Dell. These include determining and controlling the costs of material, labor, and overhead and the relationship between costs and profits. In previous chapters, you learned about the form and content of **financial statements for external users** of financial information, such as stockholders and creditors. These financial statements represent the principal product of financial accounting. Managerial accounting focuses primarily on the preparation of **reports for internal users** of financial information, such as the managers and officers of a company. Managers are evaluated on the results of their decisions. In today's rapidly changing global environment, managers often make decisions that determine their company's fate—and their own. Managerial accounting provides tools for assisting management in making decisions and for evaluating the effectiveness of those decisions.

The content and organization of this chapter are as follows.

Managerial Accounting

Managerial Accounting Basics	Managerial Cost Concepts	Manufacturing Costs in Financial Statements	Managerial Accounting Today
• Comparing managerial and financial accounting • Management functions • Business ethics	• Manufacturing costs • Product vs. period costs	• Income statement • Balance sheet • Cost concepts—A review	• Service-industry trends • Managerial accounting practices

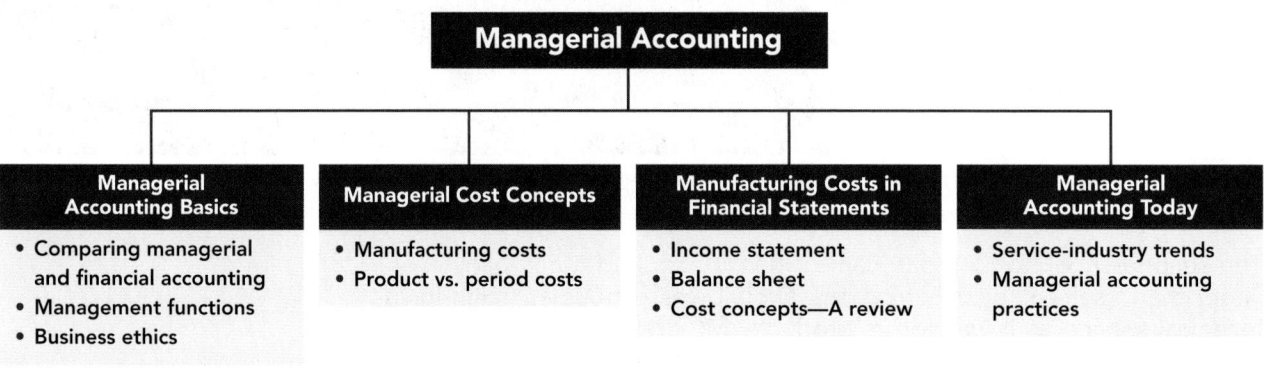

The Navigator

MANAGERIAL ACCOUNTING BASICS

Managerial accounting, also called **management accounting**, is a field of accounting that provides economic and financial information for managers and other internal users. The activities that are part of managerial accounting (and the chapters in which they are discussed in this textbook) are as follows.

1. Explaining manufacturing and nonmanufacturing costs and how they are reported in the financial statements (Chapter 19).
2. Computing the cost of providing a service or manufacturing a product (Chapters 20 and 21).
3. Determining the behavior of costs and expenses as activity levels change and analyzing cost–volume–profit relationships within a company (Chapter 22).
4. Assisting management in profit planning and formalizing these plans in the form of budgets (Chapter 23).
5. Providing a basis for controlling costs and expenses by comparing actual results with planned objectives and standard costs (Chapters 24 and 25).
6. Accumulating and presenting data for management decision making (Chapter 27).

Managerial accounting applies to all types of businesses—service, merchandising, and manufacturing. It also applies to all forms of business organizations—proprietorships, partnerships, and corporations. Managerial accounting is needed in not-for-profit entities as well as in profit-oriented enterprises.

In the past, managerial accountants were primarily engaged in cost accounting—collecting and reporting costs to management. Recently that role changed significantly. First as the business environment has become more automated, methods to determine the amount and type of cost in a product have changed. Second, managerial accountants are now held responsible for strategic cost management; that is, assisting in evaluating how well the company is employing its resources. As a result, managerial accountants now serve as team members alongside personnel from production, marketing, and engineering when critical strategic decisions are being made.

Opportunities for managerial accountants to advance within the company are considerable. Financial executives must have a background that includes an understanding of managerial accounting concepts. Whatever your position in the company—marketing, sales, or production, knowledge of managerial accounting greatly improves your opportunities for advancement. As the CEO of Microsoft noted: "If you're supposed to be making money in business and supposed to be satisfying customers and building market share, there are numbers that characterize those things. And if somebody can't sort of speak to me quantitatively about it, then I'm nervous."

Comparing Managerial and Financial Accounting

STUDY OBJECTIVE 1

Explain the distinguishing features of managerial accounting.

There are both similarities and differences between managerial and financial accounting. First, each field of accounting deals with the economic events of a business. Thus, their interests overlap. For example, determining the unit cost of manufacturing a product is part of managerial accounting. Reporting the total cost of goods manufactured and sold is part of financial accounting. In addition, both managerial and financial accounting require that a company's economic events be quantified and communicated to interested parties.

The principal differences between financial accounting and managerial accounting are summarized in Illustration 19-1. The need for various types of economic data is responsible for many of the differences.

Illustration 19-1
Differences between financial and managerial accounting

Financial Accounting		Managerial Accounting
• External users: stockholders, creditors, and regulators.	**Primary Users of Reports**	• Internal users: officers and managers.
• Financial statements. • Quarterly and annually.	**Types and Frequency of Reports**	• Internal reports. • As frequently as needed.
• General-purpose.	**Purpose of Reports**	• Special-purpose for specific decisions.
• Pertains to business as a whole. • Highly aggregated (condensed). • Limited to double-entry accounting and cost data. • Generally accepted accounting principles.	**Content of Reports**	• Pertains to subunits of the business. • Very detailed. • Extends beyond double-entry accounting to any relevant data. • Standard is relevance to decisions.
• Audit by CPA.	**Verification Process**	• No independent audits.

Management Functions

STUDY OBJECTIVE 2

Identify the three broad functions of management.

Management's activities and responsibilities can be classified into three broad functions. They are:

1. Planning.
2. Directing.
3. Controlling.

In performing these functions, managers make decisions that have a significant impact on the organization.

Planning requires management to look ahead and to establish objectives. These objectives are often diverse: maximizing short-term profits and market share, maintaining a commitment to environmental protection, and contributing to social programs. For example, Hewlett-Packard, in an attempt to gain a stronger foothold in the computer industry, has greatly reduced its prices to compete with Dell. A key objective of management is to add **value** to the business under its control. Value is usually measured by the trading price of the company's stock and by the potential selling price of the company.

Directing involves coordinating a company's diverse activities and human resources to produce a smooth-running operation. This function relates to implementing planned objectives and providing necessary incentives to motivate employees. For example, manufacturers such as Campbell Soup Company, General Motors, and Dell must coordinate purchasing, manufacturing, warehousing, and selling. Service corporations such as American Airlines, FedEx, and AT&T must coordinate scheduling, sales, service, and acquisitions of equipment and supplies. Directing also involves selecting executives, appointing managers and supervisors, and hiring and training employees.

The third management function, **controlling**, is the process of keeping the company's activities on track. In controlling operations, managers determine whether planned goals are being met. When there are deviations from targeted objectives, managers must decide what changes are needed to get back on track. Recent scandals at companies like Enron, Lucent, and Xerox attest to the fact that companies must have adequate controls to ensure that accurate information is developed.

How do managers achieve control? A smart manager in a small operation can make personal observations, ask good questions, and know how to evaluate the answers. But using this approach in a large organization would result in chaos. Imagine the president of Dell attempting to determine whether planned objectives are being met without some record of what has happened and what is expected to occur. Thus, large businesses typically use a formal system of evaluation. These systems include such features as budgets, responsibility centers, and performance evaluation reports.

MANAGEMENT INSIGHT

Automation Has Changed Management

The trend toward more automated and computerized factories has changed the way managers and employees interact. For one thing, managers have fewer direct labor employees to supervise because fewer are needed on the line. Recently, two technology giants, General Electric and Cisco Systems, joined forces to build computerized infrastructures for manufacturers. Their goal is to improve productivity by making better use of data generated by factory-automation equipment. Ultimately their systems should provide a closer link between the factory and corporate offices.

? As factories become more automated, what will managers "manage"?

Decision making is not a separate management function. Rather, it is the outcome of the exercise of good judgment in planning, directing, and controlling.

Business Ethics

As indicated in Chapter 1, all employees within an organization are expected to act ethically in their business activities. Given the importance of ethical behavior to corporations and their owners (stockholders), an increasing number of organizations provide codes of business ethics for their employees.

Despite these efforts, recent business scandals resulted in massive investment losses and numerous employee layoffs. A 2003 survey of fraud by international accounting firm KPMG reported a 13% increase in instances of corporate fraud compared to five years earlier. It noted that while employee fraud (such things as expense-account abuse, payroll fraud, and theft of assets) represented 60% of all instances of fraud, financial reporting fraud (the intentional misstatement of financial reports) was the most costly to companies. That should not be surprising given the long list of companies such as Enron, Global Crossing, WorldCom, and others that engaged in massive financial frauds which led to huge financial losses and thousands of lost jobs.

CREATING PROPER INCENTIVES

Companies like Motorola, IBM, and Nike use complex systems to control and evaluate the actions of managers. They dedicate substantial resources to monitor and effectively evaluate the actions of employees. Unfortunately, these systems and controls sometimes unwittingly create incentives for managers to take unethical actions. For example, companies prepare budgets to provide direction. Because the budget is also used as an evaluation tool, some managers try to "game" the budgeting process by underestimating their division's predicted performance so that it will be easier to meet their performance targets. On the other hand, if the budget is set at unattainable levels, managers sometimes take unethical actions to meet the targets in order to receive higher compensation or, in some cases, to keep their jobs.

For example, in recent years, airline manufacturer Boeing was plagued by a series of scandals including charges of over-billing, corporate espionage, and illegal conflicts of interest. Some long-time employees of Boeing blame the decline in ethics on a change in the corporate culture that took place after Boeing merged with McDonnell Douglas. They suggest that evaluation systems implemented after the merger to monitor results and evaluate employee performance made employees believe they needed to succeed no matter what.

As another example, manufacturing companies need to establish production goals for their processes. Again, if controls are not effective and realistic, problems develop. To illustrate, Schering-Plough, a pharmaceutical manufacturer, found that employees were so concerned with meeting production standards that they failed to monitor the quality of the product, and as a result the dosages were often wrong.

CODE OF ETHICAL STANDARDS

As noted throughout the textbook, the U.S. Congress enacted legislation to help prevent lapses in internal control. This legislation, referred to as the **Sarbanes-Oxley Act of 2002** (SOX, or Sarbox) has important implications for the financial community. One result of SOX was to clarify top management's responsibility for the company's financial statements. CEOs and CFOs must now certify that financial statements give a fair presentation of the company's operating results and its financial condition. In addition, top managers must certify that the company maintains an adequate system of internal controls to safeguard the company's assets and ensure accurate financial reports.

Another result of SOX is that companies now pay more attention to the composition of the board of directors. In particular, the audit committee of the board of directors must be comprised entirely of independent members (that is, non-employees) and must contain at least one financial expert.

Finally, to increase the likelihood of compliance with the rules that are part of the new legislation, the law substantially increases the penalties for misconduct.

To provide guidance for managerial accountants, the Institute of Management Accountants (IMA) has developed a code of ethical standards, entitled *IMA Statement of Ethical Professional Practice.* Management accountants should not commit acts in violation of these standards. Nor should they condone such acts by others within their organizations. We include the IMA code of ethical standards in Appendix E at the end of the book. Throughout the chapters on managerial accounting, we will address various ethical issues faced by managers.

Before You Go On...

REVIEW IT

1. Compare financial accounting and managerial accounting and identify the principal differences.
2. Identify and discuss the three broad functions of management.
3. What were some of the regulatory changes enacted under the Sarbanes-Oxley Act?

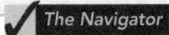

The Navigator

MANAGERIAL COST CONCEPTS

For managers at companies like Dell or Hewlett-Packard to plan, direct, and control operations effectively, they need good information. One very important type of information is related to costs. Managers should ask questions such as the following.

1. What costs are involved in making a product or providing a service?
2. If we decrease production volume, will costs decrease?
3. What impact will automation have on total costs?
4. How can we best control costs?

To answer these questions, managers need reliable and relevant cost information. We now explain and illustrate the various cost categories that management uses.

Manufacturing Costs

STUDY OBJECTIVE 3

Define the three classes of manufacturing costs.

Manufacturing consists of activities and processes that convert raw materials into finished goods. Contrast this type of operation with merchandising, which sells merchandise in the form in which it is purchased. Manufacturing costs are typically classified as shown in Illustration 19-2.

Illustration 19-2
Classifications of manufacturing costs

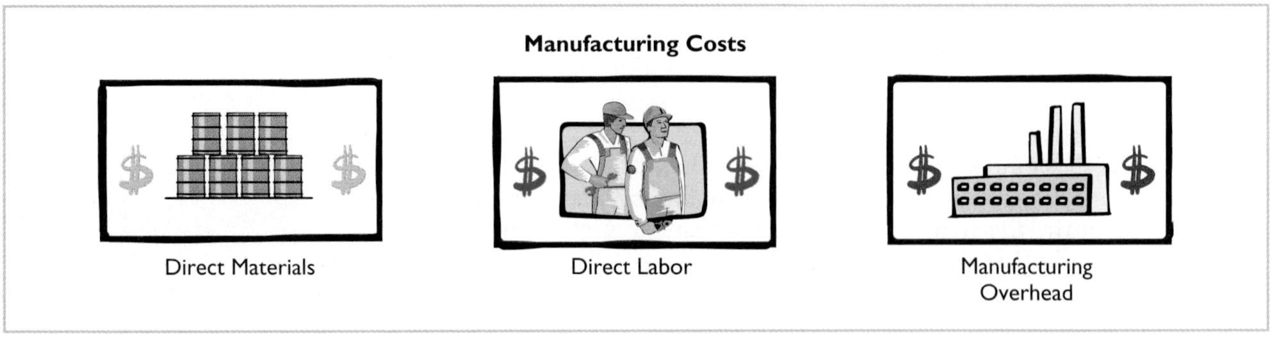

DIRECT MATERIALS

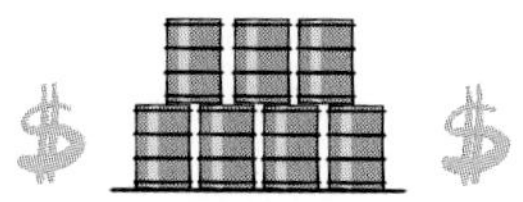

Direct Materials

To obtain the materials that will be converted into the finished product, the manufacturer purchases raw materials. **Raw materials** are the basic materials and parts used in the manufacturing process. For example, auto manufacturers such as General Motors, Ford, and DaimlerChrysler use steel, plastics, and tires as raw materials in making cars.

Raw materials that can be physically and directly associated with the finished product during the manufacturing process are called **direct materials**. Examples include flour in the baking of bread, syrup in the bottling of soft drinks, and steel in the making of automobiles. In the Feature Story, direct materials for Hewlett-Packard and Dell Computer include plastic, glass, hard drives, and processing chips.

But some raw materials cannot be easily associated with the finished product. These are called indirect materials. **Indirect materials** have one of two characteristics: Either (1) they do not physically become part of the finished product, such as lubricants and polishing compounds. Or (2) they cannot be traced because their physical association with the finished product is too small in terms of cost, such as cotter pins and lock washers. Companies account for indirect materials as part of **manufacturing overhead**.

DIRECT LABOR

Direct Labor

The work of factory employees that can be physically and directly associated with converting raw materials into finished goods is called **direct labor**. Bottlers at Coca-Cola, bakers at Sara Lee, and typesetters at TechBooks are employees whose activities are usually classified as direct labor. **Indirect labor** refers to the work of factory employees that has no physical association with the finished product, or for which it is impractical to trace costs to the goods produced. Examples include wages of maintenance people, time-keepers, and supervisors. Like indirect materials, companies classify indirect labor as **manufacturing overhead**.

MANAGEMENT INSIGHT

Productivity at Nissan

Recently a closely watched study of productivity in the automobile industry reported some encouraging improvements for U.S. auto manufacturers. For example, the U.S. unit of DaimlerChrysler improved its overall productivity 8.3%. A Nissan Motor plant in Tennessee set the standard for least amount of labor hours per vehicle: It produced Altima automobiles using only 15.74 labor hours per vehicle. Chrysler assembly plants required 28 hours per vehicle, and Ford took 26 hours.

Source: Ann Keeton, "Chrysler Leads Big Three in Productivity Gains," *Wall Street Journal*, June 18, 2003.

? Why might Nissan production require significantly fewer labor hours?

MANUFACTURING OVERHEAD

Manufacturing Overhead

Manufacturing overhead consists of costs that are indirectly associated with the manufacture of the finished product. These costs may also be manufacturing costs that cannot be classified as direct materials or direct labor. Manufacturing overhead includes indirect materials, indirect labor, depreciation on factory buildings and machines, and insurance, taxes, and maintenance on factory facilities.

One study found the following magnitudes of the three different product costs as a percentage of the total product cost: direct materials 54%, direct labor 13%, and manufacturing overhead 33%. Note that the direct labor component is the smallest. This component of product cost is dropping substantially because of automation. In some companies, direct labor has become as little as 5% of the total cost.

Allocating materials and labor costs to specific products is fairly straightforward. Good record keeping can tell a company how much plastic is used in making each type of gear, or how many hours of factory labor were used to assemble a part. But allocating overhead costs to specific products presents problems. How much of the purchasing agent's salary is attributable to the hundreds of different products made in the same plant? What about the grease that keeps the machines humming, or the computers that make sure paychecks come out on time? Boiled down to its simplest form, the question becomes: Which products cause the incurrence of which costs? In subsequent chapters we show various methods of allocating overhead to products.

ALTERNATIVE TERMINOLOGY

Terms such as *factory overhead, indirect manufacturing costs,* and *burden* are sometimes used instead of manufacturing overhead.

Product versus Period Costs

STUDY OBJECTIVE 4

Distinguish between product and period costs.

Each of the manufacturing cost components—direct materials, direct labor, and manufacturing overhead—are product costs. As the term suggests, **product costs** are costs that are a necessary and integral part of producing the finished product. Companies record product costs, when incurred, as inventory. Under the matching principle, these costs do not become expenses until the company sells the finished goods inventory. The expense is cost of goods sold.

ALTERNATIVE TERMINOLOGY

Product costs are also called *inventoriable costs.*

Period costs are costs that are matched with the revenue of a specific time period rather than included as part of the cost of a salable product. These are nonmanufacturing costs. Period costs include selling and administrative expenses. Companies deduct these costs from revenues in the period in which they are incurred in order to determine net income.

Illustration 19-3 summarizes these relationships and cost terms. Our main concern in this chapter is with product costs.

Illustration 19-3
Product versus period costs

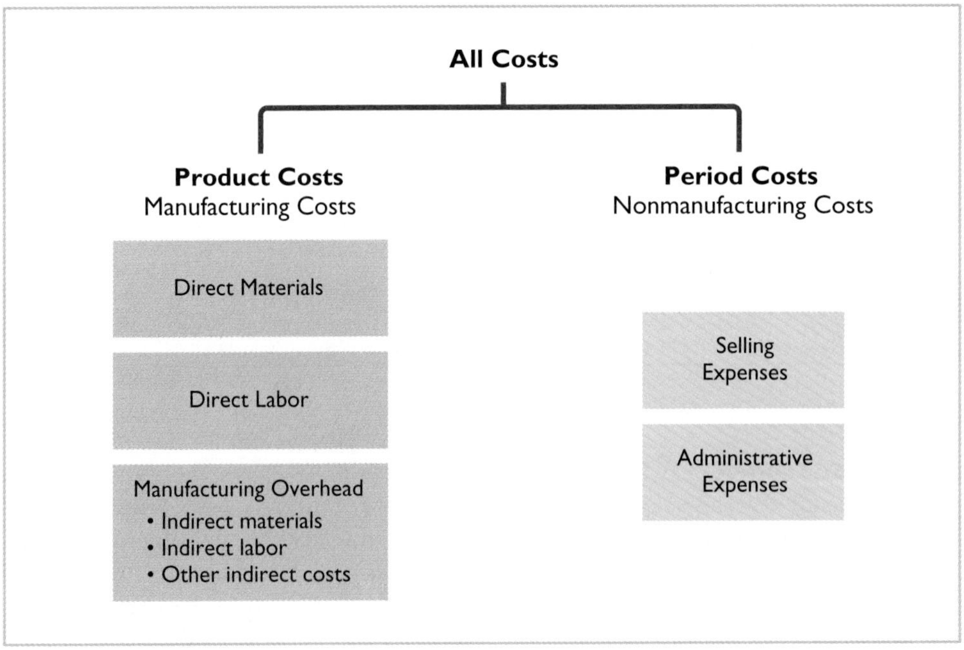

Before You Go On...

REVIEW IT

1. What are the major cost classifications involved in manufacturing a product?
2. What are product and period costs, and what is their relationship to the manufacturing process?

DO IT

A bicycle company has these costs: tires, salaries of employees who put tires on the wheels, factory building depreciation, wheel nuts, spokes, salary of factory manager, handle bars, and salaries of factory maintenance employees. Classify each cost as direct materials, direct labor, or overhead.

Action Plan

- Classify as direct materials any raw materials that can be physically and directly associated with the finished product.
- Classify as direct labor the work of factory employees that can be physically and directly associated with the finished product.
- Classify as manufacturing overhead any costs that are indirectly associated with the finished product.

Solution Tires, spokes, and handle bars are direct materials. Salaries of employees who put tires on the wheels are direct labor. All of the other costs are manufacturing overhead.

Related exercise material: BE19-4, BE19-5, BE19-6, BE19-7, E19-2, E19-3, E19-4, E19-5, E19-6, and E19-7.

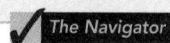

✓ The Navigator

MANUFACTURING COSTS IN FINANCIAL STATEMENTS

STUDY OBJECTIVE 5
Explain the difference between a merchandising and a manufacturing income statement.

The financial statements of a manufacturer are very similar to those of a merchandiser. For example, you will find many of the same sections and same accounts in the financial statements of Procter & Gamble that you find in those of Dick's Sporting Goods. The principal differences between their financial statements pertain to the cost of goods sold section in the income statement and the current assets section in the balance sheet.

Income Statement

Under a periodic inventory system, the income statements of a merchandiser and a manufacturer differ in the cost of goods sold section. Merchandisers compute cost of goods sold by adding the beginning merchandise inventory to the **cost of goods purchased** and subtracting the ending merchandise inventory. Manufacturers compute cost of goods sold by adding the beginning finished goods inventory to the **cost of goods manufactured** and subtracting the ending finished goods inventory. (See Illustration 19-4 on page 840.)

A number of accounts are involved in determining the cost of goods manufactured. To eliminate excessive detail, income statements typically show only the total cost of goods manufactured. The details are presented in a Cost of Goods Manufactured Schedule.

Illustration 19-4
Cost of goods sold components

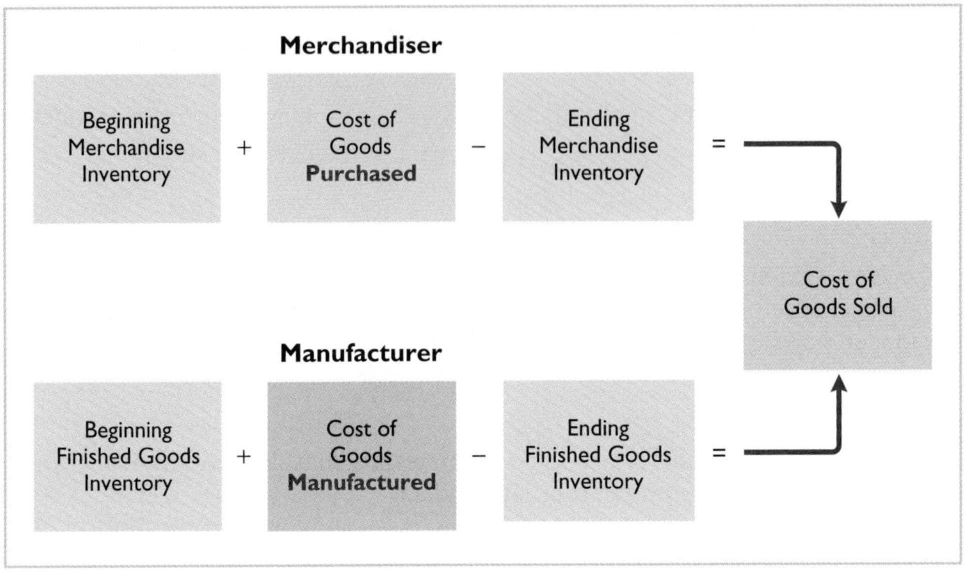

HELPFUL HINT
We assume a periodic inventory system in this illustration.

Illustration 19-5 shows the different presentations of the cost of goods sold sections for merchandising and manufacturing companies. The other sections of an income statement are similar for merchandisers and manufacturers.

Illustration 19-5
Cost of goods sold sections of merchandising and manufacturing income statements

MERCHANDISING COMPANY Income Statement (partial) For the Year Ended December 31, 2008	
Cost of goods sold	
Merchandise inventory, January 1	**$ 70,000**
Cost of goods purchased	**650,000**
Cost of goods available for sale	720,000
Merchandise inventory, December 31	**400,000**
Cost of goods sold	$320,000

MANUFACTURING COMPANY Income Statement (partial) For the Year Ended December 31, 2008	
Cost of goods sold	
Finished goods inventory, January 1	**$ 90,000**
Cost of goods manufactured (see Illustration 19-7)	**370,000**
Cost of goods available for sale	460,000
Finished goods inventory, December 31	**80,000**
Cost of goods sold	$380,000

DETERMINING THE COST OF GOODS MANUFACTURED

STUDY OBJECTIVE 6
Indicate how cost of goods manufactured is determined.

An example may help show how companies determine the cost of goods manufactured. Assume that Dell has a number of computers in various stages of production on January 1. In total, these partially completed units are called **beginning work in process inventory**. The costs assigned to beginning work in process inventory are based on the **manufacturing costs incurred in the prior period**.

The manufacturing costs incurred in the current year are used first to complete the work in process on January 1. They then are used to start the production of other computers. The sum of the direct materials costs, direct labor costs, and manufacturing overhead incurred in the current year is the **total manufacturing costs** for the current period.

We now have two cost amounts: (1) the cost of the beginning work in process and (2) the total manufacturing costs for the current period. The sum of these costs is the **total cost of work in process** for the year.

At the end of the year, some computers may be only partially completed. The costs of these units become the cost of the **ending work in process inventory**. To find the **cost of goods manufactured**, we subtract this cost from the total cost of work in process. Illustration 19-6 shows the formula for determining the cost of goods manufactured.

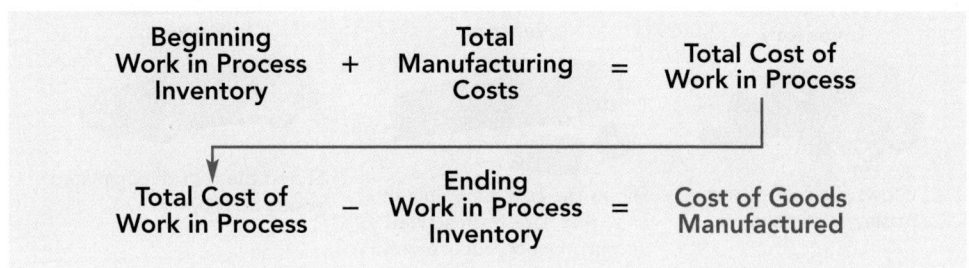

Illustration 19-6
Cost of goods manufactured formula

Beginning Work in Process Inventory + Total Manufacturing Costs = Total Cost of Work in Process

Total Cost of Work in Process − Ending Work in Process Inventory = Cost of Goods Manufactured

COST OF GOODS MANUFACTURED SCHEDULE

The **cost of goods manufactured schedule** is a report that shows cost elements used in calculating cost of goods manufactured. Illustration 19-7 shows the schedule for Olsen Manufacturing Company (using assumed data). The schedule presents detailed data for direct materials and for manufacturing overhead.

Review Illustration 19-6 and then examine the cost of goods manufactured schedule in Illustration 19-7. You should be able to distinguish between "Total manufacturing costs" and "Cost of goods manufactured." The difference is the effect of the change in work in process during the period.

Illustration 19-7
Cost of goods manufactured schedule

OLSEN MANUFACTURING COMPANY
Cost of Goods Manufactured Schedule
For the Year Ended December 31, 2008

Work in process, January 1			**$ 18,400**
Direct materials			
Raw materials inventory, January 1	$ 16,700		
Raw materials purchases	152,500		
Total raw materials available for use	169,200		
Less: Raw materials inventory, December 31	22,800		
Direct materials used		$146,400	
Direct labor		175,600	
Manufacturing overhead			
Indirect labor	14,300		
Factory repairs	12,600		
Factory utilities	10,100		
Factory depreciation	9,440		
Factory insurance	8,360		
Total manufacturing overhead		54,800	
Total manufacturing costs			**376,800**
Total cost of work in process			395,200
Less: Work in process, December 31			**25,200**
Cost of goods manufactured			**$370,000**

Balance Sheet

The balance sheet for a merchandising company shows just one category of inventory. In contrast, the balance sheet for a manufacturer may have three inventory accounts, as shown in Illustration 19-8.

Illustration 19-8
Inventory accounts for a manufacturer

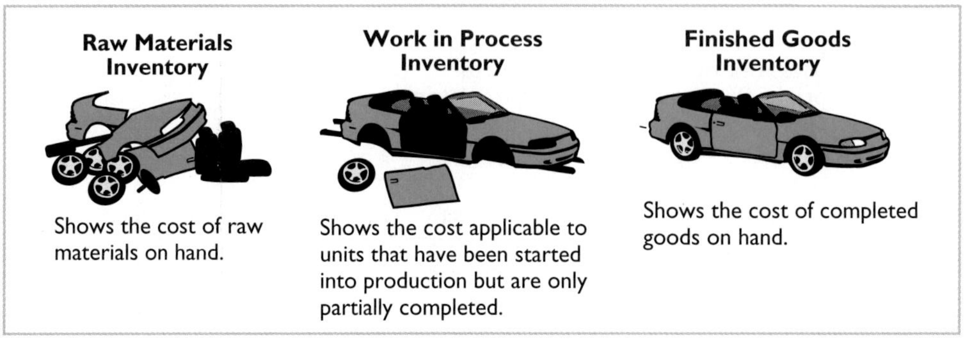

Raw Materials Inventory
Shows the cost of raw materials on hand.
Work in Process Inventory
Shows the cost applicable to units that have been started into production but are only partially completed.
Finished Goods Inventory
Shows the cost of completed goods on hand.

STUDY OBJECTIVE 7
Explain the difference between a merchandising and a manufacturing balance sheet.

Finished Goods Inventory is to a manufacturer what Merchandise Inventory is to a merchandiser. It represents the goods that are available for sale.

The current assets sections presented in Illustration 19-9 contrast the presentations of inventories for merchandising and manufacturing companies. Companies generally list manufacturing inventories in the order of their liquidity—the order in which they are expected to be realized in cash. Thus, finished goods inventory comes first. The remainder of the balance sheet is similar for the two types of companies.

Illustration 19-9
Current assets sections of merchandising and manufacturing balance sheets

MERCHANDISING COMPANY
Balance Sheet
December 31, 2008

Current assets	
Cash	$100,000
Receivables (net)	210,000
Merchandise inventory	**400,000**
Prepaid expenses	22,000
Total current assets	$732,000

MANUFACTURING COMPANY
Balance Sheet
December 31, 2008

Current assets		
Cash		$180,000
Receivables (net)		210,000
Inventories		
Finished goods	**$80,000**	
Work in process	**25,200**	
Raw materials	**22,800**	**128,000**
Prepaid expenses		18,000
Total current assets		$536,000

Each step in the accounting cycle for a merchandiser applies to a manufacturer. For example, prior to preparing financial statements, manufacturers make adjusting entries. The adjusting entries are essentially the same as those of a merchandiser. The closing entries are also similar for manufacturers and merchandisers.

For expanded coverage, go to the Student Companion site and select Chapter 19, Accounting Cycle (Worksheet) for a Manufacturing Company.

Cost Concepts—A Review

You have learned a number of cost concepts in this chapter. Because many of these concepts are new, here we provide an extended example for review.

Assume that Northridge Company manufactures and sells pre-hung metal doors. Recently, it also has decided to start selling pre-hung wood doors. The company will use an old warehouse that it owns to manufacture the new product. Northridge identifies the following costs associated with manufacturing and selling the pre-hung wood doors.

1. The material cost (wood) for each door is $10.
2. Labor costs required to construct a wood door are $8 per door.
3. Depreciation on the factory equipment used to make the wood doors is $25,000 per year.
4. Property taxes on the factory building used to make the wood doors are $6,000 per year.
5. Advertising costs for the pre-hung wood doors total $2,500 per month or $30,000 per year.
6. Sales commissions related to pre-hung wood doors sold are $4 per door.
7. Salaries for employees who maintain the factory facilities are $28,000.
8. The salary of the plant manager in charge of pre-hung wood doors is $70,000.
9. The cost of shipping pre-hung wood doors is $12 per door sold.

Illustration 19-10 shows how these manufacturing and selling costs can be assigned to the various categories.

Illustration 19-10
Assignment of costs to cost categories

	Product Costs			
Cost Item	**Direct Materials**	**Direct Labor**	**Manufacturing Overhead**	**Period Costs**
1. Material cost ($10) per door	X			
2. Labor costs ($8) per door		X		
3. Depreciation on factory equipment ($25,000 per year)			X	
4. Property taxes on factory building ($6,000 per year)			X	
5. Advertising costs ($30,000 per year)				X
6. Sales commissions ($4 per door)				X
7. Maintenance salaries (factory facilities) ($28,000 per year)			X	
8. Salary of plant manager ($70,000)			X	
9. Cost of shipping pre-hung doors ($12 per door)				X

Remember that total manufacturing costs are the sum of the **product costs**—direct materials, direct labor, and manufacturing overhead. If Northridge Company produces 10,000 pre-hung wood doors the first year, the total manufacturing costs would be $309,000 as shown in Illustration 19-11 (page 844).

Illustration 19-11
Computation of total manufacturing costs

Cost Number and Item	Manufacturing Cost
1. Material cost ($10 × 10,000)	$100,000
2. Labor cost ($8 × 10,000)	80,000
3. Depreciation on factory equipment	25,000
4. Property taxes on factory building	6,000
7. Maintenance salaries (factory facilities)	28,000
8. Salary of plant manager	70,000
Total manufacturing costs	**$309,000**

Knowing the total manufacturing costs, Northridge can compute the manufacturing cost per unit. Assuming 10,000 units, the cost to produce one pre-hung wood door is $30.90 ($309,000 ÷ 10,000 units).

We will use the cost concepts discussed in this chapter extensively in subsequent chapters. Study Illustration 19-10 carefully. If you do not understand any of these classifications, go back and reread the appropriate section in this chapter.

Before You Go On...

REVIEW IT

1. How does the content of an income statement for a merchandiser differ from that for a manufacturer?
2. How do companies report the work in process inventories in the cost of goods manufactured schedule?
3. How does the content of the balance sheet for a merchandiser differ from that for a manufacturer?

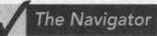

The Navigator

MANAGERIAL ACCOUNTING TODAY

STUDY OBJECTIVE 8

Identify trends in managerial accounting.

In recent years, the competitive environment for U.S. business has changed significantly. For example, the airline, financial services, and telecommunications industries have been deregulated. Global competition has intensified. The world economy now has the European Union, NAFTA, and ASEAN. Countries like China and India are becoming economic powerhouses. As indicated earlier, managerial accountants must be forward-looking, acting as advisors and information providers to different parts of the organization. Some of the issues they face are discussed below.

Service-Industry Trends

The Feature Story notes that at the peak of its success as a personal computer manufacturer, Compaq purchased Digital Equipment. Its management believed that the future of computing was in providing computer services, rather than in manufacturing computer hardware. In fact, the U.S. economy in general has shifted toward an emphasis on providing services, rather than goods. Today over 50% of U.S. workers work in service companies, and that percentage is projected to increase in coming years. Much of this chapter focused on manufacturers, but most of the techniques that you will learn in this course apply equally to service companies.

ETHICS NOTE

Do telecommunications companies have an obligation to provide service to remote or low-user areas for a fee that may be less than the cost of the service?

Managers of service companies look to managerial accounting to answer many questions. In some instances the managerial accountant may need to develop new systems for measuring the cost of serving individual customers.

In others, companies may need new operating controls to improve the quality and efficiency of specific services. Many of the examples we present in subsequent chapters will be based on service companies.

Managerial Accounting Practices

As discussed earlier, the practice of managerial accounting has changed significantly in recent years to better address the needs of managers. The following sections explain some recent managerial accounting practices.

THE VALUE CHAIN

The **value chain** refers to all activities associated with providing a product or service. For a manufacturer these include research and development, product design, acquisition of raw materials, production, sales and marketing, delivery, customer relations, and subsequent service. Illustration 19-12 depicts the value chain for a manufacturer. In recent years, companies have made huge strides in analyzing all stages of the value chain in an effort to improve productivity and eliminate waste. Japanese automobile manufacturer Toyota pioneered many of these innovations.

Illustration 19-12
A manufacturer's value chain

In the 1980s many companies purchased giant machines to replace humans in the manufacturing process. These machines were designed to produce large batches of products. In recent years these large-batch manufacturing processes have been recognized as very wasteful. They require vast amounts of inventory storage capacity and considerable movement of materials. Consequently, many companies have reengineered their manufacturing processes. As one example, the manufacturing company Pratt and Whitney has replaced many large machines with smaller, more flexible ones and has begun reorganizing its plants for more efficient flow of goods. Pratt and Whitney was able to reduce the time that its turbine engine blades spend in the grinding section of its factory from 10 days down to 2 hours. It cut the total amount of time spent making a blade from 22 days to 7 days. Analysis of the value chain has made companies far more responsive to customer needs and has improved profitability.

JUST-IN-TIME INVENTORY METHODS

Many companies have significantly lowered inventory levels and costs using **just-in-time (JIT) inventory** methods. Under a just-in-time method, goods are manufactured or purchased just in time for use. As noted in the Feature Story, Dell is famous for having developed a system for making computers in response to individual customer requests. Even though each computer is custom-made to meet each customer's particular specifications, it takes Dell less than 48 hours to assemble the computer and put it on a truck. By integrating its information systems with those of its suppliers, Dell reduced its inventories to nearly zero. This is a huge advantage in an industry where products become obsolete nearly overnight.

ETHICS NOTE

Does just-in-time inventory justify "just-in-time" employees obtained through temporary employment services?

QUALITY

JIT inventory systems require an increased emphasis on product quality. If products are produced only as they are needed, it is very costly for the company to have to stop production because of defects or machine breakdowns. Many companies have installed **total quality management (TQM)** systems to reduce defects in finished products. The goal is to achieve zero defects. These systems require timely data on defective products, rework costs, and the cost of honoring warranty contracts. Often, companies use this information to help redesign the product in a way that makes it less prone to defect. Or they may use the information to reengineer the production process to reduce setup time and decrease the potential for error. TQM systems also provide information on nonfinancial measures such as customer satisfaction, number of service calls, and time to generate reports. Attention to these measures, which employees can control, leads to increased profitability.

ACTIVITY-BASED COSTING

As discussed earlier, overhead costs have become an increasingly large component of product and service costs. By definition, overhead costs cannot be directly traced to individual products. But to determine each product's cost, overhead must be **allocated** to the various products. In order to obtain more accurate product costs, many companies now allocate overhead using **activity-based costing (ABC)**. Under ABC, companies allocate overhead based on each product's use of activities in making the product. For example, companies can keep track of their cost of setting up machines for each batch of a production process. Then companies can allocate part of the total set-up cost to a particular product based on the number of set-ups that product required.

Activity-based costing is beneficial because it results in more accurate product costing and in more careful scrutiny of all activities in the value chain. For example, if a product's cost is high because it requires a high number of set-ups, management will be motivated to determine how to produce the product using the optimal number of machine set-ups. Both manufacturing and service companies now widely use ABC. Allied Signal and Coca-Cola have both enjoyed improved results from ABC. Fidelity Investments uses ABC to identify which customers cost the most to serve.

MANAGEMENT INSIGHT

Bananas Receive Special Treatment

When it comes to total quality management, few companies can compare with Chiquita Brands International. Grocery store customers are very picky about bananas—bad bananas are consistently the number one grocery store complaint. Because bananas often account for up to 3% of a grocery store's sales, Chiquita goes to great lengths to protect the popular fruit. While bananas are in transit from Central America, "black box" recording devices attached to shipping crates ensure that they are kept in an environment of 90% humidity and an unvarying 55-degree temperature. Upon arrival in the U.S., bananas are ripened in airtight warehouses that use carefully monitored levels of ethylene gas. Regular checks are made of each warehouse using ultrasonic detectors that can detect leaks the size of a pinhole. Says one grocery store executive, "No other item in the store has this type of attention and resources devoted to it."

Source: Devon Spurgeon, "When Grocers in U.S. Go Bananas Over Bad Fruit, They Call Laubenthal," *Wall Street Journal*, August 14, 2000, p. A1.

? Why is it important to keep track of costs that are incurred to improve product quality?

BALANCED SCORECARD

As companies implement various business practice innovations, managers sometimes focus too enthusiastically on the latest innovation, to the detriment of other areas of the business. For example, in focusing on improving quality, companies sometimes have lost sight of cost/benefit considerations. Similarly, in focusing on reducing inventory levels through just-in-time, companies sometimes have lost sales due to inventory shortages. The **balanced scorecard** is a performance-measurement approach that uses both financial and nonfinancial measures to evaluate all aspects of a company's operations in an **integrated** fashion. The performance measures are linked in a cause-and-effect fashion to ensure that they all tie to the company's overall objectives.

For example, the company may desire to increase its return on assets, a common financial performance measure (calculated as net income divided by average total assets). It will then identify a series of linked goals. If the company accomplishes each goal, the ultimate result will be an increase in return on assets. For example, in order to increase return on assets, sales must increase. In order to increase sales, customer satisfaction must be increased. In order to increase customer satisfaction, product defects must be reduced. In order to reduce product defects, employee training must be increased. Note the linkage, which starts with employee training and ends with return on assets. Each objective will have associated performance measures.

The use of the balanced scorecard is widespread among well-known and respected companies. For example, Hilton Hotels Corporation uses the balanced scorecard to evaluate the performance of employees at all of its hotel chains. Wal-Mart employs the balanced scorecard, and actually extends its use to evaluation of its suppliers. For example, Wal-Mart recently awarded Welch Company the "Dry Grocery Division Supplier of the Year Award" for its balanced scorecard results. We discuss the balanced scorecard further in Chapter 25.

Before You Go On...

REVIEW IT

1. Describe, in sequence, the main components of a manufacturer's value chain.
2. Why is product quality important for companies that implement a just-in-time inventory system?
3. Explain what is meant by "balanced" in the balanced scorecard approach.

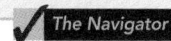

✓ The Navigator

Be sure to read **ALL ABOUT YOU: *Outsourcing and Jobs*** on page 848 for information on how topics in this chapter apply to you.

all about YOU

Outsourcing and Jobs

As noted in this chapter, because of global competition, companies have become increasingly focused on reducing costs. To reduce costs, and remain competitive, many companies are turning to outsourcing. *Outsourcing* means hiring an outside supplier to provide elements of a product rather than producing them internally.

In many instances companies outsource jobs to foreign suppliers, which has caused considerable concern about loss of U.S. jobs. Until recently, most of the debate about outsourcing related to manufacturing. Now outsourcing is taking place in professional services like engineering and accounting. This is occurring because high-speed transmission of large amounts of data over the Internet is now cheap and easy. As a consequence, jobs that once seemed safe from foreign competition are now at risk.

Some Facts

* IBM has expanded beyond information technology into providing advisory services related to outsourcing, which it believes will be a $500 billion market.
* A U.S. professional association of certified public accountants requires that its members notify clients before they share confidential client information with an outside contractor as part of an outsourcing arrangement.
* During a recent two-year period Ford Motor Co. inspected the working conditions at about 160 of the more than 2,000 foreign-owned plants in low-cost countries that supply it with outsourced parts.
* The McKinsey Global Institute predicts that white-collar overseas outsourcing will increase at a rate of 30 to 40% over the next five years. By 2015, the consultancy group Forrester predicts, roughly 3.3 million service jobs will have moved offshore, including 1.7 million "back-office" jobs such as payroll processing and accounting, and 473,000 jobs in the information technology industry.
* On the otherhand, Hewlett-Packard has begun to "insource" many of the manufacturing operations that it previously outsourced.

About the Numbers

Interestingly, foreign firms doing business in the United States also hire a lot of Americans. In a recent year, U.S. subsidiaries of foreign companies employed approximately 5.3 million Americans. In comparison, in that same year 134,000 Americans lost their jobs due to outsourcing. The following graph shows which countries are the top foreign employers in the United States.

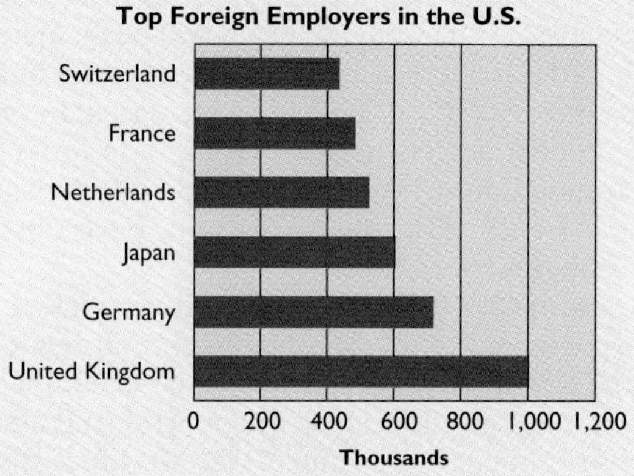

Source: Darren Dahl, "Insourcing 101," *Inc.* Magazine, April 2006, p. 50.

What Do You Think?

Suppose you are the managing partner in a CPA firm with 30 full-time staff. Larger firms in your community have begun to outsource basic tax-return preparation work to India. Should you outsource your basic tax return work to India as well? You estimate that you would have to lay off six staff members if you outsource the work.

YES: The wages paid to Indian accountants are very low relative to U.S. wages. You will not be able to compete unless you outsource.

NO: Tax-return data is highly sensitive. Many customers will be upset to learn that their data is being emailed around the world.

Sources: Jonathan Weil, "Accountants Scrutinize Outsourcing," *Wall Street Journal*, August 11, 2004, p. A2; Jeffrey McCracken, "Ford Probes Work Conditions at Part Makers in China, Mexico," *Wall Street Journal*, April 5, 2006m p. A12; Council on Foreign Affairs, "Backgrounder, Trade: Outsourcing Jobs," February 20, 2004, *cfr.org/publication* (accessed June 2006).

The authors' comments on this situation appear on page 869.

Demonstration Problem 1

WILEY PLUS

Giant Manufacturing Co. Ltd. specializes in manufacturing many different models of bicycles. Assume that a new model, the Jaguar, has been well accepted. As a result, the company has established a separate manufacturing facility to produce these bicycles. The company produces 1,000 bicycles per month. Giant's monthly manufacturing cost and other expenses data related to these bicycles are as follows.

1. Rent on manufacturing equipment (lease cost)	$2,000/month	8. Miscellaneous materials (lubricants, solders, etc.)	$1.20/bicycle
2. Insurance on manufacturing building	$750/month	9. Property taxes on manufacturing building	$2,400/year
3. Raw materials (frames, tires, etc.)	$80/bicycle	10. Manufacturing supervisor's salary	$3,000/month
4. Utility costs for manufacturing facility	$1,000/month	11. Advertising for bicycles	$30,000/year
5. Supplies for administrative office	$800/month	12. Sales commissions	$10/bicycle
6. Wages for assembly line workers in manufacturing facility	$30/bicycle	13. Depreciation on manufacturing building	$1,500/month
7. Depreciation on office equipment	$650/month		

Instructions

(a) Prepare an answer sheet with the following column headings.

	Product Costs			
Cost Item	**Direct Materials**	**Direct Labor**	**Manufacturing Overhead**	**Period Costs**

Enter each cost item on your answer sheet, placing an "X" mark under the appropriate headings.

(b) Compute total manufacturing costs for the month.

Solution to Demonstration Problem 1

(a)

	Product Costs			
Cost Item	**Direct Materials**	**Direct Labor**	**Manufacturing Overhead**	**Period Costs**
1. Rent on manufacturing equipment ($2,000/month)			X	
2. Insurance on manufacturing building ($750/month)			X	
3. Raw materials ($80/bicycle)	X			
4. Manufacturing utilities ($1,000/month)			X	
5. Office supplies ($800/month)				X
6. Wages for workers ($30/bicycle)		X		

Cost Item	Product Costs: Direct Materials	Direct Labor	Manufacturing Overhead	Period Costs
7. Depreciation on office equipment ($650/month)				X
8. Miscellaneous materials ($1.20/bicycle)			X	
9. Property taxes on manufacturing building ($2,400/year)			X	
10. Manufacturing supervisor's salary ($3,000/month)			X	
11. Advertising cost ($30,000/year)				X
12. Sales commissions ($10/bicycle)				X
13. Depreciation on manufacturing building ($1,500/month)			X	

(b)

Cost Item	Manufacturing Cost
Rent on manufacturing equipment	$ 2,000
Insurance on manufacturing building	750
Raw materials ($80 × 1,000)	80,000
Manufacturing utilities	1,000
Labor ($30 × 1,000)	30,000
Miscellaneous materials ($1.20 × 1,000)	1,200
Property taxes on manufacturing building ($2,400 ÷ 12)	200
Manufacturing supervisor's salary	3,000
Depreciation on manufacturing building	1,500
Total manufacturing costs	$119,650

The Navigator

Demonstration Problem 2

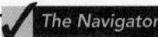

WILEY PLUS

Superior Manufacturing Company has the following cost and expense data for the year ending December 31, 2008.

Raw materials, 1/1/08	$ 30,000	Insurance, factory	$ 14,000
Raw materials, 12/31/08	20,000	Property taxes, factory building	6,000
Raw materials purchases	205,000	Sales (net)	1,500,000
Indirect materials	15,000	Delivery expenses	100,000
Work in process, 1/1/08	80,000	Sales commissions	150,000
Work in process, 12/31/08	50,000	Indirect labor	90,000
Finished goods, 1/1/08	110,000	Factory machinery rent	40,000
Finished goods, 12/31/08	120,000	Factory utilities	65,000
Direct labor	350,000	Depreciation, factory building	24,000
Factory manager's salary	35,000	Administrative expenses	300,000

Instructions

(a) Prepare a cost of goods manufactured schedule for Superior Company for 2008.
(b) Prepare an income statement for Superior Company for 2008.
(c) Assume that Superior Company's ledgers show the balances of the following current asset accounts: Cash $17,000, Accounts Receivable (net) $120,000, Prepaid Expenses $13,000, and Short-term Investments $26,000. Prepare the current assets section of the balance sheet for Superior Company as of December 31, 2008.

Solution to Demonstration Problem 2

(a)

SUPERIOR MANUFACTURING COMPANY
Cost of Goods Manufactured Schedule
For the Year Ended December 31, 2008

Work in process, 1/1			$ 80,000
Direct materials			
Raw materials inventory, 1/1	$ 30,000		
Raw materials purchases	205,000		
Total raw materials available for use	235,000		
Less: Raw materials inventory, 12/31	20,000		
Direct materials used		$215,000	
Direct labor		350,000	
Manufacturing overhead			
Indirect labor	90,000		
Factory utilities	65,000		
Factory machinery rent	40,000		
Factory manager's salary	35,000		
Depreciation on building	24,000		
Indirect materials	15,000		
Factory insurance	14,000		
Property taxes	6,000		
Total manufacturing overhead		289,000	
Total manufacturing costs			854,000
Total cost of work in process			934,000
Less: Work in process, 12/31			50,000
Cost of goods manufactured			$884,000

(b)

SUPERIOR MANUFACTURING COMPANY
Income Statement
For the Year Ended December 31, 2008

Sales (net)		$1,500,000
Cost of goods sold		
Finished goods inventory, January 1	$110,000	
Cost of goods manufactured	884,000	
Cost of goods available for sale	994,000	
Less: Finished goods inventory, December 31	120,000	
Cost of goods sold		874,000
Gross profit		626,000
Operating expenses		
Administrative expenses	300,000	
Sales commissions	150,000	
Delivery expenses	100,000	
Total operating expenses		550,000
Net income		$ 76,000

action plan

- ✓ Start with beginning work in process as the first item in the cost of goods manufactured schedule.
- ✓ Sum direct materials used, direct labor, and total manufacturing overhead to determine total manufacturing costs.
- ✓ Sum beginning work in process and total manufacturing costs to determine total cost of work in process.
- ✓ Cost of goods manufactured is the total cost of work in process less ending work in process.
- ✓ In the cost of goods sold section of the income statement, show beginning and ending finished goods inventory and cost of goods manufactured.
- ✓ In the balance sheet, list manufacturing inventories in the order of their expected realization in cash, with finished goods first.

(c)

SUPERIOR MANUFACTURING COMPANY
Balance Sheet (partial)
December 31, 2008

Current assets		
Cash		$ 17,000
Short-term investments		26,000
Accounts receivable (net)		120,000
Inventories		
Finished goods	$120,000	
Work in process	50,000	
Raw materials	20,000	190,000
Prepaid expenses		13,000
Total current assets		$366,000

The Navigator

SUMMARY OF STUDY OBJECTIVES

WILEY PLUS

1 **Explain the distinguishing features of managerial accounting.** The *primary users* of managerial accounting reports are internal users, who are officers, department heads, managers, and supervisors in the company. Managerial accounting issues internal reports as frequently as the need arises. The purpose of these reports is to provide special-purpose information for a particular user for a specific decision. The content of managerial accounting reports pertains to subunits of the business and may be very detailed and may extend beyond the double-entry accounting system. The reporting standard is relevance to the decision being made. No independent audits are required in managerial accounting.

2 **Identify the three broad functions of management.** The three functions are planning, directing, and controlling. Planning requires management to look ahead and to establish objectives. Directing involves coordinating the diverse activities and human resources of a company to produce a smooth-running operation. Controlling is the process of keeping the activities on track.

3 **Define the three classes of manufacturing costs.** Manufacturing costs are typically classified as either (1) direct materials, (2) direct labor, or (3) manufacturing overhead. Raw materials that can be physically and directly associated with the finished product during the manufacturing process are called direct materials. The work of factory employees that can be physically and directly associated with converting raw materials into finished goods is considered direct labor. Manufacturing overhead consists of costs that are indirectly associated with the manufacture of the finished product.

4 **Distinguish between product and period costs.** Product costs are costs that are a necessary and integral part of producing the finished product. Product costs are also called inventoriable costs. Under the matching principle, these costs do not become expenses until the company sells the finished goods inventory. Period costs are costs that are identified with a specific time period rather than with a salable product. These costs relate to nonmanufacturing costs and therefore are not inventoriable costs.

5 **Explain the difference between a merchandising and a manufacturing income statement.** The difference between a merchandising and a manufacturing income statement is in the cost of goods sold section. A manufacturing cost of goods sold section shows beginning and ending finished goods inventories and the cost of goods manufactured.

6 **Indicate how cost of goods manufactured is determined.** The cost of the beginning work in process is added to the total manufacturing costs for the current year to arrive at the total cost of work in process for the year. The ending work in process is then subtracted from the total cost of work in process to arrive at the cost of goods manufactured.

7 **Explain the difference between a merchandising and a manufacturing balance sheet.** The difference between a merchandising and a manufacturing balance sheet is in the current assets section. The current assets section of a manufacturing company's balance sheet presents three inventory accounts: finished goods inventory, work in process inventory, and raw materials inventory.

8 **Identify trends in managerial accounting.** Managerial accounting has experienced many changes in recent years. Among these are a shift toward addressing the needs of service companies and improving practices to better meet the needs of managers. Improved practices include a focus on managing the value chain through techniques such as just-in-time inventory and total quality management. In addition, techniques such as activity-based costing (ABC) have been developed to improve decision making. Finally, the balanced scorecard is now used by many companies in order to attain a more comprehensive view of the company's operations.

The Navigator

GLOSSARY

Activity-based costing (ABC) A method of allocating overhead based on each product's use of activities in making the product. (p. 846).

Balanced scorecard A performance-measurement approach that uses both financial and nonfinancial measures, tied to company objectives, to evaluate a company's operations in an integrated fashion. (p. 847).

Cost of goods manufactured Total cost of work in process less the cost of the ending work in process inventory. (p. 841).

Direct labor The work of factory employees that can be physically and directly associated with converting raw materials into finished goods. (p. 837).

Direct materials Raw materials that can be physically and directly associated with manufacturing the finished product. (p. 837).

Indirect labor Work of factory employees that has no physical association with the finished product, or for which it is impractical to trace the costs to the goods produced. (p. 837).

Indirect materials Raw materials that do not physically become part of the finished product or cannot be traced because their physical association with the finished product is too small. (p. 837).

Just-in-time (JIT) inventory Inventory system in which goods are manufactured or purchased just in time for use. (p. 845).

Managerial accounting A field of accounting that provides economic and financial information for managers and other internal users. (p. 832).

Manufacturing overhead Manufacturing costs that are indirectly associated with the manufacture of the finished product. (p. 837).

Period costs Costs that are matched with the revenue of a specific time period and charged to expense as incurred. (p. 838).

Product costs Costs that are a necessary and integral part of producing the finished product. (p. 838).

Total cost of work in process Cost of the beginning work in process plus total manufacturing costs for the current period. (p. 840).

Total manufacturing costs The sum of direct materials, direct labor, and manufacturing overhead incurred in the current period. (p. 840).

Total quality management (TQM) Systems implemented to reduce defects in finished products with the goal of achieving zero defects. (p. 846).

Value chain All activities associated with providing a product or service. (p. 845).

SELF-STUDY QUESTIONS

Answers are at the end of the chapter.

(SO 1) **1.** Managerial accounting:
- **a.** is governed by generally accepted accounting principles.
- **b.** places emphasis on special-purpose information.
- **c.** pertains to the entity as a whole and is highly aggregated.
- **d.** is limited to cost data.

(SO 2) **2.** The management of an organization performs several broad functions. They are:
- **a.** planning, directing, and selling.
- **b.** planning, directing, and controlling.
- **c.** planning, manufacturing, and controlling.
- **d.** directing, manufacturing, and controlling.

(SO 3) **3.** Direct materials are a:

	Product Cost	Manufacturing Overhead	Period Cost
a.	Yes	Yes	No
b.	Yes	No	No
c.	Yes	Yes	Yes
d.	No	No	No

(SO 4) **4.** Indirect labor is a:
- **a.** nonmanufacturing cost.
- **b.** raw material cost.
- **c.** product cost.
- **d.** period cost.

5. Which of the following costs would be included in manufacturing overhead of a computer manufacturer? (SO 3)
- **a.** The cost of the disk drives.
- **b.** The wages earned by computer assemblers.
- **c.** The cost of the memory chips.
- **d.** Depreciation on testing equipment.

6. Which of the following is *not* an element of manufacturing overhead? (SO 3)
- **a.** Sales manager's salary.
- **b.** Plant manager's salary.
- **c.** Factory repairman's wages.
- **d.** Product inspector's salary.

7. For the year, Redder Company has cost of goods manufactured of $600,000, beginning finished goods inventory of $200,000, and ending finished goods inventory of $250,000. The cost of goods sold is: (SO 5)
- **a.** $450,000.
- **b.** $500,000.
- **c.** $550,000.
- **d.** $600,000.

8. A cost of goods manufactured schedule shows beginning and ending inventories for: (SO 6)
- **a.** raw materials and work in process only.
- **b.** work in process only.
- **c.** raw materials only.
- **d.** raw materials, work in process, and finished goods.

(SO 7) **9.** In a manufacturer's balance sheet, three inventories may be reported: (1) raw materials, (2) work in process, and (3) finished goods. Indicate in what sequence these inventories generally appear on a balance sheet.
a. (1), (2), (3)
b. (2), (3), (1)
c. (3), (1), (2)
d. (3), (2), (1)

(SO 8) **10.** Which of the following managerial accounting techniques attempts to allocate manufacturing overhead in a more meaningful fashion?
a. Just-in-time inventory.
b. Total-quality management.
c. Balanced scorecard.
d. Activity-based costing.

Go to the book's website, **www.wiley.com/college/weygandt**, for Additional Self-Study questions.

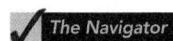

The Navigator

QUESTIONS

1. (a) "Managerial accounting is a field of accounting that provides economic information for all interested parties." Do you agree? Explain.
(b) Mary Barett believes that managerial accounting serves only manufacturing firms. Is Mary correct? Explain.

2. Distinguish between managerial and financial accounting as to (a) primary users of reports, (b) types and frequency of reports, and (c) purpose of reports.

3. How does the content of reports and the verification of reports differ between managerial and financial accounting?

4. In what ways can the budgeting process create incentives for unethical behavior?

5. Karen Fritz is studying for the next accounting mid-term examination. Summarize for Karen what she should know about management functions.

6. "Decision making is management's most important function." Do you agree? Why or why not?

7. What new rules were enacted under the Sarbanes-Oxley Act to address unethical accounting practices?

8. Stan Kaiser is studying for his next accounting examination. Explain to Stan what he should know about the differences between the income statements for a manufacturing and for a merchandising company.

9. Terry Lemay is unclear as to the difference between the balance sheets of a merchandising company and a manufacturing company. Explain the difference to Terry.

10. How are manufacturing costs classified?

11. Matt Litkee claims that the distinction between direct and indirect materials is based entirely on physical association with the product. Is Matt correct? Why?

12. Megan Neill is confused about the differences between a product cost and a period cost. Explain the differences to Megan.

13. Identify the differences in the cost of goods sold section of an income statement between a merchandising company and a manufacturing company.

14. The determination of the cost of goods manufactured involves the following factors: (A) beginning work in process inventory, (B) total manufacturing costs, and (C) ending work in process inventory. Identify the meaning of x in the following formulas:
(a) $A + B = x$
(b) $A + B - C = x$

15. Ohmie Manufacturing has beginning raw materials inventory $12,000, ending raw materials inventory $15,000, and raw materials purchases $170,000. What is the cost of direct materials used?

16. Neff Manufacturing Inc. has beginning work in process $26,000, direct materials used $240,000, direct labor $200,000, total manufacturing overhead $180,000, and ending work in process $32,000. What are total manufacturing costs?

17. Using the data in Q16, what are (a) the total cost of work in process and (b) the cost of goods manufactured?

18. In what order should manufacturing inventories be listed in a balance sheet?

19. What is the value chain? Describe, in sequence, the main components of a manufacturer's value chain.

20. Why is product quality important for companies that implement a just-in-time inventory system?

21. Explain what is meant by "balanced" in the balanced scorecard approach.

22. What is activity-based costing, and what are its potential benefits?

BRIEF EXERCISES

WILEY PLUS

Distinguish between managerial and financial accounting.
(SO 1)

BE19-1 Complete the following comparison table between managerial and financial accounting.

	Financial Accounting	Managerial Accounting
Primary users		
Types of reports		
Frequency of reports		
Purpose of reports		
Content of reports		
Verification		

BE19-2 The Sarbanes Oxley Act of 2002 (SOX) has important implications for the financial community. Explain two implications of SOX.

Identify important regulatory changes.
(SO 2)

BE19-3 Listed below are the three functions of the management of an organization.

Identify the three management functions.
(SO 2)

1. Planning 2. Directing 3. Controlling

Identify which of the following statements best describes each of the above functions.

(a) ____ require(s) management to look ahead and to establish objectives. A key objective of management is to add value to the business.
(b) ____ involve(s) coordinating the diverse activities and human resources of a company to produce a smooth-running operation. This function relates to the implementation of planned objectives.
(c) ____ is the process of keeping the activities on track. Management must determine whether goals are being met and what changes are necessary when there are deviations.

BE19-4 Determine whether each of the following costs should be classified as direct materials (DM), direct labor (DL), or manufacturing overhead (MO).

Classify manufacturing costs.
(SO 3)

(a) ____Frames and tires used in manufacturing bicycles.
(b) ____Wages paid to production workers.
(c) ____Insurance on factory equipment and machinery.
(d) ____Depreciation on factory equipment.

BE19-5 Indicate whether each of the following costs of an automobile manufacturer would be classified as direct materials, direct labor, or manufacturing overhead.

Classify manufacturing costs.
(SO 3)

(a) ____Windshield.
(b) ____Engine.
(c) ____Wages of assembly line worker.
(d) ____Depreciation of factory machinery.
(e) ____Factory machinery lubricants.
(f) ____Tires.
(g) ____Steering wheel.
(h) ____Salary of painting supervisor.

BE19-6 Identify whether each of the following costs should be classified as product costs or period costs.

Identify product and period costs.
(SO 4)

(a) ____Manufacturing overhead.
(b) ____Selling expenses.
(c) ____Administrative expenses.
(d) ____Advertising expenses.
(e) ____Direct labor.
(f) ____Direct material.

BE19-7 Presented below are Lang Company's monthly manufacturing cost data related to its personal computer products.

Classify manufacturing costs.
(SO 3)

(a) Utilities for manufacturing equipment	$116,000
(b) Raw material (CPU, chips, etc.)	$ 85,000
(c) Depreciation on manufacturing building	$880,000
(d) Wages for production workers	$191,000

Enter each cost item in the following table, placing an "X" under the appropriate headings.

	Product Costs		
	Direct Materials	**Direct Labor**	**Factory Overhead**
(a)			
(b)			
(c)			
(d)			

BE19-8 Francum Manufacturing Company has the following data: direct labor $229,000, direct materials used $180,000, total manufacturing overhead $208,000, and beginning work in process $25,000. Compute (a) total manufacturing costs and (b) total cost of work in process.

Compute total manufacturing costs and total cost of work in process.
(SO 6)

BE19-9 In alphabetical order below are current asset items for Dieker Company's balance sheet at December 31, 2008. Prepare the current assets section (including a complete heading).

Prepare current assets section.
(SO 7)

Accounts receivable	$200,000
Cash	62,000
Finished goods	71,000
Prepaid expenses	38,000
Raw materials	73,000
Work in process	87,000

Determine missing amounts in computing total manufacturing costs.

(SO 6)

BE19-10 Presented below are incomplete manufacturing cost data. Determine the missing amounts for three different situations.

	Direct Materials Used	Direct Labor Used	Factory Overhead	Total Manufacturing Costs
(1)	$25,000	$61,000	$ 50,000	?
(2)	?	$75,000	$140,000	$296,000
(3)	$55,000	?	$111,000	$310,000

Determine missing amounts in computing cost of goods manufactured.

(SO 6)

BE19-11 Use the same data from BE19–10 above and the data below. Determine the missing amounts.

	Total Manufacturing Costs	Work in Process (1/1)	Work in Process (12/31)	Cost of Goods Manufactured
(1)	?	$120,000	$82,000	?
(2)	$296,000	?	$98,000	$321,000
(3)	$310,000	$463,000	?	$715,000

EXERCISES

WILEY PLUS

Identify distinguishing features of managerial accounting.

(SO 1)

E19-1 Chris Martin has prepared the following list of statements about managerial accounting and financial accounting.

1. Financial accounting focuses on providing information to internal users.
2. Analyzing cost-volume-profit relationships is part of managerial accounting.
3. Preparation of budgets is part of financial accounting.
4. Managerial accounting applies only to merchandising and manufacturing companies.
5. Both managerial accounting and financial accounting deal with many of the same economic events.
6. Managerial accounting reports are prepared only quarterly and annually.
7. Financial accounting reports are general-purpose reports.
8. Managerial accounting reports pertain to subunits of the business.
9. Managerial accounting reports must comply with generally accepted accounting principles.
10. Although managerial accountants are expected to behave ethically, there is no code of ethical standards for managerial accountants.

Instructions

Identify each statement as true or false. If false, indicate how to correct the statement.

Classify costs into three classes of manufacturing costs.

(SO 3)

E19-2 Presented below is a list of costs and expenses usually incurred by Burrand Corporation, a manufacturer of furniture, in its factory.

1. Salaries for assembly line inspectors.
2. Insurance on factory machines.
3. Property taxes on the factory building.
4. Factory repairs.
5. Upholstery used in manufacturing furniture.
6. Wages paid to assembly line workers.
7. Factory machinery depreciation.
8. Glue, nails, paint, and other small parts used in production.
9. Factory supervisors' salaries.
10. Wood used in manufacturing furniture.

Instructions

Classify the above items into the following categories: (a) direct materials, (b) direct labor, and (c) manufacturing overhead.

E19-3 Coldplay Corporation incurred the following costs while manufacturing its product.

Identify types of cost and explain their accounting.

(SO 3, 4)

Materials used in product	$100,000	Advertising expense	$45,000
Depreciation on plant	60,000	Property taxes on plant	14,000
Property taxes on store	7,500	Delivery expense	21,000
Labor costs of assembly-line workers	110,000	Sales commissions	35,000
Factory supplies used	13,000	Salaries paid to sales clerks	50,000

Instructions

(a) Identify each of the above costs as direct materials, direct labor, manufacturing overhead, or period costs.

(b) Explain the basic difference in accounting for product costs and period costs.

E19-4 Caroline Company reports the following costs and expenses in May.

Determine the total amount of various types of costs.

(SO 3, 4)

Factory utilities	$ 11,500	Direct labor	$69,100
Depreciation on factory equipment	12,650	Sales salaries	46,400
Depreciation on delivery trucks	3,800	Property taxes on factory building	2,500
Indirect factory labor	48,900	Repairs to office equipment	1,300
Indirect materials	80,800	Factory repairs	2,000
Direct materials used	137,600	Advertising	18,000
Factory manager's salary	8,000	Office supplies used	2,640

Instructions

From the information, determine the total amount of:

(a) Manufacturing overhead.

(b) Product costs.

(c) Period costs.

E19-5 Sota Company is a manufacturer of personal computers. Various costs and expenses associated with its operations are as follows.

Classify various costs into different cost categories.

(SO 3, 4)

1. Property taxes on the factory building.
2. Production superintendents' salaries.
3. Memory boards and chips used in assembling computers.
4. Depreciation on the factory equipment.
5. Salaries for assembly line quality control inspectors.
6. Sales commissions paid to sell personal computers.
7. Electrical components used in assembling computers.
8. Wages of workers assembling personal computers.
9. Soldering materials used on factory assembly lines.
10. Salaries for the night security guards for the factory building.

The company intends to classify these costs and expenses into the following categories: (a) direct materials, (b) direct labor, (c) manufacturing overhead, and (d) period costs.

Instructions

List the items (1) through (10). For each item, indicate the cost category to which it belongs.

E19-6 The administrators of San Diego County's Memorial Hospital are interested in identifying the various costs and expenses that are incurred in producing a patient's X-ray. A list of such costs and expenses in presented below.

Classify various costs into different cost categories.

(SO 3)

1. Salaries for the X-ray machine technicians.
2. Wages for the hospital janitorial personnel.
3. Film costs for the X-ray machines.
4. Property taxes on the hospital building.
5. Salary of the X-ray technicians' supervisor.
6. Electricity costs for the X-ray department.
7. Maintenance and repairs on the X-ray machines.
8. X-ray department supplies.
9. Depreciation on the X-ray department equipment.
10. Depreciation on the hospital building.

The administrators want these costs and expenses classified as: (a) direct materials, (b) direct labor, or (c) service overhead.

Instructions

List the items (1) through (10). For each item, indicate the cost category to which the item belongs.

Classify various costs into different cost categories.

(SO 4)

E19-7 Rapid Delivery Service reports the following costs and expenses in June 2008.

Indirect materials	$ 5,400	Drivers' salaries	$11,000
Depreciation on delivery equipment	11,200	Advertising	1,600
Dispatcher's salary	5,000	Delivery equipment repairs	300
Property taxes on office building	870	Office supplies	650
CEO's salary	12,000	Office utilities	990
Gas and oil for delivery trucks	2,200	Repairs on office equipment	180

Instructions

Determine the total amount of (a) delivery service (product) costs and (b) period costs.

Compute cost of goods manufactured and sold.

(SO 5, 6)

E19-8 Coldplay Corporation incurred the following costs while manufacturing its product.

Materials used in product	$100,000	Advertising expense	$45,000
Depreciation on plant	60,000	Property taxes on plant	14,000
Property taxes on store	7,500	Delivery expense	21,000
Labor costs of assembly-line workers	110,000	Sales commissions	35,000
Factory supplies used	23,000	Salaries paid to sales clerks	50,000

Work-in-process inventory was $12,000 at January 1 and $15,500 at December 31. Finished goods inventory was $60,000 at January 1 and $55,600 at December 31.

Instructions

(a) Compute cost of goods manufactured.
(b) Compute cost of goods sold.

Determine missing amounts in cost of goods manufactured schedule.

(SO 6)

E19-9 An incomplete cost of goods manufactured schedule is presented below.

CEPEDA MANUFACTURING COMPANY
Cost of Goods Manufactured Schedule
For the Year Ended December 31, 2008

Work in process (1/1)			$210,000
Direct materials			
Raw materials inventory (1/1)	$?		
Add: Raw materials purchases	158,000		
Total raw materials available for use	?		
Less: Raw materials inventory (12/31)	12,500		
Direct materials used		$190,000	
Direct labor		?	
Manufacturing overhead			
Indirect labor	$ 18,000		
Factory depreciation	36,000		
Factory utilities	68,000		
Total overhead		122,000	
Total manufacturing costs			?
Total cost of work in process			?
Less: Work in process (12/31)			81,000
Cost of goods manufactured			$510,000

Instructions

Complete the cost of goods manufactured schedule for Cepeda Manufacturing Company.

E19-10 Manufacturing cost data for Criqui Company are presented below.

Determine the missing amount of different cost items.
(SO 6)

	Case A	Case B	Case C
Direct materials used	(a)	$58,400	$130,000
Direct labor	$ 57,000	86,000	(g)
Manufacturing overhead	46,500	81,600	102,000
Total manufacturing costs	185,650	(d)	253,700
Work in process 1/1/08	(b)	16,500	(h)
Total cost of work in process	221,500	(e)	337,000
Work in process 12/31/08	(c)	11,000	70,000
Cost of goods manufactured	185,275	(f)	(i)

Instructions
Indicate the missing amount for each letter (a) through (i).

E19-11 Incomplete manufacturing cost data for Ikerd Company for 2008 are presented as follows for four different situations.

Determine the missing amount of different cost items, and prepare a condensed cost of goods manufactured schedule.
(SO 6)

	Direct Materials Used	Direct Labor Used	Manufacturing Overhead	Total Manufacturing Costs	Work in Process 1/1	Work in Process 12/31	Cost of Goods Manufactured
(1)	$127,000	$140,000	$ 77,000	(a)	$33,000	(b)	$360,000
(2)	(c)	200,000	132,000	$450,000	(d)	$40,000	470,000
(3)	80,000	100,000	(e)	245,000	60,000	80,000	(f)
(4)	70,000	(g)	75,000	288,000	45,000	(h)	270,000

Instructions
(a) Indicate the missing amount for each letter.
(b) Prepare a condensed cost of goods manufactured schedule for situation (1) for the year ended December 31, 2008.

E19-12 Aikman Corporation has the following cost records for June 2008.

Prepare a cost of goods manufactured schedule and a partial income statement.
(SO 5, 6)

Indirect factory labor	$ 4,500	Factory utilities	$ 400
Direct materials used	20,000	Depreciation, factory equipment	1,400
Work in process, 6/1/08	3,000	Direct labor	30,000
Work in process, 6/30/08	3,800	Maintenance, factory equipment	1,800
Finished goods, 6/1/08	5,000	Indirect materials	2,200
Finished goods, 6/30/08	7,500	Factory manager's salary	3,000

Instructions
(a) Prepare a cost of goods manufactured schedule for June 2008.
(b) Prepare an income statement through gross profit for June 2008 assuming net sales are $87,100.

E19-13 Sara Collier, the bookkeeper for Danner, Cheney, and Howe, a political consulting firm, has recently completed a managerial accounting course at her local college. One of the topics covered in the course was the cost of goods manufactured schedule. Sara wondered if such a schedule could be prepared for her firm. She realized that, as a service-oriented company, it would have no Work-in-Process inventory to consider.

Classify various costs into different categories and prepare cost of services provided schedule.
(SO 4, 5, 6)

Listed below are the costs her firm incurred for the month ended August 31, 2008.

Supplies used on consulting contracts	$ 1,200
Supplies used in the administrative offices	1,500
Depreciation on equipment used for contract work	900
Depreciation used on administrative office equipment	1,050
Salaries of professionals working on contracts	12,600
Salaries of administrative office personnel	7,700
Janitorial services for professional offices	400
Janitorial services for administrative offices	500
Insurance on contract operations	800
Insurance on administrative operations	900
Utilities for contract operations	1,400
Utilities for administrative offices	1,300

Instructions

(a) Prepare a schedule of cost of contract services provided (similar to a cost of goods manufactured schedule) for the month.

(b) For those costs not included in (a), explain how they would be classified and reported in the financial statements.

Prepare a cost of goods manufactured schedule and a partial income statement.

(SO 5, 6, 7)

E19-14 The following information is available for Sassafras Company.

	January 1, 2008	2008	December 31, 2008
Raw materials inventory	$ 21,000		$30,000
Work in process inventory	13,500		17,200
Finished goods inventory	27,000		21,000
Materials purchased		$150,000	
Direct labor		200,000	
Manufacturing overhead		180,000	
Sales		900,000	

Instructions

(a) Compute cost of goods manufactured.

(b) Prepare an income statement through gross profit.

(c) Show the presentation of the ending inventories on the December 31, 2008 balance sheet.

(d) How would the income statement and balance sheet of a merchandising company be different from Sassafras's financial statements?

Indicate in which schedule or financial statement(s) different cost items will appear.

(SO 5, 6, 7)

E19-15 Corbin Manufacturing Company produces blankets. From its accounting records it prepares the following schedule and financial statements on a yearly basis.

(a) Cost of goods manufactured schedule.

(b) Income statement.

(c) Balance sheet.

The following items are found in its ledger and accompanying data.

1. Direct labor
2. Raw materials inventory, 1/1
3. Work in process inventory, 12/31
4. Finished goods inventory, 1/1
5. Indirect labor
6. Depreciation on factory machinery
7. Work in process, 1/1
8. Finished goods inventory, 12/31
9. Factory maintenance salaries
10. Cost of goods manufactured
11. Depreciation on delivery equipment
12. Cost of goods available for sale
13. Direct materials used
14. Heat and electricity for factory
15. Repairs to roof of factory building
16. Cost of raw materials purchases

Instructions

List the items (1)–(16). For each item, indicate by using the appropriate letter or letters, the schedule and/or financial statement(s) in which the item will appear.

Prepare a cost of goods manufactured schedule, and present the ending inventories of the balance sheet.

(SO 6, 7)

E19-16 An analysis of the accounts of Chamberlin Manufacturing reveals the following manufacturing cost data for the month ended June 30, 2008.

Inventories	Beginning	Ending
Raw materials	$9,000	$13,100
Work in process	5,000	7,000
Finished goods	9,000	6,000

Costs incurred: Raw materials purchases $54,000, direct labor $57,000, manufacturing overhead $19,900. The specific overhead costs were: indirect labor $5,500, factory insurance $4,000, machinery depreciation $4,000, machinery repairs $1,800, factory utilities $3,100, miscellaneous factory costs $1,500. Assume that all raw materials used were direct materials.

Instructions

(a) Prepare the cost of goods manufactured schedule for the month ended June 30, 2008.

(b) Show the presentation of the ending inventories on the June 30, 2008, balance sheet.

Determine the amount of cost to appear in various accounts, and indicate in which financial statements these accounts would appear.

(SO 5, 6, 7)

E19-17 Todd Motor Company manufactures automobiles. During September 2008 the company purchased 5,000 head lamps at a cost of $9 per lamp. Todd withdrew 4,650 lamps from the warehouse during the month. Fifty of these lamps were used to replace the head lamps in autos used by traveling sales staff. The remaining 4,600 lamps were put in autos manufactured during the month.

Of the autos put into production during September 2008, 90% were completed and transferred to the company's storage lot. Of the cars completed during the month, 75% were sold by September 30.

Instructions

(a) Determine the cost of head lamps that would appear in each of the following accounts at September 30, 2008: Raw Materials, Work in Process, Finished Goods, Cost of Goods Sold, and Selling Expenses.

(b) Write a short memo to the chief accountant, indicating whether and where each of the accounts in (a) would appear on the income statement or on the balance sheet at September 30, 2008.

E19-18 The following is a list of terms related to managerial accounting practices.

Identify various managerial accounting practices.
(SO 8)

1. Activity-based costing.
2. Just-in-time inventory.
3. Balanced scorecard.
4. Value chain.

Instructions

Match each of the terms with the statement below that best describes the term.

(a) ____ A performance-measurement technique that attempts to consider and evaluate all aspects of performance using financial and nonfinancial measures in an integrated fashion.

(b) ____ The group of activities associated with providing a product or service.

(c) ____ An approach used to reduce the cost associated with handling and holding inventory by reducing the amount of inventory on hand.

(d) ____ A method used to allocate overhead to products based on each product's use of the activities that cause the incurrence of the overhead cost.

EXERCISES: SET B

Visit the book's website at **www.wiley.com/college/weygandt**, and choose the Student Companion site, to access Exercise Set B.

PROBLEMS: SET A

P19-1A Bjerg Company specializes in manufacturing a unique model of bicycle helmet. The model is well accepted by consumers, and the company has enough orders to keep the factory production at 10,000 helmets per month (80% of its full capacity). Bjerg's monthly manufacturing cost and other expense data are as follows.

Classify manufacturing costs into different categories and compute the unit cost.
(SO 3, 4)

Rent on factory equipment	$ 7,000
Insurance on factory building	1,500
Raw materials (plastics, polystyrene, etc.)	75,000
Utility costs for factory	900
Supplies for general office	300
Wages for assembly line workers	43,000
Depreciation on office equipment	800
Miscellaneous materials (glue, thread, etc.)	1,100
Factory manager's salary	5,700
Property taxes on factory building	400
Advertising for helmets	14,000
Sales commissions	7,000
Depreciation on factory building	1,500

Instructions

(a) Prepare an answer sheet with the following column headings.

(a) DM $75,000
DL $43,000
MO $18,100
PC $22,100

	Product Costs			
Cost Item	Direct Materials	Direct Labor	Manufacturing Overhead	Period Costs

Enter each cost item on your answer sheet, placing the dollar amount under the appropriate headings. Total the dollar amounts in each of the columns.

(b) Compute the cost to produce one helmet

Classify manufacturing costs into different categories and compute the unit cost.

(SO 3, 4)

P19-2A Copa Company, a manufacturer of stereo systems, started its production in October 2008. For the preceding 3 years Copa had been a retailer of stereo systems. After a thorough survey of stereo system markets, Copa decided to turn its retail store into a stereo equipment factory.

Raw materials cost for a stereo system will total $74 per unit. Workers on the production lines are on average paid $12 per hour. A stereo system usually takes 5 hours to complete. In addition, the rent on the equipment used to assemble stereo systems amounts to $4,900 per month. Indirect materials cost $5 per system. A supervisor was hired to oversee production; her monthly salary is $3,000.

Janitorial costs are $1,300 monthly. Advertising costs for the stereo system will be $8,500 per month. The factory building depreciation expense is $7,200 per year. Property taxes on the factory building will be $9,000 per year.

Instructions

(a) Prepare an answer sheet with the following column headings.

(a) DM $96,200
DL $78,000
MO $17,050
PC $ 8,500

	Product Costs			
Cost Item	Direct Materials	Direct Labor	Manufacturing Overhead	Period Costs

Assuming that Copa manufactures, on average, 1,300 stereo systems per month, enter each cost item on your answer sheet, placing the dollar amount per month under the appropriate headings. Total the dollar amounts in each of the columns.

(b) Compute the cost to produce one stereo system.

Indicate the missing amount of different cost items, and prepare a condensed cost of goods manufactured schedule, an income statement, and a partial balance sheet.

(SO 5, 6, 7)

P19-3A Incomplete manufacturing costs, expenses, and selling data for two different cases are as follows.

	Case 1	Case 2
Direct Materials Used	$ 7,600	$ (g)
Direct Labor	5,000	8,000
Manufacturing Overhead	8,000	4,000
Total Manufacturing Costs	(a)	18,000
Beginning Work in Process Inventory	1,000	(h)
Ending Work in Process Inventory	(b)	3,000
Sales	24,500	(i)
Sales Discounts	2,500	1,400
Cost of Goods Manufactured	17,000	22,000
Beginning Finished Goods Inventory	(c)	3,300
Goods Available for Sale	18,000	(j)
Cost of Goods Sold	(d)	(k)
Ending Finished Goods Inventory	3,400	2,500
Gross Profit	(e)	7,000
Operating Expenses	2,500	(l)
Net Income	(f)	5,000

Instructions

(a) Indicate the missing amount for each letter.

(b) Ending WIP $4,600

(b) Prepare a condensed cost of goods manufactured schedule for Case 1.

(c) Prepare an income statement and the current assets section of the balance sheet for Case 1. Assume that in Case 1 the other items in the current assets section are as follows: Cash $4,000, Receivables (net) $15,000, Raw Materials $600, and Prepaid Expenses $400.

(c) Current assets $28,000

Prepare a cost of goods manufactured schedule, a partial income statement, and a partial balance sheet.

(SO 5, 6, 7)

P19-4A The following data were taken from the records of Stellar Manufacturing Company for the fiscal year ended June 30, 2008.

Raw Materials Inventory 7/1/07	$ 48,000	Factory Insurance	$ 4,600
Raw Materials Inventory 6/30/08	39,600	Factory Machinery Depreciation	16,000
Finished Goods Inventory 7/1/07	96,000	Factory Utilities	27,600
Finished Goods Inventory 6/30/08	95,900	Office Utilities Expense	8,650
Work in Process Inventory 7/1/07	19,800	Sales	554,000
Work in Process Inventory 6/30/08	18,600	Sales Discounts	4,200
Direct Labor	149,250	Plant Manager's Salary	29,000
Indirect Labor	24,460	Factory Property Taxes	9,600
Accounts Receivable	27,000	Factory Repairs	1,400
		Raw Materials Purchases	96,400
		Cash	32,000

Instructions

(a) Prepare a cost of goods manufactured schedule. (Assume all raw materials used were direct materials.)

(b) Prepare an income statement through gross profit.

(c) Prepare the current assets section of the balance sheet at June 30, 2008.

(a) CGM $367,910

(b) Gross profit $181,790

(c) Current assets $213,100

Prepare a cost of goods manufactured schedule and a correct income statement.

(SO 5, 6)

P19-5A Tombert Company is a manufacturer of computers. Its controller resigned in October 2008. An inexperienced assistant accountant has prepared the following income statement for the month of October 2008.

TOMBERT COMPANY
Income Statement
For the Month Ended October 31, 2008

Sales (net)		$780,000
Less: Operating expenses		
Raw materials purchases	$264,000	
Direct labor cost	190,000	
Advertising expense	90,000	
Selling and administrative salaries	75,000	
Rent on factory facilities	60,000	
Depreciation on sales equipment	45,000	
Depreciation on factory equipment	31,000	
Indirect labor cost	28,000	
Utilities expense	12,000	
Insurance expense	8,000	803,000
Net loss		$(23,000)

Prior to October 2008 the company had been profitable every month. The company's president is concerned about the accuracy of the income statement. As his friend, you have been asked to review the income statement and make necessary corrections. After examining other manufacturing cost data, you have acquired additional information as follows.

1. Inventory balances at the beginning and end of October were:

	October 1	October 31
Raw materials	$18,000	$34,000
Work in process	16,000	14,000
Finished goods	30,000	48,000

2. Only 70% of the utilities expense and 60% of the insurance expense apply to factory operations. The remaining amounts should be charged to selling and administrative activities.

Instructions

(a) CGM $572,200
(b) NI $ 9,000

(a) Prepare a schedule of cost of goods manufactured for October 2008.
(b) Prepare a correct income statement for October 2008.

PROBLEMS: SET B

Classify manufacturing costs into different categories and compute the unit cost.
(SO 3, 4)

P19-1B Hite Company specializes in manufacturing motorcycle helmets. The company has enough orders to keep the factory production at 1,000 motorcycle helmets per month. Hite's monthly manufacturing cost and other expense data are as follows.

Maintenance costs on factory building	$ 600
Factory manager's salary	4,000
Advertising for helmets	8,000
Sales commissions	3,000
Depreciation on factory building	700
Rent on factory equipment	6,000
Insurance on factory building	3,000
Raw materials (plastic, polystyrene, etc.)	20,000
Utility costs for factory	800
Supplies for general office	200
Wages for assembly line workers	44,000
Depreciation on office equipment	500
Miscellaneous materials (glue, thread, etc.)	2,000

Instructions

(a) DM $20,000
DL $44,000
MO $17,100
PC $11,700

(a) Prepare an answer sheet with the following column headings.

	Product Costs			
Cost Item	Direct Materials	Direct Labor	Manufacturing Overhead	Period Costs

Enter each cost item on your answer sheet, placing the dollar amount under the appropriate headings. Total the dollar amounts in each of the columns.

(b) Compute the cost to produce one motorcycle helmet.

Classify manufacturing costs into different categories and compute the unit cost.
(SO 3, 4)

P19-2B Ladoca Company, a manufacturer of tennis rackets, started production in November 2008. For the preceding 5 years Ladoca had been a retailer of sports equipment. After a thorough survey of tennis racket markets, Ladoca decided to turn its retail store into a tennis racket factory.

Raw materials cost for a tennis racket will total $23 per racket. Workers on the production lines are paid on average $13 per hour. A racket usually takes 2 hours to complete. In addition, the rent on the equipment used to produce rackets amounts to $1,300 per month. Indirect materials cost $3 per racket. A supervisor was hired to oversee production; her monthly salary is $3,500.

Janitorial costs are $1,400 monthly. Advertising costs for the rackets will be $6,000 per month. The factory building depreciation expense is $8,400 per year. Property taxes on the factory building will be $5,400 per year.

Instructions

(a) DM $46,000
DL $52,000
MO $13,350
PC $ 6,000

(a) Prepare an answer sheet with the following column headings.

	Product Costs			
Cost Item	Direct Materials	Direct Labor	Manufacturing Overhead	Period Costs

Assuming that Ladoca manufactures, on average, 2,000 tennis rackets per month, enter each cost item on your answer sheet, placing the dollar amount per month under the appropriate headings. Total the dollar amounts in each of the columns.

(b) Compute the cost to produce one racket.

P19-3B Incomplete manufacturing costs, expenses, and selling data for two different cases are as follows.

Indicate the missing amount of different cost items, and prepare a condensed cost of goods manufactured schedule, an income statement, and a partial balance sheet.

(SO 5, 6, 7)

	Case 1	Case 2
Direct Materials Used	$ 8,300	$ (g)
Direct Labor	3,000	4,000
Manufacturing Overhead	6,000	5,000
Total Manufacturing Costs	(a)	18,000
Beginning Work in Process Inventory	1,000	(h)
Ending Work in Process Inventory	(b)	2,000
Sales	22,500	(i)
Sales Discounts	1,500	1,200
Cost of Goods Manufactured	15,800	20,000
Beginning Finished Goods Inventory	(c)	4,000
Goods Available for Sale	17,300	(j)
Cost of Goods Sold	(d)	(k)
Ending Finished Goods Inventory	1,200	2,500
Gross Profit	(e)	6,000
Operating Expenses	2,700	(l)
Net Income	(f)	3,200

Instructions

(a) Indicate the missing amount for each letter.

(b) Prepare a condensed cost of goods manufactured schedule for Case 1.

(c) Prepare an income statement and the current assets section of the balance sheet for Case 1. Assume that in Case 1 the other items in the current assets section are as follows: Cash $3,000, Receivables (net) $10,000, Raw Materials $700, and Prepaid Expenses $200.

(c) Current assets $17,600

P19-4B The following data were taken from the records of Ruiz Manufacturing Company for the year ended December 31, 2008.

Prepare a cost of goods manufactured schedule, a partial income statement, and a partial balance sheet.

(SO 5, 6, 7)

Raw Materials Inventory 1/1/08	$ 47,000	Factory Insurance	$ 7,400
Raw Materials Inventory 12/31/08	44,200	Factory Machinery Depreciation	7,700
Finished Goods Inventory 1/1/08	85,000	Factory Utilities	12,900
Finished Goods Inventory 12/31/08	77,800	Office Utilities Expense	8,600
Work in Process Inventory 1/1/08	9,500	Sales	475,000
Work in Process Inventory 12/31/08	8,000	Sales Discounts	2,500
Direct Labor	145,100	Plant Manager's Salary	30,000
Indirect Labor	18,100	Factory Property Taxes	6,100
Accounts Receivable	27,000	Factory Repairs	800
		Raw Materials Purchases	67,500
		Cash	28,000

Instructions

(a) Prepare a cost of goods manufactured schedule. (Assume all raw materials used were direct materials.)

(b) Prepare an income statement through gross profit.

(c) Prepare the current assets section of the balance sheet at December 31.

(a) CGM $299,900

(b) Gross profit $165,400

(c) Current assets $185,000

P19-5B Agler Company is a manufacturer of toys. Its controller, Joyce Rotzen, resigned in August 2008. An inexperienced assistant accountant has prepared the following income statement for the month of August 2008.

Prepare a cost of goods manufactured schedule and a correct income statement.

(SO 5, 6)

AGLER COMPANY
Income Statement
For the Month Ended August 31, 2008

Sales (net)		$675,000
Less: Operating expenses		
Raw materials purchases	$200,000	
Direct labor cost	160,000	
Advertising expense	75,000	
Selling and administrative salaries	70,000	
Rent on factory facilities	60,000	
Depreciation on sales equipment	50,000	
Depreciation on factory equipment	35,000	
Indirect labor cost	20,000	
Utilities expense	10,000	
Insurance expense	5,000	685,000
Net loss		$(10,000)

Prior to August 2008 the company had been profitable every month. The company's president is concerned about the accuracy of the income statement. As her friend, you have been asked to review the income statement and make necessary corrections. After examining other manufacturing cost data, you have acquired additional information as follows.

1. Inventory balances at the beginning and end of August were:

	August 1	August 31
Raw materials	$19,500	$30,000
Work in process	25,000	21,000
Finished goods	40,000	64,000

2. Only 60% of the utilities expense and 70% of the insurance expense apply to factory operations; the remaining amounts should be charged to selling and administrative activities.

Instructions

(a) CGM $478,000
(b) NI $ 20,500

(a) Prepare a cost of goods manufactured schedule for August 2008.
(b) Prepare a correct income statement for August 2008.

PROBLEMS: SET C

Visit the book's website at **www.wiley.com/college/weygandt**, and choose the Student Companion site, to access Problem Set C.

BROADENING YOUR PERSPECTIVE

DECISION MAKING ACROSS THE ORGANIZATION

BYP19-1 Mismatch Manufacturing Company specializes in producing fashion outfits. On July 31, 2008, a tornado touched down at its factory and general office. The inventories in the warehouse and the factory were completely destroyed as was the general office nearby. Next morning, through a careful search of the disaster site, however, Ross Clarkson, the company's controller, and Catherine Harper, the cost accountant, were able to recover a small part of manufacturing cost data for the current month.

"What a horrible experience," sighed Ross. "And the worst part is that we may not have enough records to use in filing an insurance claim."

"It was terrible," replied Catherine. "However, I managed to recover some of the manufacturing cost data that I was working on yesterday afternoon. The data indicate that our direct labor cost in July totaled $240,000 and that we had purchased $345,000 of raw materials. Also, I recall that the amount of raw materials used for July was $350,000. But I'm not sure this information will help. The rest of our records are blown away."

"Well, not exactly," said Ross. "I was working on the year-to-date income statement when the tornado warning was announced. My recollection is that our sales in July were $1,260,000 and our gross profit ratio has been 40% of sales. Also, I can remember that our cost of goods available for sale was $770,000 for July."

"Maybe we can work something out from this information!" exclaimed Catherine. "My experience tells me that our manufacturing overhead is usually 60% of direct labor."

"Hey, look what I just found," cried Catherine. "It's a copy of this June's balance sheet, and it shows that our inventories as of June 30 are Finished goods $38,000, Work in process $25,000, and Raw materials $19,000."

"Super," yelled Ross. "Let's go work something out."

In order to file an insurance claim, Mismatch Company must determine the amount of its inventories as of July 31, 2008, the date of the tornado touchdown.

Instructions

With the class divided into groups, determine the amount of cost in the Raw Materials, Work in Process, and Finished Goods inventory accounts as of the date of the tornado touchdown.

MANAGERIAL ANALYSIS

BYP19-2 Love All is a fairly large manufacturing company located in the southern United States. The company manufactures tennis rackets, tennis balls, tennis clothing, and tennis shoes, all bearing the company's distinctive logo, a large green question mark on a white flocked tennis ball. The company's sales have been increasing over the past 10 years.

The tennis racket division has recently implemented several advanced manufacturing techniques. Robot arms hold the tennis rackets in place while glue dries, and machine vision systems check for defects. The engineering and design team uses computerized drafting and testing of new products. The following managers work in the tennis racket division.

Andre Agassi, Sales Manager (supervises all sales representatives).
Serena Williams, technical specialist (supervises computer programmers).
Pete Sampras, cost accounting manager (supervises cost accountants).
Andy Roddick, production supervisor (supervises all manufacturing employees).
Venus Williams, engineer (supervises all new-product design teams).

Instructions

(a) What are the primary information needs of each manager?
(b) Which, if any, financial accounting report(s) is each likely to use?
(c) Name one special-purpose management accounting report that could be designed for each manager. Include the name of the report, the information it would contain, and how frequently it should be issued.

REAL-WORLD FOCUS

BYP19-3 Anchor Glass Container Corporation, the third largest manufacturer of glass containers in the U.S., supplies beverage and food producers and consumer products manufacturers nationwide. Parent company Consumers Packaging Inc. (*Toronto Stock Exchange:* CGC) is a leading international designer and manufacturer of glass containers.

The following management discussion appeared in a recent annual report of Anchor Glass.

ANCHOR GLASS CONTAINER CORPORATION
Management Discussion

Cost of Products Sold Cost of products sold as a percentage of net sales was 89.3% in the current year compared to 87.6% in the prior year. The increase in cost of products sold as a percentage of net sales principally reflected the impact of operational problems during the second quarter of the current year at a major furnace at one of the Company's plants, higher downtime, and costs and expenses associated with an increased number of scheduled capital improvement projects, increases in labor, and certain other manufacturing costs (with no corresponding selling price increases in the current year). Reduced fixed costs from the closing of the Streator, Illinois, plant in June of the current year and productivity and efficiency gains partially offset these cost increases.

Instructions
What factors affect the costs of products sold at Anchor Glass Container Corporation?

EXPLORING THE WEB

BYP19-4 The Institute of Management Accountants (IMA) is an organization dedicated to excellence in the practice of management accounting and financial management.

Address: www.imanet.org, or go to **www.wiley.com/college/weygandt**

Instructions
At the IMA's home page, locate the answers to the following questions.

(a) How many members does the IMA have, and what are their job titles?
(b) What are some of the benefits of joining the IMA as a student?
(c) Use the chapter locator function to locate the IMA chapter nearest you, and find the name of the chapter president.

COMMUNICATION ACTIVITY

BYP19-5 Refer to Problem 19–5A and add the following requirement.

Prepare a letter to the president of the company, Sue Tombert, describing the changes you made. Explain clearly why net income is different after the changes. Keep the following points in mind as you compose your letter.

1. This is a letter to the president of a company, who is your friend. The style should be generally formal, but you may relax some requirements. For example, you may call the president by her first name.
2. Executives are very busy. Your letter should tell the president your main results first (for example, the amount of net income).
3. You should include brief explanations so that the president can understand the changes you made in the calculations.

ETHICS CASE

BYP19-6 Wayne Terrago, controller for Robbin Industries, was reviewing production cost reports for the year. One amount in these reports continued to bother him—advertising. During the year, the company had instituted an expensive advertising campaign to sell some of its slower-moving products. It was still too early to tell whether the advertising campaign was successful.

There had been much internal debate as how to report advertising cost. The vice president of finance argued that advertising costs should be reported as a cost of production, just like direct materials and direct labor. He therefore recommended that this cost be identified as manufacturing overhead and reported as part of inventory costs until sold. Others disagreed. Terrago believed that this cost should be reported as an expense of the current period, based on the conservatism principle. Others argued that it should be reported as Prepaid Advertising and reported as a current asset.

The president finally had to decide the issue. He argued that these costs should be reported as inventory. His arguments were practical ones. He noted that the company was experiencing financial difficulty and expensing this amount in the current period might jeopardize a planned bond offering. Also, by reporting the advertising costs as inventory rather than as prepaid advertising, less attention would be directed to it by the financial community.

Instructions

(a) Who are the stakeholders in this situation?
(b) What are the ethical issues involved in this situation?
(c) What would you do if you were Wayne Terrago?

"All About You" Activity

BYP19-7 The primary purpose of managerial accounting is to provide information useful for management decisions. Many of the managerial accounting techniques that you learn in this course will be useful for decisions you make in your everyday life.

Instructions

For each of the following managerial accounting techniques, read the definition provided and then provide an example of a personal situation that would benefit from use of this technique.

(a) Break-even analysis (page 968).
(b) Budgeting (page 1000).
(c) Balanced scorecard (page 847).
(d) Capital budgeting (page 1144).

Answers to Insight and Accounting Across the Organization Questions

p. 834 Automation Has Changed Management

Q: As factories become more automated, what will managers "manage"?

A: *Managers will review production and equipment utilization data to determine if quality and quantity goals are being met. Such data should indicate which equipment and operators are most reliable and efficient.*

p. 837 Productivity at Nissan

Q: Why might Nissan production require significantly fewer labor hours?

A: *Nissan's U.S. factories are probably newer than those of Daimler-Chrysler and Ford. Newer factories tend to be more highly automated with less reliance on production-line employees.*

p. 846 Bananas Receive Special Treatment

Q: Why is it important to keep track of costs that are incurred to improve product quality?

A: *Most companies are concerned about product quality, but managers need to consider the cost/benefit tradeoff. If you spend too much on improving product quality, your customers might not be willing to pay the price needed to recover costs. Therefore it is very important that Chiquita closely track all of the costs that it incurs to protect the bananas, to ensure that these costs are factored into the price that it ultimately charges for the bananas.*

Authors' Comments on *All About You*: Outsourcing and Jobs (p. 848)

This is a difficult decision. While the direct costs of outsourced tax return preparation may in fact be lower, you must also consider other issues: Will the accuracy of the returns be as high? Will your relationships with your customers suffer due to the loss of direct contact? Will customers resent having their personal information shipped overseas? While you may not want to lay off six employees, you also don't want to put your firm at risk by not remaining competitive.

Perhaps one solution would be to outsource the most basic tasks, and then provide training to the six employees so they can perform higher-skilled services such as tax planning. Many of the techniques that you learn in the remaining chapters of this text will help you evaluate the merits of your various options.

Answers to Self-Study Questions

1. b **2.** b **3.** b **4.** c **5.** d **6.** a **7.** c **8.** a **9.** d **10.** d

Remember to go back to the Navigator box on the chapter-opening page and check off your completed work.

Chapter 20

Job Order Cost Accounting

STUDY OBJECTIVES

After studying this chapter, you should be able to:

1 Explain the characteristics and purposes of cost accounting.

2 Describe the flow of costs in a job order cost accounting system.

3 Explain the nature and importance of a job cost sheet.

4 Indicate how the predetermined overhead rate is determined and used.

5 Prepare entries for jobs completed and sold.

6 Distinguish between under- and overapplied manufacturing overhead.

The Navigator

The Navigator

Scan **Study Objectives**	■
Read **Feature Story**	■
Read **Preview**	■
Read text and answer **Before You Go On** p. 874 ■ p. 884 ■ p. 889 ■	
Work **Demonstration Problem**	■
Review **Summary of Study Objectives**	■
Answer **Self-Study Questions**	■
Complete **Assignments**	■

Feature Story

" . . . AND WE'D LIKE IT IN RED"

Western States Fire Apparatus, Inc., of Cornelius, Oregon, is one of the few U.S. companies that makes fire trucks. The company builds about 25 trucks per year. Founded in 1941, the company is run by the children and grandchildren of the original founder.

"We buy the chassis, which is the cab and the frame," says Susan Scott, the company's bookkeeper. "In our computer, we set up an account into which all of the direct material that is purchased for that particular job is charged."

Other direct materials include the water pump—which can cost $10,000—the lights, the siren, ladders, and hoses.

As for direct labor, the production workers fill out time tickets that tell what jobs they worked on. Usually, the company is building four trucks at any one time. On payday, the controller allocates the payroll to the appropriate job record.

Indirect materials, such as nuts and bolts, wiring, lubricants, and abrasives, are allocated to each job in proportion to direct material dollars. Other costs, such as insurance and supervisors' salaries, are allocated based on direct labor hours. "We need to allocate overhead in order to know what kind of price we have to charge when we submit our bids," she says.

Western gets orders through a "blind-bidding" process. That is, Western submits its bid without knowing the bid prices made by its competitors. "If we bid too low, we won't make a profit. If we bid too high, we don't get the job."

Regardless of the final price for the truck, the quality had better be first-rate. "The fire departments let you know if they don't like what you did, and you usually end up fixing it."

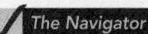

✓ The Navigator

Inside Chapter 20...

Preview of Chapter 20

The Feature Story about Western States Fire Apparatus describes the manufacturing costs used in making a fire truck. It demonstrates that accurate costing is critical to the company's success. For example, in order to submit accurate bids on new jobs and to know whether it profited from past jobs, the company needs a good costing system. This chapter illustrates how these manufacturing costs are assigned to specific jobs, such as the manufacture of individual fire trucks. We begin the discussion in this chapter with an overview of the flow of costs in a job order cost accounting system. We then use a case study to explain and illustrate the documents, entries, and accounts in this type of cost accounting system.

The content and organization of Chapter 20 are as follows.

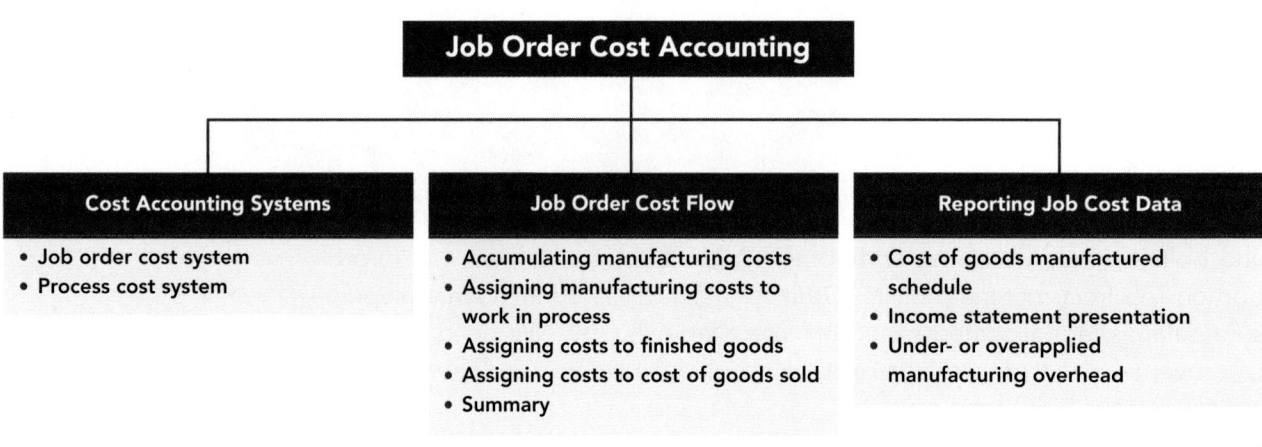

Job Order Cost Accounting

Cost Accounting Systems
- Job order cost system
- Process cost system

Job Order Cost Flow
- Accumulating manufacturing costs
- Assigning manufacturing costs to work in process
- Assigning costs to finished goods
- Assigning costs to cost of goods sold
- Summary

Reporting Job Cost Data
- Cost of goods manufactured schedule
- Income statement presentation
- Under- or overapplied manufacturing overhead

The Navigator

COST ACCOUNTING SYSTEMS

STUDY OBJECTIVE 1

Explain the characteristics and purposes of cost accounting.

Cost accounting involves the measuring, recording, and reporting of product costs. From the data accumulated, companies determine both the total cost and the unit cost of each product. The accuracy of the product cost information produced by the cost accounting system is critical to the success of the company. As you will see in later chapters, this information is used to determine which products to produce, what price to charge, and the amounts to produce. Accurate product cost information is also vital for effective evaluation of employee performance.

A **cost accounting system** consists of accounts for the various manufacturing costs. These accounts are fully integrated into the general ledger of a company. **An important feature of a cost accounting system is the use of a perpetual inventory system.** Such a system **provides immediate, up-to-date information on the cost of a product**.

There are two basic types of cost accounting systems: (1) a job order cost system and (2) a process cost system. Although cost accounting systems differ widely from company to company, most involve one of these two traditional product costing systems.

Job Order Cost System

Under a **job order cost system**, the company assigns costs to each **job** or to each **batch** of goods. An example of a job is the manufacture of a mainframe computer by IBM, the production of a movie by Disney, or the making of a fire truck by Western States. An example of a batch is the printing of 225 wedding invitations by a local print shop, or the printing of a weekly issue of *Fortune* magazine by a hi-tech printer such as Quad Graphics. Companies may complete jobs or batches to fill a specific customer order or to replenish inventory.

An important feature of job order costing is that each job (or batch) has its own distinguishing characteristics. For example, each house is custom built, each consulting engagement by a CPA firm is unique, and each printing job is different. **The objective is to compute the cost per job.** At each point in manufacturing a product or providing a service, the company can identify the job and its associated costs. A job order cost system measures costs for each completed job, rather than for set time periods. Illustration 20-1 shows the recording of costs in a job order cost system.

Illustration 20-1
Job order cost system

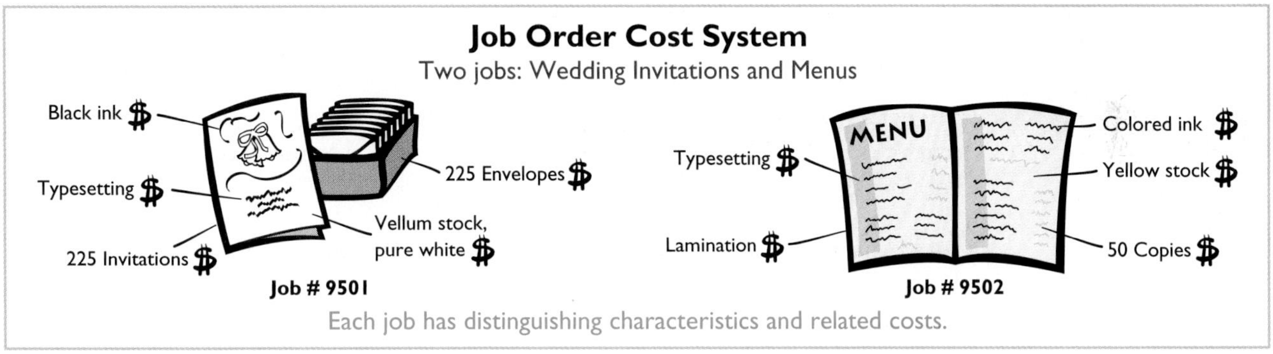

Process Cost System

A company uses a process cost system when it manufactures a large volume of similar products. Production is continuous to ensure that adequate inventories of the finished product(s) are on hand. A process cost system is used in the manufacture of cereal by Kellogg, the refining of petroleum by ExxonMobil, and the production of automobiles by General Motors. Process costing accumulates product-related costs **for a period of time** (such as a week or a month) instead of assigning costs to specific products or job orders. In process costing, companies assign the costs to departments or processes for a set period of time. Illustration 20-2 shows examples of the use of a process cost system. We will discuss the process cost system further in Chapter 21.

Illustration 20-2
Process cost system

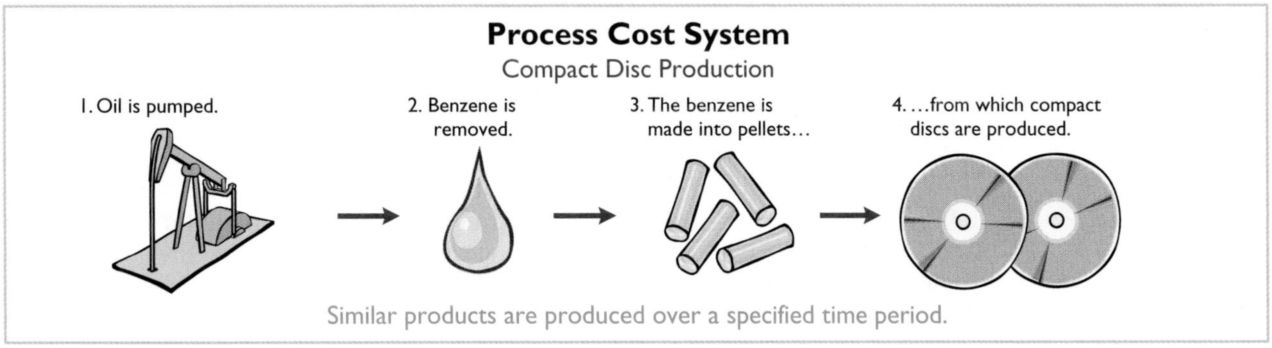

A company may use both types of cost systems. For example, General Motors uses process cost accounting for its standard model cars, such as Saturns and

Corvettes, and job order cost accounting for a custom-made limousine for the President of the United States. The objective of both systems is to provide unit cost information for product pricing, cost control, inventory valuation, and financial statement presentation. End-of-period inventory values are computed by using unit cost data.

MANAGEMENT INSIGHT

Jobs Won, Money Lost

Many companies suffer from poor cost accounting. As a result, they sometimes make products they should not be selling at all and buy others that they could more profitably make themselves. Also, inaccurate cost data lead companies to misallocate capital and frustrate efforts by plant managers to improve efficiency.

For example, consider the case of a diversified company in the business of rebuilding diesel locomotives. The managers thought they were making money, but a consulting firm found that costs had been seriously underestimated. The company bailed out of the business, and not a moment too soon. Says the consultant who advised the company, "The more contracts it won, the more money it lost." Given that situation, a company cannot stay in business very long!

What type of costs do you think the company had been underestimating?

Before You Go On...

REVIEW IT

1. What is cost accounting?
2. What does a cost accounting system consist of?
3. How does a job order cost system differ from a process cost system?

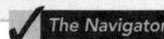

The Navigator

JOB ORDER COST FLOW

STUDY OBJECTIVE 2

Describe the flow of costs in a job order cost accounting system.

The flow of costs (direct materials, direct labor, and manufacturing overhead) in job order cost accounting parallels the physical flow of the materials as they are converted into finished goods. As shown in Illustration 20-3, companies assign manufacturing costs to the Work in Process Inventory account. When a job is completed, the cost of the job is transferred to Finished Goods Inventory. Later when the goods are sold, their cost is transferred to Cost of Goods Sold.

Illustration 20-3 provides a basic overview of the flow of costs in a manufacturing setting. A more detailed presentation of the flow of costs is shown in Illustration 20-4. It indicates that there are two major steps in the flow of costs: (1) *accumulating* the manufacturing costs incurred, and (2) *assigning* the accumulated costs to the work done. As shown, manufacturing costs incurred are accumulated in entries 1–3 by debits to Raw Materials Inventory, Factory Labor, and Manufacturing Overhead. When the company incurs these costs, it does not attempt to associate the costs with specific jobs. The remaining entries (entries 4–8) assign manufacturing costs incurred. In the remainder of this chapter, we will use a case study to explain how a job order system operates.

Illustration 20-3
Flow of costs in job order cost accounting

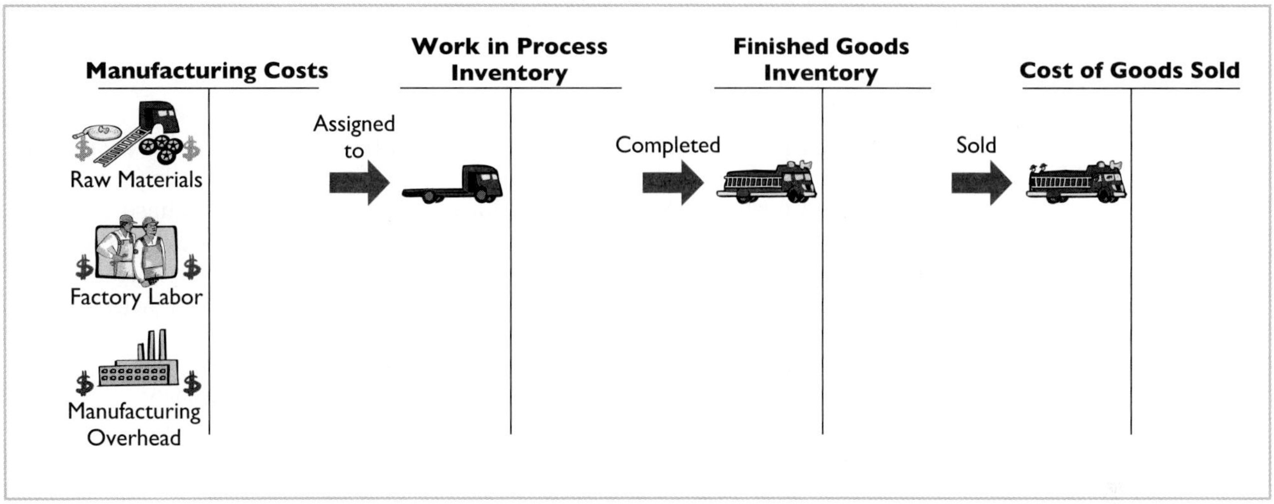

Illustration 20-4
Job order cost accounting system

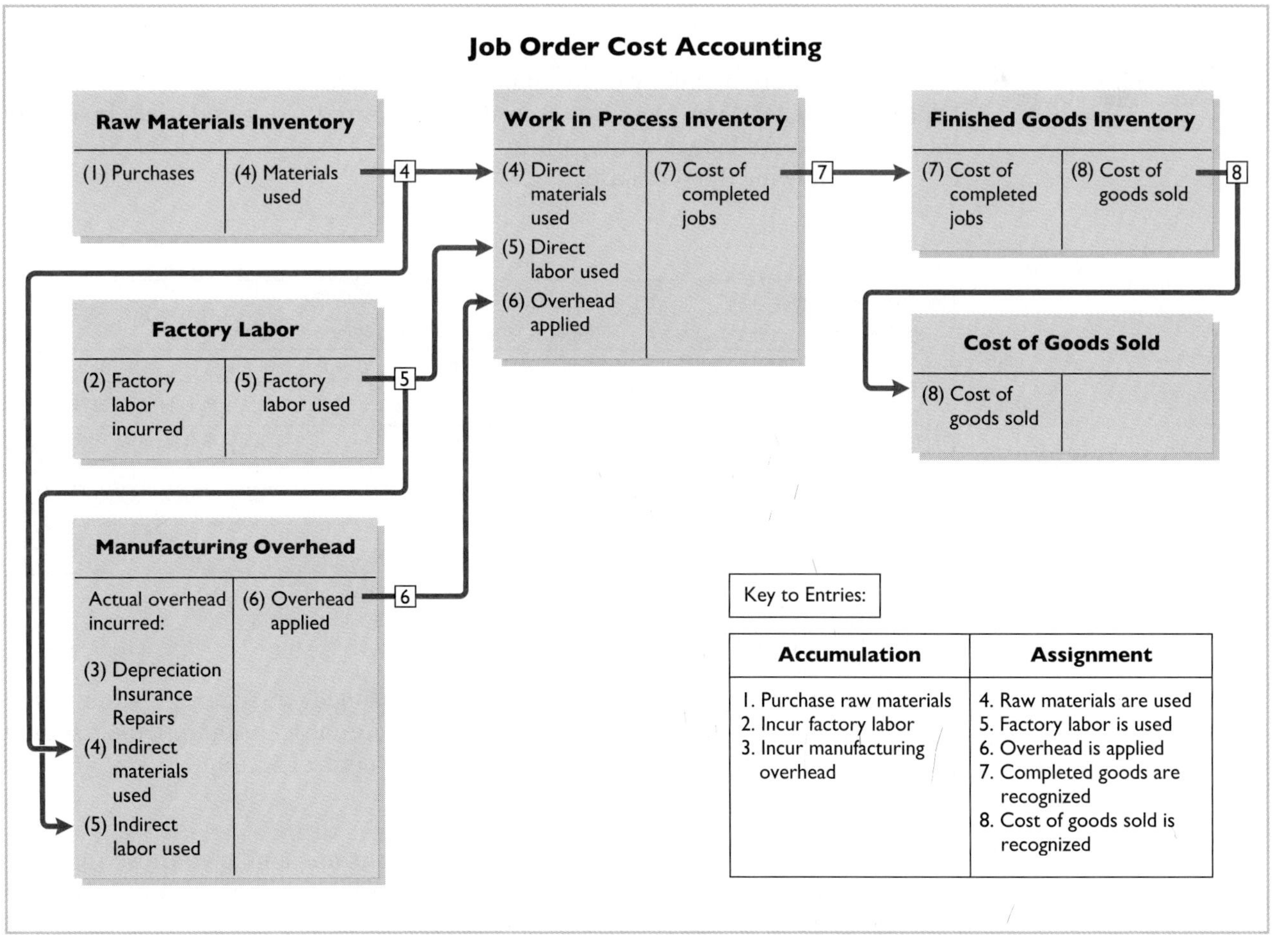

Accumulating Manufacturing Costs

In a job order cost system, companies record manufacturing costs in the period in which the costs are incurred. To illustrate, we will use the January transactions of Wallace Manufacturing Company, which makes machine tools.

RAW MATERIALS COSTS

When Wallace receives the raw materials it has purchased, **it debits the costs of the materials to Raw Materials Inventory**. This account is debited for the invoice cost and freight costs chargeable to the purchaser. It is credited for purchase discounts taken and purchase returns and allowances. Wallace makes **no effort at this point to associate the cost of materials with specific jobs or orders**. The procedures for ordering, receiving, recording, and paying for raw materials are similar to the purchasing procedures of a merchandising company.

To illustrate, assume that Wallace Manufacturing purchases 2,000 handles (Stock No. AA2746) at $5 per unit ($10,000) and 800 modules (Stock No. AA2850) at $40 per unit ($32,000) for a total cost of $42,000 ($10,000 + $32,000). The entry to record this purchase on January 4 is:

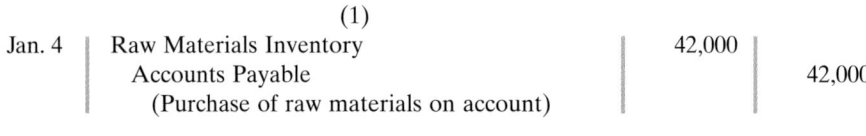

(1)

Jan. 4	Raw Materials Inventory	42,000	
	Accounts Payable		42,000
	(Purchase of raw materials on account)		

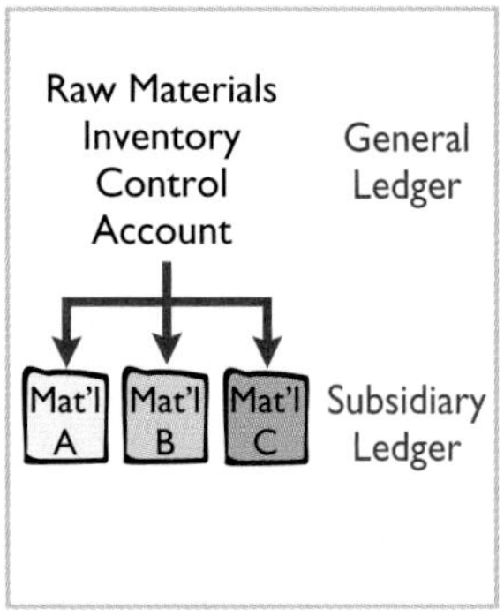

Raw Materials Inventory is a general ledger account. It is also referred to as a **control account** because it summarizes the detailed data regarding specific inventory accounts in the subsidiary ledger. The subsidiary ledger consists of individual records for each item of raw materials. The records may take the form of accounts (or cards) that are manually or mechanically prepared. Generally the records are kept as computer data files. The records are referred to as **materials inventory records** (or **stores ledger cards**). Illustration 20-5 shows the card for Stock No. AA2746, following the purchase.

Illustration 20-5
Materials inventory card

Materials Inventory.xls

File Edit View Insert Format Tools Data Window Help

	A	B	C	D	E	F	G	H	I	J
1–2	**Item: Handles**									**Part No: AA2746**
3			**Receipts**			**Issues**			**Balance**	
4	Date	Units	Cost	Total	Units	Cost	Total	Units	Cost	Total
5	1/4	2,000	$5	$10,000				2,000	$5	$10,000
6										
7										

Wallace makes postings daily to the subsidiary ledger. After all postings are completed, the sum of the balances in the raw materials subsidiary ledger should equal the balance in the Raw Materials Inventory control account.

FACTORY LABOR COSTS

The procedures for accumulating factory labor costs are similar to those for computing the payroll for a merchandising company. Companies use time clocks and time cards to determine total hours worked; gross and net earnings for each employee are listed in a payroll register; and individual employee earnings records are maintained. To help ensure the accuracy of data, a company should follow the principles of internal control.

In a manufacturing company, the cost of factory labor consists of (1) gross earnings of factory workers, (2) employer payroll taxes on these earnings, and (3) fringe benefits (such as sick pay, pensions, and vacation pay) incurred by the employer. **Companies debit labor costs to Factory Labor as they incur those costs.**

To illustrate, assume that Wallace Manufacturing incurs $32,000 of factory labor costs. Of that amount, $27,000 relates to wages payable and $5,000 relates to payroll taxes payable in January. The entry is:

	(2)		
Jan. 31	Factory Labor	32,000	
	Factory Wages Payable		27,000
	Employer Payroll Taxes Payable		5,000
	(To record factory labor costs)		

Factory labor is subsequently assigned to work in process and manufacturing overhead, as explained later in the chapter.

MANUFACTURING OVERHEAD COSTS

A company has many types of overhead costs. It may recognize these costs **daily**, as in the case of machinery repairs and the use of indirect materials and indirect labor. Or, it may record overhead costs **periodically** through adjusting entries. Property taxes, depreciation, and insurance are recorded periodically, for example. This is done using a summary entry, which summarizes the totals from multiple transactions.

Using assumed data, the summary entry for manufacturing overhead in Wallace Manufacturing Company is:

	(3)		
Jan. 31	Manufacturing Overhead	13,800	
	Utilities Payable		4,800
	Prepaid Insurance		2,000
	Accounts Payable (for repairs)		2,600
	Accumulated Depreciation		3,000
	Property Taxes Payable		1,400
	(To record overhead costs)		

Manufacturing Overhead is a control account. The subsidiary ledger consists of individual accounts for each type of cost, such as Factory Utilities, Factory Insurance, and Factory Repairs.

Assigning Manufacturing Costs to Work in Process

STUDY OBJECTIVE 3

Explain the nature and importance of a job cost sheet.

As Illustration 20-4 (page 875) shows, assigning manufacturing costs to work in process results in the following entries:

1. **Debits** are made to Work in Process Inventory.
2. **Credits** are made to Raw Materials Inventory, Factory Labor, and Manufacturing Overhead.

Journal entries to assign costs to work in process are usually made and posted **monthly**.

An essential accounting record in assigning costs to jobs is a **job cost sheet**, shown in Illustration 20-6 (page 878). A job cost sheet is a form used to record the costs chargeable to a specific job and to determine the total and unit costs of the completed job.

Illustration 20-6
Job cost sheet

Job Cost Sheet

Job No. ____________________ Quantity ____________________
Item ____________________ Date Requested ____________________
For ____________________ Date Completed ____________________

Date	Direct Materials	Direct Labor	Manufacturing Overhead

Cost of completed job
Direct materials $ ________
Direct labor ________
Manufacturing overhead ________
Total cost $ ________
Unit cost (total dollars ÷ quantity) $ ________

HELPFUL HINT
In today's electronic environment, companies typically maintain job cost sheets as computer files.

Postings to job cost sheets are made daily, directly from supporting documents.

Companies keep a separate job cost sheet for each job. The job cost sheets constitute the subsidiary ledger for the Work in Process Inventory account. **Each entry to Work in Process Inventory must be accompanied by a corresponding posting to one or more job cost sheets.**

RAW MATERIALS COSTS

HELPFUL HINT
Approvals are an important part of a materials requisition slip because they help to establish individual accountability over inventory.

Companies assign raw materials costs when the materials are issued by the storeroom. To achieve effective internal control over the issuance of materials, the storeroom worker should receive a written authorization before releasing materials to production. Such authorization for issuing raw materials is made on a prenumbered **materials requisition slip**. An authorized employee such as a department supervisor signs this form. The materials issued may be used directly on a job, or they may be considered indirect materials. As Illustration 20-7 shows, the requisition should indicate the quantity and type of materials withdrawn and the account to be charged. Direct materials will be charged to Work in Process Inventory, and indirect materials to Manufacturing Overhead.

ETHICS NOTE
The internal control principle of documentation includes prenumbering to enhance accountability.

The company prepares the requisition in duplicate. A copy is retained in the storeroom as evidence of the materials released. The original is sent to Accounting, where the cost per unit and total cost of the materials used are determined. The company may use any of the inventory costing methods (FIFO, LIFO, or average-cost) in costing the requisitions. After the requisition slips have been costed, they are posted daily to the materials inventory records. Also, **requisitions for direct materials are posted daily to the individual job cost sheets**.

Periodically, the requisitions are sorted, totaled, and journalized. For example, if Wallace Manufacturing uses $24,000 of direct materials and $6,000 of indirect materials in January, the entry is:

(4)

Jan. 31	Work in Process Inventory	24,000	
	Manufacturing Overhead	6,000	
	Raw Materials Inventory		30,000
	(To assign materials to jobs and overhead)		

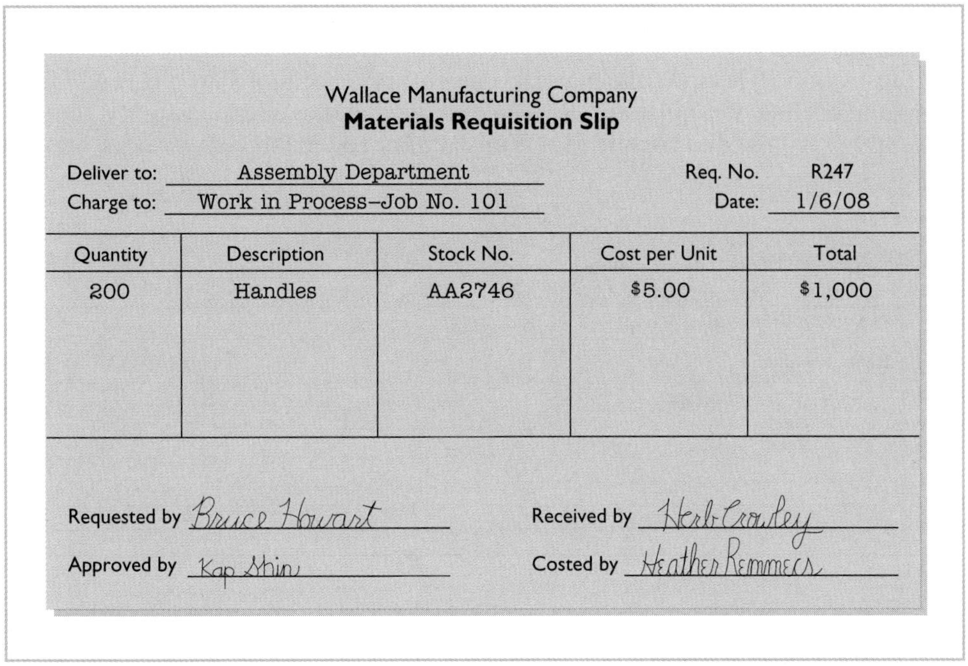
Wallace Manufacturing Company
Materials Requisition Slip

Deliver to: Assembly Department Req. No. R247
Charge to: Work in Process–Job No. 101 Date: 1/6/08

Quantity	Description	Stock No.	Cost per Unit	Total
200	Handles	AA2746	$5.00	$1,000

Requested by Bruce Howart Received by Herb Crowley
Approved by Kap Shin Costed by Heather Remmers

Illustration 20-7
Materials requisition slip

The requisition slips show total direct materials costs of $12,000 for Job No. 101, $7,000 for Job No. 102, and $5,000 for Job No. 103. Illustration 20-8 shows the posting of requisition slip R247 and other assumed postings to the job cost sheets for materials. After all postings have been completed, the sum of the direct materials

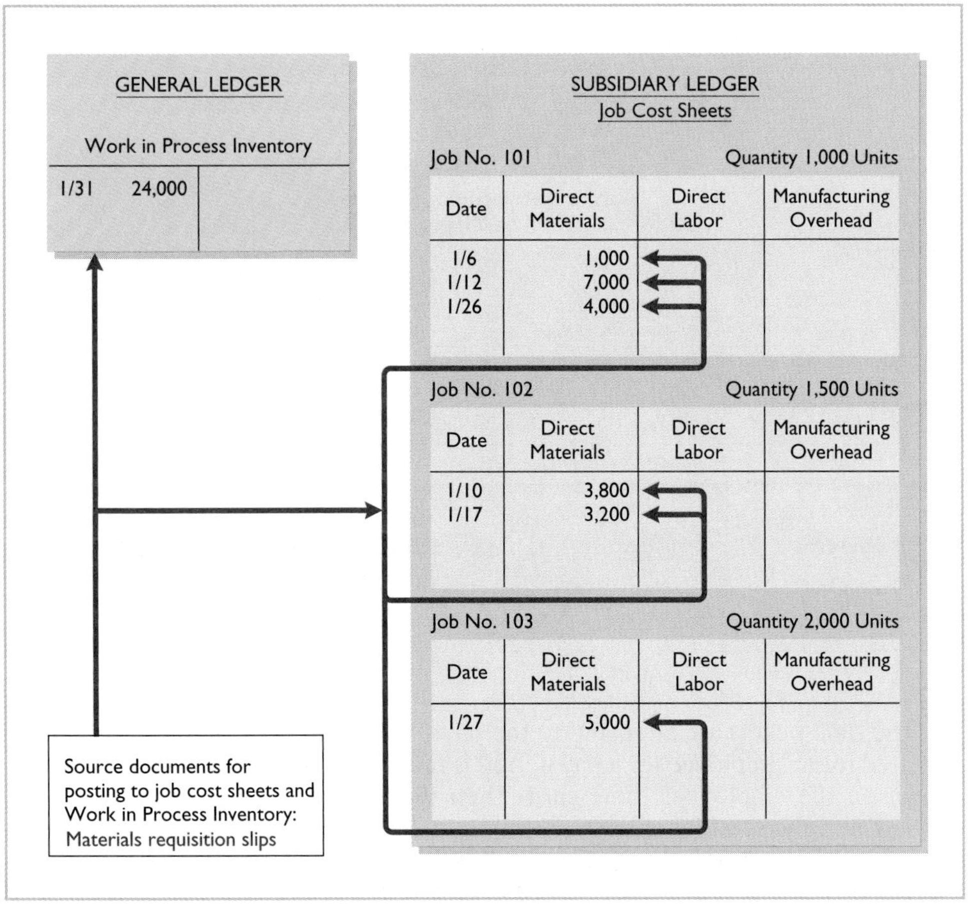

Illustration 20-8
Job cost sheets—direct materials

HELPFUL HINT
Postings to control accounts are made monthly, and postings to job cost sheets are made daily.

columns of the job cost sheets should equal the direct materials debited to Work in Process Inventory.

Illustration 20-9 shows the materials inventory record for Part No. AA2746. It shows the posting of requisition slip R247 for 200 handles and an assumed requisition slip for 760 handles costing $3,800 on January 10 for Job 102.

Illustration 20-9
Materials inventory card following issuances

Materials Inventory.xls

File Edit View Insert Format Tools Data Window Help

	A	B	C	D	E	F	G	H	I	J
1	Item: Handles									Part No: AA2746
2										
3		Receipts			Issues			Balance		
4	Date	Units	Cost	Total	Units	Cost	Total	Units	Cost	Total
5	1/4	2,000	$5	$10,000				2,000	$5	$10,000
6	1/6				200	$5	$1,000	1,800	$5	9,000
7	1/10				760	$5	3,800	1,040	$5	5,200

FACTORY LABOR COSTS

Companies assign factory labor costs to jobs on the basis of time tickets prepared when the work is performed. The time ticket indicates the employee, the hours worked, the account and job to be charged, and the total labor cost. Many companies accumulate these data through the use of bar coding and scanning devices. When they start and end work, employees scan bar codes on their identification badges and bar codes associated with each job they work on. When direct labor is involved, the job number must be indicated, as shown in Illustration 20-10. The employee's supervisor should approve all time tickets.

Illustration 20-10
Time ticket

Wallace Manufacturing Company
Time Ticket

Date: 1/6/08
Employee: John Nash — Employee No. 124
Charge to: Work in Process — Job No. 101

Time: Start	Stop	Total Hours	Hourly Rate	Total Cost
0800	1200	4	10.00	40.00

Approved by Bob Kadler — Costed by M Chen

HELPFUL HINT
Some companies use different colored time tickets for direct and for indirect labor.

The time tickets are later sent to the payroll department. There, the total time reported for an employee for a pay period is reconciled with total hours worked, as shown on the employee's time card. Then the employee's hourly wage rate is applied, and the total labor cost is computed. Finally, the time tickets are sorted, totaled, and journalized. The company debits the account Work in Process Inventory for direct labor, and debits Manufacturing Overhead for indirect labor. For example, if the $32,000 total factory labor cost consists of $28,000 of direct labor and $4,000 of indirect labor, the entry is:

	(5)		
Jan. 31	Work in Process Inventory	28,000	
	Manufacturing Overhead	4,000	
	Factory Labor		32,000
	(To assign labor to jobs and overhead)		

As a result of this entry, Factory Labor has a zero balance, and gross earnings are assigned to the appropriate manufacturing accounts.

Let's assume that the labor costs chargeable to Wallace's three jobs are $15,000, $9,000, and $4,000. Illustration 20-11 shows the Work in Process Inventory and job cost sheets after posting. As in the case of direct materials, the postings to the direct labor columns of the job cost sheets should equal the posting of direct labor to Work in Process Inventory.

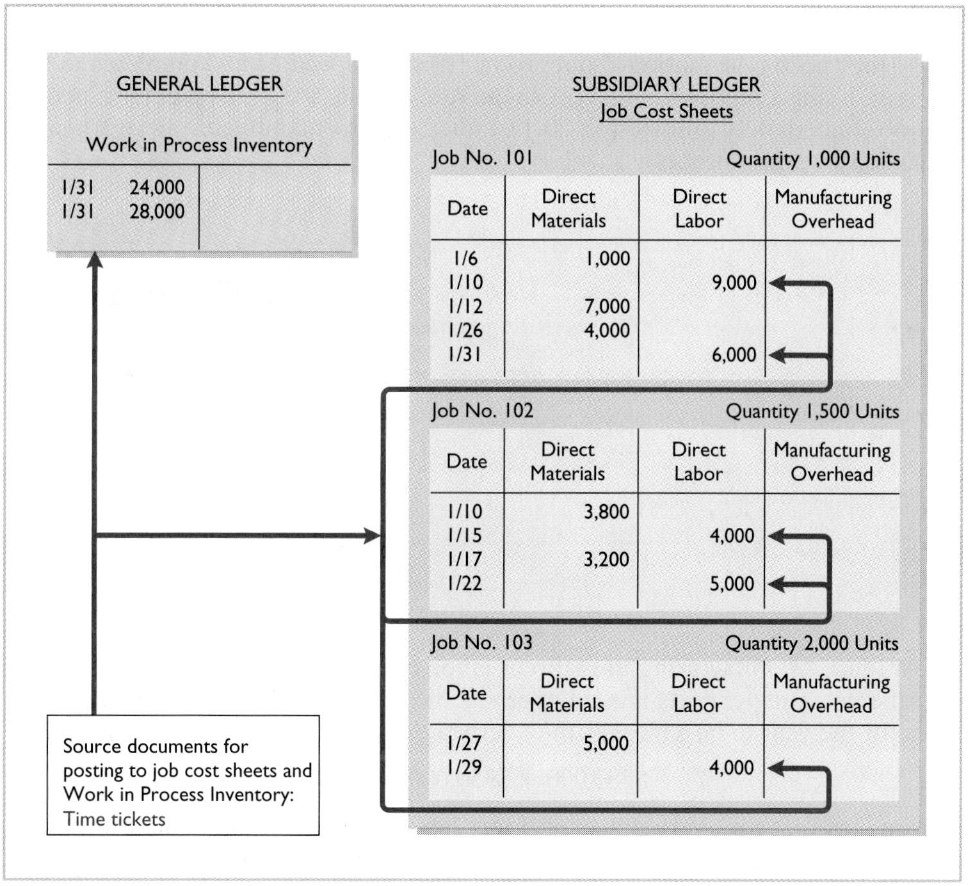

Illustration 20-11
Job cost sheets—direct labor

HELPFUL HINT
Prove the $28,000 by totaling the charges by jobs:

101	$15,000
102	9,000
103	4,000
	$28,000

MANUFACTURING OVERHEAD COSTS

STUDY OBJECTIVE 4
Indicate how the predetermined overhead rate is determined and used.

The actual costs of direct materials and direct labor are charged to specific jobs. In contrast, manufacturing **overhead** relates to production operations **as a whole**. As a result, overhead costs cannot be assigned to specific jobs on the basis of actual costs incurred. Instead, companies assign manufacturing overhead to work in process and to specific jobs **on an estimated basis through the use of a predetermined overhead rate**.

The **predetermined overhead rate** is based on the relationship between estimated annual overhead costs and expected annual operating activity. This relationship is expressed in terms of a common **activity base**. The activity may be stated in terms of direct labor costs, direct labor hours, machine hours, or any other measure that will provide an equitable basis for applying overhead costs to jobs. The predetermined overhead rate is established at the beginning of the year. Small companies often use a single, company-wide predetermined overhead rate. Large companies, however, often use rates that vary from department to department. The formula for a predetermined overhead rate is as follows.

Illustration 20-12
Formula for predetermined overhead rate

$$\text{Estimated Annual Overhead Costs} \div \text{Expected Annual Operating Activity} = \text{Predetermined Overhead Rate}$$

Overhead relates to production operations as a whole. To know what "the whole" is, the logical thing is to wait until the end of the year's operations. At that time the company knows all of its costs for the period. As a practical matter, though, managers cannot wait until the end of the year. To price products accurately, they need information about product costs of specific jobs completed during the year. Using a predetermined overhead rate enables a cost to be determined for the job immediately. Illustration 20-13 indicates how manufacturing overhead is assigned to work in process.

Illustration 20-13
Using predetermined overhead rates

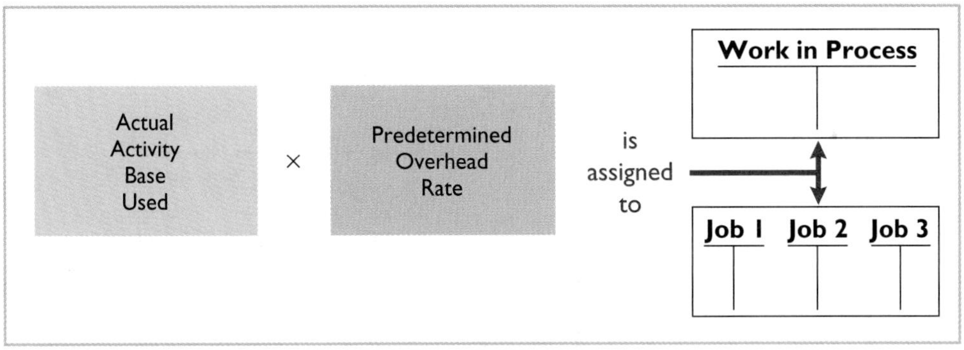

Wallace Manufacturing uses direct labor cost as the activity base. Assuming that the company expects annual overhead costs to be $280,000 and direct labor costs for the year to be $350,000, the overhead rate is 80%, computed as follows:

$$\$280{,}000 \div \$350{,}000 = 80\%$$

This means that for every dollar of direct labor, 80 cents of manufacturing overhead will be assigned to a job. The use of a predetermined overhead rate enables the company to determine the approximate total cost of each job **when the job is completed**.

Historically, companies used direct labor costs or direct labor hours as the activity base. The reason was the relatively high correlation between direct labor and manufacturing overhead. Today more companies are using **machine hours as the activity base, due to increased reliance on automation in manufacturing operations**. Or, as mentioned in Chapter 19, many companies now use activity-based costing in an attempt to more accurately allocate overhead costs based on the activities that give rise to the costs.

A company may use more than one activity base. For example, if a job is manufactured in more than one factory department, each department may have its own overhead rate. In the Feature Story about fire trucks, Western States Fire Apparatus uses two bases in assigning overhead to jobs: direct materials dollars for indirect materials, and direct labor hours for such costs as insurance and supervisors' salaries.

Companies apply manufacturing overhead to work in process when they assign direct labor costs. They also apply manufacturing overhead to specific jobs at the same time. For Wallace Manufacturing, overhead applied for January is $22,400 (direct labor cost of $28,000 × 80%). The following entry records this application.

	(6)		
Jan. 31	Work in Process Inventory	22,400	
	Manufacturing Overhead		22,400
	(To assign overhead to jobs)		

The overhead applied to each job will be 80% of the direct labor cost of the job for the month. Illustration 20-14 shows the Work in Process Inventory account and the job cost sheets after posting. Note that the debit of $22,400 to Work in Process Inventory equals the sum of the overhead applied to jobs: Job 101 $12,000 + Job 102 $7,200 + Job 103 $3,200.

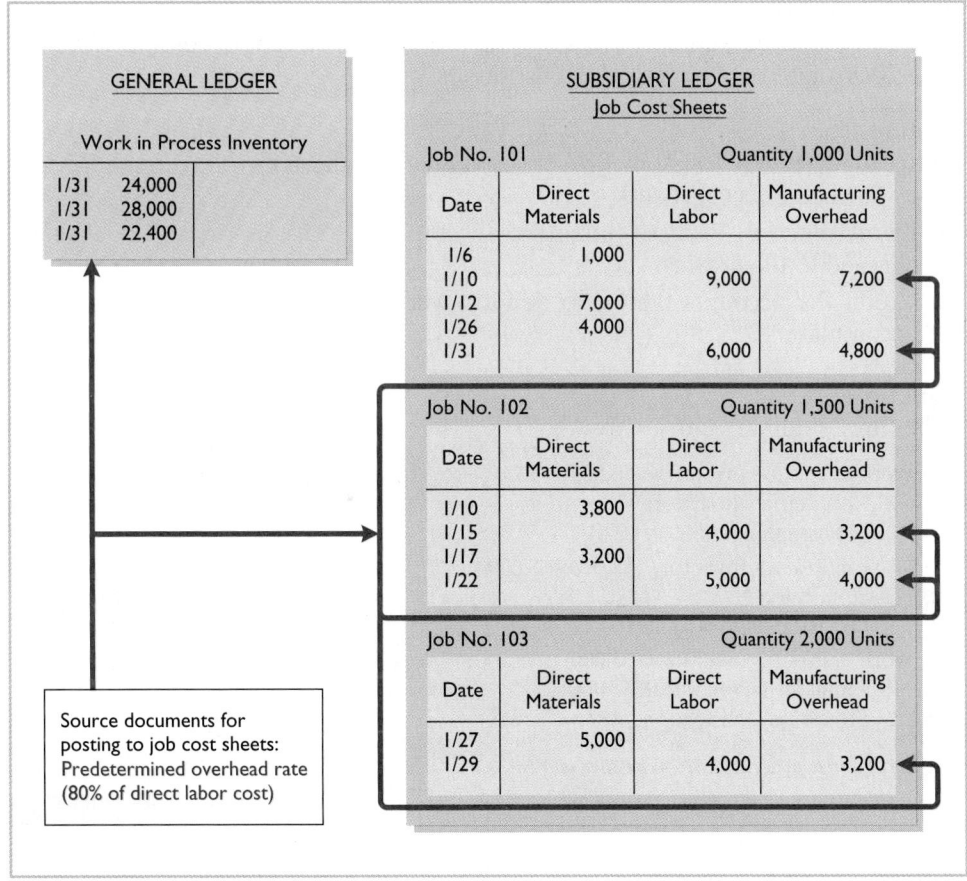

Illustration 20-14
Job cost sheets—manufacturing overhead applied

GENERAL LEDGER

Work in Process Inventory

1/31	24,000	
1/31	28,000	
1/31	22,400	

SUBSIDIARY LEDGER
Job Cost Sheets

Job No. 101 — Quantity 1,000 Units

Date	Direct Materials	Direct Labor	Manufacturing Overhead
1/6	1,000		
1/10		9,000	7,200
1/12	7,000		
1/26	4,000		
1/31		6,000	4,800

Job No. 102 — Quantity 1,500 Units

Date	Direct Materials	Direct Labor	Manufacturing Overhead
1/10	3,800		
1/15		4,000	3,200
1/17	3,200		
1/22		5,000	4,000

Job No. 103 — Quantity 2,000 Units

Date	Direct Materials	Direct Labor	Manufacturing Overhead
1/27	5,000		
1/29		4,000	3,200

Source documents for posting to job cost sheets: Predetermined overhead rate (80% of direct labor cost)

At the end of each month, **the balance in Work in Process Inventory should equal the sum of the costs shown on the job cost sheets of unfinished jobs.** Assuming that all jobs are unfinished, proof of the agreement of the control and subsidiary accounts in Wallace Manufacturing is shown in Illustration 20-15 (page 884).

Illustration 20-15
Proof of job cost sheets to work in process inventory

Work in Process Inventory			Job Cost Sheets	
Jan. 31	24,000		No. 101	$39,000
31	28,000		102	23,200
31	22,400		103	12,200
	74,400	←		**$74,400**

Before You Go On...

REVIEW IT

1. What source documents do companies use in assigning manufacturing costs to Work in Process Inventory?
2. What is a job cost sheet, and what is its primary purpose?
3. What is the formula for computing a predetermined overhead rate?

DO IT

Danielle Company is working on two job orders. The job cost sheets show the following:

Direct materials—Job 120 $6,000, Job 121 $3,600
Direct labor—Job 120 $4,000, Job 121 $2,000
Manufacturing overhead—Job 120 $5,000, Job 121 $2,500

Prepare the three summary entries to record the assignment of costs to Work in Process from the data on the job cost sheets.

Action Plan

- Recognize that Work in Process Inventory is the control account for all unfinished job cost sheets.
- Debit Work in Process Inventory for the materials, labor, and overhead charged to the job cost sheets.
- Credit the accounts that were debited when the manufacturing costs were accumulated.

Solution

The three summary entries are:

Work in Process Inventory ($6,000 + $3,600)	9,600	
Raw Materials Inventory		9,600
(To assign materials to jobs)		
Work in Process Inventory ($4,000 + $2,000)	6,000	
Factory Labor		6,000
(To assign labor to jobs)		
Work in Process Inventory ($5,000 + $2,500)	7,500	
Manufacturing Overhead		7,500
(To assign overhead to jobs)		

Related exercise material: *BE20-3, BE20-4, and BE20-7.*

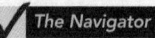

✓ The Navigator

Assigning Costs to Finished Goods

STUDY OBJECTIVE 5
Prepare entries for jobs completed and sold.

When a job is completed, Wallace summarizes the costs and completes the lower portion of the applicable job cost sheet. For example, if we assume that Wallace completes Job No. 101 on January 31, the job cost sheet appears as shown in Illustration 20-16.

Illustration 20-16
Completed job cost sheet

Job Cost Sheet

Job No.	101	Quantity	1,000
Item	Magnetic Sensors	Date Requested	February 5
For	Tanner Company	Date Completed	January 31

Date	Direct Materials	Direct Labor	Manufacturing Overhead
1/6	$ 1,000		
1/10		$ 9,000	$ 7,200
1/12	7,000		
1/26	4,000		
1/31		6,000	4,800
	$12,000	$15,000	$12,000

Cost of completed job	
Direct materials	$ 12,000
Direct labor	15,000
Manufacturing overhead	12,000
Total cost	$ 39,000
Unit cost ($39,000 ÷ 1,000)	$ 39.00

When a job is finished, Wallace makes an entry to transfer its total cost to finished goods inventory. The entry is as follows:

	(7)		
Jan. 31	Finished Goods Inventory	39,000	
	Work in Process Inventory		39,000
	(To record completion of Job No. 101)		

Finished Goods Inventory is a control account. It controls individual finished goods records in a finished goods subsidiary ledger. Postings to the receipts columns are made directly from completed job cost sheets. Illustration 20-17 (on page 886) shows the finished goods inventory record for Job No. 101.

Assigning Costs to Cost of Goods Sold

Companies recognize cost of goods sold when each sale occurs. To illustrate the entries when a completed job is sold, assume that on January 31 Wallace Manufacturing sells on account Job 101, costing $39,000, for $50,000. The entries to record the sale and recognize cost of goods sold are:

	(8)		
Jan. 31	Accounts Receivable	50,000	
	Sales		50,000
	(To record sale of Job No. 101)		
31	Cost of Goods Sold	39,000	
	Finished Goods Inventory		39,000
	(To record cost of Job No. 101)		

As Illustration 20-17 shows, Wallace records, in the issues section of the finished goods record, the units sold, the cost per unit, and the total cost of goods sold for each job sold.

Illustration 20-17
Finished goods record

Finished Goods.xls

Item: Magnetic Sensors | **Job No: 101**

Date	Receipts Units	Receipts Cost	Receipts Total	Issues Units	Issues Cost	Issues Total	Balance Units	Balance Cost	Balance Total
1/31	1,000	$39	$39,000				1,000	$39	$39,000
1/31				1,000	$39	$39,000			– 0 –

Summary of Job Order Cost Flows

Illustration 20-18 shows a completed flow chart for a job order cost accounting system. All postings are keyed to entries 1–8 in Wallace Manufacturing's accounts presented in the cost flow graphic in Illustration 20-4 (page 875).

Illustration 20-18
Flow of costs in a job order cost system

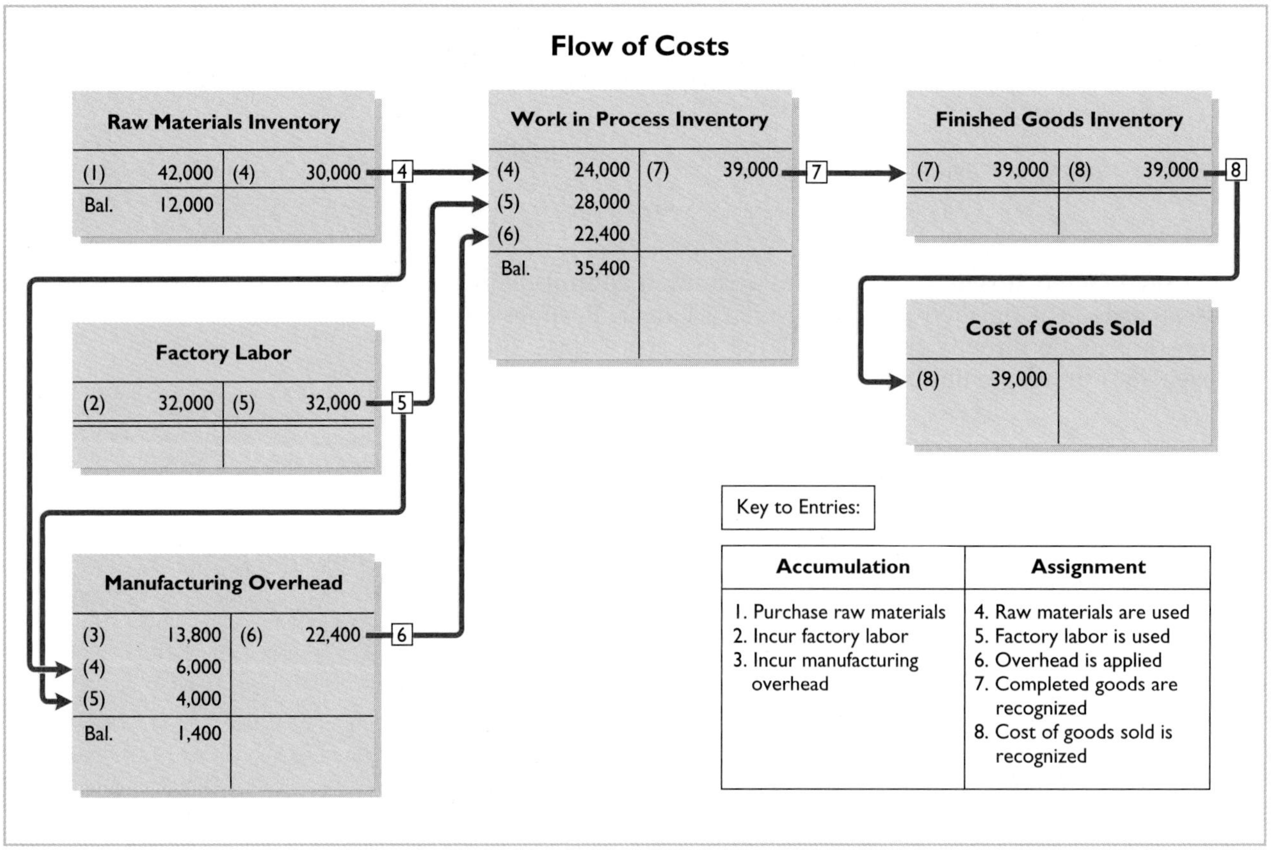

Illustration 20-19 summarizes the flow of documents in a job order cost system.

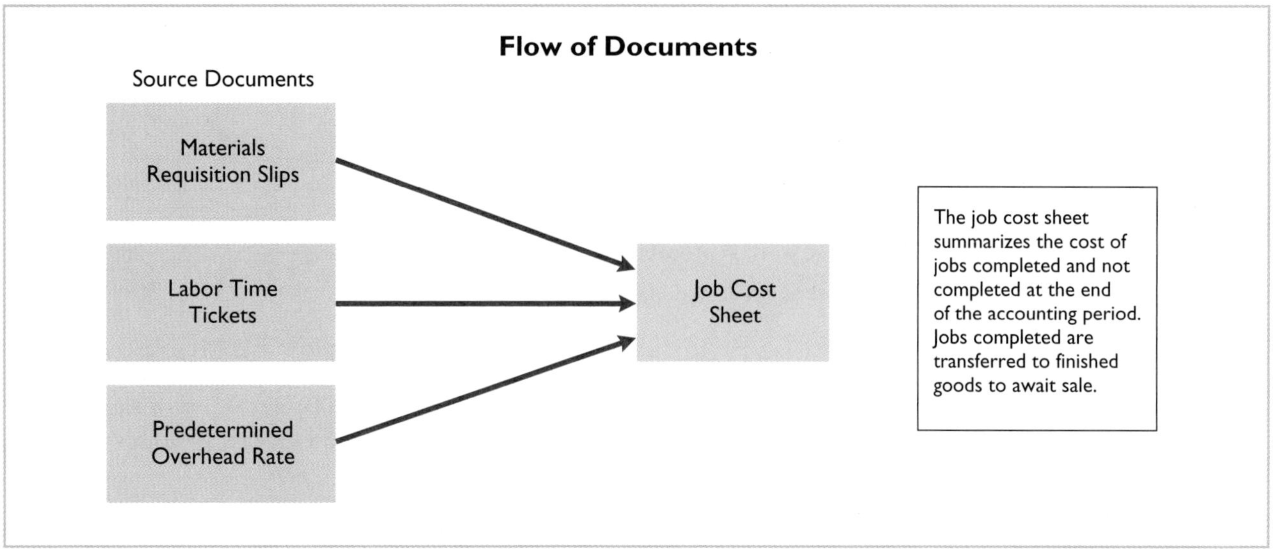
Flow of Documents
Source Documents
Materials Requisition Slips
Labor Time Tickets
Predetermined Overhead Rate
Job Cost Sheet
The job cost sheet summarizes the cost of jobs completed and not completed at the end of the accounting period. Jobs completed are transferred to finished goods to await sale.

Illustration 20-19
Flow of documents in a job order cost system

ACCOUNTING ACROSS THE ORGANIZATION

What About Service Companies?

Many of you will work for service companies. Service companies like the Mayo Clinic (health care), PriceWaterhouseCoopers (accounting firm), and Merrill Lynch (financial services firm) also use job order costing systems. The major difference in a job order costing system between a manufacturing company such as Western States Fire Apparatus and a service company such as Massachusetts General Hospital involves inventory. Service companies do not have raw materials nor finished goods inventory.

Because job order costing systems are used extensively in service industries, we provide exercises in the end-of-chapter material to help you understand how to cost various types of services.

? What types of costs will service companies report in job order cost systems?

REPORTING JOB COST DATA

At the end of a period, companies prepare financial statements that present aggregate data on all jobs manufactured and sold. The cost of goods manufactured schedule in job order costing is the same as in Chapter 19 with one exception: **The schedule shows manufacturing overhead applied, rather than actual overhead costs. Wallace adds this amount to direct materials and direct labor to determine total manufacturing costs.** The schedule is prepared directly from the Work in Process Inventory account. A condensed schedule for Wallace Manufacturing Company for January is shown in Illustration 20-20 (page 888).

HELPFUL HINT
Monthly financial statements are usually prepared for management use only.

Illustration 20-20
Cost of goods manufactured schedule

WALLACE MANUFACTURING COMPANY
Cost of Goods Manufactured Schedule
For the Month Ended January 31, 2008

Work in process, January 1		$ -0-
Direct materials used	$24,000	
Direct labor	28,000	
Manufacturing overhead applied	**22,400**	
Total manufacturing costs		74,400
Total cost of work in process		74,400
Less: Work in process, January 31		35,400
Cost of goods manufactured		$39,000

Note that the cost of goods manufactured ($39,000) agrees with the amount transferred from Work in Process Inventory to Finished Goods Inventory in journal entry no. 7 in Illustration 20-18 (page 886).

The income statement and balance sheet are the same as those illustrated in Chapter 19. For example, Illustration 20-21 shows the partial income statement for Wallace Manufacturing for the month of January.

Illustration 20-21
Partial income statement

WALLACE MANUFACTURING COMPANY
Income Statement (partial)
For the Month Ending January 31, 2008

Sales		$50,000
Cost of goods sold		
Finished goods inventory, January 1	$ -0-	
Cost of goods manufactured (See Illustration 20-20)	**39,000**	
Cost of goods available for sale	39,000	
Less: Finished goods inventory, January 31	-0-	
Cost of goods sold		39,000
Gross profit		$11,000

Under- or Overapplied Manufacturing Overhead

STUDY OBJECTIVE 6
Distinguish between under- and overapplied manufacturing overhead.

When Manufacturing Overhead has a **debit balance**, overhead is said to be underapplied. **Underapplied overhead** means that the overhead assigned to work in process is less than the overhead incurred. Conversely, when manufacturing overhead has a **credit balance**, overhead is overapplied. **Overapplied overhead** means that the overhead assigned to work in process is greater than the overhead incurred. Illustration 20-22 shows these concepts.

Illustration 20-22
Under- and overapplied overhead

Manufacturing Overhead

Manufacturing Overhead	
Actual (Costs incurred)	Applied (Costs assigned)

If actual is ***greater*** than applied, manufacturing overhead is underapplied.

If actual is ***less*** than applied, manufacturing overhead is overapplied.

YEAR-END BALANCE

At the end of the year, all manufacturing overhead transactions are complete. There is no further opportunity for offsetting events to occur. At this point, Wallace eliminates any balance in Manufacturing Overhead by an adjusting entry. It considers under- or overapplied overhead to be an **adjustment to cost of goods sold**. Thus, Wallace **debits underapplied overhead to Cost of Goods Sold**. It **credits overapplied overhead to Cost of Goods Sold**.

To illustrate, assume that Wallace Manufacturing has a $2,500 credit balance in Manufacturing Overhead at December 31. The adjusting entry for the overapplied overhead is:

Dec. 31	Manufacturing Overhead	2,500	
	Cost of Goods Sold		2,500
	(To transfer overapplied overhead to cost of goods sold)		

After Wallace posts this entry, Manufacturing Overhead has a zero balance. In preparing an income statement for the year, Wallace reports cost of goods sold **after adjusting it** for either under- or overapplied overhead.

Conceptually, it can be argued that under- or overapplied overhead at the end of the year should be allocated among ending work in process, finished goods, and cost of goods sold. The discussion of this possible allocation approach is left to more advanced courses.

ETHICS INSIGHT

"Did I Mention Our Overhead Charge?"

The State of Michigan found that auto dealers were charging service and documentary fees ranging from $18 to $445 per automobile and inspection fees from $88 to $360. Dealers often charged these fees after auto buyers had negotiated a base sales price for the car. The Attorney General of the State of Michigan ruled that auto dealers cannot charge customers additional fees for routine overhead costs. The attorney general said: "Overhead is part of the sales price of a motor vehicle. Processing paper work, dealer incurred costs, and inspection fees to qualify cars for extended warranty plans are ordinary overhead expenses."

? What implications might this ruling have on the dealerships' processing and inspection costs?

Before You Go On...

REVIEW IT

1. When are entries made to record the completion and sale of a job?
2. What costs are included in total manufacturing costs in the cost of goods manufactured schedule?

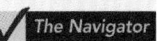

✓ The Navigator

Be sure to read **ALL ABOUT YOU: *Minding Your Own Business*** on page 890 for information on how topics in this chapter apply to you.

Minding Your Own Business

After graduating you might decide to start a small business. As discussed in this chapter, owners of any business need to know how to calculate the cost of their products. In fact, many small businesses fail because they do not accurately calculate their product costs, so they don't know if they are making money or losing money—until it is too late.

Some Facts

* There are about 17.6 million sole proprietorships in the U.S. The most common type of sole proprietorship is construction contractor.
* During a recent year, 25% of all sole proprietorships reported losses. The safest business is surveying and mapping, with only 6% of firms reporting losses. The riskiest business is hunting and trapping, with 76% of firms reporting losses.
* *Inc.* Magazine ranked the following as the top ten best places to start a business in 2006: Yuma, AZ; St. George, UT: Cape Coral–Fort Myers, FL; Fort Walton Beach–Crestview–Destin, FL; Coeur d'Alene, ID; Bellingham, WA; Port St. Lucie–Fort Pierce, FL; Naples–Marco Island, FL: Las Vegas–Paradise, NV; Idaho Fall, ID.
* About.com ranked the top ten business opportunities for 2005: business coach (motivates managers); business broker (brings together buyers and sellers of businesses); garage-organizing service; designing and producing smart (customized) clothes; medical transcription; trash removal; anti-aging spas; college admissions consulting; translation services; gaming-related businesses.

About the Numbers

Instead of starting your own business from scratch, perhaps you think it makes more sense to purchase a franchise. Initial investment varies, and annual franchise fees range from about $20,000 up to $80,000. The nearby chart of some well-known franchises shows the investment you typically need to make for these franchises. As you can see, one has to generate considerable revenue to cover the investment and related franchise fees. That's a lot of overhead.

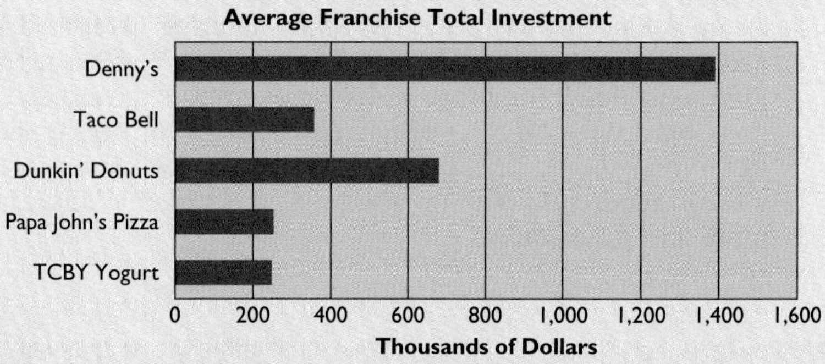

Source: AllBusiness.com, *www.allbusiness.com/franchise/listings.asp?cat=4933&sub=4970* (accessed June 2006).

What Do You Think?

Suppose that you decide to start a landscape business. You use an old pickup truck that you've fully paid for. You store the truck and other equipment in your parents' barn, and you store trees and shrubs on their land. Your parents will not charge you for the use of these facilities for the first two years, but beginning in the third year they will charge a reasonable rent. Your mother helps you by answering phone calls and providing customers with information. She doesn't charge you for this service, but she plans on doing it for only your first two years in business.

In pricing your services, should you include charges for the truck, the barn, the land, and your mother's services when calculating your product cost?

YES: If you don't include charges for these costs, your costs are understated and your profitability is overstated.

NO: At this point you are not actually incurring costs related to these activities, therefore you shouldn't record charges.

Sources: *www.bizstats.com;* Darrel Zahorsky, "10 Best Small Business Opportunities for 2005," *sbinformation.about.com* (accessed June 2006); Joel Kotkin, "Boomtowns '06," *Inc.* Magazine, May 2006, p. 97.

The authors' comments on this situation appear on page 909.

Demonstration Problem

During February, Cardella Manufacturing works on two jobs: A16 and B17. Summary data concerning these jobs are as follows.

Manufacturing Costs Incurred

Purchased $54,000 of raw materials on account.
Factory labor $76,000, plus $4,000 employer payroll taxes.
Manufacturing overhead exclusive of indirect materials and indirect labor $59,800.

Assignment of Costs

Direct materials:	Job A16 $27,000, Job B17 $21,000
Indirect materials:	$3,000
Direct labor:	Job A16 $52,000, Job B17 $26,000
Indirect labor:	$2,000

Manufacturing overhead rate: 80% of direct labor costs.

Job A16 was completed and sold on account for $150,000. Job B17 was only partially completed.

Instructions

(a) Journalize the February transactions in the sequence followed in the chapter.
(b) What was the amount of under- or overapplied manufacturing overhead?

Solution to Demonstration Problem

(a)

Date	Account Titles and Explanation	Debit	Credit
	1.		
Feb. 28	Raw Materials Inventory	54,000	
	Accounts Payable		54,000
	(Purchase of raw materials on account)		
	2.		
28	Factory Labor	80,000	
	Factory Wages Payable		76,000
	Employer Payroll Taxes Payable		4,000
	(To record factory labor costs)		
	3.		
28	Manufacturing Overhead	59,800	
	Accounts Payable, Accumulated Depreciation, and Prepaid Insurance		59,800
	(To record overhead costs)		
	4.		
28	Work in Process Inventory	48,000	
	Manufacturing Overhead	3,000	
	Raw Materials Inventory		51,000
	(To assign raw materials to production)		
	5.		
28	Work in Process Inventory	78,000	
	Manufacturing Overhead	2,000	
	Factory Labor		80,000
	(To assign factory labor to production)		
	6.		
28	Work in Process Inventory	62,400	
	Manufacturing Overhead		62,400
	(To assign overhead to jobs— 80% × $78,000)		

action plan

✔ In accumulating costs, debit three accounts: Raw Materials Inventory, Factory Labor, and Manufacturing Overhead.

✔ When Work in Process Inventory is debited, credit one of the three accounts listed above.

✔ Debit Finished Goods Inventory for the cost of completed jobs. Debit Cost of Goods Sold for the cost of jobs sold.

✔ Overhead is underapplied when Manufacturing Overhead has a debit balance.

	7.		
Feb 28	Finished Goods Inventory	120,600	
	Work in Process Inventory		120,600
	(To record completion of Job A16: direct materials $27,000, direct labor $52,000, and manufacturing overhead $41,600)		
	8.		
28	Accounts Receivable	150,000	
	Sales		150,000
	(To record sale of Job A16)		
28	Cost of Goods Sold	120,600	
	Finished Goods Inventory		120,600
	(To record cost of sale for Job A16)		

(b) Manufacturing Overhead has a debit balance of $2,400 as shown below.

Manufacturing Overhead

(3)	59,800	(6)	62,400
(4)	3,000		
(5)	2,000		
Bal.	2,400		

Thus, manufacturing overhead is underapplied for the month.

The Navigator

SUMMARY OF STUDY OBJECTIVES

WILEY PLUS

1 **Explain the characteristics and purposes of cost accounting.** Cost accounting involves the procedures for measuring, recording, and reporting product costs. From the data accumulated, companies determine the total cost and the unit cost of each product. The two basic types of cost accounting systems are job order cost and process cost.

2 **Describe the flow of costs in a job order cost accounting system.** In job order cost accounting, manufacturing costs are first accumulated in three accounts: Raw Materials Inventory, Factory Labor, and Manufacturing Overhead. The accumulated costs are then assigned to Work in Process Inventory and eventually to Finished Goods Inventory and Cost of Goods Sold.

3 **Explain the nature and importance of a job cost sheet.** A job cost sheet is a form used to record the costs chargeable to a specific job and to determine the total and unit costs of the completed job. Job cost sheets constitute the subsidiary ledger for the Work in Process Inventory control account.

4 **Indicate how the predetermined overhead rate is determined and used.** The predetermined overhead rate is based on the relationship between estimated annual overhead costs and expected annual operating activity. This is expressed in terms of a common activity base, such as direct labor cost. The rate is used in assigning overhead costs to work in process and to specific jobs.

5 **Prepare entries for jobs completed and sold.** When jobs are completed, the cost is debited to Finished Goods Inventory and credited to Work in Process Inventory. When a job is sold the entries are: (a) Debit Cash or Accounts Receivable and credit Sales for the selling price. And (b) debit Cost of Goods Sold and credit Finished Goods Inventory for the cost of the goods.

6 **Distinguish between under- and overapplied manufacturing overhead.** Underapplied manufacturing overhead means that the overhead assigned to work in process is less than the overhead incurred. Overapplied overhead means that the overhead assigned to work in process is greater than the overhead incurred.

The Navigator

GLOSSARY

WILEY PLUS

Cost accounting An area of accounting that involves measuring, recording, and reporting product costs. (p. 872)

Cost accounting system Manufacturing cost accounts that are fully integrated into the general ledger of a company. (p. 872)

Job cost sheet A form used to record the costs chargeable to a specific job and to determine the total and unit costs of the completed job. (p. 877)

Job order cost system A cost accounting system in which costs are assigned to each job or batch. (p. 872)

Materials requisition slip A document authorizing the issuance of raw materials from the storeroom to production. (p. 878)

Overapplied overhead A situation in which overhead assigned to work in process is greater than the overhead incurred. (p. 888)

Predetermined overhead rate A rate based on the relationship between estimated annual overhead costs and expected annual operating activity, expressed in terms of a common activity base. (p. 882)

Process cost system A system of accounting used when a large quantity of similar products are manufactured. (p. 873)

Summary entry A journal entry that summarizes the totals from multiple transactions. (p. 877)

Time ticket A document that indicates the employee, the hours worked, the account and job to be charged, and the total labor cost. (p. 880)

Underapplied overhead A situation in which overhead assigned to work in process is less than the overhead incurred. (p. 888)

SELF-STUDY QUESTIONS

WILEY PLUS

Answers are at the end of the chapter.

(SO 1) **1.** Cost accounting involves the measuring, recording, and reporting of:
a. product costs.
b. future costs.
c. manufacturing processes.
d. managerial accounting decisions.

(SO 2) **2.** In accumulating raw materials costs, the cost of raw materials purchased in a perpetual system is debited to:
a. Raw Materials Purchases.
b. Raw Materials Inventory.
c. Purchases.
d. Work in Process.

(SO 2) **3.** When incurred, factory labor costs are debited to:
a. Work in Process.
b. Factory Wages Expense.
c. Factory Labor.
d. Factory Wages Payable.

(SO 3) **4.** The source documents for assigning costs to job cost sheets are:
a. invoices, time tickets, and the predetermined overhead rate.
b. materials requisition slips, time tickets, and the actual overhead costs.
c. materials requisition slips, payroll register, and the predetermined overhead rate.
d. materials requisition slips, time tickets, and the predetermined overhead rate.

(SO 3) **5.** In recording the issuance of raw materials in a job order cost system, it would be *incorrect* to:
a. debit Work in Process Inventory.
b. debit Finished Goods Inventory.
c. debit Manufacturing Overhead.
d. credit Raw Materials Inventory.

(SO 3) **6.** The entry when direct factory labor is assigned to jobs is a debit to:
a. Work in Process Inventory and a credit to Factory Labor.
b. Manufacturing Overhead and a credit to Factory Labor.
c. Factory Labor and a credit to Manufacturing Overhead.
d. Factory Labor and a credit to Work in Process Inventory.

7. The formula for computing the predetermined manufacturing overhead rate is estimated annual overhead costs divided by an expected annual operating activity, expressed as: (SO 4)
a. direct labor cost.
b. direct labor hours.
c. machine hours.
d. any of the above.

8. In Crawford Company, the predetermined overhead rate is 80% of direct labor cost. During the month, $210,000 of factory labor costs are incurred, of which $180,000 is direct labor and $30,000 is indirect labor. Actual overhead incurred was $200,000. The amount of overhead debited to Work in Process Inventory should be: (SO 4)
a. $120,000.
b. $144,000.
c. $168,000.
d. $160,000.

9. In Mynex Company, Job No. 26 is completed at a cost of $4,500 and later sold for $7,000 cash. A correct entry is: (SO 5)
a. Debit Finished Goods Inventory $7,000 and credit Work in Process Inventory $7,000.
b. Debit Cost of Goods Sold $7,000 and credit Finished Goods Inventory $7,000.
c. Debit Finished Goods Inventory $4,500 and credit Work in Process Inventory $4,500.
d. Debit Accounts Receivable $7,000 and credit Sales $7,000.

10. Manufacturing overhead is underapplied if: (SO 6)
a. actual overhead is less than applied.
b. actual overhead is greater than applied.
c. the predetermined rate equals the actual rate.
d. actual overhead equals applied overhead.

Go to the book's website,
www.wiley.com/college/weygandt,
for Additional Self-Study questions.

The Navigator

QUESTIONS

1. (a) Joe Delong is not sure about the difference between cost accounting and a cost accounting system. Explain the difference to Joe. (b) What is an important feature of a cost accounting system?

2. (a) Distinguish between the two types of cost accounting systems. (b) May a company use both types of cost accounting systems?

3. What type of industry is likely to use a job order cost system? Give some examples.
4. What type of industry is likely to use a process cost system? Give some examples.
5. Your roommate asks your help in understanding the major steps in the flow of costs in a job order cost system. Identify the steps for your roommate.
6. There are three inventory control accounts in a job order system. Identify the control accounts and their subsidiary ledgers.
7. What source documents are used in accumulating direct labor costs?
8. "Entries to Manufacturing Overhead normally are only made daily." Do you agree? Explain.
9. Tony Andres is confused about the source documents used in assigning materials and labor costs. Identify the documents and give the entry for each document.
10. What is the purpose of a job cost sheet?
11. Indicate the source documents that are used in charging costs to specific jobs.
12. Differentiate between a "materials inventory record" and a "materials requisition slip" as used in a job order cost system.
13. Mel Finney believes actual manufacturing overhead should be charged to jobs. Do you agree? Why or why not?
14. What relationships are involved in computing a predetermined overhead rate?
15. How can the agreement of Work in Process Inventory and job cost sheets be verified?
16. Tina Birk believes that the cost of goods manufactured schedule in job order cost accounting is the same as shown in Chapter 19. Is Tina correct? Explain.
17. Jeff Gillum is confused about under- and overapplied manufacturing overhead. Define the terms for Jeff, and indicate the balance in the manufacturing overhead account applicable to each term.
18. "At the end of the year, under- or overapplied overhead is closed to Income Summary." Is this correct? If not, indicate the customary treatment of this amount.

BRIEF EXERCISES

WILEY PLUS

Prepare a flowchart of a job order cost accounting system, and identify transactions.
(SO 2)

BE20-1 Reyes Tool & Die begins operations on January 1. Because all work is done to customer specifications, the company decides to use a job order cost accounting system. Prepare a flow chart of a typical job order system with arrows showing the flow of costs. Identify the eight transactions.

Prepare entries in accumulating manufacturing costs.
(SO 2)

BE20-2 During January, its first month of operations, Reyes Tool & Die accumulated the following manufacturing costs: raw materials $4,000 on account, factory labor $5,000 of which $4,200 relates to factory wages payable and $800 relates to payroll taxes payable, and utilities payable $2,000. Prepare separate journal entries for each type of manufacturing cost.

Prepare entry for the assignment of raw materials costs.
(SO 2)

BE20-3 In January, Reyes Tool & Die requisitions raw materials for production as follows: Job 1 $900, Job 2 $1,200, Job 3 $700, and general factory use $600. Prepare a summary journal entry to record raw materials used.

Prepare entry for the assignment of factory labor costs.
(SO 2)

BE20-4 Factory labor data for Reyes Tool & Die is given in BE20-2. During January, time tickets show that the factory labor of $5,000 was used as follows: Job 1 $1,200, Job 2 $1,600 Job 3 $1,400, and general factory use $800. Prepare a summary journal entry to record factory labor used.

Prepare job cost sheets.
(SO 3)

BE20-5 Data pertaining to job cost sheets for Reyes Tool & Die are given in BE20-3 and BE20-4. Prepare the job cost sheets for each of the three jobs. (*Note*: You may omit the column for Manufacturing Overhead.)

Compute predetermined overhead rates.
(SO 4)

BE20-6 Marquis Company estimates that annual manufacturing overhead costs will be $800,000. Estimated annual operating activity bases are: direct labor cost $500,000, direct labor hours 50,000, and machine hours 100,000. Compute the predetermined overhead rate for each activity base.

Assign manufacturing overhead to production.
(SO 4)

BE20-7 During the first quarter, Diaz Company incurs the following direct labor costs: January $40,000, February $30,000, and March $50,000. For each month, prepare the entry to assign overhead to production using a predetermined rate of 90% of direct labor cost.

Prepare entries for completion and sale of completed jobs.
(SO 5)

BE20-8 In March, Hollaway Company completes Jobs 10 and 11. Job 10 cost $25,000 and Job 11 $30,000. On March 31, Job 10 is sold to the customer for $35,000 in cash. Journalize the entries for the completion of the two jobs and the sale of Job 10.

Prepare adjusting entries for under- and overapplied overhead.
(SO 6)

BE20-9 At December 31, balances in Manufacturing Overhead are: Lott Company—debit $1,500, Perez Company—credit $900. Prepare the adjusting entry for each company at December 31, assuming the adjustment is made to cost of goods sold.

EXERCISES

WILEY PLUS

E20-1 The gross earnings of the factory workers for Brantley Company during the month of January are $60,000. The employer's payroll taxes for the factory payroll are $8,000. The fringe benefits to be paid by the employer on this payroll are $4,000. Of the total accumulated cost of factory labor, 85% is related to direct labor and 15% is attributable to indirect labor.

Prepare entries for factory labor.

(SO 2, 3)

Instructions

(a) Prepare the entry to record the factory labor costs for the month of January.
(b) Prepare the entry to assign factory labor to production.

E20-2 Milner Manufacturing uses a job order cost accounting system. On May 1, the company has a balance in Work in Process Inventory of $3,200 and two jobs in process: Job No. 429 $2,000, and Job No. 430 $1,200. During May, a summary of source documents reveals the following.

Prepare journal entries for manufacturing costs.

(SO 2, 3, 4, 5)

Job Number	Materials Requisition Slips		Labor Time Tickets	
429	$2,500		$1,900	
430	3,500		3,000	
431	4,400	$10,400	7,600	$12,500
General use		800		1,200
		$11,200		$13,700

Milner Manufacturing applies manufacturing overhead to jobs at an overhead rate of 80% of direct labor cost. Job No. 429 is completed during the month.

Instructions

(a) Prepare summary journal entries to record: (i) the requisition slips, (ii) the time tickets, (iii) the assignment of manufacturing overhead to jobs, and (iv) the completion of Job No. 429.
(b) Post the entries to Work in Process Inventory, and prove the agreement of the control account with the job cost sheets.

E20-3 A job order cost sheet for Rolen Company is shown below.

Analyze a job cost sheet and prepare entries for manufacturing costs.

(SO 2, 3, 4, 5)

Job No. 92			For 2,000 Units
Date	Direct Materials	Direct Labor	Manufacturing Overhead
Beg. bal. Jan. 1	5,000	6,000	4,500
8	6,000		
12		8,000	6,400
25	2,000		
27		4,000	3,200
	13,000	18,000	14,100
Cost of completed job:			
Direct materials			$13,000
Direct labor			18,000
Manufacturing overhead			14,100
Total cost			$45,100
Unit cost ($45,100 ÷ 2,000)			$22.55

Instructions

(a) On the basis of the foregoing data answer the following questions.
  (1) What was the balance in Work in Process Inventory on January 1 if this was the only unfinished job?
  (2) If manufacturing overhead is applied on the basis of direct labor cost, what overhead rate was used in each year?
(b) Prepare summary entries at January 31 to record the current year's transactions pertaining to Job No. 92.

Analyze costs of manufacturing and determine missing amounts.

(SO 2, 5)

E20-4 Manufacturing cost data for Pena Company, which uses a job order cost system, are presented below.

	Case A	Case B	Case C
Direct materials used	$ (a)	$ 83,000	$ 63,150
Direct labor	50,000	120,000	(h)
Manufacturing overhead applied	42,500	(d)	(i)
Total manufacturing costs	155,650	(e)	213,000
Work in process 1/1/08	(b)	15,500	18,000
Total cost of work in process	201,500	(f)	(j)
Work in process 12/31/08	(c)	11,800	(k)
Cost of goods manufactured	192,300	(g)	222,000

Instructions

Indicate the missing amount for each letter. Assume that in all cases manufacturing overhead is applied on the basis of direct labor cost and the rate is the same.

Compute the manufacturing overhead rate and under- or overapplied overhead.

(SO 4, 6)

E20-5 Renteria Company applies manufacturing overhead to jobs on the basis of machine hours used. Overhead costs are expected to total $305,000 for the year, and machine usage is estimated at 125,000 hours.

For the year, $322,000 of overhead costs are incurred and 130,000 hours are used.

Instructions

(a) Compute the manufacturing overhead rate for the year.
(b) What is the amount of under- or overapplied overhead at December 31?
(c) Assuming the under- or overapplied overhead for the year is not allocated to inventory accounts, prepare the adjusting entry to assign the amount to cost of goods sold.

Analyze job cost sheet and prepare entry for completed job.

(SO 2, 3, 4, 5)

E20-6 A job cost sheet of Nilson Company is given below.

Job Cost Sheet

JOB NO. 469 Quantity 2,000
ITEM White Lion Cages Date Requested 7/2
FOR Tesla Company Date Completed 7/31

Date	Direct Materials	Direct Labor	Manufacturing Overhead
7/10	825		
12	900		
15		440	550
22		380	475
24	1,600		
27	1,500		
31		540	675

Cost of completed job:
Direct materials ______
Direct labor ______
Manufacturing overhead ______
Total cost ______
Unit cost ______

Instructions

(a) Answer the following questions.
(1) What are the source documents for direct materials, direct labor, and manufacturing overhead costs assigned to this job?
(2) What is the predetermined manufacturing overhead rate?
(3) What are the total cost and the unit cost of the completed job?
(b) Prepare the entry to record the completion of the job.

E20-7 Elder Corporation incurred the following transactions.

Prepare entries for manufacturing costs.
(SO 2, 3, 4, 5)

1. Purchased raw materials on account $46,300.
2. Raw Materials of $36,000 were requisitioned to the factory. An analysis of the materials requisition slips indicated that $6,800 was classified as indirect materials.
3. Factory labor costs incurred were $53,900, of which $49,000 pertained to factory wages payable and $4,900 pertained to employer payroll taxes payable.
4. Time tickets indicated that $48,000 was direct labor and $5,900 was indirect labor.
5. Overhead costs incurred on account were $80,500.
6. Manufacturing overhead was applied at the rate of 150% of direct labor cost.
7. Goods costing $88,000 were completed and transferred to finished goods.
8. Finished goods costing $75,000 to manufacture were sold on account for $103,000.

Instructions
Journalize the transactions. (Omit explanations.)

E20-8 Garnett Printing Corp. uses a job order cost system. The following data summarize the operations related to the first quarter's production.

Prepare entries for manufacturing costs.
(SO 2, 3, 4, 5)

1. Materials purchased on account $192,000, and factory wages incurred $87,300.
2. Materials requisitioned and factory labor used by job:

Job Number	Materials	Factory Labor
A20	$ 35,240	$18,000
A21	42,920	22,000
A22	36,100	15,000
A23	39,270	25,000
General factory use	4,470	7,300
	$158,000	$87,300

3. Manufacturing overhead costs incurred on account $39,500.
4. Depreciation on machinery and equipment $14,550.
5. Manufacturing overhead rate is 80% of direct labor cost.
6. Jobs completed during the quarter: A20, A21, and A23.

Instructions
Prepare entries to record the operations summarized above. (Prepare a schedule showing the individual cost elements and total cost for each job in item 6.)

E20-9 At May 31, 2008, the accounts of Hannifan Manufacturing Company show the following.

Prepare a cost of goods manufactured schedule and partial financial statements.
(SO 2, 5)

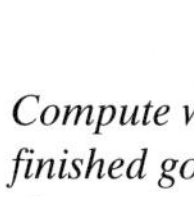

1. May 1 inventories—finished goods $12,600, work in process $14,700, and raw materials $8,200.
2. May 31 inventories—finished goods $9,500, work in process $17,900, and raw materials $7,100.
3. Debit postings to work in process were: direct materials $62,400, direct labor $32,000, and manufacturing overhead applied $40,000.
4. Sales totaled $200,000.

Instructions
(a) Prepare a condensed cost of goods manufactured schedule.
(b) Prepare an income statement for May through gross profit.
(c) Indicate the balance sheet presentation of the manufacturing inventories at May 31, 2008.

E20-10 Tomlin Company begins operations on April 1. Information from job cost sheets shows the following.

Compute work in process and finished goods from job cost sheets.
(SO 3, 5)

	Manufacturing Costs Assigned			
Job Number	April	May	June	Month Completed
10	$5,200	$4,400		May
11	4,100	3,900	$3,000	June
12	1,200			April
13		4,700	4,500	June
14		4,900	3,600	Not complete

Job 12 was completed in April. Job 10 was completed in May. Jobs 11 and 13 were completed in June. Each job was sold for 25% above its cost in the month following completion.

Instructions

(a) What is the balance in Work in Process Inventory at the end of each month?
(b) What is the balance in Finished Goods Inventory at the end of each month?
(c) What is the gross profit for May, June, and July?

Prepare entries for costs of services provided.
(SO 2, 4, 5)

E20-11 Shown below are the job cost related accounts for the law firm of Barnes, King, and Morton and their manufacturing equivalents:

Law Firm Accounts	Manufacturing Firm Accounts
Supplies	Raw Materials
Salaries Payable	Factory Wages Payable
Operating Overhead	Manufacturing Overhead
Work in Process	Work in Process
Cost of Completed Work	Cost of Goods Sold

Cost data for the month of March follow.

1. Purchased supplies on account $1,500.
2. Issued supplies $1,200 (60% direct and 40% indirect).
3. Time cards for the month indicated labor costs of $50,000 (80% direct and 20% indirect).
4. Operating overhead costs incurred for cash totaled $40,000.
5. Operating overhead is applied at a rate of 90% of direct attorney cost.
6. Work completed totaled $70,000.

Instructions

(a) Journalize the transactions for March. Omit explanations.
(b) Determine the balance of the Work in Process account. Use a T account.

Determine cost of jobs and ending balance in work in process and overhead accounts.
(SO 3, 4, 6)

E20-12 Pedro Morales and Associates, a C.P.A. firm, uses job order costing to capture the costs of its audit jobs. There were no audit jobs in process at the beginning of November. Listed below are data concerning the three audit jobs conducted during November.

	Gonzalez	Navarro	Rojas
Direct materials	$600	$400	$200
Auditor labor costs	$5,400	$6,600	$3,375
Auditor hours	72	88	45

Overhead costs are applied to jobs on the basis of auditor hours, and the predetermined overhead rate is $55 per auditor hour. The Gonzalez job is the only incomplete job at the end of November. Actual overhead for the month was $12,000.

Instructions

(a) Determine the cost of each job.
(b) Indicate the balance of the Work in Process account at the end of November.
(c) Calculate the ending balance of the Manufacturing Overhead account for November.

Determine predetermined overhead rate, apply overhead and determine whether balance under- or overapplied.
(SO 4, 6)

E20-13 Easy Decorating uses a job order costing system to collect the costs of its interior decorating business. Each client's consultation is treated as a separate job. Overhead is applied to each job based on the number of decorator hours incurred. Listed below are data for the current year.

Budgeted overhead	$960,000
Actual overhead	$982,800
Budgeted decorator hours	40,000
Actual decorator hours	40,500

The company uses Operating Overhead in place of Manufacturing Overhead.

Instructions

(a) Compute the predetermined overhead rate.
(b) Prepare the entry to apply the overhead for the year.
(c) Determine whether the overhead was under- or overapplied and by how much.

EXERCISES: SET B

Visit the book's website at **www.wiley.com/college/weygandt**, and choose the Student Companion site, to access Exercise Set B.

PROBLEMS: SET A

Prepare entries in a job cost system and job cost sheets.

(SO 2, 3, 4, 5, 6)

P20-1A Garcia Manufacturing uses a job order cost system and applies overhead to production on the basis of direct labor costs. On January 1, 2008, Job No. 50 was the only job in process. The costs incurred prior to January 1 on this job were as follows: direct materials $20,000, direct labor $12,000, and manufacturing overhead $16,000. As of January 1, Job No. 49 had been completed at a cost of $90,000 and was part of finished goods inventory. There was a $15,000 balance in the Raw Materials Inventory account.

During the month of January, Garcia Manufacturing began production on Jobs 51 and 52, and completed Jobs 50 and 51. Jobs 49 and 50 were also sold on account during the month for $122,000 and $158,000, respectively. The following additional events occurred during the month.

1. Purchased additional raw materials of $90,000 on account.
2. Incurred factory labor costs of $65,000. Of this amount $16,000 related to employer payroll taxes.
3. Incurred manufacturing overhead costs as follows: indirect materials $17,000; indirect labor $15,000; depreciation expense $19,000, and various other manufacturing overhead costs on account $20,000.
4. Assigned direct materials and direct labor to jobs as follows.

Job No.	Direct Materials	Direct Labor
50	$10,000	$ 5,000
51	39,000	25,000
52	30,000	20,000

Instructions

(a) Calculate the predetermined overhead rate for 2008, assuming Garcia Manufacturing estimates total manufacturing overhead costs of $1,050,000, direct labor costs of $700,000, and direct labor hours of 20,000 for the year.

(b) Open job cost sheets for Jobs 50, 51, and 52. Enter the January 1 balances on the job cost sheet for Job No. 50.

(c) Prepare the journal entries to record the purchase of raw materials, the factory labor costs incurred, and the manufacturing overhead costs incurred during the month of January.

(d) Prepare the journal entries to record the assignment of direct materials, direct labor, and manufacturing overhead costs to production. In assigning manufacturing overhead costs, use the overhead rate calculated in (a). Post all costs to the job cost sheets as necessary.

*The check figures you see next to **Problems** are also shown in the student's text.*

(e) Total the job cost sheets for any job(s) completed during the month. Prepare the journal entry (or entries) to record the completion of any job(s) during the month.

(e) Job 50, $70,500
Job 51, $101,500

(f) Prepare the journal entry (or entries) to record the sale of any job(s) during the month.

(g) What is the balance in the Finished Goods Inventory account at the end of the month? What does this balance consist of?

(h) What is the amount of over- or underapplied overhead?

Prepare entries in a job cost system and partial income statement.

(SO 2, 3, 4, 5, 6)

P20-2A For the year ended December 31, 2008, the job cost sheets of DeVoe Company contained the following data.

Job Number	Explanation	Direct Materials	Direct Labor	Manufacturing Overhead	Total Costs
7640	Balance 1/1	$25,000	$24,000	$28,800	$ 77,800
	Current year's costs	30,000	36,000	43,200	109,200
7641	Balance 1/1	11,000	18,000	21,600	50,600
	Current year's costs	43,000	48,000	57,600	148,600
7642	Current year's costs	48,000	55,000	66,000	169,000

Other data:

1. Raw materials inventory totaled $15,000 on January 1. During the year, $140,000 of raw materials were purchased on account.
2. Finished goods on January 1 consisted of Job No. 7638 for $87,000 and Job No. 7639 for $92,000.
3. Job No. 7640 and Job No. 7641 were completed during the year.
4. Job Nos. 7638, 7639, and 7641 were sold on account for $530,000.
5. Manufacturing overhead incurred on account totaled $120,000.
6. Other manufacturing overhead consisted of indirect materials $14,000, indirect labor $20,000, and depreciation on factory machinery $8,000.

Instructions

(a) $169,000; Job 7642: $169,000

(a) Prove the agreement of Work in Process Inventory with job cost sheets pertaining to unfinished work. *Hint:* Use a single T account for Work in Process Inventory. Calculate each of the following, then post each to the T account: (1) beginning balance, (2) direct materials, (3) direct labor, (4) manufacturing overhead, and (5) completed jobs.

(b) Amount = $4,800

(b) Prepare the adjusting entry for manufacturing overhead, assuming the balance is allocated entirely to Cost of Goods Sold.

(c) $156,600

(c) Determine the gross profit to be reported for 2008.

Prepare entries in a job cost system and cost of goods manufactured schedule.

(SO 2, 3, 4, 5)

P20-3A Enos Inc. is a construction company specializing in custom patios. The patios are constructed of concrete, brick, fiberglass, and lumber, depending upon customer preference. On June 1, 2008, the general ledger for Enos Inc. contains the following data.

Raw Materials Inventory	$4,200	Manufacturing Overhead Applied	$32,640
Work in Process Inventory	$5,540	Manufacturing Overhead Incurred	$31,650

Subsidiary data for Work in Process Inventory on June 1 are as follows.

Job Cost Sheets

	Customer Job		
Cost Element	**Fowler**	**Haines**	**Krantz**
Direct materials	$ 600	$ 800	$ 900
Direct labor	320	540	580
Manufacturing overhead	400	675	725
	$1,320	$2,015	$2,205

During June, raw materials purchased on account were $3,900, and all wages were paid. Additional overhead costs consisted of depreciation on equipment $700 and miscellaneous costs of $400 incurred on account.

A summary of materials requisition slips and time tickets for June shows the following.

Customer Job	Materials Requisition Slips	Time Tickets
Fowler	$ 800	$ 450
Elgin	2,000	800
Haines	500	360
Krantz	1,300	1,600
Fowler	300	390
	4,900	3,600
General use	1,500	1,200
	$6,400	$4,800

Overhead was charged to jobs at the same rate of $1.25 per dollar of direct labor cost. The patios for customers Fowler, Haines, and Krantz were completed during June and sold for a total of $18,900. Each customer paid in full.

Instructions

(a) Journalize the June transactions: (i) for purchase of raw materials, factory labor costs incurred, and manufacturing overhead costs incurred; (ii) assignment of direct materials, labor, and overhead to production; and (iii) completion of jobs and sale of goods.

(b) Post the entries to Work in Process Inventory.

(c) Reconcile the balance in Work in Process Inventory with the costs of unfinished jobs.
(d) Prepare a cost of goods manufactured schedule for June.

(d) Cost of goods manufactured $14,740

Compute predetermined overhead rates, apply overhead and calculate under- or overapplied overhead.

(SO 4, 6)

P20-4A Mabry Manufacturing Company uses a job order cost system in each of its three manufacturing departments. Manufacturing overhead is applied to jobs on the basis of direct labor cost in Department D, direct labor hours in Department E, and machine hours in Department K.

In establishing the predetermined overhead rates for 2008 the following estimates were made for the year.

	Department		
	D	E	K
Manufacturing overhead	$1,050,000	$1,500,000	$840,000
Direct labor costs	$1,500,000	$1,250,000	$450,000
Direct labor hours	100,000	125,000	40,000
Machine hours	400,000	500,000	120,000

During January, the job cost sheets showed the following costs and production data.

	Department		
	D	E	K
Direct materials used	$140,000	$126,000	$78,000
Direct labor costs	$120,000	$110,000	$37,500
Manufacturing overhead incurred	$ 89,000	$124,000	$74,000
Direct labor hours	8,000	11,000	3,500
Machine hours	34,000	45,000	10,400

Instructions

(a) Compute the predetermined overhead rate for each department.
(b) Compute the total manufacturing costs assigned to jobs in January in each department.
(c) Compute the under- or overapplied overhead for each department at January 31.

(a) 70%, $12, $7.00
(b) $344,000, $368,000 $188,300
(c) $5,000, $(8,000), $1,200

Analyze manufacturing accounts and determine missing amounts.

(SO 2, 3, 4, 5, 6)

P20-5A Vargas Corporation's fiscal year ends on November 30. The following accounts are found in its job order cost accounting system for the first month of the new fiscal year.

Raw Materials Inventory

Dec. 1	Beginning balance	(a)	Dec. 31	Requisitions	18,850
31	Purchases	19,225			
Dec. 31	Ending balance	7,975			

Work in Process Inventory

Dec. 1	Beginning balance	(b)	Dec. 31	Jobs completed	(f)
31	Direct materials	(c)			
31	Direct labor	8,800			
31	Overhead	(d)			
Dec. 31	Ending balance	(e)			

Finished Goods Inventory

Dec. 1	Beginning balance	(g)	Dec. 31	Cost of goods sold	(i)
31	Completed jobs	(h)			
Dec. 31	Ending balance	(j)			

Factory Labor

Dec. 31	Factory wages	12,465	Dec. 31	Wages assigned	(k)

Manufacturing Overhead

Dec. 31	Indirect materials	1,900	Dec. 31	Overhead applied	(m)
31	Indirect labor	(l)			
31	Other overhead	1,245			

Other data:

1. On December 1, two jobs were in process: Job No. 154 and Job No. 155. These jobs had combined direct materials costs of $9,750 and direct labor costs of $15,000. Overhead was applied at a rate that was 80% of direct labor cost.
2. During December, Job Nos. 156, 157, and 158 were started. On December 31, Job No. 158 was unfinished. This job had charges for direct materials $3,800 and direct labor $4,800, plus manufacturing overhead. All jobs, except for Job No. 158, were completed in December.
3. On December 1, Job No. 153 was in the finished goods warehouse. It had a total cost of $5,000. On December 31, Job No. 157 was the only job finished that was not sold. It had a cost of $4,000.
4. Manufacturing overhead was $230 overapplied in December.

(c) $16,950
(f) $57,100
(i) $58,100

Instructions

List the letters (a) through (m) and indicate the amount pertaining to each letter.

PROBLEMS: SET B

Prepare entries in a job cost system and job cost sheets.

(SO 2, 3, 4, 5, 6)

P20-1B Lowry Manufacturing uses a job order cost system and applies overhead to production on the basis of direct labor hours. On January 1, 2008, Job No. 25 was the only job in process. The costs incurred prior to January 1 on this job were as follows: direct materials $10,000; direct labor $6,000; and manufacturing overhead $9,000. Job No. 23 had been completed at a cost of $45,000 and was part of finished goods inventory. There was a $5,000 balance in the Raw Materials Inventory account.

During the month of January, the company began production on Jobs 26 and 27, and completed Jobs 25 and 26. Jobs 23 and 25 were sold on account during the month for $67,000 and $74,000, respectively. The following additional events occurred during the month.

1. Purchased additional raw materials of $45,000 on account.
2. Incurred factory labor costs of $31,500. Of this amount $7,500 related to employer payroll taxes.
3. Incurred manufacturing overhead costs as follows: indirect materials $10,000; indirect labor $7,500; depreciation expense $12,000; and various other manufacturing overhead costs on account $8,000.
4. Assigned direct materials and direct labor to jobs as follows.

Job No.	Direct Materials	Direct Labor
25	$ 5,000	$ 3,000
26	20,000	12,000
27	15,000	9,000

5. The company uses direct labor hours as the activity base to assign overhead. Direct labor hours incurred on each job were as follows: Job No. 25, 200; Job No. 26, 800; and Job No. 27, 600.

Instructions

(a) Calculate the predetermined overhead rate for the year 2008, assuming Lowry Manufacturing estimates total manufacturing overhead costs of $440,000, direct labor costs of $300,000, and direct labor hours of 20,000 for the year.

(b) Open job cost sheets for Jobs 25, 26, and 27. Enter the January 1 balances on the job cost sheet for Job No. 25.

(c) Prepare the journal entries to record the purchase of raw materials, the factory labor costs incurred, and the manufacturing overhead costs incurred during the month of January.

(d) Prepare the journal entries to record the assignment of direct materials, direct labor, and manufacturing overhead costs to production. In assigning manufacturing overhead costs, use the overhead rate calculated in (a). Post all costs to the job cost sheets as necessary.

(e) Job 25, $37,400
Job 26, $49,600

(e) Total the job cost sheets for any job(s) completed during the month. Prepare the journal entry (or entries) to record the completion of any job(s) during the month.

(f) Prepare the journal entry (or entries) to record the sale of any job(s) during the month.

(g) What is the balance in the Work in Process Inventory account at the end of the month? What does this balance consist of?

(h) What is the amount of over- or underapplied overhead?

P20-2B For the year ended December 31, 2008, the job cost sheets of Mazzone Company contained the following data.

Prepare entries in a job cost system and partial income statement.

(SO 2, 3, 4, 5, 6)

Job Number	Explanation	Direct Materials	Direct Labor	Manufacturing Overhead	Total Costs
7650	Balance 1/1	$18,000	$20,000	$25,000	$ 63,000
	Current year's costs	32,000	30,000	37,500	99,500
7651	Balance 1/1	12,000	18,000	22,500	52,500
	Current year's costs	28,000	40,000	50,000	118,000
7652	Current year's costs	40,000	68,000	85,000	193,000

Other data:

1. Raw materials inventory totaled $20,000 on January 1. During the year, $100,000 of raw materials were purchased on account.
2. Finished goods on January 1 consisted of Job No. 7648 for $98,000 and Job No. 7649 for $62,000.
3. Job No. 7650 and Job No. 7651 were completed during the year.
4. Job Nos. 7648, 7649, and 7650 were sold on account for $490,000.
5. Manufacturing overhead incurred on account totaled $126,000.
6. Other manufacturing overhead consisted of indirect materials $12,000, indirect labor $18,000 and depreciation on factory machinery $19,500.

Instructions

(a) Prove the agreement of Work in Process Inventory with job cost sheets pertaining to unfinished work. (*Hint*: Use a single T account for Work in Process Inventory.) Calculate each of the following, then post each to the T account: (1) beginning balance, (2) direct materials, (3) direct labor, (4) manufacturing overhead, and (5) completed jobs.

(a) (1) $115,500
(4) $172,500
Unfinished job 7652, $193,000

(b) Prepare the adjusting entry for manufacturing overhead, assuming the balance is allocated entirely to cost of goods sold.

(b) Amount = $3,000

(c) Determine the gross profit to be reported for 2008.

(c) $164,500

P20-3B Chris Duncan is a contractor specializing in custom-built jacuzzis. On May 1, 2008, his ledger contains the following data.

Prepare entries in a job cost system and cost of goods manufactured schedule.

(SO 2, 3, 4, 5)

Raw Materials Inventory	$30,000
Work in Process Inventory	12,400
Manufacturing Overhead	2,500 (dr.)

The Manufacturing Overhead account has debit totals of $12,500 and credit totals of $10,000. Subsidiary data for Work in Process Inventory on May 1 include:

Job Cost Sheets

Job by Customer	Direct Materials	Direct Labor	Manufacturing Overhead
Looper	$2,500	$2,000	$1,500
Carpenter	2,000	1,200	900
Ingle	900	800	600
	$5,400	$4,000	$3,000

During May, the following costs were incurred: (a) raw materials purchased on account $5,000, (b) labor paid $7,600, (c) manufacturing overhead paid $1,400.

A summary of materials requisition slips and time tickets for the month of May reveals the following.

Job by Customer	Materials Requisition Slips	Time Tickets
Looper	$ 500	$ 400
Carpenter	600	1,000
Ingle	2,300	1,300
Bennett	2,400	2,900
	5,800	5,600
General use	1,500	2,000
	$7,300	$7,600

Overhead was charged to jobs on the basis of $0.75 per dollar of direct labor cost.

The jacuzzis for customers Looper, Carpenter, and Ingle were completed during May. Each jacuzzi was sold for $12,500 cash.

Instructions

(a) Prepare journal entries for the May transactions: (i) for purchase of raw materials, factory labor costs incurred, and manufacturing overhead costs incurred; (ii) assignment of direct materials, labor, and overhead to production; and (iii) completion of jobs and sale of goods.

(b) Post the entries to Work in Process Inventory.

(c) Reconcile the balance in Work in Process Inventory with the costs of unfinished jobs.

(d) Prepare a cost of goods manufactured schedule for May.

(d) Cost of goods manufactured $20,525.

Compute predetermined overhead rates, apply overhead, and calculate under- or overapplied overhead.

(SO 4, 6)

P20-4B Eckstein Manufacturing uses a job order cost system in each of its three manufacturing departments. Manufacturing overhead is applied to jobs on the basis of direct labor cost in Department A, direct labor hours in Department B, and machine hours in Department C.

In establishing the predetermined overhead rates for 2008 the following estimates were made for the year.

	Department		
	A	B	C
Manufacturing overhead	$900,000	$800,000	$750,000
Direct labor cost	$600,000	$100,000	$600,000
Direct labor hours	50,000	40,000	40,000
Machine hours	100,000	120,000	125,000

During January, the job cost sheets showed the following costs and production data.

	Department		
	A	B	C
Direct materials used	$92,000	$86,000	$64,000
Direct labor cost	$48,000	$35,000	$50,400
Manufacturing overhead incurred	$76,000	$75,000	$72,100
Direct labor hours	4,000	3,500	4,200
Machine hours	8,000	10,500	12,600

(a) 150%, $20, $6
(b) $212,000, $191,000 $190,000
(c) $4,000, $5,000, $(3,500)

Instructions

(a) Compute the predetermined overhead rate for each department.

(b) Compute the total manufacturing costs assigned to jobs in January in each department.

(c) Compute the under- or overapplied overhead for each department at January 31.

Analyze manufacturing accounts and determine missing amounts.

(SO 2, 3, 4, 5, 6)

P20-5B Spivey Company's fiscal year ends on June 30. The following accounts are found in its job order cost accounting system for the first month of the new fiscal year.

Raw Materials Inventory

July 1	Beginning balance	19,000	July 31	Requisitions	(a)
31	Purchases	90,400			
July 31	Ending balance	(b)			

Work in Process Inventory

July 1	Beginning balance	(c)	July 31	Jobs completed	(f)
31	Direct materials	70,000			
31	Direct labor	(d)			
31	Overhead	(e)			
July 31	Ending balance	(g)			

Finished Goods Inventory

July 1	Beginning balance	(h)	July 31	Cost of goods sold	(j)
31	Completed jobs	(i)			
July 31	Ending balance	(k)			

Factory Labor

July 31	Factory wages	(l)	July 31	Wages assigned	(m)

Manufacturing Overhead

July 31	Indirect materials	8,900	July 31	Overhead applied	104,000
31	Indirect labor	16,000			
31	Other overhead	(n)			

Other data:

1. On July 1, two jobs were in process: Job No. 4085 and Job No. 4086, with costs of $19,000 and $8,200, respectively.
2. During July, Job Nos. 4087, 4088, and 4089 were started. On July 31, only Job No. 4089 was unfinished. This job had charges for direct materials $2,000 and direct labor $1,500, plus manufacturing overhead. Manufacturing overhead was applied at the rate of 130% of direct labor cost.
3. On July 1, Job No. 4084, costing $135,000, was in the finished goods warehouse. On July 31, Job No. 4088, costing $143,000, was in finished goods.
4. Overhead was $3,000 underapplied in July.

(d) $ 80,000
(f) $275,750
(l) $ 96,000

Instructions

List the letters (a) through (n) and indicate the amount pertaining to each letter. Show computations.

PROBLEMS: SET C

Visit the book's website at **www.wiley.com/college/weygandt**, and choose the Student Companion site, to access Problem Set C.

BROADENING YOUR PERSPECTIVE

DECISION MAKING ACROSS THE ORGANIZATION

BYP20-1 Pine Products Company uses a job order cost system. For a number of months there has been an ongoing rift between the sales department and the production department concerning a special-order product, TC-1. TC-1 is a seasonal product that is manufactured in batches of 1,000 units. TC-1 is sold at cost plus a markup of 40% of cost.

The sales department is unhappy because fluctuating unit production costs significantly affect selling prices. Sales personnel complain that this has caused excessive customer complaints and the loss of considerable orders for TC-1.

The production department maintains that each job order must be fully costed on the basis of the costs incurred during the period in which the goods are produced. Production personnel maintain that the only real solution to the problem is for the sales department to increase sales in the slack periods.

Regina Newell, president of the company, asks you as the company accountant to collect quarterly data for the past year on TC-1. From the cost accounting system, you accumulate the following production quantity and cost data.

	Quarter			
Costs	**1**	**2**	**3**	**4**
Direct materials	$100,000	$220,000	$ 80,000	$200,000
Direct labor	60,000	132,000	48,000	120,000
Manufacturing overhead	105,000	123,000	97,000	125,000
Total	$265,000	$475,000	$225,000	$445,000
Production in batches	5	11	4	10
Unit cost (per batch)	$ 53,000	$ 43,182	$ 56,250	$ 44,500

Instructions

With the class divided into groups, answer the following questions.

(a) What manufacturing cost element is responsible for the fluctuating unit costs? Why?
(b) What is your recommended solution to the problem of fluctuating unit cost?
(c) Restate the quarterly data on the basis of your recommended solution.

MANAGERIAL ANALYSIS

BYP20-2 In the course of routine checking of all journal entries prior to preparing year-end reports, Diane Riser discovered several strange entries. She recalled that the president's son Ron had come in to help out during an especially busy time and that he had recorded some journal entries. She was relieved that there were only a few of his entries, and even more relieved that he had included rather lengthy explanations. The entries Ron made were:

1.

Work in Process Inventory	25,000	
Cash		25,000

(This is for materials put into process. I don't find the record that we paid for these, so I'm crediting Cash, because I know we'll have to pay for them sooner or later.)

2.

Manufacturing Overhead	12,000	
Cash		12,000

(This is for bonuses paid to salespeople. I know they're part of overhead, and I can't find an account called "Non-factory Overhead" or "Other Overhead" so I'm putting it in Manufacturing Overhead. I have the check stubs, so I know we paid these.)

3.

Wages Expense	120,000	
Cash		120,000

(This is for the factory workers' wages. I have a note that payroll taxes are $15,000. I still think that's part of wages expense, and that we'll have to pay it all in cash sooner or later, so I credited Cash for the wages and the taxes.)

4.

Work in Process Inventory	3,000	
Raw Materials Inventory		3,000

(This is for the glue used in the factory. I know we used this to make the products, even though we didn't use very much on any one of the products. I got it out of inventory, so I credited an inventory account.)

Instructions

(a) How should Ron have recorded each of the four events?

(b) If the entry was not corrected, which financial statements (income statement or balance sheet) would be affected? What balances would be overstated or understated?

REAL-WORLD FOCUS

BYP20-3 Founded in 1970, Parlex Corporation is a world leader in the design and manufacture of flexible interconnect products. Utilizing proprietary and patented technologies, Parlex produces custom flexible interconnects including flexible circuits, polymer thick film, laminated cables, and value-added assemblies for sophisticated electronics used in automotive, telecommunications, computer, diversified electronics, and aerospace applications. In addition to manufacturing sites in Methuen, Massachusetts; Salem, New Hampshire; Cranston, Rhode Island; San Jose, California; Shanghai, China; Isle of Wight, UK; and Empalme, Mexico, Parlex has logistic support centers and strategic alliances throughout North America, Asia, and Europe.

The following information was provided in the company's annual report.

PARLEX COMPANY
Notes to the Financial Statements

The Company's products are manufactured on a job order basis to customers' specifications. Customers submit requests for quotations on each job, and the Company prepares bids based on its own cost estimates. The Company attempts to reflect the impact of changing costs when establishing prices. However, during the past several years, the market conditions for flexible circuits and the resulting price sensitivity haven't always allowed this to transpire. Although still not satisfactory, the Company was able to reduce the cost of products sold as a percentage of sales to 85% this year versus 87% that was experienced in the two immediately preceding years. Management continues to focus on improving operational efficiency and further reducing costs.

Instructions

(a) Parlex management discusses the job order cost system employed by their company. What are several advantages of using the job order approach to costing?

(b) Contrast the products produced in a job order environment, like Parlex, to those produced when process cost systems are used.

EXPLORING THE WEB

BYP20-4 The Institute of Management Accountants sponsors a certification for management accountants, allowing them to obtain the title of Certified Management Accountant.

Address: www.imanet.org, or go to **www.wiley.com/college/weygandt**

Steps

1. Go to the site shown above.
2. Choose **Certification**, and then, **Getting Started**.

Instructions

(a) What is the experience qualification requirement?

(b) How many hours of continuing education are required, and what types of courses qualify?

COMMUNICATION ACTIVITY

BYP20-5 You are the management accountant for Newberry Manufacturing. Your company does custom carpentry work and uses a job order cost accounting system. Newberry sends detailed job cost sheets to its customers, along with an invoice. The job cost sheets show the date materials were used, the dollar cost of materials, and the hours and cost of labor. A predetermined overhead application rate is used, and the total overhead applied is also listed.

Donna Werly is a customer who recently had custom cabinets installed. Along with her check in payment for the work done, she included a letter. She thanked the company for including the detailed cost information but questioned why overhead was estimated. She stated that she would be interested in knowing exactly what costs were included in overhead, and she thought that other customers would, too.

Instructions

Prepare a letter to Ms. Werly (address: 123 Cedar Lane, Altoona, Kansas 66651) and tell her why you did not send her information on exact costs of overhead included in her job. Respond to her suggestion that you provide this information.

ETHICS CASE

BYP20-6 SEK Printing provides printing services to many different corporate clients. Although SEK bids most jobs, some jobs, particularly new ones, are negotiated on a "cost-plus" basis. Cost-plus means that the buyer is willing to pay the actual cost plus a return (profit) on these costs to SEK.

Betty Keiser, controller for SEK, has recently returned from a meeting where SEK's president stated that he wanted her to find a way to charge most costs to any project that was on a cost-plus basis. The president noted that the company needed more profits to meet its stated goals this period. By charging more costs to the cost-plus projects and therefore fewer costs to the jobs that were bid, the company should be able to increase its profit for the current year.

Betty knew why the president wanted to take this action. Rumors were that he was looking for a new position and if the company reported strong profit, the president's opportunities would be enhanced. Betty also recognized that she could probably increase the cost of certain jobs by changing the basis used to allocate manufacturing overhead.

Instructions

(a) Who are the stakeholders in this situation?
(b) What are the ethical issues in this situation?
(c) What would you do if you were Betty Keiser?

"ALL ABOUT YOU" ACTIVITY

*

BYP20-7 Many of you will work for a small business. As noted in the ***All About You:* Minding Your Own Business** feature in this chapter, some of you will even own your own business. In order to operate a small business you will need a good understanding of managerial accounting, as well as many other skills. Much information is available to assist people who are interested in starting a new business. A great place to start is the website provided by the Small Business Administration which is an agency of the federal government whose purpose is to support small business.

Instructions

Go to **www.sba.gov** and in the Starting Your Business link, review the material under the "Are You Ready?" Answer the following questions.

(a) What are some of the characteristics required of a small business owner?
(b) What are the top 10 reasons given for business failure?

Answers to Insight and Accounting Across the Organization Questions

p. 874 Jobs Won, Money Lost

Q: What type of costs do you think the company had been underestimating?

A: *It is most likely that the company failed to estimate and track overhead. In a highly diversified company, overhead associated with the diesel locomotive jobs may have been "lost" in the total overhead pool for the entire company.*

p. 887 What About Service Companies?

Q: What types of costs will service companies report in job order cost systems?

A: *Like a manufacturing company, a service company will report direct labor and overhead charges. Although service companies do not produce inventory, many have significant material costs that are charged to each job. For example, a health-care provider would track medication and treatment supplies used by each patient.*

p. 889 "Did I Mention Our Overhead Charge?"

Q: What implications might this ruling have on the dealerships' processing and inspection costs?

A: *When these costs were tacked on after the price had been negotiated, the dealerships had little incentive to control these costs—and actually had an incentive to overstate them. But if the costs are disclosed as part of the price, dealerships will have an incentive to keep better track of the costs and try to minimize them.*

Authors' Comments on *All About You:* Minding Your Own Business (p. 890)

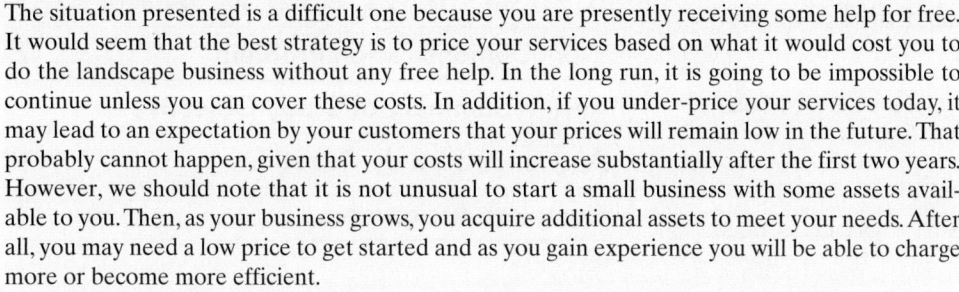

The situation presented is a difficult one because you are presently receiving some help for free. It would seem that the best strategy is to price your services based on what it would cost you to do the landscape business without any free help. In the long run, it is going to be impossible to continue unless you can cover these costs. In addition, if you under-price your services today, it may lead to an expectation by your customers that your prices will remain low in the future. That probably cannot happen, given that your costs will increase substantially after the first two years. However, we should note that it is not unusual to start a small business with some assets available to you. Then, as your business grows, you acquire additional assets to meet your needs. After all, you may need a low price to get started and as you gain experience you will be able to charge more or become more efficient.

So what to do? Let's address your old truck first. You should treat the truck as an asset owned by your business. Put it on your books at its fair value, and depreciate it over a reasonable life. This will result in an overhead charge. You need to cover the cost of that truck, as you will have to buy another one some day.

The land, barn, and your mother's services are a little more difficult. If you rented the land and barn and if you paid an assistant, all of these costs would be charged to overhead. (The assistant would be indirect labor.) You are currently getting all these services for free. This is a good situation now, and you may need this situation early in your business to help you get started. But you should recognize that even if you run your business profitably for the first two years, you may have problems starting in the third year. Thus, it would seem prudent to establish a budget based on both scenarios for the first two years. If you can charge based on your expected costs in the future, do so. If that is not realistic, because you need to establish yourself and get more experience, then charge less. But be sure from the start to cover a reasonable amount of your costs, or the business does not make sense for you financially.

Answers to Self-Study Questions

1. a **2.** b **3.** c **4.** d **5.** b **6.** a **7.** d **8.** b **9.** c **10.** b

Remember to go back to the Navigator box on the chapter-opening page and check off your completed work.

Chapter 21

Process Cost Accounting

STUDY OBJECTIVES

After studying this chapter, you should be able to:

1. Understand who uses process cost systems.
2. Explain the similarities and differences between job order cost and process cost systems.
3. Explain the flow of costs in a process cost system.
4. Make the journal entries to assign manufacturing costs in a process cost system.
5. Compute equivalent units.
6. Explain the four steps necessary to prepare a production cost report.
7. Prepare a production cost report.
8. Explain just-in-time (JIT) processing.
9. Explain activity-based costing (ABC).

The Navigator

The Navigator

- Scan **Study Objectives** ■
- Read **Feature Story** ■
- Read **Preview** ■
- Read text and answer **Before You Go On** p. 917 ■ p. 925 ■ p. 927 ■ p. 930 ■
- Work **Demonstration Problem** ■
- Review **Summary of Study Objectives** ■
- Answer **Self-Study Questions** ■
- Complete **Assignments** ■

Feature Story

BEN & JERRY'S TRACKS ITS MIX-UPS

Ben & Jerry's Homemade, Inc. (*www.benjerry.com*) is one of the "hottest" and "coolest" U.S. companies. Based in Waterbury, Vermont, the ice cream company that started out of a garage in 1978 is now a public company.

Making ice cream is a process—a movement of product from a mixing department to a prepping department to a pint department. The mixing department is where the ice cream is created. The prep area is where extras

such as cherries and walnuts are added to make plain ice cream into "Cherry Garcia," Ben & Jerry's most popular flavor. The pint department is where the ice cream is actually put into containers. As the product is processed from one department to the next, the appropriate materials, labor, and overhead are added to it.

"The incoming ingredients from the shipping and receiving departments are stored in certain locations, either in a freezer or dry warehouse," says Beecher Eurich, staff accountant. "As ingredients get added, so do the costs associated with them." How much ice cream is produced? Running plants around the clock, the company produces 18 million gallons a year.

Using a process costing system, Eurich can tell you how much a certain batch of ice cream costs to make—its materials, labor, and overhead in each of the production departments. She generates reports for the production department heads, but makes sure not to overdo it. "You can get bogged down in numbers," says Eurich. "If you're generating a report that no one can use, then that's a waste of time."

It's more likely, though, Ben & Jerry's production people want to know how efficient they are. Why? Many own stock in the company.

✓ The Navigator

Inside Chapter 21...

Preview of Chapter 21

The cost accounting system used by companies such as Ben & Jerry's is a **process cost accounting** system. In contrast to job order cost accounting, which focuses on the individual job, process cost accounting focuses on the *processes* involved in mass-producing products that are identical or very similar in nature. The primary objective of the chapter is to explain and illustrate process cost accounting.

The content and organization of this chapter are as follows.

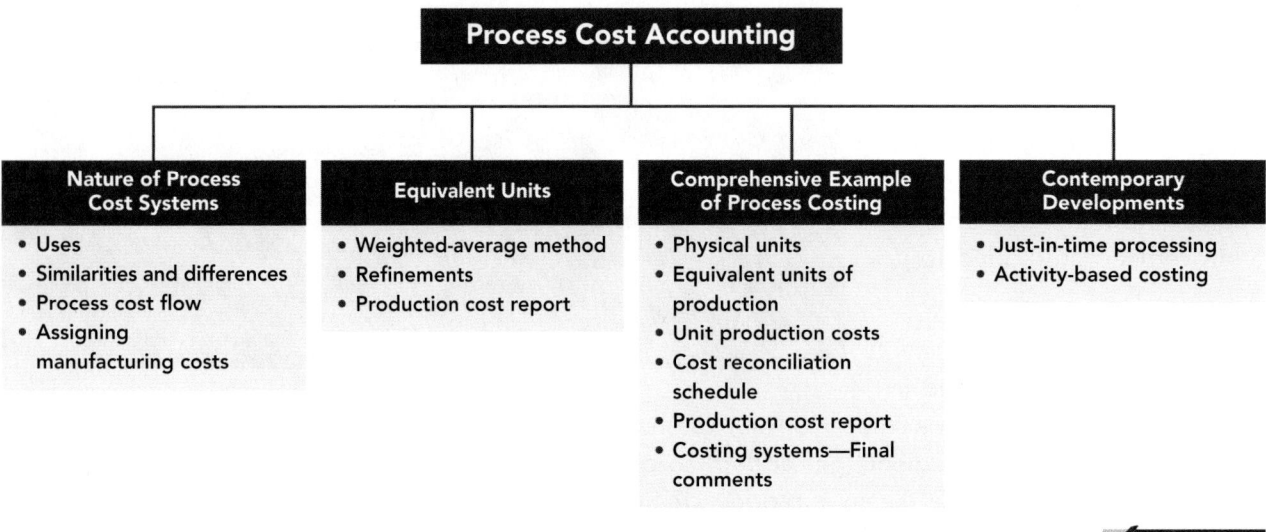

Process Cost Accounting

Nature of Process Cost Systems
- Uses
- Similarities and differences
- Process cost flow
- Assigning manufacturing costs

Equivalent Units
- Weighted-average method
- Refinements
- Production cost report

Comprehensive Example of Process Costing
- Physical units
- Equivalent units of production
- Unit production costs
- Cost reconciliation schedule
- Production cost report
- Costing systems—Final comments

Contemporary Developments
- Just-in-time processing
- Activity-based costing

The Navigator

THE NATURE OF PROCESS COST SYSTEMS

Uses of Process Cost Systems

STUDY OBJECTIVE 1

Understand who uses process cost systems.

Companies use **process cost systems** to apply costs to similar products that are mass-produced in a continuous fashion. Ben & Jerry's uses a process cost system: Production of the ice cream, once it begins, continues until the ice cream emerges, and the processing is the same for the entire run—with precisely the same amount of materials, labor, and overhead. Each finished pint of ice cream is indistinguishable from another.

A company such as USX uses process costing in the manufacturing of steel. Kellogg and General Mills use process costing for cereal production; ExxonMobil uses process costing for its oil refining. Sherwin Williams uses process costing for its paint products. At a bottling company like Coca-Cola, the manufacturing process begins with the blending of ingredients. Next, automated machinery moves the bottles into position and fills them. The bottles are then capped, packaged, and forwarded to the finished goods warehouse. Illustration 21-1 shows this process.

Illustration 21-1
Manufacturing processes

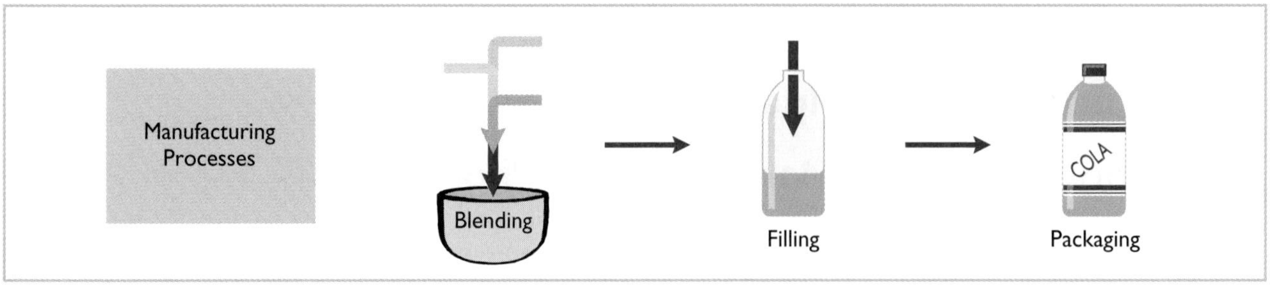

For Coca-Cola, as well as the other companies just mentioned, once the production begins, it continues until the finished product emerges, and each unit of finished product is like every other unit.

In comparison, costs in a job order cost system are assigned to a *specific job*. Examples are the construction of a customized home, the making of a motion picture, or the manufacturing of a specialized machine. Illustration 21-2 provides examples of companies that primarily use either a process cost system or a job order cost system.

Illustration 21-2
Process cost and job order cost companies and products

Process Cost System Company	Product	Job Order Cost System Company	Product
Coca-Cola, PepsiCo	Soft drinks 	Young & Rubicam, J. Walter Thompson	Advertising 
ExxonMobil, Royal Dutch Shell	Oil 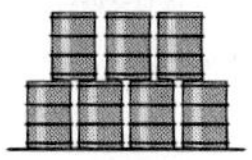	Walt Disney, Warner Brothers	Motion pictures 
Intel, Advanced Micro Devices	Computer chips 	Center Ice Consultants, Ice Pro	Ice rinks 
Dow Chemical, DuPont	Chemicals 	Kaiser, Mayo Clinic	Patient health care 

Similarities and Differences Between Job Order Cost and Process Cost Systems

STUDY OBJECTIVE 2
Explain the similarities and differences between job order cost and process cost systems.

In a job order cost system, costs are assigned to each job. In a process cost system, costs are tracked through a series of connected manufacturing processes or departments, rather than by individual jobs. Thus, companies use process cost systems when they produce a large volume of uniform or relatively homogeneous products. Illustration 21-3 shows the basic flow of costs in these two systems.

Illustration 21-3
Job order cost and process cost flow

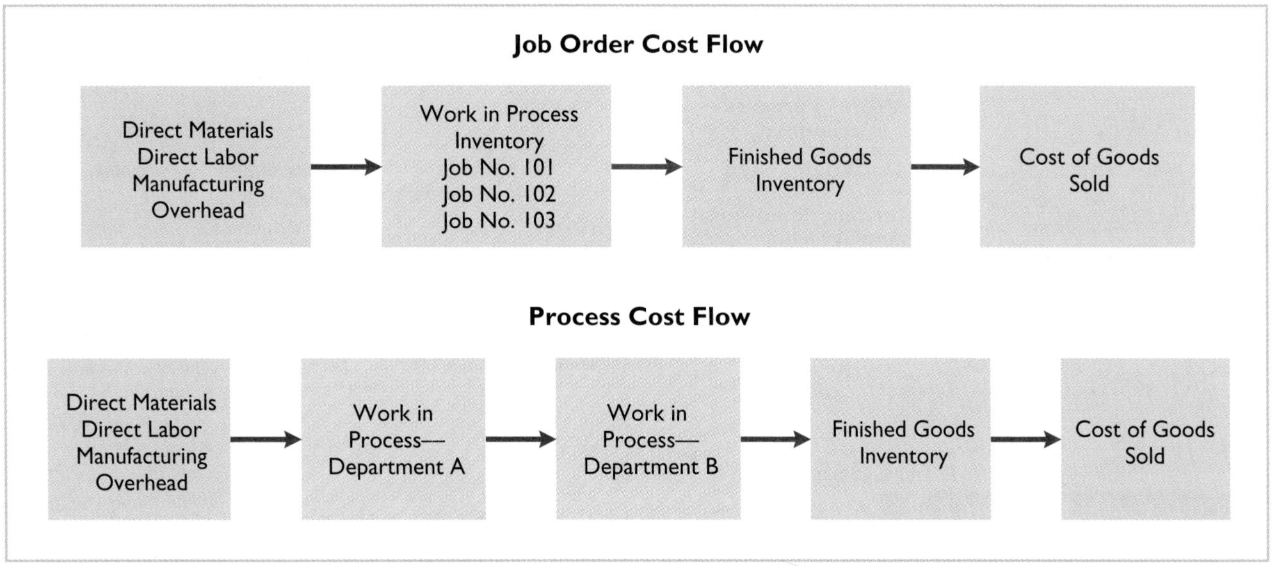

The following analysis highlights the basic similarities and differences between these two systems.

SIMILARITIES

Job order cost and process cost systems are similar in three ways:

1. **The manufacturing cost elements.** Both costing systems track three manufacturing cost elements—direct materials, direct labor, and manufacturing overhead.
2. **The accumulation of the costs of materials, labor, and overhead.** Both costing systems debit raw materials to Raw Materials Inventory; factory labor to Factory Labor; and manufacturing overhead costs to Manufacturing Overhead.
3. **The flow of costs.** As noted above, all manufacturing costs are accumulated by debits to Raw Materials Inventory, Factory Labor, and Manufacturing Overhead. These costs are then assigned to the same accounts in both costing systems—Work in Process, Finished Goods Inventory, and Cost of Goods Sold. **The methods of assigning costs, however, differ significantly.** These differences are explained and illustrated later in the chapter.

DIFFERENCES

The differences between a job order cost and a process cost system are as follows.

1. **The number of work in process accounts used.** A job order cost system uses only one Work in Process account. A process cost system uses multiple work in process accounts.
2. **Documents used to track costs.** In a job order cost system, costs are charged to individual jobs and summarized in a job cost sheet. In a process cost system, costs are summarized in a production cost report for each department.
3. **The point at which costs are totaled.** In a job order cost system, total costs are determined when the job is completed. In a process cost system, total costs are determined at the end of a period of time.
4. **Unit cost computations.** In a job order cost system, the unit cost is the total cost per job divided by the units produced. In a process cost system, the unit cost is total manufacturing costs for the period divided by the units produced during the period.

Illustration 21-4 summarizes the major differences between a job order cost and a process cost system.

Illustration 21-4
Job order versus process cost systems

Features	Job Order Cost System	Process Cost System
Work in process accounts	• One work in process account	• Multiple work in process accounts
Documents used	• Job cost sheets	• Production cost reports
Determination of total manufacturing costs	• Each job	• Each period
Unit-cost computations	• Cost of each job ÷ Units produced for the job	• Total manufacturing costs ÷ Units produced during the period

Process Cost Flow

STUDY OBJECTIVE 3
Explain the flow of costs in a process cost system.

Illustration 21-5 shows the flow of costs in the process cost system for Tyler Company. Tyler Company manufactures automatic can openers that it sells to retail outlets. Manufacturing consists of two processes: machining and assembly. The Machining Department shapes, hones, and drills the raw materials. The Assembly Department assembles and packages the parts.

Illustration 21-5
Flow of costs in process cost system

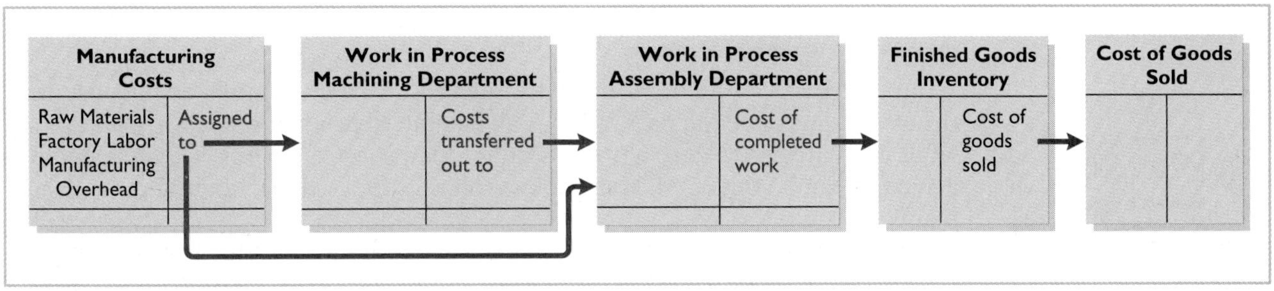

As the flow of costs indicates, the company can add materials, labor, and manufacturing overhead in both the Machining and Assembly Departments. When the Machining Department finishes its work, the partially completed units are transferred to the Assembly Department. In the Assembly Department, the goods are finished and are then transferred to the finished goods inventory. Upon sale, the goods are removed from the finished goods inventory. Within each department, a similar set of activities is performed on each unit processed.

Assigning Manufacturing Costs—Journal Entries

STUDY OBJECTIVE 4
Make the journal entries to assign manufacturing costs in a process cost system.

As indicated, the accumulation of the costs of materials, labor, and manufacturing overhead is the same in a process cost system as in a job order cost system. All raw materials are debited to Raw Materials Inventory when the materials are purchased. All factory labor is debited to Factory Labor when the labor costs are incurred. Overhead costs are debited to Manufacturing Overhead as they are incurred. However, the assignment of the three manufacturing cost elements to Work in Process in a process cost system is different from a job order cost system. Here we'll look at how companies assign these manufacturing cost elements in a process cost system.

MATERIALS COSTS

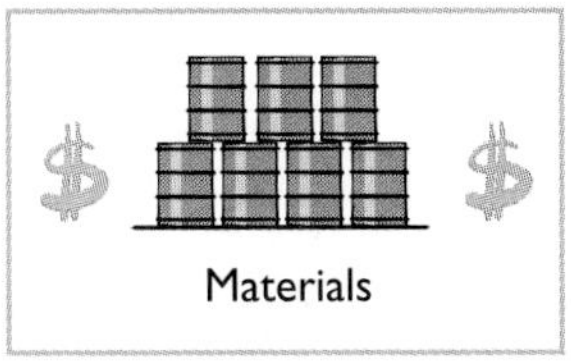

All raw materials issued for production are a materials cost to the producing department. A process cost system may use materials requisition slips but **fewer requisitions are generally required than in a job order cost system, because the materials are used for processes rather than for specific jobs**. Requisitions are issued less frequently in a process cost system because the requisitions are for larger quantities.

Materials are usually added to production at the beginning of the first process. However, in subsequent processes, other materials may be added at various points. For example, in the manufacture of Hershey candy bars, the chocolate and other ingredients are added at the beginning of the first process, and the wrappers and cartons are added at the end of the packaging process. At Tyler Company, materials are entered at the beginning of each process. The entry to record the materials used is:

Work in Process—Machining	XXXX	
Work in Process—Assembly	XXXX	
Raw Materials Inventory		XXXX
(To record materials used)		

At ice cream maker Ben & Jerry's, materials are added in three departments: milk and flavoring in the mixing department; extras such as cherries and walnuts in the prepping department; and cardboard containers in the pinting (packaging) department.

FACTORY LABOR COSTS

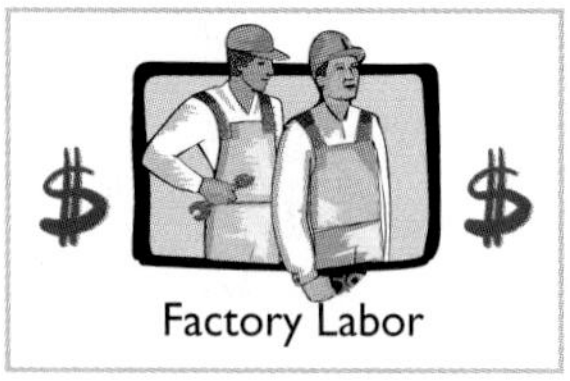

In a process cost system, as in a job order cost system, companies may use time tickets to determine the cost of labor assignable to production departments. Since labor costs are assigned to a process rather than a job, the labor cost chargeable to a process can be obtained from the payroll register or departmental payroll summaries.

Labor costs for the Machining Department will include the wages of employees who shape, hone, and drill the raw materials. The entry to assign these costs for Tyler Company is:

Work in Process—Machining	XXXX	
Work in Process—Assembly	XXXX	
Factory Labor		XXXX
(To assign factory labor to production)		

MANUFACTURING OVERHEAD COSTS

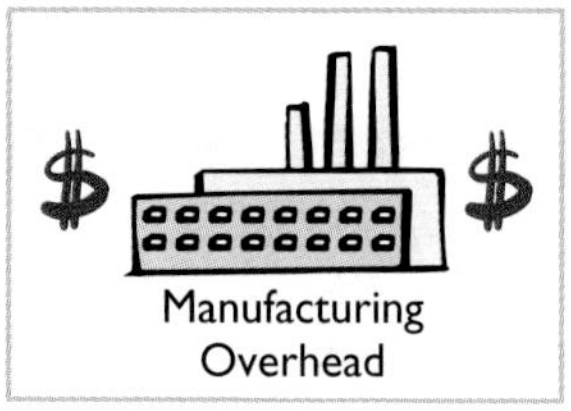

The objective in assigning overhead in a process cost system is to allocate the overhead costs to the production departments on an objective and equitable basis. That basis is the activity that "drives" or causes the costs. A primary driver of overhead costs in continuous manufacturing operations is **machine time used**, not direct labor. Thus, companies **widely use machine hours** in allocating manufacturing overhead costs. Tyler's entry to allocate overhead to the two processes is:

Work in Process—Machining	XXXX	
Work in Process—Assembly	XXXX	
Manufacturing Overhead		XXXX
(To assign overhead to production)		

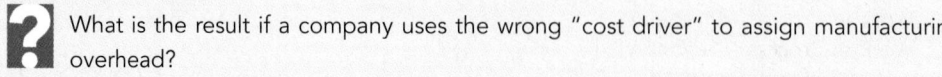

MANAGEMENT INSIGHT

Choosing a Cost Driver

In one of Caterpillar's automated cost centers, work is fed into the cost center, processed by robotic machines, and transferred to the next cost center without human intervention. One person tends all of the machines and spends more time maintaining machines than operating them. In such cases, overhead rates based on direct labor hours may be misleading. Surprisingly, some companies continue to assign manufacturing overhead on the basis of direct labor despite the fact that there is no cause-and-effect relationship between labor and overhead.

?

What is the result if a company uses the wrong "cost driver" to assign manufacturing overhead?

TRANSFER TO NEXT DEPARTMENT

At the end of the month, an entry is needed to record the cost of the goods transferred out of the department. In this case, the transfer is to the Assembly Department, and the following entry is made.

Work in Process—Assembly	XXXXX	
Work in Process—Machining		XXXXX
(To record transfer of units to the Assembly Department)		

TRANSFER TO FINISHED GOODS

The units completed in the Assembly Department are transferred to the finished goods warehouse. The entry for this transfer is as follows.

Finished Goods Inventory	XXXXX	
Work in Process—Assembly		XXXXX
(To record transfer of units to finished goods)		

TRANSFER TO COST OF GOODS SOLD

When finished goods are sold, the entry to record the cost of goods sold is as follows.

Cost of Goods Sold	XXXXX	
Finished Goods Inventory		XXXXX
(To record cost of units sold)		

Before You Go On...

REVIEW IT

1. What type of manufacturing companies might use a process cost accounting system?
2. What are the principal similarities and differences between a job order cost system and a process cost system?

DO IT

Ruth Company manufactures ZEBO through two processes: Blending and Bottling. In June, raw materials used were Blending \$18,000 and Bottling \$4,000; factory labor costs were Blending \$12,000 and Bottling \$5,000; manufacturing overhead costs were Blending \$6,000 and Bottling \$2,500. Units completed at a cost of \$19,000 in the Blending Department are transferred to the Bottling Department. Units completed at a cost of \$11,000 in the Bottling Department are transferred to Finished Goods. Journalize the assignment of these costs to the two processes and the transfer of units as appropriate.

Action Plan

- In process cost accounting, keep separate work in process accounts for each process.
- When the costs are assigned to production, debit the separate work in process accounts.
- Transfer cost of completed units to the next process or to Finished Goods.

Solution The entries are:

Work in Process—Blending	18,000	
Work in Process—Bottling	4,000	
Raw Materials Inventory		22,000
(To record materials used)		
Work in Process—Blending	12,000	
Work in Process—Bottling	5,000	
Factory Labor		17,000
(To assign factory labor to production)		
Work in Process—Blending	6,000	
Work in Process—Bottling	2,500	
Manufacturing Overhead		8,500
(To assign overhead to production)		
Work in Process—Bottling	19,000	
Work in Process—Blending		19,000
(To record transfer of units to the Bottling Department)		
Finished Goods Inventory	11,000	
Work in Process—Bottling		11,000
(To record transfer of units to finished goods)		

Related exercise material: *BE21-1, BE21-2, BE21-3, E21-2, and E21-4.*

The Navigator

EQUIVALENT UNITS

STUDY OBJECTIVE 5

Compute equivalent units.

Suppose you were asked to compute the cost of instruction per full-time equivalent student at your college. You are provided the following information.

Illustration 21-6
Information for full-time student example

Costs:	
Total cost of instruction	$9,000,000
Student population:	
Full-time students	900
Part-time students	1,000

Part-time students take 60% of the classes of a full-time student during the year. To compute the number of full-time equivalent students per year, you would make the following computation.

Illustration 21-7
Full-time equivalent unit computation

Full-time Students	+	Equivalent Units of Part-time Students	=	Full-time Equivalent Students
900	+	(60% × 1,000)	=	**1,500**

The cost of instruction per full-time equivalent student is therefore the total cost of instruction ($9,000,000) divided by the number of full-time equivalent students (1,500), which is $6,000 ($9,000,000 ÷ 1,500).

In a process cost system, the same idea, called equivalent units of production, is used. **Equivalent units of production** measure the work done during the period, expressed in fully completed units. This concept is used to determine the cost per unit of completed product.

Weighted-Average Method

The formula to compute equivalent units of production is as follows.

Units Completed and Transferred Out	+	Equivalent Units of Ending Work in Process	=	Equivalent Units of Production

Illustration 21-8
Equivalent units of production formula

To better understand this concept of equivalent units, consider the following two separate examples.

Example 1: The Blending Department's entire output during the period consists of ending work in process of 4,000 units which are 60% complete as to materials, labor, and overhead. The equivalent units of production for the Blending Department are therefore 2,400 units (4,000 × 60%).

Example 2: The Packaging Department's output during the period consists of 10,000 units completed and transferred out, and 5,000 units in ending work in process which are 70% completed. The equivalent units of production are therefore 13,500 [10,000 + (5,000 × 70%)].

This method of computing equivalent units is referred to as the **weighted-average method**. It considers the degree of completion (weighting) of the units completed and transferred out and the ending work in process.

Refinements on the Weighted-Average Method

Kellogg Company has produced Eggo® Waffles since 1970. Three departments produce these waffles: Mixing, Baking, and Freezing/Packaging. The Mixing Department combines dry ingredients, including flour, salt, and baking powder, with liquid ingredients, including eggs and vegetable oil, to make waffle batter. Illustration 21-9 provides information related to the Mixing Department at the end of June.

MIXING DEPARTMENT

		Percentage Complete	
	Physical Units	**Materials**	**Conversion Costs**
Work in process, June 1	100,000	100%	70%
Started into production	800,000		
Total units	900,000		
Units transferred out	700,000		
Work in process, June 30	200,000	100%	60%
Total units	900,000		

Illustration 21-9
Information for Mixing Department

HELPFUL HINT

Question: When are separate unit cost computations needed for materials and conversion costs? Answer: Whenever the two types of costs do not occur in the process at the same time.

Illustration 21-9 indicates that the beginning work in process is 100% complete as to materials cost and 70% complete as to conversion costs. **Conversion costs consists of the sum of labor costs and overhead costs.** In other words, both the dry and liquid ingredients (materials) are added at the beginning of the process to make Eggo® Waffles. The conversion costs (labor and overhead) related to the mixing of these ingredients were incurred uniformly and are 70% complete. The ending work in process is 100% complete as to materials cost and 60% complete as to conversion costs.

We then use the Mixing Department information to determine equivalent units. **In computing equivalent units, the beginning work in process is not part of the equivalent units of production formula.** The units transferred out to the Baking Department are fully complete as to both materials and conversion costs. The ending work in process is fully complete as to materials, but only 60% complete as to conversion costs. We therefore need to make **two equivalent unit computations:** one for materials, and the other for conversion costs. Illustration 21-10 shows these computations.

Illustration 21-10
Computation of equivalent units—Mixing Department

	Equivalent Units	
	Materials	**Conversion Costs**
Units transferred out	700,000	700,000
Work in process, June 30		
200,000 × 100%	200,000	
200,000 × 60%		120,000
Total equivalent units	900,000	820,000

We can refine the earlier formula used to compute equivalent units of production (Illustration 21-8) (page 919) to show the computations for materials and for conversion costs, as follows.

Illustration 21-11
Refined equivalent units of production formula

Units Completed and Transferred Out—Materials	+	Equivalent Units of Ending Work in Process—Materials	=	Equivalent Units of Production—Materials
Units Completed and Transferred Out—Conversion Costs	+	Equivalent Units of Ending Work in Process—Conversion Costs	=	Equivalent Units of Production—Conversion Costs

Production Cost Report

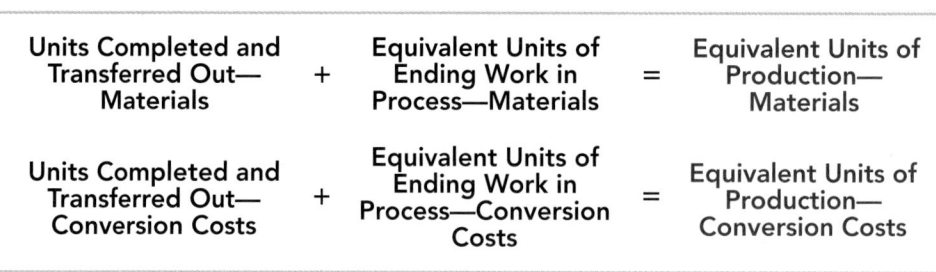

As mentioned earlier, companies prepare a production cost report for each department. A **production cost report** is the key document management uses to understand the activities in a department; it shows the production quantity and cost data related to that department. For example, in producing Eggo® Waffles, Kellogg Company uses three production cost reports: Mixing, Baking, and Freezing/Packaging. Illustration 21-12 shows the flow of costs to make an Eggo® Waffle and the related production cost reports for each department.

STUDY OBJECTIVE 6

Explain the four steps necessary to prepare a production cost report.

In order to complete a production cost report, the company must perform four steps, which as a whole, make up the process costing system.

1. Compute the physical unit flow.
2. Compute the equivalent units of production.

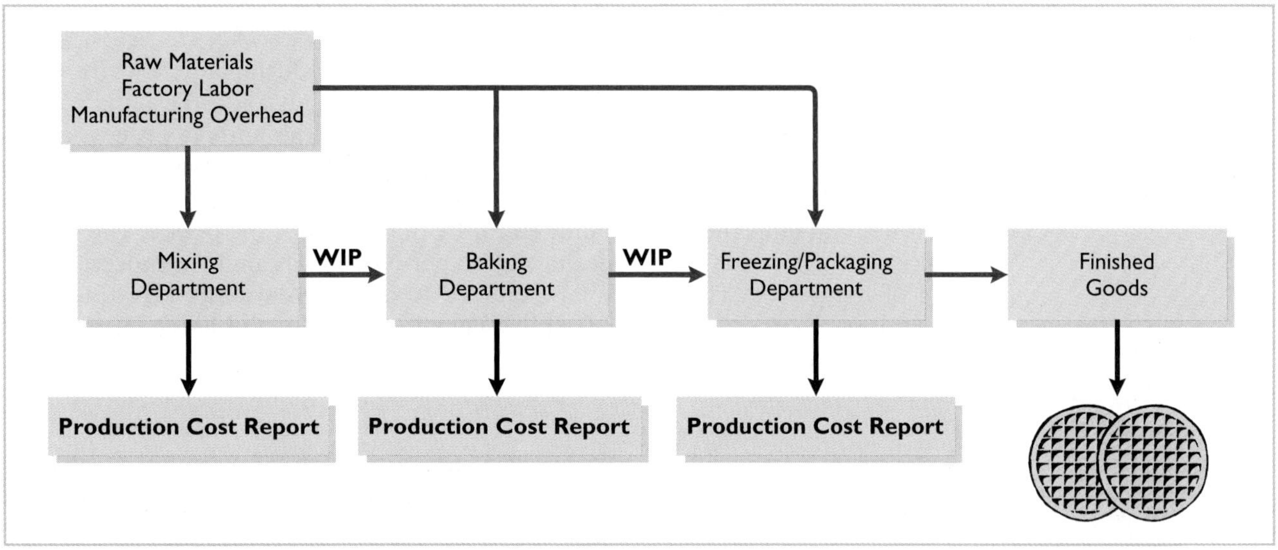

Illustration 21-12
Flow of costs in making Eggo® Waffles

3. Compute unit production costs.
4. Prepare a cost reconciliation schedule.

The next section explores these steps in an extended example.

COMPREHENSIVE EXAMPLE OF PROCESS COSTING

Illustration 21-13 shows assumed data for the Mixing Department at Kellogg Company for the month of June. We will use this information to complete a production cost report for the Mixing Department.

Illustration 21-13
Unit and cost data—Mixing Department

MIXING DEPARTMENT	
Units	
Work in process, June 1	100,000
Direct materials: 100% complete	
Conversion costs: 70% complete	
Units started into production during June	800,000
Units completed and transferred out to Baking Department	700,000
Work in process, June 30	200,000
Direct materials: 100% complete	
Conversion costs: 60% complete	
Costs	
Work in process, June 1	
Direct materials: 100% complete	$ 50,000
Conversion costs: 70% complete	35,000
Cost of work in process, June 1	$ 85,000
Costs incurred during production in June	
Direct materials	$400,000
Conversion costs	170,000
Costs incurred in June	$570,000

Compute the Physical Unit Flow (Step 1)

Physical units are the actual units to be accounted for during a period, irrespective of any work performed. To keep track of these units, add the units started (or transferred) into production during the period to the units in process at the beginning of the period. This amount is referred to as the **total units to be accounted for**.

The total units then are accounted for by the output of the period. The output consists of units transferred out during the period and any units in process at the end of the period. This amount is referred to as the **total units accounted for**. Illustration 21-14 shows the flow of physical units for Kellogg's Mixing Department for the month of June.

Illustration 21-14
Physical unit flow—Mixing Department

MIXING DEPARTMENT

	Physical Units
Units to be accounted for	
Work in process, June 1	100,000
Started (transferred) into production	800,000
Total units	**900,000**
Units accounted for	
Completed and transferred out	700,000
Work in process, June 30	200,000
Total units	**900,000**

The records indicate that 900,000 units must be accounted for in the Mixing Department. Of this sum, 700,000 units were transferred to the Baking Department and 200,000 units were still in process.

Compute Equivalent Units of Production (Step 2)

HELPFUL HINT
Materials are not always added at the beginning of the process. For example, materials are sometimes added uniformly during the process.

Once the physical flow of the units is established, it is necessary to measure the Mixing Department's productivity in terms of equivalent units of production. The Mixing Department adds materials at the beginning of the process, and incurs conversion costs uniformly during the process. Thus, two computations of equivalent units are required: one for materials, and one for conversion costs. The equivalent unit computation is as follows.

Illustration 21-15
Computation of equivalent units—Mixing Department

HELPFUL HINT
Remember that the beginning work in process is ignored in this computation.

	Equivalent Units	
	Materials	**Conversion Costs**
Units transferred out	700,000	700,000
Work in process, June 30		
200,000 × 100%	200,000	
200,000 × 60%		120,000
Total equivalent units	**900,000**	**820,000**

Compute Unit Production Costs (Step 3)

Armed with the knowledge of the equivalent units of production, we can now compute the unit production costs. **Unit production costs** are costs expressed in terms of equivalent units of production. When equivalent units of production are different for materials and conversion costs, we compute three unit costs: (1) materials, (2) conversion, and (3) total manufacturing.

The computation of total materials cost related to Eggo® Waffles is as follows.

Illustration 21-16
Total materials cost computation

Work in process, June 1	
Direct materials cost	$ 50,000
Costs added to production during June	
Direct materials cost	400,000
Total materials cost	**$450,000**

The computation of unit materials cost is as follows.

Illustration 21-17
Unit materials cost computation

Total Materials Cost	÷	Equivalent Units of Materials	=	Unit Materials Cost
$450,000	÷	900,000	=	**$0.50**

Illustration 21-18 shows the computation of total conversion costs.

Illustration 21-18
Total conversion costs computation

Work in process, June 1	
Conversion costs	$ 35,000
Costs added to production during June	
Conversion costs	170,000
Total conversion costs	**$205,000**

The computation of unit conversion cost is as follows.

Illustration 21-19
Unit conversion cost computation

Total Conversion Costs	÷	Equivalent Units of Conversion Costs	=	Unit Conversion Cost
$205,000	÷	820,000	=	**$0.25**

Total manufacturing cost per unit is therefore computed as shown in Illustration 21-20 (page 924).

Illustration 21-20
Total manufacturing cost per unit

Unit Materials Cost	+	Unit Conversion Cost	=	Total Manufacturing Cost per Unit
$0.50	+	$0.25	=	**$0.75**

Prepare a Cost Reconciliation Schedule (Step 4)

We are now ready to determine the cost of goods transferred out of the Mixing Department to the Baking Department and the costs in ending work in process. The total costs that were charged to the Mixing Department in June are as follows.

Illustration 21-21
Costs charged to Mixing Department

Costs to be accounted for	
Work in process, June 1	$ 85,000
Started into production	570,000
Total costs	**$655,000**

The total costs charged to the Mixing Department in June are therefore $655,000.

The company then prepares a cost reconciliation schedule to assign these costs to (1) units transferred out to the Baking Department and (2) ending work in process.

Illustration 21-22
Cost reconciliation schedule—Mixing Department

MIXING DEPARTMENT
Cost Reconciliation Schedule

Costs accounted for		
Transferred out (700,000 × $0.75)		$ 525,000
Work in process, June 30		
Materials (200,000 × $0.50)	$100,000	
Conversion costs (120,000 × $0.25)	30,000	130,000
Total costs		**$655,000**

The total manufacturing cost per unit, $0.75, is used in costing the **units completed** and transferred to the Baking Department. In contrast, the unit cost of materials and the unit cost of conversion are needed in costing **units in process**. The **cost reconciliation schedule** shows that the **total costs accounted for** (Illustration 21-22) equal the **total costs to be accounted for** (see Illustration 21-21).

Preparing the Production Cost Report

STUDY OBJECTIVE 7
Prepare a production cost report.

At this point, we are ready to prepare the production cost report for the Mixing Department. As indicated earlier, this report is an internal document for management that shows production quantity and cost data for a production department.

There are four steps in preparing a production cost report. They are:

(1) Prepare a physical unit schedule.

(2) Compute equivalent units.

(3) Compute unit costs.

(4) Prepare a cost reconciliation schedule.

Illustration 21-23 shows the production cost report for the Mixing Department. The report identifies the four steps.

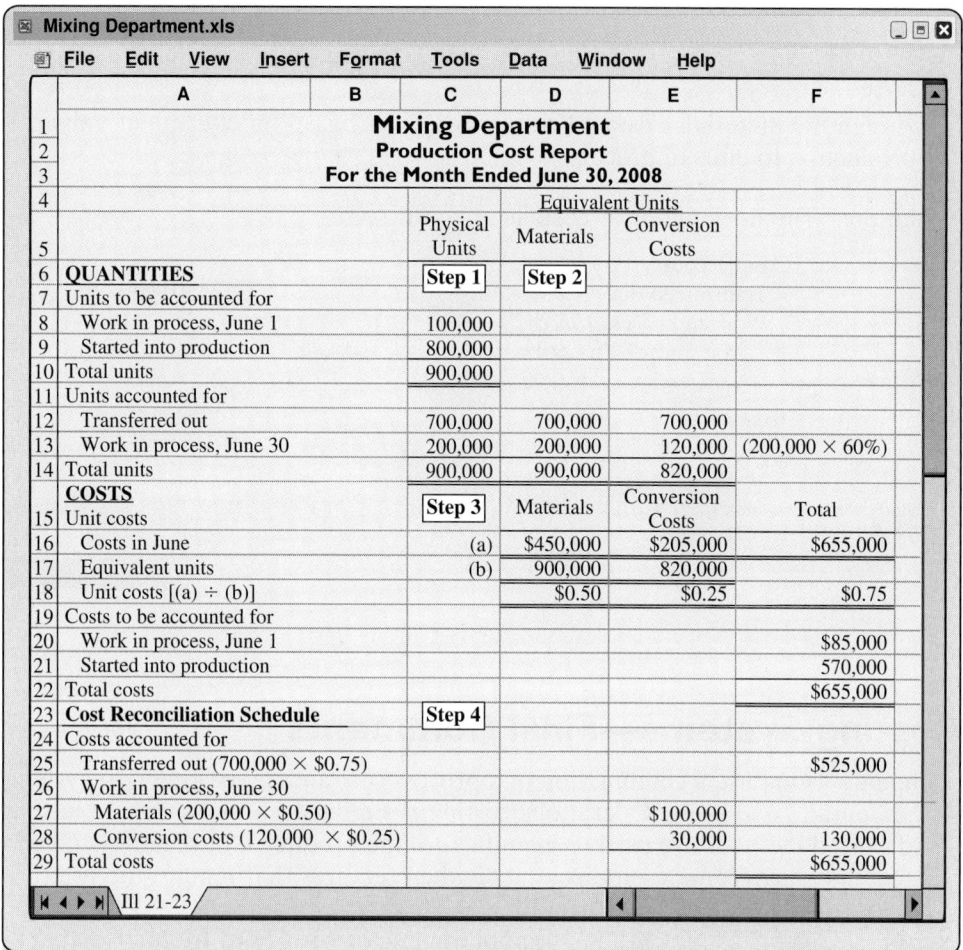

Illustration 21-23
Production cost report

Mixing Department.xls

File Edit View Insert Format Tools Data Window Help

	A	B	C	D	E	F
1	**Mixing Department**					
2	**Production Cost Report**					
3	**For the Month Ended June 30, 2008**					
4				Equivalent Units		
5			Physical Units	Materials	Conversion Costs	
6	QUANTITIES		Step 1	Step 2		
7	Units to be accounted for					
8	Work in process, June 1		100,000			
9	Started into production		800,000			
10	Total units		900,000			
11	Units accounted for					
12	Transferred out		700,000	700,000	700,000	
13	Work in process, June 30		200,000	200,000	120,000	(200,000 × 60%)
14	Total units		900,000	900,000	820,000	
15	COSTS Unit costs		Step 3	Materials	Conversion Costs	Total
16	Costs in June		(a)	$450,000	$205,000	$655,000
17	Equivalent units		(b)	900,000	820,000	
18	Unit costs [(a) ÷ (b)]			$0.50	$0.25	$0.75
19	Costs to be accounted for					
20	Work in process, June 1					$85,000
21	Started into production					570,000
22	Total costs					$655,000
23	**Cost Reconciliation Schedule**		Step 4			
24	Costs accounted for					
25	Transferred out (700,000 × $0.75)					$525,000
26	Work in process, June 30					
27	Materials (200,000 × $0.50)				$100,000	
28	Conversion costs (120,000 × $0.25)				30,000	130,000
29	Total costs					$655,000

Ill 21-23

Production cost reports provide a basis for evaluating the productivity of a department. In addition, managers can use the cost data to assess whether unit costs and total costs are reasonable. By comparing the quantity and cost data with predetermined goals, top management can also judge whether current performance is meeting planned objectives.

Before You Go On...

REVIEW IT

1. How do physical units differ from equivalent units of production?
2. What are the formulas for computing unit costs of production?
3. How are costs assigned to units transferred out and in process?
4. What are the four steps in preparing a production cost report?

DO IT

In March, Rodayo Manufacturing had the following unit production costs: materials $6 and conversion costs $9. On March 1, it had zero work in process. During March, 12,000 units were transferred out, and 800 units that were 25 percent completed as to conversion costs and 100 percent complete as to materials were in ending work in process at March 31. Assign the costs to the units transferred out and in process.

Action Plan

- Assign the total manufacturing cost of $15 per unit to the 12,000 units transferred out.
- Assign the materials cost and conversion costs based on equivalent units of production to units in process.

Solution The assignment of costs is as follows.

Costs accounted for		
Transferred out (12,000 × $15)		$180,000
Work in process, March 31		
Materials (800 × $6)	$4,800	
Conversion costs (200[a] × $9)	1,800	6,600
Total costs		$186,600

[a]800 × 25%

Related exercise material: *BE21-4, BE21-5, BE21-6, BE21-7, BE21-8, BE21-9, BE21-10, E21-5, E21-6, E21-8, E21-9, E21-10, E21-11, E21-12, and E21-14.*

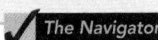

The Navigator

Costing Systems—Final Comments

Companies often use a combination of a process cost and a job order cost system, called **operations costing**. Operations costing is similar to process costing in that standardized methods are used to manufacture the product. At the same time, the product may have some customized, individual features that require the use of a job order cost system.

Consider, for example, the automobile manufacturer Ford Motor Company. Each vehicle at a given plant goes through the same assembly line, but different materials (such as seat coverings, paint, and tinted glass) may be used for different vehicles. Similarly, Kellogg's Pop-Tarts Toaster Pastries® go through numerous processes—mixing, filling, baking, frosting, and packaging. The pastry dough, though, comes in three flavors—plain, chocolate, and graham—and fillings include Smucker's® real fruit, chocolate fudge, vanilla creme, brown sugar cinnamon, and S'mores.

A cost-benefit tradeoff occurs as a company decides which costing system to use. A job order system, for example, provides detailed information related to the cost of the product. Because each job has its own distinguishing characteristics, the system can provide an accurate cost per job. This information is useful in controlling costs and pricing products. However, the cost of implementing a job order cost system is often expensive because of the accounting costs involved.

On the other hand, for a company like Intel, which makes computer chips, is there a benefit in knowing whether the cost of the one hundredth chip produced is different from the one thousandth chip produced? Probably not. An average cost of the product will suffice for control and pricing purposes.

In summary, when deciding to use one of these systems, or a combination system, a company must weigh the costs of implementing the system against the benefits from the additional information provided.

ACCOUNTING ACROSS THE ORGANIZATION

What Cost System Might Jiffy Lube Use?

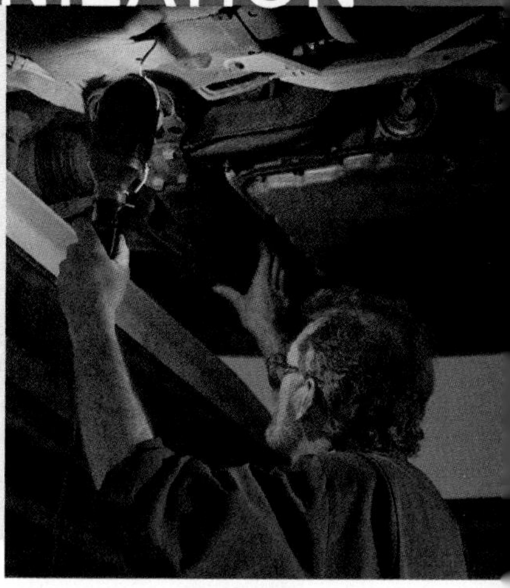

Frequently, when we think of service companies, we think of specific, nonroutine tasks, such as rebuilding an automobile engine, providing consulting services on a business acquisition, or working on a major lawsuit. However, many service companies specialize in performing repetitive, routine aspects of a particular business. For example, autocare vendors such as Jiffy Lube focus on the routine aspects of car care. H&R Block focuses on the routine aspects of basic tax practice, and many large law firms focus on routine legal services, such as uncomplicated divorces.

? What criteria should be considered when selecting a cost accounting system for a service company?

Before You Go On...

REVIEW IT

1. In what circumstances would a manufacturer use operations costing instead of process costing?
2. Describe the cost-benefit tradeoff in deciding what costing system to use.

✓ The Navigator

CONTEMPORARY DEVELOPMENTS

As indicated in Chapter 19, two contemporary developments in managerial accounting are just-in-time processing and activity-based costing. We explain these innovations in the following sections.

Just-In-Time Processing

STUDY OBJECTIVE 8

Explain just-in-time (JIT) processing.

Traditionally, continuous process manufacturing has been based on a **just-in-case** philosophy: Companies hold inventories of raw materials **just in case** some items are of poor quality or a key supplier is shut down by a strike. They manufacture and store subassembly parts **just in case** these parts are needed later in the manufacturing process. Companies complete and store finished goods **just in case** they receive unexpected and rush customer orders. This philosophy often results in a **"push approach"**: Raw materials and subassembly parts are pushed through each process. Traditional processing often results in the buildup of extensive manufacturing inventories.

Primarily in response to foreign competition, many U.S. firms have switched to **just-in-time (JIT) processing**. The goal of JIT manufacturing is to produce the right products (or parts) at the right time as they are needed. Under JIT processing, companies receive raw materials **just in time** for use in production; they complete subassembly parts **just in time** for use in finished goods; and they complete finished goods **just in time** to be sold. Illustration 21-24 (page 928) shows the sequence of activities in just-in-time processing.

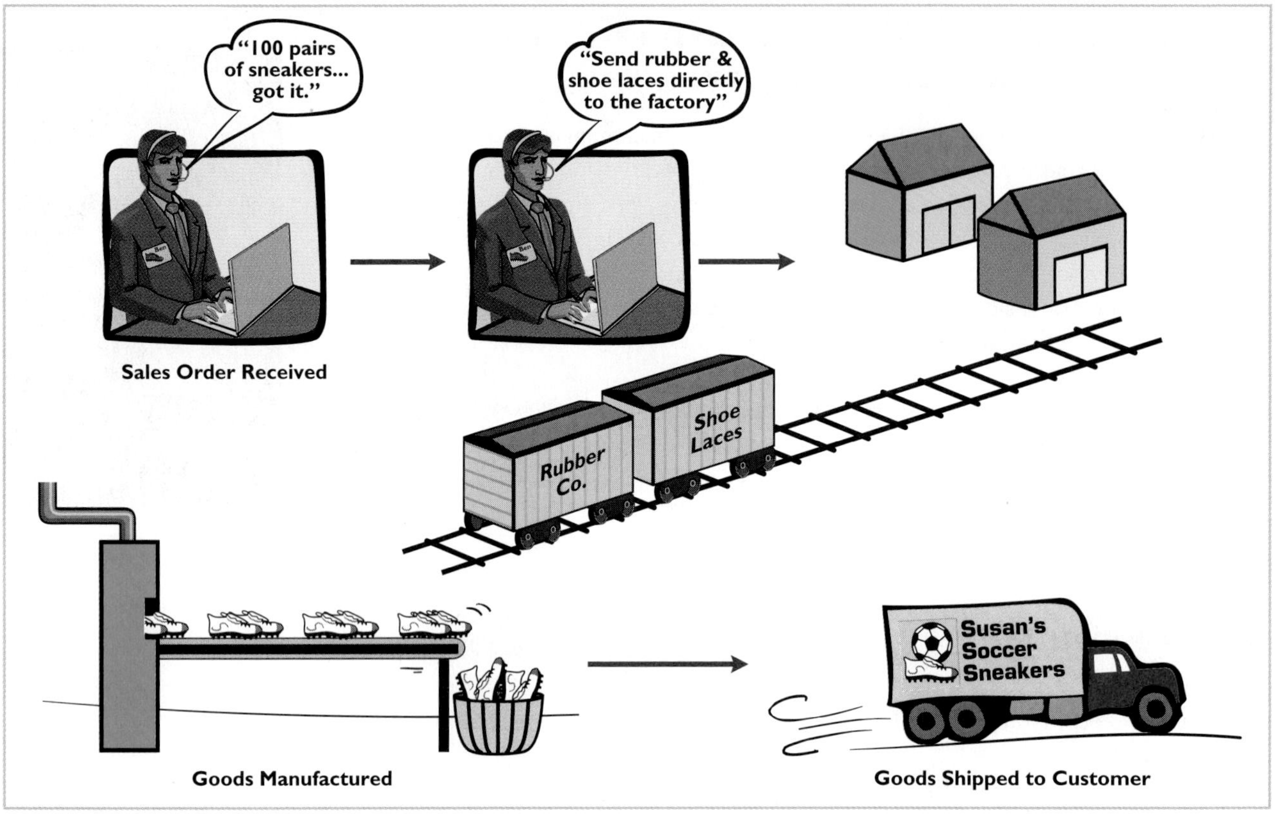

Illustration 21-24
Just-in-time processing

OBJECTIVE OF JIT PROCESSING

A primary objective of JIT is to eliminate all manufacturing inventories. Inventories have an adverse effect on net income because they tie up funds and storage space that could be made available for more productive purposes. JIT strives to eliminate inventories by using a **"pull approach"** in manufacturing: A computer at the final work station sends a signal to the preceding work station. This signal indicates the exact materials (parts and subassemblies) needed to complete the production of a specified product for a specified time period (such as an eight-hour shift). The preceding process, in turn, sends its signal to other processes back up the line. The goal is a smooth continuous flow in the manufacturing process and no buildup of inventories at any point.

ELEMENTS OF JIT PROCESSING

There are three important elements in JIT processing:

1. **Dependable suppliers**. Suppliers must be willing to deliver on short notice exact quantities of raw materials according to precise quality specifications (even including multiple deliveries within the same day). Suppliers must also be willing to deliver the raw materials at specified work stations rather than at a central receiving department. This type of purchasing requires constant and direct communication. Such communication is facilitated by an online computer linkage between the company and its suppliers.
2. A **multiskilled workforce**. Under JIT, machines are often strategically grouped around work cells or work stations. Much of the work is automated. As a result, one worker may have the responsibility to operate and maintain several different types of machines.

3. A **total quality control system.** The company must establish total quality control throughout the manufacturing operations. Total quality control means **no defects**. Since the **pull approach** signals only required quantities, any defects at any work station will shut down operations at subsequent work stations. Total quality control requires continuous monitoring by both employees and supervisors at each work station.

BENEFITS OF JIT PROCESSING

The major benefits of JIT processing are:

1. Significant reduction or elimination of manufacturing inventories.
2. Enhanced product quality.
3. Reduction or elimination of rework costs and inventory storage costs.
4. Production cost savings from the improved flow of goods through the processes.

One of the major accounting benefits of JIT is the elimination of raw materials and work in process inventory accounts. In place of these accounts is **one account**, Raw and In-Process Inventory. All materials and conversion costs are charged to this account. The reduction (or elimination) of in-process inventories results in a simplified computation of equivalent units of production.

MANAGEMENT INSIGHT

How Just-in-Time Helped Hewlett-Packard

JIT first hit the United States in the early 1980s when it was adopted by automobile companies to meet foreign competition. It is now being successfully used in many companies, including General Electric, Caterpillar, and Harley-Davidson. The effects in most cases have been dramatic. For example, after using JIT for two years, a major division of Hewlett-Packard found that work-in-process inventories (in dollars) were down 82%, scrap/rework costs were down 30%, space utilization was down 40%, and labor efficiency improved 50%. As indicated, JIT not only reduces inventory but also enables a manufacturer to produce a better product faster and with less waste.

? How could just-in-time processing contribute to a 50% improvement in labor efficiency?

Activity-Based Costing

STUDY OBJECTIVE 9

Explain activity-based costing (ABC).

Activity-based costing focuses on the activities performed in producing a product. An ABC system is similar to conventional costing systems in accounting for direct materials and direct labor, but it differs in regard to manufacturing overhead.

A conventional cost system uses a **single unit-level** basis to allocate overhead costs to products. The basis may be direct labor or machine hours used to manufacture the product. The assumption in this approach is that as volume of units produced increases, so does the cost of overhead. However, in recent years the amount of direct labor used in many industries has greatly *decreased*, and total overhead costs resulting from depreciation on expensive equipment and machinery, utilities, repairs, and maintenance have significantly *increased*.

In ABC costing, the cost of a product is equal to the sum of the costs of all activities performed to manufacture it. ABC recognizes that to have accurate and meaningful cost data, **more than one basis** of allocating activity costs to products is needed.

In selecting the allocation basis, ABC seeks to identify the **cost drivers** that measure the activities performed on the product. A **cost driver** may be any factor or activity that has a direct cause–effect relationship with the resources consumed. Examples of activities and possible cost drivers are as follows.

Illustration 21-25
Activities and cost drivers in ABC

Activity	Cost Driver
Ordering raw materials	Ordering hours; number of orders
Receiving raw materials	Receiving hours; number of shipments
Materials handling	Number of requisitions; weight of materials; handling hours
Production scheduling	Number of orders
Machine setups	Setup hours; number of setups
Machining (fabricating, assembling, etc.)	Machine hours
Quality control inspections	Number of inspections
Factory supervision	Number of employees

Two important assumptions must be met in order to obtain accurate product costs under ABC:

1. All overhead costs related to the activity must be driven by the cost driver used to assign costs to products.
2. All overhead costs related to the activity should respond proportionally to changes in the activity level of the cost driver.

For example, if there is little or no correlation between changes in the cost driver and consumption of the overhead cost, inaccurate product costs are inevitable. An example of the use of ABC is illustrated in the appendix at the end of this chapter.

Activity-based costing may be used with either a job order or a process cost accounting system. The primary benefit of ABC is more accurate and meaningful product costing. Also, improved cost data about an activity can lead to reduced costs for the activity. In sum, ABC makes managers realize that it is *activities*, and not products, that determine the profitability of a company—a realization that should lead to better management decisions.

Before You Go On...

REVIEW IT

1. What are the principal accounting effects of just-in-time (JIT) processing?
2. What are the primary differences between activity-based costing (ABC) and traditional costing?

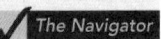

The Navigator

Be sure to read **ALL ABOUT YOU: *Wal-Mart Is on the Phone*** on the next page for information on how topics in this chapter apply to you.

Wal-Mart Is on the Phone

If you own a small business that produces a consumer product, and if Wal-Mart decides to stock your product on its shelves, it is a big, big deal. But those companies lucky enough to have this happen often find themselves in a precarious situation. The same deal that might make them fabulously wealthy might also cause the failure of the business. Suppliers to Wal-Mart sell lots of units, but Wal-Mart demands extremely low prices. You must learn to exist on razor-thin margins. Your cost accounting system had better be accurate, or you may soon be broke.

Some Facts

* Wal-Mart has 138 million weekly customers.
* In 2006 Wal-Mart had annual sales of $312 billion and net income of more than $11.2 billion.
* There are about 5,300 Wal-Mart stores worldwide. During a single recent year, it planned on adding 500 more stores, and it believes that the U.S. has room for at least 4,000 more "supercenters."
* During a recent year, 10,000 companies applied to be new suppliers to Wal-Mart. Of those, some 200 (about 2%) were accepted.
* Wal-Mart doesn't like to account for more than 30% of a supplier's total business for fear that changing an order can destroy the supplier.
* As shown in the "About the Numbers" section, Wal-Mart's "kingdom" spreads across many different countries. Recently, however, it sold all of its stores in Germany because they could not meet its desired profitability goals.

About the Numbers

Wal-Mart continues to grow across the world, but its success varies across countries. The following chart shows total store count in various countries.

Wal-Mart 2006 Worldwide Store Count

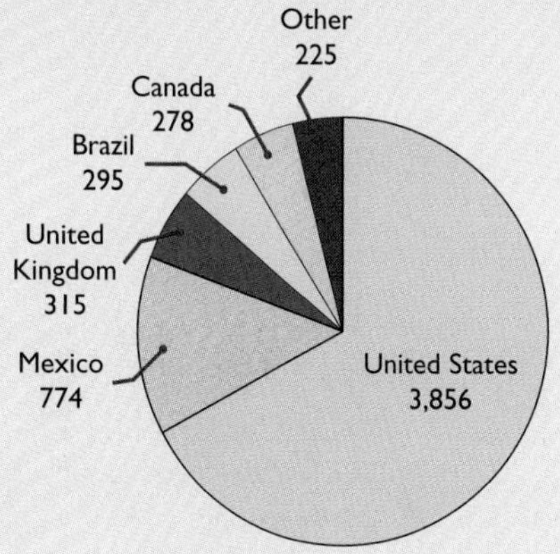

Source: Based on data from Wal-Mart 2006 Annual Report, p. 51.

What Do You Think?

Suppose that you were Colin Roche, whose PenAgain pen was recently offered a 30-day trial period at 500 Wal-Mart stores. In order for the product to pass the trial, in one month Wal-Mart needs to sell 85% of the 48,000 pens that it ordered. If it does, it will then order pens for a much wider distribution at many more of its stores. If it doesn't, the deal is off.

The PenAgain company gets between $6.49 and $12 from other retailers for the PenAgain pen, but Wal-Mart is willing to pay only $3.76. Last year total sales of PenAgain were $2,000,000. If you were Colin Roche would you accept Wal-Mart's offer?

YES: Are you kidding? If only a tiny fraction of Wal-Mart customers buy a pen, the company's sales will go through the roof. You have to take a shot at it.

NO: The risks are high on two counts. First, the company has to dramatically increase its operations in order to meet the production requirements. What will it do with this excess capacity if the deal falls through? Second, the company risks alienating the retailers that it currently supplies with pens. It could lose both Wal-Mart and its existing customers.

Sources: Gwendolyn Bounds, "One Month to Make It," *Wall Street Journal*, May 30, 2006, p. B1; Gwendolyn Bounds, "The Long Road to Wal-Mart," *Wall Street Journal*, September 19, 2005, p. R1; John Anderson, "Running the Gauntlet at Wal-Mart," *Inc.* Magazine, November 2003, p. 93.

The authors' comments on this situation appear on page 955.

Demonstration Problem

Essence Company manufactures a high-end after-shave lotion, called Eternity, in 10-ounce plastic bottles. Because the market for after-shave lotion is highly competitive, the company is very concerned about keeping its costs under control. Eternity is manufactured through three processes: mixing, filling, and corking. Materials are added at the beginning of the process, and labor and overhead are incurred uniformly throughout each process. The company uses a weighted-average method to cost its product. A partially completed production cost report for the month of May for the Mixing Department is shown below.

ESSENCE COMPANY
Mixing Department
Production Cost Report
For the Month Ended May 31, 2008

		Equivalent Units	
QUANTITIES	Physical Units	Materials	Conversion Costs
Units to be accounted for	Step 1	Step 2	
Work in process, May 1	1,000		
Started into production	2,000		
Total units	3,000		
Units accounted for			
Transferred out	2,200	?	?
Work in process, May 31	800	?	?
Total units	3,000	?	?

COSTS		Materials	Conversion Costs	Total
Unit costs Step 3				
Costs in May	(a)	?	?	?
Equivalent units	(b)	?	?	
Unit costs [(a) ÷ (b)]		?	?	?
Costs to be accounted for				
Work in process, May 1				$ 56,300
Started into production				119,320
Total costs				$175,620
Cost Reconciliation Schedule Step 4				
Costs accounted for				
Transferred out				?
Work in process, May 31				
Materials			?	
Conversion costs			?	?
Total costs				?

Additional information:

Work in process, May 1, 1000 units		
Materials cost, 1,000 units (100% complete)	$49,100	
Conversion costs, 1,000 units (70% complete)	7,200	$ 56,300
Materials cost for May, 2,000 units		$100,000

Work in process, May 31, 800 units, 100% complete as to materials and 50% complete as to conversion costs.

Instructions

(a) Prepare a production cost report for the Mixing Department for the month of May.
(b) Prepare the journal entry to record the transfer of goods from the Mixing Department to the Filling Department.
(c) Explain why Essence Company is using a process cost system to account for its costs.

Solution to Demonstration Problem

(a) A completed production cost report for the Mixing Department is shown below. Computations to support the amounts reported follow the report.

ESSENCE COMPANY
Mixing Department
Production Cost Report
For the Month Ended May 31, 2008

		Equivalent Units	
QUANTITIES	Physical Units	Materials	Conversion Costs
Units to be accounted for	Step 1	Step 2	
Work in process, May 1	1,000		
Started into production	2,000		
Total units	3,000		
Units accounted for			
Transferred out	2,200	2,200	2,200
Work in process, May 31	800	800	400 (800 × 50%)
Total units	3,000	3,000	2,600

COSTS				
Unit costs Step 3		Materials	Conversion Costs	Total
Costs in May	(a)	$149,100	$26,520	$175,620
Equivalent units	(b)	3,000	2,600	
Unit costs [(a) ÷ (b)]		$49.70	$10.20	$59.90
Costs to be accounted for				
Work in process, May 1				$ 56,300
Started into production				119,320
Total costs				$175,620

Cost Reconciliation Schedule Step 4		
Costs accounted for		
Transferred out (2,200 × $59.90)		$131,780
Work in process, May 31		
Materials (800 × $49.70)	$39,760	
Conversion costs (400 × $10.20)	4,080	43,840
Total costs		$175,620

Additional computations to support production cost report data:
Materials cost—$49,100 + $100,000
Conversion costs—$7,200 + $19,320 ($119,320 − $100,000)

(b) Work in Process—Filling	131,780	
Work in Process—Mixing		131,780

action plan

- ✓ Compute the physical unit flow—that is, the total units to be accounted for.
- ✓ Compute the equivalent units of production.
- ✓ Compute the unit production costs, expressed in terms of equivalent units of production.
- ✓ Prepare a cost reconciliation schedule, which shows that the total costs accounted for equal the total costs to be accounted for.

(c) Process cost systems are used to apply costs to similar products that are mass-produced in a continuous fashion. Essence Company uses a process cost system: Production of the after-shave lotion, once it begins, continues until the after-shave lotion emerges. The processing is the same for the entire run—with precisely the same amount of materials, labor, and overhead. Each bottle of Eternity after-shave lotion is indistinguishable from another.

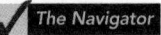

The Navigator

SUMMARY OF STUDY OBJECTIVES

WILEY PLUS

1 **Understand who uses process cost systems.** Process cost systems are used by companies that mass-produce similar products in a continuous fashion. Once production begins, it continues until the finished product emerges. Each unit of finished product is indistinguishable from every other unit.

2 **Explain the similarities and differences between job order cost and process cost systems.** Job order cost systems are similar to process cost systems in three ways: (1) Both systems track the same cost elements—direct materials, direct labor, and manufacturing overhead. (2) Costs are accumulated in the same accounts—Raw Materials Inventory, Factory Labor, and Manufacturing Overhead. (3) Accumulated costs are assigned to the same accounts—Work in Process, Finished Goods Inventory, and Cost of Goods Sold. However, the method of assigning costs differs significantly.

There are four main differences between the two cost systems: (1) A process cost system uses separate accounts for each department or manufacturing process, rather than only one work in process account used in a job order cost system. (2) In a process cost system, costs are summarized in a production cost report for each department. In a job cost system, costs are charged to individual jobs and summarized in a job cost sheet. (3) Costs are totaled at the end of a time period in a process cost system, but at the completion of a job in a job cost system. (4) In a process cost system, unit cost is calculated as: Total manufacturing costs for the period ÷ Units produced during the period. In a job cost system, unit cost is : Total cost per job ÷ Units produced.

3 **Explain the flow of costs in a process cost system.** Manufacturing costs for raw materials, labor, and overhead are assigned to work in process accounts for various departments or manufacturing processes. The costs of units completed are transferred from one department to another as those units move through the manufacturing process. The costs of completed work are transferred to Finished Goods Inventory. When inventory is sold, costs are transferred to Cost of Goods Sold.

4 **Make the journal entries to assign manufacturing costs in a process cost system.** Entries to assign the costs of raw materials, labor, and overhead consist of a credit to Raw Materials Inventory, Factory Labor, and Manufacturing Overhead, and a debit to Work in Process for each department. Entries to record the cost of goods transferred to another department are a credit to Work in Process for the department whose work is finished and a debit to the department to which the goods are transferred. The entry to record units completed and transferred to the warehouse is a credit for the department whose work is finished and a debit to Finished Goods Inventory. The entry to record the sale of goods is a credit to Finished Goods Inventory and a debit to Cost of Goods Sold.

5 **Compute equivalent units.** Equivalent units of production measure work done during a period, expressed in fully completed units. This concept is used to determine the cost per unit of completed product. Equivalent units are the sum of units completed and transferred out plus equivalent units of ending work in process.

6 **Explain the four steps necessary to prepare a production cost report.** The four steps to complete a production cost report are: (1) Compute the physical unit flow—that is, the total units to be accounted for. (2) Compute the equivalent units of production. (3) Compute the unit production costs, expressed in terms of equivalent units of production. (4) Prepare a cost reconciliation schedule, which shows that the total costs accounted for equal the total costs to be accounted for.

7 **Prepare a production cost report.** The production cost report contains both quantity and cost data for a production department. There are four sections in the report: (1) number of physical units, (2) equivalent units determination, (3) unit costs, and (4) cost reconciliation schedule.

8 **Explain just-in-time (JIT) processing.** JIT is a manufacturing technique dedicated to producing the right products at the right time as needed. One of the principal accounting effects is that a Raw and In-Process Inventory account replaces both the raw materials and work in process inventory accounts.

9 **Explain activity-based costing (ABC).** ABC is a method of product costing that focuses on the activities performed to produce products. It assigns the cost of the activities to products by using cost drivers that measure the activities performed. The primary objective of ABC is accurate and meaningful product costs.

The Navigator

GLOSSARY

Activity-based costing A cost accounting system that focuses on the activities performed in manufacturing a specific product. (p. 929).

Conversion costs The sum of labor costs and overhead costs. (p. 920).

Cost driver Any factor or activity that has a direct cause–effect relationship with the resources consumed. (p. 930).

Cost reconciliation schedule A schedule that shows that the total costs accounted for equal the total costs to be accounted for. (p. 924).

Equivalent units of production A measure of the work done during the period, expressed in fully completed units. (p. 919).

Just-in-time processing A processing system dedicated to producing the right products (or parts) as they are needed. (p. 927).

Operations costing A combination of a process cost and a job order cost system, in which products are manufactured primarily by standardized methods, with some customization. (p. 926).

Physical units Actual units to be accounted for during a period, irrespective of any work performed. (p. 922).

Process cost systems An accounting system used to apply costs to similar products that are mass-produced in a continuous fashion. (p. 912).

Production cost report An internal report for management that shows both production quantity and cost data for a production department. (p. 920).

Total units (costs) accounted for The sum of the units (costs) transferred out during the period plus the units (costs) in process at the end of the period. (pp. 922, 924).

Total units (costs) to be accounted for The sum of the units (costs) started (or transferred) into production during the period plus the units (costs) in process at the beginning of the period. (pp. 922, 924).

Unit production costs Costs expressed in terms of equivalent units of production. (p. 923).

Weighted-average method Method used to compute equivalent units of production which considers the degree of completion (weighting) of the units completed and transferred out and the ending work in process. (p. 919).

APPENDIX Example of Traditional Costing versus Activity-Based Costing

Production and Cost Data

STUDY OBJECTIVE 10
Apply activity-based costing to specific company data.

In this appendix we present an example that compares activity-based costing to traditional costing. Assume that Atlas Company produces two products, The Boot and The Club. The Boot is a high-volume item totaling 25,000 units annually. The Club is a low-volume item totaling only 5,000 units per year. Each product requires one hour of direct labor for completion. Therefore, total annual direct labor hours are 30,000 (25,000 + 5,000). Expected annual manufacturing overhead costs are $900,000. The predetermined overhead rate is $30 ($900,000 ÷ 30,000) per direct labor hour.

The direct materials cost per unit is $40 for The Boot and $30 for The Club. The direct labor cost is $12 per unit for each product.

Unit Costs Under Traditional Costing

Illustration 21A-1 shows the unit cost for each product under traditional costing.

Illustration 21A-1
Units costs—traditional costing

	Product	
Manufacturing Costs	**The Boot**	**The Club**
Direct materials	$40	$30
Direct labor	12	12
Overhead	30*	30*
Total unit cost	**$82**	**$72**

*Predetermined overhead rate × Direct labor hours ($30 × 1 hr = $30)

DETERMINING OVERHEAD RATES UNDER ABC

Analysis reveals that Atlas Company's expected annual overhead costs of $900,000 relate to three activities—machine setups, machining, and inspections. Illustration 21A-2 shows the cost driver and overhead rate for each activity.

Illustration 21A-2
Computing overhead rates—ABC

Activity	Cost Driver	Total Expected Overhead Cost	Total Expected Use of Driver	Activity Based Overhead Rate
Machine setups	Number of setups	$300,000	1,500	**$200** per setup
Machining	Machine hours	500,000	50,000	**$10** per machine hour
Inspections	Number of inspections	100,000	2,000	**$50** per inspection

ASSIGNING OVERHEAD COSTS TO PRODUCTS UNDER ABC

In assigning costs, it is necessary to know the expected number of cost drivers for each product. Because of its low volume, The Club requires more setups and inspections than The Boot. The expected number of cost drivers for each product is as follows.

Illustration 21A-3
Expected number of cost drivers

	Product		
Cost Driver	**The Boot**	**The Club**	**Total Usage**
Number of machine setups	500	1,000	1,500
Machine hours	30,000	20,000	50,000
Number of inspections	500	1,500	2,000

Using these data, Atlas can assign the expected annual overhead cost to each product as follows.

Illustration 21A-4
Assignment of overhead costs to products

	The Boot		The Club		
Activity	**Number**	**Cost**	**Number**	**Cost**	**Total Cost**
Machine setups ($200)	500	$100,000	1,000	$200,000	$300,000
Machining ($10)	30,000	300,000	20,000	200,000	500,000
Inspections ($50)	500	25,000	1,500	75,000	100,000
Total assigned costs (a)		$425,000		$475,000	$900,000
Units produced (b)		25,000		5,000	
Overhead cost per unit [(a) ÷ (b)]		$17		$95	

These data show that under ABC, overhead costs are shifted from the high-volume product (The Boot) to the low-volume product (The Club). This shift results in more accurate costing for two reasons:

1. Low-volume products often require more special handling, such as more machine setups and inspections, than high-volume products. This is true for Atlas Company. Thus, the low-volume product frequently is responsible for more overhead costs per unit than a high-volume product.
2. The overhead costs incurred by the low-volume product often are disproportionate to a traditional allocation base. For example, direct labor hours is usually a poor cost driver for assigning overhead costs to low-volume products. When overhead is properly assigned in ABC, it will usually increase the unit cost of low-volume products.

Comparing Unit Costs

A comparison of unit manufacturing costs under traditional costing and ABC shows the following significant differences.

Illustration 21A-5
Comparison of unit product costs

	The Boot		The Club	
Manufacturing Costs	**Traditional Costing**	**ABC**	**Traditional Costing**	**ABC**
Direct materials	$40	$40	$30	$ 30
Direct labor	12	12	12	12
Overhead	30	17	30	95
Total cost per unit	**$82**	**$69**	**$72**	**$137**
	Overstated $13		**Understated $65**	

The comparison shows that unit costs under traditional costing have been significantly distorted. The cost of The Boot has been overstated $13 per unit ($82−$69). The cost of The Club has been understated $65 per unit ($137−$72). The differences are attributable to how manufacturing overhead is assigned. A likely consequence of the differences is that Atlas Company has been overpricing The Boot and possibly losing market share to competitors. It also has been sacrificing profitability by underpricing The Club.

As illustrated in the above case, ABC involves the following steps.

1. Identify the major activities that pertain to the manufacture of specific products.
2. Accumulate manufacturing overhead costs by activities.
3. Identify the cost driver(s) that accurately measure(s) each activity's contribution to the finished product.
4. Assign manufacturing overhead costs for each activity to products, using the cost driver(s).

Benefits and Limitations of Activity-Based Costing

We have already seen that a primary benefit of ABC is more accurate product costing. In addition, ABC offers the following other benefits:

1. **Enhanced control over overhead costs.** Many overhead costs are incurred directly by activities. Thus, managers become more aware of their responsibility to control the activities that generate the costs.
2. **Better management decisions.** More accurate product costing should contribute to setting selling prices that will achieve desired profitability levels. The cost data also should be helpful in deciding whether to discontinue or expand a product line or whether to make or buy a component.

The principal disadvantages of ABC generally focus on two factors. First, **the expense of obtaining the cost data** required by the system is relatively high. ABC requires data that are not normally generated within a company. Examples of such data are the number of setups, inspections, orders placed, and orders received. In addition, many computations are involved in assigning overhead costs to individual products.

Second, **ABC does not eliminate arbitrary assignments** of overhead. For example, plant-wide overhead costs such as depreciation, insurance, and property taxes on the factory building should be allocated to the activity centers in determining the cost of a product. With ABC, these allocations may be more difficult to do accurately because of the increased number of activity centers. As a result, accuracy of product costs could be adversely affected.

SUMMARY OF STUDY OBJECTIVE FOR APPENDIX

WILEY PLUS

10. **Apply activity-based costing to specific company data.** In applying ABC, it is necessary to compute the overhead rate for each activity by dividing total expected overhead by the total expected usage of the cost driver. The overhead cost for each activity is then assigned to products on the basis of each product's use of the cost driver.

*Note: All **asterisked** Questions, Exercises, and Problems relate to material contained in the appendix to the chapter.

SELF-STUDY QUESTIONS

WILEY PLUS

Answers are at the end of the chapter.

(SO 1) 1. Which of the following items is *not* a characteristic of a process cost system?
a. Once production begins, it continues until the finished product emerges.
b. The products produced are heterogeneous in nature.
c. The focus is on continually producing homogeneous products.
d. When the finished product emerges, all units have precisely the same amount of materials, labor, and overhead.

(SO 2) 2. Indicate which of the following statements is *not* correct.
a. Both a job order and a process cost system track the same three manufacturing cost elements—direct materials, direct labor, and manufacturing overhead.
b. In a job order cost system, only one work in process account is used, whereas in a process cost system, multiple work in process accounts are used.
c. Manufacturing costs are accumulated the same way in a job order and in a process cost system.
d. Manufacturing costs are assigned the same way in a job order and in a process cost system.

(SO 3) 3. In a process cost system, costs are assigned only:
a. to one work in process account.
b. to work in process and finished goods inventory.
c. to work in process, finished goods, and cost of goods sold.
d. to work in process accounts.

(SO 4) 4. In making the journal entry to assign raw materials costs:
a. the debit is to Finished Goods Inventory.
b. the debit is often to two or more work in process accounts.
c. the credit is generally to two or more work in process accounts.
d. the credit is to Finished Goods Inventory.

(SO 5) 5. The Mixing Department's output during the period consists of 20,000 units completed and transferred out, and 5,000 units in ending work in process 60% complete as to materials and conversion costs. Beginning inventory is 1,000 units, 40% complete as to materials and conversion costs. The equivalent units of production are:
a. 22,600. **c.** 24,000.
b. 23,000. **d.** 25,000.

6. In RYZ Company, there are zero units in beginning work in process, 7,000 units started into production, and 500 units in ending work in process 20% completed. The physical units to be accounted for are: (SO 6)
a. 7,000. **c.** 7,600.
b. 7,360. **d.** 7,340.

7. Stock Company has 2,000 units in beginning work in process, 20% complete as to conversion costs, 23,000 units transferred out to finished goods, and 3,000 units in ending work in process 33⅓% complete as to conversion costs. The beginning and ending inventory is fully complete as to materials costs. Equivalent units for materials and conversion costs are, respectively: (SO 6)
a. 22,000, 24,000. **c.** 26,000, 24,000.
b. 24,000, 26,000. **d.** 26,000, 26,000.

8. Fortner Company has no beginning work in process; 9,000 units are transferred out and 3,000 units in ending work in process are one-third finished as to conversion costs and fully complete as to materials cost. If total materials cost is $60,000, the unit materials cost is: (SO 6)
a. $5.00.
b. $5.45 rounded.
c. $6.00.
d. No correct answer is given.

9. Largo Company has unit costs of $10 for materials and $30 for conversion costs. If there are 2,500 units in ending work in process, 40% complete as to conversion costs, and fully complete as to materials cost, the total cost assignable to the ending work in process inventory is: (SO 6)
a. $45,000. **c.** $75,000.
b. $55,000. **d.** $100,000.

10. A production cost report (SO 7)
a. is an external report.
b. shows costs charged to a department and costs accounted for.

c. shows equivalent units of production but not physical units.
d. contains six sections.

(SO 8) 11. Just-in-time processing (JIT):
a. strives to eliminate inventories.
b. uses a pull approach in manufacturing.
c. Neither of the above.
d. Both (a) and (b).

(SO 9) 12. Activity-based costing (ABC):
a. can be used only in a process cost system.
b. focuses on units of production.
c. focuses on activities performed to produce a product.
d. uses only a single basis of allocation.

*13. The overhead rate for Machine Setups is $100 per setup. Products A and B have 80 and 60 setups, respectively. The overhead assigned to each product is: (SO 10)
a. Product A $8,000, Product B $8,000.
b. Product A $8,000, Product B $6,000.
c. Product A $6,000, Product B $6,000.
d. Product A $6,000, Product B $8,000.

Go to the book's website,
www.wiley.com/college/weygandt,
for additional Self-Study Questions.

The Navigator

QUESTIONS

1. Identify which costing system—job order or process cost—the following companies would primarily use: (a) Quaker Oats, (b) Ford Motor Company, (c) Kinko's Print Shop, and (d) Warner Bros. Motion Pictures.
2. Contrast the primary focus of job order cost accounting and of process cost accounting.
3. What are the similarities between a job order and a process cost system?
4. Your roommate is confused about the features of process cost accounting. Identify and explain the distinctive features for your roommate.
5. Mel Storrer believes there are no significant differences in the flow of costs between job order cost accounting and process cost accounting. Is Storrer correct? Explain.
6. (a) What source documents are used in assigning (1) materials and (2) labor to production in a process cost system?
(b) What criterion and basis are commonly used in allocating overhead to processes?
7. At Ace Company, overhead is assigned to production departments at the rate of $5 per machine hour. In July, machine hours were 3,000 in the Machining Department and 2,400 in the Assembly Department. Prepare the entry to assign overhead to production.
8. Gary Weiss is uncertain about the steps used to prepare a production cost report. State the procedures that are required in the sequence in which they are performed.
9. Rich Mordica is confused about computing physical units. Explain to Rich how physical units to be accounted for and physical units accounted for are determined.
10. What is meant by the term "equivalent units of production"?
11. How are equivalent units of production computed?
12. Mason Company had zero units of beginning work in process. During the period, 9,000 units were completed, and there were 600 units of ending work in process. What were the units started into production?
13. Mendle Co. has zero units of beginning work in process. During the period 12,000 units were completed, and there were 800 units of ending work in process one-fifth complete as to conversion cost and 100% complete as to materials cost. What were the equivalent units of production for (a) materials and (b) conversion costs?
14. Reyes Co. started 3,000 units for the period. Its beginning inventory is 500 units one-fourth complete as to conversion costs and 100% complete as to materials cost. Its ending inventory is 200 units one-fifth complete as to conversion cost and 100% complete as to materials costs. How many units were transferred out this period?
15. Kiner Company transfers out 14,000 units and has 2,000 units of ending work in process that are 25% complete. Materials are entered at the beginning of the process and there is no beginning work in process. Assuming unit materials costs of $3 and unit conversion costs of $6, what are the costs to be assigned to units (a) transferred out and (b) in ending work in process?
16. (a) Eve Adams believes the production cost report is an external report for stockholders. Is Eve correct? Explain.
(b) Identify the sections in a production cost report.
17. What purposes are served by a production cost report?
18. At Frank Company, there are 800 units of ending work in process that are 100% complete as to materials and 40% complete as to conversion costs. If the unit cost of materials is $4 and the costs assigned to the 800 units is $6,000, what is the per-unit conversion cost?
19. What is the difference between operations costing and a process costing system?
20. How does a company decide whether to use a job order or a process cost system?
21. (a) Describe the philosophy and approach of just-in-time processing.
(b) Identify the major elements of JIT processing.
22. (a) What are the principal differences between activity-based costing (ABC) and traditional product costing?
(b) What assumptions must be met for ABC costing to be useful?
23. Dipak Co. identifies the following activities that pertain to manufacturing overhead: Materials Handling, Machine Setups, Factory Machine Maintenance, Factory Supervision, and Quality Control. For each activity identify an appropriate cost driver.
*24. (a) Identify the steps that pertain to activity-based costing.
(b) What are the advantages of ABC costing?

BRIEF EXERCISES

Journalize entries for accumulating costs. (SO 4)

BE21-1 Sanchez Manufacturing purchases $45,000 of raw materials on account, and it incurs $50,000 of factory labor costs. Journalize the two transactions on March 31 assuming the labor costs are not paid until April.

Journalize the assignment of materials and labor costs. (SO 4)

BE21-2 Data for Sanchez Manufacturing are given in BE21-1. Supporting records show that (a) the Assembly Department used $24,000 of raw materials and $30,000 of the factory labor, and (b) the Finishing Department used the remainder. Journalize the assignment of the costs to the processing departments on March 31.

Journalize the assignment of overhead costs. (SO 4)

BE21-3 Factory labor data for Sanchez Manufacturing are given in BE21-2. Manufacturing overhead is assigned to departments on the basis of 200% of labor costs. Journalize the assignment of overhead to the Assembly and Finishing Departments.

Compute physical units of production. (SO 6)

BE21-4 Bowyer Manufacturing Company has the following production data for selected months.

			Ending Work in Process	
Month	**Beginning Work in Process**	**Units Transferred Out**	**Units**	**% Complete as to Conversion Cost**
January	–0–	30,000	10,000	40%
March	–0–	40,000	8,000	75
July	–0–	40,000	16,000	25

Compute the physical units for each month.

Compute equivalent units of production. (SO 5)

BE21-5 Using the data in BE21-4, compute equivalent units of production for materials and conversion costs, assuming materials are entered at the beginning of the process.

Compute unit costs of production. (SO 6)

BE21-6 In Montego Company, total material costs are $32,000, and total conversion costs are $54,000. Equivalent units of production are materials 10,000 and conversion costs 12,000. Compute the unit costs for materials, conversion costs, and total manufacturing costs.

Assign costs to units transferred out and in process. (SO 6)

BE21-7 Hindi Company has the following production data for April: units transferred out 40,000, and ending work in process 5,000 units that are 100% complete for materials and 40% complete for conversion costs. If unit materials cost is $4 and unit conversion cost is $9, determine the costs to be assigned to the units transferred out and the units in ending work in process.

Compute unit costs. (SO 6)

BE21-8 Production costs chargeable to the Finishing Department in June in Castilla Company are materials $15,000, labor $29,500, overhead $18,000. Equivalent units of production are materials 20,000 and conversion costs 19,000. Compute the unit costs for materials and conversion costs.

Prepare cost reconciliation schedule. (SO 6)

BE21-9 Data for Castilla Company are given in BE21-8. Production records indicate that 18,000 units were transferred out, and 2,000 units in ending work in process were 60% complete as to conversion cost and 100% complete as to materials. Prepare a cost reconciliation schedule.

Compute equivalent units of production. (SO 5)

BE21-10 The Smelting Department of Massaro Manufacturing Company has the following production and cost data for November.

> Production: Beginning work in process 2,000 units that are 100% complete as to materials and 20% complete as to conversion costs; units transferred out 8,000 units; and ending work in process 5,000 units that are 100% complete as to materials and 40% complete as to conversion costs.

Compute the equivalent units of production for **(a)** materials and **(b)** conversion costs for the month of November.

Compute overhead rates for activities. (SO 10)

***BE21-11** Bristol Company identifies three activities in its manufacturing process: machine setups, machining, and inspections. Estimated annual overhead cost for each activity is $120,000, $300,000, and $70,000, respectively. The cost driver for each activity and the expected annual usage are: number of setups 1,000, machine hours 25,000, and number of inspections 2,000. Compute the overhead rate for each activity.

EXERCISES

E21-1 Doc Gibbs has prepared the following list of statements about process cost accounting.

Understand process cost accounting. (SO 1, 2)

1. Process cost systems are used to apply costs to similar products that are mass-produced in a continuous fashion.
2. A process cost system is used when each finished unit is indistinguishable from another.
3. Companies that produce soft drinks, motion pictures, and computer chips would all use process cost accounting.
4. In a process cost system, costs are tracked by individual jobs.
5. Job order costing and process costing track different manufacturing cost elements.
6. Both job order costing and process costing account for direct materials, direct labor, and manufacturing overhead.
7. Costs flow through the accounts in the same basic way for both job order costing and process costing.
8. In a process cost system, only one work in process account is used.
9. In a process cost system, costs are summarized in a job cost sheet.
10. In a process cost system, the unit cost is total manufacturing costs for the period divided by the units produced during the period.

Instructions

Identify each statement as true or false. If false, indicate how to correct the statement.

E21-2 Fernando Company manufactures pizza sauce through two production departments: Cooking and Canning. In each process, materials and conversion costs are incurred evenly throughout the process. For the month of April, the work in process accounts show the following debits.

Journalize transactions. (SO 4)

	Cooking	Canning
Beginning work in process	\$ –0–	\$ 4,000
Materials	21,000	6,000
Labor	8,500	7,000
Overhead	29,500	25,800
Costs transferred in		53,000

Instructions

Journalize the April transactions.

E21-3 The ledger of Molindo Company has the following work in process account.

Answer questions on costs and production. (SO 3, 5, 6)

Work in Process—Painting

5/1	Balance	3,590	5/31	Transferred out	?
5/31	Materials	5,160			
5/31	Labor	2,740			
5/31	Overhead	1,650			
5/31	Balance	?			

Production records show that there were 400 units in the beginning inventory, 30% complete, 1,100 units started, and 1,200 units transferred out. The beginning work in process had materials cost of \$2,040 and conversion costs of \$1,550. The units in ending inventory were 40% complete. Materials are entered at the beginning of the painting process.

Instructions

(a) How many units are in process at May 31?
(b) What is the unit materials cost for May?
(c) What is the unit conversion cost for May?
(d) What is the total cost of units transferred out in May?
(e) What is the cost of the May 31 inventory?

Journalize transactions for two processes.
(SO 4)

E21-4 Douglas Manufacturing Company has two production departments: Cutting and Assembly. July 1 inventories are Raw Materials $4,200, Work in Process—Cutting $2,900, Work in Process—Assembly $10,600, and Finished Goods $31,000. During July, the following transactions occurred.

1. Purchased $62,500 of raw materials on account.
2. Incurred $56,000 of factory labor. (Credit Wages Payable.)
3. Incurred $70,000 of manufacturing overhead; $40,000 was paid and the remainder is unpaid.
4. Requisitioned materials for Cutting $15,700 and Assembly $8,900.
5. Used factory labor for Cutting $29,000 and Assembly $27,000.
6. Applied overhead at the rate of $15 per machine hour. Machine hours were Cutting 1,680 and Assembly 1,720.
7. Transferred goods costing $67,600 from the Cutting Department to the Assembly Department.
8. Transferred goods costing $134,900 from Assembly to Finished Goods.
9. Sold goods costing $150,000 for $200,000 on account.

Instructions
Journalize the transactions. (Omit explanations.)

Compute physical units and equivalent units of production.
(SO 5, 6)

E21-5 In Ramirez Company, materials are entered at the beginning of each process. Work in process inventories, with the percentage of work done on conversion costs, and production data for its Sterilizing Department in selected months during 2008 are as follows.

	Beginning Work in Process			Ending Work in Process	
Month	**Units**	**Conversion Cost%**	**Units Transferred Out**	**Units**	**Conversion Cost%**
January	–0–	—	7,000	2,000	60
March	–0–	—	12,000	3,000	30
May	–0–	—	16,000	5,000	80
July	–0–	—	10,000	1,500	40

Instructions
(a) Compute the physical units for January and May.
(b) Compute the equivalent units of production for (1) materials and (2) conversion costs for each month.

Determine equivalent units, unit costs, and assignment of costs.
(SO 5, 6)

E21-6 The Cutting Department of Groneman Manufacturing has the following production and cost data for July.

Production	Costs	
1. Transferred out 9,000 units.	Beginning work in process	$ –0–
2. Started 3,000 units that are 60% complete as to conversion costs and 100% complete as to materials at July 31.	Materials	45,000
	Labor	16,200
	Manufacturing overhead	18,900

Materials are entered at the beginning of the process. Conversion costs are incurred uniformly during the process.

Instructions
(a) Determine the equivalent units of production for (1) materials and (2) conversion costs.
(b) Compute unit costs and prepare a cost reconciliation schedule.

Prepare a production cost report.
(SO 5, 6, 7)

E21-7 The Sanding Department of Ortiz Furniture Company has the following production and manufacturing cost data for March 2008, the first month of operation.

Production: 12,000 units finished and transferred out; 3,000 units started that are 100% complete as to materials and 20% complete as to conversion costs.
Manufacturing costs: Materials $33,000; labor $27,000; overhead $36,000.

Instructions
Prepare a production cost report.

E21-8 The Blending Department of Hancock Company has the following cost and production data for the month of April.

Determine equivalent units, unit costs, and assignment of costs.

(SO 5, 6)

Costs:	
Work in process, April 1	
Direct materials: 100% complete	$100,000
Conversion costs: 20% complete	70,000
Cost of work in process, April 1	$170,000
Costs incurred during production in April	
Direct materials	$ 800,000
Conversion costs	362,000
Costs incurred in April	$1,162,000

Units transferred out totaled 14,000. Ending work in process was 1,000 units that are 100% complete as to materials and 40% complete as to conversion costs.

Instructions
(a) Compute the equivalent units of production for (1) materials and (2) conversion costs for the month of April.
(b) Compute the unit costs for the month.
(c) Determine the costs to be assigned to the units transferred out and in ending work in process.

E21-9 Podsednik Company has gathered the following information.

Determine equivalent units, unit costs, and assignment of costs.

(SO 5, 6)

Units in beginning work in process	-0-
Units started into production	36,000
Units in ending work in process	6,000
Percent complete for conversion costs in ending work in process	40%
Costs incurred:	
Direct materials	$72,000
Direct labor	$81,000
Overhead	$97,200

Instructions
(a) Compute equivalent units of production for materials and for conversion costs.
(b) Determine the unit costs of production.
(c) Show the assignment of costs to units transferred out and in process.

E21-10 Pink Martini Company has gathered the following information.

Determine equivalent units, unit costs, and assignment of costs.

(SO 5, 6)

Units in beginning work in process	20,000
Units started into production	72,000
Units in ending work in process	24,000
Percent complete for conversion costs in ending work in process	60%
Costs incurred:	
Direct materials	$101,200
Direct labor	$164,800
Overhead	$123,600

Instructions
(a) Compute equivalent units of production for materials and for conversion costs.
(b) Determine the unit costs of production.
(c) Show the assignment of costs to units transferred out and in process.

Compute equivalent units, unit costs, and costs assigned.
(SO 5, 6)

E21-11 The Polishing Department of Estaban Manufacturing Company has the following production and manufacturing cost data for September. Materials are entered at the beginning of the process.

Production: Beginning inventory 1,600 units that are 100% complete as to materials and 30% complete as to conversion costs; units started during the period are 18,400; ending inventory of 5,000 units 10% complete as to conversion costs.

Manufacturing costs: Beginning inventory costs, comprised of $20,000 of materials and $43,180 of conversion costs; materials costs added in Polishing during the month, $177,200; labor and overhead applied in Polishing during the month, $102,680 and $257,140, respectively.

Instructions

(a) Compute the equivalent units of production for materials and conversion costs for the month of September.
(b) Compute the unit costs for materials and conversion costs for the month.
(c) Determine the costs to be assigned to the units transferred out and in process.

Explain the production cost report.
(SO 7)

E21-12 Stan Maley has recently been promoted to production manager, and so he has just started to receive various managerial reports. One of the reports he has received is the production cost report that you prepared. It showed that his department had 2,000 equivalent units in ending inventory. His department has had a history of not keeping enough inventory on hand to meet demand. He has come to you, very angry, and wants to know why you credited him with only 2,000 units when he knows he had at least twice that many on hand.

Instructions

Explain to him why his production cost report showed only 2,000 equivalent units in ending inventory. Write an informal memo. Be kind and explain very clearly why he is mistaken.

Prepare a production cost report.
(SO 5, 6, 7)

E21-13 The Welding Department of Batista Manufacturing Company has the following production and manufacturing cost data for February 2008. All materials are added at the beginning of the process.

Manufacturing Costs		
Beginning work in process		
Materials	$18,000	
Conversion costs	14,175	$32,175
Materials		180,000
Labor		32,780
Overhead		61,445

Production Data	
Beginning work in process	15,000 units
	1/10 complete
Units transferred out	49,000
Units started	60,000
Ending work in process	26,000 units
	1/5 complete

Instructions

Prepare a production cost report for the Welding Department for the month of February.

Compute overhead rates and assign overhead using ABC.
(SO 10)

***E21-14** Carmeli Instrument Inc. manufactures two products: missile range instruments and space pressure gauges. During January, 50 range instruments and 300 pressure gauges were produced, and overhead costs of $81,000 were incurred. An analysis of overhead costs reveals the following activities.

Activity	Cost Driver	Total Cost
1. Materials handling	Number of requisitions	$30,000
2. Machine setups	Number of setups	27,000
3. Quality inspections	Number of inspections	24,000

The cost driver volume for each product was as follows.

Cost Driver	Instruments	Gauges	Total
Number of requisitions	400	600	1,000
Number of setups	150	300	450
Number of inspections	200	400	600

Instructions

(a) Determine the overhead rate for each activity.

(b) Assign the manufacturing overhead costs for January to the two products using activity-based costing.

(c) Write a memo to the president of Carmeli Instrument, explaining the benefits of activity-based costing.

Compute product cost using traditional costing and ABC.

(SO 10)

***E21-15** Oakenfeld Company manufactures a number of specialized machine parts. Part Bunkka-22 uses $35 of direct materials and $15 of direct labor per unit.

Oakenfeld's estimated manufacturing overhead is as follows:

Materials handling	$100,000
Machining	200,000
Factory supervision	150,000
Total	$450,000

Overhead is applied based on direct labor costs, which were estimated at $200,000.

Oakenfeld is considering adopting activity-based costing. The cost drivers are estimated at:

Activity	Cost driver	Expected use
Materials handling	Weight of materials	50,000 pounds
Machining	Machine hours	20,000 hours
Factory supervision	Direct labor hours	12,000 hours

Instructions

(a) Compute the cost of 1,000 units of Bunkka-22 using the current traditional costing system.

(b) Compute the cost of 1,000 units of Bunkka-22 using the proposed activity-based costing system. Assume the 1,000 units use 2,500 pounds of materials, 500 machine hours, and 1,000 direct labor hours.

EXERCISES: SET B

Visit the book's website at **www.wiley.com/college/weygandt**, and choose the Student Companion site, to access Exercise Set B.

PROBLEMS: SET A

Complete four steps necessary to prepare a production cost report.

(SO 5, 6, 7)

P21-1A Kasten Company manufactures bowling balls through two processes: Molding and Packaging. In the Molding Department, the urethane, rubber, plastics, and other materials are molded into bowling balls. In the Packaging Department, the balls are placed in cartons and sent to the finished goods warehouse. All materials are entered at the beginning of each process. Labor and manufacturing overhead are incurred uniformly throughout each process. Production and cost data for the Molding Department during June 2008 are presented below.

Production Data	June
Beginning work in process units	–0–
Units started into production	20,000
Ending work in process units	2,000
Percent complete—ending inventory	60%
Cost Data	
Materials	$198,000
Labor	50,400
Overhead	112,800
Total	$361,200

Instructions

(a) Prepare a schedule showing physical units of production.
(b) Determine the equivalent units of production for materials and conversion costs.
(c) Compute the unit costs of production.
(d) Determine the costs to be assigned to the units transferred and in process for June.
(e) Prepare a production cost report for the Molding Department for the month of June.

Complete four steps necessary to prepare a production cost report.

(SO 5, 6, 7)

P21-2A Ortega Industries Inc. manufactures in separate processes furniture for homes. In each process, materials are entered at the beginning, and conversion costs are incurred uniformly. Production and cost data for the first process in making two products in two different manufacturing plants are as follows.

	Cutting Department	
	Plant 1	**Plant 2**
Production Data—July	**T12-Tables**	**C10-Chairs**
Work in process units, July 1	–0–	–0–
Units started into production	20,000	16,000
Work in process units, July 31	3,000	500
Work in process percent complete	60	80
Cost Data—July		
Work in process, July 1	$ –0–	$ –0–
Materials	380,000	288,000
Labor	234,400	125,900
Overhead	104,000	96,700
Total	$718,400	$510,600

Instructions

(a) For each plant:
  (1) Compute the physical units of production.
  (2) Compute equivalent units of production for materials and for conversion costs.
  (3) Determine the unit costs of production.
  (4) Show the assignment of costs to units transferred out and in process.
(b) Prepare the production cost report for Plant 1 for July 2008.

Journalize transactions.

(SO 3, 4)

P21-3A Fiedel Company manufactures its product, Vitadrink, through two manufacturing processes: Mixing and Packaging. All materials are entered at the beginning of each process. On October 1, 2008, inventories consisted of Raw Materials $26,000, Work in Process—Mixing $0, Work in Process—Packaging $250,000, and Finished Goods $289,000. The beginning inventory for Packaging consisted of 10,000 units that were 50% complete as to conversion costs and fully complete as to materials. During October, 50,000 units were started into production in the Mixing Department and the following transactions were completed.

1. Purchased $300,000 of raw materials on account.
2. Issued raw materials for production: Mixing $210,000 and Packaging $45,000.
3. Incurred labor costs of $248,900.
4. Used factory labor: Mixing $182,500 and Packaging $66,400.
5. Incurred $790,000 of manufacturing overhead on account.
6. Applied indirect manufacturing overhead on the basis of $22 per machine hour. Machine hours were 28,000 in Mixing and 6,000 in Packaging.
7. Transferred 45,000 units from Mixing to Packaging at a cost of $979,000.
8. Transferred 53,000 units from Packaging to Finished Goods at a cost of $1,315,000.
9. Sold goods costing $1,640,000 for $2,500,000 on account.

Instructions

Journalize the October transactions.

P21-4A Cavalier Company has several processing departments. Costs charged to the Assembly Department for November 2008 totaled $2,229,000 as follows.

Assign costs and prepare production cost report.

(SO 5, 6, 7)

Work in process, November 1		
Materials	$69,000	
Conversion costs	48,150	$ 117,150
Materials added		1,548,000
Labor		225,920
Overhead		337,930

Production records show that 35,000 units were in beginning work in process 30% complete as to conversion costs, 700,000 units were started into production, and 25,000 units were in ending work in process 40% complete as to conversion costs. Materials are entered at the beginning of each process.

Instructions

(a) Determine the equivalent units of production and the unit production costs for the Assembly Department.
(b) Determine the assignment of costs to goods transferred out and in process.
(c) Prepare a production cost report for the Assembly Department.

P21-5A Chen Company manufactures basketballs. Materials are added at the beginning of the production process and conversion costs are incurred uniformly. Production and cost data for the month of July 2008 are as follows.

Determine equivalent units and unit costs and assign costs.

(SO 5, 6, 7)

Production Data—Basketballs		**Units**	**Percent Complete**
Work in process units, July 1		500	60%
Units started into production		1,000	
Work in process units, July 31		600	30%
Cost Data—Basketballs			
Work in process, July 1			
Materials	$750		
Conversion costs	600	$1,350	
Direct materials		2,400	
Direct labor		1,580	
Manufacturing overhead		1,060	

Instructions

(a) Calculate the following.
  (1) The equivalent units of production for materials and conversion.
  (2) The unit costs of production for materials and conversion costs.
  (3) The assignment of costs to units transferred out and in process at the end of the accounting period.
(b) Prepare a production cost report for the month of July for the basketballs.

P21-6A Luther Processing Company uses a weighted-average process costing system and manufactures a single product—a premium rug shampoo and cleaner. The manufacturing activity for the month of October has just been completed. A partially completed production cost report for the month of October for the mixing and cooking department is shown on page 948.

Compute equivalent units and complete production cost report.

(SO 5, 7)

Instructions

(a) Prepare a schedule that shows how the equivalent units were computed so that you can complete the "Quantities: Units accounted for" equivalent units section shown in the production cost report, and compute October unit costs.
(b) Complete the "Cost Reconciliation Schedule" part of the production cost report on page 948.

LUTHER PROCESSING COMPANY
Mixing and Cooking Department
Production Cost Report
For the Month Ended October 31

QUANTITIES	Physical Units	Equivalent Units: Materials	Equivalent Units: Conversion Costs	
Units to be accounted for				
Work in process, October 1 (all materials, 70% conversion costs)	20,000			
Started into production	160,000			
Total units	180,000			
Units accounted for				
Transferred out	130,000	?	?	
Work in process, October 31 (60% materials, 40% conversion costs)	50,000	?	?	
Total units accounted for	180,000	?	?	
COSTS		**Materials**	**Conversion Costs**	**Total**
Unit costs				
Costs in October		$240,000	$105,000	$345,000
Equivalent units		?	?	
Unit costs		$?	+ $?	= $?
Costs to be accounted for				
Work in process, October 1				$ 30,000
Started into production				315,000
Total costs				$345,000
Cost Reconciliation Schedule				
Costs accounted for				
Transferred out				$?
Work in process, October 31				
Materials			?	
Conversion costs			?	?
Total costs				?

Assign overhead to products using ABC.
(SO 10)

***P21-7A** Darby Electronics manufactures two large-screen television models: the Royale which sells for $1,500, and a new model, the Majestic, which sells for $1,200. The production cost per unit for each model in 2008 was as follows.

	Royale	Majestic
Direct materials	$ 700	$420
Direct labor ($20 per hour)	100	80
Manufacturing overhead ($40 per DLH)	200	160
Total per unit cost	$1,000	$660

In 2008, Darby manufactured 30,000 units of the Royale and 10,000 units of the Majestic. The overhead rate of $40 per direct labor hour was determined by dividing total expected manufacturing overhead of $7,600,000 by the total direct labor hours (190,000) for the two models.

The gross profit on the model was: Royale $500 ($1,500 − $1,000) and Majestic $540 ($1,200 − $660). Because of this difference, management is considering phasing out the Royale model and increasing the production of the Majestic model.

Before finalizing its decision, management asks the controller, Marie Stumfall, to prepare an analysis using activity-based costing. Marie accumulates the following information about overhead for the year ended December 31, 2008.

Activity	Cost Driver	Total Cost	Cost Driver Volume	Overhead Rate
Purchase orders	Number of orders	$1,200,000	30,000	$40
Machine setups	Number of setups	900,000	15,000	60
Machining	Machine hours	4,800,000	160,000	30
Quality control	Number of inspections	700,000	35,000	20

The cost driver volume for each product was:

Cost Driver	Royale	Majestic	Total
Purchase orders	16,000	14,000	30,000
Machine setups	5,000	10,000	15,000
Machine hours	100,000	60,000	160,000
Inspections	10,000	25,000	35,000

Instructions

(a) Assign the total 2008 manufacturing overhead costs to the two products using activity-based costing (ABC).

(b) What was the cost per unit and gross profit of each model using ABC costing?

(c) Are management's future plans for the two models sound?

PROBLEMS: SET B

P21-1B Bicnell Corporation manufactures water skis through two processes: Molding and Packaging. In the Molding Department fiberglass is heated and shaped into the form of a ski. In the Packaging Department, the skis are placed in cartons and sent to the finished goods warehouse. Materials are entered at the beginning of both processes. Labor and manufacturing overhead are incurred uniformly throughout each process. Production and cost data for the Molding Department for January 2008 are presented below.

Complete four steps necessary to prepare a production cost report.

(SO 5, 6, 7)

Production Data	January
Beginning work in process units	–0–
Units started into production	35,000
Ending work in process units	5,000
Percent complete—ending inventory	40%

Cost Data	
Materials	$595,000
Labor	96,000
Overhead	224,000
Total	$915,000

Instructions

(a) Compute the physical units of production.
(b) Determine the equivalent units of production for materials and conversion costs.
(c) Compute the unit costs of production.
(d) Determine the costs to be assigned to the units transferred out and in process.
(e) Prepare a production cost report for the Molding Department for the month of January.

Complete four steps necessary to prepare a production cost report.

(SO 5, 6, 7)

P21-2B Atkins Corporation manufactures in separate processes refrigerators and freezers for homes. In each process, materials are entered at the beginning and conversion costs are incurred uniformly. Production and cost data for the first process in making two products in two different manufacturing plants are as follows.

	Stamping Department	
Production Data—June	**Plant A R12 Refrigerators**	**Plant B F24 Freezers**
Work in process units, June 1	–0–	–0–
Units started into production	20,000	18,000
Work in process units, June 30	4,000	2,500
Work in process percent complete	75	60
Cost Data—June		
Work in process, June 1	$ –0–	$ –0–
Materials	840,000	684,000
Labor	245,000	251,000
Overhead	420,000	191,000
Total	$1,505,000	$1,126,000

Instructions

(a) For each plant:
  (1) Compute the physical units of production.
  (2) Compute equivalent units of production for materials and for conversion costs.
  (3) Determine the unit costs of production.
  (4) Show the assignment of costs to units transferred out and in process.
(b) Prepare the production cost report for Plant A for June 2008.

Journalize transactions.

(SO 3, 4)

P21-3B McNally Company manufactures a nutrient, Everlife, through two manufacturing processes: Blending and Packaging. All materials are entered at the beginning of each process. On August 1, 2008, inventories consisted of Raw Materials $5,000, Work in Process—Blending $0, Work in Process—Packaging $3,945, and Finished Goods $7,500. The beginning inventory for Packaging consisted of 500 units, two-fifths complete as to conversion costs and fully complete as to materials. During August, 9,000 units were started into production in Blending, and the following transactions were completed.

1. Purchased $25,000 of raw materials on account.
2. Issued raw materials for production: Blending $18,930 and Packaging $7,140.
3. Incurred labor costs of $20,770.
4. Used factory labor: Blending $13,320 and Packaging $7,450.
5. Incurred $41,500 of manufacturing overhead on account.
6. Applied manufacturing overhead at the rate of $20 per machine hour. Machine hours were Blending 900 and Packaging 300.
7. Transferred 8,200 units from Blending to Packaging at a cost of $44,940.
8. Transferred 8,600 units from Packaging to Finished Goods at a cost of $67,490.
9. Sold goods costing $62,000 for $90,000 on account.

Instructions
Journalize the August transactions.

P21-4B Crosby Company has several processing departments. Costs charged to the Assembly Department for October 2008 totaled $1,354,400 as follows.

Assign costs and prepare production cost report.

(SO 5, 6, 7)

Work in process, October 1		
Materials	$29,000	
Conversion costs	26,200	$ 55,200
Materials added		1,071,000
Labor		90,000
Overhead		138,200

Production records show that 25,000 units were in beginning work in process 40% complete as to conversion cost, 415,000 units were started into production, and 40,000 units were in ending work in process 60% complete as to conversion costs. Materials are entered at the beginning of each process.

Instructions
(a) Determine the equivalent units of production and the unit production costs for the Assembly Department.
(b) Determine the assignment of costs to goods transferred out and in process.
(c) Prepare a production cost report for the Assembly Department.

P21-5B Kiley Company manufactures bicycles and tricycles. For both products, materials are added at the beginning of the production process, and conversion costs are incurred uniformly. Production and cost data for the month of May are as follows.

Determine equivalent units and unit costs and assign costs.

(SO 5, 6, 7)

Production Data—Bicycles	Units		Percent Complete
Work in process units, May 1	500		80%
Units started in production	1,000		
Work in process units, May 31	600		10%
Cost Data—Bicycles			
Work in process, May 1			
Materials	$10,000		
Conversion costs	9,280		$ 19,280
Direct materials			50,000
Direct labor			18,320
Manufacturing overhead			30,000

Instructions
(a) Calculate the following.
  (1) The equivalent units of production for materials and conversion.
  (2) The unit costs of production for materials and conversion costs.
  (3) The assignment of costs to units transferred out and in process at the end of the accounting period.
(b) Prepare a production cost report for the month of May for the bicycles.

P21-6B Windsor Cleaner Company uses a weighted-average process costing system and manufactures a single product—an all-purpose liquid cleaner. The manufacturing activity for the month of March has just been completed. A partially completed production cost report for the month of March for the mixing and blending department is shown on page 952.

Compute equivalent units and complete production cost report.

(SO 5, 7)

WINDSOR CLEANER COMPANY
Mixing and Blending Department
Production Cost Report
For the Month Ended March 31

		Equivalent Units		
QUANTITIES	Physical Units	Materials	Conversion Costs	
Units to be accounted for				
Work in process, March 1 (40% materials, 20% conversion costs)	10,000			
Started into production	100,000			
Total units	110,000			
Units accounted for				
Transferred out	95,000	?	?	
Work in process, March 31 (2/3 materials, 1/3 conversion costs)	15,000	?	?	
Total units accounted for	110,000	?	?	
COSTS				
Unit costs		Materials	Conversion Costs	Total
Costs in March		$210,000	$90,000	$300,000
Equivalent units		?	?	
Unit costs		$? +	$? =	$?
Costs to be accounted for				
Work in process, March 1				$ 15,700
Started into production				284,300
Total costs				$300,000
Cost Reconciliation Schedule				
Costs accounted for				
Transferred out				$?
Work in process, March 31				
Materials			?	
Conversion costs			?	?
Total costs				?

Instructions

(a) Prepare a schedule that shows how the equivalent units were computed so that you can complete the "Quantities: Units accounted for" equivalent units section shown in the production cost report above, and compute March unit costs.

(b) Complete the "Cost Reconciliation Schedule" part of the production cost report above.

PROBLEMS: SET C

Visit the book's website at **www.wiley.com/college/weygandt**, and choose the Student Companion site, to access Problem Set C.

BROADENING YOUR PERSPECTIVE

DECISION MAKING ACROSS THE ORGANIZATION

BYP21-1 Sunshine Beach Company manufactures suntan lotion, called Surtan, in 11-ounce plastic bottles. Surtan is sold in a competitive market. As a result, management is very cost-conscious. Surtan is manufactured through two processes: mixing and filling. Materials are entered at the beginning of each process and labor and manufacturing overhead occur uniformly throughout each process. Unit costs are based on the cost per gallon of Surtan using the weighted-average costing approach.

On June 30, 2008, Jill Ritzman, the chief accountant for the past 20 years, opted to take early retirement. Her replacement, Sid Benili, had extensive accounting experience with motels in the area but only limited contact with manufacturing accounting. During July, Sid correctly accumulated the following production quantity and cost data for the Mixing Department.

Production quantities: Work in process, July 1, 8,000 gallons 75% complete; started into production 91,000 gallons; work in process, July 31, 5,000 gallons 20% complete. Materials are added at the beginning of the process.

Production costs: Beginning work in process $88,000, comprised of $21,000 of materials costs and $67,000 of conversion costs; incurred in July: materials $573,000, conversion costs $769,000.

Sid then prepared a production cost report on the basis of physical units started into production. His report showed a production cost of $15.71 per gallon of Surtan. The management of Sunshine Beach was surprised at the high unit cost. The president comes to you, as Jill's top assistant, to review Sid's report and prepare a correct report if necessary.

Instructions

With the class divided into groups, answer the following questions.

(a) Show how Sid arrived at the unit cost of $15.71 per gallon of Surtan.
(b) What error(s) did Sid make in preparing his production cost report?
(c) Prepare a correct production cost report for July.

MANAGERIAL ANALYSIS

BYP21-2 Guion Furniture Company manufactures living room furniture through two departments: Framing and Upholstering. Materials are entered at the beginning of each process. For May, the following cost data are obtained from the two work in process accounts.

	Framing	Upholstering
Work in process, May 1	$ –0–	$?
Materials	420,000	?
Conversion costs	280,000	330,000
Costs transferred in	–0–	550,000
Costs transferred out	600,000	?
Work in process, May 31	100,000	?

Instructions

Answer the following questions.

(a) If 3,000 sofas were started into production on May 1 and 2,500 sofas were transferred to Upholstering, what was the unit cost of materials for May in the Framing Department?
(b) Using the data in (a) above, what was the per unit conversion cost of the sofas transferred to Upholstering?
(c) Continuing the assumptions in (a) above, what is the percentage of completion of the units in process at May 31 in the Framing Department?

EXPLORING THE WEB

www.wiley.com/college/weygandt

BYP21-3 Search the Internet and find the websites of two manufacturers that you think are likely to use process costing. Are there any specifics included in their websites that confirm the use of process costing for each of these companies?

COMMUNICATION ACTIVITY

BYP21-4 Carol Gorden was a good friend of yours in high school and is from your home town. While you chose to major in accounting when you both went away to college, she majored in marketing and management. You have recently been promoted to accounting manager for the Snack Foods Division of Koonce Enterprises, and your friend was promoted to regional sales manager for the same division of Koonce. Carol recently telephoned you. She explained that she was familiar with job cost sheets, which had been used by the Special Projects division where she had formerly worked. She was, however, very uncomfortable with the production cost reports prepared by your division. She faxed you a list of her particular questions:

1. Since Koonce occasionally prepares snack foods for special orders in the Snack Foods Division, why don't we track costs of the orders separately?
2. What is an equivalent unit?
3. Why am I getting four production cost reports? Isn't there one Work in Process account?

Instructions

Prepare a memo to Carol. Answer her questions, and include any additional information you think would be helpful. You may write informally, but do use proper grammar and punctuation.

ETHICS CASE

BYP21-5 R. B. Patrick Company manufactures a high-tech component that passes through two production processing departments, Molding and Assembly. Department managers are partially compensated on the basis of units of products completed and transferred out relative to units of product put into production. This was intended as encouragement to be efficient and to minimize waste.

Sue Wooten is the department head in the Molding Department, and Fred Barando is her quality control inspector. During the month of June, Sue had three new employees who were not yet technically skilled. As a result, many of the units produced in June had minor molding defects. In order to maintain the department's normal high rate of completion, Sue told Fred to pass through inspection and on to the Assembly Department all units that had defects nondetectable to the human eye. "Company and industry tolerances on this product are too high anyway," says Sue. "Less than 2% of the units we produce are subjected in the market to the stress tolerance we've designed into them. The odds of those 2% being any of this month's units are even less. Anyway, we're saving the company money."

Instructions

(a) Who are the potential stakeholders involved in this situation?

(b) What alternatives does Fred have in this situation? What might the company do to prevent this situation from occurring?

"ALL ABOUT YOU" ACTIVITY

*

BYP21-6 Many of you ultimately will work in service environments, such as medical facilities. Many service organizations have adopted activity-based management systems, which incorporate activity-based costing concepts throughout the organization.

East Valley Hospital is a primary medical health-care facility and trauma center that serves 11 small, rural Midwestern communities within a 40-mile radius. The hospital offers all the medical/surgical services of a typical small hospital. It has a staff of 18 full-time doctors and 20 part-time visiting specialists. East Valley has a payroll of 150 employees, consisting of nurses, technicians, therapists, dieticians, managers, directors, administrators, secretaries, data processors, and janitors.

Instructions

(a) Using your existing knowledge (however limited, moderate, or in-depth) of a hospital's operations, identify as many *activities* as you can that would serve as the basis for implementing an activity-based costing system.

(b) For each of the activities listed in **(a)**, identify a *cost driver* that would serve as a valid measure of the resources consumed in the activity.

Answers to Insight and Accounting Across the Organization Questions

pp. 916 What Cost Driver should Caterpillar Use?

Q: What is the result if a company uses the wrong "cost driver" to assign manufacturing overhead?

A: *Incorrect application of manufacturing overhead will result in some products receiving too much overhead and others receiving too little.*

p. 927 What Cost System Might Jiffy Lube Use?

Q: What criteria should be considered when selecting a cost accounting system for a service company?

A: *Companies that provide specific, non-routine services will probably benefit from using a job order cost system. Those that perform routine, repetitive services will probably to better off with a process cost system. In fact, since there may be little or no work in process at the end of an accounting period, applying process costing may be even easier for a service company than for a manufacturer.*

p. 929 How Just-in-Time Helped Hewlett-Packard

Q: How could just-in-time processing contribute to a 50% improvement in labor efficiency?

A: *A successful just-in-time system is based on a multi-skilled workforce and highly automated production. Both of these features should improve labor efficiency.*

Authors' Comments on All About You: Wal-Mart Is on the Phone (p. 931)

It will come as a surprise to some of you that some companies would decline this offer. The production requirements will be extreme, the necessary new investments will be high, and there is no guarantee of continued orders from Wal-Mart. While there eventually should be production efficiencies that result from the increased scale, there will certainly be many growing pains in the short run. Wal-Mart's price does not allow for any error.

By accepting Wal-Mart's order, you would be changing the nature of your company from a producer of a high-price, high-margin, lower-volume product to that of a low-price, low-margin, high-volume product. Very few companies are able to continue to sell their products at a high price in one outlet and a low price in another. As noted, because margins will be razor-thin, the company will now have to be incredibly cost-conscious. Its cost accounting system will become far more critical to its success.

See the article at the following site for a discussion of how things didn't work out well for one company that tried to be a Wal-Mart supplier: *www.inc.com/magazine/20031101/walmart.html.*

Answers to Self-Study Questions

1. b **2.** d **3.** c **4.** b **5.** b **6.** a **7.** c **8.** a **9.** b **10.** b **11.** d **12.** c **13.** b

Remember to go back to the Navigator box on the chapter-opening page and check off your completed work.

Chapter 22

Cost-Volume-Profit

STUDY OBJECTIVES

After studying this chapter, you should be able to:

1. Distinguish between variable and fixed costs.
2. Explain the significance of the relevant range.
3. Explain the concept of mixed costs.
4. List the five components of cost-volume-profit analysis.
5. Indicate what contribution margin is and how it can be expressed.
6. Identify the three ways to determine the break-even point.
7. Give the formulas for determining sales required to earn target net income.
8. Define margin of safety, and give the formulas for computing it.
9. Describe the essential features of a cost-volume-profit income statement.

The Navigator

The Navigator

- Scan **Study Objectives**
- Read **Feature Story**
- Read **Preview**
- Read text and answer **Before You Go On** p. 965 p. 971 p. 976
- Work **Demonstration Problems**
- Review **Summary of Study Objectives**
- Answer **Self-Study Questions**
- Complete **Assignments**

Feature Story

GROWING BY LEAPS AND LEOTARDS

When the last of her three children went off to school, Amy began looking for a job. At this same time, her daughter asked to take dance classes. The nearest dance studio was over 20 miles away, and Amy didn't know how she would balance a new job and drive her daughter to dance class. Suddenly it hit her—why not start her own dance studio?

Amy sketched out a business plan: A local church would rent its basement for $6 per hour. The size of the basement limited the number of students she could teach, but the rent was low. Insurance for a small studio was $50 per month. Initially she would teach classes only for young kids since that was all she felt qualified to do. She thought she could charge $2.50 for a one-hour class. There was room for 8 students per class. She wouldn't get

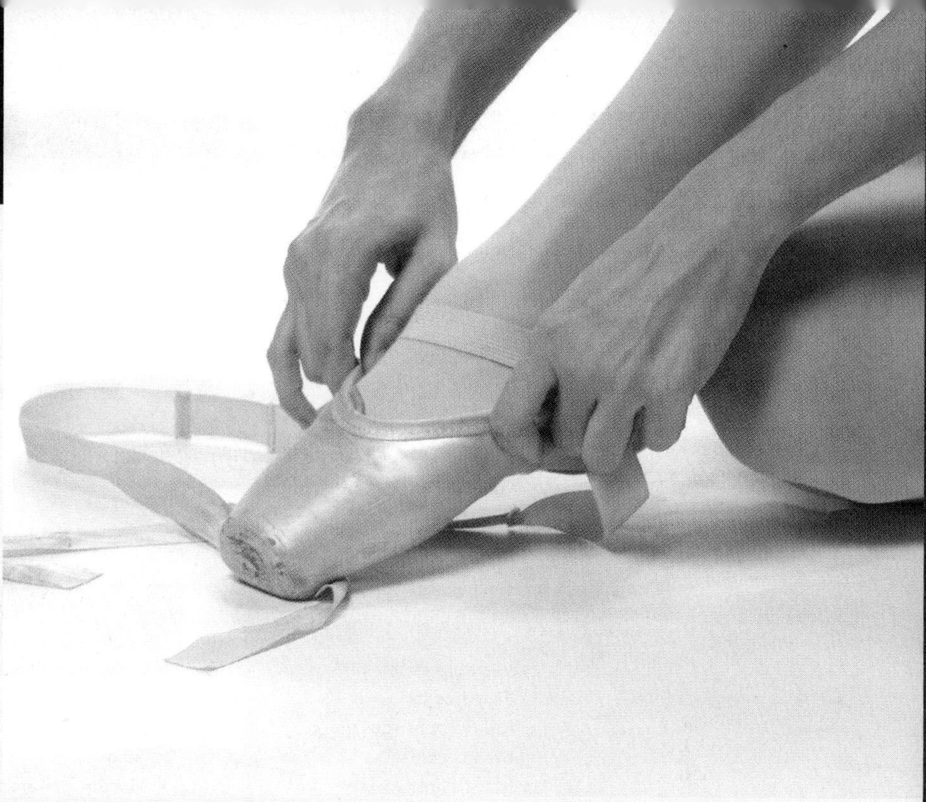

rich—but at least it would be fun, and she didn't have much at risk.

Amy soon realized that the demand for dance classes far exceeded her capacity. She considered renting a bigger space that could serve 15 students per class. But her rent would also increase significantly. Also, rather than paying rent by the hour, she would have to pay $600 per month, even during the summer months when demand for dance classes was low. She also would have to pay utilities—roughly $70 per month.

However, with a bigger space Amy could offer classes for teens and adults. Teens and adults would pay a higher fee—$5 per hour—though the number of students per class would have to be smaller, probably only 8 per class. She could hire a part-time instructor at about $18 per hour to teach advanced classes. Insurance costs could increase to $100 per month. In addition, she would need a part-time administrator at $100 per month to keep records. Amy also realized she could increase her income by selling dance supplies such as shoes, towels, and leotards.

Amy laid out a new business plan based on these estimates. If she failed, she stood to lose real money. Convinced she could make a go of it, she made the big plunge.

Her planning paid off: Within 10 years of starting her business in a church basement Amy had over 800 students, seven instructors, two administrators, and a facility with three separate studios.

The Navigator

Inside Chapter 22...

Preview of Chapter 22

As the Feature Story indicates, to manage any size business you must understand how costs respond to changes in sales volume and the effect of costs and revenues on profits. A prerequisite to understanding cost-volume-profit (CVP) relationships is knowledge of how costs behave. In this chapter, we first explain the considerations involved in cost behavior analysis. Then we discuss and illustrate CVP analysis.

The content and organization of Chapter 22 are as follows.

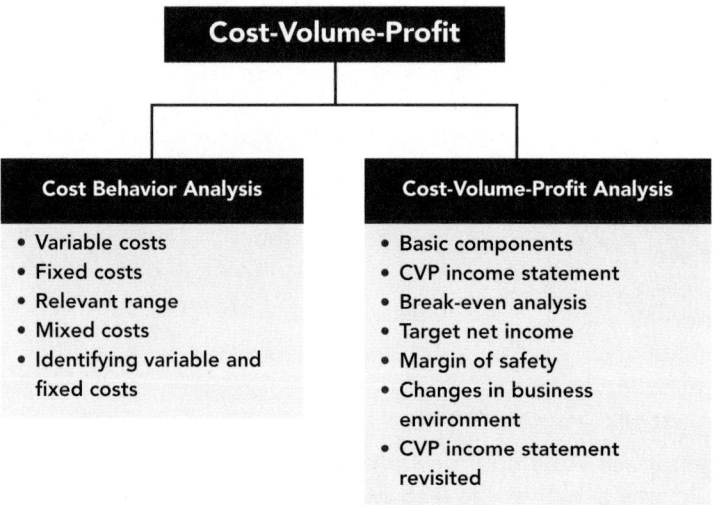

Cost-Volume-Profit

Cost Behavior Analysis

- Variable costs
- Fixed costs
- Relevant range
- Mixed costs
- Identifying variable and fixed costs

Cost-Volume-Profit Analysis

- Basic components
- CVP income statement
- Break-even analysis
- Target net income
- Margin of safety
- Changes in business environment
- CVP income statement revisited

The Navigator

COST BEHAVIOR ANALYSIS

Cost behavior analysis is the study of how specific costs respond to changes in the level of business activity. As you might expect, some costs change, and others remain the same. For example, for an airline company such as Southwest or United, the longer the flight the higher the fuel costs. On the other hand, Massachusetts General Hospital's costs to staff the emergency room on any given night are relatively constant regardless of the number of patients treated. A knowledge of cost behavior helps management plan operations and decide between alternative courses of action. Cost behavior analysis applies to all types of entities, as the Feature Story about Amy's dance studio indicates.

The starting point in cost behavior analysis is measuring the key business activities. Activity levels may be expressed in terms of sales dollars (in a retail company), miles driven (in a trucking company), room occupancy (in a hotel), or dance classes taught (by a dance studio). Many companies use more than one measurement base. A manufacturer, for example, may use direct labor hours or units of output for manufacturing costs and sales revenue or units sold for selling expenses.

For an activity level to be useful in cost behavior analysis, changes in the level or volume of activity should be correlated with changes in costs. The activity level selected is referred to as the activity (or volume) index. The **activity index** identifies the activity that causes changes in the behavior of costs. With an appropriate activity index, companies can classify the behavior of costs in response to changes in activity levels into three categories: variable, fixed, or mixed.

Variable Costs

STUDY OBJECTIVE 1

Distinguish between variable and fixed costs.

Variable costs are costs that vary **in total** directly and proportionately with changes in the activity level. If the level increases 10%, total variable costs will increase 10%. If the level of activity decreases by 25%, variable costs will decrease 25%. Examples of variable costs include direct materials and direct labor for a manufacturer; cost of goods sold, sales commissions, and freight-out for a merchandiser; and gasoline in airline and trucking companies. A variable cost may also be defined as a cost that **remains the same *per unit* at every level of activity**.

To illustrate the behavior of a variable cost, assume that Damon Company manufactures radios that contain a $10 digital clock. The activity index is the number of radios produced. As Damon manufactures each radio, the total cost of the clocks increases by $10. As shown in part (a) of Illustration 22-1, total cost of the clocks will be $20,000 if 2,000 radios are produced, and $100,000 when 10,000 radios are produced. We also can see that a variable cost remains the same per unit as the level of activity changes. As shown in part (b) of Illustration 22-1, the unit cost of $10 for the clocks is the same whether 2,000 or 10,000 radios are produced.

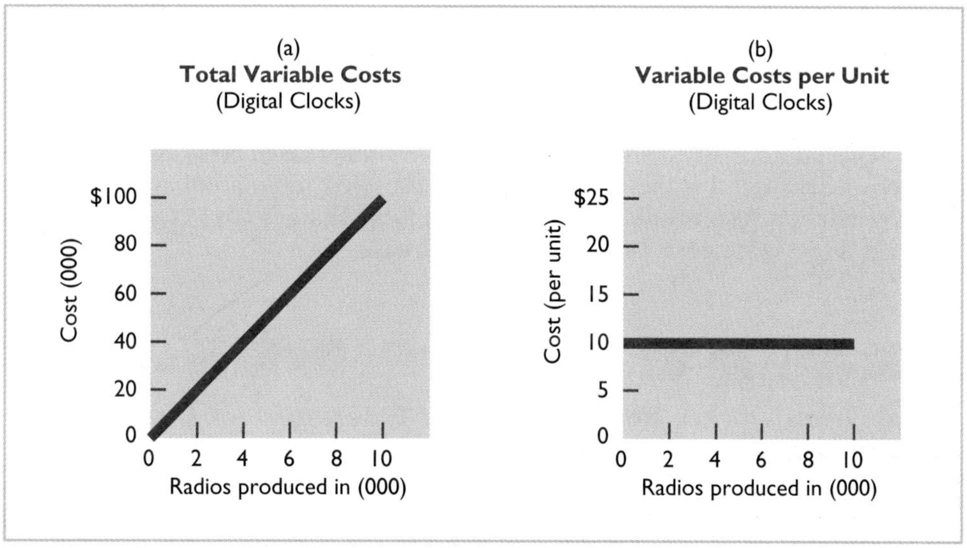

Illustration 22-1
Behavior of total and unit variable costs

HELPFUL HINT

True or false: Variable cost per unit changes directly and proportionately with changes in activity.
Answer: False. Per unit cost remains constant at all levels of activity.

Companies that rely heavily on labor to manufacture a product, such as Nike or Reebok, or to provide a service, such as Hilton or Marriott, are likely to have many variable costs. In contrast, companies that use a high proportion of machinery and equipment in producing revenue, such as AT&T or Duke Energy Co., may have few variable costs.

Fixed Costs

Fixed costs are costs that **remain the same in total** regardless of changes in the activity level. Examples include property taxes, insurance, rent, supervisory salaries, and depreciation on buildings and equipment. Because total fixed costs remain constant as activity changes, it follows that **fixed costs *per unit* vary inversely with activity: As volume increases, unit cost declines, and vice versa**.

To illustrate the behavior of fixed costs, assume that Damon Company leases its productive facilities at a cost of $10,000 per month. Total fixed costs of the facilities will remain constant at every level of activity, as shown in part (a) of Illustration 22-2 (page 960). But, on a per unit basis, the cost of rent will decline as activity increases, as shown in part (b) of Illustration 22-2. At 2,000 units, the unit cost is $5 ($10,000 ÷ 2,000). When Damon produces 10,000 radios, the unit cost is only $1 ($10,000 ÷ 10,000).

Illustration 22-2
Behavior of total and unit fixed costs

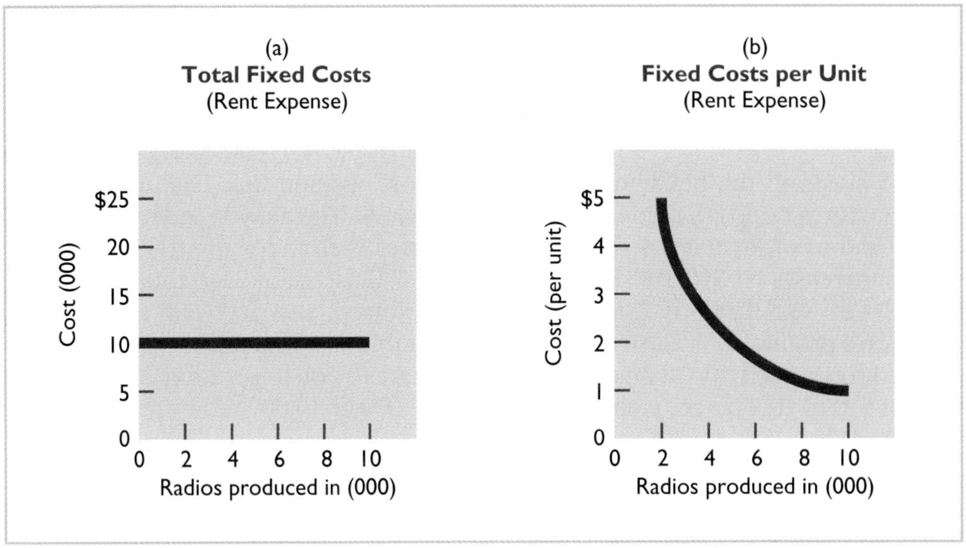

The trend for many manufacturers is to have more fixed costs and fewer variable costs. This trend is the result of increased use of automation and less use of employee labor. As a result, depreciation and lease charges (fixed costs) increase, whereas direct labor costs (variable costs) decrease.

MANAGEMENT INSIGHT

Woodworker Runs an Efficient Operation for Designing Furniture

When Thomas Moser quit teaching communications at Bates College 25 years ago, he turned to what he loved doing—furniture woodworking. Today he has over 120 employees. In a business where profit margins are seldom thicker than wood shavings, cost control is everything. Moser keeps no inventory; a 50% deposit buys the wood. Because computer-driven machines cut most of the standardized parts and joints, "we're free to be inefficient in assembly and finishing work, where the craft is most obviously expressed," says Moser. Direct labor costs are a manageable 30% of revenues. By keeping a tight lid on costs and running an efficient operation, Moser is free to spend most of his time doing what he enjoys most—designing furniture.

Source: Excerpts from "Out of the Woods," *Forbes*, April 5, 1999, p. 74.

? Are the costs associated with use of the computer-driven cutting machines fixed or variable?

Relevant Range

STUDY OBJECTIVE 2
Explain the significance of the relevant range.

In Illustration 22-1 (page 959), a straight line is drawn throughout the entire range of the activity index for total variable costs. In essence, the assumption is that the costs are **linear**. If a relationship is linear (that is, straight-line), then changes in the activity index will result in a direct, proportional change in the variable cost. For example, if the activity level doubles, the cost doubles.

It is now necessary to ask: Is the straight-line relationship realistic? Does the linear assumption produce useful data for CVP analysis?

In most business situations, a straight-line relationship **does not exist** for variable costs throughout the entire range of possible activity. At abnormally low levels of activity, it may be impossible to be cost-efficient. Small-scale operations may not allow the company to obtain quantity discounts for raw materials or to use specialized labor. In contrast, at abnormally high levels of activity, labor costs may increase sharply because of overtime pay. Also at high activity levels, materials costs may jump significantly because of excess spoilage caused by worker fatigue.

As a result, in the real world, the relationship between the behavior of a variable cost and changes in the activity level is often **curvilinear**, as shown in part (a) of Illustration 22-3. In the curved sections of the line, a change in the activity index will not result in a direct, proportional change in the variable cost. That is, a doubling of the activity index will not result in an exact doubling of the variable cost. The variable cost may more than double, or it may be less than double.

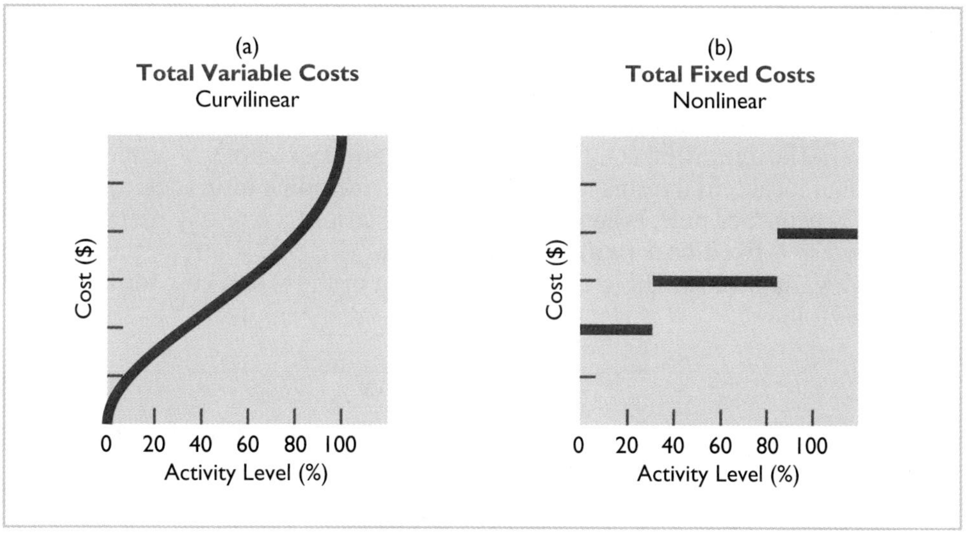

Illustration 22-3
Nonlinear behavior of variable and fixed costs

Total fixed costs also do not have a straight-line relationship over the entire range of activity. Some fixed costs will not change. But it is possible for management to change other fixed costs. For example, in the Feature Story the dance studio's rent was originally variable and then became fixed at a certain amount. It then increased to a new fixed amount when the size of the studio increased beyond a certain point. An example of the behavior of total fixed costs through all potential levels of activity is shown in part (b) of Illustration 22-3.

HELPFUL HINT
Fixed costs that may be changeable include research, such as new product development, and management training programs.

For most companies, operating at almost zero or at 100% capacity is the exception rather than the rule. Instead, companies often operate over a somewhat narrower range, such as 40–80% of capacity. The range over which a company expects to operate during a year is called the **relevant range** of the activity index. Within the relevant range, as shown in both diagrams in Illustration 22-4 (page 962), a straight-line relationship generally exists for both variable and fixed costs.

ALTERNATIVE TERMINOLOGY
The relevant range is also called the *normal* or *practical range.*

Illustration 22-4
Linear behavior within relevant range

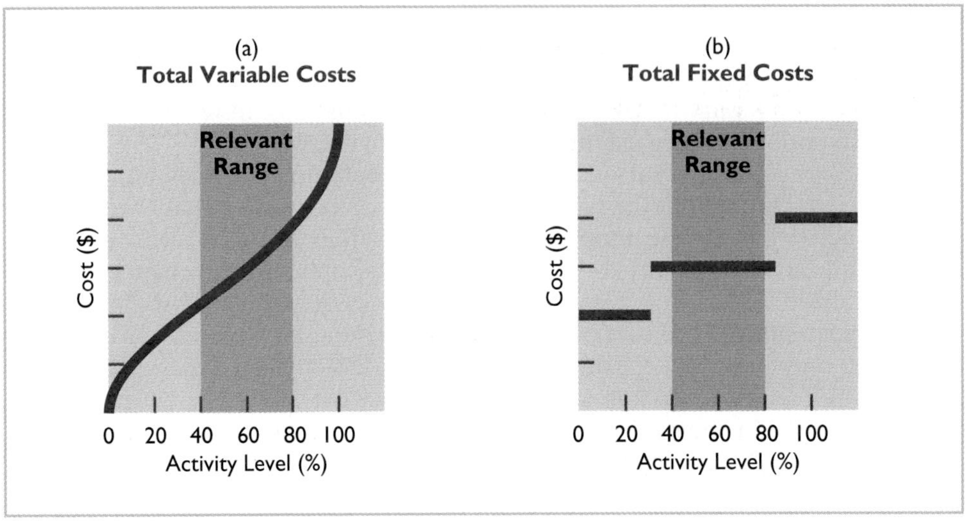

As you can see, although the linear (straight-line) relationship may not be completely realistic, **the linear assumption produces useful data for CVP analysis as long as the level of activity remains within the relevant range.**

Mixed Costs

STUDY OBJECTIVE 3
Explain the concept of mixed costs.

Mixed costs are costs that contain both a variable element and a fixed element. **Mixed costs, therefore, change in total but not proportionately with changes in the activity level.**

The rental of a U-Haul truck is a good example of a mixed cost. Assume that local rental terms for a 17-foot truck, including insurance, are $50 per day plus 50 cents per mile. When determining the cost of a one-day rental, the per day charge is a fixed cost (with respect to miles driven), whereas the mileage charge is a variable cost. The graphic presentation of the rental cost for a one-day rental is as follows.

Illustration 22-5
Behavior of a mixed cost

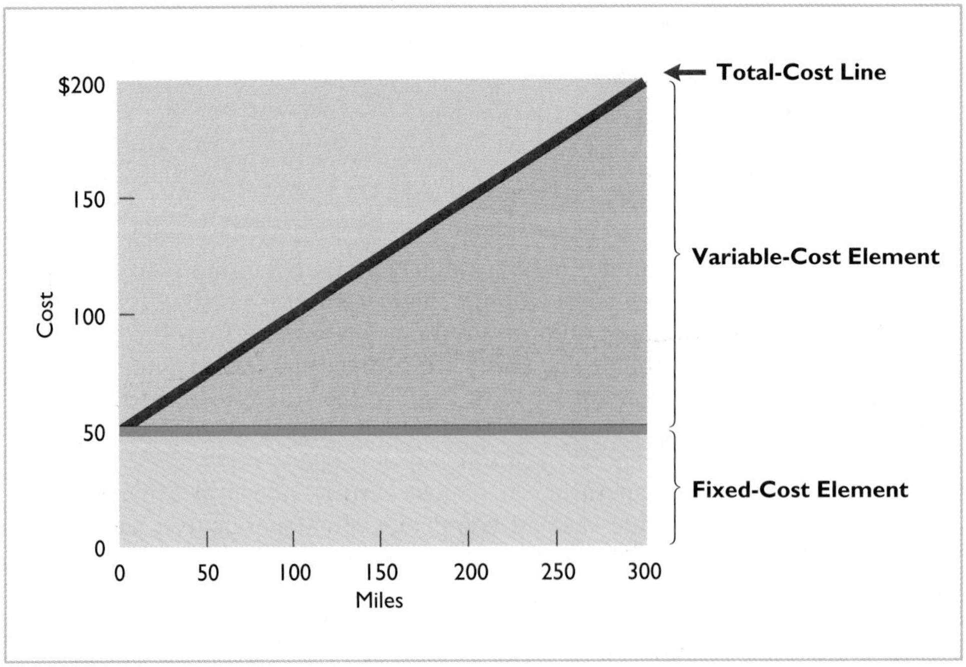

In this case, the fixed-cost element is the cost of having the service available. The variable-cost element is the cost of actually using the service. Another example of a mixed cost is utility costs (electric, telephone, and so on), where there is a flat service fee plus a usage charge.

For purposes of CVP analysis, **mixed costs must be classified into their fixed and variable elements**. How does management make the classification? One possibility is to determine the variable and fixed components each time a mixed cost is incurred. But because of time and cost constraints, this approach is rarely followed. Instead, the usual approach is to collect data on the behavior of the mixed costs at various levels of activity. An analysis then identifies the fixed and variable cost components. Companies use various types of analysis. One type of analysis, called the **high-low method**, is discussed below. Other methods, such as the scatter diagram method and least squares regression analysis, are more appropriately explained in cost accounting courses.

HIGH-LOW METHOD

The **high-low method** uses the total costs incurred at the high and low levels of activity to classify mixed costs into fixed and variable components. The difference in costs between the high and low levels represents variable costs, since only the variable cost element can change as activity levels change. The steps in computing fixed and variable costs under this method are as follows.

1. **Determine variable cost per unit from the following formula.**

Change in Total Costs	÷	High minus Low Activity Level	=	Variable Cost per Unit

Illustration 22-6
Formula for variable cost per unit using high-low method

To illustrate, assume that Metro Transit Company has the following maintenance costs and mileage data for its fleet of buses over a 4-month period.

Month	Miles Driven	Total Cost	Month	Miles Driven	Total Cost
January	**20,000**	**$30,000**	March	35,000	$49,000
February	40,000	48,000	April	**50,000**	**63,000**

Illustration 22-7
Assumed maintenance costs and mileage data

The high and low levels of activity are 50,000 miles in April and 20,000 miles in January. The maintenance costs at these two levels are $63,000 and $30,000, respectively. The difference in maintenance costs is $33,000 ($63,000 − $30,000), and the difference in miles is 30,000 (50,000 − 20,000). Therefore, for Metro Transit, variable cost per unit is $1.10, computed as follows.

$$\$33,000 \div 30,000 = \$1.10$$

2. **Determine the fixed cost by subtracting the total variable cost at either the high or the low activity level from the total cost at that activity level.**

For Metro Transit, the computations are shown in Illustration 22-8.

Illustration 22-8
High-low method computation of fixed costs

Metro Transit.xls

	A	B	C	D
1	METRO TRANSIT			
2			Activity Level	
3			High	Low
4	Total cost		$63,000	$30,000
5	Less:	Variable costs		
6		50,000 X $1.10	55,000	
7		20,000 X $1.10		22,000
8	Total fixed costs		$8,000	$8,000

Maintenance costs are therefore $8,000 per month plus $1.10 per mile. This is represented by the following formula:

$$\text{Maintenance costs} = \text{Fixed costs} + (\$1.10 \times \text{miles driven})$$

For example, at 45,000 miles, estimated maintenance costs would be $8,000 fixed and $49,500 variable ($1.10 × 45,000) for a total of $57,500.

The high-low method generally produces a reasonable estimate for analysis. However, it does not produce a precise measurement of the fixed and variable elements in a mixed cost because other activity levels are ignored in the computation.

Importance of Identifying Variable and Fixed Costs

Why is it important to segregate costs into variable and fixed elements? The answer may become apparent if we look at the following four business decisions.

1. If American Airlines is to make a profit when it reduces all domestic fares by 30%, what reduction in costs or increase in passengers will be required? **Answer**: To make a profit when it cuts domestic fares by 30%, American Airlines will have to increase the number of passengers or cut its variable costs for those flights. Its fixed costs will not change.
2. If Ford Motor Company meets workers' demands for higher wages, what increase in sales revenue will be needed to maintain current profit levels? **Answer**: Higher wages at Ford Motor Company will increase the variable costs of manufacturing automobiles. To maintain present profit levels, Ford will have to cut other variable costs or increase the price of its automobiles.
3. If United States Steel Corp.'s program to modernize plant facilities through significant equipment purchases reduces the work force by 50%, what will be the effect on the cost of producing one ton of steel? **Answer**: The modernizing of plant facilities at United States Steel Corp. changes the proportion of fixed and variable costs of producing one ton of steel. Fixed costs increase because of higher depreciation charges, whereas variable costs decrease due to the reduction in the number of steelworkers.
4. What happens if Kellogg Company increases its advertising expenses but cannot increase prices because of competitive pressure? **Answer**: Sales volume must be increased to cover the increase in fixed advertising costs.

Before You Go On...

REVIEW IT

1. What are the effects on (a) a variable cost and (b) a fixed cost due to a change in activity?
2. What is the relevant range, and how do costs behave within this range?
3. What are the steps in applying the high-low method to mixed costs?

DO IT

Helena Company reports the following total costs at two levels of production.

	10,000 units	20,000 units
Direct materials	$20,000	$40,000
Maintenance	8,000	10,000
Depreciation	4,000	4,000

Classify each cost as either variable, fixed, or mixed.

Action Plan

- Recall that a variable cost varies in total directly and proportionately with each change.
- Recall that a fixed cost remains the same in total with each change.
- Recall that a mixed cost changes in total but not proportionately with each change.

Solution Direct materials is a variable cost. Maintenance is a mixed cost. Depreciation is a fixed cost.

Related exercise material: *BE22-1, BE22-2, BE22-3, E22-1, E22-2, and E22-3.*

The Navigator

COST-VOLUME-PROFIT ANALYSIS

STUDY OBJECTIVE 4

List the five components of cost-volume-profit analysis.

Cost-volume-profit (CVP) analysis is the study of the effects of changes in costs and volume on a company's profits. CVP analysis is important in profit planning. It also is a critical factor in such management decisions as setting selling prices, determining product mix, and maximizing use of production facilities.

Basic Components

CVP analysis considers the interrelationships among the components shown in Illustration 22-9.

Illustration 22-9
Components of CVP analysis

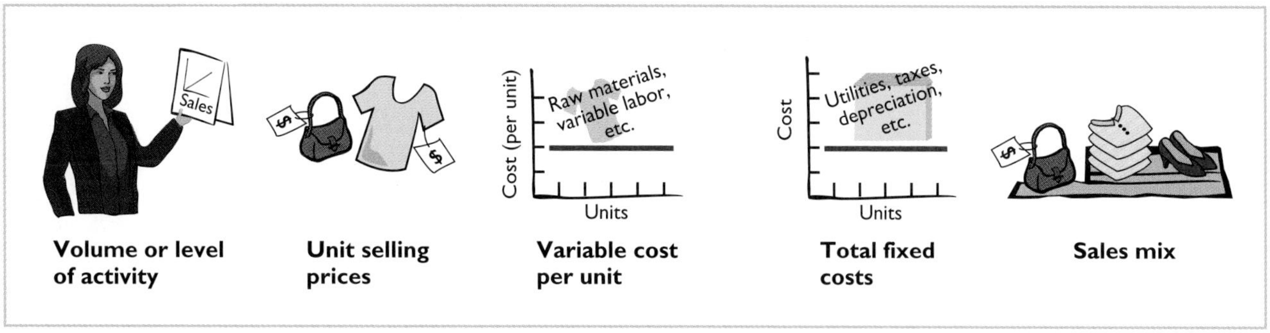

The following assumptions underlie each CVP analysis.

1. The behavior of both costs and revenues is linear throughout the relevant range of the activity index.
2. Costs can be classified accurately as either variable or fixed.
3. Changes in activity are the only factors that affect costs.
4. All units produced are sold.
5. When more than one type of product is sold, the sales mix will remain constant. That is, the percentage that each product represents of total sales will stay the same. Sales mix complicates CVP analysis because different products will have different cost relationships. In this chapter we assume a single product.

When these assumptions are not valid, the CVP analysis may be inaccurate.

CVP Income Statement

STUDY OBJECTIVE 5

Indicate what contribution margin is and how it can be expressed.

Because CVP is so important for decision making, management often wants this information reported in a **CVP income statement** format for internal use. The CVP income statement classifies costs as variable or fixed and computes a contribution margin. **Contribution margin** is the amount of revenue remaining after deducting variable costs. It is often stated both as a total amount and on a per unit basis.

We will use Vargo Video Company to illustrate a CVP income statement. Vargo Video produces a high-end, progressive-scan DVD player/recorder with up to 160-hour recording capacity and MP3 playback capability. Relevant data for the DVD players sold by this company in June 2008 are as follows.

Illustration 22-10
Assumed selling and cost data for Vargo Video

Unit selling price of DVD player	$500
Unit variable costs	$300
Total monthly fixed costs	$200,000
Units sold	1,600

The CVP income statement for Vargo Video therefore would be reported as follows.

Illustration 22-11
CVP income statement, with net income

VARGO VIDEO COMPANY
CVP Income Statement
For the Month Ended June 30, 2008

	Total	Per Unit
Sales (1,600 DVD players)	$800,000	$500
Variable costs	480,000	300
Contribution margin	**320,000**	**$200**
Fixed costs	200,000	
Net income	**$120,000**	

A traditional income statement and a CVP income statement both report the same net income of $120,000. However a traditional income statement does not classify costs as variable or fixed, and therefore a contribution margin is not reported. In addition, both a total and a per unit amount are often shown on a CVP income statement to facilitate CVP analysis.

In the applications of CVP analysis that follow, we assume that the term "cost" includes all costs and expenses related to production and sale of the product. That is, cost includes manufacturing costs plus selling and administrative expenses.

CONTRIBUTION MARGIN PER UNIT

Vargo Video's CVP income statement shows a contribution margin of $320,000, and a contribution margin per unit of $200 ($500 − $300). The formula for **contribution margin per unit** and the computation for Vargo Video are:

Unit Selling Price	−	Unit Variable Costs	=	Contribution Margin per Unit
$500	−	$300	=	**$200**

Illustration 22-12
Formula for contribution margin per unit

Contribution margin per unit indicates that for every DVD player sold, Vargo has $200 to cover fixed costs and contribute to net income. Because Vargo Video has fixed costs of $200,000, it must sell 1,000 DVD players ($200,000 ÷ $200) before it earns any net income. Vargo's CVP income statement, assuming a zero net income, is as follows.

Illustration 22-13
CVP income statement, with zero net income

VARGO VIDEO COMPANY
CVP Income Statement
For the Month Ended June 30, 2008

	Total	Per Unit
Sales (1,000 DVD players)	$500,000	$500
Variable costs	300,000	300
Contribution margin	**200,000**	**$200**
Fixed costs	200,000	
Net income	**$ -0-**	

It follows that for every DVD player sold above 1,000 units, net income increases $200. For example, assume that Vargo sold one more DVD player, for a total of 1,001 DVD players sold. In this case Vargo reports net income of $200 as shown in Illustration 22-14.

Illustration 22-14
CVP income statement, with net income

VARGO VIDEO COMPANY
CVP Income Statement
For the Month Ended June 30, 2008

	Total	Per Unit
Sales (1,001 DVD players)	$500,500	$500
Variable costs	300,300	300
Contribution margin	**200,200**	**$200**
Fixed costs	200,000	
Net income	**$ 200**	

CONTRIBUTION MARGIN RATIO

Some managers prefer to use a contribution margin ratio in CVP analysis. The **contribution margin ratio** is the contribution margin per unit divided by the unit selling price. For Vargo Video, the ratio is as follows.

Illustration 22-15
Formula for contribution margin ratio

Contribution Margin per Unit	÷	Unit Selling Price	=	Contribution Margin Ratio
$200	÷	$500	=	**40%**

The contribution margin ratio of 40% means that $0.40 of each sales dollar ($1 × 40%) is available to apply to fixed costs and to contribute to net income.

This expression of contribution margin is very helpful in determining the effect of changes in sales on net income. For example, if sales increase $100,000, net income will increase $40,000 (40% × $100,000). Thus, by using the contribution margin ratio, managers can quickly determine increases in net income from any change in sales.

We can also see this effect through a CVP income statement. Assume that Vargo Video's current sales are $500,000 and it wants to know the effect of a $100,000 increase in sales. Vargo prepares a comparative CVP income statement analysis as follows.

Illustration 22-16
Comparative CVP income statements

VARGO VIDEO COMPANY
CVP Income Statements
For the Month Ended June 30, 2008

	No Change		With Change	
	Total	**Per Unit**	**Total**	**Per Unit**
Sales	$500,000	$500	$600,000	$500
Variable costs	300,000	300	360,000	300
Contribution margin	**200,000**	**$200**	**240,000**	**$200**
Fixed costs	200,000		200,000	
Net income	**$ -0-**		**$ 40,000**	

Study these CVP income statements carefully. The concepts presented in these statements are used extensively in this and later chapters.

Break-Even Analysis

STUDY OBJECTIVE 6
Identify the three ways to determine the break-even point.

A key relationship in CVP analysis is the level of activity at which total revenues equal total costs (both fixed and variable). This level of activity is called the **break-even point**. At this volume of sales, the company will realize no income but will suffer no loss. The process of finding the break-even point is called **break-even analysis**. Knowledge of the break-even point is useful to management when it decides whether to introduce new product lines, change sales prices on established products, or enter new market areas.

The break-even point can be:

1. Computed from a mathematical equation.
2. Computed by using contribution margin.
3. Derived from a cost-volume-profit (CVP) graph.

The break-even point can be expressed either in **sales units** or **sales dollars**.

MATHEMATICAL EQUATION

Illustration 22-17 shows a common equation used for CVP analysis.

Sales	=	Variable Costs	+	Fixed Costs	+	Net Income

Illustration 22-17
Basic CVP equation

Identifying the break-even point is a special case of CVP analysis. Because at the break-even point net income is zero, **break-even occurs where total sales equal variable costs plus fixed costs**.

The break-even point **in units** can be computed directly from the equation by **using unit selling prices** and **unit variable costs**. The computation for Vargo Video is:

Sales	=	Variable Costs	+	Fixed Costs	+	Net Income
\$500Q	=	\$300Q	+	\$200,000	+	\$0

\$200Q = \$200,000
Q = **1,000 units**

where

Q = sales volume in units
\$500 = selling price
\$300 = variable cost per unit
\$200,000 = total fixed costs

Illustration 22-18
Computation of break-even point in units

Thus, Vargo Video must sell 1,000 units to break even.

To find **sales dollars** required to break even, we multiply the units sold at the break-even point times the selling price per unit, as shown below.

1,000 × \$500 = \$500,000 (break-even sales dollars)

CONTRIBUTION MARGIN TECHNIQUE

We know that contribution margin equals total revenues less variable costs. It follows that at the break-even point, **contribution margin must equal total fixed costs**. On the basis of this relationship, we can compute the break-even point using either the contribution margin per unit or the contribution margin ratio.

When a company uses the contribution margin per unit, the formula to compute break-even point in units is fixed costs divided by contribution margin per unit. For Vargo Video the computation is as follows.

Fixed Costs	÷	Contribution Margin per Unit	=	Break-even Point in Units
\$200,000	÷	\$200	=	**1,000 units**

Illustration 22-19
Formula for break-even point in units using contribution margin

One way to interpret this formula is that Vargo Video generates \$200 of contribution margin with each unit that it sells. This \$200 goes to pay off fixed costs. Therefore, the company must sell 1,000 units to pay off \$200,000 in fixed costs.

When a company uses the contribution margin ratio, the formula to compute break-even point in dollars is fixed costs divided by the contribution margin ratio. We know that the contribution margin ratio for Vargo Video is 40% ($200 ÷ $500), which means that every dollar of sales generates 40 cents to pay off fixed costs. Thus, the break-even point in dollars is:

Illustration 22-20
Formula for break-even point in dollars using contribution margin ratio

Fixed Costs	÷	Contribution Margin Ratio	=	Break-even Point in Dollars
$200,000	÷	40%	=	**$500,000**

ACCOUNTING ACROSS THE ORGANIZATION

Charter Flights Offer a Good Deal

The Internet is wringing inefficiencies out of nearly every industry. While commercial aircraft spend roughly 4,000 hours a year in the air, chartered aircraft spend only 500 hours flying. That means that they are sitting on the ground—not making any money—about 90% of the time. One company, FlightServe, saw a business opportunity in that fact. For about the same cost as a first-class ticket, FlightServe decided to match up executives with charter flights in small "private jets." The executive would get a more comfortable ride and could avoid the hassle of big airports. FlightServe noted that the average charter jet has eight seats. When all eight seats are full, the company would have an 80% profit margin. It would break even at an average of 3.3 full seats per flight.

Source: "Jet Set Go," *The Economist,* March 18, 2000, p. 68.

? How did FlightServe determine that it would break even with 3.3 seats full per flight?

GRAPHIC PRESENTATION

An effective way to find the break-even point is to prepare a break-even graph. Because this graph also shows costs, volume, and profits, it is referred to as a **cost-volume-profit (CVP) graph.**

As shown in the CVP graph in Illustration 22-21, sales volume is recorded along the horizontal axis. This axis should extend to the maximum level of expected sales. Both total revenues (sales) and total costs (fixed plus variable) are recorded on the vertical axis.

The construction of the graph, using the data for Vargo Video, is as follows.

1. Plot the total-sales line, starting at the zero activity level. For every DVD player sold, total revenue increases by $500. For example, at 200 units, sales are $100,000. At the upper level of activity (1,800 units), sales are $900,000. The revenue line is assumed to be linear through the full range of activity.
2. Plot the total fixed cost using a horizontal line. For the DVD players, this line is plotted at $200,000. The fixed cost is the same at every level of activity.
3. Plot the total-cost line. This starts at the fixed-cost line at zero activity. It increases by the variable cost at each level of activity. For each DVD player, variable costs are $300. Thus, at 200 units, total variable cost is $60,000, and the total cost is $260,000. At 1,800 units total variable cost is $540,000, and total cost

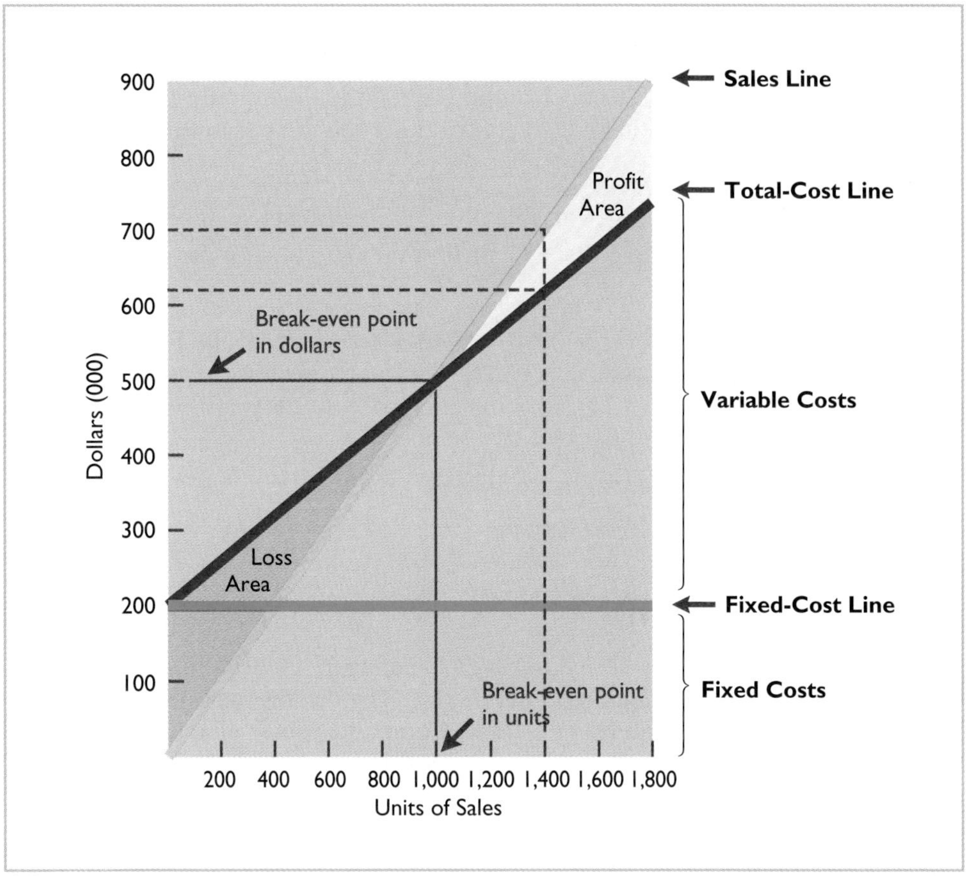

Illustration 22-21
CVP graph

is $740,000. On the graph, the amount of the variable cost can be derived from the difference between the total cost and fixed cost lines at each level of activity.

4. Determine the break-even point from the intersection of the total-cost line and the total-revenue line. The break-even point in dollars is found by drawing a horizontal line from the break-even point to the vertical axis. The break-even point in units is found by drawing a vertical line from the break-even point to the horizontal axis. For the DVD players, the break-even point is $500,000 of sales, or 1,000 units. At this sales level, Vargo Video will cover costs but make no profit.

The CVP graph also shows both the net income and net loss areas. Thus, the amount of income or loss at each level of sales can be derived from the total sales and total cost lines.

A CVP graph is useful because the effects of a change in any element in the CVP analysis can be quickly seen. For example, a 10% increase in selling price will change the location of the total revenue line. Likewise, the effects on total costs of wage increases can be quickly observed.

Before You Go On...

REVIEW IT

1. What are the assumptions that underlie each CVP application?
2. What is contribution margin, and how can it be expressed?
3. How can the break-even point be determined?

DO IT

Lombardi Company has a unit selling price of $400, variable costs per unit of $240, and fixed costs of $180,000. Compute the break-even point in units using (a) a mathematical equation and (b) contribution margin per unit.

Action Plan

- Apply the formula: Sales = Variable costs + Fixed costs + Net income.
- Apply the formula: Fixed costs ÷ Contribution margin per unit = Break-even point in units.

Solution (a) The formula is $400Q = $240Q + $180,000. The break-even point in units is 1,125 ($180,000 ÷ $160). (b) The contribution margin per unit is $160 ($400 − $240). The formula therefore is $180,000 ÷ $160, and the break-even point in units is 1,125.

Related exercise material: *BE22-5, BE22-6, E22-4, E22-7, and E22-8.*

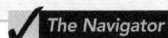

The Navigator

Target Net Income

STUDY OBJECTIVE 7

Give the formulas for determining sales required to earn target net income.

Rather than simply "breaking even," management usually sets an income objective often called **target net income**. It indicates the sales necessary to achieve a specified level of income. Companies determine the sales necessary to achieve target net income by using one of the three approaches discussed earlier.

MATHEMATICAL EQUATION

We know that at the break-even point no profit or loss results for the company. By adding an amount for target net income to the same basic equation, we obtain the following formula for determining required sales.

Illustration 22-22
Formula for required sales to meet target net income

Required Sales = Variable Costs + Fixed Costs + Target Net Income

Required sales may be expressed in either **sales units** or **sales dollars**. Assuming that target net income is $120,000 for Vargo Video, the computation of required sales in units is as follows.

Illustration 22-23
Computation of required sales

Required Sales	=	Variable Costs	+	Fixed Costs	+	Target Net Income
$500Q	=	$300Q	+	$200,000	+	$120,000

$200Q = $320,000
Q = **1,600**

where

Q = sales volume
$500 = selling price
$300 = variable costs per unit
$200,000 = total fixed costs
$120,000 = target net income

The sales dollars required to achieve the target net income is found by multiplying the units sold by the unit selling price [(1,600 × $500) = $800,000].

CONTRIBUTION MARGIN TECHNIQUE

As in the case of break-even sales, the sales required to meet a target net income can be computed in either units or dollars. The formula to compute required sales in units for Vargo Video using the contribution margin per unit is as follows.

Fixed Costs + Target Net Income	÷	Contribution Margin Per Unit	=	Required Sales in Units
($200,000 + $120,000)	÷	$200	=	**1,600 units**

Illustration 22-24
Formula for required sales in units using contribution margin per unit

This computation tells Vargo that to achieve its desired target net income of $120,000, it must sell 1,600 DVD players.

The formula to compute the required sales in dollars for Vargo Video using the contribution margin ratio is as follows.

Fixed Costs + Target Net Income	÷	Contribution Margin Ratio	=	Required Sales in Dollars
($200,000 + $120,000)	÷	40%	=	**$800,000**

Illustration 22-25
Formula for required sales in dollars using contribution margin ratio

This computation tells Vargo that to achieve its desired target net income of $120,000, it must generate sales of $800,000.

GRAPHIC PRESENTATION

The CVP graph in Illustration 22-21 (on page 971) is also used to find the sales required to meet target net income. In the profit area of the graph, the distance between the sales line and the total cost line at any point equals net income. We can find required sales by analyzing the differences between the two lines until the desired net income is found.

For example, suppose Vargo Video sells 1,400 DVD players. Illustration 22-21 shows that a vertical line drawn at 1,400 units intersects the sales line at $700,000 and the total cost line at $620,000. The difference between the two amounts represents the net income (profit) of $80,000.

Margin of Safety

STUDY OBJECTIVE 8
Define margin of safety, and give the formulas for computing it.

The margin of safety is another relationship used in CVP analysis. **Margin of safety** is the difference between actual or expected sales and sales at the break-even point. This relationship measures the "cushion" that management has, allowing it to still break even if expected sales fail to materialize. The margin of safety is expressed in dollars or as a ratio.

The formula for stating the **margin of safety in dollars** is actual (or expected) sales minus break-even sales. Assuming that actual (expected) sales for Vargo Video are $750,000, the computation is:

Actual (Expected) Sales	−	Break-even Sales	=	Margin of Safety in Dollars
$750,000	−	$500,000	=	**$250,000**

Illustration 22-26
Formula for margin of safety in dollars

Vargo's margin of safety is $250,000. Its sales must fall $250,000 before it operates at a loss.

The **margin of safety ratio** is the margin of safety in dollars divided by actual (or expected) sales. The formula and computation for determining the margin of safety ratio are:

Illustration 22-27
Formula for margin of safety ratio

Margin of Safety in Dollars	÷	Actual (Expected) Sales	=	Margin of Safety Ratio
$250,000	÷	$750,000	=	**33%**

This means that the company's sales could fall by 33% before it would be operating at a loss.

The higher the dollars or the percentage, the greater the margin of safety. Management continuously evaluates the adequacy of the margin of safety in terms of such factors as the vulnerability of the product to competitive pressures and to downturns in the economy.

MANAGEMENT INSIGHT

How a Rolling Stones' Tour Makes Money

Computation of break-even and margin of safety is important for service companies as well. Consider how the promoter for the Rolling Stones' tour used the break-even point and margin of safety. For example, one outdoor show should bring 70,000 individuals for a gross of $2.45 million. The promoter guarantees $1.2 million to the Rolling Stones. In addition, 20% of gross goes to the stadium in which the performance is staged. Add another $400,000 for other expenses such as ticket takers, parking attendants, advertising, and so on. The promoter also shares in sales of T-shirts and memorabilia for which the promoter will net over $7 million during the tour. From a successful Rolling Stones' tour, the promoter could make $35 million!

? What amount of sales dollars are required for the promoter to break even?

CVP and Changes in the Business Environment

When the personal computer was introduced, it sold for $2,500; today similar computers sell for much less. Recently, when oil prices rose, the break-even point for airline companies such as American and United rose dramatically. Because of lower prices for imported steel, the demand for domestic steel dropped significantly. The point should be clear: Business conditions change rapidly, and management must respond intelligently to these changes. CVP analysis can help.

To illustrate how CVP analysis helps in responding to change, we look at three independent situations that might occur at Vargo Video. Each case uses the original DVD player sales and cost data, which were:

Illustration 22-28
Original DVD player sales and cost data

Unit selling price	$500
Unit variable cost	$300
Total fixed costs	$200,000
Break-even sales	$500,000 or 1,000 units

Case I. A competitor is offering a 10% discount on the selling price of its DVD players. Management must decide whether to offer a similar discount. **Question**: What effect will a 10% discount on selling price have on the break-even point for DVD players? **Answer**: A 10% discount on selling price reduces the selling price per unit to $450 [$500 − ($500 × 10%)]. Variable costs per unit remain unchanged at $300. Thus, the contribution margin per unit is $150. Assuming no change in fixed costs, break-even sales are 1,333 units, computed as follows.

Illustration 22-29
Computation of break-even sales in units

Fixed Costs	÷	Contribution Margin per Unit	=	Break-even Sales
$200,000	÷	$150	=	**1,333 units (rounded)**

For Vargo Video, this change requires monthly sales to increase by 333 units, or 33⅓%, in order to break even. In reaching a conclusion about offering a 10% discount to customers, management must determine how likely it is to achieve the increased sales. Also, management should estimate the possible loss of sales if the competitor's discount price is not matched.

Case II. To meet the threat of foreign competition, management invests in new robotic equipment that will lower the amount of direct labor required to make DVD players. The company estimates that total fixed costs will increase 30% and that variable cost per unit will decrease 30%. **Question**: What effect will the new equipment have on the sales volume required to break even? **Answer**: Total fixed costs become $260,000 [$200,000 + (30% × $200,000)]. The variable cost per unit becomes $210 [$300 − (30% × $300)]. The new break-even point is approximately 897 units, computed as follows.

Illustration 22-30
Computation of break-even sales in units

Fixed Costs	÷	Contribution Margin per Unit	=	Break-even Sales
$260,000	÷	($500 − $210)	=	**897 units (rounded)**

These changes appear to be advantageous for Vargo Video. The break-even point is reduced by 10%, or 100 units.

Case III. Vargo's principal supplier of raw materials has just announced a price increase. The higher cost is expected to increase the variable cost of DVD players by $25 per unit. Management decides to hold the line on the selling price of the DVD players. It plans a cost-cutting program that will save $17,500 in fixed costs per month. Vargo is currently realizing monthly net income of $80,000 on sales of 1,400 DVD players. **Question**: What increase in units sold will be needed to maintain the same level of net income? **Answer**: The variable cost per unit increases to $325 ($300 + $25). Fixed costs are reduced to $182,500 ($200,000 − $17,500). Because of the change in variable cost, the contribution margin per unit becomes $175 ($500 − $325). The required number of units sold to achieve the target net income is computed as follows.

Illustration 22-31
Computation of required sales

Fixed Costs + Target Net Income	÷	Contribution Margin per Unit	=	Required Sales in Units
($182,500 + $80,000)	÷	$175	=	**1,500**

To achieve the required sales, 1,500 DVD players will have to be sold, an increase of 100 units. If this does not seem to be a reasonable expectation, management will either have to make further cost reductions or accept less net income if the selling price remains unchanged.

CVP Income Statement Revisited

STUDY OBJECTIVE 9

Describe the essential features of a cost-volume-profit income statement.

Earlier in the chapter we presented a simple CVP income statement. When companies prepare a CVP income statement, they provide more detail about specific variable and fixed-cost items.

To illustrate a more detailed CVP income statement, we will assume that Vargo Video reaches its target net income of $120,000 (see Illustration 22-23 on page 972). The following information is obtained on the $680,000 of costs that were incurred in June to produce and sell 1,600 units.

Illustration 22-32
Assumed cost and expense data

	Variable	Fixed	Total
Cost of goods sold	$400,000	$120,000	$520,000
Selling expenses	60,000	40,000	100,000
Administrative expenses	20,000	40,000	60,000
	$480,000	$200,000	$680,000

The detailed CVP income statement for Vargo is shown below.

Illustration 22-33
Detailed CVP income statement

VARGO VIDEO COMPANY
CVP Income Statement
For the Month Ended June 30, 2008

	Total		Per Unit
Sales		$800,000	$500
Variable expenses			
Cost of goods sold	$400,000		
Selling expenses	60,000		
Administrative expenses	20,000		
Total variable expenses		480,000	300
Contribution margin		**320,000**	**$200**
Fixed expenses			
Cost of goods sold	120,000		
Selling expenses	40,000		
Administrative expenses	40,000		
Total fixed expenses		200,000	
Net income		**$120,000**	

Before You Go On...

REVIEW IT

1. What is the formula for computing the margin of safety (a) in dollars and (b) as a ratio?
2. What is the equation to compute target net income?

The Navigator

Be sure to read **ALL ABOUT YOU: *A Hybrid Dilemma*** on the next page for information on how topics in this chapter apply to you.

all about YOU

A Hybrid Dilemma

Have high gas prices got you down? Maybe you should consider a hybrid. These half-gas and half-electric vehicles are generating a lot of interest. They burn less fuel and therefore are easier on the environment. But are they easier on your pocketbook? Is a hybrid car at least a break-even investment, or is it more likely a losing proposition?

Some Facts

* Ford plans to sell at least seven different models of hybrid cars, about 250,000 vehicles annually, by the end of the decade.
* Hybrid vehicles typically cost $3,000 to $5,000 more than their conventional counterpart, although for some models the premium is higher.
* Bank of America and Timberland offer $3,000 to employees who purchase hybrids. Google offers $5,000 to employees who purchase cars that get at least 45 miles per gallon.
* The most fuel-efficient hybrids–the Toyota Prius and the Honda Civic–can save about $660 per year in fuel costs relative to a similar conventional car. However some other hybrids provide only slight fuel savings.
* Each gallon of gasoline that is not consumed reduces carbon dioxide emissions by 19 pounds. Many believe carbon dioxide contributes to global warming.
* The federal government initially provided tax credits of up to $3,400 to buyers of hybrids. These credits are to be phased out as automakers reach sales caps determined by the Internal Revenue Service (IRS).

About the Numbers

Sales of hybrid cars started very strong in 2005, but then tapered off. The following graph shows that sales of the Toyota Prius far exceed other brands.

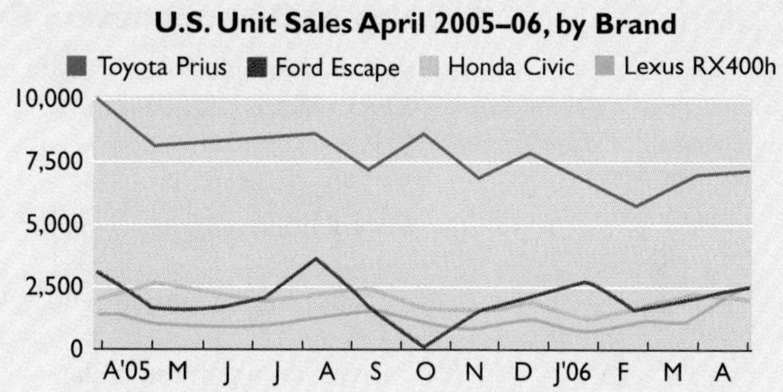

Source: J.D. Power and Associates, 2006, "Happening Hybrids," as reported in the *Wall Street Journal*, May 23, 2006.

What Do You Think?

Gas prices are depleting your wallet so fast that you might even have to give up your old car and resort to walking or riding your bike on occasion. Will making the investment in a hybrid slow the outflow from your wallet and spare your feet?

YES: At 44 miles per gallon, I can drive forever without ever having to fill up.

NO: Because of the premium price charged for hybrids, I will never drive enough miles to break even on my investment.

Sources: "The Dollars and Sense of Hybrids," *Consumer Reports*, April, 2006, pp. 18-22.; John D. Stoll and Gina Chon, "Consumer Drive for Hybrid Autos Is Slowing Down," *Wall Street Journal*, April 7, 2006, p. A2. Associated Press, "Bank Workers Get Hybrid Reward," *Wall Street Journal*, June 8, 2006, p. D2.

The authors' comments on this situation appear on page 996.

Demonstration Problem 1

WILEY PLUS

Mabo Company makes calculators that sell for $20 each. For the coming year, management expects fixed costs to total $220,000 and variable costs to be $9 per unit.

Instructions

(a) Compute break-even point in units using the mathematical equation.
(b) Compute break-even point in dollars using the contribution margin (CM) ratio.
(c) Compute the margin of safety percentage assuming actual sales are $500,000.
(d) Compute the sales required in dollars to earn net income of $165,000.

action plan

- ✔ Know the formulas.
- ✔ Recognize that variable costs change with sales volume; fixed costs do not.
- ✔ Avoid computational errors.

Solution to Demonstration Problem 1

(a) Sales = Variable costs + Fixed costs + Net income

$$\$20Q = \$9Q + \$220{,}000 + \$0$$
$$\$11Q = \$220{,}000$$
$$Q = 20{,}000 \text{ units}$$

(b) Contribution margin per unit = Unit selling price − Unit variable costs

$$\$11 = \$20 - \$9$$

Contribution margin ratio = Contribution margin per unit ÷ Unit selling price

$$55\% = \$11 \div \$20$$

Break-even point in dollars = Fixed cost ÷ Contribution margin ratio

$$= \$220{,}000 \div 55\%$$
$$= \$400{,}000$$

(c)
$$\text{Margin of safety} = \frac{\text{Actual sales} - \text{Break-even sales}}{\text{Actual sales}}$$
$$= \frac{\$500{,}000 - \$400{,}000}{\$500{,}000}$$
$$= 20\%$$

(d) Required sales = Variable costs + Fixed costs + Net income

$$\$20Q = \$9Q + \$220{,}000 + \$165{,}000$$
$$\$11Q = \$385{,}000$$
$$Q = 35{,}000 \text{ units}$$

35,000 units × $20 = $700,000 required sales

✔ The Navigator

Demonstration Problem 2

WILEY PLUS

B.T. Hernandez Company, maker of high-quality flashlights, has experienced steady growth over the last 6 years. However, increased competition has led Mr. Hernandez, the president, to believe that an aggressive campaign is needed next year to maintain the company's present growth. The company's accountant has presented Mr. Hernandez with the following data for the current year, 2008, for use in preparing next year's advertising campaign.

Cost Schedules

Variable costs	
Direct labor per flashlight	$ 8.00
Direct materials	4.00
Variable overhead	3.00
Variable cost per flashlight	$15.00

Fixed costs	
Manufacturing	$ 25,000
Selling	40,000
Administrative	70,000
Total fixed costs	$135,000
Selling price per flashlight	$25.00
Expected sales, 2008 (20,000 flashlights)	$500,000

Mr. Hernandez has set the sales target for the year 2009 at a level of $550,000 (22,000 flashlights).

Instructions

(Ignore any income tax considerations.)

(a) What is the projected operating income for 2008?
(b) What is the contribution margin per unit for 2008?
(c) What is the break-even point in units for 2008?
(d) Mr. Hernandez believes that to attain the sales target in the year 2009, the company must incur an additional selling expense of $10,000 for advertising in 2009, with all other costs remaining constant. What will be the break-even point in dollar sales for 2009 if the company spends the additional $10,000?
(e) If the company spends the additional $10,000 for advertising in 2009, what is the sales level in dollars required to equal 2008 operating income?

action plan

✓ Know the formulas.
✓ Recognize that variable costs change with sales volume; fixed costs do not.
✓ Avoid computational errors.

Solution to Demonstration Problem 2

(a)

Expected sales	$500,000
Less:	
Variable cost (20,000 flashlights × $15)	300,000
Fixed costs	135,000
Projected operating income	$ 65,000

(b)

Selling price per flashlight	$25
Variable cost per flashlight	15
Contribution margin per unit	$10

(c) Fixed costs ÷ Contribution margin per unit = Break-even point in units
$135,000 ÷ $10 = 13,500 units

(d) Fixed costs ÷ Contribution margin ratio = Break-even point in dollars
$145,000 ÷ 40% = $362,500

Fixed costs (from 2008)	$135,000
Additional advertising expense	10,000
Fixed costs (2009)	$145,000

Contribution margin per unit (b) $10
Contribution margin ratio = Contribution margin per unit ÷ Unit selling price
40% = $10 ÷ $25

(e) Required sales = (Fixed costs + Target net income) ÷ Contribution margin ratio
$525,000 = ($145,000 + $65,000) ÷ 40%

✓ The Navigator

SUMMARY OF STUDY OBJECTIVES

WILEY PLUS

1 **Distinguish between variable and fixed costs.** Variable costs are costs that vary in total directly and proportionately with changes in the activity index. Fixed costs are costs that remain the same in total regardless of changes in the activity index.

2 **Explain the significance of the relevant range.** The relevant range is the range of activity in which a company expects to operate during a year. It is important in CVP analysis because the behavior of costs is assumed to be linear throughout the relevant range.

3 **Explain the concept of mixed costs.** Mixed costs increase in total but not proportionately with changes in the activity level. For purposes of CVP analysis, mixed costs must be classified into their fixed and variable elements. One method that management may use to classify these costs is the high-low method.

4 **List the five components of cost-volume-profit analysis.** The five components of CVP analysis are (a) volume or level of activity, (b) unit selling prices, (c) variable cost per unit, (d) total fixed costs, and (e) sales mix.

5 **Indicate what contribution margin is and how it can be expressed.** Contribution margin is the amount of revenue remaining after deducting variable costs. It is identified in a CVP income statement, which classifies costs as variable or fixed. It can be expressed as a per unit amount or as a ratio.

6 **Identify the three ways to determine the break-even point.** The break-even point can be (a) computed from a mathematical equation, (b) computed by using a contribution margin technique, and (c) derived from a CVP graph.

7 **Give the formulas for determining sales required to earn target net income.** The general formula is: Required sales = Variable costs + Fixed costs + Target net income. Two other formulas are: Required sales in units = (Fixed costs + Target net income) ÷ Contribution margin per unit, and Required sales in dollars = (Fixed costs + Target net income) ÷ Contribution margin ratio.

8 **Define margin of safety, and give the formulas for computing it.** Margin of safety is the difference between actual or expected sales and sales at the break-even point. The formulas for margin of safety are: Actual (expected) sales − Break-even sales = Margin of safety in dollars; Margin of safety in dollars ÷ Actual (expected) sales = Margin of safety ratio.

9 **Describe the essential features of a cost-volume-profit income statement.** The CVP income statement classifies costs and expenses as variable or fixed and reports contribution margin in the body of the statement.

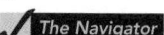

The Navigator

GLOSSARY

WILEY PLUS

Activity index The activity that causes changes in the behavior of costs. (p. 958).

Break-even point The level of activity at which total revenues equal total costs. (p. 968).

Contribution margin (CM) The amount of revenue remaining after deducting variable costs. (p. 966).

Contribution margin per unit The amount of revenue remaining per unit after deducting variable costs; calculated as unit selling price minus unit variable cost. (p. 967).

Contribution margin ratio The percentage of each dollar of sales that is available to apply to fixed costs and contribute to net income; calculated as contribution margin per unit divided by unit selling price. (p. 968).

Cost behavior analysis The study of how specific costs respond to changes in the level of business activity. (p. 958).

Cost-volume-profit (CVP) analysis The study of the effects of changes in costs and volume on a company's profits. (p. 965).

Cost-volume-profit (CVP) graph A graph showing the relationship between costs, volume, and profits. (p. 970).

Cost-volume-profit (CVP) income statement A statement for internal use that classifies costs as fixed or variable and reports contribution margin in the body of the statement. (p. 966).

Fixed costs Costs that remain the same in total regardless of changes in the activity level. (p. 959).

High-low method A mathematical method that uses the total costs incurred at the high and low levels of activity to classify mixed costs into fixed and variable components. (p. 963).

Margin of safety The difference between actual or expected sales and sales at the break-even point. (p. 973).

Mixed costs Costs that contain both a variable and a fixed cost element and change in total but not proportionately with changes in the activity level. (p. 962).

Relevant range The range of the activity index over which the company expects to operate during the year. (p. 961).

Target net income The income objective set by management. (p. 972).

Variable costs Costs that vary in total directly and proportionately with changes in the activity level. (p. 959).

APPENDIX Variable Costing

STUDY OBJECTIVE 10

Explain the difference between absorption costing and variable costing.

In earlier chapters, both variable and fixed manufacturing costs were classified as product costs. In job order costing, for example, a job is assigned the costs of direct materials, direct labor, and both variable and fixed manufacturing overhead. This costing approach is called **absorption costing** (or **full costing**). It is so named because all manufacturing costs are charged to, or absorbed by, the product.

An alternative approach is to use variable costing. Under **variable costing** only direct materials, direct labor, and variable manufacturing overhead costs are considered product costs. In this approach, companies recognize fixed manufacturing overhead costs as period costs (expenses) when incurred. Illustration 22A-1 shows the difference between absorption costing and variable costing.

Illustration 22A-1
Difference between absorption costing and variable costing

Absorption Costing		Variable Costing
Product Cost ←	Fixed Manufacturing Overhead	→ Period Cost

Selling and administrative expenses are period costs under both absorption and variable costing.

To illustrate the computation of unit production cost under absorption and variable costing, assume that Premium Products Corporation manufactures a polyurethane sealant called Fix-It for car windshields. Relevant data for Fix-It in January 2008, the first month of production, are as follows.

Illustration 22A-2
Sealant sales and cost data for Premium Products Corporation

Selling price	$20 per unit.
Units	Produced 30,000; sold 20,000; beginning inventory zero.
Variable unit costs	Manufacturing $9 (direct materials $5, direct labor $3, and variable overhead $1). Selling and administrative expenses $2.
Fixed costs	Manufacturing overhead $120,000. Selling and administrative expenses $15,000.

The per unit production cost of Fix-It under each costing approach is:

Illustration 22A-3
Computation of per unit production cost

Type of Cost	Absorption Costing	Variable Costing
Direct materials	$ 5	$5
Direct labor	3	3
Variable manufacturing overhead	1	1
Fixed manufacturing overhead ($120,000 ÷ 30,000 units produced)	4	0
Total unit cost	$13	$9

The total unit cost is $4 ($13 − $9) higher for absorption costing. This occurs because fixed manufacturing costs are a product cost under absorption costing. They are a period cost under variable costing and so are expensed, instead. Based on these data, each unit sold and each unit remaining in inventory is costed at $13 under absorption costing and at $9 under variable costing.

Effects of Variable Costing on Income

Illustrations 22A-4 and 22A-5 (page 982) show the income statements under the two costing approaches. Absorption costing uses the traditional income statement format. Variable costing uses the cost-volume-profit format. We have inserted computations parenthetically in the statements to facilitate your understanding of the amounts.

Income from operations under absorption costing (Illustration 22A-4) is \$40,000 (\$85,000 − \$45,000) higher than under variable costing (Illustration 22A-5).

As highlighted in the two income statements, there is a \$40,000 difference in the ending inventories (\$130,000 under absorption costing versus \$90,000 under variable costing). Under absorption costing, the company defers \$40,000 of the fixed overhead costs (10,000 units × \$4) to a future period as a product cost. In contrast, under variable costing the company expenses the entire fixed manufacturing costs when incurred.

Illustration 22A-4
Absorption costing income statement

HELPFUL HINT
This is the traditional statement that would result from job order and processing costing explained in Chapters 20 and 21.

PREMIUM PRODUCTS CORPORATION
Income Statement
For the Month Ended January 31, 2008
(Absorption Costing)

Sales (20,000 units × \$20)		\$400,000
Cost of goods sold		
Inventory, January 1	\$ -0-	
Cost of goods manufactured (30,000 units × \$13)	390,000	
Cost of goods available for sale	390,000	
Inventory, January 31 (10,000 units × \$13)	**130,000**	
Cost of goods sold (20,000 units × \$13)		260,000
Gross profit		140,000
Selling and administrative expenses		
(Variable 20,000 units × \$2 + fixed \$15,000)		55,000
Income from operations		**\$ 85,000**

Illustration 22A-5
Variable costing income statement

HELPFUL HINT
Note the difference in the computation of the ending inventory: \$9 per unit here, \$13 per unit in Illustration 22A-4.

PREMIUM PRODUCTS CORPORATION
Income Statement
For the Month Ended January 31, 2008
(Variable Costing)

Sales (20,000 units × \$20)		\$400,000
Variable expenses		
Variable cost of goods sold		
Inventory, January 1	\$ -0-	
Variable manufacturing costs (30,000 units × \$9)	270,000	
Cost of goods available for sale	270,000	
Inventory, January 31 (10,000 units × \$9)	**90,000**	
Variable cost of goods sold	180,000	
Variable selling and administrative expenses		
(20,000 units × \$2)	40,000	
Total variable expenses		220,000
Contribution margin		180,000
Fixed expenses		
Manufacturing overhead	120,000	
Selling and administrative expenses	15,000	
Total fixed expenses		135,000
Income from operations		**\$ 45,000**

The following relationships apply:

- When units produced exceed units sold (as shown), income under absorption costing is higher.
- When units produced are less than units sold, income under absorption costing is lower.
- When units produced and sold are the same, income from operations will be equal under the two costing approaches. In this case, there is no increase in ending inventory, so fixed overhead costs of the current period are not deferred to future periods through the ending inventory.

Illustration 22A-6 summarizes the foregoing effects of the two costing approaches on income from operations.

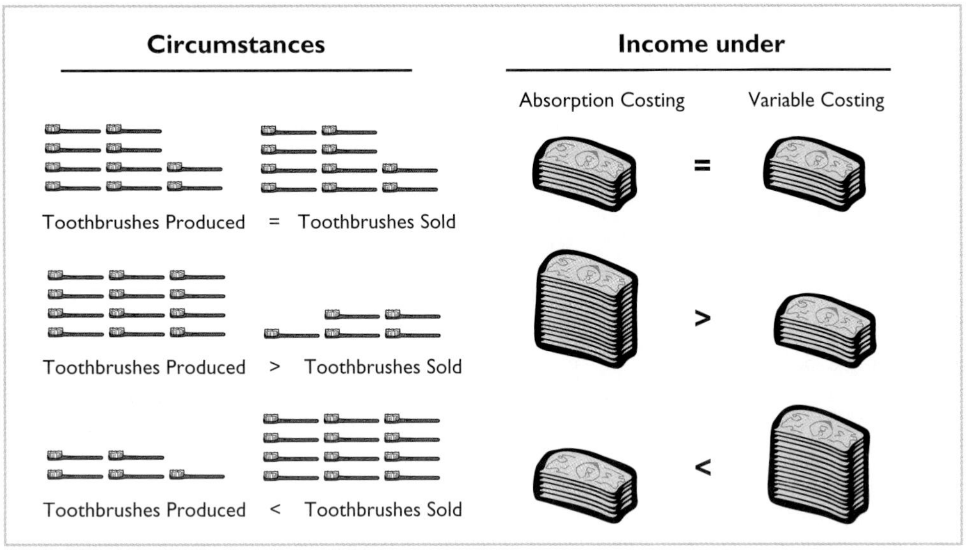

Illustration 22A-6
Summary of income effects

Rationale for Variable Costing

The purpose of fixed manufacturing costs is **to have productive facilities available for use**. A company incurs these costs whether it operates at zero or at 100% of capacity. Thus, proponents of variable costing argue that these costs are period costs and therefore should be expensed when incurred.

Supporters of absorption costing defend the assignment of fixed manufacturing overhead costs to inventory. They say that these costs are as much a cost of getting a product ready for sale as direct materials or direct labor. Accordingly, they contend, these costs should not be matched with revenues until the product is sold.

The use of variable costing is acceptable **only for internal use by management**. It cannot be used in determining product costs in financial statements prepared in accordance with generally accepted accounting principles because it understates inventory costs. To comply with the matching principle, a company must use absorption costing for its work in process and finished goods inventories. Similarly, companies must use absorption costing for income tax purposes.

SUMMARY OF STUDY OBJECTIVE FOR APPENDIX

10 Explain the difference between absorption costing and variable costing. Under absorption costing, fixed manufacturing costs are product costs. Under variable costing, fixed manufacturing costs are period costs.

GLOSSARY FOR APPENDIX

Absorption costing A costing approach in which all manufacturing costs are charged to the product. (p. 981).

Variable costing A costing approach in which only variable manufacturing costs are product costs, and fixed manufacturing costs are period costs (expenses). (p. 981).

*__Note__: All **asterisked** Questions, Exercises, and Problems relate to material in the appendix to the chapter.

SELF-STUDY QUESTIONS

Answers are at the end of the chapter.

(SO 1) **1.** Variable costs are costs that:
a. vary in total directly and proportionately with changes in the activity level.
b. remain the same per unit at every activity level.
c. Neither of the above.
d. Both (a) and (b) above.

(SO 2) **2.** The relevant range is:
a. the range of activity in which variable costs will be curvilinear.
b. the range of activity in which fixed costs will be curvilinear.
c. the range over which the company expects to operate during a year.
d. usually from zero to 100% of operating capacity.

(SO 3) **3.** Mixed costs consist of a:
a. variable cost element and a fixed cost element.
b. fixed cost element and a controllable cost element.
c. relevant cost element and a controllable cost element.
d. variable cost element and a relevant cost element.

(SO 4) **4.** One of the following is *not* involved in CVP analysis. That factor is:
a. sales mix.
b. unit selling prices.
c. fixed costs per unit.
d. volume or level of activity.

(SO 5) **5.** Contribution margin:
a. is revenue remaining after deducting variable costs.
b. may be expressed as contribution margin per unit.
c. is selling price less cost of goods sold.
d. Both (a) and (b) above.

6. Gossen Company is planning to sell 200,000 pliers for $4 per unit. The contribution margin ratio is 25%. If Gossen will break even at this level of sales, what are the fixed costs? (SO 6)
a. $100,000. **c.** $200,000.
b. $160,000. **d.** $300,000.

7. The mathematical equation for computing required sales to obtain target net income is: Required sales = (SO 7)
a. Variable costs + Target net income.
b. Variable costs + Fixed costs + Target net income.
c. Fixed costs + Target net income.
d. No correct answer is given.

8. Marshall Company had actual sales of $600,000 when break-even sales were $420,000. What is the margin of safety ratio? (SO 8)
a. 25%. **c.** 33⅓%.
b. 30%. **d.** 45%.

9. Cournot Company sells 100,000 wrenches for $12 a unit. Fixed costs are $300,000, and net income is $200,000. What should be reported as variable expenses in the CVP income statement? (SO 9)
a. $700,000. **c.** $500,000.
b. $900,000. **d.** $1,000,000.

***10.** Under variable costing, fixed manufacturing costs are classified as: (SO 10)
a. period costs. **c.** both (a) and (b).
b. product costs. **d.** neither (a) nor (b).

Go to the book's website, **www.wiley.com/college/weygandt**, for Additional Self-Study questions.

The Navigator

QUESTIONS

1. (a) What is cost behavior analysis?
(b) Why is cost behavior analysis important to management?

2. (a) Jenny Kent asks your help in understanding the term "activity index." Explain the meaning and importance of this term for Jenny.
(b) State the two ways that variable costs may be defined.

3. Contrast the effects of changes in the activity level on total fixed costs and on unit fixed costs.

4. A. J. Hernandez claims that the relevant range concept is important only for variable costs.
(a) Explain the relevant range concept.
(b) Do you agree with A. J.'s claim? Explain.

5. "The relevant range is indispensable in cost behavior analysis." Is this true? Why or why not?

6. Ryan Ricketts is confused. He does not understand why rent on his apartment is a fixed cost and rent on a Hertz rental truck is a mixed cost. Explain the difference to Ryan.

7. How should mixed costs be classified in CVP analysis? What approach is used to effect the appropriate classification?
8. At the high and low levels of activity during the month, direct labor hours are 90,000 and 40,000, respectively. The related costs are $160,000 and $100,000. What are the fixed and variable costs at any level of activity?
9. "Cost-volume-profit (CVP) analysis is based entirely on unit costs." Do you agree? Explain.
10. Jill Nott defines contribution margin as the amount of profit available to cover operating expenses. Is there any truth in this definition? Discuss.
11. Kosko Company's Speedo calculator sells for $40. Variable costs per unit are estimated to be $28. What are the contribution margin per unit and the contribution margin ratio?
12. "Break-even analysis is of limited use to management because a company cannot survive by just breaking even." Do you agree? Explain.
13. Total fixed costs are $25,000 for Haag Inc. It has a contribution margin per unit of $15, and a contribution margin ratio of 25%. Compute the break-even sales in dollars.
14. Nancy Tobias asks your help in constructing a CVP graph. Explain to Nancy (a) how the break-even point is plotted, and (b) how the level of activity and dollar sales at the break-even point are determined.
15. Define the term "margin of safety." If Peine Company expects to sell 1,250 units of its product at $12 per unit, and break-even sales for the product are $12,000, what is the margin of safety ratio?
16. Ortega Company's break-even sales are $600,000. Assuming fixed costs are $180,000, what sales volume is needed to achieve a target net income of $60,000?
17. The traditional income statement for Mallon Company shows sales $900,000, cost of goods sold $500,000, and operating expenses $200,000. Assuming all costs and expenses are 70% variable and 30% fixed, prepare a CVP income statement through contribution margin.

*18. Distinguish between absorption costing and variable costing.

*19. (a) What is the major rationale for the use of variable costing? (b) Discuss why variable costing may not be used for financial reporting purposes.

BRIEF EXERCISES

WILEY PLUS

BE22-1 Monthly production costs in Pesavento Company for two levels of production are as follows.

Classify costs as variable, fixed, or mixed.

(SO 1, 3)

Cost	3,000 units	6,000 units
Indirect labor	$10,000	$20,000
Supervisory salaries	5,000	5,000
Maintenance	4,000	7,000

Indicate which costs are variable, fixed, and mixed, and give the reason for each answer.

BE22-2 For Loder Company, the relevant range of production is 40–80% of capacity. At 40% of capacity, a variable cost is $4,000 and a fixed cost is $6,000. Diagram the behavior of each cost within the relevant range assuming the behavior is linear.

Diagram the behavior of costs within the relevant range.

(SO 2)

BE22-3 For Hunt Company, a mixed cost is $20,000 plus $16 per direct labor hour. Diagram the behavior of the cost using increments of 500 hours up to 2,500 hours on the horizontal axis and increments of $20,000 up to $80,000 on the vertical axis.

Diagram the behavior of a mixed cost.

(SO 3)

BE22-4 Deines Company accumulates the following data concerning a mixed cost, using miles as the activity level.

Determine variable and fixed cost elements using the high-low method.

(SO 3)

	Miles Driven	Total Cost		Miles Driven	Total Cost
January	8,000	$14,150	March	8,500	$15,000
February	7,500	13,600	April	8,200	14,490

Compute the variable and fixed cost elements using the high-low method.

BE22-5 Determine the missing amounts.

Determine missing amounts for contribution margin.

(SO 5)

	Unit Selling Price	Unit Variable Costs	Contribution Margin per Unit	Contribution Margin Ratio
1.	$250	$170	(a)	(b)
2.	$500	(c)	$200	(d)
3.	(e)	(f)	$300	30%

Compute the break-even point.
(SO 6)

BE22-6 Hamby Company has a unit selling price of $400, variable costs per unit of $260, and fixed costs of $210,000. Compute the break-even point in units using (a) the mathematical equation and (b) contribution margin per unit.

Compute sales for target net income.
(SO 7)

BE22-7 For Markowis Company, variable costs are 70% of sales, and fixed costs are $210,000. Management's net income goal is $60,000. Compute the required sales needed to achieve management's target net income of $60,000. (Use the mathematical equation approach.)

Compute the margin of safety and the margin of safety ratio.
(SO 8)

BE22-8 For Briggs Company actual sales are $1,200,000 and break-even sales are $900,000. Compute (a) the margin of safety in dollars and (b) the margin of safety ratio.

Prepare CVP income statement.
(SO 9)

BE22-9 Dilts Manufacturing Inc. has sales of $1,800,000 for the first quarter of 2008. In making the sales, the company incurred the following costs and expenses.

	Variable	Fixed
Cost of goods sold	$760,000	$540,000
Selling expenses	95,000	60,000
Administrative expenses	79,000	66,000

Prepare a CVP income statement for the quarter ended March 31, 2008.

Compute net income under absorption and variable costing.
(SO 10)

***BE22-10** Gore Company's fixed overhead costs are $3 per unit, and its variable overhead costs are $8 per unit. In the first month of operations, 50,000 units are produced, and 47,000 units are sold. Write a short memo to the chief financial officer explaining which costing approach will produce the higher income and what the difference will be.

EXERCISES

WILEY PLUS

Define and classify variable, fixed, and mixed costs.
(SO 1, 3)

E22-1 Dye Company manufactures a single product. Annual production costs incurred in the manufacturing process are shown below for two levels of production.

	Costs Incurred			
Production in Units	**5,000**		**10,000**	
Production Costs	**Total Cost**	**Cost/ Unit**	**Total Cost**	**Cost/ Unit**
Direct materials	$8,250	$1.65	$16,500	$1.65
Direct labor	9,500	1.90	19,000	1.90
Utilities	1,500	0.30	2,500	0.25
Rent	4,000	0.80	4,000	0.40
Maintenance	800	0.16	1,100	0.11
Supervisory salaries	1,000	0.20	1,000	0.10

Instructions

(a) Define the terms variable costs, fixed costs, and mixed costs.
(b) Classify each cost above as either variable, fixed, or mixed.

Determine fixed and variable costs using the high-low method and prepare graph.
(SO 1, 3)

E22-2 The controller of Dugan Industries has collected the following monthly expense data for use in analyzing the cost behavior of maintenance costs.

Month	Total Maintenance Costs	Total Machine Hours
January	$2,400	300
February	3,000	400
March	3,600	600
April	4,500	790
May	3,200	500
June	4,900	800

Instructions

(a) Determine the fixed and variable cost components using the high-low method.

(b) Prepare a graph showing the behavior of maintenance costs, and identify the fixed and variable cost elements. Use 200 unit increments and $1,000 cost increments.

E22-3 Black Brothers Furniture Corporation incurred the following costs.

Classify variable, fixed, and mixed costs.

(SO 1, 3)

1. Wood used in the production of furniture.
2. Fuel used in delivery trucks.
3. Straight-line depreciation on factory building.
4. Screws used in the production of furniture.
5. Sales staff salaries.
6. Sales commissions.
7. Property taxes.
8. Insurance on buildings.
9. Hourly wages of furniture craftsmen.
10. Salaries of factory supervisors.
11. Utilities expense.
12. Telephone bill.

Instructions

Identify the costs above as variable, fixed, or mixed.

E22-4 Jim Thome wants Thome Company to use CVP analysis to study the effects of changes in costs and volume on the company. Thome has heard that certain assumptions must be valid in order for CVP analysis to be useful.

Explain assumptions underlying CVP analysis.

(SO 4)

Instructions

Prepare a memo to Jim Thome concerning the assumptions that underlie CVP analysis.

E22-5 In the month of June, Barbara's Beauty Salon gave 2,700 haircuts, shampoos, and permanents at an average price of $30. During the month, fixed costs were $18,000 and variable costs were 70% of sales.

Compute contribution margin, break-even point, and margin of safety.

(SO 5, 6, 8)

Instructions

(a) Determine the contribution margin in dollars, per unit, and as a ratio.

(b) Using the contribution margin technique, compute the break-even point in dollars and in units.

(c) Compute the margin of safety in dollars and as a ratio.

E22-6 Grissom Company estimates that variable costs will be 60% of sales, and fixed costs will total $800,000. The selling price of the product is $4.

Prepare a CVP graph and compute break-even point and margin of safety.

(SO 6, 8)

Instructions

(a) Prepare a CVP graph, assuming maximum sales of $3,200,000. (*Note*: Use $400,000 increments for sales and costs and 100,000 increments for units.)

(b) Compute the break-even point in (1) units and (2) dollars.

(c) Compute the margin of safety in (1) dollars and (2) as a ratio, assuming actual sales are $2.5 million.

E22-7 In 2008, Hadicke Company had a break-even point of $350,000 based on a selling price of $7 per unit and fixed costs of $105,000. In 2009, the selling price and the variable cost per unit did not change, but the break-even point increased to $420,000.

Compute variable cost per unit, contribution margin ratio, and increase in fixed costs.

(SO 5, 6)

Instructions

(a) Compute the variable cost per unit and the contribution margin ratio for 2008.

(b) Compute the increase in fixed costs for 2009.

E22-8 NIU Company has the following information available for September 2008.

Prepare CVP income statements.

(SO 5, 6)

Unit selling price of video game consoles	$ 400
Unit variable costs	$ 270
Total fixed costs	$52,000
Units sold	620

Instructions

(a) Prepare a CVP income statement that shows both total and per unit amounts.
(b) Compute NIU's breakeven point in units.
(c) Prepare a CVP income statement for the breakeven point that shows both total and per unit amounts.

Compute various components to derive target net income under different assumptions.
(SO 6, 7)

E22-9 Lynn Company had $150,000 of net income in 2008 when the selling price per unit was $150, the variable costs per unit were $90, and the fixed costs were $570,000. Management expects per unit data and total fixed costs to remain the same in 2009. The president of Lynn Company is under pressure from stockholders to increase net income by $60,000 in 2009.

Instructions

(a) Compute the number of units sold in 2008.
(b) Compute the number of units that would have to be sold in 2009 to reach the stockholders' desired profit level.
(c) Assume that Lynn Company sells the same number of units in 2009 as it did in 2008. What would the selling price have to be in order to reach the stockholders' desired profit level?

Compute net income under different alternatives.
(SO 7)

E22-10 Moran Company reports the following operating results for the month of August: Sales $350,000 (units 5,000); variable costs $210,000; and fixed costs $90,000. Management is considering the following independent courses of action to increase net income.

1. Increase selling price by 10% with no change in total variable costs.
2. Reduce variable costs to 55% of sales.
3. Reduce fixed costs by $10,000.

Instructions

Compute the net income to be earned under each alternative. Which course of action will produce the highest net income?

Prepare a CVP income statement before and after changes in business environment.
(SO 9)

E22-11 Polzin Company had sales in 2008 of $1,500,000 on 60,000 units. Variable costs totaled $840,000, and fixed costs totaled $500,000.

A new raw material is available that will decrease the variable costs per unit by 20% (or $2.80). However, to process the new raw material, fixed operating costs will increase by $60,000. Management feels that one-half of the decline in the variable costs per unit should be passed on to customers in the form of a sales price reduction. The marketing department expects that this sales price reduction will result in a 7% increase in the number of units sold.

Instructions

Prepare a CVP income statement for 2008, assuming the changes are made as described.

Compute total product cost and prepare an income statement using variable costing.
(SO 10)

***E22-12** Titus Equipment Company manufactures and distributes industrial air compressors. The following costs are available for the year ended December 31, 2008. The company has no beginning inventory. In 2008, 1,500 units were produced, but only 1,300 units were sold. The unit selling price was $4,500. Costs and expenses were:

Variable costs per unit	
Direct materials	$ 1,000
Direct labor	1,500
Variable manufacturing overhead	300
Variable selling and administrative expenses	70
Annual fixed costs and expenses	
Manufacturing overhead	$1,400,000
Selling and administrative expenses	100,000

Instructions

(a) Compute the manufacturing cost of one unit of product using variable costing.
(b) Prepare a 2008 income statement for Titus Company using variable costing.

Prepare absorption cost and variable cost income statements.
(SO 10)

***E22-13** Cowell Corporation produces one product. Its cost includes direct materials ($10 per unit), direct labor ($8 per unit), variable overhead ($6 per unit), fixed manufacturing ($250,000), and fixed selling and administrative ($30,000). In October 2008, Cowell produced 25,000 units and sold 20,000 at $50 each.

Instructions

(a) Prepare an absorption costing income statement.
(b) Prepare a variable costing income statement.
(c) Explain the difference in net income in the two income statements.

EXERCISES: SET B

Visit the book's website at **www.wiley.com/college/weygandt**, and choose the Student Companion site, to access Exercise Set B.

PROBLEMS: SET A

Determine variable and fixed costs, compute break-even point, prepare a CVP graph, and determine net income.
(SO 1, 3, 5, 6)

P22-1A Matt Reiss owns the Fredonia Barber Shop. He employs five barbers and pays each a base rate of $1,000 per month. One of the barbers serves as the manager and receives an extra $500 per month. In addition to the base rate, each barber also receives a commission of $5.50 per haircut.

Other costs are as follows.

Advertising	$200 per month
Rent	$900 per month
Barber supplies	$0.30 per haircut
Utilities	$175 per month plus $0.20 per haircut
Magazines	$25 per month

Matt currently charges $10 per haircut.

Instructions

(a) Determine the variable cost per haircut and the total monthly fixed costs.
(b) Compute the break-even point in units and dollars.
(c) Prepare a CVP graph, assuming a maximum of 1,800 haircuts in a month. Use increments of 300 haircuts on the horizontal axis and $3,000 on the vertical axis.
(d) Determine net income, assuming 1,900 haircuts are given in a month.

Prepare a CVP income statement, compute break-even point, contribution margin ratio, margin of safety ratio, and sales for target net income.
(SO 5, 6, 7, 8, 9)

P22-2A Utech Company bottles and distributes Livit, a diet soft drink. The beverage is sold for 50 cents per 16-ounce bottle to retailers, who charge customers 75 cents per bottle. For the year 2008, management estimates the following revenues and costs.

Net sales	$1,800,000	Selling expenses—variable	$70,000
Direct materials	430,000	Selling expenses—fixed	65,000
Direct labor	352,000	Administrative expenses—variable	20,000
Manufacturing overhead—variable	316,000	Administrative expenses—fixed	60,000
Manufacturing overhead—fixed	283,000		

Instructions

(a) Prepare a CVP income statement for 2008 based on management's estimates.
(b) Compute the break-even point in (1) units and (2) dollars.
(c) Compute the contribution margin ratio and the margin of safety ratio. (Round to full percents.)
(d) Determine the sales dollars required to earn net income of $238,000.

Compute break-even point under alternative courses of action.
(SO 5, 6)

P22-3A Gorham Manufacturing's sales slumped badly in 2008. For the first time in its history, it operated at a loss. The company's income statement showed the following results from selling 600,000 units of product: Net sales $2,400,000; total costs and expenses $2,540,000; and net loss $140,000. Costs and expenses consisted of the amounts shown on the next page.

	Total	Variable	Fixed
Cost of goods sold	$2,100,000	$1,440,000	$660,000
Selling expenses	240,000	72,000	168,000
Administrative expenses	200,000	48,000	152,000
	$2,540,000	$1,560,000	$980,000

Management is considering the following independent alternatives for 2009.

1. Increase unit selling price 20% with no change in costs, expenses, and sales volume.
2. Change the compensation of salespersons from fixed annual salaries totaling $210,000 to total salaries of $60,000 plus a 5% commission on net sales.
3. Purchase new automated equipment that will change the proportion between variable and fixed cost of goods sold to 54% variable and 46% fixed.

Instructions

(a) Compute the break-even point in dollars for 2008.

(b) Compute the break-even point in dollars under each of the alternative courses of action. (Round all ratios to nearest full percent.) Which course of action do you recommend?

Compute break-even point and margin of safety ratio, and prepare a CVP income statement before and after changes in business environment.

(SO 6, 8, 9)

P22-4A Alice Shoemaker is the advertising manager for Value Shoe Store. She is currently working on a major promotional campaign. Her ideas include the installation of a new lighting system and increased display space that will add $34,000 in fixed costs to the $270,000 currently spent. In addition, Alice is proposing that a 5% price decrease ($40 to $38) will produce a 20% increase in sales volume (20,000 to 24,000). Variable costs will remain at $22 per pair of shoes. Management is impressed with Alice's ideas but concerned about the effects that these changes will have on the break-even point and the margin of safety.

Instructions

(a) Compute the current break-even point in units, and compare it to the break-even point in units if Alice's ideas are used.

(b) Compute the margin of safety ratio for current operations and after Alice's changes are introduced. (Round to nearest full percent.)

(c) Prepare a CVP income statement for current operations and after Alice's changes are introduced. Would you make the changes suggested?

Compute break-even point and margin of safety ratio, and prepare a CVP income statement before and after changes in business environment.

(SO 5, 6, 7, 8)

P22-5A Poole Corporation has collected the following information after its first year of sales. Net sales were $1,600,000 on 100,000 units; selling expenses $240,000 (40% variable and 60% fixed); direct materials $511,000; direct labor $285,000; administrative expenses $280,000 (20% variable and 80% fixed); manufacturing overhead $360,000 (70% variable and 30% fixed). Top management has asked you to do a CVP analysis so that it can make plans for the coming year. It has projected that unit sales will increase by 10% next year.

Instructions

(a) Compute (1) the contribution margin for the current year and the projected year, and (2) the fixed costs for the current year. (Assume that fixed costs will remain the same in the projected year.)

(b) Compute the break-even point in units and sales dollars for the current year.

(c) The company has a target net income of $310,000. What is the required sales in dollars for the company to meet its target?

(d) If the company meets its target net income number, by what percentage could its sales fall before it is operating at a loss? That is, what is its margin of safety ratio?

(e) The company is considering a purchase of equipment that would reduce its direct labor costs by $104,000 and would change its manufacturing overhead costs to 30% variable and 70% fixed (assume total manufacturing overhead cost is $360,000, as above). It is also considering switching to a pure commission basis for its sales staff. This would change selling expenses to 90% variable and 10% fixed (assume total selling expense is $240,000, as above). Assuming that net sales remain at first-year levels, compute (1) the contribution margin and (2) the contribution margin ratio, and recompute (3) the break-even point in sales dollars. Comment on the effect each of management's proposed changes has on the break-even point.

Prepare income statements under absorption and variable costing.

(SO 10)

***P22-6A** TLR produces plastic that is used for injection molding applications such as gears for small motors. In 2008, the first year of operations, TLR produced 6,000 tons of plastic and sold

5,000 tons. In 2009, the production and sales results were exactly reversed. In each year, selling price per ton was $1,000, variable manufacturing costs were 15% of the sales price of units produced, variable selling expenses were 10% of the selling price of units sold, fixed manufacturing costs were $2,100,000, and fixed administrative expenses were $500,000.

Instructions

(a) Prepare comparative income statements for each year using variable costing.
(b) Prepare comparative income statements for each year using absorption costing.
(c) Reconcile the differences each year in income from operations under the two costing approaches.
(d) Comment on the effects of production and sales on net income under the two costing approaches.

PROBLEMS: SET B

Determine variable and fixed costs, compute break-even point, prepare a CVP graph, and determine net income.

(SO 1, 3, 5, 6)

P22-1B The Galena Barber Shop employs four barbers. One barber, who also serves as the manager, is paid a salary of $3,200 per month. The other barbers are paid $1,400 per month. In addition, each barber is paid a commission of $3 per haircut. Other monthly costs are: store rent $700 plus 60 cents per haircut, depreciation on equipment $500, barber supplies 40 cents per haircut, utilities $300, and advertising $100. The price of a haircut is $10.

Instructions

(a) Determine the variable cost per haircut and the total monthly fixed costs.
(b) Compute the break-even point in units and dollars.
(c) Prepare a CVP graph, assuming a maximum of 1,800 haircuts in a month. Use increments of 300 haircuts on the horizontal axis and $3,000 increments on the vertical axis.
(d) Determine the net income, assuming 1,700 haircuts are given in a month.

Prepare a CVP income statement, compute break-even point, contribution margin ratio, margin of safety ratio, and sales for target net income.

(SO 5, 6, 7, 8, 9)

P22-2B Wilks Company bottles and distributes No-FIZZ, a fruit drink. The beverage is sold for 50 cents per 16-ounce bottle to retailers, who charge customers 70 cents per bottle. For the year 2008, management estimates the following revenues and costs.

Net sales	$2,000,000	Selling expenses—variable	$ 100,000
Direct materials	360,000	Selling expenses—fixed	150,000
Direct labor	590,000	Administrative expenses—variable	40,000
Manufacturing overhead—variable	270,000	Administrative expenses—fixed	78,000
Manufacturing overhead—fixed	220,000		

Instructions

(a) Prepare a CVP income statement for 2008 based on management's estimates.
(b) Compute the break-even point in (1) units and (2) dollars.
(c) Compute the contribution margin ratio and the margin of safety ratio.
(d) Determine the sales dollars required to earn net income of $272,000.

Compute break-even point under alternative courses of action.

(SO 5, 6)

P22-3B Milner Manufacturing had a bad year in 2008. For the first time in its history it operated at a loss. The company's income statement showed the following results from selling 60,000 units of product: Net sales $1,500,000; total costs and expenses $1,660,000; and net loss $160,000. Costs and expenses consisted of the following.

	Total	Variable	Fixed
Cost of goods sold	$1,200,000	$780,000	$420,000
Selling expenses	340,000	65,000	275,000
Administrative expenses	120,000	55,000	65,000
	$1,660,000	$900,000	$760,000

Management is considering the following independent alternatives for 2009.

1. Increase unit selling price 20% with no change in costs, expenses, and sales volume.
2. Change the compensation of salespersons from fixed annual salaries totaling $200,000 to total salaries of $30,000 plus a 6% commission on net sales.

3. Purchase new high-tech factory machinery that will change the proportion between variable and fixed cost of goods sold to 50:50.

Instructions

(a) Compute the break-even point in dollars for 2008.

(b) Compute the break-even point in dollars under each of the alternative courses of action. (Round all ratios to nearest full percent.) Which course of action do you recommend?

Compute break-even point and margin of safety ratio, and prepare a CVP income statement before and after changes in business environment.

(SO 6, 8, 9)

P22-4B Anne Ogilvie is the advertising manager for Thrifty Shoe Store. She is currently working on a major promotional campaign. Her ideas include the installation of a new lighting system and increased display space that will add \$51,000 in fixed costs to the \$204,000 currently spent. In addition, Anne is proposing that a 6⅔% price decrease (from \$30 to \$28) will produce an increase in sales volume from 16,000 to 21,000 units. Variable costs will remain at \$13 per pair of shoes. Management is impressed with Anne's ideas but concerned about the effects that these changes will have on the break-even point and the margin of safety.

Instructions

(a) Compute the current break-even point in units, and compare it to the break-even point in units if Anne's ideas are used.

(b) Compute the margin of safety ratio for current operations and after Anne's changes are introduced. (Round to nearest full percent.)

(c) Prepare a CVP income statement for current operations and after Anne's changes are introduced. Would you make the changes suggested?

Compute break-even point and margin of safety ratio, and prepare a CVP income statement before and after changes in business environment.

(SO 5, 6, 7, 8)

P22-5B Washington Corporation has collected the following information after its first year of sales. Net sales were \$2,400,000 on 200,000 units; selling expenses \$360,000 (30% variable and 70% fixed); direct materials \$626,500; direct labor \$507,500; administrative expenses \$420,000 (40% variable and 60% fixed); manufacturing overhead \$540,000 (50% variable and 50% fixed). Top management has asked you to do a CVP analysis so that it can make plans for the coming year. It has projected that unit sales will increase by 20% next year.

Instructions

(a) Compute (1) the contribution margin for the current year and the projected year, and (2) the fixed costs for the current year. (Assume that fixed costs will remain the same in the projected year.)

(b) Compute the break-even point in units and sales dollars for the current year.

(c) The company has a target net income of \$620,000. What is the required sales in dollars for the company to meet its target?

(d) If the company meets its target net income number, by what percentage could its sales fall before it is operating at a loss? That is, what is its margin of safety ratio?

(e) The company is considering a purchase of equipment that would reduce its direct labor costs by \$240,000 and would change its manufacturing overhead costs to 30% variable and 70% fixed (assume total manufacturing overhead cost is \$540,000, as above). It is also considering switching to a pure commission basis for its sales staff. This would change selling expenses to 80% variable and 20% fixed (assume total selling expense is \$360,000, as above). Compute (1) the contribution margin and (2) the contribution margin ratio, and recompute (3) the break-even point in sales dollars. Comment on the effect each of management's proposed changes has on the break-even point.

Prepare income statements under absorption and variable costing.

(SO 10)

***P22-6B** Yancey Metal Company produces the steel wire that goes into the production of paper clips. In 2008, the first year of operations, Yancey produced 50,000 miles of wire and sold 40,000 miles. In 2009, the production and sales results were exactly reversed. In each year, selling price per mile was \$60, variable manufacturing costs were 25% of the sales price, variable selling expenses were \$7.00 per mile sold, fixed manufacturing costs were \$1,100,000, and fixed administrative expenses were \$230,000.

Instructions

(a) Prepare comparative income statements for each year using variable costing.

(b) Prepare comparative income statements for each year using absorption costing.

(c) Reconcile the differences each year in income from operations under the two costing approaches.

(d) Comment on the effects of production and sales on net income under the two costing approaches.

PROBLEMS: SET C

Visit the book's website at **www.wiley.com/college/weygandt**, and choose the Student Companion site, to access Problem Set C.

BROADENING YOUR PERSPECTIVE

DECISION MAKING ACROSS THE ORGANIZATION

BYP22-1 Gagliano Company has decided to introduce a new product. The new product can be manufactured by either a capital-intensive method or a labor-intensive method. The manufacturing method will not affect the quality of the product. The estimated manufacturing costs by the two methods are as follows.

	Capital-Intensive	Labor-Intensive
Direct materials	\$5 per unit	\$5.50 per unit
Direct labor	\$6 per unit	\$8.00 per unit
Variable overhead	\$3 per unit	\$4.50 per unit
Fixed manufacturing costs	\$2,508,000	\$1,538,000

Gagliano's market research department has recommended an introductory unit sales price of \$30. The incremental selling expenses are estimated to be \$502,000 annually plus \$2 for each unit sold, regardless of manufacturing method.

Instructions

With the class divided into groups, answer the following.

(a) Calculate the estimated break-even point in annual unit sales of the new product if Gagliano Company uses the:
(1) capital-intensive manufacturing method.
(2) labor-intensive manufacturing method.

(b) Determine the annual unit sales volume at which Gagliano Company would be indifferent between the two manufacturing methods.

(c) Explain the circumstance under which Gagliano should employ each of the two manufacturing methods.

(CMA adapted)

MANAGERIAL ANALYSIS

BYP22-2 The condensed income statement for the Terri and Jerry partnership for 2008 is as follows.

TERRI AND JERRY COMPANY
Income Statement
For the Year Ended December 31, 2008

Sales (200,000 units)		\$1,200,000
Cost of goods sold		800,000
Gross profit		400,000
Operating expenses		
Selling	\$280,000	
Administrative	160,000	440,000
Net loss		(\$40,000)

A cost behavior analysis indicates that 75% of the cost of goods sold are variable, 50% of the selling expenses are variable, and 25% of the administrative expenses are variable.

Instructions

(Round to nearest unit, dollar, and percentage, where necessary. Use the CVP income statement format in computing profits.)

(a) Compute the break-even point in total sales dollars and in units for 2008.

(b) Terri has proposed a plan to get the partnership "out of the red" and improve its profitability. She feels that the quality of the product could be substantially improved by spending \$0.25 more per unit on better raw materials. The selling price per unit could be increased to only \$6.25 because of competitive pressures. Terri estimates that sales volume will increase by 30%. What effect would Terri's plan have on the profits and the break-even point in dollars of the partnership? (Round the contribution margin ratio to two decimal places.)

(c) Jerry was a marketing major in college. He believes that sales volume can be increased only by intensive advertising and promotional campaigns. He therefore proposed the following plan as an alternative to Terri's. (1) Increase variable selling expenses to \$0.79 per unit, (2) lower the selling price per unit by \$0.30, and (3) increase fixed selling expenses by \$35,000. Jerry quoted an old marketing research report that said that sales volume would increase by 60% if these changes were made. What effect would Jerry's plan have on the profits and the break-even point in dollars of the partnership?

(d) Which plan should be accepted? Explain your answer.

REAL-WORLD FOCUS

BYP22-3 The Coca-Cola Company hardly needs an introduction. A line taken from the cover of a recent annual report says it all: If you measured time in servings of Coca-Cola, "a billion Coca-Cola's ago was yesterday morning." On average, every U.S. citizen drinks 363 8-ounce servings of Coca-Cola products each year. Coca-Cola's primary line of business is the making and selling of syrup to bottlers. These bottlers then sell the finished bottles and cans of Coca-Cola to the consumer.

In the annual report of Coca-Cola, the following information was provided.

THE COCA-COLA COMPANY
Management Discussion

Our gross margin declined to 61 percent this year from 62 percent in the prior year, primarily due to costs for materials such as sweeteners and packaging.

The increases [in selling expenses] in the last two years were primarily due to higher marketing expenditures in support of our Company's volume growth.

We measure our sales volume in two ways: (1) gallon shipments of concentrates and syrups and (2) unit cases of finished product (bottles and cans of Coke sold by bottlers).

Instructions

Answer the following questions.

(a) Are sweeteners and packaging a variable cost or a fixed cost? What is the impact on the contribution margin of an increase in the per unit cost of sweeteners or packaging? What are the implications for profitability?

(b) In your opinion, are marketing expenditures a fixed cost, variable cost, or mixed cost to The Coca-Cola Company? Give justification for your answer.

(c) Which of the two measures cited for measuring volume represents the activity index as defined in this chapter? Why might Coca-Cola use two different measures?

EXPLORING THE WEB

BYP22-4 Ganong Bros. Ltd., located in St. Stephen, New Brunswick, is Canada's oldest independent candy company. Its products are distributed worldwide. In 1885, Ganong invented the popular "chicken bone," a cinnamon flavored, pink, hard candy jacket over a chocolate center. The home page of Ganong, listed on the next page, includes information about the company and its products.

Address: www.ganong.com/retail/chicken_bones.html, or go to **www.wiley.com/college/weygandt**

Instructions

Read the description of "chicken bones," and answer the following.

(a) Describe the steps in making "chicken bones."

(b) Identify at least two variable and two fixed costs that are likely to affect the production of "chicken bones."

COMMUNICATION ACTIVITY

BYP22-5 Your roommate asks your help on the following questions about CVP analysis formulas.

(a) How can the mathematical equation for break-even sales show both sales units and sales dollars?

(b) How do the formulas differ for contribution margin per unit and contribution margin ratio?

(c) How can contribution margin be used to determine break-even sales in units and in dollars?

Instructions

Write a memo to your roommate stating the relevant formulas and answering each question.

ETHICS CASE

BYP22-6 Kenny Hampton is an accountant for Bartley Company. Early this year Kenny made a highly favorable projection of sales and profits over the next 3 years for Bartley's hot-selling computer PLEX. As a result of the projections Kenny presented to senior management, they decided to expand production in this area. This decision led to dislocations of some plant personnel who were reassigned to one of the company's newer plants in another state. However, no one was fired, and in fact the company expanded its work force slightly.

Unfortunately Kenny rechecked his computations on the projections a few months later and found that he had made an error that would have reduced his projections substantially. Luckily, sales of PLEX have exceeded projections so far, and management is satisfied with its decision. Kenny, however, is not sure what to do. Should he confess his honest mistake and jeopardize his possible promotion? He suspects that no one will catch the error because sales of PLEX have exceeded his projections, and it appears that profits will materialize close to his projections.

Instructions

(a) Who are the stakeholders in this situation?

(b) Identify the ethical issues involved in this situation.

(c) What are the possible alternative actions for Kenny? What would you do in Kenny's position?

"ALL ABOUT YOU" ACTIVITY

BYP22-7 In the **All About You** feature in this chapter, you learned that cost-volume-profit analysis can be used in making personal financial decisions. The purchase of a new car is one of your biggest personal expenditures. It is important that you carefully analyze your options.

Suppose that you are considering the purchase of a hybrid vehicle. Let's assume the following facts: The hybrid will initially cost an additional $3,000 above the cost of a traditional vehicle. The hybrid will get 40 miles per gallon of gas, and the traditional car will get 30 miles per gallon. Also, assume that the cost of gas is $3 per gallon.

Instructions

Using the facts above, answer the following questions.

(a) What is the variable gasoline cost of going one mile in the hybrid car? What is the variable cost of going one mile in the traditional car?

(b) Using the information in part (a), if "miles" is your unit of measure, what is the "contribution margin" of the hybrid vehicle relative to the traditional vehicle? That is, express the variable cost savings on a per-mile basis.

(c) How many miles would you have to drive in order to break even on your investment in the hybrid car?
(d) What other factors might you want to consider?

Answers to Insight and Accounting Across the Organization Questions

p. 960 Woodworker Runs an Efficient Operation for Designing Furniture

Q: Are the costs associated with use of the computer-driven cutting machines fixed or variable?
A: *The cost of the cutting machine that is recognized through depreciation expense is a fixed cost. The costs of operating (electricity) and maintaining the machine are variable.*

p. 970 Charter Flights Offer a Good Deal

Q: How did FlightServe determine that it would break even with 3.3 seats full per flight?
A: *FlightServe determined its break-even point with the following formula:*
Fixed costs ÷ Contribution margin per seat occupied = Break-even point in seats.

p. 974 How a Rolling Stones' Tour Makes Money

Q: What amount of sales dollars are required for the promoter to break even?
A: Fixed costs = $1,200,000 + $400,000 = $1,600,000
Contribution margin ratio = 80%
Break-even sales = $1,600,000 ÷ .80 = $2,000,000

Authors' Comments on All About You: A Hybrid Dilemma (p. 977)

Just like the break-even analysis that a company would perform on an investment in a new piece of equipment, the break-even analysis of a hybrid car requires a lot of assumptions. After deciding on a car, you need to estimate how many miles you would drive each year and how many years you would own the car. If you trade cars every two or three years, it is unlikely, with the hybrids available today, that you will recoup your initial investment. Your chances of recouping the investment increase the longer you keep the car and the more miles you drive. You need to determine whether you will get a federal tax credit or a rebate from your employer. You also need to estimate what the car would be worth when you sell it. Based on assumed values for the average driver, *Consumer Reports* determined that only the most fuel-efficient hybrids save enough on fuel to cover their additional costs, but individual results will vary depending on the factors mentioned above.

Answers to Self-Study Questions

1. d **2.** c **3.** a **4.** c **5.** d **6.** c **7.** b **8.** b **9.** a **10.** a

Remember to go back to the Navigator box on the chapter-opening page and check off your completed work.

Chapter 23

Budgetary Planning

STUDY OBJECTIVES

After studying this chapter, you should be able to:

1 Indicate the benefits of budgeting.
2 State the essentials of effective budgeting.
3 Identify the budgets that comprise the master budget.
4 Describe the sources for preparing the budgeted income statement.
5 Explain the principal sections of a cash budget.
6 Indicate the applicability of budgeting in non-manufacturing companies.

The Navigator

The Navigator

- Scan **Study Objectives**
- Read **Feature Story**
- Read **Preview**
- Read text and answer **Before You Go On** p. 1005 p. 1009 p. 1016 p. 1018
- Work **Demonstration Problem**
- Review **Summary of Study Objectives**
- Answer **Self-Study Questions**
- Complete **Assignments**

Feature Story

THE NEXT AMAZON.COM? NOT QUITE

The bursting of the dot-com bubble resulted in countless stories of dot-com failures. Many of these ventures were half-baked, get-rich-quick schemes, rarely based on sound business practices. Initially they saw money flowing in faster than they knew what to do with—which was precisely the problem. Without proper planning and budgeting, much of the money went to waste. In some cases, failure was actually brought on by rapid, uncontrolled growth.

One such example was online discount bookseller, www.Positively-You.com. One of the Website's co-founders, Lyle Bowline, had never run a business. However, his experience as an assistant director of an entrepreneurial center had provided him with knowledge about the do's and don'ts of small business. To minimize costs, he started the company small and simple. He invested $5,000 in computer equipment and ran the business out of his basement. In the early months, even though sales were only about $2,000 a month, the company actually made a profit because it kept its costs low (a feat few other dot-coms could boast of).

Things changed dramatically when the company received national publicity in the financial press. Suddenly the company's sales increased to $50,000 a month—fully 25 times the previous level. The "simple" little business suddenly needed a business plan, a strategic plan, and a budget. It needed to rent office space and to hire employees.

Initially, members of a local book club donated time to help meet the sudden demand. Some put in so much time that eventually the company hired them. Quickly the number of paid employees ballooned. The sudden growth necessitated detailed planning and budgeting. The need for a proper budget was accentuated by the fact that the company's gross profit was only 16 cents on each dollar of goods sold. This meant that after paying for its inventory, the company had only 16 cents of every dollar to cover its remaining operating costs.

Unfortunately, the company never got things under control. Within a few months, sales had plummeted to $12,000 per month. At this level of sales the company could not meet the mountain of monthly expenses that it had accumulated in trying to grow. Ironically, the company's sudden success, and the turmoil it created, appears to have been what eventually caused the company to fail.

✓ The Navigator

Inside Chapter 23...

Preview of Chapter 23

As the Feature Story about Positively-You.com indicates, budgeting is critical to financial well-being. As a student, you budget your study time and your money. Families budget income and expenses. Governmental agencies budget revenues and expenditures. Business enterprises use budgets in planning and controlling their operations.

Our primary focus in this chapter is budgeting—specifically, how budgeting is used as a *planning tool* by management. Through budgeting, it should be possible for management to maintain enough cash to pay creditors, to have sufficient raw materials to meet production requirements, and to have adequate finished goods to meet expected sales.

The content and organization of Chapter 23 are as follows.

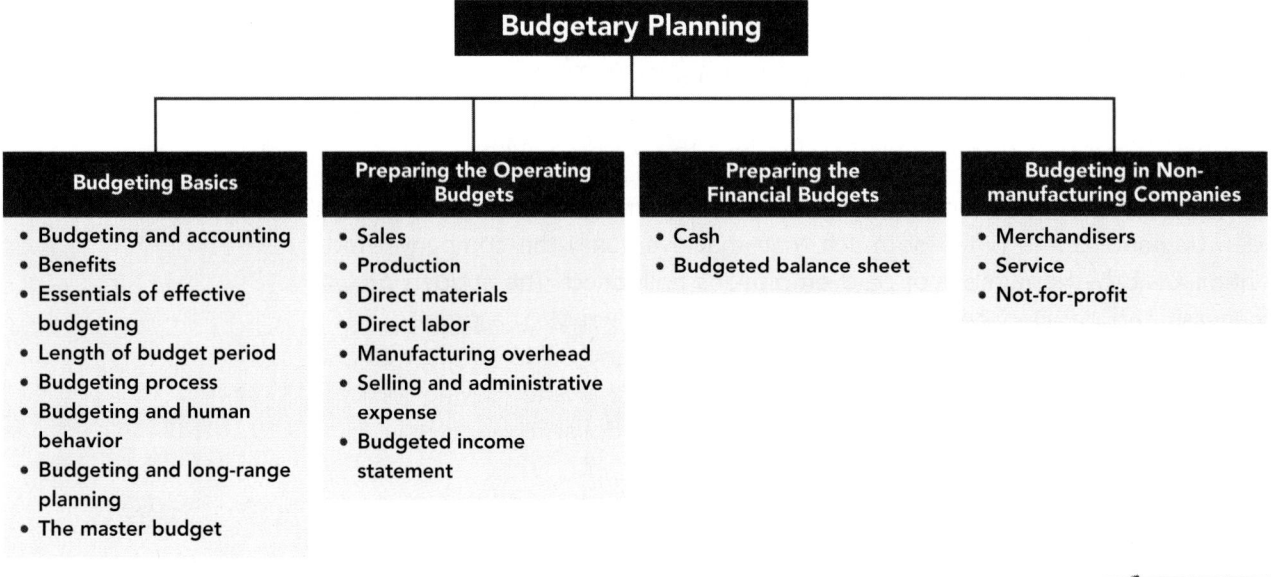

Budgetary Planning

Budgeting Basics
- Budgeting and accounting
- Benefits
- Essentials of effective budgeting
- Length of budget period
- Budgeting process
- Budgeting and human behavior
- Budgeting and long-range planning
- The master budget

Preparing the Operating Budgets
- Sales
- Production
- Direct materials
- Direct labor
- Manufacturing overhead
- Selling and administrative expense
- Budgeted income statement

Preparing the Financial Budgets
- Cash
- Budgeted balance sheet

Budgeting in Non-manufacturing Companies
- Merchandisers
- Service
- Not-for-profit

The Navigator

BUDGETING BASICS

One of management's major responsibilities is planning. As explained in Chapter 19, **planning** is the process of establishing enterprise-wide objectives. A successful organization makes both long-term and short-term plans. These plans set forth the objectives of the company and the proposed way of accomplishing them.

A **budget** is a formal written statement of management's plans for a specified future time period, expressed in financial terms. It normally represents the primary method of communicating agreed-upon objectives throughout the organization. Once adopted, a budget becomes an important basis for evaluating performance. It promotes efficiency and serves as a deterrent to waste and inefficiency. We consider the role of budgeting as a **control device** in Chapter 24.

Budgeting and Accounting

Accounting information makes major contributions to the budgeting process. From the accounting records, companies can obtain historical data on revenues, costs, and expenses. These data are helpful in formulating future budget goals.

Normally, accountants have the responsibility for presenting management's budgeting goals in financial terms. In this role, they translate management's plans and communicate the budget to employees throughout the company. They prepare periodic budget reports that provide the basis for measuring performance and comparing actual results with planned objectives. The budget itself, and the administration of the budget, however, are entirely management responsibilities.

The Benefits of Budgeting

The primary benefits of budgeting are:

STUDY OBJECTIVE 1

Indicate the benefits of budgeting.

1. It requires all levels of management to **plan ahead** and to formalize goals on a recurring basis.
2. It provides **definite objectives** for evaluating performance at each level of responsibility.
3. It creates an **early warning system** for potential problems so that management can make changes before things get out of hand.
4. It facilitates the **coordination of activities** within the business. It does this by correlating the goals of each segment with overall company objectives. Thus, the company can integrate production and sales promotion with expected sales.
5. It results in greater **management awareness** of the entity's overall operations and the impact on operations of external factors, such as economic trends.
6. It **motivates personnel** throughout the organization to meet planned objectives.

A budget is an aid to management; it is not a *substitute* for management. A budget cannot operate or enforce itself. Companies can realize the benefits of budgeting only when managers carefully administer budgets.

Essentials of Effective Budgeting

STUDY OBJECTIVE 2

State the essentials of effective budgeting.

Effective budgeting depends on a **sound organizational structure**. In such a structure, authority and responsibility for all phases of operations are clearly defined. Budgets based on **research and analysis** should result in realistic goals that will contribute to the growth and profitability of a company. And, the effectiveness of a budget program is directly related to its **acceptance by all levels of management**.

Once adopted, the budget should be an important tool for evaluating performance. Managers should systematically and periodically review variations between actual and expected results to determine their cause(s). However, individuals should not be held responsible for variations that are beyond their control.

Length of the Budget Period

The budget period is not necessarily one year in length. **A budget may be prepared for any period of time.** Various factors influence the length of the budget period. These factors include the type of budget, the nature of the organization, the need for periodic appraisal, and prevailing business conditions. For example, cash may be budgeted monthly, whereas a plant expansion budget may cover a 10-year period.

The budget period should be long enough to provide an attainable goal under normal business conditions. Ideally, the time period should minimize the impact of seasonal or cyclical fluctuations. On the other hand, the budget period should not be so long that reliable estimates are impossible.

The **most common budget period is one year**. The annual budget, in turn, is often supplemented by monthly and quarterly budgets. Many companies use **continuous 12-month budgets**. These budgets drop the month just ended and add a future month. One advantage of continuous budgeting is that it keeps management planning a full year ahead.

The Budgeting Process

The development of the budget for the coming year generally starts several months before the end of the current year. The budgeting process usually begins with the collection of data from each organizational unit of the company. Past performance is often the starting point from which future budget goals are formulated.

The budget is developed within the framework of a **sales forecast**. This forecast shows potential sales for the industry and the company's expected share of such sales. Sales forecasting involves a consideration of various factors: (1) general economic conditions, (2) industry trends, (3) market research studies, (4) anticipated advertising and promotion, (5) previous market share, (6) changes in prices, and (7) technological developments. The input of sales personnel and top management is essential to the sales forecast.

In small companies like Positively-You.com, the budgeting process is often informal. In larger companies, a **budget committee** has responsibility for coordinating the preparation of the budget. The committee ordinarily includes the president, treasurer, chief accountant (controller), and management personnel from each of the major areas of the company, such as sales, production, and research. The budget committee serves as a review board where managers can defend their budget goals and requests. Differences are reviewed, modified if necessary, and reconciled. The budget is then put in its final form by the budget committee, approved, and distributed.

ACCOUNTING ACROSS THE ORGANIZATION

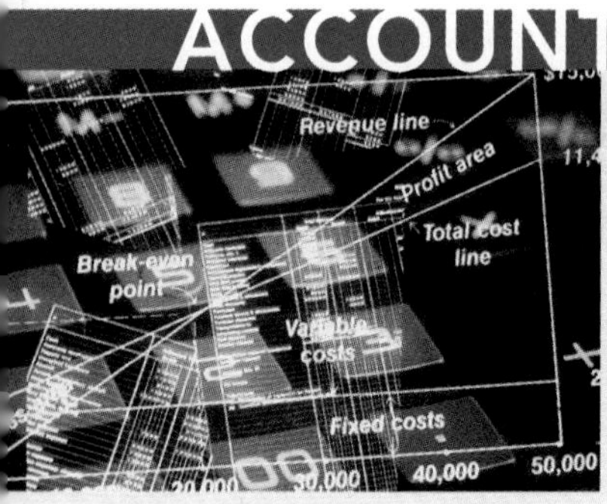

Businesses Often Feel Too Busy to Plan for the Future

A recent study by Willard & Shullman Group Ltd. found that fewer than 14% of businesses with fewer than 500 employees do an annual budget or have a written business plan. In all, nearly 60% of these businesses have no plans on paper at all. For many small businesses the basic assumption is that, "As long as I sell as much as I can, and keep my employees paid, I'm doing OK." A few small business owners even say that they see no need for budgeting and planning. Most small business owners, though, say that they understand that budgeting and planning are critical for survival and growth. But given the long hours that they already work addressing day-to-day challenges, they also say that they are "just too busy to plan for the future."

? Describe a situation in which a business "sells as much as it can" but cannot "keep its employees paid."

Budgeting and Human Behavior

A budget can have a significant impact on human behavior. It may inspire a manager to higher levels of performance. Or, it may discourage additional effort and pull down the morale of a manager. Why do these diverse effects occur? The answer is found in how the budget is developed and administered.

In developing the budget, each level of management should be invited to participate. This "bottom-to-top" approach is referred to as **participative budgeting**.

The advantages of participative budgeting are, first, that lower-level managers have more detailed knowledge of their specific area and thus are able to provide more accurate budgetary estimates. Second, when lower-level managers participate in the budgeting process, they are more likely to perceive the resulting budget as fair. The overall goal is to reach agreement on a budget that the managers consider fair and achievable, but which also meets the corporate goals set by top management. When this goal is met, the budget will provide positive motivation for the managers. In contrast, if the managers view the budget as being unfair and unrealistic, they may feel discouraged and uncommitted to budget goals. The risk of having unrealistic budgets is generally greater when the budget is developed from top management down to lower management than vice versa.

Participative budgeting does, however, have potential disadvantages. First, it is more time-consuming (and thus more costly) than a "top-down" approach, in which the budget is simply dictated to lower-level managers. A second disadvantage is that participative budgeting can foster budgetary "gaming" through budgetary slack. **Budgetary slack** occurs when managers intentionally underestimate budgeted revenues or overestimate budgeted expenses in order to make it easier to achieve budgetary goals. To minimize budgetary slack, higher-level managers must carefully review and thoroughly question the budget projections provided to them by employees whom they supervise. Illustration 23-1 graphically displays the appropriate flow of budget data from bottom to top in an organization.

Illustration 23-1
Flow of budget data from lower levels of management to top levels

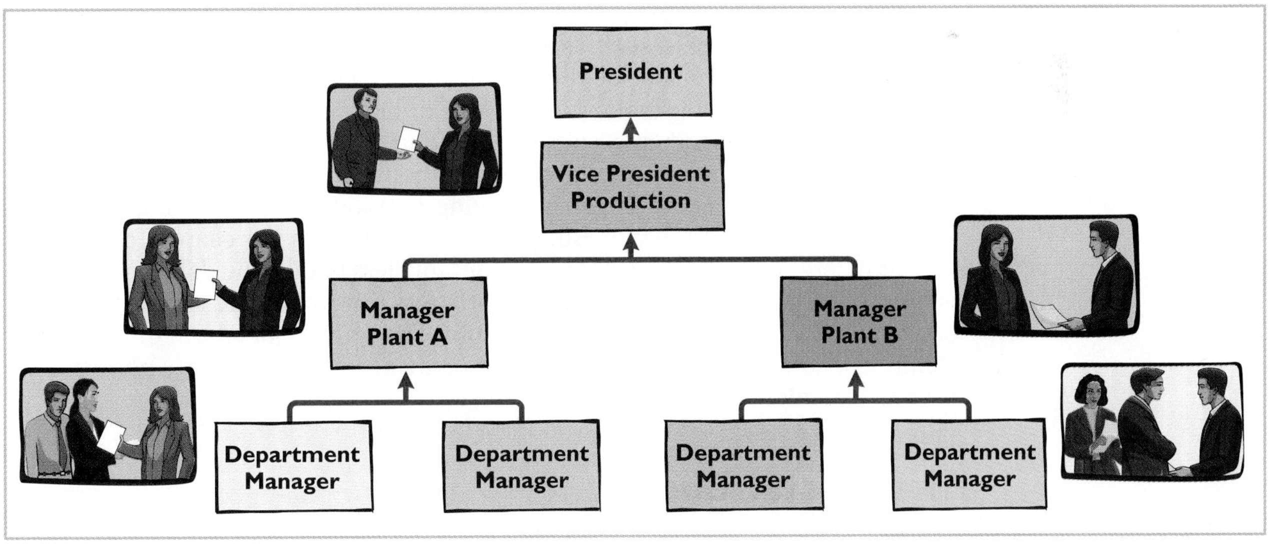

For the budget to be effective, top management must completely support the budget. The budget is an important basis for evaluating performance. It also can be used as a positive aid in achieving projected goals. The effect of an evaluation is positive when top management tempers criticism with advice and assistance. In contrast, a manager is likely to respond negatively if top management uses the budget exclusively to assess blame. A budget should not be used as a pressure device to force improved performance. In sum, a budget can be a manager's friend or a foe.

ETHICS NOTE

Unrealistic budgets can lead to unethical employee behavior such as cutting corners on the job or distorting internal financial reports.

ACCOUNTING ACROSS THE ORGANIZATION

Which Budget Approach Do You Prefer?

Not too long ago, in an effort to revive its plummeting stock, Time Warner's top management determined and publicly announced bold new financial goals for the coming year. Unfortunately, these goals were not reached.

The next year the company got a new CEO who promised, "We will not over promise, and we will deliver." The new budgets were developed with each operating unit setting what it felt were optimistic but attainable goals. In the words of one manager, using this approach created a sense of teamwork: "We're all going forward with our arms locked together."

Source: Carol J. Loomis, "AOL Time Warner's New Math," *Fortune*, February 4, 2002, pp. 98–102.

? What approach did Time Warner use to prepare the old budget? What approach did it use to prepare the new budget?

Budgeting and Long-Range Planning

Budgeting and long-range planning are not the same. One important difference is the **time period involved**. The maximum length of a budget is usually one year, and budgets are often prepared for shorter periods of time, such as a month or a quarter. In contrast, long-range planning usually encompasses a period of at least five years.

HELPFUL HINT
In comparing a budget with a long-range plan: (1) Which has more detail? (2) Which is done for a longer period of time? (3) Which is more concerned with short-term goals?
Answers: (1) Budget. (2) Long-range plan. (3) Budget.

A second significant difference is in **emphasis**. Budgeting focuses on achieving specific short-term goals, such as meeting annual profit objectives. **Long-range planning**, on the other hand, identifies long-term goals, selects strategies to achieve those goals, and develops policies and plans to implement the strategies. In long-range planning, management also considers anticipated trends in the economic and political environment and how the company should cope with them.

The final difference between budgeting and long-range planning relates to the **amount of detail presented**. Budgets, as you will see in this chapter, can be very detailed. Long-range plans contain considerably less detail. The data in long-range plans are intended more for a review of progress toward long-term goals than as a basis of control for achieving specific results. The primary objective of long-range planning is to develop the best strategy to maximize the company's performance over an extended future period.

The Master Budget

STUDY OBJECTIVE 3
Identify the budgets that comprise the master budget.

The term "budget" is actually a shorthand term to describe a variety of budget documents. All of these documents are combined into a master budget. The **master budget** is a set of interrelated budgets that constitutes a plan of action for a specified time period.

The master budget contains two classes of budgets. **Operating budgets** are the individual budgets that result in the preparation of the budgeted income statement. These budgets establish goals for the company's sales and production personnel. In contrast, **financial budgets** are the capital expenditure budget, the cash budget, and the budgeted balance sheet. These budgets focus primarily on the cash resources needed to fund expected operations and planned capital expenditures.

Illustration 23-2 pictures the individual budgets included in a master budget, and the sequence in which they are prepared. The company first develops the operating budgets, beginning with the sales budget. Then it prepares the financial budgets. We will explain and illustrate each budget shown in Illustration 23-2 except the capital expenditure budget. That budget is discussed under the topic of capital budgeting in Chapter 26.

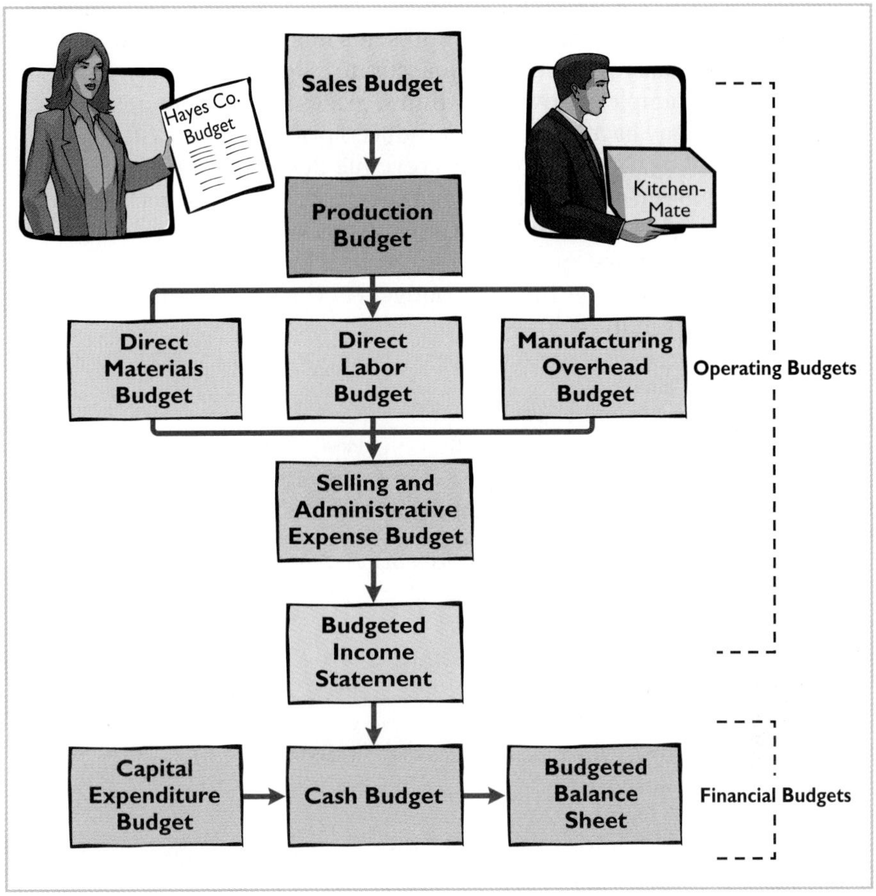

Illustration 23-2
Components of the master budget

Before You Go On...

REVIEW IT

1. What are the benefits of budgeting?
2. What are the factors essential to effective budgeting?
3. How does the budget process work?
4. How does budgeting differ from long-range planning?
5. What is a master budget?

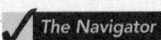

The Navigator

PREPARING THE OPERATING BUDGETS

We use a case study of Hayes Company in preparing the operating budgets. Hayes manufactures and sells a single product, Kitchen-Mate. The budgets are prepared by quarters for the year ending December 31, 2008. Hayes Company begins its annual budgeting process on September 1, 2007, and it completes the budget for 2008 by December 1, 2007.

Sales Budget

HELPFUL HINT

For a retail or manufacturing company, what is the starting point in preparing the master budget, and why? Answer: The sales budget is the starting point for the master budget. It sets the level of activity for other functions such as production and purchasing.

As shown in the master budget in Illustration 23-2, **the sales budget is the first budget prepared**. Each of the other budgets depends on the sales budget. The **sales budget** is derived from the sales forecast. It represents management's best estimate of sales revenue for the budget period. An inaccurate sales budget may adversely affect net income. For example, an overly optimistic sales budget may result in excessive inventories that may have to be sold at reduced prices. In contrast, an unduly conservative budget may result in loss of sales revenue due to inventory shortages.

The sales budget is prepared by multiplying the expected unit sales volume for each product by its anticipated unit selling price. Hayes Company expects sales volume to be 3,000 units in the first quarter, with 500-unit increases in each succeeding quarter. Illustration 23-3 shows the sales budget for the year, by quarters, based on a sales price of $60 per unit.

Illustration 23-3
Sales budget

Hayes Company Sales Budget.xls

File Edit View Insert Format Tools Data Window Help

	A	B	C	D	E	F
1	HAYES COMPANY					
2	Sales Budget					
3	For the Year Ending December 31, 2008					
4		Quarter				
5		1	2	3	4	Year
6	Expected unit sales	3,000	3,500	4,000	4,500	15,000
7	Unit selling price	× $60	× $60	× $60	× $60	× $60
8	Total sales	$180,000	$210,000	$240,000	$270,000	$900,000

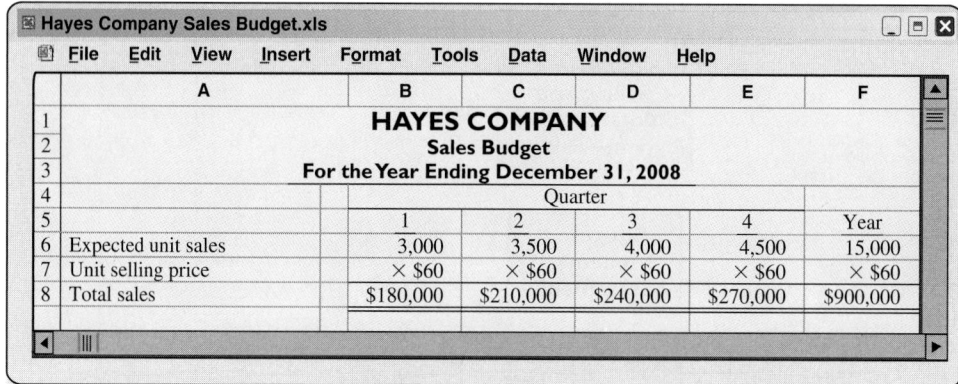

Some companies classify the anticipated sales revenue as cash or credit sales and by geographical regions, territories, or salespersons.

Production Budget

The **production budget** shows the units to produce to meet anticipated sales. Production requirements are determined from the following formula.[1]

Illustration 23-4
Production requirements formula

Budgeted Sales Units + Desired Ending Finished Goods Units − Beginning Finished Goods Units = Required Production Units

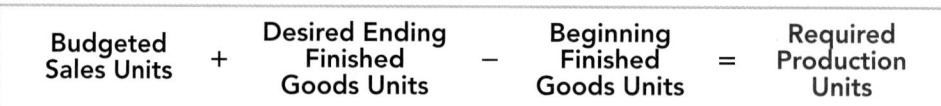

A realistic estimate of ending inventory is essential in scheduling production requirements. Excessive inventories in one quarter may lead to cutbacks in production and employee layoffs in a subsequent quarter. On the other hand, inadequate inventories may result either in added costs for overtime work or in lost

[1]This formula ignores any work in process inventories, which are assumed to be nonexistent in Hayes Company.

sales. Hayes Company believes it can meet future sales requirements by maintaining an ending inventory equal to 20% of the next quarter's budgeted sales volume. For example, the ending finished goods inventory for the first quarter is 700 units (20% × anticipated second-quarter sales of 3,500 units). Illustration 23-5 shows the production budget.

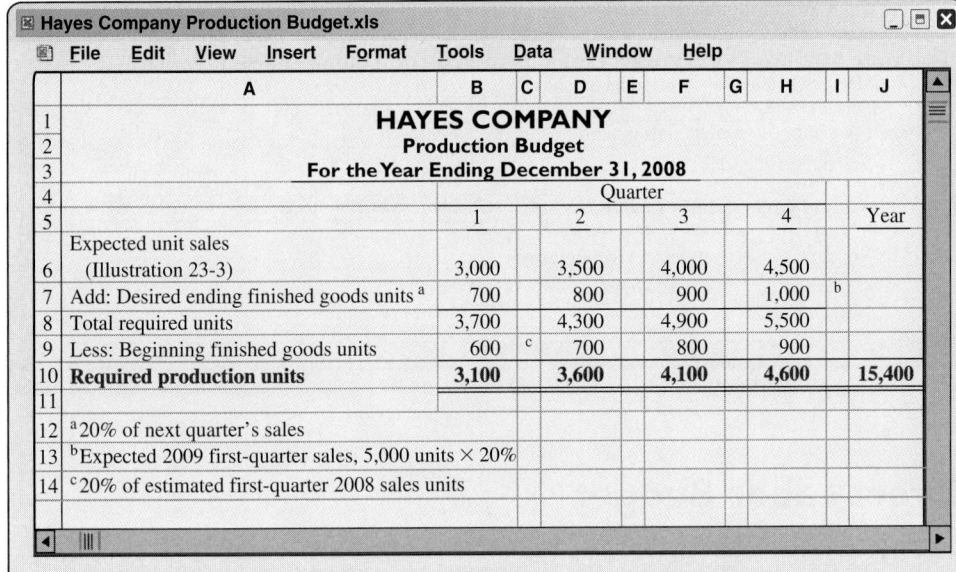

Illustration 23-5
Production budget

Hayes Company Production Budget.xls

HAYES COMPANY
Production Budget
For the Year Ending December 31, 2008

	Quarter 1	Quarter 2	Quarter 3	Quarter 4	Year
Expected unit sales (Illustration 23-3)	3,000	3,500	4,000	4,500	
Add: Desired ending finished goods units [a]	700	800	900	1,000 [b]	
Total required units	3,700	4,300	4,900	5,500	
Less: Beginning finished goods units	600 [c]	700	800	900	
Required production units	**3,100**	**3,600**	**4,100**	**4,600**	**15,400**

[a] 20% of next quarter's sales
[b] Expected 2009 first-quarter sales, 5,000 units × 20%
[c] 20% of estimated first-quarter 2008 sales units

The production budget, in turn, provides the basis for the budgeted costs for each manufacturing cost element, as explained in the following pages.

Direct Materials Budget

The **direct materials budget** shows both the quantity and cost of direct materials to be purchased. The quantities of direct materials are derived from the following formula.

Illustration 23-6
Formula for direct materials quantities

Direct Materials Units Required for Production + Desired Ending Direct Materials Units − Beginning Direct Materials Units = Required Direct Materials Units to be Purchased

The company then computes the budgeted cost of direct materials to be purchased by multiplying the required units of direct materials by the anticipated cost per unit.

The desired ending inventory is again a key component in the budgeting process. For example, inadequate inventories could result in temporary shutdowns of production. Because of its close proximity to suppliers, Hayes Company maintains an ending inventory of raw materials equal to 10% of the next quarter's production requirements. The manufacture of each Kitchen-Mate requires 2 pounds of raw materials, and the expected cost per pound is $4. Illustration 23-7 (page 1008) shows the direct materials budget. Assume that the desired ending direct materials amount is 1,020 pounds for the fourth quarter of 2008.

Illustration 23-7
Direct materials budget

Hayes Company Direct Materials Budget.xls

File Edit View Insert Format Tools Data Window Help

HAYES COMPANY
Direct Materials Budget
For the Year Ending December 31, 2008

	Quarter 1	Quarter 2	Quarter 3	Quarter 4	Year
Units to be produced (Illustration 23-5)	3,100	3,600	4,100	4,600	
Direct materials per unit	× 2	× 2	× 2	× 2	
Total pounds needed for production	6,200	7,200	8,200	9,200	
Add: Desired ending direct materials (pounds)[a]	720	820	920	1,020	
Total materials required	6,920	8,020	9,120	10,220	
Less: Beginning direct materials (pounds)	620[b]	720	820	920	
Direct materials purchases	6,300	7,300	8,300	9,300	
Cost per pound	× $4	× $4	× $4	× $4	
Total cost of direct materials purchases	**$25,200**	**$29,200**	**$33,200**	**$37,200**	**$124,800**

[a] 10% of next quarter's production requirements
[b] 10% of estimated first-quarter pounds needed for production

Direct Labor Budget

Like the direct materials budget, the **direct labor budget** contains the quantity (hours) and cost of direct labor necessary to meet production requirements. The total direct labor cost is derived from the following formula.

Illustration 23-8
Formula for direct labor cost

Units to be Produced × **Direct Labor Time per Unit** × **Direct Labor Cost per Hour** = **Total Direct Labor Cost**

Direct labor hours are determined from the production budget. At Hayes Company, two hours of direct labor are required to produce each unit of finished goods. The anticipated hourly wage rate is $10. Illustration 23-9 shows these data.

Illustration 23-9
Direct labor budget

Hayes Company Direct Labor Budget.xls

File Edit View Insert Format Tools Data Window Help

HAYES COMPANY
Direct Labor Budget
For the Year Ending December 31, 2008

	Quarter 1	Quarter 2	Quarter 3	Quarter 4	Year
Units to be produced (Illustration 23-5)	3,100	3,600	4,100	4,600	
Direct labor time (hours) per unit	× 2	× 2	× 2	× 2	
Total required direct labor hours	6,200	7,200	8,200	9,200	
Direct labor cost per hour	× $10	× $10	× $10	× $10	
Total direct labor cost	**$62,000**	**$72,000**	**$82,000**	**$92,000**	**$308,000**

The direct labor budget is critical in maintaining a labor force that can meet the expected levels of production.

Before You Go On...

REVIEW IT

1. What is the formula to determine required production units?
2. What are the inputs necessary to prepare the direct labor budget?
3. Which budget must be prepared before the direct materials budget?

DO IT

Becker Company estimates that 2008 unit sales will be 12,000 in quarter 1, 16,000 in quarter 2, and 20,000 in quarter 3, at a unit selling price of $30. Management desires to have ending finished goods inventory equal to 15% of the next quarter's expected unit sales. Prepare a production budget by quarter for the first 6 months of 2008.

Action Plan

- Begin with budgeted sales in units.
- Add desired ending finished goods inventory.
- Subtract beginning finished goods inventory.

Solution

BECKER COMPANY
Production Budget
For the Six Months Ending June 30, 2008

	Quarter		Six
	1	2	Months
Expected unit sales	12,000	16,000	
Add: Desired ending finished goods	2,400	3,000	
Total required units	14,400	19,000	
Less: Beginning finished goods inventory	1,800	2,400	
Required production units	12,600	16,600	29,200

Related exercise material: *BE23-3, E23-4, and E23-6.*

The Navigator

HELPFUL HINT
An important assumption in Illustration 23-9 is that the company can add to and subtract from its work force as needed so that the $10 per hour labor cost applies to a wide range of possible production activity.

Manufacturing Overhead Budget

The **manufacturing overhead budget** shows the expected manufacturing overhead costs for the budget period. As Illustration 23-10 (page 1010) shows, **this budget distinguishes between variable and fixed overhead costs**. Hayes Company expects variable costs to fluctuate with production volume on the basis of the following rates per direct labor hour: indirect materials $1.00, indirect labor $1.40, utilities $0.40, and maintenance $0.20. Thus, for the 6,200 direct labor hours to produce 3,100 units, budgeted indirect materials are $6,200 (6,200 × $1), and budgeted indirect labor is $8,680 (6,200 × $1.40). Hayes also recognizes that some maintenance is fixed. The amounts reported for fixed costs are assumed for our example. The accuracy of budgeted fixed overhead cost estimates can be greatly improved by employing activity-based costing.

At Hayes Company, overhead is applied to production on the basis of direct labor hours. Thus, as Illustration 23-10 shows, the annual rate is $8 per hour ($246,400 ÷ 30,800).

Selling and Administrative Expense Budget

Hayes Company combines its operating expenses into one budget, the **selling and administrative expense budget**. This budget projects anticipated selling and

Illustration 23-10
Manufacturing overhead budget

Hayes Company Manufacturing Overhead Budget.xls

File Edit View Insert Format Tools Data Window Help

	A	B	C	D	E	F
1	**HAYES COMPANY**					
2	**Manufacturing Overhead Budget**					
3	**For the Year Ending December 31, 2008**					
4		Quarter				
5		1	2	3	4	Year
6	Variable costs					
7	Indirect materials ($1.00/hour)	$ 6,200	$ 7,200	$ 8,200	$ 9,200	$ 30,800
8	Indirect labor ($1.40/hour)	8,680	10,080	11,480	12,880	43,120
9	Utilities ($0.40/hour)	2,480	2,880	3,280	3,680	12,320
10	Maintenance ($0.20/hour)	1,240	1,440	1,640	1,840	6,160
11	Total variable costs	18,600	21,600	24,600	27,600	92,400
12	Fixed costs					
13	Supervisory salaries	20,000	20,000	20,000	20,000	80,000
14	Depreciation	3,800	3,800	3,800	3,800	15,200
15	Property taxes and insurance	9,000	9,000	9,000	9,000	36,000
16	Maintenance	5,700	5,700	5,700	5,700	22,800
17	Total fixed costs	38,500	38,500	38,500	38,500	154,000
18	**Total manufacturing overhead**	**$57,100**	**$60,100**	**$63,100**	**$66,100**	**$246,400**
19	**Direct labor hours (Illustration 23-9)**	**6,200**	**7,200**	**8,200**	**9,200**	**30,800**
20	**Manufacturing overhead rate per direct labor hour ($246,400 ÷ 30,800)**					**$ 8**
21						

administrative expenses for the budget period. This budget (Illustration 23-11) also classifies expenses as either variable or fixed. In this case, the variable expense rates per unit of sales are sales commissions $3 and freight-out $1. Variable expenses per quarter are based on the unit sales from the sales budget (Illustration 23-3). For example, Hayes expects sales in the first quarter to be 3,000 units. Thus, Sales Commissions Expense is $9,000 (3,000 × $3), and Freight-out is $3,000 (3,000 × $1). Fixed expenses are based on assumed data. Illustration 23-11 shows the selling and administrative expense budget.

Illustration 23-11
Selling and administrative expense budget

Hayes Company Manufacturing Selling and Administrative Expense Budget.xls

File Edit View Insert Format Tools Data Window Help

	A	B	C	D	E	F
1	**HAYES COMPANY**					
2	**Selling and Administrative Expense Budget**					
3	**For the Year Ending December 31, 2008**					
4		Quarter				
5		1	2	3	4	Year
6	Budgeted sales in units (Illustration 23-3)	3,000	3,500	4,000	4,500	15,000
7	Variable expenses					
8	Sales commissions ($3 per unit)	$ 9,000	$10,500	$12,000	$13,500	$ 45,000
9	Freight-out ($1 per unit)	3,000	3,500	4,000	4,500	15,000
10	Total variable expenses	12,000	14,000	16,000	18,000	60,000
11	Fixed expenses					
12	Advertising	5,000	5,000	5,000	5,000	20,000
13	Sales salaries	15,000	15,000	15,000	15,000	60,000
14	Office salaries	7,500	7,500	7,500	7,500	30,000
15	Depreciation	1,000	1,000	1,000	1,000	4,000
16	Property taxes and insurance	1,500	1,500	1,500	1,500	6,000
17	Total fixed expenses	30,000	30,000	30,000	30,000	120,000
18	**Total selling and administrative expenses**	**$42,000**	**$44,000**	**$46,000**	**$48,000**	**$180,000**
19						

Budgeted Income Statement

STUDY OBJECTIVE 4

Describe the sources for preparing the budgeted income statement.

The **budgeted income statement** is the important end-product of the operating budgets. This budget indicates the expected profitability of operations for the budget period. The budgeted income statement provides the basis for evaluating company performance.

As you would expect, this budget is prepared from the various operating budgets. For example, to find the cost of goods sold, it is first necessary to determine the total unit cost of producing one Kitchen-Mate, as follows.

Illustration 23-12
Computation of total unit cost

Cost of One Kitchen-Mate

Cost Element	Illustration	Quantity	Unit Cost	Total
Direct materials	23-7	2 pounds	$ 4.00	$ 8.00
Direct labor	23-9	2 hours	$10.00	20.00
Manufacturing overhead	23-10	2 hours	$ 8.00	16.00
Total unit cost				**$44.00**

Hayes Company then determines cost of goods sold by multiplying the units sold by the unit cost. Its budgeted cost of goods sold is $660,000 (15,000 × $44). All data for the statement come from the individual operating budgets except the following: (1) interest expense is expected to be $100, and (2) income taxes are estimated to be $12,000. Illustration 23-13 shows the budgeted income statement.

Illustration 23-13
Budgeted income statement

HAYES COMPANY
Budgeted Income Statement
For the Year Ending December 31, 2008

Sales (Illustration 23-3)	$900,000
Cost of goods sold (15,000 × $44)	660,000
Gross profit	240,000
Selling and administrative expenses (Illustration 23-11)	180,000
Income from operations	60,000
Interest expense	100
Income before income taxes	59,900
Income tax expense	12,000
Net income	$ 47,900

PREPARING THE FINANCIAL BUDGETS

As shown in Illustration 23-2 (page 1005), the financial budgets consist of the capital expenditure budget, the cash budget, and the budgeted balance sheet. We will discuss the capital expenditure budget in Chapter 26; the other budgets are explained in the following sections.

Cash Budget

STUDY OBJECTIVE 5

Explain the principal sections of a cash budget.

The **cash budget** shows anticipated cash flows. Because cash is so vital, this budget is often considered to be the most important financial budget.

The cash budget contains three sections (cash receipts, cash disbursements, and financing) and the beginning and ending cash balances, as shown in Illustration 23-14.

Illustration 23-14
Basic form of a cash budget

ANY COMPANY Cash Budget	
Beginning cash balance	$X,XXX
Add: **Cash receipts** (Itemized)	X,XXX
Total available cash	X,XXX
Less: **Cash disbursements** (Itemized)	X,XXX
Excess (deficiency) of available cash over cash disbursements	X,XXX
Financing	X,XXX
Ending cash balance	$X,XXX

HELPFUL HINT

Why is the cash budget prepared after the other budgets are prepared? Answer: Because the information generated by the other budgets dictates the expected inflows and outflows of cash.

The **cash receipts section** includes expected receipts from the company's principal source(s) of revenue. These are usually cash sales and collections from customers on credit sales. This section also shows anticipated receipts of interest and dividends, and proceeds from planned sales of investments, plant assets, and the company's capital stock.

The **cash disbursements section** shows expected cash payments. Such payments include direct materials, direct labor, manufacturing overhead, and selling and administrative expenses. This section also includes projected payments for income taxes, dividends, investments, and plant assets.

The **financing section** shows expected borrowings and the repayment of the borrowed funds plus interest. Companies need this section when there is a cash deficiency or when the cash balance is below management's minimum required balance.

Data in the cash budget are prepared in sequence. The ending cash balance of one period becomes the beginning cash balance for the next period. Companies obtain data for preparing the cash budget from other budgets and from information provided by management. In practice, cash budgets are often prepared for the year on a monthly basis.

To minimize detail, we will assume that Hayes Company prepares an annual cash budget by quarters. Hayes Company's cash budget is based on the following assumptions.

1. The January 1, 2008, cash balance is expected to be $38,000.
2. Sales (Illustration 23-3, page 1006): 60% are collected in the quarter sold and 40% are collected in the following quarter. Accounts receivable of $60,000 at December 31, 2007, are expected to be collected in full in the first quarter of 2008.
3. Short-term investments are expected to be sold for $2,000 cash in the first quarter.
4. Direct materials (Illustration 23-7, page 1008): 50% are paid in the quarter purchased and 50% are paid in the following quarter. Accounts payable of

$10,600 at December 31, 2007, are expected to be paid in full in the first quarter of 2008.

5. Direct labor (Illustration 23-9, page 1008): 100% is paid in the quarter incurred.
6. Manufacturing overhead (Illustration 23-10, page 1010) and selling and administrative expenses (Illustration 23-11, page 1010): All items except depreciation are paid in the quarter incurred.
7. Management plans to purchase a truck in the second quarter for $10,000 cash.
8. Hayes makes equal quarterly payments of its estimated annual income taxes.
9. Loans are repaid in the earliest quarter in which there is sufficient cash (that is, when the cash on hand exceeds the $15,000 minimum required balance).

In preparing the cash budget, it is useful to prepare schedules for collections from customers (assumption No. 2, above) and cash payments for direct materials (assumption No. 4, above). These schedules are shown in Illustrations 23-15 and 23-16.

Illustration 23-15
Collections from customers

HAYES COMPANY
Schedule of Expected Collections from Customers

	Quarter			
	1	2	3	4
Accounts receivable, 12/31/07	$ 60,000			
First quarter ($180,000)	108,000	$ 72,000		
Second quarter ($210,000)		126,000	$ 84,000	
Third quarter ($240,000)			144,000	$ 96,000
Fourth quarter ($270,000)				162,000
Total collections	$168,000	$198,000	$228,000	$258,000

Illustration 23-16
Payments for direct materials

HAYES COMPANY
Schedule of Expected Payments for Direct Materials

	Quarter			
	1	2	3	4
Accounts payable, 12/31/07	$10,600			
First quarter ($25,200)	12,600	$12,600		
Second quarter ($29,200)		14,600	$14,600	
Third quarter ($33,200)			16,600	$16,600
Fourth quarter ($37,200)				18,600
Total payments	$23,200	$27,200	$31,200	$35,200

Illustration 23-17 (page 1014) shows the cash budget for Hayes Company. The budget indicates that Hayes will need $3,000 of financing in the second quarter to maintain a minimum cash balance of $15,000. Since there is an excess of available cash over disbursements of $22,500 at the end of the third quarter, the borrowing, plus $100 interest, is repaid in this quarter.

Hayes Company Cash Budget.xls

File Edit View Insert Format Tools Data Window Help

	A	B	C	D	E	G	I
1			**HAYES COMPANY**				
2			**Cash Budget**				
3			**For the Year Ending December 31, 2008**				
4					Quarter		
5		Assumption	1		2	3	4
6	Beginning cash balance	1	$ 38,000		$ 25,500	$ 15,000	$ 19,400
7	**Add: Receipts**						
8	Collections from customers	2	168,000		198,000	228,000	258,000
9	Sale of securities	3	2,000		0	0	0
10	Total receipts		170,000		198,000	228,000	258,000
11	Total available cash		208,000		223,500	243,000	277,400
12	**Less: Disbursements**						
13	Direct materials	4	23,200		27,200	31,200	35,200
14	Direct labor	5	62,000		72,000	82,000	92,000
15	Manufacturing overhead	6	53,300	a	56,300	59,300	62,300
16	Selling and administrative expenses	6	41,000	b	43,000	45,000	47,000
17	Purchase of truck	7	0		10,000	0	0
18	Income tax expense	8	3,000		3,000	3,000	3,000
19	Total disbursements		182,500		211,500	220,500	239,500
20	Excess (deficiency) of available cash over cash disbursements		25,500		12,000	22,500	37,900
21	**Financing**						
22	Borrowings		0		**3,000**	0	0
23	Repayments-plus $100 interest	9	0		0	**3,100**	0
24	Ending cash balance		$ 25,500		$ 15,000	$ 19,400	$ 37,900
25							
26	[a]$57,100-$3,800 depreciation						
27	[b]$42,000-$1,000 depreciation						

Illustration 23-17
Cash budget

MANAGEMENT INSIGHT

Growth and Cash Flow Often Do Not Occur Together

Douglas Roberson, president of Atlantic Network, woke up one morning to find that his company was out of cash. At that point, Roberson realized that managing cash flow is different from simply accumulating sales. He says: "If you don't do serious projections about how much cash you will need to handle sales—and how long it will take to collect on invoices—you can end up out of business no matter how fast you are growing." In fact, Roberson says, fast growth makes cash flow problems worse.

? How can fast growth make cash flow problems worse?

A cash budget contributes to more effective cash management. It shows managers when additional financing is necessary well before the actual need arises. And, it indicates when excess cash is available for investments or other purposes.

Budgeted Balance Sheet

The **budgeted balance sheet** is a projection of financial position at the end of the budget period. This budget is developed from the budgeted balance sheet for the preceding year and the budgets for the current year. Pertinent data from the budgeted balance sheet at December 31, 2007, are as follows.

Buildings and equipment	$182,000	Common stock	$225,000
Accumulated depreciation	$ 28,800	Retained earnings	$ 46,480

Illustration 23-18 show Hayes Company's budgeted balance sheet at December 31, 2008.

Illustration 23-18
Budgeted balance sheet

HAYES COMPANY Budgeted Balance Sheet December 31, 2008		
Assets		
Cash		$ 37,900
Accounts receivable		108,000
Finished goods inventory		44,000
Raw materials inventory		4,080
Buildings and equipment	$192,000	
Less: Accumulated depreciation	48,000	144,000
Total assets		$337,980
Liabilities and Stockholders' Equity		
Accounts payable		$ 18,600
Common stock		225,000
Retained earnings		94,380
Total liabilities and stockholders' equity		$337,980

The computations and sources of the amounts are explained below.

Cash: Ending cash balance $37,900, shown in the cash budget (Illustration 23-17, page 1014).

Accounts receivable: 40% of fourth-quarter sales $270,000, shown in the schedule of expected collections from customers (Illustration 23-15, page 1013).

Finished goods inventory: Desired ending inventory 1,000 units, shown in the production budget (Illustration 23-5, page 1007) times the total unit cost $44 (shown in Illustration 23-12, page 1011).

Raw materials inventory: Desired ending inventory 1,020 pounds, times the cost per pound $4, shown in the direct materials budget (Illustration 23-7, page 1008).

Buildings and equipment: December 31, 2007, balance $182,000, plus purchase of truck for $10,000.

Accumulated depreciation: December 31, 2007, balance $28,800, plus $15,200 depreciation shown in manufacturing overhead budget (Illustration 23-10, page 1010) and $4,000 depreciation shown in selling and administrative expense budget (Illustration 23-11, page 1010).

Accounts payable: 50% of fourth-quarter purchases $37,200, shown in schedule of expected payments for direct materials (Illustration 23-16, page 1013).

Common stock: Unchanged from the beginning of the year.

Retained earnings: December 31, 2007, balance $46,480, plus net income $47,900, shown in budgeted income statement (Illustration 23-13, page 1011).

After budget data are entered into the computer, Hayes prepares the various budgets (sales, cash, etc.), as well as the budgeted financial statements. Using spreadsheets, management can also perform "what if" (sensitivity) analyses based on different hypothetical assumptions. For example, suppose that sales managers project that sales will be 10% higher in the coming quarter. What impact does this change have on the rest of the budgeting process and the financing needs of the business? The impact of the various assumptions on the budget is quickly determined by the spreadsheet. Armed with these analyses, managers make more informed decisions about the impact of various projects. They also anticipate future problems and business opportunities. As seen in this chapter, budgeting is an excellent use of electronic spreadsheets.

Before You Go On...

REVIEW IT

1. What are the two classifications of the individual budgets in the master budget?
2. What is the sequence for preparing the budgets that comprise the operating budgets?
3. Identify some of the source documents that would be used in preparing each of the operating budgets.
4. What are the three principal sections of the cash budget?

DO IT

Martian Company management wants to maintain a minimum monthly cash balance of $15,000. At the beginning of March, the cash balance is $16,500, expected cash receipts for March are $210,000, and cash disbursements are expected to be $220,000. How much cash, if any, must be borrowed to maintain the desired minimum monthly balance?

Action Plan

- Write down the basic form of the cash budget, starting with the beginning cash balance, adding cash receipts for the period, deducting cash disbursements, and identifying the needed financing to achieve the desired minimum ending cash balance.
- Insert the data given into the outlined form of the cash budget.

Solution

MARTIAN COMPANY
Cash Budget
For the Month Ending March 31, 2008

Beginning cash balance	$ 16,500
Add: Cash receipts for March	210,000
Total available cash	226,500
Less: Cash disbursements for March	220,000
Excess of available cash over cash disbursements	6,500
Financing	8,500
Ending cash balance	$ 15,000

To maintain the desired minimum cash balance of $15,000, Martian Company must borrow $8,500 of cash.

Related exercise material: *BE23-9, E23-12, E23-13, and E23-14.*

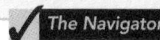

The Navigator

BUDGETING IN NON-MANUFACTURING COMPANIES

Budgeting is not limited to manufacturers. Budgets are also used by merchandisers, service enterprises, and not-for-profit organizations.

STUDY OBJECTIVE 6
Indicate the applicability of budgeting in non-manufacturing companies.

Merchandisers

As in manufacturing operations, the sales budget for a merchandiser is both the starting point and the key factor in the development of the master budget. The major differences between the master budgets of a merchandiser and a manufacturer are these:

1. A merchandiser **uses a merchandise purchases budget instead of a production budget**.
2. A merchandiser **does not use the manufacturing budgets (direct materials, direct labor, and manufacturing overhead)**.

The merchandise purchases budget shows the estimated cost of goods to be purchased to meet expected sales. The formula for determining budgeted merchandise purchases is:

Budgeted Cost of Goods Sold	+	Desired Ending Merchandise Inventory	−	Beginning Merchandise Inventory	=	Required Merchandise Purchases

Illustration 23-19
Merchandise purchases formula

To illustrate, assume that the budget committee of Lima Company is preparing the merchandise purchases budget for July 2008. It estimates that budgeted sales will be $300,000 in July and $320,000 in August. Cost of goods sold is expected to be 70% of sales—that is, $210,000 in July (.70 × $300,000) and $224,000 in August (.70 × $320,000). The company's desired ending inventory is 30% of the following month's cost of goods sold. Required merchandise purchases for July are $214,200, computed as follows.

Illustration 23-20
Merchandise purchases budget

LIMA COMPANY
Merchandise Purchases Budget
For the Month Ending July 31, 2008

Budgeted cost of goods sold ($300,000 × 70%)	$ 210,000
Add: Desired ending merchandise inventory ($224,000 × 30%)	67,200
Total	277,200
Less: Beginning merchandise inventory ($210,000 × 30%)	63,000
Required merchandise purchases for July	**$214,200**

When a merchandiser is departmentalized, it prepares separate budgets for each department. For example, a grocery store prepares sales budgets and purchases

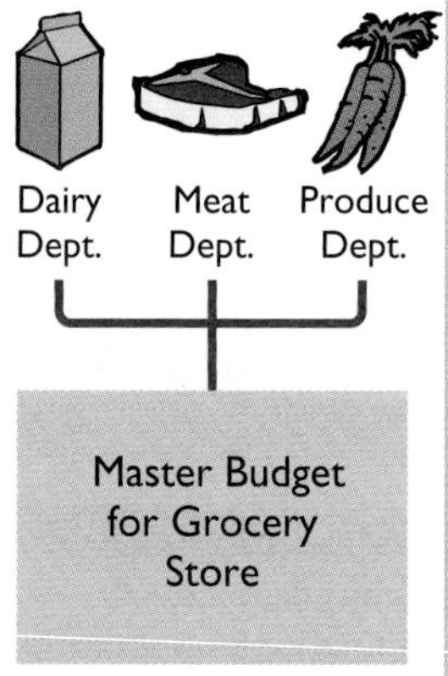

Departmentalized budgets

budgets for each of its major departments, such as meats, dairy, and produce. The store then combines these budgets into a master budget for the store. When a retailer has branch stores, it prepares separate master budgets for each store. Then it incorporates these budgets into master budgets for the company as a whole.

Service Enterprises

In a service enterprise, such as a public accounting firm, a law office, or a medical practice, the critical factor in budgeting is **coordinating professional staff needs with anticipated services**. If a firm is overstaffed, several problems may result: Labor costs are disproportionately high. Profits are lower because of the additional salaries. Staff turnover sometimes increases because of lack of challenging work. In contrast, if a service enterprise is understaffed, it may lose revenue because existing and prospective client needs for service cannot be met. Also, professional staff may seek other jobs because of excessive work loads.

Service enterprises can obtain budget data for service revenue from **expected output** or **expected input**. When output is used, it is necessary to determine the expected billings of clients for services provided. In a public accounting firm, for example, output is the sum of its billings in auditing, tax, and consulting services. When input data are used, each professional staff member projects his or her billable time. The firm then applies billing rates to billable time to produce expected service revenue.

Not-for-Profit Organizations

Budgeting is just as important for not-for-profit organizations as for profit-oriented enterprises. The budget process, however, is different. In most cases, not-for-profit entities budget **on the basis of cash flows (expenditures and receipts), rather than on a revenue and expense basis**. Further, the starting point in the process is usually expenditures, not receipts. For the not-for-profit entity, management's task generally is to find the receipts needed to support the planned expenditures. The activity index is also likely to be significantly different. For example, in a not-for-profit entity, such as a university, budgeted faculty positions may be based on full-time equivalent students or credit hours expected to be taught in a department.

For some governmental units, voters approve the budget. In other cases, such as state governments and the federal government, legislative approval is required. After the budget is adopted, it must be followed. Overspending is often illegal. In governmental budgets, authorizations tend to be on a line-by-line basis. That is, the budget for a municipality may have a specified authorization for police and fire protection, garbage collection, street paving, and so on. The line-item authorization of governmental budgets significantly limits the amount of discretion management can exercise. The city manager often cannot use savings from one line item, such as street paving, to cover increased spending in another line item, such as snow removal.

Before You Go On...

REVIEW IT

1. What is the formula for computing required merchandise purchases?
2. How does budgeting in service and not-for-profit organizations differ from budgeting for manufacturers and merchandisers?

The Navigator

Be sure to read **ALL ABOUT YOU: *Avoiding Personal Financial Disaster*** on the next page for information on how topics in this chapter apply to you.

Avoiding Personal Financial Disaster

You might hear people say that they "need to learn to live within a budget." The funny thing is that most people who say this haven't actually prepared a personal budget, nor do they intend to. Instead, what they are referring to is a vaguely defined, poorly specified, collection of rough ideas of how much they should spend on various aspects of their life. You can't live within or even outside of something that doesn't exist. With that in mind, let's take a look at personal budgets.

Some Facts

* The average American household income is $49,430, before taxes.
* The average family spends $5,375 on food each year. Of this, $3,099 is for food consumed at home, and $2,276 is for food consumed away from home.
* The average family spends $13,283 annually on housing costs. Of this amount, $7,829 is the actual cost of shelter, $2,684 is for utilities, and $1,518 is for furnishings and equipment.
* The average family spends $7,759 per year on transportation. Of this, $3,665 goes to vehicle purchase payments, and $1,235 is spent on fuel. The average family spends only $389 per year on public transportation.

About the Numbers

Obviously people spend their income in different ways. For example, the percentage of your income spent on necessities declines as your income increases. Nonetheless, it is interesting to see how the average family spends its money.

Average U.S. Household Expenditures

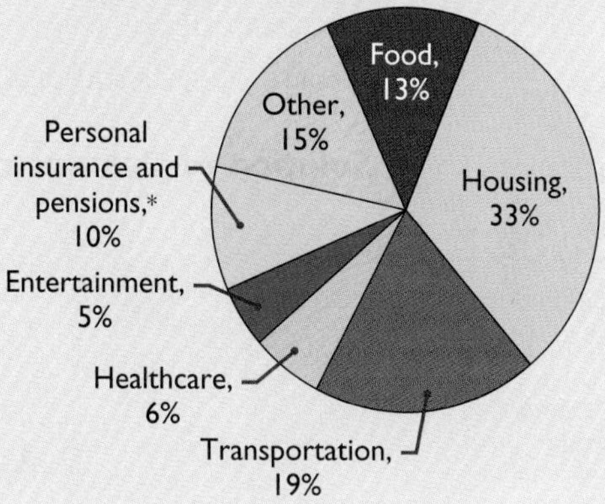

* This includes Social Security tax.

Source: "Consumer Expenditures in 2004," U.S. Department of Labor and U.S. Bureau of Labor Statistics, Report 992, April 2006.

What Do You Think?

Many worksheet templates that are provided for personal budgets for college students treat student loans as an income source. See, for example, the template provided at **http://financialplan.about.com/cs/budgeting/l/blmocolbud.htm**. Based on your knowledge of accounting, is this correct?

YES: Student loans provide a source of cash which can be used to pay costs. As the saying goes, "It all spends the same." Therefore student loans are income.

NO: Student loans must eventually be repaid; therefore they are not income. As the name suggests, they are loans.

Source: U.S. Department of Labor and U.S. Bureau of Labor Statistics, "Consumer Expenditures in 2004," April 2006, Report 992.

The authors' comments on this situation appear on page 1037.

Demonstration Problem

Soroco Company is preparing its master budget for 2008. Relevant data pertaining to its sales and production budgets are as follows:

Sales: Sales for the year are expected to total 1,200,000 units. Quarterly sales are 20%, 25%, 30%, and 25% respectively. The sales price is expected to be $50 per unit for the first three quarters and $55 per unit beginning in the fourth quarter. Sales in the first quarter of 2009 are expected to be 10% higher than the budgeted sales volume for the first quarter of 2008.

Production: Management desires to maintain ending finished goods inventories at 25% of the next quarter's budgeted sales volume.

Instructions

Prepare the sales budget and production budget by quarters for 2008.

action plan

- Know the form and content of the sales budget.
- Prepare the sales budget first as the basis for the other budgets.
- Determine the units that must be produced to meet anticipated sales.
- Know how to compute the beginning and ending finished goods units.

Solution to Demonstration Problem

SOROCO COMPANY
Sales Budget
For the Year Ending December 31, 2008

	Quarter 1	2	3	4	Year
Expected unit sales	240,000	300,000	360,000	300,000	1,200,000
Unit selling price	× $50	× $50	× $50	× $55	—
Total sales	$12,000,000	$15,000,000	$18,000,000	$16,500,000	$61,500,000

SOROCO COMPANY
Production Budget
For the Year Ending December 31, 2008

	Quarter 1	2	3	4	Year
Expected unit sales	240,000	300,000	360,000	300,000	
Add: Desired ending finished goods units	75,000	90,000	75,000	66,000[1]	
Total required units	315,000	390,000	435,000	366,000	
Less: Beginning finished goods units	60,000[2]	75,000	90,000	75,000	
Required production units	255,000	315,000	345,000	291,000	1,206,000

[1]Estimated first-quarter 2009 sales volume 240,000 + (240,000 × 10%) = 264,000; 264,000 × 25%.
[2]25% of estimated first-quarter 2008 sales units (240,000 × 25%).

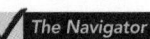

The Navigator

SUMMARY OF STUDY OBJECTIVES

1 **Indicate the benefits of budgeting.** The primary advantages of budgeting are that it (a) requires management to plan ahead, (b) provides definite objectives for evaluating performance, (c) creates an early warning system for potential problems, (d) facilitates coordination of activities, (e) results in greater management awareness, and (f) motivates personnel to meet planned objectives.

2 **State the essentials of effective budgeting.** The essentials of effective budgeting are (a) sound organizational

structure, (b) research and analysis, and (c) acceptance by all levels of management.

3 **Identify the budgets that comprise the master budget.** The master budget consists of the following budgets: (a) sales, (b) production, (c) direct materials, (d) direct labor, (e) manufacturing overhead, (f) selling and administrative expense, (g) budgeted income statement, (h) capital expenditure budget, (i) cash budget, and (j) budgeted balance sheet.

4 **Describe the sources for preparing the budgeted income statement.** The budgeted income statement is prepared from (a) the sales budget, (b) the budgets for direct materials, direct labor, and manufacturing overhead, and (c) the selling and administrative expense budget.

5 **Explain the principal sections of a cash budget.** The cash budget has three sections (receipts, disbursements, and financing) and the beginning and ending cash balances.

6 **Indicate the applicability of budgeting in nonmanufacturing companies.** Budgeting may be used by merchandisers for development of a master budget. In service enterprises budgeting is a critical factor in coordinating staff needs with anticipated services. In not-for-profit organizations, the starting point in budgeting is usually expenditures, not receipts.

The Navigator

GLOSSARY

WILEY PLUS

Budget A formal written statement of management's plans for a specified future time period, expressed in financial terms. (p. 1000).

Budget committee A group responsible for coordinating the preparation of the budget. (p. 1002).

Budgetary slack The amount by which a manager intentionally underestimates budgeted revenues or overestimates budgeted expenses in order to make it easier to achieve budgetary goals. (p. 1003).

Budgeted balance sheet A projection of financial position at the end of the budget period. (p. 1015).

Budgeted income statement An estimate of the expected profitability of operations for the budget period. (p. 1011).

Cash budget A projection of anticipated cash flows. (p. 1012).

Direct labor budget A projection of the quantity and cost of direct labor necessary to meet production requirements. (p. 1008).

Direct materials budget An estimate of the quantity and cost of direct materials to be purchased. (p. 1007).

Financial budgets Individual budgets that focus primarily on the cash resources needed to fund expected operations and planned capital expenditures. (p. 1004).

Long-range planning A formalized process of selecting strategies to achieve long-term goals and developing policies and plans to implement the strategies. (p. 1004).

Manufacturing overhead budget An estimate of expected manufacturing overhead costs for the budget period. (p. 1009).

Master budget A set of interrelated budgets that constitutes a plan of action for a specific time period. (p. 1004).

Merchandise purchases budget The estimated cost of goods to be purchased by a merchandiser to meet expected sales. (p. 1017).

Operating budgets Individual budgets that result in a budgeted income statement. (p. 1004).

Participative budgeting A budgetary approach that starts with input from lower-level managers and works upward so that managers at all levels participate. (p. 1002).

Production budget A projection of the units that must be produced to meet anticipated sales. (p. 1006).

Sales budget An estimate of expected sales revenue for the budget period. (p. 1006).

Sales forecast The projection of potential sales for the industry and the company's expected share of such sales. (p. 1002).

Selling and administrative expense budget A projection of anticipated selling and administrative expenses for the budget period. (p. 1009).

SELF-STUDY QUESTIONS

WILEY PLUS

Answers are at the end of the chapter.

(SO 1) **1.** Which of the following is not a benefit of budgeting?
  a. Management can plan ahead.
  b. An early warning system is provided for potential problems.
  c. It enables disciplinary action to be taken at every level of responsibility.
  d. The coordination of activities is facilitated.

(SO 2) **2.** The essentials of effective budgeting do *not* include:
  a. top-down budgeting.
  b. management acceptance.
  c. research and analysis.
  d. sound organizational structure.

3. Compared to budgeting, long-range planning generally has the: (SO 2)
  a. same amount of detail.
  b. longer time period.
  c. same emphasis.
  d. same time period.

4. A sales budget is: (SO 3)
  a. derived from the production budget.
  b. management's best estimate of sales revenue for the year.

c. not the starting point for the master budget.
d. prepared only for credit sales.

(SO 3) 5. The formula for the production budget is budgeted sales in units plus:
a. desired ending merchandise inventory less beginning merchandise inventory.
b. beginning finished goods units less desired ending finished goods units.
c. desired ending direct materials units less beginning direct materials units.
d. desired ending finished goods units less beginning finished goods units.

(SO 3) 6. Direct materials inventories are kept in pounds in Byrd Company, and the total pounds of direct materials needed for production is 9,500. If the beginning inventory is 1,000 pounds and the desired ending inventory is 2,200 pounds, the total pounds to be purchased is:
a. 9,400.
b. 9,500.
c. 9,700.
d. 10,700.

(SO 3) 7. The formula for computing the direct labor budget is to multiply the direct labor cost per hour by the:
a. total required direct labor hours.
b. physical units to be produced.
c. equivalent units to be produced.
d. No correct answer is given.

8. Each of the following budgets is used in preparing the budgeted income statement *except* the: (SO 4)
a. sales budget.
b. selling and administrative budget.
c. capital expenditure budget.
d. direct labor budget.

9. Expected direct materials purchases in Read Company are \$70,000 in the first quarter and \$90,000 in the second quarter. Forty percent of the purchases are paid in cash as incurred, and the balance is paid in the following quarter. The budgeted cash payments for purchases in the second quarter are: (SO 5)
a. \$96,000.
b. \$90,000.
c. \$78,000.
d. \$72,000.

10. The budget for a merchandiser differs from a budget for a manufacturer because: (SO 6)
a. a merchandise purchases budget replaces the production budget.
b. the manufacturing budgets are not applicable.
c. None of the above.
d. Both (a) and (b) above.

Go to the book's website, **www.wiley.com/college/weygandt**, for Additional Self-Study questions.

The Navigator

QUESTIONS

1. **(a)** What is a budget?
(b) How does a budget contribute to good management?
2. Karen Bay and Frank Barone are discussing the benefits of budgeting. They ask you to identify the primary advantages of budgeting. Comply with their request.
3. Tina Haworth asks your help in understanding the essentials of effective budgeting. Identify the essentials for Tina.
4. **(a)** "Accounting plays a relatively unimportant role in budgeting." Do you agree? Explain.
(b) What responsibilities does management have in budgeting?
5. What criteria are helpful in determining the length of the budget period? What is the most common budget period?
6. Megan Pedigo maintains that the only difference between budgeting and long-range planning is time. Do you agree? Why or why not?
7. What is participative budgeting? What are its potential benefits? What are its potential shortcomings?
8. What is budgetary slack? What incentive do managers have to create budgetary slack?
9. Distinguish between a master budget and a sales forecast.
10. What budget is the starting point in preparing the master budget? What may result if this budget is inaccurate?
11. "The production budget shows both unit production data and unit cost data." Is this true? Explain.
12. Cali Company has 15,000 beginning finished goods units. Budgeted sales units are 160,000. If management desires 20,000 ending finished goods units, what are the required units of production?
13. In preparing the direct materials budget for Mast Company, management concludes that required purchases are 64,000 units. If 52,000 direct materials units are required in production and there are 7,000 units of beginning direct materials, what is the desired units of ending direct materials?
14. The production budget of Rooney Company calls for 80,000 units to be produced. If it takes 30 minutes to make one unit and the direct labor rate is \$16 per hour, what is the total budgeted direct labor cost?
15. Morales Company's manufacturing overhead budget shows total variable costs of \$198,000 and total fixed costs of \$162,000. Total production in units is expected to be 160,000. It takes 15 minutes to make one unit, and the direct labor rate is \$15 per hour. Express the manufacturing overhead rate as (a) a percentage of direct labor cost, and (b) an amount per direct labor hour.
16. Elbert Company's variable selling and administrative expenses are 10% of net sales. Fixed expenses are \$50,000 per quarter. The sales budget shows expected sales of \$200,000 and \$250,000 in the first and second quarters, respectively. What are the total budgeted selling and administrative expenses for each quarter?

17. For Nolte Company, the budgeted cost for one unit of product is direct materials $10, direct labor $20, and manufacturing overhead 90% of direct labor cost. If 25,000 units are expected to be sold at $69 each, what is the budgeted gross profit?
18. Indicate the supporting schedules used in preparing a budgeted income statement through gross profit for a manufacturer.
19. Identify the three sections of a cash budget. What balances are also shown in this budget?
20. Van Gundy Company has credit sales of $500,000 in January. Past experience suggests that 45% is collected in the month of sale, 50% in the month following the sale, and 5% in the second month following the sale. Compute the cash collections from January sales in January, February, and March.
21. What is the formula for determining required merchandise purchases for a merchandiser?
22. How may expected revenues in a service enterprise be computed?

BRIEF EXERCISES

BE23-1 Noble Manufacturing Company uses the following budgets: Balance Sheet, Capital Expenditure, Cash, Direct Labor, Direct Materials, Income Statement, Manufacturing Overhead, Production, Sales, and Selling and Administrative. Prepare a diagram of the interrelationships of the budgets in the master budget. Indicate whether each budget is an operating or a financial budget.

Prepare a diagram of a master budget.
(SO 3)

BE23-2 Goody Company estimates that unit sales will be 10,000 in quarter 1; 12,000 in quarter 2; 14,000 in quarter 3; and 18,000 in quarter 4. Using a sales price of $80 per unit, prepare the sales budget by quarters for the year ending December 31, 2008.

Prepare a sales budget.
(SO 3)

BE23-3 Sales budget data for Goody Company are given in BE23-2. Management desires to have an ending finished goods inventory equal to 20% of the next quarter's expected unit sales. Prepare a production budget by quarters for the first 6 months of 2008.

Prepare a production budget for 2 quarters.
(SO 3)

BE23-4 Ortiz Company has 1,600 pounds of raw materials in its December 31, 2008, ending inventory. Required production for January and February of 2009 are 4,000 and 5,500 units, respectively. Two pounds of raw materials are needed for each unit, and the estimated cost per pound is $6. Management desires an ending inventory equal to 20% of next month's materials requirements. Prepare the direct materials budget for January.

Prepare a direct materials budget for 1 month.
(SO 3)

BE23-5 For Everly Company, units to be produced are 5,000 in quarter 1 and 6,000 in quarter 2. It takes 1.5 hours to make a finished unit, and the expected hourly wage rate is $14 per hour. Prepare a direct labor budget by quarters for the 6 months ending June 30, 2008.

Prepare a direct labor budget for 2 quarters.
(SO 3)

BE23-6 For Justus Inc. variable manufacturing overhead costs are expected to be $20,000 in the first quarter of 2008 with $4,000 increments in each of the remaining three quarters. Fixed overhead costs are estimated to be $35,000 in each quarter. Prepare the manufacturing overhead budget by quarters and in total for the year.

Prepare a manufacturing overhead budget.
(SO 3)

BE23-7 Mize Company classifies its selling and administrative expense budget into variable and fixed components. Variable expenses are expected to be $25,000 in the first quarter, and $5,000 increments are expected in the remaining quarters of 2008. Fixed expenses are expected to be $40,000 in each quarter. Prepare the selling and administrative expense budget by quarters and in total for 2008.

Prepare a selling and administrative expense budget.
(SO 3)

BE23-8 Perine Company has completed all of its operating budgets. The sales budget for the year shows 50,000 units and total sales of $2,000,000. The total unit cost of making one unit of sales is $22. Selling and administrative expenses are expected to be $300,000. Income taxes are estimated to be $150,000. Prepare a budgeted income statement for the year ending December 31, 2008.

Prepare a budgeted income statement for the year.
(SO 4)

BE23-9 Agee Industries expects credit sales for January, February, and March to be $200,000, $260,000, and $310,000, respectively. It is expected that 70% of the sales will be collected in the month of sale, and 30% will be collected in the following month. Compute cash collections from customers for each month.

Prepare data for a cash budget.
(SO 5)

BE23-10 Palermo Wholesalers is preparing its merchandise purchases budget. Budgeted sales are $400,000 for April and $475,000 for May. Cost of goods sold is expected to be 60% of sales. The company's desired ending inventory is 20% of the following month's cost of goods sold. Compute the required purchases for April.

Determine required merchandise purchases for 1 month.
(SO 6)

EXERCISES

WILEY PLUS

Explain the concept of budgeting.
(SO 1, 2, 3)

E23-1 Black Rose Company has always done some planning for the future, but the company has never prepared a formal budget. Now that the company is growing larger, it is considering preparing a budget.

Instructions

Write a memo to Jack Bruno, the president of Black Rose Company, in which you define budgeting, identify the budgets that comprise the master budget, identify the primary benefits of budgeting, and discuss the essentials of effective budgeting.

Prepare a sales budget for 2 quarters.
(SO 3)

E23-2 Zeller Electronics Inc. produces and sells two models of pocket calculators, XQ-103 and XQ-104. The calculators sell for $12 and $25, respectively. Because of the intense competition Zeller faces, management budgets sales semiannually. Its projections for the first 2 quarters of 2008 are as follows.

	Unit Sales	
Product	**Quarter 1**	**Quarter 2**
XQ-103	20,000	25,000
XQ-104	12,000	15,000

No changes in selling prices are anticipated.

Instructions

Prepare a sales budget for the 2 quarters ending June 30, 2008. List the products and show for each quarter and for the 6 months, units, selling price, and total sales by product and in total.

Prepare a sales budget for four quarters.
(SO 3, 6)

E23-3 Roche and Young, CPAs, are preparing their service revenue (sales) budget for the coming year (2008). The practice is divided into three departments: auditing, tax, and consulting. Billable hours for each department, by quarter, are provided below.

Department	Quarter 1	Quarter 2	Quarter 3	Quarter 4
Auditing	2,200	1,600	2,000	2,400
Tax	3,000	2,400	2,000	2,500
Consulting	1,500	1,500	1,500	1,500

Average hourly billing rates are: auditing $80, tax $90, and consulting $100.

Instructions

Prepare the service revenue (sales) budget for 2008 by listing the departments and showing for each quarter and the year in total, billable hours, billable rate, and total revenue.

Prepare quarterly production budgets.
(SO 3)

E23-4 Turney Company produces and sells automobile batteries, the heavy-duty HD-240. The 2008 sales budget is as follows.

Quarter	HD-240
1	5,000
2	7,000
3	8,000
4	10,000

The January 1, 2008, inventory of HD-240 is 2,500 units. Management desires an ending inventory each quarter equal to 50% of the next quarter's sales. Sales in the first quarter of 2009 are expected to be 30% higher than sales in the same quarter in 2008.

Instructions

Prepare quarterly production budgets for each quarter and in total for 2008.

Prepare a direct materials purchases budget.
(SO 3)

E23-5 Moreno Industries has adopted the following production budget for the first 4 months of 2009.

Month	Units	Month	Units
January	10,000	March	5,000
February	8,000	April	4,000

Each unit requires 3 pounds of raw materials costing $2 per pound. On December 31, 2008, the ending raw materials inventory was 9,000 pounds. Management wants to have a raw materials inventory at the end of the month equal to 30% of next month's production requirements.

Instructions
Prepare a direct materials purchases budget by month for the first quarter.

Prepare production and direct materials budgets by quarters for 6 months.

(SO 3)

E23-6 On January 1, 2009 the Batista Company budget committee has reached agreement on the following data for the 6 months ending June 30, 2009.

Sales units:	First quarter 5,000; second quarter 6,000; third quarter 7,000
Ending raw materials inventory:	50% of the next quarter's production requirements
Ending finished goods inventory:	30% of the next quarter's expected sales units
Third-quarter production:	7,250 units

The ending raw materials and finished goods inventories at December 31, 2008, follow the same percentage relationships to production and sales that occur in 2009. Three pounds of raw materials are required to make each unit of finished goods. Raw materials purchased are expected to cost $4 per pound.

Instructions
(a) Prepare a production budget by quarters for the 6-month period ended June 30, 2009.
(b) Prepare a direct materials budget by quarters for the 6-month period ended June 30, 2009.

Prepare a direct labor budget.

(SO 3)

E23-7 Neely, Inc., is preparing its direct labor budget for 2008 from the following production budget based on a calendar year.

Quarter	Units	Quarter	Units
1	20,000	3	35,000
2	25,000	4	30,000

Each unit requires 1.6 hours of direct labor.

Instructions
Prepare a direct labor budget for 2008. Wage rates are expected to be $15 for the first 2 quarters and $16 for quarters 3 and 4.

Prepare a manufacturing overhead budget for the year.

(SO 3)

E23-8 Hardin Company is preparing its manufacturing overhead budget for 2008. Relevant data consist of the following.

Units to be produced (by quarters): 10,000, 12,000, 14,000, 16,000.

Direct labor: Time is 1.5 hours per unit.

Variable overhead costs per direct labor hour: Indirect materials $0.70; indirect labor $1.20; and maintenance $0.50.

Fixed overhead costs per quarter: Supervisory salaries $35,000; depreciation $16,000; and maintenance $12,000.

Instructions
Prepare the manufacturing overhead budget for the year, showing quarterly data.

Prepare a selling and administrative expense budget for 2 quarters.

(SO 3)

E23-9 Edington Company combines its operating expenses for budget purposes in a selling and administrative expense budget. For the first 6 months of 2008, the following data are available.

1. Sales: 20,000 units quarter 1; 22,000 units quarter 2.
2. Variable costs per dollar of sales: Sales commissions 5%, delivery expense 2%, and advertising 3%.
3. Fixed costs per quarter: Sales salaries $10,000, office salaries $6,000, depreciation $4,200, insurance $1,500, utilities $800, and repairs expense $600.
4. Unit selling price: $20.

Instructions
Prepare a selling and administrative expense budget by quarters for the first 6 months of 2008.

Prepare a production and a direct materials budget.

(SO 3)

E23-10 Tyson Chandler Company's sales budget projects unit sales of part 198Z of 10,000 units in January, 12,000 units in February, and 13,000 units in March. Each unit of part 198Z requires 2 pounds of materials, which cost $3 per pound. Tyson Chandler Company desires its ending raw materials inventory to equal 40% of the next month's production requirements, and its ending finished goods inventory to equal 25% of the next month's expected unit sales. These goals were met at December 31, 2007.

Instructions

(a) Prepare a production budget for January and February 2008.
(b) Prepare a direct materials budget for January 2008.

Prepare a budgeted income statement for the year.
(SO 3, 4)

E23-11 Fuqua Company has accumulated the following budget data for the year 2008.

1. Sales: 30,000 units, unit selling price $80.
2. Cost of one unit of finished goods: Direct materials 2 pounds at $5 per pound, direct labor 3 hours at $12 per hour, and manufacturing overhead $6 per direct labor hour.
3. Inventories (raw materials only): Beginning, 10,000 pounds; ending, 15,000 pounds.
4. Raw materials cost: $5 per pound.
5. Selling and administrative expenses: $200,000.
6. Income taxes: 30% of income before income taxes.

Instructions

(a) Prepare a schedule showing the computation of cost of goods sold for 2008.
(b) Prepare a budgeted income statement for 2008.

Prepare a cash budget for 2 months.
(SO 5)

E23-12 Garza Company expects to have a cash balance of $46,000 on January 1, 2008. Relevant monthly budget data for the first 2 months of 2008 are as follows.

Collections from customers: January $85,000, February $150,000.

Payments for direct materials: January $50,000, February $70,000.

Direct labor: January $30,000, February $45,000. Wages are paid in the month they are incurred.

Manufacturing overhead: January $21,000, February $25,000. These costs include depreciation of $1,000 per month. All other overhead costs are paid as incurred.

Selling and administrative expenses: January $15,000, February $20,000. These costs are exclusive of depreciation. They are paid as incurred.

Sales of marketable securities in January are expected to realize $10,000 in cash. Garza Company has a line of credit at a local bank that enables it to borrow up to $25,000. The company wants to maintain a minimum monthly cash balance of $20,000.

Instructions

Prepare a cash budget for January and February.

Prepare a cash budget.
(SO 5)

E23-13 Pink Martini Corporation is projecting a cash balance of $31,000 in its December 31, 2007, balance sheet. Pink Martini's schedule of expected collections from customers for the first quarter of 2008 shows total collections of $180,000. The schedule of expected payments for direct materials for the first quarter of 2008 shows total payments of $41,000. Other information gathered for the first quarter of 2008 is: sale of equipment $3,500; direct labor $70,000, manufacturing overhead $35,000, selling and administrative expenses $45,000; and purchase of securities $12,000. Pink Martini wants to maintain a balance of at least $25,000 cash at the end of each quarter.

Instructions

Prepare a cash budget for the first quarter.

Prepare schedules of expected collections and payments.
(SO 5)

E23-14 NIU Company's budgeted sales and direct materials purchases are as follows.

	Budgeted Sales	Budgeted D.M. Purchases
January	$200,000	$30,000
February	220,000	35,000
March	270,000	41,000

NIU's sales are 40% cash and 60% credit. Credit sales are collected 10% in the month of sale, 50% in the month following sale, and 36% in the second month following sale; 4% are uncollectible. NIU's purchases are 50% cash and 50% on account. Purchases on account are paid 40% in the month of purchase, and 60% in the month following purchase.

Instructions

(a) Prepare a schedule of expected collections from customers for March.
(b) Prepare a schedule of expected payments for direct materials for March.

E23-15 Environmental Landscaping Inc. is preparing its budget for the first quarter of 2008. The next step in the budgeting process is to prepare a cash receipts schedule and a cash payments schedule. To that end the following information has been collected.

Prepare schedules for cash receipts and cash payments, and determine ending balances for balance sheet.

(SO 5, 6)

Clients usually pay 60% of their fee in the month that service is provided, 30% the month after, and 10% the second month after receiving service.

Actual service revenue for 2007 and expected service revenues for 2008 are: November 2007, $90,000; December 2007, $80,000; January 2008, $100,000; February 2008, $120,000; March 2008, $130,000.

Purchases on landscaping supplies (direct materials) are paid 40% in the month of purchase and 60% the following month. Actual purchases for 2007 and expected purchases for 2008 are: December 2007, $14,000; January 2008, $12,000; February 2008, $15,000; March 2008, $18,000.

Instructions

(a) Prepare the following schedules for each month in the first quarter of 2008 and for the quarter in total:
(1) Expected collections from clients.
(2) Expected payments for landscaping supplies.

(b) Determine the following balances at March 31, 2008:
(1) Accounts receivable.
(2) Accounts payable.

E23-16 Donnegal Dental Clinic is a medium-sized dental service specializing in family dental care. The clinic is currently preparing the master budget for the first 2 quarters of 2008. All that remains in this process is the cash budget. The following information has been collected from other portions of the master budget and elsewhere.

Prepare a cash budget for two quarters.

(SO 5, 6)

Beginning cash balance	$ 30,000
Required minimum cash balance	25,000
Payment of income taxes (2nd quarter)	4,000
Professional salaries:	
1st quarter	140,000
2nd quarter	140,000
Interest from investments (2nd quarter)	5,000
Overhead costs:	
1st quarter	75,000
2nd quarter	100,000
Selling and administrative costs, including $3,000 depreciation:	
1st quarter	50,000
2nd quarter	70,000
Purchase of equipment (2nd quarter)	50,000
Sale of equipment (1st quarter)	15,000
Collections from clients:	
1st quarter	230,000
2nd quarter	380,000
Interest payments (2nd quarter)	300

Instructions

Prepare a cash budget for each of the first two quarters of 2008.

E23-17 In May 2008, the budget committee of Dalby Stores assembles the following data in preparation of budgeted merchandise purchases for the month of June.

Prepare a purchases budget and budgeted income statement for a merchandiser.

(SO 6)

1. Expected sales: June $500,000, July $600,000.
2. Cost of goods sold is expected to be 70% of sales.
3. Desired ending merchandise inventory is 40% of the following (next) month's cost of goods sold.
4. The beginning inventory at June 1 will be the desired amount.

Instructions

(a) Compute the budgeted merchandise purchases for June.
(b) Prepare the budgeted income statement for June through gross profit.

EXERCISES: SET B

Visit the book's website at **www.wiley.com/college/weygandt**, and choose the Student Companion site, to access Exercise Set B.

PROBLEMS: SET A

Prepare budgeted income statement and supporting budgets.

(SO 3, 4)

P23-1A Danner Farm Supply Company manufactures and sells a pesticide called Snare. The following data are available for preparing budgets for Snare for the first 2 quarters of 2009.

1. Sales: Quarter 1, 28,000 bags; quarter 2, 42,000 bags. Selling price is $60 per bag.
2. Direct materials: Each bag of Snare requires 4 pounds of Gumm at a cost of $4 per pound and 6 pounds of Tarr at $1.50 per pound.
3. Desired inventory levels:

Type of Inventory	January 1	April 1	July 1
Snare (bags)	8,000	12,000	18,000
Gumm (pounds)	9,000	10,000	13,000
Tarr (pounds)	14,000	20,000	25,000

4. Direct labor: Direct labor time is 15 minutes per bag at an hourly rate of $14 per hour.
5. Selling and administrative expenses are expected to be 15% of sales plus $175,000 per quarter.
6. Income taxes are expected to be 30% of income from operations.

Your assistant has prepared two budgets: (1) The manufacturing overhead budget shows expected costs to be 150% of direct labor cost. (2) The direct materials budget for Tarr shows the cost of Tarr purchases to be $297,000 in quarter 1 and $421,500 in quarter 2.

Instructions

Net income $600,250
Cost per bag $33.75

Prepare the budgeted income statement for the first 6 months and all required supporting budgets by quarters. (*Note*: Use variable and fixed in the selling and administrative expense budget). Do not prepare the manufacturing overhead budget or the direct materials budget for Tarr.

Prepare sales, production, direct materials, direct labor, and income statement budgets.

(SO 3, 4)

P23-2A Larussa Inc. is preparing its annual budgets for the year ending December 31, 2009. Accounting assistants furnish the data shown below.

	Product JB 50	Product JB 60
Sales budget:		
Anticipated volume in units	400,000	200,000
Unit selling price	$20	$25
Production budget:		
Desired ending finished goods units	25,000	15,000
Beginning finished goods units	30,000	10,000
Direct materials budget:		
Direct materials per unit (pounds)	2	3
Desired ending direct materials pounds	30,000	15,000
Beginning direct materials pounds	40,000	10,000
Cost per pound	$3	$4
Direct labor budget:		
Direct labor time per unit	0.4	0.6
Direct labor rate per hour	$12	$12
Budgeted income statement:		
Total unit cost	$12	$21

An accounting assistant has prepared the detailed manufacturing overhead budget and the selling and administrative expense budget. The latter shows selling expenses of $660,000 for product JB 50 and $360,000 for product JB 60, and administrative expenses of $540,000 for product JB 50 and $340,000 for product JB 60. Income taxes are expected to be 30%.

Instructions

Prepare the following budgets for the year. Show data for each product. Quarterly budgets should not be prepared.

(a) Sales
(b) Production
(c) Direct materials
(d) Direct labor
(e) Income statement (*Note*: Income taxes are not allocated to the products.)

(a) Total sales $13,000,000
(b) Required production units: JB 50, 395,000 JB 60, 205,000
(c) Total cost of direct materials purchases $4,820,000
(d) Total direct labor cost $3,372,000
(e) Net income $1,470,000

P23-3A Colt Industries had sales in 2008 of $6,400,000 and gross profit of $1,100,000. Management is considering two alternative budget plans to increase its gross profit in 2009.

Prepare sales and production budgets and compute cost per unit under two plans.

(SO 3, 4)

Plan A would increase the selling price per unit from $8.00 to $8.40. Sales volume would decrease by 5% from its 2008 level. Plan B would decrease the selling price per unit by $0.50. The marketing department expects that the sales volume would increase by 150,000 units.

At the end of 2008, Colt has 40,000 units of inventory on hand. If Plan A is accepted, the 2009 ending inventory should be equal to 5% of the 2009 sales. If Plan B is accepted, the ending inventory should be equal to 50,000 units. Each unit produced will cost $1.80 in direct labor, $2.00 in direct materials, and $1.20 in variable overhead. The fixed overhead for 2009 should be $1,895,000.

Instructions

(a) Prepare a sales budget for 2009 under each plan.
(b) Prepare a production budget for 2009 under each plan.
(c) Compute the production cost per unit under each plan. Why is the cost per unit different for each of the two plans? (Round to two decimals.)
(d) Which plan should be accepted? (*Hint*: Compute the gross profit under each plan.)

(c) Unit cost: Plan A $7.50 Plan B $6.97
(d) Gross profit: Plan A $684,000 Plan B $503,500

P23-4A Haas Company prepares monthly cash budgets. Relevant data from operating budgets for 2009 are:

Prepare cash budget for 2 months.

(SO 5)

	January	February
Sales	$350,000	$400,000
Direct materials purchases	110,000	130,000
Direct labor	90,000	100,000
Manufacturing overhead	70,000	75,000
Selling and administrative expenses	79,000	86,000

All sales are on account. Collections are expected to be 50% in the month of sale, 30% in the first month following the sale, and 20% in the second month following the sale. Sixty percent (60%) of direct materials purchases are paid in cash in the month of purchase, and the balance due is paid in the month following the purchase. All other items above are paid in the month incurred except for selling and administrative expenses that include $1,000 of depreciation per month.

Other data:

1. Credit sales: November 2008, $260,000; December 2008, $320,000.
2. Purchases of direct materials: December 2008, $100,000.
3. Other receipts: January—Collection of December 31, 2008, notes receivable $15,000; February—Proceeds from sale of securities $6,000.
4. Other disbursements: February—Withdrawal of $5,000 cash for personal use of owner, Dewey Yaeger.

The company's cash balance on January 1, 2009, is expected to be $60,000. The company wants to maintain a minimum cash balance of $50,000.

Instructions

(a) Prepare schedules for (1) expected collections from customers and (2) expected payments for direct materials purchases.
(b) Prepare a cash budget for January and February in columnar form.

(a) January: collections $323,000 payments $106,000
(b) Ending cash balance: January $54,000 February $50,000

P23-5A The budget committee of Deleon Company collects the following data for its San Miguel Store in preparing budgeted income statements for May and June 2009.

Prepare purchases and income statement budgets for a merchandiser.

(SO 6)

1. Sales for May are expected to be $800,000. Sales in June and July are expected to be 10% higher than the preceding month.
2. Cost of goods sold is expected to be 75% of sales.
3. Company policy is to maintain ending merchandise inventory at 20% of the following month's cost of goods sold.

4. Operating expenses are estimated to be:

Sales salaries	$30,000 per month
Advertising	5% of monthly sales
Delivery expense	3% of monthly sales
Sales commissions	4% of monthly sales
Rent expense	$5,000 per month
Depreciation	$800 per month
Utilities	$600 per month
Insurance	$500 per month

(a) Purchases:
May $612,000
June $673,200
(b) Net income:
May $46,970
June $54,250

5. Income taxes are estimated to be 30% of income from operations.

Instructions

(a) Prepare the merchandise purchases budget for each month in columnar form.

(b) Prepare budgeted income statements for each month in columnar form. Show in the statements the details of cost of goods sold.

Prepare budgeted income statement and balance sheet.

(SO 4, 5)

P23-6A Glendo Industries' balance sheet at December 31, 2008, is presented below.

GLENDO INDUSTRIES
Balance Sheet
December 31, 2008

Assets

Current assets		
Cash		$ 7,500
Accounts receivable		82,500
Finished goods inventory (2,000 units)		30,000
Total current assets		120,000
Property, plant, and equipment		
Equipment	$40,000	
Less: Accumulated depreciation	10,000	30,000
Total assets		$150,000

Liabilities and Stockholders' Equity

Liabilities		
Notes payable		$ 25,000
Accounts payable		45,000
Total liabilities		70,000
Stockholders' equity		
Common stock	$50,000	
Retained earnings	30,000	
Total stockholders' equity		80,000
Total liabilities and stockholders' equity		$150,000

Additional information accumulated for the budgeting process is as follows.

Budgeted data for the year 2009 include the following.

	4th Qtr. of 2009	Year 2009 Total
Sales budget (8,000 units at $35)	$84,000	$280,000
Direct materials used	17,000	69,400
Direct labor	12,500	56,600
Manufacturing overhead applied	10,000	54,000
Selling and administrative expenses	18,000	76,000

To meet sales requirements and to have 3,000 units of finished goods on hand at December 31, 2009, the production budget shows 9,000 required units of output. The total unit cost of production is expected to be \$20. Glendo Industries uses the first-in, first-out (FIFO) inventory costing method. Selling and administrative expenses include \$4,000 for depreciation on equipment. Interest expense is expected to be \$3,500 for the year. Income taxes are expected to be 30% of income before income taxes.

All sales and purchases are on account. It is expected that 60% of quarterly sales are collected in cash within the quarter and the remainder is collected in the following quarter. Direct materials purchased from suppliers are paid 50% in the quarter incurred and the remainder in the following quarter. Purchases in the fourth quarter were the same as the materials used. In 2009, the company expects to purchase additional equipment costing \$19,000. It expects to pay \$8,000 on notes payable plus all interest due and payable to December 31 (included in interest expense \$3,500, above). Accounts payable at December 31, 2009, includes amounts due suppliers (see above) plus other accounts payable of \$5,700. In 2009, the company expects to declare and pay a \$5,000 cash dividend. Unpaid income taxes at December 31 will be \$5,000. The company's cash budget shows an expected cash balance of \$7,950 at December 31, 2009.

Instructions

Prepare a budgeted income statement for 2009 and a budgeted balance sheet at December 31, 2009. In preparing the income statement, you will need to compute cost of goods manufactured (direct materials + direct labor + manufacturing overhead) and finished goods inventory (December 31, 2009).

Net income \$35,350
Total assets \$146,550

PROBLEMS: SET B

Prepare budgeted income statement and supporting budgets.
(SO 3, 4)

P23-1B Krause Farm Supply Company manufactures and sells a fertilizer called Basic II. The following data are available for preparing budgets for Basic II for the first 2 quarters of 2008.

1. Sales: Quarter 1, 40,000 bags; quarter 2, 60,000 bags. Selling price is \$60 per bag.
2. Direct materials: Each bag of Basic II requires 6 pounds of Crup at a cost of \$4 per pound and 10 pounds of Dert at \$1.50 per pound.
3. Desired inventory levels:

Type of Inventory	January 1	April 1	July 1
Basic II (bags)	10,000	15,000	20,000
Crup (pounds)	9,000	12,000	15,000
Dert (pounds)	15,000	20,000	25,000

4. Direct labor: Direct labor time is 15 minutes per bag at an hourly rate of \$12 per hour.
5. Selling and administrative expenses are expected to be 10% of sales plus \$150,000 per quarter.
6. Income taxes are expected to be 30% of income from operations.

Your assistant has prepared two budgets: (1) The manufacturing overhead budget shows expected costs to be 100% of direct labor cost. (2) The direct materials budget for Dert which shows the cost of Dert purchases to be \$682,500 in quarter 1 and \$907,500 in quarter 2.

Instructions

Prepare the budgeted income statement for the first 6 months of 2008 and all required supporting budgets by quarters. (*Note*: Use variable and fixed in the selling and administrative expense budget.) Do not prepare the manufacturing overhead budget or the direct materials budget for Dert.

Net income \$420,000
Cost per bag \$45.00

Prepare sales, production, direct materials, direct labor, and income statement budgets.
(SO 3, 4)

P23-2B Mercer Inc. is preparing its annual budgets for the year ending December 31, 2008. Accounting assistants furnish the following data.

	Product LN 35	Product LN 40
Sales budget:		
Anticipated volume in units	300,000	180,000
Unit selling price	\$20	\$30
Production budget:		
Desired ending finished goods units	30,000	25,000
Beginning finished goods units	20,000	15,000

Table continues on next page

	Product LN 35	Product LN 40
Direct materials budget:		
Direct materials per unit (pounds)	2	3
Desired ending direct materials pounds	50,000	20,000
Beginning direct materials pounds	40,000	10,000
Cost per pound	$2	$3
Direct labor budget:		
Direct labor time per unit	0.5	0.75
Direct labor rate per hour	$12	$12
Budgeted income statement:		
Total unit cost	$11	$20

An accounting assistant has prepared the detailed manufacturing overhead budget and the selling and administrative expense budget. The latter shows selling expenses of $560,000 for product LN 35 and $440,000 for product LN 40, and administrative expenses of $420,000 for product LN 35 and $380,000 for product LN 40. Income taxes are expected to be 30%.

(a) Total sales $11,400,000
(b) Required production units: LN 35, 310,000
(c) Total cost of direct materials purchases $3,000,000
(d) Total direct labor cost $3,570,000
(e) Net income $1,890,000

Instructions

Prepare the following budgets for the year. Show data for each product. Quarterly budgets should not be prepared.

(a) Sales
(b) Production
(c) Direct materials
(d) Direct labor
(e) Income statement (*Note*: Income taxes are not allocated to the products.)

Prepare sales and production budgets and compute cost per unit under two plans.

(SO 3, 4)

P23-3B Litwin Industries has sales in 2008 of $4,900,000 (700,000 units) and gross profit of $1,187,500. Management is considering two alternative budget plans to increase its gross profit in 2009.

Plan A would increase the selling price per unit from $7.00 to $7.60. Sales volume would decrease by 10% from its 2008 level. Plan B would decrease the selling price per unit by 5%. The marketing department expects that the sales volume would increase by 100,000 units.

At the end of 2008, Litwin has 70,000 units on hand. If Plan A is accepted, the 2009 ending inventory should be equal to 90,000 units. If Plan B is accepted, the ending inventory should be equal to 100,000 units. Each unit produced will cost $2.00 in direct materials, $1.50 in direct labor, and $0.50 in variable overhead. The fixed overhead for 2009 should be $975,000.

(c) Unit cost: Plan A $5.50, Plan B $5.17
(d) Gross profit: Plan A $1,323,000 Plan B $1,184,000

Instructions

(a) Prepare a sales budget for 2009 under (1) Plan A and (2) Plan B.
(b) Prepare a production budget for 2009 under (1) Plan A and (2) Plan B.
(c) Compute the cost per unit under (1) Plan A and (2) Plan B. Explain why the cost per unit is different for each of the two plans. (Round to two decimals.)
(d) Which plan should be accepted? (*Hint*: Compute the gross profit under each plan.)

Prepare cash budget for 2 months.

(SO 5)

P23-4B Orton Company prepares monthly cash budgets. Relevant data from operating budgets for 2009 are:

	January	February
Sales	$320,000	$400,000
Direct materials purchases	80,000	110,000
Direct labor	85,000	115,000
Manufacturing overhead	60,000	75,000
Selling and administrative expenses	75,000	80,000

All sales are on account. Collections are expected to be 60% in the month of sale, 30% in the first month following the sale, and 10% in the second month following the sale. Thirty percent (30%) of direct materials purchases are paid in cash in the month of purchase, and the balance due is paid in the month following the purchase. All other items above are paid in the month incurred. Depreciation has been excluded from manufacturing overhead and selling and administrative expenses.

Other data:

1. Credit sales: November 2008, $200,000; December 2008, $280,000.
2. Purchases of direct materials: December 2008, $90,000.
3. Other receipts: January—Collection of December 31, 2008, interest receivable $3,000;
   February—Proceeds from sale of securities $5,000.
4. Other disbursements: February—payment of $20,000 for land.

The company's cash balance on January 1, 2009, is expected to be $60,000. The company wants to maintain a minimum cash balance of $50,000.

Instructions

(a) Prepare schedules for (1) expected collections from customers and (2) expected payments for direct materials purchases.

(b) Prepare a cash budget for January and February in columnar form.

(a) January: collections $296,000 payments $87,000
(b) Ending cash balance: January $52,000 February $50,000

P23-5B The budget committee of Urbina Company collects the following data for its Westwood Store in preparing budgeted income statements for July and August 2008.

Prepare purchases and income statement budgets for a merchandiser.

(SO 6)

1. Expected sales: July $400,000, August $450,000, September $500,000.
2. Cost of goods sold is expected to be 64% of sales.
3. Company policy is to maintain ending merchandise inventory at 25% of the following month's cost of goods sold.
4. Operating expenses are estimated to be:

Sales salaries	$40,000 per month
Advertising	4% of monthly sales
Delivery expense	2% of monthly sales
Sales commissions	3% of monthly sales
Rent expense	$3,000 per month
Depreciation	$700 per month
Utilities	$500 per month
Insurance	$300 per month

5. Income taxes are estimated to be 30% of income from operations.

Instructions

(a) Prepare the merchandise purchases budget for each month in columnar form.

(b) Prepare budgeted income statements for each month in columnar form. Show the details of cost of goods sold in the statements.

(a) Purchases: July $264,000 August $296,000
(b) Net income: July $44,450 August $53,900

PROBLEMS: SET C

Visit the book's website at **www.wiley.com/college/weygandt**, and choose the Student Companion site, to access Problem Set C.

BROADENING YOUR PERSPECTIVE

DECISION MAKING ACROSS THE ORGANIZATION

BYP23-1 Lanier Corporation operates on a calendar-year basis. It begins the annual budgeting process in late August when the president establishes targets for the total dollar sales and net income before taxes for the next year.

The sales target is given first to the marketing department. The marketing manager formulates a sales budget by product line in both units and dollars. From this budget, sales quotas by product line in units and dollars are established for each of the corporation's sales districts. The marketing manager also estimates the cost of the marketing activities required to support the target sales volume and prepares a tentative marketing expense budget.

The executive vice president uses the sales and profit targets, the sales budget by product line, and the tentative marketing expense budget to determine the dollar amounts that can be devoted to manufacturing and corporate office expense. The executive vice president prepares the budget for corporate expenses. She then forwards to the production department the product-line sales budget in units and the total dollar amount that can be devoted to manufacturing.

The production manager meets with the factory managers to develop a manufacturing plan that will produce the required units when needed within the cost constraints set by the executive vice president. The budgeting process usually comes to a halt at this point because the production department does not consider the financial resources allocated to be adequate.

When this standstill occurs, the vice president of finance, the executive vice president, the marketing manager, and the production manager meet together to determine the final budgets for each of the areas. This normally results in a modest increase in the total amount available for manufacturing costs and cuts in the marketing expense and corporate office expense budgets. The total sales and net income figures proposed by the president are seldom changed. Although the participants are seldom pleased with the compromise, these budgets are final. Each executive then develops a new detailed budget for the operations in his or her area.

None of the areas has achieved its budget in recent years. Sales often run below the target. When budgeted sales are not achieved, each area is expected to cut costs so that the president's profit target can be met. However, the profit target is seldom met because costs are not cut enough. In fact, costs often run above the original budget in all functional areas (marketing, production, and corporate office).

The president is disturbed that Lanier has not been able to meet the sales and profit targets. He hired a consultant with considerable experience with companies in Lanier's industry. The consultant reviewed the budgets for the past 4 years. He concluded that the product line sales budgets were reasonable and that the cost and expense budgets were adequate for the budgeted sales and production levels.

Instructions

With the class divided into groups, answer the following.

(a) Discuss how the budgeting process employed by Lanier Corporation contributes to the failure to achieve the president's sales and profit targets.

(b) Suggest how Lanier Corporation's budgeting process could be revised to correct the problems.

(c) Should the functional areas be expected to cut their costs when sales volume falls below budget? Explain your answer. (CMA adapted.)

MANAGERIAL ANALYSIS

BYP23-2 Bedner & Flott Inc. manufactures ergonomic devices for computer users. Some of their more popular products include glare screens (for computer monitors), keyboard stands with wrist rests, and carousels that allow easy access to magnetic disks. Over the past 5 years, they experienced rapid growth, with sales of all products increasing 20% to 50% each year.

Last year, some of the primary manufacturers of computers began introducing new products with some of the ergonomic designs, such as glare screens and wrist rests, already built in. As a result, sales of Bedner & Flott's accessory devices have declined somewhat. The company believes that the disk carousels will probably continue to show growth, but that the other products will probably continue to decline. When the next year's budget was prepared, increases were built in to research and development so that replacement products could be developed or the company could expand into some other product line. Some product lines being considered are general-purpose ergonomic devices including back supports, foot rests, and sloped writing pads.

The most recent results have shown that sales decreased more than was expected for the glare screens. As a result, the company may have a shortage of funds. Top management has therefore asked that all expenses be reduced 10% to compensate for these reduced sales. Summary budget information is as follows.

Direct materials	$240,000
Direct labor	110,000
Insurance	50,000
Depreciation	90,000
Machine repairs	30,000
Sales salaries	50,000
Office salaries	80,000
Factory salaries (indirect labor)	50,000
Total	$700,000

Instructions

Using the information above, answer the following questions.

(a) What are the implications of reducing each of the costs? For example, if the company reduces direct materials costs, it may have to do so by purchasing lower-quality materials. This may affect sales in the long run.

(b) Based on your analysis in (a), what do you think is the best way to obtain the $70,000 in cost savings requested? Be specific. Are there any costs that cannot or should not be reduced? Why?

REAL-WORLD FOCUS

BYP23-3 Network Computing Devices Inc. was founded in 1988 in Mountain View, California. The company develops software products such as X-terminals, Z-mail, PC X-ware, and related hardware products. Presented below is a discussion by management in its annual report.

NETWORK COMPUTING DEVICES, INC.
Management Discussion

The Company's operating results have varied significantly, particularly on a quarterly basis, as a result of a number of factors, including general economic conditions affecting industry demand for computer products, the timing and market acceptance of new product introductions by the Company and its competitors, the timing of significant orders from large customers, periodic changes in product pricing and discounting due to competitive factors, and the availability of key components, such as video monitors and electronic subassemblies, some of which require substantial order lead times. The Company's operating results may fluctuate in the future as a result of these and other factors, including the Company's success in developing and introducing new products, its product and customer mix, and the level of competition which it experiences. The Company operates with a small backlog. Sales and operating results, therefore, generally depend on the volume and timing of orders received, which are difficult to forecast. The Company has experienced slowness in orders from some customers during the first quarter of each calendar year due to budgeting cycles common in the computer industry. In addition, sales in Europe typically are adversely affected in the third calendar quarter as many European customers reduce their business activities during the month of August.

Due to the Company's rapid growth rate and the effect of new product introductions on quarterly revenues, these seasonal trends have not materially impacted the Company's results of operations to date. However, as the Company's product lines mature and its rate of revenue growth declines, these seasonal factors may become more evident. Additionally, the Company's international sales are denominated in U.S. dollars, and an increase or decrease in the value of the U.S. dollar relative to foreign currencies could make the Company's products less or more competitive in those markets.

Instructions

(a) Identify the factors that affect the budgeting process at Network Computing Devices, Inc.

(b) Explain the additional budgeting concerns created by the international operations of the company.

COMMUNICATION ACTIVITY

BYP23-4 In order to better serve their rural patients, Drs. Dan and Jack Fleming (brothers) began giving safety seminars. Especially popular were their "emergency-preparedness" talks given to farmers. Many people asked whether the "kit" of materials the doctors recommended for common farm emergencies was commercially available.

After checking with several suppliers, the doctors realized that no other company offered the supplies they recommended in their seminars, packaged in the way they described. Their wives, Julie and Amy, agreed to make a test package by ordering supplies from various medical supply companies and assembling them into a "kit" that could be sold at the seminars. When these kits proved a runaway success, the sisters-in-law decided to market them. At the advice of their accountant, they organized this venture as a separate company, called Life Protection Products (LPP), with Julie Fleming as CEO and Amy Fleming as Secretary-Treasurer.

LPP soon started receiving requests for the kits from all over the country, as word spread about their availability. Even without advertising, LPP was able to sell its full inventory every month. However, the company was becoming financially strained. Julie and Amy had about $100,000 in savings, and they invested about half that amount initially. They believed that this venture would allow them to make money. However, at the present time, only about $30,000 of the cash remains, and the company is constantly short of cash.

Julie has come to you for advice. She does not understand why the company is having cash flow problems. She and Amy have not even been withdrawing salaries. However, they have rented a local building and have hired two more full-time workers to help them cope with the increasing demand. They do not think they could handle the demand without this additional help.

Julie is also worried that the cash problems mean that the company may not be able to support itself. She has prepared the cash budget shown below. All seminar customers pay for their products in full at the time of purchase. In addition, several large companies have ordered the kits for use by employees who work in remote sites. They have requested credit terms and have been allowed to pay in the month following the sale. These large purchasers amount to about 25% of the sales at the present time. LPP purchases the materials for the kits about 2 months ahead of time. Julie and Amy are considering slowing the growth of the company by simply purchasing less materials, which will mean selling fewer kits.

The workers are paid in cash weekly. Julie and Amy need about $15,000 cash on hand at the beginning of the month to pay for purchases of raw materials. Right now they have been using cash from their savings, but as noted, only $30,000 is left.

Instructions

Write a response to Julie Fleming. Explain why LPP is short of cash. Will this company be able to support itself? Explain your answer. Make any recommendations you deem appropriate.

LIFE PROTECTION PRODUCTS
Cash Budget
For the Quarter Ending June 30, 2009

	April	May	June
Cash balance, beginning	$15,000	$15,000	$15,000
Cash received			
From prior month sales	5,000	7,500	12,500
From current sales	15,000	22,500	37,500
Total cash on hand	35,000	45,000	65,000
Cash payments			
To employees	3,000	3,000	3,000
For products	25,000	35,000	45,000
Miscellaneous expenses	5,000	6,000	7,000
Postage	1,000	1,000	1,000
Total cash payments	34,000	45,000	56,000
Cash balance	$ 1,000	$ 0	$ 9,000
Borrow from savings	$14,000	$15,000	$ 1,000
Borrow from bank?	$ 0	$ 0	$ 5,000

ETHICS CASE

BYP23-5 You are an accountant in the budgetary, projections, and special projects department of American Conductor, Inc., a large manufacturing company. The president, William Brown, asks you on very short notice to prepare some sales and income projections covering the next 2 years of the company's much heralded new product lines. He wants these projections for a series of speeches he is making while on a 2-week trip to eight East Coast brokerage firms. The president hopes to bolster American's stock sales and price.

You work 23 hours in 2 days to compile the projections, hand deliver them to the president, and are swiftly but graciously thanked as he departs. A week later you find time to go over some of your computations and discover a miscalculation that makes the projections grossly overstated. You quickly inquire about the president's itinerary and learn that he has made half of his speeches and has half yet to make. You are in a quandary as to what to do.

Instructions

(a) What are the consequences of telling the president of your gross miscalculations?
(b) What are the consequences of *not* telling the president of your gross miscalculations?
(c) What are the ethical considerations to you and the president in this situation?

"ALL ABOUT YOU" ACTIVITY

BYP23-6 The ***All About You:*** **Avoiding Personal Financial Disaster** feature in this chapter emphasizes that in order to get your personal finances under control, you need to prepare a personal budget. Assume that you have compiled the following information regarding your expected cash flows for a typical month.

Rent payment	$ 400	Miscellaneous costs	$110
Interest income	50	Savings	50
Income tax withheld	300	Eating out	150
Electricity bill	22	Telephone and Internet costs	90
Groceries	80	Student loan payments	275
Wages received (net)	2,000	Entertainment costs	250
Insurance	100	Transportation costs	150

Instructions

Using the information above, prepare a personal budget. In preparing this budget, use the format found at **http://financialplan.about.com/cs/budgeting/l/blbudget.htm**. Just skip any unused line items.

Answers to Insight and Accounting Across the Organization Questions

p. 1002 Business Often Feel Too Busy to Plan for the Future

Q: Describe a situation in which a business "sells as much as it can" but cannot "keep its employees paid."

A: *If sales are made to customers on credit and collection is slow, the company may find that it does not have enough cash to pay employees or suppliers. Without these resources, the company will fail to survive.*

p. 1004 Which Budget Approach Do You Prefer?

Q: What approach did Time Warner use to prepare the old budget? What approach did it use to prepare the new budget?

A: *Time Warner used a "top-down" approach to prepare the old budget since its goals were determined by top management. It used a participative approach to prepare the new budget since each operating unit set goals.*

p. 1014 Growth and Cash Flow Often Do Not Occur Together

Q: How can fast growth make cash flow problems worse?

A: *Fast growth in sales demands large amounts of purchases and higher payroll costs. Suppliers and employees expect to be paid even though collections from sales on account may not have taken place.*

Authors' Comments on All About You: Avoiding Personal Financial Disaster (p. 1019)

We are concerned that the personal budgets presented on websites and in financial planning textbooks often list student loans among the sources of income. This type of thinking can lead to an over-reliance on debt during college, and will result in accumulation of large amounts of debt that must be repaid. We would prefer a format that lists non-debt sources of income, then subtracts expenses, then shows debt borrowed. This format emphasizes an important point: Just like a business, in the short run you can borrow money when your cash inflows are not sufficient to meet your outflows, but in the long run you need to learn to live within your income, and your budget.

Answers to Self-Study Questions

1. c **2.** a **3.** b **4.** b **5.** d **6.** d **7.** a **8.** c **9.** c **10.** d

Remember to go back to the Navigator box on the chapter-opening page and check off your completed work.

Chapter 24

Budgetary Control and Responsibility Accounting

STUDY OBJECTIVES

After studying this chapter, you should be able to:

1 Describe the concept of budgetary control.

2 Evaluate the usefulness of static budget reports.

3 Explain the development of flexible budgets and the usefulness of flexible budget reports.

4 Describe the concept of responsibility accounting.

5 Indicate the features of responsibility reports for cost centers.

6 Identify the content of responsibility reports for profit centers.

7 Explain the basis and formula used in evaluating performance in investment centers.

The Navigator

The Navigator

Scan **Study Objectives**	■
Read **Feature Story**	■
Read **Preview**	■
Read text and answer **Before You Go On** p. 1050 ■ p. 1058 ■ p. 1062 ■	
Work **Demonstration Problem**	■
Review **Summary of Study Objectives**	■
Answer **Self-Study Questions**	■
Complete **Assignments**	■

Feature Story

TRYING TO AVOID AN ELECTRIC SHOCK

Budgets are critical to evaluating an organization's success. They are based on management's expectations of what is most likely to happen in the future. In order to be useful, they must be accurate. But what if management's expectations are wrong? Estimates are never exactly correct, and

sometimes, especially in volatile industries, estimates can be "off by a mile."

In recent years the electric utility industry has become very volatile. Deregulation, volatile prices for natural gas, coal, and oil, changes in environmental regulations, and economic swings have all contributed to large changes in the profitability of electric utility companies. This means that for planning and budgeting purposes, utilities must plan and budget based on multiple "what if" scenarios that take into account factors beyond management's control. For example, in recent years, Duke Energy Corporation (*www.duke-energy.com*), headquartered in Charlotte, North Carolina, built budgeting and planning models based on three different scenarios of what the future might hold. One scenario assumes that the U.S. economy will slow considerably. A second scenario assumes that the company will experience "pricing pressure" as the market for energy becomes more efficient as a result of more energy being traded in Internet auctions. A third scenario assumes a continuation of the current environment of rapid growth, changing regulation, and large swings in the prices for the fuels the company uses to create energy.

Compounding this budgeting challenge is the fact that changes in many indirect costs can also significantly affect the company. For example, even a tiny change in market interest rates has a huge effect on the company because it has massive amounts of outstanding debt. And finally, as a result of the California energy crisis, there is mounting pressure for government intervention and regulation. This pressure has resulted in setting "rate caps" that limit the amount that utilities and energy companies can charge, thus lowering profits. The bottom line is that for budgeting and planning purposes, utility companies must remain alert and flexible.

✓ The Navigator

Inside Chapter 24...

Preview of Chapter 24

In contrast to Chapter 23, we now consider how budgets are used by management to control operations. In the Feature Story on Duke Energy, we saw that budgeting must take into account factors beyond management's control. This chapter focuses on two aspects of management control: (1) budgetary control and (2) responsibility accounting.

The content and organization of Chapter 24 are as follows.

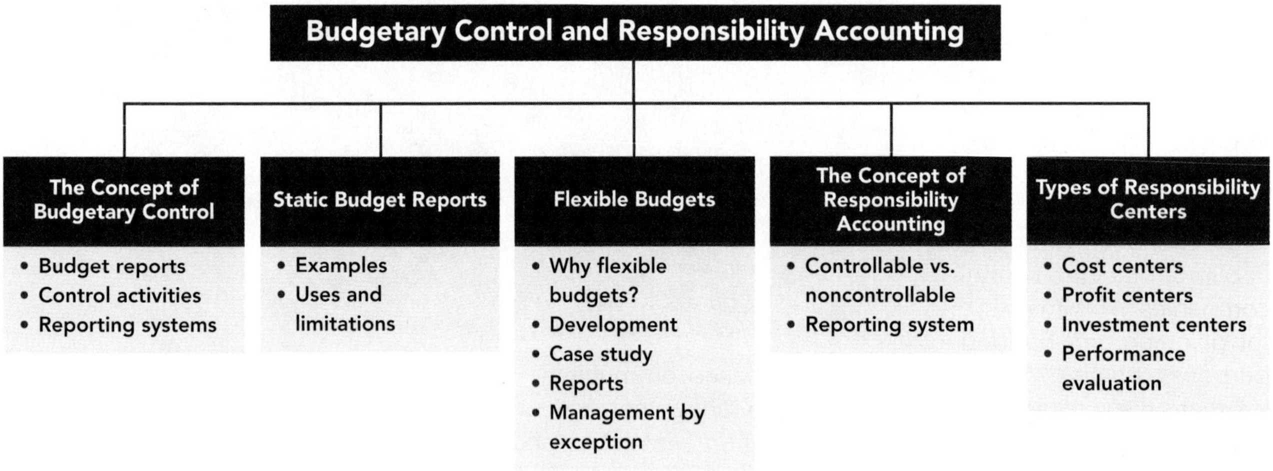

The Navigator

THE CONCEPT OF BUDGETARY CONTROL

STUDY OBJECTIVE 1

Describe the concept of budgetary control.

One of management's major functions is to control company operations. Control consists of the steps taken by management to see that planned objectives are met. We now ask: How do budgets contribute to control of operations?

The use of budgets in controlling operations is known as **budgetary control**. Such control takes place by means of **budget reports** that compare actual results with planned objectives. The use of budget reports is based on the belief that planned objectives lose much of their potential value without some monitoring of progress along the way. Just as your professors give midterm exams to evaluate your progress, so top management requires periodic reports on the progress of department managers toward their planned objectives.

Budget reports provide management with feedback on operations. The feedback for a crucial objective, such as having enough cash on hand to pay bills, may be made daily. For other objectives, such as meeting budgeted annual sales and operating expenses, monthly budget reports may suffice. Budget reports are prepared as frequently as needed. From these reports, management analyzes any differences between actual and planned results and determines their causes. Management then takes corrective action, or it decides to modify future plans.

Budgetary control involves activities shown in Illustration 24-1.

Illustration 24-1
Budgetary control activities

Budgetary control works best when a company has a formalized reporting system. The system does the following:

1. Identifies the name of the budget report, such as the sales budget or the manufacturing overhead budget.
2. States the frequency of the report, such as weekly or monthly.
3. Specifies the purpose of the report.
4. Indicates the primary recipient(s) of the report.

Illustration 24-2 provides a partial budgetary control system for a manufacturing company. Note the frequency of the reports and their emphasis on control. For example, there is a daily report on scrap and a weekly report on labor.

Illustration 24-2
Budgetary control reporting system

Name of Report	Frequency	Purpose	Primary Recipient(s)
Sales	Weekly	Determine whether sales goals are being met	Top management and sales manager
Labor	Weekly	Control direct and indirect labor costs	Vice president of production and production department managers
Scrap	Daily	Determine efficient use of materials	Production manager
Departmental overhead costs	Monthly	Control overhead costs	Department manager
Selling expenses	Monthly	Control selling expenses	Sales manager
Income statement	Monthly and quarterly	Determine whether income objectives are being met	Top management

STATIC BUDGET REPORTS

STUDY OBJECTIVE 2

Evaluate the usefulness of static budget reports.

You learned in Chapter 23 that the master budget formalizes management's planned objectives for the coming year. When used in budgetary control, each budget included in the master budget is considered to be static. A **static budget** is a projection of budget data **at one level of activity**. These budgets do not consider data for different levels of activity. As a result, companies always compare actual results with budget data at the activity level that was used in developing the master budget.

Examples

To illustrate the role of a static budget in budgetary control, we will use selected data prepared for Hayes Company in Chapter 23. Budget and actual sales data for the Kitchen-Mate product in the first and second quarters of 2008 are as follows.

Illustration 24-3
Budget and actual sales data

Sales	First Quarter	Second Quarter	Total
Budgeted	$180,000	$210,000	$390,000
Actual	179,000	199,500	378,500
Difference	$ 1,000	$ 10,500	$ 11,500

The sales budget report for Hayes Company's first quarter is shown below. The right-most column reports the difference between the budgeted and actual amounts.

Illustration 24-4
Sales budget report—first quarter

ALTERNATIVE TERMINOLOGY

The difference between budget and actual is sometimes called a *budget variance*.

HAYES COMPANY
Sales Budget Report
For the Quarter Ended March 31, 2008

Product Line	Budget	Actual	Difference Favorable F Unfavorable U
Kitchen-Mate[a]	$180,000	$179,000	**$1,000 U**

[a]In practice, each product line would be included in the report.

The report shows that sales are $1,000 under budget—an unfavorable result. This difference is less than 1% of budgeted sales ($1,000 ÷ $180,000 = .0056). Top management's reaction to unfavorable differences is often influenced by the materiality (significance) of the difference. Since the difference of $1,000 is immaterial in this case, we assume that Hayes Company management takes no specific corrective action.

Illustration 24-5 shows the budget report for the second quarter. It contains one new feature: cumulative year-to-date information. This report indicates that sales for the second quarter are $10,500 below budget. This is 5% of budgeted sales ($10,500 ÷ $210,000). Top management may now conclude that the difference between budgeted and actual sales requires investigation.

Illustration 24-5
Sales budget report—second quarter

HAYES COMPANY
Sales Budget Report
For the Quarter Ended June 30, 2008

	Second Quarter			Year-to-Date		
Product Line	Budget	Actual	Difference Favorable F Unfavorable U	Budget	Actual	Difference Favorable F Unfavorable U
Kitchen-Mate	$210,000	$199,500	**$10,500 U**	$390,000	$378,500	**$11,500 U**

Management's analysis should start by asking the sales manager the cause(s) of the shortfall. Managers should consider the need for corrective action. For example, management may decide to spur sales by offering sales incentives to customers or by increasing the advertising of Kitchen-Mates. Or, if management concludes that a downturn in the economy is responsible for the lower sales, it may modify planned sales and profit goals for the remainder of the year.

Uses and Limitations

From these examples, you can see that a master sales budget is useful in evaluating the performance of a sales manager. It is now necessary to ask: Is the master budget appropriate for evaluating a manager's performance in controlling costs? Recall that in a static budget, data are not modified or adjusted, regardless of changes in activity. It follows, then, that a static budget is appropriate in evaluating a manager's effectiveness in controlling costs when:

1. The actual level of activity closely approximates the master budget activity level, and/or
2. The behavior of the costs in response to changes in activity is fixed.

A static budget report is, therefore, appropriate for **fixed manufacturing costs** and for **fixed selling and administrative expenses**. But, as you will see shortly, static budget reports may not be a proper basis for evaluating a manager's performance in controlling variable costs.

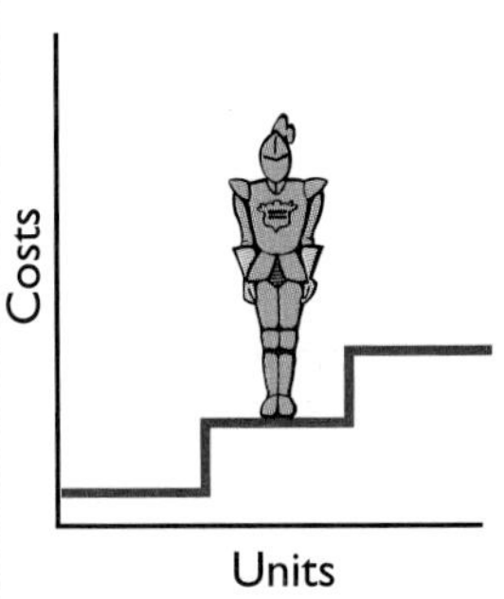

Static budgets report a single level of activity

FLEXIBLE BUDGETS

STUDY OBJECTIVE 3

Explain the development of flexible budgets and the usefulness of flexible budget reports.

In contrast to a static budget, which is based on one level of activity, a flexible budget projects budget data for various levels of activity. In essence, **the flexible budget is a series of static budgets at different levels of activity.** The flexible budget recognizes that the budgetary process is more useful if it is adaptable to changed operating conditions.

Flexible budgets can be prepared for each of the types of budgets included in the master budget. For example, Marriott Hotels can budget revenues and net income on the basis of 60%, 80%, and 100% of room occupancy. Similarly, American Van Lines can budget its operating expenses on the basis of various levels of truck miles driven. Likewise, in the Feature Story, Duke Energy can budget revenue and net income on the basis of estimated billions of kwh (kilowatt hours) of residential, commercial, and industrial electricity generated. In the following pages, we will illustrate a flexible budget for manufacturing overhead.

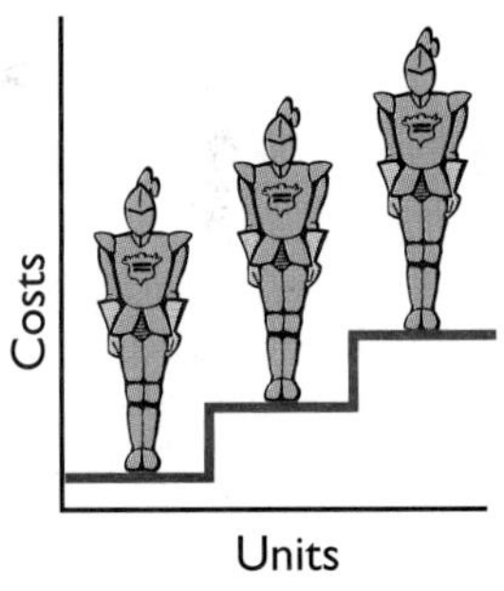

Flexible budgets are static budgets at different activity levels

Why Flexible Budgets?

Assume that you are the manager in charge of manufacturing overhead in the Forging Department of Barton Steel. In preparing the manufacturing overhead budget for 2008, you prepare the following static budget based on a production volume of 10,000 units of steel ingots.

Illustration 24-6
Static overhead budget

BARTON STEEL
Manufacturing Overhead Budget (Static)
Forging Department
For the Year Ended December 31, 2008

Budgeted production in units (steel ingots)	10,000
Budgeted costs	
Indirect materials	$ 250,000
Indirect labor	260,000
Utilities	190,000
Depreciation	280,000
Property taxes	70,000
Supervision	50,000
	$1,100,000

HELPFUL HINT

The static budget is the master budget described in Chapter 23.

Fortunately for the company, the demand for steel ingots has increased, and Barton produces and sells 12,000 units during the year, rather than 10,000. You are elated: Increased sales means increased profitability, which should mean a bonus or a raise for you and the employees in your department. Unfortunately, a comparison of Forging Department actual and budgeted costs has put you on the spot. The budget report is shown below.

Illustration 24-7
Static overhead budget report

Barton Steel.xls

BARTON STEEL
Manufacturing Overhead Budget Report (Static)
For the Year Ended December 31, 2008

	Budget	Actual	Difference Favorable - F Unfavorable - U	
Production in units	10,000	12,000		
Costs				
Indirect materials	$ 250,000	$ 295,000	**$ 45,000**	U
Indirect labor	260,000	312,000	**52,000**	U
Utilities	190,000	225,000	**35,000**	U
Depreciation	280,000	280,000	**0**	
Property taxes	70,000	70,000	**0**	
Supervision	50,000	50,000	**0**	
	$1,100,000	$1,232,000	**$132,000**	U

HELPFUL HINT
A static budget is not useful for performance evaluation if a company has substantial variable costs.

This comparison uses budget data based on the original activity level (10,000 steel ingots). It indicates that the Forging Department is significantly **over budget** for three of the six overhead costs. And, there is a total unfavorable difference of $132,000, which is 12% over budget ($132,000 ÷ $1,100,000). Your supervisor is very unhappy! Instead of sharing in the company's success, you may find yourself looking for another job. What went wrong?

When you calm down and carefully examine the manufacturing overhead budget, you identify the problem: The budget data are not relevant! At the time the budget was developed, the company anticipated that only 10,000 units of steel ingots would be produced, **not** 12,000. Comparing actual with budgeted variable costs is meaningless. As production increases, the budget allowances for variable costs should increase proportionately. The variable costs in this example are indirect materials, indirect labor, and utilities.

Analyzing the budget data for these costs at 10,000 units, you arrive at the following per unit results.

Illustration 24-8
Variable costs per unit

Item	Total Cost	Per Unit
Indirect materials	$250,000	$25
Indirect labor	260,000	26
Utilities	190,000	19
	$700,000	$70

Illustration 24-9 calculates the budgeted variable costs at 12,000 units.

Illustration 24-9
Budgeted variable costs, 12,000 units

Item	Computation	Total
Indirect materials	$25 × 12,000	$300,000
Indirect labor	26 × 12,000	312,000
Utilities	19 × 12,000	228,000
		$840,000

Because fixed costs do not change in total as activity changes, the budgeted amounts for these costs remain the same. Illustration 24-10 shows the budget report based on the flexible budget for **12,000 units** of production. (Compare this with Illustration 24-7.)

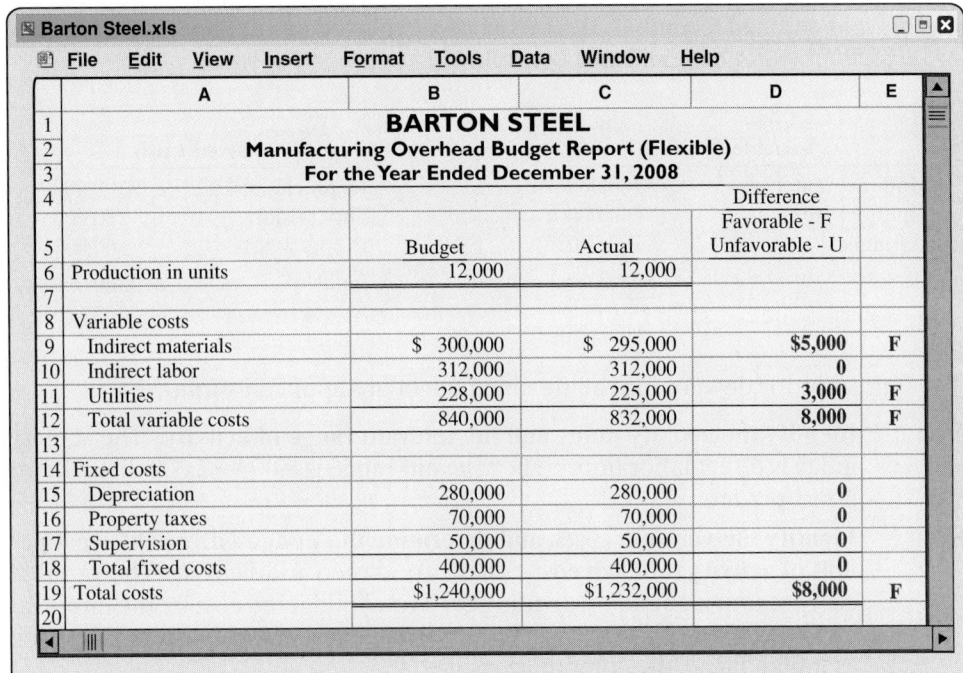

Illustration 24-10
Flexible overhead budget report

Barton Steel.xls

File Edit View Insert Format Tools Data Window Help

	A	B	C	D	E
1	**BARTON STEEL**				
2	**Manufacturing Overhead Budget Report (Flexible)**				
3	**For the Year Ended December 31, 2008**				
4				Difference	
5		Budget	Actual	Favorable - F Unfavorable - U	
6	Production in units	12,000	12,000		
7					
8	Variable costs				
9	Indirect materials	$ 300,000	$ 295,000	**$5,000**	F
10	Indirect labor	312,000	312,000	**0**	
11	Utilities	228,000	225,000	**3,000**	F
12	Total variable costs	840,000	832,000	**8,000**	F
13					
14	Fixed costs				
15	Depreciation	280,000	280,000	**0**	
16	Property taxes	70,000	70,000	**0**	
17	Supervision	50,000	50,000	**0**	
18	Total fixed costs	400,000	400,000	**0**	
19	Total costs	$1,240,000	$1,232,000	**$8,000**	F
20					

This report indicates that the Forging Department is *below budget*—a favorable difference. Instead of worrying about being fired, you may be in line for a bonus or a raise after all! As this analysis shows, the only appropriate comparison is between actual costs at 12,000 units of production and budgeted costs at 12,000 units. Flexible budget reports provide this comparison.

Developing the Flexible Budget

The flexible budget uses the master budget as its basis. To develop the flexible budget, management uses the following steps.

1. Identify the activity index and the relevant range of activity.
2. Identify the variable costs, and determine the budgeted variable cost per unit of activity for each cost.
3. Identify the fixed costs, and determine the budgeted amount for each cost.
4. Prepare the budget for selected increments of activity within the relevant range.

The activity index chosen should significantly influence the costs being budgeted. For manufacturing overhead costs, for example, the activity index is usually the same as the index used in developing the predetermined overhead rate—that is, direct labor hours or machine hours. For selling and administrative expenses, the activity index usually is sales or net sales.

The choice of the increment of activity is largely a matter of judgment. For example, if the relevant range is 8,000 to 12,000 direct labor hours, increments of 1,000 hours may be selected. The flexible budget is then prepared for each increment within the relevant range.

Flexible Budget—A Case Study

To illustrate the flexible budget, we use Fox Manufacturing Company. Fox's management uses a **flexible budget for monthly comparisons** of actual and budgeted manufacturing overhead costs of the Finishing Department. The master budget for the year ending December 31, 2008, shows expected annual operating capacity of 120,000 direct labor hours and the following overhead costs.

Illustration 24-11
Master budget data

Variable Costs		Fixed Costs	
Indirect materials	$180,000	Depreciation	$180,000
Indirect labor	240,000	Supervision	120,000
Utilities	60,000	Property taxes	60,000
Total	$480,000	Total	$360,000

The four steps for developing the flexible budget are applied as follows.

STEP 1. **Identify the activity index and the relevant range of activity.** The activity index is direct labor hours. The relevant range is 8,000–12,000 direct labor hours per month.

STEP 2. **Identify the variable costs, and determine the budgeted variable cost per unit of activity for each cost.** There are three variable costs. The variable cost per unit is found by dividing each total budgeted cost by the direct labor hours used in preparing the master budget (120,000 hours). For Fox Manufacturing, the computations are:

Illustration 24-12
Computation of variable costs per direct labor hour

Variable Cost	Computation	Variable Cost per Direct Labor Hour
Indirect materials	$180,000 ÷ 120,000	**$1.50**
Indirect labor	$240,000 ÷ 120,000	**2.00**
Utilities	$ 60,000 ÷ 120,000	**0.50**
Total		**$4.00**

STEP 3. **Identify the fixed costs, and determine the budgeted amount for each cost.** There are three fixed costs. Since Fox desires **monthly budget data**, it divides each annual budgeted cost by 12 to find the monthly amounts. For Fox Manufacturing, the monthly budgeted fixed costs are: depreciation $15,000, supervision $10,000, and property taxes $5,000.

STEP 4. **Prepare the budget for selected increments of activity within the relevant range.** Management prepares the budget in increments of 1,000 direct labor hours.

Illustration 24-13 shows Fox's flexible budget.

Illustration 24-13
Flexible monthly overhead budget

Fox Manufacturing Company.xls

File Edit View Insert Format Tools Data Window Help

FOX MANUFACTURING COMPANY
Flexible Monthly Manufacturing Overhead Budget
Finishing Department
For the Year 2008

	B	C	D	E	F
Activity level					
Direct labor hours	8,000	9,000	10,000	11,000	12,000
Variable costs					
Indirect materials	$12,000	$13,500	$15,000	$16,500	$18,000
Indirect labor	16,000	18,000	20,000	22,000	24,000
Utilities	4,000	4,500	5,000	5,500	6,000
Total variable costs	32,000	36,000	40,000	44,000	48,000
Fixed costs					
Depreciation	15,000	15,000	15,000	15,000	15,000
Supervision	10,000	10,000	10,000	10,000	10,000
Property taxes	5,000	5,000	5,000	5,000	5,000
Total fixed costs	30,000	30,000	30,000	30,000	30,000
Total costs	$62,000	$66,000	$70,000	$74,000	$78,000

Fox uses the formula below to determine total budgeted costs at any level of activity.

Illustration 24-14
Formula for total budgeted costs

Fixed Costs + **Variable Costs*** = **Total Budgeted Costs**

*Total variable cost per unit of activity × Activity level.

HELPFUL HINT
Using the data given for Fox, what amount of total costs would be budgeted for 10,600 direct labor hours? Answer: $30,000 fixed + $42,400 variable (i.e, 10,600 × $4) = $72,400 total.

For Fox, fixed costs are $30,000, and total variable cost per direct labor hour is $4. At 9,000 direct labor hours, total budgeted costs are $66,000 [$30,000 + ($4 × 9,000)]. At 8,622 direct labor hours, total budgeted costs are $64,488 [$30,000 + ($4 × 8,622)].

Total budgeted costs can also be shown graphically, as in Illustration 24-15.

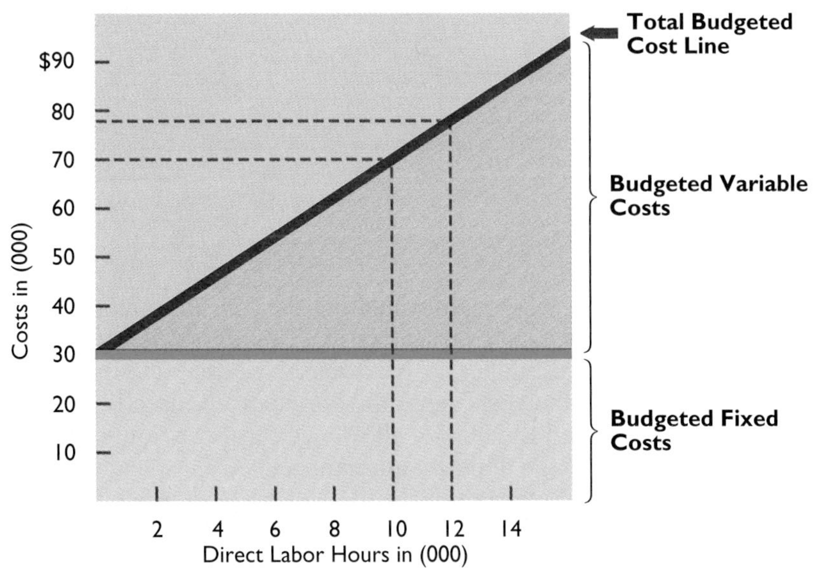

Illustration 24-15
Graphic flexible budget data highlighting 10,000 and 12,000 activity levels

In the graph, the horizontal axis represents the activity index, and costs are indicated on the vertical axis. The graph highlights two activity levels (10,000 and 12,000). As shown, total budgeted costs at these activity levels are \$70,000 [\$30,000 + (\$4 × 10,000)] and \$78,000 [\$30,000 + (\$4 × 12,000)], respectively.

Flexible Budget Reports

Flexible budget reports are another type of internal report. The flexible budget report consists of two sections: (1) production data for a selected activity index, such as direct labor hours, and (2) cost data for variable and fixed costs. The report provides a basis for evaluating a manager's performance in two areas: production control and cost control. Flexible budget reports are widely used in production and service departments.

Illustration 24-16 shows a budget report for the Finishing Department of Fox Company for the month of January. In this month, 9,000 hours are worked. The budget data are therefore based on the flexible budget for 9,000 hours in Illustration 24-13 (page 1047). The actual cost data are assumed.

Illustration 24-16
Flexible overhead budget report

Fox Manufacturing Company.xls
File Edit View Insert Format Tools Data Window Help

FOX MANUFACTURING COMPANY
Flexible Manufacturing Overhead Budget Report
Finishing Department
For the Month Ended January 31, 2008

	Budget at 9,000 DLH	Actual costs at 9,000 DLH	Difference Favorable - F Unfavorable - U	
Direct labor hours (DLH)				
Variable costs				
Indirect materials	\$13,500	\$14,000	**\$ 500**	U
Indirect labor	18,000	17,000	**1,000**	F
Utilities	4,500	4,600	**100**	U
Total variable costs	36,000	35,600	**400**	F
Fixed costs				
Depreciation	15,000	15,000	**0**	
Supervision	10,000	10,000	**0**	
Property taxes	5,000	5,000	**0**	
Total fixed costs	30,000	30,000	**0**	
Total costs	\$66,000	\$65,600	**\$ 400**	F

How appropriate is this report in evaluating the Finishing Department manager's performance in controlling overhead costs? The report clearly provides a reliable basis. Both actual and budget costs are based on the activity level worked during January. Since variable costs generally are incurred directly by the department, the difference between the budget allowance for those hours and the actual costs is the responsibility of the department manager.

In subsequent months, Fox Manufacturing will prepare other flexible budget reports. For each month, the budget data are based on the actual activity level attained. In February that level may be 11,000 direct labor hours, in July 10,000, and so on.

Note that this flexible budget is based on a single cost driver. A more accurate budget often can be developed using the activity-based costing concepts explained in Chapter 21.

ACCOUNTING ACROSS THE ORGANIZATION

Budgets and the Exotic Newcastle Disease

Exotic Newcastle Disease, one of the most infectious bird diseases in the world, kills so swiftly that many victims die before any symptoms appear. When it broke out in Southern California in 2003, it could have spelled disaster for the San Diego Zoo. "We have one of the most valuable collections of birds in the world, if not *the* most valuable," says Paula Brock, CFO of the Zoological Society of San Diego, which operates the zoo.

Bird exhibits were closed to the public for several months (the disease, which is harmless to humans, can be carried on clothes and shoes). The tires of arriving delivery trucks were sanitized, as were the shoes of anyone visiting the zoo's nonpublic areas. Zookeeper uniforms had to be changed and cleaned daily. And ultimately, the zoo, with $150 million in revenues, spent almost half a million dollars on quarantine measures in 2003.

It worked: no birds got sick. Better yet, the damage to the rest of the zoo's budget was minimized by another protective measure: the monthly budget reforecast. "When we get a hit like this, we still have to find a way to make our bottom line," says Brock. Thanks to a new planning process Brock had introduced a year earlier, the zoo's scientists were able to raise the financial alarm as they redirected resources to ward off the disease. "Because we had timely awareness," she says, "we were able to make adjustments to weather the storm."

Budget reforecasting is nothing new. (The San Diego Zoo's annual static budget was behind the times before Brock took over as CFO in 2001.) But the reaction of the zoo's staff shows the benefits of Brock's immediate efforts to link strategy to the process. It's a move long touted by consultants as a key way to improve people's involvement in budgeting.

"To keep your company on a path, it has to have some kind of map," says Brock. "The budgeting-and-planning process is that map. I cannot imagine an organization feeling in control if it didn't have that sort of discipline."

Source: Tim Reason, "Budgeting in the Real World," *CFO Magazine*, July 12, 2005, www.cfodirect.com/cfopublic.nsf/vContentPrint/649A82C8FF8AB06B85257037004 (accessed July 2005).

? What is the major benefit of tying a budget to the overall goals of the company?

Management by Exception

Management by exception means that top management's review of a budget report is focused either entirely or primarily on differences between actual results and planned objectives. This approach enables top management to focus on problem areas. Management by exception does not mean that top management will investigate every difference. For this approach to be effective, there must be guidelines for identifying an exception. The usual criteria are materiality and controllability.

MATERIALITY

Without quantitative guidelines, management would have to investigate every budget difference regardless of the amount. Materiality is usually expressed as a percentage difference from budget. For example, management may set the percentage difference at 5% for important items and 10% for other items. Managers will investigate all differences either over or under budget by the specified percentage. Costs over budget warrant investigation to determine why they were not controlled. Likewise, costs under budget merit investigation to determine whether costs critical to profitability are being curtailed. For example, if maintenance costs are budgeted at $80,000 but only $40,000 is spent, major unexpected breakdowns in productive facilities may occur in the future.

Alternatively, a company may specify a single percentage difference from budget for all items and supplement this guideline with a minimum dollar limit. For example, the exception criteria may be stated at 5% of budget or more than $10,000.

CONTROLLABILITY OF THE ITEM

Exception guidelines are more restrictive for controllable items than for items the manager cannot control. In fact, there may be no guidelines for noncontrollable items. For example, a large unfavorable difference between actual and budgeted property tax expense may not be flagged for investigation because the only possible causes are an unexpected increase in the tax rate or in the assessed value of the property. An investigation into the difference would be useless: the manager cannot control either cause.

Before You Go On...

REVIEW IT

1. What is the meaning of budgetary control?
2. When is a static budget appropriate for evaluating a manager's effectiveness in controlling costs?
3. What is a flexible budget?
4. How is a flexible budget developed?
5. What are the criteria used in management by exception?

DO IT

Your roommate asks your help in understanding how to compute total budgeted costs at any level of activity. Compute total budgeted costs at 30,000 direct labor hours, assuming that in the flexible budget graph, the fixed cost line and the total budgeted cost line intersect the vertical axis at $36,000 and that the total budget cost line is $186,000 at an activity level of 50,000 direct labor hours.

Action Plan

- Apply the formula: Fixed costs + Variable costs (Total variable costs per unit × Activity level) = Total budgeted costs.

Solution Using the graph, fixed costs are $36,000, and variable costs are $3 per direct labor hour [($186,000 − $36,000) ÷ 50,000]. Thus, at 30,000 direct labor hours, total budgeted costs are $126,000 [$36,000 + ($3 × 30,000)].

Related exercise material: *BE24-3, BE24-4, BE24-5, E24-3, E24-4, E24-5, E24-6, and E24-8.*

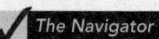

The Navigator

THE CONCEPT OF RESPONSIBILITY ACCOUNTING

STUDY OBJECTIVE 4

Describe the concept of responsibility accounting.

Like budgeting, responsibility accounting is an important part of management accounting. **Responsibility accounting** involves accumulating and reporting costs (and revenues, where relevant) on the basis of the manager who has the authority to make the day-to-day decisions about the items. Under responsibility accounting, a manager's performance is evaluated on matters directly under that manager's control. Responsibility accounting can be used at every level of management in which the following conditions exist.

1. Costs and revenues can be directly associated with the specific level of management responsibility.
2. The costs and revenues can be controlled by employees at the level of responsibility with which they are associated.
3. Budget data can be developed for evaluating the manager's effectiveness in controlling the costs and revenues.

Illustration 24-17 depicts levels of responsibility for controlling costs.

Illustration 24-17
Responsibility for controllable costs at varying levels of management

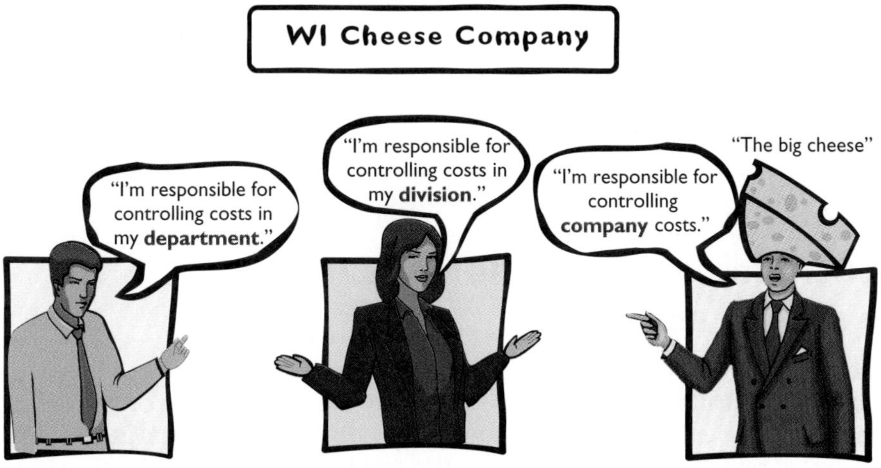

Responsibility accounting gives managers responsibility for *controllable costs* at each level of authority

Under responsibility accounting, any individual who controls a specified set of activities can be a responsibility center. Thus, responsibility accounting may extend from the lowest level of control to the top strata of management. Once responsibility is established, the company first measures and reports the effectiveness of the individual's performance for the specified activity. It then reports that measure upward throughout the organization.

HELPFUL HINT

All companies use responsibility accounting. Without some form of responsibility accounting, there would be chaos in discharging management's control function.

Responsibility accounting is especially valuable in a decentralized company. **Decentralization** means that the control of operations is delegated to many managers throughout the organization. The term **segment** is sometimes used to identify an area of responsibility in decentralized operations. Under responsibility accounting, companies prepare segment reports periodically, such as monthly, quarterly, and annually, to evaluate managers' performance.

Responsibility accounting is an essential part of any effective system of budgetary control. The reporting of costs and revenues under responsibility accounting differs from budgeting in two respects:

1. A distinction is made between controllable and noncontrollable items.
2. Performance reports either emphasize or include only items controllable by the individual manager.

Responsibility accounting applies to both profit and not-for-profit entities. For-profit entities seek to maximize net income. Not-for-profit entities wish to provide services as efficiently as possible.

MANAGEMENT INSIGHT

Who Should Do the Work?

Since devising its budgeting and control system, JKL, Inc., a large New York advertising agency, has become aware of which specific customer accounts are unprofitable and the reasons why. Account managers now feel responsible for the profitability of their accounts. They carefully monitor actual hours spent on each account to make sure the account is being run as efficiently as possible. For example, an account manager noticed a large amount of supervisory creative time being spent on one account. Further investigation showed that the supervisors, rather than the creative department, were doing the actual creative work.

? What can JKL's managers do when they find unprofitable accounts?

Controllable versus Noncontrollable Revenues and Costs

All costs and revenues are controllable at some level of responsibility within a company. This truth underscores the adage by the CEO of any organization that "the buck stops here." Under responsibility accounting, the critical issue is **whether the cost or revenue is controllable at the level of responsibility with which it is associated**. A cost over which a manager has control is called a **controllable cost**. From this definition, it follows that:

1. All costs are controllable by top management because of the broad range of its authority.
2. Fewer costs are controllable as one moves down to each lower level of managerial responsibility because of the manager's decreasing authority.

In general, **costs incurred directly by a level of responsibility are controllable at that level**. In contrast, costs incurred indirectly and allocated to a responsibility level are **noncontrollable costs** at that level.

HELPFUL HINT
Are there more or fewer controllable costs as you move to higher levels of management?
Answer: More.

HELPFUL HINT
The longer the time span, the more likely that the cost becomes controllable.

Responsibility Reporting System

A **responsibility reporting system** involves the preparation of a report for each level of responsibility in the company's organization chart. To illustrate such a system, we use the partial organization chart and production departments of Francis Chair Company in Illustration 24-18.

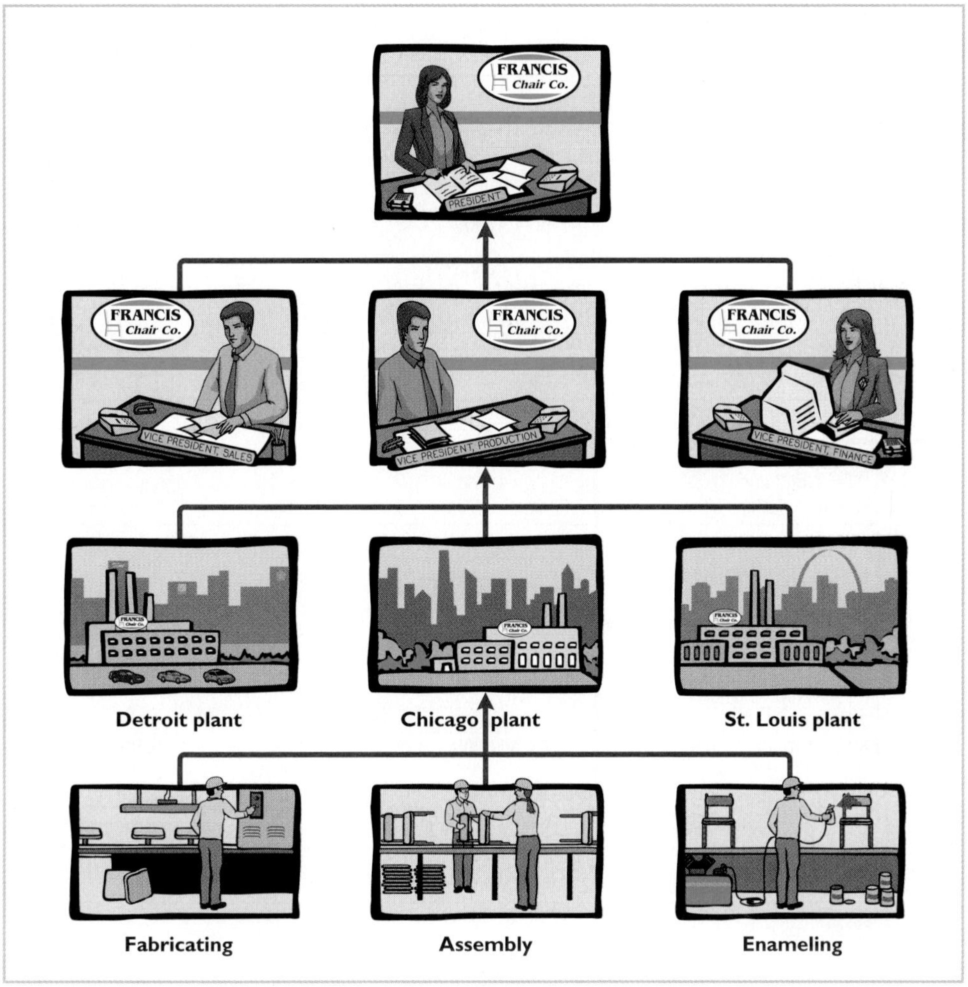

Illustration 24-18
Partial organization chart

Report A
President sees summary data of vice presidents.

Report B
Vice president sees summary of controllable costs in his/her functional area.

Report C
Plant manager sees summary of controllable costs for each department in the plant.

Report D
Department manager sees controllable costs of his/her department.

The responsibility reporting system begins with the lowest level of responsibility for controlling costs and moves upward to each higher level. Illustration 24-19 (page 1054) details the connections between levels. A brief description of the four reports for Francis Chair Company is as follows.

1. **Report D** is typical of reports that go to managers at the lowest level of responsibility shown in the organization chart—department managers. Similar reports are prepared for the managers of the Fabricating, Assembly, and Enameling Departments.
2. **Report C** is an example of reports that are sent to plant managers. It shows the costs of the Chicago plant that are controllable at the second level of responsibility. In addition, Report C shows summary data for each department that is controlled by the plant manager. Similar reports are prepared for the Detroit and St. Louis plant managers.
3. **Report B** illustrates the reports at the third level of responsibility. It shows the controllable costs of the vice president of production and summary data on the three assembly plants for which this officer is responsible. Similar reports are prepared for the vice presidents of sales and finance.
4. **Report A** is typical of reports that go to the top level of responsibility—the president. It shows the controllable costs and expenses of this office and summary data on the vice presidents that are accountable to the president.

Illustration 24-19
Responsibility reporting system

Report A
President sees summary data of vice presidents.

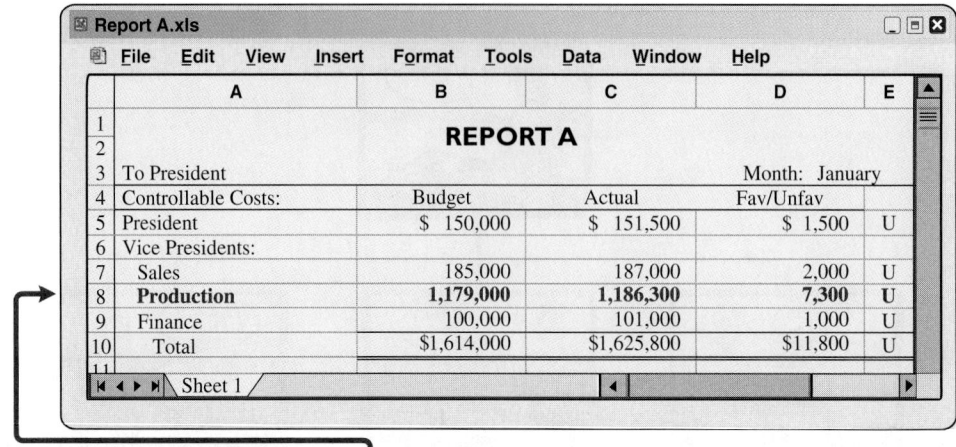

Report A.xls

Controllable Costs:	Budget	Actual	Fav/Unfav	
REPORT A				
To President			Month: January	
President	$ 150,000	$ 151,500	$ 1,500	U
Vice Presidents:				
Sales	185,000	187,000	2,000	U
Production	**1,179,000**	**1,186,300**	**7,300**	**U**
Finance	100,000	101,000	1,000	U
Total	$1,614,000	$1,625,800	$11,800	U

Report B
Vice president sees summary of controllable costs in his/her functional area.

Report B.xls

Controllable Costs:	Budget	Actual	Fav/Unfav	
REPORT B				
To Vice President Production			Month: January	
V P Production	$ 125,000	$ 126,000	$1,000	U
Assembly Plants:				
Detroit	420,000	418,000	2,000	F
Chicago	**304,000**	**309,300**	**5,300**	**U**
St. Louis	330,000	333,000	3,000	U
Total	**$1,179,000**	**$1,186,300**	**$7,300**	**U**

Report C
Plant manager sees summary of controllable costs for each department in the plant.

Report C.xls

Controllable Costs:	Budget	Actual	Fav/Unfav	
REPORT C				
To Plant Manager-Chicago			Month: January	
Chicago Plant	$110,000	$113,000	$3,000	U
Departments:				
Fabricating	**84,000**	**85,300**	**1,300**	**U**
Enameling	62,000	64,000	2,000	U
Assembly	48,000	47,000	1,000	F
Total	**$304,000**	**$309,300**	**$5,300**	**U**

Report D
Department manager sees controllable costs of his/her department.

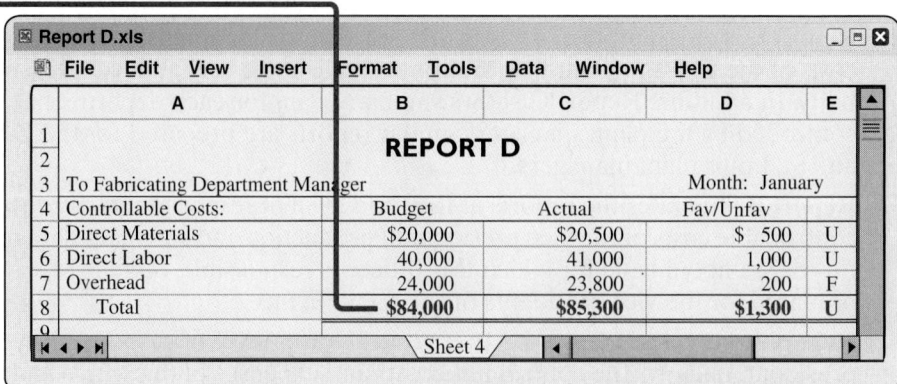

Report D.xls

Controllable Costs:	Budget	Actual	Fav/Unfav	
REPORT D				
To Fabricating Department Manager			Month: January	
Direct Materials	$20,000	$20,500	$ 500	U
Direct Labor	40,000	41,000	1,000	U
Overhead	24,000	23,800	200	F
Total	**$84,000**	**$85,300**	**$1,300**	**U**

A responsibility reporting system permits management by exception at each level of responsibility. And, each higher level of responsibility can obtain the detailed report for each lower level of responsibility. For example, the vice president of production in the Francis Chair Company may request the Chicago plant manager's report because this plant is $5,300 over budget.

This type of reporting system also permits comparative evaluations. In Illustration 24-19, the Chicago plant manager can easily rank the department managers' effectiveness in controlling manufacturing costs. Comparative rankings provide further incentive for a manager to control costs.

TYPES OF RESPONSIBILITY CENTERS

There are three basic types of responsibility centers: cost centers, profit centers, and investment centers. These classifications indicate the degree of responsibility the manager has for the performance of the center.

A cost center incurs costs (and expenses) but does not directly generate revenues. Managers of cost centers have the authority to incur costs. They are evaluated on their ability to control costs. **Cost centers are usually either production departments or service departments.** Production departments participate directly in making the product. Service departments provide only support services. In a Ford Motor Company automobile plant, the welding, painting, and assembling departments are production departments. Ford's maintenance, cafeteria, and human resources departments are service departments. All of them are cost centers.

A profit center incurs costs (and expenses) and also generates revenues. Managers of profit centers are judged on the profitability of their centers. Examples of profit centers include the individual departments of a retail store, such as clothing, furniture, and automotive products, and branch offices of banks.

Like a profit center, an investment center incurs costs (and expenses) and generates revenues. In addition, an investment center has control over decisions regarding the assets available for use. Investment center managers are evaluated on both the profitability of the center and the rate of return earned on the funds invested. Investment centers are often associated with subsidiary companies. Utility Duke Energy has operating divisions such as electric utility, energy trading, and natural gas. Investment center managers control or significantly influence investment decisions related to such matters as plant expansion and entry into new market areas. Illustration 24-20 depicts these three types of responsibility centers.

HELPFUL HINT

(1) Is the jewelry department of Macy's department store a profit center or a cost center? (2) Is the props department of a movie studio a profit center or a cost center? Answers: (1) Profit center. (2) Cost center.

Illustration 24-20
Types of responsibility centers

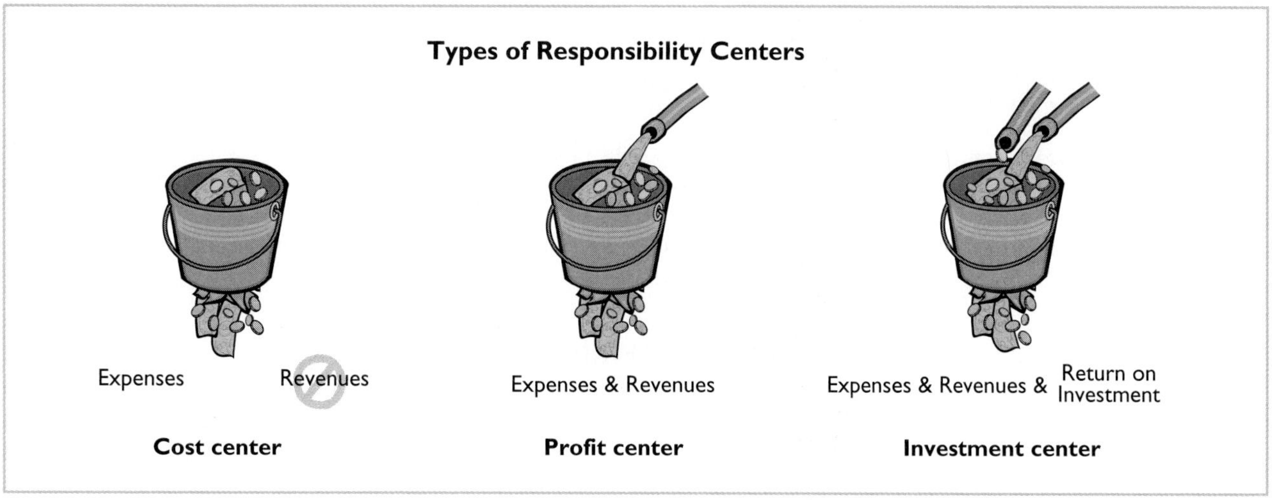

Responsibility Accounting for Cost Centers

STUDY OBJECTIVE 5

Indicate the features of responsibility reports for cost centers.

The evaluation of a manager's performance for cost centers is based on his or her ability to meet budgeted goals for controllable costs. **Responsibility reports for cost centers compare actual controllable costs with flexible budget data.**

Illustration 24-21 shows a responsibility report. The report is adapted from the flexible budget report for Fox Manufacturing Company in Illustration 24-16 on page 1048. It assumes that the Finishing Department manager is able to control all manufacturing overhead costs except depreciation, property taxes, and his own monthly salary of $6,000. The remaining $4,000 ($10,000 − $6,000) of supervision costs are assumed to apply to other supervisory personnel within the Finishing Department, whose salaries are controllable by the manager.

Illustration 24-21
Responsibility report for a cost center

Fox Manufacturing Company.xls

File Edit View Insert Format Tools Data Window Help

FOX MANUFACTURING COMPANY
Finishing Department
Responsibility Report
For the Month Ended January 31, 2008

Controllable Cost	Budget	Actual	Difference Favorable - F Unfavorable - U	
Indirect materials	$13,500	$14,000	**$ 500**	U
Indirect labor	18,000	17,000	**$1,000**	F
Utilities	4,500	4,600	**100**	U
Supervision	**4,000**	**4,000**	**0**	
	$40,000	$39,600	**$ 400**	F

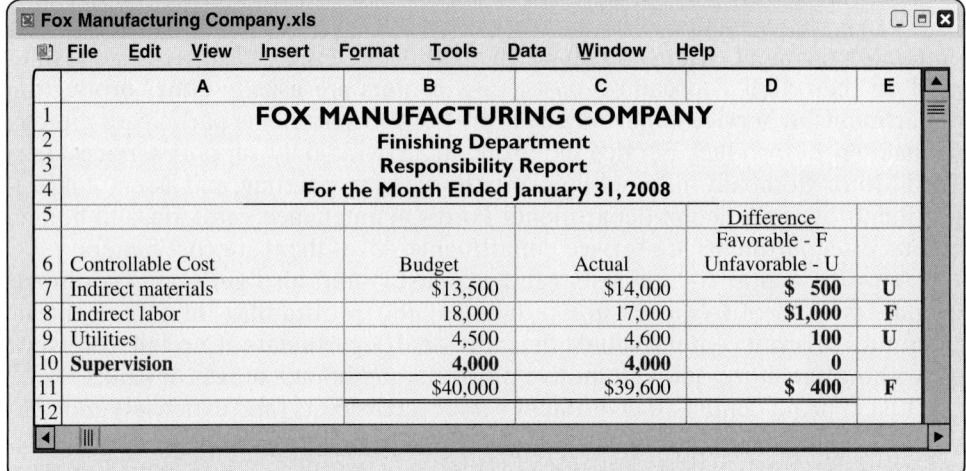

The report in Illustration 24-21 includes **only controllable costs**, and no distinction is made between variable and fixed costs. The responsibility report continues the concept of management by exception. In this case, top management may request an explanation of the $1,000 favorable difference in indirect labor and/or the $500 unfavorable difference in indirect materials.

Responsibility Accounting for Profit Centers

STUDY OBJECTIVE 6

Identify the content of responsibility reports for profit centers.

To evaluate the performance of a profit center manager, upper management needs detailed information about both controllable revenues and controllable costs. The operating revenues earned by a profit center, such as sales, are controllable by the manager. All variable costs (and expenses) incurred by the center are also controllable by the manager because they vary with sales. However, to determine the controllability of fixed costs, it is necessary to distinguish between direct and indirect fixed costs.

DIRECT AND INDIRECT FIXED COSTS

A profit center may have both direct and indirect fixed costs. **Direct fixed costs** relate specifically to one center and are incurred for the sole benefit of that center. Examples of such costs include the salaries established by the profit center manager for supervisory personnel and the cost of a timekeeping department for the center's employees.

Since these fixed costs can be traced directly to a center, they are also called **traceable costs**. **Most direct fixed costs are controllable by the profit center manager.**

In contrast, **indirect fixed costs** pertain to a company's overall operating activities and are incurred for the benefit of more than one profit center. Management allocates indirect fixed costs to profit centers on some type of equitable basis. For example, property taxes on a building occupied by more than one center may be allocated on the basis of square feet of floor space used by each center. Or, the costs of a company's human resources department may be allocated to profit centers on the basis of the number of employees in each center. Because these fixed costs apply to more than one center, they are also called **common costs**. **Most indirect fixed costs are not controllable by the profit center manager.**

RESPONSIBILITY REPORT

The responsibility report for a profit center shows budgeted and actual **controllable revenues and costs**. The report is prepared using the cost-volume-profit income statement explained in Chapter 22. In the report:

1. Controllable fixed costs are deducted from contribution margin.
2. The excess of contribution margin over controllable fixed costs is identified as **controllable margin**.
3. Noncontrollable fixed costs are not reported.

Illustration 24-22 shows the responsibility report for the manager of the Marine Division, a profit center of Mantle Manufacturing Company. For the year, the Marine Division also had $60,000 of indirect fixed costs that were not controllable by the profit center manager.

Controllable margin is considered to be the best measure of the manager's performance **in controlling revenues and costs**. The report in Illustration 24-22 shows that the manager's performance was below budgeted expectations by 10% ($36,000 ÷ $360,000). Top management would likely investigate the causes of this unfavorable result. Note that the report does not show the Marine Division's noncontrollable fixed costs of $60,000. These costs would be included in a report on the profitability of the profit center.

HELPFUL HINT
Recognize that we are emphasizing *financial* measures of performance. These days companies are also making an effort to stress *nonfinancial* performance measures such as product quality, labor productivity, market growth, materials' yield, manufacturing flexibility, and technological capability.

Illustration 24-22
Responsibility report for profit center

Mantle Manufacturing Company.xls

File Edit View Insert Format Tools Data Window Help

MANTLE MANUFACTURING COMPANY
Marine Division
Responsibility Report
For the Year Ended December 31, 2008

	Budget	Actual	Difference Favorable - F Unfavorable - U	
Sales	$1,200,000	$1,150,000	$50,000	U
Variable costs				
Cost of goods sold	500,000	490,000	10,000	F
Selling and administrative	160,000	156,000	4,000	F
Total	660,000	646,000	14,000	F
Contribution margin	540,000	504,000	36,000	U
Controllable fixed costs				
Cost of goods sold	100,000	100,000	0	
Selling and administrative	80,000	80,000	0	
Total	180,000	180,000	0	
Controllable margin	**$ 360,000**	**$ 324,000**	**$36,000**	U

Management also may choose to see monthly responsibility reports for profit centers. In addition, responsibility reports may include cumulative year-to-date results.

Before You Go On...

REVIEW IT

1. What conditions are essential for responsibility accounting?
2. What is involved in a responsibility reporting system?
3. What is the primary objective of a responsibility report for a cost center?
4. How does contribution margin differ from controllable margin in a responsibility report for a profit center?

DO IT

Midwest Division operates as a profit center. It reports the following for the year:

	Budgeted	Actual
Sales	$1,500,000	$1,700,000
Variable costs	700,000	800,000
Controllable fixed costs	400,000	400,000
Noncontrollable fixed costs	200,000	200,000

Prepare a responsibility report for the Midwest Division for December 31, 2008.

Action Plan

- Deduct variable costs from sales to show contribution margin.
- Deduct controllable fixed costs from the contribution margin to show controllable margin.
- Do not report noncontrollable fixed costs.

Solution

MIDWEST DIVISION
Responsibility Report
For the Year Ended December 31, 2008

	Budget	Actual	Difference Favorable F Unfavorable U
Sales	$1,500,000	$1,700,000	$200,000 F
Variable costs	700,000	800,000	100,000 U
Contribution margin	800,000	900,000	100,000 F
Controllable fixed costs	400,000	400,000	–0–
Controllable margin	$ 400,000	$ 500,000	$100,000 F

Related exercise material: *BE24-7 and E24-13.*

The Navigator

Responsibility Accounting for Investment Centers

STUDY OBJECTIVE 7

Explain the basis and formula used in evaluating performance in investment centers.

As explained earlier, an investment center manager can control or significantly influence the investment funds available for use. Thus, the primary basis for evaluating the performance of a manager of an investment center is **return on investment (ROI)**. The return on investment is considered to be a useful performance measurement because it shows the **effectiveness of the manager in utilizing the assets at his or her disposal**.

RETURN ON INVESTMENT (ROI)

The formula for computing ROI for an investment center, together with assumed illustrative data, is shown in Illustration 24-23.

Controllable Margin	÷	Average Operating Assets	=	Return on Investment (ROI)
$1,000,000	÷	$5,000,000	=	**20%**

Illustration 24-23
ROI formula

Both factors in the formula are controllable by the investment center manager. Operating assets consist of current assets and plant assets used in operations by the center and controlled by the manager. Nonoperating assets such as idle plant assets and land held for future use are excluded. Average operating assets are usually based on the cost or book value of the assets at the beginning and end of the year.

RESPONSIBILITY REPORT

The scope of the investment center manager's responsibility significantly affects the content of the performance report. Since an investment center is an independent entity for operating purposes, **all fixed costs are controllable by its manager**. For example, the manager is responsible for depreciation on investment center assets. Therefore, more fixed costs are identified as controllable in the performance report for an investment center manager than in a performance report for a profit center manager. The report also shows budgeted and actual ROI below controllable margin.

To illustrate this responsibility report, we will now assume that the Marine Division of Mantle Manufacturing Company is an investment center. It has budgeted and actual average operating assets of $2,000,000. The manager can control $60,000 of fixed costs that were not controllable when the division was a profit center. Illustration 24-24 shows the division's responsibility report.

Mantle Manufacturing Company.xls
File Edit View Insert Format Tools Data Window Help

	A	B	C	D	E
1	**MANTLE MANUFACTURING COMPANY**				
2	**Marine Division**				
3	**Responsibility Report**				
4	**For the Year Ended December 31, 2008**				
5				Difference	
6		Budget	Actual	Favorable - F Unfavorable - U	
7	Sales	$1,200,000	$1,150,000	$ 50,000	U
8	Variable costs				
9	Cost of goods sold	500,000	490,000	10,000	F
10	Selling and administrative	160,000	156,000	4,000	F
11	Total	660,000	646,000	14,000	F
12	Contribution margin	540,000	504,000	36,000	U
13	**Controllable fixed costs**				
14	Cost of goods sold	100,000	100,000	0	
15	Selling and administrative	80,000	80,000	0	
16	**Other fixed costs**	**60,000**	**60,000**	**0**	
17	Total	240,000	240,000	0	
18	**Controllable margin**	**$ 300,000**	**$ 264,000**	**$ 36,000**	**U**
19	**Return on investment**	**15.0%**	**13.2%**	**1.8%**	**U**
20		(a)	(b)	(c)	
21					
22		(a) $ 300,000 / $2,000,000	(b) $ 264,000 / $2,000,000	(c) $ 36,000 / $2,000,000	
23					

Illustration 24-24
Responsibility report for investment center

The report shows that the manager's performance based on ROI was below budget expectations by 1.8% (15.0% versus 13.2%). Top management would likely want an explanation of the reasons for this unfavorable result.

JUDGMENTAL FACTORS IN ROI

The return on investment approach includes two judgmental factors:

1. **Valuation of operating assets.** Operating assets may be valued at acquisition cost, book value, appraised value, or market value. The first two bases are readily available from the accounting records.
2. **Margin (income) measure.** This measure may be controllable margin, income from operations, or net income.

Each of the alternative values for operating assets can provide a reliable basis for evaluating a manager's performance as long as it is consistently applied between reporting periods. However, the use of income measures other than controllable margin will not result in a valid basis for evaluating the performance of an investment center manager.

IMPROVING ROI

The manager of an investment center can improve ROI in two ways: (1) increase controllable margin, and/or (2) reduce average operating assets. To illustrate, we will use the following assumed data for the Laser Division of Berra Manufacturing.

Illustration 24-25
Assumed data for Laser Division

Sales	$2,000,000
Variable cost	1,100,000
Contribution margin (45%)	900,000
Controllable fixed costs	300,000
Controllable margin (a)	$ 600,000
Average operating assets (b)	$5,000,000
Return on investment (a) ÷ (b)	**12%**

Increasing Controllable Margin. Controllable margin can be increased by increasing sales or by reducing variable and controllable fixed costs as follows.

1. **Increase sales 10%.** Sales will increase $200,000 ($2,000,000 × .10). Assuming no change in the contribution margin percentage of 45%, contribution margin will increase $90,000 ($200,000 × .45). Controllable margin will increase by the same amount because controllable fixed costs will not change. Thus, controllable margin becomes $690,000 ($600,000 + $90,000). The new ROI is 13.8%, computed as follows.

Illustration 24-26
ROI computation—increase in sales

$$\text{ROI} = \frac{\text{Controllable margin}}{\text{Average operating assets}} = \frac{\$690{,}000}{\$5{,}000{,}000} = \mathbf{13.8\%}$$

An increase in sales benefits both the investment center and the company if it results in new business. It would not benefit the company if the increase was achieved at the expense of other investment centers.

2. **Decrease variable and fixed costs 10%.** Total costs decrease $140,000 [($1,100,000 + $300,000) × .10]. This reduction results in a corresponding increase in controllable margin. Thus, controllable margin becomes $740,000 ($600,000 + $140,000). The new ROI is 14.8%, computed as follows.

$$\text{ROI} = \frac{\text{Controllable margin}}{\text{Average operating assets}} = \frac{\$740{,}000}{\$5{,}000{,}000} = \mathbf{14.8\%}$$

Illustration 24-27
ROI computation—decrease in costs

This course of action is clearly beneficial when waste and inefficiencies are eliminated. But, a reduction in vital costs such as required maintenance and inspections is not likely to be acceptable to top management.

Reducing Average Operating Assets. Assume that average operating assets are reduced 10% or $500,000 ($5,000,000 × .10). Average operating assets become $4,500,000 ($5,000,000 − $500,000). Since controllable margin remains unchanged at $600,000, the new ROI is 13.3%, computed as follows.

$$\text{ROI} = \frac{\text{Controllable margin}}{\text{Average operating assets}} = \frac{\$600{,}000}{\$4{,}500{,}000} = \mathbf{13.3\%}$$

Illustration 24-28
ROI computation—decrease in operating assets

Reductions in operating assets may or may not be prudent. It is beneficial to eliminate overinvestment in inventories and to dispose of excessive plant assets. However, it is unwise to reduce inventories below expected needs or to dispose of essential plant assets.

ACCOUNTING ACROSS THE ORGANIZATION

Does Hollywood Look at ROI?

If Hollywood were run like a real business, where things like return on investment mattered, there would be one unchallenged, sacred principle that studio chieftains would never violate: Make lots of G-rated movies.

No matter how you slice the movie business—by star vehicles, by budget levels, by sequels or franchises—by far the best return on investment comes from the not-so-glamorous world of G-rated films. The problem is, these movies represent only 3% of the total films made in a typical year.

Take 2003: According to Motion Picture Association of America statistics, of the 940 movies released that year, only 29 were G-rated. Yet the highest-grossing movie of the year, *Finding Nemo*, was G-rated. . . . On the flip side are the R-rated films, which dominate the total releases and yet yield the worst return on investment. A whopping 646 R-rated films were released in 2003—69% of the total output—but only four of the top-20 grossing movies of the year were R-rated films.

This trend—G-rated movies are good for business but underproduced; R-rated movies are bad for business, and yet overdone—is something that has been driving economists batty for the past several years.

Source: Grainger, David, "The Dysfunctional Family-Film Business," *Fortune*, January 10, 2005, pp. 20–21.

? What might be the reason that G-rated movies are not produced as much as R-rated movies?

Principles of Performance Evaluation

Performance evaluation is at the center of responsibility accounting. **Performance evaluation** is a management function that compares actual results with budget goals. It involves both behavioral and reporting principles.

BEHAVIORAL PRINCIPLES

The human factor is critical in evaluating performance. Behavioral principles include the following.

1. **Managers of responsibility centers should have direct input into the process of establishing budget goals of their area of responsibility.** Without such input, managers may view the goals as unrealistic or arbitrarily set by top management. Such views adversely affect the managers' motivation to meet the targeted objectives.
2. **The evaluation of performance should be based entirely on matters that are controllable by the manager being evaluated.** Criticism of a manager on matters outside his or her control reduces the effectiveness of the evaluation process. It leads to negative reactions by a manager and to doubts about the fairness of the company's evaluation policies.
3. **Top management should support the evaluation process.** As explained earlier, the evaluation process begins at the lowest level of responsibility and extends upward to the highest level of management. Managers quickly lose faith in the process when top management ignores, overrules, or bypasses established procedures for evaluating a manager's performance.
4. **The evaluation process must allow managers to respond to their evaluations.** Evaluation is not a one-way street. Managers should have the opportunity to defend their performance. Evaluation without feedback is both impersonal and ineffective.
5. **The evaluation should identify both good and poor performance.** Praise for good performance is a powerful motivating factor for a manager. This is especially true when a manager's compensation includes rewards for meeting budget goals.

REPORTING PRINCIPLES

Performance evaluation under responsibility accounting should be based on certain reporting principles. These principles pertain primarily to the internal reports that provide the basis for evaluating performance. Performance reports should:

1. Contain only data that are controllable by the manager of the responsibility center.
2. Provide accurate and reliable budget data to measure performance.
3. Highlight significant differences between actual results and budget goals.
4. Be tailor-made for the intended evaluation.
5. Be prepared at reasonable intervals.

Before You Go On...

REVIEW IT

1. What is the formula for computing return on investment (ROI)?
2. Identify three actions a manager may take to improve ROI.

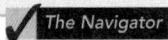

The Navigator

Be sure to read **ALL ABOUT YOU: *Budgeting for Housing Costs*** on the next page for information on how topics in this chapter apply to you.

Budgeting for Housing Costs

In Chapter 23 you learned how to prepare a budget. Budgets are great planning tools, but planning is only one purpose of budgeting. As you learned in this chapter, budgets also are used as the basis of performance evaluation. That is, a company prepares the budget to lay out what it plans on doing, and then it compares its actual results with its plan to see how well it did.

It works the same way for individual budgets. Preparing a personal budget is a great first step. But the real benefit of budgeting comes from comparing your actual results with your personal budget and then making the necessary (and sometimes unpleasant) adjustments. Although unexpected bills can create problems, most financial problems are the result of not controlling routine expenses.

Some Facts

* Most experts encourage people to keep housing costs (mortgage, insurance, and taxes) at approximately 25% to 30% of pre-tax income.
* The U.S. Department of Agriculture estimates that it will cost between $127,080 and $254,400 to raise a child born in 2002 to the age of 18. That amount *does not* include college tuition. Married couples with children file for bankruptcy twice as often as married couples without children.
* Medical bills contribute to one out of five bankruptcies. One out of seven Americans has no health insurance.
* Approximately 40% of American households do not have even $1,000 in cash available for emergencies when unexpected expenses arise.
* Increases in interest rates are causing budget problems for people with adjustable-rate mortgages. As interest rates rose from 2005 to 2006, the number of adjustable-rate mortgages that were at least 90 days past due increased by more than 140%.

About the Numbers

Housing represents the largest cost for nearly all Americans. The cost of housing as a percentage of income varies considerably across the United States. The following graph shows the percentage of homeowners with mortgages in each state who spend more than 30% of household income on housing costs.

Figure 1. Mortgaged Owners Spending 30 Percent or more of Household Income on Selected Monthly Owner Costs, 2004

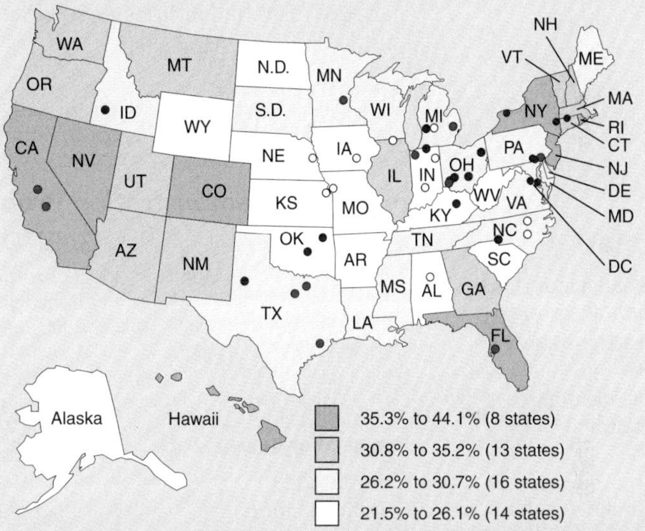

What Do You Think?

As noted above, housing is the greatest expense for most people. The percentage of people in the United States who own a home is high compared to many other countries. This is in part the result of U.S. government programs and incentives that encourage home ownership. For example, the interest on a home mortgage is deductible for tax purposes.

Suppose you have just graduated from college and are moving to a new community. Should you immediately buy a new home?

YES: The cost of housing continues to rise. By purchasing a home soon, I can make my housing cost more like a fixed cost, and thus reduce future cost increases. Also I will benefit from the appreciation in my home's value.

NO: I just moved to a new town, so I don't know the market. Also, it is likely that my income will increase in the next few years, so I will be able to afford a better house if I wait a few years. Also, house prices have increased a lot in recent years, but some experts think they may actually decline in some parts of the country. I don't want to get stuck with a house that I can't sell.

Sources: Liz Pullman Weston, "How to Survive 7 Budget Busters," *moneycentral.msn.com/content/Savinganddebt/Learntobudget/P58710.asp*; Amber Kostelac, "Housing Is Affordable in the Hoosier State," *www.incontext.indiana.edu/2005/october/pdfs/housing.pdf*, October 2005 (both accessed August 2006).

The authors' comments on this situation appear on page 1084.

Demonstration Problem

WILEY PLUS

Glenda Company uses a flexible budget for manufacturing overhead based on direct labor hours. For 2008 the master overhead budget for the Packaging Department based on 300,000 direct labor hours was as follows.

Variable Costs		Fixed Costs	
Indirect labor	$360,000	Supervision	$ 60,000
Supplies and lubricants	150,000	Depreciation	24,000
Maintenance	210,000	Property taxes	18,000
Utilities	120,000	Insurance	12,000
	$840,000		$114,000

During July, 24,000 direct labor hours were worked. The company incurred the following variable costs in July: indirect labor $30,200, supplies and lubricants $11,600, maintenance $17,500, and utilities $9,200. Actual fixed overhead costs were the same as monthly budgeted fixed costs.

Instructions

Prepare a flexible budget report for the Packaging Department for July.

Solution to Demonstration Problem

action plan

- ✓ Use budget data for actual direct labor hours worked.
- ✓ Classify each cost as variable or fixed.
- ✓ Determine the difference between budgeted and actual costs.
- ✓ Identify the difference as favorable or unfavorable.
- ✓ Determine the difference in total variable costs, total fixed costs, and total costs.

GLENDA COMPANY
Manufacturing Overhead Budget Report (Flexible)
Packaging Department
For the Month Ended July 31, 2008

Direct labor hours (DLH)	Budget 24,000 DLH	Actual Costs 24,000 DLH	Difference Favorable F Unfavorable U
Variable costs			
Indirect labor	$28,800	$30,200	$1,400 U
Supplies and lubricants	12,000	11,600	400 F
Maintenance	16,800	17,500	700 U
Utilities	9,600	9,200	400 F
Total variable	67,200	68,500	1,300 U
Fixed costs			
Supervision	$ 5,000	$ 5,000	–0–
Depreciation	2,000	2,000	–0–
Property taxes	1,500	1,500	–0–
Insurance	1,000	1,000	–0–
Total fixed	9,500	9,500	–0–
Total costs	$76,700	$78,000	$1,300 U

✓ The Navigator

SUMMARY OF STUDY OBJECTIVES

WILEY PLUS

1 **Describe the concept of budgetary control.** Budgetary control consists of (a) preparing periodic budget reports that compare actual results with planned objectives, (b) analyzing the differences to determine their causes, (c) taking appropriate corrective action, and (d) modifying future plans, if necessary.

2 Evaluate the usefulness of static budget reports. Static budget reports are useful in evaluating the progress toward planned sales and profit goals. They are also appropriate in assessing a manager's effectiveness in controlling costs when (a) actual activity closely approximates the master budget activity level, and/or (b) the behavior of the costs in response to changes in activity is fixed.

3 Explain the development of flexible budgets and the usefulness of flexible budget reports. To develop the flexible budget it is necessary to: (a) Identify the activity index and the relevant range of activity. (b) Identify the variable costs, and determine the budgeted variable cost per unit of activity for each cost. (c) Identify the fixed costs, and determine the budgeted amount for each cost. (d) Prepare the budget for selected increments of activity within the relevant range. Flexible budget reports permit an evaluation of a manager's performance in controlling production and costs.

4 Describe the concept of responsibility accounting. Responsibility accounting involves accumulating and reporting revenues and costs on the basis of the individual manager who has the authority to make the day-to-day decisions about the items. The evaluation of a manager's performance is based on the matters directly under the manager's control. In responsibility accounting, it is necessary to distinguish between controllable and noncontrollable fixed costs and to identify three types of responsibility centers: cost, profit, and investment.

5 Indicate the features of responsibility reports for cost centers. Responsibility reports for cost centers compare actual costs with flexible budget data. The reports show only controllable costs, and no distinction is made between variable and fixed costs.

6 Identify the content of responsibility reports for profit centers. Responsibility reports show contribution margin, controllable fixed costs, and controllable margin for each profit center.

7 Explain the basis and formula used in evaluating performance in investment centers. The primary basis for evaluating performance in investment centers is return on investment (ROI). The formula for computing ROI for investment centers is: Controllable margin ÷ Average operating assets.

The Navigator

GLOSSARY

WILEY PLUS

Budgetary control The use of budgets to control operations. (p. 1040).

Controllable cost A cost over which a manager has control. (p. 1052).

Controllable margin Contribution margin less controllable fixed costs. (p. 1057).

Cost center A responsibility center that incurs costs but does not directly generate revenues. (p. 1055).

Decentralization Control of operations is delegated to many managers throughout the organization. (p. 1051).

Direct fixed costs Costs that relate specifically to a responsibility center and are incurred for the sole benefit of the center. (p. 1056).

Flexible budget A projection of budget data for various levels of activity. (p. 1043).

Indirect fixed costs Costs that are incurred for the benefit of more than one profit center. (p. 1057).

Investment center A responsibility center that incurs costs, generates revenues, and has control over decisions regarding the assets available for use. (p. 1055).

Management by exception The review of budget reports by top management focused entirely or primarily on differences between actual results and planned objectives. (p. 1049).

Noncontrollable costs Costs incurred indirectly and allocated to a responsibility center that are not controllable at that level. (p. 1052).

Profit center A responsibility center that incurs costs and also generates revenues. (p. 1055).

Responsibility accounting A part of management accounting that involves accumulating and reporting revenues and costs on the basis of the manager who has the authority to make the day-to-day decisions about the items. (p. 1051).

Responsibility reporting system The preparation of reports for each level of responsibility in the company's organization chart. (p. 1052).

Return on investment (ROI) A measure of management's effectiveness in utilizing assets at its disposal in an investment center. (p. 1058).

Segment An area of responsibility in decentralized operations. (p. 1051).

Static budget A projection of budget data at one level of activity. (p. 1041).

SELF-STUDY QUESTIONS

WILEY PLUS

Answers are at the end of the chapter.

(SO 1) **1.** Budgetary control involves all but one of the following:
(a) modifying future plans.
(b) analyzing differences.
(c) using static budgets.
(d) determining differences between actual and planned results.

2. A static budget is useful in controlling costs when cost behavior is: (SO 2)
(a) mixed. **(c)** variable.
(b) fixed. **(d)** linear.

3. At zero direct labor hours in a flexible budget graph, the total budgeted cost line intersects the vertical axis at $30,000. At 10,000 direct labor hours, a horizontal line (SO 3)

drawn from the total budgeted cost line intersects the vertical axis at $90,000. Fixed and variable costs may be expressed as:
(a) $30,000 fixed plus $6 per direct labor hour variable.
(b) $30,000 fixed plus $9 per direct labor hour variable.
(c) $60,000 fixed plus $3 per direct labor hour variable.
(d) $60,000 fixed plus $6 per direct labor hour variable.

(SO 3) **4.** At 9,000 direct labor hours, the flexible budget for indirect materials is $27,000. If $28,000 of indirect materials costs are incurred at 9,200 direct labor hours, the flexible budget report should show the following difference for indirect materials:
(a) $1,000 unfavorable.
(b) $1,000 favorable.
(c) $400 favorable.
(d) $400 unfavorable.

(SO 4) **5.** Under responsibility accounting, the evaluation of a manager's performance is based on matters that the manager:
(a) directly controls.
(b) directly and indirectly controls.
(c) indirectly controls.
(d) has shared responsibility for with another manager.

(SO 4) **6.** Responsibility centers include:
(a) cost centers.
(b) profit centers.
(c) investment centers.
(d) all of the above.

(SO 5) **7.** Responsibility reports for cost centers:
(a) distinguish between fixed and variable costs.
(b) use static budget data.
(c) include both controllable and noncontrollable costs.
(d) include only controllable costs.

8. In a responsibility report for a profit center, controllable fixed costs are deducted from contribution margin to show: (SO 6)
(a) profit center margin.
(b) controllable margin.
(c) net income.
(d) income from operations.

9. In the formula for return on investment (ROI), the factors for controllable margin and operating assets are, respectively: (SO 7)
(a) controllable margin percentage and total operating assets.
(b) controllable margin dollars and average operating assets.
(c) controllable margin dollars and total assets.
(d) controllable margin percentage and average operating assets.

10. A manager of an investment center can improve ROI by: (SO 7)
(a) increasing average operating assets.
(b) reducing sales.
(c) increasing variable costs.
(d) reducing variable and/or controllable fixed costs.

Go to the book's website,
www.wiley.com/college/weygandt,
for Additional Self-Study questions.

The Navigator

QUESTIONS

1. **(a)** What is budgetary control?
   (b) Greg Gilligan is describing budgetary control. What steps should be included in Greg's description?
2. The following purposes are part of a budgetary reporting system: (a) Determine efficient use of materials. (b) Control overhead costs. (c) Determine whether income objectives are being met. For each purpose, indicate the name of the report, the frequency of the report, and the primary recipient(s) of the report.
3. How may a budget report for the second quarter differ from a budget report for the first quarter?
4. Joe Cey questions the usefulness of a master sales budget in evaluating sales performance. Is there justification for Joe's concern? Explain.
5. Under what circumstances may a static budget be an appropriate basis for evaluating a manager's effectiveness in controlling costs?
6. "A flexible budget is really a series of static budgets." Is this true? Why?
7. The static manufacturing overhead budget based on 40,000 direct labor hours shows budgeted indirect labor costs of $54,000. During March, the department incurs $65,000 of indirect labor while working 45,000 direct labor hours. Is this a favorable or unfavorable performance? Why?
8. A static overhead budget based on 40,000 direct labor hours shows Factory Insurance $6,500 as a fixed cost. At the 50,000 direct labor hours worked in March, factory insurance costs were $6,200. Is this a favorable or unfavorable performance? Why?
9. Kate Coulter is confused about how a flexible budget is prepared. Identify the steps for Kate.
10. Alou Company has prepared a graph of flexible budget data. At zero direct labor hours, the total budgeted cost line intersects the vertical axis at $25,000. At 10,000 direct labor hours, the line drawn from the total budgeted cost line intersects the vertical axis at $85,000. How may the fixed and variable costs be expressed?
11. The flexible budget formula is fixed costs $40,000 plus variable costs of $4 per direct labor hour. What is the total budgeted cost at (a) 9,000 hours and (b) 12,345 hours?
12. What is management by exception? What criteria may be used in identifying exceptions?
13. What is responsibility accounting? Explain the purpose of responsibility accounting.
14. Ann Wilkins is studying for an accounting examination. Describe for Ann what conditions are necessary for responsibility accounting to be used effectively.

15. Distinguish between controllable and noncontrollable costs.
16. How do responsibility reports differ from budget reports?
17. What is the relationship, if any, between a responsibility reporting system and a company's organization chart?
18. Distinguish among the three types of responsibility centers.
19. (a) What costs are included in a performance report for a cost center? (b) In the report, are variable and fixed costs identified?
20. How do direct fixed costs differ from indirect fixed costs? Are both types of fixed costs controllable?
21. Lori Quan is confused about controllable margin reported in an income statement for a profit center. How is this margin computed, and what is its primary purpose?
22. What is the primary basis for evaluating the performance of the manager of an investment center? Indicate the formula for this basis.
23. Explain the ways that ROI can be improved.
24. Indicate two behavioral principles that pertain to (a) the manager being evaluated and (b) top management.

BRIEF EXERCISES

WILEY PLUS

BE24-1 For the quarter ended March 31, 2008, Voorhees Company accumulates the following sales data for its product, Garden-Tools: $310,000 budget; $304,000 actual. Prepare a static budget report for the quarter.

Prepare static budget report. (SO 2)

BE24-2 Data for Voorhees Company are given in BE24-1. In the second quarter, budgeted sales were $380,000, and actual sales were $383,000. Prepare a static budget report for the second quarter and for the year to date.

Prepare static budget report for 2 quarters. (SO 2)

BE24-3 In Mussatto Company, direct labor is $20 per hour. The company expects to operate at 10,000 direct labor hours each month. In January 2008, direct labor totaling $203,000 is incurred in working 10,400 hours. Prepare (a) a static budget report and (b) a flexible budget report. Evaluate the usefulness of each report.

Show usefulness of flexible budgets in evaluating performance. (SO 3)

BE24-4 Hannon Company expects to produce 1,200,000 units of Product XX in 2008. Monthly production is expected to range from 80,000 to 120,000 units. Budgeted variable manufacturing costs per unit are: direct materials $4, direct labor $6, and overhead $8. Budgeted fixed manufacturing costs per unit for depreciation are $2 and for supervision are $1. Prepare a flexible manufacturing budget for the relevant range value using 20,000 unit increments.

Prepare a flexible budget for variable costs. (SO 3)

BE24-5 Data for Hannon Company are given in BE24-4. In March 2008, the company incurs the following costs in producing 100,000 units: direct materials $425,000, direct labor $590,000, and variable overhead $805,000. Prepare a flexible budget report for March. Were costs controlled?

Prepare flexible budget report. (SO 3)

BE24-6 In the Assembly Department of Cobb Company, budgeted and actual manufacturing overhead costs for the month of April 2008 were as follows.

Prepare a responsibility report for a cost center. (SO 5)

	Budget	Actual
Indirect materials	$15,000	$14,300
Indirect labor	20,000	20,600
Utilities	10,000	10,750
Supervision	5,000	5,000

All costs are controllable by the department manager. Prepare a responsibility report for April for the cost center.

BE24-7 Eckert Manufacturing Company accumulates the following summary data for the year ending December 31, 2008, for its Water Division which it operates as a profit center: sales—$2,000,000 budget, $2,080,000 actual; variable costs—$1,000,000 budget, $1,050,000 actual; and controllable fixed costs—$300,000 budget, $310,000 actual. Prepare a responsibility report for the Water Division.

Prepare a responsibility report for a profit center. (SO 6)

BE24-8 For the year ending December 31, 2008, Kaspar Company accumulates the following data for the Plastics Division which it operates as an investment center: contribution margin—$700,000 budget, $715,000 actual; controllable fixed costs—$300,000 budget, $309,000 actual.

Prepare a responsibility report for an investment center. (SO 7)

Average operating assets for the year were $2,000,000. Prepare a responsibility report for the Plastics Division beginning with contribution margin.

Compute return on investment using the ROI formula.
(SO 7)

BE24-9 For its three investment centers, Paige Company accumulates the following data:

	I	II	III
Sales	$2,000,000	$3,000,000	$ 4,000,000
Controllable margin	1,200,000	2,000,000	3,200,000
Average operating assets	5,000,000	8,000,000	10,000,000

Compute the return on investment (ROI) for each center.

Compute return on investment under changed conditions.
(SO 7)

BE24-10 Data for the investment centers for Paige Company are given in BE24-9. The centers expect the following changes in the next year: (I) increase sales 15%; (II) decrease costs $200,000; (III) decrease average operating assets $400,000. Compute the expected return on investment (ROI) for each center. Assume center I has a contribution margin percentage of 75%.

EXERCISES

Understand the concept of budgetary control.
(SO 1, 2, 3)

E24-1 Jim Thome has prepared the following list of statements about budgetary control.

1. Budget reports compare actual results with planned objectives.
2. All budget reports are prepared on a weekly basis.
3. Management uses budget reports to analyze differences between actual and planned results and determine their causes.
4. As a result of analyzing budget reports, management may either take corrective action or modify future plans.
5. Budgetary control works best when a company has an informal reporting system.
6. The primary recipients of the sales report are the sales manager and the vice-president of production.
7. The primary recipient of the scrap report is the production manager.
8. A static budget is a projection of budget data at one level of activity.
9. Top management's reaction to unfavorable differences is not influenced by the materiality of the difference.
10. A static budget is not appropriate in evaluating a manager's effectiveness in controlling costs unless the actual activity level approximates the static budget activity level or the behavior of the costs is fixed.

Instructions

Identify each statement as true or false. If false, indicate how to correct the statement.

Prepare and evaluate static budget report.
(SO 2)

E24-2 Pargo Company budgeted selling expenses of $30,000 in January, $35,000 in February, and $40,000 in March. Actual selling expenses were $31,000 in January, $34,500 in February, and $47,000 in March.

Instructions

(a) Prepare a selling expense report that compares budgeted and actual amounts by month and for the year to date.
(b) What is the purpose of the report prepared in (a), and who would be the primary recipient?
(c) What would be the likely result of management's analysis of the report?

Prepare flexible manufacturing overhead budget.
(SO 3)

E24-3 Raney Company uses a flexible budget for manufacturing overhead based on direct labor hours. Variable manufacturing overhead costs per direct labor hour are as follows.

Indirect labor	$1.00
Indirect materials	0.50
Utilities	0.40

Fixed overhead costs per month are: Supervision $4,000, Depreciation $1,500, and Property Taxes $800. The company believes it will normally operate in a range of 7,000–10,000 direct labor hours per month.

Instructions

Prepare a monthly flexible manufacturing overhead budget for 2008 for the expected range of activity, using increments of 1,000 direct labor hours.

Prepare flexible budget reports for manufacturing overhead costs, and comment on findings.

(SO 3)

E24-4 Using the information in E24-3, assume that in July 2008, Raney Company incurs the following manufacturing overhead costs.

Variable Costs		Fixed Costs	
Indirect labor	$8,700	Supervision	$4,000
Indirect materials	4,300	Depreciation	1,500
Utilities	3,200	Property taxes	800

Instructions

(a) Prepare a flexible budget performance report, assuming that the company worked 9,000 direct labor hours during the month.

(b) Prepare a flexible budget performance report, assuming that the company worked 8,500 direct labor hours during the month.

(c) Comment on your findings.

Prepare flexible selling expense budget.

(SO 3)

E24-5 Trusler Company uses flexible budgets to control its selling expenses. Monthly sales are expected to range from $170,000 to $200,000. Variable costs and their percentage relationship to sales are: Sales Commissions 5%, Advertising 4%, Traveling 3%, and Delivery 2%. Fixed selling expenses will consist of Sales Salaries $34,000, Depreciation on Delivery Equipment $7,000, and Insurance on Delivery Equipment $1,000.

Instructions

Prepare a monthly flexible budget for each $10,000 increment of sales within the relevant range for the year ending December 31, 2008.

Prepare flexible budget reports for selling expenses.

(SO 3)

E24-6 The actual selling expenses incurred in March 2008 by Trusler Company are as follows.

Variable Expenses		Fixed Expenses	
Sales commissions	$9,200	Sales salaries	$34,000
Advertising	7,000	Depreciation	7,000
Travel	5,100	Insurance	1,000
Delivery	3,500		

Instructions

(a) Prepare a flexible budget performance report for March using the budget data in E24-5, assuming that March sales were $170,000. Expected and actual sales are the same.

(b) Prepare a flexible budget performance report, assuming that March sales were $180,000. Expected sales and actual sales are the same.

(c) Comment on the importance of using flexible budgets in evaluating the performance of the sales manager.

Prepare flexible budget and responsibility report for manufacturing overhead.

(SO 3, 5)

E24-7 Pletcher Company's manufacturing overhead budget for the first quarter of 2008 contained the following data.

Variable Costs		Fixed Costs	
Indirect materials	$12,000	Supervisory salaries	$36,000
Indirect labor	10,000	Depreciation	7,000
Utilities	8,000	Property taxes and insurance	8,000
Maintenance	6,000	Maintenance	5,000

Actual variable costs were: indirect materials $13,800, indirect labor $9,600, utilities $8,700, and maintenance $4,900. Actual fixed costs equaled budgeted costs except for property taxes and insurance, which were $8,200.

All costs are considered controllable by the production department manager except for depreciation, and property taxes and insurance.

Instructions

(a) Prepare a flexible manufacturing overhead budget report for the first quarter.

(b) Prepare a responsibility report for the first quarter.

Prepare flexible budget report, and answer question.

(SO 2, 3)

E24-8 As sales manager, Terry Dewitt was given the following static budget report for selling expenses in the Clothing Department of Garber Company for the month of October.

GARBER COMPANY
Clothing Department
Budget Report
For the Month Ended October 31, 2008

	Budget	Actual	Difference Favorable F Unfavorable U
Sales in units	8,000	10,000	2,000 F
Variable expenses			
Sales commissions	$ 2,000	$ 2,600	$ 600 U
Advertising expense	800	850	50 U
Travel expense	3,600	4,000	400 U
Free samples given out	1,600	1,300	300 F
Total variable	8,000	8,750	750 U
Fixed expenses			
Rent	1,500	1,500	–0–
Sales salaries	1,200	1,200	–0–
Office salaries	800	800	–0–
Depreciation—autos (sales staff)	500	500	–0–
Total fixed	4,000	4,000	–0–
Total expenses	$12,000	$12,750	$ 750 U

As a result of this budget report, Terry was called into the president's office and congratulated on his fine sales performance. He was reprimanded, however, for allowing his costs to get out of control. Terry knew something was wrong with the performance report that he had been given. However, he was not sure what to do, and comes to you for advice.

Instructions

(a) Prepare a budget report based on flexible budget data to help Terry.
(b) Should Terry have been reprimanded? Explain.

Prepare and discuss a responsibility report.

(SO 3, 5)

E24-9 Pronto Plumbing Company is a newly formed company specializing in plumbing services for home and business. The owner, Paul Pronto, had divided the company into two segments: Home Plumbing Services and Business Plumbing Services. Each segment is run by its own supervisor, while basic selling and administrative services are shared by both segments.

Paul has asked you to help him create a performance reporting system that will allow him to measure each segment's performance in terms of its profitability. To that end, the following information has been collected on the Home Plumbing Services segment for the first quarter of 2008.

	Budgeted	Actual
Service revenue	$25,000	$26,000
Allocated portion of:		
Building depreciation	11,000	11,000
Advertising	5,000	4,200
Billing	3,500	3,000
Property taxes	1,200	1,000
Material and supplies	1,500	1,200
Supervisory salaries	9,000	9,400
Insurance	4,000	3,500
Wages	3,000	3,300
Gas and oil	2,700	3,400
Equipment depreciation	1,600	1,300

Instructions

(a) Prepare a responsibility report for the first quarter of 2008 for the Home Plumbing Services segment.

(b) Write a memo to Paul Pronto discussing the principles that should be used when preparing performance reports.

E24-10 Rensing Company has two production departments, Fabricating and Assembling. At a department managers' meeting, the controller uses flexible budget graphs to explain total budgeted costs. Separate graphs based on direct labor hours are used for each department. The graphs show the following.

State total budgeted cost formulas, and prepare flexible budget graph.

(SO 3)

1. At zero direct labor hours, the total budgeted cost line and the fixed cost line intersect the vertical axis at $40,000 in the Fabricating Department and $30,000 in the Assembling Department.
2. At normal capacity of 50,000 direct labor hours, the line drawn from the total budgeted cost line intersects the vertical axis at $150,000 in the Fabricating Department, and $110,000 in the Assembling Department.

Instructions

(a) State the total budgeted cost formula for each department.

(b) Compute the total budgeted cost for each department, assuming actual direct labor hours worked were 53,000 and 47,000, in the Fabricating and Assembling Departments, respectively.

(c) Prepare the flexible budget graph for the Fabricating Department, assuming the maximum direct labor hours in the relevant range is 100,000. Use increments of 10,000 direct labor hours on the horizontal axis and increments of $50,000 on the vertical axis.

E24-11 Lovell Company's organization chart includes the president; the vice president of production; three assembly plants—Dallas, Atlanta, and Tucson; and two departments within each plant—Machining and Finishing. Budget and actual manufacturing cost data for July 2008 are as follows:

Prepare reports in a responsibility reporting system.

(SO 4)

Finishing Department—Dallas: Direct materials $41,500 actual, $45,000 budget; direct labor $83,000 actual, $82,000 budget; manufacturing overhead $51,000 actual, $49,200 budget.

Machining Department—Dallas: Total manufacturing costs $220,000 actual, $216,000 budget.

Atlanta Plant: Total manufacturing costs $424,000 actual, $421,000 budget.

Tucson Plant: Total manufacturing costs $494,000 actual, $496,500 budget.

The Dallas plant manager's office costs were $95,000 actual and $92,000 budget. The vice president of production's office costs were $132,000 actual and $130,000 budget. Office costs are not allocated to departments and plants.

Instructions

Using the format on page 1054, prepare the reports in a responsibility system for:

(a) The Finishing Department—Dallas.

(b) The plant manager—Dallas.

(c) The vice president of production.

E24-12 The Mixing Department manager of Crede Company is able to control all overhead costs except rent, property taxes, and salaries. Budgeted monthly overhead costs for the Mixing Department, in alphabetical order, are:

Prepare a responsibility report for a cost center.

(SO 5)

Indirect labor	$12,000	Property taxes	$ 1,000
Indirect materials	7,500	Rent	1,800
Lubricants	1,700	Salaries	10,000
Maintenance	3,500	Utilities	5,000

Actual costs incurred for January 2008 are indirect labor $12,200; indirect materials $10,200; lubricants $1,650; maintenance $3,500; property taxes $1,100; rent $1,800; salaries $10,000; and utilities $6,500.

Instructions

(a) Prepare a responsibility report for January 2008.

(b) What would be the likely result of management's analysis of the report?

Compute missing amounts in responsibility reports for three profit centers, and prepare a report.

(SO 6)

E24-13 Gonzales Manufacturing Inc. has three divisions which are operated as profit centers. Actual operating data for the divisions listed alphabetically are as follows.

Operating Data	Women's Shoes	Men's Shoes	Children's Shoes
Contribution margin	$240,000	(3)	$180,000
Controllable fixed costs	100,000	(4)	(5)
Controllable margin	(1)	$ 90,000	96,000
Sales	600,000	450,000	(6)
Variable costs	(2)	330,000	250,000

Instructions

(a) Compute the missing amounts. Show computations.

(b) Prepare a responsibility report for the Women's Shoe Division assuming (1) the data are for the month ended June 30, 2008, and (2) all data equal budget except variable costs which are $10,000 over budget.

Prepare a responsibility report for a profit center, and compute ROI.

(SO 6,7)

E24-14 The Sports Equipment Division of Brandon McCarthy Company is operated as a profit center. Sales for the division were budgeted for 2008 at $900,000. The only variable costs budgeted for the division were cost of goods sold ($440,000) and selling and administrative ($60,000). Fixed costs were budgeted at $100,000 for cost of goods sold, $90,000 for selling and administrative and $70,000 for noncontrollable fixed costs. Actual results for these items were:

Sales	$880,000
Cost of goods sold	
Variable	409,000
Fixed	105,000
Selling and administrative	
Variable	61,000
Fixed	67,000
Noncontrollable fixed	80,000

Instructions

(a) Prepare a responsibility report for the Sports Equipment Division for 2008.

(b) Assume the division is an investment center, and average operating assets were $1,000,000. Compute ROI.

Compute ROI for current year and for possible future changes.

(SO 7)

E24-15 The Green Division of Frizell Company reported the following data for the current year.

Sales	$3,000,000
Variable costs	1,950,000
Controllable fixed costs	600,000
Average operating assets	5,000,000

Top management is unhappy with the investment center's return on investment (ROI). It asks the manager of the Green Division to submit plans to improve ROI in the next year. The manager believes it is feasible to consider the following independent courses of action.

1. Increase sales by $320,000 with no change in the contribution margin percentage.
2. Reduce variable costs by $100,000.
3. Reduce average operating assets by 4%.

Instructions

(a) Compute the return on investment (ROI) for the current year.

(b) Using the ROI formula, compute the ROI under each of the proposed courses of action. (Round to one decimal.)

Prepare a responsibility report for an investment center.

(SO 7)

E24-16 The Medina and Ortiz Dental Clinic provides both preventive and orthodontic dental services. The two owners, Martin Medina and Olga Ortiz, operate the clinic as two separate investment centers: Preventive Services and Orthodontic Services. Each of them is in charge of one of the centers: Martin for Preventive Services and Olga for Orthodontic Services. Each month they prepare an income statement on the two centers to evaluate performance and make decisions about how to improve the operational efficiency and profitability of the clinic.

Recently they have been concerned about the profitability of the Preventive Services operations. For several months it has been reporting a loss. Shown below is the responsibility report for the month of May 2008.

	Actual	Difference from Budget
Service revenue	$40,000	$1,000 F
Variable costs:		
Filling materials	5,000	100 U
Novocain	4,000	200 U
Supplies	2,000	250 F
Dental assistant wages	2,500	–0–
Utilities	500	50 U
Total variable costs	14,000	100 U
Fixed costs:		
Allocated portion of receptionist's salary	3,000	200 U
Dentist salary	10,000	500 U
Equipment depreciation	6,000	–0–
Allocated portion of building depreciation	15,000	1,000 U
Total fixed costs	34,000	1,700 U
Operating income (loss)	$ (8,000)	$ 800 U

In addition, the owners know that the investment in operating assets at the beginning of the month was $82,400, and it was $77,600 at the end of the month. They have asked for your assistance in evaluating their current performance reporting system.

Instructions

(a) Prepare a responsibility report for an investment center as illustrated in the chapter.

(b) Write a memo to the owners discussing the deficiencies of their current reporting system.

Prepare missing amounts in responsibility reports for three investment centers.

(SO 7)

E24-17 The Transamerica Transportation Company uses a responsibility reporting system to measure the performance of its three investment centers: Planes, Taxis, and Limos. Segment performance is measured using a system of responsibility reports and return on investment calculations. The allocation of resources within the company and the segment managers' bonuses are based in part on the results shown in these reports.

Recently, the company was the victim of a computer virus that deleted portions of the company's accounting records. This was discovered when the current period's responsibility reports were being prepared. The printout of the actual operating results appeared as follows.

	Planes	Taxis	Limos
Service revenue	$?	$500,000	$?
Variable costs	5,500,000	?	320,000
Contribution margin	?	200,000	480,000
Controllable fixed costs	1,500,000	?	?
Controllable margin	?	80,000	240,000
Average operating assets	25,000,000	?	1,600,000
Return on investment	12%	10%	?

Instructions

Determine the missing pieces of information above.

EXERCISES: SET B

Visit the book's website at **www.wiley.com/college/weygandt**, and choose the Student Companion site, to access Exercise Set B.

PROBLEMS: SET A

WILEY PLUS

Prepare flexible budget and budget report for manufacturing overhead.

(SO 3)

P24-1A Malone Company estimates that 360,000 direct labor hours will be worked during the coming year, 2008, in the Packaging Department. On this basis, the following budgeted manufacturing overhead cost data are computed for the year.

Fixed Overhead Costs		Variable Overhead Costs	
Supervision	$ 90,000	Indirect labor	$126,000
Depreciation	60,000	Indirect materials	90,000
Insurance	30,000	Repairs	54,000
Rent	24,000	Utilities	72,000
Property taxes	18,000	Lubricants	18,000
	$222,000		$360,000

It is estimated that direct labor hours worked each month will range from 27,000 to 36,000 hours.

During October, 27,000 direct labor hours were worked and the following overhead costs were incurred.

Fixed overhead costs: Supervision $7,500, Depreciation $5,000, Insurance $2,470, Rent $2,000, and Property taxes $1,500.

Variable overhead costs: Indirect labor $10,360, Indirect materials, $6,400, Repairs $4,000, Utilities $5,700, and Lubricants $1,640.

(a) Total costs: DLH 27,000, $45,500; DLH 36,000, $54,500

(b) Total $1,070 U

Instructions

(a) Prepare a monthly flexible manufacturing overhead budget for each increment of 3,000 direct labor hours over the relevant range for the year ending December 31, 2008.

(b) Prepare a flexible budget report for October.

(c) Comment on management's efficiency in controlling manufacturing overhead costs in October.

Prepare flexible budget, budget report, and graph for manufacturing overhead.

(SO 3)

P24-2A Fultz Company manufactures tablecloths. Sales have grown rapidly over the past 2 years. As a result, the president has installed a budgetary control system for 2008. The following data were used in developing the master manufacturing overhead budget for the Ironing Department, which is based on an activity index of direct labor hours.

Variable Costs	Rate per Direct Labor Hour	Annual Fixed Costs	
Indirect labor	$0.40	Supervision	$42,000
Indirect materials	0.50	Depreciation	18,000
Factory utilities	0.30	Insurance	12,000
Factory repairs	0.20	Rent	24,000

The master overhead budget was prepared on the expectation that 480,000 direct labor hours will be worked during the year. In June, 42,000 direct labor hours were worked. At that level of activity, actual costs were as shown below.

Variable—per direct labor hour: Indirect labor $0.43, Indirect materials $0.49, Factory utilities $0.32, and Factory repairs $0.24.

Fixed: same as budgeted.

(a) Total costs: 35,000 DLH, $57,000; 50,000 DLH, $78,000

(b) Budget $66,800
Actual $70,160

Instructions

(a) Prepare a monthly flexible manufacturing overhead budget for the year ending December 31, 2008, assuming production levels range from 35,000 to 50,000 direct labor hours. Use increments of 5,000 direct labor hours.

(b) Prepare a budget report for June comparing actual results with budget data based on the flexible budget.

(c) Were costs effectively controlled? Explain.

(d) State the formula for computing the total budgeted costs for Fultz Company.

(e) Prepare the flexible budget graph, showing total budgeted costs at 35,000 and 45,000 direct labor hours. Use increments of 5,000 direct labor hours on the horizontal axis and increments of $10,000 on the vertical axis.

P24-3A Zelmer Company uses budgets in controlling costs. The August 2008 budget report for the company's Assembling Department is as follows.

State total budgeted cost formula, and prepare flexible budget reports for 2 time periods.

(SO 2, 3)

ZELMER COMPANY
Budget Report
Assembling Department
For the Month Ended August 31, 2008

Manufacturing Costs	Budget	Actual	Difference Favorable F Unfavorable U
Variable costs			
Direct materials	$ 48,000	$ 47,000	$1,000 F
Direct labor	54,000	51,300	2,700 F
Indirect materials	24,000	24,200	200 U
Indirect labor	18,000	17,500	500 F
Utilities	15,000	14,900	100 F
Maintenance	9,000	9,200	200 U
Total variable	168,000	164,100	3,900 F
Fixed costs			
Rent	12,000	12,000	-0-
Supervision	17,000	17,000	-0-
Depreciation	7,000	7,000	-0-
Total fixed	36,000	36,000	-0-
Total costs	$204,000	$200,100	$3,900 F

The monthly budget amounts in the report were based on an expected production of 60,000 units per month or 720,000 units per year. The Assembling Department manager is pleased with the report and expects a raise, or at least praise for a job well done. The company president, however, is unhappy with the results for August, because only 58,000 units were produced.

Instructions

(a) State the total monthly budgeted cost formula.

(b) Prepare a budget report for August using flexible budget data. Why does this report provide a better basis for evaluating performance than the report based on static budget data?

(b) Budget $198,400

(c) In September, 64,000 units were produced. Prepare the budget report using flexible budget data, assuming (1) each variable cost was 10% higher than its actual cost in August, and (2) fixed costs were the same in September as in August.

(c) Budget $215,200
Actual $216,510

P24-4A Jantzen Manufacturing Inc. operates the Patio Furniture Division as a profit center. Operating data for this division for the year ended December 31, 2008, are as shown below.

Prepare responsibility report for a profit center.

(SO 6)

	Budget	Difference from Budget
Sales	$2,500,000	$60,000 F
Cost of goods sold		
Variable	1,300,000	41,000 F
Controllable fixed	200,000	6,000 U
Selling and administrative		
Variable	220,000	7,000 U
Controllable fixed	50,000	2,000 U
Noncontrollable fixed costs	70,000	4,000 U

In addition, Jantzen Manufacturing incurs $180,000 of indirect fixed costs that were budgeted at $175,000. Twenty percent (20%) of these costs are allocated to the Patio Furniture Division.

Instructions

(a) Prepare a responsibility report for the Patio Furniture Division for the year.

(b) Comment on the manager's performance in controlling revenues and costs.

(c) Identify any costs excluded from the responsibility report and explain why they were excluded.

(a) Contribution margin
$94,000 F
Controllable margin
$86,000 F

Prepare responsibility report for an investment center, and compute ROI.

(SO 7)

P24-5A Dinkle Manufacturing Company manufactures a variety of tools and industrial equipment. The company operates through three divisions. Each division is an investment center. Operating data for the Home Division for the year ended December 31, 2008, and relevant budget data are as follows.

	Actual	Comparison with Budget
Sales	$1,500,000	$100,000 favorable
Variable cost of goods sold	700,000	60,000 unfavorable
Variable selling and administrative expenses	125,000	25,000 unfavorable
Controllable fixed cost of goods sold	170,000	On target
Controllable fixed selling and administrative expenses	80,000	On target

Average operating assets for the year for the Home Division were $2,500,000 which was also the budgeted amount.

Instructions

(a) Controllable margin: Budget $410; Actual $425

(a) Prepare a responsibility report (in thousands of dollars) for the Home Division.

(b) Evaluate the manager's performance. Which items will likely be investigated by top management?

(c) Compute the expected ROI in 2009 for the Home Division, assuming the following independent changes to actual data.

(1) Variable cost of goods sold is decreased by 6%.

(2) Average operating assets are decreased by 10%.

(3) Sales are increased by $200,000, and this increase is expected to increase contribution margin by $90,000.

Prepare reports for cost centers under responsibility accounting, and comment on performance of managers.

(SO 4)

P24-6A Nieto Company uses a responsibility reporting system. It has divisions in Denver, Seattle, and San Diego. Each division has three production departments: Cutting, Shaping, and Finishing. The responsibility for each department rests with a manager who reports to the division production manager. Each division manager reports to the vice president of production. There are also vice presidents for marketing and finance. All vice presidents report to the president.

In January 2008, controllable actual and budget manufacturing overhead cost data for the departments and divisions were as shown below.

Manufacturing Overhead	Actual	Budget
Individual costs—Cutting Department—Seattle		
Indirect labor	$ 73,000	$ 70,000
Indirect materials	47,700	46,000
Maintenance	20,500	18,000
Utilities	20,100	17,000
Supervision	22,000	20,000
	$183,300	$171,000
Total costs		
Shaping Department—Seattle	$158,000	$148,000
Finishing Department—Seattle	210,000	206,000
Denver division	676,000	673,000
San Diego division	722,000	715,000

Additional overhead costs were incurred as follows: Seattle division production manager—actual costs $52,500, budget $51,000; vice president of production—actual costs $65,000, budget $64,000; president—actual costs $76,400, budget $74,200. These expenses are not allocated.

The vice presidents who report to the president, other than the vice president of production, had the following expenses.

Vice president	Actual	Budget
Marketing	$133,600	$130,000
Finance	109,000	105,000

Instructions

(a) Using the format on page 1054, prepare the following responsibility reports.
  (1) Manufacturing overhead—Cutting Department manager—Seattle division.
  (2) Manufacturing overhead—Seattle division manager.
  (3) Manufacturing overhead—vice president of production.
  (4) Manufacturing overhead and expenses—president.

(b) Comment on the comparative performances of:
  (1) Department managers in the Seattle division.
  (2) Division managers.
  (3) Vice presidents.

(a) (1) $12,300 U
(2) $27,800 U
(3) $38,800 U
(4) $48,600 U

PROBLEMS: SET B

Prepare flexible budget and budget report for manufacturing overhead.

(SO 3)

P24-1B Clarke Company estimates that 240,000 direct labor hours will be worked during 2008 in the Assembly Department. On this basis, the following budgeted manufacturing overhead data are computed.

Variable Overhead Costs		Fixed Overhead Costs	
Indirect labor	$ 72,000	Supervision	$ 72,000
Indirect materials	48,000	Depreciation	36,000
Repairs	24,000	Insurance	12,000
Utilities	50,400	Rent	9,000
Lubricants	9,600	Property taxes	6,000
	$204,000		$135,000

It is estimated that direct labor hours worked each month will range from 18,000 to 24,000 hours.

During January, 20,000 direct labor hours were worked and the following overhead costs were incurred.

Variable Overhead Costs		Fixed Overhead Costs	
Indirect labor	$ 6,200	Supervision	$ 6,000
Indirect materials	3,600	Depreciation	3,000
Repairs	1,600	Insurance	1,000
Utilities	3,300	Rent	800
Lubricants	830	Property taxes	500
	$15,530		$11,300

Instructions

(a) Prepare a monthly flexible manufacturing overhead budget for each increment of 2,000 direct labor hours over the relevant range for the year ending December 31, 2008.

(b) Prepare a manufacturing overhead budget report for January.

(c) Comment on management's efficiency in controlling manufacturing overhead costs in January.

(a) Total costs: 18,000 DLH, $26,550; 24,000 DLH, $31,650

(b) Budget, $28,250
Actual, $26,830

Prepare flexible budget, budget report, and graph for manufacturing overhead.

(SO 3)

P24-2B Flaherty Manufacturing Company produces one product, Kebo. Because of wide fluctuations in demand for Kebo, the Assembly Department experiences significant variations in monthly production levels.

The annual master manufacturing overhead budget is based on 300,000 direct labor hours. In July 27,500 labor hours were worked. The master manufacturing overhead budget for the year and the actual overhead costs incurred in July are as follows.

Overhead Costs	Master Budget (annual)	Actual in July
Variable		
Indirect labor	$ 360,000	$32,000
Indirect materials	210,000	17,000
Utilities	90,000	8,100
Maintenance	60,000	5,400

Table Continued

Overhead Costs	Master Budget (annual)	Actual in July
Fixed		
Supervision	150,000	12,500
Depreciation	120,000	10,000
Insurance and taxes	60,000	5,000
Total	$1,050,000	$90,000

Instructions

(a) Total costs: 22,500 DLH, $81,500; 30,000 DLH, $99,500

(b) Budget $93,500 Actual $90,000

(a) Prepare a monthly flexible overhead budget for the year ending December 31, 2008, assuming monthly production levels range from 22,500 to 30,000 direct labor hours. Use increments of 2,500 direct labor hours.

(b) Prepare a budget report for the month of July 2008 comparing actual results with budget data based on the flexible budget.

(c) Were costs effectively controlled? Explain.

(d) State the formula for computing the total monthly budgeted costs in the Flaherty Manufacturing Company.

(e) Prepare the flexible budget graph showing total budgeted costs at 25,000 and 27,500 direct labor hours. Use increments of 5,000 on the horizontal axis and increments of $10,000 on the vertical axis.

State total budgeted cost formula, and prepare flexible budget reports for 2 time periods.

(SO 2, 3)

P24-3B Hardesty Company uses budgets in controlling costs. The May 2008 budget report for the company's Packaging Department is as follows.

HARDESTY COMPANY
Budget Report
Packaging Department
For the Month Ended May 31, 2008

Manufacturing Costs	Budget	Actual	Difference Favorable F Unfavorable U
Variable costs			
Direct materials	$ 45,000	$ 47,000	$2,000 U
Direct labor	50,000	53,000	3,000 U
Indirect materials	15,000	15,200	200 U
Indirect labor	12,500	13,000	500 U
Utilities	7,500	7,100	400 F
Maintenance	5,000	5,200	200 U
Total variable	135,000	140,500	5,500 U
Fixed costs			
Rent	8,000	8,000	–0–
Supervision	7,000	7,000	–0–
Depreciation	5,000	5,000	–0–
Total fixed	20,000	20,000	–0–
Total costs	$155,000	$160,500	$5,500 U

The monthly budget amounts in the report were based on an expected production of 50,000 units per month or 600,000 units per year.

The company president was displeased with the department manager's performance. The department manager, who thought he had done a good job, could not understand the unfavorable results. In May, 55,000 units were produced.

Instructions

(b) Budget $168,500

(a) State the total budgeted cost formula.

(b) Prepare a budget report for May using flexible budget data. Why does this report provide a better basis for evaluating performance than the report based on static budget data?

(c) In June, 40,000 units were produced. Prepare the budget report using flexible budget data, assuming (1) each variable cost was 20% less in June than its actual cost in May, and (2) fixed costs were the same in the month of June as in May.

(c) Budget $128,000
Actual $132,400

Prepare responsibility report for a profit center.
(SO 6)

P24-4B Grider Manufacturing Inc. operates the Home Appliance Division as a profit center. Operating data for this division for the year ended December 31, 2008, are shown below.

	Budget	Difference from Budget
Sales	$2,400,000	$90,000 U
Cost of goods sold		
Variable	1,200,000	40,000 U
Controllable fixed	200,000	8,000 F
Selling and administrative		
Variable	240,000	8,000 F
Controllable fixed	60,000	6,000 U
Noncontrollable fixed costs	50,000	2,000 U

In addition, Grider Manufacturing incurs $150,000 of indirect fixed costs that were budgeted at $155,000. Twenty percent (20%) of these costs are allocated to the Home Appliance Division. None of these costs are controllable by the division manager.

Instructions

(a) Prepare a responsibility report for the Home Appliance Division (a profit center) for the year.
(b) Comment on the manager's performance in controlling revenues and costs.
(c) Identify any costs excluded from the responsibility report and explain why they were excluded.

(a) Contribution margin $122,000 U
Controllable margin $120,000 U

Prepare responsibility report for an investment center, and compute ROI.
(SO 7)

P24-5B Jeffery Manufacturing Company manufactures a variety of garden and lawn equipment. The company operates through three divisions. Each division is an investment center. Operating data for the Lawnmower Division for the year ended December 31, 2008, and relevant budget data are as follows.

	Actual	Comparison with Budget
Sales	$2,800,000	$150,000 unfavorable
Variable cost of goods sold	1,400,000	80,000 unfavorable
Variable selling and administrative expenses	300,000	50,000 favorable
Controllable fixed cost of goods sold	270,000	On target
Controllable fixed selling and administrative expenses	130,000	On target

Average operating assets for the year for the Lawnmower Division were $5,000,000 which was also the budgeted amount.

Instructions

(a) Prepare a responsibility report (in thousands of dollars) for the Lawnmower Division.
(b) Evaluate the manager's performance. Which items will likely be investigated by top management?
(c) Compute the expected ROI in 2009 for the Lawnmower Division, assuming the following independent changes.
  (1) Variable cost of goods sold is decreased by 15%.
  (2) Average operating assets are decreased by 20%.
  (3) Sales are increased by $500,000 and this increase is expected to increase contribution margin by $200,000.

(a) Controllable margin:
Budget $880
Actual $700

PROBLEMS: SET C

Visit the book's website at **www.wiley.com/college/weygandt**, and choose the Student Companion site, to access Problem Set C.

BROADENING YOUR PERSPECTIVE

DECISION MAKING ACROSS THE ORGANIZATION

BYP24-1 G-Bar Pastures is a 400-acre farm on the outskirts of the Kentucky Bluegrass, specializing in the boarding of broodmares and their foals. A recent economic downturn in the thoroughbred industry has led to a decline in breeding activities, and it has made the boarding business extremely competitive. To meet the competition, G-Bar Pastures planned in 2008 to entertain clients, advertise more extensively, and absorb expenses formerly paid by clients such as veterinary and blacksmith fees.

The budget report for 2008 is presented below. As shown, the static income statement budget for the year is based on an expected 21,900 boarding days at $25 per mare. The variable expenses per mare per day were budgeted: Feed $5, Veterinary fees $3, Blacksmith fees $0.30, and Supplies $0.55. All other budgeted expenses were either semifixed or fixed.

During the year, management decided not to replace a worker who quit in March, but it did issue a new advertising brochure and did more entertaining of clients.[1]

G-BAR PASTURES
Static Budget Income Statement
Year Ended December 31, 2008

	Actual	Master Budget	Difference
Number of mares	52	60	8*
Number of boarding days	18,980	21,900	2,920*
Sales	$379,600	$547,500	$167,900*
Less variable expenses:			
Feed	104,390	109,500	5,110
Veterinary fees	58,838	65,700	6,862
Blacksmith fees	6,074	6,570	496
Supplies	10,178	12,045	1,867
Total variable expenses	179,480	193,815	14,335
Contribution margin	200,120	353,685	153,565*
Less fixed expenses:			
Depreciation	40,000	40,000	–0–
Insurance	11,000	11,000	–0–
Utilities	12,000	14,000	2,000
Repairs and maintenance	10,000	11,000	1,000
Labor	88,000	96,000	8,000
Advertisement	12,000	8,000	4,000*
Entertainment	7,000	5,000	2,000*
Total fixed expenses	180,000	185,000	5,000
Net income	$ 20,120	$168,685	$148,565*

*Unfavorable.

Instructions

With the class divided into groups, answer the following.

(a) Based on the static budget report:

(1) What was the primary cause(s) of the loss in net income?

(2) Did management do a good, average, or poor job of controlling expenses?

(3) Were management's decisions to stay competitive sound?

[1]Data for this case are based on Hans Sprohge and John Talbott, "New Applications for Variance Analysis," *Journal of Accountancy* (AICPA, New York), April 1989, pp. 137–141.

(b) Prepare a flexible budget report for the year.
(c) Based on the flexible budget report, answer the three questions in part (a) above.
(d) What course of action do you recommend for the management of G-Bar Pastures?

MANAGERIAL ANALYSIS

BYP24-2 Fugate Company manufactures expensive watch cases sold as souvenirs. Three of its sales departments are: Retail Sales, Wholesale Sales, and Outlet Sales. The Retail Sales Department is a profit center. The Wholesale Sales Department is a cost center. Its managers merely take orders from customers who purchase through the company's wholesale catalog. The Outlet Sales Department is an investment center, because each manager is given full responsibility for an outlet store location. The manager can hire and discharge employees, purchase, maintain, and sell equipment, and in general is fairly independent of company control.

Jane Duncan is a manager in the Retail Sales Department. Richard Wayne manages the Wholesale Sales Department. Jose Lopez manages the Golden Gate Club outlet store in San Francisco. The following are the budget responsibility reports for each of the three departments.

Budget

	Retail Sales	Wholesale Sales	Outlet Sales
Sales	$ 750,000	$ 400,000	$200,000
Variable costs			
Cost of goods sold	150,000	100,000	25,000
Advertising	100,000	30,000	5,000
Sales salaries	75,000	15,000	3,000
Printing	10,000	20,000	5,000
Travel	20,000	30,000	2,000
Fixed costs			
Rent	50,000	30,000	10,000
Insurance	5,000	2,000	1,000
Depreciation	75,000	100,000	40,000
Investment in assets	$1,000,000	$1,200,000	$800,000

Actual Results

	Retail Sales	Wholesale Sales	Outlet Sales
Sales	$ 750,000	$ 400,000	$200,000
Variable costs			
Cost of goods sold	195,000	120,000	26,250
Advertising	100,000	30,000	5,000
Sales salaries	75,000	15,000	3,000
Printing	10,000	20,000	5,000
Travel	15,000	20,000	1,500
Fixed costs			
Rent	40,000	50,000	12,000
Insurance	5,000	2,000	1,000
Depreciation	80,000	90,000	60,000
Investment in assets	$1,000,000	$1,200,000	$800,000

Instructions

(a) Determine which of the items should be included in the responsibility report for each of the three managers.
(b) Compare the budgeted measures with the actual results. Decide which results should be called to the attention of each manager.

REAL-WORLD FOCUS

BYP24-3 Computer Associates International, Inc., the world's leading business software company, delivers the end-to-end infrastructure to enable e-business through innovative technology, services, and education. CA has 19,000 employees worldwide and recently had revenue of over $6 billion.

Presented below is information from the company's annual report.

COMPUTER ASSOCIATES INTERNATIONAL
Management Discussion

The Company has experienced a pattern of business whereby revenue for its third and fourth fiscal quarters reflects an increase over first- and second-quarter revenue. The Company attributes this increase to clients' increased spending at the end of their calendar year budgetary periods and the culmination of its annual sales plan. Since the Company's costs do not increase proportionately with the third- and fourth-quarters' increase in revenue, the higher revenue in these quarters results in greater profit margins and income. Fourth-quarter profitability is traditionally affected by significant new hirings, training, and education expenditures for the succeeding year.

Instructions

(a) Why don't the company's costs increase proportionately as the revenues increase in the third and fourth quarters?

(b) What type of budgeting seems appropriate for the Computer Associates situation?

EXPLORING THE WEB

BYP24-4 Genelle and Doug have recorded the story of their wedding planning. They are on a strict budget and need help in preparing what they call "a somewhat flexible budget."

Address: www.wednet.com/inspire/wedstory/story1.htm, or go to **www.wiley.com/college/weygandt**

Steps

1. Go to Genelle and Doug's Web site, and read about their trials and tribulations in planning a wedding.
2. Review the **Planning and Budgeting** section in "Part 1" of their story. They mention that this is a "somewhat flexible budget" for 250 guests, totalling $7,150. They would like to reduce their total costs to $7,000, if at all possible.

Instructions

Recast Genelle and Doug's budget into a truly flexible budget so that they can see the effects on their total costs of reducing the number of invited guests to 225 or 200.

COMMUNICATION ACTIVITY

BYP24-5 The manufacturing overhead budget for Edmonds Company contains the following items.

Variable costs		Fixed costs	
Indirect materials	$24,000	Supervision	$18,000
Indirect labor	12,000	Inspection costs	1,000
Maintenance expense	10,000	Insurance expense	2,000
Manufacturing supplies	6,000	Depreciation	15,000
Total variable	$52,000	Total fixed	$36,000

The budget was based on an estimated 2,000 units being produced. During the past month, 1,500 units were produced, and the following costs incurred.

Variable costs		Fixed costs	
Indirect materials	$24,200	Supervision	$19,300
Indirect labor	13,500	Inspection costs	1,200
Maintenance expense	8,200	Insurance expense	2,200
Manufacturing supplies	5,100	Depreciation	14,700
Total variable	$51,000	Total fixed	$37,400

Instructions

(a) Determine which items would be controllable by Mark Farris, the production manager.
(b) How much should have been spent during the month for the manufacture of the 1,500 units?
(c) Prepare a flexible manufacturing overhead budget report for Mr. Farris.
(d) Prepare a responsibility report. Include only the costs that would have been controllable by Mr. Farris. Assume that the supervision cost above includes Mr. Farris's salary of $10,000, both at budget and actual. In an attached memo, describe clearly for Mr. Farris the areas in which his performance needs to be improved.

ETHICS CASE

BYP24-6 National Products Corporation participates in a highly competitive industry. In order to meet this competition and achieve profit goals, the company has chosen the decentralized form of organization. Each manager of a decentralized investment center is measured on the basis of profit contribution, market penetration, and return on investment. Failure to meet the objectives established by corporate management for these measures has not been acceptable and usually has resulted in demotion or dismissal of an investment center manager.

An anonymous survey of managers in the company revealed that the managers feel the pressure to compromise their personal ethical standards to achieve the corporate objectives. For example, at certain plant locations there was pressure to reduce quality control to a level which could not assure that all unsafe products would be rejected. Also, sales personnel were encouraged to use questionable sales tactics to obtain orders, including gifts and other incentives to purchasing agents.

The chief executive officer is disturbed by the survey findings. In his opinion such behavior cannot be condoned by the company. He concludes that the company should do something about this problem.

Instructions

(a) Who are the stakeholders (the affected parties) in this situation?
(b) Identify the ethical implications, conflicts, or dilemmas in the above described situation.
(c) What might the company do to reduce the pressures on managers and decrease the ethical conflicts?

(CMA adapted)

"ALL ABOUT YOU" ACTIVITY

BYP24-7 It is one thing to prepare a personal budget; it is another thing to stick to it. Financial planners have suggested various mechanisms to provide support for enforcing personal budgets. One approach is called "envelope budgeting."

Instructions

Read the article provided at **http://en.wikipedia.org/wiki/Envelope_budgeting**, and answer the following questions.

(a) Summarize the process of envelope budgeting.
(b) Evaluate whether you think you would benefit from envelope budgeting. What do you think are its strengths and weaknesses relative to your situation?

Answers to Insight and Accounting Across the Organization Questions

p. 1049 Budgets and the Exotic Newcastle Disease

Q: What is the major benefit of tying a budget to the overall goals of the company?

A: *People working on a budgeting process that is clearly guided and focused by strategic goals spend less time arguing about irrelevant details and more time focusing on the items that matter.*

p. 1052 Who Should Do The Work?

Q: What can JKL's managers do when they find unprofitable accounts?

A: *Managers can drop unprofitable lines or reduce costs associated with the accounts. In the example described, managers could have the creative work performed by less expensive members of its creative team rather than by supervisory staff.*

p. 1061 Does Hollywood Look at ROI?

Q: What might be the reason that G-rated movies are not produced as much as R-rated movies?

A: *Perhaps Hollywood believes that big-name stars or large budgets, both of which are typical of R-rated movies, sell movies. However, one study recently concluded, "We can't find evidence that stars help movies, and we can't find evidence that bigger budgets increase return on investment." Some film companies are going out of their way to achieve at least a PG rating.*

Authors' Comments on *All About You:* Budgeting for Housing Costs (p. 1063)

In general, in past years it has been a wise decision to purchase a home rather than to rent. As noted, over time home prices have usually appreciated in most parts of the country. Mortgage interest provides some tax relief, and by purchasing a home you get some control over your housing costs. However, in the current environment the decision is a little more complicated. In some parts of the country, home prices have appreciated so much that some experts suggest that renting is actually a more financially prudent choice, at least in the short term.

If you do purchase a home, do not bite off more than you can chew. In addition to a higher mortgage payment, a more expensive house will result in increased maintenance and utility costs, more spent on insurance premiums, and higher property taxes. Make sure to factor all of these expenses into your budget.

Answers to Self-Study Questions

1. c **2.** b **3.** a **4.** d **5.** a **6.** d **7.** d **8.** b **9.** b **10.** d

Remember to go back to the Navigator box on the chapter-opening page and check off your completed work.

Chapter 25

Standard Costs and Balanced Scorecard

STUDY OBJECTIVES

After studying this chapter, you should be able to:

1 Distinguish between a standard and a budget.
2 Identify the advantages of standard costs.
3 Describe how companies set standards.
4 State the formulas for determining direct materials and direct labor variances.
5 State the formulas for determining manufacturing overhead variances.
6 Discuss the reporting of variances.
7 Prepare an income statement for management under a standard costing system.
8 Describe the balanced scorecard approach to performance evaluation.

The Navigator

The Navigator

- Scan **Study Objectives**
- Read **Feature Story**
- Read **Preview**
- Read text and answer **Before You Go On**
  p. 1094 p. 1097 p. 1107
- Work **Demonstration Problem**
- Review **Summary of Study Objectives**
- Answer **Self-Study Questions**
- Complete **Assignments**

Feature Story

HIGHLIGHTING PERFORMANCE EFFICIENCY

There's a very good chance that the highlighter you're holding in your hand was made by Sanford (*www.sanfordcorp.com*), a maker of permanent markers and other writing instruments. Sanford, headquartered in Illinois, annually sells hundreds of millions of dollars' worth of Accent® highlighters, fine-point pens, Sharpie permanent markers, Expo dry-erase markers for overhead projectors, and other writing instruments.

Since Sanford makes literally billions of writing utensils per year, the company must keep tight control over manufacturing costs. A very important part of Sanford's manufacturing process is determining how much direct materials, labor, and overhead should cost. The company then compares these costs to actual costs to assess performance efficiency. Raw materials for Sanford's markers include a barrel, plug, cap, ink reservoir, and a nib (tip). Machines assemble these parts to produce thousands of units per hour. A major component of manufacturing overhead is machine maintenance—some fixed, some variable.

"Labor costs are associated with material handling and equipment maintenance functions. Although the assembly process is highly automated, labor is still required to move raw materials to the machine and to package the finished product. In addition, highly skilled technicians are required to service and maintain each piece of equipment," says Mike Orr, vice president, operations.

Labor rates are predictable because the hourly workers are covered by a union contract. The story is the same with the fringe benefits and some supervisory salaries. Even volume levels are fairly predictable—demand for the product is high—so fixed overhead is efficiently absorbed. Raw material standard costs are based on the previous year's actual prices plus any anticipated inflation. For the past several years, though, inflation had been so low that the company was considering any price increase in raw material to be unfavorable because its standards remained unchanged.

✓ The Navigator

Inside Chapter 25...

Preview of Chapter 25

Standards are a fact of life. You met the admission standards for the school you are attending. The vehicle that you drive had to meet certain governmental emissions standards. The hamburgers and salads you eat in a restaurant have to meet certain health and nutritional standards before they can be sold. As described in our Feature Story, Sanford Corp. has standards for the costs of its materials, labor, and overhead. The reason for standards in these cases is very simple: They help to ensure that overall product quality is high while keeping costs under control.

In this chapter we continue the study of controlling costs. You will learn how to evaluate performance using standard costs and a balanced scorecard.

The content and organization of Chapter 25 are as follows.

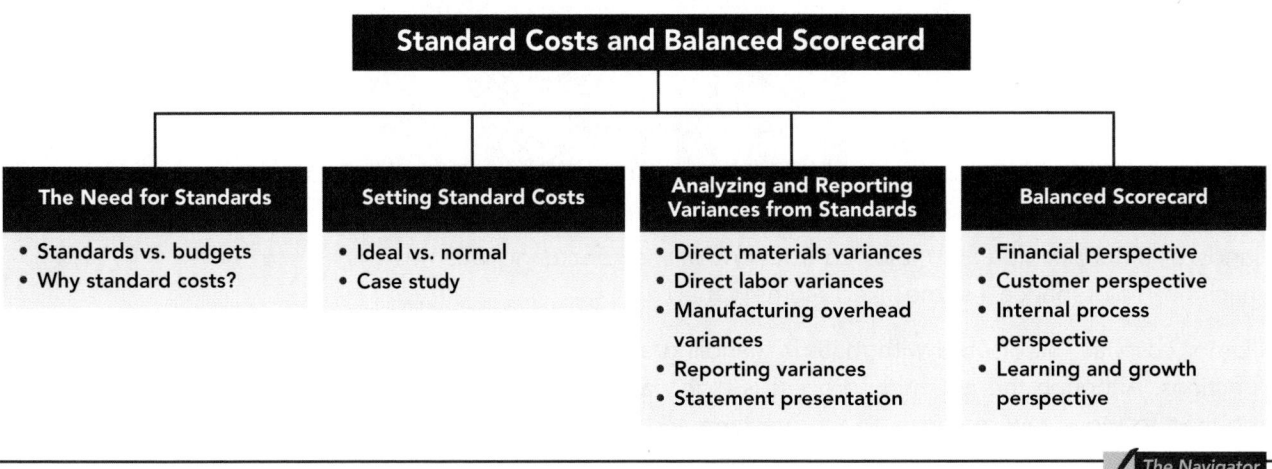

Standard Costs and Balanced Scorecard

- **The Need for Standards**
  - Standards vs. budgets
  - Why standard costs?
- **Setting Standard Costs**
  - Ideal vs. normal
  - Case study
- **Analyzing and Reporting Variances from Standards**
  - Direct materials variances
  - Direct labor variances
  - Manufacturing overhead variances
  - Reporting variances
  - Statement presentation
- **Balanced Scorecard**
  - Financial perspective
  - Customer perspective
  - Internal process perspective
  - Learning and growth perspective

The Navigator

THE NEED FOR STANDARDS

Standards are common in business. Those imposed by government agencies are often called **regulations**. They include the Fair Labor Standards Act, the Equal Employment Opportunity Act, and a multitude of environmental standards. Standards established internally by a company may extend to personnel matters, such as employee absenteeism and ethical codes of conduct, quality control standards for products, and standard costs for goods and services. In managerial accounting, **standard costs** are predetermined unit costs, which companies use as measures of performance.

We will focus on manufacturing operations in this chapter. But you should also recognize that standard costs also apply to many types of service businesses as well. For example, a fast-food restaurant such as McDonald's knows the price it should pay for pickles, beef, buns, and other ingredients. It also knows how much time it should take an employee to flip hamburgers. If the company pays too much for pickles or if employees take too much time to prepare Big Macs, McDonald's notices the deviations and takes corrective action. Not-for-profit enterprises such as universities, charitable organizations, and governmental agencies also may use standard costs.

Distinguishing between Standards and Budgets

STUDY OBJECTIVE 1

Distinguish between a standard and a budget.

Both **standards** and **budgets** are predetermined costs, and both contribute to management planning and control. There is a difference, however, in the way the terms are expressed. A standard is a **unit** amount. A budget is a **total** amount. Thus, it is customary to state that the **standard cost** of direct labor for a unit of product is, say, $10. If the company produces 5,000 units of the product, the $50,000 of direct labor is the **budgeted** labor cost. A standard is the budgeted **cost per unit** of product. A standard is therefore concerned with each individual cost component that makes up the entire budget.

There are important accounting differences between budgets and standards. Except in the application of manufacturing overhead to jobs and processes, budget data are not journalized in cost accounting systems. In contrast, as we illustrate in the appendix to this chapter, standard costs may be incorporated into cost accounting systems. Also, a company may report its inventories at standard cost in its financial statements, but it would not report inventories at budgeted costs.

Why Standard Costs?

Standard costs offer a number of advantages to an organization, as shown in Illustration 25-1.

Illustration 25-1
Advantages of standard costs

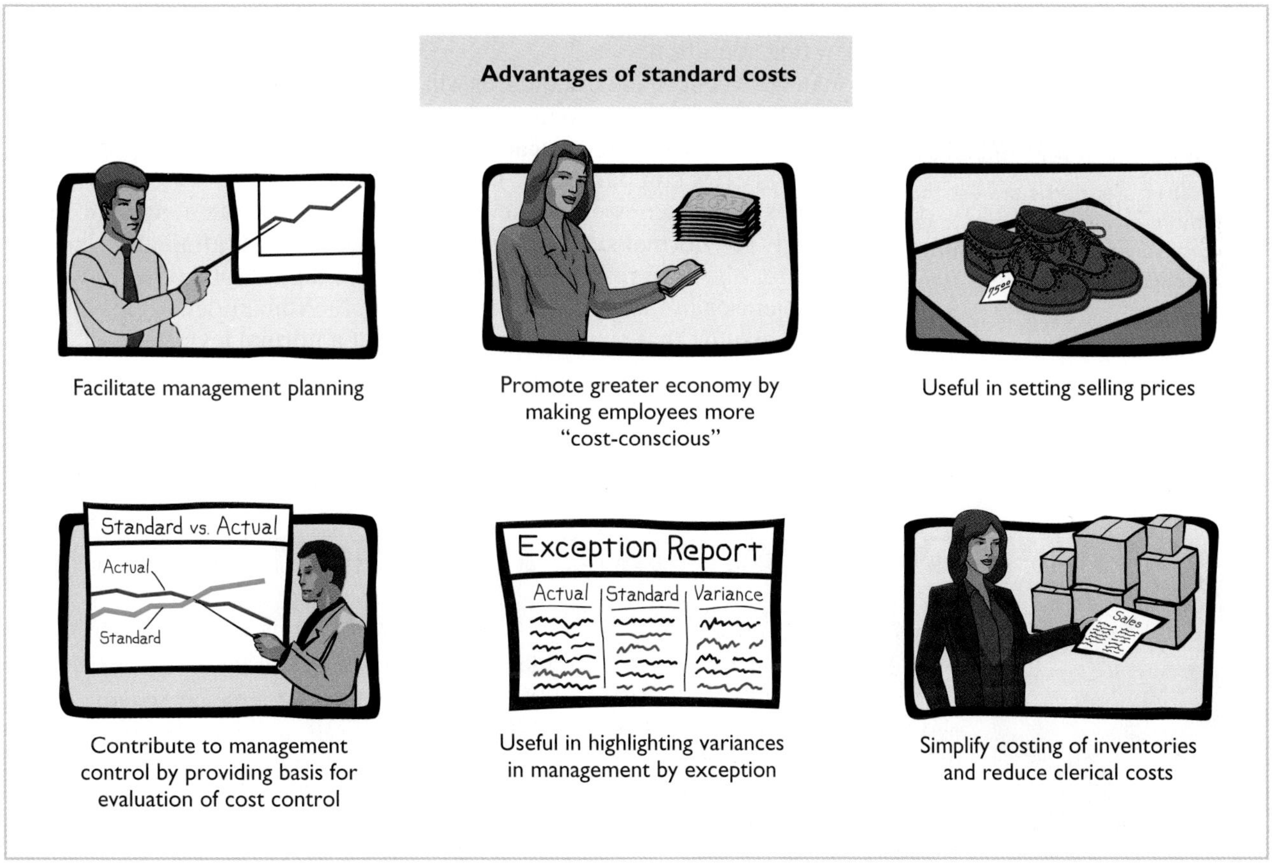
Advantages of standard costs
Facilitate management planning
Promote greater economy by making employees more "cost-conscious"
Useful in setting selling prices
Standard vs. Actual
Actual
Standard
Contribute to management control by providing basis for evaluation of cost control
Exception Report
Actual
Standard
Variance
Useful in highlighting variances in management by exception
Sales
Simplify costing of inventories and reduce clerical costs

STUDY OBJECTIVE 2

Identify the advantages of standard costs.

The organization will realize these advantages only when standard costs are carefully established and prudently used. Using standards solely as a way to place blame can have a negative effect on managers and employees. To minimize this effect, many companies offer wage incentives to those who meet the standards.

SETTING STANDARD COSTS—A DIFFICULT TASK

STUDY OBJECTIVE 3

Describe how companies set standards.

The setting of standard costs to produce a unit of product is a difficult task. It requires input from all persons who have responsibility for costs and quantities. To determine the standard cost of direct materials, management consults purchasing agents, product managers, quality control engineers, and production supervisors. In setting the cost standard for direct labor, managers obtain pay rate data from the payroll department. Industrial engineers generally determine the labor time requirements. The managerial accountant provides important input for the standard-setting process by accumulating historical cost data and by knowing how costs respond to changes in activity levels.

To be effective in controlling costs, standard costs need to be current at all times. Thus, standards are under continuous review. They should change whenever managers determine that the existing standard is not a good measure of performance. Circumstances that warrant revision of a standard include changed wage rates resulting from a new union contract, a change in product specifications, or the implementation of a new manufacturing method.

Ideal versus Normal Standards

Companies set standards at one of two levels: ideal or normal. **Ideal standards** represent optimum levels of performance under perfect operating conditions. **Normal standards** represent efficient levels of performance that are attainable under expected operating conditions.

Some managers believe ideal standards will stimulate workers to ever-increasing improvement. However, most managers believe that ideal standards lower the morale of the entire workforce because they are difficult, if not impossible, to meet. Very few companies use ideal standards.

ETHICS NOTE

When standards are set too high, employees sometimes feel pressure to consider unethical practices to meet these standards.

Most companies that use standards set them at a normal level. Properly set, normal standards should be **rigorous but attainable**. Normal standards allow for rest periods, machine breakdowns, and other "normal" contingencies in the production process. In the remainder of this chapter we will assume that standard costs are set at a normal level.

ACCOUNTING ACROSS THE ORGANIZATION

How Do Standards Help a Business?

Recently a number of organizations, including corporations, consultants, and governmental agencies, agreed to share information regarding performance standards in an effort to create a standard set of measures for thousands of business processes. The group, referred to as the Open Standards Benchmarking Collaborative, includes IBM, Procter and Gamble, the U.S. Navy, and the World Bank. Companies that are interested in participating can go to the group's Web site and enter their information.

Source: William M. Bulkeley, "Business, Agencies to Standardize Their Benchmarks," *Wall Street Journal*, May 19, 2004.

? How will the creation of such standards help a business or organization?

A Case Study

To establish the standard cost of producing a product, it is necessary to establish standards for each manufacturing cost element—direct materials, direct labor, and manufacturing overhead. The standard for each element is derived from the standard price to be paid and the standard quantity to be used.

To illustrate, we look at a case study of how standard costs are set. In this extended example, we assume that Xonic, Inc. wishes to use standard costs to measure performance in filling an order for 1,000 gallons of Weed-O, a liquid weed killer.

DIRECT MATERIALS

The **direct materials price standard** is the cost per unit of direct materials that should be incurred. This standard should be based on the purchasing department's best estimate of the **cost of raw materials**. This cost is frequently based on current purchase prices. The price standard also includes an amount for related costs such as receiving, storing, and handling. The materials price standard per pound of material for Xonic's weed killer is:

Illustration 25-2
Setting direct materials price standard

Item	Price
Purchase price, net of discounts	$2.70
Freight	0.20
Receiving and handling	0.10
Standard direct materials price per pound	**$3.00**

The **direct materials quantity standard** is the quantity of direct materials that should be used per unit of finished goods. This standard is expressed as a physical measure, such as pounds, barrels, or board feet. In setting the standard, management considers both the quality and quantity of materials required to manufacture the product. The standard includes allowances for unavoidable waste and normal spoilage. The standard quantity per unit for Xonic, Inc. is as follows.

Illustration 25-3
Setting direct materials quantity standard

Item	Quantity (Pounds)
Required materials	3.5
Allowance for waste	0.4
Allowance for spoilage	0.1
Standard direct materials quantity per unit	**4.0**

The standard direct materials cost per unit is the standard direct materials price times the standard direct materials quantity. For Xonic, Inc., the standard direct materials cost per gallon of Weed-O is $12.00 ($3.00 × 4.0 pounds).

DIRECT LABOR

The **direct labor price standard** is the rate per hour that should be incurred for direct labor. This standard is based on current wage rates, adjusted for anticipated changes such as cost of living adjustments (COLAs). The price standard also generally includes employer payroll taxes and fringe benefits, such as paid holidays and vacations. For Xonic, Inc., the direct labor price standard is as follows.

ALTERNATIVE TERMINOLOGY
The direct labor price standard is also called the *direct labor rate standard.*

Illustration 25-4
Setting direct labor price standard

Item	Price
Hourly wage rate	$ 7.50
COLA	0.25
Payroll taxes	0.75
Fringe benefits	1.50
Standard direct labor rate per hour	**$10.00**

ALTERNATIVE TERMINOLOGY

The direct labor quantity standard is also called the *direct labor efficiency standard.*

The **direct labor quantity standard** is the time that should be required to make one unit of the product. This standard is especially critical in labor-intensive companies. Allowances should be made in this standard for rest periods, cleanup, machine setup, and machine downtime. For Xonic, Inc., the direct labor quantity standard is as follows.

Illustration 25-5
Setting direct labor quantity standard

Item	Quantity (Hours)
Actual production time	1.5
Rest periods and cleanup	0.2
Setup and downtime	0.3
Standard direct labor hours per unit	**2.0**

The standard direct labor cost per unit is the standard direct labor rate times the standard direct labor hours. For Xonic, Inc., the standard direct labor cost per gallon of Weed-O is $20 ($10.00 × 2.0 hours).

MANUFACTURING OVERHEAD

For manufacturing overhead, companies use a **standard predetermined overhead rate** in setting the standard. This overhead rate is determined by dividing budgeted overhead costs by an expected standard activity index. For example, the index may be standard direct labor hours or standard machine hours.

Calculating the overhead rate

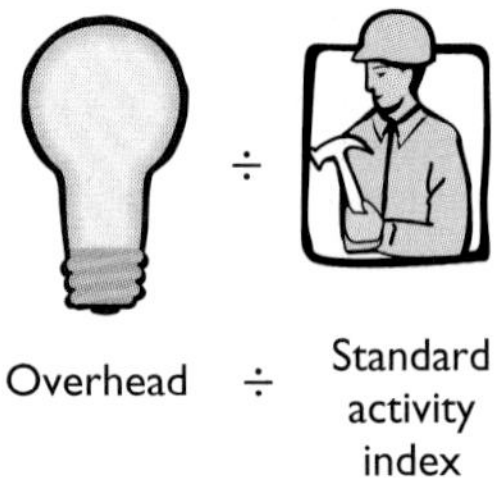

As discussed in Chapter 21, many companies employ activity-based costing (ABC) to allocate overhead costs. Because ABC uses multiple activity indices to allocate overhead costs, it results in a better correlation between activities and costs incurred than do other methods. As a result, the use of ABC can significantly improve the usefulness of standard costing for management decision making.

Xonic, Inc. uses standard direct labor hours as the activity index. The company expects to produce 13,200 gallons of Weed-O during the year at normal capacity. Since it takes 2 direct labor hours for each gallon, total standard direct labor hours are 26,400 (13,200 gallons × 2 hours). At this level of activity, overhead costs are expected to be $132,000. Of that amount, $79,200 are variable and $52,800 are fixed. Illustration 25-6 shows computation of the standard predetermined overhead rates for Xonic, Inc.

Illustration 25-6
Computing predetermined overhead rates

Budgeted Overhead Costs	Amount	÷	Standard Direct Labor Hours	=	Overhead Rate per Direct Labor Hour
Variable	$ 79,200		26,400		$3.00
Fixed	52,800		26,400		2.00
Total	$132,000		26,400		**$5.00**

The standard manufacturing overhead rate per unit is the predetermined overhead rate times the activity index quantity standard. For Xonic, Inc., which uses direct labor hours as its activity index, the standard manufacturing overhead rate per gallon of Weed-O is $10 ($5 × 2 hours).

TOTAL STANDARD COST PER UNIT

After a company has established the standard quantity and price per unit of product, it can determine the total standard cost. The total standard cost per unit is the sum of the standard costs of direct materials, direct labor, and manufacturing overhead. For Xonic, Inc., the total standard cost per gallon of Weed-O is $42, as shown on the following standard cost card.

Illustration 25-7
Standard cost per gallon of Weed-O

Product: Weed-O | **Unit Measure: Gallon**

Manufacturing Cost Elements	Standard Quantity	×	Standard Price	=	Standard Cost
Direct materials	4 pounds		$ 3.00		$12.00
Direct labor	2 hours		$10.00		$20.00
Manufacturing overhead	2 hours		$ 5.00		$10.00
					$42.00

The company prepares a standard cost card for each product. This card provides the basis for determining variances from standards.

MANAGEMENT INSIGHT

How Can We Make Susan's Chili Profitable?

Setting standards can be difficult. Consider Susan's Chili Factory, which manufactures and sells chili. The cost of manufacturing Susan's chili consists of the costs of raw materials, labor to convert the basic ingredients to chili, and overhead. We will use materials cost as an example. Managers need to develop three standards: (1) What should be the formula (mix) of ingredients for one gallon of chili? (2) What should be the normal wastage (or shrinkage) for the individual ingredients? (3) What should be the standard cost for the individual ingredients that go into the chili?

Susan's Chili Factory also illustrates how managers can use standard costs in controlling costs. Suppose that summer droughts have reduced crop yields. As a result, prices have doubled for beans, onions, and peppers. In this case, actual costs will be significantly higher than standard costs, which will cause management to evaluate the situation. Similarly, assume that poor maintenance caused the onion-dicing blades to become dull. As a result, usage of onions to make a gallon of chili tripled. Because this deviation is quickly highlighted through standard costs, managers can take corrective action promptly.

Source: Adapted from David R. Beran, "Cost Reduction Through Control Reporting," *Management Accounting*, April 1982, pp. 29–33.

How might management use this raw material cost information?

Before You Go On...

REVIEW IT

1. How do standards differ from budgets?
2. What are the advantages of standard costs to an organization?
3. Distinguish between normal standards and ideal standards. Which standard is more widely used? Why?

DO IT

The management of Arapahoe Company has decided to use standard costs. Management asks you to explain the components used in setting the standard cost per unit for direct materials, direct labor, and manufacturing overhead.

Action Plan

- Differentiate between the two components of each standard: price and quantity.

Solution The standard direct materials cost per unit is the standard direct materials price times the standard direct materials quantity. The standard direct labor cost per unit is the standard direct labor rate times the standard direct labor hours. The standard manufacturing overhead rate per unit is the standard predetermined overhead rate times the activity index quantity standard.

Related exercise material: *BE25-2, BE25-3, E25-1, E25-2, and E25-3.*

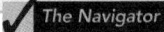

✓ The Navigator

ANALYZING AND REPORTING VARIANCES FROM STANDARDS

ALTERNATIVE TERMINOLOGY

In business, the term *variance* is also used to indicate differences between total budgeted and total actual costs.

One of the major management uses of standard costs is to identify variances from standards. **Variances** are the differences between total actual costs and total standard costs.

To illustrate, we will assume that in producing 1,000 gallons of Weed-O in the month of June, Xonic, Inc. incurred the following costs.

Illustration 25-8
Actual production costs

Direct materials	$13,020
Direct labor	20,580
Variable overhead	6,500
Fixed overhead	4,400
Total actual costs	$44,500

Companies determine total standard costs by multiplying the units produced by the standard cost per unit. The total standard cost of Weed-O is $42,000 (1,000 gallons × $42). Thus, the total variance is $2,500, as shown below.

Illustration 25-9
Computation of total variance

Actual costs	$44,500
Less: Standard costs	42,000
Total variance	**$ 2,500**

Note that the variance is expressed in total dollars, and not on a per unit basis.

When actual costs exceed standard costs, the variance is **unfavorable**. The $2,500 variance in June for Weed-O is unfavorable. An unfavorable variance has a negative connotation. It suggests that the company paid too much for one or more of the manufacturing cost elements or that it used the elements inefficiently.

If actual costs are less than standard costs, the variance is **favorable**. A favorable variance has a positive connotation. It suggests efficiencies in incurring manufacturing costs and in using direct materials, direct labor, and manufacturing overhead.

However, be careful: A favorable variance could be obtained by using inferior materials. In printing wedding invitations, for example, a favorable variance could result from using an inferior grade of paper. Or, a favorable variance might be achieved in installing tires on an automobile assembly line by tightening only half of the lug bolts. A variance is not favorable if the company has sacrificed quality control standards.

To interpret properly the significance of a variance, you must analyze it to determine the underlying factors. Analyzing variances begins by determining the cost elements that comprise the variance. **For each manufacturing cost element, a company computes a total dollar variance. It then analyzes this variance into a price variance and a quantity variance.** Illustration 25-10 depicts these relationships. We discuss each of the variances in the following sections.

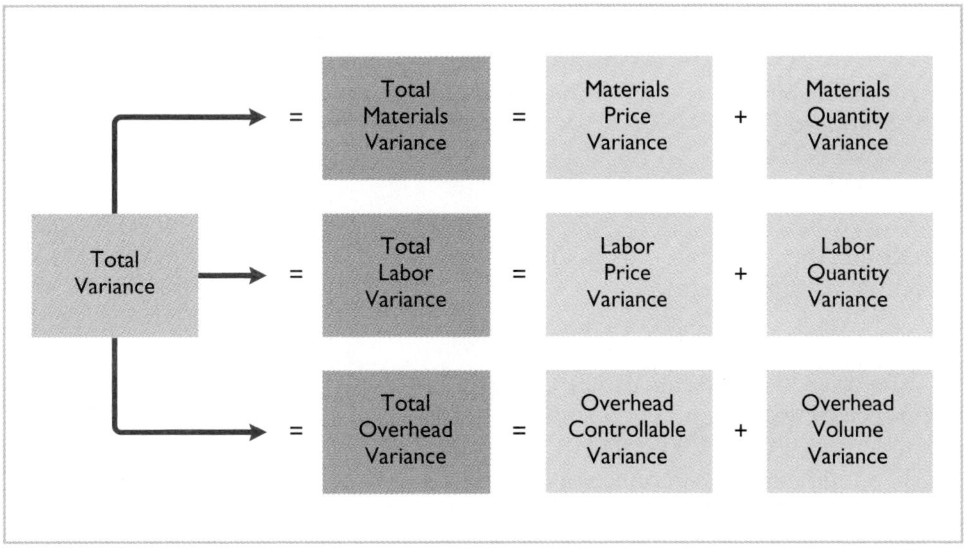

Illustration 25-10
Variance relationships

Direct Materials Variances

STUDY OBJECTIVE 4
State the formulas for determining direct materials and direct labor variances.

In completing the order for 1,000 gallons of Weed-O, Xonic used 4,200 pounds of direct materials. These were purchased at a cost of $3.10 per unit. The **total materials variance** is computed from the following formula.

$$\begin{matrix}\text{Actual Quantity} \\ \times\ \text{Actual Price} \\ (AQ) \times (AP)\end{matrix} \quad - \quad \begin{matrix}\text{Standard Quantity} \\ \times\ \text{Standard Price} \\ (SQ) \times (SP)\end{matrix} \quad = \quad \begin{matrix}\text{Total Materials} \\ \text{Variance} \\ (TMV)\end{matrix}$$

Illustration 25-11
Formula for total materials variance

For Xonic, Inc., the total materials variance is \$1,020 (\$13,020 − \$12,000) unfavorable, as shown below.

(4,200 × \$3.10) − (4,000 × \$3.00) = \$1,020 U

Next, the company analyzes the total variance to determine the amount attributable to price (costs) and to quantity (use). The **materials price variance** is computed from the following formula.[1]

Illustration 25-12
Formula for materials price variance

Actual Quantity × Actual Price (AQ) × (AP)	−	Actual Quantity × Standard Price (AQ) × (SP)	=	Materials Price Variance (MPV)

For Xonic, Inc., the materials price variance is \$420 (\$13,020 − \$12,600) unfavorable, as shown below.

(4,200 × \$3.10) − (4,200 × \$3.00) = \$420 U

HELPFUL HINT
The alternative formula is:
AQ × AP − SP = MPV

The price variance can also be computed by multiplying the actual quantity purchased by the difference between the actual and standard price per unit. The computation in this case is 4,200 × (\$3.10 − \$3.00) = \$420 U.

The **materials quantity variance** is determined from the following formula.

Illustration 25-13
Formula for materials quantity variance

Actual Quantity × Standard Price (AQ) × (SP)	−	Standard Quantity × Standard Price (SQ) × (SP)	=	Materials Quantity Variance (MQV)

For Xonic, Inc., the materials quantity variance is \$600 (\$12,600 − \$12,000) unfavorable, as shown below.

(4,200 × \$3.00) − (4,000 × \$3.00) = \$600 U

HELPFUL HINT
The alternative formula is:
SP × AQ − SQ = MQV

The price variance can also be computed by applying the standard price to the difference between actual and standard quantities used. The computation in this example is \$3.00 × (4,200 − 4,000) = \$600 U.

The total materials variance of \$1,020 U, therefore, consists of the following.

Illustration 25-14
Summary of materials variances

Materials price variance	\$ 420 U
Materials quantity variance	600 U
Total materials variance	**\$1,020 U**

Companies sometimes use a matrix to analyze a variance. **When the matrix is used, a company computes the formulas for each cost element first and then computes the variances.** Illustration 25-15 shows the completed matrix for the direct materials variance for Xonic, Inc. The matrix provides a convenient structure for determining each variance.

[1]We will assume that all materials purchased during the period are used in production and that no units remain in inventory at the end of the period.

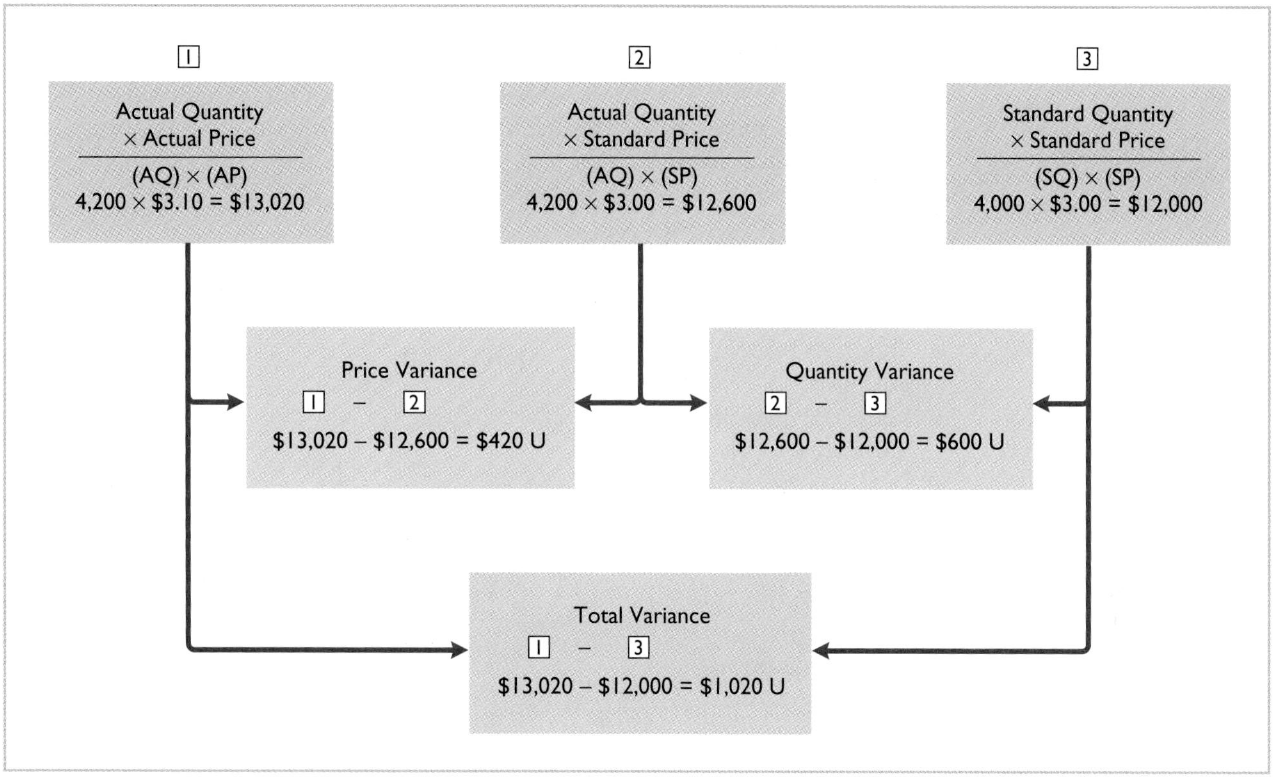

Illustration 25-15
Matrix for direct materials variances

CAUSES OF MATERIALS VARIANCES

What are the causes of a variance? The causes may relate to both internal and external factors. The investigation of a **materials price variance usually begins in the purchasing department**. Many factors affect the price paid for raw materials. These include availability of quantity and cash discounts, the quality of the materials requested, and the delivery method used. To the extent that these factors are considered in setting the price standard, the purchasing department is responsible for any variances.

However, a variance may be beyond the control of the purchasing department. Sometimes, for example, prices may rise faster than expected. Moreover, actions by groups over which the company has no control, such as the OPEC nations' oil price increases, may cause an unfavorable variance. There are also times when a production department may be responsible for the price variance. This may occur when a rush order forces the company to pay a higher price for the materials.

The starting point for determining the cause(s) of an unfavorable **materials quantity variance is in the production department**. If the variances are due to inexperienced workers, faulty machinery, or carelessness, the production department is responsible. However, if the materials obtained by the purchasing department were of inferior quality, then the purchasing department is responsible.

Before You Go On...

REVIEW IT

1. What are the three main components of the total variance from standard cost?
2. What are the formulas for computing the total, price, and quantity variances for direct materials?

DO IT

The standard cost of Product XX includes two units of direct materials at $8.00 per unit. During July, the company buys 22,000 units of direct materials at $7.50 and uses those materials to produce 10,000 units. Compute the total, price, and quantity variances for materials.

Action Plan

Use the formulas for computing each of the materials variances:

- Total materials variance = (AQ × AP) − (SQ × SP)
- Materials price variance = (AQ × AP) − (AQ × SP)
- Materials quantity variance = (AQ × SP) − (SQ × SP)

Solution Substituting amounts into the formulas, the variances are:

Total materials variance = (22,000 × $7.50) − (20,000 × $8.00) = $5,000 unfavorable.

Materials price variance = (22,000 × $7.50) − (22,000 × $8.00) = $11,000 favorable.

Materials quantity variance = (22,000 × $8.00) − (20,000 × $8.00) = $16,000 unfavorable.

Related exercise material: *BE25-4 and E25-5*

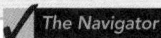

The Navigator

Direct Labor Variances

The process of determining direct labor variances is the same as for determining the direct materials variances. In completing the Weed-O order, Xonic, Inc. incurred 2,100 direct labor hours at an average hourly rate of $9.80. The standard hours allowed for the units produced were 2,000 hours (1,000 gallons × 2 hours). The standard labor rate was $10 per hour. The **total labor variance** is computed from the following formula.

Illustration 25-16
Formula for total labor variance

Actual Hours × Actual Rate (AH) × (AR)	−	Standard Hours × Standard Rate (SH) × (SR)	=	Total Labor Variance (TLV)

The total labor variance is $580 ($20,580 − $20,000) unfavorable, as shown below.

(2,100 × $9.80) − (2,000 × $10.00) = $580 U

The formula for the **labor price variance** is as follows.

Illustration 25-17
Formula for labor price variance

Actual Hours × Actual Rate (AH) × (AR)	−	Actual Hours × Standard Rate (AH) × (SR)	=	Labor Price Variance (LPV)

For Xonic, Inc., the labor price variance is $420 ($20,580 − $21,000) favorable, as shown below.

(2,100 × $9.80) − (2,100 × $10.00) = $420 F

The labor price variance can also be computed by multiplying actual hours worked by the difference between the actual pay rate and the standard pay rate. The computation in this example is 2,100 × ($10.00 − $9.80) = $420 F.

The **labor quantity variance** is derived from the following formula.

HELPFUL HINT
The alternative formula is:
AH × AR − SR = LPV

Illustration 25-18
Formula for labor quantity variance

Actual Hours × Standard Rate (AH) × (SR)	−	Standard Hours × Standard Rate (SH) × (SR)	=	Labor Quantity Variance (LQV)

For Xonic, Inc., the labor quantity variance is $1,000 ($21,000 − $20,000) unfavorable:

(2,100 × $10.00) − (2,000 × $10.00) = $1,000 U

The same result can be obtained by multiplying the standard rate by the difference between actual hours worked and standard hours allowed. In this case the computation is $10.00 × (2,100 − 2,000) = $1,000 U.

The total direct labor variance of $580 U, therefore, consists of:

HELPFUL HINT
The alternative formula is:
SR × AH − SH = LQV

Illustration 25-19
Summary of labor variances

Labor price variance	$ 420 F
Labor quantity variance	1,000 U
Total direct labor variance	**$ 580 U**

These results can also be obtained from the matrix in Illustration 25-20.

Illustration 25-20
Matrix for direct labor variances

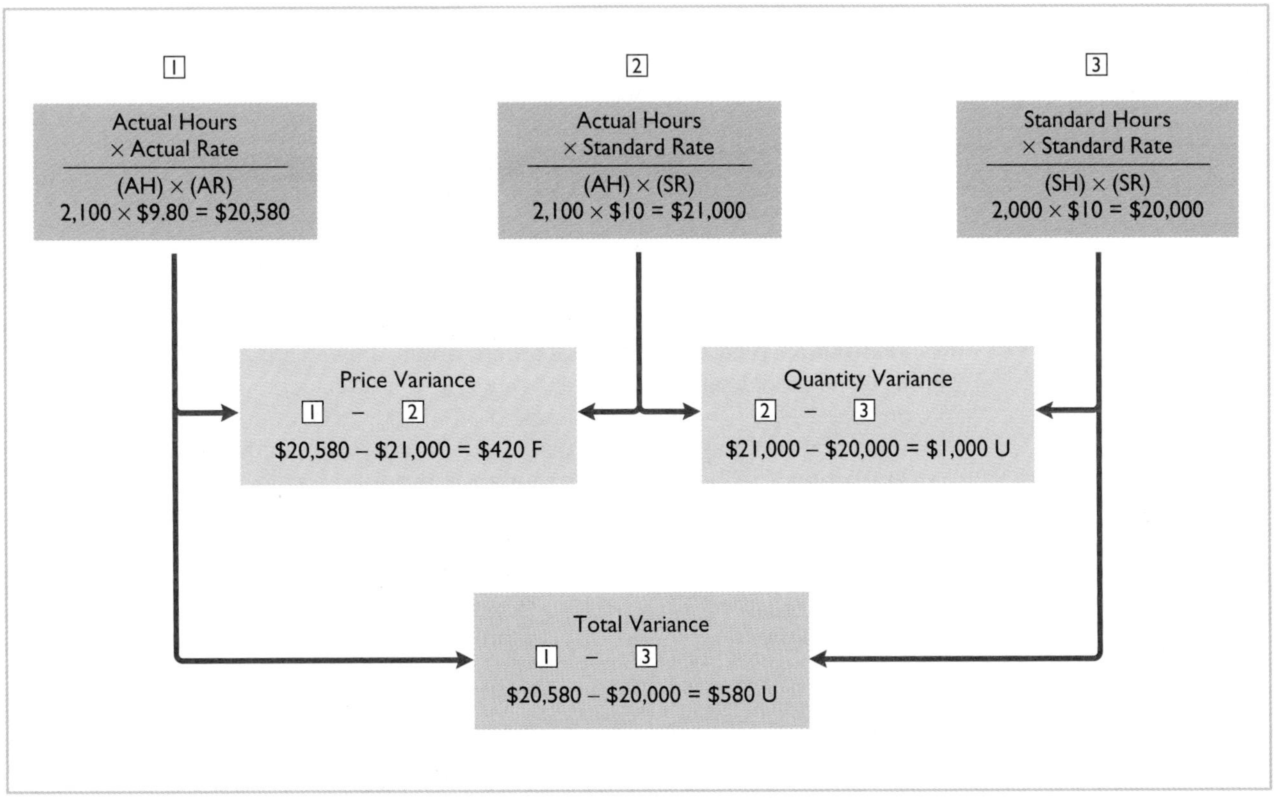

CAUSES OF LABOR VARIANCES

Labor price variances usually result from two factors: (1) paying workers **higher wages than expected**, and (2) **misallocation of workers**. In companies where pay rates are determined by union contracts, labor price variances should be infrequent. When workers are not unionized, there is a much higher likelihood of such variances. The responsibility for these variances rests with the manager who authorized the wage increase.

Misallocation of the workforce refers to using skilled workers in place of unskilled workers and vice versa. The use of an inexperienced worker instead of an experienced one will result in a favorable price variance because of the lower pay rate of the unskilled worker. An unfavorable price variance would result if a skilled worker were substituted for an inexperienced one. The production department generally is responsible for labor price variances resulting from misallocation of the workforce.

Labor quantity variances relate to the **efficiency of workers**. The cause of a quantity variance generally can be traced to the production department. The causes of an unfavorable variance may be poor training, worker fatigue, faulty machinery, or carelessness. These causes are the responsibility of the **production department**. However, if the excess time is due to inferior materials, the responsibility falls outside the production department.

Manufacturing Overhead Variances

The computation of the manufacturing overhead variances involves total overhead variance, overhead controllable variance, and overhead volume variance.

STUDY OBJECTIVE 5

State the formulas for determining manufacturing overhead variances.

TOTAL OVERHEAD VARIANCE

The **total overhead variance** is the difference between actual overhead costs and overhead costs applied to work done. We assumed earlier, in Illustration 25-8 (page 1094), that Xonic incurred overhead costs to produce 1,000 gallons of Weed-O in the month of June. The actual computation of the overhead cost is comprised of a variable and a fixed component. Illustration 25-21 shows this computation.

Illustration 25-21
Actual overhead costs

Variable overhead	$ 6,500
Fixed overhead	4,400
Total actual overhead	**$10,900**

Under a standard costing system, manufacturing overhead costs are applied to work in process on the basis of the **standard hours allowed** for the work done. **Standard hours allowed** are the hours that should have been worked for the units produced. For the 1,000-gallon Weed-O order, the standard hours allowed are 2,000 (1,000 gallons × 2 hours). The predetermined overhead rate is $5 per direct labor hour (see Illustration 25-6 on page 1092). Thus, overhead applied is $10,000 (2,000 hours × $5). Note that actual hours of direct labor (2,100) are not used in applying manufacturing overhead.

Illustration 25-22 shows the formula for the total overhead variance and the calculation for Xonic, Inc.

Illustration 25-22
Formula for total overhead variance

Actual Overhead	–	Overhead Applied*	=	Total Overhead Variance
$10,900	–	$10,000	=	**$900 U**

*Based on standard hours allowed.

Thus, for Xonic, Inc., the total overhead variance is $900 unfavorable.

The overhead variance is generally analyzed through a price variance and a quantity variance. The name usually given to the price variance is the **overhead controllable variance**; the quantity variance is referred to as the **overhead volume variance**.

OVERHEAD CONTROLLABLE VARIANCE

The **overhead controllable variance** shows whether overhead costs are effectively controlled. To compute this variance, the company compares actual overhead costs incurred with budgeted costs for the **standard hours allowed**. The budgeted costs are determined from the flexible manufacturing overhead budget presented in Chapter 24.

ALTERNATIVE TERMINOLOGY

The overhead controllable variance is also called the *budget* or *spending variance*.

For Xonic the budget formula for manufacturing overhead is variable manufacturing overhead cost of $3 per hour of labor plus fixed manufacturing overhead costs of $4,400. Illustration 25-23 shows the flexible budget for Xonic, Inc.

Illustration 25-23
Flexible budget using standard direct labor hours

Xonic, Inc.xls

File Edit View Insert Format Tools Data Window Help

	A	B	C	D	E
1	XONIC, INC				
2	Flexible Manufacturing Overhead Budget				
3	Activity Index				
4	Standard direct labor hours	1,800	**2,000**	2,200	2,400
5	Costs				
6	Variable costs				
7	Indirect materials	$1,800	**$ 2,000**	$ 2,200	$ 2,400
8	Indirect labor	2,700	**3,000**	3,300	3,600
9	Utilities	900	**1,000**	1,100	1,200
10	Total variable costs	5,400	**6,000**	6,600	7,200
11					
12	Fixed costs				
13	Supervision	3,000	**3,000**	3,000	3,000
14	Depreciation	1,400	**1,400**	1,400	1,400
15	Total fixed costs	4,400	**4,400**	4,400	4,400
16	Total costs	$9,800	**$10,400**	$11,000	$11,600
17					

As shown, the budgeted costs for 2,000 standard hours are $10,400 ($6,000 variable and $4,400 fixed).

Illustration 25-24 shows the formula for the overhead controllable variance and the calculation for Xonic, Inc.

Illustration 25-24
Formula for overhead controllable variance

Actual Overhead	–	Overhead Budgeted*	=	Overhead Controllable Variance
$10,900	–	$10,400	=	**$500 U**

*Based on standard hours allowed.

The overhead controllable variance for Xonic, Inc. is $500 unfavorable.

Most controllable variances are associated with variable costs, which are controllable costs. Fixed costs are usually known at the time the budget is prepared. Xonic, Inc. accounts for the variance by comparing the actual variable overhead costs ($6,500) with the budgeted variable costs ($6,000).

Management can compare actual and budgeted overhead for each manufacturing overhead cost that contributes to the controllable variance. In addition, management can develop cost and quantity variances for each overhead cost, such as indirect materials and indirect labor.

OVERHEAD VOLUME VARIANCE

The **overhead volume variance** is the difference between normal capacity hours and standard hours allowed times the fixed overhead rate. The overhead volume variance relates to whether fixed costs were under- or over-applied during the year. For example, the overhead volume variance answers the question of whether Xonic effectively used its fixed costs. If Xonic produces less Weed-O than normal capacity would allow, an unfavorable variance results. Conversely, if Xonic produces more Weed-O than what is considered normal capacity, a favorable variance results.

The formula for computing the overhead volume variance is as follows.

Illustration 25-25
Formula for overhead volume variance

$$\text{Fixed Overhead Rate} \times \left(\text{Normal Capacity Hours} - \text{Standard Hours Allowed}\right) = \text{Overhead Volume Variance}$$

To illustrate the fixed overhead rate computation, recall that Xonic Inc. budgeted fixed overhead cost for the year of $52,800 (Illustration 25-6 on page 1092). At normal capacity, 26,400 standard direct labor hours are required. The fixed overhead rate is therefore $2 ($52,800 ÷ 26,400 hours).

Xonic produced 1,000 units of Weed-O in June. As indicated earlier, the standard hours allowed for the 1,000 gallons produced in June is 2,000 (1,000 gallons × 2 hours). For Xonic, standard direct labor hours for June at normal capacity is 2,200 (26,400 annual hours ÷ 12 months). The computation of the overhead volume variance in this case is as follows.

Illustration 25-26
Computation of overhead volume variance for Xonic Co.

Fixed Overhead Rate	×	(Normal Capacity Hours	−	Standard Hours Allowed)	=	Overhead Volume Variance
$2	×	(2,200	−	2,000)	=	**$400 U**

In Xonic's case, a $400 unfavorable volume variance results. The volume variance is unfavorable because Xonic produced only 1,000 gallons rather than the normal capacity of 1,100 gallons in the month of June. As a result, it underapplied fixed overhead for that period.

In computing the overhead variances, it is important to remember the following.

1. Standard hours allowed are used in each of the variances.
2. Budgeted costs for the controllable variance are derived from the flexible budget.
3. The controllable variance generally pertains to variable costs.
4. The volume variance pertains solely to fixed costs.

CAUSES OF MANUFACTURING OVERHEAD VARIANCES

Since the **controllable variance** relates to variable manufacturing costs, the responsibility for the variance **rests with the production department**. The cause of an unfavorable variance may be: (1) **higher than expected use** of indirect materials, indirect labor, and factory supplies, or (2) **increases in indirect manufacturing costs**, such as fuel and maintenance costs.

The **overhead volume variance** is the responsibility of the **production department** if the cause is inefficient use of direct labor or machine breakdowns. When the cause is a **lack of sales orders**, the responsibility rests **outside the production department**.

Reporting Variances

STUDY OBJECTIVE 6

Discuss the reporting of variances.

All variances should be reported to appropriate levels of management as soon as possible. The sooner managers are informed, the sooner they can evaluate problems and take corrective action.

The form, content, and frequency of variance reports vary considerably among companies. One approach is to prepare a weekly report for each department that has primary responsibility for cost control. Under this approach, materials price variances are reported to the purchasing department, and all other variances are reported to the production department that did the work. The following report for Xonic, Inc., with the materials for the Weed-O order listed first, illustrates this approach.

Illustration 25-27
Materials price variance report

XONIC, INC.
Variance Report — Purchasing Department
For Week Ended June 8, 2008

Type of Materials	Quantity Purchased	Actual Price	Standard Price	Price Variance	Explanation
X100	4,200 lbs.	$3.10	$3.00	$420 U	Rush order
X142	1,200 units	2.75	2.80	60 F	Quantity discount
A85	600 doz.	5.20	5.10	60 U	Regular supplier on strike
Total price variance				**$420 U**	

The explanation column is completed after consultation with the purchasing department manager.

Variance reports facilitate the principle of "management by exception" explained in Chapter 24. For example, the vice president of purchasing can use the report shown above to evaluate the effectiveness of the purchasing department manager. Or, the vice president of production can use production department variance reports to determine how well each production manager is controlling costs. In using variance reports, top management normally looks for **significant variances**. These may be judged on the basis of some quantitative measure, such as more than 10% of the standard or more than $1,000.

Statement Presentation of Variances

STUDY OBJECTIVE 7

Prepare an income statement for management under a standard costing system.

In income statements **prepared for management** under a standard cost accounting system, **cost of goods sold is stated at standard cost and the variances are disclosed separately**. Illustration 25-28 (page 1104) shows this format. Based entirely on the production and sale of Weed-O, it assumes selling and administrative costs of $3,000. Observe that each variance is shown, as well as the total net variance. In this example, variations from standard costs reduced net income by $2,500.

Illustration 25-28
Variances in income statement for management

XONIC, INC.
Income Statement
For the Month Ended June 30, 2008

Sales		$60,000
Cost of goods sold (at standard)		42,000
Gross profit (at standard)		18,000
Variances		
Materials price	**$ 420**	
Materials quantity	**600**	
Labor price	**(420)**	
Labor quantity	**1,000**	
Overhead controllable	**500**	
Overhead volume	**400**	
Total variance unfavorable		**2,500**
Gross profit (actual)		15,500
Selling and administrative expenses		3,000
Net income		$12,500

Standard costs may be used in financial statements prepared for stockholders and other external users. The costing of inventories at standard costs is in accordance with generally accepted accounting principles when there are no significant differences between actual costs and standard costs. Hewlett-Packard and Jostens, Inc., for example, report their inventories at standard costs. However, if there are significant differences between actual and standard costs, the financial statements must report inventories and cost of goods sold at actual costs.

It is also possible to show the variances in an income statement prepared in the variable costing (CVP) format. To do so, it is necessary to analyze the overhead variances into variable and fixed components. This type of analysis is explained in cost accounting textbooks.

BALANCED SCORECARD

STUDY OBJECTIVE 8
Describe the balanced scorecard approach to performance evaluation.

Financial measures (measurement of dollars), such as variance analysis and return on investment (ROI), are useful tools for evaluating performance. However, many companies now supplement these financial measures with nonfinancial measures to better assess performance and anticipate future results. For example, airlines, like Delta, American, and United, use capacity utilization as an important measure to understand and predict future performance. Newspaper publishers, such as the *New York Times* and the *Chicago Tribune*, use circulation figures as another measure by which to assess performance. Illustration 25-29 (page 1105) lists some key nonfinancial measures used in various industries.

Most companies recognize that both financial and nonfinancial measures can provide useful insights into what is happening in the company. As a result, many companies now use a broad-based measurement approach, called the **balanced scorecard**, to evaluate performance. The balanced scorecard incorporates financial and nonfinancial measures in an integrated system that links performance measurement and a company's strategic goals. Nearly 50% of the largest companies in the United States including Unilever, Chase, and Wal-Mart, are using the balanced scorecard approach.

Industry		Measure
Automobiles		Capacity utilization of plants. Average age of key assets. Impact of strikes. Brand-loyalty statistics.
Computer Systems		Market profile of customer end-products. Number of new products. Employee stock ownership percentages. Number of scientists and technicians used in R&D.
Chemicals		Customer satisfaction data. Factors affecting customer product selection. Number of patents and trademarks held. Customer brand awareness.
Regional Banks		Number of ATMs by state. Number of products used by average customer. Percentage of customer service calls handled by interactive voice response units. Personnel cost per employee. Credit card retention rates.

Source: Financial Accounting Standards Board, *Business Reporting: Insights into Enhancing Voluntary Disclosures* (Norwalk, Conn.: FASB, 2001)

Illustration 25-29
Nonfinancial measures used in various industries

The balanced scorecard evaluates company performance from a series of "perspectives." The four most commonly employed perspectives are as follows.

1. The **financial perspective** is the most traditional view of the company. It employs financial measures of performance used by most firms.
2. The **customer perspective** evaluates how well the company is performing from the viewpoint of those people who buy and use its products or services. This view measures how well the company compares to competitors in terms of price, quality, product innovation, customer service, and other dimensions.
3. The **internal process perspective** evaluates the internal operating processes critical to success. All critical aspects of the value chain—including product development, production, delivery and after-sale service—are evaluated to ensure that the company is operating effectively and efficiently.
4. The **learning and growth perspective** evaluates how well the company develops and retains its employees. This would include evaluation of such things as employee skills, employee satisfaction, training programs, and information dissemination.

Within each perspective, the balanced scorecard identifies objectives that will contribute to attainment of strategic goals. Illustration 25-30 (page 1106) shows examples of objectives within each perspective.

The objectives are linked across perspectives in order to tie performance measurement to company goals. The financial objectives are normally set first, and then objectives are set in the other perspectives in order to accomplish the financial objectives.

For example, within the financial perspective, a common goal is to increase profit per dollars invested as measured by ROI. In order to increase ROI, a

Illustration 25-30
Examples of objectives within the four perspectives of balanced scorecard

Financial perspective
- Return on assets
- Net income
- Credit rating
- Share price
- Profit per employee

Customer perspective
- Percentage of customers who would recommend product
- Customer retention
- Response time per customer request
- Brand recognition
- Customer service expense per customer

Internal process perspective
- Percentage of defect-free products
- Stockouts
- Labor utilization rates
- Waste reduction
- Planning accuracy

Learning and growth perspective
- Percentage of employees leaving in less than one year
- Number of cross-trained employees
- Ethics violations
- Training hours
- Reportable accidents

customer-perspective objective might be to increase customer satisfaction as measured by the percentage of customers who would recommend the product to a friend. In order to increase customer satisfaction, an internal business process perspective objective might be to increase product quality as measured by the percentage of defect-free units. Finally, in order to increase the percentage of defect-free units, the learning and growth perspective objective might be to reduce factory employee turnover as measured by the percentage of employees leaving in under one year.

Illustration 25-31 illustrates this linkage across perspectives.

Illustration 25-31
Linked process across balanced scorecard perspectives

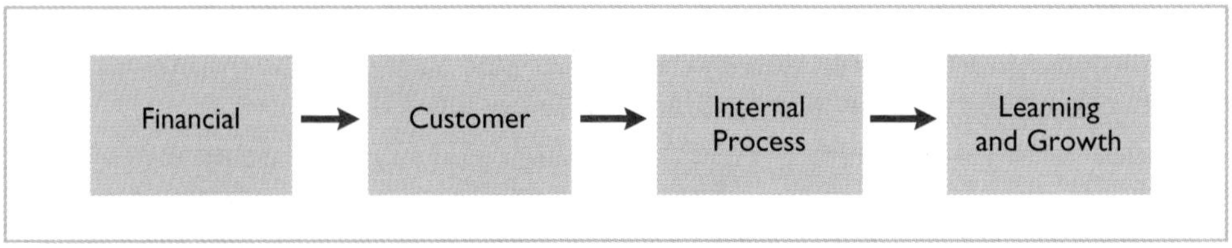

Through this linked process, the company can better understand how to achieve its goals and what measures to use to evaluate performance.

In summary, the balanced scorecard does the following:

1. Employs both financial and nonfinancial measures. (For example, ROI is a financial measure; employee turnover is a nonfinancial measure.)
2. Creates linkages so that high-level corporate goals can be communicated all the way down to the shop floor.

3. Provides measurable objectives for such nonfinancial measures as product quality, rather than vague statements such as "We would like to improve quality."
4. Integrates all of the company's goals into a single performance measurement system, so that an inappropriate amount of weight will not be placed on any single goal.

ACCOUNTING ACROSS THE ORGANIZATION

It May Be Time to Fly United Again

Many of the benefits of a balanced scorecard approach are evident in the improved operations at United Airlines. At the time it filed for bankruptcy in 2002, United had a reputation for some of the worst service in the airline business. But when Glenn Tilton took over as United's Chief Executive Officer in September 2002, he recognized that things had to change.

One thing he did was to implement an incentive program that allows all of United's 63,000 employees to earn a bonus of 2.5% or more of their wages if the company "exceeds its goals for on-time flight departures and for customer intent to fly United again." Since instituting this program the company's on-time departures are among the best, its customer complaints have been reduced considerably, and its number of customers who say that they would fly United again is at its highest level ever. While none of these things guarantees that United will survive, these improvements certainly increase its chances.

Source: Susan Carey, "Friendlier Skies: In Bankruptcy, United Airlines Forges a Path to Better Service," *Wall Street Journal*, June 15, 2004.

? Which of the perspectives of a balanced scorecard were the focus of United's CEO?

Before You Go On...

REVIEW IT

1. What are the formulas for computing the total, price, and quantity variances for direct labor?
2. What are the formulas for computing the total, controllable, and volume variances for manufacturing overhead?
3. How are standard costs and variances reported in income statements prepared for management?
4. What are the basic characteristics of the balanced scorecard?

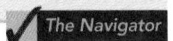

✓ The Navigator

Be sure to read **ALL ABOUT YOU: *Balancing Costs and Quality in Health Care*** on page 1108 for information on how topics in this chapter apply to you.

Balancing Costs and Quality in Health Care

Do you think that standard costs are used only in making products like wheel bearings and hamburgers? Think again. Standards influence virtually every aspect of our lives. For example, the next time you call to schedule an appointment with your doctor, ask the receptionist how many minutes the appointment is scheduled for. Doctors are under increasing pressure to see more patients each day, which means the time spent with each patient is shorter. As insurance companies and employers push for reduced medical costs, every facet of medicine has been standardized and analyzed. Doctors, nurses, and other medical staff are evaluated in every part of their operations to ensure maximum efficiency.

While keeping medical treatment affordable seems like a worthy goal, what are the potential implications for the quality of health care? Does a focus on the bottom line result in a reduction in the quality of health care? Here are some facts to think about while you are sitting in the waiting room.

Some Facts

* Medical costs for a family of four hit $13,383 in 2006, a 9.6% increase over 2005. Of this amount, the employer typically pays about $8,363, and the employee pays about $5,020. Increases have averaged about 10% per year in recent years.
* During the 1990s many health-care facilities provided bonuses to doctors based on cost-based financial incentives. By the end of the 1990s critics began to question this approach because they felt it created perverse incentives for doctors. If a doctor is under pressure to reduce costs, he or she may feel compelled to not provide necessary care.
* Two reports, *To Err Is Human* in 1999 and *Crossing the Quality Chasm* in 2001, called attention to quality and patient-safety shortcomings. As a result, the new emphasis is to align compensation policies with quality improvement.
* Some health plans have adopted compensation systems that attempt to tie pay to performance. These systems offer higher pay for doctors who meet specific goals, such as preventive care, patient satisfaction, acquisition of information technology, and cost containment. In 2004, major California health plans paid physician organizations about $40 million in performance-based bonuses.

About the Numbers

As the following graph shows, the United States spends a huge amount on health care compared to other countries. Note that we spend more on a per person basis, and as a percentage of our gross domestic product (GDP) than every other listed country. This fact makes it even more frustrating that more than 40 million Americans have no health coverage, and that on many measures of health-care quality, America falls short.

International Health Spending per Capita, 2002

In fact, the U.S. spends much more per person on healthcare than other countries, as well as a larger percent of gross domestic product (GDP).

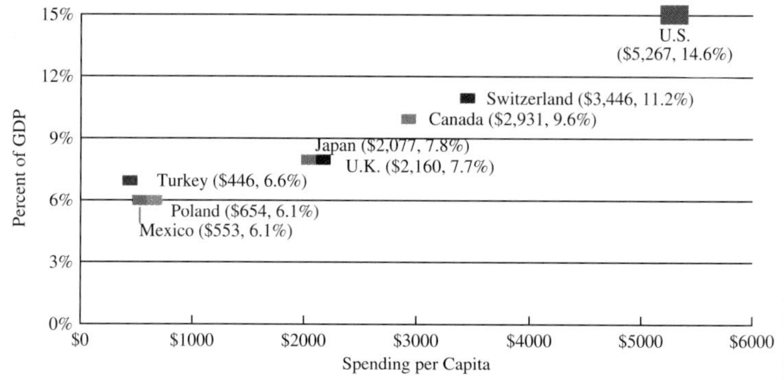

Source: BlueCross BlueShield Association, *www.bcbs.com/mcrg/chap1/ch1_Slide_4.html;* adapted from G. F. Anderson et al., *Health Affairs* (2005).

What Do You Think?

Eventually we all need to see a doctor. Therefore, we all have a vested interest in the quality of medical care. As medical costs have soared in recent years, many approaches have been tried to keep costs down. A simmering debate has centered on a very basic question: To what extent should accountants, through financial measures, influence the type of medical care that you receive?

Suppose that your local medical facility is in danger of closing because it has been losing money. Should the facility put in place incentives that provide bonuses to doctors if they meet certain standard-cost targets for the cost of treating specific ailments?

YES: If the facility is in danger of closing, then someone should take steps to change the medical practices to reduce costs. A closed medical facility is of no use to me, my family, or the community.

NO: I don't want an accountant deciding the right medical treatment for me. My family and I deserve the best medical care.

Source: Thomas Bodenheimer, et al., Can Money Buy Quality? Physician Response to Pay for Performance, Issue Brief No. 102, December 2005, *www.hschange.com/CONTENT/807/#ib1;* Bradley C. Strunk and Robert E. Hurley, "Paying for Quality: Health Plans Try Carrots Instead of Sticks, Issue Brief No. 82, May 2004.

The authors' comments on this situation appear on page 1131.

Demonstration Problem

Manlow Company makes a cologne called Allure. The standard cost for one bottle of Allure is as follows.

	Standard				
Manufacturing Cost Elements	**Quantity**	× **Price**	=	**Cost**	
Direct materials	6 oz.	× $ 0.90	=	$ 5.40	
Direct labor	0.5 hrs.	× $12.00	=	6.00	
Manufacturing overhead	0.5 hrs.	× $ 4.80	=	2.40	
				$13.80	

During the month, the following transactions occurred in manufacturing 10,000 bottles of Allure.

1. 58,000 ounces of materials were purchased at $1.00 per ounce.
2. All the materials purchased were used to produce the 10,000 bottles of Allure.
3. 4,900 direct labor hours were worked at a total labor cost of $56,350.
4. Variable manufacturing overhead incurred was $15,000 and fixed overhead incurred was $10,400.

The manufacturing overhead rate of $4.80 is based on a normal capacity of 5,200 direct labor hours. The total budget at this capacity is $10,400 fixed and $14,560 variable.

Instructions

Compute the total variance and the variances for each of the manufacturing cost elements.

Solution to Demonstration Problem

Total Variance

Actual costs incurred	
Direct materials	$ 58,000
Direct labor	56,350
Manufacturing overhead	25,400
	139,750
Standard cost (10,000 × $13.80)	138,000
Total variance	$ 1,750 U

Direct Materials Variances

Total	=	$58,000 (58,000 × $1.00)	–	$54,000 (60,000 × $0.90)	=	$4,000 U
Price	=	$58,000 (58,000 × $1.00)	–	$52,200 (58,000 × $0.90)	=	$5,800 U
Quantity	=	$52,200 (58,000 × $0.90)	–	$54,000 (60,000 × $0.90)	=	$1,800 F

Direct Labor Variances

Total	=	$56,350 (4,900 × $11.50)	–	$60,000 (5,000 × $12.00)	=	$3,650 F
Price	=	$56,350 (4,900 × $11.50)	–	$58,800 (4,900 × $12.00)	=	$2,450 F
Quantity	=	$58,800 (4,900 × $12.00)	–	$60,000 (5,000 × $12.00)	=	$1,200 F

action plan

- ✓ Check to make sure the total variance and the sum of the individual variances are equal.
- ✓ Find the price variance first, then the quantity variance.
- ✓ Base budgeted overhead costs on flexible budget data.
- ✓ Base overhead applied on standard hours allowed.
- ✓ Ignore actual hours worked in computing overhead variances.
- ✓ Relate the overhead volume variance solely to fixed costs.

Overhead Variances

Total	=	$25,400	−	$24,000	=	$ 1,400 U
		($15,000 + $10,400)		(5,000 × $4.80)		
Controllable	=	$25,400	−	$24,400	=	$ 1,000 U
		($15,000 + $10,400)		($14,000* + $10,400)		
		*$14,560 ÷ 5,200	=	$2.80; $2.80 × 5,000	=	$14,000
Volume	=	$2.00**	×	(5,200 − 5,000)	=	$ 400 U
		**$10,400 ÷ 5,200	=	$2.00		

The Navigator

SUMMARY OF STUDY OBJECTIVES

WILEY PLUS

1 Distinguish between a standard and a budget. Both standards and budgets are predetermined costs. The primary difference is that a standard is a unit amount, whereas a budget is a total amount. A standard may be regarded as the budgeted cost per unit of product.

2 Identify the advantages of standard costs. Standard costs offer a number of advantages. They (a) facilitate management planning, (b) promote greater economy, (c) are useful in setting selling prices, (d) contribute to management control, (e) permit "management by exception," and (f) simplify the costing of inventories and reduce clerical costs.

3 Describe how companies set standards. The direct materials price standard should be based on the delivered cost of raw materials plus an allowance for receiving and handling. The direct materials quantity standard should establish the required quantity plus an allowance for waste and spoilage.

The direct labor price standard should be based on current wage rates and anticipated adjustments such as COLAs. It also generally includes payroll taxes and fringe benefits. Direct labor quantity standards should be based on required production time plus an allowance for rest periods, cleanup, machine setup, and machine downtime.

For manufacturing overhead, a standard predetermined overhead rate is used. It is based on an expected standard activity index such as standard direct labor hours or standard machine hours.

4 State the formulas for determining direct materials and direct labor variances. The formulas for the direct materials variances are:

$$\begin{pmatrix}\text{Actual quantity}\\ \times\text{ Actual price}\end{pmatrix} - \begin{pmatrix}\text{Standard quantity}\\ \times\text{ Standard price}\end{pmatrix} = \begin{matrix}\text{Total}\\ \text{materials}\\ \text{variance}\end{matrix}$$

$$\begin{pmatrix}\text{Actual quantity}\\ \times\text{ Actual price}\end{pmatrix} - \begin{pmatrix}\text{Actual quantity}\\ \times\text{ Standard price}\end{pmatrix} = \begin{matrix}\text{Materials}\\ \text{price}\\ \text{variance}\end{matrix}$$

$$\begin{pmatrix}\text{Actual quantity}\\ \times\text{ Standard price}\end{pmatrix} - \begin{pmatrix}\text{Standard quantity}\\ \times\text{ Standard price}\end{pmatrix} = \begin{matrix}\text{Materials}\\ \text{quantity}\\ \text{variance}\end{matrix}$$

The formulas for the direct labor variances are:

$$\begin{pmatrix}\text{Actual hours}\\ \times\text{ Actual rate}\end{pmatrix} - \begin{pmatrix}\text{Standard hours}\\ \times\text{ Standard rate}\end{pmatrix} = \begin{matrix}\text{Total}\\ \text{labor}\\ \text{variance}\end{matrix}$$

$$\begin{pmatrix}\text{Actual hours}\\ \times\text{ Actual rate}\end{pmatrix} - \begin{pmatrix}\text{Actual hours}\\ \times\text{ Standard rate}\end{pmatrix} = \begin{matrix}\text{Labor}\\ \text{price}\\ \text{variance}\end{matrix}$$

$$\begin{pmatrix}\text{Actual hours}\\ \times\text{ Standard rate}\end{pmatrix} - \begin{pmatrix}\text{Standard hours}\\ \times\text{ Standard rate}\end{pmatrix} = \begin{matrix}\text{Labor}\\ \text{quantity}\\ \text{variance}\end{matrix}$$

5 State the formulas for determining manufacturing overhead variances. The formulas for the manufacturing overhead variances are:

$$\begin{pmatrix}\text{Actual}\\ \text{overhead}\end{pmatrix} - \begin{pmatrix}\text{Overhead}\\ \text{applied}\end{pmatrix} = \begin{matrix}\text{Total overhead}\\ \text{variance}\end{matrix}$$

$$\begin{pmatrix}\text{Actual}\\ \text{overhead}\end{pmatrix} - \begin{pmatrix}\text{Overhead}\\ \text{budgeted}\end{pmatrix} = \begin{matrix}\text{Overhead control-}\\ \text{lable variance}\end{matrix}$$

$$\begin{pmatrix}\text{Fixed}\\ \text{overhead}\\ \text{rate}\end{pmatrix} \times \begin{pmatrix}\text{Normal} & & \text{Standard}\\ \text{capacity} & - & \text{hours}\\ \text{hours} & & \text{allowed}\end{pmatrix} = \begin{matrix}\text{Overhead}\\ \text{volume}\\ \text{variance}\end{matrix}$$

6 Discuss the reporting of variances. Variances are reported to management in variance reports. The reports facilitate management by exception by highlighting significant differences.

7 Prepare an income statement for management under a standard costing system. Under a standard costing system, an income statement prepared for management will report cost of goods sold at standard cost and then disclose each variance separately.

8 Describe the balanced scorecard approach to performance evaluation. The balanced scorecard incorporates financial and nonfinancial measures in an integrated system that links performance measurement and a company's strategic goals. It employs four perspectives: financial, customer, internal processes, and learning and growth. Objectives are set within each of these perspectives that link to objectives within the other perspectives.

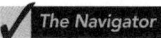

The Navigator

GLOSSARY

Balanced scorecard An approach that incorporates financial and nonfinancial measures in an integrated system that links performance measurement and a company's strategic goals. (p. 1104)

Customer perspective A viewpoint employed in the balanced scorecard to evaluate the company from the perspective of those people who buy and use its products or services. (p. 1105)

Direct labor price standard The rate per hour that should be incurred for direct labor. (p. 1091)

Direct labor quantity standard The time that should be required to make one unit of product. (p. 1092)

Direct materials price standard The cost per unit of direct materials that should be incurred. (p. 1091)

Direct materials quantity standard The quantity of direct materials that should be used per unit of finished goods. (p. 1091)

Financial perspective A viewpoint employed in the balanced scorecard to evaluate a company's performance using financial measures. (p. 1105)

Ideal standards Standards based on the optimum level of performance under perfect operating conditions. (p. 1090)

Internal process perspective A viewpoint employed in the balanced scorecard to evaluate the effectiveness and efficiency of a company's value chain, including product development, production, delivery, and after-sale service. (p. 1105)

Labor price variance The difference between the actual hours times the actual rate and the actual hours times the standard rate for labor. (p. 1098)

Labor quantity variance The difference between actual hours times the standard rate and standard hours times the standard rate for labor. (p. 1099)

Learning and growth perspective A viewpoint employed in the balanced scorecard to evaluate how well a company develops and retains its employees. (p. 1105)

Materials price variance The difference between the actual quantity times the actual price and the actual quantity times the standard price for materials. (p. 1096)

Materials quantity variance The difference between the actual quantity times the standard price and the standard quantity times the standard price for materials. (p. 1096)

Normal standards Standards based on an efficient level of performance that are attainable under expected operating conditions. (p. 1090)

Overhead controllable variance The difference between actual overhead incurred and overhead budgeted for the standard hours allowed. (p. 1101)

Overhead volume variance The difference between normal capacity hours and standard hours allowed times the fixed overhead rate. (p. 1102)

Standard costs Predetermined unit costs which companies use as measures of performance. (p. 1088)

Standard hours allowed The hours that should have been worked for the units produced. (p. 1100)

Standard predetermined overhead rate An overhead rate determined by dividing budgeted overhead costs by an expected standard activity index. (p. 1092)

Total labor variance The difference between actual hours times the actual rate and standard hours times the standard rate for labor. (p. 1098)

Total materials variance The difference between the actual quantity times the actual price and the standard quantity times the standard price of materials. (p. 1095)

Total overhead variance The difference between actual overhead costs and overhead costs applied to work done. (p. 1100)

Variances The difference between total actual costs and total standard costs. (p. 1094)

APPENDIX Standard Cost Accounting System

STUDY OBJECTIVE 9

Identify the features of a standard cost accounting system.

A **standard cost accounting system** is a double-entry system of accounting. In this system, companies use standard costs in making entries, and they formally recognize variances in the accounts. Companies may use a standard cost system with either job order or process costing.

In this appendix, we will explain and illustrate a **standard cost, job order cost accounting system**. The system is based on two important assumptions:

(1) Variances from standards are recognized at the earliest opportunity.

(2) The Work in Process account is maintained exclusively on the basis of standard costs.

In practice, there are many variations among standard cost systems. The system described here should prepare you for systems you see in the "real world."

Journal Entries

We will use the transactions of Xonic, Inc. to illustrate the journal entries. Note as you study the entries that the major difference between the entries here and those for the job order cost accounting system in Chapter 20 is the **variance accounts**.

1. Purchase raw materials on account for $13,020 when the standard cost is $12,600.

Raw Materials Inventory	12,600	
Materials Price Variance	420	
Accounts Payable		13,020
(To record purchase of materials)		

Xonic debits the inventory account for actual quantities at standard cost. This enables the perpetual materials records to show actual quantities. Xonic debits the price variance, which is unfavorable, to Materials Price Variance.

2. Incur direct labor costs of $20,580 when the standard labor cost is $21,000.

Factory Labor	21,000	
Labor Price Variance		420
Wages Payable		20,580
(To record direct labor costs)		

Like the raw materials inventory account, Xonic debits Factory Labor for actual hours worked at the standard hourly rate of pay. In this case, the labor variance is favorable. Thus, Xonic credits Labor Price Variance.

3. Incur actual manufacturing overhead costs of $10,900.

Manufacturing Overhead	10,900	
Accounts Payable/Cash/Acc. Depreciation		10,900
(To record overhead incurred)		

The controllable overhead variance is not recorded at this time. It depends on standard hours applied to work in process. This amount is not known at the time overhead is incurred.

4. Issue raw materials for production at a cost of $12,600 when the standard cost is $12,000.

Work in Process Inventory	12,000	
Materials Quantity Variance	600	
Raw Materials Inventory		12,600
(To record issuance of raw materials)		

Xonic debits Work in Process Inventory for standard materials quantities used at standard prices. It debits the variance account because the variance is unfavorable. The company credits Raw Materials Inventory for actual quantities at standard prices.

5. Assign factory labor to production at a cost of $21,000 when standard cost is $20,000.

Work in Process Inventory	20,000	
Labor Quantity Variance	1,000	
Factory Labor		21,000
(To assign factory labor to jobs)		

Xonic debits Work in Process Inventory for standard labor hours at standard rates. It debits the unfavorable variance to Labor Quantity Variance. The credit to Factory Labor produces a zero balance in this account.

6. Applying manufacturing overhead to production $10,000.

Work in Process Inventory	10,000	
Manufacturing Overhead		10,000
(To assign overhead to jobs)		

Xonic debits Work in Process Inventory for standard hours allowed multiplied by the standard overhead rate.

7. Transfer completed work to finished goods $42,000.

Finished Goods Inventory	42,000	
Work in Process Inventory		42,000
(To record transfer of completed work to finished goods)		

In this example, both inventory accounts are at standard cost.

8. The 1,000 gallons of Weed-O are sold for $60,000.

Accounts Receivable	60,000	
Cost of Goods Sold	42,000	
Sales		60,000
Finished Goods Inventory		42,000
(To record sale of finished goods and the cost of goods sold)		

The company debits Cost of Goods Sold at standard cost. Gross profit, in turn, is the difference between sales and the standard cost of goods sold.

9. Recognize unfavorable overhead variances: controllable $500; volume $400.

Overhead Controllable Variance	500	
Overhead Volume Variance	400	
Manufacturing Overhead		900
(To recognize overhead variances)		

Prior to this entry, a debit balance of $900 existed in Manufacturing Overhead. This entry therefore produces a zero balance in the Manufacturing Overhead account. The information needed for this entry is often not available until the end of the accounting period.

Ledger Accounts

Illustration 25A-1(page 1114) shows the cost accounts for Xonic, Inc., after posting the entries. Note that six variance accounts are included in the ledger. The remaining accounts are the same as those illustrated for a job order cost system in Chapter 20, in which only actual costs were used.

Illustration 25A-1
Cost accounts with variances

Raw Materials Inventory

Debit	Credit
(1) 12,600	(4) 12,600

Materials Price Variance

Debit	Credit
(1) 420	

Work in Process Inventory

Debit	Credit
(4) 12,000	(7) 42,000
(5) 20,000	
(6) 10,000	

Factory Labor

Debit	Credit
(2) 21,000	(5) 21,000

Materials Quantity Variance

Debit	Credit
(4) 600	

Finished Goods Inventory

Debit	Credit
(7) 42,000	(8) 42,000

Manufacturing Overhead

Debit	Credit
(3) 10,900	(6) 10,000
	(9) 900

Labor Price Variance

Debit	Credit
	(2) 420

Cost of Goods Sold

Debit	Credit
(8) 42,000	

Labor Quantity Variance

Debit	Credit
(5) 1,000	

Overhead Controllable Variance

Debit	Credit
(9) 500	

Overhead Volume Variance

Debit	Credit
(9) 400	

HELPFUL HINT

All debit balances in variance accounts indicate unfavorable variances; all credit balances indicate favorable variances.

SUMMARY OF STUDY OBJECTIVE FOR APPENDIX

WILEY PLUS

9 Identify the features of a standard cost accounting system. In a standard cost accounting system, companies journalize and post standard costs, and they maintain separate variance accounts in the ledger.

GLOSSARY FOR APPENDIX

WILEY PLUS

Standard cost accounting system A double-entry system of accounting in which standard costs are used in making entries and variances are recognized in the accounts. (p. 1111)

Note: All asterisked Questions, Exercises, and Problems relate to material in the appendix to the chapter.

SELF-STUDY QUESTIONS

Answers are at the end of the chapter.

(SO 1) **1.** Standards differ from budgets in that:
- **a.** budgets but not standards may be used in valuing inventories.
- **b.** budgets but not standards may be journalized and posted.
- **c.** budgets are a total amount and standards are a unit amount.
- **d.** only budgets contribute to management planning and control.

(SO 2) **2.** The advantages of standard costs include all of the following *except:*
- **a.** management by exception may be used.
- **b.** management planning is facilitated.
- **c.** they may simplify the costing of inventories.
- **d.** management must use a static budget.

(SO 3) **3.** The setting of standards is:
- **a.** a managerial accounting decision.
- **b.** a management decision.
- **c.** a worker decision.
- **d.** preferably set at the ideal level of performance.

(SO 4) **4.** Each of the following formulas is correct except:
- **a.** Labor price variance = (Actual hours × Actual rate) − (Actual hours × Standard rate).
- **b.** Overhead controllable variance = Actual overhead − Overhead budgeted.
- **c.** Materials price variance = (Actual quantity × Actual price) − (Standard quantity × Standard price).
- **d.** Overhead volume variance = Fixed overhead rate × (Normal capacity hours − Standard hours allowed).

(SO 4) **5.** In producing product AA, 6,300 pounds of direct materials were used at a cost of $1.10 per pound. The standard was 6,000 pounds at $1.00 per pound. The direct materials quantity variance is:
- **a.** $330 unfavorable.
- **b.** $300 unfavorable.
- **c.** $600 unfavorable.
- **d.** $630 unfavorable.

(SO 4) **6.** In producing product ZZ, 14,800 direct labor hours were used at a rate of $8.20 per hour. The standard was 15,000 hours at $8.00 per hour. Based on these data, the direct labor:
- **a.** quantity variance is $1,600 favorable.
- **b.** quantity variance is $1,600 unfavorable.
- **c.** price variance is $2,960 favorable.
- **d.** price variance is $3,000 unfavorable.

7. Which of the following is *correct* about overhead variances? (SO 5)
- **a.** The controllable variance generally pertains to fixed overhead costs.
- **b.** The volume variance pertains solely to variable overhead costs.
- **c.** Standard hours actually worked are used in each variance.
- **d.** Budgeted overhead costs are based on the flexible overhead budget.

8. The formula for computing the total overhead variance is: (SO 5)
- **a.** actual overhead less overhead applied.
- **b.** overhead budgeted less overhead applied.
- **c.** actual overhead less overhead budgeted.
- **d.** No correct answer given.

9. Which of the following is *incorrect* about variance reports? (SO 6)
- **a.** They facilitate "management by exception."
- **b.** They should only be sent to the top level of management.
- **c.** They should be prepared as soon as possible.
- **d.** They may vary in form, content, and frequency among companies.

10. Which of the following would *not* be an objective used in the customer perspective of the balanced scorecard approach? (SO 8)
- **a.** Percentage of customers who would recommend product to a friend.
- **b.** Customer retention.
- **c.** Brand recognition.
- **d.** Earnings per share.

***11.** Which of the following is *incorrect* about a standard cost accounting system? (SO 9)
- **a.** It is applicable to job order costing.
- **b.** It is applicable to process costing.
- **c.** It reports only favorable variances.
- **d.** It keeps separate accounts for each variance.

Go to the book's website,
www.wiley.com/college/weygandt,
for Additional Self-Study questions.

The Navigator

QUESTIONS

1. **(a)** "Standard costs are the expected total cost of completing a job." Is this correct? Explain.
(b) "A standard imposed by a governmental agency is known as a regulation." Do you agree? Explain.

2. **(a)** Explain the similarities and differences between standards and budgets.
(b) Contrast the accounting for standards and budgets.

3. Standard costs facilitate management planning. What are the other advantages of standard costs?

4. Contrast the roles of the management accountant and management in setting standard costs.

5. Distinguish between an ideal standard and a normal standard.

6. What factors should be considered in setting (a) the direct materials price standard and (b) the direct materials quantity standard?
7. "The objective in setting the direct labor quantity standard is to determine the aggregate time required to make one unit of product." Do you agree? What allowances should be made in setting this standard?
8. How is the predetermined overhead rate determined when standard costs are used?
9. What is the difference between a favorable cost variance and an unfavorable cost variance?
10. In each of the following formulas, supply the words that should be inserted for each number in parentheses.
    (a) (Actual quantity × (1)) − (Standard quantity × (2)) = Total materials variance
    (b) ((3) × Actual price) − (Actual quantity × (4)) = Materials price variance
    (c) (Actual quantity × (5)) − ((6) × Standard price) = Materials quantity variance
11. In the direct labor variance matrix, there are three factors: (1) Actual hours × Actual rate, (2) Actual hours × Standard rate, and (3) Standard hours × Standard rate. Using the numbers, indicate the formulas for each of the direct labor variances.
12. Greer Company's standard predetermined overhead rate is $8 per direct labor hour. For the month of June, 26,000 actual hours were worked, and 27,000 standard hours were allowed. Normal capacity hours were 28,000. How much overhead was applied?
13. If the $8 per hour overhead rate in question 12 includes $5 variable, and actual overhead costs were $218,000, what is the overhead controllable variance for June? Is the variance favorable or unfavorable?
14. Using the data in questions 12 and 13, what is the overhead volume variance for June? Is the variance favorable or unfavorable?
15. What is the purpose of computing the overhead volume variance? What is the basic formula for this variance?
16. Janet Finney does not understand why the overhead volume variance indicates that fixed overhead costs are under- or overapplied. Clarify this matter for Janet.
17. Nick Menke is attempting to outline the important points about overhead variances on a class examination. List four points that Nick should include in his outline.
18. How often should variances be reported to management? What principle may be used with variance reports?
19. What circumstances may cause the purchasing department to be responsible for both an unfavorable materials price variance and an unfavorable materials quantity variance?
20. What are the four perspectives used in the balanced scorecard? Discuss the nature of each, and how the perspectives are linked.
21. Tom Jones says that the balanced scorecard was created to replace financial measures as the primary mechanism for performance evaluation. He says that it uses only nonfinancial measures. Is this true?
22. What are some examples of nonfinancial measures used by companies to evaluate performance?
23. (a) How are variances reported in income statements prepared for management? (b) May standard costs be used in preparing financial statements for stockholders? Explain.

*24. (a) Explain the basic features of a standard cost accounting system. (b) What type of balance will exist in the variance account when (1) the materials price variance is unfavorable and (2) the labor quantity variance is favorable?

BRIEF EXERCISES

WILEY PLUS

Distinguish between a standard and a budget.
(SO 1)

BE25-1 Orasco Company uses both standards and budgets. For the year, estimated production of Product X is 500,000 units. Total estimated cost for materials and labor are $1,200,000 and $1,600,000. Compute the estimates for (a) a standard cost and (b) a budgeted cost.

Set direct materials standard.
(SO 3)

BE25-2 Asaki Company accumulates the following data concerning raw materials in making one gallon of finished product: (1) Price—net purchase price $2.20, freight-in $0.20 and receiving and handling $0.10. (2) Quantity—required materials 2.6 pounds, allowance for waste and spoilage 0.4 pounds. Compute the following.

(a) Standard direct materials price per gallon.
(b) Standard direct materials quantity per gallon.
(c) Total standard materials cost per gallon.

Set direct labor standard.
(SO 3)

BE25-3 Labor data for making one gallon of finished product in Asaki Company are as follows: (1) Price—hourly wage rate $12.00, payroll taxes $0.80, and fringe benefits $1.20. (2) Quantity—actual production time 1.2 hours, rest periods and clean up 0.25 hours, and setup and downtime 0.15 hours. Compute the following.

(a) Standard direct labor rate per hour.
(b) Standard direct labor hours per gallon.
(c) Standard labor cost per gallon.

Compute direct materials variances.
(SO 4)

BE25-4 Neville Company's standard materials cost per unit of output is $10 (2 pounds × $5). During July, the company purchases and uses 3,200 pounds of materials costing $16,160 in making 1,500 units of finished product. Compute the total, price, and quantity materials variances.

BE25-5 Wamser Company's standard labor cost per unit of output is $20 (2 hours × $10 per hour). During August, the company incurs 2,100 hours of direct labor at an hourly cost of $10.50 per hour in making 1,000 units of finished product. Compute the total, price, and quantity labor variances.

Compute direct labor variances. (SO 4)

BE25-6 In October, Keane Company reports 21,000 actual direct labor hours, and it incurs $115,000 of manufacturing overhead costs. Standard hours allowed for the work done is 20,000 hours. The predetermined overhead rate is $6 per direct labor hour. Compute the total overhead variance.

Compute total overhead variance. (SO 5)

BE25-7 Some overhead data for Keane Company are given in BE25-6. In addition, the flexible manufacturing overhead budget shows that budgeted costs are $4 variable per direct labor hour and $50,000 fixed. Compute the overhead controllable variance.

Compute the overhead controllable variance. (SO 5)

BE25-8 Using the data in BE25-6 and BE25-7, compute the overhead volume variance. Normal capacity was 25,000 direct labor hours.

Compute overhead volume variance. (SO 5)

BE25-9 The four perspectives in the balanced scorecard are (1) financial, (2) customer, (3) internal process, and (4) learning and growth. Match each of the following objectives with the perspective it is most likely associated with: (a) Plant capacity utilization. (b) Employee work days missed due to injury. (c) Return on assets. (d) Brand recognition.

Match balanced scorecard perspectives. (SO 8)

***BE25-10** Journalize the following transactions for Orkin Manufacturing.

Journalize materials variances. (SO 9)

(a) Purchased 6,000 units of raw materials on account for $11,100. The standard cost was $12,000.
(b) Issued 5,500 units of raw materials for production. The standard units were 5,800.

***BE25-11** Journalize the following transactions for Rogler Manufacturing.

Journalize labor variances. (SO 9)

(a) Incurred direct labor costs of $24,000 for 3,000 hours. The standard labor cost was $25,200.
(b) Assigned 3,000 direct labor hours costing $24,000 to production. Standard hours were 3,100.

EXERCISES

E25-1 Lovitz Company is planning to produce 2,000 units of product in 2008. Each unit requires 3 pounds of materials at $6 per pound and a half hour of labor at $14 per hour. The overhead rate is 70% of direct labor.

Compute budget and standard. (SO 1, 2, 3)

Instructions

(a) Compute the budgeted amounts for 2008 for direct materials to be used, direct labor, and applied overhead.
(b) Compute the standard cost of one unit of product.
(c) What are the potential advantages to a corporation of using standard costs?

E25-2 Tony Rondeli manufactures and sells homemade wine, and he wants to develop a standard cost per gallon. The following are required for production of a 50-gallon batch.

Compute standard materials costs. (SO 3)

3,000 ounces of grape concentrate at $0.04 per ounce
54 pounds of granulated sugar at $0.35 per pound
60 lemons at $0.60 each
50 yeast tablets at $0.25 each
50 nutrient tablets at $0.20 each
2,500 ounces of water at $0.004 per ounce

Tony estimates that 4% of the grape concentrate is wasted, 10% of the sugar is lost, and 20% of the lemons cannot be used.

Instructions

Compute the standard cost of the ingredients for one gallon of wine. (Carry computations to two decimal places.)

E25-3 Muhsin Company has gathered the information shown on the next page about its product.

Compute standard cost per unit. (SO 3)

Direct materials: Each unit of product contains 4.5 pounds of materials. The average waste and spoilage per unit produced under normal conditions is 0.5 pounds. Materials cost $4 per pound, but Muhsin always takes the 2% cash discount all of its suppliers offer. Freight costs average $0.25 per pound.

Direct labor: Each unit requires 2 hours of labor. Setup, cleanup, and downtime average 0.2 hours per unit. The average hourly pay rate of Muhsin's employees is $12. Payroll taxes and fringe benfits are an additional $3 per hour.

Manufacturing overhead: Overhead is applied at a rate of $6 per direct labor hour.

Instructions

Compute Muhsin's total standard cost per unit.

Compute labor quantity variance.

(SO 3, 4)

E25-4 Rapid Repair Services, Inc. is trying to establish the standard labor cost of a typical oil change. The following data have been collected from time and motion studies conducted over the past month.

Actual time spent on the oil change	1.0 hour
Hourly wage rate	$10
Payroll taxes	10% of wage rate
Setup and downtime	10% of actual labor time
Cleanup and rest periods	30% of actual labor time
Fringe benefits	25% of wage rate

Instructions

(a) Determine the standard direct labor hours per oil change.
(b) Determine the standard direct labor hourly rate.
(c) Determine the standard direct labor cost per oil change.
(d) If an oil change took 1.5 hours at the standard hourly rate, what was the direct labor quantity variance?

Compute materials price and quantity variances.

(SO 4)

E25-5 The standard cost of Product B manufactured by Mateo Company includes three units of direct materials at $5.00 per unit. During June, 28,000 units of direct materials are purchased at a cost of $4.70 per unit, and 28,000 units of direct materials are used to produce 9,000 units of Product B.

Instructions

(a) Compute the total materials variance and the price and quantity variances.
(b) Repeat (a), assuming the purchase price is $5.20 and the quantity purchased and used is 26,200 units.

Compute labor price and quantity variances.

(SO 4)

E25-6 Scheer Company's standard labor cost of producing one unit of Product DD is 4 hours at the rate of $12.00 per hour. During August, 40,800 hours of labor are incurred at a cost of $12.10 per hour to produce 10,000 units of Product DD.

Instructions

(a) Compute the total labor variance.
(b) Compute the labor price and quantity variances.
(c) Repeat (b), assuming the standard is 4.2 hours of direct labor at $12.25 per hour.

Compute materials and labor variances.

(SO 4)

E25-7 Haslett Inc., which produces a single product, has prepared the following standard cost sheet for one unit of the product.

Direct materials (8 pounds at $2.50 per pound)	$20
Direct labor (3 hours at $12.00 per hour)	$36

During the month of April, the company manufactures 230 units and incurs the following actual costs.

Direct materials purchased and used (1,900 pounds)	$4,940
Direct labor (700 hours)	$8,120

Instructions

Compute the total, price, and quantity variances for materials and labor.

Compute the materials and labor variances and list reasons for unfavorable variances.

(SO 4)

E25-8 The following direct materials and direct labor data pertain to the operations of Solario Manufacturing Company for the month of August.

Costs		Quantities	
Actual labor rate	$13 per hour	Actual hours incurred and used	4,200 hours
Actual materials price	$128 per ton	Actual quantity of materials purchased and used	1,225 tons
Standard labor rate	$12 per hour	Standard hours used	4,300 hours
Standard materials price	$130 per ton	Standard quantity of materials used	1,200 tons

Instructions

(a) Compute the total, price, and quantity variances for materials and labor.

(b) Provide two possible explanations for each of the unfavorable variances calculated above, and suggest where responsibility for the unfavorable result might be placed.

Prepare a variance report for direct labor.

(SO 4, 6)

E25-9 During March 2008, Hinton Tool & Die Company worked on four jobs. A review of direct labor costs reveals the following summary data.

Job Number	Actual Hours	Actual Costs	Standard Hours	Standard Costs	Total Variance
A257	220	$ 4,400	225	$4,500	$ 100 F
A258	450	9,900	430	8,600	1,300 U
A259	300	6,150	300	6,000	150 U
A260	115	2,070	110	2,200	130 F
Total variance					$1,220 U

Analysis reveals that Job A257 was a repeat job. Job A258 was a rush order that required overtime work at premium rates of pay. Job A259 required a more experienced replacement worker on one shift. Work on Job A260 was done for one day by a new trainee when a regular worker was absent.

Instructions

Prepare a report for the plant supervisor on direct labor cost variances for March. The report should have columns for (1) Job No., (2) Actual Hours, (3) Standard Hours, (4) Quantity Variance, (5) Actual Rate, (6) Standard Rate, (7) Price Variance, and (8) Explanation.

Compute overhead variances.

(SO 5)

E25-10 Manufacturing overhead data for the production of Product H by Norland Company are as follows.

Overhead incurred for 52,000 actual direct labor hours worked	$213,000
Overhead rate (variable $3; fixed $1) at normal capacity of 54,000 direct labor hours	$4
Standard hours allowed for work done	51,000

Instructions

Compute the total, controllable, and volume overhead variances.

Compute variances for materials.

(SO 4)

E25-11 Buerhle Company purchased (at a cost of $10,900) and used 2,300 pounds of materials during May. Buerhle's standard cost of materials per unit produced is based on 2 pounds per unit at a cost $5 per pound. Production in May was 1,070 units.

Instructions

(a) Compute the total, price, and quantity variances for materials.

(b) Assume Buerhle also had an unfavorable labor quantity variance. What is a possible scenario that would provide one cause for the variances computed in (a) and the unfavorable labor quantity variance?

Compute manufacturing overhead variances and interpret findings.

(SO 5)

E25-12 The following information was taken from the annual manufacturing overhead cost budget of Granada Company.

Variable manufacturing overhead costs	$33,000
Fixed manufacturing overhead costs	$19,800
Normal production level in labor hours	16,500
Normal production level in units	4,125
Standard labor hours per unit	4

During the year, 4,000 units were produced, 16,100 hours were worked, and the actual manufacturing overhead was $54,000. Actual fixed manufacturing overhead costs equaled budgeted fixed manufacturing overhead costs. Overhead is applied on the basis of direct labor hours.

Instructions

(a) Compute the total, fixed, and variable predetermined manufacturing overhead rates.
(b) Compute the total, controllable, and volume overhead variances.
(c) Briefly interpret the overhead controllable and volume variances computed in (b).

Compute overhead variances.
(SO 5)

E25-13 The loan department of Local Bank uses standard costs to determine the overhead cost of processing loan applications. During the current month a fire occurred, and the accounting records for the department were mostly destroyed. The following data were salvaged from the ashes.

Standard variable overhead rate per hour	$9
Standard hours per application	2
Standard hours allowed	2,000
Standard fixed overhead rate per hour	$6
Actual fixed overhead cost	$13,200
Variable overhead budget based on standard hours allowed	$18,000
Fixed overhead budget	$13,200
Overhead controllable variance	$ 1,500 U

Instructions

(a) Determine the following.
  (1) Total actual overhead cost.
  (2) Actual variable overhead cost.
  (3) Variable overhead cost applied.
  (4) Fixed overhead cost applied.
  (5) Overhead volume variance.
(b) Determine how many loans were processed.

Compute variances.
(SO 5)

E25-14 Jackson Company's overhead rate was based on estimates of $200,000 for overhead costs and 20,000 direct labor hours. Jackson's standards allow 2 hours of direct labor per unit produced. Production in May was 900 units, and actual overhead incurred in May was $18,800. The overhead budgeted for 1,800 standard direct labor hours is $17,600 ($5,000 fixed and $12,600 variable).

Instructions

(a) Compute the total, controllable, and volume variances for overhead.
(b) What are possible causes of the variances computed in part (a)?

Prepare a variance report.
(SO 4, 6)

E25-15 Imperial Landscaping plants grass seed as the basic landscaping for business campuses. During a recent month the company worked on three projects (Ames, Korman, and Stilles). The company is interested in controlling the material costs, namely the grass seed, for these plantings projects.

In order to provide management with useful cost control information, the company uses standard costs and prepares monthly variance reports. Analysis reveals that the purchasing agent mistakenly purchased poor-quality seed for the Ames project. The Korman project, however, received higher-than-standard-quality seed that was on sale. The Stilles project received standard-quality seed; however, the price had increased and a new employee was used to spread the seed.

Shown below are quantity and cost data for each project.

	Actual		Standard		Total
Project	**Quantity**	**Costs**	**Quantity**	**Costs**	**Variance**
Ames	500 lbs.	$1,175	460 lbs.	$1,150	$ 25 U
Korman	400	960	410	1,025	65 F
Stilles	500	1,300	480	1,200	100 U
Total variance					$ 60 U

Instructions

(a) Prepare a variance report for the purchasing department with the following columns: (1) Project, (2) Actual pounds purchased, (3) Actual price, (4) Standard price, (5) Price variance, and (6) Explanation.

(b) Prepare a variance report for the production department with the following columns: (1) Project, (2) Actual pounds, (3) Standard pounds, (4) Standard price, (5) Quantity variance, and (6) Explanation.

E25-16 Archangel Corporation prepared the following variance report.

Complete variance report.

(SO 6)

ARCHANGEL CORPORATION
Variance Report—Purchasing Department
for Week Ended January 9, 2009

Type of Materials	Quantity Purchased	Actual Price	Standard Price	Price Variance	Explanation
Rogue11	? lbs.	$5.20	$5.00	$5,200 ?	Price increase
Storm17	7,000 oz.	?	3.25	1,050 U	Rush order
Beast29	22,000 units	0.45	?	440 F	Bought larger quantity

Instructions

Fill in the appropriate amounts or letters for the question marks in the report.

E25-17 Cepeda Company uses a standard cost accounting system. During January, the company reported the following manufacturing variances.

Prepare income statement for management.

(SO 7)

Materials price variance	$1,250 U	Labor quantity variance	$ 725 U
Materials quantity variance	700 F	Overhead controllable	200 F
Labor price variance	525 U	Overhead volume	1,000 U

In addition, 8,000 units of product were sold at $8.00 per unit. Each unit sold had a standard cost of $6.00. Selling and administrative expenses were $6,000 for the month.

Instructions

Prepare an income statement for management for the month ended January 31, 2008.

E25-18 The following is a list of terms related to performance evaluation.

Identify performance evaluation terminology.

(SO 3, 8)

(1) Balanced scorecard
(2) Variance
(3) Learning and growth perspective
(4) Nonfinancial measures
(5) Customer perspective
(6) Internal process perspective
(7) Ideal standards
(8) Normal standards

Instructions

Match each of the following descriptions with one of the terms above.

(a) The difference between total actual costs and total standard costs.
(b) An efficient level of performance that is attainable under expected operating conditions.
(c) An approach that incorporates financial and nonfinancial measures in an integrated system that links performance measurement and a company's strategic goals.
(d) A viewpoint employed in the balanced scorecard to evaluate how well a company develops and retains its employees.
(e) An evaluation tool that is not based on dollars.
(f) A viewpoint employed in the balanced scorecard to evaluate the company from the perspective of those people who buy and use its products or services.
(g) An optimum level of performance under perfect operating conditions.
(h) A viewpoint employed in the balanced scorecard to evaluate the efficiency and effectiveness of the company's value chain.

***E25-19** Peyton Company installed a standard cost system on January 1. Selected transactions for the month of January are as follows.

Journalize entries in a standard cost accounting system.

(SO 9)

1. Purchased 18,000 units of raw materials on account at a cost of $4.50 per unit. Standard cost was $4.30 per unit.
2. Issued 18,000 units of raw materials for jobs that required 17,600 standard units of raw materials.

3. Incurred 15,200 actual hours of direct labor at an actual rate of $4.80 per hour. The standard rate is $5.50 per hour. (Credit Wages Payable)
4. Performed 15,200 hours of direct labor on jobs when standard hours were 15,400.
5. Applied overhead to jobs at the rate of 100% of direct labor cost for standard hours allowed.

Instructions
Journalize the January transactions.

Answer questions concerning missing entries and balances.
(SO 4, 5, 9)

***E25-20** Cesar Company uses a standard cost accounting system. Some of the ledger accounts have been destroyed in a fire. The controller asks your help in reconstructing some missing entries and balances.

Instructions
Answer the following questions.

(a) Materials Price Variance shows a $2,000 favorable balance. Accounts Payable shows $128,000 of raw materials purchases. What was the amount debited to Raw Materials Inventory for raw materials purchased?
(b) Materials Quantity Variance shows a $3,000 unfavorable balance. Raw Materials Inventory shows a zero balance. What was the amount debited to Work in Process Inventory for direct materials used?
(c) Labor Price Variance shows a $1,500 unfavorable balance. Factory Labor shows a debit of $140,000 for wages incurred. What was the amount credited to Wages Payable?
(d) Factory Labor shows a credit of $140,000 for direct labor used. Labor Quantity Variance shows a $900 unfavorable balance. What was the amount debited to Work in Process for direct labor used?
(e) Overhead applied to Work in Process totaled $165,000. If the total overhead variance was $1,200 unfavorable, what was the amount of overhead costs debited to Manufacturing Overhead?
(f) Overhead Controllable Variance shows a debit balance of $1,500. What was the amount and type of balance (debit or credit) in Overhead Volume Variance?

Journalize entries for materials and labor variances.
(SO 9)

***E25-21** Data for Haslett Inc. are given in E25-7.

Instructions
Journalize the entries to record the materials and labor variances.

Journalize overhead variances.
(SO 9)

***E25-22** Data for Norland Company are given in E25-10.

Instructions
(a) Journalize the incurrence of the overhead costs and the application of overhead to the job, assuming a standard cost accounting system is used.
(b) Prepare the adjusting entry for the overhead variances.

EXERCISES: SET B

Visit the book's website at **www.wiley.com/college/weygandt**, and choose the Student Companion site, to access Exercise Set B.

PROBLEMS: SET A

Compute variances.
(SO 4, 5)

P25-1A Putnam Corporation manufactures a single product. The standard cost per unit of product is shown below.

Direct materials—1 pound plastic at $7.00 per pound	$ 7.00
Direct labor—1.5 hours at $12.00 per hour	18.00
Variable manufacturing overhead	11.25
Fixed manufacturing overhead	3.75
Total standard cost per unit	$40.00

The predetermined manufacturing overhead rate is $10 per direct labor hour ($15.00 ÷ 1.5). It was computed from a master manufacturing overhead budget based on normal production of

7,500 direct labor hours (5,000 units) for the month. The master budget showed total variable costs of $56,250 ($7.50 per hour) and total fixed overhead costs of $18,750 ($2.50 per hour). Actual costs for October in producing 4,900 units were as follows.

Direct materials (5,100 pounds)	$ 37,230
Direct labor (7,000 hours)	87,500
Variable overhead	56,170
Fixed overhead	19,680
Total manufacturing costs	$200,580

The purchasing department buys the quantities of raw materials that are expected to be used in production each month. Raw materials inventories, therefore, can be ignored.

Instructions

Compute all of the materials, labor, and overhead variances.

Compute variances, and prepare income statement.

(SO 4, 5, 7)

P25-2A Dinkel Manufacturing Corporation accumulates the following data relative to jobs started and finished during the month of June 2008.

Costs and Production Data	Actual	Standard
Raw materials unit cost	$2.25	$2.00
Raw materials units used	10,600	10,000
Direct labor payroll	$122,400	$120,000
Direct labor hours worked	14,400	15,000
Manufacturing overhead incurred	$184,500	
Manufacturing overhead applied		$189,000
Machine hours expected to be used at normal capacity		42,500
Budgeted fixed overhead for June		$51,000
Variable overhead rate per hour		$3.00
Fixed overhead rate per hour		$1.20

Overhead is applied on the basis of standard machine hours. Three hours of machine time are required for each direct labor hour. The jobs were sold for $400,000. Selling and administrative expenses were $40,000. Assume that the amount of raw materials purchased equaled the amount used.

Instructions

(a) Compute all of the variances for (1) direct materials, (2) direct labor, and (3) manufacturing overhead.

(b) Prepare an income statement for management. Ignore income taxes.

Compute and identify significant variances.

(SO 4, 5, 6)

P25-3A Rapache Clothiers is a small company that manufactures tall-men's suits. The company has used a standard cost accounting system. In May 2008, 11,200 suits were produced. The following standard and actual cost data applied to the month of May when normal capacity was 14,000 direct labor hours. All materials purchased were used.

Cost Element	Standard (per unit)	Actual
Direct materials	8 yards at $4.30 per yard	$371,050 for 90,500 yards ($4.10 per yard)
Direct labor	1.2 hours at $13.50 per hour	$201,630 for 14,300 hours ($14.10 per hour)
Overhead	1.2 hours at $6.00 per hour (fixed $3.50; variable $2.50)	$49,000 fixed overhead $37,000 variable overhead

Overhead is applied on the basis of direct labor hours. At normal capacity, budgeted fixed overhead costs were $49,000, and budgeted variable overhead was $35,000.

Instructions

(a) Compute the total, price, and quantity variances for (1) materials and (2) labor, and (3) the total, controllable, and volume variances for manufacturing overhead.

(b) Which of the materials and labor variances should be investigated if management considers a variance of more than 4% from standard to be significant?

Answer questions about variances.

(SO 4, 5)

P25-4A Dorantes Manufacturing Company uses a standard cost accounting system. In 2008, 28,000 units were produced. Each unit took several pounds of direct materials and 1½ standard hours of direct labor at a standard hourly rate of $12.00. Normal capacity was 50,000 direct labor hours. During the year, 131,000 pounds of raw materials were purchased at $0.92 per pound. All materials purchased were used during the year.

Instructions

(a) If the materials price variance was $2,620 favorable, what was the standard materials price per pound?
(b) If the materials quantity variance was $4,700 unfavorable, what was the standard materials quantity per unit?
(c) What were the standard hours allowed for the units produced?
(d) If the labor quantity variance was $7,200 unfavorable, what were the actual direct labor hours worked?
(e) If the labor price variance was $10,650 favorable, what was the actual rate per hour?
(f) If total budgeted manufacturing overhead was $350,000 at normal capacity, what was the predetermined overhead rate?
(g) What was the standard cost per unit of product?
(h) How much overhead was applied to production during the year?
(i) If the fixed overhead rate was $2.00, what was the overhead volume variance?
(j) If the overhead controllable variance is $3,000 unfavorable, what were the total variable overhead costs incurred? (Assume that the overhead controllable variance relates only to variable costs.)
(k) Using one or more answers above, what were the total costs assigned to work in process?

Compute variances, prepare an income statement, and explain unfavorable variances.

(SO 4, 5, 7)

P25-5A Farm Labs, Inc. provides mad cow disease testing for both state and federal governmental agricultural agencies. Because the company's customers are governmental agencies, prices are strictly regulated. Therefore, Farm Labs must constantly monitor and control its testing costs. Shown below are the standard costs for a typical test.

Direct materials (2 test tubes @ $1.50 per tube)	$ 3
Direct labor (1 hour @ $25 per hour)	25
Variable overhead (1 hour @ $5 per hour)	5
Fixed overhead (1 hour @ $10 per hour)	10
Total standard cost per test	$43

The lab does not maintain an inventory of test tubes. Therefore, the tubes purchased each month are used that month. Actual activity for the month of November 2008, when 1,500 tests were conducted, resulted in the following:

Direct materials (3,050 test tubes)	$ 4,270
Direct labor (1,600 hours)	36,800
Variable overhead	7,400
Fixed overhead	14,000

Monthly budgeted fixed overhead is $14,000. Revenues for the month were $75,000, and selling and administrative expenses were $4,000.

Instructions

(a) Compute the price and quantity variances for direct materials and direct labor, and the controllable and volume variances for overhead.
(b) Prepare an income statement for management.
(c) Provide possible explanations for each unfavorable variance.

Journalize and post standard cost entries, and prepare income statement.

(SO 4, 5, 7, 9)

***P25-6A** Adcock Corporation uses standard costs with its job order cost accounting system. In January, an order (Job No. 12) for 1,900 units of Product B was received. The standard cost of one unit of Product B is as follows.

Direct materials	3 pounds at $1.00 per pound	$ 3.00
Direct labor	1 hour at $8.00 per hour	8.00
Overhead	2 hours (variable $4.00 per machine hour; fixed $2.25 per machine hour)	12.50
Standard cost per unit		$23.50

Normal capacity for the month was 4,200 machine hours. During January, the following transactions applicable to Job No. 12 occurred.

1. Purchased 6,250 pounds of raw materials on account at $1.06 per pound.
2. Requisitioned 6,250 pounds of raw materials for Job No. 12.
3. Incurred 2,100 hours of direct labor at a rate of $7.75 per hour.
4. Worked 2,100 hours of direct labor on Job No. 12.
5. Incurred manufacturing overhead on account $25,800.
6. Applied overhead to Job No. 12 on basis of standard machine hours used.
7. Completed Job No. 12.
8. Billed customer for Job No. 12 at a selling price of $70,000.
9. Incurred selling and administrative expenses on account $2,000.

Instructions

(a) Journalize the transactions.
(b) Post to the job order cost accounts.
(c) Prepare the entry to recognize the overhead variances.
(d) Prepare the January 2008 income statement for management.

PROBLEMS: SET B

P25-1B Loper Corporation manufactures a single product. The standard cost per unit of product is as follows.

Compute variances.
(SO 4, 5)

Direct materials—2 pounds of plastic at $5 per pound	$10
Direct labor—2 hours at $12 per hour	24
Variable manufacturing overhead	12
Fixed manufacturing overhead	6
Total standard cost per unit	$52

The master manufacturing overhead budget for the month based on normal productive capacity of 15,000 direct labor hours (7,500 units) shows total variable costs of $90,000 ($6 per labor hour) and total fixed costs of $45,000 ($3 per labor hour). Normal productive capacity is 15,000 direct labor hours. Overhead is applied on the basis of direct labor hours. Actual costs for November in producing 7,400 units were as follows.

Direct materials (15,000 pounds)	$ 73,500
Direct labor (14,900 hours)	181,780
Variable overhead	88,990
Fixed overhead	44,000
Total manufacturing costs	$388,270

The purchasing department normally buys the quantities of raw materials that are expected to be used in production each month. Raw materials inventories, therefore, can be ignored.

Instructions

Compute all of the materials, labor, and overhead variances.

P25-2B Orlanda Manufacturing Company uses a standard cost accounting system to account for the manufacture of exhaust fans. In July 2008, it accumulates the following data relative to 1,500 units started and finished.

Compute variances, and prepare income statement.
(SO 4, 5, 7)

Cost and Production Data	Actual	Standard
Raw materials		
Units purchased	17,500	
Units used	17,500	18,000
Unit cost	$3.40	$3.00
Direct labor		
Hours worked	2,900	3,000
Hourly rate	$11.80	$12.50

Table continues on the next page

Cost and Production Data	Actual	Standard
Manufacturing overhead		
Incurred	$87,500	
Applied		$93,000

Manufacturing overhead was applied on the basis of direct labor hours. Normal capacity for the month was 2,800 direct labor hours. At normal capacity, budgeted overhead costs were $20 per labor hour variable and $11 per labor hour fixed. Total budgeted fixed overhead costs were $30,800.

Jobs finished during the month were sold for $240,000. Selling and administrative expenses were $25,000.

Instructions

(a) Compute all of the variances for (1) direct materials, (2) direct labor, and (3) manufacturing overhead.

(b) Prepare an income statement for management showing variances. Ignore income taxes.

Compute and identify significant variances.

(SO 4, 5, 6)

P25-3B Goltra Clothiers manufactures women's business suits. The company uses a standard cost accounting system. In March 2008, 11,800 suits were made. The following standard and actual cost data applied to the month of March when normal capacity was 15,000 direct labor hours. All materials purchased were used in production.

Cost Element	Standard (per unit)	Actual
Direct materials	5 yards at $6.80 per yard	$410,400 for 57,000 yards ($7.20 per yard)
Direct labor	1.0 hours at $11.50 per hour	$125,440 for 11,200 hours ($11.20 per hour)
Overhead	1.0 hours at $9.30 per hour (fixed $6.30; variable $3.00)	$90,000 fixed overhead $37,000 variable overhead

Overhead is applied on the basis of direct labor hours. At normal capacity, budgeted fixed overhead costs were $94,500, and budgeted variable overhead costs were $45,000.

Instructions

(a) Compute the total, price, and quantity variances for (1) materials and (2) labor, and (3) the total, controllable, and volume variances for manufacturing overhead.

(b) Which of the materials and labor variances should be investigated if management considers a variance of more than 5% from standard to be significant? Discuss the potential causes of this variance.

Answer questions about variances.

(SO 4, 5)

P25-4B Heath Manufacturing Company uses a standard cost accounting system. In 2008, 36,000 units were produced. Each unit took several pounds of direct materials and 1⅓ standard hours of direct labor at a standard hourly rate of $12.00. Normal capacity was 42,000 direct labor hours. During the year, 142,000 pounds of raw materials were purchased at $0.90 per pound. All materials purchased were used during the year.

Instructions

(a) If the materials price variance was $7,100 unfavorable, what was the standard materials price per pound?

(b) If the materials quantity variance was $4,760 favorable, what was the standard materials quantity per unit?

(c) What were the standard hours allowed for the units produced?

(d) If the labor quantity variance was $8,400 unfavorable, what were the actual direct labor hours worked?

(e) If the labor price variance was $9,740 favorable, what was the actual rate per hour?

(f) If total budgeted manufacturing overhead was $327,600 at normal capacity, what was the predetermined overhead rate per direct labor hour?

(g) What was the standard cost per unit of product?

(h) How much overhead was applied to production during the year?

(i) If the standard fixed overhead rate was $2.50, what was the overhead volume variance?

(j) If the overhead controllable variance was $3,000 favorable, what were the total variable overhead costs incurred? (Assume that the overhead controllable variance relates only to variable costs.)

(k) Using selected answers above, what were the total costs assigned to work in process?

Compute variances, prepare an income statement, and explain unfavorable variances.

(SO 4, 5, 7)

P25-5B Hi-Tek Labs performs steroid testing services to high schools, colleges, and universities. Because the company deals solely with educational institutions, the price of each test is strictly regulated. Therefore, the costs incurred must be carefully monitored and controlled. Shown below are the standard costs for a typical test.

Direct materials (1 petrie dish @ $2 per dish)	$ 2.00
Direct labor (0.5 hours @ $20 per hour)	10.00
Variable overhead (0.5 hours @ $8 per hour)	4.00
Fixed overhead (0.5 hours @ $3 per hour)	1.50
Total standard cost per test	$17.50

The lab does not maintain an inventory of petrie dishes. Therefore, the dishes purchased each month are used that month. Actual activity for the month of May 2008, when 2,000 tests were conducted, resulted in the following.

Direct materials (2,020 dishes)	$ 4,242
Direct labor (995 hours)	20,895
Variable overhead	8,100
Fixed overhead	3,400

Monthly budgeted fixed overhead is $3,600. Revenues for the month were $45,000, and selling and administrative expenses were $2,000.

Instructions

(a) Compute the price and quantity variances for direct materials and direct labor, and the controllable and volume variances for overhead.
(b) Prepare an income statement for management.
(c) Provide possible explanations for each unfavorable variance.

Journalize and post standard cost entries, and prepare income statement.

(SO 4, 5, 7, 9)

***P25-6B** Gibsen Manufacturing Company uses standard costs with its job order cost accounting system. In January, an order (Job No. 84) was received for 4,100 units of Product D. The standard cost of 1 unit of Product D is as follows.

Direct materials—1.4 pounds at $4.00 per pound	$ 5.60
Direct labor—1 hour at $9.00 per hour	9.00
Overhead—1 hour (variable $7.40; fixed $10.00)	17.40
Standard cost per unit	$32.00

Overhead is applied on the basis of direct labor hours. Normal capacity for the month of January was 4,500 direct labor hours. During January, the following transactions applicable to Job No. 84 occurred.

1. Purchased 6,100 pounds of raw materials on account at $3.60 per pound.
2. Requisitioned 6,100 pounds of raw materials for production.
3. Incurred 3,800 hours of direct labor at $9.25 per hour.
4. Worked 3,800 hours of direct labor on Job No. 84.
5. Incurred $73,650 of manufacturing overhead on account.
6. Applied overhead to Job No. 84 on the basis of direct labor hours.
7. Transferred Job No. 84 to finished goods.
8. Billed customer for Job No. 84 at a selling price of $250,000.
9. Incurred selling and administrative expenses on account $61,000.

Instructions

(a) Journalize the transactions.
(b) Post to the job order cost accounts.
(c) Prepare the entry to recognize the overhead variances.
(d) Prepare the income statement for management for January 2008.

PROBLEMS: SET C

Visit the book's website at **www.wiley.com/college/weygandt**, and choose the Student Companion site, to access Problem Set C.

BROADENING YOUR PERSPECTIVE

DECISION MAKING ACROSS THE ORGANIZATION

BYP25-1 Colaw Professionals, a management consulting firm, specializes in strategic planning for financial institutions. Ken Comer and Mary Linden, partners in the firm, are assembling a new strategic planning model for use by clients. The model is designed for use on most personal computers and replaces a rather lengthy manual model currently marketed by the firm. To market the new model Ken and Mary will need to provide clients with an estimate of the number of labor hours and computer time needed to operate the model. The model is currently being test marketed at five small financial institutions. These financial institutions are listed below, along with the number of combined computer/labor hours used by each institution to run the model one time.

Financial Institutions	Computer/Labor Hours Required
Midland National	25
First State	45
Financial Federal	40
Pacific America	30
Lakeview National	30
Total	170
Average	34

Any company that purchases the new model will need to purchase user manuals for the system. User manuals will be sold to clients in cases of 20, at a cost of $300 per case. One manual must be used each time the model is run because each manual includes a nonreusable computer-accessed password for operating the system. Also required are specialized computer forms that are sold only by Colaw. The specialized forms are sold in packages of 250, at a cost of $50 per package. One application of the model requires the use of 50 forms. This amount includes two forms that are generally wasted in each application due to printer alignment errors. The overall cost of the strategic planning model to clients is $12,000. Most clients will use the model four times annually.

Colaw must provide its clients with estimates of ongoing costs incurred in operating the new planning model, and would like to do so in the form of standard costs.

Instructions

With the class divided into groups, answer the following.

(a) What factors should be considered in setting a standard for computer/labor hours?

(b) What alternatives for setting a standard for computer/labor hours might be used?

(c) What standard for computer/labor hours would you select? Justify your answer.

(d) Determine the standard materials cost associated with the user manuals and computer forms for each application of the strategic planning model.

MANAGERIAL ANALYSIS

BYP25-2 Ed Widner and Associates is a medium-sized company located near a large metropolitan area in the Midwest. The company manufactures cabinets of mahogany, oak, and other fine woods for use in expensive homes, restaurants, and hotels. Although some of the work is custom, many of the cabinets are a standard size.

One such non-custom model is called Luxury Base Frame. Normal production is 1,000 units. Each unit has a direct labor hour standard of 5 hours. Overhead is applied to production based on standard direct labor hours. During the most recent month, only 900 units were produced; 4,500 direct labor hours were allowed for standard production, but only 4,000 hours were used. Standard and actual overhead costs were as follows.

	Standard (1,000 units)	Actual (900 units)
Indirect materials	$ 12,000	$ 12,300
Indirect labor	43,000	51,000
(Fixed) Manufacturing supervisors salaries	22,000	22,000
(Fixed) Manufacturing office employees salaries	13,000	11,500
(Fixed) Engineering costs	27,000	25,000
Computer costs	10,000	10,000
Electricity	2,500	2,500
(Fixed) Manufacturing building depreciation	8,000	8,000
(Fixed) Machinery depreciation	3,000	3,000
(Fixed) Trucks and forklift depreciation	1,500	1,500
Small tools	700	1,400
(Fixed) Insurance	500	500
(Fixed) Property taxes	300	300
Total	$143,500	$149,000

Instructions

(a) Determine the overhead application rate.
(b) Determine how much overhead was applied to production.
(c) Calculate the controllable overhead variance and the overhead volume variance.
(d) Decide which overhead variances should be investigated.
(e) Discuss causes of the overhead variances. What can management do to improve its performance next month?

REAL-WORLD FOCUS

BYP25-3 Glassmaster Co. is organized as two divisions and one subsidiary. One division focuses on the manufacture of filaments such as fishing line and sewing thread; the other division manufactures antennas and specialty fiberglass products. Its subsidiary manufactures flexible steel wire controls and molded control panels.

The annual report of Glassmaster provides the following information.

GLASSMASTER COMPANY
Management Discussion

Gross profit margins for the year improved to 20.9% of sales compared to last year's 18.5%. All operations reported improved margins due in large part to improved operating efficiencies as a result of cost reduction measures implemented during the second and third quarters of the fiscal year and increased manufacturing throughout due to higher unit volume sales. Contributing to the improved margins was a favorable materials price variance due to competitive pricing by suppliers as a result of soft demand for petrochemical-based products. This favorable variance is temporary and will begin to reverse itself as stronger worldwide demand for commodity products improves in tandem with the economy. Partially offsetting these positive effects on profit margins were competitive pressures on sales prices of certain product lines. The company responded with pricing strategies designed to maintain and/or increase market share.

Instructions

(a) Is it apparent from the information whether Glassmaster utilizes standard costs?
(b) Do you think the price variance experienced should lead to changes in standard costs for the next fiscal year?

EXPLORING THE WEB

BYP25-4 The Balanced Scorecard Institute **(www.balancedscorecard.org)** is a great resource for information about implementing the balanced scorecard. One item of interest provided at its website is an example of a balanced scorecard for a regional airline.

Address: http://www.balancedscorecard.org/files/Regional_Airline.pdf, or go to **www.wiley.com/college/weygandt**

Instructions

Go to the address above and answer the following questions.

(a) What are the objectives identified for the airline for each perspective?
(b) What measures are used for the objective in the customer perspective?
(c) What initiatives are planned to achieve the objective in the learning perspective?

COMMUNICATION ACTIVITY

BYP25-5 The setting of standards is critical to the effective use of standards in evaluating performance.

Instructions

Explain the following in a memo to your instructor.

(a) The comparative advantages and disadvantages of ideal versus normal standards.
(b) The factors that should be included in setting the price and quantity standards for direct materials, direct labor, and manufacturing overhead.

ETHICS CASE

BYP25-6 At Camden Manufacturing Company, production workers in the Painting Department are paid on the basis of productivity. The labor time standard for a unit of production is established through periodic time studies conducted by the Lowery Management Department. In a time study, the actual time required to complete a specific task by a worker is observed. Allowances are then made for preparation time, rest periods, and clean-up time. Ron Orlano is one of several veterans in the Painting Department.

Ron is informed by Lowery Management that he will be used in the time study for the painting of a new product. The findings will be the basis for establishing the labor time standard for the next 6 months. During the test, Ron deliberately slows his normal work pace in an effort to obtain a labor time standard that will be easy to meet. Because it is a new product, the Lowery Management representative who conducted the test is unaware that Ron did not give the test his best effort.

Instructions

(a) Who was benefited and who was harmed by Ron's actions?
(b) Was Ron ethical in the way he performed the time study test?
(c) What measure(s) might the company take to obtain valid data for setting the labor time standard?

"ALL ABOUT YOU" ACTIVITY

BYP25-7 From the time you first entered school many years ago, instructors have been measuring and evaluating you by imposing standards. In addition, many of you will pursue professions that administer professional examinations to attain recognized certification. Recently a federal commission presented proposals suggesting all public colleges and universities should require standardized tests to measure their students' learning.

Instructions

Read the following article at **www.signonsandiego.com/uniontrib/20060811/news_1n11colleges.html**, and answer the following questions.

(a) What areas of concern did the panel's recommendations address?

(b) What are possible advantages of standard testing?
(c) What are possible disadvantages of standard testing?
(d) Would you be in favor of standardized tests?

Answers to Insight and Accounting Across the Organization Questions

p. 1090 How Do Standards Help a Business?

Q: How will the creation of such standards help a business or organization?

A: *A business or organization may use the data to compare its performance relative to others with regard to common practices such as processing a purchase order or filling a sales order. Armed with this information, an organization can determine which areas to focus on with improvement campaigns.*

p. 1093 How Can We Make Susan's Chili Profitable?

Q: How might management use this raw material cost information?

A: *Management might decide to increase the price of its chili. Or it might revise its recipes to use cheaper ingredients. Or it might eliminate some products until ingredients are available at costs closer to standard.*

p. 1107 It May Be Time to Fly United Again

Q: Which of the perspectives of a balanced scorecard were the focus of United's CEO?

A: *Improving on-time flight departures is an objective within the internal process perspective. Customer intent to fly United again is an objective within the customer perspective.*

Authors' Comments on *All About You:* Balancing Costs and Quality in Health Care (p. 1108)

The practice of medicine holds an unusual place in society. On the one hand, it provides a critical, life-sustaining service. We expect and demand the highest-quality service. We measure its success in terms of health improvement and lives saved. On the other hand, it is a business, and like other businesses, it must operate profitably. Some health-care providers characterize this delicate balance as "The Business of Caring."

How should we balance providing quality health care and reducing costs? In recent years, managerial accounting has played an important, although not always successful, role in this issue. As noted earlier, in the 1990s health-care providers made extensive use of managerial accounting techniques to reduce costs. By the end of that decade, a number of important studies suggested that the quality of health care had suffered as a result of concentrating too much on cost-controlling efforts and not enough on maintaining quality.

Today many health-care organizations are implementing balanced scorecards in an effort to balance the dual (and in some ways competing) goals of quality health care and reduced costs. For example, by providing incentives for preventive medicine, health-care providers can reduce costs and at the same time improve patient health. It is likely that, in order to provide health care to more Americans, we will have to reduce costs. It is hoped that successful implementation of balanced scorecard programs will result in reduced costs through increased efficiency, while increasing the quality of health care.

Answers to Self-Study Questions

1. c **2.** d **3.** b **4.** c **5.** b **6.** a **7.** d **8.** a **9.** b **10.** d ***11.** c

Remember to go back to the Navigator box on the chapter-opening page and check off your completed work.

Chapter 26

Incremental Analysis and Capital Budgeting

STUDY OBJECTIVES

After studying this chapter, you should be able to:

1. Identify the steps in management's decision-making process.
2. Describe the concept of incremental analysis.
3. Identify the relevant costs in accepting an order at a special price.
4. Identify the relevant costs in a make-or-buy decision.
5. Give the decision rule for whether to sell or process materials further.
6. Identify the factors to consider in retaining or replacing equipment.
7. Explain the relevant factors in whether to eliminate an unprofitable segment.
8. Determine which products to make and sell when resources are limited.
9. Contrast annual rate of return and cash payback in capital budgeting.
10. Distinguish between the net present value and internal rate of return methods.

The Navigator

The Navigator

- Scan **Study Objectives**
- Read **Feature Story**
- Read **Preview**
- Read text and answer **Before You Go On** p. 1143
- Work **Demonstration Problem 1**
- Read text and answer **Before You Go On** p. 1152
- Work **Demonstration Problem 2**
- Review **Summary of Study Objectives**
- Answer **Self-Study Questions**
- Complete **Assignments**

Feature Story

SOUP IS GOOD FOOD

When you hear the word *Campbell*, what is the first thing that comes to mind? Soup. Campbell *is* soup. It sells 38 percent of all the soup—including homemade—consumed in the United States.

But can a company survive on soup alone? In an effort to expand its operations and to lessen its reliance on soup, Campbell Soup Company (*www.campbellsoup.com*) in 1990 began searching for an additional line of business. Campbell's management believed it saw an opportunity in convenient meals that were low in fat, nutritionally rich, and had therapeutic value for heart patients and diabetics. This venture would require a huge investment—but the rewards were potentially tremendous.

The initial investment required building food labs, hiring nutritional scientists, researching prototype products, constructing new production facilities, and marketing the new products. Management predicted that with an initial investment of roughly $55 million, the company might generate sales of $200 million per year.

By 1994 the company had created 24 meals, and an extensive field-study revealed considerable health benefits from the products. Unfortunately, initial sales of the new product line, called Intelligent Quisine, were less than stellar. In 1997 Campbell hired a consulting firm to evaluate whether to continue the project. Product development of the new line was costing $20 million per year—a sum that some managers felt could be better spent developing new products in other divisions, or expanding overseas operations. In 1998 Campbell discontinued the project.

Campbell was not giving up on growth, but simply had decided to refocus its efforts on soup. The company's annual report stated management's philosophy: "Soup will be our growth engine." Campbell has sold off many of its non-soup businesses and in a recent year introduced 20 new soup products.

Source: Vanessa O'Connell, "Food for Thought: How Campbell Saw a Breakthrough Menu Turn into Leftovers," *Wall Street Journal*, October 6, 1998.

✓ The Navigator

Inside Chapter 26...

Preview of Chapter 26

An important purpose of management accounting is to provide relevant information for decision making. Examples of these decisions include the following: (1) Campbell Soup's decision to produce "therapeutic meals" rather than some other food product. (2) Boeing's strategic decisions to spend $5 billion to build a plane for the 21st century—the B-777—and to cancel development of a larger version of the B-747. (3) The Coca-Cola Company's decision to spend $750 million to build twelve plants in Russia.

This chapter begins with an explanation of management's decision-making process. It then considers the topics of incremental analysis and capital budgeting. The content and organization of Chapter 26 are as follows.

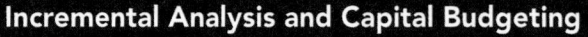

Incremental Analysis and Capital Budgeting

Incremental Analysis

- Management's decision-making process
- Types of incremental analysis

Capital Budgeting

- Evaluation process
- Annual rate of return
- Cash payback
- Discounted cash flow

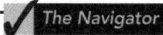

The Navigator

SECTION 1 Incremental Analysis

MANAGEMENT'S DECISION-MAKING PROCESS

STUDY OBJECTIVE 1

Identify the steps in management's decision-making process.

Making decisions is an important management function. Management's decision-making process does not always follow a set pattern, because decisions vary significantly in their scope, urgency, and importance. It is possible, though, to identify some steps that are frequently involved in the process. These steps are shown in Illustration 26-1.

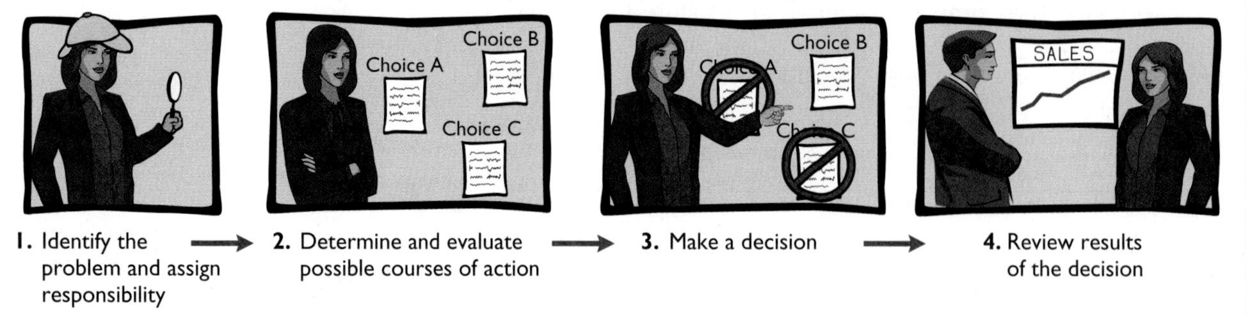

Illustration 26-1
Management's decision-making process

Accounting's contribution to the decision-making process occurs primarily in Steps 2 and 4—evaluating possible courses of action, and reviewing the results. In Step 2, for each possible course of action, accounting provides relevant revenue and cost data. These show the expected overall effect on net income. In Step 4, accounting prepares internal reports that review the actual impact of the decision.

In making business decisions, management ordinarily considers both financial and nonfinancial information. *Financial information* is related to revenues and costs and their effect on the company's overall profitability. *Nonfinancial information* relates to such factors as the effect of the decision on employee turnover, the environment, or the overall image of the company in the community. Although the nonfinancial information can be as important as the financial information, we focus primarily on financial information that is relevant to the decision.

The Incremental Analysis Approach

STUDY OBJECTIVE 2

Describe the concept of incremental analysis.

Decisions involve a choice among alternative courses of action. Suppose that you were deciding whether to purchase or lease a computer for use in doing your accounting homework. The financial data relate to the cost of leasing versus the cost of purchasing. For example, leasing involves periodic lease payments; purchasing requires "up-front" payment of the purchase price. In other words, the financial data relevant to the decision are the data that vary among the possible alternatives. The process used to identify the financial data that change under alternative courses of action is called **incremental analysis**. In some cases, when you use incremental analysis, both costs **and** revenues will change. In other cases, only costs **or** revenues will change.

ALTERNATIVE TERMINOLOGY

Incremental analysis is also called *differential analysis* because the analysis focuses on differences.

Just as your decision to buy or lease a PC affects your future, similar decisions, on a larger scale, affect a company's future. Incremental analysis identifies the probable effects of those decisions on future earnings. Such analysis inevitably involves estimates and uncertainty. Gathering data for incremental analyses may involve market analysts, engineers, and accountants. In quantifying the data, the accountant is expected to produce the most reliable information available at the time the decision must be made.

How Incremental Analysis Works

The following example illustrates the basic approach in incremental analysis.

Illustration 26-2
Basic approach in incremental analysis

Incremental Analysis.xls

File Edit View Insert Format Tools Data Window Help

	A	B	C	D
1		**Alternative A**	**Alternative B**	**Net Income Increase (Decrease)**
2	Revenues	$125,000	$110,000	**$ (15,000)**
3	Costs	100,000	80,000	**20,000**
4	Net income	$ 25,000	$ 30,000	**$ 5,000**
5				

This example compares alternative B with alternative A. The net income column shows the differences between the alternatives. In this case, incremental revenue will be $15,000 less under alternative B than under alternative A, but a $20,000 incremental cost saving will be realized.[1] Thus, alternative B will produce $5,000 more net income than alternative A.

Incremental analysis sometimes involves changes that at first glance might seem contrary to your intuition. For example, sometimes variable costs *do not change* under the alternative courses of action. Also, sometimes fixed costs *do change.* For example, direct labor, normally a variable cost, is not an incremental cost in deciding between two new factory machines if each asset requires the same amount of direct

[1]Although income taxes are sometimes important in incremental analysis, they are ignored in the chapter for simplicity's sake.

labor. In contrast, rent expense, normally a fixed cost, is an incremental cost in a decision to continue occupancy of a building or to purchase or lease a new building.

TYPES OF INCREMENTAL ANALYSIS

A number of different types of decisions involve incremental analysis. The more common types of decisions are:

1. Accept an order at a special price.
2. Make or buy.
3. Sell or process further.
4. Retain or replace equipment.
5. Eliminate an unprofitable business segment.
6. Allocate limited resources.

We consider each of these types of analysis in the following pages.

Accept an Order at a Special Price

STUDY OBJECTIVE 3

Identify the relevant costs in accepting an order at a special price.

Sometimes, a company has an opportunity to obtain additional business if it is willing to make a major price concession to a specific customer. To illustrate, assume that Sunbelt Company produces 100,000 automatic blenders per month, which is 80% of plant capacity. Variable manufacturing costs are $8 per unit. Fixed manufacturing costs are $400,000, or $4 per unit. The blenders are normally sold directly to retailers at $20 each. Sunbelt has an offer from Mexico Co. (a foreign wholesaler) to purchase an additional 2,000 blenders at $11 per unit. Acceptance of the offer would not affect normal sales of the product, and the additional units can be manufactured without increasing plant capacity. What should management do?

HELPFUL HINT

This is a good example of different costs for different purposes. In the long-run all costs are relevant, but for this decision only costs that change are relevant.

If management makes its decision on the basis of the total cost per unit of $12 ($8 + $4), the order would be rejected, because costs ($12) would exceed revenues ($11) by $1 per unit. However, since the units can be produced within existing plant capacity, the special order **will not increase fixed costs**. The relevant data for the decision, therefore, are the variable manufacturing costs per unit of $8 and the expected revenue of $11 per unit. Thus, as shown in Illustration 26-3, Sunbelt will increase its net income by $6,000 by accepting this special order.

Illustration 26-3
Incremental analysis—accepting an order at a special price

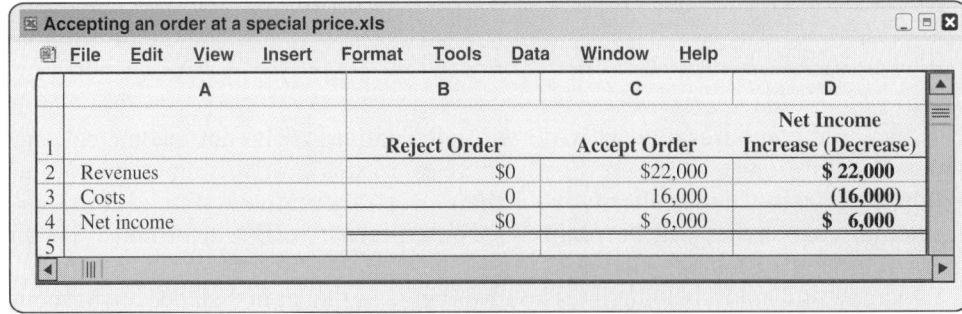

Accepting an order at a special price.xls

File Edit View Insert Format Tools Data Window Help

	A	B	C	D
1		Reject Order	Accept Order	Net Income Increase (Decrease)
2	Revenues	$0	$22,000	**$ 22,000**
3	Costs	0	16,000	**(16,000)**
4	Net income	$0	$ 6,000	**$ 6,000**
5				

Two points should be emphasized: First, we assume that sales of the product in other markets are not affected by this special order. If other sales are affected, then Sunbelt must consider the lost sales in making the decision. Second, if Sunbelt is operating at full capacity, it is likely that the special order would be rejected. Under such circumstances, the company would have to expand plant capacity. In that case, the special order would have to absorb these additional fixed manufacturing costs, as well as the variable manufacturing costs.

Make or Buy

STUDY OBJECTIVE 4

Identify the relevant costs in a make-or-buy decision.

When a manufacturer assembles component parts in producing a finished product, management must decide whether to make or buy the components. For example, General Motors Corporation may either make or buy the batteries, tires, and radios used in its cars. Similarly, Hewlett-Packard Corporation may make or buy the electronic circuitry, cases, and printer heads for its printers. The decision to make or buy components should be made on the basis of incremental analysis.

To illustrate the analysis, assume that Baron Company incurs the following annual costs in producing 25,000 ignition switches for motor scooters.

Direct materials	$ 50,000
Direct labor	75,000
Variable manufacturing overhead	40,000
Fixed manufacturing overhead	60,000
Total manufacturing costs	$225,000
Total cost per unit ($225,000 ÷ 25,000)	**$9.00**

Illustration 26-4
Annual product cost data

Or, instead of making its own switches, Baron Company might purchase the ignition switches from Ignition Inc. at a price of $8 per unit. The question again is, "What should management do?"

At first glance, it appears that management should purchase the ignition switches for $8, rather than make them at a cost of $9. However, a review of operations indicates that if Baron purchases the ignition switches from Ignition Inc., it will eliminate *all* of its variable costs but only $10,000 of its fixed manufacturing costs. Thus, $50,000 of the fixed manufacturing costs will remain if the ignition switches are purchased. The relevant costs for incremental analysis, therefore, are as follows.

Incremental Analysis - Make or buy.xls

File Edit View Insert Format Tools Data Window Help

	A	B	C	D
1		**Make**	**Buy**	**Net Income Increase (Decrease)**
2	Direct materials	$ 50,000	$ 0	**$ 50,000**
3	Direct labor	75,000	0	**75,000**
4	Variable manufacturing costs	40,000	0	**40,000**
5	Fixed manufacturing costs	60,000	50,000	**10,000**
6	Purchase price (25,000 × $8)	0	200,000	**(200,000)**
7	Total annual cost	$225,000	$250,000	**$ (25,000)**
8				

Illustration 26-5
Incremental analysis—make or buy

This analysis indicates that Baron Company will incur $25,000 of additional costs by buying the ignition switches. Therefore, Baron should continue to make the ignition switches, even though the total manufacturing cost is $1 higher than the purchase price. The reason is that if the company purchases the ignition switches, it will still have fixed costs of $50,000 to absorb.

ETHICS NOTE

In the make-or-buy decision it is important for management to take into account the social impact of its choice. For instance, buying may be the most economically feasible solution, but such action could result in the closure of a manufacturing plant that employs many good workers.

OPPORTUNITY COST

The foregoing make-or-buy analysis is complete only if the productive capacity used to make the ignition switches cannot be converted to another purpose. If there is an opportunity to use this productive capacity in some other manner, then this opportunity cost must be considered. **Opportunity cost** is the potential benefit that may be obtained by following an alternative course of action.

To illustrate, assume that through buying the switches, Baron Company can use the released productive capacity to generate additional income of $28,000. This lost income is an additional cost of continuing to make the switches in the make-or-buy decision. This opportunity cost therefore is added to the "Make" column, for comparison. As shown, it is now advantageous to buy the ignition switches.

Illustration 26-6
Incremental analysis—make or buy, with opportunity cost

Incremental Analysis - Make or buy with opportunity cost.xls

File Edit View Insert Format Tools Data Window Help

	A	B	C	D
1		**Make**	**Buy**	**Net Income Increase (Decrease)**
2	Total annual cost	$225,000	$250,000	$(25,000)
3	**Opportunity cost**	**28,000**	0	**28,000**
4	Total cost	$253,000	$250,000	$ 3,000
5				

The qualitative factors in this decision include the possible loss of jobs for employees who produce the ignition switches. In addition, management must assess how long the supplier will be able to satisfy the company's quality control standards at the quoted price per unit.

ACCOUNTING ACROSS THE ORGANIZATION

Incremental Analysis and Off-Shoring

Consider the make-or-buy decision faced by Superior Industries International, Inc., a big aluminum-wheel maker in Van Nuys, California. For years, president Steve Borick had ignored the possibility of Chinese manufacturing. Then Mr. Borick started getting a blunt message from General Motors and Ford, with whom Superior does 85% of its business: Match the prices of Chinese wheel suppliers. Both auto makers said separately that if Superior could not agree to the lower prices, they would go directly to Chinese manufacturers or turn to other North American wheel-makers.

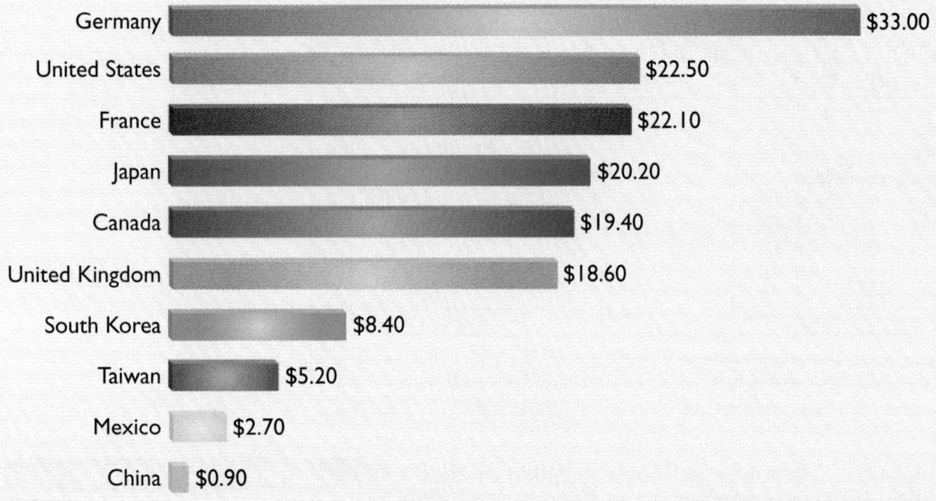

Stories like this, repeated in various industries, illustrate why manufacturers engage in overseas *off-shoring* (outsourcing). For example, compare the relative labor costs in major auto-producing nations, in dollars per hour, to see why incremental analysis often leads to outsourcing production to countries like China.

Source: Norihiko Shirouzu, "Big Three's Outsourcing Plan: Make Parts Suppliers Do It," *Wall Street Journal*, June 10, 2004, p. A1.

? What other costs should General Motors and Ford consider in regard to this possible decision?

Sell or Process Further

STUDY OBJECTIVE 5

Give the decision rule for whether to sell or process materials further.

Many manufacturers have the option of selling products at a given point in the production cycle or continuing to process with the expectation of selling them at a higher price. For example, a bicycle manufacturer such as Schwinn could sell its 10-speed bicycles to retailers either unassembled or assembled. A furniture manufacturer such as Ethan Allen could sell its dining room sets to furniture stores either unfinished or finished. The sell-or-process-further decision should be made on the basis of incremental analysis. The basic decision rule is: **Process further as long as the incremental revenue from such processing exceeds the incremental processing costs.**

Assume, for example, that Woodmasters Inc. makes tables. The cost to manufacture an unfinished table is $35, computed as follows.

Direct material	$15
Direct labor	10
Variable manufacturing overhead	6
Fixed manufacturing overhead	4
Manufacturing cost per unit	**$35**

Illustration 26-7
Per unit cost of unfinished table

The selling price per unfinished unit is $50. Woodmasters currently has unused productive capacity that is expected to continue indefinitely. Management concludes that some of this capacity can be used to finish the tables and sell them at $60 per unit. For a finished table, direct materials will increase $2 and direct labor costs will increase $4. Variable manufacturing overhead costs will increase by $2.40 (60% of direct labor). No increase is anticipated in fixed manufacturing overhead. Illustration 26-8 shows the incremental analysis on a per unit basis.

Incremental Analysis - Sell or process further.xls

File Edit View Insert Format Tools Data Window Help

	A	B	C	D
1		Sell	Process Further	Net Income Increase (Decrease)
2	Sales per unit	$50.00	$60.00	**$10.00**
3	Cost per unit			
4	Direct materials	15.00	17.00	**(2.00)**
5	Direct labor	10.00	14.00	**(4.00)**
6	Variable manufacturing overhead	6.00	8.40	**(2.40)**
7	Fixed manufacturing overhead	4.00	4.00	**0.00**
8	Total	35.00	43.40	**(8.40)**
9	Net income per unit	$15.00	$16.60	**$ 1.60**
10				

Illustration 26-8
Incremental analysis—sell or process further

HELPFUL HINT

Current net income is known. Net income from processing further is an estimate. In making its decision, management could add a "risk" factor for the estimate.

It is advantageous for Woodmaster to process the tables further. The incremental revenue of $10.00 from the additional processing is $1.60 higher than the incremental processing costs of $8.40.

Retain or Replace Equipment

STUDY OBJECTIVE 6

Identify the factors to consider in retaining or replacing equipment.

Management often has to decide whether to continue using an asset or replace it. To illustrate, assume that Jeffcoat Company has a factory machine with a book value of $40,000 and a remaining useful life of four years. A new machine is available that costs $120,000. It is expected to have zero salvage value at the end of its four-year useful life. If Jeffcoat acquires the new machine, variable manufacturing costs are expected to decrease from $160,000 to $125,000 annually, and the old unit will be scrapped. The incremental analysis for the four-year period is as follows.

Illustration 26-9
Incremental analysis—retain or replace equipment

Incremental Analysis - Retain or replace equipment.xls

	A	B	C	D	E	F
1		**Retain Equipment**		**Replace Equipment**		**Net Income Increase (Decrease)**
2	Variable manufacturing costs	$640,000	a	$500,000	b	**$140,000**
3	New machine cost			120,000		**(120,000)**
4	Total	$640,000		$620,000		**$ 20,000**
5						
6	[a](4 years × $160,000)					
7	[b](4 years × $125,000)					
8						

In this case, it is advantageous to replace the equipment. The lower variable manufacturing costs related to the new equipment more than offset its purchase cost.

One other point about Jeffcoat's decision: **The book value of the old machine does not affect the decision.** Book value is a sunk cost, which is a cost that cannot be changed by any present or future decision. Sunk costs **are not relevant in incremental analysis**. In this example, if the company retains the asset, book value is depreciated over its remaining useful life. Or, if the company acquires the new unit, book value is recognized as a loss of the current period. Thus, the effect of book value on current and future earnings is the same regardless of the replacement decision. However, **any trade-in allowance or cash disposal value of the existing asset is relevant** to the decision, because the company will not realize this value if the old asset is continued in use.

Eliminate an Unprofitable Segment

STUDY OBJECTIVE 7

Explain the relevant factors in whether to eliminate an unprofitable segment.

Management sometimes must decide whether to eliminate an unprofitable business segment. Again, the key is to focus on the relevant amounts—the data that change under the alternative courses of action. To illustrate, assume that Martina Company manufactures tennis racquets in three models: Pro, Master, and Champ. Pro and Master are profitable lines. Champ (highlighted in color in the table on the next page) operates at a loss. Condensed income statement data for the three segments are:

Illustration 26-10
Segment income data

	Pro	Master	Champ	Total
Sales	$800,000	$300,000	**$100,000**	$1,200,000
Variable expenses	520,000	210,000	**90,000**	820,000
Contribution margin	280,000	90,000	**10,000**	380,000
Fixed expenses	80,000	50,000	**30,000**	160,000
Net income	$200,000	$ 40,000	**$(20,000)**	$ 220,000

It might be expected that total net income will increase by $20,000 to $240,000 if Martina Company eliminates the unprofitable Champ line of racquets. However, **net income may decrease if that line is discontinued.** The reason is that the other products will have to absorb the fixed expenses allocated to the Champ racquets. To illustrate, assume that the $30,000 of fixed costs applicable to the unprofitable segment are allocated ⅔ and ⅓ to the Pro and Master product lines, respectively. Fixed expenses will increase to $100,000 ($80,000 + $20,000) in the Pro line and to $60,000 ($50,000 + $10,000) in the Master line. Illustration 26-11 shows the revised income statements.

HELPFUL HINT
A decision to discontinue a segment based solely on the bottom line—net loss—is inappropriate.

Illustration 26-11
Income data after eliminating unprofitable product line

	Pro	Master	Total
Sales	$800,000	$300,000	$1,100,000
Variable expenses	520,000	210,000	730,000
Contribution margin	280,000	90,000	370,000
Fixed expenses	**100,000**	**60,000**	160,000
Net income	$180,000	$ 30,000	**$ 210,000**

Total net income has decreased $10,000 ($220,000 − $210,000). This result is also obtained in the following incremental analysis of the Champ racquets.

Illustration 26-12
Incremental analysis—eliminating an unprofitable segment

Incremental Analysis - Eliminating an unprofitable segment.xls

File Edit View Insert Format Tools Data Window Help

	A	B	C	D
1		**Continue**	**Eliminate**	**Net Income Increase (Decrease)**
2	Sales	$100,000	$ 0	**$(100,000)**
3	Variable costs	90,000	0	**90,000**
4	Contribution margin	10,000	0	**(10,000)**
5	Fixed costs	30,000	30,000	**0**
6	Net income	$ (20,000)	$(30,000)	**$ (10,000)**
7				

The loss in net income is attributable to the contribution margin ($10,000) that the company will not realize if it discontinues the segment.

In deciding on the future status of an unprofitable segment, management should consider the effect of elimination on related product lines. It may be possible for continuing product lines to obtain some or all of the sales lost by the discontinued product line. In some businesses, services or products may be linked—for example, free checking accounts at a bank, or coffee at a donut shop. In addition, management should consider the effect of eliminating the product line on employees who may have to be discharged or retrained.

ACCOUNTING ACROSS THE ORGANIZATION

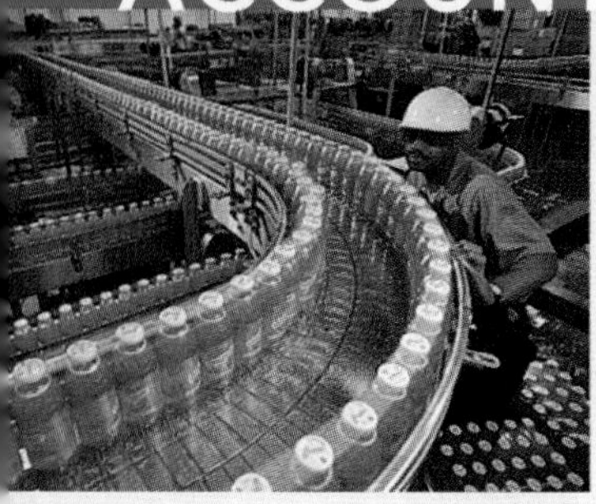

A $1.4 Billion Mistake

In 1994 Quaker Oats paid $1.7 billion for one of America's hottest new beverage companies. While some observers thought that Quaker Oats had overpaid, Quaker's management believed it was an exciting purchase because it would make a great strategic partner for the company's famous sport drink—Gatorade.

But, for a variety of reasons, the acquisition didn't work out. One of those reasons was that at about the same time, several other major beverage manufacturers decided to begin producing and selling competing fruit and tea drinks. Worse yet, the processing methods used by these other manufacturers appeared to allow them to produce their drinks much more inexpensively.

Only a few years after purchasing the beverage company, Quaker Oats sold it and took a $1.4 billion loss.

? Why might management sell the beverage company and take a $1.4 billion loss?

Allocate Limited Resources

STUDY OBJECTIVE 8

Determine which products to make and sell when resources are limited.

Companies, like individuals, face limited resources. For a retail department store, the limited resource may be floor space. For a manufacturing company, the limited resource may be raw materials, direct labor hours, or machine capacity. When a company has limited resources, management must decide which products to make and sell in order to maximize net income.

To illustrate, assume that Collins Company manufactures deluxe and standard pen and pencil sets. The limiting resource is machine capacity, which is 3,600 hours per month. Relevant data consist of the following.

Illustration 26-13
Contribution margin and machine hours

	Deluxe Sets	Standard Sets
Contribution margin per unit	$8	$6
Machine hours required	0.4	0.2

HELPFUL HINT

CM alone is not enough in this decision. The key factor is CM per unit of limited resource.

The deluxe sets may appear to be more profitable: They have a higher contribution margin ($8) than the standard sets ($6). However, the standard sets take fewer machine hours to produce than the deluxe sets. Therefore, Collins needs to find the **contribution margin per unit of limited resource**—in this case, contribution margin per machine hour. This is obtained by dividing the contribution margin per unit of each product by the number of units of the limited resource required for each product, as shown in Illustration 26-14.

Illustration 26-14
Contribution margin per unit of limited resource

	Deluxe Sets	Standard Sets
Contribution margin per unit (**a**)	$8	$6
Machine hours required (**b**)	0.4	0.2
Contribution margin per unit of limited resource [(a) ÷ (b)]	**$20**	**$30**

The computation shows that the standard sets have a higher contribution margin per unit of limited resource. This suggests that, given sufficient demand for standard sets, the company should shift the sales mix to standard sets or should increase machine capacity. If Collins Company is able to increase machine capacity from 3,600 hours to 4,200 hours, the additional 600 hours could be used to produce either the standard or deluxe pen and pencil sets. The total contribution margin under each alternative is found by multiplying the machine hours by the contribution margin per unit of limited resource, as shown below.

Illustration 26-15
Incremental analysis—computation of total contribution margin

	Produce Deluxe Sets	Produce Standard Sets
Machine hours (**a**)	600	600
Contribution margin per unit of limited resource (**b**)	$20	$30
Contribution margin [(a) × (b)]	**$12,000**	**$18,000**

From this analysis, we see that to maximize net income, Collins should use all of the increased capacity to make and sell the standard sets.

Before You Go On...

REVIEW IT

1. Give three examples of how companies might use incremental analysis.
2. What is the decision rule in deciding to sell or process products further?
3. How may the elimination of an unprofitable segment decrease the overall net income of a company?
4. What is the critical factor in allocating limited resources?

DO IT

Cobb Company incurs a cost of $28 per unit, of which $18 is variable, to make a product that normally sells for $42. A foreign wholesaler offers to buy 5,000 units at $25 each. Cobb will incur shipping costs of $1 per unit. Compute the net income (loss) Cobb will realize by accepting the special order, assuming Cobb has excess operating capacity. Should Cobb Company accept the special order?

Action Plan

- Identify all revenues that will change as a result of accepting the order.
- Identify all costs that will change as a result of accepting the order, and net this amount against the change in revenues.

Solution

	Reject	Accept	Net Income Increase (Decrease)
Revenues	$-0-	$125,000	$125,000
Costs	-0-	95,000*	(95,000)
Net income	$-0-	$ 30,000	$ 30,000

*(5,000 × $18) + (5,000 × $1)

Given the result of the above analysis, Cobb Company should accept the special order.

Related exercise material: *BE26-2, BE26-3, E26-2, and E26-3.*

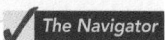

The Navigator

Demonstration Problem 1

WILEY PLUS

Juanita Company must decide whether to make or buy some of its components. The costs of producing 50,000 electrical cords for its floor lamps are as follows.

Direct materials	$60,000	Variable overhead	$12,000
Direct labor	30,000	Fixed overhead	8,000

Instead of making the electrical cords at an average cost per unit of $2.20 ($110,000 ÷ 50,000), the company has an opportunity to buy the cords at $2.15 per unit. If the company purchases the cords, all variable costs and one-half of the fixed costs will be eliminated.

Instructions

(a) Prepare an incremental analysis showing whether the company should make or buy the electrical cords.

(b) Will your answer be different if the released productive capacity will generate additional income of $25,000?

action plan

- Look for the costs that change.
- Ignore the costs that do not change.
- Use the format in the chapter for your answer.
- Recognize that opportunity cost can make a difference.

Solution to Demonstration Problem 1

(a)

	Make	Buy	Net Income Increase (Decrease)
Direct materials	$ 60,000	$ -0-	$ 60,000
Direct labor	30,000	-0-	30,000
Variable manufacturing costs	12,000	-0-	12,000
Fixed manufacturing costs	8,000	4,000	4,000
Purchase price	-0-	107,500	(107,500)
Total cost	$110,000	$111,500	$ (1,500)

This analysis indicates that Juanita Company will incur $1,500 of additional costs if it buys the electrical cords.

(b)

	Make	Buy	Net Income Increase (Decrease)
Total cost	$110,000	$111,500	$ (1,500)
Opportunity cost	25,000		25,000
Total cost	$135,000	$111,500	$ 23,500

Yes, the answer is different because the analysis shows that net income will be increased by $23,500 if Juanita Company purchases the electrical cords.

The Navigator

SECTION 2 Capital Budgeting

Individuals make capital expenditures when they buy a new home, car, or television set. Similarly, businesses make capital expenditures when they modernize plant facilities or expand operations. Companies like Campbell Soup must constantly determine how to invest their resources. Other examples: Hollywood studios recently built 25 new sound stage projects to allow for additional filming in future years. Also, Union Pacific Resources Group Inc. announced that it would cut its capital budget by 19% in order to use the funds to reduce its outstanding debt.

In business, as for individuals, the amount of possible capital expenditures usually exceeds the funds available for such expenditures. Thus, the resources available must be allocated (budgeted) among the competing alternatives. The process of making capital expenditure decisions in business is known as **capital budgeting**. Capital budgeting involves choosing among various capital projects to find the one(s) that will maximize a company's return on its financial investment.

EVALUATION PROCESS

Many companies follow a standard process in capital budgeting. At least once a year, top management requests proposals for projects from each department. A capital budgeting committee screens the proposals and submits its findings to the officers of the company. The officers, in turn, select the projects they believe to be most worthy of funding. They submit this list to the board of directors. Ultimately, the directors approve the capital expenditure budget for the year.

The involvement of top management and the board of directors in the process demonstrates the importance of capital budgeting decisions. These decisions often have a significant impact on a company's future profitability. In fact, poor capital budgeting decisions have led to the bankruptcy of some companies.

Accounting data are indispensable in assessing the probable effects of capital expenditures. To provide management with relevant data for capital budgeting decisions, you should be familiar with the quantitative techniques that may be used. The three most common techniques are: (1) annual rate of return, (2) cash payback, and (3) discounted cash flow. We demonstrate each of these techniques in the following sections. To illustrate the three quantitative techniques, assume that Tappan Company is considering an investment of $130,000 in new equipment. The new equipment is expected to last 10 years. It will have zero salvage value at the end of its useful life. Tappan uses the straight-line method of depreciation for accounting purposes. The expected annual revenues and costs of the new product that will be produced from the investment are:

Sales		$200,000
Less: Costs and expenses		
Manufacturing costs (exclusive of depreciation)	$145,000	
Depreciation expenses ($130,000 ÷ 10)	13,000	
Selling and administrative expenses	22,000	180,000
Income before income taxes		20,000
Income tax expense		7,000
Net income		$ 13,000

Illustration 26-16
Estimated annual net income from capital expenditure

ANNUAL RATE OF RETURN

STUDY OBJECTIVE 9
Contrast annual rate of return and cash payback in capital budgeting.

The **annual rate of return technique** is based directly on accounting data. It indicates **the profitability of a capital expenditure** by dividing expected annual net income by the average investment. Illustration 26-17 shows the formula for computing annual rate of return.

$$\text{Expected Annual Net Income} \div \text{Average Investment} = \text{Annual Rate of Return}$$

Illustration 26-17
Annual rate of return formula

Expected annual net income is obtained from the projected income statement. Tappan Company's expected annual net income is $13,000. Average investment is derived from the following formula.

$$\text{Average Investment} = \frac{\text{Original Investment} + \text{Value at End of Useful Life}}{2}$$

Illustration 26-18
Formula for computing average investment

The "value at the end of useful life" is the asset's salvage value, if any.

For Tappan Company, average investment is $65,000 ($130,000 + $0) ÷ 2. The expected annual rate of return for Tappan Company's investment in new equipment is therefore 20%, computed as follows:

$$\$13,000 \div \$65,000 = 20\%$$

ALTERNATIVE TERMINOLOGY

The minimum rate of return is also called the *hurdle rate* or *cutoff rate*.

Management then compares this annual rate of return with its required **minimum rate of return** for investments of similar risk. The minimum rate of return is generally based on the company's **cost of capital**. The cost of capital is the rate of return that management expects to pay on all borrowed and equity funds. The cost of capital is a company-wide (or sometimes a division-wide) rate; it does not relate to the cost of funding a specific project.

HELPFUL HINT

A capital budgeting decision based on only one technique may be misleading. It is often wise to analyze the investment from a number of different perspectives.

The annual rate of return decision rule is: **A project is acceptable if its rate of return is greater than management's minimum rate of return. It is unacceptable when the reverse is true.** When the rate of return technique is used in deciding among several acceptable projects, **the higher the rate of return for a given risk, the more attractive the investment.**

The principal advantages of this technique are simplicity of calculation and management's familiarity with the accounting terms used in the computation. A major limitation of the annual rate of return approach is that it does not consider the time value of money. For example, no consideration is given as to whether cash inflows will occur early or late in the life of the investment. As explained in Appendix C at the back of the book, recognition of the time value of money can make a significant difference between the future value and the present value of an investment.

CASH PAYBACK

The cash payback technique identifies the time period required to recover the cost of the capital investment from the annual cash inflow produced by the investment. Illustration 26-19 presents the formula for computing the cash payback period.

Illustration 26-19
Cash payback formula

Cost of Capital Investment	÷	Net Annual Cash Flow	=	Cash Payback Period

HELPFUL HINT

Net annual cash flow can also be approximated by net cash provided by operating activities from the statement of cash flows.

Net annual cash flow is approximated by taking net income and adding back depreciation expense. Depreciation expense is added back because depreciation on the capital expenditure does not involve an annual outflow of cash. Accordingly, the depreciation deducted in determining net income must be added back to determine net annual cash flows.

In the Tappan Company example, net annual cash flow is $26,000, as shown below.

Illustration 26-20
Computation of net annual cash flow

Net income	$13,000
Add: Depreciation expense	13,000
Net annual cash flow	**$26,000**

The cash payback period in this example is therefore five years, computed as follows.

$$\$130{,}000 \div \$26{,}000 = 5 \text{ years}$$

Evaluation of the payback period is often related to the expected useful life of the asset. For example, assume that at Tappan Company a project is unacceptable if the payback period is longer than 60% of the asset's expected useful life. The five-year payback period in this case is 50% of the project's expected useful life. Thus, the project is acceptable.

It follows that when companies use the payback technique to decide among acceptable alternative projects, **the shorter the payback period, the more attractive the investment.** This is true for two reasons: First, the earlier the investment is recovered, the sooner the cash funds can be used for other purposes. Second, the risk of loss from obsolescence and changed economic conditions is less in a shorter payback period.

The computation of the cash payback period above assumes equal cash flows in each year of the investment's life. In many cases, this assumption is not valid. In the case of **uneven** cash flows, the cash payback period is determined when the cumulative net cash flows from the investment equal the cost of the investment.

To illustrate, assume that Chan Company proposes an investment in a new Website that is estimated to cost $300,000. Illustration 26-21 shows the proposed investment cost, net annual cash flows, cumulative net cash flows, and the cash payback period.

Illustration 26-21
Net annual cash flow schedule

Year	Investment	Net Annual Cash Flow	Cumulative Net Cash Flow
0	$300,000		
1		$ 60,000	$ 60,000
2		90,000	150,000
3		90,000	240,000
4		120,000	360,000
5		100,000	460,000

Cash payback period = **3.5 years**

As Illustration 26-21 indicates, at the end of year 3, cumulative net cash flow of $240,000 is less than the investment cost of $300,000. However, at the end of year 4 the cumulative net cash flow of $360,000 exceeds the investment cost. The net cash flow needed in year 4 to equal the investment cost is $60,000 ($300,000 − $240,000). Assuming the net cash flow occurs evenly during year 4, we then divide this amount by the annual net cash flow in year 4 ($120,000) to determine the point during the year when the cash payback occurs. Thus, we get 0.50 ($60,000/$120,000), or half of the year, and the cash payback period is 3.5 years.

The cash payback technique may be useful as an initial screening tool. It also may be the most critical factor in the capital budgeting decision for a company that desires a fast turnaround of its investment because of a weak cash position. Like the annual rate of return, cash payback is relatively easy to compute and understand.

However, cash payback is not ordinarily the only basis for the capital budgeting decision because it ignores the expected profitability of the project. To illustrate, assume that Projects X and Y have the same payback period, but Project X's useful life is double the useful life of Project Y's. Project X's earning power, therefore, is twice as long as Project Y's. A further disadvantage of this technique is that it ignores the time value of money.

MANAGEMENT INSIGHT

Are You Ready for the 50-Inch Screen?

Building a new factory to produce 50-inch-plus TV screens can cost $4 billion at a time when prices for flat screens are tumbling. Now the makers of those giant liquid-crystal displays are wondering whether such investments are worth the gamble.

If LCD makers decide to hold off on building new factories, price declines for wide-screen TVs could slow in two or three years as production falls behind added consumer demand. Experts also say a slowdown in factory building could also bring welcome relief for the industry by reducing its volatile profit swings.

Since 2000, LCD makers have been on a nonstop construction binge, building new factories to produce the latest generation of screens arriving every 18 months or so. . . . Now, with the eighth generation of screens, the cost to build new factories is higher than ever—running between $3 billion to $4 billion each. And this generation of factories is optimized for screens measuring 50 inches or more diagonally, which so far is a much smaller potential market than that targeted by previous screen generations.

Source: Evan Ramstad, "The 50-Inch Screen Poses a Gamble," *Wall Street journal*, June 8, 2006, p. B3.

? In building factories to manufacture 50-inch TV screens, how might companies build risk factors into their financial analyses?

DISCOUNTED CASH FLOW

STUDY OBJECTIVE 10

Distinguish between the net present value and internal rate of return methods.

The **discounted cash flow technique** is generally recognized as the best conceptual approach to making capital budgeting decisions. This technique considers both the estimated total net cash flows from the investment and the time value of money. The expected total net cash flow consists of the sum of the annual net cash flows plus the estimated liquidation proceeds when the asset is sold for salvage at the end of its useful life. But because liquidation proceeds are generally immaterial, we ignore them in subsequent discussions.

Two methods are used with the discounted cash flow technique: (1) net present value, and (2) internal rate of return. **Before we discuss the methods, we recommend that you examine Appendix C if you need a review of present value concepts.**

Net Present Value Method

The **net present value method** involves discounting net cash flows to their present value and then comparing the present value with the capital outlay required by the investment. The difference between these two amounts is referred to as **net present value (NPV)**. The interest rate to be used in discounting the future net cash flows is the required minimum rate of return.

The NPV decision rule is this: **A proposal is acceptable when net present value is zero or positive.** This means that the rate of return on the investment equals or exceeds the required rate of return. When net present value is negative, the project is unacceptable. Illustration 26-22 shows the net present value decision criteria.

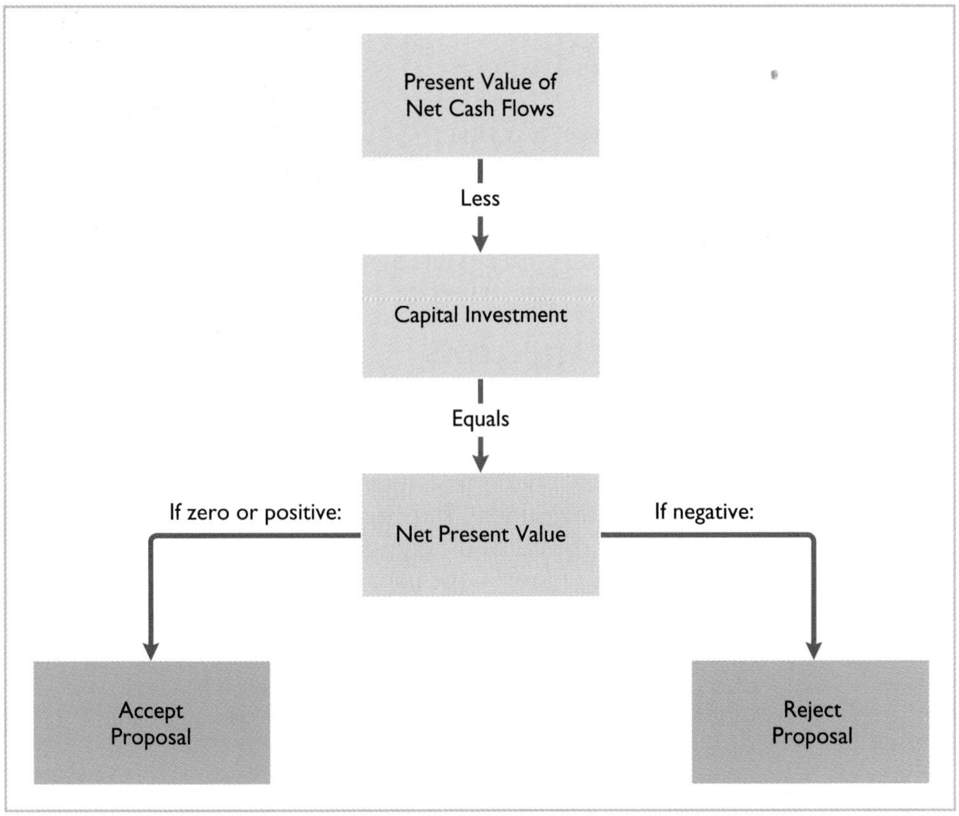

Illustration 26-22
Net present value decision criteria

When making a selection among acceptable proposals, **the higher the positive net present value, the more attractive the investment**. The next two sections demonstrate use of this method. In each case, we assume that the investment has no salvage value.

ETHICS NOTE

Discounted future cash flows may not take into account all of the important considerations needed to make an informed capital budgeting decision. Other issues, for example, could include worker safety, product quality, and environmental impact.

EQUAL NET ANNUAL CASH FLOWS

Tappan Company's net annual cash flows are $26,000. If we assume this amount **is uniform over the asset's useful life**, we can compute the present value of the net annual cash flows by using the present value of an annuity of 1 for 10 periods (in Table 2, Appendix C). The computations at rates of return of 12% and 15%, respectively, are:

Illustration 26-23
Present value of net annual cash flows

	Present Values at Different Discount Rates	
	12%	**15%**
Discount factor for 10 periods	5.65022	5.01877
Present value of net annual cash flows:		
$26,000 × 5.65022	**$146,906**	
$26,000 × 5.01877		**$130,488**

The analysis of the proposal by the net present value method is as follows:

Illustration 26-24
Computations of net present value

	12%	15%
Present value of net annual cash flows	$146,906	$130,488
Capital investment	130,000	130,000
Positive (negative) net present value	**$ 16,906**	**$ 488**

HELPFUL HINT
The ABC Co. expects equal cash flows over an asset's 5-year useful life. What discount factor should be used in determining present values if management wants (1) a 12% return or (2) a 15% return? Answer: Using Table 2, the factors are (1) 3.60478 and (2) 3.35216.

The proposed capital expenditure is acceptable at a required rate of return of both 12% and 15% because the net present values are positive.

UNEQUAL NET ANNUAL CASH FLOWS

When net annual cash flows are unequal, we cannot use annuity tables to calculate their present value. Instead, we use tables showing the **present value of a single future amount for each net annual cash flow**. To illustrate, assume that Tappan Company management expects the same aggregate net annual cash flow ($260,000) over the life of the investment. But because of a declining market demand for the new product over the life of the equipment, the net annual cash flows are higher in the early years and lower in the later years. The present value of the net annual cash flows is calculated as follows using Table 1 in Appendix C.

Illustration 26-25
Computing present value of unequal annual cash flows

		Discount Factor		Present Value	
Year	**Assumed Net Annual Cash Flows**	**12%**	**15%**	**12%**	**15%**
	(1)	(2)	(3)	(1) × (2)	(1) × (3)
1	$ 36,000	.89286	.86957	$ 32,143	$ 31,305
2	32,000	.79719	.75614	25,510	24,196
3	29,000	.71178	.65752	20,642	19,068
4	27,000	.63552	.57175	17,159	15,437
5	26,000	.56743	.49718	14,753	12,927
6	24,000	.50663	.43233	12,159	10,376
7	23,000	.45235	.37594	10,404	8,647
8	22,000	.40388	.32690	8,885	7,192
9	21,000	.36061	.28426	7,573	5,969
10	20,000	.32197	.24719	6,439	4,944
	$260,000			**$155,667**	**$140,061**

Therefore, the analysis of the proposal by the net present value method is as follows.

Illustration 26-26
Analysis of proposal using net present value method

	12%	15%
Present value of net annual cash flows	$155,667	$140,061
Capital investment	130,000	130,000
Positive (negative) net present value	**$ 25,667**	**$ 10,061**

In this example, the present values of the net annual cash flows are greater than the $130,000 capital investment. Thus, the project is acceptable at both a 12% and 15% required rate of return. The difference between the present values using the 12% rate under equal cash flows ($146,906) and unequal net annual cash flows ($155,667) is due to the pattern of the net cash flows.

Internal Rate of Return Method

The **internal rate of return method** differs from the net present value method in that it finds the **interest yield of the potential investment**. The **internal rate of return** (IRR) is the interest rate that will cause the present value of the proposed capital expenditure to equal the present value of the expected net annual cash flows. The determination of the internal rate of return involves two steps.

Step 1. Compute the internal rate of return factor. The formula for this factor is:

Capital Investment	÷	Net Annual Cash Flows	=	Internal Rate of Return Factor

Illustration 26-27
Formula for internal rate of return factor

The computation for the Tappan Company, assuming equal net annual cash flows,[2] is:

$$\$130{,}000 \div \$26{,}000 = 5.0$$

Step 2. Use the factor and the present value of an annuity of 1 table to find the internal rate of return. Table 2 of Appendix C is used in this step. The internal rate of return is the discount factor that is closest to the internal rate of return factor for the time period covered by the net annual cash flows.

For Tappan Company, the net annual cash flows are expected to continue for 10 years. Thus, it is necessary to read across the period-10 row in Table 2 to find the discount factor. The row for 10 periods is reproduced below for your convenience.

TABLE 2
PRESENT VALUE OF AN ANNUITY OF 1

(*n*) Periods	5%	6%	8%	9%	10%	11%	12%	15%
10	7.72173	7.36009	6.71008	6.41766	6.14457	5.88923	5.65022	**5.01877**

In this case, the closest discount factor to 5.0 is 5.01877, which represents an interest rate of approximately 15%. The rate of return can be further determined by interpolation, but since we are using estimated net annual cash flows, such precision is seldom required.

We then compare the internal rate of return to management's required minimum rate of return. The IRR decision rule is: **Accept the project when the internal rate of return is equal to or greater than the required rate of return. Reject the project when the internal rate of return is less than the required rate.** Illustration 26-28 (page 1152) shows these relationships. Assuming the minimum required rate of return is 10% for Tappan Company, the project is acceptable because the 15% internal rate of return is greater than the required rate.

The IRR method is widely used in practice. Most managers find the internal rate of return easy to interpret.

[2]When net annual cash flows are equal, the internal rate of return factor is the same as the cash payback period.

Illustration 26-28
Internal rate of return decision criteria

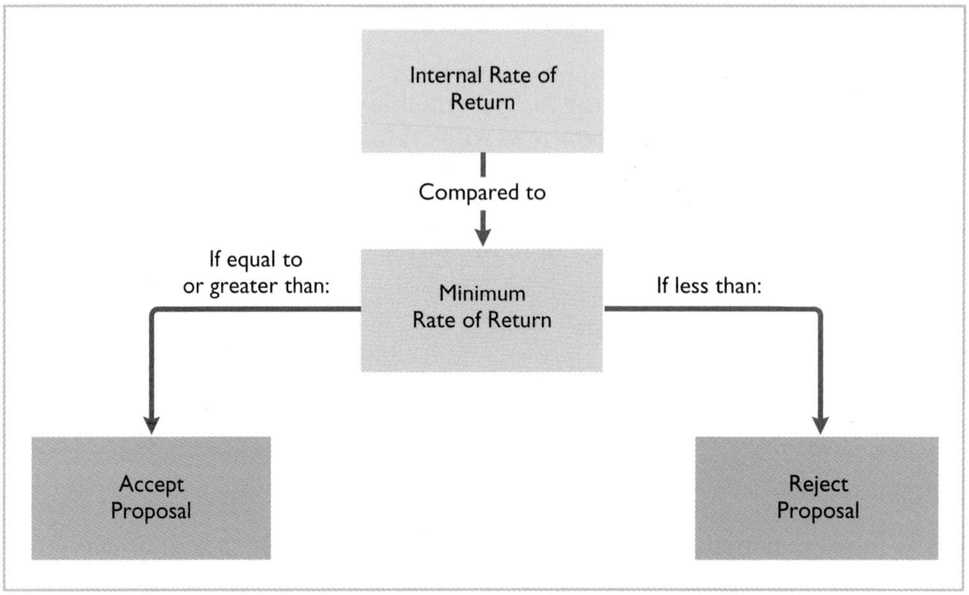

Comparison of Discounted Cash Flow Methods

Illustration 26-29 compares the two discounted cash flow methods—net present value and internal rate of return. When properly used, either method provides management with relevant quantitative data for making capital budgeting decisions.

Illustration 26-29
Comparison of discounted cash flow methods

Item	Net Present Value	Internal Rate of Return
1. Objective	Compute net present value (a dollar amount).	Compute internal rate of return (a percentage).
2. Decision rule	If net present value is zero or positive, accept the proposal. If net present value is negative, reject the proposal.	If internal rate of return is equal to or greater than the minimum required rate of return, accept the proposal. If internal rate of return is less than the minimum rate, reject the proposal.

Before You Go On...

REVIEW IT

1. What is the formula for and the decision rule in using the annual rate of return method?
2. What is the formula for the cash payback method?
3. When is a proposal acceptable under (a) the net present value method, and (b) the internal rate of return method?
4. What does PepsiCo report as its capital spending for 2004 and 2005? (See PepsiCo's financial highlights section.) The answer to this question is provided on page 1172.

The Navigator

Be sure to read **ALL ABOUT YOU: *What Is a Degree Worth?*** on the next page for information on how topics in this chapter apply to you.

What Is a Degree Worth?

It may not have occurred to you at the time, but you already made a huge decision in your life that was ideally suited to both incremental analysis and capital budgeting. No, it's not your choice of whether to have pizza or Chinese food at lunch today. We are referring to your decision to pursue a post–high-school degree. If you weren't going to college, you could be working full-time. School costs money, which is an expenditure that you could have avoided. Also, if you did not go to college, many of you would avoid mountains of school-related debt. While you cannot go back and redo your initial decision, we can look at some facts to evaluate the wisdom of your decision.

Some Facts

* Over a lifetime of work, high-school graduates earn an average of $1.2 million, associate's degree holders earn an average of $1.6 million, and people with bachelor's degrees earn about $2.1 million.
* A year of tuition at a public four-year college costs about $8,655, and a year of tuition at a public two-year college costs about $1,359.
* There has also been considerable research on other, less-tangible benefits of post–high-school education. For example, some have suggested that there is a relationship between higher education and good health. Research also suggests that college-educated people are more optimistic.
* About 600,000 students drop out of four-year colleges each year.

About the Numbers

Tuition is very expensive. As a result, many students have high "unmet needs"—the portion of college expenses not provided by family or student aid. The graph below suggests that in the coming decade an increasing number of students with high "unmet" financial needs will decide not to pursue any form of post–high-school education. This has obvious implications for their long-term personal financial well-being. It also has significant implications for the well-being of the United States as a society. Research shows that people with post–high-school degrees pay more in taxes. Also, without adequate educational training of its citizenry, the United States will be less able to compete in a high-tech world.

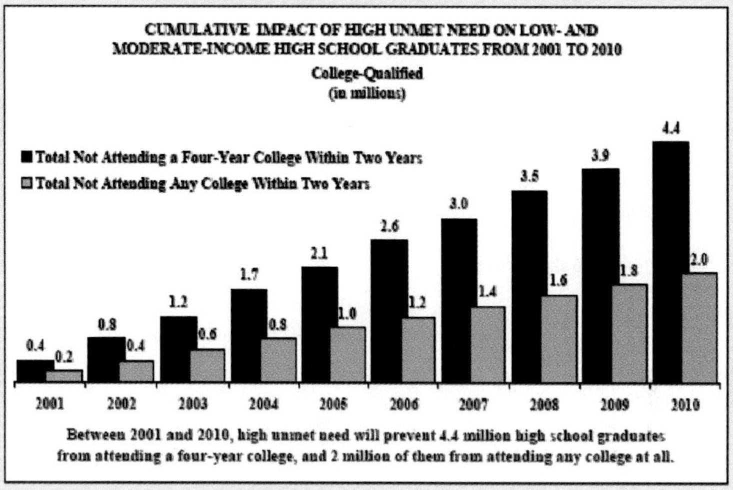

Source: "Empty Promises: The Myth of College Access in America," A Report of the Advisory Committee on Student Financial Assistance, June 2002, *www.ed.gov/about/bdscomm/list/acsfa/emptypromises.pdf*, p. 28 (accessed August 2006).

What Do You Think?

Each year many students decide to drop out of school. Many of them never return. Suppose that you are working two jobs and going to college and that you are not making ends meet. Your grades are suffering due to your lack of available study time. You feel depressed. Should you drop out of school?

YES: You can always go back to school. If your grades are bad, and you are depressed, what good is school doing you anyway?

NO: Once you drop out, it is very hard to get enough momentum to go back. Dropping out will dramatically reduce your long-term opportunities. It is better to stay in school, even if you take only one class per semester.

Sources: Kathleen Porter, "The Value of a College Degree," ERIC Clearinghouse on Higher Education, Washington DC, *www.ericdigests.org/2003-3/value.htm* (accessed August 2006).

The authors' comments on this situation appear on page 1172.

Demonstration Problem 2

Sierra Company is considering a long-term capital investment project called ZIP. The project will require an investment of $120,000, and it will have a useful life of 4 years. Annual net income for ZIP is expected to be: Year 1 $12,000; Year 2 $10,000; Year 3 $8,000; and Year 4 $6,000. Depreciation is computed by the straight-line method with no salvage value. The company's cost of capital is 12%.

Instructions

(Round all computations to two decimal places.)

(a) Compute the annual rate of return for the project.
(b) Compute the cash payback period for the project. (Round to two decimals.)
(c) Compute the net present value for the project. (Round to nearest dollar.)
(d) Should the project be accepted? Why?

action plan

✔ To compute annual rate of return, divide expected annual net income by average investment.

✔ To compute cash payback, divide cost of the investment by net annual cash flows.

✔ Recall that net annual cash flow equals annual net income plus annual depreciation expense.

✔ Be careful to use the correct discount factor in using the net present value method.

Solution to Demonstration Problem 2

(a) $9,000 ($36,000 ÷ 4) ÷ $60,000 ($120,000 ÷ 2) = 15%
(b) Depreciation expense is $120,000 ÷ 4 years = $30,000.
Net annual cash flows are:

Year 1	$12,000 + $30,000 = $42,000
Year 2	$10,000 + $30,000 = $40,000
Year 3	$8,000 + $30,000 = $38,000
Year 4	$6,000 + $30,000 = $36,000

Cumulative net cash flows would be $82,000 ($42,000 + $40,000) at the end of year 2 and $120,000 ($42,000 + $40,000 + $38,000) at the end of year 3. Since the cumulative net cash flows at the end of year 3 exactly equal the initial cash investment of $120,000, the cash payback period is 3 years.

(c)

Year	Discount Factor	Net Annual Cash Flow	Present Value
1	.89286	$42,000	$ 37,500
2	.79719	40,000	31,888
3	.71178	38,000	27,048
4	.63552	36,000	22,879
			119,315
		Capital investment	120,000
		Negative net present value	$ (685)

(d) The annual rate of return of 15% is good. However, the cash payback period is 75% of the project's useful life, and net present value is negative. The recommendation is to reject the project.

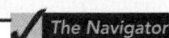

The Navigator

SUMMARY OF STUDY OBJECTIVES

1 **Identify the steps in management's decision-making process.** Management's decision-making process is: (a) identify the problem and assign responsibility, (b) determine and evaluate possible courses of action, (c) make the decision, and (d) review the results of the decision.

2 **Describe the concept of incremental analysis.** Incremental analysis identifies financial data that change under alternative courses of action. These data are relevant to the decision because they will vary in the future among the possible alternatives.

3 **Identify the relevant costs in accepting an order at a special price.** The relevant information in accepting an order at a special price is the difference between the variable costs to produce the special order and expected revenues.

4 **Identify the relevant costs in a make-or-buy decision.** In a make-or-buy decision, the relevant costs are (a) the manufacturing costs that will be saved, (b) the purchase price, and (c) opportunity costs.

5 **Give the decision rule for whether to sell or process materials further.** The decision rule for whether to sell or process materials further is: Process further as long as the incremental revenue from processing exceeds the incremental processing costs.

6 **Identify the factors to consider in retaining or replacing equipment.** The factors to consider in determining whether equipment should be retained or replaced are the effects on variable costs and the cost of the new equipment. Also, any trade-in allowance or cash disposal value of the existing asset must be considered.

7 **Explain the relevant factors in whether to eliminate an unprofitable segment.** In deciding whether to eliminate an unprofitable segment, determine the contribution margin, if any, produced by the segment and the disposition of the segment's fixed expenses.

8 **Determine which products to make and sell when resources are limited.** When a company has limited resources, find the contribution margin per unit of limited resource. Then multiply this amount by the units of limited resource to determine which product maximizes net income.

9 **Contrast annual rate of return and cash payback in capital budgeting.** The *annual rate of return* is obtained by dividing expected annual net income by the average investment. The higher the rate of return, the more attractive the investment. The *cash payback* technique identifies the time period to recover the cost of the investment. The formula is: Cost of capital expenditure divided by estimated net annual cash flow equals cash payback period. The shorter the payback period, the more attractive the investment.

10 **Distinguish between the net present value and internal rate of return methods.** Under the *net present value* method, compare the present value of future net cash flows with the capital investment to determine net present value. The NPV decision rule is: Accept the project if net present value is zero or positive. Reject the investment if net present value is negative.

Under the *internal rate of return* method, find the interest yield of the potential investment. The IRR decision rule is: Accept the project when the internal rate of return is equal to or greater than the required rate of return. Reject the project when the internal rate of return is less than the required rate.

The Navigator

GLOSSARY

WILEY PLUS

Annual rate of return technique Determines the profitability of a capital expenditure by dividing expected annual net income by the average investment. (p. 1145).

Capital budgeting The process of making capital expenditure decisions in business. (p. 1144).

Cash payback technique Identifies the time period required to recover the cost of a capital investment from the net annual cash flow produced by the investment. (p. 1146).

Cost of capital The rate of return that management expects to pay on all borrowed and equity funds. (p. 1146).

Discounted cash flow technique Considers both the estimated total net cash flows from the investment and the time value of money. (p. 1148).

Incremental analysis The process of identifying the financial data that change under alternative courses of action. (p. 1135).

Internal rate of return (IRR) The rate that will cause the present value of the proposed capital expenditure to equal the present value of the expected net annual cash flows. (p. 1151).

Internal rate of return method Finds the interest yield of the potential investment. (p. 1151).

Net present value (NPV) The difference that results when the original capital outlay is subtracted from the discounted net cash flows. (p. 1148).

Net present value method Discounts net cash flows to their present value and then compares that present value to the capital outlay required by the investment. (p. 1148).

Opportunity cost The potential benefit that may be obtained from following an alternative course of action. (p. 1137).

Sunk cost A cost that cannot be changed by any present or future decision. (p. 1140).

SELF-STUDY QUESTIONS

WILEY PLUS

Answers are at the end of the chapter.

(SO 1) 1. Three of the steps in management's decision process are: (1) Review results of decision. (2) Identify the problem. (3) Make the decision. The steps are performed in the following order.
- **a.** (1), (2), (3).
- **b.** (3), (2), (1).
- **c.** (2), (1), (3).
- **d.** (2), (3), (1).

2. Incremental analysis is the process of identifying the financial data that: (SO 2)
- **a.** do not change under alternative courses of action.
- **b.** change under alternative courses of action.
- **c.** are mixed under alternative courses of action.
- **d.** No correct answer is given.

3. It costs a company \$14 of variable costs and \$6 of fixed costs to produce product A that sells for \$30. A foreign (SO 3)

buyer offers to purchase 3,000 units at $18 each. If the special offer is accepted and produced with unused capacity, net income will:
a. decrease $6,000.
b. increase $6,000.
c. increase $12,000.
d. increase $9,000.

(SO 4) **4.** In a make-or-buy decision, relevant costs are:
a. manufacturing costs that will be saved.
b. the purchase price of the units.
c. opportunity costs.
d. all of the above.

(SO 5) **5.** The decision rule in a sell-or-process-further decision is: Process further as long as the incremental revenue from processing exceeds:
a. incremental processing costs.
b. variable processing costs.
c. fixed processing costs.
d. No correct answer is given.

(SO 6) **6.** In a decision to retain or replace equipment, the book value of the old equipment is a(n):
a. opportunity cost.
b. sunk cost.
c. incremental cost.
d. marginal cost.

(SO 7) **7.** If an unprofitable segment is eliminated:
a. net income will always increase.
b. variable expenses of the eliminated segment will have to be absorbed by other segments.
c. fixed expenses allocated to the eliminated segment will have to be absorbed by other segments.
d. net income will always decrease.

8. If the contribution margin per unit is $15 and it takes 3.0 machine hours to produce the unit, the contribution margin per unit of limited resource is: (SO 8)
a. $25.
b. $5.
c. $45.
d. No correct answer is given.

9. Which of the following is *incorrect* about the annual rate of return technique? (SO 9)
a. The calculation is simple.
b. The accounting terms used are familiar to management.
c. The timing of the net cash flows is not considered.
d. The time value of money is considered.

10. A positive net present value means that the: (SO 10)
a. project's rate of return is less than the cutoff rate.
b. project's rate of return exceeds the required rate of return.
c. project's rate of return equals the required rate of return.
d. project is unacceptable.

Go to the book's website,
www.wiley.com/college/weygandt,
for Additional Self-Study questions.

The Navigator

QUESTIONS

1. What steps are frequently involved in management's decision-making process?
2. Your roommate, Matt Mikan, contends that accounting contributes to most of the steps in management's decision-making process. Is your roommate correct? Explain.
3. "Incremental analysis involves the accumulation of information concerning a single course of action." Do you agree? Why?
4. Jerry Karr asks your help concerning the relevance of variable and fixed costs in incremental analysis. Help Jerry with his problem.
5. What data are relevant in deciding whether to accept an order at a special price?
6. Perney Company has an opportunity to buy parts at $7 each that currently cost $10 to make. What manufacturing costs are relevant to this make-or-buy decision?
7. Define the term "opportunity cost." How may this cost be relevant in a make-or-buy decision?
8. What is the decision rule in deciding whether to sell a product or process it further?
9. Your roommate, Betty Melton, is confused about sunk costs. Explain to your roommate the meaning of sunk costs and their relevance to a decision to retain or replace equipment.
10. Slocum Inc. has one product line that is unprofitable. What circumstances may cause overall company net income to be lower if the unprofitable product line is eliminated?
11. How is the contribution margin per unit of limited resources computed?
12. Describe the process a company may use in screening and approving the capital expenditure budget.
13. Your classmate, Laura Elder, is confused about the factors that are included in the annual rate of return technique. What is the formula for this technique?
14. Hector Ruiz is trying to understand the term "cost of capital." Define the term, and indicate its relevance to the decision rule under the annual rate of return technique.
15. Pete Hetzel claims the formula for the cash payback technique is the same as the formula for the annual rate of return technique. Is Pete correct? What is the formula for the cash payback technique?
16. What are the advantages and disadvantages of the cash payback technique?
17. Two types of present value tables may be used with the discounted cash flow technique. Identify the tables and the circumstance(s) when each table should be used.
18. What is the decision rule under the net present value method?

19. Identify the steps required in using the internal rate of return method.

20. Gillaspie Company uses the internal rate of return method. What is the decision rule for this method?

BRIEF EXERCISES

WILEY PLUS

BE26-1 The steps in management's decision-making process are listed in random order below. Indicate the order in which the steps should be executed.

Identify the steps in management's decision-making process. (SO 1)

—Make a decision.
—Identify the problem and assign responsibility.
—Review results of the decision.
—Determine and evaluate possible courses of action.

BE26-2 Ming Company is considering two alternatives. Alternative A will have sales of $150,000 and costs of $100,000. Alternative B will have sales of $180,000 and costs of $120,000. Compare Alternative A to Alternative B showing incremental revenues, costs, and net income.

Determine incremental changes. (SO, 2)

BE26-3 In Karnes Company it costs $30 per unit ($20 variable and $10 fixed) to make a product that normally sells for $45. A foreign wholesaler offers to buy 4,000 units at $23 each. Karnes will incur special shipping costs of $1 per unit. Assuming that Karnes has excess operating capacity, indicate the net income (loss) Karnes would realize by accepting the special order.

Determine whether to accept a special order. (SO 3)

BE26-4 Bartley Manufacturing incurs unit costs of $8 ($5 variable and $3 fixed) in making a sub-assembly part for its finished product. A supplier offers to make 10,000 of the part at $5.30 per unit. If the offer is accepted, Bartley will save all variable costs but no fixed costs. Prepare an analysis showing the total cost saving, if any, Bartley will realize by buying the part.

Determine whether to make or buy a part. (SO 4)

BE26-5 Stanton Inc. makes unfinished bookcases that it sells for $60. Production costs are $30 variable and $10 fixed. Because it has unused capacity, Stanton is considering finishing the bookcases and selling them for $72. Variable finishing costs are expected to be $8 per unit with no increase in fixed costs. Prepare an analysis on a per unit basis showing whether Stanton should sell unfinished or finished bookcases.

Determine whether to sell or process further. (SO 5)

BE26-6 Felton Company has a factory machine with a book value of $90,000 and a remaining useful life of 4 years. A new machine is available at a cost of $200,000. This machine will have a 4-year useful life with no salvage value. The new machine will lower annual variable manufacturing costs from $600,000 to $440,000. Prepare an analysis showing whether the old machine should be retained or replaced.

Determine whether to retain or replace equipment. (SO 6)

BE26-7 Derby, Inc. manufactures golf clubs in three models. For the year, the Eagle line has a net loss of $20,000 from sales $200,000, variable expenses $180,000, and fixed expenses $40,000. If the Eagle line is eliminated, $34,000 of fixed costs will remain. Prepare an analysis showing whether the Eagle line should be eliminated.

Determine whether to eliminate an unprofitable segment. (SO 7)

BE26-8 In Nevitt Company, data concerning two products are: Contribution margin per unit—Product A $11, Product B $12; machine hours required for one unit—Product A 2, Product B 2.5. Compute the contribution margin per unit of limited resource for each product.

Show allocation of limited resources. (SO 8)

BE26-9 Adler Company is considering purchasing new equipment for $300,000. It is expected that the equipment will produce annual net income of $10,000 over its 10-year useful life. Annual depreciation will be $30,000. Compute the cash payback period.

Compute the cash payback period for a capital investment. (SO 9)

BE26-10 Engles Oil Company is considering investing in a new oil well. It is expected that the oil well will increase annual revenues by $130,000 and will increase annual expenses by $80,000 including depreciation. The oil well will cost $490,000 and will have a $10,000 salvage value at the end of its 10-year useful life. Calculate the annual rate of return.

Compute annual rate of return. (SO 9)

BE26-11 Harry Company is considering two different, mutually exclusive capital expenditure proposals. Project A will cost $395,000, has an expected useful life of 10 years, a salvage value of zero, and is expected to increase net annual cash flows by $70,000. Project B will cost $270,000, has an expected useful life of 10 years, a salvage value of zero, and is expected to increase net annual cash flows by $50,000. A discount rate of 9% is appropriate for both projects. Compute the net present value of each project. Which project should be accepted?

Compute net present value. (SO 10)

Calculate internal rate of return.

(SO 10)

BE26-12 Frost Company is evaluating the purchase of a rebuilt spot-welding machine to be used in the manufacture of a new product. The machine will cost $170,000, has an estimated useful life of 7 years, a salvage value of zero, and will increase net annual cash flows by $33,740. What is its approximate internal rate of return?

Compute net present value of an investment.

(SO 10)

BE26-13 Horak Company accumulates the following data concerning a proposed capital investment: cash cost $225,000, net annual cash flow $34,000, present value factor of cash inflows for 10 years 6.71 (rounded). Determine the net present value, and indicate whether the investment should be made.

EXERCISES

WILEY PLUS

Analyze statements about decision making and incremental analysis.

(SO 1, 2)

E26-1 Pender has prepared the following list of statements about decision making and incremental analysis.

1. The first step in management's decision-making process is, "Determine and evaluate possible courses of action."
2. The final step in management's decision-making process is to actually make the decision.
3. Accounting's contribution to management's decision-making process occurs primarily in evaluating possible courses of action and in reviewing the results.
4. In making business decisions, management ordinarily considers only financial information because it is objectively determined.
5. Decisions involve a choice among alternative courses of action.
6. The process used to identify the financial data that change under alternative courses of action is called incremental analysis.
7. Costs that are the same under all alternative courses of action sometimes affect the decision.
8. When using incremental analysis, some costs will always change under alternative courses of action, but revenues will not.
9. Variable costs will change under alternative courses of action, but fixed costs will not.

Instructions

Identify each statement as true or false. If false, indicate how to correct the statement.

Make incremental analysis for special order.

(SO 3)

E26-2 Wyco Company manufactures toasters. For the first 8 months of 2009, the company reported the following operating results while operating at 75% of plant capacity.

Sales (400,000 units)	$4,000,000
Cost of goods sold	2,400,000
Gross profit	1,600,000
Operating expenses	900,000
Net income	$ 700,000

Cost of goods sold was 70% variable and 30% fixed. Operating expenses were 60% variable and 40% fixed.

In September, Wyco Company receives a special order for 40,000 toasters at $6.00 each from Salono Company of Mexico City. Acceptance of the order would result in $8,000 of shipping costs but no increase in fixed operating expenses.

Instructions

(a) Prepare an incremental analysis for the special order.

(b) Should Wyco Company accept the special order? Why or why not?

Make incremental analysis for special-order decision.

(SO 3)

E26-3 Innova Company produces golf discs which it normally sells to retailers for $7 each. The cost of manufacturing 20,000 golf discs is:

Materials	$ 10,000
Labor	30,000
Variable overhead	20,000
Fixed overhead	40,000
Total	$100,000

Innova also incurs 5% sales commission ($0.35) on each disc sold.

Mudd Corporation offers Innova $4.75 per disc for 5,000 discs. Mudd would sell the discs under its own brand name in foreign markets not yet served by Innova. If Innova accepts the offer, its fixed overhead will increase from $50,000 to $55,000 due to the purchase of a new imprinting machine. No sales commission will result from the special order.

Instructions

(a) Prepare an incremental analysis for the special order.
(b) Should Innova accept the special order? Why or why not?
(c) What assumptions underlie the decision made in part (b)?

Make incremental analysis for make-or-buy decision.
(SO 4)

E26-4 Shannon Inc. has been manufacturing its own shades for its table lamps. The company is currently operating at 100% of capacity. Variable manufacturing overhead is charged to production at the rate of 50% of direct labor cost. The direct materials and direct labor cost per unit to make the lamp shades are $4.00 and $6.00, respectively. Normal production is 40,000 table lamps per year.

A supplier offers to make the lamp shades at a price of $13.50 per unit. If Shannon Inc. accepts the supplier's offer, all variable manufacturing costs will be eliminated, but the $40,000 of fixed manufacturing overhead currently being charged to the lamp shades will have to be absorbed by other products.

Instructions

(a) Prepare the incremental analysis for the decision to make or buy the lamp shades.
(b) Should Shannon Inc. buy the lamp shades?
(c) Would your answer be different in (b) if the productive capacity released by not making the lamp shades could be used to produce income of $35,000?

Make incremental analysis for further processing of materials.
(SO 5)

E26-5 Stacy McGuire recently opened her own basketweaving studio. She sells finished baskets in addition to the raw materials needed by customers to weave baskets of their own. Stacy has put together a variety of raw material kits, each including materials at various stages of completion. Unfortunately, owing to space limitations, Stacy is unable to carry all varieties of kits originally assembled and must choose between two basic packages.

The basic introductory kit includes undyed, uncut reeds (with dye included) for weaving one basket. This basic package costs Stacy $12 and sells for $27. The second kit, called Stage 2, includes cut reeds that have already been dyed. With this kit the customer need only soak the reeds and weave the basket. Stacy is able to produce the second kit by using the basic materials included in the first kit and adding one hour of her own time (to produce two kits), which she values at $18 per hour. Because she is more efficient at cutting and dying reeds than her average customer, Stacy is able to make two kits of the dyed reeds, in one hour, from one kit of undyed reeds. The kit of dyed and cut reeds sells for $33.

Instructions

Determine whether Stacy's basketweaving shop should carry the basic introductory kit with undyed and uncut reeds, or the Stage 2 kit with reeds already dyed and cut. Prepare an incremental analysis to support your answer.

Make incremental analysis for sell-or-process-further decision.
(SO 5)

E26-6 Donkey Bikes could sell its bicycles to retailers either assembled or unassembled. The cost of an unassembled bike is as follows.

Direct materials	$150
Direct labor	70
Variable overhead (70% of direct labor)	49
Fixed overhead (30% of direct labor)	21
Manufacturing cost per unit	$290

The unassembled bikes are sold to retailers at $400 each.

Donkey currently has unused productive capacity that is expected to continue indefinitely; management has concluded that some of this capacity can be used to assemble the bikes and sell them at $450 each. Assembling the bikes will increase direct materials by $5 per bike, and direct labor by $20 per bike. Additional variable overhead will be incurred at the normal rates, but there will be no additional fixed overhead as a result of assembling the bikes.

Instructions

(a) Prepare an incremental analysis for the sell-or-process-further decision.
(b) Should Donkey sell or process further? Why or why not?

Make incremental analysis for retaining or replacing equipment.

(SO 6)

E26-7 Crone Enterprises uses a word processing computer to handle its sales invoices. Lately, business has been so good that it takes an extra 3 hours per night, plus every third Saturday, to keep up with the volume of sales invoices. Management is considering updating its computer with a faster model that would eliminate all of the overtime processing.

	Current Machine	New Machine
Original purchase cost	$15,000	$21,000
Accumulated depreciation	6,000	—
Estimated operating costs	24,000	20,000
Useful life	5 years	5 years

If sold now, the current machine would have a salvage value of $5,000. If operated for the remainder of its useful life, the current machine would have zero salvage value. The new machine is expected to have zero salvage value after 5 years.

Instructions

Should the current machine be replaced? (Ignore the time value of money.)

Make incremental analysis for elimination of division.

(SO 7)

E26-8 Judy Herzog, a recent graduate of Rolling's accounting program, evaluated the operating performance of Klumpe Company's six divisions. Judy made the following presentation to the Klumpe board of directors and suggested the Ketchum Division be eliminated. "If the Ketchum Division is eliminated," she said, "our total profits would increase by $16,870."

	The Other Five Divisions	Ketchum Division	Total
Sales	$1,664,200	$ 98,200	$1,762,400
Cost of goods sold	978,520	76,470	1,054,990
Gross profit	685,680	21,730	707,410
Operating expenses	527,940	38,600	566,540
Net income	$ 157,740	$(16,870)	$ 140,870

In the Ketchum Division, cost of goods sold is $56,000 variable and $20,470 fixed, and operating expenses are $12,000 variable and $26,600 fixed. None of the Ketchum Division's fixed costs will be eliminated if the division is discontinued.

Instructions

Is Judy right about eliminating the Ketchum Division? Prepare a schedule to support your answer.

Make incremental analysis for elimination of a product line.

(SO 7)

E26-9 Shatner Company makes three models of phasers. Information on the three products is given below.

	Stunner	Double-Set	Mega-Power
Sales	$300,000	$500,000	$200,000
Variable expenses	150,000	200,000	140,000
Contribution margin	150,000	300,000	60,000
Fixed expenses	120,000	225,000	90,000
Net income	$ 30,000	$ 75,000	$ (30,000)

Fixed expenses consist of $300,000 of common costs allocated to the three products based on relative sales, and additional fixed expenses of $30,000 (Stunner), $75,000 (Double-Set), and $30,000 (Mega-Power). The common costs will be incurred regardless of how many models are produced. The other fixed expenses would be eliminated if a model is phased out.

Jim Kirk, an executive with the company, feels the Mega-Power line should be discontinued to increase the company's net income.

Instructions

(a) Compute current net income for Shatner Company.

(b) Compute net income by product line and in total for Shatner Company if the company discontinues the Mega-Power product line. (*Hint:* Allocate the $300,000 common costs to the two remaining product lines based on their relative sales.)

(c) Should Shatner eliminate the Mega-Power product line? Why or why not?

Compute contribution margin and determine the product to be manufactured.

(SO 8)

E26-10 Freese Company manufactures and sells three products. Relevant per unit data concerning each product are given below.

	Product		
	A	B	C
Selling price	$11	$12	$15
Variable costs and expenses	$ 4	$ 8	$ 9
Machine hours to produce	2	1	2

Instructions

(a) Compute the contribution margin per unit of the limited resource (machine hour) for each product.

(b) Assuming 3,000 additional machine hours are available, which product should be manufactured?

(c) Prepare an analysis showing the total contribution margin if the additional hours are (1) divided equally among the products, and (2) allocated entirely to the product identified in (b) above.

Compute cash payback period and annual rate of return.

(SO 9)

E26-11 Carleton Service Center just purchased an automobile hoist for $15,000. The hoist has a 5-year life and an estimated salvage value of $1,080. Installation costs were $2,900, and freight charges were $820. Carleton uses straight-line depreciation.

The new hoist will be used to replace mufflers and tires on automobiles. Carleton estimates that the new hoist will enable his mechanics to replace four extra mufflers per week. Each muffler sells for $65 installed. The cost of a muffler is $35, and the labor cost to install a muffler is $10.

Instructions

(a) Compute the payback period for the new hoist.

(b) Compute the annual rate of return for the new hoist. (Round to one decimal.)

Compute cash payback period and net present value.

(SO 9, 10)

E26-12 Suzaki Manufacturing Company is considering three new projects, each requiring an equipment investment of $22,000. Each project will last for 3 years and produce the following cash inflows.

Year	AA	BB	CC
1	$ 7,000	$ 9,500	$13,000
2	9,000	9,500	10,000
3	15,000	9,500	9,000
Total	$31,000	$28,500	$32,000

The equipment's salvage value is zero. Suzaki uses straight-line depreciation. Suzaki will not accept any project with a payback period over 2 years. Suzaki's minimum required rate of return is 12%.

Instructions

(a) Compute each project's payback period, indicating the most desirable project and the least desirable project using this method. (Round to two decimals.)

(b) Compute the net present value of each project. Does your evaluation change? (Round to nearest dollar.)

Compute annual rate of return, cash payback period, and net present value.

(SO 9, 10)

E26-13 Rondello Company is considering a capital investment of $150,000 in additional productive facilities. The new machinery is expected to have a useful life of 5 years with no salvage value. Depreciation is by the straight-line method. During the life of the investment, annual net income and cash inflows are expected to be $18,000 and $48,000, respectively. Rondello has a 12% cost of capital rate, which is the minimum acceptable rate of return on the investment.

Instructions

(Round to two decimals.)

(a) Compute (1) the annual rate of return and (2) the cash payback period on the proposed capital expenditure.

(b) Using the discounted cash flow technique, compute the net present value.

Determine internal rate of return.
(SO 10)

E26-14 Omega Company is considering three capital expenditure projects. Relevant data for the projects are as follows.

Project	Investment	Annual Income	Life of Project
22A	$240,000	$13,300	6 years
23A	270,000	21,000	9 years
24A	288,000	20,000	8 years

Annual income is constant over the life of the project. Each project is expected to have zero salvage value at the end of the project. Omega Company uses the straight-line method of depreciation.

Instructions

(a) Determine the internal rate of return for each project. Round the internal rate of return factor to three decimals.

(b) If Omega Company's minimum required rate of return is 11%, which projects are acceptable?

Compute net present value and recommend project.
(SO 10)

E26-15 Vasquez Corporation is considering investing in two different projects. It could invest in both, neither, or just one of the projects. The forecasts for the projects are as follows.

	Project A	Project B
Capital investment	$200,000	$300,000
Net annual cash flows	$ 50,000	$ 65,000
Length of project	5 years	7 years

The minimum rate of return acceptable to Vasquez is 10%.

Instructions

(a) Compute the net present value of the two projects.

(b) What capital budgeting decision should Vasquez make?

(c) Project A could be modified. By spending $20,000 more initially, the net annual cash flows could be increased by $10,000 per year. Would this change Vasquez's decision?

EXERCISES: SET B

Visit the book's website at **www.wiley.com/college/weygandt**, and choose the Student Companion site, to access Exercise Set B.

PROBLEMS: SET A

Make incremental analysis for special order, and identify nonfinancial factors in decision.
(SO 3)

P26-1A Korte Company is currently producing 16,000 units per month, which is 80% of its production capacity. Variable manufacturing costs are currently $8.00 per unit. Fixed manufacturing costs are $56,000 per month. Korte pays a 9% sales commission to its sales people, has $30,000 in fixed administrative expenses per month, and is averaging $320,000 in sales per month.

A special order received from a foreign company would enable Korte Company to operate at 100% capacity. The foreign company offered to pay 75% of Korte's current selling price per unit. If the order is accepted, Korte will have to spend an extra $2.00 per unit to package the product for overseas shipping. Also, Korte Company would need to lease a new stamping machine to imprint the foreign company's logo on the product, at a monthly cost of $2,500. The special order would require a sales commission of $3,500.

Instructions

(a) Compute the number of units involved in the special order and the foreign company's offered price per unit.

(b) What is the manufacturing cost of producing one unit of Korte's product for regular customers?

(c) Prepare an incremental analysis of the special order. Should management accept the order?

(d) What is the lowest price that Korte could accept for the special order to earn net income of $1.20 per unit?

(e) What nonfinancial factors should management consider in making its decision?

P26-2A The management of Martinez Manufacturing Company has asked for your assistance in deciding whether to continue manufacturing a part or to buy it from an outside supplier. The part, called Tropica, is a component of Martinez's finished product.

Make incremental analysis related to make or buy; consider opportunity cost, and identify nonfinancial factors.

(SO 4)

An analysis of the accounting records and the production data revealed the following information for the year ending December 31, 2008.

1. The Machinery Department produced 36,000 units of Tropica.
2. Each Tropica unit requires 10 minutes to produce. Three people in the Machinery Department work full time (2,000 hours per year) producing Tropica. Each person is paid $11.00 per hour.
3. The cost of materials per Tropica unit is $2.00.
4. Manufacturing costs directly applicable to the production of Tropica are: indirect labor, $5,500; utilities, $1,300; depreciation, $1,600; property taxes and insurance, $1,000. All of the costs will be eliminated if Tropica is purchased.
5. The lowest price for a Tropica from an outside supplier is $3.90 per unit. Freight charges will be $0.30 per unit, and a part-time receiving clerk at $8,500 per year will be required.
6. If Tropica is purchased, the excess space will be used to store Martinez's finished product. Currently, Martinez rents storage space at approximately $0.60 per unit stored per year. Approximately 6,000 units per year are stored in the rented space.

Instructions

(a) Prepare an incremental analysis for the make-or-buy decision. Should Martinez make or buy the part? Why?

(b) Prepare an incremental analysis, assuming the released facilities can be used to produce $10,000 of net income in addition to the savings on the rental of storage space. What decision should now be made?

(c) What nonfinancial factors should be considered in the decision?

P26-3A Deskins Manufacturing Company has four operating divisions. During the first quarter of 2008 the company reported total income from operations of $61,000 and the following results for the divisions.

Compute contribution margin, and prepare incremental analysis concerning elimination of divisions.

(SO 7)

	Division			
	Denver	**Miami**	**San Diego**	**Tacoma**
Sales	$455,000	$730,000	$920,000	$515,000
Cost of goods sold	380,000	480,000	576,000	430,000
Selling and administrative expenses	120,000	207,000	246,000	120,000
Income (loss) from operations	$(45,000)	$ 43,000	$ 98,000	$(35,000)

Analysis reveals the following percentages of variable costs in each division.

	Denver	**Miami**	**San Diego**	**Tacoma**
Cost of goods sold	95%	80%	90%	90%
Selling and administrative expenses	80	60	70	60

Discontinuance of any division would save 60% of the fixed costs and expenses for that division.

Top management is deeply concerned about the unprofitable divisions (Denver and Tacoma). The consensus is that one or both of the divisions should be eliminated.

Instructions

(a) Compute the contribution margin for the two unprofitable divisions.

(b) Prepare an incremental analysis concerning the possible elimination of (1) the Denver Division and (2) the Tacoma Division. What course of action do you recommend for each division?

(c) Prepare a columnar condensed income statement using the CVP format for Deskins Manufacturing Company, assuming (1) the Denver Division is eliminated, and (2) the unavoidable fixed costs and expenses of the Denver Division are allocated 30% to Miami, 50% to San Diego, and 20% to Tacoma.

(d) Compare the total income from operations with the Denver Division ($61,000) to total income from operations without this division.

Compute annual rate of return, cash payback, and net present value.

(SO 9, 10)

P26-4A Timmons Corporation is considering three long-term capital investment proposals. Relevant data on each project are as follows.

	Project		
	Brown	**Red**	**Yellow**
Capital investment	$190,000	$220,000	$250,000
Annual net income:			
Year 1	25,000	20,000	26,000
2	16,000	20,000	24,000
3	13,000	20,000	23,000
4	10,000	20,000	17,000
5	8,000	20,000	20,000
Total	$ 72,000	$100,000	$110,000

Salvage value is expected to be zero at the end of each project. Depreciation is computed by the straight-line method. The company's minimum rate of return is the company's cost of capital which is 12%.

Instructions

(a) Compute the annual rate of return for each project. (Round to one decimal.)
(b) Compute the cash payback period for each project. (Round to two decimals.)
(c) Compute the net present value for each project. (Round to nearest dollar.)
(d) Rank the projects on each of the foregoing bases. Which project do you recommend?

Compute annual rate of return, cash payback, and net present value.

(SO 9, 10)

P26-5A Wendy Dobson is the managing director of the Wichita Day Care Center. Wichita is currently set up as a full-time child care facility for children between the ages of 12 months and 6 years. Wendy is trying to determine whether the center should expand its facilities to incorporate a newborn care room for infants between the ages of 6 weeks and 12 months. The necessary space already exists. An investment of $25,000 would be needed, however, to purchase cribs, high chairs, etc. The equipment purchased for the room would have a 5-year useful life with zero salvage value.

The newborn nursery would be staffed to handle 12 infants on a full-time basis. The parents of each infant would be charged $200 weekly, and the facility would operate 52 weeks of the year. Staffing the nursery would require two full-time specialists and five part-time assistants at an annual cost of $103,800. Food, diapers, and other miscellaneous supplies are expected to total $14,000 annually.

Instructions

(a) Determine (1) annual net income and (2) net cash flow for the new nursery.
(b) Compute (1) the annual rate of return and (2) the cash payback period for the new nursery. (Round to two decimals.)
(c) Assuming that Wichita can borrow the money needed for expansion at 10%, compute the net present value of the new room. (Round to the nearest dollar.)
(d) What should Wendy conclude from these computations?

Compute net present value and internal rate of return.

(SO 10)

P26-6A Aqua Tech Testing is considering investing in a new testing device. It has two options: Option A would have an initial lower cost but would require a significant expenditure for rebuilding after 5 years. Option B would require no rebuilding expenditure, but its maintenance costs would be higher. Since the option B machine is of initial higher quality, it is expected to have a salvage value at the end of its useful life. The following estimates were provided. The company's cost of capital is 9%.

	Option A	**Option B**
Initial cost	$90,000	$170,000
Net annual cash flows	$20,000	$32,000
Cost to rebuild (end of year 5)	$26,500	$0
Salvage value	$0	$27,500
Estimated useful life	8 years	8 years

Instructions

(a) Compute the (1) net present value, and (2) internal rate of return for each option. (*Hint:* To solve for internal rate of return, experiment with alternative discount rates to arrive at a net present value of zero.)
(b) Which option should be accepted?

PROBLEMS: SET B

Make incremental analysis for special order, and identify nonfinancial factors in decision.

(SO 3)

P26-1B Houston Inc. manufactures basketballs for the National Basketball Association (NBA). For the first 6 months of 2009, the company reported the following operating results while operating at 90% of plant capacity.

	Amount	Per Unit
Sales	$4,500,000	$50.00
Cost of goods sold	3,600,000	40.00
Selling and administrative expenses	360,000	4.00
Net income	$ 540,000	$ 6.00

Fixed costs for the period were: Cost of goods sold $900,000, and selling and administrative expenses $225,000.

In July, normally a slack manufacturing month, Houston receives a special order for 6,000 basketballs at $35 each from the Italian Basketball Association (IBA). Acceptance of the order would increase variable selling and administrative expenses $0.50 per unit because of shipping costs but would not increase fixed costs and expenses.

Instructions

(a) Prepare an incremental analysis for the special order.

(b) Should Houston Inc. accept the special order?

(c) What is the minimum selling price on the special order to produce net income of $3.00 per ball?

(d) What nonfinancial factors should management consider in making its decision?

Make incremental analysis related to make or buy; consider opportunity cost, and identify nonfinancial factors.

(SO 4)

P26-2B The management of Edgerton Manufacturing Company is trying to decide whether to continue manufacturing a part or to buy it from an outside supplier. The part, called WISCO, is a component of the company's finished product.

The following information was collected from the accounting records and production data for the year ending December 31, 2009.

1. 8,000 units of WISCO were produced in the Machining Department.
2. Variable manufacturing costs applicable to the production of each WISCO unit were: direct materials $4.75, direct labor $4.60, indirect labor $0.45, utilities $0.35.
3. Fixed manufacturing costs applicable to the production of WISCO were:

Cost Item	Direct	Allocated
Depreciation	$1,600	$ 900
Property taxes	400	200
Insurance	900	600
	$2,900	$1,700

All variable manufacturing and direct fixed costs will be eliminated if WISCO is purchased. Allocated costs will have to be absorbed by other production departments.

4. The lowest quotation for 8,000 WISCO units from a supplier is $88,000.
5. If WISCO units are purchased, freight and inspection costs would be $0.30 per unit, and receiving costs totaling $750 per year would be incurred by the Machining Department.

Instructions

(a) Prepare an incremental analysis for WISCO. Your analysis should have columns for (1) Make WISCO, (2) Buy WISCO, and (3) Net Income Increase/Decrease.

(b) Based on your analysis, what decision should management make?

(c) Would the decision be different if Edgerton Company has the opportunity to produce $8,000 of net income with the facilities currently being used to manufacture WISCO? Show computations.

(d) What nonfinancial factors should management consider in making its decision?

Compute contribution margin, and prepare incremental analysis concerning elimination of divisions.

(SO 7)

P26-3B Plott Manufacturing Company has four operating divisions. During the first quarter of 2009, the company reported aggregate income from operations of $155,000 and the divisional results shown on the next page.

	Division I	Division II	Division III	Division IV
Sales	$490,000	$410,000	$ 290,000	$200,000
Cost of goods sold	300,000	250,000	270,000	180,000
Selling and administrative expenses	60,000	80,000	35,000	60,000
Income (loss) from operations	$130,000	$ 80,000	$ (15,000)	$(40,000)

Analysis reveals the following percentages of variable costs in each division.

	I	II	III	IV
Cost of goods sold	70%	80%	75%	90%
Selling and administrative expenses	40	50	60	70

Discontinuance of any division would save 50% of the fixed costs and expenses for that division.

Top management is very concerned about the unprofitable divisions (III and IV). Consensus is that one or both of the divisions should be discontinued.

Instructions

(a) Compute the contribution margin for Divisions III and IV.

(b) Prepare an incremental analysis concerning the possible discontinuance of (1) Division III and (2) Division IV. What course of action do you recommend for each division?

(c) Prepare a columnar condensed income statement for Plott Manufacturing, assuming Division IV is eliminated. Use the CVP format. Division IV's unavoidable fixed costs are allocated equally to the continuing divisions.

(d) Reconcile the total income from operations ($155,000) with the total income from operations without Division IV.

Compute annual rate of return, cash payback, and net present value.

(SO 9, 10)

P26-4B Lapham Corporation is considering three long-term capital investment proposals. Each investment has a useful life of 5 years. Relevant data on each project are as follows.

	Project Tic	Project Tac	Project Toe
Capital investment	$160,000	$180,000	$200,000
Annual net income:			
Year 1	13,000	18,000	27,000
2	13,000	17,000	22,000
3	13,000	16,000	16,000
4	13,000	12,000	13,000
5	13,000	9,000	12,000
Total	$ 65,000	$ 72,000	$ 90,000

Depreciation is computed by the straight-line method with no salvage value. The company's cost of capital is 15%.

Instructions

(a) Compute the annual rate of return for each project. (Round to one decimal.)

(b) Compute the cash payback period for each project. (Round to two decimals.)

(c) Compute the net present value for each project. (Round to nearest dollar.)

(d) Rank the projects on each of the foregoing bases. Which project do you recommend?

Compute annual rate of return, cash payback, and net present value.

(SO, 9, 10)

P26-5B Marie Dunston is an accounting major at a midwestern state university located approximately 60 miles from a major city. Many of the students attending the university are from the metropolitan area and visit their homes regularly on the weekends. Marie, an entrepreneur at heart, realizes that few good commuting alternatives are available for students doing weekend travel. She believes that a weekend commuting service could be organized and run profitably from several suburban and downtown shopping mall locations. Marie has gathered the following investment information.

1. Six used vans would cost a total of $90,000 to purchase and would have a 3-year useful life with negligible salvage value. Marie plans to use straight-line depreciation.
2. Ten drivers would have to be employed at a total payroll expense of $70,000.

3. Other annual out of pocket expenses associated with running the commuter service would include Gasoline $20,000, Maintenance $2,800, Repairs $3,500, Insurance $3,200, Advertising $1,500. (Exclude interest expense.)
4. Marie has visited several financial institutions to discuss funding for her new venture. The best interest rate she has been able to negotiate is 10%. Use this rate for cost of capital.
5. Marie expects each van to make ten round trips weekly and carry an average of five students each trip. The service is expected to operate 30 weeks each years. Each student will be charged $15.00 for a round-trip ticket.

Instructions

(a) Determine the annual (1) net income, and (2) net cash flow for the commuter service.
(b) Compute (1) the annual rate of return, and (2) the cash payback period. (Round to two decimals.)
(c) Compute the net present value of the commuter service. (Round to the nearest dollar.)
(d) What should Marie conclude from these computations?

Compute net present value, and internal rate of return.

(SO 10)

P26-6B Carolina Clinic is considering investing in new heart-monitoring equipment. It has two options: Option A would have an initial lower cost but would require a significant expenditure for rebuilding after 4 years. Option B would require no rebuilding expenditure, but its maintenance costs would be higher. Since the option B machine is of initial higher quality, it is expected to have a salvage value at the end of its useful life. The following estimates were made of the cash flows. The company's cost of capital is 11%.

	Option A	**Option B**
Initial cost	$160,000	$227,000
Net annual cash flows	$40,000	$50,000
Cost to rebuild (end of year 4)	$60,000	$0
Salvage value	$0	$12,000
Estimated useful life	8 years	8 years

Instructions

(a) Compute the (1) net present value and (2) internal rate of return for each option. (*Hint:* To solve for internal rate of return, experiment with alternative discount rates to arrive at a net present value of zero.)
(b) Which option should be accepted?

PROBLEMS: SET C

Visit the book's website at **www.wiley.com/college/weygandt**, and choose the Student Companion site, to access Problem Set C.

COMPREHENSIVE PROBLEM: CHAPTERS 19 TO 26

You would like to start a business manufacturing a unique model of bicycle helmet. In preparation for an interview with the bank to discuss your financing needs, you develop answers to the following questions. A number of assumptions are required; clearly note all assumptions that you make.

Instructions

(a) Identify the types of costs that would likely be involved in making this product.
(b) Set up five columns as indicated.

	Product Costs			
Item	**Direct Materials**	**Direct Labor**	**Manufacturing Overhead**	**Period Costs**

Classify the costs you identified in (a) into the manufacturing cost classifications of product costs (direct materials, direct labor, and manufacturing overhead) and period costs.

(c) Assign hypothetical monthly dollar figures to the costs you identified in (a) and (b).

(d) Assume you have no raw materials or work in process beginning or ending inventories. Prepare a projected cost of goods manufactured schedule for the first month of operations.

(e) Project the number of helmets you expect to produce the first month of operations. Compute the cost to produce one bicycle helmet. Review the result to ensure it is reasonable; if not, return to part (c) and adjust the monthly dollar figures you assigned accordingly.

(f) What type of cost accounting system will you likely use—job order or process costing?

(g) Explain how you would assign costs in either the job order or process costing system you plan to use.

(h) Classify your costs as either variable or fixed costs. For simplicity, assign all costs to either variable or fixed, assuming there are no mixed costs, using the format shown.

Item	Variable Costs	Fixed Costs	Total Costs

(i) Compute the unit variable cost, using the production number you determined in (e).

(j) Project the number of helmets you anticipate selling the first month of operations. Set a unit selling price, and compute both the contribution margin per unit and the contribution margin ratio.

(k) Determine your break-even point in dollars and in units.

(l) Prepare projected operating budgets (sales, production, direct materials, direct labor, manufacturing overhead, selling and administrative expense, and income statement). You will need to make assumptions for each of the following:

Direct materials budget:	Quantity of direct materials required to produce one helmet; cost per unit of quantity; desired ending direct materials (assume none).
Direct labor budget:	Direct labor time required per helmet; direct labor cost per hour.
Budgeted income statement:	Income tax expense is 45% of income from operations.

(m) Prepare a cash budget for the month. Assume the percentage of sales that will be collected from customers is 75%, and the percentage of direct materials that will be paid in the current month is 75%.

(n) Determine a relevant range of activity, using the number of helmets produced as your activity index. Recast your manufacturing overhead budget into a flexible monthly budget for two additional activity levels.

(o) Identify one potential cause of materials, direct labor, and manufacturing overhead variances for your product.

(p) Assume that you wish to purchase production equipment that costs $720,000. Determine the cash payback period, utilizing the monthly cash flow that you computed in part (m) multiplied by 12 months (for simplicity).

(q) Identify any nonfinancial factors that should be considered before commencing your business venture.

BROADENING YOUR PERSPECTIVE

DECISION MAKING ACROSS THE ORGANIZATION

BYP26-1 Morganstern Company is considering the purchase of a new machine. The invoice price of the machine is $170,000, freight charges are estimated to be $4,000, and installation costs are expected to be $6,000. Salvage value of the new equipment is expected to be zero after a useful life of 4 years. Existing equipment could be retained and used for an additional 4 years if the new machine is not purchased. At that time, the salvage value of the equipment would be zero. If the new machine is purchased now, the existing machine would be scrapped. Morganstern's accountant, Diane Gallup, has accumulated the following data regarding annual sales and expenses with and without the new machine.

1. Without the new machine, Morganstern can sell 10,000 units of product annually at a per unit selling price of $100. If the new unit is purchased, the number of units produced and sold would increase by 20%. The selling price would remain the same.

2. The new machine is faster than the old machine, and it is more efficient in its usage of materials. With the old machine the gross profit rate will be 25% of sales. With the new machine the rate will be 28% of sales.
3. Annual selling expenses are $135,000 with the current equipment. Because the new equipment would produce a greater number of units to be sold, annual selling expenses are expected to increase by 10% if it is purchased.
4. Annual administrative expenses are expected to be $100,000 with the old machine and $113,000 with the new machine.
5. The current book value of the existing machine is $36,000. Morganstern uses straight-line depreciation.
6. Morganstern's management wants a minimum rate of return of 15% on its investment and a payback period of no more than 3 years.

Instructions

With the class divided into groups, answer the following. (Ignore income tax effects.)

(a) Prepare an incremental analysis for the 4 years showing whether Morganstern should keep the existing machine or buy the new machine.
(b) Calculate the annual rate of return for the new machine. (Round to two decimals.)
(c) Compute the payback period for the new machine. (Round to two decimals.)
(d) Compute the net present value of the new machine. (Round to the nearest dollar.)
(e) On the basis of the foregoing data, would you recommend that Morganstern buy the machine? Why?

MANAGERIAL ANALYSIS

BYP26-2 Barone Company manufactures private-label small electronic products, such as alarm clocks, calculators, kitchen timers, stopwatches, and automatic pencil sharpeners. Some of the products are sold as sets, and others are sold individually. Products are studied as to their sales potential, and then cost estimates are made. The Engineering Department develops production plans, and then production begins. The company has generally had very successful product introduction. Only two products introduced by the company have been discontinued.

One of the products currently sold is a multi-alarm alarm clock. The clock has four alarms that can be programmed to sound at various times and for varying lengths of time. The company has experienced a great deal of difficulty in making the circuit boards for the clocks. The production process has never operated smoothly. The product is unprofitable at the present time, primarily because of warranty repairs and product recalls. Two models of the clocks were recalled, for example, because they sometimes caused an electric shock when the alarms were being shut off. The Engineering Department is attempting to revise the manufacturing process, but the revision will take another 6 months at least.

The clocks were very popular when they were introduced, and since they are private-label, the company has not suffered much from the recalls. Presently, the company has a very large order for several items from Kmart Stores. The order includes 5,000 of the multi-alarm clocks. When the company suggested that Kmart purchase the clocks from another manufacturer, Kmart threatened to rescind the entire order unless the clocks were included.

The company has therefore investigated the possibility of having another company make the clocks for them. The clocks were bid for the Kmart order, based on an estimated $5.50 cost to manufacture, as follows.

Circuit board, 1 each @ $1.00	$1.00
Plastic case, 1 each @ $0.50	0.50
Alarms, 4 @ $0.15 each	0.60
Labor, 15 minutes @ $12/hour	3.00
Overhead, $1.60 per labor hour	0.40

Barone could purchase clocks to fill the Kmart order for $9 from Silver Star, a Korean manufacturer with a very good quality record. Silver Star has offered to reduce the price to $7.50 after Barone has been a customer for 6 months, placing an order of at least 1,000 units per month. If Barone becomes a "preferred customer" by purchasing 15,000 units per year, the price would be reduced still further to $4.50.

Sigma Products, a local manufacturer, has also offered to make clocks for Barone. They have offered to sell 5,000 clocks for $5 each. However, Sigma Products has been in business for only 6 months. They have experienced significant turnover in their labor force, and the local media have reported that the owners may soon face tax evasion charges. The owner of Sigma Products is an electronic engineer, however, and the quality of the clocks is likely to be good.

If Barone decides to purchase the clocks from either Silver Star or Sigma, all the costs to manufacturer could be avoided, except a total of $5,000 in overhead costs for machine depreciation. The machinery is fairly new, and has no alternate use.

Instructions

(a) What is the difference in profit under each of the alternatives if the clocks are to be sold for $13.00 each to Kmart?

(b) What are the most important nonfinancial factors that Barone should consider when making this decision?

(c) What should Barone do in regard to the Kmart order? What should it do in regard to continuing to manufacture the multi-alarm alarm clocks? Be prepared to defend your answer.

REAL-WORLD FOCUS

BYP26-3 Founded in 1983, the Beverly Hills Fan Company is located in Woodland Hills, California. With 23 employees and sales of less than $10 million, the company is relatively small. Management feels that there is potential for growth in the upscale market for ceiling fans and lighting. They are particularly optimistic about growth in Mexican and Canadian markets.

Presented below is information from the president's letter in the company's annual report.

BEVERLY HILLS FAN COMPANY

President's Letter

An aggressive product development program was initiated during the past year resulting in new ceiling fan models planned for introduction next year. Award winning industrial designer Ron Rezek created several new fan models for the Beverly Hills Fan and L.A. Fan lines, including a new Showroom Collection, designed specifically for the architectural and designer markets. Each of these models has received critical acclaim, and order commitments for next year have been outstanding. Additionally, our Custom Color and special order fans continued to enjoy increasing popularity and sales gains as more and more customers desire fans that match their specific interior decors. Currently, Beverly Hills Fan Company offers a product line of over 100 models of contemporary, traditional, and transitional ceiling fans.

Instructions

(a) What points did the company management need to consider before deciding to offer the special-order fans to customers?

(b) How would incremental analysis be employed to assist in this decision?

EXPLORING THE WEB

BYP26-4 Campbell Soup Company is an international provider of soup products. Management is very interested in continuing to grow the company in its core business, while "spinning off" those businesses that are not part of its core operation.

Address: www.campbellsoups.com, or go to **www.wiley.com/college/weygandt**

Steps

1. Go to the home page of Campbell Soup Company at the address shown above.
2. Choose **Our Company** and then **Investor Center**.

3. Choose **Financial Reports**.
4. Choose the 2005 annual report, or the current annual report if 2005 is no longer available.

Instructions

Review the financial statements and management's discussion and analysis, and answer the following questions.

(a) What was the total amount reported as "Purchases of Plant Assets" in the 2005 statement of cash flows? How does this amount compare with the previous year?

(b) What range of interest rates does the company report on its long-term liabilities in the notes to its financial statements?

(c) Assume that this year's capital expenditures are expected to increase cash flows by $45 million. What is the expected internal rate of return (IRR) for these capital expenditures? (Assume a 10-year period for the cash flows.)

Communication Activity

BYP26-5 Refer back to E26-11 to address the following.

Instructions

Prepare a memo to Angie Baden, your supervisor. Show your calculations from E26-11, parts **(a)** and **(b)**. In one or two paragraphs, discuss important nonfinancial considerations. Make any assumptions you believe to be necessary. Make a recommendation, based on your analysis.

Ethics Case

BYP26-6 DeVito Company operates in a state where corporate taxes and workmen's compensation insurance rates have recently doubled. DeVito's president has assigned you the task of preparing an economic analysis and making a recommendation about whether to move the company's entire operation to Missouri. The president is slightly in favor of such a move because Missouri is his boyhood home, and he also owns a fishing lodge there.

You have just completed building your dream house, moved in, and sodded the lawn. Your children are all doing well in school and sports and, along with your spouse, want no part of a move to Missouri. If the company does move, so will you because your town is a one-industry community, and you and your spouse will have to move to have employment. Moving when everyone else does will cause you to take a big loss on the sale of your house. The same hardships will be suffered by your coworkers, and the town will be devastated.

In compiling the costs of moving versus not moving, you have latitude in the assumptions you make, the estimates you compute, and the discount rates and time periods you project. You are in a position to influence the decision singlehandedly.

Instructions

(a) Who are the stakeholders in this situation?

(b) What are the ethical issues in this situation?

(c) What would you do in this situation?

"All About You" Activity

BYP26-7 Managerial accounting techniques can be used in a wide variety of settings. As we have frequently pointed out, you can use them in many personal situations. They also can be useful in trying to find solutions for societal issues that appear to be hard to solve.

*

Instructions

Read the *Fortune* article "The Toughest Customers: How Hardheaded Business Metrics Can Help the Hard-core Homeless," by Cait Murphy, available at *http://money.cnn.com/magazines/fortune/fortune_archive/2006/04/03/8373067/index.htm.* Answer the following questions.

(a) How does the article define "chronic" homelessness?

(b) In what ways does homelessness cost a city money? What are the estimated costs of a chronic homeless person to various cities?

(c) What are the steps suggested to address the problem?

(d) What is the estimated cost of implementing this program in New York? What results have been seen?

(e) In terms of incremental analysis, frame the relevant costs in this situation.

Answers to Insight and Accounting Across the Organization Questions

p. 1138 Incremental Analysis and Off-Shoring

Q: What other costs should General Motors and Ford consider in regard to this possible decision?

A: *One issue relates to whether the quality of the product will suffer if the car-makers outsource manufacture of aluminum wheels. In addition, transportation costs will also increase.*

p. 1142 A $1.4 Billion Mistake

Q: Why might management sell the beverage company and take a $1.4 billion loss?

A: *By selling the division, the company could reduce its debt burden and focus on its cereal brands and Gatorade.*

p. 1148 Are You Ready for the 50-Inch Screen?

Q: In building factories to manufacture 50-inch TV screens, how might companies build risk factors into their financial analyses?

A: *One approach is to use sensitivity analysis. Sensitivity analysis uses a number of outcome estimates to get a sense of the variability among potential returns. In addition, more distant cash flows can be discarded or given a low weighting because of their high uncertainty.*

Authors' Comments on *All About You:* What Is a Degree Worth? (p. 1153)

This is a very difficult decision. All of the evidence suggests that your short-term and long-term prospects will be far greater with some form of post–high-school degree. Because of this, we feel strongly that you should make every effort to continue your education. Many of the discussions provided in this text presented ideas on how to get control of your individual financial situation. We would encourage you to use these tools to identify ways to reduce your financial burden in order to continue your education. We also want to repeat that even taking only one course a semester is better than dropping out. Your instructors and advisors frequently provide advice to students who are faced with the decision about whether to continue with their education. If you are in this situation, we would encourage you to seek their advice since the implications of this decision can be long-lasting.

Answer to PepsiCo Review It Question 4, p. 1152

PepsiCo's capital spending for 2004 is $1,387,000,000 and for 2005 is $1,736,000,000.

Answers to Self-Study Questions

1. d **2.** b **3.** c **4.** d **5.** a **6.** b **7.** c **8.** b **9.** d **10.** b

Remember to go back to the Navigator box on the chapter-opening page and check off your completed work.

Appendix A

SPECIMEN FINANCIAL STATEMENTS: PepsiCo, Inc.

THE ANNUAL REPORT

Once each year a corporation communicates to its stockholders and other interested parties by issuing a complete set of audited financial statements. The **annual report**, as this communication is called, summarizes the financial results of the company's operations for the year and its plans for the future. Many annual reports are attractive, multicolored, glossy public relations pieces, containing pictures of corporate officers and directors as well as photos and descriptions of new products and new buildings. Yet the basic function of every annual report is to report financial information, almost all of which is a product of the corporation's accounting system.

The content and organization of corporate annual reports have become fairly standardized. Excluding the public relations part of the report (pictures, products, etc.), the following are the traditional financial portions of the annual report:

- Financial Highlights
- Letter to the Stockholders
- Management's Discussion and Analysis
- Financial Statements
- Notes to the Financial Statements
- Management's Report on Internal Control
- Management Certification of Financial Statements
- Auditor's Report
- Supplementary Financial Information

In this appendix we illustrate current financial reporting with a comprehensive set of corporate financial statements that are prepared in accordance with generally accepted accounting principles and audited by an international independent certified public accounting firm. We are grateful for permission to use the actual financial statements and other accompanying financial information from the annual report of a large, publicly held company, PepsiCo, Inc.

FINANCIAL HIGHLIGHTS

Companies usually present the financial highlights section inside the front cover of the annual report or on its first two pages. This section generally reports the total or per share amounts for five to ten financial items for the current year and one or more previous years. Financial items from the income statement and the balance sheet that typically are presented are sales, income from continuing operations, net income, net income per share, net cash provided by operating activities, dividends per common share, and the amount of capital expenditures. The financial highlights section from PepsiCo's Annual Report is shown on page A-2.

The financial information herein is reprinted with permission from the PepsiCo, Inc. 2005 Annual Report. The complete financial statements are available through a link at the book's companion website.

Financial Highlights

PEPSICO

PepsiCo, Inc. and Subsidiaries
($ in millions except per share amounts; all per share amounts assume dilution)

Net Revenue
Total: $32,562

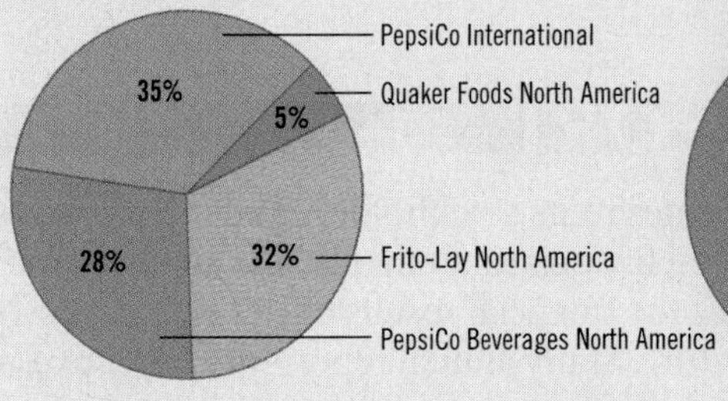

Division Operating Profit
Total: $6,710

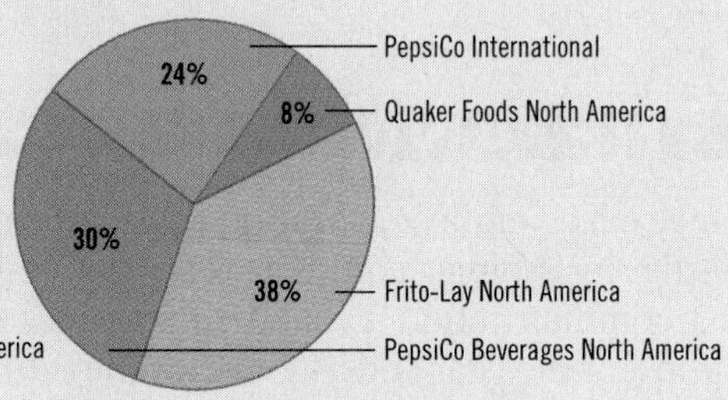

	2005	2004	% Chg[a]
Summary of Operations			
Total net revenue	$32,562	$29,261	11
Division operating profit	$6,710	$6,098	10
Total operating profit	$5,922	$5,259	13
Net income[b]	$4,536	$4,004	13
Earnings per share[b]	$2.66	$2.32	15
Other Data			
Management operating cash flow[c]	$4,204	$3,705	13
Net cash provided by operating activities	$5,852	$5,054	16
Capital spending	$1,736	$1,387	25
Common share repurchases	$3,012	$3,028	(0.5)
Dividends paid	$1,642	$1,329	24
Long-term debt	$2,313	$2,397	(3.5)

(a) Percentage changes above and in text are based on unrounded amounts.

(b) In 2005, excludes the impact of AJCA tax charge, the 53rd week and restructuring charges. In 2004, excludes certain prior year tax benefits, and restructuring and impairment charges. See page 76 for reconciliation to net income and earnings per share on a GAAP basis.

(c) Includes the impact of net capital spending. Also, see "Our Liquidity, Capital Resources and Financial Position" in Management's Discussion and Analysis.

LETTER TO THE STOCKHOLDERS

Nearly every annual report contains a letter to the stockholders from the chairman of the board or the president, or both. This letter typically discusses the company's accomplishments during the past year and highlights significant events such as mergers and acquisitions, new products, operating achievements, business philosophy, changes in officers or directors, financing commitments, expansion plans, and future prospects. The letter to the stockholders is signed by Steve Reinemund, Chairman of the Board and Chief Executive Officer, of PepsiCo.

Only a short summary of the letter is provided below. The full letter can be accessed at the book's companion website at **www.wiley.com/college/weygandt.**

Dear Shareholders:

With profitable growth across all divisions, on every continent and across both convenient food and beverage categories, PepsiCo delivered a very strong 2005. The company's continued focus on health and wellness, and innovation — coupled with its efforts to build big, muscular brands and powerful go-to-market systems — generated industry leading results.

- Volume grew 7%.
- Net revenue grew 11%.
- Division operating profit grew 10%.
- Earnings per share grew 15%.
- Total return to shareholders was 15% compared with 5% for the S&P.
- Cash flow from operations was $5.9 billion and management operating cash flow was $4.2 billion.

Steve Reinemund
Chairman and Chief Executive Officer

MANAGEMENT'S DISCUSSION AND ANALYSIS

The **management's discussion and analysis (MD&A)** section covers three financial aspects of a company: its results of operations, its ability to pay near-term obligations, and its ability to fund operations and expansion. Management must highlight favorable or unfavorable trends and identity significant events and uncertainties that affect these three factors. This discussion obviously involves a number of subjective estimates and opinions. In its MD&A section, PepsiCo breaks its discussion into three major headings: Our Business, Our Critical Accounting Policies, and Our Financial Results. PepsiCo's MD&A section is 22 pages long. You can access that section at **www.wiley.com/college/weygandt.**

FINANCIAL STATEMENTS AND ACCOMPANYING NOTES

The standard set of financial statements consists of: (1) a comparative income statement for 3 years, (2) a comparative statement of cash flows for 3 years, (3) a comparative balance sheet for 2 years, (4) a statement of stockholders' equity for 3 years, and (5) a set of accompanying notes that are considered an integral part of the financial statements. The auditor's report, unless stated otherwise, covers the financial statements and the accompanying notes. PepsiCo's financial statements and accompanying notes plus supplementary data and analyses follow.

PEPSICO

Consolidated Statement of Income

PepsiCo, Inc. and Subsidiaries
Fiscal years ended December 31, 2005, December 25, 2004 and December 27, 2003

(in millions except per share amounts)	2005	2004	2003
Net Revenue	$32,562	$29,261	$26,971
Cost of sales	14,176	12,674	11,691
Selling, general and administrative expenses	12,314	11,031	10,148
Amortization of intangible assets	150	147	145
Restructuring and impairment charges	–	150	147
Merger-related costs	–	–	59
Operating Profit	5,922	5,259	4,781
Bottling equity income	557	380	323
Interest expense	(256)	(167)	(163)
Interest income	159	74	51
Income from Continuing Operations before Income Taxes	6,382	5,546	4,992
Provision for Income Taxes	2,304	1,372	1,424
Income from Continuing Operations	4,078	4,174	3,568
Tax Benefit from Discontinued Operations	–	38	–
Net Income	$ 4,078	$ 4,212	$ 3,568
Net Income per Common Share — Basic			
Continuing operations	$2.43	$2.45	$2.07
Discontinued operations	–	0.02	–
Total	$2.43	$2.47	$2.07
Net Income per Common Share — Diluted			
Continuing operations	$2.39	$2.41	$2.05
Discontinued operations	–	0.02	–
Total	$2.39	$2.44*	$2.05

* Based on unrounded amounts.
See accompanying notes to consolidated financial statements.

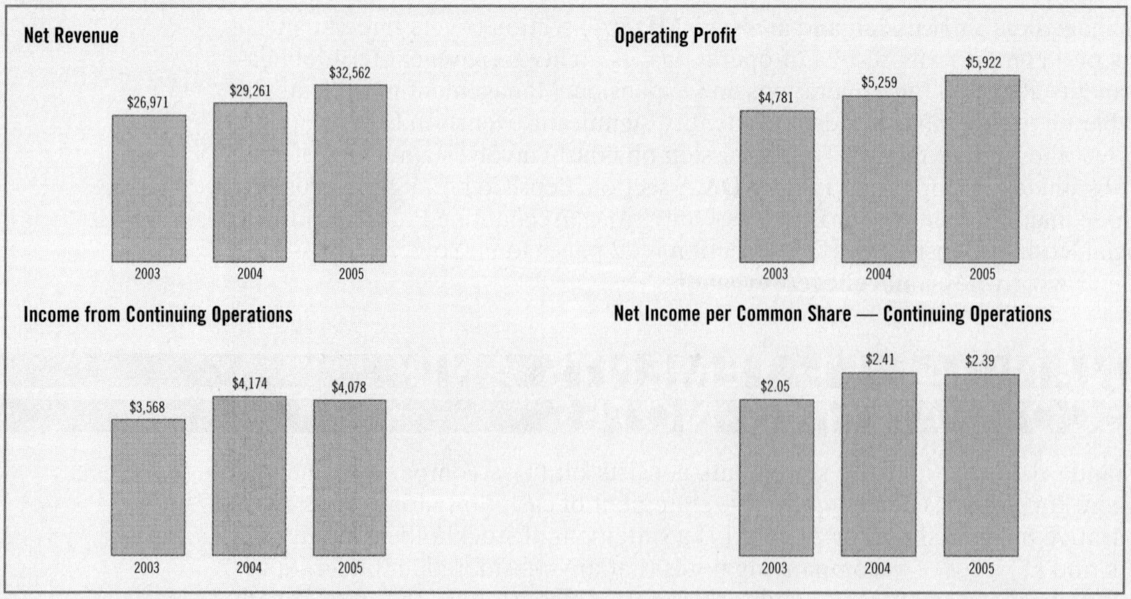

PEPSICO

Consolidated Statement of Cash Flows

PepsiCo, Inc. and Subsidiaries
Fiscal years ended December 31, 2005, December 25, 2004 and December 27, 2003

(in millions)	2005	2004	2003
Operating Activities			
Net income	**$ 4,078**	$ 4,212	$ 3,568
Adjustments to reconcile net income to net cash provided by operating activities			
Depreciation and amortization	**1,308**	1,264	1,221
Stock-based compensation expense	**311**	368	407
Restructuring and impairment charges	**–**	150	147
Cash payments for merger-related costs and restructuring charges	**(22)**	(92)	(109)
Tax benefit from discontinued operations	**–**	(38)	–
Pension and retiree medical plan contributions	**(877)**	(534)	(605)
Pension and retiree medical plan expenses	**464**	395	277
Bottling equity income, net of dividends	**(411)**	(297)	(276)
Deferred income taxes and other tax charges and credits	**440**	(203)	(286)
Merger-related costs	**–**	–	59
Other non-cash charges and credits, net	**145**	166	101
Changes in operating working capital, excluding effects of acquisitions and divestitures			
Accounts and notes receivable	**(272)**	(130)	(220)
Inventories	**(132)**	(100)	(49)
Prepaid expenses and other current assets	**(56)**	(31)	23
Accounts payable and other current liabilities	**188**	216	(11)
Income taxes payable	**609**	(268)	182
Net change in operating working capital	**337**	(313)	(75)
Other	**79**	(24)	(101)
Net Cash Provided by Operating Activities	**5,852**	5,054	4,328
Investing Activities			
Snack Ventures Europe (SVE) minority interest acquisition	**(750)**	–	–
Capital spending	**(1,736)**	(1,387)	(1,345)
Sales of property, plant and equipment	**88**	38	49
Other acquisitions and investments in noncontrolled affiliates	**(345)**	(64)	(71)
Cash proceeds from sale of PBG stock	**214**	–	–
Divestitures	**3**	52	46
Short-term investments, by original maturity			
More than three months — purchases	**(83)**	(44)	(38)
More than three months — maturities	**84**	38	28
Three months or less, net	**(992)**	(963)	(940)
Net Cash Used for Investing Activities	**(3,517)**	(2,330)	(2,271)
Financing Activities			
Proceeds from issuances of long-term debt	**25**	504	52
Payments of long-term debt	**(177)**	(512)	(641)
Short-term borrowings, by original maturity			
More than three months — proceeds	**332**	153	88
More than three months — payments	**(85)**	(160)	(115)
Three months or less, net	**1,601**	1,119	40
Cash dividends paid	**(1,642)**	(1,329)	(1,070)
Share repurchases — common	**(3,012)**	(3,028)	(1,929)
Share repurchases — preferred	**(19)**	(27)	(16)
Proceeds from exercises of stock options	**1,099**	965	689
Net Cash Used for Financing Activities	**(1,878)**	(2,315)	(2,902)
Effect of exchange rate changes on cash and cash equivalents	**(21)**	51	27
Net Increase/(Decrease) in Cash and Cash Equivalents	**436**	460	(818)
Cash and Cash Equivalents, Beginning of Year	**1,280**	820	1,638
Cash and Cash Equivalents, End of Year	**$ 1,716**	$ 1,280	$ 820

See accompanying notes to consolidated financial statements.

PEPSICO

Consolidated Balance Sheet

PepsiCo, Inc. and Subsidiaries
December 31, 2005 and December 25, 2004

(in millions except per share amounts)	2005	2004
ASSETS		
Current Assets		
Cash and cash equivalents	$ 1,716	$ 1,280
Short-term investments	3,166	2,165
	4,882	3,445
Accounts and notes receivable, net	3,261	2,999
Inventories	1,693	1,541
Prepaid expenses and other current assets	618	654
Total Current Assets	10,454	8,639
Property, Plant and Equipment, net	8,681	8,149
Amortizable Intangible Assets, net	530	598
Goodwill	4,088	3,909
Other nonamortizable intangible assets	1,086	933
Nonamortizable Intangible Assets	5,174	4,842
Investments in Noncontrolled Affiliates	3,485	3,284
Other Assets	3,403	2,475
Total Assets	$31,727	$27,987
LIABILITIES AND SHAREHOLDERS' EQUITY		
Current Liabilities		
Short-term obligations	$ 2,889	$ 1,054
Accounts payable and other current liabilities	5,971	5,599
Income taxes payable	546	99
Total Current Liabilities	9,406	6,752
Long-Term Debt Obligations	2,313	2,397
Other Liabilities	4,323	4,099
Deferred Income Taxes	1,434	1,216
Total Liabilities	17,476	14,464
Commitments and Contingencies		
Preferred Stock, no par value	41	41
Repurchased Preferred Stock	(110)	(90)
Common Shareholders' Equity		
Common stock, par value 1 2/3¢ per share (issued 1,782 shares)	30	30
Capital in excess of par value	614	618
Retained earnings	21,116	18,730
Accumulated other comprehensive loss	(1,053)	(886)
	20,707	18,492
Less: repurchased common stock, at cost (126 and 103 shares, respectively)	(6,387)	(4,920)
Total Common Shareholders' Equity	14,320	13,572
Total Liabilities and Shareholders' Equity	$31,727	$27,987

See accompanying notes to consolidated financial statements.

PEPSICO

Consolidated Statement of Common Shareholders' Equity

PepsiCo, Inc. and Subsidiaries
Fiscal years ended December 31, 2005, December 25, 2004 and December 27, 2003

(in millions)	2005		2004		2003	
	Shares	Amount	Shares	Amount	Shares	Amount
Common Stock	1,782	$ 30	1,782	$ 30	1,782	$ 30
Capital in Excess of Par Value						
Balance, beginning of year		618		548		207
Stock-based compensation expense		311		368		407
Stock option exercises[(a)]		(315)		(298)		(66)
Balance, end of year		614		618		548
Retained Earnings						
Balance, beginning of year		18,730		15,961		13,489
Net income		4,078		4,212		3,568
Cash dividends declared — common		(1,684)		(1,438)		(1,082)
Cash dividends declared — preferred		(3)		(3)		(3)
Cash dividends declared — RSUs		(5)		(2)		–
Other		–		–		(11)
Balance, end of year		21,116		18,730		15,961
Accumulated Other Comprehensive Loss						
Balance, beginning of year		(886)		(1,267)		(1,672)
Currency translation adjustment		(251)		401		410
Cash flow hedges, net of tax:						
Net derivative gains/(losses)		54		(16)		(11)
Reclassification of (gains)/losses to net income		(8)		9		(1)
Minimum pension liability adjustment, net of tax		16		(19)		7
Unrealized gain on securities, net of tax		24		6		1
Other		(2)		–		(1)
Balance, end of year		(1,053)		(886)		(1,267)
Repurchased Common Stock						
Balance, beginning of year	(103)	(4,920)	(77)	(3,376)	(60)	(2,524)
Share repurchases	(54)	(2,995)	(58)	(2,994)	(43)	(1,946)
Stock option exercises	31	1,523	32	1,434	26	1,096
Other	–	5	–	16	–	(2)
Balance, end of year	(126)	(6,387)	(103)	(4,920)	(77)	(3,376)
Total Common Shareholders' Equity		$14,320		$13,572		$11,896

	2005	2004	2003
Comprehensive Income			
Net income	$4,078	$4,212	$3,568
Currency translation adjustment	(251)	401	410
Cash flow hedges, net of tax	46	(7)	(12)
Minimum pension liability adjustment, net of tax	16	(19)	7
Unrealized gain on securities, net of tax	24	6	1
Other	(2)	–	(1)
Total Comprehensive Income	$3,911	$4,593	$3,973

(a) Includes total tax benefit of $125 million in 2005, $183 million in 2004 and $340 million in 2003.
See accompanying notes to consolidated financial statements.

PEPSICO

Notes to Consolidated Financial Statements

Note 1 — Basis of Presentation and Our Divisions

Basis of Presentation

Our financial statements include the consolidated accounts of PepsiCo, Inc. and the affiliates that we control. In addition, we include our share of the results of certain other affiliates based on our economic ownership interest. We do not control these other affiliates, as our ownership in these other affiliates is generally less than 50%. Our share of the net income of noncontrolled bottling affiliates is reported in our income statement as bottling equity income. Bottling equity income also includes any changes in our ownership interests of these affiliates. In 2005, bottling equity income includes $126 million of pre-tax gains on our sales of PBG stock. See Note 8 for additional information on our noncontrolled bottling affiliates. Our share of other noncontrolled affiliates is included in division operating profit. Intercompany balances and transactions are eliminated. In 2005, we had an additional week of results (53rd week). Our fiscal year ends on the last Saturday of each December, resulting in an additional week of results every five or six years.

In connection with our ongoing BPT initiative, we aligned certain accounting policies across our divisions in 2005. We conformed our methodology for calculating our bad debt reserves and modified our policy for recognizing revenue for products shipped to customers by third-party carriers. Additionally, we conformed our method of accounting for certain costs, primarily warehouse and freight. These changes reduced our net revenue by $36 million and our operating profit by $60 million in 2005. We also made certain reclassifications on our Consolidated Statement of Income in the fourth quarter of 2005 from cost of sales to selling, general and administrative expenses in connection with our BPT initiative. These reclassifications resulted in reductions to cost of sales of $556 million through the third quarter of 2005, $732 million in the full year 2004 and $688 million in the full year 2003, with corresponding increases to selling, general and administrative expenses in those periods. These reclassifications had no net impact on operating profit and have been made to all periods presented for comparability.

The preparation of our consolidated financial statements in conformity with generally accepted accounting principles requires us to make estimates and assumptions that affect reported amounts of assets, liabilities, revenues, expenses and disclosure of contingent assets and liabilities. Estimates are used in determining, among other items, sales incentives accruals, future cash flows associated with impairment testing for perpetual brands and goodwill, useful lives for intangible assets, tax reserves, stock-based compensation and pension and retiree medical accruals. Actual results could differ from these estimates.

See "Our Divisions" below and for additional unaudited information on items affecting the comparability of our consolidated results, see "Items Affecting Comparability" in Management's Discussion and Analysis.

Tabular dollars are in millions, except per share amounts. All per share amounts reflect common per share amounts, assume dilution unless noted, and are based on unrounded amounts. Certain reclassifications were made to prior years' amounts to conform to the 2005 presentation.

Our Divisions

We manufacture or use contract manufacturers, market and sell a variety of salty, sweet and grain-based snacks, carbonated and non-carbonated beverages, and foods through our North American and international business divisions. Our North American divisions include the United States and Canada. The accounting policies for the divisions are the same as those described in Note 2, except for certain allocation methodologies for stock-based compensation expense and pension and retiree medical expense, as described in the unaudited information in "Our Critical Accounting Policies." Additionally, beginning in the fourth quarter of 2005, we began centrally managing commodity derivatives on behalf of our divisions. Certain of the commodity derivatives, primarily those related to the purchase of energy for use by our divisions, do not qualify for hedge accounting treatment. These derivatives hedge underlying commodity price risk and were not entered into for speculative purposes. Such derivatives are marked to market with the resulting gains and losses recognized as a component of corporate unallocated expense. These gains and losses are reflected in division results when the divisions take delivery of the underlying commodity. Therefore, division results reflect the contract purchase price of the energy or other commodities.

Division results are based on how our Chairman and Chief Executive Officer evaluates our divisions. Division results exclude certain Corporate-initiated restructuring and impairment charges, merger-related costs and divested businesses. For additional unaudited information on our divisions, see "Our Operations" in Management's Discussion and Analysis.

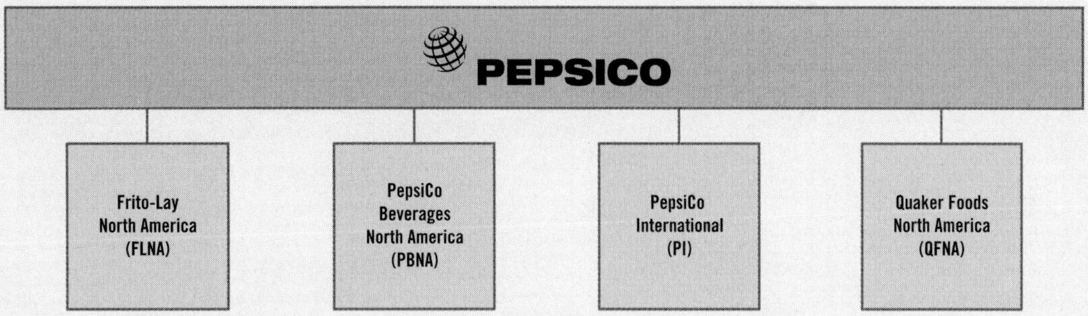

	2005	2004	2003	2005	2004	2003
		Net Revenue			Operating Profit	
FLNA	**$10,322**	$ 9,560	$ 9,091	**$2,529**	$2,389	$2,242
PBNA	**9,146**	8,313	7,733	**2,037**	1,911	1,690
PI	**11,376**	9,862	8,678	**1,607**	1,323	1,061
QFNA	**1,718**	1,526	1,467	**537**	475	470
Total division	**32,562**	29,261	26,969	**6,710**	6,098	5,463
Divested businesses	**–**	–	2	**–**	–	26
Corporate	**–**	–	–	**(788)**	(689)	(502)
	32,562	29,261	26,971	**5,922**	5,409	4,987
Restructuring and impairment charges	**–**	–	–	**–**	(150)	(147)
Merger-related costs	**–**	–	–	**–**	–	(59)
Total	**$32,562**	$29,261	$26,971	**$5,922**	$5,259	$4,781

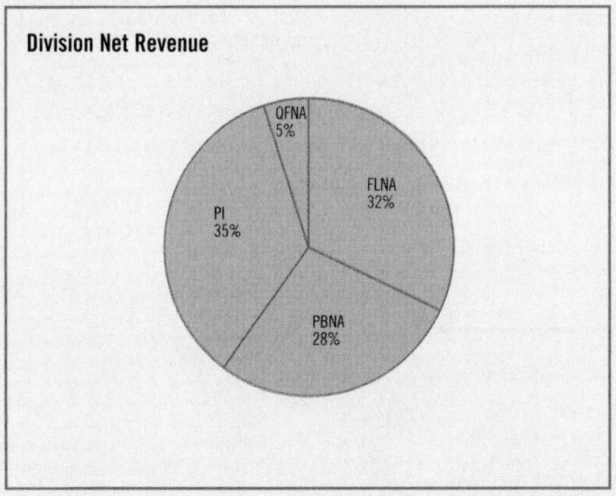

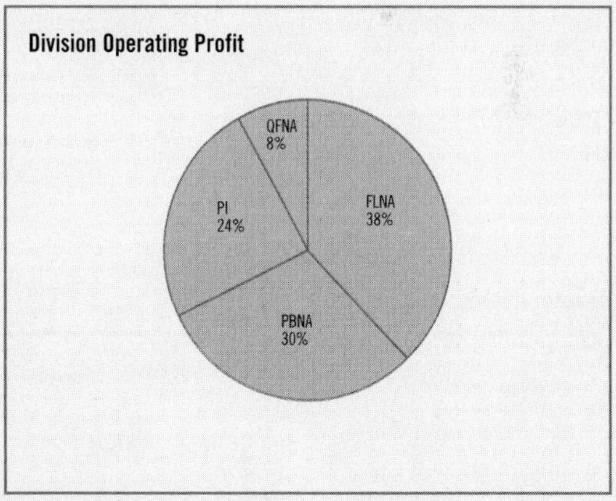

Divested Businesses
During 2003, we sold our Quaker Foods North America Mission pasta business. The results of this business are reported as divested businesses.

Corporate
Corporate includes costs of our corporate headquarters, centrally managed initiatives, such as our BPT initiative, unallocated insurance and benefit programs, foreign exchange transaction gains and losses, and certain commodity derivative gains and losses, as well as profit-in-inventory elimination adjustments for our noncontrolled bottling affiliates and certain other items.

Restructuring and Impairment Charges and Merger-Related Costs — See Note 3.

Other Division Information

	2005	2004	2003	2005	2004	2003
	Total Assets			Capital Spending		
FLNA	$ 5,948	$ 5,476	$ 5,332	$ 512	$ 469	$ 426
PBNA	6,316	6,048	5,856	320	265	332
PI	9,983	8,921	8,109	667	537	521
QFNA	989	978	995	31	33	32
Total division	23,236	21,423	20,292	1,530	1,304	1,311
Corporate(a)	5,331	3,569	2,384	206	83	34
Investments in bottling affiliates	3,160	2,995	2,651	–	–	–
	$31,727	$27,987	$25,327	$1,736	$1,387	$1,345

(a) Corporate assets consist principally of cash and cash equivalents, short-term investments, and property, plant and equipment.

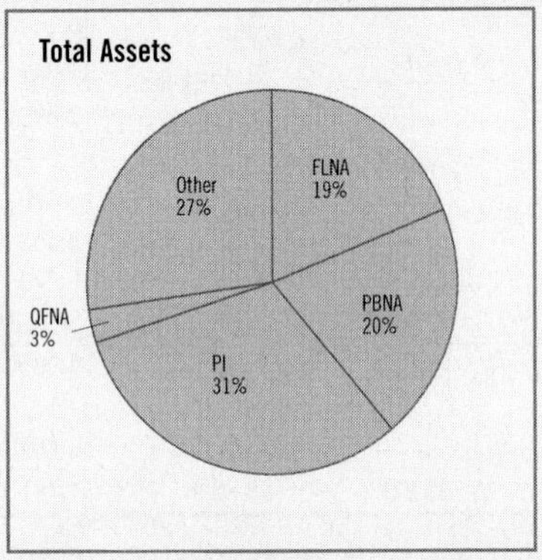

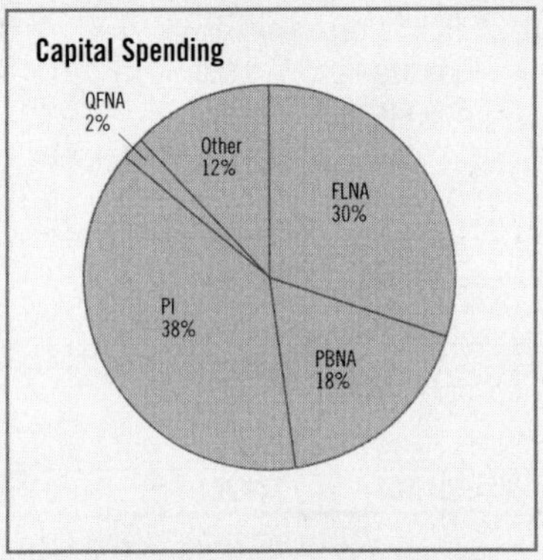

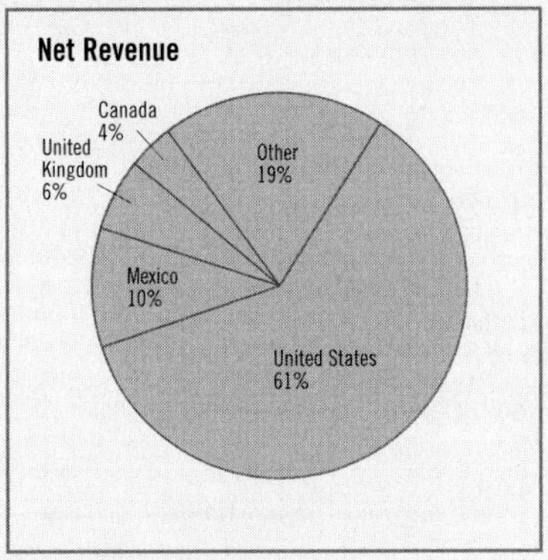

	2005	2004	2003	2005	2004	2003
	Amortization of Intangible Assets			Depreciation and Other Amortization		
FLNA	$ 3	$ 3	$ 3	$ 419	$ 420	$ 416
PBNA	76	75	75	264	258	245
PI	71	68	66	420	382	350
QFNA	–	1	1	34	36	36
Total division	150	147	145	1,137	1,096	1,047
Corporate	–	–	–	21	21	29
	$150	$147	$145	$1,158	$1,117	$1,076

	2005	2004	2003	2005	2004	2003
	Net Revenue(a)			Long-Lived Assets(b)		
U.S.	$19,937	$18,329	$17,377	$10,723	$10,212	$ 9,907
Mexico	3,095	2,724	2,642	902	878	869
United Kingdom	1,821	1,692	1,510	1,715	1,896	1,724
Canada	1,509	1,309	1,147	582	548	508
All other countries	6,200	5,207	4,295	3,948	3,339	3,123
	$32,562	$29,261	$26,971	$17,870	$16,873	$16,131

(a) Represents net revenue from businesses operating in these countries.

(b) Long-lived assets represent net property, plant and equipment, nonamortizable and net amortizable intangible assets and investments in noncontrolled affiliates. These assets are reported in the country where they are primarily used.

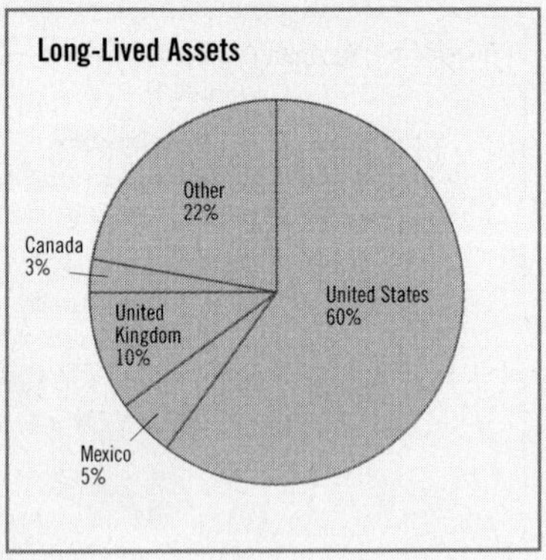

Note 2 — Our Significant Accounting Policies

Revenue Recognition

We recognize revenue upon shipment or delivery to our customers based on written sales terms that do not allow for a right of return. However, our policy for direct-store-delivery (DSD) and chilled products is to remove and replace damaged and out-of-date products from store shelves to ensure that our consumers receive the product quality and freshness that they expect. Similarly, our policy for warehouse distributed products is to replace damaged and out-of-date products. Based on our historical experience with this practice, we have reserved for anticipated damaged and out-of-date products. For additional unaudited information on our revenue recognition and related policies, including our policy on bad debts, see "Our Critical Accounting Policies" in Management's Discussion and Analysis. We are exposed to concentration of credit risk by our customers, Wal-Mart and PBG. Wal-Mart represents approximately 9% of our net revenue, including concentrate sales to our bottlers which are used in finished goods sold by them to Wal-Mart; and PBG represents approximately 10%. We have not experienced credit issues with these customers.

Sales Incentives and Other Marketplace Spending

We offer sales incentives and discounts through various programs to our customers and consumers. Sales incentives and discounts are accounted for as a reduction of revenue and totaled $8.9 billion in 2005, $7.8 billion in 2004 and $7.1 billion in 2003. While most of these incentive arrangements have terms of no more than one year, certain arrangements extend beyond one year. For example, fountain pouring rights may extend up to 15 years. Costs incurred to obtain these arrangements are recognized over the contract period and the remaining balances of $321 million at December 31, 2005 and $337 million at December 25, 2004 are included in current assets and other assets in our Consolidated Balance Sheet. For additional unaudited information on our sales incentives, see "Our Critical Accounting Policies" in Management's Discussion and Analysis.

Other marketplace spending includes the costs of advertising and other marketing activities and is reported as selling, general and administrative expenses. Advertising expenses were $1.8 billion in 2005, $1.7 billion in 2004 and $1.6 billion in 2003. Deferred advertising costs are not expensed until the year first used and consist of:

- media and personal service prepayments,
- promotional materials in inventory, and
- production costs of future media advertising.

Deferred advertising costs of $202 million and $137 million at year-end 2005 and 2004, respectively, are classified as prepaid expenses in our Consolidated Balance Sheet.

Distribution Costs

Distribution costs, including the costs of shipping and handling activities, are reported as selling, general and administrative expenses. Shipping and handling expenses were $4.1 billion in 2005, $3.9 billion in 2004 and $3.6 billion in 2003.

Cash Equivalents

Cash equivalents are investments with original maturities of three months or less which we do not intend to rollover beyond three months.

Software Costs

We capitalize certain computer software and software development costs incurred in connection with developing or obtaining computer software for internal use. Capitalized software costs are included in property, plant and equipment on our Consolidated Balance Sheet and amortized on a straight-line basis over the estimated useful lives of the software, which generally do not exceed 5 years. Net capitalized software and development costs were $327 million at December 31, 2005 and $181 million at December 25, 2004.

Commitments and Contingencies

We are subject to various claims and contingencies related to lawsuits, taxes and environmental matters, as well as commitments under contractual and other commercial obligations. We recognize liabilities for contingencies and commitments when a loss is probable and estimable. For additional information on our commitments, see Note 9.

Other Significant Accounting Policies

Our other significant accounting policies are disclosed as follows:

- *Property, Plant and Equipment and Intangible Assets* — Note 4 and, for additional unaudited information on brands and goodwill, see "Our Critical Accounting Policies" in Management's Discussion and Analysis.
- *Income Taxes* — Note 5 and, for additional unaudited information, see "Our Critical Accounting Policies" in Management's Discussion and Analysis.
- *Stock-Based Compensation Expense* — Note 6 and, for additional unaudited information, see "Our Critical Accounting Policies" in Management's Discussion and Analysis.
- *Pension, Retiree Medical and Savings Plans* — Note 7 and, for additional unaudited information, see "Our Critical Accounting Policies" in Management's Discussion and Analysis.
- *Risk Management* — Note 10 and, for additional unaudited information, see "Our Business Risks" in Management's Discussion and Analysis.

There have been no new accounting pronouncements issued or effective during 2005 that have had, or are expected to have, a material impact on our consolidated financial statements.

Note 3 — Restructuring and Impairment Charges and Merger-Related Costs

2005 Restructuring Charges

In the fourth quarter of 2005, we incurred a charge of $83 million ($55 million after-tax or $0.03 per share) in conjunction with actions taken to reduce costs in our operations, principally through headcount reductions. Of this charge, $34 million related to FLNA, $21 million to PBNA, $16 million to PI and $12 million to Corporate (recorded in corporate unallocated expenses). Most of this charge related to the termination of approximately 700 employees. We expect the substantial portion of the cash payments related to this charge to be paid in 2006.

2004 and 2003 Restructuring and Impairment Charges

In the fourth quarter of 2004, we incurred a charge of $150 million ($96 million after-tax or $0.06 per share) in conjunction with the consolidation of FLNA's manufacturing network as part of its ongoing productivity program. Of this charge, $93 million related to asset impairment, primarily reflecting the closure of four U.S. plants. Production from these plants was redeployed to other FLNA facilities in the U.S. The remaining $57 million included employee-related costs of $29 million, contract termination costs of $8 million and other exit costs of $20 million. Employee-related costs primarily reflect the termination costs for approximately 700 employees. Through December 31, 2005, we have paid $47 million and incurred non-cash charges of $10 million, leaving substantially no accrual.

In the fourth quarter of 2003, we incurred a charge of $147 million ($100 million after-tax or $0.06 per share) in conjunction with actions taken to streamline our North American divisions and PepsiCo International. These actions were taken to increase focus and eliminate redundancies at PBNA and PI and to improve the efficiency of the supply chain at FLNA. Of this charge, $81 million related to asset impairment, reflecting $57 million for the closure of a snack plant in Kentucky, the retirement of snack manufacturing lines in Maryland and Arkansas and $24 million for the closure of a PBNA office building in Florida. The remaining $66 million included employee-related costs of $54 million and facility and other exit costs of $12 million. Employee-related costs primarily reflect the termination costs for approximately 850 sales, distribution, manufacturing, research and marketing employees. As of December 31, 2005, all terminations had occurred and substantially no accrual remains.

Merger-Related Costs

In connection with the Quaker merger in 2001, we recognized merger-related costs of $59 million ($42 million after-tax or $0.02 per share) in 2003.

Note 4 — Property, Plant and Equipment and Intangible Assets

	Average Useful Life	2005	2004	2003
Property, plant and equipment, net				
Land and improvements	10 – 30 yrs.	$ 685	$ 646	
Buildings and improvements	20 – 44	3,736	3,605	
Machinery and equipment, including fleet and software	5 – 15	11,658	10,950	
Construction in progress		1,066	729	
		17,145	15,930	
Accumulated depreciation		(8,464)	(7,781)	
		$ 8,681	$ 8,149	
Depreciation expense		$1,103	$1,062	$1,020
Amortizable intangible assets, net				
Brands	5 – 40	$1,054	$1,008	
Other identifiable intangibles	3 – 15	257	225	
		1,311	1,233	
Accumulated amortization		(781)	(635)	
		$ 530	$ 598	
Amortization expense		$150	$147	$145

Depreciation and amortization are recognized on a straight-line basis over an asset's estimated useful life. Land is not depreciated and construction in progress is not depreciated until ready for service. Amortization of intangible assets for each of the next five years, based on average 2005 foreign exchange rates, is expected to be $152 million in 2006, $35 million in 2007, $35 million in 2008, $34 million in 2009 and $33 million in 2010.

Depreciable and amortizable assets are only evaluated for impairment upon a significant change in the operating or macroeconomic environment. In these circumstances, if an evaluation of the undiscounted cash flows indicates impairment, the asset is written down to its estimated fair value, which is based on discounted future cash flows. Useful lives are periodically evaluated to determine whether events or circumstances have occurred which indicate the need for revision. For additional unaudited information on our amortizable brand policies, see "Our Critical Accounting Policies" in Management's Discussion and Analysis.

Nonamortizable Intangible Assets

Perpetual brands and goodwill are assessed for impairment at least annually to ensure that discounted future cash flows continue to exceed the related book value. A perpetual brand is impaired if its book value exceeds its fair value. Goodwill is evaluated for impairment if the book value of its reporting unit exceeds its fair value. A reporting unit can be a division or business within a division. If the fair value of an evaluated asset is less than its book value, the asset is written down based on its discounted future cash flows to fair value. No impairment charges resulted from the required impairment evaluations. The change in the book value of nonamortizable intangible assets is as follows:

	Balance, Beginning 2004	Acquisition	Translation and Other	Balance, End of 2004	Acquisition	Translation and Other	Balance, End of 2005
Frito-Lay North America							
Goodwill	$ 130	$ –	$ 8	$ 138	$ –	$ 7	**$ 145**
PepsiCo Beverages North America							
Goodwill	2,157	–	4	2,161	–	3	**2,164**
Brands	59	–	–	59	–	–	**59**
	2,216	–	4	2,220	–	3	**2,223**
PepsiCo International							
Goodwill	1,334	29	72	1,435	278	(109)	**1,604**
Brands	808	–	61	869	263	(106)	**1,026**
	2,142	29	133	2,304	541	(215)	**2,630**
Quaker Foods North America							
Goodwill	175	–	–	175	–	–	**175**
Corporate							
Pension intangible	2	–	3	5	–	(4)	**1**
Total goodwill	3,796	29	84	3,909	278	(99)	**4,088**
Total brands	867	–	61	928	263	(106)	**1,085**
Total pension intangible	2	–	3	5	–	(4)	**1**
	$4,665	$29	$148	$4,842	$541	$(209)	**$5,174**

Note 5 — Income Taxes

	2005	2004	2003
Income before income taxes — continuing operations			
U.S.	$3,175	$2,946	$3,267
Foreign	3,207	2,600	1,725
	$6,382	$5,546	$4,992
Provision for income taxes — continuing operations			
Current: U.S. Federal	$1,638	$1,030	$1,326
Foreign	426	256	341
State	118	69	80
	2,182	1,355	1,747
Deferred: U.S. Federal	137	11	(274)
Foreign	(26)	5	(47)
State	11	1	(2)
	122	17	(323)
	$2,304	$1,372	$1,424
Tax rate reconciliation — continuing operations			
U.S. Federal statutory tax rate	35.0%	35.0%	35.0%
State income tax, net of U.S. Federal tax benefit	1.4	0.8	1.0
Taxes on AJCA repatriation	7.0	–	–
Lower taxes on foreign results	(6.5)	(5.4)	(5.5)
Settlement of prior years' audit	–	(4.8)	(2.2)
Other, net	(0.8)	(0.9)	0.2
Annual tax rate	36.1%	24.7%	28.5%
Deferred tax liabilities			
Investments in noncontrolled affiliates	$ 993	$ 850	
Property, plant and equipment	772	857	
Pension benefits	863	669	
Intangible assets other than nondeductible goodwill	135	153	
Zero coupon notes	35	46	
Other	169	157	
Gross deferred tax liabilities	2,967	2,732	
Deferred tax assets			
Net carryforwards	608	666	
Stock-based compensation	426	402	
Retiree medical benefits	400	402	
Other employee-related benefits	342	379	
Other	520	460	
Gross deferred tax assets	2,296	2,309	
Valuation allowances	(532)	(564)	
Deferred tax assets, net	1,764	1,745	
Net deferred tax liabilities	$1,203	$ 987	
Deferred taxes included within:			
Prepaid expenses and other current assets	$231	$229	
Deferred income taxes	$1,434	$1,216	
Analysis of valuation allowances			
Balance, beginning of year	$564	$438	$487
(Benefit)/provision	(28)	118	(52)
Other (deductions)/additions	(4)	8	3
Balance, end of year	$532	$564	$438

For additional unaudited information on our income tax policies, including our reserves for income taxes, see "Our Critical Accounting Policies" in Management's Discussion and Analysis.

Carryforwards, Credits and Allowances
Operating loss carryforwards totaling $5.1 billion at year-end 2005 are being carried forward in a number of foreign and state jurisdictions where we are permitted to use tax operating losses from prior periods to reduce future taxable income. These operating losses will expire as follows: $0.1 billion in 2006, $4.1 billion between 2007 and 2025 and $0.9 billion may be carried forward indefinitely. In addition, certain tax credits generated in prior periods of approximately $39.4 million are available to reduce certain foreign tax liabilities through 2011. We establish valuation allowances for our deferred tax assets when the amount of expected future taxable income is not likely to support the use of the deduction or credit.

Undistributed International Earnings
The AJCA created a one-time incentive for U.S. corporations to repatriate undistributed international earnings by providing an 85% dividends received deduction. As approved by our Board of Directors in July 2005, we repatriated approximately $7.5 billion in earnings previously considered indefinitely reinvested outside the U.S. in the fourth quarter of 2005. In 2005, we recorded income tax expense of $460 million associated with this repatriation. Other than the earnings repatriated, we intend to continue to reinvest earnings outside the U.S. for the foreseeable future and, therefore, have not recognized any U.S. tax expense on these earnings. At December 31, 2005, we had approximately $7.5 billion of undistributed international earnings.

Reserves
A number of years may elapse before a particular matter, for which we have established a reserve, is audited and finally resolved. The number of years with open tax audits varies depending on the tax jurisdiction. During 2004, we recognized $266 million of tax benefits related to the favorable resolution of certain open tax issues. In addition, in 2004, we recognized a tax benefit of $38 million upon agreement with the IRS on an open issue related to our discontinued restaurant operations. At the end of 2003, we entered into agreements with the IRS for open years through 1997. These agreements resulted in a tax benefit of $109 million in the fourth quarter of 2003. As part of these agreements, we also resolved the treatment of certain other issues related to future tax years.

The IRS has initiated their audits of our tax returns for the years 1998 through 2002. Our tax returns subsequent to 2002 have not yet been examined. While it is often difficult to predict the final outcome or the timing of resolution of any particular tax matter, we believe that our reserves reflect the probable outcome of known tax contingencies. Settlement of any particular issue would usually require the use of cash. Favorable resolution would be recognized as a reduction to our annual tax rate in the year of resolution. Our tax reserves, covering all federal, state and foreign jurisdictions, are presented in the balance sheet within other liabilities (see Note 14), except for any amounts relating to items we expect to pay in the coming year which are included in current income taxes payable. For further unaudited information on the impact of the resolution of open tax issues, see "Other Consolidated Results."

Note 6 — Stock-Based Compensation

Our stock-based compensation program is a broad-based program designed to attract and retain employees while also aligning employees' interests with the interests of our shareholders. Employees at all levels participate in our stock-based compensation program. In addition, members of our Board of Directors participate in our stock-based compensation program in connection with their service on our Board. Stock options and RSUs are granted to employees under the shareholder-approved 2003 Long-Term Incentive Plan (LTIP), our only active stock-based plan. Stock-based compensation expense was $311 million in 2005, $368 million in 2004 and $407 million in 2003. Related income tax benefits recognized in earnings were $87 million in 2005, $103 million in 2004 and $114 million in 2003. At year-end 2005, 51 million shares were available for future executive and SharePower grants. For additional unaudited information on our stock-based compensation program, see "Our Critical Accounting Policies" in Management's Discussion and Analysis.

SharePower Grants
SharePower options are awarded under our LTIP to all eligible employees, based on job level or classification, and in the case of international employees, tenure as well. All stock option grants have an exercise price equal to the fair market value of our common stock on the day of grant and generally have a 10-year term with vesting after three years.

Executive Grants
All senior management and certain middle management are eligible for executive grants under our LTIP. All stock option grants have an exercise price equal to the fair market value of our common stock on the day of grant and generally have a 10-year term with vesting after three years. There have been no reductions to the exercise price of previously issued awards, and any repricing of awards would require approval of our shareholders.

Beginning in 2004, executives who are awarded long-term incentives based on their performance are offered the choice of stock options or RSUs. RSU expense is based on the fair value of PepsiCo stock on the date of grant and is amortized over the vesting period, generally three years. Each restricted stock unit can be settled in a share of our stock after the vesting period. Executives who elect RSUs receive one RSU for every four stock options that would have otherwise been granted. Senior officers do not have a choice and are granted 50% stock options and 50% RSUs. Vesting of RSU awards for senior officers is contingent upon the achievement of pre-established performance targets. We granted 3 million RSUs in both 2005 and 2004 with weighted-average intrinsic values of $53.83 and $47.28, respectively.

Method of Accounting and Our Assumptions

We account for our employee stock options under the fair value method of accounting using a Black-Scholes valuation model to measure stock-based compensation expense at the date of grant. We adopted SFAS 123R, *Share-Based Payment*, under the modified prospective method in the first quarter of 2006. We do not expect our adoption of SFAS 123R to materially impact our financial statements.

Our weighted-average Black-Scholes fair value assumptions include:

	2005	2004	2003
Expected life	6 yrs.	6 yrs.	6 yrs.
Risk free interest rate	3.8%	3.3%	3.1%
Expected volatility	23%	26%	27%
Expected dividend yield	1.8%	1.8%	1.15%

Our Stock Option Activity[a]

	2005		2004		2003	
	Options	Average Price[b]	Options	Average Price[b]	Options	Average Price[b]
Outstanding at beginning of year	174,261	$40.05	198,173	$38.12	190,432	$36.45
Granted	12,328	53.82	14,137	47.47	41,630	39.89
Exercised	(30,945)	35.40	(31,614)	30.57	(25,833)	26.74
Forfeited/expired	(5,495)	43.31	(6,435)	43.82	(8,056)	43.56
Outstanding at end of year	150,149	42.03	174,261	40.05	198,173	38.12
Exercisable at end of year	89,652	40.52	94,643	36.41	97,663	32.56

Stock options outstanding and exercisable at December 31, 2005[a]

	Options Outstanding			Options Exercisable		
Range of Exercise Price	Options	Average Price[b]	Average Life[c]	Options	Average Price[b]	Average Life[c]
$14.40 to $21.54	905	$20.01	3.56 yrs.	905	$20.01	3.56 yrs.
$23.00 to $33.75	14,559	30.46	3.07	14,398	30.50	3.05
$34.00 to $43.50	82,410	39.44	5.34	48,921	39.19	4.10
$43.75 to $56.75	52,275	49.77	7.17	25,428	49.48	6.09
	150,149	42.03	5.67	89,652	40.52	4.45

(a) Options are in thousands and include options previously granted under Quaker plans. No additional options or shares may be granted under the Quaker plans.

(b) Weighted-average exercise price.

(c) Weighted-average contractual life remaining.

Our RSU Activity[a]

	2005			2004		
	RSUs	Average Intrinsic Value[b]	Average Life[c]	RSUs	Average Intrinsic Value[b]	Average Life[c]
Outstanding at beginning of year	2,922	$47.30		–	$ –	
Granted	3,097	53.83		3,077	47.28	
Converted	(91)	48.73		(18)	47.25	
Forfeited/expired	(259)	50.51		(137)	47.25	
Outstanding at end of year	5,669	50.70	1.8 yrs.	2,922	47.30	2.2 yrs.

(a) RSUs are in thousands.

(b) Weighted-average intrinsic value.

(c) Weighted-average contractual life remaining.

Other stock-based compensation data

	Stock Options			RSUs	
	2005	2004	2003	2005	2004
Weighted-average fair value of options granted	$13.45	$12.04	$11.21		
Total intrinsic value of options/RSUs exercised/converted[a]	$632,603	$667,001	$466,719	$4,974	$914
Total intrinsic value of options/RSUs outstanding[a]	$2,553,594	$2,062,153	$1,641,505	$334,931	$151,760
Total intrinsic value of options exercisable[a]	$1,662,198	$1,464,926	$1,348,658		

(a) In thousands.

At December 31, 2005, there was $315 million of total unrecognized compensation cost related to nonvested share-based compensation grants. This unrecognized compensation is expected to be recognized over a weighted-average period of 1.6 years.

Note 7 — Pension, Retiree Medical and Savings Plans

Our pension plans cover full-time employees in the U.S. and certain international employees. Benefits are determined based on either years of service or a combination of years of service and earnings. U.S. retirees are also eligible for medical and life insurance benefits (retiree medical) if they meet age and service requirements. Generally, our share of retiree medical costs is capped at specified dollar amounts, which vary based upon years of service, with retirees contributing the remainder of the costs. We use a September 30 measurement date and all plan assets and liabilities are generally reported as of that date. The cost or benefit of plan changes that increase or decrease benefits for prior employee service (prior service cost) is included in expense on a straight-line basis over the average remaining service period of employees expected to receive benefits.

The Medicare Act was signed into law in December 2003 and we applied the provisions of the Medicare Act to our plans in 2005 and 2004. The Medicare Act provides a subsidy for sponsors of retiree medical plans who offer drug benefits equivalent to those provided under Medicare. As a result of the Medicare Act, our 2005 and 2004 retiree medical costs were $11 million and $7 million lower, respectively, and our 2005 and 2004 liabilities were reduced by $136 million and $80 million, respectively. We expect our 2006 retiree medical costs to be approximately $18 million lower than they otherwise would have been as a result of the Medicare Act.

For additional unaudited information on our pension and retiree medical plans and related accounting policies and assumptions, see "Our Critical Accounting Policies" in Management's Discussion and Analysis.

	Pension						Retiree Medical		
	2005	2004	2003	**2005**	2004	2003	**2005**	2004	2003
	U.S.			International					
Weighted-average assumptions									
Liability discount rate	**5.7%**	6.1%	6.1%	**5.1%**	6.1%	6.1%	**5.7%**	6.1%	6.1%
Expense discount rate	**6.1%**	6.1%	6.7%	**6.1%**	6.1%	6.4%	**6.1%**	6.1%	6.7%
Expected return on plan assets	**7.8%**	7.8%	8.3%	**8.0%**	8.0%	8.0%	–	–	–
Rate of compensation increases	**4.4%**	4.5%	4.5%	**4.1%**	3.9%	3.8%	–	–	–
Components of benefit expense									
Service cost	**$ 213**	$ 193	$ 153	**$ 32**	$ 27	$ 24	**$ 40**	$ 38	$ 33
Interest cost	**296**	271	245	**55**	47	39	**78**	72	73
Expected return on plan assets	**(344)**	(325)	(305)	**(69)**	(65)	(54)	–	–	–
Amortization of prior service cost/(benefit)	**3**	6	6	**1**	1	–	**(11)**	(8)	(3)
Amortization of experience loss	**106**	81	44	**15**	9	5	**26**	19	13
Benefit expense	**274**	226	143	**34**	19	14	**133**	121	116
Settlement/curtailment loss	–	4	–	–	1	–	–	–	–
Special termination benefits	**21**	19	4	–	1	–	**2**	4	–
Total	**$ 295**	$ 249	$ 147	**$ 34**	$ 21	$ 14	**$135**	$125	$116

	Pension				Retiree Medical	
	2005	2004	**2005**	2004	**2005**	2004
	U.S.		International			
Change in projected benefit liability						
Liability at beginning of year	**$4,968**	$4,456	**$ 952**	$758	**$1,319**	$1,264
Service cost	**213**	193	**32**	27	**40**	38
Interest cost	**296**	271	**55**	47	**78**	72
Plan amendments	**–**	(17)	**3**	1	**(8)**	(41)
Participant contributions	**–**	–	**10**	9	**–**	–
Experience loss/(gain)	**517**	261	**203**	73	**(45)**	58
Benefit payments	**(241)**	(205)	**(28)**	(29)	**(74)**	(76)
Settlement/curtailment loss	**–**	(9)	**–**	(2)	**–**	–
Special termination benefits	**21**	18	**–**	1	**2**	4
Foreign currency adjustment	**–**	–	**(68)**	67	**–**	–
Other	**(3)**	–	**104**	–	**–**	–
Liability at end of year	**$5,771**	$4,968	**$1,263**	$952	**$1,312**	$1,319
Liability at end of year for service to date	**$4,783**	$4,164	**$1,047**	$779		
Change in fair value of plan assets						
Fair value at beginning of year	**$4,152**	$3,558	**$ 838**	$687	**$ –**	$ –
Actual return on plan assets	**477**	392	**142**	77	**–**	–
Employer contributions/funding	**699**	416	**104**	37	**74**	76
Participant contributions	**–**	–	**10**	9	**–**	–
Benefit payments	**(241)**	(205)	**(28)**	(29)	**(74)**	(76)
Settlement/curtailment loss	**–**	(9)	**–**	(2)	**–**	–
Foreign currency adjustment	**–**	–	**(61)**	59	**–**	–
Other	**(1)**	–	**94**	–	**–**	–
Fair value at end of year	**$5,086**	$4,152	**$1,099**	$838	**$ –**	$ –
Funded status as recognized in our Consolidated Balance Sheet						
Funded status at end of year	**$ (685)**	$ (817)	**$(164)**	$(113)	**$(1,312)**	$(1,319)
Unrecognized prior service cost/(benefit)	**5**	9	**17**	13	**(113)**	(116)
Unrecognized experience loss	**2,288**	2,013	**474**	380	**402**	473
Fourth quarter benefit payments	**5**	5	**4**	7	**19**	19
Net amounts recognized	**$1,613**	$1,210	**$ 331**	$ 287	**$(1,004)**	$ (943)
Net amounts as recognized in our Consolidated Balance Sheet						
Other assets	**$2,068**	$1,572	**$367**	$294	**$ –**	$ –
Intangible assets	**–**	–	**1**	5	**–**	–
Other liabilities	**(479)**	(387)	**(41)**	(37)	**(1,004)**	(943)
Accumulated other comprehensive loss	**24**	25	**4**	25	**–**	–
Net amounts recognized	**$1,613**	$1,210	**$331**	$287	**$(1,004)**	$(943)
Components of increase in unrecognized experience loss						
Decrease in discount rate	**$ 365**	$ –	**$194**	$ 4	**$ 61**	$ –
Employee-related assumption changes	**57**	196	**2**	65	**–**	109
Liability-related experience different from assumptions	**95**	65	**7**	4	**(54)**	31
Actual asset return different from expected return	**(133)**	(67)	**(73)**	(12)	**–**	–
Amortization of losses	**(106)**	(81)	**(15)**	(9)	**(26)**	(19)
Other, including foreign currency adjustments and 2003 Medicare Act	**(3)**	(5)	**(22)**	26	**(52)**	(82)
Total	**$ 275**	$108	**$ 93**	$ 78	**$(71)**	$ 39
Selected information for plans with liability for service to date in excess of plan assets						
Liability for service to date	**$(374)**	$(320)	**$(65)**	$(191)	**$(1,312)**	$(1,319)
Projected benefit liability	**$(815)**	$(685)	**$(84)**	$(227)	**$(1,312)**	$(1,319)
Fair value of plan assets	**$8**	$11	**$33**	$161	**$–**	$–

Of the total projected pension benefit liability at year-end 2005, $765 million relates to plans that we do not fund because the funding of such plans does not receive favorable tax treatment.

Future Benefit Payments

Our estimated future benefit payments are as follows:

	2006	2007	2008	2009	2010	2011-15
Pension	$235	$255	$275	$300	$330	$2,215
Retiree medical	$85	$90	$90	$95	$100	$545

These future benefits to beneficiaries include payments from both funded and unfunded pension plans.

Pension Assets

The expected return on pension plan assets is based on our historical experience, our pension plan investment guidelines, and our expectations for long-term rates of return. We use a market-related value method that recognizes each year's asset gain or loss over a five-year period. Therefore, it takes five years for the gain or loss from any one year to be fully included in the value of pension plan assets that is used to calculate the expected return. Our pension plan investment guidelines are established based upon an evaluation of market conditions, tolerance for risk and cash requirements for benefit payments. Our investment objective is to ensure that funds are available to meet the plans' benefit obligations when they are due. Our investment strategy is to prudently invest plan assets in high-quality and diversified equity and debt securities to achieve our long-term return expectation. Our target allocation and actual pension plan asset allocations for the plan years 2005 and 2004, are below.

Pension assets include approximately 5.5 million shares of PepsiCo common stock with a market value of $311 million in 2005, and 5.5 million shares with a market value of $267 million in 2004. Our investment policy limits the investment in PepsiCo stock at the time of investment to 10% of the fair value of plan assets.

		Actual Allocation	
Asset Category	Target Allocation	2005	2004
Equity securities	60%	**60%**	60%
Debt securities	40%	**39%**	39%
Other, primarily cash	–	**1%**	1%
Total	100%	**100%**	100%

Retiree Medical Cost Trend Rates

An average increase of 10% in the cost of covered retiree medical benefits is assumed for 2006. This average increase is then projected to decline gradually to 5% in 2010 and thereafter. These assumed health care cost trend rates have an impact on the retiree medical plan expense and liability. However, the cap on our share of retiree medical costs limits the impact. A 1 percentage point change in the assumed health care trend rate would have the following effects:

	1% Increase	1% Decrease
2005 service and interest cost components	$3	$(2)
2005 benefit liability	$38	$(33)

Savings Plans

Our U.S. employees are eligible to participate in 401(k) savings plans, which are voluntary defined contribution plans. The plans are designed to help employees accumulate additional savings for retirement. We make matching contributions on a portion of eligible pay based on years of service. In 2005 and 2004, our matching contributions were $52 million and $35 million, respectively.

Note 8 — Noncontrolled Bottling Affiliates

Our most significant noncontrolled bottling affiliates are PBG and PAS. Approximately 10% of our net revenue in 2005, 2004 and 2003 reflects sales to PBG.

The Pepsi Bottling Group

In addition to approximately 41% and 42% of PBG's outstanding common stock that we own at year-end 2005 and 2004, respectively, we own 100% of PBG's class B common stock and approximately 7% of the equity of Bottling Group, LLC, PBG's principal operating subsidiary. This gives us economic ownership of approximately 45% and 46% of PBG's combined operations at year-end 2005 and 2004, respectively. In 2005, bottling equity income includes $126 million of pre-tax gains on our sales of PBG stock.

PBG's summarized financial information is as follows:

	2005	2004	2003
Current assets	$ 2,412	$ 2,183	
Noncurrent assets	9,112	8,754	
Total assets	$11,524	$10,937	
Current liabilities	$2,598	$1,725	
Noncurrent liabilities	6,387	6,818	
Minority interest	496	445	
Total liabilities	$9,481	$8,988	
Our investment	$1,738	$1,594	
Net revenue	$11,885	$10,906	$10,265
Gross profit	$5,632	$5,250	$5,050
Operating profit	$1,023	$976	$956
Net income	$466	$457	$416

Our investment in PBG, which includes the related goodwill, was $400 million and $321 million higher than our ownership interest in their net assets at year-end 2005 and 2004, respectively. Based upon the quoted closing price of PBG shares at year-end 2005 and 2004, the calculated market value of our shares in PBG, excluding our investment in Bottling Group, LLC, exceeded our investment balance by approximately $1.5 billion and $1.7 billion, respectively.

PepsiAmericas

At year-end 2005 and 2004, we owned approximately 43% and 41% of PepsiAmericas, respectively, and their summarized financial information is as follows:

	2005	2004	2003
Current assets	$ 598	$ 530	
Noncurrent assets	3,456	3,000	
Total assets	$4,054	$3,530	
Current liabilities	$ 722	$ 521	
Noncurrent liabilities	1,763	1,386	
Total liabilities	$2,485	$1,907	
Our investment	$968	$924	
Net revenue	$3,726	$3,345	$3,237
Gross profit	$1,562	$1,423	$1,360
Operating profit	$393	$340	$316
Net income	$195	$182	$158

Our investment in PAS, which includes the related goodwill, was $292 million and $253 million higher than our ownership interest in their net assets at year-end 2005 and 2004, respectively. Based upon the quoted closing price of PAS shares at year-end 2005 and 2004, the calculated market value of our shares in PepsiAmericas exceeded our investment balance by approximately $364 million and $277 million, respectively.

In January 2005, PAS acquired a regional bottler, Central Investment Corporation. The table above includes the results of Central Investment Corporation from the transaction date forward.

Related Party Transactions

Our significant related party transactions involve our noncontrolled bottling affiliates. We sell concentrate to these affiliates, which is used in the production of carbonated soft drinks and non-carbonated beverages. We also sell certain finished goods to these affiliates and we receive royalties for the use of our trademarks for certain products. Sales of concentrate and finished goods are reported net of bottler funding. For further unaudited information on these bottlers, see "Our Customers" in Management's Discussion and Analysis. These transactions with our bottling affiliates are reflected in our consolidated financial statements as follows:

	2005	2004	2003
Net revenue	$4,633	$4,170	$3,699
Selling, general and administrative expenses	$143	$114	$128
Accounts and notes receivable	$178	$157	
Accounts payable and other current liabilities	$117	$95	

Such amounts are settled on terms consistent with other trade receivables and payables. See Note 9 regarding our guarantee of certain PBG debt.

In addition, we coordinate, on an aggregate basis, the negotiation and purchase of sweeteners and other raw materials requirements for certain of our bottlers with suppliers. Once we have negotiated the contracts, the bottlers order and take delivery directly from the supplier and pay the suppliers directly. Consequently, these transactions are not reflected in our consolidated financial statements. As the contracting party, we could be liable to these suppliers in the event of any nonpayment by our bottlers, but we consider this exposure to be remote.

Note 9 — Debt Obligations and Commitments

	2005	2004
Short-term debt obligations		
Current maturities of long-term debt	**$ 143**	$ 160
Commercial paper (3.3% and 1.6%)	**3,140**	1,287
Other borrowings (7.4% and 6.6%)	**356**	357
Amounts reclassified to long-term debt	**(750)**	(750)
	$2,889	$1,054
Long-term debt obligations		
Short-term borrowings, reclassified	**$ 750**	$ 750
Notes due 2006-2026 (5.4% and 4.7%)	**1,161**	1,274
Zero coupon notes, $475 million due 2006-2012 (13.4%)	**312**	321
Other, due 2006-2014 (6.3% and 6.2%)	**233**	212
	2,456	2,557
Less: current maturities of long-term debt obligations	**(143)**	(160)
	$2,313	$2,397

The interest rates in the above table reflect weighted-average rates as of year-end.

Short-term borrowings are reclassified to long-term when we have the intent and ability, through the existence of the unused lines of credit, to refinance these borrowings on a long-term basis. At year-end 2005, we maintained $2.1 billion in corporate lines of credit subject to normal banking terms and conditions. These credit facilities support short-term debt issuances and remained unused as of December 31, 2005. Of the $2.1 billion, $1.35 billion expires in May 2006 with the remaining $750 million expiring in June 2009.

In addition, $181 million of our debt was outstanding on various lines of credit maintained for our international divisions. These lines of credit are subject to normal banking terms and conditions and are committed to the extent of our borrowings.

Interest Rate Swaps

We entered into interest rate swaps in 2004 to effectively convert the interest rate of a specific debt issuance from a fixed rate of 3.2% to a variable rate. The variable weighted-average interest rate that we pay is linked to LIBOR and is subject to change. The notional amount of the interest rate swaps outstanding at December 31, 2005 and December 25, 2004 was $500 million. The terms of the interest rate swaps match the terms of the debt they modify. The swaps mature in 2007.

At December 31, 2005, approximately 78% of total debt, after the impact of the associated interest rate swaps, was exposed to variable interest rates, compared to 67% at December 25, 2004. In addition to variable rate long-term debt, all debt with maturities of less than one year is categorized as variable for purposes of this measure.

Cross Currency Interest Rate Swaps

In 2004, we entered into a cross currency interest rate swap to hedge the currency exposure on U.S. dollar denominated debt of $50 million held by a foreign affiliate. The terms of this swap match the terms of the debt it modifies. The swap matures in 2008. The unrecognized gain related to this swap was less than $1 million at December 31, 2005, resulting in a U.S. dollar liability of $50 million. At December 25, 2004, the unrecognized loss related to this swap was $3 million, resulting in a U.S. dollar liability of $53 million. We have also entered into cross currency interest rate swaps to hedge the currency exposure on U.S. dollar denominated intercompany debt of $125 million. The terms of the swaps match the terms of the debt they modify. The swaps mature over the next two years. The net unrecognized gain related to these swaps was $5 million at December 31, 2005. The net unrecognized loss related to these swaps was less than $1 million at December 25, 2004.

Long-Term Contractual Commitments

Payments Due by Period	Total	2006	2007-2008	2009-2010	2011 and beyond
Long-term debt obligations[(a)]	$2,313	$ –	$1,052	$ 876	$ 385
Operating leases	769	187	253	132	197
Purchasing commitments[(b)]	4,533	1,169	1,630	775	959
Marketing commitments	1,487	412	438	381	256
Other commitments	99	82	10	6	1
	$9,201	$1,850	$3,383	$2,170	$1,798

(a) Excludes current maturities of long-term debt of $143 million which are classified within current liabilities.

(b) Includes approximately $13 million of long-term commitments which are reflected in other liabilities in our Consolidated Balance Sheet.

The above table reflects non-cancelable commitments as of December 31, 2005 based on year-end foreign exchange rates.

Most long-term contractual commitments, except for our long-term debt obligations, are not recorded in our Consolidated Balance Sheet. Non-cancelable operating leases primarily represent building leases. Non-cancelable purchasing commitments are primarily for oranges and orange juices to be used for our Tropicana brand beverages. Non-cancelable marketing commitments primarily are for sports marketing and with our fountain customers. Bottler funding is not reflected in our long-term contractual commitments as it is negotiated on an annual basis. See Note 7 regarding our pension and retiree medical obligations and discussion below regarding our commitments to noncontrolled bottling affiliates and former restaurant operations.

Off-Balance Sheet Arrangements

It is not our business practice to enter into off-balance sheet arrangements, other than in the normal course of business, nor is it our policy to issue guarantees to our bottlers, noncontrolled affiliates or third parties. However, certain guarantees were necessary to facilitate the separation of our bottling and restaurant operations from us. In connection with these transactions, we have guaranteed $2.3 billion of Bottling Group, LLC's long-term debt through 2012 and $28 million of YUM! Brands, Inc. (YUM) outstanding obligations, primarily property leases, through 2020. The terms of our Bottling Group, LLC debt guarantee are intended to preserve the structure of PBG's separation from us and our payment obligation would be triggered if Bottling Group, LLC failed to perform under these debt obligations or the structure significantly changed. Our guarantees of certain obligations ensured YUM's continued use of certain properties. These guarantees would require our cash payment if YUM failed to perform under these lease obligations.

See "Our Liquidity, Capital Resources and Financial Position" in Management's Discussion and Analysis for further unaudited information on our borrowings.

Note 10 — Risk Management

We are exposed to the risk of loss arising from adverse changes in:

- commodity prices, affecting the cost of our raw materials and energy,
- foreign exchange risks,
- interest rates,
- stock prices, and
- discount rates affecting the measurement of our pension and retiree medical liabilities.

In the normal course of business, we manage these risks through a variety of strategies, including the use of derivatives. Certain derivatives are designated as either cash flow or fair value hedges and qualify for hedge accounting treatment, while others do not qualify and are marked to market through earnings. See "Our Business Risks" in Management's Discussion and Analysis for further unaudited information on our business risks.

For cash flow hedges, changes in fair value are deferred in accumulated other comprehensive loss within shareholders' equity until the underlying hedged item is recognized in net income. For fair value hedges, changes in fair value are recognized immediately in earnings, consistent with the underlying hedged item. Hedging transactions are limited to an underlying exposure. As a result, any change in the value of our derivative instruments would be substantially offset by an opposite change in the value of the underlying hedged items. Hedging ineffectiveness and a net earnings impact occur when the change in the value of the hedge does not offset the change in the value of the underlying hedged item. If the derivative instrument is terminated, we continue to defer the related gain or loss and include it as a component of the cost of the underlying hedged item. Upon determination that the underlying hedged item will not be part of an actual transaction, we recognize the related gain or loss in net income in that period.

We also use derivatives that do not qualify for hedge accounting treatment. We account for such derivatives at market value with the resulting gains and losses reflected in our income statement. We do not use derivative instruments for trading or speculative purposes and we limit our exposure to individual counterparties to manage credit risk.

Commodity Prices

We are subject to commodity price risk because our ability to recover increased costs through higher pricing may be limited in the competitive environment in which we operate. This risk is managed through the use of fixed-price purchase orders, pricing agreements, geographic diversity and derivatives. We use derivatives, with terms of no more than two years, to economically hedge price fluctuations related to a portion of our anticipated commodity purchases, primarily for natural gas and diesel fuel. For those derivatives that are designated as cash flow hedges, any ineffectiveness is recorded immediately. However, our commodity cash flow hedges have not had any significant ineffectiveness for all periods presented. We classify both the earnings and cash flow impact from these derivatives consistent with the underlying hedged item. During the next 12 months, we expect to reclassify gains of $24 million related to cash flow hedges from accumulated other comprehensive loss into net income.

Foreign Exchange

Our operations outside of the U.S. generate over a third of our net revenue of which Mexico, the United Kingdom and Canada comprise nearly 20%. As a result, we are exposed to foreign currency risks from unforeseen economic changes and political unrest. On occasion, we enter into hedges, primarily forward contracts with terms of no more than two years, to reduce the effect of foreign exchange rates. Ineffectiveness on these hedges has not been material.

Interest Rates

We centrally manage our debt and investment portfolios considering investment opportunities and risks, tax consequences and overall financing strategies. We may use interest rate and cross currency interest rate swaps to manage our overall interest expense and foreign exchange risk. These instruments effectively change the interest rate and currency of specific debt issuances. These swaps are entered into concurrently with the issuance of the debt that they are intended to modify. The notional amount, interest payment and maturity date of the swaps match the principal, interest payment and maturity date of the related debt. These swaps are entered into only with strong creditworthy counterparties, are settled on a net basis and are of relatively short duration.

Stock Prices
The portion of our deferred compensation liability that is based on certain market indices and on our stock price is subject to market risk. We hold mutual fund investments and prepaid forward contracts to manage this risk. Changes in the fair value of these investments and contracts are recognized immediately in earnings and are offset by changes in the related compensation liability.

Fair Value
All derivative instruments are recognized in our Consolidated Balance Sheet at fair value. The fair value of our derivative instruments is generally based on quoted market prices. Book and fair values of our derivative and financial instruments are as follows:

	2005		2004	
	Book Value	Fair Value	Book Value	Fair Value
Assets				
Cash and cash equivalents[(a)]	**$1,716**	**$1,716**	$1,280	$1,280
Short-term investments[(b)]	**$3,166**	**$3,166**	$2,165	$2,165
Forward exchange contracts[(c)]	**$19**	**$19**	$8	$8
Commodity contracts[(d)]	**$41**	**$41**	$7	$7
Prepaid forward contract[(e)]	**$107**	**$107**	$120	$120
Cross currency interest rate swaps[(f)]	**$6**	**$6**	$–	$–
Liabilities				
Forward exchange contracts[(c)]	**$15**	**$15**	$35	$35
Commodity contracts[(d)]	**$3**	**$3**	$8	$8
Debt obligations	**$5,202**	**$5,378**	$3,451	$3,676
Interest rate swaps[(g)]	**$9**	**$9**	$1	$1
Cross currency interest rate swaps[(f)]	**$–**	**$–**	$3	$3

Included in our Consolidated Balance Sheet under the captions noted above or as indicated below. In addition, derivatives are designated as accounting hedges unless otherwise noted below.

(a) Book value approximates fair value due to the short maturity.

(b) Principally short-term time deposits and includes $124 million at December 31, 2005 and $118 million at December 25, 2004 of mutual fund investments used to manage a portion of market risk arising from our deferred compensation liability.

(c) 2005 asset includes $14 million related to derivatives not designated as accounting hedges. Assets are reported within current assets and other assets and liabilities are reported within current liabilities and other liabilities.

(d) 2005 asset includes $2 million related to derivatives not designated as accounting hedges and the liability relates entirely to derivatives not designated as accounting hedges. Assets are reported within current assets and other assets and liabilities are reported within current liabilities and other liabilities.

(e) Included in current assets and other assets.

(f) Asset included within other assets and liability included in long-term debt.

(g) Reported in other liabilities.

This table excludes guarantees, including our guarantee of $2.3 billion of Bottling Group, LLC's long-term debt. The guarantee had a fair value of $47 million at December 31, 2005 and $46 million at December 25, 2004 based on an external estimate of the cost to us of transferring the liability to an independent financial institution. See Note 9 for additional information on our guarantees.

Note 11 — Net Income per Common Share from Continuing Operations

Basic net income per common share is net income available to common shareholders divided by the weighted average of common shares outstanding during the period. Diluted net income per common share is calculated using the weighted average of common shares outstanding adjusted to include the effect that would occur if in-the-money employee stock options were exercised and RSUs and preferred shares were converted into common shares. Options to purchase 3.0 million shares in 2005, 7.0 million shares in 2004 and 49.0 million shares in 2003 were not included in the calculation of diluted earnings per common share because these options were out-of-the-money. Out-of-the-money options had average exercise prices of $53.77 in 2005, $52.88 in 2004 and $48.27 in 2003.

The computations of basic and diluted net income per common share from continuing operations are as follows:

	2005		2004		2003	
	Income	Shares[a]	Income	Shares[a]	Income	Shares[a]
Net income	$4,078		$4,174		$3,568	
Preferred shares:						
Dividends	(2)		(3)		(3)	
Redemption premium	(16)		(22)		(12)	
Net income available for common shareholders	$4,060	1,669	$4,149	1,696	$3,553	1,718
Basic net income per common share	$2.43		$2.45		$2.07	
Net income available for common shareholders	$4,060	1,669	$4,149	1,696	$3,553	1,718
Dilutive securities:						
Stock options and RSUs	–	35	–	31	–	17
ESOP convertible preferred stock	18	2	24	2	15	3
Unvested stock awards	–	–	–	–	–	1
Diluted	$4,078	1,706	$4,173	1,729	$3,568	1,739
Diluted net income per common share	$2.39		$2.41		$2.05	

(a) Weighted-average common shares outstanding.

Note 12 — Preferred and Common Stock

As of December 31, 2005 and December 25, 2004, there were 3.6 billion shares of common stock and 3 million shares of convertible preferred stock authorized. The preferred stock was issued only for an employee stock ownership plan (ESOP) established by Quaker and these shares are redeemable for common stock by the ESOP participants. The preferred stock accrues dividends at an annual rate of $5.46 per share. At year-end 2005 and 2004, there were 803,953 preferred shares issued and 354,853 and 424,853 shares outstanding, respectively. Each share is convertible at the option of the holder into 4.9625 shares of common stock. The preferred shares may be called by us upon written notice at $78 per share plus accrued and unpaid dividends.

As of December 31, 2005, 0.3 million outstanding shares of preferred stock with a fair value of $104 million and 17 million shares of common stock were held in the accounts of ESOP participants. As of December 25, 2004, 0.4 million outstanding shares of preferred stock with a fair value of $110 million and 18 million shares of common stock were held in the accounts of ESOP participants. Quaker made the final award to its ESOP plan in June 2001.

	2005		2004		2003	
	Shares	Amount	Shares	Amount	Shares	Amount
Preferred stock	0.8	$41	0.8	$41	0.8	$41
Repurchased preferred stock						
Balance, beginning of year	0.4	$ 90	0.3	$63	0.2	$48
Redemptions	0.1	19	0.1	27	0.1	15
Balance, end of year	0.5	$110*	0.4	$90	0.3	$63

*Does not sum due to rounding.

Note 13 — Accumulated Other Comprehensive Loss

Comprehensive income is a measure of income which includes both net income and other comprehensive income or loss. Other comprehensive loss results from items deferred on the balance sheet in shareholders' equity. Other comprehensive (loss)/income was $(167) million in 2005, $381 million in 2004, and $405 million in 2003. The accumulated balances for each component of other comprehensive loss were as follows:

	2005	2004	2003
Currency translation adjustment	$ (971)	$(720)	$(1,121)
Cash flow hedges, net of tax[a]	27	(19)	(12)
Minimum pension liability adjustment[b]	(138)	(154)	(135)
Unrealized gain on securities, net of tax	31	7	1
Other	(2)	–	–
Accumulated other comprehensive loss	$(1,053)	$(886)	$(1,267)

(a) Includes net commodity gains of $55 million in 2005. Also includes no impact in 2005, $6 million gain in 2004 and $8 million gain in 2003 for our share of our equity investees' accumulated derivative activity. Deferred gains/(losses) reclassified into earnings were $8 million in 2005, $(10) million in 2004 and no impact in 2003.

(b) Net of taxes of $72 million in 2005, $77 million in 2004 and $67 million in 2003. Also, includes $120 million in 2005, $121 million in 2004 and $110 million in 2003 for our share of our equity investees' minimum pension liability adjustments.

Note 14 — Supplemental Financial Information

	2005	2004	2003
Accounts receivable			
Trade receivables	$2,718	$2,505	
Other receivables	618	591	
	3,336	3,096	
Allowance, beginning of year	97	105	$116
Net amounts (credited)/charged to expense	(1)	18	32
Deductions[a]	(22)	(25)	(43)
Other[b]	1	(1)	–
Allowance, end of year	75	97	$105
Net receivables	$3,261	$2,999	
Inventory[c]			
Raw materials	$ 738	$ 665	
Work-in-process	112	156	
Finished goods	843	720	
	$1,693	$1,541	
Accounts payable and other current liabilities			
Accounts payable	$1,799	$1,731	
Accrued marketplace spending	1,383	1,285	
Accrued compensation and benefits	1,062	961	
Dividends payable	431	387	
Insurance accruals	136	131	
Other current liabilities	1,160	1,104	
	$5,971	$5,599	
Other liabilities			
Reserves for income taxes	$1,884	$1,567	
Other	2,439	2,532	
	$4,323	$4,099	
Other supplemental information			
Rent expense	$228	$245	$231
Interest paid	$213	$137	$147
Income taxes paid, net of refunds	$1,258	$1,833	$1,530
Acquisitions[d]			
Fair value of assets acquired	$ 1,089	$ 78	$178
Cash paid and debt issued	(1,096)	(64)	(71)
SVE minority interest eliminated	216	–	–
Liabilities assumed	$ 209	$ 14	$107

(a) Includes accounts written off.

(b) Includes collections of previously written-off accounts and currency translation effects.

(c) Inventories are valued at the lower of cost or market. Cost is determined using the average, first-in, first-out (FIFO) or last-in, first-out (LIFO) methods. Approximately 17% in 2005 and 15% in 2004 of the inventory cost was computed using the LIFO method. The differences between LIFO and FIFO methods of valuing these inventories were not material.

(d) In 2005, these amounts include the impact of our acquisition of General Mills, Inc.'s 40.5% ownership interest in SVE for $750 million. The excess of our purchase price over the fair value of net assets acquired is $250 million and is included in goodwill. We also reacquired rights to distribute global brands for $263 million which is included in other nonamortizable intangible assets.

ADDITIONAL INFORMATION

In addition to the financial statements and accompanying notes, companies are required to provide a report on internal control over financial reporting and to have an auditor's report on the financial statements. In addition, PepsiCo has provided a report indicating that financial reporting is management's responsibility. Finally, PepsiCo also provides selected financial data it believes is useful. The two required reports are further explained below.

Management's Report on Internal Control over Financial Reporting

The Sarbanes-Oxley Act of 2002 requires managers of publicly traded companies to establish and maintain systems of internal control over the company's financial reporting processes. In addition, management must express its responsibility for financial reporting, and it must provide certifications regarding the accuracy of the financial statements.

Auditor's Report

All publicly held corporations, as well as many other enterprises and organizations engage the services of independent certified public accountants for the purpose of obtaining an objective, expert report on their financial statements. Based on a comprehensive examination of the company's accounting system, accounting records, and the financial statements, the outside CPA issues the auditor's report.

The standard auditor's report identifies who and what was audited and indicates the responsibilities of management and the auditor relative to the financial statements. It states that the audit was conducted in accordance with generally accepted auditing standards and discusses the nature and limitations of the audit. It then expresses an informed opinion as to (1) the fairness of the financial statements and (2) their conformity with generally accepted accounting principles. It also expresses an opinion regarding the effectiveness of the company's internal controls. All of this additional information for PepsiCo is provided on the following pages.

PEPSICO

Management's Responsibility for Financial Reporting

To Our Shareholders:

At PepsiCo, our actions — the actions of all our associates — are governed by our Worldwide Code of Conduct. This code is clearly aligned with our stated values — a commitment to sustained growth, through empowered people, operating with responsibility and building trust. Both the code and our core values enable us to operate with integrity — both within the letter and the spirit of the law. Our code of conduct is reinforced consistently at all levels and in all countries. We have maintained strong governance policies and practices for many years.

The management of PepsiCo is responsible for the objectivity and integrity of our consolidated financial statements. The Audit Committee of the Board of Directors has engaged independent registered public accounting firm, KPMG LLP, to audit our consolidated financial statements and they have expressed an unqualified opinion.

We are committed to providing timely, accurate and understandable information to investors. Our commitment encompasses the following:

Maintaining strong controls over financial reporting. Our system of internal control is based on the control criteria framework of the Committee of Sponsoring Organizations of the Treadway Commission published in their report titled, *Internal Control — Integrated Framework*. The system is designed to provide reasonable assurance that transactions are executed as authorized and accurately recorded; that assets are safeguarded; and that accounting records are sufficiently reliable to permit the preparation of financial statements that conform in all material respects with accounting principles generally accepted in the U.S. We maintain disclosure controls and procedures designed to ensure that information required to be disclosed in reports under the Securities Exchange Act of 1934 is recorded, processed, summarized and reported within the specified time periods. We monitor these internal controls through self-assessments and an ongoing program of internal audits. Our internal controls are reinforced through our Worldwide Code of Conduct, which sets forth our commitment to conduct business with integrity, and within both the letter and the spirit of the law.

Exerting rigorous oversight of the business. We continuously review our business results and strategies. This encompasses financial discipline in our strategic and daily business decisions. Our Executive Committee is actively involved — from understanding strategies and alternatives to reviewing key initiatives and financial performance. The intent is to ensure we remain objective in our assessments, constructively challenge our approach to potential business opportunities and issues, and monitor results and controls.

Engaging strong and effective Corporate Governance from our Board of Directors. We have an active, capable and diligent Board that meets the required standards for independence, and we welcome the Board's oversight as a representative of our shareholders. Our Audit Committee comprises independent directors with the financial literacy, knowledge and experience to provide appropriate oversight. We review our critical accounting policies, financial reporting and internal control matters with them and encourage their direct communication with KPMG LLP, with our General Auditor, and with our General Counsel. In 2005, we named a senior compliance officer to lead and coordinate our compliance policies and practices.

Providing investors with financial results that are complete, transparent and understandable. The consolidated financial statements and financial information included in this report are the responsibility of management. This includes preparing the financial statements in accordance with accounting principles generally accepted in the U.S., which require estimates based on management's best judgment.

PepsiCo has a strong history of doing what's right. We realize that great companies are built on trust, strong ethical standards and principles. Our financial results are delivered from that culture of accountability, and we take responsibility for the quality and accuracy of our financial reporting.

Peter A. Bridgman
Senior Vice President and Controller

Indra K. Nooyi
President and Chief Financial Officer

Steven S Reinemund
Chairman of the Board
and Chief Executive Officer

Management's Report on Internal Control over Financial Reporting

To Our Shareholders:

Our management is responsible for establishing and maintaining adequate internal control over financial reporting, as such term is defined in Rule 13a-15(f) of the Exchange Act. Under the supervision and with the participation of our management, including our Chief Executive Officer and Chief Financial Officer, we conducted an evaluation of the effectiveness of our internal control over financial reporting based upon the framework in *Internal Control — Integrated Framework* issued by the Committee of Sponsoring Organizations of the Treadway Commission. Based on that evaluation, our management concluded that our internal control over financial reporting is effective as of December 31, 2005.

KPMG LLP, an independent registered public accounting firm, has audited the consolidated financial statements included in this Annual Report and, as part of their audit, has issued their report, included herein, (1) on our management's assessment of the effectiveness of our internal controls over financial reporting and (2) on the effectiveness of our internal control over financial reporting.

Peter A. Bridgman
Senior Vice President and Controller

Indra K. Nooyi
President and Chief Financial Officer

Steven S Reinemund
Chairman of the Board
and Chief Executive Officer

Report of Independent Registered Public Accounting Firm

Board of Directors and Shareholders PepsiCo, Inc.:

We have audited the accompanying Consolidated Balance Sheet of PepsiCo, Inc. and Subsidiaries as of December 31, 2005 and December 25, 2004 and the related Consolidated Statements of Income, Cash Flows and Common Shareholders' Equity for each of the years in the three-year period ended December 31, 2005. We have also audited management's assessment, included in Management's Report on Internal Control over Financial Reporting, that PepsiCo, Inc. and Subsidiaries maintained effective internal control over financial reporting as of December 31, 2005, based on criteria established in *Internal Control — Integrated Framework* issued by the Committee of Sponsoring Organizations of the Treadway Commission (COSO). PepsiCo, Inc.'s management is responsible for these consolidated financial statements, for maintaining effective internal control over financial reporting, and for its assessment of the effectiveness of internal control over financial reporting. Our responsibility is to express an opinion on these consolidated financial statements, an opinion on management's assessment, and an opinion on the effectiveness of PepsiCo, Inc.'s internal control over financial reporting based on our audits.

We conducted our audits in accordance with the standards of the Public Company Accounting Oversight Board (United States). Those standards require that we plan and perform the audits to obtain reasonable assurance about whether the financial statements are free of material misstatement and whether effective internal control over financial reporting was maintained in all material respects. Our audit of financial statements included examining, on a test basis, evidence supporting the amounts and disclosures in the financial statements, assessing the accounting principles used and significant estimates made by management, and evaluating the overall financial statement presentation. Our audit of internal control over financial reporting included obtaining an understanding of internal control over financial reporting, evaluating management's assessment, testing and evaluating the design and operating effectiveness of internal control, and performing such other procedures as we considered necessary in the circumstances. We believe that our audits provide a reasonable basis for our opinions.

A company's internal control over financial reporting is a process designed to provide reasonable assurance regarding the reliability of financial reporting and the preparation of financial statements for external purposes in accordance with generally accepted accounting principles. A company's internal control over financial reporting includes those policies and procedures that (1) pertain to the maintenance of records that, in reasonable detail, accurately and fairly reflect the transactions and dispositions of the assets of the company; (2) provide reasonable assurance that transactions are recorded as necessary to permit preparation of financial statements in accordance with generally accepted accounting principles, and that receipts and expenditures of the company are being made only in accordance with authorizations of management and directors of the company; and (3) provide reasonable assurance regarding prevention or timely detection of unauthorized acquisition, use, or disposition of the company's assets that could have a material effect on the financial statements.

Because of its inherent limitations, internal control over financial reporting may not prevent or detect misstatements. Also, projections of any evaluation of effectiveness to future periods are subject to the risk that controls may become inadequate because of changes in conditions, or that the degree of compliance with the policies or procedures may deteriorate.

In our opinion, the consolidated financial statements referred to above present fairly, in all material respects, the financial position of PepsiCo, Inc. and Subsidiaries as of December 31, 2005 and December 25, 2004, and the results of their operations and their cash flows for each of the years in the three-year period ended December 31, 2005, in conformity with United States generally accepted accounting principles. Also, in our opinion, management's assessment that PepsiCo, Inc. maintained effective internal control over financial reporting as of December 31, 2005, is fairly stated, in all material respects, based on criteria established in *Internal Control — Integrated Framework* issued by COSO. Furthermore, in our opinion, PepsiCo, Inc. maintained, in all material respects, effective internal control over financial reporting as of December 31, 2005, based on criteria established in *Internal Control — Integrated Framework* issued by COSO.

KPMG LLP
New York, New York
February 24, 2006

PEPSICO

Selected Financial Data (in millions except per share amounts, unaudited)

Quarterly	First Quarter	Second Quarter	Third Quarter	Fourth Quarter
Net revenue				
2005	**$6,585**	**$7,697**	**$8,184**	**$10,096**
2004	$6,131	$7,070	$7,257	$8,803
Gross profit(a)				
2005	**$3,715**	**$4,383**	**$4,669**	**$5,619**
2004	$3,466	$4,039	$4,139	$4,943
2005 restructuring charges(b)				
2005	–	–	–	**$83**
2004 restructuring and impairment charges(c)				
2004	–	–	–	$150
AJCA tax charge(d)				
2005	–	–	**$468**	**$(8)**
Net income(e)				
2005	**$912**	**$1,194**	**$864**	**$1,108**
2004	$804	$1,059	$1,364	$985
Net income per common share — basic(e)				
2005	**$0.54**	**$0.71**	**$0.52**	**$0.66**
2004	$0.47	$0.62	$0.80	$0.58
Net income per common share — diluted(e)				
2005	**$0.53**	**$0.70**	**$0.51**	**$0.65**
2004	$0.46	$0.61	$0.79	$0.58
Cash dividends declared per common share				
2005	**$0.23**	**$0.26**	**$0.26**	**$0.26**
2004	$0.16	$0.23	$0.23	$0.23
2005 stock price per share(f)				
High	**$55.71**	**$57.20**	**$56.73**	**$60.34**
Low	**$51.34**	**$51.78**	**$52.07**	**$53.55**
Close	**$52.62**	**$55.52**	**$54.65**	**$59.08**
2004 stock price per share(f)				
High	$53.00	$55.48	$55.71	$53.00
Low	$45.30	$50.28	$48.41	$47.37
Close	$50.93	$54.95	$50.84	$51.94

The first, second, and third quarters consist of 12 weeks and the fourth quarter consists of 16 weeks in 2004 and 17 weeks in 2005.

(a) Reflects net reclassifications in all periods from cost of sales to selling, general and administrative expenses related to the alignment of certain accounting policies in connection with our ongoing BPT initiative. See Note 1.

(b) The 2005 restructuring charges were $83 million ($55 million or $0.03 per share after-tax). See Note 3.

(c) The 2004 restructuring and impairment charges were $150 million ($96 million or $0.06 per share after-tax). See Note 3.

(d) Represents income tax expense associated with the repatriation of earnings in connection with the AJCA. See Note 5.

(e) Fourth quarter 2004 net income reflects a tax benefit from discontinued operations of $38 million or $0.02 per share. See Note 5.

(f) Represents the composite high and low sales price and quarterly closing prices for one share of PepsiCo common stock.

Five-Year Summary	2005	2004	2003
Net revenue	**$32,562**	$29,261	$26,971
Income from continuing operations	**$4,078**	$4,174	$3,568
Net income	**$4,078**	$4,212	$3,568
Income per common share — basic, continuing operations	**$2.43**	$2.45	$2.07
Income per common share — diluted, continuing operations	**$2.39**	$2.41	$2.05
Cash dividends declared per common share	**$1.01**	$0.850	$0.630
Total assets	**$31,727**	$27,987	$25,327
Long-term debt	**$2,313**	$2,397	$1,702
Return on invested capital(a)	**22.7%**	27.4%	27.5%

Five-Year Summary (Cont.)	2002	2001
Net revenue	$25,112	$23,512
Net income	$3,000	$2,400
Income per common share — basic	$1.69	$1.35
Income per common share — diluted	$1.68	$1.33
Cash dividends declared per common share	$0.595	$0.575
Total assets	$23,474	$21,695
Long-term debt	$2,187	$2,651
Return on invested capital(a)	25.7%	22.1%

(a) Return on invested capital is defined as adjusted net income divided by the sum of average shareholders' equity and average total debt. Adjusted net income is defined as net income plus net interest expense after tax. Net interest expense after tax was $62 million in 2005, $60 million in 2004, $72 million in 2003, $93 million in 2002, and $99 million in 2001.

- As a result of the adoption of SFAS 142, *Goodwill and Other Intangible Assets*, and the consolidation of SVE in 2002, the data provided above is not comparable.
- Includes restructuring and impairment charges of:

	2005	2004	2003	2001
Pre-tax	$83	$150	$147	$31
After-tax	$55	$96	$100	$19
Per share	$0.03	$0.06	$0.06	$0.01

- Includes Quaker merger-related costs of:

	2003	2002	2001
Pre-tax	$59	$224	$356
After-tax	$42	$190	$322
Per share	$0.02	$0.11	$0.18

- The 2005 fiscal year consisted of fifty-three weeks compared to fifty-two weeks in our normal fiscal year. The 53rd week increased 2005 net revenue by an estimated $418 million and net income by an estimated $57 million or $0.03 per share.
- Cash dividends per common share in 2001 are those of pre-merger PepsiCo prior to the effective date of the merger.
- In the fourth quarter of 2004, we reached agreement with the IRS for an open issue related to our discontinued restaurant operations which resulted in a tax benefit of $38 million or $0.02 per share.

Appendix B

SPECIMEN FINANCIAL STATEMENTS: The Coca-Cola Company

THE COCA-COLA COMPANY AND SUBSIDIARIES
CONSOLIDATED STATEMENTS OF INCOME

Year Ended December 31,	**2005**	2004	2003
(In millions except per share data)			
NET OPERATING REVENUES	**$ 23,104**	$ 21,742	$ 20,857
Cost of goods sold	**8,195**	7,674	7,776
GROSS PROFIT	**14,909**	14,068	13,081
Selling, general and administrative expenses	**8,739**	7,890	7,287
Other operating charges	**85**	480	573
OPERATING INCOME	**6,085**	5,698	5,221
Interest income	**235**	157	176
Interest expense	**240**	196	178
Equity income — net	**680**	621	406
Other loss — net	**(93)**	(82)	(138)
Gains on issuances of stock by equity investees	**23**	24	8
INCOME BEFORE INCOME TAXES	**6,690**	6,222	5,495
Income taxes	**1,818**	1,375	1,148
NET INCOME	**$ 4,872**	$ 4,847	$ 4,347
BASIC NET INCOME PER SHARE	**$ 2.04**	$ 2.00	$ 1.77
DILUTED NET INCOME PER SHARE	**$ 2.04**	$ 2.00	$ 1.77
AVERAGE SHARES OUTSTANDING	**2,392**	2,426	2,459
Effect of dilutive securities	**1**	3	3
AVERAGE SHARES OUTSTANDING ASSUMING DILUTION	**2,393**	2,429	2,462

Refer to Notes to Consolidated Financial Statements.

The financial information herein is reprinted with permission from The Coca-Cola Company 2005 Annual Report. The accompanying Notes are an integral part of the consolidated financial statements. The complete financial statements are available through a link at the book's companion website.

THE COCA-COLA COMPANY AND SUBSIDIARIES
CONSOLIDATED BALANCE SHEETS

December 31, (In millions except par value)	2005	2004
ASSETS		
CURRENT ASSETS		
Cash and cash equivalents	**$ 4,701**	$ 6,707
Marketable securities	**66**	61
Trade accounts receivable, less allowances of $72 and $69, respectively	**2,281**	2,244
Inventories	**1,424**	1,420
Prepaid expenses and other assets	**1,778**	1,849
TOTAL CURRENT ASSETS	**10,250**	12,281
INVESTMENTS		
Equity method investments:		
Coca-Cola Enterprises Inc.	**1,731**	1,569
Coca-Cola Hellenic Bottling Company S.A.	**1,039**	1,067
Coca-Cola FEMSA, S.A. de C.V.	**982**	792
Coca-Cola Amatil Limited	**748**	736
Other, principally bottling companies	**2,062**	1,733
Cost method investments, principally bottling companies	**360**	355
TOTAL INVESTMENTS	**6,922**	6,252
OTHER ASSETS	**2,648**	2,981
PROPERTY, PLANT AND EQUIPMENT — net	**5,786**	6,091
TRADEMARKS WITH INDEFINITE LIVES	**1,946**	2,037
GOODWILL	**1,047**	1,097
OTHER INTANGIBLE ASSETS	**828**	702
TOTAL ASSETS	**$ 29,427**	$ 31,441
LIABILITIES AND SHAREOWNERS' EQUITY		
CURRENT LIABILITIES		
Accounts payable and accrued expenses	**$ 4,493**	$ 4,403
Loans and notes payable	**4,518**	4,531
Current maturities of long-term debt	**28**	1,490
Accrued income taxes	**797**	709
TOTAL CURRENT LIABILITIES	**9,836**	11,133
LONG-TERM DEBT	**1,154**	1,157
OTHER LIABILITIES	**1,730**	2,814
DEFERRED INCOME TAXES	**352**	402
SHAREOWNERS' EQUITY		
Common stock, $0.25 par value; Authorized — 5,600 shares; Issued — 3,507 and 3,500 shares, respectively	**877**	875
Capital surplus	**5,492**	4,928
Reinvested earnings	**31,299**	29,105
Accumulated other comprehensive income (loss)	**(1,669)**	(1,348)
Treasury stock, at cost — 1,138 and 1,091 shares, respectively	**(19,644)**	(17,625)
TOTAL SHAREOWNERS' EQUITY	**16,355**	15,935
TOTAL LIABILITIES AND SHAREOWNERS' EQUITY	**$ 29,427**	$ 31,441

Refer to Notes to Consolidated Financial Statements.

THE COCA-COLA COMPANY AND SUBSIDIARIES
CONSOLIDATED STATEMENTS OF CASH FLOWS

Year Ended December 31, (In millions)	**2005**	2004	2003
OPERATING ACTIVITIES			
Net income	**$ 4,872**	$ 4,847	$ 4,347
Depreciation and amortization	**932**	893	850
Stock-based compensation expense	**324**	345	422
Deferred income taxes	**(88)**	162	(188)
Equity income or loss, net of dividends	**(446)**	(476)	(294)
Foreign currency adjustments	**47**	(59)	(79)
Gains on issuances of stock by equity investees	**(23)**	(24)	(8)
Gains on sales of assets, including bottling interests	**(9)**	(20)	(5)
Other operating charges	**85**	480	330
Other items	**299**	437	249
Net change in operating assets and liabilities	**430**	(617)	(168)
Net cash provided by operating activities	**6,423**	5,968	5,456
INVESTING ACTIVITIES			
Acquisitions and investments, principally trademarks and bottling companies	**(637)**	(267)	(359)
Purchases of investments and other assets	**(53)**	(46)	(177)
Proceeds from disposals of investments and other assets	**33**	161	147
Purchases of property, plant and equipment	**(899)**	(755)	(812)
Proceeds from disposals of property, plant and equipment	**88**	341	87
Other investing activities	**(28)**	63	178
Net cash used in investing activities	**(1,496)**	(503)	(936)
FINANCING ACTIVITIES			
Issuances of debt	**178**	3,030	1,026
Payments of debt	**(2,460)**	(1,316)	(1,119)
Issuances of stock	**230**	193	98
Purchases of stock for treasury	**(2,055)**	(1,739)	(1,440)
Dividends	**(2,678)**	(2,429)	(2,166)
Net cash used in financing activities	**(6,785)**	(2,261)	(3,601)
EFFECT OF EXCHANGE RATE CHANGES ON CASH AND CASH EQUIVALENTS	**(148)**	141	183
CASH AND CASH EQUIVALENTS			
Net increase (decrease) during the year	**(2,006)**	3,345	1,102
Balance at beginning of year	**6,707**	3,362	2,260
Balance at end of year	**$ 4,701**	$ 6,707	$ 3,362

Refer to Notes to Consolidated Financial Statements.

THE COCA-COLA COMPANY AND SUBSIDIARIES
CONSOLIDATED STATEMENTS OF SHAREOWNERS' EQUITY

Year Ended December 31,	2005	2004	2003
(In millions except per share data)			
NUMBER OF COMMON SHARES OUTSTANDING			
Balance at beginning of year	**2,409**	2,442	2,471
Stock issued to employees exercising stock options	**7**	5	4
Purchases of stock for treasury[1]	**(47)**	(38)	(33)
Balance at end of year	**2,369**	2,409	2,442
COMMON STOCK			
Balance at beginning of year	**$ 875**	$ 874	$ 873
Stock issued to employees exercising stock options	**2**	1	1
Balance at end of year	**877**	875	874
CAPITAL SURPLUS			
Balance at beginning of year	**4,928**	4,395	3,857
Stock issued to employees exercising stock options	**229**	175	105
Tax benefit from employees' stock option and restricted stock plans	**11**	13	11
Stock-based compensation	**324**	345	422
Balance at end of year	**5,492**	4,928	4,395
REINVESTED EARNINGS			
Balance at beginning of year	**29,105**	26,687	24,506
Net income	**4,872**	4,847	4,347
Dividends (per share — $1.12, $1.00 and $0.88 in 2005, 2004 and 2003, respectively)	**(2,678)**	(2,429)	(2,166)
Balance at end of year	**31,299**	29,105	26,687
ACCUMULATED OTHER COMPREHENSIVE INCOME (LOSS)			
Balance at beginning of year	**(1,348)**	(1,995)	(3,047)
Net foreign currency translation adjustment	**(396)**	665	921
Net gain (loss) on derivatives	**57**	(3)	(33)
Net change in unrealized gain on available-for-sale securities	**13**	39	40
Net change in minimum pension liability	**5**	(54)	124
Net other comprehensive income adjustments	**(321)**	647	1,052
Balance at end of year	**(1,669)**	(1,348)	(1,995)
TREASURY STOCK			
Balance at beginning of year	**(17,625)**	(15,871)	(14,389)
Purchases of treasury stock	**(2,019)**	(1,754)	(1,482)
Balance at end of year	**(19,644)**	(17,625)	(15,871)
TOTAL SHAREOWNERS' EQUITY	**$ 16,355**	$ 15,935	$ 14,090
COMPREHENSIVE INCOME			
Net income	**$ 4,872**	$ 4,847	$ 4,347
Net other comprehensive income adjustments	**(321)**	647	1,052
TOTAL COMPREHENSIVE INCOME	**$ 4,551**	$ 5,494	$ 5,399

[1] Common stock purchased from employees exercising stock options numbered 0.5 shares, 0.4 shares and 0.4 shares for the years ended December 31, 2005, 2004 and 2003, respectively.

Refer to Notes to Consolidated Financial Statements.

Appendix C

Time Value of Money

STUDY OBJECTIVES

After studying this appendix, you should be able to:

1 Distinguish between simple and compound interest.
2 Identify the variables fundamental to solving present value problems.
3 Solve for present value of a single amount.
4 Solve for present value of an annuity.
5 Compute the present value of notes and bonds.

Would you rather receive $1,000 today or a year from now? You should prefer to receive the $1,000 today because you can invest the $1,000 and earn interest on it. As a result, you will have more than $1,000 a year from now. What this example illustrates is the concept of the **time value of money**. Everyone prefers to receive money today rather than in the future because of the interest factor.

NATURE OF INTEREST

Interest is payment for the use of another person's money. It is the difference between the amount borrowed or invested (called the principal) and the amount repaid or collected. The amount of interest to be paid or collected is usually stated as a **rate** over a specific period of time. The rate of interest is generally stated as an **annual rate**.

The amount of interest involved in any financing transaction is based on three elements:

1. **Principal (*p*):** The original amount borrowed or invested.
2. **Interest Rate (*i*):** An annual percentage of the principal.
3. **Time (*n*):** The number of years that the principal is borrowed or invested.

Simple Interest

STUDY OBJECTIVE 1
Distinguish between simple and compound interest.

Simple interest is computed on the principal amount only. It is the return on the principal for one period. Simple interest is usually expressed as shown in Illustration C-1 on the next page.

Illustration C-1
Interest computation

$$\text{Interest} = \underset{p}{\text{Principal}} \times \underset{i}{\text{Rate}} \times \underset{n}{\text{Time}}$$

For example, if you borrowed $5,000 for 2 years at a simple interest rate of 12% annually, you would pay $1,200 in total interest computed as follows:

$$\begin{aligned} \text{Interest} &= p \times i \times n \\ &= \$5{,}000 \times .12 \times 2 \\ &= \$1{,}200 \end{aligned}$$

Compound Interest

Compound interest is computed on principal **and** on any interest earned that has not been paid or withdrawn. It is the return on the principal for two or more time periods. Compounding computes interest not only on the principal but also on the interest earned to date on that principal, assuming the interest is left on deposit.

To illustrate the difference between simple and compound interest, assume that you deposit $1,000 in Bank Two, where it will earn *simple interest* of 9% per year, and you deposit another $1,000 in Citizens Bank, where it will earn compound interest of 9% per year *compounded annually*. Also assume that in both cases you will not withdraw any interest until three years from the date of deposit. Illustration C-2 shows the computation of interest you will receive and the accumulated year-end balances.

Illustration C-2
Simple versus compound interest

Bank Two

Simple Interest Calculation	Simple Interest	Accumulated Year-end Balance
Year 1 $1,000.00 × 9%	$ 90.00	$1,090.00
Year 2 $1,000.00 × 9%	90.00	$1,180.00
Year 3 $1,000.00 × 9%	90.00	$1,270.00
	$ 270.00	

Citizens Bank

Compound Interest Calculation	Compound Interest	Accumulated Year-end Balance
Year 1 $1,000.00 × 9%	$ 90.00	$1,090.00
Year 2 $1,090.00 × 9%	98.10	$1,188.10
Year 3 $1,188.10 × 9%	106.93	$1,295.03
	$ 295.03	

$25.03 Difference

Note in Illustration C-2 that simple interest uses the initial principal of $1,000 to compute the interest in all three years. Compound interest uses the accumulated balance (principal plus interest to date) at each year-end to compute interest in the succeeding year—which explains why your compound interest account is larger.

Obviously, if you had a choice between investing your money at simple interest or at compound interest, you would choose compound interest, all other things—especially risk—being equal. In the example, compounding provides $25.03 of additional interest income. For practical purposes, compounding assumes that unpaid interest earned becomes a part of the principal, and the accumulated balance at the end of each year becomes the new principal on which interest is earned during the next year.

Illustration C-2 indicates that you should invest your money at the bank that compounds interest annually. Most business situations use compound interest. Simple interest is generally applicable only to short-term situations of one year or less.

PRESENT VALUE VARIABLES

STUDY OBJECTIVE 2

Identify the variables fundamental to solving present value problems.

The **present value** is the value now of a given amount to be paid or received in the future, assuming compound interest. The present value is based on three variables: (1) the dollar amount to be received (future amount), (2) the length of time until the amount is received (number of periods), and (3) the interest rate (the discount rate). The process of determining the present value is referred to as **discounting the future amount**.

In this textbook, we use present value computations in measuring several items. For example, Chapter 15 computed the present value of the principal and interest payments to determine the market price of a bond. In addition, determining the amount to be reported for notes payable and lease liabilities involves present value computations.

PRESENT VALUE OF A SINGLE AMOUNT

STUDY OBJECTIVE 3

Solve for present value of a single amount.

To illustrate present value, assume that you want to invest a sum of money that will yield $1,000 at the end of one year. What amount would you need to invest today to have $1,000 one year from now? Illustration C-3 shows the formula for calculating present value.

Illustration C-3
Formula for present value

$$\text{Present Value} = \text{Future Value} \div (1 + i)^n$$

Thus, if you want a 10% rate of return, you would compute the present value of $1,000 for one year as follows:

$$\begin{aligned} PV &= FV \div (1 + i)^n \\ &= \$1{,}000 \div (1 + .10)^1 \\ &= \$1{,}000 \div 1.10 \\ &= \$909.09 \end{aligned}$$

We know the future amount ($1,000), the discount rate (10%), and the number of periods (1). These variables are depicted in the time diagram in Illustration C-4.

Illustration C-4
Finding present value if discounted for one period

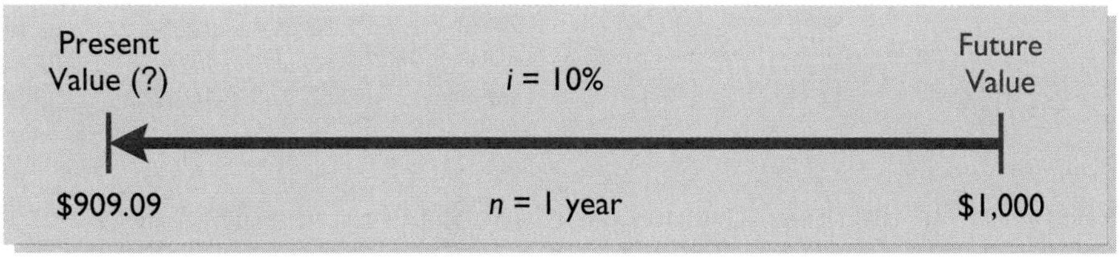

If you receive the single amount of $1,000 **in two years**, discounted at 10% [$PV = \$1{,}000 \div (1 + .10)^2$], the present value of your $1,000 is $826.45 [($1,000 ÷ 1.21), depicted as shown in Illustration C-5 on the next page.

Illustration C-5
Finding present value if discounted for two periods

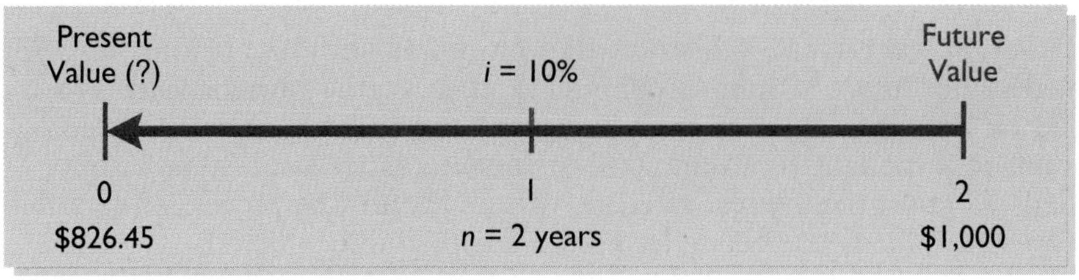

You also could find the present value of your amount through tables that show the present value of 1 for *n* periods. In Table 1, below, *n* (represented in the table's rows) is the number of discounting periods involved. The percentages (represented in the table's columns) are the periodic interest rates or discount rates. The 5-digit decimal numbers in the intersections of the rows and columns are called the **present value of 1 factors**.

When using Table 1 to determine present value, you multiply the future value by the present value factor specified at the intersection of the number of periods and the discount rate.

TABLE 1
Present Value of 1

(*n*) Periods	4%	5%	6%	8%	9%	10%	11%	12%	15%
1	.96154	.95238	.94340	.92593	.91743	.90909	.90090	.89286	.86957
2	.92456	.90703	.89000	.85734	.84168	.82645	.81162	.79719	.75614
3	.88900	.86384	.83962	.79383	.77218	.75132	.73119	.71178	.65752
4	.85480	.82270	.79209	.73503	.70843	.68301	.65873	.63552	.57175
5	.82193	.78353	.74726	.68058	.64993	.62092	.59345	.56743	.49718
6	.79031	.74622	.70496	.63017	.59627	.56447	.53464	.50663	.43233
7	.75992	.71068	.66506	.58349	.54703	.51316	.48166	.45235	.37594
8	.73069	.67684	.62741	.54027	.50187	.46651	.43393	.40388	.32690
9	.70259	.64461	.59190	.50025	.46043	.42410	.39092	.36061	.28426
10	.67556	.61391	.55839	.46319	.42241	.38554	.35218	.32197	.24719
11	.64958	.58468	.52679	.42888	.38753	.35049	.31728	.28748	.21494
12	.62460	.55684	.49697	.39711	.35554	.31863	.28584	.25668	.18691
13	.60057	.53032	.46884	.36770	.32618	.28966	.25751	.22917	.16253
14	.57748	.50507	.44230	.34046	.29925	.26333	.23199	.20462	.14133
15	.55526	.48102	.41727	.31524	.27454	.23939	.20900	.18270	.12289
16	.53391	.45811	.39365	.29189	.25187	.21763	.18829	.16312	.10687
17	.51337	.43630	.37136	.27027	.23107	.19785	.16963	.14564	.09293
18	.49363	.41552	.35034	.25025	.21199	.17986	.15282	.13004	.08081
19	.47464	.39573	.33051	.23171	.19449	.16351	.13768	.11611	.07027
20	.45639	.37689	.31180	.21455	.17843	.14864	.12403	.10367	.06110

For example, the present value factor for one period at a discount rate of 10% is .90909, which equals the $909.09 ($1,000 × .90909) computed in Illustration C-4. For two periods at a discount rate of 10%, the present value factor is .82645, which equals the $826.45 ($1,000 × .82645) computed previously.

Note that a higher discount rate produces a smaller present value. For example, using a 15% discount rate, the present value of $1,000 due one year from now is $869.57, versus $909.09 at 10%. Also note that the further removed from the present the future value is, the smaller the present value. For example, using the same discount rate of 10%, the present value of $1,000 due in **five years** is $620.92, versus the present value of $1,000 due in **one year**, which is $909.09.

The following two demonstration problems (Illustrations C-6, C-7) illustrate how to use Table 1.

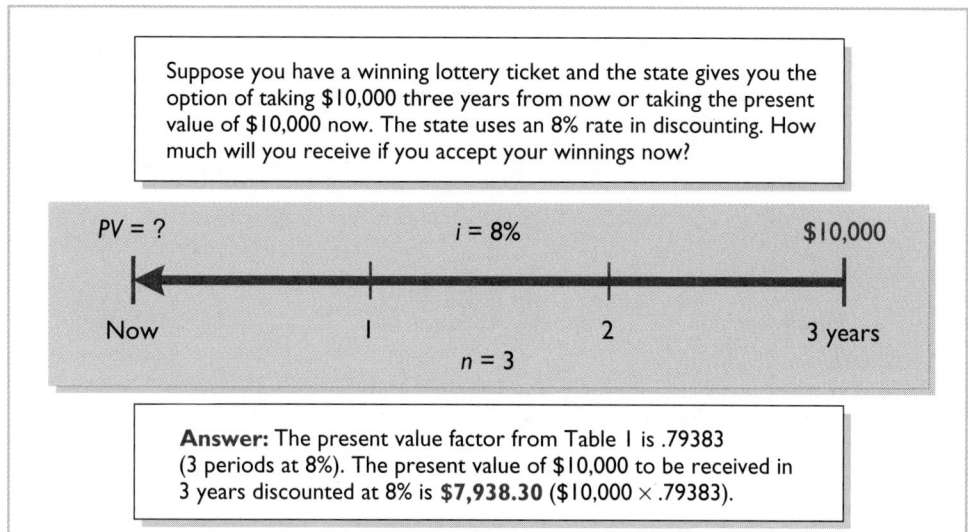

Illustration C-6
Demonstration problem—Using Table 1 for *PV* of 1

Suppose you have a winning lottery ticket and the state gives you the option of taking $10,000 three years from now or taking the present value of $10,000 now. The state uses an 8% rate in discounting. How much will you receive if you accept your winnings now?

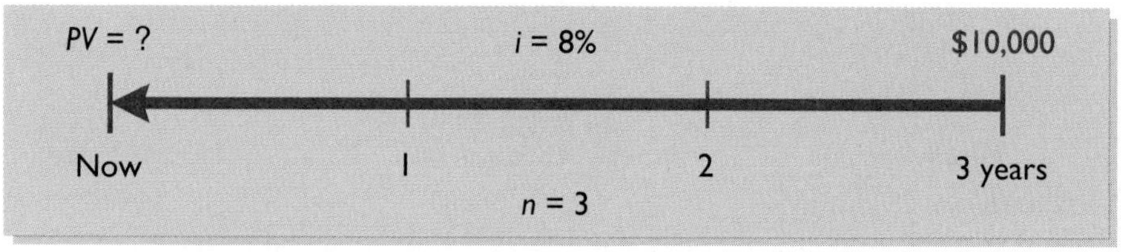

Answer: The present value factor from Table 1 is .79383 (3 periods at 8%). The present value of $10,000 to be received in 3 years discounted at 8% is **$7,938.30** ($10,000 × .79383).

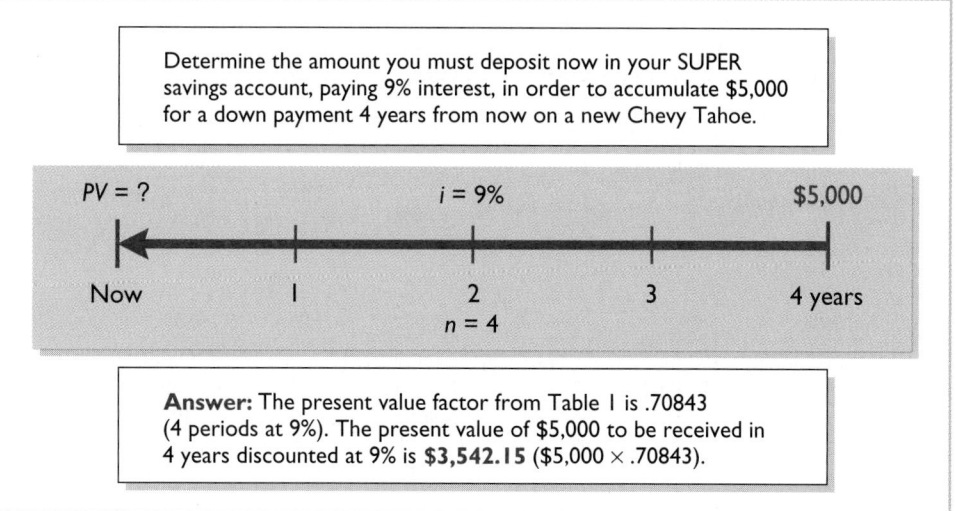

Illustration C-7
Demonstration problem—Using Table 1 for *PV* of 1

Determine the amount you must deposit now in your SUPER savings account, paying 9% interest, in order to accumulate $5,000 for a down payment 4 years from now on a new Chevy Tahoe.

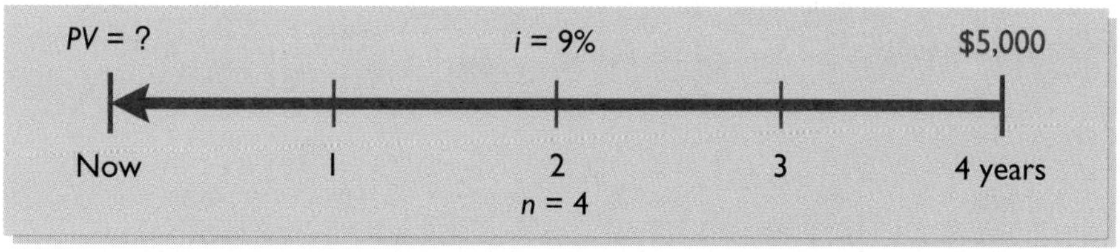

Answer: The present value factor from Table 1 is .70843 (4 periods at 9%). The present value of $5,000 to be received in 4 years discounted at 9% is **$3,542.15** ($5,000 × .70843).

PRESENT VALUE OF AN ANNUITY

STUDY OBJECTIVE 4
Solve for present value of an annuity.

The preceding discussion involved the discounting of only a single future amount. Businesses and individuals frequently engage in transactions in which a *series* of equal dollar amounts are to be received or paid periodically. Examples of a series of periodic receipts or payments are loan agreements, installment sales, mortgage notes, lease (rental) contracts, and pension obligations. As discussed in Chapter 15, these periodic receipts or payments are **annuities**.

The **present value of an annuity** is the value now of a series of future receipts or payments, discounted assuming compound interest. In computing the present value of an annuity, you need to know: (1) the discount rate, (2) the number of discount periods, and (3) the amount of the periodic receipts or payments.

To illustrate how to compute the present value of an annuity, assume that you will receive $1,000 cash annually for three years at a time when the discount rate is 10%. Illustration C-8 depicts this situation, and Illustration C-9 shows the computation of its present value.

Illustration C-8
Time diagram for a three-year annuity

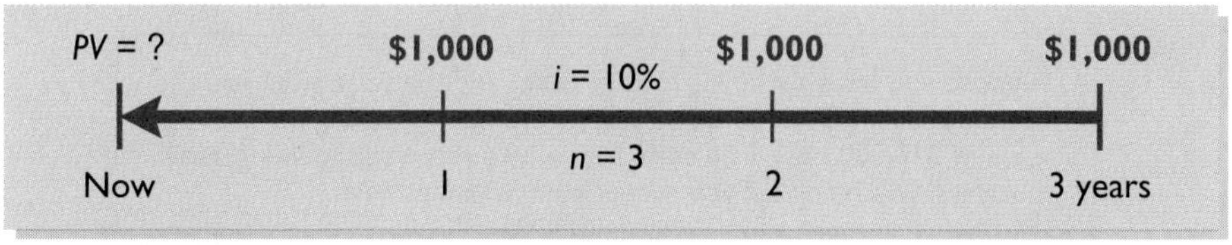

Illustration C-9
Present value of a series of future amounts computation

Future Amount	×	Present Value of 1 Factor at 10%	=	Present Value
$1,000 (one year away)		.90909		$ 909.09
1,000 (two years away)		.82645		826.45
1,000 (three years away)		.75132		751.32
		2.48686		**$2,486.86**

This method of calculation is required when the periodic cash flows are not uniform in each period. However, when the future receipts are the same in each period, there are two other ways to compute present value. First, you can multiply the annual cash flow by the sum of the three present value factors. In the previous example, $1,000 × 2.48686 equals $2,486.86. The second method is to use annuity tables. As illustrated in Table 2 below, these tables show the present value of 1 to be received periodically for a given number of periods.

TABLE 2
Present Value of an Annuity of 1

(n) Periods	4%	5%	6%	8%	9%	10%	11%	12%	15%
1	.96154	.95238	.94340	.92593	.91743	.90909	.90090	.89286	.86957
2	1.88609	1.85941	1.83339	1.78326	1.75911	1.73554	1.71252	1.69005	1.62571
3	2.77509	2.72325	2.67301	2.57710	2.53130	2.48685	2.44371	2.40183	2.28323
4	3.62990	3.54595	3.46511	3.31213	3.23972	3.16986	3.10245	3.03735	2.85498
5	4.45182	4.32948	4.21236	3.99271	3.88965	3.79079	3.69590	3.60478	3.35216
6	5.24214	5.07569	4.91732	4.62288	4.48592	4.35526	4.23054	4.11141	3.78448
7	6.00205	5.78637	5.58238	5.20637	5.03295	4.86842	4.71220	4.56376	4.16042
8	6.73274	6.46321	6.20979	5.74664	5.53482	5.33493	5.14612	4.96764	4.48732
9	7.43533	7.10782	6.80169	6.24689	5.99525	5.75902	5.53705	5.32825	4.77158
10	8.11090	7.72173	7.36009	6.71008	6.41766	6.14457	5.88923	5.65022	5.01877
11	8.76048	8.30641	7.88687	7.13896	6.80519	6.49506	6.20652	5.93770	5.23371
12	9.38507	8.86325	8.38384	7.53608	7.16073	6.81369	6.49236	6.19437	5.42062
13	9.98565	9.39357	8.85268	7.90378	7.48690	7.10336	6.74987	6.42355	5.58315
14	10.56312	9.89864	9.29498	8.24424	7.78615	7.36669	6.98187	6.62817	5.72448
15	11.11839	10.37966	9.71225	8.55948	8.06069	7.60608	7.19087	6.81086	5.84737
16	11.65230	10.83777	10.10590	8.85137	8.31256	7.82371	7.37916	6.97399	5.95424
17	12.16567	11.27407	10.47726	9.12164	8.54363	8.02155	7.54879	7.11963	6.04716
18	12.65930	11.68959	10.82760	9.37189	8.75563	8.20141	7.70162	7.24967	6.12797
19	13.13394	12.08532	11.15812	9.60360	8.95012	8.36492	7.83929	7.36578	6.19823
20	13.59033	12.46221	11.46992	9.81815	9.12855	8.51356	7.96333	7.46944	6.25933

Table 2 shows that the present value of an annuity of 1 factor for three periods at 10% is 2.48685.[1] (This present value factor is the total of the three individual present value factors, as shown in Illustration C-9.) Applying this amount to the annual cash flow of $1,000 produces a present value of $2,486.85.

The following demonstration problem (Illustration C-10) illustrates how to use Table 2.

Illustration C-10
Demonstration problem—Using Table 2 for *PV* of an annuity of 1

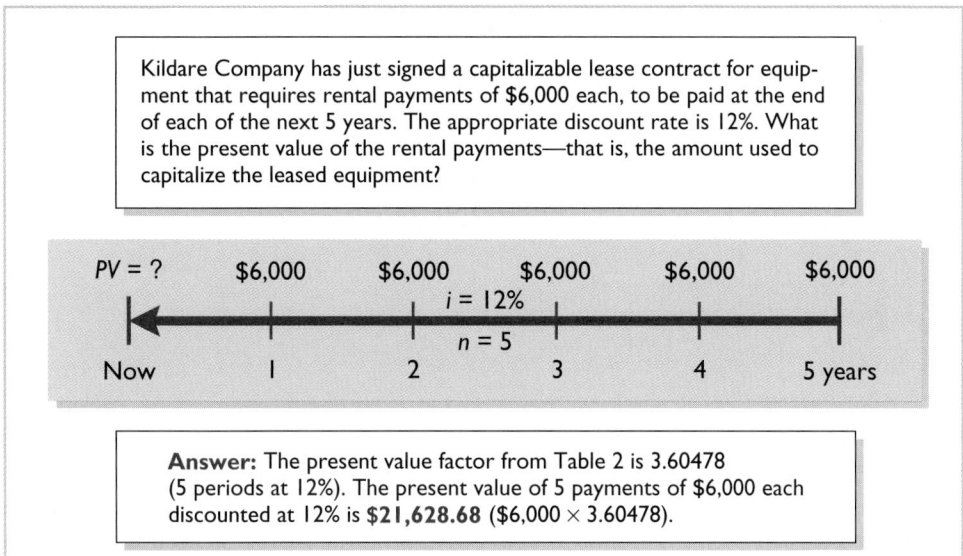

Kildare Company has just signed a capitalizable lease contract for equipment that requires rental payments of $6,000 each, to be paid at the end of each of the next 5 years. The appropriate discount rate is 12%. What is the present value of the rental payments—that is, the amount used to capitalize the leased equipment?

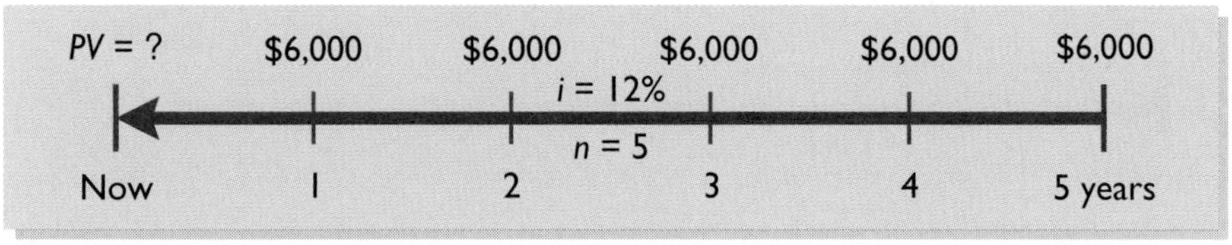

Answer: The present value factor from Table 2 is 3.60478 (5 periods at 12%). The present value of 5 payments of $6,000 each discounted at 12% is **$21,628.68** ($6,000 × 3.60478).

TIME PERIODS AND DISCOUNTING

In the preceding calculations, the discounting was done on an *annual* basis using an *annual* interest rate. Discounting may also be done over shorter periods of time such as monthly, quarterly, or semiannually.

When the time frame is less than one year, you need to convert the annual interest rate to the applicable time frame. Assume, for example, that the investor in Illustration C-8 received $500 **semiannually** for three years instead of $1,000 annually. In this case, the number of periods becomes six (3 × 2), the discount rate is 5% (10% ÷ 2), the present value factor from Table 2 is 5.07569, and the present value of the future cash flows is $2,537.85 (5.07569 × $500). This amount is slightly higher than the $2,486.86 computed in Illustration C-9 because interest is paid twice during the same year; therefore interest is earned on the first half year's interest.

COMPUTING THE PRESENT VALUE OF A LONG-TERM NOTE OR BOND

STUDY OBJECTIVE 5
Compute the present value of notes and bonds.

The present value (or market price) of a long-term note or bond is a function of three variables: (1) the payment amounts, (2) the length of time until the amounts are paid, and (3) the discount rate. Our illustration uses a five-year bond issue.

[1] The difference of .00001 between 2.48686 and 2.48685 is due to rounding.

The first variable—dollars to be paid—is made up of two elements: (1) a series of interest payments (an annuity), and (2) the principal amount (a single sum). To compute the present value of the bond, we must discount both the interest payments and the principal amount—two different computations. The time diagrams for a bond due in five years are shown in Illustration C-11.

Illustration C-11
Present value of a bond time diagram

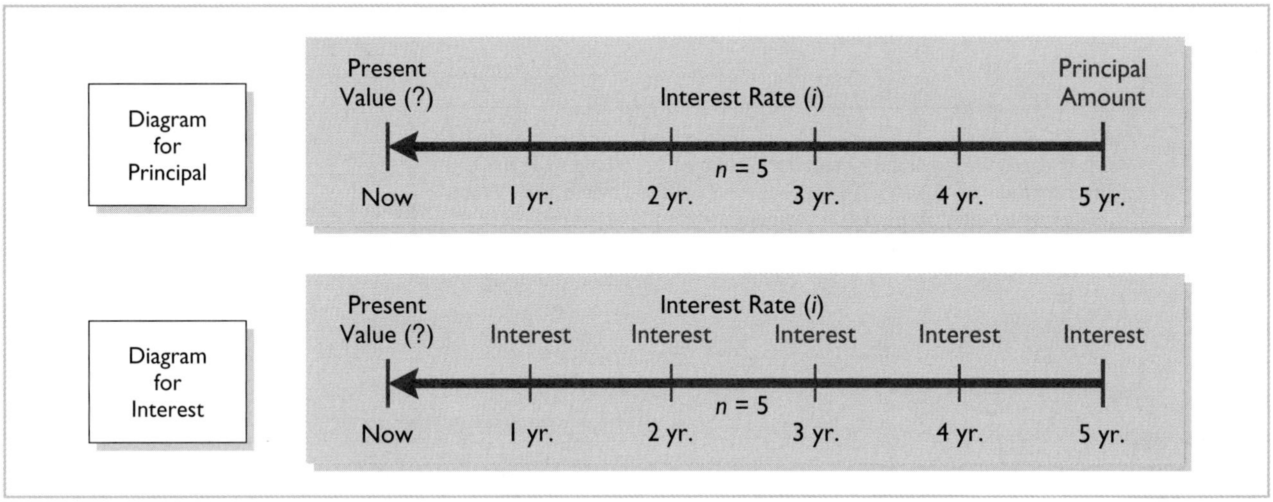

When the investor's market interest rate is equal to the bond's contractual interest rate, the present value of the bonds will *equal* the face value of the bonds. To illustrate, assume a bond issue of 10%, five-year bonds with a face value of $100,000 with interest payable **semiannually** on January 1 and July 1. If the discount rate is the same as the contractual rate, the bonds will sell at face value. In this case, the investor will receive the following: (1) $100,000 at maturity, and (2) a series of ten $5,000 interest payments [($100,000 × 10%) ÷ 2] over the term of the bonds. The length of time is expressed in terms of interest periods—in this case—10, and the discount rate per interest period, 5%. The following time diagram (Illustration C-12) depicts the variables involved in this discounting situation.

Illustration C-12
Time diagram for present value of a 10%, five-year bond paying interest semiannually

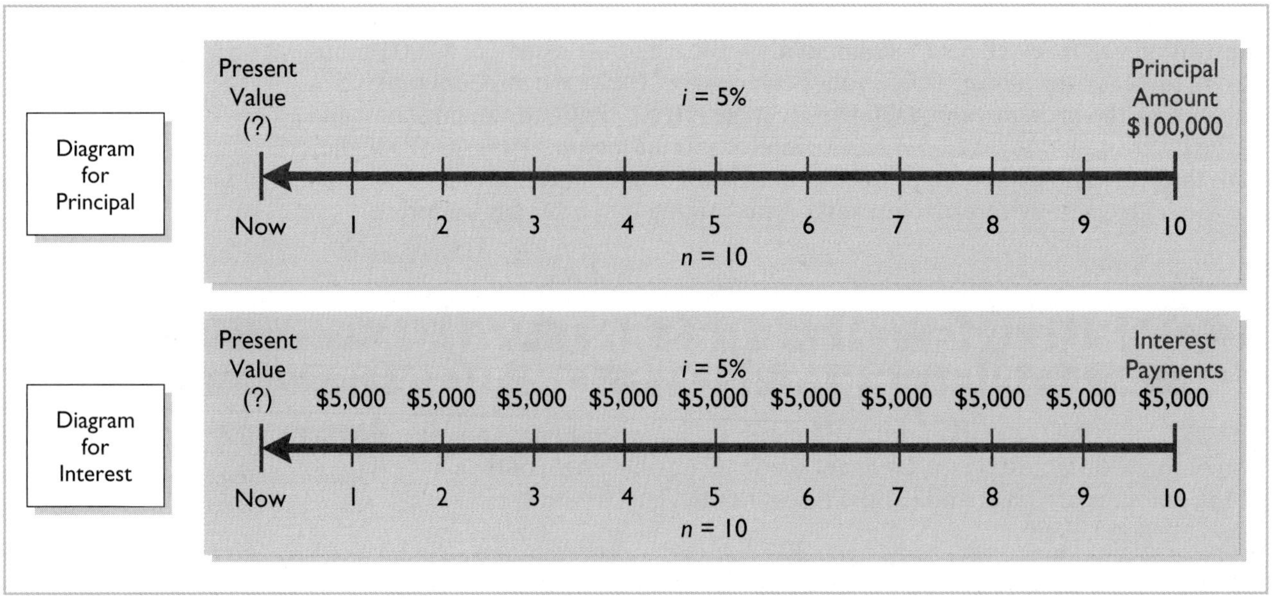

Illustration C-13 shows the computation of the present value of these bonds.

Illustration C-13
Present value of principal and interest—face value

10% Contractual Rate—10% Discount Rate	
Present value of principal to be received at maturity	
$100,000 × *PV* of 1 due in 10 periods at 5%	
$100,000 × .61391 (Table 1)	$ 61,391
Present value of interest to be received periodically over the term of the bonds	
$5,000 × *PV* of 1 due periodically for 10 periods at 5%	
$5,000 × 7.72173 (Table 2)	38,609*
Present value of bonds	**$100,000**

*Rounded

Now assume that the investor's required rate of return is 12%, not 10%. The future amounts are again $100,000 and $5,000, respectively, but now a discount rate of 6% (12% ÷ 2) must be used. The present value of the bonds is $92,639, as computed in Illustration C-14.

Illustration C-14
Present value of principal and interest—discount

10% Contractual Rate—12% Discount Rate	
Present value of principal to be received at maturity	
$100,000 × .55839 (Table 1)	$55,839
Present value of interest to be received periodically over the term of the bonds	
$5,000 × 7.36009 (Table 2)	36,800
Present value of bonds	**$92,639**

Conversely, if the discount rate is 8% and the contractual rate is 10%, the present value of the bonds is $108,111, computed as shown in Illustration C-15.

Illustration C-15
Present value of principal and interest—premium

10% Contractual Rate—8% Discount Rate	
Present value of principal to be received at maturity	
$100,000 × .67556 (Table 1)	$ 67,556
Present value of interest to be received periodically over the term of the bonds	
$5,000 × 8.11090 (Table 2)	40,555
Present value of bonds	**$108,111**

The above discussion relies on present value tables in solving present value problems. Many people use spreadsheets such as Excel or Financial calculators (some even on websites) to compute present values, without the use of tables. Many calculators, especially "financial calculators," have present value (*PV*) functions that allow you to calculate present values by merely inputting the proper amount, discount rate, and periods, and pressing the PV key. Appendix D illustrates how to use a financial calculator in various business situations.

SUMMARY OF STUDY OBJECTIVES

WILEY PLUS

1 **Distinguish between simple and compound interest.** Simple interest is computed on the principal only, while compound interest is computed on the principal and any interest earned that has not been withdrawn.

2 **Identify the variables fundamental to solving present value problems.** The following three variables are fundamental to solving present value problems: (1) the future amount, (2) the number of periods, and (3) the interest rate (the discount rate).

3 **Solve for present value of a single amount.** Prepare a time diagram of the problem. Identify the future amount, the number of discounting periods, and the discount (interest) rate. Using the present value of a single amount table, multiply the future amount by the present value factor specified at the intersection of the number of periods and the discount rate.

4 **Solve for present value of an annuity.** Prepare a time diagram of the problem. Identify the future annuity payments, the number of discounting periods, and the discount (interest) rate. Using the present value of an annuity of 1 table, multiply the amount of the annuity payments by the present value factor specified at the intersection of the number of periods and the interest rate.

5 **Compute the present value of notes and bonds.** To determine the present value of the principal amount: Multiply the principal amount (a single future amount) by the present value factor (from the present value of 1 table) intersecting at the number of periods (number of interest payments) and the discount rate.

To determine the present value of the series of interest payments: Multiply the amount of the interest payment by the present value factor (from the present value of an annuity of 1 table) intersecting at the number of periods (number of interest payments) and the discount rate. Add the present value of the principal amount to the present value of the interest payments to arrive at the present value of the note or bond.

GLOSSARY

WILEY PLUS

Annuity A series of equal dollar amounts to be paid or received periodically. (p. C5).

Compound interest The interest computed on the principal and any interest earned that has not been paid or withdrawn. (p. C2)

Discounting the future amount(s) The process of determining present value. (p. C3).

Interest Payment for the use of another's money. (p. C1).

Present value The value now of a given amount to be paid or received in the future assuming compound interest. (p. C3).

Present value of an annuity The value now of a series of future receipts or payments, discounted assuming compound interest. (p. C5).

Principal The amount borrowed or invested. (p. C1).

Simple interest The interest computed on the principal only. (p. C1).

BRIEF EXERCISES

Use present value tables.

Use tables to solve exercises.

BEC-1 For each of the following cases, indicate (a) to what interest rate columns, and (b) to what number of periods you would refer in looking up the discount rate.

1. In Table 1 (present value of 1):

	Annual Rate	Number of Years Involved	Discounts Per Year
(a)	12%	6	Annually
(b)	10%	15	Annually
(c)	8%	12	Semiannually

2. In Table 2 (present value of an annuity of 1):

	Annual Rate	Number of Years Involved	Number of Payments Involved	Frequency of Payments
(a)	8%	20	20	Annually
(b)	10%	5	5	Annually
(c)	12%	4	8	Semiannually

Determine present values.

BEC-2 **(a)** What is the present value of $30,000 due 8 periods from now, discounted at 8%? **(b)** What is the present value of $30,000 to be received at the end of each of 6 periods, discounted at 9%?

BEC-3 Ramirez Company is considering an investment that will return a lump sum of $600,000 5 years from now. What amount should Ramirez Company pay for this investment in order to earn a 10% return?

Compute the present value of a single-sum investment.

BEC-4 LaRussa Company earns 9% on an investment that will return $700,000 8 years from now. What is the amount LaRussa should invest now in order to earn this rate of return?

Compute the present value of a single-sum investment.

BEC-5 Polley Company sold a 5-year, zero-interest-bearing $36,000 note receivable to Valley Inc. Valley wishes to earn 10% over the remaining 4 years of the note. How much cash will Polley receive upon sale of the note?

Compute the present value of a single-sum zero-interest-bearing note.

BEC-6 Marichal Company issues a 3-year, zero-interest-bearing $60,000 note. The interest rate used to discount the zero-interest-bearing note is 8%. What are the cash proceeds that Marichal Company should receive?

Compute the present value of a single-sum zero-interest-bearing note.

BEC-7 Colaw Company is considering investing in an annuity contract that will return $40,000 annually at the end of each year for 15 years. What amount should Colaw Company pay for this investment if it earns a 6% return?

Compute the present value of an annuity investment.

BEC-8 Sauder Enterprises earns 11% on an investment that pays back $100,000 at the end of each of the next 4 years. What is the amount Sauder Enterprises invested to earn the 11% rate of return?

Compute the present value of an annuity investment.

BEC-9 Chicago Railroad Co. is about to issue $200,000 of 10-year bonds paying a 10% interest rate, with interest payable semiannually. The discount rate for such securities is 8%. How much can Chicago expect to receive for the sale of these bonds?

Compute the present value of bonds.

BEC-10 Assume the same information as in BEC-9 except that the discount rate is 10% instead of 8%. In this case, how much can Chicago expect to receive from the sale of these bonds?

Compute the present value of bonds.

BEC-11 Berghaus Company receives a $75,000, 6-year note bearing interest of 8% (paid annually) from a customer at a time when the discount rate is 9%. What is the present value of the note received by Berghaus Company?

Compute the present value of a note.

BEC-12 Troutman Enterprises issued 8%, 8-year, $1,000,000 par value bonds that pay interest semiannually on October 1 and April 1. The bonds are dated April 1, 2008, and are issued on that date. The discount rate of interest for such bonds on April 1, 2008 is 10%. What cash proceeds did Troutman receive from issuance of the bonds?

Compute the present value of bonds.

BEC-13 Ricky Cleland owns a garage and is contemplating purchasing a tire retreading machine for $16,280. After estimating costs and revenues, Ricky projects a net cash flow from the retreading machine of $2,800 annually for 8 years. Ricky hopes to earn a return of 11% on such investments. What is the present value of the retreading operation? Should Ricky Cleland purchase the retreading machine?

Compute the value of a machine for purposes of making a purchase decision.

BEC-14 Martinez Company issues a 10%, 6-year mortgage note on January 1, 2008, to obtain financing for new equipment. Land is used as collateral for the note. The terms provide for semiannual installment payments of $78,978. What were the cash proceeds received from the issuance of the note?

Compute the present value of a note.

BEC-15 Durler Company is considering purchasing equipment. The equipment will produce the following cash flows: Year 1, $30,000; Year 2, $40,000; Year 3, $60,000. Durler requires a minimum rate of return of 12%. What is the maximum price Durler should pay for this equipment?

Compute the maximum price to pay for a machine.

BEC-16 If Carla Garcia invests $2,745 now, she will receive $10,000 at the end of 15 years. What annual rate of interest will Carla earn on her investment? (*Hint:* Use Table 1.)

Compute the interest rate on a single sum.

BEC-17 Sara Altom has been offered the opportunity of investing $51,316 now. The investment will earn 10% per year and at the end of that time will return Sara $100,000. How many years must Sara wait to receive $100,000? (*Hint:* Use Table 1.)

Compute the number of periods of a single sum.

BEC-18 Stacy Dains purchased an investment for $11,469.92. From this investment, she will receive $1,000 annually for the next 20 years, starting one year from now. What rate of interest will Stacy's investment be earning for her? (*Hint:* Use Table 2.)

Compute the interest rate on an annuity.

BEC-19 Diana Rossi invests $8,559.48 now for a series of $1,000 annual returns, beginning one year from now. Diana will earn a return of 8% on the initial investment. How many annual payments of $1,000 will Diana receive? (*Hint:* Use Table 2.)

Compute the number of periods of an annuity.

Compute the amount to be invested.

BEC-20 Minitori Company needs $10,000 on January 1, 2011. It is starting a fund on January 1, 2008.

Instructions

Compute the amount that must be invested in the fund on January 1, 2008, to produce a $10,000 balance on January 1, 2011 if.

(a) The fund earns 8% per year compounded annually.
(b) The fund earns 8% per year compounded semiannually.
(c) The fund earns 12% per year compounded annually.
(d) The fund earns 12% per year compounded semiannually.

Compute the amount to be invested.

BEC-21 Venuchi Company needs $10,000 on January 1, 2013. It is starting a fund to produce that amount.

Instructions

Compute the amount that must be invested in the fund to produce a $10,000 balance on January 1, 2013, if:

(a) The initial investment is made January 1, 2008, and the fund earns 6% per year.
(b) The initial investment is made January 1, 2010, and the fund earns 6% per year.
(c) The initial investment is made January 1, 2008, and the fund earns 10% per year.
(d) The initial investment is made January 1, 2010, and the fund earns 10% per year.

Select the better payment option.

BEC-22 Letterman Corporation is buying new equipment. It can pay $39,500 today (option 1), or $10,000 today and 5 yearly payments of $8,000 each, starting in one year (option 2).

Instructions

Which option should Letterman select? (Assume a discount rate of 10%.)

Compute the cost of an investment, amount received, and rate of return.

BEC-23 Carmen Corporation is considering several investments.

Instructions

(a) One investment returns $10,000 per year for 5 years and provides a return of 10%. What is the cost of this investment?
(b) Another investment costs $50,000 and returns a certain amount per year for 10 years, providing an 8% return. What amount is received each year?
(c) A third investment costs $70,000 and returns $11,971 each year for 15 years. What is the rate of return on this investment?

Select the best payment option.

BEC-24 You are the beneficiary of a trust fund. The fund gives you the option of receiving $5,000 per year for 10 years, $9,000 per year for 5 years, or $30,000 today.

Instructions

If the desired rate of return is 8%, which option should you select?

Compute the semiannual car payment.

BEC-25 You are purchasing a car for $24,000, and you obtain financing as follows: $2,400 down payment, 12% interest, semiannual payments over 5 years.

Instructions

Compute the payment you will make every 6 months

Compute the present value of bonds.

BEC-26 Contreras Corporation is considering purchasing bonds of Jose Company as an investment. The bonds have a face value of $40,000 with a 10% interest rate. The bonds mature in 4 years and pay interest semiannually.

Instructions

(a) What is the most Contreras should pay for the bonds if it desires a 12% return?
(b) What is the most Contreras should pay for the bonds if it desires an 8% return?

Compute the present value of bonds.

BEC-27 Garcia Corporation is considering purchasing bonds of Fred Company as an investment. The bonds have a face value of $90,000 with a 9% interest rate. The bonds mature in 6 years and pay interest semiannually.

Instructions

(a) What is the most Garcia should pay for the bonds if it desires a 10% return?
(b) What is the most Garcia should pay for the bonds if it desires an 8% return?

Appendix D

Using Financial Calculators

STUDY OBJECTIVE

After studying this appendix, you should be able to:

1 Use a financial calculator to solve time value of money problems.

STUDY OBJECTIVE 1

Use a financial calculator to solve time value of money problems.

Business professionals, once they have mastered the underlying concepts in Appendix C, often use a financial (business) calculator to solve time value of money problems. In many cases, they must use calculators if interest rates or time periods do not correspond with the information provided in the compound interest tables.

To use financial calculators, you enter the time value of money variables into the calculator. Illustration D-1 shows the five most common keys used to solve time value of money problems.[1]

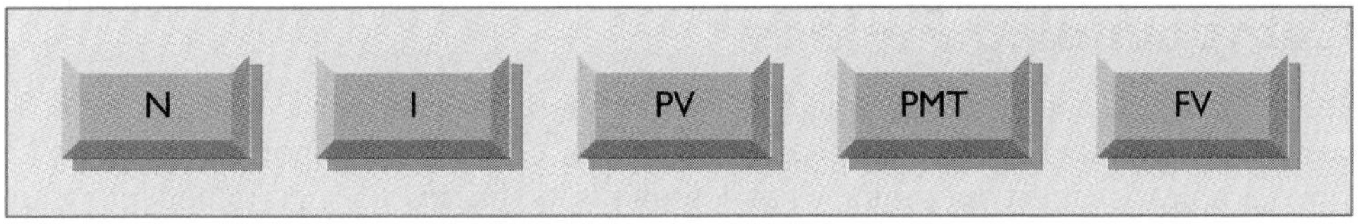

Illustration D-1
Financial calculator keys

where

N = number of periods

I = interest rate per period (some calculators use I/YR or i)

PV = present value (occurs at the beginning of the first period)

PMT = payment (all payments are equal, and none are skipped)

FV = future value (occurs at the end of the last period)

In solving time value of money problems in this appendix, you will generally be given three of four variables and will have to solve for the remaining variable. The fifth key (the key not used) is given a value of zero to ensure that this variable is not used in the computation.

PRESENT VALUE OF A SINGLE SUM

To illustrate how to solve a present value problem using a financial calculator, assume that you want to know the present value of $84,253 to be received in five years, discounted at 11% compounded annually. Illustration D-2 pictures this problem.

[1] On many calculators, these keys are actual buttons on the face of the calculator; on others they appear on the display after the user accesses a present value menu.

Illustration D-2
Calculator solution for present value of a single sum

Inputs:	5	11	?	0	84,253
	N	I	PV	PMT	FV
Answer:			**–50,000**		

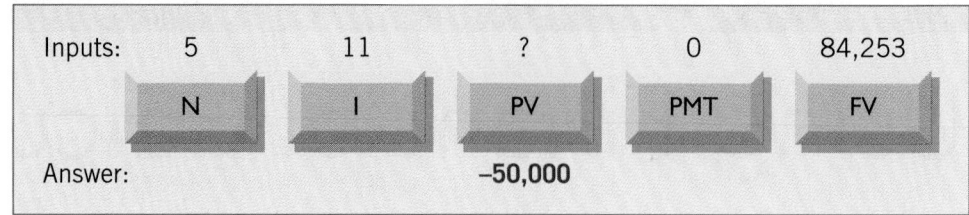

The diagram shows you the information (inputs) to enter into the calculator: N = 5, I = 11, PMT = 0, and FV = 84,253. You then press PV for the answer: −\$50,000. As indicated, the PMT key was given a value of zero because a series of payments did not occur in this problem.

Plus and Minus

The use of plus and minus signs in time value of money problems with a financial calculator can be confusing. Most financial calculators are programmed so that the positive and negative cash flows in any problem offset each other. In the present value problem above, we identified the \$84,253 future value initial investment as a positive (inflow); the answer −\$50,000 was shown as a negative amount, reflecting a cash outflow. If the 84,253 were entered as a negative, then the final answer would have been reported as a positive 50,000.

Hopefully, the sign convention will not cause confusion. If you understand what is required in a problem, you should be able to interpret a positive or negative amount in determining the solution to a problem.

Compounding Periods

In the problem above, we assumed that compounding occurs once a year. Some financial calculators have a default setting, which assumes that compounding occurs 12 times a year. You must determine what default period has been programmed into your calculator and change it as necessary to arrive at the proper compounding period.

Rounding

Most financial calculators store and calculate using 12 decimal places. As a result, because compound interest tables generally have factors only up to 5 decimal places, a slight difference in the final answer can result. In most time value of money problems, the final answer will not include more than two decimal points.

PRESENT VALUE OF AN ANNUITY

To illustrate how to solve a present value of an annuity problem using a financial calculator, assume that you are asked to determine the present value of rental receipts of \$6,000 each to be received at the end of each of the next five years, when discounted at 12%, as pictured in Illustration D-3.

Illustration D-3
Calculator solution for present value of an annuity

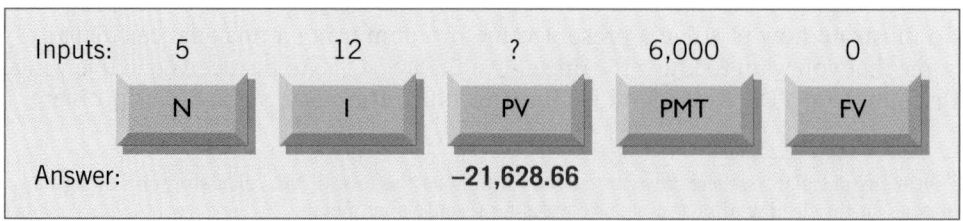

Inputs:	5	12	?	6,000	0
	N	I	PV	PMT	FV
Answer:			**–21,628.66**		

In this case, you enter N = 5, I = 12, PMT = 6,000, FV = 0, and then press PV to arrive at the answer of $21, 628.66.

USEFUL APPLICATIONS OF THE FINANCIAL CALCULATOR

With a financial calculator you can solve for any interest rate or for any number of periods in a time value of money problem. Here are some examples of these applications.

Auto Loan

Assume you are financing a car with a three-year loan. The loan has a 9.5% nominal annual interest rate, compounded monthly. The price of the car is $6,000, and you want to determine the monthly payments, assuming that the payments start one month after the purchase. This problem is pictured in Illustration D-4.

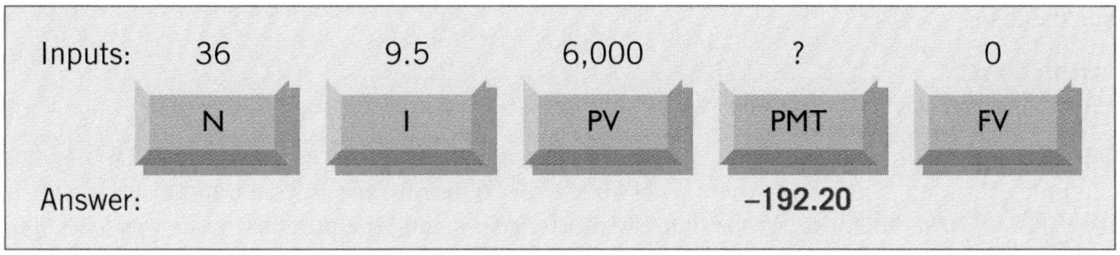

Illustration D-4
Calculator solution for auto loan payments

To solve this problem, you enter N = 36 (12 × 3), I = 9.5, PV = 6,000, FV = 0, and then press PMT. You will find that the monthly payments will be $192.20. Note that the payment key is usually programmed for 12 payments per year. Thus, you must change the default (compounding period) if the payments are other than monthly.

Mortgage Loan Amount

Let's say you are evaluating financing options for a loan on a house. You decide that the maximum mortgage payment you can afford is $700 per month. The annual interest rate is 8.4%. If you get a mortgage that requires you to make monthly payments over a 15-year period, what is the maximum purchase price you can afford? Illustration D-5 depicts this problem.

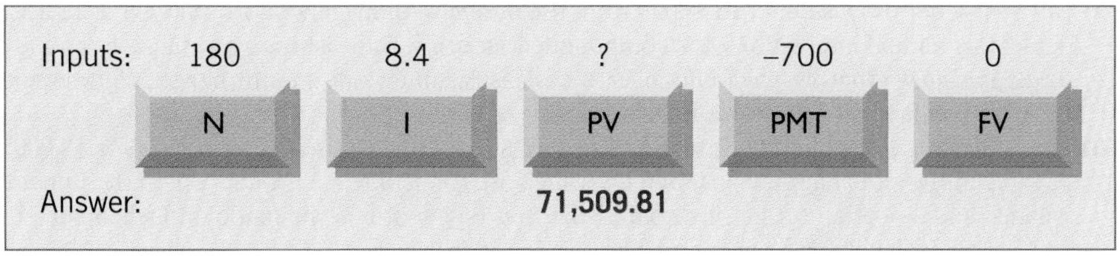

Illustration D-5
Calculator solution for mortgage amount

You enter N = 180 (12 × 15 years), I = 8.4, PMT = −700, FV = 0, and press PV. You find a present value of $71,509.81—the maximum house price you can afford, given that you want to keep your mortgage payments at $700. Note that by changing any of the variables, you can quickly conduct "what-if" analyses for different situations.

SUMMARY OF LEARNING OBJECTIVE FOR APPENDIX

1 **Use a financial calculator to solve time value of money problems.** Financial calculators can be used to solve the same and additional problems as those solved with time value of money tables. One enters into the financial calculator the amounts for all but one of the unknown elements of a time value of money problem (periods, interest rate, payments, future or present value). Particularly useful situations involve interest rates and compounding periods not presented in the tables.

BRIEF EXERCISES

Determine interest rate.

BED-1 Reba McEntire wishes to invest $19,000 on July 1, 2008, and have it accumulate to $49,000 by July 1, 2018.

Instructions
Use a financial calculator to determine at what exact annual rate of interest Reba must invest the $19,000.

Determine interest rate.

BED-2 On July 17, 2008, Tim McGraw borrowed $42,000 from his grandfather to open a clothing store. Starting July 17, 2009, Tim has to make 10 equal annual payments of $6,500 each to repay the loan.

Instructions
Use a financial calculator to determine what interest rate Tim is paying.

Determine interest rate.

BED-3 As the purchaser of a new house, Patty Loveless has signed a mortgage note to pay the Memphis National Bank and Trust Co. $14,000 every 6 months for 20 years, at the end of which time she will own the house. At the date the mortgage is signed the purchase price was $198,000, and Loveless made a down payment of $20,000. The first payment will be made 6 months after the date the mortgage is signed.

Instructions
Using a financial calculator, compute the exact rate of interest earned on the mortgage by the bank.

Various time value of money situations.

BED-4 Using a financial calculator, solve for the unknowns in each of the following situations.

(a) On June 1, 2008, Shelley Long purchases lakefront property from her neighbor, Joey Brenner, and agrees to pay the purchase price in seven payments of $16,000 each, the first payment to be payable June 1, 2009. (Assume that interest compounded at an annual rate of 7.35% is implicit in the payments.) What is the purchase price of the property?

(b) On January 1, 2008, Cooke Corporation purchased 200 of the $1,000 face value, 8% coupon, 10-year bonds of Howe Inc. The bonds mature on January 1, 2018, and pay interest annually beginning January 1, 2009. Cooke purchased the bonds to yield 10.65%. How much did Cooke pay for the bonds?

Various time value of money situations.

BED-5 Using a financial calculator, provide a solution to each of the following situations.

(a) Bill Schroeder owes a debt of $35,000 from the purchase of his new sport utility vehicle. The debt bears annual interest of 9.1% compounded monthly. Bill wishes to pay the debt and interest in equal monthly payments over 8 years, beginning one month hence. What equal monthly payments will pay off the debt and interest?

(b) On January 1, 2008, Sammy Sosa offers to buy Mark Grace's used snowmobile for $8,000, payable in five equal annual installments, which are to include 8.25% interest on the unpaid balance and a portion of the principal. If the first payment is to be made on December 31, 2008, how much will each payment be?

Appendix E

Standards of Ethical Conduct for Management Accountants

Management accountants have an obligation to the organizations they serve, their profession, the public, and themselves to maintain the highest standards of ethical conduct. In recognition of this obligation, the **Institute of Management Accountants** has published and promoted the following standards of ethical conduct for management accountants.

IMA STATEMENT OF ETHICAL PROFESSIONAL PRACTICE

Members of IMA shall behave ethically. A commitment to ethical professional practice includes: overarching principles that express our values, and standards that guide our conduct.

Principles

IMA's overarching ethical principles include: Honesty, Fairness, Objectivity, and Responsibility. Members shall act in accordance with these principles and shall encourage others within their organizations to adhere to them.

Standards

A member's failure to comply with the following standards may result in disciplinary action.

I. COMPETENCE

Each member has a responsibility to:

1. Maintain an appropriate level of professional expertise by continually developing knowledge and skills.
2. Perform professional duties in accordance with relevant laws, regulations, and technical standards.
3. Provide decision support information and recommendations that are accurate, clear, concise, and timely.
4. Recognize and communicate professional limitations or other constraints that would preclude responsible judgment or successful performance of an activity.

II. CONFIDENTIALITY

Each member has a responsibility to:

1. Keep information confidential except when disclosure is authorized or legally required.
2. Inform all relevant parties regarding appropriate use of confidential information. Monitor subordinates' activities to ensure compliance.
3. Refrain from using confidential information for unethical or illegal advantage.

III. INTEGRITY

Each member has a responsibility to:

1. Mitigate actual conflicts of interest. Regularly communicate with business associates to avoid apparent conflicts of interest. Advise all parties of any potential conflicts.
2. Refrain from engaging in any conduct that would prejudice carrying out duties ethically.
3. Abstain from engaging in or supporting any activity that might discredit the profession.

IV. CREDIBILITY

Each member has a responsibility to:

1. Communicate information fairly and objectively.
2. Disclose all relevant information that could reasonably be expected to influence an intended user's understanding of the reports, analyses, or recommendations.
3. Disclose delays or deficiencies in information, timeliness, processing, or internal controls in conformance with organization policy and/or applicable law.

Resolution of Ethical Conflict

In applying the Standards of Ethical Professional Practice, you may encounter problems identifying unethical behavior or resolving an ethical conflict. When faced with ethical issues, you should follow your organization's established policies on the resolution of such conflict. If these policies do not resolve the ethical conflict, you should consider the following courses of action:

1. Discuss the issue with your immediate supervisor except when it appears that the supervisor is involved. In that case, present the issue to the next level. If you cannot achieve a satisfactory resolution, submit the issue to the next management level. If your immediate superior is the chief executive officer or equivalent, the acceptable reviewing authority may be a group such as the audit committee, executive committee, board of directors, board of trustees, or owners. Contact with levels above the immediate superior should be initiated only with your superior's knowledge, assuming he or she is not involved. Communication of such problems to authorities or individuals not employed or engaged by the organization is not considered appropriate, unless you believe there is a clear violation of the law.
2. Clarify relevant ethical issues by initiating a confidential discussion with an IMA Ethics Counselor or other impartial advisor to obtain a better understanding of possible courses of action.
3. Consult your own attorney as to legal obligations and rights concerning the ethical conflict.

Source: Institute of Management Accountants, *www.imanct.org/pdf/981.pdf*. Reprinted by permission.

PHOTO CREDITS

Chapter 1 Page 3 Dinodia Images/Alamy Limited Page 9 Hai Wen China Tourism Press/Getty Images, Inc Page 11 Brent Holland/iStockphoto Page 24 iStockphoto

Chapter 2 Page 47 NBAE/Getty Images Page 55 Koichi Kamoshida/AsiaPac/Getty Images, Inc Page 57 Mike Stewart/Corbis Sygma Page 69 PhotoDisc, Inc./Getty Images

Chapter 3 Page 91 Witte Thomas E/Gamma Presse, Inc. Page 94 Kevin Winter/Getty Images, Inc Page 98 Chris Weeks/Getty Images, Inc Page 102 iStockphoto

Chapter 4 Page 141 Brian Bahr/Getty Images, Inc Page 153 M. Tcherevkoff/Getty Images, Inc Page 158 Christian Lagereek/iStockphoto Page 162 Digital Vision Page 162 Nikki Ward/iStockphoto Page 163 Brand X/PictureArts Page 164 iStockphoto Page 164 iStockphoto

Chapter 5 Page 193 Stone/Getty Images, Inc Page 197 Courtesy Morrow Snowboards Inc. Page 203 iStockphoto Page 211 Victor Prikhoddko/iStockphoto

Chapter 6 Page 243 Pathaithai Chungyam/iStockphoto Page 245 Bjorn Kindler/iStockphoto Page 246 iStockphoto Page 257 PhotoDisc, Inc./Getty Images Page 260 Courtesy Samsung Electronics America

Chapter 7 Page 291 Henry Chaplin/iStockphoto Page 294 Sean Locke/iStockphoto Page 297 Andrejs Zavadskis/iStockphoto

Chapter 8 Page 337 Valerie Loiseleux/iStockphoto Page 341 Gianni Dagli Orti/Corbis Images Page 342 Terence John/Retna Page 344 Nick Koudis/AFP/Getty Images Page 355 Ingvald Kaldhussaeter/iStockphoto

Chapter 9 Page 383 Jorg Greuel/AFP/Getty Images Page 386 Alice Millikan/iStockphoto Page 392 Joe Polillio/Getty Images, Inc Page 395 Michael Braun/iStockphoto Page 400 Jamie Evans/iStockphoto

Chapter 10 Page 423 David Trood/Getty Images, Inc Page 427 iStockphoto Page 436 AFP/Getty Images Page 443 Andy Lions/Photonica/Getty Images, Inc

Chapter 11 Page 471 Cary Westfall/iStockphoto Page 480 Peter Gridley/Taxi/Getty Images Page 484 Catherine dee Auvil/iStockphoto

Chapter 12 Page 513 Charles Taylor/iStockphoto Page 516 Malcolm Romain/iStockphoto Page 518 PhotoDisc/Getty Images, Inc. Page 523 Carmen Martinez/iStockphoto

Chapter 13 Page 555 David Young-Wolf/PhotoEdit Page 559 Reuters NewMedia Inc/PhotoEdit Page 563 Brandon Laufenberg/iStockphoto Page 570 Alex Fevzer/Corbis Images

Chapter 14 Page 595 Clive Brunskill/Getty Images Sport Services Page 599 Tomasz Resiak/iStockphoto Page 603 PhotoDisc, Inc./Getty Images Page 605 Arpad Benedek/iStockphoto Page 611 iStockphoto

Chapter 15 Page 631 Corporation of London/HIP/The Image Works Page 636 iStockphoto Page 644 Greg Nicholas/iStockphoto Page 647 Corbis Stock Market

Chapter 16 Page 683 Warner Bros. David James/The Kobal Collection, Ltd. Page 696 John Lamb/Stone/Getty Images, Inc

Chapter 17 Page 719 Rudi Von Briel/PhotoEdit Page 723 Darren McCollester/Getty Images News and Sport Services Page 726 Corbis Digital Stock Page 737 PhotoDisc, Inc./Getty Images

Chapter 18 Page 779 Jeremy Edwards/iStockphoto Page 789 Nora Good/Masterfile Page 797 Royalty-Free/Corbis Images Page 802 Martina Misar/iStockphoto Page 806 iStockphoto Page 806 iStockphoto

Chapter 19 Page 831 Alamy Images Page 834 iStockphoto Page 837 iStockphoto Page 846 Octavio Campos/iStockphoto

Chapter 20 Page 871 PhotoDisc, Inc./Getty Images Page 874 iStockphoto Page 887 Photodisc/Getty Images, Inc. Page 889 Corbis Stock Market

Chapter 21 Page 911 Lon C. Diehl/PhotoEdit Page 916 iStockphoto Page 927 PhotoDisc, Inc./Getty Images Page 929 Jennie Oppenheimer/Stock Illustration Source/Images.com

Chapter 22 Page 957 Tad Denson/iStockphoto Page 960 Kirill Zdorov/iStockphoto Page 970 Digital Vision/Getty Images Page 974 Yael/Retna

Chapter 23 Page 999 (c)2000 Artville, Inc Page 1002 Gary Conner/Index Stock Page 1004 Gary Buss/Taxi/Getty Images Page 1014 Corbis Digital Stock

Chapter 24 Page 1039 (c)EyeWire Page 1049 Derek Dammann/iStockphoto Page 1052 (c)2000 Artville, Inc Page 1061 Sandy Jones/iStockphoto

Chapter 25 Page 1087 Dick Luria/Taxi/Getty Images Page 1090 Wally McNamee/Corbis Images Page 1094 Hywit Dimyadi/iStockphoto Page 1107 PhotoDisc, Inc./Getty Images

Chapter 26 Page 1133 Royalty-Free/Corbis Images Page 1142 William Tautic/Corbis Stock Market Page 1148 Rebecca Ellis/iStockphoto

COMPANY INDEX

SUBJECT INDEX

RAPID REVIEW
Chapter Content

RESPONSIBILITY ACCOUNTING (Chapter 24)

Types of Responsibility Centers

Cost	Profit	Investment
Expenses only	Expenses and Revenues	Expenses and Revenues and ROI

Return on Investment

Return on investment (ROI) = Investment center controllable margin ÷ Average investment center operating assets

STANDARD COSTS (Chapter 25)

Standard Cost Variances

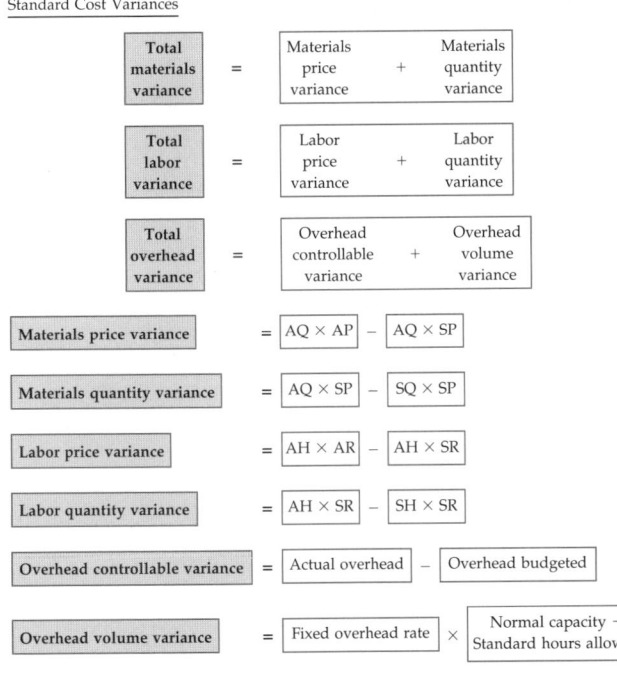

Total materials variance = Materials price variance + Materials quantity variance

Total labor variance = Labor price variance + Labor quantity variance

Total overhead variance = Overhead controllable variance + Overhead volume variance

Materials price variance = $(AQ \times AP) - (AQ \times SP)$

Materials quantity variance = $(AQ \times SP) - (SQ \times SP)$

Labor price variance = $(AH \times AR) - (AH \times SR)$

Labor quantity variance = $(AH \times SR) - (SH \times SR)$

Overhead controllable variance = Actual overhead − Overhead budgeted

Overhead volume variance = Fixed overhead rate × (Normal capacity − Standard hours allowed)

INCREMENTAL ANALYSIS AND CAPITAL BUDGETING (Chapter 26)

Annual Rate of Return

Annual rate of return = Expected annual net income ÷ Average investment

Cash Payback

Cash payback period = Cost of capital investment ÷ Annual cash inflow

Discounted Cash Flow Approaches

Net Present Value	Internal Rate of Return
Compute net present value (a dollar amount). If net present value is zero or positive, accept the proposal. If net present value is negative, reject the proposal.	Compute internal rate of return (a percentage). If internal rate of return is equal to or greater than the minimum required rate of return, accept the proposal. If internal rate of return is less than the minimum rate, reject the proposal.

Incremental Analysis

1. Identify the relevant costs associated with each alternative. Relevant costs are those costs and revenues that differ across alternatives. Choose the alternative that maximizes net income.
2. Opportunity costs are those benefits that are given up when one alternative is chosen instead of another one. Opportunity costs are relevant costs.
3. Sunk costs have already been incurred and will not be changed or avoided by any future decision. Sunk costs are not relevant costs.

RAPID REVIEW
Financial Statements

Order of Preparation

Statement Type	Date
1. Income statement	For the period ended
2. Retained earnings statement	For the period ended
3. Balance sheet	As of the end of the period
4. Statement of cash flows	For the period ended

Income Statement (perpetual inventory system)

Name of Company Income Statement For the Period Ended		
Sales revenues		
Sales	$X	
Less: Sales returns and allowances	X	
Sales discounts	X	
Net sales		$X
Cost of goods sold		X
Gross profit		X
Operating expenses		
(Examples: store salaries, advertising, delivery, rent, depreciation, utilities, insurance)		X
Income from operations		X
Other revenues and gains		
(Examples: interest, gains)	X	
Other expenses and losses		
(Examples: interest, losses)	X	X
Income before income taxes		X
Income tax expense		X
Net income		$X

Income Statement (periodic inventory system)

Name of Company Income Statement For the Period Ended			
Sales revenues			
Sales		$X	
Less: Sales returns and allowances		X	
Sales discounts		X	
Net sales			$X
Cost of goods sold			
Beginning inventory		X	
Purchases	$X		
Less: Purchase returns and allowances	X		
Net purchases	X		
Add: Freight in	X		
Cost of goods purchased		X	
Cost of goods available for sale		X	
Less: Ending inventory		X	
Cost of goods sold			X
Gross profit			X
Operating expenses			
(Examples: store salaries, advertising, delivery, rent, depreciation, utilities, insurance)			X
Income from operations			X
Other revenues and gains			
(Examples: interest, gains)		X	
Other expenses and losses			
(Examples: interest, losses)		X	X
Income before income taxes			X
Income tax expense			X
Net income			$X

Retained Earnings Statement

Name of Company Retained Earnings Statement For the Period Ended	
Retained earnings, beginning of period	$X
Add: Net income (or deduct net loss)	X
	X
Deduct: Dividends	X
Retained earnings, end of period	$X

STOP AND CHECK: Net income (loss) presented on the retained earnings statement must equal the net income (loss) presented on the income statement.

Balance Sheet

Name of Company Balance Sheet As of the End of the Period			
Assets			
Current assets			
(Examples: cash, short-term investments, accounts receivable, merchandise inventory, prepaids)			$X
Long-term investments			
(Examples: investments in bonds, investments in stocks)			X
Property, plant, and equipment			
Land		$X	
Buildings and equipment	$X		
Less: Accumulated depreciation	X	X	X
Intangible assets			X
Total assets			$X
Liabilities and Stockholders' Equity			
Liabilities			
Current liabilities			
(Examples: notes payable, accounts payable, accruals, unearned revenues, current portion of notes payable)			$X
Long-term liabilities			
(Examples: notes payable, bonds payable)			X
Total liabilities			X
Stockholders' equity			
Common stock			X
Retained earnings			X
Total liabilities and stockholders' equity			$X

STOP AND CHECK: Total assets on the balance sheet must equal total liabilities and stockholders' equity; and, ending retained earnings on the balance sheet must equal ending retained earnings on the retained earnings statement.

Statement of Cash Flows

Name of Company Statement of Cash Flows For the Period Ended	
Cash flows from operating activities	
Note: May be prepared using the direct or indirect method	
Cash provided (used) by operating activities	$X
Cash flows from investing activities	
(Examples: purchase / sale of long-term assets)	
Cash provided (used) by investing activities	X
Cash flows from financing activities	
(Examples: issue / repayment of long-term liabilities, issue of stock, payment of dividends)	
Net cash provided (used) by financing activities	X
Net increase (decrease) in cash	X
Cash, beginning of the period	X
Cash, end of the period	$X

STOP AND CHECK: Cash, end of the period, on the statement of cash flows must equal cash presented on the balance sheet.